D1299130

Features

Visit us on the Web at
http://www.census.gov/compendia/statab

ACKNOWLEDGMENTS

Jean F. Mullin was responsible for the technical supervision and coordination of this volume under the direction of **Ian R. O'Brien**, Chief, Statistical Compendia Branch. Assisting in the research and analytical phases of assigned sections and in the development aspects of new tables were **Brian Clark**, **Richard P. Kersey**, **Christine Nguyen**, **Michael Sellner**, and **Sean R. Wilburn**. **Catherine B. Lavender** provided primary editorial assistance. Other editorial assistance was rendered by **Stacey Barber**, **Alethea S. Carter**, **Jennifer Grimes**, **April C. Harris**, **Jennifer Harrison**, **Michael Lopez**, **Alexandra Nguyen**, **Juan Rodriguez**, **Melissa Swindell**, and **Kevin Younes**.

Maps were designed and produced by **Connie Beard**, **Stephen Jones**, and **Scott Wilcox** of the Cartographic Products Branch within the Geography Division.

Monique D. Lindsay, **Connie Nadzadi**, **Faye Brock**, **Christine E. Geter**, and **Taunisha Gates** of Editorial Services provided publications management and editorial review under the direction of **Janet S. Sweeney**. **Linda Chen** and **Donald Meyd** of the Administrative and Customer Services Division, **Francis Grailand Hall**, Chief, provided printing management and graphics design and composition for print and electronic media. General direction and production management were provided by **Claudette E. Bennett**, Assistant Division Chief.

The cooperation of many contributors to this volume is gratefully acknowledged. The source note below each table credits the various government and private sector agencies that have collaborated in furnishing the information for the *Statistical Abstract*.

This book is dedicated to the many branch chiefs, statisticians, editors, and information assistants who have worked on the *Statistical Abstract* through the years. Special thanks to **Lars B. Johanson**, **Glenn W. King**, and **Rosemary E. Clark**, whose advice and expertise is still sought out long after their retirements.

Statistical Abstract
of the United States: 2012

Issued August 2011

U.S. Department of Commerce
Rebecca Blank,
Acting Secretary

Vacant,
Deputy Secretary

**Economics and Statistics
Administration
Rebecca Blank,**
Under Secretary for Economic Affairs

U.S. CENSUS BUREAU
Robert M. Groves,
Director

SUGGESTED CITATION

U.S. Census Bureau,
*Statistical Abstract
of the United States:
2012*
(131st Edition)
Washington, DC,
2011

ECONOMICS
AND STATISTICS
ADMINISTRATION

**Economics
and Statistics
Administration**

Rebecca Blank,
Under Secretary for
Economic Affairs

U.S. CENSUS BUREAU

Robert M. Groves,
Director

Thomas L. Mesenbourg,
Deputy Director and
Chief Operating Officer

Ted A. Johnson,
Associate Director for
Administration and
Chief Financial Officer

Francis Grailand Hall,
Chief, Administrative and
Customer Services Division

Published in the United States of America
by Bernan Press, a wholly owned subsidiary of
The Rowman & Littlefield Publishing Group, Inc.
4501 Forbes Boulevard, Suite 200
Lanham, Maryland 20706

Bernan Press
800-865-3457
www.bernan.com

ISBN 13: 978-1-59888-503-3

Preface

The *Statistical Abstract of the United States,* published since 1878, is a comprehensive collection of statistics on the social, political, and economic organization of the United States. It is designed to serve as a convenient volume for statistical reference and as a guide to other statistical publications and sources. The latter function is served by the introductory text to each section, the source note appearing below each table, and Appendix I, which is comprised of the *Guide to Sources of Statistics*, the *Guide to State Statistical Abstracts*, and the *Guide to Foreign Statistical Abstracts*.

This volume includes a selection of data from many statistical sources, both government and private. Publications cited as sources usually contain additional statistical detail and more comprehensive discussions of definitions and concepts. Data not available in publications issued by the contributing agency, but obtained from the Internet or unpublished records are identified in the source notes. More information on the subjects covered in the tables may generally be obtained from the source.

Except as indicated, figures are for the United States as presently constituted. Although emphasis in the *Statistical Abstract* is primarily given to national data, many tables present data for regions and individual states and a smaller number for metropolitan areas and cities. Appendix II, Metropolitan and Micropolitan Statistical Areas: Concepts, Components, and Population, presents explanatory text, a complete current listing, and population data for metropolitan and micropolitan areas defined as of November 2009. Statistics for the Commonwealth of Puerto Rico and for island areas of the United States are included in many state tables and are supplemented by information in Section 29. Additional information for states, cities, counties, metropolitan areas, and other small units, as well as more historical data, are available in various supplements to the *Statistical Abstract* (see inside back cover).

Statistics in this edition are generally for the most recent year or period available by early June 2011. Each year over 1,400 tables and charts are reviewed and evaluated; new tables and charts of current interest are added, continuing series are updated, and less timely data are condensed or eliminated. Text notes and appendices are revised as appropriate. In addition two special features USA Statistics in Brief, and State Rankings can be found on our Web site: <http://www.census.gov/compendia/statab/>.

Changes in this edition—This year we have introduced 27 new tables covering a wide range of subject areas. These include new data from the 2010 Decennial Census, and the Survey of Business Owners, as well as changes to the organization and presentation of national health expenditures data from the U.S. Centers for Medicare and Medicaid. In addition, we have introduced new material on a wide variety of topics, such as, migration of college freshmen, hate crimes, judicial caseloads, hurricanes, suicides, congressional apportionment, minority-owned businesses, family farms, and horticulture sales. For a complete list of new tables, see "New Tables," p. xi.

Statistical Abstract on other media—The *Abstract* is available on the Internet and on CD-ROM. Both versions contain the same material as the book, except for a few copyrighted tables for which we did not receive permission to release in these formats. Our Internet site <http://www.census.gov/compendia/statab> contains this 2012 edition plus selected earlier editions in Adobe Acrobat .pdf format. The CD-ROM version and internet site also include spreadsheet files for each table in the book.

Statistics for states and metropolitan areas—Extensive data for the states and metropolitan areas of the United States can be found in the *State and Metropolitan Area Data Book: 2010.* This publication, as well as, selected rankings of the states and metropolitan areas, is also available on our Internet site at <http://www.census.gov/compendia/smadb>.

Statistics for counties and cities—Extensive data for counties can be found in the County and City Data Book: 2007. It features items covering everything from age and agriculture to retail trade and water use for all states and counties with U.S. totals for comparison. This publication is available on our Internet site at <www.census.gov/compendia/ccdb>.

The database for USA Counties features over 6,000 items. Files include data published for 2009 population estimates (latest) and many items from the 2000 and 2010 Census of Population and Housing, the American Community Survey 2005-2009, the 1990 census, the 1980 census and the 2007, 2002, 1997, 1992, 1987, 1982 and 1977 economic censuses.

Information in USA Counties is derived from the following general topics: Accommodation and Food Services, Age, Agriculture, Ancestry, Banking, Building Permits, Business, Civilian Labor Force, Crime, Earnings, Education, Elections, Employment, Government, Health, Households, Housing, Income, Manufacturing, Population, Poverty, Race and Hispanic or Latino Origin, Retail Trade, Social Programs, Taxes, Veterans, Vital Statistics, Water Use, and Wholesale Trade.

Files contain a collection of data from the U.S. Census Bureau and other federal agencies, such as the Bureau of Economic Analysis, the Bureau of Labor Statistics, the Federal Bureau of Investigation, the Internal Revenue Service, and the Social Security Administration.

For further information on the USA Counties database, please see <http://censtats.census.gov/usa/usa.shtml>.

Limitations of the data—The contents of this volume were taken from many sources. All data from censuses, surveys, and from administrative records are subject to error arising from a number of factors: Sampling variability (for statistics based on samples), reporting errors in the data for individual units, incomplete coverage, nonresponse, imputations, and processing error. (See also Appendix III, p. 919). The Census Bureau cannot accept responsibility for the accuracy or limitations of the data presented here, other than for those for which it collects. The responsibility for selection of the material and for proper presentation, however, rests with the Census Bureau.

For additional information on data presented—Please consult the source publications available in local libraries, on the Internet, or contact the agency indicated in the source notes. Contact the Census Bureau only if it is cited as the source.

Suggestions and comments—Users of the Statistical Abstract and its supplements (see inside back cover) are urged to make their data needs known for consideration in planning future editions. Suggestions and comments for improving coverage and presentation of data should be sent to the Director, U.S. Census Bureau, Washington, DC 20233; or e-mail us at <ACSD.US.Data@census.gov> or visit <ask.census.gov> for further information on the Abstract.

Contents

[Numbers following subjects are page numbers]

U.S. Census Bureau, Statistical Abstract of the United States: 2012

New Tables

Guide to Tabular Presentation

Example of Table Structure

Table 537. Seizure Statistics for Intellectual Property Rights (IPR) by Commodity and Trading Partner: 2009 and 2010

[In thousands of dollars (260,698 represents $260,698,000, except as indicated). Customs and Border Protection (CBP) is dedicated to protecting against the importation of goods which infringe/violate Intellectual Property Rights (IPR) by devoting substantial resources toward identifying and seizing shipments of infringing articles]

Commodity	2009	2010	Trading partner	2009	2010
Number of IPR Seizures	14,841	19,959	China	204,656	124,681
Total domestic value of IPR seizures [1]	260,698	188,125	Hong Kong	26,887	26,173
Footwear	99,779	45,750	India	3,047	1,571
Consumer electronics [2]	31,774	33,588	Taiwan	2,454	1,138
Handbags/wallets/backpacks	21,502	15,422	Korea, South	1,510	1,049
Wearing apparel	21,462	18,682	Jordan	(NA)	7,713
Watches /parts	15,534	7,848	Malaysia	(NA)	1,286
Computers/Technology Components	12,546	9,502	United Arab Emirates	(NA)	493
Media [3]	11,100	12,681	Canada	(NA)	609
Pharmaceuticals	11,058	5,662	Vietnam	604	742
All other commodities	19,941	23,377	All other countries	16,575	22,668

NA Not available. [1] Domestic value is the cost of the seized goods, plus the costs of shipping and importing the goods into the U.S. and an amount for profit. [2] Consumer electronics includes cell phones and accessories, radios, power strips, electrical tools and appliances. [3] Includes motion pictures on tape, laser disc, and DVD; interactive and computer software on CD-ROM and floppy discs; and music on CD or tape.

Source: U.S. Department of Homeland Security, Customs and Border Protection, "Import, Commercial Enforcement, Intellectual Property Rights, Seizure Statistics," <http://www.cbp.gov/xp/cgov/trade/priority_trade/ipr/pub/seizure/>.

Headnotes immediately below table titles provide information important for correct interpretation or evaluation of the table as a whole or for a major segment of it.

Footnotes below the bottom rule of tables give information relating to specific items or figures within the table.

Unit indicators show the *specified quantities* in which data items are presented. They are used for two primary reasons. Sometimes data are not available in absolute form and are estimates (as in the case of many surveys). In other cases we round the numbers in order to save space to show more data, as in the case above.

EXAMPLES OF UNIT INDICATOR INTERPRETATION FROM TABLE

Year	Item	Unit Indicator	Number shown	Multiplier
2009	Total domestic value of IPR seizures	$ Thousands	260,698	1,000

To Determine the Figure it is Necessary to Multiply the Number Shown by the Unit Indicator:

Value of seizures by Customs and Border Protection – 260,698 x $1,000 = $260,698,000 ($261 million)

When a table presents data with more than one unit indicator, they are found in the headnotes and column headings (Tables 2 and 26), spanner (Table 37), stub (Table 25), or unit column (Table 159). When the data in a table are shown in the same unit indicator, it is shown as the first part of the headnote (Table 2). If no unit indicator is shown, data presented are in absolute form (Table 1).

Vertical rules are used to separate independent sections of a table (Table 1), or in tables where the stub is continued into one or more additional columns (Table 2).

Averages—An average is a single number or value that is often used to represent the "typical value" of a group of numbers. It is regarded as a measure of "location" or "central tendency" of a group of numbers.

The *arithmetic mean* is the type of average used most frequently. It is derived by summing the individual item values of a particular group and dividing the total by the number of items. The arithmetic mean is often referred to as simply the "mean" or "average."

The *median* of a group of numbers is the middle number or value when each item in the group is arranged according to size (lowest to highest or visa versa); it generally has the same number of items above it as well as below it. If there is an even number of items in the group, the median is taken to be the average of the two middle numbers.

Per capita (or per person) quantities—a per capita figure represents an average computed for every person in a specified group (or population). It is derived by taking the total for an item (such as income,

xiii

U.S. Census Bureau, Statistical Abstract of the United States: 2012

taxes, or retail sales) and dividing it by the number of persons in the specified population.

Index numbers—An index number is the measure of difference or change, usually expressed as a percent, relating one quantity (the variable) of a specified kind to another quantity of the same kind. Index numbers are widely used to express changes in prices over periods of time, but may also be used to express differences between related subjects for a single point in time.

To compute a price index, a base year or period is selected. The base year price (of the commodity or service) is then designated as the base or reference price to which the prices for other years or periods are related. Many price indexes use the year 1982 as the base year; in tables this is shown as "1982 = 100." A method of expressing the price relationship is: The price of a set of one or more items for a related year (e.g. 1990) **divided by** the price of the same set of items for the base year (e.g. 1982). The result multiplied by 100 provides the index number. When 100 is subtracted from the index number, the result equals the percent change in price from the base year.

Average annual percent change— Unless otherwise stated in the *Abstract* (as in Section 1, Population), average annual percent change is computed by use of a *compound interest formula.* This formula assumes that the rate of change is constant throughout a specified compounding period (1 year for average annual rates of change). The formula is similar to that used to compute the balance of a savings account that receives compound interest. According to this formula, at the end of a compounding period the amount of accrued change (e.g., school enrollment or bank interest) is added to the amount that existed at the beginning of the period. As a result, over time (e.g., with each year or quarter), the same rate of change is applied to a larger and larger figure.

The *exponential formula,* which is based on continuous compounding, is often used to measure population change. It is preferred by population experts, because they view population and population-related subjects as changing without interruption, ever ongoing. Both exponential and compound interest formulas assume a constant rate of change. The former, however, applies the amount of change continuously to the base rather than at the end of each compounding period. When the average annual rates are small (e.g., less than 5 percent) both formulas give virtually the same results. For an explanation of these two formulas as they relate to population, see U.S. Census Bureau, *The Methods and Materials of Demography,* Vol. 2, 3d printing (rev.), 1975, pp. 372–381.

Current and constant dollars— Statistics in some tables in a number of sections are expressed in both current and constant dollars (see, e.g., Table 659 in Section 13, Income, Expenditures, Poverty, and Wealth). Current dollar figures reflect actual prices or costs prevailing during the specified year(s). Constant dollar figures are estimates representing an effort to remove the effects of price changes from statistical series reported in dollar terms. In general, constant dollar series are derived by dividing current dollar estimates by the appropriate price index for the appropriate period (e.g., the Consumer Price Index). The result is a series as it would presumably exist if prices were the same throughout, as in the base year—in other words, as if the dollar had constant purchasing power. Any changes in this constant dollar series would reflect only changes in real volume of output, income, expenditures, or other measure.

Explanation of Symbols

The following symbols, used in the tables throughout this book, are explained in condensed form in footnotes to the tables where they appear:

− Represents zero or rounds to less than half the unit of measurement shown.

B Base figure too small to meet statistical standards for reliability of a derived figure.

D Figure withheld to avoid disclosure pertaining to a specific organization or individual.

NA Data not enumerated, tabulated, or otherwise available separately.

S Figure does not meet publication standards for reasons other than that covered by symbol B, above.

X Figure not applicable because column heading and stub line make entry impossible, absurd, or meaningless.

Z Entry would amount to less than half the unit of measurement shown.

In many tables, details will not add to the totals shown because of rounding.

xiv

Telephone & Internet Contacts

To help Abstract users find more data and information about statistical publications, we are issuing this list of contacts for federal agencies with major statistical programs. The intent is to give a single, first-contact point-of-entry for users of statistics. These agencies will provide general information on their statistical programs and publications, as well as specific information on how to order their publications. We are also including the Internet (World Wide Web) addresses for many of these agencies. These URLs were current in July 2011.

Executive Office of the President

Office of Management and Budget
Administrator
Office of Information and Regulatory Affairs
Office of Management and Budget
725 17th Street, NW
Washington, DC 20503
Information: 202-395-3080
Internet address:
http://www.whitehouse.gov/omb

Department of Agriculture

Economic Research Service
Information Center
U.S. Department of Agriculture
1800 M Street, NW
Washington, DC 20036-5831
Information and Publications:
202-694-5050
Internet address:
http://www.ers.usda.gov/

National Agricultural Statistics Service
National Agricultural Statistics Service
USDA-NASS
1400 Independence Ave., SW
Washington, DC 20250
Information hotline: 1-800-727-9540
Internet address:
http://www.nass.usda.gov/

Department of Commerce

U.S. Census Bureau
Customer Services Branch
4600 Silver Hill Road
Washington, DC 20233
Information and Publications:
1-800-923-8282
Internet address:
http://www.census.gov/

Bureau of Economic Analysis
Bureau of Economic Analysis
1441 L Street, NW
Washington, DC 20230
Information and Publications:
202-606-9900
Internet address: http://www.bea.gov/

International Trade Administration
International Trade Administration
1401 Constitution Ave., NW
Washington, DC 20230
Information: 1-800-872-8723
Internet address: http://trade.gov/

National Oceanic and Atmospheric Administration
National Oceanic and Atmospheric Administration Central Library
U.S. Department of Commerce
1315 East-West Highway
SSMC3, 2nd Floor
Silver Spring, MD 20910
Library: 301-713-2600 x.124
Internet address:
http://www.lib.noaa.gov/

Department of Defense

Department of Defense
Office of Public Communication
1400 Defense Pentagon
Washington, DC 20301-1400
Information: 703-571-3343
Internet address:
http://www.defenselink.mil

Department of Education

National Library of Education
U.S. Department of Education
400 Maryland Avenue, SW
Washington, DC 20202
Education Information and Statistics:
1-800-872-5327
Education Publications: 1-877-433-7827
Internet address: http://www.ed.gov/

Department of Energy

Energy Information Administration
National Energy Information Center
Energy Information Administration
1000 Independence Ave., SW
Washington, DC 20585
Information and Publications:
202-586-8800
Internet address:
http://www.eia.doe.gov/

Department of Health and Human Services

Health Resources and Services Administration
HRSA Information Center
P.O. Box 2910
Merrifield, VA 22118
Information Center: 1-888-275-4772
Internet address: http://www.hrsa.gov/

Substance Abuse and Mental Health Services Administration
Substance Abuse and Mental Health Services Administration
1 Choke Cherry Road
Rockville, MD 20857
Information: 240-276-2130
Publications: 1-877-726-4727
Internet address:
http://www.samhsa.gov/

Centers for Disease Control and Prevention
Public Inquiries/MASO
1600 Clifton Road
Atlanta, GA 30333
Public Inquiries: 1-800-232-4636
Internet address: http://www.cdc.gov/

Centers for Medicare and Medicaid Services (CMS)
U.S. Department of Health and Human Services
7500 Security Boulevard
Baltimore, MD 21244
Information: 1-877-267-2323
Internet address:
http://www.cms.hhs.gov/

National Center for Health Statistics
National Center for Health Statistics
3311 Toledo Road
Hyattsville, MD 20782
Information: 1-800-232-4636
Internet address:
http://www.cdc.gov/nchs

Department of Homeland Security

Office of Public Affairs
245 Murray Lane, SW, Bldg. 410
Washington, DC 20528
Information and Publications:
 202-282-8010
Internet address: http://www.dhs.gov

Department of Housing and Urban Development

Office of the Assistant Secretary for Community Planning and Development
4517th St., SW
Washington, DC 20410
Information: 202-708-1112
Publications: 1-800-767-7468
Internet address: http://www.hud.gov/

Department of the Interior

U.S. Geological Survey
USGS National Center
12201 Sunrise Valley Drive
Reston, VA 20192
Information and Publications:
 1-888-275-8747
Internet address for minerals:
http://minerals.usgs.gov/
Internet address for other materials:
http://ask.usgs.gov/

Department of Justice

Bureau of Justice Statistics
Statistics Division
810 7th Street, NW
Washington, DC 20531
Information and Publications:
1-800-851-3420
Internet address:
http://www.ojp.usdoj.gov/bjs/

National Criminal Justice Reference Service
P.O. Box 6000
Rockville, MD 20849-6000
Publications: 1-800-851-3420
Internet address: http://www.ncjrs.gov/

Federal Bureau of Investigation
Federal Bureau of Investigations
J. Edgar Hoover Building
935 Pennsylvania Avenue, NW
Washington, DC 20535-0001
Information: 202-324-3000
Internet address: http://www.fbi.gov/

Department of Labor

Bureau of Labor Statistics
Office of Publications and Special Studies Services
Bureau of Labor Statistics
Postal Square Building
2 Mass. Ave., NE
Washington, DC 20212-0001
Information and Publications:
 202-691-5200
Internet address: http://www.bls.gov/

Employment and Training Administration
U.S. Department of Labor
Francis Perkins Building
200 Constitution Ave., NW
Washington, DC 20210
Information and Publications:
 1-877-872-5627
Internet address: http://www.doleta.gov/

Department of Transportation

Federal Aviation Administration
800 Independence Ave., SW
Washington, DC 20591
Information and Publications:
1-866-835-5322
Internet address: http://www.faa.gov/

Bureau of Transportation Statistics
  1200 New Jersey Avenue, SE
  Washington, DC 20590
  Products and Statistical Information:
  1-800-853-1351
  Internet address: http://www.bts.gov/

Federal Highway Administration
  Office of Public Affairs
  U.S. Department of Transportation
  1200 New Jersey Avenue, SE
  Washington, DC 20590
  Information: 202-366-4000
  Internet address:
  http://www.fhwa.dot.gov/

National Highway Traffic Safety
  Administration
  Office of Public & Consumer Affairs
  1200 New Jersey Avenue, SE – West
  Building
  Washington, DC 20590
  Information and Publications:
  1-888-327-4236
  Internet address:
  http://www.nhtsa.dot.gov/

Department of the Treasury
Internal Revenue Service
  Statistics of Income Division
  Internal Revenue Service
  P. O. Box 2608
  Washington, DC 20013-2608
  Information and Publications:
  202-874-0410
  Internet address:
  http://www.irs.gov/taxstats/

Department of Veterans Affairs
Department of Veterans Affairs
  Office of Public Affairs
  810 Vermont Ave., NW
  Washington, DC 20420
  Information: 202-273-6000
  Internet address: http://www.va.gov/

Independent Agencies
Administrative Office of the U.S. Courts
  Office of Public Affairs
  1 Columbus Circle, NE
  Washington, DC 20544
  Information: 202-502-2600
  Internet address:
  http://www.uscourts.gov/

*Board of Governors of the Federal Reserve
  System*
  Division of Research and Statistics
  Federal Reserve System
  20th & Constitution Avenue, NW
  Washington, DC 20551
  Information: 202-452-3000
  Publications: 202-452-3245
  Internet address:
  http://www.federalreserve.gov/

Environmental Protection Agency
  Environmental Protection Agency
  Ariel Rios Building
  1200 Pennsylvania Ave., NW
  Washington, DC 20460
  Publications: 1-800-490-9198
  Internet address: http://www.epa.gov/

National Science Foundation
  Office of Legislation and Public Affairs
  National Science Foundation
  4201 Wilson Boulevard
  Arlington, Virginia 22230
  Information: 703-292-5111
  Publications: 703-292-7827
  Internet address: http://www.nsf.gov/

Securities and Exchange Commission
  Office of Public Affairs
  Securities and Exchange Commission
  100 F Street, NE
  Washington, DC 20549
  Information: 202-942-8088
  Publications: 202-551-4040
  Internet address: http://www.sec.gov/

Social Security Administration
  Social Security Administration
  Office of Public Inquiries
  6401 Security Boulevard
  Baltimore, MD 21235
  Information and Publications:
  1-800-772-1213
  Internet Address:
  http://www.socialsecurity.gov/

Section 1
Population

This section presents statistics on the growth, distribution, and characteristics of the U.S. population. The principal source of these data is the U.S. Census Bureau, which conducts a decennial census of population, a monthly population survey, a program of population estimates and projections, and a number of other periodic surveys.

Decennial censuses—

The U.S. Constitution provides for a census of the population every 10 years, primarily to establish a basis for apportionment of members of the House of Representatives among the states. For over a century after the first census in 1790, the census organization was a temporary one, created only for each decennial census. In 1902, the Census Bureau was established as a permanent federal agency, responsible for enumerating the population and also for compiling statistics on other population and housing characteristics.

Historically, the enumeration of the population has been a complete (100 percent) count. That is, an attempt is made to account for every person, for each person's residence, and for other characteristics (sex, age, family relationships, etc.). Since the 1940 census, in addition to the complete count information, some data have been obtained from representative samples of the population. In the 1990 and 2000 censuses, variable sampling rates were employed. For most of the country, 1 in every 6 households (about 17 percent) received the long form or sample questionnaire; in governmental units estimated to have fewer than 2,500 inhabitants, every other household (50 percent) received the sample questionnaire to enhance the reliability of sample data for small areas. Exact agreement is not to be expected between sample data and the 100-percent count. For Census 2010, only the short form questionnaire was used. Sample data may be used with confidence where large numbers are involved and assumed to indicate trends and relationships where small numbers are involved.

Current Population Survey (CPS)—This is a monthly nationwide survey of a scientifically selected sample representing the noninstitutionalized civilian population. The sample is located in 824 areas with coverage in every state and the District of Columbia and is subject to sampling error. At the present time, about 60,000 occupied households are eligible for interview every month; of these, about 8 percent are, for various reasons, unavailable for interview.

While the primary purpose of the CPS is to obtain monthly statistics on the labor force, it also serves as a vehicle for inquiries on other subjects. Using CPS data, the Census Bureau issues a series of publications under the general title of *Current Population Reports.*

Estimates of population characteristics based on the CPS will not agree with the counts from the census because the CPS and the census use different procedures for collecting and processing the data for racial groups, the Hispanic population, and other topics. Caution should also be used when comparing estimates for various years because of the periodic introduction of changes into the CPS. Beginning in January 1994, a number of changes were introduced into the CPS that affect all data comparisons with prior years. These changes included the results of a major redesign of the survey questionnaire and collection methodology and the introduction of 1990 census population controls, adjusted for the estimated undercount. Beginning with the 2001 CPS Annual Demographic Supplement, the independent estimates used as control totals for the CPS are based on civilian population benchmarks consistent with Census 2000. In March 2002, the sample size of the Annual Demographic Supplement was increased to approximately 78,000. In 2003 the name of the March supplement was changed to Annual Social and Economic Supplement. These changes in population controls had relatively little impact on derived measures such as means, medians, and percent distribution, but did have a significant impact on levels.

American Community Survey (ACS)— This is a nationwide survey to obtain data about demographic, social, economic, and housing information of people, households, and housing units. The survey collects the same type of information that has been collected from the long-form questionnaire of Census 2000, which the American Community Survey has replaced. Beginning 2006, the estimates include the household population and the population living in institutions, college dormitories, and other group quarters.

Population estimates and projections—Estimates of the United States population are derived by updating the resident population enumerated in Census 2000 with information on the components of population change: births, deaths, and net international migration. The April 1, 2000, population used in these estimates reflects modifications to the Census 2000 population as documented in the Count Question Resolution program.

Registered births and deaths are estimated from data supplied by the National Center for Health Statistics. The net international migration component consists of four parts: (1) the net international migration of the foreign born, (2) the net migration of natives to and from the United States, (3) the net migration between the United States and Puerto Rico, and (4) the net overseas movement of the Armed Forces population. Data from the ACS are used to estimate the annual net migration of the foreign-born population. Estimates of the net migration of natives and net migration between Puerto Rico and the United States prior to 2005 are derived from the Demographic Analysis and Population Estimates (DAPE) project (see Population Division Working Paper Series, No. 63 and No. 64). Estimates for net migration between Puerto Rico and the U.S. for 2005 and later years are derived from the ACS and the Puerto Rico Community Survey. Estimates of the net overseas movement of the Armed Forces are derived from data collected by the Defense Manpower Data Center.

Estimates for state and county areas are based on the same components of change data and sources as the national estimates with the addition of net internal migration. Estimates of net internal migration are derived from federal income tax returns from the Internal Revenue Service, group quarters data from the Federal-State Cooperative Program, and Medicare data from the Centers for Medicare and Medicaid Services.

The population by age for April 1, 1990, reflects modifications to the 1990 census data counts. The review of detailed 1990 information indicated that respondents tended to report age as of the date of completion of the questionnaire, not as of April 1, 1990. In addition, there may have been a tendency for respondents to round up their age if they were close to having a birthday. A detailed explanation of the age modification procedure appears in 1990 Census of Population and Housing, Data Paper Listing CPH-L74.

Population estimates and projections are available on the Census Bureau Web site, see <http://www.census.gov>. These estimates and projections are consistent with official decennial census figures with no adjustment for estimated net census coverage. However, the categories for these estimates and projections by race have been modified and are not comparable to the census race categories (see section below under "Race"). For details on methodology, see the sources cited below the individual tables.

Immigration—Immigration (migration to a country) is one component of international migration; the other component is emigration (migration *from* a country). In its simplest form, international migration is defined as any movement across a national border. In the United States, federal statistics on international migration are produced primarily by the U.S. Census Bureau and the Office of Immigration Statistics of the U.S. Department of Homeland Security (DHS).

The Census Bureau collects data used to estimate international migration through its decennial censuses and numerous surveys of the U.S. population.

2 Population

The Office of Immigration Statistics publishes immigration data in annual flow reports and the *Yearbook of Immigration Statistics*. Data for these publications are collected from several administrative data sources including the DS-230 Application for Immigrant Visa and Alien Registration (U.S. Department of State) for new arrivals, and the I-485 Application to Register Permanent Residence or Adjust Status (U.S. Citizenship and Immigration Services—USCIS) for persons adjusting immigrant status.

An immigrant, or legal permanent resident, is a foreign national who has been granted lawful permanent residence in the United States. New arrivals are foreign nationals living abroad who apply for an immigrant visa at a consular office of the Department of State, while individuals adjusting status are already living in the United States and file an application for adjustment of status to lawful permanent residence with USCIS. Individuals adjusting status include refugees, asylees, and various classes of nonimmigrants. A refugee is an alien outside the United States who is unable or unwilling to return to his or her country of origin because of persecution or a well-founded fear of persecution. Asylees must meet the same criteria as refugees, but are located in the United States or at a port of entry. After 1 year of residence, refugees and asylees are eligible to adjust to legal permanent resident status. Nonimmigrants are foreign nationals granted temporary entry into the United States. The major activities for which nonimmigrant admission is authorized include temporary visits for business or pleasure, academic or vocational study, temporary employment, and to act as a representative of a foreign government or international organization. DHS collects information on the characteristics of a proportion of nonimmigrant admissions, those recorded on the I-94 Arrival/Departure Record.

U.S. immigration law gives preferential immigration status to persons with a close family relationship with a U.S. citizen or legal permanent resident, persons with needed job skills, persons who qualify as refugees or asylees, and persons who are from countries with relatively low levels of immigration to the United States. Immigration to the United States can be divided into two general categories: (1) classes of admission subject to the annual worldwide limitation and (2) classes of admission exempt from worldwide limitations. Numerical limits are imposed on visas issued and not on admissions. In 2008, the annual limit for preference visas subject to limitation was 388,704, which included a family-sponsored preference limit of 226,000 and an employment-based preference limit of 162,704. Classes of admission exempt from the worldwide limitation include immediate relatives of U.S. citizens, refugees and asylees adjusting to permanent residence, and other various classes of special immigrants.

Metropolitan and micropolitan areas—The U.S. Office of Management and Budget (OMB) defines metropolitan and micropolitan statistical areas according to published standards that are applied to Census Bureau data. The general concept of a metropolitan or micropolitan statistical area is that of a core area containing a substantial population nucleus, together with adjacent communities having a high degree of economic and social integration with that core. Currently defined metropolitan and micropolitan statistical areas are based on application of 2000 standards to 2000 decennial census data as updated by application of those standards to more recent Census Bureau population estimates. The term "metropolitan area" (MA) was adopted in 1990 and referred collectively to metropolitan statistical areas (MSAs), consolidated metropolitan statistical areas (CMSAs), and primary metropolitan statistical areas (PMSAs). The term "core-based statistical area" (CBSA) became effective in 2003 and refers collectively to metropolitan and micropolitan statistical areas. For descriptive details and a list of titles and components of metropolitan and micropolitan statistical areas, see Appendix II.

Urban and rural—For Census 2010, the Census Bureau classified as urban all territory, population, and housing units located within urbanized areas (UAs) and urban clusters (UCs). A UA consists of densely settled territory that contains 50,000 or more people, while a UC consists of densely settled territory with at least 2,500 people but fewer than 50,000 people. From the 1950 census through the 1990 census, the urban population consisted of all people living in UAs and most places outside of UAs with a census population of 2,500 or more.

UAs and UCs encompass territory that generally consists of:

- A cluster of one or more block groups or census blocks each of which has a population density of at least 1,000 people per square mile at the time.

- Surrounding block groups and census blocks each of which has a population density of at least 500 people per square mile at the time.

- Less densely settled blocks that form enclaves or indentations, or are used to connect discontiguous areas with qualifying densities.

They also may include an airport located adjacent to qualifying densely settled area if it has an annual enplanement (aircraft boarding) of at least 10,000 people. "Rural" for Census 2010 consists of all territory, population, and housing units located outside of UAs and UCs. Prior to Census 2000, rural consisted of all territory, population, and housing outside of UAs and outside of other places designated as "urban." For Census 2010, many more geographic entities, including metropolitan areas, counties, and places, contain both urban and rural territory, population, and housing units.

Residence—In determining residence, the Census Bureau counts each person as an inhabitant of a usual place of residence (i.e., the place where one lives and sleeps most of the time). While this place is not necessarily a person's legal residence or voting residence, the use of these different bases of classification would produce the same results in the vast majority of cases.

Race—For the 1990 census, the Census Bureau collected and published racial statistics as outlined in Statistical Policy Directive No. 15 issued by the OMB. This directive provided standards on ethnic and racial categories for statistical reporting to be used by all federal agencies. According to the directive, the basic racial categories were American Indian or Alaska Native, Asian or Pacific Islander, Black, and White. (The directive identified Hispanic origin as an ethnicity.) The question on race for Census 2000 was different from the one for the 1990 census in several ways. Most significantly, respondents were given the option of selecting one or more race categories to indicate their racial identities. Because of these changes, the Census 2000 data on race are not directly comparable with data from the 1990 census or earlier censuses. Caution must be used when interpreting changes in the racial composition of the United States population over time. Census 2010 adheres to the federal standards for collecting and presenting data on race and ethnicity as established by the OMB in October 1997. Starting with Census 2000, the OMB requires federal agencies to use a minimum of five race categories: White, Black or African American, American Indian or Alaska Native, Asian, and Native Hawaiian or Other Pacific Islander. Additionally, to collect data on individuals of mixed race parentage, respondents were allowed to select one or more races. For respondents unable to identify with any of these five race categories, the OMB approved and included a sixth category—"Some other race" on the Census 2000 questionnaire. The Census 2000 question on race included 15 separate response categories and three areas where respondents could write in a more specific race group. The response categories and write-in answers can be combined to create the five minimum OMB race categories plus "Some other race." People who responded to the question on race by indicating only one race are referred to as the *race alone* population, or the group that reported only one race category. Six categories make up this population: White alone, Black or African American alone, American Indian and Alaska Native alone, Asian alone, Native Hawaiian and Other Pacific Islander alone, and Some other race alone. Individuals who chose more than one of the six race categories are referred to as the *Two or More Races* population, or as the group that reported more than one race. Additionally, respondents who reported one race together with those who reported the same race plus one or more other races are combined to create the race alone or in *combination*

4 Population

categories. For example, the *White alone or in combination group* consists of those respondents who reported only White or who reported White combined with one or more other race groups, such as "White and Black or African American," or "White and Asian and American Indian and Alaska Native." Another way to think of the group who reported White alone or in combination is as the total number of people who identified entirely or partially as White. This group is also described as people who reported White, whether or not they reported any other race.

The *alone or in combination* categories are tallies of *responses* rather than *respondents*. That is, the alone or in combination categories are not mutually exclusive. Individuals who reported two races were counted in two separate and distinct alone or in combination race categories, while those who reported three races were counted in three categories, and so on. Consequently, the sum of all alone or in combination categories equals the number of races reported, which exceeds the total population.

The concept of race, as used by the Census Bureau, reflects self-identification by people according to the race or races with which they most closely identify. These categories are sociopolitical constructs and should not be interpreted as being scientific or anthropological in nature. Furthermore, the race categories include both racial and national-origin groups. Additionally, data are available for the American Indian and Alaska Native tribes. A detailed explanation of race can be found at <http://www.census.gov /prod/cen2010/doc/sf1.pdf>.

Data for the population by race for April 1, 2000, (shown in Tables 6, 10, and 11) are modified counts and are not comparable to Census 2000 race categories. These numbers were computed using Census 2000 data by race and had been modified to be consistent with the 1997 OMB's "Revisions to the Standards for the Classification of Federal Data on Race and Ethnicity," (Federal Register Notice, Vol. 62, No 210, October 1997). A detailed explanation of the race modification procedure appears at <http://www.census .gov/popest/archives/files/MRSF-01-US1 .html>.

In the CPS and other household sample surveys in which data are obtained through personal interview, respondents are asked to classify their race as: (1) White; (2) Black, African American, or Negro; (3) American Indian or Alaska Native; (4) Asian; or (5) Native Hawaiian or Other Pacific Islander. Beginning January 2003, respondents were allowed to report more than one race to indicate their mixed racial heritage.

Hispanic population—The Census Bureau collected data on the Hispanic-origin population in the 2000 and 2010 censuses by using a self-identification question. Persons of Spanish/Hispanic/ Latino origin are those who classified themselves in one of the specific Hispanic origin categories listed on the questionnaire—Mexican, Puerto Rican, Cuban, as well as those who indicated that they were of Other Spanish/ Hispanic/Latino origin (persons whose origins are from Spain, the Spanish-speaking countries of Central or South America, or the Dominican Republic).

In the CPS, information on Hispanic persons is gathered by using a self-identification question. The respondents are first asked whether or not they are of Hispanic, Spanish, or Latino origin and based on their response are further classified into the following categories: Mexican or Mexican American or Chicano; Puerto Rican; Cuban; Central or South American; or Other Hispanic, Spanish, or Latino origin group.

Traditional and current data collection and classification treat race and Hispanic origin as two separate and distinct concepts in accordance with guidelines from the OMB. Race and Hispanic origin are two separate concepts in the federal statistical system. People who are Hispanic may be any race and people in each race group may be either Hispanic or Not Hispanic. Also, each person has two attributes, their race (or races) and whether or not they are Hispanic. The overlap of race and Hispanic origin is the main comparability issue. For example, Black Hispanics (Hispanic Blacks) are included in both the number of Blacks and in the number of Hispanics. For further information, see <http://www.census.gov/population /www/socdemo/compraceho.html>.

Foreign-born and native populations—The Census Bureau separates the U.S. resident population into two groups based on whether or not a person was a U.S. citizen or U.S. national at the time of birth. Anyone born in the United States, Puerto Rico, or a U.S. Island Area (such as Guam), or born abroad to a U.S. citizen parent is a U.S. citizen at the time of birth and consequently included in the *native population.* The term *foreign-born population* refers to anyone who is not a U.S. citizen or a U.S. national at birth. This includes naturalized U.S. citizens, legal permanent resident aliens (immigrants), temporary migrants (such as foreign students), humanitarian migrants (such as refugees), and people illegally present in the United States. The Census Bureau provides a variety of demographic, social, economic, geographic, and housing information on the foreign-born population in the United States at <http://www.census.gov/population /www/socdemo/foreign/>.

Mobility status—The U.S. population is classified according to mobility status on the basis of a comparison between the place of residence of each individual at the time of the survey or census and the place of residence at a specified earlier date. Nonmovers are all persons who were living in the same house or apartment at the end of the period as at the beginning of the period. Movers are all persons who were living in a different house or apartment at the end of the period than at the beginning of the period. Movers are further classified as to whether they were living in the same or different county, state, region, or were movers from abroad. Movers from abroad include all persons whose place of residence was outside the United States (including Puerto Rico, other U.S. Island Area, or a foreign country) at the beginning of the period.

Living arrangements—Living arrangements refer to residency in households or in group quarters. A "household" comprises all persons who occupy a "housing unit," that is, a house, an apartment or other group of rooms, or a single room that constitutes "separate living quarters." A household includes the related family members and all the unrelated persons,

if any, such as lodgers, foster children, or employees who share the housing unit. A person living alone or a group of unrelated persons sharing the same housing unit is also counted as a household. See text, Section 20, Construction and Housing, for definition of housing unit.

All persons not living in housing units are classified as living in group quarters. These individuals may be institutionalized, e.g., under care or custody in juvenile facilities, jails, correctional centers, hospitals, or nursing homes; or they may be residents in noninstitutional group quarters such as college dormitories, group homes, or military barracks.

Householder—The householder is the person in whose name the home is owned or rented. If a home is owned or rented jointly by a married couple, either the husband or the wife may be listed first.

Family—The term family refers to a group of two or more persons related by birth, marriage, or adoption and residing together in a household. A family includes among its members the householder.

Subfamily—A subfamily consists of a married couple and their children, if any, or one parent with one or more never-married children under 18 years old living in a household. Subfamilies are divided into "related" and "unrelated" subfamilies. A related subfamily is related to, but does not include, the householder or the spouse of the householder. Members of a related subfamily are also members of the family with whom they live. The number of related subfamilies, therefore, is not included in the count of families. An unrelated subfamily may include persons such as guests, lodgers, or resident employees and their spouses and/or children; none of whom is related to the householder.

Married couple—A married couple is defined as a husband and wife living together in the same household, with or without children and other relatives.

Statistical reliability—For a discussion of statistical collection and estimation, sampling procedures, and measures of statistical reliability applicable to Census Bureau data, see Appendix III.

Percent Change in Population for States: April 1, 2000 to April 1, 2010

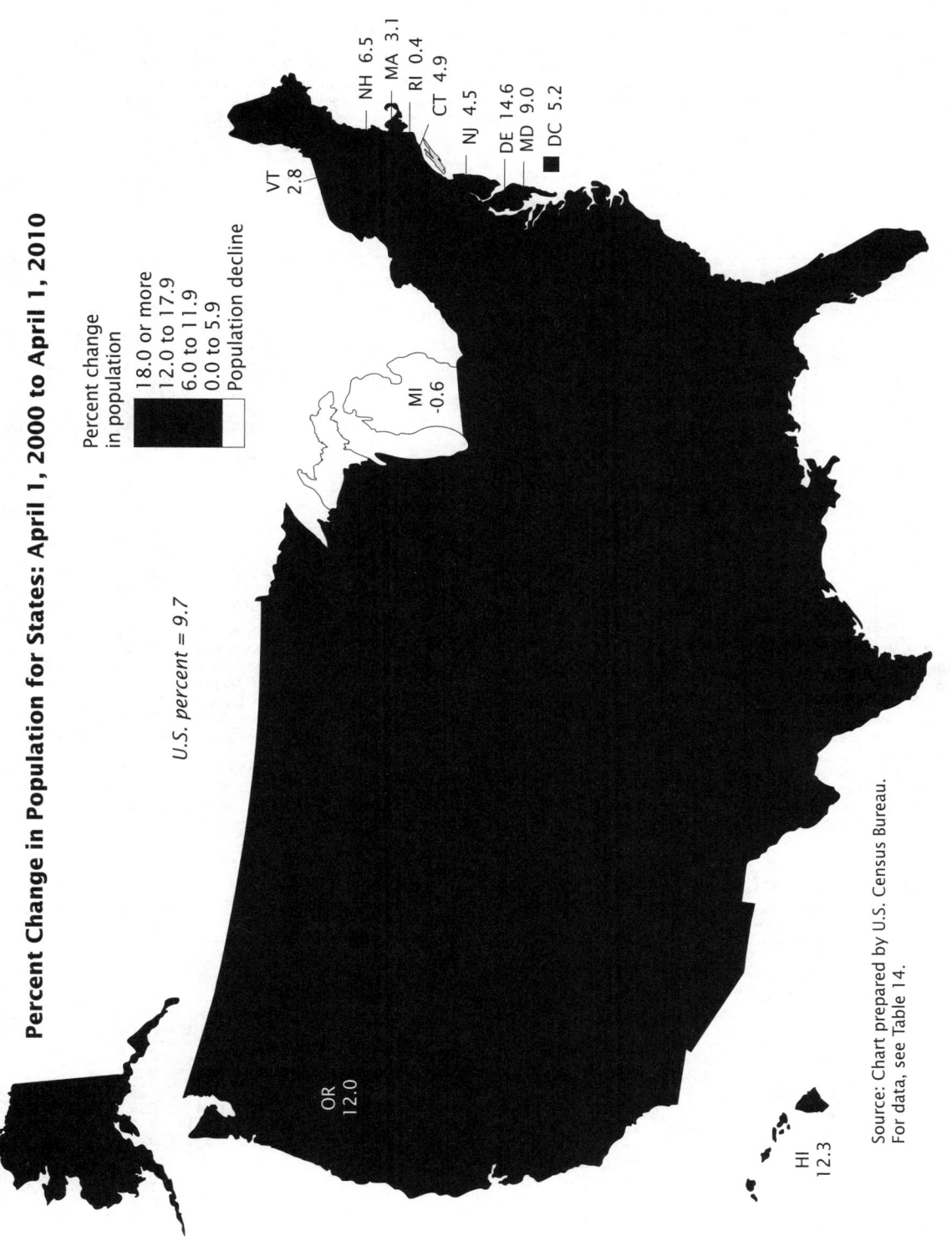

Percent change
in population

- 18.0 or more
- 12.0 to 17.9
- 6.0 to 11.9
- 0.0 to 5.9
- Population decline

U.S. percent = 9.7

NH 6.5
MA 3.1
RI 0.4
CT 4.9
NJ 4.5
DE 14.6
MD 9.0
DC 5.2

VT 2.8

MI -0.6

OR 12.0

HI 12.3

Source: Chart prepared by U.S. Census Bureau.
For data, see Table 14.

U.S. Census Bureau, Statistical Abstract of the United States: 2012

Table 1. Population and Area: 1790 to 2010

[Area figures represent area on indicated date including in some cases considerable areas not then organized or settled, and not covered by the census. Area data include Alaska beginning in 1870 and Hawaii beginning in 1900. Total area figures for 1790 to 1970 have been recalculated on the basis of the remeasurement of states and counties for the 1980 census, but not on the basis of subsequent censuses. The land and water area figures for past censuses have not been adjusted and are not strictly comparable with the total area data for comparable dates because the land areas were derived from different base data, and these values are known to have changed with the construction of reservoirs, draining of lakes, etc. Density figures are based on land area measurements as reported in earlier censuses]

Census date	Resident population				Area (square miles)		
	Number	Per square mile of land area	Increase over preceding census		Total	Land	Water [1]
			Number	Percent			
1790 (Aug. 2)	3,929,214	4.5	(X)	(X)	891,364	864,746	24,065
1800 (Aug. 4)	5,308,483	6.1	1,379,269	35.1	891,364	864,746	24,065
1810 (Aug. 6)	7,239,881	4.3	1,931,398	36.4	1,722,685	1,681,828	34,175
1820 (Aug. 7)	9,638,453	5.5	2,398,572	33.1	1,792,552	1,749,462	38,544
1830 (June 1)	12,866,020	7.4	3,227,567	33.5	1,792,552	1,749,462	38,544
1840 (June 1)	17,069,453	9.8	4,203,433	32.7	1,792,552	1,749,462	38,544
1850 (June 1)	23,191,876	7.9	6,122,423	35.9	2,991,655	2,940,042	52,705
1860 (June 1)	31,443,321	10.6	8,251,445	35.6	3,021,295	2,969,640	52,747
1870 (June 1)	[2] 39,818,449	[2] 11.2	8,375,128	26.6	3,612,299	3,540,705	68,082
1880 (June 1)	50,189,209	14.2	10,370,760	26.0	3,612,299	3,540,705	68,082
1890 (June 1)	62,979,766	17.8	12,790,557	25.5	3,612,299	3,540,705	68,082
1900 (June 1)	76,212,168	21.5	13,232,402	21.0	3,618,770	3,547,314	67,901
1910 (Apr. 15)	92,228,496	26.0	16,016,328	21.0	3,618,770	3,547,045	68,170
1920 (Jan. 1)	106,021,537	29.9	13,793,041	15.0	3,618,770	3,546,931	68,284
1930 (Apr. 1)	123,202,624	34.7	17,181,087	16.2	3,618,770	3,554,608	60,607
1940 (Apr. 1)	132,164,569	37.2	8,961,945	7.3	3,618,770	3,554,608	60,607
1950 (Apr. 1)	151,325,798	42.6	19,161,229	14.5	3,618,770	3,552,206	63,005
1960 (Apr. 1)	179,323,175	50.6	27,997,377	18.5	3,618,770	3,540,911	74,212
1970 (Apr. 1)	203,302,031	57.5	23,978,856	13.4	3,618,770	3,536,855	78,444
1980 (Apr. 1)	[3] 226,542,199	64.0	23,240,168	11.4	3,618,770	3,539,289	79,481
1990 (Apr. 1)	[4] 248,718,302	70.3	22,176,103	9.8	[5] 3,717,796	3,536,278	[5] 181,518
2000 (Apr. 1)	[6] 281,424,603	79.6	32,706,301	13.1	3,794,083	3,537,438	256,645
2010 (Apr. 1)	308,745,538	87.4	27,320,935	9.7	3,796,742	3,531,905	264,837

X Not applicable. [1] Data for 1790 to 1980 cover inland water only. Data for 1990 comprise Great Lakes, inland, and coastal water. Data for 2000 and 2010 comprise Great Lakes, inland, territorial, and coastal water. [2] Revised to include adjustments for underenumeration in southern states; unrevised number is 38,558,371 (10.9 per square mile). [3] Total population count has been revised since the 1980 census publications. Numbers by age, race, Hispanic origin, and sex have not been corrected. [4] The April 1, 1990, census count includes count question resolution corrections processed through December 1997, and does not include adjustments for census coverage errors. [5] Data reflect corrections made after publication of the results. [6] Reflects modifications to the Census 2000 population as documented in the Count Question Resolution program.

Source: U.S. Census Bureau, 2010 Census, National Summary File of Redistricting Data; 2000 Census of Population and Housing, *Population and Housing Counts*, Series PHC-3-1, United States Summary; *Notes and Errata, 2000* SF/01-ER, <http://www.census.gov/prod/cen2000/notes/errata.pdf>; *Areas of the United States: 1940*; Area data for 1990: unpublished data from TIGER ®; and Davis, Warren, personal correspondence, U.S. Census Bureau, June 23, 2006.

Table 2. Population: 1960 to 2009

[In thousands, except as indicated (180,671 represents 180,671,000). Estimates as of July 1. Civilian population excludes Armed Forces. For basis of estimates, see text, this section]

Year	Resident population, plus Armed Forces overseas		Resident population	Civilian population	Year	Resident population, including Armed Forces overseas		Resident population	Civilian population
	Population	Percent change [1]				Population	Percent change [1]		
1960	180,671	1.60	179,979	178,140	1989	247,342	0.95	246,819	245,131
1965	194,303	1.26	193,526	191,605	1990	250,132	1.13	249,623	247,983
1970	205,052	1.17	203,984	201,895	1991	253,493	1.34	252,981	251,370
1971	207,661	1.27	206,827	204,866	1992	256,894	1.34	256,514	254,929
1972	209,896	1.08	209,284	207,511	1993	260,255	1.31	259,919	258,446
1973	211,909	0.96	211,357	209,600	1994	263,436	1.22	263,126	261,714
1974	213,854	0.92	213,342	211,636	1995	266,557	1.18	266,278	264,927
1975	215,973	0.99	215,465	213,789	1996	269,667	1.17	269,394	268,108
1976	218,035	0.95	217,563	215,894	1997	272,912	1.20	272,647	271,394
1977	220,239	1.01	219,760	218,106	1998	276,115	1.17	275,854	274,633
1978	222,585	1.06	222,095	220,467	1999	279,295	1.15	279,040	277,841
1979	225,055	1.11	224,567	222,969	2000	282,385	1.11	282,172	280,927
1980	227,726	1.19	227,225	225,621	2001	285,309	1.04	285,082	283,845
1981	229,966	0.98	229,466	227,818	2002	288,105	0.98	287,804	286,537
1982	232,188	0.97	231,664	229,995	2003	290,820	0.94	290,326	289,107
1983	234,307	0.91	233,792	232,097	2004	293,463	0.91	293,046	291,785
1984	236,348	0.87	235,825	234,110	2005	296,186	0.93	295,753	294,562
1985	238,466	0.90	237,924	236,219	2006	298,996	0.95	298,593	297,413
1986	240,651	0.92	240,133	238,412	2007	302,004	1.01	301,580	300,425
1987	242,804	0.89	242,289	240,550	2008	304,798	0.93	304,375	303,202
1988	245,021	0.91	244,499	242,817	2009	307,439	0.87	307,007	305,782

[1] Percent change from immediate preceding year.

Source: U.S. Census Bureau, Population Division, 1960 to 1979: Current Population Reports P25-802 and P25-917; 1980 to 1989: "Monthly Estimates of the United States Population: April 1, 1980 to July 1, 1999, with Short-Term Projections to November 1, 2000," January 2001, <http://www.census.gov/popest/archives/1990s/nat-total.txt>; 1990 to 1999: "National Intercensal Estimates (1990–2000)," August 2004, <http://www.census.gov/popest/archives/EST90INTERCENSAL/US-EST90INT-datasets .html>; 2000 to 2009: "Monthly Population Estimates for the United States: April 1, 2000 to December 1, 2009 (NA-EST2009-01)," December 2009, <http://www.census.gov/popest/national/tables/NA-EST2009-01.xls>.

Table 3. Resident Population Projections: 2010 to 2050

[In thousands, except as indicated (310,233 represents 310,233,000). As of July 1. Projections are based on assumptions about future births, deaths, and net international migration. Data do not reflect results of 2010 Census. More information on methodology and assumptions is available at <http://www.census.gov/population/www/projections/methodstatement.html>]

Year	Population	Percent change [1]	Year	Population	Percent change [1]	Year	Population	Percent change [1]
2010......	310,233	1.0	2024......	354,235	0.9	2038......	399,184	0.8
2011......	313,232	1.0	2025......	357,452	0.9	2039......	402,415	0.8
2012......	316,266	1.0	2026......	360,667	0.9	2040......	405,655	0.8
2013......	319,330	1.0	2027......	363,880	0.9	2041......	408,906	0.8
2014......	322,423	1.0	2028......	367,090	0.9	2042......	412,170	0.8
2015......	325,540	1.0	2029......	370,298	0.9	2043......	415,448	0.8
2016......	328,678	1.0	2030......	373,504	0.9	2044......	418,743	0.8
2017......	331,833	1.0	2031......	376,708	0.9	2045......	422,059	0.8
2018......	335,005	1.0	2032......	379,912	0.9	2046......	425,395	0.8
2019......	338,190	1.0	2033......	383,117	0.8	2047......	428,756	0.8
2020......	341,387	0.9	2034......	386,323	0.8	2048......	432,143	0.8
2021......	344,592	0.9	2035......	389,531	0.8	2049......	435,560	0.8
2022......	347,803	0.9	2036......	392,743	0.8	2050......	439,010	0.8
2023......	351,018	0.9	2037......	395,961	0.8			

[1] Percent change from immediate preceding year. 2010, change from 2009.
Source: U.S. Census Bureau, Population Division, "2008 National Population Projections," August 2008, <http://www.census.gov/population/www/projections/2008projections.html>.

Table 4. Components of Population Change: 2000 to 2009

[In thousands, except as indicated (281,425 represents 281,425,000). Resident population]

Period	Population as of beginning of period	Net increase [1]		Births	Deaths	Net international migration [3]	Population as of end of period
		Total	Percent [2]				
April 1, 2000 to July 1, 2000 [4].....	281,425	747	0.3	989	561	319	282,172
July 1, 2001 to July 1, 2002......	285,082	2,722	1.0	4,007	2,430	1,078	287,804
July 1, 2002 to July 1, 2003......	287,804	2,523	0.9	4,053	2,423	822	290,326
July 1, 2003 to July 1, 2004......	290,326	2,719	0.9	4,113	2,450	986	293,046
July 1, 2004 to July 1, 2005......	293,046	2,707	0.9	4,121	2,433	948	295,753
July 1, 2005 to July 1, 2006......	295,753	2,840	1.0	4,178	2,418	1,006	298,593
July 1, 2006 to July 1, 2007......	298,593	2,987	1.0	4,305	2,425	866	301,580
July 1, 2007 to July 1, 2008......	301,580	2,795	0.9	4,283	2,439	863	304,375
July 1, 2008 to July 1, 2009......	304,375	2,632	0.9	4,263	2,486	855	307,007

[1] Net increase includes a residual. This residual represents the change in population that cannot be attributed to any specific demographic component. [2] Percent of population at beginning of period. [3] Net international migration includes the international migration of both native and foreign-born populations. Specifically, it includes: (a) the net international migration of the foreign born, (b) the net migration between the United States and Puerto Rico, (c) the net migration of natives to and from the United States, and (d) the net movement of the Armed Forces population between the United States and overseas. [4] The April 1, 2000, population estimates base reflects changes to the Census 2000 population from the Count Question Resolution program and geographic program revisions.
Source: U.S. Census Bureau, Population Division, "Population, population change and estimated components of population change: April 1, 2000 to July 1, 2009 (NST-EST2009-alldata)," December 2009, <http://www.census.gov/popest/national/files/NST_EST2009_ALLDATA.csv>.

Table 5. Components of Population Change by Race and Hispanic Origin: 2000 to 2009

[In thousands (25,582 represents 25,582,000). Resident population. Covers period April 1, 2000, to July 1, 2009. The April 1, 2000, Population Estimates base reflects changes to the Census 2000 population from the Count Question Resolution program]

Race and Hispanic origin	April 1, 2000 to July 1, 2009				
	Net increase [1]	Natural increase	Births	Deaths	Net international migration [2]
Total..............................	**25,582**	**15,876**	**38,359**	**22,483**	**8,944**
One race.................................	24,156	14,557	36,894	22,337	8,850
White..................................	16,192	9,744	28,859	19,115	5,840
Black or African American..................	3,936	3,062	5,783	2,720	777
American Indian and Alaska Native...........	487	403	513	110	77
Asian..................................	3,425	1,270	1,650	379	2,119
Native Hawaiian and Other Pacific Islander......	116	78	90	12	36
Two or more races.......................	1,426	1,318	1,464	146	95
Race alone or in combination: [3]					
White..................................	17,483	10,949	30,186	19,237	5,914
Black or African American..................	4,699	3,779	6,539	2,760	818
American Indian and Alaska Native...........	736	625	816	192	99
Asian..................................	3,983	1,779	2,204	425	2,164
Native Hawaiian and Other Pacific Islander......	231	180	210	30	48
Hispanic [4].............................	13,113	8,216	9,261	1,045	4,776
White alone, not Hispanic..................	4,274	2,435	20,573	18,138	1,343

[1] See footnote 1, Table 4. [2] See footnote 3, Table 4. [3] In combination with one or more other races. The sum of the five race groups adds to more than the total population because individuals may report more than one race. [4] Hispanic origin is considered an ethnicity, not a race. Hispanics may be of any race.
Source: U.S. Census Bureau, Population Division, "Table 5. Cumulative Estimates of the Components of Resident Population Change by Race and Hispanic Origin for the United States: April 1, 2000 to July 1, 2009 (NC-EST2009-05)," June 2010, <http://www.census.gov/popest/national/asrh/NC-EST2009/NC-EST2009-05.xls>.

Population 9

Table 6. Resident Population by Sex, Race, and Hispanic-Origin Status: 2000 to 2009

[281,425 represents 281,425,000. As of July, except as noted. Data shown are modified race counts; see text, this section]

Characteristic	Number (1,000)					Percent change, 2000 to 2009
	2000 [1] (April)	2005	2007	2008	2009	
BOTH SEXES						
Total..............................	**281,425**	**295,753**	**301,580**	**304,375**	**307,007**	**9.1**
One race..........................	277,527	291,087	296,587	299,216	301,683	8.7
White............................	228,107	237,251	240,947	242,685	244,298	7.1
Black or African American............	35,705	37,813	38,742	39,205	39,641	11.0
American Indian and Alaska Native.........	2,664	2,924	3,038	3,095	3,151	18.3
Asian............................	10,589	12,571	13,307	13,665	14,014	32.3
Native Hawaiian and Other Pacific Islander......	463	527	553	566	578	25.0
Two or more races....................	3,898	4,666	4,993	5,159	5,324	36.6
Race alone or in combination: [2]						
White............................	231,436	241,276	245,268	247,156	248,919	7.6
Black or African American............	37,105	39,618	40,723	41,277	41,804	12.7
American Indian and Alaska Native.........	4,225	4,620	4,791	4,877	4,961	17.4
Asian............................	12,007	14,294	15,156	15,578	15,990	33.2
Native Hawaiian and Other Pacific Islander......	907	1,035	1,086	1,112	1,137	25.4
Not Hispanic........................	246,118	253,201	256,071	257,396	258,587	5.1
One race..........................	242,712	249,167	251,776	252,969	254,028	4.7
White............................	195,577	198,074	199,109	199,529	199,851	2.2
Black or African American............	34,314	36,150	36,931	37,319	37,682	9.8
American Indian and Alaska Native.........	2,097	2,242	2,302	2,332	2,361	12.6
Asian............................	10,357	12,289	13,003	13,349	13,686	32.1
Native Hawaiian and Other Pacific Islander......	367	413	431	440	449	22.2
Two or more races....................	3,406	4,034	4,295	4,428	4,559	33.8
Race alone or in combination: [2]						
White............................	198,477	201,543	202,817	203,357	203,800	2.7
Black or African American............	35,499	37,670	38,596	39,058	39,495	11.3
American Indian and Alaska Native.........	3,456	3,687	3,782	3,829	3,874	12.1
Asian............................	11,632	13,828	14,647	15,047	15,437	32.7
Native Hawaiian and Other Pacific Islander......	752	845	882	900	918	22.1
Hispanic [3]........................	35,306	42,552	45,508	46,979	48,419	37.1
One race..........................	34,815	41,920	44,811	46,247	47,655	36.9
White............................	32,530	39,177	41,838	43,156	44,447	36.6
Black or African American............	1,391	1,663	1,811	1,886	1,960	40.9
American Indian and Alaska Native.........	566	682	735	763	790	39.6
Asian............................	232	282	305	316	328	41.0
Native Hawaiian and Other Pacific Islander......	95	115	122	126	130	36.1
Two or more races....................	491	632	698	731	764	55.6
Race alone or in combination: [2]						
White............................	32,959	39,732	42,451	43,799	45,119	36.9
Black or African American............	1,606	1,947	2,128	2,219	2,309	43.8
American Indian and Alaska Native.........	770	934	1,009	1,048	1,087	41.2
Asian............................	375	467	509	531	553	47.4
Native Hawaiian and Other Pacific Islander......	155	190	205	212	220	41.8
MALE						
Total..............................	**138,056**	**145,561**	**148,612**	**150,074**	**151,449**	**9.7**
One race..........................	136,146	143,262	146,147	147,525	148,817	9.3
White............................	112,478	117,433	119,428	120,366	121,236	7.8
Black or African American............	16,972	18,017	18,484	18,716	18,936	11.6
American Indian and Alaska Native.........	1,333	1,465	1,524	1,553	1,581	18.6
Asian............................	5,128	6,079	6,431	6,603	6,769	32.0
Native Hawaiian and Other Pacific Islander......	235	268	281	288	294	25.0
Two or more races....................	1,910	2,299	2,465	2,549	2,633	37.8
Race alone or in combination: [2]						
White............................	114,116	119,423	121,568	122,582	123,528	8.2
Black or African American............	17,644	18,894	19,452	19,730	19,996	13.3
American Indian and Alaska Native.........	2,088	2,288	2,375	2,419	2,462	17.9
Asian............................	5,834	6,939	7,355	7,559	7,758	33.0
Native Hawaiian and Other Pacific Islander......	456	521	547	560	573	25.6
Not Hispanic........................	119,894	123,579	125,080	125,773	126,393	5.4
Hispanic [3].........................	18,162	21,981	23,532	24,302	25,057	38.0
FEMALE						
Total..............................	**143,368**	**150,192**	**152,968**	**154,301**	**155,557**	**8.5**
One race..........................	141,381	147,825	150,440	151,691	152,866	8.1
White............................	115,628	119,818	121,519	122,319	123,063	6.4
Black or African American............	18,733	19,796	20,258	20,488	20,705	10.5
American Indian and Alaska Native.........	1,331	1,459	1,514	1,542	1,570	18.0
Asian............................	5,461	6,493	6,877	7,063	7,244	32.6
Native Hawaiian and Other Pacific Islander......	227	259	272	278	284	25.1
Two or more races....................	1,987	2,367	2,528	2,610	2,691	35.4
Race alone or in combination: [2]						
White............................	117,321	121,853	123,700	124,574	125,391	6.9
Black or African American............	19,461	20,723	21,272	21,546	21,808	12.1
American Indian and Alaska Native.........	2,137	2,332	2,415	2,458	2,499	16.9
Asian............................	6,173	7,355	7,802	8,019	8,232	33.4
Native Hawaiian and Other Pacific Islander......	451	514	539	552	565	25.3
Not Hispanic........................	126,224	129,622	130,991	131,624	132,195	4.7
Hispanic [3].........................	17,144	20,571	21,977	22,677	23,362	36.3

[1] See footnote 4, Table 4. [2] In combination with one or more other races. The sum of the five race groups adds to more than the total population because individuals may report more than one race. [3] Hispanic origin is considered an ethnicity, not a race. Hispanics may be of any race.

Source: U.S. Census Bureau, Population Division, "Table 3. Annual Estimates of the Resident Population by Sex, Race, and Hispanic Origin for the United States: April 1, 2000 to July 1, 2009 (NC-EST2009-03)," June 2010, <http://www.census.gov/popest /national/asrh/NC-EST2009/NC-EST2009-03.xls>.

Table 7. Resident Population by Sex and Age: 1980 to 2010

[In thousands, except as indicated (226,546 represents 226,546,000). As of April 1. Excludes Armed Forces overseas. For definition of median, see Guide to Tabular Presentation]

Age	1980 [1]			1990 [2]			2000 [3]			2010		
	Total	Male	Female	Total	Male	Female	Total	Male	Female	Total	Male	Female
Total............	226,546	110,053	116,493	248,791	121,284	127,507	281,425	138,056	143,368	308,746	151,781	156,964
Under 5 years	16,348	8,362	7,986	18,765	9,603	9,162	19,176	9,811	9,365	20,201	10,319	9,882
5 to 9 years	16,700	8,539	8,161	18,042	9,236	8,806	20,550	10,523	10,026	20,349	10,390	9,959
10 to 14 years	18,242	9,316	8,926	17,067	8,742	8,325	20,528	10,520	10,008	20,677	10,580	10,097
15 to 19 years	21,168	10,755	10,413	17,893	9,178	8,714	20,219	10,391	9,828	22,040	11,304	10,737
20 to 24 years	21,319	10,663	10,655	19,143	9,749	9,394	18,963	9,688	9,275	21,586	11,014	10,572
25 to 29 years	19,521	9,705	9,816	21,336	10,708	10,629	19,382	9,799	9,583	21,102	10,636	10,466
30 to 34 years	17,561	8,677	8,884	21,838	10,866	10,973	20,511	10,322	10,189	19,962	9,997	9,966
35 to 39 years	13,965	6,862	7,104	19,851	9,837	10,014	22,707	11,319	11,388	20,180	10,042	10,138
40 to 44 years	11,669	5,708	5,961	17,593	8,679	8,914	22,442	11,130	11,313	20,891	10,394	10,497
45 to 49 years	11,090	5,388	5,702	13,747	6,741	7,006	20,093	9,890	10,203	22,709	11,209	11,500
50 to 54 years	11,710	5,621	6,089	11,335	5,494	5,821	17,586	8,608	8,978	22,298	10,933	11,365
55 to 59 years	11,615	5,482	6,133	10,489	5,009	5,480	13,469	6,509	6,961	19,665	9,524	10,141
60 to 64 years	10,088	4,670	5,418	10,627	4,947	5,679	10,806	5,137	5,669	16,818	8,078	8,740
65 to 74 years	15,581	6,757	8,824	18,048	7,908	10,140	18,391	8,303	10,088	21,713	10,097	11,617
75 to 84 years	7,729	2,867	4,862	10,014	3,745	6,268	12,361	4,879	7,482	13,061	5,477	7,584
85 years and over	2,240	682	1,559	3,022	841	2,181	4,240	1,227	3,013	5,493	1,790	3,704
5 to 13 years	31,159	15,923	15,237	31,839	16,301	15,538	37,026	18,964	18,062	36,860	18,834	18,026
14 to 17 years	16,247	8,298	7,950	13,345	6,860	6,485	16,093	8,285	7,808	17,120	8,792	8,328
18 to 24 years	30,022	15,054	14,969	26,961	13,744	13,217	27,141	13,873	13,268	30,672	15,662	15,010
18 years and over ..	162,791	77,473	85,321	184,841	88,519	96,322	209,130	100,996	108,133	234,564	113,836	120,728
55 years and over ..	47,253	20,458	26,796	52,200	22,450	29,748	59,267	26,055	33,212	76,751	34,964	41,787
65 years and over ..	25,550	10,306	15,245	31,084	12,494	18,589	34,992	14,410	20,582	40,268	17,363	22,905
75 years and over ..	9,969	3,549	6,421	13,036	4,586	8,449	16,601	6,106	10,495	18,555	7,266	11,288
Median age (years)	30.0	28.8	31.3	32.8	31.6	34.0	35.3	34.0	36.5	37.2	35.8	38.5

[1] Total population count has been revised since the 1980 census publications. Numbers by age and sex have not been corrected. [2] The data shown have been modified from the official 1990 census counts. See text, this section, for explanation. The April 1, 1990, estimates base (248,790,925) includes count question resolution corrections processed through August 1997. It generally does not include adjustments for census coverage errors. However, it includes adjustments estimated for the 1995 Test Census in various localities in California, New Jersey, and Louisiana, and the 1998 census dress rehearsals in localities in California and Wisconsin. These adjustments amounted to a total of 81,052 persons. [3] The April 1, 2000 population estimates base reflects changes to the Census 2000 population from the Count Question Resolution program.

Source: U.S. Census Bureau, Current Population Reports, P25-1095; "Table US-EST90INT-04—Intercensal Estimates of the United States Resident Population by Age Groups and Sex, 1990–2000: Selected Months," September 2002, <http://www.census.gov/popest/archives/EST90INTERCENSAL/US-EST90INT-04.html>; and 2010 Census Redistricting Data (P.L. 94-171) Summary File, <http://www.census.gov/rdo/data/2010_census_redistricting_data_pl_94-171_summary_files.html>.

Table 8. Intercensal Resident Population by Sex and Age: 2001 to 2009

[In thousands, except as indicated (285,082 represents 285,082,000). As of July 1. Excludes Armed Forces overseas. For definition of median, see Guide to Tabular Presentation]

Age	2001	2002	2003	2004	2005	2006	2007	2008	2009
Total............	285,082	287,804	290,326	293,046	295,753	298,593	301,580	304,375	307,007
Under 5 years	19,430	19,668	19,940	20,243	20,484	20,613	20,921	21,153	21,300
5 to 9 years	20,238	19,985	19,778	19,655	19,632	19,831	20,054	20,313	20,610
10 to 14 years	20,898	21,112	21,193	21,113	20,837	20,579	20,319	20,104	19,974
15 to 19 years	20,370	20,456	20,574	20,808	21,120	21,367	21,562	21,628	21,538
20 to 24 years	19,802	20,317	20,685	20,959	21,081	21,161	21,217	21,322	21,540
25 to 29 years	18,899	18,830	18,971	19,372	19,866	20,511	21,018	21,442	21,678
30 to 34 years	20,685	20,716	20,551	20,260	19,846	19,433	19,353	19,516	19,889
35 to 39 years	22,245	21,766	21,284	20,896	20,818	20,959	20,993	20,847	20,538
40 to 44 years	22,820	22,898	22,903	22,943	22,726	22,320	21,858	21,394	20,992
45 to 49 years	20,694	21,245	21,714	22,053	22,402	22,696	22,787	22,802	22,831
50 to 54 years	18,649	18,673	19,004	19,447	19,940	20,407	20,962	21,432	21,761
55 to 59 years	13,930	15,073	15,706	16,460	17,315	18,170	18,209	18,541	18,975
60 to 64 years	11,101	11,495	12,100	12,573	12,981	13,340	14,459	15,082	15,812
65 to 74 years	18,342	18,310	18,381	18,502	18,666	18,936	19,389	20,139	20,792
75 to 84 years	12,624	12,817	12,968	13,077	13,176	13,207	13,213	13,211	13,148
85 years and over ...	4,354	4,444	4,574	4,684	4,862	5,063	5,264	5,450	5,631
5 to 13 years	37,085	36,980	36,774	36,396	36,162	36,159	36,180	36,297	36,487
14 to 17 years	16,221	16,401	16,544	16,854	17,104	17,239	17,239	16,980	16,761
18 to 24 years	28,001	28,489	28,912	29,286	29,405	29,541	29,734	30,090	30,412
18 years and over ...	212,345	214,755	217,068	219,553	222,004	224,583	227,240	229,945	232,458
55 years and over ...	60,352	62,139	63,729	65,296	67,000	68,715	70,535	72,423	74,358
65 years and over ...	35,320	35,571	35,923	36,263	36,704	37,206	37,867	38,800	39,571
75 years and over ...	16,978	17,261	17,542	17,762	18,038	18,270	18,478	18,661	18,779
Median age (years) ..	35.5	35.7	35.9	36.0	36.2	36.3	36.5	36.7	36.8

Source: U.S. Census Bureau, Population Division, "Annual Estimates of the Resident Population by Sex and Five-Year Age Groups for the United States: April 1, 2000 to July 1, 2009 (NC-EST2009-01)," June 2010, <http://www.census.gov/popest/national/asrh/NC-EST2009/NC-EST2009-01.xls>.

Table 9. Resident Population Projections by Sex and Age: 2010 to 2050

[In thousands, except as indicated (310,233 represents 310,233,000). As of July 1. Projections are based on assumptions about future births, deaths, and net international migration. Data do not reflect results of the 2010 Census. More information on methodology and assumptions is available at <http://www.census.gov/population/www/projections/methodstatement.html>]

Age	2010 Total	2010 Male	2010 Female	2015 Total	2015 Male	2015 Female	2020	2025	2030	2035	2040	2045	2050	Percent distribution 2010	2015	2020	2025	2050
Total	310,233	152,753	157,479	325,540	160,424	165,116	341,387	357,452	373,504	389,531	405,655	422,059	439,010	100.0	100.0	100.0	100.0	100.0
Under 5 years	21,100	10,779	10,320	22,076	11,278	10,798	22,846	23,484	24,161	25,056	26,117	27,171	28,148	6.8	6.8	6.7	6.6	6.4
5 to 9 years	20,886	10,654	10,232	21,707	11,074	10,633	22,732	23,548	24,232	24,953	25,893	26,998	28,096	6.7	6.7	6.7	6.6	6.4
10 to 14 years	20,395	10,421	9,975	21,658	11,049	10,609	22,571	23,677	24,567	25,319	26,105	27,108	28,274	6.6	6.7	6.6	6.6	6.4
15 to 19 years	21,770	11,159	10,611	21,209	10,844	10,365	22,554	23,545	24,723	25,682	26,501	27,354	28,422	7.0	6.5	6.6	6.6	6.5
20 to 24 years	21,779	11,100	10,680	22,342	11,378	10,963	21,799	23,168	24,191	25,408	26,408	27,272	28,171	7.0	6.9	6.4	6.5	6.4
25 to 29 years	21,418	10,873	10,545	22,400	11,353	11,048	22,949	22,417	23,804	24,855	26,102	27,138	28,039	6.9	6.9	6.7	6.3	6.4
30 to 34 years	20,400	10,308	10,092	22,099	11,182	10,917	23,112	23,699	23,216	24,647	25,745	27,040	28,126	6.6	6.8	6.8	6.6	6.4
35 to 39 years	20,267	10,191	10,076	20,841	10,506	10,335	22,586	23,645	24,279	23,848	25,321	26,462	27,799	6.5	6.4	6.6	6.6	6.3
40 to 44 years	21,010	10,509	10,500	20,460	10,247	10,214	21,078	22,851	23,944	24,612	24,224	25,726	26,897	6.8	6.3	6.2	6.4	6.1
45 to 49 years	22,596	11,165	11,430	21,001	10,447	10,553	20,502	21,154	22,943	24,061	24,759	24,411	25,933	7.3	6.5	6.0	5.9	5.9
50 to 54 years	22,109	10,827	11,282	22,367	10,977	11,390	20,852	20,404	21,087	22,884	24,025	24,750	24,445	7.1	6.9	6.1	5.7	5.6
55 to 59 years	19,517	9,450	10,067	21,682	10,524	11,158	21,994	20,575	20,186	20,903	22,703	23,867	24,621	6.3	6.7	6.4	5.8	5.6
60 to 64 years	16,758	8,024	8,733	18,861	9,023	9,838	21,009	21,377	20,080	19,760	20,513	22,305	23,490	5.4	5.8	6.2	6.0	5.4
65 to 69 years	12,261	5,747	6,514	15,812	7,449	8,364	17,861	19,957	20,381	19,230	18,989	19,776	21,543	4.0	4.9	5.2	5.6	4.9
70 to 74 years	9,202	4,191	5,011	11,155	5,109	6,046	14,452	16,399	18,404	18,879	17,906	17,754	18,570	3.0	3.4	4.2	4.6	4.2
75 to 79 years	7,282	3,159	4,123	7,901	3,480	4,421	9,656	12,598	14,390	16,249	16,771	16,016	15,964	2.3	2.4	2.8	3.5	3.6
80 to 84 years	5,733	2,302	3,431	5,676	2,342	3,334	6,239	7,715	10,173	11,735	13,375	13,925	13,429	1.8	1.7	1.8	2.2	3.1
85 to 89 years	3,650	1,297	2,353	3,786	1,409	2,376	3,817	4,278	5,383	7,215	8,450	9,767	10,303	1.2	1.2	1.1	1.2	2.3
90 to 94 years	1,570	473	1,097	1,856	591	1,265	1,976	2,047	2,360	3,044	4,180	5,007	5,909	0.5	0.6	0.6	0.6	1.3
95 to 99 years	452	108	344	546	142	404	669	739	795	952	1,270	1,803	2,229	0.1	0.2	0.2	0.2	0.5
100 years and over	79	15	65	105	21	84	135	175	208	239	298	409	601	(Z)	(Z)	(Z)	(Z)	0.1
5 to 13 years	37,123	18,945	18,178	39,011	19,900	19,111	40,792	42,490	43,858	45,170	46,743	48,664	50,697	12.0	12.0	11.9	11.9	11.5
14 to 17 years	16,994	8,713	8,281	17,019	8,699	8,320	18,048	18,892	19,796	20,496	21,126	21,834	22,728	5.5	5.2	5.3	5.3	5.2
18 to 24 years	30,713	15,675	15,037	30,885	15,746	15,139	30,817	32,555	34,059	35,695	37,038	38,234	39,538	9.9	9.5	9.0	9.1	9.0
16 years and over	243,639	118,739	124,900	255,864	124,858	131,006	268,722	282,014	295,595	309,084	322,265	335,328	348,811	78.5	78.6	78.7	78.9	79.5
18 years and over	235,016	114,316	120,700	247,434	120,547	126,887	259,702	272,585	285,688	298,809	311,669	324,389	337,437	75.8	76.0	76.1	76.3	76.9
16 to 64 years	203,410	101,447	101,963	209,027	104,316	104,711	213,917	218,107	223,503	231,540	241,027	250,872	260,264	65.6	64.2	62.7	61.0	59.3
55 years and over	76,504	34,766	41,737	87,381	40,090	47,291	97,807	105,860	112,358	118,206	124,455	130,628	136,658	24.7	26.8	28.6	29.6	31.1
65 years and over	40,229	17,292	22,937	46,837	20,542	26,295	54,804	63,907	72,092	77,543	81,238	84,456	88,547	13.0	14.4	16.1	17.9	20.2
75 years and over	18,766	7,354	11,412	19,870	7,985	11,885	22,492	27,551	33,308	39,435	44,343	46,926	48,434	6.0	6.1	6.6	7.7	11.0
85 years and over	5,751	1,893	3,859	6,292	2,163	4,130	6,597	7,239	8,745	11,450	14,198	16,985	19,041	1.9	1.9	1.9	2.0	4.3
Median age (years) [1]	36.9	35.5	38.2	37.1	35.9	38.4	37.7	38.2	38.7	39.0	38.9	38.9	39.0	(X)	(X)	(X)	(X)	(X)

X Not applicable. Z Less than 0.05 percent. [1] For definition of median, see Guide to Tabular Presentation.

Source: U.S. Census Bureau, "2008 National Population Projections," August 2008, <http://www.census.gov/population/www/projections/2008projections.html>.

Table 10. Resident Population by Race, Hispanic Origin, and Age: 2000 and 2009

[In thousands, except as indicated (281,425 represents 281,425,000). 2000, as of April 1, and 2009, as of July 1]

Age	Total 2000[1]	Total 2009	White alone 2000[1]	White alone 2009	Black or African American alone 2000[1]	Black or African American alone 2009	American Indian, Alaska Native alone 2000[1]	American Indian, Alaska Native alone 2009	Asian alone 2000[1]	Asian alone 2009	Native Hawaiian, Other Pacific Islander alone 2000[1]	Native Hawaiian, Other Pacific Islander alone 2009	Two or more races 2000[1]	Two or more races 2009	Hispanic origin[2] 2000[1]	Hispanic origin[2] 2009	Not Hispanic White alone 2000[1]	Not Hispanic White alone 2009
Total	281,425	307,007	228,107	244,298	35,705	39,641	2,664	3,151	10,589	14,014	463	578	3,898	5,324	35,306	48,419	195,577	199,851
Under 5 years	19,176	21,300	14,657	15,875	2,925	3,230	233	298	708	1,006	41	53	613	838	3,718	5,485	11,288	11,016
5 to 9 years	20,550	20,610	15,688	15,640	3,320	2,987	258	255	716	949	44	48	524	729	3,624	4,792	12,392	11,275
10 to 14 years	20,528	19,974	15,843	15,210	3,221	3,030	264	240	715	844	42	44	443	605	3,163	4,060	12,961	11,516
15 to 19 years	20,219	21,538	15,745	16,386	3,024	3,457	251	272	776	853	44	47	380	522	3,172	4,032	12,836	12,707
20 to 24 years	18,963	21,540	14,826	16,610	2,729	3,253	218	274	848	915	46	47	297	440	3,409	3,884	11,681	13,046
25 to 29 years	19,382	21,678	15,217	16,761	2,645	3,098	204	260	1,019	1,125	42	50	254	383	3,385	4,150	12,077	12,927
30 to 34 years	20,511	19,889	16,349	15,381	2,710	2,715	202	221	980	1,229	39	49	231	295	3,125	4,030	13,451	11,646
35 to 39 years	22,707	20,538	18,372	16,025	2,910	2,723	217	210	937	1,276	38	44	233	260	2,825	3,758	15,753	12,535
40 to 44 years	22,442	20,992	18,346	16,684	2,772	2,715	202	205	870	1,117	33	40	219	230	2,304	3,306	16,213	13,616
45 to 49 years	20,093	22,831	16,615	18,478	2,330	2,834	169	215	770	1,032	27	39	183	232	1,775	2,894	14,973	15,794
50 to 54 years	17,586	21,761	14,794	17,833	1,846	2,573	135	192	641	921	21	32	149	210	1,361	2,274	13,530	15,727
55 to 59 years	13,469	18,975	11,479	15,738	1,332	2,094	95	157	443	789	15	26	106	170	960	1,720	10,582	14,145
60 to 64 years	10,806	15,812	9,214	13,382	1,082	1,541	70	120	350	616	11	19	78	133	750	1,274	8,511	12,198
65 to 69 years	9,534	11,784	8,238	10,068	895	1,092	52	82	279	437	8	13	61	92	599	891	7,675	9,235
70 to 74 years	8,858	9,008	7,799	7,699	742	843	38	58	224	332	6	10	49	65	477	676	7,348	7,066
75 to 79 years	7,416	7,326	6,634	6,339	557	644	27	41	159	246	4	7	36	49	327	509	6,325	5,860
80 to 84 years	4,945	5,822	4,466	5,133	350	451	15	27	90	172	2	4	22	35	180	362	4,296	4,792
85 to 89 years	2,790	3,662	2,525	3,277	200	247	8	15	43	100	1	2	12	21	98	207	2,432	3,081
90 to 94 years	1,113	1,502	1,007	1,357	82	89	3	6	15	40	1	1	4	9	39	82	970	1,280
95 to 99 years	287	402	254	363	27	22	1	2	4	12	–	–	1	3	11	28	243	336
100 years and over	50	64	41	57	7	3	–	–	1	3	–	–	–	1	3	7	39	51
5 to 13 years	37,026	36,487	28,381	27,732	5,923	5,380	471	446	1,288	1,625	78	83	885	1,221	6,186	8,045	22,754	20,408
14 to 17 years	16,093	16,761	12,523	12,738	2,426	2,671	205	207	590	676	33	37	315	433	2,438	3,220	10,290	9,802
18 to 24 years	27,141	30,412	21,197	23,377	3,944	4,676	315	387	1,178	1,261	64	67	444	643	4,744	5,503	16,827	18,335
16 years and over	217,151	240,990	178,790	194,435	25,633	29,735	1,857	2,308	8,304	11,046	328	424	2,237	3,042	24,204	33,282	156,352	163,637
18 years and over	209,130	232,458	172,546	187,954	24,431	28,361	1,755	2,200	8,003	10,707	311	405	2,084	2,832	22,964	31,669	151,245	158,626
16 to 64 years	182,159	201,419	147,826	160,141	22,773	26,345	1,713	2,076	7,489	9,705	305	386	2,051	2,767	22,471	30,521	127,023	131,935
55 years and over	59,267	74,358	51,656	63,415	5,274	7,026	310	509	1,608	2,745	48	84	371	578	3,444	5,755	48,422	58,044
65 years and over	34,992	39,571	30,964	34,294	2,860	3,391	144	232	815	1,340	23	38	186	275	1,734	2,761	29,329	31,702
75 years and over	16,601	18,779	14,927	16,527	1,223	1,456	55	92	312	572	8	15	77	117	657	1,194	14,306	15,400
85 years and over	4,240	5,631	3,827	5,054	316	361	13	24	63	154	2	4	18	34	151	324	3,685	4,748
Median age (years)[3]	35.3	36.8	36.6	38.3	30.0	31.3	27.7	29.5	32.5	35.3	26.8	29.9	19.8	19.7	25.8	27.4	38.6	41.2

– Represents or rounds to zero. [1] April 1, 2000, population estimates base reflects changes to the Census 2000 population from the Count Question Resolution program. [2] Hispanic origin is considered an ethnicity, not a race. Hispanics may be any race. [3] For definition of median, see Guide to Tabular Presentation.

Source: U.S. Census Bureau, "Table 4. Annual Estimates of the Resident Population by Race, Hispanic Origin, Sex and Age for the United States: April 1, 2000 to July 1, 2009 (NC-EST2009-04)," June 2010, <http://www.census.gov/popest/national/asrh/NC-EST2009-asrh.html>.

Table 11. Resident Population by Race, Hispanic Origin, and Single Years of Age: 2009

[In thousands, except as indicated (307,007 represents 307,007,000). As of July 1. For derivation of estimates, see text, this section]

Age	Total	Race						Hispanic origin [1]	Non-Hispanic White alone
		White alone	Black or African American alone	American Indian, Alaska Native alone	Asian alone	Native Hawaiian and Other Pacific Islander alone	Two or more races		
Total.	307,007	244,298	39,641	3,151	14,014	578	5,324	48,419	199,851
Under 5 years old	21,300	15,875	3,230	298	1,006	53	838	5,485	11,016
Under 1 year old	4,261	3,163	656	62	198	11	173	1,105	2,187
1 year old.	4,298	3,183	664	62	206	11	172	1,124	2,190
2 years old.	4,336	3,226	662	62	204	11	171	1,126	2,228
3 years old.	4,224	3,163	631	57	198	10	164	1,082	2,202
4 years old.	4,181	3,140	616	56	200	10	158	1,048	2,208
5 to 9 years old	20,610	15,640	2,987	255	949	48	729	4,792	11,275
5 years old.	4,186	3,169	599	53	199	10	155	1,015	2,251
6 years old.	4,139	3,143	588	52	196	10	149	987	2,243
7 years old.	4,108	3,120	595	51	188	9	145	963	2,238
8 years old.	4,167	3,160	612	51	191	10	144	949	2,293
9 years old.	4,010	3,048	593	48	174	9	136	878	2,250
10 to 14 years old	19,974	15,210	3,030	240	844	44	605	4,060	11,516
10 years old.	3,946	3,004	588	48	167	9	130	827	2,254
11 years old.	3,941	2,997	596	47	168	9	125	813	2,258
12 years old.	3,957	3,013	598	47	169	9	119	805	2,281
13 years old.	4,033	3,077	611	48	172	9	117	808	2,341
14 years old.	4,096	3,119	637	49	169	9	113	807	2,383
15 to 19 years old	21,538	16,386	3,457	272	853	47	522	4,032	12,707
15 years old.	4,134	3,138	658	51	168	9	109	801	2,407
16 years old.	4,225	3,205	683	53	169	9	106	804	2,472
17 years old.	4,307	3,276	692	55	170	9	104	808	2,539
18 years old.	4,389	3,345	705	56	171	10	102	808	2,608
19 years old.	4,484	3,422	719	57	175	10	101	811	2,681
20 to 24 years old	21,540	16,610	3,253	274	915	47	440	3,884	13,046
20 years old.	4,340	3,322	682	56	177	10	94	775	2,613
21 years old.	4,291	3,301	659	55	177	9	90	774	2,591
22 years old.	4,266	3,295	642	54	178	9	87	771	2,588
23 years old.	4,306	3,332	638	55	187	10	85	777	2,618
24 years old.	4,336	3,361	633	54	195	10	83	787	2,636
25 to 29 years old	21,678	16,761	3,098	260	1,125	50	383	4,150	12,927
25 years old.	4,264	3,299	617	53	204	10	80	793	2,568
26 years old.	4,330	3,353	620	54	214	10	79	821	2,594
27 years old.	4,350	3,364	620	52	227	10	77	840	2,587
28 years old.	4,380	3,386	620	51	238	10	75	843	2,608
29 years old.	4,353	3,359	621	50	242	11	71	853	2,570
30 to 34 years old	19,889	15,381	2,715	221	1,229	49	295	4,030	11,646
30 years old.	4,136	3,191	581	47	241	10	66	817	2,436
31 years old.	4,013	3,107	551	45	239	10	61	812	2,356
32 years old.	3,950	3,056	539	45	243	10	58	807	2,309
33 years old.	3,844	2,971	517	43	248	9	55	798	2,231
34 years old.	3,945	3,055	527	42	258	9	54	796	2,315
35 to 39 years old	20,538	16,025	2,723	210	1,276	44	260	3,758	12,535
35 years old.	3,824	2,960	509	41	254	9	52	764	2,249
36 years old.	3,909	3,021	529	41	258	9	51	759	2,316
37 years old.	4,093	3,186	546	42	258	9	52	750	2,490
38 years old.	4,316	3,391	568	43	252	9	53	742	2,703
39 years old.	4,396	3,467	571	43	255	9	52	743	2,778
40 to 44 years old	20,992	16,684	2,715	205	1,117	40	230	3,306	13,616
40 years old.	4,156	3,293	526	41	239	8	48	689	2,654
41 years old.	4,077	3,226	528	40	230	8	45	674	2,601
42 years old.	4,084	3,254	525	40	213	8	44	647	2,654
43 years old.	4,196	3,336	551	41	215	8	45	646	2,737
44 years old.	4,479	3,575	585	44	220	8	47	651	2,971
45 to 49 years old	22,831	18,478	2,834	215	1,032	39	232	2,894	15,794
45 years old.	4,543	3,650	576	44	218	8	47	626	3,070
46 years old.	4,524	3,647	565	43	215	8	47	594	3,097
47 years old.	4,535	3,680	558	43	200	8	46	573	3,148
48 years old.	4,576	3,728	557	42	195	8	46	548	3,220
49 years old.	4,653	3,772	579	43	204	8	47	552	3,260

See footnote at end of table.

U.S. Census Bureau, Statistical Abstract of the United States: 2012

[See headnote, page 14]

Age	Total	Race						Hispanic origin [1]	Non-Hispanic White alone
		White alone	Black or African American alone	American Indian, Alaska Native alone	Asian alone	Native Hawaiian and Other Pacific Islander alone	Two or more races		
50 to 54 years old	21,761	17,833	2,573	192	921	32	210	2,274	15,727
50 years old	4,460	3,638	541	40	189	7	44	498	3,177
51 years old	4,456	3,647	529	40	189	7	44	473	3,210
52 years old	4,397	3,607	520	39	182	6	42	454	3,187
53 years old	4,218	3,462	493	37	180	6	41	429	3,065
54 years old	4,230	3,477	490	37	180	6	40	420	3,088
55 to 59 years old	18,975	15,738	2,094	157	789	26	170	1,720	14,145
55 years old	4,040	3,339	456	35	168	6	37	383	2,985
56 years old	3,898	3,235	428	33	162	5	36	359	2,903
57 years old	3,759	3,128	407	31	154	5	33	335	2,818
58 years old	3,652	3,034	402	30	148	5	32	323	2,735
59 years old	3,626	3,002	401	30	158	5	32	321	2,704
60 to 64 years old	15,812	13,382	1,541	120	616	19	133	1,274	12,198
60 years old	3,479	2,910	364	27	143	5	30	289	2,642
61 years old	3,438	2,903	341	26	135	4	29	275	2,647
62 years old	3,587	3,081	321	26	126	4	30	262	2,838
63 years old	2,666	2,252	259	20	108	4	23	230	2,039
64 years old	2,642	2,236	257	20	104	3	22	218	2,032
65 to 69 years old	11,784	10,068	1,092	82	437	13	92	891	9,235
65 years old	2,588	2,209	240	18	97	3	21	202	2,020
66 years old	2,656	2,288	236	18	90	3	21	191	2,110
67 years old	2,329	1,992	213	16	87	3	18	174	1,830
68 years old	2,145	1,828	202	15	82	2	17	163	1,675
69 years old	2,067	1,752	201	14	81	2	16	161	1,601
70 to 74 years old	9,008	7,699	843	58	332	10	65	676	7,066
70 years old	1,949	1,666	180	13	73	2	14	148	1,527
71 years old	1,893	1,617	176	12	70	2	14	142	1,485
72 years old	1,765	1,508	165	11	66	2	13	133	1,384
73 years old	1,712	1,462	162	11	62	2	12	127	1,343
74 years old	1,689	1,446	160	11	60	2	12	126	1,328
75 to 79 years old	7,326	6,339	644	41	246	7	49	509	5,860
75 years old	1,529	1,310	143	9	54	2	11	111	1,206
76 years old	1,506	1,295	138	9	53	1	10	105	1,197
77 years old	1,463	1,268	127	8	48	1	10	101	1,173
78 years old	1,422	1,241	117	7	46	1	9	97	1,150
79 years old	1,406	1,225	119	7	45	1	9	96	1,135
80 to 84 years old	5,822	5,133	451	27	172	4	35	362	4,792
80 years old	1,295	1,135	104	6	40	1	8	85	1,055
81 years old	1,249	1,099	98	6	37	1	8	79	1,025
82 years old	1,173	1,035	90	5	34	1	7	71	968
83 years old	1,083	957	83	5	31	1	6	66	895
84 years old	1,023	907	76	5	29	1	6	60	850
85 to 89 years old	3,662	3,277	247	15	100	2	21	207	3,081
90 to 94 years old	1,502	1,357	89	6	40	1	9	82	1,280
95 to 99 years old	402	363	22	2	12	–	3	28	336
100 years old and over . . .	64	57	3	–	3	–	1	7	51
Median age (years) [2]	36.8	38.3	31.3	29.5	35.3	29.9	19.7	27.4	41.2

– Represents or rounds to zero. [1] Hispanic origin is considered an ethnicity, not a race. Hispanics may be of any race.
[2] For definition of median, see Guide to Tabular Presentation
Source: U.S. Census Bureau, "Monthly Resident Population Estimates by Age, Sex, Race and Hispanic Origin for the United States: April 1, 2000 to July 1, 2009," June 2010, <http://www.census.gov/popest/national/asrh/2009-nat-res.html>.

Table 12. Resident Population Projections by Race, Hispanic-Origin Status, and Age: 2010 and 2015

[In thousands, except as indicated (310,233 represents 310,233,000). As of July 1. Projections are based on assumptions about future births, deaths, and net international migration. Data do not reflect results of the 2010 Census. More information on methodology and assumptions is available at <http://www.census.gov/population/www/projections/methodstatement.html>]

Age group	Total 2010	Total 2015	White alone 2010	White alone 2015	Black or African American alone 2010	Black or African American alone 2015	American Indian and Alaska Native alone 2010	American Indian and Alaska Native alone 2015	Asian alone 2010	Asian alone 2015	Native Hawaiian and Other Pacific Islander alone 2010	Native Hawaiian and Other Pacific Islander alone 2015	Two or more races 2010	Two or more races 2015	Hispanic origin [1] 2010	Hispanic origin [1] 2015	Not Hispanic White alone 2010	Not Hispanic White alone 2015
Total	310,233	325,540	246,630	256,306	39,909	42,137	3,188	3,472	14,415	16,527	592	662	5,499	6,435	49,726	57,711	200,853	203,208
Under 5 years	21,100	22,076	15,944	16,563	3,034	3,191	286	311	943	1,004	53	56	840	951	5,053	5,622	11,375	11,487
5 to 9 years	20,886	21,707	15,888	16,412	3,011	3,084	264	292	927	1,018	49	55	746	845	4,888	5,452	11,448	11,465
10 to 14 years	20,395	21,658	15,560	16,467	3,021	3,080	244	271	894	1,034	45	52	631	754	4,513	5,401	11,440	11,540
15 to 19 years	21,770	21,209	16,570	16,143	3,330	3,096	268	252	932	1,030	48	48	541	639	4,473	5,040	12,472	11,524
20 to 24 years	21,779	22,342	16,731	16,976	3,330	3,449	275	273	938	1,047	47	50	459	546	4,010	4,873	13,049	12,499
25 to 29 years	21,418	22,400	16,544	17,125	3,107	3,374	261	279	1,063	1,106	48	49	395	467	3,887	4,311	12,959	13,160
30 to 34 years	20,400	22,099	15,711	16,915	2,845	3,158	228	264	1,245	1,305	52	52	319	405	4,039	4,166	11,974	13,068
35 to 39 years	20,267	20,841	15,674	15,946	2,691	2,872	210	230	1,376	1,413	47	54	269	325	3,868	4,236	12,078	12,023
40 to 44 years	21,010	20,460	16,610	15,763	2,713	2,690	205	211	1,199	1,476	42	48	241	272	3,431	3,979	13,423	12,062
45 to 49 years	22,596	21,001	18,202	16,561	2,838	2,679	216	204	1,064	1,272	40	43	236	242	3,002	3,491	15,415	13,316
50 to 54 years	22,109	22,367	18,049	17,998	2,650	2,765	200	214	957	1,115	34	40	219	234	2,425	3,036	15,800	15,177
55 to 59 years	19,517	21,682	16,134	17,691	2,170	2,545	165	196	840	1,001	27	34	181	216	1,862	2,450	14,409	15,417
60 to 64 years	16,758	18,861	14,087	15,582	1,671	2,042	130	160	704	875	21	27	145	176	1,417	1,867	12,769	13,849
65 to 69 years	12,261	15,812	10,446	13,285	1,130	1,528	87	123	483	717	15	21	99	138	974	1,387	9,534	11,994
70 to 74 years	9,202	11,155	7,867	9,511	845	990	61	80	350	469	10	14	69	91	710	920	7,201	8,650
75 to 79 years	7,282	7,901	6,331	6,780	619	690	41	53	236	310	7	9	48	60	514	637	5,848	6,183
80 to 84 years	5,733	5,676	5,093	4,957	427	458	26	32	151	186	4	5	33	38	354	424	4,759	4,558
85 to 89 years	3,650	3,786	3,290	3,374	247	271	14	17	78	99	2	3	19	22	195	257	3,106	3,131
90 to 94 years	1,570	1,856	1,423	1,674	106	125	5	7	27	39	1	1	8	10	78	117	1,350	1,564
95 to 99 years	452	546	407	492	35	40	1	2	7	9	–	–	2	3	26	35	383	459
100 years and over	79	105	69	92	8	10	–	–	1	1	–	–	1	1	6	9	63	83
5 to 13 years	37,123	39,011	28,273	29,577	5,412	5,529	459	511	1,636	1,844	85	97	1,259	1,454	8,501	9,786	20,536	20,678
14 to 17 years	16,994	17,019	12,941	12,937	2,619	2,478	205	204	741	818	38	39	450	543	3,595	4,112	9,648	9,175
18 to 24 years	30,713	30,885	23,536	23,483	4,741	4,703	387	374	1,315	1,468	66	70	668	787	5,788	6,869	18,225	17,173
16 years and over	243,639	255,864	196,026	203,643	30,201	32,171	2,343	2,547	11,466	13,267	435	489	3,168	3,747	34,372	40,202	164,202	166,441
18 years and over	235,016	247,434	189,473	197,229	28,844	30,940	2,237	2,446	11,095	12,861	416	470	2,950	3,487	32,576	38,192	159,295	161,868
16 to 64 years	203,410	209,027	161,100	163,478	26,783	28,059	2,108	2,232	10,132	11,437	397	436	2,890	3,384	31,515	36,416	131,959	129,819
55 years and over	76,504	87,381	65,147	73,437	7,258	8,698	531	671	2,877	3,706	87	114	604	755	6,136	8,104	59,421	65,888
65 years and over	40,229	46,837	34,926	40,164	3,418	4,111	235	314	1,333	1,831	39	53	278	363	2,858	3,786	32,243	36,623
75 years and over	18,766	19,870	16,613	17,368	1,442	1,594	87	111	500	645	14	18	110	133	1,173	1,479	15,509	15,978
85 years and over	5,751	6,292	5,189	5,632	397	445	20	26	113	149	3	4	29	36	305	418	4,902	5,238
Median age (years) [2]	36.9	37.1	38.4	38.6	31.7	32.8	29.9	31.1	36.0	37.5	30.5	32.0	19.9	20.2	27.5	27.8	41.3	42.1

– Represents or rounds to zero. [1] Hispanic origin is considered an ethnicity, not a race. Hispanics may be of any race. [2] For definition of median, see Guide to Tabular Presentation.

Source: U.S. Census Bureau, Population Division, "2008 National Population Projections," August 2008, <http://www.census.gov/population/www/projections/2008projections.html>.

Figure 1.2.
Center of Population: 1970 to 2010

[Prior to 1960, excludes Alaska and Hawaii. The median center is located at the intersection of two median lines, a north-south line constructed so that half of the nation's population lives east and half lives west of it, and an east-west line selected so that half of the nation's population lives north and half lives south of it. The mean center of population is that point at which an imaginary, flat, weightless, and rigid map of the United States would balance if weights of identical value were placed on it so that each weight represented the location of one person on the date of the census]

Year	Median center		Mean center		
	Latitude-N	Longitude	Latitude-N	Longitude-W	Approximate location
1790 (August 2) ..	(NA)	(NA)	39 16 30	76 11 12	In Kent County, MD, 23 miles E of Baltimore MD
1850 (June 1) ...	(NA)	(NA)	38 59 00	81 19 00	In Wirt County, WV, 23 miles SE of Parkersburg, WV [1]
1900 (June 1) ...	40 03 32	84 49 01	39 09 36	85 48 54	In Bartholomew County, IN, 6 miles SE of Columbus, IN
1950 (April 1)....	40 00 12	84 56 51	38 50 21	88 09 33	In Richland County, IL, 8 miles NNW of Olney, IL
1960 (April 1)....	39 56 25	85 16 60	38 35 58	89 12 35	In Clinton County, IL, 6.5 miles NW of Centralia, IL
1970 (April 1)....	39 47 43	85 31 43	38 27 47	89 42 22	In St. Clair County, IL, 5.3 miles ESE of Mascoutah, IL
1980 (April 1)....	39 18 60	86 08 15	38 08 13	90 34 26	In Jefferson County, MO, .25 miles W of DeSoto, MO
1990 (April 1)....	38 57 55	86 31 53	37 52 20	91 12 55	In Crawford County, MO, 10 miles SE of Steelville, MO
2000 (April 1)....	38 45 23	86 55 51	37 41 49	91 48 34	In Phelps County, MO, 3 miles E of Edgar Springs, MO
2010 (April 1)....	38 28 25	87 24 37	37 31 03	92 10 23	In Texas County, MO, 2.7 miles NE of Plato, MO

NA Not available. [1] West Virginia was set off from Virginia, Dec. 31, 1862, and admitted as a state, June 19, 1863.

Figure 1.1
Percent Change in Population for States: April 1, 2000 to April 1, 2010

Percent change in population
- 18.0 or more
- 12.0 to 17.9
- 6.0 to 11.9
- 0.0 to 5.9
- Population decline

U.S. percent = 9.7

Source: Chart prepared by U.S. Census Bureau. For data, see Table 14.

U.S. Census Bureau, Statistical Abstract of the United States: 2012

Table 13. Intercensal Resident Population—States: 2001 to 2009

[In thousands (285,082 represents 285,082,000). As of July 1. Insofar as possible, population shown for all years is that of present area of state. See Appendix III]

State	2001	2002	2003	2004	2005	2006	2007	2008	2009
United States	**285,082**	**287,804**	**290,326**	**293,046**	**295,753**	**298,593**	**301,580**	**304,375**	**307,007**
Alabama	4,464	4,472	4,491	4,512	4,545	4,598	4,638	4,677	4,709
Alaska	633	643	651	662	669	677	682	688	698
Arizona	5,304	5,452	5,591	5,759	5,975	6,192	6,362	6,499	6,596
Arkansas	2,691	2,705	2,722	2,746	2,776	2,815	2,842	2,868	2,889
California	34,486	34,876	35,251	35,558	35,795	35,979	36,226	36,580	36,962
Colorado	4,433	4,504	4,549	4,600	4,661	4,753	4,842	4,935	5,025
Connecticut	3,428	3,448	3,468	3,475	3,477	3,485	3,489	3,503	3,518
Delaware	795	804	815	827	840	853	865	876	885
District of Columbia	578	580	578	580	582	584	586	590	600
Florida	16,354	16,680	16,981	17,375	17,784	18,089	18,278	18,424	18,538
Georgia	8,420	8,586	8,735	8,914	9,097	9,330	9,534	9,698	9,829
Hawaii	1,218	1,228	1,239	1,253	1,266	1,276	1,277	1,287	1,295
Idaho	1,321	1,342	1,364	1,392	1,426	1,464	1,499	1,528	1,546
Illinois	12,508	12,558	12,598	12,645	12,674	12,718	12,779	12,843	12,910
Indiana	6,125	6,149	6,182	6,214	6,253	6,302	6,346	6,388	6,423
Iowa	2,929	2,929	2,933	2,941	2,949	2,964	2,979	2,994	3,008
Kansas	2,701	2,713	2,722	2,731	2,742	2,756	2,776	2,797	2,819
Kentucky	4,069	4,091	4,119	4,148	4,182	4,219	4,256	4,288	4,314
Louisiana	4,461	4,466	4,475	4,489	4,498	4,240	4,376	4,452	4,492
Maine	1,285	1,294	1,303	1,308	1,312	1,315	1,317	1,320	1,318
Maryland	5,375	5,440	5,497	5,543	5,583	5,612	5,634	5,659	5,699
Massachusetts	6,412	6,441	6,452	6,451	6,453	6,466	6,499	6,544	6,594
Michigan	10,006	10,039	10,066	10,089	10,091	10,082	10,051	10,002	9,970
Minnesota	4,983	5,017	5,048	5,079	5,107	5,148	5,191	5,231	5,266
Mississippi	2,853	2,859	2,868	2,886	2,900	2,897	2,922	2,940	2,952
Missouri	5,644	5,681	5,715	5,758	5,807	5,862	5,910	5,956	5,988
Montana	906	910	917	926	935	946	957	968	975
Nebraska	1,718	1,725	1,734	1,742	1,752	1,760	1,770	1,782	1,797
Nevada	2,095	2,166	2,237	2,329	2,409	2,493	2,568	2,616	2,643
New Hampshire	1,257	1,271	1,282	1,293	1,301	1,312	1,317	1,322	1,325
New Jersey	8,489	8,544	8,583	8,612	8,622	8,624	8,636	8,663	8,708
New Mexico	1,829	1,850	1,870	1,892	1,917	1,943	1,969	1,987	2,010
New York	19,089	19,162	19,231	19,298	19,331	19,357	19,423	19,468	19,541
North Carolina	8,203	8,317	8,416	8,531	8,669	8,867	9,064	9,247	9,381
North Dakota	636	634	633	636	635	637	638	641	647
Ohio	11,397	11,421	11,445	11,465	11,475	11,492	11,521	11,528	11,543
Oklahoma	3,465	3,485	3,499	3,514	3,533	3,574	3,612	3,644	3,687
Oregon	3,470	3,517	3,550	3,574	3,618	3,678	3,733	3,783	3,826
Pennsylvania	12,300	12,326	12,358	12,388	12,418	12,471	12,523	12,566	12,605
Rhode Island	1,058	1,066	1,072	1,071	1,065	1,060	1,055	1,054	1,053
South Carolina	4,063	4,104	4,146	4,201	4,256	4,339	4,424	4,503	4,561
South Dakota	759	762	767	774	780	789	797	805	812
Tennessee	5,755	5,803	5,857	5,917	5,996	6,089	6,173	6,240	6,296
Texas	21,333	21,711	22,058	22,418	22,802	23,369	23,838	24,304	24,782
Utah	2,291	2,334	2,380	2,439	2,500	2,584	2,664	2,727	2,785
Vermont	612	615	617	618	619	620	620	621	622
Virginia	7,191	7,284	7,374	7,469	7,564	7,647	7,720	7,795	7,883
Washington	5,988	6,056	6,113	6,184	6,261	6,372	6,465	6,566	6,664
West Virginia	1,799	1,799	1,802	1,803	1,804	1,807	1,811	1,815	1,820
Wisconsin	5,409	5,447	5,477	5,511	5,541	5,572	5,602	5,628	5,655
Wyoming	493	497	499	503	506	513	523	533	544

Source: U.S. Census Bureau, Population Division, "Table 1: Annual Estimates of the Resident Population for the United States, Regions, States, and Puerto Rico: April 1, 2000 to July 1, 2009 (NST-EST2009-01)," December 2009, <http://www.census.gov/popest/states/NST-ann-est.html>.

Table 14. State Population—Rank, Percent Change, and Population Density: 1980 to 2010

[As of April 1. Insofar as possible, population shown for all years is that of present area of state. Data for 1990 and earlier censuses include corrections processed via the Count Question Resolution program and other official revised census counts. For area figures of states, see Table 358. Minus sign (–) indicates decrease. See Appendix III]

State	Rank				Percent change			Population per square mile of land area [1]		
	1980	1990	2000	2010	1980–1990	1990–2000	2000–2010	1990	2000	2010
United States	(X)	(X)	(X)	(X)	9.8	13.1	9.7	70.4	79.7	87.4
Alabama	22	22	23	23	3.8	10.1	7.5	79.8	87.8	94.4
Alaska	50	49	48	47	36.9	14.0	13.3	1.0	1.1	1.2
Arizona	29	24	20	16	34.8	40.0	24.6	32.3	45.2	56.3
Arkansas	33	33	33	32	2.8	13.7	9.1	45.2	51.4	56.0
California	1	1	1	1	26.0	13.8	10.0	191.0	217.4	239.1
Colorado	28	26	24	22	14.0	30.6	16.9	31.8	41.5	48.5
Connecticut	25	27	29	29	5.8	3.6	4.9	678.8	703.3	738.1
Delaware	47	46	45	45	12.1	17.6	14.6	341.9	402.1	460.8
District of Columbia	(X)	(X)	(X)	(X)	–4.9	–5.7	5.2	9,941.3	9,370.6	9,856.5
Florida	7	4	4	4	32.7	23.5	17.6	241.3	298.0	350.6
Georgia	13	11	10	9	18.6	26.4	18.3	112.6	142.3	168.4
Hawaii	39	41	42	40	14.9	9.3	12.3	172.6	188.6	211.8
Idaho	41	42	39	39	6.7	28.5	21.1	12.2	15.7	19.0
Illinois	5	6	5	5	(Z)	8.6	3.3	205.9	223.7	231.1
Indiana	12	14	14	15	1.0	9.7	6.6	154.8	169.7	181.0
Iowa	27	30	30	30	–4.7	5.4	4.1	49.7	52.4	54.5
Kansas	32	32	32	33	4.8	8.5	6.1	30.3	32.9	34.9
Kentucky	23	23	25	26	0.7	9.6	7.4	93.4	102.4	109.9
Louisiana	19	21	22	25	0.4	5.9	1.4	97.7	103.4	104.9
Maine	38	38	40	41	9.2	3.8	4.2	39.8	41.3	43.1
Maryland	18	19	19	19	13.4	10.8	9.0	492.5	545.6	594.8
Massachusetts	11	13	13	14	4.9	5.5	3.1	771.3	814.0	839.4
Michigan	8	8	8	8	0.4	6.9	–0.6	164.4	175.8	174.8
Minnesota	21	20	21	21	7.4	12.4	7.8	55.0	61.8	66.6
Mississippi	31	31	31	31	2.2	10.5	4.3	54.9	60.6	63.2
Missouri	15	15	17	18	4.1	9.3	7.0	74.4	81.4	87.1
Montana	44	44	44	44	1.6	12.9	9.7	5.5	6.2	6.8
Nebraska	35	36	38	38	0.5	8.4	6.7	20.5	22.3	23.8
Nevada	43	39	35	35	50.1	66.3	35.1	10.9	18.2	24.6
New Hampshire	42	40	41	42	20.5	11.4	6.5	123.9	138.0	147.0
New Jersey	9	9	9	11	5.2	8.9	4.5	1,051.1	1,144.2	1,195.5
New Mexico	37	37	36	36	16.3	20.1	13.2	12.5	15.0	17.0
New York	2	2	3	3	2.5	5.5	2.1	381.8	402.7	411.2
North Carolina	10	10	11	10	12.8	21.4	18.5	136.4	165.6	196.1
North Dakota	46	47	47	48	–2.1	0.5	4.7	9.3	9.3	9.7
Ohio	6	7	7	7	0.5	4.7	1.6	265.5	277.8	282.3
Oklahoma	26	28	27	28	4.0	9.7	8.7	45.9	50.3	54.7
Oregon	30	29	28	27	7.9	20.4	12.0	29.6	35.6	39.9
Pennsylvania	4	5	6	6	0.2	3.4	3.4	265.6	274.5	283.9
Rhode Island	40	43	43	43	5.9	4.5	0.4	970.6	1,014.0	1,018.1
South Carolina	24	25	26	24	11.7	15.1	15.3	116.0	133.5	153.9
South Dakota	45	45	46	46	0.8	8.5	7.9	9.2	10.0	10.7
Tennessee	17	17	16	17	6.2	16.7	11.5	118.3	138.0	153.9
Texas	3	3	2	2	19.4	22.8	20.6	65.0	79.8	96.3
Utah	36	35	34	34	17.9	29.6	23.8	21.0	27.2	33.6
Vermont	48	48	49	49	10.0	8.2	2.8	61.1	66.1	67.9
Virginia	14	12	12	12	15.8	14.4	13.0	156.7	179.2	202.6
Washington	20	18	15	13	17.8	21.1	14.1	73.2	88.7	101.2
West Virginia	34	34	37	37	–8.0	0.8	2.5	74.6	75.2	77.1
Wisconsin	16	16	18	20	4.0	9.6	6.0	90.3	99.0	105.0
Wyoming	49	50	50	50	–3.4	8.9	14.1	4.7	5.1	5.8

X Not applicable. Z Less than 0.05 percent. [1] Persons per square mile were calculated on the basis of land area data from the 2010 census.

Source: U.S. Census Bureau, United States Summary: 2000 (PHC-3-1), <http://www.census.gov/prod/cen2000/phc3-us-pt1.pdf>; 2010 Census Redistricting Data (P.L. 94-171) Summary File, <http://www.census.gov/rdo/data/2010_census_redistricting_data_pl_94-171_summary_files.html>.

Table 15. State Resident Population—Components of Change: 2000 to 2009

[Covers period April 1, 2000, to July 1, 2009. Minus sign (–) indicates net decrease or net outflow]

State	Numeric population change [1]	Births	Deaths	Natural increase (births minus deaths)	Net migration Total	Net migration International [2]	Net migration Domestic
United States	25,581,948	38,358,804	22,483,225	15,875,579	8,944,170	8,944,170	(X)
Alabama	261,326	566,363	427,844	138,519	136,452	50,742	85,710
Alaska	71,542	97,287	28,894	68,393	–724	8,308	–9,032
Arizona	1,465,171	875,726	411,488	464,238	986,764	272,410	714,354
Arkansas	216,064	361,135	258,324	102,811	112,923	36,478	76,445
California	3,090,016	5,058,440	2,179,958	2,878,482	306,925	1,816,633	–1,509,708
Colorado	722,733	641,107	272,191	368,916	357,683	144,861	212,822
Connecticut	112,681	388,331	271,426	116,905	16,608	112,936	–96,328
Delaware	101,565	106,409	66,314	40,095	66,047	19,523	46,524
District of Columbia	27,602	73,986	50,911	23,075	–17,427	24,179	–41,606
Florida	2,555,130	2,046,244	1,566,658	479,586	2,034,234	851,260	1,182,974
Georgia	1,642,430	1,301,426	616,981	684,445	849,133	281,998	567,135
Hawaii	83,640	168,965	83,575	85,390	5,843	38,951	–33,108
Idaho	251,846	211,735	95,443	116,292	134,462	22,121	112,341
Illinois.............	490,751	1,681,839	960,627	721,212	–228,888	403,978	–632,866
Indiana.............	342,593	810,225	512,148	298,077	71,633	93,367	–21,734
Iowa...............	81,476	361,766	255,370	106,396	–15,876	36,329	–52,205
Kansas.............	129,936	370,672	225,837	144,835	–17,574	52,388	–69,962
Kentucky	271,825	519,005	370,888	148,117	126,831	44,314	82,517
Louisiana...........	23,104	595,844	382,645	213,199	–285,765	33,046	–318,811
Maine..............	43,386	128,319	116,170	12,149	38,804	8,079	30,725
Maryland	402,934	698,269	405,035	293,234	95,290	191,262	–95,972
Massachusetts........	244,468	729,448	508,747	220,701	–31,623	245,145	–276,768
Michigan	31,235	1,196,297	802,544	393,753	–372,082	168,668	–540,750
Minnesota	346,722	654,294	348,464	305,830	62,426	106,388	–43,962
Mississippi..........	107,330	403,008	263,192	139,816	–18,973	17,572	–36,545
Missouri............	390,896	726,153	507,227	218,926	105,461	63,420	42,041
Montana............	72,799	108,579	77,395	31,184	42,980	3,042	39,938
Nebraska...........	85,354	241,832	139,626	102,206	–9,156	31,988	–41,144
Nevada	644,825	333,232	165,152	168,080	485,443	110,681	374,762
New Hampshire.......	88,784	135,471	92,897	42,574	53,460	18,373	35,087
New Jersey	293,361	1,038,937	664,523	374,414	–60,000	399,803	–459,803
New Mexico..........	190,630	265,766	136,175	129,591	70,558	47,343	23,215
New York	564,642	2,323,103	1,417,221	905,882	–846,993	839,590	–1,686,583
North Carolina........	1,334,478	1,143,251	685,324	457,927	889,589	214,573	675,016
North Dakota.........	4,649	76,697	53,637	23,060	–15,217	4,568	–19,785
Ohio...............	189,495	1,389,016	999,895	389,121	–247,751	120,452	–368,203
Oklahoma	236,412	481,766	325,299	156,467	92,977	53,514	39,463
Oregon.............	404,220	433,972	284,372	149,600	274,031	95,484	178,547
Pennsylvania.........	323,696	1,350,244	1,183,448	166,796	136,359	176,498	–40,139
Rhode Island	4,894	115,762	89,989	25,773	–14,632	30,017	–44,649
South Carolina........	549,410	537,443	355,877	181,566	376,441	65,869	310,572
South Dakota........	57,548	105,163	64,270	40,893	13,367	6,545	6,822
Tennessee...........	606,978	754,589	525,554	229,035	356,078	91,508	264,570
Texas..............	3,930,484	3,568,617	1,444,493	2,124,124	1,781,785	933,083	848,702
Utah...............	551,368	479,519	124,262	355,257	118,543	65,961	52,582
Vermont............	12,939	59,886	47,266	12,620	3,877	5,001	–1,124
Virginia.............	803,542	957,904	532,166	425,738	375,639	204,219	171,420
Washington	770,052	772,324	424,029	348,295	440,988	202,442	238,546
West Virginia	11,433	192,926	193,308	–382	21,653	5,635	16,018
Wisconsin	291,066	654,879	429,869	225,010	59,904	70,347	–10,443
Wyoming	50,487	65,633	38,277	27,356	25,660	3,278	22,382

X Not applicable. [1] Total population change includes a residual. This residual represents the change in population that cannot be attributed to any specific demographic component. [2] Net international migration includes the international migration of both native and foreign-born populations. Specifically, it includes: (a) the net international migration of the foreign born, (b) the net migration between the United States and Puerto Rico, (c) the net migration of natives to and from the United States, and (d) the net movement of the Armed Forces population between the United States and overseas.

Source: U.S. Census Bureau, Population Division, "Table 4. Cumulative Estimates of the Components of Resident Population Change for the United States, Regions, States, and Puerto Rico: April 1, 2000 to July 1, 2009 (NST-EST2009-04)," December 2009, <http://www.census.gov/popest/states/tables/NST-EST2009-04.xls>.

U.S. Census Bureau, Statistical Abstract of the United States: 2012

Table 16. Resident Population by Age and State: 2010

[In thousands, except percent (308,746 represents 308,746,000). As of April 1]

State	Total	Under 5 years	5 to 14 years	15 to 24 years	25 to 34 years	35 to 44 years	45 to 54 years	55 to 64 years	65 to 74 years	75 to 84 years	85 years and over	Percent 65 years old and over
U.S.	**308,746**	**20,201**	**41,026**	**43,626**	**41,064**	**41,071**	**45,007**	**36,483**	**21,713**	**13,061**	**5,493**	**13.0**
AL	4,780	305	628	679	609	620	694	588	371	212	76	13.8
AK	710	54	102	107	103	93	111	86	35	15	5	7.7
AZ	6,392	456	902	904	857	822	843	726	498	281	103	13.8
AR	2,916	198	394	403	376	366	407	351	235	134	51	14.4
CA	37,254	2,531	5,097	5,590	5,318	5,183	5,252	4,036	2,275	1,370	601	11.4
CO	5,029	344	681	688	726	700	743	598	310	170	70	10.9
CT	3,574	202	463	479	420	484	576	443	255	167	85	14.2
DE	898	56	113	127	111	116	134	111	72	41	16	14.4
DC	602	33	51	104	125	81	76	64	37	22	10	11.4
FL	18,801	1,074	2,211	2,457	2,290	2,431	2,741	2,338	1,728	1,098	434	17.3
GA	9,688	687	1,385	1,390	1,336	1,398	1,391	1,070	606	312	114	10.7
HI	1,360	87	165	182	185	176	194	176	101	64	30	14.3
ID	1,568	122	238	224	209	192	209	180	110	60	25	12.4
IL	12,831	836	1,739	1,801	1,776	1,726	1,871	1,473	850	525	235	12.5
IN	6,484	434	897	928	827	841	947	769	452	274	115	13.0
IA	3,046	202	402	430	383	365	440	373	225	154	75	14.9
KS	2,853	205	401	408	378	347	406	331	190	126	59	13.2
KY	4,339	282	567	587	566	577	643	539	325	184	69	13.3
LA	4,533	314	613	665	628	565	654	536	312	180	66	12.3
ME	1,328	70	153	168	145	171	219	192	113	69	29	15.9
MD	5,774	364	746	800	762	796	902	696	386	223	98	12.3
MA	6,548	367	791	938	845	887	1,012	803	456	301	145	13.8
MI	9,884	596	1,313	1,409	1,164	1,278	1,510	1,252	725	445	192	13.8
MN	5,304	356	708	723	716	681	808	629	354	222	107	12.9
MS	2,967	211	414	436	387	375	417	347	214	122	44	12.8
MO	5,989	390	787	837	775	749	889	723	450	274	114	14.0
MT	989	62	122	134	123	113	150	139	81	46	20	14.8
NE	1,826	132	252	258	245	221	259	213	123	84	39	13.5
NV	2,701	187	366	360	387	383	377	315	198	96	30	12.0
NH	1,316	70	162	178	144	179	226	178	97	57	25	13.5
NJ	8,792	541	1,152	1,139	1,110	1,238	1,379	1,046	611	395	180	13.5
NM	2,059	145	285	292	267	249	292	257	154	86	32	13.2
NY	19,378	1,156	2,375	2,777	2,659	2,610	2,879	2,304	1,361	866	391	13.5
NC	9,535	632	1,267	1,321	1,247	1,327	1,369	1,139	698	389	147	12.9
ND	673	45	80	106	90	75	97	82	47	34	17	14.5
OH	11,537	721	1,523	1,587	1,410	1,480	1,742	1,452	850	541	230	14.1
OK	3,751	264	513	534	507	461	526	440	280	164	62	13.5
OR	3,831	238	480	508	524	500	539	510	290	166	78	13.9
PA	12,702	730	1,545	1,779	1,511	1,616	1,940	1,622	980	674	306	15.4
RI	1,053	57	124	162	127	137	162	131	74	51	27	14.4
SC	4,625	302	593	661	592	601	659	584	369	192	71	13.7
SD	814	60	109	115	105	93	117	98	58	40	19	14.3
TN	6,346	408	831	863	824	854	926	786	487	266	100	13.4
TX	25,146	1,928	3,810	3,700	3,613	3,458	3,435	2,598	1,472	824	305	10.3
UT	2,764	264	478	448	446	332	307	240	138	80	31	9.0
VT	626	32	72	90	70	78	103	90	50	29	13	14.6
VA	8,001	510	1,023	1,123	1,090	1,109	1,214	955	550	305	122	12.2
WA	6,725	440	868	924	934	908	988	835	457	253	117	12.3
WV	1,853	104	215	237	221	237	276	265	164	98	36	16.0
WI	5,687	358	745	786	722	726	874	700	400	258	119	13.7
WY	564	40	73	78	78	67	84	74	40	22	9	12.4

Source: U.S. Census Bureau, "Demographic Profiles: Census 2010," <http://2010.census.gov/news/press-kits/demographic-profiles.html>.

Table 17. Age Dependency Ratios by State: 2000 and 2010

[As of April]

State	Age dependency ratio [1]		Child dependency ratio [2]		Old-age dependency ratio [3]	
	2000	2010	2000	2010	2000	2010
United States	**61.6**	**58.9**	**41.5**	**38.2**	**20.1**	**20.7**
Alabama	62.1	59.9	40.9	37.9	21.1	22.0
Alaska	56.5	51.8	47.6	40.0	8.9	11.7
Arizona	65.7	64.7	44.2	42.0	21.6	22.7
Arkansas	65.1	63.4	42.0	39.9	23.1	23.5
California	61.1	57.1	44.0	39.2	17.1	17.9
Colorado	54.5	54.6	39.5	37.7	14.9	16.9
Connecticut	62.7	58.8	40.2	36.3	22.5	22.5
Delaware	60.8	59.5	39.9	36.6	20.9	23.0
District of Columbia	47.8	39.3	29.7	23.3	18.1	15.9
Florida	67.7	62.9	38.3	34.7	29.5	28.2
Georgia	56.5	57.2	41.5	40.4	15.0	16.7
Hawaii	60.4	57.9	39.2	35.3	21.3	22.7
Idaho	66.1	66.1	47.4	45.5	18.7	20.6
Illinois................	61.8	58.6	42.3	38.7	19.5	19.9
Indiana...............	62.0	60.7	41.9	39.9	20.1	20.8
Iowa.................	66.6	63.3	41.8	39.0	24.8	24.3
Kansas...............	66.0	63.0	44.0	41.5	22.0	21.5
Kentucky	59.0	58.5	39.1	37.4	19.9	21.1
Louisiana..............	63.6	58.6	44.6	39.1	18.9	19.5
Maine................	61.3	57.6	38.1	32.6	23.2	25.0
Maryland	58.5	55.5	40.6	36.4	17.9	19.1
Massachusetts...........	59.2	54.9	37.6	33.6	21.6	21.4
Michigan	62.3	60.0	42.4	37.9	19.9	22.0
Minnesota	61.9	59.0	42.4	38.5	19.6	20.5
Mississippi.............	64.8	62.0	44.9	41.3	19.9	20.8
Missouri...............	64.0	60.8	41.8	38.3	22.1	22.5
Montana..............	63.7	59.8	41.7	36.1	21.9	23.7
Nebraska..............	66.3	63.0	43.8	41.0	22.6	22.0
Nevada	57.6	57.8	40.4	38.9	17.3	19.0
New Hampshire..........	58.8	54.7	39.8	33.8	19.0	20.9
New Jersey	61.4	58.7	40.0	37.3	21.4	21.4
New Mexico...........	65.6	62.4	46.3	40.9	19.3	21.5
New York	60.3	55.8	39.6	34.8	20.7	21.1
North Carolina...........	57.3	58.4	38.4	37.9	19.0	20.5
North Dakota...........	66.0	58.2	41.6	35.2	24.4	22.9
Ohio.................	63.2	60.6	41.5	38.0	21.7	22.6
Oklahoma	64.1	62.0	42.4	40.2	21.7	21.9
Oregon................	60.1	57.6	39.6	35.6	20.5	21.9
Pennsylvania	65.1	59.8	39.3	35.1	25.8	24.6
Rhode Island	61.8	55.5	38.2	33.1	23.5	22.4
South Carolina...........	59.4	58.8	40.1	37.1	19.3	21.7
South Dakota...........	70.0	64.5	45.6	41.0	24.4	23.6
Tennessee..............	58.6	58.8	39.0	37.4	19.6	21.4
Texas.................	61.7	60.4	45.7	43.8	16.1	16.6
Utah.................	68.6	68.2	54.3	53.0	14.4	15.2
Vermont...............	58.6	54.3	38.4	31.9	20.2	22.5
Virginia................	55.6	54.7	38.2	35.9	17.4	18.9
Washington	58.5	55.8	40.7	36.6	17.8	19.2
West Virginia	60.2	58.6	35.6	33.2	24.5	25.5
Wisconsin	62.9	59.3	41.6	37.5	21.3	21.8
Wyoming	60.7	57.4	41.9	37.8	18.8	19.6

[1] The age dependency ratio is derived by dividing the combined under 18 and 65-and-over populations by the 18-to-64 population and multiplying by 100. [2] The child dependency ratio is derived by dividing the population under 18 by the 18-to-64 population and multiplying by 100. [3] The old-age dependency ratio is derived by dividing the population 65 and over by the 18-to-64 population and multiplying by 100.

Source: U.S. Census Bureau, Table GCT-T6-R, "Age Dependency Ratio of the Total Population"; Table GCT-T7-R, "Child Dependency Ratio of the Total Population"; and Table GCT-T8-R, "Old-Age Dependency Ratio of the Total Population," <http://factfinder.census.gov/>, accessed May 2011.

Table 18. Resident Population by Hispanic Origin and State: 2010

[In thousands, except as indicated (308,746 represents 308,746,000). As of April 1. Hispanic origin is considered an ethnicity, not a race. Persons of Hispanic origin may be any race]

State	Total population	Hispanic Total Number	Hispanic Total Percent of total population	Mexican	Puerto Rican	Cuban	Other Hispanic	Non-Hispanic Total	Non-Hispanic White
U.S.	**308,746**	**50,478**	**16.3**	**31,798**	**4,624**	**1,786**	**12,270**	**258,268**	**196,818**
AL	4,780	186	3.9	123	12	4	46	4,594	3,204
AK	710	39	5.5	22	5	1	12	671	455
AZ	6,392	1,895	29.6	1,658	35	11	192	4,497	3,696
AR	2,916	186	6.4	138	5	1	42	2,730	2,173
CA	37,254	14,014	37.6	11,423	190	89	2,312	23,240	14,956
CO	5,029	1,039	20.7	757	23	6	252	3,991	3,521
CT	3,574	479	13.4	51	253	9	166	3,095	2,546
DE	898	73	8.2	30	23	1	19	825	587
DC	602	55	9.1	9	3	2	41	547	209
FL	18,801	4,224	22.5	630	848	1,213	1,533	14,578	10,885
GA	9,688	854	8.8	520	72	25	237	8,834	5,414
HI	1,360	121	8.9	35	44	2	40	1,239	309
ID	1,568	176	11.2	149	3	1	23	1,392	1,316
IL	12,831	2,028	15.8	1,602	183	23	220	10,803	8,168
IN	6,484	390	6.0	295	30	4	60	6,094	5,286
IA	3,046	152	5.0	117	5	1	28	2,895	2,701
KS	2,853	300	10.5	247	9	3	41	2,553	2,231
KY	4,339	133	3.1	82	11	9	30	4,207	3,746
LA	4,533	193	4.2	79	12	10	92	4,341	2,735
ME	1,328	17	1.3	5	4	1	7	1,311	1,254
MD	5,774	471	8.2	88	43	10	330	5,303	3,158
MA	6,548	628	9.6	38	266	11	312	5,920	4,985
MI	9,884	436	4.4	318	37	10	71	9,447	7,570
MN	5,304	250	4.7	176	11	4	60	5,054	4,405
MS	2,967	81	2.7	52	6	2	21	2,886	1,722
MO	5,989	212	3.5	147	12	5	48	5,776	4,851
MT	989	29	2.9	20	1	(Z)	7	961	869
NE	1,826	167	9.2	128	3	2	34	1,659	1,500
NV	2,701	717	26.5	541	21	21	133	1,984	1,462
NH	1,316	37	2.8	8	12	1	16	1,280	1,215
NJ	8,792	1,555	17.7	218	434	83	820	7,237	5,215
NM	2,059	953	46.3	591	8	4	350	1,106	834
NY	19,378	3,417	17.6	457	1,071	71	1,818	15,961	11,304
NC	9,535	800	8.4	487	72	18	223	8,735	6,224
ND	673	13	2.0	9	1	(Z)	3	659	598
OH	11,537	355	3.1	172	95	8	80	11,182	9,359
OK	3,751	332	8.9	267	12	3	50	3,419	2,575
OR	3,831	450	11.7	370	9	5	66	3,381	3,006
PA	12,702	720	5.7	130	366	18	206	11,983	10,095
RI	1,053	131	12.4	9	35	2	85	922	804
SC	4,625	236	5.1	138	26	6	65	4,390	2,963
SD	814	22	2.7	14	1	(Z)	7	792	690
TN	6,346	290	4.6	187	21	8	75	6,056	4,801
TX	25,146	9,461	37.6	7,951	131	47	1,333	15,685	11,397
UT	2,764	358	13.0	259	7	2	90	2,406	2,222
VT	626	9	1.5	3	2	1	4	617	590
VA	8,001	632	7.9	155	74	15	388	7,369	5,186
WA	6,725	756	11.2	602	26	7	121	5,969	4,877
WV	1,853	22	1.2	10	4	1	8	1,831	1,726
WI	5,687	336	5.9	244	46	4	42	5,351	4,738
WY	564	50	8.9	38	1	(Z)	11	513	484

Z Less than 500.

Source: U.S. Census Bureau, "Demographic Profiles: 2010," <http://2010.census.gov/news/press-kits/demographic-profiles.html>

Population 23

Table 19. Resident Population by Race and State: 2010

[In thousands, except as indicated (308,746 represents 308,746,000). As of April 1]

State	Number (1,000)							
		One race						
	Total population	White alone	Black or African American alone	American Indian, Alaska Native alone	Asian alone	Native Hawaiian and Other Pacific Islander alone	Some other race	Two or more races
U.S.	**308,746**	**223,553**	**38,929**	**2,932**	**14,674**	**540**	**19,107**	**9,009**
AL	4,780	3,275	1,251	28	54	3	97	71
AK	710	474	23	105	38	7	11	52
AZ	6,392	4,667	259	297	177	13	762	218
AR	2,916	2,245	450	22	36	6	100	57
CA	37,254	21,454	2,299	363	4,861	144	6,317	1,815
CO	5,029	4,089	202	56	139	7	364	172
CT	3,574	2,772	362	11	136	1	198	93
DE	898	619	192	4	29	(Z)	31	24
DC	602	231	305	2	21	(Z)	24	17
FL	18,801	14,109	3,000	71	455	12	681	473
GA	9,688	5,787	2,950	32	314	7	389	207
HI	1,360	337	21	4	525	135	17	321
ID	1,568	1,396	10	21	19	2	80	39
IL	12,831	9,178	1,866	44	587	4	861	290
IN	6,484	5,468	591	18	102	2	173	128
IA	3,046	2,782	89	11	53	2	56	53
KS	2,853	2,391	168	28	68	2	110	86
KY	4,339	3,810	338	10	49	3	56	75
LA	4,533	2,836	1,452	31	70	2	69	73
ME	1,328	1,265	16	9	14	(Z)	4	21
MD	5,774	3,359	1,700	20	319	3	207	165
MA	6,548	5,265	434	19	350	2	305	172
MI	9,884	7,803	1,400	62	238	3	147	230
MN	5,304	4,524	274	61	214	2	103	125
MS	2,967	1,755	1,098	15	26	1	38	34
MO	5,989	4,959	693	27	98	6	80	125
MT	989	885	4	63	6	1	6	25
NE	1,826	1,573	83	18	32	1	79	40
NV	2,701	1,787	219	32	195	17	325	126
NH	1,316	1,236	15	3	28	(Z)	12	21
NJ	8,792	6,029	1,205	29	726	3	560	240
NM	2,059	1,408	43	193	28	2	309	77
NY	19,378	12,741	3,074	107	1,420	9	1,442	586
NC	9,535	6,529	2,049	122	209	7	414	206
ND	673	605	8	37	7	(Z)	4	12
OH	11,537	9,539	1,408	25	192	4	130	238
OK	3,751	2,707	278	322	65	4	154	221
OR	3,831	3,205	69	53	141	13	205	145
PA	12,702	10,406	1,378	27	349	4	301	238
RI	1,053	857	60	6	30	1	64	35
SC	4,625	3,060	1,291	20	59	3	113	80
SD	814	699	10	72	8	(Z)	7	17
TN	6,346	4,922	1,057	20	91	4	142	110
TX	25,146	17,702	2,980	171	965	22	2,628	679
UT	2,764	2,380	29	33	55	25	167	76
VT	626	596	6	2	8	(Z)	2	11
VA	8,001	5,487	1,551	29	440	6	254	233
WA	6,725	5,196	240	104	481	40	350	313
WV	1,853	1,740	63	4	12	(Z)	6	27
WI	5,687	4,902	359	55	129	2	136	104
WY	564	511	5	13	4	(Z)	17	12

See footnote at end of table.

U.S. Census Bureau, Statistical Abstract of the United States: 2012

Table 19. Resident Population by Race and State: 2010—Con.

[See headnote, page 24]

State	Percent distribution						Two or more races
	One race						
	White alone	Black or African American alone	American Indian, Alaska Native alone	Asian alone	Native Hawaiian and Other Pacific Islander alone	Some other race	
U.S.	72.4	12.6	0.9	4.8	0.2	6.2	2.9
AL	68.5	26.2	0.6	1.1	0.1	2.0	1.5
AK	66.7	3.3	14.8	5.4	1.0	1.6	7.3
AZ	73.0	4.1	4.6	2.8	0.2	11.9	3.4
AR	77.0	15.4	0.8	1.2	0.2	3.4	2.0
CA	57.6	6.2	1.0	13.0	0.4	17.0	4.9
CO	81.3	4.0	1.1	2.8	0.1	7.2	3.4
CT	77.6	10.1	0.3	3.8	(Z)	5.6	2.6
DE	68.9	21.4	0.5	3.2	(Z)	3.4	2.7
DC	38.5	50.7	0.3	3.5	0.1	4.1	2.9
FL	75.0	16.0	0.4	2.4	0.1	3.6	2.5
GA	59.7	30.5	0.3	3.2	0.1	4.0	2.1
HI	24.7	1.6	0.3	38.6	10.0	1.2	23.6
ID	89.1	0.6	1.4	1.2	0.1	5.1	2.5
IL	71.5	14.5	0.3	4.6	(Z)	6.7	2.3
IN	84.3	9.1	0.3	1.6	(Z)	2.7	2.0
IA	91.3	2.9	0.4	1.7	0.1	1.8	1.8
KS	83.8	5.9	1.0	2.4	0.1	3.9	3.0
KY	87.8	7.8	0.2	1.1	0.1	1.3	1.7
LA	62.6	32.0	0.7	1.5	(Z)	1.5	1.6
ME	95.2	1.2	0.6	1.0	(Z)	0.3	1.6
MD	58.2	29.4	0.4	5.5	0.1	3.6	2.9
MA	80.4	6.6	0.3	5.3	(Z)	4.7	2.6
MI	78.9	14.2	0.6	2.4	(Z)	1.5	2.3
MN	85.3	5.2	1.1	4.0	(Z)	1.9	2.4
MS	59.1	37.0	0.5	0.9	(Z)	1.3	1.1
MO	82.8	11.6	0.5	1.6	0.1	1.3	2.1
MT	89.4	0.4	6.3	0.6	0.1	0.6	2.5
NE	86.1	4.5	1.0	1.8	0.1	4.3	2.2
NV	66.2	8.1	1.2	7.2	0.6	12.0	4.7
NH	93.9	1.1	0.2	2.2	(Z)	0.9	1.6
NJ	68.6	13.7	0.3	8.3	(Z)	6.4	2.7
NM	68.4	2.1	9.4	1.4	0.1	15.0	3.7
NY	65.7	15.9	0.6	7.3	(Z)	7.4	3.0
NC	68.5	21.5	1.3	2.2	0.1	4.3	2.2
ND	90.0	1.2	5.4	1.0	(Z)	0.5	1.8
OH	82.7	12.2	0.2	1.7	(Z)	1.1	2.1
OK	72.2	7.4	8.6	1.7	0.1	4.1	5.9
OR	83.6	1.8	1.4	3.7	0.3	5.3	3.8
PA	81.9	10.8	0.2	2.7	(Z)	2.4	1.9
RI	81.4	5.7	0.6	2.9	0.1	6.0	3.3
SC	66.2	27.9	0.4	1.3	0.1	2.5	1.7
SD	85.9	1.3	8.8	0.9	(Z)	0.9	2.1
TN	77.6	16.7	0.3	1.4	0.1	2.2	1.7
TX	70.4	11.8	0.7	3.8	0.1	10.5	2.7
UT	86.1	1.1	1.2	2.0	0.9	6.0	2.7
VT	95.3	1.0	0.4	1.3	(Z)	0.3	1.7
VA	68.6	19.4	0.4	5.5	0.1	3.2	2.9
WA	77.3	3.6	1.5	7.2	0.6	5.2	4.7
WV	93.9	3.4	0.2	0.7	(Z)	0.3	1.5
WI	86.2	6.3	1.0	2.3	(Z)	2.4	1.8
WY	90.7	0.8	2.4	0.8	0.1	3.0	2.2

Z Less than 500 or 0.05 percent.
Source: U.S. Census Bureau, 2010 Census Redistricting Data (Public Law 94-171) Summary File, Table P1,
<www.census.gov/prod/cen2010/doc/pl94-171.pdf>.

Table 20. Large Metropolitan Statistical Areas—Population: 1990 to 2010

[As of April 1. In thousands, except as indicated (658 represents 658,000). Covers metropolitan statistical areas with 250,000 and over population in 2010, as defined by the U.S. Office of Management and Budget as of November 2009. All geographic boundaries for 2000 and 2010 population are defined as of January 1, 2010. For definitions and components of all metropolitan and micropolitan areas, see Appendix II. Minus sign (−) indicates decrease]

Metropolitan statistical area	1990	2000	2010	Change 1990–2000 Number	Change 1990–2000 Percent	Change 2000–2010 Number	Change 2000–2010 Percent	Rank, 2010
Akron, OH	658	695	703	37	5.7	8	1.2	72
Albany–Schenectady–Troy, NY	810	826	871	16	2.0	45	5.4	58
Albuquerque, NM	599	730	887	130	21.7	157	21.6	57
Allentown–Bethlehem–Easton, PA–NJ	687	740	821	54	7.8	81	10.9	64
Anchorage, AK	266	320	381	54	20.1	61	19.2	133
Ann Arbor, MI	283	323	345	40	14.1	22	6.8	146
Asheville, NC	308	369	425	61	19.9	56	15.1	117
Atlanta–Sandy Springs–Marietta, GA	3,069	4,248	5,269	1,179	38.4	1,021	24.0	9
Atlantic City–Hammonton, NJ	224	253	275	28	12.6	22	8.7	166
Augusta–Richmond County, GA–SC	436	500	557	64	14.7	57	11.4	92
Austin–Round Rock, TX	846	1,250	1,716	404	47.7	467	37.3	35
Bakersfield, CA	545	662	840	117	21.4	178	26.9	62
Baltimore–Towson, MD	2,382	2,553	2,710	171	7.2	157	6.2	20
Baton Rouge, LA	624	706	802	82	13.2	97	13.7	65
Beaumont–Port Arthur, TX	361	385	389	24	6.6	4	0.9	132
Binghamton, NY	264	252	252	−12	−4.6	−1	−0.2	182
Birmingham–Hoover, AL	957	1,052	1,128	96	10.0	76	7.2	49
Boise City–Nampa, ID	320	465	617	145	45.4	152	32.6	86
Boston–Cambridge–Quincy, MA–NH	4,134	4,391	4,552	257	6.2	161	3.7	10
Boulder, CO [1]	209	270	295	61	29.1	25	9.2	160
Bremerton-Silverdale, WA	190	232	251	42	22.3	19	8.3	183
Bridgeport–Stamford–Norwalk, CT	828	883	917	55	6.6	34	3.9	56
Brownsville–Harlingen, TX	260	335	406	75	28.9	71	21.2	126
Buffalo–Niagara Falls, NY	1,189	1,170	1,136	−19	−1.6	−35	−3.0	47
Canton–Massillon, OH	394	407	404	13	3.3	−3	−0.6	128
Cape Coral–Fort Myers, FL	335	441	619	106	31.6	178	40.3	85
Cedar Rapids, IA	211	237	258	27	12.6	21	8.7	176
Charleston, WV	308	310	304	2	0.6	−5	−1.7	154
Charleston–North Charleston–Summerville, SC	507	549	665	42	8.3	116	21.1	79
Charlotte–Gastonia–Concord, NC–SC	1,025	1,330	1,758	306	29.8	428	32.1	33
Chattanooga, TN–GA	433	477	528	43	10.0	52	10.8	97
Chicago–Joliet-Naperville–Joliet, IL–IN–WI	8,182	9,098	9,461	916	11.2	363	4.0	3
Cincinnati–Middletown, OH–KY–IN	1,845	2,010	2,130	165	8.9	121	6.0	27
Clarksville, TN–KY	189	232	274	43	22.6	42	18.1	168
Cleveland–Elyria–Mentor, OH	2,102	2,148	2,077	46	2.2	−71	−3.3	28
Colorado Springs, CO	409	537	646	128	31.3	108	20.1	82
Columbia, SC	549	647	768	98	17.9	120	18.6	70
Columbus, GA–AL	266	282	295	15	5.7	13	4.6	159
Columbus, OH	1,405	1,613	1,837	208	14.8	224	13.9	32
Corpus Christi, TX	368	403	428	35	9.7	25	6.2	114
Dallas–Fort Worth–Arlington, TX	3,989	5,162	6,372	1,172	29.4	1,210	23.4	4
Davenport–Moline–Rock Island, IA–IL	368	376	380	8	2.1	4	1.0	134
Dayton, OH	844	848	842	4	0.5	−7	−0.8	61
Deltona–Daytona Beach–Ormond Beach, FL	371	443	495	73	19.6	51	11.6	103
Denver–Aurora–Broomfield, CO [1]	1,667	2,179	2,543	512	30.7	364	16.7	21
Des Moines–West Des Moines, IA	416	481	570	65	15.6	88	18.3	88
Detroit–Warren–Livonia, MI	4,249	4,453	4,296	204	4.8	−156	−3.5	12
Duluth, MN–WI	269	275	280	6	2.3	4	1.6	165
Durham–Chapel Hill, NC	345	426	504	82	23.7	78	18.3	102
El Paso, TX	592	680	801	88	14.9	121	17.8	66
Erie, PA	276	281	281	5	1.9	(−Z)	−0.1	164
Eugene–Springfield, OR	283	323	352	40	14.2	29	8.9	143
Evansville, IN–KY	325	343	359	18	5.5	16	4.6	142
Fayetteville, NC	298	337	366	39	13.1	30	8.8	139
Fayetteville–Springdale–Rogers, AR–MO	239	347	463	108	44.9	116	33.5	109
Flint, MI	430	436	426	6	1.3	−10	−2.4	115
Fort Collins–Loveland, CO	186	251	300	65	35.1	48	19.1	156
Fort Smith, AR–OK	234	273	299	39	16.7	25	9.3	158
Fort Wayne, IN	354	390	416	36	10.1	26	6.7	121
Fresno, CA	667	799	930	132	19.8	131	16.4	55

See footnotes at end of table.

U.S. Census Bureau, Statistical Abstract of the United States: 2012

Table 20. Large Metropolitan Statistical Areas—Population: 1990 to 2010—Con.

[As of April 1. In thousands, except as indicated (658 represents 658,000). Covers metropolitan statistical areas with 250,000 and over population in 2010, as defined by the U.S. Office of Management and Budget as of November 2009. All geographic boundaries for 2000 and 2010 population are defined as of January 1, 2010. For definitions and components of all metropolitan and micropolitan areas, see Appendix II. Minus sign (–) indicates decrease]

Metropolitan statistical area	1990	2000	2010	Change 1990–2000 Number	Change 1990–2000 Percent	Change 2000–2010 Number	Change 2000–2010 Percent	Rank, 2010
Gainesville, FL	191	232	264	41	21.5	32	13.7	173
Grand Rapids–Wyoming, MI	646	740	774	95	14.6	34	4.5	69
Greeley, CO [1]	132	181	253	49	37.3	72	39.7	179
Green Bay, WI	244	283	306	39	16.0	24	8.4	153
Greensboro–High Point, NC	540	643	724	103	19.1	80	12.5	71
Greenville–Mauldin–Easley, SC	472	560	637	88	18.6	77	13.8	83
Hagerstown–Martinsburg, MD–WV	193	223	269	30	15.6	46	20.8	172
Harrisburg–Carlisle, PA	474	509	549	35	7.3	40	7.9	93
Hartford–West Hartford–East Hartford, CT	1,124	1,149	1,212	25	2.2	64	5.6	45
Hickory–Lenoir–Morganton, NC	292	342	365	49	16.9	24	6.9	140
Holland–Grand Haven, MI	188	238	264	51	26.9	25	10.7	174
Honolulu, HI	836	876	953	40	4.8	77	8.8	53
Houston–Sugar Land–Baytown, TX	3,767	4,715	5,947	948	25.2	1,231	26.1	6
Huntington–Ashland, WV–KY–OH	288	289	288	(Z)	0.2	–1	–0.3	161
Huntsville, AL	293	342	418	49	16.8	75	22.0	120
Indianapolis–Carmel, IN	1,294	1,525	1,756	231	17.8	231	15.2	34
Jackson, MS	447	497	539	50	11.2	42	8.4	96
Jacksonville, FL	925	1,123	1,346	198	21.4	223	19.8	40
Kalamazoo–Portage, MI	293	315	327	21	7.3	12	3.7	148
Kansas City, MO–KS	1,637	1,836	2,035	200	12.2	199	10.9	29
Kennewick-Pasco-Richland, WA	150	192	253	42	27.9	62	32.1	178
Killeen–Temple–Fort Hood, TX	269	331	405	62	23.0	75	22.6	127
Kingsport–Bristol–Bristol, TN–VA	276	298	310	23	8.3	11	3.7	151
Knoxville, TN	535	616	698	81	15.2	82	13.3	75
Lafayette, LA	209	239	274	30	14.5	35	14.5	169
Lakeland–Winter Haven, FL	405	484	602	79	19.4	118	24.4	87
Lancaster, PA	423	471	519	48	11.3	49	10.4	99
Lansing–East Lansing, MI	433	448	464	15	3.5	16	3.6	108
Laredo, TX	133	193	250	60	44.9	57	29.6	184
Las Vegas–Paradise, NV	741	1,376	1,951	634	85.6	576	41.8	30
Lexington–Fayette, KY	348	408	472	60	17.2	64	15.6	106
Lincoln, NE	229	267	302	38	16.5	35	13.3	155
Little Rock–North Little Rock–Conway, AR	535	611	700	76	14.1	89	14.6	74
Los Angeles–Long Beach–Santa Ana, CA	11,274	12,366	12,829	1,092	9.7	463	3.7	2
Louisville/Jefferson County, KY–IN	1,056	1,162	1,284	106	10.0	122	10.5	42
Lubbock, TX	230	250	285	20	8.6	35	14.1	162
Lynchburg, VA	206	229	253	22	10.9	24	10.5	180
Madison, WI	432	502	569	69	16.1	67	13.3	89
Manchester–Nashua, NH	336	381	401	45	13.4	20	5.2	129
McAllen–Edinburg–Mission, TX	384	569	775	186	48.5	205	36.1	68
Memphis, TN–MS–AR	1,067	1,205	1,316	138	12.9	111	9.2	41
Merced, CA	178	211	256	32	18.0	45	21.5	177
Miami–Fort Lauderdale–Pompano Beach, FL	4,056	5,008	5,565	951	23.5	557	11.1	8
Milwaukee–Waukesha–West Allis, WI	1,432	1,501	1,556	69	4.8	55	3.7	39
Minneapolis–St. Paul–Bloomington, MN–WI	2,539	2,969	3,280	430	16.9	311	10.5	16
Mobile, AL	379	400	413	21	5.6	13	3.3	124
Modesto, CA	371	447	514	76	20.6	67	15.1	100
Montgomery, AL	305	347	375	41	13.6	28	8.1	136
Myrtle Beach–North Myrtle Beach–Conway, SC	144	197	269	53	36.5	73	37.0	171
Naples–Marco Island, FL	152	251	322	99	65.3	70	27.9	149
Nashville–Davidson—Murfreesboro—Franklin, TN	1,048	1,312	1,590	264	25.1	278	21.2	38
New Haven–Milford, CT	804	824	862	20	2.5	38	4.7	60
New Orleans–Metairie–Kenner, LA	1,264	1,317	1,168	52	4.1	–149	–11.3	46
New York–Northern New Jersey–Long Island, NY–NJ–PA	16,846	18,323	18,897	1,477	8.8	574	3.1	1
North Port-Bradenton-Sarasota, FL	489	590	702	100	20.5	112	19.0	73
Norwich–New London, CT	255	259	274	4	1.6	15	5.8	167
Ocala, FL	195	259	331	64	32.9	72	28.0	147
Ogden–Clearfield, UT	352	443	547	91	25.8	105	23.6	94
Oklahoma City, OK	971	1,095	1,253	124	12.8	158	14.4	44
Olympia, WA	161	207	252	46	28.6	45	21.7	181
Omaha–Council Bluffs, NE–IA	686	767	865	81	11.8	98	12.8	59
Orlando–Kissimmee-Sanford, FL	1,225	1,645	2,134	420	34.3	490	29.8	26
Oxnard–Thousand Oaks–Ventura, CA	669	753	823	84	12.6	70	9.3	63
Palm Bay–Melbourne–Titusville, FL	399	476	543	77	19.4	67	14.1	95
Pensacola–Ferry Pass–Brent, FL	344	412	449	68	19.7	37	8.9	110
Peoria, IL	359	367	379	8	2.3	12	3.3	135
Philadelphia–Camden–Wilmington, PA–NJ–DE–MD	5,436	5,687	5,965	252	4.6	278	4.9	5
Phoenix–Mesa–Glendale, AZ	2,238	3,252	4,193	1,013	45.3	941	28.9	14
Pittsburgh, PA	2,468	2,431	2,356	–37	–1.5	–75	–3.1	22

See footnotes at end of table.

Table 20. Large Metropolitan Statistical Areas—Population: 1990 to 2010—Con.

[As of April 1. In thousands, except as indicated (658 represents 658,000). Covers metropolitan statistical areas with 250,000 and over population in 2010, as defined by the U.S. Office of Management and Budget as of November 2009. All geographic boundaries for 2000 and 2010 population are defined as of January 1, 2010. For definitions and components of all metropolitan and micropolitan areas, see Appendix II. Minus sign (–) indicates decrease]

Metropolitan statistical area	1990	2000	2010	Change				Rank, 2010
				1990–2000		2000–2010		
				Number	Percent	Number	Percent	
Portland–South Portland–Biddeford, ME	441	488	514	46	10.5	27	5.4	101
Portland–Vancouver–Hillsboro, OR–WA	1,524	1,928	2,226	404	26.5	298	15.5	23
Port St. Lucie, FL	251	319	424	68	27.2	105	32.8	118
Poughkeepsie–Newburgh–Middletown, NY	567	622	670	54	9.6	49	7.8	78
Providence–New Bedford–Fall River, RI–MA	1,510	1,583	1,601	73	4.8	18	1.1	37
Provo–Orem, UT	269	377	527	107	39.9	150	39.8	98
Raleigh–Cary, NC	544	797	1,130	253	46.5	333	41.8	48
Reading, PA	337	374	411	37	11.0	38	10.1	125
Reno–Sparks, NV	257	343	425	86	33.3	83	24.1	116
Richmond, VA	949	1,097	1,258	148	15.6	161	14.7	43
Riverside–San Bernardino–Ontario, CA	2,589	3,255	4,225	666	25.7	970	29.8	13
Roanoke, VA	269	288	309	20	7.4	20	7.1	152
Rochester, NY	1,002	1,038	1,054	35	3.5	16	1.6	51
Rockford, IL	284	320	349	36	12.9	29	9.1	144
Sacramento—Arden-Arcade—Roseville, CA	1,481	1,797	2,149	316	21.3	352	19.6	24
St. Louis, MO–IL [2]	2,581	2,699	2,813	118	4.6	114	4.2	18
Salem, OR	278	347	391	69	24.9	44	12.5	131
Salinas, CA	356	402	415	46	13.0	13	3.3	122
Salt Lake City, UT	768	969	1,124	201	26.1	155	16.0	50
San Antonio–New Braunfels, TX	1,408	1,712	2,143	304	21.6	431	25.2	25
San Diego–Carlsbad–San Marcos, CA	2,498	2,814	3,095	316	12.6	281	10.0	17
San Francisco–Oakland–Fremont, CA	3,684	4,124	4,335	440	11.9	212	5.1	11
San Jose–Sunnyvale–Santa Clara, CA	1,534	1,736	1,837	202	13.1	101	5.8	31
San Luis Obispo–Paso Robles, CA	217	247	270	30	13.6	23	9.3	170
Santa Barbara–Santa Maria–Goleta, CA	370	399	424	30	8.0	25	6.1	119
Santa Cruz–Watsonville, CA	230	256	262	26	11.3	7	2.7	175
Santa Rosa–Petaluma, CA	388	459	484	70	18.1	25	5.5	104
Savannah, GA	258	293	348	35	13.6	55	18.6	145
Scranton—Wilkes-Barre, PA	575	561	564	–15	–2.6	3	0.5	91
Seattle–Tacoma–Bellevue, WA	2,559	3,044	3,440	485	18.9	396	13.0	15
Shreveport–Bossier City, LA	360	376	399	16	4.5	23	6.0	130
South Bend–Mishawaka, IN–MI	297	317	319	20	6.8	3	0.8	150
Spartanburg, SC	227	254	284	27	11.9	31	12.0	163
Spokane, WA	361	418	471	57	15.7	53	12.7	107
Springfield, MA	673	680	693	7	1.0	13	1.9	76
Springfield, MO	299	368	437	70	23.3	68	18.6	112
Stockton, CA	481	564	685	83	17.3	122	21.6	77
Syracuse, NY	660	650	663	–10	–1.5	12	1.9	80
Tallahassee, FL	259	320	367	61	23.6	47	14.7	137
Tampa–St. Petersburg–Clearwater, FL	2,068	2,396	2,783	328	15.9	387	16.2	19
Toledo, OH	654	659	651	5	0.8	–8	–1.2	81
Trenton–Ewing, NJ	326	351	367	25	7.7	16	4.5	138
Tucson, AZ	667	844	980	177	26.5	137	16.2	52
Tulsa, OK	761	860	937	99	12.9	78	9.1	54
Utica–Rome, NY	317	300	299	–17	–5.3	(–Z)	–0.2	157
Vallejo–Fairfield, CA	339	395	413	55	16.2	19	4.8	123
Virginia Beach–Norfolk–Newport News, VA–NC	1,451	1,576	1,672	126	8.7	95	6.0	36
Visalia–Porterville, CA	312	368	442	56	18.0	74	20.2	111
Washington–Arlington–Alexandria, DC–VA–MD–WV	4,122	4,796	5,582	674	16.3	786	16.4	7
Wichita, KS	511	571	623	60	11.7	52	9.1	84
Wilmington, NC	200	275	362	74	37.2	88	32.0	141
Winston–Salem, NC	361	422	478	61	16.7	56	13.2	105
Worcester, MA	710	751	799	41	5.8	48	6.3	67
York–Hanover, PA	340	382	435	42	12.4	53	13.9	113
Youngstown–Warren–Boardman, OH–PA	614	603	566	–11	–1.7	–37	–6.2	90

Z Less than 500. [1] Broomfield County, CO, was formed from parts of Adams, Boulder, Jefferson, and Weld Counties, CO, on November 15, 2001, and is coextensive with Broomfield city. For purposes of defining and presenting data for metropolitan statistical areas, Broomfield city is treated as if it were a county at the time of the 2000 census. [2] The portion of Sullivan city in Crawford County, Missouri, is legally part of the St. Louis, MO-IL MSA. Data shown here do not include this area.

Source: U.S. Census Bureau, 1990 Census, Census 2000, and 2010 Census. See also <http://www.census.gov/prod/www /abs/decennial>.

Table 21. The 50 Largest Metropolitan Statistical Areas in 2009—Components of Population Change: 2000 to 2009

[Covers period April 1, 2000 to July 1, 2009 (1,227 represents 1,227,000). Covers metropolitan statistical areas as defined by the U.S. Office of Management and Budget as of November 2008. All geographic boundaries for 2000 to 2009 population estimates are defined as of January 1, 2009. For definitions and components of all metropolitan and micropolitan areas, see Appendix II. Minus sign (–) indicates decrease or outmigration]

Metropolitan statistical area	Number (1,000)							Percent change
	Total change [1]	Natural increase			Net migration			
		Total	Births	Deaths	Total	International	Domestic migration	
Atlanta-Sandy Springs-Marietta, GA	1,227	458	724	265	643	215	429	28.9
Austin-Round Rock, TX	455	158	223	65	303	68	234	36.4
Baltimore-Towson, MD	138	106	322	216	9	46	–36	5.4
Birmingham-Hoover, AL	80	38	140	102	42	15	27	7.6
Boston-Cambridge-Quincy, MA-NH	196	190	516	326	–38	197	–236	4.5
Buffalo-Niagara Falls, NY	–46	6	118	112	–45	10	–55	–4.0
Charlotte-Gastonia-Concord, NC-SC	415	123	222	99	298	50	248	31.2
Chicago-Naperville-Joliet, IL-IN-WI	482	662	1,300	638	–184	378	–562	5.3
Cincinnati-Middletown, OH-KY-IN	162	109	274	165	5	23	–18	8.1
Cleveland-Elyria-Mentor, OH	–57	49	244	195	–108	29	–137	–2.6
Columbus, OH	189	120	239	119	75	41	34	11.7
Dallas-Fort Worth-Arlington, TX	1,286	611	921	310	652	335	317	24.9
Denver-Aurora-Broomfield, CO [2]	373	215	345	131	164	98	66	17.1
Detroit-Warren-Livonia, MI	–49	180	539	359	–270	97	–367	–1.1
Hartford-West Hartford-East Hartford, CT	47	33	126	93	22	31	–9	4.1
Houston-Sugar Land-Baytown, TX	1,152	552	836	284	543	300	244	24.4
Indianapolis-Carmel, IN	219	118	235	117	101	29	73	14.3
Jacksonville, FL	205	68	164	96	143	16	127	18.3
Kansas City, MO-KS	231	127	270	143	67	36	32	12.6
Las Vegas-Paradise, NV	527	135	247	112	400	88	311	38.3
Los Angeles-Long Beach-Santa Ana, CA	509	1,104	1,815	711	–532	833	–1,365	4.1
Louisville/Jefferson County, KY-IN	96	49	151	102	51	17	34	8.3
Memphis, TN-MS-AR	100	86	184	98	12	20	–9	8.3
Miami-Fort Lauderdale-Pompano Beach, FL	539	211	650	438	235	522	–287	10.8
Milwaukee-Waukesha-West Allis, WI	59	80	199	119	–47	28	–74	3.9
Minneapolis-St. Paul-Bloomington, MN-WI	301	248	424	176	68	87	–20	10.1
Nashville-Davidson-Murfreesboro-Franklin, TN	270	93	196	103	161	38	123	20.6
New Orleans-Metairie-Kenner, LA	–127	51	156	106	–287	15	–302	–9.6
New York-Northern New Jersey-Long Island, NY-NJ-PA	746	1,067	2,371	1,304	–846	1,116	–1,962	4.1
Oklahoma City, OK	132	73	164	91	66	25	41	12.0
Orlando-Kissimmee, FL	438	119	248	129	323	98	225	26.6
Philadelphia-Camden-Wilmington, PA-NJ-DE-MD	281	208	702	494	11	127	–116	4.9
Phoenix-Mesa-Scottsdale, AZ	1,112	356	600	243	764	220	543	34.2
Pittsburgh, PA	–76	–29	230	259	–32	20	–52	–3.1
Portland-Vancouver-Beaverton, OR-WA	314	129	267	138	196	74	122	16.3
Providence-New Bedford-Fall River, RI-MA	18	40	177	137	–13	36	–49	1.1
Raleigh-Cary, NC	329	92	139	48	233	38	194	41.2
Richmond, VA	141	54	144	90	94	18	76	12.9
Riverside-San Bernardino-Ontario, CA	888	341	577	237	563	94	469	27.3
Sacramento-Arden-Arcade-Roseville, CA	331	132	266	134	208	67	141	18.4
St. Louis, MO-IL [3]	130	106	339	234	–13	31	–44	4.8
Salt Lake City, UT	161	137	189	52	8	43	–34	16.7
San Antonio, TX	360	159	283	124	211	33	177	21.1
San Diego-Carlsbad-San Marcos, CA	240	242	423	182	–23	103	–127	8.5
San Francisco-Oakland-Fremont, CA	194	251	520	269	–81	267	–347	4.7
San Jose-Sunnyvale-Santa Clara, CA	104	174	258	84	–64	176	–240	6.0
Seattle-Tacoma-Bellevue, WA	364	197	393	196	172	131	41	12.0
Tampa-St. Petersburg-Clearwater, FL	351	28	292	265	337	77	260	14.7
Virginia Beach-Norfolk-Newport News, VA-NC	98	107	220	113	–18	2	–20	6.2
Washington-Arlington-Alexandria, DC-VA-MD-WV	680	441	721	280	213	320	–107	14.2

[1] Total population change includes residual. This residual represents the change in population that cannot be attributed to any specific demographic component of change. See "State & County terms & definitions" at <http://www.census.gov/popest/topics/terms/states.html>. [2] Broomfield County, CO, was formed from parts of Adams, Boulder, Jefferson, and Weld Counties, CO on November 15, 2001, and is coextensive with Broomfield city. For purposes of defining and presenting data for metropolitan statistical areas, Broomfield city is treated as if it were a county at the time of the 2000 census. [3] The portion of Sullivan city in Crawford County, Missouri, is legally part of the St. Louis, MO-IL MSA. Data shown here do not include this area.

Source: U.S. Census Bureau, "Table 10—Cumulative Estimates of the Components of Population Change for Metropolitan and Micropolitan Statistical Areas: April 1, 2000 to July 1, 2009 (CBSA-EST2009-10)," <http://www.census.gov/popest/metro/CBSA-est2009-comp-chg.html>.

Table 22. Metropolitan Statistical Areas With More Than 750,000 Persons in 2010—Population by Age: 2010

[In thousands (871 represents 871,000). As of April 1. Covers metropolitan statistical areas as defined by the U.S. Office of Management and Budget as of December 2009. All geographic boundaries are defined as of January 1, 2010. For definitions and components of all metropolitan and micropolitan areas, see Appendix II]

Metropolitan statistical area	Number (1,000)						Percent under 18 years	Percent 65 years and over
	Total	Under 18 years	18 to 44 years	45 to 64 years	65 to 74 years	75 years and over		
Albany-Schenectady-Troy, NY	871	186	313	249	62	60	21.4	14.0
Albuquerque, NM	887	218	323	237	61	48	24.6	12.3
Allentown-Bethlehem-Easton, PA-NJ	821	187	275	234	62	63	22.8	15.2
Atlanta-Sandy Springs-Marietta, GA	5,269	1,396	2,076	1,325	283	189	26.5	9.0
Austin-Round Rock-San Marcos, TX	1,716	435	750	392	81	58	25.3	8.1
Bakersfield-Delano, CA	840	254	324	186	44	32	30.3	9.0
Baltimore-Towson, MD	2,710	623	992	753	183	159	23.0	12.6
Baton Rouge, LA	802	198	313	205	50	37	24.7	10.7
Birmingham-Hoover, AL	1,128	270	409	304	80	66	23.9	13.0
Boston-Cambridge-Quincy, MA-NH	4,552	983	1,721	1,252	306	290	21.6	13.1
Bridgeport-Stamford-Norwalk, CT	917	227	309	256	62	62	24.8	13.5
Buffalo-Niagara Falls, NY	1,136	245	388	323	87	92	21.6	15.7
Charlotte-Gastonia-Rock Hill, NC-SC	1,758	456	688	437	102	76	25.9	10.1
Chicago-Joliet-Naperville, IL-IN-WI	9,461	2,378	3,574	2,429	579	501	25.1	11.4
Cincinnati-Middletown, OH-KY-IN	2,130	531	761	578	140	120	24.9	12.2
Cleveland-Elyria-Mentor, OH	2,077	481	682	598	159	157	23.2	15.2
Columbia, SC	768	180	299	201	50	37	23.5	11.4
Columbus, OH	1,837	455	720	468	108	86	24.8	10.6
Dallas-Fort Worth-Arlington, TX	6,372	1,774	2,506	1,532	328	233	27.8	8.8
Dayton, OH	842	193	290	233	66	60	23.0	14.9
Denver-Aurora-Broomfield, CO[1]	2,543	634	987	666	144	112	24.9	10.0
Detroit-Warren-Livonia, MI	4,296	1,044	1,471	1,215	296	271	24.3	13.2
El Paso, TX	801	241	301	177	44	38	30.1	10.3
Fresno, CA	930	278	356	204	49	44	29.8	10.0
Grand Rapids-Wyoming, MI	774	200	281	202	48	43	25.9	11.7
Hartford-West Hartford-East Hartford, CT	1,212	270	420	348	87	87	22.3	14.3
Honolulu, HI	953	211	358	246	69	70	22.1	14.5
Houston-Sugar Land-Baytown, TX	5,947	1,662	2,329	1,444	303	208	28.0	8.6
Indianapolis-Carmel, IN	1,756	460	653	453	105	86	26.2	10.9
Jacksonville, FL	1,346	321	493	369	93	70	23.8	12.1
Kansas City, MO-KS	2,035	522	730	540	130	113	25.6	12.0
Las Vegas-Paradise, NV	1,951	489	762	480	135	86	25.0	11.3
Los Angeles-Long Beach-Santa Ana, CA	12,829	3,139	5,126	3,148	756	659	24.5	11.0
Louisville/Jefferson County, KY-IN	1,284	308	455	356	90	75	24.0	12.8
McAllen-Edinburg-Mission, TX	775	268	294	140	40	33	34.7	9.3
Memphis, TN-MS-AR	1,316	350	487	340	79	60	26.6	10.5
Miami-Fort Lauderdale-Pompano Beach, FL	5,565	1,206	2,001	1,471	443	444	21.7	15.9
Milwaukee-Waukesha-West Allis, WI	1,556	383	560	417	97	99	24.6	12.6
Minneapolis-St. Paul-Bloomington, MN-WI	3,280	820	1,232	879	188	162	25.0	10.7
Nashville-Davidson—Murfreesboro—Franklin, TN	1,590	388	619	413	98	72	24.4	10.7
New Haven-Milford, CT	862	193	308	238	61	63	22.4	14.4
New Orleans-Metairie-Kenner, LA	1,168	273	431	322	79	63	23.4	12.2
New York-Northern New Jersey-Long Island, NY-NJ-PA	18,897	4,312	7,132	4,980	1,288	1,185	22.8	13.1
Oklahoma City, OK	1,253	313	477	315	82	66	25.0	11.8
Omaha-Council Bluffs, NE-IA	865	227	323	219	51	45	26.3	11.1
Orlando-Kissimmee-Sanford, FL	2,134	499	830	542	146	117	23.4	12.3
Oxnard-Thousand Oaks-Ventura, CA	823	212	298	217	51	45	25.7	11.7
Philadelphia-Camden-Wilmington, PA-NJ-DE-MD	5,965	1,391	2,160	1,622	405	388	23.3	13.3
Phoenix-Mesa-Glendale, AZ	4,193	1,108	1,581	989	289	226	26.4	12.3
Pittsburgh, PA	2,356	475	778	696	195	212	20.2	17.3
Portland-Vancouver-Hillsboro, OR-WA	2,226	527	854	593	138	114	23.7	11.3
Providence-New Bedford-Fall River, RI-MA	1,601	346	578	447	113	117	21.6	14.4
Raleigh-Cary, NC	1,130	296	453	280	60	42	26.2	9.0
Richmond, VA	1,258	294	462	350	85	68	23.3	12.1
Riverside-San Bernardino-Ontario, CA	4,225	1,215	1,589	981	244	196	28.8	10.4
Rochester, NY	1,054	238	370	298	76	72	22.6	14.1
Sacramento—Arden-Arcade—Roseville, CA	2,149	535	797	559	138	120	24.9	12.0
St. Louis, MO-IL[2]	2,813	671	990	777	196	179	23.8	13.3
Salt Lake City, UT	1,124	331	455	241	54	43	29.4	8.6
San Antonio-New Braunfels, TX	2,143	576	808	524	131	104	26.9	11.0
San Diego-Carlsbad-San Marcos, CA	3,095	724	1,259	760	181	171	23.4	11.4
San Francisco-Oakland-Fremont, CA	4,335	921	1,689	1,179	289	258	21.2	12.6
San Jose-Sunnyvale-Santa Clara, CA	1,837	446	726	463	109	93	24.3	11.0
Seattle-Tacoma-Bellevue, WA	3,440	786	1,353	929	203	169	22.8	10.8
Tampa-St. Petersburg-Clearwater, FL	2,783	590	943	770	249	231	21.2	17.2
Tucson, AZ	980	225	350	254	82	70	23.0	15.4
Tulsa, OK	937	239	333	245	67	54	25.5	12.8
Virginia Beach-Norfolk-Newport News, VA-NC	1,672	394	648	436	107	86	23.6	11.6
Washington-Arlington-Alexandria, DC-VA-MD-WV	5,582	1,332	2,212	1,480	320	238	23.9	10.0
Worcester, MA	799	187	282	227	51	51	23.4	12.8

[1] See footnote 1, Table 20. [2] The portion of Sullivan city in Crawford County, Missouri, is legally part of the St. Louis, MO-IL MSA. Data shown here do not include this area.

Source: U.S. Census Bureau, USA Counties, <http://censtats.census.gov/usa/usa.shtml>, accessed June 2011.

Table 23. Metropolitan Statistical Areas With More Than 750,000 Persons in 2010—Population by Race and Hispanic or Latino Origin: 2010

[In thousands (871 represents 871,000). As of April 1. Covers metropolitan statistical areas as defined by the U.S. Office of Management and Budget as of December 2009. All geographic boundaries are defined as of January 1, 2010. For definitions and components of all metropolitan and micropolitan areas, see Appendix II]

Metropolitan statistical area	Total	White alone	Black or African American alone	American Indian and Alaska Native alone	Asian alone	Native Hawaiian and Other Pacific Islander alone	Two or more races	Hispanic or Latino origin [1]
Albany-Schenectady-Troy, NY	871	739	67	2	27	(Z)	21	36
Albuquerque, NM	887	618	24	52	18	1	38	414
Allentown-Bethlehem-Easton, PA-NJ	821	694	41	2	20	(Z)	19	107
Atlanta-Sandy Springs-Marietta, GA	5,269	2,920	1,708	18	254	3	126	547
Austin-Round Rock-San Marcos, TX	1,716	1,250	127	13	82	1	55	538
Bakersfield-Delano, CA	840	500	49	13	35	1	38	413
Baltimore-Towson, MD	2,710	1,684	779	9	123	1	68	124
Baton Rouge, LA	802	480	286	2	14	(Z)	10	27
Birmingham-Hoover, AL	1,128	753	318	3	14	1	13	49
Boston-Cambridge-Quincy, MA-NH	4,552	3,588	331	11	295	1	118	411
Bridgeport-Stamford-Norwalk, CT	917	686	99	2	42	(Z)	24	155
Buffalo-Niagara Falls, NY	1,136	927	139	8	26	(Z)	21	46
Charlotte-Gastonia-Rock Hill, NC-SC	1,758	1,145	421	9	55	1	39	173
Chicago-Joliet-Naperville, IL-IN-WI	9,461	6,184	1,646	37	533	3	230	1,957
Cincinnati-Middletown, OH-KY-IN	2,130	1,766	256	4	40	1	39	55
Cleveland-Elyria-Mentor, OH	2,077	1,538	417	4	41	(Z)	42	98
Columbia, SC	768	464	255	3	13	1	15	39
Columbus, OH	1,837	1,424	274	4	57	1	46	66
Dallas-Fort Worth-Arlington, TX	6,372	4,161	962	43	342	6	180	1,752
Dayton, OH	842	673	126	2	15	(Z)	19	17
Denver-Aurora-Broomfield, CO [2]	2,543	1,983	143	25	94	3	91	571
Detroit-Warren-Livonia, MI	4,296	3,011	980	15	141	1	95	168
El Paso, TX	801	657	25	6	8	1	20	658
Fresno, CA	930	515	50	16	89	1	42	468
Grand Rapids-Wyoming, MI	774	643	62	4	15	(Z)	21	65
Hartford-West Hartford-East Hartford, CT	1,212	932	132	3	47	(Z)	30	151
Honolulu, HI	953	199	19	2	418	91	213	77
Houston-Sugar Land-Baytown, TX	5,947	3,581	1,026	38	389	4	180	2,099
Indianapolis-Carmel, IN	1,756	1,353	263	5	40	1	38	108
Jacksonville, FL	1,346	940	293	5	46	1	35	93
Kansas City, MO-KS	2,035	1,597	255	10	46	3	56	167
Las Vegas-Paradise, NV	1,951	1,188	204	14	169	14	99	569
Los Angeles-Long Beach-Santa Ana, CA	12,829	6,767	908	91	1,885	35	567	5,701
Louisville/Jefferson County, KY-IN	1,284	1,037	176	3	20	1	26	50
McAllen-Edinburg-Mission, TX	775	682	5	3	7	(Z)	10	702
Memphis, TN-MS-AR	1,316	631	601	3	24	1	18	65
Miami-Fort Lauderdale-Pompano Beach, FL	5,565	3,914	1,169	16	126	2	140	2,313
Milwaukee-Waukesha-West Allis, WI	1,556	1,147	261	8	46	1	36	148
Minneapolis-St. Paul-Bloomington, MN-WI	3,280	2,657	243	23	188	1	91	176
Nashville-Davidson–Murfreesboro–Franklin, TN	1,590	1,222	242	5	36	1	33	105
New Haven-Milford, CT	862	645	110	2	30	(Z)	23	130
New Orleans-Metairie-Kenner, LA	1,168	680	397	5	32	1	23	92
New York-Northern New Jersey-Long Island, NY-NJ-PA	18,897	11,178	3,363	93	1,878	9	613	4,328
Oklahoma City, OK	1,253	901	131	51	35	1	65	142
Omaha-Council Bluffs, NE-IA	865	714	68	5	18	1	22	78
Orlando-Kissimmee-Sanford, FL	2,134	1,494	345	9	85	2	69	539
Oxnard-Thousand Oaks-Ventura, CA	823	566	15	8	55	2	37	332
Philadelphia-Camden-Wilmington, PA-NJ-DE-MD	5,965	4,068	1,242	16	296	2	139	468
Phoenix-Mesa-Glendale, AZ	4,193	3,059	208	99	139	9	146	1,236
Pittsburgh, PA	2,356	2,069	197	3	41	(Z)	37	30
Portland-Vancouver-Hillsboro, OR-WA	2,226	1,804	64	21	127	10	91	242
Providence-New Bedford-Fall River, RI-MA	1,601	1,342	78	8	41	1	49	164
Raleigh-Cary, NC	1,130	763	228	6	50	(Z)	27	115
Richmond, VA	1,258	780	375	5	39	1	29	63
Riverside-San Bernardino-Ontario, CA	4,225	2,488	322	46	259	14	207	1,996
Rochester, NY	1,054	855	123	3	27	(Z)	24	65
Sacramento–Arden-Arcade–Roseville, CA	2,149	1,390	158	22	256	16	127	434
St. Louis, MO-IL [3]	2,813	2,153	516	7	60	1	51	72
Salt Lake City, UT	1,124	922	17	10	35	16	35	187
San Antonio-New Braunfels, TX	2,143	1,617	141	17	45	3	70	1,158
San Diego-Carlsbad-San Marcos, CA	3,095	1,981	158	26	336	15	158	991
San Francisco-Oakland-Fremont, CA	4,335	2,240	364	25	1,006	32	240	939
San Jose-Sunnyvale-Santa Clara, CA	1,837	872	47	14	572	7	90	510
Seattle-Tacoma-Bellevue, WA	3,440	2,475	192	37	393	28	184	309
Tampa-St. Petersburg-Clearwater, FL	2,783	2,193	329	10	81	2	73	452
Tucson, AZ	980	729	35	33	26	2	36	339
Tulsa, OK	937	665	79	77	17	1	60	78
Virginia Beach-Norfolk-Newport News, VA-NC	1,672	997	522	7	58	2	57	90
Washington-Arlington-Alexandria, DC-VA-MD-WV	5,582	3,059	1,438	23	517	4	206	771
Worcester, MA	799	683	33	2	32	(Z)	19	75

Z Less than 500. [1] Persons of Hispanic origin may be any race. [2] See footnote 1, Table 20. [3] The portion of Sullivan city in Crawford County, Missouri, is legally part of the St. Louis, MO-IL MSA. Data shown here do not include this area.
Source: U.S. Census Bureau, USA Counties, <http://censtats.census.gov/usa/usa.shtml>, accessed June 2011.

Table 24. Population by Core Based Statistical Area (CBSA) Status and State: 2010

[As of April 1. (308,746 represents 308,746,000). Covers core-based statistical areas (metropolitan and micropolitan statistical areas) as defined by the U.S. Office of Management and Budget as of November 2009. All geographic boundaries for 2000 to 2010 population estimates are defined as of January 1, 2010. For definitions and components of all metropolitan and micropolitan areas, see Appendix II. Minus sign (–) indicates decrease]

State	Total population, 2010 (1,000)	Inside Core-Based Statistical Area (metropolitan or micropolitan statistical area), 2010				Outside CBSA, 2010		Percent change, 2000–2010		
		Total		Metro-politan (1,000)	Micro-politan (1,000)	Number (1,000)	Percent	Metro-politan	Micro-politan	Outside CBSAs
		Number (1,000)	Percent							
U.S.	308,746	289,261	93.7	258,318	30,944	19,484	6.3	10.8	5.9	1.8
AL	4,780	4,291	89.8	3,415	876	489	10.2	9.0	8.0	–2.8
AK	710	537	75.6	478	58	173	24.4	18.9	–0.6	4.6
AZ	6,392	6,300	98.6	5,915	385	92	1.4	26.0	11.1	3.2
AR	2,916	2,333	80.0	1,757	575	583	20.0	15.9	1.7	–1.3
CA	37,254	36,995	99.3	36,409	587	258	0.7	10.1	6.1	6.3
CO	5,029	4,620	91.9	4,342	278	409	8.1	18.1	13.8	7.7
CT	3,574	3,574	100.0	3,266	308	–	–	4.9	5.9	–
DE	898	898	100.0	701	197	–	–	11.8	25.9	–
DC	602	602	100.0	602	–	–	–	5.2	–	–
FL	18,801	18,380	97.8	17,690	690	421	2.2	17.8	15.7	16.1
GA	9,688	8,817	91.0	7,848	969	871	9.0	20.2	9.6	12.2
HI	1,360	1,360	100.0	953	407	–	–	8.8	21.4	–38.8
ID	1,568	1,364	87.0	1,028	336	203	13.0	27.4	13.6	6.5
IL	12,831	12,222	95.3	11,159	1,063	608	4.7	4.1	–0.9	–2.5
IN	6,484	6,116	94.3	5,079	1,037	368	5.7	8.4	0.8	0.7
IA	3,046	2,240	73.5	1,722	518	807	26.5	10.1	–1.6	–3.5
KS	2,853	2,440	85.5	1,949	491	413	14.5	11.2	–0.7	–6.2
KY	4,339	3,329	76.7	2,524	806	1,010	23.3	11.1	5.5	0.4
LA	4,533	4,228	93.3	3,381	847	306	6.7	1.2	3.8	–2.2
ME	1,328	938	70.6	776	162	391	29.4	5.4	3.3	2.3
MD	5,774	5,690	98.6	5,463	227	83	1.4	8.8	15.1	5.8
MA	6,548	6,521	99.6	6,521	–	27	0.4	3.1	–	9.0
MI	9,884	9,113	92.2	8,033	1,080	771	7.8	–0.8	2.5	–1.9
MN	5,304	4,649	87.6	3,972	677	655	12.4	9.7	4.8	0.3
MS	2,967	2,331	78.6	1,331	1,000	636	21.4	11.4	–0.2	–1.9
MO	5,989	5,179	86.5	4,464	715	810	13.5	7.5	8.7	3.0
MT	989	654	66.1	349	306	335	33.9	10.7	17.8	2.3
NE	1,826	1,476	80.8	1,071	404	351	19.2	13.7	2.1	–5.9
NV	2,701	2,651	98.1	2,432	219	50	1.9	37.3	22.0	4.2
NH	1,316	1,269	96.4	819	450	48	3.6	6.3	6.6	9.5
NJ	8,792	8,792	100.0	8,792	–	–	–	4.5	–	–
NM	2,059	1,981	96.2	1,371	611	78	3.8	19.4	3.6	–5.0
NY	19,378	18,947	97.8	17,815	1,132	431	2.2	2.3	0.1	0.3
NC	9,535	8,777	92.0	6,704	2,072	759	8.0	22.2	10.9	9.2
ND	673	480	71.3	325	154	193	28.7	14.6	2.5	–7.1
OH	11,537	11,023	95.5	9,299	1,723	514	4.5	1.7	0.9	2.0
OK	3,751	3,207	85.5	2,407	799	545	14.5	11.6	5.2	2.1
OR	3,831	3,687	96.2	2,979	709	144	3.8	13.8	6.8	2.8
PA	12,702	12,314	96.9	10,686	1,629	388	3.1	3.5	3.1	1.5
RI	1,053	1,053	100.0	1,053	–	–	–	0.4	–	–
SC	4,625	4,351	94.1	3,536	815	274	5.9	17.8	11.2	–1.0
SD	814	595	73.1	369	226	219	26.9	18.1	5.4	–3.9
TN	6,346	5,708	89.9	4,660	1,048	638	10.1	13.0	9.5	4.7
TX	25,146	23,775	94.5	22,085	1,690	1,371	5.5	23.1	7.2	2.9
UT	2,764	2,623	94.9	2,449	174	141	5.1	24.3	26.4	12.3
VT	626	461	73.7	211	250	164	26.3	6.2	–	3.1
VA	8,001	7,166	89.6	6,888	278	835	10.4	14.7	6.5	3.1
WA	6,725	6,493	96.6	5,900	592	232	3.4	14.5	12.8	7.4
WV	1,853	1,398	75.4	1,033	365	455	24.6	5.0	0.2	–1.2
WI	5,687	4,912	86.4	4,142	770	775	13.6	7.1	4.6	2.1
WY	564	405	71.9	167	238	159	28.1	12.9	16.8	11.7

– Represents or rounds to zero.

Source: U.S. Census Bureau, 2010 Census Redistricting Data (P.L. 94-171) Summary File, and Census 2000, <www.census.gov/prod/cen2010/cen2010/doc/pl94-171.pdf>.

U.S. Census Bureau, Statistical Abstract of the United States: 2012

Table 25. Population in Coastal Counties: 1980 to 2010

[Population as of April 1, (3,537 represents 3,537,000). Areas as defined by U.S. National Oceanic and Atmospheric Administration, 1992. Covers 675 counties and equivalent areas with at least 15 percent of their land area either in a coastal watershed (drainage area) or in a coastal cataloging unit (a coastal area between watersheds). See Appendix III]

Year	Total	Counties in coastal regions					Balance of United States
		Total	Atlantic	Gulf of Mexico	Great Lakes	Pacific	
Land area, 2000 (1,000 sq. mi.). . . .	3,537	889	148	115	115	511	2,649
POPULATION							
1980 (mil.).	226.5	119.8	53.7	13.1	26.0	27.0	106.7
1990 (mil.).	248.7	133.4	59.0	15.2	25.9	33.2	115.3
2000 (mil.).	281.4	148.3	65.2	18.0	27.3	37.8	133.1
2010 (mil.).	308.7	159.6	70.2	20.8	27.2	41.4	149.1
1980 (percent).	100	53	24	6	11	12	47
1990 (percent).	100	54	24	6	10	13	46
2000 (percent).	100	53	23	6	10	13	47
2010 (percent).	100	52	23	7	9	13	48

Source: U.S. Census Bureau, *U.S. Summary, 1980 Census of Population*, Vol. 1, Chapter A (PC80-1-A-1); *1990 Census of Population and Housing (CPH1)*; 2010 Census, and unpublished data.

Table 26. States With Coastal Counties—Population, Housing Units, Establishments, and Employees by Coastal Region and State: 2000 to 2010

[281,422 represents 281,422,000. Population and housing as of April 1. See headnote, Table 25. Minus sign (–) indicates decrease]

Coastal region and state	Population					Housing units			Private nonfarm [2]	
	2000 (1,000)	2010				Number			Estab-lish-ments, 2008 (1,000)	Employ-ees, 2008 (1,000)
		Number (1,000)	Percent of state, total	Percent change, 2000–2010	Per square mile, 2010 [1]	2000 (1,000)	2010 (1,000)	Percent change, 2000–2010		
United States, total	281,422	308,746	(X)	9.7	87	115,905	131,705	13.6	7,601	120,904
Interior U.S.	133,102	149,148	(X)	12.1	56	55,928	64,704	15.7	3,565	58,425
Coastal counties, total . .	148,320	159,597	(X)	7.6	180	59,977	67,001	11.7	4,036	62,478
Atlantic.	65,196	70,217	(X)	7.7	475	26,820	29,908	11.5	1,874	28,339
Maine.	1,184	1,239	93.3	4.7	61	599	667	11.3	39	480
New Hampshire.	1,007	1,073	81.5	6.6	255	432	485	12.4	32	467
Massachusetts.	6,125	6,318	96.5	3.1	956	2,531	2,712	7.1	169	2,972
Rhode Island	1,048	1,053	100.0	0.4	1,007	440	463	5.4	30	430
Connecticut	3,406	3,574	100.0	4.9	738	1,386	1,488	7.4	92	1,538
New York	13,572	13,952	72.0	2.8	1,800	5,285	5,601	6.0	396	5,587
New Jersey	8,312	8,683	98.8	4.5	1,230	3,269	3,509	7.3	236	3,552
Pennsylvania	5,750	6,108	48.1	6.2	887	2,334	2,512	7.6	146	2,609
Delaware	784	898	100.0	14.6	460	343	406	18.3	25	389
Maryland	4,865	5,288	91.6	8.7	698	1,970	2,176	10.5	126	2,034
District of Columbia	572	602	100.0	5.2	9,800	275	297	8.0	21	466
Virginia.	4,794	5,426	67.8	13.2	390	1,912	2,216	15.9	135	2,242
North Carolina	1,985	2,233	23.4	12.5	114	905	1,069	18.2	48	651
South Carolina.	1,653	1,932	41.8	16.9	127	750	953	27.0	47	641
Georgia	821	945	9.8	15.1	78	346	414	19.8	20	283
Florida	9,319	10,894	57.9	16.9	582	4,043	4,940	22.2	311	4,000
Gulf of Mexico	18,003	20,761	(X)	15.3	181	7,718	9,229	19.6	463	7,028
Florida	6,248	7,435	39.5	19.0	236	3,074	3,832	24.6	185	2,321
Georgia	95	98	1.0	3.1	61	40	43	7.0	2	30
Alabama	712	765	16.0	7.3	88	319	363	13.8	18	261
Mississippi	588	629	21.2	6.9	93	246	280	13.7	12	187
Louisiana	3,510	3,548	78.3	1.1	138	1,439	1,533	6.5	83	1,309
Texas	6,850	8,288	33.0	21.0	206	2,599	3,178	22.3	163	2,921
Great Lakes.	27,324	27,190	(X)	-0.5	236	11,405	12,128	6.3	654	11,151
New York	3,650	3,635	18.8	-0.4	170	1,586	1,647	3.9	83	1,376
Pennsylvania	281	281	2.2	-0.1	350	114	119	4.2	7	119
Ohio.	4,418	4,326	37.5	-2.1	410	1,869	1,967	5.2	106	1,846
Michigan	8,859	8,797	89.0	-0.7	172	3,782	4,050	7.1	207	3,256
Indiana.	1,378	1,433	22.1	3.9	352	556	607	9.2	33	587
Illinois.	6,021	5,898	46.0	-2.0	4,233	2,322	2,441	5.1	150	2,715
Wisconsin	2,469	2,569	45.2	4.0	167	1,055	1,165	10.5	61	1,151
Minnesota	248	252	4.7	1.3	24	121	132	9.2	7	101
Pacific	37,796	41,429	(X)	9.6	81	14,034	15,737	12.1	1,044	15,960
Washington	4,587	5,229	77.8	14.0	212	1,919	2,264	18.0	146	2,072
Oregon.	1,808	1,982	51.7	9.6	94	794	895	12.8	61	822
California	29,660	32,259	86.6	8.8	415	10,650	11,803	10.8	787	12,347
Alaska	529	598	84.2	13.0	2	211	255	21.2	17	214
Hawaii	1,212	1,360	100.0	12.3	212	461	520	12.8	33	504

X Not applicable. [1] Calculated on the basis of land area data from the 2000 census. [2] Covers establishments with payroll. Excludes most government employees, railroad employees, self-employed persons. Employees are for the week including March 12.

Source: U.S. Census Bureau, *USA Counties*, <http://censtats.census.gov/usa/usa.shtml>, accessed June 2011, and "County Business Patterns," <http://www.census.gov/econ/cbp/index.html>.

Population 33

Table 27. Incorporated Places With 175,000 or More Inhabitants in 2010—Population: 1970 to 2010

[In thousands, except as indicated (275 represents 275,000). As of April 1. For 1990 and 2000, the counts relate to places as defined on January 1, 2000. Data for 1970 and 1980 refer to boundaries in effect for those censuses. For 1970 and 1980, the counts relate to places as defined at each census. Minus sign (–) indicates decrease. See Appendix III]

City	Number (1,000)					Percent change		Rank, 2010
	1970	1980	1990	2000 [1]	2010	1990 to 2000 [1]	2000 to 2010 [1]	
Akron, OH	275	237	223	217	199	–2.7	–8.3	109
Albuquerque, NM	245	332	385	449	546	16.6	21.7	32
Amarillo, TX	127	149	158	174	191	10.2	9.8	119
Anaheim, CA	166	219	267	328	336	23.0	2.5	53
Anchorage, AK	48	174	226	260	292	15.0	12.1	63
Arlington, TX	90	160	262	333	365	27.2	9.8	50
Atlanta, GA	495	425	394	416	420	5.7	0.8	40
Augusta–Richmond County, GA [2]	(NA)	[3] 48	186	200	201	7.3	0.4	107
Aurora, CO	75	159	222	276	325	24.6	17.6	55
Aurora, IL	74	81	100	143	198	43.6	38.4	111
Austin, TX	254	346	466	657	790	41.0	20.4	14
Bakersfield, CA	70	106	175	247	347	41.2	40.6	51
Baltimore, MD	905	787	736	651	621	–11.5	–4.6	23
Baton Rouge, LA	166	220	223	228	229	2.2	0.7	84
Birmingham, AL	301	284	265	243	212	–8.5	–12.6	96
Boise City, ID	75	102	126	186	206	48.0	10.7	102
Boston, MA	641	563	575	589	618	2.5	4.8	24
Brownsville, TX	53	85	114	140	175	22.6	25.3	132
Buffalo, NY	463	358	328	293	261	–10.8	–10.7	69
Chandler, AZ	14	30	90	177	236	96.5	33.7	79
Charlotte, NC	241	315	428	541	731	26.4	35.2	18
Chesapeake, VA	90	114	152	199	222	31.1	11.6	90
Chicago, IL	3,369	3,005	2,783	2,896	2,696	4.1	–6.9	3
Chula Vista, CA	68	84	135	174	244	28.4	40.5	76
Cincinnati, OH	454	385	364	331	297	–9.0	–10.4	61
Cleveland, OH	751	574	506	478	397	–5.5	–17.1	45
Colorado Springs, CO	136	215	280	361	416	28.7	15.4	41
Columbus, GA	[2] 155	[2] 169	[2] 179	[2] 186	190	[2] 3.9	1.9	121
Columbus, OH	540	565	633	711	787	12.4	10.6	15
Corpus Christi, TX	205	232	258	277	305	7.4	10.0	59
Dallas, TX	844	905	1,008	1,189	1,198	18.0	0.8	9
Denver, CO	515	493	468	555	600	18.6	8.2	27
Des Moines, IA	201	191	193	199	203	2.8	2.4	104
Detroit, MI	1,514	1,203	1,028	951	714	–7.5	–25.0	19
Durham, NC	95	101	137	187	228	36.9	22.1	85
El Paso, TX	322	425	515	564	649	9.4	15.2	20
Fayetteville, NC	54	60	76	121	201	59.5	65.7	106
Fontana, CA	21	37	88	129	196	47.3	52.1	113
Fort Wayne, IN	178	172	173	206	254	18.9	23.3	73
Fort Worth, TX	393	385	448	535	741	19.5	38.6	16
Fremont, CA	101	132	173	203	214	17.3	5.2	94
Fresno, CA	166	217	354	428	495	20.8	15.7	34
Garland, TX	81	139	181	216	227	19.4	5.1	86
Gilbert, AZ	2	6	29	110	208	276.7	90.0	100
Glendale, AZ	36	97	148	219	227	48.0	3.6	87
Glendale, CA	133	139	180	195	192	8.3	–1.7	118
Grand Prairie, TX	51	71	100	127	175	27.9	37.6	131
Grand Rapids, MI	198	182	189	198	188	4.6	–4.9	122
Greensboro, NC	144	156	184	224	270	21.8	20.4	68
Henderson, NV	16	24	65	175	258	170.0	47.0	72
Hialeah, FL	102	145	188	226	225	20.4	–0.8	89
Houston, TX	1,234	1,595	1,631	1,954	2,099	19.8	7.5	4
Huntington Beach, CA	116	171	182	190	190	4.4	0.2	120
Huntsville, AL	139	143	160	158	180	–1.0	13.8	127
Indianapolis, IN [2]	737	701	731	792	830	8.3	4.8	11
Irvine, CA	([4])	62	110	143	212	29.7	48.4	95
Irving, TX	97	110	155	192	216	23.6	12.9	93
Jacksonville, FL	504	541	635	736	822	15.8	11.7	12
Jersey City, NJ	260	224	229	240	248	5.0	3.1	74
Kansas City, MO	507	448	435	442	460	1.5	4.1	37
Knoxville, TN	175	175	165	174	179	5.4	2.9	128
Laredo, TX	69	91	123	177	236	43.7	33.7	80
Las Vegas, NV	126	165	258	478	584	85.3	22.0	30
Lexington–Fayette, KY	108	204	225	261	296	15.6	13.5	62
Lincoln, NE	150	172	192	226	258	17.5	14.5	71
Little Rock, AR	132	159	176	183	194	4.2	5.7	116
Long Beach, CA	359	361	429	462	462	7.5	0.2	36
Los Angeles, CA	2,812	2,969	3,486	3,695	3,793	6.0	2.6	2
Louisville/Jefferson County, KY [2]	[5] 362	[5] 299	[5] 270	[5] 256	741	[5] –4.9	189.2	17
Lubbock, TX	149	174	186	200	230	7.2	15.0	83
Madison, WI	172	171	191	208	233	9.1	12.1	81

See footnotes at end of table.

U.S. Census Bureau, Statistical Abstract of the United States: 2012

Table 27. Incorporated Places With 175,000 or More Inhabitants in 2010—Population: 1970 to 2010—Con.

[In thousands, except as indicated (275 represents 275,000). As of April 1. For 1990 and 2000, the counts relate to places as defined on January 1, 2000. Data for 1970 and 1980 refer to boundaries in effect for those censuses. For 1970 and 1980, the counts relate to places as defined at each census. Minus sign (–) indicates decrease. See Appendix III]

City	Number (1,000)					Percent change		Rank, 2010
	1970	1980	1990	2000 [1]	2010	1990 to 2000 [1]	2000 to 2010 [1]	
Memphis, TN	624	646	610	650	647	6.5	–0.5	21
Mesa, AZ	63	152	288	396	439	37.6	10.8	38
Miami, FL	335	347	359	362	399	1.1	10.2	44
Milwaukee, WI	717	636	628	597	595	–5.0	–0.4	28
Minneapolis, MN	434	371	368	383	383	3.9	–	48
Mobile, AL	190	200	196	199	195	1.4	–1.9	115
Modesto, CA	62	107	165	189	201	14.6	6.5	105
Montgomery, AL	133	178	188	202	206	7.5	2.1	101
Moreno Valley, CA	([4])	([4])	119	142	193	19.9	35.8	117
Nashville–Davidson, TN [2]	426	456	488	570	627	16.7	10.0	22
New Orleans, LA	593	558	497	485	344	–2.5	–29.1	52
New York, NY	7,896	7,072	7,323	8,008	8,175	9.4	2.1	1
Newark, NJ	382	329	275	274	277	–0.6	1.3	67
Newport News, VA	138	145	171	180	181	5.1	0.3	126
Norfolk, VA	308	267	261	234	243	–10.3	3.6	77
North Las Vegas, NV	46	43	48	115	217	141.4	87.9	92
Oakland, CA	362	339	372	399	391	7.3	–2.2	47
Oklahoma City, OK	368	404	445	506	580	13.8	14.6	31
Omaha, NE	347	314	336	390	409	16.2	4.9	42
Orlando, FL	99	128	165	186	238	12.9	28.2	78
Oxnard, CA	71	108	143	170	198	19.5	16.2	111
Philadelphia, PA	1,949	1,688	1,586	1,518	1,526	–4.3	0.6	5
Phoenix, AZ	584	790	983	1,321	1,446	34.3	9.4	6
Pittsburgh, PA	520	424	370	335	306	–9.5	–8.6	58
Plano, TX	18	72	128	222	260	73.6	17.0	70
Portland, OR	380	368	439	529	584	20.6	10.3	29
Providence, RI	179	157	161	174	178	8.0	2.5	129
Raleigh, NC	123	150	212	276	404	30.2	46.3	43
Reno, NV	73	101	134	180	225	34.8	24.8	88
Richmond, VA	249	219	203	198	204	–2.5	3.2	103
Riverside, CA	140	171	227	255	304	12.6	19.1	60
Rochester, NY	295	242	230	220	211	–4.6	–4.2	97
Sacramento, CA	257	276	369	407	466	10.2	14.6	35
Salt Lake City, UT	176	163	160	182	186	13.6	2.6	123
San Antonio, TX	654	786	935	1,145	1,327	22.4	16.0	7
San Bernardino, CA	107	119	165	185	210	12.6	13.2	98
San Diego, CA	697	876	1,111	1,223	1,307	10.2	6.9	8
San Francisco, CA	716	679	724	777	805	7.3	3.7	13
San Jose, CA	460	629	782	895	946	14.4	5.7	10
Santa Ana, CA	156	204	294	338	325	15.0	–4.0	56
Santa Clarita, CA	([4])	([4])	111	151	176	36.5	16.7	130
Scottsdale, AZ	68	89	130	203	217	55.8	7.2	91
Seattle, WA	531	494	516	563	609	9.1	8.0	25
Shreveport, LA	182	206	199	200	199	0.8	–0.4	108
Spokane, WA	171	171	177	196	209	10.4	6.8	99
St. Louis, MO	622	453	397	348	319	–12.2	–8.3	57
St. Paul, MN	310	270	272	287	285	5.5	–0.7	66
St. Petersburg, FL	216	239	240	248	245	3.3	–1.4	75
Stockton, CA	110	150	211	244	292	15.6	19.7	64
Tacoma, WA	154	159	177	194	198	9.6	2.5	110
Tallahassee, FL	73	82	125	151	181	20.7	20.4	124
Tampa, FL	278	272	280	303	336	8.4	10.6	54
Toledo, OH	383	355	333	314	287	–5.8	–8.4	65
Tucson, AZ	263	331	405	487	520	20.1	6.9	33
Tulsa, OK	330	361	367	393	392	7.0	–0.3	46
Virginia Beach, VA	172	262	393	425	438	8.2	3.0	39
Washington, DC	757	638	607	572	602	–5.7	5.2	26
Wichita, KS	277	280	304	344	382	13.2	11.1	49
Winston–Salem, NC	134	132	143	186	230	29.5	23.6	82
Worcester, MA	177	162	170	173	181	1.7	4.9	125
Yonkers, NY	204	195	188	196	196	4.3	–0.1	114

– Represents or rounds to zero. NA Not available. [1] Based on 2000 Census numbers as tabulated. [2] Represents the portion of a consolidated city that is not within one or more separately incorporated places. [3] Data are for the incorporated places of Athens city and Augusta city before consolidation of the city and county governments. [4] Not incorporated. [5] Data are for the incorporated place of Louisville city before consolidation of the city and county governments.

Source: U.S. Census Bureau, 1970 data: U.S. Census Bureau, *Census of Population: 1970, Vol. 1, Characteristics of the Population*. 1980 data: U.S. Census Bureau, *1980 Census of Population, Vol. 1, Characteristics of the Population*, PC80-1. 1990 data: U.S. Census Bureau, *1990 Census CP-1-1, General Population Characteristics*, and *1990 CPH-L-157 Corrected Counts*. 2000 Census data: 2000 Census of Population and Housing, *Population and Housing Unit Counts PHC-3*. 2010 Census data: *2010 Census Redistricting Data (Public Law 94-171) Summary File*, Table P1.

Table 28. Incorporated Places by Population Size: 1980 to 2010

[140.3 represents 140,300,000. See Appendix III]

Population size	Number of incorporated places				Population (mil.)				Percent of total			
	1980	1990	2000	2010	1980	1990	2000	2010	1980	1990	2000	2010
Total..............	19,097	19,262	19,452	19,540	140.3	153.1	173.5	192.0	100.0	100.0	100.0	100.0
1,000,000 or more.....	6	8	9	9	17.5	20.0	22.9	23.6	12.5	13.1	13.2	12.3
500,000 to 999,999	16	15	20	24	10.9	10.1	12.9	16.1	7.8	6.6	7.4	8.4
250,000 to 499,999	33	41	37	40	11.8	14.2	13.3	14.0	8.4	9.3	7.7	7.3
100,000 to 249,999	114	131	172	200	16.6	19.1	25.5	30.2	11.8	12.5	14.7	15.7
50,000 to 99,999	250	309	363	432	17.6	21.2	24.9	30.1	12.5	13.8	14.4	15.7
25,000 to 49,999	526	567	644	723	18.4	20.0	22.6	25.2	13.1	13.1	13.0	13.1
10,000 to 24,999	1,260	1,290	1,435	1,542	19.8	20.3	22.6	24.2	14.1	13.3	13.0	12.6
Under 10,000.........	16,892	16,901	16,772	16,570	28.0	28.2	28.7	28.7	20.0	18.4	16.5	14.9

Source: U.S. Census Bureau, *Census of Population: 1980, Vol. I*; *1990 Census of Population and Housing, Population and Housing Unit Counts (CPH-2-1)*; *Census 2000 PHC-3, Population and Housing Unit Counts*; *2010 Census Redistricting Data (Public Law 94-171) Summary File.*

Table 29. Urban and Rural Population by State: 1990 and 2000

[222,361 represents 222,361,000. As of April 1. Resident population. For urban definitions, see text, this section]

State	Urban population				Rural popula-tion, 2000 (1,000)	State	Urban population				Rural popula-tion, 2000 (1,000)
	1990		2000, current definition				1990		2000, current definition		
	Former definition (percent)	Current definition (percent)	Number (1,000)	Percent			Former definition (percent)	Current definition (percent)	Number (1,000)	Percent	
U.S., total...	75.2	78.0	222,361	79.0	59,061						
AL	60.4	56.8	2,466	55.4	1,981	MO.....	68.7	69.6	3,883	69.4	1,712
AK	67.5	61.0	411	65.6	216	MT	52.5	56.4	488	54.1	414
AZ	87.5	86.5	4,524	88.2	607	NE	66.1	67.2	1,194	69.8	518
AR	53.5	52.0	1,404	52.5	1,269	NV	88.3	87.4	1,829	91.5	170
CA	92.6	93.7	31,990	94.4	1,882	NH	51.0	57.2	732	59.3	503
CO	82.4	83.8	3,633	84.5	668	NJ	89.4	93.5	7,939	94.4	475
CT	79.1	87.0	2,988	87.7	418	NM.....	73.0	75.0	1,364	75.0	456
DE	73.0	79.2	628	80.1	156	NY	84.3	87.4	16,603	87.5	2,374
DC	100.0	100.0	572	100.0	–	NC	50.4	57.8	4,849	60.2	3,200
FL	84.8	88.0	14,270	89.3	1,712	ND	53.3	53.4	359	55.9	283
GA	63.2	68.7	5,864	71.6	2,322	OH	74.1	77.5	8,782	77.4	2,571
HI.......	89.0	90.5	1,108	91.5	103	OK	67.7	65.2	2,255	65.3	1,196
ID.......	57.4	62.2	859	66.4	434	OR	70.5	74.9	2,694	78.7	727
IL.......	84.6	86.4	10,910	87.8	1,510	PA	68.9	76.8	9,464	77.1	2,817
IN.......	64.9	69.1	4,304	70.8	1,776	RI......	86.0	89.9	953	90.9	95
IA.......	60.6	59.4	1,787	61.1	1,139	SC	54.6	61.5	2,427	60.5	1,585
KS	69.1	69.5	1,921	71.4	768	SD	50.0	50.3	391	51.9	363
KY	51.8	55.9	2,254	55.8	1,788	TN	60.9	62.7	3,620	63.6	2,069
LA	68.1	72.9	3,246	72.6	1,223	TX	80.3	81.2	17,204	82.5	3,648
ME......	44.6	42.6	513	40.2	762	UT	87.0	86.8	1,970	88.2	263
MD.....	81.3	85.0	4,559	86.1	738	VT	32.2	40.2	232	38.2	376
MA.....	84.3	90.5	5,801	91.4	548	VA	69.4	71.5	5,170	73.0	1,909
MI......	70.5	75.2	7,419	74.7	2,519	WA.....	76.4	79.9	4,831	82.0	1,063
MN.....	69.9	69.0	3,490	70.9	1,429	WV.....	36.1	46.9	833	46.1	976
MS.....	47.1	49.1	1,387	48.8	1,457	WI	65.7	67.3	3,664	68.3	1,700
						WY.....	65.0	67.1	321	65.1	172

– Represents zero.
Source: U.S. Census Bureau, 2000 Census of Population and Housing, *Population and Housing Unit Counts PHC-3*. See also <http://www.census.gov/prod/cen2000/index.html>.

U.S. Census Bureau, Statistical Abstract of the United States: 2012

Table 30. Mobility Status of the Population by Selected Characteristics: 1981 to 2010

[As of March (221,641 represents 221,641,000). For persons 1 year old and over. Based on comparison of place of residence in immediate prior year and year shown. Excludes members of the Armed Forces except those living off post or with their families on post. Based on Current Population Survey, Annual Social and Economic Supplement. See text, this section and Appendix III. For composition of regions, see map, inside front cover]

Mobility period and characteristic	Total (1,000)	Percent distribution						Movers from abroad
		Non–movers	Movers (different house in United States)					
			Total	Same county	Different county			
					Total	Same state	Different state	
1981	221,641	83	17	10	6	3	3	1
1991	244,884	83	16	10	6	3	3	1
2001	275,611	86	14	8	6	3	3	1
2010, total	300,074	87	12	9	4	2	1	–
1 to 4 years old	17,228	80	19	14	5	3	2	–
5 to 9 years old	20,785	86	14	11	4	2	2	–
10 to 14 years old	19,893	89	11	8	3	2	1	–
15 to 19 years old	21,087	88	11	8	3	2	1	–
20 to 24 years old	21,154	73	26	18	8	5	3	1
25 to 29 years old	21,453	74	25	18	7	4	3	1
30 to 44 years old	60,079	86	14	10	4	2	2	–
45 to 64 years old	79,782	93	7	5	2	1	1	–
65 to 74 years old	20,956	96	4	2	2	1	1	–
75 to 84 years old	12,964	97	3	2	1	1	–	–
85 years old and over	4,693	96	4	2	1	1	1	–
Northeast	53,976	92	8	6	2	1	1	–
Midwest	65,271	88	12	8	3	2	1	–
South	110,699	86	13	9	4	3	2	–
West	70,129	85	14	11	4	2	2	–
Persons 16 years old and over	238,095	88	12	8	3	2	1	–
Civilian labor force	153,517	87	13	9	4	2	1	–
Employed	137,753	88	12	9	3	2	1	–
Unemployed	15,764	80	19	13	6	4	2	1
Armed Forces	937	69	26	13	13	2	11	4
Not in labor force	83,641	90	9	6	3	2	1	–
Employed civilians, 16 years old and over	137,753	88	12	9	3	2	1	–
Management, business, and financial	20,997	91	9	7	3	2	1	–
Professional	30,982	89	11	7	4	2	2	–
Service	24,258	84	16	12	4	2	1	–
Sales	15,467	86	14	10	4	3	2	–
Office and administrative support	17,874	88	12	9	3	2	1	–
Farming, fishing, and forestry	905	88	10	9	2	1	1	1
Construction and extraction	6,905	87	13	9	3	2	1	–
Installation, maintenance, and repair	4,922	89	11	8	3	2	1	–
Production	7,569	88	12	9	3	2	1	–
Transportation and material moving	7,875	87	13	9	4	2	1	–
Tenure:								
Owner occupied units	206,274	95	5	3	2	1	1	–
Renter occupied units	89,982	71	28	21	8	4	3	1
No cash renter occupied units	3,817	82	18	10	7	5	3	–

– Represents or rounds to zero.

Source: U.S. Census Bureau, Current Population Survey, 2010 Annual Social and Economic Supplement, "Geographical Mobility: 2009 to 2010, Detailed Tables," <http://www.census.gov/population/www/socdemo/migrate.html>.

Table 31. Movers by Type of Move and Reason for Moving: 2010

[As of March (37,540 represents 37,540,000). For persons 1 year old and over. Based on comparison of place of residence in 2009 and 2010. Excludes members of the Armed Forces except those living off post or with their families on post. Based on Current Population Survey, Annual Social and Economic Supplement. See text, this section and Appendix III]

Reason for move	All movers	Intra-county	Inter-county	From abroad	Reason for move	All movers	Intra-county	Inter-county	From abroad
Total (1,000)	37,540	26,017	10,577	946	Housing–related reasons	43.7	52.8	24.4	8.4
					Wanted to own home/ not rent	4.6	5.4	3.1	0.3
PERCENT DISTRIBUTION					New/better house/ apartment	15.5	19.2	7.3	4.3
Total	100.0	100.0	100.0	100.0	Better neighborhood/less crime	4.1	4.8	2.8	–
Family–related reasons	30.3	30.2	30.7	28.3	Cheaper housing	10.8	13.0	6.2	1.7
Change in marital status	7.3	7.5	7.2	5.0	Other housing	8.7	10.5	5.0	1.9
To establish own household	11.2	12.6	8.3	5.7					
Other family reasons	11.7	10.1	15.3	17.5					
Work–related reasons	16.4	9.6	31.1	40.7	Other reasons	9.5	7.4	13.8	22.6
New job/job transfer	7.8	2.7	18.9	23.8	Attend/leave college	2.7	1.7	4.7	8.4
To look for work/lost job	2.6	1.3	5.1	8.8	Change of climate	0.6	0.3	1.5	0.7
Closer to work/easier commute	4.2	4.2	4.5	1.4	Health reasons	1.5	1.3	2.1	1.7
Retired	0.5	0.3	0.8	2.4	Natural disaster	0.3	0.3	0.2	0.2
Other job–related reason	1.3	1.0	1.9	4.3	Other reason	4.4	3.8	5.3	11.6

– Represents or rounds to zero.

Source: U.S. Census Bureau, Current Population Survey, 2010 Annual Social and Economic Supplement, "Geographical Mobility: 2009 to 2010, Detailed Tables," <http://www.census.gov/population/www/socdemo/migrate.html>.

Population 37

Table 32. Mobility Status of Households by Household Income: 2010

[As of March (117,572 represents 117,572,000). Covers householders 15 years old and over. Based on comparison of place of residence in 2009 and 2010. Excludes members of the Armed Forces except those living off post or with their families on post. Based on Current Population Survey, Annual Social and Economic Supplement. See text, this section and Appendix III]

| Household income in 2009 | Total (1,000) | Non–movers | Movers (different house in United States) | | Different county | | | Movers from abroad |
			Total	Same county	Total	Same state	Different state	
Householders, 15 years and over.......	**117,572**	**88**	**12**	**8**	**3**	**2**	**1**	**–**
Under $5,000 or loss...................	3,757	78	21	15	6	4	3	1
$5,000 to $9,999	4,824	81	19	14	5	3	2	–
$10,000 to $14,999	6,759	85	15	11	4	2	2	–
$15,000 to $24,999	14,024	85	15	11	4	3	1	–
$25,000 to $34,999	13,004	86	13	10	3	2	1	–
$35,000 to $49,999	16,615	87	13	9	4	2	2	–
$50,000 to $69,999	17,587	88	11	8	3	2	1	–
$70,000 to $99,999	17,246	91	9	6	3	2	1	–
$100,000 and over....................	23,756	93	6	4	2	1	1	–

– Represents or rounds to zero.

Source: U.S. Census Bureau, Current Population Survey, 2010 Annual Social and Economic Supplement, "Geographical Mobility: 2009 to 2010, Detailed Tables," <http://www.census.gov/population/www/socdemo/migrate.html>.

Table 33. Mobility Status of Resident Population by State: 2009

[In percent, except as indicated (302,952 represents 302,952,000). Based on comparison of place of residence in 2008 and 2009. The American Community Survey universe includes the household population and the population living in institutions, college dormitories, and other group quarters. Based on a sample and subject to sampling variability. See text, this section and Appendix III]

| State | Population 1 year old and over [1] (1,000) | Same house in 2008 | Different house in United States in **2008** | | State | Population 1 year old and over [1] (1,000) | Same house in 2008 | Different house in United States in **2008** | |
			Same county	Different county				Same county	Different county
U.S.....	**302,952**	**84.6**	**9.4**	**5.5**					
					MO.......	5,912	83.6	9.4	6.7
AL	4,654	84.5	9.3	5.8	MT.......	962	83.0	10.1	6.5
AK	686	77.7	12.8	8.7	NE	1,770	82.2	10.4	7.0
AZ	6,494	79.5	14.5	5.3	NV	2,607	78.8	15.6	5.0
AR	2,853	82.1	11.0	6.6	NH	1,313	86.6	7.2	5.7
CA	36,454	83.7	11.3	4.3					
					NJ	8,607	90.1	5.5	3.7
CO......	4,954	81.2	9.9	8.3	NM.......	1,980	84.2	9.5	5.8
CT	3,480	88.3	7.1	4.0	NY	19,302	88.8	6.7	3.8
DE	873	85.4	9.2	4.8	NC	9,256	84.3	8.7	6.5
DC	592	84.2	8.0	6.5	ND	637	82.4	8.9	8.4
FL	18,312	83.4	10.2	5.7					
					OH.......	11,401	85.5	9.6	4.6
GA......	9,686	83.0	8.8	7.7	OK.......	3,633	81.4	10.5	7.7
HI........	1,278	83.4	10.5	4.9	OR.......	3,779	82.1	10.8	6.5
ID........	1,521	83.0	9.6	6.9	PA.......	12,465	87.6	7.5	4.5
IL........	12,737	86.8	8.7	4.0	RI........	1,043	86.4	8.4	4.5
IN........	6,334	84.4	9.5	5.7					
					SC	4,502	85.3	8.1	6.2
IA........	2,969	84.2	9.4	6.0	SD	801	83.7	7.9	8.2
KS	2,777	82.0	10.3	7.3	TN	6,214	84.4	9.7	5.6
KY	4,258	84.3	9.2	6.1	TX	24,384	81.9	11.2	6.2
LA	4,430	85.5	8.5	5.7	UT	2,732	82.8	9.9	6.5
ME.......	1,304	87.3	7.4	5.0					
					VT	616	86.9	7.3	5.5
MD......	5,624	85.9	7.5	5.9	VA	7,783	83.9	6.8	8.6
MA......	6,521	86.6	7.6	5.0	WA......	6,578	83.0	10.7	5.7
MI.......	9,852	85.2	9.7	4.7	WV......	1,799	87.6	6.9	5.3
MN......	5,200	85.7	7.8	6.1	WI	5,586	85.5	9.2	5.1
MS.......	2,911	85.2	8.3	6.4	WY.......	537	83.3	8.6	7.7

[1] Includes persons moving from abroad, not shown separately.

Source: U.S. Census Bureau, 2009 American Community Survey, B07003, "Residence 1 Year Ago by Sex," <http://factfinder.census.gov/>, accessed December 2010.

Table 34. Persons 65 Years Old and Over—Characteristics by Sex: 1990 to 2010

[As of March, except as noted (29.6 represents 29,600,000). Covers civilian noninstitutional population. Excludes members of Armed Forces except those living off post or with their families on post. Data for 1990 are based on 1980 census population controls; 2000 data based on 1990 census population controls; beginning 2005, data based on 2000 census population controls and an expanded sample of households. Based on Current Population Survey. See text, this section and Appendix III]

Characteristic	Total				Male				Female			
	1990	2000	2005	2010	1990	2000	2005	2010	1990	2000	2005	2010
Total (million)	**29.6**	**32.6**	**35.2**	**38.6**	**12.3**	**13.9**	**15.1**	**16.8**	**17.2**	**18.7**	**20.0**	**21.8**
PERCENT DISTRIBUTION												
Marital status:												
Never married	4.6	3.9	4.1	4.3	4.2	4.2	4.4	4.1	4.9	3.6	3.9	4.5
Married	56.1	57.2	57.7	57.6	76.5	75.2	74.9	74.5	41.4	43.8	44.7	44.5
Spouse present	54.1	54.6	54.8	55.2	74.2	72.6	71.7	71.7	39.7	41.3	42.0	42.4
Spouse absent [1]	2.0	2.6	2.9	2.4	2.3	2.6	3.2	2.8	1.7	2.5	2.7	2.1
Widowed	34.2	32.1	30.3	28.1	14.2	14.4	13.7	12.7	48.6	45.3	42.9	39.9
Divorced	5.0	6.7	7.9	10.0	5.0	6.1	7.0	8.7	5.1	7.2	8.5	11.1
Educational attainment:												
Less than ninth grade	28.5	16.7	13.4	10.2	30.0	17.8	13.2	10.2	27.5	15.9	13.5	10.1
Completed 9th to 12th grade, but no high school diploma	[2] 16.1	13.8	12.7	10.3	[2] 15.7	12.7	11.9	9.7	[2] 16.4	14.7	13.3	10.8
High school graduate.	[3] 32.9	35.9	36.3	36.4	[3] 29.0	30.4	31.6	32.0	[3] 35.6	39.9	39.9	39.8
Some college or associate's degree	[4] 10.9	18.0	18.7	20.6	[4] 10.8	17.8	18.4	19.7	[4] 11.0	18.2	19.0	21.2
Bachelor's or advanced degree	[5] 11.6	15.6	18.9	22.5	[5] 14.5	21.4	24.9	28.4	[5] 9.5	11.4	14.3	18.0
Labor force participation: [6]												
Employed.	11.5	12.4	14.5	16.2	15.9	16.9	19.1	20.5	8.4	9.1	11.1	12.9
Unemployed.	0.4	0.4	0.5	1.2	0.5	0.6	0.7	1.6	0.3	0.3	0.4	0.9
Not in labor force	88.1	87.2	84.9	82.6	83.6	82.5	80.2	77.9	91.3	90.6	88.5	86.2
Percent below poverty level [7]	11.4	9.7	9.8	(NA)	7.8	6.9	7.0	(NA)	13.9	11.8	11.9	(NA)

NA Not available. [1] Includes separated. [2] Represents those who completed 1 to 3 years of high school. [3] Represents those who completed 4 years of high school. [4] Represents those who completed 1 to 3 years of college. [5] Represents those who completed 4 years of college or more. [6] Annual averages of monthly figures. Source: U.S. Bureau of Labor Statistics, *Employment and Earnings*, January issues. See footnote 2, Table 586. [7] Poverty status based on income in preceding year.

Source: Except as noted, U.S. Census Bureau, Current Population Reports, *The Older Population in the United States: March 2002*, P20-546, 2003, and earlier reports; "Educational Attainment," <http://www.census.gov/population/www/socdemo /educ-attn.html>; "Families and Living Arrangements," <http://www.census.gov/population/www/socdemo/hh-fam.html>; and "Detailed Poverty Tabulations from the CPS," <http://www.census.gov/hhes/www/cpstables/032010/pov/toc.htm>.

Table 35. Persons 65 Years and Over—Living Arrangements and Disability Status: 2009

[In thousands (39,507 represents 39,507,000), except as indicated. Based on the American Community Survey (ACS). Disability data limited to civilian noninstitutionalized population. Based on a sample and subject to sampling variability; see text, this section and Appendix III]

Relationship by household type	Number	Percent distribu- tion	Type of disability	Total	65 to 74 years old	75 years old and over
Total.	**39,507**	**100.0**	**Persons with any disability. . . . .**	**14,189**	**5,278**	**8,902**
In households	37,648	95.3				
In family households	25,950	65.7	With a hearing disability.	5,847	1,904	3,943
Householder	12,955	32.8	With a vision disability	2,696	877	1,819
Spouse	9,299	23.5	With a cognitive disability	3,600	1,117	2,483
Parent	2,125	5.4	With a ambulatory disability.	9,213	3,392	5,822
Other relatives	1,405	3.6	With a self-care disability.	3,326	953	2,374
Nonrelatives.	166	0.4	With an independent living disability	6,236	1,699	4,537
In nonfamily households	11,698	29.6				
Householder	11,190	28.3				
Living alone	10,659	27.0				
Not living alone	530	1.3				
Nonrelatives.	508	1.3				
In group quarters	1,858	4.7				

Source: U.S. Census Bureau, 2009 American Community Survey, B09017, "Relationship by Household Type (Including Living Alone) for the Population 65 Years and Over;" B18101, "Sex by Age by Disability Status;" B18102, "Sex by Age by Hearing Difficulty;" B18103, "Sex by Age by Vision Difficulty;" B18104, "Sex by Age by Cognitive Difficulty;" B18105, "Sex by Age by Ambulatory Difficulty;" B18106, "Sex by Age by Self-Care Difficulty;" B18107, "Sex by Age by Independent Living Difficulty," <http://factfinder.census.gov/>, accessed December 2010.

Table 36. Selected Characteristics of Racial Groups and Hispanic or Latino Population: 2009

[In thousands (201,952 represents 201,952,000), except as indicated. The American Community Survey universe includes the household population and the population living in institutions, college dormitories, and other group quarters. Based on a sample and subject to sampling variability; see text, this section and Appendix III]

Characteristic	Total population	White alone	Black or African American alone	American Indian, Alaska Native alone	Asian alone
EDUCATIONAL ATTAINMENT					
Persons 25 years old and over, total	**201,952**	**156,607**	**22,975**	**1,451**	**9,404**
Less than 9th grade	12,641	7,981	1,269	141	814
9th to 12th grade, no diploma	17,144	11,661	3,008	200	568
High school graduate (includes equivalency)	57,552	45,324	7,261	442	1,506
Some college, no degree	43,087	33,610	5,720	372	1,224
Associate's degree	15,192	12,140	1,673	107	623
Bachelor's degree	35,494	28,916	2,635	124	2,767
Graduate degree	20,841	16,975	1,404	64	1,902
Percent high school graduate or higher	85.3	87.5	81.4	76.4	85.3
Percent bachelor's degree or higher	27.9	29.3	17.6	13.0	49.7
OCCUPATION					
Employed civilian population, 16 years old and over, total	**140,602**	**108,748**	**15,091**	**926**	**6,750**
Management, professional, and related occupations	50,180	40,650	4,225	238	3,288
Management, business and financial operations occupations	20,038	16,653	1,495	95	1,088
Professional and related occupations	30,142	23,997	2,730	143	2,201
Service occupations	25,067	17,525	3,816	228	1,128
Sales and office occupations	35,426	27,735	3,983	210	1,457
Farming, fishing, and forestry occupations	988	748	45	12	12
Construction, extraction, and maintenance occupations	12,274	9,938	801	113	219
Construction and extraction occupations	7,573	6,072	440	79	89
Installation, maintenance, and repair occupations	4,701	3,866	362	34	129
Production, transportation, and material moving occupations	16,668	12,153	2,221	125	646
Production occupations	8,309	6,107	929	63	431
Transportation and material moving occupations	8,359	6,045	1,292	62	216
FAMILY INCOME IN THE PAST 12 MONTHS					
Total families	**75,531**	**58,832**	**8,605**	**542**	**3,227**
Less than $10,000	3,676	2,151	992	62	122
$10,000 to $19,999	5,769	3,740	1,210	69	199
$20,000 to $29,999	7,056	5,021	1,138	75	228
$30,000 to $39,999	7,199	5,369	1,004	62	226
$40,000 to $49,999	6,930	5,399	796	53	229
$50,000 to $59,999	6,450	5,138	674	42	220
$60,000 to $74,999	8,538	6,926	798	52	325
$75,000 to $99,999	10,852	8,969	891	57	467
$100,000 to $124,999	7,026	5,871	499	33	376
$125,000 to $149,999	4,136	3,476	260	15	253
$150,000 to $199,999	4,041	3,407	212	13	295
$200,000 or more	3,859	3,365	130	8	288
Median family income in the past 12 months (dol.) [2]	61,082	65,319	39,587	40,552	78,529
POVERTY STATUS IN THE PAST 12 MONTHS [3]					
Persons below poverty level	42,868	26,271	9,408	647	1,539
Percent below poverty level	14.3	11.7	25.8	27.3	11.4
Families below poverty level	7,956	4,754	1,924	123	277
Percent below poverty level	10.5	8.1	22.4	22.7	8.6
HOUSING TENURE					
Total householders	**113,616**	**89,252**	**13,521**	**788**	**4,310**
Owner-occupied	74,843	63,262	6,012	430	2,560
Renter-occupied	38,773	25,990	7,510	358	1,750

See footnotes at end of table.

U.S. Census Bureau, Statistical Abstract of the United States: 2012

[See headnote, page 40]

Characteristic	Native Hawaiian and Other Pacific Islander alone	Some other race alone	Two or more races	Hispanic or Latino origin [1]	White alone, not Hispanic or Latino
EDUCATIONAL ATTAINMENT					
Persons 25 years old and over, total	**277**	**8,227**	**3,011**	**26,107**	**139,962**
Less than 9th grade	14	2,218	204	6,142	4,284
9th to 12th grade, no diploma	25	1,406	275	4,069	9,183
High school graduate (includes equivalency)	102	2,154	761	6,830	40,969
Some college, no degree	75	1,279	808	4,402	30,771
Associate's degree	22	373	254	1,377	11,219
Bachelor's degree	29	565	458	2,259	27,323
Graduate degree	10	234	251	1,030	16,212
Percent high school graduate or higher	85.8	56.0	84.1	60.9	90.4
Percent bachelor's degree or higher	14.2	9.7	23.6	12.6	31.1
OCCUPATION					
Employed civilian population, 16 years old and over, total	**200**	**6,534**	**2,354**	**20,055**	**96,172**
Management, professional, and related occupations	47	991	740	3,728	38,108
Management, business and financial operations occupations	19	415	273	1,560	15,585
Professional and related occupations	28	576	467	2,169	22,523
Service occupations	51	1,802	517	5,277	14,313
Sales and office occupations	55	1,362	623	4,395	24,936
Farming, fishing, and forestry occupations	1	156	15	476	443
Construction, extraction, and maintenance occupations	17	996	190	2,807	8,223
Construction and extraction occupations	11	763	120	2,101	4,803
Installation, maintenance, and repair occupations	7	233	70	706	3,420
Production, transportation, and material moving occupations	28	1,227	269	3,372	10,149
Production occupations	10	642	126	1,736	5,082
Transportation and material moving occupations	17	584	143	1,636	5,067
FAMILY INCOME IN THE PAST 12 MONTHS					
Total families	**99**	**3,111**	**1,115**	**9,877**	**52,520**
Less than $10,000	5	263	82	760	1,697
$10,000 to $19,999	7	435	109	1,325	2,912
$20,000 to $29,999	10	457	127	1,446	4,101
$30,000 to $39,999	11	414	112	1,247	4,589
$40,000 to $49,999	11	338	105	1,042	4,742
$50,000 to $59,999	9	269	97	848	4,597
$60,000 to $74,999	13	305	119	969	6,303
$75,000 to $99,999	14	310	144	1,018	8,308
$100,000 to $124,999	8	155	84	547	5,504
$125,000 to $149,999	6	75	50	282	3,279
$150,000 to $199,999	4	61	48	236	3,244
$200,000 or more	2	29	37	157	3,243
Median family income in the past 12 months (dol.) [2]	57,185	39,632	52,137	41,423	68,390
POVERTY STATUS IN THE PAST 12 MONTHS [3]					
Persons below poverty level	66	3,620	1,317	11,131	19,463
Percent below poverty level	15.1	24.7	18.1	23.5	10.0
Families below poverty level	12	697	169	2,058	3,496
Percent below poverty level	11.8	22.4	15.1	20.8	6.7
HOUSING TENURE					
Total householders	**126**	**3,896**	**1,724**	**12,724**	**81,067**
Owner-occupied	55	1,630	894	6,103	59,049
Renter-occupied	71	2,266	830	6,621	22,018

[1] Persons of Hispanic origin may be any race. [2] For definition of median, see Guide to Tabular Presentation [3] For explanation of poverty level, see text, Section 13.

Source: U.S. Census Bureau, 2009 American Community Survey, B15002, "Sex by Educational Attainment for the Population 25 Years and Over"; B24010, "Sex by Occupation for the Employed Civilian Population 16 Years and Over"; B19101, "Family Income in the Past 12 Months (In 2009 Inflation-Adjusted Dollars)"; B19113, "Median Family Income in the Past 12 Months (In 2009 Inflation-Adjusted Dollars)"; B17001, "Poverty Status in the Past 12 Months by Sex by Age"; B17010, "Poverty Status in the Past 12 Months of Families by Family Type by Presence of Related Children Under 18 Years by Age of Related Children"; B25003, "Tenure," <http://factfinder.census.gov/>.

Table 37. Social and Economic Characteristics of the Hispanic Population: 2009

[As of March, except labor force status, annual average (47,485 represents 47,485,000). Excludes members of the Armed Forces except those living off post or with their families on post. Based on Current Population Survey; see text, this section and Appendix III]

Characteristic	Number (1,000)					Percent distribution				
	His-panic, total [1]	Mexi-can	Puerto Rican	Cuban	Central, South Ameri-can	His-panic, total [1]	Mexi-can	Puerto Rican	Cuban	Central, South Ameri-can
Total persons	**47,485**	**31,550**	**4,224**	**1,647**	**7,583**	**100.0**	**100.0**	**100.0**	**100.0**	**100.0**
Under 5 years old	5,396	3,919	462	85	673	11.4	12.4	10.9	5.1	8.9
5 to 14 years old	8,640	6,072	800	192	1,115	18.2	19.2	19.0	11.7	14.7
15 to 44 years old	22,648	15,174	1,907	659	3,871	47.7	48.0	45.2	40.0	51.1
45 to 64 years old	8,084	4,879	794	385	1,528	17.0	15.5	18.8	23.4	20.1
65 years old and over	2,717	1,505	262	326	396	5.7	4.8	6.2	19.8	5.2
EDUCATIONAL ATTAINMENT										
Persons 25 years old and over	**25,956**	**16,461**	**2,244**	**1,164**	**4,696**	**100.0**	**100.0**	**100.0**	**100.0**	**100.0**
High school graduate or more	16,066	9,168	1,718	914	3,160	61.9	55.7	76.6	78.5	67.3
Bachelor's degree or more	3,428	1,566	370	325	920	13.2	9.5	16.5	27.9	19.6
LABOR FORCE STATUS [2]										
Civilians 16 years old and over	**32,585**	**20,984**	**2,867**	**1,349**	**(NA)**	**100.0**	**100.0**	**100.0**	**100.0**	**100.0**
Civilian labor force	21,971	14,082	1,772	802	(NA)	67.4	67.1	61.8	59.5	(NA)
Employed	19,285	12,313	1,525	734	(NA)	59.2	58.7	53.2	54.4	(NA)
Unemployed	2,686	1,769	246	68	(NA)	8.2	8.4	8.6	5.0	(NA)
Unemployment rate [3]	12.2	12.6	13.9	8.5	(NA)	(X)	(X)	(X)	(X)	(X)
Male	13.1	13.1	16.9	8.9	(NA)	(X)	(X)	(X)	(X)	(X)
Female	11.0	11.6	10.8	7.8	(NA)	(X)	(X)	(X)	(X)	(X)
Not in labor force	10,614	6,902	1,095	547	(NA)	32.6	32.9	38.2	40.5	(NA)
HOUSEHOLDS										
Total	**13,425**	**8,335**	**1,369**	**630**	**2,362**	**100.0**	**100.0**	**100.0**	**100.0**	**100.0**
Family households	10,503	6,731	985	440	1,839	78.2	80.8	72.0	69.8	77.9
Married-couple families [4]	6,911	4,613	518	313	1,144	51.5	55.3	37.8	49.7	48.4
Male householder, no spouse present	1,021	652	89	32	208	7.6	7.8	6.5	5.1	8.8
Female householder, no spouse present	2,571	1,466	378	95	487	19.2	17.6	27.6	15.1	20.6
Nonfamily households	2,923	1,604	384	190	523	21.8	19.2	28.0	30.2	22.1
Male householder	1,578	917	186	79	293	11.8	11.0	13.6	12.5	12.4
Female householder	1,345	687	199	111	230	10.0	8.2	14.5	17.6	9.7
Size:										
One person	2,195	1,175	326	151	363	16.4	14.1	23.8	24.0	15.4
Two people	3,067	1,733	361	211	558	22.8	20.8	26.4	33.5	23.6
Three people	2,613	1,522	277	124	536	19.5	18.3	20.2	19.7	22.7
Four people	2,597	1,717	221	90	480	19.3	20.6	16.1	14.3	20.3
Five people	1,705	1,221	120	36	265	12.7	14.6	8.8	5.7	11.2
Six people	754	567	40	15	106	5.6	6.8	2.9	2.4	4.5
Seven people or more	494	400	24	4	53	3.7	4.8	1.8	0.6	2.2
FAMILY INCOME IN 2008										
Total families [5]	**10,503**	**6,731**	**985**	**440**	**1,778**	**100.0**	**100.0**	**100.0**	**100.0**	**100.0**
Less than $5,000	436	281	56	7	65	4.1	4.2	5.6	1.8	3.6
$5,000 to $14,999	1,092	741	123	40	154	10.4	11.0	12.5	9.1	8.6
$15,000 to $24,999	1,504	1,021	132	56	231	14.3	15.2	13.4	12.8	13.0
$25,000 to $34,999	1,496	1,009	131	47	238	14.2	15.0	13.3	10.6	13.4
$35,000 to $49,999	1,761	1,169	131	74	313	16.8	17.4	13.3	16.9	17.6
$50,000 to $74,999	1,867	1,143	176	70	359	17.8	17.0	17.9	15.9	20.2
$75,000 and over	2,346	1,369	236	145	418	22.3	20.3	23.9	32.9	23.5
POVERTY STATUS IN 2008										
Families below poverty level [6]	2,239	1,565	224	55	314	21.3	23.2	22.7	12.6	17.6
Persons below poverty level [6]	10,987	7,821	1,065	277	1,431	23.2	24.8	25.2	16.8	18.9
HOUSEHOLD TENURE										
Total occupied units	**13,425**	**8,335**	**1,369**	**630**	**2,280**	**100.0**	**100.0**	**100.0**	**100.0**	**100.0**
Owner occupied	6,418	4,109	515	367	920	47.8	49.3	37.6	58.2	40.3
Renter occupied [7]	7,007	4,226	854	263	1,360	52.2	50.7	62.4	41.8	59.7

NA Not available. X Not applicable. [1] Includes other Hispanic groups not shown separately. [2] Source: U.S. Bureau of Labor Statistics, "Employment and Earnings Online," January 2010, <http://stats.bls.gov/opub/ee/home.htm>. [3] Total unemployment as percent of civilian labor force. [4] In married-couple families, Hispanic origin refers to the householder. [5] Includes families in group quarters. [6] For explanation of poverty level; see text, Section 13. [7] Includes no cash rent.

Source: Except as noted, U.S. Census Bureau, "Educational Attainment," <http://www.census.gov/population/www/socdemo/educ-attn.html>; "Families and Living Arrangements," <http://www.census.gov/population/www/socdemo/hh-fam.html>; "Detailed Income Tabulations from the CPS," <http://www.census.gov/hhes/www/income/dinctabs.html>; "Detailed Poverty Tabulations from the CPS," <http://www.census.gov/hhes/www/cpstables/032009/pov/toc.htm> ; and unpublished data.

Table 38. Native and Foreign-Born Population by Place of Birth and State: 2009

[268,489 represents 268,489,000. The American Community Survey universe includes the household population and the population living in institutions, college dormitories, and other group quarters. Based on a sample and subject to sampling variability; see text, this section and Appendix III. See headnote, Table 42]

State	Native population (1,000)	Foreign-born population			State	Native population (1,000)	Foreign-born population		
		Number (1,000)	Percent of total population	Percent entered 2000 or later			Number (1,000)	Percent of total population	Percent entered 2000 or later
U.S.	268,489	38,517	12.5	31.6	MO	5,775	213	3.6	42.2
AL	4,562	147	3.1	47.6	MT	956	19	2.0	30.3
AK	650	49	7.0	35.7	NE	1,690	106	5.9	44.4
AZ	5,670	925	14.0	32.7	NV	2,137	507	19.2	32.1
AR	2,769	120	4.2	37.8	NH	1,256	68	5.2	30.8
CA	27,015	9,947	26.9	24.9	NJ	6,948	1,759	20.2	32.1
CO	4,538	487	9.7	36.0	NM	1,814	196	9.8	29.9
CT	3,059	460	13.1	34.5	NY	15,363	4,178	21.4	28.2
DE	811	74	8.4	44.3	NC	8,716	665	7.1	44.2
DC	528	72	12.0	39.6	ND	631	15	2.4	53.1
FL	15,054	3,484	18.8	31.8	OH	11,109	433	3.8	37.4
GA	8,909	920	9.4	41.4	OK	3,497	190	5.1	40.0
HI	1,071	224	17.3	26.4	OR	3,458	367	9.6	35.5
ID	1,448	98	6.3	34.1	PA	11,914	691	5.5	35.5
IL	11,170	1,741	13.5	28.4	RI	920	133	12.7	27.0
IN	6,142	281	4.4	44.8	SC	4,356	205	4.5	45.7
IA	2,892	116	3.9	39.8	SD	791	22	2.7	42.2
KS	2,647	171	6.1	39.9	TN	6,031	266	4.2	42.6
KY	4,186	128	3.0	54.0	TX	20,797	3,985	16.1	33.5
LA	4,340	152	3.4	39.5	UT	2,566	218	7.8	38.1
ME	1,274	44	3.3	33.9	VT	601	21	3.3	20.2
MD	4,969	730	12.8	36.4	VA	7,077	806	10.2	37.8
MA	5,650	943	14.3	34.2	WA	5,854	811	12.2	33.2
MI	9,356	614	6.2	36.5	WV	1,797	23	1.3	37.2
MN	4,909	358	6.8	41.8	WI	5,399	256	4.5	36.6
MS	2,892	60	2.0	48.1	WY	527	17	3.1	41.1

Source: U.S. Census Bureau, 2009 American Community Survey, C05002, "Place of Birth by Citizenship Status" and C05005, "Year of Entry by Citizenship Status," <http://factfinder.census.gov/>, accessed May 2011.

Table 39. Nativity and Place of Birth of Resident Population—25 Largest Cities: 2009

[791 represents 791,000. The American Community Survey universe includes the household population and the population living in institutions, college dormitories, and other group quarters. Based on a sample and subject to sampling variability; see text, this section and Appendix III. See headnote, Table 42]

City	Total population (1,000)	Native population			Foreign born			
		Total (1,000)	Born in United States (1,000)	Born outside United States (1,000)	Total		Entered 2000 or later	
					Number (1,000)	Percent of total population	Number (1,000)	Percent of foreign-born population
Austin, TX	791	631	619	12	159	20.2	75	46.8
Baltimore, MD	637	596	592	4	41	6.5	21	51.5
Boston, MA	645	483	468	15	162	25.1	60	37.3
Charlotte, NC.	704	608	600	7	97	13.7	48	49.9
Chicago, IL.	2,851	2,262	2,211	51	588	20.6	170	28.8
Columbus, OH.	773	690	684	6	83	10.7	44	52.5
Dallas, TX	1,300	978	965	13	322	24.8	128	39.8
Denver, CO	610	515	507	7	96	15.7	39	40.8
Detroit, MI	911	851	844	7	60	6.6	28	46.3
El Paso, TX	620	469	455	14	151	24.4	33	21.6
Fort Worth, TX	732	600	592	8	131	17.9	45	34.2
Houston, TX.	2,261	1,617	1,596	20	644	28.5	248	38.5
Indianapolis, IN [1]	808	744	740	4	63	7.8	37	59.2
Jacksonville, FL.	814	740	723	16	74	9.1	25	33.8
Los Angeles, CA	3,832	2,311	2,275	35	1,521	39.7	407	26.8
Memphis, TN	677	640	636	4	37	5.4	18	50.4
Nashville-Davidson, TN [1]	605	535	529	6	70	11.6	31	44.4
New York, NY.	8,392	5,395	5,067	328	2,997	35.7	860	28.7
Philadelphia, PA.	1,547	1,368	1,315	53	179	11.6	71	39.5
Phoenix, AZ.	1,594	1,247	1,231	16	346	21.7	124	35.8
San Antonio, TX.	1,374	1,193	1,167	26	181	13.2	51	27.9
San Diego, CA.	1,306	980	956	24	326	24.9	91	27.9
San Francisco, CA.	815	537	523	14	278	34.1	63	22.7
San Jose, CA.	965	597	587	10	368	38.1	106	28.7
Seattle, WA	617	512	499	12	105	17.1	35	33.3

[1] Represents the portion of a consolidated city that is not within one or more separately incorporated places.
Source: U.S. Census Bureau, 2009 American Community Survey, C05002, "Place of Birth by Citizenship Status" and C05005, "Year of Entry by Citizenship Status," <http://factfinder.census.gov/>, accessed June 2011.

Population 43

Table 40. Native and Foreign-Born Populations by Selected Characteristics: 2010

[In thousands (304,280 represents 304,280,000). As of March. The foreign-born population includes anyone who is not a U.S. citizen at birth. This includes legal permanent residents (immigrants), temporary migrants (such as students), humanitarian migrants (such as refugees), and persons illegally present in the United States. Based on Current Population Survey, Annual Social and Economic Supplement which includes the civilian noninstitutional population plus Armed Forces living off post or with their families on post; see text, this section, and Appendix III]

Characteristic	Total population	Native population	Foreign-born population			
			Total	Natural-ized citizen	Not U.S. citizen	Year of entry: 2000 to March 2010
Total	304,280	266,674	37,606	16,024	21,581	13,085
Under 5 years old	21,434	21,162	272	53	219	272
5 to 14 years old	40,678	39,028	1,651	314	1,337	1,415
15 to 24 years old	42,240	38,433	3,807	878	2,929	2,345
25 to 34 years old	41,085	33,507	7,577	1,974	5,603	4,106
35 to 44 years old	40,447	31,905	8,542	3,323	5,219	2,570
45 to 54 years old	44,387	37,611	6,776	3,546	3,230	1,303
55 to 64 years old	35,395	31,003	4,391	2,747	1,643	624
65 to 74 years old	20,956	18,294	2,663	1,795	868	263
75 to 84 years old	12,964	11,499	1,466	1,048	419	151
85 years old and over	4,693	4,233	460	347	114	35
Median age (years) [1]	36.7	35.4	41.3	48.9	36.2	31.0
Male	149,485	130,728	18,758	7,470	11,288	6,690
Female	154,795	135,946	18,849	8,555	10,294	6,395
MARITAL STATUS						
Persons 15 years old and over	242,168	206,485	35,683	15,658	20,025	11,398
Married	124,219	102,435	21,784	10,300	11,484	6,316
Widowed	14,356	12,605	1,751	1,078	673	267
Divorced	23,758	21,374	2,384	1,322	1,062	409
Separated	5,541	4,348	1,193	455	738	355
Never married	74,294	65,723	8,570	2,503	6,067	4,052
EDUCATIONAL ATTAINMENT						
Persons 25 years old and over	199,928	168,052	31,876	14,780	17,096	9,052
Not high school graduate	25,711	16,212	9,499	2,802	6,697	2,799
High school graduate/some college	114,376	101,203	13,174	6,785	6,389	3,359
Bachelor's degree	38,784	33,016	5,769	3,296	2,473	1,831
Advanced degree	21,056	17,620	3,434	1,897	1,537	1,062
EARNINGS IN 2009 [2]						
Persons 15 years old and over with earnings	99,270	83,790	15,480	7,459	8,020	4,524
Under $15,000	5,685	4,290	1,394	426	969	525
$15,000 to $24,999	14,845	11,294	3,551	1,075	2,475	1,422
$25,000 to $34,999	17,553	14,528	3,025	1,415	1,610	845
$35,000 to $49,999	21,591	18,931	2,660	1,522	1,138	586
$50,000 to $74,999	21,131	18,706	2,425	1,461	964	561
$75,000 and over	18,465	16,040	2,425	1,561	864	584
Median earnings (dollars) [1]	41,480	42,283	32,932	41,339	27,170	27,198
HOUSEHOLD SIZE [3]						
Total households	117,538	102,039	15,499	7,834	7,665	3,978
One person	31,399	28,615	2,784	1,626	1,158	578
Two persons	39,487	35,720	3,767	2,172	1,595	931
Three persons	18,638	15,736	2,902	1,346	1,556	885
Four persons	16,122	13,121	3,001	1,383	1,618	833
Five persons	7,367	5,709	1,658	776	882	412
Six persons	2,784	2,010	774	312	463	179
Seven persons or more	1,740	1,128	612	218	394	160
INCOME IN 2009 [3]						
Total family households	78,833	66,840	11,993	5,952	6,041	3,066
Under $15,000	6,030	4,769	1,261	410	851	431
$15,000 to $24,999	6,968	5,500	1,469	520	949	418
$25,000 to $34,999	7,795	6,274	1,522	613	908	439
$35,000 to $49,999	10,881	9,187	1,694	819	875	451
$50,000 to $74,999	15,633	13,387	2,246	1,194	1,052	534
$75,000 and over	31,525	27,724	3,801	2,395	1,406	794
Median income (dollars) [1]	61,265	63,231	50,341	61,333	39,542	41,507
POVERTY STATUS IN 2009 [4]						
Persons below poverty level	43,569	36,407	7,162	1,736	5,425	3,350
Persons at or above poverty level	260,251	229,815	30,435	14,288	16,147	9,727
HOUSEHOLD TENURE [3]						
Total households	117,539	102,039	15,500	7,834	7,666	3,978
Owner occupied unit	78,780	70,687	8,092	5,261	2,831	1,121
Renter occupied unit [5]	38,759	31,352	7,408	2,573	4,835	2,857

[1] For definition of median, see Guide to Tabular Presentation. [2] Covers only year-round, full-time workers. [3] Based on citizenship of householder. [4] Persons for whom poverty status is determined. Excludes unrelated individuals under 15 years old. [5] Includes occupiers who paid no cash rent.

Source: U.S. Census Bureau, Current Population Survey, "Annual Social and Economic Supplement," <http://www.census.gov/population/www/socdemo/foreign/datatbls.html>.

Table 41. Foreign-Born Population—Selected Characteristics by Region of Origin: 2010

[In thousands (37,606 represents 37,606,000). As of March. The term foreign-born refers to anyone who is not a U.S. citizen at birth. This includes naturalized U.S. citizens, legal permanent residents (immigrants), temporary migrants (such as foreign students), humanitarian migrants (such as refugees), and persons illegally present in the United States. Based on Current Population Survey, Annual Social and Economic Supplement; see text, this section and Appendix III]

| Characteristic | Total foreign-born | Europe | Asia | Latin America | | Central America [1] | South America | Other areas |
				Total	Caribbean			
Total	**37,606**	**4,509**	**10,126**	**20,419**	**3,649**	**14,400**	**2,370**	**2,553**
Under 5 years old	272	35	100	83	4	76	2	54
5 to 14 years old	1,651	151	466	892	152	667	73	142
15 to 24 years old	3,807	296	848	2,390	351	1,822	217	273
25 to 34 years old	7,577	544	1,868	4,620	536	3,648	436	545
35 to 44 years old	8,542	778	2,190	5,005	637	3,805	563	569
45 to 54 years old	6,776	742	1,927	3,661	805	2,329	527	446
55 to 64 years old	4,391	695	1,405	2,036	523	1,244	268	255
65 to 74 years old	2,663	683	753	1,071	352	534	184	156
75 to 84 years old	1,466	412	457	515	233	205	77	82
85 years old and over	460	171	111	147	55	69	23	31
EDUCATIONAL ATTAINMENT								
Persons 25 years old and over	**31,876**	**4,026**	**8,712**	**17,054**	**3,142**	**11,834**	**2,078**	**2,083**
Less than ninth grade	5,906	302	618	4,844	394	4,273	177	142
9th to 12th grade (no diploma)	3,593	154	438	2,909	331	2,405	173	92
High school graduate	8,138	1,102	1,836	4,725	967	3,055	703	475
Some college or associate's degree	5,035	814	1,259	2,436	748	1,245	443	526
Bachelor's degree	5,769	996	2,753	1,554	500	682	372	466
Advanced degree	3,434	659	1807	586	202	176	209	382
High school graduate or more	22,377	3,570	7,655	9,301	2,417	5,157	1,728	1,851
Bachelor's degree or more	9,204	1,654	4,561	2,141	702	857	582	848
INCOME IN 2009								
Total family households	**11,993**	**1,444**	**3,365**	**6,362**	**1,218**	**4,439**	**705**	**821**
Under $15,000	1,261	87	241	834	167	614	53	100
$15,000 to $24,999	1,469	128	249	1,035	171	798	66	57
$25,000 to $34,999	1,522	152	276	995	169	753	74	99
$35,000 to $49,999	1,694	165	373	1,050	190	768	92	107
$50,000 to $74,999	2,246	292	633	1,191	200	806	185	130
$75,000 and over	3,801	621	1,595	1,257	322	700	235	328
Median income (dol.) [2]	50,341	64,340	70,856	38,785	41,972	35,789	56,963	55,758
POVERTY STATUS IN 2009 [3]								
Persons below poverty level	7,162	442	1,325	4,957	689	3,984	285	438
Persons at or above poverty level	30,435	4,067	8,801	15,455	2,960	10,409	2,085	2,112

[1] Includes Mexico. [2] For definition of median, see Guide to Tabular Presentation. [3] Persons for whom poverty status is determined. Excludes unrelated individuals under 15 years old.
Source: U.S. Census Bureau, Current Population Survey, "Annual Social and Economic Supplement," <http://www.census.gov/population/www/socdemo/foreign/datatbls.html>.

Table 42. Foreign-Born Population by Citizenship Status and Place of Birth: 2009

[The term foreign-born refers to anyone who is not a U.S. citizen at birth. This includes naturalized U.S. citizens, legal permanent residents (immigrants), temporary migrants (such as foreign students), humanitarian migrants (such as refugees), and persons illegally present in the United States. The American Community Survey universe includes the household population and the population living in institutions, college dormitories, and other group quarters. Based on a sample and subject to sampling variability; see text, this section and Appendix III]

| Region | Foreign-born population, total | Naturalized citizen | Not U.S. citizen | |
			Number	Percent of foreign-born
Total [1]	**38,517,234**	**16,846,397**	**21,670,837**	**56.3**
Latin America	20,455,547	6,556,447	13,899,100	67.9
Caribbean	3,465,890	1,934,369	1,531,521	44.2
Central America	14,393,833	3,491,399	10,902,434	75.7
Mexico	11,478,413	2,609,110	8,869,303	77.3
Other Central America	2,915,420	882,289	2,033,131	69.7
South America	2,595,824	1,130,679	1,465,145	56.4
Asia	10,652,379	6,193,074	4,459,305	41.9
Europe	4,887,221	2,999,879	1,887,342	38.6
Africa	1,492,785	(NA)	(NA)	(NA)
Northern America	822,377	(NA)	(NA)	(NA)
Oceania	206,795	(NA)	(NA)	(NA)

NA Not available. [1] Includes persons born at sea.
Source: U.S. Census Bureau, 2009 American Community Survey, B05002, "Place of Birth by Citizenship Status"; C05006, "Place of Birth for the Foreign-Born Population"; and B05007, "Place of Birth by Year of Entry by Citizenship Status for the Foreign-Born Population," <http://factfinder.census.gov>, accessed January 2011.

Table 43. Persons Obtaining Legal Permanent Resident Status: 1901 to 2010

[8,795 represents 8,795,000. For fiscal years ending in year shown; see text, Section 8. Rates based on Census Bureau estimates as of July 1 for resident population through 1929 and for total population thereafter (excluding Alaska and Hawaii prior to 1959. 2010 based on resident population as of April 1)]

Period	Number (1,000)	Rate [1]	Year	Number (1,000)	Rate [1]
1901 to 1910	8,795	10.4	1990.	1,536	6.1
1911 to 1920	5,736	5.7	1995.	720	2.7
1921 to 1930	4,107	3.5	2000.	841	3.0
1931 to 1940	528	0.4	2003.	704	2.4
1941 to 1950	1,035	0.7	2004.	958	3.3
1951 to 1960	2,515	1.5	2005.	1,122	3.8
1961 to 1970	3,322	1.7	2006.	1,266	4.2
1971 to 1980	4,399	2.0	2007.	1,052	3.5
1981 to 1990	7,256	3.0	2008.	1,107	3.6
1991 to 2000	9,081	3.4	2009.	1,131	3.7
2001 to 2010	10,501	3.5	2010.	1,043	3.4

[1] Annual rate per 1,000 U.S. population. Rate computed by dividing sum of annual immigration totals by sum of annual U.S. population totals for same number of years.

Source: U.S. Department of Homeland Security, Office of Immigration Statistics, *2010 Yearbook of Immigration Statistics*. See also <http://www.dhs.gov/ximgtn/statistics/publications/yearbook.shtm>.

Table 44. Refugee Arrivals and Individuals Granted Asylum by Country of Nationality: 2005 to 2010

[For year ending September 30. Data shown provide information on the number of persons admitted to the United States as refugees or granted asylum in the United States in the year shown. In cases with no country of nationality, refers to country of last residence. For definitions of refugee and asylee, see text, this section. Based on data from the Bureau of Population, Refugees, and Migration of the U.S. Department of State and the Executive Office for Immigration Review of the U.S. Department of Justice]

Country of nationality	Refugee arrivals			Country of nationality	Asylees		
	2005	2009	2010		2005	2009	2010
Total.	**53,738**	**74,602**	**73,293**	Total.	**25,228**	**22,090**	**21,113**
Iraq	198	18,838	18,016	China.	5,247	6,118	6,683
Burma	1,447	18,202	16,693	Ethiopia	730	1,109	1,093
Bhutan	–	13,452	12,363	Haiti	2,935	1,000	832
Somalia	10,405	4,189	4,884	Venezuela	1,105	584	660
Cuba	6,360	4,800	4,818	Nepal	313	667	640
Iran	1,856	5,381	3,543	Colombia	3,362	993	591
Congo, Democratic Republic. .	424	1,135	3,174	Russia	487	493	548
Eritrea	327	1,571	2,570	Egypt	336	481	536
Vietnam	2,009	1,486	873	Iran	288	348	485
Ethiopia	1,663	321	668	Guatemala	389	502	465
Other countries [1]	29,049	5,227	5,691	Other countries [1]	10,036	9,795	8,580

– Represents zero. [1] Includes unknown.

Source: U.S. Department of Homeland Security, Office of Immigration Statistics, Annual Flow Report, *Refugees and Asylees: 2010*. See also <http://www.dhs.gov/xlibrary/assets/statistics/publications/ois_rfa_fr_2010.pdf>.

Table 45. Estimated Unauthorized Immigrants by Selected States and Countries of Birth: 2000 and 2010

[In thousands (8,460 represents 8,460,000). As of January. Unauthorized immigrants refers to foreign-born persons who entered the United States without inspection or who were admitted temporarily and stayed past the date they were required to leave. Unauthorized aliens who have applied for but have not yet received approval to lawfully remain in the United States are considered to be unauthorized. These estimates were calculated using a "residual method," whereby estimates of the legally resident foreign-born population were subtracted from the total foreign-born population in order to derive the unauthorized immigrant population. All of these component populations were resident in the United States on January 1, 2010, and entered during the 1980–2009 period. Persons who entered the United States prior to 1980 were assumed to be legally resident. Estimates of the legally resident foreign-born were based primarily on administrative data of the Department of Homeland Security, while estimates of the total foreign-born population were obtained from the American Community Survey of the U.S. Census Bureau. Estimates for 2000 are based on the same methodology, assumptions, and definitions with the exception that data from Census 2000 were used to estimate the foreign-born population in 2000 that entered the United States from January 1, 1980 through December 31, 1999]

State of residence	2000	2005	2010	Country of birth	2000	2005	2010
United States, total . .	**8,460**	**10,490**	**10,790**	Total.	**8,460**	**10,490**	**10,790**
California	2,510	2,770	2,570	Mexico	4,680	5,970	6,640
Texas	1,090	1,360	1,770	El Salvador	430	470	620
Florida	800	850	760	Guatemala	290	370	520
Illinois.	440	520	490	Honduras	160	180	330
Arizona	330	480	470	Philippines	200	210	280
Georgia	220	470	460	India.	120	280	200
New York	540	560	460	Ecuador	110	120	180
North Carolina	260	360	390	Brazil	100	170	180
New Jersey	350	380	370	Korea	180	210	170
Nevada	170	240	260	China.	190	230	130
Other states	1,760	2,510	2,790	Other countries	2,000	2,280	1,550

Source: U.S. Department of Homeland Security, Office of Immigration Statistics, "Estimates of the Unauthorized Immigrant Population Residing in the United States: January 2010." See also <www.dhs.gov/xlibrary/assets/statistics/publications/ois_ill_pe_2010.pdf>.

U.S. Census Bureau, Statistical Abstract of the United States: 2012

Table 46. Immigrant Orphans Adopted by U.S. Citizens by Sex, Age, Region, and Country of Birth: 2010

[For years ending September 30]

Region and country of birth	Total	Male	Female	Under 1 year old	1 to 4 years old	5 years old and over
REGION						
Total.........................	**11,100**	**4,864**	**6,236**	**2,312**	**5,874**	**2,914**
Africa............................	3,156	1,605	1,551	937	1,345	874
Asia..............................	5,409	1,984	3,425	1,246	3,267	896
Europe...........................	1,721	895	826	53	1,007	661
North America..................	433	203	230	9	133	291
Oceania..........................	28	14	14	17	6	5
South America...................	335	154	181	48	108	179
Unknown.........................	18	9	9	2	8	8
COUNTRY						
Total [1].......................	**11,100**	**4,864**	**6,236**	**2,312**	**5,874**	**2,914**
Armenia...........................	18	7	11	5	8	5
Brazil.............................	24	12	12	–	8	16
China.............................	3,361	863	2,498	498	2,292	571
Colombia.........................	233	106	127	47	81	105
Ethiopia..........................	2,548	1,301	1,247	864	1,107	577
Ghana............................	99	55	44	(D)	(D)	67
Guatemala........................	49	30	19	–	22	27
Guyana...........................	33	12	21	–	8	25
Haiti..............................	179	73	106	–	74	105
India.............................	249	83	166	14	179	56
Jamaica..........................	63	30	33	(D)	(D)	58
Japan.............................	35	19	16	28	4	3
Kazakhstan.......................	182	81	101	70	78	34
Kenya.............................	16	9	7	–	5	11
Korea, South.....................	875	573	302	464	396	15
Latvia............................	40	26	14	–	5	35
Liberia...........................	40	20	20	–	10	30
Lithuania.........................	15	4	11	–	6	9
Marshall Islands..................	18	9	9	15	3	–
Mexico............................	59	31	28	4	11	44
Morocco...........................	33	21	12	13	16	4
Nicaragua........................	12	7	5	–	4	8
Nigeria...........................	197	88	109	23	86	88
Pakistan..........................	40	17	23	28	8	4
Peru..............................	34	15	19	(D)	(D)	27
Philippines.......................	215	114	101	(D)	113	(D)
Poland............................	48	21	27	(D)	(D)	25
Russia............................	1,079	596	483	47	826	206
Rwanda...........................	42	21	21	14	22	6
Taiwan............................	277	153	124	123	89	65
Thailand..........................	57	29	28	(D)	37	(D)
Uganda...........................	64	33	31	3	30	31
Ukraine...........................	445	202	243	3	113	329
Unknown.........................	18	9	9	2	8	8

– Represents zero. D Data withheld to limit disclosure. [1] Includes unknown and countries not shown separately.
Source: U.S. Department of Homeland Security, Office of Immigration Statistics, *2010 Yearbook of Immigration Statistics*. See also <http://www.dhs.gov/ximgtn/statistics/publications/yearbook.shtm>.

Table 47. Petitions for Naturalization Filed, Persons Naturalized, and Petitions Denied: 1990 to 2010

[For fiscal years ending in year shown; see text, Section 8. Naturalizations refer to persons 18 and over who become citizens of the United States]

Year	Petitions filed	Persons naturalized				Petitions denied
		Total	Civilian	Military	Not reported	
1990.....	233,843	267,586	245,410	1,618	20,558	6,516
1995.....	959,963	485,720	472,518	3,855	9,347	46,067
1996.....	1,277,403	1,040,991	924,368	1,214	115,409	229,842
1997.....	1,412,712	596,010	532,871	531	62,608	130,676
1998.....	932,957	461,169	437,689	961	22,519	137,395
1999.....	765,346	837,418	740,718	711	95,989	379,993
2000.....	460,916	886,026	812,579	836	72,611	399,670
2001.....	501,643	606,259	575,030	758	30,471	218,326
2002.....	700,649	572,646	550,835	1,053	20,758	139,779
2003.....	523,370	462,435	449,123	3,865	9,447	91,599
2004.....	662,796	537,151	520,771	4,668	11,712	103,339
2005.....	602,972	604,280	589,269	4,614	10,397	108,247
2006.....	730,642	702,589	684,484	6,259	11,846	120,722
2007.....	1,382,993	660,477	648,005	3,808	8,664	89,683
2008.....	525,786	1,046,539	1,032,281	4,342	9,916	121,283
2009.....	570,442	743,715	726,043	7,100	10,572	109,813
2010.....	710,544	619,913	604,410	9,122	6,381	56,990

Source: U.S. Department of Homeland Security, Office of Immigration Statistics, *2010 Yearbook of Immigration Statistics*. See also <http://www.dhs.gov/ximgtn/statistics/publications/yearbook.shtm>.

Table 48. Persons Obtaining Legal Permanent Resident Status by Class of Admission: 2000 to 2010

[For years ending September 30. For definition of immigrants, see text, this section]

Class of admission	2000	2005	2007	2008	2009	2010
Total	**841,002**	**1,122,257**	**1,052,415**	**1,107,126**	**1,130,818**	**1,042,625**
New arrivals	407,279	383,955	431,368	466,558	463,042	476,049
Adjustments	433,723	738,302	621,047	640,568	667,776	566,576
Family-sponsored preferences	235,092	212,970	194,900	227,761	211,859	214,589
Unmarried sons/daughters of U.S. citizens and their children	27,635	24,729	22,858	26,173	23,965	26,998
Spouses, unmarried sons/daughters of alien residents and their children	124,540	100,139	86,151	103,456	98,567	92,088
Married sons/daughters of U.S. citizens [1]	22,804	22,953	20,611	29,273	25,930	32,817
Brothers or sisters of U.S. citizens [1]	60,113	65,149	65,280	68,859	63,397	62,686
Employment-based preferences	106,642	246,865	161,733	164,741	140,903	148,343
Priority workers [1]	27,566	64,731	26,697	36,678	40,924	41,055
Professionals with advanced degrees or aliens of exceptional ability [1]	20,255	42,597	44,162	70,046	45,552	53,946
Skilled workers, professionals, unskilled workers [1]	49,589	129,070	85,030	48,903	40,398	39,762
Special immigrants [1]	9,014	10,121	5,038	7,754	10,341	11,100
Employment creation (investors) [1]	218	346	806	1,360	3,688	2,480
Immediate relatives of U.S. citizens	346,350	436,115	494,920	488,483	535,554	476,414
Spouses	196,405	259,144	274,358	265,671	317,129	271,909
Children [2]	82,638	94,858	103,828	101,342	98,270	88,297
Parents	67,307	82,113	116,734	121,470	120,155	116,208
Refugees	56,091	112,676	54,942	90,030	118,836	92,741
Asylees	6,837	30,286	81,183	76,362	58,532	43,550
Diversity [3]	50,920	46,234	42,127	41,761	47,879	49,763
Cancellation of removal	12,154	20,785	14,927	11,128	8,156	8,180
Parolees	3,162	7,715	1,999	1,172	2,385	1,592
Nicaraguan Adjustment and Central American Relief Act (NACARA)	20,364	1,155	340	296	296	248
Children born abroad to alien residents	(NA)	571	597	637	587	716
Haitian Refugee Immigration Fairness Act (HRIFA)	435	2,820	2,448	1,580	552	386
Other	2,955	4,065	2,299	3,175	5,279	6,103

NA Not Available. [1] Includes spouses and children. [2] Includes orphans. [3] Includes categories of immigrants admitted under three laws intended to diversify immigration: P.L. 99-603, P.L. 100-658, and P.L. 101-649.
Source: U.S. Department of Homeland Security, Office of Immigration Statistics, *2010 Yearbook of Immigration Statistics*. See also <http://www.dhs.gov/ximgtn/statistics/publications/yearbook.shtm>.

Table 49. Persons Obtaining Legal Permanent Resident Status by Selected Country of Birth and Selected Characteristics: 2010

[For year ending September 30]

Age, marital status, class of admission	All countries [1]	Mexico	China	India	Philip- pines	Dominican Republic	Cuba	Vietnam	Haiti
Total	**1,042,625**	**139,120**	**70,863**	**69,162**	**58,173**	**53,870**	**33,573**	**30,632**	**22,582**
Under 18 years old	206,519	24,369	11,610	8,327	11,978	18,808	6,119	6,248	6,396
18 to 24 years old	141,388	22,287	8,246	5,224	6,537	8,625	4,355	5,212	3,146
25 to 34 years old	253,188	33,225	14,045	23,574	10,774	8,496	6,162	5,205	4,393
35 to 44 years old	195,209	26,884	17,498	15,028	9,627	8,258	7,496	5,165	3,683
45 to 54 years old	118,070	14,424	9,931	6,559	7,345	5,067	4,587	5,288	2,194
55 to 64 years old	75,817	9,477	5,119	5,963	7,397	2,821	2,690	2,565	1,385
65 years old and over	52,425	8,454	4,414	4,487	4,514	1,795	2,164	947	1,385
Unknown	9	–	–	–	1	–	–	2	–
Single	390,470	43,248	21,909	14,215	22,684	34,569	14,890	11,663	13,874
Married	596,959	89,139	45,765	51,783	32,223	17,436	13,834	17,494	7,921
Other	51,174	6,184	3,045	2,990	3,164	1,790	4,688	1,440	681
Unknown	4,022	549	144	174	102	75	161	35	106
Family-sponsored preferences	214,589	34,114	13,610	14,636	17,849	31,089	455	18,027	8,492
Employment-based preferences	148,343	11,535	17,949	31,118	6,423	396	8	360	179
Immediate relatives of U.S. citizens	476,414	88,572	24,198	21,831	33,746	22,218	3,153	11,091	10,665
Diversity programs	49,763	10	23	58	14	16	125	–	4
Refugee and asylee adjustments	136,291	397	14,943	1,324	55	72	29,804	1,032	2,817
Other	17,225	4,492	140	195	86	79	28	122	425

– Represents zero. [1] Includes other countries not shown separately.
Source: U.S. Department of Homeland Security, Office of Immigration Statistics, <http://www.dhs.gov/files/statistics/data/dslpr.shtm>.

Table 50. Persons Obtaining Legal Permanent Resident Status by Country of Birth: 1981 to 2010

[In thousands (7,256.0 represents 7,256,000). For years ending Sept. 30. Persons by country prior to 1996 are unrevised]

Region and Country of birth	1981–1990, total	1991–2000, total	2001–2009, total	2010	Region and Country of birth	1981–1990, total	1991–2000, total	2001–2009, total	2010
All countries [1]	7,256.0	9,080.5	9,458.4	1,042.6					
Europe [1]	705.6	1,226.0	1,175.2	88.7	Syria	20.6	26.1	23.3	2.6
Albania	(NA)	26.2	45.8	4.7	Taiwan [5]	([6])	106.3	81.2	6.7
Belarus	(X)	[2] 28.9	23.7	2.0	Thailand	64.4	48.4	58.9	9.4
Bosnia and Herzegovina	(X)	[2] 38.8	88.1	0.9	Turkey	20.9	26.3	36.6	4.5
Bulgaria	(NA)	23.1	36.6	2.6	Uzbekistan	(X)	[2] 22.9	31.2	4.8
France	23.1	27.4	35.8	3.9	Vietnam	401.4	420.8	275.5	30.6
Germany	70.1	67.6	70.8	6.9	**Africa** [1]	192.3	382.5	759.1	101.4
Ireland	32.8	58.9	14.0	1.5	Egypt	31.4	46.7	64.1	9.0
Italy	32.9	22.5	23.9	2.6	Ethiopia	27.2	49.3	95.5	14.3
Poland	97.4	169.5	109.2	7.6	Ghana	14.9	35.6	58.1	7.2
Portugal	40.0	22.7	10.1	0.8	Nigeria	35.3	67.2	97.8	13.4
Romania	38.9	57.5	49.6	4.0	Somalia	(NA)	20.1	59.6	4.6
Russia	(X)	[2] 127.8	133.0	6.7	**Oceania**	(NA)	47.9	52.8	5.3
Serbia and Montenegro [3, 4]	19.2	25.8	44.0	2.2	**North America** [1]	3,125.0	3,910.1	3,268.5	336.6
Soviet Union [3]	84.0	103.8	32.5	5.0	Canada	119.2	137.2	154.9	13.3
Ukraine	(X)	[2] 141.0	140.8	8.5	Mexico	1,653.3	2,250.5	1,554.1	139.1
United Kingdom	142.1	135.6	140.7	12.8	Cuba	159.2	178.7	284.8	33.6
Asia [1]	2,817.4	2,973.2	3,362.5	422.1	Dominican Republic	251.8	340.8	275.3	53.9
Armenia	(X)	[2] 26.6	27.0	3.0	Haiti	140.2	181.7	191.2	22.6
Bangladesh	15.2	66.0	91.9	14.8	Jamaica	213.8	173.4	160.9	19.8
Cambodia	116.6	18.5	32.6	3.0	Trinidad and Tobago	39.5	63.2	56.3	5.4
China [5]	[6] 388.8	424.4	591.8	70.9	El Salvador	214.6	217.3	234.0	18.8
Hong Kong	63.0	74.0	38.4	2.4	Guatemala	87.9	103.0	150.2	10.5
India	261.9	383.0	593.3	69.2	Honduras	49.5	66.7	58.9	6.4
Iran	154.8	112.5	111.7	14.2	Nicaragua	44.1	94.6	57.3	3.6
Iraq	19.6	40.7	45.2	19.9	Panama	29.0	24.0	15.8	1.5
Israel	36.3	31.9	42.1	4.5	**South America** [1]	455.9	539.3	818.8	87.2
Japan	43.2	61.4	69.8	6.3	Argentina	25.7	24.3	46.1	4.4
Jordan [7]	32.6	39.7	34.8	3.9	Brazil	23.7	52.2	111.5	12.3
Korea [8]	338.8	171.1	199.3	22.2	Colombia	124.4	130.8	228.9	22.4
Laos	145.6	43.5	15.3	1.2	Ecuador	56.0	76.3	101.1	11.5
Lebanon	41.6	43.4	36.0	3.5	Guyana	95.4	73.8	69.5	6.7
Pakistan	61.3	124.5	138.7	18.3	Peru	64.4	105.6	131.4	14.2
Philippines	495.3	505.3	529.1	58.2	Venezuela	17.9	29.9	75.0	9.4

NA Not available. X Not applicable. [1] Includes countries not shown separately. [2] Covers years 1992–2000. [3] Prior to 1992, data include independent republics; beginning in 1992, data are for unknown republic only. [4] Yugoslavia (unknown republic) prior to February 7, 2003. [5] See footnote 4, Table 1332. [6] Data for Taiwan included with China. [7] Prior to 2003, includes Palestine; beginning in 2003, Palestine included in Unknown. [8] Prior to 2009, includes a small number of cases from North Korea.
Source: U.S. Department of Homeland Security, Office of Immigration Statistics, *2010 Yearbook of Immigration Statistics*. See also <http://www.dhs.gov/ximgtn/statistics/publications/yearbook.shtm>.

Table 51. Refugees and Asylees Obtaining Legal Permanent Resident Status by Country of Birth: 1991 to 2010

[For years ending September 30]

Country of birth	1991–2000, total	2001–2009, total	2010	Country of birth	1991–2000, total	2001–2009, total	2010
Total [1]	1,016,820	1,189,074	136,291	Iraq	22,488	24,934	15,855
Europe [1]	425,047	292,024	4,770	Laos	37,203	6,366	172
Albania	3,250	10,276	629	Pakistan	1,649	7,832	507
Armenia	1,794	11,754	654	Thailand	22,716	18,129	4,276
Azerbaijan	[2] 10,566	5,910	135	Vietnam	206,530	35,958	1,032
Belarus	[2] 21,592	9,019	291	**Africa** [1]	51,469	220,205	22,634
Bosnia and Herzegovina	[2] 37,251	82,258	227	Ethiopia [6]	17,829	29,236	2,664
Croatia	1,786	9,479	19	Kenya	1,438	13,935	1,416
Moldova	[2] 10,150	10,302	511	Liberia	3,836	26,150	2,658
Poland	7,451	391	21	Sierra Leone	272	9,885	484
Romania	15,682	1,349	74	Somalia	16,737	55,354	3,715
Russia	[2] 54,488	32,006	813	Sudan	5,174	22,531	1,049
Serbia and Montenegro [3, 4]	6,242	24,973	449	**Oceania**	291	1,401	52
Soviet Union [3]	117,783	6,455	339	**North America** [1]	183,251	292,189	34,657
Ukraine	[2] 96,974	56,336	850	Cuba	142,571	246,527	29,804
Uzbekistan	[2] 17,991	13,629	418	Guatemala	2,029	6,755	644
Asia [1]	350,702	320,882	68,587	Haiti	9,354	27,007	2,817
Afghanistan	9,711	13,014	519	Nicaragua	22,468	1,939	121
Burma	721	21,459	11,445	**South America** [1]	5,840	60,550	5,362
Cambodia	6,358	1,635	113	Colombia	1,129	37,805	2,516
China [5]	7,577	96,689	14,943	Peru	2,500	6,735	523
India	2,538	22,686	1,324	Venezuela	1,390	9,412	1,314
Iran	24,251	40,780	4,735				

[1] Includes other countries and unknown not shown separately. [2] Covers years 1992–2000. [3] Prior to 1992, data include independent republics; beginning in 1992, data are for unknown republic only. [4] Yugoslavia (unknown republic) prior to February 7, 2003. [5] See footnote 4, Table 1332. [6] Prior to 1993, data include Eritrea.
Source: U.S. Department of Homeland Security, Office of Immigration Statistics, *2010 Yearbook of Immigration Statistics*. See also <http://www.dhs.gov/ximgtn/statistics/publications/yearbook.shtm\>.

Table 52. Population by Selected Ancestry Group and Region: 2009

[In thousands (307,007 represents 307,007,000), except percent. Covers single and multiple ancestries. Ancestry refers to a person's ethnic origin or descent, "roots," or heritage; or the place of birth of the person, the person's parents, or ancestors before their arrival in the United States. The American Community Survey universe includes the household population and the population living in institutions, college dormitories, and other group quarters. Based on a sample and subject to sampling variability; see text, this section, and Appendix III. For composition of regions of the United States, see map, inside front cover]

Ancestry group	Total, (1,000)	North-east	Mid-west	South	West
Total population [1]	307,007	18	22	37	23
Afghan	87	20	6	26	47
Albanian	182	55	28	11	7
American	18,699	11	20	56	12
Arab [1]	1,680	25	24	27	23
Egyptian	197	36	12	25	27
Iraqi	101	9	44	18	29
Jordanian	68	16	21	31	32
Lebanese	504	25	26	29	20
Moroccan	78	40	14	31	15
Palestinian	104	17	31	29	23
Syrian	159	38	19	25	18
Arab	286	21	28	28	23
Armenian	485	20	8	10	62
Assyrian/Chaldean/Syriac	96	3	58	4	35
Australian	93	19	16	28	37
Austrian	765	30	23	24	23
Basque	58	4	4	11	80
Belgian	398	12	54	17	17
Brazilian	373	44	4	39	13
British	1,172	16	17	38	29
Bulgarian	84	17	28	24	31
Cajun	104	4	5	81	10
Canadian	715	27	17	27	29
Croatian	434	23	40	15	23
Czech	1,615	12	45	27	17
Czechoslovakian	332	24	32	24	20
Danish	1,487	8	31	15	46
Dutch	5,024	16	35	27	23
Eastern European	457	45	14	22	19
English	27,658	17	21	37	25
European	3,197	13	19	34	34
Finnish	695	12	47	13	27
French (except Basque)	9,412	25	23	33	20
French Canadian	2,151	42	20	23	15
German	50,708	16	39	26	19
Greek	1,390	34	23	24	19
Guyanese	202	72	4	21	3
Hungarian	1,547	32	32	20	17
Iranian	470	12	6	25	57
Irish	36,915	25	24	32	18
Israeli	139	43	9	23	25
Italian	18,085	44	17	22	17
Latvian	96	27	23	21	29
Lithuanian	727	38	28	19	15
Northern European	222	12	20	23	45
Norwegian	4,643	6	49	12	33
Pennsylvania German	344	55	27	11	7
Polish	10,091	33	37	18	12
Portuguese	1,477	47	4	12	37
Romanian	519	24	28	22	27
Russian	3,163	36	17	21	25
Scandinavian	581	7	31	19	43
Scotch-Irish	3,570	12	17	51	20
Scottish	5,847	17	20	37	27
Serbian	177	20	42	17	21
Slavic	132	27	25	26	22
Slovak	801	43	34	15	8
Slovene	180	15	59	12	14
Sub-Saharan African [1]	2,855	21	18	45	16
Cape Verdean	91	83	1	11	4
Ethiopian	186	10	14	47	29
Ghanian	85	53	12	29	6
Nigerian	253	26	15	47	12
Somalian	103	11	49	12	28
African	1,793	15	19	50	16
Swedish	4,348	13	39	16	32
Swiss	1,018	15	33	21	31
Turkish	187	36	12	31	20
Ukrainian	976	39	21	18	22
Welsh	1,987	20	23	30	27
West Indian [1,2]	2,540	48	3	44	5
British West Indian	97	70	2	23	5
Haitian	830	42	2	54	2
Jamaican	951	49	4	43	5
Trinidadian and Tobagonian	185	64	2	31	3
West Indian	259	61	3	31	6
Yugoslavian	325	19	29	22	29

[1] Includes other groups, not shown separately. [2] Excludes Hispanic-origin groups.
Source: U.S. Census Bureau, 2009 American Community Survey, B04006, "People Reporting Ancestry," <http://factfinder.census.gov/>, January 2011.

Table 53. Language Spoken at Home: 2009

[The American Community Survey universe includes the household population and the population living in institutions, college dormitories, and other group quarters. Based on a sample and subject to sampling variability; see text, this section, and Appendix III]

Language	Number	Language	Number
Total population 5 years old and over	285,797,349		
Speak only English	228,699,523	Other Indic languages	668,596
Spanish or Spanish Creole	35,468,501	Other Indo-European languages	455,483
French (including Patois, Cajun)	1,305,503	Chinese	2,600,150
French Creole	659,053	Japanese	445,471
Italian	753,992	Korean	1,039,021
Portuguese or Portuguese Creole	731,282	Mon-Khmer, Cambodian	202,033
German	1,109,216	Hmong	193,179
Yiddish	148,155	Thai	152,679
Other West Germanic languages	271,227	Laotian	146,297
Scandinavian languages	126,337	Vietnamese	1,251,468
Greek	325,747	Other Asian languages	783,140
Russian	881,723	Tagalog	1,513,734
Polish	593,598	Other Pacific Island languages	371,653
Serbo-Croatian	269,333	Navajo	169,009
Other Slavic languages	298,094	Other Native North American languages	196,372
Armenian	242,836	Hungarian	90,612
Persian	396,769	Arabic	845,396
Gujarathi	341,404	Hebrew	221,593
Hindi	560,983	African languages	777,553
Urdu	355,964	Other and unspecified languages	134,670

Source: U.S. Census Bureau, 2009 American Community Survey, B16001, "Language Spoken at Home by Ability to Speak English for the Population 5 Years and Over," <http://factfinder.census.gov/>, accessed January 2011.

Table 54. Language Spoken at Home by State: 2009

[In thousands (285,797 represents 285,797,000), except percent. The American Community Survey universe includes the household population and the population living in institutions, college dormitories, and other group quarters. Based on a sample and subject to sampling variability; see text, this section, and Appendix III]

State	Population 5 years and over (1,000)	English only (1,000)	Language other than English Number (1,000)	Language other than English Percent of population 5 years and over	State	Population 5 years and over (1,000)	English only (1,000)	Language other than English Number (1,000)	Language other than English Percent of population 5 years and over
U.S.	285,797	228,700	57,098	20.0	MO.	5,583	5,260	324	5.8
AL	4,395	4,191	204	4.6	MT.	914	870	44	4.8
AK	644	538	106	16.4	NE.	1,663	1,503	159	9.6
AZ	6,079	4,396	1,684	27.7	NV.	2,441	1,746	695	28.5
AR	2,687	2,505	183	6.8	NH.	1,250	1,150	100	8.0
CA	34,212	19,462	14,751	43.1	NJ.	8,153	5,832	2,321	28.5
CO	4,660	3,883	777	16.7	NM.	1,860	1,194	666	35.8
CT	3,309	2,633	676	20.4	NY.	18,323	13,011	5,312	29.0
DE	826	731	94	11.4	NC.	8,727	7,848	879	10.1
DC	562	491	71	12.6	ND.	604	574	30	5.0
FL	17,375	12,802	4,573	26.3	OH.	10,805	10,124	681	6.3
GA	9,085	7,950	1,135	12.5	OK.	3,415	3,121	294	8.6
HI.	1,207	907	300	24.9	OR.	3,581	3,058	523	14.6
ID.	1,422	1,281	141	9.9	PA.	11,861	10,718	1,143	9.6
IL	12,018	9,416	2,602	21.7	RI.	993	783	210	21.1
IN.	5,979	5,527	452	7.6	SC.	4,250	3,981	269	6.3
IA.	2,809	2,626	184	6.5	SD.	753	705	48	6.3
KS	2,614	2,351	263	10.1	TN.	5,874	5,521	352	6.0
KY	4,024	3,843	180	4.5	TX.	22,716	14,950	7,766	34.2
LA	4,174	3,832	342	8.2	UT.	2,514	2,166	347	13.8
ME.	1,247	1,156	91	7.3	VT.	589	563	26	4.4
MD.	5,320	4,503	817	15.3	VA.	7,357	6,366	991	13.5
MA.	6,209	4,927	1,282	20.6	WA.	6,214	5,159	1,054	17.0
MI.	9,354	8,492	862	9.2	WV.	1,713	1,674	39	2.3
MN.	4,904	4,422	483	9.8	WI.	5,294	4,856	439	8.3
MS.	2,732	2,630	102	3.7	WY.	505	471	34	6.8

Source: U.S. Census Bureau, 2009 American Community Survey, C16005, "Nativity by Language Spoken at Home by Ability to Speak English for the Population 5 Years and Over," <http://factfinder.census.gov/>, accessed January 2011.

Table 55. Language Spoken at Home—25 Largest Cities: 2009

[731 represents 731,000. The American Community Survey universe includes the household population and the population living in institutions, college dormitories, and other group quarters. Based on a sample and subject to sampling variability; see text, this section, and Appendix III]

City	Population 5 years and over (1,000)	English only (1,000)	Language other than English, total [1] Number (1,000)	Language other than English, total [1] Percent of population 5 years and over	Language other than English, total [1] Speak English less than "very well" (1,000)	Spanish (1,000)	Other Indo-European languages (1,000)	Asian and Pacific Island languages (1,000)
Austin, TX	731	489	242	33.1	119	191	22	24
Baltimore, MD	592	543	50	8.4	21	18	14	7
Boston, MA	609	405	205	33.6	102	90	69	35
Charlotte, NC.	646	535	112	17.3	53	64	22	17
Chicago, IL.	2,639	1,734	905	34.3	415	614	164	93
Columbus, OH.	712	615	97	13.6	44	33	22	20
Dallas, TX	1,175	673	502	42.7	268	452	16	24
Denver, CO	559	416	143	25.6	69	111	16	12
Detroit, MI	842	747	95	11.3	39	51	19	3
El Paso, TX	561	154	407	72.5	159	394	6	6
Fort Worth, TX	659	442	217	32.9	111	188	11	13
Houston, TX.	2,058	1,135	922	44.8	491	747	66	87
Indianapolis, IN [2]	742	660	82	11.1	42	52	15	8
Jacksonville, FL	751	661	90	12.0	34	39	25	21
Los Angeles, CA	3,546	1,399	2,146	60.5	1,072	1,555	236	301
Memphis, TN.	621	574	47	7.6	21	28	6	8
Nashville-Davidson, TN [2]	560	478	82	14.6	41	40	14	13
New York, NY.	7,811	4,098	3,712	47.5	1,809	1,870	1,037	618
Philadelphia, PA.	1,437	1,137	300	20.9	130	136	82	59
Phoenix, AZ.	1,444	891	553	38.3	253	474	36	26
San Antonio, TX.	1,261	691	569	45.2	166	524	19	19
San Diego, CA.	1,216	763	454	37.3	198	263	49	129
San Francisco, CA.	774	432	342	44.2	175	92	50	196
San Jose, CA.	889	400	489	55.0	225	210	61	211
Seattle, WA	582	461	121	20.8	55	26	24	59

[1] Includes other language groups, not shown separately. [2] Represents the portion of a consolidated city that is not within one or more separately incorporated places.

Source: U.S. Census Bureau, 2009 American Community Survey, C16005, "Nativity by Language Spoken at Home by Ability to Speak English for the Population 5 Years and Over," <http://factfinder.census.gov/>, accessed January 2011.

Table 56. Marital Status of the Population by Sex, Race, and Hispanic Origin: 1990 to 2010

[In millions, except percent (181.8 represents 181,800,000). As of March. Persons 18 years old and over. Excludes members of Armed Forces except those living off post or with their families on post. Beginning 2005, population controls based on Census 2000 and an expanded sample of households. Based on Current Population Survey, see text, this section and Appendix III]

Marital status, race and Hispanic origin	Total				Male				Female			
	1990	2000	2005	2010	1990	2000	2005	2010	1990	2000	2005	2010
Total [1]	**181.8**	**201.8**	**217.2**	**229.1**	**86.9**	**96.9**	**104.8**	**111.1**	**95.0**	**104.9**	**112.3**	**118.0**
Never married	40.4	48.2	53.9	61.5	22.4	26.1	29.6	33.7	17.9	22.1	24.3	27.8
Married [2]	112.6	120.1	127.4	129.5	55.8	59.6	63.3	64.4	56.7	60.4	64.0	65.1
Widowed	13.8	13.7	13.8	14.3	2.3	2.6	2.7	3.0	11.5	11.1	11.1	11.4
Divorced	15.1	19.8	22.1	23.7	6.3	8.5	9.2	10.0	8.8	11.3	12.9	13.7
Percent of total	100.0	100.0	100.0	100.0	100.0	100.0	100.0	100.0	100.0	100.0	100.0	100.0
Never married	22.2	23.9	24.8	26.9	25.8	27.0	28.2	30.4	18.9	21.1	21.6	23.6
Married [2]	61.9	59.5	58.6	56.4	64.3	61.5	60.4	57.9	59.7	57.6	56.9	55.1
Widowed	7.6	6.8	6.4	6.3	2.7	2.7	2.6	2.7	12.1	10.5	9.9	9.6
Divorced	8.3	9.8	10.2	10.4	7.2	8.8	8.8	9.0	9.3	10.8	11.5	11.7
White, total [3]	**155.5**	**168.1**	**177.5**	**185.7**	**74.8**	**81.6**	**86.6**	**91.2**	**80.6**	**86.6**	**90.9**	**94.5**
Never married	31.6	36.0	39.7	45.1	18.0	20.3	22.6	25.7	13.6	15.7	17.0	19.4
Married [2]	99.5	104.1	108.3	109.4	49.5	51.8	54.0	54.7	49.9	52.2	54.2	54.7
Widowed	11.7	11.5	11.5	11.8	1.9	2.2	2.3	2.5	9.8	9.3	9.2	9.3
Divorced	12.6	16.5	18.1	19.4	5.4	7.2	7.6	8.3	7.3	9.3	10.4	11.1
Percent of total	100.0	100.0	100.0	100.0	100.0	100.0	100.0	100.0	100.0	100.0	100.0	100.0
Never married	20.3	21.4	22.3	24.3	24.1	24.9	26.1	28.2	16.9	18.1	18.7	20.6
Married [2]	64.0	62.0	61.0	58.9	66.2	63.5	62.4	60.0	61.9	60.3	59.7	57.9
Widowed	7.5	6.8	6.5	6.3	2.6	2.7	2.6	2.7	12.2	10.8	10.2	9.8
Divorced	8.1	9.8	10.2	10.4	7.2	8.8	8.8	9.1	9.0	10.7	11.5	11.7
Black, total [3]	**20.3**	**24.0**	**25.2**	**27.3**	**9.1**	**10.7**	**11.2**	**12.3**	**11.2**	**13.3**	**13.9**	**15.0**
Never married	7.1	9.5	10.2	11.7	3.5	4.3	4.7	5.5	3.6	5.1	5.5	6.2
Married [2]	9.3	10.1	10.3	10.6	4.5	5.0	5.0	5.2	4.8	5.1	5.2	5.3
Widowed	1.7	1.7	1.7	1.8	0.3	0.3	0.3	0.4	1.4	1.4	1.4	1.5
Divorced	2.1	2.8	2.9	3.2	0.8	1.1	1.1	1.2	1.3	1.7	1.8	2.0
Percent of total	100.0	100.0	100.0	100.0	100.0	100.0	100.0	100.0	100.0	100.0	100.0	100.0
Never married	35.1	39.4	40.6	42.8	38.4	40.2	42.0	44.5	32.5	38.3	39.5	41.4
Married [2]	45.8	42.1	41.0	38.8	49.2	46.7	45.5	42.7	43.0	38.3	37.4	35.6
Widowed	8.5	7.0	6.6	6.7	3.7	2.8	2.7	2.9	12.4	10.5	10.0	9.8
Divorced	10.6	11.5	11.7	11.7	8.8	10.3	9.8	9.9	12.0	12.8	13.3	13.2
Asian, total [3]	**(NA)**	**(NA)**	**9.4**	**10.7**	**(NA)**	**(NA)**	**4.5**	**5.1**	**(NA)**	**(NA)**	**4.9**	**5.6**
Never married	(NA)	(NA)	2.3	2.7	(NA)	(NA)	1.3	1.5	(NA)	(NA)	1.0	1.2
Married [2]	(NA)	(NA)	6.2	7.0	(NA)	(NA)	2.9	3.3	(NA)	(NA)	3.3	3.7
Widowed	(NA)	(NA)	0.4	0.5	(NA)	(NA)	0.1	0.1	(NA)	(NA)	0.3	0.5
Divorced	(NA)	(NA)	0.5	0.5	(NA)	(NA)	0.2	0.2	(NA)	(NA)	0.3	0.3
Percent of total	100.0	100.0	100.0	100.0	100.0	100.0	100.0	100.0	100.0	100.0	100.0	100.0
Never married	(NA)	(NA)	24.8	25.1	(NA)	(NA)	29.7	29.8	(NA)	(NA)	20.3	20.8
Married [2]	(NA)	(NA)	65.6	65.5	(NA)	(NA)	64.7	65.5	(NA)	(NA)	66.5	65.7
Widowed	(NA)	(NA)	4.3	4.9	(NA)	(NA)	1.3	1.3	(NA)	(NA)	6.7	8.1
Divorced	(NA)	(NA)	5.3	4.5	(NA)	(NA)	4.1	3.4	(NA)	(NA)	6.4	5.4
Hispanic, total [4]	**13.6**	**21.1**	**27.5**	**31.8**	**6.7**	**10.4**	**14.1**	**16.4**	**6.8**	**10.7**	**13.4**	**15.4**
Never married	3.7	5.9	8.6	10.9	2.2	3.4	5.2	6.5	1.5	2.5	3.4	4.4
Married [2]	8.4	12.7	15.6	17.1	4.1	6.2	7.8	8.6	4.3	6.5	7.8	8.5
Widowed	0.5	0.9	1.0	1.2	0.1	0.2	0.2	0.3	0.4	0.7	0.8	0.9
Divorced	1.0	1.6	2.2	2.6	0.4	0.7	0.9	1.1	0.6	1.0	1.3	1.5
Percent of total	100.0	100.0	100.0	100.0	100.0	100.0	100.0	100.0	100.0	100.0	100.0	100.0
Never married	27.2	28.0	31.3	34.2	32.1	32.3	36.7	39.3	22.5	23.4	25.6	28.7
Married [2]	61.7	60.2	57.0	53.8	60.9	59.7	55.6	52.2	62.4	60.7	58.7	55.6
Widowed	4.0	4.2	3.7	3.8	1.5	1.6	1.5	1.8	6.5	6.5	6.1	5.8
Divorced	7.0	7.6	7.9	8.2	5.5	6.4	6.3	6.7	8.5	9.3	9.7	9.9
Non-Hispanic White, total [3]	**(NA)**	**(NA)**	**151.9**	**156.2**	**(NA)**	**(NA)**	**73.4**	**75.9**	**(NA)**	**(NA)**	**78.5**	**80.3**
Never married	(NA)	(NA)	31.8	35.2	(NA)	(NA)	17.8	19.8	(NA)	(NA)	13.9	15.5
Married [2]	(NA)	(NA)	93.5	93.3	(NA)	(NA)	46.6	46.6	(NA)	(NA)	47.0	46.7
Widowed	(NA)	(NA)	10.6	10.6	(NA)	(NA)	2.1	2.2	(NA)	(NA)	8.5	8.4
Divorced	(NA)	(NA)	16.0	17.0	(NA)	(NA)	6.8	7.3	(NA)	(NA)	9.2	9.7
Percent of total	100.0	100.0	100.0	100.0	100.0	100.0	100.0	100.0	100.0	100.0	100.0	100.0
Never married	(NA)	(NA)	20.9	22.6	(NA)	(NA)	24.3	26.0	(NA)	(NA)	17.7	19.3
Married [2]	(NA)	(NA)	61.5	59.7	(NA)	(NA)	63.5	61.4	(NA)	(NA)	59.7	58.1
Widowed	(NA)	(NA)	6.9	6.8	(NA)	(NA)	2.8	2.9	(NA)	(NA)	10.8	10.5
Divorced	(NA)	(NA)	10.6	10.9	(NA)	(NA)	9.3	9.7	(NA)	(NA)	11.7	12.1

NA Not available. [1] Includes persons of other races not shown separately. [2] Includes persons who are married with spouse present, married with spouse absent, and separated. [3] Beginning 2005, data represent persons who selected this race group only and exclude persons reporting more than one race. The CPS in 1990 and 2000 only allowed respondents to report one race group. See also comments on race in the text for this section. [4] Hispanic persons may be any race.

Source: U.S. Census Bureau, *America's Families and Living Arrangements*, Current Population Reports, P20-537, 2001 and earlier reports. See also <http://www.census.gov/population/www/socdemo/hh-fam.html>.

Table 57. Marital Status of the Population by Sex and Age: 2010

[As of March (111,120 represents 111,120,000). Excludes members of Armed Forces except those living off post or with their families on post. Population controls based on Census 2000 and an expanded sample of households. Based on Current Population Survey, see text, this section, and Appendix III]

Sex and age	Number of persons (1,000)					Percent distribution				
	Total	Never married	Married [1]	Widowed	Divorced	Total	Never married	Married [1]	Widowed	Divorced
Male	**111,120**	**33,748**	**64,437**	**2,968**	**9,966**	**100.0**	**30.4**	**58.0**	**2.7**	**9.0**
18 to 19 years old	4,147	4,040	90	3	14	100.0	97.4	2.2	0.1	0.3
20 to 24 years old	10,677	9,469	1,155	3	49	100.0	88.7	10.8	–	0.5
25 to 29 years old	10,926	6,800	3,787	21	318	100.0	62.2	34.7	0.2	2.9
30 to 34 years old	9,759	3,561	5,577	28	593	100.0	36.5	57.1	0.3	6.1
35 to 39 years old	9,897	2,324	6,665	29	879	100.0	23.5	67.3	0.3	8.9
40 to 44 years old	10,169	2,078	6,919	52	1,119	100.0	20.4	68.0	0.5	11.0
45 to 54 years old	21,779	3,246	15,186	284	3,063	100.0	14.9	69.7	1.3	14.1
55 to 64 years old	16,980	1,545	12,545	424	2,465	100.0	9.1	73.9	2.5	14.5
65 to 74 years old	9,731	441	7,592	627	1,071	100.0	4.5	78.0	6.4	11.0
75 years old and over	7,056	244	4,922	1,497	393	100.0	3.5	69.8	21.2	5.6
Female	**118,000**	**27,792**	**65,096**	**11,364**	**13,748**	**100.0**	**23.6**	**55.2**	**9.6**	**11.7**
18 to 19 years old	4,004	3,816	162	9	18	100.0	95.3	4.0	0.2	0.4
20 to 24 years old	10,465	8,296	2,009	14	146	100.0	79.3	19.2	0.1	1.4
25 to 29 years old	10,519	5,026	5,007	39	448	100.0	47.8	47.6	0.4	4.3
30 to 34 years old	9,864	2,678	6,289	44	854	100.0	27.1	63.8	0.4	8.7
35 to 39 years old	9,982	1,768	6,923	94	1,197	100.0	17.7	69.4	0.9	12.0
40 to 44 years old	10,387	1,430	7,286	170	1,501	100.0	13.8	70.1	1.6	14.5
45 to 54 years old	22,594	2,479	15,432	794	3,889	100.0	11.0	68.3	3.5	17.2
55 to 64 years old	18,401	1,315	12,303	1,499	3,284	100.0	7.1	66.9	8.1	17.8
65 to 74 years old	11,208	576	6,270	2,686	1,676	100.0	5.1	55.9	24.0	15.0
75 years old and over	10,576	408	3,418	6,013	736	100.0	3.9	32.3	56.9	7.0

– Represents or rounds to zero. [1] Includes persons who are married with spouse present, married with spouse absent, and separated.

Source: U.S. Census Bureau, "America's Families and Living Arrangements: 2010, Table 1A. Marital Status of People 15 Years and Over, by Age, Sex, Personal Earnings, Race, and Hispanic Origin: 2010," <http://www.census.gov/population/www/socdemo/hh–fam/cps2010.html>.

Table 58. Living Arrangements of Persons 15 Years Old and Over by Race and Age: 2010

[In thousands (242,047 represents 242,047,000). As of March. See headnote, Table 57]

Living arrangement	Total	15 to 19 years old	20 to 24 years old	25 to 34 years old	35 to 44 years old	45 to 54 years old	55 to 64 years old	65 to 74 years old	75 years old and over
Total [1]	**242,047**	**21,079**	**21,142**	**41,068**	**40,435**	**44,373**	**35,381**	**20,938**	**17,631**
Alone	31,399	95	1,272	3,917	3,453	5,480	5,865	4,709	6,608
With spouse	120,768	178	2,655	18,689	25,729	28,619	23,621	13,340	7,937
With other persons	89,880	20,806	17,215	18,462	11,253	10,274	5,895	2,889	3,086
White [2]	**195,468**	**16,085**	**16,388**	**31,936**	**31,972**	**36,134**	**29,583**	**17,965**	**15,407**
Alone	25,202	71	969	2,895	2,544	4,201	4,739	3,924	5,858
With spouse	103,102	156	2,332	15,455	21,300	24,339	20,465	11,894	7,160
With other persons	67,164	15,858	13,087	13,586	8,128	7,594	4,379	2,147	2,389
Black [2]	**29,350**	**3,314**	**3,082**	**5,515**	**5,086**	**5,333**	**3,703**	**1,908**	**1,411**
Alone	4,705	18	237	689	670	1,015	913	606	557
With spouse	8,834	9	165	1,462	2,092	2,244	1,674	799	388
With other persons	15,811	3,287	2,680	3,364	2,324	2,074	1,116	503	466
Asian [2]	**11,201**	**821**	**918**	**2,353**	**2,364**	**1,948**	**1,447**	**743**	**607**
Alone	850	2	37	214	151	115	98	104	128
With spouse	6,573	1	94	1,302	1,777	1,489	1,114	484	309
With other persons	3,778	818	787	837	436	344	235	155	170
Hispanic origin [3]	**34,272**	**4,041**	**3,866**	**8,085**	**7,068**	**5,292**	**3,109**	**1,687**	**1,124**
Alone	2,054	10	133	354	279	368	349	318	242
With spouse	14,622	61	660	3,449	4,094	3,179	1,811	907	461
With other persons	17,596	3,970	3,073	4,282	2,695	1,745	949	462	421
Non-Hispanic White [2]	**163,727**	**12,429**	**12,892**	**24,486**	**25,324**	**31,263**	**26,637**	**16,344**	**14,353**
Alone	23,299	62	852	2,575	2,287	3,870	4,408	3,616	5,631
With spouse	89,315	97	1,720	12,240	17,399	21,385	18,740	11,012	6,722
With other persons	51,113	12,270	10,320	9,671	5,638	6,008	3,489	1,716	2,000

[1] Includes other races and non-Hispanic groups, not shown separately. [2] See footnote 3, Table 56. [3] Persons of Hispanic origin may be any race.

Source: U.S. Census Bureau, "America's Families and Living Arrangements: 2010, Table A2. Family Status and Household Relationship of People 15 Years and Over, by Marital Status, Age, Sex, Race, and Hispanic Origin: 2010" and unpublished data. See also <http://www.census.gov/population/www/socdemo/hh-fam/cps2010.html>.

Population 53

Table 59. Households, Families, Subfamilies, and Married Couples: 1980 to 2010

[In thousands, except as indicated (80,776 represents 80,776,000). As of March. Excludes members of Armed Forces except those living off post or with their families on post. Beginning 2005, population controls based on Census 2000 and an expanded sample of households. Based on Current Population Survey, see text, this section and Appendix III. Minus sign (–) indicates decrease]

Type of unit	1980	1990	2000	2005	2008	2009	2010	Percent change 1980 to 1990	Percent change 1990 to 2000	Percent change 2000 to 2010
Households	80,776	93,347	104,705	113,343	116,783	117,181	117,538	16	12	12
Persons per household	2.76	2.63	2.62	2.57	2.56	2.57	2.59	(X)	(X)	(X)
White [1]	70,766	80,163	87,671	92,880	95,112	95,297	95,489	13	9	9
Black [1]	8,586	10,486	12,849	13,809	14,551	14,595	14,730	22	23	15
Hispanic [2]	3,684	5,933	9,319	12,178	13,339	13,425	13,298	61	57	43
Family households	59,550	66,090	72,025	76,858	77,873	78,850	78,833	11	9	9
Married couple	49,112	52,317	55,311	57,975	58,370	59,118	58,410	7	6	6
Male householder [3]	1,733	2,884	4,028	4,901	5,100	5,252	5,580	66	40	39
Female householder [3]	8,705	10,890	12,687	13,981	14,404	14,480	14,843	25	17	17
Nonfamily households	21,226	27,257	32,680	36,485	38,910	38,331	38,705	28	20	18
Male householder	8,807	11,606	14,641	16,543	17,872	17,694	18,263	32	26	25
Female householder	12,419	15,651	18,039	19,942	21,038	20,637	20,442	26	15	13
One person	18,296	22,999	26,724	30,137	32,167	31,657	31,399	26	16	17
Families	59,550	66,090	72,025	76,858	77,873	78,850	78,833	11	9	9
Persons per family	3.29	3.17	3.17	3.13	3.15	3.15	3.16	(X)	(X)	(X)
With own children [4]	31,022	32,289	34,605	36,211	35,709	35,635	35,218	4	7	2
Without own children [4]	28,528	33,801	37,420	40,647	42,164	43,215	43,615	18	11	17
Married couple	49,112	52,317	55,311	57,975	58,370	59,118	58,410	7	6	6
With own children [4]	24,961	24,537	25,248	25,919	25,173	25,129	24,575	–2	3	–3
Without own children [4]	24,151	27,780	30,062	32,056	33,197	33,989	33,835	15	8	13
Male householder [3]	1,733	2,884	4,028	4,901	5,100	5,252	5,580	66	40	39
With own children [4]	616	1,153	1,786	2,021	2,162	2,111	2,224	87	55	25
Without own children [4]	1,117	1,731	2,242	2,880	2,937	3,141	3,356	55	30	50
Female householder [3]	8,705	10,890	12,687	13,981	14,404	14,480	14,843	25	17	17
With own children [4]	5,445	6,599	7,571	8,270	8,374	8,394	8,419	21	15	11
Without own children [4]	3,261	4,290	5,116	5,711	6,030	6,086	6,424	32	19	26
Unrelated subfamilies	360	534	571	515	526	397	484	48	7	–15
Married couple	20	68	37	62	95	46	93	(B)	(B)	(B)
Male reference persons [3]	36	45	57	61	63	41	44	(B)	(B)	(B)
Female reference persons [3]	304	421	477	392	368	311	347	38	13	–27
Related subfamilies	1,150	2,403	2,984	3,427	3,855	3,971	4,300	109	24	44
Married couple	582	871	1,149	1,336	1,664	1,681	1,881	50	32	64
Father-child [3]	54	153	201	387	335	306	313	(B)	31	56
Mother-child [3]	512	1,378	1,634	1,704	1,855	1,985	2,106	169	19	29
Married couples	49,714	53,256	56,497	59,373	60,129	60,844	60,384	7	6	7
With own household	49,112	52,317	55,311	57,975	58,370	59,118	58,410	7	6	6
Without own household	602	939	1,186	1,398	1,759	1,726	1,974	56	26	66
Percent without	1.2	1.8	2.1	2.4	2.9	2.8	3.2	(X)	(X)	(X)

B Base less than 75,000. X Not applicable. [1] Beginning with the 2003 Current Population Survey (CPS), respondents could choose more than one race. Beginning 2005, data shown represent persons who selected this race group only and exclude persons reporting more than one race. The CPS prior to 2003 only allowed respondents to report one race group. See also comments on race in the text for this section. [2] Persons of Hispanic origin may be any race. [3] No spouse present. [4] Under 18 years old.

Source: U.S. Census Bureau, "Families and Living Arrangements," <http://www.census.gov/population/www/socdemo/hh-fam.html>.

Table 60. Interracially Married Couples by Race and Hispanic Origin of Spouses: 1980 to 2010

[In thousands (49,714 represents 49,714,000). As of March. Persons 15 years old and over. Persons of Hispanic origin may be of any race. Based on Current Population Survey; see headnote, Table 59 and Appendix III]

Race and origin of spouses	1980	1990	2000	2008	2009	2010
Married couples, total [1]	**49,714**	**53,256**	**56,497**	**60,129**	**60,844**	**60,384**
Interracial married couples, total	651	964	1,464	2,340	2,437	2,413
White [2]/Black [2]	167	211	363	481	550	558
Black husband/White wife	122	150	268	317	354	390
White husband/Black wife	45	61	95	164	196	168
White [2]/other race [3]	450	720	1,051	1,737	1759	1,723
Black [2]/other race [3]	34	33	50	122	128	132
HISPANIC ORIGIN						
Hispanic/Hispanic	1,906	3,085	4,739	6,390	6,317	6,166
Hispanic/other origin (not Hispanic)	891	1,193	1,743	2,222	2,421	2,289
All other couples (not of Hispanic origin)	46,917	48,979	50,015	51,517	52,107	51,928

[1] Includes other married couples not shown separately. [2] See footnote 1, Table 59. [3] "Other race," is any race other than White or Black, such as American Indian, Japanese, Chinese, etc. This total excludes combinations of other races by other races.

Source: U.S. Census Bureau, "Families and Living Arrangements, Table MS-3. Interracial Married Couples: 1980 to 2002," and unpublished data, <http://www.census.gov/population/www/socdemo/hh-fam.html>.

Table 61. Households and Persons Per Household by Type of Household: 1990 to 2010

[As of March (93,347 represents 93,347,000). See headnote, Table 59]

Type of household	Households						Persons per household		
	Number (1,000)			Percent distribution					
	1990	2000	2010	1990	2000	2010	1990	2000	2010
Total households	**93,347**	**104,705**	**117,538**	**100**	**100**	**100**	**2.63**	**2.62**	**2.59**
Family households.	66,090	72,025	78,833	71	69	67	3.22	3.24	3.24
Married couple family	52,317	55,311	58,410	56	53	50	3.25	3.26	3.24
Male householder, no spouse present.	2,884	4,028	5,580	3	4	5	3.04	3.16	3.24
Female householder, no spouse present	10,890	12,687	14,843	12	12	13	3.10	3.17	3.23
Nonfamily households.	27,257	32,680	38,705	29	31	33	1.22	1.25	1.26
Living alone	22,999	26,724	31,399	25	26	27	1.00	1.00	1.00
Male householder	11,606	14,641	18,263	12	14	16	1.33	1.34	1.35
Living alone	9,049	11,181	13,971	10	11	12	1.00	1.00	1.00
Female householder	15,651	18,039	20,442	17	17	17	1.14	1.17	1.18
Living alone	13,950	15,543	17,428	15	15	15	1.00	1.00	1.00

Source: U.S. Census Bureau, *America's Families and Living Arrangements*, Current Population Reports, P20-537, 2001, and earlier reports. See also <http://www.census.gov/population/www/socdemo/hh-fam.html>.

Table 62. Households by Age of Householder and Size of Household: 1990 to 2010

[In millions (93.3 represents 93,300,000). As of March. Based on Current Population Survey; see headnote, Table 59]

Age of householder and size of household	1990	2000	2005	2010					
				Total [1]	White [2]	Black [2]	Asian [2]	Hispanic [3]	Non-Hispanic White
Total.	**93.3**	**104.7**	**113.3**	**117.5**	**95.5**	**14.7**	**4.7**	**13.3**	**83.2**
Age of householder:									
15 to 24 years old	5.1	5.9	6.7	6.2	4.7	1.0	0.3	1.2	3.7
25 to 29 years old	9.4	8.5	9.2	9.4	7.4	1.3	0.4	1.5	6.0
30 to 34 years old	11.0	10.1	10.1	9.8	7.5	1.4	0.6	1.6	6.0
35 to 44 years old	20.6	24.0	23.2	21.5	16.8	3.0	1.1	3.3	13.7
45 to 54 years old	14.5	20.9	23.4	24.9	20.1	3.2	1.0	2.6	17.7
55 to 64 years old	12.5	13.6	17.5	20.4	16.9	2.4	0.7	1.6	15.5
65 to 74 years old	11.7	11.3	11.5	13.2	11.2	1.3	0.4	0.9	10.4
75 years old and over	8.4	10.4	11.6	12.1	10.7	1.0	0.3	0.6	10.2
One person	23.0	26.7	30.1	31.4	25.2	4.7	0.9	2.1	23.3
Male.	9.0	11.2	12.8	14.0	11.2	2.0	0.4	1.1	10.3
Female.	14.0	15.5	17.3	17.4	14.0	2.7	0.4	1.0	13.1
Two persons	30.1	34.7	37.4	39.5	33.4	4.0	1.3	3.0	30.6
Three persons	16.1	17.2	18.3	18.6	14.7	2.5	0.9	2.5	12.3
Four persons	14.5	15.3	16.4	16.1	12.9	1.9	1.0	2.6	10.5
Five persons	6.2	7.0	7.2	7.4	5.8	0.9	0.4	1.6	4.3
Six persons	2.1	2.4	2.5	2.8	2.1	0.4	0.2	0.8	1.4
Seven persons or more	1.3	1.4	1.4	1.7	1.2	0.3	0.1	0.6	0.7

[1] Includes other races, not shown separately. [2] Beginning with the 2003 Current Population Survey (CPS), respondents could choose more than one race. 2005 and 2010 data represent persons who selected this race group only and exclude persons reporting more than one race. The CPS in prior years only allowed respondents to report one race group. See also comments on race in the text for this section. [3] Hispanic persons may be any race.
Source: U.S. Census Bureau, *America's Families and Living Arrangements*, Current Population Reports, P20-537, 2001, and earlier reports; "Families and Living Arrangements." See also <http://www.census.gov/population/www/socdemo/hh-fam.html>.

Table 63. Unmarried-Partner Households by Region and Sex of Partners: 2009

[The American Community Survey universe includes the household population and the population living in institutions, college dormitories, and other group quarters. For composition of regions, see inside front cover. Based on a sample and subject to sampling variability; see text, this section and Appendix III]

Item	Total	Northeast	Midwest	South	West
Total households	**113,616,229**	**20,770,447**	**25,917,520**	**42,080,155**	**24,848,107**
Unmarried-partner households	6,502,121	1,209,445	1,537,394	2,167,843	1,587,439
Male householder and male partner	280,410	57,817	50,026	95,829	76,738
Male householder and female partner.	3,053,290	556,884	722,160	1,028,149	746,097
Female householder and female partner. . .	300,890	59,924	61,266	98,399	81,301
Female householder and male partner	2,867,531	534,820	703,942	945,466	683,303
All other households	107,114,108	19,561,002	24,380,126	39,912,312	23,260,668

Source: U.S. Census Bureau, 2009 American Community Survey, B11009, "Unmarried-Partner Households and Household Type by Sex of Partner," <http://factfinder.census.gov/>, accessed January 2011.

Population 55

Table 64. Family Households by Number of Own Children Under 18 Years of Age: 2000 to 2010

[As of March (72,025 represents 72,025,000). Based on Current Population Survey; see headnote, Table 67]

Race, Hispanic origin, and year	Number of families (1,000)					Percent distribution				
	Total	No children	One child	Two children	Three or more children	Total	No children	One child	Two children	Three or more children
ALL FAMILIES [1]										
2000.............................	72,025	37,420	14,311	13,215	7,080	100	52	20	18	10
2005.............................	76,858	40,647	15,069	13,741	7,400	100	53	20	18	10
2010, total.....................	**78,833**	**43,615**	**15,149**	**12,947**	**7,122**	**100**	**55**	**19**	**16**	**9**
Married couple................	58,410	33,835	9,567	9,658	5,351	100	58	16	17	9
Male householder [2].............	5,580	3,356	1,375	576	273	100	60	25	10	5
Female householder [2]...........	14,843	6,424	4,207	2,714	1,499	100	43	28	18	10
WHITE FAMILIES [3]										
2000.............................	60,251	32,144	11,496	10,918	5,693	100	53	19	18	9
2005.............................	63,079	34,255	11,872	11,127	5,825	100	54	19	18	9
2010, total.....................	**64,120**	**36,464**	**11,856**	**10,275**	**5,525**	**100**	**57**	**18**	**16**	**9**
Married couple................	50,163	29,616	7,982	8,092	4,473	100	59	16	16	9
Male householder [2].............	4,194	2,518	1,045	436	196	100	60	25	10	5
Female householder [2]...........	9,762	4,331	2,829	1,747	856	100	44	29	18	9
BLACK FAMILIES [3]										
2000.............................	8,664	3,882	2,101	1,624	1,058	100	45	24	19	12
2005.............................	8,902	4,077	2,059	1,641	1,125	100	46	23	18	13
2010, total.....................	**9,358**	**4,502**	**2,142**	**1,608**	**1,106**	**100**	**48**	**23**	**17**	**12**
Married couple................	4,274	2,357	733	695	489	100	55	17	16	12
Male householder [2].............	939	541	235	104	59	100	58	25	11	6
Female householder [2]...........	4,145	1,604	1,174	809	557	100	39	28	20	13
ASIAN FAMILIES [3]										
2005.............................	3,142	1,535	730	646	230	100	49	23	21	7
2010, total.....................	**3,592**	**1,794**	**777**	**754**	**267**	**100**	**50**	**22**	**21**	**7**
Married couple................	2,888	1,327	638	678	246	100	46	22	23	8
Male householder [2].............	257	202	40	13	2	100	79	16	5	1
Female householder [2]...........	447	265	99	63	19	100	59	22	14	4
HISPANIC FAMILIES [4]										
2000.............................	7,561	2,747	1,791	1,693	1,330	100	36	24	22	18
2005.............................	9,521	3,528	2,130	2,163	1,699	100	37	22	23	18
2010, total.....................	**10,412**	**4,173**	**2,344**	**2,269**	**1,626**	**100**	**40**	**23**	**22**	**16**
Married couple................	6,589	2,497	1,366	1,576	1,149	100	38	21	24	17
Male householder [2].............	1,079	670	210	124	75	100	62	19	11	7
Female householder [2]...........	2,745	1,005	768	569	402	100	37	28	21	15
NON-HISPANIC WHITE FAMILIES [3]										
2005.............................	54,257	30,965	9,924	9,151	4,217	100	57	18	17	8
2010, total.....................	**54,445**	**32,569**	**9,691**	**8,173**	**4,012**	**100**	**60**	**18**	**15**	**7**
Married couple................	43,954	27,254	6,689	6,627	3,385	100	62	15	15	7
Male householder [2].............	3,200	1,897	851	322	130	100	59	27	10	4
Female householder [2]...........	7,291	3,418	2,152	1,224	497	100	47	29	17	7

[1] Includes other races and non-Hispanic groups, not shown separately. [2] No spouse present. [3] Beginning with the 2003 Current Population Survey (CPS), respondents could choose more than one race. 2005 and 2010 data represent persons who selected this race group only and exclude persons reporting more than one race. The CPS prior to 2003 only allowed respondents to report one race group. See also comments on race in the text for this section. [4] Hispanic persons may be any race.

Source: U.S. Census Bureau, *America's Families and Living Arrangements*, Current Population Reports, P20-553 and earlier reports; "Families and Living Arrangements," and unpublished data. See also <http://www.census.gov/population/www/socdemo/hh-fam.html>.

Table 65. Family Households With Own Children Under Age 18 by Type of Family, 2000 and 2010, and by Age of Householder, 2010

[As of March (34,605 represents 34,605,000). See headnote, Table 67]

Age of Householder	Family households with children		Married couple households with children		Male householder with children [1]		Female householder with children [1]	
	Number (1,000)	Percent of all family households	Number (1,000)	Percent of all married couple households	Number (1,000)	Percent of all male householder families [1]	Number (1,000)	Percent of all female householder families [1]
2000, total	34,605	48	25,248	46	1,786	44	7,571	60
2010, total	**35,218**	**45**	**24,575**	**42**	**2,224**	**40**	**8,419**	**57**
15 to 24 years old	1,746	51	652	58	150	18	944	66
25 to 34 years old	9,859	75	6,345	73	667	53	2,847	89
35 to 44 years old	13,672	80	10,066	81	737	66	2,869	83
45 to 54 years old	8,353	46	6,318	45	515	42	1,520	50
55 to 64 years old	1,347	10	1,028	9	128	20	191	11
65 years old and over	241	2	167	2	27	5	48	2

[1] No spouse present.

Source: U.S. Census Bureau, *America's Families and Living Arrangements*, Current Population Reports, P20-537, 2001; "America's Families and Living Arrangements: 2010," <http://www.census.gov/population/www/socdemo/hh-fam/cps2010.html>.

Table 66. Families by Type, Race, and Hispanic Origin: 2010

[In thousands (78,833 represents 78,833,000). As of March. Excludes members of Armed Forces except those living off post or with their families on post. Population controls based on Census 2000 and an expanded sample of households. Based on Current Population Survey; see text, this section and Appendix III]

Characteristic	All families	Married couple families						Female family householder[4]						Male family householder,[4] all races
		All races[1]	White[2]	Black[2]	Asian[2]	Hispanic[3]	Non-Hispanic White[2,3]	All races[1]	White[2]	Black[2]	Asian[2]	Hispanic[3]	Non-Hispanic White[2]	
All families	78,833	58,410	50,163	4,274	2,888	6,589	43,945	14,843	9,762	4,145	447	2,745	7,291	5,580
Age of householder:														
Under 25 years old	3,399	1,125	1,005	63	32	272	756	1,436	874	465	38	313	593	838
25 to 34 years old	13,093	8,634	7,207	685	526	1,477	5,832	3,199	1,949	1,042	77	715	1,311	1,260
35 to 44 years old	17,062	12,465	10,375	1,016	811	1,958	8,515	3,473	2,266	1,000	105	739	1,608	1,124
45 to 54 years old	18,177	13,895	11,858	1,083	686	1,434	10,516	3,048	2,072	805	95	483	1,640	1,233
55 to 64 years old	13,706	11,405	9,900	833	480	798	9,140	1,672	1,128	408	75	279	868	629
65 to 74 years old	8,066	6,835	6,131	404	221	436	5,707	994	686	240	28	121	575	237
75 years old and over	5,330	4,050	3,687	188	132	208	3,487	1,021	788	185	29	94	696	259
Without own children under 18 ...	43,615	33,835	29,616	2,357	1,327	2,497	27,254	6,424	4,331	1,604	265	1,005	3,418	3,356
With own children under 18 ...	35,218	24,575	20,548	1,917	1,561	4,091	16,700	8,419	5,432	2,541	182	1,739	3,873	2,224
One own child under 18 ...	15,149	9,567	7,982	733	638	1,366	6,689	4,207	2,829	1,174	99	768	2,152	1,375
Two own children under 18 ...	12,947	9,658	8,092	695	678	1,576	6,627	2,714	1,747	809	63	569	1,224	576
Three or more own children under 18 ...	7,122	5,351	4,473	489	246	1,149	3,385	1,499	856	557	19	402	497	273
Age of own children:														
Of any age	47,463	31,514	26,525	2,601	1,980	4,978	21,570	12,624	8,369	3,542	317	2,355	6,261	3,325
Under 25 years old	41,422	28,728	24,021	2,285	1,798	4,637	19,659	9,984	6,467	2,971	228	2,013	4,669	2,710
Under 12 years old	25,867	18,304	15,223	1,426	1,238	3,255	12,167	5,986	3,806	1,870	104	1,332	2,616	1,577
Under 6 years old	15,506	11,170	9,261	855	790	2,109	7,291	3,382	2,110	1,097	44	759	1,430	954
Under 3 years old	9,010	6,561	5,496	461	448	1,227	4,343	1,856	1,143	625	16	407	782	594
Under 1 year old	3,247	2,377	2,034	128	166	363	1,696	621	373	226	4	129	259	249
Members 65 and older:														
Without members 65 and older ...	61,843	45,149	38,421	3,455	2,363	5,647	33,110	12,118	7,836	3,543	331	2,386	5,699	4,575
With members 65 and older ...	16,990	13,261	11,742	819	525	942	10,843	2,725	1,926	602	116	359	1,592	1,005
Marital status of householder:														
Married, spouse present	58,410	58,410	50,163	4,274	2,888	6,589	43,945	(X)	(X)	(X)	(X)	(X)	(X)	(X)
Married, spouse absent	2,766	(X)	(X)	(X)	(X)	(X)	(X)	2,142	1,414	565	88	632	845	624
Separated	1,936	(X)	(X)	(X)	(X)	(X)	(X)	1,550	1,051	421	33	447	638	386
Other	830	(X)	(X)	(X)	(X)	(X)	(X)	592	363	144	55	185	207	238
Widowed	2,936	(X)	(X)	(X)	(X)	(X)	(X)	2,364	1,729	486	90	286	1,461	572
Divorced	6,537	(X)	(X)	(X)	(X)	(X)	(X)	4,851	3,686	889	118	668	3,095	1,686
Never married	8,185	(X)	(X)	(X)	(X)	(X)	(X)	5,486	2,933	2,205	151	1,158	1,891	2,698

X Not applicable. [1] Includes other races and non-Hispanic groups, not shown separately. [2] Beginning with the 2003 Current Population Survey (CPS), respondents could choose more than one race. Data represent persons who selected this race group only and exclude persons reporting more than one race. See also comments on race in the text for this section. [3] Persons of Hispanic origin may be any race. [4] No spouse present.

Source: U.S. Census Bureau, "America's Families and Living Arrangements: 2010" and unpublished data, <http://www.census.gov/population/www/socdemo/hh-fam/cps2010.html>.

U.S. Census Bureau, Statistical Abstract of the United States: 2012

Table 67. Family Groups With Children Under 18 Years Old by Race and Hispanic Origin: 1990 to 2010

[In thousands. As of March (34,670 represents 34,670,000). Family groups comprise family households, related subfamilies, and unrelated subfamilies. Excludes members of Armed Forces except those living off post or with their families on post. Beginning 2005, population controls based on Census 2000 and an expanded sample of households. Based on Current Population Survey, see text, this section and Appendix III]

Race and Hispanic origin of householder or reference person	Number (1,000)				Percent distribution			
	1990	2000	2005	2010	1990	2000	2005	2010
All races, total [1]	**34,670**	**37,496**	**39,317**	**38,768**	**100**	**100**	**100**	**100**
Two-parent family groups [2]	24,921	25,771	26,482	27,082	72	69	67	70
One-parent family groups	9,749	11,725	12,835	11,686	28	31	32	30
Maintained by mother	8,398	9,681	10,366	9,924	24	26	26	26
Maintained by father	1,351	2,044	2,469	1,762	4	5	6	5
White, total [3]	**28,294**	**30,079**	**30,960**	**30,186**	**100**	**100**	**100**	**100**
Two-parent family groups [2]	21,905	22,241	22,319	22,457	77	74	72	74
One-parent family groups	6,389	7,838	8,641	7,729	23	26	28	26
Maintained by mother	5,310	6,216	6,747	6,396	19	21	22	21
Maintained by father	1,079	1,622	1,894	1,333	4	5	6	4
Black, total [3]	**5,087**	**5,530**	**5,495**	**5,555**	**100**	**100**	**100**	**100**
Two-parent family groups [2]	2,006	2,135	2,065	2,275	39	39	38	41
One-parent family groups	3,081	3,396	3,430	3,280	61	61	62	59
Maintained by mother	2,860	3,060	3,037	2,977	56	55	55	54
Maintained by father	221	335	393	303	4	6	7	5
Asian, total [3]	**(NA)**	**1,469**	**1,757**	**1,986**	**100**	**100**	**100**	**100**
Two-parent family groups [2]	(NA)	1,184	1,472	1,694	(NA)	81	84	85
One-parent family groups	(NA)	285	285	292	(NA)	19	16	15
Maintained by mother	(NA)	236	222	235	(NA)	16	13	12
Maintained by father	(NA)	49	63	57	(NA)	3	4	3
Hispanic, total [4]	**3,429**	**5,503**	**6,752**	**7,355**	**100**	**100**	**100**	**100**
Two-parent family groups [2]	2,289	3,625	4,346	4,856	67	66	64	66
One-parent family groups	1,140	1,877	2,406	2,499	33	34	36	34
Maintained by mother	1,003	1,565	1,964	2,186	29	28	29	30
Maintained by father	138	313	442	313	4	6	7	4
Non-Hispanic White, total [3]	**(NA)**	**24,847**	**24,730**	**23,368**	**100**	**100**	**100**	**100**
Two-parent family groups [2]	(NA)	18,750	18,253	17,911	(NA)	75	74	77
One-parent family groups	(NA)	6,096	6,476	5,457	(NA)	25	26	23
Maintained by mother	(NA)	4,766	4,984	4,404	(NA)	19	20	19
Maintained by father	(NA)	1,331	1,492	1,053	(NA)	5	6	5

NA Not available. [1] Includes other races and non-Hispanic groups, not shown separately. [2] Beginning 2007, includes children living both with married and unmarried parents. [3] Beginning with the 2003 Current Population Survey (CPS), respondents could choose more than one race. Beginning 2005, data represent persons who selected this race group only and exclude persons reporting more than one race. The CPS prior to 2003 allowed respondents to report only one race group. See also comments on race in the text for this section. [4] Hispanic persons may be any race.

Source: U.S. Census Bureau, *Families and Living Arrangements*, Current Population Reports, P20-537, 2001 and earlier reports; and "Families and Living Arrangements," <http://www.census.gov/population/www/socdemo/hh-fam.html>.

Table 68. Parents and Children in Stay-At-Home Parent Family Groups: 1995 to 2010

[In thousands (22,973 represents 22,973,000). Family groups with children include those families that maintain their own household (family households with own children); those that live in the home of a relative (related subfamilies); and those that live in the home of a nonrelative (unrelated subfamilies). Stay-at-home family groups are married-couple family groups with children under 15 where one parent is in the labor force all of the previous year and their spouse is out of the labor force for the entire year with the reason 'taking care of home and family.' Only married couples with children under 15 are included. Based on Current Population Survey; see Appendix III]

Year	Married-couple family groups with children under 15 years old			Children under 15 years old in married-couple family groups		
	Total	With stay-at-home mothers	With stay-at-home fathers	Total	With stay-at-home mothers	With stay-at-home fathers
1995...........	22,973	4,440	64	41,008	9,106	125
1996...........	22,808	4,633	49	40,739	9,693	115
1997...........	22,779	4,617	71	40,798	9,788	140
1998...........	22,881	4,555	90	41,038	9,432	196
1999...........	22,754	4,731	71	41,003	9,796	143
2000...........	22,953	4,785	93	41,860	10,087	180
2001...........	22,922	4,934	81	41,862	10,194	148
2002...........	23,339	5,206	106	41,802	10,573	189
2003...........	23,209	5,388	98	41,654	11,028	175
2004...........	23,160	5,571	147	41,409	11,205	268
2005...........	23,305	5,584	142	41,111	11,224	247
2006...........	23,232	5,646	159	41,259	11,372	283
2007...........	23,507	5,563	165	41,559	11,193	303
2008...........	22,445	5,327	140	41,037	11,132	234
2009...........	22,523	5,095	158	41,208	10,934	290
2010...........	22,138	5,020	154	41,026	10,833	287

Source: U.S. Census Bureau, "Families and Living Arrangements, Table SHP-1. Parents and Children in Stay-At-Home Parent Family Groups: 1994 to Present," <http://www.census.gov/population/www/socdemo/hh-fam.html>.

Table 69. Children Under 18 Years Old by Presence of Parents: 2000 to 2010

[As of March (72,012 represents 72,012,000). Excludes persons under 18 years old who maintained households or family groups. Based on Current Population Survey; see headnote, Table 67]

Race, Hispanic origin, and year	Number (1,000)	Both parents [1]	Percent living with—					Father only	Neither parent
			Mother only						
			Total	Divorced	Married, spouse absent	Never married	Widowed		
ALL RACES [2]									
2000	72,012	69.1	22.4	7.9	4.5	9.2	1.0	4.2	4.2
2005	73,494	67.3	23.4	7.9	4.6	10.1	0.8	4.8	4.5
2008	74,107	69.9	22.8	7.5	4.6	9.8	0.9	3.5	3.8
2009	74,230	69.8	22.8	7.0	4.9	10.0	0.8	3.4	4.0
2010	74,718	69.4	23.1	7.1	5.1	10.1	0.8	3.4	4.1
WHITE [3]									
2000	56,455	75.3	17.3	(NA)	(NA)	(NA)	(NA)	4.3	3.1
2005	56,234	73.5	18.4	7.9	4.0	5.8	0.7	4.7	3.4
2008	56,482	76.0	17.5	7.5	3.9	5.3	0.7	3.6	2.9
2009	56,254	75.8	17.7	7.0	4.2	5.8	0.7	3.4	3.1
2010	56,416	74.9	18.3	6.9	4.5	6.1	0.8	3.5	3.4
BLACK [3]									
2000	11,412	37.6	49.0	(NA)	(NA)	(NA)	(NA)	4.2	9.2
2005	11,293	35.0	50.2	8.7	8.1	32.0	1.3	5.0	9.8
2008	11,342	37.5	51.1	8.6	8.2	32.7	1.6	3.3	8.1
2009	11,235	38.1	50.2	7.9	8.7	32.4	1.3	3.5	8.3
2010	11,272	39.2	49.7	8.6	8.4	31.5	1.2	3.6	7.5
ASIAN [3]									
2005	2,843	83.6	10.2	4.0	2.3	2.7	1.3	3.6	2.5
2008	2,980	85.1	10.2	2.7	3.5	3.2	0.9	2.3	2.4
2009	3,035	85.2	10.2	2.8	4.5	2.0	1.0	2.5	2.0
2010	3,300	85.5	10.1	3.8	3.7	2.1	0.6	2.2	2.1
HISPANIC [4]									
2000	11,613	65.1	25.1	(NA)	(NA)	(NA)	(NA)	4.4	5.4
2005	14,241	64.7	25.4	6.1	7.1	11.4	0.8	4.8	5.2
2008	15,642	69.7	24.1	5.8	7.0	10.5	0.7	2.3	3.9
2009	16,360	68.7	24.9	5.2	7.2	11.7	0.8	2.5	3.9
2010	16,941	67.0	26.3	5.8	8.1	11.7	0.7	2.7	4.0
NON-HISPANIC WHITE [3]									
2005	43,106	75.9	16.4	8.5	3.1	4.2	0.7	4.8	2.9
2008	42,052	77.8	15.5	8.1	3.0	3.7	0.7	4.1	2.6
2009	41,418	78.1	15.3	7.6	3.1	3.9	0.7	3.8	2.8
2010	41,809	77.5	15.5	7.5	3.1	4.2	0.8	3.8	3.1

NA Not available. [1] Beginning in 2007, includes children living both with married and unmarried parents. [2] Includes other races and non-Hispanic groups, not shown separately. [3] Beginning with the 2003 Current Population Survey (CPS), respondents could choose more than one race. Beginning 2005, data represent persons who selected this race group only and exclude persons reporting more than one race. The CPS prior to 2003 allowed respondents to report only one race group. See also comments on race in the text for this section. [4] Hispanic persons may be any race.
Source: U.S. Census Bureau, "Families and Living Arrangements," <http://www.census.gov/population/www/socdemo /hh-fam.html>.

Table 70. Grandparents Living With Grandchildren by Race and Sex: 2009

[In thousands (6,687 represents 6,687,000) except percent. Covers both grandparents living in own home with grandchildren present and grandparents living in grandchildren's home. The American Community Survey universe includes the household population and the population living in institutions, college dormitories, and other group quarters. Based on a sample and subject to sampling variability; see text, this section, and Appendix III]

Race, Hispanic origin, and sex	Grandparents living with own grandchildren, total	Grandparents responsible for grandchildren		
		Total	30 to 59 years old	60 years old and over
Grandparents living with own grandchildren under 18 years old (1,000)	**6,687**	**2,696**	**1,815**	**881**
PERCENT DISTRIBUTION				
Total	100.0	100.0	100.0	100.0
White alone	62.2	63.3	62.7	64.6
Black or African American alone	18.8	23.2	23.7	22.0
American Indian and Alaska Native alone	1.4	2.0	2.0	2.0
Asian alone	7.3	2.9	2.0	4.6
Native Hawaiian and Other Pacific Islander alone	0.3	0.3	0.3	0.3
Some other race alone	8.0	6.4	7.3	4.6
Two or more races	1.8	1.9	2.0	1.9
Hispanic origin [1]	24.7	20.1	22.0	16.2
White alone, not Hispanic	46.8	50.8	49.2	54.1
Male	35.9	37.1	34.7	42.1
Female	64.1	62.9	65.3	57.9

[1] Persons of Hispanic origin may be any race.
Source: U.S. Census Bureau, American Community Survey 2009, Subject Table S1002, "Grandparents," <http://factfinder.census.gov/>, accessed February 2011.

Table 71. Nonfamily Households by Sex and Age of Householder: 2010

[In thousands (18,263 represents 18,263,000). As of March. See headnote, Table 72]

Item	Male householder					Female householder				
	Total	15 to 24 yrs. old	25 to 44 yrs. old	45 to 64 yrs. old	65 yrs. old and over	Total	15 to 24 yrs. old	25 to 44 yrs. old	45 to 64 yrs. old	65 yrs. old and over
Total..............	**18,263**	**1,536**	**6,562**	**6,695**	**3,470**	**20,442**	**1,299**	**4,058**	**6,681**	**8,403**
One person (living alone) ...	13,971	723	4,466	5,582	3,198	17,428	642	2,903	5,762	8,121
Nonrelatives present	4,291	812	2,097	1,111	273	3,014	656	1,155	919	284
Never married	9,399	1,481	4,898	2,525	495	6,658	1,258	3,007	1,768	626
Married [1]	1,581	41	528	685	327	1,122	26	282	544	271
Widowed	1,871	2	30	327	1,512	7,016	4	77	1,108	5,828
Divorced	5,412	12	1,106	3,158	1,137	5,646	11	693	3,263	1,678

[1] No spouse present, includes separated.

Source: U.S. Census Bureau, "America's Families and Living Arrangements: 2010, Table A2. Family Status and Household Relationship of People 15 Years and Over, by Marital Status, Age, and Sex: 2010," <http://www.census.gov/population/www/socdemo/hh-fam/cps2010.html>.

Table 72. Persons Living Alone by Sex and Age: 1990 to 2010

[As of March (22,999 represents 22,999,000). Excludes members of Armed Forces except those living off post or with their families on post. Beginning 2005, population controls based on Census 2000 and an expanded sample of households. Based on Current Population Survey, see text, this section and Appendix III]

Sex and age	Number of persons (1,000)						Percent distribution				
				2010					2010		
	1990	2000	2005	Total	Male	Female	1990	2000	Total	Male	Female
Total.	**22,999**	**26,724**	**30,137**	**31,399**	**13,971**	**17,428**	**100**	**100**	**100**	**100**	**100**
15 to 24 years old	1,210	1,144	1,521	1,367	723	642	5	4	4	5	4
25 to 34 years old	3,972	3,848	3,836	3,917	2,293	1,624	17	14	12	16	9
35 to 44 years old	3,138	4,109	3,988	3,453	2,173	1,279	14	15	11	16	7
45 to 64 years old	5,502	7,842	10,180	11,345	5,582	5,762	24	29	36	40	33
65 to 74 years old	4,350	4,091	4,222	4,709	1,600	3,110	19	15	15	11	18
75 years old and over	4,825	5,692	6,391	6,608	1,598	5,011	21	21	21	11	29

Source: U.S. Census Bureau, *America's Families and Living Arrangements*, Current Population Reports, P20-537, 2001, and earlier reports. See also <http://www.census.gov/population/www/socdemo/hh-fam.html>.

Table 73. Group Quarters Population by Type of Group Quarter and Selected Characteristics: 2009

[In percent, except as indicated (8,277 represents 8,277,000). The American Community Survey universe includes the household population and the population living in institutions, college dormitories, and other group quarters. Based on a sample and subject to sampling variability; see text, this section, and Appendix III]

Characteristic	Total group quarters population [1]	Adult correctional facilities	Nursing facilities/ skilled nursing facilities	College/ university housing	Characteristic	Total group quarters population [1]	Adult correctional facilities	Nursing facilities/ skilled nursing facilities	College/ university housing
Total population (1,000). . .	**8,277**	**2,153**	**1,832**	**2,464**	One race (1,000)	8,073	2,085	1,821	2,398
					Two or more races (1,000)	204	69	12	67
PERCENT DISTRIBUTION					PERCENT DISTRIBUTION				
Male.	59.0	90.9	32.3	46.1	White	69.6	48.9	83.6	77.2
Female.	41.0	9.1	67.7	53.9	Black or African American . . .	22.0	41.2	12.8	12.9
					American Indian and				
Under 15 years old	0.8	(X)	(X)	(X)	Alaska Native.	1.1	1.9	0.5	0.4
15 to 17 years old	1.9	0.5	(X)	1.7	Asian	3.3	0.9	1.7	7.1
18 to 24 years old	38.4	17.9	0.2	96.5	Native Hawaiian and				
25 to 34 years old	11.9	32.4	0.7	1.6	Other Pacific Islander	0.2	0.3	0.1	0.2
35 to 44 years old	9.8	25.6	1.6	0.2	Some other race	3.9	6.8	1.3	2.2
45 to 54 years old	9.2	17.4	4.7	0.1					
55 to 64 years old	5.5	5.0	8.6	–	Hispanic origin [2].	11.0	19.8	4.3	6.6
65 to 74 years old	4.4	1.0	13.4	–	Not Hispanic	89.0	80.2	95.7	93.4
75 to 84 years old	7.5	0.2	28.6	(X)	White alone, Not Hispanic . . .	61.6	36.0	80.2	71.4
85 years old and over	10.6	–	42.2	(X)					

– Represents zero. X Not applicable. [1] Includes other types of group quarters, not shown separately. [2] Persons of Hispanic origin may be any race.

Source: U.S. Census Bureau, 2009 American Community Survey, S2601A, "Characteristics of the Group Quarters Population" and S2601B, "Characteristics of the Group Quarters Population by Group Quarters Type," <http://factfinder.census.gov/>, accessed November 2010.

Table 74. Population in Group Quarters by State: 2000 to 2010

[In thousands (7,780 represents 7,780,000). As of April. For definition of group quarters, see text, this section]

State	2000 [1]	2010	State	2000 [1]	2010	State	2000 [1]	2010
U.S.	**7,780**	**7,987**						
AL	115	116	KY	115	126	ND	24	25
AK	19	26	LA	136	127	OH	299	306
AZ	110	139	ME	35	36	OK	112	112
AR	74	79	MD	134	138	OR	77	87
CA	820	820	MA	221	239	PA	433	426
CO	103	116	MI	250	229	RI	39	43
CT	108	118	MN	136	135	SC	135	139
DE	25	24	MS	95	92	SD	28	34
DC	36	40	MO	164	174	TN	148	153
FL	389	422	MT	25	29	TX	561	581
GA	234	253	NE	51	51	UT	40	46
HI	36	43	NV	34	36	VT	21	25
ID	31	29	NH	36	40	VA	231	240
IL	322	302	NJ	195	187	WA	136	139
IN	178	187	NM	36	43	WV	43	49
IA	104	98	NY	581	586	WI	156	150
KS	82	79	NC	254	257	WY	14	14

[1] The April 1, 2000, Population Estimates base reflects changes to the Census 2000 population from the Count Question Resolution program and geographic program revisions.
Source: U.S. Census Bureau, "Annual Resident Population Estimates, Estimated Components of Resident Population Change, and Rates of the Components of Resident Population Change for States and Counties: April 1, 2000 to July 1, 2009," March 2010, <http://www.census.gov/popest/counties/files/CO-EST2009-ALLDATA.csv>, and 2010 Census Data, <http://2010.census.gov/2010census/data/>.

Table 75. Self-Described Religious Identification of Adult Population: 1990, 2001, and 2008

[In thousands (175,440 represents 175,440,000). The methodology of the American Religious Identification Survey (ARIS) 2008 replicated that used in previous surveys. The three surveys are based on random-digit-dialing telephone surveys of residential households in the continental U.S.A (48 states): 54,461 interviews in 2008, 50,281 in 2001, and 113,723 in 1990. Respondents were asked to describe themselves in terms of religion with an open-ended question. Interviewers did not prompt or offer a suggested list of potential answers. Moreover, the self-description of respondents was not based on whether established religious bodies, institutions, churches, mosques or synagogues considered them to be members. Instead, the surveys sought to determine whether the respondents regarded themselves as adherents of a religious community. Subjective rather than objective standards of religious identification were tapped by the surveys]

Religious group	Estimates (1,000)			Religious group	Estimates (1,000)		
	1990	2001	2008		1990	2001	2008
Adult population, total [1]	**175,440**	**207,983**	**228,182**	Christian Reform	40	79	381
Christian, total [2]	151,225	159,514	173,402	Foursquare Gospel	28	70	116
Catholic	46,004	50,873	57,199	Independent Christian Church	25	71	86
Baptist	33,964	33,820	36,148	Other Christian [4]	105	254	206
Protestant—no denomination supplied	17,214	4,647	5,187	Other religions, total [2]	5,853	7,740	8,796
Methodist/Wesleyan	14,174	14,039	11,366	Jewish	3,137	2,837	2,680
Lutheran	9,110	9,580	8,674	Muslim	527	1,104	1,349
Christian—no denomination supplied	8,073	14,190	16,834	Buddhist	404	1,082	1,189
Presbyterian	4,985	5,596	4,723	Unitarian/Universalist	502	629	586
Pentecostal/Charismatic	3,116	4,407	5,416	Hindu	227	766	582
Episcopalian/Anglican	3,043	3,451	2,405	Native American	47	103	186
Mormon/Latter-Day Saints	2,487	2,697	3,158	Sikh	13	57	78
Churches of Christ	1,769	2,593	1,921	Wiccan	8	134	342
Jehovah's Witness	1,381	1,331	1,914	Pagan	(NA)	140	340
Seventh-Day Adventist	668	724	938	Spiritualist	(NA)	116	426
Assemblies of God	617	1,105	810	Other unclassified [4]	991	774	1,030
Holiness/Holy	610	569	352	No religion specified, total [2]	14,331	29,481	34,169
Congregational/United Church of Christ	438	1,378	736	Atheist	(5)	902	1,621
Church of the Nazarene	549	544	358	Agnostic	[5] 1,186	991	1,985
Church of God	590	943	663	Humanist	29	49	90
Orthodox (Eastern)	502	645	824	No religion	13,116	27,486	30,427
Evangelical/Born Again [3]	546	1,088	2,154	Other no religion [4]	(NA)	57	45
Mennonite	235	346	438	Refused to reply to question	4,031	11,246	11,815
Christian Science	214	194	339				
Church of the Brethren	206	358	231				
Nondenominational [3]	194	2,489	8,032				
Disciples of Christ	144	492	263				
Reformed/Dutch Reform	161	289	206				
Apostolic/New Apostolic	117	254	970				
Quaker	67	217	130				
Full Gospel	51	168	67				

NA Not available. [1] Refers to the total number of adults in all fifty states. All other figures are based on projections from surveys conducted in the continental United States (48 states). [2] Includes other groups, not shown separately. [3] Because of the subjective nature of replies to open-ended questions, these categories are the most unstable as they do not refer to clearly identifiable denominations as much as underlying feelings about religion. Thus they may be the most subject to fluctuation over time. [4] Estimates for subpopulations smaller than 75,000 adults are aggregated to minimize sampling errors. [5] Atheist included in Agnostic.

Source: 1990 data, Barry A. Kosmin and Seymour P. Lachman, "One Nation Under God: Religion in Contemporary American Society, 1993"; 2001 data, Barry A. Kosmin and Ariela Keysar, *Religion in A Free Market: Religious and Non-Religious Americans, Who, What, Why, Where, 2006*; and 2008 data, Institute for the Study of Secularism in Society and Culture, Trinity College, Hartford, CT. See also <http://www.trincoll.edu/Academics/centers/ISSSC/Pages/ARIS-Data-Archive.aspx> and <www.AmericanReligionSurvey-ARIS.org> (copyright).

Table 76. Religious Bodies—Selected Data

[Includes the self-reported membership of religious bodies with 750,000 or more as reported to the Yearbook of American and Canadian Churches. Groups may be excluded if they do not supply information. The data are not standardized so comparisons between groups are difficult. The definition of "church member" is determined by the religious body]

Religious body	Year reported	Churches reported	Membership
African Methodist Episcopal Church	2009	4,100	2,500,000
African Methodist Episcopal Zion Church	2008	3,393	1,400,000
American Baptist Churches in the USA.................	2009	5,402	1,310,505
Assemblies of God	2009	12,371	2,914,669
Catholic Church....................................	2009	18,372	68,503,456
Christian Churches and Churches of Christ	1988	5,579	1,071,616
Christian Methodist Episcopal Church.................	2006	3,500	850,000
Church of God in Christ.............................	1991	15,300	5,499,875
Church of God (Cleveland, Tennessee)................	2009	6,654	1,076,254
Church of Jesus Christ of Latter-day Saints	2009	13,474	6,058,907
Churches of Christ.................................	2006	13,000	1,639,495
Episcopal Church	2009	6,895	2,006,343
Evangelical Lutheran Church in America	2009	10,348	4,542,868
Greek Orthodox Archdiocese of America	2006	560	1,500,000
Jehovah's Witnesses...............................	2009	13,021	1,162,686
Lutheran Church—Missouri Synod	2009	6,178	2,312,111
National Baptist Convention of America Inc............	2000	(NA)	3,500,000
National Baptist Convention, U.S.A., Inc.	2004	9,000	5,000,000
National Missionary Baptist Convention of America	1992	(NA)	2,500,000
Pentecostal Assemblies of the World, Inc.	2006	1,750	1,500,000
Presbyterian Church (U.S.A.)	2009	10,657	2,770,730
Progressive National Baptist Convention, Inc.	2009	1,500	1,010,000
Seventh Day Adventist Church	2009	4,892	1,043,606
Southern Baptist Convention........................	2009	45,010	16,160,088
United Church of Christ.............................	2009	5,287	1,080,199
United Methodist Church............................	2009	33,855	7,774,931

NA Not available.

Source: National Council of Churches USA, New York, NY, *2011 Yearbook of American & Canadian Churches*, annual (copyright). See also <http://www.ncccusa.org>, or call 888-870-3325.

Table 77. Christian Church Adherents, 2000, and Jewish Population, 2010—States

[133,377 represents 133,377,000. Christian church adherents were defined as "all members, including full members, their children and the estimated number of other regular participants who are not considered as communicant, confirmed or full members." The Jewish population includes Jews who define themselves as Jewish by religion as well as those who define themselves as Jewish in cultural or ethnic terms. Data on Jewish population are based on scientific studies and informant estimates provided by local Jewish communities]

State	Christian adherents 2000		Jewish population 2010		State	Christian adherents 2000		Jewish population 2010	
	Number (1,000)	Percent of population [1]	Number (1,000) [2]	Percent of population [1]		Number (1,000)	Percent of population [1]	Number (1,000) [2]	Percent of population [1]
U.S.	133,377	47.4	6,543,820	2.1	MO.......	2,813	50.3	59,200	1.0
AL	2,418	54.4	8,900	0.2	MT.......	401	44.4	1,350	0.1
AK	210	33.6	6,200	0.9	NE.......	995	58.2	6,850	0.4
AZ	1,946	37.9	106,400	1.7	NV.......	604	30.2	74,400	2.8
AR	1,516	56.7	1,725	0.1	NH.......	571	46.2	10,170	0.8
CA	14,328	42.3	1,219,740	3.3	NJ	4,262	50.7	504,500	5.7
CO......	1,604	37.3	90,120	1.8	NM	1,041	57.2	11,250	0.5
CT	1,828	53.7	119,280	3.3	NY	9,569	50.4	1,624,720	8.4
DE	299	38.2	15,100	1.7	NC.......	3,598	44.7	29,810	0.3
DC	331	57.8	28,000	4.7	ND.......	468	72.9	(Z)	(Z)
FL [3]	5,904	36.9	613,235	3.3	OH.......	4,912	43.3	148,355	1.3
GA......	3,528	43.1	127,670	1.3	OK.......	2,079	60.3	4,500	0.1
HI........	431	35.6	8,280	0.6	OR.......	1,029	30.1	48,350	1.3
ID........	624	48.3	1,625	0.1	PA	6,751	55.0	295,050	2.3
IL........	6,457	52.0	278,420	2.2	RI........	646	61.7	18,750	1.8
IN........	2,578	42.4	17,420	0.3	SC	1,874	46.7	11,245	0.2
IA........	1,698	58.0	6,190	0.2	SD	510	67.6	(Z)	(Z)
KS	1,307	48.6	17,875	0.6	TN	2,867	50.4	19,550	0.3
KY	2,141	53.0	11,350	0.3	TX	11,316	54.3	130,170	0.5
LA	2,599	58.2	10,675	0.2	UT	1,659	74.3	5,000	0.2
ME......	450	35.3	13,915	1.0	VT	230	37.8	5,385	0.9
MD......	2,012	38.0	241,050	4.2	VA	2,807	39.7	97,790	1.2
MA......	3,725	58.7	282,455	4.3	WA......	1,872	31.8	43,835	0.7
MI.......	3,970	39.9	87,270	0.9	WV......	646	35.7	2,335	0.1
MN......	2,974	60.5	46,685	0.9	WI.......	3,198	59.6	28,330	0.5
MS......	1,549	54.5	1,550	0.1	WY......	229	46.4	1,000	0.2

Z Fewer than 500 or .05 percent. [1] Based on U.S. Census Bureau data for resident population enumerated as of April 1, 2000 and April 1, 2010. [2] Jewish population of the United States is believed to be between 6.0 and 6.4 million. Over count is mostly due to a significant number of Jews who live in more than one state. [3] An additional 76,000 Jews live in Florida less than 8 months out of the year and are not counted here.

Source: Christian church adherents—Dale E. Jones, Sherri Doty, Clifford Grammich, James E. Horsch, Richard Houseal, John P. Marcum, Kenneth M. Sanchagrin, and Richard H. Taylor, *Religious Congregations and Membership in the United States: 2000* (copyright, 2002); Glenmary Research Center, Nashville, TN, <www.glenmary.org/grc>. Jewish population—Ira M. Sheskin (University of Miami) and Arnold Dashefsky (University of Connecticut), "Jewish Population of the United States, 2010," published by the Mandell L. Berman North American Jewish Data Bank in cooperation with the Association for the Social Scientific Study of Jewry and the Jewish Federations of North America. See also <www.jewishdatabank.org>.

Section 2
Births, Deaths, Marriages, and Divorces

This section presents vital statistics data on natality, mortality, marriages, and divorces, as well as factors that help explain fertility, such as, use of contraception, sexual activity, and prevalence of abortions and fetal deaths. Vital statistics are collected and disseminated for the nation through the National Vital Statistics System by the National Center for Health Statistics (NCHS) and published annually in *Vital Statistics of the United States, National Vital Statistics Reports (NVSR),* and other selected publications. Reports are also issued by various state bureaus participating in the National Vital Statistics System. Factors influencing fertility are collected in NCHS's National Survey of Family Growth and the U.S. Census Bureau's Current Population Survey and American Community Survey published in *Fertility of American Women.* Data on abortions are published by the Alan Guttmacher Institute in selected issues of *Perspectives on Sexual and Reproductive Health.*

Registration of vital events—The registration of births, deaths, fetal deaths, and other vital events in the United States is primarily a state and local function. There are 57 vital registration jurisdictions in the United States: the 50 states, five territories (Puerto Rico, etc.) District of Columbia, and New York City. Each of the 57 jurisdictions has a direct statistical reporting relationship with NCHS. Vital events occurring to U.S. residents outside the United States are not included in the data.

Births and deaths—The live-birth, death, and fetal-death statistics prepared by NCHS are based on vital records filed in the registration offices of all states, New York City, and the District of Columbia. The annual collection of death statistics on a national basis began in 1900 with a national death-registration area of ten states and the District of Columbia; a similar annual collection of birth statistics for a national birth-registration area began in 1915, also with ten reporting states and the District of Columbia. Since

1933, the birth- and death-registration areas have comprised the entire United States, including Alaska (beginning 1959) and Hawaii (beginning 1960). National statistics on fetal deaths were first compiled for 1918 and annually since 1922. Prior to 1951, birth statistics came from a complete count of records received in the Public Health Service (now received in NCHS). From 1951 through 1971, they were based on a 50-percent sample of all registered births (except for a complete count in 1955 and a 20- to 50-percent sample in 1967). Beginning in 1972, they have been based on a complete count for states participating in the Vital Statistics Cooperative Program (VSCP) (for details, see the technical appendix in *Vital Statistics of the United States*) and on a 50-percent sample of all other areas. Beginning in 1986, all reporting areas participated in the VSCP. Mortality data have been based on a complete count of records for each area (except for a 50-percent sample in 1972). Beginning in 1970, births to and deaths of nonresident aliens of the United States and U.S. citizens outside the United States have been excluded from the data. Fetal deaths and deaths among Armed Forces abroad are excluded. Data based on samples are subject to sampling error; for details, see annual issues of *Vital Statistics of the United States.*

Mortality statistics by cause of death are compiled in accordance with World Health Organization regulations according to the *International Classification of Diseases* (ICD). The ICD is revised approximately every 10 years. The tenth revision of the ICD was employed beginning in 1999. Deaths for prior years were classified according to the revision of the ICD in use at the time. Each revision of the ICD introduces a number of discontinuities in mortality statistics; for a discussion of those between the ninth and tenth revisions of the ICD, see *National Vital Statistics Reports*, Vol. 58, No. 19. Preliminary mortality data are based on a percentage of death records weighted up to the total number of deaths reported for the given year; for a discussion of preliminary data, see *National Vital Statistics Reports*, Vol. 59, No. 4. Information on tests of statistical significance, differences between death rates, and standard errors can also be found in the reports mentioned above. Some of the tables present age-adjusted death rates in addition to crude death rates. Age-adjusted death rates shown in this section were prepared using the direct method, in which age-specific death rates for a population of interest are applied to a standard population distributed by age. Age adjustment eliminates the differences in observed rates between points in time or among compared population groups that result from age differences in population composition.

Fertility and life expectancy—The total fertility rate, defined as the number of births that 1,000 women would have in their lifetime if, at each year of age, they experienced the birth rates occurring in the specified year, is compiled and published by NCHS. See Births: Final Data for 2008, *National Vital Statistics Reports*, Vol. 59, No. 1. Data on life expectancy, the average remaining lifetime in years for persons who attain a given age, are computed and published by NCHS. For details, see Deaths: Final Data for 2007, *National Vital Statistics Reports*, Vol. 58, No. 19 and <http://www.cdc.gov /nchs/products.htm#nvsr>.

Marriage and divorce—In 1957 and 1958 respectively, the National Office of Vital Statistics established marriage- and divorce-registration areas. Beginning in 1957, the marriage-registration area comprised 30 states, plus Alaska, Hawaii, Puerto Rico, and the Virgin Islands; it currently includes 42 states and the District of Columbia. The divorce-registration area, starting in 1958 with 14 states, Alaska, Hawaii, and the Virgin Islands, currently includes a total of 31 states and the Virgin Islands. Procedures for estimating the number of marriages and divorces in the registration states are discussed in *Vital Statistics of the United States, Vol. III—Marriage and Divorce*. Total

counts of events for registration and nonregistration states are gathered by collecting already summarized data on marriages and divorces reported by state offices of vital statistics and by county offices of registration. The collection and publication of detailed marriage and divorce statistics was suspended beginning in January 1996. For additional information, contact the National Center for Health Statistics online at <http://www.cdc.gov/nchs/datawh /datasite/frnotice.htm>.

Vital statistics rates—Except as noted, vital statistics rates computed by NCHS are based on decennial census population figures as of April 1 for 1960, 1970, 1980, 1990, and 2000; and on midyear population figures for other years, as estimated by the Census Bureau (see text, Section 1).

Race—Data by race for births, deaths, marriages, and divorces from NCHS are based on information contained in the certificates of registration. The Census Bureau's Current Population Survey obtains information on race by asking respondents to classify their race as (1) White, (2) Black, (3) American Indian or Alaska Native, (4) Native Hawaiian or Other Pacific Islander, and (5) Asian. Beginning with the 1989 data year, NCHS is tabulating its birth data primarily by race of the mother. In 1988 and prior years, births were tabulated by race of the child, which was determined from the race of the parents as entered on the birth certificate. Trend data by race shown in this section are by race of mother beginning with the 1980 data. Hispanic origin of the mother is reported and tabulated independently of race. Thus, persons of Hispanic origin may be any race. The majority of women of Hispanic origin are reported as White.

Statistical reliability—For a discussion of statistical collection, estimation, and sampling procedures and measures of reliability applicable to data from NCHS and the Census Bureau, see Appendix III.

Table 78. Live Births, Deaths, Marriages, and Divorces: 1960 to 2008

[4,258 represents 4,258,000. Beginning 1970, excludes births to, and deaths of nonresidents of the United States. See Appendix III]

Year	Number					Rate per 1,000 population				
		Deaths					Deaths			
	Births (1,000)	Total (1,000)	Infant [1] (1,000)	Marriages [2] (1,000)	Divorces [3] (1,000)	Births	Total	Infant [1]	Marriages [2]	Divorces [3]
1960........	4,258	1,712	111	1,523	393	23.7	9.5	26.0	8.5	2.2
1970........	3,731	1,921	75	2,159	708	18.4	9.5	20.0	10.6	3.5
1971........	3,556	1,928	68	2,190	773	17.2	9.3	19.1	10.6	3.7
1972........	3,258	1,964	60	2,282	845	15.6	9.4	18.5	10.9	4.0
1973........	3,137	1,973	56	2,284	915	14.8	9.3	17.7	10.8	4.3
1974........	3,160	1,934	53	2,230	977	14.8	9.1	16.7	10.5	4.6
1975........	3,144	1,893	51	2,153	1,036	14.6	8.8	16.1	10.0	4.8
1976........	3,168	1,909	48	2,155	1,083	14.6	8.8	15.2	9.9	5.0
1977........	3,327	1,900	47	2,178	1,091	15.1	8.6	14.1	9.9	5.0
1978........	3,333	1,928	46	2,282	1,130	15.0	8.7	13.8	10.3	5.1
1979........	3,494	1,914	46	2,331	1,181	15.6	8.5	13.1	10.4	5.3
1980........	3,612	1,990	46	2,390	1,189	15.9	8.8	12.6	10.6	5.2
1981........	3,629	1,978	43	2,422	1,213	15.8	8.6	11.9	10.6	5.3
1982........	3,681	1,975	42	2,456	1,170	15.9	8.5	11.5	10.6	5.1
1983........	3,639	2,019	41	2,446	1,158	15.6	8.6	11.2	10.5	5.0
1984	3,669	2,039	40	2,477	1,169	15.6	8.6	10.8	10.5	5.0
1985........	3,761	2,086	40	2,413	1,190	15.8	8.8	10.6	10.1	5.0
1986	3,757	2,105	39	2,407	1,178	15.6	8.8	10.4	10.0	4.9
1987........	3,809	2,123	38	2,403	1,166	15.7	8.8	10.1	9.9	4.8
1988........	3,910	2,168	39	2,396	1,167	16.0	8.9	10.0	9.8	4.8
1989........	4,041	2,150	40	2,403	1,157	16.4	8.7	9.8	9.7	4.7
1990........	4,158	2,148	38	2,443	1,182	16.7	8.6	9.2	9.8	4.7
1991........	4,111	2,170	37	2,371	1,187	16.2	8.6	8.9	9.4	4.7
1992........	4,065	2,176	35	2,362	1,215	15.8	8.5	8.5	9.3	4.8
1993........	4,000	2,269	33	2,334	1,187	15.4	8.8	8.4	9.0	4.6
1994	3,953	2,279	31	2,362	1,191	15.0	8.8	8.0	9.1	4.6
1995........	3,900	2,312	30	2,336	1,169	14.6	8.7	7.6	8.9	4.4
1996........	3,891	2,315	28	2,344	1,150	14.4	8.6	7.3	8.8	4.3
1997........	3,881	2,314	28	2,384	1,163	14.2	8.5	7.2	8.9	4.3
1998........	3,942	2,337	28	2,244	[4] 1,135	14.3	8.5	7.2	8.4	[4] 4.2
1999........	3,959	2,391	28	2,358	(NA)	14.2	8.6	7.1	8.6	[4] 4.1
2000........	4,059	2,403	28	2,315	[4] 944	14.4	8.5	6.9	8.3	[4] 4.1
2001........	4,026	2,416	28	2,326	[4] 940	14.1	8.5	6.8	8.2	[4] 4.0
2002........	4,022	2,443	28	2,290	[5] 955	13.9	8.5	7.0	7.8	[5] 3.9
2003........	4,090	2,448	28	2,245	[6] 927	14.1	8.4	6.9	7.7	[6] 3.8
2004........	4,112	2,398	28	2,279	[7] 879	14.0	8.2	6.8	7.8	[7] 3.7
2005........	4,138	2,448	28	2,249	[8] 847	14.0	8.3	6.9	7.6	[8] 3.6
2006........	4,266	2,426	29	[9] 2,193	[8] 872	14.2	8.1	6.7	[9] 7.4	[8] 3.7
2007........	4,316	2,424	29	2,197	[8] 856	14.3	8.0	6.8	7.3	[8] 3.6
2008........	4,248	2,473	28	2,157	[8] 844	14.0	8.1	6.6	7.1	[8] 3.5

NA Not available. [1] Infant mortality rate; infants under 1 year, excluding fetal deaths. [2] Marriages and marriage rates are by place of occurrence. Beginning 1991 data are provisional. Includes estimates for some States through 1965 and also for 1976 and 1977 and marriage licenses for some states for all years except 1973 and 1975. Beginning 1978, includes nonlicensed marriages in California. [3] Divorces and divorce rates are by place of occurrence. Includes reported annulments and some estimated state figures for all years. Beginning 1991 data are provisional. [4] Excludes data for California, Colorado, Indiana, and Louisiana. [5] Excludes data for California, Indiana, and Oklahoma. [6] Excludes data for California, Hawaii, Indiana, and Oklahoma [7] Excludes data for California, Georgia, Hawaii, Indiana, and Louisiana. [8] Excludes data for California, Georgia, Hawaii, Indiana, Louisiana, and Minnesota. [9] Excludes Louisiana.

Source: U.S. National Center for Health Statistics, Vital Statistics of the United States, and National Vital Statistics Reports (NVSR), <http://www.cdc.gov/nchs/nvss.htm>.

Table 79. Live Births, Birth Rates, and Fertility Rates by Hispanic Origin: 2000 to 2008

[4,059 represents 4,059,000. Represents registered births. Excludes births to nonresidents of the United States. Data are based on Hispanic origin and race of mother. Persons of Hispanic origin may be of any race. See Appendix III]

Hispanic-origin status and race of mother	Number of births (1,000)				Birth rate per 1,000 population				Fertility rate [1]			
	2000	2005	2007	2008	2000	2005	2007	2008	2000	2005	2007	2008
Total [2]	**4,059**	**4,138**	**4,316**	**4,248**	**14.4**	**14.0**	**14.3**	**14.0**	**65.9**	**66.7**	**69.5**	**68.6**
Hispanic	816	986	1,063	1,041	23.1	23.1	23.4	22.2	95.9	99.4	102.2	98.8
Mexican..................	582	693	722	685	25.0	24.7	24.3	22.1	105.1	107.7	107.8	98.9
Puerto Rico	58	63	68	69	18.1	17.2	17.4	16.7	73.5	72.1	73.6	71.5
Cuban	13	16	17	17	9.7	10.2	10.2	10.2	49.3	50.4	49.7	59.3
Central and South American [3]...	113	151	170	156	21.8	22.8	25.0	26.6	85.1	93.2	104.9	116.1
Other and unknown Hispanic ...	49	62	85	115	(3)	(3)	(3)	(3)	(3)	(3)	(3)	(3)
Non-Hispanic [4].................	3,200	3,123	3,222	3,174	13.2	12.4	12.7	12.5	61.1	60.4	62.9	62.4
White	2,363	2,280	2,310	2,268	12.2	11.5	11.6	11.3	58.5	58.3	60.1	59.4
Black	604	584	627	623	17.3	15.7	16.6	16.4	71.4	67.2	71.6	71.1

[1] Live births per 1,000 women aged 15 to 44 years in specified group. [2] Includes all races and Hispanic origin status not stated. [3] Rates for the Central and South American population include other and unknown Hispanic. [4] Includes other races not shown separately.

Source: U.S. National Center for Health Statistics, National Vital Statistics Reports (NVSR), *Births: Final Data for 2008*, Vol. 59, No. 1, January 2010.

U.S. Census Bureau, Statistical Abstract of the United States: 2012

Table 80. Births, Birth Rates, and Fertility Rates by Race, Sex, and Age: 1980 to 2008

[Births in thousands (3,612 represents 3,612,000). Except as indicated, births by race of mother. Excludes births to nonresidents of the United States. For population bases used to derive these data; see text, this section and Appendix III]

Item	1980	1990	2000	2001	2002	2003	2004	2005	2006	2007	2008
Live births [1]	**3,612**	**4,158**	**4,059**	**4,026**	**4,022**	**4,090**	**4,112**	**4,138**	**4,266**	**4,316**	**4,248**
White	2,936	3,290	3,194	3,178	3,175	3,226	3,223	3,229	3,310	3,337	3,274
Black	568	684	623	606	594	600	616	633	666	676	671
American Indian, Eskimo, Aleut	29	39	42	42	42	43	44	45	47	49	50
Asian or Pacific Islander	74	142	201	200	211	221	229	231	241	254	253
Male	1,853	2,129	2,077	2,058	2,058	2,094	2,105	2,119	2,184	2,208	2,173
Female	1,760	2,029	1,982	1,968	1,964	1,996	2,007	2,019	2,081	2,108	2,074
Males per 100 females (sex ratio)	105	105	105	105	105	105	105	105	105	105	105
Age of mother:											
Under 20 years	562	533	478	454	433	421	422	421	442	451	441
20 to 24 years	1,226	1,094	1,018	1,022	1,022	1,032	1,034	1,040	1,081	1,082	1,052
25 to 29 years	1,108	1,277	1,088	1,058	1,060	1,086	1,104	1,132	1,182	1,208	1,196
30 to 34 years	550	886	929	943	951	976	966	951	950	962	957
35 to 39 years	141	318	452	452	454	468	476	483	499	500	489
40 to 44 years	(NA)	(NA)	90	93	96	101	104	105	106	105	106
45 to 54 years	(NA)	(NA)	4	5	5	6	6	6	7	7	7
Mean age of mother at first birth (years)	22.7	24.2	24.9	25.0	25.1	25.2	25.2	25.2	25.0	25.0	25.1
Birth rate per 1,000 population	**15.9**	**16.7**	**14.4**	**14.1**	**13.9**	**14.1**	**14.0**	**14.0**	**14.2**	**14.3**	**14.0**
White	15.1	15.8	13.9	13.7	13.5	13.6	13.5	13.4	13.7	13.7	13.4
Black	21.3	22.4	17.0	16.3	15.7	15.7	16.0	16.2	16.8	16.9	16.6
American Indian, Eskimo, Aleut	20.7	18.9	14.0	13.7	13.8	13.8	14.0	14.2	14.9	15.3	14.5
Asian or Pacific Islander	19.9	19.0	17.1	16.4	16.5	16.8	16.8	16.5	16.6	17.2	16.8
Age of mother:											
10 to 14 years	1.1	1.4	0.9	0.8	0.7	0.6	0.7	0.7	0.6	0.6	0.6
15 to 19 years	53.0	59.9	47.7	45.3	43.0	41.6	41.1	40.4	41.9	42.5	41.5
20 to 24 years	115.1	116.5	109.7	106.2	103.6	102.6	101.7	102.2	105.9	106.3	103.0
25 to 29 years	112.9	120.2	113.5	113.4	113.6	115.6	115.5	115.5	116.7	117.5	115.1
30 to 34 years	61.9	80.8	91.2	91.9	91.5	95.1	95.3	95.8	97.7	99.9	99.3
35 to 39 years	19.8	31.7	39.7	40.6	41.4	43.8	45.4	46.3	47.3	47.5	46.9
40 to 44 years	3.9	5.5	8.0	8.1	8.3	8.7	8.9	9.1	9.4	9.5	9.8
45 to 54 years [2]	0.2	0.2	0.5	0.5	0.5	0.5	0.5	0.6	0.6	0.6	0.7
Fertility rate per 1,000 women [3]	**68.4**	**70.9**	**65.9**	**65.3**	**64.8**	**66.1**	**66.3**	**66.7**	**68.5**	**69.5**	**68.6**
White [3]	65.6	68.3	65.3	65.0	64.8	66.1	66.1	66.3	68.0	68.8	67.8
Black [3]	84.9	84.8	70.0	67.6	65.8	66.3	67.6	69.0	72.1	72.7	71.9
American Indian, Eskimo, Aleut [3]	82.7	76.2	58.7	58.1	58.0	58.4	58.9	59.9	63.1	64.9	64.6
Asian or Pacific Islander [3]	73.2	69.6	65.8	64.2	64.1	66.3	67.1	66.6	67.5	71.3	71.3

NA Not available. [1] Includes other races not shown separately. [2] The number of births shown is the total for women aged 45–54 years. The rate is computed by relating the births to women aged 45–54 years to women aged 45–49 years. [3] Number of live births per 1,000 women, 15 to 44 years old in specified group.

Source: U.S. National Center for Health Statistics, National Vital Statistics Reports (NVSR), *Births: Final Data for 2008*, Vol. 59, No. 1, December 2010.

Table 81. Births and Multiple Births by Race and Hispanic Origin of Mother: 1990 to 2008

[Represents registered births. Excludes births to nonresidents of the United States. Data are based on Hispanic origin and race of mother. Persons of Hispanic origin may be of any race. See Appendix III]

Birth order	1990 [1]	2000	2005	2006	2007	2008
All births, total number [2]	**4,158,212**	**4,058,814**	**4,138,349**	**4,265,555**	**4,316,233**	**4,247,694**
Twin births	93,865	118,916	133,122	137,085	138,961	138,660
Triplet and higher order multiple births	3,028	7,325	6,694	6,540	6,427	6,268
Multiple birth rate [3]	23.3	31.1	33.8	33.7	33.7	34.1
Twin birth rate [4]	22.6	29.3	32.2	32.1	32.2	32.6
Triplet and higher order multiple birth rate [5]	72.8	180.5	161.8	153.3	148.9	147.6
Non-Hispanic White births, total number	**2,626,500**	**2,362,968**	**2,279,768**	**2,308,640**	**2,310,333**	**2,267,817**
Twin births	60,210	76,018	82,223	83,108	83,632	82,903
Triplet and higher order multiple births	2,358	5,821	4,966	4,805	4,559	4,493
Multiple birth rate [3]	23.8	34.6	38.2	38.1	38.2	38.5
Twin birth rate [4]	22.9	32.2	36.1	36.0	36.2	36.6
Non-Hispanic Black births, total number	**661,701**	**604,346**	**583,759**	**617,247**	**627,191**	**623,029**
Twin births	17,646	20,173	21,254	22,702	23,101	22,924
Triplet and higher order multiple births	306	506	616	580	612	569
Multiple birth rate [3]	27.1	34.2	33.8	37.7	37.8	37.7
Twin birth rate [4]	26.7	33.4	32.2	36.8	36.8	36.8
Hispanic births, total number	**595,073**	**815,868**	**985,505**	**1,039,077**	**1,062,799**	**1,041,239**
Twin births	10,713	16,470	21,723	22,698	23,405	23,266
Triplet and higher order multiple births	235	659	761	787	857	834
Multiple birth rate [3]	18.4	21.0	22.8	22.6	22.8	23.1
Twin birth rate [4]	18.0	20.2	22.0	21.8	22.0	22.3

[1] Data by Hispanic-origin status exclude data for New Hampshire and Oklahoma, which did not report Hispanic origin. [2] Includes other races not shown separately. [3] Number of live births in all multiple deliveries per 1,000 live births. [4] Number of live births in twin deliveries per 1,000 live births. [5] Births in greater than twin deliveries per 100,000 live births.

Source: U.S. National Center for Health Statistics, National Vital Statistics Report (NVSR), Births: Final Data for 2008, Vol. 59, No. 1, December 2010.

Table 82. Births—Number and Rate by State and Island Areas: 2009

[Number of births, except rates. Registered births by place of residence. Excludes births to nonresidents of the United States. Based on race and Hispanic origin of mother. Preliminary data are based on 99.95 percent of registered vital records occurring in calendar year 2009. See Appendix III]

State	All races [1]	Non-Hispanic White	Non-Hispanic Black	Asian or Pacific Islander	American Indian, Eskimo, Aleut	Hispanic [2]	Birth rate [3]	Fertility rate [4]
United States	**4,131,019**	**2,211,960**	**609,552**	**250,935**	**48,660**	**999,632**	**13.5**	**66.7**
Alabama	62,476	36,902	19,230	989	217	5,134	13.3	65.7
Alaska	11,325	6,018	409	950	2,960	695	16.2	78.3
Arizona	92,816	40,044	4,136	3,442	6,271	39,176	14.1	71.5
Arkansas	39,853	26,998	7,649	669	214	4,208	13.8	70.1
California	527,011	146,392	31,090	71,457	3,669	270,239	14.3	68.5
Colorado	68,627	41,169	3,120	2,543	770	20,680	13.7	66.8
Connecticut	38,896	22,798	4,971	2,232	275	8,589	11.1	56.5
Delaware	11,562	6,183	3,178	517	22	1,648	13.1	65.4
District of Columbia	9,044	2,344	4,720	406	28	1,510	15.1	60.0
Florida	221,391	100,575	50,723	7,409	644	61,987	11.9	63.6
Georgia	141,375	61,732	46,242	5,976	360	24,595	14.4	67.7
Hawaii	18,888	4,603	411	12,562	107	3,135	14.6	75.8
Idaho	23,731	19,048	136	419	458	3,681	15.4	77.4
Illinois	171,255	90,964	29,947	9,616	269	40,425	13.3	64.7
Indiana	86,698	66,345	10,076	1,994	130	8,079	13.5	67.6
Iowa	39,700	33,381	1,907	1,060	256	3,210	13.2	68.7
Kansas	41,396	29,856	3,063	1,366	375	6,795	14.7	74.7
Kentucky	57,558	48,059	5,438	1,075	82	2,986	13.3	66.6
Louisiana	64,988	34,591	25,150	1,263	452	3,558	14.5	69.8
Maine	13,470	12,504	392	236	125	198	10.2	54.8
Maryland	75,061	34,014	24,992	5,388	201	10,612	13.2	63.8
Massachusetts	75,104	50,411	7,228	6,040	174	11,021	11.4	55.4
Michigan	117,293	81,218	22,071	4,091	824	7,921	11.8	59.8
Minnesota	70,648	51,290	6,475	5,313	1,755	5,625	13.4	67.5
Mississippi	42,905	21,510	19,043	479	339	1,514	14.5	70.9
Missouri	78,920	60,184	12,026	2,028	375	4,290	13.2	66.2
Montana	12,261	10,002	65	134	1,537	424	12.6	67.3
Nebraska	26,937	19,783	1,759	822	598	4,265	15.0	76.4
Nevada	37,627	15,939	3,602	3,146	514	14,353	14.2	71.2
New Hampshire	13,378	11,955	217	577	23	552	10.1	51.9
New Jersey	110,324	52,161	17,131	11,668	179	29,003	12.7	64.5
New Mexico	29,002	8,081	513	498	3,998	16,159	14.4	73.4
New York	248,110	119,530	40,982	23,274	748	59,791	12.7	61.7
North Carolina	126,846	70,428	30,317	4,107	1,828	20,171	13.5	66.3
North Dakota	9,001	7,319	162	159	1,035	312	13.9	70.8
Ohio	144,772	109,698	23,834	3,540	288	6,892	12.5	63.8
Oklahoma	54,574	34,734	5,086	1,365	6,391	7,273	14.8	74.9
Oregon	47,199	32,849	1,144	2,731	919	9,701	12.3	62.5
Pennsylvania	146,432	103,302	21,482	6,416	413	14,115	11.6	60.1
Rhode Island	11,443	6,979	906	662	178	2,508	10.9	53.6
South Carolina	60,632	33,985	19,480	1,236	206	5,562	13.3	66.3
South Dakota	11,935	9,118	247	153	2,018	476	14.7	77.8
Tennessee	82,213	55,446	17,405	2,107	319	7,433	13.1	64.7
Texas	402,011	137,603	45,493	16,948	1,174	201,241	16.2	77.6
Utah	53,887	42,388	548	1,629	764	8,773	19.4	88.4
Vermont	6,109	5,803	76	111	17	94	9.8	50.8
Virginia	105,056	60,404	23,021	7,780	179	13,688	13.3	64.4
Washington	89,284	56,543	4,083	9,134	2,407	17,189	13.4	66.4
West Virginia	21,270	19,962	831	146	20	231	11.7	61.7
Wisconsin	70,840	52,460	7,288	2,969	1,258	6,934	12.5	63.7
Wyoming	7,884	6,355	56	102	296	981	14.5	75.0
Puerto Rico	44,765	1,028	146	(NA)	(NA)	43,569	11.3	53.3
Virgin Islands	(NA)	(NA)	(NA)	(NA)	(NA)	(NA)	(NA)	(NA)
Guam	3,417	214	33	3,125	3	48	19.2	87.9
American Samoa	1,340	(NA)	(NA)	1,335	1	(NA)	20.4	90.4
Northern Marianas	1,110	(NA)	(NA)	–	(NA)	(NA)	21.6	77.1

– Represents or rounds to zero. NA Not available. [1] Includes persons of other groups, not shown separately. [2] Persons of Hispanic origin may be any race. [3] Per 1,000 estimated population. [4] Number of births per 1,000 women aged 15 to 44 years.
Source: U.S. National Center for Health Statistics, National Vital Statistics Reports (NVSR), *Births: Preliminary Data for 2009*, Vol.59, No. 3, December 2010.

Table 83. Total Fertility Rate by Race and Hispanic Origin: 1980 to 2008

[Based on race of mother. Excludes births to nonresidents of United States. The *total fertility rate* is the number of births that 1,000 women would have in their lifetime if, at each year of age, they experienced the birth rates occurring in the specified year. A total fertility rate of 2,110 represents "replacement level" fertility for the total population under current mortality conditions (assuming no net immigration). See Appendix III]

Race and Hispanic origin	1980	1990	2000	2004	2005	2006	2007	2008
Total [1]	**1,840**	**2,081**	**2,056**	**2,046**	**2,054**	**2,101**	**2,122**	**2,085**
White	1,773	2,003	2,051	2,055	2,056	2,096	2,112	2,067
Black	2,177	2,480	2,129	2,033	2,071	2,155	2,168	2,132
American Indian, Eskimo, Aleut	2,165	2,185	1,773	1,735	1,750	1,829	1,867	1,844
Asian or Pacific Islander	1,954	2,003	1,892	1,898	1,889	1,919	2,039	2,055
Hispanic [2]	(NA)	2,960	2,730	2,825	2,885	2,960	2,995	2,912

NA Not available. [1] For 1970 to 1991 includes births to races not shown separately. Beginning 1992 unknown race of mother is imputed. [2] Persons of Hispanic origin may be any race.

Source: U.S. National Center for Health Statistics, National Vital Statistics Report (NVSR), *Births: Final Data for 2008*, Vol. 59, No. 1, December 2010,

Table 84. Teenagers—Births and Birth Rates by Age, Race, and Hispanic Origin: 1990 to 2009

[Birth rates per 1,000 women in specified group. Based on race and Hispanic origin of mother. See text this section]

Item	Number of births					Birth rate				
	1990	2000	2005	2008	2009 [1]	1990	2000	2005	2008	2009 [1]
All races, 15 to 19 years	[2]**521,826**	**468,990**	**414,593**	**434,758**	**409,840**	**59.9**	**47.7**	**40.5**	**41.5**	**39.1**
15 to 17 years	183,327	157,209	133,191	135,664	124,256	37.5	26.9	21.4	21.7	20.1
18 to 19 years	338,499	311,781	281,402	299,094	285,584	88.6	78.1	69.9	70.6	66.2
White	354,482	333,013	295,265	306,402	(NA)	50.8	43.2	37.0	37.8	(NA)
Black	151,613	118,954	103,905	112,004	(NA)	112.8	77.4	62.0	63.4	(NA)
American Indian, Eskimo, Aleut	(NA)	8,055	7,807	8,815	8,316	81.1	58.3	52.7	58.4	55.5
Asian or Pacific Islander	(NA)	8,968	7,616	7,537	7,041	26.4	20.5	17.0	16.2	14.6
Hispanic [3]	(NA)	129,469	136,906	144,914	136,274	100.3	87.3	81.7	77.5	70.1
Non-Hispanic White	(NA)	204,056	165,005	168,684	159,526	42.5	32.6	25.9	26.7	25.6
Non-Hispanic Black	(NA)	116,019	96,813	104,559	98,425	116.2	79.2	60.9	62.8	59.0

NA Not available. [1] Preliminary data. [2] Includes races other than White and Black, not shown separately. [3] Persons of Hispanic origin may be any race.

Source: U.S. National Center for Health Statistics, National Vital Statistics Reports (NVSR), *Births: Final Data for 2008*, Vol. 59, No. 1, December 2010, and *Births: Preliminary Data for 2009*, Vol. 59, No. 3, December 2010.

Table 85. Births to Unmarried Women by Race, Hispanic Origin, and Age of Mother: 1990 to 2008

[1,165 represents 1,165,000. Excludes births to nonresidents of the United States. Persons of Hispanic origin may be any race. Marital status is inferred from a comparison of the child's and parents' surnames on the birth certificate for those states that do not report on marital status. No estimates included for misstatements on birth records or failure to register births. Based on race and Hispanic origin of mother. See also Appendix III]

Race and age of mother	Number (1,000)				Percent distribution				Birth rate [1]			
	1990	2000	2005	2008	1990	2000	2005	2008	1990	2000	2005	2008
Total live births [2]	**1,165**	**1,347**	**1,527**	**1,727**	**100.0**	**100.0**	**100.0**	**100.0**	**43.8**	**44.1**	**47.5**	**52.5**
White	670	866	1,023	1,169	57.5	64.3	67.0	67.7	32.9	38.2	43.0	48.2
Black	455	427	439	482	39.1	31.7	28.7	27.9	90.5	70.5	67.8	72.5
American Indian, Eskimo, Aleut	(NA)	(NA)	28	33	(NA)	(NA)	1.9	1.9	(NA)	(NA)	(NA)	(NA)
Asian or Pacific Islander	(NA)	(NA)	37	43	(NA)	(NA)	2.4	2.5	(NA)	20.9	24.9	28.2
Hispanic	[3]219	348	473	547	[3]18.8	25.8	31.0	31.7	[3]89.6	87.2	100.3	105.1
Non-Hispanic White	[3]443	522	578	650	[3]38.0	38.7	37.8	37.6	[3]24.4	28.0	30.1	33.7
Non-Hispanic Black	(NA)	415	408	451	(NA)	30.8	26.7	26.1	(NA)	(NA)	(NA)	(NA)
Under 15 years	11	8	7	6	0.9	0.6	0.4	0.3	(NA)	(NA)	(NA)	(NA)
15 to 19 years	350	369	345	377	30.0	27.4	22.6	21.8	42.5	39.0	34.5	37.0
20 to 24 years	404	504	585	641	34.7	37.4	38.3	37.1	65.1	72.2	74.9	79.2
25 to 29 years	230	255	332	397	19.7	18.9	21.7	23.0	56.0	58.5	71.1	76.1
30 to 34 years	118	130	162	193	10.1	9.7	10.6	11.2	37.6	39.3	50.0	59.0
35 to 39 years	44	65	76	89	3.8	4.8	5.0	5.1	17.3	19.7	24.5	30.4
40 years and over	9	16	21	24	0.7	1.2	1.4	1.4	3.6	5.0	[4]6.2	[4]7.5

NA Not available. [1] Rate per 1,000 unmarried women (never-married, widowed, and divorced) estimated as of July 1. Total rate and rates by race cover women 15 to 44 years old. [2] Includes races other than White and Black, not shown separately. [3] Excludes data for New Hampshire and Oklahoma, which did not report Hispanic origin. [4] Birth rates computed by relating births to unmarried mothers aged 40 years and over to unmarried women aged 40–44 years.

Source: U.S. National Center for Health Statistics, National Vital Statistics Reports (NVSR), *Births: Final Data for 2008*, Vol. 59, No. 1, December 2010; and earlier reports .

Table 86. Percentage of Births to Teens, Unmarried Mothers, and Births With Low Birth Weight: 1990 to 2008

[Represents registered births. Excludes births to nonresidents of the United States. Data are based on race and Hispanic origin of mother. See Appendix III]

Characteristics	1990	1995	2000	2005	2006	2007	2008
Percent of births to teenage mothers [1]	**12.8**	**13.1**	**11.8**	10.2	10.4	10.5	10.4
White	10.9	11.5	10.6	9.3	9.4	9.5	9.5
Black	23.1	23.1	19.7	16.9	17.0	17.2	17.0
American Indian, Eskimo, Aleut	19.5	21.4	19.7	17.7	17.6	18.4	18.0
Asian or Pacific Islander	5.7	5.6	4.5	3.3	3.3	3.1	3.0
Hispanic origin [2]	16.8	17.9	16.2	14.1	14.3	14.2	14.1
Mexican	17.7	18.8	17.0	14.9	15.0	14.9	14.8
Puerto Rican	21.7	23.5	20.0	17.4	17.7	17.2	17.3
Cuban	7.7	7.7	7.5	7.7	8.0	8.2	7.8
Central and South American	9.0	10.6	9.9	8.6	8.9	9.0	8.4
Other and unknown Hispanic	(NA)	20.1	18.8	17.1	16.9	17.2	17.1
Non-Hispanic	(NA)	(NA)	10.7	8.9	9.1	9.2	9.1
White	(NA)	(NA)	8.7	7.3	7.4	7.5	7.5
Black	(NA)	(NA)	19.8	17.0	17.2	17.3	17.1
Percent of births to unmarried mothers	26.6	32.2	33.2	36.9	38.5	39.7	40.6
White	16.9	25.3	27.1	31.7	33.3	34.8	35.7
Black	66.7	69.9	68.5	69.3	70.2	71.2	71.8
American Indian, Eskimo, Aleut	53.6	57.2	58.4	63.5	64.6	65.3	65.8
Asian or Pacific Islander	13.2	16.3	14.8	16.2	16.5	16.6	16.9
Hispanic origin [2]	36.7	40.8	42.7	48.0	49.9	51.3	52.6
Mexican	33.3	38.1	40.7	46.7	48.6	50.1	51.3
Puerto Rican	55.9	60.0	59.6	61.7	62.4	63.4	64.6
Cuban	18.2	23.8	27.3	36.4	39.4	41.8	44.2
Central and South American	41.2	44.1	44.7	49.2	51.5	52.7	52.3
Other and unknown Hispanic	(NA)	44.0	46.2	48.6	49.2	51.3	54.4
Non-Hispanic	(NA)	(NA)	30.8	33.4	34.8	35.9	36.7
White	(NA)	(NA)	22.1	25.3	26.6	27.8	28.7
Black	(NA)	(NA)	68.7	69.9	70.7	71.6	72.3
Percent of births with low birth weight [3]	**7.0**	**7.3**	**7.6**	**8.2**	**8.3**	**8.2**	**8.2**
White	5.7	6.2	6.5	7.2	7.2	7.2	7.1
Black	13.3	13.1	13.0	13.6	13.6	13.6	13.4
American Indian, Eskimo, Aleut	6.1	6.6	6.8	7.4	7.5	7.5	7.4
Asian or Pacific Islander	(NA)	6.9	7.3	8.0	8.1	8.1	8.2
Hispanic origin [2]	6.1	6.3	6.4	6.9	7.0	6.9	7.0
Mexican	5.5	5.8	6.0	6.5	6.6	6.5	6.5
Puerto Rican	9.0	9.4	9.3	9.9	10.1	9.8	9.9
Cuban	5.7	6.5	6.5	7.6	7.1	7.7	7.8
Central and South American	5.8	6.2	6.3	6.8	6.8	6.7	6.7
Other and unknown Hispanic	(NA)	7.5	7.8	8.3	8.5	8.6	8.2
Non-Hispanic	(NA)	(NA)	7.9	8.6	8.7	8.6	8.6
White	(NA)	(NA)	6.6	7.3	7.3	7.3	7.2
Black	(NA)	(NA)	13.1	14.0	14.0	13.9	13.7

NA Not available. [1] Mothers under 20 years. [2] Hispanic persons may be any race. [3] Births less than 2,500 grams (5 pounds–8 ounces). Source: U.S. National Center for Health Statistics, National Vital Statistics Reports (NVSR), *Births: Final Data for 2008*, Vol. 59, No. 1, December 2010.

Table 87. Births by Race, Hispanic Origin, and Method of Delivery: 1990 to 2008

[In thousands (4,111 represents 4,111,000), except rate. 1990 excludes data for Oklahoma, which did not report method of delivery on the birth certificate. Persons of Hispanic origin may be any race. See Appendix III]

Method of delivery	1990 [1]	2000	2005	2008 Total [2]	Hispanic	Non-Hispanic White	Non-Hispanic Black
Births, total	**4,111**	**4,059**	**4,138**	**4,248**	**1,041**	**2,268**	**623**
Vaginal	3,111	3,108	2,874	2,864	717	1,527	406
Cesarean deliveries	914	924	1,249	1,369	322	733	214
Not stated	85	27	16	14	3	8	2
Cesarean delivery rate [3]	22.7	22.9	30.3	32.3	31.0	32.4	34.5

[1] 1990 excludes data for Oklahoma, which did not report method of delivery on the birth certificate. [2] Includes other races, not shown separately. [3] Percent of all live births by cesarean delivery.

Source: U.S. National Center for Health Statistics, National Vital Statistics Reports (NVSR), *Births: Final Data for 2008*, Vol. 59, No. 1, December 2010, and earlier reports.

Table 88. Induction of Labor by Gestational Age: 1990 to 2008

[In percent. Data are for singleton births]

Gestational age	1990 [1]	1995	2000	2001	2002	2003	2004	2005	2006	2007	2008
All gestations	**9.6**	**16.1**	**20.1**	**20.7**	**20.9**	**20.9**	**21.6**	**22.7**	**23.0**	**23.2**	**23.1**
Under 37 weeks (preterm)	6.9	11.6	14.8	14.7	14.7	14.5	15.1	15.6	15.6	15.6	14.1
Under 32 weeks	5.0	7.8	9.2	8.9	8.8	8.6	8.7	8.9	8.9	9.0	7.8
32–33 weeks	6.4	10.6	13.3	12.8	12.8	12.8	13.0	13.4	13.5	13.5	11.6
34–36 weeks	7.5	12.6	16.2	16.2	16.2	16.0	16.7	17.3	17.2	17.2	16.0
37 weeks and over (term)	9.9	16.7	20.8	21.6	21.8	21.9	22.5	23.7	23.9	24.2	24.3
37–39 weeks	7.9	14.3	18.9	19.6	19.8	19.8	20.6	21.7	22.0	22.1	22.1
40–41 weeks	10.7	18.5	22.9	24.1	24.6	24.8	25.3	26.8	27.4	27.9	28.1
42 weeks and over	14.9	21.3	24.4	24.4	24.3	24.3	25.4	26.2	26.8	26.9	27.3

[1] Oklahoma did not report induction of labor.

Source: U.S. National Center for Health Statistics, "VitalStats," August 2010, <http://www.cdc.gov/nchs/vitalstats.htm>.

Births, Deaths, Marriages, and Divorces 69

Table 89. Percent of Births to Teenage Mothers, Unmarried Women, and Births with Low Birth Weight by State and Island Areas: 2000 to 2009

[In percent. By place of residence. Excludes nonresidents of the United States]

State and Island Area	Births to teenage mothers [1] 2000	2009 [3]	Births to unmarried women 2000	2009 [3]	Births with low birth weight [2] 2000	2009 [3]	State and Island Area	Births to teenage mothers [1] 2000	2009 [3]	Births to unmarried women 2000	2009 [3]	Births with low birth weight [2] 2000	2009 [3]
U.S. [4]	11.8	10.0	33.2	41.0	7.8	8.2	NV	12.7	10.4	36.4	43.5	7.5	8.1
AL	15.7	13.4	34.3	41.0	9.9	10.3	NH	6.8	5.7	24.7	33.4	6.3	6.9
AK	11.8	9.8	33.0	38.0	5.8	5.9	NJ	7.1	5.9	28.9	35.3	8.0	8.3
AZ	14.3	11.9	39.3	45.4	6.8	7.1	NM	17.4	15.5	45.6	53.5	8.0	8.3
AR	17.3	14.6	35.7	45.5	8.6	8.9	NY	8.2	6.7	36.6	41.5	7.9	8.2
CA	10.6	9.2	32.7	40.6	6.4	6.8	NC	13.0	11.3	33.3	42.3	9.0	9.0
CO	11.7	9.1	25.0	24.9	8.9	8.8	ND	9.2	7.4	28.3	32.7	6.3	6.4
CT	7.8	6.8	29.3	37.6	7.8	8.0	OH	12.1	10.8	34.6	44.2	8.3	8.6
DE	12.3	9.5	37.9	47.7	9.9	8.6	OK	15.9	13.8	34.3	42.0	8.0	8.4
DC	14.2	11.7	60.3	55.8	11.6	10.3	OR	11.3	8.7	30.1	35.5	5.8	6.3
FL	12.6	10.1	38.2	47.7	8.4	8.7	PA	9.9	8.9	32.7	41.0	8.2	8.3
GA	13.9	11.7	37.0	45.5	8.9	9.4	RI	10.2	9.3	35.5	44.8	7.9	8.0
HI	10.3	8.3	32.2	37.9	8.3	8.4	SC	15.3	12.8	39.8	47.6	10.0	10.0
ID	11.6	8.6	21.6	25.6	6.1	6.5	SD	11.6	9.2	33.5	38.4	7.2	5.8
IL	11.4	9.6	34.5	40.8	8.2	8.4	TN	14.7	12.8	34.5	44.5	9.2	9.2
IN	12.5	11.1	34.7	43.8	7.6	8.3	TX	15.3	13.3	30.5	42.4	7.7	8.5
IA	10.0	8.7	28.0	35.2	6.6	6.7	UT	8.9	6.3	17.3	19.4	6.4	7.0
KS	12.0	10.3	29.0	37.9	7.0	7.3	VT	8.0	6.5	28.1	39.5	6.4	6.7
KY	14.1	12.7	31.0	41.3	8.6	8.9	VA	9.9	7.9	29.9	35.8	7.9	8.4
LA	17.0	13.1	45.6	53.6	10.4	10.6	WA	10.2	7.8	28.2	33.5	5.9	6.3
ME	9.4	7.8	31.0	40.6	6.3	6.3	WV	15.9	13.5	31.7	43.6	9.0	9.2
MD	9.9	8.3	34.6	42.7	9.0	9.1	WI	10.2	8.3	29.3	37.0	6.6	7.1
MA	6.6	6.0	26.5	34.7	7.5	7.8	WY	13.5	10.4	28.8	34.0	8.4	8.4
MI	10.5	10.1	33.3	41.3	8.0	8.4							
MN	8.3	6.3	25.8	33.5	6.3	6.5	PR	(NA)	18.2	49.7	63.9	11.5	12.4
MS	18.8	16.5	46.0	55.3	11.2	12.2	VI	(NA)	(NA)	66.7	(NA)	11.8	(NA)
MO	13.1	10.9	34.6	40.9	8.0	8.1	GU	(NA)	11.6	54.8	57.9	8.0	7.7
MT	11.6	10.3	30.8	36.3	6.8	7.1	AS	(NA)	9.7	35.5	38.8	3.9	2.7
NE	10.2	8.3	27.2	34.5	7.2	7.1	MP	(NA)	9.5	(NA)	56.8	6.9	8.6

NA Not available. [1] Defined as mothers who are 20 years of age or younger. [2] Less than 2,500 grams (5 pounds–8 ounces). [3] Data are preliminary. [4] Excludes data for the territories.
Source: U.S. National Center for Health Statistics, National Vital Statistics Reports (NVSR), *Births: Preliminary Data for 2009*, Vol. 59, No. 3, December 2010.

Table 90. Women Who had a Child in the Last Year by Living Arrangement, Age, and Educational Attainment: 2010

[In percent except total. (480 represents 480,000). As of June. Based on Current Population Survey. See headnote Table 92]

Living arrangement	Less than high school 15 to 29 years old	30 to 44 years old	High school graduate 15 to 29 years old	30 to 44 years old	Some college 15 to 29 years old	30 to 44 years old	Bachelor's degree or more 15 to 29 years old	30 to 44 years old
Total (1,000)	480	141	723	281	681	336	347	697
PERCENT								
Total	100.0	100.0	100.0	100.0	100.0	100.0	100.0	100.0
Married spouse present	29.7	71.1	40.7	68.2	46.7	81.2	85.0	91.3
Cohabiting	17.8	9.7	19.7	7.2	16.9	6.2	8.0	3.7
Not living with spouse or partner	52.5	19.2	39.6	24.5	36.4	12.7	6.9	5.0

Source: U.S Census Bureau, Current Population Survey, "Fertility of American Women," <http://www.census.gov/population/www/socdemo/fertility.html>.

Table 91. Women Who Had a Child in the Last Year by Age: 1990 to 2010

[3,913 represents 3,913,000. As of June. Based on Current Population Survey. See headnote Table 92]

Age of mother	Women who had a child in last year (1,000) 1990	2000	2010	Total births per 1,000 women 1990	2000	2010	First births per 1,000 women 1990	2000	2010
Total	3,913	3,934	3,686	67.0	64.6	60.0	26.4	26.7	23.9
15 to 29 years old	2,568	2,432	2,231	90.8	85.9	71.4	43.2	43.1	35.1
15 to 19 years old	338	586	301	39.8	59.7	29.3	30.1	38.7	22.3
20 to 24 years old	1,038	850	916	113.4	91.8	87.3	51.8	47.1	44.0
25 to 29 years old	1,192	996	1,014	112.1	107.9	96.6	46.2	43.7	38.6
30 to 44 years old	1,346	1,502	1,454	44.7	46.1	48.1	10.6	12.5	12.3
30 to 34 years old	892	871	820	80.4	87.9	82.7	21.9	27.5	22.7
35 to 39 years old	377	506	503	37.3	45.1	50.7	6.5	9.6	12.7
40 to 44 years old	77	125	131	8.6	10.9	12.6	1.2	2.3	1.9

Source: U.S. Census Bureau, Current Population Reports, P20-555 and earlier reports, and unpublished data.

Table 92. Women Who Had a Child in the Last Year by Selected Characteristics: 1990 to 2010

[58,381 represents 58,381,000. As of June. Covers civilian noninstitutional population. Since the number of women who had a birth during the 12-month period was tabulated and not the actual numbers of births, some small underestimation of fertility for this period may exist due to the omission of: (1) Multiple births, (2) Two or more live births spaced within the 12-month period (the woman is counted only once), (3) Women who had births in the period and who did not survive to the survey date,(4) Women who were in institutions and therefore not in the survey universe. These losses may be somewhat offset by the inclusion in the Current Population Survey (CPS) of births to immigrants who did not have their children born in the United States and births to nonresident women. These births would not have been recorded in the vital registration system. Based on June supplement, Current Population Survey. The 2003 Current Population Survey allowed respondents to choose more than one race. Beginning 2003 data represent persons who selected this race group only and exclude persons reporting more than one race. The Current Population Survey in prior years allowed respondents to report only one race group. See also comments on race in Section 1]

| Characteristic | Total women (1,000) | Percent childless | Women who had a child in the last year | | | |
| | | | Total births | | First births | |
			Number (1,000)	Per 1,000 women	Number (1,000)	Per 1,000 women
1990.	58,381	41.6	3,913	67.0	1,540	26.4
2000.	60,873	42.8	3,934	64.6	1,626	26.7
2010, total [1]	**61,481**	**47.1**	**3,686**	**60.0**	**1,467**	**23.9**
Age:						
15 to 19 years old	10,273	94.6	301	29.3	229	22.3
20 to 24 years old	10,493	70.5	916	87.3	462	44.0
25 to 29 years old	10,501	47.6	1,014	96.6	405	38.6
30 to 34 years old	9,923	29.7	820	82.7	225	22.7
35 to 39 years old	9,917	19.7	503	50.7	126	12.7
40 to 44 years old	10,374	18.8	131	12.6	20	1.9
Race and Hispanic origin:						
White alone	47,186	47.6	2,763	58.6	1,135	24.1
White alone, non-Hispanic	37,271	49.9	2,069	55.5	868	23.3
Black alone	9,035	43.3	574	63.5	186	20.6
Asian alone	3,353	48.8	237	70.6	93	27.6
Hispanic [2]	10,845	39.0	756	69.7	296	27.3
Marital status:						
Married, husband present	25,018	18.6	2,250	89.9	765	30.6
Married, husband absent [3]	2,298	25.4	124	54.1	29	12.4
Widowed or divorced	4,518	21.3	152	33.6	48	10.6
Never married	29,648	76.8	1,160	39.1	625	21.1
Educational attainment:						
Not a high school graduate	12,380	64.1	621	50.2	230	18.6
High school, 4 years	14,763	35.9	1,004	68.0	398	27.0
Some college, no degree	12,463	50.3	667	53.6	291	23.4
Associate's degree	5,498	33.5	349	63.5	139	25.3
Bachelor's degree	11,527	48.0	688	59.7	254	22.0
Graduate or professional degree	4,851	42.7	356	73.3	154	31.7
Labor force status:						
In labor force	41,467	45.8	2,026	48.9	851	20.5
Employed	36,983	45.5	1,771	47.9	748	20.2
Unemployed	4,484	48.7	256	57.0	103	22.9
Not in labor force	20,014	49.7	1,660	82.9	616	30.8
Family income:						
Under $10,000	3,810	40.4	374	98.3	127	33.3
$10,000 to $19,999	5,327	40.3	398	74.7	156	29.3
$20,000 to $24,999	2,879	43.2	179	62.1	50	17.5
$25,000 to $29,999	3,039	45.5	202	66.4	82	26.8
$30,000 to $34,999	3,066	41.8	208	67.9	87	28.5
$35,000 to $49,999	7,336	47.9	403	55.0	171	23.3
$50,000 to $74,999	9,893	49.7	549	55.5	220	22.2
$75,000 and over	15,714	51.1	862	54.8	340	21.6

[1] Includes women of other races and women with family income not reported, not shown separately [2] Persons of Hispanic origin may be any race. [3] Includes separated women.
Source: U.S. Census Bureau, Current Population Reports, P20-555 and unpublished data.

Table 93. Women Who Had a Child in the Last Year by Age and Labor Force Status: 1980 to 2010

[3,913 represents 3,913,000. As of June. Based on Current Population Survey. See headnote, Table 92]

| Year | Total, 15 to 44 years old | | | 15 to 29 years old | | | 30 to 44 years old | | |
| | Number (1,000) | In the labor force | | Number (1,000) | In the labor force | | Number (1,000) | In the labor force | |
		Number (1,000)	Percent		Number (1,000)	Percent		Number (1,000)	Percent
1990	3,913	2,068	53	2,568	1,275	50	1,346	793	59
1995	3,696	2,034	55	2,252	1,150	51	1,444	884	61
2000	3,934	2,170	55	2,432	1,304	54	1,502	866	58
2006	3,974	2,221	56	2,399	1,273	53	1,576	948	60
2008	3,960	2,261	57	2,372	1,299	55	1,587	962	61
2010	3,686	2,026	55	2,231	1,114	50	1,454	912	63

Source: U.S. Bureau of the Census, Current Population Reports, *Fertility of American Women*, P20-563, and earlier reports, and unpublished data. See also <http://www.census.gov/prod/www/abs/p20.html>.

Table 94. Women With Births in the Past 12 Months by Citizenship Status, Educational Attainment, and Poverty Status, by State: 2009

[In percent, except for total. For women 15 to 50 years old. Based on 2009 American Community Survey (ACS). The ACS universe includes the household population and the population living in institutions, college dormitories, and other group quarters. Based on a sample and subject to sampling variability; See Appendix III]

State	Total (number)	Citizenship status		Educational attainment					Below poverty [2]
		Native born	Foreign born [1]	Less than high school graduate	High school graduate (includes equivalency)	Some college or associate's degree	Bachelor's degree	Graduate or professional degree	
United States	**4,333,485**	**79.7**	**20.3**	**17.4**	**24.4**	**30.6**	**17.8**	**9.8**	**26.6**
Alabama	69,364	94.3	5.7	18.6	29.3	32.5	13.4	6.1	33.5
Alaska	13,598	93.0	7.0	9.9	34.1	37.3	11.7	6.9	19.4
Arizona	93,353	76.0	24.0	21.3	24.6	34.3	14.0	5.8	28.6
Arkansas	41,732	92.5	7.5	17.5	29.6	34.2	13.2	5.5	31.8
California	532,289	59.9	40.1	22.4	22.6	29.3	16.6	9.0	24.1
Colorado	72,492	82.6	17.4	17.6	24.4	26.8	19.6	11.6	21.8
Connecticut	40,387	77.4	22.6	11.2	22.2	27.6	22.3	16.7	17.5
Delaware	12,190	87.1	12.9	9.7	30.2	29.3	19.1	11.7	20.8
District of Columbia ..	7,915	78.9	21.1	12.1	27.8	15.8	13.2	31.0	24.4
Florida	231,153	73.4	26.6	16.5	26.5	32.4	15.9	8.8	28.7
Georgia	149,184	82.9	17.1	19.8	24.7	30.7	15.9	8.9	29.6
Hawaii	20,598	79.1	20.9	7.6	24.7	38.9	21.3	7.6	18.3
Idaho	28,738	86.8	13.2	16.7	22.9	39.5	16.4	4.5	23.9
Illinois	185,509	77.9	22.1	16.2	22.8	29.5	18.9	12.6	24.4
Indiana	95,945	91.2	8.8	17.8	27.0	32.5	15.8	7.0	29.4
Iowa	45,083	91.7	8.3	9.4	21.4	39.1	23.2	6.9	25.8
Kansas	47,037	87.3	12.7	16.8	21.9	35.5	18.2	7.6	30.2
Kentucky	62,730	94.2	5.8	16.4	26.1	34.3	14.2	9.0	34.5
Louisiana	67,870	94.0	6.0	19.2	28.5	29.7	15.5	7.1	29.6
Maine	15,826	94.6	5.4	8.3	35.0	28.5	17.2	11.0	25.3
Maryland	84,069	76.6	23.4	13.3	21.3	26.8	22.7	15.9	18.5
Massachusetts.	77,909	75.8	24.2	11.2	20.5	22.7	24.3	21.3	19.5
Michigan	130,553	90.2	9.8	14.1	25.5	34.5	17.3	8.6	29.1
Minnesota	75,041	85.2	14.8	11.1	20.4	34.4	25.3	8.8	20.8
Mississippi	47,571	97.4	2.6	19.9	21.5	40.5	12.7	5.4	37.8
Missouri	82,624	93.0	7.0	17.5	21.3	32.9	17.4	10.8	28.8
Montana	13,406	98.5	1.5	15.8	25.9	26.4	21.9	10.1	33.9
Nebraska	33,017	87.1	12.9	16.9	22.1	29.7	22.6	8.6	28.8
Nevada	35,453	63.5	36.5	23.5	24.5	32.8	13.5	5.7	26.5
New Hampshire	14,079	91.0	9.0	8.3	22.2	26.5	33.2	9.7	17.2
New Jersey	113,145	67.9	32.1	11.7	23.3	24.2	25.7	15.1	18.8
New Mexico	31,643	85.4	14.6	21.8	21.9	40.5	11.4	4.3	34.6
New York	240,633	72.1	27.9	16.1	21.7	25.3	18.8	18.2	24.1
North Carolina	131,909	84.2	15.8	20.8	20.6	31.9	17.7	9.0	31.3
North Dakota	10,941	96.5	3.5	7.2	23.7	39.7	20.8	8.6	28.9
Ohio	152,614	93.9	6.1	15.2	24.5	33.0	17.0	10.3	29.4
Oklahoma	55,175	89.4	10.6	17.3	28.7	31.0	16.2	6.8	28.2
Oregon	47,691	82.7	17.3	19.5	20.5	37.0	12.4	10.6	28.1
Pennsylvania	151,344	89.8	10.2	12.4	27.5	26.4	21.5	12.2	24.7
Rhode Island	10,222	74.2	25.8	10.7	24.3	22.2	26.1	16.7	16.7
South Carolina	66,483	91.0	9.0	17.6	26.6	30.2	18.3	7.4	36.0
South Dakota	11,731	92.8	7.2	12.2	19.4	35.0	25.2	8.3	22.9
Tennessee	103,522	91.1	8.9	15.6	31.3	30.9	15.7	6.4	31.8
Texas	418,903	71.7	28.3	24.4	26.2	28.4	15.0	6.1	30.7
Utah	52,057	90.7	9.3	10.2	22.5	40.5	23.0	3.9	14.0
Vermont	5,642	93.5	6.5	10.2	28.3	26.8	21.1	13.6	27.9
Virginia	106,693	81.6	18.4	13.8	22.3	28.6	20.2	15.1	21.8
Washington	89,077	75.3	24.7	15.1	22.2	33.5	20.8	8.4	21.2
West Virginia	22,406	97.6	2.4	15.7	32.8	32.0	12.6	6.9	35.0
Wisconsin	76,062	90.5	9.5	12.5	25.9	32.8	20.4	8.3	24.2
Wyoming	8,877	92.8	7.2	13.0	21.1	44.5	16.0	5.4	21.9

[1] Foreign born excludes people born outside the United States to a parent who is a U.S. citzen. [2] The population universe used when determining poverty status excludes institutionalized people, people in military group quarters, people in college dormitories, and unrelated individuals under 15 years old.

Source: U.S. Census Bureau, 2009 American Community Survey, B13008, "Women 15 to 50 Years Who Had a Birth in the Past 12 Months by Marital Status and Citizenship"; B13010 "Women 15 to 50 Years Who Had a Birth in the Past 12 Months by Marital Stataus and Poverty Status in the past 12 Months"; and B13014,"Women 15 to 50 Years Who Had a Birth in the Past 12 Months by Marital Stataus and Educational Attainment," <http://factfinder.census.gov/servlet/DatasetMainPageServlet?_program=ACS&_submenuId=&_lang=en&_ts=>.

Table 95. Persons Who Have Ever Had Sexual Contact by Selected Characteristics: 2006 to 2008

[In percent except as indicated (62,199 represents 62,199,000). Based on the National Survey of Family Growth conducted from July 2006 through December 2008. See Appendix III]

Characteristic	Number (1,000)	Number of opposite-sex partners in lifetime							Any same-sex sexual contact [3]
		Any [1]	One	Two	3 to 6	7 to 14	15 or more	Median number [2]	
Males, 15 to 44 years old [4]	**62,199**	**88.8**	**15.0**	**7.6**	**26.5**	**18.1**	**21.4**	**5.1**	**5.2**
15 to 19 years old	10,777	58.0	21.2	9.4	17.6	5.4	3.1	1.8	2.5
20 to 24 years old	10,404	85.7	19.1	8.0	26.1	18.1	14.2	4.1	5.6
25 to 44 years old	41,019	97.7	12.3	7.0	28.9	21.5	27.9	6.1	5.8
25 to 29 years old	10,431	96.2	11.8	8.9	29.5	22.9	23.1	5.7	5.2
30 to 34 years old	9,575	96.9	14.2	6.1	26.6	21.7	28.3	6.4	4.0
35 to 39 years old	10,318	98.7	13.3	5.6	29.7	19.6	30.6	6.2	5.7
40 to 44 years old	10,695	98.8	10.3	7.2	29.7	21.6	30.0	6.4	8.1
Hispanic	11,724	92.0	12.5	10.2	32.6	17.8	19.1	4.6	3.8
Non-Hispanic White	37,374	88.5	16.1	7.3	25.7	18.4	20.9	5.1	6.0
Non-Hispanic Black	7,186	90.7	8.3	5.0	25.6	21.6	30.0	6.9	2.4
Currently married	24,763	100.0	19.1	7.5	30.7	20.7	22.1	4.9	3.5
Currently cohabiting	7,301	100.0	10.3	7.6	24.4	25.9	31.8	7.3	3.2
Never married, not cohabiting	27,012	74.2	14.1	8.2	23.6	12.9	14.9	4.1	7.2
Formerly married, not cohabiting	3,123	100.0	1.4	2.2	23.9	25.1	47.4	11.9	6.4
Females, 15 to 44 years old [4]	**61,865**	**89.0**	**22.2**	**10.7**	**31.6**	**16.0**	**8.3**	**3.2**	**12.5**
15 to 19 years old	10,431	53.0	22.7	8.2	15.7	4.1	1.1	1.4	11.0
20 to 24 years old	10,140	87.7	24.5	12.5	31.6	11.7	7.2	2.6	15.8
25 to 44 years old	41,294	98.4	21.4	10.9	35.6	20.1	10.4	3.6	12.0
25 to 29 years old	10,250	96.6	20.0	12.4	31.0	20.4	12.8	3.6	15.0
30 to 34 years old	9,587	98.1	20.9	10.6	31.9	21.3	13.4	4.2	14.2
35 to 39 years old	10,475	99.1	22.2	9.9	38.3	20.8	7.9	3.5	11.5
40 to 44 years old	10,982	99.7	22.4	10.8	40.5	18.0	8.0	3.4	7.9
Hispanic	10,377	89.5	35.0	16.7	26.6	6.6	4.4	1.6	6.3
Non-Hispanic White	37,660	88.4	19.2	9.7	31.4	18.9	8.9	3.7	14.6
Non-Hispanic Black	8,452	90.2	12.3	8.3	40.9	16.7	11.3	4.4	11.3
Currently married	27,006	100.0	32.2	12.3	34.4	15.0	6.1	2.5	8.3
Currently cohabiting	6,821	100.0	12.8	11.6	37.0	24.9	13.7	4.6	20.5
Never married, not cohabiting	22,847	70.1	16.4	9.1	25.2	11.9	6.9	3.2	13.4
Formerly married, not cohabiting	5,190	100.0	6.8	8.7	37.7	28.0	18.8	5.3	19.6

[1] Includes vaginal, oral, or anal sex. [2] Excludes those who have never had sexual intercourse with a person of the opposite sex. For definition of median, see Guide to Tabular Presentation. [3] For females includes oral sex or any sexual experience. For males includes oral or anal sex with male partners. [4] Includes person of other or multiple race and origin groups, not shown separately.

Source: U.S. National Center for Health Statistics, National Health Statistics Report, No.36, "Sexual Behavior, Sexual Attraction, and Sexual Identity in the United States: Data From the 2006–2008 National Survey of Family Growth," March 2011. See also <http://www.cdc.gov/nchs/nsfg/nsfg_products.htm>.

Table 96. Number and Type of Sexual Partners in the Past 12 Months: 2006 to 2008

[In percent except as indicated (62,199 represents 62,199,000). Based on the National Survey of Family Growth conducted from July 2006 through December 2008. See Appendix III]

Sex and age	Number (1,000)	Sexual partners in last 12 months [1]				
		No partner in last month	Any same-sex partners	One opposite-sex partner, but no same-sex partners	Two or more opposite-sex partners, but no same sex-partners	Did not report
Males 15 to 44 years old	**62,199**	**16.0**	**4.3**	**60.2**	**17.6**	**2.0**
15 to 19 years old	10,777	48.9	1.5	25.1	21.2	3.3
20 to 24 years old	10,404	18.3	4.6	48.0	27.2	1.9
25 to 44 years old	41,019	6.8	4.9	72.4	14.2	1.7
25 to 29 years old	10,431	7.6	4.8	65.7	20.3	1.6
30 to 34 years old	9,575	6.6	3.6	75.3	13.0	1.4
35 to 39 years old	10,318	5.1	5.0	73.7	14.2	2.0
40 to 44 years old	10,695	7.7	6.2	75.2	9.3	1.6
Females 15 to 44 years old	**61,865**	**15.9**	**11.7**	**61.3**	**9.4**	**1.7**
15 to 19 years old	10,431	51.3	9.5	24.2	13.5	1.6
20 to 24 years old	10,140	15.8	15.2	49.5	17.7	1.8
25 to 44 years old	41,294	7.0	11.4	73.6	6.3	1.8
25 to 29 years old	10,250	7.6	14.3	65.1	10.6	2.4
30 to 34 years old	9,587	5.2	13.6	73.8	6.0	1.5
35 to 39 years old	10,475	6.8	10.8	76.2	4.2	2.0
40 to 44 years old	10,982	8.3	7.1	79.0	4.5	1.1

[1] Includes vaginal, oral, or anal sex.

Source: U.S. National Center for Health Statistics, National Health Statistics Report, No.36, "Sexual Behavior, Sexual Attraction, and Sexual Identity in the United States: Data From the 2006–2008 National Survey of Family Growth," March 2011. See also <http://www.cdc.gov/nchs/nsfg/nsfg_products.htm>.

Births, Deaths, Marriages, and Divorces   73

Table 97. Sexual Identity Among Men and Women: 2006 to 2008

[In percent except as indicated (55,556 represents 55,556,000). For men and women 18 to 44 years of age. Based on the National Survey of Family Growth conducted from July 2006 through December 2008. See Appendix III]

Characteristic	Number (1,000)	Sexual identity Heterosexual or straight	Homosexual or gay	Bisexual	Something else	Did not report
Males, 18 to 44 years old [1]	**55,556**	**95.7**	**1.7**	**1.1**	**0.2**	**1.3**
18 to 19 years old	4,134	96.6	1.6	1.1	(S)	0.6
20 to 24 years old	10,404	95.1	1.2	2.0	0.4	1.3
25 to 29 years old	10,431	96.3	1.7	0.8	0.5	0.8
30 to 34 years old	9,575	96.2	1.5	0.6	(S)	1.8
35 to 44 years old	21,013	95.2	2.1	1.0	0.2	1.5
Hispanic	10,618	93.4	1.2	0.9	0.6	3.9
Non-Hispanic White..........	33,573	96.6	1.8	1.1	0.1	0.4
Non-Hispanic Black...........	6,208	97.8	1.2	(S)	(S)	0.4
Females, 18 to 44 years old [1]	**56,032**	**93.7**	**1.1**	**3.5**	**0.6**	**1.1**
18 to 19 years old	4,598	90.1	1.9	5.8	(S)	(S)
20 to 24 years old	10,140	90.4	1.3	6.3	0.9	1.2
25 to 29 years old	10,250	91.9	1.2	5.4	0.6	0.9
30 to 34 years old	9,587	94.4	1.1	2.9	0.8	1.0
35 to 44 years old	21,457	96.6	0.7	1.1	0.2	1.3
Hispanic	9,272	92.1	0.9	2.2	0.7	4.1
Non-Hispanic White..........	34,410	94.2	0.9	4.1	0.5	0.4
Non-Hispanic Black...........	7,520	93.3	1.6	3.0	1.5	0.7

S Figure does not meet publication standards [1] Includes person of other or multiple race and origin groups, not shown separately.

Source: U.S. National Center for Health Statistics, National Health Statistics Report, No.36, "Sexual Behavior, Sexual Attraction, and Sexual Identity in the United States: Data From the 2006–2008 National Survey of Family Growth," March 2011. See also <http://www.cdc.gov/nchs/nsfg/nsfg_products.htm>.

Table 98. Current Contraceptive Use by Women by Age, Race, Hispanic Origin, Marital, and Cohabitation Status: 2006 to 2008

[61,864 represents 61,864,000. Based on the National Survey of Family Growth conducted from July 2006 through December 2008. Contraceptive use reported by women 15–44 years of age during heterosexual vaginal intercourse. Women using more than one method of contraception are classified by most effective method reported]

Contraceptive status and method	Unit	All women [1]	Race/ethnicity White only, Non-His-panic	Black only, Non-His-panic	His-panic [2]	Marital and cohabitation status Never mar-ried, not cohab-iting	Cur-rently mar-ried	For-merly mar-ried, not cohab-iting	Cur-rently cohab-iting
All women........................	(1,000)...	**61,864**	**37,660**	**8,452**	**10,377**	**22,847**	**27,006**	**5,190**	**6,821**
PERCENT DISTRIBUTION									
Using contraception (contraceptors) [3]	Percent ..	61.8	64.7	54.5	58.5	39.3	78.6	60.6	71.2
Female sterilization	Percent ..	16.7	14.9	21.8	19.6	4.5	23.6	35.3	16.3
Male sterilization	Percent ..	6.1	8.3	1.1	3.4	0.3	12.7	2.3	2.2
Pill	Percent ..	17.3	21.2	11.4	11.4	18.1	16.3	11.4	23.2
Implant, Lunelle™	Percent ..	0.7	0.5	0.6	1.5	0.6	0.7	(S)	1.0
3-month injectable (Depo-Provera™)	Percent ..	2.0	1.4	4.1	2.6	2.2	1.4	2.6	3.1
Intrauterine device (IUD)	Percent ..	1.5	1.6	1.7	1.2	1.5	1.0	0.8	3.7
Diaphragm.............................	Percent ..	3.4	3.3	2.8	4.8	1.1	5.3	2.1	4.7
Condom................................	Percent ..	10.0	9.5	8.8	9.4	9.1	11.7	4.1	10.2
Periodic abstinence-calendar rhythm	Percent ..	0.5	0.5	(S)	0.6	0.2	1.0	(S)	0.4
Periodic abstinence-natural family planning ...	Percent ..	0.1	(S)	(S)	(S)	(S)	0.2	(S)	(S)
Withdrawal.............................	Percent ..	3.2	3.3	2.1	3.0	1.5	4.5	1.4	5.3
Other methods [3].	Percent ..	0.3	0.3	(S)	0.5	0.2	0.3	(S)	(S)
Not using contraception....................	Percent ..	38.2	35.3	45.5	41.5	60.7	21.4	39.4	28.8
Surgically sterile-female (noncontraceptive) ...	Percent ..	0.4	0.2	0.4	0.7	0.4	0.3	1.0	(S)
Nonsurgically sterile-female or male [4]........	Percent ..	1.7	1.6	1.8	1.8	2.1	1.0	2.7	2.2
Pregnant or postpartum...................	Percent ..	5.4	4.9	5.7	8.3	2.6	7.2	2.6	10.5
Seeking pregnancy	Percent ..	4.1	3.5	4.4	6.2	1.3	6.4	0.8	7.1
Other nonuse:									
Never had intercourse or no intercourse in 3 months before interview	Percent ..	19.2	18.3	22.6	18.8	45.6	0.9	21.1	1.8
Had intercourse in 3 months before interview ..	Percent ..	7.3	6.7	10.6	5.8	8.7	5.5	11.3	6.9

S Figure does not meet publication standards. [1] Includes other races not shown separately. [2] Persons of Hispanic origin may be any race. [3] Includes diaphragm, emergency contraception, female condom or vaginal pouch, foam, cervical cap, Today™ sponge, suppository or insert, jelly or cream, and other methods. [4] Persons sterile from illness, accident, or congenital conditions.

Source: U.S. National Center for Health Statistics, National Survey of Family Growth, "Use of Contraception in the United States: 1982–2008," Series 23, No. 29, May 2010. See also <http://cdc.gov/nchs/nsfg/>.

Table 99. Infants Who Were Ever Breastfed by Maternal Age and Race-Ethnicity: 1999 to 2006

[In percent. Covers period from 1999 through 2006. Breastfeeding was defined as ever having been breastfed or received breast milk. Based on data from National Health and Nutrition Examination Surveys (NHANES)]

Race and ethnicity	Under 20 years old	20 to 29 years old	30 years old and older
Total......................	43	65	75
Non-Hispanic White...........	40	65	77
Non-Hispanic Black...........	30	44	56
Mexican American............	66	75	76

Source: U.S. National Center for Health Statistics, Breastfeeding in the United States Findings from the National Health and Nutrition Examination Surveys: 1999–2006, NCHS Data Brief, No. 5, April 2008. See <http://www.cdc.gov/nchs/data/databriefs/db05.htm\>

Table 100. Outcomes of Assisted Reproductive Technology (ART) by Procedures: 2000 to 2006

[In 1996, Centers for Disease Control (CDC) initiated data collection regarding Assisted Reproductive Technology (ART) procedures performed in the United States, as mandated by the Fertility Clinic Success Rate and Certification Act. ARTs include those infertility treatments in which both eggs and sperm are handled in the laboratory for the purpose of establishing a pregnancy (i.e., in vitro fertilization and related procedures)]

Year	Procedures started [1]	Number of pregnancies	Live birth deliveries [2]	Live born infants
2000.................	99,629	30,557	25,228	35,025
2001.................	107,587	35,726	29,344	40,687
2002.................	115,392	40,046	33,141	45,751
2003.................	122,872	43,503	35,785	48,756
2004.................	127,977	44,774	36,760	49,458
2005.................	134,260	47,651	38,910	52,041
2006.................	138,198	50,571	41,343	54,656

[1] Excludes procedures for which new treatments were being evaluated [2] A live-birth delivery is defined as the delivery of one or more live born infants.

Source: U.S. Centers for Disease Control and Prevention, Morbidity and Mortality Weekly Report (MMWR) Surveillance Summary Reports, Assisted Reproductive Technology Surveillance—United States, 2006, Vol. 58, No. SS-5, June 2009. See also <http://www.cdc.gov/mmwr/preview/mmwrhtml/ss5805a1.htm\>.

Table 101. Abortions—Number and Rate by Race: 1990 to 2007

[58,700 represents 58,700,000]

Year	All races			White			Black			Other		
	Women 15 to 44 years old (1,000)	Abortions		Women 15 to 44 years old (1,000)	Abortions		Women 15 to 44 years old (1,000)	Abortions		Women 15 to 44 years old (1,000)	Abortions	
		Number (1,000)	Rate per 1,000 women [1]		Number (1,000)	Rate per 1,000 women [1]		Number (1,000)	Rate per 1,000 women [1]		Number (1,000)	Rate per 1,000 women [1]
1990 [2]	58,700	1,609	27.4	48,224	1,039	21.5	7,905	505	63.9	2,571	65	25.1
1991......	59,305	1,557	26.2	48,560	982	20.2	8,053	507	62.9	2,692	68	26.2
1992......	59,417	1,529	25.7	48,435	943	19.5	8,170	517	63.3	2,812	69	24.4
1993 [2]	59,712	1,495	25.0	48,497	908	18.7	8,282	517	62.4	2,933	70	23.9
1994 [2]	60,020	1,423	23.7	48,592	856	17.6	8,390	492	58.6	3,039	76	23.7
1995......	60,368	1,359	22.5	48,719	817	16.8	8,496	462	54.4	3,153	80	25.3
1996......	60,704	1,360	22.4	48,837	797	16.3	8,592	483	56.2	3,275	81	24.6
1997 [2]	61,041	1,335	21.9	48,942	777	15.9	8,694	479	55.1	3,405	79	23.1
1998 [2]	61,326	1,319	21.5	49,012	762	15.5	8,785	476	54.2	3,528	81	23.1
1999......	61,475	1,315	21.4	48,974	743	15.2	8,851	485	54.8	3,650	87	24.0
2000......	61,631	1,313	21.3	48,936	733	15.0	8,907	488	54.8	3,788	92	24.4
2001 [2]	61,673	1,291	20.9	48,868	717	14.7	8,962	476	53.1	3,843	99	25.7
2002 [2]	62,044	1,269	20.5	48,998	706	14.4	9,026	468	51.8	4,020	96	23.8
2003 [2]	61,911	1,250	20.2	48,782	695	14.2	9,054	458	50.6	4,075	97	23.8
2004......	62,033	1,222	19.7	48,758	674	13.8	9,116	453	49.7	4,160	95	22.9
2005......	62,074	1,206	19.4	48,678	662	13.6	9,177	452	49.3	4,219	92	21.9
2006 [2]	62,258	1,242	19.9	48,686	681	14.0	9,248	464	50.2	4,325	97	22.3
2007......	62,097	1,210	19.5	48,480	668	13.8	9,288	448	48.2	4,329	93	21.6

[1] Aged 15–44. [2] Total numbers of abortions have been estimated by interpolation.

Source: R.K. Jones and K. Kooistra, "Abortion Incidence and Access to Services in the United States, 2008," Perspectives on Sexual and Reproductive Health, 2011, 43(1):41-50, and unpublished data from Guttmacher Institute.

Births, Deaths, Marriages, and Divorces 75

Table 102. Abortions by Selected Characteristics: 1990 to 2007

[1,609 represents 1,609,000. Number of abortions from surveys conducted by source; characteristics from the U.S. Centers for Disease Control's (CDC) annual abortion surveillance summaries, with adjustments for changes in states reporting data to the Centers for Disease Control each year]

Characteristic	Number (1,000)			Percent distribution			Abortion rate per 1,000 women		
	1990	2000	2007	1990	2000	2007	1990	2000	2007
Total abortions................	1,609	1,313	1,210	100.0	100.0	100.0	27.4	21.3	19.5
Age of woman:									
Less than 15 years [1].............	13	9	6	0.8	0.7	0.5	7.9	4.4	3.1
15 to 19 years..................	351	235	196	21.8	17.9	16.2	40.6	24.0	18.7
20 to 24 years..................	532	430	395	33.1	32.7	32.6	56.7	45.9	38.8
25 to 29 years..................	360	303	295	22.4	23.0	24.4	34.0	31.8	28.7
30 to 34 years..................	216	190	174	13.4	14.5	14.4	19.7	18.6	18.1
35 to 39 years..................	108	110	106	6.7	8.4	8.8	10.7	9.7	10.1
40 years and over [2]..............	29	37	37	1.8	2.8	3.1	3.2	3.2	3.4
Hispanic......................	195	261	270	12.1	19.8	22.3	35.1	30.3	26.0
Non-Hispanic White.............	852	479	398	52.9	36.5	34.2	19.7	11.7	10.6
Marital status of woman: [3]									
Married	341	246	197	21.0	19.0	16.3	10.6	7.9	6.7
Unmarried	1,268	1,067	1,013	79.0	81.0	83.7	47.7	34.9	31.2
Number of prior live births:									
None	780	533	495	49.0	41.0	40.9	32.0	20.2	(NA)
One	396	361	328	25.0	28.0	27.1	36.9	32.5	(NA)
Two	280	260	231	17.0	20.0	19.1	20.5	18.9	(NA)
Three	102	104	101	6.0	8.0	8.3	15.6	14.8	(NA)
Four or more	50	56	55	3.0	4.0	4.6	14.7	16.5	(NA)
Number of prior induced abortions:									
None	891	699	652	55.0	53.0	53.9	(NA)	(NA)	(NA)
One	443	355	317	28.0	27.0	26.2	(NA)	(NA)	(NA)
Two or more..................	275	259	241	17.0	20.0	19.9	(NA)	(NA)	(NA)
Weeks of gestation:									
Less than 9 weeks...............	825	749	740	51.3	57.1	61.2	(NA)	(NA)	(NA)
9 to 10 weeks	416	269	212	25.8	20.5	17.5	(NA)	(NA)	(NA)
11 to 12 weeks	195	138	119	12.1	10.5	9.9	(NA)	(NA)	(NA)
13 weeks or more	173	156	138	10.8	11.9	11.4	(NA)	(NA)	(NA)

NA Not available. [1] Denominator of rate is women aged 14. [2] Denominator of rate is women aged 40–44. [3] Separated women are included with married.

Source: R.K. Jones and K. Kooistra, "Abortion Incidence and Access to Services in the United States, 2008," *Perspectives on Sexual and Reproductive Health*, 2011, 430(1):41-50; S.K. Henshaw and K. Kost, *Trends in the Characteristics of Women Obtaining Abortions*, 1974–2004, New York: Guttmacher Institute, 2008; and unpublished data from the Guttmacher Institute.

Table 103. Abortions—Number and Rate by State of Occurrence: 2000 to 2008

[Number of abortions by state of occurrence from surveys of hospitals, clinics, and physicians identified as providers of abortion services conducted by the Guttmacher Institute]

State	State of occurrence						State	State of occurrence					
	Number			Rate [1]				Number			Rate [1]		
	2000	2005	2008	2000	2005	2008		2000	2005	2008	2000	2005	2008
U.S....	1,312,990	1,206,200	1,211,500	21.3	19.4	19.6	MO...	7,920	8,400	7,440	6.6	7.0	6.3
AL	13,830	11,340	11,270	14.2	12.1	12.0	MT ...	2,510	2,150	2,230	13.5	11.9	12.3
AK	1,660	1,880	1,700	11.7	13.2	12.0	NE ...	4,250	3,220	2,840	11.6	9.1	8.1
AZ	17,940	19,480	19,500	16.5	16.1	15.2	NV ...	13,740	13,530	13,450	32.4	27.7	25.9
AR	5,540	4,710	4,890	9.8	8.4	8.7	NH ...	3,010	3,170	3,200	11.2	11.8	12.3
CA	236,060	208,430	214,190	31.2	26.9	27.6	NJ ...	65,780	61,150	54,160	36.3	34.5	31.3
CO....	15,530	16,120	15,960	16.0	16.2	15.7	NM ...	5,760	6,220	6,150	14.7	15.7	15.5
CT	15,240	16,780	17,030	21.1	23.8	24.6	NY ...	164,630	155,960	153,110	39.1	37.7	37.6
DE	5,440	5,150	7,070	31.3	29.2	40.0	NC ...	37,610	34,500	33,140	21.1	18.9	17.5
DC....	9,800	7,230	4,450	68.2	50.0	29.9	ND ...	1,340	1,230	1,400	9.9	9.6	11.2
FL	103,050	92,300	94,360	32.0	26.7	27.2	OH ...	40,230	35,060	33,550	16.5	14.9	14.7
GA....	32,140	33,180	39,820	16.9	16.6	19.2	OK ...	7,390	6,950	7,160	10.1	9.7	9.9
HI.....	5,630	5,350	5,630	22.2	21.3	22.6	OR ...	17,010	13,200	12,920	23.6	18.1	17.3
ID.....	1,950	1,810	1,800	7.0	6.2	6.0	PA ...	36,570	34,150	41,000	14.3	13.9	17.0
IL	63,690	50,970	54,920	23.2	18.9	20.5	RI	5,600	5,290	5,000	24.1	23.3	22.9
IN.....	12,490	11,150	10,680	9.4	8.6	8.3	SC ...	8,210	7,080	7,300	9.3	8.0	8.1
IA.....	5,970	6,370	6,560	9.8	10.9	11.3	SD ...	870	790	850	5.5	5.1	5.6
KS	12,270	10,700	10,620	21.4	19.2	19.2	TN ...	19,010	18,140	19,550	15.2	14.5	15.5
KY	4,700	3,870	4,430	5.3	4.5	5.1	TX ...	89,160	85,760	84,610	18.8	17.4	16.5
LA	13,100	11,400	14,860	13.0	11.8	16.1	UT ...	3,510	3,630	4,000	6.7	6.4	6.7
ME	2,650	2,770	2,800	9.9	10.7	11.2	VT ...	1,660	1,490	1,510	12.7	11.9	12.5
MD....	34,560	37,590	34,290	29.0	31.3	29.0	VA ...	28,780	26,520	28,520	18.1	16.4	17.6
MA....	30,410	27,270	24,900	21.4	19.8	18.3	WA...	26,200	23,260	24,320	20.3	17.8	18.3
MI.....	46,470	40,600	36,790	21.6	19.5	18.4	WV...	2,540	2,360	2,280	6.8	6.7	6.6
MN....	14,610	13,910	13,060	13.5	13.1	12.5	WI ...	11,130	9,800	8,230	9.6	8.6	7.4
MS....	3,780	3,090	2,770	6.0	5.0	4.6	WY ...	100	70	90	1.0	0.7	0.9

[1] Rate per 1,000 women, 15 to 44 years old on July 1 of specified year.

Source: R.K. Jones et al., *Abortion in the United States: Incidence and Access to Services, 2005, Perspectives on Sexual and Reproductive Health 40:6, 2008*; R.K. Jones and K. Kooistra, *Abortion Incidence and Access to Services in the United States, 2008, Perspectives on Sexual and Reproductive Health 43:1, 2011*; and unpublished data. See also <http://www.guttmacher.org/>.

Table 104. Expectation of Life at Birth, 1970 to 2008, and Projections, 2010 to 2020

[In years. Excludes deaths of nonresidents of the United States. See Appendix III]

Year	Total			White			Black		
	Total	Male	Female	Total	Male	Female	Total	Male	Female
1970............	70.8	67.1	74.7	71.7	68.0	75.6	64.1	60.0	68.3
1980..........	73.7	70.0	77.4	74.4	70.7	78.1	68.1	63.8	72.5
1981..........	74.1	70.4	77.8	74.8	71.1	78.4	68.9	64.5	73.2
1982..........	74.5	70.8	78.1	75.1	71.5	78.7	69.4	65.1	73.6
1983..........	74.6	71.0	78.1	75.2	71.6	78.7	69.4	65.2	73.5
1984..........	74.7	71.1	78.2	75.3	71.8	78.7	69.5	65.3	73.6
1985..........	74.7	71.1	78.2	75.3	71.8	78.7	69.3	65.0	73.4
1986..........	74.7	71.2	78.2	75.4	71.9	78.8	69.1	64.8	73.4
1987..........	74.9	71.4	78.3	75.6	72.1	78.9	69.1	64.7	73.4
1988..........	74.9	71.4	78.3	75.6	72.2	78.9	68.9	64.4	73.2
1989..........	75.1	71.7	78.5	75.9	72.5	79.2	68.8	64.3	73.3
1990..........	75.4	71.8	78.8	76.1	72.7	79.4	69.1	64.5	73.6
1991..........	75.5	72.0	78.9	76.3	72.9	79.6	69.3	64.6	73.8
1992..........	75.8	72.3	79.1	76.5	73.2	79.8	69.6	65.0	73.9
1993..........	75.5	72.2	78.8	76.3	73.1	79.5	69.2	64.6	73.7
1994..........	75.7	72.4	79.0	76.5	73.3	79.6	69.5	64.9	73.9
1995..........	75.8	72.5	78.9	76.5	73.4	79.6	69.6	65.2	73.9
1996..........	76.1	73.1	79.1	76.8	73.9	79.7	70.2	66.1	74.2
1997..........	76.5	73.6	79.4	77.2	74.3	79.9	71.1	67.2	74.7
1998..........	76.7	73.8	79.5	77.3	74.5	80.0	71.3	67.6	74.8
1999..........	76.7	73.9	79.4	77.3	74.6	79.9	71.4	67.8	74.7
2000 [1]	76.8	74.1	79.3	77.3	74.7	79.9	71.8	68.2	75.1
2001 [1]	76.9	74.2	79.4	77.4	74.8	79.9	72.0	68.4	75.2
2002 [1]	76.9	74.3	79.5	77.4	74.9	79.9	72.1	68.6	75.4
2003 [1,2]	77.1	74.5	79.6	77.6	75.0	80.0	72.3	68.8	75.6
2004 [1,2]	77.5	74.9	79.9	77.9	75.4	80.4	72.8	69.3	76.0
2005 [1,2]	77.4	74.9	79.9	77.9	75.4	80.4	72.8	69.3	76.1
2006 [1,2]	77.7	75.1	80.2	78.2	75.7	80.6	73.2	69.7	76.5
2007 [1,2]	77.9	75.4	80.4	78.4	75.9	80.8	73.6	70.0	76.8
2008 [1,2,3]	78.0	75.5	80.5	78.4	75.9	80.8	74.3	70.9	77.4
Projections: [4]									
2010..........	78.3	75.7	80.8	78.9	76.5	81.3	73.8	70.2	77.2
2015..........	78.9	76.4	81.4	79.5	77.1	81.8	75.0	71.4	78.2
2020..........	79.5	77.1	81.9	80.0	77.7	82.4	76.1	72.6	79.2

[1] Life expectancies for 2000–2008 were calculated using a revised methodology and may differ from those previously published. [2] Multiple-race data were bridged to the single-race categories of the 1977 OMB standards for comparability with other reporting areas. [3] Data are preliminary. [4] Based on middle mortality assumptions; for details, see source: U.S. Census Bureau, "2008 National Population Projections," released August, 2008, <http://www.census.gov/population/www/projections/2008projections.html>.

Source: Except as noted. U.S. National Center for Health Statistics, National Vital Statistics Reports (NVSR), *Deaths: Preliminary Data for 2008*, Vol. 59, No. 2, December 2010.

Table 105. Life Expectancy by Sex, Age, and Race: 2008

[Average number of years of life remaining. Excludes deaths of nonresidents of the United States. Data are preliminary]

Age	Total [1]			White			Black		
	Total	Male	Female	Total	Male	Female	Total	Male	Female
0.............	78.0	75.5	80.5	78.4	75.9	80.8	74.3	70.9	77.4
1.............	77.6	75.1	80.0	77.8	75.4	80.2	74.3	71.0	77.4
5.............	73.7	71.2	76.1	73.9	71.5	76.3	70.5	67.1	73.5
10.............	68.7	66.2	71.1	68.9	66.5	71.3	65.5	62.2	68.5
15.............	63.8	61.3	66.1	64.0	61.6	66.3	60.6	57.2	63.6
20.............	58.9	56.5	61.2	59.2	56.8	61.4	55.8	52.6	58.7
25.............	54.2	51.9	56.4	54.4	52.2	56.6	51.1	48.0	53.9
30.............	49.4	47.2	51.5	49.6	47.5	51.7	46.5	43.5	49.1
35.............	44.7	42.6	46.7	44.9	42.8	46.9	41.8	39.0	44.3
40.............	40.0	37.9	41.9	40.2	38.1	42.1	37.3	34.5	39.6
45.............	35.4	33.4	37.2	35.6	33.6	37.4	32.8	30.1	35.1
50.............	31.0	29.0	32.7	31.1	29.2	32.8	28.6	26.0	30.8
55.............	26.7	24.9	28.3	26.8	25.0	28.3	24.6	22.2	26.7
60.............	22.6	20.9	24.0	22.6	21.0	24.0	20.9	18.7	22.7
65.............	18.7	17.2	19.9	18.7	17.3	19.9	17.5	15.5	18.9
70.............	15.0	13.7	16.0	15.0	13.7	16.0	14.3	12.6	15.4
75.............	11.7	10.6	12.5	11.6	10.6	12.4	11.3	10.0	12.2
80.............	8.8	7.9	9.4	8.8	7.9	9.3	8.8	7.8	9.5
85.............	6.5	5.8	6.8	6.4	5.7	6.8	6.8	6.0	7.1
90.............	4.6	4.1	4.8	4.5	4.1	4.8	5.1	4.6	5.3
95.............	3.2	2.9	3.3	3.2	2.9	3.3	3.8	3.5	3.8
100.............	2.3	2.1	2.3	2.2	2.0	2.2	2.8	2.6	2.8

[1] Includes races other than White and Black.

Source: U.S. National Center for Health Statistics, National Vital Statistics Reports (NVSR), *Deaths: Preliminary Data for 2008*, Vol. 59, No. 2, December 2010.

Table 106. Selected Life Table Values: 1959 to 2008

[Decennial life tables are based on population data from a decennial census and reported deaths of the 3-year period surrounding the census year; the census year is the middle year. The annual tables are based on deaths in a single year, and except for census years, on postcensal population estimates. Beginning in 1970, data excludes deaths of nonresidents of the United States. See Appendix III]

Age and sex	All races						White						Black [1]					
	1959–1961	1969–1971	1979–1981	1989–1991	1999–2001	2008	1959–1961	1969–1971	1979–1981	1989–1991	1999–2001	2008	1959–1961	1969–1971	1979–1981	1989–1991	1999–2001	2008
EXPECTATION OF LIFE IN YEARS																		
At birth: Male	66.8	67.0	70.1	71.8	74.1	75.5	67.6	67.9	70.8	72.7	74.7	75.9	61.5	60.0	64.1	64.5	68.1	70.9
Female	73.2	74.6	77.6	78.8	79.5	80.5	74.2	75.5	78.2	79.5	80.0	80.8	66.5	68.3	72.9	73.7	75.1	77.4
Age 20: Male	49.8	49.5	51.9	53.3	55.2	56.5	50.3	50.2	52.5	54.0	55.7	56.8	45.8	43.5	46.5	46.7	49.8	52.6
Female	55.6	56.6	59.0	59.9	60.3	61.2	56.3	57.2	59.4	60.4	60.7	61.4	50.8	51.2	54.9	55.5	56.5	58.7
Age 40: Male	31.4	31.5	33.6	35.1	36.6	37.9	31.7	31.9	34.0	35.6	37.0	38.1	28.7	27.6	29.5	30.1	32.1	34.5
Female	36.6	37.6	39.8	40.7	41.0	41.9	37.1	38.1	40.2	41.0	41.3	42.1	32.2	33.3	36.3	37.0	37.7	39.6
Age 50: Male	23.0	23.1	25.0	26.4	27.8	29.0	23.2	23.3	25.3	26.7	28.1	29.2	21.3	20.7	22.0	22.5	24.1	26.0
Female	27.7	28.8	30.7	31.4	31.7	32.7	28.1	29.1	31.0	31.7	32.0	32.8	24.3	25.5	27.8	28.4	29.0	30.8
Age 65: Male	13.0	13.0	14.2	15.1	16.1	17.2	13.0	13.0	14.3	15.2	16.2	17.3	12.8	12.5	13.3	13.3	14.1	15.5
Female	15.8	16.8	18.4	19.0	19.1	19.9	15.9	16.9	18.6	19.1	19.2	19.9	15.1	15.7	17.1	17.4	17.7	18.9
NUMBER OF SURVIVORS OUT OF 1,000 BORN ALIVE [2]																		
At birth: Male	1,000	1,000	1,000	1,000	1,000	1,000	1,000	1,000	1,000	1,000	1,000	1,000	1,000	1,000	1,000	1,000	1,000	1,000
Female	1,000	1,000	1,000	1,000	1,000	1,000	1,000	1,000	1,000	1,000	1,000	1,000	1,000	1,000	1,000	1,000	1,000	1,000
Age 20: Male	955	961	973	979	984	986	959	965	975	981	986	987	931	941	961	963	973	980
Female	968	973	982	986	989	990	971	976	984	988	990	991	947	957	972	976	981	976
Age 40: Male	916	915	933	938	954	957	924	926	940	946	959	960	857	834	885	879	919	948
Female	946	951	965	970	975	977	953	958	969	975	978	979	897	908	941	944	956	933
Age 50: Male	862	861	890	899	918	925	874	877	901	911	926	929	772	733	801	800	856	910
Female	913	919	941	949	954	956	925	929	947	956	960	959	830	842	896	903	917	887
Age 65: Male	642	643	706	740	781	800	658	663	724	760	795	809	514	475	551	568	646	762
Female	785	797	835	851	864	876	807	816	848	863	874	883	608	647	733	750	778	703
PERCENT SURVIVING OUT OF 1,000 BORN ALIVE																		
At birth: Male	100.0	100.0	100.0	100.0	100.0	100.0	100.0	100.0	100.0	100.0	100.0	100.0	100.0	100.0	100.0	100.0	100.0	100.0
Female	100.0	100.0	100.0	100.0	100.0	100.0	100.0	100.0	100.0	100.0	100.0	100.0	100.0	100.0	100.0	100.0	100.0	100.0
Age 20: Male	95.5	96.1	97.3	97.9	98.4	98.6	95.9	96.5	97.5	98.1	98.6	98.7	93.1	94.1	96.1	96.3	97.3	98.0
Female	96.8	97.3	98.2	98.6	98.9	99.0	97.1	97.6	98.4	98.8	99.0	99.1	94.7	95.7	97.2	97.6	98.1	97.6
Age 40: Male	91.6	91.5	93.3	93.8	95.4	95.7	92.4	92.6	94.0	94.6	95.9	96.0	85.7	83.4	88.5	87.9	91.9	94.8
Female	94.6	95.1	96.5	97.0	97.5	97.7	95.3	95.8	96.9	97.5	97.8	97.9	89.7	90.8	94.1	94.4	95.6	93.3
Age 50: Male	86.2	86.1	89.0	89.9	91.8	92.5	87.4	87.7	90.1	91.1	92.6	92.9	77.2	73.3	80.1	80.0	85.6	91.0
Female	91.3	91.9	94.1	94.9	95.4	95.6	92.5	92.9	94.7	95.6	96.0	95.9	83.0	84.2	89.6	90.3	91.7	88.7
Age 65: Male	64.2	64.3	70.6	74.0	78.1	80.0	65.8	66.3	72.4	76.0	79.5	80.9	51.4	47.5	55.1	56.8	64.6	76.2
Female	78.5	79.7	83.5	85.1	86.4	87.6	80.7	81.6	84.8	86.3	87.4	88.3	60.8	64.7	73.3	75.0	77.8	70.3

[1] Prior to 1970, data for the Black population are not available. Data shown for 1959–1970 are for the Non-White population. [2] The number of persons from the original synthetic cohort of 1,000 live births, who survive the beginning of each age interval.

Source: U.S. National Center for Health Statistics, National Vital Statistics Reports (NVSR), "U.S. Decennial Life Tables for 1999–2001," United States Life Tables, Vol. 57, No. 1, August 2008; United States Life Tables, 2006, Vol. 58, No.21, June 2010, and unpublished data, <http://www.cdc.gov/nchs/products/nvsr.htm>.

Table 107. Expectation of Life and Expected Deaths by Race, Sex, and Age: 2008

[Life expectancies were calculated using a revised methodology and may differ from those previously published. The methodology uses vital statistics death rates for ages under 66 and modeled probabilities of death for ages 66 to 100 based on blended vital statistics and Medicare probabilities of dying]

Age (years)	Expectation of life in years					Expected deaths per 1,000 alive at specified age [1]				
	Total [2]	White		Black		Total [1]	White		Black	
		Male	Female	Male	Female		Male	Female	Male	Female
At birth...	78.0	75.9	80.8	70.9	77.4	6.81	6.29	5.22	14.42	11.92
1.......	77.6	75.4	80.2	71.0	77.4	0.45	0.46	0.39	0.74	0.52
2.......	76.6	74.4	79.2	70.0	76.4	0.28	0.30	0.22	0.43	0.33
3.......	75.6	73.5	78.2	69.1	75.4	0.22	0.23	0.16	0.33	0.31
4.......	74.6	72.5	77.2	68.1	74.5	0.17	0.17	0.14	0.30	0.19
5.......	73.7	71.5	76.3	67.1	73.5	0.15	0.16	0.13	0.26	0.17
6.......	72.7	70.5	75.3	66.1	72.5	0.14	0.14	0.11	0.24	0.14
7.......	71.7	69.5	74.3	65.1	71.5	0.12	0.12	0.11	0.22	0.13
8.......	70.7	68.5	73.3	64.1	70.5	0.11	0.10	0.10	0.18	0.12
9.......	69.7	67.5	72.3	63.2	69.5	0.09	0.08	0.09	0.13	0.11
10.......	68.7	66.5	71.3	62.2	68.5	0.08	0.07	0.08	0.09	0.12
11.......	67.7	65.5	70.3	61.2	67.5	0.09	0.07	0.09	0.08	0.13
12.......	66.7	64.5	69.3	60.2	66.5	0.12	0.12	0.11	0.15	0.16
13.......	65.7	63.5	68.3	59.2	65.6	0.19	0.22	0.14	0.31	0.19
14.......	64.7	62.6	67.3	58.2	64.6	0.29	0.35	0.19	0.53	0.23
15.......	63.8	61.6	66.3	57.2	63.6	0.39	0.49	0.24	0.76	0.28
16.......	62.8	60.6	65.4	56.3	62.6	0.48	0.61	0.29	0.96	0.32
17.......	61.8	59.6	64.4	55.3	61.6	0.57	0.74	0.33	1.15	0.36
18.......	60.8	58.7	63.4	54.4	60.6	0.65	0.87	0.35	1.32	0.40
19.......	59.9	57.7	62.4	53.5	59.7	0.73	1.00	0.37	1.48	0.44
20.......	58.9	56.8	61.4	52.6	58.7	0.82	1.13	0.39	1.67	0.49
21.......	58.0	55.9	60.5	51.6	57.7	0.90	1.26	0.41	1.85	0.54
22.......	57.0	54.9	59.5	50.7	56.8	0.95	1.34	0.43	1.98	0.59
23.......	56.1	54.0	58.5	49.8	55.8	0.97	1.36	0.45	2.03	0.63
24	55.1	53.1	57.5	48.9	54.8	0.96	1.33	0.46	2.01	0.66
25.......	54.2	52.2	56.6	48.0	53.9	0.95	1.29	0.48	1.97	0.69
26.......	53.2	51.2	55.6	47.1	52.9	0.94	1.26	0.49	1.94	0.72
27.......	52.3	50.3	54.6	46.2	51.9	0.94	1.24	0.51	1.92	0.75
28.......	51.3	49.4	53.7	45.3	51.0	0.95	1.24	0.52	1.95	0.80
29.......	50.4	48.4	52.7	44.4	50.0	0.96	1.26	0.54	2.00	0.85
30.......	49.4	47.5	51.7	43.5	49.1	0.99	1.28	0.57	2.07	0.91
31.......	48.5	46.5	50.7	42.6	48.1	1.02	1.30	0.60	2.14	0.98
32.......	47.5	45.6	49.8	41.7	47.2	1.05	1.33	0.64	2.24	1.06
33.......	46.6	44.7	48.8	40.8	46.2	1.10	1.38	0.69	2.26	1.13
34.......	45.6	43.7	47.8	39.9	45.3	1.14	1.42	0.74	2.30	1.21
35.......	44.7	42.8	46.9	39.0	44.3	1.20	1.48	0.79	2.35	1.29
36.......	43.8	41.9	45.9	38.1	43.4	1.27	1.56	0.85	2.43	1.38
37.......	42.8	40.9	44.9	37.2	42.4	1.35	1.64	0.93	2.53	1.50
38.......	41.9	40.0	44.0	36.3	41.5	1.45	1.75	1.01	2.67	1.65
39.......	40.9	39.1	43.0	35.4	40.6	1.57	1.88	1.11	2.86	1.83
40.......	40.0	38.1	42.1	34.5	39.6	1.70	2.02	1.22	3.06	2.03
41.......	39.1	37.2	41.1	33.6	38.7	1.85	2.18	1.34	3.30	2.23
42.......	38.1	36.3	40.2	32.7	37.8	2.03	2.38	1.48	3.57	2.46
43.......	37.2	35.4	39.3	31.8	36.9	2.24	2.63	1.64	3.87	2.72
44.......	36.3	34.5	38.3	31.0	36.0	2.46	2.90	1.81	4.21	2.99
45.......	35.4	33.6	37.4	30.1	35.1	2.69	3.17	1.99	4.54	3.27
46.......	34.5	32.7	36.5	29.3	34.2	2.92	3.44	2.16	4.91	3.55
47.......	33.6	31.8	35.5	28.4	33.4	3.17	3.74	2.33	5.36	3.84
48.......	32.7	30.9	34.6	27.6	32.5	3.44	4.06	2.51	5.93	4.16
49.......	31.8	30.1	33.7	26.8	31.7	3.73	4.42	2.69	6.60	4.50
50.......	31.0	29.2	32.8	26.0	30.8	4.05	4.80	2.90	7.33	4.87
51.......	30.1	28.4	31.9	25.2	30.0	4.37	5.19	3.12	8.06	5.24
52.......	29.2	27.5	31.0	24.4	29.1	4.70	5.58	3.34	8.80	5.61
53.......	28.4	26.7	30.1	23.6	28.3	5.02	5.97	3.56	9.53	5.94
54.......	27.5	25.9	29.2	22.9	27.5	5.35	6.36	3.79	10.26	6.25
55.......	26.7	25.0	28.3	22.2	26.7	5.69	6.76	4.03	11.04	6.58
56.......	25.8	24.2	27.5	21.5	25.9	6.06	7.21	4.31	11.84	6.93
57.......	25.0	23.4	26.6	20.8	25.1	6.48	7.69	4.65	12.56	7.33
58.......	24.2	22.6	25.7	20.1	24.3	6.94	8.21	5.06	13.16	7.78
59.......	23.4	21.8	24.9	19.4	23.5	7.44	8.78	5.55	13.67	8.29
60.......	22.6	21.0	24.0	18.7	22.7	8.00	9.38	6.09	14.18	8.88
61.......	21.8	20.3	23.2	18.1	21.9	8.58	10.02	6.66	14.76	9.53
62.......	21.0	19.5	22.3	17.4	21.2	9.20	10.69	7.25	15.44	10.21
63.......	20.2	18.7	21.5	16.8	20.4	9.84	11.39	7.85	16.24	10.87
64.......	19.4	18.0	20.7	16.1	19.7	10.53	12.15	8.48	17.12	11.51
65.......	18.7	17.3	19.9	15.5	18.9	11.31	13.01	9.20	18.05	12.17
70.......	15.0	13.7	16.0	12.6	15.4	15.71	17.98	13.41	21.52	16.03
75.......	11.7	10.6	12.4	10.0	12.2	22.88	25.49	20.76	26.01	22.27
80.......	8.8	7.9	9.3	7.8	9.5	30.58	32.38	29.96	27.35	28.25
85.......	6.5	5.7	6.8	6.0	7.1	34.98	34.17	37.38	24.52	31.42
90.......	4.6	4.1	4.8	4.6	5.3	31.07	26.79	36.44	17.49	28.56
95.......	3.2	2.9	3.3	3.5	3.8	18.50	13.21	23.65	9.05	19.11
100......	2.3	2.0	2.2	2.6	2.8	18.45	8.92	24.78	10.40	30.63

[1] Based on the proportion of the cohort who are alive at the beginning of the indicated age who will die before reaching the age shown plus 1. For example, out of every 1,000 people alive and exactly 50 years old at the beginning of the period, 4 (4.05) people will die before reaching their 51st birthdays. [2] Includes other races, not shown separately.

Source: U.S. National Expectation of Health Statistics, unpublished data.

Births, Deaths, Marriages, and Divorces 79

Table 108. Life Expectancy by Sex, Race, and State: 1979 to 1991

[Average number of years of life remaining. Excludes deaths of nonresidents of the United States. Decennial life tables are based on population data from a decennial census and reported deaths of the 3-year period surrounding the census year; the census year is the middle year. The annual tables are based on deaths in a single year, and except for census years, on postcensal population estimates]

State	Total, 1979–1981	1989–1991						
		Total	Male			Female		
			Total	White	Black	Total	White	Black
United States	**73.88**	**75.37**	**71.83**	**72.72**	**64.47**	**78.81**	**79.45**	**73.73**
Alabama	72.53	73.64	69.59	71.12	64.37	77.61	78.85	73.76
Alaska	72.24	74.83	71.60	72.82	(B)	78.60	79.40	(B)
Arizona	74.30	76.10	72.66	73.04	67.20	79.58	79.84	74.90
Arkansas	73.72	74.33	70.54	71.54	64.03	78.13	78.89	73.58
California	74.57	75.86	72.53	72.61	65.43	79.19	79.26	74.07
Colorado	75.30	76.96	73.79	73.88	68.96	80.01	80.13	75.89
Connecticut	75.12	76.91	73.62	74.25	66.04	79.97	80.37	75.44
Delaware	73.21	74.76	71.63	72.75	65.51	77.74	78.62	72.91
District of Columbia	69.20	67.99	61.97	71.36	57.53	74.23	81.06	71.61
Florida	74.00	75.84	72.10	73.19	64.26	79.60	80.46	73.28
Georgia	72.22	73.61	69.65	71.46	63.98	77.46	78.94	73.34
Hawaii	77.02	78.21	75.37	75.12	(B)	81.26	81.09	(B)
Idaho	75.19	76.88	73.88	73.90	(B)	79.93	79.93	(B)
Illinois	73.37	74.90	71.34	72.83	62.41	78.31	79.33	72.39
Indiana	73.84	75.39	71.99	72.44	65.87	78.62	79.03	73.56
Iowa	75.81	77.29	73.89	73.98	(B)	80.54	80.62	(B)
Kansas	75.31	76.76	73.40	73.72	67.48	79.99	80.25	75.04
Kentucky	73.06	74.37	70.72	71.01	66.06	77.97	78.24	74.13
Louisiana	71.74	73.05	69.10	71.15	63.84	76.93	78.54	73.16
Maine	74.59	76.35	72.98	72.98	(B)	79.61	79.61	(B)
Maryland	73.32	74.79	71.31	73.20	64.99	78.13	79.23	74.31
Massachusetts	75.01	76.72	73.32	73.54	68.17	79.80	79.95	76.50
Michigan	73.67	75.04	71.71	73.06	63.68	78.24	79.14	73.18
Minnesota	76.15	77.76	74.53	74.78	(B)	80.85	81.02	(B)
Mississippi	71.98	73.03	68.90	70.74	64.66	77.10	78.82	73.82
Missouri	73.84	75.25	71.54	72.43	63.87	78.82	79.48	73.52
Montana	73.93	76.23	73.05	73.59	(B)	79.49	79.92	(B)
Nebraska	75.49	76.92	73.57	73.87	(B)	80.17	80.44	(B)
Nevada	72.64	74.18	70.96	71.26	(B)	77.76	77.99	(B)
New Hampshire	74.98	76.72	73.52	73.48	(B)	79.77	79.74	(B)
New Jersey	74.00	75.42	72.16	73.37	63.87	78.49	79.34	72.88
New Mexico	74.01	75.74	72.20	72.66	(B)	79.33	79.53	(B)
New York	73.70	74.68	70.86	72.01	63.86	78.32	79.03	74.35
North Carolina	72.96	74.48	70.58	72.21	64.38	78.27	79.44	74.24
North Dakota	75.71	77.62	74.35	74.74	(B)	80.99	81.32	(B)
Ohio	73.49	75.32	71.99	72.70	65.80	78.45	78.95	74.29
Oklahoma	73.67	75.10	71.63	71.76	67.10	78.49	78.59	74.48
Oregon	74.99	76.44	73.21	73.28	(B)	79.67	79.73	(B)
Pennsylvania	73.58	75.38	71.91	72.81	63.33	78.66	79.28	73.02
Rhode Island	74.76	76.54	73.00	73.31	(B)	79.77	79.97	(B)
South Carolina	71.85	73.51	69.59	71.62	64.07	77.34	78.97	73.35
South Dakota	74.97	76.91	73.17	74.30	(B)	80.77	81.59	(B)
Tennessee	73.30	74.32	70.38	71.38	64.41	78.18	79.10	73.24
Texas	73.64	75.14	71.41	72.08	65.36	78.87	79.42	74.23
Utah	75.76	77.70	74.93	75.00	(B)	80.38	80.44	(B)
Vermont	74.79	76.54	73.29	73.25	(B)	79.68	79.65	(B)
Virginia	73.43	75.22	71.77	73.04	65.75	78.56	79.48	74.37
Washington	75.13	76.82	73.84	73.97	67.91	79.74	79.81	75.58
West Virginia	72.84	74.26	70.53	70.66	65.00	77.93	78.02	74.36
Wisconsin	75.35	76.87	73.61	73.99	66.42	80.03	80.27	75.27
Wyoming	73.85	76.21	73.16	73.27	(B)	79.29	79.46	(B)

B Base figure too small to meet statistical standards for reliability.

Source: U.S. National Center for Health Statistics, National Vital Statistics Reports (NVSR), *U.S. Decennial Life Tables for 1989–91*, Vol. 1, No. 3., and *Trends and Comparisons of United States Life Table Data: 1900–1991*. See also <http://cdc.gov/nchs/products/life_tables.htm#life>.

Table 109. Deaths and Death Rates by Sex, Race, and Hispanic Origin: 1970 to 2008

[1,921 represents 1,921,000. Rates are per 1,000 population for specified groups. Excludes deaths of nonresidents of the United States and fetal deaths. For explanation of age adjustment, see text, this section. Data for Hispanic origin and specified races other than White and Black should be interpreted with caution because of inconsistencies between reporting Hispanic origin and race on death certificates and censuses and surveys]

Sex and race	1970	1980	1990	2000	2002	2003	2004	2005	2006	2007	2008[1]
Deaths [2] (1,000)	**1,921**	**1,990**	**2,148**	**2,403**	**2,443**	**2,448**	**2,398**	**2,448**	**2,426**	**2,424**	**2,473**
Male [2] (1,000)	1,078	1,075	1,113	1,178	1,199	1,202	1,182	1,208	1,202	1,204	1,227
Female [2] (1,000)	843	915	1,035	1,226	1,244	1,246	1,216	1,240	1,224	1,220	1,246
White (1,000)	1,682	1,739	1,853	2,071	2,103	2,104	2,057	2,098	2,078	2,074	2,121
Male (1,000)	942	934	951	1,007	1,025	1,026	1,007	1,028	1,022	1,024	1,047
Female (1,000)	740	805	902	1,064	1,077	1,078	1,049	1,070	1,055	1,050	1,074
Black (1,000)	226	233	265	286	290	291	287	293	290	290	289
Male (1,000)	128	130	145	145	147	148	146	149	149	148	147
Female (1,000)	98	103	120	141	143	143	141	144	141	141	142
Asian or Pacific Islander (1,000)	(NA)	11	21	35	38	40	41	43	45	46	48
Male (1,000)	(NA)	7	12	19	20	21	21	23	23	24	25
Female (1,000)	(NA)	4	9	16	18	19	19	20	21	22	23
American Indian, Eskimo, Aleut (1,000)	6	7	8	11	12	13	13	14	14	14	15
Male (1,000)	3	4	5	6	7	7	7	8	8	8	8
Female (1,000)	2	3	3	5	6	6	6	6	6	6	7
Hispanic origin [3]	(NA)	(NA)	(NA)	107	117	122	122	131	133	136	140
Male (1,000)	(NA)	(NA)	(NA)	60	66	68	69	74	74	76	77
Female (1,000)	(NA)	(NA)	(NA)	47	51	54	54	57	59	60	63
Non-Hispanic, White (1,000)	(NA)	(NA)	(NA)	1,960	1,982	1,979	1,933	1,967	1,945	1,940	1,981
Male (1,000)	(NA)	(NA)	(NA)	945	958	956	938	954	948	949	969
Female (1,000)	(NA)	(NA)	(NA)	1,015	1,024	1,023	995	1,013	997	991	1,012
Death rates [2]	**9.5**	**8.8**	**8.6**	**8.5**	**8.5**	**8.4**	**8.2**	**8.3**	**8.1**	**8.0**	**8.1**
Male [2]	10.9	9.8	9.2	8.5	8.5	8.4	8.2	8.3	8.1	8.1	8.2
Female [2]	8.1	7.9	8.1	8.6	8.5	8.4	8.2	8.2	8.1	8.0	8.1
White	9.5	8.9	8.9	9.0	9.0	8.9	8.6	8.7	8.6	8.5	8.6
Male	10.9	9.8	9.3	8.9	8.8	8.8	8.5	8.6	8.5	8.5	8.6
Female	8.1	8.1	8.5	9.1	9.1	9.0	8.7	8.8	8.6	8.5	8.7
Black	10.0	8.8	8.7	7.8	7.7	7.6	7.4	7.5	7.3	7.2	7.2
Male	11.9	10.3	10.1	8.3	8.2	8.1	7.9	8.0	7.9	7.8	7.6
Female	8.3	7.3	7.5	7.3	7.2	7.2	7.0	7.0	6.8	6.8	6.7
Asian or Pacific Islander	(NA)	3.0	2.8	3.0	3.0	3.0	3.0	3.1	3.1	3.1	3.2
Male	(NA)	3.8	3.3	3.3	3.3	3.3	3.2	3.3	3.3	3.3	3.4
Female	(NA)	2.2	2.3	2.6	2.7	2.8	2.7	2.8	2.9	2.9	3.0
American Indian, Eskimo, Aleut	(NA)	4.9	4.0	3.8	4.0	4.2	4.2	4.4	4.4	4.4	4.3
Male	(NA)	6.0	4.8	4.2	4.4	4.6	4.5	4.8	4.8	4.9	4.8
Female	(NA)	3.8	3.3	3.5	3.7	3.9	3.8	4.0	4.0	4.0	3.9
Hispanic origin [3]	(NA)	(NA)	(NA)	3.0	3.0	3.1	3.0	3.1	3.0	3.0	3.0
Male	(NA)	(NA)	4.1	3.3	3.3	3.3	3.2	3.3	3.2	3.2	3.2
Female	(NA)	(NA)	2.9	2.7	2.7	2.8	2.7	2.8	2.7	2.7	2.8
Non-Hispanic, White	(NA)	(NA)	(NA)	9.9	10.0	9.9	9.7	9.8	9.7	9.6	9.8
Male	(NA)	(NA)	9.9	9.8	9.8	9.8	9.6	9.7	9.6	9.6	9.8
Female	(NA)	(NA)	9.0	10.1	10.1	10.1	9.8	9.9	9.7	9.7	9.9
Age-adjusted death rates [2],[4]	**12.2**	**10.4**	**9.4**	**8.7**	**8.5**	**8.3**	**8.0**	**8.0**	**7.8**	**7.6**	**7.6**
Male [2]	15.4	13.5	12.0	10.5	10.1	9.9	9.6	9.5	9.2	9.1	9.0
Female [2]	9.7	8.2	7.5	7.3	7.2	7.1	6.8	6.8	6.6	6.4	6.4
White	11.9	10.1	9.1	8.5	8.3	8.2	7.9	7.9	7.6	7.5	7.5
Male	15.1	13.2	11.7	10.3	9.9	9.7	9.4	9.3	9.1	8.9	8.9
Female	9.4	8.0	7.3	7.2	7.0	6.9	6.7	8.5	6.5	6.3	6.4
Black	15.2	13.1	12.5	11.2	10.8	10.7	10.3	10.2	9.8	9.6	9.4
Male	18.7	17.0	16.4	14.0	13.4	13.2	12.7	12.5	12.2	11.8	11.5
Female	12.3	10.3	9.8	9.3	9.0	8.9	8.6	8.5	8.1	7.9	7.8
Asian or Pacific Islander	(NA)	5.9	5.8	5.1	4.7	4.7	4.4	4.4	4.3	4.2	4.1
Male	(NA)	7.9	7.2	6.2	5.8	5.6	5.3	5.3	5.2	5.0	4.9
Female	(NA)	4.3	4.7	4.2	4.0	3.9	3.8	3.7	3.6	3.5	3.5
American Indian, Eskimo, Aleut	(NA)	8.7	7.2	7.1	6.8	6.9	6.5	6.6	6.4	6.3	6.1
Male	(NA)	11.1	9.2	8.4	7.9	8.0	7.6	7.8	7.4	7.4	7.2
Female	(NA)	6.6	5.6	6.0	5.8	5.9	5.6	5.7	5.6	5.3	5.2
Hispanic origin [3]	(NA)	(NA)	(NA)	6.7	6.3	6.2	5.9	5.9	5.6	5.5	5.4
Male	(NA)	(NA)	8.9	8.2	7.7	7.5	7.1	7.2	6.8	6.5	6.3
Female	(NA)	(NA)	5.4	5.5	5.2	5.2	4.9	4.9	4.7	4.5	4.5
Non-Hispanic, White	(NA)	(NA)	(NA)	8.6	8.4	8.3	8.0	8.0	7.8	7.6	7.7
Male	(NA)	(NA)	11.7	10.4	10.0	9.8	9.5	9.5	9.2	9.1	9.1
Female	(NA)	(NA)	7.3	7.2	7.1	7.0	6.8	6.8	6.6	6.5	6.5

NA Not available. [1] Data are preliminary. [2] Includes other races not shown separately. [3] Persons of Hispanic origin may be any race. [4] Age-adjusted death rates are better indicators than crude death rates for showing changes in the risk of death over time when the age distribution of the population is changing, and for comparing the mortality of population subgroups that have different age compositions. All age-adjusted death rates are standardized to the year 2000 population.

Source: U.S. National Center for Health Statistics, National Vital Statistics Reports (NVSR), Deaths: Preliminary Data for 2008, Vol. 59, No. 2, December 2010, and Deaths: Final Data for 2007, Vol.58, No. 19, May 2010.

U.S. Census Bureau, Statistical Abstract of the United States: 2012

Table 110. Death Rates by Age, Sex, and Race: 1950 to 2008

[Rates per 100,000 population]

Characteristic	All ages [1]	Under 1 year	1 to 4 years	5 to 14 years	15 to 24 years	25 to 34 years	35 to 44 years	45 to 54 years	55 to 64 years	65 to 74 years	75 to 84 years	85 years and over
MALE												
1950	1,106	3,728	152	71	168	217	429	1,067	2,395	4,931	10,426	21,636
1960	1,105	3,059	120	56	152	188	373	992	2,310	4,914	10,178	21,186
1970	1,090	2,410	93	51	189	215	403	959	2,283	4,874	10,010	17,822
1980	977	1,429	73	37	172	196	299	767	1,815	4,105	8,817	18,801
1990	918	1,083	52	29	147	204	310	610	1,553	3,492	7,889	18,057
2000	853	807	36	21	115	139	255	543	1,231	2,980	6,973	17,501
2005	827	762	33	19	118	143	243	548	1,131	2,612	6,350	14,889
2006	815	756	31	18	119	147	239	541	1,110	2,516	6,178	14,309
2007	810	748	31	17	116	144	232	530	1,101	2,457	6,038	14,006
2008 [2]	818	709	32	16	110	142	224	527	1,105	2,434	6,035	14,023
White:												
1990	931	896	46	26	131	176	268	549	1,467	3,398	7,845	18,268
2000	888	668	33	20	106	124	234	497	1,163	2,906	6,933	17,716
2005	865	640	31	17	110	131	229	509	1,068	2,553	6,343	15,157
2006	852	633	28	16	112	135	224	505	1,051	2,456	6,182	14,577
2007	848	628	28	16	108	134	218	498	1,043	2,397	6,049	14,286
2008 [2]	861	600	29	15	103	133	214	501	1,052	2,378	6,054	14,359
Black:												
1990	1,008	2,112	86	41	252	431	700	1,261	2,618	4,946	9,130	16,955
2000	834	1,568	55	28	181	261	453	1,018	2,080	4,254	8,486	16,791
2005	799	1,437	47	27	172	254	396	949	1,954	3,747	7,667	13,810
2006	787	1,407	47	25	171	254	392	922	1,892	3,669	7,393	13,206
2007	776	1,363	45	25	168	240	379	877	1,871	3,605	7,169	12,965
2008 [2]	763	1,293	48	24	159	225	348	828	1,828	3,541	7,108	12,538
Asian or Pacific Islander: [3]												
1990	334	605	45	21	76	80	131	287	789	2,041	5,009	12,446
2000	333	529	23	13	55	55	105	250	642	1,661	4,328	12,125
2005	334	465	21	14	57	56	94	242	545	1,404	3,759	9,839
2006	331	470	18	11	62	54	89	233	551	1,329	3,606	9,525
2007	331	484	25	12	61	50	89	229	523	1,305	3,538	8,918
2008 [2]	338	464	18	12	50	55	88	223	530	1,313	3,500	8,742
American Indian, Eskimo, Aleut: [3]												
1990	476	1,057	77	33	220	256	365	620	1,211	2,462	5,389	11,244
2000	416	700	45	20	136	179	295	520	1,090	2,478	5,351	10,726
2005	482	882	72	23	145	206	337	589	1,124	2,254	4,373	8,419
2006	477	1,058	58	17	156	194	339	592	1,030	2,147	4,198	7,540
2007	488	1,010	64	23	144	198	333	573	1,037	2,132	4,193	7,639
2008 [2]	478	660	38	19	151	199	315	618	1,039	2,173	4,157	6,503
FEMALE												
1950	824	2,855	127	49	89	143	290	642	1,405	3,333	8,400	19,195
1960	809	2,321	98	37	61	107	229	527	1,196	2,872	7,633	19,008
1970	808	1,864	75	32	68	102	231	517	1,099	2,580	6,678	15,518
1980	785	1,142	55	24	58	76	159	413	934	2,145	5,440	14,747
1990	812	856	41	19	49	74	138	343	879	1,991	4,883	14,274
2000	855	663	29	15	43	64	143	313	772	1,921	4,815	14,719
2005	825	619	25	14	43	64	144	320	699	1,736	4,520	13,298
2006	806	622	26	13	43	64	142	318	687	1,678	4,388	12,759
2007	797	618	26	13	42	64	137	315	670	1,633	4,304	12,442
2008 [2]	809	588	25	12	40	63	135	318	669	1,623	4,316	12,536
White:												
1990	847	690	36	18	46	62	117	309	823	1,924	4,839	14,401
2000	912	551	26	14	41	55	126	281	731	1,868	4,785	14,891
2005	883	515	23	13	42	58	130	291	664	1,700	4,519	13,498
2006	864	517	24	12	42	59	129	292	655	1,646	4,395	12,966
2007	855	517	23	12	41	60	126	291	638	1,600	4,318	12,647
2008 [2]	869	497	23	11	38	58	126	295	639	1,595	4,344	12,769
Black:												
1990	748	1,736	68	28	69	160	299	639	1,453	2,866	5,688	13,310
2000	733	1,280	45	20	58	122	272	588	1,227	2,690	5,697	13,941
2005	704	1,180	37	19	51	110	250	568	1,104	2,342	5,264	12,790
2006	684	1,195	39	17	51	107	245	548	1,076	2,240	5,029	12,197
2007	676	1,132	39	17	49	102	229	537	1,047	2,210	4,903	11,997
2008 [2]	674	1,084	36	16	50	98	222	526	1,030	2,156	4,819	11,874
Asian or Pacific Islander: [3]												
1990	234	518	32	13	29	38	70	183	483	1,089	3,128	10,254
2000	262	434	20	12	22	28	66	156	391	996	2,882	9,052
2005	283	395	18	12	26	29	58	143	353	906	2,530	7,793
2006	286	357	21	10	25	29	57	145	333	898	2,526	7,560
2007	287	398	18	10	24	28	55	136	329	833	2,471	7,334
2008 [2]	301	381	20	9	23	35	49	137	328	868	2,439	7,487
American Indian, Eskimo, Aleut: [3]												
1990	330	689	38	26	69	102	156	381	806	1,679	3,073	8,201
2000	346	492	40	18	59	85	172	285	772	1,900	3,850	9,118
2005	399	753	46	17	68	91	194	366	699	1,781	3,603	7,065
2006	400	690	51	17	64	92	205	342	687	1,657	3,746	6,634
2007	400	830	46	13	61	91	196	346	694	1,612	3,437	6,248
2008 [2]	386	498	40	17	59	99	217	343	670	1,558	3,264	5,981

[1] Figures for age not stated are included in "All ages" but not distributed among age groups. [2] Data are preliminary. [3] The death rates for specified races other than white and black should be interpreted with caution because of inconsistencies between reporting race on death certificates and censuses and surveys.

Source: U.S. National Center for Health Statistics, *Health*, United States, 2010, and unpublished data. See also <http://cdc.gov/nchs/hus.htm>.

82 Births, Deaths, Marriages, and Divorces

Table 111. Age-Adjusted Death Rates by Sex, Race, and Hispanic Origin: 1970 to 2008

[Age-adjusted rates per 100,000 population. Age-adjusted death rates are better indicators than crude death rates for showing changes in the risk of death over time when the age distribution of the population is changing, and for comparing the mortality of population subgroups that have different age compositions. Populations enumerated as of April 1 for census years and estimated as of July 1 for all other years. Excludes deaths of nonresidents of the United States. Data for Hispanic-origin and specified races other than White and Black should be interpreted with caution because of inconsistencies reporting race on death certificates and on censuses and surveys. See text this section and Appendix III]

Sex, race, and Hispanic origin	1970	1980	1990	2000	2003	2004	2005	2006	2007	2008 [1]
ALL RACES [2]										
Total	**1,223**	**1,039**	**939**	**869**	**833**	**801**	**799**	**777**	**760**	**759**
Male	1,542	1,348	1,203	1,054	994	956	951	925	906	901
Female	971	818	751	731	706	679	678	658	643	644
WHITE										
Total	**1,193**	**1,013**	**910**	**850**	**817**	**786**	**785**	**764**	**749**	**751**
Male	1,514	1,318	1,166	1,029	974	937	933	908	891	890
Female	944	796	729	715	693	667	667	648	635	637
BLACK										
Total	**1,518**	**1,315**	**1,250**	**1,121**	**1,066**	**1,027**	**1,017**	**982**	**958**	**936**
Male	1,874	1,698	1,645	1,404	1,319	1,269	1,253	1,216	1,184	1,151
Female	1,229	1,033	975	928	886	855	846	813	794	779
ASIAN OR PACIFIC ISLANDER										
Total	**(NA)**	**590**	**582**	**506**	**466**	**444**	**440**	**429**	**415**	**414**
Male	(NA)	787	716	624	563	535	534	516	499	493
Female	(NA)	426	469	417	393	376	369	363	351	354
AMERICAN INDIAN, ESKIMO, ALEUT										
Total	**(NA)**	**867**	**716**	**709**	**685**	**650**	**663**	**642**	**627**	**610**
Male	(NA)	1,112	916	842	797	758	775	740	737	718
Female	(NA)	662	562	605	592	558	568	556	533	515
HISPANIC ORIGIN [3]										
Total	**(NA)**	**(NA)**	**(NA)**	**666**	**621**	**587**	**591**	**564**	**546**	**536**
Male	(NA)	(NA)	886	818	748	707	717	676	655	635
Female	(NA)	(NA)	537	546	516	486	485	469	453	449
NON-HISPANIC, WHITE										
Total	**(NA)**	**(NA)**	**(NA)**	**856**	**826**	**797**	**797**	**777**	**763**	**766**
Male	(NA)	(NA)	1,171	1,035	984	949	945	923	907	909
Female	(NA)	(NA)	735	722	702	678	678	660	648	651

NA Not available. [1] Data are preliminary. [2] For 1970 to 1990 includes deaths among races not shown separately. [3] Persons of Hispanic origin may be any race.

Source: U.S. National Center for Health Statistics, National Vital Statistics Reports (NVSR), Deaths: Final Data for 2007, Vol.58, No. 19, May 2010, and unpublished data.

Table 112. Death Rates by Hispanic-Origin Status, Sex, and Age: 2000 to 2008

[Rates per 100,000 U.S. standard population. Rates are based on populations enumerated as of April 1 for census years and estimated as of July 1 for all other years. Excludes deaths of nonresidents of the United States. Data for Hispanic-origin should be interpreted with caution because of inconsistencies between reporting Hispanic origin and race on death certificates and censuses and surveys]

Age	Hispanic male			Hispanic female			Non-Hispanic White male			Non-Hispanic White female		
	2000	2005	2008 [1]	2000	2005	2008 [1]	2000	2005	2008 [1]	2000	2005	2008 [1]
Age adjusted [2]	818	717	635	546	485	449	1,035	945	909	722	678	651
Crude [3]	331	334	319	275	278	277	979	971	978	1,007	993	986
Under 1 year	637	670	579	554	555	482	659	626	596	531	497	489
1 to 4 years	32	33	28	28	25	22	32	30	29	24	22	23
5 to 14 years	18	15	13	13	12	11	20	17	15	14	13	11
15 to 24 years	108	120	104	32	37	31	104	106	101	43	42	39
25 to 34 years	120	116	107	43	41	43	123	134	141	57	62	62
35 to 44 years	211	182	159	101	91	83	234	236	226	128	137	134
45 to 54 years	439	417	374	224	216	201	498	517	516	285	299	307
55 to 64 years	966	876	836	548	494	480	1,171	1,080	1,067	742	677	652
65 to 74 years	2,288	2,029	1,839	1,423	1,292	1,161	2,931	2,585	2,413	1,891	1,730	1,628
75 to 84 years	5,395	4,857	4,289	3,625	3,366	3,148	6,978	6,420	6,167	4,819	4,580	4,420
85 years and over	13,086	10,141	8,475	11,203	9,068	8,343	17,853	15,401	14,721	14,972	13,683	12,997

[1] Data are preliminary. [2] Age-adjusted death rates are better indicators than crude death rates for showing changes in the risk of death over time when the age distribution of the population is changing, and for comparing the mortality of population subgroups that have different age compositions. All age-adjusted death rates are standardized to the year 2000 population. [3] The total number of deaths in a given time period divided by the total resident population as of July 1.

Source: U.S. National Center for Health Statistics, National Vital Statistics Reports (NVSR), Deaths: Final Data for 2007, Vol.58, No. 19, May 2010, and unpublished data.

Births, Deaths, Marriages, and Divorces 83

Table 113. Deaths and Death Rates by State and Island Areas: 1990 to 2008

[2,148 represents 2,148,000. By state of residence. Except as noted, excludes deaths of nonresidents of the United States. Caution should be used in comparing death rates by state; rates are affected by the population composition of the area. See also Appendix III]

State	Number of deaths (1,000)						Death rate per 1,000 population [1]						Age-adjusted rate 2008 [2,3]
	1990	1995	2000	2005	2007	2008 [2]	1990	1995	2000	2005	2007	2008 [2]	
United States	**2,148**	**2,312**	**2,403**	**2,448**	**2,424**	**2,473**	**8.6**	**8.7**	**8.5**	**8.3**	**8.0**	**8.1**	**7.6**
Alabama	39	42	45	47	47	48	9.7	10.0	10.1	10.3	10.1	10.2	9.3
Alaska	2	3	3	3	3	3	4.0	4.2	4.6	4.8	5.1	5.1	7.4
Arizona	29	35	41	46	46	46	7.9	8.4	7.9	7.7	7.2	7.0	6.5
Arkansas	25	27	28	28	28	29	10.5	10.8	10.6	10.1	9.9	10.3	9.0
California	214	224	230	237	234	234	7.2	7.1	6.8	6.6	6.4	6.4	6.6
Colorado	22	25	27	30	30	31	6.6	6.7	6.3	6.4	6.2	6.3	7.1
Connecticut	28	29	30	29	29	29	8.4	9.0	8.8	8.4	8.2	8.2	6.9
Delaware	6	6	7	7	7	8	8.7	8.8	8.8	8.9	8.5	8.7	7.8
District of Columbia . . .	7	7	6	5	5	5	12.0	12.4	10.5	10.0	8.8	8.7	8.5
Florida	134	153	164	171	168	171	10.4	10.8	10.3	9.6	9.2	9.3	6.8
Georgia	52	58	64	67	68	70	8.0	8.1	7.8	7.4	7.2	7.2	8.4
Hawaii	7	8	8	9	9	9	6.1	6.4	6.8	7.2	7.4	7.4	5.9
Idaho	7	9	10	11	11	11	7.4	7.3	7.4	7.4	7.2	7.2	7.2
Illinois	103	108	107	104	101	104	9.0	9.2	8.6	8.1	7.8	8.0	7.7
Indiana	50	53	55	56	54	57	8.9	9.2	9.1	8.9	8.5	8.9	8.4
Iowa	27	28	28	28	27	29	9.7	9.9	9.6	9.4	9.1	9.5	7.4
Kansas	22	24	25	25	24	25	9.0	9.3	9.2	9.0	8.8	8.9	7.8
Kentucky	35	37	40	40	40	41	9.5	9.6	9.8	9.6	9.5	9.7	9.0
Louisiana	38	40	41	44	40	41	8.9	9.1	9.2	9.8	9.3	9.3	9.2
Maine	11	12	12	13	12	13	9.0	9.5	9.7	9.7	9.5	9.5	7.6
Maryland	38	42	44	44	44	44	8.0	8.3	8.3	7.8	7.8	7.8	7.7
Massachusetts	53	55	57	54	53	54	8.8	9.1	8.9	8.4	8.2	8.2	7.1
Michigan	79	84	87	87	87	88	8.5	8.8	8.7	8.6	8.6	8.8	8.1
Minnesota	35	38	38	38	37	38	7.9	8.1	7.7	7.3	7.1	7.4	6.8
Mississippi	25	27	29	29	28	29	9.8	10.0	10.1	10.0	9.7	9.9	9.5
Missouri	50	54	55	55	54	57	9.8	10.2	9.8	9.4	9.2	9.6	8.5
Montana	7	8	8	9	9	9	8.6	8.8	9.0	9.1	9.0	9.2	7.9
Nebraska	15	15	15	15	15	15	9.4	9.3	8.8	8.5	8.6	8.7	7.4
Nevada	9	13	15	19	19	[4] 21	7.8	8.2	7.6	7.9	7.3	[4] 8.0	[4] 8.7
New Hampshire	8	9	10	10	10	10	7.7	8.0	7.8	7.8	7.8	7.8	7.1
New Jersey	70	74	75	72	70	70	9.1	9.3	8.9	8.3	8.0	8.1	7.2
New Mexico	11	13	13	15	15	16	7.0	7.4	7.4	7.8	7.9	8.1	7.6
New York	169	168	158	152	148	149	9.4	9.3	8.3	7.9	7.7	7.6	6.8
North Carolina	57	65	72	75	76	77	8.6	9.0	8.9	8.6	8.4	8.4	8.3
North Dakota	6	6	6	6	6	6	8.9	9.3	9.1	9.0	8.7	9.2	7.1
Ohio	99	106	108	109	107	110	9.1	9.5	9.5	9.5	9.3	9.6	8.4
Oklahoma	30	33	35	36	36	37	9.7	10.0	10.2	10.2	10.0	10.2	9.3
Oregon	25	28	30	31	31	32	8.8	9.0	8.6	8.5	8.4	8.4	7.5
Pennsylvania	122	128	131	130	125	127	10.3	10.6	10.7	10.4	10.1	10.2	8.0
Rhode Island	10	10	10	10	10	10	9.5	9.8	9.6	9.3	9.2	9.3	7.5
South Carolina	30	34	37	39	39	40	8.5	9.1	9.2	9.1	8.9	9.0	8.4
South Dakota	6	7	7	7	7	7	9.1	9.5	9.5	9.3	9.1	8.8	7.1
Tennessee	46	51	55	57	57	59	9.5	9.8	9.7	9.6	9.3	9.5	8.9
Texas	125	138	150	156	161	165	7.4	7.4	7.2	6.8	6.7	6.8	7.8
Utah	9	11	12	13	14	14	5.3	5.6	5.5	5.4	5.3	5.1	6.6
Vermont	5	5	5	5	5	5	8.2	8.5	8.4	8.1	8.3	8.4	7.2
Virginia	48	53	56	58	58	59	7.8	8.0	8.0	7.6	7.6	7.6	7.6
Washington	37	41	44	46	47	49	7.6	7.5	7.5	7.3	7.3	7.4	7.2
West Virginia	19	20	21	21	21	22	10.8	11.1	11.7	11.4	11.6	11.9	9.6
Wisconsin	43	45	46	47	46	47	8.7	8.8	8.7	8.4	8.3	8.3	7.3
Wyoming	3	4	4	4	4	4	7.1	7.7	7.9	8.0	8.2	7.9	7.7
Puerto Rico	26	30	28	30	28	29	7.3	8.1	7.2	7.5	7.4	7.3	7.0
Virgin Islands	(Z)	1	1	1	1	1	4.6	5.8	5.3	6.1	6.4	6.4	6.8
Guam	1	1	1	1	1	1	3.9	4.1	4.2	4.0	4.5	4.3	6.8
American Samoa	(NA)	(NA)	(Z)	(Z)	(Z)	(Z)	(NA)	(NA)	3.3	4.4	3.9	3.7	9.6
Northern Marianas . .	(NA)	(NA)	(Z)	(Z)	(Z)	(NA)	(NA)	(NA)	1.9	2.3	1.6	(NA)	(NA)

NA Not available. Z Less than 500. [1] Rates based on enumerated resident population as of April 1 for 1990 and 2000; estimated resident population as of July 1 for all other years. [2] Preliminary data. [3] Age-adjusted death rates are better indicators than crude death rates for showing changes in the risk of death over time when the age distribution of the population is changing, and for comparing the mortality of population subgroups that have different age compositions. See text this section. [4] Preliminary records for Nevada were missing geographic information indicating whether the decedent resided in that state, all records filed by Nevada are considered as residents of Nevada. Therefore, data shown for Nevada are approximately 8 percent higher than would be if nonresidents for that state were excluded.

Source: U.S. National Center for Health Statistics, National Vital Statistics Reports (NVSR), Deaths: Preliminary Data for 2008, Vol. 59, No. 2, December 2010, and Deaths: Final Data for 2007, Vol.58, No. 19, May 2010.

Table 114. Fetal and Infant Deaths: 1990 to 2005

[The term "fetal death" defined on an all inclusive basis to end confusion arising from the use of such terms as stillbirth, spontaneous abortion, and miscarriage have been adopted by the National Center for Health Statistics (NCHS) as the nationally recommended standard. Fetal deaths do not include induced terminations of pregnancy. See also Appendix III]

Year	Fetal deaths [1]			Infant deaths		Fetal mortality rate [2]			Perinatal mortality rate	
	Total [1]	20 to 27 weeks [3]	28 weeks or more [3]	Less than 7 days	Less than 28 days	Total [1]	20–27 weeks [3]	28 weeks or more [3]	Defi- nition I [4]	Defi- nition II [5]
1990......	31,386	13,427	17,959	19,439	23,591	7.49	3.22	4.30	8.95	13.12
1995......	27,294	13,043	14,251	15,483	19,186	6.95	3.33	3.64	7.60	11.84
1996......	27,069	12,990	14,079	14,947	18,556	6.91	3.33	3.60	7.43	11.64
1997......	26,486	12,800	13,686	14,827	18,507	6.78	3.29	3.51	7.32	11.51
1998......	26,702	13,229	13,473	15,061	18,915	6.73	3.35	3.41	7.21	11.50
1999......	26,884	13,457	13,427	14,874	18,700	6.74	3.39	3.38	7.12	11.44
2000......	27,003	13,497	13,506	14,893	18,733	6.61	3.31	3.32	6.97	11.19
2001......	26,373	13,122	13,251	14,622	18,275	6.51	3.25	3.28	6.90	11.02
2002......	25,943	13,072	12,871	15,020	18,791	6.41	3.24	3.19	6.91	11.05
2003......	25,653	13,168	12,485	15,152	18,935	6.23	3.21	3.04	6.74	10.83
2004......	25,655	12,894	12,761	14,836	18,602	6.20	3.13	3.09	6.69	10.70
2005......	25,894	13,327	12,567	15,013	18,782	6.22	3.21	3.03	6.64	10.73

[1] Fetal deaths with stated or presumed gestation of 20 weeks or more. [2] Rate per 1,000 live births and fetal deaths in specified group. [3] Not stated gestational age proportionally distributed. [4] Infant deaths of less than 7 days and fetal deaths with stated or presumed period of gestation of 28 weeks or more, per 1,000 live births and fetal deaths. [5] Infant deaths of less than 28 days and fetal deaths with stated or presumed period of gestation of 20 weeks or more per 1,000 live births and fetal deaths.

Source: U.S. National Center for Health Statistics, National Vital Statistics Reports (NVSR), *Fetal and Perinatal Mortality, U.S., 2005*, Vol. 57. No. 8, January 2009.

Table 115. Infant, Neonatal, and Maternal Mortality Rates by Race: 1980 to 2007

[Deaths per 1,000 live births, except as noted. Data based on death certificates, fetal death records, and birth certificates. Excludes deaths of nonresidents of the United States. See also Appendix III]

Race and year	Infant [1]	Neonatal [1]		Post- neonatal [1]	Fetal mortality rate [2]	Late fetal mortality rate [3]	Perinatal mortality rate [4]	Maternal mortality rate [5]
		Under 28 days	Under 7 days					
ALL RACES								
1980.........	12.6	8.5	7.1	4.1	9.1	6.2	13.2	9.2
1990.........	9.2	5.8	4.8	3.4	7.5	4.3	9.1	8.2
1995.........	7.6	4.9	4.0	2.7	7.0	3.6	7.6	7.1
2000.........	6.9	4.6	3.7	2.3	6.6	3.3	7.0	9.8
2002.........	7.0	4.7	3.7	2.3	6.4	3.2	6.9	8.9
2003.........	6.9	4.6	3.7	2.2	6.3	3.1	6.8	[6] 12.1
2004.........	6.8	4.5	3.6	2.3	6.3	3.1	6.7	[6] 13.1
2005.........	6.9	4.5	3.6	2.3	6.2	3.0	6.6	[6] 15.1
2006.........	6.7	4.5	3.5	2.2	(NA)	(NA)	(NA)	13.3
2007.........	6.8	4.4	3.5	2.3	(NA)	(NA)	(NA)	12.7
WHITE [7]								
1980.........	10.9	7.4	6.1	3.5	8.1	5.7	11.8	6.7
1990.........	7.6	4.8	3.9	2.8	6.4	3.8	7.7	5.4
1995.........	6.3	4.1	3.3	2.2	5.9	3.3	6.5	4.2
2000.........	5.7	3.8	3.0	1.9	5.6	2.9	5.9	7.5
2002.........	5.8	3.9	3.1	1.9	5.5	2.8	5.9	6.0
2003.........	5.7	3.9	3.1	1.8	5.2	2.7	5.8	[6] 8.7
2004.........	5.7	3.8	3.0	1.9	5.3	(NA)	(NA)	[6] 9.3
2005.........	5.7	3.8	3.0	1.9	5.3	(NA)	(NA)	[6] 11.1
2006.........	5.6	3.7	2.9	1.8	(NA)	(NA)	(NA)	9.5
2007.........	5.6	3.7	2.9	1.9	(NA)	(NA)	(NA)	10.0
BLACK [7]								
1980.........	22.2	14.6	12.3	7.6	14.7	9.1	21.3	21.5
1990.........	18.0	11.6	9.7	6.4	13.3	6.7	16.4	22.4
1995.........	15.1	9.8	8.2	5.3	12.7	5.7	13.8	22.1
2000.........	14.1	9.4	7.6	4.7	12.4	5.4	13.0	22.0
2002.........	14.4	9.5	7.8	4.8	11.9	5.2	12.8	24.9
2003.........	14.0	9.4	7.5	4.6	12.1	5.1	12.5	[6] 30.5
2004.........	13.8	9.1	7.3	4.7	11.6	(NA)	(NA)	[6] 34.7
2005.........	13.7	9.1	7.3	4.7	11.4	(NA)	(NA)	[6] 36.5
2006.........	13.3	8.8	7.0	4.5	(NA)	(NA)	(NA)	32.7
2007.........	13.2	8.6	6.9	4.6	(NA)	(NA)	(NA)	26.5

NA Not available. [1] Infant (under 1 year of age), neonatal (under 28 days), early neonatal (under 7 days), and postneonatal (28 days–11 months). [2] Number of fetal deaths of 20 weeks or more gestation per 1,000 live births plus fetal deaths. [3] Number of fetal deaths of 28 weeks or more gestation (late fetal deaths) per 1,000 live births plus late fetal deaths. [4] Number of late fetal deaths plus infant deaths within 7 days of birth per 1,000 live births plus fetal deaths. [5] Per 100,000 live births from deliveries and complications of pregnancy, childbirth, and the puerperium. Beginning 2000, deaths are classified according to the tenth revision of the International Classification of Diseases; earlier years classified according to the revision in use at the time; see text, this section. [6] Increase partially reflects the use of a separate item on the death certificate on pregnancy status by an increasing number of states. [7] Infant deaths are tabulated by race of decedent; fetal deaths and live births are tabulated by race of mother.

Source: U.S. National Center for Health Statistics, *Health, United States, 2010.* See also <http://cdc.gov/nchs/hus.htm>.

Table 116. Infant Mortality Rates by Race, States, and Island Areas: 1980 to 2007

[Deaths per 1,000 live births, by place of residence. Represents deaths of infants under 1 year old, exclusive of fetal deaths. Excludes deaths of nonresidents of the United States. See headnote 112 and Appendix III]

State	Total [1]				White				Black			
	1980	1990	2000	2007	1980	1990	2000	2007	1980	1990	2000	2007
United States	**12.6**	**9.2**	**6.9**	**6.8**	**10.9**	**7.6**	**5.7**	**5.6**	**22.2**	**18.0**	**14.1**	**13.2**
Alabama	15.1	10.8	9.4	9.9	11.6	8.1	6.6	8.0	21.6	16.0	15.4	14.4
Alaska	12.3	10.5	6.8	6.5	9.4	7.6	5.8	5.2	19.5	(B)	(B)	(B)
Arizona	12.4	8.8	6.7	6.8	11.8	7.8	6.2	6.5	18.4	20.6	17.6	15.0
Arkansas	12.7	9.2	8.4	7.7	10.3	8.4	7.0	6.5	20.0	13.9	13.7	13.2
California	11.1	7.9	5.4	5.2	10.6	7.0	5.1	4.9	18.0	16.8	12.9	12.4
Colorado	10.1	8.8	6.2	6.1	9.8	7.8	5.6	5.9	19.1	19.4	19.5	13.2
Connecticut	11.2	7.9	6.6	6.6	10.2	6.3	5.6	5.9	19.1	17.6	14.4	12.1
Delaware	13.9	10.1	9.2	7.5	9.8	9.7	7.9	6.1	27.9	20.1	14.8	11.8
District of Columbia	25.0	20.7	12.0	13.1	17.8	(B)	(B)	8.5	26.7	24.6	16.1	16.6
Florida	14.6	9.6	7.0	7.1	11.8	6.7	5.4	5.5	22.8	16.8	12.6	12.2
Georgia	14.5	12.4	8.5	8.0	10.8	7.4	5.9	5.6	21.0	18.3	13.9	12.8
Hawaii	10.3	6.7	8.1	6.5	11.6	6.1	6.5	6.1	(B)	(B)	(B)	(B)
Idaho	10.7	8.7	7.5	6.8	10.7	8.6	7.5	6.6	(NA)	(B)	(B)	(B)
Illinois.	14.8	10.7	8.5	6.7	11.7	7.9	6.6	5.2	26.3	22.4	17.1	14.2
Indiana.	11.9	9.6	7.8	7.6	10.5	7.9	6.9	6.6	23.4	17.4	15.8	16.0
Iowa.	11.8	8.1	6.5	5.5	11.5	7.9	6.0	5.3	27.2	21.9	21.1	11.6
Kansas.	10.4	8.4	6.8	7.9	9.5	8.0	6.4	7.0	20.6	17.7	12.2	19.0
Kentucky	12.9	8.5	7.2	6.7	12.0	8.2	6.7	6.0	22.0	14.3	12.7	12.7
Louisiana	14.3	11.1	9.0	9.2	10.5	8.1	5.9	6.1	20.6	16.7	13.3	14.1
Maine.	9.2	6.2	4.9	6.3	9.4	6.7	4.8	6.3	(B)	(B)	(B)	(B)
Maryland	14.0	9.5	7.6	8.0	11.6	6.8	4.8	4.8	20.4	17.1	13.2	13.6
Massachusetts.	10.5	7.0	4.6	4.9	10.1	6.1	4.0	4.5	16.8	11.9	9.9	8.8
Michigan	12.8	10.7	8.2	7.9	10.6	7.4	6.0	6.1	24.2	21.6	18.2	16.4
Minnesota	10.0	7.3	5.6	5.6	9.6	6.7	4.8	4.7	20.0	23.7	14.6	11.7
Mississippi.	17.0	12.1	10.7	10.0	11.1	7.4	6.8	6.7	23.7	16.2	15.3	13.9
Missouri.	12.4	9.4	7.2	7.5	11.1	7.9	5.9	5.9	20.7	18.2	14.7	16.5
Montana.	12.4	9.0	6.1	6.4	11.8	6.0	5.5	5.9	(NA)	(B)	(B)	(B)
Nebraska	11.5	8.3	7.3	6.8	10.7	6.9	6.4	6.1	25.2	18.9	20.3	14.0
Nevada	10.7	8.4	6.5	6.4	10.0	8.2	6.0	6.0	20.6	14.2	12.7	12.4
New Hampshire.	9.9	7.1	5.7	5.4	9.9	6.0	5.5	5.3	22.5	(B)	(B)	(B)
New Jersey	12.5	9.0	6.3	5.2	10.3	6.4	5.0	4.1	21.9	18.4	13.6	11.0
New Mexico	11.5	9.0	6.6	6.3	11.3	7.6	6.3	6.0	23.1	(B)	(B)	(B)
New York	12.5	9.6	6.4	5.6	10.8	7.4	5.4	5.0	20.0	18.1	10.9	8.8
North Carolina	14.5	10.6	8.6	8.5	12.1	8.0	6.3	6.4	20.0	16.5	15.7	15.1
North Dakota	12.1	8.0	8.1	7.5	11.7	7.2	7.5	6.8	27.5	(B)	(B)	(B)
Ohio.	12.8	9.8	7.6	7.7	11.2	7.8	6.3	6.3	23.0	19.5	15.4	14.8
Oklahoma	12.7	9.2	8.5	8.5	12.1	9.1	7.9	7.3	21.8	14.3	16.9	18.0
Oregon.	12.2	8.3	5.6	5.8	12.2	7.0	5.5	5.7	15.9	(B)	(B)	(B)
Pennsylvania	13.2	9.6	7.1	7.6	11.9	7.4	5.8	6.1	23.1	20.5	15.7	15.1
Rhode Island	11.0	8.1	6.3	7.4	10.9	7.0	5.9	6.5	(B)	(B)	(B)	16.0
South Carolina.	15.6	11.7	8.7	8.6	10.8	8.1	5.4	6.0	22.9	17.3	14.8	13.7
South Dakota.	10.9	10.1	5.5	6.4	9.0	8.0	4.3	5.6	(NA)	(B)	(B)	(B)
Tennessee	13.5	10.3	9.1	8.3	11.9	7.3	6.8	6.4	19.3	17.9	18.0	15.7
Texas	12.2	8.1	5.7	6.3	11.2	6.7	5.1	5.7	18.8	14.7	11.4	11.5
Utah.	10.4	7.5	5.2	5.1	10.5	6.0	5.1	5.0	27.3	(B)	(B)	(B)
Vermont	10.7	6.4	6.0	5.1	10.7	5.9	6.1	4.8	(B)	(B)	(B)	(B)
Virginia.	13.6	10.2	6.9	7.8	11.9	7.4	5.4	5.8	19.8	19.5	12.4	15.4
Washington	11.8	7.8	5.2	4.8	11.5	7.3	4.9	4.3	16.4	20.6	9.4	10.3
West Virginia	11.8	9.9	7.6	7.5	11.4	8.1	7.4	7.0	21.5	(B)	(B)	(B)
Wisconsin	10.3	8.2	6.6	6.5	9.7	7.7	5.5	5.4	18.5	19.0	17.2	15.2
Wyoming	9.8	8.6	6.7	7.4	9.3	7.5	6.5	6.7	25.9	(B)	(B)	(B)
Puerto Rico	(NA)	(NA)	9.7	8.5	(NA)	(NA)	10.2	9.1	(NA)	(NA)	(B)	(B)
Virgin Islands	(NA)	(NA)	13.4	(B)	(NA)	(NA)	(B)	(B)	(B)	(B)	(B)	(B)
Guam.	(NA)	(NA)	5.8	10.3	(NA)	(NA)	(B)	(B)	(B)	(B)	(B)	(B)
American Samoa.	(NA)	(NA)	(B)	(B)	(B)	(B)	(B)	(B)	(B)	(B)	(B)	(B)
Northern Marianas . . .	(NA)	(NA)	(B)	(B)	(B)	(B)	(B)	(B)	(B)	(B)	(B)	(B)

B Base figure too small to meet statistical standards for reliability. NA Not available. [1] Includes other races, not shown separately.

Source: U.S. National Center for Health Statistics, National Vital Statistics Reports (NVSR), *Deaths: Final Data for 2007*, Vol. 58, No. 19, May 2010, and earlier reports.

Table 117. Age-Adjusted Death Rates by Major Causes: 1960 to 2008

[Age-adjusted rates per 100,000 population. Age adjusted death rates were prepared using the direct method, in which age specific death rates for a population of interest are applied to a standard population distributed by age. Age adjustment eliminates the differences in observed rates between points in time or among compared population groups that result from age differences in population composition. Beginning 1999 deaths classified according to tenth revision of International Classification of Diseases; for earlier years, causes of death were classified according to the revisions then in use. Changes in classification of causes of death due to these revisions may result in discontinuities in cause-of-death trends. See Appendix III]

Year	Dis-eases of the heart	Malignant neo-plasms (cancer)	Cerebro-vascular diseases	Chronic lower res-piratory diseases	Acci-dents [1]	Alz-heimer's disease	Dia-betes mellitus	Influenza and pneu-monia	Nephritis, nephrotic syndrome and nephrosis	Inten-tional self-harm (suicide)
1960.....	559.0	193.9	177.9	12.5	63.1	(NA)	22.5	53.7	10.6	12.5
1961.....	545.3	193.4	173.1	12.6	60.6	(NA)	22.1	43.4	10.0	12.2
1962.....	556.9	193.3	174.0	14.2	62.9	(NA)	22.6	47.1	9.6	12.8
1963.....	563.4	194.7	173.9	16.5	64.0	(NA)	23.1	55.6	9.2	13.0
1964.....	543.3	193.6	167.0	16.3	64.1	(NA)	22.5	45.4	8.9	12.7
1965.....	542.5	195.6	166.4	18.3	65.8	(NA)	22.9	46.8	8.3	13.0
1966.....	541.2	196.5	165.8	19.2	67.6	(NA)	23.6	47.9	7.9	12.7
1967.....	524.7	197.3	159.3	19.2	66.2	(NA)	23.4	42.2	7.3	12.5
1968.....	531.0	198.8	162.5	20.7	65.5	(NA)	25.3	52.8	6.1	12.4
1969.....	516.8	198.5	155.4	20.9	64.9	(NA)	25.1	47.9	6.0	12.7
1970.....	492.7	198.6	147.7	21.3	62.2	(NA)	24.3	41.7	5.5	13.1
1971.....	492.9	199.3	147.6	21.8	60.3	(NA)	23.9	38.4	5.2	13.1
1972.....	490.2	200.3	147.3	22.8	60.2	(NA)	23.7	41.3	5.2	13.3
1973.....	482.0	200.0	145.2	23.6	59.3	(NA)	23.0	41.2	5.0	13.1
1974.....	458.8	201.5	136.8	23.2	52.7	(NA)	22.1	35.5	4.7	13.2
1975.....	431.2	200.1	123.5	23.7	50.8	(NA)	20.3	34.9	4.7	13.6
1976.....	426.9	202.5	117.4	24.9	48.7	(NA)	19.5	38.8	4.9	13.2
1977.....	413.7	203.5	110.4	24.7	48.8	(NA)	18.2	31.0	4.8	13.7
1978.....	409.9	204.9	103.7	26.3	48.9	(NA)	18.3	34.5	4.8	12.9
1979.....	401.6	204.0	97.1	25.5	46.5	(NA)	17.5	26.1	8.6	12.6
1980.....	412.1	207.9	96.4	28.3	46.4	(NA)	18.1	31.4	9.1	12.2
1981.....	397.0	206.4	89.5	29.0	43.4	0.9	17.6	30.0	9.1	12.3
1982.....	389.0	208.3	84.2	29.1	40.1	1.3	17.2	26.5	9.4	12.5
1983.....	388.9	209.1	81.2	31.6	39.1	2.2	17.6	29.8	9.6	12.4
1984.....	378.8	210.8	78.7	32.4	38.8	3.1	17.2	30.6	10.0	12.6
1985.....	375.0	211.3	76.6	34.5	38.5	4.1	17.4	34.5	10.4	12.5
1986.....	365.1	211.5	73.1	34.8	38.6	4.6	17.2	34.8	10.4	13.0
1987.....	355.9	211.7	71.6	35.0	38.2	5.5	17.4	33.8	10.4	12.8
1988.....	352.5	212.5	70.6	36.5	38.9	5.8	18.0	37.3	10.4	12.5
1989.....	332.0	214.2	66.9	36.6	37.7	6.1	20.5	35.9	9.6	12.3
1990.....	321.8	216.0	65.3	37.2	36.3	6.3	20.7	36.8	9.3	12.5
1991.....	312.5	215.2	62.9	37.9	34.7	6.3	20.7	34.7	9.3	12.3
1992.....	304.0	213.5	61.5	37.7	33.2	6.3	20.7	32.8	9.4	12.0
1993.....	308.1	213.5	62.7	40.7	34.2	7.1	21.9	35.0	9.7	12.1
1994.....	297.5	211.7	62.6	40.3	34.2	7.7	22.6	33.6	9.4	11.9
1995.....	293.4	209.9	63.1	40.1	34.4	8.4	23.2	33.4	9.5	11.8
1996.....	285.7	206.7	62.5	40.6	34.5	8.5	23.8	32.9	9.6	11.5
1997.....	277.7	203.4	61.1	41.1	34.2	8.7	23.7	33.3	9.8	11.2
1998.....	267.4	202.1	62.8	43.8	35.6	8.6	24.2	24.2	9.8	11.1
1999.....	266.5	200.8	61.6	45.4	35.3	16.5	25.0	23.5	13.0	10.5
2000.....	257.6	199.6	60.9	44.2	34.9	18.1	25.0	23.7	13.5	10.4
2001.....	247.8	196.0	57.9	43.7	35.7	19.1	25.3	22.0	14.0	10.7
2002.....	240.8	193.5	56.2	43.5	36.9	20.2	25.4	22.6	14.2	10.9
2003.....	232.3	190.1	53.5	43.3	37.3	21.4	25.3	22.0	14.4	10.8
2004.....	217.0	185.8	50.0	41.1	37.7	21.8	24.5	19.8	14.2	10.9
2005.....	211.1	183.8	46.6	43.2	39.1	22.9	24.6	20.3	14.3	10.9
2006.....	200.2	180.7	43.6	40.5	39.8	22.6	23.3	17.8	14.5	10.9
2007.....	190.9	178.4	42.2	40.8	40.0	22.7	22.5	16.2	14.5	11.3
2008 [2] ...	186.7	175.5	40.6	44.0	38.6	24.4	21.8	17.0	14.8	11.6

NA Not available. [1] Unintentional injuries. [2] Preliminary data.

Source: U.S. National Center for Health Statistics, *Health, United States, 2010.* See also <http://www.cdc.gov/nchs/hus.htm> and National Vital Statistics Reports (NVSR), *Deaths: Preliminary Data for 2008*, Vol. 59, No. 2, December 2010.

Table 118. Leading Causes of Deaths by Race: 2007

[Cause of death based on International Classification of Diseases (ICD), tenth edition)]

Cause of death	White Rank[1]	White Deaths	White Per-cent	Black Rank	Black Deaths	Black Per-cent	American Indian/ Alas-kan Native Rank	American Indian/ Alas-kan Native Deaths	American Indian/ Alas-kan Native Per-cent	Asian/ Pacific Islander Rank	Asian/ Pacific Islander Deaths	Asian/ Pacific Islander Per-cent
All causes...........	(X)	2,074,151	100.0	(X)	289,585	100.0	(X)	14,367	100.0	(X)	45,609	100.0
Diseases of heart	1	531,636	25.6	1	71,209	24.6	1	2,648	18.4	2	10,574	23.2
Malignant neoplasms......	2	483,939	23.3	2	64,049	22.1	2	2,561	17.8	1	12,326	27.0
Cerebrovascular diseases..	3	114,695	5.5	3	17,085	5.9	5	586	4.1	3	3,586	7.9
Chronic lower respiratory diseases.............	4	118,081	5.7	7	7,901	2.7	7	611	4.3	7	1,331	2.9
Accidents (unintentional injuries).............	5	106,252	5.1	4	13,559	4.7	3	1,701	11.8	4	2,194	4.8
Alzheimer's disease.......	6	68,933	3.3	14	4,760	1.6	13	191	1.3	10	748	1.6
Diabetes mellitus........	7	56,390	2.7	5	12,459	4.3	4	790	5.5	5	1,743	3.8
Influenza and pneumonia ..	8	45,947	2.2	11	5,155	1.8	9	280	1.9	6	1,335	2.9
Nephritis, nephrotic syn-drome and nephrosis	9	36,871	1.8	8	8,392	2.9	10	292	2.0	8	893	2.0
Intentional self harm (suicide)	10	31,348	1.5	16	1,958	0.7	8	392	2.7	9	900	2.0
Septicemia.............	11	27,750	1.3	10	6,297	2.2	12	230	1.6	12	551	1.2
Chronic liver disease and cirrhosis	12	25,490	1.2	15	2,558	0.9	6	709	4.9	15	408	0.9
Assault (homicide).......	20	8,914	0.4	6	8,870	3.1	11	220	1.5	14	357	0.8
Human immunodeficiency virus (HIV)............	22	4,672	0.2	9	6,470	2.2	17	78	0.5	25	75	0.2

X Not applicable. [1] Rank based on number of deaths.
Source: U.S. National Center for Health Statistics, National Vital Statistics Reports (NVSR), *Deaths: Final Data for 2007*, Vol. 58, No. 19, May 2010. See also <http://cdc.gov/NCHS/products/nvsr.htm#vol58>.

Table 119. Leading Causes of Deaths by Hispanic Origin: 2007

[Race and Hispanic origin are reported separately on death certificate. Persons of Hispanic origin may be any race. Cause of death based on International Classification of Diseases (ICD), tenth edition]

Cause of death	Hispanic Rank	Hispanic Deaths	Hispanic Per-cent	Non-Hispanic Rank	Non-Hispanic Deaths	Non-Hispanic Per-cent	Non-Hispanic White Rank	Non-Hispanic White Deaths	Non-Hispanic White Per-cent	Non-Hispanic Black Rank	Non-Hispanic Black Deaths	Non-Hispanic Black Per-cent
All causes.........	(X)	135,519	100.0	(X)	2,284,446	100.0	(X)	1,939,606	100.0	(X)	286,366	100.0
Diseases of heart	1	29,021	21.4	1	586,077	25.7	1	502,683	25.9	1	70,443	24.6
Malignant neoplasms....	2	27,660	20.4	2	534,614	23.4	2	456,576	23.5	2	63,441	22.2
Accidents (unintentional injuries).............	3	11,723	8.7	5	111,641	4.9	5	94,584	4.9	4	13,332	4.7
Cerebrovascular diseases............	4	7,078	5.2	3	128,705	5.6	4	107,678	5.6	3	16,934	5.9
Diabetes mellitus.......	5	6,417	4.7	7	64,863	2.8	7	50,046	2.6	5	12,343	4.3
Chronic liver disease and cirrhosis	6	3,913	2.9	12	25,190	1.1	12	21,598	1.1	15	2,525	0.9
Assault (homicide)......	7	3,466	2.6	16	14,798	0.6	21	5,512	0.3	6	8,746	3.1
Chronic lower respiratory diseases............	8	3,531	2.6	4	124,217	5.4	3	114,480	5.9	7	7,830	2.7
Influenza and pneumonia	9	2,735	2.0	8	49,896	2.2	8	43,219	2.2	11	5,091	1.8
Certain conditions origi-nating in the perinatal period.............	10	2,946	2.2	19	11,525	0.5	20	6,064	0.3	13	4,868	1.7
Nephritis, nephrotic syndrome and nephrosis	11	2,691	2.0	9	43,694	1.9	9	34,219	1.8	8	8,318	2.9
Alzheimer's disease.....	12	2,471	1.8	6	72,101	3.2	6	66,453	3.4	14	4,729	1.7
Intentional self harm (suicide)	13	2,465	1.8	11	32,061	1.4	10	28,897	1.5	16	1,916	0.7
Septicemia............	15	1,894	1.4	10	32,865	1.4	11	25,856	1.3	10	6,241	2.2
Human immunodeficiency virus (HIV)...........	16	1,516	1.1	21	9,726	0.4	22	3,182	0.2	9	6,398	2.2

X Not applicable.
Source: U.S. National Center for Health Statistics, National Vital Statistics Reports (NVSR), *Deaths: Final Data for 2007*, Vol. 58, No. 19, May 2010. See also <http://cdc.gov/NCHS/products/nvsr.htm#vol58>.

Table 120. Deaths and Death Rates by Selected Causes: 2006 and 2007

[Rates per 100,000 population. Figures are weighted data rounded to the nearest individual, so categories may not add to total or subtotal. Excludes deaths of nonresidents of the United States. Deaths classified according to tenth revision of International Classification of Diseases (ICD). See also Appendix III]

Cause of death	2006			2007		
	Number	Rate	Age-adjusted rate [1]	Number	Rate	Age-adjusted rate [1]
All causes [2]	**2,426,264**	**810.4**	**776.5**	**2,423,712**	**803.6**	**760.2**
Major cardiovascular diseases [2]	823,746	275.1	261.2	806,156	267.3	249.9
Diseases of heart	631,636	211.0	200.2	616,067	204.3	190.9
Acute rheumatic fever and chronic rheumatic heart disease	3,257	1.1	1.1	3,201	1.1	1.0
Hypertensive heart disease	29,788	9.9	9.4	30,780	10.2	9.5
Hypertensive heart and renal disease	2,918	1.0	0.9	2,987	1.0	0.9
Ischemic heart disease	425,425	142.1	134.9	406,351	134.7	126.0
Acute myocardial infarction	141,462	47.2	45.0	132,968	44.1	41.4
Other heart diseases	170,248	56.9	53.9	172,748	57.3	53.4
Heart failure	60,337	20.2	18.9	56,565	18.8	17.3
Essential (primary) hypertension and hypertensive renal disease	23,855	8.0	7.5	23,965	7.9	7.4
Cerebrovascular diseases	137,119	45.8	43.6	135,952	45.1	42.2
Atherosclerosis	8,652	2.9	2.7	8,232	2.7	2.5
Malignant neoplasms [2]	559,888	187.0	180.7	562,875	186.6	178.4
Malignant neoplasms of lip, oral cavity, and pharynx	7,720	2.6	2.5	8,067	2.7	2.5
Malignant neoplasms of esophagus	13,686	4.6	4.4	13,592	4.5	4.3
Malignant neoplasms of stomach	11,345	3.8	3.7	11,388	3.8	36.0
Malignant neoplasms of colon, rectum and anus	53,549	17.9	17.2	53,586	17.8	16.9
Malignant neoplasms of liver and intrahepatic bile ducts	16,525	5.5	5.3	17,146	5.7	5.4
Malignant neoplasms of pancreas	33,454	11.2	10.8	34,117	11.3	10.8
Malignant neoplasms of trachea, bronchus and lung	158,664	53.0	51.5	158,760	52.6	50.6
Malignant melanoma of skin	8,441	2.8	2.7	8,461	2.8	2.7
Malignant neoplasm of breast	41,210	13.8	13.2	40,970	13.6	12.9
Malignant neoplasm of ovary	14,857	5.0	4.8	14,621	4.8	4.6
Malignant neoplasm of prostate	28,372	9.5	9.2	29,093	9.6	9.2
Malignant neoplasms of kidney and renal pelvis	12,379	4.1	4.0	12,703	4.2	4.0
Malignant neoplasms of bladder	13,474	4.5	4.3	13,843	4.6	4.4
Malignant neoplasms of meninges, brain and other parts of central nervous system	12,886	4.3	4.2	13,234	4.4	4.2
Malignant neoplasms of lymphoid, hematopoietic and related tissue [2]	55,045	18.4	17.9	54,991	18.2	17.6
Non-Hodgkins' lymphoma	20,594	6.9	6.7	20,528	6.8	6.5
Leukemia	21,944	7.3	7.1	21,825	7.2	7.0
Accidents (unintentional injuries)	121,599	40.6	39.8	123,706	41.0	40.0
Transport accidents [2]	48,412	16.2	16.0	46,844	15.5	15.3
Motor vehicle accidents	45,316	15.1	15.0	43,945	14.6	14.4
Nontransport accidents [2]	73,187	24.4	23.8	76,862	25.5	24.6
Falls	20,823	7.0	6.6	22,631	7.5	7.0
Accidental drowning and submersion	3,579	1.2	1.2	3,443	1.1	1.1
Accidental exposure to smoke, fire and flames	3,109	1.0	1.0	3,286	1.1	1.1
Accidental poisoning and exposure to noxious substances	27,531	9.2	9.1	29,846	9.9	9.8
Chronic lower respiratory diseases [2]	124,583	41.6	40.5	127,924	42.4	40.8
Emphysema	12,551	4.2	4.1	12,790	4.2	4.1
Asthma	3,613	1.2	1.2	3,447	1.1	1.1
Influenza and pneumonia [2]	56,326	18.8	17.8	52,717	17.5	16.2
Pneumonia	55,477	18.5	17.5	52,306	17.3	16.1
Septicemia (blood poisoning)	34,234	11.4	11.0	34,828	11.5	11.0
Viral hepatitis	7,250	2.4	2.3	7,407	2.5	2.3
Human immunodeficiency virus (HIV) disease	12,113	4.0	4.0	11,295	3.7	3.7
Anemias	3,996	1.3	1.3	4,829	1.6	1.5
Diabetes mellitus	72,449	24.2	23.3	71,382	23.7	22.5
Nutritional deficiencies	2,556	0.9	0.8	2,852	0.9	0.9
Malnutrition	2,377	0.8	0.7	2,644	0.9	0.8
Parkinson's disease	19,566	6.5	6.3	20,058	6.7	6.4
Alzheimer's disease	72,432	24.2	22.6	74,632	24.7	22.7
Chronic liver disease and cirrhosis	27,555	9.2	8.8	29,165	9.7	9.1
Alcoholic liver disease	13,050	4.4	4.1	14,406	4.8	4.5
Nephritis, nephrotic syndrome, and nephrosis [2]	45,344	15.1	14.5	46,448	15.4	14.5
Renal failure	43,344	14.5	13.9	43,263	14.3	13.6
Intentional self-harm (suicide)	33,300	11.1	10.9	34,598	11.5	11.3
Intentional self-harm (suicide) by discharge of firearms	16,883	5.6	5.5	17,352	5.8	5.6
Assault (homicide)	18,573	6.2	6.2	18,361	6.1	6.1
Assault (homicide) by discharge of firearms	12,791	4.3	4.3	12,632	4.2	4.2
Events of undetermined intent	5,131	1.7	1.7	5,381	1.8	1.8
Drug-induced deaths [3]	38,396	12.8	12.7	38,371	12.7	12.6
Alcohol-induced deaths [3]	22,073	7.4	7.0	23,199	7.7	7.3

[1] See text, this section. [2] Includes other causes, not shown separately. [3] Included in selected categories.

Source: U.S. National Center for Health Statistics, National Vital Statistics Reports (NVSR), *Deaths: Final Data for 2007*, Vol. 58, No. 19, May 2010.

Table 121. Deaths by Age and Selected Causes: 2007

[Deaths are classified according to the tenth revision of the International Classification of Diseases. See Appendix III]

Cause of death	All ages[1]	Under 1 year	1 to 4 years	5 to 14 years	15 to 24 years	25 to 34 years	35 to 44 years	45 to 54 years	55 to 64 years	65 to 74 years	75 to 84 years	85 years and over
All causes[2]	2,423,712	29,138	4,703	6,147	33,982	42,572	79,606	184,686	287,110	389,238	652,682	713,647
Septicemia	34,828	283	78	74	160	297	910	2,431	4,231	6,345	10,403	9,614
Human immunodeficiency virus (HIV) disease	11,295	5	4	10	160	1,091	3,572	4,156	1,721	448	109	16
Malignant neoplasms[2]	562,875	72	364	959	1,653	3,463	13,288	50,167	103,171	138,466	163,608	87,656
Malignant neoplasm of esophagus	13,592	–	–	–	5	28	246	1,452	3,379	3,726	3,376	1,380
Malignant neoplasm of colon, rectum, and anus	53,586	–	–	1	35	275	1,302	4,793	9,058	11,634	15,417	11,069
Malignant neoplasms of liver and intrahepatic bile ducts	17,146	6	19	25	38	90	368	2,503	4,181	3,884	4,266	1,766
Malignant neoplasm of pancreas	34,117	–	–	2	5	52	538	2,808	6,507	8,671	10,317	5,217
Malignant neoplasms of trachea, bronchus, and lung	158,760	1	1	4	25	135	1,852	12,480	31,216	48,157	48,358	16,528
Malignant neoplasm of breast	40,970	–	–	–	15	344	2,184	5,990	8,756	8,179	9,075	6,426
Malignant neoplasm of ovary	14,621	–	–	–	28	79	352	1,532	2,997	3,616	3,946	2,071
Malignant neoplasm of prostate	29,093	–	1	–	1	1	21	428	2,271	5,716	11,257	9,397
Malignant neoplasm of bladder	13,843	1	–	–	–	7	93	570	1,564	2,817	5,009	3,782
Malignant neoplasms of lymphoid, hematopoietic and related tissue[2]	54,991	26	111	352	630	771	1,464	3,606	7,694	12,223	17,884	10,228
Non-Hodgkins lymphoma	20,528	2	5	33	133	206	516	1,392	2,922	4,476	6,868	3,975
Leukemia	21,825	21	106	314	428	438	657	1,362	2,801	4,611	6,858	4,228
Diabetes mellitus	71,382	7	5	21	168	610	1,984	5,753	11,304	15,112	21,189	15,227
Parkinson's disease	20,058	–	–	–	2	2	12	60	396	2,310	9,363	7,911
Alzheimer's disease	74,632	–	–	–	1	1	8	95	728	3,984	23,009	46,804
Major cardiovascular diseases[2]	806,156	571	230	338	1,369	3,950	14,867	46,280	80,797	115,623	229,050	313,044
Diseases of heart[2]	616,067	424	173	241	1,084	3,223	11,839	37,434	65,527	89,589	171,257	235,249
Hypertensive heart disease	30,780	1	1	–	44	338	1,372	3,604	4,487	4,009	6,324	10,598
Ischemic heart diseases	406,351	24	8	21	151	1,048	6,219	24,390	46,164	63,027	116,152	149,126
Acute myocardial infarction	132,968	10	4	11	54	400	2,402	9,467	17,835	23,441	37,629	41,711
Heart failure	56,565	21	11	12	43	87	317	1,073	2,758	5,749	15,935	30,558
Essential (primary) hypertension and hypertensive renal disease	23,965	1	1	–	23	85	384	1,235	2,124	3,133	6,442	10,536
Cerebrovascular diseases	135,952	132	52	83	195	505	2,133	6,385	10,500	18,007	41,979	55,975
Influenza and pneumonia	52,717	222	109	103	163	331	784	1,909	3,152	5,547	14,859	25,535
Pneumonia	52,306	209	90	68	153	322	771	1,890	3,115	5,509	14,780	25,396
Chronic lower respiratory diseases[2]	127,924	43	57	118	149	263	796	4,153	12,777	28,664	48,041	32,857
Emphysema	12,790	3	–	1	1	10	60	486	1,590	3,294	4,835	2,509
Pneumonitis due to solids and liquids	16,988	10	8	16	47	70	154	436	884	1,724	5,187	8,451
Chronic liver disease and cirrhosis	29,165	4	4	–	30	384	2,570	8,212	8,004	5,167	3,694	1,093
Nephritis, nephrotic syndrome, and nephrosis[2]	46,448	144	22	24	86	261	754	2,233	4,440	7,752	14,711	16,021
Renal failure	43,263	138	16	18	77	237	696	2,091	4,205	7,330	13,718	14,737
Accidents (unintentional injuries)[2]	123,706	1,285	1,588	2,194	15,897	14,977	16,931	20,315	12,193	8,753	13,736	15,803
Transport accidents	46,844	127	581	1,374	10,928	7,452	6,829	7,199	4,838	3,194	2,983	1,326
Motor vehicle accidents	43,945	124	551	1,285	10,568	7,087	6,370	6,530	4,359	2,940	2,845	1,277
Nontransport accidents	76,862	1,158	1,007	820	4,969	7,525	10,102	13,116	7,355	5,559	10,753	14,477
Falls	22,631	24	36	32	233	334	593	1,304	1,739	2,594	6,552	9,188
Accidental poisoning and exposure to noxious substances	29,846	19	34	81	3,159	5,700	7,575	9,006	3,120	602	355	192
Intentional self-harm (suicide)	34,598	(NA)	(NA)	184	4,140	5,278	6,722	7,778	5,069	2,444	2,119	858
Assault (homicide)	18,361	352	398	346	5,551	4,758	3,052	2,140	980	411	268	80
Assault (homicide) by discharge of firearms	12,632	15	48	201	4,669	3,751	2,038	1,159	446	185	88	23
Enterocolitis due to clostridium difficile	6,372	4	1	–	4	14	31	107	313	876	2,338	2,647

– Represents zero. NA Not available. [1] Includes persons with age not stated, not shown separately. [2] Includes other causes, not shown separately.
Source: U.S. National Center for Health Statistics, National Vital Statistics Reports, *Deaths: Final Data for 2007*, Vol. 58, No. 19, May 2010.

Table 122. Deaths and Death Rates by Leading Causes of Death and Age: 2007

[Rates per 100,000 population in specified group. Data are based on the tenth revision of the International Classification of Diseases (ICD). See Appendix III]

Age and cause of death	Number	Rate
ALL AGES [1]		
All causes	**2,423,712**	**803.6**
Diseases of heart	616,067	204.3
Malignant neoplasms	562,875	186.6
Cerebrovascular diseases	135,952	45.1
Chronic lower respiratory diseases	127,924	42.4
Accidents (unintentional injuries)	123,706	41.0
Alzheimer's disease	74,632	24.7
Diabetes mellitus	71,382	23.7
Influenza and pneumonia	52,717	17.5
Nephritis, nephrotic syndrome and nephrosis	46,448	15.4
Septicemia	34,828	11.5
1 TO 4 YEARS		
All causes	**4,703**	**28.6**
Accidents (unintentional injuries)	1,588	9.6
Congenital malformations, deformations and chromosomal abnormalities	546	3.3
Malignant neoplasms	364	2.2
Assault (homicide)	398	2.4
Diseases of heart	173	1.1
Influenza and pneumonia	109	0.7
Septicemia	78	0.5
Certain conditions originating in the perinatal period	70	0.4
In situ neoplasms, benign neoplasms and neoplasms of uncertain or unknown behavior	59	0.4
Cerebrovascular diseases	52	0.3
5 TO 14 YEARS		
All causes	**6,147**	**15.3**
Accidents (unintentional injuries)	2,194	5.5
Malignant neoplasms	959	2.4
Assault (homicide)	346	0.9
Congenital malformations, deformations and chromosomal abnormalities	374	0.9
Diseases of heart	241	0.6
Intentional self-harm (suicide)	184	0.5
Chronic lower respiratory diseases	118	0.3
In situ neoplasms, benign neoplasms and neoplasms of uncertain or unknown behavior	84	0.2
Cerebrovascular diseases	83	0.2
Septicemia	74	0.2
15 TO 24 YEARS		
All causes	**33,982**	**79.9**
Accidents (unintentional injuries)	15,897	37.4
Assault (homicide)	5,551	13.1
Intentional self-harm (suicide)	4,140	9.7
Malignant neoplasms	1,653	3.9
Diseases of heart	1,084	2.6
Congenital malformations, deformations and chromosomal abnormalities	402	0.9
Cerebrovascular diseases	195	0.5
Human immunodeficiency virus (HIV) disease (B20-B24)	160	0.4
Influenza and pneumonia	163	0.4
Pregnancy, childbirth and the puerperium	160	0.4
Diabetes mellitus	168	0.4
Septicemia	160	0.4
25 TO 34 YEARS		
All causes	**42,572**	**104.9**
Accidents (unintentional injuries)	14,977	36.9
Intentional self-harm (suicide)	5,278	13.0
Assault (homicide)	4,758	11.7
Malignant neoplasms	3,463	8.5
Diseases of heart	3,223	7.9
Human immunodeficiency virus (HIV) disease	1,091	2.7
Diabetes mellitus	610	1.5
Cerebrovascular diseases	505	1.2
Congenital malformations, deformations and chromosomal abnormalities	417	1.0
Influenza and pneumonia	331	0.8
Septicemia	297	0.7
35 TO 44 YEARS		
All causes	**79,606**	**184.4**
Accidents	16,931	39.2
Malignant neoplasms	13,288	30.8
Diseases of heart	11,839	27.4
Intentional self-harm (suicide)	6,722	15.6
Human immunodeficiency virus (HIV) disease	3,572	8.3
Assault (homicide)	3,052	7.1
Chronic liver disease and cirrhosis	2,570	6.0
Cerebrovascular diseases	2,133	4.9
Diabetes mellitus	1,984	4.6
Septicemia	910	2.1
45 TO 54 YEARS		
All causes	**184,686**	**420.9**
Malignant neoplasms	50,167	114.3
Diseases of heart	37,434	85.3
Accidents	20,315	46.3
Chronic liver disease and cirrhosis	8,212	18.7
Intentional self-harm (suicide)	7,778	17.7
Cerebrovascular diseases	6,385	14.6
Diabetes mellitus	5,753	13.1
Human immunodeficiency virus (HIV) disease	4,156	9.5
Chronic lower respiratory diseases	4,153	9.5
Viral hepatitis	2,815	6.4
Assault (homicide)	2,140	4.9
Septicemia	2,431	5.5
55 TO 64 YEARS		
All causes	**287,110**	**877.7**
Malignant neoplasms	103,171	315.4
Diseases of heart	65,527	200.3
Chronic lower respiratory diseases	12,777	39.1
Accidents (unintentional injuries)	12,193	37.3
Diabetes mellitus	11,304	34.6
Cerebrovascular diseases	10,500	32.1
Chronic liver disease and cirrhosis	8,004	24.5
Intentional self-harm (suicide)	5,069	15.5
Nephritis, nephrotic syndrome and nephrosis	4,440	13.6
Septicemia	4,231	12.9
65 TO 74 YEARS		
All causes	**389,238**	**2,011.3**
Malignant neoplasms	138,466	715.5
Diseases of heart	89,589	462.9
Chronic lower respiratory diseases	28,664	148.1
Cerebrovascular diseases	18,007	93.0
Diabetes mellitus	15,112	78.1
Accidents (unintentional injuries)	8,753	45.2
Nephritis, nephrotic syndrome and nephrosis	7,752	40.1
Septicemia	6,345	32.8
Influenza and pneumonia	5,547	28.7
Chronic liver disease and cirrhosis	5,167	26.7
75 TO 84 YEARS		
All causes	**652,682**	**5,011.6**
Diseases of heart	171,257	1,315.0
Malignant neoplasms	163,608	1,256.3
Chronic lower respiratory diseases	48,041	368.9
Cerebrovascular diseases	41,979	322.3
Alzheimer's disease	23,009	176.7
Diabetes mellitus	21,189	162.7
Influenza and pneumonia	14,859	114.1
Nephritis, nephrotic syndrome and nephrosis	14,711	113.0
Accidents (unintentional injuries)	13,736	105.5
Septicemia	10,403	79.9
85 YEARS AND OVER		
All causes	**713,647**	**12,946.5**
Diseases of heart	235,249	4,267.7
Malignant neoplasms	87,656	1,590.2
Cerebrovascular diseases	55,975	1,015.5
Alzheimer's disease	46,804	849.1
Chronic lower respiratory diseases	32,857	596.1
Influenza and pneumonia	25,535	463.2
Nephritis, nephrotic syndrome and nephrosis	16,021	290.6
Diabetes mellitus	15,227	276.2
Accidents (unintentional injuries)	15,803	286.7
Septicemia	9,614	174.4

[1] Includes deaths under 1 year of age.

Source: U.S. National Center for Health Statistics, National Vital Statistics Reports (NVSR), *Deaths: Final Data for 2007*, Vol. 58, No. 19, May 2010.

Table 123. Age-Adjusted Death Rates for Major Causes of Death—States and Island Areas: 2007

[Age adjusted rates per 100,000 resident population estimated as of July 1. By place of residence. Excludes nonresidents of the United States. Causes of death classified according to tenth revisions of International Classification of Diseases. See text, this section and Appendix III]

State and Island Areas	All causes of death	Diseases of heart	Malig- nant neo- plasms	Cerebro- vascular diseases	Chronic lower respira- tory disease	Accidents Total	Accidents Motor vehicle acci- dents	Alz- heimer's disease	Diabetes mellitus	Influ- enza and pneu- monia	Inten- tional self- harm (suicide)
U.S.	760.2	190.9	178.4	42.2	40.8	40.0	14.4	22.7	22.5	16.2	11.3
AL	930.7	235.5	197.3	54.5	50.2	53.9	25.9	30.1	26.0	17.8	12.5
AK	755.1	147.9	179.9	44.3	44.4	55.3	15.2	20.8	23.4	12.9	22.1
AZ	682.1	152.5	152.8	32.7	40.2	49.4	17.6	29.6	17.4	13.5	16.1
AR	882.8	221.8	200.4	57.4	51.7	47.6	23.7	24.6	26.5	22.3	14.3
CA	674.2	177.9	161.7	42.2	37.4	31.9	11.7	24.3	21.8	18.9	9.8
CO	700.8	145.3	153.7	39.0	49.1	44.2	12.3	27.8	16.7	14.3	16.4
CT	694.1	171.0	170.7	34.2	33.1	35.8	8.7	16.9	15.8	17.6	7.4
DE	773.6	200.2	193.9	39.4	40.1	34.8	13.6	20.9	23.4	12.2	10.7
DC	866.9	239.4	199.1	36.9	22.4	32.4	8.9	21.8	25.2	13.2	5.8
FL	685.9	162.4	166.6	33.6	36.7	46.5	18.1	16.2	21.1	8.6	13.3
GA	839.8	203.0	181.8	49.7	43.8	44.2	18.5	25.3	19.5	18.3	10.7
HI	607.4	140.2	146.2	39.6	19.3	33.3	10.3	14.1	18.5	11.6	9.7
ID	734.6	164.1	165.6	43.2	46.6	43.1	18.5	28.2	22.7	15.1	15.1
IL	759.8	192.8	185.9	43.9	36.7	33.4	10.6	19.9	21.8	18.8	8.5
IN	809.9	203.0	193.2	45.7	49.2	38.7	14.8	24.2	23.4	16.1	12.4
IA	718.6	174.8	177.7	42.1	44.7	37.3	15.0	27.9	20.5	18.0	10.6
KS	783.0	178.7	180.0	46.0	48.8	41.2	15.9	25.2	22.8	19.9	13.7
KY	896.9	220.9	213.5	48.1	59.0	55.1	20.0	27.1	24.1	20.1	15.1
LA	926.4	230.0	200.3	50.1	39.7	57.6	24.0	31.3	33.3	20.3	12.2
ME	773.6	172.9	191.9	40.3	44.8	41.5	14.7	27.9	21.9	14.1	13.7
MD	782.7	202.4	180.7	42.7	35.1	26.2	12.0	16.0	23.4	17.9	9.0
MA	707.5	165.5	179.8	36.5	31.6	30.8	6.7	20.9	16.6	19.5	7.6
MI	806.1	221.5	187.3	44.3	43.6	36.1	12.0	22.1	26.3	15.0	11.0
MN	661.5	129.8	169.7	38.1	32.8	37.4	11.7	19.6	19.6	10.2	10.8
MS	943.0	266.5	200.4	53.0	47.5	61.9	31.6	26.5	21.8	18.3	13.8
MO	826.7	214.4	191.6	48.2	47.4	48.4	17.6	24.3	22.3	18.9	13.5
MT	772.7	163.1	172.1	38.5	55.0	60.2	27.6	22.1	23.1	15.8	19.4
NE	743.7	165.3	177.3	43.1	45.8	35.7	15.7	22.9	23.3	15.1	10.2
NV	803.5	200.0	180.2	38.3	47.5	48.4	16.0	12.3	12.9	18.4	18.3
NH	727.0	174.9	184.5	34.3	44.0	38.5	10.3	28.9	20.1	14.5	11.1
NJ	724.2	191.9	180.4	35.8	31.3	26.8	8.2	18.0	24.4	13.7	6.7
NM	755.9	159.2	157.3	39.2	43.6	66.7	19.2	15.5	32.7	14.6	20.4
NY	686.4	225.1	168.0	28.2	30.8	25.3	7.4	8.8	17.5	20.0	7.0
NC	834.4	191.0	189.0	50.3	47.1	48.3	20.0	27.7	23.4	18.4	11.7
ND	679.5	164.1	165.3	37.3	32.9	39.3	17.5	40.4	28.3	14.6	14.4
OH	830.8	204.8	197.9	45.3	50.7	41.1	12.1	27.4	29.1	13.3	11.0
OK	920.4	241.6	198.2	53.8	61.2	58.4	20.4	23.0	29.3	20.1	14.7
OR	753.9	156.9	179.3	43.6	46.3	41.5	13.0	27.6	27.0	11.1	15.2
PA	790.1	199.4	188.2	42.9	38.1	40.9	12.5	19.8	22.0	15.2	11.2
RI	750.0	203.6	179.6	33.5	32.7	34.6	7.6	22.2	19.2	16.1	8.7
SC	849.7	192.9	186.7	53.4	44.0	53.0	24.2	30.9	26.2	15.8	11.7
SD	693.5	159.1	171.3	38.7	47.0	41.8	18.3	30.2	25.6	17.9	12.5
TN	885.2	220.6	200.3	53.9	49.2	52.1	21.0	35.9	26.2	22.5	13.3
TX	777.7	191.9	170.3	49.0	41.2	41.4	16.2	24.7	24.9	16.1	10.4
UT	694.2	152.1	128.8	38.9	31.9	34.4	12.4	20.5	27.6	16.0	15.4
VT	729.3	161.2	188.5	37.6	44.9	44.7	10.9	28.4	24.4	9.8	13.8
VA	770.6	182.7	182.7	44.5	37.7	38.1	13.9	23.4	19.7	16.6	11.2
WA	722.2	167.3	177.7	41.4	42.4	39.8	9.9	40.7	23.2	11.1	13.0
WV	951.7	229.4	207.6	48.9	58.6	65.9	23.6	23.1	35.5	17.8	15.9
WI	732.3	171.9	177.9	42.3	38.7	43.8	14.2	24.3	18.3	15.5	12.7
WY	802.0	178.3	174.4	39.5	56.5	57.0	25.3	21.0	26.2	20.9	19.7
PR [1]	726.7	138.4	121.3	41.3	27.9	29.9	11.0	40.7	66.5	25.6	6.9
VI [1]	700.2	234.7	109.2	36.8	(S)	30.7	(S)	(S)	45.4	(S)	(S)
GU [1]	694.9	228.4	122.3	50.1	23.2	26.2	16.0	(S)	44.0	(S)	16.0
AS [1]	1,054.4	278.0	150.1	94.2	(S)	(S)	(S)	(S)	126.1	(S)	(S)
MP [1]	913.0	167.0	239.5	(S)	(S)	(S)	(S)	(S)	(S)	(S)	(S)

S Figure does not meet standards of reliability or precision. [1] Age-adjusted death rates for Puerto Rico, Virgin Islands, American Samoa, and Northern Marianas are calculated using different age groups in the weighting procedure. See source "Technical Notes."

Source: U.S. National Center for Health Statistics, National Vital Statistics Reports, (NVSR), *Deaths: Final Data for 2007*, Vol. 58, No. 19, May 2010.

Table 124. Death Rates From Heart Disease by Selected Characteristics: 1980 to 2007

[Rates per 100,000 population. See headnote Tables 107 and 115. See Appendix III]

Characteristics	1980	1990	2000	2002	2003	2004	2005	2006	2007
All ages, age adjusted [1]	412.1	321.8	257.6	240.8	232.3	217.0	211.1	200.2	190.9
All ages, crude rate [2]	336.0	289.5	252.6	241.7	235.6	222.2	220.0	211.0	204.3
Under 1 year	22.8	20.1	13.0	12.4	11.0	10.3	8.7	8.4	10.0
1 to 4 years	2.6	1.9	1.2	1.1	1.2	1.2	0.9	1.0	1.1
5 to 14 years	0.9	0.9	0.7	0.6	0.6	0.6	0.6	0.6	0.6
15 to 24 years	2.9	2.5	2.6	2.5	2.7	2.5	2.7	2.5	2.6
25 to 34 years	8.3	7.6	7.4	7.9	8.2	7.9	8.1	8.2	7.9
35 to 44 years	44.6	31.4	29.2	30.5	30.7	29.3	28.9	28.3	27.4
45 to 54 years	180.2	120.5	94.2	93.7	92.5	90.2	89.7	88.0	85.3
55 to 64 years	494.1	367.3	261.2	241.5	233.2	218.8	214.8	207.3	200.3
65 to 74 years	1,218.6	894.3	665.6	615.9	585.0	541.6	518.9	490.3	462.9
75 to 84 years	2,993.1	2,295.7	1,780.3	1,677.2	1,611.1	1,506.3	1,460.8	1,383.1	1,315.0
85 years and over	7,777.1	6,739.9	5,926.1	5,446.8	5,278.4	4,895.9	4,778.4	4,480.8	4,267.7
Male, age adjusted [1]	538.9	412.4	320.0	297.4	286.6	267.9	260.9	248.5	237.7
White	539.6	409.2	316.7	294.1	282.9	264.6	258.0	245.2	234.8
Black	561.4	485.4	392.5	371.0	364.3	342.1	329.8	320.6	305.9
American Indian, Alaska Native	320.5	264.1	222.2	201.2	203.2	182.7	173.2	170.2	159.8
Asian, Pacific Islander	286.9	220.7	185.5	169.8	158.3	146.5	141.1	136.3	126.0
Hispanic origin [3]	(NA)	270.0	238.2	219.8	206.8	193.9	192.4	175.2	165.0
Non-Hispanic, White [3]	(NA)	413.6	319.9	297.7	286.9	268.7	262.2	250.0	239.8
Male, crude rate [2]	368.6	297.6	249.8	240.7	235.0	222.8	221.1	214.0	208.4
Under 1 year	25.5	21.9	13.3	12.9	12.1	10.9	9.4	8.8	10.9
1 to 14 years	2.8	1.9	1.4	1.1	1.1	1.1	1.0	1.1	1.0
5 to 14 years	1.0	0.9	0.8	0.7	0.7	0.6	0.6	0.7	0.6
15 to 24 years	3.7	3.1	3.2	3.3	3.4	3.2	3.6	3.3	3.2
25 to 34 years	11.4	10.3	9.6	10.5	10.5	10.5	10.8	11.2	10.5
35 to 44 years	68.7	48.1	41.4	43.1	42.8	40.9	40.7	39.5	38.6
45 to 54 years	282.6	183.0	140.2	138.4	136.2	132.3	131.5	128.9	124.6
55 to 64 years	746.8	537.3	371.7	343.4	331.7	312.8	306.9	296.8	288.8
65 to 74 years	1,728.0	1,250.0	898.3	827.1	785.3	723.8	692.3	660.5	624.9
75 to 84 years	3,834.3	2,968.2	2,248.1	2,110.1	2,030.3	1,893.6	1,829.4	1,743.5	1,656.5
85 years and over	8,752.7	7,418.4	6,430.0	5,823.5	5,621.5	5,239.3	5,143.4	4,819.9	4,621.8
Female, age adjusted [1]	320.8	257.0	210.9	197.2	190.3	177.3	172.3	162.2	154.0
White	315.9	250.9	205.6	192.1	185.4	172.9	168.2	158.6	150.5
Black	378.6	327.5	277.6	263.2	253.8	236.5	228.3	212.5	204.5
American Indian, Alaska Native	175.4	153.1	143.6	123.6	127.5	119.9	115.9	113.2	99.8
Asian, Pacific Islander	132.3	149.2	115.7	108.1	104.2	96.1	91.9	87.3	82.0
Hispanic origin [3]	(NA)	177.2	163.7	149.7	145.8	130.0	129.1	118.9	111.8
Non-Hispanic, White [3]	(NA)	252.6	206.8	193.7	187.1	175.1	170.3	160.9	153.0
Female, crude rate [2]	305.1	281.8	255.3	242.7	236.2	221.6	218.9	208.0	200.2
Under 1 year	20.0	18.3	12.5	11.8	9.8	9.7	8.0	7.9	9.0
1 to 14 years	2.5	1.9	1.0	1.0	1.3	1.2	0.9	0.9	1.1
5 to 14 years	0.9	0.8	0.5	0.6	0.5	0.6	0.6	0.6	0.6
15 to 24 years	2.1	1.8	2.1	1.7	2.1	1.7	1.7	1.8	1.9
25 to 34 years	5.3	5.0	5.2	5.2	5.7	5.2	5.3	5.1	5.3
35 to 44 years	21.4	15.1	17.2	18.0	18.6	17.7	17.1	17.0	16.2
45 to 54 years	84.5	61.0	49.8	50.6	50.2	49.6	49.2	48.5	47.2
55 to 64 years	272.1	215.7	159.3	147.2	141.9	131.5	129.1	124.1	117.9
65 to 74 years	828.6	616.8	474.0	440.1	417.5	388.6	372.7	346.3	325.4
75 to 84 years	2,497.0	1,893.8	1,475.1	1,389.7	1,331.1	1,245.6	1,210.5	1,136.7	1,079.7
85 years and over	7,350.5	6,478.1	5,720.9	5,283.3	5,126.7	4,741.5	4,610.8	4,322.1	4,099.3

NA Not available. [1] Age-adjusted death rates were prepared using the direct method, in which age-specific death rates for a population of interest are applied to a standard population distributed by age. Age adjustment eliminates the differences in observed rates between points in time or among compared population groups that result from age differences in population composition. [2] The total number of deaths in a given time period divided by the total resident population as of July 1. [3] Persons of Hispanic origin may be any race. Prior to 1997 excludes data from states lacking an Hispanic-origin item on their death certificates. See text, this section.

Source: U.S. National Center for Health Statistics, *Health, United States, 2009*. See also <http://cdc.gov/nchs/hus.htm>.

Table 125. Death Rates From Cerebrovascular Diseases by Sex and Age: 1990 to 2007

[Rates per 100,000 population. See headnote, Tables 107 and 115. See Appendix III]

Characteristics	Total				Male				Female			
	1990	2000	2005	2007	1990	2000	2005	2007	1990	2000	2005	2007
All ages, age adjusted [1]	65.3	60.9	46.6	42.2	68.5	62.4	46.9	42.5	62.6	59.1	45.6	41.3
All ages, crude rate [2]	57.8	59.6	48.4	45.1	46.7	46.9	38.8	36.4	68.4	71.8	57.8	53.5
Under 1 year	3.8	3.3	3.1	3.1	4.4	3.8	3.5	3.5	3.1	2.7	2.6	2.6
1 to 4 years	0.3	0.3	0.4	0.3	0.3	(B)	0.5	0.2	0.3	0.4	0.3	0.4
5 to 14 years	0.2	0.2	0.2	0.2	0.2	0.2	0.3	0.2	0.2	0.2	0.2	0.2
15 to 24 years	0.6	0.5	0.5	0.5	0.7	0.5	0.4	0.5	0.6	0.5	0.5	0.4
25 to 34 years	2.2	1.5	1.4	1.2	2.1	1.5	1.5	1.2	2.2	1.5	1.2	1.3
35 to 44 years	6.4	5.8	5.2	4.9	6.8	5.8	5.2	5.3	6.1	5.7	5.1	4.6
45 to 54 years	18.7	16.0	15.0	14.6	20.5	17.5	16.5	16.2	17.0	14.5	13.6	12.9
55 to 64 years	47.9	41.0	33.0	32.1	54.3	47.2	38.5	38.0	42.2	35.3	27.9	26.6
65 to 74 years	144.2	128.6	101.1	93.0	166.6	145.0	113.6	105.2	126.7	115.1	90.5	82.7
75 to 84 years	498.0	461.3	359.0	322.3	551.1	490.8	372.9	333.2	466.2	442.1	349.5	314.9
85 years and over	1,628.9	1,589.2	1,141.8	1,015.5	1,528.5	1,484.3	1,023.3	895.7	1,667.6	1,632.0	1,196.1	1,072.4

B Figure too small to meet statistical standards for reliability. [1] See footnote 1, Table 122. [2] The total number of deaths in a given time period divided by the total resident population as of July 1.

Source: U.S. National Center for Health Statistics, *Health, United States, 2009*. See also <http://cdc.gov/nchs/hus.htm>.

Births, Deaths, Marriages, and Divorces **93**

Table 126. Death Rates From Malignant Neoplasms by Selected Characteristics: 1990 to 2007

[Rates per 100,000 population. Excludes deaths of nonresidents of the United States. Beginning 1999, deaths classified according to tenth revision of International Classification of Diseases (ICD); for earlier years, causes of death were classified according to the revisions then in use. Changes in classification of causes of death due to these revisions may result in discontinuities in cause-of-death trends. For explanation of age adjustment, see text, this section. See Appendix III]

Characteristic	1990	2000	2003	2004	2005	2006	2007
All ages, age adjusted [1]	**216.0**	**199.6**	**190.1**	**185.8**	**183.8**	**180.7**	**178.4**
All ages, crude rate [2]	**203.2**	**196.5**	**191.5**	**188.6**	**188.7**	**187.0**	**186.6**
Under 1 year	2.3	2.4	1.9	1.8	1.8	1.8	1.7
1 to 4 years	3.5	2.7	2.5	2.5	2.3	2.3	2.2
5 to 14 years	3.1	2.5	2.6	2.5	2.5	2.2	2.4
15 to 24 years	4.9	4.4	4.0	4.1	4.1	3.9	3.9
25 to 34 years	12.6	9.8	9.4	9.1	9.0	9.0	8.5
35 to 44 years	43.3	36.6	35.0	33.4	33.2	31.9	30.8
45 to 54 years	158.9	127.5	122.2	119.0	118.6	116.3	114.3
55 to 64 years	449.6	366.7	343.0	333.4	326.9	321.1	315.4
65 to 74 years	872.3	816.3	770.3	755.1	742.7	727.2	715.5
75 to 84 years	1,348.5	1,335.6	1,302.5	1,280.4	1,274.8	1,263.8	1,256.3
85 years old and over	1,752.9	1,819.4	1,698.2	1,653.3	1,637.7	1,606.1	1,590.2
DEATH RATES FOR MALIGNANT NEOPLASM OF BREASTS FOR FEMALES							
All ages, age adjusted [1]	**33.3**	**29.4**	**26.6**	**24.4**	**24.1**	**23.5**	**22.9**
All ages, crude rate [2]	**34.0**	**31.3**	**28.9**	**27.5**	**27.3**	**26.9**	**26.5**
Under 25 years	(B)	(B)	(B)	(B)	(B)	(B)	(B)
25 to 34 years	2.9	2.6	2.2	2.0	1.8	1.8	1.7
35 to 44 years	17.8	14.1	12.0	11.3	11.3	10.8	10.1
45 to 54 years	45.4	38.3	32.9	29.3	28.7	27.6	26.7
55 to 64 years	78.6	66.8	59.2	55.8	54.5	53.7	51.3
65 to 74 years	111.7	98.3	88.9	81.6	79.2	76.9	77.3
75 to 84 years	146.3	137.6	128.9	119.5	119.2	119.2	116.3
85 years old and over	196.8	201.7	200.8	178.6	177.9	169.9	170.4
DEATH RATES FOR MALIGNANT NEOPLASM OF TRACHEA, BRONCHUS, AND LUNG							
All ages, age adjusted [1]	**37.1**	**41.3**	**41.3**	**40.9**	**40.5**	**40.0**	**50.6**
All ages, crude rate [2]	**39.4**	**45.4**	**46.1**	**45.9**	**45.9**	**45.7**	**52.6**
Under 25 years	(Z)	(Z)	(Z)	(Z)	(Z)	(Z)	0.1
25 to 34 years	0.5	0.5	0.4	0.3	0.3	0.4	0.3
35 to 44 years	5.2	5.3	5.1	5.2	5.1	4.5	4.3
45 to 54 years	34.5	25.0	24.4	24.2	24.5	24.6	28.4
55 to 64 years	105.0	93.3	87.1	83.9	80.7	78.2	95.4
65 to 74 years	177.6	206.9	204.8	205.0	199.6	197.0	248.8
75 to 84 years	190.1	265.6	279.4	277.0	280.9	280.3	371.3
85 years old and over	138.1	212.8	221.0	221.3	226.2	226.9	299.8

B Base figure too small to meet statistical standards for reliability of a derived figure. Z Less than 0.05. [1] Age adjusted death rates were prepared using the direct method, in which age specific death rates for a population of interest are applied to a standard population distributed by age. Age adjustment eliminates the differences in observed rates between points in time or among compared population groups that result from age differences in population composition. [2] The total number of deaths in a given time period divided by the total population as of July 1.

Source: U.S. National Center for Health Statistics, *Health, United States, 2009*. See also <http://www.cdc.gov/nchs/hus.htm>.

Table 127. Suicide Deaths and Death Rates by Age and Method: 2007

[Deaths based on tenth revison of International Classification of Diseases (ICD). Excludes deaths of nonresidents of the United States. National Safety Council analysis of National Center for Health Statistics mortality data]

Method	Total	Age						
		0–4 years [1]	5–14 years	15–24 years	25–44 years	45–64 years	65–74 years	75+ years
Number								
Total	34,598	(X)	184	4,140	12,000	12,847	2,444	2,983
Firearms	17,352	(X)	53	1,900	5,185	6,317	1,700	2,197
Hanging, strangulation, and suffocation	8,161	(X)	122	1,533	3,609	2,314	275	308
Poisoning by drugs and medicines	4,772	(X)	7	273	1,644	2,408	249	191
Poisoning by other sustances	1,586	(X)	0	89	577	754	71	95
Other means	2,727	(X)	2	345	985	1,054	149	192
Rate per 100,000								
Total	11.5	(X)	0.5	9.8	14.4	16.8	12.6	16.1
Firearms	5.8	(X)	0.1	4.5	6.2	8.2	8.8	11.8
Hanging, strangulation, and suffocation	2.7	(X)	0.3	3.6	4.3	3.0	1.4	1.7
Poisoning by drugs and medicines	1.6	(X)	(Z)	0.6	2.0	3.1	1.3	1.0
Poisoning by other sustances	0.5	(X)	(Z)	0.2	0.7	1.0	0.4	0.5
Other means	0.9	(X)	(Z)	0.8	1.2	1.4	0.8	1.0

X Not applicable. Z Entry would amount to less than half the unit of measurement. [1] It is generally accepted that children under 5 years of age cannot commit suicide.

Source: National Safety Council, Itasca, Il, *Accident Facts*, annual (copyright).

Table 128. Death Rates From Suicide by Selected Characteristics: 1990 to 2007

[Rates per 100,000 population. Excludes deaths of nonresidents of the United States. Beginning 2000, deaths classified according to tenth revision of International Classification of Diseases. See Appendix III]

Characteristic	1990	2000	2003	2004	2005	2006	2007
All ages, age adjusted [1]	**12.5**	**10.4**	**10.8**	**10.9**	**10.9**	**10.9**	**11.3**
All ages, crude rate [2]	**12.4**	**10.4**	**10.8**	**11.0**	**11.0**	**11.1**	**11.5**
Under 1 year	(X)	(X)	(X)	(X)	(X)	(X)	(X)
1 to 4 years	(X)	(X)	(X)	(X)	(X)	(X)	(X)
5 to 14 years	0.8	0.7	0.6	0.7	0.7	0.5	0.5
15 to 24 years	13.2	10.2	9.7	10.3	10.0	9.9	9.7
25 to 44 years	15.2	13.4	13.8	13.9	13.7	13.8	14.3
45 to 64 years	15.3	13.5	15.0	15.4	15.4	16.0	16.8
65 to 74 years	17.9	12.5	12.7	12.3	12.6	12.6	12.6
75 to 84 years	24.9	17.6	16.4	16.3	16.9	15.9	16.3
85 years and over	22.2	19.6	16.9	16.4	16.9	15.9	15.6
AGE-ADJUSTED RATES							
Male	21.5	17.7	18.0	18.0	18.0	18.0	18.4
Female	4.8	4.0	4.2	4.5	4.4	4.5	4.7
White male	22.8	19.1	19.6	19.6	19.6	19.6	20.2
Black male	12.8	10.0	9.2	9.6	9.2	9.4	8.8
American Indian, Alaska Native male	20.1	16.0	16.6	18.7	18.9	18.3	18.1
Asian, Pacific Islander male	9.6	8.6	8.5	8.4	7.3	7.9	9.0
Hispanic male [3]	13.7	10.3	9.7	9.8	9.4	8.8	10.1
Non-Hispanic, White male [3]	23.5	20.2	21.0	21.0	21.2	21.4	21.9
White female	5.2	4.3	4.6	5.0	4.9	5.1	5.2
Black female	2.4	1.8	1.9	1.8	1.9	1.4	1.7
American Indian, Alaska Native female	3.6	3.8	3.5	5.9	4.6	5.1	4.9
Asian, Pacific Islander female	4.1	2.8	3.1	3.5	3.3	3.4	3.5
Hispanic female [3]	2.3	1.7	1.7	2.0	1.8	1.8	1.9
Non-Hispanic, White female [3]	5.4	4.7	5.0	5.4	5.3	5.6	5.7

X Not applicable. [1] Age-adjusted death rates were prepared using the direct method, in which age-specific death rates for a population of interest are applied to a standard population distributed by age. Age adjustment eliminates the differences in observed rates between points in time or among compared population groups that result from age differences in population composition. [2] The total number of deaths in a given time period divided by the total resident population as of July 1.
[3] Persons of Hispanic origin may be any race. Excludes data from states lacking an Hispanic-origin item on their death certificates.
Source: U.S. National Center for Health Statistics, *Health, United States, 2009*. See also <http://www.cdc.gov/nchs/hus.htm>.

Table 129. Death Rates From Human Immunodeficiency Virus (HIV) Disease by Selected Characteristics

[Rates per 100,000 population. Excludes deaths of nonresidents of the United States. Beginning 2000, deaths classified according to tenth revision of International Classification of Diseases. See Appendix III]

Characteristic	1990	2000	2003	2004	2005	2006	2007
All ages, age adjusted [1]	**10.2**	**5.2**	**4.7**	**4.5**	**4.2**	**4.0**	**3.7**
All ages, crude [2]	**10.1**	**5.1**	**4.7**	**4.4**	**4.2**	**4.0**	**3.7**
Under 1 year	2.7	(B)	(B)	(B)	(B)	(B)	(B)
1 to 4 years	0.8	(B)	(B)	(B)	(B)	(B)	(B)
5 to 14 years	0.2	0.1	0.1	0.1	(B)	(B)	(B)
15 to 24 years	1.5	0.5	0.4	0.5	0.4	0.5	0.4
25 to 34 years	19.7	6.1	4.0	3.7	3.3	2.9	2.7
35 to 44 years	27.4	13.1	12.0	10.9	9.9	9.2	8.3
45 to 54 years	15.2	11.0	10.9	10.6	10.6	10.1	9.5
55 to 64 years	6.2	5.1	5.4	5.4	5.3	5.5	5.3
65 to 74 years	2.0	2.2	2.4	2.4	2.3	2.5	2.3
75 to 84 years	0.7	0.7	0.7	0.8	0.8	0.8	0.8
85 years and over	(B)	(B)	(B)	(B)	(B)	(B)	(B)
AGE-ADJUSTED RATES							
Male	18.5	7.9	7.1	6.6	6.2	5.9	5.4
Female	2.2	2.5	2.4	2.4	2.3	2.2	2.1
White male	15.7	4.6	4.2	3.8	3.6	3.4	3.1
Black male	46.3	35.1	31.3	29.2	28.2	26.3	24.5
American Indian, Alaska Native male	3.3	3.5	3.5	4.3	4.0	3.3	3.6
Asian, Pacific Islander male	4.3	1.2	1.1	1.2	1.0	1.1	0.8
Hispanic male [3]	28.8	10.6	9.2	8.2	7.5	7.0	6.3
Non-Hispanic, White male [3]	14.1	3.8	3.4	3.1	3.0	2.8	2.5
White female	1.1	1.0	0.9	0.9	0.8	0.7	0.7
Black female	10.1	13.2	12.8	13.0	12.0	12.2	11.3
American Indian, Alaska Native female	(B)	1.0	1.5	1.5	1.5	1.5	1.7
Asian, Pacific Islander female	(B)	0.2	(B)	(B)	(B)	(B)	(B)
Hispanic female [3]	3.8	2.9	2.7	2.4	1.9	1.9	1.8
Non-Hispanic, White female [3]	0.7	0.7	0.6	0.6	0.6	0.6	0.5

B Base figure too small to meet statistical standards. [1] Age-adjusted death rates were prepared using the direct method, in which age-specific death rates for a population of interest are applied to a standard population distributed by age. Age adjustment eliminates the differences in observed rates between points in time or among compared population groups that result from age differences in population composition. [2] The total number of deaths in a given time period divided by the total resident population as of July 1. [3] Persons of Hispanic origin may be any race. Excludes data from states lacking an Hispanic-origin item on their death certificates.
Source: U.S. National Center for Health Statistics, *Health, United States, 2009*. See also <http://www.cdc.gov/nchs/hus.htm>.

Births, Deaths, Marriages, and Divorces 95

Table 130. Deaths—Life Years Lost and Mortality Costs by Age, Sex, and Cause: 2009

[2,436 represents 2,436,000. Life years lost: Number of years person would have lived in absence of death. Mortality cost: value of lifetime earnings lost by persons who die prematurely]

Characteristics	Number of deaths (1,000)	Life years lost [1]		Mortality cost [2]	
		Total (1,000)	Per death	Total (mil. dol.)	Per death (dol.)
2009, total [3]	**2,436**	**38,144**	**15.7**	**527,897**	**216,678**
Under 5 years	31	2,409	77.8	35,769	1,154,815
5 to 14 years	6	385	68.5	8,201	1,457,171
15 to 24 years	30	1,752	57.9	52,410	1,732,506
25 to 44 years	117	5,002	42.8	160,080	1,370,198
45 to 64 years	371	12,466	33.6	235,767	634,991
65 years and over	1,881	16,129	8.6	35,670	18,960
Heart disease	599	7,449	12.4	80,032	133,709
Cancer	569	8,906	15.7	105,979	186,378
Cerebrovascular diseases	129	1,501	11.7	13,227	102,861
Accidents and adverse effects	117	3,518	30.0	88,668	756,947
Other	1,023	16,769	16.4	239,991	234,500
Male	**1,217**	**20,281**	**16.7**	**366,978**	**301,476**
Under 5 years	17	1,316	75.6	21,700	1,247,558
5 to 14 years	3	214	66.4	5,057	1,571,498
15 to 24 years	22	1,259	56.7	40,463	1,822,258
25 to 44 years	76	3,140	41.6	113,623	1,504,748
45 to 64 years	299	7,218	24.2	161,893	542,110
65 years and over	800	7,134	8.9	24,242	30,291
Heart disease	307	4,132	13.5	60,640	197,683
Cancer	297	4,380	14.7	63,675	214,059
Cerebrovascular diseases	52	642	12.4	8,321	160,081
Accidents and adverse effects	75	2,351	31.5	67,771	909,176
Other	487	8,776	18.0	166,571	342,366
Female	**1,219**	**17,863**	**14.7**	**160,919**	**132,003**
Under 5 years	14	1,093	80.5	14,069	1,036,025
5 to 14 years	2	172	71.2	3,144	1,304,514
15 to 24 years	8	493	61.3	11,947	1,484,814
25 to 44 years	41	1,862	45.1	46,457	1,124,317
45 to 64 years	73	5,248	72.2	73,874	1,016,751
65 years and over	1,081	8,995	8.3	11,428	10,571
Heart disease	292	3,318	11.4	19,392	66,455
Cancer	271	4,526	16.7	42,304	156,011
Cerebrovascular diseases	77	859	11.2	4,906	64,034
Accidents and adverse effects	43	1,167	27.4	20,897	490,567
Other	537	7,993	14.9	73,420	136,752

[1] Based on life expectancy at year of death. [2] Cost estimates based on the person's age, sex, life expectancy at the time of death, labor force participation rates, annual earnings, value of homemaking services, and a 3 percent discount rate by which to convert to present worth the potential aggregate earnings lost over the years. [3] Total excludes 329 deaths for which age is unknown.
Source: Wendy Max and Yanling Shi, Institute for Health & Aging, University of California San Francisco, CA., unpublished data.

Table 131. Percentage of First Marriages Reaching Stated Anniversary by Sex and Year of Marriage: 2009

[In percent except number of marriages. For currently married couples aged 15 years and over. Based on the second wave (interview) of the 2008 Survey of Income and Program Participation (SIPP), a longitudinal survey, conducted from January through April 2009]

Sex and year of marriage	Number of marriages (1,000)	Anniversary [1]							
		5th	10th	15th	20th	25th	30th	35th	40th
Men									
1960 to 1964	4,150	94.6	83.4	74.7	70.2	66.9	64.5	62.1	60.1
1965 to 1969	5,658	91.7	80.0	69.9	65.8	62.7	60.5	57.9	(X)
1970 to 1974	7,036	88.0	75.0	65.7	60.2	56.8	53.8	(X)	(X)
1975 to 1979	6,901	88.2	73.4	63.7	58.7	54.4	(X)	(X)	(X)
1980 to 1984	7,144	90.6	74.3	65.2	60.0	(X)	(X)	(X)	(X)
1985 to 1989	7,670	87.7	75.4	66.6	(X)	(X)	(X)	(X)	(X)
1990 to 1994	7,569	89.7	77.3	(X)	(X)	(X)	(X)	(X)	(X)
1995 to 1999	8,088	89.6	(X)	(X)	(X)	(X)	(X)	(X)	(X)
Women									
1960 to 1964	5,495	93.0	82.8	73.5	67.0	60.8	57.2	53.6	49.7
1965 to 1969	6,705	90.7	79.3	69.6	64.0	59.1	55.8	52.1	(X)
1970 to 1974	7,667	89.2	74.5	66.1	61.3	56.2	52.6	(X)	(X)
1975 to 1979	7,619	86.9	72.8	63.2	57.4	53.2	(X)	(X)	(X)
1980 to 1984	8,051	87.8	71.1	62.9	56.6	(X)	(X)	(X)	(X)
1985 to 1989	8,027	87.9	74.5	66.4	(X)	(X)	(X)	(X)	(X)
1990 to 1994	8,164	87.1	74.5	(X)	(X)	(X)	(X)	(X)	(X)
1995 to 1999	8,229	89.5	(X)	(X)	(X)	(X)	(X)	(X)	(X)

X Marriage cohort had not sufficient time to reach stated anniversary at time of the survey. [1] People reaching stated anniversary.
Source: U.S. Census Bureau, Current Population Reports, "Number, Timing, and Duration of Marriages and Divorces: 2009," P70-125, May 2011. See also <http://www.census.gov/hhes/socdemo/marriage/data/index.html>.

Table 132. People Who Got Married and Divorced in the Past 12 Months by State: 2009

[In thousands (2,287 represents 2,287,000). For 12 month period prior to interview date, which occurred for each month in calender year. For example, a person interviewed in January 2009 could report they got married between January 2008 and January 2009. Persons 15 years and over. Vital event is counted in state in which respondent lived at the time of survey. Based on 2009 American Community Survey (ACS). The ACS universe includes the household population and the group quarters population." Based on a sample and subject to sampling variability. See Appendix III]

| State | People who got married in the past 12 months | | | | People who got divorced in the past 12 months | | | |
	Males (1,000)	Marriage rate per 1,000 men	Females (1,000)	Marriage rate per 1,000 women	Males (1,000)	Divorce rate per 1,000 men	Females (1,000)	Divorce rate per 1,000 women
United States	**2,287**	**19.1**	**2,209**	**17.6**	**1,099**	**9.2**	**1,220**	**9.7**
Alabama	36	20.2	37	18.8	23	12.7	27	13.9
Alaska	7	26.0	7	24.7	4	12.5	4	16.2
Arizona	52	20.3	49	19.0	28	10.8	31	11.9
Arkansas	29	26.4	27	23.0	15	13.5	15	12.8
California	276	19.1	256	17.5	116	8.0	130	8.9
Colorado	47	23.5	44	22.0	23	11.6	19	9.4
Connecticut	24	17.1	24	15.9	9	6.7	16	10.7
Delaware	8	23.1	8	20.9	3	8.9	3	8.7
District of Columbia	4	17.7	5	16.9	1	6.3	2	8.3
Florida	126	17.0	118	15.2	63	8.5	77	9.9
Georgia	82	22.1	81	20.4	43	11.5	46	11.7
Hawaii	13	24.9	11	21.9	4	8.3	4	7.8
Idaho	15	25.8	15	25.1	5	7.7	6	9.7
Illinois.............	89	17.9	86	16.3	40	8.0	42	8.0
Indiana............	49	19.8	49	18.9	27	11.0	28	10.7
Iowa..............	25	21.5	27	21.5	12	10.2	13	10.8
Kansas............	24	22.1	24	20.8	12	10.6	12	10.2
Kentucky	37	22.2	37	20.5	21	12.6	24	13.5
Louisiana..........	35	20.6	33	17.6	19	11.0	19	10.0
Maine.............	7	13.5	7	12.2	7	13.0	5	9.1
Maryland	40	18.3	39	16.1	19	8.8	20	8.2
Massachusetts........	41	15.8	40	14.1	20	7.8	20	7.0
Michigan	65	16.5	64	15.6	36	9.2	38	9.3
Minnesota	32	15.3	33	15.4	15	7.4	17	7.8
Mississippi.........	21	19.3	21	17.3	12	11.1	15	12.5
Missouri............	43	18.6	46	18.7	22	9.5	26	10.4
Montana............	7	18.5	8	18.8	4	9.1	4	11.1
Nebraska..........	14	19.6	14	18.9	6	8.8	7	9.8
Nevada	24	23.2	23	22.4	13	12.3	13	12.3
New Hampshire.......	9	16.7	9	15.5	5	10.1	5	9.6
New Jersey	50	14.8	48	13.3	21	6.1	22	6.0
New Mexico.........	16	20.4	16	19.9	8	10.2	8	10.1
New York	128	16.8	122	14.8	50	6.6	60	7.3
North Carolina.......	74	20.4	74	19.0	36	9.9	40	10.3
North Dakota........	7	26.7	7	27.3	2	8.0	2	8.3
Ohio..............	76	16.9	74	15.4	43	9.5	48	10.0
Oklahoma	34	23.8	33	22.4	18	12.8	21	14.1
Oregon............	29	18.9	29	18.1	16	10.4	18	11.4
Pennsylvania	77	15.5	77	14.3	38	7.7	40	7.4
Rhode Island........	6	15.0	7	15.1	4	9.4	4	9.5
South Carolina.......	32	18.1	30	15.8	14	8.1	15	7.8
South Dakota........	6	20.1	7	20.3	3	10.9	3	8.9
Tennessee..........	47	19.4	45	17.1	28	11.4	30	11.6
Texas.............	202	21.5	195	20.4	94	10.0	114	11.9
Utah..............	30	29.6	27	26.7	10	10.2	11	10.8
Vermont	4	16.4	4	15.4	2	9.6	3	11.5
Virginia............	63	20.5	61	18.8	28	8.9	33	10.2
Washington	57	21.4	55	20.3	27	10.0	29	10.6
West Virginia	16	22.2	16	20.8	8	10.9	9	11.8
Wisconsin	39	17.2	38	16.2	19	8.3	17	7.5
Wyoming	7	30.7	6	28.7	2	10.3	2	10.7

Source: U.S. Census Bureau, 2009 American Community Survey, B12501, Marriage in the Last Year by Sex by Marital Status for the Population 15 Years and Over," B12502, "Marriages Ending in Widowhood in the Last Year by Sex by Marital Status for the Population 15 Years and Over," B12503, "Divorces in the Last Year by Sex by Marital Status for the Population 15 Years and Over," <http://factfinder.census.gov/servlet/DatasetMainPageServlet?_program=ACS&_submenuId=&_lang=en&_ts=>.

Births, Deaths, Marriages, and Divorces 97

Table 133. Marriages and Divorces—Number and Rate by State: 1990 to 2009

[(2,443 represents 2,443,000). Based on provisional counts by state of occurrence. Population enumerated as of April 1 for 1990 and 2000 and estimated as of July for 2009. See Appendix III]

State	Marriages [1]						Divorces [3]					
	Number (1,000)			Rate per 1,000 population [2]			Number (1,000)			Rate per 1,000 population [2]		
	1990	2000	2009	1990	2000	2009	1990	2000	2009	1990	2000	2009
United States [4]	2,443	2,329	2,077	9.8	8.3	6.8	1,182	(NA)	(NA)	4.7	4.1	3.4
Alabama	43.1	45.0	37.3	10.6	10.1	8.3	25.3	23.5	20.2	6.1	5.5	4.4
Alaska	5.7	5.6	5.5	10.2	8.9	7.8	2.9	2.7	3.3	5.5	3.9	4.4
Arizona [5]	36.8	38.7	35.3	10.0	7.5	5.4	25.1	21.6	23.1	6.9	4.6	3.5
Arkansas	36.0	41.1	31.6	15.3	15.4	10.7	16.8	17.9	16.3	6.9	6.4	5.7
California	237.1	196.9	213.9	7.9	5.8	5.8	128.0	(NA)	(NA)	4.3	(NA)	(NA)
Colorado	32.4	35.6	37.4	9.8	8.3	6.8	18.4	(NA)	21.2	5.5	4.7	4.2
Connecticut	26.0	19.4	19.8	7.9	5.7	5.9	10.3	6.5	10.8	3.2	3.3	3.1
Delaware	5.6	5.1	5.1	8.4	6.5	5.4	3.0	3.2	3.4	4.4	3.9	3.6
District of Columbia . . .	5.0	2.8	1.9	8.2	4.9	4.7	2.7	1.5	1.3	4.5	3.2	2.6
Florida	141.8	141.9	141.2	10.9	8.9	7.5	81.7	81.9	79.9	6.3	5.1	4.2
Georgia	66.8	56.0	63.6	10.3	6.8	6.5	35.7	30.7	(NA)	5.5	3.3	(NA)
Hawaii	18.3	25.0	22.2	16.4	20.6	17.9	5.2	4.6	(NA)	4.6	3.9	(NA)
Idaho	14.1	14.0	13.9	13.9	10.8	8.9	6.6	6.9	7.7	6.5	5.5	5.0
Illinois	100.6	85.5	72.7	8.8	6.9	5.6	44.3	39.1	32.7	3.8	3.2	2.5
Indiana	53.2	34.5	52.9	9.6	7.9	7.9	(NA)	(NA)	(NA)	(NA)	(NA)	(NA)
Iowa	24.9	20.3	21.2	9.0	6.9	7.0	11.1	9.4	7.3	3.9	3.3	2.4
Kansas	22.7	22.2	18.5	9.2	8.3	6.5	12.6	10.6	10.3	5.0	3.6	3.7
Kentucky	49.8	39.7	33.4	13.5	9.8	7.6	21.8	21.6	19.9	5.8	5.1	4.6
Louisiana	40.4	40.5	28.7	9.6	9.1	7.1	(NA)	(NA)	(NA)	(NA)	(NA)	(NA)
Maine	11.9	10.5	9.4	9.7	8.8	7.2	5.3	5.8	5.3	4.3	5.0	4.1
Maryland	46.3	40.0	32.4	9.7	7.5	5.8	16.1	17.0	15.2	3.4	3.3	2.8
Massachusetts	47.7	37.0	36.7	7.9	5.8	5.5	16.8	18.6	12.7	2.8	2.5	2.2
Michigan	76.1	66.4	53.1	8.2	6.7	5.4	40.2	39.4	32.5	4.3	3.9	3.3
Minnesota	33.7	33.4	28.4	7.7	6.8	5.3	15.4	14.8	(NA)	3.5	3.2	(NA)
Mississippi	24.3	19.7	14.5	9.4	6.9	4.8	14.4	14.4	12.2	5.5	5.0	4.1
Missouri	49.1	43.7	39.8	9.6	7.8	6.5	26.4	26.5	23.3	5.1	4.5	3.7
Montana	6.9	6.6	7.1	8.6	7.3	7.4	4.1	2.1	3.9	5.1	4.2	4.1
Nebraska	12.6	13.0	12.5	8.0	7.6	6.7	6.5	6.4	5.4	4.0	3.7	3.4
Nevada	120.6	144.3	108.2	99.0	72.2	40.9	13.3	18.1	17.7	11.4	9.9	6.7
New Hampshire	10.5	11.6	8.5	9.5	9.4	6.4	5.3	7.1	4.9	4.7	4.8	3.7
New Jersey	58.7	50.4	46.3	7.6	6.0	5.0	23.6	25.6	24.0	3.0	3.0	2.8
New Mexico [5]	13.3	14.5	10.2	8.8	8.0	5.1	7.7	9.2	8.0	4.9	5.1	4.0
New York [5]	154.8	162.0	120.1	8.6	7.1	6.4	57.9	62.8	46.1	3.2	3.0	2.6
North Carolina	51.9	65.6	65.8	7.8	8.2	6.7	34.0	36.9	36.7	5.1	4.5	3.8
North Dakota	4.8	4.6	4.3	7.5	7.2	6.6	2.3	2.0	1.6	3.6	3.4	2.9
Ohio	98.1	88.5	64.8	9.0	7.8	5.8	51.0	49.3	36.9	4.7	4.2	3.3
Oklahoma	33.2	15.6	23.5	10.6	(NA)	6.9	24.9	12.4	16.9	7.7	(NA)	4.9
Oregon	25.3	26.0	23.5	8.9	7.6	6.6	15.9	16.7	13.3	5.5	4.8	3.9
Pennsylvania	84.9	73.2	64.2	7.1	6.0	5.3	40.1	37.9	28.8	3.3	3.1	2.7
Rhode Island	8.1	8.0	6.5	8.1	7.6	5.9	3.8	3.1	3.3	3.7	2.9	3.0
South Carolina	55.8	42.7	29.2	15.9	10.6	7.4	16.1	14.4	12.2	4.5	3.8	3.0
South Dakota	7.7	7.1	5.9	11.1	9.4	7.2	2.6	2.7	2.6	3.7	3.5	3.3
Tennessee	68.0	88.2	55.2	13.9	15.5	8.4	32.3	33.8	25.8	6.5	5.9	3.9
Texas	178.6	196.4	179.8	10.5	9.4	7.1	94.0	85.2	76.9	5.5	4.0	3.3
Utah	19.4	24.1	23.9	11.2	10.8	8.2	8.8	9.7	10.7	5.1	4.3	3.6
Vermont	6.1	6.1	4.7	10.9	10.0	8.7	2.6	5.1	2.1	4.5	4.1	3.5
Virginia	71.0	62.4	54.1	11.4	8.8	7.0	27.3	30.2	28.5	4.4	4.3	3.7
Washington	46.6	40.9	40.4	9.5	6.9	6.0	28.8	27.2	26.3	5.9	4.6	3.9
West Virginia	13.0	15.7	12.4	7.2	8.7	6.9	9.7	9.3	9.2	5.3	5.1	5.2
Wisconsin	38.9	36.1	30.3	7.9	6.7	5.3	17.8	17.6	17.3	3.6	3.2	3.0
Wyoming	4.9	4.9	4.7	10.7	10.0	8.2	3.1	2.8	2.8	6.6	5.8	5.2

NA Not available. [1] Data are counts of marriages performed, except as noted. [2] Based on total population residing in area; population enumerated as of April 1 for 1990 and 2000; estimated as of July 1 for all other years. [3] Includes annulments. Includes divorce petitions filed or legal separations for some counties or states. [4] U.S. total for the number of divorces is an estimate which includes states not reporting. Beginning 2000, divorce rates based solely on the combined counts and populations for reporting states and the District of Columbia. [5] Some figures for marriages are marriage licenses issued.

Source: U.S. National Center for Health Statistics, National Vital Statistics Reports (NVSR), *Births, Marriages, Divorces, and Deaths: Provisional Data for 2009*, Vol. 58, No. 25, August 2010, and prior reports.

Section 3
Health and Nutrition

This section presents statistics on health expenditures and insurance coverage, including Medicare and Medicaid, medical personnel, hospitals, nursing homes and other care facilities, injuries, diseases, disability status, nutritional intake of the population, and food consumption. Summary statistics showing recent trends on health care and discussions of selected health issues are published annually by the U.S. National Center for Health Statistics (NCHS) in *Health, United States*. Data on national health expenditures, medical costs, and insurance coverage are compiled by the U.S. Centers for Medicare & Medicaid Services (CMS) and appear on the CMS Web site at <http://www.cms.gov/NationalHealthExpendData/> and in the annual *Medicare and Medicaid Statistical Supplement* to the *Health Care Financing Review*. Statistics on health insurance are also collected by NCHS and are published in Series 10 of *Vital and Health Statistics*. NCHS also conducts periodic surveys of nutrient levels in the population, including estimates of food and nutrient intake, overweight and obesity, hypercholesterolemia, hypertension, and clinical signs of malnutrition. Data are published in Series 10 and 11 of *Vital and Health Statistics*. Statistics on hospitals are published annually by the Health Forum, L.L.C.; an American Hospital Association (AHA) company, in AHA Hospital Statistics. The primary source for data on nutrition and on annual per capita consumption of food is *Diet Quality and Food Consumption*, issued by the U.S. Department of Agriculture. Data are available on the Web site at <http://www.ers.usda.gov/Briefing/DietQuality>.

National health expenditures—
CMS compiles estimates of national health expenditures (NHE) to measure spending for health care in the United States. The NHE accounts are structured to show spending by type of expenditure (i.e., hospital care, physician and clinical care, dental care, and other professional care; home health care; retail sales of prescription drugs; other medical non-durables; nursing home care and other personal health expenditures; plus other health expenditures such as public health activities, administration, and the net cost of private health insurance; plus medical sector investment, the sum of noncommercial medical research and capital formation in medical sector structures and equipment; and by source of funding (e.g., health insurance, out-of-pocket payments, and other third party payers and programs).

Data used to estimate health expenditures come from existing sources, which are tabulated for other purposes. The type of expenditure estimates rely upon statistics produced by such groups as the AHA, the Census Bureau, and the U.S. Department of Health and Human Services (HHS). Source of funding estimates are constructed using administrative and statistical records from the Medicare and Medicaid programs, the U.S. Department of Defense and VA medical programs, the Social Security Administration, Census Bureau's *Governmental Finances*, state and local governments, other HHS agencies, and other nongovernment sources.

Medicare, Medicaid, and CHIP—
Since July 1966, the federal Medicare program has provided two coordinated plans for nearly all people aged 65 and over: (1) a hospital insurance plan, which covers hospital and related services and (2) a voluntary supplementary medical insurance plan, financed partially by monthly premiums paid by participants, which partly covers physicians' and related medical services. Such insurance also applies, since July 1973, to disabled beneficiaries of any age after 24 months of entitlement to cash benefits under the social security or railroad retirement programs and to persons with end stage renal disease. On January 1, 2006, Medicare began to provide coverage for prescription drugs as mandated by the Medicare Prescription Drug, Improvement,

and Modernization Act of 2003 (MMA). This benefit is available on a voluntary basis to everyone with Medicare, and beneficiaries pay a monthly premium to enroll in one of Medicare's prescription drug plans.

Medicaid is a health insurance program for certain low-income people. These include: certain low-income families with children; people on supplemental security income; certain low-income pregnant women and children; and people who have very high medical bills. There are special rules for those who live in nursing homes and for disabled children living at home. Medicaid is funded and administered through a state/federal partnership. Although there are broad federal requirements for Medicaid, states have a wide degree of flexibility to design their program. The Children's Health Insurance Program Reauthorization Act of 2009 (CHIPRA or Public Law 111-3) reauthorized the Children's Health Insurance Program (CHIP). The program went into effect on April 1, 2009. CHIP replaces the State Children's Health Insurance Program (SCHIP). It will preserve coverage for the millions of children who rely on CHIP today and provides the resources for states to reach millions of additional uninsured children. CHIP was designed as a federal/state partnership, similar to Medicaid, with the goal of expanding health insurance to children whose families earn too much money to be eligible for Medicaid, but not enough money to purchase private insurance.

Health resources—Hospital statistics based on data from AHA's yearly survey are published annually in *AHA Hospital Statistics* and cover all hospitals accepted for registration by the Association. To be accepted for registration, a hospital must meet certain requirements relating to number of beds, construction, equipment, medical and nursing staff, patient care, clinical records, surgical and obstetrical facilities, diagnostic and treatment facilities, laboratory services, etc. Data obtained from NCHS cover all U.S. hospitals that meet certain criteria for inclusion. The criteria are published in *Vital*

and Health Statistics reports, Series 13. Statistics on the demographic characteristics of persons employed in the health occupations are compiled by the U.S. Bureau of Labor Statistics and reported in *Employment and Earnings* (monthly) (see Table 615, Section 12, Labor Force, Employment, and Earnings). Data based on surveys of health personnel and utilization of health facilities providing long-term care, ambulatory care, emergency room care, and hospital care are presented in NCHS Series 13, data from the National Health Interview Survey. Statistics on patient visits to health care providers, as reported in health interviews, appear in NCHS Series 10, data from the National Health Care Survey.

The CMS's *Health Care Financing Review* and its annual *Medicare and Medicaid Statistical Supplement* present data for hospitals and nursing homes as well as extended care facilities and home health agencies. These data are based on records of the Medicare program and differ from those of other sources because they are limited to facilities meeting federal eligibility standards for participation in Medicare.

Disability and illness—General health statistics, including morbidity, disability, injuries, preventive care, and findings from physiological testing are collected by NCHS in its National Health Interview Survey and its National Health and Nutrition Examination Surveys and appear in *Vital and Health Statistics*, Series 10 and 11, respectively. Annual incidence data on notifiable diseases are compiled by the Public Health Service (PHS) at its Centers for Disease Control and Prevention in Atlanta, Georgia, and are published as a supplement to its *Morbidity and Mortality Weekly Report* (MMWR). The list of diseases is revised annually and includes those which, by mutual agreement of the states and PHS, are communicable diseases of national importance.

Statistical reliability—For discussion of statistical collection, estimation, and sampling procedures and measures of reliability applicable to data from NCHS and CMS, see Appendix III.

Table 134. National Health Expenditures—Summary: 1960 to 2009

[In billions of dollars (27.3 represents $27,300,000,000). Excludes Puerto Rico and Island Areas]

Year	Total expenditures [1]	Health consumption expenditures, total [2]	Personal health care expenditures									
			Total [3]	Hospital care	Physician and clinical services	Other professional services	Dental services	Home health care	Nursing care facilities [4]	Prescription drugs	Durable medical equipment	Other nondurable medical equipment
1960	27.3	24.8	23.3	9.0	5.6	0.4	2.0	0.1	0.8	2.7	0.7	1.6
1961	29.2	26.3	24.8	9.8	5.8	0.4	2.1	0.1	0.8	2.7	0.8	1.8
1962	31.9	28.4	26.6	10.4	6.3	0.4	2.2	0.1	0.9	3.0	0.9	1.9
1963	34.7	30.9	29.0	11.5	7.1	0.5	2.3	0.1	1.0	3.2	0.9	1.9
1964	38.5	34.1	32.0	12.5	8.1	0.5	2.6	0.1	1.2	3.3	1.0	2.1
1965	41.9	37.2	34.7	13.5	8.6	0.5	2.8	0.1	1.4	3.7	1.1	2.2
1966	46.2	41.2	38.4	15.3	9.3	0.6	3.0	0.1	1.7	4.0	1.2	2.4
1967	51.7	46.5	43.5	17.8	10.4	0.6	3.4	0.2	2.2	4.2	1.1	2.5
1968	58.7	52.7	49.2	20.5	11.4	0.6	3.7	0.2	2.9	4.7	1.3	2.8
1969	66.2	59.1	55.5	23.4	12.7	0.7	4.2	0.3	3.4	5.1	1.5	3.0
1970	74.8	67.0	63.1	27.2	14.3	0.7	4.7	0.2	4.0	5.5	1.7	3.3
1971	83.2	74.3	69.4	30.2	15.9	0.8	5.2	0.2	4.6	5.9	1.8	3.5
1972	93.1	83.3	77.1	33.8	17.7	0.9	5.5	0.2	5.2	6.3	2.0	3.7
1973	103.3	93.1	86.1	37.9	19.6	1.0	6.3	0.3	6.0	6.8	2.2	4.0
1974	117.1	105.9	98.8	44.1	22.2	1.2	7.1	0.4	6.9	7.4	2.5	4.5
1975	133.5	121.1	113.2	51.2	25.3	1.3	8.0	0.6	8.0	8.1	2.8	4.9
1976	153.0	139.3	129.3	59.4	28.7	1.6	9.0	0.9	9.1	8.7	3.0	5.4
1977	173.9	159.9	146.7	67.0	33.1	2.1	10.1	1.1	10.3	9.2	3.2	6.1
1978	195.4	180.0	164.3	75.6	35.8	2.4	11.0	1.6	11.8	9.9	3.4	7.1
1979	221.6	204.6	187.2	86.2	41.2	2.8	11.9	1.9	13.3	10.7	3.8	8.5
1980	255.7	235.6	217.1	100.5	47.7	3.5	13.3	2.4	15.3	12.0	4.1	9.8
1981	296.6	273.5	251.9	117.5	55.6	4.3	15.7	2.9	17.3	13.4	4.3	11.3
1982	334.6	308.2	283.2	133.6	61.6	4.9	17.0	3.5	19.5	15.0	4.6	12.6
1983	368.8	339.6	311.8	144.7	68.7	5.7	18.3	4.2	21.7	17.3	5.3	13.8
1984	406.3	375.3	341.9	154.4	77.4	7.3	19.8	5.1	23.7	19.6	6.1	15.0
1985	444.4	413.2	376.8	164.6	90.8	8.1	21.7	5.6	26.3	21.8	7.1	16.0
1986	476.7	444.2	409.4	175.7	100.7	9.3	23.1	6.4	28.7	24.3	8.1	17.1
1987	518.9	482.9	448.3	189.5	112.9	11.4	25.3	6.7	30.7	26.9	9.5	18.3
1988	581.5	541.3	499.3	206.5	128.6	13.8	27.3	8.4	34.3	30.6	11.1	19.4
1989	647.2	603.2	551.4	226.0	143.3	14.6	29.3	10.2	38.7	34.8	11.9	20.8
1990	724.0	675.3	616.6	250.4	158.9	17.4	31.5	12.6	44.9	40.3	13.8	22.4
1991	791.2	739.2	677.4	275.8	176.5	18.7	33.3	15.2	49.4	44.4	13.1	23.2
1992	857.7	800.8	733.4	298.5	191.3	21.0	37.0	18.7	53.1	47.0	13.5	23.2
1993	921.3	860.1	781.0	315.7	202.8	23.2	38.9	22.8	56.0	49.6	14.1	23.7
1994	972.5	908.6	823.0	328.4	212.2	24.2	41.5	27.4	58.6	53.1	15.3	24.3
1995	1,027.3	961.4	872.7	339.3	222.3	27.0	44.5	32.4	64.5	59.8	15.9	25.1
1996	1,081.6	1,013.9	921.7	350.8	231.3	29.2	46.8	35.8	69.6	68.1	17.4	26.0
1997	1,142.4	1,070.2	974.5	363.4	242.9	31.7	50.2	37.0	74.4	77.6	19.2	27.6
1998	1,208.6	1,128.5	1,028.3	374.9	257.9	33.8	53.5	34.2	79.4	88.4	21.3	28.6
1999	1,286.8	1,200.0	1,088.8	393.6	271.1	35.0	57.2	32.9	80.8	104.7	23.0	30.6
2000	1,378.0	1,288.5	1,164.4	415.5	290.0	37.0	62.0	32.4	85.1	120.9	25.1	31.6
2001	1,495.3	1,401.4	1,264.1	449.4	314.7	40.6	67.5	34.4	90.8	138.7	25.1	32.3
2002	1,637.0	1,531.6	1,371.6	486.5	340.8	43.7	73.4	36.6	94.5	158.2	27.0	33.3
2003	1,772.2	1,658.2	1,479.0	525.8	368.4	46.8	76.0	39.8	100.1	175.2	27.8	35.1
2004	1,894.7	1,772.9	1,585.0	564.5	393.6	50.1	81.8	43.8	105.4	190.3	28.9	35.8
2005	2,021.0	1,890.3	1,692.6	606.5	419.6	53.1	86.8	48.7	112.1	201.7	30.4	37.2
2006	2,152.1	2,016.9	1,798.8	648.3	441.6	55.4	91.4	52.6	117.0	219.8	31.9	38.7
2007	2,283.5	2,135.1	1,904.3	686.8	462.6	59.5	97.3	57.8	126.5	230.2	34.4	41.1
2008	2,391.4	2,234.2	1,997.2	722.1	486.5	63.4	102.3	62.1	132.8	237.2	35.1	42.3
2009	2,486.3	2,330.1	2,089.9	759.1	505.9	66.8	102.2	68.3	137.0	249.9	34.9	43.3

[1] Includes Health Consumption Expenditures plus medical research, and medical structures and equipment. [2] Includes Personal Health Expenditures plus government administration, net cost of health insurance, and government public health activities. [3] Includes hospital care, physician and clinical services, dental services, other professional services, other health, residential, and personal services, home health care, nursing care facilities and continuing care retirement communities, prescription drugs, durable medical equipment, and other nondurable medical products. [4] Includes care provided in nursing care facilities (NAICS 6231), continuing care retirement communities (623311), state and local government nursing facilities, and nursing facilities operated by the Department of Veterans' Affairs (DVA).

Source: U.S. Centers for Medicare and Medicaid Services, Office of the Actuary, "National Health Statistics Group," <http://www.cms.hhs.gov/NationalHealthExpendData/>.

Health and Nutrition 101

Table 135. National Health Expenditures by Source of Funds: 1990 to 2009

[In billions of dollars (724.0 represents $724,000,000,000), except percent. Excludes Puerto Rico and Island Areas]

Type of expenditure	1990	2000	2004	2005	2006	2007	2008	2009
National health expenditure, total	**724.0**	**1,378.0**	**1,894.7**	**2,021.0**	**2,152.1**	**2,283.5**	**2,391.4**	**2,486.3**
Annual percent change [1]	11.9	7.1	6.9	6.7	6.5	6.1	4.7	4.0
Percent of gross domestic product	12.5	13.8	16.0	16.0	16.1	16.2	16.6	17.6
Out of pocket	138.8	202.1	248.8	263.8	272.1	289.4	298.2	299.3
Health insurance	439.2	918.8	1,316.2	1,410.5	1,513.7	1,597.5	1,681.8	1,767.4
Private health insurance	233.9	458.2	653.7	697.2	733.6	763.8	790.6	801.2
Medicare	110.2	224.4	311.3	339.9	403.1	431.4	465.7	502.3
Medicaid (Title XIX)	73.7	200.5	291.2	309.5	307.1	327.0	343.1	373.9
CHIP (Title XIX and Title XXI)	–	3.0	7.1	7.5	8.3	9.1	10.2	11.1
Department of Defense	10.4	13.7	24.9	26.5	29.7	32.2	33.9	36.5
Department of Veterans Affairs	10.9	19.1	28.0	29.8	31.9	34.0	38.2	42.4
Other third party payers and programs	77.4	124.5	153.9	159.8	168.5	179.5	181.2	186.1
Worksite health care	2.2	3.5	4.0	4.2	4.3	4.4	4.4	4.4
Other private revenues [2]	29.5	57.5	65.7	69.7	76.9	85.5	81.3	83.8
Indian health services	1.0	2.0	2.5	2.5	2.6	2.7	2.8	3.2
Workers' compensation	17.5	26.2	34.7	34.9	34.9	35.4	38.9	39.6
General assistance	5.0	3.9	5.9	6.2	6.7	6.9	7.1	7.1
Maternal/Child health	1.6	2.7	2.6	2.6	2.7	2.8	2.9	3.0
Vocational rehabilitation	0.3	0.4	0.5	0.5	0.5	0.5	0.5	0.5
Other federal programs [3]	1.5	4.5	6.2	6.3	6.4	6.7	6.9	7.3
Substance abuse and mental health services administration	1.4	2.6	3.2	3.1	3.2	3.3	3.2	3.2
Other state and local programs [4]	15.9	18.7	25.4	26.4	26.8	27.4	28.9	29.4
School health	1.3	2.5	3.2	3.4	3.6	3.9	4.2	4.5
Public health activity [5]	20.0	43.0	54.0	56.2	62.6	68.8	72.9	77.2
Investment	**48.7**	**89.6**	**121.8**	**130.7**	**135.2**	**148.4**	**157.2**	**156.2**
Research [6]	12.7	25.5	38.5	40.3	41.4	41.9	43.2	45.3
Structures & equipment [7]	36.0	64.1	83.3	90.4	93.8	106.4	114.0	110.9

– Represents zero. [1] Average annual growth from prior year shown. [2] The most common source of other private funds is philanthropy. Philanthropic support may be direct from individuals or may be obtained through philanthropic fund-raising organizations such as the United Way. Support may also be obtained from foundations or corporations. [3] Includes general hospital/medical, general hospital/medical NEC, non-XIX federal, and O.E.O. [4] Includes non-XIX state and local, temporary disability insurance, and state and local subsidies. [5] Governments are involved in organizing and delivering publicly provided health services such as epidemiological surveillance, inoculations, immunization/vaccination services, disease prevention programs, the operation of public health laboratories, and other such functions. In the NHEA, spending for these activities is reported in government public health activity. [6] Non-profit or government entities. Research and development expenditures by drug and medical supply and equipment manufacturers are not shown in this line, as those expenditures are treated as intermediate purchases under the definitions of national income accounting; that is, the value of that research is deemed to be recouped through product sales. [7] Structures are defined as the value of new construction by the medical sector. Includes establishments engaged in providing health care, but does not include retail establishments that sell non-durable or durable medical goods. Construction includes new buildings; additions, alterations, and major replacements; mechanical and electric installations; and site preparation.
Source: U. S. Centers for Medicare and Medicaid Services, Office of the Actuary, "National Health Expenditure Group," <http://www.cms.hhs.gov/NationalHealthExpendData/>.

Table 136. National Health Expenditures by Source of Funds and Type of Expenditure: 1990 to 2009

[In billions of dollars (724.0 represents $724,000,000,000). Excludes Puerto Rico and Island Areas]

Object of expenditure	1990	2000	2003	2004	2005	2006	2007	2008	2009
Total	**724.0**	**1,378.0**	**1,772.2**	**1,894.7**	**2,021.0**	**2,152.1**	**2,283.5**	**2,391.4**	**2,486.3**
Source of funds:									
Out-of-pocket	138.8	202.1	237.1	248.8	263.8	272.1	289.4	298.2	299.3
Health insurance [1]	439.2	918.8	1,219.2	1,316.2	1,410.5	1,513.7	1,597.5	1,681.8	1,767.4
Other third party payers and programs [2]	77.4	124.5	148.2	153.9	159.8	168.5	179.5	181.2	186.1
Public health activities [3]	20.0	43.0	53.7	54.0	56.2	62.6	68.8	72.9	77.2
Investment	48.7	89.6	114.0	121.8	130.7	135.2	148.4	157.2	156.2
Type of expenditure:									
Health consumption expenditures	675.3	1,288.5	1,658.2	1,772.9	1,890.3	2,016.9	2,135.1	2,234.2	2,330.1
Personal health care	616.6	1,164.4	1,479.0	1,585.0	1,692.6	1,798.8	1,904.3	1,997.2	2,089.9
Hospital care	250.4	415.5	525.8	564.5	606.5	648.3	686.8	722.1	759.1
Physician and clinical services	158.9	290.0	368.4	393.6	419.6	441.6	462.6	486.5	505.9
Other professional services [4]	17.4	37.0	46.8	50.1	53.1	55.4	59.5	63.4	66.8
Dental services	31.5	62.0	76.0	81.8	86.8	91.4	97.3	102.3	102.2
Other health, residential, and personal care [5]	24.3	64.7	84.0	90.7	96.5	102.1	108.3	113.3	122.6
Home health care	12.6	32.4	39.8	43.8	48.7	52.6	57.8	62.1	68.3
Nursing care facilities and continuing care retirement communities	44.9	85.1	100.1	105.4	112.1	117.0	126.5	132.8	137.0
Prescription drugs	40.3	120.9	175.2	190.3	201.7	219.8	230.2	237.2	249.9
Durable medical equipment [6]	13.8	25.1	27.8	28.9	30.4	31.9	34.4	35.1	34.9
Other nondurable medical products [7]	22.4	31.6	35.1	35.8	37.2	38.7	41.1	42.3	43.3
Investment	48.7	89.6	114.0	121.8	130.7	135.2	148.4	157.2	156.2
Research [8]	12.7	25.5	34.9	38.5	40.3	41.4	41.9	43.2	45.3
Structures & equipment [9]	36.0	64.1	79.2	83.3	90.4	93.8	106.4	114.0	110.9

[1] Includes Private Health Insurance, Medicare, Medicaid, CHIP (Titles XIX and XXI), Department of Defense, and Department of Veterans Affairs. [2] See footnote 2, Table 141. [3] See footnote 5, Table 135. [4] See footnote 5, Table 136. [5] Includes spending for Medicaid home and community based waivers, care provided in residential care facilities, ambulance services, school health and worksite health care. Generally these programs provide payments for services in non-traditional settings such as community centers, senior citizens centers, schools, and military field stations. [6] See footnote 7, Table 136. [7] Covers the "retail" sales of non-prescription drugs and medical sundries. [8] See footnote 6, Table 135. [9] See footnote 7, Table 135
Source: U.S. Centers for Medicare and Medicaid Services, Office of the Actuary, "National Health Statistics Group," <http://www.cms.hhs.gov/NationalHealthExpendData/>.

Table 137. Health Consumption Expenditures—Per Capita Spending by Type of Expenditure and Source of Funds: 1990 to 2009

[In dollars, except percent. Based on U.S. Census Bureau estimates of total U.S. resident population plus the net Census undercount. Excludes research, structures and equipment. Excludes Puerto Rico and Island Areas]

Type of expenditure and source of funds	1990	1995	2000	2004	2005	2006	2007	2008	2009
Total [1]	**2,661**	**3,578**	**4,561**	**6,043**	**6,385**	**6,746**	**7,069**	**7,329**	**7,578**
Annual percent change [2]	10.6	4.7	6.3	5.9	5.7	5.6	4.8	3.7	3.4
Hospital care	987	1,263	1,471	1,924	2,049	2,168	2,274	2,369	2,469
Physician and clinical services	626	827	1,027	1,342	1,417	1,477	1,532	1,596	1,645
Other professional services [3]	124	166	220	279	293	306	322	336	332
Dental services	69	100	131	171	179	185	197	208	217
Other health, residential, and personal care [4]	88	93	112	122	126	129	136	139	141
Home health care	96	156	229	309	326	341	359	372	399
Nursing care facilities and continuing care retirement communities	54	59	89	99	103	107	114	115	113
Prescription drugs	50	120	115	149	165	176	191	204	222
Durable medical equipment [5]	159	223	428	649	681	735	762	778	813
Other nondurable medical products [6]	177	240	301	359	379	391	419	436	445
Public health activities [7]	79	115	152	184	190	209	228	239	251
Source of funds	**2,661**	**3,578**	**4,561**	**6,043**	**6,385**	**6,746**	**7,069**	**7,329**	**7,578**
Out-of-pocket payments	547	545	715	848	891	910	958	978	974
Health insurance [8]	1,730	2,541	3,252	4,486	4,764	5,063	5,289	5,517	5,748
Other third party payers and programs [9]	305	376	441	525	540	563	594	594	605

[1] Includes other items, not shown separately. [2] Average annual growth from prior year shown. [3] See footnote 4, Table 136. [4] Includes spending for Medicaid home and community based waivers, care provided in residential care facilities, ambulance services, school health and worksite health care. Generally these programs provide payments for services in non-traditional settings such as community centers, senior citizens centers, schools, and military field stations. [5] See footnote 6, Table 136. [6] Covers the "retail" sales of non-prescription drugs and medical sundries. [7] See footnote 5, Table 135. [8] See footnote 1, Table 136. [9] See footnote 2, Table 136.

Source: U. S. Centers for Medicare and Medicaid Services, Office of the Actuary, "National Health Statistics Group," <http://www.cms.hhs.gov/NationalHealthExpendData/>.

Table 138. Health Consumption Expenditures by Type of Expenditure and Source of Funds: 2009

[In millions of dollars (2,330,064 represents $2,330,064,000,000). Excludes Puerto Rico and Island Areas. Excludes research, structures, and equipment]

Type of expenditure	Total	Out-of-pocket	Health insurance Total	Private health insurance	Medicare	Medicaid	Other health insurance programs [1]	Other third party payers and programs [2]
Total	2,330,064	299,345	1,767,416	801,190	502,289	373,941	89,997	186,090
Personal health care [3]	2,089,862	299,345	1,614,955	712,165	471,260	345,669	85,861	175,562
Hospital care	759,074	24,417	669,348	265,894	220,382	136,102	46,971	65,309
Physician and clinical services	505,888	47,943	407,336	237,674	109,434	39,947	20,281	50,609
Dental services	102,222	42,480	59,258	49,960	290	7,147	1,861	484
Other health, residential, and personal care [4]	122,623	8,918	76,780	5,814	4,588	64,403	1,976	36,925
Home health care	68,264	6,015	59,746	5,020	29,835	24,291	600	2,503
Nursing care facilities and continuing care retirement communities	136,971	39,812	87,465	10,549	27,991	44,956	3,968	9,694
Prescription drugs	249,904	52,992	193,325	108,566	54,818	19,981	9,960	3,587
Durable medical equipment [5]	34,878	18,577	15,805	3,970	7,446	4,315	74	496
Government administration [6]	29,812	–	28,434	–	6,956	18,197	3,281	1,378
Net cost of health insurance [6]	133,177	–	124,027	89,025	24,073	10,074	855	9,150
Public health activities [7]	77,213	–	–	–	–	–	–	–

– Represents zero. [1] Includes CHIP (Titles XIX and XXI), Department of Defense, and Department of Veterans Affairs. [2] See footnote 2, Table 141. [3] Includes other items, not shown separately [4] See footnote 5, Table 136. [5] See footnote 6, Table 136. [6] See source material for definitions. [7] See footnote 5, Table 135.

Source: U. S. Centers for Medicare and Medicaid Services, Office of the Actuary, "National Health Statistics Group," <http://www.cms.hhs.gov/NationalHealthExpendData/>.

Table 139. Personal Health Care Expenditures by Source of Funds: 1990 to 2009

[In billions of dollars (616.6 represents $616,600,000,000), except percent. Excludes Puerto Rico and Island Areas]

Item	1990	2000	2003	2004	2005	2006	2007	2008	2009
Personal health care expenditures	**616.6**	**1,164.4**	**1,479.0**	**1,585.0**	**1,692.6**	**1,798.8**	**1,904.3**	**1,997.2**	**2,089.9**
Out-of-pocket	138.8	202.1	237.1	248.8	263.8	272.1	289.4	298.2	299.3
Health insurance	403.0	843.5	1,102.4	1,191.5	1,278.5	1,367.6	1,444.7	1,528.1	1,615.0
Private health insurance	204.8	405.8	526.2	562.8	603.8	636.4	663.8	692.7	712.2
Medicare	107.3	215.9	273.8	300.2	326.4	381.7	407.4	440.8	471.3
Medicaid	69.7	186.9	249.8	271.2	287.7	283.7	302.5	316.5	345.7
Other health insurance [1]	21.2	34.9	52.7	52.7	60.4	65.9	71.0	78.2	85.9
Other third party payers and programs [2]	74.8	118.9	139.5	144.7	150.5	159.1	170.3	170.9	175.6

[1] Includes Children's Health Insurance Program (Titles XIX and XXI), Department of Defense, and Department of Veterans Affairs. [2] See footnote 2, Table 141.

Source: U. S. Centers for Medicare and Medicaid Services, Office of the Actuary, "National Health Statistics Group," <http://www.cms.hhs.gov/NationalHealthExpendData/>.

Table 140. National Health Expenditures by Sponsor: 1990 to 2009

[In billions of dollars (724.0 represents $724,000,000,000). Excludes Puerto Rico and Island Areas.]

Type of Sponsor	1990	2000	2004	2005	2006	2007	2008	2009
Total	**724.0**	**1,378.0**	**1,894.7**	**2,021.0**	**2,152.1**	**2,283.5**	**2,391.4**	**2,486.3**
Business, households and other private revenues	488.0	889.5	1,147.6	1,219.4	1,283.8	1,358.8	1,406.0	1,403.1
Private business [1]	178.1	345.5	451.9	478.3	492.0	511.4	521.0	518.3
Household [2,3]	253.0	434.2	559.7	595.5	634.9	671.2	707.2	708.4
Other private revenues	56.9	109.9	135.9	145.7	156.9	176.2	177.8	176.4
Governments	236.0	488.5	747.1	801.6	868.2	924.7	985.4	1,083.2
Federal government [4,5]	125.3	261.1	425.9	452.6	494.6	525.0	575.5	678.4
State and local government [6,7]	110.7	227.4	321.3	349.0	373.6	399.7	410.0	404.8

[1] Estimates for 2006–2009 exclude Retiree Drug Subsidy (RDS) payments to private plans. [2] Estimates for 2009 excludes subsidized COBRA payments. [3] Includes one-half of self-employment contribution to Medicare Hospital Insurance Trust Fund and taxation of Social Security benefits. [4] Includes RDS payments to private and state and local plans, 2006-2009. [5] Includes maternal and child health, vocational rehabilitation, Substance Abuse and Mental Health Services Administration, Indian Health Service, Office of Economic Opportunity (1965–74), Federal workers' compensation, and other federal programs, public health activities, Department of Defense, Department of Veterans Affairs, Children's Health Program (CHIP), investment (research, structures and equipment) and COBRA subsidies. [6] Includes Medicaid buy-in premiums for Medicare. [7] Includes other public and general assistance, maternal and child health, vocational rehabilitation, public health activities, hospital subsidies, other state and local programs, state phase-down payments and investment (research, structures and equipment).

Source: U.S. Centers for Medicare and Medicaid Services, Office of the Actuary, "Health Expenditures by Sponsors: Business, Household and Government," <http://www.cms.gov/NationalHealthExpendData/downloads/bhg09.pdf>.

Table 141. Hospital Care, Physician and Clinical Services, Nursing Care Facilities and Continuing Care Retirement Communities, and Prescription Drug Expenditures by Source of Funds: 1990 to 2009

[In billions of dollars (250.4 represents $250,400,000,000). Excludes Puerto Rico and Island Areas]

Source of payment	1990	2000	2004	2005	2006	2007	2008	2009
Hospital care, total	**250.4**	**415.5**	**564.5**	**606.5**	**648.3**	**686.8**	**722.1**	**759.1**
Out-of-pocket	11.2	13.4	17.6	19.0	20.3	21.6	23.2	24.4
Health insurance	206.8	358.3	493.8	532.1	567.2	598.8	634.0	669.3
Private health insurance	96.5	140.8	198.9	214.5	234.0	245.1	258.8	265.9
Medicare	67.8	124.4	165.3	179.1	187.1	195.3	208.1	220.4
Medicaid	26.7	71.2	97.7	104.8	110.2	119.7	123.6	136.1
Other health insurance [1]	15.8	21.9	32.0	33.7	36.0	38.8	43.6	47.0
Other third party payers and programs [2]	32.4	43.8	53.1	55.4	60.8	66.3	64.9	65.3
Physician and clinical services, total ...	**158.9**	**290.0**	**393.6**	**419.6**	**441.6**	**462.6**	**486.5**	**505.9**
Out-of-pocket	30.2	32.4	39.9	43.2	45.1	47.1	48.4	47.9
Health insurance	107.5	221.7	309.9	331.7	350.3	367.1	389.0	407.3
Private health insurance	67.2	137.8	190.2	204.8	214.2	223.2	233.3	237.7
Medicare	30.0	57.9	79.8	84.7	90.0	94.2	102.0	109.4
Medicaid	7.0	19.2	27.7	29.8	31.6	33.2	35.7	39.9
Other health insurance [1]	3.3	6.8	12.1	12.4	14.5	16.4	18.1	20.3
Other third party payers and programs [2]	21.2	35.9	43.9	44.7	46.2	48.4	49.0	50.6
Nursing care facilities and continuing care retirement communities, total	**44.9**	**85.1**	**105.4**	**112.1**	**117.0**	**126.5**	**132.8**	**137.0**
Out-of-pocket	18.1	27.7	32.5	34.2	35.1	38.5	40.4	39.8
Health insurance	21.9	51.5	66.3	70.5	73.9	78.0	83.2	87.5
Private health insurance	2.8	7.6	7.0	7.5	8.7	9.2	10.0	10.5
Medicare	1.7	10.1	16.9	19.0	21.0	23.4	26.0	28.0
Medicaid	16.4	31.9	39.8	41.2	41.3	42.1	43.6	45.0
Other health insurance [1]	1.0	1.9	2.7	2.8	2.8	3.3	3.7	4.0
Other third party payers and programs [2]	4.9	6.0	6.6	7.4	8.0	10.0	9.2	9.7
Prescription drugs, total	**40.3**	**120.9**	**190.3**	**201.7**	**219.8**	**230.2**	**237.2**	**249.9**
Out-of-pocket	22.9	34.0	47.7	50.6	49.9	52.5	51.8	53.0
Health insurance	16.2	84.6	138.9	147.2	165.8	173.9	181.7	193.3
Private health insurance	10.9	60.7	93.1	99.6	99.2	101.5	103.3	108.6
Medicare	0.2	2.1	3.4	3.9	39.6	45.8	50.4	54.8
Medicaid	5.1	19.8	35.7	36.3	18.9	18.1	18.9	20.0
Other health insurance [1]	0.1	2.1	6.7	7.4	8.1	8.5	9.1	10.0
Other third party payers and programs [2]	1.2	2.3	3.7	3.9	4.1	3.8	3.7	3.6

[1] Includes Children's Health Insurance Program (Titles XIX and XXI), Department of Defense, and Department of Veterans Affairs. [2] Includes worksite health care, other private revenues, Indian Health Service, workers' compensation, general assistance, maternal and child health, vocational rehabilitation, other federal programs, Substance Abuse and Mental Health Services Administration, other state and local programs, and school health.

Source: U.S. Centers for Medicare and Medicaid Services, Office of the Actuary, "National Health Statistics Group," <http://www.cms.hhs.gov/NationalHealthExpendData/>.

Table 142. Consumer Price Indexes of Medical Care Prices: 1980 to 2010

[1982–1984 = 100. Indexes are annual averages of monthly data based on components of consumer price index for all urban consumers; for explanation, see text, Section 14 and Appendix III]

Year	Medical care, total	Medical care services					Medical care commodities		Annual percent change [3]		
		Total [1]	Professional services			Hospital and related services	Total [2]	Pre-scription drugs	Medical care, total	Medical care services	Medical care com-modities
			Total [1]	Physi-cians	Dental						
1980....	74.9	74.8	77.9	76.5	78.9	69.2	75.4	72.5	11.0	11.3	9.3
1985....	113.5	113.2	113.5	113.3	114.2	116.1	115.2	120.1	6.3	6.1	7.2
1990....	162.8	162.7	156.1	160.8	155.8	178.0	163.4	181.7	9.0	9.3	8.4
1995....	220.5	224.2	201.0	208.8	206.8	257.8	204.5	235.0	4.5	5.1	1.9
2000....	260.8	266.0	237.7	244.7	258.5	317.3	238.1	285.4	4.1	4.3	3.2
2004....	310.1	321.3	271.5	278.3	306.9	417.9	269.3	337.1	4.4	5.0	2.5
2005....	323.2	336.7	281.7	287.5	324.0	439.9	276.0	349.0	4.2	4.8	2.5
2006....	336.2	350.6	289.3	291.9	340.9	468.1	285.9	363.9	4.0	4.1	3.6
2007....	351.1	369.3	300.8	303.2	358.4	498.9	290.0	369.2	4.4	5.3	1.4
2008....	364.1	384.9	311.0	311.3	376.9	534.0	296.0	378.3	3.7	4.2	2.1
2009....	375.6	397.3	319.4	320.8	388.1	567.9	305.1	391.1	3.2	3.2	3.1
2010....	388.4	411.2	328.2	331.3	398.8	607.7	314.7	407.8	3.4	3.5	3.1

[1] Includes other services not shown separately. [2] Includes other commodities not shown separately. [3] Percent change from the immediate prior year.

Source: Bureau of Labor Statistics, "CPI Detailed Report, Data for January 2011," <http://www.bls.gov/cpi/cpi_dr.htm>. See also "Monthly Labor Review Online," <http://www.bls.gov/opub/mlr/>.

Table 143. Average Annual Expenditures Per Consumer Unit for Health Care: 2007 to 2009

[In dollars, except percent. See text, Section 13 and headnote, Table 680. For composition of regions, see map, inside front cover]

Item	Health care, total		Health insur-ance	Medical services	Drugs and medical sup-plies [1]	Percent distribution		
	Amount	Percent of total expendi-tures				Health insur-ance	Medical services	Drugs and medical sup-plies [1]
2007...................	2,853	5.7	1,545	709	599	54.2	24.9	21.0
2008...................	2,976	5.9	1,653	727	596	55.5	24.4	20.0
2009...................	3,126	6.4	1,785	736	605	57.1	23.5	19.4
Age of reference person:								
Under 25 years old	676	2.4	381	167	127	56.4	24.7	18.8
25 to 34 years old	1,805	3.9	1,083	466	256	60.0	25.8	14.2
35 to 44 years old	2,520	4.4	1,436	650	435	57.0	25.8	17.3
45 to 54 years old	3,173	5.4	1,688	862	624	53.2	27.2	19.7
55 to 64 years old	3,895	7.4	2,017	1,054	823	51.8	27.1	21.1
65 to 74 years old	4,906	11.4	3,042	818	1,046	62.0	16.7	21.3
75 years old and over	4,779	15.1	3,011	824	945	63.0	17.2	19.8
Race of reference person:								
White and other....................	3,314	6.5	1,875	797	642	56.6	24.0	19.4
Black	1,763	5.0	1,133	294	336	64.3	16.7	19.1
Origin of reference person:								
Hispanic...........................	1,568	3.7	848	418	302	54.1	26.7	19.3
Non-Hispanic.......................	3,335	6.7	1,910	779	645	57.3	23.4	19.3
Region of residence:								
Northeast..........................	3,132	5.8	1,916	625	592	61.2	20.0	18.9
Midwest...........................	3,272	7.0	1,845	780	647	56.4	23.8	19.8
South.............................	3,030	6.6	1,730	672	629	57.1	22.2	20.8
West..............................	3,128	5.9	1,703	889	536	54.4	28.4	17.1
Size of consumer unit:								
One person	2,007	6.8	1,169	446	393	58.2	22.2	19.6
Two or more persons.................	3,578	6.3	2,034	854	691	56.8	23.9	19.3
Two persons......................	4,021	7.8	2,332	855	834	58.0	21.3	20.7
Three persons	3,273	5.8	1,890	783	600	57.7	23.9	18.3
Four persons	3,300	5.0	1,772	981	546	53.7	29.7	16.5
Five persons or more..............	2,960	4.7	1,628	781	551	55.0	26.4	18.6
Income before taxes:								
Quintiles of income:								
Lowest 20 percent..................	1,628	7.5	978	323	327	60.1	3.3	20.1
Second 20 percent.................	2,491	7.9	1,524	437	530	61.2	3.3	21.3
Third 20 percent...................	3,069	7.5	1,825	642	602	59.5	3.2	19.6
Fourth 20 percent	3,762	6.6	2,080	995	687	55.3	4.0	18.3
Highest 20 percent	4,677	5.0	2,516	1,283	877	53.8	4.4	18.8
Education:								
Less than a high school graduate	2,010	6.6	1,215	364	432	60.4	18.1	21.5
High school graduate...................	2,913	7.5	1,712	624	577	58.8	21.4	19.8
High school graduate with some college.....	2,917	6.5	1,635	691	592	56.1	23.7	20.3
Associate's degree	3,000	5.9	1,660	729	611	55.3	24.3	20.4
Bachelor's degree	3,778	5.7	2,121	974	682	56.1	25.8	18.1
Master's, professional, doctoral degree......	4,503	5.9	2,544	1,177	782	56.5	26.1	17.4

[1] Includes prescription and nonprescription drugs.

Source: U.S. Bureau of Labor Statistics, Consumer Expenditure Survey, annual, <http://www.bls.gov/cex/>.

Health and Nutrition 105

Table 144. Medicare Disbursements by Type of Beneficiary: 1990 to 2010

[In millions of dollars (109,709 represents $109,709,000,000). For years ending Sept. 30. Distribution of benefits by type is estimated and subject to change. See headnote, Table 149]

Selected type of beneficiary	1990	1995	2000	2005	2007	2008 [1]	2009	2010
Total disbursements	**109,709**	**180,096**	**219,276**	**336,876**	**434,823**	**455,069**	**498,213**	**521,141**
HI, Part A disbursements [2]	**66,687**	**114,883**	**130,284**	**184,142**	**202,827**	**230,240**	**238,001**	**248,978**
Benefits..............................	65,722	113,394	125,992	181,934	203,990	226,276	234,302	245,180
Aged	58,503	100,107	110,067	155,772	172,847	183,846	196,766	205,180
Disabled...........................	7,218	13,288	15,925	26,161	31,142	33,946	37,536	40,001
SMI, Part B disbursements [2]	**43,022**	**65,213**	**88,992**	**151,537**	**179,651**	**177,709**	**203,421**	**208,380**
Benefits..............................	41,498	63,490	88,875	147,449	172,698	174,805	200,169	204,885
Aged	36,837	54,830	76,340	122,905	142,841	151,386	164,266	167,540
Disabled...........................	4,661	8,660	12,535	24,544	29,858	31,903	35,903	37,345
SMI, Part D disbursements [2]	**(X)**	**(X)**	**(X)**	**1,198**	**52,345**	**47,120**	**56,791**	**63,783**
Benefits..............................	(X)	(X)	(X)	73	51,331	46,728	56,559	63,525
Transitional assistance benefit payments	(X)	(X)	(X)	1,125	10	–	–	–

– Represents or rounds to zero. X Not applicable. [1] A transfer of expenditures between Parts A and B took place during 2008 that corrected for accounting errors that happened during FY 2005–2007. The transfer is reflected in the "Benefits" data and is the sum of "Aged, Disabled, and Transfer." The Part A "Benefits" total increased by $8,484,000,000 while Part B "Benefits" total decreased by the same amount. [2] Other types, not shown separately.

Source: U.S. Centers for Medicare and Medicaid Services, Trustees Report and Trust Funds, and unpublished data. See also <http://www.cms.hhs.gov/ReportsTrustFunds/>.

Table 145. Children's Health Insurance Program (CHIP)—Enrollment and Expenditures by State: 2000 and 2010

[3,357.4 represents 3,357,400. For year ending September 30. This program provides health benefits coverage to children living in families whose incomes exceed the eligibility limits for Medicaid. Although it is generally targeted to families with incomes at or below 200 percent of the federal poverty level, each state may set its own income eligibility limits, within certain guidelines. For explanation of poverty level, see text, Section 13. States have three options: they may expand their Medicaid programs, develop a separate child health program that functions independently of Medicaid, or do a combination of both. See text, this section, regarding the change from SCHIP to CHIP]

State	Enrollment [1] (1,000) 2000	2010	Expenditures [2] (mil. dol.) 2000	2010	State	Enrollment [1] (1,000) 2000	2010	Expenditures [2] (mil. dol.) 2000	2010
U.S.	**3,357.4**	**7,718.4**	**1,928.8**	**7,913.1**	MO......	72.8	91.4	41.2	107.0
AL	37.6	137.5	31.9	128.4	MT......	8.3	25.2	4.3	36.5
AK	13.4	12.6	18.1	18.7	NE......	11.4	47.9	6.1	36.7
AZ	59.6	39.6	29.4	57.8	NV......	15.9	31.6	9.0	22.7
AR	1.9	100.8	1.5	85.8	NH......	4.3	10.6	1.6	12.2
CA	484.4	1,731.6	187.3	1,186.8	NJ	89.0	187.2	46.9	562.4
CO......	34.9	106.6	13.9	115.6	NM......	8.0	9.7	3.4	230.6
CT	19.9	21.0	12.8	29.7	NY......	769.5	539.6	401.0	499.4
DE......	4.5	12.9	1.5	12.9	NC......	103.6	254.0	65.5	359.2
DC......	2.3	8.1	5.8	11.3	ND......	2.6	6.7	1.8	14.4
FL	227.5	403.3	125.7	308.5	OH......	118.3	253.7	53.1	264.0
GA......	120.6	248.3	48.7	225.4	OK......	57.7	122.9	51.3	113.0
HI.......	(Z)	27.3	0.4	31.4	OR......	37.1	64.7	12.5	86.1
ID........	12.4	42.2	7.5	34.1	PA	119.7	273.2	70.7	305.6
IL........	62.5	329.1	32.7	259.4	RI.......	11.5	23.3	10.4	28.8
IN........	44.4	141.5	53.7	89.8	SC......	60.4	73.4	46.6	92.5
IA........	20.0	64.0	15.5	71.6	SD......	5.9	15.9	3.1	18.9
KS	26.3	56.4	12.8	52.7	TN	14.9	89.3	41.7	127.0
KY	55.6	79.4	60.0	122.9	TX	131.1	928.5	41.4	776.3
LA	50.0	157.0	25.3	175.7	UT......	25.3	62.1	12.8	59.5
ME......	22.7	33.0	11.4	33.7	VT......	4.1	7.0	1.4	5.5
MD......	93.1	118.9	92.2	160.3	VA	37.7	173.5	18.6	165.4
MA......	113.0	142.3	44.2	301.0	WA......	2.6	35.9	0.6	42.7
MI.......	55.4	69.8	36.2	114.9	WV......	21.7	37.5	9.7	39.2
MN......	(Z)	5.2	(Z)	19.5	WI......	47.1	161.5	21.4	97.6
MS......	12.2	95.6	21.1	152.4	WY......	2.5	8.3	1.0	9.3

Z Less than 50 or $50,000. [1] Number of children ever enrolled during the year in Children's Health Insurance Program. [2] Expenditures for which states are entitled to federal reimbursement under Title XXI and which reconciles any advance of Title XXI federal funds made on the basis of estimates.

Source: U.S. Centers for Medicare & Medicaid Services, *The Children's Health Insurance Program (CHIP), Annual Enrollment Report* and the Statement of Expenditures for the CHIP Program (CMS-21). See also <http://www.cms.hhs.gov/NationalSCHIPPolicy/SCHIPER/list.asp> and <http://www.cms.hhs.gov/medicaid/mbes/default.asp>.

Table 146. Medicare Enrollees: 1990 to 2010

[In millions (34.3 represents 34,300,000). As of July 1. Includes Puerto Rico and Island Areas and enrollees in foreign countries and unknown place of residence. SMI is Supplemental Medical Insurance. See headnote, Table 149]

Item	1990	1995	2000	2005	2006	2007	2008	2009	2010
Total	**34.3**	**37.6**	**39.7**	**42.6**	**43.4**	**44.4**	**45.5**	**46.6**	**47.5**
Aged	31.0	33.2	34.3	35.8	36.3	37.0	37.9	38.8	39.6
Disabled	3.3	4.4	5.4	6.8	7.1	7.4	7.6	7.8	7.9
Hospital insurance, Part A	**33.7**	**37.2**	**39.3**	**42.2**	**43.1**	**44.0**	**45.1**	**46.2**	**47.1**
Aged	30.5	32.7	33.8	35.4	36.0	36.6	37.6	38.4	39.2
Disabled	3.3	4.4	5.4	6.8	7.1	7.4	7.6	7.8	7.9
SMI, Part B	**32.6**	**35.6**	**37.3**	**39.8**	**40.4**	**41.1**	**42.0**	**42.9**	**43.8**
Aged	29.6	31.7	32.6	33.8	34.1	34.6	35.3	36.0	36.7
Disabled	2.9	3.9	4.8	6.0	6.2	6.4	6.6	6.9	7.1
SMI, Part D	(X)	(X)	(X)	1.8	30.5	31.2	32.4	33.5	34.5
Medicare Advantage [1]	1.3	2.7	6.2	5.8	7.3	8.7	10.0	11.1	11.7

X Not applicable. [1] Prior to 2004, Medicare Advantage was referred to as Medicare + Choice.

Source: U.S. Centers for Medicare and Medicaid Services, Office of the Actuary, CMS Statistics Medicare Enrollment, "National Trends," and unpublished data, <http://www.cms.hhs.gov/MedicareEnrpts/>.

Table 147. Medicare—Enrollment by State and Other Areas: 2000 to 2009

[In thousands (39,620 represents 39,620,000). Hospital (HI) and/or supplementary medical insurance (SMI) enrollment as of July 1]

State and area	2000	2005	2008	2009	State and area	2000	2005	2008	2009
All areas [1]	**39,620**	**42,395**	**45,412**	**46,521**	MT	137	146	160	165
U.S.	**38,762**	**41,003**	**44,385**	**45,467**	NE	254	259	271	276
AL	685	740	809	828	NV	240	294	330	343
AK	42	51	60	63	NH	170	185	212	217
AZ	675	777	870	899	NJ	1,203	1,215	1,283	1,304
AR	439	464	509	520	NM	234	261	294	304
CA	3,901	4,158	4,492	4,620	NY	2,715	2,758	2,891	2,937
CO	467	513	579	602	NC	1,133	1,255	1,405	1,448
CT	515	520	549	558	ND	103	103	107	108
DE	112	125	141	145	OH	1,701	1,731	1,841	1,870
DC	75	72	75	77	OK	508	531	578	592
FL	2,804	3,008	3,212	3,289	OR	489	532	584	602
GA	916	1,016	1,153	1,194	PA	2,095	2,108	2,221	2,252
HI	165	180	194	200	RI	172	171	178	180
ID	165	188	214	222	SC	568	637	724	749
IL	1,635	1,674	1,775	1,806	SD	119	123	132	134
IN	852	893	964	985	TN	829	903	1,004	1,031
IA	477	484	506	512	TX	2,265	2,491	2,802	2,900
KS	390	397	418	425	UT	206	231	264	274
KY	623	668	728	743	VT	89	95	105	108
LA	602	630	656	671	VA	893	981	1,079	1,110
ME	216	233	253	259	WA	736	807	903	938
MD	645	687	745	764	WV	338	351	373	377
MA	961	961	1,019	1,039	WI	783	818	874	892
MI	1,403	1,468	1,580	1,615	WY	65	70	76	78
MN	654	691	749	767	Outlying areas [2]	537	622	(NA)	653
MS	419	449	479	488	Pending state				
MO	861	901	966	985	designations [3]	321	769	(NA)	(NA)

NA Not available. [1] Includes outlying areas and pending state designation. [2] Includes American Samoa, Federated States of Micronesia, Guam, Marshall Islands, Northern Marianas, Puerto Rico, Virgin Islands, and Wake Island. [3] Include foreign countries and unknown places of residence.

Source: U.S. Centers for Medicare and Medicaid Services, "Data Compendium," <http://www.cms.gov/DataCompendium/>.

Table 148. Medicaid—Selected Characteristics of Persons Covered: 2009

[In thousands, except percent (47,469 represents 47,469,000). Represents number of persons as of March of following year who were enrolled at any time in year shown. Excludes unrelated individuals under age 15. Persons did not have to receive medical care paid for by Medicaid in order to be counted. For explanation of poverty level, see text, Section 13. See headnote, Table 567]

Poverty status	Total [1]	White alone [2]	Black alone [3]	Asian alone [4]	His- panic [5]	Under 18 years	18–44 years	45–64 years	65 years and over
Persons covered, total	**47,469**	**32,599**	**10,408**	**1,949**	**12,906**	**25,042**	**12,235**	**6,543**	**3,649**
Below poverty level	19,919	12,633	5,404	666	5,905	11,265	5,254	2,436	965
Above poverty level	27,550	19,966	5,004	1,283	7,001	13,777	6,981	4,107	2,684
Percent of population covered	**15.6**	**13.5**	**27.0**	**13.9**	**26.4**	**33.6**	**11.0**	**8.2**	**9.5**
Below poverty level	45.7	42.3	54.3	38.1	47.8	72.9	31.0	31.5	28.1
Above poverty level	10.6	9.4	17.5	10.5	19.2	23.3	7.4	5.7	7.6

[1] Includes other races, not shown separately. [2] White alone refers to people who reported White and did not report any other race category. [3] Black alone refers to people who reported Black and did not report any other race category. [4] Asian alone refers to people who reported Asian and did not report any other race category. [5] Persons of Hispanic origin may be of any race.

Source: U.S. Census Bureau, Income, Poverty, and Health Insurance Coverage in the United States: 2009, Current Population Reports, P60-238, 2010; Table HI02, "Health Insurance Coverage Status and Type of Coverage by Selected Characteristics for People in the Poverty Universe: 2009" and Table HI03, "Health Insurance Coverage Status and Type of Coverage by Selected Characteristics for Poor People in the Poverty Universe: 2009." See also <http://www.census.gov/hhes/www/cpstables/032010/health/toc.htm>.

Table 149. Medicare Benefits by Type of Provider: 1990 to 2010

[In millions of dollars (65,721 represents $65,721,000,000). For years ending Sept. 30. Distribution of benefits by type is estimated and subject to change. The Medicare program has two components: Hospital Insurance (HI) or Medicare Part A and Supplementary Medical Insurance (SMI) consisting of Medicare Part B (medical insurance) and Part D (prescription drug plans). See text in this section for details. See footnote 1, Table 144, for 2008 data changes]

Type of provider	1990	1995	2000	2005	2007	2008	2009	2010
Hospital insurance benefits (Part A), total	**65,721**	**113,395**	**125,992**	**181,934**	**203,990**	**217,791**	**234,302**	**245,180**
Inpatient hospital	57,012	81,095	86,561	122,718	125,533	128,851	132,768	137,834
Skilled nursing facility	2,761	8,684	10,269	18,644	22,432	24,117	25,826	27,047
Home health agency	3,295	15,715	4,880	5,892	6,313	6,537	6,942	7,138
Hospice	318	1,854	2,818	7,678	10,482	11,137	11,977	12,910
Managed care	2,335	6,047	21,463	27,001	39,230	47,150	56,789	60,253
Supplementary medical insurance benefits (Part B), total	**41,498**	**63,490**	**88,876**	**147,449**	**172,698**	**183,289**	**200,169**	**204,885**
Physician fee schedule	(NA)	31,110	35,958	57,211	58,780	59,396	62,462	63,442
Durable medical equipment	(NA)	3,576	4,577	7,894	8,188	8,454	8,209	8,131
Carrier lab [1]	(NA)	2,819	2,194	3,521	4,050	4,141	4,639	4,924
Other carrier [2]	(NA)	4,513	7,154	15,195	15,698	16,390	17,269	17,199
Hospital [3]	(NA)	8,448	8,516	18,974	22,882	23,435	26,447	26,800
Home health	(NA)	223	4,281	6,750	9,053	10,100	11,326	12,087
Intermediary lab [4]	(NA)	1,437	1,748	2,820	3,019	2,912	3,274	3,235
Other intermediary [5]	(NA)	5,110	6,099	11,350	13,305	12,775	14,375	14,330
Managed care	(NA)	6,253	18,348	23,735	37,724	45,686	52,167	54,739
Supplementary medical insurance benefits (Part D), total [6]	**(X)**	**(X)**	**(X)**	**1,198**	**51,341**	**46,728**	**56,559**	**63,525**

NA Not available. X Not applicable. [1] Lab services paid under the lab fee schedule performed in a physician's office lab or an independent lab. [2] Includes free-standing ambulatory surgical centers facility costs, ambulance, and supplies. [3] Includes the hospital facility costs for Medicare Part B services which are predominantly in the outpatient department. The physician reimbursement associated with these services is included on the "Physician Fee Schedule" line. [4] Lab fee services paid under the lab fee schedule performed in a hospital outpatient department. [5] Includes End Stage Renal Disease (ESRD) free-standing dialysis facility payments and payments to rural health clinics and federally qualified health centers. [6] Starting with 2006, Part D provides subsidized access to drug insurance coverage on a voluntary basis for all beneficiaries and premium and cost-sharing subsidies for low-income enrollees. Benefits prior to 2006 were for transitional assistance to beneficiaries with low income.

Source: U.S. Centers for Medicare and Medicaid Services, unpublished data. See also <http://www.cms.hhs.gov/ReportsTrustFunds/>.

Table 150. Medicare Insurance Trust Funds: 1990 to 2010

[In billions of dollars (126.3 represents $126,300,000,000). SMI is Supplemental Medical Insurance. See headnote, Table 149]

Type of trust fund	1990	1995	2000	2005	2006	2007	2008	2009	2010
TOTAL MEDICARE									
Total income	126.3	175.3	257.1	357.5	437.0	462.1	480.8	508.2	486.0
Total expenditures	111.0	184.2	221.8	336.4	408.3	431.7	468.1	509.0	522.8
Assets, end of year	114.4	143.4	221.5	309.8	338.5	368.9	381.6	380.8	344.0
HOSPITAL INSURANCE (Part A)									
Net contribution income [1]	72.1	103.3	154.5	182.6	194.3	205.4	213.5	206.3	199.3
Interest received [2]	8.5	10.8	11.7	16.1	16.4	17.4	16.3	17.0	15.9
Benefit payments [3]	66.2	116.4	126.8	180.0	189.0	200.2	232.3	239.3	244.5
Assets, end of year	98.9	130.3	177.5	285.8	305.4	326.0	321.3	304.2	271.9
SMI (Part B)									
Net premium income	11.3	19.7	20.6	37.5	42.9	46.8	50.2	56.0	52.0
Transfers from general revenue	33.0	39.0	65.9	118.1	132.7	139.6	146.8	162.8	153.5
Interest received [2]	1.6	1.6	3.5	1.4	1.8	2.2	3.5	3.0	3.1
Benefit payments [3]	42.5	65.0	88.9	149.9	166.2	176.4	180.3	202.6	209.7
Assets, end of year	15.5	13.1	44.0	24.0	32.3	42.1	59.4	75.5	71.4
SMI (Part D)									
Net premium income	(X)	(X)	(X)	–	3.5	4.0	5.0	6.3	6.5
Transfers from general revenue [4]	(X)	(X)	(X)	1.1	39.2	38.8	37.3	47.1	51.1
Interest received	(X)	(X)	(X)	–	–	–	–	–	–
Benefit payments [4]	(X)	(X)	(X)	1.1	47.0	48.8	49.0	60.5	61.7
Assets, end of year	(X)	(X)	(X)	–	0.8	0.8	0.9	1.1	0.7

– Represents zero. X Not applicable. [1] Includes income from taxation of benefits beginning in 1994. Includes premiums from aged ineligibles enrolled in Hospital Insurance (HI). [2] Includes recoveries of amounts reimbursed from the trust fund. [3] Beginning 1998, monies transferred to the SMI trust fund for home health agency costs, as provided for by P.L. 105-33, are included in HI benefit payments but excluded from SMI benefit payments. [4] The amount for 2005 includes amounts transferred for transitional assistance for Part D of Medicare

Source: U.S. Centers for Medicare and Medicaid Services, *2011 Annual Report of the Board of Trustees of the Federal Hospital Insurance and Federal Supplementary Medical Insurance Trust Funds.* See also <http://www.cms.hhs.gov/ReportsTrustFunds/>.

Table 151. Medicaid—Beneficiaries and Payments: 2000 to 2009

[For year ending September 30. 42,887 represents 42,887,000]

Basis of eligibility and type of service	Beneficiaries (1,000) [1]				Payments (mil. dol.)			
	2000	2005	2008	2009 [2]	2000	2005	2008	2009 [2]
Total	42,887	57,651	58,771	61,825	168,443	274,851	296,830	317,982
Age 65 and over	3,730	4,395	4,147	4,180	44,560	63,415	61,131	62,887
Blind/Disabled	6,890	8,211	8,694	8,927	72,772	119,305	129,040	137,149
Children........................	19,018	26,341	27,111	28,348	23,490	41,863	51,200	56,082
Adults..........................	8,671	12,533	12,903	13,970	17,671	32,162	37,185	43,383
Foster care children...........	761	874	960	937	3,309	5,286	5,936	5,971
Unknown	3,817	5,268	4,912	5,416	6,639	12,539	11,825	11,927
BCCA WOMEN [3]	(NA)	29	44	47	(NA)	281	513	583
All service categories:								
Capitated care [4]	21,292	33,496	38,151	40,334	25,026	46,421	68,130	78,687
Clinic services	7,678	11,918	11,857	12,560	6,138	8,921	9,152	9,952
Dental services	5,922	9,317	9,821	10,773	1,413	3,040	3,819	4,386
Home health services	1,007	1,195	1,144	1,159	3,133	5,362	6,620	6,986
ICF/MR services [5]	119	109	102	102	9,376	11,709	12,558	12,668
Inpatient hospital services......	4,913	5,480	5,259	5,360	24,131	35,131	37,245	38,733
Lab and X-ray services	11,439	15,959	15,612	16,396	1,292	2,917	2,931	3,112
Mental health facility services [6]	100	120	108	115	1,769	2,301	2,374	2,516
Nursing facility services...........	1,706	1,711	1,616	1,643	34,528	44,790	47,718	48,020
Other care [7]	9,022	12,346	12,264	12,165	14,755	26,421	34,257	36,733
Outpatient hospital services	13,170	16,234	14,789	16,253	7,082	10,011	10,881	11,475
Other practitioner services..........	4,758	5,893	5,165	5,535	664	1,180	884	943
PCCM services [8]	5,649	8,723	8,728	9,043	177	232	276	320
Prescribed drugs................	20,325	28,390	24,579	26,561	19,898	42,849	23,515	25,036
Physician services................	18,965	24,238	21,661	22,369	6,809	11,269	10,506	10,927
Personal support services [9]	4,559	6,807	6,371	6,869	11,629	20,657	24,539	26,380
Sterilizations	137	178	138	132	128	211	143	151
Unknown	74	73	90	122	496	1,428	1,282	957

NA Not available. [1] Beneficiaries data do not add due to number of beneficiaries that are reported in more than one category.
[2] 2009 data not available for the District of Columbia, Florida, Hawaii, Massachusetts, Missouri, North Dakota, Pennsylvania, Texas, Utah, Vermont, and Wisconsin; 2008 data are reported. [3] Women-Breast and Cervical Cancer Assistance. [4] HMO payments and prepaid health plans. [5] Intermediate care facilities and or for mentally retarded. [6] Inpatient mental health-aged and inpatient mental health-under 21. [7] Includes beneficiaries of, and payments for, other care not shown separately. [8] Primary Care Case Management Services. [9] Includes personal care services, rehabilitative services, physical occupational targeted case management services, speech therapies, hospice services, nurse midwife services, nurse practitioner services, private duty nursing services, and religious nonmedical health care institutions.

Source: U.S. Centers for Medicare and Medicaid Services, "Medicaid Program Statistics, Medicaid Statistical Information System," <http://www.cms.gov/MedicaidDataSourcesGenInfo/MSIS/list.asp>.

Table 152. Medicaid—Summary by State: 2000 and 2009

[42,887 represents 42,887,000. For year ending September 30]

State	Beneficiaries [1] (1,000)		Payments [2] (mil. dol.)		State	Beneficiaries [1] (1,000)		Payments [2] (mil. dol.)	
	2000	2009 [3]	2000	2009 [3]		2000	2009 [3]	2000	2009 [3]
U.S.	42,887	61,825	168,443	317,982	MO........	890	1,054	3,274	5,225
AL	619	877	2,393	3,626	MT........	104	113	422	714
AK	96	119	473	1,067	NE	229	256	960	1,590
AZ	681	1,588	2,112	8,617	NV	138	281	516	1,196
AR	489	825	1,543	3,579	NH	97	141	651	995
CA	7,918	11,519	17,105	35,224	NJ	822	1,151	4,714	8,293
CO.......	381	678	1,809	3,288	NM.......	376	562	1,249	2,913
CT	420	558	2,839	5,289	NY	3,420	4,985	26,148	44,883
DE	115	209	529	1,264	NC	1,214	1,782	4,834	9,665
DC	139	168	793	1,739	ND	63	74	358	551
FL	2,373	2,871	7,433	13,224	OH	1,305	2,238	7,115	13,972
GA	1,369	1,805	3,624	7,376	OK	507	809	1,604	3,574
HI	194	236	600	1,014	OR	558	564	1,714	2,797
ID	131	253	594	1,351	PA	1,492	2,134	6,366	12,501
IL	1,519	2,626	7,807	11,774	RI	179	203	1,070	1,556
IN	706	1,109	2,977	5,390	SC	689	906	2,765	4,712
IA	314	482	1,477	2,877	SD	102	141	402	732
KS	263	355	1,227	2,316	TN	1,568	1,479	3,491	7,262
KY	764	942	2,921	5,017	TX	2,633	3,993	9,277	16,657
LA	761	1,184	2,632	5,430	UT	225	296	960	1,643
ME.......	194	315	1,310	1,481	VT	139	162	480	883
MD......	626	846	3,003	6,325	VA	627	917	2,479	5,548
MA.......	1,060	1,230	5,413	8,991	WA.......	896	1,177	2,435	5,734
MI.......	1,352	1,890	4,881	10,171	WV.......	342	386	1,394	2,589
MN.......	558	802	3,280	7,030	WI.......	577	1,532	2,968	4,589
MS.......	605	932	1,808	3,198	WY.......	46	72	215	552

[1] Persons who had payments made on their behalf at any time during the fiscal year. [2] Payments are for fiscal year and reflect federal and state contribution payments. Data exclude disproportionate share hospital payments. Disproportionate share hospitals receive higher medicaid reimbursement than other hospitals because they treat a disproportionate share of Medicaid patients. [3] 2009 data not available for the District of Columbia, Florida, Hawaii, Massachusetts, Missouri, North Dakota, Pennsylvania, Texas, Utah, Vermont, and Wisconsin; 2008 data are reported.

Source: U.S. Centers for Medicare and Medicaid Services, "Medicaid, Program Statistics, Medicaid Statistical Information System," <http://www.cms.gov/MedicaidDataSourcesGenInfo/MSIS/list.asp>.

Health and Nutrition 109

Table 153. Medicaid Managed Care Enrollment by State and Other Areas: 1995 to 2009

[For year ending June 30. 33,373 represents 33,373,000]

State and other areas	Total enrollment [1] (1,000)	Managed care enrollment [2] Number (1,000)	Percent of total	State and other areas	Total enrollment [1] (1,000)	Managed care enrollment [2] Number (1,000)	Percent of total	State and other areas	Total enrollment [1] (1,000)	Managed care enrollment [2] Number (1,000)	Percent of total
1995....	33,373	9,800	29.4	HI.....	235	228	97.0	NY.....	4,422	2,927	66.2
2000....	33,690	18,786	55.8	ID.....	198	167	84.1	NC.....	1,442	1,012	70.2
2004....	44,356	26,914	60.7	IL.....	2,321	1,278	55.1	ND.....	60	41	67.6
2005....	45,392	28,576	63.0	IN.....	962	712	74.0	OH.....	1,952	1,375	70.4
2006....	45,653	29,830	65.3	IA.....	398	330	82.9	OK.....	626	553	88.5
2007....	45,962	29,463	64.1	KS.....	297	257	86.6	OR.....	475	418	88.1
2008....	47,143	33,428	70.1	KY.....	769	638	83.0	PA.....	1,920	1,577	82.1
2009,				LA.....	1,007	692	68.7	RI.....	178	111	62.1
Total...	**50,472**	**36,202**	**71.7**	ME.....	280	178	63.7	SC.....	763	763	100.0
U.S.....	**49,451**	**35,225**	**71.2**	MD.....	787	620	78.7	SD.....	107	85	79.7
AL......	812	540	66.5	MA.....	1,227	731	59.6	TN.....	1,231	1,231	100.0
AK......	102	–	–	MI.....	1,630	1,447	88.8	TX.....	3,343	2,161	64.6
AZ.....	1,223	1,096	89.6	MN.....	675	426	63.1	UT.....	238	205	85.9
AR.....	645	511	79.2	MS.....	674	513	76.1	VT.....	157	137	87.8
CA.....	6,956	3,633	52.2	MO.....	895	883	98.7	VA.....	815	521	63.9
CO.....	468	445	95.1	MT.....	85	56	66.6	WA.....	1,103	949	86.0
CT.....	456	343	75.2	NE.....	215	180	83.6	WV.....	326	150	46.0
DE.....	171	126	73.9	NV.....	213	179	83.7	WI.....	1,005	607	60.4
DC.....	154	150	66.0	NH.....	124	97	77.6	WY.....	64	–	–
FL.....	2,426	1,601	92.0	NJ.....	969	726	74.9	PR.....	1,013	978	96.5
GA.....	1,386	1,275	92.0	NM.....	465	345	74.2	VI.....	8	–	–

– Represents zero. [1] The unduplicated Medicaid enrollment figures include individuals in state health care reform programs that expand eligibility beyond traditional Medicaid eligibility standards. [2] The unduplicated managed care enrollment figures include enrollees receiving comprehensive and limited benefits.

Source: U.S. Centers for Medicare and Medicaid Services, "2009 Medicaid Managed Care Enrollment Report," <http://www.cms.hhs.gov/MedicaidDataSourcesGenInfo/04_MdManCrEnrllRep.asp>.

Table 154. Persons Enrolled in Health Maintenance Organizations (HMOs) by State: 2007 and 2008

[As of January 1 (74,698 represents 74,698,000). Data are based on a census of health maintenance organizations]

State	Number 2008 (1,000)	Percent of population 2007	2008	State	Number 2008 (1,000)	Percent of population 2007	2008	State	Number 2008 (1,000)	Percent of population 2007	2008
U.S....	**74,698**	**24.7**	**24.8**	KY.....	408	8.1	9.6	ND.....	10	0.2	1.5
AL.....	201	3.6	4.3	LA.....	352	8.6	8.2	OH.....	2,466	20.3	21.5
AK.....	7	1.0	1.1	ME.....	152	29.4	11.5	OK.....	263	7.2	7.3
AZ.....	1,942	29.2	30.6	MD.....	1,701	29.3	30.3	OR.....	1,007	25.3	26.9
AR.....	106	3.4	3.7	MA.....	2,964	48.1	46.0	PA.....	3,744	30.6	30.1
CA.....	16,415	44.6	44.9	MI.....	2,841	28.1	28.2	RI.....	223	22.6	21.0
CO.....	1,053	23.8	21.7	MN.....	939	14.1	18.1	SC.....	417	7.8	9.5
CT.....	1,349	41.2	38.5	MS.....	54	0.9	1.8	SD.....	148	17.7	18.5
DE.....	201	26.0	23.3	MO.....	1,164	23.0	19.8	TN.....	1,897	31.1	30.8
DC.....	377	64.0	64.1	MT.....	62	5.1	6.5	TX.....	3,702	12.8	15.5
FL.....	4,400	24.1	24.1	NE.....	135	6.9	7.6	UT.....	970	35.1	36.7
GA.....	2,099	26.5	22.0	NV.....	608	23.0	23.7	VT.....	86	19.9	13.8
HI.....	650	46.7	50.6	NH.....	219	23.2	16.7	VA.....	1,665	21.5	21.6
ID.....	86	4.6	5.7	NJ.....	2,284	26.5	26.3	WA.....	1,423	20.0	22.0
IL.....	1,762	13.9	13.7	NM.....	591	23.3	30.0	WV.....	277	11.3	15.3
IN.....	1,098	24.1	17.3	NY.....	6,500	32.3	33.7	WI.....	1,507	23.8	26.9
IA.....	327	9.7	11.0	NC.....	838	8.3	9.2	WY.....	21	2.6	4.1
KS.....	471	14.9	17.0								

Source: HealthLeaders-InterStudy, Nashville, TN, *The Competitive Edge* (copyright). See also <http://www.interstudypublications.com/>.

U.S. Census Bureau, Statistical Abstract of the United States: 2012

Table 155. Health Insurance Coverage Status by Selected Characteristics: 2008 and 2009

[301,483 represents 301,483,000. Persons as of following year for coverage in the year shown. Government health insurance includes Medicare, Medicaid, and military plans. Based on Current Population Survey, Annual Social and Economic Supplement (ASEC); see text, Section 1 and Appendix III]

Characteristic	Number (1,000)							Percent			
	Total persons	Covered by private or government health insurance					Not covered by health insur- ance	Covered by private or government health insurance			Not covered by health insur- ance
		Total [1]	Private		Government			Total [1]	Private	Medic- aid	
			Total	Group health [2]	Medi- care	Medic- aid					
2008.	301,483	255,143	200,992	176,332	43,029	42,641	46,340	84.6	66.7	14.1	15.4
2009.	304,280	253,606	194,545	169,689	43,440	47,758	50,674	83.3	63.9	15.7	16.7
Age:											
Under 18 years	75,040	67,527	45,288	41,892	543	25,331	7,513	90.0	60.4	33.8	10.0
Under 6 years	25,542	23,192	14,137	13,282	194	10,090	2,350	90.8	55.3	39.5	9.2
6 to 11 years	24,613	22,268	15,077	14,167	193	8,294	2,344	90.5	61.3	33.7	9.5
12 to 17 years	24,885	22,066	16,074	14,442	157	6,946	2,819	88.7	64.6	27.9	11.3
18 to 24 years	29,313	20,389	16,308	12,802	199	4,437	8,923	69.6	55.6	15.1	30.4
25 to 34 years	41,085	29,122	24,708	22,612	547	4,236	11,963	70.9	60.1	10.3	29.1
35 to 44 years	40,447	31,689	27,962	26,125	934	3,562	8,759	78.3	69.1	8.8	21.7
45 to 54 years	44,387	36,481	32,147	29,867	1,796	3,552	7,906	82.2	72.4	8.0	17.8
55 to 64 years	35,395	30,462	25,718	23,245	3,318	2,991	4,933	86.1	72.7	8.5	13.9
65 years and over	38,613	37,937	22,414	13,146	36,102	3,649	676	98.2	58.0	9.5	1.8
Sex:											
Male.	149,485	122,022	95,046	83,774	19,088	21,824	27,463	81.6	63.6	14.6	18.4
Female.	154,795	131,584	99,498	85,915	24,352	25,934	23,211	85.0	64.3	16.8	15.0
Race: White alone [3]	242,403	204,004	161,513	139,809	36,807	32,814	38,399	84.2	66.6	13.5	15.8
Black alone [3]	38,624	30,522	18,813	17,275	4,598	10,459	8,102	79.0	48.7	27.1	21.0
Asian alone [3]	14,011	11,602	9,352	8,180	1,304	1,951	2,409	82.8	66.7	13.9	17.2
Hispanic origin [4].	48,901	33,081	19,453	17,830	3,274	12,959	15,820	67.6	39.8	26.5	32.4
Household income:											
Less than $25,000.	58,159	42,675	15,795	9,350	14,986	21,693	15,483	73.4	27.2	37.3	26.6
$25,000–$49,999.	71,340	56,062	38,211	31,199	13,821	14,363	15,278	78.6	53.6	20.1	21.4
$50,000–$74,999.	58,381	49,029	41,689	37,376	6,640	6,066	9,352	84.0	71.4	10.4	16.0
$75,000 or more	116,400	105,839	98,849	91,765	7,993	5,636	10,561	90.9	84.9	4.8	9.1
Persons below poverty . .	43,569	29,666	8,599	5,437	4,996	19,919	13,903	68.1	19.7	45.7	31.9

[1] Includes other government insurance, not shown separately. Persons with coverage counted only once in total, even though they may have been covered by more than one type of policy. [2] Related to employment of self or other family members. [3] Refers to people who reported specified race and did not report any other race category. [4] Persons of Hispanic origin may be any race.

Source: U.S. Census Bureau, Income, Poverty, and Health Insurance Coverage in the United States: 2009, Current Population Reports, P60-238, 2010, Table HI01, "Health Insurance Data, Health Insurance Coverage Status and Type of Coverage by Selected Characteristics: 2009" and Table HI03, "Health Insurance Coverage Status and Type of Coverage by Selected Characteristics for Poor People in the Poverty Universe: 2009." See also <http://www.census.gov/hhes/www/cpstables/032010/health/toc.htm>.

Table 156. Persons With and Without Health Insurance Coverage by State: 2009

[253,606 represents 253,606,000. Based on the Current Population Survey, Annual Social and Economic Supplement (ASEC), see text, Section 1 and Appendix III]

State	Total persons covered (1,000)	Total persons not covered		Children not covered		State	Total persons covered (1,000)	Total persons not covered		Children not covered	
		Number (1,000)	Percent of total	Number (1,000)	Percent of total			Number (1,000)	Percent of total	Number (1,000)	Percent of total
U.S.	253,606	50,674	16.7	7,513	10.0	MO.	5,055	914	15.3	139	9.7
AL	3,880	789	16.9	86	7.9	MT	823	149	15.4	23	10.4
AK	568	122	17.7	19	9.9	NE	1,574	205	11.5	31	6.7
AZ	5,239	1,273	19.6	229	13.4	NV	2,086	546	20.8	89	13.3
AR	2,304	548	19.2	81	11.5	NH	1,176	138	10.5	11	3.8
CA	29,449	7,345	20.0	1,012	10.7	NJ	7,309	1,371	15.8	190	9.2
CO	4,209	762	15.3	119	9.6	NM	1,548	430	21.7	72	14.0
CT	3,062	418	12.0	62	7.7	NY	16,347	2,837	14.8	335	7.5
DE	766	118	13.4	19	8.8	NC	7,663	1,685	18.0	276	11.8
DC	522	74	12.4	9	8.0	ND	565	67	10.7	9	5.9
FL	14,287	4,118	22.4	724	17.9	OH.	9,819	1,643	14.3	237	8.7
GA	7,687	1,985	20.5	293	11.3	OK.	2,977	659	18.1	117	12.6
HI.	1,149	102	8.2	11	3.5	OR.	3,156	678	17.7	103	11.9
ID.	1,294	232	15.2	43	10.2	PA	11,004	1,409	11.4	193	6.8
IL	10,875	1,891	14.8	291	9.1	RI.	906	127	12.3	14	6.0
IN.	5,462	902	14.2	141	8.6	SC	3,740	766	17.0	136	12.3
IA.	2,654	342	11.4	42	5.9	SD	693	108	13.5	17	8.4
KS	2,380	365	13.3	58	8.1	TN	5,290	963	15.4	98	6.6
KY	3,588	694	16.2	84	8.2	TX	18,224	6,433	26.1	1,150	16.5
LA	3,741	711	16.0	97	8.4	UT	2,385	415	14.8	99	11.3
ME.	1,167	133	10.2	11	4.0	VT	557	61	9.9	7	5.6
MD.	4,874	793	14.0	94	7.0	VA	6,764	1,014	13.0	144	7.5
MA.	6,337	295	4.4	43	2.9	WA.	5,845	869	12.9	75	4.8
MI.	8,465	1,350	13.8	132	5.6	WV.	1,552	253	14.0	24	6.2
MN.	4,747	456	8.8	68	5.5	WI	5,037	527	9.5	61	4.7
MS.	2,349	502	17.6	85	10.9	WY.	455	86	15.8	13	9.6

Source: U.S. Census Bureau, Income, Poverty, and Health Insurance Coverage in the United States: 2009, Current Population Reports, P60-236, 2010, Table HI05, "Health Insurance Coverage Status and Type of Coverage by State for All People: 2009." See also <http://www.census.gov/hhes/www/cpstables/032010/health/toc.htm>.

Health and Nutrition 111

Table 157. People Without Health Insurance for the Entire Year by Selected Characteristics: 2008 and 2009

[In thousands, except as noted (301,483 represents 301,483,000). Based on the Current Population Survey; Annual Social and Economic Supplement (ASEC); see text, Section 1 and Appendix III]

Characteristic	2008			2009		
	Total persons	Uninsured Persons		Total persons	Uninsured Persons	
		Number	Percent distribution		Number	Percent distribution
Total [1]	301,483	46,340	100.0	304,280	50,674	100.0
Under 18 years	74,510	7,348	15.9	75,040	7,513	14.8
18 to 24 years	28,688	8,200	17.7	29,313	8,923	17.6
25 to 34 years	40,520	10,754	23.2	41,085	11,963	23.6
35 to 44 years	41,322	8,035	17.3	40,447	8,759	17.3
45 to 64 years	78,655	11,355	24.5	79,782	12,840	25.3
65 years and over	37,788	646	1.4	38,613	676	1.3
Male........................	148,094	25,208	54.4	149,485	27,463	54.2
Female......................	153,388	21,131	45.6	154,795	23,211	45.8
White alone [2]	240,852	34,890	75.3	242,403	38,399	75.8
White alone or in combination	245,920	35,680	77.0	247,660	39,118	77.2
Black alone [2]	38,076	7,284	15.7	38,624	8,102	16.0
Black alone or in combination	40,216	7,602	16.4	40,957	8,414	16.6
Asian alone [2]	13,315	2,344	5.1	14,011	2,409	4.8
Asian alone or in combination	14,548	2,484	5.4	15,281	2,503	4.9
Hispanic [3]...................	47,485	14,558	31.4	48,901	15,820	31.2
White alone, not Hispanic	197,159	21,322	46.0	197,436	23,658	46.7

[1] Includes other races, not shown separately. [2] Refers to people who reported specified race and did not report any other race category. [3] Persons of Hispanic origin may be any race.

Source: U.S. Census Bureau, *Income, Poverty, and Health Insurance Coverage in the United States: 2009*, Current Population Reports, P60-238, 2010, and "Health Insurance Coverage Status and Type of Coverage by Selected Characteristics: 2009." See also <http://www.census.gov/prod/www/abs/p60.html> and <http://www.census.gov/hhes/www/cpstables/032010/health/toc.htm>.

Table 158. Percentage of Workers Participating in Health Care Benefit Programs and Percentage of Participants Required to Contribute: 2010

[Based on National Compensation Survey, a sample survey of 8,782 private industry establishments of all sizes, representing about 108 million workers; see Appendix III. See also Table 656. For more information, see <www.bls.gov/ncs/ebs/benefits/2010/benefits.htm>]

Characteristic	Percent of workers participating—				Single coverage medical plans		Family coverage medical plans	
	Medical care	Dental care	Vision care	Out-patient prescription drug coverage	Employee contributions required (percent)	Average monthly contribution [1] (dol.)	Employee contributions required (percent)	Average monthly contribution [1] (dol.)
Total........................	51	36	20	50	80	99.07	89	383.12
Worker characteristics:								
Management, professional, and related ...	66	50	28	65	82	97.05	91	377.11
Management, business, and financial	74	56	30	73	83	98.89	91	376.96
Professional and related	63	47	26	61	82	96.06	91	377.19
Service	27	19	11	27	83	100.12	91	420.31
Sales and office....................	50	35	18	49	84	101.75	92	397.12
Sales and related..................	41	28	15	40	85	110.63	93	417.51
Office and administrative support	56	39	20	55	83	97.37	92	387.14
Natural resources, construction, and maintenance	60	37	25	58	66	104.28	79	405.30
Production, transportation, and material moving.....................	59	39	24	57	77	95.33	84	336.64
Production	65	42	24	63	79	93.10	86	316.67
Transportation, and material moving ...	52	35	23	51	75	98.32	82	363.28
Full-time [2].......................	64	44	25	62	80	98.11	89	379.65
Part-time [2].......................	14	10	6	13	78	112.75	86	434.40
Union [3].........................	77	63	47	75	55	89.05	63	316.92
Nonunion.........................	48	33	17	47	85	100.22	93	390.83
Average hourly wage: [4]								
Less than $8.10....................	12	7	5	12	86	101.39	93	399.35
$8.10 to under $10.63	22	13	8	21	84	102.46	93	425.40
$10.63 to under $15.70	52	35	18	51	83	100.62	92	396.72
$15.70 to under $24.53	66	44	25	65	79	97.43	89	375.88
$24.53 to under $37.02	72	56	33	70	77	97.91	85	361.75
$37.02 or greater...................	72	59	34	71	80	96.12	87	350.16

[1] The average is presented for all covered workers and excludes workers without the plan provision. Averages are for plans stating a flat monthly cost. [2] Employees are classified as working either a full-time or part-time schedule based on the definition used by each establishment. [3] Union workers are those whose wages are determined through collective bargaining. [4] The National Compensation Survey—Benefits program presents wage data in percentiles rather than dollar amounts; see "Technical Note" in source.

Source: U.S. Bureau of Labor Statistics, *National Compensation Survey: Employee Benefits in Private Industry in the United States–March 2010*, September 2010. See also <http://www.bls.gov/ncs/ebs/publications.htm>.

Table 159. Retail Prescription Drug Sales: 1995 to 2010

[2,125 represents 2,125,000,000]

Sales outlet	Unit	1995	2000	2004	2005	2006	2007	2008	2009	2010
Number of prescriptions	Mil.........	2,125	2,865	3,274	3,279	3,419	3,530	3,559	3,633	3,676
Traditional chain............	Mil.........	908	1,335	1,494	1,513	1,599	1,652	1,677	1,731	1,760
Independent................	Mil.........	672	698	744	719	738	753	739	730	729
Mass merchant	Mil.........	238	293	353	359	375	390	400	423	433
Supermarkets	Mil.........	221	394	470	465	476	478	481	488	490
Mail order.................	Mil.........	86	146	214	223	232	257	262	261	264
Percent distribution of brand/generic mix:										
Brand drugs................	Percent	59.8	57.6	54.1	50.6	44.8	40.8	35.5	32.6	28.8
Generic drugs	Percent	40.2	42.4	45.9	49.4	55.2	59.2	64.5	67.4	71.2
Retail sales	Bil. dol......	72.2	145.6	216.7	226.1	243.2	249.2	249.2	261.3	266.4
Traditional chain............	Bil. dol......	27.8	59.1	86.7	90.7	96.0	100.5	101.2	105.3	106.6
Independent................	Bil. dol......	22.0	33.4	44.2	45.4	46.7	45.3	43.3	43.6	44.7
Mass merchant	Bil. dol......	7.7	13.5	16.8	17.5	21.6	23.6	24.2	25.6	26.6
Supermarkets	Bil. dol......	7.4	17.4	26.4	26.9	28.1	27.3	25.2	25.9	25.9
Mail order.................	Bil. dol......	7.4	22.1	42.7	45.5	50.9	52.5	55.4	61.3	62.6
Average prices [1]										
All prescriptions............	Dollars	30.01	45.79	62.64	63.87	66.97	68.77	71.69	75.66	79.39
Brand drugs................	Dollars	40.22	65.29	91.80	97.65	112.24	121.26	137.98	151.06	166.61
Generic drugs	Dollars	14.84	19.33	28.23	29.21	30.17	32.60	35.21	39.25	44.14

[1] Excludes mail order.

Source: National Association of Chain Drug Stores, Alexandria, VA, *NACDS Foundation Chain Pharmacy Industry Profile, 2010,* (copyright). See also <http://www.nacds.org>.

Table 160. Annual Revenue for Health Care Industries: 2007 to 2009

[In millions of dollars (1,668,276 represents $1,668,276,000,000). For taxable and tax-exempt employer firms. Estimates have been adjusted to the results of the 2007 Economic Census. Based on the Service Annual Survey and administrative data; see Appendix III. All firms in NAICS 6211, 6212, 6213, and 6215 are defined as taxable]

Kind of business	2002 NAICS code [1]	Total, all firms [2]			Taxable employer firms		
		2007	2008	2009	2007	2008	2009
Health care and social assistance........	62	**1,668,276**	**1,756,177**	**1,835,384**	**818,395**	**871,130**	**904,683**
Ambulatory health care services [3]............	621	668,452	706,368	729,255	604,742	639,808	659,034
Offices of physicians	6211	336,282	352,700	359,853	336,282	352,700	359,853
Offices of dentists	6212	93,930	98,707	99,087	93,930	98,707	99,087
Offices of other health practitioners............	6213	50,318	54,169	56,853	50,318	54,169	56,853
Offices of chiropractors	62131	9,980	10,143	10,356	9,980	10,143	10,356
Offices of optometrists....................	62132	10,316	11,072	11,361	10,316	11,072	11,361
Offices of mental health practitioners	62133	5,132	5,560	6,203	5,132	5,560	6,203
Offices of PT/OT/speech therapy & audiology [4]....	62134	17,785	19,831	21,084	17,785	19,831	21,084
Outpatient care centers	6214	74,092	79,290	84,513	35,834	39,871	42,579
Medical & diagnostic laboratories	6215	40,077	42,638	44,939	40,077	42,638	44,939
Home health care services	6216	47,617	50,860	55,243	32,614	34,862	38,386
Other ambulatory health care services	6219	26,136	28,004	28,767	15,687	16,861	17,337
Hospitals [3]...............................	622	702,960	736,888	781,471	80,831	88,487	96,911
General medical & surgical hospitals	6221	657,319	688,313	729,870	67,124	72,656	79,294
Psychiatric & substance abuse hospitals	6222	17,189	18,131	18,761	3,468	3,987	4,330
Other specialty hospitals	6223	28,452	30,444	32,840	10,239	11,844	13,287
Nursing and residential care facilities [3]...........	623	169,061	177,565	183,968	101,404	108,596	112,635
Nursing care facilities	6231	92,517	97,513	100,821	70,139	74,882	77,422
Residential mental retardation/health facilities	6232	26,967	29,002	30,557	7,947	8,887	9,569
Residential mental retardation facilities..........	62321	18,275	19,755	21,047	5,189	5,623	6,125
Community care facilities for the elderly	6233	41,238	42,618	44,504	22,065	23,445	24,269
Continuing care retirement communities.........	623311	26,030	26,891	28,410	10,247	11,043	11,514
Homes for the elderly	623312	15,208	15,727	16,094	11,818	12,402	12,755
Other residential care facilities	6239	8,339	8,432	8,086	1,253	1,382	1,375
Social assistance [3].........................	624	127,803	135,356	140,690	31,418	34,239	36,103
Individual and family services	6241	63,063	66,252	68,978	11,603	12,842	14,065
Community food and housing, and emergency relief services	6242	23,519	25,822	26,713	382	500	477
Vocational rehabilitation services................	6243	11,536	12,029	12,649	1,700	1,843	1,911
Child day care services	6244	29,685	31,253	32,350	17,733	19,054	19,650

[1] North American Industry Classification System (NAICS), 2002; see text, Section 15. [2] Excludes taxable nonemployer firms. [3] Includes other kinds of business, not shown separately. [4] Offices of physical, occupational, and speech therapists, and audiologists.

Source: U.S. Census Bureau, "Service Annual Survey 2009: Health Care and Social Assistance Sector Services," January 2011, <http://www.census.gov/services/index.html>.

Table 161. Revenue for Selected Health Care Industries by Source of Revenue: 2008 and 2009

[In millions of dollars (352,700 represents $352,700,000,000). For taxable and tax-exempt employer firms. Estimates have been adjusted to the results of the 2007 Economic Census. Based on Service Annual Survey and administrative data; see Appendix III]

Source of revenue	Offices of physicians (NAICS 6211)[1]		Offices of dentists (NAICS 6212)[1]		Hospitals (NAICS 622)[1]		Nursing and residential care facilities (NAICS 623)[1]	
	2008	2009	2008	2009	2008	2009	2008	2009
Total..................	352,700	359,853	98,707	99,087	736,888	781,471	177,565	183,968
Medicare	70,576	73,155	815	936	186,622	195,737	29,891	31,379
Medicaid	18,416	18,128	3,974	4,376	72,212	77,067	64,251	66,301
Other government [2]	5,236	5,743	601	716	39,990	41,689	12,739	13,402
Worker's compensation.....	7,156	7,577	101	112	7,254	7,341	(S)	(S)
Private insurance..........	180,050	184,823	44,355	45,047	310,831	333,174	8,357	9,113
Patient (out-of-pocket) [3]	36,444	35,954	44,369	42,359	33,895	36,948	43,329	44,274
Other patient care sources, n.e.c [4]................	19,615	19,499	3,579	4,534	25,101	26,747	7,039	7,519
Nonpatient care revenue	15,207	14,974	913	1,007	60,983	62,768	11,570	11,574

S Figure does not meet publication standards. [1] North American Industry Classification System (NAICS), 2002; see text Section 15. [2] Veterans, National Institute of Health, Indian Affairs, etc. [3] Represents payment from patients and their families plus patients' assigned social security benefits. [4] n.e.c. represents not elsewhere classified.

Source: U.S. Census Bureau, "Service Annual Survey 2009: Health Care and Social Assistance Sector Services," January 2011, <http://www.census.gov/services/index.html>.

Table 162. Employment in the Health Service Industries: 1990 to 2010

[In thousands (9,296 represents 9,296,000). See headnote, Table 632. Based on the 2007 North American Industry Classification System (NAICS); see text, Section 15. For more information on the NAICS changes, please see <http://stats.bls.gov/ces /cesnaics07.htm>]

Industry	2007 NAICS code	1990	2000	2005	2006	2007	2008	2009	2010
Health care and social assistance [1]...	62	9,296	12,718	14,536	14,925	15,380	15,798	16,103	16,415
Ambulatory health care services [1]........	621	2,842	4,320	5,114	5,286	5,474	5,647	5,793	5,976
Offices of physicians	6211	1,278	1,840	2,094	2,148	2,202	2,253	2,279	2,316
Offices of dentists	6212	513	688	774	786	808	818	818	829
Offices of other health practitioners......	6213	276	438	549	573	600	627	647	673
Medical and diagnostic laboratories	6215	129	162	198	204	211	217	219	226
Home health care services	6216	288	633	821	866	914	961	1,027	1,081
Hospitals [1]........................	622	3,513	3,954	4,345	4,423	4,515	4,627	4,667	4,685
General medical and surgical hospitals...	6221	3,305	3,745	4,096	4,163	4,242	4,337	4,367	4,375
Psychiatric and substance abuse hospitals	6222	113	86	93	98	99	102	104	106
Other hospitals	6223	95	123	156	163	174	188	196	205
Nursing and residential care facilities [1]	623	1,856	2,583	2,855	2,893	2,958	3,016	3,082	3,129
Nursing care facilities	6231	1,170	1,514	1,577	1,581	1,603	1,619	1,645	1,661

[1] Includes other industries, not shown separately.

Source: U.S. Bureau of Labor Statistics, Current Employment Statistics, "Employment, Hours, and Earnings—National," <http://www.bls.gov/ces/data.htm>, accessed May 2011.

Table 163. Osteopathic Physicians: 2001 to 2010

[As of May 31. Osteopathic physicians are fully qualified physicians licensed to practice medicine and to perform surgery. Osteopathic medicine has a strong emphasis on the interrelationship of the body's nerves, muscles, bones and organs. Doctors of osteopathic medicine, or D.O.s, apply the philosophy of treating the whole person to the prevention, diagnosis and treatment of illness, disease, and injury]

Characteristics	2001	2005	2010	Characteristics	2001	2005	2010
Total number of DOs	46,990	56,512	70,480	Unknown.........................	28	318	412
Female................	10,875	15,147	22,537	Self-identified practice specialty [1]	31,996	38,442	50,355
Male.................	36,115	41,365	47,942	Family and general practice..............	14,102	17,800	19,720
				General internal Medicine	2,592	3,107	5,641
Age:				General pediatrics/adolescent medicine ...	958	1,176	2,211
Less than 35 years old ...	9,866	12,983	16,277	Obstetrics and gynecology	1,219	1,465	2,165
35 to 44 years old	14,798	16,179	20,118	Pediatric specialties...................	320	348	380
45 to 54 years old	12,754	13,845	15,950	Osteopathic specialties [2]	414	464	902
55 to 64 years old	4,706	7,998	11,195	Other specialties	12,001	13,431	18,984
65 years old and over	4,838	5,189	6,528	Unknown	390	651	352

[1] DOs are assumed to be in active practice if they are under age 65 and have not informed the AOA that they have retired or are inactive. DOs are assumed to be in postdoctoral training (internship, residency or fellowship) if they graduated within the last 3 years or if the AOA has received information that they are in a postdoctoral program. [2] Osteopathic self-identified practice specialties include FOM (Family Practice/OMT), FPO (Family Practice/OMM), NMO (Neuromusculoskeletal Med/OMM), NMS (Neuromusculoskeletal Med/OMT), OM1 (Osteopathic Manipulative Med +1), OMM (Spec Prof in Osteo Manip Med), OMS (Sports Medicine-OMM), and OMT (Osteo Manipulative Medicine). OMT is the therapeutic application of manually guided forces by an osteopathic physician to improve physiologic function and/or support homeostasis that has been altered by somatic dysfunction. OMM is the application of osteopathic philosophy, structural diagnosis, and use of OMT in the patient's diagnosis and management.

Source: American Osteopathic Association, Chicago, IL, *AOA Annual Statistics*, annual. See also <http://www.osteopathic.org>.

Table 164. Physicians by Sex and Specialty: 1980 to 2009

[In thousands (467.7 represents 467,700). As of Dec. 31, except 1990 as of Jan. 1, and as noted. Includes Puerto Rico and Island Areas]

Activity	1980 Total	1980 Office-based	1990 Total	1990 Office-based	2000 Total	2000 Office-based	2009 Total	2009 Office-based
Doctors of medicine, total [1]	**467.7**	**272.0**	**615.4**	**361.0**	**813.8**	**490.4**	**972.4**	**560.4**
Place of medical education:								
U.S. medical graduates	370.0	226.2	483.7	286.2	616.8	376.5	720.3	421.8
International medical graduates [2]	97.7	45.8	131.8	74.8	197.0	113.9	252.1	138.6
Sex:								
Male.	413.4	251.4	511.2	311.7	618.2	382.3	684.7	399.1
Female.	54.3	20.6	104.2	49.2	195.5	108.1	287.7	161.2
Allergy/immunology	1.5	1.4	3.4	2.5	4.0	3.1	4.3	3.4
Anesthesiology	16.0	11.3	26.0	17.8	35.7	27.6	42.7	31.3
Cardiovascular diseases	9.8	6.7	15.9	10.7	21.0	16.3	22.8	17.4
Child psychiatry	3.3	2.0	4.3	2.6	6.2	4.3	7.4	5.3
Dermatology	5.7	4.4	7.6	6.0	9.7	8.0	11.2	9.2
Diagnostic radiology	7.0	4.2	15.4	9.8	21.1	14.6	25.6	17.1
Emergency medicine	5.7	3.4	14.2	8.4	23.1	14.5	32.4	20.0
Family practice.	27.5	18.4	47.6	37.5	71.6	54.2	86.8	68.8
Gastroenterology	4.0	2.7	7.5	5.2	10.6	8.5	13.0	10.3
General practice	32.5	29.6	22.8	20.5	15.2	13.0	9.2	7.7
General surgery	34.0	22.4	38.4	24.5	36.7	24.5	38.0	24.7
Internal medicine	71.5	40.6	98.3	58.0	134.5	89.7	162.4	109.3
Neurological surgery	3.3	2.5	4.4	3.1	5.0	3.7	5.6	4.0
Neurology	5.7	3.3	9.2	5.6	12.3	8.6	15.5	10.4
Obstetrics and gynecology	26.3	19.5	33.7	25.5	40.2	31.7	42.9	34.1
Ophthalmology	13.0	10.6	16.1	13.1	18.1	15.6	18.3	15.7
Orthopedic surgery	14.0	10.7	19.1	14.2	22.3	17.4	25.0	19.2
Otolaryngology	6.6	5.3	8.1	6.4	9.4	7.6	10.3	8.0
Pathology.	13.6	6.1	16.6	7.5	18.8	10.6	19.8	10.9
Pediatrics.	29.5	18.2	41.9	27.1	63.9	43.2	78.1	53.6
Physical med./rehab	2.1	1.0	4.1	2.2	6.5	4.3	8.8	6.3
Plastic surgery.	3.0	2.4	4.6	3.8	6.2	5.3	7.3	6.1
Psychiatry	27.5	16.0	35.2	20.1	39.5	25.0	40.6	26.2
Pulmonary diseases	3.7	2.0	6.1	3.7	8.7	5.9	10.9	7.7
Radiology.	11.7	7.8	8.5	6.1	8.7	6.7	9.2	6.8
Urological surgery	7.7	6.2	9.4	7.4	10.3	8.5	10.5	8.7
Unspecified	12.3	5.0	8.1	1.6	8.3	3.8	9.6	3.6
Not classified	20.6	(X)	12.7	(X)	45.1	(X)	57.4	(X)
Other categories [3]	32.1	(X)	55.4	(X)	75.2	(X)	122.1	(X)

X Not applicable. [1] Includes other categories not shown. [2] International medical graduates received their medical education in schools outside the United States and Canada. [3] Includes inactive and address unknown.

Source: Except as noted, American Medical Association, *Physician Characteristics and Distribution in the U.S.*, Chicago, IL, annual (copyright).

Table 165. Active Physicians and Nurses by State: 2009

[As of December 31. Excludes doctors of osteopathy, physicians with addresses unknown, and inactive status. Includes all physicians not classified according to activity status. As of May. Nurses data comes from the Bureau of Labor Statistics]

State	Physicians Total	Physicians Rate [1]	Nurses Total	Nurses Rate [1]	State	Physicians Total	Physicians Rate [1]	Nurses Total	Nurses Rate [1]
United States	**838,453**	**273**	**2,583,770**	**842**	Missouri.	14,789	247	62,130	1,038
Alabama	10,265	218	42,880	911	Montana.	2,138	219	8,340	855
Alaska	1,574	225	5,010	717	Nebraska.	4,511	251	18,930	1,054
Arizona	14,051	213	38,570	585	Nevada	4,967	188	16,100	609
Arkansas	5,902	204	23,050	798	New Hampshire. . .	3,828	289	13,330	1,006
California	100,131	271	233,030	630	New Jersey	27,433	315	74,730	858
Colorado	13,047	260	41,750	831	New Mexico	4,877	243	12,340	614
Connecticut	13,370	380	35,790	1,017	New York	77,042	394	165,730	848
Delaware	2,177	246	10,220	1,155	North Carolina	24,072	257	88,190	940
District of Columbia . . .	4,900	817	8,890	1,483	North Dakota	1,617	250	6,260	968
Florida	46,645	252	150,940	814	Ohio.	31,315	271	117,870	1,021
Georgia	21,269	216	65,370	665	Oklahoma	6,467	175	27,340	742
Hawaii	4,800	371	8,930	689	Oregon.	10,753	281	30,730	803
Idaho	2,649	171	10,540	682	Pennsylvania	38,676	307	129,810	1,030
Illinois.	36,528	283	116,340	901	Rhode Island	4,020	382	11,630	1,104
Indiana	13,938	217	57,880	901	South Carolina. . . .	10,403	228	38,020	834
Iowa	5,696	189	30,750	1,022	South Dakota.	1,818	224	10,530	1,296
Kansas.	6,436	228	26,320	934	Tennessee	16,754	266	61,980	984
Kentucky	10,076	234	43,250	1,003	Texas	53,546	216	168,020	678
Louisiana	11,974	267	39,560	881	Utah.	5,903	212	17,670	635
Maine.	3,663	278	14,410	1,093	Vermont.	2,313	372	5,680	914
Maryland	24,118	423	51,620	906	Virginia.	21,931	278	60,230	764
Massachusetts.	31,252	474	83,060	1,260	Washington	18,090	271	54,260	814
Michigan	25,697	258	84,620	849	West Virginia	4,295	236	17,340	953
Minnesota	15,620	297	57,560	1,093	Wisconsin	14,816	262	53,510	946
Mississippi	5,281	179	28,030	950	Wyoming	1,020	187	4,700	864

[1] Per 100,000 resident population. Based on U.S. Census Bureau estimates as of July 1.

Source: Physicians: American Medical Association, *Physician Characteristics and Distribution in the U.S.*, Chicago, IL, annual (copyright); Nurses: Bureau of Labor Statistics, Occupational Employment Statistics, Occupational Employment and Wages, "May 2009 Wage and Employment Statistics," <http://www.bls.gov/oes/home.htm#data>.

Health and Nutrition 115

Table 166. Percent Distribution of Number of Visits to Health Care Professionals by Selected Characteristics: 2000 and 2009

[Covers ambulatory visits to doctor's offices and emergency departments, and home health care visits during a 12-month period. Based on the redesigned National Health Interview Survey, a sample survey of the civilian noninstitutionalized population]

Characteristic	None		1–3 visits		4–9 visits		10 or more visits	
	2000	2009	2000	2009	2000	2009	2000	2009
All persons [1,2]	**16.7**	**15.4**	**45.4**	**46.7**	**24.6**	**24.7**	**13.3**	**13.2**
SEX [2]								
Male	21.7	20.3	45.9	47.1	22.3	22.0	10.1	10.6
Female	11.9	10.5	44.8	46.4	27.0	27.4	16.3	15.7
AGE								
Under 18 years old	12.3	9.1	53.8	56.9	26.2	27.4	7.6	6.5
18 to 44 years old	23.5	22.7	45.2	45.7	19.1	19.3	12.2	12.3
45 to 64 years old	15.0	15.4	43.4	43.6	25.7	24.9	15.9	16.1
65 to 74 years old	9.0	5.6	34.5	37.6	34.5	34.6	22.1	22.2
75 years old and over	5.8	3.7	29.3	31.1	39.3	38.0	25.6	27.2
RACE [2,3]								
Race alone:								
White	16.1	15.1	45.1	46.5	25.2	25.0	13.6	13.5
Black or African American	17.2	14.6	46.7	46.8	23.4	24.8	12.6	13.8
American Indian or Alaska Native	21.3	21.7	43.0	50.1	20.0	18.4	15.7	9.9
Asian	20.3	20.8	49.2	50.6	20.8	20.7	9.7	8.0
Two or more races	12.1	16.2	41.7	41.4	28.2	28.9	18.0	13.4
HISPANIC ORIGIN AND RACE [2,3,4]								
Hispanic or Latino	26.8	23.8	41.8	44.3	19.8	21.2	11.6	10.8
Mexican	31.0	25.9	40.8	44.5	17.8	20.1	10.3	9.5
Not Hispanic or Latino	15.2	13.7	45.9	47.2	25.3	25.5	13.6	13.7
White, non-Hispanic	14.5	12.9	45.4	47.0	25.9	25.9	14.1	14.2
Black, non-Hispanic	17.1	14.4	46.8	46.6	23.5	25.2	12.6	13.8

[1] Includes other categories not shown separately. [2] Estimates are age adjusted to the year 2000 standard using six age groups: Under 18 years, 18–44 years, 45–54 years, 55–64 years, 65–74 years, and 75 years and over. [3] Estimates by race and Hispanic origin are tabulated using the 1997 standards for federal data on race and ethnicity. Estimates for specific race groups are shown when they meet requirements for statistical reliability and confidentiality. The categories "White only," "Black or African American only," "American Indian and Alaska Native (AI/AN) only," and "Asian only" include persons who reported only one racial group; and the category "2 or more races" includes persons who reported more than one of the five racial groups in the 1997 standards or one of the five racial groups and "Some other race." [4] Persons of Hispanic or Latino origin may be any race.

Source: U.S. National Center for Health Statistics, *Health, United States, 2010.* See also <www.cdc.gov/nchs/hus.htm>.

Table 167. Adults 18 Years and Over Who Used Complementary and Alternative Medicine (CAM) in the Past 12 Months by Type of Therapy: 2002 and 2007

[The denominators for statistics shown exclude persons with unknown CAM information. Estimates were age adjusted to the year 2000 U.S. standard population using four age groups: 18 to 24 years, 25 to 44 years, 45 to 64 years, and 65 years and over]

Therapy	2002		2007	
	Number (1,000)	Percent	Number (1,000)	Percent
Alternative medical systems:				
Acupuncture	2,136	1.1	3,141	1.4
Homeopathic treatment	3,433	1.7	3,909	1.8
Biologically based therapies:				
Nonvitamin, nonmineral, natural products [1]	38,183	18.9	38,797	17.7
Diet-based therapies [2,3]	7,099	3.5	7,893	3.6
Vegetarian diet	3,184	1.6	3,351	1.5
Atkins diet	3,417	1.7	2,673	1.2
South Beach	(X)	(X)	2,334	1.1
Megavitamin therapy	5,739	2.8	(X)	(X)
Manipulative and body-based therapies:				
Chiropractic care [4]	15,226	7.5	(X)	(X)
Chiropractic or osteopathic manipulation [4]	(X)	(X)	18,740	8.6
Massage	10,052	5.0	18,068	8.3
Movement therapies	(X)	(X)	3,146	1.5
Pilates	(X)	(X)	3,015	1.4
Mind-body therapies:				
Meditation	15,336	7.6	20,541	9.4
Guided imagery	4,194	2.1	4,866	2.2
Progressive relaxation	6,185	3.0	6,454	2.9
Deep breathing exercises	23,457	11.6	27,794	12.7
Yoga	10,386	5.1	13,172	6.1
Tai chi	2,565	1.3	2,267	1.0
Energy healing therapy/Reiki	1,080	0.5	1,216	0.5

X Not applicable. [1] While questions were asked about nonvitamin, nonmineral, natural products in both 2002 and 2007, the data are not comparable due primarily to question order and the specific nonvitamin, nonmineral, natural product covered. [2] The totals of the numbers and percents of the categories listed under "Diet-based therapies" are greater than the number and percent of their respective category heading because respondents could choose more than one of the categories. [3] While questions were asked about Diet-based therapies in both 2002 and 2007, the data are not comparable because respondents were asked about the South Beach Diet in 2007, but not in 2002. [4] While questions were asked about chiropractic therapy in both 2002 and 2007, the data are not comparable because respondents were asked about chiropractic care in 2002 and chiropractic or osteopathic manipulation in 2007.

Source: U.S. National Center for Health Statistics, *Complementary and Alternative Medicine Use Among Adults and Children: United States, 2007*, National Health Statistics Reports, Number 12, 2008. See also <http://www.cdc.gov/nchs/data/nhsr/nhsr012.pdf>.

Table 168. Ambulatory Care Visits to Physicians' Offices and Hospital Outpatient and Emergency Departments: 2008

[1,189.6 represents 1,189,600,000. Based on the annual National Ambulatory Medical Care Survey and National Hospital Ambulatory Medical Care Survey and subject to sampling error; see source for details]

Characteristic	Number of visits (mil.)				Visits per 100 persons			
	Total	Physician offices	Out-patient dept.	Emer-gency dept.	Total	Physician offices	Out-patient dept.	Emer-gency dept.
Total..........................	1,189.6	956.0	109.9	123.8	398.3	320.1	36.8	41.4
Age:								
Under 15 years old	192.7	147.2	22.3	23.2	315.5	241.0	36.6	37.9
15 to 24 years old	105.3	73.9	11.6	19.8	253.3	177.8	27.8	47.7
25 to 44 years old	256.0	194.6	26.2	35.2	314.8	239.4	32.2	43.3
45 to 64 years old	341.6	284.1	31.1	26.3	440.7	366.5	40.2	34.0
65 to 74 years old	144.9	127.1	10.3	7.5	728.8	639.5	51.7	37.6
75 years old and over	149.2	129.0	8.4	11.8	859.7	743.5	48.3	67.9
Sex:								
Male...........................	482.5	383.3	42.5	56.7	329.9	262.1	29.1	38.8
Female.........................	707.1	572.7	67.4	67.0	463.9	375.7	44.2	44.0
Race: [1]								
White	970.9	802.4	79.2	89.4	406.5	335.9	33.1	37.4
Black/African American	158.4	104.0	25.4	29.0	420.9	276.4	67.5	77.0
Asian	43.9	38.4	2.9	2.6	325.7	285.1	21.6	19.0
Native Hawaiian/Other Pacific Islander ...	[2] 5.6	[2] 4.5	0.3	[2] 0.8	[2]1,019.4	[2] 820.7	[2] 60.3	[2] 138.4
American Indian/Alaska Native	4.4	3.0	[2] 0.4	[2] 1.1	145.1	98.9	[2] 13.3	[2] 32.9
More than one race reported	6.4	3.6	[2] 1.7	[2] 1.1	124.3	71.1	[2] 32.5	[2] 20.6
Expected sources of payment: [3]								
Private insurance	729.3	631.6	45.8	51.9	(X)	(X)	(X)	(X)
Medicare	275.1	231.4	20.9	22.8	(X)	(X)	(X)	(X)
Medicaid/SCHIP [4]	175.9	111.6	34.6	29.7	(X)	(X)	(X)	(X)
Worker's compensation	13.1	10.5	1.0	1.6	(X)	(X)	(X)	(X)
No insurance: [5]	71.3	43.5	8.7	19.1	(X)	(X)	(X)	(X)
Self pay	64.0	40.1	6.1	17.9	(X)	(X)	(X)	(X)
No charge	7.7	3.6	[2] 2.7	1.5	(X)	(X)	(X)	(X)
Other	39.7	27.5	6.5	5.7	(X)	(X)	(X)	(X)
Unknown	39.1	28.7	2.9	7.5	(X)	(X)	(X)	(X)

X Not applicable. [1] Race data were missing for 30.2 percent of ambulatory care visits, including 33.0 percent of visits to physician offices, 21.1 percent of visits to hospital outpatient departments, and 16.0 percent of visits to emergency departments. Missing data were imputed, and readers are advised to treat the resulting estimates with caution. More information is available at the Web site below. [2] Figure does not meet standards of reliability or precision. [3] Estimates include all expected sources of payment reported at the visit. [4] SCHIP is State Children's Health Insurance Program. [5] "No insurance" is defined as having only "self-pay" or "no charge/charity" as payment sources.

Source: U.S. National Center for Health Statistics, *National Health Statistics Reports*, <http://www.cdc.gov/nchs/ahcd.htm>.

Table 169. Visits to Office-Based Physicians and Hospital Outpatient Departments by Diagnosis: 2003 and 2008

[405.5 represents 405,500,000. Based on the International Classification of Diseases, 9th Revision, Clinical Modification, (ICD-9-CM). See headnote, Table 168]

Leading diagnosis	Number (mil.)		Rate per 1,000 persons [1]		Leading diagnosis	Number (mil.)		Rate per 1,000 persons [1]	
	2003	2008	2003	2008		2003	2008	2003	2008
Male, all ages	**405.5**	**425.8**	**2,908**	**2,911**	**Female, all ages ....**	**595.1**	**640.1**	**4,074**	**4,199**
Under 15 years old [2]	**89.1**	**89.6**	**2,870**	**2,869**	**Under 15 years old [2] ....**	**78.0**	**79.9**	**2,630**	**2,679**
Routine infant or child health check	16.8	23.1	541	740	Routine infant or child health check	14.0	21.9	472	733
Acute upper respiratory infections [3]	7.8	8.1	250	259	Acute upper respiratory infections [3]	7.8	7.1	262	239
Otitis media and Eustachian tube disorders	8.4	7.4	269	236	Otitis media and Eustachian tube disorders	6.4	6.2	217	209
Acute pharyngitis.............	2.1	3.4	66	107	Acute pharyngitis.............	3.3	3.1	110	105
15 to 44 years old [2]	**104.0**	**93.4**	**1,710**	**1,524**	**15 to 44 years old [2] ....**	**208.3**	**212.8**	**3,386**	**3,458**
General medical examination ..	4.4	4.8	72	78	Normal pregnancy.............	25.6	24.7	415	401
Acute upper respiratory infections [3]	4.0	3.2	65	53	Gynecological examination	9.8	10.1	160	165
Spinal disorders.............	3.4	3.2	56	52	Complications of pregnancy, childbirth, and the puerperium..	7.4	7.7	121	124
Essential hypertension	2.1	2.8	35	46					
45 to 64 years old [2]	**112.6**	**127.2**	**3,404**	**3,376**	**45 to 64 years old [2] ....**	**167.9**	**188.1**	**4,781**	**4,720**
Essential hypertension	7.6	8.6	231	227	Essential hypertension	8.2	12.0	234	302
Diabetes mellitus.............	5.2	6.4	156	171	Arthropathies and related disorders	8.1	7.9	231	198
Spinal disorders.............	4.7	5.4	143	144	Rheumatism, excluding back....	6.0	6.4	170	161
Arthropathies and related disorders	4.5	4.1	135	110					
65 years old and over [2]	**99.8**	**115.5**	**6,881**	**7,211**	**65 years old and over [2] ....**	**140.9**	**159.3**	**7,123**	**7,509**
Essential hypertension	7.2	8.8	496	546	Essential hypertension	11.1	15.4	563	728
Heart disease [4]	3.7	6.7	256	416	Arthropathies and related disorders	8.1	7.7	408	364
Malignant neoplasms..........	6.3	6.3	434	392	Heart disease [4]	4.3	6.9	218	328
Ischemic heart disease	3.6	6.0	250	376					

[1] Based on U.S. Census Bureau estimated civilian population as of July 1. [2] Includes other first-listed diagnoses, not shown separately. [3] Excluding pharyngitis. [4] Excluding ischemic.

Source: U.S. National Center for Health Statistics, *National Health Statistics Reports*, <http://www.cdc.gov/nchs/ahcd.htm>.

Health and Nutrition 117

Table 170. Visits to Hospital Emergency Departments by Diagnosis: 2008

[56,742 represents 56,742,000. See headnote, Tables 168 and 169]

Leading diagnosis	Number (1,000)	Rate per 1,000 persons [1]	Leading diagnosis	Number (1,000)	Rate per 1,000 persons [1]
MALE			**FEMALE**		
All ages............	56,742	388	All ages............	67,020	440
Under 15 years old [2]............	12,762	409	**Under 15 years old [2]**............	10,395	348
Acute upper respiratory infections [3].....	1,129	36	Acute respiratory infections [3]..........	916	31
Otitis media and eustachian tube disorders............	826	26	Otitis media and Eustachian tube disorders............	696	23
Open wound of head............	742	24	Pyrexia of unknown origin............	650	22
Pyrexia of unknown origin............	718	23	Contusion with intact skin surface......	363	12
Contusion with intact skin surface......	577	18	Acute pharyngitis............	308	10
15 to 44 years old [2]............	23,246	379	**15 to 44 years old [2]**............	31,763	516
Open wound, excluding head.........	1,264	21	Abdominal pain............	2,103	34
Contusion with intact skin surfaces.....	1,186	19	Complications of pregnancy, childbirth and the puerperium............	1,394	23
Cellulitis and abscess............	921	15	Contusion with intact skin surface.....	1,121	18
Chest pain............	869	14	Chest pain............	1,121	18
Sprains and strains, excluding ankle and back............	765	12	Spinal disorders............	1,048	17
45 to 64 years old [2]............	12,542	333	**45 to 64 years old [2]**............	13,793	346
Chest pain............	786	21	Chest pain............	850	21
Open wound, excluding head.........	565	15	Abdominal pain............	701	18
Spinal disorders............	512	14	Spinal disorders............	512	13
Abdominal pain............	452	12	Contusion with intact skin surface.....	433	11
Cellulitis and abscess............	373	10	Cellulitis and abscess............	389	10
65 years old and over [2]............	8,192	511	**65 years old and over [2]**............	11,069	522
Chest pain............	456	28	Chest pain............	628	30
Heart disease, excluding ischemic......	442	28	Contusion with intact skin surface......	541	25
Pneumonia............	356	22	Heart disease, excluding ischemic.....	537	25
Contusion with intact skin surface.....	254	16	Abdominal pain............	459	22
Chronic and unspecified bronchitis.....	241	15	Urinary tract infection site not specified..	316	15

[1] Based on U.S. Census Bureau estimated civilian noninstitutional population as of July 1. [2] Includes other first-listed diagnosis, not shown separately. [3] Excluding pharyngitis.

Source: U.S. National Center for Health Statistics, *National Health Statistics Reports*, <http://www.cdc.gov/nchs/ahcd.htm>.

Table 171. Procedures for Inpatients Discharged From Short-Stay Hospitals: 1990 to 2008

[23,051 represents 23,051,000. Procedure categories are based on the International Classification of Diseases, 9th Revision, Clinical Modification. See headnote, Table 176]

Sex and type of procedure	Number of procedures (1,000)				Rate per 1,000 population [1]			
	1990	1995	2000	2008	1990	1995	2000	2008
Surgical procedures, total [2]............	23,051	22,530	23,244	28,704	92.4	86.2	83.6	94.8
Cesarean section............	945	785	855	1,351	3.8	3.0	3.1	4.5
Repair of current obstetric laceration............	795	964	1,136	1,325	3.2	3.7	4.1	4.4
Cardiac catheterization............	995	1,068	1,221	1,108	4.0	4.1	4.4	3.7
Reduction of fracture [3]............	609	577	628	716	2.4	2.2	2.3	2.4
Male, total [2]............	8,538	8,388	8,689	11,317	70.6	65.9	63.9	76.0
Cardiac catheterization............	620	660	732	648	5.1	5.2	5.4	4.4
Coronary artery bypass graft [4]............	286	423	371	329	2.4	3.3	2.7	2.2
Reduction of fracture [3]............	300	251	285	362	2.5	2.0	2.1	2.4
Female, total [2]............	14,513	14,142	14,556	17,387	113.0	105.3	102.4	112.9
Cesarean section............	945	785	855	1,351	7.4	5.8	6.0	8.8
Repair of current obstetric laceration............	795	964	1,136	1,325	6.2	7.2	8.0	8.6
Hysterectomy............	591	583	633	584	4.6	4.3	4.5	3.8
Diagnostic and other nonsurgical procedures [5]....	17,455	17,278	16,737	18,634	70.0	66.1	60.2	61.5
Angiocardiography and arteriography [6]............	1,735	1,834	2,005	1,996	7.0	7.0	7.2	6.6
Respiratory therapy............	1,164	1,127	991	1,182	4.7	4.3	3.6	3.9
Manual assisted delivery............	750	866	898	1,308	3.0	3.3	3.2	4.3
Diagnostic ultrasound............	1,608	1,181	886	895	6.4	4.5	3.2	3.0
Fetal electrocardiogram (EKG) and fetal monitoring.....	1,377	935	750	1,024	5.6	3.6	2.7	3.4
Male, total [5]............	7,378	7,261	6,965	7,473	61.0	57.1	51.2	50.2
Angiocardiography and arteriography [6]............	1,051	1,076	1,157	1,094	8.7	8.5	8.5	7.3
Respiratory therapy............	586	572	507	610	4.9	4.5	3.7	4.1
Computerized Axial Tomographic scan [7]............	736	473	345	278	6.1	3.7	2.5	1.9
Female, total [5]............	10,077	10,016	9,772	11,161	78.5	74.6	68.8	72.5
Manual assisted delivery............	750	866	898	1,308	5.9	6.5	6.3	8.5
Fetal electrocardiogram (EKG) and fetal monitoring.....	1,377	935	750	1,024	10.8	7.0	5.5	6.7
Respiratory therapy............	578	555	484	572	4.5	4.1	3.4	3.7
Diagnostic ultrasound............	941	682	501	476	7.3	5.1	3.5	3.1

[1] Based on Census Bureau estimated civilian population as of July 1. Population estimates based on the 1990 census were used to calculate rates for 1990 through 2000. Population estimates based on the 2000 census were used to calculate rates for 2001 through 2008. [2] Includes other types of surgical procedures, not shown separately. [3] Excluding skull, nose, and jaw. [4] It is possible for a discharge to have more than one of these recorded. [5] Includes other nonsurgical procedures, not shown separately. [6] Using contrast material. [7] Also known as CAT scan.

Source: U.S. National Center for Health Statistics, *Vital and Health Statistics*, Series 13, and unpublished data, <http://www.cdc.gov/nchs/products/series.htm> and <http://www.cdc.gov/nchs/nhds.htm>.

Table 172. Hospitals—Summary Characteristics: 1990 to 2009

[For beds, (1,213 represents 1,213,000). Covers hospitals accepted for registration by the American Hospital Association; see text, this section. Short-term hospitals have an average patient stay of less than 30 days; long-term, an average stay of longer duration. Special hospitals include obstetrics and gynecology; eye, ear, nose, and throat; rehabilitation; orthopedic; chronic and other special hospitals except psychiatric, tuberculosis, alcoholism, and chemical dependency hospitals]

Item	1990	1995	2000	2004	2005	2006	2007	2008	2009
Number:									
All hospitals	6,649	6,291	5,810	5,759	5,756	5,747	5,708	5,815	5,795
With 100 beds or more	3,620	3,376	3,102	2,972	2,942	2,928	2,901	2,884	2,861
Nonfederal [1]	6,312	5,992	5,565	5,520	5,530	5,526	5,495	5,602	5,584
Community hospitals [2]	5,384	5,194	4,915	4,919	4,936	4,927	4,897	5,010	5,008
Nongovernmental nonprofit	3,191	3,092	3,003	2,967	2,958	2,919	2,913	2,923	2,918
For profit	749	752	749	835	868	889	873	982	998
State and local government	1,444	1,350	1,163	1,117	1,110	1,119	1,111	1,105	1,092
Long term general and special	131	112	131	108	115	127	135	128	115
Psychiatric	757	657	496	466	456	462	444	447	444
Tuberculosis	4	3	4	4	3	2	1	1	2
Federal	337	299	245	239	226	221	213	213	211
Beds (1,000): [3]									
All hospitals	1,213	1,081	984	956	947	947	945	951	944
Rate per 1,000 population [4]	4.9	4.1	3.5	3.3	3.2	3.2	3.1	3.1	3.1
Beds per hospital	182	172	169	166	165	165	166	164	163
Nonfederal [1]	1,113	1,004	931	908	901	901	899	905	900
Community hospitals [2]	927	873	824	808	802	802	801	808	806
Rate per 1,000 population [4]	3.7	3.3	2.9	2.8	2.7	2.7	2.7	2.7	2.6
Nongovernmental nonprofit	657	610	583	567	561	559	554	557	556
For profit	102	106	110	112	114	115	116	121	122
State and local government	169	157	131	127	128	128	131	131	127
Long term general and special	25	19	18	15	15	16	17	16	16
Psychiatric	158	110	87	86	82	84	79	79	76
Tuberculosis	(Z)	(Z)	(Z)	(Z)	(Z)	(Z)	(Z)	(Z)	(Z)
Federal	98	78	53	47	46	46	46	46	45
Average daily census (1,000): [5]									
All hospitals	844	710	650	658	656	653	645	649	641
Community hospitals [2]	619	548	526	541	540	538	533	536	528
Nongovernmental nonprofit	455	393	382	388	388	384	380	380	375
For profit	54	55	61	68	68	67	66	70	70
State and local government	111	100	83	84	85	86	87	86	83
Expenses (bil. dol.): [6]									
All hospitals	234.9	320.3	395.4	533.8	570.5	607.3	638.5	690.0	726.7
Nonfederal [1]	219.6	300.0	371.5	499.0	533.7	569.8	599.7	646.1	676.6
Community hospitals [2]	203.7	285.6	356.6	481.2	515.7	551.8	581.0	626.6	656.2
Nongovernmental nonprofit	150.7	209.6	267.1	359.4	386.0	412.8	435.5	468.1	492.9
For profit	18.8	26.7	35.0	48.9	51.8	54.9	55.8	61.8	64.4
State and local government	34.2	49.3	54.5	72.8	77.9	83.9	89.8	96.7	98.9
Long term general and special	2.7	2.2	2.8	3.6	3.6	4.0	3.9	4.5	4.2
Psychiatric	12.9	11.7	11.9	13.8	13.9	15.0	14.5	14.7	15.1
Tuberculosis	0.1	0.4	(Z)	(Z)	(Z)	(Z)	(Z)	(Z)	(Z)
Federal	15.2	20.2	23.9	34.8	36.8	37.5	38.8	44.0	50.1
Personnel (1,000): [7]									
All hospitals	4,063	4,273	4,454	4,695	4,790	4,907	5,024	5,116	5,178
Nonfederal [1]	3,760	3,971	4,157	4,379	4,479	4,569	4,699	4,775	4,814
Community hospitals [2]	3,420	3,714	3,911	4,147	4,260	4,343	4,465	4,550	4,585
Nongovernmental nonprofit	2,533	2,702	2,919	3,076	3,154	3,207	3,286	3,340	3,369
For profit	273	343	378	405	421	423	432	450	464
State and local government	614	670	614	665	681	713	747	760	751
Long term general and special	55	38	41	42	38	43	44	41	37
Psychiatric	280	215	200	185	182	180	187	182	183
Tuberculosis	1	1	1	1	1	1	1	(Z)	(Z)
Federal	303	301	297	315	311	339	325	341	364
Outpatient visits (mil.)	368.2	483.2	592.7	662.1	673.7	690.4	693.5	710.0	742.0
Emergency	92.8	99.9	106.9	116.9	118.9	122.6	124.7	126.7	131.4

Z Less than 500 or $50 million. [1] Includes hospital units of institutions. [2] Short-term (average length of stay less than 30 days) general and special (e.g., obstetrics and gynecology; eye, ear, nose and throat; rehabilitation, etc. except psychiatric, tuberculosis, alcoholism, and chemical dependency). Excludes hospital units of institutions. [3] Number of beds at end of reporting period. [4] Based on Census Bureau estimated resident population as of July 1. 1990 and 2000 based on enumerated resident population as of April 1. Other years are estimates, which reflect revisions based on the 2000 Census of Population. [5] The average number of people served on an inpatient basis on a single day during the reporting period. [6] Excludes new construction. [7] Includes full-time equivalents of part-time personnel.

Source: Health Forum, An American Hospital Association Company, Chicago, IL, *AHA Hospital Statistics 2011 Edition*, and prior years (copyright). See also <www.ahadata.com>.

Table 173. Average Cost to Community Hospitals Per Patient: 1990 to 2009

[In dollars, except percent. Covers non-federal short-term general or special hospitals (excluding psychiatric or tuberculosis hospitals and hospital units of institutions). Total cost per patient based on total hospital expenses (payroll, employee benefits, professional fees, supplies, etc.). Data have been adjusted for outpatient visits]

Type of expense and hospital	1990	1995	2000	2003	2004	2005	2006	2007	2008	2009
Average cost per day, total	**687**	**968**	**1,149**	**1,379**	**1,450**	**1,522**	**1,612**	**1,690**	**1,782**	**1,853**
Annual percent change [1]	7.8	4.0	4.2	6.9	5.1	5.0	5.9	4.8	5.4	4.0
Nongovernmental nonprofit	692	994	1,182	1,429	1,501	1,585	1,686	1,772	1,876	1,957
For profit	752	947	1,057	1,264	1,362	1,412	1,472	1,519	1,556	1,574
State and local government	635	878	1,064	1,238	1,291	1,329	1,400	1,460	1,552	1,611
Average cost per stay, total	**4,947**	**6,216**	**6,649**	**7,796**	**8,166**	**8,793**	**8,970**	**9,342**	**9,788**	**10,043**
Nongovernmental nonprofit	5,001	6,279	6,717	7,905	8,266	8,670	9,190	9,574	10,081	10,379
For profit	4,727	5,425	5,642	6,590	7,139	7,351	7,422	7,740	7,985	8,037
State and local government	4,838	6,445	7,106	8,205	8,473	8,793	9,147	9,446	9,827	10,068

[1] Change from immediate prior year.

Source: Health Forum, An American Hospital Association Company, Chicago, IL, *AHA Hospital Statistics 2011 Edition*, and prior years (copyright). See also <www.ahadata.com>.

Table 174. Community Hospitals—States: 2000 and 2009

[In thousands, (823.6 represents 823,600). For definition of community hospitals see footnote 2, Table 172]

State	Number of hospitals 2000	Number of hospitals 2009	Beds (1,000) 2000	Beds (1,000) 2009	Patients admitted (1,000) 2000	Patients admitted (1,000) 2009	Average daily census [1] (1,000) 2000	Average daily census [1] (1,000) 2009	Outpatient visits (mil.) 2000	Outpatient visits (mil.) 2009	Average cost per day (dol.) 2000	Average cost per day (dol.) 2009
United States	**4,915**	**5,008**	**823.6**	**805.6**	**33,089**	**35,527**	**525.7**	**527.9**	**521.4**	**642.0**	**1,149**	**1,853**
Alabama	108	108	16.4	15.3	680	666	9.8	9.5	8.0	9.2	980	1,319
Alaska	18	22	1.4	1.5	47	57	0.8	0.9	1.3	1.8	1,495	2,163
Arizona	61	72	10.9	13.5	539	705	6.8	8.8	5.3	7.1	1,311	2,106
Arkansas	83	86	9.8	9.6	368	380	5.7	5.4	4.4	5.0	908	1,428
California	389	343	72.7	68.7	3,315	3,433	47.8	48.2	44.9	48.3	1,438	2,419
Colorado	69	81	9.4	10.4	397	445	5.4	6.1	6.7	8.9	1,280	2,156
Connecticut	35	35	7.7	7.9	349	408	5.8	6.4	6.7	8.2	1,373	2,077
Delaware	5	7	1.8	2.2	83	102	1.4	1.6	1.5	1.7	1,311	2,154
District of Columbia	11	10	3.3	3.5	129	138	2.5	2.5	1.3	2.4	1,512	2,514
Florida	202	210	51.2	53.3	2,119	2,453	31.0	33.6	21.8	24.9	1,161	1,776
Georgia	151	152	23.9	25.4	863	957	15.0	16.6	11.2	14.4	978	1,354
Hawaii	21	25	3.1	3.0	100	112	2.3	2.1	2.5	2.2	1,088	1,892
Idaho	42	41	3.5	3.4	123	130	1.8	1.7	2.2	3.1	1,003	1,887
Illinois	196	189	37.3	33.9	1,531	1,558	22.4	21.3	25.1	32.1	1,278	1,948
Indiana	109	123	19.2	17.3	700	713	10.8	10.1	14.1	17.5	1,132	1,955
Iowa	115	118	11.8	10.3	360	355	6.8	6.0	9.2	11.0	740	1,204
Kansas	129	133	10.8	10.1	310	316	5.7	5.5	5.3	6.7	837	1,271
Kentucky	105	104	14.8	14.1	582	597	9.1	8.5	8.7	10.1	929	1,543
Louisiana	123	128	17.5	15.9	654	639	9.8	9.6	10.0	12.4	1,075	1,510
Maine	37	37	3.7	3.6	147	150	2.4	2.3	3.2	5.8	1,148	1,881
Maryland	49	49	11.2	11.9	587	715	8.2	8.9	6.0	8.3	1,315	2,271
Massachusetts	80	78	16.6	15.5	740	820	11.7	11.5	16.7	21.4	1,467	2,351
Michigan	146	158	26.1	25.9	1,106	1,220	16.9	17.3	24.9	29.3	1,211	1,905
Minnesota	135	132	16.7	15.6	571	624	11.2	10.2	7.3	10.8	932	1,667
Mississippi	95	97	13.6	12.9	425	413	8.0	7.1	3.7	4.7	719	1,231
Missouri	119	125	20.1	19.1	773	825	11.7	11.7	14.8	19.2	1,185	1,934
Montana	52	48	4.3	3.8	99	101	2.9	2.4	2.6	3.3	579	1,190
Nebraska	85	87	8.2	7.4	209	210	4.8	4.3	3.4	4.7	743	1,402
Nevada	22	35	3.8	5.1	199	246	2.7	3.6	2.2	2.8	1,285	1,912
New Hampshire	28	28	2.9	2.9	111	123	1.7	1.8	2.8	4.7	1,201	1,980
New Jersey	80	74	25.3	21.1	1,074	1,095	17.3	15.3	16.3	18.4	1,299	2,147
New Mexico	35	37	3.5	3.9	174	183	2.0	2.3	3.1	4.6	1,388	1,989
New York	215	189	66.4	60.4	2,416	2,534	52.1	47.9	46.4	54.2	1,118	1,820
North Carolina	113	115	23.1	22.8	971	1,034	16.0	15.9	12.4	18.3	1,061	1,641
North Dakota	42	41	3.9	3.4	89	93	2.3	2.1	1.7	2.4	747	1,140
Ohio	163	183	33.8	33.9	1,404	1,531	20.6	21.2	26.9	34.2	1,198	2,021
Oklahoma	108	116	11.1	11.3	429	442	6.2	6.6	4.7	5.6	1,031	1,489
Oregon	59	58	6.6	6.5	330	324	3.9	3.9	7.3	8.9	1,461	2,596
Pennsylvania	207	194	42.3	39.2	1,796	1,842	28.8	27.0	31.8	37.9	1,080	1,837
Rhode Island	11	11	2.4	2.5	119	127	1.7	1.8	2.1	2.6	1,313	2,235
South Carolina	63	70	11.5	12.5	495	528	8.0	8.1	7.8	6.3	1,101	1,792
South Dakota	48	53	4.3	4.1	99	102	2.8	2.8	1.7	1.9	476	985
Tennessee	121	137	20.6	21.0	737	859	11.5	13.2	10.3	11.6	1,078	1,464
Texas	403	428	55.9	62.1	2,367	2,621	33.1	37.3	29.4	36.0	1,274	1,923
Utah	42	44	4.3	5.0	194	226	2.4	2.8	4.5	5.5	1,375	2,071
Vermont	14	14	1.7	1.3	52	51	1.1	0.9	1.2	3.4	888	1,586
Virginia	88	90	16.9	17.5	727	793	11.4	12.0	9.5	14.2	1,057	1,747
Washington	84	87	11.1	11.3	505	589	6.6	7.3	9.6	11.5	1,511	2,696
West Virginia	57	56	8.0	7.4	288	280	4.8	4.5	5.2	6.7	844	1,134
Wisconsin	118	126	15.3	13.6	558	609	9.1	8.6	10.9	14.9	1,055	1,935
Wyoming	24	24	1.9	2.0	48	52	1.1	1.1	0.9	1.1	677	1,025

[1] The average number of people served on an inpatient basis on a single day during the reporting period.

Source: Health Forum, An American Hospital Association Company, Chicago, IL, *AHA Hospital Statistics 2011 Edition*, and prior years (copyright). See also <www.ahadata.com>.

Table 175. Hospital Utilization Rates by Type of Hospital: 1990 to 2009

Type of hospital	1990	1995	2000	2005	2006	2007	2008	2009
Community hospitals: [1]								
Admissions per 1,000 population [2]	125	116	117	119	118	117	118	116
Admissions per bed.	34	35	40	44	44	43	44	44
Average length of stay (days) [3]	7.2	6.5	5.8	5.6	5.5	5.5	5.5	5.4
Outpatient visits per admission	9.7	13.4	15.8	16.6	16.9	17.1	17.5	18.1
Outpatient visits per 1,000 population [2]	1,207	1,556	1,852	1,976	2,002	2,000	2,053	2,091
Surgical operations (million [4])	21.9	23.2	26.1	27.5	28.1	28.1	27.5	27.5
Number per admission	0.7	0.7	0.8	0.8	0.7	0.8	0.8	0.8
Nonfederal psychiatric:								
Admissions per 1,000 population [2]	2.9	2.7	2.4	2.5	2.3	2.3	2.4	2.5
Days in hospital per 1,000 population [2]	190	122	93	89	83	82	80	80

[1] Short term (average length of stay less than 30 days) general and special (e.g., obstetrics and gynecology; eye, ear, nose and throat; rehabilitation, etc., except psychiatric, tuberculosis, alcoholism and chemical dependency). Excludes hospital units of institutions. [2] Based on U.S. Census Bureau estimated resident population as of July 1. Estimates reflect revisions based on the 2000 Census of Population. 1990 and 2000 based on enumerated resident population as of April 1. [3] Number of inpatient days divided by number of admissions. [4] 21.9 represents 21,900,000.

Source: Health Forum, An American Hospital Association Company, *AHA Hospital Statistics 2011 Edition*, Chicago, IL, and prior years (copyright). See also <www.ahadata.com>.

Table 176. Hospital Utilization Rates by Sex: 1990 to 2008

[30,788 represents 30,788,000. Represents estimates of inpatients discharged from noninstitutional, short-stay hospitals, exclusive of federal hospitals. Excludes newborn infants. Based on sample data collected from the National Hospital Discharge Survey, a sample survey of hospital records of patients discharged in year shown; subject to sampling variability]

Item and sex	1990	1995	2000	2003	2004	2005	2006	2007	2008
Patients discharged (1,000).	30,788	30,722	31,706	34,738	34,864	34,667	34,854	34,369	35,697
Patients discharged per 1,000 persons, total [1] . . .	122	116	113	120	119	117	117	114	118
Male.	100	94	91	98	97	96	95	94	96
Female.	143	136	134	141	141	138	138	134	139
Days of care per 1,000 persons, total [1]	784	620	555	578	574	562	558	554	577
Male.	694	551	486	507	505	498	495	494	518
Female.	869	686	620	646	641	624	619	612	635
Average stay (days).	6.4	5.4	4.9	4.8	4.8	4.8	4.8	4.8	4.9
Male.	6.9	5.8	5.3	5.2	5.2	5.2	5.2	5.3	5.4
Female.	6.1	5.0	4.6	4.6	4.5	4.5	4.5	4.6	4.6

[1] Rates are computed using Census Bureau estimates of the civilian population as of July 1. Rates for 1990 and 1995 were based on population estimates adjusted for the net underenumeration in the 1990 census. Rates for 2000 and later were calculated using 2000-based postcensal estimates.

Source: U.S. National Center for Health Statistics, *Vital and Health Statistics*, Series 13 and unpublished data. See also <http://www.cdc.gov/nchs/products/series.htm#sr13>.

Table 177. Hospital Utilization Measures for HIV Patients: 1990 to 2008

[HIV represents human immunodeficiency virus. See headnote, Table 176]

Measure of utilization	Unit	1990	1995	2000	2005	2006	2007	2008
Number of patients discharged . . .	1,000	146	249	173	185	223	221	215
Male.	1,000	114	183	115	113	145	146	133
Female.	1,000	32	66	58	72	78	75	81
Rate of patient discharges [1]	Rate.	5.8	9.4	6.2	6.3	7.5	7.4	7.1
Number of days of care	1,000	2,188	2,326	1,257	1,244	1,418	1,483	1,342
Male.	1,000	1,777	1,649	895	751	907	1,009	875
Female.	1,000	411	677	362	493	511	474	468
Rate of days of care [1]	Rate.	86.9	87.6	45.2	42.2	47.6	49.3	44.3
Average length of stay	Days	14.9	9.3	7.3	6.7	6.3	6.7	6.3
Male.	Days	15.5	9.0	7.8	6.7	6.2	6.9	6.6
Female.	Days	12.9	10.3	6.3	6.8	6.5	6.3	5.7

[1] Per 10,000 population. Based on Census Bureau estimated civilian population as of July 1. Rates for 1990 and 1995 were based on population estimates adjusted for the net undernumeration in the 1990 census. Populations for 2000 and later were 2000-based postcensal estimates.

Source: U.S. National Center for Health Statistics, *Vital and Health Statistics*, Series 13 and unpublished data. See also <http://www.cdc.gov/nchs/products/series.htm#sr13> and <http://www.cdc.gov/nchs/nhds.htm>.

Health and Nutrition 121

Table 178. Hospital Discharges and Days of Care: 2003 and 2008

[(34,738 represents 34,738,000). See headnote, Table 176. For composition of regions, see map, inside front cover]

Age, race, and region	Discharges Number (1,000) 2003	2008	Discharges Per 1,000 persons [1] 2003	2008	Days of care per 1,000 persons [1] 2003	2008	Average stay (days) 2003	2008
Total [2]	34,738	35,697	120	118	578	577	4.8	4.9
Age:								
Under 1 year old	833	715	208	166	1,218	940	5.9	5.7
1 to 4 years old	751	563	48	34	149	102	3.1	3.0
5 to 14 years old	986	707	24	18	108	75	4.5	4.3
15 to 24 years old	3,138	2,950	77	70	268	233	3.5	3.3
25 to 34 years old	4,011	4,066	102	100	353	346	3.5	3.4
35 to 44 years old	3,683	3,453	83	82	359	331	4.3	4.0
45 to 64 years old	8,120	9,341	118	120	582	628	4.9	5.2
65 to 74 years old	4,861	5,094	265	253	1,429	1,391	5.4	5.5
75 years old and over	8,356	8,808	475	470	2,776	2,735	5.8	5.8
Race:								
White	21,292	20,487	91	85	437	421	4.8	5.0
Black	4,102	4,665	111	120	611	642	5.5	5.3
Asian/Pacific Islander	550	591	44	42	231	[3] 213	5.2	5.1
American Indian/Eskimo/Aleut	120	[3] 194	43	[3] 63	224	[3] 259	5.2	4.1
Region:								
Northeast	7,267	7,574	134	138	735	771	5.5	5.6
Midwest	7,786	8,062	119	121	520	543	4.4	4.5
South	13,055	13,366	126	120	610	584	4.9	4.9
West	6,631	6,695	100	95	455	450	4.5	4.7

[1] Rates were calculated using U.S. Census Bureau 2000-based postcensal estimates of the civilian population as of July 1.
[2] Includes other races not shown separately. [3] Figure does not meet standard of reliability or precision.

Source: U.S. National Center for Health Statistics, Vital and Health Statistics, Series 13 and unpublished data. See also <http://www.cdc.gov/nchs/products/series.htm#sr13>.

Table 179. Hospital Discharges and Days of Care by Selected Diagnosis: 2008

[(14,371 represents 14,371,000). Represents estimates of inpatients discharged from noninstitutional, short-stay hospitals, exclusive of federal hospitals. Excludes newborn infants. Diagnostic categories are based on the International Classification of Diseases, Ninth Revision, Clinical Modification. See headnote, Table 176]

Sex, age, and selected first-listed diagnosis [1]	Discharges Number (1,000)[2]	Per 1,000 persons[2]	Average stay (days)[2]	Sex, age, and selected first-listed diagnosis [1]	Discharges Number (1,000)[2]	Per 1,000 persons[2]	Average stay (days)[2]
MALE				**FEMALE**			
All ages [3]	**14,371**	**96.5**	**5.4**	**All ages, [3]**	**21,326**	**138.5**	**4.6**
Under 18 years [3]	1,336	35.3	4.7	Under 18 years [3]	1,203	33.3	3.9
Injury	131	3.5	3.4	Childbirth	138	3.8	2.7
Pneumonia	95	2.5	5.2	Injury	76	2.1	2.4
Asthma	82	2.2	2.3	Schizophrenia, mood disorders, delusional disorders,			
18-44 years [3]	2,486	43.9	4.7	nonorganic psychoses [5]	[4] 67	[4] 1.8	7.5
Injury	399	7.1	4.6	18-44 years [3]	7,430	133.9	3.2
Schizophrenia, mood disorders, delusional disorders,				Childbirth	3,998	72.0	2.7
nonorganic psychoses [5]	263	4.6	7.2	Schizophrenia, mood disorders, delusional disorders,			
Heart disease	157	2.8	3.7	nonorganic psychoses [5]	293	5.3	7.2
Alcohol and drug [6]	118	2.1	3.8	Injury	175	3.1	4.3
45-64 years [3]	4,619	121.4	5.4	Uterine fibroids	108	1.9	2.2
Heart disease	774	20.3	3.9	45-64 years [3]	4,722	118.2	5.1
Injury	271	7.1	5.2	Heart disease	436	10.9	4.3
Cancer, all	255	6.7	6.3	Cancer, all	267	6.7	5.9
65-74 years [3]	2,410	260.2	5.6	Osteoarthritis	225	5.6	3.3
Heart disease	491	53.0	4.4	65-74 years [3]	2,683	247.1	5.4
Cancer, all	152	16.4	6.9	Heart disease	424	39.0	4.5
Stroke	110	11.8	5.1	Osteoarthritis	178	16.4	4.0
Pneumonia	93	10.0	6.1	Cancer, all	141	13.0	6.5
75-84 years [3]	2,400	449.8	5.8	Pneumonia	93	8.6	6.0
Heart disease	475	89.0	4.8	75-84 years [3]	3,087	401.5	5.8
Cancer, all	130	24.4	7.6	Heart disease	526	68.5	5.1
Pneumonia	130	24.3	5.6	Injury	204	26.5	5.2
Stroke	126	23.6	4.8	Pneumonia	160	20.8	6.0
85 years and over [3]	1,119	600.4	6.2	Stroke	160	20.8	5.2
Heart disease	230	123.4	4.9	85 years and over [3]	2,202	570.6	5.7
Pneumonia	90	48.2	6.4	Heart disease	384	99.5	5.3
Injury	69	37.0	6.6	Injury	239	62.0	5.3
				Pneumonia	123	31.9	5.4

[1] The first-listed diagnosis is the one specified as the principal diagnosis or the first diagnosis listed on the face sheet or discharge summary of the medical record. It is usually the main cause of the hospitalization. The number of first-listed diagnoses is the same as the number of discharges. [2] Crude estimates. [3] Includes discharges with first-listed diagnoses not shown in table. [4] Estimates are considered unreliable. [5] These estimates are for nonfederal short-stay hospitals only and do not include mental illness discharges from other types of facilities such as Veterans Affairs hospitals. [6] Includes abuse, dependence, and withdrawal. These estimates are for non-federal short-stay hospitals only and do not include alcohol and drug discharges from other types of facilities or or programs such as the Department of Veterans Affairs or day treatment programs.

Source: Centers for Disease Control and Prevention, National Center for Health Statistics, National Hospital Discharge Survey, <http://www.cdc.gov/nchs/nhds.htm>.

Table 180. Selected Cosmetic Plastic Surgical and Nonsurgical Procedures: 2003 to 2009

[In thousands (8,252.0 represents 8,252,000). As of December 31. The final data are projected to reflect nationwide statistics and are based on a survey of doctors who have been certified by the American Board of Medical Specialties recognized boards, including but not limited to the American Board of Plastic Surgery. Data for the procedures include but are not limited to those performed by American Society for Aesthetic Plastic Surgery (ASAPS) members. ASAPS members are plastic surgeons certified by the American Board of Plastic Surgery who specialize in cosmetic surgery of the face and the entire body. Procedures are ranked by total number in the most current year]

Procedure	2003	2004	2005	2006	2007	2008	2009
Total all procedures	**8,252.0**	**11,855.0**	**11,428.8**	**11,456.8**	**11,701.0**	**10,258.6**	**9,993.7**
Total surgical procedures	**1,819.5**	**2,120.0**	**2,131.0**	**1,922.8**	**2,079.0**	**1,766.7**	**1,471.6**
Breast augmentation	280.4	334.1	364.6	383.9	399.4	355.7	312.0
Lipoplasty (Liposuction)	384.6	478.3	455.5	403.7	456.8	341.1	283.7
Blepharoplasty (eyelid surgery)	267.6	290.3	231.5	210.0	240.8	195.1	149.9
Rhinoplasty (nose reshaping)	172.4	166.2	200.9	141.9	151.8	152.4	138.3
Abdominoplasty (tummy tuck)	117.7	151.0	169.3	172.5	185.3	147.4	127.9
Total nonsurgical procedures	**6,432.5**	**9,735.0**	**9,297.7**	**9,534.0**	**9,622.0**	**8,491.9**	**8,522.1**
Botox injection [1]	2,272.1	2,837.3	3,294.8	3,181.6	2,775.2	2,464.1	2,557.1
Hyaluronic acid [2]	116.2	882.5	1,194.2	1,593.6	1,448.7	1,262.8	1,313.0
Laser hair removal	923.2	1,411.9	1,566.9	1,475.3	1,412.7	1,281.0	1,280.0
Microdermabrasion [3]	858.3	1,098.3	1,023.9	993.1	829.7	557.1	621.9
Chemical peel	722.2	1110.4	556.2	558.4	575.1	591.8	529.3
Total female procedures	**7,177.9**	**10,681.4**	**10,443.8**	**10,516.7**	**10,602.5**	**9,394.8**	**9,058.5**
Total surgical procedures	**1,559.4**	**1,887.3**	**1,918.1**	**1,730.5**	**1,877.1**	**1,600.7**	**1,310.7**
Breast augmentation	280.4	334.1	364.6	383.9	399.4	355.7	312.0
Lipoplasty (Liposuction)	323.0	416.6	402.9	350.4	398.8	309.7	243.2
Blepharoplasty (eyelid surgery)	216.8	249.3	198.1	182.4	208.2	166.4	124.9
Abdominoplasty (tummy tuck)	112.7	145.3	164.1	164.8	180.5	143.0	123.0
Breast reduction	147.2	144.4	160.5	145.8	153.1	139.9	113.5
Total nonsurgical procedures	**5,618.6**	**8,794.1**	**8,525.7**	**8,786.2**	**8,725.4**	**7,794.1**	**7,747.8**
Botox injection [1]	1,963.0	2,525.4	2,990.7	2,881.1	2,445.7	2,239.0	2,299.3
Hyaluronic acid [2]	104.7	838.9	1,149.2	1,519.9	1,364.5	1,200.4	1,221.8
Laser hair removal	695.2	1,215.1	1,334.7	1,308.7	1,227.0	1,101.3	1,114.0
Microdermabrasion [3]	774.3	999.1	939.5	922.0	743.7	517.3	565.0
Chemical peel	640.1	977.3	533.0	530.1	536.0	554.5	492.3
Laser skin resurfacing	116.5	520.3	432.6	528.1	479.8	532.0	463.3
Sclerotherapy (Spider veins)	431.3	479.2	548.0	541.3	467.8	417.5	442.0
IPL laser treatment [4]	(X)	(X)	(X)	(X)	584.5	479.9	404.5
Total male procedures	**1,074.1**	**1,173.6**	**984.9**	**940.0**	**1,098.6**	**863.7**	**935.2**
Total surgical procedures	**260.1**	**232.7**	**212.9**	**192.3**	**202.0**	**166.0**	**160.9**
Lipoplasty (Liposuction)	61.6	61.6	52.5	53.3	58.0	31.5	40.5
Rhinoplasty (nose reshaping)	53.4	39.0	45.9	33.1	31.7	30.2	32.7
Blepharoplasty (eyelid surgery)	50.8	41.1	33.4	27.6	32.6	28.7	25.0
Gynecomastia (male breast reduction)	22.0	19.6	17.7	23.7	20.3	19.1	16.8
Hair transplantation	14.9	19.5	11.2	11.2	16.5	18.1	13.1
Facelift	13.6	11.8	13.0	14.1	12.4	13.4	10.5
Total nonsurgical procedures	**814.0**	**932.6**	**772.0**	**747.7**	**896.6**	**697.8**	**774.4**
Botox injection [1]	309.1	311.9	304.1	300.5	329.5	225.1	257.8
Laser hair removal	228.0	196.8	232.2	166.6	185.7	179.7	166.0
Hyaluronic acid [2]	11.5	43.6	45.0	73.6	84.2	62.4	91.2
Microdermabrasion [3]	84.0	99.2	84.4	71.1	85.9	39.8	56.9
Laser skin resurfacing	11.0	69.4	43.1	48.5	30.1	38.9	49.0
IPL laser treatment [4]	(X)	(X)	(X)	(X)	63.2	46.9	47.7

X Not applicable. [1] As of 2009, includes Dysport. [2] In 2003, the FDA has approved hyaluronan injections for filling soft tissue defects such as facial wrinkles. [3] Procedure for reducing fine lines, "crow's feet," age spots, and acne scars. [4] IPL is intense pulse light. One of the procedures available for facial rejuvenation.

Source: The American Society for Aesthetic Plastic Surgery, *Statistics*, annual (copyright), <http://www.surgery.org/media/statistics>.

Table 181. Organ Transplants: 1990 to 2010

[As of end of year. Based on reports of procurement programs and transplant centers in the United States, except as noted]

Procedure	Number of procedures						Number of centers		Number of people waiting, 2010	1-year patient survival rates, 2009 (percent)
	1990	1995	2000	2005	2009	2010	1990	2010		
Transplant: [1]										
Heart	2,095	2,342	2,172	2,125	2,212	2,333	148	132	3,182	86.7
Heart-lung	52	69	47	35	29	41	79	50	67	67.6
Lung	203	869	955	1,406	1,661	1,770	70	66	1,774	80.6
Liver	2,631	3,818	4,816	6,443	6,320	6,291	85	132	16,954	86.4
Kidney	9,358	10,957	13,258	16,481	16,829	16,898	232	238	94,598	94.6
Kidney-pancreas	459	915	910	903	854	828	(NA)	(NA)	2,281	94.7
Pancreas	60	103	420	541	379	350	84	144	1,385	93.4
Intestine	1	21	29	178	180	151	(NA)	43	266	74.4
Multi-organ	71	124	213	518	(NA)	(NA)	(NA)	(NA)	(NA)	(NA)

NA Not available. [1] Kidney-pancreas and heart-lung transplants are each counted as one procedure. All other multiorgan transplants, excluding kidney-pancreas and heart-lung, are included in the multiorgan row. Based on the Organ Procurement and Transplant Network (OPTN) as of May 20, 2011. The data have been supplied by UNOS under contract with Health and Human Services (HHS). This work was supported in part by Health Resources and Services Administration contract 231-00-0015. The authors alone are responsible for the reporting and interpretation of these data. Data subject to change based on future data submission or correction.

Source: U.S. Department of Health and Human Services, Health Resources and Services Administration, Office of Special Programs, Division of Transplantation, Rockville, MD; United Network for Organ Sharing (UNOS), Richmond, VA; University Renal Research and Education Association, Ann Arbor, MI; American Association of Tissue Banks, McLean, VA; and unpublished data. See also <http://optn.transplant.hrsa.gov/>.

Table 182. Cancer—Estimated New Cases, 2010, and Survival Rates: 1990–2007

[1,530 represents 1,530,000. The 5-year relative survival rate, which is derived by adjusting the observed survival rate for expected mortality, represents the likelihood that a person will not die from causes directly related to their cancer within 5 years. Survival data shown are based on those patients diagnosed while residents of an area listed below during the time periods shown. Data are based on information collected as part of the National Cancer Institute's Surveillance, Epidemiology and End Results (SEER) program, a collection of 9 population-based registries in five states (Connecticut, Hawaii, Iowa, New Mexico, Utah) and four metropolitan areas (Atlanta, Detroit, San Francisco-Oakland, and Seattle-Puget Sound)]

Site	Estimated new cases,[1] 2010 (1,000)			5-year relative survival rates (percent)							
				White				Black			
	Total	Male	Female	1990– 1992	1993– 1995	1996– 2000	2001– 2007	1990– 1992	1993– 1995	1996– 2000	2001– 2007
All sites [2]...............	1,530	790	740	61.5	62.5	65.4	68.6	47.9	52.7	56.0	59.4
Lung.....................	223	117	106	14.0	14.6	15.2	16.7	10.4	12.8	12.6	13.3
Breast [3]................	209	2	207	86.6	87.8	90.2	91.4	71.7	72.7	77.5	77.4
Colon and rectum	143	72	70	62.2	60.8	64.5	67.1	53.0	52.1	53.8	56.3
Colon..................	103	49	53	63.0	60.8	64.4	66.5	53.5	51.5	53.5	54.8
Rectum	40	23	17	60.2	60.8	65.0	68.7	51.3	54.0	54.8	60.9
Prostate..................	218	218	(X)	94.4	96.1	98.9	99.9	84.6	91.7	95.6	97.9
Bladder	71	53	18	80.6	81.4	80.3	81.1	63.4	60.0	62.6	64.1
Corpus uteri..............	43	(X)	43	86.4	85.9	86.6	86.3	56.0	60.5	63.4	62.0
Non-Hodgkin's lymphoma [4]....	66	35	30	51.7	53.4	61.4	70.7	42.1	41.9	53.6	62.1
Oral cavity and pharynx.......	37	25	11	58.1	60.3	60.9	65.1	32.5	38.0	39.8	44.7
Leukemia [4]................	43	25	18	46.4	48.3	49.0	57.1	36.0	41.1	38.3	50.3
Melanoma of skin	68	39	29	89.3	89.5	91.5	93.0	61.8	68.2	72.7	73.4
Pancreas..................	43	21	22	4.4	3.9	4.3	5.9	3.7	3.4	4.6	3.8
Kidney	58	35	23	60.8	62.0	63.0	71.0	57.2	57.5	65.6	68.4
Stomach	21	13	8	18.8	19.9	21.0	26.1	22.9	19.5	22.1	27.2
Ovary....................	22	(X)	22	40.5	40.7	42.9	43.3	36.2	41.7	37.6	36.0
Cervix uteri [5]	12	(X)	12	70.9	74.2	73.8	70.3	57.9	63.0	66.6	60.9

X Not applicable. [1] Estimates provided by American Cancer Society, <www.cancer.org>, are based on rates from the National Cancer Institute's SEER program. [2] Includes other sites, not shown separately. [3] Survival rates for female only. [4] All types combined. [5] Invasive cancer only.

Source: U.S. National Institutes of Health, National Cancer Institute, <http://seer.cancer.gov/csr/1975_2008/>.

Table 183. Cancer—Estimated New Cases and Deaths by State: 2011

[In thousands (1,596.7 represents 1,596,700). Excludes basal and squamous cell skin cancers and in situ carcinomas, except urinary bladder]

State	New cases [1]			Deaths			State	New cases [1]			Deaths		
	Total [2]	Female breast	Lung & bron- chus	Total [2]	Female breast	Lung & bron- chus		Total [2]	Female breast	Lung & bron- chus	Total [2]	Female breast	Lung & bron- chus
U.S...	1,596.7	230.5	221.1	572.0	39.5	156.9	MO....	32.7	4.1	5.5	12.7	0.9	4.0
AL	25.5	3.7	4.2	10.2	0.7	3.2	MT....	5.7	0.8	0.8	2.0	0.1	0.6
AK	3.1	0.5	0.4	0.9	0.1	0.3	NE....	9.4	1.2	1.3	3.5	0.2	0.9
AZ	31.6	4.2	3.8	10.8	0.8	2.7	NV....	12.8	1.4	1.5	4.7	0.3	1.3
AR	16.1	2.1	2.7	6.5	0.4	2.0	NH....	8.2	1.2	1.1	2.7	0.2	0.8
CA	163.5	25.5	17.7	56.0	4.0	12.5	NJ	49.1	7.4	6.2	16.4	1.3	4.2
CO....	22.4	3.4	2.3	7.0	0.5	1.7	NM....	9.6	1.3	1.0	3.5	0.2	0.8
CT	21.4	3.3	2.7	6.8	0.5	1.8	NY....	107.3	15.7	14.2	34.4	2.5	8.6
DE	5.1	0.8	0.8	1.9	0.1	0.6	NC....	48.9	7.4	7.3	19.8	1.4	5.8
DC....	2.8	0.5	0.4	0.9	0.1	0.2	ND....	3.6	0.4	0.4	1.3	0.1	0.3
FL	113.4	15.3	17.2	41.0	2.7	11.5	OH....	65.1	9.0	10.1	24.9	1.7	7.2
GA....	44.6	7.0	6.4	15.9	1.1	4.7	OK....	19.0	2.7	3.3	7.8	0.5	2.4
HI.....	6.7	1.0	0.8	2.4	0.1	0.6	OR....	21.2	3.4	2.9	7.6	0.5	2.1
ID.....	7.5	1.0	0.9	2.6	0.2	0.6	PA	78.0	10.6	10.9	28.6	2.0	8.0
IL.....	65.6	9.5	9.2	23.1	1.8	6.4	RI.....	6.1	0.9	0.9	2.2	0.1	0.6
IN.....	34.1	4.8	5.5	13.0	0.9	4.0	SC	25.5	3.7	3.9	9.3	0.7	2.9
IA.....	17.5	2.1	2.5	6.4	0.4	1.8	SD	4.4	0.6	0.6	1.7	0.1	0.5
KS	14.1	1.9	2.0	5.4	0.4	1.6	TN	34.8	5.0	5.9	13.8	0.9	4.6
KY	25.0	3.5	4.9	9.8	0.6	3.4	TX	105.0	15.1	13.9	36.8	2.6	9.6
LA	22.8	2.9	3.6	8.4	0.6	2.5	UT	10.5	1.4	0.6	2.9	0.3	0.5
ME....	8.8	1.3	1.4	3.2	0.2	1.0	VT	4.0	0.6	0.5	1.3	0.1	0.4
MD....	28.9	4.9	4.0	10.2	0.8	2.7	VA	38.7	6.5	5.7	14.3	1.1	4.1
MA....	37.5	5.6	5.0	12.9	0.8	3.5	WA....	35.4	5.6	4.5	11.7	0.8	3.1
MI.....	57.0	7.9	8.1	20.8	1.3	5.8	WV....	11.1	1.5	2.1	4.7	0.3	1.5
MN....	27.6	3.4	3.3	9.2	0.6	2.5	WI	30.5	4.4	4.0	11.4	0.7	2.9
MS....	15.0	2.2	2.4	6.1	0.4	2.0	WY....	2.7	0.4	0.3	1.0	0.1	0.3

[1] Estimates are offered as a rough guide and should be interpreted with caution. [2] Includes other types of cancer, not shown separately.

Source: American Cancer Society, Inc., *Cancer Facts and Figures—2011*, Atlanta, GA, (copyright). See also <http://www.cancer.org/docroot/STT/stt_0.asp>.

Table 184. Selected Notifiable Diseases—Cases Reported: 1980 to 2009

[190.9 represents 190,900. As of June 30, 2010. Figures should be interpreted with caution. Although reporting of some of these diseases is incomplete, the figures are of value in indicating trends of disease incidence. Includes cases imported from outside the United States]

Disease	1980	1990	1995	2000	2005	2006	2007	2008	2009
AIDS [1]	(2)	41,595	71,547	40,758	41,120	38,423	37,503	39,202	(1)
Botulism [3]	89	92	97	138	135	165	144	145	118
Brucellosis (undulant fever)	183	85	98	87	120	121	131	80	115
Chickenpox (Varicella) [4] (1,000)	190.9	173.1	120.6	27.4	32.2	48.4	40.1	30.4	20.5
Coccidoidomycosis	(2)	(2)	(2)	2,867	6,542	8,917	8,121	7,523	12,926
Cryptosporidiosis	(2)	(2)	(2)	3,128	5,659	6,071	11,170	9,113	7,654
Domestic arboviral diseases: [5]									
West Nile: neuroinvasive	(2)	(2)	(2)	(2)	1,309	1,495	1,227	689	386
nonneuroinvasive	(2)	(2)	(2)	(2)	1,691	2,774	2,403	667	334
Enterohemorrhagic Escherichia coli 0157:H7	(2)	(2)	2,139	4,528	2,621	(2)	(2)	(2)	(2)
Giardiasis	(2)	(2)	(2)	(2)	19,733	18,953	19,417	18,908	19,399
Haemophilus influenza	(2)	(2)	1,180	1,398	2,304	2,436	2,541	2,886	3,022
Hansen disease (Leprosy)	223	198	144	91	87	66	101	80	103
Hepatitis: A (infectious) (1,000) [6]	29.1	31.4	31.6	13.4	4.5	3.6	3.0	2.6	2.0
B (serum) (1,000)	19.0	21.1	10.8	8.0	5.1	4.7	4.5	4.0	3.4
C/Non-A, non-B	(2)	2,600	4,576	3,197	652	766	845	877	782
Legionellosis	(2)	1,370	1,241	1,127	2,301	2,834	2,716	3,181	3,522
Lyme disease	(2)	(2)	11,700	17,730	23,305	19,931	27,444	35,198	38,468
Malaria	2,062	1,292	1,419	1,560	1,494	1,474	1,408	1,255	1,451
Meningococcal infections	2,840	2,451	3,243	2,256	1,245	1,194	1,077	1,172	980
Mumps (1,000)	8.6	5.3	0.9	0.3	0.3	6.6	0.8	0.5	2.0
Pertussis [7] (1,000)	1.7	4.6	5.1	7.9	25.6	15.6	10.5	13.3	16.9
Psittacosis	124	113	64	17	16	21	12	8	9
Rabies, animal	6,421	4,826	7,811	6,934	5,915	5,534	5,862	4,196	5,343
Rocky Mountain spotted fever	1,163	651	590	495	1,936	2,288	2,221	2,563	1,815
Rubella [8]	3,904	1,125	128	176	11	11	12	16	3
Salmonellosis [9] (1,000)	33.7	48.6	46.0	39.6	45.3	45.8	48.0	51.0	49.2
Shigellosis [10] (1,000)	19.0	27.1	32.1	22.9	16.2	15.5	19.8	22.6	15.9
Streptococcal disease, invasive, Group A	(2)	(2)	(2)	3,144	4,715	5,407	5,294	5,674	5,279
Streptococcus pneumoniae, invasive:									
Drug-resistant	(2)	(2)	(2)	4,533	2,996	3,308	3,329	3,448	3,370
Age less than 5 years	(2)	(2)	(2)	(2)	1,495	1,861	563	532	583
Tetanus	95	64	41	35	27	41	28	19	18
Toxic-shock syndrome	(2)	322	191	135	90	101	92	71	74
Trichinosis	131	129	29	16	16	15	5	39	13
Tuberculosis [11] (1,000)	27.7	25.7	22.9	16.4	14.1	13.8	13.3	12.9	11.5
Typhoid fever	510	552	369	377	324	353	434	449	397
Sexually transmitted diseases:									
Chlamydia (1,000)	(2)	(2)	478	702	976	1,031	1,108	1,211	1,244
Gonorrhea (1,000)	1,004	690	393	359	340	358	356	337	301
Syphilis (1,000)	69	134	69	32	33	37	41	46	45

[1] Acquired immunodeficiency syndrome was not a notifiable disease until 1984. Includes all cases reported to the Division of HIV/AIDS Prevention, National Center for HIV/AIDS, Viral Hepatitis, STD, and TB Prevention. In 2008 CDC published a revised HIV case definition, see Table 185. [2] Disease was not notifiable. [3] Includes foodborne, infant, wound, and unspecified cases. [4] Chickenpox was taken off the nationally notifiable list in 1991 but many states continue to report. [5] The national surveillance case definitions for the arboviral diseases was revised in 2005, and nonneuroinvasive arboviral diseases were added to the list of nationally notifiable infectious diseases. [6] Data on chronic hepatitis B and hepatitis C virus infection (past or present) are not included because they are undergoing data quality review. [7] Whooping cough. [8] German measles. Excludes congenital syndrome. [9] Excludes typhoid fever. [10] Bacillary dysentery. [11] Newly reported active cases.

Source: Centers for Disease Control and Prevention, *Summary of Notifiable Diseases, United States, 2009, Morbidity and Mortality Weekly Report*, Vol. 58, No. 53, 2011. See also <http://www.cdc.gov/mmwr/mmwr_nd/index.html>.

Table 185. HIV Diagnoses, Chlamydia, and Lyme Disease Cases Reported by State: 2009

State	HIV diagnon- ses [1]	Chla- mydia [2]	Lyme disease	State	HIV diagnon- ses [1]	Chla- mydia [2]	Lyme disease	State	HIV diagnon- ses [1]	Chla- mydia [2]	Lyme disease
U.S.	36,870	1,244,180	38,468								
AL	594	25,929	3	KY	289	13,293	1	ND	12	1,957	15
AK	18	5,166	7	LA	1,223	27,628	-	OH	914	48,239	58
AZ	540	26,002	7	ME	48	2,431	970	OK	123	15,023	2
AR	133	14,354	−	MD	1,057	23,747	2,024	OR	203	11,497	38
CA	3,776	146,796	117	MA	307	19,315	5,256	PA	1,469	43,068	5,722
CO	348	19,998	1	MI	731	45,714	103	RI	100	3,615	235
CT	308	12,127	4,156	MN	358	14,197	1,543	SC	727	26,654	42
DE	144	4,718	984	MS	549	23,589	−	SD	20	3,015	1
DC	556	6,549	61	MO	504	25,868	3	TN	902	29,711	37
FL	5,401	72,931	110	MT	27	2,988	3	TX	3,115	105,910	276
GA	1,606	39,828	40	NE	77	5,443	5	UT	107	6,145	9
HI	34	6,026	(NA)	NV	333	10,045	13	VT	4	1,186	408
ID	32	3,842	16	NH	38	2,102	1,415	VA	869	30,903	908
IL	1,202	60,542	136	NJ	908	23,974	4,973	WA	467	21,387	16
IN	425	21,732	83	NM	148	9,493	5	WV	72	3,604	201
IA	123	9,406	108	NY	3,962	92,069	5,651	WI	292	20,906	2,589
KS	136	10,510	18	NC	1,521	41,045	96	WY	18	1,963	3

− Represents zero. NA Not available. [1] Total number of HIV diagnoses reported to the Division of HIV/AIDS Prevention, National Center for HIV/AIDS, Viral Hepatitis, STD, and TB Prevention (NCIRD), as of December 31, 2009. [2] As of May 7, 2010.

Source: Centers for Disease Control and Prevention, Summary of Notifiable Diseases, United States, 2009, *Morbidity and Mortality Weekly Report*, Vol. 58, No. 53, 2011. See also <http://www.cdc.gov/mmwr/mmwr_nd/index.html>.

Health and Nutrition 125

Table 186. Estimated Numbers of AIDS Diagnoses Among Adults and Adolescents by Sex and Transmission Category: 2006 to 2009

[All data are provisional. Data are included for 50 states, the District of Columbia, Puerto Rico, the U.S. Virgin Islands, Guam, and the U.S. Pacific Islands. Estimated numbers resulted from statistical adjustment that accounted for reporting delays and missing risk-factor information, but not for incomplete reporting. Acquired immunodeficiency syndrome (AIDS) is a specific group of diseases or conditions which are indicative of severe immunosuppression related to infection with the human immunodeficiency virus (HIV). Data are subject to retrospective changes and may differ from those data in Table 184. For information on HIV death rates, go to Table 129]

Transmission category	2006	2007	2008	2009	Cumulative through 2009 [1]
Persons 13 years old and over, total [2]	**36,987**	**36,213**	**35,512**	**34,980**	**1,132,836**
Males, total	**27,067**	**26,435**	**26,175**	**26,102**	**903,661**
Male-to-male sexual contact	16,665	16,680	16,637	17,171	535,570
Injection drug use	4,126	3,744	3,554	3,207	199,565
Male-to-male sexual contact and injection drug use	1,994	1,841	1,729	1,608	79,693
Heterosexual contact [3]	4,080	4,004	4,066	3,956	75,901
Other [4]	202	167	190	159	12,931
Females, total	**9,920**	**9,777**	**9,337**	**8,879**	**229,173**
Injection drug use	2,553	2,453	2,192	1,982	90,102
Heterosexual contact [3]	7,172	7,139	7,007	6,740	131,886
Other [4]	195	185	137	157	7,185

[1] From the beginning of the epidemic through 2009. [2] Because column totals for estimated numbers were calculated independently of the values for the subpopulations, the values in each column may not sum to the column total. [3] Heterosexual contact with a person known to have, or to be at high risk for, HIV infection. [4] Includes hemophilia, blood transfusion, perinatal exposure, and risk factor not reported or not identified.

Source: U.S. Centers for Disease Control and Prevention, Atlanta, GA, *HIV Surveillance Report, 2009*, Vol. 21, <http://www.cdc.gov/hiv/surveillance/resources/reports/2009report>.

Table 187. Estimated Numbers of Persons Living With an AIDS Diagnosis by Selected Characteristics: 2000 to 2008

[See headnote, Table 186]

Age and characteristic	2000	2005	2006	2007	2008
Total [1,2]	**323,679**	**432,846**	**452,235**	**471,749**	**490,696**
AGE AS OF END OF YEAR					
Less than 13 years old	2,954	1,506	1,211	942	720
13 and 14 years old	528	811	766	700	624
15 to 24 years old	5,158	7,806	8,281	8,873	9,521
25 to 34 years old	56,129	45,923	45,070	44,904	45,509
35 to 44 years old	146,206	164,551	161,547	156,302	149,198
45 to 54 years old	85,474	149,284	162,424	175,766	188,896
55 to 64 years old	21,717	50,376	58,267	67,048	76,362
65 years old and over	5,513	12,589	14,669	17,213	19,865
RACE/ETHNICITY					
American Indian/Alaska Native	1,035	1,506	1,571	1,635	1,733
Asian [3]	2,293	3,777	4,095	4,472	4,883
Black/African American	131,826	183,083	191,618	200,281	209,175
Hispanic/Latino [4]	66,271	90,836	95,532	100,344	104,791
Native Hawaiian/Other Pacific Islander	174	331	374	418	449
White	118,189	147,585	153,055	158,383	163,286
Multiple races	3,719	5,566	5,831	6,056	6,222
Transmission category:					
MALE ADULT/ADOLESCENT					
Males 13 years old and over, total	251,286	330,239	344,327	358,519	372,528
Male-to-male sexual contact	143,594	196,973	207,449	218,049	228,727
Injection drug use	58,437	65,366	66,042	66,741	67,287
Male-to-male sexual contact and injection drug use	25,635	30,289	30,831	31,368	31,822
Heterosexual contact [5]	20,922	34,563	36,898	39,209	41,467
Other [6]	2,698	3,048	3,106	3,151	3,224
FEMALE ADULT/ADOLESCENT					
Females 13 years old and over, total	68,423	98,500	103,819	109,164	114,123
Injection drug use	28,644	34,207	34,872	35,547	35,981
Heterosexual contact [5]	38,269	62,252	66,803	71,364	75,831
Other [6]	1,510	2,041	2,144	2,252	2,311
(CHILD LESS THAN 13 YEARS OLD AT DIAGNOSIS)					
Total	3,971	4,107	4,088	4,064	4,043
Perinatal	3,756	3,889	3,875	3,857	3,835
Other [6]	215	218	213	207	208

[1] Total numbers include persons of unknown race/ethnicity. [2] Because column totals were calculated independently of the values for the subpopulations, the values in each column may not sum to the column total. [3] Includes Asian/Pacific Islander legacy cases. [4] Hispanics/Latinos can be of any race. [5] Heterosexual contact with a person known to have, or to be at high risk for, HIV infection. [6] Includes hemophilia, blood transfusion, perinatal exposure, and risk factor not reported or not identified.

Source: U.S. Centers for Disease Control and Prevention, Atlanta, GA, *HIV Surveillance Report, 2009*, Vol. 21, <http://www.cdc.gov/hiv/surveillance/resources/reports/2009report>.

Table 188. Learning Disability or Attention Deficit Hyperactivity Disorder for Children 3 to 17 Years of Age by Selected Characteristics: 2009

[In thousands, except percent (61,638 represents 61,638,000). Learning disability is based on the question, "Has a representative from a school or a health professional ever told you that (child's name) had a learning disability?" Attention Deficit Hyperactivity Disorder is based on the question, "Has a doctor or health professional ever told you that (child's name) had Attention Hyperactivity Disorder or Attention Deficit Disorder?"]

| Selected characteristic | Total | Ever told had— | | | |
| | | Learning disability | | Attention deficit hyperactivity disorder | |
		Number [1]	Percent [2]	Number [1]	Percent [2]
Total [3]	**61,638**	**5,059**	**8.2**	**5,288**	**8.6**
SEX [4]					
Male	31,356	3,321	10.6	3,689	11.8
Female	30,281	1,738	5.8	1,599	5.3
AGE					
3 to 4 years old	8,776	245	2.8	[6] 133	[6] 1.5
5 to 11 years old	27,943	2,120	7.6	2,121	7.6
12 to 17 years old	24,918	2,695	10.8	3,035	12.2
RACE					
Race Alone [4, 5]	59,450	4,771	8.1	5,012	8.5
White	46,717	3,759	8.1	4,057	8.7
Black or African American	9,232	863	9.3	904	9.8
American Indian or Alaska Native	683	(B)	[6] 11	(B)	(B)
Asian	2,588	78	3.0	[6] 21	[6] 0.8
Native Hawaiian or Other Pacific Islander	230	(B)	(B)	(B)	(B)
Two or more races [4, 7]	2,188	289	13.9	277	13.4
Black or African American and White	1,019	[6] 147	[6] 14.8	[6] 158	16.8
American Indian or Alaska Native and White	441	[6] 104	21.7	[6] 74	[6] 16.1
HISPANIC ORIGIN AND RACE [4, 8]					
Hispanic or Latino	13,308	940	7.3	659	5.1
Mexican or Mexican American	9,279	571	6.4	395	4.4
Not Hispanic or Latino	48,329	4,119	8.5	4,629	9.5
White, single race	34,724	2,963	8.5	3,460	9.9
Black or African American, single race	8,653	793	9.1	857	10.0

B Base figure too small to meet statistical standards for reliability of a derived figure. [1] Unknowns for the columns are not included in the frequencies, but they are included in the "Total" column. [2] Unknowns for the column variables are not included in the denominators when calculating percentages. [3] Includes other races not shown separately. [4] Percents are age-adjusted to the 2000 projected U.S. standard population using age groups 3–4 years, 5–11 years, and 12–17 years. [5] Refers to persons who indicated only a single race group. [6] Figures do not meet standard of reliability or precision. [7] Refers to all persons who indicated more than one race group. [8] Persons of Hispanic or Latino origin may be any race.

Source: National Center for Health Statistics, *Summary Health Statistics for U.S. Children: National Health Interview Survey, 2009*, Vital and Health Statistics, Series 10, Number 247, 2010. See also <http://www.cdc.gov/nchs/data/series/sr_10/sr10_247 .pdf>.

Table 189. Children and Youth With Disabilities Served by Selected Programs: 1995 to 2009

[In thousands (5,078.8 represents 5,078,800). As of fall. For children and youth aged 6 to 21 served under the Individuals with Disabilities Education Act (IDEA) Part B. Includes outlying areas]

Disability	1995	2000	2004	2005	2006	2007	2008	2009
Total	**5,078.8**	**5,773.9**	**6,116.4**	**6,113.5**	**6,085.6**	**5,999.2**	**5,889.8**	**5,882.2**
Specific learning disabilities	2,601.8	2,881.6	2,839.3	2,782.8	2,711.8	2,616.3	2,525.9	2,486.4
Speech or language impairments	1,026.9	1,093.4	1,149.6	1,156.9	1,162.1	1,151.9	1,122.0	1,107.4
Mental retardation	585.6	613.4	567.6	546.0	523.5	497.5	476.1	461.3
Emotional disturbance	439.2	474.3	484.5	472.5	458.8	439.7	418.1	405.5
Multiple disabilities	94.5	122.9	133.4	134.0	133.8	132.5	124.1	124.5
Hearing impairments	68.0	70.8	72.6	72.4	72.8	72.0	70.8	70.7
Orthopedic impairments	63.2	73.0	65.4	63.1	62.0	60.5	62.4	58.0
Other health impairments	134.2	294.0	512.2	561.6	600.4	630.7	648.4	679.0
Visual impairments	25.5	26.0	26.1	26.0	26.5	26.4	25.8	25.8
Autism	29.1	79.6	166.5	193.8	224.6	258.0	292.8	333.2
Deaf-blind	1.4	1.3	1.7	1.6	1.4	1.4	1.7	1.4
Traumatic brain injury	9.6	14.9	23.3	23.5	23.8	23.9	24.9	24.4
Developmental delay [1]	(X)	28.6	74.4	79.1	84.0	88.6	96.9	104.5

X Not applicable. [1] States had the option of reporting children aged 3 to 9 under developmental delay beginning 1997.
Source: U.S. Department of Education, Office of Special Education, <http://www.ideadata.org/index.html>.

Table 190. Children Under 18 Years of Age Receiving Special Education or Early Intervention Services: 2009

[In thousands, except percent (73,994 represents 73,994,000). Receiving special education or early intervention services is based on the question, "Do any of the following (family members under 18 years of age) receive special education or early intervention services?"]

Selected Characteristic	Total	Persons under 18 years who were receiving special education early intervention services	
		Number [1]	Percent [2]
Total [3]	**73,994**	**5,279**	**7.1**
SEX [4]			
Male.........................	37,818	3,494	9.3
Female.......................	36,177	1,786	4.9
AGE			
Under 12 years	49,374	3,204	6.5
12 to 17 years	24,621	2,076	8.4
RACE			
Race Alone [4, 5]	71,350	5,064	7.1
White.......................	55,943	3,998	7.1
Black or African American.....	11,353	863	7.6
American Indian or Alaska Native	708	[6] 68	[6] 9.5
Asian.......................	3,041	130	4.3
Native Hawaiian or Other Pacific Islander	306	(B)	(B)
Two or more races [4, 7].......	2,644	215	8.6
HISPANIC ORIGIN AND RACE [4, 8]			
Hispanic or Latino	16,521	938	5.7
Mexican or Mexican American. ...	11,543	587	5.1
Not Hispanic or Latino.........	57,473	4,342	7.5
White, single race	41,069	3,206	7.8
Black or African American, single race	10,612	794	7.4

B Base figure too small to meet statistical standards for reliability of a derived figure. [1] Unknowns for the columns are not included in the frequencies, but they are included in the "Total" column. [2] Unknowns for the column variables are not included in the denominators when calculating percentages. [3] Includes other races not shown separately. [4] Percents are age-adjusted to the 2000 projected U.S. standard population using two age groups 0-11 years, and 12-17 years. [5] Refers to persons who indicated only a single race group. [6] Figures do not meet standard of reliability or precision. [7] Refers to all persons who indicated more than one race group. [8] Persons of Hispanic or Latino origin may be any race.
Source: National Center for Health Statistics, *Summary Health Statistics for the U.S. Population: National Health Interview Survey, 2009*, Vital and Health Statistics, Series 10, Number 248, 2010. See also <http://www.cdc.gov/nchs/data/series/sr_10/sr10_248.pdf>.

Table 191. Disabilities Tallied by Age Group and by State: 2009

[In thousands (35,992 represents 35,992,000). Based on data from the American Community Survey (ACS). Disability data limited to civilian noninstitutionalized population. People aged 5 to 14 were classified as having a disability if they were reported to have any one of the five limitations: hearing difficulty, vision difficulty, cognitive difficulty, ambulatory difficulty, or self-care difficulty. People aged 15 and over were classified as having a disability if they reported any one of the five limitations listed above or independent living difficulty. Based on a sample and subject to sampling variability. See text, Section 1 and Appendix III]

State	Total	5 to 17 years	18 to 64 years	65 years and over	State	Total	5 to 17 years	18 to 64 years	65 years and over
U.S.	**35,992**	**2,749**	**19,055**	**14,189**	MO.	823	62	454	307
AL	758	57	425	276	MT.	127	8	68	51
AK	79	7	49	23	NE	190	14	96	79
AZ	751	58	380	312	NV	264	22	139	102
AR	489	35	279	175	NH	149	10	76	62
CA	3,618	253	1,851	1,514	NJ	862	68	415	379
CO........	474	37	258	180	NM.	269	16	144	109
CT	359	29	184	146	NY	2,116	150	1,083	882
DE	111	8	59	44	NC.......	1,181	91	646	444
DC........	72	6	42	24	ND.......	72	4	36	32
FL........	2,319	141	1,071	1,107	OH.......	1,513	122	830	560
GA........	1,095	90	620	386	OK.......	563	40	322	201
HI........	130	6	59	65	OR.......	487	37	260	190
ID........	181	13	100	68	PA.......	1,622	131	832	660
IL........	1,279	99	638	542	RI........	126	10	68	48
IN........	794	68	427	299	SC	607	37	330	239
IA........	335	28	168	139	SD.......	88	6	45	38
KS........	336	28	178	130	TN.......	922	59	525	337
KY	710	56	416	238	TX	2,765	260	1,490	1,015
LA	633	54	351	228	UT	243	25	131	87
ME........	209	15	116	78	VT	84	7	46	30
MD........	563	48	294	221	VA.......	830	63	441	326
MA........	725	61	377	286	WA.......	789	55	437	297
MI........	1,313	107	731	476	WV.......	336	16	195	125
MN........	513	43	270	201	WI	598	48	312	238
MS........	455	35	256	165	WY.......	68	5	37	26

Source: U.S. Census Bureau, 2009 American Community Survey, B18101, "Sex by Age by Disability Status," <http://www.factfinder.census.gov/>, accessed February 2011.

Table 192. Children Immunized Against Specified Diseases: 1995 to 2009

[In percent. Covers civilian noninstitutionalized population aged 19 months to 35 months. Based on estimates from the National Immunization Survey. The health care providers of the children are contacted to verify and/or complete vaccination information. Results are based on race/ethnic status of the child]

Vaccination	1995, total	2000, total	2009 [1] Total	White [2]	Black [2]	Hispanic [3]	American Indian/ Alaska Native only [2]	Asian [2]
Diphtheria-tetanus-pertussis (DTP) diphtheria-tetanus:								
3+ doses..........................	95.0	94.0	95.0	95.6	93.3	94.6	94.5	95.9
4+ doses..........................	79.0	82.0	83.9	85.8	78.6	82.9	82.1	86.6
Polio: 3+ doses	88.0	90.0	92.8	93.3	90.9	92.5	92.2	94.0
Measles, mumps, rubella vaccine	90.0	91.0	90.0	90.8	88.2	89.3	94.9	90.7
Hib: 3+ doses [4]	92.0	93.0	92.4	92.3	91.6	92.6	92.5	93.1
Hepatitis B: 3+ doses................	68.0	90.0	92.4	92.3	91.6	92.6	92.5	93.1
Varicella [5]...........................	(NA)	68.0	89.6	89.2	88.2	90.7	89.2	89.5
PCV: 3+ doses [6].....................	(X)	(X)	92.6	93.2	91.5	92.7	94.4	88.5
4+ DTP/3+ polio/1+ MMR/3+ Hib [7]	74.0	76.0	73.4	73.9	68.9	74.7	77.4	73.3
4+ DTP/3+ polio/1+ MMR/3+ Hib/3+ HepB [8]	55.1	72.8	71.9	71.9	67.9	73.9	76.8	72.0

NA Not available. X Not applicable. [1] Children in the first quarter 2009—fourth quarter 2009 National Immunization Survey were born between January 2006 and June 2008. [2] Non-Hispanic. [3] Children of Hispanic origin may be any race. [4] Haemophilus influenzae type B. [5] Data collection for varicella (chicken pox) began in July 1996. [6] PCV = Pneumococcal conjugate vaccine. [7] MMR = Measles, mumps, and rubella. [8] Children are considered immunized with this series.
Source: U.S. Centers for Disease Control and Prevention, Atlanta, GA, National Immunization Program, Data and Statistics, *Immunization Coverage in the U.S.* See also <http://www.cdc.gov/vaccines/stats-surv/imz-coverage.htm#nis>.

Table 193. Asthma Incidence Among Children Under 18 Years of Age by Selected Characteristics: 2009

[In thousands, except percent (73,996 represents 73,996,000). Based on the National Health Interview Survey, a sample survey of the civilian noninstitutionalized population; see Appendix III]

Selected characteristic	Total	Ever told had asthma Number [1]	Ever told had asthma Percent [2]	Still have asthma Number [1]	Still have asthma Percent [2]
Total [3]	**73,996**	**10,196**	**13.8**	**7,111**	**9.6**
SEX [4]					
Male..	37,818	6,210	16.6	4,268	11.4
Female.....................................	36,177	3,986	11.1	2,843	7.9
AGE					
0 to 4 years old	21,134	1,668	7.9	1,332	6.3
5 to 11 years old	27,943	4,246	15.2	2,997	10.7
12 to 17 years old	24,918	4,282	17.2	2,781	11.2
RACE					
Race Alone [4, 5]............................	71,276	9,719	13.8	6,734	9.5
White.....................................	55,807	6,829	12.3	4,544	8.2
Black or African American...................	11,293	2,441	21.9	1,893	17.0
American Indian or Alaska Native	795	75	[6] 10.1	[6] 57	[6] 7.5
Asian	3,023	347	11.3	232	7.6
Native Hawaiian or Other Pacific Islander	358	[6] 27	[6] 11.3	(B)	(B)
Two or more races [4, 7]	2,720	476	18.1	377	14.1
HISPANIC ORIGIN AND RACE [4, 8]					
Hispanic or Latino	16,522	2,051	12.9	1,276	7.9
Mexican or Mexican American.................	11,476	1,153	10.4	757	6.7
Not Hispanic or Latino........................	57,474	8,145	14.2	5,835	10.2
White, single race	40,952	5,056	12.3	3,473	8.4
Black or African American, single race	10,544	2,300	22.1	1,788	17.3

B Figure too small to meet statistical standards for reliability of a derived figure. [1] Unknowns for the columns are not included in the frequencies, but they are included in the "Total" column. [2] Unknowns for the column variables are not included in the denominators when calculating percentages. [3] Includes other races, not shown separately. [4] Estimates are age-adjusted to the 2000 projected U.S. standard population using age groups 0–4 years, 5–11 years, and 12–17 years. [5] Refers to persons who indicated only a single race group. [6] Figures do not meet standard of reliability or precision. [7] Refers to all persons who indicated more than one race group. [8] Persons of Hispanic or Latino origin may be any race or combination of races.
Source: National Center for Health Statistics, Summary Health Statistics for U.S. Children: *National Health Interview Survey, 2009*, Vital and Health Statistics, Series 10, Number 247, 2010. See also <http://www.cdc.gov/nchs/data/series/sr_10/sr10_247 .pdf>.

Table 194. Nursing Homes, Beds, Residents, and Occupancy Rate by State: 2009

[Based on a census of certified nursing facilities]

State	Nursing homes	Beds	Residents	Occupancy rate [1]	State	Nursing homes	Beds	Residents	Occupancy rate [1]
U.S.....	**15,700**	**1,705,808**	**1,401,718**	**82.2**	MO.......	513	55,361	37,588	67.9
AL.......	231	26,854	23,186	86.3	MT.......	90	7,053	5,077	72.0
AK.......	15	716	633	88.4	NE.......	225	16,214	12,627	77.9
AZ.......	135	16,073	11,908	74.1	NV.......	49	5,719	4,699	82.2
AR.......	230	24,413	17,801	72.9	NH.......	80	7,742	6,941	89.7
CA......	1,252	121,699	102,747	84.4	NJ.......	360	51,159	45,788	89.5
CO......	210	19,867	16,288	82.0	NM.......	70	6,760	5,569	82.4
CT......	240	29,306	26,253	89.6	NY.......	640	121,769	109,867	90.2
DE......	46	4,953	4,256	85.9	NC.......	423	44,106	37,587	85.2
DC......	19	2,765	2,531	91.5	ND.......	84	6,339	5,777	91.1
FL......	676	81,887	71,657	87.5	OH.......	961	93,359	80,185	85.9
GA......	360	39,993	34,899	87.3	OK.......	316	29,269	19,209	65.6
HI.......	47	4,241	3,841	90.6	OR.......	137	12,313	7,708	62.6
ID.......	79	6,176	4,419	71.6	PA......	711	88,861	80,562	90.7
IL.......	794	102,123	75,673	74.1	RI.......	86	(NA)	8,040	91.2
IN.......	504	57,450	39,190	68.2	SC.......	177	19,085	17,148	89.9
IA.......	447	33,301	25,814	77.5	SD.......	109	6,900	6,476	93.9
KS......	341	25,732	19,029	74.0	TN......	318	37,185	31,876	85.7
KY......	287	25,996	23,318	89.7	TX......	1,165	128,984	90,534	70.2
LA......	282	35,602	25,077	70.4	UT.......	96	8,027	5,358	66.8
ME......	109	7,113	6,485	91.2	VT.......	40	3,293	2,980	90.5
MD......	231	29,100	25,025	86.0	VA......	281	31,972	28,392	88.8
MA......	429	49,126	43,227	88.0	WA......	233	22,050	18,188	82.5
MI.......	428	47,271	40,306	85.3	WV......	128	10,843	9,613	88.7
MN......	385	32,956	30,073	91.3	WI......	391	36,482	31,619	86.7
MS......	202	18,458	16,294	88.3	WY......	38	2,974	2,380	80.0

NA Not available. [1] Percentage of beds occupied (number of nursing home residents per 100 nursing home beds).
Source: U.S. National Center for Health Statistics, *Health, United States, 2010*. See also <http://www.cdc.gov/nchs/hus.htm>.

Table 195. Insufficient Rest or Sleep by Number of Days and Selected Characteristics: 2008

[In percent. Age-adjusted to 2000 projected U.S. population. Respondents were asked, "During the past 30 days, for about how many days have you felt you did not get enough sleep?"]

Characteristic	Number [1]	Days without enough rest or sleep			
		0 days	1–13 days	14–29 days	30 days
Total.....................	**403,981**	**30.7**	**41.3**	**16.8**	**11.1**
Sex:					
Male...................	152,513	33.6	40.9	15.6	9.9
Female.................	251,468	28.1	41.5	18	12.4
Age:					
18 to 24 years old.....	13,881	23.2	45.5	19.7	11.6
25 to 34 years old.....	38,978	21.8	44.1	20.4	13.8
35 to 44 years old.....	61,350	22.8	45.2	20.1	12.0
45 to 64 years old.....	169,906	30.5	42.4	16.3	10.9
65 years old or over....	119,866	56.7	28.3	7.6	7.4
Race/ethnicity:					
White, non-Hispanic.....	318,694	27.9	42.7	18.2	11.2
Black, non-Hispanic.....	31,513	30.4	40.4	16.0	13.3
Other, non-Hispanic [2].	22,108	35.4	37.2	15.8	11.6
Hispanic [3]............	28,045	38.8	37.7	13.0	10.5
Employment status:					
Employed...............	215,127	28.7	44.2	17.1	9.9
Unemployed............	16,797	32.5	36.7	16.9	13.9
Retired................	106,325	43.8	33.2	13.4	9.5
Unable to work.........	25,956	24.3	28.4	21.6	25.8
Homemaker or student..	38,395	31.3	41.7	15.9	11.1
Education:					
Less than high school...	39,395	37.9	33.6	14.2	14.3
High school or GED [4]..	121,346	33.8	37.3	15.7	13.2
Some college or college graduate.........	242,194	28.0	44.5	17.9	9.6
Marital status:					
Married................	226,418	30.9	42.1	15.9	11.1
Divorced, widowed, or separated.........	119,372	30.4	35.1	18.6	16.0
Member of unmarried couple.............	8,945	28.4	42.8	16.7	12.1
Never married.........	48,016	31.6	41.0	16.7	10.6

[1] Unweighted sample. Categories may not sum to total due to missing responses. [2] Asian, Hawaiian or other Pacific Islander, American Indian/Alaska Native, or multiracial. [3] Persons of Hispanic origin may be any race. [4] General Education Development certificate.
Source: U.S. Centers for Disease Control and Prevention, Atlanta, GA, *Morbidity and Mortality Weekly Report*, Vol. 58, No. 42, 2009. See also <http://www.cdc.gov/mmwr/index2009.html>.

130 Health and Nutrition

Table 196. Persons 18 Years of Age and Over With Selected Diseases and Conditions by Selected Characteristics: 2009

[In thousands (227,371 represents 227,371,000). Based on National Health Interview Survey, a sample survey of the civilian noninstitutionalized population; see Appendix III]

Selected characteristics	Total persons	Persons with selected diseases and conditions					
		Diabetes [1,2]	Ulcers [1]	Kidney disease [3,4]	Liver disease [3]	Arthritis diagnosis [5]	Chronic joint symptoms [5]
Total [6]	**227,371**	**20,490**	**17,665**	**4,483**	**3,287**	**52,107**	**64,929**
SEX							
Male	109,844	10,447	7,903	2,142	1,651	20,775	29,071
Female	117,527	10,043	9,762	2,342	1,637	31,332	35,858
AGE							
18 to 44 years	110,337	3,234	5,242	1,053	901	8,963	18,476
45 to 64 years	79,195	9,886	7,711	1,551	1,832	23,844	29,155
65 to 74 years	20,597	4,107	2,691	761	337	9,974	8,883
75 years and over	17,242	3,263	2,020	1,118	217	9,326	8,415
RACE							
Race alone [7]	224,290	20,148	17,208	4,398	3,181	51,335	63,747
White	183,739	15,894	14,762	3,639	2,805	43,929	54,751
Black or African American	27,374	3,269	1,746	617	250	5,938	6,871
American Indian or Alaska Native	1,856	174	148	[8] 43	(B)	329	561
Asian	10,763	779	527	[8] 98	118	1,098	1,462
Native Hawaiian or other Pacific Islander	558	[8] 33	(B)	–	–	[8] 41	[8] 102
Two or more races [9]	3,082	342	457	[8] 85	106	771	1,183
HISPANIC ORIGIN [10]							
Hispanic or Latino	31,312	2,879	1,605	623	557	3,793	5,784
Mexican or Mexican American	19,687	1,865	1,017	340	331	2,159	3,538

– Represents zero. B Figure too small to meet statistical standards for reliability of a derived figure. [1] Respondents were asked if they had ever been told by a health professional that they had an ulcer or diabetes. A person may be represented in more than one column. [2] Excludes borderline diabetes. [3] Respondents were asked if they had been told in the last 12 months by a health professional that they had weak or failing kidneys or any kind of liver condition. [4] Excludes kidney stones, bladder infections, or incontinence. [5] Respondents were asked if they had ever been told by a health professional that they had some form of arthritis, rheumatoid arthritis, gout, lupus or fibromyalgia. Those that answered "yes" were classified as having an arthritis diagnosis. Respondents with joint symptoms (excluding back and neck) that began more than 3 months prior to interview were classified as having chronic joint symptoms. [6] Total includes other races not shown separately. [7] Refers to persons who indicated only a single race group. [8] Figures do not meet standard of reliability or precision. [9] Refers to all persons who indicated more than one race group. [10] Persons of Hispanic or Latino origin may be of any race or combination of races.

Source: National Center for Health Statistics, *Summary Health Statistics for U.S. Adults: National Health Interview Survey, 2009*, Vital and Health Statistics, Series 10, Number 249, 2010, <http://www.cdc.gov/nchs/data/series/sr_10/sr10_249.pdf>.

Table 197. Persons 18 Years of Age and Over With Selected Circulatory Diseases by Selected Characteristics: 2009

[In thousands (227,371 represents 227,371,000). In separate questions, respondents were asked if they had ever been told by a doctor or other health professional that they had: hypertension (or high blood pressure); coronary heart disease, angina (or angina pectoris); heart attack (or myocardial infarction); any other heart condition or disease not already mentioned; or a stroke. A person may be represented in more than one column. Based on National Health Interview Survey, a sample survey of the civilian noninstitutionalized population; see Appendix III]

Characteristic	Total persons	Selected circulatory diseases			
		Heart disease		Hypertension [3]	Stroke
		All types [1]	Coronary [2]		
Total [4]	**227,371**	**26,845**	**14,740**	**56,582**	**6,011**
SEX					
Male	109,844	14,185	8,909	26,935	2,678
Female	117,527	12,659	5,832	29,647	3,333
AGE					
18 to 44 years	110,337	4,885	1,258	9,558	627
45 to 64 years	79,195	10,323	5,683	25,755	1,992
65 to 74 years	20,597	5,299	3,445	11,081	1,317
75 years and over	17,242	6,338	4,354	10,188	2,076
RACE					
Race alone [5]	224,290	26,450	14,521	55,800	5,936
White	183,739	22,925	12,478	45,178	4,923
Black or African American	27,374	2,825	1,637	8,283	901
American Indian or Alaska Native	1,856	[6] 115	[6] 59	366	(B)
Asian	10,763	579	347	1,892	106
Native Hawaiian or Other Pacific Islander	558	(B)	–	[6] 81	–
Two or more races [7]	3,082	395	219	782	[6] 75
HISPANIC ORIGIN [8]					
Hispanic or Latino	31,312	1,947	1,188	5,088	418
Mexican or Mexican American	19,687	1,110	688	2,957	268

B Figure too small to meet statistical standards for reliability of a derived figure. [1] Heart disease includes coronary heart disease, angina pectoris, heart attack, or any other heart condition or disease. [2] Coronary heart disease includes coronary heart disease, angina pectoris, or heart attack. [3] Persons had to have been told on two or more different visits that they had hypertension, or high blood pressure, to be classified as hypertensive. [4] Includes other races not shown separately. [5] Refers to persons who indicated only a single race group. [6] Figures do not meet standard of reliability or precision. [7] Refers to all persons who indicated more than one race group. [8] Persons of Hispanic or Latino origin may be any race or combination of races.

Source: National Center for Health Statistics, *Summary Health Statistics for the U.S. Population: National Health Interview Survey*, 2009, Vital and Health Statistics, Series 10, Number 249, 2010. See also <http://www.cdc.gov/nchs/data/series/sr_10/sr10_249.pdf>.

Table 198. Selected Respiratory Diseases Among Persons 18 Years of Age and Over by Selected Characteristics: 2009

[In thousands (227,371 represents 227,371,000). Respondents were asked in two separate questions if they had ever been told by a doctor or other health professional that they had emphysema or asthma. Respondents who had been told they had asthma were asked if they still had asthma. Respondents were asked in three separate questions if they had been told by a doctor or other health professional in the past 12 months that they had hay fever, sinusitis, or bronchitis. Based on the National Health Interview Survey, a sample survey of the civilian noninstitutionalized population; see Appendix III]

Selected characteristic	Total persons	Emphy-sema	Asthma Ever	Asthma Still	Hay fever	Sinusitis	Chronic bronchitis
Total [2]	**227,371**	**4,895**	**29,734**	**17,456**	**17,738**	**29,305**	**9,908**
SEX							
Male.	109,844	2,578	12,311	6,058	7,546	10,555	3,189
Female.	117,527	2,317	17,423	11,398	10,192	18,750	6,718
AGE							
18 to 44 years	110,337	369	15,743	8,368	7,106	11,342	3,093
45 to 64 years	79,195	2,065	9,706	6,182	7,932	12,792	4,411
65 to 74 years	20,597	1,194	2,466	1,720	1,629	3,028	1,329
75 years and over	17,242	1,268	1,819	1,186	1,072	2,142	1,074
RACE							
Race alone [3]	224,290	4,825	29,056	17,061	17,406	28,819	9,750
White	183,739	4,357	23,880	13,990	15,061	24,447	8,386
Black or African American.	27,374	360	3,854	2,380	1,551	3,513	1,082
American Indian or Alaska Native	1,856	(B)	275	[4] 177	[4] 104	155	[4] 78
Asian	10,763	[4] 59	968	490	670	694	184
Native Hawaiian or other Pacific Islander	558	(B)	(B)	[4] 25	(B)	(B)	(B)
Two or more races [5].	3,082	[4] 70	678	394	332	486	158
HISPANIC ORIGIN AND RACE [6]							
Hispanic or Latino	31,312	200	3,225	1,721	1,648	2,584	820
Mexican or Mexican American.	19,687	107	1,557	826	980	1,561	362
Not Hispanic or Latino.	196,059	4,696	26,509	15,735	16,090	26,721	9,088
White, single race	155,185	4,173	21,035	12,484	13,532	22,123	7,647
Black or African American, single race	26,213	350	3,675	2,281	1,497	3,393	1,046

B Figure too small to meet statistical standards for reliability of a derived figure. [1] A person may be represented in more than one column. [2] Total includes other races not shown separately. [3] Refers to persons who indicated only a single race group. [4] Figure does not meet standard of reliability or precision. [5] Refers to all persons who indicated more than one race group. [6] Persons of Hispanic or Latino origin may be any race or combination of races.

Source: National Center for Health Statistics, *Summary Health Statistics for the U.S. Population: National Health Interview Survey, 2009*, Vital and Health Statistics, Series 10, Number 249, 2010. See also <http://www.cdc.gov/nchs/data/series /sr_10/sr10_249.pdf>.

Table 199. Persons 18 Years of Age and Over With Migraines and Pains in the Neck, Lower Back, Face, or Jaw by Selected Characteristics: 2009

[In thousands (227,371 represents 227,371,000). Based on National Health Interview Survey, a sample survey of the civilian noninstitutionalized population, Appendix III]

Selected characteristic	Total persons	Migraine or severe headache [2]	Pain in neck [3]	Pain in lower back [3]	Pain in face or jaw [3]
Total [4]	**227,371**	**35,973**	**34,954**	**64,810**	**11,501**
SEX					
Male.	109,844	11,098	14,095	28,842	3,654
Female.	117,527	24,875	20,859	35,968	7,847
AGE					
18 to 44 years	110,337	21,706	14,306	26,973	5,752
45 to 64 years	79,195	11,893	15,147	25,795	4,400
65 to 74 years	20,597	1,415	3,136	6,198	799
75 years and over	17,242	959	2,365	5,843	550
RACE					
Race alone [5]	224,290	35,295	34,355	63,689	11,213
White	183,739	29,118	29,430	53,817	9,599
Black or African American.	27,374	4,811	3,569	7,286	1,115
American Indian or Alaska Native	1,856	429	363	566	171
Asian	10,763	902	935	1,879	303
Native Hawaiian or other Pacific Islander	558	[6] 33	[6] 57	[6] 141	(B)
Two or more races [7].	3,082	678	598	1,121	288
HISPANIC ORIGIN AND RACE [8]					
Hispanic or Latino	31,312	5,362	4,341	7,905	1,345
Mexican or Mexican American.	19,687	3,297	2,446	4,319	818
Not Hispanic or Latino.	196,059	30,611	30,613	56,905	10,156
White, single race	155,185	24,379	25,497	46,665	8,423
Black or African American, single race	26,213	4,546	3,426	6,982	1,065

B Figure to small to meet statistical standards for reliability of a derived figure. [1] A person may be represented in more than one column. [2] Respondents were asked, "During the past 3 months, did you have a severe headache or migraine?" Respondents were instructed to report pain that had lasted a whole day or more and, conversely, not to report fleeting or minor aches or pains. [3] Respondents were asked, "During the past 3 months, did you have a neck pain; or low back pain; or facial ache or pain in the jaw muscles or the joint in front of the ear?" Respondents were instructed to report pain that had lasted a whole day or more and, conversely, not to report fleeting or minor aches or pains. [4] Total includes other races not shown separately. [5] Refers to persons who indicated only a single race group. [6] Figure does not meet standard of reliability or precision. [7] Refers to all persons who indicated more than one race group. [8] Persons of Hispanic or Latino origin may be any race or combination of races.

Source: National Center for Health Statistics, *Summary Health Statistics for the U.S. Adults: National Health Interview Survey, 2009*, Vital and Health Statistics, Series 10, Number 249, 2010. See also <http://www.cdc.gov/nchs/data/series /sr_10/sr10_249.pdf>.

Table 200. Injury and Poisoning Episodes and Conditions by Age and Sex: 2009

[36,836 represents 36,836,000. Covers all medically attended injuries and poisonings occurring during the 5–week period prior to the survey interview. Age adjustment is used to adjust for differences in the age distribution of populations being compared. There may be more than one condition per episode. Based on the National Health Interview Survey, a sample survey of the civilian noninstitutionalized population; see Appendix III]

External cause and nature of injury	Both sexes								Male	Female
	Total	Total, age-adjusted [1]	Under 12 years	12 to 21 years	22 to 44 years	45 to 64 years	65 years and over		Male	Female
EPISODES										
Number (1,000)	36,836	(X)	4,576	6,829	10,304	9,599	5,528		17,999	18,837
Annual rate per 1,000 population, total [2]	122.2	122.0	92.7	165.1	110.1	121.4	145.5		121.9	122.6
Fall	45.8	45.2	51.2	48.4	24.5	48.7	82.6		38.2	53.2
Struck by or against a person or an object	16.5	16.8	12.9	32.5	17.9	10.9	[4] 11.9		19.1	14.0
Transportation [3]	13.4	13.4	[4] 7.2	23.4	13.1	13.0	[4] 11.8		13.4	13.4
Overexertion	15.3	15.2	[4] 2.1	[4] 13.4	22.9	18.3	[4] 9.5		15.6	15.0
Cutting, piercing instruments . .	8.3	8.5	[4] 5.0	[4] 14.4	10.8	[4] 7.0	[4] 3.1		12.8	[4] 4.1
Poisoning [5]	2.4	2.3	[4] 3.5	[4] 4.4	[4] 0.8	[4] 2.5	[4] 2.4		[4] 2.6	[4] 2.2
CONDITIONS										
Annual rate per 1,000 population, total [2]	166.9	166.1	116.8	203.6	153.3	175.6	207.4		156.0	177.4
Sprains/strains	47.1	46.7	14.7	60.5	54.6	55.1	39.1		43.1	50.9
Open wounds	20.2	20.6	34.2	27.0	18.5	12.7	14.7		28.7	12.1
Fractures	24.1	24.1	20.0	38.6	15.0	21.3	42.2		21.4	26.8
Contusions	27.0	26.5	14.5	24.8	19.5	33.8	50.4		17.6	36.1

X Not applicable. [1] Data were age-adjusted using the 2000 standard population using age groups: under 12 years, 12–21 years, 22–44 years, 45–64 years, and 65 years and over. [2] Includes other items not shown separately. [3] Includes the categories "Motor vehicle traffic"; "Pedal cycle, other"; "Pedestrian, other"; and "Transport, other." [4] Figure does not meet standard of reliability or precision. [5] Poisoning episodes are assumed to have a single condition resulting from the episode.

Source: U.S. National Center for Health Statistics, Vital and Health Statistics, unpublished data.

Table 201. Injuries Associated With Selected Consumer Products: 2009

[Estimates calculated from a representative sample of hospitals with emergency treatment departments in the United States. Data are estimates of the number of emergency room treated cases nationwide associated with various products. Product involvement does not necessarily mean the product caused the accident. Products were selected from the U.S. Consumer Product Safety Commission's National Electronic Injury Surveillance System (NEISS)]

Product	Number	Product	Number
Home workshop equipment:		Floors or flooring materials	1,334,455
Saws (hand or power)	86,617	Other doors [2]	322,951
Hammers	32,933	Home entertainment equipment:	
Household packaging and containers:		Televisions	68,486
Household containers and packaging	224,227	Computers (equip. & electronic games)	32,434
Bottles and jars	75,340	Personal use items:	
Housewares:		Footwear	169,208
Knives	409,590	Wheelchairs	129,001
Tableware and flatware	97,389	Crutches, canes, walkers	108,751
Drinking glasses	81,552	Jewelry	83,535
Home furnishing		Yard and garden equipment:	
Beds	613,870	Lawn mowers	86, 272
Chairs	352,691	Sports and recreation equipment:	
Tables [1]	344,036	Bicycles	544,470
Household cabinets, racks, and shelves . . .	289,311	Skateboards	144,416
Bathtubs and showers	274,109	Trampolines	97,908
Home structures, construction:		Minibikes or trail bikes	74,913
Stairs or steps	1,266,319	Swings or swing sets	66,018

[1] Excludes baby-changing and television tables or stands. [2] Excludes glass doors and garage doors.

Source: National Safety Council, Itasca, IL, *Injury Facts*, annual (copyright). See also <http://www.nsc.org/Pages/Home.aspx>.

Table 202. Costs of Unintentional Injuries: 2009

[693.5 represents $693,500,000,000. Covers costs of deaths or disabling injuries together with vehicle accidents and fires]

Cost	Amount (bil. dol.)					Percent distribution				
	Total [1]	Motor vehicle	Work	Home	Other	Total [1]	Motor vehicle	Work	Home	Other
Total	**693.5**	**244.7**	**168.9**	**192.2**	**108.2**	**100.0**	**100.0**	**100.0**	**100.0**	**100.0**
Wage and productivity losses [2]	357.4	83.1	82.4	126.4	69.2	51.5	34.0	48.8	65.8	64.0
Medical expense	147.3	41.9	38.3	42.2	27.0	21.2	17.1	22.7	22.0	25.0
Administrative expenses [3]	117.2	78.3	33.1	11.1	7.0	16.9	32.0	19.6	5.8	6.5
Motor vehicle damage	39.4	39.4	2.0	(NA)	(NA)	5.7	16.1	1.2	(NA)	(NA)
Employer uninsured cost [4]	19.7	2.0	10.3	4.6	3.2	2.8	0.8	6.1	2.4	3.0
Fire loss	12.5	(NA)	2.8	7.9	1.8	1.8	(NA)	1.7	4.1	1.7

NA Not available. [1] Excludes duplication between work and motor vehicle: $20.5 billion in 2009. [2] Actual loss of wages and household production, and the present value of future earnings lost. [3] Home and other costs may include costs of administering medical treatment claims for some motor vehicle injuries filed through health insurance plans. [4] Estimate of the uninsured costs incurred by employers, representing the money value of time lost by noninjured workers.

Source: National Safety Council, Itasca, IL, Injury Facts, annual (copyright). See also <http://www.nsc.org/Pages/Home.aspx>.

Health and Nutrition 133

Table 203. Use of Mammography for Women 40 Years Old and Over by Patient Characteristics: 2000 to 2008

[Percent of women having a mammogram within the past 2 years. Covers civilian noninstitutional population. Based on National Health Interview Survey; see Appendix III]

Characteristic	2000 [1]	2005 [1]	2008 [1]	Characteristic	2000 [1]	2005 [1]	2008 [1]
Total [2]	**70.4**	**66.8**	**67.6**	Years of school completed:			
40 to 49 years old	64.3	63.5	61.5	No high school diploma or GED . . .	57.7	52.8	53.8
50 years old and over	73.6	68.4	70.5	High school diploma or GED.	69.7	64.9	65.2
50 to 64 years old	78.7	71.8	74.2	Some college or more	76.2	72.7	73.4
65 years old and over	67.9	63.8	65.5				
White, non-Hispanic	72.2	68.4	68.7	Poverty status: [4]			
Black, non-Hispanic.	67.9	65.2	68.3	Below poverty	54.8	48.5	51.4
Hispanic origin [3].	61.2	58.8	61.2	At or above poverty	72.1	68.8	(NA)

NA Not available. [1] Adjusted data—data have been reweighted using the 2000 Census population controls. [2] Includes other races not shown separately and unknown education level and poverty status. [3] Persons of Hispanic origin may be any race or combination of races. [4] For explanation of poverty level, see text, Section 13.

Source: U.S. National Center for Health Statistics, *Health, United States, 2010*. See also <http://www.cdc.gov/nchs/hus.htm>.

Table 204. Current Cigarette Smoking: 1990 to 2009

[In percent. Prior to 1992, a current smoker is a person who has smoked at least 100 cigarettes and who now smokes. Beginning 1992, definition includes persons who smoke only "some days." Excludes unknown smoking status. For definition of age adjustment, see text, Section 2. Based on National Health Interview Survey; for details, see Appendix III]

Sex, age, and race	1990 [1]	2000	2005	2009	Sex, age, and race	1990 [1]	2000	2005	2009
Total smokers,					Black, total	32.5	26.2	26.5	23.7
age-adjusted [2]	**25.3**	**23.1**	**20.8**	**20.6**	18 to 24 years	21.3	20.9	21.6	18.9
Male.	28.0	25.2	23.4	23.2	25 to 34 years	33.8	23.2	29.8	24.1
Female.	22.9	21.1	18.3	18.1	35 to 44 years	42.0	30.7	23.3	24.0
					45 to 64 years	36.7	32.2	32.4	28.9
White male.	27.6	25.4	23.3	23.6	65 years and over	21.5	14.2	16.8	14.0
Black male.	32.8	25.7	25.9	23.1	Female, total	22.8	20.9	18.1	17.9
					18 to 24 years	22.5	24.9	20.7	15.6
White female	23.5	22.0	19.1	18.7	25 to 34 years	28.2	22.3	21.5	21.8
Black female	20.8	20.7	17.1	18.5	35 to 44 years	24.8	26.2	21.3	21.2
					45 to 64 years	24.8	21.7	18.8	19.5
Total smokers [3]	**25.5**	**23.2**	**20.9**	**20.6**	65 years and over	11.5	9.3	8.3	9.5
Male, total	28.4	25.6	23.9	23.5	White, total.	23.4	21.4	18.7	18.3
18 to 24 years	26.6	28.1	28.0	28.0	18 to 24 years	25.4	28.5	22.6	16.7
25 to 34 years	31.6	28.9	27.7	27.6	25 to 34 years	28.5	24.9	23.1	22.7
35 to 44 years	34.5	30.2	26.0	25.4	35 to 44 years	25.0	26.6	22.2	22.9
45 to 64 years	29.3	26.4	25.2	24.5	45 to 64 years	25.4	21.4	18.9	19.4
65 years and over	14.6	10.2	8.9	9.5	65 years and over	11.5	9.1	8.4	9.6
White, total.	28.0	25.7	23.6	23.6	Black, total.	21.2	20.8	17.3	18.8
18 to 24 years	27.4	30.4	29.7	30.0	18 to 24 years	[4] 10.0	14.2	14.2	13.3
25 to 34 years	31.6	29.7	27.7	28.4	25 to 34 years	29.1	15.5	16.9	20.1
35 to 44 years	33.5	30.6	26.3	26.3	35 to 44 years	25.5	30.2	19.0	20.0
45 to 64 years	28.7	25.8	24.5	24.0	45 to 64 years	22.6	25.6	21.0	22.7
65 years and over	13.7	9.8	7.9	9.3	65 years and over	11.1	10.2	10.0	11.5

[1] Data prior to 1997 are not strictly comparable with data for later years due to the 1997 questionnaire redesign. [2] Data are age-adjusted to the year 2000 standard using five age groups: 18–24 years, 25–34 years, 35–44 years, 45–64 years, 65 years and over. [3] Crude, not age-adjusted. [4] Figure does not meet standard of reliability or precision.

Source: U.S. National Center for Health Statistics, *Health, United States, 2010*. See also <http://www.cdc.gov/nchs/hus.htm>.

Table 205. Current Cigarette Smoking by Sex and State: 2009

[In percent. Current cigarette smoking is defined as persons 18 years and older who reported having smoked 100 or more cigarettes during their lifetime and who currently smoke every day or some days. Based on the Behavioral Risk Factor Surveillance System, a telephone survey of health behaviors of the civilian, noninstitutionalized U.S. population, 18 years old and over; for details, see source]

State	Total	Male	Female	State	Total	Male	Female	State	Total	Male	Female
U.S. [1] . . .	**20.6**	**23.5**	**17.9**								
AL	22.5	25.7	19.7	KY	25.6	27.1	24.2	ND	18.6	19.3	17.9
AK	20.6	20.7	20.5	LA	22.1	25.1	19.3	OH	20.3	21.2	19.5
AZ	16.1	18.0	14.3	ME	17.3	18.9	15.8	OK	25.5	27.1	24.0
AR	21.5	21.0	21.9	MD	15.2	16.7	13.8	OR	17.9	18.5	17.2
CA	12.9	15.6	10.2	MA	15.0	16.1	14.0	PA	20.2	21.5	19.1
CO	17.1	19.5	14.6	MI	19.6	21.1	18.2	RI	15.1	15.3	14.9
CT	15.4	16.2	14.7	MN	16.8	18.6	14.9	SC	20.4	21.5	19.3
DE	18.3	20.2	16.6	MS	23.3	27.2	19.8	SD	17.5	16.9	18.1
DC	15.3	15.8	14.8	MO	23.1	24.3	21.9	TN	22.0	24.6	19.6
FL	17.1	18.0	16.3	MT	16.8	16.4	17.3	TX	17.9	22.1	13.8
GA	17.7	20.0	15.5	NE	16.7	18.5	15.0	UT	9.8	11.9	7.7
HI	15.4	16.8	13.9	NV	22.0	22.7	21.3	VT	17.1	19.4	15.0
ID	16.3	18.7	13.9	NH	15.8	17.3	14.3	VA	19.0	22.5	15.8
IL	18.6	20.6	16.7	NJ	15.8	17.6	14.2	WA	14.9	16.1	13.8
IN	23.1	24.9	21.5	NM	17.9	19.9	16.1	WV	25.6	27.7	23.6
IA	17.2	19.6	14.8	NY	18.0	19.3	16.8	WI	18.8	20.3	17.3
KS	17.8	18.6	17.1	NC	20.3	23.1	17.7	WY	19.9	20.1	19.7

[1] Represents median value among the states and DC. For definition of median, see Guide to Tabular Presentations.
Source: U.S. Centers for Disease Control and Prevention, *Morbidity and Mortality Weekly Report*, Vol. 59, No. 43, 2010. See also <http://www.cdc.gov/mmwr>.

Table 206. Substance Abuse Treatment Facilities and Clients: 1995 to 2010

[As of October 2 (1995), as of October 1 (1997–2000), as of March 31 (2003–2006), as of March 30 (2007), and as of March 31 (2008–2010). Based on the Uniform Facility Data Set (UFDS)/National Survey of Substance Abuse Treatment Services (N-SSATS) survey, a census of all known facilities that provide substance abuse treatment in the United States and associated jurisdictions. Selected missing data for responding facilities were imputed]

Primary focus	Number	Primary focus	Number	Type of care and type of problem	Number of clients
FACILITIES		CLIENTS		2010, total [1, 2]	1,184,415
1995.	10,746	1995.	1,009,127		
2000.	13,428	2000.	1,000,896	Outpatient rehabilitation.	1,042,496
2004.	13,454	2004.	1,072,251	Outpatient detoxification	13,216
2005.	13,371	2005.	1,081,049	24-hour rehabilitation.	104,905
2006.	13,771	2006.	1,130,881	24-hour detoxification	14,025
2007.	13,648	2007.	1,135,425		
2008.	13,688	2008.	1,192,490	2010, total [1, 2]	1,181,830
2009.	13,513	2009.	1,182,077	Drug only.	461,359
2010, total [2]	13,337	2010, total [2]	1,184,415	Alcohol only.	217,005
Substance abuse treatment services	8,099	Substance abuse treatment services	783,203	Both alcohol & drug.	503,466
Mental health services.	853	Mental health services. . . .	45,105	Total with a drug problem [3]	964,825
General health care.	168	General health care.	15,965		
Both substance abuse and mental health.	4,112	Both substance abuse and mental health.	335,928	Total with an alcohol problem [4]	720,471
Other	105	Other	4,214		

[1] Excludes clients at facilities that did not provide data on type of substance abuse problem treated. [2] Data for 2010 is based on preliminary data and is subject to change. [3] The sum of clients with a drug problem and clients with both diagnoses. [4] The sum of clients with an alcohol problem and clients with both diagnoses.

Source: U.S. Substance Abuse and Mental Health Services Administration, Uniform Facility Data Set (UFDS),1995–1999, and Center for Behavioral Health Statistics and Quality, Substance Abuse and Mental Health Services Administration, National Survey of Substance Abuse Treatment Services (N-SSATS), 2000–2010, <http://www.samhsa.gov/dataOutcomes/>.

Table 207. Drug Use by Type of Drug and Age Group: 2003 and 2008

[In percent. Data comes from the National Survey on Drug Use and Health (NSDUH). Current users are those who used drugs at least once within month prior to this study. Based on a representative sample of the U.S. population 12 years old and over, including persons living in households and in some group quarters such as dormitories and homeless shelters. Estimates are based on computer-assisted interviews of about 68,000 respondents. Subject to sampling variability; see source]

Age and type of drug	Ever used 2003	Ever used 2008	Current user 2003	Current user 2008	Age and type of drug	Ever used 2003	Ever used 2008	Current user 2003	Current user 2008
12 YEARS OLD AND OVER					**18 TO 25 YEARS OLD**				
Any illicit drug [1]	46.4	47.0	8.2	8.0	Any illicit drug [1]	60.5	56.6	20.3	19.6
Marijuana and hashish	40.6	41.0	6.2	6.1	Marijuana and hashish	53.9	50.4	17.0	16.5
Cocaine.	14.7	14.7	1.0	0.7	Cocaine.	15.0	14.4	2.2	1.5
Crack.	3.3	3.4	0.3	0.1	Hallucinogens	23.3	17.7	1.7	1.7
Heroin	1.6	1.5	0.1	0.1	Inhalants	14.9	10.4	0.4	0.3
Hallucinogens	14.5	14.4	0.4	0.4	Any psychotherapeutic [2, 3]	29.0	29.2	6.0	5.9
LSD	10.3	9.4	(NA)	0.1	Alcohol.	87.1	85.6	61.4	61.2
Ecstasy	4.6	5.2	0.2	0.2	"Binge" alcohol use [4]	(NA)	(NA)	41.6	41.8
Inhalants	9.7	8.9	0.2	0.3	Cigarettes	70.2	64.2	40.2	35.7
Any psychotherapeutic [2, 3]	20.1	20.8	2.7	2.5	Smokeless tobacco	22.0	20.3	4.7	5.4
Pain relievers.	13.1	14.0	2.0	1.9	Cigars	45.2	41.4	11.4	11.3
Tranquilizers.	8.5	8.6	0.8	0.7	**26 TO 34 YEARS OLD**				
Stimulants [3]	8.8	8.5	0.5	0.4	Any illicit drug [1]	57.3	58.2	10.7	11.2
Methamphetamine [3].	6.4	5.0	0.3	0.1	Marijuana and hashish	51.0	51.3	8.4	8.8
Sedatives.	4.0	3.6	0.1	0.1	Cocaine.	18.1	16.7	1.5	1.5
Alcohol.	83.1	82.2	50.1	51.6	Hallucinogens	20.3	22.2	0.5	0.6
"Binge" alcohol use [4]	(NA)	(NA)	22.6	23.3	Inhalants	13.6	12.8	–	0.1
Cigarettes	68.7	65.1	25.4	23.9	Any psychotherapeutic [2, 3]	24.7	28.0	3.4	3.2
Smokeless tobacco	19.4	18.4	3.3	3.5	**35 YEARS OLD AND OVER**				
Cigars	37.1	35.8	5.4	5.3	Any illicit drug [1]	43.4	45.7	4.4	4.7
Pipe tobacco	16.9	14.6	0.7	0.8	Marijuana and hashish	38.9	40.6	3.0	3.2
12 TO 17 YEARS OLD					Cocaine.	15.9	16.4	0.6	0.4
Any illicit drug [1]	30.5	26.2	11.2	9.3	Hallucinogens	12.8	13.6	0.1	0.0
Marijuana and hashish	19.6	16.5	7.9	6.7	Inhalants	7.4	7.7	0.1	0.1
Cocaine.	2.6	1.9	0.6	0.4	Any psychotherapeutic [2, 3]	18.3	18.9	1.5	1.6
Hallucinogens	5.0	3.9	1.0	1.0	**26 YEARS OLD AND OVER**				
Inhalants	10.7	9.3	1.3	1.1	Alcohol.	88.0	87.3	52.5	54.8
Any psychotherapeutic [2, 3]	13.4	11.1	4.0	2.9	"Binge" alcohol use [4]	(NA)	(NA)	21.0	22.1
Alcohol.	42.9	38.3	17.7	14.6	Cigarettes	73.6	70.7	24.7	23.8
"Binge" alcohol use [4]	(NA)	(NA)	10.6	8.8	Smokeless tobacco	20.6	19.5	3.2	3.3
Cigarettes	31.0	22.9	12.2	9.1	Cigars	38.7	37.8	4.5	4.4
Smokeless tobacco	7.6	7.2	2.0	2.2					
Cigars	15.1	12.4	4.5	3.8					

NA Not available. – Represents or rounds to zero. [1] Illicit drugs include marijuana/hashish, cocaine (including crack), heroin, hallucinogens, inhalants, or prescription-type psychotherapeutics used nonmedically. [2] Nonmedical use of prescription-type psychotherapeutics includes the nonmedical use of pain relievers, tranquilizers, stimulants, or sedatives and does not include over-the-counter drugs. [3] Includes data from new methamphetamine items added in 2006 and 2007. Previous estimates have been adjusted to be comparable with new data and differ from those in reports prior to the 2007 data year. [4] Binge alcohol use is defined as drinking five or more drinks on the same occasion (i.e., at the same time or within a couple of hours of each other) on at least 1 day in the past 30 days.

Source: U.S. Substance Abuse and Mental Health Services Administration, National Survey on Drug Use and Health, 2003 and 2008, <http://oas.samhsa.gov/nhsda.htm>.

Table 208. Estimated Use of Selected Drugs by State: 2007 to 2008

[19,966 represents 19,966,000. Data in this table cover a 2-year period. Data is based on the National Survey on Drug Use and Health (NSDUH). Current users are those persons 12 years old and over who used drugs at least once within month prior to this study. Based on national sample of respondents (see also headnote, Table 207). The state estimates were produced by combining the prevalence rate based on the state sample data and the prevalence rate based on a national regression model applied to local-area county and census block group/tract-level estimates from the state (i.e., a survey-weighted hierarchical Bayes estimation approach). The parameters of the regression model are estimated from the entire national sample. For comparison purposes, the data shown here display estimates for all 50 states and the District of Columbia utilizing the modeled estimates for all 51 areas]

State	Estimated current users (1,000)					Current users as percent of population				
	Any illicit drug [1]	Mari-juana	Any illicit drug other than mari-juana [1]	Ciga-rettes	Binge alcohol [2]	Any illicit drug [1]	Mari-juana	Any illicit drug other than mari-juana [1]	Ciga-rettes	Binge alcohol [2]
U.S. . . .	19,966	14,825	8,917	59,918	57,938	8.0	6.0	3.6	24.1	23.3
AL	258	175	146	1,040	733	6.7	4.6	3.8	27.2	19.2
AK	64	50	21	131	131	11.8	9.2	3.9	24.2	24.2
AZ	463	300	230	1,240	1,202	9.0	5.8	4.5	23.9	23.2
AR	185	127	100	723	503	8.0	5.5	4.3	31.1	21.6
CA	2,715	1,998	1,179	5,794	6,466	9.1	6.7	3.9	19.4	21.6
CO	470	370	183	1,007	1,072	11.7	9.2	4.6	25.1	26.7
CT	240	189	95	638	760	8.2	6.5	3.3	21.9	26.1
DE	66	51	30	189	176	9.1	7.1	4.2	26.4	24.5
DC	61	48	23	136	151	12.1	9.6	4.5	27.0	29.9
FL	1,193	853	535	3,677	3,500	7.8	5.6	3.5	24.0	22.9
GA	560	415	236	2,001	1,671	7.3	5.4	3.1	26.0	21.7
HI	104	71	44	227	241	9.9	6.7	4.2	21.6	23.0
ID	97	69	43	262	228	8.0	5.7	3.5	21.7	18.8
IL	758	574	311	2,667	2,824	7.2	5.4	3.0	25.2	26.7
IN	458	326	219	1,437	1,201	8.8	6.3	4.2	27.6	23.0
IA	102	80	45	588	674	4.1	3.2	1.8	23.7	27.2
KS	153	115	80	572	563	6.8	5.1	3.6	25.3	24.9
KY	295	196	154	1,129	696	8.4	5.6	4.4	32.2	19.9
LA	253	177	139	936	840	7.2	5.0	3.9	26.5	23.8
ME	102	92	34	297	244	9.1	8.2	3.0	26.4	21.7
MD	339	249	150	998	1,030	7.3	5.4	3.2	21.5	22.1
MA	484	388	184	1,087	1,404	8.9	7.1	3.4	19.9	25.7
MI	748	587	298	2,130	2,040	9.0	7.0	3.6	25.5	24.4
MN	356	307	133	1,087	1,297	8.2	7.1	3.1	25.2	30.1
MS	151	103	73	595	467	6.4	4.4	3.1	25.3	19.9
MO	358	264	188	1,321	1,154	7.4	5.4	3.9	27.2	23.8
MT	81	67	31	188	215	10.0	8.3	3.9	23.3	26.8
NE	93	72	42	357	367	6.4	5.0	2.9	24.7	25.3
NV	196	130	93	560	508	9.4	6.2	4.5	26.6	24.2
NH	119	100	40	249	289	10.7	9.0	3.6	22.3	25.9
NJ	464	350	197	1,614	1,645	6.4	4.8	2.7	22.4	22.8
NM	141	99	57	365	353	8.7	6.2	3.6	22.7	21.9
NY	1,469	1,130	576	3,463	3,784	9.0	6.9	3.5	21.3	23.3
NC	576	446	261	1,976	1,593	7.8	6.0	3.5	26.6	21.4
ND	31	27	12	133	173	5.9	5.0	2.3	25.1	32.6
OH	724	557	314	2,678	2,430	7.6	5.9	3.3	28.1	25.5
OK	237	140	142	802	633	8.1	4.8	4.9	27.3	21.6
OR	385	271	174	769	739	12.2	8.6	5.5	24.4	23.4
PA	685	499	325	2,592	2,539	6.6	4.8	3.1	24.8	24.3
RI	119	97	52	220	247	13.3	10.9	5.9	24.7	27.7
SC	244	181	113	992	782	6.7	5.0	3.1	27.3	21.5
SD	41	34	15	160	186	6.3	5.2	2.3	24.6	28.5
TN	421	298	219	1,448	958	8.2	5.8	4.3	28.3	18.7
TX	1,194	845	629	4,465	4,427	6.3	4.4	3.3	23.4	23.2
UT	130	89	65	320	315	6.2	4.3	3.1	15.3	15.1
VT	62	54	21	120	135	11.6	10.2	4.0	22.5	25.3
VA	462	365	197	1,465	1,492	7.3	5.8	3.1	23.2	23.7
WA	518	399	202	1,224	1,140	9.6	7.4	3.7	22.7	21.1
WV	104	73	58	447	296	6.8	4.8	3.8	29.1	19.3
WI	406	302	194	1,281	1,317	8.7	6.5	4.2	27.4	28.2
WY	30	24	13	119	107	6.8	5.6	3.0	27.3	24.7

[1] Illicit drugs include marijuana/hashish, cocaine (including crack), heroin, hallucinogens, inhalants, or prescription-type psychotherapeutics used nonmedically. [2] Binge alcohol use is defined as drinking five or more drinks on the same occasion (i.e., at the same time or within a couple of hours of each other) on at least 1 day in the past 30 days.

Source: U.S. Substance Abuse and Mental Health Services Administration, *National Survey on Drug Use and Health, 2007 and 2008.* See also <http://www.oas.samhsa.gov/nhsda.htm>.

Table 209. Cumulative Percent Distribution of Population by Height and Sex: 2007 to 2008

[Data are based on National Health and Nutrition Examination Survey (NHANES), a sample of the civilian noninstitutional population. For this survey, the respondent participates in an interview and a physical examination. For persons 20 years old and over. Height was measured without shoes. Based on sample and subject to sampling variability; see source]

Height	Males						Females					
	20–29 years	30–39 years	40–49 years	50–59 years	60–69 years	70–79 years	20–29 years	30–39 years	40–49 years	50–59 years	60–69 years	70–79 years
Percent under—												
4'10"	–	–	–	(B)	–	–	–	¹1.7	–	¹1.0	–	¹3.3
4'11"	–	–	–	(B)	(B)	–	¹2.6	3.1	¹1.6	2.1	¹3.6	8.7
5'	(B)	–	–	(B)	(B)	–	5.7	6.0	5.0	8.0	9.0	16.0
5'1"	(B)	(B)	(B)	(B)	¹0.4	(B)	12.3	11.6	10.8	16.7	14.7	26.0
5'2"	(B)	(B)	(B)	(B)	(B)	(B)	20.8	19.7	19.8	23.3	23.4	36.9
5'3"	(B)	¹3.1	¹1.9	(B)	¹2.3	(B)	30.4	31.3	30.8	36.3	38.4	51.9
5'4"	3.7	¹4.4	3.8	¹4.3	4.4	5.8	43.5	46.6	46.0	50.7	52.8	69.9
5'5"	7.2	6.7	5.6	7.6	7.8	12.8	54.1	61.2	58.0	68.4	66.6	82.8
5'6"	11.6	13.1	9.8	12.2	14.7	23.0	72.4	74.0	72.2	79.7	83.3	89.3
5'7"	20.6	19.6	19.4	18.6	23.7	35.1	82.3	84.9	83.0	88.4	93.3	95.4
5'8"	33.1	32.2	30.3	30.3	37.7	47.7	90.3	91.8	91.2	95.2	97.0	98.4
5'9"	42.2	45.4	40.4	41.2	50.2	60.3	94.1	96.1	94.7	97.3	97.8	99.6
5'10"	58.6	58.1	54.4	54.3	65.2	75.2	97.6	98.9	97.8	98.9	99.6	99.6
5'11"	70.7	69.4	69.6	70.0	75.0	85.8	99.6	98.9	99.4	100.0	99.8	100.0
6'	79.9	78.5	79.1	81.2	84.3	91.0	100.0	99.4	99.5	100.0	99.9	100.0
6'1"	89.0	89.0	87.4	91.6	93.6	94.9	100.0	99.9	99.5	100.0	99.9	100.0
6'2"	94.1	94.0	92.5	93.7	97.8	98.6	100.0	100.0	99.5	100.0	100.0	100.0
6'3"	98.3	95.8	97.7	96.6	99.9	100.0	100.0	100.0	99.5	100.0	100.0	100.0
6'4"	100.0	97.6	99.0	99.5	100.0	100.0	100.0	100.0	99.5	100.0	100.0	100.0
6'5"	100.0	99.4	99.4	99.6	100.0	100.0	100.0	100.0	100.0	100.0	100.0	100.0
6'6"	100.0	99.5	99.9	100.0	100.0	100.0	100.0	100.0	100.0	100.0	100.0	100.0

– Represents zero. B Base figure too small to meet statistical standards of reliability of a derived figure. ¹ Figure does not meet standard for reliability or precision.

Source: U.S. National Center for Health Statistics, unpublished data, <http://www.cdc.gov/nchs/nhanes.htm>.

Table 210. Cumulative Percent Distribution of Population by Weight and Sex: 2007 to 2008

[See headnote, Table 209. Data are based on National Health and Nutrition Examination Survey (NHANES). Weight was measured without shoes. Pregnant females were excluded from the analyses. Based on sample and subject to sampling variability; see source]

Weight	Males						Females					
	20–29 years	30–39 years	40–49 years	50–59 years	60–69 years	70–79 years	20–29 years	30–39 years	40–49 years	50–59 years	60–69 years	70–79 years
Percent under—												
100 lbs	–	–	(B)	(B)	–	–	¹2.0	1.3	(B)	¹0.4	0.2	(B)
110 lbs	(B)	–	(B)	(B)	(B)	(B)	4.9	4.7	3.7	¹4.0	(B)	6.1
120 lbs	(B)	(B)	(B)	¹1.1	(B)	1.5	16.3	10.5	7.8	7.9	7.2	12.4
130 lbs	4.3	¹2.1	¹2.5	¹2.3	2.8	3.5	27.8	18.9	16.0	17.1	13.5	22.5
140 lbs	11.1	6.4	4.7	5.6	5.3	5.2	39.4	29.8	26.4	27.3	27.4	30.1
150 lbs	20.9	11.5	7.6	8.6	10.0	9.7	49.7	40.6	37.5	38.7	37.4	43.1
160 lbs	31.3	20.4	15.1	13.9	16.5	17.7	57.5	51.1	49.8	49.7	46.1	53.7
170 lbs	43.6	30.5	21.3	22.0	24.9	27.4	63.2	59.8	59.3	56.9	58.9	65.6
180 lbs	55.7	40.9	33.6	33.2	33.4	40.1	72.6	68.7	65.6	63.7	72.4	74.0
190 lbs	65.0	50.6	43.7	44.5	42.6	50.1	76.3	73.6	75.0	70.3	79.4	81.2
200 lbs	73.5	59.3	58.0	55.7	55.5	65.7	80.0	79.4	80.0	75.3	84.6	87.3
210 lbs	79.4	70.0	66.2	64.6	64.4	71.6	82.8	83.7	82.8	81.9	88.4	90.5
220 lbs	83.8	76.1	75.6	74.0	73.4	80.0	84.9	89.0	87.2	85.9	91.1	93.4
230 lbs	86.5	81.7	84.6	78.8	81.2	83.5	88.6	91.3	90.6	89.5	93.7	96.4
240 lbs	89.7	85.5	88.1	85.6	85.1	87.3	90.0	94.1	93.0	91.4	95.6	97.0
250 lbs	93.2	89.6	89.7	88.0	88.2	90.6	92.3	95.2	95.5	92.9	96.7	98.4
260 lbs	94.7	92.0	92.8	91.3	90.7	93.1	93.3	95.8	96.7	96.5	97.6	98.6
270 lbs	95.1	93.3	94.6	93.5	93.0	96.4	95.7	96.4	97.5	97.2	98.0	98.6
280 lbs	96.1	95.1	95.4	94.2	94.8	97.5	97.0	97.2	97.8	98.2	99.0	99.4
290 lbs	96.8	96.4	96.4	95.8	97.2	98.5	97.2	97.5	98.2	98.9	99.0	99.6
300 lbs	97.5	96.9	98.1	98.1	97.8	99.4	97.7	98.4	98.3	99.4	99.3	100.0
320 lbs	98.1	98.2	98.8	99.0	98.5	99.4	98.9	99.1	98.7	99.7	99.9	100.0
340 lbs	99.5	98.8	98.8	99.1	99.0	100.0	99.6	99.5	99.4	99.8	99.9	100.0
360 lbs	99.5	99.4	99.3	99.8	99.0	100.0	99.6	99.7	99.8	99.9	99.9	100.0
380 lbs	99.7	99.7	99.5	99.8	99.1	100.0	99.6	99.9	99.8	100.0	100.0	100.0
400 lbs	99.7	99.7	99.5	99.9	99.5	100.0	99.6	100.0	99.8	100.0	100.0	100.0
420 lbs	99.7	99.7	99.5	100.0	99.5	100.0	99.6	100.0	99.9	100.0	100.0	100.0
440 lbs	99.8	99.9	99.5	100.0	99.5	100.0	99.6	100.0	100.0	100.0	100.0	100.0

– Represents zero. B Base figure too small to meet statistical standards of reliability of a derived figure. ¹ Figure does not meet standard of reliability or precision.

Source: U.S. National Center for Health Statistics, unpublished data, <http://www.cdc.gov/nchs/nhanes.htm>.

Table 211. Age-Adjusted Percent Distribution of Body Mass Index (BMI) Among Persons 18 Years Old and Over by Selected Characteristics: 2007 to 2008

[See headnote, Table 209. Body Mass Index (BMI) is a measure that adjusts body weight for height. It is calculated as weight in kilograms divided by height in meters squared. For both men and women, underweight is indicated by a BMI under 18.5; healthy weight is indicated by a BMI greater than or equal to 18.5 and less than 25.0; overweight is greater than or equal to 25.0 and less than 30.0; obesity is indicated by a BMI greater than or equal to 30.0. BMI is calculated from the measurement of the participants' weight and height during the examination. For definition of age adjustment, see text, Section 2. Based on the National Health and Nutrition Examination Survey (NHANES)]

Selected characteristic	Underweight	Healthy weight	Above healthy weight		
			Total	Overweight	Obese
Total [1] (age-adjusted)	**1.8**	**31.6**	**66.6**	**33.9**	**32.6**
Total [1] (crude)	**1.8**	**31.2**	**67.0**	**34.0**	**33.0**
Age: [2]					
18 to 44 years old	2.1	35.5	62.4	32.2	30.3
45 to 64 years old	[3] 1.6	26.9	71.5	34.2	37.3
65 to 74 years old	(B)	25.7	73.3	36.5	36.8
75 years old and over	1.7	30.3	68.0	41.7	26.2
Sex:					
Male	1.1	28.2	70.7	39.9	30.8
Female	2.5	34.8	62.7	28.2	34.5
Race/ethnicity and sex:					
Not Hispanic or Latino:					
White, male	[3] 1.2	27.8	71.1	40.5	30.5
White, female	2.6	37.3	60.0	27.7	32.3
Black alone or African American, male	[3] 1.6	31.4	67.0	31.1	36.0
Black alone or African American, female	2.8	21.1	76.0	27.9	48.1
Mexican or Mexican American, male	(B)	20.9	78.6	44.0	34.6
Mexican or Mexican American, female	(B)	25.2	73.6	31.0	42.6
Education: [4]					
Less than a high school diploma	2.2	25.1	72.6	34.4	38.3
High school diploma or GED [5]	1.5	27.6	70.9	36.1	34.8
Some college, bachelor's degree, or higher	1.0	31.6	67.4	35.1	32.3

B Base figure too small to meet statistical standards for reliability of a derived figure. [1] Total includes other race/ethnicities not shown separately and persons with unknown race/ethnicity. [2] Estimates for age groups are not age adjusted. [3] Figure does not meet standard of reliability or precision. [4] Education is shown only for persons 25 years old and over. [5] General Education Development certificate.

Source: U.S. National Center for Health Statistics, unpublished data, <http://www.cdc.gov/nchs/nhanes.htm>.

Table 212. Age-Adjusted Percentage of Persons Engaging in Physical Activity and Fitness by Selected Characteristics: 2008

[In percent. Covers persons 18 years old and over. Based on the National Health Interview Survey, a sample survey of the civilian noninstitutionalized population. Leisure-time physical activity is assessed by asking respondents a series of questions about participation in moderate and vigorous-intensity physical activities. For definition of age adjustment, see text, Section 2. To assess muscle-strengthening activities, respondents were asked about leisure-time physical activities specifically designed to strengthen their muscles]

Characteristic	No leisure-time physical activity [1]	Regular physical activity-moderate or vigorous [2]	Muscular strength and endurance [3]	Characteristic	No leisure-time physical activity [1]	Regular physical activity-moderate or vigorous [2]	Muscular strength and endurance [3]
Total	**36.2**	**32.5**	**21.9**	Two or more races	32.3	29.2	23.0
SEX				HISPANIC ORIGIN AND RACE			
Male	33.9	34.7	25.7				
Female	38.2	30.5	18.3	Hispanic or Latino [5]	47.4	25.1	15.0
AGE [4]				Not Hispanic or Latino	34.3	33.8	23.2
18 to 29 years old	28.7	38.4	29.3	White, non-Hispanic	31.9	35.8	24.2
30 to 44 years old	31.7	35.5	24.6	Black, non-Hispanic	47.9	24.8	19.2
45 to 64 years old	37.2	31.7	19.9				
65 to 74 years old	45.8	26.1	16.3	Education level (persons aged 25 years and over):			
75 years old and over	55.9	18.4	11.5	Less than 9th grade	64.3	14.6	6.3
RACE				Grades 9 thru 11	56.3	18.0	9.2
Race alone				High School graduate	47.0	25.0	14.4
White	34.6	33.8	22.6	Some college or AA degree [6]	33.0	31.8	22.4
Black or African American	47.3	25.0	19.4	College graduate or above	20.7	45.2	31.8
American Indian or Alaska Native	49.2	25.0	11.2				
Asian or Pacific Islander	(NA)	(NA)	(NA)				

NA Not available. [1] Persons with no moderate- or vigorous-intensity activity for at least 10 minutes at a time. [2] Regular physical activity is moderate-intensity physical activity at least 5 times a week for 30 minutes at a time or vigorous-intensity physical activity for at least 3 times a week for 20 minutes at a time. [3] Persons who participated in muscle strengthening activities at least 2 times a week. [4] Age data are not age-adjusted. [5] Persons of Hispanic or Latino origin may be any race. [6] Associate of Arts degree.

Source: National Center for Health Statistics, National Health Interview Survey—United States, 2008, Hyattsville, MD. See also <http://wonder.cdc.gov/data2010/>.

138 Health and Nutrition

Table 213. High School Students Engaged in Physical Activity by Sex: 2009

[In percent. For students in grades 9 to 12. Based on the Youth Risk Behavior Survey, a school-based survey and subject to sampling error; for details, see source]

Characteristic	Participated in 60+ min. of physical activity on 5 of last 7 days [1]	Participated in 60+ min. of physical activity on all 7 days [2]	Did not participate in 60+ min. of physical activity on any day [3]	Attended physical education class		Played on at least one sports team [6]	Used computers 3 or more hours/ day [7]	Watched three or more hours/ day of TV [8]
				Total [4]	Attended daily [5]			
All students	**37.0**	**18.4**	**23.1**	**56.4**	**33.3**	**58.3**	**24.9**	**32.8**
Male.	45.6	24.8	17.0	57.7	34.6	63.8	28.3	33.5
Grade 9	47.5	28.0	17.4	70.7	45.5	65.9	32.2	36.3
Grade 10	47.4	25.3	15.7	58.6	34.9	66.8	28.2	35.7
Grade 11	46.2	23.3	16.4	50.9	29.7	63.4	27.2	31.8
Grade 12	40.4	21.9	18.5	46.9	25.2	57.9	24.5	28.4
Female	27.7	11.4	29.9	55.0	31.9	52.3	21.2	32.1
Grade 9	30.8	13.6	26.9	74.3	48.2	56.6	24.6	33.9
Grade 10	30.5	12.7	30.3	56.4	32.3	56.4	22.5	33.6
Grade 11	26.0	10.3	29.8	45.3	25.5	51.3	19.3	29.6
Grade 12	22.4	8.6	33.0	40.7	19.6	44.1	17.7	31.0

[1] Were physically active doing any kind of physical activity that increased their heart rate and made them breathe hard some of the time for a total of at least 60 minutes/day for at least 5 or more days out of the 7 days preceding the survey. [2] Participate in 60 or more minutes of any kind of physical activity that increased their heart rate and made them breathe hard some of the time on all 7 days before the survey. [3] Did not participate in 60 or more minutes of any kind of physical activity that increased their heart rate and made them breathe hard some of the time on at least 1 day during the 7 days before the survey. [4] On one or more days in an average week when they were in school. [5] Five days in an average week when they were in school. [6] Run by their school or community groups during the 12 months before the survey. [7] Played video or computer games or used computer for something that was not school work on an average day. [8] On an average school day.

Source: U.S. Centers for Disease Control and Prevention, Atlanta, GA, "Youth Risk Behavior Surveillance—United States, 2009," Surveillance Series, June 2010, *Morbidity and Mortality Weekly Report 2010*, Vol. 59 (SS-5). See also <http://www.cdc.gov/mmwr/pdf/ss/ss5905.pdf>.

Table 214. Households and Persons Having Problems With Access to Food: 2005 to 2009

[114,437 represents 114,437,000. Food-secure means that a household had access at all times to enough food for an active healthy life for all household members, with no need for recourse to socially unacceptable food sources or extraordinary coping behaviors to meet their basic food needs. Food-insecure households had limited or uncertain ability to acquire acceptable foods in socially acceptable ways. Households with very low food security (a subset of food-insecure households) were those in which food intake of one or more household members was reduced and normal eating patterns disrupted due to inadequate resources for food. The severity of food insecurity in households is measured through a series of questions about experiences and behaviors known to characterize households that are having difficulty meeting basic food needs. These experiences and behaviors generally occur in an ordered sequence as the severity of food insecurity increases. As resources become more constrained, adults in typical households first worry about having enough food, then they stretch household resources and juggle other necessities, then decrease the quality and variety of household members' diets, then decrease the frequency and quantity of adults' food intake, and finally decrease the frequency and quantity of children's food intake. All questions refer to the previous 12 months and include a qualifying phrase reminding respondents to report only those occurrences that resulted from inadequate financial resources. Restrictions to food intake due to dieting or busy schedules are excluded. The omission of homeless persons may be a cause of underreporting. Data are from the Food Security Supplement to the Current Population Survey (CPS); for details about the CPS, see text, Section 1 and Appendix III]

Household food	Number (1,000)					Percent distribution				
	2005	2006	2007	2008	2009	2005	2006	2007	2008	2009
Households, total.	**114,437**	**115,609**	**117,100**	**117,565**	**118,174**	**100.0**	**100.0**	**100.0**	**100.0**	**100.0**
Food-secure	101,851	102,961	104,089	100,416	100,820	89.0	89.1	88.9	85.4	85.3
Food-insecure	12,586	12,648	13,011	17,149	17,354	11.0	10.9	11.1	14.6	14.7
With low food security [1]	8,158	8,031	8,262	10,426	10,601	7.1	6.9	7.0	8.9	9.0
With very low food security [2]	4,428	4,617	4,749	6,723	6,753	3.9	4.0	4.1	5.7	5.7
With very low food security among children [3]	270	221	323	506	469	0.7	0.6	0.8	1.3	1.2
Adult members	**217,897**	**220,423**	**223,467**	**225,461**	**227,543**	**100.0**	**100.0**	**100.0**	**100.0**	**100.0**
In food-secure households	195,172	197,536	199,672	193,026	194,579	89.6	89.6	89.4	85.6	85.5
In food-insecure households	22,725	22,887	23,795	32,435	32,964	10.4	10.4	10.6	14.4	14.5
With low food security	15,146	15,193	15,602	20,320	20,741	7.0	6.9	7.0	9.0	9.1
With very low food security [2]	7,579	7,694	8,193	12,115	12,223	3.5	3.5	3.7	5.4	5.4
Child members.	**73,604**	**73,587**	**73,575**	**74,106**	**74,207**	**100.0**	**100.0**	**100.0**	**100.0**	**100.0**
In food-secure households	61,201	60,959	61,140	57,433	57,010	83.1	82.8	83.1	77.5	76.8
In food-insecure households	12,403	12,628	12,435	16,673	17,197	16.9	17.2	16.9	22.5	23.2
With very low food security among children [3]	606	430	691	1,077	988	0.8	0.6	0.9	1.5	1.3

[1] Prior to 2006, USDA described these households as food insecure without hunger. [2] Food intake of one or more members in these households was reduced and normal eating patterns disrupted at some time during the year because of the household's food insecurity. Prior to 2006, USDA described these households as food insecure with hunger. [3] Percentages omit households with no children. The food security survey measures food security status at the household level. Not all children residing in food-insecure households were directly affected by the households' food insecurity. Similarly, not all children in households classified as having very low food security among children were subject to the reductions in food intake and disruptions in eating patterns that characterize this condition. Young children, in particular, are often protected from effects of the households' food insecurity.

Source: U.S. Department of Agriculture, Economic Research Service, *Household Food Security in the United States, 2009*, Economic Research Report Number 108, 2010. See also <http://www.ers.usda.gov/publications/err108/>.

Health and Nutrition **139**

Table 215. Per Capita Consumption of Selected Beverages by Type: 1980 to 2009

[In gallons. See headnote, Table 217. Per capita consumption uses U.S. resident population, July 1, for all beverages except coffee, tea, and fruit juices which use U.S. total population (Resident plus Armed Forces overseas), July 1]

Beverages	1980	1990	1995	2000	2005	2006	2007	2008	2009
Nonalcoholic	104.0	112.6	107.5	114.8	(NA)	(NA)	(NA)	(NA)	(NA)
Milk (plain and flavored).	27.5	25.7	23.9	22.5	21.0	21.0	20.6	20.8	20.6
Whole.	17.0	10.5	8.6	8.1	7.0	6.7	6.4	6.1	5.9
Reduced-fat, light, and skim	10.5	15.2	15.3	14.4	14.1	14.2	14.3	14.6	14.6
Tea.	7.3	6.9	7.9	7.8	8.0	8.4	8.4	8.0	9.0
Coffee	26.7	26.8	20.2	26.3	24.3	24.4	24.6	24.2	23.3
Carbonated soft drinks	35.1	46.2	47.4	49.3	(NA)	(NA)	(NA)	(NA)	(NA)
Diet	5.1	10.7	10.9	11.6	(NA)	(NA)	(NA)	(NA)	(NA)
Regular	29.9	35.6	36.5	37.7	(NA)	(NA)	(NA)	(NA)	(NA)
Fruit juices	7.4	7.0	8.1	8.9	8.1	7.9	7.9	6.9	7.4

NA Not available.

Source: U.S. Department of Agriculture, Economic Research Service, *Food Consumption, Prices, and Expenditures,* annual; Food Consumption (Per Capita) Data System, <http://www.ers.usda.gov/data/foodconsumption/>.

Table 216. Nutrition—Nutrients in Foods Available for Civilian Consumption Per Capita Per Day: 1970 to 2006

[Computed by the Center for Nutrition Policy and Promotion (CNPP). Based on Economic Research Service (ERS) estimates of per capita quantities of food available for consumption from "Food Consumption, Prices, and, Expenditures," on imputed consumption data for foods no longer reported by ERS, and on CNPP estimates of quantities of produce from home gardens. Food supply estimates do not reflect loss of food or nutrients from further marketing or home processing. Enrichment and fortification levels of iron, zinc, thiamin, riboflavin, niacin, folate, vitamin A, vitamin B_6, vitamin B_{12}, and Vitamin C are included]

Nutrient	Unit	1970–79	1980–89	1990–99	2000	2006
Food energy	Kilocalories	3,200	3,400	3,600	3,900	3,900
Carbohydrate.	Grams	395	421	478	495	474
Fiber	Grams	20	22	24	24	25
Protein.	Grams	96	100	108	111	111
Total fat [1]	Grams	143	151	150	169	178
Saturated.	Grams	49	50	48	52	54
Monounsaturated.	Grams	57	61	64	75	77
Polyunsaturated.	Grams	27	30	31	35	39
Cholesterol	Milligrams	430	420	400	410	420
Vitamin A	Micrograms RAE [2]	1,050	1,050	1,100	1,090	940
Carotene	Micrograms	560	600	710	690	690
Vitamin E	Milligrams a-TE [3]	14	16	17	20	21
Vitamin C	Milligrams	109	115	118	121	106
Thiamin	Milligrams	2	3	3	3	3
Riboflavin.	Milligrams	3	3	3	3	3
Niacin.	Milligrams	25	29	31	32	32
Vitamin B_6	Milligrams	2	2	2	2	2
Folate [4].	Micrograms DFE [5]	341	383	504	902	874
Vitamin B_{12}.	Micrograms	9	8	8	8	8
Calcium	Milligrams	930	930	980	980	960
Phosphorus	Milligrams	1,540	1,590	1,690	1,720	1,700
Magnesium	Milligrams	340	360	390	400	400
Iron	Milligrams	17	20	23	23	23
Zinc	Milligrams	13	14	15	15	16
Copper.	Milligrams	2	2	2	2	2
Potassium	Milligrams	3,510	3,550	3,720	3,780	3,620
Sodium [6]	Milligrams	1,210	1,210	1,240	1,230	1,150
Selenium	Micrograms	133	143	163	179	181

[1] Includes other types of fat not shown separately. [2] Retinol activity equivalents. [3] Alpha-Tocopherol equivalents. [4] Reflects new terminology from Institute of Medicine's Dietary Reference Intakes reports. [5] Dietary Folate Equivalents (DFE). [6] Does not include amount from processed foods; underestimates actual availability.

Source: U.S. Department of Agriculture, Center for Nutrition Policy and Promotion, *Nutrient Content of the U.S. Food Supply, 1909–2006.* Data also published by Economic Research Service, *Food Consumption, Prices, and Expenditures*, annual. See also <http://www.usda.gov/cnpp/>.

Table 217. Per Capita Consumption of Major Food Commodities: 1980 to 2009

[In pounds, retail weight, except as indicated. Consumption represents the residual after exports, nonfood use and ending stocks are subtracted from the sum of beginning stocks, domestic production, and imports. Based on Census Bureau estimated resident population plus Armed Forces overseas for most commodities. For commodities not shipped overseas in substantial amounts, such as fluid milk and cream, the resident population is used]

Commodity	Unit	1980	1990	1995	2000	2005	2008	2009
Red meat, total (boneless, trimmed weight) [1, 2]	Pounds....	126.4	112.2	113.6	113.7	110.2	106.6	105.7
Beef	Pounds....	72.1	63.9	63.5	64.5	62.5	59.6	58.1
Veal	Pounds...	1.3	0.9	0.8	0.5	0.4	0.3	0.3
Lamb and mutton	Pounds...	1.0	1.0	0.9	0.8	0.8	0.7	0.7
Pork	Pounds...	52.1	46.4	48.4	47.8	46.6	45.9	46.6
Poultry (boneless, trimmed weight) [2]	Pounds...	40.8	56.2	62.1	67.9	73.7	72.6	69.4
Chicken	Pounds...	32.7	42.4	48.2	54.2	60.5	58.7	56.0
Turkey	Pounds...	8.1	13.8	13.9	13.7	13.2	13.9	13.3
Fish and shellfish (boneless, trimmed weight)	Pounds...	12.4	14.9	14.8	15.2	16.2	16.0	15.8
Eggs	Number ...	271	234	232	251	256	247	246.1
Shell	Number ...	236	186	172	172	173	170	173
Processed	Number ...	35	48	60	79	83	77	73
Dairy products, total [3]	Pounds...	543.1	568.0	576.2	591.1	597.5	603.7	607.1
Fluid milk products [4]	Gallons ...	27.9	26.2	24.6	23.2	22.2	22.1	22.0
Beverage milks	Gallons ...	27.6	25.7	23.9	22.5	21.0	20.7	20.6
Plain whole milk	Gallons ...	16.5	10.2	8.3	7.7	6.6	5.9	5.7
Plain reduced-fat milk (2%)	Gallons ...	6.3	9.1	8.0	7.1	6.9	7.3	7.3
Reduced fat milk (1%) and skim milk	Gallons ...	3.1	4.9	6.1	6.1	5.6	5.7	5.7
Flavored whole milk	Gallons ...	0.6	0.3	0.3	0.4	0.3	0.2	0.2
Flavored milks other than whole	Gallons ...	0.6	0.8	0.8	1.0	1.4	1.4	1.4
Buttermilk	Gallons ...	0.5	0.4	0.3	0.3	0.2	0.2	0.2
Yogurt (excl. frozen)	1/2 pints...	4.6	7.8	11.4	12.0	19.1	21.8	23.1
Fluid cream products [5]	1/2 pints...	10.5	14.3	15.6	18.3	24.0	23.8	23.6
Cream [6]	1/2 pints...	6.3	8.7	9.4	11.6	14.9	15.1	15.0
Sour cream and dips	1/2 pints...	3.4	4.7	5.4	6.1	8.3	7.9	7.8
Condensed and evaporated milks	Pounds...	7.0	7.9	6.8	5.8	5.9	7.3	7.1
Whole milk	Pounds...	3.8	3.1	2.3	2.0	2.2	2.2	2.2
Skim milk	Pounds...	3.3	4.8	4.5	3.8	3.7	5.1	5.0
Cheese [7]	Pounds...	17.5	24.6	26.9	29.8	31.7	32.7	32.8
American [8]	Pounds...	9.6	11.1	11.7	12.7	12.6	13.1	13.4
Cheddar	Pounds...	6.8	9.0	9.0	9.7	10.3	10.1	10.1
Italian [8]	Pounds...	4.4	9.0	10.3	12.1	13.3	13.9	13.9
Mozzarella	Pounds...	3.0	6.9	8.0	9.3	10.2	10.6	10.6
Other [8]	Pounds...	3.3	4.3	5.0	5.0	5.6	5.6	5.5
Swiss	Pounds...	1.3	1.4	1.1	1.0	1.3	1.1	1.2
Cream and Neufchatel	Pounds...	0.9	1.6	2.2	2.4	2.4	2.5	2.5
Cottage cheese, total	Pounds...	4.5	3.4	2.7	2.6	2.6	2.3	2.4
Lowfat	Pounds...	0.8	1.2	1.2	1.3	1.4	1.3	1.3
Frozen dairy products	Pounds...	26.4	28.5	29.0	30.0	25.7	25.2	24.4
Ice cream	Pounds...	17.5	15.8	15.5	16.7	14.6	13.8	13.4
Lowfat ice cream	Pounds...	7.1	7.7	7.4	7.3	6.7	6.9	6.8
Sherbet	Pounds...	1.2	1.2	1.3	1.2	1.2	1.2	1.1
Frozen yogurt	Pounds...	(NA)	2.8	3.4	2.0	1.3	1.2	1.1
Fats and oils:								
Total, fat content only	Pounds...	56.9	62.3	64.2	81.7	85.5	85.2	78.6
Butter (product weight)	Pounds...	4.5	4.4	4.4	4.5	4.6	5.0	4.9
Margarine (product weight)	Pounds...	11.3	10.9	9.1	8.2	4.0	4.2	3.7
Lard (direct use)	Pounds...	2.3	0.9	0.4	0.8	1.6	1.0	1.5
Edible beef tallow (direct use)	Pounds...	1.1	0.6	2.7	4.0	3.8	2.9	0.7
Shortening	Pounds...	18.2	22.2	22.2	31.5	29.0	18.0	15.9
Salad and cooking oils	Pounds...	21.2	25.2	26.5	33.7	42.7	54.2	51.9
Other edible fats and oils	Pounds...	1.5	1.2	1.6	1.5	1.6	1.6	1.7
Flour and cereal products [9]	Pounds...	144.9	181.0	188.7	199.3	191.3	196.6	194.5
Wheat flour	Pounds...	116.9	135.9	140.0	146.3	134.3	136.5	134.6
Rice, milled	Pounds...	9.5	15.8	17.1	19.1	19.9	21.2	21.2
Corn products	Pounds...	12.9	21.4	24.9	28.4	31.4	33.0	33.0
Oat products	Pounds...	3.9	6.5	5.5	4.3	4.6	4.8	4.6
Caloric sweeteners, total [10]	Pounds...	120.2	132.4	144.1	148.9	142.2	136.1	130.7
Sugar, refined cane and beet	Pounds...	83.6	64.4	64.9	65.5	63.1	65.5	63.5
Corn sweeteners [11]	Pounds...	35.3	66.8	77.9	81.8	77.6	69.1	65.7
High-fructose corn syrup	Pounds...	19.0	49.6	57.6	62.6	59.1	53.0	50.1
Other:								
Cocoa beans	Pounds...	3.4	5.4	4.5	5.9	6.5	5.6	5.5
Coffee (green beans)	Pounds...	10.3	10.3	7.9	10.3	9.5	9.5	9.1
Peanuts (shelled)	Pounds...	5.1	6.1	5.7	5.8	6.6	6.3	6.5
Tree nuts (shelled)	Pounds...	1.8	2.5	1.9	2.6	2.6	3.5	3.7

NA Not available. [1] Excludes edible offals. [2] Excludes shipments to Puerto Rico and the other U.S. possessions. [3] Milk-equivalent, milk-fat basis. Includes butter. [4] Fluid milk figures are aggregates of commercial sales and milk produced and consumed on farms. [5] Includes eggnog, not shown separately. [6] Heavy cream, light cream, and half-and-half. [7] Excludes full-skim American, cottage, pot, and baker's cheese. [8] Includes other cheeses, not shown separately. [9] Includes rye flour and barley products, not shown separately. Excludes quantities used in alcoholic beverages. [10] Dry weight. Includes edible syrups (maple, molasses, etc.) and honey, not shown separately. [11] Includes glucose and dextrose, not shown separately.

Source: U.S. Department of Agriculture, Economic Research Service, "Food Consumption, Prices, and Expenditures, Food Availability (Per Capita) Data System," <http://www.ers.usda.gov/Data/FoodConsumption/>.

Health and Nutrition 141

Table 218. Per Capita Utilization of Selected Commercially Produced Fruits and Vegetables: 1980 to 2009

[In pounds, farm weight. Domestic food use of fresh fruits and vegetables reflects the fresh-market share of commodity production plus imports and minus exports. Based on Census Bureau estimated resident population as of April 1; 2004 to 2008 as of July 1]

Commodity	1980	1990	1995	2000	2005	2006	2007	2008	2009
Fruits and vegetables, total [1]	**603.4**	**648.4**	**688.2**	**710.9**	**684.5**	**672.2**	**667.9**	**649.1**	**647.9**
Fruits, total	264.9	256.8	273.7	286.0	269.9	268.6	261.4	256.6	257.0
Fresh fruits	106.2	116.5	123.1	128.5	125.3	127.8	123.5	126.6	127.5
Noncitrus	80.1	95.2	99.3	105.0	103.7	106.2	105.5	106.0	106.8
Apples	19.2	19.6	18.7	17.5	16.7	17.7	16.4	15.9	16.4
Bananas	20.8	24.3	27.1	28.4	25.2	25.1	26.0	25.0	24.7
Cantaloupes	5.8	9.2	9.0	11.1	9.6	9.3	9.6	8.9	9.3
Grapes	4.0	7.8	7.4	7.4	8.6	7.6	8.0	8.5	7.9
Peaches and nectarines	7.1	5.5	5.3	5.3	4.8	4.6	4.5	5.1	4.4
Pears	2.6	3.2	3.4	3.4	2.9	3.2	3.1	3.1	3.2
Pineapples	1.5	2.0	1.9	3.2	4.9	5.2	5.0	5.1	5.1
Plums and prunes	1.5	1.5	0.9	1.2	1.1	1.0	1.0	0.9	0.7
Strawberries	2.0	3.2	4.1	4.9	5.8	6.1	6.3	6.4	7.2
Watermelons	10.7	13.3	15.2	13.8	13.5	15.1	14.4	15.6	15.3
Other [2]	5.1	5.4	6.3	8.7	10.5	11.3	11.4	11.4	12.5
Fresh citrus	26.1	21.4	23.8	23.5	21.6	21.6	17.9	20.6	20.7
Oranges	14.3	12.4	11.8	11.7	11.4	10.2	7.5	9.9	9.1
Grapefruit	7.3	4.4	6.0	5.1	2.6	2.3	2.8	3.2	2.8
Other [3]	4.5	4.6	6.0	6.7	7.5	9.1	7.6	7.5	8.8
Processed fruits	158.7	140.3	150.7	157.5	144.6	140.8	137.9	130.0	129.5
Frozen fruits [4]	3.3	4.3	4.3	4.6	5.2	5.0	5.3	4.9	4.9
Dried fruits [5]	11.2	12.1	12.7	10.4	10.0	10.5	9.8	9.8	9.2
Canned fruits [6]	24.4	20.8	17.2	17.5	16.5	15.4	16.0	15.5	15.5
Fruit juices [7]	119.0	102.7	116.2	124.6	112.3	109.2	106.3	99.0	99.2
Vegetables, total	338.6	391.6	414.5	424.9	414.6	403.7	406.6	392.5	390.9
Fresh vegetables	151.6	176.4	188.1	200.7	196.5	194.0	194.0	188.9	184.8
Asparagus (all uses)	0.3	0.6	0.6	1.0	1.1	1.1	1.2	1.2	1.3
Broccoli	1.4	3.4	4.3	5.9	5.3	5.8	5.6	6.0	6.1
Cabbage	8.0	8.3	8.1	8.9	7.8	7.8	8.0	8.1	7.3
Carrots	6.2	8.3	11.2	9.2	8.7	8.1	8.0	8.1	7.4
Cauliflower	1.1	2.2	1.6	1.7	1.8	1.7	1.7	1.6	1.5
Celery (all uses)	7.4	7.2	6.9	6.3	5.9	6.1	6.3	6.2	6.1
Corn	6.5	6.7	7.8	9.0	8.7	8.3	9.2	9.1	9.0
Cucumbers	3.9	4.7	5.6	6.4	6.2	6.1	6.4	6.4	6.6
Head lettuce	25.6	27.7	22.2	23.5	20.9	20.1	18.4	16.8	17.1
Mushrooms	1.2	2.0	2.0	2.6	2.6	2.6	2.5	2.4	2.4
Onions	11.4	15.1	17.8	18.9	20.9	19.9	21.6	20.9	19.3
Snap beans	1.3	1.1	1.6	2.0	1.8	2.1	2.2	2.0	1.6
Bell peppers (all uses)	2.9	5.9	7.0	8.2	9.2	9.5	9.4	9.6	9.4
Potatoes	51.1	46.7	49.2	47.1	41.3	38.6	38.7	37.8	36.4
Sweet potatoes (all uses)	4.4	4.4	4.2	4.2	4.5	4.6	5.1	5.0	5.3
Tomatoes	12.8	15.5	16.8	19.0	20.2	19.8	19.2	18.5	19.3
Other fresh vegetables [8]	6.1	16.6	21.1	27.0	29.7	32.0	30.6	29.1	28.8
Processed vegetables	187.0	215.2	226.4	224.1	218.1	209.7	212.6	203.7	206.1
Selected vegetables for freezing [9]	51.5	66.8	78.8	79.3	76.4	75.0	75.8	72.6	71.3
Selected vegetables for canning [10]	102.5	110.3	108.2	103.2	104.8	94.4	96.7	94.6	100.4
Vegetables for dehydrating [11]	10.5	14.6	14.5	17.3	13.9	14.2	14.1	13.9	13.7
Potatoes for chips	16.5	16.4	16.4	15.9	16.0	18.6	18.6	15.7	13.7
Pulses [12]	5.9	7.2	8.4	8.5	6.9	7.4	7.4	6.9	6.9

[1] Excludes wine grapes. [2] Apricots, avocados, cherries, cranberries, kiwifruit, mangoes, papayas, and honeydew melons. [3] Lemons, limes, tangerines, and tangelos. [4] Apples, apricots, blackberries, blueberries, boysenberries, cherries, loganberries, peaches, plums, prunes, raspberries, and strawberries. [5] Apples, apricots, dates, figs, peaches, pears, prunes, and raisins. [6] Apples, apricots, cherries, olives, peaches, pears, pineapples, plums, and prunes. [7] Apple, cranberry, grape, grapefruit, lemon, lime, orange, pineapple, and prunes. [8] Artichokes, brussels sprouts, eggplant, escarole, endive, garlic, romaine, leaf lettuce, radishes, spinach, and squash. Beginning 2000, includes collard greens, kale, mustard greens, okra, pumpkin, and turnip greens. [9] Asparagus, snap beans, lima beans, broccoli, carrots, cauliflower, sweet corn, green peas, potatoes, spinach, and miscellaneous vegetables. [10] Asparagus, snap beans, beets, cabbage, carrots, chili peppers, sweet corn, cucumbers for pickling, green peas, lima beans, mushrooms, spinach, and tomatoes. [11] Onions and potatoes. [12] Dry peas, lentils, and dry edible beans.

Source: U.S. Department of Agriculture, Economic Research Service, "Food Consumption, Prices, and Expenditures, Food Availability (Per Capita) Data System," <http://www.ers.usda.gov/data/foodconsumption/>.

U.S. Census Bureau, Statistical Abstract of the United States: 2012

Section 4
Education

This section presents data primarily concerning formal education as a whole, at various levels, and for public and private schools. Data shown relate to the school–age population and school enrollment, educational attainment, education personnel, and financial aspects of education. In addition, data are shown for charter schools, homeschooling, security measures used in schools, technology usage in schools, and academic libraries. The chief sources are the decennial census of population and the Current Population Survey (CPS), both conducted by the U.S. Census Bureau (see text, Section 1, Population); annual, biennial, and other periodic surveys conducted by the National Center for Education Statistics (NCES), a part of the U.S. Department of Education; and surveys conducted by the National Education Association.

The censuses of population have included data on school enrollment since 1840 and on educational attainment since 1940. The CPS has reported on school enrollment annually since 1945 and on educational attainment periodically since 1947.

The NCES is continuing the pattern of statistical studies and surveys conducted by the U.S. Office of Education since 1870. The annual *Digest of Education Statistics* provides summary data on pupils, staff, finances, including government expenditures, and organization at the elementary, secondary, and higher education levels. It is also a primary source for detailed information on federal funds for education, projections of enrollment, graduates, and teachers. The *Condition of Education*, issued annually, presents a summary of information on education of particular interest to policymakers. NCES also conducts special studies periodically.

The census of governments, conducted by the Census Bureau every 5 years (for the years ending in "2" and "7"), provides data on school district finances and state and local government expenditures for education. Reports published by the Bureau of

Labor Statistics contain data relating civilian labor force experience to educational attainment (see also Tables 593, 619, and 627 in Section 12, Labor Force, Employment, and Earnings).

Types and sources of data— The statistics in this section are of two general types. One type, exemplified by data from the Census Bureau, is based on direct interviews with individuals to obtain information about their own and their family members' education. Data of this type relate to school enrollment and level of education attained, classified by age, sex, and other characteristics of the population. The school enrollment statistics reflect attendance or enrollment in any regular school within a given period; educational attainment statistics reflect the highest grade completed by an individual, or beginning 1992, the highest diploma or degree received.

Beginning in 2001, the CPS used Census 2000 population controls. From 1994 to 2000, the CPS used 1990 census population controls plus adjustment for undercount. Also the survey changed from paper to computer-assisted technology. For years 1981 through 1993, 1980 census population controls were used; 1971 through 1980, 1970 census population controls had been used. These changes had little impact on summary measures (e.g., medians) and proportional measures (e.g., enrollment rates); however, use of the controls may have significant impact on absolute numbers.

The second type, generally exemplified by data from the NCES and the National Education Association, is based on reports from administrators of educational institutions and of state and local agencies having jurisdiction over education. Data of this type relate to enrollment, attendance, staff, and finances for the nation, individual states, and local areas.

Unlike the NCES, the Census Bureau does not regularly include specialized

U.S. Census Bureau, Statistical Abstract of the United States: 2012

vocational, trade, business, or correspondence schools in its surveys. The NCES includes nursery schools and kindergartens that are part of regular grade schools in their enrollment figures. The Census Bureau includes all nursery schools and kindergartens. At the higher education level, the statistics of both agencies are concerned with institutions granting degrees or offering work acceptable for degree–credit, such as junior colleges.

School attendance—All states require that children attend school. While state laws vary as to the ages and circumstances of compulsory attendance, generally they require that formal schooling begin by age 6 and continue to age 16.

Schools—The NCES defines a school as "a division of the school system consisting of students composing one or more grade groups or other identifiable groups, organized as one unit with one or more teachers to give instruction of a defined type, and housed in a school plant of one or more buildings. More than one school may be housed in one school plant, as is the case when the elementary and secondary programs are housed in the same school plant."

Regular schools are those which advance a person toward a diploma or degree. They include public and private nursery schools, kindergartens, graded schools, colleges, universities, and professional schools.

Public schools are schools controlled and supported by local, state, or federal governmental agencies; private schools are those controlled and supported mainly by religious organizations or by private persons or organizations.

The Census Bureau defines *elementary* schools as including grades 1 through 8; *high* schools as including grades 9 through 12; and *colleges* as including junior or community colleges, regular 4-year colleges, and universities and graduate or professional schools. Statistics reported by the NCES and the National Education Association by type of organization, such as elementary level and secondary level, may not be strictly comparable with those from the Census Bureau because the grades included at the two levels vary, depending on the level assigned to the middle or junior high school by the local school systems.

School year—Except as otherwise indicated in the tables, data refer to the school year which, for elementary and secondary schools, generally begins in September of the preceding year and ends in June of the year stated. For the most part, statistics concerning school finances are for a 12-month period, usually July 1 to June 30. Enrollment data generally refer to a specific point in time, such as fall, as indicated in the tables.

Statistical reliability—For a discussion of statistical collection, estimation, and sampling procedures and measures of statistical reliability applicable to the Census Bureau and the NCES data, see Appendix III.

U.S. Census Bureau, Statistical Abstract of the United States: 2012

Table 219. School Enrollment: 1980 to 2020

[In thousands (58,306 represents 58,306,000). As of fall]

Year	All levels			Pre-kindergarten through grade 8		Grades 9 through 12		College[3]	
	Total	Public	Private	Public	Private[1,2]	Public	Private[1]	Public	Private
1980.	58,305	50,335	7,971	27,647	3,992	13,231	1,339	9,457	2,640
1985.	57,226	48,901	8,325	27,034	4,195	12,388	1,362	9,479	2,768
1990.	60,683	52,061	8,622	29,876	4,512	11,341	1,136	10,845	2,974
1991.	62,087	53,357	8,730	30,506	4,518	11,541	1,163	11,310	3,049
1992.	62,987	54,208	8,779	31,088	4,528	11,735	1,148	11,385	3,102
1993.	63,438	54,654	8,784	31,504	4,536	11,961	1,132	11,189	3,116
1994.	64,385	55,245	9,139	31,896	4,856	12,215	1,138	11,134	3,145
1995.	65,020	55,933	9,087	32,338	4,756	12,502	1,163	11,092	3,169
1996.	65,911	56,732	9,180	32,762	4,755	12,849	1,178	11,121	3,247
1997.	66,574	57,323	9,251	33,071	4,759	13,056	1,185	11,196	3,306
1998.	67,033	57,676	9,357	33,344	4,776	13,195	1,212	11,138	3,369
1999.	67,667	58,167	9,500	33,486	4,789	13,371	1,229	11,309	3,482
2000.	68,685	58,956	9,729	33,686	4,906	13,517	1,264	11,753	3,560
2001.	69,920	59,905	10,014	33,936	5,023	13,736	1,296	12,233	3,695
2002.	71,015	60,935	10,080	34,114	4,915	14,069	1,306	12,752	3,860
2003.	71,551	61,399	10,152	34,201	4,788	14,339	1,311	12,859	4,053
2004.	72,154	61,776	10,379	34,178	4,756	14,618	1,331	12,980	4,292
2005.	72,674	62,135	10,539	34,204	4,724	14,909	1,349	13,022	4,466
2006.	73,066	62,496	10,570	34,235	4,631	15,081	1,360	13,180	4,579
2007.	73,451	62,783	10,668	34,205	4,546	15,087	1,364	13,491	4,757
2008.	74,075	63,237	10,838	34,285	4,335	14,980	1,373	13,972	5,131
2009, proj.[4]	75,198	64,092	11,106	34,440	4,151	14,842	1,337	14,811	5,617
2010, proj.	75,286	64,231	11,054	34,637	4,092	14,668	1,306	14,926	5,657
2011, proj.	75,435	64,420	11,014	34,892	4,057	14,530	1,266	14,998	5,691
2012, proj.	75,633	64,665	10,968	35,129	4,034	14,512	1,229	15,023	5,704
2013, proj.	76,082	65,093	10,988	35,368	4,025	14,545	1,194	15,180	5,769
2014, proj.	76,775	65,713	11,063	35,579	4,027	14,689	1,160	15,445	5,875
2015, proj.	77,488	66,342	11,146	35,829	4,042	14,830	1,134	15,682	5,970
2016, proj.	78,182	66,947	11,234	36,161	4,073	14,877	1,103	15,909	6,059
2017, proj.	78,869	67,545	11,324	36,491	4,110	14,939	1,077	16,115	6,137
2018, proj.	79,556	68,133	11,422	36,803	4,146	15,000	1,060	16,330	6,217
2019, proj.	80,260	68,736	11,523	37,121	4,181	15,083	1,052	16,532	6,290
2020, proj.	80,955	69,342	11,612	37,444	4,216	15,222	1,056	16,676	6,340

[1] Since the biennial Private School Universe Survey (PSS) is collected in the fall of odd numbered years, even numbered years are estimated based on data from the PSS. [2] Includes private nursery and prekindergarten enrollment in schools that offer kindergarten or higher grades. [3] Data beginning 1996 based on new classification system. See footnote 1, Table 278. [4] Pre-K through 12 are projections; college data are actual.

Source: U.S. National Center for Education Statistics, *Digest of Education Statistics*, annual, and *Projections of Education Statistics*, annual. See also <http://www.nces.ed.gov/annuals>.

Table 220. School Expenditures by Type of Control and Level of Instruction in Constant (2009 to 2010) Dollars: 1980 to 2010

[In millions of dollars (446,896 represents $446,896,000,000). For school years ending in year shown. Data shown reflect historical revisions. Total expenditures for public elementary and secondary schools include current expenditures, interest on school debt and capital outlay. Data deflated by the Consumer Price Index, all urban consumers, on a school-year basis (supplied by the National Center for Education Statistics). See also Appendix III. Based on survey of state education agencies; see source for details]

Year	Total	Elementary and secondary schools			Colleges and universities [1]		
		Total	Public	Private	Total	Public	Private
1980.	446,896	288,005	267,904	20,101	158,891	105,440	53,451
1985.	490,472	306,147	280,737	25,410	184,326	119,497	64,829
1990.	624,431	394,586	363,179	31,407	229,845	146,403	83,442
1992.	655,411	410,479	378,017	32,461	244,933	155,010	89,923
1993.	668,607	417,328	384,633	32,695	251,279	159,018	92,261
1994.	682,973	426,018	393,260	32,758	256,955	162,028	94,927
1995.	699,119	435,465	402,034	33,431	263,654	166,383	97,271
1996.	713,363	446,161	411,932	34,229	[2] 267,203	167,671	[2] 99,532
1997.	734,944	462,296	427,107	35,189	[2] 272,648	171,822	[2] 100,826
1998.	764,434	484,566	447,984	36,582	279,868	178,015	101,854
1999.	795,388	506,646	468,710	37,935	288,742	185,118	103,625
2000.	831,291	528,149	488,846	39,303	303,141	195,013	108,128
2001.	872,694	550,603	508,516	42,086	322,092	210,859	111,233
2002.	915,606	574,172	529,534	44,638	341,434	223,113	118,321
2003.	946,988	586,512	541,405	45,107	360,476	234,489	125,987
2004.	967,013	598,104	552,333	45,771	368,909	238,837	130,072
2005.	990,428	611,642	564,833	46,809	378,787	243,986	134,801
2006.	1,008,252	623,149	575,879	47,270	385,103	246,750	138,353
2007 [2]	1,044,757	646,044	596,887	49,157	398,713	253,567	145,146
2008 [2,3]	1,079,263	661,061	610,794	50,267	418,201	267,252	150,949
2009 [2,3]	1,090,450	655,280	605,806	49,474	435,170	275,642	159,529
2010 [2,3]	1,111,000	650,000	602,000	48,000	461,000	289,000	172,000

[1] Data beginning 1996 based on new classification system. See footnote 1, Table 278. [2] Estimated. [3] Detail may not add to total due to rounding.

Source: U.S. National Center for Education Statistics, *Digest of Education Statistics*, annual. See also <http://www.nces.ed.gov/programs/digest/>.

Table 221. School Enrollment, Faculty, Graduates, and Finances—Projections: 2010 to 2016

[As of fall, except as indicated (54,770 represents 54,770,000)]

Item	Unit	2010	2011	2012	2013	2014	2015	2016
ELEMENTARY AND SECONDARY SCHOOLS								
School enrollment, total	1,000	54,770	54,704	54,746	54,905	55,133	55,455	55,836
Pre-kindergarten through grade 8	1,000	38,592	38,729	38,949	39,163	39,394	39,606	39,872
Grades 9 through 12	1,000	16,179	15,975	15,797	15,742	15,739	15,849	15,964
Public	1,000	49,282	49,306	49,422	49,642	49,914	50,268	50,659
Pre-kindergarten through grade 8	1,000	34,440	34,637	34,892	35,129	35,368	35,579	35,829
Grades 9 through 12	1,000	14,842	14,668	14,530	14,512	14,545	14,689	14,830
Private	1,000	5,488	5,398	5,324	5,263	5,219	5,187	5,176
Pre-kindergarten through grade 8	1,000	4,151	4,092	4,057	4,034	4,025	4,027	4,042
Grades 9 through 12	1,000	1,337	1,306	1,266	1,229	1,194	1,160	1,134
Classroom teachers, total FTE [1]	1,000	3,644	3,668	3,679	3,696	3,725	3,752	3,782
Public	1,000	3,207	3,240	3,253	3,274	3,306	3,334	3,364
Private	1,000	437	428	426	422	419	419	418
High school graduates, total [2]	1,000	3,321	3,282	3,220	3,197	3,154	3,132	3,165
Public	1,000	3,013	2,982	2,926	2,912	2,875	2,867	2,904
Public schools: [2]								
Average daily attendance (ADA)	1,000	46,041	46,063	46,172	46,377	46,631	46,962	47,328
Current dollars: [3]								
Current school expenditure	Bil. dol	517	526	536	550	570	(NA)	(NA)
Per pupil in fall enrollment	Dollar	10,482	10,670	10,855	11,081	11,410	(NA)	(NA)
Constant (2008–2009) dollars: [3,4]								
Current school expenditure	Bil. dol	511	514	515	518	525	541	557
Per pupil in fall enrollment	Dollar	10,377	10,425	10,428	10,434	10,524	10,760	10,987
HIGHER EDUCATION								
Enrollment, total	1,000	20,428	20,582	20,688	20,727	20,948	21,320	21,651
Male	1,000	8,770	8,862	8,896	8,894	8,941	9,028	9,100
Full-time	1,000	5,671	5,689	5,709	5,705	5,730	5,787	5,834
Part-time	1,000	3,099	3,172	3,186	3,189	3,211	3,242	3,266
Female	1,000	11,658	11,720	11,793	11,833	12,008	12,291	12,551
Full-time	1,000	7,052	7,095	7,145	7,151	7,232	7,371	7,495
Part-time	1,000	4,606	4,625	4,648	4,682	4,776	4,921	5,056
Public	1,000	14,811	14,926	14,998	15,023	15,180	15,445	15,682
Four-year institutions	1,000	7,709	7,771	7,817	7,833	7,913	8,048	8,167
Two-year institutions	1,000	7,101	7,155	7,181	7,190	7,266	7,397	7,515
Private	1,000	5,617	5,657	5,691	5,704	5,769	5,875	5,970
Four-year institutions	1,000	5,197	5,238	5,271	5,285	5,346	5,445	5,533
Two-year institutions	1,000	420	419	420	420	423	430	437
Undergraduate	1,000	17,565	17,699	17,786	17,801	17,965	18,255	18,512
Postbaccalaureate	1,000	2,862	2,884	2,903	2,927	2,984	3,065	3,140
Full-time equivalent	1,000	12,723	12,784	12,854	12,856	12,962	13,158	13,329
Public	1,000	8,530	8,564	8,607	8,604	8,670	8,797	8,908
2-year	1,000	2,881	2,876	2,884	2,878	2,898	2,941	2,979
4-year	1,000	5,650	5,688	5,724	5,726	5,772	5,856	5,928
Private	1,000	4,192	4,220	4,247	4,252	4,291	4,361	4,422
2-year	1,000	368	368	369	368	371	377	382
4-year	1,000	3,824	3,852	3,878	3,883	3,920	3,984	4,039
Degrees conferred, total [2]	1,000	3,365	3,464	3,586	3,615	3,656	3,701	3,756
Associate's	1,000	835	863	895	899	906	915	927
Bachelor's	1,000	1,673	1,715	1,781	1,791	1,805	1,817	1,835
Master's	1,000	691	712	730	741	756	776	795
Doctoral	1,000	70	74	77	80	83	87	90
First-professional	1,000	95	100	103	104	105	107	109

NA Not available. [1] Full-time equivalent. [2] For school year ending in June the following year. [3] Limited financial projections are shown due to the uncertain behavior of inflation over the long term. [4] Based on the Consumer Price Index (CPI) for all urban consumers, U.S. Bureau of Labor Statistics. CPI adjusted to a school year basis by NCES.

Source: U.S. National Center for Education Statistics, *Projections of Education Statistics to 2020*. See also <http://www.nces.ed.gov/surveys/AnnualReports/>.

Table 222. Federal Funds for Education and Related Programs: 2005 to 2010

[In millions of dollars (146,207.0 represents $146,207,000,000), except percent. For fiscal years ending in September. Figures represent on-budget funds]

Level, agency, and program	2005	2009	2010[1]
Total, all programs	**146,207.0**	**163,070.7**	**(NA)**
Percent of federal budget outlays	5.9	4.6	(NA)
Elementary/secondary education programs	**68,957.7**	**88,133.6**	**115,404.3**
Department of Education[2]	37,477.6	52,468.1	76,932.5
Grants for the disadvantaged	14,635.6	15,880.5	22,134.3
School improvement programs	7,918.1	19,600.5	34,267.4
Indian education	121.9	118.2	109.9
Special education	10,940.3	12,768.8	16,450.6
Vocational and adult education	1,967.1	2,034.2	1,944.4
Education reform—Goals 2000	−35.0	(X)	(X)
Department of Agriculture[2]	12,577.3	15,273.4	17,277.4
Child nutrition programs	[3]11,901.9	[3]13,714.9	[3]15,500.9
Agricultural Marketing Service—commodities[3]	399.3	1,237.0	1,354.9
Department of Defense[2]	1,786.3	1,907.7	2,048.9
Overseas dependents schools	1,060.9	1,110.5	1,186.6
Section VI schools[4]	410.2	418.5	435.1
Department of Health and Human Services	8,043.3	9,738.0	8,539.3
Head Start	6,842.3	8,499.1	7,235.2
Social security student benefits	1,161.0	1,238.9	1,304.1
Department of Homeland Security[2]	0.5	2.6	2.9
Department of the Interior[2]	938.5	782.5	784.5
Mineral Leasing Act and other funds	140.0	78.1	74.5
Indian Education	797.5	703.4	709.1
Department of Justice	554.5	821.1	882.1
Inmate programs	554.5	820.0	881.0
Department of Labor	5,654.0	6,073.0	7,811.0
Job Corps	1,521.0	1,612.0	1,850.0
Department of Veterans Affairs	1,815.0	919.1	967.2
Vocational rehab for disabled veterans	1,815.0	919.1	967.0
Other agencies and programs	153.2	148.1	158.5
Higher education programs	**38,587.3**	**36,394.2**	**47,888.8**
Department of Education[2]	31,420.0	27,626.6	33,673.3
Student financial assistance	15,209.5	23,040.2	31,796.1
Federal Family Education Loans[5]	10,777.5	526.9	−1,003.6
Department of Agriculture	62.0	73.2	80.7
Department of Commerce	(NA)	(NA)	(NA)
Department of Defense	1,858.3	2,262.8	2,243.4
Tuition assistance for military personnel	608.1	657.7	627.5
Service academies[6]	300.8	371.2	376.9
Senior ROTC	537.5	653.6	661.9
Professional development education	411.9	580.3	577.0
Department of Health and Human Services[2]	1,433.5	1,235.9	1,345.8
Health professions training programs	581.7	354.3	406.7
National Health Service Corps scholarships	45.0	40.0	41.0
National Institutes of Health training grants[7]	756.0	776.3	824.4
Department of Homeland Security	36.4	52.7	59.0
Department of the Interior	249.2	147.9	159.5
Shared revenues, Mineral Leasing Act and other receipts—estimated education share	146.2	15.7	14.9
Indian programs	103.0	132.1	144.6
Department of State	424.0	537.0	610.0
Department of Transportation[2]	73.0	69.0	104.0
Department of Veterans Affairs[2]	2,478.6	3,682.3	8,810.6
Post-Vietnam veterans	1.1	0.4	0.1
All-volunteer-force educational assistance	2,071.0	3,013.6	8,253.2
Other agencies and programs[2]	552.2	707.0	802.6
National Endowment for the Humanities	29.3	40.8	40.0
National Science Foundation	490.0	629.0	728.0
Other education programs	**6,908.5**	**8,211.0**	**10,630.5**
Department of Education[2]	3,538.9	4,551.4	5,592.7
Administration	548.8	1,339.0	1,418.4
Rehabilitative services and handicapped research	2,973.3	3,185.7	4,145.2
Department of Agriculture	468.6	542.8	565.4
Department of Health and Human Services	313.0	331.0	34.0
Department of Homeland Security	278.2	351.1	1,920.0
Department of Justice	26.1	29.0	29.6
Department of State	109.3	118.5	118.0
Other agencies and programs[2]	2,174.3	2,287.1	2,370.5
Agency for International Development	574.0	612.0	614.0
Library of Congress	430.0	468.0	420.0
National Endowment for the Arts	2.5	3.0	4.0
National Endowment for the Humanities	88.0	93.7	93.0
Research programs at universities and related institutions[2]	**31,753.5**	**30,331.9**	**(NA)**
Department of Agriculture	709.7	538.8	(NA)
Department of Defense	2,675.9	2,507.7	(NA)
Department of Commerce	(NA)	2,883.7	(NA)
Department of Energy	4,339.9	2,883.7	(NA)
Department of Health and Human Services	16,358.0	17,165.5	(NA)
National Aeronautics and Space Administration	2,763.1	1,655.4	(NA)
National Science Foundation	3,503.2	4,405.5	(NA)

NA Not available. X Not applicable. [1] Estimated except U.S. Department of Education, which are actual budget reports. [2] Includes other programs and agencies, not shown separately. [3] Purchased under Section 32 of the Act of August 1935 for use in child nutrition programs. [4] Program provides for the education of dependents of federal employees residing on federal property where free public education is unavailable in the nearby community. [5] Includes Federal Direct Loans. [6] Instructional costs only including academics, audiovisual, academic computer center, faculty training, military training, physical education, and libraries. [7] Includes alcohol, drug abuse, and mental health training programs.

Source: U.S. National Center for Education Statistics, *Digest of Education Statistics*, annual. See also <http://www.nces.ed.gov/programs/digest/>.

Education 147

Table 223. School Enrollment by Age: 1970 to 2009

[As of October (60,357 represents 60,357,000). Covers civilian noninstitutional population enrolled in nursery school and above. Based on Current Population Survey; see text, Section 1 and Appendix III]

Age	1970	1980	1985	1990	1995	2000	2005	2007	2008	2009
ENROLLMENT (1,000)										
Total, 3 to 34 years old.......	**60,357**	**57,348**	**58,013**	**60,588**	**66,939**	**69,560**	**72,768**	**72,970**	**73,275**	**73,905**
3 and 4 years old.............	1,461	2,280	2,801	3,292	4,042	4,097	4,383	4,491	4,458	4,475
5 and 6 years old.............	7,000	5,853	6,697	7,207	7,901	7,648	7,486	7,792	7,651	7,783
7 to 13 years old	28,943	23,751	22,849	25,016	27,003	28,296	27,936	27,532	27,681	27,609
14 and 15 years old...........	7,869	7,282	7,362	6,555	7,651	7,885	8,375	8,137	7,965	7,789
16 and 17 years old...........	6,927	7,129	6,654	6,098	6,997	7,341	8,472	8,205	8,202	7,939
18 and 19 years old...........	3,322	3,788	3,716	4,044	4,274	4,926	5,109	5,566	5,607	5,935
20 and 21 years old...........	1,949	2,515	2,708	2,852	3,025	3,314	4,069	3,916	4,052	4,163
22 to 24 years old	1,410	1,931	2,068	2,231	2,545	2,731	3,254	3,375	3,488	3,818
25 to 29 years old	1,011	1,714	1,942	2,013	2,216	2,030	2,340	2,577	2,764	2,819
30 to 34 years old	466	1,105	1,218	1,281	1,284	1,292	1,344	1,379	1,407	1,576
35 years old and over	(NA)	1,290	1,766	2,439	2,830	2,653	3,013	2,997	3,079	3,383
ENROLLMENT RATE										
Total, 3 to 34 years old.......	**56.4**	**49.7**	**48.3**	**50.2**	**53.7**	**55.8**	**56.5**	**56.1**	**56.2**	**56.5**
3 and 4 years old.............	20.5	36.7	38.9	44.4	48.7	52.1	53.6	54.5	52.8	52.4
5 and 6 years old.............	89.5	95.7	96.1	96.5	96.0	95.6	95.4	94.7	93.8	94.1
7 to 13 years old	99.2	99.3	99.2	99.6	98.9	98.2	98.6	98.4	98.7	98.2
14 and 15 years old...........	98.1	98.2	98.1	99.0	98.9	98.7	98.0	98.7	98.6	98.0
16 and 17 years old...........	90.0	89.0	91.7	92.5	93.6	92.8	95.1	94.3	95.2	94.6
18 and 19 years old...........	47.7	46.4	51.6	57.3	59.4	61.2	67.6	66.8	66.0	68.9
20 and 21 years old...........	31.9	31.0	35.3	39.7	44.9	44.1	48.7	48.4	50.1	51.7
22 to 24 years old	14.9	16.3	16.9	21.0	23.2	24.6	27.3	27.3	28.2	30.4
25 to 29 years old	7.5	9.3	9.2	9.7	11.6	11.4	11.9	12.4	13.2	13.5
30 to 34 years old	4.2	6.4	6.1	5.8	6.0	6.7	6.9	7.2	7.3	8.1
35 years old and over	(NA)	1.4	1.6	2.1	2.2	1.9	2.0	1.9	2.0	2.1

NA Not available.

Source: U.S. Census Bureau, Current Population Reports, PPL-148, P-20, and earlier reports, and "School Enrollment," <http://www.census.gov/population/www/socdemo/school.html>.

Table 224. School Enrollment by Race, Hispanic Origin, and Age: 2000 to 2009

[(54,257 represents 54,257,000). See headnote, Table 223]

Age	White [1]			Black [1]			Hispanic [2]		
	2000	2005	2009	2000	2005	2009	2000	2005	2009
ENROLLMENT (1,000)									
Total, 3 to 34 years old............	**54,257**	**55,715**	**56,080**	**11,115**	**10,885**	**11,110**	**9,928**	**12,502**	**14,121**
3 and 4 years old	3,091	3,380	3,228	725	655	787	518	773	912
5 and 6 years old	5,959	5,707	5,926	1,219	1,144	1,117	1,390	1,532	1,878
7 to 13 years old	22,061	21,310	21,035	4,675	4,317	4,098	4,373	5,394	5,931
14 and 15 years old	6,176	6,429	5,981	1,260	1,321	1,177	1,093	1,431	1,482
16 and 17 years old	5,845	6,520	6,052	1,106	1,281	1,250	959	1,357	1,367
18 and 19 years old	3,924	4,006	4,532	716	707	878	617	681	959
20 and 21 years old	2,688	3,262	3,276	416	430	532	311	447	521
22 to 24 years old	2,101	2,411	2,825	393	475	577	309	419	459
25 to 29 years old	1,473	1,740	2,108	353	307	417	198	310	385
30 to 34 years old	939	950	1,117	252	248	277	160	158	227
35 years old and over	2,087	2,299	2,505	387	499	638	235	307	407
ENROLLMENT RATE									
Total, 3 to 34 years old............	**55.1**	**55.9**	**55.7**	**59.0**	**58.4**	**58.5**	**51.3**	**50.9**	**52.8**
3 and 4 years old	50.2	54.2	51.1	59.9	52.2	57.7	35.9	43.0	41.9
5 and 6 years old	95.3	95.3	94.0	96.3	95.9	93.6	94.3	93.8	93.7
7 to 13 years old	98.2	98.6	98.3	98.0	98.6	98.1	97.5	97.6	97.3
14 and 15 years old	98.4	98.3	98.1	99.6	95.8	97.8	96.2	97.3	97.9
16 and 17 years old	92.8	95.4	94.4	91.4	93.1	94.1	87.0	92.6	92.6
18 and 19 years old	61.3	68.0	68.7	57.2	62.8	65.2	49.5	54.3	57.1
20 and 21 years old	44.9	49.3	52.6	36.6	37.6	44.7	26.1	30.0	37.2
22 to 24 years old	23.7	26.0	28.9	24.2	28.0	31.9	18.2	19.5	20.4
25 to 29 years old	10.4	11.3	12.9	14.3	11.7	14.6	7.4	7.8	9.5
30 to 34 years old	6.0	6.2	7.3	9.6	10.0	11.0	5.6	4.2	5.6
35 years old and over	1.8	1.8	1.9	2.6	3.1	3.7	2.0	2.0	2.2

[1] Starting 2005, data are for persons who selected this race group only. See footnote 2, Table 229. [2] Persons of Hispanic origin may be any race.

Source: U.S. Census Bureau, Current Population Reports, PPL-148, P-20, and earlier reports, and "School Enrollment," <http://www.census.gov/population/www/socdemo/school.html>.

148 Education

Table 225. Enrollment in Public and Private Schools: 1970 to 2009

[In millions (52.2 represents 52,200,000), except percent. As of October. For civilian noninstitutional population. For 1970 to 1985, persons 3 to 34 years old; beginning 1990, for 3 years old and over. For enrollment 35 years old and over, see Table 223]

Year	Public						Private					
	Total	Nursery	Kinder-garten	Elemen-tary	High school	College	Total	Nursery	Kinder-garten	Elemen-tary	High school	College
1970.........	52.2	0.3	2.6	30.0	13.5	5.7	8.1	0.8	0.5	3.9	1.2	1.7
1975.........	52.8	0.6	2.9	27.2	14.5	7.7	8.2	1.2	0.5	3.3	1.2	2.0
1980.........	(NA)	0.6	2.7	24.4	(NA)	(NA)	(NA)	1.4	0.5	3.1	(NA)	(NA)
1985.........	49.0	0.9	3.2	23.8	12.8	8.4	9.0	1.6	0.6	3.1	1.2	2.5
1990 [1].......	53.8	1.2	3.3	26.6	11.9	10.7	9.2	2.2	0.6	2.7	0.9	2.9
1993.........	56.0	1.2	3.5	27.7	12.6	10.9	9.4	1.8	0.7	2.9	1.0	3.0
1994.........	58.6	1.9	3.3	28.1	13.5	11.7	10.7	2.3	0.6	3.4	1.1	3.3
1995.........	58.7	2.0	3.2	28.4	13.7	11.4	11.1	2.4	0.7	3.4	1.2	3.3
1996.........	59.5	1.9	3.4	28.1	14.1	12.0	10.8	2.3	0.7	3.4	1.2	3.2
1997.........	61.6	2.3	3.3	29.3	14.6	12.1	10.5	2.2	0.7	3.1	1.2	3.3
1998.........	60.8	2.3	3.1	29.1	14.3	12.0	11.3	2.3	0.7	3.4	1.2	3.6
1999.........	60.8	2.3	3.2	29.2	14.4	11.7	11.4	2.3	0.7	3.6	1.3	3.5
2000.........	61.2	2.2	3.2	29.4	14.4	12.0	11.0	2.2	0.7	3.5	1.3	3.3
2001.........	62.4	2.2	3.1	29.8	14.8	12.4	10.8	2.1	0.6	3.4	1.2	3.5
2002.........	62.8	2.2	3.0	29.7	15.1	12.8	11.3	2.2	0.6	3.5	1.3	3.7
2003.........	63.8	2.6	3.1	29.2	15.8	13.1	11.1	2.4	0.6	3.4	1.3	3.5
2004.........	64.3	2.5	3.4	29.2	15.5	13.7	11.3	2.3	0.6	3.4	1.3	3.7
2005.........	64.2	2.5	3.3	29.0	15.8	13.4	11.5	2.1	0.6	3.4	1.4	4.0
2006.........	64.1	2.5	3.6	29.0	15.6	13.5	11.1	2.2	0.5	3.1	1.5	3.8
2007.........	65.1	2.6	3.7	29.1	15.8	14.1	10.8	2.1	0.5	3.1	1.3	3.9
2008.........	65.5	2.6	3.6	29.2	15.4	14.7	10.8	2.0	0.5	3.2	1.3	4.0
2009.........	66.9	2.7	3.8	29.4	15.3	15.7	10.4	2.0	0.4	2.9	1.2	4.0
Percent White:												
1970.........	84.5	59.5	84.4	83.1	85.6	90.7	93.4	91.1	88.2	94.1	96.1	92.8
1980........	(NA)	68.2	80.7	80.9	(NA)	(NA)	(NA)	89.0	87.0	90.7	(NA)	(NA)
1990........	79.8	71.7	78.3	78.9	79.2	84.1	87.4	89.6	83.2	88.2	89.4	85.0
2000........	77.0	69.4	77.3	76.7	78.0	78.0	83.5	84.9	82.8	85.9	84.6	79.8
2005 [2].....	75.7	71.3	78.0	75.2	76.0	76.7	81.4	83.6	79.0	83.0	83.6	78.4
2007 [2].....	75.4	73.2	77.6	75.3	75.2	77.1	80.4	80.9	81.3	82.1	86.1	76.6
2008 [2].....	75.7	69.5	76.8	75.4	75.2	77.6	79.9	83.2	79.5	80.6	83.6	76.4
2009 [2].....	75.2	66.8	75.9	75.8	74.8	76.0	79.3	80.0	80.3	80.7	85.5	76.2

NA Not available. [1] Beginning 1990, based on a revised edit and tabulation package. [2] Beginning 2005, for persons who selected this race group only. See footnote 2, Table 229.
Source: U.S. Census Bureau, Current Population Reports, PPL-148, P-20, and earlier reports, and "School Enrollment," <http://www.census.gov/population/www/socdemo/school.html>.

Table 226. School Enrollment by Sex and Level: 1970 to 2009

[In millions (60.4 represents 60,400,000). As of October. For the civilian noninstitutional population. Prior to 1980, persons 3 to 34 years old; beginning 1980, 3 years old and over. Elementary includes kindergarten and grades 1–8; high school, grades 9–12; and college, 2-year and 4-year colleges, universities, and graduate and professional schools. Data for college represent degree-credit enrollment. See headnote, Table 223]

Year	All levels [1]			Elementary			High school			College		
	Total	Male	Female	Total	Male	Female	Total	Male	Female	Total	Male	Female
1970......	60.4	31.4	28.9	37.1	19.0	18.1	14.7	7.4	7.3	7.4	4.4	3.0
1980......	58.6	29.6	29.1	30.6	15.8	14.9	14.6	7.3	7.3	11.4	5.4	6.0
1985......	59.8	30.0	29.7	30.7	15.7	15.0	14.1	7.2	6.9	12.5	5.9	6.6
1990 [2].....	63.0	31.5	31.5	33.2	17.1	16.0	12.8	6.5	6.4	13.6	6.2	7.4
1992......	64.6	32.2	32.3	34.3	17.7	16.6	13.3	6.8	6.5	14.0	6.2	7.8
1993......	65.4	32.9	32.5	34.8	17.9	16.9	13.6	7.0	6.6	13.9	6.3	7.6
1994......	69.3	34.6	34.6	35.4	18.2	17.2	14.6	7.4	7.2	15.0	6.8	8.2
1995......	69.8	35.0	34.8	35.7	18.3	17.4	15.0	7.7	7.3	14.7	6.7	8.0
1996......	70.3	35.1	35.2	35.5	18.3	17.3	15.3	7.9	7.4	15.2	6.8	8.4
1997......	72.0	35.9	36.2	36.3	18.7	17.6	15.8	8.0	7.7	15.4	6.8	8.6
1998......	72.1	36.0	36.1	36.4	18.7	17.7	15.6	7.9	7.6	15.5	6.9	8.6
1999......	72.4	36.3	36.1	36.7	18.8	17.9	15.9	8.2	7.7	15.2	7.0	8.2
2000......	72.2	35.8	36.4	36.7	18.9	17.9	15.8	8.1	7.7	15.3	6.7	8.6
2001......	73.1	36.3	36.9	36.9	19.0	17.9	16.1	8.2	7.8	15.9	6.9	9.0
2002......	74.0	36.8	37.3	36.7	18.9	17.8	16.4	8.3	8.0	16.5	7.2	9.3
2003......	74.9	37.3	37.6	36.3	18.7	17.6	17.1	8.6	8.4	16.6	7.3	9.3
2004......	75.5	37.4	38.0	36.5	19.0	17.6	16.8	8.4	8.4	17.4	7.6	9.8
2005......	75.8	37.4	38.4	36.4	18.6	17.7	17.4	8.9	8.5	17.5	7.5	9.9
2006......	75.2	37.2	38.0	36.1	18.5	17.6	17.1	8.8	8.4	17.2	7.5	9.7
2007......	76.0	37.6	38.4	36.3	18.6	17.7	17.1	8.8	8.3	18.0	7.8	10.1
2008......	76.3	37.8	38.6	36.4	18.6	17.7	16.8	8.5	8.2	18.6	8.3	10.3
2009......	77.3	38.0	39.3	32.2	16.5	15.7	16.4	8.4	8.1	19.8	8.6	11.1

[1] Includes nursery schools, not shown separately. [2] Data beginning 1990, based on a revised edit and tabulation package.
Source: U.S. Census Bureau, Current Population Reports, PPL-148, P20, and earlier reports, and "School Enrollment," <http://www.census.gov/population/www/socdemo/school.html>.

Table 227. School Enrollment by Control and Level: 1980 to 2010

[In thousands (58,305 represents 58,305,000). As of fall. Data below college level are for regular day schools and exclude subcollegiate departments of colleges, federal schools, and home-schooled children. College data include degree-credit and nondegree-credit enrollment. Based on survey of state education agencies; see source for details. For more projections, see Tables 219 and 221]

Control of school and level	1980	1990	1995	2000	2005	2006	2007	2008	2009, proj.	2010, proj.
Total	**58,305**	**60,683**	**65,020**	**68,685**	**72,674**	**73,066**	**73,451**	**74,075**	**75,198**	**75,286**
Public.	50,335	52,061	55,933	58,956	62,135	62,496	62,783	63,237	64,092	64,231
Private	7,971	8,622	9,087	9,729	10,539	10,570	10,668	10,838	11,106	11,054
Pre-kindergarten through 8	31,639	34,388	37,094	38,592	38,928	38,866	38,751	38,620	38,592	38,729
Public.	27,647	29,876	32,338	33,686	34,204	34,235	34,205	34,285	34,440	34,637
Private	3,992	[1] 4,512	4,756	[1] 4,906	4,724	[1] 4,631	4,546	[1] 4,335	4,151	4,092
Grades 9 through 12	14,570	12,476	13,665	14,781	16,258	16,441	16,451	16,352	16,179	15,975
Public.	13,231	11,341	12,502	13,517	14,909	15,081	15,087	14,980	14,842	14,668
Private	1,339	1,136	1,163	[1] 1,264	1,349	[1] 1,360	1,364	[1] 1,373	1,337	1,306
College [2]	12,097	13,819	14,262	15,312	17,487	17,759	18,248	19,103	20,428	20,582
Public.	9,457	10,845	11,092	11,753	13,022	13,180	13,491	13,972	14,811	[3] 14,926
Private	2,640	2,974	3,169	3,560	4,466	4,579	4,757	5,131	5,617	5,657
Not-for-profit	2,528	2,760	2,929	3,109	3,455	3,513	3,571	3,662	3,765	(NA)
For profit	112	214	240	450	1,011	1,066	1,186	1,469	1,852	(NA)

NA Not available. [1] Estimated. [2] Data beginning 2000, reflects new classification system. See footnote 1, Table 278. [3] Data are actual.

Source: U.S. National Center for Education Statistics, *Digest of Education Statistics*, annual, and *Projections of Education Statistics*, annual. See also <http://www.nces.ed.gov/annuals>.

Table 228. Students Who Are Foreign Born or Who Have Foreign-Born Parents: 2009

[In thousands (48,684 represents 48,684,000), except percent. As of October. Covers civilian noninstitutional population enrolled in elementary school and above. Based on Current Population Survey, see text, Section 1 and Appendix III]

Characteristic	All students	Students with at least one foreign-born parent					
		Total		Foreign-born student		Native student	
		Number	Percent	Number	Percent	Number	Percent
ELEMENTARY AND HIGH SCHOOL							
Total [1]	**48,684**	**10,965**	**22.5**	**2,355**	**4.8**	**8,610**	**17.7**
White [2]	37,001	7,584	20.5	1,500	4.1	6,084	16.4
White, non-Hispanic.	27,817	1,806	6.5	314	1.1	1,492	5.4
Black [2]	7,429	1,052	14.2	313	4.2	739	9.9
Asian [2,3]	1,878	1,660	88.4	475	25.3	1,185	63.1
Hispanic [4]	10,200	6,287	61.6	1,274	12.5	5,014	49.2
COLLEGE, 1 TO 4 YEARS							
Total [1]	**16,012**	**3,617**	**22.6**	**1,534**	**9.6**	**2,083**	**13.0**
White [2]	12,235	2,198	18.0	879	7.2	1,319	10.8
White, non-Hispanic.	10,252	916	8.9	355	3.5	561	5.5
Black [2]	2,410	482	20.0	262	10.9	219	9.1
Asian [2,3]	850	776	91.3	376	44.2	400	47.1
Hispanic [4]	2,169	1,375	63.4	548	25.3	827	38.1
GRADUATE SCHOOL							
Total [1]	**3,752**	**1,068**	**28.5**	**637**	**17.0**	**431**	**11.5**
White [2]	2,792	483	17.3	247	8.8	236	8.5
White, non-Hispanic.	2,574	345	13.4	173	6.7	172	6.7
Black [2]	479	167	34.9	109	22.8	58	12.1
Asian [2,3]	381	366	96.1	273	71.7	93	24.4
Hispanic [4]	265	170	64.2	81	30.6	88	33.2

[1] Includes other races not shown separately. [2] For persons who selected this race group only. See footnote 2, Table 229. [3] Data are for Asians only, excludes Pacific Islanders. [4] Persons of Hispanic origin may be any race.

Source: U.S. Census Bureau, Current Population Survey, unpublished data, <http://www.census.gov/population/www/socdemo/school.html>.

Table 229. Educational Attainment by Race and Hispanic Origin: 1970 to 2010

[In percent. For persons 25 years old and over. 1970 and 1980 data as of April 1 and based on sample data from the censuses of population. Other years as of March and based on the Current Population Survey; see text, Section 1 and Appendix III. See Table 230 for data by sex]

Year	Total [1]	White [2]	Black [2]	Asian and Pacific Islander [2]	Hispanic [3]			
					Total [4]	Mexican	Puerto Rican	Cuban
HIGH SCHOOL GRADUATE OR MORE [5]								
1970............	52.3	54.5	31.4	62.2	32.1	24.2	23.4	43.9
1980............	66.5	68.8	51.2	74.8	44.0	37.6	40.1	55.3
1990............	77.6	79.1	66.2	80.4	50.8	44.1	55.5	63.5
1995............	81.7	83.0	73.8	(NA)	53.4	46.5	61.3	64.7
2000............	84.1	84.9	78.5	85.7	57.0	51.0	64.3	73.0
2005............	85.2	85.8	81.1	[6] 87.6	58.5	52.2	72.4	73.3
2007............	85.7	86.2	82.3	87.8	60.3	53.9	73.5	79.8
2008............	86.6	87.1	83.0	88.7	62.3	55.2	76.4	80.0
2009............	86.7	87.1	84.1	88.2	61.9	55.7	76.6	78.5
2010............	87.1	87.6	84.2	88.9	62.9	57.4	74.8	81.4
COLLEGE GRADUATE OR MORE [5]								
1970............	10.7	11.3	4.4	20.4	4.5	2.5	2.2	11.1
1980............	16.2	17.1	8.4	32.9	7.6	4.9	5.6	16.2
1990............	21.3	22.0	11.3	39.9	9.2	5.4	9.7	20.2
1995............	23.0	24.0	13.2	(NA)	9.3	6.5	10.7	19.4
2000............	25.6	26.1	16.5	43.9	10.6	6.9	13.0	23.0
2005............	27.7	28.1	17.6	[6] 50.2	12.0	8.2	13.8	24.6
2007............	28.7	29.1	18.5	52.1	12.7	9.0	16.4	27.2
2008............	29.4	29.8	19.6	52.6	13.3	9.1	15.5	28.1
2009............	29.5	29.9	19.3	52.3	13.2	9.5	16.5	27.9
2010............	29.9	30.3	19.8	52.4	13.9	10.6	17.5	26.2

NA Not available. [1] Includes other races not shown separately. [2] Beginning 2005, for persons who selected this race group only. The 2003 Current Population Survey (CPS) allowed respondents to choose more than one race. Beginning 2003, data represent persons who selected this race group only and exclude persons reporting more than one race. The CPS in prior years only allowed respondents to report one race group. See also comments on race in the text for Section 1. [3] Persons of Hispanic origin may be any race. [4] Includes persons of other Hispanic origin not shown separately. [5] Through 1990, completed 4 years of high school or more and 4 years of college or more. [6] Starting in 2005, data are for Asians only, excludes Pacific Islanders.
Source: U.S. Census Bureau, U.S. Census of Population, 1970 and 1980, Vol. 1; Current Population Reports, P20-550, and earlier reports; and "Educational Attainment," <http://www.census.gov/population/www/socdemo/educ-attn.html>.

Table 230. Educational Attainment by Race, Hispanic Origin, and Sex: 1970 to 2010

[In percent. See Table 229 for headnote and totals for both sexes]

Year	All races [1]		White [2]		Black [2]		Asian and Pacific Islander [2]		Hispanic [3]	
	Male	Female	Male	Female	Male	Female	Male	Female	Male	Female
HIGH SCHOOL GRADUATE OR MORE [4]										
1970..............	51.9	52.8	54.0	55.0	30.1	32.5	61.3	63.1	37.9	34.2
1980..............	67.3	65.8	69.6	68.1	50.8	51.5	78.8	71.4	45.4	42.7
1990..............	77.7	77.5	79.1	79.0	65.8	66.5	84.0	77.2	50.3	51.3
1995..............	81.7	81.6	83.0	83.0	73.4	74.1	(NA)	(NA)	52.9	53.8
2000..............	84.2	84.0	84.8	85.0	78.7	78.3	88.2	83.4	56.6	57.5
2005..............	84.9	85.5	85.2	86.2	81.0	81.2	[5] 90.4	[5] 85.2	57.9	59.1
2007..............	85.0	86.4	85.3	87.1	81.9	82.6	89.8	85.9	58.2	62.5
2008..............	85.9	87.2	86.3	87.8	81.8	84.0	90.8	86.9	60.9	63.7
2009..............	86.2	87.1	86.5	87.7	84.0	84.1	90.4	86.2	60.6	63.3
2010..............	86.6	87.6	86.9	88.2	83.6	84.6	91.2	87.0	61.4	64.4
COLLEGE GRADUATE OR MORE [4]										
1970..............	13.5	8.1	14.4	8.4	4.2	4.6	23.5	17.3	7.8	4.3
1980..............	20.1	12.8	21.3	13.3	8.4	8.3	39.8	27.0	9.4	6.0
1990..............	24.4	18.4	25.3	19.0	11.9	10.8	44.9	35.4	9.8	8.7
1995..............	26.0	20.2	27.2	21.0	13.6	12.9	(NA)	(NA)	10.1	8.4
2000..............	27.8	23.6	28.5	23.9	16.3	16.7	47.6	40.7	10.7	10.6
2005..............	28.9	26.5	29.4	26.8	16.0	18.8	[5] 54.0	[5] 46.8	11.8	12.1
2007..............	29.5	28.0	29.9	28.3	18.0	19.0	55.2	49.3	11.8	13.7
2008..............	30.1	28.8	30.5	29.1	18.7	20.4	55.8	49.8	12.6	14.1
2009..............	30.1	29.1	30.6	29.3	17.8	20.6	55.7	49.3	12.5	14.0
2010..............	30.3	29.6	30.8	29.9	17.7	21.4	55.6	49.5	12.9	14.9

NA Not available. [1] Includes other races not shown separately. [2] Beginning 2005, for persons who selected this race group only. See footnote 2, Table 229. [3] Persons of Hispanic origin may be any race. [4] Through 1990, completed 4 years of high school or more and 4 years of college or more. [5] Starting in 2005, data are for Asians only, excludes Pacific Islanders.
Source: U.S. Census Bureau, U.S. Census of Population, 1970 and 1980, Vol. 1; Current Population Reports P20-550, and earlier reports; and "Educational Attainment," <http://www.census.gov/population/www/socdemo/educ-attn.html>.

Table 231. Educational Attainment by Selected Characteristics: 2010

[For persons 25 years old and over (199,928 represents 199,928,000). As of March. Based on the Current Population Survey; see text, Section 1 and Appendix III. For composition of regions, see map inside front cover]

Characteristic	Population (1,000)	Percent of population—					
		Not a high school graduate	High school graduate	Some college, but no degree	Associate's degree [1]	Bachelor's degree	Advanced degree
Total persons	**199,928**	**12.9**	**31.2**	**16.8**	**9.1**	**19.4**	**10.5**
Age:							
25 to 34 years old	41,085	11.6	27.2	18.9	9.5	24.0	8.9
35 to 44 years old	40,447	11.7	28.6	16.3	10.3	21.9	11.2
45 to 54 years old	44,387	10.4	32.8	16.7	10.6	19.0	10.4
55 to 64 years old	35,395	10.4	31.3	17.3	9.2	18.6	13.1
65 to 74 years old	20,956	17.0	35.4	15.7	6.6	14.1	11.1
75 years old or over	17,657	24.6	37.6	14.0	4.6	11.9	7.3
Sex:							
Male	96,325	13.4	31.9	16.5	8.0	19.4	10.9
Female	103,603	12.4	30.7	17.1	10.2	19.4	10.2
Race:							
White [2]	163,083	12.4	31.3	16.7	9.2	19.6	10.7
Black [2]	22,969	15.8	35.2	19.8	9.4	13.3	6.5
Other	13,876	13.0	23.5	13.0	8.1	26.6	15.7
Hispanic origin:							
Hispanic	26,375	37.1	29.6	12.9	6.5	10.1	3.8
Non-Hispanic	173,553	9.2	31.5	17.4	9.5	20.8	11.5
Region:							
Northeast	36,834	11.4	33.7	13.0	8.4	20.6	12.9
Midwest	43,380	10.1	34.6	17.6	10.0	18.2	9.5
South	73,682	14.5	31.9	16.9	8.7	18.1	9.8
West	46,032	14.0	25.0	19.0	9.5	21.6	10.8
Marital status:							
Never married	35,956	14.0	30.4	17.5	8.4	21.2	8.6
Married, spouse present	117,966	10.5	30.0	16.2	9.5	21.2	12.6
Married, spouse absent [3]	3,104	26.5	31.3	12.4	6.5	14.6	8.7
Separated	5,081	23.3	34.4	18.0	8.6	10.6	5.2
Widowed	14,317	25.3	38.6	14.5	6.2	9.9	5.5
Divorced	23,504	11.3	33.7	21.0	10.5	15.7	7.7
Civilian labor force status:							
Employed	121,119	8.2	28.2	17.0	10.5	23.2	13.0
Unemployed	11,903	16.3	38.7	18.2	8.4	13.5	4.8
Not in the labor force	66,905	20.9	35.6	16.2	6.8	13.5	7.0

[1] Includes vocational degrees. [2] For persons who selected this race group only. See footnote 2, Table 229. [3] Excludes those separated.

Source: U.S. Census Bureau, Current Population Survey, unpublished data, <http://www.census.gov/population/www/socdemo/educ-attn.html>.

Table 232. Mean Earnings by Highest Degree Earned: 2009

[In dollars. For persons 18 years old and over with earnings. Persons as of March 2010. Based on Current Population Survey; see text, Section 1 and Appendix III. For definition of mean, see Guide to Tabular Presentation]

Characteristic	Total persons	Mean earnings by level of highest degree (dollars)							
		Not a high school graduate	High school graduate only	Some college, no degree	Associate's	Bachelor's	Master's	Professional	Doctorate
All persons [1]	**42,469**	**20,241**	**30,627**	**32,295**	**39,771**	**56,665**	**73,738**	**127,803**	**103,054**
Age:									
25 to 34 years old	36,595	19,415	27,511	31,392	35,544	45,692	58,997	86,440	74,626
35 to 44 years old	49,356	24,728	33,614	39,806	42,353	65,346	80,593	136,366	108,147
45 to 54 years old	51,956	23,725	36,090	44,135	46,413	69,548	86,532	148,805	112,134
55 to 64 years old	50,372	24,537	34,583	42,547	42,192	59,670	76,372	149,184	110,895
65 years old and over	37,544	19,395	28,469	29,602	33,541	44,147	45,138	95,440	95,585
Sex:									
Male	50,186	23,036	35,468	39,204	47,572	69,479	90,964	150,310	114,347
Female	33,797	15,514	24,304	25,340	33,432	43,589	58,534	89,897	83,708
White [2]	43,337	20,457	31,429	33,119	40,632	57,762	73,771	127,942	104,533
Male	51,287	23,353	36,418	40,352	48,521	71,286	91,776	149,149	115,497
Female	34,040	15,187	24,615	25,537	33,996	43,309	58,036	89,526	85,682
Black [2]	33,362	18,936	26,970	29,129	33,734	47,799	60,067	102,328	82,510
Male	37,553	21,828	30,723	33,969	41,142	55,655	68,890	(B)	(B)
Female	29,831	15,644	22,964	25,433	29,464	42,587	54,523	(B)	(B)
Hispanic [3]	29,565	19,816	25,998	29,836	33,783	49,017	71,322	79,228	88,435
Male	32,279	21,588	28,908	35,089	38,768	58,570	80,737	(B)	89,956
Female	25,713	16,170	21,473	24,281	29,785	39,566	61,843	(B)	(B)

B Base figure too small to meet statistical standards for reliability of a derived figure. [1] Includes other races not shown separately. [2] For persons who selected this race group only. See footnote 2, Table 229. [3] Persons of Hispanic origin may be any race.

Source: U.S. Census Bureau, Current Population Survey, unpublished data, <http://www.census.gov/population/www/socdemo/educ-attn.html>.

Table 233. Educational Attainment by State: 1990 to 2009

[In percent. 1990 and 2000 as of April. 2009 represents annual averages for calendar year. For persons 25 years old and over. Based on the 1990 and 2000 Census of Population and the 2009 American Community Survey, which includes the household population and the population living in institutions, college dormitories, and other group quarters. See text, Section 1 and Appendix III. For margin of error data, see source]

State	1990			2000			2009		
	High school graduate or more	Bachelor's degree or more	Advanced degree or more	High school graduate or more	Bachelor's degree or more	Advanced degree or more	High school graduate or more	Bachelor's degree or more	Advanced degree or more
United States	75.2	20.3	7.2	80.4	24.4	8.9	85.3	27.9	10.3
Alabama	66.9	15.7	5.5	75.3	19.0	6.9	82.1	22.0	7.7
Alaska	86.6	23.0	8.0	88.3	24.7	8.6	91.4	26.6	9.0
Arizona	78.7	20.3	7.0	81.0	23.5	8.4	84.2	25.6	9.3
Arkansas	66.3	13.3	4.5	75.3	16.7	5.7	82.4	18.9	6.1
California	76.2	23.4	8.1	76.8	26.6	9.5	80.6	29.9	10.7
Colorado	84.4	27.0	9.0	86.9	32.7	11.1	89.3	35.9	12.7
Connecticut	79.2	27.2	11.0	84.0	31.4	13.3	88.6	35.6	15.5
Delaware	77.5	21.4	7.7	82.6	25.0	9.4	87.4	28.7	11.4
District of Columbia	73.1	33.3	17.2	77.8	39.1	21.0	87.1	48.5	28.0
Florida	74.4	18.3	6.3	79.9	22.3	8.1	85.3	25.3	9.0
Georgia	70.9	19.3	6.4	78.6	24.3	8.3	83.9	27.5	9.9
Hawaii	80.1	22.9	7.1	84.6	26.2	8.4	90.4	29.6	9.9
Idaho	79.7	17.7	5.3	84.7	21.7	6.8	88.4	23.9	7.5
Illinois	76.2	21.0	7.5	81.4	26.1	9.5	86.4	30.6	11.7
Indiana	75.6	15.6	6.4	82.1	19.4	7.2	86.6	22.5	8.1
Iowa	80.1	16.9	5.2	86.1	21.2	6.5	90.5	25.1	7.4
Kansas	81.3	21.1	7.0	86.0	25.8	8.7	89.7	29.5	10.2
Kentucky	64.6	13.6	5.5	74.1	17.1	6.9	81.7	21.0	8.5
Louisiana	68.3	16.1	5.6	74.8	18.7	6.5	82.2	21.4	6.9
Maine	78.8	18.8	6.1	85.4	22.9	7.9	90.2	26.9	9.6
Maryland	78.4	26.5	10.9	83.8	31.4	13.4	88.2	35.7	16.0
Massachusetts	80.0	27.2	10.6	84.8	33.2	13.7	89.0	38.2	16.4
Michigan	76.8	17.4	6.4	83.4	21.8	8.1	87.9	24.6	9.4
Minnesota	82.4	21.8	6.3	87.9	27.4	8.3	91.5	31.5	10.3
Mississippi	64.3	14.7	5.1	72.9	16.9	5.8	80.4	19.6	7.1
Missouri	73.9	17.8	6.1	81.3	21.6	7.6	86.8	25.2	9.5
Montana	81.0	19.8	5.7	87.2	24.4	7.2	90.8	27.4	8.3
Nebraska	81.8	18.9	5.9	86.6	23.7	7.3	89.8	27.4	8.8
Nevada	78.8	15.3	5.2	80.7	18.2	6.1	83.9	21.8	7.6
New Hampshire	82.2	24.4	7.9	87.4	28.7	10.0	91.3	32.0	11.2
New Jersey	76.7	24.9	8.8	82.1	29.8	11.0	87.4	34.5	12.9
New Mexico	75.1	20.4	8.3	78.9	23.5	9.8	82.8	25.3	10.4
New York	74.8	23.1	9.9	79.1	27.4	11.8	84.7	32.4	14.0
North Carolina	70.0	17.4	5.4	78.1	22.5	7.2	84.3	26.5	8.8
North Dakota	76.7	18.1	4.5	83.9	22.0	5.5	90.1	25.8	6.7
Ohio	75.7	17.0	5.9	83.0	21.1	7.4	87.6	24.1	8.8
Oklahoma	74.6	17.8	6.0	80.6	20.3	6.8	85.6	22.7	7.4
Oregon	81.5	20.6	7.0	85.1	25.1	8.7	89.1	29.2	10.4
Pennsylvania	74.7	17.9	6.6	81.9	22.4	8.4	87.9	26.4	10.2
Rhode Island	72.0	21.3	7.8	78.0	25.6	9.7	84.7	30.5	11.7
South Carolina	68.3	16.6	5.4	76.3	20.4	6.9	83.6	24.3	8.4
South Dakota	77.1	17.2	4.9	84.6	21.5	6.0	89.9	25.1	7.3
Tennessee	67.1	16.0	5.4	75.9	19.6	6.8	83.1	23.0	7.9
Texas	72.1	20.3	6.5	75.7	23.2	7.6	79.9	25.5	8.5
Utah	85.1	22.3	6.8	87.7	26.1	8.3	90.4	28.5	9.1
Vermont	80.8	24.3	8.9	86.4	29.4	11.1	91.0	33.1	13.3
Virginia	75.2	24.5	9.1	81.5	29.5	11.6	86.6	34.0	14.1
Washington	83.8	22.9	7.0	87.1	27.7	9.3	89.7	31.0	11.1
West Virginia	66.0	12.3	4.8	75.2	14.8	5.9	82.8	17.3	6.7
Wisconsin	78.6	17.7	5.6	85.1	22.4	7.2	89.8	25.7	8.4
Wyoming	83.0	18.8	5.7	87.9	21.9	7.0	91.8	23.8	7.9

Source: U.S. Census Bureau, 1990 Census of Population, CPH-L-96; 2000 Census of Population, P37. "Sex by Educational Attainment for the Population 25 Years and Over"; 2009 American Community Survey, R1501, "Percent of Persons 25 Years and Over Who Have Completed High School (Includes Equivalency)," R1502, "Percent of Persons 25 Years and Over Who Have Completed a Bachelor's Degree," and R1503, "Percent of Persons 25 Years and Over Who Have Completed an Advanced Degree," <http://factfinder.census.gov/>, accessed February 2011.

Education 153

Table 234. Children With Parental Involvement in Home Literacy Activities: 1993 and 2007

[In percent, except number of children (8,579 represents 8,579,000). For children 3 to 5 years old not yet enrolled in kindergarten who participated in activities with a family member. Based on the School Readiness Early Childhood Program Participation Surveys of the National Household Education Surveys Program; see source and Appendix III. See also Table 231]

Characteristic	Children (1,000)		Read to [1]		Told a story [1]		Taught letters, words, or numbers [1]		Visited a library [2]	
	1993	2007	1993	2007	1993	2005	1993	2005	1993	2007
Total............	8,579	8,686	78	83	43	54	58	77	38	36
Age:										
3 years old................	3,889	3,755	79	84	46	54	57	75	34	36
4 years old................	3,713	3,738	78	83	41	53	58	77	41	35
5 years old................	976	1,193	76	83	36	55	58	80	38	39
Race/ethnicity:										
White, non-Hispanic............	5,902	4,664	85	91	44	53	58	76	42	41
Black, non-Hispanic............	1,271	1,312	66	78	39	54	63	81	29	25
Hispanic [3]................	1,026	1,899	58	68	38	50	54	74	26	27
Other.................	381	812	73	87	50	64	59	82	43	46
Mother's home language: [4]										
English..............	7,805	7,244	81	88	44	55	58	78	39	38
Not English	603	1,312	42	57	36	45	52	69	26	24
Mother's highest education: [4]										
Less than high school	1,036	808	60	56	37	39	56	70	22	20
High school	3,268	2,048	76	74	41	51	56	78	31	29
Vocational ed or some college............	2,624	2,658	83	86	45	57	60	79	44	33
College degree	912	1,849	90	95	48	56	56	75	55	43
Graduate/professional training or degree	569	1,194	90	95	50	64	60	76	59	53

[1] Three or more times in the past week. [2] At least once in the past month. [3] Persons of Hispanic origin may be any race. [4] Excludes children with no mother in the household and no female guardian.

Source: U.S. National Center for Education Statistics, Statistical Brief, NCES 2000–026, November 1999; the Early Childhood Program Participation Survey, National Household Education Surveys Program (NHES), 2005, unpublished data; and the NHES School Readiness Survey, 2007, unpublished data, <http://nces.ed.gov/nhes>.

Table 235. Children's School Readiness Skills: 1993 and 2007

[In percent. For children 3 to 5 years old not yet enrolled in kindergarten. Based on the School Readiness Surveys of the National Household Education Survey Program; see source for details. See also Table 234]

Characteristic	Recognizes all letters		Counts to 20 or higher		Writes name		Reads or pretends to read storybooks		Has 3 to 4 skills	
	1993	2007	1993	2007	1993	2007	1993	2005	1993	2005
Total	21	32	52	63	50	60	72	70	35	42
Age:										
3 years old.....................	11	17	37	47	22	34	66	67	15	24
4 years old.....................	28	38	62	73	70	76	75	73	49	55
5 years old.....................	36	59	78	84	84	88	81	72	65	66
Sex:										
Male.........................	19	31	49	61	47	56	68	70	32	40
Female........................	23	33	56	65	53	63	76	71	39	45
Race/ethnicity:										
White, non-Hispanic..............	23	36	56	69	52	64	76	75	39	47
Black, non-Hispanic..............	18	37	53	69	45	58	63	67	31	44
Hispanic [1].......................	10	15	32	41	42	49	59	55	22	26
Other..........................	22	39	49	69	52	61	70	79	36	48
Mother's employment status: [2]										
Employed.......................	23	34	57	66	52	63	75	72	39	46
Unemployed.....................	17	14	41	42	46	41	67	61	29	32
Not in the labor force	18	31	49	60	47	58	68	69	32	39
Family type:										
Two parents	22	33	54	64	51	62	74	72	37	44
None or one parent	18	27	49	57	47	52	65	65	31	36
Poverty status: [3]										
Above threshold..................	24	35	57	67	53	64	74	75	40	47
Below threshold..................	12	21	41	48	41	46	64	54	23	26

[1] Persons of Hispanic origin may be any race. [2] Excludes children with no mother in the household and no female guardian. [3] Children are considered poor if they lived in households with incomes below the poverty threshold, which is a dollar amount determined by the federal government to meet the household's need, given its size and composition. For more information about the poverty threshold, see text, section 13.

Source: U.S. Department of Education, U.S. National Center for Education Statistics, *Home Literacy Activities and Signs of Children's Emerging Literacy*, 1993, NCES 2000–026, November 1999; the Early Childhood Program Participation Survey, National Household Education Surveys Program (NHES), 2005, unpublished data; and the NHES School Readiness Survey, 2007, unpublished data, <http://nces.ed.gov/nhes>.

Table 236. Children Who Speak a Language Other Than English at Home by Region: 2009

[In thousands (11,227 represents 11,227,000), except percent. For children 5 to 17 years old. For more on languages spoken at home, see Tables 54–55. Based on the American Community Survey; see text Section 1, and Appendix III. For composition of regions, see map inside front cover]

Characteristic	U.S.	Northeast	Midwest	South	West
Children who speak another language at home	11,227	1,888	1,359	3,661	4,318
Percent of children 5 to 17 years old	21.1	20.9	11.8	18.4	33.6
Speak Spanish	8,067	1,023	816	2,889	3,339
Speak English "very well"	6,131	808	611	2,177	2,535
Speak English less than "very well"	1,936	215	205	713	803
Speak other Indo-European languages	1,487	516	286	385	299
Speak English "very well"	1,206	411	228	320	247
Speak English less than "very well"	281	105	58	66	52
Speak Asian and Pacific Island languages	1,242	248	159	286	549
Speak English "very well"	914	186	111	215	403
Speak English less than "very well"	327	62	48	71	146
Speak other languages	431	101	99	100	131
Speak English "very well"	342	79	75	83	104
Speak English less than "very well"	90	23	23	17	27
Have difficulty speaking English [1]	2,634	405	334	867	1,028
Language spoken at home in linguistically isolated households [2]	2,960	468	333	989	1,170
Speak only English	170	35	21	58	57
Speak Spanish	2,134	254	207	777	896
Speak other Indo-European languages	226	79	39	61	46
Speak Asian and Pacific Island languages	352	82	42	78	150
Speak other languages	78	18	25	15	21

[1] Children aged 5 to 17 who speak English less than "very well." [2] A household in which no person aged 14 or over speaks English at least "very well."

Source: U.S. Census Bureau, 2009 American Community Survey, B16003, "Age by Language Spoken at Home for the Population 5 Years and Over in Linguistically Isolated Households" and C16004, "Age by Language Spoken at Home by Ability to Speak English for the Population 5 Years and Over," <http://factfinder.census.gov/\>, accessed January 2011.

Table 237. Preprimary School Enrollment—Summary: 1970 to 2009

[As of October. Civilian noninstitutional population (10,949 represents 10,949,000). Includes public and nonpublic nursery school and kindergarten programs. Excludes 5-year-olds enrolled in elementary school. Based on Current Population Survey. See text, Section 1 and Appendix III]

Item	1970	1980	1990	1995	2000	2005	2007	2008	2009
NUMBER OF CHILDREN (1,000)									
Population, 3 to 5 years old	10,949	9,284	11,207	12,518	11,858	12,134	12,325	12,583	12,718
Total enrolled [1]	4,104	4,878	6,659	7,739	7,592	7,801	8,056	7,928	8,076
Nursery	1,094	1,981	3,378	4,331	4,326	4,529	4,569	4,570	4,648
Public	332	628	1,202	1,950	2,146	2,409	2,532	2,609	2,703
Private	762	1,353	2,177	2,381	2,180	2,120	2,037	1,961	1,945
Kindergarten	3,010	2,897	3,281	3,408	3,266	3,272	3,487	3,358	3,428
Public	2,498	2,438	2,767	2,799	2,701	2,804	3,087	2,982	3,144
Private	511	459	513	608	565	468	400	376	284
White [2]	3,443	3,994	5,389	6,144	5,861	6,025	6,191	6,011	5,943
Black [2]	586	725	964	1,236	1,265	1,148	1,213	1,231	1,337
Hispanic [3]	(NA)	370	642	1,040	1,155	1,494	1,751	1,645	1,721
3 years old	454	857	1,205	1,489	1,540	1,715	1,717	1,654	1,776
4 years old	1,007	1,423	2,086	2,553	2,556	2,668	2,774	2,804	2,698
5 years old	2,643	2,598	3,367	3,697	3,496	3,418	3,565	3,470	3,601
ENROLLMENT RATE									
Total enrolled [1]	37.5	52.5	59.4	61.8	64.0	64.3	65.4	63.0	65.3
White [2]	37.8	52.7	59.7	63.0	63.2	65.1	68.7	65.1	64.5
Black [2]	34.9	51.8	57.8	58.9	68.5	62.0	69.7	66.2	68.6
Hispanic [3]	(NA)	43.3	49.0	51.1	52.6	56.1	63.0	57.6	56.8
3 years old	12.9	27.3	32.6	35.9	39.2	41.3	41.5	39.3	40.7
4 years old	27.8	46.3	56.0	61.6	64.9	66.2	67.8	66.1	64.6
5 years old	69.3	84.7	88.8	87.5	86.4	86.4	87.1	83.8	91.5

NA Not available. [1] Includes races not shown separately. [2] Beginning 2005, for persons who selected this race group only. See footnote 2, Table 229. [3] Persons of Hispanic origin may be any race. The method of identifying Hispanic children was changed in 1980 from allocation based on status of mother to status reported for each child. The number of Hispanic children using the new method is larger.

Source: U.S. Census Bureau, Current Population Reports, PPL-148; earlier PPL and P-20 reports and unpublished data; and "School Enrollment," <http://www.census.gov/population/www/socdemo/school.html>.

Education 155

Table 238. Type of School Attended by Student and Household Characteristics: 1996 and 2007

[In percent, except total in thousands (34,600 represent 34,600,000). For students in grades 1 to 12. Includes homeschooled students enrolled in public or private school 9 or more hours per week. Based on the Parent and Family Involvement Survey of the National Household Education Survey Program; see source and Appendix III for details]

Characteristic	Public Assigned 1996	Public Assigned 2007	Public Chosen 1996	Public Chosen 2007	Private Church related 1996	Private Church related 2007	Private Not church related 1996	Private Not church related 2007
Total students (1,000)	**34,600**	**34,700**	**6,200**	**7,400**	**3,700**	**4,100**	**1,000**	**1,200**
Percent distribution	76.0	73.2	13.7	15.5	8.0	8.7	2.3	2.6
Grade level:								
1 to 5	74.1	71.4	14.8	17.0	8.9	8.7	2.2	2.8
6 to 8	79.4	77.0	11.2	11.9	7.4	8.6	2.0	2.5
9 to 12	75.9	72.6	14.1	16.4	7.3	8.6	2.7	2.3
Race/ethnicity:								
White, non-Hispanic	77.1	73.6	11.1	12.5	9.2	10.8	2.7	3.1
Black, non-Hispanic	72.9	68.9	21.5	23.7	4.2	5.5	1.4	1.8
Other, non-Hispanic	69.3	72.7	19.0	17.4	9.5	6.4	2.2	3.5
Hispanic [1]	76.4	75.8	16.1	17.4	6.3	5.6	1.3	1.2
Family type:								
Two-parent household	76.3	72.7	11.7	14.4	9.5	10.0	2.4	2.9
One-parent household	74.6	74.9	18.4	17.7	5.0	5.4	1.9	2.0
Nonparent guardians	80.2	72.8	14.6	22.7	2.3	3.9	2.9	0.6
Parents' education:								
Less than high school	78.8	85.4	17.4	12.4	2.0	1.5	1.8	0.6
High school diploma or equivalent	82.1	79.8	12.3	15.4	5.0	3.5	0.7	1.3
Some college, including vocational/technical . . .	76.4	75.4	14.7	16.3	7.1	7.3	1.8	1.0
Bachelor's degree	70.7	70.7	13.1	15.3	13.0	11.6	3.3	2.4
Graduate/professional degree	66.1	62.2	12.6	15.8	15.3	15.1	6.0	6.8
Region: [2]								
Northeast	74.3	72.3	12.9	13.3	9.2	10.9	3.6	3.4
South	78.7	75.2	12.5	14.0	6.4	8.5	2.4	2.3
Midwest	75.4	73.6	12.4	15.0	10.9	9.9	1.3	1.5
West	74.0	70.6	17.7	20.1	6.3	6.1	2.0	3.3

[1] Persons of Hispanic origin may be of any race. [2] For composition of regions see map, inside front cover.
Source: U.S. National Center for Education Statistics, *Condition of Education, 2009*, NCES 2009-081, June 2009.

Table 239. Public Charter and Traditional Schools—Selected Characteristics: 2007 to 2008

[47,432 represents 47,432,000. For school year ending in 2008. A public charter school is a public school that, in accordance with an enabling state statute, has been granted a charter exempting it from selected state and local rules and regulations]

Characteristic	All schools Traditional	All schools Public charter	Elementary Traditional	Elementary Public charter	Secondary Traditional	Secondary Public charter	Combined Traditional	Combined Public charter
Number of schools	87,190	3,560	60,390	2,050	20,720	920	6,080	590
Enrollment (1,000)	47,432	1,047	29,194	619	16,513	229	1,725	200
PERCENT DISTRIBUTION OF STUDENTS								
Race/ethnicity	100.0	100.0	100.0	100.0	100.0	100.0	100.0	100.0
White, non-Hispanic	58.2	41.0	56.2	35.9	60.3	43.5	71.3	54.0
Black, non-Hispanic	15.7	29.0	15.8	36.1	15.8	(S)	12.2	17.6
Hispanic [1]	20.3	23.8	22.1	21.6	18.0	31.5	11.5	22.0
Asian/Pacific Islander	4.4	3.8	4.5	3.8	4.7	3.5	1.3	(S)
American Indian/Alaska Native	1.4	2.3	1.4	2.6	1.2	1.5	3.8	(S)
PERCENT DISTRIBUTION OF SCHOOLS								
Size of enrollment	100.0	100.0	100.0	100.0	100.0	100.0	100.0	100.0
Less than 300 students	28.1	64.2	24.1	59.3	28.9	81.1	65.8	54.9
300 to 599 students	40.6	25.8	49.2	29.2	20.8	14.8	22.8	31.2
600 to 999 students	20.8	7.4	22.5	10.0	19.9	(S)	7.5	6.9
1,000 students or more	10.5	2.7	4.3	(S)	30.4	(S)	4.0	(S)
Percent minority enrollment	100.0	100.0	100.0	100.0	100.0	100.0	100.0	100.0
Less than 10.0	28.7	(S)	27.7	(S)	30.2	(S)	33.8	(S)
10.0 to 24.9	17.9	17.0	18.1	15.7	18.4	(S)	14.5	30.7
25.0 to 49.9	19.7	18.0	19.5	15.1	21.3	20.8	17.4	23.9
50.0 to 74.9	12.6	14.1	13.1	11.8	11.4	20.7	12.2	(S)
75.0 or more	21.0	42.7	21.7	50.4	18.7	39.2	22.1	21.2
Percent of students eligible for free or reduced-price lunch [2]	100.0	100.0	100.0	100.0	100.0	100.0	100.0	100.0
Less than 15.0	4.0	24.5	1.7	16.2	8.5	35.8	11.0	35.3
15.0 to 29.9	27.6	9.9	27.4	9.4	32.7	(S)	11.9	(S)
30.0 to 49.9	27.7	18.8	26.5	16.6	30.9	28.7	28.6	(S)
50.0 to 74.9	21.4	21.4	23.2	25.9	15.6	(S)	22.6	27.5
75.0 or more	19.4	25.5	21.2	31.9	12.2	16.6	25.9	16.9

S Figure does not meet publication standards. [1] Persons of Hispanic origin may be any race. [2] Excludes data for schools not providing information on eligibility for free or reduced-price lunch.
Source: U.S. National Center for Education Statistics, School and Staffing Survey (SASS), "Public School Questionnaire," 2007-08 and "Public Teacher Questionnaire," 2007-08; <http://www.nces.ed.gov/>.

Table 240. Students Who Are Homeschooled by Selected Characteristics: 2007

[As of spring. (51,135 represents 51,135,000). For students 5 to 17 with a grade equivalent of K–12. Homeschoolers are students whose parents reported them to be schooled at home instead of a public or private school. Excludes students who were enrolled in school for more than 25 hours a week or were homeschooled due to a temporary illness. Based on the Parent and Family Involvement Survey of the National Household Education Surveys Program; see source and Appendix III for details]

Characteristic	Number of students			Percent distribution		
	Total (1,000)	Home-schooled (1,000)	Percent home-schooled	Total	Home-schooled	Non-Home-schooled
Total.	51,135	1,508	2.9	100.0	100.0	100.0
Grade equivalent: [1]						
K–5	23,529	717	3.0	46.0	47.6	46.0
Kindergarten	3,669	114	3.1	7.2	7.6	7.2
Grades 1 to 3.	11,965	406	3.4	23.4	26.9	23.3
Grades 4 to 5.	7,895	197	2.5	15.4	13.1	15.5
Grades 6 to 8.	12,435	359	2.9	24.3	23.8	24.3
Grades 9 to 12.	15,161	422	2.8	29.6	28.0	29.7
Sex:						
Male.	26,286	633	2.4	51.4	41.9	51.7
Female.	24,849	875	3.5	48.6	58.1	48.3
Race/ethnicity:						
White, non-Hispanic.	29,815	1,159	3.9	58.3	76.8	57.7
Black, non-Hispanic.	7,523	61	0.8	14.7	4.0	15.0
Hispanic [2].	9,589	147	1.5	18.8	9.8	19.0
Other	4,208	141	3.3	8.2	9.3	8.2
Number of children in the household:						
One child	8,463	187	2.2	16.6	12.4	16.7
Two children.	20,694	412	2.0	40.5	27.3	40.9
Three or more children	21,979	909	4.1	43.0	60.3	42.5
Number of parents in the household:						
Two parents.	37,262	1,348	3.6	72.9	89.4	72.4
One parent.	11,734	115	1.0	22.9	7.6	23.4
Nonparental guardians	2,139	45	2.1	4.2	3.0	4.2
Parents' participation in the labor force:						
Two parents—one in labor force	26,075	509	2.0	51.0	33.8	51.5
Two parents—both in labor force	10,776	808	7.5	21.1	53.6	20.1
One parent in labor force.	9,989	127	1.3	19.5	8.4	19.9
No parent in labor force.	4,296	64	1.5	8.4	4.3	8.5
Household income:						
$25,000 or less	11,544	239	2.1	22.6	15.9	22.8
$25,001 to 50,000	10,592	364	3.4	20.7	24.1	20.6
$50,001 to 75,000	10,289	405	3.9	20.1	26.8	19.9
$75,001 or more	18,710	501	2.7	36.6	33.2	36.7
Parents' highest educational attainment:						
High school diploma or less.	14,303	206	1.4	28.0	13.7	28.4
Voc/tech degree or some college	14,584	549	3.8	28.5	36.4	28.3
Bachelor's degree	12,321	502	4.1	24.1	33.3	23.8
Graduate/professional school	9,927	251	2.5	19.4	16.6	19.5

[1] Excludes those ungraded. [2] Persons of Hispanic origin may be of any race.
Source: U.S. National Center for Education Statistics, "Parent and Family Involvement in Education Survey," National Household Education Surveys Program, 2007, unpublished data. See also <http://nces.ed.gov/nhes>.

Table 241. Public Elementary and Secondary Schools by Type and Size of School: 2008 to 2009

[Enrollment in thousands (49,054 represents 49,054,000). For school year ending in 2009. Data reported by schools, rather than school districts. Based on the Common Core of Data Survey; see source for details]

Enrollment size of school	Number of schools					Enrollment [1]				
	Total	Elemen-tary [2]	Second-ary [3]	Com-bined [4]	Other [5]	Total	Elemen-tary [2]	Second-ary [3]	Com-bined [4]	Other [5]
Total	98,706	67,148	24,348	5,623	1,587	49,054	31,446	16,055	1,520	32
PERCENT										
Total.	100.00	100.00	100.00	100.00	100.00	100.00	100.00	100.00	100.00	100.00
Under 100 students	10.51	5.88	17.76	38.56	44.26	0.94	0.63	1.11	5.33	8.45
100 to 199 students.	9.53	8.30	11.42	17.27	14.75	2.76	2.68	2.38	8.12	12.18
200 to 299 students.	11.42	12.46	8.62	10.00	16.94	5.56	6.71	3.04	7.91	23.68
300 to 399 students.	13.76	16.20	7.89	7.76	13.11	9.31	12.08	3.88	8.79	26.30
400 to 499 students.	13.86	16.87	6.60	6.72	8.20	12.00	16.09	4.19	9.73	20.36
500 to 599 students.	11.30	13.67	5.78	5.06	1.64	11.95	15.90	4.51	9.04	5.20
600 to 699 students.	8.33	9.78	5.14	3.60	1.09	10.40	13.44	4.73	7.59	3.84
700 to 799 students.	5.74	6.53	4.09	2.79	–	8.27	10.36	4.35	6.77	–
800 to 999 students.	6.42	6.50	6.98	3.08	–	11.00	12.20	8.87	8.82	–
1,000 to 1,499 students. . .	5.39	3.43	11.66	3.20	–	12.49	8.47	20.40	12.43	–
1,500 to 1,999 students. . .	2.03	0.31	7.33	1.01	–	6.78	1.08	18.05	5.58	–
2,000 to 2,999 students. . .	1.41	0.06	5.57	0.51	–	6.45	0.31	18.72	4.00	–
3,000 or more students . . .	0.31	0.01	1.17	0.43	–	2.11	0.06	5.77	5.90	–
Average enrollment [1]	517	470	704	308	177	517	470	704	308	177

– Represents zero. [1] Exclude data for schools not reporting enrollment. [2] Includes schools beginning with grade 6 or below and with no grade higher than 8. [3] Includes schools with no grade lower than 7. [4] Includes schools beginning with grade 6 or below and ending with grade 9 or above. [5] Includes special education, alternative, and other schools not classified by grade span.

Source: U.S. National Center for Education Statistics, *Digest of Education Statistics*, annual. See also <http://www.nces.ed.gov/programs/digest/>.

Education 157

Table 242. Public Elementary and Secondary Schools—Summary: 1980 to 2009

[For school year ending in year shown, except as indicated (48,041 represents 48,041,000). Data are estimates]

Item	Unit	1980	1990	2000	2005	2007	2008	2009
School districts, total	Number	**16,044**	**15,552**	**15,403**	**15,731**	**15,496**	**15,581**	**15,609**
ENROLLMENT								
Population 5–17 years old [1]	1,000	48,041	44,949	52,811	53,249	53,397	53,419	53,277
Percent of resident population..........	Percent ...	21.4	18.2	18.8	18.2	17.9	17.7	17.5
Fall enrollment [2]	1,000	41,778	40,527	46,577	48,417	48,860	49,011	49,036
Percent of population 5–17 years old.....	Percent ...	87.0	90.2	88.2	90.9	91.5	91.7	92.0
Elementary [3]	1,000	24,397	26,253	29,243	29,632	29,762	29,903	30,016
Secondary [4]	1,000	17,381	14,274	17,334	18,784	19,098	19,108	19,020
Average daily attendance (ADA)	1,000	38,411	37,573	43,313	45,088	45,695	45,870	46,374
High school graduates.................	1,000	2,762	2,327	2,544	2,803	2,905	2,996	3,060
INSTRUCTIONAL STAFF								
Total [5]	1,000	**2,521**	**2,685**	**3,273**	**3,509**	**3,613**	**3,654**	**3,697**
Classroom teachers...................	1,000	2,211	2,362	2,891	3,072	3,157	3,186	3,228
Average salaries:								
Instructional staff...................	Dollar.....	16,715	32,638	43,837	49,135	52,770	54,589	56,314
Classroom teachers..................	Dollar.....	15,970	31,367	41,807	47,516	51,068	52,800	54,274
REVENUES								
Revenue receipts......................	Mil. dol....	97,635	208,656	369,754	477,371	535,516	560,140	564,928
Federal............................	Mil. dol....	9,020	13,184	26,346	42,908	46,158	47,547	57,255
State	Mil. dol....	47,929	100,787	183,986	225,142	255,241	269,993	261,512
Local	Mil. dol....	40,686	94,685	159,421	209,321	234,118	242,599	246,161
EXPENDITURES								
Total...........................	**Mil. dol.**...	**96,105**	**209,698**	**374,782**	**496,199**	**548,039**	**579,683**	**591,785**
Current expenditures (day schools)........	Mil. dol....	85,661	186,583	320,954	422,346	467,418	495,475	505,694
Other current expenditures [6]	Mil. dol....	1,859	3,341	6,618	8,710	9,292	9,753	11,212
Capital outlay........................	Mil. dol....	6,504	16,012	37,552	48,757	54,049	57,105	56,111
Interest on school debt	Mil. dol....	2,081	3,762	9,659	16,385	17,280	17,350	18,769
In current dollars:								
Revenue receipts per pupil enrolled	Dollar.....	2,337	5,149	7,939	9,860	10,960	11,429	11,521
Current expenditures per pupil enrolled ...	Dollar.....	2,050	4,604	6,891	8,723	9,567	10,110	10,313
In constant (2009) dollars: [7]								
Revenue receipts per pupil enrolled	Dollar.....	6,376	8,582	9,927	10,888	11,341	11,388	11,521
Current expenditures per pupil enrolled ...	Dollar.....	5,594	7,674	8,617	9,633	9,898	10,074	10,313

[1] Estimated resident population as of July 1 of the previous year, except 1980, 1990, and 2000 population enumerated as of April 1. Estimates reflect revisions based on the 2000 Census of Population. [2] Fall enrollment of the previous year. [3] Kindergarten through grade 6. [4] Grades 7 through 12. [5] Full-time equivalent. [6] Current expenses for summer schools, adult education, post-high school vocational education, personnel retraining, etc., when operated by local school districts and not part of regular public elementary and secondary day-school program. [7] Compiled by U.S. Census Bureau. Deflated by the Consumer Price Index, all urban consumers (for school year July through June) supplied by U.S. National Center for Education Statistics.

Source: Except as noted, National Education Association, Washington, DC, Estimates of School Statistics Database (copyright).

Table 243. Public Elementary and Secondary School Enrollment by Grade: 1980 to 2008

[In thousands (40,877 represents 40,877,000). As of fall of year. Based on survey of state education agencies; see source for details]

Grade	1980	1990	1995	2000	2002	2003	2004	2005	2006	2007	2008
Pupils enrolled [1]	**40,877**	**41,217**	**44,840**	**47,204**	**48,183**	**48,540**	**48,795**	**49,113**	**49,299**	**49,293**	**49,266**
Pre-kindergarten to 8 [1]	27,647	29,878	32,341	33,688	34,116	34,202	34,178	34,205	34,221	34,205	34,286
Pre-K and Kindergarten.....	2,689	3,610	4,173	4,158	4,349	4,453	4,534	4,656	4,706	4,691	4,819
First	2,894	3,499	3,671	3,636	3,594	3,613	3,663	3,691	3,750	3,750	3,708
Second	2,800	3,327	3,507	3,634	3,565	3,544	3,560	3,606	3,640	3,704	3,699
Third.....................	2,893	3,297	3,445	3,676	3,623	3,611	3,580	3,586	3,627	3,659	3,708
Fourth	3,107	3,248	3,431	3,711	3,669	3,619	3,612	3,578	3,585	3,624	3,647
Fifth	3,130	3,197	3,438	3,707	3,711	3,685	3,635	3,633	3,601	3,600	3,629
Sixth.....................	3,038	3,110	3,395	3,663	3,788	3,772	3,735	3,670	3,660	3,628	3,614
Seventh	3,085	3,067	3,422	3,629	3,821	3,841	3,818	3,777	3,715	3,701	3,653
Eighth	3,086	2,979	3,356	3,538	3,709	3,809	3,825	3,802	3,765	3,709	3,692
Grades 9 to 12 [1]	13,231	11,338	12,500	13,340	14,067	14,338	14,617	14,909	15,078	15,087	14,980
Ninth	3,377	3,169	3,704	3,963	4,105	4,190	4,281	4,287	4,260	4,200	4,123
Tenth	3,368	2,896	3,237	3,491	3,584	3,675	3,750	3,866	3,881	3,863	3,822
Eleventh..................	3,195	2,612	2,826	3,083	3,229	3,277	3,369	3,455	3,551	3,558	3,548
Twelfth	2,925	2,381	2,487	2,803	2,990	3,046	3,094	3,180	3,276	3,375	3,400

[1] Includes unclassified students not shown separately.

Source: U.S. National Center for Education Statistics, *Digest of Education Statistics*, annual. See also <http://www.nces.ed.gov /programs/digest/>.

Table 244. Public Elementary and Secondary Schools and Enrollment—States: 2008 to 2009

[For school year ending in 2009. For total number of students (49,136 represents 49,136,000). Based on the Common Core of Data Program; see source for details]

State	Total number of schools with member-ship [1]	Total number of students (1,000)	Type of school							
			Regular		Special education [2]		Vocational education [3]		Alternative education [4]	
			Number of schools	Percent of students	Number of schools	Percent of students	Number of schools	Percent of students	Number of schools	Percent of students
Total.............	98,817	49,136	89,018	98.2	2,089	0.4	1,417	0.3	6,293	1.2
Alabama	1,600	749	1,370	99.5	41	0.1	72	(Z)	117	0.4
Alaska..............	506	132	450	89.3	2	0.1	3	0.6	51	10.0
Arizona	2,248	1,076	1,939	98.5	20	0.1	207	0.3	82	1.0
Arkansas...........	1,120	481	1,082	99.6	4	(Z)	23	–	11	0.3
California..........	10,068	6,177	8,472	96.7	146	0.4	75	(Z)	1,375	2.8
Colorado	1,793	832	1,683	98.0	9	0.1	6	0.1	95	1.8
Connecticut	1,165	564	1,049	96.9	56	0.6	16	1.9	44	0.6
Delaware	217	125	182	91.9	19	1.4	6	5.7	10	1.0
District of Columbia	233	69	208	95.5	10	2.2	4	1.4	11	0.9
Florida	4,043	2,635	3,398	97.6	170	0.7	53	0.1	422	1.6
Georgia	2,461	1,668	2,248	99.3	72	0.5	1	–	140	0.2
Hawaii	289	180	285	99.9	3	(Z)	–	(X)	1	0.1
Idaho	742	276	633	98.1	15	(Z)	11	(Z)	83	1.8
Illinois.............	4,405	2,097	4,017	99.2	147	0.4	53	(Z)	188	0.4
Indiana.............	1,961	1,047	1,875	99.7	38	0.1	29	–	19	0.2
Iowa...............	1,468	482	1,410	99.2	7	0.1	–	(X)	51	0.7
Kansas.............	1,419	469	1,407	99.9	10	0.1	1	–	1	(Z)
Kentucky	1,542	676	1,238	99.0	10	0.1	124	–	170	0.9
Louisiana	1,488	691	1,260	94.5	38	0.2	6	–	184	5.4
Maine..............	649	184	619	100.0	1	(Z)	27	–	2	(Z)
Maryland	1,447	848	1,321	97.6	40	0.5	24	1.0	62	0.9
Massachusetts........	1,836	957	1,755	95.4	23	0.5	39	3.7	19	0.4
Michigan	3,879	1,618	3,332	95.8	197	1.9	38	0.1	312	2.2
Minnesota	2,433	837	1,666	96.3	276	1.8	11	(Z)	480	1.9
Mississippi..........	1,085	492	928	100.0	3	(Z)	90	–	64	–
Missouri............	2,427	917	2,181	98.7	68	0.5	66	0.5	112	0.3
Montana............	828	142	822	99.9	2	(Z)	–	(X)	4	0.1
Nebraska...........	1,120	295	1,087	99.8	28	0.2	–	(X)	5	0.0
Nevada.............	636	429	593	98.4	10	0.2	1	(Z)	32	1.4
New Hampshire.......	484	197	484	100.0	–	(X)	–	(X)	–	(X)
New Jersey	2,590	1,387	2,359	97.6	73	0.7	55	1.6	103	0.2
New Mexico..........	855	333	808	98.4	6	0.2	1	0.1	40	1.3
New York	4,730	2,766	4,591	98.7	105	0.8	6	0.2	28	0.3
North Carolina.......	2,550	1,477	2,531	99.9	14	(Z)	1	(Z)	4	(Z)
North Dakota	517	93	474	100.0	34	(Z)	9	–	–	(X)
Ohio...............	3,796	1,762	3,653	99.5	64	0.3	73	0.1	6	0.1
Oklahoma	1,795	655	1,786	99.8	4	(Z)	–	(X)	5	0.1
Oregon.............	1,301	554	1,256	99.0	2	(Z)	–	(X)	43	1.0
Pennsylvania	3,244	1,762	3,132	98.8	12	0.1	87	1.0	13	0.1
Rhode Island	321	144	298	97.3	3	0.1	11	1.2	9	1.4
South Carolina.......	1,206	723	1,136	99.8	10	0.1	39	–	21	0.1
South Dakota........	714	124	676	98.9	7	0.1	4	(Z)	27	1.0
Tennessee	1,772	973	1,704	99.4	19	0.2	21	0.1	28	0.2
Texas	8,619	4,850	7,518	98.4	25	(Z)	–	(X)	1,076	1.6
Utah...............	1,046	583	862	97.6	86	1.0	6	–	92	1.3
Vermont............	323	86	307	100.0	–	(X)	15	–	1	(Z)
Virginia............	2,164	1,245	1,883	99.7	42	(Z)	49	–	190	0.2
Washington	2,318	1,035	1,885	95.0	103	0.4	15	(Z)	315	4.5
West Virginia	759	283	693	99.6	3	0.1	31	(Z)	32	0.3
Wisconsin	2,242	872	2,136	99.3	9	(Z)	8	0.1	89	0.6
Wyoming	363	88	336	98.6	3	(Z)	–	(X)	24	1.4

– Represents zero. X Not applicable. Z Less than 0.05 percent. [1] Membership is the count of students enrolled on October 1 of the reported school year. Individual state total number of students is included only if the state or jurisdiction reports data for regular, special education, vocational education, and alternative education school types. [2] Focuses on special education with materials and instructional approaches adapted to meet the students' needs. [3] Focuses on vocational, technical, or career education and provides education and training in at least one semi-skilled or technical occupation. [4] Addresses the needs of students that typically cannot be met in the regular school setting and provides nontraditional education.

Source: U.S. National Center for Education Statistics, Common Core of Data, "Public Elementary/Secondary School Universe Survey," 2009–10, Version 1a; <http://www.nces.ed.gov/ccd/>.

Table 245. Selected Statistics for the Largest Public School Districts: 2007 to 2008

[For the 50 largest districts by enrollment size. For school year ending in 2008. Based on reports from state education agencies in the spring 2008. Data from the Common Core Data Program; see source for details. School district boundaries are not necessarily the same as city or county boundaries]

School district	City	County	Number of students [1]	Number of full-time equivalent (FTE) teachers	Number of 2005–06 completers [2]	Number of schools
New York City Public Schools, NY	New York	New York	981,690	71,824	49,978	1,436
Los Angeles Unified, CA	Los Angeles	Los Angeles	687,534	35,084	27,004	860
City of Chicago School District, IL	Chicago	Cook	421,430	21,512	18,263	630
Dade County School District, FL	Miami	Miami-Dade	345,525	22,384	18,030	496
Clark County School District, NV	Las Vegas	Clark	312,761	15,348	10,943	350
Broward County School District, FL	Fort Lauderdale	Broward	256,351	18,729	14,201	303
Houston Independent School District, TX	Houston	Harris	200,225	11,994	7,645	296
Hillsborough County School District, FL	Tampa	Hillsborough	192,007	13,986	9,858	285
Hawaii Department of Education, HI	Honolulu	Honolulu	179,478	11,294	11,063	290
Orange County School District, FL	Orlando	Orange	172,257	10,975	9,178	236
Palm Beach County School District, FL	West Palm Beach	Palm Beach	170,757	13,213	9,472	247
Fairfax County Public Schools, VA	Falls Church	Fairfax	169,030	9,274	11,492	193
Philadelphia City School District, PA	Philadelphia	Philadelphia	159,867	10,258	8,663	274
Dallas Independent School District, TX	Dallas	Dallas	157,352	10,937	5,874	232
Gwinnett County, GA	Lawrenceville	Gwinnett	157,219	10,978	7,441	115
Montgomery County Public Schools, MD	Rockville	Montgomery	139,282	9,401	10,037	204
Wake County Schools, NC	Raleigh	Wake	138,443	9,317	6,788	156
Charlotte-Mecklenburg Schools, NC	Charlotte	Mecklenburg	135,064	9,312	5,912	166
San Diego Unified, CA	San Diego	San Diego	132,256	6,855	6,335	218
Prince George's County Public Schools, MD . .	Upper Marlboro	Prince George's	127,977	8,870	8,226	215
Duval County School District, FL	Jacksonville	Duval	122,606	7,973	5,999	175
Memphis City School District, TN	Memphis	Shelby	111,954	7,201	5,741	200
Cobb County, GA	Marietta	Cobb	106,747	8,215	6,298	118
Pinellas County School District, FL	Largo	Pinellas	106,061	7,878	6,134	173
Baltimore County Public Schools, MD	Baltimore	Baltimore	103,180	7,339	7,415	172
Cypress-Fairbanks Independent School District, TX	Houston	Harris	100,685	6,411	5,069	78
DeKalb County, GA	Decatur	Dekalb	99,775	6,902	4,730	146
Jefferson County, KY	Louisville	Jefferson	98,774	6,144	5,032	174
Detroit City School District, MI	Detroit	Wayne	97,577	5,953	6,185	197
Albuquerque Public Schools, NM	Albuquerque	Bernalillo	95,934	6,542	3,831	174
Polk County School District, FL	Bartow	Polk	94,657	7,548	4,243	156
Northside Independent School District, TX	San Antonio	Bexar	89,000	5,782	4,300	101
Fulton County, GA	Atlanta	Fulton	88,299	6,530	4,328	98
Long Beach Unified, CA	Long Beach	Los Angeles	87,509	4,017	4,654	92
Jefferson County, CO	Golden	Jefferson	85,946	4,959	5,580	162
Milwaukee, WI	Milwaukee	Milwaukee	85,381	5,158	4,425	215
Austin Independent School District, TX	Austin	Travis	83,483	5,890	3,595	120
Baltimore City Public Schools, MD	Baltimore	Baltimore	82,266	5,839	4,118	194
Jordan District, UT	Sandy	Salt Lake	81,485	3,221	4,632	99
Lee County School District, FL	Fort Myers	Lee	79,434	5,034	3,801	117
Fort Worth Independent School District, TX . . .	Fort Worth	Tarrant	79,285	5,167	3,407	147
Fresno Unified, CA	Fresno	Fresno	76,621	3,922	3,450	106
Davidson County School District, TN.	Nashville	Davidson	74,312	5,307	3,601	139
Denver County, CO	Viera	Brevard	74,189	4,356	2,814	143
Prince William County, CO	Denver	Denver	73,917	3,845	3,922	83
Anne Arundel County Public Schools, MD	Annapolis	Anne Arundel	73,653	4,939	5,077	124
Brevard School District, FL	Viera	Brevard	73,098	5,290	4,761	121
Guilford County Schools, NC	Greensboro	Guilford	72,951	5,091	4,238	119
Virginia Beach City Public Schools, VA	Virginia Beach	Virginia Beach	71,554	3,984	4,660	84
Greenville County Schools, SC	Greenville	Greenville	70,441	4,542	3,229	94

[1] Number of students receiving educational services from the school district. [2] Includes high school diploma recipients and other completers (for example certificates of attendance) but does not include high school equivalents (GEDs).

Source: U.S. Department of Education, National Center for Education Statistics, Common Core of Data (CCD), "Public Elementary/Secondary School Universe Survey," 2008–09, "Local Education Agency Universe Survey," 2008–09, and "Local Education Agency-Level Public-Use Data File on Public School Dropouts: School Year 2006–07"; <http://www.nces.ed.gov/ccd/>.

Table 246. Public Elementary and Secondary School Enrollment by State: 1990 to 2008

[In thousands (29,878 represents 29,878,000), except rate. As of fall. Includes unclassified students. Based on survey of state education agencies; see source for details]

State	Prekindergarten through grade 8 [1]					Grades 9 through 12 [1]				
	1990	2000	2005	2007	2008	1990	2000	2005	2007	2008
United States	**29,878**	**33,688**	**34,205**	**34,205**	**34,286**	**11,338**	**13,515**	**14,908**	**15,087**	**14,980**
Alabama	527	539	529	527	528	195	201	212	218	218
Alaska	85	94	91	89	89	29	39	42	42	41
Arizona	479	641	740	771	772	161	237	355	316	316
Arkansas	314	318	336	340	342	123	132	138	139	137
California	3,615	4,408	4,466	4,329	4,306	1,336	1,733	1,971	2,015	2,016
Colorado	420	517	550	566	580	154	208	230	236	238
Connecticut	347	406	400	394	392	122	156	175	177	175
Delaware	73	81	85	85	87	27	34	36	38	39
District of Columbia	61	54	56	56	51	19	15	21	23	18
Florida	1,370	1,760	1,873	1,856	1,849	492	675	802	811	782
Georgia	849	1,060	1,145	1,179	1,186	303	385	453	471	470
Hawaii	123	132	127	126	126	49	52	55	54	54
Idaho	160	170	183	191	194	61	75	79	81	81
Illinois.............	1,310	1,474	1,480	1,473	1,479	512	575	631	640	641
Indiana.............	676	703	724	730	730	279	286	311	317	316
Iowa...............	345	334	326	330	336	139	161	157	156	152
Kansas.............	320	323	321	327	331	117	147	147	142	140
Kentucky	459	471	487	469	472	177	194	192	197	198
Louisiana	586	547	482	500	504	199	197	172	181	181
Maine..............	155	146	133	131	129	60	61	62	66	64
Maryland	527	609	589	576	576	188	244	271	269	267
Massachusetts........	604	703	675	667	667	230	273	297	296	292
Michigan	1,145	1,222	1,191	1,137	1,119	440	498	551	556	541
Minnesota	546	578	558	558	560	211	277	281	279	276
Mississippi..........	372	364	358	354	352	131	134	137	141	140
Missouri	588	645	635	632	635	228	268	283	285	282
Montana............	111	105	98	96	97	42	50	48	46	45
Nebraska	198	195	195	200	203	76	91	92	91	90
Nevada	150	251	296	308	308	51	90	116	122	125
New Hampshire.......	126	147	139	134	133	46	61	67	66	65
New Jersey	784	968	971	954	957	306	346	425	428	425
New Mexico..........	208	225	230	230	231	94	95	97	99	99
New York	1,828	2,029	1,909	1,856	1,843	770	853	906	909	898
North Carolina	783	945	1,003	1,072	1,059	304	348	413	417	430
North Dakota	85	72	66	63	64	33	37	33	32	31
Ohio...............	1,258	1,294	1,261	1,241	1,239	514	541	578	586	578
Oklahoma	425	445	457	463	468	154	178	178	179	177
Oregon.............	340	379	380	384	395	132	167	173	182	180
Pennsylvania	1,172	1,258	1,228	1,205	1,194	496	556	603	597	581
Rhode Island	102	114	104	99	98	37	44	50	48	47
South Carolina........	452	493	498	505	508	170	184	204	208	211
South Dakota.........	95	88	84	83	87	34	41	38	38	39
Tennessee	598	668	677	682	685	226	241	277	283	287
Texas..............	2,511	2,943	3,268	3,375	3,447	872	1,117	1,257	1,300	1,306
Utah...............	325	333	358	410	404	122	148	151	166	155
Vermont	71	70	65	63	63	25	32	32	31	31
Virginia.............	728	816	841	850	855	270	329	372	380	381
Washington	613	694	699	697	705	227	310	333	333	332
West Virginia	224	201	197	199	199	98	85	84	84	83
Wisconsin	566	595	584	585	590	232	285	291	289	284
Wyoming	71	60	57	59	61	27	30	27	27	27

[1] Includes unclassified.

Source: U.S. National Center for Education Statistics, *Digest of Education Statistics*, annual. See also <http://www.nces.ed.gov/programs/digest/>.

U.S. Census Bureau, Statistical Abstract of the United States: 2012

Table 247. Public Schools Reporting Incidents of Crime by Incident Type and Selected School Characteristics: 2007 to 2008

[For school year ending in 2008. Includes incidents that happen in school buildings, on school grounds, on school buses, and at places that hold school-sponsored events or activities. Based on sample; see source for details]

School characteristic	Total number of schools	Percent of schools with—				Rate per 1,000 students			
		Violent inci- dents [1]	Serious violent incidents [2]	Theft [3]	Other incidents [4]	Violent inci- dents [1]	Serious violent incidents [2]	Theft [3]	Other incidents [4]
All public schools [5]	**83,000**	**75.5**	**17.2**	**47.3**	**67.4**	**27.9**	**1.2**	**5.6**	**9.2**
Level: [6]									
Primary	49,200	65.1	13.0	30.6	55.1	25.6	1.0	2.1	4.9
Middle	15,300	94.3	22.0	69.5	84.0	41.3	1.9	8.3	12.3
High school	11,900	94.0	28.9	83.7	93.5	22.3	1.1	9.9	14.8
Enrollment size:									
Less than 300	19,200	60.6	12.3	33.3	47.6	34.4	[7] 1.8	5.4	9.1
300 to 499	24,300	69.1	11.4	35.6	62.1	24.3	0.8	3.2	6.5
500 to 999	30,200	83.4	19.8	54.0	75.5	30.0	1.2	5.1	7.7
1,000 or more	9,300	97.0	34.0	84.9	95.5	25.5	1.4	8.3	13.4
Percent minority enrollment: [8]									
Less than 5 percent	13,700	66.7	15.0	46.1	60.6	21.7	0.8	5.9	7.4
5 to 20 percent.	21,400	72.7	13.7	43.0	62.0	18.8	0.6	5.5	7.3
20 to 50 percent.	20,300	77.3	15.2	45.8	70.0	27.1	0.8	5.2	8.4
50 percent or more	27,600	80.5	22.5	52.4	72.9	36.6	2.0	5.9	11.7

[1] Violent incidents include rape, sexual battery other than rape, physical attack or fight with or without a weapon, threat of physical attack with or without a weapon, and robbery with or without a weapon. [2] Serious violent incidents include rape, sexual battery other than rape, physical attack or fight with a weapon, threat of physical attack with a weapon, and robbery with or without a weapon. [3] Theft or larceny (taking things worth over $10 without personal confrontation). Includes pocket picking, stealing purse or backpack (if left unattended or no force was used to take from owner), theft from motor vehicles, etc. [4] Other incidents include possession of a firearm or explosive device, possession of knife or sharp object, distribution of illegal drugs, possession or use of alcohol or illegal drugs, and vandalism. [5] Includes combined schools, not shown separately, which include all other combination of grades, including K–12 schools. [6] Primary schools are defined as schools in which the lowest grade is not higher than grade 3 and the highest grade is not higher than grade 8. Middle schools are defined as schools in which the lowest grade is not lower than grade 4 and the highest grade is not higher than grade 9. High schools are defined as schools in which the lowest grade is not lower than grade 9 and the highest grade is not higher than grade 12. [7] Interpret data with caution. [8] These estimates exclude data from Tennessee because schools in this state did not report estimates of student race.

Source: U.S. Department of Education, National Center for Education Statistics, "2007–08 School Survey on Crime and Safety," 2008.

Table 248. Percentage of Public Schools Reporting Selected Types of Disciplinary Problems Occurring at School by Selected School Characteristics: 2007 to 2008

[In percent. For school year. "At school" includes activities that happen in school buildings, on school grounds, on school buses, and at places that hold school-sponsored events or activities. Based on sample; see source for details]

School characteristic	Happens daily or at least once a day						Happens at all	
	Student racial tensions	Student bullying	Student sexual harass- ment of other students [1]	Student verbal abuse of teachers	Wide- spread disorder in classrooms	Student acts of dis- respect for teachers	Undesir- able gang activities [2]	Undesir- able cult or extremist group activities [3]
All public schools	**3.7**	**25.3**	**3.0**	**6.0**	**10.5**	**4.0**	**19.8**	**2.6**
Level: [4]								
Primary	2.6	20.5	[5] 1.3	3.7	7.7	3.1	10.0	[5] 0.6
Middle	5.6	43.5	6.5	9.8	17.7	6.6	35.4	3.1
High school	5.3	21.7	5.7	12.1	16.9	4.8	43.1	8.0
Combined	[5] 4.3	24.9	(S)	[5] 2.9	[5] 3.8	(S)	14.3	[5] 6.4
Enrollment size:								
Less than 300	[5] 3.2	18.7	[5] 2.7	[5] 4.5	[5] 5.6	[5] 3.2	9.8	[5] 1.3
300 to 499	[5] 1.4	20.8	[5] 1.8	3.1	8.4	[5] 2.6	12.8	[5] 1.0
500 to 999	5.3	30.6	3.4	6.4	11.9	5.1	21.8	2.6
1,000 or more	5.5	33.2	5.7	15.3	22.0	6.1	52.4	9.4
Percent minority enrollment: [6]								
Less than 5 percent	[5] 1.2	25.6	[5] 2.7	[5] 2.8	5.6	[5] 2.0	3.9	(S)
5 to 20 percent.	2.7	24.9	2.5	2.6	5.6	2.1	9.9	[5] 1.7
20 to 50 percent.	3.0	22.1	2.2	5.5	11.5	[5] 2.3	21.3	2.7
50 percent or more	6.2	27.6	4.2	10.5	16.1	7.8	34.2	3.6

S Figure does not meet publication standards. [1] Sexual harassment includes "unsolicited, offensive behavior that inappropriately asserts sexuality over another person. This behavior may be verbal or nonverbal." [2] Gang includes an "ongoing loosely organized association of three or more persons, whether formal or informal, that has a common name, signs, symbols, or colors, whose members engage, either individually or collectively, in violent or other forms of illegal behavior." [3] Cult or extremist group includes "a group that espouses radical beliefs and practices, which may include a religious component, that are widely seen as threatening the basic values and cultural norms of society at large." [4] Primary schools are defined as schools in which the lowest grade is not higher than grade 3 and the highest grade is not higher than grade 8. Middle schools are defined as schools in which the lowest grade level is not lower than grade 4 and the highest grade is not higher than grade 9. High schools are defined as schools in which the lowest grade is not lower than grade 9 and the highest grade is not higher than grade 12. Combined schools include all other combinations of grades, including K–12 schools. [5] Intepret data with caution. [6] These estimates exclude data from Tennessee because schools in this state did not report estimates of student race.

Source: U.S. Department of Education, National Center for Education Statistics, "2007–08 School Survey on Crime and Safety," 2008.

Table 249. Students Who Reported Being Threatened or Injured With a Weapon on School Property by Selected Student Characteristics: 1995 to 2009

[In percent. For students in grades 9 to 12. Data are for previous 12 months. "On school property" was not defined for survey respondents]

Characteristic	1995	1997	1999	2001	2003	2005	2007	2009
Total	**8.4**	**7.4**	**7.7**	**8.9**	**9.2**	**7.9**	**7.8**	**7.7**
Sex:								
Male	10.9	10.2	9.5	11.5	11.6	9.7	10.2	9.6
Female	5.8	4.0	5.8	6.5	6.5	6.1	5.4	5.5
Race/ethnicity: [1]								
White	7.0	6.2	6.6	8.5	7.8	7.2	6.9	6.4
Black	11.0	9.9	7.6	9.3	10.9	8.1	9.7	9.4
Hispanic	12.4	9.0	9.8	8.9	9.4	9.8	8.7	9.1
Asian	([2])	([2])	7.7	11.3	11.5	4.6	[3]7.6	5.5
American Indian/Alaska Native	[3]11.4	[3]12.5	[3]13.2	[3]15.2	22.1	9.8	5.9	16.5
Pacific Islander/Native Hawaiian	([2])	([2])	15.6	24.8	16.3	[3]14.5	[3]8.1	12.5
More than one race	([2])	([2])	9.3	10.3	18.7	10.7	13.3	9.2
Grade:								
9th	9.6	10.1	10.5	12.7	12.1	10.5	9.2	8.7
10th	9.6	7.9	8.2	9.1	9.2	8.8	8.4	8.4
11th	7.7	5.9	6.1	6.9	7.3	5.5	6.8	7.9
12th	6.7	5.8	5.1	5.3	6.3	5.8	6.3	5.2

[1] Race categories exclude persons of Hispanic ethnicity. [2] The response categories for race/ethnicity changed in 1999 making comparisons of some categories with earlier years problematic. In 1995 and 1997, Asian students and Pacific Islander students were not categorized separately and students were not given the option of choosing more than one race. [3] Interpret data with caution.

Source: U.S. National Center for Education Statistics and U.S. Department of Justice, Bureau of Justice Statistics, *Indicators of School Crime and Safety: 2010*, NCES 2011-002, November 2010. See also <http://nces.ed.gov/programs/crimeindicators /crimeindicators2010/>.

Table 250. Public Schools Using Selected Safety and Security Measures by School Characteristics: 2000 to 2008

[In percent. For school year ending in year shown. Based on survey of principals or persons knowledgeable about discipline issues at the school. Refers only to those times during normal school hours or when school activities or events were in session. Based on the School Survey on Crime and Safety and subject to sampling error; for details see source]

Measure	2000	2004	2006	2008
Controlled access during school hours:				
Buildings (locked or monitored doors)	74.6	83.0	84.9	89.5
Grounds (locked or monitored gates)	33.7	36.2	41.1	42.6
Closed the campus for most students during lunch	64.6	66.0	66.1	65.0
Drug testing:				
Any students	4.1	5.3	(NA)	(NA)
Athletes	(NA)	4.2	5.0	6.4
Students in extracurricular activities other than athletes	(NA)	2.6	3.4	4.5
Any other students	(NA)	(NA)	3.0	3.0
Prohibited all tobacco use on school grounds	90.1	88.8	90.3	91.4
Required to wear badges or picture IDs:				
Students	3.9	6.4	6.1	7.6
Faculty and staff	25.4	48.0	47.8	58.3
Metal detector checks on students:				
Random checks [1]	7.2	5.6	4.9	5.3
Required to pass through daily	0.9	1.1	1.1	1.3
Sweeps and technology:				
Random dog sniffs to check for drugs [1]	20.6	21.3	23.0	21.5
Random sweeps for contraband [1,2]	11.8	12.8	13.1	11.4
Provided telephones in most classrooms	44.6	60.8	66.8	71.6
Used security cameras to monitor school [1]	19.4	36.0	42.8	55.0
Provided two-way radios	(NA)	71.2	70.8	73.1
Visitor requirements:				
Sign-in or check-in	96.6	98.3	97.6	98.7
Pass through metal detectors	0.9	0.9	1.0	(NA)
Dress code:				
Required students to wear uniforms	11.8	13.8	13.8	17.5
Enforced a strict dress code	47.4	55.1	55.3	54.8
School supplies and equipment:				
Required clear book bags or banned book bags on school grounds	5.9	6.2	6.4	6.0
Provided school lockers to students	46.5	49.5	50.6	48.9

NA Not available. [1] One or more check, sweep, or camera. [2] For example, drugs or weapons. Does not include dog sniffs.
Source: U.S. National Center for Education Statistics and U.S. Department of Justice, Bureau of Justice Statistics, *Indicators of School Crime and Safety, 2009*, December 2009, NCES 2010-012. See also <http://www.nces.ed.gov/programs/crimeindicators /crimeindicators2009/>.

Table 251. Students Who Reported Being Bullied at School or Cyber-Bullied by Student Characteristics: 2007

[In percent. For students aged 12 through 18. For school year ending in 2007. "At school" includes the school building, on school property, on a school bus, or going to and from school. For more information, see Appendix A of source]

| Characteristic | Total [1] | Bullied at school | | | | | Cyber-bullying anywhere [2] |
		Total bullying at school	Made fun of, called names, or insulted	Subject of rumors	Threatened with harm	Pushed, shoved, tripped, spit on	
Total	**32.2**	**31.7**	**21.0**	**18.1**	**5.8**	**11.0**	**3.7**
Sex:							
Male	30.6	30.3	20.3	13.5	6.0	12.2	2.0
Female	33.7	33.2	21.7	22.8	5.6	9.7	5.3
Race/ethnicity: [3]							
White	34.6	34.1	23.5	20.3	6.3	11.5	4.2
Black	30.9	30.4	19.5	15.7	5.8	11.3	3.2
Hispanic	27.6	27.3	16.1	14.4	4.9	9.9	2.9
Asian	18.1	18.1	10.6	8.2	(S)	[4] 3.8	(S)
Other	34.6	34.1	20.1	20.8	7.7	14.4	[4] 2.4
Grade:							
6th	42.9	42.7	31.2	21.3	7.0	17.6	3.1
7th	35.7	35.6	27.6	20.2	7.4	15.8	3.4
8th	37.3	36.9	25.1	19.7	6.9	14.2	3.3
9th	30.8	30.6	20.3	18.1	4.6	11.4	2.5
10th	28.4	27.7	17.7	15.0	5.8	8.6	4.6
11th	29.3	28.5	15.3	18.7	4.9	6.5	5.1
12th	23.5	23.0	12.1	14.1	4.3	4.1	3.5

S Reporting standards not met. [1] Bullying types do not sum to total because students could have experienced more than one type of bullying. Also, total includes other types of bullying not shown separately. [2] Cyber-bullied includes students who responded that another student "made unwanted contact, for example, threatened or insulted (the respondent) via text (SMS) messaging." This category did not meet reporting standards to be reported separately. [3] Race categories exclude persons of Hispanic ethnicity. Other includes American Indian, Alaska Native, Pacific Islander, and more than one race. [4] Interpret data with caution.

Source: U.S. National Center for Education Statistics and U.S. Department of Justice, Bureau of Justice Statistics, *Indicators of School Crime and Safety: 2009*, December 2009, NCES 2010-012 . See also <http://www.nces.ed.gov/programs/crimeindicators /crimeindicators2009/>.

Table 252. Parent Participation in School-Related Activities by Selected School, Student, and Family Characteristics: 2007

[In percent, except as noted (51,600 represents 51,600,000). For school year ending in 2007. Covers parents with children in kindergarten through grade 12. Homeschooled students are excluded]

| Characteristic | Number of students in grades K through 12 (thousands) | Participation in school activities by parent or other household member | | | | |
		Attended a general school or PTO/PTA [1] meeting	Attended regularly scheduled parent-teacher conference	Attended a school or class event	Volunteered or served on school committee	Participated in school fundraising
Total	**51,600**	**89**	**78**	**74**	**46**	**65**
School type: [2]						
Public, assigned	37,168	89	76	72	42	63
Public, chosen	7,951	88	81	74	45	62
Private, religious	4,560	96	86	86	73	85
Private, nonreligious	1,438	97	90	86	68	72
Student's sex:						
Male	26,875	89	79	71	45	65
Female	24,725	90	77	78	48	66
Student's race/ethnicity:						
White, non-Hispanic	29,832	91	78	80	54	72
Black, non-Hispanic	7,837	87	77	65	35	58
Hispanic [3]	9,767	87	80	65	32	51
Asian or Pacific Islander, non-Hispanic	1,566	90	80	72	46	62
Other, non-Hispanic	2,598	90	74	76	47	62
Student's grade level: [4]						
K–2nd grade	11,516	93	90	78	63	72
3rd–5th grade	11,519	94	92	83	57	71
6th–8th grade	12,058	91	76	72	38	63
9th–12th grade	16,503	83	61	68	34	57
Parents' highest education level:						
Less than high school	3,504	75	70	48	20	34
High school graduate or equivalent	11,070	84	74	65	33	55
Vocational/technical or some college	14,844	89	77	72	42	67
Bachelor's degree	11,353	94	81	83	56	72
Graduate or professional school	10,829	95	82	87	64	77
Parents' language at home:						
Both/only parent(s) speak(s) English	45,219	90	78	77	49	69
One of two parents speaks English	1,022	82	75	63	42	54
No parent speaks English	5,359	84	82	57	22	38

[1] Parent Teacher Organization (PTO) or Parent Teacher Association (PTA) meeting. [2] Variables for school characteristics (school type and school size) have a certain number of missing cases due to school non-report; therefore, the number of students across the categories for each school variable does not sum to the total number of students. [3] Persons of Hispanic origin may be any race. [4] Students whose parents reported the student's grade equivalent as "ungraded" were excluded from the analyses of grade level.

Source: U.S. Department of Education, National Center for Education Statistics, Parent and Family Involvement in Education Survey of the National Household Education Surveys Program (NHES), 2007.

164 Education

Table 253. School Enrollment Below Postsecondary—Summary by Sex, Race, and Hispanic Origin: 2009

[In thousands (57,523 represents 57,523,000), except percent and rate. As of October. Covers civilian noninstitutional population enrolled in nursery school through high school. Based on Current Population Survey, see text, Section 1 and Appendix III]

| Characteristic | Total | | | Race and Hispanic origin | | | | |
| | | | | White [2] | | | | |
	Number [1]	Male	Female	Total	Non-Hispanic	Black [2]	Asian [2]	Hispanic [3]
All students	**57,523**	**29,363**	**28,162**	**43,558**	**32,664**	**8,859**	**2,285**	**12,095**
Nursery	4,708	2,331	2,377	3,404	2,575	811	239	930
Full day	2,438	1,177	1,261	1,564	1,167	617	135	459
Part day	2,270	1,154	1,117	1,840	1,408	194	105	471
Kindergarten	4,132	2,135	1,997	3,154	2,252	619	167	965
Elementary	32,238	16,504	15,734	24,575	18,244	4,749	1,296	7,058
High school	16,445	8,393	8,053	12,425	9,573	2,680	582	3,142
Students in public schools	51,145	26,101	25,043	38,368	28,031	8,234	1,954	11,419
Nursery	2,744	1,356	1,388	1,832	1,188	640	107	717
Full day	1,418	693	725	817	525	478	42	334
Part day	1,326	663	663	1,015	663	162	66	384
Kindergarten	3,767	1,961	1,806	2,860	1,990	578	146	933
Elementary	29,365	15,005	14,359	22,257	16,198	4,424	1,170	6,716
High school	15,269	7,779	7,490	11,419	8,655	2,592	530	3,052
Population 15 to 17 years old	12,391	6,334	6,057	9,495	7,437	1,943	421	2,254
Percent below modal grade [4]	29.5	33.2	25.6	28.6	27.8	34.8	20.0	32.1
Students, 10th to 12th grade	11,651	5,798	5,853	8,886	6,944	1,797	426	2,129
Annual dropout rate	3.2	3.3	3.1	3.0	2.3	4.5	1.7	5.3
Population 18 to 24 years old	29,223	14,677	14,546	22,606	17,750	4,346	1,181	5,332
Percent dropouts	9.4	10.7	8.0	9.1	5.8	11.6	2.2	20.8
Percent high school graduates	84.3	82.5	86.2	85.1	89.2	79.6	91.4	70.3
Percent enrolled in college	41.3	38.4	44.2	41.3	45.0	36.9	65.0	27.5

[1] Includes other races not shown separately. [2] For persons who selected this race group only. See footnote 2, Table 229. [3] Persons of Hispanic origin may be any race. [4] The modal grade is the grade most common for a given age.
Source: U.S. Census Bureau, Current Population Survey, unpublished data, <http://www.census.gov/population/www/socdemo/school.html>.

Table 254. Elementary and Secondary Schools—Teachers, Enrollment, and Pupil-Teacher Ratio: 1970 to 2009

[In thousands (2,292 represents 2,292,000), except ratios. As of fall. Data are for full-time equivalent teachers. Based on surveys of state education agencies and private schools; see source for details]

| Year | Teachers | | | Enrollment | | | Pupil-teacher ratio | | |
	Total	Public	Private	Total	Public	Private	Total	Public	Private
1970	2,292	2,059	233	51,257	45,894	5,363	22.4	22.3	23.0
1975	2,453	2,198	255	49,819	44,819	5,000	20.3	20.4	19.6
1980	2,485	2,184	301	46,208	40,877	5,331	18.6	18.7	17.7
1984	2,508	2,168	340	44,908	39,208	5,700	17.9	18.1	16.8
1985	2,549	2,206	343	44,979	39,422	5,557	17.6	17.9	16.2
1986	2,592	2,244	348	45,205	39,753	5,452	17.4	17.7	15.7
1987	2,631	2,279	352	45,487	40,008	5,479	17.3	17.6	15.6
1988	2,668	2,323	345	45,430	40,189	5,242	17.0	17.3	15.2
1989	2,713	2,357	356	45,741	40,543	5,198	17.0	17.2	15.7
1990	2,759	2,398	361	46,451	41,217	5,234	17.0	17.2	15.6
1991	2,797	2,432	365	47,728	42,047	5,681	17.1	17.3	15.6
1992	2,827	2,459	368	48,500	42,823	5,677	17.2	17.4	15.4
1993	2,874	2,504	370	49,133	43,465	5,668	17.1	17.4	15.3
1994 [1]	2,925	2,552	373	49,898	44,111	5,787	17.1	17.3	15.5
1995	2,974	2,598	376	50,759	44,840	5,918	17.1	17.3	15.7
1996 [1]	3,051	2,667	384	51,544	45,611	5,933	16.9	17.1	15.5
1997	3,138	2,746	391	52,071	46,127	5,944	16.6	16.8	15.2
1998 [1]	3,230	2,830	400	52,525	46,539	5,988	16.3	16.4	15.0
1999	3,319	2,911	408	52,876	46,857	6,018	15.9	16.1	14.7
2000 [1]	3,366	2,941	424	53,373	47,204	6,169	15.9	16.0	14.5
2001	3,440	3,000	441	53,992	47,672	6,320	15.7	15.9	14.3
2002 [1]	3,476	3,034	442	54,403	48,183	6,220	15.7	15.9	14.1
2003	3,490	3,049	441	54,639	48,540	6,099	15.7	15.9	13.8
2004 [1]	3,536	3,091	445	54,882	48,795	6,087	15.5	15.8	13.7
2005	3,593	3,143	450	55,187	49,113	6,073	15.4	15.6	13.5
2006 [1]	3,622	3,166	456	55,307	49,316	5,991	15.3	15.6	13.2
2007	3,634	3,178	456	55,203	49,293	5,910	15.2	15.5	13.0
2008 [1]	3,674	3,219	455	55,235	49,266	5,969	15.0	15.3	13.1
2009 [2]	3,617	3,161	457	55,282	49,312	5,970	15.3	15.6	13.1

[1] Private school numbers are estimated based on data from the Private School Universe Survey. [2] Projection.
Source: U.S. National Center for Education Statistics, *Digest of Education Statistics*, annual, and *Projections of Educational Statistics*. See also <http://www.nces.ed.gov/annuals>.

Table 255. Public Elementary and Secondary School Teachers—Selected Characteristics: 2007 to 2008

[For school year (612 represents 612,000). Based on the 2007-2008 Schools and Staffing Survey and subject to sampling error; for details, see source Web site at <http://nces.ed.gov/surveys/sass/>. Excludes prekindergarten teachers. See Table 266 for similar data on private school teachers]

Characteristic	Unit	Age					Sex		Race/ethnicity		
		Under 30 years old	30 to 39 years old	40 to 49 years old	50 to 59 years old	Over 60 years old	Male	Female	White [1]	Black [1]	His-panic [2]
Total teachers [3]	**1,000**	**612**	**898**	**808**	**879**	**207**	**821**	**2,584**	**2,829**	**239**	**240**
Highest degree held:											
Bachelor's	Percent	70.1	46.8	43.7	38.4	35.0	47.0	47.5	46.8	47.0	56.3
Master's	Percent	28.0	46.1	47.3	50.4	51.1	43.9	44.8	45.7	41.4	34.1
Education specialist	Percent	1.5	6.0	7.3	8.7	9.6	5.5	6.7	6.0	8.7	7.7
Doctorate	Percent	(S)	0.4	0.7	1.5	3.2	1.6	0.7	0.8	2.0	1.1
Full-time teaching experience:											
Less than 3 years	Percent	44.1	10.3	7.4	3.4	2.9	13.6	13.4	13.0	13.1	18.0
3 to 9 years	Percent	55.9	53.5	25.1	11.4	8.5	33.2	33.7	32.6	38.0	39.0
10 to 20 years	Percent	(S)	36.3	40.9	26.3	20.0	26.6	27.5	27.6	24.9	26.7
20 years or more	Percent	−	(S)	26.6	59.0	68.6	26.6	25.5	26.8	24.1	16.3
Full-time teachers	1,000	572	828	739	803	185	776	2,351	2,579	229	230
Earned income	Dollars	41,790	48,380	52,850	58,760	59,610	53,910	50,790	51,530	51,110	51,520
Salary	Dollars	39,760	46,320	50,870	56,760	57,910	50,560	49,230	49,570	48,910	49,260

− Represents or rounds to zero. S Reporting standards not met, the standard error for this estimate is 50% or more of the estimate's value. [1] Non-Hispanic. [2] Persons of Hispanic origin may be any race. [3] Includes teachers with no degrees and associate's degrees not shown separately.

Source: U.S. Department of Education, National Center for Education Statistics, Schools and Staffing Survey (SASS), "Public School Teacher Data Files," 2007–08.

Table 256. Public Elementary and Secondary Schools—Number and Average Salary of Classroom Teachers, 1990 to 2009, and by State, 2009

[Estimates for school year ending in June of year shown (2,362 represents 2,362,000). Schools classified by type of organization rather than by grade-group; elementary includes kindergarten]

Year and state	Teachers [1] (1,000)			Avg. salary ($1,000)			Year and state	Teachers (1,000) [1]			Avg. salary ($1,000)		
	Total	Ele-men-tary	Sec-ond-ary	All teach-ers	Ele-men-tary	Sec-ond-ary		Total	Ele-men-tary	Sec-ond-ary	All teach-ers	Ele-men-tary	Sec-ond-ary
1990	2,362	1,390	972	31.4	30.8	32.0	MD	59.8	34.9	24.9	62.8	62.6	63.4
1995	2,565	1,517	1,048	36.7	36.1	37.5	MA	70.9	46.9	24.1	67.6	67.6	67.6
2000	2,891	1,696	1,195	41.8	41.3	42.5	MI	96.0	48.9	47.1	57.3	57.3	57.3
2002	2,992	1,751	1,240	44.7	44.2	45.3	MN	51.8	26.3	25.5	52.4	52.4	52.4
2003	3,020	1,769	1,251	45.7	45.4	46.1	MS	34.8	20.6	14.2	44.5	44.5	44.5
2004	3,042	1,782	1,260	46.5	46.2	47.0	MO	68.8	34.9	33.9	44.2	44.2	44.2
2005	3,072	1,799	1,273	47.5	47.1	47.7	MT	10.4	7.0	3.4	44.4	44.4	44.4
2006	3,125	1,811	1,313	49.1	48.6	49.5	NE	21.9	14.2	7.7	45.0	45.0	45.0
2007	3,172	1,848	1,324	51.1	50.7	51.5	NV	23.6	13.7	9.9	50.1	50.1	50.1
2008	3,201	1,860	1,341	52.8	52.4	53.3	NH	15.6	10.6	5.0	50.1	50.1	50.1
2009, U.S.	**3,228**	**1,884**	**1,344**	**54.3**	**53.9**	**54.8**	NJ	114.4	44.4	70.0	63.1	62.3	64.8
AL	47.8	25.5	22.2	46.9	46.3	47.4	NM	21.8	15.0	6.8	45.8	45.5	46.3
AK	8.7	5.9	2.8	58.4	58.4	58.4	NY	229.9	101.8	128.1	69.1	69.5	68.8
AZ	54.6	38.6	16.0	46.4	45.1	49.3	NC	99.1	70.0	29.1	48.5	48.5	48.5
AR	35.4	17.2	18.1	45.7	45.7	45.7	ND	7.7	5.3	2.4	41.7	41.9	41.1
CA	298.9	205.8	93.0	67.0	67.0	67.0	OH	111.3	72.0	39.3	54.7	55.4	54.2
CO	48.6	25.2	23.4	48.5	48.1	48.9	OK	42.1	28.7	13.4	43.8	43.5	44.6
CT	43.5	29.2	14.3	63.2	63.2	63.2	OR	29.9	19.3	10.5	54.1	53.8	54.7
DE	8.3	4.1	4.2	56.7	56.6	56.7	PA	125.0	62.5	62.5	57.8	57.8	57.8
DC	5.7	3.8	1.9	62.6	62.6	62.6	RI	11.2	6.9	4.2	58.4	58.4	58.4
FL	169.0	87.0	82.0	46.9	46.9	46.9	SC	49.3	34.4	14.9	47.4	45.7	46.5
GA	119.0	72.3	46.6	52.9	52.5	53.5	SD	8.9	6.4	2.5	35.1	33.9	37.7
HI	11.6	6.2	5.4	55.0	55.0	55.0	TN	63.8	44.4	19.3	45.5	45.5	45.5
ID	15.1	7.9	7.2	45.2	45.1	45.3	TX	327.7	167.2	160.5	47.2	46.7	47.6
IL	146.8	100.5	46.2	61.3	58.9	66.7	UT	25.2	14.0	11.2	45.9	45.9	45.9
IN	62.2	33.4	28.8	49.6	50.6	50.9	VT	8.9	4.6	4.3	47.9	47.9	47.9
IA	35.6	23.5	12.1	48.6	48.9	48.1	VA	103.4	60.9	42.5	48.4	48.1	48.7
KS	35.4	17.6	17.8	46.2	46.2	46.2	WA	54.6	30.0	24.6	52.6	52.4	52.7
KY	41.3	29.2	12.0	47.9	47.7	48.4	WV	19.8	14.3	5.5	44.7	44.4	45.4
LA	49.0	34.4	14.6	48.6	48.6	48.6	WI	59.5	40.8	18.7	51.1	51.2	51.0
ME	16.9	11.4	5.6	44.7	44.7	44.7	WY	7.0	3.6	3.4	54.6	54.4	54.9

[1] Full-time equivalent.

Source: National Education Association, Washington, DC, Estimates of School Statistics Database (copyright).

Table 257. Teacher Stayers, Movers, and Leavers by Selected Characteristics: 2000 to 2001 and 2008 to 2009

[2,994.7 represents 2,994,700. Data compare the teaching status of teacher between one school year and the prior year. Stayers are teachers who were teaching in the same school in both years. Movers are teachers who were still teaching in the current school year but in a different school. Leavers are teachers who left the teaching profession. Based on the School and Staffing Survey; see source for details]

Characteristic	Public				Private			
	Total [1]	Stayers	Movers	Leavers	Total [1]	Stayers	Movers	Leavers
NUMBER (1,000)								
2000-01	2,994.7	2,542.2	231.0	221.4	448.6	354.8	37.6	56.2
2008-09	3,380.3	2,854.9	255.7	269.8	487.3	386.0	24.0	77.3
PERCENT DISTRIBUTION								
Total, 2008-09	100.0	84.5	7.6	8.0	100.0	79.2	4.9	15.9
Age:								
Less than 30 years old	100.0	76.1	14.7	9.2	100.0	68.9	10.0	21.1
30 to 39 years old	100.0	84.4	7.3	8.4	100.0	76.9	4.9	18.2
40 to 49 years old	100.0	89.6	6.6	3.9	100.0	83.7	5.4	10.9
50 to 59 years old	100.0	85.9	5.7	8.4	100.0	85.2	2.4	12.4
60 years old and over	100.0	82.4	[2] 2.0	15.6	100.0	77.7	[2] 2.7	19.6
Sex:								
Male	100.0	84.4	7.8	7.9	100.0	80.0	5.7	14.3
Female	100.0	84.5	7.5	8.0	100.0	78.9	4.7	16.4
Race/ethnicity:								
White, non-Hispanic	100.0	85.0	7.0	8.0	100.0	80.7	4.6	14.7
Black, non-Hispanic	100.0	80.5	10.4	9.0	100.0	67.2	[2] 8.6	[2] 24.2
Hispanic, single or more than one race	100.0	83.8	10.7	[2] 5.6	100.0	69.2	(S)	[2] 23.7
Asian, Native Hawaiian, or Other Pacific Islander, non-Hispanic	100.0	80.1	(S)	[2] 8.0	100.0	[2] 58.7	(S)	(S)
American Indian/Alaska Native, non-Hispanic	100.0	[2] 82.5	(S)	(S)	100.0	(S)	(S)	(S)
More than one race, non-Hispanic	100.0	82.5	(S)	(S)	100.0	100.0	–	–
Years as a teacher:								
3 or fewer	100.0	76.2	14.1	9.7	100.0	70.5	6.5	22.9
4 to 9	100.0	83.4	8.6	7.9	100.0	74.8	7.8	17.4
10 to 19	100.0	90.4	5.2	4.4	100.0	84.3	2.8	12.9
20 or more	100.0	84.0	5.2	10.8	100.0	85.8	2.7	11.4
Main assignment field:								
Early childhood/general elementary	100.0	87.0	7.4	5.6	100.0	79.7	6.5	13.8
Special education	100.0	78.0	9.8	12.3	100.0	62.9	(S)	[2] 27.5
Arts/music	100.0	88.4	7.5	4.1	100.0	87.9	(S)	9.0
English/language arts	100.0	81.8	7.7	10.5	100.0	80.5	[2] 2.9	16.5
Mathematics	100.0	85.6	6.7	7.7	100.0	85.3	(S)	[2] 12.7
Natural sciences	100.0	83.9	7.1	[2] 9.0	100.0	80.6	[2] 4.8	[2] 14.6
Social sciences	100.0	84.2	[2] 8.2	7.6	100.0	83.3	[2] 4.3	[2] 12.4
Other	100.0	84.2	6.7	9.1	100.0	72.3	4.9	22.8

– Represents or rounds to zero. S Reporting standards not met. [1] Total teachers prior school year. [2] Interpret data with caution. The standard error for this estimate is equal to 30 percent or more of the estimate's value.

Source: U.S. National Center for Education Statistics, Teacher Follow-up Survey (TFS), "Current Teacher Data File" and "Former Teacher Data File," 2008–09.

Table 258. Public and Private School Teachers Who Moved to a Different School or Left Teaching by Reason: 2008 to 2009

[In percent. Movers are teachers who were still teaching in the current year but had moved to a different school after the 2007–08 school year. Leavers are teachers who left the teaching profession after the 2007–08 school year. Based on the School and Staffing Survey; see source for details]

Primary reason for moving	Movers		Primary reason for leaving	Leavers	
	Public	Private		Public	Private
Contract was not renewed	10.7	12.7	Contract was not renewed	5.3	13.0
Primary reason for moving, other than contract was not renewed:			Primary reason for leaving, other than contract was not renewed:		
Personal life factors	26.2	16.0	Personal life factors	42.9	27.8
Assignment and credential factors	[1] 7.5	(S)	Assignment and credential factors	[1] 1.2	[1] 1.6
Salary and other job benefits	[1] 4.0	23.2	Salary and other job benefits	[1] 4.0	[1] 10.7
Classroom factors	1.8	(S)	Classroom factors	(S)	(S)
School factors	16.1	18.9	School factors	9.8	12.1
Student performance factors	[1] 1.6	(S)	Student performance factors	3.5	(S)
Other factors	32.0	24.3	Other career factors	14.8	22.8
			Other factors	17.1	10.3

S Reporting standards not met. [1] Interpret data with caution. The standard error of this estimate is equal to 30 percent or more of the estimate's value.

Source: U.S. National Center for Education Statistics, Teacher Attrition and Mobility: Results from the 2008-09 Teacher Follow-up Survey, NCES 2010-353, August 2010.

Education 167

Table 259. Average Salary and Wages Paid in Public School Systems: 1985 to 2011

[In dollars. For school year ending in year shown. Data reported by a stratified sample of school systems enrolling 300 or more pupils. Data represent unweighted means of average salaries paid school personnel reported by each school system]

Position	1985	1990	1995	2000	2005	2008	2009	2010	2011
ANNUAL SALARY									
Central-office administrators:									
Superintendent (contract salary)	56,954	75,425	90,198	112,158	128,770	148,387	155,634	159,634	161,992
Deputy/assoc. superintendent	52,877	69,623	81,266	97,251	116,186	134,245	136,832	139,463	138,061
Assistant superintendent	48,003	62,698	75,236	88,913	103,212	116,833	119,755	123,509	122,333
Administrators for—									
Finance and business	40,344	52,354	61,323	73,499	83,678	96,490	98,590	100,306	101,347
Instructional services.	43,452	56,359	66,767	79,023	88,950	99,748	102,322	103,974	103,025
Public relations/information	35,287	44,926	53,263	60,655	70,502	80,534	83,235	86,567	84,629
Staff personnel services	44,182	56,344	65,819	76,608	86,966	98,190	100,620	102,269	101,578
Technology.	(X)	(X)	(X)	(X)	76,308	86,085	87,898	90,530	90,914
Subject area supervisors.	34,422	45,929	54,534	63,103	68,714	78,309	80,290	80,964	80,534
School building administrators:									
Principals:									
Elementary	36,452	48,431	58,589	69,407	76,182	85,907	88,062	89,673	89,591
Junior high/middle	39,650	52,163	62,311	73,877	81,514	91,334	93,478	95,003	95,426
Senior high	42,094	55,722	66,596	79,839	86,938	97,486	99,365	102,387	102,191
Assistant principals:									
Elementary	30,496	40,916	48,491	56,419	63,140	71,192	71,893	73,181	71,764
Junior high/middle	33,793	44,570	52,942	60,842	67,600	76,053	77,476	79,164	78,131
Senior high	35,491	46,486	55,556	64,811	71,401	79,391	81,083	83,074	82,027
Classroom teachers.	23,587	31,278	37,264	42,213	45,884	51,329	52,900	54,370	54,220
Auxiliary professional personnel:									
Counselors	27,593	35,979	42,486	48,195	52,500	57,618	58,775	60,142	60,188
Librarians.	24,981	33,469	40,418	46,732	50,720	56,933	57,974	59,495	59,093
School nurses	19,944	26,090	31,066	35,540	40,520	46,025	46,476	48,032	48,044
Secretarial/clerical personnel:									
Central office:									
Secretaries	15,343	20,238	23,935	28,405	32,716	36,657	37,785	38,601	38,606
Accounting/payroll clerks.	15,421	20,088	24,042	28,498	33,217	37,732	39,031	39,895	39,790
Typists/data entry clerks	12,481	16,125	18,674	22,853	26,214	30,072	31,718	32,555	32,636
School building level:									
Secretaries	12,504	16,184	19,170	22,630	25,381	28,810	29,480	30,474	30,226
Library clerks.	9,911	12,152	14,381	16,509	18,443	21,004	21,190	21,639	21,142
HOURLY WAGE RATE									
Other support personnel:									
Teacher aides:									
Instructional.	5.89	7.43	8.77	10.00	11.35	12.86	13.23	13.48	13.55
Noninstructional.	5.60	7.08	8.29	9.77	11.23	12.70	13.13	13.59	13.58
Custodians.	6.90	8.54	10.05	11.35	12.61	14.19	14.59	15.04	14.92
Cafeteria workers	5.42	6.77	7.89	9.02	10.33	11.60	11.94	12.18	12.23
Bus drivers.	7.27	9.21	10.69	12.48	14.18	16.56	16.44	16.62	16.61

X Not applicable.

Source: Educational Research Service, Arlington, VA, *National Survey of Salaries and Wages in Public Schools*, annual (copyright).

Table 260. Public School Employment: 1990 and 2008

[In thousands (3,181 represents 3,181,000). Covers all public elementary-secondary school districts with 100 or more full-time employees]

Occupation	1990					2008				
	Total	Male	Female	White [1]	Black [1]	Total	Male	Female	White [1]	Black [1]
All occupations [2].	**3,181**	**914**	**2,267**	**2,502**	**463**	**4,772**	**1,213**	**3,559**	**3,562**	**617**
Officials, administrators	43	28	15	37	4	76	36	41	60	8
Principals and assistant principals	90	56	34	70	13	190	86	104	125	35
Classroom teachers [3]	1,746	468	1,278	1,469	192	2,544	613	1,930	2,055	240
Elementary schools	875	128	747	722	103	1,218	152	1,066	978	107
Secondary schools	662	304	358	570	66	1,007	394	614	828	92
Other professional staff	227	58	170	187	30	386	71	315	298	49
Teachers' aides [4]	324	54	270	208	69	555	72	483	372	96
Clerical, secretarial staff	226	5	221	181	24	323	11	312	230	37
Service workers [5].	524	245	279	348	129	761	352	409	454	164

[1] Excludes individuals of Hispanic origin. [2] 2008 Includes other occupations not shown separately. [3] Includes other classroom teachers not shown separately. [4] Includes technicians. [5] Includes craftworkers and laborers.

Source: U.S. Equal Employment Opportunity Commission, *Elementary-Secondary Staff Information (EEO-5)*, biennial.

Table 261. Public Elementary and Secondary School Finances by Enrollment-Size Group: 2008 to 2009

[In millions of dollars (590,948 represents $590,948,000,000). Data are based on the Annual Government Finance Survey. For details, see source. See also Appendix III]

Item	All school systems	School systems with enrollment of—						
		50,000 or more	25,000 to 49,999	15,000 to 24,999	7,500 to 14,999	5,000 to 7,499	3,000 to 4,999	Under 3,000
TOTAL								
General revenue	590,948	124,377	73,579	53,837	84,808	52,690	70,586	131,070
From federal sources	55,900	13,217	7,260	5,136	7,815	4,019	5,476	12,977
Through state	51,997	12,473	6,873	4,908	7,172	3,758	5,143	11,671
Child nutrition programs	10,687	2,567	1,576	1,111	1,521	827	1,108	1,979
Direct	3,903	744	387	228	643	261	333	1,307
From state sources [1]	276,154	55,190	36,080	27,980	41,018	23,262	30,977	61,648
General formula assistance	187,040	33,747	25,454	19,677	28,671	16,101	21,031	42,360
Compensatory programs	6,224	1,340	1,045	680	1,034	491	568	1,066
Special education	16,471	3,951	1,705	1,281	2,090	1,381	2,000	4,063
From local sources	258,894	55,970	30,239	20,721	35,976	25,410	34,134	56,445
Taxes	175,902	29,474	21,069	14,744	25,922	18,710	25,027	40,958
Contributions from parent government	45,826	19,519	4,868	2,817	5,073	3,595	4,762	5,192
From other local governments	5,924	501	696	398	626	527	837	2,339
Current charges	14,666	2,474	1,700	1,282	2,129	1,311	1,798	3,972
School lunch	6,968	1,052	815	663	1,107	707	952	1,672
Other	16,575	4,002	1,905	1,480	2,226	1,267	1,710	3,984
General expenditure	604,856	129,807	76,570	55,800	86,336	53,811	70,578	131,953
Current spending	517,708	109,271	64,047	47,150	74,088	46,358	61,489	115,304
By function:								
Instruction	311,891	68,224	38,283	28,422	44,746	28,170	37,112	66,935
Support services	178,694	35,357	22,315	16,142	25,509	15,933	21,328	42,109
Other current spending	27,124	5,689	3,449	2,586	3,833	2,255	3,050	6,260
By object:								
Total salaries and wages	310,334	65,516	39,818	29,189	45,011	27,825	36,658	66,317
Total employee benefits	109,188	23,834	12,305	9,838	16,051	10,397	13,138	23,626
Other	98,186	19,921	11,925	8,123	13,026	8,136	11,693	25,362
Capital outlay	68,045	16,147	9,959	6,919	9,543	5,613	6,943	12,921
Interest on debt	17,141	4,090	2,468	1,693	2,476	1,594	1,914	2,904
Payments to other governments	1,963	298	96	38	229	247	231	824
Debt outstanding	399,118	91,379	55,310	40,491	58,440	36,694	46,664	70,140
Long-term	390,652	90,050	54,584	39,896	57,347	35,815	45,563	67,398
Short-term	8,466	1,329	726	595	1,092	879	1,101	2,743
Long-term debt issued	42,396	9,485	5,606	4,121	6,521	3,685	5,132	7,846
Long-term debt retired	28,521	5,919	3,298	2,498	4,260	2,775	3,817	5,955
PER PUPIL								
Fall enrollment (1,000)	48,239	10,055	6,611	4,880	7,272	4,256	5,625	9,541
General revenue	12,250	12,369	11,130	11,033	11,663	12,381	12,548	13,738
From federal sources	1,159	1,314	1,098	1,053	1,075	944	973	1,360
From state sources [1]	5,725	5,489	5,458	5,734	5,641	5,466	5,507	6,462
General formula assistance	3,877	3,356	3,850	4,032	3,943	3,783	3,739	4,440
Special education	341	393	258	263	287	324	355	426
From local sources [1]	5,367	5,566	4,574	4,247	4,947	5,971	6,068	5,916
Taxes	3,646	2,931	3,187	3,022	3,565	4,396	4,449	4,293
Contributions from parent government	950	1,941	736	577	698	845	847	544
Current charges	304	246	257	263	293	308	320	416
School lunch	144	105	123	136	152	166	169	175
General expenditure [1]	12,305	12,650	11,369	11,251	11,671	12,391	12,311	13,571
Current spending	10,499	10,608	9,475	9,479	9,987	10,639	10,696	11,826
By function:								
Instruction	6,369	6,669	5,698	5,766	6,071	6,487	6,490	6,928
Support services	3,704	3,516	3,376	3,308	3,508	3,744	3,791	4,414
By object:								
Total salaries and wages	6,433	6,516	6,023	5,982	6,190	6,538	6,517	6,951
Total employee benefits	2,263	2,370	1,861	2,016	2,207	2,443	2,335	2,476
Capital outlay	1,411	1,606	1,506	1,418	1,312	1,319	1,234	1,354
Interest on debt	355	407	373	347	341	375	340	304
Debt outstanding	8,274	9,088	8,367	8,298	8,037	8,622	8,295	7,352
Long-term	8,098	8,956	8,257	8,176	7,886	8,415	8,100	7,064

[1] Includes other sources not shown separately.

Source: U.S. Census Bureau, *Public Education Finances, 2009*, May 2011, <http://www.census.gov/govs/school>.

Table 262. Public Elementary and Secondary Estimated Finances: 1980 to 2009, and by State, 2009

[In millions of dollars (101,724 represents $101,724,000,000), except as noted. For school years ending in June of year shown]

Year and state	Receipts						Expenditures				
		Revenue receipts							Current expenditures		
			Source						Elementary and secondary day schools	Average per pupil in ADA [4]	
	Total	Total	Federal	State	Local	Non–revenue receipts [1]	Total [2]	Per capita [3] (dol.)		Amount (dol.)	Rank
1980............	101,724	97,635	9,020	47,929	40,686	4,089	96,105	428	85,661	2,230	(X)
1985............	146,976	141,013	9,533	69,107	62,373	5,963	139,382	591	127,230	3,483	(X)
1990............	218,126	208,656	13,184	100,787	94,685	9,469	209,698	850	186,583	4,966	(X)
1995............	288,501	273,255	18,764	129,958	124,533	15,246	276,584	1,051	242,995	5,957	(X)
2000............	390,861	369,754	26,346	183,986	159,421	21,106	374,782	1,343	320,954	7,410	(X)
2005............	519,291	477,371	42,908	225,142	209,321	41,921	496,199	1,693	422,346	9,367	(X)
2006............	549,853	505,753	45,950	236,977	222,826	44,100	521,129	1,762	443,032	9,731	(X)
2007............	581,645	535,516	46,158	255,241	234,118	46,129	548,039	1,835	467,418	10,229	(X)
2008............	602,989	560,140	47,547	269,993	242,599	42,850	579,683	1,922	495,475	10,802	(X)
2009, total......	**602,159**	**564,928**	**57,255**	**261,512**	**246,161**	**37,232**	**591,785**	**1,944**	**505,694**	**10,905**	**(X)**
Alabama........	7,790	7,201	761	4,166	2,273	590	7,763	1,660	6,634	9,321	40
Alaska..........	1,560	1,387	174	881	332	173	1,531	2,225	1,425	12,198	15
Arizona.........	9,334	9,334	730	4,892	3,712	–	7,746	1,192	6,393	6,385	50
Arkansas........	5,156	4,866	563	2,717	1,587	289	5,208	1,816	4,726	12,512	14
California........	78,639	68,700	11,342	36,520	20,838	9,938	72,202	1,974	57,668	9,472	38
Colorado........	9,194	8,359	593	3,682	4,084	836	9,183	1,861	7,642	10,069	35
Connecticut......	8,945	8,932	603	3,384	4,946	13	8,931	2,549	7,976	14,099	10
Delaware........	2,055	1,847	147	1,160	540	208	2,034	2,321	1,635	14,612	6
District of Columbia......	910	910	112	–	798	–	1,283	2,174	1,008	13,331	(X)
Florida..........	27,451	26,429	2,669	9,048	14,712	1,022	29,243	1,587	23,135	9,374	39
Georgia.........	18,563	18,105	1,688	7,724	8,693	458	17,467	1,801	16,834	10,590	29
Hawaii..........	2,689	2,689	392	2,205	92	–	2,422	1,881	2,225	13,417	11
Idaho...........	2,495	2,265	220	1,519	526	230	2,569	1,682	2,126	8,230	46
Illinois..........	24,862	23,190	2,908	4,357	15,924	1,673	26,541	2,067	23,074	11,811	18
Indiana.........	11,396	10,782	921	5,662	4,199	614	12,240	1,916	10,225	10,514	30
Iowa...........	5,585	5,283	379	2,530	2,373	302	5,339	1,783	4,487	10,116	33
Kansas..........	6,618	5,649	414	3,287	1,949	969	5,825	2,082	4,685	11,324	24
Kentucky........	6,774	6,765	732	3,936	2,097	9	6,595	1,538	6,021	10,117	32
Louisiana........	9,323	8,095	1,264	3,740	3,091	1,229	8,537	1,918	7,277	11,413	23
Maine...........	2,822	2,645	286	1,017	1,342	177	2,824	2,140	2,588	14,576	7
Maryland........	13,382	13,224	832	5,839	6,553	158	12,767	2,256	11,365	14,325	9
Massachusetts....	15,158	15,156	1,276	6,090	7,790	2	14,858	2,271	13,980	15,502	5
Michigan........	19,636	19,286	1,675	11,338	6,272	351	20,281	2,028	18,842	11,874	17
Minnesota.......	11,435	10,108	838	7,660	1,609	1,327	11,422	2,184	9,008	11,663	19
Mississippi.......	4,416	4,316	694	2,304	1,318	100	4,107	1,397	3,710	7,814	48
Missouri.........	11,304	10,020	997	3,152	5,870	1,284	9,128	1,533	7,907	9,318	41
Montana.........	1,476	1,450	182	693	575	25	1,374	1,419	1,326	11,180	25
Nebraska........	2,939	2,914	201	1,148	1,565	25	3,073	1,725	2,673	10,063	36
Nevada.........	5,241	3,338	261	1,099	1,977	1,903	4,357	1,666	3,331	7,777	49
New Hampshire...	2,697	2,650	147	980	1,522	47	2,564	1,940	2,430	13,130	12
New Jersey......	23,100	23,098	750	8,203	14,145	1	23,120	2,669	22,392	15,983	3
New Mexico......	4,337	3,771	572	2,643	556	566	4,222	2,125	3,363	10,819	26
New York........	46,238	46,207	3,704	20,863	21,640	31	48,595	2,496	43,377	14,429	8
North Carolina....	12,633	12,633	1,352	8,132	3,150	–	13,995	1,513	12,500	9,175	43
North Dakota.....	1,147	1,102	161	408	533	44	1,147	1,788	961	10,805	27
Ohio............	18,697	18,697	1,537	8,493	8,668	–	17,783	1,543	17,783	10,796	28
Oklahoma.......	6,250	5,764	778	3,038	1,947	486	5,526	1,517	4,977	8,249	45
Oregon.........	7,073	6,224	670	3,112	2,442	850	6,250	1,652	5,713	11,501	22
Pennsylvania.....	26,618	26,418	1,780	10,102	14,536	200	25,799	2,053	21,742	12,865	13
Rhode Island.....	2,388	2,388	204	960	1,224	–	2,217	2,104	2,130	16,127	2
South Carolina....	8,498	7,717	762	3,680	3,275	781	8,480	1,883	6,688	10,093	34
South Dakota.....	1,324	1,242	203	410	628	82	1,260	1,566	1,080	9,243	42
Tennessee.......	8,253	7,966	900	3,865	3,201	287	7,993	1,281	7,585	9,894	37
Texas...........	53,550	46,899	5,015	19,973	21,911	6,651	54,120	2,227	40,709	9,143	44
Utah...........	4,848	4,520	565	2,363	1,592	328	4,684	1,717	3,617	8,141	47
Vermont........	1,565	1,542	123	1,334	85	23	1,511	2,433	1,364	18,913	1
Virginia.........	16,434	15,344	949	6,364	8,031	1,090	16,154	2,072	13,320	11,643	20
Washington......	12,542	11,734	1,385	7,146	3,202	808	13,076	1,991	10,057	10,399	31
West Virginia.....	3,609	3,259	426	1,940	892	350	3,595	1,981	3,030	11,537	21
Wisconsin.......	11,512	10,832	1,302	4,809	4,720	680	11,186	1,988	9,673	11,998	16
Wyoming........	1,699	1,677	111	945	622	21	1,658	3,111	1,275	15,742	4

– Represents or rounds to zero. X Not applicable. [1] Amount received by local education agencies from the sales of bonds and real property and equipment, loans, and proceeds from insurance adjustments. [2] Includes interest on school debt and other current expenditures not shown separately. [3] Based on U.S. Census Bureau estimated resident population, as of July 1, the previous year, except 1990, and 2000 population enumerated as of April 1. [4] Average daily attendance.

Source: National Education Association, Washington, DC, Estimates of School Statistics Database (copyright).

U.S. Census Bureau, Statistical Abstract of the United States: 2012

Table 263. Public Elementary and Secondary Schools by School Type, Racial/Ethnic Concentration of Students, and Eligibility of Students for Free or Reduced-Price Lunch: 2000 and 2008

[For school year ending in June of year shown]

Characteristic	2000				2008			
	Total	Elemen-tary	Second-ary	Com-bined	Total	Elemen-tary	Second-ary	Com-bined
Total number of schools [1]	89,599	63,851	21,431	4,317	94,775	66,420	22,855	5,500
Percent [1]	100.0	71.3	23.9	4.8	100.0	70.1	24.1	5.8
PERCENT								
School type	100.0	100.0	100.0	100.0	100.0	100.0	100.0	100.0
Regular	93.8	98.7	87.2	55.0	92.2	98.4	83.8	52.7
Special education	1.8	0.8	1.2	19.5	1.9	0.8	1.5	17.2
Vocational	0.4	–	1.3	1.4	0.3	–	1.2	0.3
Alternative	4.0	0.5	10.3	24.0	5.6	0.8	13.5	29.8
Charter school [2]	1.7	1.3	1.7	6.8	4.5	3.5	5.1	14.8
Title I school [3]	52.4	62.3	26.4	33.1	65.2	72.9	45.7	52.8
Magnet school/program [4]	2.4	2.6	1.9	1.1	4.1	4.3	4.2	2.2
Racial/ethnic concentration: [5]								
More than 50 percent White	70.9	70.0	75.4	61.6	63.1	62.2	66.9	56.8
More than 50 percent Black	11.1	11.6	8.7	15.6	11.4	11.2	10.6	16.9
More than 50 percent Hispanic	8.8	9.4	7.3	7.2	13.0	13.9	11.1	10.2
Percentage of students in school eligible for free or reduced-price lunch	100.0	100.0	100.0	100.0	100.0	100.0	100.0	100.0
0–25 percent	31.5	27.8	42.6	30.6	25.0	23.7	29.6	22.4
26–50 percent	26.3	26.2	28.0	19.6	27.8	26.3	33.5	22.9
51–75 percent	17.3	19.3	11.3	17.5	22.9	24.1	19.3	23.4
76–100 percent	12.2	14.7	4.6	13.3	17.0	19.5	9.4	18.3
Missing/school did not participate	12.7	12.0	13.4	19.0	7.2	6.4	8.2	13.1

– Represents or rounds to zero. [1] Schools reporting membership are those which report at least one student enrolled on October 1 of the school year. In any given year, some small schools will not have any students. The Common Core of Data (CCD) allows a student to be reported for only a single school or agency. For example, a vocational school (identified as a "shared time" school) may provide classes for students from a number of districts and show no membership. [2] A charter school is a school that provides free public elementary and/or secondary education to eligible students under a specific charter granted by the state legislature or other appropriate authority and that is designated by such authority to be a charter school. The 2000 estimates exclude one state for lack of complete data. [3] A Title I School is designated under appropriate state and federal regulations as a high-poverty school that is eligible for participation in programs authorized by Title I of P.L. 107-110. The 2000 estimates exclude six states for lack of complete data. [4] A magnet school or program is a special school or program designed to attract students of different racial/ethnic backgrounds in an effort to reduce, prevent, or eliminate racial isolation and/or provide an academic or social focus on a particular theme. The 2000 estimates exclude 13 states for lack of complete data, and the 2008 estimates exclude 17 states. [5] The 2000 estimates exclude 2,220 schools for lack of complete data, and the 2008 estimates exclude 3 schools. Race categories exclude persons of Hispanic ethnicity.

Source: U.S. Department of Education, National Center for Education Statistics, Common Core of Data (CCD), "Public Elementary/Secondary School Universe Survey," 1999–2000 (version 1b) and 2007–08 (version 1a).

Table 264. Public School Districts Offering Various Technology Resources to All or Some Students by District Characteristics: 2008

[In percent. As of Fall. Percents are based on the percent of public school districts with students at that level (97 percent of districts have elementary students and 88 percent have secondary students). For composition of regions, see map, inside front cover]

Characteristic	Electronic storage space on a server				Online access to the library catalogue				Online curriculum			
	Elementary		Secondary		Elementary		Secondary		Elementary		Secondary	
	All	Some	All	Some	All	Some	All	Some	All	Some	All	Some
All public school districts	62	17	83	7	72	6	82	2	47	19	53	25
District enrollment size:												
Less than 2,500	63	15	85	3	69	5	80	[1] 1	46	17	53	23
2,500 to 9,999	59	22	78	14	79	7	87	3	50	23	54	28
10,000 or more	58	23	74	17	84	7	87	6	49	26	51	34
Community type:												
City	52	32	75	16	80	14	89	5	47	28	46	36
Suburban	67	15	84	7	76	7	87	2	40	23	46	30
Town	63	18	84	7	82	4	88	2	44	26	51	31
Rural	60	16	83	6	66	5	77	1	52	14	57	20
Region:												
Northeast	73	16	90	4	78	8	88	3	41	22	42	36
Southeast	43	20	64	18	74	4	82	3	52	16	59	20
Central	67	14	91	2	71	4	82	(S)	45	20	56	21
West	53	22	75	10	69	6	77	2	55	17	54	23
Poverty concentration:												
Less than 10 percent	76	12	92	3	82	6	92	[1] 1	45	22	51	30
10 to 19 percent	60	19	85	7	69	5	82	2	44	20	51	28
20 percent or more	50	21	72	10	66	6	72	2	54	14	56	18

S Reporting standards not met. [1] Interpret data with caution; the coefficient of variation is greater than 50 percent.
Source: U.S. National Center for Education Statistics, Educational Technology in Public School Districts: Fall 2008, NCES 2010-003, December 2009.

Table 265. Private Schools: 2009 to 2010

[5,488 represents 5,488,000. Based on the Private School Survey, conducted every 2 years; see source for details. For composition of regions, see map inside front cover]

Characteristic	Schools				Students (1,000)				Teachers (1,000) [1]			
	Number	Elementary	Secondary	Combined	Total	Elementary	Secondary	Combined	Total	Elementary	Secondary	Combined
Total	**33,366**	**21,425**	**2,776**	**9,165**	**5,488**	**2,937**	**786**	**1,766**	**437**	**194**	**68**	**175**
School type:												
Catholic	7,115	5,679	1,097	339	2,160	1,455	587	118	143	89	43	10
Parochial	3,111	2,893	145	73	856	762	67	28	53	46	5	2
Diocesan	2,969	2,384	487	98	909	613	261	35	58	37	18	3
Private	1,035	402	465	168	395	80	259	55	31	6	20	6
Other religious	15,616	8,903	776	5,937	2,076	884	107	1,086	172	63	11	98
Conservative Christian	4,614	1,645	147	2,823	737	209	18	511	60	15	2	43
Affiliated	2,882	1,789	259	834	516	246	43	226	45	19	5	21
Unaffiliated	8,120	5,470	370	2,280	823	429	46	349	67	29	5	33
Nonsectarian	10,635	6,842	903	2,889	1,252	599	92	562	123	43	13	67
Regular	5,231	3,899	319	1,014	818	361	64	392	76	24	9	43
Special emphasis	3,821	2,703	322	797	328	223	16	89	29	17	2	10
Special education	1,582	240	263	1,079	107	14	12	81	18	2	2	14
Program emphasis:												
Regular elem/sec	22,565	13,812	2,048	6,705	4,648	2,366	742	1,541	367	161	61	144
Montessori	2,653	2,438	8	207	213	193	1	19	15	13	(Z)	2
Special program emphasis	917	411	102	405	128	50	12	66	15	5	1	9
Special education	1,779	278	276	1,225	118	16	12	90	20	3	2	15
Vocational/tech	2	–	1	1	1	–	(Z)	1	(Z)	–	(Z)	(Z)
Alternative	1,327	363	341	623	95	26	19	50	10	3	2	6
Early childhood	4,122	4,122	(X)	–	285	285	(X)	–	10	10	(X)	–
Size:												
Less than 50	11,065	7,113	842	3,110	296	198	19	79	34	17	4	13
50 to 149	10,469	7,160	541	2,767	950	656	48	245	82	46	6	30
150 to 299	6,695	4,742	446	1,506	1,423	1,004	99	320	107	64	10	33
300 to 499	3,013	1,770	382	861	1,155	676	150	329	87	43	13	30
500 to 749	1,276	536	284	456	769	312	176	281	57	18	13	25
750 or more	848	104	279	464	896	91	294	511	70	5	20	44
Region:												
Northeast	7,643	4,982	923	1,739	1,310	686	270	353	115	47	25	43
Midwest	8,419	6,226	636	1,557	1,296	840	212	243	92	53	16	23
South	10,483	5,618	601	4,263	1,842	807	159	876	153	56	14	83
West	6,821	4,600	616	1,605	1,041	604	144	293	77	38	12	27

– Represents zero. X Not applicable. Z Less than 500. [1] Full-time equivalents.

Source: U.S. National Center for Education Statistics, Private School Universe Survey, 2009-2010; <http://nces.ed.gov/surveys/pss/>.

Table 266. Private Elementary and Secondary School Teachers—Selected Characteristics: 2007 to 2008

[For school year (80 represents 80,000). Based on the 2007–08 Schools and Staffing Survey Private School Teacher Questionnaire, and subject to sampling error; for details, see source at <http://nces.ed.gov/surveys/sass/>. Excludes prekindergarten teachers. See Table 255 for similar data on public school teachers]

Characteristic	Unit	Age					Sex		Race/ethnicity		
		Under 30 years old	30 to 39 years old	40 to 49 years old	50 to 59 years old	60 years old and over	Male	Female	White [1]	Black [1]	Hispanic [2]
Total teachers [3]	**1,000**	**80**	**109**	**116**	**128**	**56**	**127**	**362**	**423**	**20**	**29**
Highest degree held:											
Bachelor's	Percent	68.3	52.9	54.4	49.8	43.6	45.7	56.8	53.5	55.3	59.3
Master's	Percent	19.1	33.7	30.1	39.8	39.9	37.6	31.1	34.2	22.2	20.9
Education specialist	Percent	1.2	2.3	2.9	2.7	6.5	4.2	2.4	2.9	1.6	3.7
Doctorate	Percent	–	1.9	3.5	2.0	5.1	5.4	1.3	2.4	(S)	(S)
Full–time teaching experience:											
Less than 3 years	Percent	55.5	24.4	20.4	13.2	7.2	24.1	23.5	22.5	30.2	31.9
3 to 9 years	Percent	44.2	49.7	30.4	17.8	7.5	29.5	31.6	30.6	40.6	29.8
10 to 20 years	Percent	(S)	25.8	34.3	25.8	17.2	22.2	22.8	22.6	16.4	25.9
20 years or more	Percent	–	(S)	14.9	43.2	68.1	24.2	22.2	24.3	12.7	12.3
Full–time teachers	1,000	69	90	89	99	41	99	289	334	17	23
School related income	Dol	31,800	36,380	36,780	41,310	44,280	42,960	35,940	38,000	32,630	36,120
Annual salary	Dol	30,090	34,650	35,270	39,850	42,740	40,380	34,700	36,500	30,300	34,070

– Represents or rounds to zero. S Reporting standards not met. The standard error for this estimate is 50 percent or more of the estimate's value. [1] Non-Hispanic. [2] Persons of Hispanic origin may be any race. [3] Includes teachers with no degrees and associate's degrees, not shown separately.

Source: U.S. Department of Education, National Center for Education Statistics, Schools and Staffing Survey (SASS), "Private School Teacher Data Files," 2007–08.

Table 267. SAT Scores and Characteristics of College-Bound Seniors: 1970 to 2010

[For school year ending in year shown. Data are for the SAT I: Reasoning Tests. SAT I: Reasoning Test replaced the SAT in March 1994. Scores between the two tests have been equated to the same 200–800 scale and are thus comparable. Scores for 1995 and prior years have been recentered and revised]

Type of test and characteristic	Unit	1970	1980	1990	1995	2000	2005	2007	2008	2009	2010
AVERAGE TEST SCORES [1]											
Critical reading, total [2]	Point.....	537	502	500	504	505	508	502	502	501	501
Male	Point.....	536	506	505	505	507	513	504	504	503	503
Female	Point.....	538	498	496	502	504	505	502	500	498	498
Math, total [2]	Point.....	512	492	501	506	514	520	515	515	515	516
Male	Point.....	531	515	521	525	533	538	533	533	534	534
Female	Point.....	493	473	483	490	498	504	499	500	499	500
Writing	Point.....	(X)	(X)	(X)	(X)	(X)	(X)	494	494	493	492
Male	Point.....	(X)	(X)	(X)	(X)	(X)	(X)	489	488	486	486
Female	Point.....	(X)	(X)	(X)	(X)	(X)	(X)	500	501	499	498
PARTICIPANTS											
Total [3]	1,000....	(NA)	922	1,026	1,068	1,260	1,476	1,495	1,519	1,530	1,548
Male	Percent	(NA)	48.2	47.8	46.4	46.2	46.5	46.4	46.4	46.5	46.6
White	Percent..	(NA)	82.1	73.0	69.2	66.4	62.3	60.8	59.8	58.1	54.1
Black	Percent..	(NA)	9.1	10.0	10.7	11.2	11.6	11.7	12.1	12.8	12.7
Obtaining scores [1] of—											
600 or above:											
Critical reading	Percent..	(NA)	(NA)	20.3	21.9	21.1	22.5	21.2	21.0	20.5	20.5
Math	Percent..	(NA)	(NA)	20.4	23.4	24.2	26.5	24.5	25.0	25.7	25.2
Writing	Percent..	(X)	(X)	(X)	(X)	(X)	(X)	18.4	18.3	18.7	18.4
Below 400:											
Critical reading	Percent..	(NA)	(NA)	17.3	16.4	15.9	15.5	16.5	17.0	17.4	17.5
Math	Percent..	(NA)	(NA)	15.8	16.0	14.7	13.8	14.8	15.0	15.3	14.9
Writing	Percent..	(X)	(X)	(X)	(X)	(X)	(X)	18.4	18.5	19.4	19.4

NA Not available. X Not applicable. [1] Minimum score, 200; maximum score, 800. [2] 1970 estimates based on total number of persons taking SAT. For 2010, based on 1,547,990 test takers. [3] 922 represents 922,000.
Source: The College Board, *College-Bound Seniors 2010* (copyright 1967 to 2010), <http://www.collegeboard.com>. Reproduced with permission.

Table 268. ACT Program Scores and Characteristics of College-Bound Students: 1970 to 2010

[For academic year ending in year shown. Except as indicated, test scores and characteristics of college-bound students. Through 1980, data based on 10 percent sample; thereafter, based on all ACT tested graduating seniors]

Type of test and characteristic	Unit	1970	1980	1990 [1]	1995 [1]	2000 [1]	2005 [1]	2007 [1]	2008 [1]	2009 [1]	2010 [1]
TEST SCORES [2]											
Composite	Point......	19.9	18.5	20.6	20.8	21.0	20.9	21.2	21.1	21.1	21.0
Male	Point......	20.3	19.3	21.0	21.0	21.2	21.1	21.2	21.2	21.3	21.2
Female	Point......	19.4	17.9	20.3	20.7	20.9	20.9	21.0	21.0	20.9	20.9
English	Point......	18.5	17.9	20.5	20.2	20.5	20.4	20.7	20.6	20.6	20.5
Male	Point......	17.6	17.3	20.1	19.8	20.0	20.0	20.2	20.1	20.2	20.1
Female	Point......	19.4	18.3	20.9	20.6	20.9	20.8	21.0	21.0	20.9	20.8
Math	Point......	20.0	17.4	19.9	20.2	20.7	20.7	21.0	21.0	21.0	21.0
Male	Point......	21.1	18.9	20.7	20.9	21.4	21.3	21.6	21.6	21.6	21.6
Female	Point......	18.8	16.2	19.3	19.7	20.2	20.2	20.4	20.4	20.4	20.5
Reading [3]	Point......	19.7	17.2	(NA)	21.3	21.4	21.3	21.5	21.4	21.4	21.3
Male	Point......	20.3	18.2	(NA)	21.1	21.2	21.0	21.2	21.2	21.3	21.1
Female	Point......	19.0	16.4	(NA)	21.4	21.5	21.5	21.6	21.5	21.4	21.4
Science reasoning [4]	Point......	20.8	21.1	(NA)	21.0	21.0	20.9	21.0	20.8	20.9	20.9
Male	Point......	21.6	22.4	(NA)	21.6	21.6	21.4	21.4	21.3	21.4	21.4
Female	Point......	20.0	20.0	(NA)	20.5	20.6	20.5	20.5	20.4	20.4	20.5
PARTICIPANTS [5]											
Total [6]	1,000.....	788	822	817	945	1,065	1,186	1,301	1,422	1,480	1,587
Male	Percent...	52	45	46	44	43	44	45	45	45	45
White	Percent...	(NA)	83	73	69	72	66	60	63	64	62
Black	Percent...	4	8	9	9	10	12	12	13	13	14
Obtaining composite scores of—[7]											
27 or above	Percent...	14	13	12	13	14	14	15	16	16	16
18 or below	Percent...	21	33	35	34	32	34	32	33	34	35

NA Not available. [1] Beginning 1990, not comparable with previous years because a new version of the ACT was introduced. Estimated average composite scores for prior years: 1989, 20.6; 1988, 1987, and 1986, 20.8. [2] Minimum score, 1; maximum score, 36. [3] Prior to 1990, social studies; data not comparable with previous years. [4] Prior to 1990, natural sciences; data not comparable with previous years. [5] Beginning 1985, data are for seniors who graduated in year shown and had taken the ACT in their junior or senior years. Data by race are for those responding to the race question. [6] 788 represents 788,000. [7] Prior to 1990, 26 or above and 15 or below.
Source: ACT, Inc., Iowa City, IA, *High School Profile Report*, annual.

Table 269. Proficiency Levels on Selected NAEP Tests for Students in Public Schools by State: 2009

[Represents percent of public school students scoring at or above basic and proficient levels. Basic denotes mastery of the knowledge and skills that are fundamental for proficient work at a given grade level. Proficient represents solid academic performance. Students reaching this level demonstrated competency over challenging subject matter. For more detail, see <http://www.nagb.org/pubs/pubs.html>. Based on the National Assessment of Educational Progress (NAEP) tests which are administered to a representative sample of students in public schools, private schools, and Department of Defense schools. Data shown here are for public school students only]

State	Grade 4 Math		Grade 8 Math		Grade 4 Reading		Grade 8 Reading	
	At or above Basic	At or above Proficient	At or above Basic	At or above Proficient	At or above Basic	At or above Proficient	At or above Basic	At or above Proficient
U.S. average	**82**	**39**	**73**	**34**	**67**	**33**	**75**	**32**
Alabama	70	24	58	20	62	28	66	24
Alaska	78	38	75	33	59	27	72	27
Arizona	71	28	67	29	56	25	68	27
Arkansas	80	36	67	27	63	29	69	27
California	72	30	59	23	54	24	64	22
Colorado	84	45	76	40	72	40	78	32
Connecticut	86	46	78	40	76	42	81	43
Delaware	84	36	75	32	73	35	78	31
District of Columbia	56	17	40	11	44	17	51	14
Florida	86	40	70	29	73	36	76	32
Georgia	78	34	67	27	63	29	72	27
Hawaii	77	37	65	25	57	26	67	22
Idaho	85	41	78	38	69	32	77	33
Illinois	80	38	73	33	65	32	77	33
Indiana	87	42	78	36	70	34	79	32
Iowa	87	41	76	34	69	34	77	32
Kansas	89	46	79	39	72	35	80	33
Kentucky	81	37	70	27	72	36	79	33
Louisiana	72	23	62	20	51	18	64	20
Maine	87	45	78	35	70	35	80	35
Maryland	85	44	75	40	70	37	77	36
Massachusetts	92	57	85	52	80	47	83	43
Michigan	78	35	68	31	64	30	72	31
Minnesota	89	54	83	47	70	37	82	38
Mississippi	69	22	54	15	55	22	62	19
Missouri	83	41	77	35	70	36	79	34
Montana	88	45	82	44	73	35	84	38
Nebraska	82	38	75	35	70	35	80	35
Nevada	79	32	63	25	57	24	65	22
New Hampshire	92	56	82	43	77	41	81	39
New Jersey	88	49	80	44	76	40	83	42
New Mexico	72	26	59	20	52	20	66	22
New York	83	40	73	34	71	36	75	33
North Carolina	87	43	74	36	65	32	70	29
North Dakota	91	45	86	43	76	35	86	34
Ohio	85	45	76	36	71	36	80	37
Oklahoma	82	33	68	24	65	28	73	26
Oregon	80	37	75	37	65	31	76	33
Pennsylvania	84	46	78	40	70	37	81	40
Rhode Island	81	39	68	28	69	36	72	28
South Carolina	78	34	69	30	62	28	68	24
South Dakota	86	42	83	42	70	33	84	37
Tennessee	74	28	65	25	63	28	73	28
Texas	85	38	78	36	65	28	73	27
Utah	81	41	75	35	67	31	78	33
Vermont	89	51	81	43	75	41	84	41
Virginia	85	43	76	36	74	38	78	32
Washington	84	43	78	39	68	33	78	36
West Virginia	77	28	61	19	62	26	67	22
Wisconsin	85	45	79	39	67	33	78	34
Wyoming	87	40	78	35	72	33	82	34

Source: National Center for Education Statistics, National Assessment of Educational Progress (NAEP), 2009 Mathematics and Reading Assessments. See also <http://nces.ed.gov/nationsreportcard/>, accessed April 2010.

Table 270. Public High School Graduates by State: 1980 to 2009

[In thousands (2,747.7 represents 2,747,700). For school year ending in year shown]

State	1980	1990	2000	2009, proj.	State	1980	1990	2000	2009, proj.
United States	**2,747.7**	**2,320.3**	**2,553.8**	**3,004.6**					
Alabama	45.2	40.5	37.8	40.2	Missouri	62.3	49.0	52.8	61.4
Alaska	5.2	5.4	6.6	8.2	Montana	12.1	9.4	10.9	10.0
Arizona	28.6	32.1	38.3	57.2	Nebraska	22.4	17.7	20.1	20.3
Arkansas	29.1	26.5	27.3	28.7	Nevada	8.5	9.5	14.6	18.2
California	249.2	236.3	309.9	383.3	New Hampshire	11.7	10.8	11.8	14.1
Colorado	36.8	33.0	38.9	48.2	New Jersey	94.6	69.8	74.4	96.1
Connecticut	37.7	27.9	31.6	37.7	New Mexico	18.4	14.9	18.0	17.7
Delaware	7.6	5.6	6.1	7.6	New York	204.1	143.3	141.7	170.8
District of Columbia [1]	5.0	3.6	2.7	3.5	North Carolina	70.9	64.8	62.1	80.6
Florida	87.3	88.9	106.7	152.7	North Dakota	9.9	7.7	8.6	7.0
Georgia	61.6	56.6	62.6	81.0	Ohio	144.2	114.5	111.7	122.9
Hawaii	11.5	10.3	10.4	11.2	Oklahoma	39.3	35.6	37.6	37.6
Idaho	13.2	12.0	16.2	16.7	Oregon	29.9	25.5	30.2	35.8
Illinois	135.6	108.1	111.8	131.7	Pennsylvania	146.5	110.5	114.0	122.8
Indiana	73.1	60.0	57.0	64.0	Rhode Island	10.9	7.8	8.5	10.0
Iowa	43.4	31.8	33.9	34.6	South Carolina	38.7	32.5	31.6	37.0
Kansas	30.9	25.4	29.1	29.6	South Dakota	10.7	7.7	9.3	8.1
Kentucky	41.2	38.0	36.8	41.7	Tennessee	49.8	46.1	41.6	54.4
Louisiana	46.3	36.1	38.4	34.2	Texas	171.4	172.5	212.9	260.1
Maine	15.4	13.8	12.2	14.6	Utah	20.0	21.2	32.5	34.0
Maryland	54.3	41.6	47.8	57.3	Vermont	6.7	6.1	6.7	7.0
Massachusetts	73.8	55.9	53.0	64.0	Virginia	66.6	60.6	65.6	78.4
Michigan	124.3	93.8	97.7	115.9	Washington	50.4	45.9	57.6	63.4
Minnesota	64.9	49.1	57.4	59.3	West Virginia	23.4	21.9	19.4	17.8
Mississippi	27.6	25.2	24.2	25.7	Wisconsin	69.3	52.0	58.5	64.8
					Wyoming	6.1	5.8	6.5	5.5

[1] Beginning in 1990, graduates from adult programs are excluded.
Source: U.S. National Center for Education Statistics, *Digest of Education Statistics*, annual. See also <http://www.nces.ed.gov/programs/digest/>.

Table 271. High School Dropouts by Race and Hispanic Origin: 1980 to 2009

[In percent. As of October]

Item	1980	1985	1990 [1]	1995	2000	2003	2004	2005	2006	2007	2008	2009
EVENT DROPOUTS [2]												
Total [3]	6.0	5.2	4.5	5.4	4.5	3.8	4.4	3.6	3.5	3.3	3.3	3.1
White [4]	5.6	4.8	3.9	5.1	4.3	3.7	4.2	3.1	3.5	2.8	2.8	3.0
Male	6.4	4.9	4.1	5.4	4.7	3.9	4.9	3.4	3.9	2.8	2.7	3.3
Female	4.9	4.7	3.8	4.8	4.0	3.4	3.5	2.7	3.1	2.7	2.8	2.8
Black [4]	8.3	7.7	7.7	6.1	5.6	4.5	5.2	6.9	3.7	4.3	6.0	4.5
Male	8.0	8.3	6.9	7.9	7.6	4.1	4.8	7.5	3.2	4.9	4.6	4.4
Female	8.5	7.2	8.6	4.4	3.8	4.9	5.7	6.2	4.3	3.6	7.6	4.6
Hispanic [5]	11.5	9.7	7.7	11.6	6.8	6.5	8.0	4.7	6.4	5.5	4.9	5.3
Male	16.9	9.3	7.6	10.9	7.1	7.7	11.5	5.6	6.3	5.5	4.2	5.3
Female	6.9	9.8	7.7	12.5	6.5	5.4	4.6	3.9	6.6	5.6	5.6	5.4
STATUS DROPOUTS [6]												
Total [3]	15.6	13.9	14.4	13.9	12.4	11.8	12.1	11.3	11.0	10.2	9.3	9.4
White [4]	14.4	13.5	14.1	13.6	12.2	11.6	11.9	11.3	10.8	10.0	8.8	9.1
Male	15.7	14.7	15.4	14.3	13.5	13.3	13.7	13.2	12.4	11.7	9.8	10.5
Female	13.2	12.3	12.8	13.0	10.9	9.8	10.0	9.4	9.2	8.3	7.8	7.7
Black [4]	23.5	17.6	16.4	14.4	15.3	14.2	15.1	12.9	13.0	10.2	12.0	11.6
Male	26.0	18.8	18.6	14.2	17.4	16.7	17.9	14.8	11.2	10.0	10.2	13.9
Female	21.5	16.6	14.5	14.6	13.5	12.0	12.7	11.2	14.7	10.3	13.7	9.5
Hispanic [5]	40.3	31.5	37.7	34.7	32.3	28.4	28.0	27.3	26.2	25.3	22.3	20.8
Male	42.6	35.8	40.3	34.2	36.8	31.7	33.5	32.1	31.0	29.2	24.3	22.5
Female	38.1	27.0	35.0	35.4	27.3	24.7	21.7	21.8	21.0	21.1	20.2	19.1

[1] Beginning 1990, reflects new editing procedures for cases with missing data on school enrollment. [2] Percent of students who drop out in a single year without completing high school. For grades 10 to 12. [3] Includes other races, not shown separately. [4] Beginning 2003, for persons who selected this race group only. See footnote 2, Table 229. [5] Persons of Hispanic origin may be any race. [6] Percent of the population who have not completed high school and are not enrolled, regardless of when they dropped out. For persons 18 to 24 years old.
Source: U.S. Census Bureau, Current Population Reports, PPL-148, P20 and earlier reports, and "School Enrollment," <http://www.census.gov/population/www/socdemo/school.html>.

Table 272. High School Dropouts by Age, Race, and Hispanic Origin: 1980 to 2009

[As of October (5,212 represents 5,212,000). For persons 14 to 24 years old. See Table 274 for definition of dropouts. Based on Current Population Survey; see text, Section 1 and Appendix III]

Age and race	Number of dropouts (1,000)					Percent of population				
	1980	1990	2000	2005	2009	1980	1990	2000	2005	2009
Total dropouts [1, 2]	**5,212**	**3,854**	**3,883**	**3,597**	**3,185**	**12.0**	**10.1**	**9.1**	**7.9**	**7.0**
16 to 17 years	709	418	460	303	452	8.8	6.3	5.8	3.4	2.7
18 to 21 years	2,578	1,921	2,005	1,669	1,519	15.8	13.4	12.9	10.5	9.1
22 to 24 years	1,798	1,458	1,310	1,485	1,214	15.2	13.8	11.8	12.4	9.7
White [2, 3]	4,169	3,127	3,065	2,785	2,421	11.3	10.1	9.1	7.9	6.9
16 to 17 years	619	334	366	223	362	9.2	6.4	5.8	3.3	2.9
18 to 21 years	2,032	1,516	1,558	1,299	1,097	14.7	13.1	12.6	10.4	8.6
22 to 24 years	1,416	1,235	1,040	1,167	962	14.0	14.0	11.7	12.6	9.8
Black [2, 3]	934	611	705	616	570	16.0	10.9	10.9	9.2	8.2
16 to 17 years	80	73	84	64	66	6.9	6.9	7.0	4.7	2.5
18 to 21 years	486	345	383	281	330	23.0	16.0	16.0	12.4	13.0
22 to 24 years	346	185	232	231	175	24.0	13.5	14.3	13.6	9.7
Hispanic [2, 4]	919	1,122	1,499	1,467	1,237	29.5	26.8	23.5	18.6	14.7
16 to 17 years	92	89	121	93	125	16.6	12.9	11.0	6.3	4.1
18 to 21 years	470	502	733	672	548	40.3	32.9	30.0	24.5	17.8
22 to 24 years	323	523	602	663	564	40.6	42.8	35.5	30.8	25.0

[1] Includes other groups not shown separately. [2] Includes persons 14 to 15 years not shown separately. [3] Beginning 2005, for persons who selected this race group only. See footnote 2, Table 229. [4] Persons of Hispanic origin may be any race.

Source: U.S. Census Bureau, Current Population Reports, PPL-148, P-20 and earlier reports, and "School Enrollment," <http://www.census.gov/population/www/socdemo/school.html>.

Table 273. Enrollment Status by Race, Hispanic Origin, and Sex: 2000 and 2009

[As of October (15,553 represents 15,553,000). For persons 18 to 21 years old. For the civilian noninstitutional population. Based on the Current Population Survey; see text, Section 1 and Appendix III]

Characteristic	Total persons 18 to 21 years old (1,000)		Percent distribution								
			Enrolled in high school		High school graduates				Not high school graduates and not enrolled in high school	
					Total		In college			
	2000	2009	2000	2009	2000	2009	2000	2009	2000	2009
Total [1]	**15,553**	**16,662**	**9.4**	**10.5**	**77.6**	**80.2**	**43.5**	**50.0**	**12.9**	**9.1**
White [2]	12,383	12,826	8.9	9.7	78.5	81.6	44.4	51.0	12.6	8.6
Black [2]	2,389	2,538	12.6	13.9	71.3	73.0	34.7	41.5	16.0	13.1
Hispanic [3]	2,439	3,080	12.5	14.4	57.2	67.7	25.3	33.5	30.0	17.9
Male [1]	7,814	8,501	11.0	11.4	74.7	78.1	38.9	45.5	14.3	10.5
White [2]	6,313	6,578	10.6	10.4	75.7	79.6	39.8	46.3	13.7	10.0
Black [2]	1,096	1,277	14.9	15.5	66.0	69.0	27.4	36.1	19.1	15.5
Hispanic [3]	1,269	1,600	14.4	13.4	51.8	67.9	21.9	28.9	33.7	18.7
Female [1]	7,739	8,161	7.9	9.6	80.6	82.5	48.1	54.6	11.5	7.9
White [2]	6,070	6,248	7.1	9.0	81.3	83.7	49.3	56.0	11.4	7.3
Black [2]	1,293	1,261	10.7	12.3	75.9	77.0	40.9	47.0	13.5	10.7
Hispanic [3]	1,169	1,480	10.6	15.4	63.1	67.4	28.9	38.4	26.1	17.2

[1] Includes other races not shown separately. [2] For 2008, for persons who selected this race group only. See footnote 2, Table 229. [3] Persons of Hispanic origin may be any race.

Source: U.S. Census Bureau, Current Population Reports, PPL-148, P-20 and earlier reports, and "School Enrollment," <http://www.census.gov/population/www/socdemo/school.html>.

Table 274. Employment Status of High School Graduates and Dropouts Not Enrolled in School by Sex and Race: 1980 to 2010

[In thousands (11,622 represents 11,622,000), except percent. As of October. For civilian noninstitutional population 16 to 24 years old. Based on Current Population Survey; see text, Section 1 and Appendix III]

Employment status, sex, and race	Graduates [1]				Dropouts [3]			
	1980	1990	2000 [2]	2010 [2]	1980	1990	2000 [2]	2010 [2]
Civilian population	**11,622**	**8,370**	**7,351**	**6,999**	**5,254**	**3,800**	**3,776**	**2,816**
In labor force	9,795	7,107	6,195	5,407	3,549	2,506	2,612	1,817
Percent of population	84.3	84.9	84.3	77.3	67.5	66.0	69.2	64.5
Employed	8,567	6,279	5,632	4,201	2,651	1,993	2,150	1,290
Percent of labor force	87.5	88.3	90.9	77.7	74.7	79.5	82.3	71.0
Unemployed	1,228	828	563	1,206	898	513	463	527
Unemployment rate, total [4]	12.5	11.7	9.1	22.3	25.3	20.5	17.7	29.0
Male	13.5	11.1	9.3	21.7	23.5	18.8	16.3	27.7
Female	11.5	12.3	8.8	23.3	28.7	23.5	20.3	31.4
White [5]	10.8	9.0	7.2	19.5	21.6	17.0	15.0	25.5
Black [5]	26.1	26.0	18.1	33.9	43.9	43.3	33.2	46.6
Not in labor force	1,827	1,262	1,156	1,592	1,705	1,294	1,163	999
Percent of population	15.7	15.1	15.7	22.7	32.5	34.1	30.8	35.5

[1] For persons not enrolled in college who have completed 4 years of high school only. [2] Data not strictly comparable with data for earlier years. See text, this section, and February 2000 and 2010 issues of Employment and Earnings. [3] For persons not in regular school and who have not completed the 12th grade nor received a general equivalency degree. [4] Includes other races not shown separately. [5] 2010 data are for persons who selected this race group only. See footnote 2, Table 229.

Source: U.S. Bureau of Labor Statistics, News Release, USDL 11-0462, April 2011, and unpublished data. See also <http://www.bls.gov/news.release/hsgec.toc.htm>.

Table 275. General Educational Development (GED) Credentials Issued: 1980 to 2009

[GEDs issued in thousands (479 represents 479,000). For the 50 states and DC]

Year	GEDs issued	Percent distribution of GED test takers				
		16 to 18 years old [1]	19 to 24 years old [1]	25 to 29 years old	30 to 34 years old	35 years old and over
1980.............	479	37	27	13	8	15
1985.............	413	32	26	15	10	16
1990.............	410	22	39	13	10	15
1995.............	504	27	36	13	9	15
2000.............	487	33	37	11	7	13
2003.............	387	35	37	10	7	11
2004.............	406	35	38	11	6	10
2005.............	424	34	37	12	7	11
2006.............	398	35	36	12	6	11
2007.............	429	35	35	12	7	11
2008.............	469	34	35	13	7	11
2009.............	448	31	36	13	8	12

[1] For 1985 and prior years, 19-year-olds are included with the 16- to 18-year-olds instead of the 19- to 24-year-olds.

Source: U.S. National Center for Education Statistics, *Digest of Education Statistics*, annual. See also <http://www.nces.ed.gov/programs/digest/>.

Table 276. College Enrollment of Recent High School Completers: 1970 to 2009

[2,758 represents 2,758,000. For persons 16 to 24 years old who graduated from high school in the preceding 12 months. Includes persons receiving GEDs. Based on surveys and subject to sampling error; data will not agree with data in other tables]

Year	Number of high school completers (1,000)						Percent enrolled in college [5]					
	Total [1]	Male	Female	White [2]	Black [2,3]	His-panic [3,4]	Total [1]	Male	Female	White [2]	Black [2,3]	His-panic [3,4]
1970...	2,758	1,343	1,415	2,461	(NA)	(NA)	52	55	49	52	(NA)	(NA)
1975...	3,185	1,513	1,672	2,701	302	132	51	53	49	51	42	58
1980...	3,088	1,498	1,589	2,554	350	130	49	47	52	50	43	52
1985...	2,668	1,287	1,381	2,104	332	141	58	59	57	60	42	51
1990...	2,362	1,173	1,189	1,819	331	121	60	58	62	63	47	43
1995...	2,599	1,238	1,361	1,861	349	288	62	63	61	64	51	54
2000...	2,756	1,251	1,505	1,938	393	300	63	60	66	66	55	53
2001...	2,549	1,277	1,273	1,834	381	241	62	60	63	64	55	52
2002...	2,796	1,412	1,384	1,903	382	344	65	62	68	69	59	54
2003...	2,677	1,306	1,372	1,832	327	314	64	61	67	66	58	59
2004...	2,752	1,327	1,425	1,854	398	286	67	61	72	69	63	62
2005...	2,675	1,262	1,414	1,799	345	390	69	67	70	73	56	54
2006...	2,692	1,328	1,363	1,805	318	382	66	66	66	69	55	58
2007...	2,955	1,511	1,444	2,043	416	355	67	66	68	70	56	64
2008...	3,151	1,640	1,511	2,091	416	458	69	66	72	72	56	64
2009...	2,937	1,407	1,531	1,863	415	459	70	66	74	71	70	59

NA Not available. [1] Includes other races not shown separately. [2] Beginning 2003, for persons of this race group only. See footnote 2, Table 229. [3] Due to small sample size, data are subject to relatively large sampling errors. [4] Persons of Hispanic origin may be any race. [5] As of October.

Source: U.S. National Center for Education Statistics, *Digest of Education Statistics*, annual. See also <http://www.nces.ed.gov/programs/digest/>.

Table 277. College Enrollment by Sex and Attendance Status: 2005 to 2010

[As of fall. In thousands (17,487 represents 17,487,000). Includes enrollment at branch campuses, some additional (primarily 2-year) colleges and excludes a few institutions that did not award degrees. Includes enrollment at institutions that were eligible to participate in Title IV federal financial aid programs. Includes unclassified students, (students taking courses for credit, but are not candidates for degrees)]

Sex and age	2005		2007		2008		2009		2010 proj.	
	Total	Part-time	Total	Part-time	Total	Part-time	Total	Part-time	Total	Part-time
Total.................	**17,487**	**6,690**	**18,248**	**6,979**	**19,103**	**7,355**	**20,428**	**7,705**	**20,550**	**7,849**
Male.................	7,456	2,653	7,816	2,787	8,189	2,955	8,770	3,099	8,904	3,172
14 to 17 years old	78	41	75	17	92	19	98	22	90	22
18 to 19 years old	1,592	235	1,805	273	1,850	278	1,798	178	1,987	315
20 to 21 years old	1,778	318	1,633	288	1,792	342	1,854	315	1,987	377
22 to 24 years old	1,355	405	1,551	544	1,558	485	1,666	441	1,700	535
25 to 29 years old	978	539	1,020	435	1,177	602	1,357	725	1,276	622
30 to 34 years old	545	306	659	430	640	414	713	441	704	442
35 years old and over	1,130	809	1,074	799	1,080	814	1,284	976	1,161	859
Female.................	10,032	4,038	10,432	4,192	10,914	4,401	11,658	4,606	11,645	4,678
14 to 17 years old	121	27	104	9	101	12	102	7	118	21
18 to 19 years old	2,018	338	2,173	327	2,240	357	2,250	282	2,387	385
20 to 21 years old	2,000	430	2,129	452	2,137	409	2,037	308	2,330	460
22 to 24 years old	1,717	571	1,811	685	1,922	703	2,025	651	2,028	747
25 to 29 years old	1,406	709	1,502	824	1,560	818	1,702	844	1,646	860
30 to 34 years old	809	499	770	449	842	547	1,006	668	893	554
35 years old and over	1,960	1,464	1,943	1,446	2,112	1,554	2,537	1,846	2,243	1,650

Source: U.S. National Center for Education Statistics, *Digest of Education Statistics*, annual. See also <http://www.nces.ed.gov/programs/digest/>.

Education 177

Table 278. Higher Education—Institutions and Enrollment 1980 to 2009

[As of fall (686 represents 686,000). Covers universities, colleges, professional schools, junior and teachers' colleges, both publicly and privately controlled, regular session. Includes estimates for institutions not reporting. See also Appendix III]

Item	Unit	1980	1990	2000	2005	2006	2007	2008	2009
ALL INSTITUTIONS									
Number of institutions [1]	Number...	3,231	3,559	4,182	4,276	4,314	4,352	4,409	4,495
4-year	Number...	1,957	2,141	2,450	2,582	2,629	2,675	2,719	2,774
2-year	Number...	1,274	1,418	1,732	1,694	1,685	1,677	1,690	1,721
Instructional staff—									
(lecturer or above) [2]	1,000.....	686	817	(NA)	1,290	(NA)	1,371	(NA)	1,439
Percent full-time	Percent...	66	61	(NA)	52	(NA)	51	(NA)	51
Total enrollment [3,4]	1,000.....	12,097	13,819	15,312	17,487	17,759	18,248	19,103	20,428
Male	1,000.....	5,874	6,284	6,722	7,456	7,575	7,816	8,189	8,770
Female	1,000.....	6,223	7,535	8,591	10,032	10,184	10,432	10,914	11,658
4-year institutions	1,000.....	7,571	8,579	9,364	10,999	11,240	11,630	12,131	12,906
2-year institutions	1,000.....	4,526	5,240	5,948	6,488	6,519	6,618	6,971	7,521
Full-time	1,000.....	7,098	7,821	9,010	10,797	10,957	11,270	11,748	12,723
Part-time	1,000.....	4,999	5,998	6,303	6,690	6,802	6,978	7,355	7,705
Public	1,000.....	9,457	10,845	11,753	13,022	13,180	13,491	13,972	14,811
Private	1,000.....	2,640	2,974	3,560	4,466	4,579	4,757	5,131	5,617
Not-for-profit	1,000.....	2,528	2,760	3,109	3,455	3,513	3,571	3,662	3,765
For profit	1,000.....	112	213	450	1,011	1,066	1,186	1,469	1,852
Undergraduate [4]	1,000.....	10,475	11,959	13,155	14,964	15,184	15,604	16,366	17,565
Men	1,000.....	5,000	5,380	5,778	6,409	6,513	6,728	7,067	7,595
Women	1,000.....	5,475	6,579	7,377	8,555	8,671	8,876	9,299	9,970
First-time freshmen	1,000.....	2,588	2,257	2,428	2,657	2,707	2,776	3,025	3,210
First professional	1,000.....	278	273	307	337	343	351	(NA)	(NA)
Men	1,000.....	199	167	164	170	174	178	(NA)	(NA)
Women	1,000.....	78	107	143	167	170	173	(NA)	(NA)
Graduate [4]	1,000.....	1,343	1,586	1,850	2,186	2,231	2,294	(NA)	(NA)
Men	1,000.....	675	737	780	877	887	910	(NA)	(NA)
Women	1,000.....	670	849	1,071	1,309	1,344	1,383	(NA)	(NA)
2-YEAR INSTITUTIONS									
Number of institutions [1]	Number...	1,274	1,418	1,732	1,694	1,685	1,677	1,690	1,721
Public	Number...	945	972	1,076	1,053	1,045	1,032	1,024	1,000
Private	Number...	329	446	656	641	640	645	666	721
Instructional staff—									
(lecturer or above) [2]	1,000.....	192	(NA)	(NA)	373	(NA)	381	(NA)	401
Enrollment [3,4]	1,000.....	4,526	5,240	5,948	6,488	6,519	6,618	6,971	7,521
Public	1,000.....	4,329	4,996	5,697	6,184	6,225	6,324	6,640	7,101
Private	1,000.....	198	244	251	304	293	294	331	420
Male	1,000.....	2,047	2,233	2,559	2,680	2,705	2,771	2,936	3,197
Female	1,000.....	2,479	3,007	3,390	3,808	3,814	3,847	4,035	4,325
4-YEAR INSTITUTIONS									
Number of institutions [1]	Number...	1,957	2,141	2,450	2,582	2,629	2,675	2,719	2,774
Public	Number...	552	595	622	640	643	653	652	672
Private	Number...	1,405	1,546	1,828	1,942	1,986	2,022	2,067	2,102
Instructional staff—									
(lecturer or above) [2]	1,000.....	494	(NA)	(NA)	917	(NA)	991	(NA)	1,038
Enrollment [3,4]	1,000.....	7,571	8,579	9,364	10,999	11,240	11,630	12,131	12,906
Public	1,000.....	5,129	5,848	6,055	6,838	6,955	7,167	7,332	7,709
Private	1,000.....	2,442	2,730	3,308	4,162	4,285	4,464	4,800	5,197
Male	1,000.....	3,827	4,051	4,163	4,776	4,870	5,045	5,253	5,573
Female	1,000.....	3,743	4,527	5,201	6,224	6,370	6,585	6,878	7,333

NA Not available. [1] Number of institutions includes count of branch campuses. Due to revised survey procedures, data beginning 1990 are not comparable with previous years. Beginning 2000, data reflect a new classification of institutions; this classification includes some additional, primarily 2-year, colleges and excludes a few institutions that did not award degrees. Includes institutions that were eligible to participate in Title IV federal financial aid programs. Includes schools accredited by the National Association of Trade and Technical Schools. [2] Due to revised survey methods, data beginning 1990 not comparable with previous years. [3] Branch campuses counted according to actual status, e.g., 2-year branch in 2-year category. [4] Includes unclassified students. (Students taking courses for credit, but are not candidates for degrees.)

Source: U.S. National Center for Education Statistics, *Digest of Education Statistics*, annual, and unpublished data. See also <http://www.nces.ed.gov/programs/digest/>.

Table 279. College Enrollment by Selected Characteristics: 1990 to 2009

[In thousands (13,818.6 represents 13,818,600). As of fall. Nonresident alien students are not distributed among racial/ethnic groups]

Characteristic	1990	2000 [1]	2005 [1]	2006 [1]	2007 [1]	2008 [1]	2009 [1]
Total	**13,818.6**	**15,312.3**	**17,487.5**	**17,758.9**	**18,248.1**	**19,102.8**	**20,427.7**
Male	6,283.9	6,721.8	7,455.9	7,574.8	7,815.9	8,188.9	8,769.5
Female	7,534.7	8,590.5	10,031.6	10,184.1	10,432.2	10,913.9	11,658.2
Public	10,844.7	11,752.8	13,021.8	13,180.1	13,490.8	13,972.2	14,810.6
Private	2,973.9	3,559.5	4,465.6	4,578.7	4,757.3	5,130.7	5,617.1
2-year	5,240.1	5,948.4	6,488.1	6,518.5	6,617.9	6,971.4	7,521.4
4-year	8,578.6	9,363.9	10,999.4	11,240.3	11,630.2	12,131.4	12,906.3
Undergraduate	11,959.2	13,155.4	14,964.0	15,184.3	15,603.8	16,365.7	17,565.3
Graduate	1,586.2	1,850.3	2,186.5	2,231.1	2,293.6	(NA)	(NA)
First professional	273.4	306.6	337.0	343.4	350.8	(NA)	(NA)
White [2]	10,722.5	10,462.1	11,495.4	11,572.4	11,756.2	12,088.8	12,730.8
Male	4,861.0	4,634.6	5,007.2	5,046.2	5,146.1	5,302.9	5,594.4
Female	5,861.5	5,827.5	6,488.2	6,526.2	6,610.1	6,785.9	7,136.4
Public	8,385.4	7,963.4	8,518.2	8,540.5	8,640.3	8,817.7	9,234.6
Private	2,337.0	2,498.7	2,977.3	3,032.0	3,116.0	3,271.1	3,496.2
2-year	3,954.3	3,804.1	3,998.6	3,969.1	3,975.2	4,101.6	4,373.4
4-year	6,768.1	6,658.0	7,496.9	7,603.4	7,781.0	7,987.1	8,357.4
Undergraduate	9,272.6	8,983.5	9,828.6	9,885.4	10,046.6	10,339.2	10,915.3
Graduate	1,228.4	1,258.5	1,428.7	1,445.3	1,465.0	(NA)	(NA)
First professional	221.5	220.1	238.1	241.7	244.7	(NA)	(NA)
Black [2]	1,247.0	1,730.3	2,214.6	2,279.6	2,383.4	2,584.5	2,919.8
Male	484.7	635.3	774.1	795.4	838.1	911.8	1,037.1
Female	762.3	1,095.0	1,440.4	1,484.2	1,545.3	1,672.7	1,882.7
Public	976.4	1,319.2	1,580.4	1,612.6	1,667.6	1,759.2	1,937.2
Private	270.6	411.1	634.2	667.0	715.7	825.3	982.7
2-year	524.3	734.9	901.1	917.9	941.7	1,019.5	1,152.8
4-year	722.8	995.4	1,313.4	1,361.7	1,441.7	1,565.0	1,767.0
Undergraduate	1,147.2	1,548.9	1,955.4	2,005.7	2,092.6	2,269.3	2,577.4
Graduate	83.9	157.9	233.2	247.2	263.5	(NA)	(NA)
First professional	15.9	23.5	26.0	26.8	27.3	(NA)	(NA)
Hispanic	782.4	1,461.8	1,882.0	1,964.3	2,076.2	2,272.9	2,546.7
Male	353.9	627.1	774.6	810.0	861.6	946.7	1,066.3
Female	428.5	834.7	1,107.3	1,154.3	1,214.5	1,326.1	1,480.4
Public	671.4	1,229.3	1,525.6	1,594.3	1,685.4	1,832.4	2,017.7
Private	111.0	232.5	356.4	370.1	390.7	440.5	529.0
2-year	424.2	843.9	981.5	1,014.3	1,067.4	1,180.7	1,309.0
4-year	358.2	617.9	900.5	950.0	1,008.7	1,092.2	1,237.7
Undergraduate	724.6	1,351.0	1,733.6	1,810.1	1,915.9	2,103.5	2,362.5
Graduate	47.2	95.4	130.7	135.8	140.9	(NA)	(NA)
First professional	10.7	15.4	17.7	18.4	19.3	(NA)	(NA)
American Indian/ Alaska Native	102.8	151.2	176.3	181.1	190.0	193.3	207.9
Male	43.1	61.4	68.4	71.2	74.4	76.9	83.4
Female	59.7	89.7	107.9	110.0	115.6	116.4	124.5
Public	90.4	127.3	143.0	145.9	153.3	153.0	161.8
Private	12.4	23.9	33.3	35.2	36.7	40.3	46.1
2-year	54.9	74.7	80.7	81.1	81.4	85.5	90.3
4-year	47.9	76.5	95.6	100.0	108.6	108.6	117.7
Undergraduate	95.5	138.5	160.4	164.2	171.3	175.6	189.4
Graduate	6.2	10.3	13.4	14.5	16.1	(NA)	(NA)
First professional	1.1	2.3	2.5	2.5	2.6	(NA)	(NA)
Asian/Pacific Islander	572.4	978.2	1,134.4	1,165.5	1,217.9	1,302.8	1,337.7
Male	294.9	465.9	522.0	536.0	562.5	597.4	621.5
Female	277.5	512.3	612.4	629.5	655.4	705.4	716.1
Public	461.0	770.5	881.9	903.8	942.5	982.9	1,018.5
Private	111.5	207.7	252.4	261.7	275.4	319.9	319.1
2-year	215.2	401.9	434.4	442.8	456.4	479.4	495.7
4-year	357.2	576.3	700.0	722.7	761.5	823.4	842.0
Undergraduate	500.5	845.5	971.4	997.9	1,042.1	1,117.9	1,142.3
Graduate	53.2	95.8	118.4	121.9	127.8	(NA)	(NA)
First professional	18.7	36.8	44.6	45.7	48.0	(NA)	(NA)
Nonresident alien	391.5	528.7	584.8	595.9	624.5	660.6	684.8
Male	246.3	297.3	309.5	316.1	333.2	353.3	366.7
Female	145.2	231.4	275.3	279.8	291.2	307.3	318.1
Public	260.0	343.1	372.8	383.1	401.7	427.0	440.8
Private	131.4	185.6	212.0	212.8	222.8	233.6	244.0
2-year	67.1	89.0	91.8	93.4	95.8	104.7	100.2
4-year	324.3	439.7	493.1	502.5	528.7	555.9	584.6
Undergraduate	218.7	288.0	314.7	321.0	335.3	360.3	378.4
Graduate	167.3	232.3	262.1	266.4	280.3	(NA)	(NA)
First professional	5.4	8.4	8.1	8.4	8.8	(NA)	(NA)

NA Not available. [1] Data beginning 2000 reflect a new classification of institutions; see footnote 1, Table 278. [2] Non-Hispanic.
Source: U.S. National Center for Education Statistics, *Digest of Education Statistics*, annual. See also <http://www.nces.ed.gov/programs/digest/>.

Table 280. Degree-Granting Institutions, Number and Enrollment by State: 2008

[19,103 represents 19,103,000. Number of institutions beginning in academic year. Opening fall enrollment of resident and extension students attending full-time or part-time. Excludes students taking courses for credit by mail, radio, or TV, and students in branches of U.S. institutions operated in foreign countries. See Appendix III]

State	Number of institutions [1]	Enrollment (1,000) Total	Male	Female	Public	Private	Full-time	White [2]	Minority Total [3]	Minority Black [2]	Minority Hispanic	Non-resident alien
United States......	4,495	19,103	8,189	10,914	13,972	5,131	11,748	12,089	4,857	2,584	2,273	661
Alabama	72	311	132	179	245	66	205	200	98	90	7	6
Alaska	7	31	12	19	29	2	13	21	2	1	1	1
Arizona	78	704	265	439	331	373	500	430	208	101	107	21
Arkansas	50	158	64	94	141	18	101	115	35	30	5	4
California	436	2,652	1,186	1,466	2,239	413	1,322	1,066	981	217	764	88
Colorado	82	325	142	183	235	90	204	240	61	23	38	7
Connecticut	45	184	78	106	119	65	120	129	38	21	18	8
Delaware	10	53	21	32	39	14	35	36	13	11	2	2
District of Columbia ...	18	126	49	77	6	121	66	56	56	49	7	6
Florida	207	973	403	570	710	263	549	527	376	179	197	30
Georgia	131	477	192	285	376	100	321	271	170	154	16	14
Hawaii	20	70	29	41	54	17	40	17	4	2	2	5
Idaho	15	80	36	45	61	19	54	70	5	1	5	2
Illinois..........	181	859	371	489	560	299	508	544	234	128	105	28
Indiana..........	106	402	179	223	297	105	278	324	52	39	13	15
Iowa..........	65	287	115	172	157	130	177	218	29	19	11	8
Kansas..........	67	199	89	110	173	26	119	156	24	13	11	10
Kentucky	75	258	110	147	209	49	160	221	28	24	4	4
Louisiana	87	236	96	141	203	33	164	145	78	71	6	7
Maine..........	30	68	28	40	48	20	43	62	2	1	1	1
Maryland	59	339	141	198	281	58	183	188	111	96	15	14
Massachusetts.......	125	477	204	273	206	271	329	335	74	40	34	30
Michigan	105	653	283	370	528	125	386	490	111	92	19	25
Minnesota	117	411	169	242	257	154	249	324	51	41	10	12
Mississippi	41	160	62	99	144	16	123	91	65	63	2	2
Missouri..........	132	396	165	231	229	168	241	307	64	51	12	12
Montana..........	23	48	22	26	44	4	35	40	1	(Z)	1	1
Nebraska..........	43	130	59	71	100	31	84	110	12	6	6	4
Nevada	21	120	54	66	109	12	56	70	31	10	21	3
New Hampshire......	28	72	30	41	42	30	50	64	4	2	2	2
New Jersey	65	410	183	227	329	81	255	236	119	58	61	18
New Mexico.........	41	142	61	81	133	9	72	59	63	4	59	4
New York	305	1,235	524	710	676	559	857	726	321	173	149	78
North Carolina.......	137	529	214	315	435	94	331	349	146	129	17	13
North Dakota........	22	51	25	27	44	7	37	43	2	1	1	3
Ohio..........	213	654	284	369	476	178	445	519	98	83	15	19
Oklahoma	61	207	90	116	178	29	132	143	28	19	9	9
Oregon..........	60	220	98	122	182	39	132	175	20	6	14	7
Pennsylvania........	257	740	322	419	405	335	537	569	108	80	28	27
Rhode Island........	13	84	37	47	43	41	62	64	12	5	7	3
South Carolina.......	71	231	92	138	187	43	159	154	68	64	5	3
South Dakota.......	25	50	22	29	40	11	33	44	1	1	1	1
Tennessee..........	106	308	127	180	214	93	222	226	68	61	7	6
Texas..............	240	1,327	577	751	1,163	164	724	647	547	170	377	52
Utah..............	40	217	109	108	158	59	133	185	16	4	13	6
Vermont............	25	43	20	23	26	17	32	39	2	1	1	1
Virginia..........	119	501	214	286	383	118	303	327	126	103	23	14
Washington	81	363	159	203	312	50	224	266	43	17	26	12
West Virginia	45	125	61	65	89	37	80	107	13	9	4	3
Wisconsin	77	353	154	199	280	72	228	297	33	21	12	8
Wyoming	11	36	17	19	34	2	19	32	2	(Z)	2	1
U.S. military [4].......	5	16	13	3	16	(X)	16	12	2	1	1	(Z)

X Not applicable. Z Fewer than 500. [1] Branch campuses counted as separate institutions. [2] Non-Hispanic. [3] Includes other races not shown separately. [4] Service schools.

Source: U.S. National Center for Education Statistics, *Digest of Education Statistics*, annual. See also <http://www.nces.ed.gov/programs/digest/>.

Table 281. College Enrollment by Sex, Age, Race, and Hispanic Origin: 1980 to 2009

[In thousands (11,387 represents 11,387,000). As of October for the civilian noninstitutional population, 14 years old and over. Based on the Current Population Survey; see text, Section 1 and Appendix III]

Characteristic	1980	1990 [1]	1995	2000	2003	2004	2005	2006	2007	2008	2009
Total [2]	**11,387**	**13,621**	**14,715**	**15,314**	**16,638**	**17,383**	**17,472**	**17,020**	**17,770**	**18,632**	**19,764**
Male [3]	5,430	6,192	6,703	6,682	7,318	7,575	7,539	7,427	7,749	8,311	8,642
18 to 24 years	3,604	3,922	4,089	4,342	4,697	4,866	4,972	4,874	5,156	5,383	5,640
25 to 34 years	1,325	1,412	1,561	1,361	1,590	1,604	1,486	1,571	1,625	1,806	1,843
35 years old and over	405	772	985	918	970	1,033	1,019	982	968	989	1,069
Female [3]	5,957	7,429	8,013	8,631	9,319	9,808	9,933	9,593	10,021	10,321	11,123
18 to 24 years	3,625	4,042	4,452	5,109	5,667	5,742	5,859	5,712	6,004	6,083	6,432
25 to 34 years	1,378	1,749	1,788	1,846	1,904	2,091	2,115	2,087	2,212	2,207	2,450
35 years old and over	802	1,546	1,684	1,589	1,660	1,850	1,838	1,793	1,804	1,922	2,124
White [3,4]	9,925	11,488	12,021	11,999	12,870	13,381	13,467	13,112	13,693	14,405	15,027
18 to 24 years	6,334	6,635	7,011	7,566	8,150	8,354	8,499	8,298	8,780	9,141	9,327
25 to 34 years	2,328	2,698	2,686	2,339	2,545	2,748	2,647	2,725	2,769	2,859	3,163
35 years old and over	1,051	2,023	2,208	1,978	2,075	2,143	2,090	2,144	2,234	2,234	2,377
Male	4,804	5,235	5,535	5,311	5,714	5,944	5,844	5,772	5,989	6,570	6,681
Female	5,121	6,253	6,486	6,689	7,155	7,438	7,624	7,340	7,705	7,834	8,346
Black [3,4]	1,163	1,393	1,772	2,164	2,144	2,301	2,297	2,304	2,473	2,481	2,889
18 to 24 years	688	894	988	1,216	1,225	1,238	1,229	1,321	1,395	1,349	1,604
25 to 34 years	289	258	426	567	503	522	520	502	629	646	663
35 years old and over	156	207	334	361	388	502	448	480	449	451	587
Male	476	587	710	815	798	776	864	886	1,006	919	1,058
Female	686	807	1,062	1,349	1,346	1,525	1,435	1,418	1,468	1,562	1,831
Hispanic origin [3,5]	443	748	1,207	1,426	1,714	1,975	1,942	1,914	2,131	2,227	2,434
18 to 24 years	315	435	745	899	1,115	1,223	1,216	1,182	1,375	1,338	1,465
25 to 34 years	118	168	250	309	380	460	438	461	487	500	590
35 years old and over	(NA)	130	193	195	207	271	257	271	269	338	336
Male	222	364	568	619	703	852	804	789	864	1,042	1,080
Female	221	384	639	807	1,011	1,123	1,139	1,125	1,267	1,185	1,354

NA Not available. [1] Beginning 1990, based on a revised edit and tabulation package. [2] Includes other races not shown separately. [3] Includes persons 14 to 17 years old not shown separately. [4] Beginning 2003, for persons who selected this race group only. See footnote 2, Table 229. [5] Persons of Hispanic origin may be any race.

Source: U.S. Census Bureau, Current Population Reports, PPL-148, P-20 and earlier reports, and "School Enrollment," <http://www.census.gov/population/www/socdemo/school.html>.

Table 282. Foreign (Nonimmigrant) Student Enrollment in College: 1980 to 2010

[In thousands (286 represents 286,000). For fall of the previous year]

Region of origin	1980	1990	1995	1999	2000	2001	2002	2003	2004	2005	2006	2007	2008	2009	2010
All regions	**286**	**387**	**453**	**491**	**515**	**548**	**583**	**586**	**573**	**565**	**565**	**583**	**624**	**672**	**691**
Africa	36	25	21	26	30	34	38	40	38	36	36	36	36	37	37
Nigeria	16	4	2	3	4	4	4	6	6	6	6	6	6	6	7
Asia [1,2]	165	245	292	308	315	339	363	367	356	356	346	367	405	444	469
China [3]	1	33	39	51	54	60	63	65	62	63	63	68	81	98	128
Taiwan [3]	18	31	36	31	29	29	29	28	26	26	28	29	29	28	27
Hong Kong	10	11	13	9	8	8	8	8	7	7	8	8	8	8	8
India	9	26	34	37	42	55	67	75	80	80	77	84	95	103	105
Indonesia	2.	9	12	12	11	12	12	10	9	8	8	7	8	8	7
Iran	51	7	3	2	2	2	2	2	2	2	3	3	4	5	
Japan	12	30	45	46	47	46	47	46	41	42	39	35	34	29	25
Malaysia	4	14	14	12	9	8	7	7	6	6	6	5	5	6	6
Saudi Arabia	10	4	4	5	5	5	6	4	4	3	3	8	10	13	16
South Korea	5	22	34	39	41	46	49	52	52	53	59	62	69	75	72
Thailand	7	7	11	12	11	11	12	10	9	9	9	9	9	9	9
Europe [4]	23	46	65	74	78	81	82	78	74	72	85	83	84	88	85
Latin America [1,5]	42	48	47	55	62	64	68	69	66	68	65	65	64	68	66
Mexico	6	7	9	10	11	11	13	13	13	13	14	14	15	15	13
Venezuela	10	3	4	5	5	5	6	5	6	5	5	5	4	5	5
North America	16	19	23	23	24	26	27	27	28	29	29	29	29	30	29
Canada	15	18	23	23	24	25	27	27	27	28	28	28	29	30	28
Oceania	4	4	4	4	5	5	5	5	5	4	5	4	5	5	5

[1] Includes countries not shown separately. [2] Beginning 2006, excludes Cyprus and Turkey. [3] With the establishment of diplomatic relations with China on January 1, 1979, the U.S. government recognized the People's Republic of China as the sole legal government of China and acknowledged the Chinese position that there is only one China and that Taiwan is part of China. [4] Beginning 2006, includes Cyprus and Turkey. [5] Includes Mexico, Central America, Caribbean, and South America.

Source: Institute of International Education, New York, NY, *Open Doors Report on International Educational Exchange*, annual (copyright).

Table 283. College Enrollment—Summary by Sex, Race, and Hispanic Origin: 2009

[In thousands (19,764 represents 19,764,000), except percent. As of October. Covers civilian noninstitutional population 15 years old and over enrolled in colleges and graduate schools. Based on Current Population Survey. See text, Section 1 and Appendix III]

Characteristic	Total			Race and Hispanic origin				
				White [2]				
	Number [1]	Male	Female	Total	Non-Hispanic	Black [2]	Asian [2]	Hispanic [3]
Total enrollment	**19,764**	**8,642**	**11,123**	**15,027**	**12,826**	**2,889**	**1,231**	**2,434**
15 to 17 years old	206	89	116	160	120	34	11	43
18 to 19 years old	4,289	1,928	2,361	3,337	2,842	559	243	550
20 to 21 years old	4,034	1,943	2,091	3,205	2,755	495	216	482
22 to 24 years old	3,749	1,770	1,980	2,784	2,385	550	308	433
25 to 29 years old	2,769	1,194	1,575	2,066	1,736	410	197	373
30 to 34 years old	1,524	649	875	1,097	913	253	114	217
35 years old and over	3,193	1,069	2,124	2,377	2,074	587	141	336
Type of school:								
2-year	5,551	2,363	3,188	4,210	3,278	920	257	1,001
15 to 19 years old	1,636	688	948	1,250	967	246	78	313
20 to 24 years old	1,773	885	888	1,341	1,017	292	91	346
25 years old and over	2,141	790	1,352	1,618	1,294	383	88	341
4-year	10,461	4,758	5,703	8,025	6,974	1,490	593	1,168
15 to 19 years old	2,827	1,317	1,510	2,224	1,972	343	172	280
20 to 24 years old	5,040	2,403	2,637	3,925	3,446	671	287	515
25 years old and over	2,594	1,038	1,556	1,876	1,556	475	134	374
Graduate school	3,752	1,521	2,232	2,792	2,574	479	381	265
15 to 24 years old	1,002	437	565	746	701	87	151	55
25 to 34 years old	1,556	667	890	1,130	1,016	212	160	145
35 years old and over	1,194	417	777	915	856	180	70	65
Public	15,722	6,890	8,833	11,948	10,022	2,322	950	2,122
2-year	5,095	2,199	2,895	3,897	3,022	826	227	937
4-year	8,262	3,754	4,508	6,279	5,389	1,203	490	981
Graduate	2,366	937	1,430	1,772	1,610	293	232	204
Percent of students:								
Employed full-time	15.4	14.0	16.6	15.5	15.7	17.0	12.1	14.5
Employed part-time	21.7	19.2	23.9	23.6	25.0	14.0	17.4	17.2

[1] Includes other races not shown separately. [2] For persons who selected this race group only. See footnote 2, Table 229. [3] Persons of Hispanic origin may be any race.

Source: U.S. Census Bureau, unpublished data.

Table 284. Higher Education Enrollment in Languages Other Than English: 1970 to 2009

[As of fall (1,111.5 represents 1,111,500). For credit enrollment]

Enrollment	1970	1980	1986	1990	1995	1998	2002	2006	2009
Registrations [1] (1,000)	**1,111.5**	**924.8**	**1,003.2**	**1,184.1**	**1,138.8**	**1,193.8**	**1,397.3**	**1,577.8**	**1,682.6**
By selected language (1,000):									
Spanish	389.2	379.4	411.3	533.9	606.3	656.6	746.3	823.0	865.0
French	359.3	248.4	275.3	272.5	205.4	199.1	202.0	206.4	216.4
German	202.6	126.9	121.0	133.3	96.3	89.0	91.1	94.3	96.3
American Sign Language	(NA)	(NA)	(NA)	1.6	4.3	11.4	60.8	78.8	91.8
Italian	34.2	34.8	40.9	49.7	43.8	49.3	63.9	78.4	80.8
Japanese	6.6	11.5	23.5	45.7	44.7	43.1	52.2	66.6	73.4
Chinese	6.2	11.4	16.9	19.5	26.5	28.5	34.2	51.6	61.0
Arabic	1.3	3.5	3.4	3.5	4.4	5.5	10.6	24.0	35.1
Latin	27.6	25.0	25.0	28.2	25.9	26.1	29.8	32.2	32.6
Russian	36.2	24.0	34.0	44.6	24.7	23.8	23.9	24.8	26.9
Hebrew	16.6	19.4	15.6	13.0	13.1	15.8	22.8	23.8	22.1
Ancient Greek	16.7	22.1	17.6	16.4	16.3	16.4	20.4	22.8	20.7
Portuguese	5.1	4.9	5.1	6.2	6.5	6.9	8.4	10.3	11.4
Korean	0.1	0.4	0.9	2.3	3.3	4.5	5.2	7.1	8.5
Index (1965 = 100)	107.3	89.3	96.8	114.3	109.9	115.2	134.9	152.3	162.4

NA Not available. [1] Includes other languages, not shown separately.

Source: Furman, Nelly, David Goldberg, and Natalia Lusin. Enrollments in Languages Other Than English in United States Institutions of Higher Education, Fall 2009. Modern Language Association, December 2010 (copyright). For 1970 to 2006, consult prior Association of Departments of Foreign Languages (ADFL) Bulletins.

Table 285. Students Reported Disability Status by Selected Characteristic: 2007 to 2008

[20,928 represents 20,928,000. Disabled students reported that they had one or more of the following conditions: a specific learning disability, a visual handicap, hard of hearing, deafness, a speech disability, an orthopedic handicap, or a health impairment. Based on the 2007–2008 National Postsecondary Student-Aid Study; see source for details. Includes Puerto Rico. See also Appendix III]

Student characteristic	Undergraduate			Graduate and first-professional		
	All students	Disabled students	Nondisabled students	All students	Disabled students	Nondisabled students
Total students (1,000)	**20,928**	**2,266**	**18,662**	**3,456**	**261**	**3,195**
PERCENT DISTRIBUTION						
Total.......................	**100.0**	**10.8**	**89.2**	**100.0**	**7.6**	**92.4**
Age:						
15 to 23 years old	59.7	54.0	60.4	11.4	7.8	11.7
24 to 29 years old	17.3	20.1	17.0	39.9	36.2	40.2
30 years or older	23.0	25.9	22.7	48.7	56.0	48.1
Sex:						
Male........................	43.1	42.7	43.1	40.1	39.2	40.2
Female......................	56.9	57.3	56.9	59.9	60.8	59.8
Race/ethnicity of student:						
White, non-Hispanic.............	61.8	66.3	61.2	66.6	63.6	66.9
Black, non-Hispanic.............	14.0	12.7	14.1	11.7	19.0	11.1
Hispanic.....................	14.1	12.3	14.4	8.0	7.4	8.0
Asian/Pacific Islander	6.6	4.8	6.8	11.1	7.3	11.4
American Indian/Alaska Native	0.8	0.8	0.9	0.3	0.5	0.3
Other	2.7	3.2	2.6	2.3	2.3	2.3
Attendance status:						
Full-time, full-year	39.3	34.7	39.8	34.1	32.6	34.2
Part-time or part-year	60.7	65.3	60.2	65.9	67.4	65.8
Student housing status:						
On-campus	14.2	11.1	14.5	(NA)	(NA)	(NA)
Off-campus	54.0	56.3	53.7	(NA)	(NA)	(NA)
With parents or relatives	31.9	32.6	31.8	(NA)	(NA)	(NA)
Dependency status:						
Dependent...................	53.0	46.8	53.7	(S)	(S)	(S)
Independent, unmarried	15.3	19.5	14.7	50.0	52.7	49.8
Independent, married	6.4	6.9	6.3	16.9	12.9	17.2
Independent with dependents	25.4	26.7	25.2	33.1	34.4	33.0

NA Not available. S Figure does not meet publication standards.
Source: U.S. National Center for Education Statistics, *Digest of Education Statistics*, annual.

Table 286. College Freshmen—Summary Characteristics: 1980 to 2010

[In percent, except as indicated (24.5 represents $24,500). As of fall for first-time full-time freshmen in 4-year colleges and universities. Based on sample survey and subject to sampling error; see source]

Characteristic	1980	1990	1995	2000	2005	2007	2008	2009	2010
Sex:									
Male........................	48.8	46.9	45.6	45.2	45.0	45.2	45.4	45.9	44.3
Female......................	51.2	53.1	54.4	54.8	55.0	54.8	54.6	54.1	55.7
Applied to more than three colleges	31.5	42.9	44.4	50.5	55.4	56.5	60.1	61.9	64.1
Average grade in high school:									
A– to A+.....................	26.6	29.4	36.1	42.9	46.6	45.9	47.2	48.1	48.4
B– to B+.....................	58.2	57.0	54.2	50.5	48.0	49.0	48.0	47.5	47.5
C to C+	14.9	13.4	9.6	6.5	5.4	5.0	4.7	4.4	4.1
D	0.2	0.2	0.1	0.1	0.1	0.1	0.1	0.1	0.1
Political orientation:									
Liberal......................	21.0	24.6	22.9	24.8	27.1	29.3	31.0	29.0	27.3
Middle of the road	57.0	51.7	51.3	51.9	45.0	43.4	43.3	44.4	46.4
Conservative	19.0	20.6	21.8	18.9	22.6	23.1	20.7	21.8	21.7
Probable field of study:									
Biological sciences	4.5	4.9	8.3	6.6	7.6	8.6	9.3	9.7	10.8
Business	21.2	21.1	15.4	16.7	17.4	17.7	16.8	14.3	13.7
Education....................	8.4	10.3	10.1	11.0	9.9	9.2	8.2	8.1	7.2
Engineering..................	11.2	9.7	8.1	8.7	8.3	7.5	9.4	9.7	10.3
Physical science	3.2	2.8	3.1	2.6	3.1	3.2	3.2	3.4	2.7
Social science	8.2	11.0	9.9	10.0	10.7	11.1	11.5	11.7	8.9
Data processing/computer programming	1.7	0.7	0.8	1.5	0.5	0.6	0.5	0.6	0.5
Other [1]	41.6	39.5	44.3	42.9	42.5	42.1	41.1	42.5	45.9
Communications	2.4	2.9	1.8	2.7	2.0	1.8	1.8	1.9	1.8
Computer science	2.6	1.7	2.2	3.7	1.1	1.1	1.0	1.0	1.0
Personal objectives—very important or essential:									
Being very well off financially..............	62.5	72.3	72.8	73.4	74.5	74.4	76.8	78.1	77.4
Developing a meaningful philosophy of life	62.5	45.9	45.4	42.4	45.0	49.2	51.4	48.0	46.9
Keeping up to date with political affairs	45.2	46.6	32.3	28.1	36.4	37.2	39.5	36.0	33.2
Median family income ($1,000)	24.5	46.6	54.8	64.4	73.2	77.9	77.5	76.6	76.1

[1] Includes other fields not shown separately.
Source: The Higher Education Research Institute, University of California, Los Angeles, CA, *The American Freshman: National Norms*, annual.

Table 287. Residence and Migration of College Freshmen by State: 2008

[As of fall. Includes first-time postsecondary students who had graduated from high school in the previous 12 months and were enrolled at public and private not-for-profit 4-year degree-granting institutions that participated in Title IV federal financial aid programs. Excludes respondents for whom state residence and/or migration are unknown. Also excludes U.S. Service Academies (Air Force Academy, Coast Guard Academy, Merchant Marine Academy, Military Academy, and Naval Academy)]

State	Total freshmen enrollment in institutions located in the state	Ratio of in-state students to freshmen enrollment	Ratio of in-state students to residents enrolled in any state[1]	State	Total freshmen enrollment in institutions located in the state	Ratio of in-state students to freshmen enrollment	Ratio of in-state students to residents enrolled in any state[1]
U.S.	1,444,239	0.73	0.74	MO	28,854	0.72	0.77
AL	23,996	0.66	0.86	MT	5,324	0.68	0.75
AK	2,342	0.90	0.60	NE	11,117	0.75	0.80
AZ	22,004	0.62	0.81	NV	7,603	0.85	0.74
AR	15,112	0.73	0.87	NH	9,032	0.40	0.42
CA	116,252	0.88	0.82	NJ	26,223	0.84	0.41
CO	24,467	0.72	0.72	NM	7,393	0.79	0.79
CT	19,656	0.54	0.43	NY	108,398	0.72	0.73
DE	4,905	0.39	0.50	NC	45,861	0.73	0.85
DC	8,659	0.06	0.24	ND	6,239	0.48	0.77
FL	70,373	0.81	0.84	OH	66,257	0.82	0.81
GA	44,482	0.84	0.79	OK	17,572	0.73	0.86
HI	3,846	0.68	0.49	OR	14,633	0.63	0.70
ID	7,510	0.61	0.70	PA	86,833	0.65	0.78
IL	53,440	0.75	0.63	RI	11,393	0.27	0.53
IN	45,913	0.71	0.87	SC	22,095	0.65	0.86
IA	19,022	0.58	0.78	SD	5,715	0.65	0.74
KS	14,746	0.73	0.78	TN	29,351	0.75	0.80
KY	22,576	0.74	0.86	TX	84,742	0.92	0.82
LA	23,928	0.79	0.90	UT	18,188	0.66	0.91
ME	7,541	0.59	0.59	VT	6,460	0.27	0.42
MD	19,922	0.64	0.45	VA	41,853	0.69	0.74
MA	50,540	0.51	0.59	WA	22,786	0.75	0.72
MI	51,283	0.87	0.85	WV	11,998	0.60	0.89
MN	26,776	0.72	0.61	WI	34,522	0.74	0.78
MS	9,353	0.66	0.81	WY	1,601	0.54	0.55

[1] Students residing in a particular state when admitted to an institution anywhere, either in their home state or another state.
Source: U.S. Department of Education, National Center for Education Statistics, Fall 2008 Integrated Postsecondary Education Data System (IPEDS), Spring 2009.

Table 288. Average Total Price of Attendance of Undergraduate Education: 2007 to 2008

[In dollars. For school year ending in 2008. Excludes students attending more than one institution. Price of attendance includes tuition and fees, books and supplies, room and board, transportation, and personal and other expenses allowed for federal cost of attendance budgets. Based on the 2007–2008 National Postsecondary Student-Aid Study; see source for details. Includes Puerto Rico. See also Appendix III]

Student characteristic	All institutions[1]	Public 2-year	Public 4-year — Non-doctorate	Public 4-year — Doctorate	Private not-for-profit 4-year — Non-doctorate	Private not-for-profit 4-year — Doctorate	Private for-profit
Total	14,006	7,033	12,657	16,615	25,194	31,628	20,636
Age:[2]							
18 years or younger	17,065	12,630	16,664	19,888	32,586	38,311	19,868
19 to 23 years	16,059	6,830	10,128	12,513	17,861	22,540	20,376
24 to 29 years	11,551	8,035	11,188	13,833	17,823	21,294	20,275
30 to 39 years	10,994	3,854	5,739	7,319	8,446	10,419	21,305
40 years or older	9,269	8,268	14,912	18,501	31,809	37,581	21,265
Sex:							
Male	13,957	7,406	13,778	17,661	30,099	35,206	21,765
Female	14,044	6,856	10,701	13,005	17,458	20,772	20,133
Race:							
One race:							
White	14,446	6,546	9,690	12,452	15,561	17,839	20,888
Black or African American	13,235	5,992	9,062	10,623	14,722	14,452	20,141
Asian	15,122	7,121	12,668	16,486	25,512	31,163	22,203
American Indian/Alaska Native	12,150	7,013	13,170	16,707	26,717	32,236	25,013
Native Hawaiian or other Pacific Islander	12,904	6,974	12,824	15,891	21,412	26,817	23,122
Other race	12,788	6,990	10,511	15,513	19,548	27,808	24,076
More than one race	15,077	7,313	13,285	18,271	29,162	36,973	23,245
Hispanic or Latino[3]	12,419	6,920	12,644	16,757	24,765	32,182	19,753
Attendance pattern:							
Full-time, full-year	22,368	7,330	10,436	15,078	27,614	(S)	28,638
Full-time, part-year	12,227	6,718	12,988	16,878	18,659	40,521	16,653
Part-time, full-year	10,655	6,759	10,879	15,650	16,534	(S)	19,259
Part-time, part-year	5,231	7,495	13,028	17,256	28,172	34,460	11,810

S Data do not meet publication standards. [1] Includes public less-than-2-year and private not-for-profit less-than-4-year. [2] As of December 31, 2007. [3] Persons of Hispanic origin may be any race.
Source: U.S. National Center for Education Statistics, "Student Financial Aid Estimates for 2007–08," NCES 2009-166, April 2009, <http://nces.ed.gov/surveys/npsas/>.

Table 289. Average Out-of-Pocket Net Price of Attendance for Undergraduates: 2007 to 2008

[In dollars. For school year ending in 2008. Excludes students attending more than one institution. Net Price of attendance is the price that students pay to receive postsecondary education after taking financial aid into account. Based on net tuition and net price for all students. Based on the 2007–2008 National Postsecondary Student-Aid Study; see source for details. Includes Puerto Rico. See also Appendix III]

| Student characteristic | All institu-tions [1] | Type of Institution | | | | | |
| | | Public 2-year | Public 4-year | | Private not-for-profit 4 year | | Private for-profit |
			Non-doctorate	Doctorate	Non-doctorate	Doctorate	
Total.	**8,769**	**5,645**	**7,801**	**10,627**	**12,772**	**18,103**	**11,647**
Age: [2]							
18 years or younger.	10,219	6,612	8,927	11,313	15,067	20,967	9,974
19 to 23 years	9,974	5,995	8,488	11,509	14,672	20,217	11,460
24 to 29 years	7,160	5,303	6,559	7,508	9,755	11,380	11,239
30 to 39 years	7,073	5,168	5,916	7,360	8,858	9,832	12,353
40 years or older	6,487	4,998	5,933	7,180	9,365	8,822	12,379
Sex:							
Male.	8,985	5,705	8,061	11,042	12,946	19,016	11,942
Female.	8,603	5,599	7,586	10,248	12,644	17,313	11,517
Race:							
One race:							
White.	9,211	5,674	8,266	11,196	13,550	18,899	11,858
Black or African American.	7,286	5,192	6,039	7,318	10,564	12,319	11,109
Asian.	10,613	6,386	9,518	12,615	17,147	24,543	12,809
American Indian/Alaska Native	7,715	5,493	6,047	8,115	(S)	(S)	16,623
Native Hawaiian or other Pacific Islander	8,445	5,627	8,840	9,499	7,855	29,807	11,896
Other race	8,286	5,435	(S)	7,968	(S)	(S)	15,868
More than one race	8,867	5,854	7,581	10,100	11,828	17,450	13,817
Hispanic or Latino [3]	7,567	5,638	6,941	8,657	9,761	12,824	11,028
Attendance pattern:							
Full-time, full-year	13,218	9,428	9,654	12,419	15,659	21,293	16,875
Full-time, part-year	7,751	5,442	6,672	8,522	10,386	14,220	8,825
Part-time, full-year	7,410	6,544	7,588	9,030	9,561	12,597	9,174
Part-time, part-year	3,906	3,348	4,193	5,297	5,498	6,791	5,933

S Date do not meet publication standards. [1] Includes public less-than-2-year and private not-for-profit less-than-4-year. [2] As of December 2007. [3] Persons of Hispanic origin may be of any race.

Source: U.S. National Center for Education Statistics, "Student Financial Aid Estimates for 2007–08," NCES 2009-166, April 2009, <http://nces.ed.gov/surveys/npsas/>.

Table 290. Higher Education Price Indexes: 2002 to 2010

[1983 = 100. For years ending June 30. The Higher Education Price Index (HEPI), calculated for the July–June academic fiscal year, reflects prices paid by colleges and universities for the following eight cost factors: faculty salaries, administrative salaries, clerical and service employees, fringe benefits, miscellaneous services, supplies and materials, and utilities. Minus sign (−) indicates decrease]

| Item and year | Total | Personnel compensation | | | | | Contracted services, supplies, and equipment | | |
		Faculty salaries	Admin-istrative salaries	Clerical salaries	Service employ-ees salaries	Fringe benefits	Miscel-laneous services	Supplies and materials	Utilities
INDEXES									
2002.	212.7	222.7	236.4	205.4	189.6	277.1	205.8	128.2	118.1
2003.	223.5	229.4	255.7	211.1	193.9	292.3	209.5	132.2	157.6
2004.	231.7	234.2	263.3	217.1	197.6	312.8	216.4	135.6	176.4
2005.	240.8	240.7	274.0	223.4	201.4	327.2	222.7	145.5	200.2
2006.	253.1	248.2	287.7	229.5	205.5	343.7	228.8	158.1	255.7
2007.	260.3	257.6	299.2	237.7	213.6	360.8	238.3	165.3	220.6
2008.	273.2	268.1	314.0	245.0	220.4	380.7	246.5	180.0	252.0
2009.	279.3	277.3	330.9	251.6	226.7	394.4	253.1	181.6	213.8
2010.	281.8	280.6	337.6	255.2	230.0	402.8	255.8	179.3	193.6
ANNUAL PERCENT CHANGE [1]									
2002.	3.0	3.8	3.1	3.9	3.8	5.9	3.0	−2.7	−30.5
2003.	5.1	3.0	8.2	2.8	2.3	5.5	1.8	3.1	33.5
2004.	3.7	2.1	3.0	2.8	1.9	7.0	3.3	2.6	11.9
2005.	3.9	2.8	4.1	2.9	1.9	4.6	2.9	7.3	13.5
2006.	5.1	3.1	5.0	2.7	2.0	5.0	2.7	8.7	27.7
2007.	2.8	3.8	4.0	3.6	4.0	5.0	4.2	4.5	−13.7
2008.	5.0	4.1	5.0	3.1	3.2	5.5	3.4	8.9	14.2
2009.	2.3	3.4	5.4	2.7	2.9	3.6	2.7	0.9	−15.1
2010.	0.9	1.2	2.0	1.4	1.4	2.1	1.1	−1.3	−9.5

[1] Percent change from the immediate prior year.

Source: The Commonfund Institute, Wilton, CT, (copyright), <http://www.commonfund.org>.

Table 291. Federal Student Financial Assistance: 1995 to 2011

[For award years July 1 of year shown to the following June 30 (35,477 represents $35,477,000,000). Funds utilized exclude operating costs, etc., and represent funds given to students]

Type of assistance	1995	2000	2005	2008	2009	2010, est.	2011, est.
FUNDS UTILIZED (mil. dol.)							
Total........................	**35,477**	**44,007**	**72,634**	**97,478**	**130,549**	**144,977**	**155,102**
Federal Pell Grants	5,472	7,956	12,693	18,291	29,992	36,515	35,773
Academic Competitiveness Grants	(X)	(X)	(X)	340	479	548	(X)
SMART [1] Grants	(X)	(X)	(X)	200	359	384	(X)
TEACH Grants [2]...................	(X)	(X)	(X)	25	72	109	131
Federal Supplemental Educational Opportunity Grant ...	764	907	1,084	1,039	1,066	959	959
Federal Work-Study......................	764	939	1,050	1,113	1,246	1,171	1,171
Federal Perkins Loan......................	1,029	1,144	1,593	961	818	971	971
Federal Direct Student Loan (FDSL)...............	8,296	10,348	12,930	18,213	29,738	84,704	116,098
Federal Family Education Loans (FFEL)..............	19,152	22,712	43,284	57,296	66,778	19,618	(X)
NUMBER OF AWARDS (1,000)							
Total........................	**13,667**	**15,043**	**21,317**	**25,713**	**32,188**	**34,257**	**35,730**
Federal Pell Grants	3,612	3,899	5,167	6,157	8,094	8,873	9,413
Academic Competitiveness Grants	(X)	(X)	(X)	438	613	786	(X)
SMART [1] Grants	(X)	(X)	(X)	64	115	150	(X)
TEACH Grants [2]...................	(X)	(X)	(X)	8	31	36	44
Federal Supplemental Educational Opportunity Grant ...	1,083	1,175	1,419	1,451	1,593	1,339	1,339
Federal Work-Study......................	702	713	710	678	733	713	713
Federal Perkins Loan......................	688	639	727	488	441	493	493
Federal Direct Student Loan (FDSL)...............	2,339	2,739	2,971	3,730	6,109	16,647	23,728
Federal Family Education Loans (FFEL)..............	5,243	5,878	10,323	12,698	14,459	5,220	(X)
AVERAGE AWARD (dol.)							
Total........................	**2,596**	**2,925**	**3,407**	**3,791**	**4,056**	**4,232**	**4,341**
Federal Pell Grants	1,515	2,041	2,456	2,971	3,706	4,115	3,800
Academic Competitiveness Grants/SMART [1] Grants	(X)	(X)	(X)	774	760	697	(X)
SMART [1] Grants	(X)	(X)	(X)	3,107	3,125	2,560	(X)
TEACH Grants [2]...................	(X)	(X)	(X)	3,125	2,369	2,966	2,966
Federal Supplemental Educational Opportunity Grant ...	705	772	764	716	669	716	716
Federal Work-Study......................	1,088	1,318	1,478	1,642	1,700	1,642	1,642
Federal Perkins Loan......................	1,496	1,790	2,190	1,968	1,852	1,968	1,968
Federal Direct Student Loan (FDSL)...............	3,547	3,778	4,352	4,882	4,867	5,088	4,893
Federal Family Education Loans (FFEL)..............	3,653	3,864	4,193	4,512	4,618	3,758	(X)
COHORT DEFAULT RATE [3]							
Federal Perkins Loan......................	12.6	9.9	8.1	10.4	10.1	(NA)	(NA)

NA Not available. X Not applicable. [1] National Science and Mathematics Access to Retain Talent. Funding for Academic Competitiveness Grants and SMART Grants was terminated in 2011. [2] Teacher Education Assistance for College and Higher Education (TEACH) Grant Program. [3] As of June 30. Represents the percent of borrowers entering repayment status in year shown who defaulted in the following year.

Source: U.S. Department of Education, Office of Postsecondary Education, unpublished data.

Table 292. State and Local Financial Support for Higher Education by State: 2009 to 2010

[For 2009–2010 fiscal year (11,618.0 represents 11,618,000). Data for the 50 states]

State	2009–2010 FTE enrollment [1] (1,000)	2009–2010 Educational appropriations per FTE enrollment [2] (dollars)	State	2009–2010 FTE enrollment [1] (1,000)	2009–2010 Educational appropriations per FTE enrollment [2] (dollars)
Total	**11,618.0**	**6,454**			
AL	204.0	5,574	MT	38.9	4,892
AK	20.3	14,940	NE	84.9	7,149
AZ	251.6	6,653	NV	68.8	7,507
AR	121.4	5,814	NH	39.6	3,229
CA	1,926.4	6,065	NJ	268.1	7,199
CO	182.9	4,511	NM	98.7	7,569
CT	85.0	10,459	NY	571.4	8,431
DE	32.4	7,039	NC	421.0	8,413
FL	596.0	5,764	ND	37.7	6,525
GA	370.7	6,901	OH	443.4	4,604
HI	39.9	11,569	OK	142.0	6,914
ID	49.3	7,208	OR	160.6	4,676
IL	401.3	8,288	PA	371.3	5,326
IN	265.3	4,951	RI	32.1	5,250
IA	127.1	5,835	SC	166.8	5,005
KS	137.4	5,715	SD	32.3	4,806
KY	154.2	6,743	TN	190.3	6,924
LA	178.9	6,567	TX	863.5	7,622
ME	37.5	6,331	UT	118.4	5,678
MD	233.5	7,101	VT	21.8	3,073
MA	165.2	7,240	VA	312.6	5,065
MI	431.6	5,310	WA	254.9	6,105
MN	215.0	5,957	WV	78.8	4,899
MS	123.1	6,473	WI	237.4	6,773
MO	187.2	6,278	WY	25.6	11,657

[1] Full-time equivalent. Includes degree enrollment and enrollment in public postsecondary programs resulting in a certificate or other formal recognition. Includes summer sessions. Excludes medical enrollments. [2] State and local appropriations for general operating expenses of public postsecondary education. Includes American Recovery and Reinvestment Act of 2009 (ARRA) funds, state-funded financial aid to students attending in-state public institutions. Excludes sums for research, agricultural extension, and teaching hospitals and medical schools.

Source: State Higher Education Executive Officers, Boulder, CO (copyright), <http://www.sheeo.org>.

Table 293. Institutions of Higher Education—Average Charges: 1985 to 2010

[In dollars. Estimated. For the entire academic year ending in year shown. Figures are average charges per full-time equivalent student. Room and board are based on full-time students]

Academic control and year	Tuition and required fees [1]				Board rates [2]				Dormitory charges			
	All institutions	2-yr. colleges	4-yr. universities	Other 4-yr. schools	All institutions	2-yr. colleges	4-yr. universities	Other 4-yr. schools	All institutions	2-yr. colleges	4-yr. universities	Other 4-yr. schools
Public:												
1985	971	584	1,386	1,117	1,241	1,302	1,276	1,201	1,196	921	1,237	1,200
1990	1,356	756	2,035	1,608	1,635	1,581	1,728	1,561	1,513	962	1,561	1,554
1995	2,057	1,192	2,977	2,499	1,949	1,712	2,108	1,866	1,959	1,232	1,992	2,044
2000	2,506	1,338	3,768	3,091	2,364	1,834	2,628	2,239	2,440	1,549	2,516	2,521
2005	3,629	1,849	5,939	4,512	2,931	2,353	3,222	2,809	3,304	2,174	3,427	3,413
2006	3,874	1,935	6,399	4,765	3,035	2,306	3,372	2,899	3,545	2,251	3,654	3,672
2007	4,102	2,018	6,842	5,020	3,191	2,390	3,498	3,083	3,757	2,407	3,875	3,881
2008	4,291	2,061	7,173	5,285	3,331	2,409	3,668	3,221	3,952	2,506	4,079	4,083
2009	4,512	2,136	7,624	5,610	3,554	2,769	3,911	3,417	4,190	2,664	4,344	4,322
2010, prel. . . .	4,751	2,285	8,123	5,964	3,653	2,574	4,018	3,578	4,399	2,845	4,571	4,561
Private:												
1985	5,315	3,485	6,843	5,135	1,462	1,294	1,647	1,405	1,426	1,424	1,753	1,309
1990	8,147	5,196	10,348	7,778	1,948	1,811	2,339	1,823	1,923	1,663	2,411	1,774
1995	11,111	6,914	14,537	10,653	2,509	2,023	3,035	2,362	2,587	2,233	3,469	2,347
2000	14,081	8,235	19,307	13,361	2,882	2,922	3,157	2,790	3,224	2,808	4,070	2,976
2005	18,154	12,122	25,643	17,050	3,485	3,728	3,855	3,370	4,171	4,243	5,263	3,854
2006	18,862	12,450	26,954	17,702	3,647	4,726	4,039	3,517	4,380	3,994	5,517	4,063
2007	20,048	12,708	28,580	18,848	3,785	3,429	4,166	3,672	4,606	4,613	5,691	4,302
2008	21,462	13,126	30,251	20,190	3,992	4,074	4,376	3,875	4,804	4,484	6,006	4,466
2009	22,299	13,562	31,968	20,948	4,209	4,627	4,622	4,080	5,025	4,537	6,254	4,688
2010, prel. . . .	22,604	14,876	33,315	21,244	4,331	4,390	4,765	4,205	5,249	5,217	6,539	4,897

[1] For public institutions, data are for in-state students. [2] Beginning 1990, rates reflect 20 meals per week, rather than meals served 7 days a week.

Source: U.S. National Center for Education Statistics, *Digest of Education Statistics*, annual. See also <http://www.nces.ed.gov/programs/digest/>.

Table 294. Voluntary Financial Support of Higher Education: 1990 to 2010

[For school years ending in years shown (9,800 represents $9,800,000,000). Voluntary support, as defined in Gift Reporting Standards, excludes income from endowment and other invested funds as well as all support received from federal, state, and local governments and their agencies and contract research]

Item	Unit	1990	1995	2000	2005	2007	2008	2009	2010
Estimated support, total.	Mil. dol.	9,800	12,750	23,200	25,600	29,750	31,600	27,850	28,000
Individuals	Mil. dol.	4,770	6,540	12,220	12,100	13,920	14,820	12,125	12,020
Alumni	Mil. dol.	2,540	3,600	6,800	7,100	8,270	8,700	7,130	7,100
Business corporations	Mil. dol.	2,170	2,560	4,150	4,400	4,800	4,900	4,620	4,730
Foundations	Mil. dol.	1,920	2,460	5,080	7,000	8,500	9,100	8,235	8,400
Fundraising consortia and other organizations	Mil. dol.	700	940	1,380	1,730	2,150	2,400	2,545	2,545
Religious organizations	Mil. dol.	240	250	370	370	380	380	325	305
Current operations.	Mil. dol.	5,440	7,230	11,270	14,200	16,100	17,070	16,955	17,000
Capital purposes	Mil. dol.	4,360	5,520	11,930	11,400	13,650	14,530	10,895	11,000
Support per student.	Dollars	724	893	1,568	1,482	1,675	1,732	1,458	1,414
In 2010 dollars.	Dollars	1,206	1,276	1,984	1,653	1,760	1,752	1,480	1,414
Expenditures, higher education	Bil. dol.	134.7	183.0	236.8	335.0	375.5	408.0	432.0	444.8
Expenditures per student.	Dollars	9,946	12,814	16,008	19,397	21,147	22,358	22,614	22,455
In 2010 dollars.	Dollars	16,576	18,314	20,249	21,633	22,215	22,620	22,960	22,455
Institutions reporting support	Number	1,056	1,086	945	997	1,023	1,052	1,027	996
Total support reported	Mil. dol.	8,214	10,992	19,419	20,953	25,247	27,323	23,693	23,487
Private 4-year institutions	Mil. dol.	5,072	6,500	11,047	11,011	13,675	14,296	12,351	12,189
Public 4-year institutions	Mil. dol.	3,056	4,382	8,254	9,780	11,321	12,766	11,141	11,114
2-year colleges	Mil. dol.	85	110	117	163	251	261	201	185

Source: Council for Aid to Education, New York, NY, *Voluntary Support of Education*, annual.

Table 295. Average Salaries for College Faculty Members: 2009 to 2011

[In thousands of dollars (77.0 represents $77,000). For academic year ending in year shown. Figures are for 9 months teaching for full-time faculty members in 2-year and 4-year institutions with ranks. Fringe benefits averaged in 2009, $21,691 in public institutions and $25,374 in private institutions; in 2010, $22,258 in public institutions and $25,516 in private institutions and in 2011, $23,103 in public institutions and $26,211 in private institutions]

Type of control and academic rank	2009	2010	2011	Type of control and academic rank	2009	2010	2011
Public: All ranks	77.0	78.0	78.3	Private: [1] All ranks	92.3	92.9	94.6
Professor	104.5	105.7	105.8	Professor	128.3	128.7	131.6
Associate professor	75.2	75.7	76.2	Associate professor	82.9	82.9	84.6
Assistant professor	63.4	64.0	64.7	Assistant professor	69.0	69.5	71.0
Instructor	44.7	46.5	45.7	Instructor	51.6	52.8	53.6

[1] Excludes church-related colleges and universities.

Source: American Association of University Professors, Washington, DC, *AAUP Annual Report on the Economic Status of the Profession*.

Table 296. Employees in Higher Education Institutions by Sex and Occupation: 1995 to 2009

[In thousands (2,662.1 represents 2,662,100). As of fall. Based on complete census taken every other year; see source]

Year and status	Total	Professional staff										Non-profes- sional staff, total
		Total	Executive, administrative, and managerial		Faculty [1]		Graduate assistants		Other			
			Male	Female	Male	Female	Male	Female	Male	Female		
1995, total.....	**2,662.1**	**1,744.9**	**82.1**	**65.3**	**562.9**	**368.8**	**124.0**	**91.9**	**177.2**	**272.7**		**917.2**
Full–time.....	1,801.4	1,066.5	79.2	61.8	360.2	190.7	–	–	151.5	223.2		734.9
Part–time.....	860.7	678.4	2.9	3.6	202.7	178.1	124.0	91.9	25.6	49.5		182.3
2005, total [2]....	**3,379.1**	**2,459.9**	**95.2**	**101.1**	**714.5**	**576.0**	**167.5**	**149.6**	**262.8**	**393.2**		**919.2**
Full–time.....	2,179.9	1,432.1	92.9	97.2	401.5	274.1	–	–	231.4	335.0		747.8
Part–time.....	1,199.2	1,027.8	2.4	3.9	312.9	301.9	167.5	149.6	31.4	58.2		171.4
2009, total.....	**3,723.4**	**2,782.1**	**106.9**	**123.7**	**761.0**	**678.1**	**180.9**	**161.5**	**305.0**	**465.0**		**941.3**
Full–time.....	2,381.7	1,619.5	103.8	118.5	415.8	313.2	–	–	268.6	399.7		762.2
Part–time.....	1,341.7	1,162.6	3.1	5.2	345.2	365.0	180.9	161.5	36.4	65.3		179.1

– Represents zero. [1] Instruction and research. [2] Beginning 2005, data reflect the new classification of institutions. See footnote 1, Table 278.

Source: U.S. National Center for Education Statistics, *Digest of Education Statistics*, annual. See also <http://www.nces.ed.gov/programs/digest>.

Table 297. Faculty in Institutions of Higher Education: 1980 to 2009

[In thousands (686 represents 686,000), except percent. As of fall. Based on complete census taken every other year; see source]

Year	Total	Employment status		Control		Level		Percent		
		Full-time	Part-time	Public	Private	4-Year	2-Year or less	Part-time	Public	2-Year or less
1980 [1]...	686	450	236	495	191	494	192	34	72	28
1985 [1]...	715	459	256	503	212	504	211	36	70	30
1991 [2]...	826	536	291	581	245	591	235	35	70	28
1995.....	932	551	381	657	275	647	285	41	70	31
1999 [3]...	1,028	591	437	713	315	714	314	43	69	31
2001 [3]...	1,113	618	495	771	342	764	349	44	69	31
2003 [3]...	1,174	630	544	792	382	814	359	46	67	31
2005 [3]...	1,290	676	615	841	449	917	373	48	65	29
2007 [3,4]..	1,371	703	668	877	494	991	381	49	64	28
2009 [3,4]..	1,439	729	710	914	525	1,038	401	49	63	28

[1] Estimated on the basis of enrollment. [2] Data beginning 1991 not comparable to prior years. [3] Beginning 1997, data reflect the new classification of institutions. See footnote 1, Table 278. [4] Beginning in 2007, data include institutions with fewer than 15 full-time employees; these institutions did not report staff data prior to 2007.

Source: U.S. National Center for Education Statistics, *Digest of Education Statistics*, annual. See also <http://www.nces.ed.gov/programs/digest/>.

Table 298. Salary Offers to Candidates for Degrees: 2005 to 2010

[In dollars. Data are average beginning salaries based on offers made by business, industrial, government, nonprofit, and educational employers to graduating students. Data from representative colleges throughout the United States]

Field of study	Bachelor's			Master's [1]			Doctoral		
	2005	2009	2010	2005	2009	2010	2005	2009	2010
Accounting..............	42,940	48,471	48,378	45,992	48,760	[3] 49,254	(NA)	(NA)	(NA)
Business administration/ management [2]..........	39,480	44,607	43,991	[3] 50,513	[3] 63,615	[3] 49,875	[3] 66,500	[3] 82,429	[3] 103,667
Marketing..............	36,409	42,260	41,670	[3] 47,000	(NA)	[3] 40,933	(NA)	(NA)	(NA)
Engineering:									
Civil.................	43,774	52,287	51,321	48,619	[3] 53,311	[3] 57,225	[3] 59,216	[3] 60,351	[3] 58,964
Chemical.............	53,639	65,675	64,889	62,845	[3] 70,484	[3] 90,333	[3] 73,317	[3] 85,250	[3] 82,488
Computer.............	52,242	60,844	60,396	58,631	[3] 72,771	[3] 69,389	[3] 69,625	[3] 104,286	[3] 92,556
Electrical.............	51,773	60,509	59,512	64,781	70,921	[3] 67,844	[3] 75,066	[3] 89,715	[3] 81,188
Mechanical..........	50,175	59,222	58,110	60,223	66,961	67,234	69,757	[3] 75,186	[3] 73,036
Nuclear [4]..........	[3] 51,225	60,209	[3] 57,417	[3] 59,059	[3] 69,100	[3] 69,467	(NA)	(NA)	(NA)
Petroleum	62,236	85,417	77,278	[3] 65,000	(NA)	[3] 96,000	(NA)	(NA)	(NA)
Engineering technology....	45,790	55,023	52,756	(NA)	(NA)	(NA)	(NA)	(NA)	(NA)
Chemistry	38,635	39,354	39,404	(NA)	[3] 49,800	[3] 58,000	55,874	62,785	[3] 64,249
Mathematics	43,304	50,461	48,499	[3] 34,500	[3] 58,200	[3] 53,200	[3] 55,047	[3] 70,226	[3] 61,888
Physics	[3] 44,700	[3] 53,939	[3] 52,487	[3] 62,500	[3] 98,425	[3] 65,500	[3] 54,897	[3] 74,333	[3] 59,008
Humanities.............	31,565	[3] 38,292	[3] 34,982	[3] 35,212	[3] 42,380	[3] 49,250	[3] 43,728	[3] 47,491	[3] 53,000
Social sciences [5].........	31,621	36,217	36,433	[3] 40,575	[3] 47,000	[3] 46,030	[3] 46,838	[3] 54,870	[3] 57,320
Computer science	50,664	61,467	60,473	64,840	[3] 68,627	[3] 69,753	[3] 84,025	[3] 84,080	[3] 69,112

NA Not available. [1] Candidates with 1 year or less of full-time nonmilitary employment. [2] For master's degree, offers are after nontechnical undergraduate degree. [3] Fewer than 50 offers reported. [4] Includes engineering physics. [5] Excludes economics.

Source: National Association of Colleges and Employers, Bethlehem, PA (copyright). Reprinted with permission from Fall 2005, 2009, and 2010 Salary Survey. All rights reserved.

Table 299. Degrees Earned by Level and Sex: 1960 to 2009

[In thousands (477 represents 477,000), except percent. Based on survey; see Appendix III]

Year ending	All degrees Total	All degrees Percent male	Associate's Male	Associate's Female	Bachelor's Male	Bachelor's Female	Master's Male	Master's Female	First professional Male	First professional Female	Doctoral Male	Doctoral Female
1960 [1]	477	65.8	(NA)	(NA)	254	138	51	24	(NA)	(NA)	9	1
1970.	1,271	59.2	117	89	451	341	126	83	33	2	26	4
1975.	1,666	56.0	191	169	505	418	162	131	49	7	27	7
1980.	1,731	51.1	184	217	474	456	151	147	53	17	23	10
1985.	1,828	49.3	203	252	483	497	143	143	50	25	22	11
1990.	1,940	46.6	191	264	492	560	154	171	44	27	24	14
1993.	2,167	45.5	212	303	533	632	169	200	45	30	26	16
1994.	2,206	45.1	215	315	532	637	176	211	45	31	27	17
1995.	2,218	44.9	218	321	526	634	179	219	45	31	27	18
1996 [2]	2,248	44.2	220	336	522	642	179	227	45	32	27	18
1997 [2]	2,288	43.6	224	347	521	652	181	238	46	33	27	19
1998 [2]	2,298	43.2	218	341	520	664	184	246	45	34	27	19
1999 [2]	2,323	42.7	218	342	519	682	186	254	44	34	25	19
2000 [2]	2,385	42.6	225	340	530	708	192	265	44	36	25	20
2001 [2]	2,416	42.4	232	347	532	712	194	274	43	37	25	20
2002 [2]	2,494	42.2	238	357	550	742	199	283	43	38	24	20
2003 [2]	2,621	42.1	253	380	573	775	211	301	42	39	24	22
2004 [2]	2,755	41.8	260	405	595	804	230	329	42	41	25	23
2005 [2]	2,850	41.6	268	429	613	826	234	341	44	43	27	26
2006 [2]	2,936	41.3	270	443	631	855	238	356	44	44	29	27
2007 [2]	3,007	41.2	275	453	650	875	238	366	45	45	30	30
2008 [2]	3,093	41.2	283	468	668	895	246	379	46	45	31	32
2009 [2]	3,205	41.3	298	489	685	916	260	397	47	45	32	35

NA Not available. [1] First-professional degrees are included with bachelor's degrees. [2] Beginning 1996, data reflect the new classification of institutions. See footnote 1, Table 278.

Source: U.S. National Center for Education Statistics, *Digest of Education Statistics*, annual. See also <http://www.nces.ed.gov/programs/digest/>.

Table 300. Degrees Earned by Level and Race/Ethnicity: 1990 to 2009

[For school year ending in year shown. Based on survey; see Appendix III]

Level of degree and race/ethnicity	Total 1990	Total 2000 [1]	Total 2005 [1]	Total 2008 [1]	Total 2009 [1]	Percent distribution 1990	Percent distribution 2000 [1]	Percent distribution 2009 [1]
Associate's degrees, total.	**455,102**	**564,933**	**696,660**	**750,164**	**787,325**	**100.0**	**100.0**	**100.0**
White, non-Hispanic.	376,816	408,772	475,513	501,079	522,985	82.8	72.4	66.4
Black, non-Hispanic.	34,326	60,221	86,402	95,702	101,487	7.5	10.7	12.9
Hispanic.	21,504	51,573	78,557	91,274	97,921	4.7	9.1	12.4
Asian or Pacific Islander	13,066	27,782	33,669	38,843	40,914	2.9	4.9	5.2
American Indian/Alaska Native	3,430	6,497	8,435	8,849	8,834	0.8	1.2	1.1
Nonresident alien.	5,960	10,088	14,084	14,417	15,184	1.3	1.8	1.9
Bachelor's degrees, total	**1,051,344**	**1,237,875**	**1,439,264**	**1,563,069**	**1,601,368**	**100.0**	**100.0**	**100.0**
White, non-Hispanic.	887,151	929,106	1,049,141	1,122,675	1,144,612	84.4	75.1	71.5
Black, non-Hispanic.	61,046	108,013	136,122	152,457	156,615	5.8	8.7	9.8
Hispanic.	32,829	75,059	101,124	123,048	129,526	3.1	6.1	8.1
Asian or Pacific Islander	39,230	77,912	97,209	109,058	112,510	3.7	6.3	7.0
American Indian/Alaska Native	4,390	8,719	10,307	11,509	12,222	0.4	0.7	0.8
Nonresident alien.	26,698	39,066	45,361	44,322	45,883	2.5	3.2	2.9
Master's degrees, total	**324,301**	**457,056**	**574,618**	**625,023**	**656,784**	**100.0**	**100.0**	**100.0**
White, non-Hispanic.	254,299	320,485	379,350	409,312	424,188	78.4	70.1	64.6
Black, non-Hispanic.	15,336	35,874	54,482	65,062	70,010	4.7	7.8	10.7
Hispanic.	7,892	19,253	31,485	36,801	39,439	2.4	4.2	6.0
Asian or Pacific Islander	10,439	23,218	32,783	37,408	39,944	3.2	5.1	6.1
American Indian/Alaska Native	1,090	2,246	3,295	3,758	3,759	0.3	0.5	0.6
Nonresident alien.	35,245	55,980	73,223	72,682	79,444	10.9	12.2	12.1
Doctoral degrees, total	**38,371**	**44,808**	**52,631**	**63,712**	**67,716**	**100.0**	**100.0**	**100.0**
White, non-Hispanic.	26,221	27,843	30,261	36,390	39,648	68.3	62.1	58.6
Black, non-Hispanic.	1,149	2,246	3,056	3,906	4,434	3.0	5.0	6.5
Hispanic.	780	1,305	1,824	2,279	2,540	2.0	2.9	3.8
Asian or Pacific Islander	1,225	2,420	2,911	3,618	3,875	3.2	5.4	5.7
American Indian/Alaska Native	98	160	237	272	332	0.3	0.4	0.5
Nonresident alien.	8,898	10,834	14,342	17,247	16,887	23.2	24.2	24.9
First-professional degrees, total . . .	**70,988**	**80,057**	**87,289**	**91,309**	**92,004**	**100.0**	**100.0**	**100.0**
White, non-Hispanic.	60,487	59,637	63,429	65,383	65,439	85.2	74.5	71.1
Black, non-Hispanic.	3,409	5,555	6,313	6,400	6,571	4.8	6.9	7.1
Hispanic.	2,425	3,865	4,445	4,840	5,089	3.4	4.8	5.5
Asian or Pacific Islander	3,362	8,584	10,501	11,846	12,182	4.7	10.7	13.2
American Indian/Alaska Native	257	564	564	675	659	0.4	0.7	0.7
Nonresident alien.	1,048	1,852	2,037	2,165	2,064	1.5	2.3	2.2

[1] Beginning 2000, data reflect the new classification of institutions. See footnote 1, Table 278.

Source: U.S. National Center for Education Statistics, *Digest of Education Statistics*, annual. See also <http://www.nces.ed.gov/programs/digest/>.

Table 301. Degrees and Awards Earned Below Bachelor's by Field: 2009

[For school year ending in 2009. Covers associate's degrees and other awards based on postsecondary curriculums of less than 4 years in institutions of higher education. Based on survey; see Appendix III]

Field of study	Less than 1-year awards		1- to less than 4-year awards		Associate degree	
	Total	Women	Total	Women	Total	Women
Total [1]	**285,277**	**158,888**	**216,379**	**133,830**	**787,325**	**489,184**
Agriculture and natural resources, total	3,167	810	1,817	623	5,724	1,969
Architecture and related services	256	82	72	27	596	322
Area, ethnic, cultural, and gender studies	434	335	102	64	173	122
Biological and biomedical sciences	118	64	26	17	2,364	1,608
Business, management, and marketing	31,869	21,470	15,588	11,398	111,521	73,653
Communications and communications technologies	1,465	669	1,324	525	7,525	2,901
Computer and information sciences	10,436	3,297	5,783	1,960	30,006	7,453
Construction trades	9,102	441	8,334	312	4,252	217
Education	2,788	2,559	2,647	2,261	14,123	12,083
Engineering and engineering technologies	10,345	1,613	7,034	825	32,615	4,602
English language and literature/letters	1,218	756	252	145	1,525	984
Family and consumer sciences	11,816	9,898	2,738	2,409	9,020	8,664
Foreign languages and literatures	881	653	512	454	1,627	1,366
Health professions and related sciences	120,911	97,284	101,312	86,849	165,163	140,893
Nursing	2,156	1,934	3,540	3,064	77,929	67,933
Legal professions and studies	1,457	1,241	2,281	1,928	9,062	8,125
Liberal arts and sciences, general studies, and humanities	613	441	10,684	6,479	263,853	161,635
Library science	184	163	66	52	116	101
Mathematics	10	3	2	–	930	295
Mechanics and repairers	20,219	1,116	22,341	961	16,066	890
Military technologies	3	–	–	–	721	158
Multi/interdisciplinary studies	845	396	1,154	663	15,459	9,504
Parks, recreation, leisure, and fitness studies	346	174	327	197	1,587	641
Personal and culinary services	8,829	6,735	10,981	8,742	16,327	8,460
Philosophy and religion	68	36	35	22	191	55
Physical sciences and science technologies	227	86	453	189	3,617	1,497
Precision production trades	9,530	556	6,639	335	2,126	138
Psychology	81	66	38	34	3,949	3,205
Public administration and social services	1,006	818	549	453	4,178	3,595
Security and protective services	19,113	4,493	5,251	1,382	33,033	15,803
Social sciences and history	333	163	183	74	9,142	5,889
Theology and religious vocations	135	80	360	200	675	338
Transportation and material moving	14,848	925	584	40	1,430	182
Visual and performing arts	2,624	1,465	6,910	4,210	18,629	11,836

– Represents zero. [1] Includes other fields of study, not shown separately.

Source: U.S. National Center for Education Statistics, *Digest of Education Statistics*, annual. See also <http://www.nces.ed.gov/programs/digest>.

Table 302. Bachelor's Degrees Earned by Field: 1980 to 2009

[The new Classification of Instructional Programs was introduced in 2002–2003. Data for previous years has been reclassified where necessary to conform to the new classifications. Based on survey; see Appendix III]

Field of study	1980	1990	2000	2005	2008	2009
Total [1]	**929,417**	**1,051,344**	**1,237,875**	**1,439,264**	**1,563,069**	**1,601,368**
Agriculture and natural resources	22,802	12,900	24,238	23,002	24,113	24,988
Architecture and related services	9,132	9,364	8,462	9,237	9,805	10,119
Area, ethnic, cultural, and gender studies	2,840	4,447	6,212	7,569	8,454	8,772
Biological and biomedical sciences	46,190	37,204	63,005	64,611	77,854	80,756
Business	186,264	248,568	256,070	311,574	335,254	347,985
Communication, journalism, and related programs [2]	28,616	51,572	57,058	75,238	81,048	83,109
Computer and information sciences	11,154	27,347	37,788	54,111	38,476	37,994
Education	118,038	105,112	108,034	105,451	102,582	101,708
Engineering and engineering technologies	69,387	82,480	73,419	79,743	83,853	84,636
English language and literature/letters	32,187	46,803	50,106	54,379	55,038	55,462
Family and consumer sciences/human sciences	18,411	13,514	16,321	20,074	21,870	21,905
Foreign languages, literatures, and linguistics	12,480	13,133	15,886	18,386	20,977	21,158
Health professions and related clinical sciences	63,848	58,983	80,863	80,685	111,478	120,488
Legal professions and studies	683	1,632	1,969	3,161	3,771	3,822
Liberal arts and sciences, general studies, and humanities	23,196	27,985	36,104	43,751	46,940	47,096
Mathematics and statistics	11,378	14,276	11,418	14,351	15,192	15,496
Multi/interdisciplinary studies	11,457	16,557	28,561	30,243	36,149	37,444
Parks, recreation, leisure, and fitness studies	5,753	4,582	17,571	22,888	29,931	31,667
Philosophy and religious studies	7,069	7,034	8,535	11,584	12,257	12,444
Physical sciences and science technologies	23,407	16,056	18,331	18,905	21,934	22,466
Psychology	42,093	53,952	74,194	85,614	92,587	94,271
Public administration and social services	16,644	13,908	20,185	21,769	23,493	23,851
Security and protective services	15,015	15,354	24,877	30,723	40,235	41,800
Social sciences and history	103,662	118,083	127,101	156,892	167,363	168,500
Theology and religious vocations	6,170	5,185	6,789	9,284	8,992	8,940
Transportation and materials moving	213	2,387	3,395	4,904	5,203	5,189
Visual and performing arts	40,892	39,934	58,791	80,955	87,703	89,140

[1] Includes other fields of study, not shown separately. [2] Includes technologies.

Source: U.S. National Center for Education Statistics, *Digest of Education Statistics*, annual and unpublished data. See also <http://www.nces.ed.gov/programs/digest/>.

Table 303. Master's and Doctoral Degrees Earned by Field: 1980 to 2009

[The new Classification of Instructional Programs was introduced in 2002–2003. Data for previous years has been reclassified where necessary to conform to the new classifications. Based on survey; see Appendix III]

Field of study	1980	1990	2000	2005	2008	2009
MASTER'S DEGREES						
Total [1]	**298,081**	**324,301**	**457,056**	**574,618**	**625,023**	**656,784**
Agriculture and natural resources	3,976	3,382	4,360	4,746	4,684	4,877
Architecture and related services	3,139	3,499	4,268	5,674	6,065	6,587
Area, ethnic, cultural, and gender studies	852	1,191	1,544	1,755	1,778	1,779
Biological and biomedical sciences	6,322	4,906	6,781	8,199	9,565	9,898
Business	55,008	76,676	111,532	142,617	155,637	168,375
Communication, journalism, and related programs [2]	3,082	4,353	5,525	7,195	7,546	7,567
Computer and information sciences	3,647	9,677	14,990	18,416	17,087	17,907
Education	101,819	84,890	123,045	167,490	175,880	178,564
Engineering and engineering technologies	16,765	25,294	26,726	35,133	34,592	38,205
English language and literature/letters	6,026	6,317	7,022	8,468	9,161	9,261
Family and consumer sciences/human sciences	2,690	1,679	1,882	1,827	2,199	2,453
Foreign languages, literatures, and linguistics	3,067	3,018	3,037	3,407	3,565	3,592
Health professions and related clinical sciences	15,374	20,406	42,593	46,703	58,120	62,620
Legal professions and studies	1,817	1,888	3,750	4,170	4,754	5,150
Liberal arts and sciences, general studies, and humanities	2,646	1,999	3,256	3,680	3,797	3,728
Library science	5,374	4,341	4,577	6,213	7,162	7,091
Mathematics and statistics	2,860	3,624	3,208	4,477	4,980	5,211
Multi/interdisciplinary studies	2,494	3,182	3,487	4,252	5,289	5,344
Parks, recreation, leisure, and fitness studies	647	529	2,322	3,740	4,440	4,822
Philosophy and religious studies	1,204	1,327	1,376	1,647	1,879	1,859
Physical sciences and science technologies	5,167	5,410	4,810	5,678	5,899	5,658
Psychology	9,938	10,730	15,740	18,830	21,431	23,415
Public administration and social services	17,560	17,399	25,594	29,552	33,029	33,933
Security and protective services	1,805	1,151	2,609	3,991	5,760	6,128
Social sciences and history	12,176	11,634	14,066	16,952	18,495	19,240
Theology and religious vocations	3,872	4,941	5,534	5,815	6,996	7,541
Visual and performing arts	8,708	8,481	10,918	13,183	14,164	14,918
DOCTORAL DEGREES						
Total [1]	**32,615**	**38,371**	**44,808**	**52,631**	**63,712**	**67,716**
Agriculture and natural resources	991	1,295	1,168	1,173	1,257	1,328
Architecture and related services	79	103	129	179	199	212
Area, ethnic, cultural, and gender studies	151	125	205	189	270	239
Biological and biomedical sciences	3,527	3,837	5,180	5,578	6,918	6,957
Business	767	1,093	1,194	1,498	2,084	2,123
Communication, journalism, and related programs [2]	193	272	357	468	496	533
Computer and information sciences	240	627	779	1,119	1,698	1,580
Education	7,314	6,503	6,409	7,681	8,491	9,028
Engineering and engineering technologies	2,546	5,030	5,421	6,601	8,167	7,990
English language and literature/letters	1,196	986	1,470	1,212	1,262	1,271
Family and consumer sciences/human sciences	192	273	327	331	323	333
Foreign languages, literatures, and linguistics	857	816	1,086	1,027	1,078	1,111
Health professions and related clinical sciences	821	1,449	2,053	5,868	9,886	12,112
Legal professions and studies	40	111	74	98	172	259
Liberal arts and sciences, general studies, and humanities	192	63	83	109	76	67
Mathematics and statistics	724	917	1,075	1,176	1,360	1,535
Multi/interdisciplinary studies	318	442	792	983	1,142	1,273
Parks, recreation, leisure, and fitness studies	21	35	134	207	228	285
Philosophy and religious studies	374	445	598	586	635	686
Physical sciences and science technologies	3,044	4,116	3,963	4,114	4,804	5,048
Psychology	3,395	3,811	4,731	5,106	5,296	5,477
Public administration and social services	342	508	537	673	760	812
Security and protective services	18	38	52	94	88	97
Social sciences and history	3,230	3,010	4,095	3,819	4,059	4,234
Theology and religious vocations	1,315	1,317	1,630	1,422	1,446	1,520
Visual and performing arts	655	849	1,127	1,278	1,453	1,569

[1] Includes other fields of study, not shown separately. [2] Includes technologies.

Source: U.S. National Center for Education Statistics, *Digest of Education Statistics*, annual and unpublished data. See also <http://www.nces.ed.gov/programs/digest/>.

Table 304. First Professional Degrees Earned in Selected Professions: 1970 to 2009

[First professional degrees include degrees which require at least 6 years of college work for completion (including at least 2 years of preprofessional training). Based on survey; see Appendix III]

Type of degree and sex of recipient	1970	1980	1985	1990	1995	2000	2005	2007	2008	2009
Medicine (M.D.):										
Institutions conferring degrees	86	112	120	124	119	118	120	120	120	120
Degrees conferred, total	8,314	14,902	16,041	15,075	15,537	15,286	15,461	15,730	15,646	15,987
Percent to women	8.4	23.4	30.4	34.2	38.8	42.7	47.3	49.2	49.3	48.9
Dentistry (D.D.S. or D.M.D.):										
Institutions conferring degrees	48	58	59	57	53	54	53	55	55	55
Degrees conferred, total	3,718	5,258	5,339	4,100	3,897	4,250	4,454	4,596	4,795	4,918
Percent to women	0.9	13.3	20.7	30.9	36.4	40.1	43.8	44.6	44.5	46.4
Law (LL.B. or J.D.):										
Institutions conferring degrees	145	179	181	182	183	190	198	200	201	203
Degrees conferred, total	14,916	35,647	37,491	36,485	39,349	38,152	43,423	43,486	43,769	44,045
Percent to women	5.4	30.2	38.5	42.2	42.6	45.9	48.7	47.6	47.0	45.8
Theological (B.D., M.Div., M.H.L.):										
Institutions conferring degrees	(NA)	(NA)	(NA)	(NA)	192	198	(NA)	(NA)	(NA)	(NA)
Degrees conferred, total	5,298	7,115	7,221	5,851	5,978	6,129	5,533	5,990	5,751	5,362
Percent to women	2.3	13.8	18.5	24.8	25.7	29.2	35.6	33.2	34.3	33.1

NA Not available.
Source: U.S. National Center for Education Statistics, *Digest of Education Statistics*, annual. See also <http://www.nces.ed.gov/programs/digest/>.

Table 305. Academic Libraries by Selected Characteristics: 2008

[As of Fall of year shown. For information on public libraries, see Tables 1152 and 1153]

Institution characteristic	Number of libraries	Circulation (1,000)		Expenditures (mil. dol.)	Paid staff [1]			
		General collection	Reserve collection		Total [2]	Librarians	Other professional staff	Student assistants
All U.S. academic libraries . . .	**3,827**	**138,103**	**40,663**	**6,786**	**93,438**	**27,030**	**7,491**	**24,110**
Control:								
Public.	1,576	88,140	27,745	4,031	56,019	15,666	4,355	13,572
Private	2,251	49,962	12,918	2,754	37,419	11,364	3,136	10,537
Level: [3]								
Total 4-year and above	2,393	120,659	34,859	6,145	80,431	22,797	6,433	21,315
Doctor's	721	88,575	24,553	4,751	56,617	15,367	4,964	13,822
Master's	911	21,614	6,789	991	16,716	5,143	984	5,158
Bachelor's	730	10,168	3,333	355	6,572	2,093	456	2,200
Less than 4-year	1,434	17,444	5,805	640	13,007	4,233	1,058	2,794
Size (FTE enrollment): [4]								
Less than 1,000.	1,455	7,255	1,310	329	6,692	2,331	640	2,232
1,000 to 2,999	1,136	19,700	6,072	856	14,630	4,534	1,018	4,569
3,000 to 4,999	475	11,348	3,803	558	9,298	2,955	670	2,414
5,000 to 9,999	405	17,603	7,147	1,017	14,665	4,443	976	3,610
10,000 to 19,999	238	30,325	10,942	1,642	20,625	5,541	1,586	4,838
20,000 or more	118	51,872	11,389	2,384	27,528	7,226	2,601	6,446

[1] Full-time equivalent (FTE) staff is calculated by dividing the total number of hours for all part-time positions by the number of hours the library defines as a full-time position. [2] Includes other staff not shown separately. [3] Level refers to the highest level of any degree offered by the institution. Doctoral, master's, and bachelor's level institutions do not sum to total number of 4-year and above institutions because there are 4-year and above institutions that grant "other" degrees and are thus not included in the breakdown. [4] Full-time equivalent (FTE) enrollment is calculated by adding one-third of part-time enrollment to full-time enrollment.

Source: U.S. National Center for Education Statistics, Academic Libraries Survey (ALS), 2008. See also <http://nces.ed.gov/surveys/libraries/academic.asp>.

Section 5
Law Enforcement, Courts, and Prisons

This section presents data on crimes committed, victims of crimes, arrests, and data related to criminal violations and the criminal justice system. The major sources of these data are the Bureau of Justice Statistics (BJS), the Federal Bureau of Investigation (FBI), and the Administrative Office of the U.S. Courts. BJS issues many reports—see our Guide to Sources for a complete listing. The Federal Bureau of Investigation's major annual reports are *Crime in the United States, Law Enforcement Officers Killed and Assaulted*, annual, and *Hate Crimes*, annual, which present data on reported crimes as gathered from state and local law enforcement agencies.

Legal jurisdiction and law enforcement—
Law enforcement is, for the most part, a function of state and local officers and agencies. The U.S. Constitution reserves general police powers to the states. By act of Congress, federal offenses include only offenses against the U.S. government and against or by its employees while engaged in their official duties and offenses which involve the crossing of state lines or an interference with interstate commerce. Excluding the military, there are 52 separate criminal law jurisdictions in the United States: one in each of the 50 states, one in the District of Columbia, and the federal jurisdiction. Each of these has its own criminal law and procedure and its own law enforcement agencies. While the systems of law enforcement are quite similar among the states, there are often substantial differences in the penalties for like offenses.

Law enforcement can be divided into three parts: Investigation of crimes and arrests of persons suspected of committing them; prosecution of those charged with crime; and the punishment or treatment of persons convicted of crime.

Crime—
The U.S. Department of Justice administers two statistical programs to measure the magnitude, nature, and impact of crime in the nation: the Uniform Crime Reporting (UCR) Program and the National Crime Victimization Survey (NCVS). Each of these programs produces valuable information about aspects of the nation's crime problem. Because the UCR and NCVS programs are conducted for different purposes, use different methods, and focus on somewhat different aspects of crime, the information they produce together provides a more comprehensive panorama of the nation's crime problem than either could produce alone.

Uniform Crime Reports (UCR)—
The FBI's UCR Program, which began in 1929, collects information on the following crimes reported to law enforcement authorities—Part 1 offenses (detail data reported): murder and nonnegligent manslaughter, forcible rape, robbery, aggravated assault, burglary, larceny-theft, motor vehicle theft, and arson. For Part 2 offenses, law enforcement agencies report only arrest data for 21 additional crime categories. For UCR definitions of criminal offenses (including those listed), please go to: <www.fbi.gov/ucr/cius2009/about/offense_definitions.html>.

The UCR Program compiles data from monthly law enforcement reports or individual crime incident records transmitted directly to the FBI or to centralized state agencies that then report to the FBI. The Program thoroughly examines each report it receives for reasonableness, accuracy, and deviations that may indicate errors. Large variations in crime levels may indicate modified records procedures, incomplete reporting, or changes in a jurisdiction's boundaries. To identify any unusual fluctuations in an agency's crime counts, the Program compares monthly reports to previous submissions of the agency and with those for similar agencies.

The UCR Program presents crime counts for the nation as a whole, as well as for regions, states, counties, cities, towns, tribal law enforcement, and colleges and universities. This permits studies among neighboring jurisdictions and among

U.S. Census Bureau, Statistical Abstract of the United States: 2011

those with similar populations and other common characteristics.

The UCR Program annually publishes its findings in a preliminary release in the spring of the following calendar year, followed by a detailed annual report, *Crime in the United States*, issued in the fall. In addition to crime counts and trends, this report includes data on crimes cleared, persons arrested (age, sex, and race), law enforcement personnel (including the number of sworn officers killed or assaulted), and the characteristics of homicides (including age, sex, and race of victims and offenders; victim-offender relationships; weapons used; and circumstances surrounding the homicides). Other periodic reports are also available from the UCR Program.

National Crime Victimization Survey (NCVS)—A second perspective on crime is provided by this survey of the Bureau of Justice Statistics (BJS). The NCVS is an annual data collection (interviews of persons aged 12 or older), conducted by the U.S. Census Bureau for the BJS. As an ongoing survey of households, the NCVS measures crimes of violence and property both reported and not reported to police. It produces national rates and levels of personal and property victimization. No attempt is made to validate the information against police records or any other source.

The NCVS measures rape/sexual assault, robbery, assault, pocket-picking, purse snatching, burglary, and motor vehicle theft. The NCVS includes crimes reported to the police, as well as those not reported. Murder and kidnapping are not covered. The so-called victimless crimes, such as drunkenness, drug abuse, and prostitution, also are excluded, as are crimes for which it is difficult to identify knowledgeable respondents or to locate data records.

Crimes of which the victim may not be aware also cannot be measured effectively. Buying stolen property may fall into this category, as may some instances of embezzlement. Attempted crimes of many types probably are under recorded for this reason. Events in which the victim

has shown a willingness to participate in illegal activity also are excluded.

In any encounter involving a personal crime, more than one criminal act can be committed against an individual. For example, a rape may be associated with a robbery, or a household offense, such as a burglary, can escalate into something more serious in the event of a personal confrontation. In classifying the survey measured crimes, each criminal incident has been counted only once—by the most serious act that took place during the incident and ranked in accordance with the seriousness classification system used by the FBI. The order of seriousness for crimes against persons is as follows: rape, robbery, assault, and larceny. Personal crimes take precedence over household offenses.

A *victimization*, basic measure of the occurrence of crime, is a specific criminal act as it affects a single victim. The number of victimizations is determined by the number of victims of such acts. Victimization counts serve as key elements in computing rates of victimization. For crimes against persons, the rates are based on the total number of individuals aged 12 and over or on a portion of that population sharing a particular characteristic or set of traits. As general indicators of the danger of having been victimized during the reference period, the rates are not sufficiently refined to represent true measures of risk for specific individuals or households.

An *incident* is a specific criminal act involving one or more victims; therefore the number of incidents of personal crimes is lower than that of victimizations.

Courts—Statistics on criminal offenses and the outcome of prosecutions are incomplete for the country as a whole, although data are available for many states individually.

Since 1982, through its National Judicial Reporting Program, the BJS has surveyed a nationally representative sample of 300 counties every 2 years and collected detailed information on demographic characteristics of felons, conviction offenses, type of sentences, sentence lengths, and time from arrest to conviction and sentencing.

The bulk of civil and criminal litigation in the country is commenced and determined in the various state courts. Only when the U.S. Constitution and acts of Congress specifically confer jurisdiction upon the federal courts may civil or criminal litigation be heard and decided by them. Generally, the federal courts have jurisdiction over the following types of cases: suits or proceedings by or against the United States; civil actions between private parties arising under the Constitution, laws, or treaties of the United States; civil actions between private litigants who are citizens of different states; civil cases involving admiralty, maritime, or private jurisdiction; and all matters in bankruptcy.

There are several types of courts with varying degrees of legal jurisdiction. These jurisdictions include original, appellate, general, and limited or special. A court of original jurisdiction is one having the authority initially to try a case and pass judgment on the law and the facts; a court of appellate jurisdiction is one with the legal authority to review cases and hear appeals; a court of general jurisdiction is a trial court of unlimited original jurisdiction in civil and/or criminal cases, also called a "major trial court"; a court of limited or special jurisdiction is a trial court with legal authority over only a particular class of cases, such as probate, juvenile, or traffic cases.

The 94 federal courts of original jurisdiction are known as the U.S. district courts. One or more of these courts is established in every state and one each in the District of Columbia, Puerto Rico, the Virgin Islands, the Northern Mariana Islands, and Guam. Appeals from the district courts are taken to intermediate appellate courts of which there are 13, known as U.S. courts of appeals and the United States Court of Appeals for the Federal Circuit. The Supreme Court of the United States is the final and highest appellate court in the federal system of courts.

Juvenile offenders—For statistical purposes, the FBI and most states classify as juvenile offenders persons under the age of 18 years who have committed a crime or crimes.

Delinquency cases are all cases of youths referred to a juvenile court for violation of a law or ordinance or for seriously "antisocial" conduct. Several types of facilities are available for those adjudicated delinquents, ranging from the short-term physically unrestricted environment to the long-term very restrictive atmosphere.

Prisoners and jail inmates—
BJS started to collect annual data in 1979 on prisoners in federal and state prisons and reformatories. Adults convicted of criminal activity may be given a prison or jail sentence. A *prison* is a confinement facility having custodial authority over adults sentenced to confinement of more than 1 year. A *jail* is a facility, usually operated by a local law enforcement agency, holding persons detained pending adjudication and/or persons committed after adjudication to 1 year or less.

Data on inmates in local jails were collected by the BJS for the first time in 1970. Since then, BJS has conducted censuses of facilities and inmates every 5 to 6 years. In 1984, BJS initiated an annual survey of jails conducted in noncensus years.

Statistical reliability—For discussion of statistical collection, estimation and sampling procedures, and measures of statistical reliability pertaining to the National Crime Victimization Survey and Uniform Crime Reporting Program, see Appendix III.

Law Enforcement, Courts, and Prisons 195

Table 306. Crimes and Crime Rates by Type of Offense: 1980 to 2009

[(13,408 represents 13,408,000). For year ending March 31. Data include offenses reported to law enforcement, offense estimations for nonreporting and partially reporting agencies within each state. Rates are based on Census Bureau estimated resident population as of July 1; 1980, 1990, and 2000, enumerated as of April 1. See source for details]

Item and year	All crimes	Violent crime					Property crimes			
		Total	Murder [1]	Forcible rape	Robbery	Aggravated assault	Total	Burglary	Larceny/ theft	Motor vehicle theft
Number of offenses (1,000):										
1980	13,408	1,345	23.0	83.0	566	673	12,064	3,795	7,137	1,132
1985	12,430	1,328	19.0	87.7	498	723	11,103	3,073	6,926	1,103
1990	14,476	1,820	23.4	102.6	639	1,055	12,655	3,074	7,946	1,636
1995	13,863	1,799	21.6	97.5	581	1,099	12,064	2,594	7,998	1,472
1996	13,494	1,689	19.6	96.3	536	1,037	11,805	2,506	7,905	1,394
1997	13,195	1,636	18.2	96.2	499	1,023	11,558	2,461	7,744	1,354
1998	12,486	1,534	17.0	93.1	447	977	10,952	2,333	7,376	1,243
1999	11,634	1,426	15.5	89.4	409	912	10,208	2,101	6,956	1,152
2000	11,608	1,425	15.6	90.2	408	912	10,183	2,051	6,972	1,160
2001 [2]	11,877	1,439	16.0	90.9	424	909	10,437	2,117	7,092	1,228
2002	11,879	1,424	16.2	95.2	421	891	10,455	2,151	7,057	1,247
2003	11,827	1,384	16.5	93.9	414	859	10,443	2,155	7,027	1,261
2004	11,679	1,360	16.1	95.1	401	847	10,319	2,144	6,937	1,238
2005	11,565	1,391	16.7	94.3	417	862	10,175	2,155	6,783	1,236
2006	11,467	1,436	17.3	94.8	450	874	10,031	2,196	6,637	1,198
2007	11,295	1,422	17.2	91.9	447	866	9,873	2,187	6,587	1,098
2008	11,168	1,393	16.4	90.5	444	842	9,775	2,228	6,588	959
2009	10,639	1,318	15.2	88.1	408	807	9,321	2,199	6,327	795
Rate per 100,000 population:										
1980	5,950	597	10.2	36.8	251	299	5,353	1,684	3,167	502
1985	5,225	558	8.0	36.8	209	304	4,666	1,292	2,911	464
1990	5,803	730	9.4	41.1	256	423	5,073	1,232	3,185	656
1995	5,276	685	8.2	37.1	221	418	4,591	987	3,043	560
1996	5,087	637	7.4	36.3	202	391	4,451	945	2,980	526
1997	4,930	611	6.8	35.9	186	382	4,316	919	2,892	506
1998	4,619	568	6.3	34.5	166	361	4,053	863	2,730	460
1999	4,267	523	5.7	32.8	150	334	3,744	770	2,551	423
2000	4,125	507	5.5	32.0	145	324	3,618	729	2,477	412
2001 [2]	4,163	505	5.6	31.8	149	319	3,658	742	2,486	431
2002	4,125	494	5.6	33.1	146	310	3,631	747	2,451	433
2003	4,067	476	5.7	32.3	143	295	3,591	741	2,417	434
2004	3,977	463	5.5	32.4	137	289	3,514	730	2,362	422
2005	3,899	469	5.6	31.8	141	291	3,432	727	2,288	417
2006	3,838	481	5.8	31.7	151	293	3,358	735	2,221	401
2007	3,749	472	5.7	30.5	148	287	3,277	726	2,186	365
2008	3,669	458	5.4	29.7	146	277	3,212	732	2,165	315
2009	3,466	429	5.0	28.7	133	263	3,036	716	2,061	259

[1] Includes nonnegligent manslaughter. [2] The murder and nonnegligent homicides that occurred as a result of the events of September 11, 2001, were not included in this table.

Source: U.S. Department of Justice, Federal Bureau of Investigation, "Crime in the United States," September 2010, <http://www2.fbi.gov/ucr/cius2009/index.html>

Table 307. Crimes and Crime Rates by Type and Geographic Community: 2009

[In thousands (1,318.4 represents 1,318,400), except rate. Rate per 100,000 population. For year ending March 31. See headnote, Table 306]

Type of crime	United States		Metropolitan statistical area [1]		Cities outside metropolitan areas		Nonmetropolitan counties	
	Total	Rate	Total	Rate	Total	Rate	Total	Rate
Violent crime	1,318.4	429.4	1,177.8	458.7	79.4	396.4	61.2	202.4
Murder [2]	15.2	5.0	13.4	5.2	0.8	4.0	1.0	3.4
Forcible rape	88.1	28.7	72.4	28.2	8.3	41.2	7.4	24.6
Robbery	408.2	133.0	390.5	152.1	12.6	63.1	5.1	16.9
Aggravated assault	806.8	262.8	701.5	273.2	57.8	288.2	47.6	157.6
Property crime	9,321.0	3,036.1	8,113.2	3,160.2	733.2	3,658.5	474.6	1,569.8
Burglary	2,199.1	716.3	1,867.2	727.3	164.9	822.6	167.1	552.8
Larceny-theft	6,327.2	2,060.9	5,511.9	2,146.9	539.7	2,693.2	275.6	911.7
Motor vehicle theft	794.6	258.8	734.2	286.0	28.6	142.6	31.8	105.3

[1] For definition, see Appendix II. [2] Includes nonnegligent manslaughter.

Source: U.S. Department of Justice, Federal Bureau of Investigation, "Crime in the United States," September 2010, <http://www2.fbi.gov/ucr/cius2009/index.html/>

Table 308. Crime Rates by State, 2008 and 2009, and by Type, 2009

[For year ending December 31. Rates per 100,000 population. Offenses reported to law enforcement . Based on Census Bureau estimated resident population as of July 1]

State	Violent crime						Property crime				
	2008 total	2009					2008 total	2009			
		Total	Murder	Forcible rape	Robbery	Aggra-vated assault		Total	Burglary	Larceny/ theft	Motor vehicle theft
United States	467.2	439.7	5.1	28.5	137.6	268.6	3,248.0	3,071.5	724.9	2,080.6	266.0
Alabama	465.7	459.9	7.1	32.8	142.5	277.5	4,192.6	3,877.6	1,058.9	2,574.0	244.8
Alaska	654.4	632.6	3.2	73.4	94.0	462.0	2,920.4	2,934.5	514.2	2,178.9	241.5
Arizona	478.6	423.2	5.5	32.7	123.9	261.1	3,805.5	3,302.0	817.3	2,087.6	397.1
Arkansas	516.4	530.3	6.3	48.7	93.5	381.8	3,911.0	3,885.1	1,224.1	2,445.5	215.6
California	503.8	473.4	5.4	23.6	173.7	270.8	2,940.3	2,728.2	622.1	1,662.5	443.6
Colorado	344.1	340.9	3.2	45.4	67.9	224.5	2,818.5	2,683.6	532.5	1,900.5	250.6
Connecticut	306.7	300.5	3.0	18.7	113.6	165.2	2,490.8	2,345.8	431.1	1,702.7	212.0
Delaware	708.6	645.1	4.6	44.6	189.7	406.2	3,594.7	3,351.7	784.0	2,352.3	215.4
District of Columbia [1] ...	1,437.7	1,348.9	24.2	25.0	734.4	565.3	5,104.6	4,751.9	616.4	3,213.0	922.5
Florida	688.9	612.6	5.5	29.7	166.8	410.6	4,141.3	3,841.1	981.2	2,588.7	271.2
Georgia	496.1	432.6	6.0	23.7	157.0	245.9	4,068.7	3,748.0	1,025.2	2,368.9	354.0
Hawaii	272.5	274.1	1.8	29.7	79.5	163.1	3,566.5	3,668.7	713.7	2,580.0	375.0
Idaho	239.3	238.5	1.5	37.2	16.5	183.4	2,089.0	2,017.1	429.3	1,493.0	94.8
Illinois [2,3]	(NA)	(NA)	8.4	(NA)	260.7	349.1	3,497.9	3,185.7	720.6	2,188.1	276.9
Indiana............	375.5	366.4	5.3	27.2	129.4	204.4	3,571.2	3,305.6	815.9	2,256.3	233.4
Iowa..............	298.2	294.5	1.3	30.9	42.2	220.2	2,522.2	2,436.4	570.1	1,730.4	136.0
Kansas............	415.1	412.0	4.7	42.7	66.7	297.9	3,384.8	3,249.4	690.0	2,341.3	218.2
Kentucky	306.6	265.5	4.3	35.3	86.8	139.0	2,705.1	2,558.5	697.8	1,718.2	142.4
Louisiana..........	658.4	628.4	12.3	29.5	142.3	444.3	3,780.3	3,820.8	1,036.4	2,517.3	267.1
Maine.............	119.4	119.9	2.0	28.4	30.3	59.2	2,463.7	2,405.1	510.4	1,817.1	77.5
Maryland	628.2	590.0	7.7	20.3	210.7	351.3	3,516.0	3,198.4	647.5	2,206.7	344.2
Massachusetts.......	466.2	465.6	2.7	26.4	114.1	322.4	2,393.3	2,329.2	524.1	1,624.4	180.7
Michigan	522.2	504.4	6.3	45.3	126.5	326.5	2,969.8	2,856.3	768.1	1,790.5	297.7
Minnesota [3]	(NA)	(NA)	1.5	(NA)	70.4	142.3	2,893.1	2,653.6	489.6	2,002.0	162.0
Mississippi..........	328.7	306.7	6.9	37.0	117.3	145.4	3,286.7	3,335.9	1,085.2	2,037.7	213.0
Missouri............	505.2	500.3	6.6	27.3	127.1	339.2	3,682.3	3,422.6	733.5	2,392.9	296.2
Montana...........	302.0	283.9	3.2	35.7	22.9	222.0	2,733.1	2,544.0	374.1	2,007.6	162.2
Nebraska...........	323.3	305.5	2.5	35.5	74.7	192.8	2,951.6	2,878.4	499.4	2,171.8	207.1
Nevada	727.5	704.6	5.9	38.6	228.0	432.1	3,456.4	3,060.4	835.7	1,756.1	468.6
New Hampshire.......	166.0	169.5	0.9	31.2	37.2	100.1	2,217.5	2,283.4	383.7	1,810.2	89.5
New Jersey	326.1	311.3	3.7	12.0	133.7	162.0	2,291.4	2,075.2	424.2	1,472.9	178.1
New Mexico.........	670.6	652.8	10.0	53.9	98.7	490.3	3,923.6	3,866.0	1,117.3	2,409.4	339.3
New York	401.8	385.5	4.0	13.2	144.5	223.7	2,004.8	1,927.5	321.6	1,493.6	112.3
North Carolina.......	486.6	414.0	5.4	25.2	131.6	251.8	4,155.9	3,729.7	1,165.6	2,345.1	219.0
North Dakota.........	200.5	223.6	2.0	43.5	17.2	161.0	2,142.7	2,008.6	375.7	1,497.9	135.0
Ohio.............	385.1	358.1	5.0	37.7	167.6	147.8	3,597.0	3,337.0	952.6	2,173.3	211.1
Oklahoma	539.7	510.4	6.5	42.1	92.9	369.0	3,525.3	3,637.8	1,044.7	2,305.4	287.7
Oregon............	265.0	261.2	2.3	31.4	65.3	162.3	3,349.5	2,987.3	513.0	2,212.8	261.5
Pennsylvania	417.0	388.9	5.4	28.4	142.4	212.6	2,424.8	2,219.2	439.2	1,635.5	144.5
Rhode Island.........	252.8	254.3	3.0	28.1	74.5	148.6	2,845.0	2,616.6	546.2	1,842.3	228.1
South Carolina.......	726.2	675.1	6.7	36.5	126.0	506.0	4,211.4	3,887.1	991.7	2,596.7	298.7
South Dakota........	300.6	201.0	3.6	59.5	14.9	123.1	1,880.6	1,825.2	324.0	1,394.2	107.1
Tennessee..........	721.6	666.0	7.4	32.1	153.3	473.2	4,028.1	3,766.6	1,013.8	2,514.3	238.5
Texas..............	508.2	491.4	5.4	33.5	153.6	299.0	3,985.6	4,017.2	967.4	2,740.9	308.9
Utah..............	225.6	216.2	1.4	33.7	47.3	133.8	3,395.3	3,308.8	548.7	2,509.0	251.1
Vermont...........	140.8	135.1	1.3	21.5	18.0	94.3	2,620.3	2,442.1	562.8	1,806.2	73.2
Virginia............	258.1	230.0	4.7	19.9	80.2	125.2	2,535.5	2,456.1	404.8	1,903.4	148.0
Washington.........	332.1	338.3	2.8	38.5	103.4	193.5	3,783.6	3,745.6	791.9	2,597.1	356.5
West Virginia	300.4	331.2	4.9	28.4	56.2	241.7	2,717.9	2,706.2	698.4	1,842.9	164.9
Wisconsin	276.9	259.7	2.6	19.8	87.7	149.6	2,770.2	2,612.6	475.5	1,978.1	159.1
Wyoming	245.5	219.3	2.0	31.7	14.3	171.3	2,720.2	2,613.9	399.8	2,075.1	139.0

NA Not Available. [1] Includes offenses reported by the Zoological Police and the Metro Transit Police. [2] Limited data for 2008 and 2009 were available for Illinois. [3] The data collection methodology for the offense of forcible rape used by the Illinois and the Minnesota state Uniform Crime Reporting (UCR) Programs (with the exception of Rockford, Illinois, and Minneapolis and St. Paul, Minnesota) does not comply with national UCR guidelines. Consequently, their state figures for forcible rape and violent crime (of which forcible rape is a part) are not published in this table.

Source: U.S. Department of Justice, Federal Bureau of Investigation, Uniform Crime Reports, Return A Master Files.

U.S. Census Bureau, Statistical Abstract of the United States: 2012

Table 309. Crime Rates by Type—Selected Large Cities: 2009

[For year ending December 31. Rates per 100,000 population, offenses reported to law enforcement. Based on U.S. Census Bureau estimated resident population as of July 1]

Cities ranked by population size, 2009	Violent crime					Property crime			
	Total	Murder	Forcible rape	Robbery	Aggravated assault	Total	Burglary	Larceny/ theft	Motor vehicle theft
New York, NY	552	5.6	9.9	221	315	1,690	224	1,339	127
Los Angeles, CA	625	8.1	23.5	317	276	2,449	479	1,492	478
Chicago, IL	(¹)	16.1	(¹)	557	552	4,227	930	2,754	543
Houston, TX	1,126	12.6	36.2	500	577	5,319	1,288	3,389	642
Phoenix, AZ	547	7.6	32.7	235	271	4,108	1,019	2,482	607
Philadelphia, PA	1,238	19.5	57.9	584	577	3,611	709	2,452	451
Las Vegas MPD, NV	947	8.1	50.7	326	562	3,461	981	1,832	648
San Antonio, TX	571	7.2	45.7	195	323	6,671	1,322	4,926	422
San Diego, CA	451	3.1	24.2	145	279	2,453	509	1,373	570
Dallas, TX	792	12.9	37.6	426	315	5,531	1,506	3,215	810
San Jose, CA	360	2.9	27.0	107	223	2,385	392	1,429	564
Detroit, MI	1,992	40.0	36.8	661	1,254	5,606	2,117	2,070	1,419
Honolulu, HI	280	1.5	26.8	96	156	3,679	661	2,607	411
Indianapolis, IN	1,200	12.2	56.5	483	648	5,829	1,871	3,407	551
Jacksonville, FL	836	12.2	26.9	291	506	5,158	1,396	3,426	336
San Francisco, CA	736	5.6	22.1	423	285	4,262	642	3,013	607
Charlotte-Mecklenburg, NC	723	7.5	39.0	302	375	4,955	1,262	3,263	429
Austin, TX	523	2.9	34.5	184	302	6,245	1,138	4,819	289
Columbus, OH	708	10.8	78.9	448	171	6,454	1,925	3,977	552
Fort Worth, TX	587	6.1	52.4	200	328	4,965	1,409	3,262	295
Memphis, TN	1,809	19.8	58.0	620	1,111	7,080	2,091	4,361	629
Baltimore, MD	1,513	37.3	24.7	580	871	4,566	1,221	2,621	724
Louisville Metro, KY	597	9.8	36.4	249	302	4,262	1,122	2,866	274
Boston, MA	992	8.0	43.1	365	576	3,324	473	2,484	366
El Paso, TX	457	1.9	29.4	73	353	2,994	322	2,367	305
Nashville, TN	1,140	12.9	42.4	323	762	4,775	1,036	3,456	283
Denver, CO	578	5.8	56.4	154	358	3,451	786	2,088	577
Milwaukee, WI	1,102	11.9	33.6	525	531	5,770	1,087	3,878	805
Seattle, WA	641	3.7	16.9	297	323	5,824	1,113	4,165	545
Washington, DC	1,265	24.0	25.0	667	549	4,504	616	3,004	884
Portland, OR	554	3.4	44.9	185	320	4,724	659	3,499	566
Oklahoma City, OK	930	11.7	52.8	224	642	6,098	1,902	3,509	687
Atlanta, GA	1,150	14.5	24.4	493	618	6,213	1,648	3,529	1,036
Tucson, AZ	650	6.4	37.2	227	379	(²)	924	(²)	650
Albuquerque, NM	769	10.6	61.4	208	489	5,492	1,202	3,649	641
Kansas City, MO	1,300	20.6	56.9	406	816	5,508	1,492	3,288	728
Fresno, CA	609	8.7	17.9	225	357	4,369	919	2,775	675
Mesa, AZ	425	3.0	26.1	130	266	3,415	653	2,485	277
Sacramento, CA	886	6.4	38.1	341	500	4,465	1,092	2,492	882
Long Beach, CA	681	8.6	28.2	298	347	2,725	672	1,544	509
Omaha, NE	533	6.8	43.3	201	282	4,129	729	2,920	480
Virginia Beach, VA	205	4.4	15.1	103	83	3,077	468	2,479	130
Cleveland, OH	1,396	19.3	88.5	828	460	5,639	2,152	2,545	942
Miami, FL	1,189	14.1	15.5	500	660	4,957	1,158	3,193	605
Raleigh, NC	493	3.4	24.4	205	260	3,403	785	2,422	196
Oakland, CA	1,679	25.7	80.6	716	857	4,986	1,186	2,183	1,617
Colorado Springs, CO	490	3.7	86.1	130	270	3,662	822	2,576	264
Tulsa, OK	1,116	17.7	66.0	290	742	6,034	1,722	3,773	539
Minneapolis, MN ¹	1,109	4.7	107.9	435	561	4,668	1,239	2,959	470
Arlington, TX	615	3.2	40.1	177	394	5,412	1,290	3,742	380
Wichita, KS	885	6.8	71.3	143	664	5,347	1,103	3,789	455
St. Louis, MO	2,070	40.3	70.4	766	1,193	8,332	1,924	5,011	1,397
Tampa, FL	752	5.8	23.2	263	460	3,754	1,014	2,346	394
Santa Ana, CA	509	7.4	22.7	256	223	2,004	342	1,228	434
New Orleans, LA	777	51.7	29.1	277	419	3,846	1,136	1,934	776
Anaheim, CA	352	2.7	21.4	150	178	2,379	434	1,664	281
Cincinnati, OH	1,194	16.5	72.2	681	424	6,120	1,886	3,765	469
Bakersfield, CA	634	8.2	14.8	213	399	4,716	1,175	2,823	718
Aurora, CO	469	5.9	66.0	171	227	3,095	633	2,102	360
Pittsburgh, PA	989	12.5	37.2	438	501	3,771	900	2,605	266
Riverside, CA	512	5.0	32.7	222	252	3,198	674	2,081	444
Lexington, KY	594	4.4	36.1	195	358	3,416	819	2,414	183
Stockton, CA	1,267	11.3	28.1	431	797	5,279	1,362	3,174	744
Toledo, OH	1,117	11.3	56.7	420	629	(²)	2,771	(²)	459
Corpus Christi, TX	823	4.2	73.7	160	585	5,604	1,035	4,361	208
Anchorage, AK	878	4.9	99.5	188	585	3,641	569	2,766	306
St. Paul, MN	763	4.6	28.9	248	451	4,080	1,045	2,396	638
Newark, NJ	930	28.7	24.4	472	405	3,160	697	1,354	1,108
Plano, TX	173	1.5	16.9	52	103	2,940	543	2,224	172
Buffalo, NY	1,459	22.3	52.5	609	775	5,390	1,472	3,330	588
Henderson, NV	234	1.5	21.4	98	113	1,975	539	1,199	236
Chandler, AZ	289	2.0	18.0	80	189	2,912	537	2,186	189
Glendale, AZ	450	7.1	21.2	165	257	4,896	1,000	3,220	676
Lincoln, NE	458	2.0	49.5	77	329	3,933	636	3,182	116
Greensboro, NC	766	9.5	30.0	359	368	6,044	1,891	3,818	334
Fort Wayne, IN	348	7.2	29.8	193	118	3,728	902	2,656	170
Mobile, AL ³	810	9.7	15.0	348	437	5,737	1,510	3,842	386

¹ The data collection methodology for the offense of forcible rape used by the Illinois and Minnesota state programs (with the exception of Rockford, Illinois, and Minneapolis and St Paul, Minnesota) does not comply with national Uniform Crime Reporting (UCR) Program guidelines. Consequently, their figures for forcible rape and violent crime (of which forcible rape is a part) are not published in this table. ² It was determined that the agency did not follow the national UCR program guidelines for reporting an offense. Consequently, this figure is not included in this table. ³ The population for the city of Mobile, Alabama, includes 60,536 inhabitants from the jurisdiction of the Mobile County Sheriff's Department.

Source: U.S. Department of Justice, Federal Bureau of Investigation, Uniform Crime Reporting Program, Return A Master Files.

Table 310. Murder Victims—Circumstances and Weapons Used or Cause of Death: 2000 to 2009

[For year ending December 31. The FBI's Uniform Crime Reporting (UCR) Program defines murder and nonnegligent manslaughter as the willful (nonnegligent) killing of one human being by another. The classification of this offense is based solely on police investigation as opposed to the determination of a court, medical examiner, coroner, jury, or other judicial body. The UCR Program does not include the following situations in this offense classification: deaths caused by negligence, suicide, or accident; justifiable homicides; and attempts to murder, which are scored as aggravated assaults]

Characteristic	2000	2005	2008	2009	Characteristic	2000	2005	2008	2009
Murders, total	**13,230**	**14,965**	**14,299**	**13,756**	Gangland killings	65	96	133	177
					Juvenile gang killings	653	756	711	715
CIRCUMSTANCES					Institutional killings	10	12	15	12
Felonies, total	2,229	2,189	2,101	2,051	Sniper attack	8	2	4	1
Rape	58	45	23	24	Other—not specified	1,901	1,938	2,014	1,996
Robbery	1,077	930	924	858	Unknown	4,070	5,635	5,000	4,846
Burglary	76	91	87	110					
Larceny-theft	23	12	16	13	TYPE OF WEAPON OR				
Motor vehicle theft	25	32	19	23	CAUSE OF DEATH				
Arson	81	39	26	38	Total firearms	8,661	10,158	9,484	9,203
					Handguns	6,778	7,565	6,755	6,503
Prostitution and					Rifles	411	445	375	352
commercialized vice	6	13	7	6	Shotguns	485	522	444	424
Other sex offenses	10	9	11	10	Other not specified or				
Narcotic drug laws	589	597	501	495	type unknown	53	138	79	96
Gambling	12	2	10	5	Firearms, type not stated	934	1,488	1,831	1,828
Other—not specified	272	419	477	469	Knives or cutting				
					instruments	1,782	1,920	1,897	1,836
Suspected felony type	60	45	104	56	Blunt objects [1]	617	608	614	623
Other[1] than felony total	6,871	7,096	7,014	6,803	Personal weapons [2]	927	905	861	815
Romantic triangle	122	118	104	89	Poison	8	9	10	7
Child killed by babysitter	30	26	51	29	Explosives	9	2	10	2
Brawl due to influence of					Fire	134	125	86	98
alcohol	188	123	125	117	Narcotics	20	46	33	52
Brawl due to influence of					Drowning	15	20	15	8
narcotics	99	97	68	94	Strangulation	166	118	88	122
Argument over money or					Asphyxiation	92	96	89	84
property	206	210	192	205	All other [3]	799	958	993	905
Other arguments	3,589	3,718	3,586	3,368					

[1] Refers to club, hammer, etc. [2] Hands, fists, feet, pushed, etc. [3] Includes poison, explosives, narcotics, drowning, and unknown.

Source: U.S. Department of Justice, Federal Bureau of Investigation, Uniform Crime Reporting Program, Return A Master Files.

Table 311. Murder Victims by Age, Sex, and Race: 2008

[See headnote, Table 310]

Age	Total	Sex			Race			
		Male	Female	Unknown	White	Black	Other	Unknown
Murders, total	**13,756**	**10,582**	**3,158**	**16**	**6,655**	**6,587**	**365**	**149**
Percent of total	100.0	76.9	23.1	0.1	48.4	47.9	2.7	1.1
Under 18 years old [1]	1,363	921	442	–	669	640	44	10
18 years old and over [1]	12,393	9,661	2,716	16	5,986	5,947	321	139
Infant (under 1 year old)	201	106	95	–	113	74	9	5
1 to 4 years old	305	163	142	–	164	131	9	1
5 to 8 years old	74	35	39	–	42	27	4	1
9 to 12 years old	70	35	35	–	44	21	5	–
13 to 16 years old	398	317	81	–	189	198	9	2
17 to 19 years old	1,250	1,072	178	–	477	742	22	9
20 to 24 years old	2,432	2,087	344	1	934	1,409	65	24
25 to 29 years old	1,955	1,616	338	1	799	1,101	39	16
30 to 34 years old	1,545	1,221	324	–	654	848	25	18
35 to 39 years old	1,221	963	258	–	581	588	41	12
40 to 44 years old	1,016	741	274	1	552	419	35	10
45 to 49 years old	941	655	286	–	571	340	23	7
50 to 54 years old	708	526	181	1	425	247	27	9
55 to 59 years old	466	314	152	–	293	147	22	4
60 to 64 years old	321	224	97	–	216	90	12	3
65 to 69 years old	231	153	78	–	169	57	4	1
70 to 74 years old	135	86	49	–	105	26	1	3
75 years old and over	294	144	150	–	231	53	10	–
Age unknown	193	124	57	12	96	69	3	24

– Represents zero. [1] Does not include unknown ages.

Source: U.S. Department of Justice, Federal Bureau of Investigation, Uniform Crime Reporting Program Return A Master Files.

Law Enforcement, Courts, and Prisons 199

Table 312. Homicide Trends: 1980 to 2008

[Based on Federal Bureau of Investigation's Uniform Crime Reports Supplementary Homicide Reports. Homicide includes murder and nonnegligent manslaughter, which is the willful killing of one human being by another. Excludes deaths caused by negligence, suicide, or accident; justifiable homicides; and attempts to murder. Justifiable homicides based on the reports of law enforcement agencies are analyzed separately. Deaths from the terrorist attacks of 9/11/01 are not included. Data based solely on police investigation, as opposed to the determination of a court, medical examiner, coroner, jury, or other judicial body]

Year	Number of victims						Rate [1]					
	Total	Male	Female	White	Black	Other	Total	Male	Female	White	Black	Other
1980.......	23,040	17,803	5,237	12,275	9,767	327	10.2	16.1	4.5	6.3	37.7	5.7
1985.......	18,980	14,095	4,885	10,590	7,891	399	7.9	12.2	4.0	5.2	27.6	5.5
1990.......	23,440	18,320	5,121	11,278	11,489	400	9.4	15.1	4.0	5.4	37.6	4.2
1995.......	21,610	16,579	5,030	10,376	10,444	581	8.2	12.7	3.7	4.8	31.6	4.9
1996.......	19,650	15,175	4,475	9,483	9,476	512	7.4	11.5	3.3	4.3	28.3	4.1
1997.......	18,210	14,079	4,132	8,620	8,842	524	6.8	10.5	3.0	3.9	26.0	4.1
1998.......	16,970	12,812	4,158	8,389	7,931	393	6.3	9.5	3.0	3.8	23.0	2.9
1999.......	15,522	11,718	3,804	7,777	7,139	458	5.7	8.6	2.7	3.5	20.5	3.3
2000.......	15,586	11,844	3,742	7,560	7,425	399	5.5	8.6	2.6	3.3	20.3	2.7
2001.......	16,037	12,256	3,782	7,884	7,522	424	5.6	8.8	2.6	3.4	20.2	2.8
2002.......	16,204	12,432	3,772	7,784	7,759	437	5.6	8.8	2.6	3.3	20.6	2.8
2003.......	16,528	12,828	3,700	7,932	7,893	468	5.7	9.0	2.5	3.4	20.7	2.9
2004.......	16,148	12,596	3,552	7,944	7,562	417	5.5	8.7	2.4	3.3	19.6	2.5
2005.......	16,740	13,169	3,571	8,045	8,015	443	5.6	9.0	2.4	3.3	20.5	2.6
2006.......	17,030	13,433	3,597	7,906	8,428	461	5.7	9.1	2.4	3.3	21.3	2.6
2007.......	16,929	13,286	3,643	7,924	8,352	402	5.6	8.9	2.4	3.3	20.9	2.2
2008.......	16,272	12,731	3,541	7,995	7,901	376	5.4	8.5	2.3	3.3	19.6	2.0

[1] Rate is per 100,000 inhabitants.

Source: U.S. Department of Justice, Bureau of Justice Statistics, "Homicide Trends in the United States, 1980–2008." See also <http://bjs.ojp.usdoj.gov/content/homicide/homtrnd.cfm>.

Table 313. Homicide Victims by Race and Sex: 1980 to 2007

[Excludes deaths to nonresidents of United States. Effective with data for 1999, causes of death are classified by The Tenth Revision International Classification of Diseases (ICD-10), replacing the Ninth Revision (ICD-9) used for 1979–98 data. In ICD-9, the category Homicide also includes death as a result of legal intervention. ICD-10 has two separate categories for these two causes of death. Some caution should be used in comparing data. See text, Section 2]

Year	Homicide victims					Homicide rate [2]				
	Total [1]	White		Black		Total [1]	White		Black	
		Male	Female	Male	Female		Male	Female	Male	Female
1980.......	24,278	10,381	3,177	8,385	1,898	10.7	10.9	3.2	66.6	13.5
1985.......	19,893	8,122	3,041	6,616	1,666	8.3	8.2	2.9	48.4	11.0
1990.......	24,932	9,147	3,006	9,981	2,163	10.0	9.0	2.8	69.2	13.5
1995.......	22,895	8,336	3,028	8,847	1,936	8.7	7.8	2.7	56.3	11.1
1996.......	20,971	7,570	2,747	8,183	1,800	7.9	7.0	2.5	51.5	10.2
1997.......	19,846	7,343	2,570	7,601	1,652	7.4	6.7	2.3	47.1	9.3
1998.......	18,272	6,707	2,534	6,873	1,547	6.8	6.1	2.2	42.1	8.6
1999.......	16,889	6,162	2,466	6,214	1,434	6.2	5.6	2.2	37.5	7.8
2000.......	16,765	5,925	2,414	6,482	1,385	6.1	5.3	2.1	38.6	7.5
2001.......	20,308	8,254	3,074	6,780	1,446	7.1	7.2	2.6	38.3	7.4
2002.......	17,638	6,282	2,403	6,896	1,391	6.1	5.4	2.0	38.4	7.0
2003.......	17,732	6,337	2,372	7,083	1,309	6.1	5.4	2.0	38.9	6.6
2004.......	17,357	6,302	2,341	6,839	1,296	5.9	5.3	1.9	37.1	6.4
2005.......	18,124	6,457	2,313	7,412	1,257	6.1	5.4	1.9	39.7	6.2
2006.......	18,573	6,514	2,346	7,677	1,355	6.2	5.4	1.9	40.6	6.6
2007.......	18,361	6,541	2,373	7,584	1,286	6.1	5.4	1.9	39.7	6.2

[1] Includes races not shown separately. [2] Rates per 100,000 resident population in specified group. Based on enumerated population figures as of April 1 for 1980, 1990, and 2000; estimated resident population as of July 1 for other years.

Source: U.S. National Center for Health Statistics, *Deaths: Final Data for 2007*, Vol. 58, No.19, May 2010, and earlier reports. See <http://www.cdc.gov/nchs/products/nvsr.htm>.

Table 314. Forcible Rape—Number and Rate: 1990 to 2009

[For year ending December 31. Forcible rape, as defined in the FBI's Uniform Crime Reporting (UCR) Program, is the carnal knowledge of a female forcibly and against her will. Attempts or assaults to commit rape by force or threat of force are also included; however, statutory rape (without force) and other sex offenses are excluded]

Item	1990 [1]	2000 [1]	2001	2002	2003	2004	2005	2006	2007	2008	2009
NUMBER											
Total................	102,560	90,186	79,365	81,953	80,371	82,835	82,725	83,480	82,000	81,009	81,280
By force	86,541	81,111	71,626	74,570	73,483	76,015	75,930	76,773	75,545	74,901	75,720
Attempt	16,019	9,075	7,739	7,383	6,888	6,820	6,795	6,707	6,455	6,108	5,560
RATE											
Per 100,000 population	41.1	32.0	32.7	32.9	33.10	33.10	32.50	32.10	30.80	30.10	29.80
Per 100,000 females	80.5	62.7	54.7	56.0	54.40	55.60	55.10	55.10	53.60	52.50	52.30

[1] 2001–2009 contain actual reported data; no estimates or annual averages. It is noted that the estimations are considerably higher than actual reported values because estimations are performed against total U.S. population and not just female population.

Source: U.S. Department of Justice, Federal Bureau of Investigation, Uniform Crime Reporting Program, Return A Master Files.

Table 315. Criminal Victimizations and Victimization Rates: 1995 to 2009

[(39,926 represents 39,926,000). Based on National Crime Victimization Survey (NCVS); see text, this section and Appendix III]

Type of crime	Number of victimizations (1,000)				Victimization rates [1]			
	1995	2000	2005	2009	1995	2000	2005	2009
All crimes, total	**39,926**	**25,893**	**23,441**	**20,057**	(X)	(X)	(X)	(X)
Population: Aged 12 or older	*215,709*	*226,805*	*244,505*	*254,106*	*(X)*	*(X)*	*(X)*	*(X)*
Personal crimes [2]	**10,436**	**6,597**	**5,401**	**4,477**	**46.2**	**29.1**	**22.1**	**17.6**
Crimes of violence...............	10,022	6,323	5,174	4,343	44.5	27.9	21.2	17.1
Completed violence...........	2,960	2,044	1,659	1,383	12.9	9.0	6.8	5.4
Attempted/threatened violence ...	7,061	4,279	3,515	2,960	31.6	18.9	14.4	11.6
Rape/sexual assault	363	261	192	126	1.6	1.2	0.8	0.5
Rape/attempted rape...........	252	147	130	88	1.1	0.6	0.5	0.3
Rape	153	92	69	37	0.7	0.4	0.3	0.1
Attempted rape	99	55	61	50	0.4	0.2	0.2	0.2
Sexual assault...............	112	114	62	38	0.5	0.5	0.3	0.2
Robbery......................	1,171	732	625	534	5.3	3.2	2.6	2.1
Completed/property taken.......	753	520	415	368	3.5	2.3	1.7	1.4
With injury...............	224	160	143	153	1.0	0.7	0.6	0.6
Without injury.............	529	360	272	215	2.4	1.6	1.1	0.8
Attempted to take property	418	212	210	166	1.8	0.9	0.9	0.7
With injury...............	84	66	64	63	0.4	0.3	0.3	0.2
Without injury.............	335	146	145	103	1.4	0.6	0.6	0.4
Assault........................	8,487	5,330	4,357	3,684	37.6	23.5	17.8	14.5
Aggravated	2,050	1,293	1,052	823	8.8	5.7	4.3	3.2
With injury...............	533	346	331	313	2.4	1.5	1.4	1.2
Threatened with weapon.......	1,517	946	722	510	6.4	4.2	3.0	2.0
Simple	6,437	4,038	3,305	2,860	28.9	17.8	13.5	11.3
With minor injury	1,426	989	795	638	6.0	4.4	3.3	2.5
Without injury.............	5,012	3,048	2,510	2,222	22.9	13.4	10.3	8.7
Personal theft [3]	414	274	227	133	1.7	1.2	0.9	0.5
Total number of households (1,000)	*101,888*	*108,353*	*117,100*	*122,328*	*(X)*	*(X)*	*(X)*	*(X)*
Property crimes..............	**29,490**	**19,297**	**18,040**	**15,581**	**279.5**	**178.1**	**154.0**	**127.4**
Household burglary..............	5,004	3,444	3,456	3,135	47.4	31.8	29.5	25.6
Completed	4,232	2,909	2,900	2,604	40.0	26.9	24.8	21.3
Attempted forcible entry..........	773	534	556	531	7.4	4.9	4.7	4.3
Motor vehicle theft...............	1,717	937	978	736	16.2	8.6	8.4	6.0
Completed...................	1,163	642	775	570	10.8	5.9	6.6	4.7
Attempted...................	554	295	203	166	5.5	2.7	1.7	1.4
Theft	22,769	14,916	13,606	11,710	215.9	137.7	116.2	95.7
Completed [4].................	21,857	14,300	13,116	11,219	207.6	132.0	112.0	91.7
Attempted...................	911	616	489	491	8.4	5.7	4.2	4.0

X Not applicable. [1] Per 1,000 persons age 12 or older for "Personal crime"; per 1,000 households for "Property crime." [2] The victimization survey cannot measure murder because of the inability to question the victim. [3] Includes pocket picking, purse snatching, and attempted purse snatching. [4] Includes thefts in which the amount taken was not ascertained.

Source: U.S. Department of Justice, Bureau of Justice Statistics, *Criminal Victimization*, 2009, NCJ 231327, October 2010, annual. See also <http://bjs.ojp.usdoj.gov/index.cfm?ty=pbdetail&iid=2217>.

Table 316. Victimization Rates by Type of Crime and Characteristics of the Victim: 2009

[Rate per 1,000 persons age 12 years or older. Based on the National Crime Victimization Survey. See text, this section and Appendix III]

Characteristic of the victim	Personal crimes	Crimes of violence							Personal theft [1]
		Total	Rape/sex-ual assault	Robbery	Assault				
					Total	Aggravated	Simple		
Total	**17.6**	**17.1**	**0.5**	**2.1**	**14.5**	**3.2**	**11.3**		**0.5**
Male..................	18.8	18.4	[2] 0.2	2.7	15.6	4.3	11.3		0.4
Female................	16.5	15.8	0.8	1.6	13.5	2.3	11.2		0.6
12 to 15 years old	37.3	36.8	[2] 0.9	3.1	32.8	6.9	25.9		[2] 0.4
16 to 19 years old	32.3	30.3	[2] 0.6	5.2	24.6	5.3	19.3		[2] 1.9
20 to 24 years old	28.8	28.1	[2] 0.8	3.5	23.8	7.5	16.3		[2] 0.7
25 to 34 years old	22.1	21.5	[2] 0.8	2.8	17.9	4.5	13.4		[2] 0.7
35 to 49 years old	16.3	16.1	[2] 0.4	2.0	13.7	2.6	11.1		[2] 0.2
50 to 64 years old	11.0	10.7	[2] 0.3	1.1	9.3	1.9	7.5		[2] 0.4
65 years old and over ...	3.7	3.2	[2] 0.2	[2] 0.4	2.5	[2] 0.3	2.2		[2] 0.5
White..................	16.3	15.8	0.4	1.6	13.7	2.7	11.0		0.5
Black..................	27.8	26.8	1.2	5.6	19.9	6.8	13.0		[2] 1
Other [3]	9.8	9.8	(Z)	[2] 0.5	9.3	[2] 1.9	7.4		(Z)
Two or more races......	43.3	42.1	(Z)	[2] 5.2	36.9	[2] 9.3	27.5		[2] 1.2
Hispanic...............	18.6	18.1	[2] 0.5	3.4	14.2	3.2	11.0		[2] 0.5
Non-Hispanic...........	17.5	17.0	0.5	1.9	14.6	3.3	11.3		0.5
Household income:									
Less than $7,500........	49.0	47.7	[2] 3.9	7.3	36.5	15.5	21.0		[2] 1.2
$7,500 to $14,999	40.4	40.0	[2] 1.8	5.7	32.6	6.0	26.6		[2] 0.4
$15,000 to $24,999	23.3	22.3	[2] 0.9	3.8	17.6	4.0	13.5		[2] 1.0
$25,000 to $34,999	18.7	18.6	[2] (Z)	2.0	16.6	3.9	12.8		[2] 0.2
$35,000 to $49,999	16.7	16.6	[2] 0.3	2.0	14.3	4.5	9.8		[2] 0.1
$50,000 to $74,999	13.0	12.6	[2] 0.2	[2] 0.9	11.5	2.0	9.5		[2] 0.4
$75,000 or more	12.4	11.5	[2] 0.2	1.1	10.2	2.1	8.1		0.9

Z Rounds to less than 0.05 victimizations per 1,000 persons. [1] Includes pocket picking, completed purse snatching, and attempted purse snatching. [2] Based on 10 or fewer sample cases. [3] Includes American Indians, Alaska Natives, Asians, Native Hawaiians, and other Pacific Islanders.

Source: U.S. Department of Justice, Bureau of Justice Statistics, *Criminal Victimization, 2009*, NCJ 231327, October 2010. See also <http://bjs.ojp.usdoj.gov/index.cfm?ty=pbdetail&iid=2217>.

Table 317. Violent Crimes by Characteristics of Incident: 2009

[In percent, except as indicated. Based on National Crime Victimization Survey; see text, this section, and Appendix III]

Selected characteristics of incident	Number of incidents	Crimes of violence					
		Total	Rape/ sexual assault	Robbery	Assault		
					Total	Aggra-vated [1]	Simple
Total.....................	**4,343,450**	**100**	**100**	**100**	**100**	**100**	**100**
Victim/offender relationship: [2]							
Relatives	523,670	12.1	[3] 6.6	13.3	12.1	[3] 3.7	14.5
Well-known	1,126,240	25.9	39.4	11.5	27.6	27.8	27.5
Casual acquaintance...............	552,530	12.7	[3] 22.4	[3] 2.3	13.9	14.3	13.8
Stranger.......................	1,813,850	41.8	[3] 29.1	56.8	40.0	46.2	38.3
Time of day: [4]							
6 a.m. to 6 p.m...................	2,264,520	54.8	43.9	49.2	56.1	43.0	59.5
6 p.m. to midnight	1,183,920	28.7	[3] 26.8	32.3	28.2	39.0	25.3
Midnight to 6 a.m..................	488,190	11.8	[3] 21.8	13.2	11.2	15.7	10.1
Location of crime:							
At or near victim's home or lodging	1,649,510	40.0	56.2	43.1	38.9	33.5	40.4
Friend's/relative's/neighbor's home	323,110	7.8	[3] 11.2	[3] 5.3	8.1	12.5	6.9
Commercial places	397,910	9.7	[3] 1.6	[3] 6.3	10.4	10.9	10.2
Parking lots/garages	214,000	5.2	[3] 2.5	8.9	4.7	6.0	4.4
School	540,780	13.1	[3] 3.2	[3] 6.9	14.4	6.3	16.5
Streets other than near victim's home ...	575,950	13.9	[3] 11.9	26.7	12.1	20.6	9.9
Other [5]	428,870	10.3	[3] 13.4	2.7	11.8	10.1	11.7
Victim's activity: [6]							
At work or traveling to or from work......	668,280	16.2	[3] 9.8	10.0	(NA)	15.1	17.9
School	576,590	14.0	[3] 8.1	11.3	(NA)	9.7	15.9
Activities at home	1,151,300	27.9	37.1	20.6	(NA)	20.6	30.8
Shopping/errands	206,430	5.0	[3] 2.5	13.1	(NA)	[3] 3.4	4.0
Leisure activities away from home......	901,550	21.8	[3] 21.9	23.1	(NA)	34.8	18.1
Traveling.......................	292,520	7.1	[3] 6.8	13.6	(NA)	9.0	5.4
Other [7]	285,080	6.9	[3] 11.8	7.8	(NA)	6.7	6.6
Distance from victim's home: [8]							
Inside home or lodging	884,320	21.4	51.2	25.1	19.8	11.9	21.9
Near victim's home	749,310	18.1	[3] 10.8	11.0	19.5	18.6	19.7
1 mile or less....................	749,020	18.1	[3] 12.9	28.2	16.8	26.3	14.3
5 miles or less	890,500	21.6	[3] 14.7	17.2	22.5	22.6	22.4
50 miles or less	709,520	17.2	[3] 10.4	15.7	17.6	15.7	18.2
More than 50 miles	127,840	3.1	[3] –	[3] 2.8	3.2	[3] 4.9	2.8
Weapons:							
No weapons present	2,999,560	72.6	84.7	47.5	75.9	11.3	93.2
Weapons present..................	904,820	21.9	[3] 10.3	46.9	18.6	88.2	[3] –

– Represents zero. NA Not available. [1] An aggravated assault is any assault in which an offender possesses or uses a weapon or inflicts serious injury. [2] Excludes "don't know" relationships. [3] Based on 10 or fewer sample cases. [4] Excludes "not known and not available" time of day. [5] Includes areas on public transportation or inside station, in apartment yard, park, field, playground, or other areas. [6] Excludes "don't know" and "not available" victim activity. [7] Includes sleeping. [8] Excludes "don't know" and "not available" distance from victim's home.

Source: U.S. Department of Justice, Bureau of Justice Statistics, *Criminal Victimization, 2009*, NCJ 231327, October 2010. See also <http://bjs.ojp.usdoj.gov/index.cfm?ty=pbdetail&iid=2217>.

Table 318. Violent Crime Between Intimate Partners by Sex of Victims: 2008

[Violence includes rape and sexual assault, robbery, aggravated assault, simple assault and homicide. Intimate partners are defined as spouses, ex-spouses, current boy/girlfriends, and ex-boy/girlfriends. Based on the National Crime Victimization Survey, for 2000 to 2008, and the Federal Bureau of Investigation's (FBI) Uniform Crime Reporting Program's Supplementary Homicide Reports for 2000 to 2007; see text, this section and Appendix III]

Year and type of crime	All persons		Female victims		Male victims	
	Number	Rate per 1,000 [1]	Number	Rate per 1,000 [1]	Number	Rate per 1,000 [1]
2000.....................	684,970	3.0	584,390	5.0	100,580	0.9
2005.....................	519,130	2.1	410,970	3.3	108,160	0.9
2006 [2]	823,360	3.3	665,600	5.3	157,760	1.3
2007.....................	663,780	2.7	587,680	4.6	76,100	0.6
2008, total..............	**652,660**	**2.6**	**551,590**	**4.3**	**101,060**	**0.8**
Rape or sexual assault	44,000	0.2	(B)	(B)	(B)	(B)
Robbery..................	(B)	(B)	(B)	(B)	(B)	(B)
Aggravated assault	111,530	0.4	70,550	0.5	(B)	(B)
Simple assault.............	458,310	1.8	406,530	3.1	51,770	0.4
Homicide	(NA)	(NA)	(NA)	(NA)	(NA)	(NA)

B Base figure too small to meet statistical standards for reliability of derived figure. NA Not available. [1] Rates are the number of victimizations per 1,000 persons. Rates are not available for all categories. Except for Homicide, the number of victimizations is per 100,000 persons aged 12 or older. [2] Due to changes in methodology, the 2006 national crime victimization rates are not comparable to previous years and cannot be used for yearly trend comparisons. However, the overall patterns of victimization at the national level can be examined.

Source: U.S. Department of Justice, Bureau of Justice Statistics, *Female Victims of Violence*, NCJ-228356, September 2009; See also <http://bjs.ojp.usdoj.gov/index.cfm?ty=pbdetail&iid=2020>.

Table 319. Stalking and Harassment Victimization in the United States: 2006

[Survey based on population of persons aged 18 or older. The survey defines stalking as a course of conduct directed at a specific person that would cause a reasonable person to feel fear. The survey characterizes individuals as victims of harassment who experience the behaviors associated with stalking but neither reported feeling fear as a result of such conduct nor experienced actions that would cause a reasonable person to feel fear]

Characteristic	Number			Rate per 1,000 persons		
	All	Stalking	Harassment	All	Stalking	Harassment
All victims [1]	**5,857,030**	**3,424,100**	**2,432,930**	**23.8**	**13.9**	**9.9**
Male.	2,032,460	892,340	1,140,120	16.9	7.4	9.5
Female.	3,824,570	2,531,770	1,292,800	30.3	20.0	10.2
18 to 19 years old	379,610	238,990	140,620	47.2	29.7	17.5
20 to 24 years old	929,710	576,870	352,840	45.7	28.4	17.3
25 to 34 years old	1,198,195	805,260	392,930	30.1	20.2	9.9
35 to 49 years old	1,971,290	1,139,320	831,970	29.9	17.3	12.6
50 to 64 years old	1,046,650	534,870	511,780	20.4	10.4	10.0
65 years old and over . . .	331,580	128,790	202,790	9.3	3.6	5.7
White.	4,835,270	2,860,810	1,974,460	24.1	14.2	9.8
Black.	678,230	363,280	314,950	22.7	12.2	10.5
American Indian/						
Alaska Native	55,890	[2] 33,150	[2] 22,740	33.0	[2] 19.6	[2] 13.4
Asian/Pacific Islander	151,670	79,790	71,890	13.4	7.0	6.4
More than one race [3]	135,960	87,080	48,880	49.3	31.6	17.7
Hispanic origin						
Hispanic.	487,320	312,490	174,830	16.5	10.6	5.9
Non-Hispanic.	5,308,010	3,089,570	2,218,440	24.7	14.4	10.3
Marital status						
Never married	2,143,400	1,321,870	821,530	26.9	16.6	10.3
Married	2,078,830	1,071,630	1,007,200	16.8	8.7	8.1
Divorced or separated. . .	1,363,540	895,620	467,920	51.8	34.0	17.8
Widowed	229,450	107,730	121,720	16.0	7.5	8.5
Household Income						
Less than $7,500.	395,740	266,800	128,940	47.0	31.7	15.3
$7,500 to $14,999	583,840	399,620	184,210	40.1	27.4	12.6
$15,000 to $24,999	724,270	474,220	250,050	32.3	21.1	11.1
$25,000 to $34,999	625,680	362,180	263,500	27.4	15.8	11.5
$35,000 to $49,999	765,580	480,750	284,830	25.2	15.8	9.4
$50,000 to $74,999	877,660	476,420	401,230	23.1	12.6	10.6
$75,000 or more	1,063,860	542,730	521,130	18.8	9.6	9.2

[1] Table excludes missing data. [2] Based on 10 or fewer sample cases. [3] Includes all persons of any race, including persons who identify two or more races.

Source: U.S. Department of Justice, Bureau of Justice Statistics, National Crime Victimization Survey, Supplemental Victimization Survey, *Stalking Victimization in the United States*, Series NCJ-224527, January 2009. See also <http://bjs.ojp.usdoj.gov/index.cfm?ty=dcdetail&iid=245>.

Table 320. Property Crime by Selected Household Characteristics: 2009

[(122,328 represents 122,328,000). Households headed by person aged 12 years or older. Based on National Crime Victimization Survey (NCVS); see text, this section and Appendix III]

Characteristic	Number of house- holds (1,000)	Property crimes							
		Number of victimizations (1,000)				Victimization rate per 1,000 households			
		Total	Burglary	Motor vehicle theft	Theft	Total	Burglary	Motor vehicle theft	Theft
Total	**122,328**	**15,581**	**3,135**	**736**	**11,710**	**127.4**	**25.6**	**6.0**	**95.7**
Race:									
White	99,433	12,320	2,317	536	9,467	123.9	23.3	5.4	95.2
Black	15,798	2,359	639	151	1,569	149.4	40.5	9.6	99.4
Other	5,911	596	103	[1] 36	457	100.8	17.5	[1] 6.1	77.3
Two or more races	1,200	306	75	[1] 13	218	254.8	62.9	[1] 10.5	181.4
Ethnicity:									
Hispanic.	13,852	2,351	451	217	1,683	169.7	32.6	15.7	121.5
Non-Hispanic.	108,164	13,202	2,674	519	10,009	122.1	24.7	4.8	92.5
Household income:									
Less than $7,500.	4,063	817	180	[1] 25	612	201.1	44.4	[1] 6.0	150.7
$7,500 to $14,999	6,770	1,063	314	56	693	157.0	46.3	8.3	102.4
$15,000 to $24,999	10,188	1,442	360	66	1,017	141.6	35.3	6.5	99.8
$25,000 to $34,999	10,327	1,384	334	67	984	134.1	32.3	6.5	95.3
$35,000 to $49,999	13,868	1,937	370	141	1,426	139.7	26.7	10.2	102.8
$50,000 to $74,999	14,819	1,779	286	67	1,425	120.0	19.3	4.5	96.2
$75,000 or more	23,765	2,969	358	101	2,511	124.9	15.1	4.2	105.6
Number of persons in household:									
1.	35,317	3,243	947	131	2,164	91.8	26.8	3.7	61.3
2 or 3	60,992	7,235	1,390	350	5,495	118.6	22.8	5.7	90.1
4 or 5	22,414	4,139	598	192	3,348	184.6	26.7	8.6	149.4
6 or more	3,604	964	200	62	703	267.5	55.4	17.1	195.0

[1] Based on 10 or fewer sample cases.

Source: U.S. Department of Justice, Bureau of Justice Statistics, Criminal Victimization, 2009, NCJ 231327, October 2010, annual, See also <http://bjs.ojp.usdoj.gov/index.cfm?ty=pbdetail&iid=2217>.

Table 321. Robbery and Property Crimes by Type and Average Value Lost: 1990 to 2009

[639 represents 639,000. For year ending December 31]

Characteristic of offense	Number of offenses (1,000)				Rate per 100,000 population				Average value lost (dol.)			
	1990	2000	2005	2009	1990	2000	2005	2009	1990	2000	2005	2009
Robbery, total [1]	**639**	**408**	**417**	**342**	**256.3**	**144.9**	**140.7**	**125.1**	**631**	**1,127**	**1,239**	**1,246**
Type of crime:												
Street or highway	359	188	184	146	144.2	66.7	62.1	53.5	511	858	1,020	865
Commercial house	73	57	60	46	29.5	20.1	20.1	16.9	945	1,685	1,662	1,774
Gas station	18	12	12	8	7.1	4.1	4.0	3.0	423	679	1,104	862
Convenience store	39	26	24	18	15.6	9.3	8.0	6.7	344	566	677	717
Residence	62	50	59	58	25.1	17.7	20.0	21.1	828	1,243	1,332	1,674
Bank	9	9	9	7	3.8	3.1	3.0	2.7	2,885	4,379	4,113	4,202
Weapon used:												
Firearm	234	161	175	131	94.1	57.0	59.0	55.3	(NA)	(NA)	(NA)	(NA)
Knife or cutting instrument	76	36	37	24	30.7	12.8	12.5	9.9	(NA)	(NA)	(NA)	(NA)
Other weapon	61	53	39	27	24.5	18.9	13.2	11.3	(NA)	(NA)	(NA)	(NA)
Strong-arm	268	159	166	126	107.7	56.4	56.0	53.3	(NA)	(NA)	(NA)	(NA)
Burglary, total	**3,074**	**2,050**	**2,154**	**1,955**	**1,232.2**	**728.4**	**726.7**	**715.7**	**1,014**	**1,458**	**1,771**	**2,087**
Forcible entry [2]	2,150	1,297	1,310	1,224	864.5	460.7	440.0	448.1	(NA)	(NA)	(NA)	(NA)
Unlawful entry [2]	678	615	701	655	272.8	218.7	237.5	239.7	(NA)	(NA)	(NA)	(NA)
Attempted forcible entry [2]	245	138	133	129	98.7	49.0	45.2	47.4	(NA)	(NA)	(NA)	(NA)
Residence [2]	2,033	1,335	1,417	1,127	817.4	474.3	477.9	412.9	1,037	1,378	1,813	2,709
Nonresidence [2]	1,041	715	738	407	418.5	254.1	248.8	148.8	967	1,610	1,687	2,521
Occurred during the night [2]	1,135	699	708	625	456.4	248.3	238.9	229.0	(NA)	(NA)	(NA)	(NA)
Occurred during the day [2]	1,151	836	890	910	462.8	297.2	328.8	332.8	(NA)	(NA)	(NA)	(NA)
Larceny-theft, total	**7,946**	**6,972**	**6,783**	**5,560**	**3,185.1**	**2,477.3**	**2,286.3**	**2,035.1**	**426**	**727**	**857**	**865**
Pocket picking	81	36	29	24	32.4	12.7	9.8	8.8	384	437	346	489
Purse snatching	82	37	42	27	32.8	13.2	14.2	9.8	228	387	404	440
Shoplifting	1,291	959	940	1,002	519.1	340.7	317.0	366.9	104	185	184	178
From motor vehicles	1,744	1,754	1,752	1,520	701.3	623.3	590.6	556.5	461	692	704	737
Motor vehicle accessories	1,185	677	693	501	476.3	240.6	233.6	183.2	297	451	482	528
Bicycles	443	312	249	187	178.2	110.9	83.9	67.6	188	273	267	345
From buildings	1,118	914	852	620	449.4	324.6	287.3	226.8	673	1,184	1,738	1,233
From coin-operated machines	63	46	41	22	25.4	16.2	13.8	8.1	144	272	232	348
Other	1,940	2,232	2,184	1,660	780.0	793.0	736.1	607.5	615	957	1,137	1,439
Motor vehicles, total [3]	**1,636**	**1,160**	**1,236**	**731**	**655.8**	**412.2**	**417.4**	**258.6**	**5,117**	**6,581**	**6,204**	**6,495**
Automobiles	1,304	877	907	527	524.3	311.5	304.5	193.0	(NA)	(NA)	(NA)	(NA)
Trucks and buses	238	209	219	205	95.5	74.1	76.2	74.9	(NA)	(NA)	(NA)	(NA)

NA Not available. [1] Includes other crimes, not shown separately. [2] Unknown data not included. [3] Includes other types of motor vehicles, not shown separately.
Source: U.S. Department of Justice, Federal Bureau of Investigation, Uniform Crime Reports, Return A and Supplement to Return A Master Files.

U.S. Census Bureau, Statistical Abstract of the United States: 2012

Table 322. Hate Crimes—Number of Incidents, Offenses, Victims, and Known Offenders by Bias Motivation: 2000 to 2008

[The FBI collected statistics on hate crimes from 14,422 law enforcement agencies representing over an estimated 278 million people in 2009. Not all law enforcement agencies participated in the Hate Crimes Statistics Proigram. Hate crime offenses cover incidents motivated by race, religion, sexual orientation, ethnicity/national origin, and disability. See Source and Appendix III]

Bias motivation	Incidents reported	Offenses	Victims [1]	Known offenders [2]
2000.	8,213	9,619	10,117	7,690
2005.	7,163	8,380	8,804	6,804
2009, total	**6,604**	**7,789**	**8,336**	**6,225**
Bias motive:				
Race, total	**3,199**	**3,816**	**4,057**	**3,241**
Anti-White	545	652	668	753
Anti-Black	2,284	2,724	2,902	2,160
Anti-American Indian/Alaska native	65	84	87	88
Anti-Asian/Pacific Islander	126	147	149	108
Anti-multiracial group	179	209	251	132
Ethnicity/national origin, total	**777**	**1,050**	**1,109**	**934**
Anti-Hispanic	483	654	692	649
Anti-other ethnicity/national origin	294	396	417	285
Religion, total	**1,303**	**1,376**	**1,575**	**586**
Anti-Jewish	931	964	1,132	353
Anti-Catholic	51	55	59	25
Anti-Protestant	38	40	42	17
Anti-Islamic	107	128	132	95
Anti-other religious group	109	119	131	51
Anti-multi-religious group	57	60	68	38
Anti-atheism/agnosticism/etc.	10	10	11	7
Sexual orientation, total	**1,223**	**1,436**	**1,482**	**1,394**
Anti-male homosexual	682	798	817	817
Anti-female homosexual	185	216	227	197
Anti-homosexual	312	376	391	349
Anti-heterosexual	21	21	21	14
Anti-bisexual	23	25	26	17
Disability, total	**96**	**97**	**99**	**64**
Anti-physical	25	25	25	25
Anti-mental	71	72	74	39
Multiple bias [3]	**6**	**14**	**14**	**6**

[1] The term "victim" may refer to a person, business, institution, or a society as a whole. [2] The term "known offender" does not imply that the identity of the suspect is known, but only that an attribute of the suspect has been identified which distinguishes him/her from an unknown offender. [3] In a "multiple-bias incident" two conditions must be met: more than one offense type must occur in the incident and at least two offense types must be motivated by different biases.

Source: U.S. Department of Justice, Federal Bureau of Investigation, "Hate Crime Statistics, 2009," <http://www2.fbi.gov/ucr/hc2009/index.html>.

Table 323. Hate Crimes by Bias Motivation and Location of Incident: 2009

[See headnote, Table 322]

Location	Total incidents	Bias motivation					Multiple-bias incidents [1]
		Race	Religion	Sexual orientation	Ethnicity/ national origin	Disability	
Total	6,604	3,199	1,303	1,223	777	96	6
Air/bus/train terminal	55	29	9	13	2	2	–
Bank/savings and loan	8	3	1	2	1	1	–
Bar/nightclub	133	59	2	62	10	0	–
Church/synagogue/temple	283	41	229	9	2	2	–
Commercial office building	123	55	38	16	11	3	–
Construction site	13	6	3	1	3	–	–
Convenience store	64	32	9	5	18	–	–
Department/discount store	59	37	10	8	4	–	–
Drug store/Doctor's office/hospital	50	27	16	2	5	–	–
Field/woods	95	59	10	11	12	3	–
Government/public building	108	60	23	12	12	1	–
Grocery/supermarket	44	24	6	2	11	1	–
Highway/road/alley/street	1,135	602	92	261	169	11	–
Hotel/motel/etc.	35	21	2	6	6	–	–
Jail/prison	48	28	5	10	4	1	–
Lake/waterway	12	5	–	4	3	–	–
Liquor store	12	6	1	1	4	–	–
Parking lot/garage	403	212	36	84	64	7	–
Rental storage facility	7	5	1	–	1	–	–
Residence/home	2,070	1,064	324	381	253	46	2
Restaurant	107	53	10	27	16	–	1
School/college	754	396	168	123	64	2	1
Service/gas station	42	17	2	7	15	1	–
Specialty store (TV, furniture, etc.)	64	31	19	8	6	–	–
Other/unknown	877	327	287	168	80	15	–
Multiple locations	3	–	–	–	1	–	2

– Represents zero. [1] See footnote 3, Table 322.

Source: U.S. Department of Justice, Federal Bureau of Investigation, "Hate Crime Statistics, 2009," <http://www2.fbi.gov/ucr/hc2009/index.html>.

Law Enforcement, Courts, and Prisons **205**

Table 324. Arrests by Sex and Age: 2009

[In thousands (11,062.6 represents 11,062,600) For year ending December 31. Based on Uniform Crime Reporting (UCR) Program. Represents arrests reported (not charged) by 12,910 agencies with a total population of 247,526,916 as estimated by the FBI. Some persons may be arrested more than once during a year, therefore, the data in this table, in some cases, could represent multiple arrests of the same person. See text, this section and source]

Offense charged	Total			Male			Female		
	Total	Under 18 years	18 years and over	Total	Under 18 years	18 years and over	Total	Under 18 years	18 years and over
Total	**11,062.6**	**1,540.0**	**9,522.6**	**8,263.3**	**1,071.6**	**7,191.7**	**2,799.2**	**468.3**	**2,330.9**
Violent crime	**467.9**	**69.1**	**398.8**	**380.2**	**56.5**	**323.7**	**87.7**	**12.6**	**75.2**
Murder and nonnegligent manslaughter	10.0	0.9	9.1	9.0	0.9	8.1	1.1	–	1.0
Forcible rape	17.5	2.6	14.9	17.2	2.5	14.7	–	–	–
Robbery	102.1	25.5	76.6	90.0	22.9	67.1	12.1	2.5	9.5
Aggravated assault	338.4	40.1	298.3	264.0	30.2	233.8	74.4	9.9	64.5
Property crime	**1,396.4**	**338.7**	**1,057.7**	**875.9**	**210.8**	**665.1**	**608.2**	**127.9**	**392.6**
Burglary	240.9	60.3	180.6	205.0	53.4	151.7	35.9	6.9	29.0
Larceny-theft	1,080.1	258.1	822.0	608.8	140.5	468.3	471.3	117.6	353.6
Motor vehicle theft	65.6	16.0	49.6	53.9	13.3	40.7	11.7	2.7	8.9
Arson	9.8	4.3	5.5	8.1	3.7	4.4	1.7	0.6	1.1
Other assaults	1,061.3	175.3	886.1	785.4	115.4	670.0	276.0	59.9	216.1
Forgery and counterfeiting	68.9	1.7	67.2	42.9	1.2	41.7	26.0	0.5	25.5
Fraud	173.7	5.1	168.5	98.4	3.3	95.0	75.3	1.8	73.5
Embezzlement	14.6	–	14.1	7.2	–	6.9	7.4	–	7.2
Stolen property [1]	84.3	15.1	69.2	66.7	12.2	54.5	17.6	2.8	14.7
Vandalism	217.4	72.7	144.7	178.1	62.8	115.3	39.3	9.9	29.4
Weapons; carrying, possessing, etc.	132.9	27.1	105.8	122.1	24.3	97.8	10.8	2.8	8.0
Prostitution and commercialized vice	56.9	1.1	55.8	17.3	–	17.1	39.6	0.8	38.7
Sex offenses [2]	61.5	10.7	50.7	56.1	9.6	46.5	5.4	1.1	4.3
Drug abuse violations	1,333.0	136.6	1,196.4	1,084.3	115.2	969.1	248.7	21.4	227.3
Gambling	8.2	1.4	6.8	7.2	1.4	5.9	0.9	–	0.9
Offenses against the family and children	92.4	3.7	88.7	68.9	2.4	66.6	23.4	1.3	22.1
Driving under the influence	1,158.5	109.2	1,147.5	895.8	8.2	887.6	262.7	2.7	260.0
Liquor laws	48.2	90.2	368.0	326.8	55.4	271.4	131.4	34.7	96.6
Drunkenness	488.1	11.4	476.8	406.8	8.5	398.3	81.3	2.9	78.4
Disorderly conduct	529.5	136.1	393.3	387.1	90.8	296.2	142.4	45.3	97.1
Vagrancy	26.6	2.2	24.4	20.9	1.6	19.3	5.7	0.6	5.1
All other offenses (except traffic)	306.1	263.4	2,800.8	2,337.1	194.2	2,142.9	727.0	69.2	657.9
Suspicion	1.6	–	1.4	1.2	–	1.0	–	–	–
Curfew and loitering law violations	91.0	91.0	(X)	63.1	63.1	(X)	28.0	28.0	(X)
Runaways	75.8	75.8	(X)	34.0	34.0	(X)	41.8	41.8	(X)

– Represents zero. X Not applicable. [1] Buying, receiving, possessing stolen property. [2] Except forcible rape and prostitution.
Source: U.S. Department of Justice, Federal Bureau of Investigation, Uniform Crime Reports, Arrests Master Files.

Table 325. Arrests by Race: 2009

[Based on Uniform Crime Reporting (UCR) Program. Represents arrests reported (not charged) by 12,371 agencies with a total population of 239,839,971 as estimated by the FBI. See headnote, Table 324]

Offense charged	Total	White	Black	American Indian/Alaskan Native	Asian Pacific Islander
Total	**10,690,561**	**7,389,208**	**3,027,153**	**150,544**	**123,656**
Violent crime	**456,965**	**268,346**	**177,766**	**5,608**	**5,245**
Murder and nonnegligent manslaughter	9,739	4,741	4,801	100	97
Forcible rape	16,362	10,644	5,319	169	230
Robbery	100,496	43,039	55,742	726	989
Aggravated assault	330,368	209,922	111,904	4,613	3,929
Property crime	**1,364,409**	**922,139**	**406,382**	**17,599**	**18,289**
Burglary	234,551	155,994	74,419	2,021	2,117
Larceny-theft	1,056,473	719,983	306,625	14,646	15,219
Motor vehicle theft	63,919	39,077	23,184	817	841
Arson	9,466	7,085	2,154	115	112
Other assaults	1,032,502	672,865	332,435	15,127	12,075
Forgery and counterfeiting	67,054	44,730	21,251	345	728
Fraud	161,233	108,032	50,367	1,315	1,519
Embezzlement	13,960	9,208	4,429	75	248
Stolen property; buying, receiving, possessing	82,714	51,953	29,357	662	742
Vandalism	212,173	157,723	48,746	3,352	2,352
Weapons—carrying, possessing, etc.	130,503	74,942	53,441	951	1,169
Prostitution and commercialized vice	56,560	31,699	23,021	427	1,413
Sex offenses [1]	60,175	44,240	14,347	715	873
Drug abuse violations	1,301,629	845,974	437,623	8,588	9,444
Gambling	8,046	2,290	5,518	27	211
Offenses against the family and children	87,232	58,068	26,850	1,690	624
Driving under the influence	1,105,401	954,444	121,594	14,903	14,460
Liquor laws	444,087	373,189	50,431	14,876	5,591
Drunkenness	469,958	387,542	71,020	8,552	2,844
Disorderly conduct	515,689	326,563	176,169	8,783	4,174
Vagrancy	26,347	14,581	11,031	543	192
All other offenses (except traffic)	2,929,217	1,937,221	911,670	43,880	36,446
Suspicion	1,513	677	828	1	7
Curfew and loitering law violations	89,578	54,439	33,207	872	1,060
Runaways	73,616	48,343	19,670	1,653	3,950

[1] Except forcible rape and prostitution.
Source: U.S. Department of Justice, Federal Bureau of Investigation, "Crime in the United States, Arrests," September 2010, <http://www.fbi.gov/ucr/cius2009/arrests/index.html>.

Table 326. Juvenile Arrests for Drug Abuse Offenses: 1980 to 2009

[For year ending December 31. Juveniles are persons under 18 years of age. Some persons may be arrested more than once during a year. Therefore, this table could, in some cases, represent multiple arrests of the same person]

Offense	1980	1990	2000	2003	2004	2005	2006	2007	2008	2009
Drug arrests, total	**86,685**	**66,300**	**146,594**	**134,746**	**135,056**	**137,809**	**145,153**	**143,270**	**134,661**	**130,317**
Sale and manufacturing	13,004	24,575	26,432	21,987	21,136	21,607	22,466	21,493	19,467	18,840
Heroin/cocaine	1,318	17,511	11,000	7,848	7,852	7,863	8,261	7,334	6,288	4,975
Marijuana	8,876	4,372	11,792	10,463	9,743	9,845	10,333	10,640	9,678	9,871
Synthetic narcotics	465	346	945	1,043	1,119	1,071	1,262	1,162	1,093	1,170
Dangerous nonnarcotic drugs	2,345	2,346	2,695	2,633	2,422	2,828	2,610	2,357	2,408	2,824
Possession	73,681	41,725	120,432	112,759	113,920	116,202	122,687	121,777	115,194	111,477
Heroin/cocaine	2,614	15,194	12,586	9,932	10,805	11,131	12,024	9,756	7,944	6,208
Marijuana	64,465	20,940	95,962	87,909	87,717	88,909	95,120	97,671	93,042	90,927
Synthetic narcotics	1,524	1,155	2,052	2,872	3,279	3,235	3,337	3,142	3,286	3,385
Dangerous nonnarcotic drugs	5,078	4,436	9,832	12,046	12,119	12,927	12,206	11,208	10,922	10,957

Source: U.S. Department of Justice, Federal Bureau of Investigation Uniform Crime Reports, Arrests Master File.

Table 327. Drug Arrest Rates for Drug Abuse Violations, 1990 to 2005, and by Region: 2009

[Rate per 100,000 population. For year ending December 31. Based on Census Bureau estimated resident population as of July 1, except 1990 and 2000, enumerated as of April 1. For composition of regions, see map, inside front cover]

Offense	1990	2000	2005	2009 Total	2009 Region North-east	2009 Region Mid-west	2009 Region South	2009 Region West
Drug arrest rate, total	**435.3**	**587.1**	**600.9**	**416.0**	**382.5**	**295.3**	**425.8**	**538.9**
Sale and/or manufacture	139.0	122.7	109.9	76.9	85.4	57.9	76.9	87.9
Heroin or cocaine [1]	93.7	60.8	47.8	29.5	48.6	15.0	29.1	28.7
Marijuana	26.4	34.2	29.6	25.2	24.4	26.1	21.7	30.4
Synthetic or manufactured drugs	2.7	6.4	8.6	7.5	5.5	3.9	13.2	3.3
Other dangerous nonnarcotic drugs	16.2	21.3	23.9	14.8	6.9	12.9	13.0	25.5
Possession	296.3	464.4	490.9	339.1	297.1	237.4	348.9	451.0
Heroin or cocaine [1]	144.4	138.7	131.5	72.8	71.8	31.6	71.9	113.5
Marijuana	104.9	244.4	228.9	190.0	179.5	157.7	216.5	186.1
Synthetic or manufactured drugs	6.6	12.0	21.0	15.6	10.8	11.4	21.3	14.2
Other dangerous nonnarcotic drugs	40.4	69.4	109.6	60.7	35.0	36.6	39.2	137.3

[1] Includes other derivatives such as morphine, heroin, and codeine.
Source: U.S. Department of Justice, Federal Bureau of Investigation, Uniform Crime Reports, Arrests Master Files and unpublished data.

Table 328. Federal Drug Arrests and Seizures by Type of Drug: 2000 to 2010

[For fiscal years ending in year shown. The data have all been revised. In years past, the data for the amount of drugs seized at the Federal level was obtained from the Federal-wide Drug Seizure System (FDSS). A new system has been created called the National Seizure System (NSS). This system will broaden the scope of data collected for the amount of drugs seized (in pounds) at the national level. The data for "Seizure in (pounds)" for years shown are from NSS]

Drug	2000	2003	2004	2005	2006	2007	2008	2009	2010
Number of Arrests, total [1, 2]	**36,845**	**26,021**	**26,863**	**28,118**	**27,326**	**27,493**	**25,783**	**27,115**	**27,200**
Heroin	3,622	2,527	2,491	2,453	2,361	2,169	2,610	3,063	2,991
Cocaine	16,375	11,389	11,979	13,045	13,104	12,885	12,168	11,738	10,726
Cannabis [3]	8,572	6,032	6,312	6,115	6,003	6,887	6,271	7,511	8,108
Methamphetamine	8,276	6,073	6,081	6,505	5,858	5,552	4,734	4,803	5,375
Seizure in (pounds), total	**1,451,412**	**3,746,766**	**3,248,585**	**2,907,197**	**3,007,207**	**3,973,738**	**3,397,766**	**4,575,249**	**4,499,621**
Cocaine	61,051	106,530	104,836	112,076	142,859	124,713	108,838	127,789	137,823
Heroin	1,590	5,968	4,159	4,005	4,404	3,633	4,114	4,941	6,234
Cannabis [3]	1,383,189	3,622,057	3,126,441	2,777,560	2,847,150	3,832,127	3,271,081	4,428,160	4,333,348
Methamphetamine	5,582	12,211	13,149	13,556	12,794	13,265	13,733	14,359	22,216

[1] Domestic Arrests are for the Drug Enforcement Administration only. [2] Includes other drug-related arrests not shown. [3] Includes Hashish.
Source: U.S. Drug Enforcement Administration, "Stats and Facts," <www.usdoj.gov/dea/statistics.html>, and unpublished data from the National Seizure System (NSS).

Table 329. Background Checks for Firearm Transfers: 1994 to 2009

[In thousands (12,740 represents 12,740,000), except rates. The Brady Handgun Violence Prevention Act (Brady Act) requires a background check on an applicant for a firearm purchase from a dealer who is a Federal Firearms Licensee]

Inquiries and rejections	Interm period 1994–1998 [1]	Permanent Brady [2]									
		2000	2001	2002	2003	2004	2005	2006	2007	2008	2009
Applications and denials:											
Applications received.........	12,740	7,699	7,958	7,806	7,831	8,084	8,278	8,612	8,658	9,901	10,764
Applications denied..........	312	153	151	136	126	126	132	135	136	147	150
Denied (percent)...........	2.4	2.0	1.9	1.7	1.6	1.6	1.6	1.6	1.6	1.5	1.4
Selective reasons for rejection:											
Felony indictment/conviction ...	44	88	87	65	53	53	57	52	49	77	67
Other....................	18	65	64	71	73	73	75	83	87	70	83
Felony denials per 1,000 applications......	(NA)	11.4	10.9	8.3	6.8	6.6	6.9	6.0	5.7	7.2	6.2

NA Not available. [1] Background checks on applicants were conducted by state and local agencies, mainly on handgun transfers. See "Presale Handgun Checks, the Brady Interim Period, 1994–98" (NCJ 175034). [2] The period beginning November 30, 1998 is the effective date for the Brady Handgun Violence Prevention Act, P.L. 103–159, 1993. The National Instant Criminal Background Check System (NICS) began operations. Checks on handgun and long gun transfers are conducted by the Federal Bureau of Investigation (FBI), and by state and local agencies. Totals combine Firearm Inquiry Statistics (FIST) estimates for state and local agencies with transactions and denials reported by the FBI.

Source: U.S. Department of Justice, Office of Justice Programs, Bureau of Justice Statistics, "Background Checks for Firearm Transfers—Statistical Tables, 2009," Series NCJ 231679, October 2010. See also <http://bjs.ojp.usdoj.gov /index.cfm?ty=pbdetail&iid=1706>.

Table 330. Law Enforcement Officers Killed and Assaulted: 1990 to 2009

[The statistics presented in this table are based on information collected by the staff of the FBI's Law Enforcement Officers Killed and Assaulted (LEOKA) Program from law enforcement agencies throughout the Nation and U.S. Territories. It contains statistics on line-of-duty felonious deaths, accidental deaths, and assaults of duly sworn local, state, tribal, and federal law enforcement officers. For composition of regions, see map, inside front cover]

Item	1990	1995	2000	2004	2005	2006	2007	2008	2009
OFFICERS KILLED									
Total killed	132	133	134	139	122	114	141	109	96
Geographical region:									
Northeast....................	13	16	13	18	12	12	13	14	13
Midwest.....................	20	19	32	25	23	20	20	14	14
South.......................	68	63	67	66	58	48	78	52	42
West	23	32	19	24	24	31	28	26	25
Puerto Rico..................	8	2	3	5	5	3	1	2	2
Island Areas, foreign countries ...	–	1	–	1	–	–	1	1	–
Total feloniously killed	65	74	51	57	55	48	58	41	48
Firearms	56	63	47	54	50	46	56	35	45
Handgun	47	44	33	36	42	36	39	25	28
Rifle.....................	8	14	10	13	3	8	8	6	15
Shotgun..................	1	5	4	5	5	2	8	4	2
Type of firearm not reported ...	–	–	–	–	–	–	1	–	–
Blunt instrument.............	–	–	–	–	–	–	–	–	–
Bomb......................	–	8	–	–	–	–	–	2	–
Knife/cutting instrument........	3	1	1	1	–	–	–	–	–
Personal weapons [1]..........	2	–	–	–	–	–	–	–	–
Vehicle....................	1	2	3	2	5	2	2	4	3
Other......................	3	–	–	–	–	–	–	–	–
Total accidentally killed	67	59	83	82	67	66	83	68	48
OFFICERS ASSAULTED									
Population covered (1,000) [2]	197,426	191,759	204,599	226,273	222,874	227,361	234,734	238,731	243,764
Number of—									
Reporting agencies	9,343	8,503	8,940	10,589	10,119	10,596	10,973	10,835	11,451
Officers employed	410,131	428,379	452,531	501,462	489,393	504,147	523,944	541,906	556,155
Total assaulted.............	72,091	57,762	58,398	59,692	57,820	59,396	61,257	61,087	57,268
Firearm	3,651	2,354	1,749	2,114	2,157	2,290	2,216	2,292	1,994
Knife/cutting instrument........	1,647	1,356	1,015	1,123	1,059	1,055	1,028	958	880
Other dangerous weapon	7,423	6,414	8,132	8,645	8,379	8,611	8,692	8,466	7,801
Personal weapons [1]...........	59,370	47,638	47,502	47,810	46,225	47,440	49,321	49,371	46,593

– Represents zero. [1] Includes hands, fists, feet, etc. [2] Represents the number of persons covered by agencies shown.
Source: U.S. Department of Justice, Federal Bureau of Investigation, Crime Statistics Management Unit, LEOKA Program.

Table 331. U.S. Supreme Court—Cases Filed and Disposition: 1980 to 2010

[Statutory term of court begins first Monday in October]

Action	1980	1990	1995	2000	2005	2007	2008	2009	2010
Total cases on docket	**5,144**	**6,316**	**7,565**	**8,965**	**9,608**	**9,602**	**8,966**	**9,302**	**9,066**
Appellate cases on docket.	2,749	2,351	2,456	2,305	2,025	1,969	1,941	1,908	1,895
From prior term	527	365	361	351	354	355	345	328	337
Docketed during present term	2,222	1,986	2,095	1,954	1,671	1,614	1,596	1,580	1,558
Cases acted upon	2,324	2,042	2,130	2,024	1,703	1,666	1,654	1,607	1,618
Granted review	167	114	92	85	63	85	78	69	76
Denied, dismissed, or withdrawn.	1,999	1,802	1,945	1,842	1,554	1,529	1,505	1,452	1,461
Summarily decided	90	81	62	63	46	30	29	45	45
Cases not acted upon	425	309	326	281	322	303	287	301	277
Pauper cases on docket	2,371	3,951	5,098	6,651	7,575	7,628	7,021	7,388	7,167
Cases acted upon [1]	2,027	3,436	4,514	5,736	6,533	6,753	6,214	6,524	6,250
Granted review	17	27	13	14	15	10	9	8	14
Denied, dismissed, or withdrawn.	1,968	3,369	4,439	5,658	6,459	6,562	6,136	6,465	6,195
Summarily decided	32	28	55	61	58	175	65	46	37
Cases not acted upon	344	515	584	915	1,042	875	807	864	917
Original cases on docket	24	14	11	9	8	5	4	6	4
Cases disposed of during term	7	3	5	2	4	1	1	2	2
Total cases available for argument. . . .	**264**	**201**	**145**	**138**	**122**	**125**	**136**	**125**	**131**
Cases disposed of.	162	131	93	89	87	78	88	86	88
Cases argued	154	125	90	86	88	75	87	82	86
Cases dismissed or remanded without argument	8	6	3	3	1	3	1	4	2
Cases remaining	102	70	52	49	31	47	48	40	43
Cases decided by signed opinion	144	121	87	83	82	72	83	77	83
Cases decided by per curiam opinion	8	4	3	4	5	2	3	4	3
Number of signed opinions	123	112	75	77	69	67	74	73	75

[1] Includes cases granted review and carried over to next term, not shown separately.

Source: Office of the Clerk, Supreme Court of the United States, unpublished data.

Table 332. Judicial Officers and Judicial Caseloads for the Federal Judiciary: 2000 to 2010

[For 12 month period ending June 30]

Judicial caseload	2000	2005	2006	2007	2008	2009	2010
U.S. Courts of Appeals:							
Cases filed.	54,642	67,999	68,313	58,809	59,406	59,399	56,097
Cases terminated	56,509	59,577	67,772	63,916	59,152	60,144	59,343
Cases pending.	40,815	57,349	57,996	51,849	52,478	50,954	47,708
U.S. District Courts Civil:							
Cases filed.	263,049	282,758	244,343	272,067	256,354	257,204	285,215
Cases terminated	260,277	280,455	264,734	249,960	230,930	255,361	295,909
Cases pending.	247,973	266,938	245,667	260,769	295,414	298,493	[1] 287,799
Criminal (includes transfers):							
Cases filed.	62,523	69,876	67,872	67,503	70,024	75,324	78,213
Defendants filed.	84,147	92,356	89,956	88,006	91,782	96,718	100,031
Cases terminated	57,543	65,239	67,448	67,791	69,008	74,478	77,633
Cases pending.	46,796	70,692	72,417	73,419	75,566	78,186	78,766
U.S. Bankruptcy Courts:							
Cases filed.	1,276,922	1,637,254	1,484,570	751,056	967,831	1,306,315	1,572,597
Cases terminated	1,271,300	1,583,959	1,821,396	862,382	929,206	1,109,993	1,441,419
Cases pending.	1,396,916	1,748,038	1,423,342	1,312,016	1,325,220	1,527,073	1,658,318
Post-conviction supervision:							
Persons under supervision	99,577	113,008	113,697	115,930	120,051	123,839	126,642
Pretrial services:							
Total cases activated	86,067	98,946	99,508	95,955	98,862	103,610	110,666
Pretrial services cases activated . . .	84,107	97,045	97,800	94,384	97,315	102,434	109,711
Pretrial diversion cases activated. . .	1,960	1,901	1,708	1,571	1,547	1,176	965
Total released on supervision.	31,607	34,348	33,816	32,361	32,460	29,937	29,748
Pretrial supervision.	31,927	32,438	32,112	30,865	31,089	28,754	28,440
Diversion supervision	2,166	1,910	1,704	1,496	1,371	1,183	1,308

[1] Data have been revised.

Source: Administrative Office of the United States Courts, *Statistical Tables for the Federal Judiciary*, <http://www.uscourts.gov/Statistics/StatisticalTablesForTheFederalJudiciary.aspx>.

U.S. Census Bureau, Statistical Abstract of the United States: 2012

Table 333. U.S. District Courts—Civil Cases Filed, Terminated, and Pending by Basis of Jurisdiction and Nature of Suit: 2009 and 2010

[For years ending June 30]

Type of case	Cases filed		Cases terminated		Cases pending	
	2009	2010	2009	2010	2009	2010
Cases total [1]	**257,204**	**285,215**	**255,361**	**295,909**	**297,257**	**287,799**
BASIS OF JURISDICTION						
U.S. cases:						
U.S. plaintiff	9,030	8,427	9,569	8,849	7,672	7,099
U.S. defendant	33,286	34,306	33,348	32,358	30,259	31,763
Private cases:						
Federal question	133,697	137,776	133,684	137,889	137,309	135,724
Diversity of citizenship	81,188	104,703	78,758	116,807	121,955	113,205
NATURE OF SUIT						
Contract actions [1]	35,229	31,461	35,828	33,643	30,019	27,467
Recovery of overpayments [2]	3,214	3,079	3,245	3,088	1,625	1,551
Real property actions [1]	5,413	6,809	5,170	6,153	4,719	5,448
Foreclosure	2,639	3,836	2,277	3,103	1,599	2,291
Tort actions	61,936	87,256	60,584	98,184	116,918	109,939
Personal injury	57,332	82,057	56,612	93,158	111,747	104,803
Personal injury product liability [1]	43,055	66,958	40,772	78,754	86,662	79,230
Other personal injury [1]	14,277	15,099	15,840	14,404	25,085	25,573
Medical malpractice	1,076	1,120	1,142	1,127	1,274	1,256
Personal property damage	4,604	5,199	3,972	5,026	5,171	5,136
Actions under statutes [1]	154,572	159,683	153,688	157,897	145,512	144,925
Bankruptcy suits	2,334	2,615	2,588	2,352	1,570	1,767
Civil rights [1]	33,188	34,427	32,156	33,351	35,629	36,226
Employment	13,778	14,343	13,714	13,875	15,500	15,786
Environmental matters	735	826	718	903	1,236	1,146
Prisoner petitions	52,237	51,748	52,254	52,074	46,080	44,787
Forfeiture and penalty	2,322	2,297	2,471	2,332	2,066	1,990
Labor laws	17,153	18,878	17,298	18,527	14,954	15,112
Immigration	2,166	1,853	1,689	1,553	852	896
Protected property rights [3]	8,714	8,519	9,452	8,487	8,234	8,105
Securities commodities and exchanges	1,720	1,442	1,781	1,938	3,469	2,891
Social security laws	13,222	13,725	13,143	13,277	13,216	13,581
Tax suits	1,411	1,171	1,452	1,337	1,306	1,124
Freedom of information	279	315	273	313	370	367
Other actions	54	6	91	32	89	20

[1] Includes other types not shown separately. [2] Includes enforcement of judgments in student loan cases, and overpayments of veterans' benefits. [3] Includes copyright, patent, and trademark rights.
Source: Administrative Office of the United States Courts, "Statistical Tables for the Federal Judiciary,"
<http://www.uscourts.gov/Statistics/StatisticalTablesForTheFederalJudiciary.aspx>.

Table 334. U.S. Courts of Appeals—Nature of Suit or Offense in Cases Arising From the U.S. District Courts: 2000 to 2010

[For 12-month periods ending June 30. Excludes data for the U.S. Court of Appeals for the Federal Circuit. Includes appeals reopened, remanded, and reinstated (after being terminated due to procedural defaults) as well as original appeals]

Nature of suit and offense	2000	2005	2006	2007	2008	2009	2010
Total cases	**46,682**	**48,907**	**47,743**	**43,789**	**43,671**	**45,490**	**43,880**
Criminal cases	10,570	15,831	15,426	13,583	13,011	14,259	12,863
Civil cases	36,112	33,076	32,317	30,206	30,660	31,231	31,017
U.S cases	8,707	9,055	8,791	7,541	7,688	8,536	7,772
U.S. plaintiff	615	356	359	387	386	382	435
U.S. defendant	8,092	8,699	8,432	7,154	7,302	8,154	7,337
Private cases	27,405	24,021	23,526	22,665	22,972	22,695	23,245
Federal question	24,155	21,000	20,826	19,998	20,289	20,044	20,599
Diversity of citizenship	3,239	3,020	2,698	2,664	2,678	2,651	2,646
General local jurisdiction	11	1	–	3	5	–	–
Criminal cases	10,570	15,831	15,426	13,583	13,011	14,259	12,863
Violent offenses	683	768	805	703	637	653	621
Property offenses	1,520	1,974	1,788	1,626	1,585	1,526	1,624
Drug offenses	4,388	5,962	5,966	5,237	5,125	6,519	5,066
Firearms, explosives offenses	1,029	2,488	2,404	2,057	1,947	1,997	1,927
Sex offenses	190	403	491	520	611	657	651
Justice system offenses	179	216	201	185	166	172	142
Immigration offenses	1,109	2,888	2,635	2,198	1,663	1,644	1,787
General offenses	579	553	573	574	484	432	411
Other	893	579	563	483	793	659	1,045

– Represents or rounds to zero.
Source: Administrative Office of the United States Courts, "Statistical Tables for the Federal Judiciary,"
<http://www.uscourts.gov/Statistics/StatisticalTablesForTheFederalJudiciary.aspx>.

U.S. Census Bureau, Statistical Abstract of the United States: 2012

Table 335. Total Incoming Caseloads in State Trial Courts by Case Category: 2008

[Represents total incoming caseloads (i.e., new filings, plus reopened and reactivated cases when provided) as reported to the Court Statistics Project for 2008. Some figures may be incomplete and/or overinclusive. Since state court caseload statistics should only be viewed in the context of each state's court structure, comparisons of the data reported here should not be made without additional information]

State	Total	Civil [1]	Domestic relations [2]	Criminal [3]	Juvenile [4]	Traffic/ violations [5]
United States	**106,091,588**	**19,400,641**	**5,665,558**	**21,264,621**	**2,078,773**	**57,681,995**
Alabama	2,091,345	224,447	90,902	275,075	59,012	1,441,909
Alaska	155,868	25,616	13,034	39,414	2,853	74,951
Arizona	2,907,386	343,888	133,695	763,038	21,355	1,645,410
Arkansas	1,453,913	140,867	51,655	580,700	25,357	655,334
California	9,552,781	1,163,889	443,531	1,724,310	148,920	6,072,131
Colorado	1,023,124	324,301	51,197	187,796	22,157	437,673
Connecticut	887,407	260,218	36,118	167,483	30,611	392,977
Delaware	546,659	65,265	40,090	402,491	8,062	30,751
District of Columbia	125,549	69,104	12,466	36,018	4,407	3,554
Florida	5,431,345	1,419,204	503,648	1,503,985	196,204	1,808,304
Georgia	3,478,995	1,029,507	161,156	649,760	117,371	1,521,201
Hawaii	607,461	32,116	13,282	112,209	18,063	431,791
Idaho	488,252	82,253	22,549	133,695	16,150	233,605
Illinois.	4,301,942	642,701	140,183	512,133	29,248	2,977,677
Indiana.	2,041,939	512,956	104,980	307,275	59,584	1,057,144
Iowa.	1,049,323	184,370	44,179	91,962	12,215	716,597
Kansas.	977,869	195,021	38,117	57,866	20,025	666,840
Kentucky	1,048,240	284,899	84,059	251,252	43,850	384,180
Louisiana	1,908,961	288,155	56,528	364,760	45,264	1,154,254
Maine.	282,265	43,593	15,144	71,218	4,809	147,501
Maryland	2,335,335	1,014,391	100,127	310,788	40,007	870,022
Massachusetts.	912,769	424,672	135,878	51,940	44,760	255,519
Michigan	4,397,286	824,665	124,925	1,012,366	59,787	2,375,543
Minnesota	1,541,192	236,782	47,886	176,570	53,287	1,026,667
Mississippi	121,134	69,439	50,881	(NA)	814	(NA)
Missouri.	2,222,379	318,115	108,767	189,227	15,270	1,591,000
Montana.	362,368	64,779	13,318	52,247	2,420	229,604
Nebraska.	475,496	119,386	26,305	141,814	12,623	175,368
Nevada	920,049	187,511	56,395	156,489	26,275	493,379
New Hampshire.	212,535	54,519	5,641	77,774	2,206	72,395
New Jersey	7,859,400	918,527	233,652	757,009	76,420	5,873,792
New Mexico.	424,844	93,370	39,739	114,182	7,576	169,977
New York	4,492,488	1,852,112	669,874	749,317	76,389	1,144,796
North Carolina	3,472,479	591,007	134,273	1,853,505	40,945	852,749
North Dakota	187,330	33,727	17,071	39,962	9,806	86,764
Ohio.	4,130,751	915,127	243,594	901,902	166,671	1,903,457
Oklahoma	579,951	209,142	37,432	110,209	15,706	207,462
Oregon.	611,641	202,283	45,318	93,433	17,152	253,455
Pennsylvania	3,926,852	463,311	370,109	553,290	63,302	2,476,840
Rhode Island	230,096	67,518	12,010	42,283	9,878	98,407
South Carolina.	2,540,989	346,478	58,486	823,309	16,617	1,296,099
South Dakota.	251,819	58,416	13,946	28,410	11,787	139,260
Tennessee	483,341	70,240	86,445	173,196	136,178	17,282
Texas	13,303,834	913,184	378,271	2,565,242	49,235	9,397,902
Utah.	852,682	133,650	22,052	121,922	50,570	524,488
Vermont.	191,072	25,545	21,034	17,862	2,042	124,589
Virginia.	4,172,951	1,017,606	347,319	1,163,226	100,315	1,544,485
Washington	2,637,545	307,898	66,323	358,463	46,364	1,858,497
West Virginia	428,779	81,166	52,903	144,496	9,571	140,643
Wisconsin	1,018,228	300,005	52,644	144,501	19,748	501,330
Wyoming	186,057	36,782	1,222	30,592	1,708	115,753
Puerto Rico	247,292	116,918	35,205	76,655	7,827	10,687

NA Not available. [1] Includes tort, contract, real property, small claims, probate, mental health, and civil appeals cases.
[2] Includes divorce/dissolution, paternity, custody, support, visitation, adoption, and civil protection/restraining order cases. [3] Includes felony, misdemeanor, and appeals from limited jurisdiction courts. [4] Includes delinquency, dependency, and status offense petitions.
[5] Includes non-criminal traffic violations (infractions), parking violations, and ordinance violations.

Source: National Center for State Courts, "State Court Caseload Statistics, An Analysis of 2008 State Court Caseloads," November 2010, <http://www.courtstatistics.org>.

Law Enforcement, Courts, and Prisons 211

Table 336. U.S. District Courts—National Petit and Grand Juror Service: 2006 to 2010

[For years ending September 30. Includes data on jury selection days only. Data on juror service after the selection day are not included]

Juror service	2006	2007	2008	2009	2010
PETIT JUROR SERVICE					
Jurors present for jury selection or orientation.	323,928	307,204	297,820	282,668	262,376
Percent selected	24.5	23.3	23.0	22.2	22.7
Percent challenged	38.8	38.6	39.8	37.9	38.5
Percent not selected or challenged	36.7	38.1	37.3	39.9	38.7
Voir Dire [1]	24.5	24.0	24.2	24.9	24.9
Non-Voir Dire [2]	13.7	13.3	13.2	15.0	13.9
Total juries selected.	6,839	6,139	6,039	5,378	5,332
GRAND JUROR SERVICE					
Juries serving	758	733	749	766	784
Sessions convened	9,399	9,279	9,357	9,257	9,277
Jurors in session	187,646	185,083	186,586	186,194	186,020
Average per session	20.0	19.9	19.9	20.1	20.1
Hours in session	45,718	45,197	44,731	44,676	44,845
Average per session	4.9	4.9	4.8	4.8	4.8

[1] Jurors who completed pre-screening questionaires or were in the courtroom during the conducting of voir dire. [2] Other jurors not selected or challenged who were not called to the courtroom or otherwise did not participate in the actual voir dire.

Source: Administrative Office of the United States Courts, *Judicial Business of the United States Courts*, annual. See also <http://www.uscourts.gov/Statistics/JudicialBusiness.aspx>.

Table 337. Fraud and Identity Theft—Consumer Complaints by State: 2010

[Rate per 100,000 population. As of December 31. Rates based on 2010 Census results. The Consumer Sentinel Network (CSN) is a secure online database of consumer complaints available only to law enforcement. Based on unverified complaints reported by consumers. Excludes complaints outside of the United States and excludes North Carolina Department of Justice, Idaho and Mississippi Attorneys General, and the Minnesota Department of Public Safety]

State	Fraud and other complaints [1]		Identity theft victims [1]		State	Fraud and other complaints [1]		Identity theft victims [1]	
	Number	Rate	Number	Rate		Number	Rate	Number	Rate
U.S.	**1,088,411**	**352.5**	**250,854**	**81.2**	MO.	19,175	320.2	3,920	65.5
AL	13,457	281.5	3,339	69.9	MT	3,108	314.1	392	39.6
AK	2,731	384.5	342	48.2	NE	5,005	274.0	860	47.1
AZ	23,999	375.5	6,549	102.5	NV	10,757	398.3	2,423	89.7
AR	6,712	230.2	1,667	57.2	NH	4,702	357.2	503	38.2
CA	124,072	333.0	38,148	102.4	NJ	27,227	309.7	6,807	77.4
CO	21,012	417.8	3,961	78.8	NM	6,053	294.0	1,773	86.1
CT	10,054	281.3	2,330	65.2	NY	52,113	268.9	16,494	85.1
DE	3,255	362.5	664	73.9	NC	27,415	287.5	5,986	62.8
DC	3,374	560.7	923	153.4	ND	1,235	183.6	199	29.6
FL	70,858	376.9	21,581	114.8	OH	32,847	284.7	6,844	59.3
GA	31,225	322.3	9,404	97.1	OK	10,038	267.6	2,234	59.6
HI	4,479	329.3	589	43.3	OR	13,508	352.6	2,256	58.9
ID	4,674	298.2	729	46.5	PA	38,024	299.3	9,025	71.0
IL	37,691	293.8	10,345	80.6	RI	2,865	272.2	579	55.0
IN	17,962	277.0	3,560	54.9	SC	12,982	280.7	2,726	58.9
IA	6,397	210.0	1,111	36.5	SD	1,766	216.9	200	24.6
KS	8,177	286.6	1,717	60.2	TN	19,271	303.7	4,175	65.8
KY	10,184	234.7	1,847	42.6	TX	71,164	283.0	24,158	96.1
LA	11,953	263.7	2,896	63.9	UT	8,151	294.9	1,488	53.8
ME	3,343	251.7	425	32.0	VT	1,654	264.3	245	39.2
MD	23,581	408.4	4,784	82.9	VA	28,369	354.6	5,065	63.3
MA	18,936	289.2	4,044	61.8	WA	24,627	366.2	4,646	69.1
MI.	27,111	274.3	6,880	69.6	WV	4,249	229.3	750	40.5
MN	14,770	278.5	2,612	49.2	WI	14,716	258.8	2,553	44.9
MS	6,473	218.1	1,992	67.1	WY	1,652	293.1	290	51.5

[1] Includes non-U.S. residents and people who did not report residence.

Source: U.S. Federal Trade Commission, *Consumer Sentinel Network Data Book*, for January–December 2010, March 2011, <http://www.ftc.gov/sentinel/reports.shtml>.

Table 338. Federal Prosecutions of Public Corruption: 1990 to 2009

[As of Dec. 31. Prosecution of persons who have corrupted public office in violation of Federal Criminal Statutes]

Prosecution status	1990			2000			2005			2009		
	Charged	Con-victed	Await-ing trial	Charged	Con-victed	Await-ing trial	Charged	Con-victed	Await-ing trial	Charged	Con-victed	Await-ing trial
Total [1]	1,176	1,084	300	1,000	938	327	1,163	1,027	451	1,082	1,061	473
Federal officials . . .	615	583	103	441	422	92	445	390	118	425	426	107
State officials	96	79	28	92	91	37	96	94	51	93	102	57
Local officials.	257	225	98	211	183	89	309	232	148	270	257	148
Others involved . . .	208	197	71	256	242	109	313	311	134	294	276	161

[1] Includes individuals who are neither public officials nor employees, but were involved with public officials or employees in violating the law, not shown separately.

Source: U.S. Department of Justice, Criminal Division, *Report to Congress on the Activities and Operations of the Public Integrity Section*. See also <http://www.justice.gov/criminal/pin/>.

Table 339. Financial Crimes: 2003 to 2009

[For the year ending September 30. The FBI focuses its financial crimes investigations on such criminal activities as corporate fraud, securities and commodities fraud, health care fraud, financial institution fraud, mortgage fraud, insurance fraud, mass marketing fraud, and money laundering]

Type of financial fraud	Unit indicator	2003	2004	2005	2006	2007	2008	2009
Corporate fraud:								
Cases pending...........	Number.....	279	332	423	486	529	545	592
Indictments...........	Number.....	150	192	178	176	183	160	161
Convictions...........	Number.....	143	126	150	134	181	134	162
Restitution...........	Bil. dol.....	–	0.4	5.6	1.1	12.6	8.2	6.1
Recoveries...........	1,000 dol....	37.0	28.0	68.0	41,400.0	27,400.0	6,590.0	16,100.0
Fines...........	Mil. dol.....	3.0	117.1	122.4	14.2	38.6	193.7	5.3
Seizures...........	Mil. dol.....	(NA)	20.8	12.6	82.4	70.1	9.3	40.6
Securities/Commodities fraud:								
Cases pending...........	Number.....	937	987	1,139	1,165	1,217	1,210	1510
Indictments...........	Number.....	358	393	327	320	408	359	412
Convictions...........	Number.....	320	305	363	279	321	302	309
Restitution...........	Bil. dol.....	1.6	0.9	2.3	2.1	1.5	3.0	2.1
Recoveries...........	Mil. dol.....	28.6	13.0	76.3	20.6	25.4	43.7	47.3
Fines...........	Mil. dol.....	16.7	12.5	14.8	80.7	202.8	128.5	7.4
Seizures...........	Mil. dol.....	(NA)	11.9	281.9	41.8	83.0	77.5	85.0
Insurance fraud:								
Cases pending...........	Number.....	326	289	270	233	209	177	152
Indictments...........	Number.....	111	100	72	56	39	73	43
Convictions...........	Number.....	172	77	79	66	47	60	42
Restitution...........	Mil. dol.....	101.9	121.6	171.7	30.4	27.6	553.7	22.9
Recoveries...........	1,000 dol....	115.0	34,200.0	913.0	14.0	21.0	10,400.0	31,400.0
Fines...........	1,000 dol....	810.0	330.0	112.0	212.0	447.0	31.0	138.0
Seizures...........	Mil. dol.....	0.3	15.7	10.7	3.5	15.9	25.3	2.2
Mass marketing fraud:								
Cases pending...........	Number.....	236	192	161	147	127	100	92
Indictments...........	Number.....	94	66	28	15	13	50	9
Convictions...........	Number.....	93	64	43	46	11	23	23
Restitution...........	Mil. dol.....	154.2	23.0	503.8	273.2	30.6	4.2	4.4
Recoveries...........	1,000 dol....	125.0	1,900.0	4.0	468.0	542.0	173.0	–
Fines...........	1,000 dol....	4,900.0	11,100.0	362.0	86,900.0	121.0	23.0	2.1
Seizures...........	Mil. dol.....	9.6	1.8	8.1	12.7	(Z)	–	(Z)
Health care fraud:								
Cases pending...........	Number.....	2,262	2,468	2,547	2,423	2,493	2,434	2,494
Indictments...........	Number.....	523	693	589	588	847	851	982
Convictions...........	Number.....	414	564	550	535	642	707	674
Restitution...........	Bil. dol.....	1.1	1.0	1.1	0.4	1.1	1.1	1.3
Recoveries...........	Mil. dol.....	10.0	28.8	115.0	1,600.0	439.8	102.4	517.1
Fines...........	Mil. dol.....	78.8	543.0	42.4	172.8	33.7	25.6	68.9
Seizures...........	Mil. dol.....	79.7	60.4	52.7	28.9	86.1	48.3	55.7
Money laundering:								
Cases pending...........	Number.....	496	509	507	473	443	404	350
Indictments...........	Number.....	105	127	126	264	140	114	63
Convictions...........	Number.....	61	69	91	112	115	134	96
Restitution...........	Mil. dol.....	13.2	282.9	313.0	17.1	69.4	222.4	81.9
Recoveries...........	Mil. dol.....	2.9	0.8	9.3	3.2	2.7	20.9	0.6
Fines...........	Mil. dol.....	2.4	0.9	0.3	0.4	11.4	34.1	1.5
Seizures...........	Mil. dol.....	8.2	5.1	7.8	6.4	10.9	24.2	4.5
Mortgage fraud:								
Cases pending...........	Number.....	(NA)	(NA)	721	881	1,211	1,644	2,794
Indictments...........	Number.....	(NA)	(NA)	93	138	328	574	822
Convictions...........	Number.....	(NA)	(NA)	60	123	283	354	494
Restitution...........	Mil. dol.....	(NA)	(NA)	151.2	308.3	600.6	825.2	2,540.0
Recoveries...........	Mil. dol.....	(NA)	(NA)	(Z)	1.2	21.8	3.3	7.5
Fines...........	Mil. dol.....	(NA)	(NA)	44.0	300.8	1.6	3.1	58.4
Seizures...........	Mil. dol.....	(NA)	(NA)	(NA)	(NA)	5.1	6.6	5.0
Suspicious Activity Reports (SARs) [1,2]								
Mortgage fraud related—								
Number of violations:								
Mortgage fraud...........	Number.....	6,936	17,127	21,994	35,617	46,717	63,713	67,190
Commercial loan...........	Number.....	1,850	1,724	2,126	2,409	3,240	4,189	4,514
False statement...........	Number.....	4,569	6,784	11,611	21,023	28,692	37,622	38,159
Dollars losses reported on:								
Mortgage fraud SARs...........	Bil. dol.....	0.2	0.4	1.0	0.9	0.8	1.5	2.8
Reported on commercial loan SARs....	Bil. dol.....	1.0	1.1	0.7	0.5	1.0	1.9	1.7
False statement SARs...........	Bil. dol.....	0.4	0.5	1.0	1.4	0.8	2.5	2.1

– Represents zero. NA Not available. Z represents a value less than 50 thousand. [1] Reports filed by federally-insured financial institutions. [2] SARs are cataloged according to the year in which they are submitted and the information contained within them may describe activity that occurred in previous month or years.

Source: U.S. Department of Justice, Federal Bureau of Investigation, *Financial Crimes Report to the Public* and *2009 Mortgage Fraud Report, Year in Review*. See also <http://www.fbi.gov/stats-services/publications/financial-crimes-report-2009 /financial-crimes-report-2009> and <http://www.fbi.gov/stats-services/publications/mortgage-fraud-2009>.

Table 340. Delinquency Cases Disposed by Juvenile Courts by Type of Offense: 1990 to 2008

[In thousands (1,337 represents 1,337,000), except rate. A delinquency offense is an act committed by a juvenile for which an adult could be prosecuted in a criminal court. Disposition of a case involves taking a definite action such as waiving the case to criminal court, dismissing the case, placing the youth on probation, placing the youth in a facility for delinquents, or such actions as fines, restitution, and community service]

Type of offense	1990	1995	1999	2000	2001	2002	2003	2004	2005	2006	2007	2008
All delinquency offenses ...	**1,337**	**1,800**	**1,730**	**1,710**	**1,687**	**1,678**	**1,687**	**1,689**	**1,696**	**1,647**	**1,658**	**1,653**
Case rate [1]	52.1	62.9	57.2	55.6	54.2	53.5	53.5	53.5	53.7	52.3	53.2	53.6
Person offenses [2]	256	398	405	397	402	403	410	417	431	413	410	403
Criminal homicide	2	3	2	1	1	1	1	1	1	1	1	1
Forcible rape	4	6	4	4	4	4	4	4	4	4	4	4
Robbery	28	42	26	22	21	21	21	21	25	29	31	33
Aggravated assault	53	73	54	51	49	47	48	49	51	50	49	48
Property offenses [2]	776	901	723	697	660	653	643	630	611	586	600	617
Burglary	146	149	124	116	112	110	110	104	101	105	106	109
Larceny-theft	344	429	327	322	299	298	291	289	273	245	260	281
Motor vehicle theft	70	53	38	38	38	38	38	34	32	29	27	23
Arson	7	10	9	9	9	9	8	9	8	9	8	8
Drug law violations	71	161	183	186	190	183	183	184	184	181	184	180
Public order offenses [2]	233	340	418	431	436	439	451	458	471	466	464	454
Obstruction of justice	88	135	201	214	213	209	215	210	212	212	213	212
Disorderly conduct	56	91	100	106	111	119	123	131	137	131	131	127
Weapons offenses	30	47	37	34	33	32	34	39	43	44	41	39
Liquor law violations	18	17	19	25	24	24	25	25	24	25	26	24
Nonviolent sex offenses	11	10	13	14	14	14	14	14	13	12	12	12

[1] Number of cases disposed per 1,000 juveniles (ages 10 to upper age of juvenile court jurisiction). The upper age of juvenile court jurisdiction is defined by statute in each state. [2] Total include other offenses not shown.

Source: National Center for Juvenile Justice, Pittsburgh, PA, Juvenile Court Statistics, annual. See also <http://ojjdp.ncjrs.gov/ojstatbb/default.asp>.

Table 341. Delinquency Cases Disposed by Juvenile Courts by Type of Offense, Sex, and Race: 1995 to 2008

[See headnote, Table 340]

Sex, race, and offense	Number of cases disposed				Case rate [1]			
	1995	2000	2005	2008	1995	2000	2005	2008
Male, total	**1,396,000**	**1,275,600**	**1,229,300**	**1,203,600**	**94.7**	**80.9**	**76.0**	**76.2**
Person	300,500	286,400	302,500	284,400	20.4	18.2	18.7	18.0
Property	699,800	519,300	442,800	443,900	47.5	32.9	27.4	28.1
Drugs	138,200	155,100	147,700	148,100	9.4	9.8	9.1	9.4
Public order	257,500	314,800	336,200	327,200	17.5	20.0	20.8	20.7
Female, total	**404,200**	**434,700**	**466,700**	**449,700**	**28.9**	**29.1**	**30.3**	**29.9**
Person	99,200	110,800	128,100	118,900	7.1	7.4	8.3	7.9
Property	204,100	177,300	168,000	172,800	14.6	11.9	10.9	11.5
Drugs	23,600	30,400	35,900	31,400	1.7	2.0	2.3	2.1
Public order	77,200	116,100	134,800	126,700	5.5	7.8	8.8	8.4
White, total	**1,209,700**	**1,164,300**	**1,085,500**	**1,043,600**	**52.9**	**48.2**	**44.3**	**43.6**
Person	237,400	248,200	244,800	226,400	10.4	10.3	10.0	9.5
Property	646,800	488,900	412,500	405,900	28.3	20.2	16.8	17.0
Drugs	106,400	136,300	134,400	131,200	4.7	5.6	5.5	5.5
Public order	219,100	291,000	293,900	280,100	9.6	12.0	12.0	11.7
Black, total	**541,400**	**496,300**	**561,300**	**563,500**	**124.3**	**102.6**	**108.4**	**113.1**
Person	152,300	138,900	175,100	167,100	35.0	28.7	33.8	33.5
Property	228,900	183,000	177,500	191,200	52.6	37.9	34.3	38.4
Drugs	52,600	44,900	44,300	43,500	12.1	9.3	8.5	8.7
Public order	107,500	129,500	164,400	161,600	24.7	26.8	31.8	32.4
American Indian, total	**26,200**	**26,000**	**25,000**	**23,500**	**69.6**	**57.0**	**54.5**	**53.7**
Person	5,200	5,300	5,700	5,200	13.7	11.7	12.4	11.9
Property	15,200	12,700	10,200	9,400	40.2	27.8	22.2	21.4
Drugs	1,500	2,500	2,900	2,700	4.0	5.5	6.3	6.2
Public order	4,400	5,500	6,200	6,200	11.8	12.1	13.6	14.2
Asian, total	**22,900**	**23,600**	**24,100**	**22,700**	**20.5**	**18.3**	**17.1**	**15.5**
Person	4,800	4,800	5,000	4,500	4.3	3.7	3.6	3.1
Property	13,100	12,000	10,600	10,200	11.8	9.3	7.5	6.9
Drugs	1,200	1,900	2,100	2,000	1.1	1.4	1.5	1.4
Public order	3,700	4,900	6,500	6,000	3.3	3.8	4.6	4.0

[1] Cases per 1,000 juveniles (aged 10 to 17).

Source: National Center for Juvenile Justice, Pittsburgh, PA, Juvenile Court Statistics, annual. See also <http://ojjdp.ncjrs.gov/ojstatbb/default.asp>.

Table 342. Child Abuse and Neglect Victims by Selected Characteristics: 2000 to 2009

[Based on State submissions to National Child Abuse and Neglect Data System (NCANDS) of alleged child abuse and neglect. NCANDS collects case level data on children who received child protective services response in the form of an investigative or alternative response. Each state has its own definition of child abuse and neglect based on standards set by federal law. Child abuse is defined as any recent act or failure to act on the part of a parent or caretaker which results in death, serious physical or emotional harm, sexual abuse or exploitation; or an act or failure to act which presents an imminent risk or serious harm. See source for more information]

Item	2000		2005		2008		2009	
	Number	Percent	Number	Percent	Number	Percent	Number	Percent
TYPES OF MALTREATMENT [1]								
Victims, total [2]	864,837	116.5	900,642	113.1	773,792	115.0	762,940	116.2
Neglect	517,118	59.8	566,277	62.9	549,399	71.0	548,508	71.9
Physical abuse.............	167,713	19.4	149,328	16.6	125,971	16.3	124,863	16.4
Sexual abuse..............	87,770	10.2	83,786	9.3	71,162	9.2	67,032	8.8
Emotional maltreatment.......	66,965	7.7	63,438	7.0	55,236	7.1	53,326	7.0
Medical neglect	25,498	3.0	17,653	2.0	16,783	2.2	17,133	2.2
Other and unknown	146,184	16.9	137,946	15.3	71,237	9.2	75,561	9.9
SEX OF VICTIM [3]								
Victims, total [2]	864,837	100.0	882,239	100.0	770,868	100.0	762,940	99.4
Male....................	413,744	47.8	426,019	48.3	373,889	48.5	368,380	48.3
Female..................	446,230	51.6	456,220	51.7	396,979	51.5	389,936	51.1
AGE OF VICTIM [3]								
Victims, total [2]	864,837	100.0	881,058	100.0	770,907	100.0	760,607	100.0
1 year and younger	133,094	15.4	154,399	17.3	150,866	19.6	148,834	19.6
2 to 5 years old	205,790	23.8	222,387	24.7	194,342	25.2	196,650	25.9
6 to 9 years old	212,186	24.5	193,089	21.4	168,055	21.8	163,500	21.5
10 to 13 years old	176,071	20.4	171,776	19.0	135,838	17.6	132,560	17.4
14 to 17 years old	126,207	14.6	138,934	15.4	121,164	15.7	118,407	15.6
18 years old and over	992	0.1	473	0.1	642	0.1	656	0.1

[1] A child may be a victim of more than one maltreatment. Therefore, the total for this item adds up to more than 100 percent. [2] Duplicate count of child victims counts a child each time he or she was found to be a victim. [3] Unknown data not shown.

Source: U.S. Department of Health and Human Services, Administration for Children and Families, Administration on Children, Youth and Families, Children's Bureau, *Child Maltreatment 2009,* annual. See also <http://www.acf.hhs.gov/programs/cb/stats_research/index.htm#can>.

Table 343. Child Abuse and Neglect Cases Reported, Investigated, and Number of Child Victims by State: 2009

[See headnote, Table 342. Duplicate counts of child victims]

State and outlying area	Population under 18 years old	Number of reports [1]	Number of children subject of an investi- gation [2][3]	Number of child victims [3]	State and outlying area	Population under 18 years old	Number of reports [1]	Number of children subject of an investi- gation [2][3]	Number of child victims [3]
U.S.	75,512,062	2,000,488	3,635,686	762,940	MT	219,828	8,148	13,901	1,628
AL	1,128,864	18,651	27,629	8,295	NE	451,641	13,532	31,375	5,448
AK	183,546	6,100	10,752	3,959	NV	681,033	12,241	25,192	4,708
AZ	1,732,019	32,136	75,064	3,922	NH	289,071	7,880	11,649	984
AR	709,968	30,381	64,124	10,556	NJ	2,045,848	55,909	86,379	9,293
CA	9,435,682	235,812	449,388	79,799	NM	510,238	14,535	23,277	5,368
CO	1,227,763	33,978	52,510	11,881	NY	4,424,083	168,658	282,373	90,031
CT	807,985	24,937	36,946	9,756	NC	2,277,967	67,652	138,229	24,506
DE	206,993	5,862	13,936	2,071	ND	143,971	3,886	6936	1254
DC	114,036	6,593	16,710	3,407	OH	2,714,341	78,098	119306	34,084
FL	4,057,773	153,733	339,289	49,078	OK	918,849	29,408	51,809	7,621
GA	2,583,792	28,095	67,686	23,921	OR	872,811	28584	46,592	11802
HI	290,361	2,871	5,404	2,072	PA	2,775,132	25,839	25,839	4,084
ID	419,190	6,966	11,027	1,634	RI	226,825	6,110	9,319	3,065
IL	3,177,377	68,591	150,304	29,836	SC	1,080,732	17,721	40,966	12,707
IN	1,589,365	67,505	104,677	24,108	SD	199,616	3,920	7,186	1,513
IA	713,155	24,940	38,623	13,007	TN	1,493,252	57,143	90,857	9,186
KS	704,951	17,942	26,645	1,363	TX	6,895,969	170,576	292,109	69,169
KY	1,014,323	47,633	73,029	17,470	UT	868,824	20,534	32,518	13,706
LA	1,123,386	22,804	37,255	9,660	VT	126,275	3,215	4,109	762
ME	271,176	6,288	10,596	4,073	VA	1,847,182	30,364	62,596	6,068
MD	1,351,935	28,929	41,611	16,771	WA	1,569,592	30,405	44,900	6,560
MA	1,433,002	42,447	84,424	38,958	WV	386,449	22,249	50,280	5,473
MI	2,349,892	75,441	188,341	32,463	WI	1,310,250	25,543	37,550	4,947
MN	1,260,797	17,678	25,083	4,961	WY	132,025	2,669	5,541	727
MS	767,742	19,717	31,284	7,883					
MO	1,431,338	49,755	71,849	5,451	PR	963,847	19,884	40,712	11,891

[1] Once an allegation of abuse and neglect is received by a child protective services agency (CPS), it is either screened in for further attention by CPS agency or it is screened out. A screened-in referral is called a report. [2] The number of "Children Subject of an Investigation" is based on the total number of children who were included in an investigation or assessment. [3] Maltreatment acted upon by a CPS agency in the form of an investigative or alternative response.

Source: U.S. Department of Health and Human Services, Administration for Children and Families, Administration on Children, Youth and Families, Children's Bureau, *Child Maltreatment 2009,* annual. See also <http://www.acf.hhs.gov/programs/cb/stats_research/index.htm#can>.

Table 344. Employment by State and Local Law Enforcement Agencies by Type of Agency and Employee: 2008

[As of September 30. Based on census of all state and local law enforcement agencies operating nationwide, conducted every 4 years]

Type of agency	Number of agencies	Number of employees					
		Full-time			Part-time		
		Total	Sworn	Civilian	Total	Sworn	Civilian
Total [1]	**17,985**	**1,133,905**	**765,237**	**368,668**	**100,340**	**44,062**	**56,278**
Local police	12,501	593,003	461,054	131,949	58,129	27,810	30,319
Sheriffs' offices	3,063	353,461	182,979	170,482	26,052	11,334	14,718
Primary State.	50	93,148	60,772	32,376	947	54	893
Special jurisdiction.	1,733	90,262	56,968	33,294	14,681	4,451	10,230
Constable/marshal.	638	4,031	3,464	567	531	413	118

[1] Excludes agencies with less than one full-time officer or the equivalent in part-time officers.
Source: U.S. Bureau of Justice Statistics, "Census of State and Local Law Enforcement Agencies, 2008," <http://bjs.ojp.usdoj.gov/index.cfm?ty=dcdetail&iid=249>.

Table 345. State and Local Government Expenditures Per Capita by Criminal Justice Function and State: 2007

[In dollars. Based on Census Bureau's Annual Government Finance Survey and Annual Survey of Public Employment. Based on Census Bureau resident population as of July 1. See Appendix III]

State	Total justice system	Police protec-tion	Judicial and legal	Correc-tions	State	Total justice system	Police protec-tion	Judicial and legal	Correc-tions
Total.	**633**	**279**	**129**	**225**	Missouri	452	238	78	136
Alabama	463	211	87	165	Montana.	539	215	134	189
Alaska	980	347	280	353	Nebraska	471	202	85	184
Arizona	709	322	143	243	Nevada	803	385	159	259
Arkansas	400	169	73	158	New Hampshire. . .	443	225	93	125
California	963	381	236	347	New Jersey	747	353	159	235
Colorado	618	278	98	243	New Mexico	686	304	143	239
Connecticut	626	259	177	189	New York	861	393	176	291
Delaware	835	346	181	309	North Carolina. . . .	485	225	67	193
District of Columbia . . .	1,373	851	139	384	North Dakota	402	166	96	140
Florida	697	345	119	232	Ohio.	538	258	139	142
Georgia	552	224	96	232	Oklahoma	467	200	83	185
Hawaii	613	239	220	154	Oregon.	628	259	104	265
Idaho	483	200	102	180	Pennsylvania	579	215	119	245
Illinois.	566	317	104	146	Rhode Island	640	311	120	209
Indiana.	400	175	71	154	South Carolina. . . .	416	205	61	150
Iowa	444	197	101	146	South Dakota	426	171	79	176
Kansas.	480	244	98	138	Tennessee	467	221	91	154
Kentucky	402	148	98	155	Texas	505	220	88	198
Louisiana	647	277	128	242	Utah	509	217	113	179
Maine.	397	176	79	142	Vermont	508	228	97	183
Maryland	744	317	132	296	Virginia.	574	247	101	226
Massachusetts.	634	282	153	199	Washington	577	219	113	245
Michigan	572	233	104	236	West Virginia	412	148	114	151
Minnesota	555	272	121	162	Wisconsin	611	267	100	244
Mississippi	416	196	72	148	Wyoming	836	335	174	327

Source: U.S. Department of Justice, Bureau of Justice Statistics, "Justice Expenditure and Employment Extracts 2007," Series NCJ 231540, September 2010, <http://bjs.ojp.usdoj.gov/index.cfm?ty=pbdetail&iid=2315>.

Table 346. Felony Convictions in State Courts: 2000 to 2006

[In 2006, an estimated 1,205,273 persons were convicted of a felony (federal and state courts). Of that number, 1,132,290 were convicted in state courts, the vast majority (94 percent) of whom pleaded guilty. At the time of sentencing, about 3 out of 4 felons sentenced (77 percent) were sentenced for a single felony]

Most serious conviction	Felony convictions in state courts							
	2000		2002		2004		2006	
	Number	Percent	Number	Percent	Number	Percent	Number	Percent
All offenses	924,700	100.0	1,051,000	100.0	1,078,920	100.0	1,132,290	100.0
Violent offenses	173,200	18.7	197,030	18.8	194,570	18.0	206,140	18.2
Murder [1]	8,600	0.9	8,990	0.9	8,400	0.8	8,670	0.8
Rape/Sexual assault	31,500	3.4	35,500	3.4	33,190	3.1	33,200	2.9
Robbery	36,800	4.0	38,430	3.7	38,850	3.6	41,740	3.7
Aggravated assault	79,400	8.6	95,600	9.1	94,380	8.7	100,560	8.9
Other violent [2]	17,000	1.8	18,510	1.8	19,750	1.8	21,980	1.9
Property offenses	262,000	28.3	325,200	30.9	310,680	28.8	321,570	28.4
Burglary	79,300	8.6	100,640	9.6	93,870	8.7	99,910	8.8
Larceny [3]	100,000	10.8	124,320	11.8	119,340	11.1	125,390	11.1
Fraud/forgery [4]	82,700	8.9	100,240	9.5	97,470	9.0	96,260	8.5
Drug offenses	319,700	34.6	340,330	32.4	362,850	33.6	377,860	33.4
Possession	116,300	12.6	127,530	12.1	161,090	14.9	165,360	14.6
Trafficking.	203,400	22.0	212,810	20.2	201,760	18.7	212,490	18.8
Weapon offenses	28,200	3.1	32,470	3.1	33,010	3.1	38,010	3.4
Other offenses [5]	141,600	15.3	155,970	14.8	177,810	16.5	188,730	16.7

[1] A small number of cases were classified as nonnegligent manslaughter when it was unclear if the conviction offense was murder or nonnegligent manslaughter. [2] Includes offenses such as negligent manslaughter and kidnapping. [3] When vehicle theft could not be distinguished from other theft, the case was coded as "other theft." This results in a conservative estimate of vehicle thefts. [4] Includes embezzlement. [5] Composed of nonviolent offenses such as receiving stolen property and vandalism.
Source: U.S. Department of Justice, Office of Justice Programs, Bureau of Justice Statistics, *Criminal Sentencing Statistics*, Series NCJ 226846, December 2009. See <http://bjs.ojp.usdoj.gov/index.cfm?ty=pbdetail&iid=2152>.

Table 347. Prisoners Under Jurisdiction of Federal or State Correctional Authorities—Summary by State: 1990 to 2009

[For years ending December 31. Jurisdiction refers to the legal authority over a prisoner, regardless of where held]

State	1990	2000	2005	2008	2009	State	1990	2000	2005	2008	2009
U.S. [1]	**773,919**	**1,391,261**	**1,527,929**	**1,609,759**	**1,613,740**						
Federal. ...	65,526	145,416	187,618	201,280	208,118	MS	8,375	20,241	20,515	22,754	21,482
State	708,393	1,245,845	1,340,311	1,408,479	1,405,622	MO	14,943	27,543	30,823	30,186	30,563
						MT	1,425	3,105	3,532	3,545	3,605
AL	15,665	26,332	27,888	30,508	31,874	NE	2,403	3,895	4,455	4,520	4,474
AK [2]	2,622	4,173	4,812	5,014	5,285	NV [6]	5,322	10,063	11,782	12,743	12,482
AZ [3]	14,261	26,510	33,565	39,589	40,627	NH	1,342	2,257	2,530	2,702	2,731
AR	7,322	11,915	13,541	14,716	15,208	NJ	21,128	29,784	27,359	25,953	25,382
CA	97,309	163,001	170,676	173,670	171,275	NM	3,187	5,342	6,571	6,402	6,519
CO	7,671	16,833	21,456	23,274	22,795	NY	54,895	70,199	62,743	60,347	58,687
CT [2]	10,500	18,355	19,442	20,661	19,716	NC	18,411	31,266	36,365	39,482	39,860
DE [2]	3,471	6,921	6,966	7,075	6,794	ND	483	1,076	1,385	1,452	1,486
DC [4, 5]	9,947	7,456	(NA)	(NA)	(NA)	OH	31,822	45,833	45,854	51,686	51,606
FL	44,387	71,319	89,768	102,388	103,915	OK	12,285	23,181	26,676	25,864	26,397
GA [3]	22,411	44,232	48,749	52,719	53,371	OR	6,492	10,580	13,411	14,167	14,403
HI [2]	2,533	5,053	6,146	5,955	5,891	PA	22,290	36,847	42,380	49,215	51,429
ID	1,961	5,535	6,818	7,290	7,400	RI [2]	2,392	3,286	3,654	4,045	3,674
IL	27,516	45,281	44,919	45,474	45,161	SC	17,319	21,778	23,160	24,326	24,288
IN	12,736	20,125	24,455	28,322	28,808	SD	1,341	2,616	3,463	3,342	3,434
IA [3]	3,967	7,955	8,737	8,766	8,813	TN	10,388	22,166	26,369	27,228	26,965
KS	5,775	8,344	9,068	8,539	8,641	TX	50,042	166,719	169,003	172,506	171,249
KY	9,023	14,919	19,662	21,706	21,638	UT	2,496	5,637	6,382	6,552	6,533
LA	18,599	35,207	36,083	38,381	39,780	VT [2]	1,049	1,697	2,078	2,116	2,220
ME	1,523	1,679	2,023	2,195	2,206	VA	17,593	30,168	35,344	38,276	38,092
MD	17,848	23,538	22,737	23,324	22,255	WA	7,995	14,915	17,382	17,926	18,233
MA	8,345	10,722	10,701	11,408	11,316	WV	1,565	3,856	5,312	6,059	6,367
MI	34,267	47,718	49,546	48,738	45,478	WI	7,465	20,754	22,697	23,379	23,153
MN	3,176	6,238	9,281	9,910	9,986	WY	1,110	1,680	2,047	2,084	2,075

NA Not available. [1] U.S. total includes federal prisoners not distributed by state and prison system. [2] Data include both total jail and prison population. Prisons and jails form one integrated system. [3] Numbers are for custody rather than jurisdiction counts. [4] The transfer of responsibility for sentenced felons from the District of Columbia to the federal system was completed by the year end 2001. [5] The District of Columbia inmates sentenced to more than 1 year are now under the responsibility of the Bureau of Prisons. [6] Prison population for yearend 2008 is as of January 2, 2009.

Source: Source: U.S. Department of Justice, Bureau of Justice Statistics, *Prisoners in 2009*, Series NCJ 231675, and earlier reports. See also <http://bjs.ojp.usdoj.gov/index.cfm?ty=pbdetail&iid=2232>.

Table 348. Adults Under Correctional Supervision: 1980 to 2009

[As of December 31, except jail counts as of June 30]

Year	Estimated total [1, 2, 3]	Percent of adults under correctional supervision	Community supervision		Incarceration		Male [2, 3, 4]	Female [2, 3, 4]
			Probation	Parole	Jail [3]	Prison		
1980	1,840,400	1.1	1,118,097	220,438	182,288	319,598	(NA)	(NA)
1985	3,011,500	1.7	1,968,712	300,203	254,986	487,593	2,606,000	405,500
1990	4,348,000	2.3	2,670,234	531,407	403,019	743,382	3,756,100	592,000
1995	5,335,100	2.8	3,077,861	679,421	499,300	1,078,542	4,513,000	822,100
1996	5,482,700	2.8	3,164,996	679,733	510,400	1,127,528	4,629,300	853,400
1997 [5]	5,725,800	2.9	3,296,513	694,787	557,974	1,176,564	4,823,200	902,600
1998 [5]	6,126,100	3.1	3,670,441	696,385	584,372	1,224,469	5,132,600	993,400
1999	6,331,400	3.1	3,779,922	714,457	596,485	1,287,172	5,280,300	1,051,000
2000	6,437,400	3.1	3,826,209	723,898	613,534	1,316,333	5,366,600	1,070,800
2001	6,574,100	3.1	3,931,731	732,333	623,628	1,330,007	5,458,700	1,115,400
2002	6,750,500	3.1	4,024,067	750,934	658,228	1,367,547	5,566,500	1,184,100
2003 [6]	6,917,700	3.2	4,120,012	769,925	684,431	1,390,279	5,711,500	1,206,100
2004	6,987,900	3.2	4,143,792	771,852	706,907	1,421,345	5,756,100	1,231,800
2005	7,045,100	3.1	4,166,757	780,616	740,770	1,448,344	5,810,400	1,234,700
2006	7,176,000	3.2	4,215,361	799,875	759,717	1,492,973	5,875,000	1,301,000
2007 [7]	7,267,500	3.2	4,234,471	821,177	773,341	1,517,867	5,975,100	1,292,500
2008 [7]	7,274,600	3.1	4,244,046	824,834	777,852	1,522,834	5,973,700	1,300,800
2009 [8]	7,225,800	3.1	4,203,967	819,308	760,400	1,524,513	5,927,200	1,298,600

NA Not available. [1] Detail may not sum to total due to rounding and/or individuals having multiple correctional statuses. [2] Estimates were rounded to the nearest 100. [3] In 2009, the 2000–2009 jail counts were revised to exclude juveniles held as adults; therefore, these counts may not be comparable to those published in prior years. [4] The 1990–2009 gender estimates were revised based on a new method of estimation. [5] Probation coverage was expanded and the additional probationers resulting from the expansion of coverage are reflected in these estimates. See "Methodology" in the BJS report, *Correctional Populations in the United States, 2009*, for more details. [6] Due to changes in reporting in a few states, total probation and parole counts include estimated counts. See the BJS report, *Probation and Parole in the United States, 2004*, for more details. [7] Includes counts estimated by BJS because some states were unable to provide data. See "Methodology" in *Correctional Populations in the United States, 2009*, for more details. [8] Preliminary data.

Source: U.S. Department of Justice, Bureau of Justice Statistics (BJS), *Correctional Populations in the United States, 2009*; *Prisoners in 2009*; *Jail inmates at Midyear 2009—Statistical Tables*; and *Probation and Parole in the United States, 2009*. See also <http://bjs.ojp.usdoj.gov/index.cfm?ty=tp&tid=1>.

Table 349. Jail Inmates by Sex, Race, and Hispanic Origin: 1990 to 2009

[As of the last week day in June. Data for 2000 and 2007 – 2009 are based on the Annual Survey of Jails]

Characteristic	1990	1995	2000	2005	2007	2008	2009
Total inmates [1,2]	405,320	507,044	621,149	747,529	780,174	785,536	767,434
Incarceration rate per 100,000							
U.S. residents	163	193	220	252	259	258	250
Rated capacity [3,4]	389,171	545,763	677,787	786,954	810,543	828,714	849,895
Adult	403,019	499,300	613,534	740,770	773,341	777,832	760,216
Male	365,821	448,000	543,120	646,807	673,346	678,660	667,039
Female	37,198	51,300	70,414	93,963	99,995	99,172	93,176
Juveniles [5]	2,301	7,800	7,615	6,759	6,833	7,703	7,218
White, non-Hispanic	169,600	203,300	260,500	331,000	338,200	333,300	326,400
Black, non-Hispanic	172,300	220,600	256,300	290,500	301,700	308,000	300,500
Hispanic/Latino [6]	58,100	74,400	94,100	111,900	125,500	128,500	124,000
Other [6]	5,400	8,800	10,200	13,000	13,900	14,000	14,800

[1] Total does not include offenders who were supervised outside of jail facilities. [2] Race and Hispanic Origin data do not include the Two or More Race data. [3] Beginning 1995, rated capacity subject to sampling error. [4] Rated capacity is the number of beds or inmates assigned by a rating official to facilities within each jurisdiction. [5] Juveniles are persons held under the age of 18. Includes juveniles who were tried or awaiting trial as adults. [6] Persons of Hispanic Origin may be any race. [7] Excludes persons of Hispanic or Latino origin. Includes American Indians, Alaska Natives, Asians, and Pacific Islanders.

Source: U.S. Department of Justice, Bureau of Justice Statistics, *Jail Inmates at Midyear 2009*, annual, Series NCJ 230112, June 2010. See also <http://bjs.ojp.usdoj.gov/index.cfm?ty=pbdetail&iid=2273>.

Table 350. Prisoners Under Federal or State Jurisdiction by Sex: 1980 to 2009

[Prisoners, as of December 31. Represents prisoners sentenced to more than one year under jurisdiction of federal or state authorities rather than those in the custody of such authorities]

Year	Total [1]	Rate [2]	State	Male	Female	Year	Total [1]	Rate [2]	State	Male	Female
1980	315,974	139	295,363	303,643	12,331	2001	1,345,217	470	1,208,708	1,260,033	85,184
1985	480,568	202	447,873	459,223	21,345	2002	1,380,516	476	1,237,476	1,291,450	89,066
1990	739,980	297	689,577	699,416	40,564	2003	1,408,361	482	1,256,442	1,315,790	92,571
1995	1,085,022	411	1,001,359	1,021,059	63,963	2004	1,433,728	486	1,274,591	1,337,730	95,998
1996	1,137,722	427	1,048,907	1,068,123	69,599	2005	1,462,866	491	1,296,693	1,364,178	98,688
1997	1,195,498	445	1,100,511	1,121,663	73,835	2006	1,504,660	501	1,331,127	1,401,317	103,343
1998	1,245,402	461	1,141,720	1,167,802	77,600	2007	1,532,850	506	1,353,646	1,427,064	105,786
1999	1,304,074	476	1,189,799	1,221,611	82,463	2008	1,547,742	504	1,365,409	1,441,384	106,358
2000	1,331,278	[3] 470	1,204,323	1,246,234	85,044	2009	1,548,721	502	1,360,835	1,443,524	105,197

[1] Includes prisoners under the legal authority of state or federal correctional officials. [2] Rate per 100,000 estimated population. Based on U.S. Census Bureau estimated resident population. [3] Decrease in incarceration rate from 1999 to 2000 due to use of new Census numbers.

Source: U.S. Department of Justice, Bureau of Justice Statistics, *Prisoners in 2009*, Series NCJ 231675, December 2010. See also <bjs.ojp.usdoj.gov/index.cfm?ty=pbdetail&iid=2232>.

Table 351. Prisoners Under Sentence of Death by Characteristic: 1980 to 2009

[As of December 31. Excludes prisoners under sentence of death who remained within local correctional systems pending exhaustion of appellate process or who had not been committed to prison]

Characteristic	1980	1990	2000	2001	2002	2003	2004	2005	2006	2007	2008	2009
Total [1,2]	688	2,346	3,601	3,577	3,562	3,377	3,320	3,245	3,233	3,215	3,210	3,173
White	418	1,368	1,989	1,968	1,939	1,882	1,856	1,802	1,806	1,806	1,795	1,780
Black and other	270	978	1,612	1,609	1,623	1,495	1,464	1,443	1,427	1,409	1,415	1,393
Under 20 years old	11	8	11	4	4	1	1	–	–	1	–	–
20 to 24 years old	173	168	237	192	153	133	95	61	51	42	44	39
25 to 34 years old	334	1,110	1,103	1,099	1,058	965	896	816	735	680	610	564
35 to 54 years old	186	1,006	2,019	2,043	2,069	1,969	1,977	2,012	2,043	2,060	2,076	2,062
55 years old and over	10	64	223	243	273	306	345	365	399	437	477	508
Years of school completed:												
7 years or less	68	178	214	212	215	213	207	192	186	183	176	176
8 years	74	186	233	236	234	227	221	206	195	189	185	180
9 to 11 years	204	775	1,157	1,145	1,130	1,073	1,053	1,030	1,015	989	977	950
12 years	162	729	1,184	1,183	1,173	1,108	1,091	1,105	1,098	1,089	1,094	1,097
More than 12 years	43	209	315	304	294	270	262	256	248	248	247	238
Unknown	163	279	490	501	511	483	480	465	486	522	528	532
Marital status:												
Never married	268	998	1,749	1,763	1,746	1,641	1,622	1,586	1,577	1,558	1,552	1,531
Married	229	632	739	716	709	684	658	649	626	635	630	613
Divorced [3]	217	726	1,105	1,102	1,102	1,049	1,034	1,019	1,025	1,027	1,025	1,029
Time elapsed since sentencing:												
Less than 12 months	185	231	208	151	147	137	117	122	105	110	106	103
12 to 47 months	389	753	786	734	609	495	421	399	382	352	339	329
48 to 71 months	102	438	507	476	468	451	388	299	262	262	244	237
72 months and over	38	934	2,092	2,220	2,333	2,291	2,388	2,434	2,479	2,496	2,518	2,504
Legal status at arrest:												
Not under sentence	384	1,345	2,202	2,189	2,165	2,048	2,026	1,979	1,952	1,963	1,961	1,931
Parole or probation [4]	115	578	921	918	909	845	809	792	778	760	753	739
Prison or escaped	45	128	126	135	141	137	145	144	142	143	146	156
Unknown	170	305	344	339	342	344	334	339	356	354	347	347

– Represents zero. [1] Revisions to the total number of prisoners were not carried to the characteristics except for race. [2] Includes races not shown separately. [3] Includes persons married but separated, widows, widowers, and unknown. [4] Includes prisoners on mandatory conditional release, work release, other leave, AWOL, or bail. Covers 28 prisoners in 1990; 17 in 2001, 2002, and 2003; 15 in 2004; 14 in 2005, 2006, 2007, and 2009; and 12 in 2008.

Source: U.S. Department of Justice, Bureau of Justice Statistics, *Capital Punishment, 2009*, Series NCJ 231676, December 2010. See also <http://bjs.gov/index.cfm?ty=pbdetail&iid=2215>.

Table 352. Prisoners Executed Under Civil Authority by Sex and Race: 1930 to 2010

[Excludes executions by military authorities]

Year or period	Total [1]	Male	Female	White	Black	Executed for murder Total [1]	Executed for murder White	Executed for murder Black
All years, 1930–2009 . . .	**5,093**	**5,049**	**44**	**2,544**	**2,492**	**4,568**	**2,457**	**2.056**
1960 to 1967	191	190	1	98	93	155	87	68
1968 to 1976	–	–	–	–	–	–	–	–
1977 to 2010	1,234	1,222	12	793	426	1,234	793	426
1985	18	18	–	11	7	18	11	7
1990	23	23	–	16	7	23	16	7
1995	56	56	–	33	22	56	33	22
2000	85	83	2	49	35	85	49	35
2001	66	63	3	48	17	66	48	17
2002	71	69	2	53	18	71	53	18
2003	65	65	–	44	20	65	44	20
2004	59	59	–	39	19	59	39	19
2005	60	59	1	41	19	60	41	19
2006	53	53	–	32	21	53	32	21
2007	42	42	–	28	14	42	28	14
2008	37	37	–	20	17	37	20	17
2009	52	52	–	31	21	52	31	21
2010	46	45	1	34	12	46	34	12

– Represents zero. [1] Includes races other than White or Black.
Source: Through 1978, U.S. Law Enforcement Assistance Administration; thereafter, U.S. Department of Justice, Bureau of Justice Statistics, *Capital Punishment, 2009*, Series NCJ 231676, December 2010. See also <http://bjs.gov/index .cfm?ty=pbdetail&iid=2215>.

Table 353. Prisoners Executed Under Civil Authority by State: 1977 to 2010

[Alaska, District of Columbia, Hawaii, Iowa, Maine, Massachusetts, Michigan, Minnesota, New Jersey, North Dakota, Rhode Island, Vermont, West Virginia, and Wisconsin are jurisdictions without a death penalty. New Mexico abolished the death penalty for offenses committed after July 1, 2009; two men under previously imposed death sentences are still subject to execution]

State	1977 to 2010	2000	2005	2008	2009	2010	State	1977 to 2010	2000	2005	2008	2009	2010	State	1977 to 2010	2000	2005	2008	2009	2010
U.S. .	**1,234**	**85**	**60**	**37**	**52**	**46**	IL . . .	12	–	–	–	–	–	OH . .	41	–	4	2	5	8
							IN . .	20	–	5	–	1	–	OK . .	94	11	4	2	3	3
AL . . .	49	4	4	–	6	–	KY . .	3	–	–	1	–	–	OR . .	2	–	–	–	–	–
AZ . . .	24	3	–	–	–	1	LA . .	28	1	–	–	–	1	PA . .	3	–	–	–	–	–
AR . . .	27	2	1	–	–	–	MD . .	5	–	1	–	–	–	SC . .	42	1	3	3	2	–
CA . . .	13	1	2	–	–	–	MS . .	13	–	1	2	–	3	SD . .	1	–	–	–	–	–
CO . . .	1	–	–	–	–	–	MO . .	67	5	5	–	1	–	TN . .	6	1	–	–	2	–
CT . . .	1	–	1	–	–	–	MT . .	3	–	–	–	–	–	TX . .	464	40	19	18	24	17
DE . . .	14	1	1	–	–	–	NE . .	3	–	–	–	–	–	UT . .	7	–	–	–	–	1
FL . . .	69	6	1	2	2	1	NV . .	12	–	–	–	–	–	VA . .	108	8	–	4	3	3
GA . . .	48	–	3	3	3	2	NM . .	1	–	–	–	–	–	WA . .	5	–	–	–	–	1
ID	1	–	–	–	–	–	NC . .	43	1	5	–	–	–	WY . .	1	–	–	–	–	–

– Represents zero.
Source: Through 1978, U.S. Law Enforcement Assistance Administration; thereafter, U.S. Department of Justice, Bureau of Justice Statistics, *Capital Punishment, 2009*, Series NCJ 231676, December 2010. See also <http://bjs.gov/index .cfm?ty=pbdetail&iid=2215>.

Table 354. Fire Losses—Total and Per Capita: 1980 to 2009

[5,579 represents $5,579,000,000. Includes allowances for FAIR Plan and uninsured losses]

Year	Total (mil. dol.)	Per capita [1] (dol.)	Year	Total (mil. dol.)	Per capita [1] (dol.)	Year	Total (mil. dol.)	Per capita [1] (dol.)
1980	5,579	24.56	1995	11,887	45.23	2004	17,344	[3] 59.22
1985	7,753	32.70	1996	12,544	47.29	2005	20,427	[3] 69.11
1988	9,626	39.11	1997	12,940	48.32	2006	20,340	[3] 68.17
1989	9,514	38.33	1998	11,510	45.59	2007	[3] 24,399	[3] 80.98
1990	9,495	38.07	1999	12,428	45.58	2008	30,561	[3] 100.51
1991	11,302	44.82	2000	13,457	47.69	2009	28,070	91.43
1992	13,588	53.28	2001 [2]	17,118	[3] 60.05			
1993	11,331	43.96	2002	17,586	[3] 61.12			
1994	12,778	49.08	2003	21,129	[3] 72.81			

[1] Based on U.S. Census Bureau estimated resident population as of July 1. Enumerated population as of April 1 for 1980, 1990, and 2000. [2] Does not include insured fire losses related to terrorism. [3] Data have been revised.
Source: ISO; Insurance Information Institute, New York, NY. *The III Insurance Fact Book*, annual, and *Financial Services Fact Book*, annual (copyright). Data from ISO. See also <http://www.iii.org>.

Table 355. The U.S. Fire Service: Departments and Personnel: 1990 to 2009

[(In thousands 1,025.7 represents 1,025,700.) A fire department is a public or private organization that provides fire prevention, fire suppression, and associated emergency and non-emergency services to a jurisdiction such as a county, municipality, or organized fire district. For 2009, there was an estimated 30,165 fire departments in the United States. These fire departments have an estimated 52,050 fire stations, 68,400 pumpers, 6,750 aerial apparatus and 74,250 other suppression vehicles. A fire department responds to a fire every 23 seconds]

Items	1990	1995	2000	2004	2005	2006	2007	2008	2009
Total....................	30,391	31,197	30,339	30,400	30,300	30,635	30,185	30,170	30,165
Fire departments (Number):									
All career	1,949	1,831	2,178	1,917	2,087	2,321	2,263	2,315	2,457
Mostly career...............	1,338	1,660	1,667	1,242	1,766	1,731	1,765	1,790	1,752
Mostly volunteer	4,000	4,581	4,523	4,084	4,902	5,134	4,989	4,830	5,099
All volunteer...............	23,104	23,125	23,971	23,157	21,575	21,449	21,168	21,235	20,857
Fire Department personnel (1,000)...	1,025.7	1,098.9	1,064.2	1,100.8	1,136.7	1,140.9	1,148.5	1,148.9	1,148.1
Career [1]...................	253.0	260.9	286.8	305.2	313.3	317.0	323.4	321.7	336.0
Volunteer [2].................	772.7	838.0	777.4	795.6	823.7	824.0	825.5	827.2	812.1

[1] Career firefighters include full-time uniform firefighters regardless of assignment (i.e., suppression, administrative, prevention/inspection, etc.). Career firefighters do not include firefighters who work for the state or federal government or in private fire brigades. [2] Volunteer firefighters include any active part-time (call or volunteer) firefighters.

Source: National Fire Protection Association, Quincy, MA, *Annual Fire Department Profile Report*, October 2010, and prior issues (copyright).

Table 356. Fires—Number and Loss by Type and Property Use: 2006 to 2009

[(1,642 represents 1,642,000)and property loss of 11,307 represents $11,307,000,000. Based on annual sample survey of fire departments. No adjustments were made for unreported fires and losses]

Type and property use	Number (1,000)				Direct property loss (mil. dol.) [1]			
	2006	2007	2008	2009	2006	2007	2008	2009
Fires, total	1,642	1,557	1,451	1,349	11,307	14,639	15,478	12,531
Structure	524	531	515	481	9,636	10,638	12,361	10,842
Outside of structure [2]...........	82	85	71	69	262	707	129	254
Brush and rubbish.............	627	561	523	477	–	–	–	–
Vehicle......................	278	257	236	219	1,319	1,411	1,494	1,361
Other........................	131	123	106	103	90	[3] 1,883	[4] 1,494	74
Structure by property use:								
Public assembly..............	13	15	14	14	444	498	518	757
Educational	6	6	6	6	105	100	66	83
Institutional	8	7	7	6	42	41	22	32
Stores and offices	20	21	20	16	691	642	684	713
Residential...................	413	414	403	377	6,990	7,546	8,550	7,796
1–2 family homes [5]	304	300	291	273	5,936	6,225	6,892	6,391
Apartments	92	99	96	90	896	1,164	1,351	1,225
Other residential [6]	17	15	16	14	158	157	307	180
Storage	29	31	30	30	650	670	661	796
Industry, utility, defense [7]........	12	12	10	10	573	779	[8] 1,401	572
Special structures	23	25	25	22	141	362	459	98

– Represents zero. [1] Direct property damage figures do not include indirect losses, like business interruption, and adjustments for inflation. [2] Includes outside storage, crops, timber, etc. [3] Includes California Fire Storm 2007 with an estimated $1.8 billion in property loss. [4] Includes California Wildfires 2008 with an estimated $1.4 billion in property loss. [5] Includes mobile homes. [6] Includes hotels and motels, college dormitories, boarding houses, etc. [7] Data underreported as some incidents were handled by private fire brigades or fixed suppression systems which do not report. [8] Includes three industrial property incidents that resulted in $775 million in property loss.

Source: National Fire Protection Association, Quincy, MA, "2009 U.S. Fire Loss," *NFPA Journal*, September 2010, and prior issues (copyright). See also <http://www.nfpa.org/categoryList.asp?categoryID=15&URL=Research>

Table 357. Fires and Property Loss for Incendiary and Suspicious Fires and Civilian Fire Deaths and Injuries by Selected Property Type: 2006 to 2009

[In thousands, 524 represents 524,000, except as indicated. Based on sample survey of fire departments]

Characteristic	2006	2007	2008	2009	Characteristic	2006	2007	2008	2009
NUMBER (1,000)					One- and two-family dwellings	2,155	2,350	2,365	2,100
Structure fires, total........	524	531	515	481	Apartments	425	515	390	465
Structure fires that were intentionally set	31	32	31	27	Vehicles.............	490	385	365	280
PROPERTY LOSS [1] (mil. dol.)					CIVILIAN FIRE INJURIES				
Structure fires, total........	9,636	10,638	12,361	10,842	Injuries, total [2]	16,400	17,675	16,705	17,050
Structure fires that were intentionally set	775	773	866	684	Residential property ...	12,925	14,000	13,560	13,050
					One- and two-family dwellings	8,800	9,650	9,185	9,300
CIVILIAN FIRE DEATHS					Apartments	3,700	3,950	3,975	3,350
Deaths, total [2]..............	3,245	3,430	3,320	3,010					
Residential property	2,620	2,895	2,780	2,590	Vehicles.............	1,200	1,675	1,065	1,610

[1] Direct property loss only. [2] Includes other not shown separately.

Source: National Fire Protection Association, Quincy, MA, "2009 U.S. Fire Loss," *NFPA Journal*, September 2010, and prior issues (copyright). See also <http://www.nfpa.org/categoryList.asp?categoryID=15&URL=Research>

Section 6
Geography and Environment

This section presents a variety of information on the physical environment of the United States, starting with basic area measurement data and ending with climatic data for selected weather stations around the country. The subjects covered between those points are mostly concerned with environmental trends but include related subjects such as land use, water consumption, air pollutant emissions, toxic releases, oil spills, hazardous waste sites, municipal waste and recycling, threatened and endangered wildlife, and the environmental industry.

The information in this section is selected from a wide range of federal agencies that compile the data for various administrative or regulatory purposes, such as the Environmental Protection Agency (EPA), U.S. Geological Survey (USGS), National Oceanic and Atmospheric Administration (NOAA), Natural Resources Conservation Service (NRCS), and National Atlas® of the United States. New data on 11 coastline counties most frequently hit by hurricanes may be found in Table 362.

Area—2008 Area measurements are the latest available. These measurements were calculated by computer based on the information contained in a single, consistent geographic database, the Topologically Integrated Geographic Encoding & Referencing system (TIGER®) database. The 2008 area measurements may be found in Table 358.

Geography—The USGS conducts investigations, surveys, and research in the fields of geography, geology, topography, geographic information systems, mineralogy, hydrology, and geothermal energy resources as well as natural hazards. The USGS provides United States cartographic data through the Earth Sciences Information Center, water resources data through the *Water Resources of the United States* at <http://water.usgs.gov/pubs/>. In a joint project with the U.S. Census Bureau, during the 1980s, the USGS provided the basic information on geographic features

for input into a national geographic and cartographic database prepared by the Census Bureau, called TIGER® database. Since then, using a variety of sources, the Census Bureau has updated these features and their related attributes (names, descriptions, etc.) and inserted current information on the boundaries, names, and codes of legal and statistical geographic entities. The 2008 area measures, land and water, including their classifications, reflect base feature updates made in the Master Address File (MAF)/TIGER database through May 1, 2008. The boundaries of the states and equivalent areas are as of January 1, 2008. Maps prepared by the Census Bureau using the TIGER® database show the names and boundaries of entities and are available on a current basis.

An inventory of the nation's land resources by type of use/cover was conducted by the National Resources Inventory Conservation Services (NRCS) every 5 years beginning in 1977 through 2003. The most recent survey results, which were published for the year 2003, covered all nonfederal land for the contiguous 48 states.

Environment —The principal federal agency responsible for pollution abatement and control activities is the Environmental Protection Agency (EPA). It is responsible for establishing and monitoring national air quality standards, water quality activities, solid and hazardous waste disposal, and control of toxic substances. Many of these series now appear in the Envirofacts portion of the EPA Web site at <http://www.epa.gov/enviro/>.

The Clean Air Act, which was last amended in 1990, requires the EPA to set National Ambient Air Quality Standards (NAAQS) (40 CFR part 50) for pollutants considered harmful to public health and the environment. The Clean Air Act established two types of national air quality standards. **Primary standards** set limits to protect public health, including the health of "sensitive" populations such as asthmatics, children, and the elderly. **Secondary standards** set limits to protect public welfare, including protection against decreased visibility, damage to animals, crops vegetation, and buildings. See <http://www.epa.gov/air/criteria.html>. The EPA Office of Air Quality Planning and Standards (OAQPS) has set National Ambient Air Quality Standards for six principal pollutants, which are called "criteria" pollutants. These pollutants are: Carbon Monoxide, Lead, Nitrogen Dioxide, Particulate Matter (PM2.5 and 10), Ozone, and Sulfur Dioxide. NAAQS are periodically reviewed and revised to include any additional or new health or welfare data. Table 372 gives some of the health-related standards for the six air pollutants having NAAQS. Data gathered from state networks are periodically submitted to EPA's National Aerometric Information Retrieval System (AIRS) for summarization in annual reports on the nationwide status and trends in air quality. For details, see "Air Trends" on the EPA Web site at <http://www.epa.gov /airtrends/index .html>.

The Toxics Release Inventory (TRI), published by the EPA, is a valuable source of information on approximately 650 chemicals that are being used, manufactured, treated, transported, or released into the environment. Sections 313 of the Emergency Planning and Community Right-to- Know Act (EPCRA) and 6607 of the Pollution Prevention Act (PPA), mandate that a publicly-accessible

toxic chemical database be developed and maintained by EPA. This database, known as the TRI, contains information concerning waste management activities and the release of toxic chemicals by facilities that manufacture, process, or otherwise use said materials. Data on the release of these chemicals are collected from about 21,000 facilities and facilities added in 1998 that have the equivalent of 10 or more full time employees and meet the established thresholds for manufacturing, processing, or "other use" of listed chemicals. Facilities must report their releases and other waste management quantities. Since 1994 federal facilities have been required to report their data regardless of industry classification. In May 1997, EPA added seven new industry sectors that reported to the TRI for the first time in July 1999 for the 1998 reporting year. More current information on this program can be found at <http://www.epa.gov /tri>.

Climate—NOAA, through the National Weather Service and the National Environmental Satellite, Data, and Information Service, is responsible for climate data. NOAA maintains about 11,600 weather stations, of which over 3,000 produce autographic precipitation records, about 600 take hourly readings of a series of weather elements, and the remainder record data once a day. These data are reported monthly in the Climatological Data and Storm Data, published monthly and annually in the Local Climatological Data (published by location for major cities). Data can be found in tables 388 and 391–396.

Table 358. Land and Water Area of States and Other Entities: 2008

[One square mile = 2.59 square kilometers. The area measurements were derived from the Census Bureau's Master Address File/Topologically Integrated Geographic Encoding and Referencing (MAF/TIGER) geographic database. The boundaries of the states and equivalent areas are as of January 1, 2008. The land and water areas, including their classifications, reflect base feature updates made in the MAF/TIGER database through May 1, 2008. These updates show increases in total water area and decrease in land area for nearly every state. For more details, see <http://www.census.gov/geo/www/tiger/tgrshp2008/tgrshp2008.html>]

State and other areas	Total area Sq. mi.	Total area Sq. km.	Land area Sq. mi.	Land area Sq. km.	Water area Total Sq. mi.	Water area Total Sq. km.	Water area Inland (sq. mi.)	Water area Coastal (sq. mi.)	Water area Great Lakes (sq. mi.)	Water area Territorial (sq. mi.)
Total...........	3,805,142	9,855,318	3,535,846	9,157,841	269,296	697,477	86,478	43,201	59,959	76,392
United States	3,795,951	9,831,513	3,531,822	9,147,420	264,129	684,094	86,409	43,185	59,959	74,575
Alabama	52,420	135,768	50,644	131,168	1,776	4,600	1,057	518	(X)	201
Alaska...........	664,988	1,722,319	570,665	1,478,022	94,323	244,297	20,028	28,162	(X)	46,133
Arizona	113,990	295,235	113,595	294,211	396	1,026	396	–	(X)	–
Arkansas.........	53,178	137,732	52,030	134,758	1,149	2,976	1,149	–	(X)	–
California	163,694	423,967	155,766	403,434	7,928	20,534	2,842	222	(X)	4,864
Colorado	104,094	269,604	103,641	268,430	454	1,176	454	–	(X)	–
Connecticut	5,544	14,358	4,840	12,536	703	1,821	164	539	(X)	–
Delaware	2,489	6,445	1,949	5,048	539	1,396	74	372	(X)	93
District of Columbia........	68	177	61	158	7	18	7	–	(X)	–
Florida	65,758	170,312	53,603	138,832	12,154	31,479	5,373	1,128	(X)	5,653
Georgia	59,425	153,911	57,501	148,928	1,924	4,983	1,420	49	(X)	455
Hawaii	10,926	28,300	6,428	16,649	4,499	11,652	40	–	(X)	4,459
Idaho...........	83,568	216,442	82,643	214,045	926	2,398	926	–	(X)	–
Illinois..........	57,916	150,002	55,518	143,792	2,398	6,211	836	–	1,562	–
Indiana..........	36,417	94,321	35,823	92,782	594	1,538	361	–	233	–
Iowa............	56,273	145,746	55,858	144,672	415	1,075	415	–	(X)	–
Kansas..........	82,278	213,101	81,762	211,764	516	1,336	516	–	(X)	–
Kentucky	40,411	104,665	39,492	102,284	919	2,380	919	–	(X)	–
Louisiana........	51,988	134,649	43,199	111,885	8,789	22,764	4,433	1,951	(X)	2,405
Maine...........	35,384	91,644	30,841	79,878	4,543	11,766	2,282	613	(X)	1,647
Maryland	12,406	32,131	9,705	25,136	2,700	6,993	736	1,854	(X)	111
Massachusetts.....	10,554	27,336	7,801	20,205	2,754	7,133	461	977	(X)	1,316
Michigan	96,713	250,486	56,528	146,408	40,185	104,079	2,164	–	38,021	–
Minnesota	86,935	225,163	79,607	206,182	7,328	18,980	4,782	–	2,546	–
Mississippi........	48,432	125,438	46,920	121,523	1,512	3,916	772	591	(X)	149
Missouri.........	69,702	180,529	68,716	177,974	987	2,556	987	–	(X)	–
Montana.........	147,039	380,831	145,541	376,951	1,498	3,880	1,498	–	(X)	–
Nebraska........	77,349	200,334	76,825	198,977	524	1,357	524	–	(X)	–
Nevada..........	110,572	286,382	109,780	284,330	792	2,051	792	–	(X)	–
New Hampshire....	9,348	24,210	8,952	23,186	396	1,026	328	–	(X)	68
New Jersey	8,723	22,592	7,354	19,047	1,369	3,546	458	402	(X)	509
New Mexico.......	121,590	314,919	121,297	314,159	293	759	293	–	(X)	–
New York	54,555	141,298	47,126	122,056	7,429	19,241	1,979	977	3,990	482
North Carolina	53,819	139,391	48,619	125,923	5,200	13,468	4,044	–	(X)	1,157
North Dakota	70,698	183,109	69,001	178,713	1,697	4,395	1,697	–	(X)	–
Ohio............	44,825	116,097	40,858	105,822	3,967	10,275	467	–	3,500	–
Oklahoma	69,899	181,038	68,603	177,682	1,296	3,357	1,296	–	(X)	–
Oregon..........	98,379	254,801	95,985	248,601	2,394	6,200	1,063	74	(X)	1,256
Pennsylvania	46,055	119,281	44,739	115,874	1,316	3,408	567	–	749	–
Rhode Island	1,545	4,001	1,034	2,678	511	1,323	187	9	(X)	315
South Carolina....	32,021	82,934	30,070	77,881	1,951	5,053	1,044	74	(X)	832
South Dakota.....	77,116	199,730	75,811	196,350	1,305	3,380	1,305	–	(X)	–
Tennessee	42,144	109,154	41,235	106,799	910	2,357	910	–	(X)	–
Texas	268,597	695,666	261,226	676,575	7,371	19,091	5,607	406	(X)	1,358
Utah............	84,897	219,883	82,191	212,875	2,706	7,009	2,706	–	(X)	–
Vermont	9,616	24,906	9,217	23,872	400	1,036	400	–	(X)	–
Virginia..........	42,775	110,787	39,493	102,287	3,282	8,500	1,106	1,729	(X)	447
Washington	71,298	184,661	66,449	172,103	4,849	12,559	1,646	2,537	(X)	666
West Virginia	24,230	62,755	24,038	62,258	192	497	192	–	(X)	–
Wisconsin	65,496	169,636	54,154	140,259	11,342	29,376	1,984	–	9,358	–
Wyoming	97,812	253,334	97,088	251,458	724	1,875	724	–	(X)	–
Puerto Rico	5,325	13,791	3,424	8,868	1,901	4,924	68	16	(X)	1,817
Island Areas:	3,866	10,013	600	1,554	3,266	8,459	(NA)	(NA)	(X)	(NA)
American Samoa...	583	1,510	77	199	506	1,311	(NA)	(NA)	(X)	(NA)
Guam............	571	1,479	210	544	361	935	(NA)	(NA)	(X)	(NA)
No. Mariana Islands..........	1,975	5,115	179	464	1,796	4,652	(NA)	(NA)	(X)	(NA)
U.S. Virgin Islands..........	738	1,911	134	347	604	1,564	(NA)	(NA)	(X)	(NA)

– Represents or rounds to zero. NA Not available. X Not applicable.
Source: U.S. Census Bureau, unpublished data from the Census TIGER "R" database.

Table 359. Great Lakes Profile

[The Great Lakes contain the largest supply of freshwater in the world, holding about 18% of the world's total freshwater and about 90% of the United States' total freshwater. The Lakes are a series of five interconnecting large lakes, one small lake, four connecting channels, and the St. Lawrence Seaway. Combined, the lakes cover an area of over 94,000 square miles (245,000 square kilometers) and contain over 5,400 cubic miles (23,000 cubic kilometers) of water]

Characteristics	Unit	Lake Superior	Lake Michigan	Lake Huron	Lake Erie	Lake Ontario
Length	Miles	350	307	206	241	193
Breadth	Miles	160	118	183	57	53
Depth						
Average	Feet	489	279	159	62	283
Maximum	Feet	1,333	923	750	210	802
Volume	Cubic miles	2,935	1,180	849	116	393
Water Surface Area [1]	Square miles	31,700	22,300	23,000	9,910	7,340
Surface area in U.S	Square miles	20,598	22,300	9,111	4,977	3,560
Retention/Replacement Time [2]	Years	191	99	22	3	6

[1] Includes surface area in both U.S. and Canada. [2] The amount of time it takes for lakes to get rid of pollutants.
Source: Department of Commerce, National Oceanic and Atmospheric Administration, Great Lakes Environmental Research Laboratory, "About Our Great Lakes, Lake by Lake Profiles," June 2004, <http://www.glerl.noaa.gov/pr/ourlakes/intro.html\>.

Table 360. Great Lakes Length of Shoreline in Separate Basin

[In statute miles]

	Total	Canada	U.S.	MI	MN	WI	IL	IN	OH	PA	NY
Total	10,368	5,127	5,241	3,288	189	820	63	45	312	51	473
Lake Superior	2,980	1,549	1,431	917	189	325	–	–	–	–	–
St. Marys River	297	206	91	91	–	–	–	–	–	–	–
Lake Michigan	1,661	–	1,661	1,058	–	495	63	45	–	–	–
Lake Huron	3,350	2,416	934	934	–	–	–	–	–	–	–
St. Clair River	128	47	81	81	–	–	–	–	–	–	–
Lake St. Clair	160	71	89	89	–	–	–	–	–	–	–
Detroit River	107	43	64	64	–	–	–	–	–	–	–
Lake Erie	860	366	494	54	–	–	–	–	312	51	77
Niagara River	99	34	65	–	–	–	–	–	–	–	65
Lake Ontario	726	395	331	–	–	–	–	–	–	–	331

– Represents zero.
Source: State of Michigan, Department of Environment Quality, "Great Lakes, Shorelines of the Great Lakes," <http://www.michigan.gov/deq/0,1607,7-135-3313_3677---,00.html\>.

Table 361. Largest Lakes in the United States

[The list of lakes include manmade lakes and those that are only partially within the United States]

Lake	Location	Area in sq. mi.	Lake	Location	Area in sq. mi.
Lake Superior	MI-MN-WI-Ontario	31,700	Lake Pontchartrain	Louisiana	631
Lake Huron	MI-Ontario	23,000	Lake Sakakawea [1]	North Dakota	520
Lake Michigan	IL-IN-MI-WI	22,300	Lake Champlain	NY-VT-Quebec	490
Lake Erie	MI-NY-OH-PA-Ontario	9,910	Becharof Lake	Alaska	453
Lake Ontario	NY-Ontario	7,340	Lake St. Clair	MI-Ontario	430
Great Salt Lake	Utah	2,117	Red Lake	Minnesota	427
Lake of the Woods	MN-Manitoba-Ontario	1,485	Selawik Lake	Alaska	404
Iliamna Lake	Alaska	1,014	Fort Peck Lake [1]	Montana	393
Lake Oahe [1]	ND-SD	685	Salton Sea	California	347
Lake Okeechobee	Florida	662	Rainy Lake	MN-Ontario	345

[1] Manmade lakes.
Source: U.S. Geological Survey, 2003, and National Oceanic and Atmospheric Administration, "Great Lakes, 2002" and The National Atlas of the United States of America, *Lakes*, <http://nationalatlas.gov/articles/mapping/a_general.html\>.

Table 362. Coastline Counties Most Frequently Hit by Hurricanes: 1960 to 2008

[Hurricane is a type of tropical cyclone, an intense tropical weather system of strong thunderstorms with a well-defined surface circulation and maximum sustained winds of 74 miles per hour or higher]

County and State	Coastline region	Number of hurricanes	Percent change in population		Percent change in housing units	
			1960 to 2008	2000 to 2008	1960 to 2008	2000 to 2008
Monore Conty, FL	Gulf of Mexico	15	50.8	–9.2	221.8	4.3
Lafourche Parish, LA	Gulf of Mexico	14	67.2	2.9	151.5	8.9
Carteret County, NC	Atlantic	14	104.3	6.4	366.4	12.4
Dare County, NC	Atlantic	13	465.9	12.1	709.6	22.8
Hyde County, NC	Atlantic	13	–10.1	–11.1	83.7	5.8
Jefferson Parish, LA	Gulf of Mexico	12	108.9	–4.2	201.4	–3.5
Palm Beach County, FL	Atlantic	12	454.7	11.9	616.9	15.2
Miami-Dade County, FL	Atlantic	11	156.5	6.4	180.6	14.9
St. Bernard Parish, LA	Gulf of Mexico	11	17.2	–43.9	–2.6	–67.9
Cameron Parish, LA	Gulf of Mexico	11	4.8	–27.6	87.7	–8.1
Terrebonne Parish, LA	Gulf of Mexico	11	78.7	3.9	179.4	11.0

Source: National Oceanic and Atmospheric Administration (NOAA), Coastal Services Center, Historical Hurricane Tracks: 1851 to to 2008, U.S. Census Bureau, Current Population Reports, P25-1139, Population Estimates and Projections, "Coastline Population Trends in the United States: 1960 to 2008," Issued May 2010.

Table 363. U.S.–Canada and U.S.–Mexico Border Lengths

[In statue miles. Each statue mile equals one mile. For 2010, there were over 56 million personal vehicle passengers entering the United States from Canada, and almost 125 million personal vehicle passengers entering the United States from Mexico]

State	Length of international border	State	Length of international border
United States–Canada total	**5,525**	Ohio	146
Alaska	1,538	Pennsylvania	42
Idaho	45	Vermont	90
Maine	611	Washington	427
Michigan	721		
Minnesota	547	**United States–Mexico total**	**1,933**
Montana	545	Arizona	373
New Hampshire	58	California	140
New York	445	New Mexico	180
North Dakota	310	Texas	1,241

Source: U.S.–Canada lengths: International Boundary Commission, 2003; U.S. Mexico lengths: U.S. Geological Survey; and The National Atlas of the United States, 1976, *Borders*, <http://nationalatlas.gov/articles/mapping/a_general.html>.

Table 364. Coastline and Shoreline of the United States by State

[In statue miles. Each statue mile equals one mile. The term **coastline** is used to describe the general outline of the seacoast. For the table below, United States coastline measurements were made from small-scale maps, and the coastline was generalized. The coastlines of large sounds and bays were included. Measurements were made in 1948. **Shoreline** is the term used to describe a more detailed measure of the seacoast. The tidal shoreline figures in the table below were obtained in 1939–1940 from the largest-scale charts and maps then available. Shoreline of the outer coast, offshore islands, sounds, and bays was included, as well as the tidal portion of rivers and creeks. Only states with coastline or shoreline are included in the following table]

State	General coastline	Tidal shoreline	State	General coastline	Tidal shoreline
United States	**12,383**	**88,633**	Mississippi	44	359
Alabama	53	607	New Hampshire	13	131
Alaska	6,640	33,904	New Jersey	130	1,792
California	840	3,427	New York	127	1,850
Connecticut	–	618	North Carolina	301	3,375
Delaware	28	381	Oregon	296	1,410
Florida	1,350	8,426	Pennsylvania	–	89
Georgia	100	2,344	Rhode Island	40	384
Hawaii	750	1,052	South Carolina	187	2,876
Louisiana	397	7,721	Texas	367	3,359
Maine	228	3,478	Virginia	112	3,315
Maryland	31	3,190	Washington	157	3,026
Massachusetts	192	1,519			

– Represents zero.

Source: National Oceanic Atmospheric Administration, 1975 and The National Atlas of the United States, *Coastline and Shoreline*, <http://nationalatlas.gov/articles/mapping/a_general.html>.

Table 365. Flows of Largest U.S. Rivers—Length, Discharge, and Drainage Area

River	Location of mouth	Source stream (name and location)	Length (miles) [1]	Average discharge at mouth (1,000 cubic feet per second)	Drainage area (1,000 sq. miles)
Missouri	Missouri	Red Rock Creek, MT	[3] 2,540	76.2	[2] 529
Mississippi	Louisiana	Mississippi River, MN	2,340	[4] 593	[2,5] 1,150
Yukon	Alaska	McNeil River, Canada	1,980	225	[2] 328
St. Lawrence	Canada	North River, MN	1,900	348	[2] 396
Rio Grande	Mexico-Texas	Rio Grande, CO	1,900	[7]	336
Arkansas	Arkansas	East Fork Arkansas River, CO	1,460	41	161
Colorado	Mexico	Colorado River, CO	1,450	[7]	246
Atchafalaya [6]	Louisiana	Tierra Blanca Creek, NM	1,420	58	95.1
Ohio	Illinois-Kentucky	Allegheny River, PA	1,310	281	203
Red [6]	Louisiana	Tierra Blanca Creek, NM	1,290	56	93.2
Brazos	Texas	Blackwater Draw, NM	1,280	[7]	45.6
Columbia	Oregon-Washington	Columbia River, Canada	1,240	265	[2] 258
Snake	Washington	Snake River, WY	1,040	56.9	108
Platte	Nebraska	Grizzly Creek, CO	990	[7]	84.9
Pecos	Texas	Pecos River, NM	926	[7]	44.3
Canadian	Oklahoma	Canadian River, CO	906	[7]	46.9
Tennessee	Kentucky	Courthouse Creek, NC	886	68	40.9

[1] From source to mouth. [2] Drainage area includes both the United States and Canada. [3] The length from the source of the Missouri River to the Mississippi River and thence to the Gulf of Mexico is about 3,710 miles. [4] Includes about 167,000 cubic feet per second diverted from the Mississippi into the Atchafalaya River but excludes the flow of the Red River. [5] Excludes the drainage areas of the Red and Atchafalaya Rivers. [6] In east-central Louisiana, the Red River flows into the Atchafalaya River, a distributary of the Mississippi River. Data on average discharge, length, and drainage area include the Red River, but exclude all water diverted into the Atchafalaya from the Mississippi River. [7] Less than 15,000 cubic feet per second.

Source: U.S. Geological Survey, *Largest Rivers in the United States*, September 2005, <http://pubs.usgs.gov/of/1987/ofr87-242\>.

Table 366. Extreme and Mean Elevations by State and Other Areas

[One foot = .305 meter. There are 2,130 square miles of the United States below sea level (Death Valley is the lowest point). There are 20,230 square miles above 10,000 feet (Mount McKinley is the highest point in the United States). Minus sign (−) indicates below sea level]

State and other areas	Highest point Name	Highest point Elevation Feet	Highest point Elevation Meters	Lowest point Name	Lowest point Elevation Feet	Lowest point Elevation Meters	Approximate mean elevation Feet	Approximate mean elevation Meters
U.S.	Mt. McKinley (AK)	20,320	6,198	Death Valley (CA)	−282	−86	2,500	763
AL	Cheaha Mountain	2,407	734	Gulf of Mexico	(¹)	(¹)	500	153
AK	Mount McKinley	20,320	6,198	Pacific Ocean.	(¹)	(¹)	1,900	580
AZ	Humphreys Peak	12,633	3,853	Colorado River.	70	21	4,100	1,251
AR	Magazine Mountain	2,753	840	Ouachita River.	55	17	650	198
CA	Mount Whitney.	14,494	4,419	Death Valley.	−282	−86	2,900	885
CO	Mt. Elbert.	14,433	4,402	Arikaree River	3,315	1,011	6,800	2,074
CT	Mt. Frissell on south slope	2,380	726	Long Island Sound.	(¹)	(¹)	500	153
DE ²	Ebright Road ²	448	137	Atlantic Ocean	(¹)	(¹)	60	18
DC	Tenleytown at Reno Reservoir. . .	410	125	Potomac River	1	(Z)	150	46
FL	Britton Hill	345	105	Atlantic Ocean	(¹)	(¹)	100	31
GA	Brasstown Bald	4,784	1,459	Atlantic Ocean	(¹)	(¹)	600	183
HI.	Pu'u Wekiu, Mauna Kea	13,796	4,208	Pacific Ocean.	(¹)	(¹)	3,030	924
ID.	Borah Peak	12,662	3,862	Snake River	710	217	5,000	1,525
IL	Charles Mound	1,235	377	Mississippi River	279	85	600	183
IN.	Hoosier Hill	1,257	383	Ohio River	320	98	700	214
IA.	Hawkeye Point.	1,670	509	Mississippi River	480	146	1,100	336
KS	Mount Sunflower	4,039	1,232	Verdigris River	679	207	2,000	610
KY	Black Mountain	4,145	1,264	Mississippi River	257	78	750	229
LA	Driskill Mountain	535	163	New Orleans	−8	−2	100	31
ME	Mount Katahdin	5,268	1,607	Atlantic Ocean	(¹)	(¹)	600	183
MD	Hoye Crest.	3,360	1,025	Atlantic Ocean	(¹)	(¹)	350	107
MA	Mount Greylock	3,491	1,065	Atlantic Ocean	(¹)	(¹)	500	153
MI.	Mount Arvon	1,979	604	Lake Erie	571	174	900	275
MN	Eagle Mountain	2,301	702	Lake Superior	601	183	1,200	366
MS.	Woodall Mountain	806	246	Gulf of Mexico	(¹)	(¹)	300	92
MO.	Taum Sauk Mountain.	1,772	540	St. Francis River	230	70	800	244
MT.	Granite Peak	12,799	3,904	Kootenai River	1,800	549	3,400	1,037
NE	Panorama Point	5,424	1,654	Missouri River	840	256	2,600	793
NV	Boundary Peak	13,140	4,007	Colorado River	479	146	5,500	1,678
NH	Mount Washington.	6,288	1,918	Atlantic Ocean	(¹)	(¹)	1,000	305
NJ	High Point	1,803	550	Atlantic Ocean	(¹)	(¹)	250	76
NM.	Wheeler Peak	13,161	4,014	Red Bluff Reservoir	2,842	867	5,700	1,739
NY	Mount Marcy	5,344	1,630	Atlantic Ocean	(¹)	(¹)	1,000	305
NC	Mount Mitchell	6,684	2,039	Atlantic Ocean	(¹)	(¹)	700	214
ND	White Butte	3,506	1,069	Red River of the North. . .	750	229	1,900	580
OH	Campbell Hill	1,550	473	Ohio River	455	139	850	259
OK	Black Mesa	4,973	1,517	Little River	289	88	1,300	397
OR.	Mount Hood.	11,239	3,428	Pacific Ocean.	(¹)	(¹)	3,300	1,007
PA	Mount Davis.	3,213	980	Delaware River	(¹)	(¹)	1,100	336
RI.	Jerimoth Hill	812	248	Atlantic Ocean	(¹)	(¹)	200	61
SC	Sassafras Mountain.	3,560	1,086	Atlantic Ocean	(¹)	(¹)	350	107
SD	Harney Peak	7,242	2,209	Big Stone Lake	966	295	2,200	671
TN	Clingmans Dome.	6,643	2,026	Mississippi River	178	54	900	275
TX	Guadalupe Peak	8,749	2,668	Gulf of Mexico	(¹)	(¹)	1,700	519
UT	Kings Peak.	13,528	4,126	Beaverdam Wash	2,000	610	6,100	1,861
VT	Mount Mansfield	4,393	1,340	Lake Champlain.	95	29	1,000	305
VA	Mount Rogers	5,729	1,747	Atlantic Ocean	(¹)	(¹)	950	290
WA.	Mount Rainier	14,411	4,395	Pacific Ocean.	(¹)	(¹)	1,700	519
WV.	Spruce Knob	4,863	1,483	Potomac River	240	73	1,500	458
WI	Timms Hill	1,951	595	Lake Michigan	579	177	1,050	320
WY	Gannett Peak.	13,804	4,210	Belle Fourche River	3,099	945	6,700	2,044
Other areas:								
Puerto Rico	Cerro de Punta	4,390	1,339	Atlantic Ocean	(¹)	(¹)	1,800	549
American Samoa	Lata Mountain	3,160	964	Pacific Ocean.	(¹)	(¹)	1,300	397
Guam	Mount Lamlam.	1,332	406	Pacific Ocean.	(¹)	(¹)	330	101
U.S. Virgin Islands	Crown Mountain	1,556	475	Atlantic Ocean	(¹)	(¹)	750	229

Z Less than .5 meter. ¹ Sea level. ² At DE–PA state line.

Source: For highest and lowest points, see U.S. Geological Survey, "Elevations and Distances in the United States," <http://egsc.usgs.gov/isb/pubs/booklets/elvadist/elvadist.html\>, released April 2005. For mean elevations, see *Elevations and Distances in the United States*, 1983 edition.

Table 367. Land Cover/Use by Type: 1982 to 2003

[In millions of acres (1,937.7 represents 1,937,700,000), except percent. Excludes Alaska, Hawaii, and District of Columbia. For inventory-specific glossary of key terms, see <http://www.nrcs.usda.gov/technical/NRI/glossaries.html>]

Year	Total surface area	Nonfederal rural land						Developed land	Water areas	Federal land
		Rural land total [1]	Crop-land	Pasture-land	Range-land	Forest land	Other rural land			
Land										
1982..............	1,937.7	1,417.2	420.4	131.4	414.5	402.6	48.3	72.8	48.6	399.1
1992..............	1,937.6	1,400.2	381.2	125.1	406.6	404.0	49.3	86.5	49.4	401.5
2001..............	1,937.7	1,379.3	369.6	116.9	404.7	404.9	51.4	106.3	50.3	401.8
2002..............	1,937.7	1,378.1	368.4	117.3	405.3	404.9	50.6	107.3	50.4	401.9
2003..............	1,937.7	1,377.3	367.9	117.0	405.1	405.6	50.2	108.1	50.4	401.9
Percent of total land										
1982..............	100.0	73.1	21.7	6.8	21.4	20.8	2.5	3.8	2.5	20.6
1992..............	100.0	72.3	19.7	6.5	21.0	20.9	2.5	4.5	2.5	20.7
2001..............	100.0	71.2	19.1	6.0	20.9	20.9	2.7	5.5	2.5	20.7
2002..............	100.0	71.1	19.0	6.1	20.9	20.9	2.6	5.5	2.6	20.7
2003..............	100.0	71.1	19.0	6.0	20.9	20.9	2.6	5.6	2.6	20.7

[1] Includes Conservation Reserve Program (CRP) land not shown separately. CRP is a federal program established under the Food Security Act of 1985 to assist private landowners to convert highly erodible cropland to vegetative cover for 10 years.
Source: U.S. Department of Agriculture, Natural Resources and Conservation Service, *2003 Annual National Resources Inventory.* See also <http://www.nrcs.usda.gov/technical/NRI>.

Table 368. Wetlands on Nonfederal Land and Water Areas by Land Cover/Use and Farm Production Region: 2003

[In thousands of acres (110,760 represents 110,760,000). Represents palustrine and estuarine wetlands; see source]

Farm production region [1]	Total	Cropland [2]	Forest land	Range-land	Other rural land	Developed land	Water area
Wetlands, total	**110,760**	**16,730**	**65,440**	**7,740**	**15,800**	**1,590**	**3,460**
Lake states	22,460	2,710	15,480	–	3,880	160	230
Southeast	22,360	940	16,010	970	3,460	420	560
Delta states	17,950	3,240	11,020	270	2,730	190	500
Northeast.	14,150	1,250	10,890	–	1,550	240	220
Northern plains	7,640	3,020	210	2,870	1,090	80	370
Appalachian.	7,460	400	6,080	–	570	110	300
Southern plains	5,590	970	2,350	970	520	230	550
Mountain	4,780	1,570	220	2,010	820	30	130
Corn belt	4,690	1,330	2,440	–	380	100	440
Pacific	3,680	1,300	740	650	800	30	160

– Represents or rounds to zero. [1] Ten regions established by USDA, Economic Research Service, that group states according to differences in soils, slope of land, climate, distance to market, and storage and marketing facilities. [2] Includes pastureland and Conservation Reserve Program (CRP) lands.
Source: U.S. Department of Agriculture, Natural Resources Conservation Service, *2003 Annual National Resources Inventory.* See also <http://www.nrcs.usda.gov/technical/NRI/>.

Table 369. Land Cover/Use by State: 2003

[In thousands of acres (1,937,664 represents 1,937,664,000), except percent. Excludes Alaska, District of Columbia, Hawaii, and Island Areas]

State	Total surface area	Selected nonfederal rural land, percent of total			State	Total surface area	Selected nonfederal rural land, percent of total		
		Crop-land	Range-land	Forest land			Crop-land	Range-land	Forest land
United States	**1,937,664**	**19.0**	**20.9**	**20.9**					
Alabama	33,424	7.5	0.2	64.4	Nebraska	49,510	39.5	46.6	1.6
Arizona	72,964	1.3	44.2	5.7	Nevada	70,763	0.9	11.7	0.4
Arkansas	34,037	22.1	0.1	44.1	New Hampshire	5,941	2.1	–	65.6
California	101,510	9.3	17.5	13.7	New Jersey	5,216	10.1	–	30.8
Colorado	66,625	12.5	37.2	4.9	New Mexico	77,823	2.0	51.3	7.0
Connecticut	3,195	5.4	–	53.4	New York	31,361	17.1	–	56.1
Delaware	1,534	29.8	–	22.2	North Carolina	33,709	16.4	–	45.9
Florida	37,534	7.7	7.2	33.9	North Dakota	45,251	53.6	24.5	1.0
Georgia	37,741	11.0	–	58.0	Ohio	26,445	42.5	–	27.3
Idaho	53,488	10.2	12.0	7.5	Oklahoma	44,738	20.1	31.6	16.5
Illinois	36,059	66.5	–	11.0	Oregon	62,161	6.0	15.1	20.5
Indiana	23,158	57.5	–	16.5	Pennsylvania	28,995	17.7	–	53.9
Iowa	36,017	70.8	–	6.4	Rhode Island	813	2.5	–	45.9
Kansas	52,661	50.3	30.1	2.9	South Carolina	19,939	11.9	–	56.0
Kentucky	25,863	21.2	–	40.6	South Dakota	49,358	34.6	44.7	1.0
Louisiana	31,377	17.3	0.9	42.5	Tennessee	26,974	17.6	–	44.3
Maine	20,966	1.8	–	84.0	Texas	171,052	14.9	56.2	6.2
Maryland	7,870	19.3	–	30.1	Utah	54,339	3.1	19.6	3.5
Massachusetts	5,339	4.7	–	49.9	Vermont	6,154	9.5	–	67.1
Michigan	37,349	21.7	–	44.7	Virginia	27,087	10.6	–	48.7
Minnesota	54,010	39.1	–	30.3	Washington	44,035	14.7	13.3	28.9
Mississippi	30,527	16.3	–	54.9	West Virginia	15,508	5.3	–	68.1
Missouri	44,614	30.7	0.2	28.1	Wisconsin	35,920	28.7	–	40.4
Montana	94,110	15.4	39.0	5.7	Wyoming	62,603	3.5	44.0	1.5

– Represents zero.
Source: U.S. Department of Agriculture, Natural Resources and Conservation Service, *Summary Report, 2003 Annual National Resources Inventory.* See also <http://www.nrcs.usda.gov/technical/NRI/>.

Table 370. U.S. Wetland Resources and Deepwater Habitats by Type: 1998 to 2004

[In thousands of acres (148,618.8 represents 148,618,800). Wetlands and deepwater habitats are defined separately because the term wetland does not include permanent water bodies. Deepwater habitats are permanently flooded land lying below the deepwater boundary of wetlands. Deepwater habitats include environments where surface water is permanent and often deep, so that water, rather than air, is the principal medium within which the dominant organisms live, whether or not they are attached to the substrate. As in wetlands, the dominant plants are hydrophytes; however, the substrates are considered nonsoil because the water is too deep to support emergent vegetation. In general terms, wetlands are lands where saturation with water is the dominant factor determining the nature of soil development and the types of plant and animal communities living in the soil and on its surface. The single feature that most wetlands share is soil or substrate that is at least periodically saturated with or covered by water. Wetlands are lands transitional between terrestrial and aquatic systems where the water table is usually at or near the surface or the land is covered by shallow water. For more information on wetlands, see the "Classification of Wetlands and Deepwater Habitats of the United States" at <http://www.fws.gov/wetlands/_documents/gNSDI/ClassificationWetlandsDeepwaterHabitatsUS.pdf>]

Wetland or deepwater category	Estimated area, 1998	Estimated area, 2004	Change, 1998 to 2004
All wetlands and deepwater habitats, total	**148,618.8**	**149,058.5**	**439.7**
All deepwater habitats, total	41,046.6	41,304.5	247.9
Lacustrine [1]	16,610.5	16,773.4	162.9
Riverine [2]	6,765.5	6,813.3	47.7
Estuarine Subtidal [3]	17,680.5	17,717.8	37.3
All wetlands, total	107,562.3	107,754.0	191.8
Intertidal wetlands [4]	5,328.7	5,300.3	−28.4
Marine intertidal	130.4	128.6	−1.9
Estuarine intertidal nonvegetated	594.1	600.0	5.9
Estuarine intertidal vegetated	4,604.2	4,571.7	−32.4
Freshwater wetlands	102,233.6	102,453.8	220.2
Freshwater nonvegetated	5,918.7	6,633.9	715.3
Freshwater vegetated	96,414.9	95,819.8	−495.1
Freshwater emergent [5]	26,289.6	26,147.0	−142.6
Freshwater forested [6]	51,483.1	52,031.4	548.2
Freshwater shrub [7]	18,542.2	17,641.4	−900.8

[1] The lacustrine system includes deepwater habitats with all of the following characteristics: (1) situated in a topographic depression or a dammed river channel; (2) lacking trees, shrubs, persistent emergents, emergent mosses or lichens with greater than 30 percent coverage; and (3) total area exceeds 20 acres (8 hectares). [2] The riverine system includes deepwater habitats contained within a channel, with the exception of habitats with water containing ocean derived salts in excess of 0.5 parts per thousand. [3] The estuarine system consists of deepwater tidal habitats and adjacent tidal wetlands that are usually semi-enclosed by land but have open, partly obstructed, or sporadic access to the open ocean, and in which ocean water is at least occasionally diluted by freshwater runoff from the land. Subtidal is where the substrate is continuously submerged by marine or estuarine waters. [4] Intertidal is where the substrate is exposed and flooded by tides. Intertidal includes the splash zone of coastal waters. [5] Emergent wetlands are characterized by erect, rooted, herbaceous hydrophytes, excluding mosses and lichens. This vegetation is present for most of the growing season in most years. These wetlands are usually dominated by perennial plants. [6] Forested wetlands are characterized by woody vegetation that is 20 feet tall or taller. [7] Shrub wetlands include areas dominated by woody vegetation less than 20 feet tall. The species include true shrubs, young trees, and trees or shrubs that are small or stunted because of environmental conditions.

Source: U.S. Fish and Wildlife Service, *Status and Trends of Wetlands in the Conterminous United States, 1998 to 2004*, December 2005. See also <http://www.fws.gov/wetlands/_documents/gSandT/NationalReports /StatusTrendsWetlandsConterminousUS1998to2004.pdf>.

Table 371. U.S. Water Withdrawals Per Day by End Use: 1950 to 2005

[(180 represents 180,000,000,000). Includes the District of Columbia, Puerto Rico and U.S. Virgin Islands. Withdrawal signifies water physically withdrawn from a source. Includes fresh and saline water; excludes water used for hydroelectric power. For information on "Changes for the 2005 report," see "Trends in Estimated Water Use in the United States, Table 14"]

Year	Total withdrawals	Public supply	Rural domestic and livestock			Thermo electric power	Other			
			Self supplied domestic	Live-stock	Irri-gation		Self supplied domestic	Mining	Com-mercial	Aqua-culture
1950 [1]	180	14	2.1	1.5	89	40	37	(5)	(5)	(5)
1955 [2]	240	17	2.1	1.5	110	72	39	(5)	(5)	(5)
1960 [3]	270	21	2.0	1.6	110	100	38	(5)	(5)	(5)
1965 [4]	310	24	2.3	1.7	120	130	46	(5)	(5)	(5)
1970 [4]	370	27	2.6	1.9	130	170	47	(5)	(5)	(5)
1975 [3]	420	29	2.8	2.1	140	200	45	(5)	(5)	(5)
1980 [3]	430	33	3.4	2.2	150	210	45	(5)	(5)	(5)
1985 [3]	397	36.4	3.32	2.23	135	187	25.9	3.44	1.23	2.24
1990 [3]	404	38.8	3.39	2.25	134	194	22.6	4.93	2.39	2.25
1995 [3]	399	40.2	3.39	2.28	130	190	22.4	3.72	2.89	3.22
2000 [3]	413	43.2	3.58	2.38	139	195	19.7	4.50	(NA)	5.77
2005 [3]	410	44.2	3.83	2.14	128	201	18.2	4.02	(NA)	8.78

NA Not available. [1] Population covered: 48 states, District of Columbia, and Hawaii. [2] Population covered: 48 states, [3] Population covered: 50 states, District of Columbia, Puerto Rico, and the Virgin Islands. [4] Population covered: 50 states, District of Columbia, and Puerto Rico. [5] Included in "Self-Supplied Industrial."

Source: 1940–1960, U.S. Bureau of Domestic Business Development, based principally on committee prints, *Water Resources Activities in the United States*, for the Senate Committee on National Water Resources, U.S. Senate, thereafter, U.S. Geological Survey, *Estimated Use of Water in the United States in 2005*, circular 1344. See also <http://pubs.usgs.gov/circ/1344/> (October 2009).

Table 372. National Ambient Air Pollutant Concentrations by Type of Pollutant: 2003 to 2009

[Data represent annual composite averages of pollutant based on daily 24-hour averages of monitoring stations, except carbon monoxide which is based on the second-highest, nonoverlapping, 8-hour average; ozone, the fourth-highest maximum 8-hour value; and lead, the maximum quarterly average of ambient lead levels. Based on data from the Air Quality System. µmg/m³ = micrograms of pollutant per cubic meter of air; ppm = parts per million]

Pollutant	Unit	Monitoring stations, number	Air quality standard [1]	2003	2004	2005	2006	2007	2008	2009
Carbon monoxide	ppm	300	[2] 9	2.7	2.5	2.3	2.2	2.0	1.9	1.8
Ozone	ppm	1,011	[3] 0.075	0.080	0.074	0.079	0.077	0.077	0.073	0.069
Sulfur dioxide	ppm	384	[4] 0.03	0.0043	0.0041	0.0041	0.0037	0.0035	0.0032	0.0027
Particulates (PM-10)	µmg/m³	722	[5] 150	90.5	70.4	69.4	76.0	69.4	67.3	59.7
Fine particulates (PM2.5) annual average	µmg/m³	741	[6] 15	12.3	11.9	12.8	11.6	11.9	10.9	9.9
Fine particulates (PM2.5) daily average	µmg/m³	741	[7] 35	31.1	31.0	33.6	28.8	31.3	27.1	24.9
Nitrogen dioxide	ppm	311	[8] 0.053	0.014	0.013	0.013	0.013	0.012	0.011	0.011
Lead	µmg/m³	109	[9] 0.15	0.16	0.20	0.15	0.14	0.15	0.19	0.11

[1] Refers to the primary National Ambient Air Quality Standard. [2] Based on 8-hour standard of 9 ppm. [3] Based on 8-hour standard of 0.075 ppm. On March 12, 2008, EPA revised the level of the primary and secondary 8-hour ozone standards to 0.075 ppm. [4] Based on annual standard of 0.03 ppm. [5] Based on 24-hour (daily) standard of 150 mg/m³. The particulates (PM-10) standard replaced the previous standard for total suspended particulates in 1987. In 2006, EPA revoked the annual PM-10 standard. [6] Based on annual standard of 15 mg/m³. The PM-2.5 national monitoring network was deployed in 1999. National trend data prior to that time is not available. [7] Based on daily standard of 35 mg/m³. The PM-2.5 national monitoring network was deployed in 1999. National trend data prior to that time is not available. [8] Based on annual standard of 0.053 ppm. [9] Based on 3-month standard of 1.5 µmg/m³. On October 15, 2008, EPA revised the form of the primary and secondary lead standards and revised the level to 0.15 mg/m³.

Source: U.S. Environmental Protection Agency, *Latest Findings on National Air Quality—Status and Trends through 2009*, <http://www.epa.gov/air/airtrends/2010/index.html>.

Table 373. Selected National Air Pollutant Emissions: 1970 to 2008

[In thousands of tons (4,320 represents 4,320,000), except as indicated. The methodology used to estimate emission data for 1970 thru 1984 and for 1985 thru the current year is different. Beginning with 1985, the methodology for more recent years is described in the document available at <http://www.epa.gov/ttn/chief/net/2005inventory.html>]

Year	Ammonia	Carbon monoxide	Nitrogen oxide	PM-10 [1]	PM-10 [2]	PM-2.5 [1]	PM-2.5 [2]	Sulfur dioxide	V.O.C. [3]
1970	(NA)	204,042	26,882	13,022	13,022	(NA)	(NA)	31,218	34,659
1980	(NA)	185,408	27,080	7,013	7,013	(NA)	(NA)	25,926	31,107
1990	4,320	154,188	25,527	27,753	27,753	7,560	7,560	23,077	24,108
2000	4,907	114,465	22,599	23,748	22,962	7,287	6,503	16,348	17,511
2004	4,138	99,041	19,793	21,211	18,321	5,497	3,044	14,820	19,789
2005	4,143	93,034	19,122	21,153	18,266	5,457	3,013	14,844	18,422
2006	4,135	87,915	18,110	19,037	16,150	5,269	2,862	13,656	17,590
2007	4,131	82,801	17,321	16,921	14,034	5,080	2,639	13,006	16,759
2008	4,043	77,685	16,339	14,805	11,918	4,892	2,449	11,429	15,927

NA Not available. [1] PM=Particular Matter; PM-10 is equal to or less than ten microns in diameter; PM-2.5 to or less than 2.5 microns effective diameter. [2] Without condensibles. [3] Volatile organic compound.

Source: U.S. Environmental Protection Agency, *National Emissions Inventory (NEI) Air Pollutant Emissions Trends Data*, 1970–2008 Average annual emissions, all criteria pollutants, <http://www.epa.gov/ttn/chief/trends/index.html#tables>.

Table 374. Selected Air Pollutant Emissions by Pollutant and Source: 2008

[In thousands of tons, except as indicated (4,043 represents 4,043,000). See headnote, Table 373]

Source	Ammonia	Carbon monoxide	Nitrogen oxide	PM-10 [1]	PM-2.5 [1]	Sulfur dioxide	V.O.C. [2]
Total emissions	**4,043**	**77,685**	**16,339**	**14,805**	**4,892**	**11,429**	**15,927**
Fuel combustion, stationary sources	68	5,283	5,597	1,330	1,006	9,872	1,450
Electric utilities	34	699	3,007	534	410	7,552	50
Industrial	16	1,216	1,838	330	175	1,670	130
Other fuel combustion	18	3,369	727	466	421	578	1,269
Industrial processes	206	3,767	1,047	1,461	751	1,025	7,142
Chemical and allied product manufacturing	22	265	67	39	29	255	228
Metals processing	3	947	68	78	52	203	46
Petroleum and related industries	3	355	350	24	17	206	561
Other	151	500	418	967	355	329	404
Solvent utilization	–	2	6	8	7	–	4,226
Storage and transport	1	115	18	57	22	4	1,303
Waste disposal and recycling	26	1,584	120	288	267	27	374
Highway vehicles	308	38,866	5,206	171	110	64	3,418
Off highway [3]	3	18,036	4,255	304	283	456	2,586
Miscellaneous [4]	3,457	11,731	260	11,540	2,742	85	1,332

– Rounds to zero. [1] See footnote 1, Table 373. [2] Volatile organic compound. [3] Includes emissions from farm tractors and other farm machinery, construction equipment, industrial machinery, recreational marine vessels, and small general utility engines such as lawn mowers. [4] Includes emissions such as from forest fires and other kinds of burning, various agricultural activities, fugitive dust from paved and unpaved roads, and other construction and mining activities, and natural sources.

Source: U.S. Environmental Protection Agency, *National Emissions Inventory (NEI) Air Pollutant Emissions Trends Data*, 1970–2008 Average annual emissions, all criteria pollutants, <http://www.epa.gov/ttn/chief/trends/index.html#tables>.

Table 375. Emissions of Greenhouse Gases by Type and Source: 1990 to 2009

[In millions of metric tons (6,133.2 represents 6,133,200,000). Metric ton = 2,204.6 lbs. Emission estimates were mandated by Congress through Section 1605(a) of the Energy Policy Act of 1992 (Title XVI). Data shown below, by type and source, are measured in terms of their carbon dioxide equivalent]

Type and source	1990	2000	2004	2005	2006	2007	2008	2009 [1]
Total emissions	**6,133.2**	**6,935.3**	**7,071.9**	**7,109.4**	**7,027.4**	**7,150.4**	**6,983.1**	**6,575.5**
Carbon dioxide, total	5,040.9	5,900.3	6,031.3	6,055.2	5,961.6	6,059.5	5,865.5	5,446.8
From energy use by sector								
Residential	963.4	1,185.1	1,227.8	1,261.5	1,192.0	1,242.0	1,229.0	1,162.2
Commercial	792.6	1,022.0	1,053.5	1,069.0	1,043.4	1,078.6	1,073.5	1,003.6
Industrial	1,695.1	1,788.1	1,731.1	1,675.2	1,661.1	1,661.6	1,597.6	1,405.4
Transportation	1,587.7	1,872.0	1,962.3	1,990.7	2,021.9	2,039.6	1,937.9	1,854.5
Adjustments to energy [2]	-82.9	-64.7	-45.3	-44.6	-62.7	-67.5	-76.1	-66.0
Adjusted energy subtotal	4,955.9	5,802.6	5,929.3	5,951.8	5,855.7	5,954.2	5,761.9	5,359.6
Other sources	85.1	97.8	102.0	103.5	105.9	105.3	103.6	87.3
Methane	768.8	663.1	661.6	669.2	678.5	690.9	724.2	730.9
Energy sources	293.1	281.7	280.0	277.0	279.8	285.8	299.3	303.0
Agricultural sources	190.6	201.2	204.0	209.9	211.8	212.3	219.7	215.9
Waste management	280.6	174.6	172.0	177.3	181.9	187.6	200.6	207.9
Industrial processes	4.5	5.6	5.6	5.0	5.1	5.1	4.6	4.2
Nitrous oxide	221.4	217.8	222.0	223.6	223.7	228.6	223.5	219.6
Agricultural sources	148.7	144.3	154.1	156.9	157.8	162.1	161.1	161.0
Energy use	40.2	52.1	49.7	48.2	47.2	47.3	45.1	42.5
Industrial processes	28.5	16.7	13.3	13.6	13.6	14.1	12.1	10.8
Waste management	4.0	4.7	4.9	5.0	5.1	5.2	5.2	5.3
High-GWP gases [3]	102.1	154.0	157.0	161.3	163.6	171.4	169.9	178.2

[1] 2009 preliminary data. [2] Carbon dioxide emissions from U.S. Territories are added to the U.S. total, and carbon dioxide emissions from fuels used for international transport (both ocean-going vessels and airplanes) are subtracted to derive total U.S. greenhouse as emissions. [3] High global warming potential gases: hyrdofluorocarbons (HFCs), perfluorocarbons (PFCs), and sulfur hexafluoride (SF6).

Source: U.S. Energy Information Administration, Environment, *Greenhouse Gas Emissions in the United States, 2009*, Series DOE/EIA-0573 (2009), annual. See also <http://www.eia.gov/environment/emissions/ghg_report/>.

Table 376. Carbon Dioxide Emissions by Sector and Source: 1990 to 2009

[In million metric tons (5,040.9 represents 5,040,900,000), except as noted. Data below measured in terms of carbon dioxide equivalent. Data have been revised for years shown]

Sector	1990	2000	2004	2005	2006	2007	2008	2009 [1]
Total [2]	5,040.9	5,900.3	6,031.3	6,055.2	5,961.6	6,059.5	5,865.5	5,446.8
Total [3]	**5,038.7**	**5,867.2**	**5,974.7**	**5,996.4**	**5,918.3**	**6,021.8**	**5,838.0**	**5,425.6**
Petroleum	2,186.6	2,460.6	2,608.6	2,627.6	2,602.5	2,603.2	2,443.5	2,318.8
Coal	1,821.4	2,155.5	2,160.2	2,181.9	2,146.9	2,172.2	2,139.4	1,876.8
Natural gas	1,024.8	1,240.6	1,194.4	1,175.2	1,157.0	1,234.7	1,243.0	1,218.0
Residential	**963.4**	**1,185.1**	**1,227.8**	**1,261.5**	**1,192.0**	**1,242.0**	**1,229.0**	**1,162.2**
Petroleum	98.4	108.0	106.0	100.9	85.0	86.8	84.9	82.9
Coal	3.0	1.1	1.1	0.8	0.6	0.7	0.7	0.6
Natural gas	238.3	270.8	264.3	262.4	237.5	257.3	265.8	259.1
Electricity [4]	623.7	805.2	856.4	897.3	868.9	897.2	877.5	819.5
Commercial	**792.6**	**1,022.0**	**1,053.5**	**1,069.0**	**1,043.4**	**1,078.6**	**1,073.5**	**1,003.6**
Petroleum [5]	72.5	57.9	58.3	54.9	47.6	46.6	46.1	43.6
Coal	12.0	8.8	9.8	9.3	6.2	6.7	6.5	5.8
Natural gas	142.3	172.5	169.8	163.1	154.0	164.2	171.3	169.1
Electricity [4]	565.9	782.8	815.6	841.8	835.6	861.1	849.5	785.1
Industrial [6]	**1,695.1**	**1,788.1**	**1,731.1**	**1,675.2**	**1,661.1**	**1,661.6**	**1,597.6**	**1,405.4**
Petroleum	365.5	370.4	418.6	416.8	430.4	415.4	376.2	343.1
Coal	258.4	210.8	190.5	182.9	179.4	174.6	168.2	130.9
Natural gas	432.4	480.8	431.5	397.5	394.2	406.3	406.9	383.1
Electricity [4]	638.3	718.6	674.7	672.8	650.2	662.3	641.8	551
Transportation [6]	**1,587.7**	**1,872.0**	**1,962.3**	**1,990.7**	**2,021.9**	**2,039.6**	**1,937.9**	**1,854.5**
Petroleum	1,548.4	1,832.8	1,925.6	1,952.7	1,984.0	1,999.0	1,896.3	1,815.7
Natural gas	36.1	35.7	31.9	33.1	33.2	35.3	36.7	34.1
Electricity [4]	3.2	3.6	4.8	5.0	4.7	5.3	4.9	4.7
Electric power sector [7]	**1,831.0**	**2,310.2**	**2,351.5**	**2,416.9**	**2,359.5**	**2,425.9**	**2,373.7**	**2,160.3**
Petroleum	101.8	91.5	100.1	102.3	55.6	55.3	40.0	33.6
Coal	1,547.6	1,927.4	1,943.1	1,983.8	1,953.7	1,987.3	1,959.4	1,742.2
Natural gas	175.5	280.9	296.8	319.1	338.2	371.7	362.3	372.6

[1] Preliminary. [2] Emissions from nonfuel uses, adjustments to energy, and other sources are included. [3] Emissions from renewables are included in total. [4] Share of total electric power sector carbon dioxide emissions weighted by sales to this sector. [5] Includes small amounts of petroleum coke. [6] Includes emissions from nonfuel uses of fossil fuels. [7] Emissions from the electric power sector are apportioned to each end-use sector according to their share of electricity sales.

Source: U.S. Energy Information Administration, Environment, *Greenhouse Gas Emissions in the United States, 2009*, Series DOE/EIA-0573 (2009), annual. See also <http://www.eia.gov/environment/emissions/ghg_report/>.

Table 377. Municipal Solid Waste Generation, Materials Recovery, Combustion With Energy Recovery, and Discards: 1980 to 2009

[In millions of tons (151.6 represents 151,600,000), except as indicated. Covers post-consumer residential and commercial solid wastes which comprise the major portion of typical municipal collections. Excludes mining, agricultural and industrial processing, demolition and construction wastes, sewage sludge and junked autos and obsolete equipment wastes. Based on material-flows estimating procedure and wet weight as generated]

Item and material	1980	1990	2000	2005	2007	2008	2009
Waste generated	151.6	208.3	242.5	252.4	255.0	251.0	243.0
Per person per day (lb.)	3.7	4.6	4.7	4.7	4.6	4.5	4.3
Total materials recovery	14.5	33.2	69.5	79.9	84.8	83.9	82.0
Per person per day (lb.)	0.4	0.7	1.4	1.5	1.5	1.5	1.5
Recovery for recycling	14.5	29.0	53.0	59.3	63.1	61.8	61.3
Per person per day (pounds)	0.35	0.6	1.0	1.1	1.2	1.1	1.1
Recovery for composting [1]	(Z)	4.2	16.5	20.6	21.7	22.1	20.8
Per person per day (pounds)	(Z)	0.1	0.3	0.4	0.4	0.4	0.4
Combustion with energy recovery	2.7	29.7	33.7	31.6	32.0	31.6	29.0
Per person per day (lb.)	0.07	0.7	0.7	0.6	0.6	0.6	0.5
Discards to landfill, other disposal	134.4	145.3	139.4	140.9	138.2	135.6	131.9
Per person per day (lb.)	3.2	3.2	2.7	2.6	2.5	2.4	2.4
PERCENT DISTRIBUTION OF GENERATION							
Percent of total generation	71.8	70.3	73.7	73.2	72.9	72.1	70.6
Paper and paperboard	36.4	34.9	36.2	33.6	32.4	30.8	28.2
Glass	10.0	6.3	5.3	5.0	4.9	4.8	4.8
Metals	10.2	7.9	7.8	8.0	8.2	8.4	8.6
Plastics	4.5	8.2	10.5	11.6	12.1	12.0	12.3
Rubber and leather	2.8	2.8	2.8	2.9	3.0	3.0	3.1
Textiles	1.7	2.8	3.9	4.5	4.7	5.0	5.2
Wood	4.6	5.9	5.6	5.9	6.0	6.2	6.5
Other	1.7	1.5	1.6	1.7	1.8	1.9	1.9
Total other waste	28.2	29.7	26.3	26.8	27.1	27.9	29.4
Food scraps	8.6	11.5	12.3	12.7	12.8	13.3	14.1
Yard trimmings	18.1	16.8	12.6	12.7	12.8	13.1	13.7
Miscellaneous organic wastes	1.5	1.4	1.4	1.5	1.5	1.5	1.6

Z Less than 5,000 tons or 0.05 percent. [1] Composting of yard trimmings, food scraps, and other municipal solid waste organic material. Does not include backyard composting..

Source: Franklin Associates, a Division of ERG, Prairie Village, KS, *Municipal Solid Waste in the United States: 2009 Facts and Figures.* Prepared for the U.S. Environmental Protection Agency. See also <www.epa.gov/osw/nonhaz/municipal/msw99.htm>.

Table 378. Generation and Recovery of Selected Materials in Municipal Solid Waste: 1980 to 2009

[In millions of tons (151.6 represents 151,600,000), except as indicated. Covers post-consumer residential and commercial solid wastes which comprise the major portion of typical municipal collections. Excludes mining, agricultural and industrial processing, demolition and construction wastes, sewage sludge, and junked autos and obsolete equipment wastes. Based on material-flows estimating procedure and wet weight as generated]

Item and material	1980	1990	2000	2005	2007	2008	2009
Waste generated, total [1]	**151.6**	**205.2**	**242.6**	**252.4**	**255.0**	**251.0**	**243.0**
Paper and paperboard	55.2	72.7	87.7	84.8	82.5	77.4	68.4
Glass	15.1	13.1	12.8	12.5	12.5	12.2	11.8
Metals: Ferrous	12.6	12.6	14.1	15.0	15.6	15.7	15.6
Aluminum	1.7	2.8	3.2	3.3	3.4	3.4	3.4
Other nonferrous	1.2	1.1	1.6	1.9	1.9	2.0	1.9
Plastics	6.8	17.1	25.5	29.3	30.8	30.1	29.8
Food scraps	13.0	20.8	26.8	32.0	32.6	33.3	34.3
Yard trimmings	27.5	35.0	30.5	32.1	32.6	32.9	33.2
Materials recovered, total [1]	**14.5**	**33.2**	**69.4**	**79.9**	**84.8**	**83.9**	**82.0**
Paper and paperboard	11.7	20.2	37.6	42.0	44.5	42.9	42.5
Glass	0.8	2.6	2.9	2.6	2.9	2.8	3.0
Metals: Ferrous	0.4	2.2	4.7	5.0	5.3	5.3	5.2
Aluminum	0.3	1.0	0.9	0.7	0.7	0.7	0.7
Other nonferrous	0.5	0.7	1.1	1.3	1.3	1.4	1.3
Plastics	0.2	0.4	1.5	1.8	2.1	2.1	2.1
Food scraps	(Z)	(Z)	0.7	0.7	0.8	0.8	0.9
Yard trimings	(Z)	4.2	15.8	19.9	20.9	21.3	19.9
Percent of generation recovered, total [1]	**9.6**	**16.2**	**29.7**	**31.6**	**33.3**	**33.4**	**33.8**
Paper and paperboard	21.3	27.8	42.8	49.5	53.9	55.5	62.1
Glass	5.0	20.1	22.6	20.7	23.0	23.1	25.5
Metals: Ferrous	2.9	17.6	33.2	33.6	33.8	33.8	33.5
Aluminum	17.9	35.9	26.9	20.7	21.7	21.1	20.3
Other nonferrous	46.6	66.4	66.3	68.8	69.1	69.4	68.8
Plastics	0.3	2.2	5.8	6.0	6.8	7.1	7.1
Food scraps	(Z)	(Z)	2.5	2.2	2.5	2.4	2.5
Yard trimmings	(Z)	12.0	51.7	61.9	64.1	64.7	59.9

Z Less than 5,000 tons or 0.05 percent. [1] Includes products not shown separately.

Source: Franklin Associates, a Division of ERG, Prairie Village, KS, *Municipal Solid Waste in the United States: 2009 Facts and Figures.* Prepared for the U.S. Environmental Protection Agency. See also <www.epa.gov/osw/nonhaz/municipal /msw99.htm>.

Geography and Environment 231

Table 379. Municipal Solid Waste—Generation, Recovery, and Discards by Selected Type of Product: 2009

[See headnote, Table 378]

Type of product	Generation (1,000 tons)	Recovery Products recovered (1,000 tons)	Recovery Percent of generation	Discards (1,000 tons)
Paper and paperboard products [1]	68,420	42,500	62.1	25,920
Nondurable goods	33,480	17,430	52.1	16,050
Newsprint	5,060	4,490	88.7	570
Groundwood inserts	2,700	2,350	87.0	350
Magazines	1,450	780	53.8	670
Office-type papers	5,380	3,990	74.2	1,390
Standard mail	4,650	2,950	63.4	1,700
Other commercial printing	3,490	2,310	66.2	1,180
Containers and packaging	34,940	25,070	71.8	9,870
Corrugated boxes	27,190	22,100	81.3	5,090
Folding cartons	4,980	2,490	50.0	2,490
Glass products [1]	11,780	3,000	25.5	8,780
Containers and packaging	9,660	3,000	31.1	6,660
Beer and soft drink bottles	6,000	2,340	39.0	3,660
Wine and liquor bottles	1,710	310	18.1	1,400
Food and other bottles and jars	1,950	350	17.9	1,600
Metal products [1,2]	20,910	7,220	34.5	13,690
Ferrous	13,340	3,720	27.9	9,620
Aluminum	1,350	(Z)	(Z)	1,350
Other nonferrous	540	(Z)	(Z)	540
Plastics [1]	29,830	2,120	7.1	27,710
Plastics in durable goods	10,650	400	3.8	10250
Plastics in nondurable goods	6,650	(Z)	(Z)	6,650
Plastics in containers and packaging	12,530	1,720	13.7	10,810
Rubber and leather [1]	7,490	1,070	14.3	6,420
Rubber in tires	3,040	1,070	35.2	1,970

Z Less than 5,000 tons or 0.05 percent. [1] Includes products not shown separately. [2] Metals in durable goods only.

Source: Franklin Associates, a Division of ERG, Prairie Village, KS, *Municipal Solid Waste in the United States: 2009 Facts and Figures.* Prepared for the U.S. Environmental Protection Agency. See also <www.epa.gov/osw/nonhaz/municipal/msw99.htm>.

Table 380. Environmental Industry—Revenues and Employment by Industry Segment: 2000 to 2010

[211.2 represents $211,200,000,000. Covers approximately 30,000 private and public companies engaged in revenue-generating environmental activities]

Industry segment	Revenue (bil. dol.) 2000	2005	2009	2010	Employment 2000	2005	2009	2010
Industry total	**211.2**	**255.0**	**304.6**	**316.3**	**1,371,600**	**1,469,600**	**1,621,300**	**1,657,300**
Analytical services [1]	1.8	1.8	1.9	1.8	20,200	20,000	19,600	19,200
Wastewater treatment works [2]	28.7	35.6	44.1	46.9	118,800	141,100	169,000	178,900
Solid waste management [3]	39.4	47.8	51.1	52.4	221,400	256,500	265,300	271,200
Hazardous waste management [4]	8.2	8.7	8.6	8.7	44,800	45,000	42,100	42,000
Remediation/industrial services	10.1	11.0	11.9	12.2	100,200	96,600	99,600	101,000
Consulting and engineering	17.4	22.4	25.7	26.2	184,000	220,800	240,500	242,900
Water equipment and chemicals	19.8	24.8	26.6	27.2	130,500	153,000	157,300	159,300
Instrument manufacturing	3.8	4.7	5.2	5.5	30,200	34,600	36,100	37,500
Air pollution control equipment [5]	19.0	18.8	15.8	14.9	129,600	123,400	101,800	95,600
Waste management equipment [6]	10.0	10.1	11.0	11.1	75,500	72,900	73,800	73,700
Process and prevention technology	1.2	1.5	1.8	1.9	29,000	28,100	26,500	26,400
Water utilities [7]	29.9	35.1	40.6	42.1	130,000	145,200	162,000	167,200
Resource recovery [8]	16.0	21.0	24.5	25.2	127,000	78,900	88,200	91,500
Clean energy systems and power [9]	5.9	11.9	35.8	40.1	30,400	53,500	139,500	150,900

[1] Covers environmental laboratory testing and services. [2] Mostly revenues collected by municipal entities for sewage or wastewater plants. [3] Covers such activities as collection, transportation, transfer stations, disposal, landfill ownership and management for solid waste and recyclables. [4] Transportation and disposal of hazardous, medical, and nuclear waste. [5] Includes stationary and mobile sources. [6] Includes vehicles, containers, liners, processing, and remediation equipment. [7] Revenues generated from the sale of water, majority in public sector. [8] Revenues generated from the sale of recovered metals, paper, plastic, etc. [9] Revenues generated from the sale of equipment and systems and electricity.

Source: Environmental Business International, Inc., San Diego, CA, *Environmental Business Journal*, monthly (copyright). See also <http://www.ebiusa.com/>.

Table 381. Toxic Chemical Releases and Transfers by Media: 2004 to 2009

[In millions of pounds (4,253.6 represents 4,253,600,000), except as indicated. Based on reports filed as required by Section 313 of the Emergency Planning and Community Right-to-Know Act (EPCRA, or Title III of the Superfund Amendments and Reauthorization Act of 1986), Public Law 99-499. The Pollution Prevention Act (PPA)of 1990 mandates collection of data on toxic chemicals that are treated on-site, recycled, and combusted for energy recovery. Owners and operators of facilities that are classified within North American Industrial Classification Code groups 31 through 33, 2121, 2122, 2211, 4246, 4247 and 562; have 10 or more full-time employees, and that manufacture, process, or otherwise use any listed toxic chemical in quantities greater than the established threshold in the course of a calendar year are covered and required to report. Includes all Persistent, Toxic (PBT) chemicals and vanadium and vanadium compounds. Does not include off-site disposal or other releases transferred to other TRI facilities that reported the amounts as on-site disposal or other releases]

Media	2004	2005	2006	2007	2008 [1]	2009
Total facilities reporting	24,428	24,140	23,543	22,775	22,319	21,020
Total on- and off-site disposal or other releases	4,253.6	4,364.7	4,322.7	4,118.7	3,872.5	3,386.4
On-site releases	3,738.1	3,829.5	3,784.6	3,559.8	3,383.8	3,015.3
Air emissions [2]	1,544.1	1,516.4	1,413.5	1,319.8	1,151.2	915.3
Surface water discharges	253.3	256.7	250.0	238.7	249.3	204.8
Underground injection class I	210.3	211.5	199.8	184.1	174.1	153.2
Underground injection class II-V	27.7	20.2	20.1	21.5	18.2	26.3
RCRA subtitle C landfills [3]	151.9	155.2	151.8	150.6	123.9	71.7
Other landfills............................	267.8	266.9	263.1	267.2	282.1	280.4
Land treatment/application farming	21.5	23.7	26.8	22.0	24.9	17.1
Surface impoundments	719.3	782.0	822.2	764.9	738.6	746.8
Other land disposal	542.1	596.9	637.3	590.9	621.6	599.7
Off-site releases	515.5	535.2	538.1	558.8	488.6	371.1
Total transfers offsite for further waste management	4,006.4	3,944.6	3,989.0	3,885.1	3,511.4	2,842.4
Tranfers to recycling........................	2,085.0	2,095.8	2,181.6	2,142.3	1,970.4	1,628.9
Transfers to energy recovery	650.4	609.0	555.3	525.4	450.9	365.0
Transfers to treatment	326.6	335.4	328.1	286.5	257.4	229.1
Transfers to POTWs (non metals)[4]...........	259.9	264.6	260.1	252.5	256.7	216.4
Transfers to POTWs metal and metal compounds [4]	1.7	1.8	1.8	2.0	1.2	3.3
Other off-site transfers.....................	71.5	0.4	0.5	0.2	0.2	(Z)
Transfers off-site for disposal or other releases	611.3	637.6	661.5	676.3	574.5	399.8
Total production-related waste managed	25,863.8	24,863.3	24,305.5	24,377.3	22,990.2	20,390.7
Recycled on-site	7,135.9	6,719.6	6,822.9	6,878.2	6,807.9	6,035.9
Recycled off-site	2,085.3	2,100.7	2,185.2	2,121.5	1,968.9	1,615.1
Energy recovery on-site....................	2,617.1	2,462.9	2,392.7	2,286.9	2,269.4	1,871.7
Energy recovery off-site....................	649.5	608.9	554.6	523.3	449.7	367.0
Treated on-site...........................	8,447.8	7,918.0	7,314.6	7,755.4	7,050.5	6,644.4
Treated off-site..........................	566.2	574.9	555.7	515.1	484.1	423.2
Quantity disposed or otherwise release of on- and off-site	4,362.1	4,478.3	4,479.9	4,296.9	3,959.8	3,433.5
Non-production-related waste managed	19.3	24.1	18.1	14.3	34.0	11.5

[1] Data have been revised. [2] Air emissions include both fugitive and point source. [3] RCRA=Resource Conservation and Recovery Act. [4] POTW (Publicly Owned Treatment Work) is a wastewater treatment facility that is owned by a state or municipality.

Source: U.S. Environmental Protection Agency, Toxic Release Inventory (TRI) Program, 2009 TRI National Analysis. See also <http://www.epa.gov/tri/tridata/tri09/national_analysis/index.htm>, 2009 data as of April 18, 2011.

Table 382. Toxic Chemical Releases by Industry: 2009

[In millions of pounds (3,386.4 represents 3,386,400,000), except as indicated. See headnote, Table 381]

Industry	2002 NAICS [1] code	Total on- and off-site releases	On-site releases Total	Air emissions	Other surface impound- ments	Off-site releases/ transfers to disposal [2]
Total [3]	(X)	3,386.4	3,015.3	915.3	744.8	371.1
Coal mining....................	2121	11.3	11.3	0.4	1.8	(Z)
Metal mining...................	2122	1,137.0	1,135.5	3.1	563.7	(Z)
Electric utilities................	2211	797.0	730.1	386.4	128.0	1.5
Food/beverages/tobacco	311/312	142.5	134.8	40.7	0.1	66.9
Textiles.......................	313/314	1.8	1.3	1.2	0.1	7.7
Apparel	315	(Z)	(Z)	(Z)	–	0.4
Leather	316	0.6	0.2	0.2	–	(Z)
Wood products	321	8.6	8.0	7.9	(Z)	0.4
Paper........................	322	175.0	167.6	128.8	3.8	0.6
Printing and publishing	323/51	9.9	9.7	9.7	–	7.4
Petroleum	324	63.9	58.7	35.2	(Z)	0.2
Chemicals	325	420.3	377.5	157.5	15.8	5.2
Plastics and rubber	326	39.9	32.0	31.4	(Z)	42.8
Stone/clay/glass	327	23.2	20.8	15.0	0.1	7.8
Cement	32731	5.4	5.3	4.2	(Z)	2.4
Primary metals	331	305.9	148.6	31.2	29.2	0.1
Fabricated metals	332	44.3	22.8	21.2	(Z)	157.3
Machinery	333	5.6	3.5	3.5	–	21.5
Computers/electronic products	334	5.2	3.0	1.4	–	2.1
Electrical equipment	335	5.1	1.8	1.8	(Z)	2.2
Transportation equipment	336	30.3	21.5	21.1	(Z)	3.3
Furniture	337	4.4	4.3	4.3	–	8.7
Miscellaneous Manufacturing	339	4.7	2.8	2.8	–	0.1
Chemical wholesalers	4246	1.3	1.2	1.1	–	1.9
Petroleum bulk terminals........	4247	3.2	3.1	3.1	(Z)	0.1
Hazardous waste...............	562	108.3	79.8	0.5	1.2	0.1
No codes [3]	(X)	32.0	30.1	1.7	1.0	28.4
						1.9

– Represents zero. X Not applicable. Z less than 50,000 lbs. [1] North American Industry Classification System, see text, Section 12. [2] Includes off-site disposal to underground injection for Class I wells, Class II to V wells, other surface impoundments, land releases, and other releases, not shown separately. [3] Includes industries with no specific industry identified.

Source: U.S. Environmental Protection Agency, 2009 TRI National Analysis. See also <http://www.epa.gov/tri/tridata/tri09/national_analysis/index.htm>. Data as of April 18, 2011.

Geography and Environment 233

Table 383. Toxic Chemical Releases by State and Outlying Area: 2009

[In millions of pounds (3,386.4 represents 3,386,400,000). Based on reports filed as required by Section 313 of the EPCRA. See headnote, Table 381]

State and outlying areas	Total on-and off-site releases	On-site Releases or other Disposal Total [1]	Air emis-sions	Other surface im-pound-ments	Off-site releases/trans-fers to disposal	State and outlying areas	Total on-and off-site releases	On-site Releases or other Disposal Total [1]	Air emis-sions	Other surface im-pound-ments	Off-site releases/trans-fers to disposal
Total.....	3,386.4	3,015.3	915.3	744.8	371.1	MO......	76.1	74.0	15.4	42.6	2.1
U.S. total...	3,379.1	3,009.3	909.7	744.8	369.7	MT........	41.2	39.8	2.3	7.6	1.3
AL.......	91.1	77.5	34.7	14.1	13.6	NE........	29.6	26.8	5.5	(Z)	2.7
AK.......	699.1	698.8	0.5	279.3	0.3	NV........	183.4	181.2	1.7	114.0	2.2
AZ......	60.9	60.0	2.7	9.2	0.9	NH........	2.9	2.7	2.7	–	0.2
AR.......	34.0	30.2	14.4	2.1	3.8	NJ........	13.1	10.7	4.5	–	2.4
CA.......	36.7	32.6	9.5	(Z)	4.1	NM.......	15.3	15.1	1.1	1.0	0.2
CO.......	20.2	17.1	2.2	2.4	3.1	NY.......	23.3	18.3	8.9	(Z)	5.0
CT......	3.3	2.2	1.9	(Z)	1.1	NC.......	62.7	56.3	34.2	2.8	6.3
DE......	8.1	5.3	3.2	(Z)	2.8	ND.......	21.2	13.3	3.6	5.2	8.0
DC......	0.0	0.0	(Z)	(Z)	(Z)	OH.......	158.7	130.2	75.1	10.2	28.4
FL.......	85.0	80.4	52.6	0.8	4.6	OK........	29.6	28.2	14.8	0.8	1.4
GA......	80.2	78.3	50.4	13.0	1.9	OR........	17.3	12.2	6.1	(Z)	5.0
HI.......	2.9	2.6	2.2	–	0.3	PA........	123.3	74.3	54.1	1.2	48.9
ID.......	47.9	45.5	3.2	15.6	2.4	RI........	0.4	0.2	0.2	–	0.2
IL.......	95.1	52.6	29.3	8.3	42.5	SC........	49.4	43.7	32.6	3.1	5.7
IN.......	132.5	91.5	45.2	8.4	41.0	SD........	4.6	4.3	1.4	(Z)	0.3
IA.......	43.3	30.3	18.2	0.5	13.1	TN........	89.2	79.1	32.0	26.4	10.0
KS......	21.1	18.2	8.0	0.3	2.9	TX........	196.4	171.4	62.6	6.4	25.1
KY......	142.6	133.1	45.6	33.8	9.6	UT........	147.4	145.1	6.9	103.6	2.3
LA......	119.5	112.5	45.6	4.7	7.0	VT........	0.3	0.2	(Z)	–	0.1
ME......	8.5	7.7	3.9	–	0.8	VA........	56.0	50.9	28.4	1.5	5.1
MD......	35.9	33.0	30.2	(Z)	2.9	WA........	15.7	13.9	7.0	3.4	1.8
MA......	5.4	3.3	3.3	(Z)	2.1	WV........	43.0	37.8	27.0	2.2	5.2
MI.......	71.4	54.1	33.2	6.0	17.2	WI........	32.9	19.5	14.6	(Z)	13.4
MN.......	22.2	19.7	8.5	2.0	2.5	WY........	25.0	23.6	2.1	1.9	1.3
MS......	54.3	50.0	16.4	10.3	4.4	PR	6.5	5.1	5.1	–	1.3

– Represents zero. Z Less than 50,000 lbs. [1] Includes other types of release, not shown separately.
Source: U.S. Environmental Protection Agency, Toxic Release Inventory (TRI) Program, *2009 TRI National Analysis*. See also <http://www.epa.gov/tri/tridata/tri09/national_analysis/index.htm>. Data as of April 18, 2011.

Table 384. Hazardous Waste Sites on the National Priority List by State and Outlying Area: 2008

[As of December 31. Includes both proposed and final sites listed on the National Priorities List for the Superfund program as authorized by the Comprehensive Environmental Response, Compensation, and Liability Act (CERCLA) of 1980 and the Superfund Amendments and Reauthorization Act (SARA) of 1986. For information on CERCLA and SARA, see also <http://www.epa.gov/superfund/policy/cercla.htm>]

State and outlying areas	Total sites	Rank	Per-cent distri-bution	Federal	Non-fed-eral	State and outlying areas	Total sites	Rank	Per-cent distri-bution	Fed-eral	Non-fed-eral
Total.............	1,318	(X)	(X)	163	1,155	Missouri.........	29	16	2.3	3	26
United States	1,301	(X)	(X)	161	1,140	Nebraska.........	13	32	1.0	1	12
Alabama	15	26	1.2	3	12	Nevada	1	49	0.1	–	1
Alaska	5	45	0.4	5	–	New Hampshire...	21	19	1.7	1	20
Arizona	9	39	0.7	2	7	New Jersey......	116	1	9.3	8	108
Arkansas	9	40	0.7	–	9	New Mexico......	14	29	1.1	1	13
California	97	2	7.8	24	73	New York	86	4	6.9	4	82
Colorado	20	20	1.6	3	17	North Carolina....	32	13	2.6	2	30
Connecticut	15	24	1.2	1	14	North Dakota.....	–	50	–	–	–
Delaware	14	27	1.1	1	13	Ohio.............	40	10	3.2	5	35
District of Columbia ...	1	(X)	0.1	1	–	Oklahoma	9	42	0.7	1	8
Florida	52	6	4.2	6	46	Oregon...........	12	36	1.0	2	10
Georgia	16	23	1.3	2	14	Pennsylvania	96	3	7.7	6	90
Hawaii	3	46	0.2	2	1	Rhode Island.....	12	37	1.0	2	10
Idaho	9	41	0.7	2	7	South Carolina....	26	17	2.1	2	24
Illinois.............	49	7	3.9	5	44	South Dakota.....	2	47	0.2	1	1
Indiana.............	31	14	2.5	–	31	Tennessee.......	14	30	1.1	4	10
Iowa...............	12	33	1.0	1	11	Texas...........	49	8	3.9	4	45
Kansas.............	12	34	1.0	1	11	Utah.............	19	22	1.5	4	15
Kentucky	14	28	1.1	1	13	Vermont.........	11	38	0.9	0	11
Louisiana...........	13	31	1.0	1	12	Virginia..........	30	15	2.4	11	19
Maine..............	12	35	1.0	3	9	Washington	48	9	3.8	13	35
Maryland	19	21	1.5	10	9	West Virginia.....	9	43	0.7	2	7
Massachusetts.......	32	12	2.6	6	26	Wisconsin	38	11	3.0	–	38
Michigan	67	5	5.4	1	66	Wyoming	2	48	0.2	1	1
Minnesota	25	18	2.0	2	23						
Mississippi..........	6	44	0.5	–	6	Puerto Rico	13	(X)	(X)	1	12

– Represents zero. X Not applicable.
Source: U.S. Environmental Protection Agency, Supplementary Materials: CERCLIS3/WasteLan Database, published July 2009. See also <http://www.epa.gov/osw/inforesources/data/biennialreport/>.

234 Geography and Environment

Table 385. Hazardous Waste Generated, Shipped, and Received by State and Other Areas: 2009

[In thousands of tons (35,331.4 represents 35,331,400).Covers hazardous waste regulated under the Resource Conservation and Recovery Act (RCRA)of 1976 as amended. The data have been revised. See source for exclusions of data from the 2009 National Biennial RCRA Hazardous Waste Report]

State and other areas	Hazardous waste quantity (1,000) tons			State and other areas	Hazardous waste quantity (1,000) tons		
	Generated	Shipped	Received		Generated	Shipped	Received
Total.	**35,331.4**	**6,144.7**	**7,282.7**	Nebraska	28.2	31.2	32.8
				Nevada	11.1	17.2	62.7
United States	**35,285.3**	**6,098.0**	**7,281.0**	New Hampshire	4.5	4.5	–
				New Jersey	555.8	546.5	349.7
Alabama	2,063.6	166.6	220.0	New Mexico	1,078.7	6.2	5.0
Alaska	1.9	1.3	–	New York	1,032.6	218.8	185.9
Arizona	21.1	18.0	16.2	North Carolina	71.8	72.7	10.7
Arkansas	273.2	235.3	289.1	North Dakota	530.5	1.3	0.3
California	699.6	828.5	1,143.4	Ohio	1,300.8	463.1	583.1
Colorado	41.5	31.6	38.8	Oklahoma	41.9	26.0	82.8
Connecticut	21.1	27.2	13.2	Oregon	61.9	51.5	88.4
Delaware	19.8	19.5	0.1	Pennsylvania	290.8	210.2	442.5
District of Columbia	0.9	0.9	–	Rhode Island	4.5	9.2	6.6
Florida	168.9	31.3	9.4	South Carolina	102.0	106.7	128.6
Georgia	4,024.5	90.2	5.0	South Dakota	1.2	1.3	0.1
Hawaii	1.0	1.0	0.2	Tennessee	78.6	49.3	1.3
Idaho	4.8	8.3	334.0	Texas	13,461.9	581.4	637.9
Illinois	1,045.4	182.7	472.9	Utah	59.4	79.3	111.5
Indiana	778.5	313.1	367.7	Vermont	1.5	2.1	1.3
Iowa	40.3	40.1	0.7	Virginia	51.0	50.4	3.6
Kansas	222.8	111.1	195.0	Washington	317.2	97.6	33.6
Kentucky	132.7	162.3	70.2	West Virginia	92.4	68.7	9.3
Louisiana	3,878.8	527.7	475.9	Wisconsin	223.4	152.7	45.8
Maine	3.7	3.7	0.2	Wyoming	3.5	3.5	–
Maryland	33.7	42.0	34.6				
Massachusetts	32.5	41.5	11.8	Guam	0.4	0.4	0.1
Michigan	284.3	189.1	341.8	Navajo Nation	–	–	–
Minnesota	106.8	34.5	249.6	Puerto Rico	43.0	43.2	1.6
Mississippi	1,702.4	63.4	24.4	Virgin Islands	2.6	3.0	–
Missouri	238.2	69.5	143.4				
Montana	37.8	6.3	–				

– Represents or rounds to zero.
Source: U.S. Environmental Protection Agency, *The National Biennial RCRA Hazardous Waste Report (Based on 2009 data)*, Series EPA530-R-10-014a, November 2010. See also <http://www.epa.gov/epawaste/inforesources/data/biennialreport/index.htm>.

Table 386. Oil Spills in U.S. Water—Number and Volume: 2000 to 2009

[These summary statistics are based on reported discharges of oil and petroleum based products into U.S. navigable waters, including territorial waters (extending 3 to 12 miles from the coastline), tributaries, the contiguous zone, onto shoreline, or into other waters that threaten the marine environment. Spills associated with Hurricanes Katrina and Rita have been excluded]

Spill characteristic	Number of spills				Spill volume (millions)			
	2000	2005	2008	2009	2000	2005	2008	2009
Total.	**8,354**	**4,073**	**3,633**	**3,492**	**1,431,370**	**2,364,169**	**777,039**	**195,189**
Size of spill (gallons):								
1 to 100	8,058	3,857	3,474	3,351	39,355	33,041	25,335	24,428
101 to 1,000	219	166	130	123	78,779	62,357	50,486	46,062
1,001 to 3,000	37	26	12	9	67,529	46,019	22,130	20,907
3,001 to 5,000	12	9	8	2	45,512	36,803	30,396	6,872
5,001 to 10,000	16	7	3	3	112,415	58,453	21,800	21,400
10,001 to 50,000	6	5	3	4	108,400	106,870	73,600	75,520
50,001 to 100,000	4	1	1	–	266,380	84,000	82,274	–
100,001 to 1,000,000	2	1	2	–	713,000	110,000	471,018	–
1,000,000 and over	–	1	–	–	–	1,826,626	–	–
Source:								
Tankship	111	40	36	34	608,176	2,975	1,338	14,415
Tankbarge	229	130	184	166	133,540	2,006,774	288,029	5,678
All other vessels	5,220	1,789	1,577	1,585	291,927	115,906	263,632	92,388
Facilities	1,054	996	1,048	963	311,604	92,399	170,299	38,299
Pipelines	25	20	18	17	17,021	111,253	14,494	1,739
All other nonvessels	566	264	297	312	45,136	13,422	29,056	27,557
Unknown	1,149	834	473	415	23,966	21,440	10,191	15,113

– Represents zero.
Source: U.S. Coast Guard, *Pollution Incidents In and Around U.S. Waters, A Spill/Release Compendium: 1969–2004*, and *2004–2009: U.S. Coast Guard Marine Information for Safety and Law Enforcement (MISLE)*. Data are unpublished. See <http://homeport.uscg.mil/mycg/portal/ep/home.do\>.

Table 387. Threatened and Endangered Wildlife and Plant Species: 2011

[As of April. Endangered species: One in danger of becoming extinct throughout all or a significant part of its natural range. Threatened species: One likely to become endangered in the foreseeable future]

Item	Mammals	Birds	Reptiles	Amphibians	Fishes	Snails	Clams	Crustaceans	Insects	Arachnids	Plants
Total listings.............	359	300	119	33	151	37	75	22	64	12	795
Endangered species, total ...	325	271	79	22	83	26	67	19	54	12	645
United States.............	70	77	13	14	72	25	65	19	50	12	644
Foreign	255	194	66	8	11	1	2	–	4	–	1
Threatened species, total	34	29	40	11	68	11	8	3	10	0	150
United States.............	14	16	24	10	67	11	8	3	10	0	148
Foreign	20	13	16	1	1	–	–	–	–	–	2

– Represents zero.

Source: U.S. Fish and Wildlife Service, *Endangered Species Bulletin*, bimonthly. See also <http://ecos.fws.gov/tess_public/pub/listedanimals.jsp>, accessed May 2011.

Table 388. Tornadoes, Floods, Tropical Storms, and Lightning: 2000 to 2010

Weather type	2000	2002	2003	2004	2005	2006	2007	2008	2009	2010
Tornadoes: [1]										
Number	1,071	941	1,376	1,819	1,264	1,106	1,098	1,691	1,156	1,282
Lives lost	41	55	54	35	38	67	81	126	21	45
Injuries................	882	968	1,087	396	537	990	659	1,714	351	699
Property loss (mil. dol.)	424	801	1,263	537	422	752	1,408	1,844	566	1,107
Floods and flash floods:										
Lives lost	38	49	85	82	43	76	70	82	56	113
Injuries................	47	88	65	128	38	23	51	46	27	310
Property loss (mil. dol.)	1,255	655	2,541	1,696	1,538	3,768	1,278	3,406	1,050	3,927
North Atlantic tropical cyclones and hurricanes: [2]..	15	12	21	16	27	9	17	17	11	21
Hurricanes	8	4	7	9	15	5	6	8	3	12
Lives lost.............	–	51	14	34	1,016	–	1	12	2	(NA)
Property loss (bil.dol.).....	8.1	1.1	1.9	18.9	93.0	2.4	38.8	7.6	0.9	(NA)
Lightning:										
Deaths................	51	51	44	32	38	48	45	27	34	29
Injuries................	364	256	237	280	309	246	138	216	201	182

– Represents zero. NA Not available. [1] Source: U.S. National Weather Service, <http://www.spc.noaa.gov/climo/torn/monthlytornstats.html>. A violent, rotating column of air descending from a cumulonimbus cloud in the form of a tubular- or funnel-shaped cloud, usually characterized by movements along a narrow path and wind speeds from 100 to over 300 miles per hour. Also known as a "twister" or "waterspout." [2] Tropical cyclones include depressions, storms and hurricanes. For data on individual hurricanes, see National Hurricane Center (NHC) at <http://www.nhc.noaa.gov/>.

Source: Except as noted, U.S. National Oceanic and Atmospheric Administration (NOAA), National Weather Service (NWS), *Office of Climate, Water, and Weather Services, Natural Hazard Statistics*, monthly. See also <http://www.nws.noaa.gov/om/hazstats.shtml>.

Table 389. Number of Earthquakes in the United States: 2000 to 2010

[The United States Geological Survey (USGS) detects but does not generally locate mine blasts (explosions) throughout the United States on any given business day. For more information, see "Routine United States Mining Seismicity." For information on "Top Earthquake States," see <http://earthquake.usgs.gov/earthquakes/states/top_states.php>]

Magnitude	2000	2002	2003	2004	2005	2006	2007	2008	2009	2010 [1]	Top earthquake states	1974–2003 [2]
Total	2,342	3,876	2,946	3,550	3,685	2,783	2,791	3,618	4,264	8,444	Total	21,080
8.0 to 9.9	–	–	–	–	–	–	–	–	–	–	AK	[3] 12,053
7.0 to 7.9	–	1	2	–	1	–	1	–	–	1	CA	4,895
6.0 to 6.9	6	4	7	2	4	7	9	9	4	8	HI	1,533
5.0 to 5.9	63	63	54	25	47	51	72	85	58	71	NE	778
4.0 to 4.9	281	536	541	284	345	346	366	432	289	648	WA	424
3.0 to 3.9	917	1,535	1,303	1,362	1,475	1,213	1,137	1,486	1,492	3,581	ID	404
2.0 to 2.9	660	1,228	704	1,336	1,738	1,145	1,173	1,573	2,380	4,087	WY	217
1.0 to 1.9	–	2	2	1	2	7	11	13	26	37	MT	186
0.1 to 0.9	–	–	–	–	–	1	–	–	1	–	UT	139
No magnitude ...	415	507	333	540	73	13	22	20	14	11	OR	73

– Represents zero. [1] Data are as of March 3, 2011. [2] The total number represents earthquakes of a magnitude range of 3.5 and greater. [3] The number of earthquakes is underreported. Events in the magnitude range of 3.5 to 4.0 in the Aleutian Islands are not recorded on enough seismograph stations to be located.

Source: U.S. Geological Survey, *Earthquake Facts and Statistics*. See <http://earthquake.usgs.gov/earthquakes/eqarchives/>.

U.S. Census Bureau, Statistical Abstract of the United States: 2012

Table 390. Wildland Fires, Number, and Acres: 1970 to 2010

[In thousands (3,279 represents 3,279,000), except as indicated. As of December 31. There are three distinct types of wildland fires: wildfire, wildland fire use, and prescribed fire. Wildland fire is any nonstructure fire that occurs in the wildland]

Year	Total [1] Fires (number)	Total [1] Acres (1,000)	Year	Total [1] Fires (number)	Total [1] Acres (1,000)
1970.....	121,736	3,279	2000.....	92,250	7,393
1975.....	134,872	1,791	2001.....	84,079	3,571
1980.....	234,892	5,261	2002.....	73,457	7,185
1985.....	82,591	2,896	2003.....	63,629	3,961
1990.....	66,481	4,622	2004 [3]	65,461	8,098
1994.....	79,107	4,074	2005.....	66,753	8,689
1995.....	82,234	1,841	2006.....	96,385	9,874
1996.....	96,363	6,066	2007.....	85,705	9,328
1997.....	66,196	2,857	2008.....	78,979	5,292
1998.....	81,043	1,330	2009.....	78,792	5,922
1999.....	92,487	5,626	2010.....	71,971	3,423

State	Wildland [1] Fires	Wildland [1] Acres	Prescribed [2] Fires	Prescribed [2] Acres
Total	71,971	3,422,724	16,882	2,423,862
AK	689	1,125,419	6	505
ID	984	642,997	223	36,652
NM......	998	233,056	63	61,403
TX	6,748	210,320	144	166,006
CA	6,554	109,529	970	725,565
OR	1,315	93,731	836	114,716
OK......	1,735	85,770	21	10,064
WY	533	80,382	58	27,013
AZ	1,601	76,318	255	86,826
UT	1,050	64,781	124	22,657

[1] Data are for wildland fires only. The data do not include wildland fire use and prescribed fires. [2] Prescribed fire is any fire which are ignited by management action under certain predetermined conditions to meet specific objectives related to hazardous fuels or habitat improvement. [3] 2004 fires and acres do not include state lands for North Carolina.

Source: National Interagency Coordination Center, Fire Information, Statisics, 2010 Statistics and Summary, Fires and acres. See also <http://www.predictiveservices.nifc.gov/intelligence/2010_statssumm/2010Stats&Summ.html\>, accessed June 3, 2011.

Table 391. Highest and Lowest Temperatures by State Through 2010

State	Highest temperatures Station	Highest temperatures Temperature (F)	Highest temperatures Date	Lowest temperatures Station	Lowest temperatures Temperature (F)	Lowest temperatures Date
AL	Centerville...........	112	Sep. 5, 1925	New Market...........	−27	Jan. 30, 1966
AK	Fort Yukon...........	100 [1]	Jun. 27, 1915	Prospect Creek Camp...	−80	Jan. 23, 1971
AZ	Lake Havasu City.......	128	Jun. 29, 1994	Hawley Lake..........	−40	Jan. 7, 1971
AR	Ozark...............	120	Aug. 10, 1936	Pond...............	−29	Feb. 13, 1905
CA	Greenland Ranch.......	134	Jul. 10, 1913	Boca...............	−45	Jan. 20, 1937
CO	Sedgwick............	114 [1]	Jul. 11, 1954	Maybell.............	−61	Feb. 1, 1985
CT	Danbury.............	106 [1]	Jul. 15, 1995	Coventry............	−32 [1]	Jan. 22, 1961
DE	Millsboro............	110	Jul. 21, 1930	Millsboro............	−17	Jan. 17, 1893
FL	Monticello...........	109	Jun. 29, 1931	Tallahassee..........	−2	Feb. 13, 1899
GA	Greenville 2 NNW......	112 [1]	Aug. 20, 1983	CCC Camp F-16.......	−17 [1]	Jan. 27, 1940
HI	Pahala..............	100	Apr. 27, 1931	Mauna Kea Obs. 111.2 ..	12	May 17, 1979
ID	Orofino.............	118	Jul. 28, 1934	Island Park Dam.......	−60	Jan. 18, 1943
IL	East St. Louis........	117	Jul. 14, 1954	Congerville..........	−36	Jan. 5, 1999
IN	Collegeville..........	116	Jul. 14, 1936	New Whiteland........	−36	Jan. 19, 1994
IA	Keokuk.............	118	Jul. 20, 1934	Elkader.............	−47 [1]	Feb. 3, 1996
KS	Alton...............	121	Jul. 24, 1936	Lebanon............	−40	Feb. 13, 1905
KY	Greensburg..........	114	Jul. 28, 1930	Shelbyville..........	−37	Jan. 19, 1994
LA	Plain Dealing.........	114	Aug. 10, 1936	Minden.............	−16	Feb. 13, 1899
ME	North Bridgton........	105	Jul. 10, 1911	Van Buren...........	−48	Jan. 16, 2009
MD	Cumberland & Frederick ...	109 [1]	Jul. 10, 1936	Oakland............	−40	Jan. 13, 1912
MA	New Bedford & Chester....	107 [1]	Aug. 2, 1975	Chester............	−35 [1]	Jan. 12, 1981
MI	Mio................	112	Jul. 13, 1936	Vanderbilt...........	−51	Feb. 9, 1934
MN	Moorhead...........	115	Jul. 29, 1917	Tower..............	−60	Feb. 2, 1996
MS	Holly Springs.........	115	Jul. 29, 1930	Corinth.............	−19	Jan. 30, 1966
MO	Warsaw & Union.......	118 [1]	Jul. 14, 1954	Warsaw............	−40	Feb. 13, 1905
MT	Medicine Lake........	117 [1]	Jul. 5, 1937	Rogers Pass.........	−70	Jan. 20, 1954
NE	Minden.............	118 [1]	Jul. 24, 1936	Oshkosh............	−47 [1]	Dec. 22, 1989
NV	Laughlin............	125 [1]	Jun. 29, 1994	San Jacinto..........	−50	Jan. 8, 1937
NH	Nashua.............	106	Jul. 4, 1911	Mt. Washington.......	−47	Jan. 22, 1885
NJ	Runyon.............	110	Jul. 10, 1936	River Vale...........	−34	Jan. 5, 1904
NM	Waste Isolat Pilot Plt	122	Jun. 27, 1994	Gavilan............	−50	Feb. 1, 1951
NY	Troy...............	108	Jul. 22, 1926	Old Forge...........	−52	Feb. 18, 1979
NC	Fayetteville..........	110	Aug. 21, 1983	Mt. Mitchell..........	−34	Jan. 21, 1985
ND	Steele..............	121	Jul. 6, 1936	Parshall............	−60	Feb. 15, 1936
OH	Gallipolis (near).......	113	Jul. 21, 1934	Milligan............	−39	Feb. 10, 1899
OK	Tipton..............	120 [1]	Jun. 27, 1994	Watts..............	−27 [1]	Jan. 4, 1947
OR	Pendleton...........	119 [1]	Aug. 10, 1898	Seneca............	−54 [1]	Feb. 10, 1933
PA	Phoenixville..........	111	Jul. 10, 1936	Smethport..........	−42 [1]	Jan. 5, 1904
RI	Providence...........	104	Aug. 2, 1975	Greene.............	−25	Jan. 11, 1942
SC	Camden.............	111 [1]	Jun. 28, 1954	Caesars Head........	−19	Jan. 21, 1985
SD	Fort Pierre..........	120 [1]	Jul. 15, 2006	McIntosh...........	−58	Feb. 17, 1936
TN	Perryville...........	113	Aug. 9, 1930	Mountain City.........	−32	Dec. 30, 1917
TX	Monahans...........	120 [1]	Jun. 28, 1994	Seminole...........	−23	Feb. 8, 1933
UT	Saint George.........	117	Jul. 5, 1985	Peter's Sink.........	−69	Jan. 5, 1913
VT	Vernon.............	107	Jul. 7, 1912	Bloomfield..........	−50	Dec. 30, 1933
VA	Balcony Falls.........	110	Jul. 15, 1954	Mtn. Lake Bio. Stn.	−30	Jan. 22, 1985
WA	Ice Harbor Dam.......	118 [1]	Aug. 5, 1961	Mazama & Winthrop	−48 [1]	Dec. 30, 1968
WV	Martinsburg..........	112 [1]	Jul. 10, 1936	Lewisburg...........	−37	Dec. 30, 1917
WI	Wisconsin Dells........	114	Jul. 13, 1936	Couderay...........	−55	Feb. 4, 1996
WY	Diversion Dam.........	115 [1]	Mar. 5 1998	Riverside R.S........	−66	Feb. 9, 1933

[1] Also on earlier dates at the same or other places.

Source: U.S. National Oceanic and Atmospheric Administration, National Environmental Satellite, Data, and Information Services (NESDIS), National Climatic Data Center (NCDC), *Temperature Extremes and Drought*,<http://www.ncdc.noaa.gov /Extremes/scec/searchrecs.php>.>.

Geography and Environment 237

Table 392. Major U.S. Weather Disasters: 2008 to 2010

[3.0 represents $3,000,000,000. Covers only weather-related disasters costing $1 billion or more]

Event	Description	Time period	Estimated cost [1] (bil.dol.)	Deaths (number)
2010 Midwest Tornadoes and Severe Weather	An outbreak of tornadoes, hail, and severe thunderstorms occurred across OK, KS, and TX. Oklahoma was hardest hit with over 1.5 billion in damages.	May, 2010	Over 3.0	3
Mid-South Flooding and Severe Weather	Flooding, hail, tornadoes, and severe thunderstorms occurred across TN, AR, AL, KY, MS, and GA. Flooding in the Nashville, TN area alone contributed over 1.0 billion in damages. Western and Middle Tennessee were hardest hit with local rainfall amounts of 18–20 inches to the south and west of Greater Nashville.	April–May 2010	Over 2.3	32
Northeast Flooding	Heavy rainfall over portions of the Northeast in late March caused extensive flooding across RI, CT, MA, NJ, NY, and PA. The event caused the worst flooding in Rhode Island's history.	March, 2010	Over 1.5	11
2009 Southwest/Great Plains drought	Drought conditions occurred during much of the year causing agricultural losses in TX, OK, KS, CA, NM, and AZ. The largest losses occurred in TX and CA.	Entire year 2009	Over 5.0	–
Western wildfires	Residual and sustained drought conditions across western and south-central states resulted in thousands of fires. Most affected states include CA, AZ, NM, TX, OK, and UT.	Summer–Fall 2009	Over 1.0	10
Midwest, South, and Eastern Severe weather	Sustained outbreak of thunderstorms and high winds in TX, OK, MO, NE, KS, AR, AL, MS, TN, NC, SC, KY, and PA.	June, 2009	Over 1.1	–
South/Southeast Tornadoes/Severe weather	Outbreak of tornadoes, hail and severe thunderstorms in AL, AR, GA, KY, MO, SC, TN; with 85 tornadoes confirmed.	April, 2009	Over 1.2	6
Midwest/Southeast Tornadoes	Outbreak of tornadoes in NE, KS, OK, IA, TX LA, MS, AL, GA, TN, KY; with 56 tornadoes confirmed.	March, 2009	Over 1.0	–
Southeast/Ohio Valley Severe weather	Complex of severe thunderstorms and high winds in TN, KY, OK, OH, VA, WV, and PA. The majority of the damage occurred in OK and OH.	February, 2009	Over 1.4	10
2008 Widespread drought	Severe drought and heat caused agricultural losses in areas of the south and west. Record low lake levels. Includes states of CA, GA, NC, SC, TN, and TX.	Entire year 2008	Over 2.0	–
Hurricane Ike	Category 2 hurricane made landfall in Texas as the largest(in size) Atlantic hurricane on record, causing wind and considerable surge in coastal and significant flooding damage in AR, IL, IN, KY, LA, MO, OH, PA, and TX.	September, 2008	Over 27.0	82
Hurricane Gustav	Category 2 hurricane made landfall in Louisiana causing significant wind, storm surge and flood damage in AL, AR, LA, and MS.	September 2008	5.0	43
Hurricane Dolly	Category 2 hurricane made landfall in southern Texas causing considerable wind and flooding damage in TX and NM.	July, 2008	Over 1.2	3
U.S. wildfires	Drought conditions across numerous western, central and southeastern states(15) resulted in thousands of wildfires, national acreage burned exceeding 5.2 million acres (mainly in the west).	Summer–Fall 2008	Over 2.0	16
Midwest flood	Heavy rainfall and flooding caused significant agricultural loss and property damage in seven states with Iowa being hardest hit with widespread rainfall totals ranging from 4 to 16 inches.	June, 2008	Over 15.0	24
Midwest/Mid-Atlantic storms	An outbreak of tornadoes and thunderstorms over the states of IA, IL, IN, KS, NE, MD, MI, MN, MO, OK, VA, WI, WV.	June, 2008	Over 1.1	18
Midwest/Ohio Valley storms	Outbreak of tornadoes over the Midwest/Ohio Valley over the region (IL, IN, IA KS, MN, NE, OK, WY, and CO). with 235 tornadoes confirmed.	May, 2008	Over 2.4	13
Southeast/Midwest tornadoes	Series of tornadoes and severe thunderstorms across the Southeast and Midwest states (AL, AR, IN, KY, MS, OH, TN, TX) with 87 tornadoes confirmed.	February, 2008	Over 1.0	57

– Represents zero. [1] Represents actual dollar costs at the time of event and is not adjusted for inflation.

Source: U.S. National Oceanic and Atmospheric Administration, National Climatic Data Center, "Billion Dollar U.S. Weather Disasters, 1980–2010" (released January 2011). See also <http://www.ncdc.noaa.gov /oa/reports/billionz.html>.

Table 393. Highest Temperature of Record—Selected Cities

[In Fahrenheit degrees. Airport data, except as noted. For period of record through 2009]

State	Station	Length of record (years)	Jan.	Feb.	Mar.	Apr.	May	June	July	Aug.	Sept.	Oct.	Nov.	Dec.	Annual[1]
AL	Mobile	68	84	82	90	94	100	102	104	105	99	93	87	81	105
AK	Juneau	65	57	57	61	74	82	86	90	84	73	61	56	54	90
AZ	Phoenix	72	88	92	100	105	113	122	121	116	118	107	96	88	122
AK	Little Rock	68	83	85	91	95	98	105	112	109	106	97	86	80	112
CA	Los Angeles	74	91	92	95	102	97	104	97	98	110	106	101	94	110
	Sacramento	59	74	76	88	95	105	115	114	110	108	104	87	72	115
	San Diego	69	88	90	93	98	96	101	99	98	111	107	97	88	111
	San Francisco	82	72	78	85	92	97	106	105	100	103	99	85	75	106
CO	Denver	67	73	77	84	90	96	104	105	104	97	89	80	75	105
CT	Hartford	55	72	73	89	96	99	100	102	102	99	91	81	76	102
DE	Wilmington	62	75	78	86	94	96	100	102	101	100	91	85	75	102
DC	Washington	68	79	82	89	95	99	101	104	105	101	94	86	79	105
FL	Jacksonville	68	85	88	91	95	100	103	105	102	100	96	88	84	105
	Miami	67	88	89	93	96	96	98	98	98	97	95	91	89	98
GA	Atlanta	61	79	80	89	93	95	101	105	104	98	95	84	79	105
HI	Honolulu	40	88	88	88	91	93	92	94	93	95	94	93	89	95
ID	Boise	70	63	71	81	92	99	109	111	110	102	94	78	65	111
IL	Chicago	51	65	72	88	91	93	104	104	101	99	91	78	71	104
	Peoria	70	70	72	86	92	94	105	104	103	100	93	81	71	105
IN	Indianapolis	70	71	76	85	89	93	102	104	102	100	91	81	74	104
IA	Des Moines	70	67	73	91	93	98	103	105	108	101	95	81	69	108
KS	Wichita	57	75	87	89	96	100	110	113	110	108	97	86	83	113
KY	Louisville	62	77	77	86	91	95	102	106	105	104	93	84	76	106
LA	New Orleans	63	83	85	89	92	96	101	101	102	101	94	87	84	102
ME	Portland	69	67	64	88	92	94	98	99	103	95	88	74	71	103
MD	Baltimore	59	75	79	89	94	98	101	104	105	100	94	83	77	105
MA	Boston	58	69	70	89	94	95	100	102	102	100	90	79	76	102
MI	Detroit	51	64	70	81	89	93	104	102	100	98	91	77	69	104
	Sault Ste. Marie	69	45	49	75	85	89	93	97	98	95	81	68	62	98
MN	Duluth	68	52	55	78	88	90	94	97	97	95	86	71	55	97
	Minneapolis-St. Paul	71	58	61	83	95	97	102	105	102	98	90	77	68	105
MS	Jackson	46	83	85	89	94	99	105	106	107	104	95	88	84	107
MO	Kansas City	37	71	78	86	93	95	105	107	109	106	95	82	74	109
	St. Louis	52	76	85	89	93	94	102	107	107	104	94	85	76	107
MT	Great Falls	72	67	70	78	89	93	101	105	106	98	91	76	69	106
NE	Omaha	73	69	78	89	97	99	105	114	110	104	96	83	72	114
NV	Reno	68	71	75	83	89	97	103	108	105	101	91	77	70	108
NH	Concord	68	69	67	89	95	97	98	102	101	98	90	80	73	102
NJ	Atlantic City	66	78	75	87	94	99	106	104	103	99	90	84	77	106
NM	Albuquerque	70	69	76	85	89	98	107	105	101	100	91	77	72	107
NY	Albany	63	71	68	89	92	94	99	100	99	100	89	82	71	100
	Buffalo	66	72	71	81	94	91	96	97	99	98	87	80	74	99
	New York[2]	141	72	75	86	96	99	101	106	104	102	94	84	75	106
NC	Charlotte	70	79	81	90	93	100	103	103	104	104	98	85	80	104
	Raleigh	65	80	84	92	95	97	104	105	105	104	98	88	81	105
ND	Bismarck	70	63	69	81	93	98	111	112	109	105	95	79	65	112
OH	Cincinnati	48	73	75	84	89	93	102	103	102	98	91	81	75	103
	Cleveland	68	74	74	83	88	92	104	103	102	101	90	82	77	104
	Columbus	70	74	75	85	89	94	102	100	101	100	91	80	76	102
OK	Oklahoma City	56	80	92	93	100	104	105	110	110	108	96	87	86	110
OR	Portland	69	66	71	80	90	100	102	107	107	105	92	73	65	107
PA	Philadelphia	68	74	74	87	95	97	100	104	101	100	96	81	73	104
	Pittsburgh	57	72	76	82	89	91	98	103	100	97	87	82	74	103
RI	Providence	56	69	72	85	98	95	97	102	104	100	86	78	77	104
SC	Columbia	62	84	84	91	94	101	107	107	107	101	101	90	83	107
SD	Sioux Falls	64	66	70	87	94	100	110	108	108	104	94	81	63	110
TN	Memphis	68	79	81	86	94	99	104	108	107	103	95	86	81	108
	Nashville	70	78	84	86	91	97	106	107	106	105	94	84	79	107
TX	Dallas-Fort Worth	56	88	95	96	101	103	113	110	109	111	102	89	89	113
	El Paso	70	80	83	89	98	105	114	112	108	104	96	87	80	114
	Houston	40	84	91	91	95	99	104	104	107	109	96	89	85	109
UT	Salt Lake City	81	63	69	78	89	99	104	107	106	100	89	75	69	107
VT	Burlington	66	66	62	84	91	93	100	100	101	98	85	75	67	101
VA	Norfolk	61	80	82	88	97	100	101	103	104	99	95	86	80	104
	Richmond	80	81	83	93	96	100	104	105	104	103	99	86	81	105
WA	Seattle-Tacoma	65	64	70	78	85	93	96	103	99	98	89	74	64	100
	Spokane	62	59	63	71	90	96	101	103	108	98	86	67	56	108
WV	Charleston	62	79	79	89	94	93	98	104	104	102	93	85	80	104
WI	Milwaukee	69	63	68	82	91	93	101	103	103	98	89	77	68	103
WY	Cheyenne	74	66	71	74	83	91	100	100	98	95	83	75	69	100
PR	San Juan	55	92	96	96	97	96	97	95	97	97	98	96	94	98

[1] Represents the highest observed temperature in any month. [2] City office data.
Source: U.S. National Oceanic and Atmospheric Administration, *Comparative Climatic Data*. See also <http://www.ncdc.noaa.gov/oa/climate/online/ccd/hghtmp.txt>.

Geography and Environment 239

Table 394. Lowest Temperature of Record—Selected Cities

[In Fahrenheit degrees. Airport data, except as noted. For period of record through 2009]

State	Station	Length of record (years)	Jan.	Feb.	Mar.	Apr.	May	June	July	Aug.	Sept.	Oct.	Nov.	Dec.	Annual [1]
AL	Mobile	68	3	11	21	32	43	49	60	59	42	30	22	8	3
AK	Juneau.............	65	−22	−22	−15	6	25	31	36	27	23	11	−5	−21	−22
AZ	Phoenix	72	17	22	25	32	40	50	61	60	47	34	25	22	17
AR	Little Rock	68	−4	−5	11	28	40	46	54	52	37	29	17	−1	−5
CA	Los Angeles.........	74	23	32	34	39	43	48	49	51	47	41	34	32	23
	Sacramento	59	21	23	26	31	36	41	48	49	42	36	26	18	18
	San Diego	69	29	36	39	41	48	51	55	57	51	43	38	34	29
	San Francisco	82	24	25	30	31	36	41	43	42	38	34	25	20	20
CO	Denver	67	−25	−30	−11	−2	21	30	43	41	17	3	−8	−25	−30
CT	Hartford	55	−26	−21	−6	9	28	35	44	36	30	17	1	−14	−26
DE	Wilmington..........	62	−14	−6	2	18	30	41	48	43	36	24	14	−7	−14
DC	Washington	68	−5	4	11	24	34	47	54	49	39	29	16	1	−5
FL	Jacksonville	68	7	19	23	31	45	47	61	59	48	33	21	11	7
	Miami..............	67	30	32	32	43	53	60	69	68	68	51	39	30	30
GA	Atlanta.............	61	−8	5	10	26	37	46	53	55	36	28	3	0	−8
HI	Honolulu	40	53	53	55	57	60	65	66	65	66	61	57	54	53
ID	Boise	70	−17	−15	6	19	22	31	35	34	23	11	−3	−25	−25
IL	Chicago............	51	−27	−19	−8	7	24	36	40	41	28	17	1	−25	−27
	Peoria	70	−25	−19	−10	14	25	39	47	41	26	19	−2	−23	−25
IN	Indianapolis	70	−27	−21	−7	16	28	37	44	41	28	17	−2	−23	−27
IA	Des Moines	70	−24	−26	−22	9	30	38	47	40	26	14	−4	−22	−26
KS	Wichita.............	57	−12	−21	−2	15	31	43	51	48	31	18	1	−16	−21
KY	Louisville	62	−22	−19	−1	22	31	42	50	46	33	23	−1	−15	−22
LA	New Orleans	63	14	16	25	32	41	50	60	60	42	35	24	11	11
ME	Portland	69	−26	−39	−21	8	23	33	40	33	23	15	3	−21	−39
MD	Baltimore	59	−7	−3	6	20	32	40	50	45	35	25	13	0	−7
MA	Boston	58	−12	−4	5	16	34	45	50	47	38	28	15	−7	−12
MI	Detroit	51	−21	−15	−4	10	25	36	41	38	29	17	9	−10	−21
	Sault Ste. Marie.......	69	−36	−35	−24	−2	18	26	36	29	25	16	−10	−31	−36
MN	Duluth	69	−39	−39	−29	−5	17	27	35	32	22	8	−23	−34	−39
	Minneapolis-St. Paul ...	71	−34	−32	−32	2	18	34	43	39	26	13	−17	−29	−34
MS	Jackson	46	2	10	15	27	38	47	51	54	35	26	17	4	2
MO	Kansas City	37	−17	−19	−10	12	30	42	51	43	31	17	1	−23	−23
	St. Louis............	52	−18	−12	−5	22	31	43	51	47	36	23	1	−16	−18
MT	Great Falls	72	−37	−35	−29	−8	12	31	36	30	16	−11	−25	−43	−43
NE	Omaha.............	73	−23	−21	−16	5	27	38	44	43	25	13	−9	−23	−23
NV	Reno	68	−16	−16	−2	13	18	21	33	24	20	8	1	−16	−16
NH	Concord	68	−33	−37	−16	8	21	30	35	29	21	10	−5	−22	−37
NJ	Atlantic City	66	−10	−11	3	12	25	37	42	40	32	20	10	−7	−11
NM	Albuquerque	70	−17	−5	8	19	16	40	52	50	37	21	−7	−7	−17
NY	Albany	63	−28	−21	−21	10	26	36	40	34	24	16	5	−22	−28
	Buffalo.............	66	−16	−20	−7	12	26	35	43	38	32	20	9	−10	−20
	New York [2]	141	−6	−15	3	12	32	44	52	50	39	28	5	−13	−15
NC	Charlotte	70	−5	5	4	21	32	45	53	50	39	24	11	2	−5
	Raleigh	65	−9	0	11	23	31	38	48	46	37	19	11	4	−9
ND	Bismarck	70	−44	−43	−31	−12	15	30	35	33	11	−10	−30	−43	−44
OH	Cincinnati...........	48	−25	−11	−11	15	27	39	47	43	31	16	1	−20	−25
	Cleveland...........	68	−20	−15	−5	10	25	31	41	38	32	19	3	−15	−20
	Columbus	70	−22	−13	−6	14	25	35	43	39	31	20	5	−17	−22
OK	Oklahoma City.......	56	−4	−3	3	20	37	47	53	51	36	16	11	−8	−8
OR	Portland	69	−2	−3	19	29	29	39	43	44	34	26	13	6	−3
PA	Philadelphia.........	68	−7	−4	7	19	28	44	51	44	35	25	15	1	−7
	Pittsburgh	57	−22	−12	−1	14	26	34	42	39	31	16	−1	−12	−22
RI	Providence..........	56	−13	−7	1	14	29	41	48	10	33	20	6	−10	−13
SC	Columbia	62	−1	5	4	26	34	44	54	53	40	23	12	4	−1
SD	Sioux Falls	64	−36	−31	−23	5	17	33	38	34	22	9	−17	−28	−36
TN	Memphis	68	−4	−11	12	28	38	48	52	48	36	25	9	−13	−13
	Nashville	70	−17	−13	2	23	34	42	51	47	36	26	−1	−10	−17
TX	Dallas-Fort Worth	56	4	7	15	29	41	51	59	56	43	29	20	−1	−1
	El Paso	70	−8	8	14	23	31	46	57	56	41	25	1	5	−8
	Houston............	40	12	3	22	31	44	52	62	60	48	29	19	7	3
UT	Salt Lake City	81	−22	−30	2	14	25	35	40	37	27	16	−14	−21	−30
VT	Burlington	66	−30	−30	−20	2	24	33	39	35	25	15	−2	−26	−30
VA	Norfolk.............	61	−3	8	18	28	36	45	54	49	45	27	20	7	−3
	Richmond	80	−12	−10	10	23	31	40	51	46	35	21	10	−1	−12
WA	Seattle-Tacoma	65	0	1	11	29	28	38	43	44	35	28	6	6	0
	Spokane	62	−22	−24	−7	17	24	33	37	35	22	7	−21	−25	−25
WV	Charleston..........	62	−16	−12	0	19	26	33	46	41	34	17	6	−12	−16
WI	Milwaukee	69	−26	−26	−10	12	21	33	40	44	28	18	−5	−20	−26
WY	Cheyenne	74	−29	−34	−21	−8	16	25	38	36	8	−1	−16	−28	−34
PR	San Juan	55	61	62	60	64	66	69	69	70	69	46	66	59	46

[1] Represents the lowest observed temperature in any month. [2] City office data.
Source: U.S. National Oceanic and Atmospheric Administration, *Comparative Climatic Data*. See also <http://www.ncdc.noaa.gov/oa/climate/online/ccd/lowtmp.txt>.

Table 395. Snow, Hail, Ice Pellets, and Sleet—Selected Cities

[In inches. Airport data, except as noted. For period of record through 2009. T denotes trace. Stations may show snowfall (hail) during the warm months]

State	Station	Length of record (years)	Jan.	Feb.	Mar.	Apr.	May	June	July	Aug.	Sept.	Oct.	Nov.	Dec.	Annual
AL	Mobile	67	0.1	0.1	0.1	T	T	–	T	–	–	–	T	0.1	0.4
AK	Juneau	65	26.7	18.9	15.5	3.5	T	T	–	–	T	1.1	12.4	21.2	98.2
AZ	Phoenix	62	T	–	T	T	T	–	–	–	–	T	–	T	–
AR	Little Rock	58	2.4	1.5	0.5	T	T	T	–	–	–	T	0.2	0.6	5.2
CA	Los Angeles	62	T	T	T	–	–	–	–	–	–	–	–	T	–
	Sacramento	50	T	T	T	–	T	–	–	–	–	–	–	–	–
	San Diego	60	T	–	T	T	–	–	–	–	–	–	–	T	–
	San Francisco	69	–	–	T	T	–	–	–	–	–	–	T	T	–
CO	Denver	65	8.0	7.4	12.2	8.6	1.6	–	T	T	1.6	4.0	8.8	7.9	59.9
CT	Hartford	52	13.2	12.3	10.0	1.5	–	–	–	–	–	0.1	2.1	10.9	50.3
DE	Wilmington	59	6.6	6.5	3.3	0.2	T	T	T	–	–	0.1	0.9	3.7	21.1
DC	Washington	66	5.2	5.4	2.3	2.3	T	T	T	T	–	–	0.8	3.2	19.2
FL	Jacksonville	60	T	–	–	T	–	T	T	–	–	–	–	–	–
	Miami	59	–	–	–	–	T	–	–	–	–	–	–	–	–
GA	Atlanta	70	1.0	0.5	0.5	T	–	–	T	–	–	T	T	0.2	2.1
HI	Honolulu	52	–	–	–	–	–	–	–	–	–	–	–	–	–
ID	Boise	70	6.4	3.7	1.7	0.6	0.1	T	T	T	T	0.1	2.3	5.9	20.7
IL	Chicago	50	11.4	8.1	6.5	1.6	0.1	T	T	T	T	0.4	2.1	8.8	38.8
	Peoria	66	6.6	5.3	4.2	0.8	T	T	T	–	T	0.1	2.1	6.4	25.3
IN	Indianapolis	78	7.0	5.7	3.5	0.5	T	T	–	T	–	0.2	1.9	5.5	24.2
IA	Des Moines	66	8.4	7.5	6.0	1.9	T	T	T	T	T	0.3	3.1	7.0	33.9
KS	Wichita	56	4.0	4.1	2.8	0.2	T	T	T	T	T	–	1.4	3.6	16.0
KY	Louisville	62	5.2	4.2	3.2	0.1	T	T	T	T	T	0.1	1.0	2.5	16.2
LA	New Orleans	51	T	0.1	T	T	T	–	–	–	–	–	T	0.1	0.2
ME	Portland	69	19.1	16.6	13.3	3.1	0.2	–	T	–	T	0.2	3.3	15.1	70.8
MD	Baltimore	59	6.0	7.0	3.6	0.1	T	T	T	–	–	T	1.0	3.6	21.2
MA	Boston	72	12.9	11.9	8.1	0.9	–	T	T	T	–	–	1.3	8.3	43.2
MI	Detroit	51	11.3	9.4	7.0	2.0	T	T	T	–	T	0.2	2.5	10.2	42.3
	Sault Ste. Marie	62	29.2	18.8	14.4	5.9	0.5	–	–	T	0.1	2.4	15.6	31.2	118.4
MN	Duluth	66	17.6	12.2	14.0	6.8	0.7	T	T	T	0.1	1.6	12.3	16.2	81.7
	Minneapolis-St. Paul	67	10.4	8.1	10.6	2.8	0.1	T	T	T	T	0.5	7.6	9.8	49.8
MS	Jackson	38	0.5	0.2	0.2	T	–	–	–	–	–	–	T	0.1	1.0
MO	Kansas City	75	5.3	4.5	3.4	0.8	T	T	T	T	T	0.1	1.3	4.6	20.0
	St. Louis	73	5.3	4.5	3.8	0.5	T	T	T	–	–	T	1.4	4.1	19.7
MT	Great Falls	72	9.3	8.6	10.6	7.6	1.9	0.4	T	0.1	1.5	3.5	7.4	8.4	58.9
NE	Omaha	74	7.6	6.9	6.2	1.1	0.1	T	T	T	T	0.3	2.6	6.0	30.5
NV	Reno	60	6.0	5.1	4.2	1.2	0.8	–	–	–	–	0.3	2.5	4.8	24.9
NH	Concord	68	18.1	14.4	11.6	2.8	0.1	T	–	–	T	0.1	3.8	14.5	65.1
NJ	Atlantic City	60	5.0	5.6	2.6	0.3	T	T	T	–	–	T	0.4	2.6	16.2
NM	Albuquerque	70	2.5	2.1	1.8	0.6	T	T	T	T	T	0.1	1.2	3.0	11.3
NY	Albany	63	16.9	13.4	11.5	2.8	0.1	T	T	–	T	0.2	3.9	14.9	64.0
	Buffalo	66	24.3	17.9	12.5	3.2	0.2	T	T	T	T	0.7	10.9	24.4	94.3
	New York [1]	141	7.7	8.7	5.1	0.9	T	–	T	–	–	T	0.9	5.6	28.9
NC	Charlotte	70	2.2	1.8	1.2	T	T	T	–	–	T	0.1	0.5	5.8	
	Raleigh	65	2.8	2.6	1.3	T	T	T	T	–	–	0.1	0.8	7.6	
ND	Bismarck	70	7.7	6.9	8.6	3.9	0.9	T	T	T	0.2	1.9	6.8	7.6	44.0
OH	Cincinnati	62	7.2	5.6	4.2	0.5	–	T	T	T	–	0.3	2.0	3.8	23.5
	Cleveland	68	14.7	12.7	11.0	2.9	0.1	T	T	–	T	0.6	5.0	12.5	59.3
	Columbus	62	8.9	6.2	4.8	1.0	T	T	T	–	T	0.1	2.2	5.4	28.4
OK	Oklahoma City	70	3.2	2.4	1.5	T	T	T	T	T	T	T	0.6	2.1	9.6
OR	Portland	55	3.2	1.1	0.4	T	–	T	–	T	T	–	0.4	1.4	6.5
PA	Philadelphia	67	6.0	7.0	3.5	0.3	T	T	–	–	–	T	0.7	3.7	20.8
	Pittsburgh	57	12.0	9.5	8.1	1.8	0.1	T	T	T	T	0.4	3.4	8.3	43.5
RI	Providence	56	9.7	9.7	7.4	0.7	0.2	–	–	–	–	0.1	1.3	7.6	36.3
SC	Columbia	61	0.6	0.8	0.2	T	T	–	T	T	–	–	T	0.3	1.9
SD	Sioux Falls	64	6.9	7.9	9.3	3.3	T	T	T	T	T	0.9	6.0	7.4	41.5
TN	Memphis	52	2.2	1.4	0.9	T	T	T	–	–	–	T	0.1	0.6	5.2
	Nashville	63	3.6	3.0	1.5	–	–	T	–	T	–	0	0.4	1.4	10.0
TX	Dallas-Fort Worth	51	1.1	1.0	0.2	T	–	T	–	–	–	T	0.1	0.3	2.6
	El Paso	60	1.3	0.8	0.4	0.3	T	T	T	–	T	T	1.0	1.7	5.4
	Houston	75	0.2	0.2	T	T	T	T	–	–	–	–	T	–	0.4
UT	Salt Lake City	81	13.4	10.0	9.0	4.9	0.6	T	T	T	0.1	1.3	6.8	12.3	58.3
VT	Burlington	66	19.4	16.9	13.8	4.0	0.2	–	T	T	T	0.2	6.6	19.0	80.3
VA	Norfolk	59	3.0	2.9	1.0	T	T	T	T	–	–	–	–	1.0	7.9
	Richmond	70	4.9	3.8	2.5	0.1	T	–	T	–	–	T	0.4	2.1	13.6
WA	Seattle-Tacoma	53	4.9	1.6	1.3	0.1	T	–	T	–	T	–	1.1	2.4	11.4
	Spokane	62	15.5	7.3	4.1	0.8	0.1	T	–	–	T	0.4	6.2	14.8	49.2
WV	Charleston	55	10.7	8.6	5.3	0.9	–	T	T	T	T	0.2	2.4	5.4	33.2
WI	Milwaukee	69	13.9	9.7	8.6	2.0	0.1	T	T	T	T	0.2	3.0	11.1	48.5
WY	Cheyenne	74	6.1	6.4	11.8	9.5	3.4	0.2	T	T	1.1	4.1	7.2	6.8	55.8
PR	San Juan	54	–	–	–	–	–	–	–	–	–	T	–	–	–

– Represents zero. [1] City office data.

Source: U.S. National Oceanic and Atmospheric Administration, *Comparative Climatic Data*, annual. See also <http://www.ncdc.noaa.gov/oa/climate/online/ccd/avgsnf.txt>.

Table 396. Cloudiness, Average Wind Speed, Heating and Cooling Degree Days, and Average Relative Humidity—Selected Cities

[Airport data, except as noted. For period of record through 2009, except as noted. M=morning. A=afternoon]

State	Station	Cloudiness-average percentage of days [1]		Average wind speed (miles per hour, m.p.h.)				Heating degree days	Cooling degree days	Average relative humidity (percent)						
		Length of record (yr.)	Annual	Length of record (yr.)	Annual	Jan.	July			Length of record (yr.)	Annual M	Annual A	Jan. M	Jan. A	July M	July A
AL	Mobile	47	72.1	61	8.8	10.1	6.9	1,681	2,539	47	86	66	81	67	89	68
AK	Juneau.	47	87.9	64	8.2	8.0	7.5	8,574	–	43	80	70	78	75	79	67
AZ	Phoenix	57	42.3	64	6.2	5.3	7.1	1,027	4,364	49	49	22	63	61	42	19
AR	Little Rock	35	67.5	67	7.7	8.4	6.7	3,084	2,086	45	82	63	78	66	84	62
CA	Los Angeles.	60	59.8	61	7.5	6.7	7.9	1,274	679	50	79	66	71	61	86	68
	Sacramento	49	48.5	59	7.8	6.8	8.9	2,666	1,248	23	83	46	90	69	77	29
	San Diego	55	60.0	69	7.0	6.0	7.1	1,063	866	49	77	63	71	58	82	66
	San Francisco	68	56.2	82	10.6	7.2	13.6	2,862	142	50	84	63	86	68	86	60
CO	Denver	61	68.5	53	8.7	8.7	8.3	6,128	696	41	67	41	62	49	67	33
CT	Hartford	41	77.5	55	8.4	8.9	7.3	6,104	759	50	77	53	72	56	78	51
DE	Wilmington.	47	73.4	61	9.0	9.8	7.8	4,888	1,125	62	78	55	75	59	79	54
DC	Washington	48	73.8	61	9.4	10.0	8.3	4,055	1,531	49	74	53	70	55	75	53
FL	Jacksonville	47	74.2	60	7.8	8.1	7.0	1,354	2,627	73	89	56	87	57	88	58
	Miami.	46	79.7	60	9.2	9.5	7.9	149	4,361	45	83	61	83	59	82	63
GA	Atlanta	61	69.9	71	9.1	10.4	7.7	2,827	1,810	49	82	56	78	58	87	58
HI	Honolulu	47	75.3	60	11.2	9.4	13.1	–	4,561	40	71	56	79	61	67	51
ID	Boise	56	67.1	70	8.7	7.9	8.4	5,727	807	70	69	43	80	70	53	20
IL	Chicago	37	77.0	51	10.3	11.6	8.4	6,498	830	51	79	65	77	70	80	62
	Peoria	52	73.9	66	9.8	10.9	7.8	6,097	998	50	82	67	79	72	85	66
IN	Indianapolis	64	76.0	61	9.6	10.9	7.5	5,521	1,042	50	83	61	81	70	85	59
IA	Des Moines	46	71.3	60	10.7	11.4	8.9	6,436	1,052	48	79	66	76	70	82	64
KS	Wichita.	39	64.9	56	12.2	11.9	11.2	4,765	1,658	56	79	61	78	66	78	56
KY	Louisville	47	74.6	62	8.3	9.5	6.8	4,352	1,443	49	81	58	77	64	83	57
LA	New Orleans	47	72.3	61	8.2	9.3	6.1	1,417	2,773	61	86	67	83	69	90	70
ME	Portland	54	72.3	69	8.7	9.0	7.6	7,318	347	69	78	59	75	60	79	59
MD	Baltimore	45	71.2	59	8.7	9.1	7.5	4,720	1,147	56	77	53	72	56	79	52
MA	Boston	60	73.2	52	12.3	13.7	11.0	5,630	777	45	72	58	68	57	73	57
MI	Detroit	37	79.5	51	10.2	11.7	8.5	6,422	736	51	81	59	79	68	82	53
	Sault Ste. Marie . . .	54	81.9	68	9.2	9.5	7.8	9,224	145	68	85	66	80	73	87	61
MN	Duluth	47	79.0	60	11.0	11.6	9.4	9,724	189	48	80	68	77	73	84	66
	Minneapolis-St. Paul .	57	74.0	71	10.5	10.5	9.4	7,876	699	50	77	65	75	70	79	61
MS	Jackson	30	69.6	46	6.9	8.1	5.2	2,401	2,264	46	89	66	84	69	92	67
MO	Kansas City	23	67.1	37	10.6	11.1	9.1	5,249	1,325	37	80	67	76	69	83	67
	St. Louis.	47	72.4	60	9.6	10.6	8.0	4,758	1,561	49	80	65	79	69	81	62
MT	Great Falls	57	78.4	68	12.5	14.8	10.0	7,828	288	48	68	46	66	60	67	30
NE	Omaha.	49	69.6	73	10.5	10.9	8.8	6,311	1,095	45	80	66	78	69	83	66
NV	Reno	53	56.7	67	6.6	5.6	7.2	5,600	493	46	67	31	79	50	57	18
NH	Concord	54	75.3	67	6.7	7.2	5.7	7,478	442	44	81	53	76	58	82	51
NJ	Atlantic City	37	74.2	51	9.8	10.6	8.3	5,113	935	45	81	56	77	58	82	56
NM	Albuquerque	56	54.2	70	8.9	8.0	8.9	4,281	1,290	49	58	29	66	38	58	27
NY	Albany	57	81.1	71	8.9	9.8	7.5	6,860	544	44	79	57	77	63	80	55
	Buffalo	52	85.2	70	11.8	13.9	10.2	6,692	548	49	79	63	79	72	78	55
	New York [2]	42	70.8	72	9.1	10.4	7.5	4,754	1,151	75	72	56	67	59	74	55
NC	Charlotte	49	70.2	60	7.4	7.8	6.6	3,162	1,681	49	82	53	77	54	85	55
	Raleigh	47	69.7	60	7.5	8.2	6.7	3,465	1,521	45	84	53	78	54	87	57
ND	Bismarck	56	74.5	70	10.2	10.0	9.2	8,802	471	50	80	63	76	72	82	56
OH	Cincinnati.	44	77.8	62	9.0	10.4	7.2	5,148	1,064	47	82	60	79	68	85	57
	Cleveland.	54	81.9	68	10.5	12.2	8.6	6,121	702	49	79	62	78	70	80	56
	Columbus	46	80.3	60	8.3	9.8	6.5	5,492	951	50	80	58	77	67	83	55
OK	Oklahoma City.	44	61.9	61	12.2	12.5	10.8	3,663	1,907	44	78	62	76	64	78	58
OR	Portland	47	81.3	61	7.9	9.9	7.6	4,400	390	69	85	59	85	75	81	44
PA	Philadelphia	55	74.5	69	9.5	10.3	8.2	4,759	1,235	50	76	54	72	58	77	53
	Pittsburgh	43	83.8	57	9.0	10.4	7.3	5,829	726	49	79	58	77	66	82	54
RI	Providence.	42	73.2	56	10.4	10.9	9.4	5,754	714	46	75	55	71	56	76	56
SC	Columbia	48	68.5	61	6.8	7.2	6.3	2,594	2,074	43	85	51	81	53	87	53
SD	Sioux Falls	50	71.2	61	11.0	10.9	9.8	7,812	747	46	81	67	78	72	83	63
TN	Memphis	43	67.7	61	8.8	10.0	7.5	3,041	2,187	70	79	61	77	65	82	62
	Nashville	54	72.0	68	8.0	9.1	6.5	3,677	1,652	44	82	64	77	66	86	64
TX	Dallas-Fort Worth .	42	63.0	56	10.7	11.0	9.7	2,370	2,568	46	79	62	77	65	76	56
	El Paso	53	47.1	67	8.8	8.3	8.3	2,543	2,254	49	55	27	63	33	60	29
	Houston	26	75.3	40	7.6	8.1	6.6	1,525	2,893	40	88	69	84	70	90	67
UT	Salt Lake City	69	65.8	80	8.8	7.5	9.5	5,631	1,066	49	67	43	79	69	50	21
VT	Burlington	52	84.1	66	9.0	9.7	8.0	7,665	489	44	77	58	73	64	78	53
VA	Norfolk.	47	71.0	61	10.5	11.4	8.9	3,368	1,612	61	78	58	74	58	81	59
	Richmond	50	72.7	61	7.7	8.1	6.9	3,919	1,435	75	82	53	79	56	84	55
WA	Seattle-Tacoma . . .	51	84.2	61	8.8	9.5	8.1	4,797	173	50	84	62	82	75	81	48
	Spokane	48	76.4	62	8.9	8.7	8.6	6,820	394	50	78	52	86	80	64	26
WV	Charleston.	47	82.2	62	5.8	6.9	4.8	4,644	978	62	84	56	78	63	90	59
WI	Milwaukee	55	75.3	69	11.5	12.6	9.7	7,087	616	49	79	68	75	70	80	66
WY	Cheyenne	60	71.0	52	12.9	15.1	10.4	7,388	273	50	65	45	57	50	68	37
PR	San Juan	40	80.0	54	8.3	8.3	9.6	–	5,426	54	79	65	81	65	78	67

– Represents zero. [1] Percent of days that are either partly cloudy or cloudy. [2] Airport data for sunshine.

Source: U.S. National Oceanic and Atmospheric Administration, *Comparative Climatic Data*, annual. See also
<http://www.ncdc.noaa.gov/oa/climate/online/ccd/clpcdy.txt>; <http://www.ncdc.noaa.gov/oa/climate/online/ccd/wndspd.txt>;
<http://www.ncdc.noaa.gov/oa/climate/online/ccd/nrmhdd.txt>; <http://www.ncdc.noaa.gov/oa/climate/online/ccd/nrmcdd.txt>;
<http://www.ncdc.noaa.gov/oa/climate/online/ccd/relhum.txt>.

242 Geography and Environment

Section 7
Elections

This section relates primarily to presidential, congressional, and gubernatorial elections. Also presented are summary tables on congressional legislation; state legislatures; Hispanic and female office-holders; population of voting age; voter participation; and campaign finances.

Official statistics on federal elections, collected by the Clerk of the House, are published biennially in *Statistics of the Presidential and Congressional Election and Statistics of the Congressional Election*. Federal and state elections data appear also in *America Votes*, a biennial volume published by CQ Press (a division of Congressional Quarterly, Inc.), Washington, DC. Federal elections data also appear in the U.S. Congress, *Congressional Directory*, and in official state documents. Data on reported registration and voting for social and economic groups are obtained by the U.S. Census Bureau as part of the Current Population Survey (CPS) and are published in Current Population Reports, Series P20 (see text, Section 1).

Almost all federal, state, and local governmental units in the United States conduct elections for political offices and other purposes. The conduct of elections is regulated by state laws or, in some cities and counties, by local charter. An exception is that the U.S. Constitution prescribes the basis of representation in Congress and the manner of electing the president and grants to Congress the right to regulate the times, places, and manner of electing federal officers. Amendments to the Constitution have prescribed national criteria for voting eligibility. The 15th Amendment, adopted in 1870, gave all citizens the right to vote regardless of race, color, or previous condition of servitude. The 19th Amendment, adopted in 1919, further extended the right to vote to all citizens regardless of sex. The payment of poll taxes as a prerequisite to voting in federal elections was banned by the 24th Amendment in 1964. In 1971, as a result of the 26th Amendment, eligibility to vote in national elections was extended to all citizens, 18 years old and over.

Presidential election— The Constitution specifies how the president and vice president are selected. Each state elects, by popular vote, a group of electors equal in number to its total of members of Congress. The 23rd Amendment, adopted in 1961, grants the District of Columbia three presidential electors, a number equal to that of the least populous state. Subsequent to the election, the electors meet in their respective states to vote for president and vice president. Usually, each elector votes for the candidate receiving the most popular votes in his or her state. A majority vote of all electors is necessary to elect the president and vice president. If no candidate receives a majority, the House of Representatives, with each state having one vote, is empowered to elect the president and vice president, again, with a majority of votes required.

The 22nd Amendment to the Constitution, adopted in 1951, limits presidential tenure to two elective terms of 4 years each or to one elective term for any person who, upon succession to the presidency, has held the office or acted as President for more than 2 years.

Congressional election— The Constitution provides that representatives be apportioned among the states according to their population, that a census of population be taken every 10 years as a basis for apportionment, and that each state have at least one representative. At the time of each apportionment, Congress decides what the total number of representatives will be. Since 1912, the total has been 435, except during 1960 to 1962 when it increased to 437, adding one representative each for Alaska and Hawaii. The total reverted to 435 after reapportionment following the 1960 census. Members are elected for 2-year terms, all terms covering the same period. The District of Columbia, American

Samoa, Guam, and the Virgin Islands each elect one nonvoting delegate, and Puerto Rico elects a nonvoting resident commissioner.

The Senate is composed of 100 members, two from each state, who are elected to serve for a term of 6 years. One-third of the Senate is elected every 2 years. Senators were originally chosen by the state legislatures. The 17th Amendment to the Constitution, adopted in 1913, prescribed that senators be elected by popular vote.

Voter eligibility and participation— The Census Bureau publishes estimates of the population of voting age and the percent casting votes in each state for presidential and congressional election years. These voting-age estimates include a number of persons who meet the age requirement but are not eligible to vote, (e.g. aliens and some institutionalized persons). In addition, since 1964, voter participation and voter characteristics data have been collected during November of election years as part of the CPS. These survey data include noncitizens in the voting- age population estimates, but exclude members of the Armed Forces and the institutional population.

Statistical reliability— For a discussion of statistical collection and estimation, sampling procedures, and measures of statistical reliability applicable to Census Bureau data, see Appendix III.

Table 397. Participation in Elections for President and U.S. Representatives: 1932 to 2010

[75,768 represents 75,768,000. As of November, except as noted. Estimated resident population 21 years old and over, 1932–70, except as noted, and 18 years old and over thereafter; includes Armed Forces stationed in the U.S. Prior to 1958, excludes Alaska and prior to 1960, excludes Hawaii. District of Columbia is included in votes cast for President beginning 1964]

Year	Resident population (includes aliens) of voting age [1] (1,000)	Votes cast				Year	Resident population (includes aliens) of voting age [1] (1,000)	Votes cast			
		For President (1,000)	Percent of voting-age population	For U.S. Representatives (1,000)	Percent of voting-age population			For President (1,000)	Percent of voting-age population	For U.S. Representatives (1,000)	Percent of voting-age population
1932...	75,768	39,817	52.6	(NA)	(NA)	1972...	140,777	77,625	55.1	71,188	50.6
1934...	77,997	(X)	(X)	32,804	42.1	1974...	146,338	(X)	(X)	52,313	35.7
1936...	80,174	45,647	56.9	(NA)	(NA)	1976...	152,308	81,603	53.6	74,259	48.8
1938...	82,354	(X)	(X)	(NA)	(NA)	1978...	158,369	(X)	(X)	54,584	34.5
1940...	84,728	49,815	58.8	(NA)	(NA)	1980...	163,945	86,497	52.8	77,874	47.5
1942...	86,465	(X)	(X)	28,074	32.5	1982...	169,643	(X)	(X)	63,881	37.7
1944...	85,654	48,026	56.1	45,110	52.7	1984...	173,995	92,655	53.3	82,422	47.4
1946...	92,659	(X)	(X)	34,410	37.1	1986...	177,922	(X)	(X)	59,758	33.6
1948...	95,573	48,834	51.1	46,220	48.4	1988...	181,956	91,587	50.3	81,682	44.9
1950...	98,134	(X)	(X)	40,430	41.2	1990...	185,812	(X)	(X)	62,355	33.6
1952...	99,929	61,552	61.6	57,571	57.6	1992...	189,493	104,600	55.2	97,198	51.3
1954...	102,075	(X)	(X)	42,583	41.7	1994...	193,010	(X)	(X)	70,494	36.5
1956...	104,515	62,027	59.3	58,886	56.3	1996...	196,789	96,390	49.0	90,233	45.9
1958...	106,447	(X)	(X)	45,719	43.0	1998...	201,270	(X)	(X)	66,605	33.1
1960...	109,672	68,836	62.8	64,124	58.5	2000...	[2] 209,787	105,594	50.3	98,800	47.1
1962...	112,952	(X)	(X)	51,242	45.4	2002...	[2] 214,755	(X)	(X)	74,707	34.8
1964...	114,090	70,098	61.4	65,879	57.7	2004...	[2] 219,553	122,349	55.7	113,192	51.6
1966...	116,638	(X)	(X)	52,902	45.4	2006...	[2] 224,583	(X)	(X)	80,976	36.1
1968...	120,285	73,027	60.7	66,109	55.0	2008...	[2] 229,945	131,407	57.1	122,586	53.3
1970...	124,498	(X)	(X)	54,259	43.6	2010...	[3] 234,564	(X)	(X)	86,785	37.0

NA Not available. X Not applicable. [1] Population 18 and over in Georgia, 1944-70, and in Kentucky, 1956–70; 20 and over in Alaska and 20 and over in Hawaii, 1960–70. Source: Through 1990, U.S. Census Bureau, "Table 4. Participation in Elections for President and U.S. Representatives: 1930 to 1992," May 1994, <http://www.census.gov/population/socdemo/voting/p25-1117 /tab03-04.pdf>. For 1992–1998, "Estimates and Projections of the Voting-Age Population, 1992 to 2000, and Percent Casting Votes for President, by State: November 1992 and 1996," July 2000, <http://www.census.gov/population/socdemo/voting/proj00/tab03. txt>. Starting 2000, "Annual Estimates of the Resident Population by Sex and Selected Age Groups for the United States: April 1, 2000 to July 1, 2009," (NC-EST2009-02), June 2010, <http://www.census.gov/popest/national/asrh/NC-EST2009/NC-EST2009-02 .xls>. [2] As of July 1. Based on results of the 2000 Census. [3] As of April 1, 2010, from 2010 Census Redistricting Data (Public Law 94-171) Summary File.

Source: Except as noted, U.S. House of Representatives, Office of the Clerk, *Statistics of the Presidential and Congressional Election*, biennial. See also <http://clerk.house.gov/member_info/election.aspx>.

Table 398. Resident Population of Voting Age and Percent Casting Votes— States: 2000 to 2010

[219,553 represents 219,553,000. Estimated population, 18 years old and over. 2010 based on 2010 Census as of April 1. Includes Armed Forces stationed in each state, aliens, and institutional population]

State	Voting-age population (1,000) [1]				Percent casting votes for—					
					Presidential electors			U.S. Representatives		
	2004 [2]	2006 [2]	2008 [2]	2010	2000 [2]	2004 [2]	2008 [2]	2006 [2]	2008 [2]	2010
U.S........	**219,553**	**224,583**	**229,945**	**234,564**	**50.3**	**55.7**	**57.1**	**36.1**	**53.3**	**37.0**
AL	3,403	3,476	3,548	3,647	50.0	55.3	59.2	32.8	52.3	37.5
AK	475	493	508	523	65.3	65.8	64.3	47.6	62.5	48.6
AZ	4,232	4,550	4,782	4,763	40.4	47.6	48.0	32.8	45.1	35.7
AR	2,063	2,117	2,161	2,204	46.1	51.1	50.3	36.0	36.4	35.1
CA	26,078	26,534	27,156	27,959	44.4	47.6	49.9	31.3	45.4	34.5
CO	3,448	3,576	3,725	3,804	54.1	61.8	64.5	43.0	61.3	46.4
CT	2,632	2,656	2,689	2,757	56.8	60.0	61.3	40.5	56.8	41.3
DE	627	649	669	692	55.4	59.9	61.6	38.8	57.6	44.2
DC	464	469	477	501	44.2	49.1	55.7	(X)	(X)	(X)
FL	13,455	14,023	14,353	14,799	48.1	56.6	58.5	27.5	51.7	34.6
GA	6,550	6,852	7,132	7,196	42.7	50.4	55.0	30.2	51.2	34.3
HI	959	985	998	1,056	40.1	44.7	45.7	34.3	45.7	34.1
ID	1,010	1,064	1,112	1,139	54.0	59.3	58.9	41.8	57.4	39.3
IL	9,417	9,514	9,660	9,701	51.6	56.0	57.2	36.3	54.3	38.1
IN	4,639	4,715	4,796	4,876	48.7	53.2	57.4	35.4	55.8	35.8
IA	2,229	2,253	2,281	2,318	61.6	67.6	67.4	45.9	64.9	47.7
KS	2,031	2,060	2,097	2,126	54.2	58.5	58.9	41.0	57.6	39.3
KY	3,153	3,213	3,272	3,316	50.6	57.0	55.8	39.0	53.5	40.8
LA	3,319	3,175	3,331	3,415	54.3	58.6	58.9	28.9	31.4	30.3
ME	1,017	1,031	1,044	1,054	66.8	72.8	70.0	52.0	68.0	53.6
MD	4,158	4,236	4,302	4,421	51.2	57.3	61.2	40.2	58.1	41.3
MA	4,966	5,009	5,105	5,129	56.2	58.9	60.8	44.8	60.8	43.4
MI	7,548	7,598	7,610	7,540	57.5	64.1	65.7	48.0	63.2	42.4
MN	3,808	3,883	3,968	4,020	66.9	74.3	73.3	56.1	70.6	52.0
MS	2,122	2,137	2,173	2,212	47.9	53.7	59.4	28.1	58.2	35.7
MO	4,335	4,429	4,521	4,563	56.5	63.0	64.7	47.4	62.4	42.1
MT	706	727	748	766	61.0	63.8	65.6	55.9	64.3	47.1
NE	1,296	1,315	1,334	1,367	55.2	60.0	60.1	45.3	58.1	35.5
NV	1,729	1,848	1,939	2,036	40.6	48.0	49.9	31.1	46.8	34.5
NH	985	1,009	1,028	1,029	61.2	68.9	69.2	39.9	65.6	43.7
NJ	6,495	6,536	6,610	6,727	50.3	55.6	58.5	32.7	52.0	31.5
NM	1,394	1,442	1,481	1,541	45.6	54.3	56.1	38.9	55.0	38.7
NY	14,677	14,819	15,015	15,053	48.6	50.7	51.4	31.6	51.4	31.5
NC	6,446	6,703	6,993	7,254	47.7	54.3	61.5	29.0	60.3	36.7
ND	489	493	498	523	59.9	63.9	63.5	44.1	63.0	45.2
OH	8,642	8,710	8,789	8,806	55.5	65.1	64.9	45.5	61.1	43.4
OK	2,633	2,682	2,737	2,822	48.2	55.6	53.4	33.8	48.9	28.1
OR	2,725	2,817	2,912	2,965	59.4	67.4	62.8	48.2	57.8	48.2
PA	9,530	9,641	9,771	9,910	52.4	60.5	61.5	41.6	59.2	39.9
RI	825	823	824	829	51.0	53.0	57.3	45.3	53.2	40.5
SC	3,172	3,289	3,428	3,545	45.9	51.0	56.0	33.0	54.7	37.8
SD	578	591	606	611	57.2	67.2	63.0	56.4	62.5	52.2
TN	4,486	4,622	4,749	4,850	48.2	54.3	54.7	37.1	48.5	32.1
TX	16,159	16,851	17,538	18,280	42.6	45.9	46.1	24.6	42.9	26.0
UT	1,679	1,781	1,877	1,893	50.6	55.2	50.7	32.0	49.9	33.8
VT	479	486	492	497	63.6	65.2	66.0	54.0	60.5	48.0
VA	5,662	5,818	5,957	6,147	51.1	56.4	62.5	39.5	58.7	35.6
WA	4,662	4,835	5,008	5,143	56.6	61.3	60.6	42.5	58.2	48.2
WV	1,414	1,419	1,427	1,466	46.1	53.5	50.0	32.0	45.2	35.1
WI	4,170	4,243	4,311	4,347	64.9	71.9	69.2	48.6	64.4	49.2
WY	380	389	404	428	58.5	64.1	63.1	50.4	61.8	44.6

X Not applicable. [1] As of July 1. Source: U.S. Census Bureau, "Annual Estimates of the Resident Population by Sex and Age for States: April 1, 2000 to July 1, 2009," (SC-EST2009-02), June 2010, <http://www.census.gov/popest/states/asrh /SC-EST2009-02.html>. [2] Based on results of the 2000 Census.

Source: Except as noted, U.S. House of Representatives, Office of the Clerk, *Statistics of the Presidential and Congressional Election*, biennial. See also <http://clerk.house.gov/member_info/electionInfo/index.html>.

Elections 245

Table 399. Voting-Age Population—Reported Registration and Voting by Selected Characteristics: 1996 to 2010

[198.2 represents 198,200,000. As of November. Covers civilian noninstitutional population 18 years old and over. Includes aliens. Figures are based on Current Population Survey (see text, Section 1 and Appendix III) and differ from those in Table 397 based on population estimates and official vote counts]

Characteristic	Voting-age population (mil.)							Percent reporting they registered							Percent reporting they voted						
								Presidential election years				Congressional election years			Presidential election years				Congressional election years		
	1998	2000	2002	2004	2006	2008	2010	1996	2000	2004	2008	2002	2006	2010	1996	2000	2004	2008	2002	2006	2010
Total [1]	**198.2**	**202.6**	**210.4**	**215.7**	**220.6**	**225.5**	**229.7**	**65.9**	**63.9**	**65.9**	**64.9**	**60.9**	**61.6**	**59.8**	**54.2**	**54.7**	**58.3**	**58.2**	**42.3**	**43.6**	**41.8**
18 to 20 years old	11.4	11.9	11.7	11.5	11.6	11.7	12.2	45.6	40.5	50.7	49.3	32.6	37.0	34.4	31.2	28.4	41.0	41.0	15.1	17.1	16.4
21 to 24 years old	14.1	14.9	15.6	16.4	16.2	16.6	16.7	51.2	49.3	52.1	56.2	42.5	44.9	47.2	33.4	35.4	42.5	46.6	18.7	21.9	22.0
25 to 34 years old	38.6	37.3	38.5	39.0	39.4	40.2	41.2	56.9	54.7	55.6	56.5	50.2	50.3	49.8	43.1	43.7	46.9	48.5	27.1	28.3	26.9
35 to 44 years old	44.4	44.5	43.7	43.1	42.6	41.5	39.9	66.5	63.8	64.2	61.4	60.0	59.3	57.3	54.9	55.0	56.9	55.2	40.2	40.1	37.7
45 to 64 years old	57.4	61.4	66.9	71.0	75.0	78.1	80.7	73.5	71.2	72.7	70.4	69.4	69.6	66.3	64.4	64.1	66.6	65.0	53.1	54.3	51.1
65 years old and over	32.3	32.8	33.9	34.7	35.8	37.5	39.0	77.0	76.1	76.9	75.0	75.8	75.4	72.5	67.0	67.6	68.9	68.1	61.0	60.5	58.9
Male	95.2	97.1	100.9	103.8	106.5	109.0	111.1	64.4	62.2	64.0	62.6	58.9	59.5	57.9	52.8	53.1	56.3	55.7	41.4	42.4	40.9
Female	103.0	105.5	109.5	111.9	114.1	116.5	118.6	67.3	65.6	67.6	67.0	62.8	63.5	61.5	55.5	56.2	60.1	60.4	43.0	44.7	42.7
White [2]	165.8	168.7	174.1	176.6	179.9	183.2	185.8	67.7	65.6	67.9	66.6	63.1	64.0	61.6	56.0	56.4	60.3	59.6	44.1	45.8	43.4
Black [2]	23.3	24.1	24.4	24.9	25.7	26.5	27.4	63.5	63.6	64.4	65.5	58.8	57.4	58.8	50.6	53.5	56.3	60.8	39.7	38.6	40.7
Asian [2,3]	(NA)	8.0	9.6	9.3	9.9	10.5	11.0	(NA)	30.7	34.9	37.3	30.7	32.9	34.1	(NA)	25.4	29.8	32.1	19.4	21.8	21.3
Hispanic [4]	20.3	21.6	25.2	27.1	29.0	30.9	32.5	35.7	34.9	34.3	37.6	32.6	32.1	33.8	26.7	27.5	28.0	31.6	18.9	19.3	20.5
Region: [5]																					
Northeast	38.5	38.9	41.1	41.0	41.2	41.5	42.3	64.7	63.7	65.3	63.7	60.8	60.3	59.7	54.5	55.2	58.6	57.4	41.4	42.8	41.6
Midwest	45.9	46.4	48.8	48.4	49.1	49.4	50.1	71.6	70.2	72.8	70.6	66.5	68.3	65.0	59.3	60.9	65.0	63.4	47.1	50.7	45.1
South	70.1	71.8	74.2	77.2	80.0	82.4	84.2	65.9	64.5	65.5	65.5	61.6	62.0	59.4	52.2	53.5	56.4	57.7	41.6	40.3	39.3
West	43.7	45.5	46.3	49.1	50.4	52.2	53.2	60.8	56.9	60.1	59.4	54.0	55.4	55.5	51.8	49.9	54.4	54.6	39.0	42.4	42.7
School years completed:																					
8 years or less	13.3	12.9	12.3	12.6	12.1	11.1	11.1	40.7	36.1	32.5	30.1	32.4	29.5	27.0	28.1	26.8	23.6	23.4	19.4	17.1	15.8
High school:																					
Less than high school graduate	21.0	20.1	20.9	20.7	20.2	19.1	18.8	47.9	45.9	45.8	43.2	41.6	39.6	37.8	33.8	33.6	34.6	33.7	23.3	22.8	20.8
High school graduate or GED [6]	65.6	66.3	68.9	68.5	70.0	70.4	71.0	62.2	60.1	61.5	59.5	57.1	57.5	54.0	49.1	49.4	52.4	50.9	37.1	37.6	35.2
College:																					
Some college or associate's degree	52.9	55.3	57.3	58.9	60.2	63.8	65.3	72.9	70.0	73.7	72.0	66.7	68.3	65.5	60.5	60.3	66.1	65.0	45.8	47.3	44.4
Bachelor's or advanced degree	45.4	48.0	51.0	54.9	58.2	61.1	63.5	80.4	77.3	78.1	76.8	74.4	73.9	72.5	73.0	72.0	74.2	73.3	58.5	59.5	57.1
Employed	130.5	133.4	134.9	138.8	143.8	143.2	138.3	67.0	64.7	67.1	66.4	61.7	62.7	61.5	55.2	55.5	60.0	60.1	42.1	43.9	42.5
Unemployed	5.2	4.9	7.7	7.3	6.2	9.5	13.9	52.5	46.1	56.3	57.2	48.1	48.5	52.3	37.2	35.1	46.4	48.8	27.2	28.0	31.6
Not in labor force	62.5	64.2	67.8	69.6	70.5	72.8	77.5	65.1	63.8	64.4	62.9	60.9	60.7	58.0	54.1	54.5	56.2	55.5	44.2	44.3	42.3

NA Not available. [1] Includes other races, not shown separately. [2] Beginning with the 2003 Current Population Survey (CPS), respondents could choose more than one race. 2004, 2006, 2008, and 2010 data represent persons who selected this race group only and exclude persons reporting more than one race. The CPS in prior years only allowed respondents to report one race group. See also comment on race in the text for Section 1. [3] Prior to 2004, this category was "Asian and Pacific Islanders," therefore rates are not comparable with prior years. [4] Persons of Hispanic origin may be any race. [5] For composition of regions, see map, inside cover. [6] The General Educational Development (GED) Test measures how well a non-high school graduate has mastered the skills and general knowledge that are acquired in a 4-year high school education. Successfully passing the exam is a credential generally considered to be equivalent to a high school diploma.

Source: U.S. Census Bureau, *Voting and Registration in the Election of November 2010*, Current Population Reports, P20-562, 2010, and earlier reports, and unpublished data, <http://www.census.gov/hhes/www/socdemo/voting/index.html>.

Table 400. Persons Reported Registered and Voted by State: 2010

[229,690 represents 229,690,000. As of November. See headnote, Table 399]

State	Voting-age population (1,000)	Percent of voting-age population Registered	Percent of voting-age population Voted	State	Voting-age population (1,000)	Percent of voting-age population Registered	Percent of voting-age population Voted
U.S.	229,690	59.8	41.8	MO	4,506	66.9	44.5
AL	3,526	63.1	42.8	MT	753	65.2	51.3
AK	498	63.8	48.6	NE	1,323	60.8	38.7
AZ	4,831	60.7	44.9	NV	1,957	50.9	37.3
AR	2,140	58.7	39.3	NH	1,024	65.0	45.9
CA	27,381	50.6	39.2	NJ	6,581	55.6	36.2
CO	3,768	61.0	48.4	NM	1,489	50.1	38.9
CT	2,648	62.0	45.9	NY	14,974	56.1	38.4
DE	667	62.6	48.5	NC	6,998	63.7	43.0
DC	489	60.3	40.8	ND	488	73.9	54.5
FL	14,227	56.2	39.2	OH	8,642	64.8	44.2
GA	7,119	57.2	40.2	OK	2,695	59.5	39.4
HI	965	48.3	39.9	OR	2,974	67.4	53.6
ID	1,114	59.8	44.7	PA	9,631	62.6	42.6
IL	9,619	60.5	41.5	RI	812	62.8	42.9
IN	4,777	59.4	38.2	SC	3,453	66.7	49.2
IA	2,278	67.9	50.2	SD	602	67.4	53.5
KS	2,059	65.5	45.2	TN	4,745	60.1	36.1
KY	3,250	65.0	45.5	TX	17,847	53.2	31.4
LA	3,314	73.2	48.8	UT	1,929	56.8	36.0
ME	1,034	75.4	58.4	VT	490	72.7	54.0
MD	4,279	58.6	42.1	VA	5,873	60.4	38.4
MA	5,097	63.4	48.1	WA	5,095	66.1	52.8
MI	7,513	68.2	45.2	WV	1,420	62.2	40.9
MN	3,982	69.2	52.8	WI	4,291	67.8	52.6
MS	2,113	72.5	46.5	WY	411	58.2	46.1

Source: U.S. Census Bureau, Current Population Reports, "*Voting and Registration in the Election of November 2010*" and unpublished data, <http://www.census.gov/hhes/www/socdemo/voting/index.html>.

Table 401. Reported Voting and Registration Among Native and Naturalized Citizens by Race and Hispanic Origin: 2010

[In thousands, except percent. (210,800 represents 210,800,000). As of November]

Nativity status, race, and Hispanic origin	Total citizen population (1,000)	U.S. Citizen Reported registered Number (1,000)	U.S. Citizen Reported registered Percent	U.S. Citizen Not registered Number (1,000)	U.S. Citizen Not registered Percent	U.S. Citizen Reported voted Number (1,000)	U.S. Citizen Reported voted Percent	U.S. Citizen Did not vote Number (1,000)	U.S. Citizen Did not vote Percent
Total:									
All races [1]	210,800	137,263	65.1	73,537	34.9	95,987	45.5	114,813	54.5
White alone [2]	172,447	114,482	66.4	57,965	33.6	80,554	46.7	91,893	53.3
Black alone [2]	25,632	16,101	62.8	9,531	37.2	11,149	43.5	14,483	56.5
Asian alone [2]	7,639	3,765	49.3	3,874	50.7	2,354	30.8	5,285	69.2
Hispanic [3]	21,285	10,982	51.6	10,303	48.4	6,646	31.2	14,639	68.8
Native citizen:									
All races [1]	193,897	128,098	66.1	65,799	33.9	89,740	46.3	104,157	53.7
White alone [2]	162,609	109,074	67.1	53,535	32.9	76,696	47.2	85,913	52.8
White alone, non-Hispanic	148,465	101,758	68.5	46,707	31.5	72,495	48.8	75,970	51.2
Black alone [2]	23,780	15,003	63.1	8,777	36.9	10,385	43.7	13,395	56.3
Asian alone [2]	2,748	1,273	46.3	1,475	53.7	842	30.6	1,906	69.4
Hispanic [3]	15,535	7,938	51.1	7,597	48.9	4,541	29.2	10,994	70.8
White alone or in combination [4]	165,166	110,661	67.0	54,505	33.0	77,715	47.1	87,451	52.9
Black alone or in combination [4]	24,713	15,562	63.0	9,151	37.0	10,717	43.4	13,996	56.6
Asian alone or in combination [4]	3,333	1,628	48.9	1,705	51.1	1,089	32.7	2,244	67.3
Naturalized citizen:									
All races [1]	16,903	9,165	54.2	7,738	45.8	6,247	37.0	10,656	63.0
White alone [2]	9,838	5,408	55.0	4,430	45.0	3,858	39.2	5,980	60.8
White alone, non-Hispanic	4,464	2,558	57.3	1,906	42.7	1,877	42.0	2,587	58.0
Black alone [2]	1,852	1098	59.3	754	40.7	763	41.2	1,089	58.8
Asian alone [2]	4,890	2,492	51.0	2,398	49.0	1,512	30.9	3,378	69.1
Hispanic [3]	5,750	3,044	52.9	2,706	47.1	2,106	36.6	3,644	63.4
White alone or in combination [4]	9,924	5,454	55.0	4,470	45.0	3,899	39.3	6,025	60.7
Black alone or in combination [4]	1,889	1122	59.4	767	40.6	781	41.3	1,108	58.7
Asian alone or in combination [4]	4,913	2,508	51.1	2,405	48.9	1,525	31.0	3,388	69.0

[1] Includes other races, not shown separately. [2] Beginning with the 2003 Current Population Survey (CPS), respondents could choose more than one race. Data shown represent persons who selected this race group only and exclude persons reporting more than one race. [3] Persons of Hispanic origin may be any race. [4] In combination with one or more races.
Source: U.S. Census Bureau, *Voting and Registration in the Election of November 2010,* Current Population Reports P20-562, 2010. See also <http://www.census.gov/hhes/www/socdemo/voting/index.html>.

Table 402. Vote Cast for President by Major Political Party: 1952 to 2008

[In thousands (61,552 represents 61,552,000), except percent and electoral vote. Prior to 1960, excludes Alaska and Hawaii; prior to 1964, excludes DC. Vote cast for major party candidates includes the votes of minor parties cast for those candidates]

Year	Candidates for President		Vote cast for President						
				Democratic			Republican		
			Total popular vote [1] (1,000)	Popular vote		Electoral vote	Popular vote		Electoral vote
	Democratic	Republican		Number (1,000)	Percent		Number (1,000)	Percent	
1952....	Stevenson	Eisenhower ...	61,552	27,315	44.4	89	33,779	54.9	442
1956....	Stevenson	Eisenhower ...	62,027	26,739	43.1	73	35,581	57.4	457
1960....	Kennedy......	Nixon........	68,836	34,227	49.7	303	34,108	49.5	219
1964....	Johnson......	Goldwater	70,098	42,825	61.1	486	27,147	38.7	52
1968....	Humphrey	Nixon........	73,027	30,989	42.4	191	31,710	43.4	301
1972....	McGovern	Nixon........	77,625	28,902	37.2	17	46,740	60.2	520
1976....	Carter	Ford........	81,603	40,826	50.0	297	39,148	48.0	240
1980....	Carter	Reagan	86,497	35,481	41.0	49	43,643	50.5	489
1984....	Mondale......	Reagan	92,655	37,450	40.4	13	54,167	58.5	525
1988....	Dukakis	Bush	91,587	41,717	45.5	111	48,643	53.1	426
1992....	Clinton	Bush	104,600	44,858	42.9	370	38,799	37.1	168
1996....	Clinton	Dole........	96,390	47,402	49.2	379	39,198	40.7	159
2000....	Gore........	Bush	105,594	50,996	48.3	266	50,465	47.8	271
2004....	Kerry	Bush	122,349	58,895	48.1	251	61,873	50.6	286
2008....	Obama.......	McCain	131,407	69,498	52.9	365	59,948	45.6	173

[1] Include votes for minor party candidates, independents, unpledged electors, and scattered write-in votes.
Source: U.S. House of Representatives, Office of the Clerk, *Statistics of the Presidential and Congressional Election*, biennial. See also <http://clerk.house.gov/member_info/election.html>.

Table 403. Vote Cast for Leading Minority Party Candidates for President: 1952 to 2008

[In thousands (135 represents 135,000). See headnote, Table 402. Data do not include write-ins, scatterings, or votes for candidates who ran on party tickets not shown]

Year	Candidate	Party	Popular vote (1,000)	Candidate	Party	Popular vote (1,000)
1952.....	Vincent Hallinan......	Progressive	135	Stuart Hamblen	Prohibition	73
1956 [1] ...	T. Coleman Andrews ..	States' Rights	91	Eric Hass...........	Socialist Labor.....	41
1960.....	Eric Hass...........	Socialist Labor........	46	Rutherford Decker	Prohibition	46
1964.....	Eric Hass...........	Socialist Labor........	43	Clifton DeBerry	Socialist Workers...	22
1968.....	George Wallace......	American Independent ..	9,446	Henning Blomen	Socialist Labor.....	52
1972 [1] ...	John Schmitz........	American............	993	Benjamin Spock......	People's..........	9
1976.....	Eugene McCarthy	Independent.........	680	Roger McBride.......	Libertarian	172
1980.....	John Anderson	Independent.........	5,251	Ed Clark...........	Libertarian	920
1984.....	David Bergland	Libertarian	227	Lyndon H. LaRouche..	Independent.	79
1988.....	Ron Paul	Libertarian	410	Lenora B. Fulani	New Alliance	129
1992.....	H. Ross Perot.......	Independent.........	19,722	Andre Marrou........	Libertarian	281
1996.....	H. Ross Perot.......	Reform.............	7,137	Ralph Nader	Green............	527
2000.....	Ralph Nader	Green.............	2,530	Pat Buchanan	Reform...........	324
2004.....	Ralph Nader	Independent.........	156	Michael Badnarik.....	Libertarian	369
2008.....	Ralph Nader	Independent.........	739	Bob Barr	Libertarian	515

[1] Data include write-ins, scatterings, and/or votes for candidates who ran on party tickets not shown.
Source: U.S. House of Representatives, Office of the Clerk, *Statistics of the Presidential and Congressional Election*, biennial. See also <http://clerk.house.gov/member_info/election.html>.

Table 404. Democratic and Republican Percentages of Two-Party Presidential Vote by Selected Characteristics of Voters: 2004 and 2008

[In percent. Covers citizens of voting age living in private housing units in the contiguous United States. Percentages for Democratic Presidential vote are computed by subtracting the percentage Republican vote from 100 percent; third-party or independent votes are not included as valid data. Data are from the National Election Studies and are based on a sample and subject to sampling variability; for details, see source]

Characteristic	2004		2008		Characteristic	2004		2008	
	Demo-cratic	Republi-can	Demo-cratic	Republi-can		Demo-cratic	Republi-can	Demo-cratic	Republi-can
Total [1]	**50**	**50**	**55**	**45**	Race:				
					White	42	58	44	56
Year of birth:					Black	90	10	99	1
1975 or later	66	34	65	35	Education:				
1959 to 1974	45	55	56	44	Less than high school...	69	31	72	28
1943 to 1958	44	56	54	46	High school diploma/				
1927 to 1942	51	49	41	59	equivalent	46	54	57	43
1911 to 1926	52	48	52	48	Some college,				
1895 to 1910	–	–	–	–	no degree	47	53	53	47
					College	50	50	51	49
Sex:									
Male...........	46	54	52	48	Union household	64	36	60	40
Female..........	53	47	57	43	Nonunion household	46	54	54	46

– Represents zero. [1] Includes other characteristics, not shown separately.
Source: American National Election Studies, <http://www.electionstudies.org/>.

Table 405. Electoral Vote Cast for President by Major Political Party—States: 1968 to 2008

[D = Democratic, R = Republican. For composition of regions, see map, inside front cover]

State	1968 [1]	1972 [2]	1976 [3]	1980	1984	1988 [4]	1992	1996	2000 [5]	2004 [6]	2008 [7]
Democratic......	**191**	**17**	**297**	**49**	**13**	**111**	**370**	**379**	**266**	**251**	**365**
Republican......	**301**	**520**	**240**	**489**	**525**	**426**	**168**	**159**	**271**	**286**	**173**
Northeast:											
Democratic	102	14	86	4	–	53	106	106	102	101	101
Republican........	24	108	36	118	113	60	–	–	4	–	–
Midwest:											
Democratic	31	–	58	10	10	29	100	100	68	57	97
Republican........	118	145	87	135	127	108	29	29	61	66	27
South:											
Democratic	45	3	149	31	3	8	68	80	15	16	71
Republican........	77	165	20	138	174	168	116	104	168	173	118
West:											
Democratic	13	–	4	4	–	21	96	93	81	77	96
Republican........	82	102	97	98	111	90	23	26	38	47	28
AL	(¹)	R-9	D-9	R-9	R-9	R-9	R-9	R-9	R-9	R-9	R-9
AK	R-3	R-3	R-3	R-3	R-3	R-3	R-3	R-3	R-3	R-3	R-3
AZ	R-5	R-6	R-6	R-6	R-7	R-7	R-8	R-8	R-8	R-10	R-10
AR	(¹)	R-6	D-6	R-6	R-6	R-6	D-6	D-6	R-6	R-6	R-6
CA	R-40	R-45	R-45	R-45	R-47	R-47	D-54	D-54	D-54	D-55	D-55
CO	R-6	R-7	R-7	R-7	R-8	R-8	D-8	R-8	R-8	R-9	D-9
CT	D-8	R-8	R-8	R-8	R-8	R-8	D-8	D-8	D-8	D-7	D-7
DE	R-3	R-3	D-3	R-3	R-3	R-3	D-3	D-3	D-3	D-3	D-3
DC	D-3	D-3	D-3	D-3	D-3	D-3	D-3	D-3	D-3	D-3	D-3
FL	R-14	R-17	D-17	R-17	R-21	R-21	R-25	D-25	⁵ D-2	R-27	D-27
GA	(¹)	R-12	D-12	D-12	R-12	R-12	D-13	R-13	R-13	R-15	R-15
HI	D-4	R-4	D-4	D-4	R-4	D-4	D-4	D-4	D-4	D-4	D-4
ID	R-4	R-4	R-4	R-4	R-4	R-4	R-4	R-4	R-4	R-4	R-4
IL	R-26	R-26	R-26	R-26	R-24	R-24	D-22	D-22	D-22	D-21	D-21
IN	R-13	R-13	R-13	R-13	R-12	R-12	R-12	R-12	R-12	R-11	D-11
IA	R-9	R-8	R-8	R-8	R-8	D-8	D-7	D-7	D-7	R-7	D-7
KS	R-7	R-7	R-7	R-7	R-7	R-7	R-6	R-6	R-6	R-6	R-6
KY	R-9	R-9	D-9	R-9	R-9	R-9	D-8	D-8	R-8	R-8	R-8
LA	(¹)	R-10	D-10	R-10	R-10	R-10	D-9	D-9	R-9	R-9	R-9
ME	D-4	R-4	R-4	R-4	R-4	R-4	D-4	D-4	D-4	D-4	D-4
MD	D-10	R-10	D-10	D-10	R-10	R-10	D-10	D-10	D-10	D-10	D-10
MA	D-14	D-14	D-14	R-14	R-13	D-13	D-12	D-12	D-12	D-12	D-12
MI	D-21	R-21	R-21	R-21	R-20	R-20	D-18	D-18	D-18	D-17	D-17
MN	D-10	R-10	D-10	D-10	D-10	D-10	D-10	D-10	D-10	⁶ D-9	D-10
MS	(¹)	R-7	D-7	R-7	R-7	R-7	R-7	R-7	R-7	R-6	R-6
MO	R-12	R-12	D-12	R-12	R-11	R-11	D-11	D-11	R-11	R-11	R-11
MT	R-4	R-4	R-4	R-4	R-4	R-4	D-3	R-3	R-3	R-3	R-3
NE	R-5	R-5	R-5	R-5	R-5	R-5	R-5	R-5	R-5	R-5	⁷ R-4
NV	R-3	R-3	R-3	R-3	R-4	R-4	D-4	D-4	R-4	R-5	D-5
NH	R-4	R-4	R-4	R-4	R-4	R-4	D-4	D-4	R-4	D-4	D-4
NJ	R-17	R-17	R-17	R-17	R-16	R-16	D-15	D-15	D-15	D-15	D-15
NM	R-4	R-4	R-4	R-4	R-5	R-5	D-5	D-5	D-5	R-5	D-5
NY	D-43	R-41	D-41	R-41	R-36	D-36	D-33	D-33	D-33	D-31	D-31
NC	¹ R-12	R-13	D-13	R-13	R-13	R-13	R-14	R-14	R-14	R-15	D-15
ND	R-4	R-3	R-3	R-3	R-3	R-3	R-3	R-3	R-3	R-3	R-3
OH	R-26	R-25	D-25	R-25	R-23	R-23	D-21	D-21	R-21	R-20	D-20
OK	R-8	R-8	R-8	R-8	R-8	R-8	R-8	R-8	R-8	R-7	R-7
OR	R-6	R-6	R-6	R-6	R-7	D-7	D-7	D-7	D-7	D-7	D-7
PA	D-29	R-27	D-27	R-27	R-25	R-25	D-23	D-23	D-23	D-21	D-21
RI	D-4	R-4	D-4	D-4	R-4	D-4	D-4	D-4	D-4	D-4	D-4
SC	R-8	R-8	D-8	R-8	R-8	R-8	R-8	R-8	R-8	R-8	R-8
SD	R-4	R-4	R-4	R-4	R-3	R-3	R-3	R-3	R-3	R-3	R-3
TN	R-11	R-10	D-10	R-10	R-11	R-11	D-11	D-11	R-11	R-11	R-11
TX	D-25	R-26	D-26	R-26	R-29	R-29	R-32	R-32	R-32	R-34	R-34
UT	R-4	R-4	R-4	R-4	R-5	R-5	R-5	R-5	R-5	R-5	R-5
VT	R-3	² R-3	R-3	R-3	R-3	R-3	D-3	D-3	D-3	D-3	D-3
VA	R-12	² R-11	R-12	R-12	R-12	R-12	R-13	R-13	R-13	R-13	D-13
WA	D-9	R-9	³ R-8	R-9	R-10	D-10	D-11	D-11	D-11	D-11	D-11
WV	D-7	R-6	D-6	D-6	R-6	⁴ D-5	D-5	D-5	R-5	R-5	R-5
WI	R-12	R-11	D-11	R-11	R-11	D-11	D-11	D-11	R-5	R-5	D-10
WY	R-3	R-3	R-3	R-3	R-3	R-3	R-3	R-3	R-3	R-3	R-3

– Represents zero. ¹ Excludes 46 electoral votes cast for American Independent George C. Wallace as follows: AL 10, AR 6, GA 12, LA 10, MS 7, and NC 1. ² Excludes one electoral vote cast for Libertarian John Hospers in Virginia. ³ Excludes one electoral vote cast for Ronald Reagan in Washington. ⁴ Excludes one electoral vote cast for Lloyd Bentsen for President in West Virginia. ⁵ Excludes one electoral vote left blank by a Democratic elector in the District of Columbia. ⁶ Excludes one electoral vote cast for Democratic vice presidential nominee John Edwards in Minnesota. ⁷ Excludes one electoral vote for Barack Obama in Nebraska.

Source: U.S. House of Representatives, Office of the Clerk, *Statistics of the Presidential and Congressional Election*, biennial. See also <http://clerk.house.gov/member_info/election.html>.

U.S. Census Bureau, Statistical Abstract of the United States: 2012

Table 406. Popular Vote Cast for President by Political Party—States: 2004 and 2008

[In thousands (122,349 represents 122,349,000), except percent]

State	2004					2008				
				Percent of total vote					Percent of total vote	
	Total [1]	Demo-cratic party	Republi-can party	Demo-cratic party	Republi-can party	Total [1]	Demo-cratic party	Republi-can party	Demo-cratic party	Republi-can party
United States	**122,349**	**58,895**	**61,873**	**48.1**	**50.6**	**131,407**	**69,498**	**59,948**	**52.9**	**45.6**
Alabama	1,883	694	1,176	36.8	62.5	2,100	813	1,267	38.7	60.3
Alaska	313	111	191	35.5	61.1	326	124	194	37.9	59.4
Arizona	2,013	894	1,104	44.4	54.9	2,293	1,035	1,230	45.1	53.6
Arkansas	1,055	470	573	44.5	54.3	1,087	422	638	38.9	58.7
California	12,421	6,745	5,510	54.3	44.4	13,562	8,274	5,012	61.0	37.0
Colorado	2,130	1,002	1,101	47.0	51.7	2,401	1,289	1,074	53.7	44.7
Connecticut	1,579	857	694	54.3	43.9	1,647	998	629	60.6	38.2
Delaware	375	200	172	53.3	45.8	412	255	152	61.9	36.9
District of Columbia . . .	228	203	21	89.2	9.3	266	246	17	92.5	6.5
Florida	7,610	3,584	3,965	47.1	52.1	8,391	4,282	4,046	51.0	48.2
Georgia	3,302	1,366	1,914	41.4	58.0	3,924	1,844	2,049	47.0	52.2
Hawaii	429	232	194	54.0	45.3	456	326	121	71.5	26.4
Idaho	598	181	409	30.3	68.4	655	236	403	36.1	61.5
Illinois.	5,274	2,892	2,346	54.8	44.5	5,522	3,419	2,031	61.9	36.8
Indiana.	2,468	969	1,479	39.3	59.9	2,751	1,374	1,346	49.9	48.9
Iowa	1,507	742	752	49.2	49.9	1,537	829	682	53.9	44.4
Kansas.	1,188	435	736	36.6	62.0	1,236	515	700	41.7	56.6
Kentucky	1,796	713	1,069	39.7	59.5	1,827	752	1,048	41.2	57.4
Louisiana	1,943	820	1,102	42.2	56.7	1,961	783	1,148	39.9	58.6
Maine.	741	397	330	53.6	44.6	731	422	295	57.7	40.4
Maryland	2,384	1,334	1,025	56.0	43.0	2,632	1,629	960	61.9	36.5
Massachusetts.	2,927	1,804	1,071	61.6	36.6	3,103	1,904	1,109	61.4	35.7
Michigan	4,839	2,479	2,314	51.2	47.8	5,002	2,873	2,049	57.4	41.0
Minnesota	2,828	1,445	1,347	51.1	47.6	2,910	1,573	1,275	54.1	43.8
Mississippi	1,140	458	673	40.2	59.0	1,290	555	725	43.0	56.2
Missouri	2,731	1,259	1,456	46.1	53.3	2,925	1,442	1,446	49.3	49.4
Montana.	450	174	266	38.6	59.1	490	232	243	47.3	49.5
Nebraska	778	254	513	32.7	65.9	801	333	453	41.6	56.5
Nevada	830	397	419	47.9	50.5	968	534	413	55.1	42.7
New Hampshire	678	341	331	50.2	48.8	711	385	317	54.1	44.5
New Jersey	3,612	1,911	1,670	52.9	46.2	3,868	2,215	1,613	57.3	41.7
New Mexico	756	371	377	49.0	49.8	830	472	347	56.9	41.8
New York	7,448	4,181	2,807	56.1	37.7	7,722	4,805	2,753	62.2	35.6
North Carolina	3,501	1,526	1,961	43.6	56.0	4,298	2,143	2,128	49.8	49.5
North Dakota	313	111	197	35.5	62.9	317	141	169	44.6	53.3
Ohio.	5,628	2,741	2,860	48.7	50.8	5,708	2,940	2,678	51.5	46.9
Oklahoma	1,464	504	960	34.4	65.6	1,463	502	960	34.4	65.6
Oregon.	1,837	943	867	51.3	47.2	1,828	1,037	738	56.7	40.4
Pennsylvania	5,770	2,938	2,794	50.9	48.4	6,013	3,276	2,656	54.5	44.2
Rhode Island	437	260	169	59.4	38.7	472	297	165	62.9	35.1
South Carolina.	1,618	662	938	40.9	58.0	1,921	862	1,035	44.9	53.9
South Dakota.	388	149	233	38.4	59.9	382	171	203	44.7	53.2
Tennessee	2,437	1,036	1,384	42.5	56.8	2,600	1,087	1,479	41.8	56.9
Texas	7,411	2,833	4,527	38.2	61.1	8,078	3,529	4,479	43.7	55.5
Utah.	928	241	664	26.0	71.5	952	328	596	34.4	62.6
Vermont	312	184	121	58.9	38.8	325	219	99	67.5	30.4
Virginia.	3,195	1,455	1,717	45.5	53.7	3,723	1,960	1,725	52.6	46.3
Washington	2,859	1,510	1,305	52.8	45.6	3,037	1,751	1,229	57.7	40.5
West Virginia	756	327	424	43.2	56.1	713	304	397	42.6	55.7
Wisconsin	2,997	1,490	1,478	49.7	49.3	2,983	1,677	1,262	56.2	42.3
Wyoming	244	71	168	29.0	68.7	255	83	165	32.5	64.7

[1] Includes other parties.

Source: U.S. House of Representatives, Office of the Clerk, *Statistics of the Presidential and Congressional Election*, biennial. See also <http://clerk.house.gov/member_info/election.html>.

U.S. Census Bureau, Statistical Abstract of the United States: 2012

Table 407. Vote Cast for U.S. Senators, 2008 and 2010, and Incumbent Senators, 2011—States

[2,060 represents 2,060,000. D = Democrat, R = Republican, I = Independent]

State	2008 Total [2] (1,000)	2008 Percent for leading party	2010 Total [2] (1,000)	2010 Percent for leading party	Incumbent senators and year term expires [1] — Name, party, and year	Name, party, and year
Alabama	2,060	R-63.4	1,485	R-65.2	Jeff Sessions (R) 2015	Richard C. Shelby (R) 2017
Alaska	318	D-47.8	256	R-35.6	Lisa Murkowski (R) 2017	Mark Begich (D) 2015
Arizona	(X)	(X)	1,708	R-58.9	Jon Kyl (R) 2013	John McCain (R) 2017
Arkansas	1,012	D-79.5	780	R-57.9	John Boozman (R) 2017	Mark L. Pryor (D) 2015
California	(X)	(X)	10,000	D-52.2	Barbara Boxer (D) 2017	Dianne Feinstein (D) 2013
Colorado	2,332	D-52.8	1,772	D-48.1	Mark Udall (D) 2015	Michael F. Bennett (D) 2017
Connecticut	(X)	(X)	1,153	D-52.5	Richard Blumenthal (D) 2017	Joseph I. Lieberman (I) 2013
Delaware	398	D-64.7	307	D-56.6	Christopher Coons (D) 2015	Thomas R. Carper (D) 2013
Florida	(X)	(X)	5,411	R-48.9	Marco Rubio (R) 2017	Bill Nelson (D) 2013
Georgia	2,266	R-54.2	2,555	R-58.3	Saxby Chambliss (R) 2015	Johnny Isakson (R) 2017
Hawaii	(X)	(X)	371	D-74.8	Daniel K. Akaka (D) 2013	Daniel K. Inouye (D) 2017
Idaho	645	R-57.7	450	R-71.2	James E. Risch (R) 2015	Mike Crapo (R) 2017
Illinois	5,330	D-67.8	3,704	R-48.0	Richard J. Durbin (D) 2015	Mark Kirk (R) 2017
Indiana	(X)	(X)	1,744	R-54.6	Daniel Coats (R) 2017	Richard G. Lugar (R) 2013
Iowa	1,503	D-62.7	1,116	R-64.4	Chuck Grassley (R) 2017	Tom Harkin (D) 2015
Kansas	1,211	R-60.1	838	R-70.1	Jerry Moran (R) 2017	Pat Roberts (R) 2015
Kentucky	1,801	R-53.0	1,356	R-55.7	Rand Paul (R) 2017	Mitch McConnell (R) 2015
Louisiana [3]	1,897	D-52.1	1,265	R-56.6	Mary L. Landrieu (D) 2015	David Vitter (R) 2017
Maine	724	R-61.3	(X)	(X)	Susan M. Collins (R) 2015	Olympia J. Snowe (R) 2013
Maryland	(X)	(X)	1,834	D-62.2	Barbara A. Mikulski (D) 2017	Benjamin L. Cardin (D) 2013
Massachusetts	3,103	D-63.6	(X)	(X)	Scott P. Brown [4] (R) 2013	John F. Kerry (D) 2015
Michigan	4,849	D-62.7	(X)	(X)	Carl Levin (D) 2015	Debbie Stabenow (D) 2013
Minnesota	2,888	D-42.0	(X)	(X)	Al Franken (D) 2015	Amy Klobuchar (D) 2013
Mississippi	1,247	R-61.4	(X)	(X)	Thad Cochran (R) 2015	Roger F. Wicker (R) 2013
Missouri	(X)	(X)	1,944	R-54.2	Roy Blunt (R) 2017	Claire McCaskill (D) 2013
Montana	478	D-72.9	(X)	(X)	Max Baucus (D) 2015	John Tester (D) 2013
Nebraska	793	R-57.5	(X)	(X)	Mike Johanns (R) 2015	Ben Nelson (D) 2013
Nevada	(X)	(X)	721	D-50.3	Dean Heller [5] (R) 2013	Harry Reid (D) 2017
New Hampshire	695	D-51.6	455	R-60.1	Kelly Ayotte (R) 2017	Jeanne Shaheen (D) 2015
New Jersey	3,482	D-56.0	(X)	(X)	Robert Menendez (D) 2013	Frank R. Lautenberg (D) 2015
New Mexico	824	D-61.3	(X)	(X)	Jeff Bingaman (D) 2013	Tom Udall (D) 2015
New York	(X)	(X)	4,764	D-64.0	Kirsten E. Gillibrand [6] (D) 2013	Charles E. Schumer (D) 2017
North Carolina	4,272	D-52.7	2,660	R-54.8	Richard Burr (R) 2017	Kay R. Hagan (D) 2015
North Dakota	(X)	(X)	239	R-76.2	Kent Conrad (D) 2013	John Hoeven (R) 2017
Ohio	(X)	(X)	3,815	R-56.8	Sherrod Brown (D) 2013	Rob Portman (R) 2017
Oklahoma	1,347	R-56.7	1,017	R-70.6	Tom Coburn (R) 2017	James M. Inhofe (R) 2015
Oregon	1,768	D-48.9	1,443	D-57.2	Jeff Merkley (D) 2015	Ron Wyden (D) 2017
Pennsylvania	(X)	(X)	3,978	R-51.0	Robert P. Casey Jr. (D) 2013	Patrick J. Toomey (R) 2017
Rhode Island	439	D-73.1	(X)	(X)	Sheldon Whitehouse (D) 2013	Jack Reed (D) 2015
South Carolina	1,871	R-57.5	1,319	R-61.5	Jim DeMint (R) 2017	Lindsey Graham (R) 2015
South Dakota	381	D-62.5	228	R-100.0	Tim Johnson (D) 2015	John Thune (R) 2017
Tennessee	2,425	R-65.1	(X)	(X)	Lamar Alexander (R) 2015	Bob Corker (R) 2013
Texas	7,912	R-54.8	(X)	(X)	John Cornyn (R) 2015	Kay Hutchinson (R) 2013
Utah	(X)	(X)	585	R-61.6	Mike Lee (R) 2017	Orrin G. Hatch (R) 2013
Vermont	(X)	(X)	235	D-64.3	Bernard Sanders (I) 2013	Patrick J. Leahy (D) 2017
Virginia	3,643	D-65.0	(X)	(X)	Jim Webb (D) 2013	Mark R. Warner (D) 2015
Washington	(X)	(X)	2,511	D-52.4	Maria Cantwell (D) 2013	Patty Murray (D) 2017
West Virginia	702	D-63.7	(X)	(X)	Joe Manchin III (D) 2013	John D. Rockefeller IV (D) 2015
Wisconsin	(X)	(X)	2,171	R-51.9	Ronald H. Johnson (R) 2017	Herb Kohl (D) 2013
Wyoming	250	D-75.6	(X)	(X)	Michael B. Enzi (R) 2015	John Barrasso (R) 2013

X Not applicable. [1] As of June 3, 2011. See source note, Table 412. [2] Includes vote cast for minor parties. [3] Louisiana holds an open-primary election with candidates from all parties running on the same ballot. Any candidate who receives a majority is elected. [4] Elected in the January 19, 2010 special election to fill seat previously held by appointed Senator Paul G. Kirk, Jr. 2006 data represents votes cast for Edward M. Kennedy. [5] Appointed April 27, 2011, to fill vacancy due to resignation of John Ensign, May 3, 2011. [6] Appointed January 23, 2009, to fill vacancy due to resignation of Hillary Rodham Clinton, January 21, 2009.

Source: U.S. House of Representatives, Office of the Clerk, Statistics of the Presidential and Congressional Election, biennial. See also <http://clerk.house.gov/member_info/election.html>.

Table 408. Apportionment of Membership in House of Representatives by State: 1800 to 2010

[Total membership includes Representatives assigned to newly admitted States after the apportionment acts. Population figures used for apportionment purposes are those determined for States by each decennial census. No reapportionment based on 1920 population census. For method of calculating apportionment and a short history of apportionment, see House Report 91-1314, 91st Congress, 2d session, The Decennial Population Census and Congressional Apportionment]

State	Membership based on census of—																				
	1800	1820	1830	1840	1850	1860	1870	1880	1890	1900	1910	1920	1930	1940	1950	1960	1970	1980	1990	2000	2010
U.S.	**142**	**213**	**242**	**232**	**237**	**243**	**293**	**332**	**357**	**391**	**435**	**435**	**435**	**435**	**437**	**435**	**435**	**435**	**435**	**435**	**435**
AL ..	(X)	3	5	7	7	6	8	8	9	9	10	10	9	9	9	8	7	7	7	7	7
AK ..	(X)	(X)	(X)	(X)	(X)	(X)	(X)	(X)	(X)	(X)	(X)	(X)	(X)	(X)	¹1	1	1	1	1	1	1
AZ ..	(X)	(X)	(X)	(X)	(X)	(X)	(X)	(X)	(X)	(X)	²1	1	1	2	2	3	4	5	6	8	9
AR ..	(X)	(X)	¹1	1	2	3	4	5	6	7	7	7	7	7	6	4	4	4	4	4	4
CA ..	(X)	(X)	(X)	¹2	2	3	4	6	7	8	11	11	20	23	30	38	43	45	52	53	53
CO..	(X)	(X)	(X)	(X)	(X)	(X)	¹1	1	2	3	4	4	4	4	4	4	5	6	6	7	7
CT ..	7	6	6	4	4	4	4	4	4	5	5	5	6	6	6	6	6	6	6	5	5
DE ..	1	1	1	1	1	1	1	1	1	1	1	1	1	1	1	1	1	1	1	1	1
FL ..	(X)	(X)	(X)	¹1	1	1	2	2	2	3	4	4	5	6	8	12	15	19	23	25	27
GA ..	4	7	9	8	8	7	9	10	11	11	12	12	10	10	10	10	10	10	11	13	14
HI...	(X)	(X)	(X)	(X)	(X)	(X)	(X)	(X)	(X)	(X)	(X)	(X)	(X)	(X)	¹1	2	2	2	2	2	2
ID...	(X)	(X)	(X)	(X)	(X)	(X)	(X)	¹1	1	1	2	2	2	2	2	2	2	2	2	2	2
IL...	(X)	1	3	7	9	14	19	20	22	25	27	27	27	26	25	24	24	22	20	19	18
IN...	(X)	3	7	10	11	11	13	13	13	13	13	13	12	11	11	11	11	10	10	9	9
IA...	(X)	(X)	(X)	¹2	2	6	9	11	11	11	11	11	9	8	8	7	6	6	5	5	4
KS ..	(X)	(X)	(X)	(X)	(X)	1	3	7	8	8	8	8	7	6	6	5	5	5	4	4	4
KY ..	6	12	13	10	10	9	10	11	11	11	11	11	9	9	8	7	7	7	6	6	6
LA ..	(X)	3	3	4	4	5	6	6	6	7	8	8	8	8	8	8	8	8	7	7	6
ME ..	(X)	7	8	7	6	5	5	4	4	4	4	4	3	3	3	2	2	2	2	2	2
MD..	9	9	8	6	6	5	6	6	6	6	6	6	6	6	7	8	8	8	8	8	8
MA..	17	13	12	10	11	10	11	12	13	14	16	16	15	14	14	12	12	11	10	10	9
MI...	(X)	(X)	¹1	3	4	6	9	11	12	12	13	13	17	17	18	19	19	18	16	15	14
MN..	(X)	(X)	(X)	(X)	¹2	2	3	5	7	9	10	10	9	9	9	8	8	8	8	8	8
MS..	(X)	1	2	4	5	5	6	7	7	8	8	8	7	7	6	5	5	5	5	4	4
MO..	(X)	1	2	5	7	9	13	14	15	16	16	16	13	13	11	10	10	9	9	9	8
MT..	(X)	(X)	(X)	(X)	(X)	(X)	(X)	¹1	1	1	2	2	2	2	2	2	2	2	1	1	1
NE ..	(X)	(X)	(X)	(X)	(X)	¹1	1	3	6	6	6	6	5	4	4	3	3	3	3	3	3
NV ..	(X)	(X)	(X)	(X)	(X)	¹1	1	1	1	1	1	1	1	1	1	1	1	2	2	3	4
NH ..	5	6	5	4	3	3	3	2	2	2	2	2	2	2	2	2	2	2	2	2	2
NJ ..	6	6	6	5	5	5	7	7	8	10	12	12	14	14	14	15	15	14	13	13	12
NM..	(X)	(X)	(X)	(X)	(X)	(X)	(X)	(X)	(X)	(X)	²1	1	1	2	2	2	2	3	3	3	3
NY..	17	34	40	34	33	31	33	34	34	37	43	43	45	45	43	41	39	34	31	29	27
NC..	12	13	13	9	8	7	8	9	9	10	10	10	11	12	12	11	11	11	12	13	13
ND..	(X)	(X)	(X)	(X)	(X)	(X)	(X)	¹1	1	2	3	3	2	2	2	2	1	1	1	1	1
OH..	¹1	14	19	21	21	19	20	21	21	21	22	22	24	23	23	24	23	21	19	18	16
OK..	(X)	(X)	(X)	(X)	(X)	(X)	(X)	(X)	(X)	¹5	8	8	9	8	6	6	6	6	6	5	5
OR..	(X)	(X)	(X)	(X)	¹1	1	1	1	2	2	3	3	3	4	4	4	4	5	5	5	5
PA ..	18	26	28	24	25	24	27	28	30	32	36	36	34	33	30	27	25	23	21	19	18
RI...	2	2	2	2	2	2	2	2	2	2	3	3	2	2	2	2	2	2	2	2	2
SC..	8	9	9	7	6	4	5	7	7	7	7	7	6	6	6	6	6	6	6	6	7
SD ..	(X)	(X)	(X)	(X)	(X)	(X)	(X)	¹2	2	2	3	3	2	2	2	2	2	1	1	1	1
TN ..	3	9	13	11	10	8	10	10	10	10	10	10	9	10	9	9	8	9	9	9	9
TX ..	(X)	(X)	(X)	¹2	2	4	6	11	13	16	18	18	21	21	22	23	24	27	30	32	36
UT ..	(X)	(X)	(X)	(X)	(X)	(X)	(X)	(X)	¹1	1	2	2	2	2	2	2	2	3	3	3	4
VT ..	4	5	5	4	3	3	3	2	2	2	2	2	1	1	1	1	1	1	1	1	1
VA ..	22	22	21	15	13	11	9	10	10	10	10	10	9	9	10	10	10	10	11	11	11
WA..	(X)	(X)	(X)	(X)	(X)	(X)	(X)	¹1	2	3	5	5	6	6	7	7	7	8	9	9	10
WV..	(X)	(X)	(X)	(X)	(X)	3	4	4	5	6	6	6	6	6	6	5	4	4	3	3	3
WI ..	(X)	(X)	(X)	¹2	3	6	8	9	10	11	11	11	10	10	10	10	9	9	9	8	8
WY..	(X)	(X)	(X)	(X)	(X)	(X)	(X)	¹1	1	1	1	1	1	1	1	1	1	1	1	1	1

X Not applicable. ¹ Assigned after apportionment. ² Included in apportionment in anticipation of statehood.

Source: U.S. Census Bureau, Congressional Apportionment, Census 2010, <http://www.census.gov/population/apportionment/>.

U.S. Census Bureau, Statistical Abstract of the United States: 2012

Table 409. Vote Cast for U.S. Representatives by Major Political Party—States: 2006 to 2010

[In thousands (80,976 represents 80,976,000), except percent. R = Republican, D = Democrat, and I = Independent. In each state, totals represent the sum of votes cast in each Congressional District or votes cast for Representative-at-Large in states where only one member is elected. In all years there are numerous districts within the state where either the Republican or Democratic party had no candidate. In some states the Republican and Democratic vote includes votes cast for the party candidate by endorsing parties]

State	2006				2008				2010			
	Total [1]	Demo-cratic	Republi-can	Percent for leading party	Total [1]	Demo-cratic	Republi-can	Percent for leading party	Total [1]	Demo-cratic	Republi-can	Percent for leading party
U.S.	80,976	42,082	35,675	D-52.0	122,586	64,888	51,953	D-52.9	86,785	38,854	44,594	R-51.4
AL	1,140	502	628	R-55.0	1,855	718	1,121	R-60.4	1,368	419	914	R-66.9
AK	235	94	133	R-56.6	317	143	159	R-50.1	254	78	175	R-69.0
AZ	1,493	627	771	R-51.7	2,156	1,055	1,022	D-49.0	1,698	712	901	R-53.0
AR [2]	763	457	306	D-59.8	787	415	215	D-52.8	774	318	435	R-56.2
CA	8,296	4,720	3,314	D-56.9	12,322	7,381	4,516	D-59.9	9,648	5,149	4,195	D-53.4
CO	1,539	833	624	D-54.1	2,284	1,260	991	D-55.2	1,763	801	884	R-50.1
CT	1,075	649	420	D-60.4	1,527	909	505	D-59.5	1,138	635	458	D-55.8
DE	252	98	144	R-57.2	385	146	235	R-61.1	306	174	125	D-56.8
FL [2]	3,852	1,600	2,183	R-56.7	7,421	3,435	3,792	R-51.1	5,117	1,854	3,004	R-58.7
GA	2,070	932	1,138	R-55.0	3,655	1,858	1,797	D-50.8	2,469	940	1,528	R-61.9
HI	338	220	118	D-65.0	456	320	83	D-70.2	360	226	129	D-62.9
ID	445	177	248	R-55.7	638	260	377	R-59.2	447	151	264	R-59.0
IL	3,453	1,986	1,423	D-57.5	5,248	3,176	1,961	D-60.5	3,696	1,876	1,720	D-50.8
IN	1,667	812	832	R-49.9	2,677	1,389	1,241	D-51.9	1,748	679	973	R-55.7
IA	1,033	493	522	R-50.6	1,482	759	698	D-51.3	1,107	480	597	R-54.0
KS	845	369	459	R-54.3	1,208	470	690	R-57.1	836	275	528	R-63.2
KY	1,254	602	612	R-48.8	1,750	761	955	R-54.6	1,354	506	844	R-62.3
LA [2]	916	309	580	R-63.3	1,046	398	594	R-56.8	1,036	311	675	R-65.2
ME	536	351	163	D-65.4	710	432	278	D-60.8	564	316	248	D-56.0
MD	1,701	1,099	547	D-64.6	2,498	1,677	763	D-67.2	1,825	1,104	674	D-60.5
MA	2,244	1,632	199	D-72.7	3,103	2,246	318	D-72.4	2,224	1,336	808	D-60.1
MI.	3,646	1,923	1,625	D-52.7	4,811	2,517	2,114	D-52.3	3,195	1,415	1,672	R-52.3
MN	2,179	1,153	925	D-52.9	2,803	1,612	1,069	D-57.5	2,091	1,002	971	D-47.9
MS	601	260	304	R-50.7	1,265	732	527	D-57.9	789	351	424	R-53.7
MO	2,097	992	1,049	R-50.0	2,821	1,413	1,313	D-50.1	1,921	708	1,103	R-57.4
MT	406	159	239	R-58.9	481	156	308	R-64.1	360	122	218	R-60.4
NE	596	262	334	R-56.1	775	265	511	R-65.8	486	138	328	R-67.5
NV	575	288	260	D-50.1	908	457	384	D-50.4	703	318	357	R-50.9
NH	403	209	190	D-52.0	675	365	295	D-54.1	450	201	230	R-51.2
NJ	2,137	1,208	903	D-56.5	3,438	1,912	1,462	D-55.6	2,122	1,025	1,055	R-49.7
NM	561	313	248	D-55.8	815	457	321	D-56.1	597	308	289	D-51.6
NY	4,687	2,538	1,160	D-54.1	7,722	4,006	1,800	D-51.9	4,744	2,515	1,613	D-53.0
NC	1,941	1,027	914	D-52.9	4,215	2,294	1,902	D-54.4	2,663	1,205	1,441	R-54.1
ND	218	143	75	D-65.7	314	195	119	D-62.0	236	107	130	R-54.9
OH	3,961	2,082	1,870	D-52.6	5,374	2,752	2,491	D-51.2	3,825	1,611	2,053	R-53.7
OK	905	373	518	R-57.2	1,337	504	803	R-60.0	793	222	520	R-65.5
OR	1,357	766	557	D-56.4	1,683	1,036	436	D-61.6	1,429	733	657	D-51.3
PA	4,013	2,229	1,732	D-55.5	5,788	3,209	2,521	D-55.4	3,956	1,882	2,034	R-51.4
RI	373	265	42	D-71.0	438	304	119	D-69.3	335	186	127	D-55.4
SC	1,086	473	600	R-55.2	1,874	920	940	R-50.1	1,340	537	754	R-56.3
SD	334	230	98	D-69.1	379	256	123	D-67.6	319	147	154	R-48.1
TN	1,715	861	800	D-50.2	2,302	1,196	978	D-51.9	1,559	542	955	R-61.3
TX	4,141	1,831	2,094	R-50.6	7,529	2,979	4,204	R-55.8	4,746	1,450	3,058	R-64.4
UT	570	244	292	R-51.3	937	394	504	R-53.8	640	218	391	R-61.0
VT	263	140	117	D-53.2	298	248	(X)	D-83.2	239	154	76	D-64.6
VA	2,297	947	1,223	R-53.2	3,495	1,853	1,591	D-53.0	2,190	911	1,186	R-54.2
WA	2,054	1,244	798	D-60.6	2,914	1,725	1,189	D-59.2	2,479	1,297	1,135	D-52.3
WV	455	264	191	D-58.0	646	432	213	D-66.9	514	228	283	R-55.0
WI	2,063	1,003	1,040	R-50.4	2,775	1,384	1,275	D-49.9	2,140	939	1,166	R-54.5
WY	196	92	93	R-47.6	250	107	131	R-52.6	191	46	132	R-69.0

X Not applicable. [1] Includes votes cast for minor parties. [2] State law does not require tabulation of votes for unopposed candidates.

Source: U.S. House of Representatives, Office of the Clerk, *Statistics of the Presidential and Congressional Election,* biennial. See also <http://clerk.house.gov/member_info/election.html>.

Table 410. Vote Cast for U.S. Representatives by Major Political Party—Congressional Districts: 2010

[As of December 2010. Does not include special elections, see <http://clerk.house.gov/member_info/vacancies.html>. In some states the Democratic and Republican vote includes votes cast for the party candidate by endorsing parties]

State and district	Democratic candidate Name	Percent of total	Republican candidate Name	Percent of total	State and district	Democratic candidate Name	Percent of total	Republican candidate Name	Percent of total
AL.....	(X)	(X)	(X)	(X)	47th...	Sanchez	52.98	Tran	39.27
1st....	(¹)	(¹)	Bonner	82.58	48th...	Krom	36.45	Campbell	59.94
2d....	Bright	48.79	Roby	50.97	49th...	Katz	31.48	Issa	62.78
3d....	Segrest	40.48	Rogers	59.42	50th...	Busby	38.96	Bilbray	56.65
4th....	(¹)	(¹)	Aderholt	98.82	51st...	Filner	60.05	Popaditch	39.95
5th....	Raby	42.03	Brooks	57.89	52d....	Lutz	32.06	Hunter	63.09
6th....	(¹)	(¹)	Bachus	98.05	53d....	Davis	62.26	Crimmins	34.00
7th....	Sewell	72.43	Chamberlain	27.50	CO....	(X)	(X)	(X)	(X)
AK.....	Crawford	30.51	Young	68.96	1st....	DeGette	67.42	Fallon	28.76
AZ.....	(X)	(X)	(X)	(X)	2d....	Polis	57.41	Bailey	37.90
1st....	Kirkpatrick	43.73	Gosar	49.72	3d....	Salazar	45.76	Tipton	50.10
2d....	Thrasher	31.06	Franks	64.88	4th....	Markey	41.35	Gardner	52.48
3d....	Hulburd	41.14	Quayle	52.24	5th....	Bradley	29.27	Lamborn	65.75
4th....	Pastor	66.94	Contreras	27.53	6th....	Flerlage	31.46	Coffman	65.68
5th....	Mitchell	43.23	Schweikert	52.00	7th....	Perlmutter	53.44	Fraizer	41.76
6th....	Schneider	29.12	Flake	66.42	CT....	(X)	(X)	(X)	(X)
7th....	Grijalva	50.23	McClung	44.23	1st....	Larson	57.75	Brickley	37.20
8th....	Giffords	48.76	Kelly	47.30	2d....	Courtney	57.08	Peckinpaugh	38.76
AR.....	(X)	(X)	(X)	(X)	3d....	DeLauro	60.97	Labriola	33.58
1st....	Causey	43.48	Crawford	51.79	4th....	Himes	50.94	Debicella	46.93
2d....	Elliot	38.27	Griffin	57.90	5th....	Murphy	52.01	Caligiuri	44.91
3d....	Whitaker	27.56	Womack	72.44	DE....	Carney	56.78	Urquhart	41.04
4th....	Ross	57.53	Rankin	40.15	FL....	(X)	(X)	(X)	(X)
CA.....	(X)	(X)	(X)	(X)	1st....	(¹)	(¹)	Miller	80.00
1st....	Thompson	62.79	Hanks	31.03	2d....	Boyd	41.35	Southerland	53.60
2d....	Reed	42.85	Herger	57.15	3d....	Brown	63.04	Yost	33.89
3d....	Bera	43.19	Lungren	50.08	4th....	(¹)	(¹)	Crenshaw	77.21
4th....	Curtis	31.44	McClintock	61.27	5th....	Piccillo	32.57	Nugent	67.43
5th....	Matsui	72.05	Smith	25.28	6th....	(¹)	(¹)	Stearns	71.46
6th....	Woolsey	65.94	Judd	29.62	7th....	Beaven	30.97	Mica	69.03
7th....	Miller	68.32	Tubbs	31.68	8th....	Grayson	38.22	Webster	56.11
8th....	Pelosi	80.10	Dennis	15.12	9th....	Palma	28.57	Bilirakis	71.43
9th....	Lee	84.27	Hashimoto	10.77	10th...	Justice	34.08	Young	65.92
10th...	Garamendi	58.84	Clift	37.86	11th...	Castor	59.63	Prendergast	40.37
11th...	McNerney	47.97	Harmer	46.86	12th...	Edwards	41.14	Ross	48.14
12th...	Speier	75.58	Moloney	22.11	13th...	Golden	31.14	Buchanan	68.86
13th...	Stark	71.95	Baker	27.73	14th...	Roach	27.13	Mack	68.56
14th...	Eshoo	69.09	Chapman	27.83	15th...	Roberts	35.27	Posey	64.73
15th...	Honda	67.60	Kirkland	32.40	16th...	Horn	33.09	Rooney	66.85
16th...	Lofgren	67.82	Sahagun	24.29	17th...	Wilson	86.21	(¹)	(¹)
17th...	Farr	66.65	Taylor	29.85	18th...	Banciella	31.11	Ros-Lehtinen	68.89
18th...	Cardoza	58.48	Berryhill	41.52	19th...	Deutch	62.59	Budd	37.30
19th...	Goodwin	35.15	Denham	64.55	20th...	Schultz	60.15	Harrington	38.10
20th...	Costa	51.70	Vidak	48.30	21st...	(¹)	(¹)	Diaz-Balart	(²)
21st...	(¹)	(¹)	Nunes	100.00	22d....	Klein	45.64	West	54.36
22d....	(¹)	(¹)	McCarthy	98.76	23d....	Hastings	79.12	Sansaricq	20.88
23d....	Capps	57.77	Watson	37.60	24th...	Kosmas	40.32	Adams	59.64
24th...	Allison	40.06	Gallegly	59.94	25th...	Garcia	42.59	Rivera	52.15
25th...	Conaway	38.17	McKeon	61.83	GA....	(X)	(X)	(X)	(X)
26th...	Warner	36.52	Dreier	54.13	1st....	Harris II	28.37	Kingston	71.63
27th...	Sherman	65.15	Reed	34.85	2d....	Bishop, Jr.	51.44	Keown	48.56
28th...	Berman	69.54	Froyd	22.42	3d....	Saunders	30.52	Westmoreland	69.48
29th...	Schiff	64.78	Colbert	31.98	4th....	Johnson, Jr	74.67	Carter	25.33
30th...	Waxman	64.63	Wilkerson	31.94	5th....	Lewis	73.72	Little	26.28
31st...	Becerra	83.82	Smith	16.18	6th....	(¹)	(¹)	Price	99.91
32d....	Chu	71.04	Schmerling	28.96	7th....	Heckman	32.93	Woodall	67.07
33d....	Bass	86.08	Andion	13.92	8th....	Marshall	47.30	Scott	52.70
34th...	Roybal-Allard	77.23	Miller	22.77	9th....	(¹)	(¹)	Graves	100.00
35th...	Waters	79.33	Brown	20.66	10th...	Edwards	32.64	Broun	67.36
36th...	Harman	59.62	Fein	34.74	11th...	(¹)	(¹)	Gingrey	100.00
37th...	Richardson	68.36	Parker	23.23	12th...	Barrow	56.59	McKinney	43.41
38th...	Napolitano	73.45	Vaughn	26.55	13th...	Scott	69.43	Crane	30.57
39th...	Sanchez	63.27	Andre	32.60	HI....	(X)	(X)	(X)	(X)
40th...	Avalos	33.21	Royce	66.79	1st....	Hanabusa	53.23	Djou	46.77
41st...	Meagher	36.78	Lewis	63.21	2d....	Hirono	72.19	Willoughby	25.32
42d....	Williamson	31.86	Miller	62.21	ID....	(X)	(X)	(X)	(X)
43d....	Baca	65.50	Folkens	34.50	1st....	Minnick	41.28	Labrador	51.02
44th...	Hedrick	44.39	Calvert	55.61	2d.....	Crawford	24.41	Simpson	68.83
45th...	Pougnet	42.14	Mack	51.49					
46th...	Arnold	37.79	Rohrabacher	62.20					

See footnotes at end of table.

U.S. Census Bureau, Statistical Abstract of the United States: 2012

State and district	Democratic candidate Name	Percent of total	Republican candidate Name	Percent of total
IL	(X)	(X)	(X)	(X)
1st	Rush	80.36	Wardingley	15.87
2d	Jackson, Jr.	80.52	Hayes	13.83
3d	Lipinski	69.69	Bendas	24.29
4th	Gutierrez	77.36	Vasquez	14.32
5th	Quigley	70.62	Ratowitz	25.38
6th	Lowe	36.35	Roskam	63.65
7th	Davis	81.50	Weiman	16.09
8th	Bean	48.32	Walsh	48.47
9th	Schakowsky	66.34	Pollak	31.14
10th	Seals	48.92	Dold	51.08
11th	Halvorson	42.65	Kinzinger	57.35
12th	Costello	59.83	Newman	36.53
13th	Harper	36.19	Biggert	63.81
14th	Foster	45.04	Hultgren	51.31
15th	Gill	35.68	Johnson	64.32
16th	Gaulrapp	31.04	Manzullo	65.00
17th	Hare	42.96	Schilling	52.58
18th	Hirner	25.79	Schock	69.12
19th	Bagwell	28.78	Shimkus	71.22
IN	(X)	(X)	(X)	(X)
1st	Visclosky	58.56	Leyva	38.63
2d	Donnelly	48.18	Walorski	46.84
3d	Hayhurst	33.11	Stutzman	62.76
4th	Sanders	26.28	Rokita	68.57
5th	Crawford	25.39	Burton	62.14
6th	Welsh	29.92	Pence	66.57
7th	Carson	58.90	Scott	37.81
8th	VanHaaften	37.43	Bucshon	57.55
9th	Hill	42.28	Young	52.34
IA	(X)	(X)	(X)	(X)
1st	Braley	49.51	Lange	47.52
2d	Loebsack	50.99	Miller-Meeks	45.92
3d	Boswell	50.73	Zaun	46.49
4th	Maske	31.95	Latham	65.62
5th	Campbell	32.35	King	65.75
KS	(X)	(X)	(X)	(X)
1st	Jilka	22.85	Huelskamp	73.76
2d	Hudspeth	32.33	Jenkins	63.13
3d	Moore	38.66	Yoder	58.40
4th	Goyle	36.45	Pompeo	58.79
KY	(X)	(X)	(X)	(X)
1st	Hathett	28.75	Whitfield	71.25
2d	Marksberry	32.11	Guthrie	67.89
3d	Yarmuth	54.68	Lally	44.01
4th	Waltz	30.52	Davis	69.48
5th	Holbert	22.58	Rogers	77.42
6th	Chandler	50.08	Barr	49.81
LA[3]	(X)	(X)	(X)	(X)
1st	Katz	19.19	Scalise	78.52
2d[4]	Richmond	64.59	Cao	33.47
3d	Sangisetty	36.23	Landry	63.77
4th[4]	Melville	32.35	Fleming	62.34
5th	(1)	(1)	Alexander	78.57
6th	McDonald, Sr	34.37	Cassidy	65.63
7th	(1)	(1)	Boustany, Jr.	(2)
ME	(X)	(X)	(X)	(X)
1st	Pingree	56.82	Scontras	43.17
2d	Michaud	55.13	Levesque	44.87
MD	(X)	(X)	(X)	(X)
1st	Kratovil, Jr	41.98	Harris	54.08
2d	Ruppersberger	64.21	Cardarelli	33.28
3d	Sarbanes	61.07	Wilhelm	36.01
4th	Edwards	83.44	Broadus	16.39
5th	Hoyer	64.26	Lollar	34.62
6th	Duck	33.22	Bartlett	61.45
7th	Cummings	75.18	Mirabile	22.84
8th	Hollen	73.27	Philips	25.00
MA	(X)	(X)	(X)	(X)
1st	Olver	60.00	Gunn	34.88
2d	Neal	57.33	Wesley	42.60
3d	McGovern	56.46	Lamb	39.16
4th	Frank	53.90	Bielat	43.36
5th	Tsongas	54.84	Golnik	42.25
6th	Tierney	56.85	Hudak	42.99
7th	Markey	66.42	Dembrowski	33.49
8th	Capuano	98.05	(1)	(1)
9th	Lynch	68.30	Harrison	26.08
10th	Keating	46.87	Perry	42.38
MI	(X)	(X)	(X)	(X)
1st	McDowell	40.87	Benishek	51.94
2d	Johnson	31.62	Huizenga	65.27
3d	Miles	37.47	Amash	59.68
4th	Campbell	30.51	Camp	66.20
5th	Kildee	53.04	Kupiec	44.34
6th	Cooney	33.58	Upton	61.98
7th	Schauer	45.38	Walberg	50.16
8th	Enderle	34.33	Rogers	64.08
9th	Peters	49.76	Reczkowski	47.23
10th	Yanez	25.02	Miller	71.97
11th	Mosher	38.49	McCotter	59.27
12th	Levin	61.08	Volaric	34.97
13th	Clarke	79.39	Hauler	18.46
14th	Conyers, Jr	76.76	Ukrainec	19.87
15th	Dingell	56.81	Steele	40.08
MN	(X)	(X)	(X)	(X)
1st	Walz	49.34	Demmer	44.05
2d	Madore	36.59	Kline	63.31
3d	Meffert	36.57	Paulsen	58.80
4th	McCollum	59.09	Collett	34.63
5th	Ellison	67.69	Demos	24.14
6th	Clark	39.79	Bachmann	52.51
7th	Peterson	55.20	Byberg	37.60
8th	Oberstar	46.59	Cravaack	48.18
MS	(X)	(X)	(X)	(X)
1st	Childers	40.80	Nunnelee	55.26
2d	Thompson	61.47	Marcy	37.64
3d	Gill	31.19	Harper	67.99
4th	Taylor	46.83	Palazzo	51.93
MO	(X)	(X)	(X)	(X)
1st	Clay	73.55	Hamlin	23.62
2d	Lieber	29.16	Akin	67.94
3d	Carnahan	48.94	Martin	46.66
4th	Skelton	45.11	Hartzler	50.43
5th	Cleaver	53.32	Turk	44.18
6th	Hylton	30.54	Graves	69.44
7th	Eckersley	30.37	Long	63.39
8th	Sowers	28.76	Emerson	65.56
9th	(1)	(1)	Luetkemeyer	77.36
MT	McDonald	33.84	Rehberg	60.41
NE	(X)	(X)	(X)	(X)
1st	Harper	28.73	Fortenberry	71.27
2d	White	39.19	Terry	60.81
3d	Davis	17.90	Smith	70.12
NV	(X)	(X)	(X)	(X)
1st	Berkley	61.75	Wegner	35.28
2d	Price	32.66	Heller	63.30
3d	Titus	47.47	Heck	48.13
NH	(X)	(X)	(X)	(X)
1st	Shea-Porter	42.42	Guinta	54.04
2d	Kuster	46.76	Bass	48.34
NJ	(X)	(X)	(X)	(X)
1st	Andrews	63.19	Glading	34.80
2d	Stein	30.93	LoBiondo	65.50
3d	Adler	47.32	Runyan	50.03
4th	Kleinhendler	27.88	Smith	69.41
5th	Theise	32.79	Garrett	64.94
6th	Pallone, Jr	54.75	Little	43.71
7th	Potosnak	40.63	Lance	59.37
8th	Pascrell, Jr.	62.66	Straten	36.13
9th	Rothman	60.72	Agosta	37.84
10th	Payne	85.18	Alonso	12.83
11th	Herbert	30.51	Frelinghuysen	67.19
12th	Holt	53.05	Sipprelle	45.90
13th	Sires	74.11	Dwyer	23.04

See footnotes at end of table.

Table 410. Vote Cast for U.S. Representatives by Major Political Party— Congressional Districts: 2010—Con.

[See headnote, page 254]

State and district	Democratic candidate Name	Percent of total	Republican candidate Name	Percent of total	State and district	Democratic candidate Name	Percent of total	Republican candidate Name	Percent of total
NM	(X)	(X)	(X)	(X)	3d.	Blumenauer	70.02	Lopez	24.55
1st	Heinrich	51.80	Barela	48.20	4th	DeFazio	54.49	Robinson	43.58
2d	Teague	44.60	Pearce	55.40	5th	Schrader	51.25	Bruun	45.96
3d	Lujan	56.99	Mullins	43.01	PA	(X)	(X)	(X)	(X)
NY	(X)	(X)	(X)	(X)	1st	Brady	100.00	(¹)	(¹)
1st	Bishop	48.67	Altschuler	38.76	2d	Fattah	89.30	Hellberg	10.70
2d	Israel	54.21	Gomez	33.54	3d	Dahlkemper	44.28	Kelly	55.72
3d	Kudler	27.64	King	70.88	4th	Altmire	50.81	Rothfus	49.19
4th	McCarthy	53.61	Becker, Jr.	39.33	5th	Pipe	28.23	Thompson	68.69
5th	Ackerman	59.74	Milano	30.48	6th	Trivedi	42.90	Gerlach	57.10
6th	Meeks	76.27	Taub	9.01	7th	Lentz	43.98	Meehan	54.94
7th	Crowley	72.72	Reynolds	14.04	8th	Murphy	46.48	Fitzpatrick	53.52
8th	Nadler	69.06	Kone	20.62	9th	Conners	26.94	Shuster	73.06
9th	Weiner	56.98	Turner	32.10	10th	Carney	44.82	Marino	55.18
10th	Towns	79.66	Muniz	6.19	11th	Kanjorski	45.30	Barletta	54.70
11th	Clarke	83.50	Carr	7.30	12th	Critz	50.78	Burns	49.22
12th	Velazquez	79.10	(¹)	(¹)	13th	Schwartz	56.34	Adcock	43.66
13th	McMahon	46.24	Grimm	42.47	14th	Doyle	68.79	Haluszczak	28.17
14th	Maloney	71.32	Brumberg	21.31	15th	Callahan	39.00	Dent	53.55
15th	Rangel	71.80	Faulkner	8.40	16th	Herr	34.61	Pitts	65.39
16th	Serrano	86.40	Della Valle	3.16	17th	Holden	55.50	Argall	44.50
17th	Engel	68.53	Mele	21.41	18th	Connolly	32.67	Murphy	67.33
18th	Lowey	61.71	Russell	32.30	19th	Sanders	23.31	Platts	71.91
19th	Hall	45.78	Hayworth	41.13	RI	(X)	(X)	(X)	(X)
20th	Murphy	43.75	Gibson	45.27	1st	Cicilline	50.54	Loughlin	44.49
21st	Tonko	56.92	Danz, Jr	32.00	2d	Langevin	59.79	Zaccaria	31.72
22d	Hinchey	51.03	Phillips	39.08	SC	(X)	(X)	(X)	(X)
23d	Owens	45.06	Doheny	40.35	1st	Fraiser	28.67	Scott	65.37
24th	Arcuri	45.25	Hanna	43.19	2d	Miller	43.76	Wilson	53.48
25th	Maffei	48.21	Buerkle	37.74	3d	Dyer	32.90	Duncan	62.46
26th	Fedele	24.49	Lee	68.29	4th	Corden	28.79	Gowdy	63.45
27th	Higgins	57.84	Roberto	30.61	5th	Spratt, Jr	44.81	Mulvaney	55.12
28th	Slaughter	61.00	Rowland	27.15	6th	Clyburn	62.86	Pratt	36.41
29th	(¹)	(¹)	Reed II	44.33	SD	Sandlin	45.89	Noem	48.12
NC	(X)	(X)	(X)	(X)	TN	(X)	(X)	(X)	(X)
1st	Butterfield	59.31	Woolard	40.69	1st	Clark	17.12	Roe	80.84
2d	Etheridge	48.69	Ellmers	49.47	2d	Hancock	14.65	Duncan, Jr	81.78
3d	Rouse	25.75	Jones	71.86	3d	Wolfe	28.01	Fleischmann	56.79
4th	Price	57.16	Lawson	42.84	4th	Davis	38.56	DesJarlais	57.07
5th	Kennedy	34.11	Foxx	65.89	5th	Cooper	56.23	Hall	42.07
6th	Turner	24.79	Coble	75.21	6th	Carter	29.38	Black	67.26
7th	McIntyre	53.68	Pantano	46.32	7th	Rabidoux	24.75	Blackburn	72.37
8th	Kissell	53.02	Johnson	43.67	8th	Herron	38.80	Fincher	58.99
9th	Doctor	31.03	Myrick	68.97	9th	Cohen	74.00	Bergmann	25.11
10th	Gregory	28.82	McHenry	71.18	TX	(X)	(X)	(X)	(X)
11th	Shuler	54.34	Miller	45.66	1st	(¹)	(¹)	Gohmert	89.73
12th	Watt	63.88	Dority	34.14	2d	(¹)	(¹)	Poe	88.61
13th	Miller	55.50	Randall	44.50	3d	Lingenfelder	31.34	Johnson	66.28
ND	Pomeroy	45.08	Berg	54.92	4th	Hathcox	22.00	Hall	73.19
OH	(X)	(X)	(X)	(X)	5th	Berry	27.52	Hensarling	70.53
1st	Driehaus	45.99	Chabot	51.49	6th	Cozad	31.20	Barton	65.91
2d	Yalamanchili	34.66	Schmidt	58.45	7th	(¹)	(¹)	Culberson	81.45
3d	Roberts	31.89	Turner	68.11	8th	Hargett	17.25	Brady	80.27
4th	Litt	24.74	Jordan	71.49	9th	Green	75.74	Mueller	22.88
5th	Finkenbiner	26.47	Latta	67.82	10th	Ankrum	33.05	McCaul	64.67
6th	Wilson	45.15	Johnson	50.19	11th	Quillian	15.44	Conaway	80.84
7th	Conner	32.25	Austria	62.17	12th	Smith	25.13	Granger	71.86
8th	Coussoule	30.30	Boehner	65.64	13th	(¹)	(¹)	Thornberry	87.05
9th	Kaptur	59.35	Iott	40.65	14th	Pruett	24.01	Paul	75.99
10th	Kucinich	53.05	Corrigan	43.87	15th	Hinojosa	55.73	Zamora	41.59
11th	Fudge	82.93	Pekarek	17.07	16th	Reyes	58.07	Besco	36.58
12th	Brooks	40.98	Tiberi	55.79	17th	Edwards	36.57	Flores	61.80
13th	Sutton	55.73	Ganley	44.27	18th	Jackson-Lee	70.15	Faulk	27.26
14th	O'Neill	31.45	LaTourette	64.92	19th	Wilson	19.06	Neugebauer	77.78
15th	Kilroy	41.29	Stivers	54.16	20th	Gonzalez	63.62	Trotter	34.45
16th	Boccieri	41.26	Renacci	52.08	21st	Melnick	27.87	Smith	68.88
17th	Ryan	53.89	Graham	30.08	22d	Rogers	29.82	Olson	67.49
18th	Space	40.49	Gibbs	53.86	23d	Rodriguez	44.44	Canseco	49.40
OK	(X)	(X)	(X)	(X)	24th	(¹)	(¹)	Marchant	81.57
1st	(¹)	(¹)	Sullivan	76.80	25th	Doggett	52.82	Campbell	44.84
2d	Boren	56.52	Thompson	43.48	26th	Durrance	30.70	Burgess	67.05
3d	Robbins	22.01	Lucas	77.99	27th	Ortiz	47.10	Farenthold	47.85
4th	(¹)	(¹)	Cole	(²)	28th	Cuellar	56.35	Underwood	41.96
5th	Coyle	34.54	Lankford	62.52	29th	Green	64.61	Morales	34.09
OR	(X)	(X)	(X)	(X)	30th	Johnson	75.74	Broden	21.64
1st	Wu	54.75	Cornilles	41.94	31st	(¹)	(¹)	Carter	82.54
2d	Segers	25.87	Walden	73.91	32d	Raggio	34.88	Sessions	62.61

See footnotes at end of table.

U.S. Census Bureau, Statistical Abstract of the United States: 2012

Table 410. Vote Cast for U.S. Representatives by Major Political Party—Congressional Districts: 2010—Con.

[See headnote, page 254]

State and district	Democratic candidate Name	Percent of total	Republican candidate Name	Percent of total	State and district	Democratic candidate Name	Percent of total	Republican candidate Name	Percent of total
UT	(X)	(X)	(X)	(X)	4th ...	Clough......	32.36	Hastings..........	67.64
1st	Bowen	23.93	Bishop	69.19	5th ...	Romeyn	36.33	McMorris	63.67
2d.	Matheson...	50.49	Philpot	46.06	6th ...	Dicks	58.04	Cloud............	41.96
3d.	Hyer.......	22.94	Chaffetz	72.32	7th ...	McDermott...	82.97	(¹)............	(¹)
VT	Welch......	64.57	Beaudry	32.03	8th ...	DelBene.....	47.95	Reichert..........	52.05
VA	(X)	(X)	(X)	(X)	9th ...	Smith	54.85	Muri	45.15
1st	Ball.......	34.78	Wittman	63.87	**WV** ...	(X)	(X)	McKinley	50.40
2d.	Nye	42.45	Ringell	53.12	1st ...	Oliverio	49.60	Capito	68.46
3d.	Scott......	70.01	Smith.......	27.18	2d. ...	Graf	29.69	Maynard..........	43.96
4th	LeGrow	37.45	Forbes	62.33	3d. ...	Rahall II	56.04	(X)	(X)
5th	Perriello ...	46.99	Hurt	50.81	**WI** ...	(X)	(X)	Ryan	68.21
6th	(¹)	(¹)	Goodlatte....	76.27	1st ...	Heckenlively..	30.10	Lee.............	38.16
7th	Waugh, Jr ..	34.11	Cantor	59.22	2d. ...	Baldwin	61.77	Kapanke	46.49
8th	Moran	61.03	Murray	37.30	3d. ...	Kind	50.28	Sebring	29.57
9th	Boucher....	46.41	Griffith	51.21	4th ...	Moore	68.98	Sensenbrenner, Jr...	69.32
10th	Barnett.....	34.81	Wolf	62.87	5th ...	Kolosso	27.36	Petri	70.66
11th	Connolly....	49.23	Fimian	48.79	6th ...	Kallas......	29.27	Duffy	52.11
WA	(X)	(X)	(X)	(X)	7th ...	Lassa.......	44.43	Ribble	54.77
1st	Inslee......	57.67	Watkins	42.33	8th ...	Kagen	45.12	Lummis	69.00
2d.	Larsen	51.07	Koster	48.93	**WY**	Wendt	23.98		
3d.	Heck	47.03	Herrera	52.97					

X Not applicable. ¹ No candidate. ² According to state law, it is not required to tabulate votes for unopposed candidates. ³ Louisiana holds an open-primary election with candidates from all parties running on the same ballot. Any candidate who receives a majority is elected; if no candidate receives 50 percent, there is a run-off election in November between the top two finishers.
Source: U.S. House of Representatives, Office of the Clerk, *Statistics of the Presidential and Congressional Election*, biennial. See also <http://clerk.house.gov/member_info/election.html>.

Table 411. Composition of Congress by Political Party: 1975 to 2011

[D = Democratic, R = Republican. As of beginning of first session of each Congress. Data reflect immediate result of elections. Vacancies and third party candidates are noted]

Year	Party and president	Congress	House Majority party	House Minority party	Other	Senate Majority party	Senate Minority party	Other
1975 [1]	R (Ford)........	94th	D-291	R-144	–	D-61	R-37	2
1977 [2]	D (Carter)	95th	D-292	R-143	–	D-61	R-38	1
1979 [2]	D (Carter)	96th	D-277	R-158	–	D-58	R-41	1
1981 [2]	R (Reagan)	97th	D-242	R-192	1	R-53	D-46	1
1983...............	R (Reagan)	98th	D-269	R-166	–	R-54	D-46	–
1985...............	R (Reagan)	99th	D-253	R-182	–	R-53	D-47	–
1987...............	R (Reagan)	100th	D-258	R-177	–	D-55	R-45	–
1989...............	R (Bush)	101st	D-260	R-175	–	D-55	R-45	–
1991 [3]	R (Bush)	102d.	D-267	R-167	1	D-56	R-44	–
1993 [3]	D (Clinton)	103d.	D-258	R-176	1	D-57	R-43	–
1995 [3]	D (Clinton)	104th	R-230	D-204	1	R-52	D-48	–
1997 [4]	D (Clinton)	105th	R-226	D-207	2	R-55	D-45	–
1999 [3]	D (Clinton)	106th	R-223	D-211	1	R-55	D-45	–
2001 [4]	R (Bush)	107th	R-221	D-212	2	D-50	R-50	–
2003 [5, 6]	R (Bush)	108th	R-229	D-204	1	R-51	D-48	1
2005 [5]	R (Bush)	109th	R-232	D-202	1	R-55	D-44	1
2007 [7]	R (Bush)	110th	D-233	R-202	–	D-49	R-49	2
2009 [6, 7, 8]	D (Obama)......	111th	D-256	R-178	–	D-55	R-41	2
2011 [7]	D (Obama)......	112th	D-193	R-242	–	D-51	R-47	2

– Represents zero. [1] Senate had one Independent and one Conservative-Republican. [2] Senate had one Independent. [3] House had one Independent-Socialist. [4] House had one Independent-Socialist and one Independent. [5] House and Senate each had one Independent. [6] House had one vacancy. [7] Senate had two Independents. [8] Senate had two vacancies.
Source: U.S. House of Representatives, Office of the Clerk, *Official List of Members, 2011*, annual. See also <http://clerk.house.gov/member_info/olm_112.pdf>.

Table 412. Composition of Congress by Political Party Affiliation—States: 2005 to 2011

[Figures are for the beginning of the first session, except as noted. Dem. = Democratic; Rep. = Republican]

State	Representatives								Senators							
	109th Cong.,[1,2,3] 2005		110th Cong., 2007		111th Cong.,[4] 2009		112th Cong., 2011		109th Cong.,[3,5] 2005		110th Cong.,[6] 2007		111th Cong.,[6,7] 2009		112th Cong.,[6] 2011	
	Dem.	Rep.	Dem.	Rep.	Dem.	Rep.	Dem.	Rep.	Dem.	Rep.	Dem.	Rep.	Dem.	Rep.	Dem.	Rep.
U.S.	202	231	233	202	256	178	193	242	44	55	49	49	55	41	51	47
AL	2	5	2	5	3	4	1	6	–	2	–	2	–	2	–	2
AK	–	1	–	1	–	1	–	1	–	2	–	2	1	1	1	1
AZ	2	6	4	4	5	3	3	5	–	2	–	2	–	2	–	2
AR	3	1	3	1	3	1	1	3	2	–	2	–	2	–	1	1
CA	33	20	34	19	34	19	34	19	2	–	2	–	2	–	2	–
CO	3	4	4	3	5	2	3	4	1	1	1	1	2	–	2	–
CT	2	3	4	1	5	–	5	–	2	–	1	–	1	–	1	–
DE	–	1	–	1	–	1	1	–	2	–	2	–	2	–	2	–
FL	7	18	9	16	10	15	6	19	1	1	1	1	1	1	1	1
GA	6	7	6	7	6	7	5	8	–	2	–	2	–	2	–	2
HI	2	–	2	–	2	–	2	–	2	–	2	–	2	–	2	–
ID	–	2	–	2	1	1	–	2	–	2	–	2	–	2	–	2
IL	10	9	10	9	11	7	8	11	2	–	2	–	1	–	1	1
IN	2	7	5	4	5	4	3	6	1	1	1	1	1	1	–	2
IA	1	4	3	2	3	2	3	2	1	1	1	1	1	1	1	1
KS	1	3	2	2	1	3	–	4	–	2	–	2	–	2	–	2
KY	1	5	2	4	2	4	2	4	–	2	–	2	–	2	–	2
LA	2	5	2	5	1	6	1	6	1	1	1	1	1	1	1	1
ME	2	–	2	–	2	–	2	–	–	2	–	2	–	2	–	2
MD	6	2	6	2	7	1	6	2	2	–	2	–	2	–	2	–
MA	10	–	10	–	10	–	10	–	2	–	2	–	2	–	1	1
MI	6	9	6	9	8	7	6	9	2	–	2	–	2	–	2	–
MN	4	4	5	3	5	3	4	4	1	1	1	1	1	–	2	–
MS	2	2	2	2	3	1	1	3	–	2	–	2	–	2	–	2
MO	4	5	4	5	4	5	3	6	–	2	1	1	1	1	1	1
MT	–	1	–	1	–	1	–	1	1	1	2	–	2	–	2	–
NE	–	3	–	3	–	3	–	3	1	1	1	1	1	1	1	1
NV	1	2	1	2	2	1	1	2	1	1	1	1	1	1	1	1
NH	–	2	2	–	2	–	–	2	–	2	–	2	1	1	1	1
NJ	7	6	7	6	8	5	7	6	2	–	2	–	2	–	2	–
NM	1	2	1	2	3	–	2	1	1	1	1	1	2	–	2	–
NY	20	9	23	6	26	3	21	8	2	–	2	–	2	–	2	–
NC	6	7	7	6	8	5	7	6	–	2	–	2	1	1	1	1
ND	1	–	1	–	1	–	–	1	2	–	2	–	2	–	1	1
OH	6	11	7	11	10	8	5	13	–	2	1	1	1	1	1	1
OK	1	4	1	4	1	4	1	4	–	2	–	2	–	2	–	2
OR	4	1	4	1	4	1	4	1	1	1	1	1	2	–	2	–
PA	7	12	11	8	12	7	7	12	–	2	1	1	1	1	1	1
RI	2	–	2	–	2	–	2	–	1	1	2	–	2	–	2	–
SC	2	4	2	4	2	4	1	5	–	2	–	2	–	2	–	2
SD	1	–	1	–	1	–	–	1	1	1	1	1	1	1	1	1
TN	5	4	5	4	5	4	2	7	–	2	–	2	–	2	–	2
TX	11	21	13	19	12	20	9	23	–	2	–	2	–	2	–	2
UT	1	2	1	2	1	2	1	2	–	2	–	2	–	2	–	2
VT	–	–	1	–	1	–	1	–	1	–	1	–	1	–	1	–
VA	3	8	3	8	6	5	3	8	–	2	1	1	2	–	2	–
WA	6	3	6	3	6	3	5	4	2	–	2	–	2	–	2	–
WV	2	1	2	1	2	1	1	2	2	–	2	–	2	–	2	–
WI	4	4	5	3	5	3	3	5	2	–	2	–	2	–	1	1
WY	–	1	–	1	–	1	–	1	–	2	–	2	–	2	–	2

– Represents zero. [1] Vermont had one Independent-Socialist representative. [2] Ohio had one vacancy due to the resignation of Rob Portman, April 29, 2005. [3] As of June 28, 2005. [4] One vacancy due to the resignation of Rahm Emanuel, January 6, 2009. [5] Vermont had one Independent senator. [6] Vermont and Connecticut both had one Independent senator. [7] Two vacancies—one in Illinois due to the resignation of Barack Obama, November 16, 2008, and one in Minnesota due to election dispute between Norm Coleman and Al Franken.

Source: U.S. House of Representatives, Office of the Clerk, *Official List of Members*, annual. See also <http://clerk.house.gov/member_info/olm_112.pdf>.

Table 413. Members of Congress—Selected Characteristics: 1995 to 2009

[As of beginning of first session of each Congress, except as noted. Figures for Representatives exclude vacancies]

Members of Congress and year	Male	Female	Black[1]	API[2]	His-panic[3]	Under 40	40 to 49	50 to 59	60 to 69	70 and over	Less than 2 yrs.	2 to 9 yrs.	10 to 19 yrs.	20 to 29 yrs.	30 yrs. or more
						Age[4] (in years)					Seniority[5,6]				
REPRESENTATIVES															
104th Cong., 1995...	388	47	[7]40	7	17	53	155	135	79	13	92	188	110	36	9
106th Cong., 1999...	379	56	[7]39	6	19	23	116	173	87	35	41	236	104	46	7
107th Cong., 2001...	376	59	[7]39	7	19	14	97	167	117	35	44	155	158	63	14
108th Cong., 2003...	376	59	[7]39	5	22	19	86	174	121	32	54	178	140	48	13
109th Cong., 2005...	369	65	[7]42	4	23	22	96	175	113	28	37	173	158	48	18
110th Cong., 2007...	361	74	[7]42	4	23	20	91	172	118	34	62	159	160	37	17
111th Cong., 2009...	366	72	[7]41	8	(NA)	24	84	156	126	44	66	166	142	42	18
SENATORS															
104th Cong., 1995...	92	8	1	2	–	1	14	41	27	17	12	38	30	15	5
106th Cong., 1999...	91	9	–	2	–	–	14	38	35	13	8	39	33	14	6
107th Cong., 2001...	87	13	–	2	–	–	8	39	33	18	11	34	30	14	9
108th Cong., 2003...	86	14	–	2	–	1	12	29	34	24	9	42	29	13	7
109th Cong., 2005...	86	14	1	2	2	–	17	29	33	21	9	41	29	14	7
110th Cong., 2007...	84	16	1	2	3	–	11	31	34	24	12	42	24	13	9
111th Cong., 2009[8]...	83	17	1	1	(NA)	–	7	31	38	22	9	34	28	17	10

– Represents zero. NA Not available. [1] Source: Joint Center for Political and Economic Studies, Washington, DC, *Black Elected Officials: Statistical Summary*, annual (copyright). [2] Asian and Pacific Islanders. Source: Prior to 2005, Library of Congress, Congressional Research Service, "Asian Pacific Americans in the United States Congress," Report 94-767 GOV; starting 2005, U.S. House of Representatives, "House Press Gallery," <http://www.house.gov/daily/> (as of May 25, 2009) and U.S. Senate, "Minorities in the Senate," <http://www.senate.gov/artandhistory/history/common/briefing/minority_senators.htm> (August 30, 2010). [3] Source: National Association of Latino Elected and Appointed Officials, Washington, DC, *National Roster of Hispanic Elected Officials*, annual. [4] Some members do not provide date of birth. [5] Represents consecutive years of service. [6] Some members do not provide years of service. [7] Includes District of Columbia and Virgin Islands delegate. [8] Excludes vacancies.

Source: Except as noted, compiled by U.S. Census Bureau from data published in *Congressional Directory*, biennial. See also <http://www.gpoaccess.gov/cdirectory/browse.html>.

Table 414. U.S. Congress—Measures Introduced and Enacted and Time in Session: 1993 to 2010

[Excludes simple and concurrent resolutions]

Item	103d Cong., 1993–94	104th Cong., 1995–96	105th Cong., 1997–98	106th Cong., 1999–00	107th Cong., 2001–02	108th Cong., 2003–04	109th Cong., 2005–06	110th Cong., 2007–08	111th Cong., 2009–10
Measures introduced........	8,544	6,808	7,732	9,158	9,130	8,625	10,703	11,228	10,778
Bills..................	7,883	6,545	7,532	8,968	8,953	8,468	10,560	11,081	10,629
Joint resolutions..........	661	263	200	190	177	157	143	147	149
Measures enacted.........	473	337	404	604	337	504	590	460	385
Public[1]................	465	333	394	580	331	498	589	460	383
Private[2]...............	8	4	10	24	6	6	1	–	2
HOUSE OF REPRESENTATIVES									
Number of days...........	265	290	251	272	265	243	241	283	286
Number of hours...........	1,887	2,445	2,001	2,179	1,694	1,894	1,917	2,138	2,126
Number of hours per day.....	7.1	8.4	8.0	8.0	6.4	7.8	8.0	7.6	7.4
SENATE									
Number of days...........	291	343	296	303	322	300	297	374	349
Number of hours...........	2,514	2,876	2,188	2,200	2,279	2,486	2,250	2,364	2,495
Number of hours per day.....	8.6	8.4	7.4	7.3	7.1	8.3	7.6	6.3	7.1

– Represents zero. [1] Laws on public matters that apply to all persons. [2] Laws designed to provide legal relief to specified persons or entities adversely affected by laws of general applicability.

Source: U.S. Congress, *Congressional Record and Daily Calendar*, selected issues. See also <http://www.senate.gov/pagelayout/reference/two_column_table/Resumes.htm>.

Table 415. Congressional Bills Vetoed: 1961 to 2011

Period	President	Total vetoes	Regular vetoes	Pocket vetoes	Vetoes sustained	Bills passed over veto
1961–63..............	John F. Kennedy......	21	12	9	21	–
1963–69..............	Lyndon B. Johnson....	30	16	14	30	–
1969–74..............	Richard M. Nixon......	43	26	17	36	7
1974–77..............	Gerald R. Ford.......	66	48	18	54	12
1977–81..............	Jimmy Carter........	31	13	18	29	2
1981–89..............	Ronald W. Reagan.....	78	39	39	69	9
1989–93..............	George Bush.........	44	29	15	43	1
1993–2001............	William J. Clinton.....	37	36	1	34	2
2001–2009............	George W. Bush.......	10	10	–	7	3
2009–2011[1].........	Barack Obama.......	2	–	–	2	–

– Represents zero. [1] For the period January 20, 2009 through June 6, 2011.

Source: U.S. Congress, Senate Library, *Presidential Vetoes ... 1789–1968*; U.S. Congress, *Calendars of the U.S. House of Representatives and History of Legislation*, annual. See also <http://clerk.house.gov/art_history/house_history/vetoes.html>.

Table 416. Number of Governors by Political Party Affiliation: 1975 to 2011

[Reflects figures after inaugurations for each year]

Year	Demo-cratic	Republi-can	Inde-pendent/other	Year	Demo-cratic	Republi-can	Inde-pendent/other	Year	Demo-cratic	Republi-can	Inde-pendent/other
1975....	36	13	1	2000....	18	30	2	2006....	22	28	–
1980....	31	19	–	2001....	19	29	2	2007....	28	22	–
1985....	34	16	–	2002....	22	27	1	2008....	28	22	–
1990....	29	21	–	2003....	23	27	–	2009....	28	22	–
1995....	19	30	1	2004....	22	28	–	2010....	26	24	–
1999....	17	31	1	2005....	22	28	–	2011....	20	29	1

– Represents zero.

Source: National Governors Association, Washington, DC, 1970–87 and 1991–2011, *Directory of Governors of the American States, Commonwealths & Territories*, annual, and 1988–90, *Directory of Governors*, annual (copyright).

Table 417. Vote Cast for and Governor Elected by State: 2007 to 2010

[D = Democratic, R = Republican, I = Independent]

State	Current governor [1]	Year of election	Total vote [2]	Republican	Democratic	Percent leading party
Alabama	Robert Bentley	2010	1,485,324	860,272	625,052	R-57.9
Alaska	Sean Parnell	2010	256,192	151,318	96,519	R-59.1
Arizona	Jan Brewer	2010	1,728,081	938,934	733,935	R-54.3
Arkansas	Mike Beebe	2010	781,333	262,784	503,336	D-64.4
California	Jerry Brown	2010	10,095,185	4,127,391	5,428,149	D-53.8
Colorado	John Hickenlooper	2010	1,787,730	199,034	912,005	D-51.0
Connecticut	Dan Malloy	2010	1,145,799	560,874	567,278	D-49.5
Delaware	Jack Markell	2008	395,204	126,662	266,861	D-67.5
Florida	Rick Scott	2010	5,359,735	2,619,335	2,557,785	R-48.9
Georgia	Nathan Deal	2010	2,576,161	1,365,832	1,107,011	R-53.0
Hawaii	Neil Abercrombie	2010	382,583	157,311	222,724	D-58.2
Idaho	C.L. "Butch" Otter	2010	452,535	267,483	148,680	R-59.1
Illinois	Pat Quinn	2010	3,729,989	1,713,385	1,745,219	D-46.8
Indiana	Mitch Daniels	2008	2,703,752	1,563,885	1,082,463	R-57.8
Iowa	Terry Branstad	2010	1,122,013	592,494	484,798	R-52.8
Kansas	Sam Brownback	2010	838,790	530,760	270,166	R-63.3
Kentucky	Steven L. Beshear	2007	1,055,325	435,773	619,552	D-58.7
Louisiana	Bobby Jindal	2007	1,297,840	699,275	397,755	R-53.9
Maine	Paul LePage	2010	572,766	218,065	109,387	R-38.1
Maryland	Martin O'Malley	2010	1,857,880	776,319	1,044,961	D-56.2
Massachusetts	Deval Patrick	2010	2,297,039	964,866	1,112,293	D-48.4
Michigan	Rick Snyder	2010	3,226,088	1,874,834	1,287,320	R-58.1
Minnesota	Mark Dayton	2010	2,107,021	910,462	919,232	D-43.6
Mississippi	Haley Barbour	2007	744,039	430,807	313,232	R-57.9
Missouri	Jay Nixon	2008	2,877,778	1,136,364	1,680,611	D-58.4
Montana	Brian Schweitzer	2008	486,734	158,268	318,670	D-65.5
Nebraska	Dave Heineman	2010	487,988	360,645	127,343	R-73.9
Nevada	Brian Sandoval	2010	716,529	382,350	298,171	R-53.4
New Hampshire	John Lynch	2010	456,588	205,616	240,346	D-52.6
New Jersey	Chris Christie	2009	2,423,684	1,174,445	1,087,731	R-48.5
New Mexico	Susana Martinez	2010	602,827	321,219	280,614	R-53.3
New York	Andrew Cuomo	2010	4,654,352	1,548,184	2,911,721	D-62.6
North Carolina	Beverly Perdue	2008	4,268,941	2,001,168	2,146,189	D-50.3
North Dakota	Jack Dalrymple [3]	2008	315,692	235,009	74,279	R-74.4
Ohio	John Kasich	2010	3,852,469	1,889,186	1,812,059	R-49.0
Oklahoma	Mary Fallin	2010	1,034,767	625,506	409,261	R-60.4
Oregon	John Kitzhaber	2010	1,453,548	694,287	716,525	D-49.3
Pennsylvania	Tom Corbett	2010	3,987,551	2,172,763	1,814,788	R-54.5
Rhode Island	Lincoln Chafee	2010	342,290	114,911	78,896	I-43.4
South Carolina	Nikki R. Haley	2010	1,344,198	690,525	630,534	R-51.4
South Dakota	Dennis Daugaard	2010	317,083	195,046	122,037	R-61.5
Tennessee	Bill Haslam	2010	1,601,549	1,041,545	529,851	R-65.0
Texas	Rick Perry	2010	4,979,870	2,737,481	2,106,395	R-55.0
Utah	Gary R. Herbert [4]	2010	643,307	412,151	205,246	R-64.1
Vermont	Peter Shumlin	2010	241,605	115,212	119,543	D-49.5
Virginia	Bob McDonnell	2009	1,982,424	1,163,523	818,901	R-58.7
Washington	Chris Gregoire	2008	3,002,862	1,404,124	1,598,738	D-53.2
West Virginia	Earl Ray Tomblin [5]	2008	705,795	181,612	492,697	D-69.8
Wisconsin	Scott Walker	2010	2,133,244	1,128,941	1,004,303	R-52.3
Wyoming	Matthew Mead	2010	188,463	123,780	43,240	R-65.7

[1] As of 8 March 2011. Source: National Governors Association, Washington, DC. See also <http://www.nga.org>. [2] Includes minor party and scattered votes. [3] North Dakota Lt. Governor Jack Dalrymple became governor 7 December 2010, completing the unexpired term of Governor John Hoeven following his election to the U.S. Senate. [4] Utah Lt. Governor Gary Herbert became governor 11 August 2009, following Governor Jon Huntsman Jr.'s appointment as U.S. Ambassador to China. [5] West Virginia Senate President Earl Ray Tomblin became governor 15 November 2010, completing the unexpired term of Governor Joe Manchin, III following his election to the U.S. Senate.

Source: Except as noted, The Council of State Governments, Lexington, KY, *The Book of States 2011*, annual (copyright).

260 Elections

Table 418. Political Party Control of State Legislatures by Party: 1985 to 2011

[As of beginning of year. Nebraska has a nonpartisan legislature]

Year	Democratic control	Split control or tie	Republican control	Year	Democratic control	Split control or tie	Republican control	Year	Democratic control	Split control or tie	Republican control
1985....	27	11	11	1997....	20	11	18	2005....	19	10	20
1990....	29	11	9	1999....	20	12	17	2006....	19	10	20
1992....	29	14	6	2000....	16	15	18	2007....	22	12	15
1993....	25	16	8	2001....	16	15	18	2008....	23	14	12
1994....	24	17	8	2002....	17	15	17	2009....	27	8	14
1995....	18	12	19	2003....	16	12	21	2010....	27	8	14
1996....	16	15	18	2004....	17	11	21	2011....	15	8	26

Source: National Conference of State Legislatures, Denver, CO, *State Legislatures*, periodic.

Table 419. Composition of State Legislatures by Political Party Affiliation: 2010 and 2011

[Data as of March and reflect February election results in year shown, except as noted. Figures reflect immediate results of elections, including holdover members in state houses which do not have all of their members running for reelection. Dem. = Democrat, Rep. = Republican, Vac. = Vacancies. In general, Lower House refers to body consisting of state representatives and Upper House of state senators]

State	Lower House 2010 Dem.	Rep.	Other	Vac.	Lower House 2011 Dem.	Rep.	Other	Vac.	Upper House 2010 Dem.	Rep.	Other	Vac.	Upper House 2011 Dem.	Rep.	Other	Vac.
U.S........	3,028	2,356	21	6	2,453	2,924	22	12	1,026	893	2	1	881	1,032	5	4
AL [1]	60	45	–	–	39	65	–	1	21	14	–	–	12	22	1	–
AK [2]	18	22	–	–	16	24	–	–	10	10	–	–	10	10	–	–
AZ [3]	25	35	–	–	20	40	–	–	12	18	–	–	9	21	–	–
AR [2]	71	28	1	–	54	44	–	2	27	8	–	–	20	15	–	–
CA [2]	49	29	1	1	52	27	–	1	25	14	–	1	25	15	–	–
CO [2]	38	27	–	–	32	33	–	–	21	14	–	–	20	15	–	–
CT [3]	114	37	–	–	98	52	–	1	24	12	–	–	22	14	–	–
DE [2]	24	17	–	–	26	15	–	–	15	6	–	–	14	7	–	–
FL [2]	44	76	–	–	38	81	–	1	14	26	–	–	12	28	–	–
GA [3]	74	105	1	–	63	116	1	–	22	34	–	–	20	36	–	–
HI [2]	45	6	–	–	43	8	–	–	23	2	–	–	24	1	–	–
ID [3]	18	52	–	–	13	57	–	–	7	28	–	–	7	28	–	–
IL [4]	70	48	–	–	64	54	–	–	37	22	–	–	34	24	–	1
IN [2]	52	48	–	–	40	60	–	–	17	33	–	–	13	37	–	–
IA [2]	56	44	–	–	40	60	–	–	32	18	–	–	26	24	–	–
KS [2]	49	76	–	–	33	92	–	–	9	31	–	–	8	32	–	–
KY [2]	65	35	–	–	58	42	–	–	17	20	1	–	15	22	1	–
LA [1]	52	50	3	–	47	52	4	2	24	15	–	–	19	20	–	–
ME [3]	96	54	1	–	72	78	1	–	20	15	–	–	14	20	1	–
MD [1]	104	36	1	–	98	43	–	–	33	14	–	–	35	12	–	–
MA [3]	143	16	1	–	128	31	–	1	35	5	–	–	36	4	–	–
MI [2]	66	43	–	1	47	63	–	–	16	22	–	–	12	26	–	–
MN [2]	87	47	–	–	62	72	–	–	46	21	–	–	30	37	–	–
MS [1]	74	48	–	–	69	53	–	–	27	25	–	–	25	27	–	–
MO [2]	74	88	–	1	57	106	–	–	11	23	–	–	7	26	–	1
MT [2]	50	50	–	–	32	68	–	–	23	27	–	–	22	28	–	–
NE [5]	(5)	(5)	(5)	(5)	(5)	(5)	(5)	(5)	(5)	(5)	(5)	(5)	(5)	(5)	(5)	(5)
NV [2]	28	14	–	–	26	16	–	–	12	9	–	–	11	10	–	–
NH [3]	225	175	–	–	102	296	1	1	14	10	–	–	5	19	–	–
NJ [2]	47	33	–	–	47	33	–	–	23	17	–	–	24	16	–	–
NM [2]	45	25	–	–	37	33	–	–	27	15	–	–	27	15	–	–
NY [3]	105	43	2	–	98	51	1	–	32	30	–	–	30	32	–	–
NC [3]	68	52	–	–	51	67	1	1	30	20	–	–	19	31	–	–
ND [1]	36	58	–	–	25	69	–	–	21	26	–	–	12	35	–	–
OH [2]	53	46	–	–	40	59	–	–	12	21	–	–	10	23	–	–
OK [2]	40	61	–	–	31	70	–	–	22	26	–	–	16	32	–	–
OR [2]	36	24	–	–	30	30	–	–	18	12	–	–	16	14	–	–
PA [2]	103	97	–	3	91	112	–	–	20	30	–	–	19	30	–	1
RI [3]	69	6	–	–	65	10	–	–	33	4	1	–	29	8	1	–
SC [2]	51	73	–	–	48	76	–	–	19	27	–	–	19	26	–	1
SD [3]	24	46	–	–	19	50	1	–	14	21	–	–	5	30	–	–
TN [2]	48	51	–	–	34	64	1	–	14	19	–	–	13	20	–	–
TX [2]	73	77	–	–	49	101	–	–	12	19	–	–	12	19	–	–
UT [2]	22	53	–	–	17	58	–	–	8	21	–	–	7	22	–	–
VT [3]	95	48	7	–	94	48	8	–	23	7	–	–	21	8	1	–
VA [2]	39	59	2	–	39	58	2	1	22	18	–	–	22	18	–	–
WA [2]	61	37	–	–	56	42	–	–	31	18	–	–	27	22	–	–
WV [2]	71	29	–	–	65	35	–	–	26	8	–	–	28	6	–	–
WI [2]	52	46	1	–	38	60	1	–	18	15	–	–	14	19	–	–
WY [2]	19	41	–	–	10	50	–	–	7	23	–	–	4	26	–	–

– Represents zero. [1] Members of both houses serve 4-year terms. [2] Upper House members serve 4-year terms and Lower House members serve 2-year terms. [3] Members of both houses serve 2-year terms. [4] Illinois—4- and 2-year term depending on district. [5] Nebraska—4-year term and only state to have a nonpartisan legislature.

Source: The Council of State Governments, Lexington, KY, *The Book of States 2011*, annual (copyright).

Table 420. Women Holding State Public Offices by Office and State: 2010

[As of January. For data on women in U.S. Congress, see Table 413]

State	Total	Statewide elective executive office [1]	State legislature Total	Percent [2]	State	Total	Statewide elective executive office [1]	State legislature Total	Percent [2]
U.S.	1,880	71	1,809	25	MO.	46	2	44	22
					MT.	43	4	39	26
AL	24	6	18	13	NE	11	1	10	20
AK	13	–	13	22	NV	23	3	20	32
AZ	32	3	29	32	NH	156	–	156	37
AR	32	1	31	23	NJ	35	1	34	28
CA	33	1	32	27	NM	37	3	34	30
CO	40	2	38	38	NY	51	–	51	24
CT	64	4	60	32	NC	50	6	44	26
DE	18	2	16	26	ND	24	1	23	16
FL	39	1	38	24	OH	31	2	29	22
GA	46	–	46	19	OK	21	4	17	11
HI.	26	1	25	33	OR	28	2	26	29
ID	28	1	27	26	PA	39	–	39	15
IL	51	1	50	28	RI	26	1	25	22
IN	33	1	32	21	SC	17	–	17	10
IA.	36	1	35	23	SD	21	–	21	20
KS	51	1	50	30	TN	25	–	25	19
KY	23	1	22	16	TX	45	2	43	24
LA	23	–	23	16	UT	23	–	23	22
ME	54	–	54	29	VT	68	1	67	37
MD	59	–	59	31	VA	27	–	27	19
MA	52	1	51	26	WA	49	1	48	33
MI.	39	2	37	25	WV.	23	1	22	16
MN	73	3	70	35	WI	31	2	29	22
MS	25	–	25	14	WY.	16	1	15	17

– Represents zero. [1] Excludes women elected to the judiciary, women appointed to state cabinet-level positions, women elected to executive posts by the legislature, and elected members of university Board of Trustees or Board of Education.
[2] Calculated by U.S. Census Bureau based on total (male and female) state legislature (both upper and lower houses) data from Table 419.

Source: Center for the American Woman and Politics, Eagleton Institute of Politics, Rutgers University, New Brunswick, NJ, information releases, (copyright).

Table 421. Hispanic Public Elected Officials by Office, 1985 to 2008, and State, 2008

[As of January of year shown. For states not shown, no Hispanic public officials had been identified]

State	Total	State executives and legislators [1]	County and municipal officials	Judicial and law enforcement	Education and school boards	State	Total	State executives and legislators [1]	County and municipal officials	Judicial and law enforcement	Education and school boards
1985.	3,147	129	1,316	517	1,185	MD.	11	4	6	–	1
1990.	4,004	144	1,819	583	1,458	MA.	20	4	9	–	7
2000.	5,019	217	1,852	447	2,503	MI.	14	3	2	4	5
2001.	5,205	223	1,846	454	2,682	MN.	5	3	1	1	–
2002.	4,303	227	1,960	532	1,603	MO.	2	1	1	–	–
2003.	4,432	231	1,958	549	1,694	MT.	3	1	–	2	–
2004.	4,651	253	2,059	638	1,723	NE	3	1	1	–	1
2005.	4,853	266	2,149	678	1,760	NV	12	6	2	3	1
2006.	4,932	244	2,151	693	1,835	NH	4	3	1	–	–
2007.	4,954	270	2,152	685	1,847	NJ	117	10	61	–	46
2008.	**5,240**	**283**	**2,266**	**738**	**1,952**	NM.	654	49	338	105	162
AK	1	–	1	–	–	NY	61	19	27	13	2
AZ	362	19	135	53	155	NC	4	2	2	–	–
CA	1,127	35	416	42	634	ND	1	–	1	–	–
CO.	152	9	104	8	31	OH.	6	–	5	1	–
CT	28	6	18	–	4	OK.	2	–	–	–	2
DE	2	1	1	–	–	OR.	12	2	5	5	–
FL	150	21	87	35	7	PA	9	1	5	2	1
GA	6	3	1	2	–	RI.	7	3	4	–	–
HI.	2	1	1	–	–	SC	1	1	–	–	–
ID.	2	2	–	–	–	TN	3	1	2	–	–
IL.	111	13	60	8	30	TX	2,245	44	918	441	842
IN.	17	1	11	3	2	UT	8	3	3	2	–
IA.	1	–	1	–	–	VA	3	1	1	–	1
KS	10	4	6	–	–	WA.	35	3	19	–	13
KY	2	–	1	–	1	WI	9	1	3	4	1
LA	10	–	3	4	3	WY.	5	2	3	–	–

– Represents zero. [1] Includes U.S. Senators and Representatives, not shown separately.

Source: National Association of Latino Elected and Appointed Officials (NALEO) Educational Fund, Washington, DC, *National Directory of Latino Elected Officials*, annual.

Table 422. Political Action Committees—Number by Committee Type: 1980 to 2009

[As of December 31, except 2009 as of May 22]

Committee type	1980	1990	1995	2000	2005	2006	2007	2008	2009
Total...................	2,551	4,172	4,016	3,907	4,210	4,183	4,234	4,611	4,481
Corporate	1,206	1,795	1,674	1,545	1,622	1,582	1,601	1,598	1,574
Labor.......................	297	346	334	317	290	273	273	272	275
Trade/membership/health ...	576	774	815	860	925	937	925	995	1,104
Nonconnected...............	374	1,062	1,020	1,026	1,233	1,254	1,300	1,594	1,390
Cooperative.................	42	59	44	41	37	37	38	49	43
Corporation without stock	56	136	129	118	103	100	97	103	95

Source: U.S. Federal Election Commission, press release, May 2009.

Table 423. Political Action Committees—Financial Activity Summary by Committee Type: 2003 to 2008

[In millions of dollars (915.7 represents $915,700,000). Covers financial activity during 2-year calendar period indicated]

Committee type	Receipts			Disbursements [1]			Contributions to candidates		
	2003–04	2005–06	2007–08	2003–04	2005–06	2007–08	2003–04	2005–06	2007–08
Total....................	915.7	477.4	1,212.4	842.9	394.1	1,180.0	310.5	141.1	412.8
Corporate	239.0	131.2	313.4	221.6	116.3	298.6	115.6	56.5	158.3
Labor.....................	191.7	100.3	262.1	182.9	73.1	265.0	52.1	21.1	62.7
Trade/membership/health	181.8	95.4	372.7	170.1	74.6	364.6	83.2	38.0	66.6
Nonconnected..............	289.4	141.6	241.0	255.2	122.6	229.5	52.5	22.0	112.9
Cooperative................	4.2	2.7	10.3	3.9	1.9	9.9	2.9	1.4	6.9
Corporation without stock	9.6	6.1	13.0	9.2	5.7	12.4	4.2	2.1	5.5

[1] Comprises contributions to candidates, independent expenditures, and other disbursements.
Source: U.S. Federal Election Commission, *FEC Reports on Financial Activity, Final Report, Party and Non-party Political Committees*, biennial.

Table 424. Presidential Campaign Finances—Federal Funds for General Election: 1996 to 2008

[In millions of dollars (152.6 represents $152,600,000). Based on FEC certifications, audit reports, and Dept. of Treasury reports]

1996		2000		2004		2008	
Candidate	Amount	Candidate	Amount	Candidate	Amount	Candidate	Amount
Total........	152.6	Total.......	147.7	Total.......	150.1	Total.......	84.2
Clinton.......	61.8	Bush	67.6	Bush	74.6	Obama........	–
Dole.........	61.8	Gore........	67.6	Kerry	74.6	McCain	84.1
Perot	29.0	Buchanan ...	12.6	Nader........	0.9	Nader.......	0.1

– Represents zero.
Source: U.S. Federal Election Commission, periodic press releases.

Table 425. Presidential Campaign Finances—Primary Campaign Receipts and Disbursements: 1999 to 2008

[In millions of dollars (351.6 represents $351,600,000). Covers campaign finance activity during 2-year calendar period indicated. Covers candidates who received federal matching funds or who had significant financial activity]

Item	Total [1]			Democratic			Republican		
	1999–00	2003–04	2007–08 [2, 3]	1999–00	2003–04	2007–08 [2]	1999–00	2003–04	2007–08 [3]
Receipts, total [4]	351.6	673.9	1,346.6	96.6	401.8	950.1	236.7	269.6	392.6
Individual contributions	238.2	611.4	1,325.6	66.7	351.0	932.6	159.1	258.9	390.0
Federal matching funds.....	61.6	28.0	21.0	29.3	27.2	17.5	26.5	–	2.6
Disbursements..........	343.5	661.1	1,414.6	92.2	389.7	1,043.9	233.2	268.9	450.2

– Represents zero. [1] Includes other parties, not shown separately. [2] Obama activity includes both Primary and General election funds because he used a single committee for both elections. Dodd received $1,961,742 in matching funds; however his committee reported the receipt of $1,447,568. Gravel received an additional $115,966 in matching funds in early 2009. [3] Tancredo received an additional $83,775 in matching funds in early 2009. [4] Includes other types of receipts, not shown separately.
Source: U.S. Federal Election Commission, *FEC Reports on Financial Activity, Final Report, Presidential Pre-Nomination Campaigns*, quadrennial.

Table 426. Congressional Campaign Finances—Receipts and Disbursements: 2003 to 2008

[708.5 represents $708,500,000. Covers all campaign finance activity during 2-year calendar period indicated for primary, general, run-off, and special elections. Data have been adjusted to eliminate transfers between all committees within a campaign. For further information on legal limits of contributions, see Federal Election Campaign Act of 1971, as amended]

Item	House of Representatives						Senate					
	Amount (mil. dol.)			Percent distribution			Amount (mil. dol.)			Percent distribution		
	2003–04	2005–06	2007–08	2003–04	2005–06	2007–08	2003–04	2005–06	2007–08	2003–04	2005–06	2007–08
Total receipts [1]	**708.5**	**875.4**	**1,005.2**	**100**	**100**	**100**	**497.6**	**564.6**	**434.1**	**100**	**100**	**100**
Individual contributions	396.7	478.9	538.8	56	55	54	324.1	383.2	267.0	65	68	62
Other committees	225.4	279.8	300.4	32	32	30	63.7	68.9	78.2	13	12	18
Candidate loans.	47.4	56.1	77.6	7	6	8	39.8	47.0	24.2	8	8	6
Candidate contributions.	7.8	14.7	32.4	1	2	3	38.2	37.5	5.7	8	7	1
Democrats	307.4	417.5	561.0	43	48	56	250.6	291.8	237.3	50	52	55
Republicans	399.2	453.6	440.8	56	52	44	246.1	245.8	196.1	49	44	45
Others	1.9	4.2	3.4	(Z)	(Z)	(Z)	0.9	26.9	0.7	(Z)	5	(Z)
Incumbents	452.6	532.6	581.7	64	61	58	171.7	278.4	234.1	35	49	54
Challengers	118.2	188.7	252.2	17	22	25	79.5	186.6	135.0	16	33	31
Open seats [2]	137.8	154.1	171.3	19	18	17	246.4	99.6	65.1	50	18	15
Total disbursements	**660.3**	**854.8**	**929.9**	**100**	**100**	**100**	**496.4**	**562.9**	**449.4**	**100**	**100**	**100**
Democrats	288.5	395.5	491.0	44	46	53	254.6	288.6	229.6	51	51	51
Republicans	370.0	455.2	435.6	56	53	47	241.0	249.3	202.0	49	44	45
Others	1.8	4.1	3.3	(Z)	(Z)	(Z)	0.8	25.0	17.9	(Z)	4	4
Incumbents	410.1	519.2	527.6	62	61	57	171.7	274.3	251.2	35	49	56
Challengers	116.6	185.6	246.7	18	22	27	76.6	187.1	132.9	15	33	30
Open seats [2]	133.6	150.0	155.6	20	18	17	248.1	101.5	65.4	50	18	15

Z Less than 0.5 percent. [1] Includes other types of receipts, not shown separately. [2] Elections in which an incumbent did not seek reelection.

Source: U.S. Federal Election Commission, *FEC Reports on Financial Activity, Final Report, U.S. Senate and House Campaigns*, biennial.

Table 427. Contributions to Congressional Campaigns by Political Action Committees (PAC) by Type of Committee: 1997 to 2008

[In millions of dollars (158.7 represents $158,700,000). Covers amounts given to candidates in primary, general, run-off, and special elections during the 2-year calendar period indicated. For number of political action committees, see Table 422]

Type of committee	Total [1]	Democrats	Republicans	Incumbents	Challengers	Open seats [2]
HOUSE OF REPRESENTATIVES						
1997–98.	158.7	77.6	80.9	124.0	14.9	19.8
1999–00.	193.4	98.2	94.7	150.5	19.9	23.0
2001–02.	206.9	102.6	104.2	161.0	13.8	32.1
2003–04.	225.4	98.6	126.6	187.3	15.6	22.5
2005–06.	279.8	125.0	154.8	232.0	24.4	23.5
2007–08, total [3]	**300.4**	**184.3**	**116.1**	**245.7**	**35.8**	**18.9**
Corporate	108.0	56.7	51.3	99.4	5.0	3.6
Trade association [4]	85.6	47.6	38.0	73.6	7.2	4.8
Labor	53.4	49.7	3.7	37.5	11.3	4.6
Nonconnected [5]	43.9	25.1	18.8	27.0	11.6	5.4
SENATE						
1997–98.	48.1	20.7	27.3	34.3	6.6	7.2
1999–00.	51.9	18.7	33.2	33.5	7.1	11.3
2001–02.	59.2	25.4	33.8	37.0	14.2	8.1
2003–04.	63.7	28.4	35.3	39.3	5.6	18.8
2005–06.	68.9	28.6	37.5	50.0	9.9	8.7
2007–08, total [3]	**78.2**	**33.5**	**44.3**	**56.6**	**12.8**	**9.0**
Corporate	32.4	11.2	21.2	26.8	2.5	3.1
Trade association [4]	19.4	7.2	12.2	14.9	2.5	2.0
Labor	7.0	6.5	0.5	2.8	2.9	1.2
Nonconnected [5]	17.5	7.8	9.7	10.7	4.4	2.5

[1] Includes other parties, not shown separately. [2] Elections in which an incumbent did not seek reelection. [3] Includes other types of political action committees, not shown separately. [4] Includes membership organizations and health organizations. [5] Represents "ideological" groups as well as other issue groups not necessarily ideological in nature.

Source: U.S. Federal Election Commission, *FEC Reports on Financial Activity, Party and Non-Party Political Committees, Final Report*, biennial.

State and Local Government Finances and Employment

This section presents data on revenues, expenditures, debt, and employment of state and local governments. Nationwide statistics relating to state and local governments, their numbers, finances, and employment are compiled primarily by the U.S. Census Bureau through a program of censuses and surveys. Every fifth year (for years ending in "2" and "7"), the Census Bureau conducts a census of governments involving collection of data for all governmental units in the United States. In addition, the Census Bureau conducts annual surveys which cover all the state governments and a sample of local governments.

Annually, the Census Bureau releases information on the Internet which presents financial data for the federal government, nationwide totals for state and local governments, and state-local data by states. Also released annually is a series on state, city, county, and school finances and on state and local public employment. There is also a series of quarterly data releases covering tax revenue and finances of major public employee retirement systems.

Basic information for Census Bureau statistics on governments is obtained by mail canvass from state and local officials; however, financial data for each of the state governments and for many of the large local governments are compiled from their official records and reports by Census Bureau personnel. In over two-thirds of the states, all or part of local government financial data are obtained through central collection arrangements with state governments. Financial data on the federal government are primarily based on the *Budget* published by the Office of Management and Budget (see text, Section 9, Federal Government Finances and Employment).

Governmental units—The governmental structure of the United States includes, in addition to the federal government and the states, thousands of local governments—counties, municipalities, townships, school districts, and many "special districts." In 2007, 89,476 local governments were identified by the census of governments (see Tables 428–429). As defined by the census, governmental units include all agencies or bodies having an organized existence, governmental character, and substantial autonomy. While most of these governments can impose taxes, many of the special districts—such as independent public housing authorities and numerous local irrigation, power, and other types of districts—are financed from rentals, charges for services, benefit assessments, grants from other governments, and other non-tax sources. The count of governments excludes semi-autonomous agencies through which states, cities, and counties sometimes provide for certain functions—for example, "dependent" school systems, state institutions of higher education, and certain other "authorities" and special agencies which are under the administrative or fiscal control of an established governmental unit.

Finances—The financial statistics relate to government fiscal years ending June 30 or at some date within the 12 previous months. The following governments are exceptions and are included as though they were part of the June 30 group; ending September 30, the state governments of Alabama and Michigan, the District of Columbia, and Alabama school districts; and ending August 31, the state governments of Nebraska, Texas, and Chicago school districts. New York State ends its fiscal year on March 31. The federal government ended the fiscal year June 30 until 1976 when its fiscal year, by an act of

Congress, was revised to extend from Oct. 1 to Sept. 30. A 3-month quarter (July 1 to Sept. 30, 1976) bridged the transition.

Nationwide government finance statistics have been classified and presented in terms of uniform concepts and categories, rather than according to the highly diverse terminology, organization, and fund structure utilized by individual governments.

Statistics on governmental finances distinguish among general government, utilities, liquor stores, and insurance trusts. *General government* comprises all activities except utilities, liquor stores, and insurance trusts. Utilities include government water supply, electric light and power, gas supply, and transit systems. Liquor stores are operated by 17 states and by local governments in 6 states. Insurance trusts relate to employee retirement, unemployment compensation, and other social insurance systems administered by the federal, state, and local governments.

Data for cities or counties relate only to municipal or county and their dependent agencies and do not include amounts for other local governments in the same geographic location. Therefore, expenditure figures for "education" do not include spending by the separate school districts which administer public schools within most municipal or county areas. Variations in the assignment of governmental responsibility for public assistance, health, hospitals, public housing, and other functions to a lesser degree also have an important effect upon reported amounts of city or county expenditure, revenue, and debt.

Employment and payrolls—These data are based mainly on mail canvassing of state and local governments. Payroll includes all salaries, wages, and individual fee payments for the month specified, and employment relates to all persons on governmental payrolls during a pay period of the month covered—including paid officials, temporary help, and (unless otherwise specified) part-time as well as full-time personnel. Effective with the 1997 Census of Governments, the reference period for measuring government employment was changed from October of the calendar year to March of the calendar year. As a result, there was no annual survey of government employment covering the October 1996 period. The prior reference month of October was used from 1958 to 1995. Figures shown for individual governments cover major dependent agencies such as institutions of higher education, as well as the basic central departments and agencies of the government.

Statistical reliability—For a discussion of statistical collection and estimation, sampling procedures, and measures of statistical reliability applicable to Census Bureau data, see Appendix III.

Table 428. Number of Governmental Units by Type: 1962 to 2007

Type of government	1962	1967	1972	1977	1982	1987	1992	1997	2002	2007
Total units.........	**91,237**	**81,299**	**78,269**	**79,913**	**81,831**	**83,237**	**85,006**	**87,504**	**87,576**	**89,527**
U.S. government	1	1	1	1	1	1	1	1	1	1
State government	50	50	50	50	50	50	50	50	50	50
Local governments	91,186	81,248	78,218	79,862	81,780	83,186	84,955	87,453	87,525	89,476
County............	3,043	3,049	3,044	3,042	3,041	3,042	3,043	3,043	3,034	3,033
Municipal..........	18,000	18,048	18,517	18,862	19,076	19,200	19,279	19,372	19,429	19,492
Township and town ...	17,142	17,105	16,991	16,822	16,734	16,691	16,656	16,629	16,504	16,519
School district	34,678	21,782	15,781	15,174	14,851	14,721	14,422	13,726	13,506	13,051
Special district.......	18,323	21,264	23,885	25,962	28,078	29,532	31,555	34,683	35,052	37,381

Source: U.S. Census Bureau, *Census of Governments*, Volume 1, Number 1, Government Organization, Series GC07(1)-1), quinquennial. See also <http://www.census.gov/govs/cog/>.

Table 429. Number of Local Governments by Type—States: 2007

[Governments in existence in January. Limited to governments actually in existence. Excludes, therefore, a few counties and numerous townships and "incorporated places" existing as areas for which statistics can be presented as to population and other subjects, but lacking any separate organized county, township, or municipal government. See Appendix III]

State	All govern- mental units [1]	County	Municipal	Township [1]	School district	Special district [2] Total [3]	Natural resources	Fire protection	Housing [4]
United States	**89,476**	**3,033**	**19,492**	**16,519**	**13,051**	**37,381**	**7,227**	**5,873**	**3,463**
Alabama	1,185	67	458	–	131	529	69	11	150
Alaska	177	14	148	–	–	15	–	–	14
Arizona	645	15	90	–	239	301	78	150	–
Arkansas	1,548	75	502	–	247	724	250	81	119
California	4,344	57	478	–	1,044	2,765	473	353	70
Colorado	2,416	62	270	–	180	1,904	180	252	89
Connecticut	649	–	30	149	17	453	1	72	114
Delaware	338	3	57	–	19	259	238	–	3
District of Columbia	2	–	1	–	–	1	–	–	–
Florida	1,623	66	411	–	95	1,051	125	61	94
Georgia	1,439	154	535	–	180	570	38	2	191
Hawaii	19	3	1	–	–	15	14	–	–
Idaho	1,240	44	200	–	116	880	174	150	10
Illinois.............	6,994	102	1,299	1,432	912	3,249	1,026	841	113
Indiana.............	3,231	91	567	1,008	293	1,272	139	1	65
Iowa...............	1,954	99	947	–	380	528	247	66	23
Kansas.............	3,931	104	627	1,353	316	1,531	258	1	197
Kentucky	1,346	118	419	–	175	634	126	156	13
Louisiana	526	60	303	–	68	95	8	3	–
Maine..............	850	16	22	466	98	248	15	–	34
Maryland	256	23	157	–	–	76	38	–	20
Massachusetts........	861	5	45	306	82	423	16	16	252
Michigan	2,893	83	533	1,242	579	456	79	25	–
Minnesota	3,526	87	854	1,788	341	456	144	–	162
Mississippi..........	1,000	82	296	–	164	458	249	33	55
Missouri............	3,723	114	952	312	536	1,809	329	357	124
Montana............	1,273	54	129	–	332	758	132	220	13
Nebraska...........	2,659	93	530	454	288	1,294	83	417	168
Nevada	198	16	19	–	17	146	33	18	5
New Hampshire.......	545	10	13	221	164	137	10	16	21
New Jersey	1,383	21	324	242	549	247	15	196	–
New Mexico..........	863	33	101	–	96	633	576	–	6
New York	3,403	57	618	929	680	1,119	3	891	–
North Carolina........	963	100	548	–	–	315	145	–	94
North Dakota.........	2,699	53	357	1,320	198	771	78	281	35
Ohio...............	3,702	88	938	1,308	668	700	106	85	77
Oklahoma	1,880	77	594	–	567	642	100	30	137
Oregon.............	1,546	36	242	–	234	1,034	204	271	21
Pennsylvania	4,871	66	1,016	1,546	515	1,728	5	–	90
Rhode Island	134	–	8	31	4	91	4	37	25
South Carolina........	698	46	268	–	85	299	48	83	43
South Dakota........	1,983	66	309	916	166	526	103	84	49
Tennessee	928	92	347	–	14	475	109	1	96
Texas	4,835	254	1,209	–	1,081	2,291	442	139	387
Utah...............	599	29	242	–	40	288	82	18	17
Vermont............	733	14	45	237	293	144	14	16	10
Virginia.............	511	95	229	–	1	186	47	–	–
Washington	1,845	39	281	–	296	1,229	178	375	43
West Virginia	663	55	232	–	55	321	14	–	37
Wisconsin	3,120	72	592	1,259	441	756	251	–	177
Wyoming	726	23	99	–	55	549	131	64	–

– Represents zero. [1] Includes "town" governments in the six New England States and in Minnesota, New York, and Wisconsin.
[2] Single function districts. [3] Includes other special districts not shown separately. [4] Includes community development.
Source: U.S. Census Bureau, *Census of Governments*, Volume 1, Number 1, Government Organization, Series GC07(1)–1), quinquennial. See also <http://www.census.gov/cog/>.

Table 430. State and Local Government Current Receipts and Expenditures in the National Income and Product Accounts: 1990 to 2010

[In billions of dollars (738.0 represents $738,000,000,000). For explanation of national income, see text, Section 13. Minus sign (–) indicates net loss]

Item	1990	1995	2000	2005	2006	2007	2008	2009	2010
Current receipts.................	**738.0**	**991.9**	**1,322.6**	**1,730.4**	**1,829.7**	**1,923.1**	**1,967.2**	**2,005.8**	**2,128.1**
Current tax receipts.................	519.1	672.1	893.2	1,163.1	1,249.0	1,313.6	1,332.5	1,267.0	1,331.2
Personal current taxes..............	122.6	158.1	236.7	276.7	302.5	323.1	335.4	287.3	291.7
Income taxes...................	109.6	141.7	217.4	251.7	276.1	295.9	308.0	259.1	262.6
Other.......................	13.0	16.4	19.4	25.0	26.4	27.2	27.5	28.2	29.1
Taxes on production and imports......	374.1	482.4	621.3	831.4	887.4	932.7	949.1	930.3	951.9
Sales taxes....................	184.3	242.7	316.8	402.2	430.4	447.1	442.7	421.1	429.9
Property taxes..................	161.5	202.6	254.7	346.9	370.1	396.0	411.7	425.2	436.3
Other.......................	28.3	37.0	49.8	82.3	86.9	89.7	94.7	84.0	85.7
Taxes on corporate income	22.5	31.7	35.2	54.9	59.2	57.8	48.0	49.4	87.6
Contributions for government social insurance.....................	10.0	13.6	10.8	24.8	21.8	18.9	19.7	21.6	22.4
Income receipts on assets............	68.5	68.5	94.3	88.3	103.5	114.5	115.2	116.0	118.1
Interest receipts..................	64.1	63.0	86.7	76.4	90.9	100.6	99.5	98.8	98.8
Dividends.....................	0.2	1.0	1.4	2.1	2.3	2.4	2.5	2.7	3.0
Rents and royalties	4.2	4.5	6.3	9.8	10.3	11.5	13.2	14.5	16.3
Current transfer receipts	133.5	224.2	313.9	454.3	456.7	485.1	512.7	610.2	665.5
Federal grants-in-aid	111.4	184.2	247.3	361.2	359.0	380.8	396.2	484.6	529.6
From business (net)...............	7.1	13.5	28.6	36.5	38.4	41.3	46.8	50.4	54.9
From persons...................	14.9	26.5	38.0	56.5	59.2	63.1	69.7	75.2	81.0
Current surplus of government enterprises.....................	6.9	13.5	10.4	0.1	–1.3	–9.1	–13.0	–9.0	–9.0
Current expenditures	**731.8**	**982.7**	**1,281.3**	**1,704.5**	**1,778.6**	**1,910.8**	**2,014.6**	**2,025.9**	**2,095.2**
Consumption expenditures	547.0	701.3	930.6	1,212.0	1,282.3	1,368.9	1,448.2	1,424.4	1,447.2
Government social benefit payments to persons	127.7	217.6	271.4	404.8	402.9	433.7	455.2	492.1	534.7
Interest payments	56.8	63.5	78.8	87.3	93.0	101.1	108.2	108.0	111.8
Subsidies......................	0.4	0.3	0.5	0.4	0.4	7.1	3.0	1.4	1.6
Net state and local government saving......................	**6.2**	**9.2**	**41.3**	**25.9**	**51.0**	**12.2**	**–47.4**	**–20.1**	**32.9**
Social insurance funds	2.0	4.0	2.0	7.4	4.7	1.9	1.7	2.6	2.6
Other.........................	4.2	5.1	39.3	18.5	46.4	10.4	–49.1	–22.7	30.3

Source: U.S. Bureau of Economic Analysis, *Survey of Current Business*, April 2011. See also <http://www.bea.gov/national/nipaweb/SelectTable.asp?selected=N>.

Table 431. Federal Grants–in–Aid to State and Local Governments: 1990 to 2011

[135,325 represents $135,325,000,000, except as indicated. For year ending Sept. 30. Minus sign (–) indicates decrease]

Year	Current dollars							Constant (2000) dollars	
			Grants to individuals		Grants as percent of—				
	Total grants (mil. dol.)	Annual percent change [1]	Grants to individuals, total (mil. dol.)	Percent of total grants	State and local government expenditures from own sources [2]	Federal outlays	Gross domestic product	Total grants (bil. dol.)	Annual percent change [1]
1990......	135,325	11.0	77,264	57.1	25.2	10.8	2.4	198.1	6.2
1995......	224,991	6.8	144,427	64.2	31.5	14.8	3.1	283.6	3.9
1997	234,160	2.8	148,236	63.3	30.2	14.6	2.9	283.1	0.9
1998......	246,128	5.1	160,305	65.1	30.3	14.9	2.8	293.9	3.8
1999......	267,886	8.8	172,384	64.3	31.2	15.7	2.9	314.8	7.1
2000......	285,874	6.7	182,592	63.9	27.4	16.0	2.9	326.8	3.8
2001......	318,542	11.4	203,920	64.0	28.4	17.1	3.1	354.9	8.6
2002......	352,895	10.8	227,373	64.4	29.5	17.5	3.3	387.4	9.2
2003......	388,542	10.1	246,570	63.5	30.5	18.0	3.5	416.2	7.4
2004......	407,512	4.9	262,177	64.3	30.9	17.8	3.5	424.3	1.9
2005......	428,018	5.0	273,898	64.0	30.8	17.3	3.4	428.0	0.9
2006......	434,099	1.4	272,585	62.8	29.7	16.3	3.3	417.3	–2.5
2007......	443,797	2.2	284,362	64.1	28.4	16.3	3.2	412.4	–1.2
2008......	461,317	3.9	300,820	65.2	27.4	15.5	3.2	411.0	–0.3
2009......	537,991	16.6	356,692	66.3	33.1	15.3	3.8	476.6	16.0
2010	608,390	13.1	384,480	63.2	37.5	17.6	4.2	527.1	10.6
2011, est ..	625,211	2.8	392,506	62.8	(NA)	16.4	4.1	532.7	1.1

NA Not available. [1] Average annual percent change from prior year shown. For explanation, see Guide to Tabular Presentation. For 1990, change from 1989. [2] Expenditures from own sources as defined in the national income and product accounts.
Source: U.S. Office of Management and Budget, *Budget of the United States Government, Historical Tables*, annual. See also <http://www.whitehouse.gov/omb/budget>.

Table 432. Total Outlays for Grants to State and Local Governments—Selected Agencies and Programs: 1990 to 2011

[In millions of dollars (135,325 represents $135,325,000,000). For year ending Sept. 30. Includes trust funds]

Program	1990	2000	2005	2007	2008	2009	2010	2011, est.
Total outlays for grants	135,325	285,874	428,018	443,797	461,317	537,991	608,390	625,211
Energy.	461	433	636	667	524	999	2,656	5,728
Natural resources and environment	3,745	4,595	5,858	6,047	5,902	6,285	9,132	9,093
Environmental Protection Agency [1]	2,874	3,490	3,734	4,016	3,854	3,580	6,883	6,463
Agriculture	1,285	724	933	803	862	937	843	965
Transportation	19,174	32,222	43,370	47,945	51,216	55,438	60,981	61,095
Grants for airports [1]	1,220	1,624	3,530	3,874	3,808	3,759	3,156	3,299
Federal-aid highways [2]	13,854	24,711	30,915	33,222	35,429	36,049	30,385	35,036
Urban mass transportation [1]	3,728	5,262	8,114	8,984	9,847	11,182	12,939	13,235
Community and regional development	4,965	8,665	20,167	20,653	19,221	17,368	18,818	18,637
Rural community advance program.	139	479	814	760	5	–	–	–
Community development fund	2,818	4,955	4,985	10,867	8,935	6,408	7,043	8,056
Homeland Security	1,184	2,439	13,541	8,267	8,630	9,068	8,393	5,931
State and local programs.	–	–	2,116	2,385	2,870	2,529	3,247	1,992
Firefighter assistance grants	–	–	1,185	499	–	–	–	–
Operations, planning, and support	11	192	132	–	–	–	–	–
Mitigation grants	–	13	39	32	33	11	–	–
Disaster relief.	1,173	2,234	10,069	5,351	5,724	6,525	5,141	3,934
Education, training, employment, social services	21,780	36,672	57,247	58,077	58,904	73,986	97,586	101,455
Education for the disadvantaged [3]	4,437	8,511	14,539	14,409	14,799	15,797	19,515	23,661
School improvement programs [3].	1,080	2,394	6,569	5,299	5,208	5,247	5,184	5,456
Special education	1,485	4,696	10,661	11,585	12,078	12,536	17,075	17,359
Social services-block grant.	2,749	1,827	1,822	1,956	1,843	1,854	2,035	2,011
Children and family services programs . . .	2,618	5,843	8,490	8,496	8,633	8,793	10,473	10,990
Training and employment services	3,042	2,957	3,372	3,006	3,052	3,768	4,592	4,053
Health	43,890	124,843	197,848	208,311	218,025	268,320	290,168	295,535
Substance abuse and mental health services [3].	1,241	1,931	3,203	3,179	2,847	2,888	2,846	2,964
Grants to states for Medicaid [3].	41,103	117,921	181,720	190,624	201,426	250,924	272,771	276,249
State children's health insurance fund [3]. . .	–	1,220	5,129	6,000	6,900	7,547	7,887	9,069
Income security	36,768	68,653	90,885	90,971	96,102	103,169	115,156	116,479
SNAP (formerly Food Stamp Program) [3] . . .	2,130	3,508	4,385	4,602	4,935	5,624	5,739	6,105
Child nutrition programs [3]	4,871	9,060	11,726	12,871	13,761	15,083	16,259	18,451
Temporary assistance for needy families [3]. .	–	15,464	17,357	16,876	17,532	17,861	17,513	17,048
Veterans benefits and services [3]	134	434	552	639	695	809	836	980
Administration of justice.	574	5,263	4,784	4,603	4,201	4,810	5,086	5,576

– Represents zero. [1] Grants include trust funds. [2] Trust funds. [3] Includes grants for payments to individuals.

Source: U.S. Office of Management and Budget, *Budget of the United States Government, Historical Tables*, annual. See also <http://www.whitehouse.gov/omb/budget>.

Table 433. Federal Aid to State and Local Governments by State: 2005 to 2009

[In millions of dollars (403,660 represents $403,660,000,000). For fiscal year ending September 30]

State	2005	2007	2008	2009	State	2005	2007	2008	2009
U.S.	403,660	439,794	469,773	552,108	MO.	7,407	7,955	8,273	10,293
AL	6,306	6,869	6,994	7,610	MT	2,021	1,835	2,109	2,566
AK	2,671	2,431	2,604	3,624	NE	2,256	2,328	2,439	2,826
AZ	7,965	8,672	9,940	12,997	NV	2,213	2,320	2,450	3,143
AR	4,179	4,474	4,733	5,598	NH	1,483	1,626	1,692	1,986
CA	46,029	49,976	53,818	61,971	NJ	10,479	11,929	11,580	13,515
CO	4,538	4,900	5,321	6,333	NM	4,097	4,347	5,381	6,635
CT	4,539	4,963	5,279	6,759	NY	43,438	43,297	44,454	52,183
DE	1,142	1,225	1,363	1,679	NC	11,568	12,448	12,906	15,308
DC	3,450	2,137	11,946	9,659	ND	1,394	1,281	1,402	1,806
FL	19,046	20,033	20,659	22,686	OH	13,726	15,731	15,230	19,115
GA	8,914	10,465	10,675	12,953	OK	4,935	5,516	5,922	7,828
HI	1,731	1,971	2,120	2,560	OR	4,808	5,003	5,498	6,807
ID	1,814	2,031	2,688	2,458	PA	18,103	18,981	18,832	21,796
IL	14,616	16,141	16,267	20,941	RI	1,937	2,105	2,037	2,310
IN	6,483	7,258	8,272	10,194	SC	5,326	5,863	6,035	6,863
IA	3,594	3,688	4,014	5,033	SD	1,336	1,280	1,473	2,068
KS	2,872	3,415	3,514	3,965	TN	9,083	9,031	9,201	10,210
KY	5,779	6,370	6,867	8,245	TX	25,622	28,104	30,580	35,330
LA	7,148	13,278	12,457	11,534	UT	2,633	2,845	3,160	3,942
ME	2,623	2,546	2,695	3,399	VT	1,213	1,546	1,441	1,671
MD.	6,800	7,372	7,473	9,405	VA	6,330	7,173	7,724	8,970
MA	9,989	11,224	11,402	15,200	WA	7,681	8,050	8,668	10,631
MI	12,113	12,822	13,587	16,580	WV	3,482	3,571	3,557	4,031
MN	5,878	7,001	7,533	9,304	WI	6,563	6,719	7,000	9,556
MS	5,168	8,239	7,484	7,642	WY	2,243	1,898	2,334	2,214

Source: U.S. Census Bureau, Federal Aid to States, <http://www.census.gov/prod/2010pubs/fas-09.pdf\>.

Table 434. Federal Aid to State and Local Governments—Selected Programs by State: 2009

[In millions of dollars (552,108 represents 552,108,000,000). For fiscal year ending September 30. Negative amounts (–) are refunds (from the recipients) of advances from a prior year, or represent reductions in the amount of funds originally obligated to the recipients for the particular program or program category during the fiscal year]

State and Island Areas	Federal aid total [1]	Department of Agriculture					Department of Education				
		Total	Food and Nutrition Service			Other	Total	Special education pro- grams	Office of Elementary and Secondary Education		Other
			Child nutri- tion pro- grams	Supple- mental Nutrition Assis- tance Program (SNAP)[2]	Special supple- mental food program (WIC)				No Child Left Behind Act	Title 1 pro- grams	
United States, total ..	552,108	30,775	14,932	5,356	6,445	4,042	45,168	10,869	4,794	12,452	17,052
Alabama	7,610	489	269	46	103	71	620	183	87	227	123
Alaska	3,624	140	42	12	24	62	180	–	4	–	176
Arizona	12,997	624	325	55	156	88	958	212	106	289	351
Arkansas	5,598	348	190	32	69	58	478	123	66	161	129
California	61,971	3,808	1,881	559	1,031	337	5,666	1,496	774	1,898	1,499
Colorado	6,333	345	153	44	69	79	816	169	65	137	445
Connecticut	6,759	204	110	28	46	21	389	143	46	125	75
Delaware	1,679	98	46	21	15	16	134	36	22	37	38
District of Columbia	9,659	75	32	19	15	9	132	17	25	35	55
Florida	22,686	1,418	831	87	361	139	2,201	679	256	703	563
Georgia	12,953	1,108	641	75	274	119	734	4	6	–	725
Hawaii	2,560	124	50	18	33	23	280	69	21	48	141
Idaho	2,458	177	70	13	30	63	186	53	27	44	61
Illinois	20,941	1,012	554	130	227	101	2,990	486	206	680	1,618
Indiana	10,194	535	283	84	99	69	1,350	300	72	277	700
Iowa	5,033	275	131	29	50	64	519	150	43	81	245
Kansas.	3,965	276	148	16	49	63	292	13	4	–	275
Kentucky	8,245	479	253	49	96	82	656	172	84	216	184
Louisiana	11,534	617	320	89	121	88	65	1	7	–	57
Maine.	3,399	109	50	15	19	24	258	62	30	51	114
Maryland	9,405	391	192	55	98	47	801	216	79	184	323
Massachusetts.	15,200	412	229	53	88	42	1,201	296	89	242	573
Michigan	16,580	827	392	139	173	124	1,882	427	173	494	788
Minnesota	9,304	474	221	79	93	81	552	177	74	127	174
Mississippi	7,642	453	244	37	90	82	498	126	73	181	117
Missouri	10,293	522	277	69	84	92	260	2	9	–	249
Montana	2,566	131	43	16	14	58	242	43	32	45	122
Nebraska.	2,826	185	95	17	32	41	250	75	36	51	88
Nevada	3,143	162	84	16	40	22	403	68	31	88	216
New Hampshire	1,986	69	29	8	15	16	173	48	29	38	57
New Jersey	13,515	559	297	98	118	46	1,111	313	86	208	504
New Mexico.	6,635	333	165	41	52	75	523	97	47	115	263
New York	52,183	1,877	943	370	421	143	3,008	759	414	1,143	693
North Carolina	15,308	886	478	90	191	127	1,195	384	114	370	327
North Dakota	1,806	91	32	10	12	37	161	31	26	34	69
Ohio.	19,115	917	463	163	185	107	240	3	10	–	227
Oklahoma	7,828	479	241	59	95	84	698	225	66	190	217
Oregon.	6,807	509	159	90	75	185	669	155	59	142	313
Pennsylvania	21,796	892	438	162	185	107	1,427	440	183	614	189
Rhode Island	2,310	79	40	10	18	11	72	2	–	–	70
South Carolina.	6,863	442	258	23	101	60	640	193	86	192	168
South Dakota	2,068	108	42	15	16	35	157	1	3	–	153
Tennessee	10,210	580	339	59	102	80	884	244	89	239	312
Texas	35,330	2,692	1,685	211	582	215	3,577	1,028	442	1,306	801
Utah	3,942	243	113	29	44	56	568	108	37	67	356
Vermont.	1,671	81	23	26	13	19	138	28	27	33	50
Virginia	8,970	466	214	91	91	69	872	290	91	208	282
Washington	10,631	524	238	54	131	101	1,174	223	84	196	671
West Virginia	4,031	207	93	25	40	50	281	82	46	101	52
Wisconsin	9,556	419	210	50	86	73	1,331	237	97	214	783
Wyoming	2,214	58	21	7	9	22	137	29	28	34	47
Island Areas:											
American Samoa.	180	35	19	5	8	3	34	8	1	–	26
Micronesia.	98	–	–	–	–	–	4	4	–	–	–
Guam.	342	22	8	2	9	4	40	16	–	–	24
Marshall Islands.	136	–	–	–	–	–	2	2	–	–	–
Northern Marianas . . .	128	21	6	10	4	1	19	5	–	–	14
Palau	23	–	–	–	–	–	4	1	–	–	3
Puerto Rico	6,135	2,221	202	1,734	235	51	1,031	114	180	586	152
Virgin Islands	302	49	21	14	8	6	7	–	–	–	7
Undistributed amounts. .	2,832	93	–	–	–	93	–	–	–	–	–

See footnotes at end of table.

U.S. Census Bureau, Statistical Abstract of the United States: 2012

Table 434. Federal Aid to State and Local Governments—Selected Programs by State: 2009—Con.

[See headnote, page 270]

State and Island Areas	FEMA [3] total	Department of Housing and Urban Development						Department of Labor			
		Total	Community development block grants	Public housing programs			Other	State unemployment insurance and employment service Total	Work-force investment	Other	
				Low rent housing assistance	Housing certificate program	Capital program					
United States, total	6,185	47,065	6,617	28,003	1,572	3,651	7,223	9,828	4,052	3,929	1,847
Alabama	51	645	76	367	8	92	101	116	53	38	25
Alaska	8	152	21	52	2	3	73	58	33	15	10
Arizona	6	495	75	218	4	16	182	148	50	55	44
Arkansas..............	179	315	30	224	6	31	24	100	38	39	23
California..............	212	6,171	1,572	3,624	121	113	742	1,255	580	512	163
Colorado	8	457	34	330	12	22	59	119	54	43	22
Connecticut	1	862	51	612	66	52	81	130	72	36	22
Delaware	2	112	8	61	16	7	20	28	14	9	5
District of Columbia	12	3,992	74	2,033	275	755	854	175	18	11	146
Florida..............	395	1,731	217	1,133	29	76	277	338	159	135	44
Georgia..............	33	1,207	99	712	14	129	254	211	95	100	17
Hawaii	7	211	20	137	3	14	36	48	23	10	15
Idaho..............	3	93	14	51	6	1	20	54	29	12	12
Illinois..............	66	2,345	170	1,516	118	281	260	435	195	175	65
Indiana..............	125	613	77	429	12	39	56	189	74	75	40
Iowa..............	282	262	68	150	5	11	28	101	41	38	22
Kansas..............	182	210	28	129	7	17	29	67	28	27	12
Kentucky..............	95	519	50	339	6	57	67	148	47	74	28
Louisiana..............	1,641	1,083	487	415	12	66	103	142	48	81	14
Maine..............	19	229	23	142	29	8	27	54	23	16	14
Maryland	4	1,098	75	704	35	71	214	237	93	42	102
Massachusetts..............	29	2,048	120	1,525	140	87	175	208	93	86	29
Michigan..............	13	1,112	124	645	128	59	156	571	201	282	87
Minnesota	20	671	59	387	81	55	90	155	68	58	29
Mississippi..............	366	871	595	206	7	27	36	182	59	92	32
Missouri..............	107	622	76	390	14	51	90	136	39	81	16
Montana..............	19	96	15	52	1	3	25	38	14	10	15
Nebraska..............	41	161	20	100	3	13	24	36	21	9	7
Nevada..............	5	217	27	150	1	6	33	71	44	19	8
New Hampshire..............	25	190	18	131	10	10	21	34	20	10	4
New Jersey	9	1,643	103	1,122	123	137	158	227	128	70	29
New Mexico..............	12	179	23	103	3	7	43	64	24	21	20
New York..............	96	5,496	446	3,894	89	462	606	580	271	234	74
North Carolina..............	17	859	74	575	15	89	106	264	114	94	56
North Dakota..............	25	106	9	72	–	4	21	27	14	8	5
Ohio..............	62	1,636	157	1,128	29	111	211	420	141	228	51
Oklahoma	91	375	38	200	7	27	102	75	34	25	15
Oregon..............	25	382	42	266	3	15	55	167	63	67	37
Pennsylvania..............	16	1,944	238	1,133	127	200	246	371	191	124	56
Rhode Island..............	–	124	18	83	–	–	23	41	19	15	7
South Carolina..............	11	217	34	137	1	–	46	153	53	81	19
South Dakota..............	14	83	14	40	–	–	28	28	11	11	6
Tennessee..............	12	274	51	174	–	–	48	165	62	81	22
Texas..............	1,376	1,692	472	1,003	–	62	155	591	211	288	92
Utah..............	9	104	25	65	–	–	15	66	36	16	15
Vermont..............	9	67	10	46	–	–	12	26	11	9	7
Virginia..............	309	579	70	323	–	91	95	257	68	42	147
Washington	32	523	67	377	–	–	79	244	117	78	49
West Virginia..............	19	104	36	62	–	–	6	51	23	20	9
Wisconsin	48	266	55	162	–	–	49	191	91	58	42
Wyoming..............	3	26	6	11	–	–	9	24	14	6	4
Island Areas:											
American Samoa........	–	2	1	–	–	–	–	2	–	1	1
Micronesia..............	2	–	–	–	–	–	–	–	–	–	–
Guam..............	12	43	3	36	–	3	2	6	–	4	1
Marshall Islands........	–	–	–	–	–	–	–	–	–	–	–
Northern Marianas	1	4	1	2	–	–	–	2	–	1	–
Palau	–	–	–	–	–	–	–	0	–	–	–
Puerto Rico..............	20	346	119	164	2	–	60	191	28	155	8
Virgin Islands..............	2	13	2	10	–	–	2	10	3	4	3
Undistributed amounts.....	–	1,187	179	−154	–	271	–	–	–	–	–

See footnotes at end of table.

U.S. Census Bureau, Statistical Abstract of the United States: 2012

Table 434. Federal Aid to State and Local Governments—Selected Programs by State: 2009—Con.

[See headnote, page 270]

State and Island Areas	Department of Health and Human Services						Department of Transportation				Other, federal aid [4]
	Administration for Children and Families				Centers for Medi-care and Medic-aid Ser-vices						
	Total	Children & family services (Head Start)	Foster care and adop-tion assis-tance	Tempo-rary assis-tance for needy families		Other	Total	High-way trust fund	Federal Transit Admin-istration	Other	
United States, total ...	324,765	8,722	6,850	18,045	256,124	35,025	57,048	35,607	11,298	10,144	31,274
Alabama	4,304	140	52	108	3,576	428	933	725	67	142	452
Alaska	1,876	48	22	34	759	1,013	720	335	77	308	489
Arizona	9,005	182	139	267	6,855	1,562	947	605	218	124	814
Arkansas	3,369	86	54	69	2,895	264	564	419	27	118	244
California	37,740	1,067	1,587	3,936	27,888	3,262	4,472	2,494	1,459	520	2,647
Colorado	3,165	219	86	189	2,225	446	809	470	167	172	614
Connecticut	4,235	71	103	268	3,380	414	693	487	156	49	245
Delaware	935	17	6	29	777	106	235	181	26	27	135
District of Columbia	1,914	53	51	108	1,369	332	2,126	133	398	1,595	1,234
Florida	13,573	343	229	655	10,822	1,524	2,038	1,518	231	289	990
Georgia	7,508	220	129	369	6,030	761	1,610	1,265	189	156	542
Hawaii	1,355	38	36	124	1,015	142	355	214	54	87	181
Idaho	1,364	44	16	33	1,085	186	311	258	12	41	269
Illinois	10,765	344	283	595	8,374	1,169	2,496	1,370	732	394	833
Indiana	5,860	127	191	228	4,790	524	1,193	942	105	146	331
Iowa	2,621	77	67	128	2,065	284	661	453	49	160	312
Kansas	2,245	73	41	90	1,780	262	469	383	22	65	223
Kentucky	5,203	145	92	192	4,345	429	685	505	59	121	459
Louisiana	6,178	180	72	189	5,267	470	1,108	619	94	395	701
Maine	2,261	42	32	79	1,912	195	261	148	18	95	209
Maryland	5,627	115	104	270	4,128	1,010	802	497	223	83	443
Massachusetts	9,453	156	99	459	7,854	885	1,247	866	274	107	601
Michigan	9,986	307	227	669	7,766	1,018	1,453	1,100	154	199	735
Minnesota	5,984	121	81	293	4,854	635	999	563	189	247	449
Mississippi	4,237	200	19	114	3,523	382	634	430	20	184	403
Missouri	6,797	165	107	250	5,763	512	1,343	981	184	178	505
Montana	1,164	45	20	43	719	337	502	387	19	96	375
Nebraska	1,557	59	53	64	1,127	253	383	275	16	92	214
Nevada	1,362	39	51	70	960	243	539	374	93	73	383
New Hampshire	1,021	24	23	56	789	129	252	178	16	58	223
New Jersey	7,816	157	156	404	6,260	838	1,581	791	683	108	570
New Mexico	4,195	83	36	152	3,051	873	407	277	59	70	922
New York	35,467	586	672	2,595	28,922	2,691	3,976	1,779	2,003	193	1,683
North Carolina	10,129	274	122	363	8,480	891	1,411	1,117	105	190	547
North Dakota	708	36	16	30	436	190	323	245	14	64	365
Ohio	13,491	322	405	985	10,641	1,137	1,600	1,181	246	173	749
Oklahoma	4,581	140	71	193	3,093	1,083	1,044	798	39	206	485
Oregon	3,731	120	132	181	2,832	465	814	416	248	150	510
Pennsylvania	14,019	298	183	669	11,719	1,150	2,223	1,478	515	230	905
Rhode Island	1,554	27	23	99	1,259	146	268	189	44	35	172
South Carolina	4,460	108	56	111	3,788	398	568	476	35	56	372
South Dakota	1,008	50	10	21	567	359	343	226	20	97	327
Tennessee	6,687	160	83	247	5,640	556	938	634	85	218	671
Texas	20,208	679	340	648	16,621	1,921	3,601	2,503	618	481	1,592
Utah	1,866	62	28	90	1,424	263	694	317	281	96	391
Vermont	1,008	24	20	48	814	102	220	137	21	62	121
Virginia	4,714	140	94	208	3,701	570	1,151	845	190	117	623
Washington	6,121	181	157	459	4,464	860	1,240	640	347	253	773
West Virginia	2,521	70	59	122	2,052	217	583	475	26	81	266
Wisconsin	5,814	143	107	322	4,599	644	1,040	806	77	158	447
Wyoming	491	21	6	28	348	88	331	226	9	96	1,142
Island Areas:											
American Samoa	30	6	–	–	14	10	18	8	–	9	58
Micronesia	3	–	–	–	–	3	–	–	–	–	89
Guam	52	6	–	2	20	24	65	26	–	39	102
Marshall Islands	2	–	–	–	–	2	57	–	–	57	75
Northern Marianas	27	1	–	–	22	4	10	–	–	10	45
Palau	4	2	–	–	–	3	–	–	–	–	15
Puerto Rico	1,339	262	1	86	652	338	224	127	57	40	762
Virgin Islands	47	12	–	4	12	19	14	9	1	5	160
Undistributed amounts...	9	4	–	–	–	5	1,460	704	228	529	82

– Represents or rounds to zero. [1] Total includes programs, not shown separately. [2] For Puerto Rico, amount shown is for nutritional assistance grant program, all other amounts are grant payments for food stamp administration. [3] FEMA = Federal Emergency Management Agency. FEMA is part of the U.S. Department of Homeland Security. [4] Represents aid for other programs, not shown.

Source: U.S. Census Bureau, Federal Aid to States for Fiscal Year 2009. See also <http://www.census.gov/prod/2009pubs/fas-09.pdf>.

Table 435. State and Local Governments—Summary of Finances: 1990 to 2008

[In millions of dollars (1,032,115 represents $1,032,115,000,000) except as indicated. For fiscal year ending in year shown; see text, this section. Local government amounts are estimates subject to sampling variation; see Appendix III and source]

Item	1990	2000	2005	2006	2007	2008
Revenue [1]	**1,032,115**	**1,942,328**	**2,528,912**	**2,736,542**	**3,072,645**	**2,660,475**
From federal government	**136,802**	**291,950**	**438,432**	**452,233**	**467,949**	**481,380**
Public welfare	59,961	148,549	225,691	225,605	237,220	247,325
Highways	14,368	24,414	33,672	34,559	36,295	37,187
Education	23,233	45,873	74,136	79,397	79,514	80,647
Health and hospitals	5,904	15,611	22,725	23,819	24,555	25,976
Housing and community development	9,655	17,690	28,018	29,121	32,766	34,952
Other and unallocable	23,683	39,812	54,191	59,732	57,599	55,293
From state and local sources	**895,313**	**1,650,379**	**2,090,479**	**2,284,309**	**2,604,695**	**2,179,095**
General, net intergovernmental	712,700	1,249,373	1,588,292	1,733,785	1,867,945	1,944,398
Taxes	501,619	872,351	1,099,200	1,195,254	1,283,283	1,330,412
Property	155,613	249,178	335,981	359,109	389,573	409,686
Sales and gross receipts	177,885	309,290	384,383	412,114	439,586	448,689
Individual income	105,640	211,661	242,273	268,599	289,827	304,627
Corporation net income	23,566	36,059	43,138	52,931	60,592	57,810
Other	38,915	66,164	93,425	102,500	103,705	109,601
Charges and miscellaneous	211,081	377,022	489,093	538,531	584,662	613,987
Utility and liquor stores	58,642	89,546	119,607	131,642	141,234	146,385
Water supply system	17,674	30,515	37,377	40,274	43,652	45,418
Electric power system	29,268	42,436	59,157	65,387	70,494	72,669
Gas supply system	5,216	8,049	6,937	8,724	8,698	8,930
Transit system	3,043	3,954	10,146	10,881	11,568	12,125
Liquor stores	3,441	4,592	5,990	6,377	6,823	7,243
Insurance trust revenue [2]	123,970	311,460	382,580	418,881	595,516	88,312
Employee retirement	94,268	273,881	316,576	352,521	532,154	26,273
Unemployment compensation	18,441	23,366	38,362	35,367	36,989	34,186
Direct expenditure	**972,695**	**1,742,914**	**2,368,692**	**2,500,583**	**2,661,210**	**2,834,075**
By function:						
Direct general expenditure [2]	831,573	1,502,768	2,012,422	2,121,946	2,258,229	2,400,204
Education [2]	288,148	521,612	689,057	727,967	774,373	826,063
Elementary and secondary	202,009	365,181	473,406	500,528	534,905	565,631
Higher education	73,418	134,352	182,146	191,758	204,706	223,294
Highways	61,057	101,336	124,602	135,412	144,713	153,515
Public welfare	107,287	233,350	362,932	370,325	384,769	404,624
Health	24,223	51,366	66,971	71,110	74,196	79,704
Hospitals	50,412	75,976	103,404	110,455	118,876	128,853
Police protection	30,577	56,798	74,727	79,066	84,088	89,676
Fire protection	13,186	23,102	31,439	34,167	36,828	39,683
Natural resources	12,330	20,235	25,057	25,482	28,717	29,917
Sanitation and sewerage	28,453	45,261	58,069	61,900	67,016	70,436
Housing and community development	15,479	26,590	39,969	41,980	45,937	50,974
Parks and recreation	14,326	25,038	31,941	34,769	37,526	40,646
Financial administration	16,217	29,300	36,519	37,441	39,631	40,995
Interest on general debt [3]	49,739	69,814	81,119	85,660	93,586	100,055
Utility and liquor stores [3]	77,801	114,916	160,682	174,679	189,330	199,287
Water supply system	22,101	35,789	45,799	47,752	54,331	55,215
Electric power system	30,997	39,719	58,612	66,308	69,736	76,667
Gas supply system	2,989	3,724	7,075	9,064	12,073	10,527
Transit system	18,788	31,883	44,310	46,327	47,587	50,944
Liquor stores	2,926	3,801	4,885	5,228	5,603	5,934
Insurance trust expenditure [2]	63,321	125,230	195,588	203,958	213,652	234,584
Employee retirement	38,355	95,679	145,796	156,180	166,975	180,058
Unemployment compensation	16,499	18,648	29,849	28,097	28,934	35,568
By character and object:						
Current operation	700,131	1,288,746	1,764,453	1,863,023	1,977,229	2,095,772
Capital outlay	123,102	217,063	277,200	295,368	324,467	348,827
Construction	89,144	161,694	216,254	229,529	253,858	268,298
Equipment, land, and existing structures	33,958	55,369	60,947	65,839	70,608	80,529
Assistance and subsidies	27,227	31,375	39,469	41,035	39,802	41,961
Interest on debt (general and utility)	58,914	80,499	91,981	97,198	106,061	112,931
Insurance benefits and repayments	63,321	125,230	195,588	203,958	213,652	234,584
Expenditure for salaries and wages [4]	*340,654*	*548,796*	*693,146*	*721,255*	*761,991*	*800,892*
Debt outstanding, year end	**858,006**	**1,451,815**	**2,085,597**	**2,200,892**	**2,411,298**	**2,550,934**
Long-term	838,700	1,427,524	2,054,838	2,167,684	2,379,359	2,506,350
Short-term	19,306	24,291	30,759	33,208	31,939	44,585
Long-term debt:						
Issued	108,468	184,831	321,960	339,333	386,465	373,615
Retired	64,831	121,897	223,862	227,682	227,545	244,740

[1] Aggregates exclude duplicative transactions between state and local governments; see source. [2] Includes amounts not shown separately. [3] Interest on utility debt included in "utility and liquor stores expenditure." For total interest on debt, see "Interest on debt (general and utility)." [4] Included in items above.

Source: U.S. Census Bureau; Federal, State and Local Governments, "State and Local Government Finances," June 2011. See also <http://www.census.gov/govs/>.

Table 436. State and Local Governments—Revenue and Expenditures by Function: 2007 and 2008

[In millions of dollars (3,072.645 represents $3,072,645,000,000) For fiscal year ending in year shown; see text, this section. Local government amounts are estimates subject to sampling variation; see Appendix III and source]

Item	2007			2008		
	Total	State	Local	Total	State	Local
Revenue [1]	**3,072,645**	**2,000,366**	**1,539,014**	**2,660,475**	**1,619,128**	**1,530,814**
Intergovernmental revenue [1]	467,949	430,278	504,407	481,380	446,109	524,738
Total revenue from own sources [1]	2,604,695	1,570,088	1,034,607	2,179,095	1,173,019	1,006,076
General revenue from own sources	1,867,945	1,027,524	840,421	1,944,398	1,067,795	876,604
Taxes [2]	1,283,283	757,471	525,813	1,330,412	781,647	548,765
Property	389,573	12,621	376,952	409,686	12,691	396,995
Individual income	289,827	265,863	23,964	304,627	278,373	26,255
Corporation income	60,592	52,915	7,677	57,810	50,759	7,051
Sales and gross receipts	439,586	352,706	86,880	448,689	358,522	90,166
General sales	299,650	238,304	61,346	304,435	241,008	63,427
Selective sales [2]	139,936	114,402	25,534	144,254	117,515	26,739
Motor fuel	37,904	36,543	1,361	37,902	36,477	1,425
Alcoholic beverages	5,620	5,166	453	5,763	5,293	471
Tobacco products	15,834	15,299	535	16,576	16,068	508
Public utilities	27,105	14,333	12,772	28,130	14,794	13,336
Motor vehicle and operators' licenses	23,195	21,613	1,582	23,515	21,882	1,633
Death and gift	5,111	4,924	187	5,345	5,101	244
Charges and miscellaneous [2]	584,662	270,054	314,608	613,987	286,148	327,839
Current charges [2]	351,824	141,573	210,251	373,669	151,002	222,667
Education [2]	103,736	80,180	23,557	110,512	85,551	24,960
School lunch sales	6,920	22	6,898	7,000	31	6,969
Higher education	88,433	79,060	9,373	94,665	84,417	10,248
Natural resources	4,047	2,480	1,567	4,009	2,543	1,465
Hospitals	91,432	33,838	57,594	97,270	36,268	61,001
Sewerage	36,157	44	36,113	38,064	45	38,019
Solid waste management	14,458	432	14,025	15,269	457	14,812
Parks and recreation	8,812	1,495	7,317	9,620	1,593	8,027
Housing and community development	5,435	675	4,760	5,646	676	4,970
Airports	16,583	1,216	15,366	17,781	1,326	16,455
Sea and inland port facilities	3,867	1,137	2,730	4,139	1,221	2,917
Highways	10,640	6,086	4,554	11,167	6,419	4,748
Interest earnings	92,170	47,199	44,971	93,370	47,298	46,072
Special assessments	8,157	889	7,268	7,928	967	6,961
Sale of property	4,590	1,142	3,448	4,440	1,110	3,329
Utility and liquor store revenue	141,234	22,535	118,699	146,385	22,650	123,734
Insurance trust revenue	595,516	520,029	75,487	88,312	82,574	5,738
Expenditure [1]	**2,665,881**	**1,635,747**	**1,499,268**	**2,838,836**	**1,733,862**	**1,593,088**
Intergovernmental expenditure [1]	4,671	459,605	14,200	4,761	477,085	15,790
Direct expenditure [1]	2,661,210	1,176,142	1,485,068	2,834,075	1,256,777	1,577,298
General expenditure [2]	2,258,229	964,590	1,293,639	2,400,204	1,024,666	1,375,539
Education [2]	774,373	213,868	560,505	826,063	232,212	593,851
Elementary and secondary education	534,905	8,305	526,600	565,631	8,243	557,388
Higher education	204,706	170,801	33,905	223,294	186,830	36,463
Public welfare	384,769	336,510	48,259	404,624	354,048	50,576
Hospitals	118,876	47,953	70,923	128,853	51,938	76,916
Health	74,196	37,321	36,875	79,704	40,033	39,671
Highways	144,713	88,333	56,380	153,515	90,645	62,870
Police protection	84,088	11,383	72,706	89,676	12,034	77,642
Fire protection	36,828	-	36,828	39,683	-	39,683
Corrections	68,092	44,021	24,071	72,904	47,239	25,665
Natural resources	28,717	19,752	8,964	29,917	19,942	9,974
Sewerage	44,197	1,364	42,834	46,679	1,273	45,406
Solid waste management	22,819	2,226	20,593	23,757	2,439	21,318
Housing and community development	45,937	8,712	37,225	50,974	10,857	40,118
Governmental administration	119,396	49,236	70,160	126,997	52,102	74,895
Parks and recreation	37,526	5,181	32,345	40,646	5,510	35,136
Interest on general debt	93,586	41,594	51,992	100,055	44,719	55,336
Utility	183,727	24,530	159,196	193,353	26,073	167,280
Liquor store expenditure	5,603	4,664	939	5,934	4,945	989
Insurance trust expenditure	213,652	182,358	31,294	234,584	201,094	33,490
By character and object:						
Current operation	1,977,229	809,535	1,167,694	2,095,772	863,372	1,232,399
Capital outlay	324,467	110,044	214,423	348,827	113,021	235,806
Construction	253,858	90,788	163,070	268,298	92,068	176,230
Equipment, land, and existing structures	70,608	19,256	51,352	80,529	20,953	59,576
Assistance and subsidies	39,802	30,621	9,181	41,961	32,573	9,388
Interest on debt (general and utility)	106,061	43,584	62,476	112,931	46,717	66,214
Insurance benefits and repayments	213,652	182,358	31,294	234,584	201,094	33,490
Expenditure for salaries and wages [3]	*761,991*	*217,018*	*544,973*	*800,892*	*229,819*	*571,073*

- Represents or rounds to zero. [1] Aggregates exclude duplicative transactions between levels of government; see source. [2] Includes other items, not shown separately. [3] Included in items shown above.

Source: U.S. Census Bureau, Federal, State, and Local Governments, "State and Local Government Finances: 2007–08," June 2011. See also <http://www.census.gov/govs/\>.

Table 437. State and Local Governments—Capital Outlays: 1990 to 2008

[In millions of dollars (123,102 represents $123,102,000,000), except percent. For fiscal year ending in year shown; see text, this section. Local government amounts are subject to sampling variation; see Appendix III and source]

Level and function	1990	2000	2003	2004	2005	2006	2007	2008
State & local governments: Total	**123,102**	**217,063**	**263,198**	**269,976**	**277,200**	**295,368**	**324,467**	**348,827**
Percent of direct expenditure.	12.7	12.5	12.2	11.9	11.7	11.8	12.2	12.3
By function:								
Education [1]	25,997	60,968	70,813	74,597	77,779	82,505	91,466	97,855
Elementary and secondary	18,057	45,150	51,118	52,977	54,509	59,256	65,467	70,283
Higher education	7,441	15,257	19,044	21,121	22,782	22,798	25,356	26,953
Highways	33,867	56,439	65,523	65,964	69,642	76,371	83,289	88,218
Health and hospitals	3,848	5,502	7,158	7,241	7,711	8,538	9,737	11,217
Natural resources	2,545	4,347	4,244	4,657	4,543	4,473	6,372	6,755
Housing and community development. . .	3,997	6,184	7,660	7,578	7,880	8,130	7,991	9,191
Air transportation	3,434	6,717	9,066	9,731	9,326	9,064	9,851	10,386
Sea and inland port facilities [2]	924	1,618	3,721	1,798	1,598	1,850	2,140	2,149
Sewerage.	8,356	10,093	12,467	14,068	14,170	15,336	17,683	18,777
Parks and recreation	3,877	6,916	9,224	7,866	8,151	9,267	10,085	11,672
Utilities.	16,601	24,847	34,538	37,432	34,879	36,795	38,230	41,348
Water.	6,873	10,542	13,536	13,651	14,402	14,356	16,960	16,295
Electric.	3,976	4,177	6,438	7,173	6,055	7,793	7,981	11,637
Gas	310	400	422	582	544	520	508	520
Transit	5,443	9,728	14,142	16,026	13,879	14,126	12,781	12,897
Other	19,657	33,431	38,784	39,044	41,520	43,039	47,624	51,260
State governments: Total	**45,524**	**76,233**	**91,943**	**90,950**	**94,181**	**101,432**	**110,044**	**113,021**
Percent of direct expenditure.	11.5	10.1	9.4	8.9	8.8	9.0	9.4	9.0
By function:								
Education [1]	7,253	14,077	17,727	19,632	20,632	20,623	23,752	24,705
Elementary and secondary	388	521	643	716	442	580	1,734	1,592
Higher education	6,366	12,995	16,433	18,417	19,702	19,593	21,375	22,494
Highways	24,850	41,651	48,719	48,566	51,578	57,025	61,218	61,705
Health and hospitals	1,531	2,228	2,930	2,763	3,278	3,469	3,972	4,500
Natural resources	1,593	2,758	2,788	2,957	2,670	2,588	3,324	3,024
Housing and community development. . .	119	860	774	222	338	196	505	321
Air transportation.	339	561	846	795	615	519	655	764
Sea and inland port facilities [2]	202	310	410	388	367	493	573	524
Sewerage.	333	403	405	881	486	650	740	601
Parks and recreation	601	1,044	1,098	945	931	1,146	1,176	1,192
Utilities.	2,605	4,232	7,084	5,211	4,319	5,907	4,859	5,936
Water.	20	197	174	321	83	83	89	57
Electric.	464	296	964	1,089	685	1,826	983	2,738
Gas	–	–	–	–	–	–	–	–
Transit	2,121	3,740	5,945	3,800	3,550	3,998	3,788	3,140
Other	6,098	8,108	9,163	8,589	8,967	8,817	9,272	9,749
Local governments: Total	**77,578**	**140,830**	**171,255**	**179,026**	**183,020**	**193,936**	**214,423**	**235,806**
Percent of direct expenditure.	13.5	14.3	14.5	14.4	14.1	14.1	14.4	15.0
By function:								
Education [1]	18,744	46,890	53,087	54,965	57,147	61,882	67,714	73,150
Elementary and secondary	17,669	44,629	50,475	52,261	54,068	58,677	63,733	68,691
Higher education	1,076	2,261	2,612	2,704	3,079	3,205	3,981	4,459
Highways	9,017	14,789	16,804	17,398	18,064	19,346	22,071	26,513
Health and hospitals	2,316	3,274	4,228	4,478	4,433	5,069	5,765	6,717
Natural resources	952	1,589	1,456	1,699	1,873	1,885	3,048	3,731
Housing and community development. . .	3,878	5,324	6,886	7,356	7,542	7,934	7,486	8,871
Air transportation.	3,095	6,156	8,221	8,936	8,712	8,545	9,196	9,622
Sea and inland port facilities [2]	722	1,308	3,310	1,410	1,231	1,357	1,567	1,626
Sewerage.	8,023	9,690	12,062	13,186	13,684	14,687	16,943	18,176
Parks and recreation	3,276	5,872	8,126	6,921	7,221	8,122	8,909	10,479
Utilities.	13,996	20,615	27,455	32,221	30,560	30,888	33,371	35,412
Other	13,559	25,323	29,621	30,454	32,553	34,222	38,352	41,510

– Represents or rounds to zero. [1] Includes other education, not shown separately. [2] Includes terminals.

Source: U.S Census Bureau, "State and Local Government Finances, 2007–08," June 2011, and unpublished data. See also <http://www.census.gov/govs/>.

Table 438. State and Local Governments—Expenditures for Public Works: 2000 to 2008

[In millions of dollars (230,569 represents $230,569,000,000), except percent. Public works include expenditures for current operations and capital outlays on highways, airports, Sea and inland port facilities, sewerage, solid waste management, water supply, and mass transit systems. Represents direct expenditures excluding intergovernmental grants]

Item	Total	Highways	Air transportation	Sea and inland port facilities	Sewerage	Solid waste management	Water supply	Mass transit
2000, Total.	**230,569**	**101,336**	**13,160**	**3,141**	**28,052**	**17,208**	**35,789**	**31,883**
State	74,974	61,942	1,106	863	955	2,347	354	7,407
Local	155,595	39,394	12,054	2,277	27,098	14,861	35,435	24,476
Capital expenditures (percent) . . .	41.9	55.7	51.0	51.5	36.0	8.9	29.5	30.5
2005, Total.	**294,638**	**124,602**	**17,962**	**3,896**	**36,599**	**21,469**	**45,799**	**44,310**
State	92,823	76,575	1,406	1,156	1,109	3,184	319	9,074
Local	201,815	48,026	16,556	2,740	35,491	18,285	45,480	35,237
Capital expenditures (percent) . . .	42.4	55.9	51.9	41.0	38.7	9.3	31.4	31.3
2008, Total.	**356,314**	**153,515**	**21,264**	**4,940**	**46,679**	**23,757**	**55,215**	**50,944**
State	108,226	90,645	1,758	1,492	1,273	2,439	354	10,267
Local	248,087	62,870	19,507	3,448	45,406	21,318	54,860	40,677
Capital expenditures (percent) . . .	42.4	57.5	48.8	43.5	40.2	10.0	29.5	25.3

Source: U.S. Census Bureau, Federal, State, and Local Governments, Finance, "State and Local Government Finances, 2007–08," June 2011, and unpublished data. See also <http://www.census.gov/govs>.

Table 439. State and Local Governments—Indebtedness: 1990 to 2008

[In billions of dollars (858.0 represents $858,000,000,000). For fiscal year ending in year shown; see text, this section. Local government amounts are estimates subject to sampling variation; see Appendix III and source]

Item	Debt outstanding						Long-term		
	Total	Cash and security holdings	Long-term		All other	Short-term	Net long-term [1]	Debt issued	Debt retired
			Total	Public debt for private purposes					
1990: Total......	858.0	1,490.8	838.7	294.1	544.6	19.3	474.4	108.5	64.8
State	318.3	963.3	315.5	154.4	161.1	2.8	125.5	43.5	22.9
Local	539.8	527.5	523.2	139.7	383.5	16.5	348.9	65.0	42.0
1995: Total......	1,115.4	2,058.5	1,088.3	300.6	787.7	27.0	697.3	129.3	95.1
State	427.2	1,393.9	421.1	176.8	244.4	6.1	205.3	52.6	37.5
Local	688.1	664.6	667.2	123.9	543.3	20.9	491.9	76.8	57.6
1997: Total......	1,224.5	2,546.9	1,207.9	329.0	878.9	16.6	797.7	151.3	109.3
State	456.7	1,785.1	454.5	193.7	260.8	2.1	222.6	54.4	41.1
Local	767.9	761.8	753.4	135.3	618.1	14.5	575.1	96.8	68.2
1998: Total......	1,283.6	2,890.2	1,266.3	335.8	930.5	17.3	842.6	204.4	144.6
State	483.1	2,058.6	480.9	202.3	278.7	2.2	237.2	83.4	58.1
Local	800.4	831.6	785.4	133.6	651.8	15.1	605.4	120.9	86.5
1999: Total......	1,369.3	3,168.5	1,351.4	351.1	1,000.3	17.8	907.3	229.4	153.1
State	510.5	2,265.9	507.8	213.9	293.9	2.7	249.4	83.2	55.6
Local	858.8	902.5	843.6	137.2	706.4	15.2	657.9	146.2	97.5
2000: Total......	1,451.8	3,503.7	1,427.5	372.6	1,054.9	24.3	959.6	184.8	121.9
State	547.9	2,518.9	541.5	227.3	314.2	6.4	266.9	75.0	44.4
Local	903.9	984.8	886.0	145.3	740.7	17.9	692.7	109.8	77.5
2001: Total......	1,554.0	3,592.1	1,531.9	395.1	1,136.8	22.1	1,038.6	199.6	130.6
State	576.5	2,537.7	572.8	238.2	334.7	3.7	287.4	81.3	50.7
Local	977.5	1,054.3	959.1	157.0	802.1	18.5	751.2	118.3	79.9
2002: Total......	1,681.4	3,650.7	1,638.1	417.7	1,220.5	43.2	1,121.0	262.7	161.9
State	636.8	2,555.4	618.2	258.5	359.6	18.6	311.8	104.2	64.9
Local	1,044.6	1,095.3	1,020.0	159.2	860.8	24.6	809.2	158.5	97.0
2003: Total......	1,812.7	3,696.1	1,772.2	431.4	1,340.8	40.5	1,242.7	345.8	215.2
State	697.9	2,594.2	681.8	267.3	414.5	16.1	366.2	148.8	85.9
Local	1,114.7	1,101.9	1,090.4	164.1	926.3	24.3	876.5	196.9	129.3
2004: Total......	1,951.7	4,120.1	1,913.3	448.4	1,464.9	38.4	1,349.6	346.8	241.1
State	754.2	2,930.1	740.4	268.4	472.0	13.7	412.2	158.4	107.1
Local	1,197.5	1,189.9	1,172.9	180.0	992.9	24.6	937.4	188.5	134.0
2005: Total......	2,085.6	4,439.4	2,054.8	480.6	1,574.2	30.8	1,441.1	322.0	231.8
State	813.8	3,156.4	808.3	296.1	512.2	5.6	444.7	131.5	101.8
Local	1,271.8	1,283.0	1,246.5	184.5	1,062.0	25.2	996.4	190.5	130.0
2006: Total......	2,200.9	4,807.1	2,167.7	505.1	1,662.6	33.2	1,519.5	339.3	227.7
State	870.9	3,436.4	860.3	315.9	544.4	10.6	473.4	147.0	95.0
Local	1,330.0	1,370.7	1,307.4	189.1	1,118.2	22.6	1,046.0	192.4	132.7
2007: Total......	2,411.3	5,470.7	2,379.4	553.8	1,825.6	31.9	1,673.3	386.5	227.5
State	936.5	3,922.4	929.9	354.7	575.3	6.6	499.7	161.4	92.7
Local	1,474.8	1,548.3	1,449.4	199.1	1,250.3	25.4	1,173.6	225.0	134.8
2008: Total......	2,550.9	5,379.0	2,506.3	588.2	1,918.2	44.6	1,762.1	373.6	244.7
State	1,004.2	3,826.4	990.0	379.0	611.0	14.2	530.3	151.7	93.2
Local	1,546.8	1,552.5	1,516.3	209.2	1,307.1	30.4	1,231.8	222.0	151.5

[1] Net long-term debt outstanding is the amount of long-term debt held by a government for which no funds have been set aside for its repayment.

Source: U.S. Census Bureau, 1990, Government Finances, Series GF, No. 5, annual; thereafter, Federal, State, and Local Governments, Finance, "State and Local Government Finances, 2007–08," June 2011, and unpublished data. See also <http://www.census.gov/govs/>.

Table 440. New Security Issues, State and Local Governments: 1990 to 2010

[In billions of dollars (122.9 represents 122,900,000,000)]

Type of issue, issuer, or use	1990	1995	2000	2004	2005	2006	2007	2008	2009	2010
All issues, new and refunding [1]	122.9	145.7	180.4	357.9	409.6	389.5	426.2	394.5	414.3	434.5
By type of issue:										
General obligation..................	39.5	57.0	64.5	130.5	145.8	115.1	130.5	115.5	157.6	150.6
Revenue	83.3	88.7	115.9	227.4	263.8	274.4	295.7	279.0	256.7	283.9
By type of issuer:										
State	15.0	14.7	19.9	47.4	31.6	28.3	35.0	35.1	63.5	55.5
Special district of statutory authority [2]	75.9	93.5	121.2	234.2	298.6	293.4	315.3	286.2	270.8	292.9
Municipality, county, or township	32.0	37.5	39.3	76.3	79.4	67.9	75.9	73.2	80.0	86.2
Issues for new capital	97.9	102.4	154.3	228.4	223.8	262.5	275.3	217.4	265.6	284.7
By use of proceeds:										
Education..........................	17.1	24.0	38.7	65.4	71.0	70.3	70.9	56.4	61.7	66.8
Transportation	11.8	11.9	19.7	20.5	25.4	30.2	27.9	25.0	35.7	48.6
Utilities and conservation.	10.0	9.6	11.9	9.2	9.9	7.8	11.4	14.5	12.5	13.2
Industrial aid	6.6	6.6	7.1	19.1	18.6	35.0	38.1	24.9	33.2	47.8
Other purposes	31.7	30.8	47.3	80.4	60.6	72.7	82.9	66.1	94.4	89.9

[1] Par amounts of long-term issues based on date of sale. [2] Includes school districts.

Source: Board of Governors of the Federal Reserve System, *Statistical Supplement to the Federal Reserve Bulletin*, monthly. Based on data from Securities Data Company. See also <http://www.federalreserve.gov/econresdata/releases/govsecure/current.htm>.

Table 441. State and Local Governments—Total Revenue and Expenditures by State: 2000 to 2008

[In millions of dollars (1,942,328 represents $1,942,328,000,000), except as indicated. For fiscal year ending in year shown; see text, this section. These data cannot be used to compute the deficit or surplus for any single government, as these are estimates for all state and local governments within a state area. For further information, see the 2006 Government Finance and Employment Classification Manual at <http://www.census.gov/govs/classification/>]

State	Revenue				Expenditures			
	2000	2005	2007	2008	2000	2005	2007	2008
United States	**1,942,328**	**2,529,193**	**3,072,645**	**2,660,475**	**1,746,943**	**2,373,408**	**2,665,881**	**2,838,836**
Alabama	25,726	33,377	40,959	31,834	25,319	33,241	36,198	38,201
Alaska	10,525	11,404	15,460	18,793	8,628	10,027	11,663	12,903
Arizona	27,778	41,103	51,271	47,675	27,293	39,300	47,164	52,533
Arkansas	13,833	18,866	22,543	19,633	12,245	17,224	19,124	20,172
California	270,380	381,910	473,951	354,000	236,645	344,704	390,452	415,437
Colorado	29,603	38,915	46,709	47,108	26,173	35,063	40,478	42,537
Connecticut	25,828	30,490	37,417	33,284	24,011	29,649	32,672	35,081
Delaware	6,224	7,637	9,227	8,407	5,153	7,595	8,702	9,072
District of Columbia	6,383	9,919	11,389	11,790	6,527	8,787	10,585	12,949
Florida	92,402	135,562	172,872	147,940	84,301	130,858	148,513	158,175
Georgia	49,310	60,297	76,001	73,064	43,517	58,905	73,615	77,709
Hawaii	8,488	11,000	13,575	11,933	8,254	10,534	12,274	13,215
Idaho	7,590	10,004	12,347	10,547	6,404	8,915	9,967	10,781
Illinois.	80,695	99,826	120,026	104,194	74,727	97,745	108,910	115,627
Indiana.	32,716	44,261	49,162	46,431	31,250	42,048	46,814	49,266
Iowa.	17,220	23,204	27,670	24,980	17,275	21,486	24,248	25,785
Kansas.	16,235	19,990	24,269	22,672	14,419	18,948	21,799	23,473
Kentucky	25,200	28,044	33,817	29,467	21,473	26,963	31,716	34,359
Louisiana	27,109	35,858	46,815	44,211	25,018	32,578	39,298	45,938
Maine	8,554	11,383	12,481	10,756	7,652	10,207	10,862	11,175
Maryland	33,949	45,075	54,271	45,445	30,598	41,373	47,764	51,225
Massachusetts.	46,103	62,109	70,530	73,472	44,362	59,312	64,752	67,895
Michigan	70,112	81,055	91,423	68,603	61,506	75,980	81,004	83,962
Minnesota	38,785	45,465	54,341	45,666	35,424	42,936	47,216	50,844
Mississippi	16,672	21,113	29,627	23,637	15,379	20,041	24,768	25,171
Missouri.	31,635	41,340	49,755	42,180	27,953	37,186	42,037	45,102
Montana.	5,643	7,438	9,183	8,520	4,983	6,412	7,448	8,116
Nebraska	11,650	15,905	18,271	17,757	10,831	14,332	16,839	18,351
Nevada	11,885	18,953	23,207	19,961	11,230	17,405	20,017	21,462
New Hampshire.	6,948	8,911	10,366	9,632	6,222	8,679	9,416	9,968
New Jersey	62,331	79,126	95,276	85,935	54,590	79,845	87,088	91,729
New Mexico	13,073	16,656	20,972	16,911	11,195	15,596	18,123	19,264
New York	188,907	234,681	292,764	243,901	171,858	226,951	249,961	263,437
North Carolina	50,542	64,813	75,949	77,178	46,135	60,747	68,131	72,873
North Dakota	4,495	5,239	6,346	6,678	4,041	4,794	5,234	5,616
Ohio.	80,074	102,498	121,412	100,926	68,418	91,959	100,220	102,920
Oklahoma	18,760	24,552	30,228	26,781	15,962	22,005	26,062	27,430
Oregon.	28,644	32,406	41,861	28,988	24,086	29,084	32,261	34,561
Pennsylvania	80,546	103,692	121,211	109,732	75,624	101,484	106,958	111,863
Rhode Island	7,427	9,731	11,244	9,437	6,432	9,226	10,021	10,576
South Carolina.	23,467	33,278	39,435	35,414	23,436	33,011	36,645	39,741
South Dakota.	4,277	5,857	7,034	5,190	3,760	4,973	5,552	5,833
Tennessee	33,625	44,863	52,613	48,026	32,010	42,708	49,098	49,128
Texas	120,666	162,748	195,732	196,508	109,634	151,927	171,092	188,686
Utah.	14,954	19,183	23,380	22,973	13,044	17,269	19,985	22,204
Vermont.	4,019	5,393	6,366	6,085	3,766	5,179	5,806	6,039
Virginia.	44,175	56,658	70,485	58,223	38,092	51,529	59,041	63,272
Washington	46,372	57,510	72,165	63,207	41,794	55,800	62,268	66,692
West Virginia	10,760	14,576	14,814	13,710	9,990	12,120	12,612	13,686
Wisconsin	43,003	48,235	55,882	41,701	34,559	43,146	46,692	49,283
Wyoming	7,030	7,084	8,539	9,378	3,743	5,619	6,719	7,520

Source: U.S. Census Bureau, Federal, State, and Local Governments, Finance, "State and Local Government Finances, 2007–08," June 2011. See also <http://www.census.gov/govs/>.

Table 442. State and Local Governments—Revenue by State: 2008

[In millions of dollars (2,660,475 represents $2,660,475,000,000). For fiscal year ending in year shown; see text, this section]

State	Total revenue	General revenue from own sources — Total	Intergovernmental from federal government	General revenue from own sources	Select taxes — Total [1]	Property	Sales and gross receipt	Individual income	Corporation income	Other taxes
United States ...	2,660,475	2,425,778	481,380	1,944,398	1,330,412	409,686	448,689	304,627	57,810	88,256
Alabama	31,834	32,456	8,060	24,396	14,041	2,306	6,579	3,188	525	1,209
Alaska	18,793	18,352	2,444	15,908	9,735	1,068	567	–	982	7,050
Arizona	47,675	42,896	9,689	33,207	22,992	6,705	11,117	3,409	785	734
Arkansas	19,633	18,411	4,772	13,639	9,406	1,462	4,838	2,345	343	278
California	354,000	327,817	57,720	270,097	186,015	52,759	53,487	55,746	11,849	9,456
Colorado	47,108	37,222	5,633	31,589	19,636	6,130	6,789	5,068	508	846
Connecticut	33,284	32,439	4,735	27,705	23,115	8,325	5,815	7,504	604	666
Delaware	8,407	7,893	1,343	6,551	3,712	605	492	1,064	309	1,197
District of Columbia	11,790	10,023	3,011	7,012	5,398	1,728	1,388	1,355	420	474
Florida	147,940	136,072	23,272	112,800	73,351	30,261	34,470	–	2,209	5,246
Georgia	73,064	63,897	14,044	49,853	33,633	10,220	12,652	8,845	943	676
Hawaii	11,933	11,663	2,291	9,372	6,737	1,253	3,470	1,545	105	126
Idaho	10,547	9,991	2,120	7,870	4,940	1,181	1,772	1,439	190	228
Illinois..........	104,194	95,513	17,369	78,144	57,834	21,295	19,280	10,320	3,116	2,431
Indiana..........	46,431	44,245	8,565	35,680	22,954	6,935	8,496	5,386	909	970
Iowa............	24,980	23,149	4,816	18,333	11,541	3,719	3,729	2,931	347	392
Kansas..........	22,672	21,327	3,683	17,644	11,877	3,687	4,088	2,947	528	440
Kentucky	29,467	28,240	7,022	21,217	14,157	2,780	5,254	4,534	656	678
Louisiana........	44,211	42,360	15,145	27,215	17,951	2,838	9,497	3,170	703	1,653
Maine...........	10,756	10,629	2,555	8,074	5,933	2,157	1,710	1,563	185	234
Maryland	45,445	45,173	8,229	36,943	27,651	6,611	6,808	11,184	735	1,871
Massachusetts....	73,472	58,939	11,239	47,700	33,997	11,665	6,225	12,496	2,180	1,143
Michigan	68,603	73,119	14,877	58,241	37,650	14,127	12,203	7,642	1,778	1,007
Minnesota	45,666	43,400	7,854	35,546	24,724	6,635	7,709	7,777	1,040	1,048
Mississippi.......	23,637	23,085	8,189	14,896	9,213	2,299	4,331	1,551	385	524
Missouri.........	42,180	39,046	9,130	29,916	19,873	5,480	7,286	5,473	384	967
Montana.........	8,520	7,494	2,101	5,393	3,448	1,175	549	870	162	541
Nebraska........	17,757	14,107	2,774	11,334	7,508	2,485	2,486	1,726	233	419
Nevada	19,961	18,015	2,261	15,755	10,588	3,216	5,898	–	–	1,304
New Hampshire....	9,632	8,933	1,748	7,185	4,963	3,057	793	118	615	286
New Jersey	85,935	81,331	11,503	69,828	53,791	22,708	12,641	12,606	2,820	2,585
New Mexico	16,911	17,232	4,527	12,705	7,747	1,124	3,579	1,214	355	1,283
New York	243,901	228,845	44,739	184,106	138,288	39,069	33,891	46,454	11,330	6,563
North Carolina....	77,178	64,558	15,181	49,377	33,208	7,870	11,148	10,994	1,206	1,344
North Dakota......	6,678	6,176	1,360	4,816	3,174	740	980	317	162	886
Ohio............	100,926	87,189	18,654	68,534	46,660	13,573	14,693	14,015	892	2,523
Oklahoma	26,781	24,931	5,940	18,991	12,315	2,113	4,738	2,787	360	1,680
Oregon..........	28,988	27,185	5,859	21,326	12,532	4,257	1,099	4,975	543	1,173
Pennsylvania.....	109,732	96,014	19,083	76,931	54,110	15,537	15,914	14,333	2,204	5,308
Rhode Island......	9,437	8,973	2,072	6,901	4,874	2,064	1,395	1,092	146	126
South Carolina.....	35,414	31,271	7,006	24,265	13,163	4,299	4,592	2,864	320	926
South Dakota.....	5,190	5,391	1,431	3,959	2,500	859	1,361	–	70	152
Tennessee........	48,026	39,204	8,850	30,354	19,000	4,670	10,999	291	1,006	1,621
Texas	196,508	164,175	33,062	131,113	86,383	33,540	40,497	–	–	10,492
Utah............	22,973	18,933	3,811	15,122	9,371	2,218	3,584	2,593	395	302
Vermont.........	6,085	5,562	1,476	4,087	2,936	1,177	867	623	85	105
Virginia..........	58,223	56,564	7,969	48,595	32,707	10,569	8,576	10,115	787	2,156
Washington	63,207	52,690	9,321	43,369	28,590	7,809	17,908	–	–	2,354
West Virginia	13,710	13,519	3,382	10,137	6,428	1,238	2,380	1,519	539	666
Wisconsin	41,701	41,996	7,373	34,623	24,372	8,830	6,692	6,641	863	940
Wyoming	9,378	8,129	2,090	6,040	3,694	1,260	1,377	–	–	982

See footnotes at end of table.

Table 442. State and Local Governments—Revenue by State: 2008—Con.

[See headnote page 278. Minus sign (–) indicates decrease]

State	General revenue from own sources—Con.								Utility and liquor stores	Insur-ance trust revenue
	Current charges and miscellaneous revenue									
	Current charges				Miscellaneous revenue					
	Total	Total [1]	Educa-tion	Hospi-tals	Sewer-age	Total [1]	Interest earnings	Special assess-ments		
United States	613,987	373,669	110,512	97,270	38,064	240,318	93,370	7,928	146,385	88,312
Alabama	10,355	7,429	2,528	3,533	387	2,926	902	42	2,866	–3,487
Alaska	6,173	1,148	195	211	78	5,026	1,604	7	297	144
Arizona	10,215	5,311	1,988	673	655	4,903	1,675	153	4,206	572
Arkansas	4,233	2,887	1,113	989	220	1,347	559	27	852	370
California	84,082	55,062	9,955	13,579	5,472	29,020	12,430	1,467	26,734	–551
Colorado	11,953	7,509	2,722	1,579	703	4,444	1,899	197	2,313	7,573
Connecticut	4,589	2,658	1,072	426	293	1,932	832	36	754	90
Delaware	2,838	1,356	600	18	138	1,482	368	392	391	123
District of Columbia	1,614	485	64	8	186	1,129	215	–	875	893
Florida	39,449	23,978	4,395	5,546	2,508	15,471	5,771	1,556	8,563	3,305
Georgia	16,221	11,235	2,693	4,278	1,101	4,986	1,545	63	4,454	4,713
Hawaii	2,636	1,689	316	446	234	947	333	22	273	–3
Idaho	2,931	2,052	450	798	173	879	364	40	328	228
Illinois.........	20,310	11,498	4,397	1,256	1,021	8,812	4,061	526	3,357	5,324
Indiana.........	12,726	7,995	3,334	2,625	936	4,731	1,723	47	2,028	158
Iowa.........	6,792	4,776	1,650	2,025	353	2,016	857	24	1,095	736
Kansas.........	5,767	3,896	1,266	1,587	302	1,871	770	90	1,192	152
Kentucky	7,061	4,708	1,598	1,514	424	2,353	1,141	13	1,475	–248
Louisiana	9,265	5,007	1,136	2,155	343	4,258	1,835	25	1,235	616
Maine.........	2,142	1,169	464	75	145	973	322	5	127	–
Maryland	9,292	5,590	2,625	168	770	3,702	1,165	65	913	–640
Massachusetts.........	13,703	6,807	2,265	880	927	6,896	2,736	409	3,186	11,347
Michigan	20,592	13,067	5,158	2,953	1,543	7,525	2,626	245	3,098	–7,613
Minnesota	10,822	6,612	2,334	1,438	618	4,211	1,534	396	2,300	–35
Mississippi.........	5,684	4,350	1,106	2,553	203	1,334	512	7	1,053	–501
Missouri.........	10,044	6,066	2,345	1,746	617	3,978	1,850	61	1,819	1,315
Montana.........	1,945	1,050	500	63	77	895	356	70	183	843
Nebraska.........	3,826	2,606	826	833	156	1,220	521	70	3,487	163
Nevada.........	5,167	3,215	599	644	387	1,952	806	61	974	972
New Hampshire.........	2,222	1,218	606	12	105	1,004	483	4	566	133
New Jersey	16,037	9,807	3,465	1,184	1,392	6,230	2,346	13	1,821	2,784
New Mexico.........	4,958	1,904	657	614	131	3,054	1,103	24	500	–821
New York	45,818	24,003	4,516	6,411	1,780	21,816	7,408	117	13,068	1,988
North Carolina.........	16,169	11,338	3,148	4,642	1,090	4,831	1,931	7	4,310	8,310
North Dakota.........	1,642	973	440	5	43	669	355	67	116	385
Ohio.........	21,874	13,726	5,716	2,969	1,821	8,148	3,156	242	3,230	10,507
Oklahoma	6,676	4,228	1,818	1,083	268	2,448	817	11	1,398	452
Oregon.........	8,795	4,991	1,477	1,081	735	3,803	1,017	104	1,714	89
Pennsylvania	22,822	13,477	4,874	1,962	2,038	9,345	3,946	125	4,145	9,573
Rhode Island.........	2,028	948	451	5	95	1,079	437	8	200	264
South Carolina.........	11,102	8,168	2,155	4,198	466	2,934	1,017	96	2,990	1,152
South Dakota.........	1,460	734	313	41	65	726	371	26	265	–465
Tennessee.........	11,354	6,641	1,860	2,393	597	4,713	954	123	8,324	498
Texas.........	44,730	25,602	8,295	7,456	2,682	19,128	9,024	182	10,272	22,061
Utah.........	5,750	3,746	1,249	991	306	2,004	797	38	2,034	2,007
Vermont.........	1,151	680	477	–	53	471	208	3	255	268
Virginia.........	15,888	10,135	3,430	2,665	1,010	5,753	2,044	202	2,302	–644
Washington	14,780	10,184	2,480	2,810	1,526	4,596	1,905	261	6,398	4,119
West Virginia.........	3,709	2,048	803	343	190	1,660	422	25	285	–94
Wisconsin.........	10,251	6,682	2,395	1,054	646	3,569	1,605	126	1,529	–1,824
Wyoming	2,346	1,225	194	748	54	1,121	715	11	235	1,014

– Represents or rounds to zero. [1] Includes items not shown separately.

Source: U.S. Census Bureau; Federal, State and Local Governments, "State Government Finances 2007–2008," June 2011, <http://www.census.gov/govs>.

Table 443. State and Local Governments—Expenditures and Debt by State: 2008

[In millions of dollars (2,838,836 represents $2,838,836,000,000), except as indicated. For fiscal year ending in year shown; see text, this section]

State	Total expenditures	General expenditures Total¹	Direct general expenditures Total¹	Education	Public welfare	Health	Hospitals	Highways	Police protection	Corrections
United States	2,838,836	2,404,966	2,400,204	826,063	404,624	79,704	128,853	153,515	89,676	72,904
Alabama	38,201	32,627	32,627	13,021	4,569	1,043	3,860	1,980	1,044	703
Alaska	12,903	11,523	11,523	3,010	1,415	200	257	1,521	262	249
Arizona	52,533	43,224	43,224	14,041	7,231	1,792	1,216	3,002	2,155	1,644
Arkansas	20,172	17,890	17,890	6,986	3,785	281	993	1,198	493	499
California	415,437	338,922	335,283	103,871	50,989	13,941	17,959	15,702	14,892	13,727
Colorado	42,537	35,595	35,591	12,603	4,198	960	1,922	2,349	1,452	1,144
Connecticut	35,081	30,415	30,415	11,126	5,185	765	1,385	1,344	996	713
Delaware	9,072	8,076	8,075	2,878	1,443	418	63	579	289	281
District of Columbia . . .	12,949	10,677	10,677	2,227	2,405	564	232	411	591	267
Florida	158,175	138,485	138,485	41,310	19,520	4,533	7,732	10,586	6,736	4,751
Georgia	77,709	65,290	65,290	25,651	9,354	2,298	5,116	3,886	2,293	2,300
Hawaii	13,215	11,705	11,704	3,394	1,628	716	531	578	335	219
Idaho	10,781	9,697	9,697	3,169	1,642	205	803	880	321	310
Illinois	115,627	96,219	96,219	32,736	16,235	2,898	2,432	6,787	4,242	1,977
Indiana	49,266	44,442	44,442	15,419	8,348	809	3,065	2,832	1,223	1,063
Iowa	25,785	23,031	23,031	8,690	3,891	508	2,387	1,826	614	441
Kansas	23,473	20,893	20,893	7,506	3,204	467	1,744	1,856	684	464
Kentucky	34,359	29,473	29,471	10,633	6,127	805	1,629	2,527	702	734
Louisiana	45,938	41,362	41,362	11,810	5,758	816	3,150	2,964	1,327	1,243
Maine	11,175	10,322	10,309	3,189	2,506	505	131	714	233	213
Maryland	51,225	45,740	45,740	17,202	7,331	1,725	495	2,885	1,842	1,684
Massachusetts	67,895	56,802	56,606	17,306	12,382	1,168	1,769	2,865	1,843	1,408
Michigan	83,962	72,284	72,284	28,311	11,649	3,641	3,264	3,713	2,425	2,462
Minnesota	50,844	44,064	44,064	14,802	10,017	1,109	1,837	3,741	1,527	915
Mississippi	25,171	22,454	22,454	7,155	4,245	420	2,867	1,687	601	488
Missouri	45,102	39,260	39,260	13,939	6,355	1,504	2,676	2,830	1,632	875
Montana	8,116	7,258	7,258	2,523	904	406	109	769	226	196
Nebraska	18,351	13,747	13,715	5,090	2,143	418	876	1,201	528	323
Nevada	21,462	18,233	18,232	6,227	1,827	391	955	1,451	1,079	768
New Hampshire	9,968	8,927	8,927	3,419	1,637	152	60	651	317	168
New Jersey	91,729	78,875	78,875	30,503	12,620	1,676	2,434	3,750	3,087	2,062
New Mexico	19,264	17,273	17,273	5,912	3,673	541	881	1,195	603	554
New York	263,437	213,004	212,375	64,743	43,948	5,799	12,264	9,696	8,164	5,794
North Carolina	72,873	63,365	63,365	22,785	10,476	2,880	5,599	3,561	2,217	1,772
North Dakota	5,616	5,119	5,119	1,845	810	91	18	618	120	84
Ohio	102,920	86,449	86,440	30,882	16,651	4,183	3,436	4,758	3,157	1,969
Oklahoma	27,430	24,048	24,005	9,145	4,812	690	1,074	1,968	763	705
Oregon	34,561	28,142	28,142	9,674	4,103	862	1,422	1,905	1,009	1,016
Pennsylvania	111,863	94,854	94,697	33,107	20,255	4,048	2,444	7,480	2,840	3,051
Rhode Island	10,576	8,993	8,965	2,936	2,154	187	88	305	317	227
South Carolina	39,741	33,653	33,653	12,253	5,451	1,187	4,502	1,395	980	725
South Dakota	5,833	5,223	5,223	1,753	819	156	102	669	141	153
Tennessee	49,128	37,817	37,817	12,376	8,189	1,590	2,892	2,012	1,474	957
Texas	188,686	163,012	163,012	65,970	22,711	3,481	9,982	14,307	5,626	5,210
Utah	22,204	18,716	18,716	7,471	2,268	566	878	1,428	640	507
Vermont	6,039	5,436	5,436	2,215	1,254	172	20	437	141	119
Virginia	63,272	57,091	57,091	22,693	8,069	1,344	3,081	3,552	2,011	2,080
Washington	66,692	53,595	53,590	18,042	7,742	2,239	3,817	3,846	1,448	1,732
West Virginia	13,686	12,420	12,420	4,684	2,544	356	355	1,088	313	272
Wisconsin	49,283	42,440	42,440	15,592	7,480	1,838	1,274	3,510	1,552	1,447
Wyoming	7,520	6,802	6,802	2,240	671	362	774	722	170	240

See footnotes at end of table.

U.S. Census Bureau, Statistical Abstract of the United States: 2012

Table 443. State and Local Governments—Expenditures and Debt by State: 2008—Con.

[See headnote, page 280]

State	General expenditures—Con.								Utility and liquor store expenditures	Insurance trust expenditures	Total debt outstanding
	Direct general expenditures—Con.										
	Natural resources	Parks and recreation	Housing and community development	Sewerage	Solid waste	Governmental administration	Interest on general debt	Other direct general expenditures			
United States....	29,917	40,646	50,974	46,679	23,757	126,997	100,055	216,073	199,287	234,584	2,550,934
Alabama	320	485	415	329	263	1,417	973	1,946	2,962	2,612	28,008
Alaska	291	143	271	105	91	788	433	2,646	467	912	9,960
Arizona	703	1,079	537	1,284	390	2,629	1,658	3,603	5,873	3,436	43,583
Arkansas	246	211	173	313	192	956	480	1,106	948	1,334	12,939
California	6,741	6,234	10,285	6,147	3,754	22,430	13,553	34,719	35,889	40,626	341,094
Colorado	364	1,503	708	771	118	2,307	1,885	3,025	3,073	3,868	49,971
Connecticut	126	278	666	443	367	1,762	1,602	3,275	1,198	3,468	36,789
Delaware	100	92	118	199	126	620	336	604	489	506	7,943
District of Columbia	26	662	571	195	319	506	407	1,119	2,117	155	9,581
Florida	4,305	3,273	2,436	2,853	2,433	8,329	5,004	15,625	10,759	8,930	142,129
Georgia	528	1,049	1,239	1,405	618	3,382	1,365	4,305	7,081	5,338	50,562
Hawaii	120	249	199	262	226	766	617	1,830	544	966	10,445
Idaho	263	138	53	195	133	677	257	771	301	784	5,730
Illinois...........	538	2,561	2,012	1,620	524	4,416	5,444	10,142	6,826	12,582	124,163
Indiana..........	376	765	660	1,039	268	2,031	1,665	4,482	2,380	2,443	46,548
Iowa............	345	373	164	360	189	973	692	1,723	1,195	1,560	15,457
Kansas..........	266	268	189	329	153	1,057	942	1,765	1,211	1,369	20,973
Kentucky	404	281	295	458	206	1,415	1,538	1,701	1,791	3,095	38,395
Louisiana	793	721	5,423	499	307	2,015	1,511	3,296	1,371	3,206	31,887
Maine...........	170	75	245	164	119	511	348	1,226	127	726	7,796
Maryland	674	850	1,042	836	597	2,568	1,654	4,134	1,703	3,782	37,965
Massachusetts.....	315	433	1,763	1,102	403	2,638	4,208	6,302	4,690	6,403	92,828
Michigan	430	817	1,010	2,087	597	3,084	3,047	5,230	3,830	7,848	75,247
Minnesota	600	1,012	846	642	339	2,089	1,647	3,183	2,582	4,199	41,651
Mississippi........	311	193	232	202	158	889	491	2,604	1,053	1,665	13,334
Missouri..........	434	661	619	640	149	1,487	1,845	3,409	2,195	3,647	41,124
Montana..........	308	93	111	120	69	501	273	857	203	655	6,472
Nebraska........	268	214	204	263	88	619	334	1,241	4,005	600	14,014
Nevada	298	783	235	261	24	1,449	829	1,452	1,774	1,455	24,898
New Hampshire....	73	101	190	113	117	499	488	840	509	532	10,526
New Jersey	515	1,190	1,188	1,343	1,179	3,511	3,527	9,810	3,865	8,989	87,972
New Mexico.......	285	334	159	164	157	1,004	523	1,312	631	1,360	13,253
New York	687	2,693	4,661	3,927	2,798	11,005	9,847	24,123	24,712	25,720	269,742
North Carolina.....	777	1,064	869	1,209	746	2,661	1,988	4,677	4,721	4,787	51,202
North Dakota......	180	109	77	45	43	230	237	746	147	350	3,656
Ohio............	395	1,104	2,138	2,612	510	5,147	3,201	5,151	3,580	12,890	68,659
Oklahoma	221	365	215	401	186	1,211	678	1,354	1,436	1,945	16,943
Oregon...........	545	572	486	890	132	1,721	1,128	2,676	2,231	4,188	29,416
Pennsylvania	773	978	1,917	2,014	777	5,354	4,916	4,863	5,923	11,086	118,611
Rhode Island	44	58	202	123	98	546	504	949	302	1,281	11,395
South Carolina.....	319	363	446	484	332	2,007	1,285	1,891	3,313	2,775	36,554
South Dakota.....	150	147	93	135	31	305	197	475	298	312	5,247
Tennessee........	419	516	650	596	340	1,790	1,032	2,774	9,000	2,311	35,775
Texas...........	1,286	2,191	1,920	2,943	1,069	5,806	8,272	11,213	14,308	11,366	215,878
Utah............	242	494	273	394	143	1,312	523	1,523	2,319	1,169	16,729
Vermont..........	77	38	123	68	44	246	209	310	307	296	4,342
Virginia..........	283	963	1,036	1,024	701	3,049	1,943	4,449	2,701	3,480	54,700
Washington	783	973	1,147	1,798	616	2,291	2,168	4,692	7,844	5,254	64,548
West Virginia	181	156	157	318	69	774	400	848	383	883	9,837
Wisconsin	797	590	284	847	384	1,765	1,852	3,413	1,850	4,994	42,120
Wyoming	220	150	21	106	66	450	96	660	271	448	2,346

[1] Includes items not shown separately.

Source: U.S. Census Bureau; Federal, State, and Local Governments, "State and Local Government Finances, 2007–2008," June 2011. See also <http://www.census.gov/govs/>.

U.S. Census Bureau, Statistical Abstract of the United States: 2012

Table 444. State Resources, Expenditures, and Balances: 2009 and 2010

[In millions of dollars (1,546,804 represents $1,546,804,000,000). For fiscal year ending in year shown; see text; this section. General funds exclude special funds earmarked for particular purposes, such as highway trust funds and federal funds; they support most on-going broad-based state services, and are available for appropriation to support any governmental activity]

State	Total, 2009 actual	Expenditures by fund source 2010 [1] estimated			State general fund Resources [3,4]		Expenditures [4]		Balance [5,6]	
		Total [2]	General fund	Federal fund	2009	2010 [1]	2009	2010 [1]	2009	2010 [1]
United States ...	1,546,804	1,624,666	618,191	563,692	670,301	628,901	660,946	612,600	29,006	$27,589
Alabama	19,760	24,458	6,847	10,181	7,501	6,742	7,735	7,275	179	55
Alaska	13,524	9,746	5,375	3,178	5,457	5,615	5,732	4,606	8,898	10,497
Arizona	27,080	27,511	9,079	10,655	8,274	7,844	8,754	7,852	3	–
Arkansas	18,193	20,249	4,207	7,091	4,435	4,323	4,435	4,323	–	–
California	195,476	217,842	86,465	95,398	85,086	81,545	90,940	86,349	–	–
Colorado	28,806	29,003	7,326	8,920	7,830	6,851	7,386	6,705	444	146
Connecticut	25,799	26,062	17,251	3,099	15,880	17,687	16,806	17,238	1,382	103
Delaware	8,741	8,720	3,077	1,607	3,674	3,614	3,296	3,077	186	186
Florida	60,674	66,505	21,195	22,744	24,292	22,765	23,661	21,581	274	275
Georgia	38,970	38,621	14,870	13,066	19,235	17,110	17,497	15,971	217	193
Hawaii	11,822	10,948	4,838	2,391	5,338	4,817	5,375	4,838	60	63
Idaho	6,314	7,130	2,349	2,952	2,721	2,442	2,959	2,507	128	31
Illinois...........	46,469	47,426	17,244	14,686	29,285	27,370	26,797	22,675	276	276
Indiana..........	25,719	26,662	12,915	10,333	14,113	13,656	13,019	12,877	365	–
Iowa............	17,477	18,546	5,302	6,642	5,934	5,634	5,934	5,298	519	419
Kansas..........	13,960	14,497	5,451	4,544	6,114	5,341	6,064	5,408	–	–
Kentucky	24,057	25,837	8,348	10,477	9,263	8,604	9,158	8,452	7	–
Louisiana	25,654	29,612	9,011	14,798	10,370	8,576	9,382	7,951	854	644
Maine...........	8,092	8,257	2,866	3,151	3,100	2,921	3,018	2,849	–	–
Maryland	31,797	33,409	13,428	9,795	14,396	13,773	14,309	13,429	692	612
Massachusetts.....	48,993	53,410	28,912	5,722	33,587	32,444	32,570	31,693	841	657
Michigan	45,759	45,723	8,110	19,238	8,633	7,772	8,456	7,772	2	2
Minnesota	29,897	31,502	15,567	10,400	17,308	15,141	16,861	14,799	–	–
Mississippi	16,328	19,384	4,597	8,832	4,991	4,439	4,984	4,899	334	250
Missouri..........	23,094	24,811	7,565	8,743	8,712	7,707	8,449	7,522	260	252
Montana..........	5,526	6,049	1,628	2,285	2,250	2,026	1,858	1,716	–	–
Nebraska.........	9,139	9,591	3,313	2,973	3,752	3,610	3,329	3,313	576	467
Nevada	9,039	7,875	3,291	2,705	3,989	3,418	3,777	3,250	1	–
New Hampshire....	4,978	5,465	1,401	2,073	1,393	1,435	1,418	1,408	9	9
New Jersey	46,677	48,975	29,862	14,045	30,926	28,867	30,312	28,362	–	–
New Mexico.......	15,505	14,351	5,468	5,580	6,747	5,960	6,046	5,471	389	253
New York	121,571	130,937	54,262	44,843	56,555	54,504	54,607	54,262	1,206	1,206
North Carolina.....	43,090	31,792	13,765	10,492	19,745	18,750	19,653	18,513	150	150
North Dakota......	3,941	4,710	1,551	1,767	1,807	1,898	1,237	1,316	325	325
Ohio............	57,794	57,640	24,141	13,029	28,367	25,685	27,632	25,174	–	–
Oklahoma	21,430	21,559	6,036	10,899	6,568	5,163	6,542	5,119	597	373
Oregon...........	24,524	27,920	5,969	8,725	5,889	6,004	5,889	6,431	113	16
Pennsylvania	62,644	70,376	25,177	29,363	25,054	24,648	27,084	25,138	755	1
Rhode Island	7,101	8,162	2,887	3,096	2,939	2,883	3,001	2,862	80	112
South Carolina.....	21,074	22,567	5,275	10,117	5,869	5,363	5,748	5,117	–	111
South Dakota......	3,546	3,769	1,129	1,718	1,154	1,132	1,153	1,132	107	107
Tennessee........	29,118	29,136	10,671	12,903	10,841	10,071	10,675	9,738	557	453
Texas............	89,965	97,867	44,156	38,001	44,763	38,838	42,411	32,734	6,276	7,736
Utah............	11,795	12,927	4,441	3,672	5,037	4,462	4,817	4,441	419	209
Vermont..........	5,617	5,822	1,109	1,845	1,168	1,090	1,146	1,088	60	57
Virginia..........	40,024	40,773	14,989	9,327	16,104	14,919	15,943	14,787	575	295
Washington	33,714	32,543	15,036	8,662	14,807	14,494	14,617	15,036	21	95
West Virginia	20,447	20,247	3,779	4,418	4,479	4,240	3,980	3,677	473	556
Wisconsin	38,442	40,085	12,824	11,531	12,817	12,963	12,744	12,824	–	–
Wyoming	7,648	7,657	3,836	1,430	1,755	1,750	1,750	1,750	398	398

– Represents zero. [1] Estimated. [2] Includes bonds and other state funds, not shown separately. [3] Includes funds budgeted, adjustments, and balances from previous year. [4] May or may not include budget stabilization fund transfers, depending on state accounting practices. [5] Resources less expenditures. [6] Ending balance is held in a budget stabilization fund.

Source: National Association of State Budget Officers, Washington, DC, *2009 State Expenditure Report*, and *State General Fund from NASBO, Fiscal Survey of the States, semiannual* (copyright), <http://www.nasbo.org/publications.php>.

Table 445. Bond Ratings for State Governments by State: 2010

[As of fourth quarter. Key to investment grade ratings are in declining order of quality. The ratings from AA to CCC may be modified by the addition of a (+) or (–) sign to show relative standing within the major rating categories. *S&P*: AAA, AA, A, BBB, BB, B, CCC, CC, C; *Moody's*: Aaa, Aa, A, Baa, Ba, B, Caa, Ca, C; Numerical modifiers 1, 2, and 3 are added to letter–rating. *Fitch*: AAA, AA, A, BBB, BB, B, CCC, CC, C]

State	Standard & Poor's	Moody's	Fitch	State	Standard & Poor's	Moody's	Fitch
Alabama	AA	Aa2	AA+	Montana	AA	Aa2	AA+
Alaska	AA+	A1	AA+	Nebraska	[1] AA+ (ICR)	([2])	(NA)
Arizona	[1] AA–	A1	(NA)	Nevada	AA+	Aa2	AA+
Arkansas	AA	Aa2	(WD)	New Hampshire	AA	Aa2	AA+
California	A	Baa1	A–	New Jersey	AA	Aa3	AA
Colorado	[1] AA (ICR)	Aa2	(NA)	New Mexico	AA+	Aa1	N/A
Connecticut	AA	Aa3	AA	New York	AA	Aa3	AA
Delaware	AAA	Aaa	AAA	North Carolina	AAA	Aaa	AAA
Florida	AAA	Aa1	AAA	North Dakota	[1] AA+ (ICR)	Aa2	N/A
Georgia	AAA	Aaa	AAA	Ohio	AA+	Aa2	AA+
Hawaii	AA	Aa2	AA+	Oklahoma	AA+	Aa3	AA+
Idaho	[1] AA+ (ICR)	Aa2	(NA)	Oregon	AA	Aa2	AA+
Illinois	A+	A2	A	Pennsylvania	AA	Aa2	AA+
Indiana	[1] AAA (ICR)	Aa1	(NA)	Rhode Island	AA	Aa3	AA
Iowa	[1] AAA (ICR)	Aa1	AAA	South Carolina	AA+	Aaa	AAA
Kansas	[1] AA+ (ICR)	Aa1	(NA)	South Dakota	[1] AA (ICR)	([2])	(NA)
Kentucky	[1] AA– (ICR)	Aa2	(NA)	Tennessee	AA+	Aa1	AAA
Louisiana	AA–	A1	AA	Texas	AA+	Aa1	AAA
Maine	AA	Aa3	AA+	Utah	AAA	Aaa	AAA
Maryland	AAA	Aaa	AAA	Vermont	AA+	Aaa	AAA
Massachusetts	AA	Aa2	AA+	Virginia	AAA	Aaa	AAA
Michigan	AA–	Aa3	AA–	Washington	AA+	Aa1	AA+
Minnesota	AAA	Aa1	AAA	West Virginia	AA	Aa3	AA
Mississippi	AA	Aa3	AA+	Wisconsin	AA	Aa3	AA
Missouri	AAA	Aaa	AAA	Wyoming	[1] AA+ (ICR)	([2])	(NA)

NA Not available. WD Withdrawn. [1] Standard and Poor's Issue Credit Rating (ICR) is a current opinion of an obliger with respect to a specific financial obligation, a specific class of financial obligations, or a specific financial program. [2] Not rated.
Source: Standard & Poor's, New York, NY (copyright), <http://www2.standardandpoors.com/portal/site/sp/en/us/page.home /home/0,0,0,0,0,0,0,0,0,0,0,0,0,0,0,0,0.html>; Moody's Investors Service, New York, NY (copyright), <http://www.moodys.com/cust /default_alt.asp>; Fitch Ratings, New York, NY (copyright), <http://www.fitchratings.com>.

Table 446. Bond Ratings for City Governments by Largest Cities: 2010

[As of fourth quarter. See headnote in Table 445]

Cities ranked by 2000 population	Standard & Poor's	Moody's	Fitch	Cities ranked by 2000 population	Standard & Poor's	Moody's	Fitch
New York, NY	AA	Aa3	AA	Oakland, CA	AA–	A1	AA–
Los Angeles, CA	AA–	Aa2	AA–	Mesa, AZ	AA	A1	(WD)
Chicago, IL	A+	Aa3	AA–	Tulsa, OK	AA	Aa2	(NA)
Houston, TX	AA	Aa3	AA	Omaha, NE	AAA	Aa1	(NA)
Philadelphia, PA	BBB	Baa1	A–	Minneapolis, MN	AAA	Aa1	AAA
Phoenix, AZ	AAA	Aa1	(NA)	Honolulu, HI	AA	Aa2	AA+
San Diego, CA	A	A2	AA–	Miami, FL	A–	A2	A
Dallas, TX	AA+	Aa1	(NA)	St. Louis, MO	A+	A2	(NA)
San Antonio, TX	AAA	Aa1	AAA	Wichita, KS	AA+	Aa2	(WD)
Detroit, MI	BB	Ba3	BB	Santa Ana, CA	([1])	([2])	(NA)
San Jose, CA	AAA	Aa1	AAA	Pittsburgh, PA	BBB	Baa1	A
Indianapolis, IN	AA	Aa1	(NA)	Arlington, TX	AA+	Aa2	(NA)
San Francisco, CA	AA	Aa2	AA	Cincinnati, OH	AA+	Aa1	(NA)
Jacksonville, FL	AA–	Aa2	AA+	Anaheim, CA	AA	Aa2	(NA)
Columbus, OH	AAA	Aaa	AAA	Toledo, OH	A	Baa1	(WD)
Austin, TX	AAA	Aa1	(NA)	Tampa, FL	([1])	Aa2	(NA)
Baltimore, MD	AA–	Aa3	(WD)	Buffalo, NY	A–	Baa2	A+
Memphis, TN	AA	A1	AA–	St. Paul, MN	AAA	Aa2	(WD)
Milwaukee, WI	AA	Aa2	AA+	Corpus Christi, TX	AA–	A1	AA
Boston, MA	AA+	Aa1	AA+	Aurora, CO	AA	Aa2	(NA)
Washington, DC	A+	A1	AA–	Raleigh, NC	AA+	Aaa	AAA
El Paso, TX	AA	Aa3	AA	Newark, NJ	AA	Baa2	(WD)
Seattle, WA	AAA	Aaa	AA+	Lexington-Fayette, KY	([1])	Aa2	(NA)
Denver, CO	AAA	Aa1	AAA	Anchorage, AK	AA	Aa3	AA+
Nashville-Davidson, TN	AA	Aa2	AA	Louisville, KY	(\1)	Aa2	(NA)
Charlotte, NC	AAA	Aaa	AAA	Riverside, CA	AA–	([2])	AA+
Fort Worth, TX	AA+	Aa2	AA+	St Petersburg, FL	([1])	A1	(NA)
Portland, OR	([1]1)	Aaa	(NA)	Bakersfield, CA	([1])	([2])	(NA)
Oklahoma City, OK	AAA	Aa1	(NA)	Stockton CA	A	A2	(NA)
Tucson, AZ	AA–	Aa3	AA	Birmingham, AL	AA	Aa3	AA
New Orleans, LA	BBB	Baa3	A–	Jersey City, NJ	AA	Baa2	A–
Las Vegas, NV	AA	Aa2	AA	Norfolk, VA	AA	A1	AA+
Cleveland, OH	A (LEASE)	A2	AA–	Baton Rouge, LA	([1])	Aa3	AA+
Long Beach, CA	AA–	Aa3	(NA)	Hialeah, FL	([1])	([2])	A+
Albuquerque, NM	AAA	Aa2	AA+	Lincoln, NE	AAA	Aaa	(NA)
Kansas City, MO	AA	Aa3	AA	Greensboro, NC	AAA	Aaa	AAA
Fresno, CA	AA	A1	AA	Plano, TX	AAA	Aaa	AAA
Virginia Beach, VA	AAA	Aa1	AAA	Rochester, NY	A	A2	(NA)
Atlanta, GA	A	A1	(WD)				
Sacramento, CA	A+	Aa3	(NA)				

NA Not available. WD Withdrawn. [1] Not reviewed. [2] Issuer Rating/No General Obligation.
Source: Standard & Poor's, New York, NY (copyright),<http://www2.standardandpoors.com/portal/site/sp/en/us/page.home /home/0,0,0,0,0,0,0,0,0,0,0,0,0,0,0,0,0.html>; Moody's Investors Service, New York, NY (copyright); <http://www.moodys.com/cust /default_alt.asp>; Fitch Ratings, New York, NY (copyright), <http://www.fitchratings.com>.

State and Local Government Finances and Employment **283**

Table 447. Estimated State and Local Taxes Paid by a Family of Three for Largest City in Selected States: 2009

[Data based on average family of three (two wage earners and one school age child) owning their own home and living in a city where taxes apply. Comprises state and local sales, income, auto, and real estate taxes. For definition of median, see Guide to Tabular Presentation]

City	Total taxes paid by gross family income level (dollars)					Total taxes paid as percent of income				
	$25,000	$50,000	$75,000	$100,000	$150,000	$25,000	$50,000	$75,000	$100,000	$150,000
Albuquerque, NM......	2,487	4,182	6,197	8,431	11,358	9.9	8.4	8.3	8.4	7.6
Anchorage, AK	2,186	2,355	2,832	3,199	3,978	8.7	4.4	3.8	3.2	2.7
Atlanta, GA	3,270	4,535	7,040	9,837	13,969	13.1	9.1	9.4	9.8	9.3
Baltimore, MD	2,174	5,797	7,851	10,755	15,271	8.7	11.6	10.5	10.8	10.2
Boston, MA	3,032	5,031	6,947	9,135	12,185	12.1	10.1	9.3	9.1	8.1
Charlotte, NC.........	3,353	5,311	7,738	10,868	15,374	13.4	10.6	10.3	10.9	10.2
Chicago, IL...........	3,282	5,462	7,308	9,508	11,945	13.1	10.9	9.7	9.5	8.0
Columbus, OH........	2,983	4,559	7,224	10,048	14,514	11.9	9.1	9.6	10.0	9.7
Denver, CO	2,815	3,559	5,426	7,956	10,709	11.3	7.1	7.2	8.0	7.1
Detroit, MI	3,068	5,722	8,366	11,280	15,515	12.3	11.4	11.2	11.3	10.3
Honolulu, HI..........	3,283	3,476	5,480	7,767	11,598	13.1	7.0	7.3	7.8	7.7
Houston, TX..........	2,497	3,003	4,210	5,586	6,588	10.0	6.0	5.6	5.6	4.4
Indianapolis, IN	3,147	4,334	6,320	8,751	11,962	12.6	8.7	8.4	8.8	8.0
Jacksonville, FL.......	2,656	2,445	3,330	4,532	5,597	10.6	4.9	4.4	4.5	3.7
Kansas City, MO	3,203	5,062	7,524	10,243	14,352	12.8	10.1	10.0	10.2	9.6
Las Vegas, NV........	2,502	3,257	4,118	5,372	6,203	10.0	6.5	5.5	5.4	4.1
Los Angeles, CA	2,757	5,278	7,574	10,263	15,497	11.0	10.6	10.1	10.3	10.3
Memphis, TN	2,740	2,959	4,182	5,515	6,439	11.0	5.9	5.6	5.5	4.3
Milwaukee, WI	2,479	5,405	7,878	10,771	14,929	9.9	10.8	10.5	10.8	10.0
New Orleans, LA	2,695	3,310	5,122	7,233	9,815	10.8	6.6	6.8	7.2	6.5
New York City, NY	2,950	5,169	8,173	11,663	18,186	11.8	10.3	10.9	11.7	12.1
Oklahoma City, OK	2,731	4,079	6,162	8,580	11,738	10.9	8.2	8.2	8.6	7.8
Omaha, NE	2,422	4,494	6,901	10,061	14,329	9.7	9.0	9.2	10.1	9.6
Philadelphia, PA.......	4,109	6,859	9,310	12,130	16,349	16.4	13.7	12.4	12.1	10.9
Phoenix, AZ..........	3,200	3,491	5,037	7,351	9,696	12.8	7.0	6.7	7.4	6.5
Portland, OR	2,612	5,235	8,082	11,430	16,376	10.4	10.5	10.8	11.4	10.9
Seattle, WA	2,861	3,770	4,915	6,070	6,530	11.4	7.5	6.6	6.1	4.4
Virginia Beach, VA......	2,540	4,182	6,046	8,428	11,571	10.2	8.4	8.1	8.4	7.7
Washington, DC........	2,585	3,884	6,277	9,076	13,438	10.3	7.8	8.4	9.1	9.0
Wichita, KS	2,383	3,813	6,119	8,898	13,009	9.5	7.6	8.2	8.9	8.7
Average [1]..........	$2,750	$4,364	$6,392	$8,757	$12,165	11.0	8.7	8.5	8.8	8.1
Median [1]...........	$2,700	$4,182	$6,320	$8,906	$12,851	10.8	8.4	8.4	8.9	8.6

[1] Based on selected cities and District of Columbia. For complete list of cities, see Table 448.
Source: Government of the District of Columbia, Office of the Chief Financial Officer, "Tax Rates and Revenues, Tax Burden Comparisons, Nationwide Comparison," annual. See also <http://www.cfo.dc.gov/cfo>.

Table 448. Residential Property Tax Rates for Largest City in Each State: 2009

[The real property tax is a function of housing values, real estate tax rates, assessment levels, homeowner exemptions and credits. Effective rate is the amount each jurisdiction considers based upon assessment level used. Assessment level is ratio of assessed value to assumed market value. Nominal rates represent the "announced" rates levied by the jurisdiction]

City	Effective tax rate per $100		Assessment level (percent)	Nominal rate per $100	City	Effective tax rate per $100		Assessment level (percent)	Nominal rate per $100
	Rank	Rate				Rank	Rate		
Indianapolis, IN	1	2.75	100.0	2.75	Atlanta, GA	28	1.35	40.0	3.37
Bridgeport, CT.......	2	2.71	70.0	3.87	Sioux Falls, SD	29	1.27	85.0	1.49
Philadelphia, PA.......	3	2.64	32.0	8.26	Louisville, KY.........	30	1.26	100.0	1.26
Milwaukee, WI	4	2.56	100.0	2.56	Oklahoma City, OK	31	1.25	11.0	11.34
Houston, TX	5	2.52	100.0	2.52	Minneapolis, MN	32	1.24	96.8	1.28
Baltimore, MD	6	2.38	100.0	2.38	Salt Lake City, UT	33	1.15	100.0	1.15
Providence, RI	7	2.37	100.0	2.37	Las Vegas, NV	34	1.15	35.0	3.28
Des Moines, IA	8	2.29	118.0	1.94	Portland, OR	35	1.15	54.3	2.11
Detroit, MI	9	2.11	32.1	6.58	Los Angeles, CA	36	1.11	100.0	1.11
Omaha, NE	10	2.05	96.0	2.13	Charlotte, NC	37	1.08	82.9	1.30
Burlington, VT	11	2.00	100.0	2.00	Boston, MA	38	1.06	100.0	1.06
Memphis, TE	12	1.80	25.0	7.22	Columbia, SC	39	1.00	4.0	25.00
Portland, ME	13	1.79	100.0	1.79	Phoenix, AR..........	40	0.89	10.0	8.86
Columbus, OH	14	1.75	35.0	5.01	Charleston, WV	41	0.86	60.0	1.43
Manchester, NH	15	1.74	100.0	1.74	Washington, DC	42	0.85	100.0	0.85
Jacksonville, FL	16	1.73	100.0	1.73	Birmingham, AL.......	43	0.80	10.0	8.02
Jackson, MS	17	1.70	10.0	17.04	Seattle, WA	44	0.79	89.3	0.88
Fargo, ND	18	1.70	4.5	38.09	Billings, MT	45	0.78	26.8	2.93
Newark, NJ	19	1.63	59.7	2.74	Virginia Beach, VA.....	46	0.75	100.0	0.75
Boise, ID	20	1.60	108.4	1.47	Cheyenne, WY	47	0.67	9.5	7.10
Anchorage, AK	21	1.55	100.0	1.55	New York City, NY	48	0.62	3.7	16.70
Wilmington, DE	22	1.54	47.2	3.27	Denver, CO	49	0.53	8.0	6.68
Kansas City, MO	23	1.49	19.0	7.84	Chicago, IL.	50	0.52	10.0	5.17
Albuquerque, NM	24	1.44	33.3	4.32	Honolulu, HI.	51	0.34	100.0	0.34
Little Rock, AR	25	1.41	20.0	7.04					
New Orleans, LA	26	1.40	10.0	13.98	Unweighted average ...	(X)	1.46	60.2	5.45
Wichita, KS	27	1.38	11.5	12.04	Median.	(X)	1.40	60.0	2.74

X Not applicable.
Source: Government of the District of Columbia, Office of the Chief Financial Officer, "Tax Rates and Revenues, Tax Burden Comparisons, Nationwide Comparison" annual. See also <http://www.cfo.dco.gov/cfo>.

[In millions of dollars (78,521.2 represents $78,521,200,000). For fiscal years; see text, this section]

State	2006, total gross revenue	2007, total gross revenue	2008 Total gross revenue	2008 Amusement taxes [1]	2008 Pari-mutuel taxes	2008 Lottery revenue — Apportionment of funds: Total [2]	Prizes	Administration	Proceeds available from ticket sales
United States ...	78,521.2	82,218.1	59,388.2	6,376.6	225.5	52,786.1	32,211.4	2,391.7	18,183.1
Alabama	3.3	3.1	2.8	0.1	2.7	–	–	–	–
Alaska	2.4	2.4	9.5	9.5	(X)	–	–	–	–
Arizona	438.7	432.1	442.6	0.6	0.4	441.6	262.5	35.5	143.7
Arkansas	5.5	8.1	12.0	6.7	5.3	–	–	–	–
California	3,371.3	3,123.3	2,872.4	(X)	34.9	2,837.4	1,619.5	158.2	1,059.8
Colorado	533.1	568.9	578.4	108.2	2.7	467.4	313.8	33.5	120.1
Connecticut	1,383.2	1,377.8	1,402.3	451.8	8.3	942.2	608.2	41.9	292.1
Delaware	7,144.4	7,904.3	438.5	(X)	0.1	438.4	65.9	50.3	322.2
Florida	3,739.9	3,923.4	3,967.2	(X)	28.1	3,939.1	2,476.0	153.9	1,309.2
Georgia	2,751.9	2,957.8	3,045.6	(X)	(X)	3,045.6	2,049.5	135.8	860.3
Hawaii	(X)	(X)	(X)	(X)	(X)	–	–	–	–
Idaho	122.5	121.9	128.0	(X)	1.7	126.3	81.5	8.8	36.1
Illinois	2,656.7	2,839.6	2,772.1	706.4	8.4	2,057.3	1,199.0	59.6	798.6
Indiana	1,569.9	1,557.2	1,585.2	817.6	4.2	763.3	503.3	50.1	210.0
Iowa	486.6	499.2	532.1	294.5	4.1	233.6	144.7	31.7	57.2
Kansas	216.0	229.3	225.3	0.5	1.9	222.9	133.0	24.3	65.6
Kentucky	710.5	702.5	734.0	0.2	5.7	728.1	493.1	40.0	195.0
Louisiana	970.5	1,065.3	1,100.1	742.8	4.5	352.8	192.8	30.7	129.3
Maine	227.9	235.6	237.7	20.4	3.0	214.3	144.0	20.3	50.1
Maryland	1,470.9	1,474.7	1,571.8	14.8	1.8	1,555.2	956.9	58.2	540.1
Massachusetts	4,208.9	4,196.0	4,424.5	3.5	3.5	4,417.5	3,419.7	101.4	896.5
Michigan	2,191.4	2,511.1	2,468.1	129.7	8.2	2,330.2	1,350.7	66.6	912.9
Minnesota	453.1	429.6	455.2	43.2	1.0	411.0	295.0	23.6	92.4
Mississippi	145.7	185.8	194.0	194.0	(X)	–	–	–	–
Missouri	1,201.2	1,217.0	1,280.4	345.8	(X)	934.6	641.1	35.2	258.3
Montana	94.9	94.4	104.5	63.2	0.1	41.3	22.8	7.4	11.0
Nebraska	112.1	113.1	120.4	5.7	0.2	114.5	69.2	15.0	30.3
Nevada	1,045.8	1,089.1	1,047.8	1,047.8	(X)	–	–	–	–
New Hampshire	252.1	253.0	250.0	0.2	2.9	246.9	154.7	17.1	75.0
New Jersey	2,774.6	2,669.8	2,810.1	413.0	(X)	2,397.1	1,432.4	77.4	887.3
New Mexico	201.7	214.9	197.6	56.1	0.7	140.8	83.4	17.0	40.3
New York	6,321.7	6,608.5	6,871.8	1.0	30.9	6,840.0	3,952.8	299.6	2,587.6
North Carolina	225.2	839.5	1,017.0	14.3	(X)	1,002.7	618.2	48.5	336.0
North Dakota	31.1	30.8	30.8	9.2	0.5	21.1	11.4	3.7	6.0
Ohio	2,091.7	2,131.6	2,191.9	(X)	10.7	2,181.2	1,397.0	109.3	675.0
Oklahoma	195.3	214.6	213.6	11.0	1.8	200.9	112.8	15.5	72.5
Oregon	2,216.4	2,665.4	997.0	0.1	3.7	993.3	231.4	76.1	685.9
Pennsylvania	2,838.2	3,103.4	3,655.8	791.6	23.2	2,841.0	1,845.4	81.7	913.9
Rhode Island	1,542.7	1,619.7	510.5	(X)	2.8	507.7	147.6	9.5	350.6
South Carolina	1,100.2	956.2	960.0	38.0	(X)	922.1	620.5	40.2	261.4
South Dakota	580.6	587.0	161.1	8.3	0.3	152.4	23.9	7.0	121.4
Tennessee	930.9	989.2	995.2	(X)	(X)	995.2	676.7	51.4	267.1
Texas	3,619.8	3,618.3	3,522.2	26.5	10.0	3,485.8	2,281.1	167.2	1,037.4
Utah	(X)	(X)	(X)	(X)	(X)	–	–	–	–
Vermont	98.7	98.4	96.0	(X)	(X)	96.0	64.8	8.9	22.4
Virginia	1,289.2	1,286.0	1,386.5	0.1	(X)	1,386.4	792.3	72.6	521.5
Washington	449.5	463.5	492.0	0.0	3.2	488.7	314.9	42.2	131.6
West Virginia	14,027.7	14,545.6	813.3	(X)	2.9	810.4	121.2	32.7	656.5
Wisconsin	475.4	460.0	463.1	0.4	0.9	461.8	286.7	32.2	143.0
Wyoming	0.2	–	0.2	(X)	0.2	–	–	–	–

– Represents or rounds to zero. X Not applicable. [1] Represents nonlicense taxes. [2] Excludes commissions.
Source: U.S. Census Bureau, Federal, State and Local Governments, State Government Finances, Lottery, and unpublished data, <http://www.census.gov/govs/state/08lottery.html>.

Table 450. Lottery Sales—Type of Game and Use of Proceeds: 1990 to 2010

[In millions of dollars (20,017 represents $20,017,000,000). For fiscal years]

Game	1990	1995	2000	2005	2007	2008	2009	2010
Total ticket sales	20,017	31,931	37,201	47,364	52,414	53,360	53,062	54,196
Instant [1]	5,204	11,511	15,459	25,946	29,736	30,471	30,324	30,711
Three-digit [2]	4,572	5,737	5,341	5,428	5,586	5,544	5,518	5,415
Four-digit [2]	1,302	1,941	2,711	3,300	3,499	3,605	3,781	3,884
Lotto [3]	8,563	10,594	9,160	9,707	10,014	10,292	9,989	10,554
Other [4]	376	2,148	4,530	2,983	3,579	3,448	3,451	3,632
State proceeds (net income) [5]	7,703	11,100	11,404	15,779	17,627	17,877	17,601	17,972

[1] Player scratches a latex section on ticket which reveals instantly whether ticket is a winner. [2] Players choose and bet on three or four digits, depending on game, with various payoffs for different straight order or mixed combination bets. [3] Players typically select six digits out of a large field of numbers. Varying prizes are offered for matching three through six numbers drawn by lottery. [4] Includes break-open tickets, spiel, keno, video lottery, etc. [5] Sales minus prizes and expenses equal net government income.

Source: TLF Publications, Inc., Boyds, MD, 2010 World Lottery Almanac (copyright). See <http://www.lafleurs.com>.

Table 451. State Governments—Summary of Finances: 1990 to 2008

[In millions of dollars (673,119 represents $673,119,000,000). For fiscal year ending in year shown; see text, this section]

Item	1990	2000	2003	2004	2005	2006	2007	2008
Borrowing and revenue.......	**673,119**	**1,336,798**	**1,430,303**	**1,727,347**	**1,757,221**	**1,906,455**	**2,138,574**	**1,763,725**
Borrowing	632,172	1,260,829	134,644	140,682	115,264	133,247	138,208	144,597
Total revenue...............	517,429	984,783	1,295,659	1,586,665	1,641,957	1,773,208	2,000,366	1,619,128
General revenue	300,489	539,655	1,112,349	1,194,056	1,286,714	1,385,376	1,457,803	1,513,904
Taxes	147,069	252,147	548,991	590,414	650,612	710,864	757,471	781,647
Sales and gross receipts	99,702	174,461	273,811	293,326	312,584	332,972	352,706	358,522
General	19,379	29,968	184,597	197,949	212,921	226,712	238,304	241,008
Motor fuels...............	3,191	4,104	32,269	33,762	34,567	35,702	36,543	36,477
Alcoholic beverages........	5,541	8,391	4,399	4,593	4,706	4,925	5,166	5,293
Tobacco products...........	19,256	35,222	11,482	12,303	12,917	14,499	15,299	16,068
Other	18,842	32,598	41,065	44,718	47,474	51,134	57,393	59,677
Licenses	9,848	15,099	35,863	39,679	42,584	45,241	46,697	49,551
Motor vehicles	3,099	6,460	16,009	17,336	18,221	19,015	19,470	19,719
Corporations in general......	5,895	11,039	6,129	6,339	7,148	7,579	8,570	10,306
Other	96,076	194,573	13,725	16,004	17,216	18,648	18,657	19,527
Individual income.........	21,751	32,522	181,933	196,255	221,597	245,883	265,863	278,373
Corporation net income.......	5,848	10,996	28,384	30,229	38,691	47,466	52,915	50,759
Property..................	10,902	16,819	10,471	10,714	11,342	11,794	12,621	12,691
Other	90,612	170,747	18,529	20,211	23,813	27,509	26,668	31,751
Charges and miscellaneous	126,329	274,382	201,741	209,029	228,242	255,369	270,054	286,148
Intergovernmental revenue	118,353	259,114	361,617	394,613	407,860	419,143	430,278	446,109
From federal government......	59,397	147,150	343,308	374,694	386,283	397,597	410,184	423,150
Public welfare	21,271	42,086	196,954	214,528	222,909	222,916	233,479	243,513
Education...............	13,931	23,790	56,362	64,913	68,275	73,493	73,411	74,233
Highways...............	5,475	14,223	29,481	29,606	32,677	33,536	35,173	35,690
Health and hospitals	18,279	31,865	19,559	20,377	20,443	21,144	21,592	22,602
Other	7,976	15,268	40,951	45,270	41,980	46,508	46,530	47,113
From local governments	3,305	4,513	18,309	19,919	21,576	21,546	20,094	22,959
Utility revenue	2,907	3,895	12,518	12,955	14,627	15,816	16,736	16,522
Liquor store revenue	108,530	267,639	4,518	4,866	5,118	5,430	5,799	6,128
Insurance trust revenue [1].......	78,898	230,166	166,274	374,788	335,498	366,586	520,029	82,574
Employee retirement	18,370	23,260	110,839	308,896	269,617	300,350	456,789	20,664
Unemployment compensation...	18,370	23,260	35,191	38,230	35,243	36,864	34,063	34,360
Expenditure and debt redemption	**592,213**	**1,125,828**	**1,426,715**	**1,497,114**	**1,555,611**	**1,627,579**	**1,710,221**	**1,811,483**
Total expenditure	572,318	1,084,097	1,359,048	1,406,175	1,471,936	1,551,555	1,635,747	1,733,862
General expenditure	508,284	964,723	1,163,968	1,209,436	1,277,979	1,347,130	1,424,195	1,501,750
Education.................	184,935	346,465	411,094	429,341	454,364	481,877	514,147	546,806
Public welfare	104,971	238,890	314,407	339,409	370,219	378,605	393,690	412,130
Health	20,029	42,066	50,221	49,559	48,957	51,121	57,388	60,224
Hospitals	22,637	32,578	38,395	40,426	43,103	44,800	48,916	53,025
Highways.................	44,249	74,415	85,726	86,166	91,063	99,519	103,201	106,877
Police protection	5,166	9,788	11,144	10,766	11,426	12,233	12,876	13,594
Corrections	17,266	35,129	39,188	39,314	40,592	42,720	46,498	49,747
Natural resources	9,909	15,967	18,577	18,652	18,850	20,034	22,038	22,435
Housing and community development	2,856	4,726	8,112	7,191	7,708	7,918	12,475	14,576
Other and unallocable	96,267	164,698	187,106	188,613	191,697	208,302	212,964	222,336
Utility expenditure	7,131	10,723	22,405	21,676	21,824	24,904	24,530	26,073
Liquor store expenditure	2,452	3,195	3,697	3,924	4,082	4,338	4,664	4,945
Insurance trust expenditure [1].....	54,452	105,456	168,979	171,139	168,052	175,183	182,358	201,094
Employee retirement	29,562	75,971	103,049	111,376	118,333	127,493	135,760	146,665
Unemployment compensation...	16,423	18,583	51,411	43,174	29,776	28,009	28,854	35,471
By character and object:								
Intergovernmental expenditure ...	175,028	327,070	382,197	389,706	403,488	428,925	459,605	477,085
Direct expenditure	397,291	757,027	976,852	1,016,469	1,068,449	1,122,631	1,176,142	1,256,777
Current operation............	258,046	523,114	656,989	691,652	739,988	774,651	809,535	863,372
Capital outlay................	45,524	76,233	91,943	90,950	94,181	101,432	110,044	113,021
Construction	34,803	59,681	72,374	73,372	77,039	83,858	90,788	92,068
Land and existing structure	3,471	4,681	6,945	6,576	6,259	6,135	19,256	20,953
Equipment................	7,250	11,871	12,623	11,002	10,883	11,440	(NA)	(NA)
Assistance and subsidies	16,902	22,136	25,901	28,104	30,181	31,644	30,621	32,573
Interest on debt	22,367	30,089	33,040	34,624	36,047	39,720	43,584	46,717
Insurance benefits [2]...........	54,452	105,456	168,979	171,139	168,052	175,183	182,358	201,094
Debt redemption	19,895	41,730	67,666	90,939	83,675	76,024	74,474	77,621
Debt outstanding, year-end ...	**318,254**	**547,876**	**697,929**	**754,150**	**813,846**	**870,939**	**936,524**	**1,004,181**
Long-term [3]	315,490	541,497	681,796	740,414	808,293	860,310	929,947	990,000
Full-faith and credit	74,972	138,525	179,372	209,385	(NA)	(NA)	(NA)	(NA)
Nonguaranteed	240,518	402,972	502,424	531,030	(NA)	(NA)	(NA)	(NA)
Short-term..................	2,764	6,379	16,133	13,736	5,553	10,629	6,577	14,181
Net long-term [4]................	125,524	266,870	366,207	412,194	444,685	473,447	499,709	530,312
Full-faith and credit only	63,481	128,384	170,137	200,295	(NA)	(NA)	(NA)	(NA)

NA Not available. [1] Includes other items not shown separately. [2] Includes repayments. [3] As of fiscal year 2005, the Census Bureau no longer collects government debt information by the character of long-term debt. For further information, see the 2006 Government Finance and Employment Classification Manual at <http://www.census.gov/govs/www/classification/>. [4] Less cash and investment assets specifically held for redemption of long-term debt.

Source: U.S. Census Bureau, "Survey of State Government Finances, 2008." See also <http://www.census.gov/govs>.

Table 452. State Governments—Revenue by State: 2008

[In millions of dollars (1,619,128 represents $1,619,128,000,000), except as noted. For fiscal year ending in year shown. See text, this section. Includes local shares of state imposed taxes. Minus sign (–) indicates decrease]

State	Total revenue [1,2]	General revenue							Utilities and liquor store revenue	Insurance trust revenue
		Total	Intergovernmental revenue		General revenue from own sources					
			Total [1]	From federal govern- ment	Total	Total taxes	Current charges	Miscel- laneous general revenue		
United States ...	**1,619,128**	**1,513,904**	**446,109**	**423,150**	**1,067,795**	**781,647**	**151,002**	**135,146**	**22,650**	**82,574**
Alabama	18,354	21,974	7,713	7,146	14,261	9,071	3,473	1,718	249	–3,869
Alaska	16,028	15,875	2,191	2,186	13,684	8,425	555	4,704	17	136
Arizona	27,698	27,088	8,887	8,667	18,200	13,706	1,747	2,747	28	582
Arkansas	15,107	14,761	4,534	4,511	10,227	7,531	1,930	767	–	346
California	201,070	194,296	51,915	49,366	142,381	117,362	14,960	10,060	5,406	1,367
Colorado	26,503	19,599	4,945	4,853	14,654	9,625	2,892	2,138	–	6,904
Connecticut	22,160	22,068	4,345	4,333	17,723	14,598	1,682	1,443	28	64
Delaware	6,658	6,565	1,336	1,284	5,229	2,931	1,025	1,273	13	80
Florida	68,621	67,717	19,876	19,387	47,841	35,850	6,016	5,975	18	886
Georgia	41,154	36,672	13,090	12,871	23,581	18,070	3,263	2,248	4	4,478
Hawaii	9,299	9,302	2,093	2,089	7,209	5,148	1,243	819	–	–3
Idaho	7,107	6,764	2,005	1,986	4,759	3,652	592	515	116	227
Illinois	58,524	55,256	14,740	14,278	40,516	31,891	4,264	4,362	–	3,267
Indiana	29,315	29,244	8,349	8,163	20,895	15,116	3,323	2,455	–	71
Iowa	15,940	15,014	4,630	4,396	10,383	6,892	2,181	1,310	192	735
Kansas.	13,542	13,505	3,496	3,460	10,009	7,160	1,990	860	–	37
Kentucky	20,582	20,851	6,631	6,609	14,220	10,056	2,778	1,386	–	–269
Louisiana	30,308	29,869	14,181	14,111	15,688	11,004	1,913	2,771	8	431
Maine	7,656	7,656	2,428	2,416	5,228	3,786	634	808	–	–
Maryland	28,423	28,815	7,525	7,167	21,290	15,714	2,963	2,613	117	–510
Massachusetts.....	51,760	41,607	10,048	9,594	31,560	21,909	3,712	5,940	195	9,958
Michigan	42,259	49,151	13,359	13,143	35,792	24,782	6,290	4,721	768	–7,660
Minnesota	29,707	29,682	7,256	7,114	22,426	18,321	2,246	1,859	–	25
Mississippi........	16,278	16,530	7,719	7,623	8,811	6,771	1,391	650	249	–501
Missouri	25,243	24,212	8,501	8,303	15,711	10,965	2,422	2,324	–	1,032
Montana.	6,403	5,491	1,919	1,909	3,571	2,458	525	588	69	843
Nebraska.........	8,388	8,358	2,561	2,497	5,797	4,229	899	669	–	30
Nevada	10,439	9,398	1,858	1,719	7,541	6,116	685	740	68	972
New Hampshire....	6,285	5,707	1,830	1,603	3,877	2,251	811	815	463	114
New Jersey	55,046	51,396	11,218	10,625	40,178	30,617	5,231	4,331	865	2,785
New Mexico.......	12,893	13,713	4,322	4,202	9,391	5,646	1,174	2,571	–	–821
New York	147,340	133,010	46,624	39,342	86,386	65,371	8,209	12,807	7,807	6,524
North Carolina.....	51,421	43,097	13,650	12,966	29,447	22,781	3,846	2,820	–	8,324
North Dakota	5,019	4,655	1,233	1,195	3,422	2,312	703	406	–	364
Ohio.............	65,615	54,436	17,094	16,551	37,343	26,128	7,036	4,178	713	10,465
Oklahoma	18,657	17,826	5,706	5,581	12,121	8,331	2,108	1,681	458	372
Oregon.	17,138	16,648	4,835	4,820	11,813	7,279	2,278	2,256	402	88
Pennsylvania	71,142	60,800	16,170	15,968	44,630	32,124	7,065	5,441	1,413	8,929
Rhode Island	6,691	6,387	2,088	1,933	4,299	2,761	621	917	33	271
South Carolina.....	23,119	20,519	7,019	6,604	13,500	7,979	3,910	1,611	1,453	1,147
South Dakota......	2,910	3,426	1,256	1,240	2,170	1,321	307	541	–	–516
Tennessee........	25,699	25,178	8,308	8,187	16,870	11,538	2,044	3,288	–	521
Texas	119,095	98,975	33,603	29,487	65,371	44,676	10,114	10,582	–	20,120
Utah.............	15,408	13,183	3,442	3,360	9,741	6,109	2,400	1,232	218	2,007
Vermont..........	5,149	4,857	1,421	1,418	3,436	2,544	510	382	43	249
Virginia.	36,232	36,141	7,403	6,859	28,738	18,408	6,367	3,962	533	–442
Washington	36,660	32,273	8,304	7,998	23,969	17,960	3,690	2,320	547	3,841
West Virginia	10,724	10,754	3,274	3,194	7,480	4,882	1,279	1,319	75	–105
Wisconsin	25,644	27,976	7,014	6,838	20,962	15,089	3,531	2,342	–	–2,332
Wyoming	6,718	5,624	2,165	1,997	3,460	2,405	174	880	80	1,014

– Represents or rounds to zero. [1] Includes amounts for categories not shown separately. [2] Duplicate intergovernmental transactions are excluded.

Source: U.S. Census Bureau, Federal, State, and Local Governments, Finance, "Survey of State Government Finances, 2008." See also <http://www.census.gov/govs/>.

Table 453. State Government Tax Collections by State: 2008

[In millions of dollars (781,647 represents $781,647,000,000)]

State	All taxes	Total prop- erty taxes	Total general sales and gross receipts		Selective sales and gross receipts						
			Total	Total general sales and gross receipts	Selective sales tax						
					Total [1]	Alcoholic bever- age sales	Insur- ance premi- ums	Motor fuels sales	Public utilities	Tobacco products	Other
United States	781,647	12,691	358,522	241,008	117,515	5,293	15,718	36,477	14,794	16,068	29,165
Alabama	9,071	301	4,433	2,287	2,146	165	294	546	782	145	214
Alaska	8,425	82	280	–	280	39	55	42	4	73	66
Arizona	13,706	902	8,146	6,433	1,713	65	470	731	38	407	1
Arkansas	7,531	682	3,778	2,808	970	43	147	471	–	147	161
California	117,362	2,279	39,808	31,973	7,835	327	2,173	3,421	755	1,037	121
Colorado	9,625	–	3,520	2,313	1,207	35	191	637	12	221	111
Connecticut	14,598	–	5,813	3,546	2,267	47	199	490	242	335	954
Delaware	2,931	–	485	–	485	15	94	118	50	125	83
Florida	35,850	2	29,297	21,518	7,779	609	714	2,289	3,159	444	563
Georgia	18,070	82	7,689	5,797	1,892	166	348	1,011	–	233	134
Hawaii	5,148	–	3,302	2,620	683	46	99	94	127	89	227
Idaho	3,652	–	1,743	1,347	396	8	83	240	2	55	9
Illinois...........	31,891	59	15,472	7,935	7,536	158	316	1,335	1,920	614	3,194
Indiana...........	15,116	7	8,396	5,739	2,657	45	189	856	215	520	833
Iowa.............	6,892	–	2,961	1,841	1,120	14	112	442	–	253	299
Kansas...........	7,160	79	3,091	2,265	826	106	134	432	1	118	35
Kentucky	10,056	503	4,719	2,876	1,843	108	152	618	57	179	730
Louisiana.........	11,004	47	5,539	3,459	2,080	55	478	604	14	146	782
Maine............	3,786	37	1,705	1,061	645	17	97	230	33	150	117
Maryland	15,714	631	6,249	3,749	2,500	29	414	809	134	376	738
Massachusetts......	21,909	4	6,056	4,098	1,958	72	396	673	24	437	356
Michigan	24,782	2,264	11,920	8,226	3,695	139	223	995	21	1,076	1,240
Minnesota	18,321	712	7,433	4,551	2,882	73	347	649	–	419	1,395
Mississippi........	6,771	50	4,229	3,135	1,094	42	194	442	2	58	356
Missouri..........	10,965	29	4,771	3,228	1,542	31	284	736	–	109	382
Montana..........	2,458	220	544	–	544	27	65	206	49	94	103
Nebraska..........	4,229	2	2,035	1,534	501	26	37	294	57	75	12
Nevada	6,116	192	4,930	3,077	1,853	40	257	312	12	135	1,097
New Hampshire.....	2,251	388	793	–	793	13	86	137	79	170	309
New Jersey	30,617	3	12,520	8,916	3,604	104	543	563	930	789	674
New Mexico.......	5,646	58	2,663	1,950	714	41	144	250	36	48	194
New York	65,371	–	20,150	11,295	8,855	205	1,137	528	764	973	5,248
North Carolina.....	22,781	–	8,930	5,270	3,660	260	506	1,582	389	248	674
North Dakota......	2,312	2	873	530	343	7	37	143	34	24	97
Ohio.............	26,128	–	12,745	7,866	4,880	93	444	1,843	1,142	951	408
Oklahoma	8,331	–	3,034	2,096	938	86	147	385	30	252	36
Oregon...........	7,279	22	761	–	761	16	50	414	23	255	4
Pennsylvania.......	32,124	59	15,306	8,873	6,433	277	698	2,102	1,355	1,026	974
Rhode Island.......	2,761	1	1,381	847	534	11	53	127	100	114	129
South Carolina......	7,979	10	4,279	3,052	1,228	150	126	534	26	31	360
South Dakota......	1,321	–	1,072	732	340	14	62	130	3	64	67
Tennessee.........	11,538	–	8,612	6,833	1,779	116	402	873	10	272	106
Texas.............	44,676	–	33,365	21,669	11,696	784	1,405	3,103	1,016	1,447	3,941
Utah.............	6,109	–	2,644	1,964	680	40	132	377	31	62	38
Vermont...........	2,544	810	855	339	516	20	57	92	11	59	278
Virginia...........	18,408	22	6,093	3,657	2,437	176	397	920	150	168	626
Washington	17,960	1,742	14,401	11,345	3,056	267	415	1,170	468	413	323
West Virginia	4,882	5	2,267	1,110	1,157	9	114	404	158	115	356
Wisconsin	15,089	125	6,317	4,268	2,049	55	172	1,001	327	485	8
Wyoming	2,405	279	1,116	981	135	2	26	75	3	27	1

See footnotes at end of table.

Table 453. State Government Tax Collections by State: 2008—Con.

[See headnote, page 288]

State	License taxes Total [1]	Selected license taxes Corporation	Motor vehicle operators	Occupancy and business, n.e.c. [2]	Income taxes Total	Individual income	Corporation net income	Other taxes Total [1]	Selected other taxes Death and gift	Severance
United States	**49,551**	**10,306**	**2,163**	**12,526**	**329,132**	**278,373**	**50,759**	**31,751**	**5,101**	**18,278**
Alabama	488	103	18	122	3,602	3,078	525	246	–	198
Alaska	143	1	–	42	982	–	982	6,939	–	6,939
Arizona	421	23	27	99	4,193	3,409	785	44	–	44
Arkansas	307	23	15	97	2,687	2,345	343	75	–	28
California	7,642	61	235	3,795	67,595	55,746	11,849	38	6	32
Colorado	377	13	14	34	5,576	5,068	508	152	–	151
Connecticut	355	17	39	80	8,108	7,504	604	322	166	–
Delaware	1,033	619	3	245	1,316	1,007	309	98	–	–
Florida	1,875	220	162	247	2,209	–	2,209	2,467	12	56
Georgia	496	32	65	70	9,789	8,845	943	14	–	–
Hawaii	157	2	–	26	1,650	1,545	105	38	–	–
Idaho	270	2	7	60	1,629	1,439	190	10	–	7
Illinois	2,475	234	67	751	13,436	10,320	3,116	450	373	–
Indiana	800	3	226	44	5,747	4,838	909	166	166	–
Iowa	640	40	15	106	3,196	2,848	347	96	80	–
Kansas	304	55	17	27	3,473	2,945	528	213	44	169
Kentucky	470	76	20	114	4,017	3,483	534	348	51	293
Louisiana	499	253	11	108	3,873	3,170	703	1,047	11	1,036
Maine	231	8	12	96	1,747	1,563	185	65	40	–
Maryland	697	74	29	133	7,675	6,940	735	461	243	–
Massachusetts	685	24	93	168	14,676	12,496	2,180	487	254	–
Michigan	1,354	20	52	151	8,959	7,181	1,778	284	–	114
Minnesota	1,011	7	50	330	8,818	7,777	1,040	346	116	32
Mississippi	419	130	34	84	1,936	1,551	385	136	1	135
Missouri	651	89	16	155	5,503	5,119	384	12	3	–
Montana	311	3	8	90	1,032	870	162	350	–	347
Nebraska	207	7	9	63	1,959	1,726	233	25	7	5
Nevada	542	72	16	173	–	–	–	451	–	74
New Hampshire	216	39	13	47	733	118	615	122	–	–
New Jersey	1,452	313	38	568	15,425	12,606	2,820	1,216	699	–
New Mexico	258	20	5	25	1,568	1,214	355	1,099	–	1,090
New York	1,356	70	145	148	41,602	36,564	5,038	2,263	1,038	–
North Carolina	1,412	448	134	185	12,200	10,994	1,206	239	176	2
North Dakota	166	–	4	57	479	317	162	792	–	792
Ohio	2,710	1,016	80	647	10,602	9,848	755	71	61	9
Oklahoma	891	53	15	82	3,148	2,787	360	1,258	55	1,185
Oregon	917	13	32	307	5,446	4,969	477	133	110	12
Pennsylvania	2,823	813	62	717	12,600	10,408	2,191	1,336	803	–
Rhode Island	96	4	1	35	1,238	1,092	146	46	35	–
South Carolina	434	78	45	132	3,184	2,864	320	72	–	–
South Dakota	172	3	3	79	70	–	70	7	–	7
Tennessee	1,288	645	44	271	1,297	291	1,006	341	103	2
Texas	7,174	4,453	116	872	–	–	–	4,137	6	4,131
Utah	371	4	14	38	2,988	2,593	395	106	–	106
Vermont	125	5	5	27	708	623	85	46	16	–
Virginia	653	55	45	159	10,902	10,115	787	738	153	2
Washington	953	25	62	246	–	–	–	864	111	44
West Virginia	193	7	4	42	2,058	1,519	539	359	–	348
Wisconsin	910	18	36	312	7,504	6,641	863	234	159	5
Wyoming	121	11	2	19	–	–	–	889	1	884

– Represents zero or rounds to zero. [1] Includes other items not shown separately. [2] n.e.c. means not elsewhere classified.
Source: U.S. Census Bureau, *Tax collections, State government tax collections*, annual. See also <http://www.census.gov/govs/statetax>.

Table 454. State Governments—Expenditures and Debt by State: 2008

[In millions of dollars (1,733,862 represents $1,733,862,000,000) except as indicated. For fiscal year ending in year shown; see text, this section]

State	Total expenditures	General expenditures								
		Total	Inter-governmental	Direct expenditures						
				Total	Education	Public welfare	Health	Hospitals	Highways	Police protection
United States ...	1,733,862	1,501,750	477,085	1,024,666	232,212	354,048	40,033	51,938	90,645	12,034
Alabama	24,893	22,171	6,721	15,450	5,284	4,521	668	1,346	1,162	154
Alaska	10,116	9,149	1,488	7,661	1,229	1,409	135	32	1,313	76
Arizona	30,779	27,569	10,242	17,327	3,668	6,958	1,548	71	1,557	258
Arkansas	15,656	14,355	4,392	9,963	2,529	3,772	248	811	751	81
California	246,684	208,783	93,644	115,139	23,379	35,097	3,436	6,865	8,250	1,616
Colorado	22,806	19,291	6,228	13,063	4,044	3,411	673	438	966	137
Connecticut	23,529	20,057	4,231	15,826	2,952	5,082	617	1,385	793	217
Delaware	7,152	6,561	1,172	5,389	1,217	1,442	381	63	489	111
Florida	77,195	69,156	19,703	49,453	7,923	18,031	3,591	831	6,533	453
Georgia	41,165	36,165	10,415	25,750	7,004	9,143	1,159	805	2,287	317
Hawaii	10,534	9,567	138	9,429	3,394	1,564	670	531	408	12
Idaho	7,675	6,807	2,038	4,769	1,124	1,614	146	47	565	49
Illinois...........	63,368	54,310	14,750	39,560	7,412	15,665	2,168	1,005	3,799	397
Indiana..........	30,783	28,418	7,969	20,448	5,734	7,855	586	198	1,959	253
Iowa............	16,523	14,830	4,143	10,687	2,762	3,789	136	1,088	930	90
Kansas..........	14,969	13,646	4,214	9,431	2,064	3,166	214	973	1,052	99
Kentucky	25,422	22,363	4,701	17,662	4,796	6,074	474	1,092	2,067	168
Louisiana........	33,004	29,983	6,023	23,960	4,761	5,723	641	1,021	2,053	248
Maine...........	8,151	7,425	1,335	6,090	929	2,471	467	56	451	70
Maryland	34,030	30,328	8,509	21,819	4,475	7,115	1,305	495	1,981	340
Massachusetts.....	45,635	40,398	9,252	31,146	4,766	12,319	1,049	467	2,043	432
Michigan	56,869	49,825	19,513	30,312	8,835	10,540	988	2,299	1,499	308
Minnesota	34,284	30,255	11,189	19,066	5,088	8,388	486	405	1,385	265
Mississippi.......	18,643	16,777	5,112	11,665	2,213	4,219	320	953	1,091	107
Missouri.........	26,789	23,621	5,639	17,983	3,591	6,175	1,136	1,322	1,740	215
Montana.........	6,138	5,424	1,319	4,105	962	858	309	45	590	41
Nebraska........	8,443	8,024	1,982	6,042	1,602	2,068	337	239	624	66
Nevada	10,845	9,320	3,860	5,460	1,594	1,492	248	234	508	101
New Hampshire....	6,602	5,672	1,452	4,220	926	1,435	123	60	404	50
New Jersey	58,539	46,810	10,928	35,883	8,433	11,547	1,270	1,920	2,559	461
New Mexico.......	15,793	14,413	4,348	10,064	2,060	3,559	491	750	864	124
New York	157,398	128,221	52,821	75,401	10,830	33,428	2,117	4,896	4,371	779
North Carolina....	46,707	41,820	13,196	28,624	7,992	8,935	1,323	1,461	3,013	494
North Dakota	4,126	3,790	805	2,984	830	759	54	16	360	27
Ohio............	67,789	54,581	18,106	36,475	9,187	13,737	1,463	2,090	2,547	252
Oklahoma	19,518	17,209	4,392	12,817	3,567	4,773	556	227	1,196	160
Oregon..........	22,387	18,076	5,641	12,435	2,741	3,834	307	1,154	1,088	156
Pennsylvania	71,635	60,486	17,801	42,685	8,462	16,473	715	2,436	5,845	759
Rhode Island	7,496	6,228	1,054	5,175	823	2,143	181	88	202	57
South Carolina.....	27,594	22,988	5,719	17,269	4,606	5,416	1,019	1,685	958	195
South Dakota......	3,698	3,400	680	2,720	570	806	120	61	393	30
Tennessee........	26,253	24,415	6,510	17,906	4,020	8,054	1,235	408	1,274	156
Texas...........	99,127	88,765	25,158	63,607	16,980	22,432	1,684	2,914	7,603	714
Utah............	14,294	12,967	3,050	9,917	3,234	2,177	347	823	1,000	127
Vermont.........	5,070	4,707	1,341	3,366	832	1,253	163	20	268	73
Virginia..........	39,765	36,301	11,032	25,269	7,308	6,665	533	2,850	2,703	301
Washington	39,690	34,092	9,144	24,948	6,805	7,607	1,257	1,744	2,282	231
West Virginia......	10,597	9,669	2,130	7,539	1,869	2,540	293	106	1,006	65
Wisconsin	32,625	27,996	10,088	17,908	4,307	5,856	374	1,106	1,341	126
Wyoming	5,082	4,564	1,769	2,795	502	656	273	2	521	16

See footnotes at end of table.

U.S. Census Bureau, Statistical Abstract of the United States: 2012

Table 454. State Governments—Expenditures and Debt by State: 2008—Con.

[See headnote, page 290]

State	General expenditures—Con. Direct expenditures—Con.								Expenditures			
	Corrections	Parks and recreation	Housing and community development	Sewerage	Solid waste management	Governmental administration	Interest on general debt	Other	Utility and liquor store	Insurance trust	Cash and security holdings	Total debt outstanding
United States...	**47,239**	**5,510**	**10,857**	**1,273**	**2,439**	**52,102**	**44,719**	**79,618**	**31,018**	**201,094**	**3,826,448**	**1,004,181**
Alabama	496	49	11	–	1	574	329	854	235	2,487	40,282	8,472
Alaska	244	15	142	–	–	570	310	2,185	82	885	68,098	6,492
Arizona	974	74	81	–	4	722	491	920	31	3,179	50,786	10,519
Arkansas	361	46	11	–	9	591	194	557	–	1,301	24,149	4,283
California	8,454	421	277	169	1,256	8,782	5,651	11,487	5,225	32,676	541,497	121,930
Colorado	841	67	78	2	2	739	827	837	27	3,488	68,209	15,879
Connecticut	713	28	157	–	167	1,113	1,266	1,336	405	3,066	43,739	27,554
Delaware	281	52	59	–	94	475	270	456	124	467	13,293	5,723
Florida	2,770	192	76	–	220	2,972	1,604	4,256	86	7,954	185,490	42,321
Georgia	1,535	209	236	6	42	810	598	1,596	34	4,966	76,804	13,072
Hawaii	219	78	129	18	–	481	441	1,486	1	966	17,234	6,028
Idaho	236	33	14	–	–	360	162	418	86	782	17,133	3,379
Illinois..........	1,234	112	248	18	39	1,147	2,867	3,450	–	9,058	131,651	58,437
Indiana.........	677	65	274	7	6	639	968	1,229	44	2,322	55,122	19,916
Iowa...........	288	51	28	–	2	539	392	592	135	1,558	34,551	7,236
Kansas.........	312	36	67	–	4	447	334	662	–	1,323	18,478	5,837
Kentucky	508	117	153	–	23	811	503	874	–	3,058	42,818	12,210
Louisiana.......	633	336	4,949	–	–	909	904	1,784	5	3,015	59,236	16,388
Maine..........	142	11	124	2	2	315	258	791	–	726	17,198	5,296
Maryland	1,336	249	249	112	20	1,239	1,046	1,857	714	2,987	59,309	23,070
Massachusetts....	1,109	210	398	289	11	1,665	3,627	2,762	235	5,002	103,791	71,892
Michigan	1,826	85	516	–	9	949	1,310	1,150	622	6,422	97,950	29,065
Minnesota	467	171	89	–	20	843	497	962	160	3,869	61,291	9,539
Mississippi.......	328	37	15	–	–	323	239	1,822	202	1,665	32,296	6,331
Missouri.........	711	37	178	–	10	507	1,046	1,316	–	3,167	68,868	19,709
Montana.........	168	14	44	–	1	315	209	547	59	655	16,241	4,924
Nebraska........	219	29	1	5	12	205	108	527	–	419	14,273	2,719
Nevada	365	45	8	–	–	296	203	366	70	1,455	26,673	4,249
New Hampshire...	112	15	96	1	10	231	381	375	407	523	12,578	7,909
New Jersey	1,436	494	330	3	53	1,796	2,053	3,527	2,750	8,979	117,590	52,785
New Mexico......	377	92	60	–	–	528	393	766	20	1,360	48,222	7,764
New York	3,020	510	358	–	150	5,770	3,790	5,382	13,077	16,099	361,160	114,240
North Carolina....	1,321	210	178	–	12	1,165	676	1,845	125	4,763	98,410	19,605
North Dakota.....	61	25	25	–	–	120	164	543	–	336	11,840	1,952
Ohio............	1,506	111	278	471	35	1,705	1,441	1,654	445	12,763	202,397	26,885
Oklahoma	600	93	14	6	10	495	461	658	419	1,890	37,066	9,130
Oregon.........	607	86	101	2	5	888	450	1,016	217	4,094	70,998	11,647
Pennsylvania.....	1,685	219	57	1	22	2,462	1,948	1,600	1,330	9,819	152,816	40,100
Rhode Island.....	199	8	44	32	52	362	420	564	139	1,128	16,356	8,912
South Carolina....	508	100	133	–	–	1,051	591	1,006	1,832	2,773	40,977	15,213
South Dakota.....	109	42	40	–	–	168	136	245	–	298	12,286	3,408
Tennessee.......	583	143	39	19	13	716	214	1,031	–	1,838	37,293	4,366
Texas..........	3,415	98	29	3	63	1,475	1,190	5,008	140	10,222	273,877	33,299
Utah...........	333	59	81	10	–	701	276	749	158	1,169	30,171	5,907
Vermont.........	119	14	73	11	12	156	181	190	73	290	7,082	3,372
Virginia.........	1,214	123	164	48	3	985	883	1,490	629	2,835	81,476	21,875
Washington	1,205	79	96	–	14	756	1,039	1,833	520	5,077	95,856	23,524
West Virginia	242	57	15	34	9	399	255	649	76	852	16,357	6,366
Wisconsin	976	27	25	–	16	641	1,061	2,052	7	4,622	95,054	22,107
Wyoming	164	34	10	–	3	193	62	358	70	448	20,125	1,343

– Represents or rounds to zero.
Source: U.S. Census Bureau, "Survey of State Government Finances, 2008," June 2011. See also <http://www.census.gov/govs>.

U.S. Census Bureau, Statistical Abstract of the United States: 2012

Table 455. Local Governments—Revenue by State: 2008

[In millions of dollars (1,530,814 represents $1,530,814,000,000), except as noted. For fiscal year ending in year shown; see text, this section. Minus sign (–) indicates decrease]

State	Total revenue	General revenue, total	Inter–governmental revenue	General revenue from own sources — Total	Taxes — Total	Property	Sales and gross receipt	Individual income	Corporation income	Other taxes
United States	**1,530,814**	**1,401,341**	**524,738**	**876,604**	**548,765**	**396,995**	**90,166**	**26,255**	**7,051**	**28,298**
Alabama	20,313	17,314	7,179	10,134	4,970	2,005	2,146	111	–	709
Alaska	4,060	3,771	1,547	2,224	1,310	987	287	–	–	36
Arizona	29,767	25,599	10,592	15,007	9,286	5,803	2,971	–	–	513
Arkansas	8,756	7,879	4,468	3,412	1,875	780	1,060	–	–	36
California	246,099	226,689	98,973	127,716	68,653	50,480	13,679	–	–	4,494
Colorado	25,974	22,992	6,057	16,935	10,012	6,130	3,269	–	–	612
Connecticut	15,432	14,680	4,698	9,982	8,517	8,325	2	–	–	190
Delaware	3,033	2,612	1,291	1,321	781	605	7	57	–	112
District of Columbia	11,790	10,023	3,011	7,012	5,398	1,728	1,388	1,355	420	507
Florida	101,399	90,435	25,476	64,959	37,501	30,258	5,173	–	–	2,070
Georgia	43,030	38,345	12,073	26,272	15,562	10,138	4,963	–	–	462
Hawaii	2,891	2,618	455	2,163	1,589	1,253	168	–	–	168
Idaho	5,510	5,297	2,186	3,112	1,288	1,181	29	–	–	78
Illinois	62,476	57,062	19,435	37,628	25,943	21,236	3,809	–	–	899
Indiana	25,252	23,137	8,351	14,786	7,838	6,928	100	548	–	262
Iowa	13,366	12,462	4,513	7,950	4,649	3,719	768	83	–	78
Kansas	13,009	11,701	4,066	7,635	4,718	3,608	997	2	–	110
Kentucky	13,397	11,901	4,904	6,997	4,100	2,276	536	1,051	122	116
Louisiana	19,755	18,343	6,816	11,527	6,947	2,791	3,958	–	–	197
Maine	4,499	4,372	1,526	2,846	2,147	2,120	5	–	–	22
Maryland	24,459	23,794	8,141	15,653	11,937	5,980	559	4,244	–	1,154
Massachusetts	31,489	27,109	10,968	16,140	12,089	11,661	169	–	–	259
Michigan	44,641	42,264	19,814	22,450	12,868	11,862	283	461	–	262
Minnesota	26,406	24,166	11,046	13,120	6,403	5,922	276	–	–	204
Mississippi	11,881	11,078	4,992	6,085	2,442	2,249	101	–	–	92
Missouri	22,657	20,555	6,350	14,205	8,907	5,451	2,515	354	–	587
Montana	3,283	3,169	1,348	1,821	990	955	5	–	–	30
Nebraska	11,348	7,728	2,191	5,537	3,279	2,483	451	–	–	346
Nevada	14,371	13,465	5,251	8,214	4,472	3,024	968	–	–	481
New Hampshire	4,976	4,854	1,546	3,308	2,712	2,670	–	–	–	42
New Jersey	43,230	42,276	12,626	29,650	23,174	22,705	121	–	–	348
New Mexico	8,053	7,553	4,239	3,314	2,101	1,066	916	–	–	119
New York	151,229	150,504	52,784	97,720	72,917	39,069	13,741	9,890	6,293	3,925
North Carolina	38,507	34,211	14,281	19,930	10,427	7,870	2,218	–	–	338
North Dakota	2,405	2,267	872	1,395	862	738	107	–	–	17
Ohio	54,536	51,977	20,786	31,192	20,532	13,573	1,948	4,168	138	706
Oklahoma	12,370	11,351	4,481	6,870	3,984	2,113	1,704	–	–	167
Oregon	17,225	15,912	6,399	9,513	5,253	4,236	338	7	66	607
Pennsylvania	58,524	55,148	22,847	32,301	21,986	15,478	608	3,924	13	1,963
Rhode Island	4,089	3,929	1,327	2,602	2,112	2,063	14	–	–	36
South Carolina	17,786	16,244	5,479	10,765	5,183	4,289	313	–	–	581
South Dakota	2,938	2,622	833	1,789	1,179	859	289	–	–	31
Tennessee	28,423	20,121	6,638	13,484	7,461	4,670	2,386	–	–	405
Texas	108,196	95,982	30,241	65,741	41,707	33,540	7,132	–	–	1,035
Utah	10,682	8,866	3,485	5,381	3,262	2,218	940	–	–	104
Vermont	2,359	2,128	1,477	650	391	367	12	–	–	13
Virginia	32,818	31,250	11,392	19,857	14,298	10,547	2,482	–	–	1,269
Washington	36,468	30,339	10,938	19,400	10,630	6,067	3,507	–	–	1,055
West Virginia	5,030	4,809	2,152	2,657	1,546	1,233	113	–	–	200
Wisconsin	26,142	24,104	10,443	13,661	9,284	8,705	375	–	–	204
Wyoming	4,486	4,331	1,751	2,580	1,289	981	262	–	–	46

See footnotes at end of table.

U.S. Census Bureau, Statistical Abstract of the United States: 2012

Table 455. Local Governments—Revenue by State: 2008—Con.

[See headnote, page 292]

State	Current charges and miscellaneous general revenue	General revenue—Con. General revenue from own sources—Con. Current charges				Miscelleneous general revenue			Utility revenue	Liquor store revenue	Insurance trust revenue
		Total [1]	Education	Hospitals	Sewerage	Total [1]	Interest earnings	Special assessment			
United States	327,839	222,667	24,960	61,001	38,019	105,172	46,072	6,961	122,620	1,114	5,738
Alabama	5,164	3,957	384	2,463	387	1,207	423	42	2,617	–	382
Alaska...	914	592	28	208	78	321	179	7	269	11	9
Arizona...	5,721	3,565	540	673	655	2,156	932	153	4,178	–	–10
Arkansas	1,537	957	147	186	220	580	264	26	852	–	24
California	59,063	40,102	2,701	8,646	5,472	18,961	8,708	1,269	21,327	–	–1,918
Colorado	6,924	4,617	429	1,256	703	2,307	880	197	2,313	–	670
Connecticut	1,464	975	148	–	293	489	182	36	726	–	26
Delaware	540	331	18	–	138	209	60	31	378	–	43
District of Columbia . . .	1,614	485	64	8	186	1,129	215	0	875	–	893
Florida	27,458	17,962	2,270	5,134	2,508	9,496	3,828	1,556	8,545	–	2,419
Georgia	10,709	7,971	553	3,899	1,101	2,738	1,153	63	4,450	–	235
Hawaii	574	446	–	–	234	128	82	13	273	–	–
Idaho	1,824	1,460	90	772	173	364	128	40	212	–	1
Illinois.	11,685	7,235	1,313	764	1,021	4,450	1,971	526	3,357	–	2,057
Indiana.	6,947	4,672	368	2,616	936	2,276	579	47	2,028	–	87
Iowa.	3,301	2,595	523	1,173	353	706	303	24	903	–	1
Kansas.	2,918	1,906	370	712	302	1,012	477	90	1,192	–	115
Kentucky	2,897	1,930	132	474	424	967	695	13	1,475	–	21
Louisiana	4,580	3,094	62	1,726	343	1,487	800	25	1,227	–	185
Maine.	699	535	50	72	145	164	68	5	127	–	–
Maryland	3,716	2,627	665	–	770	1,089	314	65	591	205	–130
Massachusetts.	4,052	3,095	306	879	927	957	324	37	2,991	–	1,389
Michigan	9,581	6,777	1,200	845	1,543	2,804	1,288	245	2,330	–	47
Minnesota	6,717	4,366	472	1,257	618	2,351	937	396	1,991	309	–60
Mississippi	3,643	2,959	398	1,993	203	684	261	7	804	–	–
Missouri	5,298	3,644	695	1,161	617	1,653	721	61	1,819	–	283
Montana.	831	525	71	56	77	307	100	70	114	–	–
Nebraska.	2,258	1,707	222	643	156	551	240	70	3,487	–	133
Nevada	3,742	2,530	120	620	387	1,212	456	59	905	–	–
New Hampshire.	597	408	55	–	105	189	70	2	103	–	18
New Jersey	6,475	4,576	1,180	442	1,369	1,899	659	13	955	–	–2
New Mexico	1,213	730	103	98	131	482	206	24	500	–	–
New York	24,803	15,794	1,454	3,567	1,780	9,009	3,295	117	5,261	–	–4,535
North Carolina	9,503	7,492	581	3,793	1,090	2,011	840	7	3,742	568	–14
North Dakota	533	270	47	–	43	263	81	67	116	–	22
Ohio.	10,660	6,690	1,116	1,011	1,818	3,970	1,973	242	2,517	–	42
Oklahoma	2,887	2,120	308	823	268	767	311	11	939	–	80
Oregon.	4,260	2,713	494	256	735	1,547	547	104	1,311	–	1
Pennsylvania	10,315	6,412	891	29	2,038	3,904	2,094	125	2,732	–	644
Rhode Island	490	327	33	–	94	162	43	8	168	–	–8
South Carolina.	5,581	4,258	252	2,812	466	1,323	516	96	1,537	–	5
South Dakota.	611	427	68	41	65	184	83	26	243	22	50
Tennessee.	6,023	4,597	385	2,338	597	1,426	609	123	8,324	–	–23
Texas	24,034	15,488	2,157	4,331	2,668	8,546	5,195	182	10,272	–	1,942
Utah.	2,119	1,347	84	52	306	772	348	37	1,816	–	–
Vermont.	259	170	24	–	53	89	33	3	212	–	19
Virginia.	5,559	3,768	395	258	1,010	1,791	704	202	1,769	–	–201
Washington	8,771	6,495	353	1,831	1,526	2,276	1,033	261	5,851	–	278
West Virginia	1,111	769	35	284	187	342	136	25	210	–	11
Wisconsin	4,377	3,150	531	53	646	1,227	627	103	1,529	–	508
Wyoming	1,291	1,051	74	747	54	240	100	11	155	–	–

– Represents or rounds to zero. [1] Includes items not shown separately.
Source: U.S. Census Bureau; Federal, State and Local Governments, "State Government Finances, 2008," June 2011.
See also <http://www.census.gov/govs/>.

Table 456. Local Governments—Expenditures and Debt by State: 2008

[In millions of dollars (1,593,088 represents $1,593,088,000,000), except as indicated. For fiscal year ending in year shown; see text, this section]

State	Total expendi-tures	General expenditures							
		Total [1]	Direct expenditures						
			Total	Educa-tion	Public welfare	Health	Hospi-tals	High-ways	Police protec-tion
United States	**1,593,088**	**1,391,329**	**1,375,539**	**593,851**	**50,576**	**39,671**	**76,916**	**62,870**	**77,642**
Alabama	20,046	17,194	17,177	7,737	48	375	2,513	818	890
Alaska	4,275	3,863	3,862	1,781	6	65	225	208	186
Arizona	32,218	26,119	25,897	10,373	273	244	1,145	1,444	1,897
Arkansas	8,916	7,935	7,927	4,457	14	34	183	446	412
California	259,359	220,745	220,144	80,492	15,892	10,505	11,094	7,452	13,275
Colorado	25,992	22,566	22,528	8,559	787	286	1,484	1,382	1,315
Connecticut	15,787	14,592	14,588	8,175	103	148	–	550	779
Delaware	3,097	2,692	2,686	1,662	–	36	–	90	178
District of Columbia	12,949	10,677	10,677	2,227	2,405	564	232	411	591
Florida	100,978	89,329	89,033	33,386	1,489	943	6,901	4,053	6,282
Georgia	46,997	39,579	39,540	18,646	212	1,139	4,310	1,598	1,976
Hawaii	2,819	2,275	2,275	–	64	46	–	170	323
Idaho	5,147	4,931	4,928	2,045	28	60	756	315	271
Illinois	67,016	56,666	56,658	25,324	570	730	1,427	2,988	3,844
Indiana	26,557	24,099	23,994	9,685	493	223	2,867	873	970
Iowa	13,498	12,436	12,343	5,928	102	372	1,299	897	524
Kansas	12,727	11,471	11,462	5,443	38	253	771	804	585
Kentucky	13,645	11,817	11,809	5,837	53	331	537	459	534
Louisiana	18,971	17,415	17,401	7,049	35	175	2,129	912	1,079
Maine	4,351	4,225	4,219	2,260	34	38	75	262	163
Maryland	25,914	24,130	23,921	12,727	216	420	–	904	1,502
Massachusetts	32,175	26,318	25,459	12,540	63	119	1,302	822	1,411
Michigan	46,856	42,221	41,972	19,476	1,110	2,652	965	2,215	2,118
Minnesota	27,867	25,115	24,997	9,714	1,628	622	1,432	2,356	1,261
Mississippi	11,642	10,791	10,789	4,942	26	101	1,914	596	494
Missouri	23,955	21,281	21,278	10,348	181	368	1,354	1,090	1,417
Montana	3,298	3,154	3,153	1,560	46	97	64	179	185
Nebraska	11,860	7,674	7,673	3,488	75	81	636	577	462
Nevada	14,488	12,785	12,773	4,633	334	143	721	942	978
New Hampshire	4,901	4,790	4,707	2,494	202	29	–	247	266
New Jersey	44,513	43,388	42,992	22,070	1,073	406	514	1,190	2,626
New Mexico	7,850	7,239	7,209	3,852	115	50	131	331	479
New York	167,709	146,453	136,975	53,913	10,519	3,682	7,368	5,325	7,385
North Carolina	40,095	35,474	34,741	14,794	1,541	1,557	4,139	548	1,724
North Dakota	2,310	2,149	2,135	1,015	51	36	2	258	93
Ohio	53,634	50,371	49,965	21,696	2,914	2,720	1,347	2,211	2,905
Oklahoma	12,261	11,189	11,188	5,577	39	134	846	772	603
Oregon	17,830	15,722	15,707	6,933	269	555	268	816	854
Pennsylvania	58,221	52,361	52,012	24,645	3,782	3,333	8	1,635	2,081
Rhode Island	4,106	3,790	3,790	2,114	10	6	–	103	260
South Carolina	17,894	16,412	16,384	7,646	35	169	2,817	436	785
South Dakota	2,815	2,503	2,503	1,183	13	36	41	276	111
Tennessee	29,387	19,914	19,912	8,356	136	355	2,484	738	1,318
Texas	115,903	100,591	99,405	48,990	278	1,797	7,068	6,705	4,912
Utah	10,975	8,814	8,800	4,236	91	220	54	429	513
Vermont	2,310	2,070	2,070	1,383	1	8	–	168	68
Virginia	34,561	31,844	31,822	15,385	1,405	811	231	849	1,711
Washington	36,191	28,691	28,642	11,237	134	982	2,073	1,565	1,216
West Virginia	5,224	4,886	4,881	2,815	4	62	249	82	248
Wisconsin	26,791	24,577	24,532	11,285	1,624	1,463	168	2,169	1,426
Wyoming	4,208	4,007	4,006	1,738	15	89	771	201	154

See footnotes at end of table.

U.S. Census Bureau, Statistical Abstract of the United States: 2012

State	General expenditures—Con. Direct expenditures—Con.								Utility expenditures	Insurance trust expenditures	Debt outstanding
	Corrections	Sewerage	Solid waste	Parks and recreation	Housing and community development	Governmental administration	Interest on general debt	Other			
United States	25,665	45,406	21,318	35,136	40,118	74,895	55,336	176,139	168,269	33,490	1,546,753
Alabama	206	329	262	436	404	843	644	1,672	2,727	125	19,536
Alaska	5	105	91	127	129	218	123	592	385	27	3,469
Arizona	670	1,284	386	1,005	457	1,907	1,167	3,644	5,842	257	33,064
Arkansas	138	313	183	165	162	364	286	771	948	33	8,656
California	5,273	5,978	2,498	5,813	10,008	13,649	7,903	30,312	30,663	7,950	219,164
Colorado	303	768	116	1,436	630	1,568	1,058	2,835	3,046	380	34,091
Connecticut	–	443	199	250	510	649	336	2,447	793	402	9,235
Delaware	–	199	31	40	59	145	67	179	365	40	2,220
District ofColumbia . . .	267	195	319	662	571	506	407	1,323	2,117	155	9,581
Florida	1,981	2,853	2,214	3,081	2,360	5,357	3,399	14,733	10,673	976	99,808
Georgia	764	1,399	576	840	1,003	2,572	767	3,737	7,047	371	37,489
Hawaii	–	244	226	171	70	285	176	500	543	–	4,417
Idaho	74	195	133	105	40	317	95	493	214	2	2,351
Illinois.	742	1,602	485	2,449	1,764	3,270	2,577	8,886	6,826	3,524	65,726
Indiana	386	1,032	262	699	387	1,392	698	4,027	2,336	121	26,632
Iowa.	153	360	186	321	136	434	300	1,331	1,060	2	8,221
Kansas.	152	329	148	231	122	610	607	1,367	1,211	46	15,136
Kentucky	226	457	183	164	141	603	1,035	1,248	1,791	36	26,185
Louisiana	610	499	307	385	475	1,106	608	2,033	1,365	190	15,499
Maine.	71	162	116	64	121	197	90	565	127	–	2,500
Maryland	348	725	578	601	793	1,328	608	3,171	989	795	14,894
Massachusetts.	299	813	392	224	1,365	973	581	4,555	4,455	1,402	20,936
Michigan	636	2,087	588	732	494	2,135	1,737	5,027	3,208	1,426	46,182
Minnesota	448	642	319	841	757	1,246	1,151	2,580	2,422	330	32,113
Mississippi	160	202	158	156	217	566	253	1,003	851	–	7,003
Missouri.	165	640	139	624	441	980	799	2,733	2,195	479	21,415
Montana.	28	120	68	79	67	186	64	410	144	–	1,548
Nebraska	104	258	76	185	203	414	226	888	4,005	181	11,295
Nevada	403	261	24	738	227	1,154	626	1,588	1,704	–	20,649
New Hampshire	56	112	107	86	94	267	107	640	102	9	2,617
New Jersey	626	1,340	1,126	696	859	1,715	1,474	7,278	1,115	10	35,187
New Mexico	178	164	157	242	99	476	130	804	611	–	5,489
New York	2,774	3,927	2,648	2,184	4,304	5,235	6,057	21,653	11,635	9,622	155,502
North Carolina	451	1,208	735	854	690	1,496	1,312	3,693	4,596	24	31,597
North Dakota	23	45	43	84	53	111	73	248	147	14	1,704
Ohio.	463	2,141	475	993	1,860	3,442	1,760	5,039	3,135	128	41,773
Oklahoma	104	395	176	273	201	716	217	1,135	1,017	55	7,814
Oregon.	409	888	128	486	385	833	678	2,205	2,014	94	17,769
Pennsylvania	1,365	2,012	755	759	1,860	2,892	2,968	3,916	4,593	1,267	78,511
Rhode Island	28	92	46	51	158	183	84	655	163	153	2,483
South Carolina.	217	484	332	263	313	956	694	1,236	1,481	2	21,341
South Dakota.	44	135	31	106	52	137	60	277	298	14	1,839
Tennessee	374	577	328	373	611	1,073	818	2,371	9,000	473	31,408
Texas.	1,795	2,940	1,006	2,093	1,891	4,331	7,082	8,518	14,168	1,144	182,578
Utah.	174	383	143	435	192	612	247	1,071	2,160	–	10,822
Vermont	–	57	31	24	49	90	28	162	234	6	970
Virginia.	867	976	698	840	871	2,064	1,061	4,055	2,071	645	32,824
Washington	526	1,798	602	894	1,051	1,535	1,129	3,900	7,324	176	41,024
West Virginia	30	283	60	99	142	376	145	286	307	31	3,472
Wisconsin	470	847	368	563	260	1,124	791	1,973	1,843	372	20,012
Wyoming	76	106	62	115	11	257	34	377	201	–	1,003

– Represents or rounds to zero. [1] Includes other items not shown seperately.

Source: U.S. Census Bureau, "Survey of State Government Finances, 2008," June 2011. See also <http://www.census.gov/govs>.

Table 457. City Governments—Revenue for Largest Cities: 2006

[In millions of dollars (83,520 represents $83,520,000,000). For fiscal years ending in year shown; see text, this section. Cities ranked by estimated resident population as of July 1. Data reflect inclusion of fiscal activity of dependent school systems where applicable. Regarding intercity comparisons, see text, this section. See Appendix III]

Cities ranked by 2006 population	Total revenue	General revenue Total	Intergovernmental Total	From federal govern-ment	From state/ local govern-ment	From local govern-ment	General revenue from own sources Total	Taxes Total[1]	Property	Sales and gross receipts Total[1]	General sales	Public utilities	Current charges Total[1]	Parks and rec-reation	Sewer-age	Miscellaneous Total[1]	Interest earn-ings	Utility rev-enue[2]	Insur-ance trust revenue
New York, NY[3]	83,520	70,823	25,957	3,722	22,045	191	44,866	35,104	12,754	5,953	4,439	516	6,380	63	1,151	3,382	1,153	3,472	9,224
Los Angeles, CA	14,199	7,863	952	282	670	–	6,911	3,233	1,090	1,362	552	673	2,413	105	599	1,264	461	3,143	3,193
Chicago, IL	8,812	7,257	1,325	449	876	–	5,933	2,179	429	1,454	275	555	2,872	–	144	881	248	347	1,207
Houston, TX	4,449	3,119	550	195	328	27	2,569	1,492	781	664	423	187	808	26	330	269	153	341	989
Phoenix, AZ	3,377	2,903	1,115	581	488	46	1,788	1,023	261	692	537	84	581	26	232	184	137	288	186
Philadelphia, PA[3]	7,345	5,809	2,478	653	1,712	113	3,332	2,450	394	225	125	–	698	1	240	184	105	1,007	529
San Antonio, TX	3,283	1,469	191	54	120	17	1,278	612	292	287	200	27	431	24	280	234	107	1,573	242
San Diego, CA	3,266	2,100	411	175	216	20	1,690	744	313	323	173	45	694	63	396	252	110	332	833
Dallas, TX	3,027	2,277	164	123	36	6	2,112	857	488	329	198	89	861	35	240	394	144	207	543
San Jose, CA	1,924	1,498	217	50	141	27	1,281	660	285	238	106	112	440	15	185	181	100	20	406
Honolulu, HI[3]	1,483	1,337	197	117	79	–	1,140	807	591	114	–	62	284	23	241	50	29	146	–
Detroit, MI	3,184	2,132	694	97	543	54	1,439	867	309	218	–	61	452	4	351	119	47	314	739
Jacksonville, FL[3]	3,292	1,829	323	72	251	–	1,506	745	365	371	213	106	383	16	158	379	207	1,187	276
Indianapolis, IN	3,749	3,014	646	86	550	10	2,367	1,638	1,486	47	–	1	506	26	74	224	94	687	48
San Francisco, CA[3]	7,955	5,647	2,155	87	1,664	404	3,492	2,047	923	598	327	91	1,045	25	165	400	178	426	1,882
Columbus, OH	1,227	1,058	198	82	103	13	860	560	40	20	–	7	228	11	172	72	26	169	–
Austin, TX	2,272	1,037	108	54	30	24	929	457	255	186	124	30	378	23	166	94	26	1,032	203
Louisville/Jefferson, KY[3]	1,090	975	170	73	89	8	805	515	124	55	–	4	117	11	–	173	93	115	–
Memphis, TN	3,777	1,882	1,149	63	557	529	733	449	301	135	99	5	150	11	102	134	86	1,587	308
Ft. Worth, TX	1,132	712	56	–	56	–	656	417	236	144	102	32	153	5	120	85	32	184	237
Baltimore, MD[3]	3,339	2,922	1,504	262	1,205	38	1,418	1,023	558	87	–	56	261	10	149	134	48	109	308
Charlotte City, NC	1,613	1,507	351	76	114	161	1,157	366	286	39	2	–	398	–	199	392	50	80	26
El Paso, TX	822	627	91	74	17	–	535	339	178	141	107	32	134	3	71	62	20	81	115
Boston, MA	3,626	3,103	1,368	100	1,264	3	1,735	1,333	1,255	40	–	–	194	–	122	209	48	112	411
Seattle, WA	2,481	1,424	144	41	100	3	1,279	784	284	307	146	124	387	42	288	108	23	882	176
Washington, DC	9,248	8,674	2,589	2,589	–	–	6,085	4,545	1,214	1,257	817	214	574	26	178	966	205	96	369
Milwaukee, WI	1,392	931	442	69	306	67	489	250	237	–	–	–	191	4	109	48	17	59	402
Denver, CO[3]	2,472	2,121	237	17	219	2	1,884	849	226	534	460	26	810	45	70	225	72	166	185
Las Vegas, NV	883	882	401	22	272	107	481	233	121	60	–	54	185	11	78	63	15	–	–
Nashville-Davidson, TN[3]	3,237	1,955	446	8	438	–	1,509	1,101	720	327	271	15	236	9	82	172	99	1,008	275
Oklahoma City, OK	1,069	950	96	56	39	2	854	451	45	358	319	31	268	12	84	135	33	78	41
Portland, OR	1,053	961	181	54	71	56	780	419	254	65	–	49	294	24	205	67	33	91	1
Tucson, AZ	953	756	265	79	170	15	492	305	54	243	196	28	149	21	38	37	6	126	72
Albuquerque, NM	1,146	1,047	321	28	259	33	727	414	102	248	219	19	239	15	98	74	43	98	98
Atlanta, GA	1,696	1,517	323	118	114	90	1,194	354	186	110	–	38	650	31	148	190	155	146	34

– Represents or rounds to zero. [1] Includes revenue sources not shown separately. [2] Includes water, electric, and transit. [3] Represents, in effect, city-county consolidated government.
Source: U.S. Census Bureau, State and Local Governments, *State Government Finances, 2006,* July 2009. See also <http://www.census.gov/govs/>.

Table 458. City Governments—Expenditures and Debt for Largest Cities: 2006

[In millions of dollars (82,454 represents $82,454,000,000). For fiscal year ending in year shown; see headnote, Table 457]

Cities ranked by 2006 population	Total expenditures [1]	Total direct expenditures	General expenditures — Total [1]	Education	Housing and community development	Public welfare	Health and hospitals	Police protection	Fire protection	Corrections	Highways	Parks and recreation	Sewerage	Solid waste management	Governmental administration [2]	Interest on general debt	Utility expenditures [3]	Insurance trust expenditures	Debt outstanding
New York, NY [4]	82,454	77,456	66,237	17,472	3,710	9,811	8,976	3,971	1,519	1,314	1,526	559	2,161	1,100	1,178	3,205	8,699	7,517	85,234
Los Angeles, CA	12,315	12,315	7,252	–	275	–	202	1,659	589	–	561	332	498	238	842	410	3,675	1,388	15,723
Chicago, IL	7,622	7,544	6,033	1	257	135	178	1,175	390	–	454	77	101	183	153	756	316	1,272	15,862
Houston, TX	3,982	3,953	3,295	–	255	–	98	571	381	20	139	129	384	67	139	357	307	381	11,403
Phoenix, AZ	3,362	3,349	2,592	18	100	–	–	367	187	13	127	577	198	99	114	251	672	97	7,373
Philadelphia, PA [4]	6,745	6,660	5,077	23	234	555	1,292	510	172	350	71	94	189	98	332	114	1,054	614	5,825
San Antonio, TX	3,625	3,625	1,546	45	35	43	43	242	161	–	112	157	248	57	52	81	2,010	70	6,055
San Diego, CA	2,431	2,418	1,803	–	339	–	44	336	160	9	82	142	290	52	88	70	413	215	2,795
Dallas, TX	2,713	2,704	2,194	–	41	7	27	268	143	8	121	124	196	67	80	229	276	242	8,557
San Jose, CA	1,894	1,866	1,703	–	186	–	15	227	116	–	95	138	144	79	192	204	36	156	4,368
Honolulu, HI [4]	1,473	1,473	1,228	–	46	–	26	180	82	–	107	100	159	137	98	100	246	–	3,155
Detroit, MI	3,349	3,248	2,168	35	98	16	66	447	192	62	146	79	402	107	157	147	627	554	7,515
Jacksonville, FL [4]	3,474	3,343	1,847	–	33	47	84	206	96	75	200	77	198	86	97	217	1,447	180	11,022
Indianapolis, IN	3,412	3,398	2,592	–	268	91	619	188	70	170	110	149	301	40	173	193	741	79	4,125
San Francisco, CA [4]	6,908	6,908	5,305	102	148	605	1,246	317	211	10	143	200	155	–	714	406	1,008	595	8,738
Columbus, OH	1,152	1,144	1,012	–	8	10	32	212	144	–	94	60	193	34	72	93	140	110	1,703
Austin, TX	2,304	2,304	1,159	–	35	17	124	176	88	41	83	96	137	43	58	80	1,036	–	3,887
Louisville/Jefferson, KY [4]	925	924	868	–	39	–	75	130	47	–	15	38	–	18	31	102	57	191	2,520
Memphis, TN	3,508	3,479	1,815	999	36	–	11	180	132	–	65	56	33	43	45	80	1,502	83	2,747
Ft. Worth, TX	1,047	1,047	766	–	21	–	15	161	81	–	85	58	76	35	31	26	197	259	1,231
Baltimore, MD [4]	3,289	3,212	2,930	1,029	86	2	147	348	134	–	192	391	147	69	128	58	101	16	2,287
Charlotte City, NC	1,448	1,436	1,019	–	42	–	5	151	77	–	96	52	253	40	21	44	413	61	2,665
El Paso, TX	725	725	476	–	22	–	16	81	52	–	35	25	44	13	27	25	187	357	1,005
Boston, MA	3,341	3,038	2,813	950	82	150	184	279	160	106	51	34	215	58	55	57	171	93	1,459
Seattle, WA	2,424	2,311	1,400	–	45	36	14	190	135	13	113	195	175	114	67	52	932	118	3,465
Washington, DC	8,543	8,291	8,256	1,478	560	1,846	669	493	176	206	96	332	237	266	434	320	169	203	7,824
Milwaukee, WI	1,302	1,274	1,026	–	123	–	32	218	99	–	132	4	66	76	37	37	72	106	1,199
Denver, CO [4]	2,415	2,357	2,110	–	103	98	55	165	87	75	86	216	79	–	132	289	199	–	5,845
Las Vegas, NV [4]	747	600	745	–	18	1	3	124	105	39	90	80	40	5	117	16	1	–	352
Nashville-Davidson, TN [4]	3,270	3,269	2,046	679	–	28	168	158	101	52	38	72	109	21	105	148	1,084	140	3,837
Oklahoma City, OK	1,115	1,115	960	–	9	–	–	125	111	–	91	83	146	31	137	30	138	17	1,049
Portland, OR	1,210	1,210	1,059	–	54	–	–	137	79	–	162	89	192	3	52	85	71	80	2,524
Tucson, AZ	874	874	694	–	43	–	–	134	56	49	70	71	–	36	71	46	146	35	1,090
Albuquerque, NM	843	843	760	–	32	19	9	122	66	36	55	107	29	45	31	37	83	–	777
Atlanta, GA	2,025	1,979	1,552	–	5	–	–	152	66	–	43	103	185	45	61	87	407	65	6,425

– Represents or rounds to zero. [1] Includes expenditure sources, not shown separately. [2] Excludes public buildings. [3] Includes water, electric, and transit. [4] Represents, in effect, city-county consolidated government.

Source: U.S. Census Bureau, *State Government Finances, 2006*, July 2009. See also <http://www.census.gov/govs/>.

Table 459. County Governments—Revenue for Largest Counties: 2006

[In millions of dollars (21,586 represents $21,586,000,000). For fiscal year ending in year shown; see text, this section. See Appendix III]

Counties ranked by 2006 population	Total revenue[1] Total	General revenue — Total	Intergovernmental — Total	From federal govt — Total[1]	Housing and community development	From state govt — Total[1]	Public welfare	Health and hospitals	From local government	Gen. revenue from own sources — Total	Taxes — Total[1]	Property	Sales and gross receipts — Total	General sales	Current charges — Total[1]	Parks and recreation	Sanitation[2]	Hospitals	Miscellaneous general revenue — Total[1]	Interest earnings
Los Angeles, CA	21,586	17,015	9,177	386	4	8,556	4,815	1,311	235	7,838	3,285	3,009	127	42	3,802	95	83	2,220	751	235
Cook, IL	3,378	2,851	606	41	–	564	287	–	1	2,245	1,536	810	702	358	577	47	–	333	132	49
Harris, TX	3,165	3,165	647	91	23	471	174	216	85	2,518	1,318	1,232	56	–	815	3	–	256	385	245
Maricopa, AZ	2,015	2,015	952	55	9	869	167	27	28	1,062	781	604	144	144	80	4	–	–	202	128
Orange, CA	4,439	3,464	1,926	51	8	1,800	650	172	75	1,538	626	536	46	43	622	42	114	–	289	181
San Diego, CA	5,117	4,027	2,880	167	120	2,447	986	473	266	1,147	686	585	27	18	259	3	24	–	201	110
Dade, FL	6,528	6,263	1,353	896	254	413	–	55	44	4,910	1,871	1,283	480	119	2,477	36	508	1,084	562	289
Dallas, TX	1,662	1,623	254	9	–	233	150	19	12	1,369	649	597	12	–	608	7	–	545	111	29
Riverside, CA	3,399	3,399	1,898	61	13	1,683	904	208	154	1,502	666	534	43	35	581	7	71	184	255	99
San Bernardino, CA	3,919	3,290	2,043	134	18	1,826	918	240	83	1,247	383	326	25	17	680	7	73	331	183	62
Wayne, MI	1,991	1,848	1,117	122	8	862	14	522	134	731	448	423	16	–	229	4	75	10	54	19
King, WA	2,239	2,108	520	135	16	266	–	178	119	1,588	1,005	446	534	431	499	7	333	–	84	51
Broward, FL	2,326	2,270	466	119	10	203	38	23	144	1,804	927	780	124	113	676	16	172	475	201	111
Clark, NV	4,446	3,980	1,051	87	16	792	38	180	173	2,928	1,333	577	484	140	1,082	66	96	688	513	83
Santa Clara, CA	3,497	3,497	1,717	37	3	1,603	971	180	78	1,779	800	605	143	140	872	4	3	146	107	37
Tarrant, TX	1,150	1,150	273	51	24	219	7	189	4	877	515	478	15	–	203	–	–	–	158	124
Bexar, TX	1,113	1,113	203	6	2	188	101	44	9	909	396	363	27	–	421	–	24	389	93	70
Suffolk, NY	2,744	2,592	580	29	7	538	275	153	13	2,012	1,701	556	1,119	1,114	174	10	–	–	137	50
Alameda, CA	3,198	2,696	1,468	31	3	1,399	737	311	38	1,228	480	399	26	15	609	13	83	341	139	66
Sacramento, CA	3,235	2,559	1,563	46	–	1,457	811	202	60	997	428	275	89	63	373	23	2	247	195	65
Nassau, NY	3,347	3,347	769	73	21	696	397	136	0	2,578	1,903	906	965	953	431	2	5	–	244	39
Cuyahoga, OH	2,170	2,170	964	20	19	940	503	260	4	1,206	565	336	184	169	383	5	199	–	258	198
Palm Beach, FL	1,873	1,823	239	102	9	136	–	–	1	1,584	967	685	154	–	421	13	18	–	196	37
Allegheny, PA	1,486	1,419	1,026	63	47	961	282	467	2	393	302	262	38	23	64	4	–	–	27	6
Oakland, MI	1,162	1,051	574	201	6	218	6	61	155	477	350	326	9	–	85	9	18	4	42	15
Hillsborough, FL	1,836	1,663	259	75	32	183	45	169	1	1,404	901	605	274	199	395	2	78	0	108	44
Hennepin, MN	1,843	1,843	854	50	8	785	353	128	19	989	478	459	–	–	388	4	70	284	123	30
Franklin, OH	1,158	1,156	459	14	4	419	193	128	26	696	459	334	104	85	97	4	3	–	140	124
Orange, FL	1,753	1,704	285	85	–	199	5	–	5	1,420	941	506	225	79	322	47	146	–	156	95
Contra Costa, CA	2,506	2,071	899	113	102	705	391	113	81	1,173	406	342	24	10	670	24	24	404	96	33
Fairfax, VA	5,137	4,343	1,024	122	68	874	146	76	28	3,319	2,673	2,117	326	155	426	45	232	–	220	127
St Louis, MO	727	683	71	17	11	54	1	5	–	612	512	152	347	312	78	1	4	–	21	6
Salt Lake, UT	532	532	76	15	–	51	32	14	9	456	346	203	112	79	70	7	12	–	40	5
Fulton, GA	1,162	1,000	102	29	23	70	32	14	3	898	733	522	178	164	71	–	46	–	94	37
Westchester, NY	2,468	2,459	508	14	–	484	245	116	10	1,951	1,041	607	426	407	838	31	30	563	73	46

– Represents or rounds to zero. [1] Includes revenue sources, not shown separately. [2] Includes fee for sewerage and solid waste management.

Source: U.S. Census Bureau, Survey of State & Local Government Finances, 2006, July 2009, <http://www.census.gov/govs/>.

Table 460. County Governments—Expenditures and Debt for Largest Counties: 2006

[In millions of dollars (18,720 represents $18,720,000,000). For fiscal year ending in year shown; see text, this section and Appendix III]

Counties ranked by 2006 population	Total expenditures [1]	Total direct expenditures [1]	General expenditures — Total [1]	Education	Housing and community development	Public welfare	Health	Hospitals	Police protection	Correction	Highways	Parks and recreation	Natural resources	Sewage and solid waste management	Governmental administration	General public building	Interest on general debt	Utility expenditures [2]	Employee retirement expenditures	Debt outstanding
Los Angeles, CA	18,720	18,439	16,859	890	5	4,515	1,925	2,454	1,213	1,128	273	248	424	66	1,572	114	63	1,798	2,713	3
Cook, IL	3,048	3,036	2,665	–	10	8	41	916	85	350	119	118	–	–	620	149	–	383	3,246	3
Harris, TX	3,207	3,207	3,207	–	12	43	208	888	364	70	266	24	142	–	329	450	–	–	8,538	8
Maricopa, AZ	1,813	1,517	1,813	34	13	376	81	–	69	354	138	8	90	6	391	108	8	–	1,880	2
Orange, CA	3,482	3,428	3,217	244	14	764	328	–	282	263	54	–	67	100	433	174	–	265	2,856	3
San Diego, CA	4,205	3,843	3,879	425	102	989	518	–	207	297	175	20	20	29	523	125	–	326	1,845	2
Dade, FL	6,931	6,921	6,344	–	295	298	71	1,380	425	229	153	278	47	502	273	620	587	–	10,985	10
Dallas, TX	1,547	1,547	1,533	4	32	7	42	1,010	32	99	43	3	–	1	131	22	–	13	423	–
Riverside, CA	3,156	2,994	3,156	367	78	660	325	271	265	177	162	10	66	66	277	74	–	–	1,298	2
San Bernardino, CA	3,335	3,187	3,131	379	9	799	219	376	242	203	74	18	56	71	247	116	–	204	1,912	2
Wayne, MI	1,828	1,771	1,717	–	8	153	474	49	35	250	124	67	46	67	330	50	–	111	643	1
King, WA	2,226	2,180	1,785	–	30	2	344	1	121	127	112	53	9	413	246	163	441	–	3,167	3
Broward, FL	2,215	2,160	2,068	–	15	46	99	–	353	190	43	127	19	149	183	165	147	–	3,225	3
Clark, NV	4,013	3,953	3,487	–	22	187	60	495	467	136	483	319	11	42	268	218	526	–	5,865	5
Santa Clara, CA	3,350	3,274	3,350	214	9	624	365	905	105	258	102	31	4	3	336	58	–	–	910	1
Tarrant, TX	1,034	1,034	1,034	–	23	7	95	446	34	98	35	–	1	–	136	114	–	–	1,981	2
Bexar, TX	1,029	1,004	1,029	161	1	43	52	578	42	73	11	2	1	–	89	67	–	–	933	1
Suffolk, NY	2,750	2,454	2,568	39	7	504	337	–	431	124	42	43	32	79	116	65	182	–	1,797	1
Alameda, CA	2,563	2,559	2,303	154	6	557	319	394	87	271	27	1	36	–	281	41	44	216	1,327	1
Sacramento, CA	2,804	2,741	2,603	181	10	741	430	–	224	233	133	34	4	94	240	81	18	183	2,167	3
Nassau, NY	3,633	3,243	3,631	–	23	573	298	380	688	215	127	61	2	111	189	153	2	–	3,532	3
Cuyahoga, OH	2,131	2,112	2,131	–	20	438	327	576	26	94	54	–	7	13	260	201	–	–	3,338	3
Palm Beach, FL	1,777	1,690	1,686	32	57	72	50	–	216	102	112	92	37	169	193	63	91	60	1,818	2
Allegheny, PA	1,477	1,385	1,416	10	63	351	461	8	32	76	29	62	–	–	106	24	–	–	613	1
Oakland, MI	988	964	926	–	9	7	266	–	52	102	123	9	30	98	131	24	–	36	339	–
Hillsborough, FL	1,911	1,781	1,718	–	32	89	134	–	165	132	109	78	55	75	222	13	27	–	2,174	2
Hennepin, MN	1,856	1,847	1,849	–	23	458	288	480	85	83	108	3	–	52	112	56	193	–	544	2
Franklin, OH	1,164	1,126	1,160	–	7	289	320	–	30	58	47	20	–	6	162	25	7	–	2,178	1
Orange, FL	1,689	1,652	1,675	–	30	79	42	–	142	153	159	36	20	232	128	118	3	–	3,074	2
Contra Costa, CA	2,253	2,198	2,054	127	106	379	189	437	89	116	100	–	28	23	155	128	14	198	1,106	3
Fairfax, VA	4,831	4,759	4,328	2,195	162	227	178	–	196	37	37	144	9	259	174	58	197	–	3,701	1
St Louis, MO	725	495	696	–	10	24	47	–	77	20	83	30	–	4	66	177	4	306	410	4
Salt Lake, UT	519	519	519	–	1	46	26	78	32	63	25	78	5	14	92	16	–	25	197	–
Fulton, GA	1,111	909	952	–	8	62	35	–	65	83	26	4	1	62	259	6	100	59	749	1
Westchester, NY	2,629	2,311	2,586	95	–	455	277	591	41	134	43	56	1	146	107	53	44	–	1,594	1

– Represents or rounds to zero. [1] Includes expenditure categories, not shown separately. [2] Includes water, gas, electric, and transit.
Source: U.S. Census Bureau, Federal, State, and Local Governments, *State & Local Government Finances, 2006*, July 2009, <http://www.census.gov/govs/>.

State and Local Government Finances and Employment 299

Table 461. Governmental Employment and Payrolls: 1982 to 2009

[Employees in thousands (15,841 represents 15,841,000), payroll in millions of dollars (23,173 represents $23,173,000,000). Data are for the month of October through 1992. Beginning with the 1997 survey, data are for the month of March. Covers both full-time and part-time employees. Local government data are estimates subject to sampling variation; see Appendix III and source]

Type of government	1982	1987	1992	1997	2000	2005	2006	2007	2008	2009
EMPLOYEES (1,000)										
Total..............	15,841	17,212	18,745	19,540	20,876	21,725	22,048	22,116	22,462	22,632
Federal (civilian) [1]	2,848	3,091	3,047	2,807	2,899	2,720	2,721	2,730	2,769	2,824
State and local	12,993	14,121	15,698	16,733	17,976	19,004	19,327	19,386	19,693	19,809
Percent of total	82	82	84	86	86	87	88	88	88	88
State	3,744	4,116	4,595	4,733	4,877	5,078	5,128	5,200	5,270	5,329
Local	9,249	10,005	11,103	12,000	13,099	13,926	14,199	14,186	14,423	14,480
Counties	1,824	1,963	2,253	2,425	(NA)	(NA)	(NA)	(NA)	(NA)	(NA)
Municipalities	2,397	2,493	2,665	2,755	(NA)	(NA)	(NA)	(NA)	(NA)	(NA)
School districts	4,194	4,627	5,134	5,675	(NA)	(NA)	(NA)	(NA)	(NA)	(NA)
Townships	356	393	424	455	(NA)	(NA)	(NA)	(NA)	(NA)	(NA)
Special districts	478	529	627	691	(NA)	(NA)	(NA)	(NA)	(NA)	(NA)
PAYROLLS (mil. dol.)										
Total..............	23,173	32,669	43,120	49,156	58,166	71,599	74,638	78,583	83,268	85,214
Federal (civilian) [1]	5,959	7,924	9,937	9,744	11,485	13,475	13,896	14,427	15,472	15,106
State and local	17,214	24,745	33,183	39,412	46,681	58,123	60,741	64,156	67,796	70,108
Percent of total	74	76	77	80	80	81	81	82	81	82
State	5,022	7,263	9,828	11,413	13,279	16,062	16,769	17,789	18,726	19,388
Local	12,192	17,482	23,355	27,999	33,402	42,062	43,972	46,368	49,070	50,720
Counties	2,287	3,270	4,698	5,750	(NA)	(NA)	(NA)	(NA)	(NA)	(NA)
Municipalities	3,428	4,770	6,207	7,146	(NA)	(NA)	(NA)	(NA)	(NA)	(NA)
School districts	5,442	7,961	10,394	12,579	(NA)	(NA)	(NA)	(NA)	(NA)	(NA)
Townships	370	522	685	869	(NA)	(NA)	(NA)	(NA)	(NA)	(NA)
Special districts	665	959	1,370	1,654	(NA)	(NA)	(NA)	(NA)	(NA)	(NA)

NA Not available. [1] Includes employees outside the United States.

Source: U.S. Census Bureau, Federal, State, and Local Governments, "Government Employment and Payroll Data," May 2011, <http://www.census.gov/govs/apes/>.

Table 462. All Governments—Employment and Payroll by Function: 2009

[Employees in thousands (22,632 represents 22,632,000); payroll in millions of dollars (85,214 represents $85,214,000,000). See headnote, Table 461]

Function	Employees, total	Federal (civilian) [1]	Employees (1,000) State and local Total	State	Local	Payrolls (mil. dol.) Federal (civilian) [1]	Total	State and local Total	State	Local
Total	22,632	2,824	19,809	5,329	14,480	85,214	15,106	70,108	19,388	50,720
National defense [2]	729	729	(X)	(X)	(X)	3,100	3,100	(X)	(X)	(X)
Postal Service	704	704	(X)	(X)	(X)	3,236	3,236	(X)	(X)	(X)
Space research and technology	18	18	(X)	(X)	(X)	168	168	(X)	(X)	(X)
Elem. and secondary education	8,037	(X)	8,037	67	7,970	26,725	–	26,725	243	26,482
Higher education	3,093	(X)	3,093	2,487	606	9,226	(X)	9,226	7,655	1,571
Other education..................	105	10	95	95	(X)	449	70	379	379	(X)
Health	627	152	475	191	284	2,855	1,058	1,797	776	1,021
Hospitals	1,283	193	1,090	446	644	5,653	1,244	4,408	1,827	2,581
Public welfare	557	8	549	247	303	2,015	69	1,946	887	1,060
Social insurance administration......	148	65	83	83	(X)	734	404	330	328	2
Police protection	1,195	179	1,017	107	909	5,882	1,084	4,797	543	4,255
Fire protection	429	(X)	429	(X)	429	1,929	(X)	1,929	(X)	1,929
Correction	800	37	763	489	274	3,264	203	3,061	1,970	1,091
Streets & highways	563	3	560	240	320	2,228	22	2,206	1,016	1,190
Air transportation.................	97	47	50	3	47	644	418	227	16	211
Water transport/terminals	18	5	14	5	9	80	13	67	24	43
Solid waste management	122	(X)	122	2	120	422	(X)	422	11	411
Sewerage.......................	136	(X)	136	2	134	572	(X)	572	10	562
Parks & recreation................	434	25	409	40	369	1,021	132	889	116	773
Natural resources	388	181	208	159	49	1,858	1,102	756	591	165
Housing & community development ..	136	15	120	–	120	572	108	464	–	464
Water supply	183	–	183	1	183	751	–	751	4	747
Electric power	82	–	82	4	78	483	–	483	27	455
Gas supply......................	12	–	12	–	12	50	–	50	–	50
Transit	248	(X)	248	33	215	1,200	(X)	1,200	192	1,008
Libraries........................	198	4	194	1	193	460	27	433	2	431
State liquor stores	10	(X)	10	10	(X)	24	(X)	24	24	(X)
Financial administration............	556	124	432	173	258	2,434	734	1,700	721	979
Other government administration	453	25	429	62	366	1,380	146	1,234	256	978
Judicial and legal.................	518	62	456	183	273	2,481	427	2,055	898	1,157
Other & unallocable...............	752	238	514	201	313	3,316	1,340	1,976	872	1,105

– Represents or rounds to zero. X Not applicable. [1] Includes employees outside the United States. [2] Includes international relations.

Source: U.S. Census Bureau, Federal, State, and Local Governments, "2009 Annual Survey of Public Employment and Payroll," May 2011. See also <http://www.census.gov/govs/apes/>.

Table 463. State and Local Government—Employer Costs Per Hour Worked: 2011

[In dollars. As of March. Based on a sample; see source for details. Collection of severance pay and supplemental unemployment plans, which comprised "other benefits" and was published in all tables, was discontinued beginning with the March 2006 estimates]

Occupation and industry	Total compensation	Wages and salaries	Benefit cost					
			Total	Paid leave	Supplemental pay	Insurance	Retirement and savings	Legally required benefits
Total workers	**40.54**	**26.55**	**13.99**	**3.03**	**0.33**	**4.88**	**3.32**	**2.44**
Occupational group:								
Management, professional, and related	49.19	33.50	15.69	3.37	0.24	5.41	3.88	2.79
Professional and related	48.28	33.06	15.22	3.04	0.23	5.40	3.83	2.72
Teachers [1]	55.78	39.41	16.37	2.84	0.14	5.91	4.45	3.04
Primary, secondary, and special education school teachers	56.38	39.62	16.76	2.58	0.15	6.48	4.62	2.92
Sales and office	28.04	17.04	11.00	2.50	0.19	4.43	2.12	1.77
Office and administrative support	28.28	17.13	11.15	2.53	0.19	4.50	2.15	1.77
Service	30.22	18.04	12.17	2.65	0.56	3.96	2.98	2.03
Industry group:								
Education and health services	42.58	28.85	13.72	2.73	0.21	5.10	3.27	2.41
Educational services	43.55	29.75	13.80	2.66	0.15	5.17	3.41	2.42
Elementary and secondary schools	43.08	29.54	13.54	2.29	0.16	5.33	3.42	2.35
Junior colleges, colleges, and universities	45.36	30.64	14.72	3.84	0.13	4.68	3.40	2.66
Health care and social assistance	35.75	22.57	13.19	3.28	0.61	4.62	2.35	2.32
Hospitals	38.04	24.05	14.00	3.54	0.74	4.94	2.37	2.41
Public administration	38.54	23.49	15.05	3.66	0.55	4.68	3.65	2.51

[1] Includes postsecondary teachers; primary, secondary, and special education teachers; and other teachers and instructors.
Source: U.S. Bureau of Labor Statistics, *National Compensation Survey, Benefits, Archives, 2011 National Survey Compensation Publications List, Employer Costs for Employee Compensation*, News Release, March 2011, <http://www.bls.gov/ncs/ncspubs.htm>.

Table 464. State and Local Government—Full-Time Employment and Salary by Sex and Race and Ethnic Group: 1980 to 2009

[As of June 30. (2,350 represents 2,350,000). Excludes school systems and educational institutions. Based on reports from state governments (42 in 1980; 47 in 1983; 42 in 1980; 47 in 1983; 49 in 1981 and 1984 through 1987; 49 in 1981 and 1984 through 1987; and 50 in 1989 through 1991) and a sample of county, municipal, township, and special district jurisdictions employing 15 or more nonelected, nonappointed full-time employees. Beginning 1993, only for state and local governments with 100 or more employees. For definition of median, see Guide to Tabular Presentation]

Year and occupation	Employment (1,000)						Median annual salary ($1,000)					
					Minority						Minority	
	Male	Female	White [1]	Total [2]	Black [1]	Hispanic [3]	Male	Female	White [1]	Total [2]	Black [1]	Hispanic [3]
1980	2,350	1,637	3,146	842	619	163	15.2	11.4	13.8	11.8	11.5	12.3
1983	2,674	1,818	3,423	1,069	768	219	20.1	15.3	18.5	15.9	15.6	17.3
1984	2,700	1,880	3,458	1,121	799	233	21.4	16.2	19.6	17.4	16.5	18.4
1985	2,789	1,952	3,563	1,179	835	248	22.3	17.3	20.6	18.4	17.5	19.2
1986	2,797	1,982	3,549	1,230	865	259	23.4	18.1	21.5	19.6	18.7	20.2
1987	2,818	2,031	3,600	1,249	872	268	24.2	18.9	22.4	20.9	19.3	21.1
1989	3,030	2,227	3,863	1,394	961	308	26.1	20.6	24.1	22.1	20.7	22.7
1990	3,071	2,302	3,918	1,456	994	327	27.3	21.8	25.2	23.3	22.0	23.8
1991	3,110	2,349	3,965	1,494	1,011	340	28.4	22.7	26.4	23.8	22.7	24.5
1993	2,820	2,204	3,588	1,436	948	341	30.6	24.3	28.5	25.9	24.2	26.8
1995	2,960	2,355	3,781	1,534	993	379	33.5	27.0	31.4	26.3	26.8	28.6
1997	2,898	2,307	3,676	1,529	973	392	34.6	27.9	32.2	30.2	27.4	29.5
1999	2,939	2,393	3,723	1,609	1,012	417	37.0	29.9	34.8	31.1	29.6	31.2
2001	3,080	2,554	3,888	1,746	1,077	471	39.8	32.1	37.5	34.0	31.5	33.8
2003	3,134	2,610	3,919	1,826	1,097	508	42.2	34.7	40.0	35.9	33.6	36.6
2005	3,185	2,644	3,973	1,856	1,100	532	44.1	36.4	41.5	37.7	35.3	38.9
2007	3,383	2,823	4,156	(NA)	(NA)	(NA)	(NA)	(NA)	(NA)	(NA)	(NA)	(NA)
2009, total	3,239	2,742	3,978	2,004	1,145	601	50	41	48	(NA)	40.3	44.8
Officials/administrators	230	153	303	79	45	22	72	70	71	(NA)	70.8	71.3
Professionals	671	923	1,109	484	261	117	62	53	57	(NA)	50.7	55.8
Technicians	268	206	324	151	76	48	50	40	47	(NA)	39.8	44.7
Protective service	998	239	857	380	217	134	51	41	50	(NA)	42.2	54.2
Paraprofessionals	(NA)	(NA)	(NA)	(NA)	(NA)	(NA)	(NA)	(NA)	(NA)	(NA)	32.0	36.6
Admininstrative support	125	774	562	337	183	116	37	35	35	(NA)	35.0	36.3
Skilled craft	407	23	305	125	68	43	45	39	35	(NA)	42.0	46.9
Service/maintenance	434	142	299	277	180	79	37	29	29	(NA)	29.1	35.9

NA Not available [1] Non-Hispanic. [2] Includes other minority groups, not shown separately. [3] Persons of Hispanic origin may be any race.
Source: U.S. Equal Employment Opportunity Commission, 1980–1991, "State and Local Government Information Report," annual; beginning 1993, biennial, <www.eeoc.gov>.

Table 465. State and Local Government Full-Time Equivalent Employment by Selected Function and State: 2009

[In thousands (1,814.0 represents 1,814,000). For March. Local government amounts are estimates subject to sampling variation; see Appendix III and source]

State	Total [1] State	Total [1] Local	Education — Elementary and secondary State	Education — Elementary and secondary Local	Education — Higher education State	Education — Higher education Local	Public welfare State	Public welfare Local	Health State	Health Local	Hospitals State	Hospitals Local
United States	1,814.0	7,231.0	53.0	6,884.0	1,673.8	347.0	242.0	284.2	184.4	254.8	417.6	585.0
Alabama	41.5	104.6	–	104.6	38.4	–	4.2	1.5	6.1	5.6	12.0	26.6
Alaska	8.8	17.1	3.3	17.0	5.2	0.1	1.9	0.2	0.7	0.4	0.2	0.7
Arizona	31.1	144.3	–	130.8	28.1	13.6	4.9	2.3	3.0	3.0	0.8	2.5
Arkansas	26.0	71.6	–	71.4	24.5	0.2	3.8	0.1	4.9	0.3	5.8	1.8
California	159.1	754.7	–	681.3	154.8	73.4	3.8	66.6	13.4	45.1	43.1	70.7
Colorado	40.7	108.4	–	106.2	39.4	2.1	2.2	6.1	1.3	4.3	5.4	10.4
Connecticut	20.8	92.5	–	92.5	18.2	–	6.3	1.8	4.4	1.3	7.3	–
Delaware	8.2	15.5	–	15.5	7.8	–	1.8	–	2.2	0.4	1.8	–
District of Columbia	(X)	9.2	(X)	8.2	(X)	1.0	(X)	2.2	(X)	0.9	(X)	1.7
Florida	58.8	360.9	–	333.0	55.6	28.0	9.7	6.2	20.9	7.0	3.7	49.6
Georgia	55.5	255.2	–	255.2	52.4	–	8.4	1.7	4.7	10.8	7.0	19.5
Hawaii	37.6	–	28.2	–	9.3	–	0.7	0.2	2.4	0.2	4.4	–
Idaho	8.8	32.7	–	31.3	8.3	1.5	1.9	0.1	1.2	1.0	0.9	4.7
Illinois...............	66.4	305.4	–	280.4	64.4	25.0	9.9	6.5	2.5	7.9	11.5	12.3
Indiana..............	57.9	147.3	–	147.3	56.8	–	5.0	1.1	1.9	3.3	2.6	27.3
Iowa................	23.7	81.8	–	72.8	22.5	9.0	3.2	1.2	0.5	2.2	8.4	11.2
Kansas..............	20.6	102.5	–	93.4	20.0	9.1	2.5	0.8	1.2	3.6	3.1	8.9
Kentucky	38.9	113.1	–	113.1	36.4	–	6.0	0.5	2.3	5.2	5.6	4.5
Louisiana	36.0	100.2	1.9	100.2	30.3	–	6.0	0.9	4.0	1.7	14.9	18.7
Maine................	7.6	37.1	–	37.1	7.4	–	3.1	0.4	1.0	0.2	0.6	0.8
Maryland	29.2	135.9	–	124.6	26.9	11.3	6.7	3.5	6.9	4.6	4.6	–
Massachusetts.........	31.9	154.6	0.1	154.5	30.7	0.1	7.1	2.5	7.6	3.1	7.2	3.1
Michigan	71.1	215.3	–	199.7	70.6	15.6	10.8	2.8	1.9	9.3	18.8	10.1
Minnesota	41.3	120.7	–	120.7	37.4	–	2.9	10.4	2.4	3.4	5.1	9.4
Mississippi............	21.0	82.1	–	76.1	19.4	6.0	2.7	0.3	3.1	0.3	12.0	19.5
Missouri..............	30.3	147.3	–	139.8	28.6	7.5	8.1	3.2	2.8	3.6	11.6	12.6
Montana.............	7.6	22.8	–	22.5	7.2	0.4	1.7	0.6	0.9	0.9	0.6	0.8
Nebraska	13.0	50.6	–	47.2	12.4	3.4	2.6	0.8	0.7	0.7	3.9	4.7
Nevada	11.6	46.1	–	46.1	11.4	–	1.6	0.9	1.3	1.0	1.4	4.8
New Hampshire........	6.9	37.0	–	37.0	6.6	–	1.6	2.8	1.0	0.2	0.8	–
New Jersey	55.4	225.7	18.9	214.8	33.5	10.9	9.0	11.3	4.5	4.4	18.4	2.5
New Mexico...........	20.4	52.4	–	48.9	19.4	3.5	1.9	1.0	2.4	0.6	7.4	1.0
New York	57.8	522.2	–	498.6	53.2	23.6	5.3	50.2	10.1	19.3	46.1	53.5
North Carolina	60.1	243.1	–	222.0	58.6	21.0	1.6	16.0	5.2	16.8	20.0	39.8
North Dakota	8.8	15.4	–	15.4	8.5	–	0.5	0.9	1.4	0.6	0.9	–
Ohio................	73.6	257.5	–	253.3	71.1	4.2	2.8	24.1	3.6	18.3	15.5	11.9
Oklahoma	32.4	94.0	–	93.5	30.4	0.4	7.1	0.4	5.9	1.4	3.0	10.2
Oregon..............	23.7	80.2	–	71.5	23.0	8.7	6.4	0.9	1.4	4.3	5.1	2.6
Pennsylvania	64.5	272.4	–	265.6	60.5	6.7	11.8	20.8	1.8	5.5	11.7	0.8
Rhode Island	6.7	20.8	0.6	20.8	5.7	–	1.3	0.1	1.1	0.1	1.0	–
South Carolina	32.4	103.6	–	103.6	29.8	–	4.6	0.4	6.0	2.3	7.3	22.2
South Dakota	5.5	22.0	–	21.4	5.2	0.6	1.1	0.3	0.7	0.3	1.0	0.3
Tennessee...........	35.5	132.9	–	132.9	33.4	–	8.8	2.3	4.9	4.3	5.7	21.8
Texas...............	126.8	742.8	–	697.6	121.9	45.2	25.1	3.7	11.8	25.6	30.6	53.1
Utah................	24.8	55.1	–	55.1	23.6	–	3.2	0.7	1.8	1.4	7.0	0.7
Vermont.............	5.5	19.6	–	19.6	4.9	–	1.4	–	0.6	0.1	0.3	–
Virginia..............	56.2	203.3	–	201.4	53.2	1.9	2.8	8.4	5.3	6.0	15.2	2.4
Washington	57.7	108.7	–	108.7	55.6	–	10.0	1.7	5.7	4.1	10.4	15.1
West Virginia	14.5	43.3	–	43.3	13.2	0.0	3.3	0.0	0.8	1.2	1.6	2.5
Wisconsin	35.6	128.5	–	117.3	34.6	11.2	2.0	12.6	1.5	6.3	3.6	1.3
Wyoming	4.1	21.2	–	19.3	3.8	1.9	0.8	0.1	0.8	0.5	0.9	6.4

See footnote at end of table.

U.S. Census Bureau, Statistical Abstract of the United States: 2012

Table 465. State and Local Government Full-Time Equivalent Employment by Selected Function and State: 2009—Con.

[See headnote, page 302]

States	Highways		Police protection		Fire protection		Corrections		Parks and recreation	
	State	Local	State	Local	State	Local	State	Local	State	Local
United States	**235.5**	**306.5**	**106.0**	**848.1**	**(X)**	**348.6**	**484.4**	**267.1**	**34.0**	**242.0**
Alabama	4.7	6.9	1.7	12.3	(X)	5.8	5.3	3.4	0.5	3.8
Alaska	3.0	0.7	0.5	1.3	(X)	0.8	1.9	0.1	0.1	0.7
Arizona	2.8	4.8	2.1	19.4	(X)	8.4	10.5	6.2	0.3	6.1
Arkansas	3.6	3.9	1.2	7.2	(X)	2.9	5.2	2.3	0.8	1.2
California	21.7	22.3	12.1	94.1	(X)	34.2	64.5	33.6	3.6	36.6
Colorado	3.2	5.6	1.3	13.7	(X)	6.0	7.4	3.8	0.3	7.1
Connecticut	3.1	3.6	2.1	8.8	(X)	4.7	7.9	–	0.2	2.1
Delaware	1.6	1.2	1.0	2.3	(X)	0.2	3.0	–	0.3	0.3
District of Columbia	(X)	0.9	(X)	4.7	(X)	1.9	(X)	1.4	(X)	1.0
Florida	7.8	15.1	4.4	62.2	(X)	30.1	30.0	17.3	1.4	19.5
Georgia	5.6	8.7	2.1	25.9	(X)	12.8	18.2	10.5	1.9	5.9
Hawaii	0.9	0.9	–	3.9	(X)	1.9	2.5	–	0.2	2.0
Idaho	1.7	1.7	0.5	3.7	(X)	1.4	2.0	1.4	0.2	0.9
Illinois	6.8	13.8	3.8	44.8	(X)	17.2	12.1	10.0	0.5	18.0
Indiana	4.2	5.8	2.1	15.5	(X)	8.3	7.4	5.8	0.2	3.4
Iowa	2.4	5.6	1.0	6.2	(X)	2.0	3.4	1.5	0.1	2.1
Kansas	3.4	5.3	1.1	8.3	(X)	3.5	3.6	3.1	0.6	2.6
Kentucky	4.2	3.1	2.4	7.7	(X)	4.1	4.1	3.7	1.3	2.1
Louisiana	4.8	5.4	1.7	15.4	(X)	5.3	7.7	5.7	1.1	4.4
Maine	2.4	1.7	0.4	2.4	(X)	1.6	1.3	0.8	0.1	0.6
Maryland	4.9	5.0	2.4	16.7	(X)	6.7	12.8	3.5	0.4	7.0
Massachusetts	3.6	6.1	6.2	18.9	(X)	13.8	6.2	2.9	0.6	2.6
Michigan	3.0	9.2	2.7	19.9	(X)	7.4	16.1	5.6	0.3	4.7
Minnesota	4.6	7.5	1.0	11.0	(X)	2.7	4.2	5.4	0.6	4.5
Mississippi	3.4	4.8	1.2	8.1	(X)	3.4	3.7	2.0	0.4	1.2
Missouri	6.3	6.8	2.4	16.4	(X)	7.1	12.8	3.3	0.7	4.7
Montana	2.2	1.3	0.5	2.1	(X)	0.9	1.3	0.7	0.1	0.4
Nebraska	2.1	2.9	0.8	4.3	(X)	1.7	3.0	1.4	0.3	1.1
Nevada	1.8	1.3	0.8	7.6	(X)	2.9	3.7	2.9	0.2	3.9
New Hampshire	1.8	1.7	0.5	3.5	(X)	2.1	1.3	0.7	0.2	0.5
New Jersey	6.9	10.9	4.5	32.2	(X)	8.2	9.9	7.0	2.2	5.9
New Mexico	2.6	2.0	0.7	5.5	(X)	2.3	4.1	2.3	0.8	2.3
New York	12.7	30.0	6.7	83.2	(X)	24.9	33.7	25.3	2.5	12.4
North Carolina	11.0	4.1	3.3	23.6	(X)	8.7	22.4	5.0	1.2	6.3
North Dakota	1.1	1.1	0.2	1.3	(X)	0.4	0.7	0.3	0.2	0.9
Ohio	7.0	13.3	2.6	30.0	(X)	17.1	16.0	9.3	0.6	9.1
Oklahoma	3.1	5.6	2.0	9.4	(X)	4.3	5.8	1.5	0.9	1.9
Oregon	3.8	4.0	1.4	8.1	(X)	4.0	5.5	3.6	0.4	3.4
Pennsylvania	13.1	10.9	6.4	27.4	(X)	6.1	17.7	13.3	1.7	3.4
Rhode Island	0.7	0.9	0.4	3.3	(X)	2.5	1.6	0.3	0.1	0.9
South Carolina	5.0	2.6	1.9	11.8	(X)	4.8	7.8	3.0	0.5	3.2
South Dakota	1.0	1.7	0.3	1.7	(X)	0.5	0.9	0.6	0.1	0.5
Tennessee	4.1	6.9	2.2	17.3	(X)	7.8	7.1	6.4	1.1	3.5
Texas	14.7	22.6	4.4	66.3	(X)	25.5	44.1	28.8	1.3	15.7
Utah	1.7	1.9	0.8	5.7	(X)	2.4	3.3	2.1	0.3	3.2
Vermont	1.0	1.2	0.6	0.9	(X)	0.4	1.1	0.0	0.1	0.2
Virginia	8.5	4.5	3.0	19.0	(X)	10.6	14.5	9.3	0.9	8.3
Washington	7.6	7.7	2.3	13.6	(X)	9.8	10.0	5.3	0.6	5.5
West Virginia	5.1	0.8	1.0	2.8	(X)	1.0	3.4	0.1	0.6	0.8
Wisconsin	1.4	9.2	0.9	14.9	(X)	4.9	10.8	4.0	0.2	3.0
Wyoming	1.9	0.9	0.3	1.8	(X)	0.5	1.0	0.7	0.1	0.9

- Represents or rounds to zero. X Not applicable. [1] Includes other categories, not shown separately.
Source: U.S. Census Bureau, "2009 Annual Survey of Public Employment and Payroll," May 2011. See also <http://www.census.gov/govs/apes/>.

Table 466. State and Local Government Employment and Average Monthly Earnings by State: 2000 to 2009

[4,083 represents 4,083,000. As of March. Full-time equivalent employment is a derived statistic that provides an estimate of a government's total full-time employment by converting part-time employees to a full-time amount]

State	Full-time equivalent employment (1,000)						Average monthly earnings [2] (dol.)					
	State			Local [1]			State			Local [1]		
	2000	2008	2009	2000	2008	2009	2000	2008	2009	2000	2008	2009
United States	4,083	4,363	4,399	10,995	12,305	12,408	3,374	4,445	4,565	3,169	4,124	4,234
Alabama	80	89	89	182	199	200	2,841	3,990	4,067	2,431	3,155	3,201
Alaska	23	26	26	25	28	28	3,842	4,659	5,078	3,818	4,652	4,819
Arizona	65	73	69	182	251	241	3,055	4,257	4,215	2,942	4,161	4,100
Arkansas	49	61	61	96	105	108	2,842	3,459	3,663	2,175	2,866	3,045
California	355	394	411	1,322	1,452	1,434	4,451	5,913	5,714	4,062	5,652	5,782
Colorado	66	69	73	164	195	203	3,779	4,901	5,033	3,076	4,067	4,118
Connecticut	66	66	66	111	125	129	3,909	5,480	5,825	3,856	4,843	4,769
Delaware	24	27	27	21	24	23	3,222	4,177	4,227	3,163	4,494	4,502
District of Columbia	(X)	(X)	(X)	45	47	46	(X)	(X)	(X)	3,923	5,403	5,025
Florida	185	189	186	580	720	703	3,149	3,808	3,859	2,865	4,010	4,116
Georgia	120	130	123	334	409	411	2,899	3,724	3,915	2,677	3,391	3,447
Hawaii	55	60	60	14	15	15	2,926	4,065	4,249	3,352	4,791	4,891
Idaho	23	23	23	51	59	56	3,022	4,106	4,202	2,478	3,258	3,313
Illinois	128	129	137	493	519	525	3,441	4,914	5,077	3,307	4,272	4,451
Indiana	83	91	92	232	263	258	2,990	4,073	4,175	2,711	3,423	3,503
Iowa	55	55	52	121	128	130	3,656	5,165	5,376	2,727	3,511	3,733
Kansas.............	43	46	45	128	149	159	3,071	3,895	4,112	2,491	3,242	3,349
Kentucky	74	81	81	149	165	163	3,051	3,878	3,946	2,339	2,996	3,022
Louisiana	95	92	92	185	190	186	2,807	4,007	4,131	2,278	3,104	3,347
Maine..............	21	23	21	51	55	53	2,983	3,967	4,141	2,609	3,280	3,407
Maryland	91	89	90	182	211	214	3,312	4,492	4,606	3,535	4,910	5,129
Massachusetts........	96	98	97	232	245	247	3,683	4,823	4,924	3,403	4,518	4,773
Michigan	142	141	143	351	334	340	3,934	4,746	5,023	3,518	4,417	4,515
Minnesota	73	79	81	206	201	204	3,892	5,070	5,282	3,255	4,265	4,310
Mississippi	56	57	58	133	134	137	2,752	3,365	3,450	2,121	2,865	2,982
Missouri	91	89	90	208	239	239	2,678	3,291	3,398	2,678	3,307	3,441
Montana	18	20	21	34	35	36	2,931	3,822	3,949	2,546	3,261	3,488
Nebraska............	30	32	32	78	85	87	2,514	3,695	3,868	2,779	3,669	3,765
Nevada	22	28	30	61	86	87	3,444	4,752	5,016	3,817	4,942	5,027
New Hampshire	19	20	20	46	52	54	3,079	4,367	4,453	2,830	3,776	3,743
New Jersey	133	156	154	316	350	360	4,075	5,580	5,686	3,967	5,158	5,183
New Mexico..........	48	49	49	70	81	82	2,811	3,767	3,938	2,494	3,191	3,454
New York	251	255	257	924	981	994	3,859	5,052	5,282	3,961	4,858	5,052
North Carolina	123	146	148	328	421	415	3,012	3,931	4,032	2,708	3,496	3,593
North Dakota	16	18	18	23	23	25	2,826	3,639	3,952	2,778	3,662	3,478
Ohio................	136	143	143	459	478	477	3,369	4,635	4,902	3,118	3,897	4,010
Oklahoma	64	72	72	134	144	149	2,821	3,699	3,774	2,280	2,924	3,129
Oregon.............	53	60	63	124	130	136	3,269	4,463	4,524	3,332	4,210	4,222
Pennsylvania	150	162	164	388	434	442	3,436	4,188	4,338	3,296	4,021	4,082
Rhode Island.........	20	20	20	36	32	33	3,772	4,853	5,184	3,550	4,631	4,673
South Carolina........	79	78	77	155	183	180	2,741	3,530	3,579	2,474	3,374	3,484
South Dakota	13	13	14	28	30	33	2,777	3,591	3,749	2,359	3,028	3,127
Tennessee	81	86	84	218	242	245	2,786	3,794	3,794	2,631	3,276	3,359
Texas	269	290	300	909	1,081	1,130	3,095	4,057	4,208	2,643	3,465	3,545
Utah	49	51	52	73	84	90	2,880	4,152	4,293	2,836	3,857	3,797
Vermont.............	14	15	15	23	25	25	3,153	4,333	4,389	2,534	3,525	3,611
Virginia	119	128	126	269	323	324	3,229	4,163	4,246	2,928	3,829	3,899
Washington	112	123	125	193	227	235	3,551	4,581	4,772	3,835	5,050	5,369
West Virginia	32	39	40	61	63	63	2,694	3,347	3,479	2,517	2,942	3,130
Wisconsin	64	69	70	220	214	215	3,710	4,780	4,878	3,210	3,958	4,233
Wyoming	11	13	14	29	36	38	2,589	3,727	3,922	2,660	3,858	4,094

X Not applicable. [1] Estimates subject to sampling variation; see Appendix III and source. [2] For full-time employees.
Source: U.S. Census Bureau, "2009 Annual Survey of Public Employment and Payroll," May 2011. See also <http://www.census.gov/govs/apes/>.

Table 467. City Government Employment and Payroll—Largest Cities: 1999 to 2009

[In thousands (447.0 represents 447,000), except as noted. As of March. See headnote, Table 466 for full-time equivalent employment definition]

Cities ranked by 2007 population [1]	Total employment (1,000)			Full-time equivalent employment total (1,000)			Payroll (mil. dol.)			Average earnings for full-time employees (dol.)		
	1999	2008	2009	1999	2008	2009	1999	2008	2009	1999	2008	2009
New York, NY	447.0	467.0	453.9	416.4	430.3	423.6	1,485.9	2,166.3	2,315.1	3,694	5,091	5,535
Los Angeles, CA	47.2	56.2	57.6	46.2	52.1	53.2	207.4	364.5	393.4	4,534	7,264	7,675
Chicago, IL	41.9	38.7	38.7	41.9	37.9	37.8	195.8	191.5	192.2	4,670	5,072	5,102
Houston, TX	22.9	22.1	23.0	22.7	21.7	22.6	64.0	89.2	98.6	2,813	4,100	4,353
Phoenix, AZ	13.1	18.1	16.2	12.7	17.2	15.6	48.9	104.8	82.7	3,909	6,285	5,413
Philadelphia, PA	30.2	31.1	31.3	29.4	30.3	30.4	102.4	144.3	142.8	3,511	4,786	4,705
San Antonio, TX	16.5	16.1	16.0	15.3	15.5	15.5	43.6	60.6	63.8	2,927	3,998	4,184
San Diego, CA	11.7	11.4	11.4	11.0	10.6	10.5	43.8	60.2	61.3	4,072	5,847	6,022
Dallas, TX	15.4	15.7	17.2	15.0	15.3	16.7	49.6	71.8	75.4	3,326	4,763	4,576
San Jose, CA	7.4	7.8	7.9	6.7	6.8	7.0	33.2	50.8	52.9	5,227	7,847	7,966
Detroit, MI	18.5	13.8	13.8	18.1	13.7	13.7	59.5	57.6	60.9	3,301	4,225	4,487
Honolulu And, HI	9.7	9.7	10.0	9.0	8.9	9.3	30.9	42.1	45.1	3,479	4,827	4,937
Jacksonville, FL	9.2	14.5	9.8	9.2	13.7	9.6	29.7	61.3	40.1	3,238	4,533	4,230
Indianapolis, IN	11.4	15.5	14.0	11.2	14.6	13.4	30.2	55.4	52.3	2,756	3,803	3,878
San Francisco, CA	26.7	30.8	28.5	26.7	29.1	27.2	119.6	210.6	195.5	4,487	7,482	7,465
Columbus, OH	8.9	8.8	8.4	8.6	8.4	8.1	28.5	40.9	40.8	3,369	4,904	5,093
Austin, TX	10.9	13.0	13.1	10.1	12.6	12.7	30.9	58.9	59.9	3,121	4,718	4,731
Louisville, KY	5.0	7.9	8.5	4.6	7.6	8.2	11.8	29.1	32.3	2,674	3,909	4,001
Ft Worth, TX	6.4	7.0	6.5	6.1	6.7	6.5	18.5	29.2	29.2	3,159	4,446	4,538
Memphis, TN	26.3	25.9	25.8	25.2	24.7	24.6	73.6	84.0	91.0	2,973	3,459	3,770
Charlotte, NC	5.0	6.7	7.3	4.9	6.5	6.8	15.6	28.2	31.2	3,188	4,377	4,613
Baltimore, MD	30.9	28.4	30.1	29.5	26.9	28.4	92.4	128.0	129.9	3,229	4,866	4,675
El Paso, TX	6.2	5.9	6.2	6.1	5.8	6.0	15.6	21.1	22.5	2,596	3,703	3,796
Milwaukee, WI	8.0	7.2	7.1	7.9	7.0	6.8	28.6	34.6	34.4	3,636	5,036	5,097
Boston, MA	22.7	21.8	21.8	21.3	20.5	21.1	73.9	107.0	110.5	3,526	5,283	5,319
Seattle, WA	10.0	14.0	13.7	9.6	12.6	12.4	42.8	67.7	71.5	4,462	5,556	5,918
Nashville, TN	24.2	23.3	23.3	20.0	21.6	21.6	46.8	87.2	91.0	2,353	4,167	4,399
Denver, CO	14.4	13.6	13.4	14.0	12.7	12.6	45.9	68.8	64.6	3,324	5,549	5,227
Washington, DC	36.5	38.9	36.6	34.9	37.3	35.1	129.3	193.7	166.7	3,725	5,309	4,842
Las Vegas, NV	2.6	3.3	3.1	2.5	3.1	2.9	10.8	20.0	21.1	4,512	6,687	7,499
Portland, OR	6.0	6.9	6.8	5.3	6.0	5.9	22.6	32.8	33.9	4,390	5,680	5,989
Oklahoma City, OK	5.1	4.6	4.8	4.8	4.4	4.6	16.0	21.6	22.9	3,482	5,033	5,149
Tucson, AZ	6.3	6.4	6.0	5.4	5.9	5.6	17.0	27.4	25.4	3,181	4,836	4,740
Atlanta, GA	8.3	7.9	7.9	8.2	7.9	7.9	23.2	29.8	30.9	2,831	3,749	3,901
Albuquerque, NM	7.8	7.2	7.1	7.1	6.8	6.8	17.2	23.1	23.7	2,494	3,507	3,612
Fresno, CA	3.6	4.7	4.6	3.3	4.4	4.3	12.2	22.2	22.2	3,829	5,350	5,403
Long Beach, CA	5.9	6.4	6.8	5.5	6.0	6.3	24.3	32.8	36.1	4,720	5,806	5,973
Sacramento, CA	4.3	5.6	5.6	4.3	4.9	4.9	16.0	30.0	24.8	3,733	6,537	5,469
Mesa, AZ	3.3	4.0	3.7	3.2	3.8	3.6	12.0	20.7	20.6	3,819	5,494	5,845
Kansas, MO	6.6	6.8	6.8	6.6	6.9	6.8	19.7	29.2	29.3	3,023	4,283	4,349
Cleveland, OH	9.9	8.1	7.8	9.3	7.9	7.7	26.8	35.4	34.2	2,899	4,470	4,472
Virginia Beach, VA	18.3	19.3	19.4	16.0	17.8	18.0	41.0	60.9	62.2	2,744	3,724	3,778
Omaha, NE	3.2	3.0	3.1	2.9	2.8	2.9	10.4	13.5	14.0	3,778	5,147	5,193
Miami, FL	3.6	4.1	4.5	3.3	4.0	4.2	14.2	23.0	24.4	4,398	5,977	5,992
Oakland, CA	5.5	5.4	5.4	5.0	5.4	5.3	22.3	37.7	37.7	5,084	7,044	7,109
Tulsa, OK	4.5	4.4	4.4	4.4	4.3	4.3	13.5	17.2	17.8	3,118	4,062	4,204
Minneapolis, MN	10.4	5.5	5.5	6.3	5.2	5.2	21.7	25.1	25.8	3,654	4,957	5,084
Colorado Springs, CO	6.9	7.7	8.6	6.6	7.2	7.9	21.5	34.8	38.4	3,371	4,905	4,941
Raleigh, NC	3.2	4.1	4.3	2.9	3.6	3.8	8.4	13.9	15.2	3,036	4,040	4,248
Arlington, TX	3.2	2.9	2.9	2.6	2.5	2.6	7.4	11.8	12.2	3,069	4,941	4,975
Wichita, KS	3.4	4.0	3.9	3.2	3.3	3.4	9.2	13.3	13.7	2,928	4,165	4,175
St Louis, MO	8.6	6.8	6.8	8.1	6.5	6.5	24.6	27.1	26.9	3,033	4,170	4,122
Santa Ana, CA	2.5	2.1	2.1	2.1	1.8	1.8	9.3	13.3	13.8	5,315	7,813	8,101
Tampa, FL	4.2	4.6	4.3	4.1	4.5	4.2	13.3	20.5	22.3	3,272	4,589	5,387
Anaheim, CA	3.2	3.7	3.6	2.6	2.8	2.7	11.4	17.5	17.8	5,038	7,591	7,797
Cincinnati, OH	6.4	5.9	6.0	6.3	5.6	5.7	20.5	26.4	24.9	3,399	4,967	4,518
Bakersfield, CA	1.4	1.6	1.5	1.3	1.6	1.5	5.2	8.3	8.3	4,389	5,400	5,586
Aurora, CO	2.4	2.7	2.6	2.3	2.7	2.6	8.4	13.7	13.6	3,572	5,105	5,271
Pittsburgh, PA	4.4	5.1	4.2	4.3	5.1	4.2	15.3	23.6	18.2	3,610	4,712	4,374
Toledo, OH	3.0	3.0	2.9	3.0	3.0	2.9	11.3	13.2	12.7	3,751	4,406	4,406
Riverside, CA	2.0	2.7	2.6	1.8	2.5	2.3	7.5	14.5	14.5	4,348	6,325	6,575
Stockton, CA	2.3	2.2	2.0	1.9	1.8	1.8	6.5	10.6	9.7	3,846	6,187	5,759
Corpus Christi, TX	3.4	3.2	3.3	3.2	3.2	3.3	7.9	11.5	12.0	2,507	3,608	3,707
Newark, NJ	5.5	4.4	4.3	5.2	3.7	3.6	21.4	17.5	17.7	4,177	4,926	5,104
Anchorage, AK	9.8	10.9	11.1	8.4	9.8	10.0	29.4	45.8	48.5	3,571	4,760	4,938
Lexington, KY	3.8	4.9	5.1	3.5	4.3	4.4	9.6	15.6	16.6	2,827	4,008	4,099
St Paul, MN	3.5	3.3	3.3	3.2	3.0	3.0	12.1	15.2	15.3	3,961	5,283	5,356
Buffalo, NY	12.0	10.8	10.5	10.7	9.9	9.9	40.4	45.4	45.4	3,999	4,747	4,694
Plano, TX	1.9	2.6	2.6	1.7	2.3	2.2	5.8	10.5	10.6	3,499	4,843	4,934
Glendale, AZ	1.5	2.1	2.1	1.4	2.1	2.1	5.5	10.6	10.6	3,997	5,231	5,128
Ft Wayne, IN	1.9	2.2	2.1	1.9	2.1	2.0	5.4	8.5	8.0	2,882	4,170	4,109
Henderson, NV	1.9	2.9	2.8	1.4	2.3	2.3	5.0	13.7	14.1	4,348	6,798	6,957
Lincoln, NE	2.7	2.9	2.8	2.5	2.6	2.6	8.1	12.0	12.1	3,394	4,734	4,869
Greensboro, NC	4.2	3.3	3.4	3.5	3.0	3.1	11.0	11.2	12.0	3,553	3,799	3,994
St Petersburg, FL	3.0	4.1	3.2	2.8	3.9	3.0	9.3	16.5	13.5	3,264	4,405	4,663
Chandler, AZ	1.4	1.9	1.9	1.3	1.8	1.7	3.9	9.7	9.6	3,140	5,724	5,692

[1] 2007 based on estimated resident population as of July 1.

Source: U.S. Census Bureau, "2009 Annual Survey of Public Employment and Payroll," May 2011. See also <http://www.census.gov/govs/apes/>.

Table 468. County Government Employment and Payroll—Largest Counties: 1999 to 2009

[In thousands (93.3 represents 93,300). As of March. See text, this section. See headnote, Table 466, for full-time equivalent employment definition]

Counties ranked by 2007 population [1]	Total employment (1,000)			Total full-time equivalent employment (1,000)		Payroll (mil. dol.)			Average monthly earnings for full-time employees (dol.)	
	1999	2008	2009	1999	2009	1999	2008	2009	1999	2009
Los Angeles, CA	93.3	109.5	109.7	89.7	105.8	368.6	594.1	610.1	4,165	5,837
Cook, IL	27.4	22.7	22.8	27.4	22.8	91.2	108.6	110.1	3,333	4,828
Harris, TX.	19.4	24.1	26.7	19.1	25.5	56.8	102.9	111.5	2,981	4,335
Maricopa, AZ	14.6	14.6	13.9	14.5	13.6	36.9	58.7	56.3	2,562	4,208
Orange, CA	22.8	22.8	19.2	21.4	18.4	71.1	110.4	108.1	3,358	5,902
San Diego, CA.	19.1	24.4	22.1	18.1	20.5	62.8	115.5	104.8	3,513	5,148
Dade, FL	36.6	46.9	47.3	35.6	46.4	123.3	274.3	288.6	3,546	6,328
Dallas, TX	12.5	15.8	16.7	11.9	16.1	34.2	66.7	76.2	2,881	4,701
Riverside, CA.	14.7	21.9	21.3	14.3	20.7	51.9	114.0	116.8	3,688	5,641
San Bernardino, CA. . . .	18.1	21.6	21.5	16.8	20.1	58.2	103.4	102.4	3,553	5,236
Wayne, MI	6.7	5.6	5.3	6.6	5.2	24.0	28.1	24.8	3,658	4,756
King, WA	16.1	14.8	14.4	14.2	13.7	52.9	76.1	78.1	3,867	5,911
Clark, NV.	15.6	22.3	22.1	14.2	20.0	54.8	120.2	120.8	3,982	6,212
Broward, FL.	10.7	13.3	13.2	10.5	12.8	33.5	59.0	59.2	3,220	4,684
Santa Clara, CA.	15.2	19.2	19.2	14.6	18.3	62.3	125.2	128.5	4,342	7,179
Tarrant, TX.	6.6	10.4	11.6	6.4	11.3	17.1	41.2	47.1	2,717	4,190
Bexar, TX.	9.2	11.4	10.9	8.9	10.6	22.4	41.0	41.0	2,545	3,863
Alameda, CA	11.5	12.9	13.2	10.6	12.6	45.4	83.3	87.2	4,263	6,969
Suffolk, NY.	12.7	15.9	17.0	11.8	15.0	49.1	80.9	84.5	4,300	5,839
Sacramento, CA	12.7	14.7	13.8	11.7	13.7	46.7	75.4	78.0	3,963	5,696
Nassau, NY	18.5	21.1	17.6	17.4	15.7	73.5	92.1	85.0	4,518	5,596
Cuyahoga, OH.	15.7	16.6	16.1	15.7	15.7	46.2	69.3	70.4	2,939	4,385
Palm Beach, FL.	8.4	11.5	11.6	8.2	11.2	26.0	58.1	60.1	3,193	5,483
Allegheny, PA.	7.3	6.9	6.9	7.2	6.8	18.0	22.3	24.6	2,530	3,682
Oakland, MI	4.7	6.2	4.7	4.4	4.4	15.2	25.4	20.5	3,537	4,761
Hillsborough, FL	14.5	11.7	11.9	12.4	11.4	30.2	46.9	48.2	2,640	4,277
Hennepin, MN	12.9	8.7	7.6	10.9	7.5	40.0	44.3	38.8	3,705	5,299
Franklin, OH.	7.1	6.7	6.7	6.8	6.4	18.1	23.6	25.0	2,727	3,905
Orange, FL	9.4	12.4	11.8	8.8	10.9	26.1	50.2	44.7	2,986	4,131
Contra Costa, CA	9.9	9.9	9.0	9.1	8.3	41.0	57.0	50.2	4,620	6,066
Fairfax, VA	34.3	43.2	47.3	31.5	39.5	107.5	181.9	204.8	3,514	5,254
Salt Lake, UT.	5.6	6.0	6.1	4.2	4.6	12.2	16.3	17.3	3,176	4,105
St Louis, MO	4.1	4.0	4.1	4.0	4.0	12.0	15.7	16.0	3,052	4,040
Fulton, GA	7.9	8.9	9.0	7.6	8.6	23.5	37.6	37.4	3,203	4,558
Travis, TX.	3.6	5.0	5.2	3.5	5.1	10.4	20.1	21.6	2,949	4,226
Pima, AZ	7.9	8.4	7.9	7.1	7.4	18.8	30.1	28.7	2,717	4,014
Westchester, NY	10.4	11.5	11.8	9.8	10.6	40.0	43.4	48.3	4,067	4,495
Milwaukee, WI	8.2	7.4	7.6	7.8	7.1	25.9	30.1	30.7	3,374	4,338
Montgomery, MD	36.8	43.4	42.6	28.5	35.5	116.3	214.4	220.8	4,401	6,659
Du Page, IL	3.6	3.6	3.6	3.4	3.4	10.3	12.6	12.9	3,097	3,819
Pinellas, FL	5.7	7.0	6.5	5.6	6.4	16.2	30.2	28.9	2,915	4,539
Erie, NY	12.3	11.4	11.7	10.6	10.1	35.5	42.1	42.4	3,538	4,341
Shelby, TN	13.6	14.5	14.5	12.9	14.0	36.2	53.2	51.0	2,825	3,666
Fresno, CA.	7.5	9.1	8.9	7.2	8.4	22.3	37.1	37.7	3,190	4,465
Bergen, NJ.	5.7	5.6	5.8	4.1	4.8	13.2	25.2	25.0	3,273	5,456
Mecklenburg, NC.	23.1	29.4	28.6	20.4	25.9	54.0	101.7	92.8	2,722	3,559
Hamilton, OH.	6.0	6.1	5.4	5.8	5.3	15.0	22.1	19.8	2,604	3,767
Wake, NC	16.9	24.2	25.8	14.9	23.3	39.5	85.8	90.3	2,686	3,900
Macomb, MI.	3.0	3.3	3.4	2.8	3.1	8.7	12.7	13.1	3,245	4,351
Prince Georges, MD . . .	30.0	37.6	34.7	27.2	29.5	84.6	154.6	155.6	3,195	5,453
Ventura, CA.	8.3	9.1	9.5	8.1	9.1	30.2	54.2	56.7	3,754	6,430
Kern, CA	9.0	11.2	11.2	8.7	10.6	29.4	50.1	55.0	3,426	5,240
Baltimore, MD	25.7	30.0	29.7	22.6	25.4	66.5	114.7	118.2	3,172	4,928
Middlesex, NJ	5.5	4.7	5.1	4.9	4.3	16.9	19.8	22.1	3,528	5,261
Gwinnett, GA.	3.7	5.4	5.4	3.5	5.1	10.7	21.3	21.9	3,090	4,346
Montgomery, PA	3.7	4.1	4.1	3.5	4.1	9.0	12.4	12.9	2,690	3,270
Essex, NJ	6.5	5.4	5.4	5.8	4.9	20.2	23.7	24.8	3,573	5,227
Pierce, WA.	3.4	3.9	3.9	3.2	3.7	13.7	20.1	21.3	4,367	5,840
Dekalb, GA	6.2	7.6	7.6	6.1	7.4	18.1	27.2	27.8	3,000	3,778
El Paso, TX	3.7	5.0	5.1	3.6	4.9	9.0	18.5	20.1	2,573	4,120
Collin, TX.	1.0	1.8	2.0	1.0	1.9	2.7	7.1	7.6	2,617	3,908
Monroe, NY	6.9	6.9	6.9	6.0	6.0	18.9	24.2	25.7	3,157	4,371
Hidalgo, TX	1.6	2.7	2.7	1.6	2.7	3.3	8.1	8.6	2,040	3,219
Lake, IL	2.9	3.3	3.3	2.7	3.0	8.5	13.7	13.8	3,180	4,668
San Mateo, CA	6.1	7.8	7.7	5.8	7.2	23.9	42.3	42.4	4,346	6,779
Multnomah, OR	5.7	4.9	4.8	4.6	4.4	12.6	20.3	22.4	2,990	5,161
Oklahoma City, OK	2.4	2.3	2.4	2.3	2.3	4.2	6.1	6.5	1,834	2,929
Cobb, GA.	4.0	6.1	5.1	3.8	4.7	10.7	20.5	17.5	2,933	3,900
Snohomish, WA.	2.4	3.0	2.9	2.4	2.8	8.6	15.1	15.1	3,643	5,327
Will, IL	1.9	2.3	2.4	1.8	2.3	5.5	9.6	10.0	3,052	4,372
San Joaquin, CA	7.1	8.1	8.2	6.5	7.2	20.7	37.3	37.7	3,364	5,286
Jackson, MO	1.9	1.9	2.0	1.8	1.9	4.4	5.9	6.1	2,403	3,199
Jefferson, AL	4.9	4.4	4.4	4.8	4.4	14.6	16.4	18.3	3,054	4,203
Norfolk, MA	0.9	0.5	0.5	0.9	0.5	2.5	2.4	2.2	2,810	4,995

[1] 2007 based on estimated resident population as of July 1.
Source: U.S. Census Bureau Federal, State, and Local Governments "2008 Annual Survey of Public Employment and Payroll," May 2010. See also <http://www.census.gov/govs/apes/>.

U.S. Census Bureau, Statistical Abstract of the United States: 2012

Section 9
Federal Government Finances and Employment

This section presents statistics relating to the financial structure and the civilian employment of the federal government. The fiscal data cover taxes, other receipts, outlays, and debt. The principal sources of fiscal data are the *Budget of the United States Government* and related documents, published annually by the Office of Management and Budget (OMB), and the U.S. Department of the Treasury's *United States Government Annual Report* and its *Appendix*. Detailed data on tax returns and collections are published annually by the Internal Revenue Service. The personnel data relate to staffing and payrolls. They are published by the Office of Personnel Management and the Bureau of Labor Statistics. Data on federally owned land and real property are collected by the General Services Administration and presented in its annual "Federal Real Property Report."

Budget concept—Under the unified budget concept, all federal monies are included in one comprehensive budget. These monies comprise both federal funds and trust funds. Federal funds are derived mainly from taxes and borrowing and are not restricted by law to any specific government purpose. Trust funds, such as the Unemployment Trust Fund, collect certain taxes and other receipts for use in carrying out specific purposes or programs in accordance with the terms of the trust agreement or statute. Fund balances include both cash balances with the Treasury and investments in U.S. securities. Part of the balance is obligated, part unobligated. Prior to 1985, the budget totals, under provisions of law, excluded some federal activities—including the Federal Financing Bank, the Postal Service, the Synthetic Fuels Corporation, and the lending activities of the Rural Electrification Administration. The Balanced Budget and Emergency Deficit Control Act of 1985 (P.L.99-177) repealed the off-budget status of these entities and placed social security (Federal Old-Age and Survivors Insurance and the federal disability insurance trust funds) off-budget. Though social security is now off-budget and, by law, excluded from coverage of the congressional budget resolutions, it continues to be a federal program. Receipts arising from the government's sovereign powers are reported as governmental receipts and all other receipts, i.e., from business-type or market-oriented activities, are offset against outlays. Outlays are reported on a checks-issued (net) basis (i.e., outlays are recorded at the time the checks to pay bills are issued).

Debt concept—For most of U.S. history, the total debt consisted of debt borrowed by the Treasury (i.e., public debt). The present debt series includes both public debt and agency debt. The *gross federal debt* includes money borrowed by the Treasury and by various federal agencies; it is the broadest generally used measure of the federal debt. *Total public debt* is covered by a statutory debt limitation and includes only borrowing by the Treasury.

Treasury receipts and outlays—All receipts of the government, with a few exceptions, are deposited to the credit of the U.S. Treasury regardless of ultimate disposition. Under the Constitution, no money may be withdrawn from the Treasury unless appropriated by the Congress.

The day-to-day cash operations of the federal government clearing through the accounts of the U.S. Treasury are reported in the *Daily Treasury Statement*. Extensive detail on the public debt is published in the *Monthly Statement of the Public Debt of the United States*.

Budget receipts such as taxes, customs duties, and miscellaneous receipts, which are collected by government agencies, and outlays represented by checks issued and cash payments made by disbursing officers as well as government agencies are reported in the *Daily Treasury Statement of Receipts and Outlays of the United States Government* and in the Treasury's *United States Government Annual Report* and its *Appendix*. These deposits

U.S. Census Bureau, Statistical Abstract of the United States: 2012

in and payments from accounts maintained by government agencies are on the same basis as the unified budget.

The quarterly *Treasury Bulletin* contains data on fiscal operations and related Treasury activities, including financial statements of government corporations and other business-type activities.

Income tax returns and tax collections—Tax data are compiled by the Internal Revenue Service of the Treasury Department. The annual *Internal Revenue Service Data Book* gives a detailed account of tax collections by kind of tax. The agency's annual *Statistics of Income* reports present detailed data from individual income tax returns and corporation income tax returns. The quarterly *Statistics of Income Bulletin* presents data on such diverse subjects as tax-exempt organizations, unincorporated businesses, fiduciary income tax and estate tax returns, sales of capital assets by individuals, international income and taxes reported by corporations and individuals, and estate tax wealth.

Employment and payrolls—The Office of Personnel Management collects employment and payroll data from all departments and agencies of the federal government, except the Central Intelligence Agency, the National Security Agency, and the Defense Intelligence Agency. Employment figures represent the number of persons who occupied civilian positions at the end of the report month shown and who are paid for personal services rendered for the federal government, regardless of the nature of appointment or method of payment. Federal payrolls include all payments for personal services rendered during the report month and payments for accumulated annual leave of employees who separate from the service. Since most federal employees are paid on a biweekly basis, the calendar month earnings are partially estimated on the basis of the number of work days in each month where payroll periods overlap.

Federal employment and payroll figures are published by the Office of Personnel Management in its *Federal Civilian Workforce Statistics—Employment and Trends*. It also publishes biennial employment data for minority groups, data on occupations of white- and blue-collar workers, and data on employment by geographic area; reports on salary and wage distribution of federal employees are published annually. General schedule is primarily white-collar; wage system primarily blue-collar. Data on federal employment are also issued by the Bureau of Labor Statistics in its *Monthly Labor Review* and in Employment and Earnings and by the U.S. Census Bureau in its annual publication *Public Employment*.

Figure 9.1

Federal Budget Summary: 1990 to 2011

Receipts, outlays, and surplus or deficit

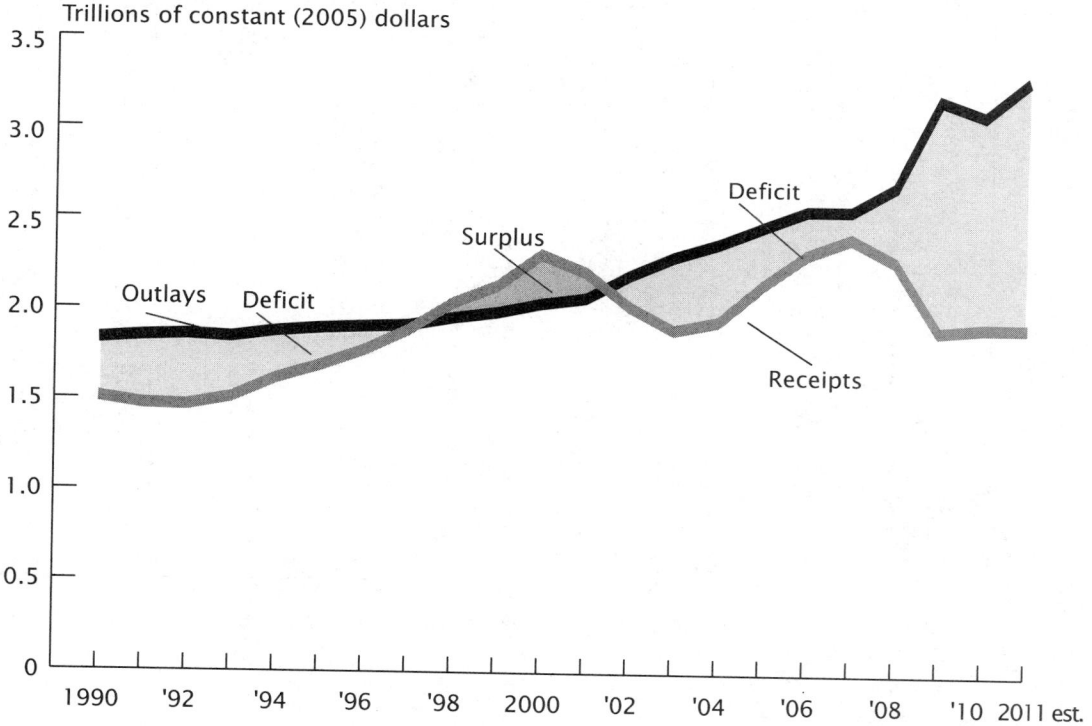

Outlays and federal debt as a percent of gross domestic product (GDP)

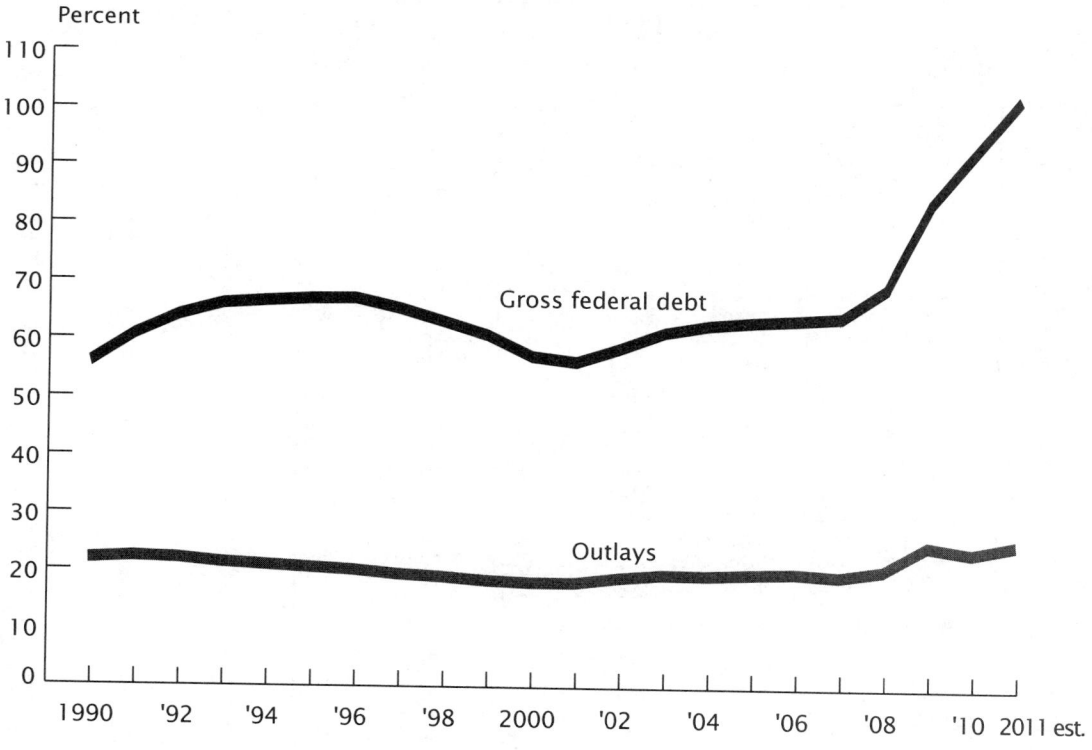

Source: Charts prepared by U.S. Census Bureau. For data, see Tables 469 & 470.

Federal Government Finances and Employment 309

Table 469. Federal Budget—Receipts and Outlays: 1960 to 2011

[92.5 represents $92,500,000,000. For fiscal years ending in year shown; see text, Section 8. See also headnote, Table 471]

Fiscal year	In current dollars (bil dol.)			In constant (2005) dollars (bil dol.)			As percentage of GDP [1]		
	Receipts	Outlays	Surplus or deficit (−)	Receipts	Outlays	Surplus or deficit (−)	Receipts	Outlays	Surplus or deficit (−)
1960	92.5	92.2	0.3	630.9	628.9	2.1	17.8	17.8	0.1
1970	192.8	195.6	−2.8	968.4	982.7	−14.3	19.0	19.3	−0.3
1980	517.1	590.9	−73.8	1,197.6	1,368.6	−171.0	19.0	21.7	−2.7
1985	734.0	946.3	−212.3	1,250.9	1,612.7	−361.8	17.7	22.8	−5.1
1990	1,032.0	1,253.0	−221.0	1,508.7	1,831.9	−323.2	18.0	21.9	−3.9
1991	1,055.0	1,324.2	−269.2	1,473.0	1,849.0	−375.9	17.8	22.3	−4.5
1992	1,091.2	1,381.5	−290.3	1,467.5	1,857.9	−390.4	17.5	22.1	−4.7
1993	1,154.3	1,409.4	−255.1	1,511.5	1,845.5	−334.0	17.5	21.4	−3.9
1994	1,258.6	1,461.8	−203.2	1,617.7	1,878.9	−261.2	18.0	21.0	−2.9
1995	1,351.8	1,515.7	−164.0	1,691.4	1,896.6	−205.1	18.4	20.6	−2.2
1996	1,453.1	1,560.5	−107.4	1,775.5	1,906.7	−131.3	18.8	20.2	−1.4
1997	1,579.2	1,601.1	−21.9	1,889.9	1,916.1	−26.2	19.2	19.5	−0.3
1998	1,721.7	1,652.5	69.3	2,040.9	1,958.8	82.1	19.9	19.1	0.8
1999	1,827.5	1,701.8	125.6	2,136.4	1,989.5	146.8	19.8	18.5	1.4
2000	2,025.2	1,789.0	236.2	2,310.0	2,040.5	269.5	20.6	18.2	2.4
2001	1,991.1	1,862.8	128.2	2,215.3	2,072.6	142.7	19.5	18.2	1.3
2002	1,853.1	2,010.9	−157.8	2,028.6	2,201.3	−172.7	17.6	19.1	−1.5
2003	1,782.3	2,159.9	−377.6	1,901.1	2,303.9	−402.8	16.2	19.7	−3.4
2004	1,880.1	2,292.8	−412.7	1,949.5	2,377.5	−428.0	16.1	19.6	−3.5
2005	2,153.6	2,472.0	−318.3	2,153.6	2,472.0	−318.3	17.3	19.9	−2.6
2006	2,406.9	2,655.0	−248.2	2,324.1	2,563.8	−239.6	18.2	20.1	−1.9
2007	2,568.0	2,728.7	−160.7	2,411.9	2,562.9	−150.9	18.5	19.6	−1.2
2008	2,524.0	2,982.5	−458.6	2,286.8	2,702.3	−415.5	17.5	20.7	−3.2
2009	2,105.0	3,517.7	−1,412.7	1,898.3	3,172.2	−1,274.0	14.9	25.0	−10.0
2010	2,162.7	3,456.2	−1,293.5	1,919.0	3,066.7	−1,147.7	14.9	23.8	−8.9
2011, est.	2,173.7	3,818.8	−1,645.1	1,901.9	3,341.3	−1,439.4	14.4	25.3	−10.9

[1] Gross domestic product; see text, Section 13.

Source: U.S. Office of Management and Budget, *Budget of the United States Government, Historical Tables*, annual. See also <http://www.whitehouse.gov/omb/budget>.

Table 470. Federal Budget Debt: 1960 to 2011

[290.5 represents $290,500,000,000. As of the end of the fiscal year. See text, Section 8]

Fiscal year	Total (bil. dol.)					As percentages of GDP [1]				
	Gross federal debt	Federal government accounts	Held by the public			Gross federal debt	Federal government accounts	Held by the public		
			Total	Federal Reserve System	Other			Total	Federal Reserve System	Other
1960	290.5	53.7	236.8	26.5	210.3	56.0	10.3	45.6	5.1	40.5
1970	380.9	97.7	283.2	57.7	225.5	37.6	9.6	28.0	5.7	22.3
1980	909.0	197.1	711.9	120.8	591.1	33.4	7.2	26.1	4.4	21.7
1985	1,817.4	310.2	1,507.3	169.8	1,337.5	43.8	7.5	36.4	4.1	32.3
1987	2,346.0	456.2	1,889.8	212.0	1,677.7	50.4	9.8	40.6	4.6	36.1
1988	2,601.1	549.5	2,051.6	229.2	1,822.4	51.9	11.0	41.0	4.6	36.4
1989	2,867.8	677.1	2,190.7	220.1	1,970.6	53.1	12.5	40.6	4.1	36.5
1990	3,206.3	794.7	2,411.6	234.4	2,177.1	55.9	13.9	42.1	4.1	38.0
1991	3,598.2	909.2	2,689.0	258.6	2,430.4	60.7	15.3	45.3	4.4	41.0
1992	4,001.8	1,002.1	2,999.7	296.4	2,703.3	64.1	16.1	48.1	4.7	43.3
1993	4,351.0	1,102.6	3,248.4	325.7	2,922.7	66.1	16.7	49.3	4.9	44.4
1994	4,643.3	1,210.2	3,433.1	355.2	3,077.9	66.6	17.3	49.2	5.1	44.1
1995	4,920.6	1,316.2	3,604.4	374.1	3,230.3	67.0	17.9	49.1	5.1	44.0
1996	5,181.5	1,447.4	3,734.1	390.9	3,343.1	67.1	18.8	48.4	5.1	43.3
1997	5,369.2	1,596.9	3,772.3	424.5	3,347.8	65.4	19.4	45.9	5.2	40.8
1998	5,478.2	1,757.1	3,721.1	458.2	3,262.9	63.2	20.3	43.0	5.3	37.7
1999	5,605.5	1,973.2	3,632.4	496.6	3,135.7	60.9	21.4	39.4	5.4	34.1
2000	5,628.7	2,218.9	3,409.8	511.4	2,898.4	57.3	22.6	34.7	5.2	29.5
2001	5,769.9	2,450.3	3,319.6	534.1	2,785.5	56.4	24.0	32.5	5.2	27.2
2002	6,198.4	2,658.0	3,540.4	604.2	2,936.2	58.8	25.2	33.6	5.7	27.8
2003	6,760.0	2,846.6	3,913.4	656.1	3,257.3	61.6	25.9	35.6	6.0	29.7
2004	7,354.7	3,059.1	4,295.5	700.3	3,595.2	62.9	26.2	36.8	6.0	30.8
2005	7,905.3	3,313.1	4,592.2	736.4	3,855.9	63.5	26.6	36.9	5.9	31.0
2006	8,451.4	3,622.4	4,829.0	768.9	4,060.0	63.9	27.4	36.5	5.8	30.7
2007	8,950.7	3,915.6	5,035.1	779.6	4,255.5	64.4	28.2	36.2	5.6	30.6
2008	9,986.1	4,183.0	5,803.1	491.1	5,311.9	69.4	29.1	40.3	3.4	36.9
2009	11,875.9	4,331.1	7,544.7	769.2	6,775.5	84.2	30.7	53.5	5.5	48.1
2010	13,528.8	4,509.9	9,018.9	811.7	8,207.3	93.2	31.1	62.2	5.6	56.6
2011, est.	15,476.2	4,619.8	10,856.5	(NA)	(NA)	102.6	30.6	72.0	(NA)	(NA)

NA Not available. [1] Gross domestic product; see text, Section 13.

Source: U.S. Office of Management and Budget, *Budget of the United States Government, Historical Tables*, annual. See also <http://www.whitehouse.gov/omb/budget>.

U.S. Census Bureau, Statistical Abstract of the United States: 2012

Table 471. Federal Budget Outlays by Type: 1990 to 2011

[1,253.0 represents $1,253,000,000,000. For years ending September 30. Given the inherent imprecision in deflating outlays, the data shown in constant dollars present a reasonable perspective—not precision. The deflators and the categories that are deflated are as comparable over time as feasible. Minus sign (–) indicates offset]

Type	Unit	1990	2000	2005	2008	2009	2010	2011, est.
Current dollar outlays	Bil. dol	**1,253.0**	**1,789.0**	**2,472.0**	**2,982.5**	**3,517.7**	**3,456.2**	**3,818.8**
National defense [1]	Bil. dol	299.3	294.4	495.3	616.1	661.0	693.6	768.2
Nondefense, total	Bil. dol	953.7	1,494.6	1,976.7	2,366.5	2,856.6	2,762.6	3,050.6
Payments for individuals	Bil. dol	585.7	1,054.5	1,490.2	1,824.6	2,093.0	2,285.6	2,410.7
Direct payments [2]	Bil. dol	507.0	867.7	1,212.1	1,520.0	1,732.2	1,893.3	2,010.3
Grants to State and local governments	Bil. dol	78.7	186.8	278.1	304.7	360.7	392.3	400.5
All other grants	Bil. dol	56.4	99.1	149.9	156.6	177.2	216.0	224.7
Net interest [2]	Bil. dol	184.3	222.9	184.0	252.8	186.9	196.2	206.7
All other [2]	Bil. dol	163.9	160.7	217.8	218.7	492.2	146.9	298.2
Undistributed offsetting receipts [2]	Bil. dol	–36.6	–42.6	–65.2	–86.2	–92.6	–82.1	–89.7
Constant (2005) dollar outlays	Bil. dol	**1,831.9**	**2,040.6**	**2,472.0**	**2,702.3**	**3,172.2**	**3,066.7**	**3,341.3**
National defense [1]	Bil. dol	461.2	361.3	495.3	548.1	588.2	612.3	669.5
Nondefense, total	Bil. dol	1,370.6	1,679.3	1,976.7	2,154.3	2,584.0	2,454.4	2,672.0
Payments for individuals	Bil. dol	815.4	1,172.3	1,490.2	1,666.5	1,906.9	2,037.5	2,119.4
Direct payments [2]	Bil. dol	705.7	964.4	1,212.1	1,388.5	1,578.6	1,688.5	1,768.0
Grants to state and local governments	Bil. dol	109.6	207.9	278.1	278.0	328.3	349.1	351.4
All other grants	Bil. dol	87.9	118.5	149.9	133.3	148.5	178.4	181.8
Net interest [2]	Bil. dol	255.7	250.8	184.0	231.9	169.2	176.3	183.3
All other [2]	Bil. dol	278.8	190.5	217.8	200.0	441.4	134.5	265.3
Undistributed offsetting receipts [2]	Bil. dol	–67.1	–52.9	–65.2	–77.5	–82.1	–72.2	–77.8
Outlays as percent of GDP [3]	Percent	**21.9**	**18.2**	**19.9**	**20.7**	**25.0**	**23.8**	**25.3**
National defense [1]	Percent	5.2	3.0	4.0	4.3	4.7	4.8	5.1
Nondefense, total	Percent	16.6	15.2	15.9	16.4	20.3	19.0	20.2
Payments for individuals	Percent	10.2	10.7	12.0	12.7	14.8	15.8	16.0
Direct payments [2]	Percent	8.8	8.8	9.7	10.6	12.3	13.0	13.3
Grants to state and local governments	Percent	1.4	1.9	2.2	2.1	2.6	2.7	2.7
All other grants	Percent	1.0	1.0	1.2	1.1	1.3	1.5	1.5
Net interest [2]	Percent	3.2	2.3	1.5	1.8	1.3	1.4	1.4
All other [2]	Percent	2.9	1.6	1.7	1.5	3.5	1.0	2.0
Undistributed offsetting receipts [2]	Percent	–0.6	–0.4	–0.5	–0.6	–0.7	–0.6	–0.6

[1] Includes a small amount of grants to state and local governments and direct payments for individuals. [2] Includes some off-budget amounts; most of the off-budget amounts are direct payments for individuals (social security benefits). [3] Gross domestic product; see text, Section 13.

Source: U.S. Office of Management and Budget, *Budget of the United States Government, Historical Tables*, annual. See also <http://www.whitehouse.gov/omb/budget>.

Table 472. Federal Budget Outlays by Agency: 1990 to 2011

[In billions of dollars (1,253.0 represents $1,253,000,000,000). For years ending September 30]

Department or other unit	1990	2000	2005	2008	2009	2010	2011, est.
Outlays, total [1]	**1,253.0**	**1,789.0**	**2,472.0**	**2,982.5**	**3,517.7**	**3,456.2**	**3,818.8**
Legislative Branch	2.2	2.9	4.0	4.4	4.7	5.8	4.9
The Judiciary Branch	1.6	4.1	5.5	6.3	6.6	7.2	7.4
Agriculture	45.9	75.1	85.3	90.8	114.4	129.5	152.1
Commerce	3.7	7.8	6.1	7.7	10.7	13.2	11.9
Defense—Military	289.7	281.0	474.4	594.7	636.8	666.7	739.7
Education	23.0	33.5	72.9	66.0	53.4	92.9	79.4
Energy	12.1	15.0	21.3	21.4	23.7	30.8	44.6
Health and Human Services	175.5	382.3	581.4	700.4	796.3	854.1	909.7
Homeland Security	7.2	13.2	38.7	40.7	51.7	44.5	48.1
Housing and Urban Development	20.2	30.8	42.5	49.1	61.0	60.1	60.8
Interior	5.8	8.0	9.3	9.8	11.8	13.2	13.0
Justice	5.9	16.8	22.4	26.5	27.7	29.6	33.5
Labor	26.1	31.9	46.9	58.8	138.2	173.1	148.0
State	4.8	6.7	12.7	17.5	21.4	23.8	28.9
Transportation	25.6	41.6	56.6	64.9	73.0	77.8	79.5
Treasury	253.9	390.5	410.2	548.8	701.8	444.3	532.3
Veterans Affairs	29.0	47.0	69.8	84.7	95.5	108.3	141.1
Corps of Engineers	3.3	4.2	4.7	5.1	6.8	9.9	10.6
Other Defense—Civil Programs	21.7	32.8	43.5	45.8	57.3	54.0	59.2
Environmental Protection Agency	5.1	7.2	7.9	7.9	8.1	11.0	11.1
Executive Office of the President	0.2	0.3	7.7	1.2	0.7	0.6	0.5
International Assistance Programs	10.1	12.1	15.0	11.4	14.8	20.0	25.2
National Aeronautics and Space Administration	12.4	13.4	15.6	17.8	19.2	18.9	19.5
National Science Foundation	1.8	3.4	5.4	5.8	6.0	6.7	8.6
Office of Personnel Management	31.9	48.7	59.5	64.4	72.3	69.9	80.6
Social Security Administration (on-budget)	17.3	45.1	54.6	58.6	78.7	70.8	170.5
Social Security Administration (off-budget)	245.0	396.2	506.8	599.2	648.9	683.4	630.9
Undistributed offsetting receipts	–98.9	–173.0	–226.2	–277.8	–274.2	–267.9	–269.7

[1] Includes other agencies, not shown separately.

Source: U.S. Office of Management and Budget, *Budget of the United States Government, Historical Tables*, annual. See also <http://www.whitehouse.gov/omb/budget>.

Table 473. Federal Budget Outlays by Detailed Function: 1990 to 2011

[In billions of dollars (1,253.0 represents $1,253,000,000,000). For years ending September 30. Minus sign (–) indicates decrease]

Superfunction and function	1990	2000	2005	2006	2007	2008	2009	2010	2011, est.
Total outlays	**1,253.0**	**1,789.0**	**2,472.0**	**2,655.1**	**2,728.7**	**2,982.5**	**3,517.7**	**3,456.2**	**3,818.8**
National defense [1]	299.3	294.4	495.3	521.8	551.3	616.1	661.0	693.6	768.2
Department of Defense—Military	289.7	281.0	474.1	499.3	528.5	594.6	636.7	666.7	739.7
Military personnel	75.6	76.0	127.5	127.5	127.5	138.9	147.3	155.7	157.0
Operation and maintenance	88.3	105.8	188.1	203.8	216.6	244.8	259.3	276.0	311.9
Procurement	81.0	51.7	82.3	89.8	99.6	117.4	129.2	133.6	151.9
Research, development, test, and evaluation	37.5	37.6	65.7	68.6	73.1	75.1	79.0	77.0	80.7
Military construction	5.1	5.1	5.3	6.2	7.9	11.6	17.6	21.2	20.9
Atomic energy defense activities	9.0	12.1	18.0	17.5	17.1	17.1	17.6	19.3	21.2
International affairs [1]	13.8	17.2	34.6	29.5	28.5	28.9	37.5	45.2	55.2
International development and humanitarian assistance	5.5	6.5	17.7	16.7	15.5	14.1	22.1	19.0	28.6
International security assistance	8.7	6.4	7.9	7.8	8.0	9.5	6.2	11.4	11.6
Conduct of foreign affairs	3.0	4.7	9.1	8.6	8.4	10.4	12.2	13.6	15.0
General science, space, and technology	14.4	18.6	23.6	23.6	25.5	27.7	29.4	31.0	33.4
General science and basic research	2.8	6.2	8.8	9.1	10.3	10.5	11.1	12.7	14.7
Space flight, research, and supporting activities	11.6	12.4	14.8	14.5	15.3	17.2	18.4	18.4	18.7
Energy	3.3	–0.8	0.4	0.8	–0.9	0.6	4.7	11.6	27.9
Energy supply	2.0	–1.8	–0.9	0.2	–2.0	–0.4	2.0	5.8	13.7
Natural resources and environment [1]	17.1	25.0	28.0	33.0	31.7	31.8	35.6	43.7	49.0
Water resources	4.4	5.1	5.7	8.0	5.1	6.1	8.1	11.7	12.5
Conservation and land management	4.0	6.8	6.2	7.8	9.6	8.7	9.8	10.8	13.9
Recreational resources	1.4	2.5	3.0	3.0	3.0	3.2	3.6	3.9	4.1
Pollution control and abatement	5.2	7.4	8.1	8.6	8.4	8.1	8.3	10.8	10.9
Agriculture	11.8	36.5	26.6	26.0	17.7	18.4	22.2	21.4	25.1
Farm income stabilization	9.7	33.4	22.0	21.4	13.1	13.8	17.6	16.6	19.7
Agricultural research and services	2.1	3.0	4.5	4.6	4.6	4.6	4.6	4.8	5.4
Commerce and housing credit [1]	67.6	3.2	7.6	6.2	0.5	27.9	291.5	–82.3	17.4
Mortgage credit	3.8	–3.3	–0.9	–0.6	–5.0	–	99.8	35.8	35.5
Postal service	2.1	2.1	–1.2	–1.0	–3.2	–3.1	–1.0	–0.7	0.8
Deposit insurance	57.9	–3.1	–1.4	–1.1	–1.5	18.8	22.6	–32.0	–4.1
Transportation [1]	29.5	46.9	67.9	70.2	72.9	77.6	84.3	92.0	94.5
Ground transportation	19.0	31.7	42.3	45.2	46.8	50.0	54.1	60.8	62.0
Air transportation	7.2	10.6	18.8	18.0	18.1	19.4	20.8	21.4	21.6
Water transportation	3.2	4.4	6.4	6.7	7.7	8.1	9.1	9.4	10.3
Community and regional development [1]	8.5	10.6	26.3	54.5	29.6	24.0	27.7	23.8	25.7
Community development	3.5	5.5	5.9	5.8	11.8	10.2	7.7	9.9	11.2
Disaster relief and insurance	2.1	2.6	17.7	46.0	15.2	11.2	16.7	10.7	11.5
Education, training, employment, and social services [1]	37.2	53.8	97.6	118.5	91.7	91.3	79.7	127.7	115.1
Elementary, secondary, and vocational education	9.9	20.6	38.3	39.7	38.4	38.9	53.2	73.3	78.2
Higher education	11.1	10.1	31.4	50.5	24.6	23.6	–3.3	20.0	0.8
Research and general education aids	1.6	2.5	3.1	3.0	3.2	3.2	3.5	3.6	4.0
Training and employment	5.6	6.8	6.9	7.2	7.1	7.2	7.7	9.9	9.1
Social services	8.1	12.6	16.3	16.5	16.7	16.8	17.0	19.2	20.9
Health	57.7	154.5	250.5	252.7	266.4	280.6	334.3	369.1	387.6
Health care services	47.6	136.2	219.6	220.8	233.9	247.7	300.0	330.7	347.0
Health research and training	8.6	16.0	28.1	28.8	29.3	29.9	30.6	34.2	36.1
Consumer and occupational health and safety	1.5	2.3	2.9	3.1	3.2	3.0	3.8	4.1	4.5
Medicare	98.1	197.1	298.6	329.9	375.4	390.8	430.1	451.6	494.3
Income security [1]	148.7	253.7	345.8	352.5	366.0	431.3	533.2	622.2	622.7
General retirement and disability insurance (excluding social security)	5.1	5.2	7.0	4.6	7.8	8.9	8.2	6.6	7.6
Federal employee retirement and disability	52.0	77.2	93.4	98.3	103.9	109.0	118.1	119.9	127.1
Unemployment compensation	18.9	23.0	35.4	33.8	35.1	45.3	122.5	160.1	134.8
Housing assistance	15.9	28.9	37.9	38.3	39.7	40.6	50.9	58.7	69.4
Food and nutrition assistance	24.0	32.5	50.8	53.9	54.5	60.7	79.1	95.1	107.2
Social security	248.6	409.4	523.3	548.5	586.2	617.0	683.0	706.7	748.4
Veterans benefits and services [1]	29.0	47.0	70.1	69.8	72.8	84.7	95.4	108.4	141.4
Income security for veterans	15.3	24.9	35.8	35.8	35.7	41.3	46.0	49.2	72.9
Veterans education, training, and rehabilitation	0.2	1.3	2.8	2.6	2.7	2.7	3.5	8.1	10.7
Hospital and medical care for veterans	12.1	19.5	28.8	29.9	32.3	37.0	41.9	45.7	49.6
Veterans housing	0.5	0.4	0.9	–1.2	–0.9	–0.4	–0.6	0.5	1.3
Administration of justice	10.2	28.5	40.0	41.0	41.2	47.1	51.5	53.4	60.7
Federal law enforcement activities	4.8	12.1	19.9	20.0	19.6	24.6	27.6	27.8	31.8
Federal litigative and judicial activities	3.6	7.8	9.6	10.1	11.0	11.8	12.1	13.1	13.5
Federal correctional activities	1.3	3.7	5.9	6.2	6.3	6.9	7.3	7.7	7.9
Criminal justice assistance	0.5	4.9	4.6	4.8	4.3	3.9	4.6	4.8	7.5
General government	10.5	13.0	17.0	18.2	17.4	20.3	22.0	23.0	32.1
Net interest [1]	184.3	222.9	184.0	226.6	237.1	252.8	186.9	196.2	206.7
Interest on Treasury debt securities (gross)	264.7	361.9	352.3	405.9	430.0	451.1	383.1	413.9	430.4
Interest received by on-budget trust funds	–46.3	–69.3	–69.2	–71.6	–72.0	–77.8	–63.6	–67.3	–64.3
Interest received by off-budget trust funds	–16.0	–59.8	–91.8	–97.7	–106.0	–113.7	–118.0	–118.5	–115.7
Allowances	–	–	–	–	–	–	–	–	3.1
Undistributed offsetting receipts	–36.6	–42.6	–65.2	–68.3	–82.2	–86.2	–92.6	–82.1	–89.7

– Represents or rounds to zero. [1] Includes functions not shown separately.

Source: U.S. Office of Management and Budget, *Budget of the United States Government, Historical Tables*, annual. See also <http://www.whitehouse.gov/omb/budget>.

Table 474. Outlays for Payments for Individuals by Category and Major Program: 1990 to 2011

[In billions of dollars (585.7 represents 585,700,000,000). For fiscal years ending September 30]

Category and program	1990	2000	2005	2007	2008	2009	2010	2011, est.
Total, payments for individuals.	**585.7**	**1,054.5**	**1,490.9**	**1,690.4**	**1,825.8**	**2,094.1**	**2,286.7**	**2,411.8**
Social security and railroad retirement	250.5	410.5	523.4	586.7	617.4	681.0	706.5	747.7
Social security:								
Old age and survivors insurance.	221.9	351.4	434.0	483.3	506.6	561.4	576.6	612.4
Disability insurance	24.4	54.4	84.2	97.5	104.7	115.5	123.5	128.6
Railroad retirement (excl. social security)	4.1	4.6	5.3	5.8	6.1	4.1	6.5	6.8
Federal employees retirement and insurance . . .	64.1	100.3	126.9	138.0	148.2	161.7	166.5	196.9
Military retirement	21.5	32.8	39.0	43.5	45.8	50.0	50.6	55.3
Civil service retirement	31.0	45.1	54.7	60.9	63.5	67.5	69.4	72.1
Veterans service-connected compensation. . . .	10.7	20.8	30.9	31.1	36.3	40.4	43.4	66.4
Other	0.8	1.7	2.4	2.6	2.7	3.8	3.1	3.1
Unemployment assistance	17.4	21.1	33.1	33.2	43.4	119.8	158.3	132.7
Medical care	164.3	362.7	562.5	682.4	714.9	813.8	865.5	926.4
Medicare:								
Hospital insurance.	65.9	127.9	182.8	204.9	223.6	240.0	250.2	265.0
Supplementary medical insurance	41.5	87.2	151.0	230.1	231.1	257.6	268.9	301.1
State children's health insurance.	–	1.2	5.1	6.0	6.9	7.5	7.9	9.2
Medicaid	41.1	117.9	181.7	190.6	201.4	250.9	272.8	276.2
Indian health	1.1	2.4	3.1	3.3	3.3	3.6	4.4	4.5
Hospital and medical care for veterans	12.0	19.3	23.1	30.5	31.1	35.3	38.2	41.1
Health resources and services	1.4	3.9	5.9	5.9	6.3	6.5	7.1	7.1
Substance abuse and mental health services. .	1.2	2.5	3.2	3.2	3.1	3.4	3.3	3.4
Health care tax credit.	–	–	0.1	0.1	0.1	0.1	0.2	0.2
Uniformed Services retiree health care fund. . .	–	–	6.3	7.6	7.9	8.4	8.4	9.5
Other	(Z)	0.3	0.2	0.2	0.2	0.5	4.1	3.5
Assistance to students.	11.2	10.9	32.1	31.0	31.1	30.6	55.5	57.7
Veterans education benefits	0.8	1.6	3.2	3.4	3.6	4.3	8.7	11.2
Student assistance, Department of Education								
and other	10.4	9.2	28.9	27.5	27.5	26.3	46.8	46.5
Housing assistance	15.9	24.1	31.8	33.0	33.4	43.6	50.0	59.2
Food and nutrition assistance	23.9	32.4	50.7	54.3	60.5	78.9	95.0	106.4
Food stamp program (including Puerto Rico) . .	15.9	18.3	32.6	34.9	39.3	55.6	70.5	78.5
Child nutrition and special milk programs	5.0	9.2	11.9	13.0	13.9	15.3	16.4	18.6
Supplemental feeding programs								
(WIC[1] and CSFP[2])	2.1	4.0	5.0	5.3	6.2	6.5	6.5	7.7
Commodity donations and other	0.8	0.9	1.2	1.1	1.1	1.6	1.6	1.6
Public assistance and related programs	34.9	88.3	123.3	126.3	168.6	156.0	183.1	178.5
Supplemental security income program	11.5	29.5	35.3	32.8	38.0	41.4	43.9	49.3
Family support payments to states and								
TANF[3]	12.2	18.4	21.3	21.1	21.8	22.2	21.9	20.7
Low income home energy assistance	1.3	1.5	2.1	2.5	2.7	4.5	4.6	5.1
Earned income tax credit.	4.4	26.1	34.6	38.3	40.6	42.4	54.7	44.9
Legal services	0.3	0.3	0.3	5.1	5.0	5.3	5.9	5.4
Payments to states for daycare assistance	–	3.3	4.9	3.4	3.8	4.2	4.4	5.0
Veterans non-service-connected pensions	3.6	3.0	3.7	6.6	6.8	6.9	7.0	6.9
Payments to states for foster care/adoption								
assistance	1.6	5.5	6.4	16.2	34.0	24.3	22.7	22.9
Payment where child credit exceeds tax								
liability	–	0.8	14.6	–	–	0.7	1.0	0.6
Other public assistance	–	–	(Z)	0.4	16.0	4.1	17.1	17.7
All other payments for individuals	3.5	4.3	7.1	5.6	8.1	8.7	6.3	6.2
Coal miners and black lung benefits	1.5	1.0	0.7	0.6	0.6	3.0	0.5	0.5
Veterans insurance and burial benefits	1.4	1.4	1.4	1.3	1.4	1.4	1.3	1.4
D.C. employee retirement	–	0.4	2.2	–	–	–	–	–
Aging services programs.	–	0.9	1.4	1.4	1.4	1.5	1.5	1.5
Energy employees compensation fund	–	–	0.6	1.0	1.1	1.0	1.1	1.0
September 11th victim compensation	–	–	(Z)	–	–	–	–	–
Refugee assistance and other.	0.6	0.6	0.8	1.3	3.7	1.8	1.9	1.9

– Represents zero. Z Less than $50,000,000. [1] WIC means Women, Infants, and Children. [2] CSFP means Commodity Supplemental Food Program. [3] TANF means Temporary Assistance for Needy Families.

Source: U.S. Office of Management and Budget, *Budget of the United States Government, Historical Tables,* annual. See also <http://www.whitehouse.gov/omb/budget>.

U.S. Census Bureau, Statistical Abstract of the United States: 2012

Table 475. Federal Budget Receipts by Source: 1990 to 2011

[In billions of dollars (1,032.0 represents $1,032,000,000,000). For years ending September 30. Receipts reflect collections. Covers both federal funds and trust funds; see text, this section]

Source	1990	2000	2005	2007	2008	2009	2010	2011, est.
Total federal receipts	**1,032.0**	**2,025.2**	**2,153.6**	**2,568.0**	**2,524.0**	**2,105.0**	**2,162.7**	**2,173.7**
Individual income taxes	466.9	1,004.5	927.2	1,163.5	1,145.7	915.3	898.5	956.0
Corporation income taxes	93.5	207.3	278.3	370.2	304.3	138.2	191.4	198.4
Social insurance and retirement receipts	380.0	652.9	794.1	869.6	900.2	890.9	864.8	806.8
Excise taxes	35.3	68.9	73.1	65.1	67.3	62.5	66.9	74.1
Other	56.2	91.7	80.9	99.6	106.4	98.1	141.0	138.4
Social insurance and retirement receipts	**380.0**	**652.9**	**794.1**	**869.6**	**900.2**	**890.9**	**864.8**	**806.8**
Employment and general retirement	0.4	0.6	0.7	0.8	0.9	0.8	0.8	0.9
Old–age and survivors insurance (off–budget)	255.0	411.7	493.6	542.9	562.5	559.1	540.0	478.6
Disability insurance (off–budget)	26.6	68.9	83.8	92.2	95.5	94.9	91.7	80.8
Hospital insurance	68.6	135.5	166.1	184.9	194.0	190.7	180.1	187.2
Railroad retirement/pension fund	2.3	2.7	2.3	2.3	2.4	2.3	2.3	2.3
Unemployment insurance funds	21.6	27.6	42.0	41.1	39.5	37.9	44.8	51.8
Other retirement	4.5	4.8	4.5	4.3	4.2	4.1	4.1	4.3
Federal employees retirement—employee share	4.4	4.7	4.4	4.2	4.1	4.1	4.1	4.3
Excise taxes, total	**35.3**	**68.9**	**73.1**	**65.1**	**67.3**	**62.5**	**66.9**	**74.1**
Federal funds [1]	15.6	22.7	22.5	11.1	15.7	13.9	18.3	21.1
Alcohol	5.7	8.1	8.1	8.6	9.3	9.9	9.2	9.2
Tobacco	4.1	7.2	7.9	7.6	7.6	12.8	17.2	17.5
Telephone	3.0	5.7	6.0	–2.1	1.0	1.1	1.0	0.8
Ozone–depleting chemicals/products	0.4	0.1	–	–	–	–	–	–
Transportation fuels	–	0.8	–0.8	–3.3	–5.1	–10.3	–11.0	–9.4
Trust funds [1]	19.8	46.2	50.5	54.0	51.6	48.6	48.7	53.0
Highway	13.9	35.0	37.9	39.4	36.4	35.0	35.0	37.5
Airport and airway	3.7	9.7	10.3	11.5	12.0	10.6	10.6	10.1
Black lung disability	0.7	0.5	0.6	0.6	0.7	0.6	0.6	0.6
Inland waterway	0.1	0.1	0.1	0.1	0.1	0.1	0.1	0.1
Oil spill liability	0.1	0.2	–	0.5	0.3	0.4	0.5	0.5
Aquatic resources	0.2	0.3	0.4	0.6	0.6	0.6	0.6	0.6
Tobacco assessments	–	–	0.9	0.9	1.1	1.0	0.9	1.0
Vaccine injury compensation	0.2	0.1	0.1	0.2	0.3	0.2	0.2	0.2

– Represents zero. [1] Includes other funds, not shown separately.
Source: U.S. Office of Management and Budget, *Budget of the United States Government, Historical Tables*, annual. See also <http://www.whitehouse.gov/omb/budget>.

Table 476. Federal Trust Fund Income, Outlays, and Balances: 2010 to 2012

[In billions of dollars (10.9 represents $10,900,000,000). For years ending September 30. Receipts deposited. Outlays on a checks-issued basis less refunds collected. Balances: That which have not been spent. See text, this section, for discussion of the budget concept and trust funds. Minus sign (-) indicates negative balance]

Description	Income 2010	Income 2011, est.	Income 2012, est.	Outlays 2010	Outlays 2011, est.	Outlays 2012, est.	Balances [1] 2010	Balances [1] 2011, est.	Balances [1] 2012, est.
Airport and airway trust fund	10.9	10.5	10.6	10.3	10.8	12.1	9.4	9.1	7.6
Federal civilian employees' retirement funds	95.7	95.3	95.1	69.5	72.2	74.8	780.4	803.4	823.8
Federal employees' health benefits fund	39.8	43.1	45.5	39.0	42.9	45.8	16.2	16.3	16.1
Foreign military sales trust fund	24.0	28.0	27.7	23.6	26.9	27.4	17.6	18.7	19.0
Highway trust fund	54.8	37.8	64.7	39.7	45.0	60.3	29.2	22.0	26.4
Medicare:									
Hospital insurance (HI) trust fund	222.9	229.8	243.0	253.9	269.2	271.4	280.1	240.7	212.2
Supplemental medical insurance trust fund	283.1	297.1	313.2	272.5	304.6	307.8	72.0	64.5	69.9
Military retirement fund	93.7	98.2	106.4	50.6	55.3	48.3	318.6	361.5	419.7
Railroad retirement trust funds	11.6	10.2	10.2	11.2	11.3	11.6	21.6	20.5	19.2
Social security: Old-age, survivors and disability insurance trust funds	799.4	804.8	855.1	717.7	745.5	779.4	2,585.5	2,644.9	2,720.6
Unemployment trust funds	122.3	107.2	80.8	151.3	134.7	97.7	20.0	17.0	19.5
Veterans' life insurance trust funds	1.0	0.9	0.8	1.6	1.6	1.5	10.2	9.5	8.8
Other trust funds	18.2	17.5	24.9	13.2	14.3	14.6	78.0	80.8	90.6

[1] Balances available on a cash basis (rather than an authorization basis) at the end of the year. Balances are primarily invested in federal debt securities.
Source: U.S. Office of Management and Budget, Budget of the United States Government, Analytical Perspectives, annual. See also <http://www.whitehouse.gov/omb/budget>.

Table 477. Tax Expenditures Estimates Relating to Individual and Corporate Income Taxes by Selected Function: 2010 to 2013

[In millions of dollars (12,740 represents $12,740,000,000). For years ending September 30. Tax expenditures are defined as revenue losses attributable to provisions of the federal tax laws which allow a special exclusion, exemption, or deduction from gross income or which provide a special credit, a preferential rate of tax, or a deferral of liability. Minus sign (-) indicates decrease]

Function and provision	2010	2011	2012	2013
National defense:				
Exclusion of benefits and allowances to armed forces personnel	12,740	13,290	13,710	12,200
International affairs:				
Exclusion of income earned abroad by U.S. citizens	6,800	5,550	5,400	5,800
Exclusion of certain allowances for Federal employees abroad	970	1,020	1,070	1,120
Inventory property sales source rules exception	2,680	2,910	3,160	3,430
Deferral of income from controlled foreign corporations (normal tax method)	38,130	41,410	42,000	41,810
Deferred taxes for financial firms on certain income earned overseas	2,330	–	–	–
General science, space, and technology:				
Expensing of research and experimentation expenditures (normal tax method)	3,560	4,610	5,770	6,730
Credit for increasing research activities	5,890	3,850	3,080	2,460
Energy:				
Alternative fuel production credit	170	170	120	90
Energy production credit	1,540	1,620	1,740	1,900
Energy investment credit	130	170	960	1,690
Bio–diesel and small agri–biodiesel producer tax credits	20	10	–	–
Commerce and housing:				
Financial institutions and insurance:				
Exclusion of interest on life insurance savings	19,910	21,210	22,660	24,220
Housing:				
Deductibility of mortgage interest on owner–occupied homes	79,150	88,720	98,550	110,660
Deductibility of state and local property tax on owner–occupied homes	15,120	19,320	24,910	27,000
Capital gains exclusion on home sales	22,160	27,650	35,200	38,880
Exclusion of net imputed rental income	41,200	46,950	50,640	51,080
Exception from passive loss rules for $25,000 of rental loss	8,790	10,860	13,110	14,830
Credit for low–income housing investments	5,650	5,990	6,290	7,130
Accelerated depreciation on rental housing (normal tax method)	–1,490	–1,670	–1,580	–1,370
Commerce:				
Capital gains (except agriculture, timber, iron ore, and coal)	36,300	37,560	38,490	43,260
Step–up basis of capital gains at death	39,520	50,940	61,480	66,090
Accelerated depreciation of machinery and equipment (normal tax method)	39,790	17,540	24,450	44,290
Expensing of certain small investments (normal tax method)	950	6,710	–710	–2,820
Graduated corporation income tax rate (normal tax method)	3,000	3,280	3,220	3,300
Deduction for U.S. production activities	13,140	13,800	14,630	15,510
Transportation:				
Exclusion of reimbursed employee parking expenses	2,970	3,050	3,180	3,320
Education, training, employment, and social services:				
Education:				
HOPE tax credit	–	540	5,410	5,510
Lifetime Learning tax credit	3,490	3,880	5,530	5,660
Exclusion of interest on bonds for private nonprofit educational facilities	2,340	2,400	2,840	3,360
Parental personal exemption for students age 19 years or over	2,960	2,990	3,400	3,210
Deductibility of charitable contributions (education)	3,930	4,520	4,900	5,290
Training, employment, and social services:				
Child credit	23,030	18,330	10,580	10,290
Credit for child and dependent care expenses	3,470	1,900	1,710	1,660
Deductibility of charitable contributions, other than education and health	34,080	39,610	43,110	46,570
Health:				
Exclusion of employer contributions for medical insurance premiums [1]	160,110	173,750	184,460	196,220
Self–employed medical insurance premiums	5,680	6,210	6,690	7,200
Deductibility of medical expenses	9,090	10,030	10,010	9,930
Exclusion of interest on hospital construction bonds	3,530	3,630	4,290	5,080
Deductibility of charitable contributions (health)	3,850	4,470	4,870	5,250
Income security:				
Exclusion of workers' compensation benefits	6,770	7,050	7,410	7,790
Net exclusion of pension contributions and earnings:				
Employer plans	39,580	42,200	45,230	46,460
401(k) plans	52,240	62,850	67,590	69,060
Individual Retirement Accounts	12,630	13,930	15,610	16,020
Keogh plans	13,820	15,030	17,070	19,580
Exclusion of other employee benefits:				
Premiums on group term life insurance	1,950	1,980	2,080	2,120
Earned income tax credit	4,910	7,510	8,500	8,730
Exclusion of unemployment insurance benefits	5,220	–	–	–
Social security:				
Exclusion of social security benefits:				
Social security benefits for retired workers	21,440	20,300	21,830	23,350
Social security benefits for disabled	7,040	7,180	7,510	7,840
Social security benefits for dependents and survivors	3,850	3,160	3,270	3,300
Veterans' benefits and services:				
Exclusion of veterans' death benefits and disability compensation	4,130	4,510	5,010	5,520
General purpose fiscal assistance:				
Exclusion of interest on public purpose state and local bonds	30,440	31,260	36,960	43,720
Deductibility of nonbusiness state and local taxes other than on owner–occupied homes	26,890	37,720	48,640	54,030
Interest:				
Deferral of interest on U.S. savings bonds	1,180	1,220	1,300	1,320
Addendum: Aid to state and local governments:				
Deductibility of:				
Property taxes on owner–occupied homes	15,120	19,320	24,910	27,000
Nonbusiness state and local taxes other than on owner–occupied homes	26,890	37,720	48,640	54,030
Exclusion of interest on state and local bonds for:				
Public purposes	30,440	31,260	36,960	43,720
Private nonprofit educational facilities	2,340	2,400	2,840	3,360
Hospital construction	3,530	3,630	4,290	5,080

– Represents zero. [1] Includes medical care.

Source: U.S. Office of Management and Budget, Budget of the United States Government, Analytical Perspectives, annual. See also \<http://www.whitehouse.gov/omb/budget/>.

Table 478. U.S. Savings Bonds: 1990 to 2010

[In billions of dollars (122.5 represents $122,500,000,000), except percent. As of September 30]

Item	Unit	1990	1995	2000	2003	2004	2005	2006	2007	2008	2009	2010
Amounts outstanding, total [1] . . .	Bil. dol	122.5	181.5	177.7	192.6	194.1	189.9	189.2	181.5	177.8	175.6	172.3
Sales	Bil. dol	7.8	7.2	5.6	13.2	10.3	6.5	8.5	3.6	3.6	3.0	2.6
Accrued discounts	Bil. dol	8.0	9.5	6.9	7.3	6.9	6.7	7.5	7.2	7.1	6.9	5.2
Redemptions [2]	Bil. dol	7.5	11.8	14.5	12.2	14.6	13.8	16.0	10.8	10.7	9.9	7.8
Percent of total outstanding . . .	Percent . . .	6.1	6.5	8.2	6.3	7.5	7.3	8.5	6.0	6.0	5.7	4.6

[1] Interest-bearing debt only for amounts at end of year. [2] Matured and unmatured bonds.
Source: U.S. Department of the Treasury, Bureau of Public Debt, <http://www.treasurydirect.gov/govt/reports/pd/pd_sbntables_downloadable_files.htm>.

Table 479. Federal Funds—Summary Distribution by State: 2009

[In millions of dollars (3,238,360 represents $3,328,360,000,000), except as indicated. For year ending September 30. Data for grants, salaries and wages, and direct payments to individuals are on an expenditures basis; procurement data are on an obligation basis]

State and Island Areas	Federal funds		Agency		Object category			
	Total	Per capita [1] (dollars)	Defense	Non-defense	Direct payments	Procure-ment	Grants	Salaries and wages
United States [2]	3,238,360	10,396	534,889	2,703,471	762,924	550,803	744,115	299,413
Alabama	54,674	11,611	12,266	42,408	12,119	10,396	10,008	4,704
Alaska	14,215	20,351	6,043	8,171	875	4,968	3,706	3,128
Arizona	63,029	9,556	15,099	47,930	12,138	13,932	14,479	4,618
Arkansas	27,302	9,449	2,071	25,231	7,065	993	6,937	2,240
California	345,970	9,360	59,330	286,640	80,814	68,979	90,919	23,462
Colorado	47,806	9,514	11,333	36,473	8,644	11,123	8,854	6,845
Connecticut	42,589	12,105	12,860	29,729	9,226	13,005	8,829	1,766
Delaware	8,137	9,193	899	7,238	1,795	621	2,125	655
District of Columbia	49,889	83,196	4,923	44,967	4,980	7,750	12,022	22,290
Florida	175,684	9,477	23,186	152,498	50,666	18,531	31,979	12,215
Georgia	83,917	8,538	16,421	67,497	18,197	7,705	19,185	13,631
Hawaii	24,610	19,001	7,546	17,064	9,155	1,819	3,258	6,156
Idaho	14,898	9,638	1,157	13,741	2,848	3,427	3,099	1,151
Illinois	116,070	8,990	9,090	106,981	32,976	11,510	31,485	7,529
Indiana	61,149	9,520	8,946	52,203	17,353	7,936	13,346	3,709
Iowa	29,369	9,764	2,332	27,036	8,899	2,323	7,578	1,663
Kansas	34,705	12,312	5,922	28,784	13,775	3,004	5,386	4,339
Kentucky	50,012	11,593	10,316	39,696	10,655	6,972	11,366	6,692
Louisiana	48,357	10,765	5,550	42,808	12,616	4,036	15,249	3,842
Maine	14,242	10,803	2,043	12,199	2,883	1,431	4,084	1,073
Maryland	92,155	16,169	23,162	68,993	14,331	34,339	11,805	13,231
Massachusetts	83,890	12,723	16,641	67,249	20,570	18,892	22,382	4,266
Michigan	92,003	9,228	7,445	84,557	26,237	9,316	21,120	4,478
Minnesota	45,691	8,676	4,170	41,521	12,443	4,776	11,744	3,074
Mississippi	32,848	11,127	6,082	26,766	7,456	4,988	8,305	2,633
Missouri	67,942	11,347	15,361	52,581	16,212	13,508	13,568	6,179
Montana	10,925	11,206	748	10,178	3,135	508	2,940	1,099
Nebraska	16,526	9,199	1,876	14,650	4,917	1,164	3,656	1,597
Nevada	18,894	7,148	2,738	16,156	4,293	2,065	3,757	1,812
New Hampshire	11,844	8,942	2,052	9,792	2,315	1,921	2,612	847
New Jersey	80,647	9,262	10,877	69,770	22,745	12,051	16,785	5,193
New Mexico	27,472	13,670	2,792	24,680	3,806	7,736	6,953	2,523
New York	194,975	9,978	13,640	181,335	53,965	14,507	62,419	12,422
North Carolina	84,830	9,043	12,542	72,288	18,450	5,203	20,942	11,640
North Dakota	8,618	13,323	788	7,829	3,065	474	2,254	959
Ohio	107,975	9,354	10,206	97,768	33,135	9,103	25,414	6,637
Oklahoma	37,516	10,175	6,071	31,445	8,869	3,149	8,554	4,710
Oregon	33,594	8,781	2,610	30,983	8,382	2,469	8,705	2,409
Pennsylvania	135,687	10,765	13,938	121,749	40,010	18,098	27,363	8,324
Rhode Island	11,517	10,936	1,143	10,374	3,079	689	3,609	911
South Carolina	46,904	10,283	6,726	40,178	10,177	8,211	9,249	3,865
South Dakota	9,499	11,693	897	8,603	3,051	569	2,467	968
Tennessee	68,546	10,887	4,208	64,337	17,106	10,425	17,064	3,562
Texas	227,108	9,164	46,736	180,372	49,452	39,311	55,671	24,373
Utah	20,702	7,435	3,926	16,776	3,478	3,636	4,945	2,848
Vermont	7,092	11,407	1,064	6,029	1,346	1,075	2,162	578
Virginia	155,554	19,734	67,051	88,503	15,515	81,797	12,670	18,253
Washington	66,560	9,988	11,798	54,762	13,108	9,214	15,261	9,229
West Virginia	19,808	10,885	900	18,907	4,676	822	4,922	1,870
Wisconsin	61,280	10,837	9,215	52,066	13,772	9,514	19,219	2,662
Wyoming	6,278	11,534	419	5,858	1,165	260	2,604	669

[1] Based on U.S. Census Bureau estimated resident population as of July 1. [2] Includes Island Areas, not shown separately.
Source: U.S. Census Bureau, *Consolidated Federal Funds Report for Fiscal Year 2009,* July 2010.
See also <http://www.census.gov/gov/cffr/index.html>.

U.S. Census Bureau, Statistical Abstract of the United States: 2012

Table 480. Internal Revenue Gross Collections by Type of Tax: 2005 to 2010

[2,269 represents $2,269,000,000,000. For years ending September 30. See text, this section, for information on taxes]

Type of tax	Gross collections (bil. dol.)						Percent of total					
	2005	2006	2007	2008	2009	2010	2005	2006	2007	2008	2009	2010
United States, total	**2,269**	**2,519**	**2,692**	**2,745**	**2,345**	**2,345**	**100.0**	**100.0**	**100.0**	**100.0**	**100.0**	**100.0**
Individual income taxes.......	1,108	1,236	1,366	1,400	1,175	1,164	48.8	49.1	50.8	51.0	50.1	50.1
Withheld by employers.......	787	849	929	971	881	900	34.7	33.7	34.5	35.4	37.6	38.4
Tax payments [1]............	321	387	438	430	295	264	14.1	15.4	16.3	15.7	12.6	11.3
Estate and trust income tax....	(NA)	(NA)	(NA)	26	15	12	(NA)	(NA)	(NA)	0.9	0.6	0.5
Employment taxes	771	815	850	883	858	824	34.0	32.4	31.6	32.2	36.6	35.1
Old-age and disability insurance...............	760	803	838	871	847	813	33.5	31.9	31.1	31.7	36.1	34.7
Unemployment insurance	7	8	7	7	7	7	0.3	0.3	0.3	0.3	0.3	0.3
Railroad retirement	5	5	5	5	5	5	0.2	0.2	0.2	0.2	0.2	0.2
Business income taxes [2]	307	381	396	354	225	278	13.5	15.1	14.7	12.9	9.6	11.9
Estate and gift taxes	24	27	25	27	22	20	1.0	1.1	0.9	1.0	0.9	0.8
Excise taxes	57	58	53	52	47	47	2.5	2.3	2.0	1.9	2.0	2.0

NA Not available. [1] Includes estimated income tax collections and payments made with tax filings. Also includes estate and trust income tax for 2004–2007. [2] Includes corporation income tax and tax-exempt organization unrelated business income tax.

Source: U.S. Internal Revenue Service, *IRS Data Book* (Publication 55B), annual. See also <http://www.irs.gov/taxstats /index.html>.

Table 481. Individual Income Tax Returns Filed—Examination Coverage: 1995 to 2010

[114,683 represents 114,683,000. See the annual *IRS Data Book* (Publication 55B) for a detailed explanation]

Year	Returns filed [1] (1,000)	Returns examined		Total recommended additional tax [3] ($1,000)	Average recommended additional tax per return (dol.) [3]
		Total [2] (1,000)	Percent coverage		
1995.................	114,683	1,919	1.7	7,756,954	4,041
1997.................	118,363	1,519	1.3	8,363,918	5,505
1998.................	120,342	1,193	1.0	6,095,698	5,110
1999.................	122,547	1,100	0.9	4,458,474	4,052
2000.................	124,887	618	0.5	3,388,905	5,486
2001.................	127,097	732	0.6	3,301,860	4,512
2002.................	129,445	744	0.6	3,636,486	4,889
2003.................	130,341	849	0.7	4,559,902	5,369
2004.................	130,134	997	0.8	6,201,693	6,220
2005.................	130,577	1,199	0.9	13,355,087	11,138
2006.................	132,276	1,284	1.0	13,045,221	10,160
2007.................	134,543	1,385	1.0	15,705,155	11,343
2008.................	137,850	1,392	1.0	12,462,770	8,956
2009 [4]...............	138,950	1,426	1.0	14,940,892	10,478
2010.................	142,823	1,581	1.1	15,066,486	9,527

[1] Returns generally filed in previous calendar year. [2] Includes taxpayer examinations by correspondence. [3] For 1995 to 1997, amount includes associated penalties. [4] Excludes returns filed by individuals only to receive an Economic Stimulus Payment and who had no other reason to file.

Source: U.S. Internal Revenue Service, *IRS Data Book* (Publication 55B), annual. See also <http://www.irs.gov/taxstats /index.html>.

Table 482. Federal Individual Income Tax Returns—Adjusted Gross Income, Taxable Income, and Total Income Tax: 2007 and 2008

[142,979 represents 142,979,000. For tax years. Based on a sample of returns, see source and Appendix III]

Year	2007		2008		Percent change in amount, 2007-08
	Number of returns (1,000)	Amount (mil. dol.)	Number of returns (1,000)	Amount (mil. dol.)	
Adjusted gross income (less deficit)	142,979	8,687,719	142,451	8,262,860	−4.9
Exemptions [1]	282,613	943,171	282,929	980,977	4.0
Taxable income	110,533	6,063,264	107,995	5,652,925	−6.8
Total income tax.....................	96,270	1,115,602	90,660	1,031,581	−7.5
Alternative minimum tax	4,109	24,110	3,935	25,649	6.4

[1] The number of returns columns represent the number of exemptions.

Source: U.S. Internal Revenue Service, *Statistics of Income Bulletin*, fall issues. See also <http://www.irs.gov/taxstats /index.html>.

Table 483. Federal Individual Income Tax Returns—Adjusted Gross Income (AGI) by Selected Source of Income and Income Class: 2008

[In millions of dollars ($8,262,860 represents $8,262,860,000,000), except as indicated. Fot the tax year. Minus sign (–) indicates net loss was greater than net income. Based on sample; see Appendix III]

Item	Total [1]	Under $10,000	$10,000 to $19,999	$20,000 to $29,999	$30,000 to $39,999	$40,000 to $49,999	$50,000 to $99,999	$100,000 and over
Number of all returns (1,000)	142,451	26,268	22,778	18,610	14,554	11,087	30,926	18,227
Adjusted gross income [2]	8,262,860	–42,352	339,856	461,556	506,107	496,891	2,193,691	4,307,111
Salaries and wages...........	5,950,635	122,516	254,845	378,495	420,338	406,847	1,729,618	2,637,976
Interest received	303,113	20,007	10,553	10,527	10,247	10,855	51,998	188,926
Dividends in AGI	219,331	8,828	4,859	4,810	9,946	10,573	30,071	160,817
Business, profession, net profit less loss	264,234	39,489	37,221	23,892	19,901	18,557	48,404	148,767
Sales of property, net gain less loss [3]...........	466,579	13,973	613	444	871	927	11,849	437,901
Pensions and annuities in AGI....	506,269	11,147	32,466	36,496	38,913	39,282	181,093	166,872
Rents and royalties, net income less loss [4]	32,940	–8,619	–671	–725	–858	–1,398	–1,374	46,585

[1] Includes a small number of returns with no adjusted gross income. [2] Includes other sources, not shown separately. [3] Includes sales of capital assets and other property; net gain less loss. [4] Excludes rental passive losses disallowed in the computation of AGI; net income less loss.

Source: U.S. Internal Revenue Service, *Statistics of Income*, fall issues. See also <http://www.irs.gov/taxstats/index.html>.

Table 484. Federal Individual Income Tax Returns—Total and Selected Sources of Adjusted Gross Income: 2007 and 2008

[142,979 represents 142,979,000. For tax years. Based on a sample of returns, see source and Appendix III. Minus sign (–) indicates decrease]

Item	2007		2008		Change in amount, 2007–08	
	Number of returns (1,000)	Amount (mil. dol.)	Number of returns (1,000)	Amount (mil. dol.)	Net change (mil. dol.)	Percent change
Adjusted gross income (less deficit) [1]	142,979	8,687,719	142,451	8,262,860	–424,859	–4.9
Salaries and wages...........................	120,845	5,842,270	119,579	5,950,635	108,365	1.9
Taxable interest	64,505	268,058	62,450	223,291	–44,767	–16.7
Ordinary dividends	32,006	237,052	31,043	219,331	–17,721	–7.5
Qualified dividends	27,145	155,872	26,409	158,975	3,103	2
Business or profession net income (less loss)........	22,629	279,736	22,112	264,234	–15,502	–5.5
Net capital gain	27,156	907,656	23,731	469,273	–438,383	–48.3
Capital gain distributions [2].....................	15,714	86,397	11,544	21,954	–64,444	–74.6
Sales of property other than capital assets, net gain (less loss).....................	1,751	4,357	1,723	–7,811	–12,168	–279.3
Sales of property other than capital assets, net gain	893	15,113	773	12,953	–2,160	–14.3
Taxable social security benefits....................	15,012	167,187	15,015	168,110	924	0.6
Total rental and royalty net income (less net loss) [3].....	10,334	20,639	10,545	32,940	12,301	59.6
Partnership and S corporation net income (less loss)...	7,945	414,705	7,909	366,965	–47,740	–11.5
Estate and trust net income (less loss)	591	18,107	604	18,150	43	0.2
Farm net income (less loss)	1,978	–14,693	1,948	–14,847	–153	–1
Farm net income	556	9,931	549	11,749	1,818	18.3
Unemployment compensation.....................	7,622	29,415	9,533	43,675	14,260	48.5
Taxable pensions and annuities....................	25,181	490,581	25,540	506,269	15,688	3.2
Taxable Individual Retirement Account distributions....	10,683	147,959	11,259	162,150	14,191	9.6
Other net income (less loss) [4]	(NA)	36,140	(NA)	34,267	–1,873	–5.2
Gambling earnings	2,009	30,139	1,890	27,197	–2,942	–9.8

NA Not available. [1] Includes sources of income, not shown separately. [2] Includes both Schedule D and non-Schedule D capital gain distributions. [3] Includes farm rental net income (less loss). [4] Other net income (less loss) represents data reported on Form 1040, line 21, except net operating loss, the foreign-earned income exclusion, and gambling earnings.

Source: U.S. Internal Revenue Service, *Statistics of Income Bulletin*, fall issues. See also <http://www.irs.gov/taxstats/index.html>.

Table 485. Federal Individual Income Tax Returns—Net Capital Gains and Capital Gain Distributions From Mutual Funds: 1989 to 2008

[14,288 represents 14,288,000. For tax years. Based on a sample of returns, see source and Appendix III. Minus sign (–) indicates decrease]

Tax year	Net capital gain (less loss)				Capital gain distributions [2]			
	Number of returns (1,000)	Current dollars (mil. dol.)	Constant (1982–1984) dollars [1]		Number of returns (1,000)	Current dollars (mil. dol.)	Constant (1982–1984) dollars [1]	
			Amount (mil. dol.)	Percent change			Amount (mil. dol.)	Percent change
1989.....	15,060	145,631	117,444	–9.6	5,191	5,483	4,422	34.9
1990.....	14,288	114,231	87,400	–25.6	5,069	3,905	2,988	–32.4
1991.....	15,009	102,776	75,460	–13.7	5,796	4,665	3,425	14.6
1992.....	16,491	118,230	84,269	11.7	5,917	7,426	5,293	54.5
1993.....	18,409	144,172	99,773	18.4	9,998	11,995	8,301	56.8
1994.....	18,823	142,288	96,011	–3.8	9,803	11,322	7,640	–8.0
1995.....	19,963	170,415	111,821	16.5	10,744	14,391	9,443	23.6
1996.....	22,065	251,817	160,495	43.5	12,778	24,722	15,757	66.9
1997.....	24,240	356,083	221,859	38.2	14,969	45,132	28,120	78.5
1998.....	25,690	446,084	273,671	23.4	16,070	46,147	28,311	0.7
1999.....	27,701	542,758	325,785	19.0	17,012	59,473	35,698	26.1
2000.....	29,521	630,542	366,169	12.4	17,546	79,079	45,923	28.6
2001.....	25,956	326,527	184,375	–49.6	12,216	13,609	7,685	–83.3
2002.....	24,189	238,789	132,734	–28.0	7,567	5,343	2,970	–61.4
2003.....	22,985	294,354	159,975	20.5	7,265	4,695	2,552	–14.1
2004.....	25,267	473,662	250,747	56.7	10,733	15,336	8,119	218.1
2005.....	26,196	668,015	342,046	36.4	13,393	35,581	18,219	124.4
2006.....	26,668	779,462	386,638	13.0	14,511	59,417	29,473	61.8
2007.....	27,156	907,656	437,758	13.2	15,714	86,397	41,669	41.4
2008.....	23,731	469,273	217,959	–50.2	11,544	21,954	10,197	–75.5

[1] Constant dollars were calculated using the U.S. Bureau of Labor Statistics consumer price index for urban consumers (CPI-U, 1982–84 = 100). See Table 725. [2] Capital gain distributions are included in net capital gain (less loss). For 1989–1996, and 1999 and later years, capital gain distributions from mutual funds are the sum of the amounts reported on the Form 1040 and Schedule D. For 1997 and 1998, capital gain distributions were reported entirely on the Schedule D.

Source: U.S. Internal Revenue Service, *Statistics of Income Bulletin*, fall issues. See also <http://www.irs.gov/taxstats/index.html>.

Table 486. Alternative Minimum Tax: 1986 to 2008

[609 represents 609,000. For tax years. Based on a sample of returns, see source and Appendix III]

Tax year	Highest statutory alternative minimum tax rate (percent)	Alternative minimum tax		Tax year	Highest statutory alternative minimum tax rate (percent)	Alternative minimum tax	
		Number of returns (1,000)	Amount (mil. dol.)			Number of returns (1,000)	Amount (mil. dol.)
1986......	20	609	6,713	1998......	[1] 28	853	5,015
1987......	21	140	1,675	1999......	[1] 28	1,018	6,478
1988......	21	114	1,028	2000......	[1] 28	1,304	9,601
1989......	21	117	831	2001......	[1] 28	1,120	6,757
1990......	21	132	830	2002......	[1] 28	1,911	6,854
1991......	24	244	1,213	2003......	[1] 28	2,358	9,470
1992......	24	287	1,357	2004......	[1] 28	3,096	13,029
1993......	28	335	2,053	2005......	[1] 28	4,005	17,421
1994......	28	369	2,212	2006......	[1] 28	3,967	21,565
1995......	28	414	2,291	2007......	[1] 28	4,109	24,110
1996......	28	478	2,813	2008......	[1] 28	3,935	25,649
1997......	28	618	4,005				

[1] Top rate on most long-term capital gains was 20 percent; beginning 2003, the rate was 15 percent.

Source: U.S. Internal Revenue Service, *Statistics of Income Bulletin*, fall issue. See also <http://www.irs.gov/taxstats/index.html>

Table 487. Federal Individual Income Tax Returns—Sources of Net Losses Included in Adjusted Gross Income: 2006 to 2008

[5,447 represents 5,447,000. For tax years. Based on a sample of returns, see source and Appendix III

Item	2006 Number of returns (1,000)	2006 Amount (mil. dol.)	2007 Number of returns (1,000)	2007 Amount (mil. dol.)	2008 Number of returns (1,000)	2008 Amount (mil. dol.)
Total net losses	**(NA)**	**343,271**	**(NA)**	**390,035**	**(NA)**	**477,538**
Business or profession net loss...........	5,447	48,738	5,697	54,849	5,677	60,646
Net capital loss [1]	8,642	18,752	7,558	16,508	12,357	28,568
Net loss, sales of property other than capital assets........................	884	9,819	858	10,756	949	20,764
Total rental and royalty net loss [2]	4,658	49,927	4,886	56,288	4,936	57,145
Partnership and S corporation net loss.....	2,597	102,747	2,799	132,696	2,959	175,489
Estate and trust net loss	45	1,942	47	2,505	48	3,748
Farm net loss...........................	1,406	23,015	1,422	24,625	1,399	26,596
Net operating loss [3]	917	80,796	923	86,369	920	97,019
Other net loss [4]	347	7,535	228	5,438	244	7,564

NA Not available. [1] Includes only the portion of capital losses allowable in the calculation of adjusted gross income. Only $3,000 of net capital loss per return ($1,500 for married filing separately) are allowed to be included in negative total income. Any excess is carried forward to future years. [2] Includes farm rental net loss. [3] Net operating loss is a carryover of the loss from a business when taxable income from a prior year was less than zero. [4] Other net loss represents losses reported on Form 1040, line 21, except net operating loss and the foreign-earned income exclusion.

Source: U.S. Internal Revenue Service, *Statistics of Income Bulletin*, fall issues. See also <http://www.irs.gov/taxstats/index.html>.

Table 488. Federal Individual Income Tax Returns—Number, Income Tax, and Average Tax by Size of Adjusted Gross Income: 2000 and 2008

[129,374 represents 129,374,000. Based on sample of returns; see Appendix III]

Size of adjusted gross income	Number of returns (1,000) 2000	2008	Adjusted gross income (AGI) (bil. dol.) 2000	2008	Income tax total [1] (bil. dol.) 2000	2008	Taxes as a percent of AGI (for taxable returns only) 2000	2008	Average tax (for taxable returns only) (dol.) 2000	2008
Total.	**129,374**	**142,451**	**6,365**	**8,263**	**981**	**1,032**	**16**	**14**	**10,129**	**7,242**
Less than $1,000 [2]......	2,966	4,412	−58	−163	−	−	(X)	(X)	648	16
$1,000 to $2,999	5,385	4,585	11	9	−	−	7	3	134	4
$3,000 to $4,999	5,599	5,132	22	20	−	−	4	6	179	12
$5,000 to $6,999	5,183	4,918	31	29	1	−	5	2	297	23
$7,000 to $8,999	4,972	4,906	40	39	1	−	4	3	331	50
$9,000 to $10,999	5,089	4,540	51	45	1	−	5	3	470	78
$11,000 to $12,999	4,859	4,828	58	58	2	1	6	3	704	124
$13,000 to $14,999	4,810	4,649	67	65	3	1	6	3	883	165
$15,000 to $16,999	4,785	4,477	76	72	3	1	7	3	1,052	224
$17,000 to $18,999	4,633	4,435	83	80	4	2	7	4	1,279	349
$19,000 to $21,999	6,502	6,224	133	127	7	3	8	5	1,565	507
$22,000 to $24,999	5,735	5,806	135	136	8	4	8	5	1,815	714
$25,000 to $29,999	8,369	8,744	229	240	16	9	8	6	2,248	1,042
$30,000 to $39,999	13,548	14,554	471	506	40	26	9	7	3,094	1,756
$40,000 to $49,999	10,412	11,087	466	497	46	31	10	8	4,462	2,832
$50,000 to $74,999	17,076	19,196	1,045	1,180	116	93	11	9	6,824	4,827
$75,000 to $99,999	8,597	11,729	738	1,014	100	92	14	9	11,631	7,835
$100,000 to $199,999 ...	8,083	13,851	1,066	1,845	184	232	17	13	22,783	16,769
$200,000 to $499,999 ...	2,136	3,477	614	993	146	194	24	20	68,628	55,713
$500,000 to $999,999 ...	396	578	269	393	76	94	28	24	192,092	162,563
$1,000,000 or more.....	240	321	817	1,076	226	249	28	23	945,172	775,052

− Represents or rounds to zero. X Not applicable. [1] Consists of income tax after credits (including alternative minimum tax). [2] In addition to low income taxpayers, this size class (and others) includes taxpayers with "tax preferences," not reflected in adjusted gross income or taxable income which are subject to the "alternative minimum tax" (included in total income tax).

Source: U.S. Internal Revenue Service, *Statistics of Income Bulletin*, quarterly and fall issues. See also <http://www.irs.gov/taxstats/index.html>.

Table 489. Federal Individual Income Tax Returns—Selected Itemized Deductions and the Standard Deduction: 2007 and 2008

[50,544 represents 50,544,000. For tax years. Based on a sample of returns, see source and Appendix III. Minus sign (–) indicates decrease]

Item	2007		2008		Percent change, 2007–08	
	Number of returns [1] (1,000)	Amount (mil. dol.)	Number of returns [1] (1,000)	Amount (mil. dol.)	Number of returns [1] (percent)	Amount (percent)
Total itemized deductions before limitation ...	**50,544**	**1,372,138**	**48,167**	**1,339,354**	**–4.7**	**–2.4**
Medical and dental expenses after 7.5 percent AGI limitation..............................	10,520	76,347	10,155	76,387	–3.5	0.1
Taxes paid [2]	50,119	465,881	47,836	467,212	–4.6	0.3
State and local income taxes................	36,683	269,351	35,403	270,958	–3.5	0.6
State and local general sales taxes...........	11,936	18,522	11,045	17,686	–7.5	–4.5
Interest paid [3]..............................	41,283	524,790	39,200	497,618	–5	–5.2
Home mortgage interest	40,777	491,432	38,684	470,408	–5.1	–4.3
Charitable contributions [4]......................	41,119	193,604	39,250	172,936	–4.5	–10.7
Other than cash contributions	23,854	58,747	23,027	40,421	–3.5	–31.2
Casualty and theft losses	107	2,337	337	4,348	213.3	86.1
Miscellaneous deductions after 2-percent AGI limitation..............................	12,734	85,218	12,437	89,924	–2.3	5.5
Total unlimited miscellaneous deductions	1,692	23,961	1,642	30,929	–3	29.1
Itemized deductions in excess of limitation	7,131	39,102	6,783	17,077	–4.9	–56.3
Total itemized deductions after limitation.........	50,544	1,333,037	48,167	1,322,276	–4.7	–0.8
Total standard deduction....................	90,511	654,182	91,781	695,488	1.4	6.3
Total deductions (after itemized deduction limitation)	141,055	1,987,218	139,948	2,017,764	–0.8	1.5

[1] Returns with no adjusted gross income are excluded from the deduction counts. For this reason, the sum of the number of returns with total itemized deductions and the number of returns with total standard deduction is less than the total number of returns for all filers. [2] Includes real estate taxes, personal property taxes, and other taxes, not shown separately. [3] Includes investment interest and deductible mortgage "points," not shown separately. [4] For more information, see Table 584.

Source: U.S. Internal Revenue Service, *Statistics of Income Bulletin*, fall issues. See also <http://www.irs.gov/taxstats /index.html>.

Table 490. Federal Individual Income Tax Returns—Statutory Adjustments: 2007 and 2008

[36,050 represents 36,050,000. For tax years. Based on a sample of returns, see source and Appendix III. Minus sign (–) indicates decrease]

Item	2007		2008		Percent change in amount, 2007–08
	Number of returns (1,000)	Amount (mil. dol.)	Number of returns (1,000)	Amount (mil. dol.)	
Total statutory adjustments	**36,050**	**123,020**	**35,774**	**121,599**	**–1.2**
Payments to an Individual Retirement Account........	3,300	12,877	2,740	11,666	–9.4
Educator expenses deduction.....................	3,654	926	3,753	947	2.3
Moving expenses adjustment	1,119	2,903	1,113	3,003	3.5
Student loan interest deduction...................	9,091	7,464	9,136	7,731	3.6
Tuition and fees deduction.......................	4,543	10,579	4,577	11,002	4
Self-employment tax deduction...................	17,840	24,760	17,411	24,286	–1.9
Self-employment health insurance deduction	3,839	21,283	3,618	21,194	–0.4
Payments to a self-employed retirement (Keogh) plan ..	1,191	22,262	1,010	20,262	–9
Forfeited interest penalty........................	1,164	353	1,311	389	10.3
Alimony paid	600	9,497	580	9,621	1.3
Other adjustment [1]............................	(NA)	1,415	(NA)	1,862	31.6

NA Not available. [1] Includes foreign housing adjustment, Medical Savings Accounts deduction, jury duty pay deduction, and other adjustments for 2007 and 2008.

Source: U.S. Internal Revenue Service, *Statistics of Income Bulletin*, Fall issues. See also <http://www.irs.gov/taxstats /index.html>.

Table 491. Federal Individual Income Tax Returns—Itemized Deductions and Statutory Adjustments by Size of Adjusted Gross Income: 2008

[48,167 represents 48,167,000. Based on a sample of returns; see Appendix III]

Item	Unit	Total	Under $10,000	$10,000 to $19,999	$20,000 to $29,999	$30,000 to $39,999	$40,000 to $49,999	$50,000 to $99,999	$100,000 and over
Returns with itemized deductions:									
Number of returns [1,2]	1000....	48,167	1,019	2,065	2,980	3,886	4,199	17,942	16,076
Amount [1,2]	Mil. dol..	1,322,276	16,268	32,889	47,082	61,809	71,336	370,996	721,896
Medical and dental expenses: [3]									
Returns	1000....	10,155	660	1,200	1,279	1,297	1,173	3,453	1,094
Amount	Mil. dol..	76,387	5,410	9,189	8,938	7,851	7,785	24,825	12,389
Taxes paid:									
Returns [2]	1000....	47,836	961	2,001	2,933	3,846	4,163	17,874	16,059
Amount, total	Mil. dol..	467,212	3,013	5,965	9,613	13,920	16,955	108,307	309,439
State and local income taxes: [4]									
Returns	1000....	46,448	832	1,844	2,757	3,704	4,007	17,445	15,860
Amount	Mil. dol..	288,644	669	1,599	3,081	5,408	7,409	55,155	215,325
Real estate taxes:									
Returns	1000....	41,643	727	1,479	2,234	3,037	3,373	15,819	14,976
Amount	Mil. dol..	167,905	2,231	4,124	6,008	7,838	8,853	49,653	89,198
Interest paid:									
Returns	1000....	39,200	641	1,280	2,089	2,920	3,248	15,082	13,940
Amount	Mil. dol..	497,618	6,342	12,552	19,237	26,280	30,352	161,734	241,121
Home mortgage interest:									
Returns	1000....	38,684	624	1,256	2,057	2,894	3,223	14,973	13,658
Amount	Mil. dol..	470,408	6,206	12,280	18,893	25,733	29,710	158,552	219,034
Charitable contributions:									
Returns	1000....	39,250	583	1,338	2,008	2,756	3,155	14,756	14,654
Amount	Mil. dol..	172,936	636	2,416	4,122	5,862	7,165	39,792	112,943
Unreimbursed employee business expenses:									
Returns	1000....	15,791	92	339	773	1,288	1,504	6,715	5,080
Amount	Mil. dol..	82,226	375	1,509	4,003	6,816	7,930	33,474	28,118
Returns with statutory adjustments:									
Number of returns [2]									
Amount of adjustments	1000....	35,774	4,621	4,485	3,295	3,191	2,888	9,702	7,592
Payments to IRAs: [4]	Mil. dol..	121,599	7,539	6,341	6,148	6,219	6,313	25,136	63,903
Returns	1000....	2,740	85	142	260	317	283	1,017	636
Amount	Mil. dol..	11,666	266	411	860	1,085	1,043	4,262	3,739
Deduction for self-employment tax:									
Returns	1000....	17,411	3,282	3,102	1,559	1,233	1,086	3,652	3,497
Amount	Mil. dol..	24,286	1,454	2,428	1,572	1,311	1,248	5,059	11,214
Self-employment health insurance:									
Returns	1000....	3,618	403	320	325	252	244	826	1,248
Amount	Mil. dol..	21,194	1,583	1,147	1,326	1,161	1,151	4,381	10,444
Payments to Keogh plans:									
Returns	1000....	1,010	17	15	26	26	33	179	714
Amount	Mil. dol..	20,262	149	128	145	193	225	1,664	17,758

[1] After limitations. [2] Includes other deductions and adjustments, not shown separately. [3] Before limitation. [4] State and local taxes include income taxes and sales taxes.

Source: U.S. Internal Revenue Service, *Statistics of Income Bulletin*, Fall issues. See also <http://www.irs.gov/taxstats/index.html>.

Table 492. Federal Individual Income Tax Returns—Selected Tax Credits: 2006 to 2008

[46,092 represents 46,092,000. For tax years. Based on a sample of returns, see source and Appendix III]

Item	2006 Number of returns (1,000)	2006 Amount (mil. dol.)	2007 Number of returns (1,000)	2007 Amount (mil. dol.)	2008 Number of returns (1,000)	2008 Amount (mil. dol.)
Total tax credits [1]	**46,092**	**58,939**	**48,091**	**63,779**	**55,229**	**75,352**
Child care credit	6,467	3,487	6,492	3,483	6,587	3,527
Earned income credit [2]	2,960	797	3,420	934	3,382	971
Foreign tax credit	6,418	10,958	7,643	15,435	6,708	16,572
General business credit	387	1,302	231	846	304	1,649
Minimum tax credit	359	1,032	395	1,035	416	945
Child tax credit [3]	25,742	31,742	25,889	31,556	25,174	30,538
Education credits	7,725	7,022	7,435	6,910	7,741	7,633
Retirement savings contribution credit	5,192	894	5,862	977	5,961	977

[1] Includes credits not shown separately. [2] Represents portion of earned income credit used to offset income tax before credits. [3] Excludes refundable portion.

Source: U.S. Internal Revenue Service, *Statistics of Income Bulletin*, fall issues. See also <http://www.irs.gov/taxstats/index.html>.

Table 493. Federal Individual Income Tax Returns by State: 2008

[143,490 represents 143,490,000. For tax year. Data will not agree with data in other tables due to differing survey methodology used to derive state data]

State	Total number of returns (1,000)	Adjusted gross income (mil. dol.)			Itemized deductions (mil. dol.)				Income tax (mil. dol.)
		Total [1]	Salaries and wages	Net capital gain [2]	Total [1]	State and local income tax	Real estate taxes	Mortgage interest paid	
U.S.	143,490	8,178,369	5,949,953	416,936	1,360,124	277,502	172,270	470,565	1,039,754
AL	2,076	99,244	73,161	3,878	13,498	2,335	658	4,621	10,910
AK	360	20,828	14,252	639	1,972	26	317	967	2,721
AZ	2,714	141,788	104,465	6,606	22,822	3,520	2,109	11,652	16,050
AR	1,224	54,403	39,749	2,307	7,072	1,694	355	1,970	5,868
CA	16,478	1,029,474	752,121	52,799	228,505	53,899	25,038	90,958	133,856
CO	2,341	143,080	102,587	9,037	24,579	4,422	1,941	10,754	18,024
CT	1,742	143,947	102,517	8,377	24,853	7,016	4,462	7,661	23,459
DE	425	24,263	17,512	973	3,845	858	294	1,624	2,850
DC	303	22,495	15,900	1,333	4,699	1,412	295	1,362	3,577
FL	8,875	472,430	311,910	37,501	76,018	2,479	10,708	29,582	62,461
GA	4,560	230,079	166,296	17,928	41,257	8,161	3,708	17,157	27,393
HI	694	35,510	23,977	2,881	5,978	1,251	315	2,906	3,998
ID	722	33,553	22,380	3,445	5,602	1,215	420	2,342	3,608
IL	6,559	392,665	267,880	38,792	56,849	8,421	10,518	23,185	54,217
IN	3,243	150,942	109,317	9,067	18,995	4,046	1,990	7,165	17,043
IA	1,415	71,528	51,896	2,568	8,446	2,221	1,000	2,333	7,633
KS	1,329	70,891	51,429	2,834	9,641	2,405	1,074	2,738	8,397
KY	1,869	85,904	63,788	2,903	12,079	3,286	939	3,833	8,917
LA	1,984	106,362	72,793	6,799	12,244	2,458	579	3,531	13,814
ME	634	29,683	21,692	1,071	4,192	1,181	635	1,603	3,028
MD	2,776	185,109	139,474	5,806	41,069	10,780	4,362	14,914	23,104
MA	3,198	226,476	164,888	11,748	38,129	9,966	5,533	12,998	32,674
MI	4,626	231,683	170,351	5,347	35,338	6,498	5,531	12,302	26,212
MN	2,570	151,774	113,388	6,151	26,787	6,801	3,028	9,543	18,474
MS	1,255	52,322	39,301	1,798	7,175	1,113	391	1,915	5,250
MO	2,739	139,188	101,955	6,293	19,921	4,462	1,989	6,499	16,159
MT	477	21,407	14,289	1,443	3,350	722	303	1,105	2,296
NE	858	43,895	31,996	1,911	6,043	1,358	809	1,631	4,890
NV	1,272	71,051	50,801	5,286	13,962	395	1,178	5,828	8,788
NH	669	40,336	30,146	2,127	5,812	461	1,403	2,492	5,056
NJ	4,305	315,972	236,237	12,164	60,977	14,997	13,336	18,967	45,765
NM	923	41,548	29,760	1,666	5,478	931	424	2,176	4,558
NY	9,204	630,575	443,418	43,230	120,053	42,074	17,800	26,660	95,489
NC	4,180	209,057	155,381	7,992	36,694	9,070	3,190	12,452	22,636
ND	323	16,859	11,179	989	1,438	219	194	394	2,013
OH	5,563	270,208	202,686	6,851	37,588	10,404	5,197	12,608	30,126
OK	1,605	82,100	56,921	4,081	10,611	2,137	725	2,729	9,947
OR	1,754	88,955	63,283	3,960	18,312	4,855	1,967	6,766	9,587
PA	6,130	334,702	244,861	12,280	46,313	10,577	7,278	14,949	41,487
RI	511	28,211	20,764	937	4,812	1,082	814	1,719	3,393
SC	2,047	93,513	68,519	3,395	14,666	3,290	964	5,336	9,541
SD	390	19,074	12,694	1,361	1,706	57	200	544	2,299
TN	2,843	134,951	101,709	5,299	15,892	517	1,433	6,092	15,503
TX	10,792	639,971	455,903	42,467	71,788	1,443	12,381	21,877	88,794
UT	1,145	60,032	45,019	3,234	11,898	2,113	822	4,438	6,174
VT	320	15,950	11,258	868	2,366	526	430	740	1,757
VA	3,728	238,154	177,885	9,905	43,980	9,172	4,755	17,658	30,099
WA	3,186	194,218	139,443	11,746	29,814	832	4,045	14,101	24,555
WV	786	34,938	25,893	986	3,005	896	166	1,060	3,692
WI	2,768	145,009	107,497	5,508	23,012	5,874	3,905	7,238	16,238
WY	274	17,865	11,312	1,966	1,871	107	136	626	2,623
Other [3]	1,794	88,035	83,920	10,207	6,378	1,796	494	1,302	11,431

[1] Includes other items, not shown separately. [2] Less loss. [3] Includes returns filed from Army Post Office and Fleet Post Office addresses by members of the armed forces stationed overseas; returns by other U.S. citizens abroad; and returns filed by residents of Puerto Rico with income from sources outside of Puerto Rico or with income earned as U.S. government employees.

Source: U.S. Internal Revenue Service, Statistics of Income Bulletin, Spring issues. See also <http://www.irs.gov/taxstats/index.html>.

Table 494. Federal Individual Income Tax—Tax Liability and Effective and Marginal Tax Rates for Selected Income Groups: 2000 to 2010

[Refers to income after exclusions but before deductions for itemized or standard deductions and for personal exemptions. Tax liability is after reductions for tax credits. As a result of the tax credits, tax liability can be negative, which means that the taxpayer receives a payment from the government. The effective rate represents tax liability, which may be negative as a result of the tax credits, divided by stated income. The marginal tax rate is the percentage of the first additional dollar of income which would be paid in income tax. Tax credits which increase with income can result in negative marginal tax rates. Computations assume itemized deductions (in excess of floors) of 18 percent of adjusted gross income or the standard deduction, whichever is greater. All income is assumed to be from wages and salaries. Does not include social security and Medicare taxes imposed on most wages and salaries]

Adjusted gross income	2000	2005	2007	2008 [1]	2009	2010
TAX LIABILITY (dol.)						
Single person, no dependents:						
$5,000	[2]-353	[2]-383	[2]-383	[1,2]-683	[2,5]-693	[2,5]-693
$10,000	[2]391	[2]46	[2]-73	[1,2]-415	[2,5]-598	[2,5]-600
$20,000	1,920	1,405	1,296	[1]656	[5]780	[5]779
$30,000	3,270	2,845	2,789	2,156	[5]2,280	[5]2,279
$40,000	4,988	4,075	4,019	3,394	[5]3,555	[5]3,554
$50,000	7,284	6,115	5,824	5,119	[5]5,125	[5]5,119
$75,000	13,024	11,240	10,949	10,244	[5]10,250	[5]10,244
$100,000	19,233	16,571	16,119	15,969	[5]15,775	[5]15,769
Married couple, two dependents, with one spouse working:						
$5,000	-2,000	[2]-2,000	[2]-2,000	[1,2]-3,200	-2,610	[2,4,5]-2,610
$10,000	-3,888	[2]-4,000	[2]-4,000	[1,2,4]-5,425	-5,670	[2,4,5]-5,670
$20,000	-2,349	[2,4]-4,986	[2,5]-5,404	[1,2,4]-7,484	-7,828	[2,4,5]-7,836
$30,000	475	[2,3,4]-2,810	[2,4,5]-3,490	[1,2,3,4]-5,143	-5,621	[2,3,4,5]-5,637
$40,000	2,218	[3,4]-150	[4,5]-428	[1,2,3,4]-2,637	-2,515	[2,3,4,5]-2,531
$50,000	3,470	[3]1,350	[4]1,073	[1,3]-838	-35	[3,5]-37
$75,000	7,384	[3]4,575	[4]4,403	[1,3]2,523	3,400	[3,5]3,398
$100,000	13,124	[3]8,630	[4]7,948	[1,3]5,888	6,475	[3,5]6,473
EFFECTIVE RATE (percent)						
Single person, no dependents:						
$5,000	-7.1	[2]-7.7	[2]-7.7	[1,2]-13.7	[2,5]-13.9	[2,5]-13.9
$10,000	3.9	[2]0.5	[2]-0.7	[1,2]-4.2	[2,5]-6	[2,5]-6
$20,000	9.6	7.0	6.5	[1]3.3	[5]3.9	[5]3.9
$30,000	10.9	9.5	9.3	[1]7.2	[5]7.6	[5]7.6
$40,000	12.5	10.2	10.1	[1]8.5	[5]8.9	[5]8.9
$50,000	14.6	12.2	11.6	[1]10.2	[5]10.3	[5]10.2
$75,000	17.4	15	14.6	[1]13.7	[5]13.7	[5]13.7
$100,000	19.2	16.6	16.1	16.0	15.8	15.8
Married couple, two dependents, with one spouse working:						
$5,000	[2]-40.0	[2]-40.0	[2]-40.0	[1,2]-64	[2,4,5]-52.2	[2,4,5]-52.2
$10,000	[2]-38.9	[2]-40.0	[2]-40.0	[1,2,4]-54.3	[2,4,5]-56.7	[2,4,5]-56.7
$20,000	[2,3]-11.7	[2,4]-24.9	[2,5]-27.0	[1,2,4]-37.4	[2,4,5]-39.1	[2,4,5]-39.2
$30,000	[2,3]1.6	[2,3,4]-9.4	[2,4,5]-11.6	[1,2,3,4]-17.1	[2,3,4,5]-18.7	[2,3,4,5]-18.8
$40,000	[3]5.5	[3,4]-0.4	[4,5]-1.1	[1,2,3,4]-6.6	[2,3,4,5]-6.3	[2,3,4,5]-6.3
$50,000	[3]6.9	[3]2.7	[4]2.1	[1,3]-1.7	[3,5]-0.1	[3,5]-0.1
$75,000	[3]9.8	[3]6.1	[4]5.9	[1,3]3.4	[3,5]4.5	[3,5]4.5
$100,000	[3]13.1	[3]8.6	[4]7.9	[1,3]5.9	[3,5]6.5	[3,5]6.5
MARGINAL TAX RATE (percent)						
Single person, no dependents:						
$5,000	–	[2]-7.7	[2]-7.7	[2]-7.7	[2,5]-13.9	[2,5]-13.9
$10,000	[2]22.7	[2]17.7	[2]17.7	[2]17.7	[2]17.7	[2]17.7
$20,000	15.0	15.0	15.0	15.0	15.0	15
$30,000	15.0	15.0	15.0	15.0	15.0	15
$40,000	28.0	15.0	15.0	15.0	15.0	15
$50,000	28.0	25.0	25.0	25.0	25.0	25
$75,000	28.0	25.0	25.0	25.0	[5]27.0	[5]27
$100,000	31.0	28.0	28.0	25.0	25.0	25
Married couple, two dependents, with one spouse working:						
$5,000	[2]-40.0	[2]-40.0	[2]-40.0	[2]-40.0	[2,4,5]-61.2	[2,4,5]-61.2
$10,000	–	[2]-40.0	[2]-40.0	[2,4]-55	[2,4,5]-61.2	[2,4,5]-61.2
$20,000	[2,3]21.1	[2,4]6.1	[2,5]6.1	[2,4]6.1	–	–
$30,000	[2]36.1	[2,3,4]31.1	[2,4,5]31.1	[2,3,4]31.1	[2]31.1	[2]31.1
$40,000	15.0	[3,4]15	[4,5]15	[2,3,4]31.1	[2]31.1	[2]31.1
$50,000	15.0	15.0	15.0	15.0	15.0	15
$75,000	28.0	15.0	15.0	15.0	15.0	15
$100,000	28.0	25.0	25.0	25.0	15.0	15

– Represents zero. [1] Includes effect of the Recovery Rebate paid in 2008 under the Economic Stimulus Act of 2008 (P.L. 110–185). [2] Includes effect from the refundable earned income credit. [3] Includes effect from the child tax credit. [4] Includes effect from the additional (refundable) child tax credit. [5] Includes effect from the (refundable) Making Work Pay tax credit.
Source: U.S. Department of the Treasury, Office of Tax Analysis, unpublished data.

Table 495. Federal Individual Income Tax—Current Income Equivalent to 2000 Constant Income for Selected Income Groups: 2000 to 2010

[Constant 2000 incomes calculated by using the U.S. Bureau of Labor Statistics Consumer Price Index for Urban Consumers (CPI–U); see Table 725, Section 14. See also headnote, Table 494]

Adjusted gross income (constant 2000 dollars)	2000	2005	2007	2008 [1]	2009	2010
REAL INCOME EQUIVALENT (dol.)						
$5,000	5,000	5,670	6,020	6,250	6,230	6,330
$10,000	10,000	11,340	12,040	12,500	12,460	12,660
$20,000	20,000	22,680	24,080	25,010	24,920	25,330
$30,000	30,000	34,020	36,120	37,510	37,380	37,990
$40,000	40,000	45,370	48,160	50,010	49,830	50,650
$50,000	50,000	56,710	60,200	62,520	62,290	63,310
$75,000	75,000	85,060	90,310	93,770	93,440	94,970
$100,000	100,000	113,410	120,410	125,030	124,590	126,630
TAX LIABILITY (dol.)						
Single person, no dependents:						
$5,000	[2] −353	[2] −399	[2] −428	[1,2] −738	[2,5] −843	[2,5] −850
$10,000	[2] 391	[2] 283	[2] 287	[1,2] −29	[2,5] −164	[2,5] −130
$20,000	1,920	1,807	1,908	[1] 1,408	[5] 1,518	[5] 1,578
$30,000	3,270	3,339	3,542	[1] 3,087	[5] 3,233	[5] 3,307
$40,000	4,988	5,166	5,447	[1] 5,121	[5] 5,090	[5] 5,252
$50,000	7,284	7,491	7,915	[1] 7,685	[5] 7,644	[5] 7,847
$75,000	13,024	13,302	14,087	[1] 14,692	[5] 14,399	[5] 14,737
$100,000	19,233	19,649	20,805	[1] 21,705	[5] 21,304	21,761
Married couple, 2 dependents with one spouse working:						
$5,000	[2] −2,000	[2] −2,268	[2] −2,408	[1,2] −3,700	[2,4,5] −3,363	[2,4,5] −3,424
$10,000	[2] −3,888	[2,4] −4,451	[2] −4,624	[1,2,4] −6,624	[2,4,5] −7,176	[2,4,5] −7,270
$20,000	[2,3] −2,349	[2,4] −4,823	[2,4] −5,157	[1,2,3,4] −6,693	[2,4,5] −7,091	[2,4,5] −7,021
$30,000	[2,3] 475	[2,3,4] −1,561	[2,3,4] −1,589	[1,2,3,4] −3,410	[2,3,4,5] −3,329	[2,4,5] −3,156
$40,000	[3] 2,218	[3] 656	[3,4] 796.5	[1,3] −836	[3,5] −60	3,560
$50,000	[3] 3,470	[3] 2,325	[3] 2,582	[1,3] 987	[3,5] 1,809	[3,5] 1,959
$75,000	[3] 7,384	[3] 5,812	[3] 6,286	[1,3] 4,831	[3,5] 5,668	[3,5] 5,854
$100,000	[3] 13,124	[3] 11,579	[3] 12,682	[1,3] 11,819	[3,5] 12,216	[3,5] 12,722
EFFECTIVE TAX RATE (percent)						
Single person, no dependents:						
$5,000	[2] −7.1	[2] −7	[2] −7.10	[1,2] −11.8	[2,5] −13.5	[2,5] −13.4
$10,000	[2] 3.9	[2] 2.5	[2] 2.38	[1,2] −0.2	[2,5] −1.3	[2,5] −1
$20,000	9.6	8.0	7.9	[1] 5.6	[5] 6.1	[5] 6.2
$30,000	10.9	9.8	9.8	[1] 8.2	[5] 8.6	[5] 8.7
$40,000	12.5	11.4	11.3	[1] 10.2	[5] 10.2	[5] 10.4
$50,000	14.6	13.2	13.1	[1] 12.3	[5] 12.3	[5] 12.4
$75,000	17.4	15.6	15.6	[1] 15.7	[5] 15.4	[5] 15.5
$100,000	19.2	17.3	17.3	[1] 17.4	17.1	17.2
Married couple, 2 dependents with one spouse working:						
$5,000	[2] −40	[2] −40	[2] −40	[1,2] −59.2	[2,4,5] −54	[2,4,5] −54.1
$10,000	[2] −38.9	[2,4] −39.3	[2] −39.5	[1,2,4] −53	[2,4,5] −57.6	[2,4,5] −57.4
$20,000	[2,3] −11.7	[2,4] −21.3	[2,4] −21.4	[1,2,3,4] −26.8	[2,4,5] −28.5	[2,4,5] −27.7
$30,000	[2,3] 1.6	[2,3,4] −4.6	[2,3,4] −4.40	[1,2,3,4] −9.1	[2,3,4,5] −8.9	[2,4,5] −8.3
$40,000	[3] 5.5	[3] 1.4	[3,4] 1.65	[1,3] −1.7	[3,5] −0.1	[3,5] 0.1
$50,000	[3] 6.9	[3] 4.1	[3] 4.28	[1,3] 1.6	[3,5] 2.9	[3,5] 3.1
$75,000	[3] 9.8	[3] 6.8	[3] 6.96	[1,3] 5.2	[3,5] 6.1	[3,5] 6.2
$100,000	[3] 13.1	[3] 10.2	[3] 10.5	[1,3] 9.5	[3,5] 9.8	[3,5] 10
MARGINAL TAX RATE (percent)						
Single person, no dependents:						
$5,000	−	−	−	−	[5] −6.2	[5] −6.2
$10,000	[2] 22.7	[2] 17.7	[2] 17.7	[2] 7.7	[2] 17.7	[2] 17.7
$20,000	15.0	15.0	15.0	15.0	15.0	15.0
$30,000	15.0	15.0	15.0	15.0	15.0	15.0
$40,000	28.0	25.0	25.0	25.0	25.0	25.0
$50,000	28.0	25.0	25.0	25.0	25.0	25.0
$75,000	28.0	25.0	25.0	25.0	[5] 27	[5] 27
$100,000	31.0	28.0	28.0	28.0	28.0	28.0
Married couple, 2 dependents with one spouse working:						
$5,000	[2] −40.0	[2] −40.0	[2] −40.0	[2] −40.0	[2,4,5] −61.2	[2,4,5] −61.2
$10,000	−	[4] −15.0	[4] −15.0	[4] −15.0	[2,4,5] −61.2	[2,4,5] −21.2
$20,000	[2,3] 21.1	[2,4] 6.1	[2,3,4] 6.1	[2,3,4] 31.1	[2] 21.1	[2] 21.1
$30,000	[2] 36.1	[2,3,4] 31.1	[2,3,4] 31.1	[2,3,4] 31.1	[2] 31.1	[2] 31.1
$40,000	15.0	15.0	15.0	15.0	15.0	15.0
$50,000	15.0	15.0	15.0	15.0	15.0	15.0
$75,000	28.0	15.0	15.0	15.0	15.0	15.0
$100,000	28.0	[3] 30.1	[3] 30.1	[3] 30.1	[3] 30.1	[3] 30.1

− Represents zero. [1] Includes effect of the Recovery Rebate paid in 2008 under the Economic Stimulus Act of 2008 (P.L. 110–185). [2] Includes effect from the refundable earned income credit. [3] Includes effect from the child tax credit. [4] Includes effect from the additional (refundable) child tax credit. [5] Includes effect from the (refundable) Making Work Pay tax credit.

Source: U.S. Department of the Treasury, Office of Tax Analysis, unpublished data.

Table 496. Federal Civilian Employment and Annual Payroll by Branch: 1970 to 2010

[2,997 represents 2,997,000. For fiscal year ending in year shown. See text, Section 8. Includes employees in U.S. territories and foreign countries. Data represent employees in active-duty status, including intermittent employees. Annual employment figures are averages of monthly figures. Excludes Central Intelligence Agency, National Security Agency, and as of November 1984, the Defense Intelligence Agency; and as of October 1996, the National Imagery and Mapping Agency]

Year	Employment						Payroll (mil. dol.)				
	Total (1,000)	Percent of U.S. em-ployed [1]	Executive (1,000)		Legis-lative (1,000)	Judicial (1,000)	Total	Executive		Legis-lative	Judicial
			Total	Defense				Total	Defense		
1970....	[2] 2,997	3.81	2,961	1,263	29	7	27,322	26,894	11,264	338	89
1975....	2,877	3.35	2,830	1,044	37	10	39,126	38,423	13,418	549	154
1980....	[2] 2,987	3.01	2,933	971	40	14	58,012	56,841	18,795	883	288
1985....	3,001	2.80	2,944	1,080	39	18	80,599	78,992	28,330	1,098	509
1990....	[2] 3,233	2.72	3,173	1,060	38	23	99,138	97,022	31,990	1,329	787
1995....	2,943	2.36	2,880	852	34	28	118,304	115,328	31,753	1,598	1,379
2003....	2,743	1.99	2,677	669	31	34	143,380	139,506	29,029	1,908	1,966
2004....	2,714	1.95	2,649	668	30	34	148,037	144,134	29,128	1,977	1,927
2005....	2,709	1.91	2,645	671	30	34	152,222	148,275	29,331	2,048	1,900
2006....	2,700	1.87	2,636	676	30	34	160,570	156,543	29,580	2,109	1,918
2007....	2,695	1.85	2,632	674	30	33	161,394	157,010	29,025	2,119	2,265
2008....	2,730	1.88	2,666	682	30	34	167,166	162,675	29,749	2,162	2,328
2009....	2,804	2.00	2,740	714	30	34	174,804	170,349	30,995	2,203	2,252
2010....	2,841	2.00	2,777	773	31	34	150,321	147,554	32,377	2,515	2,251

[1] Civilian employed only. See Table 586, Section 12. [2] Includes temporary census workers.

Source: U.S. Office of Personnel Management, *Federal Civilian Workforce Statistics—Employment and Trends*, bimonthly, and unpublished data, <http://www.opm.gov/feddata>.

Table 497. Full-Time Federal Civilian Employment—Employees and Average Pay by Pay System: 2000 to 2010

[As of March 31 (1,671 represents 1,671,000). Excludes employees of Congress and federal courts, maritime seamen of U.S. Department of Commerce, and small number for whom rates were not reported. See text, this section, for explanation of general schedule and wage system]

Pay system	Employees (1,000)				Average annual pay (dol.)			
	2000	2008	2009	2010	2000	2008	2009	2010
Total, excluding postal ...	**1,671**	**1,885**	**1,798**	**1,865**	**50,429**	**69,061**	**63,678**	**73,908**
General Schedule	1,216	1,265	1,083	1,162	49,428	68,674	59,330	70,426
Wage system.............	205	200	189	196	37,082	47,652	50,223	50,862
Other	250	420	526	507	66,248	80,444	77,433	90,383
Postal pay system [1]	788	663	623	584	37,627	50,294	49,951	53,304

[1] Source: Career employees—U.S. Postal Service, *Annual Report of the Postmaster General*. See also <http://www.usps.com/financials/cspo/welcome.html>. Average pay—U.S. Postal Service, *Comprehensive Statement of Postal Operations*, annual.

Source: Except as noted, U.S. Office of Personnel Management, "Pay Structure of the Federal Civil Service," annual (publication discontinued) and unpublished data, <http://www.opm.gov/feddata>.

Table 498. Paid Civilian Employment in the Federal Government by State: 2000 and 2009

[As of December 31. In thousands (2,766 represents 2,766,000). Excludes Central Intelligence Agency, Defense Intelligence Agency, seasonal and on-call employees, and National Security Agency]

State	2000	2009	State	2000	2009	State	2000	2009
U.S. [1]	**2,766**	**1,992**	KY	30	25	OH.......	84	52
AL	48	41	LA	33	22	OK.......	43	38
AK	14	13	ME.......	13	11	OR.......	29	21
AZ	43	42	MD.......	130	124	PA	107	71
AR	20	15	MA.......	53	29	RI........	10	7
CA	248	169	MI........	58	30	SC	26	22
CO.......	51	40	MN.......	34	18	SD	9	8
CT	21	9	MS.......	24	19	TN	50	28
DE	5	3	MO.......	54	39	TX	162	140
DC.......	181	157	MT.......	11	11	UT	30	29
FL	113	89	NE	15	10	VT	6	5
GA	89	79	NV	13	11	VA	145	147
HI........	23	25	NH	8	4	WA	62	56
ID........	11	9	NJ	62	31	WV.......	18	19
IL........	94	52	NM.......	25	27	WI	30	15
IN........	37	25	NY	134	72	WY.......	6	6
IA........	18	9	NC	57	43			
KS	25	17	ND.......	8	7			

[1] Includes employees outside the United States and in states not specified, not shown separately.

Source: U.S. Office of Personnel Management, "Employment by Geographic Area," biennial (publication discontinued) and unpublished data, <http://www.opm.gov/feddata>.

Table 499. Federal Civilian Employment by Branch and Agency: 1990 to 2010

[For years ending September 30. Annual averages of monthly figures. Excludes Central Intelligence Agency, National Security Agency; the Defense Intelligence Agency; and as of October 1996, the National Imagery and Mapping Agency]

Agency	1990	2000	2005	2008	2009	2010
Total, all agencies	**3,128,267**	**2,708,101**	**2,708,753**	**2,730,040**	**2,803,909**	**2,841,143**
Legislative Branch	37,495	31,157	30,303	29,919	29,997	30,643
Judicial Branch	23,605	32,186	33,690	33,682	33,754	33,756
Executive Branch	3,067,167	2,644,758	2,644,764	2,666,440	2,740,158	2,776,744
Executive Office of the President	1,731	1,658	1,736	1,717	1,723	1,965
Executive Departments	2,065,542	1,592,200	1,689,914	1,740,979	1,850,913	1,937,291
State	25,288	27,983	33,808	35,779	36,762	39,016
Treasury	158,655	143,508	114,194	111,335	110,686	110,099
Defense	1,034,152	676,268	670,790	682,142	714,483	772,601
Justice	83,932	125,970	105,102	107,970	111,214	117,916
Interior	77,679	73,818	73,599	70,515	71,536	70,231
Agriculture	122,594	104,466	104,989	98,720	97,803	106,867
Commerce [1]	69,920	47,652	38,927	41,339	74,305	56,856
Labor	17,727	16,040	15,599	16,269	16,316	17,592
Health & Human Services [2]	123,959	62,605	60,944	62,344	65,389	69,839
Housing & Urban Development	13,596	10,319	10,086	9,599	9,636	9,585
Transportation [3]	67,364	63,598	55,975	54,676	56,310	57,972
Energy	17,731	15,692	15,050	14,857	15,613	16,145
Education	4,771	4,734	4,429	4,210	4,097	4,452
Veterans Affairs	248,174	219,547	236,363	265,390	289,335	304,665
Homeland Security [3]	(X)	(X)	149,977	165,839	177,428	183,455
Independent agencies [4]	999,894	1,050,900	953,113	923,744	887,522	837,488
Board of Governors Federal Reserve System	1,525	2,372	1,851	1,873	1,873	1,873
Environmental Protection Agency	17,123	18,036	17,964	18,127	18,301	18,740
Equal Employment Opportunity Commission	2,880	2,780	2,421	2,209	2,226	2,543
Federal Communications Commission	1,778	1,965	1,936	1,809	1,849	1,838
Federal Deposit Insurance Corporation	17,641	6,958	4,998	4,726	5,478	6,436
Federal Trade Commission	988	1,019	1,046	1,131	1,131	1,131
General Services Administration	20,277	14,334	12,685	11,929	12,157	12,820
National Archives & Records Administration	3,120	2,702	3,048	3,068	3,298	3,523
National Aeronautics & Space Administration	24,872	18,819	19,105	18,531	18,441	18,664
National Labor Relations Board	2,263	2,054	1,822	1,670	1,631	1,715
National Science Foundation	1,318	1,247	1,325	1,383	1,430	1,474
Nuclear Regulatory Commission	3,353	2,858	3,230	3,833	4,114	4,240
Office of Personnel Management	6,636	3,780	4,333	5,375	5,408	5,892
Peace Corps	1,178	1,065	1,064	1,035	978	1,082
Railroad Retirement Board	1,772	1,176	1,010	977	957	981
Securities & Exchange Commission	2,302	2,955	3,933	3,562	3,715	3,917
Small Business Administration	5,128	4,150	4,288	3,813	4,087	4,037
Smithsonian Institution	5,092	5,065	4,981	4,929	4,930	4,984
Social Security Administration [2]	(X)	64,474	65,861	62,337	65,085	69,975
Tennessee Valley Authority	28,392	13,145	12,721	11,727	11,688	12,457
U.S. Information Agency	8,555	2,436	2,212	2,052	1,959	1,953
U.S. International Development Cooperation Agency	4,698	2,552	2,644	2,515	2,515	2,515
U.S. Postal Service	816,886	860,726	767,972	744,405	703,658	643,420

X Not applicable. [1] Includes enumerators for the 1990 and 2000 census. [2] Sizeable changes in 1995 due to the Social Security Administration which was separated from the Department of Health and Human Services to become an independent agency effective April 1995. [3] See text, Section 10, National Security and Veteran Affairs, concerning the development of the Department of Homeland Security. [4] Includes agencies with fewer than 1,000 employees in 2005, not shown separately.

Source: U.S. Office of Personnel Management, Federal Civilian Workforce Statistics—Employment and Trends, bimonthly. See <http://www.opm.gov/feddata>.

Table 500. Federal Employees—Summary Characteristics: 1990 to 2008

[As of September 30. In percent, except as indicated. For civilian employees, excluding U.S. Postal Service employees]

Characteristics	1990	1995	2000	2003	2004	2005	2006	2007	2008
Average age (years) [1]	42.3	44.3	46.3	46.7	46.8	46.9	46.9	47.0	46.8
Average length of service (years)	13.4	15.5	17.1	16.8	16.6	16.4	16.3	16.1	15.5
Retirement eligible: [2]									
Civil Service Retirement System	8	10	17	27	30	33	37	41	46
Federal Employees Retirement System	3	5	11	12	13	13	13	13	13
Bachelor's degree or higher	35	39	41	41	42	43	43	45	44
Sex: Male	57	56	55	55	56	56	56	56	56
Female	43	44	45	45	44	44	44	44	44
Race and national origin:									
Total minorities	27.4	28.9	30.4	31.1	31.4	31.7	32.1	32.5	33.0
Black	16.7	16.8	17.1	17.0	17.0	17.0	17.2	17.3	17.5
Hispanic	5.4	5.9	6.6	7.1	7.3	7.4	7.5	7.6	7.7
Asian/Pacific Islander	3.5	4.2	4.5	4.8	5.0	5.1	5.1	5.4	5.2
American Indian/Alaska Native	1.8	2.0	2.2	2.1	2.1	2.1	2.1	2.1	2.1
Disabled	7.0	7.0	7.0	7.0	7.0	7.0	7.0	7.0	7.0
Veterans preference	30.0	26.0	24.0	22.0	22.0	22.0	22.0	22.0	22.0
Vietnam era veterans	17.0	17.0	14.0	13.0	12.0	11.0	10.0	9.0	8.0
Retired military	4.9	4.2	3.9	4.6	4.9	5.4	5.7	6.0	6.3
Retired officers	0.5	0.5	0.5	0.8	0.9	1.0	1.1	1.2	1.3

[1] For full-time permanent employees. [2] Represents full-time permanent employees under the Civil Service Retirement System (excluding hires since January 1984), and the Federal Employees Retirement System (since January 1984).

Source: U.S. Office of Personnel Management, Office of Workforce Information, The Fact Book, Federal Civilian Workforce Statistics, annual. See also <http://www.opm.gov/feddata>.

Table 501. Federal Executive Branch (Nonpostal) Employment by Race and National Origin: 1990 to 2008

[As of September 30. Covers total employment for only executive branch agencies participating in OPM's Central Personnel Data File (CPDF). For information on the CPDF, see <http://www.opm.gov/feddata/acpdf.pdf>]

Pay system	1990	1995	2000	2005	2006	2007	2008
All personnel [1]	**2,150,359**	**1,960,577**	**1,755,689**	**1,856,966**	**1,848,339**	**1,862,404**	**1,916,726**
White, non-Hispanic	1,562,846	1,394,690	1,224,836	1,267,922	1,254,308	1,254,131	1,297,772
General schedule and related	1,218,188	1,101,108	961,261	973,767	948,740	878,182	858,050
Grades 1 to 4	132,028	79,195	55,067	46,671	43,450	42,135	44,324
Grades 5 to 8	337,453	288,755	239,128	227,387	219,168	208,180	211,004
Grades 9 to 12	510,261	465,908	404,649	408,111	399,400	367,195	351,302
Grades 13 to 15	238,446	267,250	262,417	291,598	286,722	260,672	251,420
Total executive/senior pay levels	9,337	13,307	14,332	16,409	16,118	20,718	21,793
Wage pay system	244,220	186,184	146,075	135,383	133,942	132,290	134,933
Other pay systems	91,101	94,091	103,168	142,363	155,508	222,941	282,996
Black	356,867	327,302	298,701	315,644	317,697	323,470	337,742
General schedule and related	272,657	258,586	241,135	246,691	246,248	236,721	236,525
Grades 1 to 4	65,077	41,381	26,895	19,774	18,326	17,692	18,286
Grades 5 to 8	114,993	112,962	99,937	94,655	93,717	89,903	90,410
Grades 9 to 12	74,985	79,795	82,809	90,809	91,869	88,042	86,054
Grades 13 to 15	17,602	24,448	31,494	41,453	42,336	41,084	41,775
Total executive/senior pay levels	479	942	1,180	1,270	1,218	1,510	1,565
Wage pay system	72,755	55,637	42,590	37,666	37,378	37,685	38,540
Other pay systems	10,976	12,137	13,796	30,017	32,853	47,554	61,973
Hispanic	115,170	115,964	115,247	138,507	138,596	141,968	136,167
General schedule and related	83,218	86,762	89,911	104,927	105,236	102,613	95,016
Grades 1 to 4	15,738	11,081	8,526	7,768	6,854	6,454	5,459
Grades 5 to 8	28,727	31,152	31,703	33,653	33,834	33,738	31,261
Grades 9 to 12	31,615	34,056	36,813	46,268	46,951	45,309	42,542
Grades 13 to 15	7,138	10,473	12,869	17,238	17,597	17,112	15,754
Total executive/senior pay levels	154	382	547	682	699	1,070	1,109
Wage pay system	26,947	22,128	16,926	15,945	15,822	15,652	15,639
Other pay systems	4,851	6,692	7,863	16,953	16,839	22,633	28,646
American Indian, Alaska Native, Asian, and Pacific Islander	115,476	122,621	116,905	134,893	136,593	141,138	145,045
General schedule and related	81,499	86,768	86,074	97,866	97,870	95,008	93,197
Grades 1 to 4	15,286	11,854	9,340	8,357	7,877	7,938	7,608
Grades 5 to 8	24,960	26,580	25,691	27,417	26,986	26,292	26,046
Grades 9 to 12	31,346	33,810	33,167	38,276	38,492	36,664	35,259
Grades 13 to 15	9,907	14,524	17,876	23,816	24,515	24,114	24,284
Total executive/senior pay levels	148	331	504	804	873	2,630	2,851
Wage pay system	24,927	21,553	17,613	16,938	16,728	16,661	17,022
Other pay systems	8,902	13,969	12,714	19,285	21,122	26,839	33,834

[1] Beginning 2006, includes persons classified as multiracial, not shown separately.
Source: U.S. Office of Personnel Management, "Central Personnel Data File," <http://www.opm.gov/feddata>.

Table 502. Area of Federally Owned Buildings in the United States by State: 2009

[3,260.7 represents 3,260,700,000. As of September 30. For executive branch agencies. For data on federal land by state, see Table 366]

State	Total building area [1] (mil. sq. ft.)	Owned building area (mil. sq. ft.)	Leased building area (mil. sq. ft.)	State	Total building area [1] (mil. sq. ft.)	Owned building area (mil. sq. ft.)	Leased building area (mil. sq. ft.)
U.S. [2]	**3,260.7**	**2,589.0**	**550.6**	MO	52.9	41.8	8.8
AL	47.6	47.6	4.0	MT	18.1	15.1	2.2
AK	47.6	43.4	3.6	NE	15.2	12.3	1.7
AZ	56.2	49.9	5.2	NV	31.9	28.5	2.6
AR	24.7	19.0	1.5	NH	94.0	2.5	0.6
CA	317.1	258.6	54.1	NJ	46.9	39.3	5.3
CO	56.7	49.1	7.0	NM	61.9	55.6	4.9
CT	15.9	10.8	3.5	NY	95.6	79.9	11.0
DE	6.1	5.0	0.4	NC	89.7	73.0	14.4
DC	88.0	63.5	23.9	ND	23.0	20.3	1.1
FL	109.9	90.3	16.2	OH	69.8	61.6	5.5
GA	109.5	98.9	8.7	OK	65.5	52.2	11.1
HI	59.3	45.6	12.9	OR	24.9	19.8	2.5
ID	22.6	18.9	3.0	PA	77.1	65.6	8.4
IL	73.0	59.7	9.6	RI	12.5	11.5	0.5
IN	36.0	30.6	3.0	SC	56.1	47.4	6.6
IA	16.6	11.9	1.7	SD	18.1	14.6	2.0
KS	36.5	32.0	2.7	TN	65.6	57.3	5.2
KY	48.9	43.2	3.5	TX	196.9	170.3	22.7
LA	45.2	32.7	5.7	UT	34.1	28.9	3.2
ME	12.4	10.6	0.9	VT	4.2	2.5	1.1
MD	124.1	98.0	23.9	VA	171.8	133.2	37.2
MA	36.1	30.1	3.5	WA	87.4	73.5	12.3
MI	33.3	24.2	4.4	WV	20.8	15.8	2.9
MN	21.4	14.6	2.0	WI	24.1	19.0	2.5
MS	42.4	33.0	3.4	WY	15.3	13.5	0.8

[1] Includes otherwised managed square feet, not shown separately. [2] Includes location not reported, not shown separately.
Source: U.S. General Services Administration, Federal Real Property Council, "Federal Real Property Report 2009." See also <http://www.gsa.gov/portal/content/102880>.

Section 10
National Security and Veterans Affairs

This section displays data for national security (national defense and homeland security) and benefits for veterans. Data are presented on national defense and its human and financial costs; active and reserve military personnel; and federally sponsored programs and benefits for veterans, and funding, budget and selected agencies for homeland security. The principal sources of these data are the annual *Selected Manpower Statistics* and the *Atlas/Data Abstract for the United States, Annual Report of Secretary of Veterans Affairs*, U.S. Department of Veterans Affairs (VA), Budget in Brief, U.S. Department of Homeland Security; and *The Budget of the United States Government*, Office of Management and Budget. For data on international expenditures and personnel, see Table 1406, Section 30.

Department of Defense (DoD)—
The U.S. Department of Defense is responsible for providing the military forces of the United States. It includes the Office of the Secretary of Defense, the Joint Chiefs of Staff, the Army, the Navy, the Air Force, and the defense agencies. The President serves as Commander-in-Chief of the Armed Forces; from him, the authority flows to the Secretary of Defense and through the Joint Chiefs of Staff to the commanders of unified and specified commands (e.g., U.S. Strategic Command).

Reserve components—
The Reserve Components of the Armed Forces consist of the Army National Guard of the United States, Army Reserve, Naval Reserve, Marine Corps Reserve, Air National Guard, Air Force Reserve, and Coast Guard Reserve. They provide trained personnel and units available for active duty in the Armed Forces during times of war or national emergency, and at such other times as national security may require. The National Guard has dual federal/state responsibilities and uses jointly provided equipment, facilities, and budget support. The President is empowered to mobilize the National Guard and to use such of the Armed Forces as he considers necessary to enforce federal authority in any state. There is in each Armed Force a ready reserve, a standby reserve, and a retired reserve. The Ready Reserve includes the Selected Reserve, which provides trained and ready units and individuals to augment the active forces during times of war or national emergency, or at other times when required; and the Individual Ready Reserve, which is a manpower pool that can be called to active duty during times of war or national emergency and would normally be used as individual fillers for active, guard, and reserve units, and as a source of combat replacements. Most of the Ready Reserve serves in an active status. See Table 513 for Standby Reserve and Retired Reserve detail.

Department of Veterans Affairs (VA)—
A veteran is someone 18 years and older (there are a few 17-year-old veterans) who is not currently on active duty, but who once served on active duty in the United States Army, Navy, Air Force, Marine Corps, or Coast Guard, or who served in the Merchant Marine during World War II. There are many groups whose active service makes them veterans including: those who incurred a service-connected disability during active duty for training in the Reserves or National Guard, even though that service would not otherwise have counted for veteran status; members of a national guard or reserve component who have been ordered to active duty by order of the President or who have a full-time military job. The latter are called AGRs (Active Guard and Reserve). No one who has received a dishonorable discharge is a veteran.

The VA administers laws authorizing benefits for eligible former and present members of the Armed Forces and for the beneficiaries of deceased members. Veterans' benefits available under various acts of Congress include compensation for service-connected disability or death; pensions for non-service-connected disability or death; vocational rehabilitation, education and training; home loan insurance; life insurance; health care; special housing and automobiles or other conveyances for certain disabled veterans; burial and plot allowances; and educational assistance to families of deceased or totally disabled veterans, servicemen missing in action, or prisoners of war. Since these benefits are legislated by Congress, the dates they were enacted and the dates they apply to veterans may be different from the actual dates the conflicts occurred. VA estimates of veterans cover all persons discharged from active U.S. military service under conditions other than dishonorable.

Department of Homeland Security (DHS)—The creation of DHS, which began operations in March 2003, represents a fusion of 22 federal agencies (legacy agencies, Coast Guard and Secret Service remained intact) to coordinate and centralize the leadership of many homeland security activities under a single department. The largest organizations under DHS include: Customs and Border Protection (CBP), Immigration and Customs Enforcement (ICE), Transportation Security Administration (TSA), Federal Emergency Management Agency (FEMA), and the Coast Guard.

Coast Guard—With more than 218 years of service to the Nation, the Coast Guard is a military, multi-mission, maritime organization that promotes safety and safeguards U.S. economic and security interests throughout the maritime environment. As one of the five Armed Services of the United States, it is the only military organization within the DHS. Unlike its sister services in the Department of Defense (DoD), the Coast Guard is also a law enforcement and regulatory agency with broad domestic authorities.

Federal Emergency Management Agency (FEMA)—FEMA manages and coordinates the federal response to and recovery from major domestic disasters and emergencies of all types in accordance with the Robert T. Stafford Disaster Relief and Emergency Assistance Act. The agency ensures the effectiveness of emergency response providers at all levels of government in responding to terrorist attacks, major disasters, and other emergencies. Through the Disaster Relief Fund, FEMA provides individual and public assistance to help families and communities impacted by declared disasters rebuild and recover. FEMA is also the principal component for preparing state and local governments to prevent or respond to threats or incidents of terrorism and other catastrophic events, through their state and local programs.

The Customs and Border Protection (CBP) is responsible for managing, securing, and controlling U.S. borders. This includes carrying out traditional border-related responsibilities, such as stemming the tide of illegal drugs and illegal aliens; securing and facilitating legitimate global trade and travel; and protecting the food supply and agriculture industry from pests and disease. CBP is composed of the Border Patrol and Inspections (both moved from INS) along with Customs (absorbed from the U.S. Department of Treasury) and Animal and Plant Health Inspections Services (absorbed from the U.S. Department of Agriculture).

The Immigration and Customs Enforcement (ICE) mission is to protect America and uphold public safety by targeting the people, money, and materials crossing the nation's borders that support terrorist and criminal activities. ICE is the largest investigation arm of DHS. ICE is composed of five law enforcement divisions: Investigations, Intelligence, Federal Protective Service, International Affairs, and Detention and Removal Operations. ICE investigates a wide range of national security, financial and smuggling violations including drug smuggling, human trafficking, illegal arms exports, financial crimes, commercial fraud, human smuggling, document fraud, money laundering, child pornography/exploitation, and immigration fraud.

The Transportation Security Administration (TSA) was created as part of the Aviation and Transportation Security Act on November 19, 2001. TSA was originally part of the U.S. Department of Transportation, but was moved to DHS. TSA's mission is to provide security to our nation's transportation systems with a primary focus on aviation security.

Figure 10.1
Officers and Enlisted Personnel by Military Branch: 2010

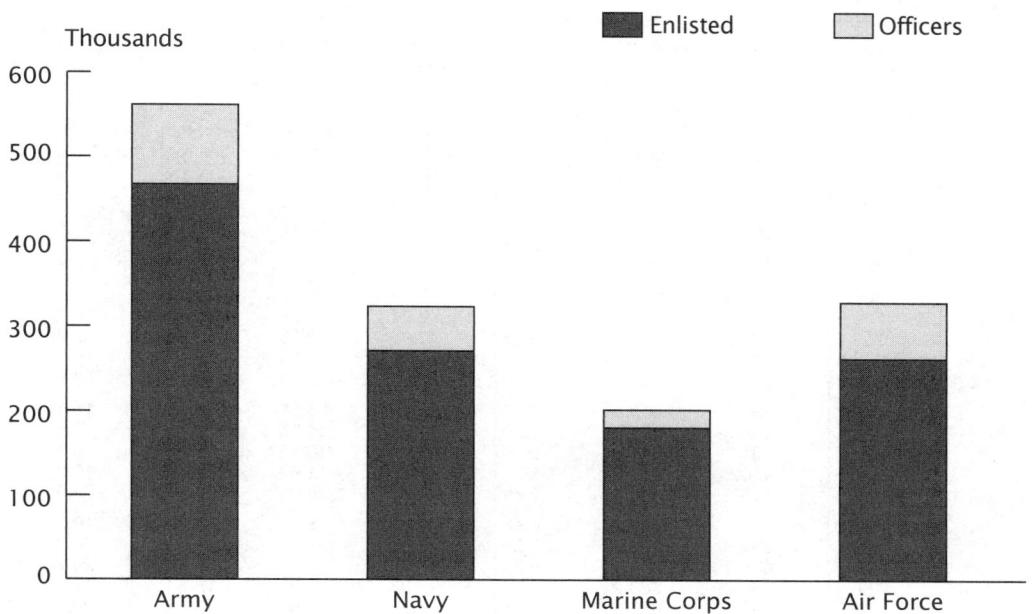

Source: Chart prepared by U.S. Census Bureau. For data, see Table 510.

Figure 10.2
Department of Defense Personnel by Sex: 2010

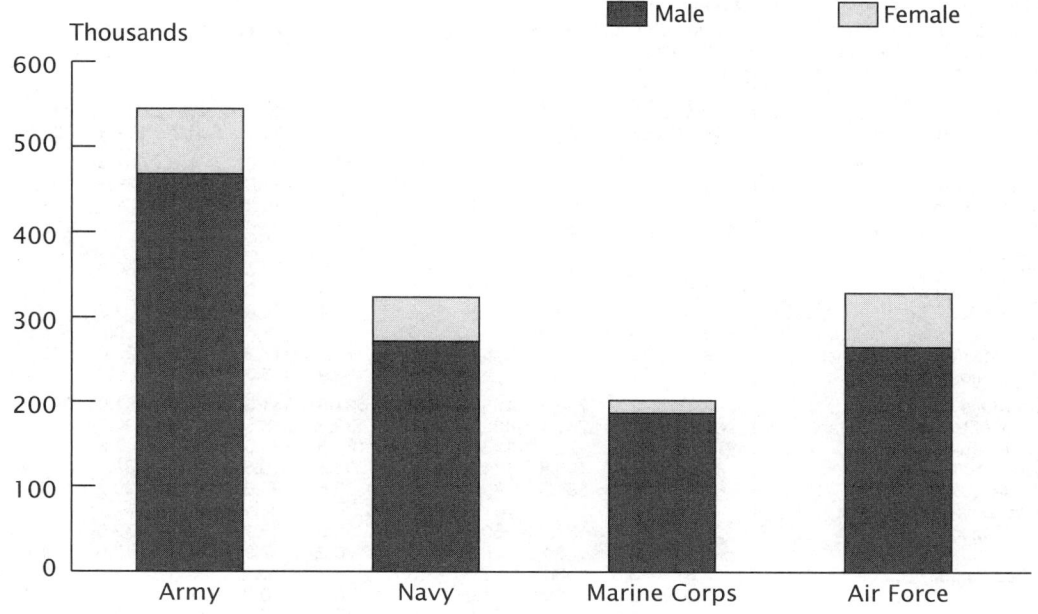

Source: Chart prepared by U.S. Census Bureau. For data, see Table 510.

National Security and Veterans Affairs 331

Table 503. National Defense Outlays and Veterans' Benefits: 1960 to 2012

[In billions of dollars (53.6 represents $53,600,000,000), except percent. For fiscal year ending in year shown, see text, Section 8. Includes outlays of Department of Defense, Department of Veterans Affairs, and other agencies for activities primarily related to national defense and veterans programs. For explanation of average annual percent change, see Guide to Tabular Presentation. Minus sign (–) indicates decrease]

Year	National defense and veterans' outlays				Annual percent change [1]			Defense outlays, percent of—	
		Defense outlays							
	Total outlays	Current dollars	Constant (FY2005) dollars	Veterans' outlays	Total outlays	Defense outlays	Veterans' outlays	Federal outlays	Gross domestic product [2]
1960.........	53.6	48.1	369.4	5.4	2.50	2.40	3.10	52.2	9.3
1970.........	90.4	81.7	463.9	8.7	0.26	–0.98	13.60	41.8	8.1
1980.........	155.2	134.0	330.1	21.2	13.88	15.17	6.30	22.7	4.9
1985.........	279.0	252.7	433.1	26.3	10.28	11.14	2.64	26.7	6.1
1990.........	328.4	299.3	461.2	29.0	–1.56	–1.39	–3.23	23.9	5.2
1995.........	309.9	272.1	375.6	37.9	–2.91	–3.40	0.81	17.9	3.7
1997.........	309.8	270.5	354.6	39.3	2.34	1.79	6.30	16.9	3.3
1998.........	309.9	268.2	346.1	41.7	0.05	–0.85	6.26	16.2	3.1
1999.........	317.9	274.8	347.6	43.2	2.58	2.45	3.39	16.1	3.0
2000.........	341.4	294.4	361.3	47.0	7.37	7.13	8.88	16.5	3.0
2001.........	349.7	304.7	363.1	45.0	2.45	3.52	–4.29	16.4	3.0
2002.........	399.4	348.5	401.7	50.9	14.21	14.35	13.24	17.3	3.3
2003.........	461.7	404.7	444.6	57.0	15.61	16.15	11.89	18.7	3.7
2004.........	515.6	455.8	480.3	59.7	11.66	12.62	4.85	19.9	3.9
2005.........	565.4	495.3	495.3	70.1	9.67	8.66	17.36	20.0	4.0
2006.........	591.6	521.8	499.3	69.8	4.64	5.35	–0.44	19.7	3.9
2007.........	624.1	551.3	509.2	72.8	5.48	5.64	4.31	20.2	4.0
2008.........	700.7	616.1	548.1	84.7	12.28	11.76	16.25	20.7	4.3
2009.........	756.5	661.0	588.2	95.4	7.96	7.30	12.73	18.8	4.7
2010.........	802.0	693.6	612.3	108.4	6.01	4.92	13.58	20.1	4.8
2011, est......	909.6	768.2	669.5	141.4	13.42	10.76	30.47	20.1	5.1
2012, est......	862.2	737.5	633.2	124.7	–5.21	–3.99	–11.85	19.8	4.7

[1] Change from immediate prior year; for 1960, change from 1955. [2] Represents fiscal year GDP; for definition, see text, Section 13.

Source: U.S. Office of Management and Budget, "Budget of the United States Government, Historical Tables," annual, <http://www.whitehouse.gov/omb/budget/>.

Table 504. National Defense Budget Authority and Outlays for Defense Functions: 1990 to 2011

[In billions of dollars (303.3 represents $303,300,000,000). For year ending September 30. Data includes defense budget authority and outlays by other departments. Minus sign (–) indicates decrease]

Function	1990	1995	2000	2004	2005	2006	2007	2008	2009	2010	2011 est.
Total budget authority..........	**303.3**	**266.4**	**304.0**	**490.5**	**505.8**	**556.3**	**625.8**	**696.2**	**697.8**	**721.3**	**739.3**
Department of Defense—Military	293.0	255.7	290.3	470.9	483.8	532.9	603.0	674.7	667.5	695.6	712.7
Military personnel	78.9	71.6	73.8	116.1	121.3	128.5	131.8	139.0	149.3	157.1	156.8
Operation and maintenance	88.4	93.7	108.7	189.8	179.2	213.5	240.2	256.2	271.6	293.6	294.9
Procurement	81.4	43.6	55.0	83.1	96.6	105.4	133.8	165.0	135.4	135.8	134.2
Research, development, test, and evaluation	36.5	34.5	38.7	64.6	68.8	72.9	77.5	79.6	80.0	80.2	80.9
Military construction.............	5.1	5.4	5.1	6.1	7.3	9.5	14.0	22.1	26.8	22.6	17.3
Family housing.................	3.1	3.4	3.5	3.8	4.1	4.4	4.0	2.9	3.9	2.3	2.3
Other........................	–0.4	3.4	5.5	7.4	6.6	–1.3	1.6	9.9	0.6	4.0	26.3
Atomic energy defense activities.....	9.7	10.1	12.4	16.8	17.9	17.4	17.2	16.6	23.0	18.2	19.0
Defense-related activities	0.7	1.0	1.3	2.8	4.0	5.9	5.7	4.9	7.3	7.4	7.6
Total outlays..............	**299.3**	**272.1**	**294.4**	**455.8**	**495.3**	**521.8**	**551.3**	**616.1**	**661.0**	**693.6**	**768.2**
Department of Defense—Military	289.8	259.4	281.1	436.4	474.1	499.3	528.5	594.6	636.7	666.7	739.7
Military personnel	75.6	70.8	76.0	113.6	127.5	127.5	127.5	138.9	147.3	155.7	157.0
Operation and maintenance	88.3	91.0	105.8	174.0	188.1	203.8	216.6	244.8	259.3	276.0	311.9
Procurement	81.0	55.0	51.7	76.2	82.3	89.8	99.6	117.4	129.2	133.6	151.9
Research, development, test, and evaluation	37.5	34.6	37.6	60.8	65.7	68.6	73.1	75.1	79.0	77.0	80.7
Military construction.............	5.1	6.8	5.1	6.3	5.3	6.2	7.9	11.6	17.6	21.2	20.9
Family housing.................	3.5	3.6	3.4	3.9	3.7	3.7	3.5	3.6	2.7	3.2	3.4
Other........................	–1.2	–2.4	1.5	1.6	1.5	–0.4	0.2	3.2	1.5	0.1	13.8
Atomic energy activities...........	9.0	11.8	12.1	16.6	18.0	17.5	17.1	17.1	17.6	19.3	21.2
Defense-related activities	0.6	0.9	1.2	2.8	3.2	5.1	5.7	4.3	6.8	7.6	7.3

Source: U.S. Office of Management and Budget, "Budget of the United States Government, Historical Tables, Budget Authority by Function and Subfunction, Outlay by Function and Subfunction," annual, <http://www.whitehouse.gov/omb/budget>.

Table 505. Military Expenditures: 2000 to 2009

[In millions of dollars (229,072 represents $229,072,000,000). For year ending September 30. For definitions, see headnote, Tables 506 and 508]

Item	2000	2005	2006	2007	2008	2009
Expenditures, total	**229,072**	**381,290**	**408,249**	**455,769**	**501,032**	**527,824**
Payroll outlays	103,447	141,018	146,858	154,326	146,781	195,170
Active duty military pay	36,872	50,482	55,829	61,918	52,159	84,460
Civilian pay	29,935	43,798	45,105	43,587	46,170	49,736
Reserve and National Guard pay	4,646	11,087	10,123	12,325	11,068	22,759
Retired military pay	31,994	35,651	35,801	36,496	37,384	38,216
Total contracts [1]	123,295	236,986	257,456	297,363	349,557	327,462
Army	32,615	74,432	79,962	98,171	139,437	109,995
Navy & Marine Corps	38,963	62,775	70,351	82,321	92,679	91,868
Air Force	35,369	51,671	58,552	66,240	59,262	63,946
Other Defense activities	16,348	48,108	48,592	50,630	58,178	61,653
Grants	2,330	3,285	3,934	4,080	4,694	5,192

[1] Represents contract awards over $25,000.

Source: U.S. Department of Defense, DoD Personnel and Procurement Statistics, Personnel, Publications, *Atlas/Data Abstract for the United States and Selected Areas*, annual, <http://siadapp.dmdc.osd.mil>.

Table 506. Department of Defense Payroll and Contract Awards—States: 2009

[(In millions of dollars (195,170 represents $195,170,000,000). For year ending September 30. Payroll outlays include the gross earnings of civilian, active duty military personnel, reserve and national guard, and retired military for services rendered to the government and for cash allowances or benefits. Excludes employer's share of employee benefits, accrued military retirement benefits and most permanent change of station costs. Contracts refer to awards made in year specified; expenditures relating to awards may extend over several years. Military awards for supplies, services, and construction. Net value of contracts of over $25,000 for work in each state and DC. Figures reflect impact of prime contracting on state distribution of defense work. The state in which a prime contractor is located is not often the state where the subcontracted work is done. Undistributed civilians and military personnel, their payrolls, and prime contract awards for performance in classified locations are excluded]

State	Payroll Total	Payroll Active duty military	Contract awards	Grants	State	Payroll Total	Payroll Active duty military	Contract awards	Grants
U.S.	**195,170**	**84,460**	**303,355**	**4,971**	MO	3,787	1,311	10,454	40
AL	4,724	1,255	9,502	66	MT	541	188	289	24
AK	2,660	2,078	2,180	49	NE	1,152	435	931	59
AZ	3,138	1,263	12,065	106	NV	1,415	600	1,819	35
AR	1,622	435	986	66	NH	411	73	1,568	36
CA	14,568	5,183	41,698	477	NJ	2,671	543	8,227	122
CO	5,125	2,966	5,544	56	NM	1,626	571	1,604	40
CT	720	198	11,818	100	NY	4,819	2,701	8,545	199
DE	537	216	315	24	NC	10,558	7,012	3,995	125
DC	3,599	1,907	4,741	66	ND	631	336	437	32
FL	9,418	2,816	13,189	195	OH	3,834	640	6,249	172
GA	11,495	6,668	7,039	74	OK	4,100	1,679	2,880	124
HI	6,344	4,529	2,377	79	OR	1,051	141	1,546	99
ID	709	262	166	59	PA	4,210	574	12,363	216
IL	3,129	738	5,937	172	RI	743	120	662	26
IN	2,338	351	6,795	55	SC	3,683	1,530	5,299	39
IA	747	140	1,285	57	SD	514	198	445	68
KS	3,668	2,465	3,158	42	TN	2,235	282	3,083	44
KY	5,681	4,339	6,534	70	TX	19,299	11,128	22,484	300
LA	2,688	1,417	6,408	54	UT	2,116	432	2,206	39
ME	847	113	1,407	128	VT	262	64	550	17
MD	6,538	2,013	12,912	477	VA	18,071	6,214	38,372	131
MA	1,491	320	13,347	244	WA	8,224	4,407	5,174	127
MI	1,827	264	5,332	130	WV	617	107	396	50
MN	1,208	206	1,530	69	WI	1,152	222	7,674	72
MS	2,224	629	3,447	18	WY	405	177	140	21

Source: U.S. Department of Defense, DoD Personnel and Procurement Statistics, Personnel, Publications, *Atlas/Data Abstract for the United States and Selected Areas*, annual, <http://siadapp.dmdc.osd.mil/>.

Table 507. Expenditures and Personnel by Selected Major Locations: 2009

[In thousands of dollars (8,406,173 represents $8,406,173,000), except for personnel. For year ending September 30. See headnote, Table 508]

Major locations	Expenditures Total	Expenditures Payroll outlays	Expenditures Contracts/ grants	Major locations	Military and civilian personnel Total	Military and civilian personnel Active duty military	Military and civilian personnel Civilian
Washington, DC	8,406,173	3,599,245	4,806,928	Fort Hood, TX	60,309	54,309	6,000
Fort Hood, TX	6,478,403	6,075,895	402,508	Camp Pendleton, CA	49,114	46,242	2,872
San Diego, CA	6,413,361	1,884,891	4,528,470	Camp Lejeune, NC	44,286	40,789	3,497
Oshkosh, WI	5,780,785	20,929	5,759,856	Fayetteville, NC	36,223	36,198	25
Huntsville, AL	5,744,462	366,537	5,377,925	Fort Lewis, WA	35,250	32,220	3,030
Arlington, VA	5,279,716	2,946,069	2,333,647	Fort Campbell, KY	33,971	32,799	1,172
Tucson, AZ	4,879,568	326,019	4,553,549	Fort Carson, CO	26,759	23,796	2,963
Fayetteville, NC	4,658,633	4,623,376	35,257	Arlington, VA	26,335	9,305	17,030
St. Louis, MO	4,623,210	203,614	4,419,596	Fort Benning, GA	26,101	22,123	3,978
Louisville, KY	4,436,075	167,250	4,268,825	Fort Bragg, NC	23,843	15,580	8,263

Source: U.S. Department of Defense, DoD Personnel and Procurement Statistics, Personnel, Publications, *Atlas/Data Abstract for the United States and Selected Areas,* annual, <http://siadapp.dmdc.osd.mil/>.

Table 508. Military and Civilian Personnel in Installations: 2009

[As of September 30. Civilian personnel includes United States citizens and foreign national direct-hire civilians subject to Office of Management and Budget (OMB) ceiling controls and civilian personnel involved in civil functions in the United States. Excludes indirect-hire civilians and those direct-hire civilians not subject to OMB ceiling controls. Military personnel include active duty personnel based ashore or afloat, excludes personnel temporarily shore-based in a transient status]

State	Active military personnel				Reserve and National Guard, total [1]	Civilian personnel			
	Total [1]	Army	Navy/ Marine Corps	Air Force		Total [1]	Army	Navy/ Marine Corps	Air Force
United States	1,088,465	537,407	264,375	286,683	819,318	709,265	274,140	186,135	160,339
Alabama	11,896	8,121	403	3,372	22,099	24,794	19,768	84	2,472
Alaska	23,178	14,087	113	8,978	4,747	5,356	3,049	20	1,938
Arizona	21,343	5,531	4,118	11,694	13,728	9,591	4,471	637	3,408
Arkansas	6,717	1,219	109	5,389	13,051	4,168	3,073	6	973
California	117,806	11,097	88,370	18,339	57,792	61,365	9,278	34,798	10,720
Colorado	35,404	25,471	715	9,218	12,491	11,585	4,187	65	5,675
Connecticut	1,914	624	1,172	118	6,369	2,625	618	1,120	257
Delaware	3,870	246	15	3,609	4,881	1,622	292	5	1,248
District of Columbia ...	13,424	7,831	3,040	2,553	6,378	16,088	4,708	9,617	853
Florida	42,642	5,363	13,782	23,497	34,653	28,429	4,070	11,871	10,297
Georgia	73,988	59,892	3,724	10,372	29,358	37,012	14,169	4,757	15,222
Hawaii	40,874	22,435	13,642	4,797	9,276	18,400	5,532	9,605	2,188
Idaho	4,967	526	41	4,400	5,892	1,716	893	51	711
Illinois...........	10,111	2,212	2,805	5,094	25,084	15,770	9,016	1,842	3,688
Indiana...........	3,108	2,612	209	287	21,073	10,932	2,403	3,243	952
Iowa.............	1,296	997	118	181	12,390	1,733	1,157	8	525
Kansas...........	25,482	21,994	117	3,371	11,479	7,800	6,296	6	1,103
Kentucky	43,138	42,532	279	327	13,126	8,962	7,655	164	248
Louisiana	17,398	10,223	1,553	5,622	18,011	6,647	4,045	793	1,476
Maine............	730	334	265	131	4,153	6,946	402	5,580	287
Maryland	29,160	8,239	12,652	8,269	16,000	34,966	14,460	15,826	2,384
Massachusetts......	3,205	1,157	574	1,474	15,335	6,918	2,632	192	3,171
Michigan	2,858	1,708	743	407	17,618	8,972	6,456	46	892
Minnesota	1,897	1,291	378	228	19,256	2,752	1,766	23	798
Mississippi.........	9,895	1,443	1,394	7,058	17,332	9,124	3,878	2,428	2,515
Missouri...........	17,925	12,053	2,028	3,844	23,769	9,982	7,569	490	1,246
Montana...........	3,623	397	12	3,214	4,748	1,596	686	1	862
Nebraska..........	6,845	653	450	5,742	7,498	3,785	1,468	15	2,197
Nevada	10,034	545	584	8,905	6,087	2,319	561	285	1,316
New Hampshire......	675	307	198	170	4,251	1,047	568	34	304
New Jersey	6,673	1,538	277	4,858	17,312	15,217	10,798	2,122	1,575
New Mexico	11,038	1,094	166	9,778	5,199	7,029	3,041	46	3,460
New York	29,553	26,568	1,676	1,309	30,362	12,318	7,561	151	2,528
North Carolina	116,073	53,231	54,942	7,900	22,542	20,426	8,975	7,669	1,472
North Dakota	7,209	416	14	6,779	4,669	1,910	617	3	1,214
Ohio.............	8,261	1,939	684	5,638	28,523	25,001	1,884	91	13,671
Oklahoma	21,673	12,216	926	8,531	15,640	22,115	5,739	91	14,794
Oregon...........	1,615	815	336	464	10,470	3,561	2,893	26	615
Pennsylvania	5,215	3,270	1,443	502	32,297	27,107	10,606	6,469	1,290
Rhode Island	1,490	420	905	165	4,438	4,372	289	3,777	209
South Carolina......	32,518	11,074	12,613	8,831	19,102	10,406	3,875	3,868	1,912
South Dakota.......	3,910	406	1	3,503	4,982	1,388	565	3	775
Tennessee.........	3,511	1,610	1,422	479	20,606	7,967	4,767	1,202	1,227
Texas	131,548	88,346	4,606	38,596	56,367	48,057	27,585	1,404	15,271
Utah..............	6,237	1,614	170	4,453	11,999	14,818	2,470	45	11,244
Vermont...........	565	347	32	186	3,952	729	403	3	290
Virginia...........	63,160	24,386	25,171	13,603	25,109	89,713	23,532	39,844	4,983
Washington	46,161	34,557	4,907	6,697	19,470	27,980	9,471	15,577	1,980
West Virginia	1,199	677	317	205	9,303	2,146	1,431	97	605
Wisconsin	2,046	1,522	163	361	15,833	2,810	2,138	34	522
Wyoming	3,407	221	1	3,185	3,218	1,193	374	1	776

[1] Includes Other Defense Activities (ODA), not shown separately.

Source: U.S. Department of Defense, DoD Personnel and Procurement Statistics, Personnel, Publications, *Atlas/Data Abstract for the United States and Selected Areas*, annual, <http://siadapp.dmdc.osd.mil/>.

Table 509. Military Personnel on Active Duty by Location: 1980 to 2010

[In thousands (2,051 represents 2,051,000). As of September 30]

Location	1980	1990	1995	2000	2005	2006	2007	2008	2009	2010
Total................	2,051	2,046	1,518	1,384	1,389	1,385	1,380	1,402	1,419	1,431
Shore-based [1]	1,840	1,794	1,351	1,237	1,262	1,263	1,264	1,294	1,313	1,328
Afloat [2]	211	252	167	147	127	121	115	108	105	103
United States [3].........	1,562	1,437	1,280	1,127	1,098	1,100	1,085	1,113	1,156	1,134
Foreign countries........	489	609	238	258	291	285	295	289	263	297

[1] Includes Navy personnel temporarily on shore. [2] Includes Marine Corps. [3] Includes Puerto Rico and Island Areas.

Source: U.S. Department of Defense, DoD Personnel and Procurement Statistics, Personnel, Publications, *Atlas/Data Abstract for the United States and Selected Areas*, annual, <http://siadapp.dmdc.osd.mil>.

Table 510. Department of Defense Personnel: 1960 to 2010

[In thousands (2,475 represents 2,475,000). As of end of fiscal year; see text, Section 8. Includes National Guard, Reserve, and retired regular personnel on extended or continuous active duty. Excludes Coast Guard. Other officer candidates are included under enlisted personnel]

Year	Total [1,2]	Army Total [1]	Army Male Officers	Army Male Enlisted	Army Female Officers	Army Female Enlisted	Navy [2] Total [1]	Navy Male Officers	Navy Male Enlisted	Navy Female Officers	Navy Female Enlisted	Marine Corps Total [1]	MC Male Officers	MC Male Enlisted	MC Female Officers	MC Female Enlisted	Air Force Total [1]	AF Male Officers	AF Male Enlisted	AF Female Officers	AF Female Enlisted
1960	2,475	873	97	762	4.3	8.3	617	67	540	2.7	5.4	171	16	153	0.1	1.5	815	126	677	3.7	5.7
1965	2,654	969	108	846	3.8	8.5	670	75	583	2.6	5.3	190	17	172	0.1	1.4	825	128	685	4.1	4.7
1970	3,065	1,323	162	1,142	5.2	11.5	691	78	600	2.9	5.8	260	25	233	0.3	2.1	791	125	648	4.7	9.0
1975	2,128	784	98	640	4.6	37.7	535	62	449	3.7	17.5	196	19	174	0.3	2.8	613	100	478	5.0	25.2
1980	2,051	777	91	612	7.6	61.7	527	58	430	4.9	30.1	189	18	164	0.5	6.2	558	90	404	8.5	51.9
1983	2,123	780	97	602	9.5	66.5	558	62	444	6.3	40.8	194	19	166	0.6	8.3	592	94	428	10.6	55.3
1984	2,138	780	98	601	10.2	67.1	565	62	448	6.6	42.6	196	19	167	0.6	8.6	597	95	430	11.2	55.9
1985	2,151	781	99	599	10.8	68.4	571	64	449	6.9	45.7	198	19	169	0.6	9.0	602	96	431	11.9	58.1
1986	2,169	781	99	597	11.3	69.7	581	65	457	7.3	47.2	200	19	170	0.7	9.2	608	97	434	12.4	61.2
1987	2,174	781	96	596	11.6	71.6	587	65	462	7.2	47.7	197	19	170	0.6	9.1	607	94	432	12.6	63.2
1988	2,138	772	95	588	11.8	72.0	593	65	466	7.3	49.7	197	19	168	0.6	9.1	576	92	405	12.9	61.5
1989	2,130	770	95	584	12.2	74.3	593	65	464	7.5	52.1	197	19	168	0.7	9.0	571	91	399	13.4	63.7
1990	2,044	732	92	553	12.4	71.2	579	64	451	7.8	52.1	194	19	168	0.7	9.0	535	87	370	13.3	60.8
1991	1,986	711	91	535	12.5	67.8	570	63	444	8.0	51.4	185	18	166	0.7	8.7	510	84	350	13.3	59.1
1992	1,807	610	83	449	11.7	61.7	542	61	417	8.3	51.0	178	17	157	0.6	8.3	470	77	320	12.7	56.1
1993	1,705	572	77	420	11.1	60.2	510	58	390	8.3	49.3	174	17	153	0.6	7.9	444	72	302	12.3	54.5
1994	1,610	541	74	394	10.9	59.0	469	54	355	8.0	47.9	175	17	149	0.6	7.2	426	69	287	12.3	54.0
1995	1,518	509	72	365	10.8	57.3	435	51	324	7.9	47.9	175	17	150	0.7	7.0	400	66	266	12.1	52.1
1996	1,472	491	70	347	10.6	59.0	417	50	308	7.8	46.9	174	17	149	0.8	7.4	389	64	256	12.0	52.8
1997	1,439	492	69	346	10.4	62.4	396	48	290	7.8	44.8	174	17	148	0.8	7.8	377	62	246	12.0	53.8
1998	1,407	484	68	340	10.4	61.4	382	47	280	7.8	42.9	173	17	146	0.9	8.5	368	60	237	12.0	54.2
1999	1,386	479	67	337	10.5	61.5	373	46	271	7.7	43.9	173	17	145	0.9	8.9	361	58	232	11.8	54.6
2000	1,384	482	66	339	10.8	62.9	373	46	272	7.8	43.8	173	17	146	1.0	9.3	356	57	227	11.8	55.0
2001	1,385	481	65	337	11.0	63.4	378	46	273	8.0	46.6	174	18	146	1.0	9.5	354	57	224	12.0	55.6
2002	1,414	487	66	341	11.5	63.2	385	47	279	8.2	47.3	178	18	149	1.1	9.6	368	59	233	12.9	58.6
2003	1,434	499	68	352	12.0	63.5	382	47	276	8.1	47.3	178	18	149	1.1	9.5	375	61	237	13.5	60.0
2004	1,427	500	69	358	12.3	61.0	373	46	273	7.8	46.1	180	18	151	1.0	9.6	377	61	242	13.6	60.2
2005	1,389	493	69	353	12.4	57.9	363	45	266	7.6	44.5	180	18	151	1.1	9.7	354	60	225	13.4	55.6
2006	1,385	505	69	365	12.5	58.5	350	44	255	7.6	43.2	186	18	156	1.1	9.8	349	58	223	12.8	55.8
2007	1,380	522	71	379	13.0	58.8	338	44	244	7.6	42.2	199	19	167	1.1	10.0	333	54	214	11.8	53.4
2008	1,402	544	74	392	13.5	59.7	332	44	235	7.7	41.4	203	19	170	1.2	10.5	327	53	207	11.9	51.4
2009	1,419	553	76	399	14.3	59.4	329	44	231	7.9	42.2	203	19	170	1.2	11.7	333	53	211	12.1	52.0
2010	1,431	566	79	407	15.1	60.3	328	44	228	8.2	43.4	202	18	169	3.0	12.2	334	54	212	12.4	50.9

[1] Includes cadets, midshipmen, and others, not shown separately. [2] Beginning 1980, excludes Navy Reserve personnel on active duty for Training and Administration of Reserves (TARS).

Source: U.S. Department of Defense, *Selected Manpower Statistics*, annual, and unpublished data.

National Security and Veterans Affairs 335

Table 511. Military Personnel on Active Duty by Rank or Grade: 1990 to 2010

[In thousands (2,043.7 represents 2,043,700). As of September 30]

Rank/grade	1990	2000	2005	2007	2008	2009	2010
Total	**2,043.7**	**1,384.3**	**1,389.4**	**1,379.6**	**1,401.8**	**1,418.5**	**1,431.0**
Total Officers	**296.6**	**217.2**	**226.6**	**221.3**	**223.7**	**228.3**	**234.0**
General-Admiral	(Z)	(Z)	(Z)	(Z)	(Z)	(Z)	(Z)
Lieutenant General-Vice Admiral	0.1	0.1	0.1	0.1	0.1	0.2	0.2
Major General-Rear Admiral (U)	0.4	0.3	0.3	0.3	0.3	0.3	0.3
Brigadier General-Rear Admiral (L)	0.5	0.4	0.4	0.4	0.5	0.5	0.5
Colonel-Captain	14.0	11.3	11.4	11.3	11.6	12.0	12.2
Lieutenant Colonel-Commander	32.3	27.5	28.1	27.7	28.1	28.4	28.8
Major-LT Commander	53.2	43.2	44.4	44.2	43.4	43.9	45.3
Captain-Lieutenant	106.6	68.1	72.5	70.6	71.0	72.5	75.0
1st Lieutenant-Lieutenant (JG)	37.9	24.7	27.5	23.4	23.9	24.9	25.5
2nd Lieutenant-Ensign	31.9	26.4	25.9	26.0	26.4	26.9	27.1
Chief Warrant Officer W-5	(Z)	0.1	0.5	0.6	0.6	0.7	0.7
Chief Warrant Officer W-4	3.0	2.0	2.2	2.9	3.1	3.1	3.2
Chief Warrant Officer W-3	5.0	3.8	4.6	4.6	4.7	4.7	4.8
Chief Warrant Officer W-2	8.4	6.7	6.2	5.7	6.4	7.1	7.5
Warrant Officer W-1	3.2	2.1	2.5	3.4	3.4	3.2	2.9
Total Enlisted	**1,733.8**	**1,154.6**	**1,149.9**	**1,145.0**	**1,164.7**	**1,176.7**	**1,183.2**
E-9	15.3	10.2	10.5	10.6	10.5	10.4	10.2
E-8	38.0	26.0	27.1	27.4	27.4	27.4	27.3
E-7	134.1	97.7	97.8	97.1	97.2	98.5	97.1
E-6	239.1	164.9	172.4	168.4	170.3	170.5	170.9
E-5	361.5	229.5	248.5	247.4	249.0	248.5	250.0
E-4	427.8	251.0	261.7	260.1	266.1	280.2	279.3
E-3	280.1	196.3	201.7	192.5	194.9	205.9	228.2
E-2	140.3	99.0	70.8	79.9	83.6	84.8	75.2
E-1	97.6	80.0	59.5	61.7	65.6	50.4	45.1
Cadets and Midshipmen	**13.3**	**12.5**	**12.9**	**13.2**	**13.4**	**13.6**	**13.8**

Z Fewer than 50.

Source: U.S. Department of Defense, DoD Personnel and Procurement Statistics, Personnel, Military, *Military Personnel Statistics*, annual, <http://siadapp.dmdc.osd.mil\>.

Table 512. Military Retirement System: 2010

[Payment in millions of dollars (3,959 represents $3,959,000,000). As of September 30. The data published in this report are produced from the files maintained by the Defense Manpower Data Center (DMDC). This report compiles data primarily from the "Retiree Pay and Survivor Pay" files. Any grouping of members by address reflects mailing, not necessarily residence address. Only those members in plans administered by the Department of Defense (DoD) are included in this table. The data are preliminary because of reporting delays due to the information about many members who retired or died within one month of the September 30 reporting date. These data were not processed in time to be included in this report. For more information, please see Introduction and Overview of source publication, "Statistical Report on the Military Retirement System; Fiscal Year 2010"]

State	Retired military personnel [1]			Monthly payment	State	Retired military personnel [1]			Monthly payment
	Total	Disabled [2]	Non-disabled			Total	Disabled [2]	Non-disabled	
Total [3]	**2,076,987**	**189,662**	**1,887,325**	**3,959**	MO	37,144	3,886	33,258	62
U.S.	2,035,921	186,193	1,849,728	3,887	MT	8,788	840	7,948	15
AL	56,793	4,664	52,129	107	NE	14,012	1,066	12,946	27
AK	9,748	684	9,064	18	NV	27,386	1,882	25,504	53
AZ	54,286	4,672	49,614	107	NH	9,544	815	8,729	18
AR	25,713	2,453	23,260	44	NJ	20,176	2,610	17,566	31
CA	165,501	15,651	149,850	322	NM	21,456	1,711	19,745	43
CO	49,052	4,116	44,936	108	NY	38,390	5,959	32,431	54
CT	10,674	1,307	9,367	18	NC	86,179	7,597	78,582	167
DE	8,331	563	7,768	15	ND	4,921	380	4,541	8
DC	2,816	400	2,416	6	OH	44,789	5,687	39,102	75
FL	186,220	15,382	170,838	380	OK	34,967	2,991	31,976	61
GA	90,554	7,782	82,772	170	OR	21,105	2,544	18,561	36
HI	16,371	1,092	15,279	34	PA	49,964	5,926	44,038	82
ID	12,967	1,150	11,817	23	RI	5,525	524	5,001	10
IL	35,986	4,563	31,423	63	SC	55,878	4,341	51,537	104
IN	24,453	3,151	21,302	38	SD	7,413	589	6,824	13
IA	12,063	1,325	10,738	18	TN	51,778	4,764	47,014	92
KS	21,012	1,832	19,180	40	TX	189,762	16,753	173,009	383
KY	27,086	2,953	24,133	46	UT	15,409	1,188	14,221	28
LA	25,694	2,763	22,931	45	VT	3,787	344	3,443	6
ME	12,104	1,131	10,973	20	VA	148,023	8,106	139,917	377
MD	52,019	3,899	48,120	110	WA	70,983	5,399	65,584	139
MA	19,156	2,515	16,641	30	WV	10,940	1,356	9,584	17
MI	28,259	4,224	24,035	42	WI	20,137	2,434	17,703	30
MN	18,000	2,067	15,933	27	WY	5,069	429	4,640	9
MS	26,472	2,264	24,208	44					

[1] Represents military personnel (officers and enlisted) receiving and not receiving pay from DoD. [2] A disabled military member is entitled to disability retired pay if the disability is not the result of the member's intentional misconduct or willful neglect, was not incurred during a period of unauthorized absence, and either: (1) the member has at least 20 years of service; or (2) at the time of determination, the disability is at least 30 percent (under a standard schedule of rating disabilities by the Veterans Administration) and one of three additional conditions are met. For the continuation of this footnote, see U.S. Census Bureau, Statistical Abstract, National Security and Veterans Affairs, Military Personnel and Expenditures, Military Retirement System, <http://www.census.gov /compendia/statab/>. [3] Includes states, U.S. territories, and retirees living in foreign countries.

Source: U.S. Department of Defense, Office of the Actuary, *Statistical Report, Fiscal Year 2010* (issued May 2011), <http://www.defenselink.mil/actuary/>.

Table 513. Military Reserve Personnel: 1995 to 2010

[As of September 30. The Ready Reserve data include the Selected Reserve which is scheduled to augment active during times of war or national emergency, would be used to fill out Active, forces during times of war or national emergency, and the Individual Ready Reserve, which, guard, and Reserve uits, and which would be a source for casualty replacements; Ready Reservists serve in an active status (except for the Inactive National Guard—a very small pool within the Army National Guard). The Standby Reserve cannot be called to active duty, other than for training, unless authorized by Congress under "full mobilization," and a determination is made that there are not enough qualified members in the Ready Reserve in the required categories who are readily available. The Retired Reserve represents a lower potential for involuntary mobilization]

Reserve status and branch of service	1995	2000	2005	2007	2008	2009	2010
Total reserves [1].........	1,674,164	1,276,843	1,136,200	1,109,805	1,099,915	1,094,071	1,102,863
Ready reserve...........	1,648,388	1,251,452	1,113,427	1,088,587	1,080,617	1,079,627	1,078,621
Army [2].................	999,462	725,771	636,355	621,422	626,892	645,394	651,098
Navy.................	267,356	184,080	140,821	128,421	123,159	109,271	102,349
Marine Corps..............	103,668	99,855	99,820	100,787	95,748	95,199	97,087
Air Force [3].............	263,011	229,009	223,551	226,806	224,545	220,364	218,350
Coast Guard	14,891	12,737	12,880	11,151	10,273	9,399	9,737
Standby reserve..........	25,776	25,391	22,773	21,218	19,298	25,808	24,242
Army	1,128	701	1,668	[4] 5,294	2,136	2,072	1,673
Navy	12,707	7,213	4,038	3,046	3,310	[4]10,036	9,742
Marine Corps..............	216	895	1,129	1,372	1,691	1,205	1,278
Air Force	11,453	16,429	15,897	10,154	10,384	10,530	10,213
Coast Guard	272	153	41	1,352	1,777	1,965	1,336
Retired reserve	505,905	573,305	627,424	648,346	658,251	707,060	716,228
Army	259,553	296,004	321,312	330,121	334,258	378,603	383,220
Navy	97,532	109,531	117,093	120,859	122,000	123,292	124,870
Marine Corps..............	11,319	12,937	14,693	15,264	15,558	15,948	16,277
Air Force	137,501	154,833	174,326	182,102	186,435	189,217	191,861

[1] Less retired reserves. [2] Includes Army National Guard. [3] Includes Air National Guard. [4] The Army for FY2007 and the Navy for FY2009 did a "scrub" of their Individual Ready Reserve (IRR) category and dropped personnel awaiting retirement or discharge into the Standby Reserve. This action was done in order to give them a better perspective on actual IRR members cleared for mobilization, if required.

Source: U.S. Department of Defense, DoD Personnel and Procurement Statistics, Personnel, Publications, *Atlas/Data Abstract for the United States and Selected Areas, Selected Manpower Statistics.* See also <http://siadapp.dmdc.osd.mil>.

Table 514. Ready Reserve Personnel by Race, Hispanic Origin, and Sex: 1990 to 2010

[In thousands (1,658.7 represents 1,658,700). As of September 30]

Year	Total [1]	Race						His-panic [2]	Sex			
		White	Black	Asian	Ameri-can Indian	Pacific Islander	Other Unknown		Officer		Enlisted	
									Male	Female	Male	Female
1990.....	1,658.7	1,304.6	272.3	14.9	7.8	(NA)	59.1	83.1	226.8	40.5	1,204.7	186.7
1995.....	1,648.4	1,267.7	274.5	22.0	8.8	(NA)	75.4	96.2	209.9	44.7	1,196.8	196.9
1999.....	1,288.8	980.0	202.6	22.6	7.6	(NA)	76.0	88.9	166.2	38.4	911.2	173.1
2000.....	1,251.5	942.2	199.6	26.7	8.4	(NA)	74.6	91.8	159.4	36.9	879.9	175.3
2001.....	1,224.1	912.7	198.4	27.9	8.5	(NA)	76.7	94.3	158.0	36.6	852.2	177.3
2002.....	1,199.3	891.3	193.2	27.9	8.8	(NA)	78.2	96.0	152.1	35.6	835.2	176.4
2003.....	1,167.1	865.7	187.5	25.4	8.5	(NA)	80.1	98.0	145.1	34.0	813.7	174.3
2004.....	1,145.0	845.3	181.3	26.2	9.1	3.6	79.6	100.2	141.9	33.6	799.7	169.8
2005.....	1,113.4	825.4	169.9	26.9	9.5	4.1	77.6	99.8	139.2	33.3	778.0	162.9
2006.....	1,101.6	822.4	163.5	27.7	10.1	4.5	73.4	101.1	136.7	33.1	769.4	162.3
2007.....	1,088.6	818.1	156.6	28.1	10.8	4.8	70.3	102.7	130.0	31.8	766.5	160.2
2008.....	1,080.7	815.2	153.4	29.0	10.9	5.3	66.9	102.6	128.0	31.2	760.8	160.6
2009.....	1,070.2	810.6	149.4	30.1	10.8	5.8	63.7	99.9	126.4	30.8	754.3	158.7
2010.....	1,068.9	809.8	148.2	31.0	10.9	6.1	62.8	99.6	125.9	30.7	754.2	158.1

[1] Includes other races, not shown separately. [2] Persons of Hispanic origin may be any race.

Source: U.S. Department of Defense, DoD Personnel and Procurement Statistics, Personnel, Publications, *Atlas/Data Abstract for the United States and Selected Areas,* annual, <http://siadapp.dmdc.osd.mil>.

Table 515. National Guard by Sex and Race: 1995 to 2010

[In thousands (375 represents 375,000). As of September 30]

Year	Army National Guard					Air National Guard				
	Total	Male [1]	Female	White	Black	Total	Male [1]	Female	White	Black
1995.....	375	344	31	299	59	110	94	16	96	9
2000.....	353	313	40	278	55	106	88	18	90	10
2004.....	343	299	44	271	50	107	88	19	89	10
2005.....	333	290	43	264	46	106	87	19	89	9
2006.....	346	300	47	276	47	106	87	19	88	9
2007.....	353	304	49	283	47	106	87	19	88	9
2008.....	360	309	51	288	49	108	88	20	89	9
2009.....	358	308	50	288	47	109	89	20	90	9
2010.....	362	310	52	291	48	108	88	20	89	9

[1] Male population includes unknown sex.

Source: U.S. Department of Defense, DoD Personnel and Procurement Statistics, Personnel, Publications, *Atlas/Data Abstract for the United States and Selected Areas, Selected Manpower Statistics,* annual. See also <http://siadapp.dmdc.osd.mil>.

Table 516. U.S. Active Duty Military Deaths by Manner of Death: 1980 to 2010

[As of December 31]

Manner of death	1980–2010	1980	1990	1995	2000	2004	2005	2006	2007	2008	2009	2010
Deaths, total	**48,968**	**2,392**	**1,507**	**1,040**	**841**	**1,874**	**1,943**	**1,881**	**1,953**	**1,439**	**1,515**	**1,483**
Accident	25,063	1,556	880	538	430	607	648	561	560	501	462	406
Hostile action	4,842	–	–	–	–	738	739	768	847	351	346	455
Homicide	2,332	174	74	67	37	46	54	47	52	47	77	36
Illness	8,631	419	277	174	181	272	291	257	237	242	273	235
Pending	158	–	–	–	–	1	1	8	23	16	44	64
Self-inflicted	6,898	231	232	250	159	202	183	213	211	257	288	271
Terrorist attack	421	1	1	7	17	–	–	–	–	1	–	–
Undetermined	623	11	43	4	17	8	27	27	23	24	25	16
Deaths per 100,000 of personnel strength	**(X)**	**110.7**	**66.8**	**62.5**	**49.5**	**109.6**	**116.7**	**116.7**	**121.3**	**85.6**	**92.4**	**88.0**
Accident	(X)	72.0	39.0	32.4	28.1	35.5	38.9	34.8	34.8	29.7	28.2	24.1
Hostile action	(X)	–	–	–	–	43.1	44.4	47.6	52.7	20.9	21.1	27.0
Homicide	(X)	8.1	3.3	4.0	2.4	2.7	3.2	2.9	3.2	2.8	4.6	2.1
Illness	(X)	19.4	12.3	10.5	11.8	15.9	17.5	15.9	14.7	14.4	16.6	13.9
Pending	(X)	–	–	–	–	0.1	0.1	0.5	1.4	1.1	3.0	3.8
Self-inflicted	(X)	10.7	10.3	15.0	10.4	11.8	11.0	13.2	13.1	15.2	17.4	14.4
Terrorist attack	(X)	–	–	0.4	1.1	–	–	–	–	–	–	–
Undetermined	(X)	0.5	1.9	0.2	1.1	0.5	1.6	1.7	1.4	1.4	1.5	0.9

– Represents zero. X Not applicable.
Source: Department of Defense Personnel and Procurement, DoD Personnel and Military Casualty Statistics, "Military Casualty Information," <http://siadapp.dmdc.osd.mil/personnel/CASUALTY/castop.htm>.

Table 517. U.S. Military Personnel on Active Duty in Selected Foreign Countries: 1995 to 2010

[As of September 30]

Country	1995	2000	2005	2006	2007	2008	2009	2010
In foreign countries [1]	**238,064**	**257,817**	**290,997**	**284,967**	**295,003**	**288,550**	**262,793**	**297,286**
Ashore	208,836	212,858	268,214	262,586	272,124	269,260	242,291	277,151
Afloat	29,228	44,959	22,783	22,381	22,879	19,290	20,502	20,135
Australia	314	175	196	347	140	140	139	130
Bahrain	618	949	1,641	1,357	1,495	1,545	1,507	1,349
Belgium	1,689	1,554	1,366	1,361	1,328	1,266	1,267	1,252
Bosnia and Herzegovina	1	5,708	263	232	209	14	11	8
Canada	214	156	150	133	141	134	128	127
Colombia	44	224	52	104	123	114	77	62
Cuba (Guantanamo)	5,129	688	950	953	932	969	926	913
Diego Garcia [2]	897	625	683	157	260	244	253	238
Djibouti	7	2	622	1,375	2,100	1,780	1,207	1,379
Egypt	1,123	499	410	360	250	284	265	275
Germany	73,280	69,203	66,418	64,319	57,080	55,140	52,658	53,951
Greece	489	678	428	395	363	366	361	338
Greenland	131	125	146	137	126	134	144	133
Honduras	193	351	438	414	403	429	416	403
Italy	12,007	11,190	11,841	10,449	9,855	9,601	9,707	9,646
Japan	39,134	40,159	35,571	33,453	32,803	33,286	35,965	34,385
Korea, South	36,016	36,565	30,983	29,086	27,014	25,062	(NA)	(NA)
Kuwait	771	4,602	(3)	(3)	(3)	(3)	(3)	(3)
Netherlands	687	659	583	591	579	547	510	442
Portugal	1,066	1,005	970	922	826	783	716	703
Qatar	2	52	463	446	411	433	463	555
Saudi Arabia	1,077	7,053	258	282	243	284	269	239
Senegal	13	10	42	7	11	7	9	9
Singapore	166	411	169	164	125	129	125	132
Spain	2,799	2,007	1,660	1,521	1,286	1,220	1,365	1,240
Turkey	3,111	2,006	1,780	1,810	1,594	1,575	1,616	1,530
United Kingdom	12,131	11,207	10,752	10,331	9,825	9,426	9,199	9,229
DEPLOYMENTS								
Operation Enduring Freedom (OEF) [4]	(X)	(X)	19,500	21,500	25,240	32,300	66,400	105,900
Operation New Dawn (OND) [5]	(X)	(X)	192,600	185,500	218,500	190,400	164,100	96,200

X Not applicable. NA Not available. [1] Includes items not shown separately. [2] British Indian Ocean Territory. [3] Military personnel data for Kuwait are included with the Operation New Dawn (OND) data. [4] Total (in/around Afghanistan as of September 30) includes Reserve/National Guard. [5] Total (in/around Iraq as of September 30) includes Reserve/National Guard.
Source: U.S. Department of Defense, DoD Personnel and Procurement Statistics, "Active Duty Military Personnel Strengths by Regional Area and by Country." See <http://siadapp.dmdc.osd.mil>.

Table 518. U.S. Military Sales and Assistance to Foreign Governments: 1995 to 2009

[In millions of dollars (8,495 represents $8,495,000,000). For year ending September 30. Department of Defense (DoD) sales deliveries cover deliveries against sales orders authorized under Arms Export Control Act, as well as earlier and applicable legislation. For details regarding individual programs, see source]

Item	1995	2000	2003	2004	2005	2006	2007	2008	2009
Military sales agreements	8,495	10,685	12,702	13,399	9,484	17,906	18,448	28,777	30,661
Military construction sales agreements . . .	24	284	223	682	308	173	430	187	1,021
Military sales deliveries [1]	12,100	10,867	9,735	11,401	11,153	11,549	12,529	11,828	12,522
Military construction sales deliveries	(NA)	183	245	281	349	323	197	267	204
Military financing program	3,712	4,333	5,955	4,584	4,956	4,450	4,519	4,506	4,580
Commercial exports licensed under arms export control act [2]	(NA)	478	2,728	7,895	30,146	31,605	8,874	33,510	(NA)
Military assistance program delivery [3]	20	5	186	45	71	11	(NA)	(NA)	(NA)
IMET program/deliveries [4]	26	50	79	89	86	83	83	83	90

NA Not available. [1] Includes military construction sales deliveries. [2] The total dollar value of deliveries made against purchases of munitions-controlled items by foreign governments directly from U.S. manufacturers. [3] Includes Military Assistance Service Funded (MASF) program data and Section 506(a) drawdown authority. [4] International Military Education & Training. Includes military assistance service funded and emergency drawdowns.

Source: U.S. Department of Defense, Defense Security Cooperation Agency, "DSCA Data and Statistics." See <http://www.dsca.osd.mil/data_stats.htm>.

Table 519. U.S. Military Sales Deliveries by Selected Country: 1995 to 2009

[In millions of dollars (12,100 represents $12,100,000,000). For year ending September 30. Represents Department of Defense military sales]

Country	1995	2000	2003	2004	2005	2006	2007	2008	2009
Total [1]	**12,100**	**10,886**	**9,739**	**11,404**	**11,184**	**11,602**	**12,566**	**11,828**	**12,522**
Afghanistan	(NA)	–	17	110	169	173	18	7	2
Argentina	(NA)	10	4	4	4	6	8	23	10
Australia	303	332	208	193	350	350	780	916	375
Bahrain	40	55	90	88	65	55	84	42	101
Belgium	8	61	71	42	49	53	49	44	39
Brazil	(NA)	61	13	14	11	28	62	55	46
Canada	127	84	155	144	150	183	247	468	530
Colombia	(NA)	14	10	53	41	86	199	124	110
Denmark	54	43	14	22	40	49	63	57	43
Ecuador	(NA)	1	1	3	4	6	7	3	2
Egypt	1,479	1,092	1,078	1,513	1,422	1,195	1,225	856	879
El Salvador	(NA)	13	2	3	3	2	2	6	13
Finland	(NA)	690	40	46	38	74	28	86	84
France	64	217	276	99	69	42	45	57	61
Georgia	(NA)	3	10	7	12	11	25	72	18
Germany	257	131	241	264	208	149	205	173	162
Greece	220	389	1,324	1,225	468	180	204	198	1,292
India	(NA)	–	21	7	100	49	92	40	15
Iraq	(NA)	–	–	–	–	2	177	683	707
Israel	327	585	927	1,202	1,524	1,284	1,316	1,407	747
Italy	54	52	185	281	127	288	153	76	93
Japan	693	448	430	392	410	769	647	609	860
Jordan	47	52	69	104	140	102	170	263	173
Kenya	(NA)	1	3	4	7	2	2	1	6
Korea, South	442	1,399	560	601	591	599	732	797	479
Kuwait	471	321	143	209	278	542	463	246	255
Malaysia	(NA)	411	9	11	49	22	19	17	23
Mexico	(NA)	9	12	6	4	8	6	4	5
Morocco	(NA)	5	9	9	17	41	8	4	10
Netherlands	153	278	224	277	178	232	240	253	252
Nigeria	(NA)	–	3	3	7	3	4	–	3
Norway	25	64	123	80	106	92	163	88	296
Pakistan	(NA)	–	5	36	61	121	196	271	119
Poland	(NA)	13	17	64	84	393	1,483	731	157
Portugal	88	20	116	30	84	57	46	45	101
Saudi Arabia	3,567	1,968	1,008	1,223	981	978	1,014	895	1,716
Singapore	59	131	168	205	229	355	173	167	182
Spain	193	141	159	433	126	104	149	169	185
Taiwan [2]	1,332	784	709	917	1,400	1,068	777	618	647
Thailand	356	114	153	180	92	83	46	40	47
Turkey	368	216	277	290	189	247	184	306	309
United Arab Emirates	345	42	87	155	169	201	70	84	119
United Kingdom	419	347	350	453	382	294	424	297	761
Venezuela	(NA)	13	12	12	8	8	1	–	–

– Represents or rounds to zero. [1] Includes countries not shown. [2] See footnote 2, Table 1296.

Source: U.S. Department of Defense, Defense Security Cooperation Agency, "DSCA Data and Statistics." See also <http://www.dsca.osd.mil/data_stats.htm/>.

Table 520. Veterans by Selected Period of Service and State: 2010

[In thousands (22,448 represents 22,448,000). As of September 30. VetPop2007 is the Department of Veterans Affairs (VA) latest official estimate and projection of the veteran population. It is based on detailed tabulations of Census 2000 data (prepared for the VA Office of the Actuary by the Census Bureau) and on recent American Community Survey data. VetPop2007 also uses administrative data and projections of service member separations from active duty provided by the Department of Defense (the Defense Manpower Data Center and the Office of the Actuary), as well as VA administrative data on veterans benefits]

State	Total [1,2]	Gulf War [3]	Vietnam era	State	Total [1,2]	Gulf War [3]	Vietnam era
United States	**22,448**	**5,690**	**7,459**	Missouri.........	506	120	172
Alabama	406	115	137	Montana.........	102	25	35
Alaska	77	28	27	Nebraska........	145	37	50
Arizona	557	138	180	Nevada	244	62	86
Arkansas..........	255	66	87	New Hampshire...	128	25	46
California.........	1,972	505	640	New Jersey	443	79	140
Colorado	421	116	152	New Mexico......	175	51	57
Connecticut........	230	41	78	New York	950	178	306
Delaware..........	78	19	25	North Carolina....	766	224	251
District of Columbia...	37	10	12	North Dakota.....	56	16	18
Florida.............	1,651	400	511	Ohio............	890	194	303
Georgia	774	243	259	Oklahoma	325	95	108
Hawaii.............	116	36	36	Oregon..........	334	72	119
Idaho	137	37	47	Pennsylvania.....	964	184	320
Illinois.............	783	191	251	Rhode Island.....	71	14	24
Indiana............	492	112	166	South Carolina....	407	117	139
Iowa..............	235	52	80	South Dakota.....	72	19	23
Kansas............	225	62	74	Tennessee.......	496	127	175
Kentucky	336	89	114	Texas...........	1,694	523	564
Louisiana..........	305	93	95	Utah............	154	40	51
Maine.............	139	30	50	Vermont.........	52	9	19
Maryland	471	138	149	Virginia..........	822	302	258
Massachusetts.......	394	70	129	Washington	632	173	223
Michigan	704	138	249	West Virginia	167	40	56
Minnesota	381	69	140	Wisconsin	418	88	141
Mississippi.........	206	61	66	Wyoming	56	16	21

[1] Veterans serving in more than one period of service are counted only once in the total. [2] Current civilians discharged from active duty, other than for training only without service-connected disability. [3] Service from August 2, 1990 to the present.

Source: U.S. Department of Veterans Affairs, Veteran Data and Information, Veteran Demographics, <http://www1.va.gov/vetdata/index.asp>.

Table 521. Veterans Living by Period of Service, Age, and Sex: 2010

[In thousands (22,658 represents 22,658,000). As of September 30. Includes those veterans living outside the United States]

Age	Total veterans	Wartime veterans					Peacetime veterans
		Total [1]	Gulf War [2]	Vietnam era	Korean conflict	World War II	
Total.................	**22,658**	**16,866**	**5,737**	**7,526**	**2,448**	**1,981**	**5,792**
Under 20 years old	8	8	8	–	–	–	–
20 to 24 years old	301	301	301	–	–	–	–
25 to 29 years old	768	768	768	–	–	–	–
30 to 34 years old	887	887	887	–	–	–	–
35 to 39 years old	1,023	996	996	–	–	–	26
40 to 44 years old	1,461	1,033	1,033	–	–	–	429
45 to 49 years old	1,790	692	692	–	–	–	1,098
50 to 54 years old	1,922	648	477	189	–	–	1,274
55 to 59 years old	2,005	1,589	312	1,415	–	–	416
60 to 64 years old	3,327	3,208	184	3,153	–	–	119
65 to 69 years old	2,470	1,944	56	1,935	–	–	525
70 to 74 years old	1,904	640	16	509	151	–	1,264
75 to 79 years old	1,877	1,350	5	188	1,270	6	527
80 to 84 years old	1,522	1,431	1	98	891	637	91
85 years & over	1,393	1,370	–	40	137	1,338	23
Female, total..........	**1,840**	**1,295**	**918**	**251**	**61**	**98**	**545**

– Represents or rounds to zero. [1] Veterans who served in more than one wartime period are counted only once in the total. [2] Service from August 2, 1990 to the present.

Source: U.S. Department of Veterans Affairs, VA Office of the Actuary, *VetPop 2007*, <http://www1.va.gov/vetdata/>.

Table 522. Veterans Status by Sex, Race, and Hispanic Origin: 2009

[Data are based on the American Community Survey (ACS). The survey universe includes the household population and the population living in institutions, college dormitories, and other group quarters. Based on a sample and subject to sampling variability; see text, this section and Appendix III]

Characteristics	Total number	18 to 64 years	65 years and over
Total.	**21,854,374**	**12,842,337**	**9,012,037**
Male.	20,374,557	11,615,529	8,759,028
Female.	1,479,817	1,226,808	253,009
White alone	18,536,634	10,302,627	8,234,007
Male	17,442,462	9,438,034	8,004,428
Female.	1,094,172	864,593	229,579
Black or African American alone	2,296,781	1,767,371	529,410
Male.	2,015,941	1,500,673	515,268
Female.	280,840	266,698	14,142
American Indian/Alaska Native alone	153,203	116,081	37,122
Male.	137,722	101,831	35,891
Female.	15,481	14,250	1,231
Asian alone	258,183	169,671	88,512
Male.	234,528	148,649	85,879
Female.	23,655	21,022	2,633
Native Hawaiian and Other Pacific Islander alone...	30,110	24,374	5,736
Male.	26,422	21,010	5,412
Female.	3,688	3,364	324
Some other race alone	262,044	217,383	44,661
Male.	237,107	193,831	43,276
Female.	24,937	23,552	1,385
Two or more races.	317,419	244,830	72,589
Male.	280,375	211,501	68,874
Female.	37,044	33,329	3,715
Hispanic or Latino origin [1]	1,129,904	846,906	282,998
Male.	1,032,983	757,181	275,802
Female.	96,921	89,725	7,196

[1] Persons of Hispanic or Latino origin may be any race.
Source: U.S. Census Bureau, 2009 American Community Survey, B21001, B21001A, B21001B, B21001C, B21001D, B21001E, B21001F, B21001G, and B21001I (accessed March 2011).

Table 523. Veterans Benefits—Expenditures by Program and Compensation for Service-Connected Disabilities: 1990 to 2010

[In millions of dollars (28,998 represents $28,998,000,000). For years ending September 30. Minus sign (–) indicates decrease]

Program	1990	1995	2000	2005	2007	2008	2009	2010
Total expenditures	**28,998**	**37,775**	**47,086**	**69,667**	**72,805**	**84,855**	**95,559**	**108,761**
Medical programs	11,582	16,255	19,637	29,433	33,705	38,396	43,400	46,923
Construction	661	641	466	483	704	1,088	1,325	1,671
General operating expenses	811	954	1,016	1,294	1,476	1,628	1,840	1,897
Compensation and pension.	14,674	17,765	22,012	34,694	34,600	40,241	44,735	47,901
Vocational rehabilitation and education	452	1,317	1,610	2,937	3,180	3,210	3,875	8,317
All other [1]	818	844	2,345	826	−860	292	384	2,052
Compensation for service-connected disabilities [2]	9,284	11,644	15,511	24,515	28,200	31,393	35,340	37,960

[1] Includes insurance, indemnities, and miscellaneous funds and expenditures and offsets from public receipts. (Excludes expenditures from personal funds of patients.) [2] Represents veterans receiving compensation for service-connected disabilities.
Source: U.S. Department of Veterans Affairs, *Expenditures and Workload*, annual; see also <http://www1.va.gov/vetdata/>.

Table 524. Veterans Compensation and Pension Benefits—Number on Rolls by Period of Service and Status: 1990 to 2010

[In thousands (3,584 represents 3,584,000), except as indicated. As of September 30. Living refers to veterans receiving compensation for disability incurred or aggravated while on active duty and war veterans receiving pension and benefits for nonservice-connected disabilities. Deceased refers to deceased veterans whose dependents were receiving pensions and compensation benefits]

Period of service and veteran status	1990	1995	2000	2005	2007	2008	2009	2010
Total.	**3,584**	**3,330**	**3,236**	**3,503**	**3,691**	**3,801**	**3,919**	**4,070**
Living veterans	2,746	2,669	2,672	2,973	3,167	3,268	3,384	3,524
Service-connected.	2,184	2,236	2,308	2,637	2,844	2,952	3,070	3,210
Nonservice-connected.	562	433	364	336	323	316	314	314
Deceased veterans	838	662	564	530	524	533	535	546
Service-connected.	320	307	307	323	330	338	341	347
Nonservice-connected.	518	355	257	207	195	196	194	199
World War I	198	89	34	13	9	8	7	6
Living.	18	3	(Z)	(Z)	(Z)	(Z)	(Z)	(Z)
World War II.	1,723	1,307	968	718	634	598	559	529
Living.	1,294	961	676	466	397	362	329	298
Korean conflict [1].	390	368	323	295	287	282	276	275
Living.	305	290	255	231	223	218	213	209
Vietnam era [2].	774	868	969	1,218	1,305	1,347	1,393	1,447
Living.	685	766	848	1,068	1,142	1,175	1,214	1,261
Gulf War [3]	(X)	138	334	630	819	923	1,028	1,140
Living.	(X)	134	326	617	802	904	1,007	1,117
Peacetime.	495	559	607	627	637	644	655	673
Living.	444	514	567	591	602	609	621	638

X Not applicable. Z Fewer than 500. [1] Service during period June 27, 1950 to January 31, 1955. [2] Service from August 5, 1964 to May 7, 1975. [3] Service from August 2, 1990 to the present.
Source: U.S. Department of Veterans Affairs, 1990 to 1995, *Annual Report of the Secretary of Veterans Affairs*; beginning 2000, *Annual Accountability Report* and unpublished data, see also <http://www1.va.gov/vetdata/>.

Table 525. Homeland Security Funding by Agency: 2005 to 2011

[In millions of dollars. (52,657 represents 52,657,000,000). A total of 31 agencies comprise federal homeland security funding. Department of Homeland Security (DHS) is the designated department to coordinate and centralize the leadership of many homeland security activities under a single department. In addition to DHS, the Departments of Defense (DoD), Energy (DoE), Justice (DoJ), Health and Human Services (HHS), and the U.S. State Department account for most of the total government-wide homeland security funding]

Agency	2005	2007	2008	2009	2010	2011 [1]
Total budget authority, excluding BioShield [2, 3]...	52,657	56,926	61,228	70,445	70,009	69,069
Department of Agriculture....................	596	541	575	513	614	604
Department of Commerce.....................	167	205	207	259	284	259
Department of Defense	16,108	16,538	17,374	19,414	19,054	17,626
Department of Education.....................	24	26	27	32	29	30
Department of Energy.......................	1,562	1,719	1,827	1,939	2,016	1,969
Department of Health and Human Services	4,229	4,327	4,301	4,627	7,196	4,227
Department of Homeland Security [4]	23,980	26,858	29,756	36,037	32,609	35,985
Department of Housing and Urban Development	2	2	2	5	5	4
Department of the Interior	65	48	50	50	52	66
Department of Justice	2,691	3,306	3,278	3,650	4,094	4,072
Department of Labor	56	49	48	49	40	42
Department of State	824	1,242	1,719	1,809	1,793	2,131
Department of Transportation	219	206	205	221	228	248
Department of the Treasury....................	101	127	120	133	125	122
Department of Veterans Affairs	249	260	309	310	427	421
Corps of Engineers	89	42	42	40	36	36
Environmental Protection Agency	106	167	138	157	154	154
Executive Office of the President................	30	21	21	19	12	12
General Services Administration	65	168	143	125	214	50
National Aeronautics and Space Administration	221	199	205	214	218	183
National Science Foundation...................	342	385	365	377	390	390
Office of Personnel Management	3	3	2	2	2	(NA)
Social Security Administration..................	155	194	184	182	190	211
District of Columbia	15	9	3	39	15	15
Federal Communications Commission	2	2	2	2	1	(NA)
Intelligence Community Management Account......	72	56	122	33	14	13
National Archives and Records Administration	17	18	18	20	20	20
Nuclear Regulatory Commission................	59	72	72	73	65	65
Securities and Exchange Commission	5	14	13	15	6	7
Smithsonian Institution	75	81	91	92	99	99
United States Holocaust Memorial Museum	8	8	8	9	10	10

NA Not available. [1] When the 2012 edition of Analytical Perspectives was published, none of the full-year appropriations bills for 2011 was enacted. For those programs and activities, data for 2011 reflect the annualized level provided by the continuing resolution. [2] The federal spending estimates are for the Executive Branch's homeland security efforts. These estimates do not include the efforts of the Legislative or Judicial Branches. [3] The Department of Homeland Security Appropriations Act, 2004, provided $5.6 billion for Project BioShield, to remain available through 2013. Including this uneven funding stream can distort year-over-year comparisons. [4] Not all activities carried out by DHS constitute homeland security funding (e.g. response to natural disasters and Coast Guard search and rescue activities). DHS estimates in this table do not represent the entire DHS budget. See Table 526.

Source: U.S. Office of Management and Budget, Budget of the United States Government Fiscal Year 2012, *The Budget Documents, Analytical Perspectives*, and Budget of the United States Government Fiscal Year 2012, *Crosscutting Programs, Homeland Security Funding Analysis*, <http://www.whitehouse.gov/omb/budget/>.

Table 526. Department of Homeland Security Total Budget Authority and Personnel by Organization: 2010 and 2011

[In thousands of dollars (56,169,614 represents $56,169,614,000). For the fiscal year ending September 30. Not all activities carried out by the Department of Homeland Security (DHS) constitute homeland security funding (e.g., Coast Guard search and rescue activities)]

Organization	Budget authority		Full-time employees	
	2010	2011 [1]	2010	2011 [1]
Total..	56,169,614	55,728,760	219,622	220,512
Departmental operations [2].........................	802,531	800,931	1,615	1,882
Analysis and operations	333,030	335,030	682	793
Office of the Inspector General	113,874	129,874	632	665
U.S. Customs & Border Protection	11,846,401	11,544,660	58,223	58,954
U.S. Immigration & Customs Enforcement	5,821,752	5,748,339	20,505	20,417
Transportation Security Administration	7,656,066	7,649,666	51,628	54,831
U.S. Coast Guard.............................	11,150,079	10,447,046	49,926	51,114
U.S. Secret Service	1,719,131	1,722,644	7,055	7,054
National Protection and Program Directorate	1,317,755	1,317,755	1,352	1,552
Office of Health Affairs.............................	136,850	139,250	84	95
Federal Emergency Management Agency (FEMA) [3]......	15,459,468	10,346,918	7,838	10,054
FEMA Grants [4]....................................	4,165,200	4,165,200	(5)	(5)
U.S. Citizenship & Immigration Services	2,881,597	3,029,829	10,835	11,421
Federal Law Enforcement Training Center..............	290,912	282,812	1,103	1,103
Science & Technology Directorate (S&T)	1,006,471	1,006,471	447	447
Domestic Nuclear Detection Office	383,037	383,037	130	130

[1] Continuing resolution. [2] Departmental operations is comprised of the Office of the Secretary & Executive Management, the Office of the Federal Coordinator for Gulf Coast Rebuilding, the Office of the Undersecretary for Management, the Office of the Chief Financial Officer, and the Office of the Chief Information Officer. [3] Supplemental appropriations funding was added to the 2010 budget. [4] Includes the following FEMA appropriations: State and Local Programs & Emergency Management Perf. Grants, and Assistance to Firefighters Grants. [5] Employee data are included in the FEMA full-time employees.

Source: U.S. Department of Homeland Security, "Budget-in-Brief, Fiscal Year 2012," <http://www.dhs.gov/xabout/budget/>, accessed May 2011.

Table 527. Homeland Security Grants by State/Territories: 2009 and 2010

[In thousands of dollars (1,714,172 represents 1,714,172,000). For years ending September 30. Grants consist of the following programs: State Homeland Security Program (SHSP), Data for Operation Stone Garden (OPSG) funding not included. Urban Areas Security Initiative (UASI), Metropolitan Medical Response System (MMRS), and Citizen Corps Program (CCP)]

State/territory	2009	2010	State/territory	2009	2010	State/territory	2009	2010
Total......	1,714,172	1,726,360	KY..........	11,668	11,045			
			LA..........	24,735	23,694	OR..........	15,360	15,402
U.S.........	1,698,443	1,710,436	ME..........	6,671	6,739	PA..........	54,042	57,856
AL..........	12,062	11,294	MD..........	28,544	27,342	RI..........	11,750	11,814
AK..........	7,296	7,358	MA..........	31,243	35,713	SC..........	9,026	8,412
AZ..........	29,997	30,087	MI..........	35,561	34,076	SD..........	6,657	6,726
AR..........	7,036	7,094	MN..........	20,134	19,908	TN..........	20,417	19,564
CA..........	262,998	268,685	MS..........	7,038	7,096	TX..........	138,552	143,037
CO..........	19,190	19,210	MO..........	28,431	28,169	UT..........	9,925	9,991
CT..........	15,631	14,955	MT..........	6,661	6,730	VT..........	6,652	6,722
DE..........	6,659	6,728	NE..........	7,327	8,398	VA..........	32,347	30,915
DC..........	68,543	69,574	NV..........	17,068	16,493	WA..........	30,479	30,616
FL..........	72,345	71,140	NH..........	6,993	7,056	WV..........	6,686	6,751
GA..........	35,171	33,716	NJ..........	61,845	62,036	WI..........	15,358	14,610
HI..........	11,746	11,810	NM..........	7,011	7,072	WY..........	6,649	6,720
ID..........	6,677	6,744	NY..........	271,463	277,151	AS [1]........	1,468	1,502
IL..........	86,917	87,934	NC..........	21,651	21,273	GU [1]........	1,471	1,505
IN..........	19,671	19,314	ND..........	6,652	6,722	NM [1]........	1,469	1,502
IA..........	7,040	7,097	OH..........	42,083	40,438	PR [1]........	9,850	9,911
KS..........	8,112	7,410	OK..........	14,674	13,999	VI [1]........	1,470	1,503

[1] AS—American Samoa, GU—Guam, NM—Northern Mariana Islands, PR—Puerto Rico, VI—Virgin Islands.
Source: U.S. Department of Homeland Security, State Contacts and Grants Award Administration; FY 2011 HSGP Guidance and Application Kit <http://www.dhs.gov/xgovt/grants/index.shtm>, released June 2010.

Table 528. Urban Areas Security Initiative (UASI) Grant Program: 2010

[In thousands of dollars (832,520 represents $832,520,000). For year ending September 30. The UASI Program provides financial assistance to address the unique multi-disciplinary planning, operations, equipment, training, and exercise needs of high-threat, high-density urban areas. The 60 highest risk urban areas were eligible for funding. The ten highest risk urban areas are designated Tier 1. For a listing of all grant programs and their descriptions, see <http://www.dhs.gov/xgovt/grants/index.shtm>]

State/territory	Urban area	Amount	State/territory	Urban area	Amount	State/territory	Urban area	Amount
Total ..		832,520						
TIER 1				Jacksonville	5,355	OH....	Cincinnati	4,978
CA....	Bay Area	42,828		Miami	11,040		Cleveland	5,094
	Los Angeles/Long Beach	69,922		Orlando	5,090		Columbus	4,247
DC....	National Capital	59,392		Tampa	7,815		Toledo	2,292
IL.....	Chicago	54,654	GA.....	Atlanta	13,523	OK....	Oklahoma City	4,405
MA....	Boston	18,934	HI.....	Honolulu	4,755		Tulsa	2,164
NJ.....	Jersey City/Newark	37,292	IN.....	Indianapolis	7,105	OR....	Portland	7,179
NY....	New York City	151,579	KY....	Louisville	2,206	PA....	Pittsburgh	6,399
PA....	Philadelphia	23,336						
TX....	Dallas/Fort Worth/Arlington	25,097	LA....	Baton Rouge	2,979			
	Houston	41,453		New Orleans	5,440	PR....	San Juan	3,108
TIER 2			MD....	Baltimore	10,975	RI.....	Providence	4,764
AZ....	Phoenix	10,833				TN....	Memphis	4,169
	Tucson	4,515	MI.....	Detroit	13,482		Nashville	2,844
CA....	Anaheim/Santa Ana	12,773	MN....	Twin Cities	8,263	TX....	Austin	2,932
	Bakersfield	1,015		Kansas City	7,706		El Paso	5,390
	Oxnard	2,508	MO....	St. Louis	8,533		San Antonio	6,230
	Riverside	5,286		Las Vegas	8,150			
	Sacramento	3,947	NV....	Albany	1,011	UT....	Salt Lake City	2,900
	San Diego	16,209	NY....	Buffalo	5,545	VA....	Norfolk	7,372
CO....	Denver	7,064		Rochester	2,315		Richmond	2,676
CT....	Bridgeport	2,812		Syracuse	1,010	WA....	Seattle	11,054
	Hartford	2,752	NC....	Charlotte	4,584	WI....	Milwaukee	4,160
FL....	Fort Lauderdale	6,067						

Source: Department of Homeland Security, FEMA, FY 2010 Homeland Security Grant Program (HSGP), <http://www.dhs.gov/xgovt/grants/index.shtm>, released June 2010.

Table 529. Preparedness Grant Programs: 2007 to 2009

[In dollars. For years ending September 30. Program formally called the Infrastructure Protection Programs]

Program [1]	2007	2008	2009
Total	655,230,003	803,916,250	968,585,000
Transit Security Grant Program..............	257,770,670	388,600,000	348,600,000
Freight Rail Security Grant Program..........	–	15,000,000	15,000,000
Intercity passenger Rail (AMTRAK)..........	13,409,537	25,000,000	25,000,000
Port Security Grant Program.................	312,269,796	388,600,000	388,600,000
Intercity Bus Security Grant Program..........	11,640,000	11,172,250	11,658,000
Trucking Security Program...................	11,640,000	15,544,000	7,772,000
Buffer Zone Protection Program..............	48,500,000	48,575,000	48,575,000

– Represents zero. [1] Total includes programs not listed.
Source: U.S. Department of Homeland Security, State Contacts and Grants Award Administration, <http://www.fema.gov/pdf/government/grant/2010/fy_10_grants_overview.pdf>.

Table 530. Deportable Aliens Located by Program and Border Patrol Sector: 2000 to 2009

[As of the end of September. For purposes of statistical reporting there is no difference between the terms "apprehension" and "deportable alien located." For definitions for Immigration statistics, see <http://www.dhs.gov/files/statistics/dtadefstd.shtm>]

Program and sector	2000	2005	2006	2007	2008	2009
Total	**1,814,729**	**1,291,142**	**1,206,457**	**960,756**	**791,568**	**613,003**
Investigations [1].	138,291	102,034	101,854	53,562	33,573	21,877
Detention and Removal Operations [2]	(X)	(X)	15,467	30,407	34,155	35,094
Border Patrol	1,676,438	1,189,108	1,089,136	876,787	723,840	556,032
All southwest sectors	**1,643,679**	**1,171,428**	**1,072,018**	**858,722**	**705,022**	**540,851**
San Diego, CA.	151,681	126,909	142,122	152,459	162,392	118,712
El Centro, CA.	238,126	55,726	61,469	55,881	40,962	33,520
Yuma, AZ.	108,747	138,438	118,537	37,994	8,363	6,952
Tucson, AZ.	616,346	439,090	392,104	378,323	317,709	241,667
El Paso, TX.	115,696	122,689	122,261	75,464	30,310	14,998
Marfa, TX.	13,689	10,536	7,517	5,537	5,390	6,357
Del Rio, TX	157,178	68,510	42,634	22,919	20,761	17,082
Laredo, TX.	108,973	75,342	74,843	56,715	43,659	40,571
Rio Grande Valley, TX	133,243	134,188	110,531	73,430	75,476	60,992
All other sectors	**32,759**	**17,680**	**17,118**	**18,065**	**18,818**	**15,181**
Blaine, WA.	2,581	1,001	809	749	951	844
Buffalo, NY.	1,570	400	1,517	2,190	3,338	2,672
Detroit, MI	2,057	1,792	1,282	902	961	1,157
Grand Forks, ND	562	754	517	500	542	472
Havre, MT	1,568	949	567	486	427	283
Houlton, ME.	489	233	175	95	81	60
Livermore, CA [3]	6,205	117	(X)	(X)	(X)	(X)
Miami, FL.	6,237	7,243	6,032	7,121	6,020	4,429
New Orleans, LA	6,478	1,358	3,054	4,018	4,303	3,527
Ramey, PR.	1,731	1,619	1,436	548	572	418
Spokane, WA.	1,324	279	185	337	340	277
Swanton, VT.	1,957	1,935	1,544	1,119	1,283	1,042

X Not applicable. [1] The Immigration and Customs Enforcement (ICE) Office of Investigations focuses on the enforcement of a wide variety of laws that include immigration and customs statutes. [2] Includes arrests of fugitive and nonfugitive aliens under the Office of Detention and Removal Operations (DRO), National Fugitive Operations Program. [3] Livermore sector closed July 30, 2004.

Source: U.S. Department of Homeland Security, Office of Immigration Statistics, *Yearbook of Immigration Statistics, 2009.* See also <http://www.dhs.gov/files/statistics/publications/>.

Table 531. U.S. Border Patrol Apprehensions by Border, Gender, Age, and Leading Country of Nationality: 2005 to 2008

[As of the end of September. See headnote, Table 530]

Characteristic	2005		2006		2007		2008	
	Number	Percent	Number	Percent	Number	Percent	Number	Percent
Border total	**1,189,031**	**100.0**	**1,089,096**	**100.0**	**876,803**	**100.0**	**723,840**	**100.0**
Southwest	1,171,391	98.5	1,071,979	98.4	858,737	97.9	705,022	97.4
Coastal	10,291	0.9	10,521	1.0	11,687	1.3	10,895	1.5
Northern	7,349	0.6	6,596	0.6	6,379	0.7	7,923	1.1
Gender								
Total	**1,189,031**	**100.0**	**1,089,096**	**100.0**	**876,803**	**100.0**	**723,840**	**100.0**
Male.	969,879	81.6	893,380	82.0	730,217	83.3	606,761	83.8
Female.	219,123	18.4	195,699	18.0	146,574	16.7	117,061	16.2
Unknown	29	–	17	–	12	–	18	–
Age								
Total	**1,189,031**	**100.0**	**1,089,096**	**100.0**	**876,803**	**100.0**	**723,840**	**100.0**
17 years and under	114,222	9.6	101,778	9.3	77,778	8.9	59,578	8.2
18 to 24 years	442,755	37.2	403,320	37.0	325,901	37.2	257,409	35.6
25 to 34 years	411,743	34.6	377,401	34.7	301,002	34.3	255,261	35.3
35 to 44 years	162,069	13.6	151,422	13.9	127,285	14.5	112,941	15.6
45 to 54 years	47,158	4.0	45,001	4.1	36,661	4.2	32,003	4.4
55 years and over	9,569	0.8	9,093	0.8	7,384	0.8	6,235	0.9
Unknown	1,515	0.1	1,081	0.1	792	0.1	413	0.1
Country of Nationality								
Total	**1,189,031**	**100.0**	**1,089,096**	**100.0**	**876,803**	**100.0**	**723,840**	**100.0**
Mexico	1,023,888	86.1	981,069	90.1	808,773	92.2	661,773	91.4
Honduras.[1]	52,741	4.4	28,709	2.6	22,914	2.6	19,351	2.7
Guatemala.	22,594	1.9	19,925	1.8	17,337	2.0	16,395	2.3
El Salvador [1]	39,309	3.3	41,391	3.8	14,114	1.6	12,684	1.8
Cuba	3,263	0.3	4,021	0.4	4,295	0.5	3,351	0.5
Ecuador.	1,343	0.1	1,143	0.1	958	0.1	1,579	0.2
Nicaragua	3,921	0.3	2,736	0.3	1,646	0.2	1,467	0.2
Brazil [1]	31,063	2.6	1,460	0.1	1,214	0.1	977	0.1
China, People's Republic.	2,200	0.2	2,179	0.2	837	0.1	836	0.1
Dominican Republic.	1,406	0.1	1,023	0.1	562	0.1	819	0.1
Canada	1,020	0.1	876	0.1	554	0.1	610	0.1
Other	6,283	0.5	4,564	0.4	3,599	0.4	3,998	0.6

– Represents zero. [1] Between 2005 and 2008, the percentage of persons apprehended who were from Honduras, El Salvador, and Brazil declined substantially. These decreases reflect the end of "catch and release," the practice of apprehending illegal aliens from countries other than Mexico and releasing them on their own recognizance pending a removal hearing.

Source: U.S. Dept. of Homeland Security, Office of Immigration Statistics, *Fact Sheets*, see also <http://www.dhs.gov/xlibrary/assets/statistics/publications/ois_apprehensions_fs_2005-2008.pdf>.

Table 532. Deportable Aliens Located: 1925 to 2009

[See headnote, Table 530. Detention and Removal Operations (DRO) data are included beginning in Fiscal Year 2006]

Year	Number	Year	Number	Year	Number	Year	Number
1925.	22,199	1974.	788,145	1986.	1,767,400	1998.	1,679,439
1930.	20,880	1975.	766,600	1987.	1,190,488	1999.	1,714,035
1935.	11,016	1976 [1]	1,097,739	1988.	1,008,145	2000.	1,814,729
1940.	10,492	1977.	1,042,215	1989.	954,243	2001.	1,387,486
1945.	69,164	1978.	1,057,977	1990.	1,169,939	2002.	1,062,279
1950.	468,339	1979.	1,076,418	1991.	1,197,875	2003.	1,046,422
1955.	254,096	1980.	910,361	1992.	1,258,481	2004.	1,264,232
1960.	70,684	1981.	975,780	1993.	1,327,261	2005.	1,291,142
1965.	110,371	1982.	970,246	1994.	1,094,719	2006.	1,206,457
1970.	345,353	1983.	1,251,357	1995.	1,394,554	2007.	960,756
1972.	505,949	1984.	1,246,981	1996.	1,649,986	2008.	791,568
1973.	655,968	1985.	1,348,749	1997.	1,536,520	2009.	613,003

[1] Includes the 15 months from July 1, 1975 to September 30, 1976, because the end date of fiscal years was changed from June 30 to September 30.

Source: U.S. Department of Homeland Security, Office of Immigration Statistics, *Yearbook of Immigration Statistics, 2009.* See also <http://www.dhs.gov/files/statistics/publications/>.

Table 533. Aliens Returned or Removed by Crime Categories and Country of Nationality: 2004 to 2009

[For definitions of immigration enforcement terms, see "Immigration Enforcement Actions, 2009 Yearbook of Immigration Statistics"; "Crime categories" and "Countries of nationality" ranked by latest data year]

Crime category and country of nationality	2004	2005	2006	2007	2008	2009
Total aliens returned or removed:	**1,407,241**	**1,343,351**	**1,324,355**	**1,210,772**	**1,170,149**	**973,396**
Returns [1]	1,166,576	1,096,920	1,043,381	891,390	811,263	580,107
Removals [2]	240,665	246,431	280,974	319,382	358,886	393,289
Noncriminal	148,285	154,210	182,484	216,988	253,783	264,944
Criminal [3]	92,380	92,221	98,490	102,394	105,103	128,345
Leading crime categories:						
Dangerous drugs.	34,071	34,215	33,485	33,449	34,882	37,993
Immigration	15,174	17,106	23,176	21,538	17,542	19,807
Assault.	9,654	9,633	9,574	11,048	7,485	9,436
Burglary.	3,406	3,351	3,506	3,466	3,292	3,795
Robbery.	2,924	3,023	2,915	2,908	3,101	3,252
Larceny	2,830	2,742	2,757	2,878	3,282	4,228
Sexual assault	2,777	2,649	2,571	2,786	2,929	2,792
Family offenses	2,478	2,172	2,262	2,410	2,343	2,611
Stolen vehicles	1,797	1,806	1,934	1,875	(NA)	(NA)
Sex offenses	1,984	1,922	1,868	1,874	(NA)	(NA)
Other	13,808	13,106	13,371	15,692	18,170	21,161
Leading country of nationality of criminals removed:						
Mexico	71,570	70,779	73,171	76,967	77,426	96,965
Honduras.	2,544	2,704	5,752	5,236	5,471	6,890
El Salvador	2,805	2,827	3,850	4,949	5,549	6,220
Guatemala.	2,176	2,143	3,850	3,917	5,130	6,432
Dominican Republic.	2,479	2,308	2,206	2,044	2,040	2,133
Colombia	1,456	1,367	1,307	1,191	1,074	1,085
Jamaica.	1,614	1,475	1,234	1,139	1,212	1,219
Nicaragua	520	462	423	411	345	370
Canada	401	356	592	508	532	601
Brazil	761	1,431	563	352	366	367
Other	16	14	13	13	23	34

NA Not available. [1] Returns are the confirmed movement of an inadmissible or deportable alien out of the United States not based on an order of removal. Most of the voluntary departures are of Mexican nationals who have been apprehended by the U.S. Border Patrol and are returned to Mexico. [2] Removals are the compulsory and confirmed movement of an inadmissible or deportable alien out of the United States based on an order of removal. An alien who is removed has administrative or criminal consequences placed on subsequent reentry owing to the fact of the removal. [3] Refers to persons removed based on a criminal charge or those with a criminal conviction.

Source: U.S. Department of Homeland Security, Office of Immigration Statistics, *2009 Yearbook of Immigration Statistics.*, Deportable Alien Control System (DACS), Enforcement Case Tracking System (ENFORCE), July 2009. See also <http://www.dhs.gov/files/statistics/publications/yearbook.shtm>.

Table 534. Coast Guard Migrant Interdictions by Nationality of Alien: 2000 to 2011

[For the year ending September 30]

Year	Total	Haiti	Dominican Republic	China [1]	Cuba	Mexico	Ecuador	Other
2000.	4,210	1,113	499	261	1,000	49	1,244	44
2005.	9,455	1,850	3,612	32	2,712	55	1,149	45
2007.	6,338	1,610	1,469	73	2,868	26	125	167
2008.	4,825	1,583	688	1	2,216	47	220	65
2009.	3,467	1,782	727	35	799	77	6	41
2010.	2,088	1,377	140	–	422	61	–	88
2011.	1,241	667	105	–	388	66	–	15

– Represents zero. [1] See footnote 4, Table 1332.

Source: U.S. Department of Homeland Security, United States Coast Guard, "USCG Migrant Interdiction Statistics," <http://www.uscg.mil/hq/cg5/cg531/amio/flowstats/currentstats.asp/>, accessed May 15, 2011.

Table 535. Customs and Border Protection (CBP)—Processed and Cleared Passengers, Planes, Vehicles, and Containers: 2000 to 2007

[In thousands (80,519 represents 80,519,000). For year ending September 30]

Characteristic	2000	2001	2002	2003	2004	2005	2006	2007
Air								
Passengers	80,519	79,676	71,608	72,959	80,866	86,123	87,906	91,574
Commercial planes [1] . . .	829	839	769	790	824	866	881	916
Private planes	146	126	129	132	140	135	139	139
Land								
Passengers [2, 3]	397,312	381,477	333,652	329,998	326,693	317,765	289,048	299,004
Autos [2]	127,095	129,603	118,307	120,376	121,419	121,654	119,372	112,428
Rail containers.	2,157	2,257	2,430	2,472	2,588	2,655	2,735	2,737
Truck containers [4]	10,397	11,001	11,129	11,163	11,252	11,308	11,489	11,459
Sea								
Passengers [5]	10,990	11,291	12,224	15,127	22,234	26,228	26,223	27,059
Vessels [6]	211	215	212	204	142	113	168	170
Vessel containers [7]	5,813	5,944	7,248	9,092	9,796	11,341	11,622	11,703

[1] A commercial aircraft is any aircraft transporting passengers and/or cargo for some payment or other consideration, including money or services rendered. [2] See Table 1270 for more details. [3] Includes pedestrians. [4] Truck containers—number of trucks entering the U.S. [5] Does not include passengers on ferries. [6] Includes every description of water craft or other contrivance used or capable of being used as a means of transportation on water, does not include aircraft. [7] Number of vessel containers.

Source: U.S. Department of Homeland Security, Customs and Border Protection, *About CBP, Statistics and Accomplishments, National Workload Statistics, 2000–2007.* See Internet site <http://www.cbp.gov/xp/cgov/about/accomplish/previous_year/national _workload_stats.xml>.

Table 536. Prohibited Items Intercepted at U.S. Airport Screening Checkpoints: 2004 to 2008

[Passengers boarding aircraft in thousands (702,921 represents 702,921,000). For the calendar year. Transportation Security Administration (TSA) assumed responsibility for airport security on February 17, 2002, and by November 19, 2002, TSA assumed control over all passenger screenings from private contractors]

Year	2004	2005	2006	2007	2008
Passengers boarding aircraft, total [1]	**702,921**	**738,327**	**744,242**	**769,370**	**741,450**
Domestic.	640,698	670,418	671,796	693,374	664,714
International.	62,222	67,908	72,445	75,996	76,735
Total prohibited items (number)	**7,104,095**	**15,886,404**	**13,709,684**	**6,516,026**	**(NA)**
Knife [2]	2,055,404	1,822,892	1,607,125	1,056,691	(9)
Other cutting items [3]	3,409,888	3,276,941	163,419	101,387	(9)
Club [4]	28,998	20,531	12,296	9,443	(9)
Box cutter	22,430	21,319	15,999	11,908	(9)
Firearm [5]	254	850	820	1,416	902
Incendiary [6]	697,606	374,487	94,097	73,670	116,200
Lighters [7]	178	9,420,991	11,616,688	5,124,344	(9)
Other [8]	889,337	949,243	200,060	137,167	(9)

NA Not available. [1] Data come from the Air Transport Association. Data are for U.S. passenger and cargo airlines only. [2] Knife includes any length and type except round-bladed, butter, and plastic cutlery. [3] Other cutting instruments refer to, e.g., scissors, screwdrivers, swords, sabers, and ice picks. [4] Club refers to baseball bats, night sticks, billy clubs, bludgeons, etc. [5] Firearm refers to items like pistols, revolvers, rifles, automatic weapons, shotguns, parts of guns and firearms. [6] Incendiaries refer to categories of ammunition and gunpowder, flammables/irritants, and explosives. [7] As of April 14, 2005, passengers are prohibited from carrying all lighters on their person or in carry-on luggage or onboard an airplane. [8] Other refers to categories of ammunition and gunpower, dangerous objects, fireworks, replica weapons, and tools. [9] The data for this prohibited item category are no longer collected as of August 8, 2008.

Source: U.S. Department of Homeland Security, Transportation Security Administration, unpublished data, June 2009, <http://www.tsa.gov>; Air Transport Association of America, Washington, DC; Annual Traffic and Operations: U.S. Airlines, <http://www.airlines.org/pages/home.aspx/>.

Table 537. Seizure Statistics for Intellectual Property Rights (IPR) by Commodity and Trading Partner: 2009 and 2010

[In thousands of dollars (260,698 represents $260,698,000, except as indicated). Customs and Border Protection (CBP) is dedicated to protecting against the importation of goods which infringe/violate Intellectual Property Rights (IPR) by devoting substantial resources toward identifying and seizing shipments of infringing articles]

Commodity	2009	2010	Trading partner	2009	2010
Number of IPR Seizures	14,841	19,959	China.	204,656	124,681
Total domestic value of IPR seizures [1]	260,698	188,125	Hong Kong.	26,887	26,173
Footwear	99,779	45,750	India.	3,047	1,571
Consumer electronics [2]	31,774	33,588	Taiwan.	2,454	1,138
Handbags/wallets/backpacks	21,502	15,422	Korea, South	1,510	1,049
Wearing apparel	21,462	18,682	Jordan	(NA)	7,713
Watches /parts.	15,534	7,848	Malaysia	(NA)	1,286
Computers/Technology Components . . .	12,546	9,502	United Arab Emirates	(NA)	493
Media [3]	11,100	12,681	Canada	(NA)	609
Pharmaceuticals	11,058	5,662	Vietnam	604	742
All other commodities	19,941	23,377	All other countries	16,575	22,668

NA Not available. [1] Domestic value is the cost of the seized goods, plus the costs of shipping and importing the goods into the U.S. and an amount for profit. [2] Consumer electronics includes cell phones and accessories, radios, power strips, electrical tools and appliances. [3] Includes motion pictures on tape, laser disc, and DVD; interactive and computer software on CD-ROM and floppy discs; and music on CD or tape.

Source: U.S. Department of Homeland Security, Customs and Border Protection, "Import, Commercial Enforcement, Intellectual Property Rights, Seizure Statistics," <http://www.cbp.gov/xp/cgov/trade/priority_trade/ipr/pub/seizure/>.

This section presents data related to governmental expenditures for social insurance and human services; governmental programs for Old-Age, Survivors, Disability, and Health Insurance (OASDHI); governmental employee retirement; private pension plans; government unemployment and temporary disability insurance; federal supplemental security income payments and aid to the needy; child and other welfare services; and federal food programs. Also included here are selected data on workers' compensation and vocational rehabilitation, child support, child care, charity contributions, and philanthropic trusts and foundations.

The principal source for these data is the Social Security Administration's *Annual Statistical Supplement to the Social Security Bulletin* which presents current data on many of the programs.

Social insurance under the Social Security Act—

Programs established by the Social Security Act provide protection against wage loss resulting from retirement, prolonged disability, death, or unemployment, and protection against the cost of medical care during old age and disability. The federal OASDI program provides monthly benefits to retired or disabled insured workers and their dependents and to survivors of insured workers. To be eligible, a worker must have had a specified period of employment in which OASDI taxes were paid. The age of eligibility for full retirement benefits had been 65 years old for many years. However, for persons born in 1938 or later that age gradually increases until it reaches age 67 for those born after 1959. Reduced benefits may be obtained as early as age 62. The worker's spouse is under the same limitations. Survivor benefits are payable to dependents of deceased insured workers. Disability benefits are payable to an insured worker under full retirement age with a prolonged disability and to the disabled worker's dependents on the

same basis as dependents of retired workers. Disability benefits are provided at age 50 to the disabled widow or widower of a deceased worker who was fully insured at the time of death. Disabled children, aged 18 or older, of retired, disabled, or deceased workers are also eligible for benefits. A lump sum benefit is generally payable on the death of an insured worker to a spouse or minor children. For information on the Medicare program, see Section 3, Health and Nutrition.

Retirement, survivors, disability, and hospital insurance benefits are funded by a payroll tax on annual earnings (up to a maximum of earnings set by law) of workers, employers, and the self-employed. The maximum taxable earnings are adjusted annually to reflect increasing wage levels (see Table 544). Effective January 1994, there is no dollar limit on wages and self-employment income subject to the hospital insurance tax. Tax receipts and benefit payments are administered through federal trust funds. Special benefits for uninsured persons; hospital benefits for persons aged 65 and over with specified amounts of social security coverage less than that required for cash benefit eligibility; and that part of the cost of supplementary medical insurance not financed by contributions from participants are financed from federal general revenues.

Unemployment insurance is presently administered by the U.S. Employment and Training Administration and each state's employment security agency. By agreement with the U.S. Secretary of Labor, state agencies also administer unemployment compensation for eligible ex-military personnel and federal employees. Under state unemployment insurance laws, benefits related to the individual's past earnings are paid to unemployed eligible workers. State laws vary concerning the length of time benefits are paid and their amount. In most states, benefits are payable for 26 weeks

U.S. Census Bureau, Statistical Abstract of the United States: 2012

and, during periods of high unemployment, extended benefits are payable under a federal-state program to those who have exhausted their regular state benefits. Some states also supplement the basic benefit with allowances for dependents.

Unemployment insurance is funded by a federal unemployment tax levied on the taxable payrolls of most employers. Taxable payroll under the federal act and 12 state laws is the first $7,000 in wages paid each worker during a year. Forty-one states have taxable payrolls above $7,000. Employers are allowed a percentage credit of taxable payroll for contributions paid to states under state unemployment insurance laws. The remaining percent of the federal tax finances administrative costs, the federal share of extended benefits, and advances to states. About 97 percent of wage and salary workers are covered by unemployment insurance.

Retirement programs for government employees—

The Civil Service Retirement System (CSRS) and the Federal Employees' Retirement System (FERS) are the two major programs providing age and service, disability, and survivor annuities for federal civilian employees. In general, employees hired after December 31, 1983, are covered under FERS and the social security program (OASDHI), and employees on staff prior to that date are members of CSRS and are covered under Medicare. CSRS employees were offered the option of transferring to FERS during 1987 and 1998. There are separate retirement systems for the uniformed services (supplementing OASDHI) and for certain special groups of federal employees. State and local government employees are covered for the most part by state and local retirement systems similar to the federal programs. In many jurisdictions these benefits supplement OASDHI coverage.

Workers' compensation—

All states provide protection against work-connected injuries and deaths, although some states exclude certain workers (e.g., domestic workers). Federal laws cover federal employees,

private employees in the District of Columbia, and longshoremen and harbor workers. In addition, the Department of Labor administers "black lung" benefits programs for coal miners disabled by pneumoconiosis and for specified dependents and survivors. Specified occupational diseases are compensable to some extent. In most states, benefits are related to the worker's salary. The benefits may or may not be augmented by dependents' allowances or automatically adjusted to prevailing wage levels.

Income support—

Income support programs are designed to provide benefits for persons with limited income and resources. The Supplemental Security Income (SSI) program and Temporary Assistance for Needy Families (TANF) program are the major programs providing monthly payments. In addition, a number of programs provide money payments or in-kind benefits for special needs or purposes. Several programs offer food and nutritional services. Also, various federal-state programs provide energy assistance, public housing, and subsidized housing to individuals and families with low incomes. General assistance may also be available at the state or local level.

The SSI program, administered by the Social Security Administration, provides income support to persons aged 65 or older and blind or disabled adults and children. Eligibility requirements and federal payment standards are nationally uniform. Most states supplement the basic SSI payment for all or selected categories of persons.

The Personal Responsibility and Work Opportunity Reconciliation Act of 1996 contained provisions that replaced the Aid to Families With Dependent Children (AFDC), Job Opportunities and Basic Skills (JOBS), and Emergency Assistance programs with the Temporary Assistance for Needy Families block grant program. This law contains strong work requirements, comprehensive child support enforcement, support for families moving from welfare to work, and other features. The TANF became effective as soon as each state submitted a complete plan implementing TANF, but no later than

U.S. Census Bureau, Statistical Abstract of the United States: 2012

July 1, 1997. The AFDC program provided cash assistance based on need, income, resources, and family size.

Federal food stamp program—

Under the food stamp program, single persons and those living in households meeting nationwide standards for income and assets may receive coupons redeemable for food at most retail food stores or provides benefits through electronic benefit transfer. The monthly amount of benefits or allotments a unit receives is determined by household size and income. Households without income receive the determined monthly cost of a nutritionally adequate diet for their household size. This amount is updated to account for food price increases. Households with income receive the difference between the amount of a nutritionally adequate diet and 30 percent of their income, after certain allowable deductions.

To qualify for the program, a household must have less than $2,000 in disposable assets ($3,000 if one member is aged 60 or older), gross income below 130 percent of the official poverty guidelines for the household size, and net income below 100 percent of the poverty guidelines. Households with a person aged 60 or older or a disabled person receiving SSI, social security, state general assistance, or veterans' disability benefits may have gross income exceeding 130 percent of the poverty guidelines. All households in which all members receive TANF or SSI are categorically eligible for food stamps without meeting these income or resource criteria. Households are certified for varying lengths of time, depending on their income sources and individual circumstances.

Health and welfare services—

Programs providing health and welfare services are aided through federal grants to states for child welfare services, vocational rehabilitation, activities for the aged, maternal and child health services, maternity and infant care projects, comprehensive health services, and a variety of public health activities. For information about the Medicaid program, see Section 3, Health and Nutrition.

Noncash benefits—

The U.S. Census Bureau annually collects data on the characteristics of recipients of noncash (in-kind) benefits to supplement the collection of annual money income data in the Current Population Survey (see text, Section 1, Population, and Section 13, Income, Expenditures, Poverty, and Wealth). Noncash benefits are those benefits received in a form other than money which serve to enhance or improve the economic well-being of the recipient. As for money income, the data for noncash benefits are for the calendar year prior to the date of the interview. The major categories of noncash benefits covered are public transfers (e.g., food stamps, school lunch, public housing, and Medicaid) and employer or union-provided benefits to employees.

Statistical reliability—

For discussion of statistical collection, estimation, and sampling procedures and measures of statistical reliability applicable to HHS and Census Bureau data, see Appendix III.

U.S. Census Bureau, Statistical Abstract of the United States: 2012

Table 538. Selected Payments to Individuals by Function: 1970 to 2009

[In billions of dollars (108 represents $108,000,000,000). The employee benefit system is composed of voluntary and mandatory programs which are employment-based and financed primarily from employment-based contributions]

Source and sector	1970	1980	1990	1995	2000	2001	2002	2003	2004	2005	2006	2007	2008	2009
All benefits	**108**	**422**	**1,027**	**1,493**	**1,909**	**2,077**	**2,251**	**2,393**	**2,559**	**2,721**	**2,912**	**3,107**	**3,327**	**3,641**
Retirement income benefits	51	202	482	660	864	920	977	1,023	1,092	1,158	1,265	1,359	1,422	1,520
Social security—old-age, survivors, and disability insurance	31	119	244	328	401	425	447	464	486	513	544	576	606	664
Private employer pension and profit sharing	7	35	136	191	271	290	311	323	355	376	433	476	487	502
Public employer retirement plans	12	48	102	141	192	205	219	237	252	269	287	308	329	354
Federal civilian employee retirement [1]	3	16	32	39	50	52	53	55	58	62	67	72	74	78
State and local government retirement	4	15	41	65	100	110	121	133	142	151	162	174	189	206
Military retirement [2]	3	13	22	28	33	35	36	41	43	46	49	52	55	59
Railroad retirement	2	5	7	8	8	8	9	9	9	9	10	10	10	11
Health benefits	22	99	300	456	596	655	705	767	834	901	986	1,044	1,111	1,170
Medicare hospital insurance and supplementary medical insurance	7	36	108	181	219	243	259	277	305	332	399	428	463	500
Group health insurance	15	62	191	274	376	411	444	488	528	567	585	614	645	667
Military health insurance [3]	–	–	2	1	1	1	2	2	2	2	3	2	3	3
Other employee benefits	17	51	88	103	113	129	156	162	148	147	148	155	181	269
Unemployment insurance [4]	4	16	18	22	21	32	54	53	36	32	30	33	51	129
Workers' compensation [5]	3	13	38	43	48	52	53	56	57	56	55	57	60	62
Group life insurance	3	7	12	16	17	17	18	18	18	19	20	20	20	20
Miscellaneous disability [6]	1	3	4	3	4	4	4	4	5	5	5	6	6	7
Veterans' benefits [7]	7	13	16	19	23	25	28	30	32	35	37	40	44	50
Public assistance [8]	18	70	157	275	336	373	413	441	485	515	513	549	613	682

– Represents or rounds to zero. [1] Consists of civil service, foreign service, Public Health Service officers, Tennessee Valley Authority, and several small retirement programs. [2] Includes the U.S. Coast Guard. [3] Consists of payments for medical services for dependents of active duty military personnel at nonmilitary facilities. [4] Consists of state, railroad employee, and federal employee unemployment benefits; special unemployment benefits; and supplemental unemployment benefits. [5] Includes payments from private, federal, and state and local workers' compensation funds. [6] Includes federal black-lung payments and payments from state and local temporary disability insurance. [7] Consists of pension and disability, readjustment, and other veterans' benefits. [8] Consists of federal benefits (food stamp benefits, Supplemental Security Income, direct relief, earned income credit, payments to nonprofit institutions, aid to students, and payments for medical services for retired military personnel and their dependents at nonmilitary facilities) and state benefits (medical care, Aid to Families with Dependent Children, Supplemental Security Income, general assistance, emergency assistance, and medical insurance premium payments on behalf of indigents). Financed from state and federal general revenues.

Source: Employee Benefit Research Institute, Washington, DC, *EBRI Databook on Employee Benefits, 12th Ed.,* and unpublished data (copyright). EBRI tabulations based on U.S. Department of Commerce, Bureau of Economic Analysis. See also <http://www.ebri.org/publications/books/index.cfm?fa=databook>.

350 Social Insurance and Human Services

Table 539. Government Transfer Payments to Individuals—Summary: 1990 to 2009

[In billions of dollars (566.1 represents $566,100,000,000)]

Year	Transfer payments, total	Retirement and disability insurance benefits	Medical payments	Income maintenance benefits	Unemployment insurance benefits	Veterans benefits	Federal education and training assistance payments [1]	Other [2]
1990......	566.1	263.9	188.8	63.5	18.2	17.7	12.3	1.7
1995......	849.8	350.0	338.6	100.4	21.8	20.5	17.2	1.2
1998......	940.9	391.2	383.4	101.1	19.9	23.3	20.5	1.6
1999......	975.7	402.4	400.7	104.8	20.7	24.1	21.3	1.7
2000......	1,027.8	424.5	427.2	106.3	21.0	25.0	21.9	2.0
2001......	1,126.7	449.8	480.8	109.4	32.1	26.6	25.4	2.6
2002......	1,232.1	474.4	523.8	120.7	53.7	29.5	27.9	2.1
2003......	1,299.0	493.5	555.8	133.2	53.6	31.8	28.5	2.7
2004......	1,381.2	517.1	610.3	144.2	37.1	34.0	31.2	7.3
2005......	1,465.1	545.4	653.2	159.6	32.3	36.4	33.8	4.5
2006......	1,565.6	576.9	717.0	163.4	30.9	38.9	35.9	2.7
2007......	1,669.8	609.1	771.4	172.3	33.4	41.7	39.5	2.6
2008......	1,824.1	639.6	822.1	185.8	52.0	45.1	45.6	33.8
2009......	2,076.1	699.5	892.4	217.9	130.1	51.4	56.7	28.0

[1] See footnote 9, Table 540. [2] See footnote 10, Table 540.

Source: U.S. Bureau of Economic Analysis, "Regional Accounts Data, Annual State Personal Income," <http://www.bea.gov/regional/spi/>, accessed March 2011.

Table 540. Government Transfer Payments to Individuals by Type: 1990 to 2009

[In millions of dollars (566,100 represents $566,100,000,000)]

Item	1990	2000	2005	2006	2007	2008	2009
Total...........................	566,100	1,027,827	1,465,125	1,565,646	1,669,795	1,824,122	2,076,109
Retirement & disability insurance benefit payments...........	263,888	424,461	545,361	576,904	609,100	639,619	699,519
Old-age, survivors, & disability insurance.......	244,135	401,393	512,728	544,096	575,648	605,530	664,287
Railroad retirement and disability.............	7,221	8,267	9,191	9,519	9,813	10,068	10,630
Workers' compensation payments (federal & state)...........	8,618	10,898	15,866	15,650	15,794	16,120	16,434
Other government disability insurance & retirement [1]........	3,914	3,903	7,576	7,639	7,845	7,901	8,168
Medical payments.............	188,808	427,194	653,193	717,010	771,361	822,111	892,410
Medicare...................	107,638	219,117	331,924	399,193	427,556	462,773	500,254
Public assistance medical care [2].........	78,176	205,021	315,032	310,977	336,884	351,846	383,614
Military medical insurance [3]......	2,994	3,056	6,237	6,840	6,921	7,492	8,542
Income maintenance benefit payments..........	63,481	106,285	159,624	163,418	172,255	185,846	217,858
Supplemental Security Income (SSI)...........	16,670	31,675	38,285	39,892	42,285	44,150	47,534
Family assistance [4]................	19,187	18,440	18,216	18,226	18,334	19,255	20,088
Food stamps................	14,741	14,565	29,492	29,390	30,920	36,987	54,574
Other income maintenance [5]........	12,883	41,605	73,631	75,910	80,716	85,454	95,662
Unemployment insurance benefit payments......	18,208	20,989	32,276	30,900	33,381	52,022	130,141
State unemployment insurance compensation...	17,644	20,223	31,001	29,594	32,006	50,318	127,915
Unemployment compensation for federal civilian employees.....	215	226	224	218	216	255	439
Unemployment compensation for railroad employees.......	89	81	72	78	83	84	179
Unemployment compensation for veterans......	144	181	446	449	406	467	840
Other unemployment compensation [6].........	116	278	533	561	670	898	768
Veterans benefit payments...........	17,687	25,004	36,371	38,877	41,676	45,125	51,429
Veterans pension and disability............	15,550	21,966	32,505	35,018	37,721	40,798	45,391
Veterans readjustment [7]........	257	1,322	2,256	2,290	2,421	2,783	4,518
Veterans life insurance benefits.............	1,868	1,706	1,596	1,554	1,517	1,523	1,493
Other assistance to veterans [8]...........	12	10	14	15	17	21	27
Federal education & training assistance payments [9]...........	12,286	21,851	33,796	35,859	39,450	45,577	56,747
Other payments to individuals [10]........	1,742	2,043	4,504	2,678	2,572	33,822	28,005

[1] Consists largely of temporary disability payments, pension benefit guaranty payments, and black lung payments. [2] Consists of medicaid and other medical vendor payments. [3] Consists of payments made under the TriCare Management Program (formerly called CHAMPUS) for the medical care of dependents of active duty military personnel and of retired military personnel and their dependents at nonmilitary medical facilities. [4] Through 1990, consists of emergency assistance and aid to families with dependent children. Beginning with 2000, consists of benefits—generally known as temporary assistance for needy families—provided under the Personal Responsibility and Work Opportunity Reconciliation Act of 1996. [5] Consists largely of general assistance, expenditures for food under the supplemental program for women, infants, and children; refugee assistance; foster home care and adoption assistance; earned income tax credits; and energy assistance. [6] Consists of trade readjustment allowance payments, Redwood Park benefit payments, public service employment benefit payments, and transitional benefit payments. [7] Consists largely of veterans' readjustment benefit payments, educational assistance to spouses and children of disabled or deceased veterans, payments to paraplegics, and payments for autos and conveyances for disabled veterans. [8] Consists largely of state and local government payments to veterans. [9] Excludes veterans. Consists largely of federal fellowship payments (National Science Foundation fellowships and traineeships, subsistence payments to state maritime academy cadets, and other federal fellowships), interest subsidy on higher education loans, basic educational opportunity grants, and Job Corps payments. [10] Consists largely of Bureau of Indian Affairs payments, education exchange payments, Alaska Permanent Fund dividend payments, compensation of survivors of public safety officers, compensation of victims of crime, disaster relief payments, compensation for Japanese internment, and other special payments to individuals.

Source: U.S. Bureau of Economic Analysis, "Regional Accounts Data, Annual State Personal Income," <http://www.bea.gov/regional/spi/>, accessed March 2011.

Table 541. Government Transfer Payments to Individuals by State: 2000 to 2009

[In millions of dollars (1,027,827 represents $1,027,827,000,000).]

State	2000, total	2008, total	2009							
			Total	Retirement and disability insurance benefits	Medical payments	Income maintenance benefits	Unemployment insurance benefits	Veterans benefits	Federal education and training assistance payments [1]	Other [2]
U.S........	1,027,827	1,824,122	2,076,109	699,519	892,410	217,858	130,141	51,429	56,747	28,005
AL........	16,803	30,730	34,052	12,529	13,621	4,119	1,073	1,283	977	450
AK........	2,950	5,162	4,520	932	1,801	497	212	171	47	861
AZ........	15,948	36,614	42,393	14,271	18,765	3,910	1,597	1,134	2,108	607
AR........	10,168	19,232	21,509	7,738	8,820	2,229	1,013	796	626	287
CA........	114,879	202,068	230,848	70,126	99,718	28,597	18,890	4,173	6,085	3,258
CO........	11,144	21,355	25,018	9,153	9,850	2,211	1,733	960	771	340
CT........	14,222	23,088	26,657	8,807	12,526	1,994	2,086	362	549	332
DE........	2,908	5,710	6,428	2,356	2,891	481	313	141	169	77
DC........	2,695	4,199	4,714	883	2,707	644	197	74	142	68
FL........	64,580	119,157	134,551	48,429	57,616	12,827	5,941	4,035	3,981	1,721
GA........	24,190	47,795	54,136	18,284	20,501	7,340	3,395	1,984	1,853	779
HI........	3,887	7,088	7,974	2,867	3,083	996	551	263	116	97
ID........	3,868	7,728	8,909	3,502	3,337	778	626	285	246	135
IL........	42,291	70,802	82,984	27,705	34,817	8,788	6,901	1,212	2,395	1,167
IN........	20,472	37,115	42,400	16,069	16,481	3,864	3,184	826	1,379	596
IA........	10,242	17,485	19,746	7,664	7,725	1,666	1,117	412	902	260
KS........	9,091	15,281	17,437	6,621	7,095	1,578	1,096	432	384	231
KY........	16,058	28,333	32,513	11,156	13,329	3,732	1,752	924	1,207	413
LA........	16,744	29,270	31,802	9,523	15,395	4,090	704	831	908	350
ME........	5,351	9,585	10,794	3,601	5,057	1,003	397	435	183	120
MD........	17,140	30,948	35,055	11,607	16,091	3,355	1,835	860	915	392
MA........	26,575	45,701	51,890	14,844	24,873	5,183	4,624	879	877	610
MI........	36,987	65,097	75,135	26,743	29,526	7,950	6,594	1,233	2,006	1,084
MN........	16,106	30,252	34,804	11,664	15,304	2,925	2,548	854	1,062	447
MS........	10,916	20,067	21,825	7,116	9,713	2,957	607	554	594	283
MO........	21,121	37,002	41,739	15,005	18,562	3,754	1,799	1,026	1,064	530
MT........	3,197	5,539	6,299	2,585	2,392	504	302	257	166	93
NE........	5,753	9,725	10,657	4,143	4,486	884	289	427	303	125
NV........	5,580	12,230	14,603	5,215	5,350	1,272	1,770	471	261	264
NH........	4,003	7,127	8,053	3,309	3,335	509	388	243	175	94
NJ........	33,512	54,779	62,879	21,688	26,626	4,741	6,781	854	1,346	843
NM........	6,035	12,376	13,981	4,314	6,225	1,676	539	580	398	250
NY........	96,578	149,551	168,208	46,190	87,139	19,058	8,301	1,886	3,912	1,722
NC........	28,335	55,185	63,751	21,939	26,355	6,775	4,283	2,174	1,312	914
ND........	2,339	3,668	4,049	1,637	1,639	339	124	130	116	65
OH........	43,906	74,252	84,403	30,200	35,222	8,657	4,768	1,559	2,955	1,042
OK........	12,064	22,636	25,320	9,026	10,619	2,601	869	1,257	644	304
OR........	12,330	22,057	26,223	9,842	9,526	2,525	2,585	840	510	394
PA........	55,370	89,367	101,019	35,475	44,030	8,007	7,937	1,709	2,535	1,325
RI........	4,702	7,736	8,725	2,807	3,908	816	696	171	219	108
SC........	14,601	28,566	32,430	11,719	12,536	3,545	1,748	1,164	1,263	456
SD........	2,499	4,316	4,754	1,858	1,984	423	85	189	119	95
TN........	21,977	39,817	44,281	15,618	18,292	5,439	1,902	1,258	1,199	573
TX........	60,244	120,807	136,469	42,627	61,045	16,665	6,069	4,833	3,495	1,734
UT........	5,025	9,825	11,479	4,383	4,284	1,197	678	280	494	163
VT........	2,308	4,299	4,876	1,605	2,204	490	265	123	133	57
VA........	20,239	38,547	43,390	16,621	17,114	4,339	1,662	1,899	1,236	520
WA........	21,190	37,005	43,630	16,239	15,593	4,818	3,708	1,438	1,267	568
WV........	8,909	14,021	15,665	5,969	6,489	1,568	518	576	353	182
WI........	18,185	30,947	37,882	13,953	15,543	3,346	2,898	864	701	577
WY........	1,613	2,880	3,259	1,363	1,269	199	191	107	87	43

[1] Excludes veterans. Consists largely of federal fellowship payments (National Science Foundation, fellowships and traineeships, subsistence payments to state maritime academy cadets, and other federal fellowships), interest subsidy on higher education loans, basic educational opportunity grants, and Job Corps payments. [2] Consists largely of Bureau of Indian Affairs payments, education exchange payments, Alaska Permanent Fund dividend payments, compensation of survivors of public safety officers, compensation of victims of crime, disaster relief payments, compensation for Japanese internment, and other special payments to individuals.

Source: U.S. Bureau of Economic Analysis, "Regional Accounts Data, Annual State Personal Income," <http://www.bea.gov/regional/spi>, accessed March 2011.

Table 542. Number of Persons With Income by Specified Sources of Income: 2009

[In thousands (211,254 represents 211,254,000). Persons 15 years old and over as of March of following year. Based on Current Population Survey; see text, Sections 1 and 13, and Appendix III. N.e.c.=not elsewhere classified]

Source of income	Total persons with income	Under 65 years	65 years and over	White [1]	Black [2]	Hispanic origin [3]
Total..........................	211,254	173,947	37,307	173,161	23,973	26,954
Earnings..........................	154,906	147,268	7,638	127,017	16,956	21,795
Wages and salary....................	145,725	139,177	6,549	119,035	16,400	20,536
Nonfarm self-employment..............	11,887	10,816	1,071	10,296	803	1,486
Farm self-employment.................	1,920	1,686	234	1,728	115	102
Unemployment compensation............	12,960	12,501	458	10,337	1,828	1,784
State or local only...................	12,167	11,751	416	9,700	1,725	1,692
Combinations.......................	793	750	42	637	103	92
Workers' compensation................	1,517	1,364	153	1,221	199	228
State payments.....................	550	498	52	439	78	98
Employment insurance................	593	542	51	469	77	88
Own insurance......................	40	40	–	34	5	1
Other..............................	398	338	60	335	43	59
Social Security.......................	43,630	10,580	33,050	37,383	4,451	3,106
SSI (Supplemental Security Income).....	5,460	4,334	1,127	3,557	1,445	819
Public Assistance, Total...............	2,028	1,973	55	1,204	647	454
TANF/Welfare (AFDC) only [4]..........	1,377	1,352	25	806	468	334
Other assistance only................	607	578	30	368	166	112
Both..............................	44	44	–	30	13	8
Veterans' benefits....................	2,771	1,662	1,109	2,284	372	180
Disability only......................	1,690	1,163	527	1,413	215	112
Survivors only......................	235	44	191	195	24	18
Pension only.......................	555	255	300	438	94	29
Education only......................	62	62	–	43	13	8
Other only.........................	104	62	43	88	13	4
Combinations.......................	124	77	47	107	12	9
Means-tested.......................	541	320	221	429	90	36
Nonmeans-tested....................	2,229	1,342	887	1,855	282	144
Survivors benefits [5].................	2,918	900	2,018	2,612	199	117
Company or union...................	1,344	293	1,051	1,216	91	57
Federal government.................	300	73	228	244	44	4
Military retirement..................	188	38	150	161	15	6
Disability Benefits [5].................	1,546	1,358	187	1,233	220	205
Workers' compensation..............	114	90	24	81	23	22
Company or union...................	378	340	38	317	43	35
Federal government.................	116	86	30	93	18	15
Military retirement..................	56	50	6	41	14	5
State or local government............	301	276	26	224	52	51
Pension Income [5]...................	16,637	5,073	11,564	14,611	1,445	632
Company or union retirement.........	11,307	2,998	8,309	10,035	920	424
Federal government retirement........	1,768	565	1,204	1,503	179	76
Military retirement..................	1,210	653	557	1,013	147	70
State or local government retirement....	4,496	1,820	2,676	3,895	431	197
Property Income [5]..................	94,476	74,313	20,162	82,926	5,704	5,641
Interest...........................	88,449	69,549	18,900	77,690	5,324	5,191
Dividends..........................	29,778	23,059	6,719	26,973	1,082	974
Rents, royalties, estates or trusts......	10,802	7,969	2,832	9,572	527	717
Educational Assistance [5]............	8,634	8,601	33	6,483	1,436	1,046
Pell grant only......................	2,547	2,542	5	1,769	588	394
Other government only...............	1,363	1,356	7	999	255	174
Scholarships only...................	2,353	2,346	7	1,892	250	247
Child support........................	4,826	4,785	41	3,679	921	660
Alimony............................	349	301	48	316	14	35
Financial assistance from outside the household......	2,305	2,170	135	1,799	300	257
Other income, n.e.c...................	1,105	912	193	896	103	79
Combinations of income types:						
Government transfer payments..................	69,319	34,752	34,567	56,750	9,044	6,629
Public assistance or SSI or both.................	7,228	6,064	1,164	4,605	2,003	1,225

– Represents or rounds to zero. [1] Beginning with the 2003, CPS respondents could choose one or more races. For example, "White" refers to people who reported White and did not report any other race category. The use of this single-race population does not imply that it is the preferred method of presenting or analyzing data. Information on people who reported more than one race, such as "Asian and Black or African American," is available from Census 2000 through American FactFinder. [2] "Black" refers to people who reported Black and did not report any other race category. [3] Persons of Hispanic origin may be of any race. [4] TANF— Temporary Assistance for Needy Families Program; AFDC—Aid to Families With Dependent Children Program. [5] Includes other sources not shown separately. [6] Includes estates and trusts reported as survivor benefits.

Source: U.S. Census Bureau: "Table PINC-09. Source of Income in 2009—Number With Income and Mean Income of Specified Type in 2009 of People 15 Years Old and Over, by Race, Hispanic Origin and Sex," published October 2010; <http://www.census .gov/hhes/www/cpstables/032010/perinc/new09_006.htm>.

Table 543. Persons Living in Households Receiving Selected Noncash Benefits: 2009

[In thousands (303,820 represents 303,820,000), except percent. Persons, as of March 2010, who lived with someone (a nonrelative or a relative) who received aid. Not every person tallied here received the aid themselves. Persons living in households receiving more than one type of aid are counted only once. Excludes members of the Armed Forces except those living off post or with their families on post. Population controls for 2009 based on Census 2000 and an expanded sample of households. Based on Current Population Survey; see text, Section 1 and Appendix III]

Age, sex, and race	Total	In household that received means-tested assistance [1]		In household that received means-tested cash assistance		In household that received food stamps		In household in which one or more persons were covered by Medicaid		Lived in public or authorized housing	
		Number	Percent	Number	Percent	Number	Percent	Number	Percent	Number	Percent
Total.............	303,820	92,005	30.3	19,608	6.5	34,377	11.3	74,457	24.5	11,098	3.7
Under 18 years	74,579	33,565	45.0	5,666	7.6	13,917	18.7	27,748	37.2	3,989	5.3
18 to 24 years	29,313	9,886	33.7	1,985	6.8	3,786	12.9	8,119	27.7	1,251	4.3
25 to 34 years	41,085	13,081	31.8	2,337	5.7	5,230	12.7	10,839	26.4	1,366	3.3
35 to 44 years	40,447	11,519	28.5	2,131	5.3	3,836	9.5	9,035	22.3	1,027	2.5
45 to 54 years	44,387	10,174	22.9	2,754	6.2	3,450	7.8	8,051	18.1	1,070	2.4
55 to 59 years	19,172	3,693	19.3	1,425	7.4	1,227	6.4	2,949	15.4	475	2.5
60 to 64 years	16,223	2,921	18.0	1,120	6.9	941	5.8	2,302	14.2	427	2.6
65 years and over	38,613	7,167	18.6	2,190	5.7	1,990	5.2	5,414	14.0	1,493	3.9
65 to 74 years	20,956	3,901	18.6	1,229	5.9	1,127	5.4	3,046	14.5	727	3.5
75 years and over ...	17,657	3,266	18.5	962	5.4	862	4.9	2,367	13.4	766	4.3
Male..............	149,237	43,163	28.9	9,087	6.1	15,242	10.2	34,954	23.4	4,388	2.9
Female.............	154,582	48,842	31.6	10,521	6.8	19,135	12.4	39,503	25.6	6,710	4.3
White alone [2]........	242,047	64,190	26.5	12,420	5.1	21,966	9.1	52,480	21.7	5,618	2.3
Black alone [2]........	38,556	19,606	50.9	5,252	13.6	9,666	25.1	15,197	39.4	4,445	11.5
Asian alone [2]........	14,005	3,907	27.9	788	5.6	801	5.7	3,254	23.2	353	2.5
Hispanic [3]...........	48,811	26,037	53.3	4,246	8.7	9,200	18.8	21,359	43.8	2,311	4.7
White alone, Non-Hispanic [2]......	197,164	40,398	20.5	8,688	4.4	13,664	6.9	32,967	16.7	3,667	1.9

[1] Means-tested assistance includes means-tested cash assistance, food stamps, Medicaid, and public or authorized housing.
[2] Refers to people who reported specific race and did not report any other race category. [3] People of Hispanic origin may be of any race.
Source: U.S. Census Bureau, Current Population Reports, P60-238. See also <http://www.census.gov/prod/2010pubs/p60-238.pdf>.

Table 544. Social Security—Covered Employment, Earnings, and Contribution Rates: 1990 to 2010

[164.4 represents 164,400,000. Includes Puerto Rico, Virgin Islands, American Samoa, and Guam. Represents all reported employment. Data are estimated. OASDHI = Old-age, survivors, disability, and health insurance; SMI = Supplementary medical insurance]

Item	Unit	1990	1995	2000	2005	2006	2007	2008	2009	2010
Workers with insured status [1]	Million ...	164.4	173.6	185.7	195.9	198.2	200.6	202.7	204.6	206.5
Male......................	Million ...	86.7	90.6	96.0	100.4	101.4	102.4	103.4	104.2	105.0
Female....................	Million ...	77.7	83.0	89.7	95.6	96.8	98.2	99.4	100.4	101.4
Under 25 years	Million ...	21.2	18.9	20.8	20.1	20.1	20.1	20.0	19.7	19.4
25 to 34 years	Million ...	41.6	39.4	36.6	36.4	36.5	36.8	37.3	37.8	38.2
35 to 44 years	Million ...	36.4	40.7	42.6	41.0	40.6	39.9	39.3	38.7	38.2
45 to 54 years	Million ...	23.0	29.7	36.0	40.4	41.2	41.8	42.3	42.6	42.6
55 to 59 years	Million ...	8.9	9.9	12.4	16.3	16.8	17.0	17.5	18.0	18.6
60 to 64 years	Million ...	8.7	8.6	9.6	11.9	12.6	13.5	14.1	14.7	15.5
65 to 69 years	Million ...	8.1	8.0	7.9	8.9	9.3	9.8	10.3	10.7	11.1
70 years and over	Million ...	16.5	18.5	19.8	20.9	21.2	21.5	21.9	22.4	22.8
Workers reported with—										
Taxable earnings [2]	Million ...	133	141	154	159	161	163	162	158	158
Maximum earnings [2]	Million ...	8	8	10	10	10	10	10	8	9
Earnings in covered employment [2]	Bil. dol ...	2,716	3,408	4,842	5,700	6,050	6,390	6,507	6,182	6,326
Reported taxable [2]...........	Bil. dol ...	2,223	2,755	3,799	4,488	4,752	4,970	5,141	4,991	5,033
Percent of total.............	Percent ..	86.8	85.7	82.8	83.7	83.4	82.3	83.5	85.3	85.3
Average per worker:										
Total earnings [2]	Dollars ...	20,413	24,194	31,343	35,935	37,564	39,225	40,072	39,200	40,099
Taxable earnings [2]	Dollars ...	16,702	19,557	24,589	28,296	29,504	30,506	31,656	31,648	31,904
Annual maximum taxable earnings [3]...................	Dollars ...	51,300	61,200	76,200	90,000	94,200	97,500	102,000	106,800	106,800
Contribution rates for OASDHI: [4]										
Each employer and employee ..	Percent ..	7.65	7.65	7.65	7.65	7.65	7.65	7.65	7.65	7.65
Self-employed [5].............	Percent ..	15.30	15.30	15.30	15.30	15.30	15.30	15.30	15.30	15.30
SMI, monthly premium [6]	Dollars ...	28.60	46.10	45.50	78.20	88.50	93.50	96.40	96.40	110.50

[1] Estimated number fully insured for retirement and/or survivor benefits as of end of year. [2] Includes self-employment. Averages per worker computed with unrounded earnings and worker amounts and may not agree with rounded table and amounts.
[3] Beginning 1995, upper limit on earnings subject to HI taxes was repealed. [4] As of January 1, 2006, each employee and employer pays 7.65 percent and the self-employed pay 15.3 percent. [5] Self-employed pays 15.3 percent and half of the tax is deductible for income tax purposes and for computing self-employment income subject to social security tax. [6] As of January 1.
Source: U.S. Social Security Administration, *Annual Statistical Supplement to the Social Security Bulletin*, March 2011, and unpublished data. See also <http://www.ssa.gov/policy/docs/statcomps/supplement/2010>.

Table 545. Social Security (OASDI)—Benefits by Type of Beneficiary: 1990 to 2010

[39,832 represents 39,832,000. A person eligible to receive more than one type of benefit is generally classified or counted only once as a retired-worker beneficiary. OASDI = Old-age, survivors, and disability insurance. See also headnote, Table 546, and Appendix III]

Type of beneficiary	1990	1995	2000	2004	2005	2006	2007	2008	2009	2010
Number of benefits [1] (1,000)	**39,832**	**43,387**	**45,415**	**47,688**	**48,434**	**49,123**	**49,865**	**50,898**	**52,523**	**54,032**
Retired workers [2] (1,000)...........	24,838	26,673	28,499	29,953	30,461	30,976	31,528	32,274	33,514	34,593
Disabled workers [3] (1,000)............	3,011	4,185	5,042	6,198	6,519	6,807	7,099	7,427	7,788	8,204
Wives and husbands [2,4] (1,000)	3,367	3,290	2,963	2,722	2,680	2,632	2,585	2,525	2,502	2,477
Children (1,000)......................	3,187	3,734	3,803	3,986	4,025	4,041	4,051	4,132	4,231	4,313
Under age 18................	2,497	2,956	2,976	3,097	3,130	3,133	3,120	3,118	3,158	3,209
Disabled children [5]...............	600	686	729	759	769	777	795	871	921	949
Students [6]	89	92	98	130	127	131	136	142	152	155
Of retired workers	422	442	459	483	488	490	494	525	561	580
Of deceased workers	1,776	1,884	1,878	1,905	1,903	1,899	1,892	1,915	1,921	1,913
Of disabled workers	989	1,409	1,466	1,599	1,633	1,652	1,665	1,692	1,748	1,820
Widowed mothers [7] (1,000)............	304	275	203	184	178	171	165	160	160	158
Widows and widowers [2,8] (1,000)......	5,111	5,226	4,901	4,643	4,569	4,494	4,436	4,380	4,327	4,286
Parents [2] (1,000)	6	4	3	2	2	2	2	2	2	2
Special benefits [9] (1,000)...........	7	1	(Z)	(Z)	(Z)	(Z)	(Z)	(Z)	(Z)	(Z)
AVERAGE MONTHLY BENEFIT, CURRENT DOLLARS										
Retired workers [2]	603	720	844	955	1,002	1,044	1,079	1,153	1,164	1,176
Retired worker and wife [2]............	1,027	1,221	1,420	1,586	1,660	1,726	1,776	1,894	1,913	1,930
Disabled workers [3].................	587	682	786	894	938	978	1,004	1,063	1,064	1,068
Wives and husbands [2,4].............	298	354	416	464	485	502	516	551	556	561
Children of retired workers	259	322	395	465	493	518	538	568	570	577
Children of deceased workers	406	469	550	625	656	684	704	745	747	752
Children of disabled workers	164	183	228	265	279	290	299	318	318	318
Widowed mothers [7]	409	478	595	689	725	757	782	835	842	849
Widows and widowers, nondisabled [2]	556	680	810	920	967	1,008	1,040	1,112	1,124	1,134
Parents [2]	482	591	704	810	851	892	918	979	988	998
Special benefits [9].................	167	192	217	238	247	256	261	276	276	276
AVERAGE MONTHLY BENEFIT, CONSTANT (2010) DOLLARS [10]										
Retired workers [2]	988	1,028	1,064	1,100	1,116	1,134	1,126	1,202	1,182	1,176
Retired worker and wife [2]............	1,682	1,744	1,789	1,827	1,849	1,875	1,854	1,975	1,942	1,930
Disabled workers [3].................	962	974	991	1,030	1,045	1,062	1,048	1,109	1,081	1,068
Wives and husbands [2,4].............	488	506	524	534	540	546	538	575	564	561
Children of deceased workers...........	665	670	693	720	731	743	735	777	759	752
Widowed mothers [7]	670	683	750	794	807	822	816	871	854	849
Widows and widowers, nondisabled [2]	911	971	1,021	1,060	1,077	1,095	1,086	1,160	1,141	1,134
Number of benefits awarded (1,000)	**3,717**	**3,882**	**4,290**	**4,459**	**4,672**	**4,621**	**4,711**	**5,135**	**5,728**	**5,697**
Retired workers [2]	1,665	1,609	1,961	1,883	2,000	1,999	2,036	2,279	2,740	2,634
Disabled workers [3].................	468	646	622	796	830	799	805	877	971	1,027
Wives and husbands [2,4].............	379	322	385	367	379	378	364	395	429	409
Children	695	809	777	859	908	897	902	961	1,008	1,045
Widowed mothers [7]	58	52	40	40	38	36	34	33	33	32
Widows and widowers [2,8].............	452	445	505	514	517	512	570	590	547	550
Parents [2]	(Z)	(Z)	(Z)	(Z)	(Z)	(Z)	(Z)	(Z)	(Z)	(Z)
Special benefits [9].................	(Z)	(Z)	(Z)	(Z)	(Z)	(Z)	(Z)	(Z)	(Z)	(Z)
BENEFIT PAYMENTS DURING YEAR (bil. dol.)										
Total [11]	**247.8**	**332.6**	**407.6**	**493.3**	**520.8**	**552.8**	**585.0**	**615.4**	**675.5**	**701.6**
Monthly benefits [12].................	247.6	332.4	407.4	493.1	520.6	552.6	584.8	615.2	675.3	701.4
Retired workers [2].................	156.8	205.3	253.5	304.3	321.7	342.9	364.3	384.0	424.0	443.4
Disabled workers [3].................	22.1	36.6	49.8	71.7	78.4	85.0	91.3	98.1	109.5	115.1
Wives and husbands [2,4].............	14.5	17.9	19.4	20.6	20.5	21.5	22.1	22.6	24.2	24.6
Children	12.0	16.1	19.3	23.3	24.5	25.8	27.0	28.2	30.2	30.7
Under age 18....................	9.0	11.9	14.1	17.0	17.9	18.8	19.5	20.1	21.2	21.4
Disabled children [5]...............	2.5	3.6	4.6	5.5	5.8	6.1	6.5	6.9	7.8	8.0
Students [6]	0.5	0.6	0.7	0.9	0.8	1.0	1.0	1.1	1.2	1.3
Of retired workers	1.3	1.7	2.1	2.7	2.9	3.1	3.3	3.5	3.9	4.1
Of deceased workers...............	8.6	10.7	12.5	14.5	15.1	15.8	16.5	17.0	18.1	18.0
Of disabled workers...............	2.2	3.7	4.7	6.1	6.5	6.9	7.3	7.7	8.2	8.5
Widowed mothers [7]	1.4	1.6	1.4	1.5	1.5	1.6	1.6	1.6	1.6	1.6
Widows and widowers [2,8].............	40.7	54.8	63.9	71.7	73.4	75.9	78.5	80.7	85.6	86.0
Parents [2]	(Z)	(Z)	(Z)	(Z)	(Z)	(Z)	(Z)	(Z)	(Z)	(Z)
Special benefits [9].................	(Z)	(Z)	(Z)	(Z)	(Z)	(Z)	(Z)	(Z)	(Z)	(Z)
Lump sum	0.2	0.2	0.2	0.2	0.2	0.2	0.2	0.2	0.2	0.2

Z Fewer than 500 or less than $50 million. [1] Number of benefit payments in current-payment status, i.e., actually being made at a specified time with no deductions or with deductions amounting to less than a month's benefit. [2] 62 years and over. [3] Disabled workers under age 65. [4] Includes wife beneficiaries with entitled children in their care and entitled divorced wives. [5] 18 years old and over. Disability began before age 18. [6] Full-time students aged 18 and 19. [7] Includes surviving divorced mothers with entitled children in their care and widowed fathers with entitled children in their care. [8] Includes widows aged 60–61,surviving divorced wives aged 60 and over, disabled widows and widowers aged 50 and over; and widowers aged 60–61. [9] Benefits for persons aged 72 and over not insured under regular or transitional provisions of Social Security Act. [10] Constant dollar figures are based on the consumer price index (CPI-U) for December as published by the U.S. Bureau of Labor Statistics. [11] Represents total disbursements of benefit checks by the U.S. Department of the Treasury during the years specified. [12] Distribution by type estimated.

Source: U.S. Social Security Administration, *Annual Statistical Supplement to the Social Security Bulletin*, March 2011, and unpublished data. See also <http://www.ssa.gov/policy/docs/statcomps/supplement/2010>.

Table 546. Social Security—Beneficiaries, Annual Payments, and Average Monthly Benefit, 1990 to 2010, and by State and Other Areas, 2010

[Number of beneficiaries in current-payment status (39,832 represents 39,832,000) and average monthly benefit as of December. Data based on 10-percent sample of administrative records. See also headnote, Table 545, and Appendix III]

Year, state, and other area	Number of beneficiaries (1,000)				Annual payments [2] (mil. dol.)				Average monthly benefit (dol.)		
	Total	Retired workers and dependents [1]	Survivors	Disabled workers and dependents	Total	Retired workers and dependents [1]	Survivors	Disabled workers and dependents	Retired workers [3]	Disabled workers	Widows and widowers [4]
1990.............	39,832	28,369	7,197	4,266	247,796	172,042	50,951	24,803	603	587	557
2000.............	45,417	31,761	6,981	6,675	407,431	274,645	77,848	54,938	845	787	810
2005.............	48,446	33,488	6,650	8,307	520,561	345,094	90,073	85,394	1,002	938	967
2007.............	49,865	34,454	6,495	8,916	584,764	389,123	96,555	99,086	1,079	1,004	1,040
2008.............	50,898	35,169	6,456	9,273	615,152	409,503	99,348	106,301	1,153	1,063	1,112
2009.............	52,523	36,419	6,410	9,694	685,299	451,579	105,380	118,329	1,164	1,064	1,124
2010, total [5]	54,032	37,489	6,358	10,184	701,436	471,505	105,740	124,191	1,176	1,068	1,134
United States	52,641	36,570	6,135	9,936	689,916	464,961	103,299	121,656	(NA)	(NA)	(NA)
Alabama	1,012	608	133	271	12,716	7,456	2,045	3,215	1,144	1,048	1,052
Alaska	78	53	10	15	959	632	145	182	1,120	1,057	1,087
Arizona	1,068	779	111	178	14,128	9,982	1,876	2,270	1,200	1,109	1,174
Arkansas	635	389	77	169	7,749	4,649	1,152	1,948	1,109	1,018	1,049
California	4,979	3,624	548	807	64,379	44,796	9,298	10,285	1,166	1,091	1,150
Colorado	693	503	76	114	8,931	6,221	1,298	1,412	1,161	1,073	1,154
Connecticut	622	464	62	95	8,903	6,507	1,175	1,221	1,287	1,106	1,271
Delaware	172	123	18	32	2,395	1,662	318	415	1,251	1,128	1,233
District of Columbia ..	74	51	9	15	876	584	125	167	1,056	950	962
Florida	3,784	2,807	384	594	49,163	35,295	6,512	7,356	1,169	1,075	1,161
Georgia	1,468	977	183	308	18,714	12,101	2,852	3,761	1,157	1,067	1,096
Hawaii	228	178	22	28	2,940	2,224	362	354	1,164	1,099	1,106
Idaho	269	192	29	49	3,398	2,341	488	569	1,146	1,042	1,164
Illinois	2,033	1,443	250	340	27,533	18,847	4,427	4,259	1,211	1,091	1,206
Indiana	1,192	813	145	234	16,192	10,827	2,540	2,825	1,235	1,073	1,216
Iowa	584	427	69	87	7,662	5,409	1,224	1,029	1,172	1,019	1,172
Kansas	489	346	58	85	6,523	4,500	1,008	1,015	1,204	1,039	1,206
Kentucky	894	522	120	252	11,047	6,223	1,848	2,976	1,120	1,043	1,049
Louisiana	791	470	137	184	9,642	5,421	2,077	2,144	1,099	1,048	1,045
Maine	300	199	31	70	3,634	2,344	501	789	1,089	988	1,092
Maryland	850	612	99	140	11,445	7,963	1,699	1,783	1,208	1,098	1,168
Massachusetts	1,141	790	115	236	15,046	10,174	2,038	2,834	1,188	1,055	1,181
Michigan	1,965	1,336	233	395	27,354	18,175	4,201	4,978	1,268	1,124	1,231
Minnesota	882	647	93	142	11,694	8,327	1,644	1,723	1,197	1,058	1,171
Mississippi	597	354	82	160	7,201	4,182	1,177	1,842	1,100	1,018	1,017
Missouri	1,166	778	138	250	14,991	9,753	2,269	2,969	1,160	1,040	1,145
Montana	193	139	22	32	2,403	1,662	367	374	1,116	1,019	1,134
Nebraska	309	224	36	49	4,000	2,803	626	571	1,159	1,011	1,162
Nevada	408	301	40	67	5,352	3,796	672	884	1,175	1,129	1,175
New Hampshire	255	177	23	55	3,410	2,342	411	657	1,221	1,085	1,218
New Jersey	1,472	1,085	156	231	21,276	15,264	2,899	3,113	1,300	1,172	1,247
New Mexico	360	244	43	72	4,354	2,852	653	849	1,102	1,025	1,052
New York	3,281	2,318	348	615	44,751	30,813	6,128	7,810	1,235	1,108	1,189
North Carolina	1,757	1,190	188	379	22,604	15,005	2,942	4,657	1,168	1,061	1,097
North Dakota	120	87	17	16	1,487	1,014	284	189	1,097	993	1,087
Ohio	2,125	1,450	289	385	27,896	18,355	5,007	4,534	1,180	1,037	1,165
Oklahoma	705	466	91	149	8,895	5,680	1,451	1,764	1,135	1,036	1,109
Oregon	712	523	73	117	9,367	6,621	1,290	1,456	1,181	1,070	1,193
Pennsylvania	2,578	1,803	310	465	34,820	23,636	5,522	5,662	1,212	1,072	1,190
Rhode Island	204	142	19	42	2,674	1,840	329	505	1,183	1,033	1,180
South Carolina	925	617	105	202	11,915	7,766	1,633	2,516	1,171	1,080	1,089
South Dakota	154	113	19	21	1,880	1,328	305	247	1,095	995	1,074
Tennessee	1,252	814	154	284	15,913	10,129	2,406	3,378	1,159	1,039	1,096
Texas	3,440	2,301	469	670	43,212	27,797	7,506	7,909	1,146	1,053	1,099
Utah	324	233	38	54	4,197	2,932	636	629	1,187	1,057	1,208
Vermont	129	90	13	26	1,647	1,134	219	294	1,175	999	1,146
Virginia	1,285	890	147	248	16,755	11,259	2,430	3,066	1,180	1,076	1,117
Washington	1,090	786	112	192	14,679	10,272	1,996	2,411	1,223	1,079	1,214
West Virginia	444	261	65	118	5,749	3,191	1,065	1,493	1,159	1,102	1,098
Wisconsin	1,062	765	114	182	14,203	9,986	2,031	2,186	1,207	1,061	1,199
Wyoming	91	66	10	14	1,193	838	179	176	1,176	1,060	1,176
Puerto Rico	800	462	116	224	7,195	3,710	1,206	2,279	786	940	693
Guam.............	14	9	3	2	123	74	29	20	788	913	772
American Samoa....	6	2	1	2	47	18	13	16	770	831	671
Virgin Islands.......	19	15	2	2	217	160	29	28	1,028	1,071	893
Northern Mariana Islands...........	3	2	1	(Z)	17	10	5	2	652	702	538
Abroad............	548	429	97	17	3,921	2,572	1,159	190	628	979	699

NA Not available. Z Less than 500. [1] Includes special benefits for persons aged 72 years and over not insured under regular or transitional provisions of Social Security Act. [2] Unnegotiated checks not deducted. 1990 and 1995 include lump-sum payments to survivors of deceased workers. [3] Excludes persons with special benefits. [4] Nondisabled only. [5] Includes those with state or area unknown.

Source: U.S. Social Security Administration, Annual Statistical Supplement to the Social Security Bulletin, March 2011. See also <http://www.ssa.gov/policy/docs/statcomps/supplement/2010>.

Table 547. Social Security Trust Funds: 1990 to 2010

[In billions of dollars (272.4 represents $272,400,000,000)]

Type of trust fund	1990	1995	2000	2005	2006	2007	2008	2009	2010
Old-age and survivors insurance (OASI):									
Net contribution income [1,2]	272.4	310.1	433.0	520.7	534.8	560.9	574.6	570.4	546.9
Interest received [2]	16.4	32.8	57.5	84.0	91.8	97.0	105.3	107.9	108.2
Benefit payments [3]	223.0	291.6	352.7	435.4	454.5	489.1	509.3	557.2	577.4
Assets, end of year	214.2	458.5	931.0	1,663.0	1,844.3	2,023.6	2,202.9	2,336.8	2,429.0
Disability insurance (DI):									
Net contribution income [1,2]	28.7	54.7	71.8	87.2	90.8	95.2	97.8	96.9	92.9
Interest received [2]	0.9	2.2	6.9	10.3	10.6	13.2	11.0	10.5	9.3
Benefit payments [3]	24.8	40.9	55.0	85.4	91.7	95.9	106.0	118.3	124.2
Assets, end of year	11.1	37.6	118.5	195.6	203.8	214.9	215.8	203.6	179.9

[1] Includes deposits by states and deductions for refund of estimated employee-tax overpayment. Includes government contributions on deemed wage credits for military service 1957–2001. Includes taxation of benefits. [2] In 1990, includes interest on advance tax transfers. Includes interest on reimbursement for unnegotiated checks. [3] Includes payments for vocational rehabilitation services furnished to disabled persons receiving benefits because of their disabilities. Amounts reflect deductions for unnegotiated benefit checks.

Source: U.S. Social Security Administration, *Annual Report of Board of Trustees, OASI, DI, HI, and SMI Trust Funds*; <http://www.ssa.gov/OACT/TR/2010/index.html>. Also published in *Social Security Bulletin*, quarterly.

Table 548. Public Employee Retirement Systems—Participants and Finances: 1980 to 2009

[4,629 represents 4,629,000. For fiscal year of retirement system, except data for the Thrift Savings Plan are for calendar year. For a definition of defined benefit, see headnote, Table 552]

Retirement plan	Unit	1980	1990	2000	2004	2005	2006	2007	2008	2009, proj.
TOTAL PARTICIPANTS [1]										
Federal retirement systems:										
Defined benefit:										
Civil Service Retirement System	1,000	4,629	4,167	3,256	3,035	2,958	2,878	2,789	2,650	2,575
Federal Employees Retirement System [2]	1,000	(X)	1,180	1,935	2,104	2,196	2,290	2,371	2,572	2,748
Military Service Retirement System [3]	1,000	3,380	3,763	3,397	3,545	3,536	3,560	3,585	3,657	2,196
Thrift Savings Plan [4]	1,000	(X)	1,625	2,500	3,400	3,600	3,700	3,900	4,000	3,676
State and local retirement systems [5,6]	1,000	(NA)	16,858	16,834	17,890	17,932	18,484	18,583	19,097	(NA)
ACTIVE PARTICIPANTS										
Federal retirement systems:										
Defined benefit:										
Civil Service Retirement System	1,000	2,700	1,826	978	788	722	650	580	477	426
Federal Employees Retirement System [2]	1,000	(X)	1,136	1,668	1,882	1,952	2,014	2,066	2,195	2,330
Military Service Retirement System [3]	1,000	2,050	2,130	1,437	1,480	1,445	1,443	1,438	1,461	1,480
Thrift Savings Plan [4]	1,000	(X)	1,419	1,900	2,500	2,800	2,600	2,600	2,700	2,800
State and local retirement systems [5,6]	1,000	(NA)	11,345	13,917	14,181	14,116	14,529	14,422	14,701	(NA)
ASSETS										
Total	Bil. dol.	258	1,047	2,950	3,472	3,697	4,023	4,533	4,380	(NA)
Federal retirement systems	Bil. dol.	73	326	782	977	1,039	1,111	1,156	1,190	1,292
Defined benefit	Bil. dol.	73	318	684	825	866	904	924	987	1,048
Civil Service Retirement System	Bil. dol.	73	220	395	433	440	442	426	423	422
Federal Employees Retirement System [2]	Bil. dol.	(X)	18	126	204	228	254	280	311	348
Military Service Retirement System [3]	Bil. dol.	(7)	80	163	188	198	208	218	253	278
Thrift Savings Plan [4]	Bil. dol.	(X)	8	98	152	173	207	232	203	244
State and local retirement systems [5]	Bil. dol.	185	721	2,168	2,495	2,658	2,912	3,377	3,190	(NA)
CONTRIBUTIONS										
Total	Bil. dol.	83	103	143	187	189	205	224	260	(NA)
Federal retirement systems	Bil. dol.	19	61	78	95	98	108	117	141	148
Defined benefit	Bil. dol.	19	59	69	79	82	88	96	119	125
Civil Service Retirement System	Bil. dol.	19	28	33	34	33	34	36	35	36
Federal Employees Retirement System [2]	Bil. dol.	(X)	4	8	13	13	15	17	19	20
Military Service Retirement System [3]	Bil. dol.	(7)	27	28	32	38	39	43	65	69
Thrift Savings Plan [4]	Bil. dol.	(X)	2	9	16	16	20	21	22	23
State and local retirement systems [5]	Bil. dol.	64	42	65	92	91	97	107	119	(NA)
BENEFITS										
Total	Bil. dol.	39	89	172	226	240	258	282	295	(NA)
Federal retirement systems	Bil. dol.	27	53	81	93	99	106	120	120	124
Defined benefit	Bil. dol.	27	53	78	89	94	99	112	112	117
Civil Service Retirement System	Bil. dol.	15	31	44	50	52	55	57	59	63
Federal Employees Retirement System [2]	Bil. dol.	(X)	(Z)	1	2	3	3	4	4	5
Military Service Retirement System [3]	Bil. dol.	12	22	33	37	39	41	43	49	49
Thrift Savings Plan [4]	Bil. dol.	(X)	(Z)	3	4	5	7	8	8	7
State and local retirement systems [5]	Bil. dol.	12	36	91	133	141	152	162	175	(NA)

NA Not available. X Not applicable. Z Less than $500 million. [1] Includes active, separated vested, retired employees and survivors. [2] The Federal Employees Retirement System was established June 6, 1986. [3] Includes nondisability and disability retirees, surviving families, and all active personnel with the exception of active reserves. [4] The Thrift Savings Plan (a defined contribution plan) was established April 1, 1987. [5] Excludes state and local plans that are fully supported by employee contributions. [6] Not adjusted for double counting of individuals participating in more than one plan. [7] The Military Retirement System was unfunded until October 1, 1984.

Source: Employee Benefit Research Institute, Washington, DC, *EBRI Databook on Employee Benefits*, 12th ed., and unpublished data (copyright). See also <http://www.ebri.org>.

Table 549. Federal Civil Service Retirement: 1990 to 2010

[As of September 30 or for year ending September 30 (2,945 represents 2,945,000). Covers both Civil Service Retirement System and Federal Employees Retirement System]

Item	Unit	1990	1995	2000	2005	2006	2007	2008	2009	2010
Employees covered [1]	1,000....	2,945	2,668	2,764	2,674	2,611	2,618	2,613	2,672	2,756
Annuitants, total	1,000....	**2,143**	**2,311**	**2,376**	**2,433**	**2,449**	**2,463**	**2,471**	**2,481**	**2,479**
Age and service	1,000....	1,288	1,441	1,501	1,568	1,602	1,625	1,643	1,662	1,674
Disability	1,000....	297	263	242	229	226	222	218	216	210
Survivors	1,000....	558	607	633	636	621	616	610	603	595
Receipts, total [2]	Mil. dol ..	**52,689**	**65,684**	**75,967**	**83,691**	**87,164**	**89,860**	**90,892**	**93,061**	**95,662**
Employee contributions	Mil. dol ..	4,501	4,498	4,637	4,353	4,304	4,205	4,111	4,083	4,015
Federal government contributions	Mil. dol ..	27,368	33,130	37,722	43,093	46,427	48,397	49,547	51,789	55,019
Disbursements, total [3]	Mil. dol ..	**31,416**	**38,435**	**45,194**	**54,790**	**57,983**	**78,146**	**63,687**	**67,669**	**69,452**
Age and service annuitants [4]	Mil. dol ..	26,495	32,070	37,546	46,029	48,895	68,776	54,202	57,782	59,594
Survivors	Mil. dol ..	4,366	5,864	7,210	8,338	8,642	8,905	9,011	9,463	9,532
Average monthly benefit:										
Age and service	Dollars...	1,369	1,643	1,885	2,240	2,363	2,473	2,550	2,710	2,723
Disability	Dollars...	1,008	1,164	1,240	1,327	1,366	1,394	1,409	1,469	1,453
Survivors	Dollars...	653	819	952	1,106	1,157	1,200	1,232	1,309	1,315
Cash and security holdings	Bil. dol...	238.0	366.2	508.1	660.8	690.0	701.7	728.9	754.3	780.4

[1] Excludes employees in leave-without-pay status. [2] Includes interest on investments. [3] Includes refunds, death claims, and administration. [4] Includes disability annuitants.

Source: U.S. Office of Personnel Management, *Civil Service Retirement and Disability Trust Fund Annual Report.*

Table 550. State and Local Government Retirement Systems—Beneficiaries and Finances: 1990 to 2008

[In billions of dollars (111.3 represents $111,300,000,000), except as indicated. For fiscal years closed during the 12 months ending June 30. Minus sign (–) indicates negative earnings on investment]

Year and level of government	Number of beneficiaries (1,000)	Receipts					Benefits and withdrawals			Cash and security holdings
		Total	Employee contributions	Government contributions State	Local	Earnings on investments	Total	Benefits	Withdrawals	
1990: All systems	4,026	111.3	13.9	14.0	18.6	64.9	38.4	36.0	2.4	721
State-administered	3,232	89.2	11.6	14.0	11.5	52.0	29.6	27.6	2.0	575
Locally administered	794	22.2	2.2	(Z)	7.0	12.9	8.8	8.4	0.4	145
1995: All systems	4,979	148.8	18.6	16.6	24.4	89.2	61.5	58.8	2.7	1,118
State-administered	4,025	123.3	15.7	16.2	15.4	76.0	48.0	45.8	2.2	914
Locally administered	954	25.5	2.9	0.4	9.0	13.3	13.5	13.0	0.5	204
2000: All systems	6,292	297.0	25.0	17.5	22.6	231.9	95.7	91.3	4.4	2,169
State-administered	4,786	247.4	20.7	17.2	16.7	192.8	76.0	72.2	3.8	1,798
Locally administered	1,506	49.7	4.3	0.4	5.9	39.1	19.8	19.1	0.7	371
2005: All systems	6,946	353.5	31.5	24.0	35.7	262.2	156.0	142.1	3.7	2,672
State-administered	5,846	293.4	26.8	23.6	22.1	220.9	126.8	115.2	3.1	2,226
Locally administered	1,100	60.1	4.8	0.4	13.6	41.3	29.3	26.9	0.5	445
2007: All systems	7,464	580.5	34.1	30.6	42.3	473.5	183.0	162.7	5.2	3,377
State-administered	6,353	486.8	29.1	30.0	26.4	401.3	148.4	131.2	4.6	2,819
Locally administered	1,110	93.7	5.0	0.6	15.9	72.2	34.6	31.5	0.7	558
2008: All systems	7,744	79.6	36.9	36.3	45.7	–39.3	193.8	175.4	4.6	3,190
State-administered	6,596	56.4	31.6	35.8	28.1	–39.1	157.4	143.5	3.2	2,664
Locally administered	1,148	23.2	5.3	0.5	17.6	–0.2	36.4	32.0	1.4	526

Z Less than $50 million.

Source: U.S. Census Bureau, through 1990, *Finances of Employee-Retirement Systems of State and Local Governments*, Series GF, No. 2, annual; beginning 2000, "Federal, State, and Local Governments, State and Local Government Public Employee Retirement Systems," <http://www.census.gov/govs/retire>.

Table 551. Percent of Workers Participating in Retirement Benefits by Worker Characteristics: 2005 to 2010

[Based on National Compensation Survey, a sample survey of 10,370 private industry establishments of all sizes, representing over 105 million workers; see Appendix III. Survey covers all 50 states and the District of Columbia. For a definition of defined benefit and defined contribution, see headnote, Table 552. See also Table 656]

Characteristic	Total [1]				Defined benefit				Defined contribution			
	2005	2008	2009	2010	2005	2008	2009	2010	2005	2008	2009	2010
Total	**50**	**51**	**51**	**50**	**21**	**20**	**20**	**19**	**42**	**43**	**43**	**41**
White-collar occupations	61	68	69	68	24	28	28	25	53	60	60	60
Blue-collar occupations	51	52	53	51	26	25	26	26	38	41	41	40
Service occupations	22	25	26	23	7	8	8	7	18	20	21	18
Full-time	60	60	61	59	25	24	24	22	50	51	51	50
Part-time	19	23	22	21	9	10	9	8	14	18	16	15
Union	85	80	82	82	72	67	66	67	43	42	44	44
Nonunion	46	48	48	46	15	15	15	13	41	43	43	41

[1] Total is less than the sum of the individual retirement items because many employees participated in both types of plans.

Source: U.S. Bureau of Labor Statistics, *Employee Benefits in Private Industry in the United States,* March 2011. See also <http://www.bls.gov/ncs/ebs/benefits/2010/ownership_private.htm>.

Table 552. Private Pension Plans—Summary by Type of Plan: 1990 to 2008

[712.3 represents 712,300. **"Pension plan"** is defined by the Employee Retirement Income Security Act (ERISA) as "any plan, fund, or program which was heretofore or is hereafter established or maintained by an employer or an employee organization, or by both, to the extent that such plan (a) provides retirement income to employees, or (b) results in a deferral of income by employees for periods extending to the termination of covered employment or beyond, regardless of the method of calculating the contributions made to the plan, the method of calculating the benefits under the plan, or the method of distributing benefits from the plan." A **defined benefit** plan provides a definite benefit formula for calculating benefit amounts—such as a flat amount per year of service or a percentage of salary times years of service. A **defined contribution** plan is a pension plan in which the contributions are made to an individual account for each employee. The retirement benefit is dependent upon the account balance at retirement. The balance depends upon amounts contributed, investment experience, and, in the case of profit sharing plans, amounts which may be allocated to the account due to forfeitures by terminating employees. Employee Stock Ownership Plans (ESOP) and 401(k) plans are included among defined contribution plans. Data are based on Form 5500 series reports filed with the U.S. Department of Labor and exclude (1) most pension plans qualified under sections 403(b), 457(b) and 457(f) of the Internal Revenue Code, (2) most SARSEP, SEP and SIMPLE IRA plans, (3) unfunded excess benefit plans, (4) most church plans, (5) top hat plans, (6) individual retirement accounts, and (7) governmental plans]

Item	Unit	Total				Defined contribution plan				Defined benefit plan			
		1990	2000	2005	2008	1990	2000	2005	2008	1990	2000	2005	2008
Number of plans [1]	1,000	712.3	735.7	679.1	717.5	599.2	686.9	631.5	669.2	113.1	48.8	47.6	48.4
Total participants [2]	Million ...	76.9	103.3	117.4	124.9	38.6	61.7	75.5	82.5	38.8	41.6	41.9	42.3
Active participants [3] ..	Million ...	61.5	73.1	82.7	86.2	35.6	50.9	62.4	67.3	26.2	22.2	20.3	19.0
Assets [4]	Bil. dol ...	1,674	4,203	5,062	4,704	834	2,216	2,808	2,663	962	1,986	2,254	2,041
Contributions [5]	Bil. dol ...	98.8	231.9	341.4	419.0	80.9	198.5	248.8	311.7	24.7	33.4	92.7	107.3
Benefits [6]	Bil. dol ...	129.4	341.0	354.5	431.1	64.0	213.5	218.0	265.1	66.4	127.5	136.6	166.0

[1] Excludes all plans covering only one participant. [2] Includes active, retired, and separated vested participants not yet in pay status. Also includes double counting of workers in more than one plan. [3] Includes any workers currently in employment covered by a plan and who are earning or retaining credited service under a plan. Also includes any nonvested former employees who have not yet incurred breaks in service. [4] Asset amounts shown exclude funds held by life insurance companies under allocated group insurance contracts for payment of retirement benefits. These excluded funds make up roughly 10 to 15 percent of total private fund assets. [5] Includes both employer and employee contributions. [6] Includes benefits paid directly from trust and premium payments made from plans to insurance carriers. Excludes benefits paid directly by insurance carriers.

Source: U.S. Department of Labor, Employee Benefits Security Administration, *Private Pension Plan Bulletin*. See also <http://www.dol.gov/ebsa/pdf/1975–2008historicaltables.pdf>.

Table. 553. Defined Benefit Retirement Plans—Selected Features: 2009

[In percent. Covers full-time employees in private industry. Based on National Compensation Survey, a sample survey of 3,227 private industry establishments of all sizes, representing over 102 million workers; see Appendix III. For definition of defined benefit, see headnote, Table 552. See also Table 656]

Feature	All workers	Goods producing	Service producing	1 to 99 workers	100 workers or more	Union	Nonunion
Benefit formula:							
Percent of terminal earnings	35	27	37	38	33	22	42
Percent of career earnings	11	3	(NA)	15	(NA)	6	14
Dollar amount formula	24	39	19	17	27	45	(NA)
Percent of contribution formula	6	15	(NA)	11	(NA)	13	(NA)
Cash balance...................	23	13	27	18	25	11	31
Pension equity	(NA)	(NA)	(NA)	(NA)	(NA)	(NA)	(NA)

NA Not available.

Source: U.S. Bureau of Labor Statistics, *National Compensation Survey: Employee Benefits in Private Industry in the United States* and unpublished data.

U.S. Census Bureau, Statistical Abstract of the United States: 2012

Table 554. Percent of U.S. Households Owning Individual Retirement Accounts (IRAs): 2000 to 2010

[Incidence of IRA ownership is based on an annual tracking survey of 3,000 randomly selected, representative U.S. households; see source for details]

Year and characteristic	Any type of IRA [1]	Traditional IRA	Roth IRA	Employer-sponsored IRA [2]	Year and characteristic	Any type of IRA [1]	Traditional IRA	Roth IRA	Employer-sponsored IRA [2]
2000	35.7	28.7	9.2	6.8	2008	40.5	32.1	15.9	8.6
2001	36.2	28.9	9.8	8.0	2009	39.3	31.2	14.5	8.2
2002	34.8	28.2	10.8	7.7	**2010, total [3]**	**41.4**	**32.8**	**16.6**	**8.0**
2003	36.7	29.6	12.5	7.5	Under 35 years	31.0	21.0	15.0	6.0
2004	36.5	29.6	11.6	8.0	35 to 44 years	40.0	27.0	20.0	9.0
2005	37.9	30.0	12.8	7.4	45 to 54 years	47.0	37.0	18.0	11.0
2006	38.3	31.7	13.4	7.7	55 to 64 years	50.0	43.0	22.0	9.0
2007	39.8	32.5	14.9	7.9	65 years and over	41.0	37.0	9.0	5.0

[1] Excludes ownership of Coverdell Education Savings Accounts, which were referred to as Education IRAs before July 2001. [2] Employer-sponsored IRAs include SEP IRAs, SAR-SEP IRAs, and SIMPLE IRAs. [3] Age is based on the age of the sole or co-decisionmaker for household saving and investing.
Source: Investment Company Institute, Washington, DC, Research Fundamentals, "Appendix: Additional Data on IRA Ownership in 2010", Vol. 19, No. 8A, December 2010 (copyright). See also <http://www.ici.org>.

Table 555. Characteristics of U.S. Households Owning Individual Retirement Accounts (IRAs): 2010

[Incidence of IRA ownership is based on an annual tracking survey of 3,000 randomly selected, representative U.S. households; see source for details]

Characteristic	Unit	Households owning IRAs				Households not owning IRAs
		Total [1]	Traditional IRA	Roth IRA	Employer-sponsored [1]	
MEDIAN PER HOUSEHOLD						
Age of household sole or co-decisionmaker for investing	Years	51	53	47	47	47
Household income [2]	Dollars	73,000	75,000	87,000	78,000	35,000
Household financial assets [3]	Dollars	150,000	200,000	200,000	200,000	25,000
Household financial assets in all types of IRAs	Dollars	36,000	50,000	40,000	50,000	(X)
Share of household financial assets in type of IRA indicated	Percent	34	27	10	10	(X)
PERCENT OF HOUSEHOLDS						
Household has defined contribution account or defined benefit plan coverage (total) [4]	Percent	80	82	84	76	50
Defined contribution retirement plan account	Percent	70	71	77	70	41
Defined benefit plan coverage	Percent	47	50	49	36	23
Types of IRAs owned: [4]						
Traditional IRA	Percent	79	100	63	58	(X)
Roth IRA	Percent	40	32	100	38	(X)
Employer-sponsored IRA [1]	Percent	19	14	18	100	(X)

X Not applicable. [1] Employer-sponsored IRAs include SIMPLE IRAs, SEP IRAs, and SAR-SEP IRAs. [2] Total reported is household income before taxes in 2009. [3] Household financial assets include assets in employer-sponsored retirement plans but exclude the household's primary residence. [4] Multiple responses are included.
Source: Investment Company Institute, Washington, DC, *Research Fundamentals*, "Appendix: Additional Data on IRA Ownership in 2010," Vol. 19, No. 8A, December 2010 (copyright). See also <http://www.ici.org>.

Table 556. Percent Distribution of Assets in Individual Retirement Accounts (IRAs) by Type of IRA: 2010

[Incidence of IRA ownership is based on an annual tracking survey of 3,000 randomly selected, representative U.S. households; see source for details]

Assets in type of IRA	Unit	Total assets in IRAs	Type of IRA owned	
			Traditional IRAs	Roth IRAs
PERCENT DISTRIBUTION OF ASSETS IN IRAs				
Less than $10,000.............................	Percent	21	20	36
$10,000 to $24,999	Percent	20	20	29
$25,000 to $49,999	Percent	15	16	14
$50,000 to $99,999	Percent	17	17	12
$100,000 to $249,999	Percent	17	16	7
$250,000 or more	Percent	10	11	2
TOTAL ASSETS IN IRAs				
Mean......................................	Dollars........	100,800	102,000	39,700
Median....................................	Dollars........	36,000	40,000	14,000

Source: Investment Company Institute, Washington, DC, *Research Fundamentals*, "Appendix: Additional Data on IRA Ownership in 2010," Vol. 19, No. 8A, December 2010 (copyright). See also <http://www.ici.org>.

Table 557. 401(k) Plans—Participants, Assets, Contributions, and Benefits by Type of Plan: 2008

Type of plan [1]	Total plans [2]	Total participants (thousands) [3]	Total assets (mil.)	Total contributions (mil.) [4]	Total benefits (mil.) [5]
Total	**511,582**	**73,155**	**2,230,188**	**285,768**	**233,440**
Profit sharing and thrift-savings.........	510,103	71,942	2,172,649	280,210	228,239
Stock bonus........................	280	847	45,495	4,455	4,250
Target benefit.......................	200	13	632	65	58
Money purchase	734	343	11,333	1,014	889
Annuity—403(b)(1)	196	8	48	20	2
Custodial account—403(b)(7)	46	1	22	3	2

[1] About 1 percent of defined contribution plans report more than one plan type. [2] Excludes plans covering only one participant. [3] Includes active, retired, and separated vested participants not yet in pay status. [4] Includes both employer and employee contributions. [5] Amounts shown include benefits paid directly from trust funds and premium payments made by plans to insurance carriers.

Source: U.S. Department of Labor, *Private Pension Plan Bulletin: 2008*, December 2010. See also <http://www.dol.gov/ebsa /PDF/2008pensionplanbulletin.pdf>.

Table 558. State Unemployment Insurance—Summary: 1990 to 2008

[2,522 represents 2,522,000. Includes unemployment compensation for state and local government employees where covered by state law]

Item	Unit	1990	1995	2000	2003	2004	2005	2006	2007	2008
Insured unemployment, average weekly...	1,000	2,522	2,572	2,110	3,531	2,950	2,661	2,475	2,571	3,306
Percent of covered employment [1]	Percent	2.4	2.3	1.7	2.8	2.3	2.1	1.9	2.0	2.5
Percent of civilian unemployed	Percent	35.8	34.7	37.6	40.7	36.8	35.7	35.3	36.3	36.3
Unemployment benefits, average weekly ..	Dollars	161	187	221	262	263	267	277	288	233
Percent of weekly wage...............	Percent	36.0	35.5	32.9	36.5	35.2	34.6	34.3	35.1	35.1
Weeks compensated..................	Million	116.2	118.3	96.0	163.2	135.1	121.2	112.2	116.3	149.5
Beneficiaries, first payments	1,000	8,629	8,035	7,033	9,935	8,369	7,922	7,350	7,641	10,053
Average duration of benefits [2]	Weeks	13.4	14.7	13.7	16.4	16.1	15.3	15.2	15.3	14.9
Claimants exhausting benefits...........	1,000	2,323	2,662	2,144	4,417	3,532	2,856	2,676	2,670	3,424
Percent of first payment [3]	Percent	29.4	34.3	31.8	43.4	39.0	35.9	35.4	35.3	41.5
Contributions collected [4]	Bil. dol......	15.2	22.0	19.9	25.3	31.2	34.8	34.1	34.5	30.0
Benefits paid	Bil. dol......	18.1	21.2	20.5	41.4	34.4	31.2	29.8	30.1	40.7
Funds available for benefits [5]	Bil. dol......	37.9	35.4	53.4	23.4	23.0	29.0	35.8	32.5	29.0
Average employer contribution rate [6]	Percent	1.95	2.44	1.75	2.20	2.68	2.86	2.68	2.61	2.25

[1] Insured unemployment as percent of average covered employment in preceding year. [2] Weeks compensated divided by first payment. [3] Based on first payments for 12-month period ending June 30. [4] Contributions from employers; also employees in states which tax workers. [5] End of year. Sum of balances in state clearing accounts, benefit-payment accounts, and state accounts in federal unemployment trust funds. [6] As percent of taxable wages.

Source: U.S. Department of Labor, Employment and Training Administration, *Unemployment Insurance Financial Data Handbook*. See also <http://www.ows.doleta.gov/unemploy/hb394.asp>.

Table 559. State Unemployment Insurance by State and Other Areas: 2009

[14,173 represents 14,173,000. See headnote, Table 558. For state data on insured unemployment, see Table 629]

State and other areas	Beneficiaries, first payments (1,000)	Benefits paid (mil. dol.)	Avg. weekly unemploy-ment benefits (dol.)	State and other areas	Beneficiaries, first payments (1,000)	Benefits paid (mil. dol.)	Avg. weekly unemploy-ment benefits (dol.)
Total.......	**14,173**	**79,550**	**317**	MT........	42	209	270
AL..........	196	651	208	NE........	61	219	249
AK..........	34	170	235	NV........	182	1,095	317
AZ..........	243	1,001	220	NH........	57	269	283
AR.........	142	620	282	NJ........	470	3,659	396
CA..........	1,779	11,455	311	NM........	63	362	300
CO..........	186	1,062	361	NY........	804	4,970	315
CT..........	223	1,313	342	NC........	544	2,555	307
DE..........	35	208	262	ND........	22	99	311
DC..........	34	217	303	OH........	504	2,942	321
FL..........	680	3,098	238	OK........	108	574	295
GA..........	410	1,718	283	OR........	260	1,625	313
HI..........	51	390	423	PA........	783	4,827	352
ID..........	92	396	275	RI........	56	409	383
IL..........	662	4,418	328	SC........	224	946	250
IN..........	354	1,831	307	SD........	17	66	254
IA..........	165	792	320	TN........	280	1,099	226
KS..........	123	744	354	TX........	714	3,837	325
KY..........	191	1,064	308	UT........	99	489	321
LA..........	137	455	231	VT........	38	196	306
ME..........	55	259	282	VA........	230	1,073	304
MD..........	187	1,089	311	WA........	346	2,597	402
MA..........	353	2,755	419	WV........	77	343	272
MI..........	653	3,785	309	WI........	448	1,932	288
MN..........	252	1,691	360	WY........	29	166	347
MS..........	102	345	196	PR........	132	304	115
MO..........	241	1,140	256	VI........	3	20	327

Source: U.S. Employment and Training Administration, *Unemployment Insurance Financial Data Handbook*. See also <http://www.ows.doleta.gov/unemploy/hb394.asp>.

Table 560. Persons With Work Disability by Selected Characteristics: 2008

[In thousands, except percent (20,213 represents 20,213,000). As of March. Covers civilian noninstitutional population and members of Armed Forces living off post or with their families on post. Persons are classified as having a work disability if they (1) have a health problem or disability which prevents them from working or which limits the kind or amount of work they can do; (2) have a service-connected disability or ever retired or left a job for health reasons; (3) did not work in survey reference week or previous year because of long-term illness or disability; or (4) are under age 65, and are covered by Medicare or receive supplemental security income. Based on Current Population Survey; see text, Section 1 and Appendix III]

Age and participation status in assistance programs	Total [1]	Male	Female	White alone [2]	Black alone [3]	Hispanic [4]
Persons with work disability	**20,213**	**9,861**	**10,352**	**15,219**	**3,841**	**2,255**
16 to 24 years old	1,562	757	805	1,073	380	230
25 to 34 years old	2,176	1,083	1,094	1,509	536	290
35 to 44 years old	3,522	1,764	1,758	2,621	698	472
45 to 54 years old	5,711	2,679	3,032	4,289	1,100	597
55 to 64 years old	7,242	3,578	3,664	5,727	1126	666
Percent work disabled of total population—						
16 to 24 years old	4.2	4.0	4.3	3.7	6.8	3.5
25 to 34 years old	5.5	5.4	5.5	4.9	10.3	3.6
35 to 44 years old	8.4	8.5	8.3	7.9	13.4	6.9
45 to 54 years old	13.0	12.5	13.5	12.0	21.3	12.2
55 to 64 years old	21.8	22.3	21.3	20.5	33.4	23.9
Percent of work disabled—						
Receiving social security income.	35.5	36.0	35.0	36.7	31.7	26.7
Receiving food stamps	19.3	15.0	23.3	16.6	29.5	22.6
Covered by Medicaid...................	65.4	68.9	62.0	67.8	60.7	56.6
Residing in public housing...............	5.9	4.7	7.1	4.4	11.1	7.5
Residing in subsidized housing	3.4	2.3	4.4	2.7	6.1	4.4

[1] Includes other races, not shown separately. [2] Beginning with the 2003 Current Population Survey asked respondents to choose one or more races. White alone refers to people who reported White and did not report any other race category. The use of this single-race population does not imply reported more than one race, such as "White and American Indian and Alaska Native" or "Asian and Black or African American," is available from Census 2000 through American FactFinder. About 2.6 percent of people reported more than one race in 2000. [3] Black alone refers to people who reported Black and did not report any other race category. [4] Hispanic persons may be of any race.

Source: U.S. Census Bureau, unpublished data.

Table 561. Workers' Compensation Payments: 1990 to 2008

[In billions of dollars, except as indicated (53.1 represents $53,100,000,000). See headnote, Table 562]

Item	1990	1995	2000	2002	2003	2004	2005	2006	2007	2008
Workers covered (mil.)............	106.0	112.8	127.1	125.6	124.7	125.9	128.2	130.3	131.7	130.6
Premium amounts paid [1]........	**53.1**	**57.1**	**60.1**	**72.6**	**80.6**	**84.2**	**89.6**	**87.6**	**85.9**	**80.3**
Private carriers [1]	35.1	31.6	35.7	41.3	45.3	47.4	51.0	51.9	51.7	47.1
State funds	8.0	10.5	8.8	13.7	16.4	17.5	18.2	15.7	13.7	12.6
Federal programs [2]	2.2	2.6	3.6	3.9	4.0	4.1	4.1	4.1	4.2	4.3
Self-insurers	7.9	12.5	11.9	13.7	14.9	15.2	16.3	15.8	16.3	16.3
Annual benefits paid [1]..........	**38.2**	**42.1**	**47.7**	**52.3**	**54.7**	**56.1**	**55.6**	**54.3**	**55.2**	**57.6**
By private carriers [1]	22.2	20.1	26.9	28.1	28.4	28.6	28.5	27.3	28.5	30.2
From state funds [3]	8.8	10.8	10.3	9.1	10.4	11.1	11.0	10.6	10.3	10.5
Employers' self-insurance [4]	7.2	11.2	10.5	11.9	12.7	13.1	12.9	12.6	13.1	13.6
Type of benefit:										
Medical/hospitalization	15.2	16.7	20.9	24.2	25.7	26.1	26.0	26.0	26.7	29.1
Compensation payments...........	23.1	25.4	26.8	28.1	29.0	30.1	29.6	28.3	28.5	28.5
Percent of covered payroll: [1]										
Workers' compensation costs [5,6]	2.18	1.82	1.34	1.57	1.71	1.70	1.72	1.58	1.47	1.35
Benefits [6]	1.53	1.34	1.06	1.13	1.16	1.13	1.07	0.98	0.94	0.97

[1] Premium and benefit amounts include estimated payments under insurance policy deductible provisions. Deductible benefits are allocated to private carriers and state funds. [2] Years 1990–1995 includes federal employer compensation program and that portion of federal black lung benefits program financed from employer contributions. Years 1997–2000 includes federal employer compensation program only due to changes in reporting methods. [3] Net cash and medical benefits paid by competitive and exclusive state funds and by federal workers' compensation programs. [4] Cash and medical benefits paid by self-insurers, plus value of medical benefits paid by employers carrying workers' compensation policies that exclude standard medical coverage. [5] Premiums written by private carriers and state funds, and benefits paid by self-insurers increased by 5–10 prior to 1995 and by 11 percent for 1995–2002 for administrative costs. Also includes benefits paid and administrative costs of federal system for government employees. [6] Excludes programs financed from general revenue—black lung benefits and supplemental pensions in some states.

Source: National Academy of Social Insurance, Washington, DC, *Workers' Compensation: Benefits, Coverage, and Costs*, annual. See also <http://www.nasi.org>.

Table 562. Workers' Compensation Payments by State: 2000 to 2008

[In millions of dollars (47,699 represents $47,699,000,000). Calendar-year data. Payments represent compensation and medical benefits and include insurance losses paid by private insurance carriers (compiled from state workers' compensation agencies and A.M. Best Co.); disbursements of state funds (compiled from the A.M. Best Co. and state workers' compensation agencies); and self-insurance payments (compiled from state workers' compensation agencies and authors' estimates)]

State	2000	2005	2006	2007	2008	State	2000	2005	2006	2007	2008
Total............	**47,699**	**55,630**	**54,274**	**55,217**	**57,633**	Montana...........	155	227	234	243	253
Alabama	529	565	563	585	648	Nebraska..........	230	310	276	291	345
Alaska	139	183	187	188	205	Nevada............	347	386	394	378	393
Arizona	498	543	608	647	649	New Hampshire.....	177	229	220	204	239
Arkansas	214	193	197	206	215	New Jersey	1,378	1,567	1,748	1,847	1,916
California	9,449	10,832	9,914	9,509	9,426	New Mexico........	144	231	238	242	272
Colorado	810	895	864	836	875	New York	2,761	3,154	3,251	3,137	3,537
Connecticut	638	709	709	726	781	North Carolina......	865	1,387	1,317	1,349	1,526
Delaware	118	186	208	197	209	North Dakota	70	82	81	95	106
District of Columbia ..	78	90	89	84	81	Ohio.............	2,099	2,447	2,384	2,478	2,490
Florida	2,577	2,914	2,672	2,716	2,787	Oklahoma	485	640	675	702	782
Georgia	965	1,379	1,370	1,482	1,602	Oregon............	425	553	567	586	602
Hawaii	231	251	243	247	246	Pennsylvania	2,379	2,741	2,759	2,804	2,902
Idaho	114	243	254	267	280	Rhode Island	127	137	149	152	158
Illinois...........	1,944	2,425	2,440	2,737	2,994	South Carolina......	515	917	989	885	915
Indiana...........	545	565	560	597	624	South Dakota.......	63	86	109	119	114
Iowa.............	343	489	489	496	575	Tennessee	774	823	881	775	828
Kansas...........	323	390	391	394	418	Texas.............	2,160	1,549	1,385	1,415	1,514
Kentucky	584	693	626	638	696	Utah..............	172	254	258	283	301
Louisiana	547	597	610	614	734	Vermont...........	101	122	124	119	127
Maine............	245	272	285	273	262	Virginia............	597	854	807	1,069	1,148
Maryland	641	784	829	844	936	Washington	1,527	1,848	1,927	1,996	2,193
Massachusetts......	801	904	905	886	843	West Virginia.......	661	818	482	634	603
Michigan	1,474	1,474	1,471	1,508	1,405	Wisconsin	765	1,170	1,043	1,094	1,011
Minnesota	798	942	937	952	1,007	Wyoming	89	117	117	127	137
Mississippi.........	293	312	338	329	361	**Federal total** [1].....	**2,957**	**3,258**	**3,270**	**3,340**	**3,424**
Missouri	780	894	832	892	937	Federal employees ..	2,119	2,462	2,455	2,587	2,676

[1] Federal benefits include: those paid under the Federal Employees' Compensation Act for civilian employees; the portion of the Black Lung benefit program that is financed by employers; and a portion of benefits under the Longshore and Harbor Workers' Compensation Act that are not reflected in state data, namely, benefits paid by self-insured employers and by special funds under the LHWCA. See Appendix H of source for more information about federal programs.

Source: National Academy of Social Insurance, Washington, DC, *Workers' Compensation: Benefits, Coverage, and Costs*, annual. See also <http://www.nasi.org>.

Table 563. Supplemental Security Income—Recipients and Payments: 1990 to 2009

[In thousands (4,817 represents 4,817,000), except as noted. Recipients and monthly payment as of December. Payments for calendar year. Persons with a federal SSI payment and/or federally administered state supplementation. See also Appendix III]

Program	Unit	1990	1995	2000	2004	2005	2006	2007	2008	2009
Recipients, total.........	1,000	**4,817**	**6,514**	**6,602**	**6,988**	**7,114**	**7,236**	**7,360**	**7,521**	**7,677**
Aged	1,000	1,454	1,446	1,289	1,211	1,214	1,212	1,205	1,203	1,186
Blind...................	1,000	84	84	79	76	75	73	72	70	69
Disabled...............	1,000	3,279	4,984	5,234	5,701	5,825	5,951	6,083	6,247	6,421
Payments, total [1]	Mil. dol. .	**16,133**	**27,037**	**30,672**	**36,065**	**37,236**	**38,889**	**41,205**	**43,040**	**46,592**
Aged	Mil. dol. ..	3,559	4,239	4,540	4,894	4,965	5,116	5,301	5,379	5,569
Blind...................	Mil. dol. ..	329	367	386	412	414	409	419	416	427
Disabled...............	Mil. dol. ..	12,245	22,431	25,746	30,745	31,857	33,364	35,485	37,246	40,597
Average monthly payment, total.........	Dollars ..	**276**	**335**	**379**	**428**	**439**	**455**	**468**	**478**	**499**
Aged	Dollars...	208	250	300	351	360	373	384	393	399
Blind...................	Dollars...	319	355	413	463	475	488	500	508	520
Disabled...............	Dollars...	303	358	398	444	455	471	485	494	517

[1] Includes payments not distributed by reason for eligibility.
Source: U.S. Social Security Administration, *Social Security Bulletin,* quarterly, and *Annual Statistical Supplement to the Social Security Bulletin,* March 2011. See also <http://www.ssa.gov/policy/docs/statcomps/supplement/2010>.

Table 564. Supplemental Security Income (SSI)—Recipients and Payments by State and Other Area: 2000 to 2009

[Recipients as of December; payments for calendar year (6,602 represents 6,602,000). Data cover federal SSI payments and/or federally administered state supplementation. For explanation of methodology, see Appendix III]

State and other area	Recipients (1,000)		Payments for the year (mil. dol.)			State and other area	Recipients (1,000)		Payments for the year (mil. dol.)		
	2000	2009	2000	2005	2009		2000	2009	2000	2005	2009
Total [1].......	**6,602**	**7,677**	**30,672**	**37,236**	**46,592**	MO..........	112	128	471	573	738
U.S...........	**6,601**	**7,676**	**30,669**	**37,232**	**46,586**	MT..........	14	17	57	70	92
AL	159	169	659	776	960	NE	21	25	85	103	136
AK	9	12	37	53	67	NV	25	39	108	163	218
AZ	81	106	355	482	612	NH	12	17	49	67	93
AR	85	103	333	407	573	NJ	146	163	672	763	957
CA	1,088	1,250	6,386	8,146	9,082	NM..........	47	59	193	248	327
CO	54	62	228	264	350	NY	617	668	3,197	3,561	4,336
CT	49	56	216	260	325	NC	191	213	732	894	1,187
DE	12	15	50	66	87	ND	8	8	30	33	41
DC	20	24	93	113	143	OH	240	274	1,114	1,295	1,695
FL	377	464	1,621	2,031	2,596	OK	72	91	302	381	515
GA	197	220	785	944	1,264	OR	52	70	228	298	406
HI	21	24	104	119	151	PA	284	347	1,367	1,659	2,142
ID	18	26	76	106	146	RI	28	32	130	161	189
IL	249	269	1,174	1,337	1,622	SC	107	109	429	488	617
IN	88	113	382	488	673	SD	13	14	48	55	71
IA	40	47	158	193	256	TN	164	169	664	752	967
KS	36	44	151	187	260	TX	409	590	1,575	2,191	3,126
KY	174	189	741	862	1,077	UT	20	27	87	110	151
LA	166	170	715	771	947	VT	13	15	51	63	82
ME..........	30	35	116	146	189	VA	132	144	535	632	790
MD..........	88	103	400	481	623	WA	101	131	484	616	818
MA..........	168	187	807	902	1,152	WV..........	71	80	318	376	462
MI..........	210	243	988	1,157	1,479	WI..........	85	104	357	437	594
MN..........	64	83	272	355	488	WY..........	6	6	23	26	33
MS..........	129	124	512	572	681	N. Mariana...	1	1	3	4	6

[1] Includes Northern Mariana.
Source: U.S. Social Security Administration, *Annual Statistical Supplement to the Social Security Bulletin,* March 2011, see also <http://www.ssa.gov/policy/docs/statcomps/supplement/2010>.

Table 565. Temporary Assistance for Needy Families (TANF)—Families and Recipients: 1980 to 2009

[In thousands (3,712 represents 3,712,000). Average monthly families and recipients for calendar year. Prior to TANF, the cash assistance program to families was called Aid to Families with Dependent Children (1980–1996). Under the new welfare law (Personal Responsibility and Work Opportunity Reconciliation Act of 1996), the program became TANF. See text, this section. Includes Puerto Rico, Guam, and Virgin Islands]

Year	Families	Recipients	Year	Families	Recipients	Year	Families	Recipients
1980......	3,712	10,774	1994......	5,033	14,161	2002......	2,048	5,069
1985......	3,701	10,855	1995......	4,791	13,418	2003......	2,024	4,929
1988......	3,749	10,915	1996......	4,434	12,321	2004......	1,979	4,748
1989......	3,799	10,993	1997......	3,740	10,376	2005......	1,894	4,469
1990......	4,057	11,695	1998......	3,050	8,347	2006......	1,777	4,148
1991......	4,497	12,930	1999......	2,554	6,824	2007......	1,674	3,897
1992......	4,829	13,773	2000......	2,215	5,778	2008......	1,635	3,801
1993......	5,012	14,205	2001......	2,104	5,359	2009......	1,769	4,154

Source: U.S. Department of Health and Human Services, Administration for Children and Families. For more information, see <http://www.acf.hhs.gov/programs/ofa/>.

Table 566. Temporary Assistance for Needy Families (TANF)—Recipients by State and Other Areas: 2000 to 2009

[In thousands (2,265 represents 2,265,000). Average monthly families and recipients for calendar year. See headnote, Table 565]

State or other area	Families 2000	Families 2005	Families 2009	Recipients 2000	Recipients 2005	Recipients 2009	State or other area	Families 2000	Families 2005	Families 2009	Recipients 2000	Recipients 2005	Recipients 2009
Total¹	2,265	1,921	1,783	5,943	4,549	4,193	MT	5	4	4	13	12	9
U.S.	2,181	1,876	1,769	5,678	4,418	4,154	NE	9	10	8	24	25	18
AL	19	20	19	45	47	45	NV	6	6	9	16	15	23
AK	7	4	3	21	11	9	NH	6	6	6	14	14	12
AZ	33	42	38	84	96	83	NJ	50	43	33	125	104	78
AR	12	8	9	29	18	19	NM	23	18	17	69	45	46
CA	489	461	547	1,262	1,078	1,340	NY	250	140	118	695	321	264
CO	11	15	10	28	39	25	NC	45	33	26	98	64	51
CT	27	19	17	64	39	34	ND	3	3	2	7	7	5
DE	6	6	5	12	13	13	OH	95	82	94	235	177	214
DC	17	17	9	45	41	20	OK	14	11	9	35	26	20
FL	65	58	57	142	100	103	OR	17	19	23	38	44	58
GA	52	39	21	125	82	38	PA	88	97	49	241	254	119
HI	14	8	8	46	19	22	RI	16	10	8	44	26	20
ID	1	2	2	2	3	2	SC	18	16	18	42	36	41
IL	78	38	20	234	96	54	SD	3	3	3	7	6	6
IN	37	44	39	101	124	101	TN	57	70	60	147	184	153
IA	20	17	17	53	42	43	TX	129	82	48	347	189	108
KS	13	18	14	32	46	35	UT	8	9	6	21	22	16
KY	38	34	30	87	74	60	VT	6	5	3	16	11	6
LA	27	15	10	71	36	23	VA	31	10	33	69	28	76
ME	11	9	11	28	25	25	WA	56	57	61	148	136	147
MD	29	23	23	71	53	56	WV	13	12	9	33	26	21
MA	43	48	48	100	102	95	WI	17	19	19	38	44	41
MI	72	81	64	198	215	164	WY	1	–	–	1	1	1
MN	39	28	22	114	71	48	PR	30	15	12	88	41	34
MS	15	15	12	34	33	24	GU	3	3	2	10	9	4
MO	47	40	35	125	96	85	VI	1	–	–	3	1	1

– Represents or rounds to zero. ¹ Includes Puerto Rico, Guam, and the Virgin Islands.
Source: U.S. Department of Health and Human Services, Administration for Children and Families.
See also <http://www.acf.hhs.gov/programs/ofa/data-reports/index.htm>.

Table 567. Temporary Assistance for Needy Families (TANF)—Expenditures by State: 2000 to 2009

[In millions of dollars (24,781 represents $24,781,000,000). Represents federal and state funds expended in fiscal year]

State	2000, total	2005, total	2009 Total¹	2009 Expenditures on assistance	State	2000, total	2005, total	2009 Total¹	2009 Expenditures on assistance
U.S.	24,781	25,580	30,578	10,511	MO	321	299	314	104
AL	96	123	147	48	MT	44	44	42	20
AK	93	74	70	41	NE	79	78	90	26
AZ	261	299	387	138	NV	69	70	128	51
AR	139	67	136	17	NH	73	63	83	40
CA	6,481	5,882	6,526	4,040	NJ	321	994	1,110	225
CO	205	214	330	57	NM	149	127	168	67
CT	436	459	478	96	NY	3,512	3,970	5,092	1,828
DE	55	61	53	23	NC	440	448	637	90
DC	157	156	172	23	ND	33	34	36	20
FL	781	868	856	204	OH	995	990	1,317	440
GA	386	520	521	92	OK	130	174	218	56
HI	162	128	336	72	OR	169	269	313	166
ID	43	40	34	6	PA	1,327	1,190	973	213
IL	879	998	1,091	64	RI	172	168	102	46
IN	342	307	314	109	SC	245	230	186	49
IA	163	162	180	76	SD	21	30	26	18
KS	151	154	170	69	TN	293	233	346	167
KY	203	216	221	145	TX	727	851	801	127
LA	118	186	203	44	UT	100	108	128	46
ME	108	127	132	101	VT	62	68	73	28
MD	336	349	516	107	VA	418	290	255	79
MA	690	689	1,056	325	WA	535	525	1,452	318
MI	1,264	1,175	1,421	382	WV	134	124	147	95
MN	381	392	490	90	WI	382	446	569	113
MS	62	79	101	30	WY	34	32	31	13

¹ Includes other items not shown separately.
Source: U.S. Administration for Children and Families, Temporary Assistance for Needy Families (TANF) Program, Annual Report to Congress. See also <http://www.acf.hhs.gov/programs/cb/stats_research>.

Table 568. Child Support—Award and Recipiency Status of Custodial Parents: 2007

[In thousands except as noted (13,743 represents 13,743,000). Custodial parents 15 years and older with own children under 21 years of age present from absent parents as of spring 2008. Covers civilian noninstitutionalized population. Based on Current Population Survey; see text, Section 1 and Appendix III. For definition of mean, see Guide to Tabular Presentation]

Award and recipiency status	All custodial parents				Custodial parents below the poverty level			
	Total				Total			
	Number	Percent distribu-tion	Mothers	Fathers	Number	Percent distribu-tion	Mothers	Fathers
Total.	**13,743**	**(X)**	**11,356**	**2,387**	**3,375**	**(X)**	**3,067**	**308**
With child support agreement or award [1]	7,428	(X)	6,463	965	1,580	(X)	1,464	116
Supposed to receive payments in 2007.	6,375	100.0	5,551	825	1,278	100.0	1,185	93
Actually received payments in 2007	4,864	76.3	4,253	611	886	69.3	811	75
Received full amount.	2,986	46.8	2,615	371	514	40.2	471	43
Received partial payments	1,878	29.5	1,638	240	372	29.1	340	32
Did not receive payments in 2007	1,511	23.7	1,298	213	392	30.7	374	18
Child support not awarded.	6,315	(X)	4,893	1,422	1,796	(X)	1,603	193
MEAN INCOME AND CHILD SUPPORT								
Received child support payments in 2007:								
Mean total money income (dol.)	34,068	(X)	32,271	46,574	8,849	(X)	8,652	10,966
Mean child support received (dol.)	4,395	(X)	4,379	4,510	3,393	(X)	3,413	3,177
Received the full amount due:								
Mean total money income (dol.)	37,266	(X)	35,135	52,294	9,309	(X)	9,115	11,430
Mean child support received (dol.)	5,736	(X)	5,694	6,032	4,462	(X)	4,481	4,259
Received partial payments:								
Mean total money income (dol.)	28,983	(X)	27,696	37,751	8,213	(X)	8,011	10,347
Mean child support received (dol.)	2,264	(X)	2,279	2,163	1,916	(X)	1,934	1,734
Received no payments in 2007:								
Mean total money income (dol.)	29,261	(X)	27,377	40,712	8,598	(X)	8,523	10,142
Without child support agreement or award:								
Mean total money income (dol.)	28,515	(X)	23,242	46,659	6,934	(X)	6,793	8,103

X Not applicable. [1] As of April of following year (e.g., 2007 data is as of April 2008).
Source: U.S. Census Bureau, unpublished data, <http://www.census.gov/hhes/www/childsupport/cs07.html>.

Table 569. Child Support Enforcement Program—Caseload and Collections: 1990 to 2010

[For years ending September 30 (12,796 represents 12,796,000). Includes Puerto Rico, Guam, and the Virgin Islands. The child support enforcement program locates absent parents, establishes paternity of children born out of wedlock, and establishes and enforces support orders. By law, these services are available to all families that need them. The program is operated at the state and local government level, but 66 percent of administrative costs are paid by the federal government. Child support (CS) collected for families not receiving Temporary Assistance for Needy Families (TANF) goes to the family to help it remain self–sufficient. Most of the child support collected on behalf of TANF families goes to federal and state governments to offset TANF payments. Some states pass–through a portion of the CS collections to help families become self–sufficient. Based on data reported by state agencies. Minus sign (–) indicates net outlay]

Item	Unit	1990	2000	2005	2006	2007	2008	2009	2010, prel.
Total cases [1]	1,000	12,796	17,334	15,861	15,844	15,755	15,676	15,798	15,859
Paternities established, total [2]	1,000	393	867	690	675	640	629	643	620
Support orders established, total [3]	1,000	1,022	1,175	1,180	1,159	1,178	1,193	1,267	1,297
FINANCES									
Collections, total	Mil. dol.	6,010	17,854	23,006	23,933	24,855	26,561	26,386	26,556
TANF/FC collections [4]	Mil. dol.	1,750	2,593	2,191	2,112	2,050	2,254	1,971	1,925
State share	Mil. dol.	620	1,080	911	875	852	948	741	716
Estimated incentive payments to states	Mil. dol.	264	353	365	402	431	615	446	448
Federal share [5]	Mil. dol.	533	968	1,129	1,086	1,054	1,170	945	891
Current assistance medical support collections.	Mil. dol.	(NA)	27	11	12	11	12	13	19
Current assistance payments to families or foster care.	Mil. dol.	(NA)	165	140	139	133	124	155	165
Non–TANF collections	Mil. dol.	4,260	15,261	20,815	21,822	22,804	24,307	24,415	24,630
Administrative expenditures, total	Mil. dol.	1,606	4,526	5,353	5,561	5,594	5,870	5,850	5,776
State share	Mil. dol.	545	1,519	1,813	1,884	1,902	2,200	1,963	1,964
Federal share.	Mil. dol.	1,061	3,006	3,540	3,677	3,692	3,671	3,887	3,811
Program savings, total.	Mil. dol.	–190	–2,125	–3,312	–3,600	–3,687	–3,780	(NA)	(NA)
State share	Mil. dol.	338	–87	–537	–607	–619	–700	(NA)	(NA)
Federal share.	Mil. dol.	–528	–2,038	–2,776	–2,993	–3,068	–3,080	(NA)	(NA)

NA Not available. [1] Passage of the Personal Responsibility and Work Opportunity Reconciliation Act of 1996 (PRWORA) mandated new categories in 1999 and cases were no longer double counted resulting in a 2 million case reduction. [2] Does not include in–hospital paternities. [3] Includes modifications to orders. [4] Collections for current assistance cases where the children are: (1) recipients of TANF under title IV–A of the Social Security Act or (2) entitled to foster care (FC) maintenance under title IV–E of the Social Security Act plus collections distributed as assistance reimbursements. Includes assistance reimbursements, which are collections that will be divided between the state and federal governments to reimburse their respective shares of either Title IV–A assistance payments or Title IV–E foster care maintenance payments. [5] Prior to fiscal year 2002, incentives were paid out of the federal share of collections and the net federal share was reported.
Source: U.S. Department of Health and Human Services, Office of Child Support Enforcement, *Annual Report to Congress*.

Table 570. Federal Food Programs: 1990 to 2010

[20.0 represents 20,000,000, except as noted. For years ending September 30. Program data include Puerto Rico, Virgin Islands, Guam, American Samoa, Northern Marianas, and the former Trust Territory when a federal food program was operated in these areas. Participation data are average monthly figures except as noted. Participants are not reported for programs. Cost data are direct federal benefits to recipients; they exclude federal administrative payments and applicable state and local contributions. Federal costs for commodities and cash in-lieu of commodities are shown separately from direct cash benefits for those programs receiving both]

Program	Unit	1990	2000	2005	2006	2007	2008	2009	2010
Supplemental nutrition assistance program (SNAP): [1]									
Participants	Million ..	20.0	17.2	25.6	26.5	26.3	28.2	33.5	40.3
Federal cost	Mil. dol..	14,143	14,983	28,568	30,187	30,373	34,608.0	50,369	64,701
Monthly average coupon value per recipient ..	Dollars ..	58.78	72.62	92.89	94.75	96.18	102.19	125.31	133.79
Nutrition assistance program for Puerto Rico: [2]									
Federal cost	Mil. dol.	937	1,268	1,495	1,518	1,551	1,623	2,001	1,746
National school lunch program (NSLP):									
Free lunches served	Million ..	1,662	2,205	2,477	2,496	2,506	2,611	2,724	2,928
Reduced-price lunches served	Million ..	273	409	479	488	501	521	519	502
Children participating [3]	Million ..	24.1	27.3	29.6	30.1	30.5	31.0	31.3	32.0
Federal cost	Mil. dol..	3,214	5,493	7,055	7,389	7,707	8,265	8,873	9,933
School breakfast (SB):									
Children participating [3]	Million ..	4.1	7.6	9.4	9.8	10.1	10.6	11.1	12.0
Federal cost	Mil. dol..	596	1,393	1,927	2,043	2,164	2,366	2,582	2,895
Special supplemental food program (WIC): [4]									
Participants	Million ..	4.5	7.2	8.0	8.1	8.3	8.7	9.1	9.2
Federal cost	Mil. dol..	1,637	2,853	3,603	3,598	3,882	4,534	4,642	4,702
Child and adult care (CAC): [5]									
Participants [6]	Million ..	1.5	2.7	3.1	3.1	3.2	3.3	3.3	3.8
Federal cost	Mil. dol..	719	1,500	1,904	1,944	2,023	2,169	2,289	2,546
Federal cost of commodities donated to— [7] Child nutrition (NSLP, CACFP, SFS, and SBP) [8]	Mil. dol..	644	704	1,045	875	1,110	1,138	1,237	1,283
Emergency feeding [9]	Mil. dol..	282	182	314	243	198	227	250	248

[1] The program name was changed from Food Stamp to Supplemental Nutrition Assistance (SNAP) in October 2008. [2] Puerto Rico receives a grant in lieu of SNAP benefits. [3] Average monthly participation (excluding summer months of June through August). Includes children in public and private elementary and secondary schools and in residential child care institutes. [4] WIC serves pregnant and postpartum women, infants, and children up to age 5. [5] CACFP provides year-round subsidies to feed preschool children in child care centers and family day care homes. Certain care centers serving disabled or elderly adults also receive meal subsidies. [6] Average quarterly daily attendance at participating institutions. [7] Includes the federal cost of commodity entitlements, cash-in-lieu of commodities, and bonus foods. [8] Includes NSLP, CACFP and Summer Food Service. [9] Provides free (bonus) commodities to needy persons for home consumption through food banks, hunger centers, soup kitchens, and similar nonprofit agencies. Includes The Emergency Food Assistance Program (TEFAP), the commodity purchases for soup kitchens/food banks program (FY 1989–96), and commodity disaster relief. Does not include SNAP disaster assistance.

Source: U.S. Department of Agriculture, Food and Nutrition Service, "Food and Nutrition Service, Program Data," <http://www.fns.usda.gov/pd>, updated monthly.

Table 571. Federal Supplemental Nutrition Assistance Program by State: 2000 to 2010

[17,194 represents 17,194,000. Participation data are average monthly number participating in year ending September 30. Food stamp costs are for benefits only and exclude administrative expenditures]

State	Persons (1,000)			Benefits (mil. dol.)			State	Persons (1,000)			Benefits (mil. dol.)		
	2000	2005	2010	2000	2005	2010		2000	2005	2010	2000	2005	2010
Total [1]	17,194	25,628	40,302	14,983	28,568	64,705	MO	423	677	901	358	736	1,361
U.S.	17,156	25,588	40,244	14,927	28,493	64,565	MT	59	81	114	51	89	177
AL	396	559	805	344	616	1,226	NE	82	117	163	61	120	238
AK	38	56	76	46	80	159	NV	61	122	278	57	129	415
AZ	259	550	1,018	240	634	1,588	NH	36	52	104	28	51	152
AR	247	374	467	206	401	686	NJ	345	392	622	304	437	1,030
CA	1,831	1,992	3,239	1,639	2,315	5,694	NM	169	241	357	140	251	542
CO	156	246	405	127	313	688	NY	1,439	1,755	2,758	1,361	2,136	4,985
CT	165	204	336	138	223	570	NC	488	800	1,346	403	856	2,072
DE	32	62	113	31	65	171	ND	32	42	60	25	45	95
DC	81	89	118	77	103	196	OH	610	1,007	1,607	520	1,155	2,734
FL	882	1,382	2,603	771	1,598	4,417	OK	253	424	582	208	440	900
GA	559	921	1,591	489	1,048	2,565	OR	234	429	705	198	456	1,067
HI	118	94	138	166	156	358	PA	777	1,043	1,575	656	1,105	2,333
ID	58	93	194	46	103	300	RI	74	76	139	59	79	238
IL	817	1,158	1,646	777	1,400	2,784	SC	295	521	797	249	566	1,256
IN	300	556	813	268	627	1,291	SD	43	56	95	37	61	153
IA	123	207	340	100	220	526	TN	496	850	1,224	415	942	1,966
KS	117	178	270	83	180	403	TX	1,333	2,442	3,552	1,215	2,659	5,447
KY	403	570	778	337	611	1,186	UT	82	133	247	68	141	367
LA	500	808	826	448	979	1,286	VT	41	45	86	32	45	124
ME	102	153	230	81	162	356	VA	336	488	786	263	500	1,213
MD	219	289	561	199	320	878	WA	295	508	956	241	539	1,387
MA	232	368	749	182	363	1,166	WV	227	262	341	185	258	487
MI	603	1,048	1,776	457	1,099	2,809	WI	193	346	715	129	317	1,000
MN	196	260	430	165	275	625	WY	22	25	35	19	27	52
MS	276	435	576	226	463	847							

[1] Includes Guam and the Virgin Islands. Several outlying areas receive nutrition assistance grants in lieu of food stamps (Puerto Rico, American Samoa, and the Northern Marianas).

Source: U.S. Department of Agriculture, Food and Nutrition Service, "Food and Nutrition Service, Program Data," <http://www.fns.usda.gov/pd>, updated monthly.

U.S. Census Bureau, Statistical Abstract of the United States: 2012

Table 572. Selected Characteristics of Food Stamp Households and Participants: 1990 to 2009

[7,811 represents 7,811,000. For years ending September 30. Data for 1990 exclude Guam and the Virgin Islands. Based on a sample of households from the Food Stamp Quality Control System]

Year	Households				Participants		
	Total [1] (1,000)	Percent of total			Total (1,000)	Percent of total	
		With children	With elderly [2]	With disabled [3]		Children	Elderly [2]
1990........	7,811	60.3	18.1	8.9	20,440	49.6	7.7
1995........	10,883	59.7	16.0	18.9	26,955	51.5	7.1
2000........	7,335	53.9	21.0	27.5	17,091	51.3	10.0
2005........	10,852	53.7	17.1	23.0	24,794	49.9	8.2
2006........	11,313	52.0	17.9	23.1	25,472	49.1	8.7
2007........	11,561	51.0	17.8	23.8	25,775	48.9	8.8
2008........	12,464	50.6	18.5	22.6	27,607	48.4	9.1
2009........	14,981	49.9	16.6	21.2	32,889	47.5	8.3

[1] Total does not include those who are ineligible or those receiving disaster benefits. [2] Persons 60 years old and over. [3] The substantial increase in 1995 and decrease in 2000 are due in part to the changes in definition of a disabled household. Prior to 1995, disabled households were defined as households with SSI income but no members over age 59. In 1995, that definition changed to households with at least one member under 65 who received SSI, or at least one member aged 18–61 who received Social Security, veterans' benefits, or other government benefits as a result of a disability. Because of changes to the QC data in 2000, the definition of a disabled household changed to households with either SSI income or a medical expense deduction and without an elderly person, and households containing a nonelderly adult who does not appear to be working and who is receiving Social Security, veterans' benefits, or workers' compensation.

Source: U.S. Department of Agriculture, Food and Nutrition Service. Percentages obtained from *Characteristics of Food Stamp Households: Fiscal Year 2009*, September 2010. See also <http://www.fns.usda.gov/ora/MENU/Published/snap/SNAPParthh.htm>.

Table 573. Supplemental Nutrition Assistance Program Households and Participants—Summary: 2009

[14,981 represents 14,981,000. For years ending September 30. Based on a sample of households from the Supplemental Nutrition Assistance Program Quality Control (QC) System. Figures are lower than official participation counts because they do not include ineligible participants or those receiving disaster food stamp assistance]

Household type and income source	Households		Age, sex, race, and Hispanic origin	Participants	
	Number (1,000)	Percent		Number (1,000)	Percent
Total.....................	14,981	100.0	Total.....................	32,889	100.0
With children	7,474	49.9	Children.....................	15,617	47.5
Single-parent households	4,367	29.2	Under 5 years old	5,403	16.4
Married-couple households......	1,340	8.9	5 to 17 years old	10,214	31.1
Other	1,767	11.8	Adults.....................	17,272	52.5
With elderly	2,486	16.6	18 to 35 years old	7,490	22.8
Living alone..................	1,947	12.4	36 to 59 years old	7,054	21.4
Not living alone	539	3.6	60 years old and over	2,728	8.3
Disabled.....................	3,172	21.2			
Living alone..................	1,864	13.0	Male.......................	14,035	42.7
Not living alone	1,307	3.6	Female.....................	18,854	57.3
Earned income	4,412	29.5			
Wages and salaries...........	3,883	25.9	White, non-Hispanic	10,586	32.2
			Black, non-Hispanic.............	7,393	22.5
Unearned income	9,475	63.2	Hispanic.....................	5,103	15.5
TANF [1]	1,446	9.7	Asian.......................	934	2.8
Supplemental security income....	3,539	23.6	Native American	1,400	4.3
Social security................	3,358	22.4	Other [2]	7,474	22.7
No income....................	2,635	17.6			

[1] Temporary Assistance for Needy Families (TANF) program. [2] For FY 2009, this category includes respondents who recorded more than one race, and those with no racial/ethnic data.

Source: U.S. Department of Agriculture, Food and Nutrition Service, *Characteristics of SNAP Households: Fiscal Year 2009*, September 2010. See also <http://www.fns.usda.gov/oane/MENU/Published/snap/snap.htm>.

Table 574. Head Start—Summary: 1980 to 2009

[For years ending September 30 (376 represents 376,000)]

Year	Enrollment (1,000)	Appropriation (mil. dol.)	Age and race	Enrollment, 2009 (percent)	Item	Number
1980......	376	735	Under 3 years old	10	Average cost per child:	
1990......	541	1,552	3 years old............	36	1995................	$4,534
1995......	751	3,534	4 years old............	51	2000................	$5,951
1999......	826	4,658	5 years old and over	3	2009................	$7,600
2000......	858	5,267				
2001......	905	6,200	White...............	40	Paid staff (1,000):	
2002......	912	6,537	Black...............	30	1995................	147
2003	910	6,668	Hispanic..............	36	2000................	180
2004......	906	6,775	American Indian/		2009................	212
2005......	907	6,843	Alaska Native	4	Volunteers (1,000):	
2006......	909	6,872	Asian	2	1995................	1,235
2007......	908	6,888	Hawaiian/		2000................	1,252
2008......	907	6,878	Pacific Islander	1	2009................	1,274
2009......	904	7,113				

Source: U.S. Department of Health and Services, Administration for Children and Families, "Head Start Statistical Fact Sheet"; <http://www.acf.hhs.gov/programs/ohs/about>.

Table 575. Number of Emergency and Transitional Beds in Homeless Assistance Systems Nationwide: 2009

[Data include beds located in Puerto Rico, Guam, and the Virgin Islands. Data are based on a nationally representative sample of 80 jurisdictions that collect data from emergency shelters and transitional providers. The data estimate homeless persons who used emergency shelters or transitional housing from January 1 through June 30, 2009. As a compliment to the survey, a "Continuum of Care" community was derived from each jurisdiction in order to estimate the number of unsheltered homeless persons and the number of emergency shelter and transitional housing beds available on a single night in January 2009. The data do not include homeless individuals living outside a sampled jurisdiction or homeless individuals not using an emergency shelter or a transitional housing program. For more information on data collection and methodology, see Appendix B of source]

Homeless programs	Year-round units/beds [1]			Total year-round beds	Other beds	
	Family units	Family beds	Individual beds		Seasonal beds [2]	Overflow/ voucher [3]
Emergency shelters..............	31,964	103,531	110,894	214,425	20,419	30,565
Transitional housing..............	35,119	110,064	97,525	207,589	(NA)	(NA)
Total inventory	67,083	213,595	210,447	424,042	20,419	30,565
Permanent supportive housing	30,649	87,718	131,663	219,381	(NA)	(NA)

NA Not available. [1] Year-round beds are available for use throughout the year and are considered part of the stable inventory of beds for homeless persons. [2] Seasonal beds are typically available during particularly high-demand seasons of the year (e.g. winter months in the North or summer months in the South) to accommodate increased need for emergency shelters to prevent illness or death due to the weather. [3] Overflow beds are typically used during unanticipated emergencies (e.g., precipitous temperature drops or a natural disaster that displaces residents). Voucher beds are made available in a hotel or motel, and often function like overflow beds.

Source: U.S. Department of Housing and Urban Development, *The Fourth Annual Homeless Assessment Report to Congress.* See also <http://www.hudhre.info/documents/4thHomelessAssessmentReport.pdf>.

Table 576. Social Assistance Services—Revenue for Employer Firms: 2000 to 2009

[In millions of dollars (77,032 represents $77,032,000,000). Estimates have been adjusted to the results of the 2007 Economic Census. Based on the Service Annual Survey and administrative data; see Appendix III]

Kind of business	2002 NAICS code [1]	2000, total	2005, total	2009		
				Total	Taxable firms	Tax-exempt firms
Social assistance, total...................	**624**	**77,032**	**110,483**	**140,690**	**36,103**	**104,587**
Individual and family services	6241	37,311	52,797	68,978	14,065	54,913
Child and youth services	62411	7,517	10,397	11,232	1,132	10,100
Services for elderly and disabled persons.........	62412	12,804	19,309	28,869	8,849	20,020
Other individual and family services	62419	16,990	23,091	28,877	4,084	24,793
Community, emergency and other relief services	6242	12,281	18,934	26,713	477	26,236
Community food services	62421	2,835	3,784	6,022	121	5,901
Community housing services..................	62422	4,888	6,683	11,065	298	10,767
Emergency and other relief services.............	62423	4,558	8,467	9,626	58	9,568
Vocational rehabilitation services	6243	9,458	13,921	12,649	1,911	10,738
Child day care services........................	6244	17,982	24,831	32,350	19,650	12,700

[1] Based on the North American Industry Classification System, 2002, ; see text, Section 15.
Source: U.S. Census Bureau, "Service Annual Survey" 2009, January 2011, <http://www.census.gov/services/index.html>.

Table 577. Social Assistance Services—Nonemployer Establishments and Receipts: 2000 to 2008

[Receipts in millions of dollars (7,539 represents $7,539,000,000). Includes only firms subject to federal income tax. Nonemployers are businesses with no paid employees. Data for 2000 based on the North American Industry Classification System (NAICS), 1997; 2005 data based on NAICS 2002; 2008 data based on NAICS 1997; see text, Section 15]

Kind of business	NAICS code	Establishments			Receipts		
		2000	2005	2008	2000	2005	2008
Social assistance, total.....................	**624**	**642,946**	**807,729**	**844,923**	**7,539**	**10,265**	**12,087**
Individual and family services	6241	72,433	112,909	124,797	1,106	1,920	2,379
Community/emergency and other relief services	6242	3,560	5,533	5,936	54	81	103
Vocational rehabilitation services	6243	7,314	11,022	11,293	151	245	286
Child day care services........................	6244	559,639	678,265	702,897	6,228	8,018	9,320

Source: U.S. Census Bureau, "Nonemployer Statistics," July 2010, <http://www.census.gov/econ/nonemployer/index.html>.

Table 578. Child Care Arrangements of Preschool Children by Type of Arrangement: 1991 to 2005

[In percent, except as indicated (8,428 represents 8,428,000). Estimates are based on children 3 to 5 years old who have not entered kindergarten. Based on interviews from a sample survey of the civilian, noninstitutionalized population in households with telephones; see source for details. See also Appendix III]

Characteristic	Children		Type of nonparental arrangement [1] (percent)			With parental care only (percent)
	Number (1,000)	Percent distribution	In relative care	In non-relative care	In center-based program [2]	
1991, total	8,428	100.0	16.9	14.8	52.8	31.0
1995, total	9,232	100.0	19.4	16.9	55.1	25.9
2005, total	**9,066**	**100.0**	**22.6**	**11.6**	**57.2**	**26.3**
Age:						
3 years old	4,070	44.9	24.0	14.4	42.5	33.4
4 years old	3,873	42.7	20.8	9.2	69.2	20.6
5 years old	1,123	12.4	23.8	9.9	68.7	20.4
Race-ethnicity:						
White, non-Hispanic	5,177	57.1	21.4	15.0	59.1	24.1
Black, non-Hispanic	1,233	13.6	25.0	5.2	66.5	19.5
Hispanic	1,822	20.1	22.7	8.1	43.4	38.0
Other	834	9.2	26.4	8.1	61.5	24.7
Household income:						
Less than $10,001	795	8.8	25.1	8.6	53.4	33.4
$10,001 to $20,000	978	10.8	26.0	7.8	49.2	27.2
$20,001 to $30,000	1,183	13.1	25.4	6.3	43.9	38.5
$30,001 to $40,000	1,124	12.4	23.8	6.9	48.7	33.4
$40,001 to $50,000	808	8.9	21.8	11.6	50.0	35.4
$50,001 to $75,000	1,849	20.4	21.1	13.3	57.1	25.5
$75,001 or more	2,329	25.7	19.8	18.0	75.1	11.4

[1] Columns do not add to 100.0 because some children participated in more than one type of nonparental arrangement.
[2] Center-based programs include day care centers, Head Start programs, preschools, prekindergarten, and nursery schools.
Source: U.S. Department of Education, National Center for Education Statistics, Early Childhood Program Participation Survey of the National Household Education Surveys Program (NHES), 2005.

Table 579. Children in Foster Care and Awaiting Adoption: 2000 to 2009

[Data are preliminary and cover the period from October 1 of prior year through September 30 of year shown]

Characteristic	In foster care		Entered foster care		Exited foster care		Waiting to be adopted		Adopted from foster care	
	2000	2009	2000	2009 [1]	2000	2009 [1]	2000	2009 [1]	2000	2009 [1]
Total	**552,000**	**423,773**	**293,000**	**255,418**	**272,000**	**276,266**	**131,000**	**114,556**	**51,000**	**69,947**
AGE										
Under 1 year	22,839	24,505	37,996	40,931	11,025	12,409	3,957	10,092	939	1,136
1 to 5 years	134,378	124,691	72,365	74,041	70,667	90,319	44,126	41,980	23,135	31,170
6 to 10 years	136,003	83,587	63,346	46,881	63,228	55,064	44,980	29,966	17,831	15,538
11 to 15 years	160,077	101,110	86,555	60,638	65,550	51,021	33,143	12,632	7,946	7,776
16 to 20 years [1]	98,701	89,401	32,737	31,814	61,531	66,303	4,793	539	1,149	1,824
RACE										
White [2]	207,970	167,235	136,214	110,933	121,322	118,422	44,898	43,918	19,462	25,418
Black [2]	217,615	127,821	84,460	64,690	84,065	74,264	57,345	34,088	19,566	14,211
Asian [2]	4,370	2,603	3,565	2,189	3,307	2,111	664	535	290	280
Hispanic [3]	81,823	86,581	42,769	51,628	39,909	55,200	17,050	25,231	7,430	11,878
Two or more	8,043	21,584	5,362	12,566	4,026	13,573	2,277	6,807	951	3,754
SEX										
Male	289,187	222,685	(NA)	(NA)	(NA)	(NA)	68,620	60,287	25,472	29,146
Female	262,813	200,999	(NA)	(NA)	(NA)	(NA)	62,380	54,269	25,528	28,306
LENGTH OF STAY										
Mean months	32.3	26.7	(X)	(X)	22.7	22.0	43.5	38.0	(X)	(X)
Median months	19.8	15.4	(X)	(X)	12.0	13.7	35.1	29.0	(X)	(X)

NA Not available. X Not applicable. [1] Preliminary data. [2] Beginning with the 2000 census, respondents could choose more than one race. Data represent persons who selected this race group only and exclude persons reporting more than one race. The census in prior years only allowed respondents to report one race group. See also comments on race in the text for section 1. [3] Hispanic persons of origin may be any race.
Source: U.S. Department of Health and Human Services, Administration for Children and Families, Adoption and Foster Care Analysis and Reporting System Reports, annual. See also <http://www.acf.hhs.gov/programs/cb/stats_research/index.htm#afcars>.

Table 580. Private Philanthropy Funds by Source and Allocation: 1990 to 2009

[In billions of dollars (101.4 represents $101,400,000,000). Estimates for sources of funds based on U.S. Internal Revenue Service reports of individual charitable deductions and household surveys of giving by Independent Sector and the Center on Philanthropy at Indiana University. For corporate giving, data are corporate charitable deductions from the U.S. Internal Revenue Service and the contributions made by corporate foundations as reported by the Foundation Center. Data about foundation donations are based upon surveys of foundations and data provided by the Foundation Center. Estimates of the allocation of funds were derived from surveys of nonprofits conducted by various sources]

Source and allocation	1990	1995	2000	2001	2002	2003	2004	2005	2006	2007	2008	2009
Total funds	101.4	123.7	229.7	231.1	231.5	236.3	260.5	293.8	294.9	306.4	307.7	303.8
Individuals	81.0	95.4	174.5	172.4	172.8	180.2	202.2	221.4	223.0	229.0	229.3	227.4
Foundations [1]	7.2	10.6	24.6	27.2	27.0	26.8	28.4	32.4	34.9	38.5	41.2	38.4
Corporations	5.5	7.4	10.7	11.6	10.8	11.1	11.4	16.6	15.4	15.7	14.5	14.1
Charitable bequests...........	7.6	10.4	19.9	19.8	20.9	18.2	18.5	23.5	21.7	23.2	22.7	23.8
Allocation:												
Religion	49.8	58.1	77.0	79.9	82.9	84.6	88.0	93.0	97.7	102.3	106.9	101.0
Health	9.9	13.9	16.4	18.3	17.8	17.8	20.2	22.5	22.0	23.2	21.6	22.5
Education..................	12.4	15.6	29.7	32.7	30.0	30.0	33.8	37.3	40.7	43.3	40.9	40.0
Human service	11.8	9.7	20.0	21.8	24.4	24.4	24.4	26.1	27.4	29.6	25.9	27.1
Arts, culture, and humanities....	7.9	5.7	10.5	11.4	10.8	10.8	11.8	11.8	12.7	13.7	12.8	12.3
Public/societal benefit	4.9	11.3	15.4	16.5	18.0	16.4	18.8	21.3	21.4	22.7	23.8	22.8
Environment/wildlife...........	2.5	2.3	4.8	5.3	5.3	5.4	5.5	6.0	6.3	7.0	6.6	6.2
International.................	1.3	3.0	7.2	8.3	8.7	9.8	11.6	15.2	11.4	13.2	13.3	8.9
Gifts to foundations [1]	3.8	8.5	24.7	25.7	19.2	21.6	20.3	27.5	30.6	27.7	32.7	31.0
Unallocated [2]	−3.0	−4.4	24.2	11.3	14.6	13.8	26.2	33.2	24.8	23.7	19.4	28.6

[1] Data are from the Foundation Center through 2001. [2] Money deducted as a charitable contribution by donors but not allocated to sources. May include gifts to governmental entities, in-kind giving, and gifts to new charities.

Source: Giving USA Foundation 2010, Glenview, IL, researched and written by the Center on Philanthropy at Indiana University, *Giving USA*, annual (copyright).

Table 581. Foundations—Number and Finances by Asset Size: 1990 to 2009

[Figures are for latest year reported by foundations (142,500 represents $142,500,000,000). Covers nongovernmental nonprofit organizations with funds and programs managed by their own trustees or directors, whose goals were to maintain or aid social, educational, religious, or other activities deemed to serve the common good. Excludes organizations that make general appeals to the public for funds, act as trade associations for industrial or other special groups, or do not currently award grants]

Asset size	Number	Assets (mil. dol.)	Gifts received (mil. dol.)	Total giving [1] (mil. dol.)
1990........................	32,401	142,500	5,000	8,700
2000........................	56,582	486,100	27,600	27,600
2005........................	71,095	550,600	31,500	36,400
2008........................	75,595	564,951	39,554	46,781
2009, Total	76,544	590,188	40,862	45,778
Under $50,000.................	12,551	193	2,354	2,590
$50,000–$99,999...............	4,958	367	154	207
$100,000–$249,999.............	10,153	1,703	409	573
$250,000–$499,999.............	9,738	3,557	396	589
$500,000–$999,999.............	10,980	7,952	968	1,345
$1,000,000–$4,999,999..........	17,887	40,844	2,790	4,098
$5,000,000–$9,999,999..........	4,214	29,857	2,194	2,660
$10,000,000–$49,999,999........	4,558	96,565	7,185	8,659
$50,000,000–$99,999,999........	762	52,417	3,920	4,530
$100,000,000–$249,999,999......	483	71,981	4,876	4,749
$250,000,000 or more...........	260	284,754	15,616	15,777

[1] Includes grants, scholarships, and employee matching gifts; excludes set-asides, loans, program-related investments (PRIs), and program expenses.

Source: The Foundation Center, New York, NY, *Foundation Yearbook 2011*, annual (copyright).

Table 582. Domestic Private Foundations—Information Returns: 1990 to 2007

[In billions (122.4 represents $122,400,000,000), except for number of returns. Minus sign (–) indicates loss]

Item	1990	1995	1999	2000	2001	2002	2003	2004	2005	2006	2007
Number of returns	40,105	47,917	62,694	66,738	70,787	73,255	76,348	76,897	79,535	81,850	84,613
Nonoperating foundations [1]	36,880	43,966	58,840	61,501	63,650	67,101	70,004	70,613	72,800	74,364	77,457
Operating foundations [2]	3,226	3,951	3,854	5,238	7,137	6,154	6,344	6,284	6,734	7,486	7,156
Total assets, book value	122.4	195.6	384.6	409.5	413.6	383.5	418.5	455.5	481.8	569.3	591.2
Total assets, fair market value	151.0	242.9	466.9	471.6	455.4	413.0	475.0	509.9	545.9	645.8	652.4
Investments in securities	115.0	190.7	363.4	361.4	329.4	294.4	344.3	361.2	373.1	403.7	400.3
Total revenue	19.0	30.8	83.3	72.8	45.3	27.8	48.4	58.7	76.4	94.1	107.3
Total expenses...................	11.3	17.2	33.9	37.4	36.7	34.4	35.1	36.6	42.8	48.8	58.8
Contributions, gifts, and grants paid..................	8.6	12.3	22.8	27.6	27.4	26.3	26.7	27.6	31.9	34.9	42.6
Excess of revenue over expenses (net).................	7.7	13.6	49.4	35.3	8.6	-6.6	13.3	22.1	33.5	45.3	48.6
Net investment income [3]	11.9	20.4	57.1	48.8	25.7	17.6	25.2	34.0	44.3	54.2	62.8

[1] Generally provide charitable support through grants and other financial means to charitable organizations; the majority of foundations are nonoperating. [2] Generally conduct their own charitable activities, e.g., museums. [3] Represents income not considered related to a foundation's charitable purpose, e.g., interest, dividends, and capital gains. Foundations could be subject to an excise tax on such income.

Source: Source: Internal Revenue Service, Statistics of Income, SOI Tax Stats—Domestic Private Foundation and Charitable Trust Statistics, <http://www.irs.gov/taxstats/charitablestats/article/0,,id=96996,00.html#2\>, accessed February 2011.

Social Insurance and Human Services **371**

Table 583. Nonprofit Charitable Organizations—Information Returns: 2000 and 2007

[In billions of dollars (1,562.5 represents $1,562,500,000,000), except as indicated. Categories based on The National Taxonomy of Exempt Entities (NTEE), a classification system that uses 26 major field areas that are aggregated into 10 categories. Includes data reported by organizations described in Internal Revenue Code, Section 501(3), excluding private foundations and most religious organizations. Organizations with receipts under $25,000 were not required to file]

Year and major category	Number of returns (1,000)	Total assets (billions)	Total fund balance or net worth (billions)	Revenue Total	Revenue Program service revenue [1]	Revenue Contributions, gifts, and grants	Total expenses (billions)	Excess of revenue over expenses (net)
2000.	230.2	1,562.5	1,023.2	866.2	579.1	199.1	796.4	69.8
2007, total	**313.1**	**2,683.4**	**1,674.4**	**1,445.9**	**980.3**	**324.5**	**1,317.2**	**128.7**
Arts, culture, and humanities. . .	31.8	102.2	82.1	34.0	8.3	18.5	28.3	5.7
Education.	55.4	939.8	663.6	293.1	149.1	92.2	243.9	49.2
Environment, animals	14.4	39.9	33.4	14.8	3.0	9.7	11.4	3.3
Health	36.5	1,015.1	542.6	801.0	697.4	60.2	758.7	42.3
Human services.	120.0	290.3	141.6	187.8	98.8	72.0	178.8	9.0
International, foreign affairs. . . .	5.1	23.7	17.2	22.6	1.8	19.6	21.6	1.0
Mutual, membership benefit . . .	0.7	18.3	8.9	3.3	2.0	0.2	2.5	0.8
Public, societal benefit.	29.4	228.4	164.6	78.6	18.4	44.6	62.7	15.9
Religion related	19.9	25.8	20.4	10.9	1.6	7.6	9.4	1.6

[1] Represents fees collected by organizations in support of their tax-exempt purposes, and income such as tuition and fees at educational institutions, hospital patient charges, and admission and activity fees collected by museums and other nonprofit organizations or institutions.

Source: Internal Revenue Service, Statistics of Income, *SOI Tax Stats—Charities and Other Tax-Exempt Organizations Statistics.* See also <http://www.irs.gov/taxstats/charitablestats/article/0,,id=97176,00.html#3>.

Table 584. Individual Charitable Contributions by State: 2008

[In millions of dollars (170,397 represents 170,397,000,000), except as indicated. For tax year. Data will not agree with data in other tables due to differing survey methodology used to derive state data]

State	Charitable contribution Number of returns (1,000)	Charitable contribution Amount (mil. dol.)	State	Charitable contribution Number of returns (1,000)	Charitable contribution Amount (mil. dol.)	State	Charitable contribution Number of returns (1,000)	Charitable contribution Amount (mil. dol.)	State	Charitable contribution Number of returns (1,000)	Charitable contribution Amount (mil. dol.)
U.S.[1,2] . . .	**39,235**	**170,397**	IL	1,742	7,123	NE . . .	215	1,006	SD . . .	59	417
AL	538	2,908	IN	668	2,733	NV . . .	348	1,289	TN . . .	570	3,380
AK	68	303	IA	353	1,296	NH . . .	182	505	TX . . .	2,133	13,660
AZ	804	2,912	KS . . .	330	1,568	NJ . . .	1,603	5,340	UT . . .	386	2,849
AR	241	1,316	KY . . .	450	1,813	NM . . .	181	690	VT . . .	71	247
CA	4,968	20,777	LA . . .	374	2,112	NY . . .	2,899	13,732	VA . . .	1,241	5,677
CO	747	2,982	ME . . .	148	402	NC . . .	1,244	5,362	WA . . .	886	3,615
CT	640	2,617	MD . . .	1,140	4,693	ND . . .	49	226	WV . . .	106	457
DE	128	465	MA . . .	1,054	3,757	OH . . .	1,389	4,676	WI . . .	811	2,454
DC	102	647	MI . . .	1,308	4,693	OK . . .	359	2,602	WY . . .	46	412
FL	2,116	9,596	MN . . .	871	3,296	OR . . .	550	1,923			
GA	1,338	6,177	MS . . .	253	1,466	PA . . .	1,556	5,778			
HI	175	569	MO . . .	668	2,810	RI . . .	157	420			
ID	181	813	MT . . .	112	478	SC . . .	545	2,561			

[1] The sum for the states does not add to the total because other components are not shown in this table. [2] U.S. totals do not agree with Table 489 in Section 9 because this table also includes (1) "substitutes for returns," whereby the IRS constructs returns for certain nonfilers on the basis of available information and imposes and income tax on the resulting estimate of the tax base and (2) returns of nonresident or departing aliens. In addition, in this table, income tax includes the alternative minimum tax, but differs from total income tax in Table 489 in that it is after subtraction of all tax credits except a portion of the earned income credit.

Source: Internal Revenue Service, *Statistics of Income Bulletin,* Spring issue. See also <http://www.irs.gov/taxstats/article/0,,id=117514,00.html>.

Table 585. Volunteers by Selected Characteristics: 2010

[In percent, except as noted. Data on volunteers relate to persons who performed unpaid volunteer activities for an organization at any point from September 1, 2009 through September 2010. Data represent the percent of the population involved in the activity]

Type of main organization [1]	Total, both sexes	Sex Male	Sex Female	Educational attainment [2] Less than a high school diploma	Educational attainment [2] High school graduate, no college [3]	Educational attainment [2] Less than a bachelor's degree [4]	Educational attainment [2] College graduates
Total volunteers (1,000)	**62,790**	**26,787**	**36,004**	**2,231**	**10,887**	**15,505**	**25,870**
Percent of population	26.3	23.2	29.3	8.8	17.9	29.2	42.3
Median annual hours [5]	52	52	52	52	52	52	56
Civic and political [6]	5.3	6.4	4.5	3.3	5.1	5.5	5.7
Educational or youth service	26.5	25.4	27.2	23.9	23.7	25.2	27.3
Environmental or animal care . . .	2.4	2.4	2.5	0.4	1.5	2.4	2.7
Hospital or other health	7.9	6.5	9.0	4.7	8.1	8.4	7.6
Public safety	1.3	2.2	0.6	1.0	1.8	1.7	0.7
Religious	33.8	32.9	34.5	49.7	39.0	34.3	31.9
Social or community service	13.6	14.2	13.1	11.1	12.9	13.2	14.3
Sport and hobby [7]	3.3	3.9	2.8	1.2	2.5	3.1	3.9

[1] Main organization is defined as the organization for which the volunteer worked the most hours during the year. See headnote for more details. [2] Data refer to persons 25 years and over. [3] Includes high school diploma or equivalent. [4] Includes the categories, "some college, no degree" and "associate's degree." [5] At all organizations. For those reporting annual hours. [6] Includes professional and/or international. [7] Includes cultural and/or arts.

Source: U.S. Bureau of Labor Statistics, News release, USDL 11–0084, January 2011. See also <http://www.bls.gov/news.release/pdf/volun.pdf>.

Labor Force, Employment, and Earnings

This section presents statistics on the labor force; its distribution by occupation and industry affiliation; and the supply of, demand for, and conditions of labor. The chief source of these data is the Current Population Survey (CPS) conducted by the U.S. Census Bureau for the Bureau of Labor Statistics (BLS). Comprehensive historical and current data are available from the BLS Internet site at <http://www .bls.gov /cps/>. These data are published on a current basis in the BLS monthly publication *Employment and Earnings Online.* Detailed data on the labor force are also available from the Census Bureau's decennial census of population.

Types of data—Most statistics in this section are obtained by two methods: household interviews or questionnaires and reports of establishment payroll records. Each method provides data that the other cannot suitably supply. Population characteristics, for example, are readily obtainable only from the household survey, while detailed industrial classifications can be readily derived only from establishment records.

CPS data are obtained from a monthly sample survey of the population. The CPS is used to gather data for the calendar week, generally the week including the 12th of the month, and provides current comprehensive data on the labor force (see text, Section 1, Population). The CPS provides information on the work status of the population without duplication since each person is classified as employed, unemployed, or not in the labor force. Employed persons holding more than one job are counted only once, according to the job at which they worked the most hours during the survey week.

Monthly, quarterly, and annual data from the CPS are published by the BLS in *Employment and Earnings Online.* Data presented include national totals of the number of persons in the civilian labor force by sex, disability status, race, Hispanic origin, and age; the number employed; hours of work; industry and occupational groups; usual weekly earnings; and the number unemployed, reasons for, and duration of unemployment. Annual data shown in this section are averages of monthly figures for each calendar year, unless otherwise specified. Historical national CPS data are available at <http://www.bls.gov/cps/>.

The CPS also produces annual estimates of employment and unemployment for each state, 50 large metropolitan statistical areas, and selected cities. These estimates are published by the BLS in its annual *Geographic Profile of Employment and Unemployment* available at <http://www.bls.gov/gps/>. More detailed geographic data (e.g., for counties and cities) are provided by the decennial population censuses.

Data based on establishment records are compiled by the BLS and cooperating state agencies as part of an ongoing Current Employment Statistics program. The BLS collects survey data monthly from a probability-based sample of nonfarm, business establishments through internet electronic data interchange, touchtone data entry, and computer-assisted telephone interviews, Internet, other electronic media, fax, transcript, or mail. CES data are adjusted annually to data from government unemployment insurance administrative records, which are supplemented by data from other government agencies. The estimates exclude self-employed persons, private household workers, unpaid family workers, agricultural workers, and members of the Armed Forces. In March 2010, reporting establishments employed 2.8 million manufacturing workers (25 percent of the total manufacturing employment at the time), 20.6 million workers in private nonmanufacturing industries (21.8 percent of the total in private nonmanufacturing), and 15.6 million federal, state, and local government employees (68 percent of total government).

U.S. Census Bureau, Statistical Abstract of the United States: 2012

The establishment survey counts workers each time they appear on a payroll during the reference period (the payroll period that includes the 12th of the month). Thus, unlike the CPS, a person with two jobs is counted twice. The establishment survey is designed to provide estimates of nonfarm wage and salary employment, average weekly hours, and average hourly and weekly earnings by detailed industry for the nation, states, and selected metropolitan areas. Establishment survey data also are published in *Employment and Earnings Online*. Historical national data are available at <http://www.bls.gov /ces/>. Historical data for states and metropolitan areas are available at <http://www.bls.gov/sae/>. CES estimates are currently classified by the 2007 North American Industry Classification System (NAICS). All published series for the nation have a NAICS–based history extending back to at least 1990. Employment series for total nonfarm and other high-level aggregates start in 1939.

For more information on data concepts, sample design, and estimating methods for the CES Survey, see the BLS Handbook of Methods, Chater 2 <http://bls.gov /opub/hom/homch2.htm>.

The completion of the sample redesign and the conversion to NAICS for state and metropolitan area establishment survey data were implemented in March 2003 with the release of January 2003 estimates. For a discussion of the changes to the state and area establishment survey data, see "Revisions to the Current Employment Statistics State and Area Estimates Effective January 2003" in the March 2003 issue of *Employment and Earnings Online*.

Labor force—According to the CPS definitions, the civilian labor force comprises all civilians in the noninstitutionalized population 16 years and over classified as "employed" or "unemployed" according to the following criteria: Employed civilians comprise (a) all civilians, who, during the reference week, did any work for pay or profit (minimum of an hour's work) or worked 15 hours

or more as unpaid workers in a family enterprise and (b) all civilians who were not working but who had jobs or businesses from which they were temporarily absent for noneconomic reasons (illness, weather conditions, vacation, labor-management dispute, etc.) whether they were paid for the time off or were seeking other jobs. Unemployed persons comprise all civilians who had no employment during the reference week, who made specific efforts to find a job within the previous 4 weeks (such as applying directly to an employer or to a public employment service or checking with friends) and who were available for work during that week, except for temporary illness. Persons on layoff from a job and expecting recall also are classified as unemployed. All other civilian persons, 16 years old and over, are classified as "not in the labor force."

Various breaks in the CPS data series have occurred over time due to the introduction of population adjustments and other changes. For details on these breaks in series and the effect that they had on the CPS data, see the BLS Web site at <www.bls.gov.cps/documentation .htm#concepts.>.

Beginning in January of each year, the CPS data reflect the introduction of revised population controls. For additional information on the effects of revised population controls on estimates from the CPS, see <www.bls.gov.cps/documentation .htm#pop>.

Hours and earnings—Average hourly earnings, based on establishment data, are gross earnings (i.e., earnings before payroll deductions) and include overtime premiums; they exclude irregular bonuses and value of payments in kind. Hours are those for which pay was received. Annual wages and salaries from the CPS consist of total monies received for work performed by an employee during the income year. It includes wages, salaries, commissions, tips, piece-rate payments, and cash bonuses earned before deductions were made for taxes, bonds, union dues, etc. Persons who worked 35 hours or more are classified as working full-time.

Industry and occupational groups—Industry data derived from the CPS for 1983–91 utilize the 1980 census industrial classification developed from the 1972 SIC. CPS data from 1971 to 1982 were based on the 1970 census classification system, which was developed from the 1967 SIC. Most of the industry categories were not affected by the change in classification.

The occupational classification system used in the 1980 census and in the CPS for 1983–91, evolved from the 1980 Standard Occupational Classification (SOC) system, first introduced in 1977. Occupational categories used in the 1980 census classification system are so radically different from the 1970 census system used in the CPS through 1982 that their implementation represented a break in historical data series.

Beginning in January 1992, the occupational and industrial classification systems used in the 1990 census were introduced into the CPS. (These systems were largely based on the 1980 SOC and the 1987 SIC systems, respectively.)

Beginning in 2003, the 2002 occupational and industrial classification systems were introduced into the CPS. These systems were derived from the 2000 SOC and the 2002 NAICS. The composition of detailed occupational and industrial classifications in the new classification systems was substantially changed from the previous systems in use, as was the structure for aggregating them into broad groups. Consequently, the use of the new classification systems created breaks in existing data series at all levels of aggregation. CPS data using the new classification systems are available beginning 2000. Additional information on the occupational and industrial classifications systems used in the CPS, including changes over time, appear on the BLS Web site at <www.bls.gov/cps/documentation .htm#oi >. Establishments responding to the establishment survey are classified according to the 2007 NAICS. Previously they were classified according to the SIC manual. See text, Section 15, Business Enterprise, for information about the SIC manual and NAICS.

Productivity—BLS publishes data on productivity as measured by output per hour (labor productivity), output per combined unit of labor and capital input (multifactor productivity), and, for industry groups and industries, output per combined unit of capital, labor, energy, materials, and purchased service inputs. Labor productivity and related indexes are published for the business sector as a whole and its major subsectors: nonfarm business, manufacturing, and nonfinancial corporations, and for over 200 detailed industries. Productivity indexes that take into account capital, labor, energy, materials, and service inputs are published for 18 major manufacturing industry groups, 86 detailed manufacturing industries, utility services, and air and railroad transportation. The major sector data are published in the BLS quarterly news release *Productivity and Costs* and in the annual *Multifactor Productivity Trends* release. Industry productivity measures are updated and published annually in the news releases *Productivity and Costs by Industry* and *Multifactor Productivity Trends by Industry*. The latest data are available at the Labor Productivity and Costs Web site at <http://www.bls.gov/lpc/> and the Multifactor Productivity Web site at <http://www.bls.gov/mfp>. Detailed information on methods, limitations, and data sources appears in the BLS *Handbook of Methods*, BLS Bulletin 2490 (1997), Chapters 10 and 11 at <http://www.bls .gov/opub/hom /home.htm>.

Unions—As defined here, unions include traditional labor unions and employee associations similar to labor unions. Data on union membership status provided by BLS are for employed wage and salary workers and relate to their principal job. Earnings by union membership status are usual weekly earnings of full-time wage and salary workers. The information is collected through the Current Population Survey.

Work stoppages—Work stoppages include all strikes and lockouts known to BLS that last for at least 1 full day or shift and involve 1,000 or more workers. All stoppages, whether or not authorized by a union, legal or illegal, are counted. Excluded are work slow-downs and instances where employees report to work late or leave early to attend mass meetings or mass rallies.

Seasonal adjustment—Many economic statistics reflect a regularly recurring seasonal movement that can be estimated on the basis of past experience. By eliminating that part of the change which can be ascribed to usual seasonal variation (e.g., climate or school openings and closings), it is possible to observe the cyclical and other nonseasonal movements in the series. However, in evaluating deviations from the seasonal pattern—that is, changes in a seasonally adjusted series—it is important to note that seasonal adjustment is merely an approximation based on past experience. Seasonally adjusted estimates have a broader margin of possible error than the original data on which they are based, since they are subject not only to sampling and other errors, but also are affected by the uncertainties of the adjustment process itself. Consistent with BLS practices, annual estimates will be published only for not seasonally-adjusted data.

Statistical reliability—For discussion of statistical collection, estimation, sampling procedures, and measures of statistical reliability applicable to Census Bureau and BLS data, see Appendix III.

Table 586. Civilian Population—Employment Status: 1970 to 2010

[In thousands (137,085 represents 137,085,000), except as indicated. Annual averages of monthly figures. Civilian noninstitutionalized population 16 years old and over. Based on Current Population Survey; see text, Section 1 and Appendix III]

Year	Civilian noninsti-tutional population	Civilian labor force				Unemployed		Not in labor force	
		Total	Percent of population	Employed	Employ-ment/ population ratio [1]	Number	Percent of labor force	Number	Percent of population
1970..........	137,085	82,771	60.4	78,678	57.4	4,093	4.9	54,315	39.6
1980..........	167,745	106,940	63.8	99,303	59.2	7,637	7.1	60,806	36.2
1990 [2]	189,164	125,840	66.5	118,793	62.8	7,047	5.6	63,324	33.5
1995..........	198,584	132,304	66.6	124,900	62.9	7,404	5.6	66,280	33.4
1996..........	200,591	133,943	66.8	126,708	63.2	7,236	5.4	66,647	33.2
1997 [2]	203,133	136,297	67.1	129,558	63.8	6,739	4.9	66,836	32.9
1998 [2]	205,220	137,673	67.1	131,463	64.1	6,210	4.5	67,547	32.9
1999 [2]	207,753	139,368	67.1	133,488	64.3	5,880	4.2	68,385	32.9
2000 [2]	212,577	142,583	67.1	136,891	64.4	5,692	4.0	69,994	32.9
2001..........	215,092	143,734	66.8	136,933	63.7	6,801	4.7	71,359	33.2
2002..........	217,570	144,863	66.6	136,485	62.7	8,378	5.8	72,707	33.4
2003 [2]	221,168	146,510	66.2	137,736	62.3	8,774	6.0	74,658	33.8
2004 [2]	223,357	147,401	66.0	139,252	62.3	8,149	5.5	75,956	34.0
2005 [2]	226,082	149,320	66.0	141,730	62.7	7,591	5.1	76,762	34.0
2006 [2]	228,815	151,428	66.2	144,427	63.1	7,001	4.6	77,387	33.8
2007 [2]	231,867	153,124	66.0	146,047	63.0	7,078	4.6	78,743	34.0
2008 [2]	233,788	154,287	66.0	145,362	62.2	8,924	5.8	79,501	34.0
2009 [2]	235,801	154,142	65.4	139,877	59.3	14,265	9.3	81,659	34.6
2010 [2]	237,830	153,889	64.7	139,064	58.5	14,825	9.6	83,941	35.3

[1] Civilian employed as a percent of the civilian noninstitutional population. [2] Data not strictly comparable with data for earlier years. See text, this section, and February 1994, March 1996, February 1997–99, and February 2003–11 issues of Employment and Earnings.
Source: U.S. Bureau of Labor Statistics, "Employment and Earnings Online," January 2011 issue, March 2011, <http://www.bls.gov/opub/ee/home.htm> and <http://www.bls.gov/cps/home.htm>.

Table 587. Civilian Labor Force and Participation Rates With Projections: 1980 to 2018

[106.9 represents 106,900,000. Civilian noninstitutionalized population 16 years old and over. Annual averages of monthly figures. Rates are based on annual average civilian noninstitutional population of each specified group and represent proportion of each specified group in the civilian labor force. Based on Current Population Survey; see text, Section 1 and Appendix III]

Race, Hispanic origin, sex, and age	Civilian labor force (mil.)						Participation rate (percent) [1]					
	1980	1990 [2]	2000 [2]	2005 [2]	2010 [2]	2018, proj.	1980	1990 [2]	2000 [2]	2005 [2]	2010 [2]	2018, proj.
Total [3]	106.9	125.8	142.6	149.3	153.9	166.9	63.8	66.5	67.1	66.0	64.7	64.5
White [4]	93.6	107.4	118.5	122.3	125.1	132.5	64.1	66.9	67.3	66.3	65.1	64.5
Male.............	54.5	59.6	64.5	66.7	67.7	71.7	78.2	77.1	75.5	74.1	72.0	71.1
Female............	39.1	47.8	54.1	55.6	57.4	60.8	51.2	57.4	59.5	58.9	58.5	58.2
Black [4]	10.9	13.7	16.4	17.0	17.9	20.2	61.0	64.0	65.8	64.2	62.2	63.3
Male.............	5.6	6.8	7.7	8.0	8.4	9.6	70.3	71.0	69.2	67.3	65.0	65.7
Female............	5.3	6.9	8.7	9.0	9.4	10.7	53.1	58.3	63.1	61.6	59.9	61.2
Asian [4,5]	(NA)	(NA)	6.3	6.5	7.2	9.3	(NA)	(NA)	67.2	66.1	64.7	65.0
Male.............	(NA)	(NA)	3.4	3.5	3.9	4.9	(NA)	(NA)	76.1	74.8	73.2	73.7
Female............	(NA)	(NA)	2.9	3.0	3.4	4.4	(NA)	(NA)	59.2	58.2	57.0	57.4
Hispanic [6]...........	6.1	10.7	16.7	19.8	22.7	29.3	64.0	67.4	69.7	68.0	67.5	67.3
Male.............	3.8	6.5	9.9	12.0	13.5	17.1	81.4	81.4	81.5	80.1	77.8	78.2
Female............	2.3	4.2	6.8	7.8	9.2	12.3	47.4	53.1	57.5	55.3	56.5	56.4
Male..............	61.5	69.0	76.3	80.0	82.0	88.7	77.4	76.4	74.8	73.3	71.2	70.6
16 to 19 years	5.0	4.1	4.3	3.6	3.0	2.9	60.5	55.7	52.8	43.2	34.9	33.2
20 to 24 years	8.6	7.9	7.5	8.1	7.9	8.1	85.9	84.4	82.6	79.1	74.5	75.2
25 to 34 years	17.0	19.9	17.8	17.8	18.4	20.2	95.2	94.1	93.4	91.7	89.7	90.6
35 to 44 years	11.8	17.5	20.1	19.5	18.1	19.1	95.5	94.3	92.7	92.1	91.5	92.0
45 to 54 years	9.9	11.1	16.3	18.1	18.9	18.0	91.2	90.7	88.6	87.7	86.8	87.1
55 to 64 years	7.2	6.6	7.8	10.0	12.1	14.5	72.1	67.8	67.3	69.3	70.0	71.2
65 years and over ...	1.9	2.0	2.5	3.0	3.7	5.9	19.0	16.3	17.7	19.8	22.1	26.7
Female.............	45.5	56.8	66.3	69.3	71.9	78.2	51.5	57.5	59.9	59.3	58.6	58.7
16 to 19 years	4.4	3.7	4.0	3.6	2.9	2.9	52.9	51.6	51.2	44.2	35.0	34.4
20 to 24 years	7.3	6.8	6.7	7.1	7.2	7.2	68.9	71.3	73.1	70.1	68.3	67.3
25 to 34 years	12.3	16.1	14.9	14.5	15.3	16.6	65.5	73.5	76.1	73.9	74.7	74.2
35 to 44 years	8.6	14.7	17.5	16.5	15.2	15.7	65.5	76.4	77.2	75.8	75.2	74.6
45 to 54 years	7.0	9.1	14.8	16.3	17.1	16.3	59.9	71.2	76.8	76.0	75.7	76.6
55 to 64 years	4.7	4.9	6.6	8.9	11.2	14.3	41.3	45.2	51.9	57.0	60.2	65.3
65 years and over ...	1.2	1.5	1.8	2.3	3.0	5.2	8.1	8.6	9.4	11.5	13.8	18.9

NA Not available. [1] Civilian labor force as a percent of the civilian noninstitutional population. [2] See footnote 2, Table 586. [3] Includes other races, not shown separately. [4] The 2005 Current Population Survey (CPS) allowed respondents to choose more than one race. Beginning 2005, data represent persons who selected this race group only and exclude persons reporting more than one race. Prior to 2005 the CPS only allowed respondents to report one race group. See also comments on race in the text for Section 1. [5] Prior to 2005, includes Pacific Islanders. [6] Persons of Hispanic origin may be any race.
Source: U.S. Bureau of Labor Statistics,"Employment and Earnings Online," January 2011; "Monthly Labor Review," November 2009; and "Employment Projections Program," <http://www.bls.gov/emp/ep_data_labor_force.htm>.

Table 588. Civilian Population—Employment Status by Sex, Race, and Ethnicity: 1970 to 2009

[In thousands (64,304 represents 64,304,000), except as indicated. Annual averages of monthly figures. See Table 586 for U.S. totals and coverage]

Year, sex, race, and Hispanic origin	Civilian noninstitutionalized population	Civilian labor force				Unemployed		Not in labor force	
		Total	Percent of population	Employed	Employment/population ratio [1]	Number	Percent of labor force	Number	Percent of population
Male:									
1970	64,304	51,228	79.7	48,990	76.2	2,238	4.4	13,076	20.3
1980	79,398	61,453	77.4	57,186	72.0	4,267	6.9	17,945	22.6
1990 [2]	90,377	69,011	76.4	65,104	72.0	3,906	5.7	21,367	23.6
2000 [2]	101,964	76,280	74.8	73,305	71.9	2,975	3.9	25,684	25.2
2005 [2]	109,151	80,033	73.3	75,973	69.6	4,059	5.1	29,119	26.7
2008 [2]	113,113	82,520	73.0	77,486	68.5	5,033	6.1	30,593	27.0
2009 [2]	114,136	82,123	72.0	73,670	64.5	8,453	10.3	32,013	28.0
2010 [2]	115,174	81,985	71.2	73,359	63.7	8,626	10.5	33,189	28.8
Female:									
1970	72,782	31,543	43.3	29,688	40.8	1,855	5.9	41,239	56.7
1980	88,348	45,487	51.5	42,117	47.7	3,370	7.4	42,861	48.5
1990 [2]	98,787	56,829	57.5	53,689	54.3	3,140	5.5	41,957	42.5
2000 [2]	110,613	66,303	59.9	63,586	57.5	2,717	4.1	44,310	40.1
2005 [2]	116,931	69,288	59.3	65,757	56.2	3,531	5.1	47,643	40.7
2008 [2]	120,675	71,767	59.5	67,876	56.2	3,891	5.4	48,908	40.5
2009 [2]	121,665	72,019	59.2	66,208	54.4	5,811	8.1	49,646	40.8
2010 [2]	122,656	71,904	58.6	65,705	53.6	6,199	8.6	50,752	41.4
White: [3]									
1980	146,122	93,600	64.1	87,715	60.0	5,884	6.3	52,523	35.9
1990 [2]	160,625	107,447	66.9	102,261	63.7	5,186	4.8	53,178	33.1
2000 [2]	176,220	118,545	67.3	114,424	64.9	4,121	3.5	57,675	32.7
2005 [2]	184,446	122,299	66.3	116,949	63.4	5,350	4.4	62,148	33.7
2008 [2]	189,540	125,635	66.3	119,126	62.8	6,509	5.2	63,905	33.7
2009 [2]	190,902	125,644	65.8	114,996	60.2	10,648	8.5	65,258	34.2
2010 [2]	192,075	125,084	65.1	114,168	59.4	10,916	8.7	66,991	34.9
Black: [3]									
1980	17,824	10,865	61.0	9,313	52.2	1,553	14.3	6,959	39.0
1990 [2]	21,477	13,740	64.0	12,175	56.7	1,565	11.4	7,737	36.0
2000 [2]	24,902	16,397	65.8	15,156	60.9	1,241	7.6	8,505	34.2
2005 [2]	26,517	17,013	64.2	15,313	57.7	1,700	10.0	9,504	35.8
2008 [2]	27,843	17,740	63.7	15,953	57.3	1,788	10.1	10,103	36.3
2009 [2]	28,241	17,632	62.4	15,025	53.2	2,606	14.8	10,609	37.6
2010 [2]	28,708	17,862	62.2	15,010	52.3	2,852	16.0	10,846	37.8
Asian: [3, 4]									
2000.	9,330	6,270	67.2	6,043	64.8	227	3.6	3,060	32.8
2005 [2]	9,842	6,503	66.1	6,244	63.4	259	4.0	3,339	33.9
2008 [2]	10,751	7,202	67.0	6,917	64.3	285	4.0	3,549	33.0
2009 [2]	10,842	7,156	66.0	6,635	61.2	522	7.3	3,685	34.0
2010 [2]	11,199	7,248	64.7	6,705	59.9	543	7.5	3,951	35.3
Hispanic: [5]									
1980	9,598	6,146	64.0	5,527	57.6	620	10.1	3,451	36.0
1990 [2]	15,904	10,720	67.4	9,845	61.9	876	8.2	5,184	32.6
2000 [2]	23,938	16,689	69.7	15,735	65.7	954	5.7	7,249	30.3
2005 [2]	29,133	19,824	68.0	18,632	64.0	1,191	6.0	9,310	32.0
2008 [2]	32,141	22,024	68.5	20,346	63.3	1,678	7.6	10,116	31.5
2009 [2]	32,891	22,352	68.0	19,647	59.7	2,706	12.1	10,539	32.0
2010 [2]	33,713	22,748	67.5	19,906	59.0	2,843	12.5	10,964	32.5
Mexican:									
1990 [2]	9,752	6,707	68.8	6,146	63.0	561	8.4	3,045	31.2
2000 [2]	15,333	10,783	70.3	10,144	66.2	639	5.9	4,550	29.7
2005 [2]	18,523	12,671	68.4	11,887	64.2	784	6.2	5,851	31.6
2008 [2]	20,474	14,009	68.4	12,931	63.2	1,078	7.7	6,465	31.6
2009 [2]	20,923	14,210	67.9	12,478	59.6	1,732	12.2	6,713	32.1
2010 [2]	21,267	14,403	67.7	12,622	59.4	1,781	12.4	6,864	32.3
Puerto Rican:									
1990 [2]	1,718	960	55.9	870	50.6	91	9.5	758	44.1
2000 [2]	2,193	1,411	64.3	1,318	60.1	92	6.6	783	35.7
2005 [2]	2,654	1,619	61.0	1,492	56.2	126	7.8	1,035	39.0
2008 [2]	2,854	1,822	63.9	1,634	57.3	188	10.3	1,032	36.2
2009 [2]	2,962	1,850	62.4	1,594	53.8	256	13.8	1,113	37.6
2010 [2]	3,110	1,906	61.3	1,612	51.8	293	15.4	1,204	38.7
Cuban:									
1990 [2]	918	603	65.7	559	60.9	44	7.2	315	34.3
2000 [2]	1,174	740	63.1	707	60.3	33	4.5	434	37.0
2005 [2]	1,259	755	60.0	730	58.0	25	3.3	503	40.0
2008 [2]	1,422	897	63.1	841	59.1	57	6.3	525	36.9
2009 [2]	1,442	877	60.8	795	55.1	82	9.4	565	39.2
2010 [2]	1,549	970	62.6	850	54.9	120	12.4	579	37.4

[1] Civilian employed as a percent of the civilian noninstitutional population. [2] See footnote 2, Table 586. [3] The 2005 Current Population Survey (CPS) allowed respondents to choose more than one race. Beginning 2005, data represent persons who selected this race group only and exclude persons reporting more than one race. The CPS in prior years only allowed respondents to report one race group. See also comments on race in the text for Section 1. [4] Prior to 2005, includes Pacific Islanders. [5] Persons of Hispanic origin may be any race. Includes persons of other Hispanic or Latino ethnicity, not shown separately.

Source: U.S. Bureau of Labor Statistics, "Employment and Earnings Online," January 2011 issue, March 2011, <www.bls.gov/opub/ee/home.htm> and <http://www.bls.gov/cps/home.htm>.

Table 589. Foreign-Born and Native-Born Populations—Employment Status by Selected Characteristics: 2010

[237,830 represents 237,830,000. For civilian noninstitutional population 16 years old and over, except as indicated. The foreign born are persons who reside in the United States but who were born outside the country or one of its outlying areas to parents who were not U.S. citizens. The foreign born include legally admitted immigrants, refugees, temporary residents such as students and temporary workers and undocumented immigrants. Annual averages of monthly figures. Based on Current Population Survey; see text, Section 1 and Appendix III]

Characteristic	Civilian noninstitutionalized population (1,000)	Civilian labor force					Not in the labor force
		Total (1,000)	Participation rate [1]	Employed (1,000)	Unemployed		
					Number (1,000)	Unemployment rate	
Total	**237,830**	**153,889**	**64.7**	**139,064**	**14,825**	**9.6**	**83,941**
Male	115,174	81,985	71.2	73,359	8,626	10.5	33,189
Female	122,656	71,904	58.6	65,705	6,199	8.6	50,752
FOREIGN BORN							
Total [2]	**35,869**	**24,356**	**67.9**	**21,969**	**2,387**	**9.8**	**11,514**
Male	17,936	14,375	80.1	12,946	1,429	9.9	3,561
Female	17,934	9,981	55.7	9,023	958	9.6	7,953
Age:							
16 to 24 years old	3,533	1,975	55.9	1,661	314	15.9	1,559
25 to 34 years old	7,714	5,936	77.0	5,387	550	9.3	1,778
35 to 44 years old	8,470	6,884	81.3	6,265	619	9.0	1,586
45 to 54 years old	6,949	5,719	82.3	5,172	547	9.6	1,231
55 to 64 years old	4,528	3,011	66.5	2,727	284	9.4	1,517
65 years old and over	4,674	831	17.8	757	74	8.9	3,843
Race and Hispanic ethnicity:							
White non-Hispanic	7,363	4,470	60.7	4,138	332	7.4	2,893
Black non-Hispanic	2,898	2,162	74.6	1,893	269	12.4	736
Asian non-Hispanic	8,073	5,315	65.8	4,928	386	7.3	2,758
Hispanic [3]	17,162	12,152	70.8	10,776	1,376	11.3	5,010
Educational attainment:							
Total, 25 years old and over	32,336	22,381	69.2	20,308	2,073	9.3	9,955
Less than a high school diploma	9,620	5,930	61.6	5,219	712	12.0	3,690
High school graduates, no college [4]	8,284	5,663	68.4	5,087	576	10.2	2,621
Some college or associate's degree	5,200	3,818	73.4	3,463	355	9.3	1,382
Bachelor's degree and higher [5]	9,232	6,970	75.5	6,539	431	6.2	2,263
NATIVE BORN							
Total [2]	**201,960**	**129,533**	**64.1**	**117,095**	**12,438**	**9.6**	**72,427**
Male	97,238	67,610	69.5	60,414	7,196	10.6	29,628
Female	104,722	61,923	59.1	56,682	5,242	8.5	42,799
Age:							
16 to 24 years old	34,415	18,960	55.1	15,417	3,543	18.7	15,455
25 to 34 years old	33,189	27,678	83.4	24,842	2,836	10.2	5,511
35 to 44 years old	31,620	26,482	83.8	24,398	2,084	7.9	5,138
45 to 54 years old	37,348	30,242	81.0	28,019	2,223	7.4	7,106
55 to 64 years old	31,357	20,286	64.7	18,909	1,377	6.8	11,072
65 years old and over	34,032	5,886	17.3	5,511	375	6.4	28,145
Race and Hispanic ethnicity:							
White non-Hispanic	153,448	99,478	64.8	91,483	7,994	8.0	53,971
Black non-Hispanic	24,691	14,996	60.7	12,529	2,467	16.5	9,695
Asian non-Hispanic	2,900	1,782	61.5	1,641	141	7.9	1,117
Hispanic [3]	16,551	10,596	64.0	9,130	1,467	13.8	5,955
Educational attainment:							
Total, 25 years and over	167,546	110,573	66.0	101,679	8,895	8.0	56,972
Less than a high school diploma	16,046	5,949	37.1	4,896	1,053	17.7	10,097
High school graduates, no college [4]	53,753	32,573	60.6	29,206	3,367	10.3	21,180
Some college or associate's degree	47,022	33,022	70.2	30,284	2,738	8.3	14,000
Bachelor's degree and higher [5]	50,724	39,029	76.9	37,293	1,736	4.4	11,696

[1] Civilian labor force as a percent of the civilian noninstitutionalized population. [2] Includes other races, not shown separately. [3] Persons of Hispanic origin may be any race. [4] Includes persons with a high school diploma or equivalent. [5] Includes persons with bachelor's, master's, professional, and doctoral degrees.

Source: U.S. Bureau of Labor Statistics, *Foreign-Born Workers: Labor Force Characteristics in 2010*, News Release, USDL-11-0763, May 2011. See also <http://www.bls.gov/news.release/forbrn.toc.htm>.

Table 590. Employment Status of Veterans by Period of Service and Sex: 2010

[In thousands (228,886 represents 228,886,000). For civilian noninstitutional population 18 years old and over. Veterans are defined as men and women who have previously served on active duty in the U.S. Armed Forces and who were civilians at the time they were surveyed. See text, Section 10. Annual averages of monthly figures. Based on Current Population Survey; see text, Section 1 and Appendix III]

Veteran status, period of service, and sex	Civilian non-institutionalized population	Civilian labor force						Not in labor force
		Total	Percent of population	Employed		Unemployed		
				Total	Percent of population	Total	Percent of labor force	
Total, 18 years and over.............	**228,886**	**151,888**	**66.4**	**137,646**	**60.1**	**14,242**	**9.4**	**76,998**
Veterans	22,011	11,758	53.4	10,738	48.8	1,020	8.7	10,253
Gulf War era, total	5,091	4,311	84.7	3,911	76.8	399	9.3	780
Gulf War era I [1]	2,922	2,528	86.5	2,334	79.9	194	7.7	394
Gulf War era II [2]	2,169	1,783	82.2	1,577	72.7	205	11.5	386
WW II, Korean War, and Vietnam era [3] ...	11,006	3,993	36.3	3,662	33.3	331	8.3	7,013
Other service periods [4]	5,914	3,455	58.4	3,165	53.5	290	8.4	2,459
Nonveterans [5]	206,875	140,130	67.7	126,908	61.3	13,222	9.4	66,745
Male, 18 years and over	**110,634**	**80,995**	**73.2**	**72,684**	**65.7**	**8,311**	**10.3**	**29,639**
Veterans	20,225	10,650	52.7	9,717	48.0	933	8.8	9,575
Gulf War era, total	4,272	3,703	86.7	3,358	78.6	345	9.3	569
Gulf War era I [1]	2,472	2,181	88.2	2,009	81.3	171	7.8	291
Gulf War era II [2]	1,800	1,523	84.6	1,348	74.9	174	11.4	278
WW II, Korean War, and Vietnam era [3] ...	10,638	3,880	36.5	3,555	33.4	324	8.4	6,758
Other service periods [4]	5,315	3,067	57.7	2,804	52.8	263	8.6	2,248
Nonveterans [5]	90,409	70345	77.8	62,967	69.6	7,378	10.5	20,064
Female, 18 years and over	**118,252**	**70,893**	**60.0**	**64,962**	**54.9**	**5,931**	**8.4**	**47,359**
Veterans	1,786	1,108	62.1	1,021	57.2	87	7.9	678
Gulf War era, total	819	607	74.2	554	67.6	54	8.9	212
Gulf War era I [1]	450	347	77.1	325	72.1	23	6.5	103
Gulf War era II [2]	369	260	70.6	229	62.2	31	12.0	108
WW II, Korean War, and Vietnam era [3] ...	368	113	30.7	107	29.0	6	5.5	255
Other service periods [4]	599	388	64.8	361	60.2	27	7.0	211
Nonveterans [5]	116,466	69,785	59.9	63,941	54.9	5,844	8.4	46,681

[1] Gulf War era I: August 1990–August 2001. [2] Gulf War era II: September 2001–present. [3] World War II: December 1941–December 1945. Korean War: July 1950–January 1955. Vietnam era: August 1964–April 1975. [4] Other service periods; all other time periods. [5] Nonveterans are men and women who never served on active duty in the U.S Armed Forces.
Source: Bureau of Labor Statistics, *Employment Situation of Veterans—2010*, New Release, USDL-11-0306, March 2011. See also <http://www.bls.gov/news.release/vet.nr0.htm>.

Table 591. Labor Force Status of Persons With and Without a Disability: 2010

[26,592 represents 26,592,000. For civilian noninstitutionalized population 16 years old and over, except as indicated. Persons with a disability are those who have a physical, mental, or emotional condition that causes serious difficulty with their daily activities. Annual averages of monthly figures. Based on Current Population Survey; see text, Section 1 and Appendix III]

Characteristic	Civilian non-institutionalized population (1,000)	Civilian labor force					Not in the labor force
		Total (1,000)	Participation rate [1]	Employed (1,000)	Unemployed		
					Number (1,000)	Unemployment rate	
WITH DISABILITY							
Total	**26,592**	**5,795**	**21.8**	**4,939**	**857**	**14.8**	**20,797**
Male [2].................	12,147	3,142	25.9	2,665	477	15.2	9,005
Female [2]...............	14,445	2,653	18.4	2,274	379	14.3	11,792
Both Sexes 65 and over....	11,862	800	6.7	729	71	8.9	11,062
WITHOUT DISABILITY							
Total	**211,238**	**148,094**	**70.1**	**134,125**	**13,968**	**9.4**	**63,144**
Male [2].................	103,027	78,842	76.5	70,694	8,148	10.3	24,184
Female [2]...............	108,211	69,251	64.0	63,431	5,820	8.4	38,960
Both Sexes 65 and over....	26,844	5,918	22.0	5,539	378	6.4	20,926

[1] Civilian labor force as a percent of the civilian noninstitutionalized population. [2] For ages 16 to 64.
Source: U.S. Bureau of Labor Statistics, Current Population Survey, "Data on the Employment Status of People With a Disability," <http://www.bls.gov/cps/cpsdisability.htm>, and unpublished data.

Table 592. Civilian Labor Force—Percent Distribution by Sex and Age: 1980 to 2010

[106,940 represents 106,940,000. Civilian noninstitutionalized population 16 years old and over. Annual averages of monthly figures. Based on Current Population Survey; see text, Section 1 and Appendix III]

Year and sex	Civilian labor force (1,000)	16 to 19 years	20 to 24 years	25 to 34 years	35 to 44 years	45 to 54 years	55 to 64 years	65 years and over
		Percent distribution						
Total: 1980	106,940	8.8	14.9	27.3	19.1	15.8	11.2	2.9
1990 [1]	125,840	6.2	11.7	28.6	25.5	16.1	9.2	2.7
2000 [1]	142,583	5.8	10.0	23.0	26.3	21.8	10.1	3.0
2005 [1]	149,320	4.8	10.1	21.7	24.1	23.0	12.7	3.5
2010 [1]	153,889	3.8	9.8	21.8	21.7	23.4	15.1	4.4
Male: 1980	61,453	8.1	14.0	27.6	19.3	16.1	11.8	3.1
1990 [1]	69,011	5.9	11.4	28.8	25.3	16.1	9.6	2.9
2000 [1]	76,280	5.6	9.9	23.4	26.3	21.3	10.2	3.3
2005 [1]	80,033	4.5	10.1	22.3	24.4	22.6	12.6	3.7
2010 [1]	81,985	3.6	9.6	22.4	22.1	23.0	14.8	4.5
Female: 1980	45,487	9.6	16.1	26.9	19.0	15.4	10.4	2.6
1990 [1]	56,829	6.5	12.0	28.3	25.8	16.1	8.7	2.6
2000 [1]	66,303	6.0	10.2	22.5	26.4	22.3	9.9	2.7
2005 [1]	69,288	5.2	10.2	20.9	23.9	23.6	12.9	3.3
2010 [1]	71,904	4.1	10.0	21.2	21.2	23.8	15.6	4.2

[1] See footnote 2, Table 586.

Source: U.S. Bureau of Labor Statistics, "Employment and Earnings Online," January 2011 issue, March 2011, <http://www.bls.gov/opub/ee/home.htm> and <http://www.bls.gov/cps/home.htm>.

Table 593. Civilian Labor Force and Participation Rates by Educational Attainment, Sex, Race, and Hispanic Origin: 2000 to 2010

[120,061 represents 120,061,000. Civilian noninstitutional population 25 years old and over. Annual averages of monthly figures. See Table 627 for unemployment data. Rates are based on annual average civilian noninstitutional population of each specified group and represent proportion of each specified group in the civilian labor force]

Year, sex, and race	Total (1,000)	Civilian labor force — Percent distribution				Participation rate (percent) [1]				
		Less than a high school diploma	High school graduate, no college	Less than a bachelor's degree	College graduate	Total	Less than a high school diploma	High school graduate, no college	Less than a bachelor's degree	College graduate
Total: [2]										
2000 [3]	120,061	10.4	31.4	27.7	30.5	67.3	43.5	64.4	73.9	79.4
2005 [3]	127,030	10.0	30.1	27.5	32.4	67.1	45.5	63.2	72.5	77.9
2009 [3]	132,781	9.1	28.8	27.7	34.4	67.0	46.5	62.1	71.2	77.5
2010 [3]	132,955	8.9	28.8	27.7	34.6	66.5	46.3	61.6	70.5	76.7
Male:										
2000 [3]	64,490	11.8	31.1	25.9	31.2	76.1	56.0	75.1	80.9	84.4
2005 [3]	68,389	11.7	30.9	25.4	32.1	75.4	58.6	73.6	79.3	82.9
2009 [3]	71,058	10.9	30.2	25.7	33.3	74.6	59.2	72.1	77.5	81.8
2010 [3]	71,129	10.6	30.4	25.6	33.4	74.1	59.1	71.4	76.7	81.3
Female:										
2000 [3]	55,572	8.8	31.8	29.7	29.7	59.4	32.3	55.5	68.0	74.0
2005 [3]	58,641	8.0	29.2	30.0	32.8	59.4	32.9	53.8	66.8	72.9
2009 [3]	61,723	7.2	27.1	30.1	35.6	59.9	33.8	52.8	65.9	73.3
2010 [3]	61,825	7.0	26.9	30.1	36.0	59.5	33.5	52.4	65.4	72.4
White: [4]										
2000 [3]	99,964	10.1	31.4	27.5	31.0	67.0	44.1	63.6	73.1	79.0
2005 [3]	104,240	9.8	29.9	27.6	32.7	66.9	46.4	62.5	72.0	77.5
2009 [3]	108,354	9.1	28.8	27.6	34.6	66.9	48.0	61.7	70.8	77.0
2010 [3]	108,274	8.9	28.7	27.5	34.9	66.5	47.7	61.2	70.1	76.5
Black: [4]										
2000 [3]	13,582	12.4	36.0	31.2	20.5	68.2	39.3	69.9	79.3	84.4
2005 [3]	14,252	11.2	36.4	30.2	22.2	67.2	39.8	67.9	75.6	82.0
2009 [3]	14,941	9.3	33.3	32.4	24.3	66.2	38.2	64.6	73.4	80.9
2010 [3]	15,114	9.4	33.3	32.8	24.5	65.8	38.8	63.8	73.5	79.5
Asian: [4, 5]										
2000 [3]	5,402	9.1	20.7	20.2	50.1	70.9	46.0	65.6	76.4	79.1
2005 [3]	5,805	8.0	17.7	17.3	57.0	69.4	45.3	61.8	71.6	77.5
2009 [3]	6,540	7.5	17.0	16.9	58.7	69.9	44.6	60.8	71.8	78.4
2010 [3]	6,601	7.3	18.8	17.1	56.7	68.7	44.1	62.8	70.6	75.9
Hispanic: [6]										
2000 [3]	12,975	36.7	29.3	20.6	13.4	71.5	61.9	75.0	80.8	83.5
2005 [3]	16,135	35.5	29.4	20.9	14.2	70.8	61.4	74.3	78.8	81.7
2009 [3]	18,643	32.5	30.3	21.6	15.5	71.3	62.1	73.1	78.9	81.7
2010 [3]	18,987	31.4	30.8	21.7	16.0	71.4	61.9	73.9	77.8	81.7

[1] See footnote 1, Table 587. [2] Includes other races, not shown separately. [3] See footnote 2, Table 586. [4] Beginning 2005, for persons in this race group only. See footnote 4, Table 587. [5] 2000 data include Pacific Islanders. [6] Persons of Hispanic origin may be any race.

Source: U.S. Bureau of Labor Statistics, "Employment and Earnings Online," January 2011 issue, March 2011, <http://www.bls.gov/opub/ee/home.htm> and <http://www.bls.gov/cps/home.htm>.

Table 594. Characteristics of the Civilian Labor Force by State: 2010

[In thousands (153,889 represents 153,889,000), except ratio and rate. Civilian noninstitutionalized population 16 years old and over. Annual averages of monthly figures. Data for states may not sum to national totals due to rounding]

State	Total Number	Total Female	Employed Total	Employed Female	Employ-ment/population ratio [1]	Unemployed Total Number	Unemployed Total Female	Unemployed Rate [2] Total	Unemployed Rate [2] Male	Unemployed Rate [2] Female	Participation rate [3] Male	Participation rate [3] Female
United States	153,889	71,904	139,064	65,705	58.5	14,825	6,199	9.6	10.5	8.6	71.2	58.6
Alabama	2,180	1,042	1,952	943	53.5	228	99	10.5	11.3	9.5	65.8	54.3
Alaska	360	167	331	155	64.0	29	11	8.0	9.0	6.8	73.7	65.3
Arizona	3,180	1,430	2,850	1,296	56.7	331	134	10.4	11.2	9.4	70.4	56.3
Arkansas	1,343	632	1,228	577	55.3	116	55	8.6	8.6	8.7	66.5	54.9
California	18,195	8,197	15,976	7,271	56.5	2,219	926	12.2	12.9	11.3	71.9	57.0
Colorado	2,720	1,236	2,482	1,133	63.7	238	103	8.7	9.1	8.3	76.7	63.0
Connecticut	1,892	902	1,719	827	62.2	173	76	9.2	9.9	8.4	74.5	62.8
Delaware	428	207	392	192	56.5	37	15	8.5	9.7	7.3	67.3	56.8
District of Columbia	341	172	310	157	62.5	31	15	9.2	9.7	8.6	74.1	64.4
Florida	9,089	4,278	8,083	3,863	54.9	1,006	415	11.1	12.3	9.7	67.8	56.0
Georgia	4,744	2,210	4,238	2,000	57.3	506	211	10.7	11.7	9.5	71.8	57.2
Hawaii	623	296	579	278	58.6	43	18	7.0	7.8	6.1	67.9	58.3
Idaho	759	342	691	314	59.4	68	28	9.0	9.7	8.1	72.4	58.2
Illinois.............	6,645	3,073	5,970	2,801	60.1	675	271	10.2	11.3	8.8	74.1	60.1
Indiana............	3,153	1,472	2,818	1,330	57.1	334	142	10.6	11.4	9.7	70.1	57.9
Iowa..............	1,673	797	1,571	754	66.9	102	44	6.1	6.6	5.5	76.1	66.6
Kansas............	1,497	702	1,385	655	64.6	111	47	7.4	8.1	6.7	75.7	64.0
Kentucky	2,056	978	1,844	886	55.0	212	92	10.3	11.1	9.4	67.0	56.1
Louisiana..........	2,092	1,007	1,928	927	56.4	164	80	7.8	7.7	8.0	67.1	55.9
Maine.............	690	338	633	314	59.4	57	24	8.2	9.3	7.1	68.6	61.0
Maryland	3,055	1,477	2,819	1,368	63.5	236	109	7.7	8.0	7.4	75.1	63.1
Massachusetts........	3,493	1,703	3,194	1,576	60.5	298	127	8.5	9.6	7.5	70.6	62.0
Michigan	4,821	2,276	4,232	2,052	54.4	589	224	12.2	14.3	9.9	67.6	56.7
Minnesota	2,935	1,390	2,721	1,310	66.2	214	80	7.3	8.6	5.8	76.0	66.9
Mississippi.........	1,296	624	1,155	564	52.2	141	60	10.9	12.1	9.6	64.7	53.2
Missouri...........	3,032	1,477	2,745	1,347	59.1	287	130	9.5	10.1	8.8	69.9	61.1
Montana...........	490	231	452	218	58.5	38	14	7.7	9.3	5.9	67.6	59.2
Nebraska..........	976	471	929	450	67.5	47	21	4.8	5.2	4.4	74.8	67.2
Nevada............	1,322	580	1,131	507	56.1	191	74	14.4	15.8	12.7	73.1	58.0
New Hampshire........	747	357	702	338	66.1	44	18	5.9	6.7	5.1	75.1	65.6
New Jersey.........	4,520	2,102	4,100	1,917	60.2	420	185	9.3	9.7	8.8	73.6	59.6
New Mexico.........	921	429	843	400	54.9	79	29	8.5	10.1	6.8	66.3	54.1
New York	9,654	4,596	8,832	4,242	57.2	822	353	8.5	9.3	7.7	68.6	57.1
North Carolina........	4,573	2,165	4,094	1,968	56.9	479	197	10.5	11.7	9.1	70.3	57.4
North Dakota.........	372	175	358	169	70.2	14	6	3.8	4.1	3.5	77.7	68.4
Ohio..............	5,853	2,812	5,263	2,572	58.6	590	239	10.1	11.5	8.5	70.5	60.3
Oklahoma	1,745	815	1,621	761	57.8	125	53	7.2	7.7	6.6	68.9	56.2
Oregon............	2,000	943	1,780	852	58.5	221	91	11.0	12.3	9.7	71.0	60.8
Pennsylvania	6,317	2,968	5,774	2,743	57.8	543	226	8.6	9.5	7.6	69.9	57.1
Rhode Island	572	281	508	251	60.1	65	30	11.3	12.0	10.5	72.1	63.7
South Carolina.........	2,134	1028	1,899	930	53.8	235	99	11.0	12.3	9.6	66.3	55.2
South Dakota.........	443	212	420	203	67.2	23	9	5.1	6.0	4.2	75.1	66.8
Tennessee	3,077	1,443	2,788	1,332	56.7	289	111	9.4	10.9	7.7	69.6	56.3
Texas.............	12,122	5,391	11,149	4,967	60.5	974	424	8.0	8.2	7.9	74.6	57.4
Utah..............	1,385	603	1,271	564	63.3	114	40	8.2	9.5	6.6	77.8	60.2
Vermont............	361	175	339	166	66.4	22	9	6.2	7.1	5.2	74.6	67.1
Virginia............	4,108	1,972	3,800	1,839	62.5	308	133	7.5	8.2	6.7	73.6	62.1
Washington	3,541	1,662	3,180	1,514	60.6	361	148	10.2	11.4	8.9	72.7	62.4
West Virginia	795	362	724	336	49.6	71	26	9.0	10.5	7.1	61.2	48.2
Wisconsin	3,082	1,481	2,813	1,368	63.4	268	114	8.7	9.7	7.7	73.3	65.6
Wyoming	298	136	278	128	65.9	20	8	6.6	7.0	6.1	76.2	64.8

[1] Civilian employment as a percent of civilian noninstitutionalized population. [2] Percent unemployed of the civilian labor force.
[3] Percent of civilian noninstitutionalized population of each specified group in the civilian labor force.

Source: U.S. Bureau of Labor Statistics, Local Area Unemployment Statistics, "Geographic Profile of Employment and Unemployment, 2010 Annual Averages," <http://www.bls.gov/gps/>.

Table 595. Civilian Labor Force Status by Selected Metropolitan Areas: 2010

[153,889 represents 153,889,000. Civilian noninstitutional population 16 years old and over. Annual averages of monthly figures. Data are derived from the Local Area Unemployment Statistics program, a Federal-State cooperative effort in which monthly estimates of total employment and unemployment are prepared for approximately 7,300 areas. For metro areas with a Census 2000 population of one million or more. For definitions of metropolitan areas, see Appendix II. Metropolitan areas defined as of December 2009]

Metropolitan area ranked by population, 2000	Civilian labor force (1,000)	Unemployment rate [1]	Metropolitan area ranked by population, 2000	Civilian labor force (1,000)	Unemployment rate [1]
U.S. total, 2010	**153,889**	**9.6**	Portland-Vancouver-Hillsboro, OR-WA	1,190	10.6
			Kansas City, MO-KS	1,037	9.1
New York-Northern New Jersey-Long Island, NY-NJ-PA	9,470	8.9	Sacramento—Arden-Arcade—Roseville, CA	1,041	12.6
Los Angeles-Long Beach-Santa Ana, CA	6,460	11.9	San Jose-Sunnyvale-Santa Clara, CA	900	11.3
Chicago-Joliet-Naperville, IL-IN-WI	4,870	10.2	San Antonio-New Braunfels, TX	989	7.3
Philadelphia-Camden-Wilmington, PA-NJ-DE-MD	2,956	9.0	Orlando-Kissimmee-Sanford, FL	1,122	11.4
Dallas-Fort Worth-Arlington, TX	3,212	8.3	Columbus, OH	967	8.6
Miami-Fort Lauderdale-Pompano Beach, FL	2,877	11.5	Virginia Beach-Norfolk-Newport News, VA-NC	826	7.4
Washington-Arlington-Alexandria, DC-VA-MD-WV	3,064	6.2	Indianapolis-Carmel, IN	889	9.2
Houston-Sugar Land-Baytown, TX	2,896	8.5	Milwaukee-Waukesha-West Allis, WI	794	8.7
Boston-Cambridge-Quincy, MA-NH NECTA [2]	2,548	7.7	Las Vegas-Paradise, NV	969	15.2
Detroit-Warren-Livonia, MI	2,070	13.5	Charlotte-Gastonia-Rock Hill, NC-SC	862	11.6
Atlanta-Sandy Springs-Marietta, GA	2,663	10.2	New Orleans-Metairie-Kenner, LA	544	7.4
San Francisco-Oakland-Fremont, CA	2,240	10.3	Nashville-Davidson—Murfreesboro—Franklin, TN	816	8.6
Riverside-San Bernardino-Ontario, CA	1,769	14.5	Providence-Fall River-Warwick, RI-MA NECTA [2]	714	11.7
Phoenix-Mesa-Glendale, AZ	2,126	9.2	Austin-Round Rock-San Marcos, TX	908	7.1
Seattle-Tacoma-Bellevue, WA	1,890	9.3	Memphis, TN-MS-AR	609	10.0
Minneapolis-St. Paul-Bloomington, MN-WI	1,845	7.2	Buffalo-Niagara Falls, NY	578	8.4
San Diego-Carlsbad-San Marcos, CA	1,558	10.5	Louisville-Jefferson County, KY-IN	637	10.3
St. Louis, MO-IL	1,437	10.0	Jacksonville, FL	688	11.2
Baltimore-Towson, MD	1,395	7.9	Richmond, VA	655	7.7
Pittsburgh, PA	1,213	8.0	Oklahoma City, OK	569	6.6
Tampa-St. Petersburg-Clearwater, FL	1,303	12.1	Hartford-West Hartford-East Hartford, CT NECTA [2]	600	9.2
Denver-Aurora-Broomfield, CO	1,381	9.0	Birmingham-Hoover, AL	516	9.0
Cleveland-Elyria-Mentor, OH	1,077	9.2	Rochester, NY	527	8.1
Cincinnati-Middletown, OH-KY-IN	1,119	9.7			

[1] Percent unemployed of the civilian labor force. [2] New England City and Town Areas. See Appendix II.
Source: U.S. Bureau of Labor Statistics, Local Area Unemployment Statistics (LAUS), <http://www.bls.gov/lau/home.htm>.

Table 596. School Enrollment and Labor Force Status: 2010

[In thousands (37,949 represents 37,949,000), except percent. As of October. Based on Current Population Survey; see text, Section 1 and Appendix III]

Characteristic	Population	Civilian labor force	Employed	Unemployed Total	Unemployed Rate [1]	Not in labor force
Total, 16 to 24 years [2]	**37,949**	**21,144**	**17,347**	**3,797**	**18.0**	**16,805**
Enrolled in school [2]	22,021	8,491	7,065	1,426	16.8	13,530
Enrolled in high school	9,598	2,120	1,509	611	28.8	7,478
Male	4,976	1,003	687	315	31.4	3,973
Female	4,622	1,117	822	296	26.5	3,505
Enrolled in college	12,423	6,372	5,556	815	12.8	6,052
Enrolled in 2 year college	3,938	2,303	1,933	370	16.1	1,635
Enrolled in 4 year college	8,485	4,068	3,623	445	10.9	4,417
Race/ethnicity:						
White: [3]						
Enrolled in high school	7,311	1,759	1,322	436	24.8	5,552
Enrolled in college	9,466	5,055	4,453	602	11.9	4,410
Black or African American: [3]						
Enrolled in high school	1,553	250	127	123	49.3	1,304
Enrolled in college	1,721	830	667	164	19.7	891
Asian: [3]						
Enrolled in high school	289	22	17	5	(5)	267
Enrolled in college	843	305	281	24	7.9	538
Hispanic: [4]						
Enrolled in high school	1,909	266	179	87	32.7	1,643
Enrolled in college	1,850	953	817	136	14.3	897
Not enrolled [2]	15,928	12,653	10,281	2,371	18.7	3,275
White [3]	12,375	10,043	8,416	1,627	16.2	2,332
Black [3]	2,486	1,834	1,283	551	30.0	653
Asian [3]	460	340	269	71	20.8	120
Hispanic [4]	3,433	2,599	2,057	542	20.8	834

[1] Percent unemployed of civilian labor force in each category. [2] Includes other races, not shown separately.
[3] Data for persons in this race group only. See footnote 4, Table 587. [4] Persons of Hispanic origin may be any race.
[5] Data not shown where base is less than 75,000.
Source: U.S. Bureau of Labor Statistics, *College Enrollment and Work Activity of High School Graduates*, News Release, USDL 11-0462, April 2011. See also <http://www.bls.gov/news.release/hsgec.toc.htm>.

Table 597. Labor Force Participation Rates by Marital Status, Sex, and Age: 1970 to 2010

[In percent. For the civilian noninstitutional population 16 years old and over. Annual averages of monthly figures. Participation rate is the civilian labor force as a percent of the civilian noninstitutional population. Based on Current Population Survey; see text, Section 1 and Appendix III]

Marital status and year	Male participation rate							Female participation rate						
	Total	16–19 years	20–24 years	25–34 years	35–44 years	45–64 years	65 years and over	Total	16–19 years	20–24 years	25–34 years	35–44 years	45–64 years	65 years and over
Single:														
1970......	65.5	54.6	73.8	87.9	86.2	75.7	25.2	56.8	44.7	73.0	81.4	78.6	73.0	19.7
1980......	72.6	59.9	81.3	89.2	82.2	66.9	16.8	64.4	53.6	75.2	83.3	76.9	65.6	13.9
1990 [1]	74.8	55.1	81.6	89.9	84.5	67.3	15.7	66.7	51.7	74.5	80.9	80.8	66.2	12.1
2000 [1]	73.6	52.5	80.5	89.4	82.9	69.7	17.3	68.9	51.1	76.1	83.9	80.9	69.9	10.8
2003 [1]	70.4	44.0	77.9	87.7	82.9	67.6	19.4	66.2	44.8	72.9	82.2	79.8	69.9	15.2
2004 [1]	70.2	43.6	77.7	87.9	82.7	67.8	20.3	65.9	43.8	73.1	81.8	80.5	70.9	14.7
2005 [1]	70.1	42.9	77.0	87.9	82.9	68.6	18.8	66.0	44.2	72.6	81.4	80.7	70.9	15.5
2006 [1]	70.7	43.4	77.8	87.7	83.5	69.9	19.3	65.7	43.7	71.8	81.4	79.8	70.5	15.0
2007 [1]	70.1	40.8	76.9	88.5	84.0	70.3	22.6	65.3	41.4	72.6	82.1	78.0	70.4	18.4
2008 [1]	69.9	39.8	77.1	87.9	84.3	69.5	24.7	65.3	40.3	71.9	82.6	79.6	70.4	20.5
2009 [1]	68.3	37.1	74.6	86.5	83.7	68.5	26.1	64.2	37.5	71.4	81.6	79.5	69.3	19.7
2010 [1]	67.3	34.6	73.1	85.8	83.7	67.6	25.0	63.3	34.9	69.8	81.3	78.2	69.4	20.1
Married: [2]														
1970......	86.1	92.3	94.7	98.0	98.1	91.2	29.9	40.5	37.8	47.9	38.8	46.8	44.0	7.3
1980......	80.9	91.3	96.9	97.5	97.2	84.3	20.5	49.8	49.3	61.4	58.8	61.8	46.9	7.3
1990 [1]	78.6	92.1	95.6	96.9	96.7	82.6	17.5	58.4	49.5	66.1	69.6	74.0	56.5	8.5
2000 [1]	77.3	79.5	94.1	96.7	95.8	83.0	19.2	61.1	53.2	63.8	70.3	74.8	65.4	10.1
2003 [1]	77.3	76.6	93.2	95.3	95.1	83.5	19.9	61.0	46.7	62.6	68.5	73.3	67.4	11.3
2004 [1]	77.1	77.4	92.4	95.6	95.1	83.1	20.4	60.5	41.1	60.9	67.6	72.7	67.0	11.6
2005 [1]	77.2	71.4	93.4	95.3	95.2	83.6	21.4	60.7	44.1	61.1	68.4	73.0	67.2	12.5
2006 [1]	77.1	79.2	93.3	95.5	95.2	83.6	21.8	61.0	39.6	59.8	69.0	73.3	67.8	12.4
2007 [1]	76.9	86.9	92.9	95.7	95.3	83.6	21.8	61.0	43.3	61.7	68.6	73.1	67.7	13.6
2008 [1]	76.8	83.4	92.0	95.3	95.2	84.0	22.8	61.4	38.0	62.3	69.5	73.8	68.3	14.1
2009 [1]	76.3	75.8	91.2	94.7	94.8	83.8	23.3	61.4	44.7	61.8	69.4	73.7	68.6	14.9
2010 [1]	75.8	78.2	89.3	94.3	94.5	83.6	23.5	61.0	40.2	60.9	68.8	72.8	68.8	15.2
Other: [3]														
1970......	60.7	(B)	90.4	93.7	91.1	78.5	19.3	40.3	48.6	60.3	64.6	68.8	61.9	10.0
1980......	67.5	(B)	92.6	94.1	91.9	73.3	13.7	43.6	50.0	68.4	76.5	77.1	60.2	8.2
1990 [1]	68.9	(B)	93.1	93.0	90.7	74.9	12.0	47.2	53.9	65.4	77.0	82.1	65.0	8.4
2000 [1]	66.8	60.5	88.1	93.2	89.9	73.9	12.9	49.0	46.0	74.0	83.1	82.9	69.8	8.7
2003 [1]	65.0	45.6	88.0	91.4	89.3	72.4	14.3	49.6	44.1	71.4	79.1	81.9	70.7	9.8
2004 [1]	64.9	53.1	87.2	90.6	88.6	72.8	14.3	49.6	48.7	70.0	79.4	81.7	69.8	10.4
2005 [1]	64.9	54.9	86.4	90.4	89.4	72.7	15.1	49.4	46.8	67.4	78.1	80.9	69.4	10.5
2006 [1]	65.6	47.8	86.0	91.5	88.9	73.8	16.3	49.6	45.3	71.5	78.2	80.9	69.3	10.9
2007 [1]	65.6	43.4	82.5	92.1	89.4	73.7	16.1	49.5	44.6	63.8	78.4	81.4	69.3	11.4
2008 [1]	65.0	43.2	84.9	90.7	89.4	73.2	16.8	49.2	39.7	64.9	77.4	81.4	69.1	12.1
2009 [1]	63.7	42.6	78.6	88.5	88.5	71.8	17.0	49.3	39.0	68.3	78.2	80.5	68.8	12.1
2010 [1]	63.0	37.6	78.8	89.0	88.5	71.8	17.2	48.8	35.2	66.3	77.7	80.7	68.8	12.1

B Percentage not shown where base is less than 50,000. [1] See footnote 2, Table 586. [2] Spouse present. [3] Widowed, divorced, and married (spouse absent).

Source: U.S. Bureau of Labor Statistics, Bulletin 2217 and Basic Tabulations, Table 12.

Table 598. Marital Status of Women in the Civilian Labor Force: 1970 to 2010

[31,543 represents 31,543,000. For civilian noninstitutional population 16 years and over. Annual averages of monthly figures. Based on the Current Population Survey; see text, Section 1 and Appendix III]

Year	Female civilian labor force (1,000)				Female participation rate (percent) [3]			
	Total	Never married	Married [1]	Other [2]	Total	Never married	Married [1]	Other [2]
1970.......	31,543	7,265	18,475	5,804	43.3	56.8	40.5	40.3
1980.......	45,487	11,865	24,980	8,643	51.5	64.4	49.8	43.6
1990 [4]	56,829	14,612	30,901	11,315	57.5	66.7	58.4	47.2
2000 [4]	66,303	17,849	35,146	13,308	59.9	68.9	61.1	49.0
2001.......	66,848	18,021	35,236	13,592	59.8	68.1	61.2	49.0
2002.......	67,363	18,203	35,477	13,683	59.6	67.4	61.0	49.2
2003 [4]	68,272	18,397	36,046	13,828	59.5	66.2	61.0	49.6
2004 [4]	68,421	18,616	35,845	13,961	59.2	65.9	60.5	49.6
2005 [4]	69,288	19,183	35,941	14,163	59.3	66.0	60.7	49.4
2006 [4]	70,173	19,474	36,314	14,385	59.4	65.7	61.0	49.6
2007 [4]	70,988	19,745	36,881	14,362	59.3	65.3	61.0	49.5
2008 [4]	71,767	20,231	37,194	14,342	59.5	65.3	61.4	49.2
2009 [4]	72,019	20,224	37,264	14,531	59.2	64.2	61.4	49.3
2010 [4]	71,904	20,592	36,742	14,570	58.6	63.3	61.0	48.8

[1] Husband present. [2] Widowed, divorced, or separated. [3] Civilian labor force as a percent of the civilian noninstitutional population. [4] See footnote 2, Table 586.

Source: U.S. Bureau of Labor Statistics, *Women in the Labor Force: A Databook*, Report 1026, December 2010, and Basic Tabulations, Table 12. See also <http://www.bls.gov/cps/wlf-databook2010.htm>.

Table 599. Employment Status of Women by Marital Status and Presence and Age of Children: 1970 to 2009

[As of March (7.0 represents 7,000,000). Annual Social and Economic Supplement (ASEC) includes Civilian noninstitutionalized population, 16 years old and over. Based on the Current Population Survey; see text, Section 1 and Appendix III]

Item	Total			With any children								
				Total			Children 6 to 17 years only			Children under 6 years		
	Single	Mar-ried[1]	Other[2]	Single	Mar-ried[1]	Other[2]	Single	Mar-ried[1]	Other[2]	Single	Mar-ried[1]	Other[2]
IN LABOR FORCE (mil.)												
1970	7.0	18.4	5.9	(NA)	10.2	1.9	(NA)	6.3	1.3	(NA)	3.9	0.6
1980	11.2	24.9	8.8	0.6	13.7	3.6	0.2	8.4	2.6	0.3	5.2	1.0
1990	14.0	31.0	11.2	1.5	16.5	4.2	0.6	9.3	3.0	0.9	7.2	1.2
2000	17.8	35.0	13.2	3.1	18.2	4.5	1.2	10.8	3.4	1.8	7.3	1.1
2005[3]	18.6	35.7	14.3	3.4	18.0	4.6	1.4	10.8	3.4	1.9	7.2	1.2
2008[3]	19.9	37.1	14.6	3.5	17.9	4.5	1.5	10.6	3.3	2.0	7.3	1.2
2009[3]	19.8	37.5	14.5	3.7	18.0	4.5	1.5	10.8	3.3	2.1	7.2	1.1
PARTICIPATION RATE[4]												
1970	53.0	40.8	39.1	(NA)	39.7	60.7	(NA)	49.2	66.9	(NA)	30.3	52.2
1980	61.5	50.1	44.0	52.0	54.1	69.4	67.6	61.7	74.6	44.1	45.1	60.3
1990	66.4	58.2	46.8	55.2	66.3	74.2	69.7	73.6	79.7	48.7	58.9	63.6
2000	68.6	62.0	50.2	73.9	70.6	82.7	79.7	77.2	84.9	70.5	62.8	76.6
2005[3]	65.1	60.2	49.8	72.9	68.1	79.8	79.7	75.0	82.2	68.5	59.8	73.5
2008[3]	64.6	61.7	49.5	71.0	69.4	79.4	78.7	76.2	81.5	66.0	61.6	73.9
2009[3]	63.7	61.7	49.0	72.0	69.8	79.2	78.9	76.7	83.0	67.8	61.6	69.8
EMPLOYMENT (mil.)												
1970	6.5	17.5	5.6	(NA)	9.6	1.8	(NA)	6.0	1.2	(NA)	3.6	0.6
1980	10.1	23.6	8.2	0.4	12.8	3.3	0.2	8.1	2.4	0.2	4.8	0.9
1990	12.9	29.9	10.5	1.2	15.8	3.8	0.5	8.9	2.7	0.7	6.9	1.1
2000	16.4	34.0	12.7	2.7	17.6	4.3	1.1	10.6	3.2	1.6	7.1	1.1
2005[3]	17.0	34.6	13.5	2.9	17.4	4.3	1.3	10.4	3.2	1.6	7.0	1.1
2008[3]	18.4	35.9	13.8	3.1	17.3	4.3	1.4	10.3	3.2	1.7	7.0	1.1
2009[3]	17.7	35.5	13.2	3.1	17.0	4.0	1.4	10.2	3.0	1.8	6.8	1.0
UNEMPLOYMENT RATE[5]												
1970	7.1	4.8	4.8	(NA)	6.0	7.2	(NA)	4.8	5.9	(NA)	7.9	9.8
1980	10.3	5.3	6.4	23.2	5.9	9.2	15.6	4.4	7.9	29.2	8.3	12.8
1990	8.2	3.5	5.7	18.4	4.2	8.5	14.5	3.8	7.7	20.8	4.8	10.2
2000	7.3	2.7	4.3	11.0	2.9	5.1	8.7	2.6	4.8	12.6	3.5	5.9
2005[3]	8.9	3.0	5.3	15.1	3.1	6.9	10.9	2.9	5.8	18.2	3.4	9.8
2008[3]	7.6	3.1	5.4	11.5	3.4	6.0	8.3	3.1	5.3	14.0	3.9	8.0
2009[3]	10.5	5.3	8.9	15.4	5.4	11.2	11.9	5.1	9.9	17.9	5.9	15.1

NA Not available. [1] Husband present. [2] Widowed, divorced, or separated (including married, spouse absent). [3] See footnote 2, Table 586. [4] Percent of women in each specific category in the labor force. [5] Unemployed as a percent of civilian labor force in specified group.
Source: U.S. Bureau of Labor Statistics, Bulletin 2307 and unpublished data.

Table 600. Labor Force Participation Rates for Wives, Husband Present, by Age of Own Youngest Child: 1990 to 2009

[In percent. As of March. Annual Social and Economic Supplement (ASEC) includes Civilian noninstitutionalized population, 16 years old and over, and military personnel who live in households with at least one other civilian adult. Armed Forces includes only those Armed Forces members living on or off post with their families; all other members of the Armed Forces are excluded. Data refer to persons in primary families. Based on Current Population Survey; see text, Section 1 and Appendix III]

Presence and age of child	1990	2000[1]	2005[1]	2008[1]	2009[1]				
					Total	White[2]	Black[2]	Asian[2,3]	Hispanic[4]
Wives, total	**58.3**	**62.2**	**60.4**	**61.9**	**61.9**	**61.5**	**67.2**	**62.4**	**55.8**
No children under 18 years	51.1	54.8	54.1	56.1	55.9	55.6	59.0	59.1	52.8
With children under 18 years	66.5	70.9	68.3	69.7	70.1	69.8	77.1	65.5	57.6
Under 6 years, total	59.1	63.1	60.3	62.0	62.0	61.7	71.1	58.0	48.3
Under 3 years	55.9	59.4	57.3	59.1	60.3	60.2	65.9	57.2	45.3
1 year or under	53.9	58.4	55.8	58.9	57.7	57.3	63.8	57.6	39.9
2 years	60.9	61.9	60.8	59.5	60.9	60.6	73.4	57.8	46.4
3 to 5 years	64.1	68.6	64.8	66.3	64.6	63.8	78.3	59.3	52.5
3 years	63.0	66.0	62.7	65.3	62.9	61.4	82.7	61.2	50.5
4 years	65.0	69.6	64.9	66.5	64.1	62.7	80.3	60.6	51.9
5 years	64.4	70.7	67.5	67.2	67.1	67.8	71.8	54.2	55.6
6 to 13 years	73.1	76.0	73.2	74.8	75.3	74.8	82.7	70.2	65.3
14 to 17 years	75.0	80.8	79.6	79.2	79.9	80.2	78.1	79.4	72.1

[1] See footnote 2, Table 586. [2] Beginning 2005, for persons in this race group only. See footnote 4, Table 587. [3] Excludes Pacific Islanders. [4] Persons of Hispanic origin may be any race.
Source: U.S. Bureau of Labor Statistics, Bulletin 2307 and unpublished data.

Table 601. Married Couples by Labor Force Status of Spouses: 1990 to 2010

[As of March. (52,317 represents 52,317,000). Annual Social and Economic Supplement (ASEC). Based on the Current Population Survey, for details see source and Appendix III]

Year	Number (1,000)					Percent distribution				
		In labor force			Husband and wife not in labor force		In labor force			Husband and wife not in labor force
	All married couples	Husband and wife	Husband only	Wife only		All married couples	Husband and wife	Husband only	Wife only	
TOTAL										
1990...............	52,317	28,056	13,013	2,453	8,794	100.0	53.6	24.9	4.7	16.8
2000...............	55,311	31,095	11,815	3,301	9,098	100.0	56.2	21.4	6.0	16.4
2003...............	57,320	31,951	12,443	3,553	9,373	100.0	55.7	21.7	6.2	16.4
2004...............	57,719	31,536	12,980	3,684	9,519	100.0	54.6	22.5	6.4	16.5
2005...............	57,975	31,398	13,385	3,641	9,551	100.0	54.2	23.1	6.3	16.5
2006...............	58,179	31,783	12,990	3,754	9,652	100.0	54.6	22.3	6.5	16.6
2007...............	60,676	33,337	13,351	4,031	9,958	100.0	54.9	22.0	6.6	16.4
2008...............	60,129	32,988	13,141	4,118	9,882	100.0	54.8	21.8	6.8	16.4
2009...............	60,844	33,249	13,207	4,314	10,074	100.0	54.6	21.7	7.1	16.6
2010...............	60,384	32,731	13,074	4,526	10,053	100.0	53.6	21.7	7.5	16.6
WITH CHILDREN UNDER 18										
1990...............	24,537	15,768	7,667	558	544	100.0	64.3	31.2	2.3	2.2
2000...............	25,248	17,116	6,950	795	387	100.0	67.8	27.5	3.1	1.5
2003...............	25,914	17,065	7,499	893	457	100.0	65.9	28.9	3.4	1.8
2004...............	25,793	16,691	7,715	952	433	100.0	64.7	29.9	3.7	1.7
2005...............	25,919	16,789	7,806	925	400	100.0	64.8	30.1	3.6	1.5
2006...............	25,982	16,909	7,754	900	420	100.0	65.1	29.9	3.5	1.6
2007...............	26,802	17,670	7,743	920	469	100.0	65.9	28.9	3.4	1.7
2008...............	25,778	16,977	7,398	932	471	100.0	65.9	28.7	3.6	1.8
2009...............	25,799	17,054	7,284	963	501	100.0	66.1	28.2	3.7	1.9
2010...............	25,317	16,710	7,220	962	425	100.0	66.0	28.5	3.8	1.7
WITH CHILDREN UNDER 6										
1990...............	12,051	6,932	4,692	192	235	100.0	57.5	38.9	1.6	2.0
2000...............	11,393	6,984	4,077	211	121	100.0	61.3	35.8	1.9	1.1
2003...............	11,743	6,747	4,507	298	191	100.0	57.5	38.4	2.5	1.6
2004...............	11,711	6,657	4,579	317	158	100.0	56.8	39.1	2.7	1.3
2005...............	11,802	6,813	4,553	299	137	100.0	57.7	38.6	2.5	1.2
2006...............	11,984	6,939	4,572	324	149	100.0	57.9	38.2	2.7	1.2
2007...............	12,468	7,337	4,633	331	167	100.0	58.8	37.2	2.7	1.3
2008...............	11,848	6,976	4,382	321	168	100.0	58.9	37.1	2.7	1.4
2009...............	11,760	6,917	4,330	329	185	100.0	58.8	36.8	2.8	1.6
2010...............	11,599	6,924	4,181	335	159	100.0	59.7	36.0	2.9	1.4

Source: U.S. Census Bureau, Families and Living Arrangements, Detailed Table MC-1, "Married Couples by Labor Force Status of Spouses: 1986 to Present," November 2010, <http://www.census.gov/population/www/socdemo/hh-fam.html>.

Table 602. Employed Civilians and Weekly Hours: 1980 to 2010

[In thousands (99,303 represents 99,303,000), except as indicated. Annual averages of monthly figures. Civilian noninstitutionalized population 16 years old and over. Based on Current Population Survey; see text, Section 1 and Appendix III]

Item	1980	1990 [1]	2000 [1]	2005 [1]	2008 [1]	2009 [1]	2010 [1]
Total employed.................	**99,303**	**118,793**	**136,891**	**141,730**	**145,362**	**139,877**	**139,064**
Age:							
16 to 19 years old	7,710	6,581	7,189	5,978	5,573	4,837	4,378
20 to 24 years old	14,087	13,401	13,229	13,792	13,629	12,764	12,699
25 to 34 years old	27,204	33,935	31,549	30,680	31,383	30,014	30,229
35 to 44 years old	19,523	30,817	36,433	34,630	33,457	31,517	30,663
45 to 54 years old	16,234	19,525	30,310	33,207	34,529	33,613	33,191
55 to 64 years old	11,586	11,189	14,002	18,349	20,812	21,019	21,636
65 years old and over	2,960	3,346	4,179	5,094	5,979	6,114	6,268
Class of worker:							
Nonagricultural industries	95,938	115,570	134,427	139,532	143,194	137,775	136,858
Wage and salary worker [2]	88,525	106,598	125,114	129,931	133,882	128,713	127,914
Self-employed	7,000	8,719	9,205	9,509	9,219	8,995	8,860
Unpaid family workers	413	253	108	93	93	66	84
Agriculture and related industries	3,364	3,223	2,464	2,197	2,168	2,103	2,206
Wage and salary worker [2]	1,425	1,740	1,421	1,212	1,279	1,242	1,353
Self-employed	1,642	1,378	1,010	955	860	836	821
Unpaid family workers	297	105	33	30	28	25	33
Weekly hours:							
Nonagricultural industries:							
Wage and salary workers [2]	38.1	39.2	39.6	39.1	39.0	38.0	38.3
Self-employed	41.2	40.8	39.7	38.4	37.0	35.6	35.6
Unpaid family workers	34.7	34.0	32.5	32.2	33.4	30.7	33.3
Agriculture and related industries:							
Wage and salary workers [2]	41.6	41.2	43.2	43.6	42.3	41.8	41.6
Self-employed	49.3	46.8	45.3	44.0	44.2	42.6	42.0
Unpaid family workers	38.6	38.5	38.3	41.1	41.0	36.1	42.1

[1] See footnote 2, Table 586. [2] Includes the incorporated self-employed.
Source: U.S. Bureau of Labor Statistics, "Employment and Earnings Online," January 2011 issue, March 2011, <http://www.bls.gov/opub/ee/home.htm> and <http://www.bls.gov/cps/home.htm>.

Table 603. Persons at Work by Hours Worked: 2010

[In thousands (134,004 represents 134,004,000), except as indicated. Annual averages of monthly figures. Persons "at work" are a subgroup of employed persons "at work," excluding those absent from their jobs during reference period for reasons such as vacation, illness, or industrial dispute. Civilian noninstitutionalized population 16 years old and over. Based on Current Population Survey; see text, Section 1, and Appendix III. See headnote Table 606, regarding industries]

Hours of work	Persons at work (1,000)			Percent distribution		
	Total	Agriculture and related industries	Non-agricultural industries	Total	Agriculture and related industries	Non-agricultural industries
Total...............................	134,004	2,113	131,891	100.0	100.0	100.0
1 to 34 hours.....................	35,097	592	34,505	26.2	28.0	26.2
1 to 4 hours.....................	1,559	53	1,506	1.2	2.5	1.1
5 to 14 hours....................	5,488	137	5,351	4.1	6.5	4.1
15 to 29 hours...................	17,272	260	17,012	12.9	12.3	12.9
30 to 34 hours...................	10,778	142	10,636	8.0	6.7	8.1
35 hours and over................	98,907	1,521	97,386	73.8	72.0	73.8
35 to 39 hours...................	9,695	111	9,584	7.2	5.3	7.3
40 hours.........................	56,478	591	55,886	42.1	28.0	42.4
41 hours and over................	32,734	818	31,916	24.4	38.7	24.2
41 to 48 hours...................	11,370	152	11,218	8.5	7.2	8.5
49 to 59 hours...................	12,530	238	12,292	9.4	11.3	9.3
60 hours and over................	8,834	428	8,406	6.6	20.3	6.4
Average weekly hours: Persons at work ...	38.2	41.8	38.1	(X)	(X)	(X)
Persons usually working full-time [1]	42.2	47.7	42.2	(X)	(X)	(X)

X Not applicable. [1] Full-time workers are those who usually worked 35 hours or more (at all jobs).
Source: U.S. Bureau of Labor Statistics, "Employment and Earnings Online," January 2011 issue, March 2011, <http://www.bls.gov/opub/ee/home.htm> and <http://www.bls.gov/cps/home.htm>.

Table 604. Persons With a Job, But Not at Work: 1980 to 2010

[In thousands (5,881 represents 5,881,000), except percent. For civilian noninstitutionalized population 16 years old and over. Annual averages of monthly figures. Based on Current Population Survey; see text, Section 1 and Appendix III]

Reason for not working	1980	1990 [1]	2000 [1]	2003 [1]	2004 [1]	2005 [1]	2006 [1]	2007 [1]	2008 [1]	2009 [1]	2010 [1]
All industries, number	5,881	6,160	5,681	5,469	5,482	5,511	5,746	5,719	5,539	5,434	5,060
Percent of employed	5.9	5.2	4.2	4.0	3.9	3.9	4.0	3.9	3.8	3.9	3.6
Reason for not working:											
Vacation.................	3,320	3,529	3,109	2,922	2,923	2,892	3,101	3,056	2,916	2,806	2,487
Illness	1,426	1,341	1,156	1,090	1,058	1,088	1,096	1,064	1,026	993	942
Bad weather	155	90	89	123	133	145	117	140	141	126	172
Industrial dispute	105	24	14	18	10	6	7	10	7	6	8
All other...............	876	1,177	1,313	1,316	1,358	1,381	1,425	1,449	1,449	1,503	1,451

[1] Data not strictly comparable with data for earlier years. See text, this section, and February 1994, March 1996, February 1997–99, and February 2003–11 issues of "Employment and Earnings Online."
Source: U.S. Bureau of Labor Statistics, unpublished data, <http://www.bls.gov/cps/home.htm>.

Table 605. Class of Worker by Sex and Selected Characteristics: 2010

[In percent, except as indicated (9,681 represents 9,681,000). Civilian noninstitutionalized population 16 years old and over. Annual averages of monthly figures. Based on Current Population Survey; see text, Section 1 and Appendix III]

Characteristic	Unincorporated self-employed			Incorporated self-employed			Wage and salary workers [1]		
	Total	Male	Female	Total	Male	Female	Total	Male	Female
Total (1,000)	9,681	6,070	3,611	5,191	3,709	1,483	124,076	63,531	60,544
PERCENT DISTRIBUTION	100.0	100.0	100.0	100.0	100.0	100.0	100.0	100.0	100.0
Age:									
16 to 19 years old	0.8	0.9	0.6	0.1	0.1	0.1	3.4	3.2	3.7
20 to 24 years old	2.7	2.9	2.5	1.0	1.1	0.7	10.0	9.8	10.1
25 to 34 years old	13.8	13.8	13.9	9.9	9.9	9.8	22.9	23.8	21.8
35 to 44 years old	21.5	21.3	21.8	23.3	23.1	24.0	22.0	22.7	21.3
45 to 54 years old	27.5	27.4	27.9	31.6	31.1	32.7	23.3	22.7	23.8
55 to 64 years old	22.4	22.1	22.8	24.2	24.2	24.2	14.7	14.0	15.4
65 years old and over	11.2	11.6	10.6	9.9	10.5	8.4	3.8	3.7	3.8
Race/ethnicity:									
White [2]	87.6	88.2	86.6	88.5	89.2	86.6	81.4	82.7	80.0
Black [2]	5.9	5.9	6.0	4.5	4.2	5.1	11.4	10.0	13.0
Asian [2]	4.4	3.9	5.1	6.0	5.6	6.9	4.7	4.9	4.7
Hispanic [3]	13.0	14.4	10.5	6.6	6.8	6.2	14.7	16.8	12.6
Country of birth: U.S. born.............	82.3	81.3	83.9	84.9	84.8	84.8	84.3	82.3	86.5
Foreign-born	17.7	18.7	16.1	15.2	15.2	15.1	15.7	17.7	13.5

[1] Excludes the incorporated self-employed. [2] For persons in this race group only. [3] Persons of Hispanic origin may be any race.
Source: U.S. Bureau of Labor Statistics, Current Population Survey, unpublished data.

Table 606. Self-Employed Workers by Industry and Occupation: 2000 to 2010

[In thousands (10,214 represents 10,214,000). Civilian noninstitutionalized population 16 years old and over. Annual averages of monthly figures. Data represent the unincorporated self-employed; the incorporated self-employed are considered wage and salary workers. Based on the occupational and industrial classification derived from those used in the 2000 census. See text, this section. Based on the Current Population Survey; see text, Section 1 and Appendix III]

Item	2000	2005 [1]	2007 [1]	2008 [1]	2009 [1]	2010 [1]
Total self-employed	10,214	10,464	10,413	10,080	9,831	9,681
Industry:						
Agriculture and related industries	1,010	955	856	860	836	821
Mining	12	11	19	15	18	20
Construction	1,728	1,830	1,890	1,817	1,701	1,699
Manufacturing	334	327	348	308	324	304
Wholesale and retail trade..........................	1,221	1,251	1,116	1,059	963	962
Transportation and utilities..........................	348	442	405	405	402	360
Information..	139	126	135	125	145	139
Financial activities [2]...............................	735	785	829	749	667	641
Professional and business services [2]	1,927	1,957	2,009	1,980	1,996	1,999
Education and health services [2]	1,107	1,071	1,102	1,071	1,102	1,100
Leisure and hospitality [2]..........................	660	674	679	693	636	610
Other services [3]....................................	993	1,036	1,026	997	1,039	1,028
Occupation:						
Management, professional, and related occupations ...	4,169	4,085	4,024	4,043	4,079	3,928
Service occupations	1,775	1,774	1,872	1,847	1,879	1,885
Sales and office occupations.......................	1,982	1,986	1,936	1,771	1,663	1,586
Natural resources, construction, and maintenance occupations	1,591	1,864	1,860	1,707	1,535	1,635
Production, transportation, and material moving occupations	698	756	721	712	674	647

[1] Data not strictly comparable with data for earlier years. See text, this section, and February 1994, March 1996, February 1997–99, and February 2003–11 issues of "Employment and Earnings." [2] For composition of industries, see Table 625. [3] Includes private households.

Source: U.S. Bureau of Labor Statistics, "Employment and Earnings Online," January 2011 issue, March 2011, <http://www.bls.gov/opub/ee/home.htm> and <http://www.bls.gov/cps/home.htm>.

Table 607. Type of Work Flexibility Provided to Employees: 2008

[In percent. The National Study of Employers does not ask employers to report on whether they have "written policies," but rather whether their organization "allows employees to" ... or "provides the following benefits or programs ..." The wording is used for two reasons. First, employers may have written policies, but not "allow" employees to use them. Second, smaller employers are less likely to have written policies than larger ones. For methodology, see source]

Type of work flexibility provided (to employee)	Employer allows all or most employees	Employer size	
		50 to 99 employees	1,000 or more employees
FLEX TIME AND PLACE			
Periodically change starting and quitting times within some range of hours	37	40	37
Change starting and quitting times on a daily basis	10	11	7
Compress workweek by working longer hours on fewer days for at least part of the year ...	8	10	5
Work some regular paid hours at home occasionally	3	3	2
Work some regular paid hours at home on regular basis	1	1	1
CHOICES IN MANAGING TIME			
Have control over when to take breaks	55	54	51
Have choices about and control over which shifts to work	16	16	16
Have control over paid and unpaid overtime hours	13	14	15
REDUCED TIME			
Move from full time to part time and back again while remaining in same position or level ...	13	12	12
Share jobs..	8	9	5
Work part year (work reduced time on annual basis)	11	10	11
CAREGIVING LEAVE			
Return to work gradually after childbirth or adoption.................	57	56	54
TIME OFF			
Family or personal time off without loss of pay	45	46	47
Compensatory time off program	18	21	9
Do volunteer work during regular work hours	21	24	20
FLEX CAREERS			
Phase into retirement by working reduced hours overtime prior to full retirement ...	25	25	20
Take sabbaticals (paid or unpaid for six months or more)	21	24	14
Take paid or unpaid time off for education or job training skills	40	41	33
Take extended career breaks for caregiving or other personal or family reasons ...	47	48	44
Receive special consideration when returning to the organization after an extended career break. ...	28	29	21

Source: Families and Work Institute, "2008 National Study of Employers" (copyright), <http://familiesandwork.org/site/research/reports/main.html>.

Table 608. Persons on Flexible Schedules: 2004

[In thousands (99,778 represents 99,778,000), except percent. As of May. For employed full-time wage and salary workers 16 years old and over. Excludes all self-employed persons, regardless of whether or not their businesses were incorporated. Data related to the primary job. Based on the Current Population Survey; see text, Section 1 and Appendix III]

Item	Total			Male			Female		
		With flexible schedules [2]			With flexible schedules [2]			With flexible schedules [2]	
	Total [1]	Number	Percent	Total [1]	Number	Percent	Total [1]	Number	Percent
Total..................	99,778	27,411	27.5	56,412	15,853	28.1	43,366	11,558	26.7
AGE									
16 to 19 years old	1,427	336	23.6	903	185	20.5	524	151	28.9
20 years and over	98,351	27,075	27.5	55,509	15,668	28.2	42,842	11,406	26.6
20 to 24 years old	9,004	2,058	22.9	5,147	1,065	20.7	3,856	993	25.8
25 to 34 years old	24,640	6,902	28.0	14,358	4,051	28.2	10,283	2,851	27.7
35 to 44 years old	26,766	7,807	29.2	15,424	4,605	29.9	11,342	3,202	28.2
45 to 54 years old	24,855	6,651	26.8	13,440	3,769	28.0	11,415	2,882	25.2
55 to 64 years old	11,745	3,181	27.1	6,383	1,865	29.2	5,361	1,316	24.5
65 years old and over	1,341	475	35.4	757	314	41.4	585	161	27.6
RACE AND HISPANIC ORIGIN									
White [3]..........................	80,498	23,121	28.7	46,222	13,582	29.4	34,276	9,539	27.8
Black [3]..........................	12,578	2,476	19.7	6,447	1,193	18.5	6,131	1,283	20.9
Asian [3]..........................	4,136	1,132	27.4	2,300	720	31.3	1,836	412	22.4
Hispanic [4].......................	14,110	2,596	18.4	8,621	1,430	16.6	5,489	1,166	21.2
MARITAL STATUS									
Married, spouse present	57,630	16,270	28.2	34,926	10,382	29.7	22,704	5,888	25.9
Not married	42,148	11,141	26.4	21,486	5,471	25.5	20,662	5,670	27.4
Never married	25,144	6,693	26.6	14,469	3,605	24.9	10,676	3,088	28.9
Other marital status	17,004	4,448	26.2	7,018	1,866	26.6	9,986	2,582	25.9
PRESENCE AND AGE OF CHILDREN									
Without own children under 18	61,761	16,759	27.1	34,680	9,410	27.1	27,081	7,349	27.1
With own children under 18.........	38,018	10,652	28.0	21,733	6,443	29.6	16,285	4,209	25.8
With youngest child 6 to 17........	21,739	5,960	27.4	11,477	3,341	29.1	10,262	2,619	25.5
With youngest child under 6	16,279	4,692	28.8	10,256	3,102	30.2	6,023	1,590	26.4

[1] Includes persons who did not provide information on flexible schedules. [2] Allowed to vary or make changes in time work begins or ends. [3] For persons in the race group only. See footnote 4, Table 587. [4] Persons of Hispanic origin may be any race.

Source: U.S. Bureau of Labor Statistics, *Workers on Flexible and Shift Schedules in May 2004*, News Release, USDL 05-1198, July 2005. See also <http://www.bls.gov/bls/newsrels.htm#OEUS>.

Table 609. Employed Workers With Alternative and Traditional Work Arrangements: 2005

[In thousands (138,952 represents 138,952,000). As of February. For employed workers 16 years old and over. Based on the Current Population Survey; see text, Section 1 and Appendix III]

Characteristic	Total employed [1]	Workers with alternative arrangements				Workers with traditional arrangements
		Independent contractors	On-call workers	Temporary help agency workers	Workers provided by contract firms	
Total employed................	138,952	10,342	2,454	1,217	813	123,843
16 to 19 years old	5,510	89	133	33	7	5,194
20 to 24 years old	13,114	356	355	202	87	12,055
25 to 34 years old	30,103	1,520	535	362	205	27,427
35 to 44 years old	34,481	2,754	571	253	196	30,646
45 to 54 years old	32,947	2,799	417	200	186	29,324
55 to 64 years old	17,980	1,943	267	135	114	15,496
65 years old and over	4,817	881	175	33	18	3,701
Male........................	73,946	6,696	1,241	574	561	64,673
16 to 19 years old	2,579	32	82	24	7	2,389
20 to 24 years old	6,928	194	200	107	61	6,331
25 to 34 years old	16,624	1,006	299	185	138	14,950
35 to 44 years old	18,523	1,824	252	120	140	16,130
45 to 54 years old	17,193	1,764	209	71	143	15,003
55 to 64 years old	9,485	1,287	108	52	70	7,954
65 years old and over	2,615	589	91	16	3	1,917
Female.......................	65,006	3,647	1,212	643	252	59,170
16 to 19 years old	2,931	57	52	9	–	2,805
20 to 24 years old	6,186	162	155	95	27	5,724
25 to 34 years old	13,480	514	236	177	67	12,477
35 to 44 years old	15,958	930	319	133	57	14,516
45 to 54 years old	15,754	1,035	208	129	43	14,322
55 to 64 years old	8,495	656	158	83	44	7,542
65 years old and over	2,202	292	84	17	15	1,785
Full-time workers..............	113,798	7,732	1,370	979	695	102,889
Part-time workers	25,154	2,611	1,084	238	119	20,954

– Represents zero. [1] Includes day laborers (an alternative arrangement) and a small number of workers who were both "on call" and "provided by contract firms," not shown separately.

Source: U.S. Bureau of Labor Statistics, *Contingent and Alternative Employment Arrangements, February 2005*, News Release, USDL 05–1443, July 2005. See also <http://www.bls.gov/bls/newsrels.htm#OEUS>.

Labor Force, Employment, and Earnings 389

Table 610. Multiple Jobholders: 2010

[Annual average of monthly figures (6,878 represents 6,878,000). Civilian noninstitutionalized population 16 years old and over. Multiple jobholders are employed persons who, either 1) had jobs as wage or salary workers with two employers or more; 2) were self-employed and also held a wage and salary job; or 3) were unpaid family workers and also held a wage and salary job. Based on the Current Population Survey; see text, Section 1 and Appendix III]

Characteristic	Total		Male		Female	
	Number (1,000)	Percent of employed	Number (1,000)	Percent of employed	Number (1,000)	Percent of employed
Total [1]	**6,878**	**4.9**	**3,326**	**4.5**	**3,552**	**5.4**
Age:						
16 to 19 years old	167	3.8	61	2.9	106	4.7
20 to 24 years old	695	5.5	289	4.5	406	6.5
25 to 54 years old	4,797	5.1	2,374	4.7	2,423	5.5
55 to 64 years old	1,021	4.7	490	4.4	531	5.1
65 years old and over	197	3.1	112	3.2	86	3.0
Race and Hispanic ethnicity:						
White [2]	5,857	5.1	2,861	4.7	2,996	5.7
Black [2]	653	4.3	298	4.3	354	4.3
Asian [2]	202	3.0	96	2.7	106	3.4
Hispanic [3]	638	3.2	360	3.1	278	3.4
Marital status:						
Married, spouse present	3,644	4.7	2,015	4.7	1,629	4.7
Widowed, divorced, or separated	1,233	5.5	416	4.5	817	6.2
Single, never married.................	2,000	5.2	895	4.3	1,105	6.2
Full- or part-time status:						
Primary job full-time, secondary job part-time...	3,591	(X)	1,926	(X)	1,665	(X)
Both jobs part-time	1,805	(X)	589	(X)	1,216	(X)
Both jobs full-time	263	(X)	172	(X)	91	(X)
Hours vary on primary or secondary job	1,182	(X)	621	(X)	562	(X)

X Not applicable. [1] Includes a small number of persons who work part-time on their primary job and full-time on their secondary job(s), not shown separately. Includes other races, not shown separately. [2] For persons who selected this race group only. See footnote 4, Table 587. [3] Persons of Hispanic origin may be any race.

Source: U.S. Bureau of Labor Statistics, "Employment and Earnings Online," January 2011 issue, March 2011, <http://www.bls.gov/opub/ee/home.htm> and <http://www.bls.gov/cps/home.htm>.

Table 611. Average Number of Jobs Held From Ages 18 to 44: 1978 to 2008

[For persons aged 43 to 52 in 2008–09 (and who were ages 14 to 22 when first interviewed in 1979). A job is an uninterrupted period of work with a particular employer. Educational attainment as of 2008–09. Based on the National Longitudinal Survey of Youth 1979; see source for details]

Sex and educational attainment	Total [1]	Number of jobs held by age				
		18 to 22 years	23 to 27 years	28 to 32 years	33 to 38 years	39 to 44 years
Total [2]	**11.0**	**4.4**	**3.2**	**2.6**	**2.4**	**2.0**
Less than a high school diploma	11.8	4.0	3.4	2.7	2.6	1.9
High school graduates, no college.	10.4	4.1	2.9	2.5	2.4	2.0
Some college or associate's degree	11.4	4.4	3.3	2.7	2.5	2.1
Bachelor's degree or more	11.3	4.9	3.5	2.6	2.3	2.0
Male.	11.4	4.5	3.4	2.8	2.5	2.0
Less than a high school diploma	13.3	4.6	4.0	3.0	2.7	2.1
High school graduate, no college	10.7	4.3	3.2	2.7	2.4	1.9
Some college or associate's degree	11.8	4.6	3.5	2.9	2.5	2.1
Bachelor's degree or more	11.0	4.6	3.5	2.6	2.5	2.0
Female.	10.7	4.2	3.1	2.4	2.4	2.0
Less than a high school diploma	9.7	3.1	2.5	2.2	2.3	1.7
High school graduate, no college	10.0	3.8	2.7	2.3	2.4	2.0
Some college or associate's degree	11.1	4.3	3.2	2.5	2.5	2.1
Bachelor's degree or more	11.7	5.2	3.6	2.6	2.2	1.9
White, non-Hispanic.	11.1	4.6	3.3	2.6	2.4	2.0
Less than a high school diploma	12.7	4.4	3.7	2.8	2.7	2.0
High school graduate, no college	10.4	4.2	3.0	2.5	2.3	1.9
Some college or associate's degree	11.4	4.6	3.4	2.7	2.5	2.0
Bachelor's degree or more	11.3	5.0	3.5	2.6	2.3	1.9
Black, non-Hispanic.	10.7	3.5	3.1	2.7	2.5	2.1
Less than a high school diploma	9.7	2.8	2.8	2.3	2.2	1.7
High school graduate, no college	10.3	3.3	2.9	2.7	2.6	2.0
Some college or associate's degree	11.5	3.9	3.2	2.8	2.7	2.3
Bachelor's degree or more	11.5	4.0	3.6	2.8	2.8	2.3
Hispanic [3]	10.7	4.0	3.0	2.5	2.4	2.1
Less than a high school diploma	10.4	3.6	2.8	2.4	2.4	2.0
High school graduate, no college	10.4	4.0	2.9	2.4	2.3	2.0
Some college or associate's degree	11.4	4.2	3.1	2.7	2.4	2.3
Bachelor's degree or more	10.7	4.2	3.3	2.7	2.5	2.0

[1] Jobs held in more than one age category were counted in each category, but only once in the total. [2] Includes other races, not shown separately. [3] Persons of Hispanic origin may be any race.

Source: U.S. Bureau of Labor Statistics, "Number of Jobs Held, Labor Market Activity, and Earnings Growth Among the Youngest Baby Boomers: Results from a Longitudinal Survey," News Release, USDL 10-1243, September, 2010. See also <http://www.bls.gov/news.release/nlsoy.toc.htm>.

Table 612. Distribution of Workers by Tenure With Current Employer by Selected Characteristics: 2010

[121,931 represents 121,931,000. As of January from the 2010 Displaced Worker Supplement. For employed wage and salary workers 16 years old and over. Data exclude the incorporated and unincorporated self-employed. Based on the Current Population Survey; see source and Appendix III]

Characteristic	Number employed (1,000)	Percent distribution by tenure with current employer								Median years [1]
		12 months or less	13 to 23 months	2 years	3 to 4 years	5 to 9 years	10 to 14 years	15 to 19 years	20 years or more	
Total [2]	**121,931**	**19.0**	**7.0**	**5.8**	**18.9**	**20.5**	**12.2**	**6.1**	**10.5**	**4.4**
AGE AND SEX										
16 to 19 years old	3,984	66.7	12.7	10.7	9.6	0.3	–	–	–	–
20 to 24 years old	11,835	45.1	13.3	12.1	22.4	7.0	0.1	–	–	1.5
25 to 34 years old	27,756	23.3	9.8	7.5	27.7	24.4	6.6	0.8	–	3.1
35 to 44 years old	27,205	14.4	6.3	4.8	19.2	24.7	18.2	8.0	4.3	5.1
45 to 54 years old	28,841	10.6	4.4	4.1	14.6	21.5	16.0	9.8	18.9	7.8
55 to 64 years old	17,740	7.8	3.6	2.9	12.8	19.7	15.6	9.6	27.9	10.0
65 years old and over	4,570	6.9	2.9	2.7	12.9	21.4	15.3	9.8	28.0	9.9
Male	61,495	18.5	6.6	5.7	18.3	20.8	12.4	6.1	11.5	4.6
16 to 19 years old	1,850	65.8	12.4	10.2	11.3	0.3	–	–	–	–
20 to 24 years old	5,746	44.2	12.7	11.9	22.8	8.3	0.1	–	–	1.6
25 to 34 years old	14,604	22.9	9.2	7.3	26.6	25.4	7.6	1.0	–	3.2
35 to 44 years old	14,160	14.0	5.8	4.7	18.4	24.7	19.4	8.3	4.7	5.3
45 to 54 years old	14,239	10.8	3.9	4.1	13.1	20.7	15.4	10.5	21.4	8.5
55 to 64 years old	8,655	7.2	3.4	2.7	12.3	19.4	14.5	9.0	31.4	10.4
65 years old and over	2,242	6.8	4.0	2.5	13.9	20.9	15.3	7.0	29.6	9.7
Female	60,435	19.4	7.4	5.9	19.5	20.2	12.0	6.0	9.5	4.2
16 to 19 years old	2,135	67.4	12.9	11.2	8.2	0.3	–	–	–	–
20 to 24 years old	6,089	46.0	13.9	12.2	22.0	5.8	0.1	–	–	1.5
25 to 34 years old	13,151	23.8	10.4	7.7	28.8	23.2	5.5	0.5	–	3.0
35 to 44 years old	13,045	14.8	7.0	4.8	20.1	24.7	17.0	7.7	3.9	4.9
45 to 54 years old	14,602	10.5	4.9	4.1	16.1	22.3	16.6	9.2	16.4	7.1
55 to 64 years old	9,085	8.2	3.7	3.1	13.3	20.0	16.7	10.2	24.6	9.7
65 years old and over	2,328	7.0	1.9	2.8	12.0	21.9	15.4	12.5	26.5	10.1
RACE AND HISPANIC ORIGIN										
White [3]	99,768	18.6	7.1	5.7	18.4	20.4	12.4	6.4	11.1	4.5
Male	51,081	18.1	6.7	5.6	17.7	20.6	12.6	6.5	12.3	4.8
Female	48,687	19.2	7.6	5.8	19.1	20.1	12.1	6.3	9.8	4.3
Black [3]	13,508	20.7	6.1	6.1	20.9	20.4	11.6	4.9	9.3	4.1
Male	5,969	20.4	5.1	6.6	20.7	21.1	11.9	4.8	9.4	4.2
Female	7,539	20.9	6.9	5.8	21.0	19.8	11.3	5.0	9.2	4.0
Asian [3]	5,598	18.1	7.0	6.8	22.1	25.4	11.8	3.3	5.5	4.0
Male	2,922	18.7	7.1	5.8	23.6	25.1	11.5	3.5	4.7	3.9
Female	2,677	17.4	6.8	7.8	20.5	25.7	12.2	3.2	6.4	4.1
Hispanic [4]	18,016	22.5	7.0	7.4	23.2	20.4	9.8	4.2	5.6	3.4
Male	10,279	22.5	6.7	7.0	23.1	19.9	10.2	4.3	6.3	3.5
Female	7,737	22.4	7.4	7.8	23.3	21.1	9.1	4.1	4.7	3.3

– Represents zero. [1] For definition of median, see Guide to Tabular Presentation. [2] Includes other races, not shown separately. [3] For persons in this race group only. See footnote 4, Table 587. [4] Persons of Hispanic origin may be any race.
Source: U. S. Bureau of Labor Statistics, *Employee Tenure in 2010*, News Release, USDL 10–1278, September 2010.
See also <http://www.bls.gov/news.release/tenure.toc.htm>.

Table 613. Part-Time Workers by Reason: 2010

[In thousands (35,097 represents 35,097,000), except hours. For persons working 1 to 34 hours per week. For civilian noninstitutionalized population 16 years old and over. Annual average of monthly figures. Based on the Current Population Survey; see text, Section 1 and Appendix III]

Reason	All industries			Nonagricultural industries		
		Usually work—			Usually work—	
	Total	Full-time	Part-time	Total	Full-time	Part-time
Total working fewer than 35 hours	**35,097**	**10,217**	**24,880**	**34,505**	**10,033**	**24,471**
Economic reasons	8,874	2,245	6,629	8,744	2,183	6,561
Slack work or business conditions	6,174	2,004	4,170	6,087	1,962	4,126
Could find only part time work	2,375	(S)	2,375	2,358	(S)	2,358
Seasonal work	207	123	84	184	107	77
Job started or ended during the week	118	118	(S)	115	115	(S)
Noneconomic reasons	26,223	7,972	18,251	25,761	7,850	17,911
Child-care problems	800	61	739	793	61	732
Other family or personal obligations	4,634	623	4,010	4,562	613	3,949
Health or medical limitations	737	(S)	737	722	(S)	722
In school or training	5,470	70	5,400	5,412	70	5,342
Retired or social security limit on earnings	2,184	(S)	2,184	2,074	(S)	2,074
Vacation or personal day	3,395	3,395	(S)	3,351	3,351	(S)
Holiday, legal, or religious	854	854	(S)	849	849	(S)
Weather-related curtailment	656	656	(S)	627	627	(S)
Other	7,493	2,312	5,180	7,370	2,280	5,092
Average hours per week:						
Economic reasons	22.5	23.5	22.1	22.5	23.5	22.1
Noneconomic reasons	21.3	24.9	19.7	21.4	25.0	19.8

S No data or data do not meet publication standards.
Source: U.S. Bureau of Labor Statistics, "Employment and Earnings Online," January 2011 issue, March 2011,
<http://www.bls.gov/opub/ee/home.htm> and <http://www.bls.gov/cps/home.htm>.

Labor Force, Employment, and Earnings **391**

Table 614. Displaced Workers by Selected Characteristics: 2010

[In percent, except total (6,938 represents 6,938,000). As of January from the 2010 Displaced Worker Supplement. For persons 20 years old and over with tenure of 3 years or more who lost or left a job between January 2007 and December 2009 because of plant closings or moves, slack work, or the abolishment of their positions. Based on Current Population Survey; see source and Appendix III]

Characteristic	Total (1,000)	Employment status in January 2010			Reason for job loss, 2007–2009		
		Employed	Unemployed	Not in the labor force	Plant or company closed down or moved	Slack/ insufficient work	Position or shift abolished
Total [1]	**6,938**	**48.8**	**36.1**	**15.2**	**30.6**	**42.8**	**26.6**
20 to 24 years old	227	54.8	29.8	15.4	35.9	52.6	11.5
25 to 54 years old	4,923	53.4	35.6	11.0	30.4	43.8	25.8
55 to 64 years old	1,395	38.7	39.9	21.4	32.5	38.6	28.9
65 years old and over	392	22.5	32.4	45.1	23.7	39.9	36.4
Males	4,183	49.0	39.1	11.9	29.8	47.9	22.3
20 to 24 years old	144	54.2	38.7	7.1	25.4	66.6	8.0
25 to 54 years old	3,031	53.1	38.4	8.4	29.5	49.2	21.3
55 to 64 years old	810	38.4	41.4	20.2	33.2	40.7	26.1
65 years old and over	198	24.3	41.2	34.5	25.2	43.4	31.3
Females	2,754	48.5	31.4	20.1	31.8	35.1	33.1
20 to 24 years old	84	55.8	14.6	29.7	54.1	28.6	17.3
25 to 54 years old	1,892	53.9	31.0	15.1	31.8	35.1	33.1
55 to 64 years old	585	39.2	37.8	23.0	31.6	35.6	32.8
65 years old and over	194	20.7	23.3	56.0	22.1	36.3	41.5
White [2]	5,716	50.3	35.0	14.8	29.7	42.9	27.3
Male	3,518	50.8	37.8	11.4	28.4	48.2	23.4
Female	2,198	49.5	30.4	20.2	31.9	34.5	33.7
Black [2]	761	42.9	41.2	15.9	33.9	41.7	24.4
Male	410	39.7	48.4	12.0	35.9	47.9	16.2
Female	351	46.7	32.8	20.4	31.5	34.6	34.0
Asian [2]	294	37.8	47.8	14.3	34.0	44.4	21.6
Male	160	34.8	51.5	13.7	36.4	42.2	21.4
Female	135	41.5	43.4	15.1	31.2	47.0	21.8
Hispanic [3]	993	48.7	38.0	13.4	32.4	57.0	10.6
Male	696	52.3	38.9	8.8	31.8	59.8	8.4
Female	297	40.1	35.8	24.1	33.8	50.4	15.8

[1] Includes other races, not shown separately. [2] For persons in this race group only. See footnote 3, Table 587. [3] Persons of Hispanic origin may be of any race.

Source: U.S. Bureau of Labor Statistics, *Worker Displacement, 2007–2009*, News Release, USDL 10-1174, August 2010. See also <http://www.bls.gov/news.release/disp.toc.htm>.

Table 615. Persons Not in the Labor Force: 2010

[In thousands (83,941 represents 83,941,000). For civilian noninstitutional population 16 years old and over. Annual average of monthly figures. Based on the Current Population Survey; see text, Section 1, and Appendix III]

Status and reason	Total	Age			Sex	
		16 to 24 years old	25 to 54 years old	55 years old and over	Male	Female
Total not in the labor force	**83,941**	**17,014**	**22,350**	**44,577**	**33,189**	**50,752**
Do not want a job now [1]	77,882	14,990	19,659	43,233	30,309	47,573
Want a job now	6,059	2,024	2,691	1,344	2,880	3,179
In the previous year—						
Did not search for a job	2,948	968	1,189	791	1,279	1,669
Did search for a job [2]	3,111	1,056	1,502	553	1,601	1,510
Not available for work now	623	274	284	65	264	359
Available for work now, not looking for work [3]	2,487	782	1,218	487	1,337	1,151
Reason for not currently looking for work:						
Discouraged over job prospects [4]	1,173	291	595	287	731	442
Family responsibilities	286	49	171	66	83	203
In school or training	350	262	81	7	191	158
Ill health or disability	50	4	21	25	21	29
Other [5]	629	176	350	102	311	318

[1] Includes some persons who are not asked if they want a job. [2] Persons who had a job in the prior 12 months must have searched since the end of that job. [3] Persons who have searched for work in the previous year and are available to work now also are referred to as "marginally attached to the labor force." [4] Includes such things as believes no work available, could not find work, lacks necessary schooling or training, employer thinks too young or old, and other types of discrimination. [5] Includes such things as child care and transportation problems.

Source: U.S. Bureau of Labor Statistics, "Employment and Earnings Online," January 2011 issue, March 2011, <http://www.bls.gov/opub/ee/home.htm> and <http://www.bls.gov/cps/tables.htm#annual>.

Table 616. Employed Civilians by Occupation, Sex, Race, and Hispanic Origin: 2010

[139,064 represents 139,064,000. Civilian noninstitutionalized population 16 years old and over. Annual average of monthly figures. Based on Current Population Survey; see text, Section 1 and Appendix III. Occupational classifications are those used in the 2000 census]

Occupation	Total employed (1,000)	Percent of total			
		Female	Black [1]	Asian [1]	Hispanic [2]
Total, 16 years and over..................................	139,064	47.2	10.8	4.8	14.3
Management, professional and related occupations	**51,743**	**51.5**	**8.4**	**6.1**	**7.3**
Management, business, and financial operations occupations	20,938	43.0	7.3	4.8	7.5
Management occupations [3]	15,001	38.2	6.4	4.4	7.6
Chief executives..	1,505	25.5	2.8	3.2	4.8
General and operations managers.........................	1,007	29.9	5.8	3.3	5.9
Marketing and sales managers............................	959	45.2	5.9	5.0	5.1
Administrative services managers.........................	104	34.4	9.0	5.5	9.5
Computer and information systems managers	537	29.9	6.8	9.0	7.2
Financial managers	1,141	53.2	6.7	6.9	8.1
Human resources managers	268	69.3	9.1	3.0	7.9
Industrial production managers	254	17.9	3.0	4.4	9.4
Purchasing managers	203	46.1	7.6	2.8	7.8
Transportation, storage, and distribution managers............	278	17.4	9.5	2.8	11.7
Farm, ranch, and other agricultural managers................	237	18.1	0.6	0.8	9.8
Farmers and ranchers	713	24.6	0.6	0.7	1.5
Construction managers	1,083	6.8	3.5	2.0	8.5
Education administrators	830	63.0	11.1	2.0	6.4
Engineering managers	113	7.7	5.4	13.3	3.5
Food service managers	960	47.4	8.5	10.8	14.6
Lodging managers..	143	48.4	5.1	11.3	5.8
Medical and health services managers	549	72.5	12.4	3.2	7.2
Property, real estate, and community association managers........	604	49.2	7.7	2.6	11.4
Social and community service managers.....................	326	70.2	13.1	1.6	7.0
Business and financial operations occupations [3]	5,937	54.9	9.8	5.7	7.1
Wholesale and retail buyers, except farm products	180	52.1	4.4	2.2	9.7
Purchasing agents, except wholesale, retail, and farm products.....	235	54.9	8.0	3.2	5.7
Claims adjusters, appraisers, examiners, and investigators	282	57.4	13.8	3.3	7.4
Compliance officers, except agriculture, construction, health and safety, and transportation....................	188	47.0	11.5	2.2	7.8
Cost estimators	115	11.6	1.5	0.6	7.5
Human resources, training, and labor relations specialists	824	70.3	14.0	2.6	10.2
Management analysts	658	43.7	7.2	7.6	6.7
Accountants and auditors.................................	1,646	60.1	8.6	9.1	5.8
Appraisers and assessors of real estate	79	34.0	3.0	1.8	2.5
Financial analysts..	97	35.7	11.6	6.9	3.0
Personal financial advisors................................	369	30.8	5.2	4.9	3.5
Insurance underwriters....................................	125	59.3	13.2	4.2	4.7
Loan counselors and officers..............................	363	51.8	9.9	4.6	10.6
Tax preparers	106	71.1	13.0	6.1	11.1
Professional and related occupations	30,805	57.4	9.2	7.0	7.1
Computer and mathematical occupations [3]	3,531	25.8	6.7	16.1	5.5
Computer scientists and systems analysts	784	30.5	7.3	14.9	5.1
Computer programmers	470	22.0	5.1	12.4	6.5
Computer software engineers	1,026	20.9	5.1	28.0	3.9
Computer support specialists.............................	388	27.6	11.3	7.9	6.9
Database administrators	101	36.4	9.0	11.8	8.6
Network and computer systems administrators	229	16.5	5.6	9.4	6.0
Network systems and data communications analysts	366	26.2	6.6	7.4	6.7
Operations research analysts.............................	107	46.2	10.7	5.8	8.4
Architecture and engineering occupations [3]	2,619	12.9	5.2	9.0	6.8
Architects, except naval	184	24.4	2.1	1.9	7.8
Aerospace engineers	126	10.8	6.7	3.7	3.8
Civil engineers	318	9.7	4.9	8.9	6.9
Computer hardware engineers............................	70	10.3	3.1	26.7	7.3
Electrical and electronics engineers.......................	307	7.2	5.3	16.7	7.0
Industrial engineers, including health and safety	159	20.0	5.0	10.2	7.8
Mechanical engineers	293	6.7	3.2	11.0	3.7
Drafters	143	21.4	3.6	4.1	11.3
Engineering technicians, except drafters	374	13.2	8.2	4.6	8.9
Life, physical, and social science occupations [3]	1,409	46.5	6.3	10.8	6.0
Biological scientists	113	45.8	8.0	9.8	6.2
Medical scientists	143	53.7	7.0	28.4	7.5
Chemists and materials scientists	103	33.5	9.9	18.2	4.3
Environmental scientists and geoscientists	108	26.2	5.4	3.0	2.9
Market and survey researchers	150	55.7	5.1	7.7	2.8
Psychologists...	179	66.7	3.9	3.3	7.3
Community and social services occupations [3]	2,337	64.2	19.3	3.3	9.8
Counselors...	702	71.2	21.4	3.8	9.5
Social workers	771	80.8	22.8	3.3	11.3
Miscellaneous community and social service specialists..........	297	68.0	21.6	1.7	13.0
Clergy..	429	17.5	12.6	2.9	6.3

See footnotes at end of table.

U.S. Census Bureau, Statistical Abstract of the United States: 2012

Table 616. Employed Civilians by Occupation, Sex, Race, and Hispanic Origin: 2010—Con.

[139,064 represents 139,064,000. Civilian noninstitutional population 16 years old and over. Annual average of monthly figures. Based on Current Population Survey; see text, Section 1, and Appendix III. Occupational classifications are those used in the 2000 census]

Occupation	Total employed (1,000)	Percent of total			
		Female	Black [1]	Asian [1]	Hispanic [2]
Legal occupations	1,716	48.8	6.5	3.4	5.5
Lawyers	1,040	31.5	4.3	3.4	3.4
Judges, magistrates, and other judicial workers	71	36.4	12.5	3.9	7.8
Paralegals and legal assistants	345	85.8	8.8	2.4	9.6
Miscellaneous legal support workers	259	72.6	10.4	4.4	7.7
Education, training, and library occupations [3]	8,628	73.8	9.4	3.8	8.0
Postsecondary teachers	1,300	45.9	6.3	11.0	5.0
Preschool and kindergarten teachers	712	97.0	13.4	2.7	9.6
Elementary and middle school teachers	2,813	81.8	9.3	2.4	7.3
Secondary school teachers	1,221	57.0	8.0	1.6	6.7
Special education teachers	387	85.1	6.8	2.0	6.2
Other teachers and instructors	806	66.5	9.6	4.8	8.0
Librarians	216	82.8	9.2	1.7	5.2
Teacher assistants	966	92.4	12.7	2.9	15.1
Arts, design, entertainment, sports, and media occupations [3]	2,759	46.2	5.5	4.3	8.8
Artists and related workers	195	47.1	2.7	3.6	6.6
Designers	793	53.7	3.3	5.2	9.0
Producers and directors	152	37.7	9.1	5.5	10.9
Athletes, coaches, umpires, and related workers	260	34.6	7.3	4.1	10.6
Musicians, singers, and related workers	182	31.9	13.9	2.1	8.7
News analysts, reporters and correspondents	81	46.9	3.0	6.0	7.2
Public relations specialists	148	58.8	2.8	2.6	8.7
Editors	162	53.2	4.9	5.0	3.9
Writers and authors	199	63.5	3.8	2.3	1.5
Miscellaneous media and communication workers	83	67.9	6.6	10.6	32.5
Broadcast and sound engineering technicians and radio operators	102	9.9	5.7	4.1	10.8
Photographers and editors	161	39.4	6.5	3.3	8.1
Healthcare practitioner and technical occupations [3]	7,805	74.3	10.8	7.8	6.2
Dentists	175	25.5	0.3	13.7	5.7
Dietitians and nutritionists	105	92.3	14.9	9.1	5.2
Pharmacists	255	53.0	5.2	15.1	4.3
Physicians and surgeons	872	32.3	5.8	15.7	6.8
Physician assistants	99	68.7	5.0	5.8	9.2
Registered nurses	2,843	91.1	12.0	7.5	4.9
Occupational therapists	109	87.8	2.5	2.6	6.1
Physical therapists	187	68.5	5.8	7.6	5.4
Speech-language pathologists	132	96.3	2.9	0.7	6.1
Clinical laboratory technologists and technicians	342	76.8	15.1	10.3	7.4
Dental hygienists	141	95.1	4.3	5.9	3.0
Diagnostic-related technologists and technicians	349	73.3	7.2	4.8	7.7
Emergency medical technicians and paramedics	179	34.1	4.4	0.9	3.7
Health diagnosing and treating practitioner support technicians	505	75.9	13.6	6.8	10.8
Licensed practical and licensed vocational nurses	573	91.7	24.4	3.8	6.2
Medical records and health information technicians	118	87.6	19.9	6.5	12.7
Service occupations	**24,634**	**56.8**	**15.3**	**4.9**	**21.3**
Healthcare support occupations [3]	3,332	88.9	25.5	4.1	15.2
Nursing, psychiatric, and home health aides	1,928	88.2	34.6	4.0	14.7
Massage therapists	162	87.1	5.3	4.9	6.0
Dental assistants	296	97.5	5.7	5.6	20.0
Medical assistants and other healthcare support occupations	850	89.7	17.8	3.5	16.4
Protective service occupations [3]	3,289	21.4	17.8	2.4	13.3
First-line supervisors/managers of police and detectives	103	15.4	8.7	2.5	7.4
Fire-fighters	301	3.6	6.4	0.5	9.6
Bailiffs, correctional officers, and jailers	465	26.1	22.0	1.2	13.3
Detectives and criminal investigators	159	22.8	10.6	3.7	13.3
Police and sheriff's patrol officers	714	13.0	12.1	2.7	15.2
Private detectives and investigators	89	37.6	5.7	3.2	12.1
Security guards and gaming surveillance officers	993	20.8	28.8	3.4	15.9
Lifeguards and other protective service workers	166	54.4	4.2	2.2	6.7
Food preparation and serving related occupations	7,660	55.1	11.3	5.6	22.2
Chefs and head cooks	337	19.0	12.0	16.5	17.9
First-line supervisors/managers of food preparation and serving workers	551	56.6	15.4	3.0	14.9
Cooks	1,951	40.5	15.0	5.0	32.5
Food-preparation workers	717	59.2	13.4	5.3	23.7
Bartenders	393	55.2	3.8	2.1	10.7
Combined food preparation and serving workers, including fast food	294	61.3	12.8	4.6	16.6
Counter attendants, cafeteria, food concession, and coffee shop	269	65.7	11.3	5.7	18.5
Waiters and waitresses	2,067	71.1	7.1	6.1	16.6
Food servers, nonrestaurant	174	64.9	18.6	6.5	16.3
Dining room and cafeteria attendants and bartender helpers	371	47.9	10.7	7.0	29.0
Dishwashers	246	21.1	10.5	4.2	38.5
Hosts and hostesses, restaurant, lounge, and coffee shop	284	84.7	8.1	4.0	14.3

See footnotes at end of table.

Table 616. Employed Civilians by Occupation, Sex, Race, and Hispanic Origin: 2010—Con.

[139,064 represents 139,064,000. Civilian noninstitutional population 16 years old and over. Annual average of monthly figures. Based on Current Population Survey; see text, Section 1, and Appendix III. Occupational classifications are those used in the 2000 census]

Occupation	Total employed (1,000)	Percent of total			
		Female	Black [1]	Asian [1]	Hispanic [2]
Building and grounds cleaning and maintenance occupations	5,328	40.6	13.6	3.1	35.2
First-line supervisors/managers of housekeeping and janitorial workers.........................	234	41.7	13.3	2.8	19.8
First-line supervisors/managers of landscaping, lawn service, and groundskeeping workers	229	7.3	3.8	1.1	20.5
Janitors and building cleaners.............................	2,186	33.2	17.1	3.2	30.9
Maids and housekeeping cleaners	1,407	89.0	16.3	5.0	40.8
Pest control workers.....................................	76	3.3	5.3	1.7	15.9
Grounds maintenance workers	1,195	5.8	6.3	1.3	43.8
Personal care and service occupations [3]...............	5,024	78.3	14.8	7.8	14.6
First-line supervisors/managers of gaming workers	136	52.2	5.4	8.3	8.9
First-line supervisors/managers of personal service workers	185	71.6	7.7	14.5	9.0
Nonfarm animal caretakers	169	71.7	2.7	2.0	12.7
Gaming services workers...............................	121	38.1	5.0	29.6	10.5
Barbers	96	17.9	37.2	1.2	12.1
Hairdressers, hairstylists, and cosmetologists.............	770	91.9	10.6	4.7	12.7
Miscellaneous personal appearance workers	273	86.6	7.5	51.4	10.9
Baggage porters, bellhops, and concierges................	77	17.9	29.8	6.9	25.8
Transportation attendants................................	110	71.6	12.2	4.9	16.6
Child care workers......................................	1,247	94.7	16.0	3.4	19.1
Personal and home care aides	973	86.1	23.8	6.4	17.6
Recreation and fitness workers	379	67.2	11.3	1.8	6.9
Sales and office occupations.........................	**33,433**	**62.9**	**11.3**	**4.2**	**12.6**
Sales and related occupations [3]	15,386	49.9	9.8	5.0	11.8
First-line supervisors/managers of retail sales workers.........	3,132	43.9	7.9	5.4	10.3
First-line supervisors/managers of non retail sales workers	1,131	28.0	5.9	5.6	9.6
Cashiers...	3,109	73.7	16.1	6.8	16.3
Counter and rental clerks................................	150	49.0	7.9	6.9	12.7
Parts salespersons.....................................	129	12.5	3.7	0.5	12.9
Retail salespersons	3,286	51.9	11.3	4.1	13.7
Advertising sales agents	214	47.6	6.3	2.7	4.9
Insurance sales agents	513	49.4	6.6	3.2	10.1
Securities, commodities, and financial services sales agents	308	30.8	6.4	8.0	4.8
Travel agents	76	84.0	9.9	6.5	8.7
Sales representatives, services, all other	524	34.4	9.6	4.9	9.9
Sales representatives, wholesale and manufacturing	1,284	25.0	4.0	3.3	9.3
Real estate brokers and sales agents	854	54.0	5.3	3.8	7.1
Telemarketers...	118	68.3	25.0	1.2	11.9
Door-to-door sales workers, news and street vendors, and related workers	203	64.3	12.9	3.6	15.7
Office and administrative support occupations [3]	18,047	73.9	12.5	3.6	13.4
First-line supervisors/managers of office and administrative support workers	1,507	68.7	9.7	3.8	11.1
Bill and account collectors..............................	216	65.4	17.5	2.9	18.9
Billing and posting clerks and machine operators	472	92.2	13.7	4.1	14.0
Bookkeeping, accounting, and auditing clerks..............	1,297	90.9	6.5	3.4	8.8
Payroll and timekeeping clerks	167	90.8	10.4	1.9	10.7
Tellers..	453	88.0	11.3	5.2	14.0
Court, municipal, and license clerks	95	75.9	17.9	3.1	12.1
Customer service representatives	1,896	66.6	17.5	3.9	15.2
File clerks...	334	82.0	16.0	3.9	14.3
Hotel, motel, and resort desk clerks	129	69.1	15.3	4.4	11.6
Interviewers, except eligibility and loan	210	76.0	17.3	5.8	12.0
Library assistants, clerical	115	77.1	5.9	3.2	12.3
Loan interviewers and clerks............................	127	78.3	11.5	4.7	11.0
Order clerks	117	68.0	8.0	6.4	16.2
Receptionists and information clerks......................	1,281	92.7	9.8	3.3	16.8
Reservation and transportation ticket agents and travel clerks ...	100	58.2	24.0	3.9	14.9
Couriers and messengers	270	15.4	16.4	2.4	15.6
Dispatchers...	293	60.9	13.5	1.6	14.4
Postal service clerks....................................	124	45.3	29.5	8.3	11.1
Postal service mail carriers	321	37.7	11.7	6.6	11.1
Postal service mail sorters, processors, and processing machine operators...................	76	48.8	30.5	16.2	7.5
Production, planning, and expediting clerks	259	54.9	9.5	3.4	7.2
Shipping, receiving, and traffic clerks	558	27.5	12.5	3.6	21.9
Stock clerks and order fillers	1,456	36.0	16.7	3.4	19.3
Weighers, measurers, checkers, and samplers, recordkeeping...	70	38.3	10.8	3.1	22.3
Secretaries and administrative assistants	3,082	96.1	8.6	1.9	9.4
Computer operators.....................................	122	48.5	10.8	9.1	11.8
Data entry keyers.......................................	338	80.5	13.2	4.2	11.4
Word processors and typists	144	92.5	12.3	2.5	13.9
Insurance claims and policy processing clerks	231	82.6	16.5	2.3	11.5
Mail clerks and mail machine operators, except postal service...	94	51.3	21.4	3.5	18.1
Office clerks, general...................................	994	84.2	13.0	5.2	15.6

See footnotes at end of table.

U.S. Census Bureau, Statistical Abstract of the United States: 2012

Table 616. Employed Civilians by Occupation, Sex, Race, and Hispanic Origin: 2010—Con.

[139,064 represents 139,064,000. Civilian noninstitutional population 16 years old and over. Annual average of monthly figures. Based on Current Population Survey; see text, Section 1, and Appendix III. Occupational classifications are those used in the 2000 census]

Occupation	Total employed (1,000)	Percent of total			
		Female	Black [1]	Asian [1]	Hispanic [2]
Natural resources, construction, and maintenance occupations...	**13,073**	**4.6**	**6.7**	**2.0**	**25.0**
Farming, fishing, and forestry occupations [3]	987	23.5	5.2	1.9	41.8
Construction and extraction occupations [3]	7,175	2.6	6.1	1.4	29.1
First-line supervisors/managers of construction trades and extraction workers	659	3.9	4.9	1.0	16.5
Brickmasons, blockmasons, and stonemasons	162	0.1	6.7	0.8	35.5
Carpenters	1,242	1.4	4.0	1.4	25.7
Carpet, floor, and tile installers and finishers	209	0.5	3.8	3.3	39.5
Cement masons, concrete finishers, and terrazzo workers	88	0.3	12.0	–	51.5
Construction laborers	1,267	2.7	9.0	2.2	43.1
Operating engineers and other construction equipment operators ...	363	1.5	4.7	1.1	13.7
Drywall installers, ceiling tile installers, and tapers	171	2.5	2.5	0.3	58.6
Electricians	691	1.5	7.0	1.6	14.0
Painters, construction and maintenance	578	7.2	4.8	1.3	41.0
Pipelayers, plumbers, pipefitters, and steamfitters	526	1.5	7.2	1.3	20.8
Roofers	214	1.0	4.0	1.3	46.4
Sheet metal workers	108	4.0	5.8	0.4	18.8
Construction and building inspectors	104	8.7	8.3	2.3	9.0
Highway maintenance workers	110	2.5	14.2	2.6	11.0
Installation, maintenance, and repair occupations [3]	4,911	3.9	7.8	2.9	15.7
First-line supervisors/managers of mechanics, installers, and repairers	381	6.3	7.5	1.9	9.9
Computer, automated teller, and office machine repairers	305	11.0	10.0	8.0	10.1
Radio and telecommunications equipment installers and repairers...	166	9.1	9.3	6.2	10.4
Aircraft mechanics and service technicians	136	2.3	7.1	7.1	15.3
Automotive body and related repairers	168	1.2	6.3	0.8	22.6
Automotive service technicians and mechanics	802	1.6	6.8	3.5	20.3
Bus and truck mechanics and diesel engine specialists	339	0.7	7.6	1.6	13.2
Heavy vehicle and mobile equipment service technicians and mechanics	235	1.2	4.6	1.1	14.1
Heating, air conditioning, and refrigeration mechanics and installers	392	0.6	8.0	2.2	17.2
Industrial and refractory machinery mechanics	447	3.5	8.1	2.2	14.4
Maintenance and repair workers, general	347	3.8	11.1	2.7	18.0
Electrical power-line installers and repairers	124	0.4	8.2	0.7	10.3
Telecommunications line installers and repairers	163	7.5	9.4	1.6	17.5
Production, transportation, and material moving occupations	**16,180**	**21.2**	**13.9**	**4.2**	**21.0**
Production occupations [3]	7,998	27.6	11.4	5.5	21.9
First-line supervisors/managers of production and operating workers	702	18.1	7.3	5.5	15.7
Electrical, electronics, and electromechanical assemblers	151	54.9	15.1	22.6	17.1
Bakers	206	57.0	9.8	5.8	30.6
Butchers and other meat, poultry, and fish processing workers	331	21.2	14.0	10.4	36.2
Food batchmakers	107	55.5	9.7	2.6	27.6
Cutting, punching, and press machine setters, operators, and tenders, metal and plastic	78	21.1	11.1	2.6	15.2
Machinists	408	3.9	4.3	5.5	15.1
Welding, soldering, and brazing workers	479	5.4	7.0	3.6	22.7
Printing machine operators	162	21.5	13.7	1.8	19.6
Laundry and dry-cleaning workers	195	55.8	15.9	9.3	30.1
Sewing machine operators	170	78.5	13.3	10.8	40.2
Tailors, dressmakers, and sewers	76	70.0	4.9	20.9	19.6
Stationary engineers and boiler operators	91	1.7	9.8	5.3	14.5
Water and liquid waste treatment plant and system operators	77	5.9	6.8	3.4	10.1
Crushing, grinding, polishing, mixing, and blending workers	90	15.7	16.0	2.2	23.2
Inspectors, testers, sorters, samplers, and weighers	669	34.3	11.1	5.3	16.9
Medical, dental, and ophthalmic laboratory technicians	92	49.0	5.5	7.8	12.5
Packaging and filling machine operators and tenders	255	47.6	16.4	4.1	42.3
Painting workers	139	7.9	9.3	0.5	26.4
Transportation and material-moving occupations [3]	8,182	15.0	16.4	2.8	20.0
Supervisors, transportation and material-moving workers	263	23.4	18.3	3.0	15.1
Aircraft pilots and flight engineers	110	5.2	1.0	1.0	6.3
Bus drivers	600	47.0	25.1	2.2	12.3
Driver/sales workers and truck drivers	3,028	4.6	13.6	1.5	17.5
Taxi drivers and chauffeurs	390	14.4	26.6	13.0	15.7
Parking lot attendants	75	6.3	25.7	12.8	18.0
Service station attendants	77	13.5	8.6	4.0	17.1
Industrial truck and tractor operators	499	6.2	22.0	1.2	32.0
Cleaners of vehicles and equipment	333	15.0	14.8	3.7	35.6
Laborers and freight, stock, and material movers, hand	1,700	17.4	16.9	3.0	21.3
Packers and packagers, hand	403	56.5	17.3	4.2	41.3
Refuse and recyclable material collectors	88	7.9	23.9	0.2	21.2

– Represents or rounds to zero. [1] The Current Population Survey (CPS) allows respondents to choose more than one race. Data represent persons who selected this race group only and exclude persons reporting more than one race. The CPS in prior years only allowed respondents to report one race group. See comments on race in the text for Section 1. [2] Persons of Hispanic origin may be any race. [3] Includes other occupations, not shown separately.

Source: U.S. Bureau of Labor Statistics, "Employment and Earnings Online," January 2011 issue, March 2011, <http://www.bls.gov/opub/ee/home.htm> and <http://www.bls.gov/cps/home.htm>.

U.S. Census Bureau, Statistical Abstract of the United States: 2012

Table 617. Employed Civilians by Occupation—States: 2010

[In thousands (139,064 represents 139,064,000). Based on the Current Population Survey see text, Section 1 and Appendix III]

State	Total	Management, professional, and related occupations		Service occupations	Sales and office occupations		Natural resources, construction, and maintenance occupations			Production, transportation, and material-moving occupations	
		Management, business, and financial operations	Professional and related occupations		Sales and related occupations	Office and administrative occupations	Farming, fishing, and forestry occupations	Construction and extraction occupations	Installation, maintenance, and repair occupations	Production occupations	Transportation and material-moving occupations
Total....	139,064	20,938	30,805	24,634	15,386	18,047	987	7,175	4,911	7,998	8,182
AL	1,952	215	408	316	198	262	14	128	87	183	142
AK	331	49	66	62	32	44	4	24	18	12	22
AZ	2,850	454	617	506	371	392	6	165	93	124	120
AR	1,228	161	245	193	129	164	16	65	51	117	88
CA	15,976	2,507	3,597	2,909	1,838	2,014	222	747	500	812	830
CO......	2,482	441	623	392	274	295	10	133	81	100	132
CT......	1,719	297	443	288	191	211	3	73	56	84	73
DE......	392	59	81	69	42	61	3	21	13	18	25
DC......	310	79	114	50	19	30	(Z)	5	3	3	7
FL	8,083	1,231	1,763	1,554	1,022	1,069	36	389	308	250	458
GA	4,238	696	860	696	531	528	19	236	159	218	296
HI	579	75	110	134	70	79	4	38	22	18	29
ID	691	100	125	123	85	97	18	37	31	37	38
IL	5,970	894	1,249	1,049	693	784	17	231	180	435	437
IN	2,818	382	555	473	317	346	13	143	103	287	200
IA	1,571	219	309	265	165	211	13	82	60	136	111
KS	1,385	234	308	235	137	173	12	68	50	88	80
KY	1,844	244	396	320	189	220	20	104	69	143	138
LA	1,928	280	394	337	218	262	20	111	72	110	125
ME	633	93	143	112	66	82	8	35	25	35	35
MD	2,819	487	767	470	275	376	9	145	93	82	117
MA	3,194	557	875	531	320	382	8	137	88	149	148
MI	4,232	589	1,006	749	441	568	45	161	130	311	230
MN	2,721	458	635	434	279	366	31	112	84	165	158
MS	1,155	133	231	190	105	168	16	72	52	106	82
MO	2,745	386	534	486	295	417	8	159	104	185	170
MT	452	78	90	90	47	53	9	28	16	17	23
NE	929	153	206	139	100	119	11	46	31	76	48
NV	1,131	156	183	305	138	143	4	56	41	36	69
NH	702	115	177	108	82	83	2	31	26	44	33
NJ	4,100	700	962	688	463	551	10	179	127	158	261
NM	843	124	203	156	78	106	4	66	32	34	40
NY	8,832	1,230	2,134	1,800	951	1,186	8	428	246	362	486
NC	4,094	602	958	703	447	481	18	231	163	281	210
ND	358	63	70	64	36	42	7	24	15	18	19
OH	5,263	702	1,074	966	558	730	24	257	199	426	328
OK	1,621	244	316	281	176	222	17	109	77	86	93
OR	1,780	292	390	325	204	213	32	75	48	97	104
PA	5,774	854	1,291	978	607	770	50	285	210	340	389
RI	508	72	131	95	53	63	1	20	16	32	25
SC	1,899	227	393	346	230	244	10	82	97	157	113
SD	420	73	77	73	42	57	9	21	15	29	25
TN	2,788	384	556	499	313	373	15	141	111	215	181
TX	11,149	1,541	2,204	2,014	1,243	1,415	69	805	490	645	722
UT	1,271	193	264	186	153	186	5	82	42	84	76
VT	339	53	87	54	36	40	4	20	11	19	16
VA	3,800	680	968	598	413	432	21	196	124	174	192
WA	3,180	499	783	546	313	383	52	162	101	158	182
WV	724	99	157	132	73	98	1	48	32	38	46
WI	2,813	420	588	468	287	395	22	124	88	240	181
WY	278	39	52	48	22	36	3	29	16	12	22

Z Less than 500.

Source: U.S. Bureau of Labor Statistics, *Geographic Profile of Employment and Unemployment, 2010*, Bulletin 2748, July 2011. See also <http://www.bls.gov/opub/gp/gpsec11.htm>.

Table 618. Employment Projections by Occupation: 2008 to 2018

[In thousands (16.0 represents 16,000), except percent and rank. Estimates based on the Current Employment Statistics Program; the Occupational Employment Statistics Survey; and the Current Population Survey. See source for methodological assumptions. Occupations based on the 2000 Standard Occupational Classification system]

Occupation	Employment (1,000)		Change, 2008–2018		Quartile rank by 2008 median annual earnings [1]	Most significant source of postsecondary education or training
	2008	2018	Number (1,000)	Percent		
FASTEST GROWING						
Biomedical engineers	16.0	27.6	11.6	72.0	VH	Bachelor's degree
Network systems and data communications analyst	292.0	447.8	155.8	53.4	VH	Bachelor's degree
Home health aides	921.7	1,382.6	460.9	50.0	VL	Short-term on-the-job training
Personal and home care aides	817.2	1,193.0	375.8	46.0	VL	Short-term on-the-job training
Financial examiners	27.0	38.1	11.1	41.2	VH	Bachelor's degree
Medical scientists, except epidemiologists	109.4	153.6	44.2	40.4	VH	Doctoral degree
Physician assistants	74.8	103.9	29.2	39.0	VH	Master's degree
Skin care specialists	38.8	53.5	14.7	37.9	L	Postsecondary vocational award
Biochemists and biophysicists	23.2	31.9	8.7	37.4	VH	Doctoral degree
Athletic trainers	16.3	22.4	6.0	37.0	H	Bachelor's degree
Physical therapist aides	46.1	62.8	16.7	36.3	L	Short-term on-the-job training
Dental hygienists	174.1	237.0	62.9	36.1	VH	Associate degree
Veterinary technologists and technicians	79.6	108.1	28.5	35.8	L	Associate degree
Dental assistants	295.3	400.9	105.6	35.8	L	Moderate-term on-the-job training
Computer software engineers, applications	514.8	689.9	175.1	34.0	VH	Bachelor's degree
Medical assistants	483.6	647.5	163.9	33.9	L	Moderate-term on-the-job training
Physical therapist assistants	63.8	85.0	21.2	33.3	H	Associate degree
Veterinarians	59.7	79.4	19.7	33.0	VH	First professional degree
Self-enrichment education teachers	253.6	334.9	81.3	32.0	H	Work experience in a related occupation
Compliance officers, except agriculture, construction, health and safety, and transportation	260.2	341.0	80.8	31.1	H	Long-term on-the-job training
Occupational therapist aides	7.8	10.2	2.4	30.7	L	Short-term on-the-job training
Environmental engineers	54.3	70.9	16.6	30.6	VH	Bachelor's degree
Pharmacy technicians	326.3	426.0	99.8	30.6	L	Moderate-term on-the-job training
Computer software engineers, systems software	394.8	515.0	120.2	30.4	VH	Bachelor's degree
Survey researchers	23.4	30.5	7.1	30.4	H	Bachelor's degree
Physical therapists	185.5	241.7	56.2	30.3	VH	Master's degree
Personal financial advisors	208.4	271.2	62.8	30.1	VH	Bachelor's degree
Environmental engineering technicians	21.2	27.5	6.4	30.1	H	Associate degree
Occupational therapist assistants	26.6	34.6	7.9	29.8	H	Associate degree
Fitness trainers and aerobics instructors	261.1	337.9	76.8	29.4	L	Postsecondary vocational award
LARGEST JOB GROWTH						
Registered nurses	2,618.7	3,200.2	581.5	22.2	VH	Associate degree
Home health aides	921.7	1,382.6	460.9	50.0	VL	Short-term on-the-job training
Customer service representatives	2,252.4	2,651.9	399.5	17.7	L	Moderate-term on-the-job training
Combined food preparation and serving workers, including fast food	2,701.7	3,096.0	394.3	14.6	VL	Short-term on-the-job training
Personal and home care aides	817.2	1,193.0	375.8	46.0	VL	Short-term on-the-job training
Retail salespersons	4,489.2	4,863.9	374.7	8.4	VL	Short-term on-the-job training
Office clerks, general	3,024.4	3,383.1	358.7	11.9	L	Short-term on-the-job training
Accountants and auditors	1,290.6	1,570.0	279.4	21.7	VH	Bachelor's degree
Nursing aides, orderlies, and attendants	1,469.8	1,745.8	276.0	18.8	L	Postsecondary vocational award
Postsecondary teachers	1,699.2	1,956.1	256.9	15.1	VH	Doctoral degree
Construction laborers	1,248.7	1,504.6	255.9	20.5	L	Moderate-term on-the-job training
Elementary school teachers, except special education	1,549.5	1,793.7	244.2	15.8	H	Bachelor's degree
Truck drivers, heavy and tractor-trailer	1,798.4	2,031.3	232.9	13.0	H	Short-term on-the-job training
Landscaping and groundskeeping workers	1,205.8	1,422.9	217.1	18.0	L	Short-term on-the-job training
Bookkeeping, accounting, and auditing clerks	2,063.8	2,276.2	212.4	10.3	H	Moderate-term on-the-job training
Executive secretaries and administrative assistants	1,594.4	1,798.8	204.4	12.8	H	Work experience in a related occupation
Management analysts	746.9	925.2	178.3	23.9	VH	Bachelor's or higher degree, plus work experience
Computer software engineers, applications	514.8	689.9	175.1	34.0	VH	Bachelor's degree
Receptionists and information clerks	1,139.2	1,312.1	172.9	15.2	L	Short-term on-the-job training
Carpenters	1,284.9	1,450.3	165.4	12.9	H	Long-term on-the-job training
Medical assistants	483.6	647.5	163.9	33.9	L	Moderate-term on-the-job training
First-line supervisors/managers of office and administrative support workers	1,457.2	1,617.5	160.3	11.0	H	Work experience in a related occupation
Network systems and data communications analysts	292.0	447.8	155.8	53.4	VH	Bachelor's degree
Licensed practical and licensed vocational nurses	753.6	909.2	155.6	20.7	H	Postsecondary vocational award

[1] Quartile ranks based on the Occupational Employment Statistics annual wages. VH = very high ($51,540 and over), H = high ($32,390 to $51,530), L = low ($21,590 to $32,380), and VL = very low (under $21,590). The rankings were based on quartiles using one-fourth of total employment to define each quartile. Wages are for wage and salary workers.

Source: U.S. Bureau of Labor Statistics "Occupational employment projections to 2018," *Monthly Labor Review*, Volume 132, Number 11, November 2009, <http://www.bls.gov/opub/mlr/2009/11/art5exc.htm>.

Table 619. Occupations of the Employed by Selected Characteristic: 2010

[In thousands (121,987 represents 121,987,000). Annual averages of monthly figures. Civilian noninstitutional population 25 years old and over. Based on Current Population Survey; see text, Section 1 and Appendix III. See headnote, Table 606, regarding occupations]

Race and educational attainment	Total employed	Managerial, professional, and related	Service	Sales and office	Natural resources, construction, and maintenance	Production, transportation, and material-moving
Total [1]	**121,987**	**48,913**	**19,226**	**27,833**	**11,675**	**14,339**
Less than a high school diploma	10,115	655	3,292	1,280	2,310	2,578
High school graduates, no college	34,293	5,639	7,334	9,235	5,150	6,935
Less than a bachelor's degree	33,747	11,138	5,899	9,866	3,243	3,601
College graduates	43,832	31,481	2,701	7,452	972	1,225
White [2]	100,100	40,920	14,448	23,027	10,343	11,362
Less than a high school diploma	8,290	548	2,523	1,008	2,099	2,112
High school graduates, no college	28,128	4,891	5,319	7,801	4,593	5,525
Less than a bachelor's degree	27,506	9,352	4,473	8,054	2,826	2,802
College graduates	36,176	26,130	2,133	6,165	826	923
Black [2]	13,092	4,118	3,164	2,980	810	2,021
Less than a high school diploma	1,103	54	490	170	118	271
High school graduates, no college	4,234	517	1,388	947	357	1,025
Less than a bachelor's degree	4,346	1,211	1,018	1,274	261	582
College graduates	3,409	2,336	268	589	74	143
Asian [2]	6,155	2,993	1,070	1,234	240	618
Less than a high school diploma	431	33	185	56	29	129
High school graduates, no college	1,149	130	421	286	81	232
Less than a bachelor's degree	1,037	305	220	312	74	125
College graduates	3,538	2,525	244	580	57	132
Hispanic [3]	16,946	3,449	4,325	3,266	2,907	2,999
Less than a high school diploma	5,183	174	1,813	463	1,398	1,336
High school graduates, no college	5,175	534	1,425	1,141	986	1,088
Less than a bachelor's degree	3,725	981	771	1,163	391	419
College graduates	2,862	1,760	316	499	132	155

[1] Includes other races, not shown separately. [2] For persons in this race group only. See footnote 4, Table 587. [3] Persons of Hispanic origin may be any race.

Source: U.S. Bureau of Labor Statistics, Current Population Survey, unpublished data.

Table 620. Employment by Industry: 2000 to 2010

[In thousands (136,891 represents 136,891,000), except percent. See headnote, Table 606]

Industry	2000	2005 [1]	2009 [1]	2010 [1]	2010, percent [1] Female	Black [2]	Asian [2]	Hispanic [3]
Total employed	**136,891**	**141,730**	**139,877**	**139,064**	**47.2**	**10.8**	**4.8**	**14.3**
Agriculture and related industries	2,464	2,197	2,103	2,206	24.5	2.7	1.1	21.8
Mining	475	624	707	731	13.8	5.1	1.1	15.3
Construction	9,931	11,197	9,702	9,077	8.9	5.4	1.7	24.4
Manufacturing	19,644	16,253	14,202	14,081	28.0	9.0	5.7	15.5
Durable goods	12,519	10,333	8,927	8,789	24.4	7.6	6.1	13.0
Nondurable goods	7,125	5,919	5,275	5,293	34.1	11.3	5.1	19.7
Wholesale trade	4,216	4,579	3,808	3,805	28.6	7.5	4.8	14.8
Retail trade	15,763	16,825	15,877	15,934	49.4	10.6	4.6	13.6
Transportation and utilities	7,380	7,360	7,245	7,134	22.9	15.9	3.8	14.4
Transportation and warehousing	6,096	6,184	6,012	5,880	23.1	17.1	4.2	15.4
Utilities	1,284	1,176	1,233	1,253	21.7	10.5	1.9	9.8
Information	4,059	3,402	3,239	3,149	40.9	10.9	5.5	9.9
Financial activities	9,374	10,203	9,622	9,350	54.3	9.0	5.3	10.3
Finance and insurance	6,641	7,035	6,826	6,605	57.3	9.3	6.1	8.9
Real estate and rental and leasing	2,734	3,168	2,796	2,745	47.1	8.2	3.6	13.5
Professional and business services	13,649	14,294	15,008	15,253	41.3	8.7	5.7	14.5
Professional and technical services	8,266	8,584	9,159	9,115	43.2	5.6	7.8	7.1
Management, administrative, and waste services	5,383	5,709	5,849	6,138	38.6	13.2	2.5	25.5
Education and health services	26,188	29,174	31,819	32,062	74.7	14.1	4.8	10.4
Educational services	11,255	12,264	13,188	13,155	68.6	10.2	3.9	9.5
Health care and social assistance	14,933	16,910	18,632	18,907	79.0	16.8	5.4	10.9
Hospitals	5,202	5,719	6,265	6,249	76.5	16.3	7.1	8.7
Health services, except hospitals	7,009	8,332	9,213	9,406	78.7	16.4	4.9	11.1
Social assistance	2,722	2,860	3,154	3,252	84.6	18.6	3.7	14.8
Leisure and hospitality	11,186	12,071	12,736	12,530	51.4	10.7	6.4	19.6
Arts, entertainment, and recreation	2,539	2,765	3,018	2,966	46.6	8.9	5.1	11.2
Accommodation and food services	8,647	9,306	9,717	9,564	52.9	11.2	6.8	22.2
Other services	6,450	7,020	6,935	6,769	51.6	9.2	6.3	16.8
Other services, except private households	5,731	6,208	6,152	6,102	47.3	9.3	6.6	14.3
Private households	718	812	783	667	90.9	8.7	3.3	39.5
Government workers	6,113	6,530	6,875	6,983	45.0	15.4	3.3	10.8

[1] See footnote 2, Table 586. [2] Persons in this race group only. See footnote 4, Table 587. [3] Persons of Hispanic origin may be any race.

Source: U.S. Bureau of Labor Statistics, "Employment and Earnings Online," January 2011 issue, March 2011, <http://www.bls.gov/opub/ee/home.htm> and <http://www.bls.gov/cps/home.htm>.

Labor Force, Employment, and Earnings 399

Table 621. Employment Projections by Industry: 2008 to 2018

[7,214.9 represents 7,214,900. Estimates based on the Current Employment Statistics program. See source for methodological assumptions. Minus sign (–) indicates decline]

Industry	2007 NAICS code [1]	Employment 2008 (1,000)	Employment 2018 (1,000)	Change, 2008–2018 (1,000)	Average annual rate of change 2008–2018
LARGEST GROWTH					
Construction	23	7,214.9	8,552.0	1,337.1	1.7
Offices of health practitioners	6211, 6212, 6213	3,713.3	4,978.6	1,265.3	3.0
Management, scientific, and technical consulting services	5416	1,008.9	1,844.1	835.2	6.2
Food services and drinking places	722	9,631.9	10,370.7	738.8	0.7
Computer systems design and related services	5415	1,450.3	2,106.7	656.4	3.8
Retail trade	44, 45	15,356.4	16,010.4	654.0	0.4
General local government educational services compensation	(X)	8,075.6	8,728.3	652.7	0.8
Nursing and residential care facilities	623	3,008.0	3,644.8	636.8	1.9
Employment services	5613	3,144.4	3,744.1	599.7	1.8
Hospitals	622	4,641.2	5,191.9	550.7	1.1
Individual and family services	6241	1,108.6	1,638.8	530.2	4.0
Home health care services	6216	958.0	1,399.4	441.4	3.9
Services to buildings and dwellings	5617	1,847.1	2,182.6	335.5	1.7
Architectural, engineering, and related services	5413	1,444.7	1,769.5	324.8	2.0
Other educational services	6114–7	578.9	894.9	316.0	4.5
Outpatient, laboratory, and other ambulatory care services	6214, 6215, 6219	989.5	1,297.9	308.4	2.8
Wholesale trade	42	5,963.9	6,219.8	255.9	0.4
Junior colleges, colleges, universities, and professional schools	6112, 6113	1,602.7	1,857.4	254.7	1.5
Legal services	5411	1,163.7	1,416.8	253.1	2.0
General government, other compensation	(X)	4,224.1	4,464.0	239.9	0.6
FASTEST GROWTH					
Management, scientific, and technical consulting services	5416	1,008.9	1,844.1	835.2	6.2
Other educational services	6114–7	578.9	894.9	316.0	4.5
Individual and family services	6241	1,108.6	1,638.8	530.2	4.0
Home health care services	6216	958.0	1,399.4	441.4	3.9
Specialized design services	5414	143.1	208.7	65.6	3.8
Data processing, hosting, related services, and other information services	518, 519	395.2	574.1	178.9	3.8
Computer systems design and related services	5415	1,450.3	2,106.7	656.4	3.8
Lessors of nonfinancial intangible assets (except copyright works)	533	28.2	37.9	9.7	3.0
Offices of health practitioners	6211, 6212, 6213	3,713.3	4,978.6	1,265.3	3.0
Personal care services	8121	621.6	819.1	197.5	2.8
Outpatient, laboratory, and other ambulatory care services	6214, 6215, 6219	989.5	1,297.9	308.4	2.8
Facilities support services	5612	132.7	173.6	40.9	2.7
Software publishers	5112	263.7	342.8	79.1	2.7
Independent artists, writers, and performers	7115	50.4	64.8	14.4	2.5
Local government passenger transit	(X)	268.6	342.6	74.0	2.5
Elementary and secondary schools	6111	854.9	1,089.7	234.8	2.5
Scientific research and development services	5417	621.7	778.9	157.2	2.3
Waste management and remediation services	562	360.2	451.0	90.8	2.3
Other miscellaneous manufacturing	3399	321.0	399.4	78.4	2.2
Community and vocational rehabilitation services	6242, 6243	540.9	672.0	131.1	2.2
MOST RAPIDLY DECLINING					
Cut and sew apparel manufacturing	3152	155.2	66.7	–88.5	–8.1
Apparel knitting mills	3151	26.2	12.5	–13.7	–7.1
Textile and fabric finishing and fabric coating mills	3133	48.3	23.5	–24.8	–7.0
Fabric mills	3132	65.4	35.0	–30.4	–6.1
Audio and video equipment manufacturing	3343	27.0	14.6	–12.4	–6.0
Apparel accessories and other apparel manufacturing	3159	17.0	9.2	–7.8	–6.0
Fiber, yarn, and thread mills	3131	37.4	20.7	–16.7	–5.7
Textile furnishings mills	3141	75.4	41.9	–33.5	–5.7
Railroad rolling stock manufacturing	3365	28.4	17.5	–10.9	–4.7
Footwear manufacturing	3162	15.8	10.0	–5.8	–4.5
Pulp, paper, and paperboard mills	3221	126.1	81.9	–44.2	–4.2
Basic chemical manufacturing	3251	152.1	99.9	–52.2	–4.1
Semiconductor and other electronic component manufacturing	3344	432.4	286.8	–145.6	–4.0
Computer and peripheral equipment manufacturing	3341	182.8	124.7	–58.1	–3.8
Other textile product mills	3149	72.2	49.4	–22.8	3.0
Federal enterprises except the Postal Service and electric utilities	(X)	63.5	44.9	–18.6	–3.4
Leather and hide tanning and finishing, and other leather and allied product manufacturing	3161, 3169	17.8	13.0	–4.8	–3.1
Cutlery and handtool manufacturing	3322	49.1	35.9	–13.2	–3.1
Manufacturing and reproducing magnetic and optical media	3346	34.9	26.0	–8.9	–2.9
Ventilation, heating, air–conditioning, and commercial refrigeration equipment manufacturing	3334	149.5	112.8	–36.7	–2.8

X Not applicable. [1] Based on the North American Industry Classification System, 2007; see text, Section 15.

Source: U.S. Bureau of Labor Statistics, "Industry output and employment projections to 2018," *Monthly Labor Review*, Vol. 132, No. 11, November 2009, <http://www.bls.gov/opub/mlr/2009/11/art4exc.htm>.

Table 622. Unemployed Workers—Summary: 1990 to 2010

[In thousands (7,047 represents 7,047,000), except as indicated. For civilian noninstitutionalized population 16 years old and over. Annual averages of monthly figures. Based on the Current Population Survey; see text, Section 1 and Appendix III. For data on unemployment insurance, see Table 629]

Item	1990 [1]	2000 [1]	2005 [1]	2006 [1]	2007 [1]	2008 [1]	2009 [1]	2010 [1]
UNEMPLOYED								
Total [2]	**7,047**	**5,692**	**7,591**	**7,001**	**7,078**	**8,924**	**14,265**	**14,825**
16 to 19 years old	1,212	1,081	1,186	1,119	1,101	1,285	1,552	1,528
20 to 24 years old	1,299	1,022	1,335	1,234	1,241	1,545	2,207	2,329
25 to 34 years old	1,995	1,207	1,661	1,521	1,544	1,949	3,284	3,386
35 to 44 years old	1,328	1,133	1,400	1,279	1,225	1,604	2,722	2,703
45 to 54 years old	723	762	1,195	1,094	1,135	1,473	2,592	2,769
55 to 64 years old	386	355	630	595	642	803	1,487	1,660
65 years and over	105	132	184	159	190	264	421	449
Male	3,906	2,975	4,059	3,753	3,882	5,033	8,453	8,626
16 to 19 years old	667	599	667	622	623	736	898	863
20 to 24 years old	715	547	775	705	721	920	1,329	1,398
25 to 34 years old	1,092	602	844	810	856	1,119	1,988	1,993
35 to 44 years old	711	557	715	642	634	875	1,600	1,534
45 to 54 years old	413	398	624	569	591	804	1,558	1,614
55 to 64 years old	249	189	331	318	349	425	840	962
65 years and over	59	83	102	88	108	153	241	262
Female	3,140	2,717	3,531	3,247	3,196	3,891	5,811	6,199
16 to 19 years old	544	483	519	496	478	549	654	665
20 to 24 years old	584	475	560	530	520	625	878	931
25 to 34 years old	902	604	817	711	688	830	1,296	1,392
35 to 44 years old	617	577	685	637	591	730	1,121	1,169
45 to 54 years old	310	364	571	524	544	669	1,034	1,156
55 to 64 years old	137	165	299	277	293	377	647	698
65 years and over	46	50	82	71	81	111	180	187
White [3]	5,186	4,121	5,350	5,002	5,143	6,509	10,648	10,916
Black [3]	1,565	1,241	1,700	1,549	1,445	1,788	2,606	2,852
Asian [3, 4]	(NA)	227	259	205	229	285	522	543
Hispanic [5]	876	954	1,191	1,081	1,220	1,678	2,706	2,843
UNEMPLOYMENT RATE [6] (percent)								
Total [2]	**5.6**	**4.0**	**5.1**	**4.6**	**4.6**	**5.8**	**9.3**	**9.6**
16 to 19 years old	15.5	13.1	16.6	15.4	15.7	18.7	24.3	25.9
20 to 24 years old	8.8	7.2	8.8	8.2	8.2	10.2	14.7	15.5
25 to 34 years old	5.6	3.7	5.1	4.7	4.7	5.8	9.9	10.1
35 to 44 years old	4.1	3.0	3.9	3.6	3.4	4.6	7.9	8.1
45 to 54 years old	3.6	2.5	3.5	3.1	3.2	4.1	7.2	7.7
55 to 64 years old	3.3	2.5	3.3	3.0	3.1	3.7	6.6	7.1
65 years and over	3.0	3.1	3.5	2.9	3.3	4.2	6.4	6.7
Male	5.7	3.9	5.1	4.6	4.7	6.1	10.3	10.5
16 to 19 years old	16.3	14.0	18.6	16.9	17.6	21.2	27.8	28.8
20 to 24 years old	9.1	7.3	9.6	8.7	8.9	11.4	17.0	17.8
25 to 34 years old	5.5	3.4	4.7	4.5	4.7	6.1	10.9	10.9
35 to 44 years old	4.1	2.8	3.7	3.3	3.3	4.6	8.6	8.5
45 to 54 years old	3.7	2.4	3.5	3.1	3.1	4.2	8.2	8.6
55 to 64 years old	3.8	2.4	3.3	3.0	3.2	3.8	7.2	8.0
65 years and over	3.0	3.3	3.4	2.8	3.4	4.5	6.7	7.1
Female	5.5	4.1	5.1	4.6	4.5	5.4	8.1	8.6
16 to 19 years old	14.7	12.1	14.5	13.8	13.8	16.2	20.7	22.8
20 to 24 years old	8.5	7.1	7.9	7.6	7.3	8.8	12.3	13.0
25 to 34 years old	5.6	4.1	5.6	4.9	4.6	5.5	8.6	9.1
35 to 44 years old	4.2	3.3	4.1	3.9	3.6	4.5	7.1	7.7
45 to 54 years old	3.4	2.5	3.5	3.1	3.2	3.9	6.0	6.8
55 to 64 years old	2.8	2.5	3.3	2.9	3.0	3.7	6.0	6.2
65 years and over	3.1	2.7	3.5	3.0	3.1	3.9	6.1	6.2
White [3]	4.8	3.5	4.4	4.0	4.1	5.2	8.5	8.7
Black [3]	11.4	7.6	10.0	8.9	8.3	10.1	14.8	16.0
Asian [3, 4]	(NA)	3.6	4.0	3.0	3.2	4.0	7.3	7.5
Hispanic [5]	8.2	5.7	6.0	5.2	5.6	7.6	12.1	12.5
Percent without work for—								
Fewer than 5 weeks	46.3	44.9	35.1	37.3	35.9	32.8	22.2	18.7
5 to 14 weeks	32.0	31.9	30.4	30.3	31.5	31.4	26.8	22.0
15 weeks and over...	21.6	23.2	34.5	32.4	32.5	35.7	51.0	59.3
15 to 26 weeks	11.7	11.8	14.9	14.7	15.0	16.0	19.5	16.0
27 weeks and over.	10.0	11.4	19.6	17.6	17.6	19.7	31.5	43.3
Unemployment duration, average (weeks)	12.0	12.6	18.4	16.8	16.8	17.9	24.4	33.0

NA Not available. [1] See footnote 2, Table 586. [2] Includes other races not shown separately. [3] See footnote 4, Table 587. [4] Prior to 2004, includes Pacific Islanders. [5] Persons of Hispanic or Latino origin may be any race. [6] Unemployed as percent of civilian labor force in specified group.

Source: U.S. Bureau of Labor Statistics, "Employment and Earnings Online," January 2011 issue, March 2011, <http://www.bls.gov/opub/ee/home.htm> and <http://www.bls.gov/cps/home.htm>.

Table 623. Unemployed Jobseekers' Job Search Activities: 2010

[14,825 represents 14,825,000. For the civilian noninstitutionalized population 16 years old and over. Annual averages of monthly data. Based on the Current Population Survey; see text, Section 1 and Appendix III]

Characteristic	Population (1,000)		Jobseekers' job search methods (percent)								Average number of methods used
	Total unem- ployed	Total jobseek- ers [1]	Em- ployer directly	Sent out a resume or filled out applica- tions	Placed or answer- ed ads	Friends or relatives	Public employ- ment agency	Private employ- ment agency	Other activi- ties	
Total, 16 years and over [2] **...**	**14,825**	**13,394**	**53.6**	**55.2**	**18.4**	**28.8**	**22.2**	**8.9**	**15.4**	**2.03**
16 to 19 years old	1,528	1,460	50.4	61.9	11.7	19.3	9.4	3.6	10.1	1.67
20 to 24 years old	2,329	2,174	54.3	57.8	17.1	25.0	19.2	7.3	14.1	1.95
25 to 34 years old	3,386	3,057	55.1	56.3	18.2	28.4	24.2	9.0	14.8	2.07
35 to 44 years old	2,703	2,391	53.4	52.6	20.0	31.7	26.2	10.6	17.1	2.12
45 to 54 years old	2,769	2,462	54.9	53.5	21.4	32.5	26.1	11.6	17.0	2.18
55 to 64 years old	1,660	1,467	52.2	52.6	20.3	32.8	23.6	9.6	18.5	2.11
65 years old and over	449	384	49.3	43.6	15.8	31.0	17.4	7.0	16.5	1.81
Male..................	8,626	7,638	54.9	52.7	18.1	30.4	23.0	9.0	15.7	2.04
16 to 19 years old	863	821	50.7	61.0	12.0	21.0	10.7	3.9	9.6	1.69
20 to 24 years old	1,398	1,288	55.0	56.0	17.2	26.7	20.3	7.9	13.9	1.98
25 to 34 years old	1,993	1,749	56.8	53.4	17.7	29.6	25.0	9.1	14.5	2.07
35 to 44 years old	1,534	1,313	54.9	49.3	19.8	34.0	27.3	11.0	18.3	2.15
45 to 54 years old	1,614	1,404	56.0	50.4	21.0	34.6	26.4	11.2	17.8	2.18
55 to 64 years old	962	837	53.8	50.1	19.2	33.7	23.7	9.6	18.9	2.10
65 years old and over	262	226	50.6	43.3	16.2	30.9	17.2	6.3	17.7	1.83
Female................	6,199	5,756	52.0	58.5	18.8	26.7	21.2	8.8	15.1	2.02
16 to 19 years old	665	638	49.9	63.0	11.4	17.1	7.8	3.2	10.8	1.63
20 to 24 years old	931	886	53.2	60.3	17.1	22.6	17.5	6.4	14.4	1.92
25 to 34 years old	1,392	1,308	52.8	60.1	18.8	26.7	23.0	8.9	15.3	2.07
35 to 44 years old	1,169	1,078	51.6	56.6	20.1	29.0	24.8	10.1	15.6	2.09
45 to 54 years old	1,156	1,057	53.5	57.6	22.0	29.7	25.7	12.2	16.0	2.18
55 to 64 years old	698	630	50.2	55.9	21.8	31.7	23.5	9.6	18.0	2.11
65 years old and over	187	158	47.5	44.1	15.2	31.2	17.7	8.1	14.9	1.80
White [3]	10,916	9,713	53.6	55.3	19.0	28.9	21.1	8.7	16.0	2.03
Male..................	6,476	5,628	55.1	52.7	18.6	30.4	22.0	8.8	16.4	2.05
Female................	4,440	4,085	51.6	58.9	19.5	26.8	19.9	8.6	15.4	2.02
Black [3]	2,852	2,698	53.9	54.4	16.9	27.6	26.9	9.3	13.2	2.03
Male..................	1,550	1,459	54.6	52.0	16.9	29.2	27.1	9.3	13.0	2.03
Female................	1,302	1,239	53.0	57.2	16.9	25.7	26.7	9.3	13.4	2.03
Asian [3]	543	511	52.3	55.1	17.2	36.6	18.9	11.1	18.2	2.11
Male..................	305	288	53.5	55.6	15.7	38.3	20.4	12.2	17.1	2.14
Female................	238	223	50.8	54.5	19.0	34.5	17.0	9.6	19.5	2.06
Hispanic [4]	2,843	2,534	55.5	47.0	14.6	32.5	21.9	9.1	12.6	1.94
Male..................	1,711	1,495	57.2	44.2	14.6	34.2	22.7	9.0	12.7	1.95
Female................	1,132	1,039	53.2	51.0	14.8	30.1	20.8	9.2	12.5	1.92

[1] Excludes persons on temporary layoff. The percent using each method will always total more than 100 because many jobseekers use more than one method. [2] Includes other races not shown separately. [3] Data for this race group only. See footnote 4, Table 587. [4] Persons of Hispanic or Latino origin may be any race.

Source: U.S. Bureau of Labor Statistics, "Employment and Earnings Online," January 2011 issue, March 2011, <http://www.bls.gov/opub/ee/home.htm> and <http://www.bls.gov/cps/home.htm>.

Table 624. Unemployed Persons by Sex and Reason: 1990 to 2010

[In thousands (3,906 represents 3,906,000). For civilian noninstitutionalized population 16 years old and over. Annual averages of monthly figures. Based on Current Population Survey; see text, Section 1 and Appendix III]

Sex and reason	1990 [1]	2000 [1]	2001	2002	2003 [1]	2004 [1]	2005 [1]	2006 [1]	2007 [1]	2008 [1]	2009 [1]	2010 [1]
Male, total	**3,906**	**2,975**	**3,690**	**4,597**	**4,906**	**4,456**	**4,059**	**3,753**	**3,882**	**5,033**	**8,453**	**8,626**
Job losers [2]	2,257	1,516	2,119	2,820	3,024	2,603	2,188	2,021	2,175	3,055	5,967	5,919
Job leavers	528	387	422	434	422	437	445	406	408	458	438	457
Reentrants.........	806	854	925	1,068	1,141	1,070	1,067	1,015	956	1,128	1,504	1,608
New entrants	315	217	223	274	320	346	359	312	343	393	545	641
Female, total.....	**3,140**	**2,717**	**3,111**	**3,781**	**3,868**	**3,694**	**3,531**	**3,247**	**3,196**	**3,891**	**5,811**	**6,199**
Job losers [2]	1,130	1,001	1,356	1,787	1,814	1,595	1,479	1,300	1,340	1,735	3,193	3,331
Job leavers	513	393	413	432	397	421	427	421	385	438	444	432
Reentrants.........	1,124	1,107	1,105	1,300	1,336	1,338	1,319	1,223	1,186	1,345	1,683	1,858
New entrants	373	217	237	262	321	340	306	304	285	374	491	579

[1] Data not strictly comparable with data for earlier years. See text, this section, and February 1994, March 1996, February 1997–99, and February 2003–11 issues of Employment and Earnings. [2] Beginning 2000, persons who completed temporary jobs are identified separately and are included as job losers.

Source: U.S. Bureau of Labor Statistics, "Employment and Earnings Online," January 2011 issue, March 2011, <http://www.bls.gov/opub/ee/home.htm> and <http://www.bls.gov/cps/home.htm>.

Table 625. Unemployment Rates by Industry and by Sex: 2000 to 2010

[In percent. Civilian noninstitutionalized population 16 years old and over. Annual averages of monthly figures. Rate represents unemployment as a percent of labor force in each specified group. Based on Current Population Survey; see text, Section 1 and Appendix III. See also headnote, Table 606, regarding industries]

Industry	2000	2005 [1]	2009 [1]	2010 [1]	Male 2009 [1]	Male 2010 [1]	Female 2009 [1]	Female 2010 [1]
All employed [2]	**4.0**	**5.1**	**9.3**	**9.6**	**10.3**	**10.5**	**8.1**	**8.6**
Wage and salary workers:								
Agriculture and related industries	9.0	8.3	14.3	13.9	14.1	13.2	15.3	16.4
Mining, quarrying, and oil and gas extraction	4.4	3.1	11.6	9.4	12.2	9.5	7.2	8.4
Construction	6.2	7.4	19.0	20.6	19.6	21.1	13.8	16.0
Manufacturing	3.5	4.9	12.1	10.6	11.8	9.9	12.7	12.4
Wholesale trade	3.3	4.0	7.2	7.3	6.9	7.2	7.8	7.7
Retail trade	4.6	5.7	9.5	10.0	9.6	10.0	9.3	10.1
Transportation and utilities	3.4	4.1	8.9	8.4	8.9	8.3	8.9	8.8
Transportation and warehousing	3.8	4.5	9.7	9.4	9.9	9.3	9.0	9.8
Utilities	1.9	1.9	4.8	3.4	3.9	3.3	8.6	3.7
Information	3.2	5.0	9.2	9.7	8.5	9.4	10.3	10.2
Telecommunications	2.3	5.2	8.4	9.2	7.4	8.3	10.0	10.8
Financial activities	2.4	2.9	6.4	6.9	6.5	7.0	6.3	6.8
Finance and insurance	2.2	2.7	5.8	6.6	5.6	6.6	5.9	6.6
Real estate and rental and leasing	3.1	3.3	8.1	7.6	8.5	7.8	7.7	7.3
Professional and business services	4.8	6.2	10.8	10.8	10.2	10.6	11.6	11.1
Professional and technical services	2.5	3.5	6.7	6.5	6.0	5.7	7.6	7.5
Management, administrative, and waste services	8.1	10.2	16.7	16.8	15.8	16.7	18.3	17.0
Education and health services	2.5	3.4	5.3	5.8	5.5	5.9	5.2	5.7
Educational services	2.4	3.7	6.6	6.4	6.8	6.9	6.6	6.2
Health care and social assistance	2.5	3.3	4.9	5.6	5.0	5.4	4.9	5.7
Leisure and hospitality	6.6	7.8	11.7	12.2	11.6	12.4	11.8	11.9
Arts, entertainment, and recreation	5.9	6.9	11.1	11.6	11.6	13.4	10.5	9.4
Accommodation and food services	6.8	8.0	11.8	12.3	11.6	12.1	12.0	12.5
Other services [3]	3.9	4.8	7.5	8.5	8.3	9.3	6.8	7.8
Government workers	2.1	2.6	3.6	4.4	3.9	4.5	3.4	4.3

[1] See footnote 2, Table 586. [2] Includes the self-employed, unpaid family workers, and persons with no previous work experience, not shown separately. [3] Includes private household workers.

Source: U.S. Bureau of Labor Statistics, "Employment and Earnings Online," January 2011 issue, March 2011, <http://www.bls.gov/opub/ee/home.htm> and <http://www.bls.gov/cps/home.htm>.

Table 626. Unemployment by Occupation: 2000 to 2010

[5,692 represents 5,692,000. Civilian noninstitutionalized population 16 years old and over. Annual averages of monthly data. Rate represents unemployment as a percent of the labor force for each specified group. Based on Current Population Survey; see text, Section 1 and Appendix III. See also headnote, Table 606, regarding occupations]

Occupation	Number (1,000) 2000	Number (1,000) 2009 [1]	Number (1,000) 2010 [1]	Unemployment rate 2000	Unemployment rate 2009 [1]	2010 [1] Total	2010 [1] Male	2010 [1] Female
Total [2]	**5,692**	**14,265**	**14,825**	**4.0**	**9.3**	**9.6**	**10.5**	**8.6**
Management, professional, and related occupations	827	2,531	2,566	1.8	4.6	4.7	4.8	4.7
Management, business, and financial operations	320	1,105	1,117	1.6	4.9	5.1	4.7	5.6
Management	214	740	762	1.5	4.6	4.8	4.6	5.3
Business and financial operations	106	365	355	2.0	5.7	5.6	5.1	6.1
Professional and related occupations	507	1,427	1,449	1.9	4.4	4.5	4.9	4.2
Computer and mathematical	74	192	195	2.2	5.2	5.2	5.1	5.7
Architecture and engineering	51	203	173	1.7	6.9	6.2	5.8	8.9
Life, physical, and social science	18	63	69	1.4	4.5	4.6	3.9	5.4
Community and social services	40	105	114	2.0	4.3	4.6	4.2	4.9
Legal	18	60	48	1.2	3.4	2.7	1.9	3.6
Education, training, and library	136	368	379	1.8	4.1	4.2	4.5	4.1
Arts, design, entertainment, sports, and media	97	251	269	3.5	8.4	8.9	9.8	7.8
Healthcare practitioner and technical	73	184	203	1.2	2.3	2.5	1.9	2.8
Service occupations	1,132	2,605	2,819	5.2	9.6	10.3	11.0	9.7
Healthcare support	101	240	276	4.0	6.8	7.6	8.1	7.6
Protective service	70	177	207	2.7	5.3	5.9	5.2	8.6
Food preparation and serving-related	469	1,011	1,079	6.6	11.6	12.4	13.0	11.8
Building and grounds cleaning and maintenance	301	736	780	5.8	12.1	12.8	13.7	11.4
Personal care and service	190	441	477	4.4	8.0	8.7	10.6	8.1
Sales and office occupations	1,446	3,143	3,315	3.8	8.5	9.0	9.0	9.1
Sales and related	673	1,501	1,596	4.1	8.8	9.4	8.3	10.5
Office and administrative support	773	1,642	1,719	3.6	8.3	8.7	10.0	8.2
Natural resources, construction, and maintenance	758	2,464	2,504	5.3	15.6	16.1	16.0	17.0
Farming, fishing, and forestry	133	179	193	10.2	16.2	16.3	15.4	19.1
Construction and extraction	507	1,825	1,809	6.2	19.7	20.1	20.1	21.8
Installation, maintenance, and repair	119	459	503	2.4	8.5	9.3	9.3	8.6
Production, transportation, and material moving occupations	1,081	2,453	2,365	5.1	13.3	12.8	12.2	14.7
Production	575	1,322	1,206	4.8	14.7	13.1	12.2	15.4
Transportation and material moving	505	1,131	1,159	5.6	12.0	12.4	12.2	13.4

[1] See footnote 2, Table 586. [2] Includes persons with no previous work experience and those whose last job was in the Armed Forces.

Source: U.S. Bureau of Labor Statistics, "Employment and Earnings Online," January 2011 issue, March 2011, <http://www.bls.gov/opub/ee/home.htm> and <http://www.bls.gov/cps/home.htm>.

Table 627. Unemployed and Unemployment Rates by Educational Attainment, Sex, Race, and Hispanic Origin: 2000 to 2010

[3,589 represents 3,589,000. Annual averages of monthly figures. Civilian noninstitutionalized population 25 years old and over. See Table 593 for civilian labor force and participation rate data. Based on Current Population Survey; see text, Section 1 and Appendix III]

Year, sex, and race	Unemployed (1,000)					Unemployment rate [1]				
	Total	Less than a high school diploma	High school graduate, no college	Some college or associate's degree	Bachelor's degree or more	Total	Less than a high school diploma	High school graduate, no college	Some college or associate's degree	Bachelor's degree or more
Total: [2]										
2000 [3]	3,589	791	1,298	890	610	3.0	6.3	3.4	2.7	1.7
2005 [3]	5,070	967	1,798	1,349	955	4.0	7.6	4.7	3.9	2.3
2010 [3]	10,968	1,765	3,943	3,093	2,167	8.2	14.9	10.3	8.4	4.7
Male:										
2000 [3]	1,829	411	682	427	309	2.8	5.4	3.4	2.6	1.5
2005 [3]	2,617	514	973	636	494	3.8	6.4	4.6	3.7	2.3
2010 [3]	6,365	1,137	2,452	1,646	1,130	8.9	15.0	11.3	9.0	4.8
Female:										
2000 [3]	1,760	380	616	463	301	3.2	7.8	3.5	2.8	1.8
2005 [3]	2,453	453	826	713	461	4.2	9.7	4.8	4.0	2.4
2010 [3]	4,603	628	1,492	1,447	1,037	7.4	14.6	9.0	7.8	4.7
White: [4]										
2000 [3]	2,644	564	924	667	489	2.6	5.6	2.9	2.4	1.6
2005 [3]	3,627	669	1,257	973	729	3.5	6.5	4.0	3.4	2.1
2010 [3]	8,174	1,337	2,937	2,278	1,622	7.5	13.9	9.5	7.6	4.3
Black: [4]										
2000 [3]	731	179	315	169	68	5.4	10.7	6.4	4.0	2.5
2005 [3]	1,075	231	440	295	110	7.5	14.4	8.5	6.9	3.5
2010 [3]	2,022	321	795	614	292	13.4	22.5	15.8	12.4	7.9
Asian: [4,5]										
2000 [3]	146	28	34	35	49	2.7	5.7	3.0	3.2	1.8
2005 [3]	203	26	47	32	99	3.5	5.5	4.6	3.2	3.0
2010 [3]	446	54	95	92	205	6.8	11.1	7.6	8.1	5.5
Hispanic: [6]										
2000 [3]	569	297	150	85	38	4.4	6.2	3.9	3.2	2.2
2005 [3]	773	354	216	138	66	4.8	6.2	4.5	4.1	2.9
2010 [3]	2,041	787	674	399	182	10.8	13.2	11.5	9.7	6.0

[1] Percent unemployed of the civilian labor force. [2] Includes other races, not shown separately. [3] See footnote 2, Table 586. [4] Beginning 2005 data are for persons in this race group only. See footnote 4, Table 587. [5] 2000 data include Pacific Islanders. [6] Persons of Hispanic origin may be any race.
Source: U.S. Bureau of Labor Statistics, "Employment and Earnings Online," January 2011 issue, March 2011, <http://www.bls.gov/opub/ee/home.htm> and <http://www.bls.gov/cps/home.htm>.

Table 628. Unemployed Persons by Reason for Unemployment: 2010

[14,825 represents 14,825,000. Annual averages of monthly data. Based on Current Population Survey; see text, Section 1 and Appendix III]

Age, sex, and reason	Total unemployed (1,000)	Percent distribution by duration				
		Less than 5 weeks	5 to 14 weeks	15 weeks and over		
				Total	15 to 26 weeks	27 weeks or longer
Total 16 years old and over..............	14,825	18.7	22.0	59.3	16.0	43.3
16 to 19 years old	1,528	29.7	31.2	39.1	16.3	22.8
Total 20 years old and over..............	13,297	17.4	21.0	61.6	16.0	45.6
Males......................	7,763	17.2	20.5	62.4	15.6	46.7
Job losers and persons who completed temporary jobs........................	5,773	17.4	20.2	62.4	15.8	46.6
On temporary layoff.....................	946	43.0	31.3	25.7	13.9	11.8
Not on temporary layoff.................	4,827	12.4	18.0	69.6	16.1	53.5
Permanent job losers...................	3,905	10.1	16.2	73.6	16.0	57.7
Persons who completed temporary jobs	922	21.9	25.6	52.5	16.7	35.8
Job leavers	433	22.8	25.7	51.5	13.9	37.7
Reentrants............................	1,346	15.3	20.1	64.6	15.4	49.2
New entrants	211	11.5	19.5	69.0	17.2	51.7
Females	5,534	17.8	21.7	60.5	16.4	44.1
Job losers and persons who completed temporary jobs........................	3,257	17.8	20.3	62.0	15.8	46.2
On temporary layoff.....................	416	49.8	30.9	19.4	10.9	8.4
Not on temporary layoff.................	2,840	13.1	18.7	68.2	16.5	51.7
Permanent job losers...................	2,396	11.5	17.3	71.1	16.4	54.7
Persons who completed temporary jobs	444	21.5	26.0	52.5	16.9	35.6
Job leavers	413	22.1	26.2	51.7	19.1	32.6
Reentrants............................	1,633	16.8	23.0	60.2	17.0	43.2
New entrants	231	17.0	25.3	57.7	16.3	41.3

Source: U.S. Bureau of Labor Statistics, "Employment and Earnings Online," January 2011 issue, March 2011, <http://www.bls.gov/opub/ee/home.htm> and <http://www.bls.gov/cps/home.htm>.

Table 629. Total Unemployed and Insured Unemployed by State: 2000 to 2010

[5,692 represents 5,692,000. Civilian noninstitutionalized population 16 years old and over. Annual averages of monthly figures. State total unemployment estimates come from the Local Area Unemployment Statistics program, while U.S. totals come from the Current Population Survey; see text, Section 1 and Appendix III. U.S. totals derived by independent population controls; therefore state data may not add to U.S. totals. Unemployment data are based on population controls from Census 2000]

| State | Total unemployed | | | | | | | | Insured unemployed [1] | | | |
| | Number (1,000) | | | | Percent [2] | | | | Number (1,000) | | Percent [3] | |
	2000 [4]	2005 [4]	2009 [4]	2010 [4]	2000 [4]	2005 [4]	2009 [4]	2010 [4]	2000	2010	2000	2010
United States	5,692	7,591	14,265	14,825	4.0	5.1	9.3	9.6	[5] 2,130.2	[5] 4,543.1	[5] 1.7	[5] 3.6
Alabama	87	81	211	202	4.1	3.8	9.7	9.5	29.4	53.3	1.6	3.0
Alaska	20	24	28	29	6.2	6.9	7.8	8.0	12.2	17.3	4.9	5.8
Arizona	100	134	306	316	4.0	4.7	9.7	10.0	20.5	80.0	1.0	3.3
Arkansas	53	69	100	107	4.2	5.1	7.4	7.9	24.2	44.1	2.2	4.0
California	833	953	2,063	2,260	4.9	5.4	11.3	12.4	339.6	662.4	2.4	4.6
Colorado	65	133	226	240	2.7	5.1	8.3	8.9	14.7	65.0	0.7	3.0
Connecticut	39	88	157	173	2.3	4.9	8.3	9.1	28.9	70.1	1.8	4.4
Delaware	14	17	35	36	3.3	4.0	8.0	8.5	6.0	13.0	1.5	3.2
District of Columbia ...	18	21	32	33	5.7	6.5	9.6	9.9	5.5	11.9	1.3	2.5
Florida	300	330	930	1,065	3.8	3.8	10.2	11.5	70.8	225.9	1.1	3.2
Georgia	148	241	464	480	3.5	5.2	9.7	10.2	34.8	117.7	0.9	3.2
Hawaii	24	17	43	42	4.0	2.8	6.8	6.6	8.4	17.4	1.7	3.1
Idaho	31	27	58	71	4.6	3.7	7.7	9.3	12.3	26.2	2.3	4.3
Illinois.	291	371	660	681	4.5	5.8	10.0	10.3	105.7	223.5	1.8	4.1
Indiana.	92	172	332	320	2.9	5.4	10.4	10.2	32.3	79.4	1.1	2.9
Iowa.	45	70	94	103	2.8	4.3	5.6	6.1	19.5	40.8	1.4	2.8
Kansas.	53	75	107	106	3.8	5.1	7.1	7.0	15.9	38.2	1.3	2.9
Kentucky	83	121	222	218	4.2	6.0	10.7	10.5	25.4	49.9	1.5	3.0
Louisiana	101	139	136	155	5.0	6.7	6.6	7.5	24.2	56.1	1.3	3.1
Maine.	22	34	57	55	3.3	4.9	8.2	7.9	8.9	18.1	1.6	3.2
Maryland	100	122	215	223	3.6	4.1	7.1	7.5	29.0	72.4	1.3	3.1
Massachusetts.	92	164	286	297	2.7	4.8	8.2	8.5	59.9	117.0	1.9	3.8
Michigan	190	346	648	597	3.7	6.8	13.3	12.5	83.3	161.3	1.9	4.3
Minnesota	87	120	238	217	3.1	4.2	8.1	7.3	31.8	80.1	1.3	3.1
Mississippi	74	103	125	137	5.7	7.8	9.6	10.4	19.9	37.2	1.8	3.5
Missouri.	98	162	283	289	3.3	5.4	9.3	9.6	43.8	83.2	1.7	3.2
Montana.	22	17	31	36	4.8	3.6	6.3	7.2	7.7	17.7	2.2	4.3
Nebraska	27	38	47	45	2.8	3.9	4.8	4.7	7.4	18.7	0.9	2.1
Nevada	48	55	170	201	4.5	4.5	12.5	14.9	19.6	53.9	2.1	4.7
New Hampshire	19	26	47	45	2.7	3.6	6.3	6.1	3.1	17.9	0.5	3.0
New Jersey	157	197	410	426	3.7	4.5	9.1	9.5	84.6	164.4	2.3	4.4
New Mexico.	42	47	66	80	5.0	5.2	7.0	8.4	9.5	26.3	1.4	3.4
New York	416	474	813	824	4.5	5.0	8.4	8.6	147.4	291.9	1.8	3.5
North Carolina	155	229	490	476	3.7	5.3	10.8	10.6	55.0	157.6	1.5	4.1
North Dakota	10	12	16	15	2.9	3.4	4.3	3.9	3.9	5.2	1.3	1.5
Ohio.	234	344	601	595	4.0	5.9	10.1	10.1	72.8	153.3	1.4	3.1
Oklahoma	52	77	116	124	3.1	4.5	6.6	7.1	12.2	34.5	0.9	2.4
Oregon.	93	115	221	215	5.1	6.2	11.1	10.8	41.6	83.9	2.7	5.3
Pennsylvania	255	312	514	549	4.2	5.0	8.1	8.7	131.4	266.0	2.5	4.9
Rhode Island	23	28	61	67	4.2	5.1	10.8	11.6	12.3	18.4	2.8	4.2
South Carolina.	71	140	247	242	3.6	6.8	11.3	11.2	27.6	71.8	1.6	4.1
South Dakota.	11	16	22	21	2.7	3.7	5.0	4.8	2.1	4.7	0.6	1.2
Tennessee	115	164	317	297	4.0	5.6	10.4	9.7	42.9	68.4	1.7	2.7
Texas	452	599	900	994	4.4	5.4	7.6	8.2	107.4	221.5	1.2	2.2
Utah.	38	53	98	106	3.4	4.1	7.1	7.7	10.7	29.6	1.1	2.7
Vermont.	9	12	25	22	2.7	3.5	6.9	6.2	4.8	10.4	1.7	3.6
Virginia.	82	138	284	289	2.3	3.5	6.8	6.9	22.5	64.2	0.7	1.9
Washington	151	180	329	340	5.0	5.5	9.3	9.6	70.1	111.5	2.7	4.0
West Virginia	44	39	62	71	5.5	4.9	7.7	9.1	14.2	21.8	2.1	3.2
Wisconsin	101	146	271	255	3.4	4.8	8.7	8.3	54.1	123.1	2.0	4.7
Wyoming	10	10	19	20	3.8	3.7	6.5	7.0	2.9	5.2	1.3	2.5

[1] Number of jobless workers who are receiving state unemployment benefits. Source: U.S. Employment and Training Administration, Unemployment Insurance, Financial Handbook, annual updates. See <http://www.ows.doleta.gov/unemploy/claims.asp>. [2] Total unemployment as percent of civilian labor force. [3] Those currently collecting unemployment insurance as a percent of the total number of eligible workers. [4] See footnote 2, Table 586. [5] U.S. totals include Puerto Rico and the Virgin Islands.

Source: Except as noted, U.S. Bureau of Labor Statistics, Local Area Unemployment Statistics program <http://www.bls.gov/lau/>.

Table 630. Nonfarm Establishments—Employees, Hours, and Earnings by Industry: 1990 to 2010

[Annual averages of monthly data. (109,487 represents 109,487,000). Based on data from establishment reports. Includes all full- and part-time employees who worked during, or received pay for, any part of the pay period reported. Excludes proprietors, the self-employed, farm workers, unpaid family workers, private household workers, and Armed Forces. Establishment data shown here conform to industry definitions in the 2007 North American Industry Classification System (NAICS) and are adjusted to March 2010 employment benchmarks. Based on the Current Employment Statistics Program; see source and Appendix III]

Item and year	Total nonfarm	Private industry Total[1]	Construction	Manufacturing	Wholesale trade	Retail trade	Transportation and warehousing	Utilities	Information	Finance and insurance	Real estate and rental and leasing	Professional, scientific, and technical services	Administrative and waste services	Educational services	Health care and social assistance	Arts, entertainment and recreation	Accommodations and food services	Government
EMPLOYEES (1,000)																		
1990	109,487	91,072	5,263	17,695	5,268	13,182	3,476	740	2,688	4,976	1,637	4,538	4,643	1,688	9,296	1,132	8,156	18,415
2000	131,785	110,995	6,787	17,263	5,933	15,280	4,410	601	3,630	5,677	2,011	6,702	8,168	2,390	12,718	1,788	10,074	20,790
2005	133,703	111,899	7,336	14,226	5,764	15,280	4,361	554	3,061	6,019	2,134	7,025	8,170	2,836	14,536	1,892	10,923	21,804
2007	137,598	115,380	7,630	13,879	6,015	15,520	4,541	553	3,032	6,132	2,169	7,660	8,416	2,941	15,380	1,969	11,457	22,218
2008	136,790	114,281	7,162	13,406	5,943	15,283	4,508	559	2,984	6,015	2,130	7,799	8,032	3,040	15,798	1,970	11,466	22,509
2009	130,807	108,252	6,016	11,847	5,587	14,522	4,236	560	2,804	5,775	1,994	7,509	7,203	3,090	16,103	1,916	11,162	22,555
2010	129,818	107,337	5,526	11,524	5,456	14,414	4,184	552	2,711	5,691	1,939	7,424	7,401	3,150	16,415	1,909	11,111	22,482
WEEKLY EARNINGS[2] (dol.)																		
1990	(NA)	349.75	513.43	436.16	444.48	235.62	471.72	670.40	479.50	(NA)	(NA)	504.83	273.60	(NA)	319.80	219.02	147.89	(NA)
2000	(NA)	481.01	685.78	590.77	631.40	333.38	562.31	955.66	700.86	(NA)	(NA)	745.77	387.49	(NA)	449.27	273.79	207.44	(NA)
2005	(NA)	544.33	750.22	673.33	685.00	377.58	618.58	1,095.90	805.08	(NA)	(NA)	862.79	431.92	(NA)	560.43	330.19	226.48	(NA)
2007	(NA)	590.04	816.66	711.56	748.94	385.11	654.95	1,182.65	874.65	(NA)	(NA)	956.42	485.15	(NA)	606.74	354.52	251.52	(NA)
2008	(NA)	607.95	842.61	724.46	769.62	386.21	670.37	1,230.69	908.99	(NA)	(NA)	995.66	500.14	(NA)	630.06	359.71	259.93	(NA)
2009	(NA)	617.18	851.76	726.12	784.49	388.57	677.56	1,239.37	931.08	(NA)	(NA)	1,036.36	517.27	(NA)	643.19	364.06	261.87	(NA)
2010	(NA)	636.91	891.85	765.08	816.15	399.74	710.63	1,263.33	938.89	(NA)	(NA)	1,073.49	536.40	(NA)	660.82		266.78	(NA)
WEEKLY HOURS[2]																		
1990	(NA)	34.3	38.3	40.5	38.4	30.6	37.7	41.5	35.8	(NA)	(NA)	36.1	32.3	(NA)	31.8	26.1	25.9	(NA)
2000	(NA)	34.3	39.2	41.3	38.8	30.7	37.4	42.0	36.8	(NA)	(NA)	36.2	33.1	(NA)	32.1	25.6	26.2	(NA)
2005	(NA)	33.8	38.6	40.7	37.7	30.6	37.0	41.1	36.5	(NA)	(NA)	35.7	32.8	(NA)	32.9	25.7	25.7	(NA)
2007	(NA)	33.9	39.0	41.2	38.2	30.2	37.0	42.4	36.7	(NA)	(NA)	36.0	33.5	(NA)	32.8	24.7	25.6	(NA)
2008	(NA)	33.6	38.5	40.8	38.2	30.0	36.4	42.7	36.6	(NA)	(NA)	35.8	33.6	(NA)	32.8	24.1	25.4	(NA)
2009	(NA)	33.1	37.6	39.8	37.6	29.9	36.0	42.0	36.6	(NA)	(NA)	35.7	33.4	(NA)	32.4	23.8	25.0	(NA)
2010	(NA)	33.4	38.4	41.1	37.9	30.2	37.1	42.1	36.3	(NA)	(NA)	35.9	33.9	(NA)	32.3	23.8	25.0	(NA)
HOURLY EARNINGS[2] (dol.)																		
1990	(NA)	10.20	13.42	10.78	11.58	7.71	12.50	16.14	13.40	(NA)	(NA)	13.99	8.48	(NA)	10.05	8.41	5.70	(NA)
2000	(NA)	14.02	17.48	14.32	16.28	10.86	15.05	22.75	19.07	(NA)	(NA)	20.61	11.69	(NA)	13.98	10.68	7.92	(NA)
2005	(NA)	16.13	19.46	16.56	18.16	12.36	16.70	26.68	22.06	(NA)	(NA)	24.15	13.16	(NA)	17.05	12.85	8.80	(NA)
2007	(NA)	17.43	20.95	17.26	19.59	12.75	17.72	27.88	23.96	(NA)	(NA)	26.58	14.47	(NA)	18.48	14.10	9.82	(NA)
2008	(NA)	18.08	21.87	17.75	20.13	12.87	18.41	28.83	24.78	(NA)	(NA)	27.82	14.87	(NA)	19.23	14.73	10.23	(NA)
2009	(NA)	18.63	22.66	18.24	20.84	13.01	18.81	29.48	25.45	(NA)	(NA)	29.03	15.51	(NA)	19.83	15.08	10.49	(NA)
2010	(NA)	19.07	23.22	18.61	21.53	13.24	19.17	30.04	25.86	(NA)	(NA)	29.93	15.82	(NA)	20.43	15.28	10.68	(NA)

NA Not available. [1] Includes other industries not shown separately. [2] Average hours and earnings of production workers for mining and logging, manufacturing, and construction; average hours and earnings of nonsupervisory workers for the service-providing industries.

Source: U.S. Bureau of Labor Statistics, Current Employment Statistics, "Employment, Hours, and Earnings—National," <http://www.bls.gov/ces/home.htm>.

Table 631. Employees in Nonfarm Establishments—States: 2010

[In thousands (129,818 represents 129,818,000). Includes all full- and part-time employees who worked during, or received pay for, any part of the pay period reported. Excludes proprietors, the self-employed, farm workers, unpaid family workers, private household workers, and Armed Forces. National totals differ from the sum of the state figures because of differing benchmarks among states and differing industrial and geographic stratification. Compiled from data supplied by cooperating state agencies. Based on North American Industry Classification System, 2007; see text, section 15]

State	Total [1]	Con-struction	Manu-facturing	Trade, transpor-tation and utilities	Infor-mation	Fin-ancial activi-ties [2]	Profes-sional and business ser-vices [3]	Educa-tion and health ser-vices [4]	Leisure and hospita-lity [5]	Other ser-vices [6]	Govern-ment
U.S.	**129,818**	**5,526**	**11,524**	**24,605**	**2,711**	**7,630**	**16,688**	**19,564**	**13,020**	**5,364**	**22,482**
AL	1,869.0	87.5	236.1	360.1	24.0	91.9	208.3	214.4	167.9	79.9	386.8
AK	324.4	16.0	12.7	62.8	6.4	15.0	26.2	41.7	31.5	11.5	85.2
AZ	2,377.3	111.1	147.8	467.8	36.4	162.5	339.4	344.0	252.5	88.4	416.5
AR	1,163.2	48.5	160.1	234.4	15.5	48.8	118.0	165.9	99.9	43.5	218.2
CA	13,891.8	559.8	1,242.4	2,616.9	429.0	759.8	2,069.4	1,786.9	1,493.7	484.7	2,422.5
CO	2,220.1	114.9	125.2	397.2	71.4	143.7	329.2	264.8	263.1	92.9	393.4
CT	1,608.0	49.6	166.0	289.1	31.7	135.0	189.9	307.1	133.8	60.6	244.7
DE	412.7	[7] 19.3	26.2	73.9	6.0	42.7	54.5	64.8	41.9	19.7	63.8
DC	710.9	[7] 10.5	1.3	27.1	18.6	26.6	148.7	108.4	59.4	64.6	245.7
FL	7,174.9	345.6	306.9	1,454.6	135.4	469.7	1,035.5	1,079.0	917.7	310.8	1,114.5
GA	3,826.3	148.6	344.4	808.3	101.3	203.6	519.4	486.1	373.9	153.4	678.1
HI	586.9	[7] 28.8	12.9	109.4	10.2	26.9	71.4	75.8	100.0	26.4	125.2
ID	602.9	31.3	53.0	120.9	9.6	28.9	73.4	84.0	58.1	21.3	118.9
IL	5,610.7	198.6	558.8	1,124.5	101.7	360.8	799.0	832.5	514.2	254.4	857.0
IN	2,793.0	115.3	446.2	541.3	35.7	130.1	275.4	425.0	272.1	107.3	438.0
IA	1,469.2	61.6	200.1	299.9	28.6	101.4	121.6	213.5	129.9	57.0	253.6
KS	1,323.0	53.5	159.6	251.0	31.2	70.8	141.8	180.4	113.1	51.5	262.0
KY	1,769.8	67.7	209.1	359.2	26.1	86.0	179.7	250.0	167.8	70.6	331.4
LA	1,884.4	121.9	137.7	364.2	26.2	92.7	192.5	271.1	194.0	66.0	366.3
ME	592.5	24.3	50.9	116.8	9.1	31.3	55.6	119.0	59.8	19.8	103.4
MD	2,513.2	[7] 144.1	114.6	437.6	43.9	142.6	385.8	400.0	228.8	114.9	500.9
MA	3,186.3	106.4	254.0	543.8	85.5	207.5	461.0	664.4	305.8	118.7	438.1
MI	3,861.4	121.7	474.4	708.9	54.9	186.7	514.3	617.0	374.0	166.6	635.8
MN	2,637.2	86.4	292.1	490.4	54.3	171.1	313.4	458.4	233.9	114.6	416.7
MS	1,089.5	48.9	135.8	212.7	12.4	44.9	91.8	132.3	118.5	34.8	248.9
MO	2,647.1	105.4	242.7	510.3	58.1	163.3	318.6	405.8	271.1	117.0	450.5
MT	428.2	22.7	16.4	86.9	7.4	21.2	39.0	63.8	55.8	16.9	90.5
NE	939.4	[7] 42.5	91.6	196.0	16.9	68.5	101.2	135.6	80.7	37.0	169.4
NV	1,115.6	59.1	37.7	208.8	12.5	52.1	135.7	99.9	308.9	33.8	155.0
NH	622.6	21.2	65.7	132.2	11.6	35.5	64.3	110.3	62.9	21.3	96.8
NJ	3,854.5	129.5	257.7	808.0	79.7	253.5	582.2	605.5	334.6	160.1	642.5
NM	801.6	44.0	29.0	133.3	14.4	32.9	98.2	119.9	83.7	28.5	199.3
NY	8,553.3	305.5	456.8	1,456.7	252.0	665.9	1,100.0	1,703.7	732.9	364.8	1,509.9
NC	3,861.9	176.0	431.1	710.6	68.2	199.2	481.0	539.2	390.4	156.2	704.3
ND	375.6	21.3	22.7	80.3	7.3	20.4	28.4	54.9	34.4	15.6	79.9
OH	5,030.6	167.6	619.7	946.5	77.5	274.1	622.7	842.6	475.5	211.0	782.3
OK	1,526.4	66.9	123.1	276.5	25.0	80.0	169.1	203.9	138.3	60.7	339.6
OR	1,599.9	67.8	163.8	308.2	32.2	92.7	181.3	228.4	161.8	57.5	299.5
PA	5,615.5	216.3	560.6	1,079.6	93.4	311.9	685.1	1,136.0	498.8	250.3	756.9
RI	458.8	15.9	40.4	73.2	10.1	30.5	53.2	101.9	49.6	22.1	61.8
SC	1,805.2	78.9	207.4	344.4	25.7	97.4	213.9	212.8	206.9	68.5	345.2
SD	402.8	[7] 20.9	36.9	80.6	6.6	28.7	27.3	64.4	43.1	15.7	78.7
TN	2,612.5	[7] 105.4	297.8	554.7	44.9	137.8	304.6	372.9	261.9	100.5	431.9
TX	10,342.0	569.7	810.7	2,049.5	195.3	622.5	1,273.1	1,387.6	1,006.1	360.9	1,860.3
UT	1,181.0	65.1	111.3	229.4	29.2	67.9	152.5	155.0	110.1	33.8	216.4
VT	297.5	13.4	30.9	55.8	5.4	12.2	23.1	59.2	32.3	9.9	54.6
VA	3,627.2	182.7	230.4	619.9	76.3	177.7	647.8	456.2	338.0	185.1	702.8
WA	2,777.4	141.1	257.8	516.5	102.9	135.1	326.0	375.2	265.8	104.5	546.7
WV	746.1	32.6	49.1	134.5	10.3	28.2	60.7	120.7	72.3	55.0	152.6
WI	2,735.3	94.0	430.6	508.3	46.6	157.5	268.0	418.3	250.9	137.6	420.6
WY	282.6	22.5	8.7	51.5	3.9	10.8	17.2	26.3	32.4	11.5	72.6

[1] Includes mining and logging, not shown separately. [2] Finance and insurance; real estate and rental and leasing.
[3] Professional, scientific, and technical services; management of companies and enterprises; administrative and support and waste management and remediation services. [4] Education services; health care and social assistance. [5] Arts, entertainment, and recreation; accommodations and food services. [6] Includes repair and maintenance; personal and laundry services; and membership associations and organizations. [7] Mining and logging included with construction.

Source: U.S. Bureau of Labor Statistics, Current Employment Statistics, "State and Metro Area Employment, Hours, and Earnings (SAE)," <http://www.bls.gov/sae/data.htm>.

Table 632. Nonfarm Industries—Employees and Earnings: 1990 to 2010

[Annual averages of monthly figures (109,487 represents 109,487,000). Covers all full- and part-time employees who worked during, or received pay for, any part of the pay period including the 12th of the month. See also headnote, Table 630]

Industry	2007 NAICS code [1]	All employees (1,000)					Average hourly earnings [2] (dol.)		
		1990	2000	2005	2009	2010	2000	2005	2010
Total nonfarm	(X)	109,487	131,785	133,703	130,807	129,818	(NA)	(NA)	(NA)
Goods-producing [3]	(X)	23,723	24,649	22,190	18,557	17,755	15.27	17.60	20.28
Service-providing [4]	(X)	85,764	107,136	111,513	112,249	112,064	(NA)	(NA)	(NA)
Total private	(X)	91,072	110,995	111,899	108,252	107,337	14.02	16.13	19.07
Mining and logging	(X)	765	599	628	694	705	16.55	18.72	23.83
Logging	1133	85	79	65	50	50	13.70	15.74	18.84
Mining	21	680	520	562	643	656	16.94	19.04	24.24
Oil and gas extraction	211	190	125	126	160	159	19.43	19.34	27.36
Mining, except oil and gas	212	302	225	213	208	203	18.07	20.18	24.64
Support activities for mining	213	188	171	224	275	294	14.55	17.89	22.96
Construction	23	5,263	6,787	7,336	6,016	5,526	17.48	19.46	23.22
Construction of buildings	236	1,413	1,633	1,712	1,357	1,232	16.74	19.05	22.74
Residential building	2361	673	823	960	638	572	15.18	17.72	19.80
Nonresidential building	2362	741	809	752	719	660	18.18	20.55	25.13
Heavy and civil engineering construction [5]	237	813	937	951	851	829	16.80	19.60	23.77
Highway, street, and bridge construction	2373	289	340	351	291	289	18.17	20.12	23.76
Specialty trade contractors	238	3,037	4,217	4,673	3,808	3,466	17.91	19.55	23.22
Building foundation and exterior contractors	2381	703	919	1,083	779	690	16.93	18.44	21.19
Building equipment contractors	2382	1,282	1,897	1,918	1,758	1,633	19.52	21.01	24.89
Building finishing contractors	2383	665	857	992	722	629	16.44	18.82	22.07
Manufacturing	31-33	17,695	17,263	14,226	11,847	11,524	14.32	16.56	18.61
Durable goods	(X)	10,737	10,877	8,956	7,284	7,067	14.92	17.33	19.80
Wood products	321	541	613	559	359	341	11.63	13.16	14.85
Nonmetallic mineral products	327	528	554	505	394	372	14.53	16.61	17.49
Cement and concrete products	3273	195	234	240	185	172	14.64	16.68	17.86
Primary metals	331	689	622	466	362	361	16.64	18.94	20.11
Iron and steel mills and ferroalloy production	3311	187	135	96	85	85	20.97	23.55	25.66
Foundries	3315	214	217	164	113	111	14.72	17.50	18.21
Fabricated metal products	332	1,610	1,753	1,522	1,312	1,285	13.77	15.80	17.94
Architectural and structural metals	3323	357	428	398	345	320	13.43	15.10	17.47
Machine shops and threaded products	3327	309	365	345	309	312	14.53	16.43	18.68
Machinery	333	1,410	1,457	1,166	1,029	993	15.21	17.02	18.96
Agricultural, construction, and mining machinery	3331	229	222	208	214	208	14.21	15.91	18.95
Heating, ventilation and air conditioning, and commercial refrigeration equipment	3334	165	194	154	129	123	13.10	14.60	16.16
Metalworking machinery	3335	267	274	202	158	153	16.66	17.86	20.00
Computer and electronic products	334	1,903	1,820	1,316	1,137	1,100	14.73	18.39	22.79
Computer and peripheral equipment	3341	367	302	205	166	162	18.39	22.75	23.25
Communications equipment	3342	223	239	141	121	118	14.39	18.05	23.88
Semiconductors and electronic components	3344	574	676	452	378	370	13.46	17.03	20.35
Electronic instruments	3345	635	488	441	422	406	15.80	17.71	24.82
Electrical equipment and appliances	335	633	591	434	374	361	13.23	15.24	16.87
Household appliances	3352	114	106	85	60	61	(NA)	(NA)	(NA)
Electrical equipment	3353	244	210	152	145	136	13.28	15.31	16.51
Transportation equipment	336	2,135	2,057	1,772	1,348	1,330	18.89	22.09	25.22
Motor vehicles	3361	271	291	248	146	151	24.45	29.01	29.04
Motor vehicle parts	3363	653	840	678	414	415	17.95	21.10	20.66
Aerospace products and parts	3364	841	517	455	492	477	20.52	24.82	33.65
Ship and boat building	3366	174	154	154	131	126	14.84	17.26	21.23
Furniture and related products	337	604	683	568	386	357	11.73	13.45	15.05
Household and institutional furniture	3371	401	443	383	244	223	11.39	13.15	14.74
Miscellaneous manufacturing	339	686	728	647	584	568	11.93	14.07	16.55
Medical equipment and supplies	3391	283	305	300	307	302	12.70	14.71	17.56
Nondurable goods	(X)	6,958	6,386	5,271	4,563	4,457	13.31	15.27	16.80
Food manufacturing	311	1,507	1,553	1,478	1,456	1,447	11.77	13.04	14.40
Fruit and vegetable preserving and specialty	3114	218	197	174	172	171	11.89	12.81	14.55
Dairy products	3115	145	136	132	131	128	14.85	16.73	18.92
Animal slaughtering and processing	3116	427	507	504	497	490	10.27	11.47	12.69
Bakeries and tortilla manufacturing	3118	292	306	280	273	276	11.45	12.57	14.43
Beverages and tobacco products [5]	312	218	207	192	187	182	17.40	18.76	21.78
Beverages	3121	173	175	167	169	166	(NA)	(NA)	(NA)
Textile mills	313	492	378	218	124	119	11.23	12.38	13.55
Textile product mills	314	236	230	176	126	119	10.31	11.61	11.80
Apparel	315	903	484	251	168	158	8.61	10.26	11.43
Cut and sew apparel	3152	750	380	193	132	125	8.40	10.06	11.33
Leather and allied products	316	133	69	40	29	28	10.35	11.50	13.03
Paper and paper products	322	647	605	484	407	397	15.91	17.99	20.03
Pulp, paper, and paperboard mills	3221	238	191	142	117	113	20.62	22.99	25.12
Converted paper products	3222	409	413	343	290	284	13.58	15.71	17.82
Printing and related support activities	323	809	807	646	522	487	14.09	15.74	16.92
Petroleum and coal products	324	153	123	112	115	114	22.80	24.47	31.34
Chemicals	325	1,036	980	872	804	784	17.09	19.67	21.08
Basic chemicals	3251	249	188	150	145	142	21.06	23.80	24.93
Resin, rubber, and artificial fibers	3252	158	136	108	92	90	17.09	19.03	21.11
Pharmaceuticals and medicines	3254	207	274	288	284	277	17.27	21.31	21.95
Plastics and rubber products	326	825	951	802	625	623	12.70	14.80	15.71
Plastics products	3261	618	737	634	502	500	12.04	14.01	15.47
Rubber products	3262	207	214	168	123	124	14.83	17.58	16.64

See footnotes at end of table.

U.S. Census Bureau, Statistical Abstract of the United States: 2012

Table 632. Nonfarm Industries—Employees and Earnings: 1990 to 2010—Con.

[Annual averages of monthly figures (109,487 represents 109,487,000). Covers all full- and part-time employees who worked during, or received pay for, any part of the pay period including the 12th of the month. See also headnote, Table 630]

Industry	2007 NAICS code [1]	All employees (1,000)					Average hourly earnings [2] (dol.)		
		1990	2000	2005	2009	2010	2000	2005	2010
Trade, transportation, and utilities	(X)	22,666	26,225	25,959	24,906	24,605	13.31	14.92	16.83
Wholesale trade	42	5,268	5,933	5,764	5,587	5,456	16.28	18.16	21.53
Durable goods	423	2,834	3,251	2,999	2,810	2,719	16.71	18.88	20.95
Motor vehicles and parts	4231	309	356	344	315	309	14.27	16.18	17.61
Lumber and construction supplies	4233	181	227	254	205	191	13.61	16.78	18.46
Commercial equipment	4234	597	722	639	617	605	20.29	23.67	25.03
Electric goods	4236	357	425	342	322	311	19.43	21.78	23.14
Hardware and plumbing	4237	216	247	245	230	219	15.07	16.47	19.81
Machinery and supplies	4238	690	725	659	634	607	16.47	18.71	21.02
Nondurable goods	424	1,900	2,065	2,022	1,966	1,932	14.33	16.15	19.62
Paper and paper products	4241	162	177	152	129	127			
Druggists' goods	4242	136	192	213	198	190	18.98	19.20	23.39
Apparel and piece goods	4243	152	163	148	138	138	14.58	17.53	21.35
Grocery and related products	4244	623	689	699	710	704	13.57	15.38	19.07
Alcoholic beverages	4248	115	128	147	163	162	15.72	18.30	20.01
Electronic markets and agents and brokers	425	535	618	743	811	805	20.79	20.71	28.31
Retail trade	44,45	13,182	15,280	15,280	14,522	14,414	10.86	12.36	13.24
Motor vehicle and parts dealers	441	1,494	1,847	1,919	1,638	1,625	14.94	16.33	17.06
Automobile dealers	4411	983	1,217	1,261	1,018	1,006	16.95	17.85	18.23
Auto parts, accessories, and tire stores	4413	418	499	491	483	490	11.04	12.74	14.54
Furniture and home furnishings stores	442	432	544	576	449	436	12.33	14.23	15.25
Furniture stores	4421	244	289	298	224	217	13.37	14.87	16.17
Home furnishings stores	4422	188	254	278	226	220	11.06	13.46	14.04
Electronics and appliance stores	443	382	564	536	491	498	13.67	17.73	16.99
Building material and garden supply stores	444	891	1,142	1,276	1,156	1,126	11.25	13.14	14.11
Building material and supplies dealers	4441	753	982	1,134	1,028	1,001	11.30	13.24	14.12
Food and beverage stores	445	2,779	2,993	2,818	2,830	2,811	9.76	10.85	12.04
Grocery stores	4451	2,406	2,582	2,446	2,479	2,464	9.71	10.80	12.12
Specialty food stores	4452	232	270	236	214	211	9.97	11.04	11.13
Beer, wine, and liquor stores	4453	141	141	136	137	136	10.40	11.48	11.89
Health and personal care stores	446	792	928	954	986	979	11.68	14.03	16.99
Gasoline stations	447	910	936	871	826	816	8.05	8.92	10.24
Clothing & clothing accessories stores	448	1,313	1,322	1,415	1,364	1,377	9.96	11.07	11.57
Clothing stores	4481	930	954	1,066	1,048	1,063	9.88	10.63	10.90
Shoe stores	4482	216	193	180	179	183	8.96	10.05	11.80
Jewelry, luggage, and leather goods stores	4483	167	175	169	137	131	11.48	14.10	15.57
Sporting goods, hobby, book, and music stores	451	532	686	647	614	601	9.33	10.35	11.67
Sporting goods and musical instrument stores	4511	352	437	447	460	460	9.55	10.68	11.82
Book, periodical, and music stores	4512	180	249	200	154	140	8.91	9.59	11.11
General merchandise stores	452	2,500	2,820	2,934	2,966	2,971	9.22	10.53	10.98
Department stores	4521	1,494	1,755	1,595	1,473	1,488	(NA)	(NA)	(NA)
Miscellaneous store retailers	453	738	1,007	900	782	760	10.20	11.22	12.50
Florists	4531	121	130	101	75	68	8.95	9.88	11.05
Office supplies, stationery, and gift stores	4532	358	471	391	317	305	10.46	11.65	13.06
Used merchandise stores	4533	56	107	113	120	124	8.07	8.96	10.72
Nonstore retailers	454	419	492	435	421	416	13.22	14.56	17.71
Electronic shopping and mail-order houses	4541	157	257	240	244	244	13.38	14.52	18.19
Transportation and warehousing	48,49	3,476	4,410	4,361	4,236	4,184	15.05	16.70	19.17
Air transportation	481	529	614	501	463	464	13.57	17.77	24.56
Scheduled air transportation	4811	503	570	456	419	422	(NA)	(NA)	(NA)
Rail transportation	482	272	232	228	218	215	(NA)	(NA)	(NA)
Water transportation	483	57	56	61	63	63	18.07	19.04	22.45
Truck transportation	484	1,122	1,406	1,398	1,268	1,244	15.86	16.74	18.62
General freight trucking	4841	807	1,013	981	885	862	16.37	17.20	18.51
Specialized freight trucking	4842	315	393	417	383	382	14.51	15.60	18.89
Transit and ground passenger transportation	485	274	372	389	422	432	11.88	13.00	14.98
Urban, interurban, rural, and charter bus transportation	4851, 2,5	72	97	91	93	93	(NA)	(NA)	(NA)
Taxi and limousine service	4853	57	72	66	67	68	(NA)	(NA)	(NA)
School and employee bus transportation	4854	114	152	169	185	191	11.42	12.74	14.92
Pipeline transportation	486	60	46	38	43	42	19.86	24.33	29.54
Scenic and sightseeing transportation	487	16	28	29	28	27	12.49	13.75	15.87
Support activities for transportation	488	364	537	552	549	540	14.57	17.67	21.08
Support activities for air transportation	4881	96	141	148	154	152	13.42	15.07	17.04
Support activities for water transportation	4883	91	97	94	91	90	19.57	27.07	35.16
Support activities for road transportation	4884	35	66	79	82	81	13.98	15.41	15.68
Freight transportation arrangement	4885	111	178	177	174	169	13.46	16.94	21.24
Couriers and messengers	492	375	605	571	546	527	13.51	15.33	17.67
Couriers and express delivery services	4921	340	546	522	499	481	(NA)	(NA)	(NA)
Warehousing and storage	493	407	514	595	637	628	14.46	15.06	15.50
Utilities	22	740	601	554	560	552	22.75	26.68	30.04
Power generation and supply	2211	550	434	401	404	397	23.13	27.63	31.25
Natural gas distribution	2212	155	121	107	109	108	23.41	26.86	28.36
Water, sewage and other systems	2213	35	46	45	47	47	16.93	17.70	23.73

See footnotes at end of table.

U.S. Census Bureau, Statistical Abstract of the United States: 2012

Table 632. Nonfarm Industries—Employees and Earnings: 1990 to 2010—Con.

[Annual averages of monthly figures (109,487 represents 109,487,000). Covers all full- and part-time employees who worked during, or received pay for, any part of the pay period including the 12th of the month. See also headnote, Table 630]

Industry	2007 NAICS code [1]	All employees (1,000)					Average hourly earnings [2] (dol.)		
		1990	2000	2005	2009	2010	2000	2005	2010
Information.........................	**51**	**2,688**	**3,630**	**3,061**	**2,804**	**2,711**	**19.07**	**22.06**	**25.86**
Publishing industries, except Internet	511	871	1,035	904	796	761	20.18	24.20	26.75
Newspaper, book, and directory publishers........	5111	773	774	666	539	501	15.06	18.57	20.98
Software publishers...........................	5112	98	261	238	258	260	28.48	38.11	36.41
Motion picture and sound recording industries	512	255	383	378	358	372	21.25	18.75	22.11
Broadcasting, except Internet	515	284	344	328	301	295	16.74	21.22	24.01
Radio and television broadcasting...............	5151	232	253	239	215	211	(NA)	(NA)	(NA)
Cable and other subscription programming........	5152	52	91	89	85	84	(NA)	(NA)	(NA)
Telecommunications	517	1,009	1,397	1,071	966	900	18.59	22.13	26.24
Wired telecommunications carriers	5171	760	922	690	635	599	18.62	22.46	25.99
Wireless telecommunications carriers (except satellite).............................	5172	36	186	191	187	171	14.40	20.40	25.35
Data processing, hosting and related services	518	211	316	263	249	242	16.97	19.97	27.03
Financial activities......................	**(X)**	**6,614**	**7,687**	**8,153**	**7,769**	**7,630**	**14.98**	**17.95**	**21.49**
Finance and insurance	**52**	**4,976**	**5,677**	**6,019**	**5,775**	**5,691**	**(NA)**	**(NA)**	**(NA)**
Monetary authorities—central bank..............	521	24	23	21	21	21	(NA)	(NA)	(NA)
Credit intermediation and related activities	522	2,425	2,548	2,869	2,590	2,545	13.14	15.85	18.22
Depository credit intermediation [5]..............	5221	1,909	1,681	1,769	1,754	1,733	11.97	14.13	17.55
Commercial banking	52211	1,362	1,251	1,296	1,317	1,308	11.83	13.79	17.56
Nondepository credit intermediation	5222	398	644	770	572	557	15.30	19.24	20.07
Activities related to credit intermediation.........	5223	119	222	330	265	254	15.39	16.48	18.28
Securities, commodity contracts, investments......	523	458	805	786	811	801	20.20	26.59	31.79
Securities and commodity contracts brokerage and exchanges................................	5231,2	338	566	499	476	469	20.07	27.68	31.79
Other financial investment activities	5239	120	239	287	336	332	20.48	24.69	31.79
Insurance carriers and related activities	524	2,016	2,221	2,259	2,264	2,238	17.37	20.66	24.58
Insurance carriers	5241	1,338	1,433	1,386	1,377	1,368	17.92	21.67	25.97
Insurance agencies, brokerages, and related services	5242	678	788	874	887	871	16.28	18.88	22.20
Funds, trusts, and other financial vehicles........	525	54	81	84	88	87	17.68	21.09	21.33
Insurance and employee benefit funds	5251	33	46	46	49	49	(NA)	(NA)	(NA)
Other investment pools and funds..............	5259	20	35	37	39	38	(NA)	(NA)	(NA)
Real estate and rental and leasing..............	**53**	**1,637**	**2,011**	**2,134**	**1,994**	**1,939**	**(NA)**	**(NA)**	**(NA)**
Real estate	531	1,109	1,316	1,461	1,420	1,396	12.26	14.69	17.37
Lessors of real estate	5311	566	610	603	576	565	11.19	13.81	16.52
Offices of real estate agents and brokers	5312	217	281	356	305	284	12.57	14.90	17.10
Activities related to real estate.................	5313	327	424	502	539	546	13.60	15.64	18.38
Rental and leasing services	532	514	667	646	547	518	11.69	14.05	15.91
Automotive equipment rental and leasing	5321	163	208	199	168	163	10.70	13.64	14.10
Consumer goods rental......................	5322	220	292	275	221	201	9.53	12.39	14.48
Machinery and equipment rental and leasing	5324	84	103	111	116	114	14.95	17.12	19.83
Lessors of nonfinancial intangible assets	533	14	28	27	27	25	17.68	20.06	32.82
Professional and business services	**(X)**	**10,848**	**16,666**	**16,954**	**16,579**	**16,688**	**15.52**	**18.08**	**22.78**
Professional and technical services [5]	**54**	**4,538**	**6,702**	**7,025**	**7,509**	**7,424**	**20.61**	**24.15**	**29.93**
Legal services..............................	5411	944	1,066	1,168	1,125	1,114	21.38	23.96	31.05
Accounting and bookkeeping services	5412	664	866	849	914	888	14.42	17.45	21.05
Architectural and engineering services	5413	942	1,238	1,311	1,325	1,277	20.49	23.96	30.21
Specialized design services	5414	82	132	131	124	111	15.32	20.29	22.35
Computer systems design and related services	5415	410	1,254	1,195	1,423	1,442	27.13	31.64	37.15
Management and technical consulting services	5416	305	673	824	995	991	20.83	23.97	28.50
Scientific research and development services	5417	494	515	577	616	620	21.39	28.33	35.68
Advertising and related services	5418	382	497	446	422	408	16.99	19.49	24.61
Management of companies and enterprises.......	**55**	**1,667**	**1,796**	**1,759**	**1,867**	**1,863**	**15.28**	**18.08**	**23.79**
Administrative and waste services	**56**	**4,643**	**8,168**	**8,170**	**7,203**	**7,401**	**11.69**	**13.16**	**15.82**
Administrative and support services [5]	561	4,413	7,855	7,833	6,852	7,044	11.53	12.93	15.61
Office administrative services	5611	211	264	345	401	412	14.68	17.82	23.56
Facilities support services.....................	5612	58	97	120	133	134	16.73	18.02	20.97
Employment services [5].......................	5613	1,512	3,849	3,607	2,481	2,717	11.89	13.04	16.23
Temporary help services	56132	1,156	2,636	2,549	1,823	2,079	11.79	12.00	14.23
Business support services.....................	5614	505	787	766	820	806	11.08	13.14	14.49
Travel arrangement and reservation services	5615	250	299	224	194	187	12.72	14.55	17.11
Investigation and security services	5616	507	689	737	789	777	9.78	11.64	14.15
Services to buildings and dwellings..............	5617	1,175	1,571	1,738	1,753	1,743	10.02	11.44	12.97
Waste management and remediation services [5]	562	229	313	338	352	357	15.29	17.69	19.30
Waste collection............................	5621	82	100	124	138	142	12.97	15.54	17.50
Waste treatment and disposal..................	5622	77	119	103	97	95	15.02	17.76	20.29

See footnotes at end of table.

Table 632. Nonfarm Industries—Employees and Earnings: 1990 to 2010—Con.

[Annual averages of monthly figures (109,487 represents 109,487,000). Covers all full- and part-time employees who worked during, or received pay for, any part of the pay period including the 12th of the month. See also headnote, Table 630]

Industry	2007 NAICS code [1]	All employees (1,000)					Average hourly earnings [2] (dol.)		
		1990	2000	2005	2009	2010	2000	2005	2010
Education and health services	(X)	**10,984**	**15,109**	**17,372**	**19,193**	**19,564**	**13.95**	**16.71**	**20.12**
Educational services	61	**1,688**	**2,390**	**2,836**	**3,090**	**3,150**	**(NA)**	**(NA)**	**(NA)**
Elementary and secondary schools	6111	461	716	837	856	851	(NA)	(NA)	(NA)
Junior colleges	6112	44	79	100	84	102	(NA)	(NA)	(NA)
Colleges and universities	6113	939	1,196	1,393	1,560	1,592	(NA)	(NA)	(NA)
Business, computer, and management training	6114	60	86	77	77	78	(NA)	(NA)	(NA)
Technical and trade schools	6115	72	91	102	119	126	(NA)	(NA)	(NA)
Other schools and instruction	6116	96	184	250	298	299	(NA)	(NA)	(NA)
Educational support services	6117	17	39	78	96	101	(NA)	(NA)	(NA)
Health care and social assistance	62	**9,296**	**12,718**	**14,536**	**16,103**	**16,415**	**13.98**	**17.05**	**20.43**
Health care	621,2,3	8,211	10,858	12,314	13,543	13,790	13.98	17.05	20.43
Ambulatory health care services	621	2,842	4,320	5,114	5,793	5,976	14.63	17.98	21.72
Offices of physicians	6211	1,278	1,840	2,094	2,279	2,316	14.99	17.86	21.68
Offices of dentists	6212	513	688	774	818	829	15.65	18.95	24.03
Offices of other health practitioners	6213	276	438	549	647	673	15.96	19.40	22.65
Outpatient care centers	6214	261	386	473	558	600	14.24	16.70	20.50
Medical and diagnostic laboratories	6215	129	162	198	219	226	15.29	18.96	22.67
Home health care services	6216	288	633	821	1,027	1,081	15.74	18.67	23.48
Hospitals	622	3,513	3,954	4,345	4,667	4,685	12.86	14.42	16.64
General medical and surgical hospitals	6221	3,305	3,745	4,096	4,367	4,375	16.71	21.30	26.12
Psychiatric and substance abuse hospitals	6222	113	86	93	104	106	16.75	21.40	26.33
Nursing and residential care facilities	623	1,856	2,583	2,855	3,082	3,129	14.97	17.79	20.06
Nursing care facilities	6231	1,170	1,514	1,577	1,645	1,661	10.67	12.37	14.21
Residential mental health facilities	6232	269	437	497	559	569	11.08	13.08	15.26
Community care facilities for the elderly	6233	330	478	615	716	737	9.96	11.30	13.06
Social assistance	624	1,085	1,860	2,222	2,560	2,624	9.83	11.33	12.89
Individual and family services	6241	389	678	921	1,166	1,215	9.78	11.35	12.88
Emergency and other relief services	6242	67	117	129	138	144	10.57	12.44	13.49
Vocational rehabilitation services	6243	242	370	383	403	414	10.95	13.48	14.41
Child day care services	6244	388	696	790	853	852	9.57	10.67	12.47
Leisure and hospitality	(X)	**9,288**	**11,862**	**12,816**	**13,077**	**13,020**	**8.32**	**9.38**	**11.31**
Arts, entertainment, and recreation	71	**1,132**	**1,788**	**1,892**	**1,916**	**1,909**	**10.68**	**12.85**	**15.28**
Performing arts and spectator sports	711	273	382	376	397	410	13.11	18.67	20.97
Museums, historical sites, zoos, and parks	712	68	110	121	129	127	12.20	13.67	15.60
Amusements, gambling, and recreation	713	791	1,296	1,395	1,389	1,371	9.86	11.08	13.37
Accommodation and food services	72	**8,156**	**10,074**	**10,923**	**11,162**	**11,111**	**7.92**	**8.80**	**10.68**
Accommodation	721	1,616	1,884	1,819	1,763	1,759	9.48	10.75	13.02
Traveler accommodation and other longer-term accommodation	7211	1,582	1,837	1,765	1,708	1,702	9.49	10.78	13.07
Food services and drinking places	722	6,540	8,189	9,104	9,399	9,352	7.49	8.34	10.14
Full-service restaurants	7221	3,070	3,845	4,316	4,473	4,466	7.78	8.84	10.93
Limited-service eating places	7222	2,765	3,462	3,889	4,053	4,001	6.87	7.49	8.96
Special food services	7223	392	491	538	528	540	9.45	10.48	11.83
Drinking places, alcoholic beverages	7224	312	391	361	344	345	7.24	7.89	10.15
Other services	81	**4,261**	**5,168**	**5,395**	**5,367**	**5,364**	**12.73**	**14.34**	**17.08**
Repair and maintenance	811	1,009	1,242	1,236	1,150	1,137	13.28	14.82	16.82
Automotive repair and maintenance	8111	659	888	886	806	800	12.45	14.11	15.55
Electronic equipment repair and maintenance	8112	100	107	103	98	98	16.31	16.65	19.38
Commercial machinery repair and maintenance	8113	161	161	170	176	171	15.53	16.89	21.03
Personal and laundry services	812	1,120	1,243	1,277	1,281	1,265	10.18	11.81	13.43
Personal care services	8121	430	490	577	605	600	10.18	12.44	13.98
Death care services	8122	123	136	137	133	132	13.04	15.34	17.46
Dry-cleaning and laundry services	8123	371	388	347	311	302	9.17	10.18	11.80
Dry-cleaning and laundry services, except coin-operated	81232	215	211	180	151	147	8.14	9.14	10.56
Other personal services	8129	196	229	216	232	231	10.52	11.29	12.43
Pet care services, except veterinary	81291	23	31	44	58	62	12.12	10.61	12.82
Parking lots and garages	81293	68	93	103	111	111	8.81	9.89	11.17
Membership associations & organizations	813	2,132	2,683	2,882	2,936	2,962	13.66	15.20	18.76
Grantmaking and giving services	8132	113	116	137	162	189	14.65	18.80	23.62
Social advocacy organizations	8133	126	143	174	201	206	12.08	13.89	17.36
Civic and social organizations	8134	377	404	409	398	394	9.85	11.16	12.16
Professional and similar organizations	8139	379	473	492	485	492	15.98	18.60	22.47
Government	(X)	**18,415**	**20,790**	**21,804**	**22,555**	**22,482**	**(NA)**	**(NA)**	**(NA)**
Federal	(X)	3,196	2,865	2,732	2,832	2,968	(NA)	(NA)	(NA)
State	(X)	4,305	4,786	5,032	5,169	5,142	(NA)	(NA)	(NA)
Local	(X)	10,914	13,139	14,041	14,554	14,372	(NA)	(NA)	(NA)

NA Not available. X Not applicable. [1] Based on the North American Industry Classification System, 2007. See text, Section 15. [2] Production employees in the goods-producing industries and nonsupervisory employees in service-providing industries. See footnotes 3 and 4. [3] Mining and logging, construction, and manufacturing. [4] Trade, transportation and utilities, information, financial activities, professional and business services, education and health services, leisure and hospitality, other services, and government. [5] Includes other industries, not shown separately.

Source: U.S. Bureau of Labor Statistics, Current Employment Statistics, "Employment, Hours, and Earnings—National," <http://www.bls.gov/ces/data.htm\>.

Table 633. Women Employees on Nonfarm Payrolls by Major Industry: 1980 to 2010

[37,813 represents 37,813,000. Annual averages of monthly data. For coverage, see headnote, Table 630]

Industry	Women employees (1,000)				Percent of total employees			
	1980	1990	2000	2010	1980	1990	2000	2010
Total nonfarm [1]	37,813	51,587	63,223	64,648	41.8	47.1	48.0	49.8
Total private	29,783	41,732	51,452	51,857	40.2	45.8	46.4	48.3
Construction	458	656	846	724	10.3	12.5	12.5	13.1
Manufacturing	5,676	5,702	5,359	3,268	30.3	32.2	31.0	28.4
Trade, transportation, and utilities	6,799	9,363	10,859	10,001	36.9	41.3	41.4	40.6
Wholesale trade	1,179	1,611	1,827	1,642	25.9	30.6	30.8	30.1
Retail trade	4,980	6,696	7,680	7,219	48.6	50.8	50.3	50.1
Transportation and warehousing	506	879	1,202	1,002	17.1	25.3	27.3	24.0
Utilities	134	177	151	138	20.6	24.0	25.1	25.1
Information	1,118	1,324	1,697	1,106	47.4	49.3	46.7	40.8
Financial activities	2,848	4,055	4,638	4,491	56.7	61.3	60.3	58.9
Professional and business services	3,096	5,105	7,680	7,438	41.0	47.1	46.1	44.6
Professional and technical services	(NA)	2,209	3,146	3,516	(NA)	48.7	46.9	47.4
Management of companies and enterprises	(NA)	849	924	934	(NA)	50.9	51.4	50.1
Administrative and waste services	(NA)	2,048	3,610	2,988	(NA)	44.1	44.2	40.4
Education and health services	5,459	8,422	11,586	15,089	77.2	76.7	76.7	77.1
Educational services	(NA)	958	1,417	1,926	(NA)	56.8	59.3	61.1
Health care and social assistance	(NA)	7,464	10,168	13,164	(NA)	80.3	79.9	80.2
Leisure and hospitality	3,021	4,829	6,082	6,804	44.9	52.0	51.3	52.3
Arts, entertainment, and recreation	(NA)	516	815	884	(NA)	45.6	45.6	46.3
Accommodation and food services	(NA)	4,312	5,267	5,920	(NA)	52.9	52.3	53.3
Other services	1,185	2,164	2,614	2,839	43.0	50.8	50.6	52.9
Government	8,029	9,855	11,771	12,792	49.0	53.5	56.6	56.9
Federal	1,136	1,378	1,231	1,288	37.9	43.1	43.0	43.4
State government	1,641	2,137	2,464	2,643	45.5	49.6	51.5	51.4
Local government	5,252	6,340	8,076	8,861	53.8	58.1	61.5	61.7

NA Not available [1] Includes other industries, not shown separately.
Source: U.S. Bureau of Labor Statistics, Current Employment Statistics, "Employment, Hours, and Earnings—National," <http://www.bls.gov/ces/data.htm>.

Table 634. Private Nonfarm Extended Mass Layoff Activity by Industry and Reason for Layoff: 2000 to 2010

[Covers layoffs of at least 31 days duration that involve 50 or more individuals from a single employer. Based on administrative records of unemployment filings and establishment classifications, supplemented with employer confirmation of layoffs, plant closings, and additional employer provided data. See source for more information]

Industry	2007 NAICS code [1]	Extended mass layoff events	Separations	Initial claimants [2]
2000	(X)	4,591	915,962	846,267
2005	(X)	4,881	884,661	834,533
2006	(X)	4,885	935,969	951,155
2007	(X)	5,363	965,935	978,712
2008	(X)	8,259	1,516,978	1,670,042
2009	(X)	11,824	2,108,202	2,442,000
Total, 2010	(X)	7,247	1,256,606	1,412,386
Mining, quarrying, and gas extraction	21	59	7,940	8,246
Utilities	22	17	2,795	3,266
Construction	23	1,623	197,436	251,417
Manufacturing	31–33	1,412	224,173	257,712
Wholesale trade	42	149	17,274	17,319
Retail trade	44,45	479	122,576	152,959
Transportation and warehousing	48,49	486	95,564	105,099
Information	51	220	54,081	76,222
Finance and Insurance	52	251	47,888	53,291
Real estate and rental and leasing	53	68	10,035	9,575
Professional and technical services	54	298	58,797	63,189
Management of companies and enterprises	55	30	5,338	4,815
Administrative and waste services	56	747	150,042	172,897
Educational services	61	87	11,817	13,284
Health care and social assistance	62	384	48,501	49,243
Arts, entertainment, and recreation	71	228	48,590	34,023
Accommodation and food services	72	564	134,814	120411
Other services	81	145	18,945	19,418
Unclassified	(X)	–	–	–
Reason for layoff:				
Business demand	(X)	2,515	384,564	509,089
Disaster/safety	(X)	24	3,202	3,225
Financial issues	(X)	511	86,637	103,762
Organizational changes	(X)	397	79,784	80,192
Production specific	(X)	54	7,830	8,459
Seasonal	(X)	2,417	429,846	442,596
Other/miscellaneous	(X)	1,329	264,743	265,063

– Represents zero. X Not applicable. [1] Based on North American Industry Classification System, 2007. See text, Section 15.
[2] A person who files any notice of unemployment to initiate a request either for a determination of entitlement to and eligibility for compensation, or for a subsequent period of unemployment within a benefit year or period of eligibility.
Source: U.S. Bureau of Labor Statistics, "Mass Layoff Statistics," May 2011, <http://www.bls.gov/mls/home.htm>.

Table 635. Private Sector Gross Job Gains and Job Losses: 2000 to 2010

[In thousands (16,096 represents 16,096,000). For year ending in March. Based on the Quarterly Census of Employment and Wages (QCEW). Excludes self-employed and certain nonprofit organizations. Minus sign (–) indicates a decrease in employment and come from either closing establishments or contracting establishments. See source]

Year and industry	Gross job gains			Gross job losses			Net change [1]
	Total	Expanding establishments	Opening establishments	Total	Contracting establishments	Closing establishments	
2000...........................	16,096	10,618	5,478	13,118	8,284	4,834	2,978
2001...........................	15,177	10,147	5,030	14,330	9,249	5,081	847
2002...........................	13,630	8,631	4,999	16,359	11,027	5,332	−2,729
2003...........................	13,196	8,604	4,592	13,928	9,290	4,638	−732
2004...........................	13,310	8,951	4,359	12,432	8,237	4,195	878
2005...........................	13,766	9,410	4,356	11,774	7,671	4,103	1,992
2006...........................	14,019	9,625	4,394	11,438	7,711	3,727	2,581
2007...........................	13,441	9,238	4,203	11,941	8,246	3,695	1,500
2008...........................	12,704	8,714	3,990	12,609	8,772	3,837	95
2009...........................	10,048	6,664	3,384	15,912	11,703	4,209	−5,864
2010, Total private	**9,953**	**6,822**	**3,131**	**12,645**	**9,094**	**3,551**	**−2,692**
Goods producing..................	1,662	1,235	427	3,202	2,442	760	−1,540
Natural resources and mining........	204	151	53	257	195	62	−53
Construction...................	798	538	260	1,546	1,097	449	−748
Manufacturing.................	660	546	114	1,399	1,150	249	−739
Service providing.................	8,292	5,589	2,703	9,441	6,651	2,790	−1,149
Wholesale trade.................	453	321	132	678	481	197	−225
Retail trade....................	1,179	804	375	1,383	965	418	−204
Transportation and warehousing......	305	220	85	479	352	127	−174
Utilities.......................	23	19	4	27	23	4	−4
Information....................	206	152	54	341	270	71	−135
Financial activities..............	656	457	199	920	646	274	−264
Professional and business services...	2,109	1,538	571	2,352	1,675	677	−243
Education and health services.......	1,430	1,075	355	1,145	828	317	285
Leisure and hospitality............	1,367	740	627	1,590	1,082	508	−223
Other services.................	396	253	143	481	322	159	−85

[1] Net change is the difference between total gross job gains and total gross job losses.
Source: Bureau of Labor Statistics, Business Employment Dynamics, "Annual Business Employment Dynamics Data," <http://www.bls.gov/bdm/bdmann.htm#TOTAL>.

Table 636. Private Sector Gross Job Gains and Job Losses by State: 2010

[In thousands (9,953 represents 9,953,000). For year ending in March. Based on the Quarterly Census of Employment and Wages (QCEW). Excludes self-employed and certain nonprofit organizations. Minus sign (–) indicates a decrease in employment and come from either closing establishments or contracting establishments. For more information, see source]

State	Gross job gains			Gross job losses			Net change [1]	State	Gross job gains			Gross job losses			Net change [1]
	Total	Expanding establishments	Opening establishments	Total	Contracting establishments	Closing establishments			Total	Expanding establishments	Opening establishments	Total	Contracting establishments	Closing establishments	
U.S ..	**9,953**	**6,822**	**3,131**	**12,645**	**9,094**	**3,551**	**−2,692**	MO...	202	133	69	267	188	79	−65
AL ...	142	100	42	186	135	51	−43	MT ...	32	22	10	38	27	11	−6
AK ...	23	16	7	24	17	7	−1	NE ...	57	42	15	73	56	17	−17
AZ ...	203	136	67	282	201	81	−79	NV ...	98	69	29	148	113	36	−50
AR ...	90	62	28	106	75	31	−16	NH ...	47	34	14	58	43	15	−11
CA ...	1,202	814	388	1600	1,106	494	−398	NJ ...	308	201	106	368	260	108	−60
CO ...	175	116	59	241	168	73	−66	NM ...	58	39	19	75	55	20	−17
CT ...	100	76	24	146	105	41	−45	NY ...	625	426	199	718	503	215	−93
DE ...	30	20	10	41	30	12	−11	NC ...	305	206	99	400	283	117	−94
DC ...	44	30	14	46	34	12	−2	ND ...	27	19	7	24	18	6	3
FL ...	694	410	283	875	566	310	−182	OH ...	338	252	87	460	349	111	−121
GA ...	339	212	127	431	291	140	−92	OK ...	109	71	38	158	111	47	−49
HI....	41	28	13	55	38	17	−13	OR ...	120	85	35	152	107	44	−32
ID ...	51	35	16	62	42	20	−12	PA ...	379	279	100	454	342	112	−75
IL	359	252	107	498	373	125	−139	RI....	34	23	11	38	28	11	−4
IN....	210	159	51	244	178	66	−35	SC ...	141	96	45	175	130	45	−34
IA....	93	68	25	116	90	26	−23	SD ...	25	18	7	32	24	8	−7
KS ...	91	62	29	131	100	31	−40	TN ...	196	142	55	247	188	58	−50
KY ...	130	95	35	156	118	38	−26	TX ...	819	574	245	996	766	230	−177
LA ...	158	106	52	202	147	55	−44	UT ...	101	67	34	128	90	38	−28
ME...	41	27	14	47	33	13	−6	VT ...	20	14	6	23	16	7	−3
MD...	198	137	61	238	169	69	−39	VA ...	267	184	82	323	234	89	−56
MA...	218	156	62	250	185	65	−32	WA...	207	150	57	278	210	68	−71
MI....	301	204	97	383	270	113	−82	WV...	53	38	15	65	47	18	−12
MN...	182	122	60	229	166	63	−46	WI ...	167	124	43	223	168	54	−56
MS...	83	57	26	105	77	28	−22	WY ..	19	12	7	31	24	7	−12

[1] Net change is the difference between total gross job gains and total gross job losses.
Source: Bureau of Labor Statistics, Business Employment Dynamics, "Annual Business Employment Dynamics Data," <http://www.bls.gov/bdm/bdmann.htm#TOTAL>.

U.S. Census Bureau, Statistical Abstract of the United States: 2012

Table 637. Hires and Separations Affecting Establishment Payrolls: 2007 to 2010

[63,326 represents 63,326,000. Hires represent any additions to payrolls, including new and rehired employees, full- and part-time workers, short-term and seasonal workers, etc. Separations represent terminations of employment, including quits, layoffs, and discharges, etc. Based on a monthly survey of private nonfarm establishments and governmental entities]

Industry	Annual hires (1,000)				Annual separations (1,000)			
	2007	2008	2009	2010	2007	2008	2009	2010
Total	**63,326**	**53,986**	**45,372**	**47,234**	**62,173**	**57,525**	**50,544**	**46,347**
Total private industry	58,760	50,286	41,966	43,299	57,924	54,042	47,035	42,125
Mining and logging	345	349	185	280	311	317	294	210
Construction	4,815	4,370	3,627	3,923	4,980	5,111	4,714	4,139
Manufacturing	4,605	3,561	2,718	3,100	4,882	4,449	4,153	3,000
Durable goods	2,682	2,046	1,399	1,771	2,886	2,686	2,519	1,637
Nondurable goods	1,922	1,513	1,318	1,330	1,995	1,765	1,636	1,366
Trade, transportation, and utilities	13,199	11,105	9,256	9,356	12,896	12,260	10,365	9,116
Wholesale trade	2,206	1,807	1,423	1,347	2,127	2,058	1,763	1,346
Retail trade	9,109	7,564	6,214	6,481	8,940	8,331	6,761	6,317
Transportation, warehousing, and utilities	1,884	1,736	1,621	1,532	1,829	1,869	1,839	1,456
Information	981	747	663	614	994	865	843	659
Financial activities	3,137	2,421	1,863	1,884	3,274	2,657	2,197	1,939
Finance and insurance	2,071	1,550	1,094	1,235	2,191	1,720	1,306	1,267
Real estate and rental and leasing	1,067	871	769	651	1,084	940	891	671
Professional and business services	11,467	9,702	8,001	8,942	11,192	10,515	8,735	8,540
Education and health services	6,428	6,290	5,816	5,678	5,920	5,843	5,502	5,282
Educational services	916	914	849	860	854	815	805	788
Health care and social assistance	5,514	5,378	4,966	4,820	5,068	5,026	4,695	4,494
Leisure and hospitality	11,193	9,491	7,600	7,475	10,938	9,720	7,894	7,298
Arts, entertainment, and recreation	1,639	1,410	1,166	1,277	1,592	1,440	1,232	1,242
Accommodation and food services	9,552	8,081	6,433	6,201	9,345	8,279	6,658	6,056
Other services	2,590	2,247	2,236	2,038	2,534	2,305	2,340	1,939
Government workers	4,567	3,698	3,406	3,936	4,255	3,485	3,507	4,223
Federal	846	336	501	1,083	823	330	446	1,056
State and local	3,720	3,363	2,907	2,854	3,430	3,155	3,063	3,167

Source: U.S. Bureau of Labor Statistics, *Job Openings and Labor Turnover*, News Release, USDL 11-0307, March 2011. See also <http://www.bls.gov/jlt/news.htm>.

Table 638. Type of Separations Affecting Establishment Payrolls: 2010

[21,296 represents 21,964,000. Covers all private nonfarm establishments. Separations are the total number of terminations of employment occurring at any time during the reference month, and are reported by type of separation—quits, layoffs and discharges, and other separations. Annual rate estimates are computed by dividing annual levels by the Current Employment Statistics (CES) annual average employment level, see Table 632, and multiplying that quotient by 100]

Industry	Number (1,000)			Rate (percent) [1]		
	Annual quits level [2]	Annual layoffs and discharge levels [3]	Annual other separations [4]	Annual quits level [2]	Annual layoffs and discharge levels [3]	Annual other separations [4]
Total	**21,296**	**21,243**	**3,810**	**16.4**	**16.4**	**2.9**
Private industry	19,951	19,156	3,019	18.6	17.8	2.8
Mining and logging	91	93	25	12.9	13.2	3.5
Construction	857	3,138	144	15.5	56.8	2.6
Manufacturing	1,114	1,643	245	9.7	14.3	2.1
Durable goods	548	929	159	7.8	13.1	2.2
Nondurable goods	564	713	87	12.7	16.0	2.0
Trade, transportation, and utilities	4,695	3,621	802	19.1	14.7	3.3
Wholesale trade	516	713	116	9.5	13.1	2.1
Retail trade	3,547	2,274	498	24.6	15.8	3.5
Transportation, warehousing, and utilities	631	634	186	13.3	13.4	3.9
Information	330	271	59	12.2	10.0	2.2
Financial activities	947	730	266	12.4	9.6	3.5
Finance and insurance	630	423	213	11.1	7.4	3.7
Real estate and rental and leasing	315	305	54	16.2	15.7	2.8
Professional and business services	3,823	4,113	606	22.9	24.6	3.6
Education and health services	2,855	2,022	406	14.6	10.3	2.1
Educational services	346	388	53	11.0	12.3	1.7
Health care and social assistance	2,509	1,632	353	15.3	9.9	2.2
Leisure and hospitality	4,285	2,663	349	32.9	20.5	2.7
Arts, entertainment, and recreation	433	774	36	22.7	40.5	1.9
Accommodation and food services	3,853	1,891	312	34.7	17.0	2.8
Other services	958	864	120	17.9	16.1	2.2
Government workers	1,343	2,087	788	6.0	9.3	3.5
Federal	166	763	128	5.6	25.7	4.3
State and local	1,180	1,325	660	6.0	6.8	3.4

[1] As a percent of total employment. [2] Quits are voluntary separations by employees (except for retirements, which are reported as other separations). [3] Layoffs and discharges are involuntary seperations initiated by the employer and include layoffs with no intent to rehire; formal layoffs lasting or expected to last more than seven days; discharges resulting from mergers, downsizing, or closings, firings or other discharges for cause; terminations of permanent or short term employees; and terminations of seasonal employees. [4] Other seperations include retirements, transfers to other locations, deaths, and seperations due to disability.

Source: U.S. Bureau of Labor Statistics, *Job Openings and Labor Turnover*, News Release, USDL 11-0307, March 2011. See also <http://www.bls.gov/jlt/news.htm>.

Table 639. Average Hours Per Week Spent Doing Unpaid Household Work and Paid Work by Sex and Age: 2003–2007

[In hours. Data for persons in the civilian noninstitutionalized population 15 years old and over for 2003 through 2007. Unpaid household work is defined as activities that are unpaid, for which market substitutes exist, and done for one's own household]

Type of work	Total, 15 years and over	Age						
		15–24 years	25–34 years	35–44 years	45–54 years	55–64 years	65–74 years	75 years and over
MEN								
Total paid work and unpaid household work ...	**47.4**	**29.9**	**57.2**	**60.0**	**57.6**	**47.9**	**30.2**	**21.2**
Unpaid household work....................	15.9	8.9	15.8	18.3	17.0	17.8	19.9	18.1
Household activities....................	9.2	4.6	7.4	9.1	10.6	12.3	13.4	12.8
Food and drink preparation	1.9	0.8	1.7	2.2	2.1	2.2	2.3	3.0
Cleaning	1.2	0.9	1.2	1.3	1.2	1.2	1.2	1.4
Laundry and sewing	0.4	0.3	0.5	0.5	0.5	0.4	0.4	0.4
Household management................	0.8	0.4	0.6	0.8	0.9	1.1	1.2	1.2
Lawn and garden care.................	1.9	0.5	1.0	1.5	2.2	3.2	3.9	3.6
Maintenance and repair...............	2.4	1.4	1.8	2.3	2.8	3.2	3.5	2.3
Caring for and helping household members.......	2.0	0.7	3.4	4.1	1.6	0.6	0.6	0.7
Purchasing goods and services	2.4	1.9	2.5	2.4	2.2	2.6	3.3	2.7
Travel related to unpaid household work	2.4	1.8	2.4	2.7	2.5	2.3	2.6	1.9
Paid work.............................	31.4	20.9	41.4	41.7	40.6	30.1	10.3	3.1
WOMEN								
Total paid work and unpaid household work ...	**47.7**	**33.4**	**58.0**	**60.4**	**55.8**	**48.0**	**33.7**	**25.1**
Unpaid household work....................	26.7	15.9	31.7	33.1	26.7	26.2	28.1	23.8
Household activities....................	15.5	7.1	13.9	17.0	17.3	18.1	20.9	18.8
Food and drink preparation	5.3	2.2	5.3	6.1	5.6	5.9	7.0	6.4
Cleaning	4.0	2.3	4.2	4.4	4.0	4.3	5.0	4.5
Laundry and sewing	2.5	0.9	2.0	2.8	3.0	2.9	3.6	3.1
Household management................	1.1	0.8	0.8	1.1	1.2	1.3	1.6	1.5
Lawn and garden care.................	0.9	0.2	0.5	0.8	1.1	1.5	1.7	1.6
Maintenance and repair...............	0.8	0.4	0.5	0.8	1.1	1.1	0.9	0.7
Caring for and helping household members.......	4.4	3.1	10.3	8.1	2.4	1.1	0.8	0.5
Purchasing goods and services	3.7	3.3	3.8	4.1	3.8	4.1	3.9	2.8
Travel related to unpaid household work	3.1	2.4	3.7	4.0	3.1	2.9	2.5	1.7
Paid work.............................	21.0	17.4	26.3	27.3	29.1	21.8	5.7	1.2

Source: U.S. Bureau of Labor Statistics, "Measuring time spent in unpaid household work: results from the American Time Use Survey," Monthly Labor Review, July 2009, Vol. 132, No. 7, <http://www.bls.gov/opub/mlr/2009/07/contents.htm>.

Table 640. Average Hours Worked Per Day by Employed Persons: 2010

[147,746 represents 147,746,000. Civilian noninstitutionalized population 15 years old and over, except as indicated. Includes work at main and any other job(s). Excludes travel related to work. Based on the American Time Use Survey. See source for details]

Characteristic	Total employed (1,000)	Employed persons who worked on their diary day [1]								
		Number (1,000)	Percent of employed	Hours of work	Worked at workplace			Worked at home [2]		
					Number (1,000)	Percent of employed [3]	Hours of work	Number (1,000)	Percent of employed [3]	Hours of work
Total	**147,746**	**100,837**	**68.2**	**7.50**	**83,512**	**82.8**	**7.76**	**23,805**	**23.6**	**2.96**
Work status: [4]										
Full-time workers [5].....	113,036	81,985	72.5	8.00	69,147	84.3	8.17	18,943	23.1	3.10
Part-time workers [5]	34,701	18,851	54.3	5.37	14,365	76.2	5.80	4,862	25.8	2.41
Male [4]...............	77,569	54,551	70.3	7.82	46,072	84.5	7.96	12,476	22.9	2.91
Full-time workers [5].....	64,043	47,201	73.7	8.17	40,324	85.4	8.28	10,647	22.6	2.98
Part-time workers [5]	13,526	7,351	54.3	5.53	5,748	78.2	5.74	1,829	24.9	2.47
Female [4].............	70,178	46,285	66.0	7.14	37,439	80.9	7.52	11,329	24.5	3.02
Full-time workers [5].....	48,993	34,785	71.0	7.75	28,823	82.9	8.02	8,296	23.8	3.25
Part-time workers [5]	21,175	11,501	54.3	5.27	8,617	74.9	5.84	3,033	26.4	2.37
Jobholding status:										
Single jobholders......	134,253	90,351	67.3	7.51	75,312	83.4	7.78	19,725	21.8	2.97
Multiple jobholders.....	13,484	10,486	77.8	7.48	8,200	78.2	7.60	4,081	38.9	2.93
Educational attainment: [6]										
Less than high school ..	10,054	6,639	66.0	7.74	6,090	91.7	7.84	688	10.4	2.64
High school diploma [7] ..	36,218	24,311	67.1	7.75	20,892	85.9	7.89	4,039	16.6	3.82
Some college.........	31,814	21,792	68.5	7.64	18,299	84.0	7.93	4,965	22.8	2.99
Bachelor's degree or higher.............	49,407	36,323	73.5	7.40	27,412	75.5	7.84	13,118	36.1	2.67

[1] Individuals may have worked at more than one location. [2] "Working at home" includes any time persons did work at home and is not restricted to persons whose usual workplace is their home. [3] Percent of employed who worked on their diary day. [4] Includes workers whose hours vary. [5] Full-time workers usually worked 35 or more hours per week at all jobs combined; part-time workers fewer than 35 hours per week. [6] For those 25 years old and over. [7] Includes persons with a high school diploma or equivalent.

Source: U.S. Bureau of Labor Statistics, American Time Use Survey—2010 Results, News Release, USDL 11-0919, June 2011. See also <http://www.bls.gov/tus/home.htm#news>.

Table 641. Productivity and Related Measures for Selected NAICS Industries: 1987 to 2009 and 2001 to 2009

[For a discussion of productivity measures and methodology, see text, this section and BLS Handbook of Methods, <http://www.bls.gov/opub/hom/homch11.htm>. Minus sign (–) indicates decrease]

Industry	2007 NAICS code [1]	Average annual percent change [2]							
		1987–2009 [3]				2001–2009			
		Output per hour	Output	Hours	Unit labor costs	Output per hour	Output	Hours	Unit labor costs
Mining	21	0.2	–0.2	–0.4	4.8	–2.3	–0.6	1.8	8.0
Oil and gas extraction	2111	0.7	–0.5	–1.2	5.7	–3.0	–0.2	2.9	8.7
Mining, except oil and gas	212	1.8	0.2	–1.6	1.7	–0.8	–1.7	–0.9	5.0
Support activities for mining	2131	2.6	4.1	1.4	3.3	3.2	6.9	3.6	2.8
Utilities:									
Power generation and supply	2211	2.2	0.9	–1.3	1.9	–	–0.8	–0.8	4.1
Natural gas distribution	2212	2.5	1.1	–1.3	2.3	0.7	0.2	–0.5	3.1
Manufacturing:									
Food	311	1.2	1.3	0.2	1.6	1.2	0.6	–0.6	1.8
Animal slaughtering and processing	3116	1.0	2.2	1.2	1.4	2.0	1.5	–0.5	1.7
Bakeries and tortilla manufacturing	3118	0.5	0.2	–0.3	1.9	–0.3	–1.0	–0.6	1.0
Beverages and tobacco products	312	0.7	–0.7	–1.4	1.8	0.3	–2.5	–2.8	2.6
Textile mills	313	3.4	–3.3	–6.5	–	4.3	–7.8	–11.6	–0.4
Textile product mills	314	0.5	–2.2	–2.7	2.2	–1.4	–7.2	–5.9	2.8
Apparel	315	–2.3	–9.3	–7.1	3.5	–11.6	–20.3	–9.8	10.0
Leather and allied products	316	1.4	–5.5	–6.9	2.1	–2.4	–10.0	–7.9	4.0
Wood products	321	1.1	–1.2	–2.3	2.4	1.9	–4.5	–6.3	1.9
Paper and paper products	322	1.9	–0.3	–2.2	1.4	2.5	–2.1	–4.5	0.6
Converted paper products	3222	1.5	–0.1	–1.6	1.8	2.5	–1.8	–4.3	0.7
Printing and related support activities	3231	1.2	–0.6	–1.8	1.5	2.3	–2.9	–5.0	0.5
Petroleum and coal products	3241	2.6	1.0	–1.5	2.7	1.4	0.5	–0.8	4.6
Chemicals	325	1.4	0.5	–0.9	2.4	1.3	–1.0	–2.3	2.6
Pharmaceuticals and medicines	3254	0.4	2.5	2.1	3.5	–0.6	–0.6	–	5.1
Plastics and rubber products	326	1.9	0.8	–1.1	1.4	1.1	–3.3	–4.4	1.5
Plastics products	3261	1.8	1.1	–0.7	1.6	0.9	–3.2	–4.1	1.8
Nonmetallic mineral products	327	0.8	–0.5	–1.3	1.9	0.6	–3.5	–4.1	2.2
Primary metals	331	1.9	–1.2	–3.0	1.3	2.4	–3.8	–6.0	1.5
Fabricated metal products	332	1.2	0.2	–1.0	2.0	0.9	–2.4	–3.3	2.5
Architectural and structural metals	3323	0.7	0.5	–0.1	2.5	0.1	–2.5	–2.6	3.8
Machine shops and threaded products	3327	1.8	1.8	–	1.6	0.1	–1.8	–1.9	2.0
Other fabricated metal products	3329	1.3	–0.2	–1.5	1.7	2.7	–0.8	–3.5	1.3
Machinery	333	2.1	0.6	–1.5	1.0	2.1	–1.7	–3.7	1.1
Agriculture, construction, and mining machinery	3331	2.3	2.2	–0.1	0.6	2.2	2.1	–	1.0
Other general purpose machinery	3339	2.4	0.8	–1.6	1.5	3.1	–1.1	–4.1	1.4
Computer and electronic products	334	11.2	8.4	–2.5	–7.0	6.3	1.0	–5.0	–3.5
Semiconductors and electronic components	3344	15.9	13.6	–2.0	–10.9	8.2	1.3	–6.3	–5.4
Electronic instruments	3345	3.9	1.7	–2.1	0.2	4.0	2.5	–1.4	0.4
Electrical equipment and appliances	335	2.3	–0.6	–2.8	1.5	1.2	–3.7	–4.9	2.3
Transportation equipment	336	2.7	0.5	–2.1	0.2	3.5	–1.2	–4.6	0.2
Motor vehicles	3361	3.0	–0.6	–3.5	–0.2	3.6	–4.8	–8.1	–0.6
Motor vehicle parts	3363	2.7	0.6	–2.1	–0.8	2.7	–5.3	–7.8	–1.0
Aerospace products and parts	3364	2.0	–0.2	–2.1	1.1	2.0	1.6	–0.4	2.1
Furniture and related products	337	1.3	–0.8	–2.1	1.9	1.2	–4.9	–6.0	1.7
Household and institutional furniture	3371	1.2	–1.2	–2.4	2.0	0.8	–5.7	–6.4	2.0
Miscellaneous manufacturing	339	2.9	2.4	–0.4	1.5	3.1	0.7	–2.3	1.5
Medical equipment and supplies	3391	3.4	4.6	1.2	1.0	3.3	3.6	0.3	1.2
Other miscellaneous manufacturing	3399	2.1	0.4	–1.7	2.0	2.3	–2.4	–4.6	2.0
Wholesale trade	42	2.6	2.9	0.3	1.3	1.2	0.5	–0.7	1.9
Durable goods	423	4.4	4.4	–	–0.3	2.7	1.1	–1.6	–
Nondurable goods	424	1.0	1.1	0.1	3.4	0.8	–0.1	–0.9	2.7
Electronic markets and agents and brokers	4251	0.6	2.9	2.3	1.5	–4.9	–0.9	4.2	8.4
Retail trade	44–45	2.9	3.3	0.3	0.1	2.8	1.7	–1.1	–0.3
Motor vehicle and parts dealers	441	1.8	2.1	0.2	0.9	0.1	–1.6	–1.7	1.1
Automobile dealers	4411	1.8	1.9	0.1	0.9	0.2	–2.0	–2.1	0.7
Other motor vehicle dealers	4412	3.2	4.1	0.8	0.3	2.2	1.9	–0.3	–0.2
Auto parts, accessories, and tire stores	4413	1.7	2.0	0.3	1.1	0.3	–0.8	–1.1	2.7
Furniture and home furnishings stores	442	3.8	3.3	–0.5	–0.7	4.3	0.8	–3.4	–2.1
Furniture stores	4421	3.2	2.8	–0.4	–0.6	3.3	0.4	–2.8	–2.1
Home furnishings stores	4422	4.6	4.0	–0.6	–0.9	5.5	1.2	–4.1	–2.1
Electronics and appliance stores	4431	13.5	14.2	0.6	–9.0	15.4	12.8	–2.2	–12.2
Building material and garden supply stores	444	2.5	3.4	0.9	0.2	1.3	0.6	–0.7	1.3
Building material and supplies dealers	4441	2.2	3.3	1.1	0.4	0.9	0.4	–0.5	1.8
Lawn and garden equipment and supplies stores	4442	4.3	3.5	–0.7	–1.3	4.5	2.6	–1.8	–1.8
Food and beverage stores	445	0.4	0.2	–0.2	3.0	1.9	–	–1.8	1.6
Grocery stores	4451	0.2	0.1	–0.1	3.2	1.6	–0.2	–1.7	2.4
Specialty food stores	4452	0.5	–0.1	–0.5	1.7	4.5	1.8	–2.6	–3.9
Beer, wine, and liquor stores	4453	2.0	0.7	–1.3	1.5	3.8	1.8	–2.0	–2.1
Health and personal care stores	4461	2.5	3.7	1.2	1.5	2.6	3.1	0.4	1.9
Gasoline stations	4471	1.9	1.0	–0.8	1.4	1.4	–0.4	–1.7	1.0
Clothing and clothing accessories stores	448	4.7	4.1	–0.5	–1.3	4.6	3.4	–1.1	–1.5
Clothing stores	4481	5.0	4.7	–0.4	–1.6	5.4	4.2	–1.1	–1.9
Shoe stores	4482	3.4	2.3	–1.1	–0.8	2.4	1.5	–0.9	–1.0
Jewelry, luggage, and leather goods stores	4483	3.9	3.2	–0.7	–0.6	2.5	1.3	–1.2	0.4
Sporting goods, hobby, book, and music stores	451	4.1	4.2	0.1	–0.8	4.4	1.9	–2.4	–2.1
Sporting goods and musical instrument stores	4511	4.8	5.1	0.3	–1.4	5.3	4.1	–1.2	–3.1

See footnotes at end of table.

Table 641. Productivity and Related Measures for Selected NAICS Industries: 1987 to 2009 and 2001 to 2009—Con.

[For a discussion of productivity measures and methodology, see text, this section and BLS Handbook of Methods, <http://www.bls.gov/opub/hom/homch11.htm>. Minus sign (−) indicates decrease]

Industry	2007 NAICS code [1]	Average annual percent change [2]							
		1987–2009 [3]				2001–2009			
		Output per hour	Output	Hours	Unit labor costs	Output per hour	Output	Hours	Unit labor costs
Retail Trade—Con.									
Book, periodical, and music stores	4512	2.5	2.1	−0.4	0.6	2.3	−3.2	−5.4	0.4
General merchandise stores	452	3.5	5.1	1.6	−1.2	2.8	4.4	1.6	−0.8
Department stores	4521	0.7	1.7	1.0	0.7	−0.1	−1.3	−1.2	1.4
Other general merchandise stores	4529	6.7	9.0	2.2	−3.1	4.0	8.9	4.7	−0.7
Miscellaneous store retailers	453	4.0	3.8	−0.2	−1.4	4.0	0.2	−3.6	−1.6
Florists	4531	3.7	0.4	−3.2	−0.4	6.7	−1.9	−8.1	−2.2
Office supplies, stationery, and gift stores	4532	6.4	5.6	−0.8	−3.1	7.7	2.0	−5.3	−5.0
Used merchandise stores	4533	4.8	5.9	1.0	−1.9	5.2	3.4	−1.7	−2.8
Other miscellaneous store retailers	4539	1.5	2.6	1.1	−0.3	−0.3	−1.4	−1.0	1.7
Nonstore retailers	454	8.8	8.9	0.1	−4.9	9.0	7.8	−1.1	−4.5
Electronic shopping and mail-order houses	4541	11.4	15.2	3.4	−6.7	11.2	11.7	0.5	−6.3
Vending machine operators	4542	0.8	−1.9	−2.6	2.9	2.1	−3.0	−5.0	1.2
Direct selling establishments	4543	3.6	1.7	−1.8	−0.4	2.3	0.2	−2.0	1.6
Transportation and warehousing:									
Air transportation	481	2.8	2.7	−0.1	0.1	5.6	1.8	−3.6	−3.4
Line-haul railroads	482111	4.0	1.4	−2.4	−0.5	1.7	−0.2	−1.9	1.8
Truck transportation	484	0.1	1.2	1.1	1.2	−	−0.8	−0.8	0.9
General freight trucking	4841	0.8	1.8	1.0	1.4	0.2	−0.7	−0.9	1.4
Used household and office goods moving	48421	−0.5	−1.0	−0.4	2.9	1.6	−3.6	−5.1	−0.1
Postal service	4911	1.0	0.1	−0.8	3.4	0.7	−2.9	−3.5	4.2
Couriers and messengers	492	−0.4	1.6	2.0	2.6	0.4	−2.6	−3.0	0.9
Warehousing and storage	4931	2.6	5.5	2.8	−	0.2	3.4	3.1	2.1
General warehousing and storage	49311	5.0	7.9	2.8	−1.7	1.3	4.7	3.4	0.9
Refrigerated warehousing and storage	49312	−0.6	2.8	3.4	1.6	−0.2	1.9	2.0	2.7
Information:									
Publishing	511	3.7	3.6	−0.1	1.5	2.7	−1.0	−3.6	1.3
Newspaper, book, and directory publishers	5111	−0.1	−1.6	−1.5	4.4	−0.4	−4.8	−4.4	4.4
Software publishers	5112	13.9	20.9	6.2	−7.7	5.3	3.4	−1.8	−2.1
Motion picture and video exhibition	51213	1.6	2.0	0.4	1.6	2.9	−	−2.9	2.6
Broadcasting, except Internet	515	1.6	2.5	0.9	2.2	4.5	3.6	−0.9	−0.2
Radio and television broadcasting	5151	0.5	0.4	−0.1	3.2	2.4	1.2	−1.1	0.2
Cable and other subscription programming	5152	3.5	7.9	4.2	2.6	7.3	7.0	−0.3	2.7
Wired telecommunications carriers	5171	4.1	3.4	−0.7	−0.9	4.0	−1.0	−4.8	−0.1
Wireless telecommunications carriers	5172	10.2	21.8	10.5	−6.3	16.3	14.4	−1.7	−7.5
Finance and insurance:									
Commercial banking	52211	3.6	3.5	−0.1	2.0	2.4	2.8	0.4	3.4
Real estate and rental and leasing:									
Passenger car rental	532111	1.8	2.2	0.4	2.5	2.5	−1.8	−4.3	1.3
Truck, trailer, and RV rental and leasing	53212	2.9	2.1	−0.8	0.9	−	−2.2	−2.2	3.6
Video tape and disc rental	53223	4.3	3.2	−1.0	−0.9	4.7	−4.3	−8.7	−0.1
Professional and technical services:									
Tax preparation services	541213	0.4	2.9	2.5	1.3	−0.5	0.6	1.2	4.4
Architectural services	54131	1.3	2.6	1.2	2.0	1.0	−0.4	−1.5	1.6
Engineering services	54133	1.2	3.0	1.8	3.3	2.0	2.6	0.6	2.6
Advertising agencies	54181	1.8	2.0	0.1	2.4	3.7	3.0	−0.7	−2.1
Photography studios, portrait	541921	−0.2	2.0	2.2	2.2	−1.0	0.2	1.2	1.0
Administrative and waste services:									
Employment placement agencies	561311	6.8	6.9	0.1	−1.5	11.5	6.5	−4.5	−8.0
Travel agencies	56151	5.5	3.6	−1.8	−0.6	12.2	5.0	−6.4	−7.9
Janitorial services	56172	1.9	3.6	1.7	1.9	1.3	1.9	0.6	1.3
Health care and social assistance:									
Medical and diagnostic laboratories	6215	3.7	6.7	2.8	−0.6	1.9	4.9	2.9	1.2
Arts, entertainment, and recreation:									
Amusement and theme parks	71311	−0.3	2.5	2.7	3.5	1.6	0.8	−0.8	1.9
Bowling centers	71395	0.2	−1.8	−2.0	3.0	2.0	−1.0	−2.9	1.9
Accommodation and food services	72	0.8	2.1	1.2	2.9	0.8	1.3	0.6	2.1
Accommodation	721	1.5	2.3	0.8	2.2	1.3	0.8	−0.5	0.8
Traveler accommodation	7211	1.6	2.4	0.8	2.2	1.3	0.8	−0.5	0.9
Food services and drinking places	722	0.6	2.0	1.4	3.1	0.7	1.5	0.8	2.5
Full-service restaurants	7221	0.6	2.0	1.4	3.9	0.2	1.1	0.9	3.2
Limited-service eating places	7222	0.6	2.2	1.6	2.8	1.0	2.2	1.2	2.0
Special food services	7223	1.4	2.4	0.9	1.1	0.8	1.5	0.6	2.0
Drinking places, alcoholic beverages	7224	−0.4	−0.8	−0.4	3.0	3.2	−0.5	−3.6	0.8
Other services:									
Automotive repair and maintenance	8111	0.7	1.1	0.4	2.6	−1.0	−2.6	−1.6	3.9
Reupholstery and furniture repair	81142	−0.7	−3.2	−2.4	3.6	−2.0	−7.0	−5.1	4.9
Hair, nail, and skin care services	81211	1.9	2.9	0.9	2.3	1.3	2.3	1.0	2.4
Funeral homes and funeral services	81221	−0.6	−0.5	−	4.5	−0.1	−2.7	−2.7	3.9
Drycleaning and laundry services	8123	1.3	0.4	−0.9	2.3	1.9	−1.0	−2.8	1.9
Photofinishing	81292	1.5	−5.0	−6.4	2.1	6.3	−7.9	−13.3	−3.4

− Represents or rounds to zero. [1] North American Industry Classification System, 2007 (NAICS); see text, section 15.
[2] Average annual percent changes based on compound rate formula. Rates of change are calculated using index numbers to three decimal places. [3] For NAICS industries 484, 4841, 4931, 49311, and 49312, annual percent changes are for 1992–2009, and for NAICS industries 561311, 6215, annual percent changes are for 1994–2009.
Source: U.S. Bureau of Labor Statistics, Labor Productivity and Costs, <http://www.bls.gov/lpc/data.htm>, accessed May 2011.

Labor Force, Employment, and Earnings 417

Table 642. Productivity and Related Measures: 1980 to 2010

[See text, this section. Minus sign (–) indicates decrease]

Item	1980	1990	2000	2005	2006	2007	2008	2009	2010
INDEXES (2005=100)									
Output per hour, business sector	58.0	69.0	85.6	100.0	100.9	102.5	103.6	107.4	111.6
Nonfarm business	59.4	69.6	85.9	100.0	100.9	102.5	103.6	107.4	111.5
Manufacturing	(NA)	53.8	80.4	100.0	100.8	105.0	104.6	104.2	110.3
Output, [1] business sector	42.7	60.0	87.7	100.0	103.1	105.2	104.2	100.4	104.1
Nonfarm business	42.9	60.0	87.7	100.0	103.1	105.3	104.2	100.3	104.0
Manufacturing	(NA)	67.0	98.9	100.0	101.5	104.0	99.4	86.2	91.2
Hours, [2] business sector	73.6	86.9	102.4	100.0	102.1	102.6	100.5	93.4	93.3
Nonfarm business	72.2	86.3	102.2	100.0	102.2	102.7	100.6	93.4	93.3
Manufacturing	(NA)	124.5	123.1	100.0	100.7	99.0	95.1	82.7	82.7
Compensation per hour, [3] business sector	33.1	55.2	82.3	100.0	103.8	108.1	111.5	113.7	116.2
Nonfarm business	33.4	55.5	82.5	100.0	103.8	107.9	111.4	113.7	116.2
Manufacturing	(NA)	55.2	81.2	100.0	102.0	105.3	109.4	115.6	118.0
Real hourly compensation, [3] business sector	74.6	80.0	93.3	100.0	100.5	101.8	101.1	103.5	104.1
Nonfarm business	75.4	80.3	93.5	100.0	100.5	101.6	101.0	103.5	104.1
Manufacturing	(NA)	80.0	92.0	100.0	98.8	99.2	99.2	105.3	105.6
Unit labor costs, [4] business sector	57.0	80.0	96.1	100.0	102.8	105.4	107.6	105.9	104.2
Nonfarm business	56.2	79.7	96.1	100.0	102.8	105.3	107.6	105.9	104.2
Manufacturing	(NA)	102.7	101.0	100.0	101.2	100.3	104.6	111.0	107.0
ANNUAL PERCENT CHANGE [5]									
Output per hour, business sector	−0.2	2.1	3.5	1.7	0.9	1.5	1.1	3.7	3.9
Nonfarm business	−0.3	1.8	3.4	1.6	0.9	1.6	1.0	3.7	3.9
Manufacturing	(NA)	2.2	4.4	4.7	0.8	4.2	−0.4	−0.4	5.9
Output, [1] business sector	−1.1	1.5	4.5	3.4	3.1	2.0	−0.9	−3.7	3.7
Nonfarm business	−1.1	1.4	4.4	3.4	3.1	2.1	−1.1	−3.8	3.7
Manufacturing	(NA)	−0.3	3.1	3.6	1.5	2.4	−4.4	−13.3	5.8
Hours, [2] business sector	−0.9	−0.6	1.0	1.7	2.1	0.5	−2.0	−7.1	−0.2
Nonfarm business	−0.8	−0.4	1.0	1.7	2.2	0.6	−2.1	−7.2	−0.2
Manufacturing	(NA)	−2.5	−1.3	−1.1	0.7	−1.7	−4.0	−13.0	–
Compensation per hour, [3] business sector	10.7	6.4	7.4	3.9	3.8	4.1	3.2	2.0	2.2
Nonfarm business	10.7	6.2	7.4	3.9	3.8	4.0	3.3	2.0	2.2
Manufacturing	(NA)	4.8	7.7	3.3	2.0	3.2	3.9	5.7	2.0
Real hourly compensation, [3] business sector	−0.4	1.4	3.9	0.5	0.5	1.2	−0.6	2.4	0.5
Nonfarm business	−0.4	1.1	4.0	0.6	0.5	1.1	−0.6	2.4	0.6
Manufacturing	(NA)	−0.1	4.2	0.0	−1.2	0.4	0.1	6.1	0.4
Unit labor costs, [4] business sector	10.9	4.2	3.7	2.2	2.8	2.5	2.1	−1.6	−1.6
Nonfarm business	11.0	4.3	3.9	2.3	2.8	2.4	2.2	−1.6	−1.6
Manufacturing	(NA)	2.6	3.2	−1.3	1.2	−0.9	4.3	6.1	−3.6

– Represents zero. NA Not available. [1] Refers to gross sectoral product, a chain–type, current–weighted index.
[2] Hours at work of all persons engaged in the business and nonfarm business sectors (employees, proprietors, and unpaid family workers); employees' and proprietors' hours in manufacturing. [3] Wages and salaries of employees plus employers' contributions for social insurance and private benefit plans. Also includes an estimate of same for self–employed. Real compensation deflated by the consumer price index research series, see text, Section 14. [4] Hourly compensation divided by output per hour. [5] All changes are from the immediate prior year.

Source: U.S. Department of Labor, Bureau of Labor Statistics, *Productivity and Costs*, News Release, USDL 11–0808, June 2011. See also <http://www.bls.gov/lpc/home.htm>.

Table 643. Annual Total Compensation and Wages and Salary Accruals Per Full-Time Equivalent Employee by Industry: 2000 to 2009

[In dollars. Wage and salary accruals include executives' compensation, bonuses, tips, and payments-in-kind; total compensation includes in addition to wages and salaries, employer contributions for social insurance, employer contributions to private and welfare funds, director's fees, jury and witness fees, etc. Based on the 2002 North American Industry Classification System (NAICS); see text, section 15]

Industry	Total annual compensation				Annual salary and wages			
	2000	2005	2008	2009	2000	2005	2008	2009
Compensation of employees	47,059	56,620	63,095	64,552	39,243	45,729	51,301	51,888
Domestic industries	46,946	56,371	62,784	64,197	39,157	45,537	51,059	51,615
Private industries	45,772	54,139	60,056	61,051	38,862	44,717	50,144	50,462
Agriculture, forestry, fishing, and hunting	25,799	34,322	39,876	41,367	22,154	28,600	33,129	34,159
Mining	69,644	86,560	102,270	102,647	57,983	73,161	88,615	87,214
Utilities	80,304	104,284	117,264	120,795	64,742	77,409	86,667	87,578
Construction	46,145	53,139	61,047	63,578	38,563	43,948	51,226	52,321
Manufacturing	53,285	64,534	71,318	74,477	43,933	50,909	56,373	57,374
Wholesale trade	59,059	68,006	75,567	75,888	50,853	57,922	65,089	64,896
Retail trade	31,110	35,468	37,223	37,807	26,585	29,230	30,861	31,195
Transportation and warehousing	47,985	55,737	60,257	61,376	39,057	43,865	48,286	48,453
Information	71,023	83,067	92,766	94,182	62,582	68,330	76,747	77,231
Finance and insurance	75,339	92,949	104,472	102,051	64,561	77,981	88,034	84,555
Real estate and rental and leasing	43,195	50,768	55,113	54,825	37,146	43,708	47,849	47,290
Professional, scientific, and technical services	71,541	81,862	91,704	93,221	62,568	69,767	79,266	80,077
Management of companies and enterprises [1]	89,918	106,577	122,431	118,437	74,201	87,971	101,450	96,586
Administrative and waste management services	28,934	36,942	41,921	43,158	25,035	31,370	35,961	36,761
Educational services	34,085	41,730	46,521	48,315	29,243	34,844	39,221	40,785
Health care and social assistance	41,701	51,850	56,897	58,373	35,269	42,286	47,071	48,354
Arts, entertainment, and recreation	37,296	43,210	50,123	49,860	32,479	37,149	43,746	43,219
Accommodation and food services	20,801	24,809	26,745	27,162	18,047	21,018	23,121	23,405
Other services, except government	30,118	35,781	39,727	40,600	25,989	30,465	34,217	34,885
Government	53,344	68,229	77,185	79,770	40,767	49,894	55,891	57,320
Federal	69,842	99,230	111,845	117,780	46,470	64,184	70,785	73,765
State and local	48,707	60,161	68,265	69,913	39,164	46,174	52,058	53,056

[1] Consists of offices of bank and other holding companies and of corporate, subsidiary, and regional managing offices.
Source: U.S. Bureau of Economic Analysis, *Survey of Current Business*, April 2011. See also <http://www.bea.gov/national/nipaweb/Index.asp>.

Table 644. Average Hourly and Weekly Earnings by Private Industry Group: 1990 to 2010

[In dollars. Average earnings include overtime. Data are for production employees in mining and logging, manufacturing, and construction, and nonsupervisory employees in the service providing industries. See headnote, Table 630]

Private industry group	Current dollars					Constant (1982–84) dollars [1]				
	1990	2000	2005	2009	2010	1990	2000	2005	2009	2010
AVERAGE HOURLY EARNINGS										
Total private	10.20	14.02	16.13	18.63	19.07	7.91	8.30	8.45	8.89	8.91
Mining and logging	13.40	16.55	18.72	23.29	23.83	10.39	9.80	9.80	11.11	11.14
Construction	13.42	17.48	19.46	22.66	23.22	10.40	10.35	10.19	10.81	10.85
Manufacturing	10.78	14.32	16.56	18.24	18.61	8.36	8.48	8.67	8.70	8.70
Trade, transportation, and utilities [2]	9.83	13.31	14.92	16.48	16.83	7.62	7.88	7.81	7.86	7.87
Information	13.40	19.07	22.06	25.45	25.86	10.39	11.29	11.55	12.14	12.09
Financial activities [2]	9.99	14.98	17.95	20.85	21.49	7.74	8.87	9.40	9.95	10.04
Professional and business services [2]	11.14	15.52	18.08	22.35	22.78	8.64	9.19	9.47	10.66	10.65
Education and health services [2]	10.00	13.95	16.71	19.49	20.12	7.75	8.26	8.75	9.30	9.40
Leisure and hospitality [2]	6.02	8.32	9.38	11.12	11.31	4.67	4.93	4.91	5.30	5.29
Other services	9.08	12.73	14.34	16.59	17.08	7.04	7.54	7.51	7.91	7.98
AVERAGE WEEKLY EARNINGS										
Total private	350	481	544	617	637	271	285	285	294	298
Mining and logging	603	735	854	1,007	1,063	467	435	447	480	497
Construction	513	686	750	852	892	398	406	393	406	417
Manufacturing	436	591	673	726	765	338	350	353	346	358
Trade, transportation, and utilities	332	450	498	542	560	257	266	261	258	262
Information	480	701	805	931	939	372	415	422	444	439
Financial activities [2]	355	537	645	752	777	275	318	338	359	363
Professional and business services [2]	381	535	619	776	799	295	317	324	370	373
Education and health services [2]	319	449	545	628	647	248	266	285	300	302
Leisure and hospitality [2]	156	217	241	276	281	121	129	126	132	131
Other services	298	413	443	506	524	231	245	232	242	245

[1] Earnings in current dollars divided by the Consumer Price Index (CPI-W) on a 1982–84 base; see text, Section 14.
[2] For composition of industries, see Table 625.
Source: U.S. Bureau of Labor Statistics, Current Employment Statistics, "Employment, Hours, and Earnings—National." See also <http://www.bls.gov/ces/data.htm>.

Table 645. Mean Hourly Earnings and Weekly Hours by Selected Characteristics: 2010

[Based on the National Compensation Survey (NCS). Covers civilian workers in private industry establishments and state and local governments in the 50 states and DC. Excludes private households, federal government and agriculture. The NCS obtained data from 35,408 establishments representing over 121 million workers. See source and Appendix III]

Item	Mean hourly earnings (dollars) [1]			Mean weekly hours [2]		
	Total	Private industry	State and local government	Total	Private industry	State and local government
Total	21.29	20.47	26.08	35.1	34.9	36.2
WORKER CHARACTERISTIC						
Management, professional and related	34.49	34.99	33.02	36.7	37.0	35.9
Management, business, and financial	38.81	39.42	35.32	39.3	39.7	37.4
Professional and related	32.55	32.57	32.50	35.6	35.7	35.6
Service	12.14	10.62	19.32	30.7	29.7	36.4
Sales and office	16.44	16.35	17.39	34.7	34.5	36.4
Sales and related	17.11	17.11	16.65	32.3	32.3	33.9
Office and administrative support	16.09	15.90	17.42	36.1	36.0	36.5
Natural resources, construction, and maintenance	21.21	21.24	20.97	39.0	39.0	38.8
Construction and extraction	21.18	21.31	20.13	39.0	39.0	38.7
Installation, maintenance, and repair	21.40	21.34	21.98	39.2	39.2	39.2
Production, transportation, and material moving	16.00	15.88	19.52	37.1	37.2	34.4
Production	16.26	16.18	21.69	38.9	38.8	39.5
Transportation and material moving	15.73	15.55	18.86	35.4	35.6	33.1
Full-time [3]	22.77	22.02	26.75	39.5	39.6	38.9
Part-time [3]	12.10	11.78	16.39	20.7	21.0	18.3
Union [4]	26.04	23.13	29.72	36.6	36.3	37.0
Nonunion	20.46	20.19	23.12	34.8	34.8	35.6
Time [5]	21.06	20.16	26.07	34.9	34.7	36.2
Incentive [5]	26.04	26.03	(S)	38.4	38.4	(S)
ESTABLISHMENT CHARACTERISTIC						
Goods producing [6]	(S)	22.04	(S)	(NA)	39.4	(NA)
Service providing [6]	(S)	20.09	(S)	(NA)	34.0	(NA)
1 to 49 workers	17.86	17.80	19.61	33.5	33.6	33.0
50 to 99 workers	19.24	19.10	21.40	34.3	34.2	35.8
100 to 499 workers	20.88	20.42	24.31	35.9	35.8	36.0
500 workers or more	27.02	26.65	27.68	36.9	37.0	36.7

NA Not available. S Figure does not meet publication standards. [1] Earnings are straight time hourly wages or salary, including incentive pay, cost-of-living adjustments, and hazard pay. Excludes premium pay for overtime, vacations and holidays, nonproduction bonuses and tips. [2] Mean weekly hours are the hours an employee is sched+++uled to work in a week exclusive of overtime [3] Based on definition used by each establishment. [4] Workers whose wages are determined through collective bargaining. [5] Time worker wages are based solely on an hourly rate or salary. Incentive workers wages are based at least in part on productivity payments such as piece rates or commissions. [6] For private industry only. See footnotes 3 and 4, Table 632, for composition of goods and service producing industries.
Source: U.S. Bureau of Labor Statistics, National Compensation Survey: Occupational Earnings in the United States, 2010, Bulletin 2753, May 2011. See also <http://www.bls.gov/ncs/ncswage2010.htm>.

Labor Force, Employment, and Earnings **419**

Table 646. Employment and Wages: 2000 to 2009

[(7,879 represents 7,879,000). See headnote, Table 647]

Employment and wages	Unit	2000	2004	2005	2006	2007	2008	2009
Establishments:								
Total............................	1,000	**7,879**	**8,365**	**8,571**	**8,784**	**8,972**	**9,082**	**9,003**
Excluding federal	1,000	7,829	8,313	8,518	8,731	8,908	9,018	8,938
Private	1,000	7,622	8,093	8,295	8,505	8,681	8,789	8,709
State government	1,000	65	65	66	67	67	68	67
Local governments	1,000	141	155	157	159	160	161	161
Federal government............	1,000	50	52	53	53	64	64	66
Average annual employment:								
Total	1,000	**129,877**	**129,278**	**131,572**	**133,834**	**135,366**	**134,806**	**128,608**
Excluding federal..............	1,000	127,006	126,539	128,838	131,105	132,640	132,044	125,781
Private..........................	1,000	110,015	108,490	110,611	112,719	114,012	113,189	106,947
State government	1,000	4,370	4,485	4,528	4,566	4,611	4,643	4,640
Local governments	1,000	12,620	13,564	13,699	13,820	14,016	14,212	14,194
Federal government............	1,000	2,871	2,740	2,734	2,729	2,726	2,762	2,827
Annual wages:								
Total	Bil. dol.	**4,588**	**5,088**	**5,352**	**5,693**	**6,018**	**6,142**	**5,859**
Excluding federal..............	Bil. dol.....	4,455	4,929	5,188	5,523	5,841	5,959	5,668
Private..........................	Bil. dol.....	3,888	4,246	4,480	4,781	5,058	5,135	4,829
State government	Bil. dol.....	159	184	191	200	212	223	226
Local governments	Bil. dol.....	409	499	517	541	572	601	612
Federal government............	Bil. dol.....	133	158	164	170	177	183	192
Average annual wage per employee:								
Total	Dol.	**35,323**	**39,354**	**40,677**	**42,535**	**44,458**	**45,563**	**45,559**
Excluding federal..............	Dol.	35,077	38,955	40,270	42,124	44,038	45,129	45,060
Private..........................	Dol.	35,337	39,134	40,505	42,414	44,362	45,371	45,155
State government	Dol.	36,296	41,118	42,249	43,875	45,903	47,980	48,742
Local governments	Dol.	32,387	36,805	37,718	39,179	40,790	42,274	43,140
Federal government............	Dol.	46,228	57,782	59,864	62,274	64,871	66,293	67,756
Average weekly wage per employee:								
Total	Dol.	**679**	**757**	**782**	**818**	**855**	**876**	**876**
Excluding federal..............	Dol.	675	749	774	810	847	868	867
Private..........................	Dol.	680	753	779	816	853	873	868
State government	Dol.	698	791	812	844	883	923	937
Local governments	Dol.	623	708	725	753	784	813	830
Federal government............	Dol.	889	1,111	1,151	1,198	1,248	1,275	1,303

Source: U.S. Bureau of Labor Statistics, "Employment and Wages Annual Averages, 2009," <http://www.bls.gov/cew/cewbultn09.htm>.

Table 647. Average Annual Wage, by State: 2008 and 2009

[In dollars, except percent change. Based on federal-state cooperative program, The Quarterly Census of Employment and Wages (QCEW), also referenced as ES-202. Includes workers covered by state unemployment insurance laws and for federal civilian workers covered by unemployment compensation for federal employees, approximately 97 percent of employees on nonfarm payrolls in 2009. Excludes most agricultural workers on small farms, all Armed Forces, elected officials in most states, railroad employees, most domestic workers, most student workers at school, value of meals and lodging, and tips and other gratuities. Minus sign (–) indicates decrease]

State	Average wage per employee		Percent change,	State	Average wage per employee		Percent change,
	2008	2009	2008–2009		2008	2009	2008–2009
United States	**45,563**	**45,559**	**–0.01**	Missouri..........	40,361	40,022	–0.84
Alabama	38,734	39,422	1.78	Montana..........	33,305	33,762	1.37
Alaska............	45,805	47,103	2.83	Nebraska..........	36,243	36,644	1.11
Arizona...........	42,518	42,832	0.74	Nevada...........	42,984	42,743	–0.56
Arkansas..........	34,919	35,692	2.21	New Hampshire.....	44,912	44,932	0.04
California..........	51,487	51,566	0.15	New Jersey	55,280	55,168	–0.20
Colorado	46,614	46,861	0.53	New Mexico........	37,910	38,529	1.63
Connecticut........	58,395	57,771	–1.07	New York.........	60,288	57,739	–4.23
Delaware	47,569	47,770	0.42	North Carolina......	39,740	39,844	0.26
District of Columbia...	76,518	77,483	1.26	North Dakota.......	35,075	35,970	2.55
Florida............	40,568	40,970	0.99	Ohio.............	40,784	40,900	0.28
Georgia	42,585	42,902	0.74	Oklahoma	37,284	37,238	–0.12
Hawaii	40,675	41,328	1.61	Oregon...........	40,500	40,757	0.63
Idaho............	33,897	34,124	0.67	Pennsylvania	44,381	44,829	1.01
Illinois............	48,719	48,358	–0.74	Rhode Island.......	43,029	43,439	0.95
Indiana...........	38,403	38,270	–0.35	South Carolina......	36,252	36,759	1.40
Iowa.............	36,964	37,158	0.52	South Dakota.......	32,822	33,352	1.61
Kansas...........	38,178	38,154	–0.06	Tennessee	39,996	40,242	0.62
Kentucky	37,434	37,996	1.50	Texas............	45,939	45,692	–0.54
Louisiana..........	40,381	40,579	0.49	Utah.............	37,980	38,614	1.67
Maine............	36,317	36,617	0.83	Vermont..........	38,328	38,778	1.17
Maryland	49,535	50,579	2.11	Virginia...........	47,241	48,239	2.11
Massachusetts.......	56,746	56,267	–0.84	Washington........	46,569	47,470	1.93
Michigan..........	44,245	43,645	–1.36	West Virginia	35,987	36,897	2.53
Minnesota	45,826	45,319	–1.11	Wisconsin	39,119	39,131	0.03
Mississippi..........	33,508	33,847	1.01	Wyoming	41,487	40,709	–1.88

Source: U.S. Bureau of Labor Statistics, "Employment and Wages Online Annual Averages, 2009," <http://www.bls.gov/cew/cewbultn09.htm>.

Table 648. Full-Time Wage and Salary Workers—Number and Earnings: 2000 to 2010

[In current dollars of usual weekly earnings. Data represent annual averages (101,210 represents 101,210,000). Full time workers are those who usually worked 35 hours or more at all jobs combined. Based on the Current Population Survey; see text, Section 1 and Appendix III. For definition of median, see Guide to Tabular Presentation]

Characteristic	Number of workers (1,000)			Median weekly earnings (dollars)		
	2000	2005 [1]	2010 [1]	2000	2005 [1]	2010 [1]
All workers [2]	**101,210**	**103,560**	**99,531**	**576**	**651**	**747**
Male	57,107	58,406	55,059	641	722	824
Female	44,103	45,154	44,472	493	585	669
White [3]	83,228	84,110	80,656	590	672	765
Black [3]	12,410	12,388	11,658	474	520	611
Asian [3, 4]	4,598	4,651	4,946	615	753	855
Hispanic [5]	12,761	14,673	14,837	399	471	535
OCCUPATION						
Management, professional and related occupations	34,831	36,908	39,145	810	937	1,063
Management, business, and financial operations	14,240	14,977	15,648	877	997	1,155
Professional and related occupations	20,590	21,931	23,497	770	902	1,008
Computer and mathematical occupations	3,051	2,924	3,202	938	1,132	1,289
Architecture and engineering occupations	2,781	2,509	2,366	949	1,105	1,255
Life, physical, and social science occupations	989	1,164	1,127	811	965	1,062
Community and social services occupations	1,641	1,797	1,909	629	725	1,909
Legal occupations	1,039	1,162	1,248	919	1,052	1,213
Education, training, and library occupations	5,467	6,066	6,535	704	798	913
Arts, design, entertainment, sports, and media	1,488	1,488	1,431	724	819	920
Healthcare practitioner and technical occupations	4,134	4,821	5,678	727	878	986
Service occupations	12,595	14,123	14,424	365	413	479
Healthcare support occupations	1,731	2,085	2,219	358	410	471
Protective service occupations	2,281	2,549	2,872	591	678	747
Food preparation and serving-related occupations	3,483	4,007	3,823	317	356	406
Building and grounds cleaning and maintenance	3,354	3,425	3,310	351	394	446
Personal care and service occupations	1,746	2,057	2,199	351	409	455
Sales and office occupations	25,606	25,193	23,060	492	575	631
Sales and related occupations	9,650	10,031	9,121	525	622	666
Office and administrative support occupations	15,956	15,161	13,939	480	550	619
Natural resources, construction, and maintenance occupations	10,958	12,086	9,869	582	623	719
Farming, fishing, and forestry occupations	842	755	729	310	372	416
Construction and extraction occupations	5,852	6,826	5,020	580	604	709
Installation, maintenance, and repair occupations	4,263	4,504	4,120	628	705	794
Production, transportation, and material-moving occupations	17,221	15,251	13,034	475	540	599
Production occupations	10,378	8,403	6,861	471	538	599
Transportation and material-moving occupations	6,843	6,848	6,172	481	543	599

[1] See footnote 2, Table 586. [2] Includes other races, not shown separately. [3] Beginning 2005, for persons in this race group only. See footnote 4, Table 587. [4] 2000, includes Pacific Islanders. [5] Persons of Hispanic origin may be any race.
Source: U.S. Bureau of Labor Statistics, "Employment and Earnings Online," January 2011 issue, March 2011, <http://www.bls.gov/opub/ee/home.htm> and <http://www.bls.gov/cps/home.htm>.

Table 649. Median Usual Weekly Earnings of Full-Time Wage and Salary Workers: 1980 to 2010

[In current dollars, except as indicated. For wage and salary workers 25 years and over. Based on Current Population Survey; see text, Section 1 and Appendix III. Wages and salaries are collected before taxes and other deductions and include overtime pay, commissions, or tips usually received at principal job. Earnings reported on basis other than weekly are converted to a weekly equivalent. Excludes all incorporated and unincorporated self employed]

Year and sex	Total	Less than a high school diploma	High school, no college [1]	Some college or associate's degree	Bachelor's degree and higher [2]
CURRENT DOLLARS					
Male:					
1980	339	267	327	358	427
1990 [3]	512	349	459	542	741
2000 [3]	693	406	591	691	1,020
2010 [3]	874	486	710	845	1,330
Female:					
1980	213	164	201	231	290
1990 [3]	369	240	315	395	535
2000 [3]	516	304	420	505	756
2010 [3]	704	388	543	638	986
WOMEN'S EARNINGS AS PERCENT OF MEN'S					
1980	62.8	61.4	61.5	64.5	67.9
1990 [3]	72.1	68.8	68.6	72.9	72.2
2000 [3]	74.5	74.9	71.1	73.1	74.1
2010 [3]	80.5	79.8	76.5	75.5	74.1

[1] Includes persons with a high school diploma or equivalent. [2] Includes persons with a bachelor's, master's, professional, or doctoral degree. [3] Data not strictly comparable to data for earlier years. See text this section and <http://www.bls.gov/cps/eetech_methods.pdf>.
Source: U.S. Bureau of Labor Statistics, "Highlights of Women's Earnings in 2010," Report 1031, July 2011, <http://www.bls.gov/cps/cpswom2010.pdf>.

Table. 650. Workers With Earnings by Occupation of Longest Held Job and Sex: 2009

[As of March. 72,972 represents 72,972,000. For definition of median, see Guide to Tabular Presentation. Beginning with 2009 income data, the Census Bureau expanded the income intervals used to calculate medians to $250,000 or more. Medians falling in the upper open-ended interval are plugged with "$250,000." Before 2009, the upper open-ended interval was $100,000 and a plug of "$100,000" was used. Based on Annual Social and Economic Supplement (ASEC) of Current Population Survey; includes Civilian noninstitutional population, 15 years old and over, and military personnel who live in households with at least one other civilian adult. See text, Section 1, and Appendix III]

Major occupation group of longest job held in 2009	All workers				Full-time, year-round			
	Female		Male		Female		Male	
	Number (1,000)	Median earnings (dol.)	Number (1,000)	Median earnings (dol.)	Number (1,000)	Median earnings (dol.)	Number (1,000)	Median earnings (dol.)
Total....................	72,972	26,030	81,934	36,331	43,217	36,278	56,053	47,127
Management, business, and financial occupations...........	9,380	45,591	12,737	61,495	7,347	51,014	10,633	70,183
Professional and related occupations.................	19,051	39,890	13,890	57,496	12,037	48,856	10,574	66,369
Service occupations	16,128	14,298	11,915	20,564	7,179	23,302	6,660	30,953
Sales and office occupations......	23,642	24,119	13,619	32,168	14,002	31,770	9,271	42,284
Natural resources, construction, and maintenance..............	800	17,535	14,926	31,032	398	30,731	8,988	40,712
Production, transportation, and material-moving occupations.....	3,872	20,028	14,060	30,021	2,192	25,322	9,225	36,678
Armed Forces	98	33,277	789	42,355	62	(B)	703	47,589

B Data not shown where base is less than 75,000.

Source: U.S. Census Bureau, *Income, Poverty and Health Insurance in the United States: 2009*, Current Population Reports, P60-238, and Detailed Tables—Table PINC-06, September 2009. See also <http://www.census.gov/hhes/www/cpstables/032010/perinc/toc.htm>.

Table. 651. Employment Cost Index (ECI) by Total Compensation and Occupation and Industry: 2007 to 2010

[As of December. (2005 = 100). The ECI is a measure of the rate of change in compensation (wages, salaries, and employer costs for employee benefits). Data are not seasonally adjusted. Based on North American Industry Classification System (NAICS) for classifying by industry. Based on the 2000 Standard Occupational Classification (SOC) for classifying by occupation]

Occupational group and industry	Indexes (December 2005 = 100)				Percent change for 12 months ending December			
	2007	2008	2009	2010	2007	2008	2009	2010
Civilian workers [1]...........................	**106.7**	**109.5**	**111.0**	**113.2**	**3.3**	**2.6**	**1.4**	**2.0**
State and local government	**108.4**	**111.6**	**114.2**	**116.2**	**4.1**	**3.0**	**2.3**	**1.8**
Workers, by occupational group:								
Management, professional and related occupations....	108.3	111.6	113.8	115.5	4.1	3.0	2.0	1.5
Sales and office occupations......................	108.6	111.3	114.4	116.6	4.3	2.5	2.8	1.9
Service occupations	109.1	112.4	115.3	118.0	4.4	3.0	2.6	2.3
Workers, by industry division:								
Service-providing industries: [2]								
Education and health services	108.2	111.5	113.9	115.6	3.7	3.0	2.2	1.5
Schools	108.0	111.2	113.7	115.3	3.7	3.0	2.2	1.4
Health care and social assistance................	109.3	113.2	115.4	117.9	3.4	3.6	1.9	2.2
Hospitals	108.2	111.3	114.3	117.0	3.7	2.9	2.7	2.4
Public administration [3]	109.1	112.0	114.6	116.8	5.1	2.7	2.3	1.9
Private industry workers [4].....................	**106.3**	**108.9**	**110.2**	**112.5**	**3.0**	**2.4**	**1.2**	**2.1**
Workers, by occupational group:								
Management, professional, and related occupations ...	106.8	109.9	110.7	113.0	3.2	2.9	0.7	2.1
Sales and office occupations......................	106.1	107.9	109.2	111.6	3.1	1.7	1.2	2.2
Natural resources, construction, and maintenance occupations	106.7	109.6	111.2	113.3	3.0	2.7	1.5	1.9
Production, transportation, and material moving occupations...............................	104.5	106.9	108.9	111.5	2.2	2.3	1.9	2.4
Service occupations	107.0	109.8	111.8	113.5	3.8	2.6	1.8	1.5
Workers, by industry division:								
Goods-producing industries [5]	105.0	107.5	108.6	111.1	2.4	2.4	1.0	2.3
Construction	107.6	110.9	111.7	112.7	3.9	3.1	0.7	0.9
Manufacturing	103.8	105.9	107.0	110.0	2.0	2.0	1.0	2.8
Service-providing industries [2]	106.7	109.4	110.8	113.0	3.2	2.5	1.3	2.0
Trade, transportation, and utilities	105.5	107.5	108.8	111.4	2.4	1.9	1.2	2.4
Information...................................	106.1	107.4	108.3	110.0	2.8	1.2	0.8	1.6
Financial activities	105.6	107.1	108.6	111.4	3.0	1.4	1.4	2.6
Professional and business services	107.5	111.6	112.4	114.6	3.9	3.8	0.7	2.0
Education and health services	107.7	110.6	112.8	114.7	3.5	2.7	2.0	1.7
Leisure and hospitality..........................	108.1	111.4	112.7	114.1	4.2	3.1	1.2	1.2
Bargaining status:								
Union..	105.1	108.0	111.1	114.8	2.0	2.8	2.9	3.3
Nonunion.....................................	106.5	109.1	110.1	112.1	3.2	2.4	0.9	1.8

[1] Includes private industry and state and local government workers and excludes farm, household, and federal government workers. [2] Includes all other service industries not shown seperately. For a description of NAICS industries, see text, this section.
[3] Consists of executive, legislative, judicial, administrative, and regulatory activities. [4] Excludes farm and household workers.
[5] Includes the following NAICS industries: construction and manufacturing.

Source: U.S. Bureau of Labor Statistics, "Employment Cost Index Historical Listing Current-dollar," <http://www.bls.gov/ncs/ect/home.htm>.

Table 652. Federal and State Minimum Wage Rates: 1940 to 2011

[In current dollars. As of January 31, 2011. Where an employee is subject to both the state and federal minimum wage laws, the employee is entitled to the higher minimum wage rate]

Year	Federal minimum wage rates per hour	State	2011 minimum wage rates per hour	State	2011 minimum wage rates per hour	State	2011 minimum wage rates per hour
1940........	0.30	AL.........	(1)	KY.........	7.25	ND.........	7.25
1945........	0.40	AK.........	7.75	LA.........	(1)	OH.........	[8] 7.40
1950........	0.75	AZ.........	7.35	ME.........	7.50	OK.........	[9] 7.25/2.00
1955........	0.75	AR.........	[2] 6.25	MD.........	7.25	OR.........	8.50
1960........	1.00	CA.........	8.00	MA.........	8.00	PA.........	7.25
1965........	1.25	CO.........	7.36	MI.........	[4] 7.40	RI.........	7.40
1970........	1.60	CT.........	8.25	MN.........	[5] 6.15/5.25	SC.........	(1)
1975........	2.10	DE.........	7.25	MS.........	(1)	SD.........	7.25
1980........	3.10	DC.........	8.25	MO.........	7.25	TN.........	(1)
1985........	3.35	FL.........	7.25	MT.........	[6] 7.35	TX.........	7.25
1990........	3.80	GA.........	[3] 5.15	NE.........	[2] 7.25	UT.........	7.25
1995........	4.25	HI.........	7.25	NV.........	[7] 7.25/8.25	VT.........	8.15
2000........	5.15	ID.........	7.25	NH.........	7.25	VA.........	[2] 7.25
2005........	5.15	IL.........	[2] 8.25	NJ.........	7.25	WA.........	8.67
2006........	5.15	IN.........	[4] 7.25	NM.........	7.50	WV.........	[3] 7.25
2007........	5.85	IA.........	7.25	NY.........	7.25	WI.........	7.25
2008........	6.55	KS.........	7.25	NC.........	7.25	WY.........	5.15
2009........	7.25						
2010........	7.25						
2011........	7.25						

[1] No state minimum wage law. [2] Employers of 4 or more, Illinois excluding family members. [3] Employers of 6 or more. [4] Employers of 2 or more. [5] Large employer (receipts of $625,000 or more) and small employer (with annual receipts of less than $625,000). [6] Except businesses with gross annual sales of $110,000 or less. [7] $8.25 with no health insurance benefits provided by employer. $7.25 with health insurance provided by employer and received by employee. [8] $7.25 for those employers grossing $271,000 or less. [9] Employees of 10 or more full time employees at any one location and employers with gross sales over $100,000 regardless of number of full-time employees. All other employers $2.00.

Source: U.S. Department of Labor, Wage and Hour Division, "Minimum Wage Laws in the States—January 1, 2011," <http://www.dol.gov/esa/minwage/america.htm>.

Table 653. Workers Paid Hourly Rates by Selected Characteristics: 2010

[Data are annual averages (72,902 represents 72,902,000). For employed wage and salary workers, excluding the incorporated self-employed. Based on the Current Population Survey; see text, Section 1 and Appendix III]

Characteristic	Number of workers paid hourly rates (1,000)				Percent of workers paid hourly rates			
		At or below federal minimum wage				At or below federal minimum wage		
	Total	Total	Below prevailing federal minimum wage	At prevailing federal minimum wage	Total	Total	Below prevailing federal minimum wage	At prevailing federal minimum wage
Total, 16 years and over [1]	72,902	4,360	2,541	1,820	6.0	3.5	2.5	
16 to 24 years	14,061	2,135	1,180	955	15.2	8.4	6.8	
25 years and over	58,842	2,225	1,360	865	3.8	2.3	1.5	
Male, 16 years old and over	35,498	1,612	943	669	4.5	2.7	1.9	
16 to 24 years	6,913	850	438	413	12.3	6.3	6.0	
25 years and over	28,585	762	505	257	2.7	1.8	0.9	
Female, 16 years old and over ...	37,404	2,748	1,598	1,151	7.3	4.3	3.1	
16 to 24 years	7,148	1,285	743	543	18.0	10.4	7.6	
25 years and over	30,256	1,463	855	608	4.8	2.8	2.0	
White [2]	58,529	3,429	2,015	1,414	5.9	3.4	2.4	
Men	28,949	1,254	716	538	4.3	2.5	1.9	
Women	29,580	2,174	1,299	875	7.4	4.4	3.0	
Black [2]	9,436	650	349	301	6.9	3.7	3.2	
Men	4,137	244	152	92	5.9	3.7	2.2	
Women	5,299	406	197	209	7.7	3.7	3.9	
Asian [2]	2,920	140	104	36	4.8	3.6	1.2	
Men	1,406	60	47	12	4.2	3.3	0.9	
Women	1,513	80	57	24	5.3	3.8	1.6	
Hispanic [3]	12,977	822	462	360	6.3	3.6	2.8	
Men	7,474	355	201	154	4.7	2.7	2.1	
Women	5,503	468	261	207	8.5	4.7	3.8	
Full-time workers...........	52,803	1,634	1,039	595	3.1	2.0	1.1	
Men	28,574	699	444	255	2.4	1.6	0.9	
Women	24,229	934	595	340	3.9	2.5	1.4	
Part-time workers [4]	19,994	2,716	1,496	1,220	13.6	7.5	6.1	
Men	6,871	911	498	413	13.3	7.2	6.0	
Women	13,123	1,806	998	807	13.8	7.6	6.1	
Private sector industries	63,201	4,089	2,378	1,711	6.5	3.8	2.7	
Public sector industries	9,701	271	163	109	2.8	1.7	1.1	

[1] Includes races not shown separately. Also includes a small number of multiple jobholders whose full- or part-time status cannot be determined for their principal job. [2] For persons in this race group only. See footnote 4, Table 587. [3] Persons of Hispanic or Latino origin may be any race. [4] Working fewer than 35 hours per week.

Source: U.S. Bureau of Labor Statistics, CPS Reports and Summaries, "Characteristics of Minimum Wage Workers: 2010," February 2011, <http://www.bls.gov/cps/minwage2010.htm>.

Labor Force, Employment, and Earnings 423

Table 654. Employer Costs for Employee Compensation Per Hour Worked: 2010

[In dollars. As of December. Based on the National Compensation Survey (NCS). See Appendix III]

Compensation component	Total civilian workers	State and local government workers	Private Industry workers						
			Total	Goods producing [1]	Service providing [2]	Union workers	Non-union workers	1–99 workers	100 workers or more
Total compensation	**29.72**	**40.28**	**27.75**	**32.50**	**26.78**	**37.35**	**26.72**	**22.91**	**33.26**
Wages and salaries	20.71	26.42	19.64	21.73	19.21	22.86	19.30	16.95	22.70
Total benefits	9.02	13.86	8.11	10.77	7.57	14.49	7.43	5.96	10.56
Paid leave	2.07	3.03	1.89	2.11	1.84	2.77	1.79	1.28	2.58
Vacation	0.99	1.14	0.96	1.12	0.93	1.43	0.91	0.64	1.33
Holiday	0.64	0.89	0.60	0.74	0.56	0.81	0.57	0.43	0.79
Sick	0.32	0.78	0.24	0.18	0.25	0.38	0.22	0.16	0.33
Supplemental pay	0.69	0.33	0.75	1.17	0.67	1.08	0.72	0.55	0.99
Overtime [3]	0.24	0.17	0.25	0.55	0.19	0.72	0.20	0.18	0.33
Insurance	2.62	4.81	2.22	3.07	2.04	4.90	1.93	1.51	3.02
Health insurance	2.49	4.66	2.08	2.87	1.92	4.60	1.81	1.43	2.83
Retirement and savings	1.33	3.27	0.97	1.53	0.86	2.60	0.80	0.57	1.43
Defined benefit	0.81	2.93	0.41	0.89	0.32	1.91	0.25	0.21	0.65
Defined contributions	0.52	0.34	0.56	0.64	0.54	0.70	0.54	0.37	0.77
Legally required	2.30	2.42	2.28	2.90	2.15	3.14	2.19	2.05	2.55
Social security and Medicare	1.68	1.87	1.64	1.85	1.60	2.00	1.60	1.40	1.92
Social security [4]	1.34	1.45	1.32	1.49	1.28	1.62	1.29	1.13	1.53
Medicare	0.34	0.42	0.32	0.36	0.32	0.39	0.32	0.27	0.38
Federal unemployment	0.03	–	0.03	0.03	0.03	0.03	0.03	0.04	0.03
State unemployment	0.17	0.09	0.18	0.25	0.17	0.24	0.18	0.18	0.18
Workers' compensation	0.43	0.46	0.42	0.78	0.35	0.86	0.38	0.42	0.42

– Represents or rounds to zero. [1] Based on the North American Industry Classification System, 2002 (NAICS). See text, this section. Includes mining, construction, and manufacturing. The agriculture, forestry, farming, and hunting sector is excluded. [2] Based on the 2002 NAICS. Includes utilities; wholesale and retail trade; transportation and warehousing; information; finance and insurance; real estate and rental and leasing; professional and technical services; management of companies and enterprises, administrative and waste services; education services; health care and social assistance; arts, entertainment, and recreation; accommodations and food services; and other services, except public administration. [3] Includes premium pay for work in addition to regular work schedule, such as, overtime, weekends, and holidays. [4] Comprises the Old-Age, Survivors, and Disability Insurance Program (OASDI).

Source: U.S. Bureau of Labor Statistics, *Employer Costs for Employee Compensation—December 2010*, News Release, USDL 11-0304, March 2011. See also <http://www.bls.gov/schedule/archives/ecec_nr.htm#2011>.

Table 655. Percent of Workers in Private Industry With Access to Retirement and Health Care Benefits by Selected Characteristics: 2010

[In percent (All workers = 100 percent) As of March. Based on National Compensation Survey (NCS). See headnote, Table 656, and Appendix III]

Characteristic	Retirement benefits			Healthcare benefits			
	All plans [1]	Defined benefit [2]	Defined contribution [2]	Medical care	Dental care	Vision care	Outpatient prescription drug coverage
Total	**65**	**20**	**59**	**71**	**46**	**26**	**69**
WORKER CHARACTERISTICS							
Management, professional, and related occupations	80	28	75	87	61	35	85
Service occupations	42	8	38	44	28	16	44
Sales and office occupations	70	19	65	72	46	23	70
Natural resources, construction, and maintenance occupations	64	26	56	76	44	31	74
Production, transportation, and material moving occupations	66	25	55	76	48	29	74
Full-time [3]	74	24	68	86	56	32	84
Part-time [3]	39	11	33	24	15	9	23
Union [4]	88	69	55	91	73	56	89
Nonunion [4]	62	15	59	68	43	23	67
AVERAGE HOURLY WAGE [5]							
Less than $8.10	30	4	27	23	13	8	23
$8.10 to under $10.63	40	7	36	38	20	11	37
$10.63 to under $15.70	67	16	61	76	47	24	74
$15.70 to under $24.53	75	24	68	86	55	32	84
$24.53 to under $37.02	84	38	76	90	67	42	89
$37.02 or greater	87	38	81	92	70	42	90
ESTABLISHMENT CHARACTERISTIC							
1 to 99 workers	51	10	47	59	30	18	57
100 or more workers	81	33	72	84	64	36	83
Goods producing [6]	72	29	65	85	55	33	83
Service producing [6]	63	19	58	68	44	25	66

[1] Employees may have access to both defined benefit and defined contribution plans. Total excludes duplication. [2] A defined benefit plan is a retirement plan that uses a specific, predetermined formula to calculate the amount of an employee's guaranteed future benefit. A defined contribution plan is a type of retirement plan in which the employer makes specified contributions to individual employee accounts, but the amount of the retirement benefit is not specified. [3] Employees are classified as working either a full-time or part-time schedule based on the definition used by each establishment. [4] See footnote 6, Table 656. [5] The National Compensation Survey—Benefits program presents wage data in percentiles rather than dollar amounts; for calculation detail, see "Technical Note" in source. [6] See Table 632 for composition of goods and service producing industries.

Source: U.S. Bureau of Labor Statistics, *Employee Benefits in the United States, March 2010*, News Release, USDL 10-1044, July 2010. See also <http://www.bls.gov/ncs/ebs/home.htm>.

Table 656. Percent of Workers In Private Industry With Access to Selected Employee Benefits: 2010

[As of March. Based on National Compensation Survey (NCS). The NCS benefits survey obtained data from 9,018 private industry establishments of all sizes, representing over 98 million workers. Excludes agricultural establishments, private households, and the self-employed. An employee has access to a benefit plan if the plan is made available by the employer, regardless of whether the employee participates in the plan. See Appendix III]

Characteristic	Leave benefits						Quality of life benefits			Nonproduction bonuses	
					Family leave [1]		Employer assistance for child care [2]	Flexible workplace [3]	Subsidized commuting [4]	All non-production bonuses [5]	End of year bonus
	Paid holidays	Paid sick leave	Paid vacation	Paid jury duty leave	Paid	Unpaid					
Total	**78**	**62**	**77**	**68**	**10**	**85**	**9**	**5**	**5**	**44**	**11**
WORKER CHARACTERISTIC											
Management, professional, and related occupations	89	86	87	85	17	90	18	13	11	52	13
Service occupations	54	42	59	49	6	79	9	1	2	30	6
Sales and office occupations	81	67	80	72	11	86	7	5	5	48	12
Natural resources, construction, and maintenance occupations	79	51	78	57	7	77	4	2	3	47	14
Production, transportation, and material moving occupations	84	54	83	69	5	85	5	1	3	44	10
Full-time [6]	90	74	91	77	12	88	11	6	7	50	13
Part-time [6]	40	26	37	42	5	76	6	2	2	27	6
Union [7]	88	71	87	85	10	91	14	1	6	37	4
Nonunion [7]	76	61	76	66	10	84	9	5	5	45	12
AVERAGE HOURLY WAGE [8]											
Less than $8.10	35	19	39	33	3	72	6	(Z)	1	24	5
$8.10 to under $10.63	52	32	53	44	4	78	5	1	1	30	6
$10.63 to under $15.70	85	66	84	71	9	85	7	3	3	46	11
$15.70 to under $24.53	90	75	89	78	12	88	9	6	7	51	13
$24.53 to under $37.02	89	84	89	85	16	90	17	12	11	54	14
$37.02 or greater	89	86	89	87	18	91	19	16	14	56	15
ESTABLISHMENT CHARACTERISTIC											
Goods producing [9]	88	54	88	70	8	86	7	4	2	52	14
Service producing [9]	75	64	75	68	11	84	10	5	6	43	10
GEOGRAPHIC AREA [10]											
New England	76	69	75	80	12	88	9	7	9	47	9
Middle Atlantic	80	67	77	78	9	83	9	6	6	42	11
East North Central	79	58	78	69	11	83	11	5	4	45	12
West North Central	75	62	76	66	9	86	11	5	5	45	13
South Atlantic	78	60	79	69	11	83	9	5	5	47	10
East South Central	79	55	77	69	6	90	9	3	4	48	13
West South Central	80	63	78	69	9	82	(NA)	3	2	46	13
Mountain	75	62	77	65	9	82	8	5	3	44	9
Pacific	75	65	76	59	12	87	10	4	9	39	11

NA Not available. Z Less than 0.5 percent. [1] Some workers may have access to both types of plans. [2] A workplace program that provides for either the full or partial cost of caring for an employee's children in a nursery, day care center, or a baby sitter in facilities either on or off the employer's premises. [3] Permits employees to set their own schedules within a general set of parameters. Employees generally are required to work a minimum number of core hours each day. [4] Employers subsidize employees' cost of commuting to and from work via public transportation, company-sponsored van pool, discounted subway fares, for example. [5] All nonproduction bonuses include cash profit sharing bonuses, employee recognition bonuses, holiday bonuses, end of year bonuses, payment in lieu of benefits bonuses referral bonuses, and others bonuses. [6] Employees are classified as working either a full-time or part-time schedule based on the definition used by each establishment. [7] Union workers are those whose wages are determined through collective bargaining. [8] The National Compensation Survey—Benefits program presents wage data in percentiles rather than dollar amounts; see "Technical Note" in source. [9] See Table 632, for composition of goods and service producing industries. [10] Composition of divisions: New England = Connecticut, Maine, Massachusetts, New Hampshire, Rhode Island, and Vermont; Middle Atlantic = New Jersey, New York, and Pennsylvania; East North Central = Illinois, Indiana, Michigan, Ohio, and Wisconsin; West North Central = Iowa, Kansas, Minnesota, Nebraska, North Dakota, and Missouri; South Atlantic = Delaware, District of Columbia, Florida, Georgia, Maryland, North Carolina, South Carolina, Virginia, and West Virginia; East South Central = Alabama, Kentucky, Mississippi, and Tennessee; West South Central = Arkansas, Louisiana, Oklahoma, and Texas; Mountain = Arizona, Colorado, Idaho, Montana, Nevada, New Mexico, Utah, and Wyoming; and Pacific = Alaska, California, Hawaii, Oregon, and Washington.

Source: U.S. Bureau of Labor Statistics, Employee Benefits in the United States, March 2010, Bulletin 2752, September 2010. See also <http://www.bls.gov/ncs/ebs/benefits/2010/>.

Table 657. Workers Killed or Disabled on the Job: 1970 to 2009

[Data for 2009 are preliminary estimates (1.7 represents 1,700). Excludes homocides and suicides. Estimates based on data from the U.S. National Center for Health Statistics, state vital statistics departments, state industrial commissions and beginning 1995, Bureau of Labor Statistics, Census of Fatal Occupational Injuries. Numbers of workers based on data from the U.S. Bureau of Labor Statistics]

Year	Manufacturing		Nonmanufacturing		Disabling injuries [2] (millions)	Year and industry group	Deaths, 2009		Medically consulted injuries, [3] 2009 (1,000)
	Number (1,000)	Rate [1]	Number (1,000)	Rate [1]			Number	Rate	
1970....	1.7	9	12.1	21	2.2	Total [4]	3,582	2.8	5,100
1980 ...	1.7	8	11.5	15	2.2	Agriculture [5].................	527	25.4	110
1990...	1.0	5	9.1	9	3.9	Mining [6].....................	101	12.8	20
1995....	0.6	3	4.4	4	3.6	Construction	776	9.3	360
1998....	0.6	3	4.5	4	3.8	Manufacturing	280	2.0	600
1999....	0.6	3	4.6	4	3.8	Wholesale trade..............	165	4.3	130
2000....	0.6	3	4.4	4	3.9	Retail trade	133	1.0	580
2001....	0.5	3	4.5	4	3.9	Transportation and warehousing.....	526	11.0	250
2002....	0.5	3	4.2	3	3.7	Utilities.....................	17	1.8	30
2003...	0.4	3	4.3	4	3.4	Information..................	28	1.0	60
2004 ...	0.4	3	4.6	4	3.7	Financial activities [7].........	53	0.6	140
2005....	0.4	2	4.6	4	3.7	Professional & business services [7] ...	341	2.5	240
2006....	0.4	3	4.7	4	3.7	Educational & health services.......	92	0.5	920
2007....	0.4	2	4.4	3	3.5	Leisure & hospitality [7]	110	1.1	390
2008....	0.4	2	4.0	3	3.2	Other services [8].................	103	1.7	170
2009....	0.3	2	3.3	3	[3] 5.1	Government....................	336	1.8	1,100

[1] See footnote 2, Table 657. [2] See footnote 3, Table 657. [3] Beginning with 2009 data, the concept of medically consulted injury was adopted in place of disabling injury. A medically consulted injury is an injury serious enough that a medical professional was consulted. Medically consulted injuries are not comparable to previous disabling injury estimates. [4] Includes deaths where industry is not known. [5] Includes forestry, fishing, and hunting. [6] Includes oil and gas extraction. [7] For composition of industry, see Table 632. [8] Excludes public service administration.

Source: National Safety Council, Itasca, IL, *Accident Facts*, annual through 1998 edition; thereafter, *Injury Facts*, annual (copyright).

Table 658. Worker Deaths, Injuries, and Production Time Lost: 2000 to 2009

[47.0 represents 47,000. Data may not agree with Table 660 because data here are not revised]

Item	Deaths (1,000)			Disabling injuries [1] (mil.)			Production time lost (mil. days)					
							In current year			In future years [3]		
	2000	2005	2009	2000	2005	2009 [2]	2000	2005	2009	2000	2005	2009
All accidents	**47.0**	**54.3**	**59.4**	**10.5**	**11.9**	**19.5**	**240**	**275**	**310**	**460**	**535**	**590**
On the job	5.2	5.0	3.6	3.9	3.7	5.1	80	80	55	60	65	45
Off the job	41.8	49.3	55.8	6.6	8.2	14.4	160	195	255	400	470	545
Motor vehicle.....	22.8	24.1	18.2	1.2	1.3	1.8	(NA)	(NA)	(NA)	(NA)	(NA)	(NA)
Public nonmotor vehicle....	8.3	10.0	8.7	2.8	3.3	3.3	(NA)	(NA)	(NA)	(NA)	(NA)	(NA)
Home.................	10.7	15.2	28.9	2.6	3.6	9.3	(NA)	(NA)	(NA)	(NA)	(NA)	(NA)

NA Not available. [1] See footnote 2, Table 657. [2] See footnote 3, Table 657. [3] Based on an average of 5,850 days lost in future years per fatality and 565 days lost in future years per permanent injury.

Source: National Safety Council, Itasca, IL, *Injury Facts*, annual (copyright).

Table 659. Industries With the Highest Total Case Incidence Rates for Nonfatal Injuries and Illnesses: 2009

[Rates per 100 full-time employees. Private industry unless otherwise noted. Incidence rates refer to any Occupational Safety & Health Administration (OSHA)-recordable occupational injury or illness, whether or not it resulted in days away from work, job transfer, or restriction. Incidence rates were calculated as: Number of injuries and illnesses divided by total hours worked by all employees during the year multiplied by 200,000 as base for 100 full-time equivalent workers (working 40 hours per week, 50 weeks per year)]

Industry	2007 NAICS code [1]	Incidence rate	Industry	2007 NAICS code [1]	Incidence rate
All Industries, including State and local government [2].....................	**(X)**	**3.9**	Iron and steel pipe and tube manufacturing from purchased steel	33121	9.5
			Scheduled passenger air transportation	481111	9.5
Fire protection [3].......................	92216	15.3	Light truck and utility vehicle manufacturing .	336112	9.4
Pet and pet supplies stores..........	45391	13.6	Veterinary services	54194	9.4
Heavy and civil engineering construction [3] ...	237	13.1	Animal (except poultry) slaughtering.......	311611	9.3
Police protection [3]...................	92212	12.7	Soft drink manufacturing	312111	9.1
Iron foundries.......................	331511	11.3	Aluminum foundries (except die-casting)....	331524	9.0
Nursing and residential care facilities [3]	623	11.1	Nursing care facilities	6231	8.9
Hospitals [4]	622	11.0	Other metal container manufacturing	332439	8.6
Skiing facilities......................	71392	10.5	Other residential care facilities	6239	8.6
Travel trailer and camper manufacturing	336214	10.2	Psychiatric and substance abuse hospitals..	6222	8.5
Beet sugar manufacturing..............	311313	10.0	Fluid milk manufacturing	311511	8.4
Ambulance services	62191	9.9	Truck trailer manufacturing...............	336212	8.4

X Not applicable [1] Based on the North American Industry Classification System, 2007 (NAICS). See text, this section. [2] Excludes farms with fewer than 11 employees. [3] Local Government. [4] State Government.

Source: U.S. Bureau of Labor Statistics, News Release, *Workplace Injuries and Illnesses—2009*, News Release USDL 10-1451, October 2010. See also <http://www.bls.gov/iif/oshsum.htm#09Summary%20News%20Release>.

Table 660. Nonfatal Occupational Injuries and Illnesses by Industry: 2009

[4,140.7 represents 4,140,700. Rates per 100 full-time employees. Except as noted, data refer to any Occupational Safety and Health Administration (OSHA) recordable occupational injury or illness, whether or not it resulted in days away from work, job transfer, or restriction. Incidence rates were calculated as: number of injuries and illnesses divided by total hours worked by all employees during the year multiplied by 200,000 as base for 100 full-time equivalent workers (working 40 hours, per week, 50 weeks per year)]

Industry	2007 NAICS code [1]	Annual average employment [2]	Number of cases (1,000)	Incidence rate of cases
Total [3]	(X)	130,315.8	4,140.7	3.9
Private industry	(X)	111,469.1	3,277.7	3.6
Agriculture, forestry, fishing, hunting	11	977.7	44.9	5.3
Mining [4]	21	689.1	17.7	2.4
Construction	23	6,700.5	251.0	4.3
Manufacturing	31–33	12,696.5	528.6	4.3
Wholesale trade	42	5,850.7	185.9	3.3
Retail trade	44–45	15,058.9	487.2	4.2
Transportation and warehousing [5]	48–49	4,171.2	206.9	5.2
Utilities	22	567.6	18.4	3.3
Information	51	2,932.2	49.3	1.9
Finance and insurance	52	5,813.6	45.3	0.8
Real estate and rental and leasing	53	2,091.3	59.3	3.3
Professional, scientific, and technical services	54	7,832.1	82.2	1.2
Management of companies and enterprises	55	1,933.4	30.3	1.7
Administrative and support and waste management and remediation services	56	7,601.4	134.3	2.9
Educational services	61	2,454.9	41.0	2.4
Health care and social assistance	62	15,904.6	667.3	5.4
Arts, entertainment, and recreation	71	2,106.0	63.2	4.9
Accommodation and food services	72	11,480.3	277.4	3.7
Other services, except public administration	81	4,607.1	87.4	2.9
State and local government [3]	(X)	18,846.7	862.9	5.8
State government	(X)	4,883.2	193.0	4.6
Local government	(X)	13,963.6	670.0	6.3

X Not applicable. [1] North American Industry Classification System, 2007; see text, this section. [2] Employment figure primarily derived from Quarterly Census of Employment and Wages (QCEW). [3] Excludes farms with fewer than 11 employees. [4] Data for Mining (Sector 21 in the North American Industry Classification System—United States, 2007) include establishments not governed by the Mine Safety and Health Administration rules and reporting, such as those in Oil and Gas Extraction and related support activities. Data for mining operators in coal, metal, and nonmetal mining are provided to BLS by the Mine Safety and Health Administration, U.S. Department of Labor. Independent mining contractors are excluded from the coal, metal, and nonmetal mining industries. These data do not reflect the changes the Occupational Safety and Health Administration made to its recordkeeping requirements effective January 1, 2002; therefore, estimates for these industries are not comparable to estimates in other industries. [5] Data for employers in railroad transportation are provided to BLS by the Federal Railroad Administration, U.S. Department of Transportation.

Source: U.S. Bureau of Labor Statistics, News Release, *Workplace Injuries and Illnesses—2009*, News Release, USDL 10-1451, October 2010. See also <http://www.bls.gov/iif/oshsum.htm#09Summary%20News%20Release>.

Table 661. Fatal Work Injuries by Event or Exposure: 2009

[For the 50 states and the District of Columbia. Based on the Census of Fatal Occupational Injuries. For details, see source. Due to methodological differences, data differ from National Safety Council data]

Event or exposure	Number of fatalities	Percent distribution	Event or exposure	Number of fatalities	Percent distribution
Total	4,551	100	Contacts with objects and equipment [1]	741	16
			Struck by object or equipment [1]	420	9
Transportation incidents [1]	1,795	39	Struck by falling object or equipment	272	6
Highway incident [1]	985	22	Struck by flying object	41	1
Collision between vehicles, mobile equipment	466	10	Caught in or compressed by equipment or objects	233	5
Noncollision incidents	240	5	Caught in or crushed in collapsing materials	80	2
Nonhighway incident (farm, industrial premises)	261	6	Falls	645	14
Aircraft accidents	159	3	Exposure to harmful substances or environments [1]	404	9
Pedestrians struck by a vehicle, mobile equipment	268	6	Contact with electric current	170	4
Water vehicle accidents	86	2	Exposure to caustic, noxious or allergenic substances	129	3
Railway accidents	34	1	Oxygen deficiency	62	1
Assaults and violent acts [1]	837	18	Drowning, submersion	51	1
Homicides [1]	542	12	Fires and explosions	113	2
Shooting	434	10	Other events and exposures	16	(Z)
Stabbing	49	1			
Self-inflicted injury	263	6			

Z Less than 0.5 percent. [1] Includes other causes, not shown separately.

Source: U.S. Bureau of Labor Statistics, "Census of Fatal Occupational Injuries (CFOI)—Current and Revised Data," <http://www.bls.gov/iif/oshcfoi1.htm>.

Table 662. Workplace Violence Incidents and Security Measures: 2005

[In percent. Covers period September 2004 to June 2006. Based on establishment survey; see source for details]

Incident or security measure	Total	Industry			Employment size				
		Private industry [1]	State government	Local government	1 to 10 employees	11 to 49 employees	50 to 249 employees	250 to 999 employees	1,000 or more employees
Any workplace violence incidents	5.3	4.8	32.2	14.7	2.4	9.1	16.0	28.8	49.9
Criminal	2.2	2.1	8.7	3.7	1.4	3.5	4.7	6.8	17.2
Customer or client	2.2	1.9	15.4	10.3	1.0	3.9	6.4	12.2	28.3
Co-worker	2.3	2.1	17.7	4.3	0.6	4.6	8.1	16.8	34.1
Domestic violence	0.9	0.8	5.5	2.1	0.1	2.0	2.9	9.0	24.1
No incident	92.1	92.5	65.3	85.1	95.6	87.8	77.8	63.9	43.8
Selected types of security provided:									
Intruder/burglar systems	41.8	42.1	29.1	35.5	35.7	53.9	57.5	54.2	61.0
Surveillance cameras	22.6	22.2	45.2	32.7	17.0	29.2	47.9	69.1	77.9
Motion detectors	26.9	27.1	14.8	21.3	24.0	32.9	33.7	28.3	36.4
Metal detectors	0.9	0.7	16.0	4.3	0.5	1.1	2.5	7.2	15.7
Electronic badges [2]	6.3	6.0	35.6	9.0	3.9	7.2	20.8	45.1	60.1
Security guards	9.5	9.1	48.6	10.5	6.4	11.7	24.8	53.9	65.3
Limited access [3]	30.7	30.0	58.0	50.7	26.0	35.9	52.5	68.3	83.2
Physical barriers [4]	13.4	13.1	27.2	23.6	10.2	18.2	24.5	33.5	46.5
Lighting of work areas	39.1	38.7	55.8	48.5	32.2	50.0	62.1	71.9	80.4
Workplace violence training provided:									
Any training	20.8	20.2	58.0	32.3	14.6	29.1	45.7	64.2	67.8
No training	78.4	78.9	42.0	67.6	84.3	70.5	54.0	35.6	32.0

[1] Excludes farms with fewer than 11 employees. [2] Or ID scanner at entry or exit. [3] Secured entry/locked doors [4] Between work areas and the public.

Source: U.S. Bureau Labor Statistics, *Survey of Workplace Violence and Prevention—2005*, News Release, USDL 06-1860, October 2006. See also <http://www.bls.gov/iif/home.htm>.

Table 663. Work Stoppages: 1960 to 2010

[896 represents 896,000. Excludes work stoppages involving fewer than 1,000 workers and lasting less than 1 day. The term "major work stoppage" includes both worker-initiated strikes and employer-initiated lockouts that involve 1,000 workers or more. Information is based on reports of labor disputes appearing in daily newspapers, trade journals, and other public sources. The parties to the disputes are contacted by telephone, when necessary, to clarify details of the stoppages]

Year	Number of work stoppages [1]	Workers involved [2] (1,000)	Days idle		Year	Number of work stoppages [1]	Workers involved [2] (1,000)	Days idle	
			Number [3] (1,000)	Percent estimated working time [4]				Number [3] (1,000)	Percent estimated working time [4]
1960.	222	896	13,260	0.09	1992.	35	364	3,989	0.01
1970.	381	2,468	52,761	0.29	1993.	35	182	3,981	0.01
1975.	235	965	17,563	0.09	1994.	45	322	5,021	0.02
1976.	231	1,519	23,962	0.12	1995.	31	192	5,771	0.02
1977.	298	1,212	21,258	0.10	1996.	37	273	4,889	0.02
1978.	219	1,006	23,774	0.11	1997.	29	339	4,497	0.01
1979.	235	1,021	20,409	0.09	1998.	34	387	5,116	0.02
1980.	187	795	20,844	0.09	1999.	17	73	1,996	0.01
1981.	145	729	16,908	0.07	2000.	39	394	20,419	0.06
1982.	96	656	9,061	0.04	2001.	29	99	1,151	(Z)
1983.	81	909	17,461	0.08	2002.	19	46	660	(Z)
1984.	62	376	8,499	0.04	2003.	14	129	4,091	0.01
1985.	54	324	7,079	0.03	2004.	17	171	3,344	0.01
1986.	69	533	11,861	0.05	2005.	22	100	1,736	0.01
1987.	46	174	4,481	0.02	2006.	20	70	2,688	0.01
1988.	40	118	4,381	0.02	2007.	21	189	1,265	(Z)
1989.	51	452	16,996	0.07	2008.	15	72	1,954	0.01
1990.	44	185	5,926	0.02	2009.	5	13	124	(Z)
1991.	40	392	4,584	0.02	2010.	11	45	302	(Z)

Z Less than 0.005 percent. [1] Beginning in year indicated. [2] Workers counted more than once if involved in more than one stoppage during the year. [3] Resulting from all stoppages in effect in a year, including those that began in an earlier year. [4] Agricultural and government employees are included in the total working time; private household and forestry and fishery employees are excluded.

Source: U.S. Bureau of Labor Statistics, *Major Work Stoppages in 2010*, News Release, USDL 11-0153, February 2011. See also <http://www.bls.gov/news.release/wkstp.toc.htm>.

Table 664. Labor Union Membership by Sector: 1985 to 2010

[Annual averages of monthly figures (16,996 represents 16,996,000). For wage and salary workers in agriculture and non-agriculture. Data represent union members by place of residence. Based on the Current Population Survey and subject to sampling error. For methodological details, see source]

Sector	1985	1990	1995	2000	2005	2007	2008	2009	2010
TOTAL (1,000)									
Wage and salary workers:									
Union members..............	16,996	16,740	16,360	16,258	15,685	15,670	16,098	15,327	14,715
Covered by unions.............	19,358	19,058	18,346	17,944	17,223	17,243	17,761	16,904	16,290
Public sector workers:									
Union members..............	5,743	6,485	6,927	7,111	7,430	7,557	7,832	7,897	7,623
Covered by unions.............	6,921	7,691	7,987	7,976	8,262	8,373	8,676	8,678	8,406
Private sector workers:									
Union members..............	11,253	10,255	9,432	9,148	8,255	8,114	8,265	7,431	7,092
Covered by unions.............	12,438	11,366	10,360	9,969	8,962	8,870	9,084	8,226	7,884
PERCENT									
Wage and salary workers:									
Union members..............	18.0	16.1	14.9	13.5	12.5	12.1	12.4	12.3	11.9
Covered by unions.............	20.5	18.3	16.7	14.9	13.7	13.3	13.7	13.6	13.1
Public sector workers:									
Union members..............	35.7	36.5	37.7	37.5	36.5	35.9	36.8	37.4	36.2
Covered by unions.............	43.1	43.3	43.5	42.0	40.5	39.8	40.7	41.1	40.0
Private sector workers:									
Union members..............	14.3	11.9	10.3	9.0	7.8	7.5	7.6	7.2	6.9
Covered by unions.............	15.9	13.2	11.3	9.8	8.5	8.2	8.4	8.0	7.7

Source: The Bureau of National Affairs, Inc., Arlington, VA, *Union Membership and Earnings Data Book: Compilations from the Current Population Survey* (2011 edition), (copyright by The Bureau of National Affairs, BNA PLUS); authored by Barry Hirsch of Georgia State University and David Macpherson of Trinity University. See also <http://bnaplus.bna.com/LaborReports.aspx> and <http://unionstats.gsu.edu/>.

Table 665. Union Members by Selected Characteristics: 2010

[Annual averages of monthly data (124,073 represents 124,073,000). Covers employed wage and salary workers 16 years old and over. Excludes self-employed workers whose businesses are incorporated although they technically qualify as wage and salary workers. Based on Current Population Survey, see text, Section 1 and Appendix III]

Characteristic	Employed wage and salary workers			Median usual weekly earnings [3] (dollars)			
		Percent					
	Total (1,000)	Union members [1]	Repre-sented by union [2]	Total	Union members [1]	Repre-sented by union [2]	Not repre-sented by union
Total [4]	**124,073**	**11.9**	**13.1**	**747**	**917**	**911**	**717**
AGE							
16 to 24 years old	16,638	4.3	5.0	432	585	580	423
25 to 34 years old	28,363	10.1	11.2	682	847	840	657
35 to 44 years old	27,356	12.8	14.2	824	961	954	792
45 to 54 years old	28,860	15.0	16.5	844	955	950	813
55 to 64 years old	18,199	15.7	17.2	860	975	971	828
65 years and over	4,657	9.3	10.4	684	823	821	665
SEX							
Men	63,531	12.6	13.8	824	967	964	789
Women	60,542	11.1	12.4	669	856	847	639
RACE							
White [5].........................	101,042	11.7	13.0	765	943	936	736
Men	52,565	12.5	13.7	850	988	985	817
Women	48,477	10.9	12.2	684	882	872	651
Black [5]	14,195	13.4	14.9	611	772	766	589
Men	6,347	14.8	16.2	633	829	827	606
Women	7,848	12.2	13.8	592	729	720	574
Asian [5]	5,900	10.9	12.1	855	909	918	842
Men	3,112	9.4	10.4	936	924	941	936
Women	2,787	12.6	13.9	773	904	909	749
HISPANIC OR LATINO ETHNICITY							
Hispanic [6].......................	18,263	10.0	11.1	535	771	766	512
Men	10,646	10.2	11.2	560	804	800	525
Women	7,616	9.6	10.8	508	729	724	489
INDUSTRY [7]							
Private sector	103,040	6.9	7.7	717	864	855	703
Mining	695	8.0	8.8	1,032	1,076	1,053	1,026
Construction.....................	6,103	13.1	13.7	735	1,051	1,046	692
Manufacturing....................	13,252	10.7	11.6	767	828	817	759
Wholesale and retail trade	17,800	4.8	5.3	612	669	657	610
Transportation and utilities	5,195	21.8	23.2	823	1,000	994	765
Information	2,743	9.6	10.9	912	1,018	998	895
Financial activities	8,072	2.0	2.5	849	806	799	852
Professional and business services ...	11,738	2.7	3.3	855	751	754	859
Education and health services	19,804	8.1	9.4	731	849	846	717
Leisure and hospitality	11,111	2.7	3.0	469	580	575	461
Other services	5,397	2.9	3.4	615	866	862	609
Public sector	21,033	36.2	40.0	878	961	956	801

[1] Members of a labor union or an employee association similar to a labor union. [2] Members of a labor union or an employee association similar to a union as well as workers who report no union affiliation but whose jobs are covered by a union or an employee association contract. [3] For full-time employed wage and salary workers. [4] Includes races not shown separately. Also includes a small number of multiple jobholders whose full- and part-time status cannot be determined for their principal job. [5] For persons in this race group only. See footnote 4, Table 587. [6] Persons of Hispanic origin may be any race. [7] For composition of industries, see Table 632.

Source: U.S. Bureau of Labor Statistics, *Union Members in 2010*, News Release, USDL-11-0063, January 2011. See also <http://www.bls.gov/news.release/union2.toc.htm>.

Labor Force, Employment, and Earnings 429

Table 666. Labor Union Membership by State: 1985 and 2010

[Annual averages of monthly figures (16,996.1 represents 16,996,100). For wage and salary workers in agriculture and non-agriculture. Data represent union members by place of residence. Based on the Current Population Survey and subject to sampling error. For methodological details, see source]

State	Union members (1,000)		Workers covered by unions (1,000)		Percent of workers					
					Union members		Covered by unions		Private sector union members	
	1985	2010	1985	2010	1985	2010	1985	2010	1985	2010
United States	**16,996.1**	**14,715.1**	**19,358.1**	**16,289.5**	**18.0**	**11.9**	**20.5**	**13.1**	**14.3**	**6.9**
Alabama [1]	226.6	183.3	254.9	202.8	15.7	10.1	17.6	11.2	13.5	5.7
Alaska	47.7	67.6	53.4	73.0	25.0	22.9	28.0	24.8	17.0	11.2
Arizona [1]	115.6	161.0	145.7	203.0	9.5	6.4	12.0	8.1	7.9	3.6
Arkansas [1]	91.6	43.6	108.4	58.6	11.2	4.0	13.3	5.4	9.5	2.7
California	2,123.1	2,431.3	2,485.8	2,577.8	20.4	17.5	23.9	18.6	15.8	9.3
Colorado	165.2	140.4	191.1	170.9	11.8	6.6	13.7	8.0	8.9	3.8
Connecticut	306.5	258.3	325.9	269.7	20.9	16.7	22.2	17.4	14.4	8.3
Delaware	45.6	40.2	50.9	43.9	16.6	11.4	18.5	12.5	12.8	5.8
District of Columbia	45.2	25.9	58.2	30.0	16.5	9.0	21.2	10.5	13.9	5.9
Florida [1]	395.2	391.8	515.7	488.0	9.1	5.6	11.9	6.9	5.3	2.3
Georgia [1]	239.5	153.3	273.1	191.3	10.0	4.0	11.4	5.0	9.1	2.5
Hawaii	109.6	111.3	121.2	120.3	27.8	21.8	30.8	23.5	19.7	14.6
Idaho [1]	41.7	41.5	48.4	50.1	11.7	7.1	13.6	8.6	9.8	3.6
Illinois.............	1,031.7	843.8	1,124.9	891.2	22.2	15.5	24.3	16.4	19.2	9.5
Indiana.............	476.7	278.6	524.4	312.8	21.3	10.9	23.4	12.2	20.8	8.2
Iowa [1].............	181.7	158.2	212.8	191.8	17.0	11.4	20.0	13.8	14.5	7.1
Kansas [1]	129.0	83.7	157.3	111.0	12.8	6.8	15.6	9.1	11.4	4.5
Kentucky	219.2	146.5	250.8	166.1	16.5	8.9	18.8	10.1	16.4	7.2
Louisiana [1]	147.9	75.6	172.8	96.0	9.6	4.3	11.2	5.5	7.9	3.2
Maine..............	77.5	62.9	90.0	70.7	17.1	11.6	19.8	13.0	11.2	5.1
Maryland	329.9	296.1	412.9	328.8	16.7	11.6	20.9	12.9	13.0	6.1
Massachusetts........	495.4	414.8	548.4	446.4	18.5	14.5	20.4	15.6	13.0	7.0
Michigan	1,004.5	627.3	1,071.0	658.7	28.4	16.5	30.3	17.3	23.5	11.1
Minnesota	407.5	384.6	452.7	397.3	22.6	15.6	25.1	16.1	16.7	8.4
Mississippi [1]	81.3	46.3	94.5	58.3	9.3	4.5	10.8	5.6	8.4	3.7
Missouri............	378.3	244.3	418.9	274.4	18.7	9.9	20.7	11.1	19.1	8.5
Montana............	57.3	46.1	66.9	52.2	19.4	12.7	22.7	14.4	14.9	5.6
Nebraska [1]	78.8	75.3	99.0	95.6	12.7	9.3	16.0	11.8	10.3	4.8
Nevada [1]	89.7	151.3	102.1	169.9	21.6	15.0	24.6	16.8	19.5	10.8
New Hampshire.......	48.8	63.2	54.8	72.6	10.7	10.2	12.0	11.7	6.9	4.4
New Jersey	821.0	636.9	937.2	660.0	24.9	17.1	28.4	17.7	19.0	9.0
New Mexico	49.4	54.8	62.4	72.4	10.0	7.3	12.7	9.7	8.9	2.6
New York	2,102.3	1,958.7	2,298.3	2,098.6	30.2	24.2	33.0	26.0	21.3	13.7
North Carolina [1]	167.0	116.7	209.5	179.6	6.4	3.2	8.0	4.9	4.7	1.8
North Dakota [1]	27.9	23.0	34.2	28.4	11.4	7.4	14.0	9.1	6.4	4.6
Ohio...............	999.0	654.9	1,090.9	701.9	23.6	13.7	25.7	14.7	20.7	8.4
Oklahoma [2]	128.4	77.4	151.0	98.5	10.5	5.5	12.3	6.9	8.2	3.5
Oregon..............	231.6	245.1	260.8	267.9	22.7	16.2	25.6	17.7	16.7	9.1
Pennsylvania.........	1,055.4	770.2	1,174.7	831.4	22.8	14.7	25.4	15.9	19.1	9.3
Rhode Island	90.2	74.9	97.7	79.4	21.1	16.4	22.9	17.4	12.7	8.4
South Carolina [1].......	58.8	79.6	72.5	106.8	4.5	4.6	5.6	6.2	3.8	2.7
South Dakota [1]........	27.9	20.0	34.5	23.5	11.2	5.6	13.8	6.6	7.5	3.0
Tennessee [1]..........	236.8	115.5	281.8	142.5	13.1	4.7	15.6	5.8	10.9	2.2
Texas [1]	474.8	545.4	626.2	676.7	7.4	5.4	9.7	6.7	5.6	3.2
Utah [1]...............	69.9	74.6	91.9	95.6	11.4	6.5	14.9	8.4	8.0	3.9
Vermont............	28.5	34.2	35.4	39.5	12.8	11.8	15.9	13.6	7.1	5.3
Virginia [1]	236.0	160.6	296.7	196.4	9.7	4.6	12.2	5.7	8.6	2.9
Washington	405.8	551.8	469.2	605.2	25.0	19.4	28.9	21.3	18.6	10.7
West Virginia	134.7	99.9	148.3	111.4	22.7	14.8	25.0	16.5	22.2	11.2
Wisconsin	435.9	354.9	463.9	379.8	22.3	14.2	23.8	15.1	17.8	8.4
Wyoming [1]	26.8	18.1	34.2	20.7	13.8	7.4	17.6	8.4	11.2	4.9

[1] Right to work state. [2] Passed right to work law in 2001.

Source: The Bureau of National Affairs (BNA), Inc., Arlington, VA, *Union Membership and Earnings Data Book: Compilations from the Current Population Survey* (2011 edition), (copyright by BNA PLUS); authored by Barry Hirsch of Georgia State University and David Macpherson of Trinity University. See also <http://unionstats.gsu.edu> and <http://bnaplus.bna.com/LaborReports.aspx>.

U.S. Census Bureau, Statistical Abstract of the United States: 2012

Section 13
Income, Expenditures, Poverty, and Wealth

This section presents data on gross domestic product (GDP), gross national product (GNP), national and personal income, saving and investment, money income, poverty, and national and personal wealth. The data on income and expenditures measure two aspects of the U.S. economy. One aspect relates to the National Income and Product Accounts (NIPA), a summation reflecting the entire complex of the nation's economic income and output and the interaction of its major components; the other relates to the distribution of money income to families and individuals or consumer income.

The primary source for data on GDP, GNP, national and personal income, gross saving and investment, and fixed assets and consumer durables is the *Survey of Current Business*, published monthly by the Bureau of Economic Analysis (BEA). A comprehensive revision to the NIPA was released beginning in July 2009. Discussions of the revision appeared in the March, August, September, October, and November 2009 issues of the *Survey of Current Business*. Summary historical estimates appeared in the August 2009 issue of the *Survey of Current Business*. Detailed historical data can be found on BEA's Web site at <http://www.bea.gov/>.

Sources of income distribution data are the decennial censuses of population, the Current Population Survey (CPS), and the American Community Survey, all products of the U.S. Census Bureau (see text, Section 1 and Section 4). Annual data on income of families, individuals, and households are presented in *Current Population Reports, Consumer Income,* P60 Series, in print. Many data series are also found on the Census Web site at <http://www.census.gov/hhes /www/income/income.html>. Data on the household sector's saving and assets are published by the Board of Governors of the Federal Reserve System in the quarterly statistical release *Flow of Funds Accounts*. The Federal Reserve Board also periodically conducts the *Survey of Consumer Finances*, which presents financial information on family assets and net worth. The most recent survey is available at <http://www.federalreserve.gov/pubs /oss/oss2/scfindex.html>. Detailed information on personal wealth is published periodically by the Internal Revenue Service (IRS) in *SOI Bulletin*.

National income and product—
GDP is the total output of goods and services produced by labor and property located in the United States, valued at market prices. GDP can be viewed in terms of the expenditure categories that comprise its major components: personal consumption expenditures, gross private domestic investment, net exports of goods and services, and government consumption expenditures and gross investment. The goods and services included are largely those bought for final use (excluding illegal transactions) in the market economy. A number of inclusions, however, represent imputed values, the most important of which is the rental value of owner–occupied housing. GDP, in this broad context, measures the output attributable to the factors of production located in the United States. GDP by state is the gross market value of the goods and services attributable to labor and property located in a state. It is the state counterpart of the nation's GDP.

The featured measure of real GDP is an index based on chain-type annual weights. Changes in this measure of real output and prices are calculated as the average of changes based on weights for the current and preceding years. (Components of real output are weighted by price, and components of prices are weighted by output.) These annual changes are "chained" (multiplied) together to form a time series that allows for the effects of changes in relative prices and changes in the composition of output over time. Quarterly and monthly changes are based on quarterly and monthly weights, respectively.

U.S. Census Bureau, Statistical Abstract of the United States: 2012

The output indexes are expressed as 2005 = 100, and for recent years, in 2005 dollars; the price indexes are also based to 2005 = 100. For more information on chained–dollar indexes, see the article on this subject in the November 2003 issue of the *Survey of Current Business*.

Chained (2005) dollar estimates of most components of GDP are not published for periods prior to 1990, because during periods far from the base period, the levels of the components may provide misleading information about their contributions to an aggregate. Values are published in index form (2005 = 100) for 1929 to the present to allow users to calculate the percent changes for all components, which are accurate for all periods. In addition, BEA publishes estimates of contributions of major components to the percent change in GDP for all periods.

Gross national product measures the output attributable to all labor and property supplied by United States residents. GNP differs from "national income" mainly in that GNP includes allowances for depreciation—that is, consumption of fixed capital.

National income includes all net incomes net of consumption of fixed capital (CFC), earned in production. National income is the sum of compensation of employees, proprietors' income with inventory valuation adjustment (IVA) and capital consumption adjustment (CCAdj), rental income of persons with CCAdj, corporate profits with IVA and CCAdj, net interest and miscellaneous payments, taxes on production and imports, business current transfer payments (net), and current surplus of government enterprises, less subsidies.

Capital consumption adjustment for corporations and for nonfarm sole proprietorships and partnerships is the difference between capital consumption based on income tax returns and capital consumption measured using empirical evidence on prices of used equipment and structures in resale markets, which have shown that depreciation for most types of assets approximates a geometric pattern. The tax return data are valued at historical costs and reflect changes over time in service lives and depreciation patterns as permitted by tax regulations. Inventory valuation adjustment represents the difference between the book value of inventories used up in production and the cost of replacing them.

Personal income is the current income received by persons from all sources minus their personal contributions for government social insurance. Classified as "persons" are individuals (including owners of unincorporated firms), nonprofit institutions that primarily serve individuals, private trust funds, and private noninsured welfare funds. Personal income includes personal current transfer receipts (payments not resulting from current production) from government and business such as social security benefits, public assistance, etc., but excludes transfers among persons. Also included are certain nonmonetary types of income chiefly, estimated net rental value to owner-occupants of their homes and the value of services furnished without payment by financial intermediaries. Capital gains (and losses) are excluded.

Disposable personal income is personal income less personal current taxes. It is the income available to persons for spending or saving. Personal current taxes are tax payments (net of refunds) by persons (except personal contributions for government social insurance) that are not chargeable to business expense. Personal taxes include income taxes, personal property taxes, motor vehicle licenses, and other miscellaneous taxes.

Gross domestic product by industry—The BEA also prepares estimates of value added by industry. *Value added* is a measure of the contribution of each private industry and of government to the nation's GDP. It is defined as an industry's gross output (which consists of sales or receipts and other operating income, commodity taxes, and inventory change) minus its intermediate inputs (which consists of energy, raw materials, semi-finished goods, and services that are purchased from domestic industries or from foreign sources). These estimates of value added are produced for

U.S. Census Bureau, Statistical Abstract of the United States: 2012

61 private industries and for 4 government classifications—federal general government and government enterprises and state and local general government and government enterprises.

The estimates by industry are available in current dollars and are derived from the estimates of gross domestic income, which consists of three components—the compensation of employees, gross operating surplus, and taxes on production and imports, less subsidies. Real, or inflation-adjusted, estimates are also prepared.

Regional Economic Accounts—
These accounts consist of estimates of state and local area personal income and of gross domestic product by state and are consistent with estimates of personal income and gross domestic product in the Bureau's national economic accounts. BEA's estimates of state and local area personal income provide a framework for analyzing individual state and local economies, and they show how the economies compare with each other. The *personal income* of a state and/or local area is the income received by, or on behalf of, the residents of that state or area. Estimates of labor and proprietors' earnings by place of work indicate the economic activity of business and government within that area, and estimates of personal income by place of residence indicate the income within the area that is available for spending. BEA prepares estimates for states, counties, metropolitan areas, and BEA economic areas.

Gross domestic product by state estimates measure the value added to the nation's production by the labor and property in each state. GDP by state is often considered the state counterpart of the nation's GDP. The GDP by state estimates provide the basis for analyzing the regional impacts of national economic trends. GDP by state is measured as the sum of the distributions by industry and state of the components of gross domestic income; that is, the sum of the costs incurred and incomes earned in the production of GDP by state. The GDP estimates are presented in current dollars and in real (chained dollars) for 63 industries.

Consumer Expenditure Survey—
The Consumer Expenditure Survey program began in 1980. The principal objective of the survey is to collect current consumer expenditure data, which provide a continuous flow of data on the buying habits of American consumers. The data are necessary for future revisions of the Consumer Price Index.

The survey conducted by the Census Bureau for the Bureau of Labor Statistics consists of two components: (1) an interview panel survey in which the expenditures of consumer units are obtained in five interviews conducted every 3 months, and (2) a diary or recordkeeping survey completed by participating households for two consecutive 1-week periods.

Each component of the survey queries an independent sample of consumer units representative of the U.S. total population. Each quarter of the year, approximately 3,200 consumer units are sampled for the diary survey. Each consumer unit keeps a diary for two 1-week periods yielding approximately 6,400 diaries a year. The interview sample is selected on a rotating panel basis, targeted at 15,000 consumer units. Data are collected in 91 areas of the country that are representative of the U.S. total population. The survey includes students in student housing. Data from the two surveys are combined; integration is necessary to permit analysis of total family expenditures because neither the diary nor quarterly interview survey was designed to collect a complete account of consumer spending.

Distribution of money income to families and individuals—
Money income statistics are based on data collected in various field surveys of income conducted since 1936. Since 1947, the Census Bureau has collected the data on an annual basis and published them in *Current Population Reports*, P60 Series. In each of the surveys, field representatives interview samples of the population with respect to income received during the previous year. *Money income* as defined by the Census Bureau differs from the BEA concept of "personal income." Data on consumer income

Income, Expenditures, Poverty, and Wealth 433

collected in the CPS by the Census Bureau cover money income received (exclusive of certain money receipts such as capital gains) before payments for personal income taxes, social security, union dues, medicare deductions, etc. Therefore, money income does not reflect the fact that some families receive part of their income in the form of noncash benefits (see Section 11) such as food stamps, health benefits, and subsidized housing; that some farm families receive noncash benefits in the form of rent-free housing and goods produced and consumed on the farm; or that noncash benefits are also received by some nonfarm residents, which often take the form of the use of business transportation and facilities, full or partial payments by business for retirement programs, medical and educational expenses, etc. These elements should be considered when comparing income levels. None of the aggregate income concepts (GDP, national income, or personal income) is exactly comparable with money income, although personal income is the closest. For a definition of families and households, see text, Section 1.

Poverty—Families and unrelated individuals are classified as being above or below poverty following the Office of Management and Budget's Statistical Policy Directive 14. The Census Bureau uses a set of thresholds that vary by family size and composition.

The poverty calculation is based solely on money income and does not reflect the fact that many low-income persons receive noncash benefits such as food stamps, medicaid, and public housing.

The original thresholds were based on the U.S. Department of Agriculture's 1961 Economy Food Plan and reflected the different consumption requirements of families. The poverty thresholds are updated every year to reflect changes in the Consumer Price Index. The following technical changes to the thresholds were made in 1981: (1) distinctions based on sex of householder were eliminated, (2) separate thresholds for farm families were dropped, and (3) the matrix was expanded to families of nine or more persons from the old cutoff of seven or more persons. These changes were incorporated in the calculation of poverty data beginning with 1981. Besides the Census Bureau Web site at <http://www.census.gov/hhes/www/poverty/poverty.html>, information on poverty guidelines and research may be found at the U.S. Department of Human Services Web site at <http://aspe.hhs.gov/poverty/index.shtml>.

In the recent past, the Census Bureau has published a number of technical papers and reports that presented experimental poverty estimates based on income definitions that counted the value of selected government noncash benefits. The Census Bureau has also published reports on after-tax income.

Statistical reliability—For a discussion of statistical collection and estimation, sampling procedures, and measures of statistical reliability pertaining to Census Bureau data, see Appendix III.

Table 667. Gross Domestic Product in Current and Chained (2005) Dollars: 1970 to 2010

[In billions of dollars (1,038 represents $1,038,000,000,000). For explanation of gross domestic product and chained dollars, see text, this section. Minus sign (−) indicates decline in inventories or net imports]

Item	1970	1980	1990	1995	1998	1999	2000	2001	2002	2003	2004	2005	2006	2007	2008	2009	2010
CURRENT DOLLARS																	
Gross domestic product	**1,038**	**2,788**	**5,801**	**7,415**	**8,794**	**9,354**	**9,952**	**10,286**	**10,642**	**11,142**	**11,868**	**12,638**	**13,399**	**14,062**	**14,369**	**14,119**	**14,660**
Personal consumption expenditures	648	1,756	3,836	4,987	5,919	6,343	6,830	7,149	7,439	7,804	8,285	8,819	9,323	9,806	10,105	10,001	10,349
Durable goods	90	226	497	636	780	857	916	946	992	1,015	1,062	1,106	1,133	1,159	1,084	1,027	1,089
Nondurable goods	229	573	994	1,180	1,330	1,433	1,543	1,588	1,618	1,713	1,831	1,968	2,089	2,198	2,296	2,204	2,336
Services	330	956	2,344	3,172	3,809	4,053	4,371	4,615	4,829	5,077	5,393	5,745	6,101	6,449	6,725	6,771	6,923
Gross private domestic investment	152	479	861	1,144	1,511	1,642	1,772	1,662	1,647	1,730	1,969	2,172	2,327	2,295	2,097	1,589	1,828
Fixed investment	150	486	846	1,113	1,447	1,581	1,718	1,700	1,635	1,713	1,904	2,122	2,267	2,266	2,138	1,716	1,756
Change in private inventories	2	−6	15	31	64	61	55	−38	12	16	65	50	60	29	−41	−127	72
Net exports of goods and services	4	−13	−78	−91	−162	−262	−382	−371	−427	−504	−619	−723	−769	−714	−710	−386	−516
Exports	60	281	552	812	954	989	1,093	1,028	1,003	1,041	1,180	1,305	1,471	1,662	1,843	1,578	1,838
Imports	56	294	630	903	1,116	1,251	1,475	1,399	1,430	1,545	1,799	2,028	2,240	2,376	2,554	1,965	2,354
Government consumption expenditures and gross investment	234	566	1,182	1,374	1,526	1,631	1,731	1,846	1,983	2,113	2,233	2,370	2,518	2,674	2,878	2,915	3,000
Federal	113	244	508	519	531	555	576	612	681	757	825	876	932	976	1,080	1,140	1,214
National defense	88	168	374	349	346	361	371	393	438	498	551	589	625	662	737	772	818
Nondefense	26	76	134	170	185	194	205	219	243	259	274	287	307	314	343	368	397
State and local	120	322	674	855	995	1,076	1,155	1,235	1,303	1,356	1,408	1,494	1,587	1,698	1,799	1,775	1,786
CHAINED (2005) DOLLARS																	
Gross domestic product	**4,270**	**5,839**	**8,034**	**9,094**	**10,284**	**10,780**	**11,226**	**11,347**	**11,553**	**11,841**	**12,264**	**12,638**	**12,976**	**13,229**	**13,229**	**12,881**	**13,248**
Personal consumption expenditures	2,740	3,766	5,316	6,079	6,866	7,241	7,608	7,814	8,022	8,248	8,533	8,819	9,074	9,290	9,265	9,154	9,314
Durable goods	(NA)	(NA)	(NA)	512	667	754	820	864	930	986	1,051	1,106	1,150	1,199	1,136	1,095	1,178
Nondurable goods	(NA)	(NA)	(NA)	1,438	1,580	1,661	1,715	1,746	1,780	1,846	1,905	1,968	2,024	2,064	2,041	2,017	2,073
Services	(NA)	(NA)	(NA)	4,208	4,662	4,853	5,093	5,219	5,318	5,418	5,578	5,745	5,900	6,028	6,082	6,033	6,065
Gross private domestic investment	475	718	994	1,259	1,695	1,844	1,970	1,832	1,807	1,872	2,058	2,172	2,230	2,162	1,957	1,516	1,775
Fixed investment	(NA)	(NA)	(NA)	1,236	1,630	1,782	1,914	1,878	1,798	1,856	1,993	2,122	2,171	2,133	1,997	1,631	1,695
Change in private inventories	(NA)	(NA)	(NA)	32	72	69	60	−42	13	17	66	50	59	28	−38	−113	63
Net exports of goods and services	(NA)	(NA)	(NA)	−99	−253	−357	−452	−472	−549	−604	−688	−723	−729	−655	−504	−363	−423
Exports	176	352	600	846	1,049	1,094	1,188	1,122	1,099	1,117	1,223	1,305	1,422	1,554	1,648	1,491	1,666
Imports	237	345	673	945	1,301	1,451	1,640	1,594	1,648	1,721	1,911	2,028	2,151	2,209	2,152	1,854	2,088
Government consumption expenditures and gross investment	1,234	1,359	1,864	1,889	1,985	2,056	2,098	2,178	2,280	2,331	2,362	2,370	2,402	2,434	2,503	2,543	2,568
Federal	(NA)	(NA)	(NA)	704	681	695	698	727	780	831	865	876	895	906	972	1,028	1,077
National defense	(NA)	(NA)	(NA)	477	448	456	454	471	505	549	580	589	598	612	658	693	720
Nondefense	(NA)	(NA)	(NA)	228	234	239	244	256	274	282	285	287	297	294	314	335	357
State and local	(NA)	(NA)	(NA)	1,184	1,304	1,362	1,400	1,452	1,501	1,500	1,497	1,494	1,507	1,528	1,533	1,519	1,497
Residual	−118	−11	−67	−176	−88	−50	−24	−29	−20	−12	−4	–	−2	−1	16	38	11

− Represents or rounds to zero. NA Not available.

Source: U.S. Bureau of Economic Analysis, Survey of Current Business, April 2011. See also <http://www.bea.gov/national/nipaweb/SelectTable.asp?Selected=N>.

Income, Expenditures, Poverty, and Wealth 435

Table 668. Real Gross Domestic Product, Chained (2005) Dollars—Annual Percent Change: 1990 to 2010

[Change from immediate previous year; for example, 1990, change from 1989. Minus sign (–) indicates decrease]

Component	1990	2000	2003	2004	2005	2006	2007	2008	2009	2010
Gross domestic product (GDP)	**1.9**	**4.1**	**2.5**	**3.6**	**3.1**	**2.7**	**1.9**	**–**	**–2.6**	**2.9**
Personal consumption expenditures	2.0	5.1	2.8	3.5	3.4	2.9	2.4	–0.3	–1.2	1.7
Durable goods	–0.4	8.8	6.0	6.6	5.2	4.1	4.2	–5.2	–3.7	7.7
Nondurable goods	1.2	3.2	3.7	3.2	3.4	2.8	2.0	–1.1	–1.2	2.7
Services	3.0	5.0	1.9	2.9	3.0	2.7	2.2	0.9	–0.8	0.5
Gross private domestic investment	–3.4	6.8	3.6	10.0	5.5	2.7	–3.1	–9.5	–22.6	17.1
Fixed investment	–2.1	7.4	3.2	7.3	6.5	2.3	–1.8	–6.4	–18.3	3.9
Nonresidential	0.5	9.8	0.9	6.0	6.7	7.9	6.7	0.3	–17.1	5.7
Structures	1.5	7.8	–3.8	1.1	1.4	9.2	14.1	5.9	–20.4	–13.7
Equipment and software	–	10.5	2.5	7.7	8.5	7.4	3.7	–2.4	–15.3	15.3
Residential	–8.6	1.0	8.2	9.8	6.2	–7.3	–18.7	–24.0	–22.9	–3.0
Exports	9.0	8.6	1.6	9.5	6.7	9.0	9.3	6.0	–9.5	11.7
Goods	8.4	11.1	1.8	8.5	7.5	9.4	9.8	6.3	–12.0	14.7
Services	10.5	2.7	1.2	11.9	5.0	7.9	8.3	5.3	–3.9	5.7
Imports	3.6	13.0	4.4	11.0	6.1	6.1	2.7	–2.6	–13.8	12.6
Goods	2.9	13.4	4.9	11.0	6.8	5.9	2.9	–3.5	–15.8	14.8
Services	6.5	11.0	1.9	11.2	2.8	7.1	1.4	2.4	–4.2	3.5
Government consumption expenditures and gross investment	3.2	2.0	2.2	1.4	0.3	1.4	1.3	2.8	1.6	1.0
Federal	2.0	0.5	6.6	4.1	1.3	2.1	1.2	7.3	5.7	4.8
National defense	–	–0.5	8.7	5.7	1.5	1.6	2.2	7.5	5.4	3.9
Nondefense	8.2	2.4	2.8	1.0	0.9	3.2	–0.8	6.7	6.5	6.6
State and local	4.1	2.8	–0.1	–0.2	–0.2	0.9	1.4	0.3	–0.9	–1.4

– Represents or rounds to zero.
Source: U.S. Bureau of Economic Analysis, *Survey of Current Business*, April 2011. See also <http://www.bea.gov/national/nipaweb/SelectTable.asp?Selected=N>.

Table 669. Gross Domestic Product in Current and Chained (2005) Dollars by Type of Product and Sector: 1990 to 2010

[In billions of dollars (5,801 represents $5,801,000,000,000). For explanation of chained dollars, see text, this section]

Type of product and sector	1990	2000	2004	2005	2006	2007	2008	2009	2010
CURRENT DOLLARS									
Gross domestic product	**5,801**	**9,952**	**11,868**	**12,638**	**13,399**	**14,062**	**14,369**	**14,119**	**14,660**
PRODUCT									
Goods	1,923	3,125	3,334	3,473	3,661	3,837	3,764	3,687	4,067
Durable goods	981	1,770	1,785	1,891	1,977	2,069	2,006	1,802	2,070
Nondurable goods	942	1,355	1,549	1,582	1,683	1,768	1,758	1,886	1,997
Services [1]	3,344	5,878	7,319	7,802	8,286	8,792	9,251	9,321	9,570
Structures	534	949	1,215	1,363	1,453	1,433	1,355	1,111	1,024
SECTOR									
Business [2]	4,454	7,716	9,085	9,696	10,284	10,771	10,864	10,521	11,018
Nonfarm [3]	4,377	7,642	8,966	9,594	10,191	10,657	10,732	10,417	10,894
Farm	77	74	118	102	93	115	131	104	125
Households and institutions	624	1,157	1,424	1,506	1,603	1,686	1,808	1,838	1,841
General government [4]	723	1,079	1,359	1,437	1,512	1,605	1,698	1,760	1,801
Federal	259	315	412	439	461	486	517	552	579
State and local	464	764	947	998	1,051	1,119	1,181	1,209	1,222
CHAINED (2005) DOLLARS									
Gross domestic product	**8,034**	**11,226**	**12,264**	**12,638**	**12,976**	**13,229**	**13,229**	**12,881**	**13,248**
PRODUCT									
Goods	1,920	3,056	3,326	3,473	3,653	3,803	3,784	3,642	4,047
Durable goods	(NA)	1,625	1,778	1,891	1,989	2,111	2,093	1,883	2,201
Nondurable goods	(NA)	1,430	1,548	1,582	1,663	1,694	1,693	1,748	1,845
Services [1]	5,269	6,919	7,613	7,802	7,985	8,170	8,291	8,278	8,345
Structures	942	1,245	1,326	1,363	1,341	1,267	1,167	974	904
SECTOR									
Business [2]	5,815	8,501	9,380	9,696	9,992	10,195	10,100	9,731	10,091
Nonfarm [3]	5,760	8,418	9,282	9,594	9,892	10,105	9,995	9,620	9,977
Farm	56	84	98	102	99	90	102	109	111
Households and institutions	1,010	1,376	1,457	1,506	1,540	1,572	1,630	1,622	1,625
General government [4]	1,266	1,349	1,427	1,437	1,445	1,463	1,497	1,521	1,529
Federal	484	411	436	439	438	442	459	486	503
State and local	789	939	991	998	1,007	1,021	1,038	1,035	1,027

NA Not available. [1] Includes government consumption expenditures, which are for services (such as education and national defense) produced by government. In current dollars, these services are valued at their cost of production. [2] Equals gross domestic product excluding gross value added of households and institutions and of general government. [3] Equals gross domestic business value added excluding gross farm value added. [4] Equals compensation of general government employees plus general government consumption of fixed capital.
Source: U.S. Bureau of Economic Analysis, *Survey of Current Business*, April 2011. See also <http://www.bea.gov/national/nipaweb/SelectTable.asp?Selected=N>.

Table 670. Gross Domestic Product in Current and Chained (2005) Dollars by Industry: 2000 to 2010

[In billions of dollars (9,952 represents $9,952,000,000,000). Data are based on the 2002 North American Industry Classification System (NAICS); see text, Section 15. Data include nonfactor charges (capital consumption allowances, indirect business taxes, etc.) as well as factor charges against gross product; corporate profits and capital consumption allowances have been shifted from a company to an establishment basis]

Industry	Current dollars				Chained (2005) dollars			
	2000	2005	2009	2010	2000	2005	2009	2010
Gross domestic product	**9,952**	**12,638**	**14,119**	**14,660**	**11,226**	**12,638**	**12,881**	**13,248**
Private industries	8,736	11,053	12,197	12,697	9,786	11,053	11,198	11,521
Agriculture, forestry, fishing, and hunting	96	127	133	154	104	127	136	137
Farms	74	102	104	(NA)	84	102	109	(NA)
Agricultural services	22	25	29	(NA)	21	25	27	(NA)
Mining	109	192	241	281	233	192	263	271
Oil and gas extraction	68	129	142	(NA)	155	129	200	(NA)
Mining, except oil and gas	28	36	49	(NA)	45	36	36	(NA)
Mining support activities	14	27	50	(NA)	29	27	35	(NA)
Utilities	174	206	268	276	223	206	207	209
Construction	467	612	538	506	655	612	447	431
Manufacturing	1,416	1,568	1,585	1,718	1,397	1,568	1,470	1,554
Durable goods	839	878	867	961	748	878	857	943
Wood products	28	33	21	(NA)	33	33	28	(NA)
Nonmetallic mineral products	42	45	38	(NA)	45	45	32	(NA)
Primary metals	46	54	43	(NA)	62	54	45	(NA)
Fabricated metal products	121	120	122	(NA)	130	120	94	(NA)
Machinery	111	110	113	(NA)	111	110	95	(NA)
Computer and electronic products	172	183	206	(NA)	82	183	294	(NA)
Electrical equipment, appliances, and components	44	40	52	(NA)	43	40	42	(NA)
Motor vehicles, bodies & trailers, & parts	117	113	78	(NA)	94	113	77	(NA)
Other transportation equipment	66	76	91	(NA)	78	76	82	(NA)
Furniture and related products	34	34	24	(NA)	35	34	20	(NA)
Miscellaneous manufacturing	58	70	79	(NA)	60	70	74	(NA)
Nondurable goods	577	690	718	756	650	690	613	618
Food & beverage & tobacco	165	172	206	(NA)	176	172	175	(NA)
Textile mills and textile product mills	28	24	18	(NA)	27	24	16	(NA)
Apparel and leather and allied products	21	16	12	(NA)	20	16	12	(NA)
Paper products	62	54	56	(NA)	58	54	42	(NA)
Printing and related support activities	40	38	33	(NA)	38	38	32	(NA)
Petroleum and coal products	44	139	120	(NA)	74	139	128	(NA)
Chemical products	152	183	217	(NA)	170	183	164	(NA)
Plastics and rubber products	65	66	57	(NA)	66	66	45	(NA)
Wholesale trade	618	725	781	808	606	725	811	844
Retail trade	686	839	820	863	751	839	790	831
Transportation and warehousing	301	370	390	407	318	370	342	348
Air transportation	53	56	62	(NA)	43	56	50	(NA)
Rail transportation	23	27	31	(NA)	27	27	23	(NA)
Water transportation	8	9	14	(NA)	7	9	22	(NA)
Truck transportation	97	119	113	(NA)	107	119	105	(NA)
Transit & ground passenger transport	18	21	23	(NA)	21	21	20	(NA)
Pipeline transportation	9	10	12	(NA)	9	10	9	(NA)
Other transportation & support	68	92	95	(NA)	76	92	80	(NA)
Warehousing and storage	26	35	39	(NA)	29	35	36	(NA)
Information	418	593	639	670	397	593	659	691
Publishing industries (includes software)	100	151	148	(NA)	102	151	141	(NA)
Motion picture and sound recording	37	56	60	(NA)	43	56	56	(NA)
Broadcasting and telecommunications	257	311	356	(NA)	227	311	380	(NA)
Information and data processing services	24	74	76	(NA)	24	74	83	(NA)
Finance and insurance	762	1,029	1,172	1,235	841	1,029	1,094	1,129
Real estate and rental and leasing	1,236	1,578	1,869	1,859	1,422	1,578	1,701	1,713
Professional, scientific, and technical services	662	876	1,069	1,104	745	876	951	972
Legal services	139	195	219	(NA)	176	195	177	(NA)
Computer systems design, related services	114	129	170	(NA)	102	129	174	(NA)
Miscellaneous services	410	552	680	(NA)	467	552	604	(NA)
Management of companies & enterprises	171	218	247	256	215	218	217	220
Admin/support waste management/remediation services	283	369	386	412	312	369	348	367
Educational services	86	120	155	163	116	120	122	122
Health care and social assistance	592	833	1,058	1,112	709	833	933	959
Ambulatory health care services	288	406	514	(NA)	326	406	462	(NA)
Hospitals, nursing, residential care	253	354	453	(NA)	322	354	392	(NA)
Social assistance	52	73	91	(NA)	62	73	79	(NA)
Arts, entertainment, and recreation	99	117	127	131	115	117	115	121
Performing arts, spectator sports, museums, and related activities	48	64	71	(NA)	59	64	62	(NA)
Amusements, gambling, & recreation	50	54	56	(NA)	55	54	53	(NA)
Accommodation and food services	283	364	386	400	328	364	324	335
Accommodation	89	109	109	(NA)	100	109	99	(NA)
Food services and drinking places	194	256	277	(NA)	227	256	225	(NA)
Other services, except government	278	319	335	344	347	319	284	288
Government	1,215	1,586	1,923	1,964	1,507	1,586	1,653	1,660
Federal	378	502	612	638	483	502	533	549
State and local	837	1,084	1,311	1,326	1,025	1,084	1,119	1,112

NA Not available.

Source: U.S. Bureau of Economic Analysis, *Survey of Current Business*, May 2011. See also <http://www.bea.gov/newsreleases/industry/gdpindustry/gdpindnewsrelease.htm>.

Table 671. Gross Domestic Product by State in Current and Chained (2005) Dollars: 2000 to 2009

[In billions of dollars (9,884.2 represents $9,884,200,000,000). For definition of gross domestic product by state or chained dollars, see text, this section]

State	Current dollars					Chained (2005) dollars				
	2000	2005	2007	2008	2009	2000	2005	2007	2008	2009
United States [1]	**9,884.2**	**12,554.5**	**13,969.4**	**14,269.8**	**14,027.7**	**11,223.1**	**12,554.5**	**13,144.1**	**13,101.2**	**12,781.2**
Alabama	116.0	151.1	165.8	170.7	168.4	132.6	151.1	155.7	156.6	152.5
Alaska	25.9	37.8	44.5	49.7	46.7	34.1	37.8	40.7	41.1	44.6
Arizona	161.9	223.0	260.4	261.5	254.1	179.3	223.0	245.2	241.6	230.9
Arkansas	68.1	88.2	97.2	100.2	100.8	77.3	88.2	91.2	91.8	91.8
California	1,317.3	1,692.0	1,881.8	1,925.5	1,884.5	1,470.4	1,692.0	1,775.1	1,779.2	1,736.9
Colorado	171.9	217.4	243.9	255.2	250.9	195.2	217.4	229.6	234.0	232.1
Connecticut	163.9	197.1	222.1	222.2	220.4	185.3	197.1	209.9	205.3	198.4
Delaware	41.0	54.7	58.5	58.4	59.3	46.9	54.7	55.6	54.0	54.2
District of Columbia	58.3	82.8	92.4	96.8	99.2	69.8	82.8	85.8	87.8	87.8
Florida	481.1	680.3	758.0	747.8	729.5	548.8	680.3	712.6	690.0	660.9
Georgia	294.5	363.2	399.9	402.1	393.4	329.7	363.2	378.3	372.7	356.3
Hawaii	41.4	56.9	64.3	66.0	65.7	48.7	56.9	59.8	60.1	58.7
Idaho	36.1	48.7	54.3	55.5	53.5	39.4	48.7	51.5	51.8	49.6
Illinois.	474.4	569.5	629.3	635.1	621.1	537.1	569.5	591.4	584.3	560.0
Indiana.	198.0	239.6	262.3	263.7	257.5	221.9	239.6	248.7	244.8	232.3
Iowa.	93.3	120.3	134.4	136.0	136.3	105.3	120.3	127.2	126.0	124.1
Kansas.	85.7	105.2	121.0	124.9	123.4	97.9	105.2	113.8	114.9	112.5
Kentucky	113.1	139.3	151.8	155.9	154.6	128.3	139.3	142.5	143.1	138.7
Louisiana	131.4	197.2	204.7	211.5	208.4	168.0	197.2	184.4	181.1	192.1
Maine.	36.4	45.6	49.4	50.5	50.6	41.6	45.6	46.5	46.5	45.5
Maryland	183.0	248.1	273.2	280.5	283.8	209.7	248.1	256.6	258.4	256.0
Massachusetts.	272.7	323.3	353.4	363.1	362.4	301.3	323.3	334.3	337.1	329.8
Michigan	336.8	375.3	387.0	376.2	361.1	371.2	375.3	368.3	353.2	327.4
Minnesota	188.4	238.4	254.8	262.0	257.6	211.2	238.4	239.9	242.3	234.9
Mississippi	65.6	81.5	91.6	95.7	95.1	76.0	81.5	85.5	87.3	86.3
Missouri.	181.0	216.6	232.5	239.7	236.7	204.8	216.6	219.1	221.2	213.1
Montana.	21.6	30.1	35.1	35.8	35.6	25.8	30.1	32.2	31.9	32.0
Nebraska.	57.2	72.5	82.2	84.6	84.6	65.2	72.5	77.1	77.5	76.5
Nevada	75.9	114.8	132.3	132.1	125.1	88.1	114.8	122.6	119.8	111.9
New Hampshire	44.1	53.7	57.9	58.8	58.9	48.7	53.7	54.9	54.8	53.7
New Jersey	349.3	430.0	473.6	484.3	478.4	393.3	430.0	446.1	446.2	434.0
New Mexico	50.3	67.8	74.3	78.0	74.4	58.5	67.8	69.6	69.9	69.1
New York	770.6	961.9	1,087.2	1,110.7	1,085.1	863.2	961.9	1,020.4	1,016.3	976.6
North Carolina	281.4	355.0	395.3	404.4	398.9	316.4	355.0	377.6	376.2	360.6
North Dakota	18.3	24.7	28.4	31.1	31.6	21.2	24.7	26.3	28.1	29.1
Ohio.	381.2	444.7	469.8	472.3	466.0	429.1	444.7	443.6	437.3	420.4
Oklahoma	91.3	120.7	139.9	151.5	154.3	110.3	120.7	129.5	133.3	147.0
Oregon.	113.0	143.3	167.2	169.5	165.2	121.2	143.3	162.9	164.5	158.5
Pennsylvania	395.8	482.3	533.2	546.1	547.9	452.4	482.3	499.8	500.5	492.0
Rhode Island	33.5	44.2	47.2	47.6	47.6	38.4	44.2	44.4	43.8	42.9
South Carolina.	115.4	141.9	157.6	159.7	158.0	130.8	141.9	148.0	146.8	140.7
South Dakota.	24.0	31.6	35.2	38.0	38.8	26.9	31.6	33.1	35.0	36.0
Tennessee	177.6	224.5	241.9	246.4	241.9	198.1	224.5	230.1	229.9	219.3
Texas	733.0	971.0	1,144.9	1,196.8	1,141.3	872.6	971.0	1,069.9	1,065.9	1,066.4
Utah.	69.5	90.7	109.3	112.7	112.7	79.6	90.7	102.1	103.0	102.4
Vermont	18.0	22.8	24.2	25.0	25.1	20.0	22.8	23.0	23.3	22.9
Virginia.	261.9	356.9	389.3	400.5	406.3	298.2	356.9	367.0	369.8	367.4
Washington	227.8	279.4	325.5	336.3	336.3	259.1	279.4	306.3	311.0	305.8
West Virginia	41.4	52.0	57.8	61.3	62.3	49.6	52.0	52.0	53.1	54.3	54.8
Wisconsin	177.6	218.9	238.2	241.2	239.1	199.2	218.9	225.5	224.1	215.7
Wyoming	17.0	26.2	33.5	38.9	37.5	23.1	26.2	29.7	31.4	35.5

[1] For chained (2005) dollar estimates, states will not add to U.S. total.

Source: U.S. Bureau of Economic Analysis, "Gross Domestic Product by State," February 2011, <http://www.bea.gov/regional/gsp/>.

Table 672. Gross Domestic Product by Selected Industries and State: 2009

[In billions of dollars (14,027.7 represents $14,027,700,000,000). Preliminary data. For definition of gross domestic product by state, see text, this section. Industries based on 2002 North American Industry Classification System; see text, Section 15]

State	Total [1]	Manu-facturing	Whole-sale trade	Retail trade	Infor-mation	Finance and insur-ance	Real estate, rental, and leasing	Profes-sional and technical services	Health care and social assis-tance	Govern-ment [2]
United States	14,027.7	1,584.8	780.8	819.6	639.4	1,171.6	1,868.7	1,068.5	1,057.9	1,831.1
Alabama	168.4	26.8	9.4	11.9	3.9	9.8	17.0	11.0	12.5	29.3
Alaska	46.7	1.6	1.1	1.8	1.1	1.7	4.2	2.0	2.6	9.0
Arizona	254.1	20.5	13.5	19.2	7.1	22.3	39.6	15.1	20.3	34.4
Arkansas	100.8	14.5	6.8	7.0	4.1	4.8	10.5	3.9	8.0	14.7
California	1,884.5	224.3	99.6	108.2	123.5	113.9	312.7	169.4	120.6	225.5
Colorado	250.9	18.0	12.4	13.6	22.2	16.5	33.7	23.9	15.4	32.2
Connecticut	220.4	26.2	11.4	11.1	8.3	36.2	33.1	16.5	17.6	21.6
Delaware	59.3	4.1	2.0	2.3	1.1	21.2	6.4	3.9	3.8	5.7
District of Columbia	99.2	0.2	0.9	1.0	5.5	5.0	7.9	20.8	4.5	34.6
Florida	729.5	36.7	45.0	52.5	31.0	52.4	126.2	50.2	58.7	94.4
Georgia	393.4	41.1	28.7	23.8	26.1	25.2	48.4	28.4	26.2	57.8
Hawaii	65.7	1.3	2.0	4.4	1.5	2.8	12.1	3.2	4.3	15.8
Idaho	53.5	5.8	2.8	4.2	1.2	2.9	7.0	3.9	4.2	8.0
Illinois............	621.1	69.3	41.6	32.5	22.7	65.4	82.9	54.9	45.5	64.1
Indiana............	257.5	64.5	13.4	15.5	5.9	17.3	26.0	10.6	21.0	27.7
Iowa..............	136.3	23.7	7.6	7.8	4.1	18.4	13.7	4.5	9.5	16.2
Kansas............	123.4	16.9	7.8	7.7	7.1	8.0	12.3	6.5	9.5	18.8
Kentucky	154.6	25.1	9.6	9.6	4.2	8.7	14.5	6.9	13.3	25.4
Louisiana	208.4	41.8	9.3	12.7	4.3	7.9	18.4	9.8	13.2	24.3
Maine.............	50.6	5.3	2.5	4.2	1.3	3.8	7.2	2.7	6.0	7.3
Maryland	283.8	15.4	13.3	15.3	10.5	17.0	48.7	30.6	22.5	52.6
Massachusetts........	362.4	33.3	18.9	16.1	17.4	39.1	52.9	43.0	36.4	33.9
Michigan	361.1	51.7	21.3	23.7	9.3	24.4	47.6	28.1	32.9	46.4
Minnesota	257.6	32.0	16.7	13.8	9.3	26.2	33.3	16.4	23.9	28.0
Mississippi	95.1	16.3	4.4	7.2	2.0	4.7	8.8	3.5	7.0	17.8
Missouri............	236.7	27.7	14.4	15.2	12.7	16.0	25.9	15.7	20.0	31.4
Montana...........	35.6	2.0	1.8	2.3	0.9	2.0	4.4	1.8	3.4	5.9
Nebraska...........	84.6	9.2	4.8	4.9	2.7	7.8	8.4	4.3	6.5	11.6
Nevada	125.1	5.3	4.7	7.9	2.4	13.4	17.4	6.2	6.7	14.0
New Hampshire.......	58.9	6.6	3.4	4.3	2.2	5.3	9.2	4.3	5.8	6.2
New Jersey	478.4	38.8	35.3	27.7	22.3	42.0	83.9	44.4	36.4	54.0
New Mexico..........	74.4	4.1	2.6	4.8	2.2	2.9	9.0	6.5	5.7	15.4
New York	1,085.1	58.8	52.6	52.8	77.6	168.5	158.0	100.7	85.2	123.4
North Carolina.......	398.9	72.9	20.7	21.3	12.6	44.0	41.6	21.5	27.8	60.5
North Dakota	31.6	2.8	2.3	2.0	1.0	2.2	3.5	1.1	2.7	4.4
Ohio..............	466.0	73.4	27.7	29.5	13.5	44.1	52.7	28.2	42.6	55.4
Oklahoma	154.3	17.6	7.0	9.0	4.3	7.4	13.9	6.3	10.0	26.4
Oregon.............	165.2	31.6	10.0	8.1	5.4	9.2	23.5	8.6	13.5	21.4
Pennsylvania	547.9	68.5	31.3	30.4	20.5	49.9	67.6	43.9	55.1	56.4
Rhode Island	47.6	4.0	2.3	2.5	1.9	5.7	7.2	2.7	4.8	6.4
South Carolina........	158.0	24.2	8.5	11.5	4.3	8.7	18.8	8.0	10.2	28.6
South Dakota........	38.8	3.3	2.1	2.5	0.9	8.1	3.5	1.1	3.3	4.6
Tennessee	241.9	34.9	15.6	17.9	8.2	17.3	26.5	14.7	24.0	28.3
Texas..............	1,141.3	146.8	74.2	65.2	47.5	75.2	106.3	80.0	69.9	139.5
Utah..............	112.7	13.0	5.3	7.6	3.9	12.0	14.1	7.4	6.6	15.9
Vermont............	25.1	2.9	1.2	2.0	0.7	1.6	3.5	1.6	2.7	3.7
Virginia............	406.3	30.9	15.8	20.9	19.4	29.6	56.2	52.8	23.9	76.6
Washington	336.3	38.9	18.1	22.1	28.2	17.3	49.1	22.7	22.5	50.6
West Virginia	62.3	5.6	2.8	4.4	1.4	3.0	6.0	2.5	6.0	12.4
Wisconsin	239.1	42.3	13.2	14.1	7.6	21.8	30.1	11.1	22.1	27.5
Wyoming	37.5	2.3	1.2	1.8	0.5	1.0	3.1	1.0	1.4	5.0

[1] Includes industries not shown separately. [2] Includes federal civilian and military and state and local government.
Source: U.S. Bureau of Economic Analysis, "Gross Domestic Product by State," February 2011, <http://www.bea.gov/regional/gsp/>.

Income, Expenditures, Poverty, and Wealth 439

Table 673. Relation of GDP, GNP, Net National Product, National Income, Personal Income, Disposable Personal Income, and Personal Saving: 1990 to 2010

[In billions of dollars (5,801 represents $5,801,000,000,000). For definitions, see text, this section. Minus sign (–) indicates deficit or net disbursement]

Item	1990	2000	2005	2006	2007	2008	2009	2010
Gross domestic product (GDP)	5,801	9,952	12,638	13,399	14,062	14,369	14,119	14,660
Plus: Income receipts from the rest of the world	189	381	573	721	871	839	630	706
Less: Income payments to the rest of the world	154	343	476	649	748	665	484	518
Equals: Gross national product (GNP)	5,835	9,989	12,736	13,471	14,185	14,544	14,265	14,849
Less: Consumption of fixed capital	691	1,184	1,541	1,661	1,768	1,849	1,861	1,869
Equals: Net national product	5,144	8,805	11,194	11,811	12,418	12,694	12,404	12,980
Less: Statistical discrepancy	84	−134	−80	−221	21	137	179	152
Equals: National income	5,060	8,939	11,274	12,031	12,396	12,558	12,225	12,828
Less: Corporate profits [1]	434	819	1,456	1,608	1,511	1,263	1,258	1,625
Taxes on production and imports less subsidies	398	663	869	936	973	992	964	1,000
Contributions for government social insurance	410	706	873	922	960	987	970	1,004
Net interest and miscellaneous payments on assets	444	539	543	652	732	813	784	738
Business current transfer payments (net)	40	87	96	83	103	122	134	132
Current surplus of government enterprises	2	9	−4	−4	−12	−17	−13	−13
Wage accruals less disbursements	–	–	5	1	−6	−5	5	
Plus: Personal income receipts on assets	921	1,361	1,542	1,830	2,057	2,109	1,920	1,908
Personal current transfer receipts	595	1,083	1,509	1,605	1,719	1,879	2,133	2,296
Equals: Personal income	4,847	8,559	10,486	11,268	11,912	12,391	12,175	12,547
Less: Personal current taxes	593	1,232	1,209	1,352	1,489	1,438	1,140	1,167
Equals: Disposable personal income	4,254	7,327	9,277	9,916	10,424	10,953	11,035	11,380
Less: Personal outlays	3,977	7,114	9,150	9,681	10,209	10,505	10,380	10,721
Equals: Personal saving	277	213	128	235	215	448	655	659

– Represents or rounds to zero. [1] Corporate profits with inventory valuation and capital consumption adjustments.

Source: U.S. Bureau of Economic Analysis, *Survey of Current Business*, April 2011. See also <http://www.bea.gov/national/nipaweb/SelectTable.asp?Selected=N>.

Table 674. Gross Saving and Investment: 1990 to 2010

[In billions of dollars (918 represents $918,000,000,000)]

Item	1990	2000	2005	2006	2007	2008	2009	2010
Gross saving	918	1,800	1,903	2,174	2,014	1,785	1,534	1,704
Net saving	226	616	362	514	246	−64	−327	−165
Net private saving	397	389	619	667	479	600	945	1,135
Personal saving	277	213	128	235	215	448	655	659
Undistributed corporate profits with IVA and CCA [1]	120	176	486	430	271	157	284	476
Wage accruals less disbursements	–	–	5	1	−6	−5	5	
Net government saving	−170	227	−257	−153	−233	−664	−1,272	−1,299
Federal	−176	185	−283	−204	−245	−616	−1,252	−1,332
State and local	6	41	26	51	12	−47	−20	33
Consumption of fixed capital	691	1,184	1,541	1,661	1,768	1,849	1,861	1,869
Private	560	987	1,291	1,391	1,476	1,537	1,536	1,534
Domestic business	470	824	1,046	1,123	1,191	1,245	1,245	1,242
Households and institutions	91	163	245	268	286	292	291	293
Government	131	198	251	269	291	312	325	335
Federal	68	88	100	107	113	120	124	130
State and local	63	110	150	163	179	193	201	205
Gross domestic investment, capital acct. transactions, and net lending	1,002	1,666	1,824	1,954	2,035	1,922	1,713	1,856
Gross domestic investment	1,077	2,077	2,564	2,752	2,752	2,592	2,093	2,337
Gross private domestic investment	861	1,772	2,172	2,327	2,295	2,097	1,589	1,828
Gross government investment	216	304	392	425	457	496	503	510
Capital account transactions (net) [2]	7	–	−13	2	–	−5	1	1
Net lending or net borrowing	−82	−411	−728	−801	−717	−665	−380	−482
Statistical discrepancy	84	−134	−80	−221	21	137	179	152
Addenda:								
Gross private saving	957	1,376	1,910	2,058	1,955	2,137	2,480	2,669
Gross government saving	−40	424	−7	117	58	−351	−947	−964
Federal	−109	273	−183	−97	−133	−497	−1,127	−1,203
State and local	69	151	176	214	191	145	181	238
Net domestic investment	386	892	1,023	1,092	984	743	232	468
Gross saving as a percentage of gross national income	16.0	17.8	14.9	15.9	14.2	12.4	10.9	11.6
Net saving as a percentage of gross national income	3.9	6.1	2.8	3.8	1.7	−0.4	−2.3	−1.1

– Represents or rounds to zero. [1] IVA and CCA = Inventory valuation adjustment and capital consumption adjustment.

[2] Consists of capital transfers and the acquisition and disposal of nonproduced nonfinancial assets.

Source: U.S. Bureau of Economic Analysis, *Survey of Current Business*, April 2011. See also <http://www.bea.gov/national/nipaweb/SelectTable.asp?Selected=N>.

Table 675. Flow of Funds Accounts—Composition of Individuals' Savings: 1990 to 2010

[In billions of dollars (518.6 represents $518,600,000,000). Combined statement for households, farm business, and nonfarm noncorporate business. Minus sign (−) indicates decrease]

Composition of savings	1990	2000	2005	2006	2007	2008	2009	2010
Net acquisition of financial assets.	**518.6**	**371.0**	**1,209.1**	**1,232.5**	**1,528.7**	**723.4**	**−115.9**	**460.3**
Foreign deposits	1.4	7.6	2.4	5.2	15.4	−24.1	−10.3	4.9
Checkable deposits and currency	−8.5	−74.2	−50.5	30.9	−5.0	240.5	33.5	−58.5
Time and savings deposits	33.1	348.8	510.5	506.8	492.1	193.0	61.9	233.4
Money market fund shares	39.2	152.4	47.6	168.4	235.4	235.1	−274.6	−185.0
Securities	200.9	−633.3	14.4	−309.3	−112.6	−159.4	209.1	330.3
Open market paper	5.8	12.4	14.7	19.0	−10.2	−101.3	28.7	28.8
U.S. savings bonds	8.5	−1.7	0.7	−2.7	−6.0	−2.4	−2.8	−3.3
Other Treasury securities	88.8	−205.8	−97.3	−90.2	−34.5	151.8	383.4	270.2
Agency and GSE-backed securities [1]	35.3	34.1	97.0	−65.0	335.5	95.6	−624.6	−5.1
Municipal securities	34.7	4.5	78.7	52.1	23.5	7.0	106.7	85.2
Corporate and foreign bonds	47.1	84.3	119.6	197.0	218.4	−213.3	−150.3	−228.7
Corporate equities [2]	−50.8	−637.5	−372.5	−585.0	−847.9	−111.9	104.4	−103.2
Mutual fund shares	31.5	76.3	173.5	165.4	208.5	15.2	363.7	286.4
Life insurance reserves	26.5	50.2	16.1	65.6	34.2	67.0	26.5	62.6
Pension fund reserves	191.8	263.0	275.4	250.6	200.8	112.7	111.6	118.6
Miscellaneous and other assets	34.1	256.5	393.2	514.3	668.5	58.6	−273.8	−46.0
Gross investment in tangible assets	**797.3**	**1,492.4**	**2,037.9**	**2,067.3**	**2,010.0**	**1,801.5**	**1,576.4**	**1,639.0**
Minus: Consumption of fixed capital	*571.2*	*913.5*	*1,208.9*	*1,281.0*	*1,352.4*	*1,393.9*	*1,404.0*	*1,388.3*
Equals: Net investment in tangible assets	**226.1**	**578.9**	**829.0**	**786.3**	**657.6**	**407.5**	**172.3**	**250.8**
Net increase in liabilities.	**229.9**	**929.5**	**1,701.0**	**1,847.1**	**1,511.4**	**302.0**	**−412.6**	**−320.2**
Mortgage debt on nonfarm homes	207.1	422.8	1,106.5	1,064.9	708.8	−96.3	−197.6	−304.8
Other mortgage debt [3]	−1.9	108.8	118.1	235.8	299.0	204.3	−57.7	−104.8
Consumer credit	15.1	176.5	100.4	95.4	139.3	38.8	−115.3	−44.2
Policy loans	4.1	2.8	0.8	3.3	3.6	5.9	0.7	3.5
Security credit	−3.7	7.2	−31.6	59.7	33.4	−160.7	38.1	75.2
Other liabilities [3]	9.3	211.3	406.8	387.9	327.3	310.0	−80.9	55.0
Personal saving with consumer durables [4]	530.5	56.0	302.1	188.5	677.9	817.0	457.0	1,006.4
Personal saving without consumer durables [4]	450.8	−181.8	62.5	−39.2	458.9	689.2	393.9	870.5
Personal saving (NIPA, excludes consumer durables) [5]	276.7	213.1	127.7	235.0	214.7	447.9	655.3	655.7

[1] GSE = government-sponsored enterprises. [2] Only directly held and those in closed-end and exchange-traded funds. Other equities are included in mutual funds and life insurance and pension reserves. [3] Includes corporate farms. [4] Flow of Funds measure. [5] National Income and Product Accounts measure.

Source: Board of Governors of the Federal Reserve System, "Federal Reserve Statistical Release, Z.1, Flow of Funds Accounts of the United States," March, 2011, <http://www.federalreserve.gov/releases/z1/20100311/>.

Table 676. Government Consumption Expenditures and Gross Investment by Level of Government and Type: 2000 to 2010

[In billions of dollars (1,731.0 represents $1,731,000,000,000). Government consumption expenditures are services (such as education and national defense) produced by government that are valued at their cost of production. Excludes government sales to other sectors and government own-account investment (construction and software). Gross government investment consists of general government and government enterprise expenditures for fixed assets; inventory investment is included in government consumption expenditures. For explanation of national income and chained dollars, see text, Section 13]

Item	Current Dollars				Chained (2005) dollars			
	2000	2005	2009	2010	2000	2005	2009	2010
Government consumption expenditures and gross investment, total	**1,731.0**	**2,369.9**	**2,914.9**	**3,000.2**	**2,097.8**	**2,369.9**	**2,542.6**	**2,568.3**
Consumption expenditures	1,426.6	1,977.9	2,411.5	2,490.6	1,750.6	1,977.9	2,112.3	2,132.2
Gross investment.	304.3	392.0	503.4	509.6	347.5	392.0	430.3	436.1
Structures	189.6	246.5	316.6	309.2	239.4	246.5	248.6	243.5
Equipment and software	114.7	145.5	186.8	200.5	109.8	145.5	184.5	197.6
Federal	**576.1**	**876.3**	**1,139.6**	**1,214.3**	**698.1**	**876.3**	**1,027.6**	**1,076.9**
Consumption expenditures	496.0	765.8	987.1	1,043.4	616.4	765.8	882.3	915.2
Gross investment.	80.1	110.5	152.4	170.9	82.0	110.5	145.9	163.1
Structures	13.7	15.7	28.0	34.2	17.2	15.7	23.6	29.1
Equipment and software	66.4	94.7	124.4	136.7	65.2	94.7	121.9	133.1
National defense	**371.0**	**589.0**	**771.6**	**817.7**	**453.5**	**589.0**	**693.0**	**720.2**
Consumption expenditures	321.8	514.8	664.1	698.2	403.9	514.8	591.7	608.7
Gross investment.	49.2	74.2	107.5	119.5	50.3	74.2	101.9	112.6
Structures	5.4	7.5	15.9	19.0	6.9	7.5	13.5	16.2
Equipment and software	43.8	66.8	91.5	100.4	43.6	66.8	87.9	95.7
Nondefense	**205.0**	**287.3**	**368.0**	**396.6**	**244.4**	**287.3**	**334.6**	**356.7**
Consumption expenditures	174.2	251.0	323.0	345.2	212.4	251.0	290.6	306.6
Gross investment.	30.9	36.3	45.0	51.4	31.6	36.3	44.0	50.4
Structures	8.3	8.3	12.1	15.2	10.4	8.3	10.1	12.9
Equipment and software	22.6	28.0	32.9	36.2	21.5	28.0	33.9	37.3
State and local	**1,154.9**	**1,493.6**	**1,775.3**	**1,786.0**	**1,400.1**	**1,493.6**	**1,518.8**	**1,497.4**
Consumption expenditures	930.6	1,212.0	1,424.4	1,447.2	1,133.7	1,212.0	1,232.1	1,220.0
Gross investment.	224.3	281.6	351.0	338.7	266.6	281.6	286.8	277.6
Structures	176.0	230.8	288.5	275.0	222.2	230.8	225.4	215.2
Equipment and software	48.3	50.8	62.4	63.8	44.3	50.8	62.5	64.3

Source: U.S. Bureau of Economic Analysis, *Survey of Current Business*, April 2011. See also <http://www.bea.gov/national/nipaweb/SelectTable.asp?Selected=N>.

Table 677. Personal Consumption Expenditures by Function: 2000 to 2009

[In billions of dollars (6,830.4 represents $6,830,400,000,000). For definition of "chained" dollars, see text, this section]

Function	Current dollars				Chained (2005) dollars			
	2000	2005	2008	2009	2000	2005	2008	2009
Personal consumption expenditures [1]	**6,830.4**	**8,819.0**	**10,104.5**	**10,001.3**	**7,608.1**	**8,819.0**	**9,265.0**	**9,153.9**
Food and nonalcoholic beverages purchased for off-premises consumption	463.1	569.5	662.6	664.0	519.1	569.5	586.6	581.9
Alcoholic beverages purchased for off-premises consumption	74.0	95.1	112.1	113.5	81.1	95.1	104.6	102.7
Clothing, footwear, and related services	297.3	331.8	352.1	339.5	276.8	331.8	357.6	341.4
Clothing	250.4	280.3	297.0	286.2	230.3	280.3	303.2	290.0
Footwear [2]	46.9	51.5	55.1	53.3	46.6	51.5	54.4	51.4
Housing [1]	1,010.5	1,328.9	1,533.2	1,581.6	1,174.2	1,328.9	1,389.8	1,407.8
Rental of tenant-occupied nonfarm housing [3]	227.9	264.7	326.3	346.1	267.9	264.7	291.8	302.7
Imputed rental of owner-occupied nonfarm housing [4]	768.9	1,044.5	1,184.5	1,211.9	890.7	1,044.5	1,080.1	1,087.1
Household utilities and fuels	204.0	275.0	328.1	317.6	265.4	275.0	265.6	269.7
Water supply and sanitation	50.4	63.6	76.5	80.0	61.9	63.6	65.5	64.5
Electricity, gas, and other fuels	153.5	211.4	251.5	237.6	203.4	211.4	200.1	205.3
Furnishings, household equipment, and routine household maintenance [1]	342.5	423.9	445.2	419.5	332.4	423.9	441.9	414.3
Furniture, furnishings, and floor coverings [5]	114.4	143.0	141.1	130.0	106.2	143.0	147.2	136.3
Household appliances [6]	37.6	47.6	49.3	46.4	36.7	47.6	45.8	42.6
Tools and equipment for house and garden	17.1	22.3	22.6	20.8	17.1	22.3	22.5	20.6
Medical products, appliances, and equipment	191.2	285.5	335.5	349.8	224.0	285.5	311.9	316.0
Pharmaceutical and other medical products [7]	159.0	247.3	291.2	305.9	189.6	247.3	269.8	274.5
Therapeutic appliances and equipment	32.2	38.2	44.3	43.9	34.1	38.2	42.2	41.4
Outpatient services	436.6	636.5	745.4	772.4	490.2	636.5	690.1	699.2
Physician services [8]	229.2	332.4	382.5	396.2	248.7	332.4	360.2	364.3
Dental services	63.6	89.0	104.5	105.0	79.7	89.0	89.8	87.6
Paramedical services	143.8	215.1	258.4	271.1	162.6	215.1	240.5	247.9
Hospital and nursing home services	481.8	679.5	801.9	850.9	592.8	679.5	720.0	741.2
Transportation	798.4	979.3	1,033.5	890.7	901.0	979.3	890.6	846.1
Motor vehicles	321.4	361.6	291.0	269.4	311.4	361.6	301.5	280.7
New motor vehicles	210.7	248.9	184.9	165.3	202.8	248.9	191.0	169.1
Net purchases of used motor vehicles	110.7	112.7	106.1	104.1	108.5	112.7	110.4	111.9
Motor vehicle operation [1]	404.0	541.0	658.0	544.3	524.9	541.0	511.6	491.3
Motor vehicle parts and accessories	41.8	48.0	52.2	50.3	45.2	48.0	46.1	42.8
Motor vehicle fuels, lubricants, and fluids	172.9	283.8	383.3	280.8	261.3	283.8	265.3	265.3
Motor vehicle maintenance and repair	127.4	154.9	159.7	154.4	148.7	154.9	141.4	131.3
Public transportation	73.0	76.8	84.5	77.0	72.7	76.8	72.9	68.5
Telephone and facsimile equipment	5.5	7.5	9.0	9.7	3.3	7.5	11.1	12.6
Postal and delivery services	9.9	9.3	9.8	9.0	11.9	9.3	8.5	7.6
Recreation [1]	639.9	807.4	916.0	897.1	600.6	807.4	937.0	929.3
Video and audio equipment	83.1	107.8	115.6	107.1	59.1	107.8	156.4	163.7
Information processing equipment	44.1	55.9	65.8	64.7	(NA)	(NA)	(NA)	(NA)
Services related to video and audio goods and computers	57.2	75.7	92.0	93.4	66.9	75.7	85.4	85.1
Sports and recreational goods and related services	147.9	188.4	203.0	196.9	135.6	188.4	207.3	202.3
Membership clubs, sports centers, parks, theaters, and museums	91.9	110.6	129.3	126.5	106.9	110.6	117.7	113.9
Magazines, newspapers, books, and stationery	81.0	93.1	104.9	105.1	84.8	93.1	100.9	97.9
Pets, pet products, and related services	39.7	53.1	65.7	67.1	45.8	53.1	56.3	54.0
Education [1]	134.3	180.7	220.5	232.9	188.2	180.7	185.1	185.2
Higher education	76.8	108.8	135.1	145.5	109.9	108.8	112.1	113.9
Food services	354.9	455.3	527.3	527.7	408.0	455.3	472.1	456.5
Accommodations [9]	55.2	70.0	84.0	75.9	62.4	70.0	75.4	71.2
Financial services	370.0	427.2	534.0	505.3	405.0	427.2	486.2	470.1
Insurance	199.9	285.4	314.1	308.6	259.6	285.4	284.9	273.1
Personal care [10]	132.2	169.1	193.9	193.1	142.8	169.1	179.5	174.4
Personal items [11]	63.7	72.6	79.1	77.4	57.3	72.6	69.1	66.6
Social services and religious activities [12]	85.0	118.7	141.7	145.7	98.7	118.7	129.4	131.0
Legal services	65.4	89.7	104.0	102.5	81.7	89.7	91.9	88.2
Funeral and burial services	15.8	19.0	19.0	18.9	19.2	19.0	16.4	15.7
Tobacco	68.5	71.1	75.7	87.9	80.3	71.1	64.7	60.7
Net foreign travel and expenditures abroad by U.S. residents [1]	−13.3	−0.1	−12.5	−11.3	−3.0	−0.1	−17.4	−10.5
Foreign travel by U.S. residents	84.3	99.8	119.8	105.4	106.8	99.8	99.5	95.3
Less: Expenditures in the United States by nonresidents	100.8	104.9	138.7	124.5	115.0	104.9	121.4	111.8

NA Not available. [1] Includes other expenditures not shown separately. [2] Consists of shoes and other footwear, and of repair and hire of footwear. [3] Consists of space rent (see footnote 4) and rent for appliances, furnishings, and furniture. [4] Consists of rent for space and for heating and plumbing facilities, water heaters, lighting fixtures, kitchen cabinets, linoleum, storm windows and doors, window screens, and screen doors, but excludes rent for appliances and furniture and purchases of fuel and electricity. [5] Includes clocks, lamps, lighting fixtures, and other household decorative items; also includes repair of furniture, furnishings, and floor coverings. [6] Consists of major household appliances, small electric household appliances, and repair of household appliances. [7] Excludes drug preparations and related products dispensed by physicians, hospitals, and other medical services. [8] Consists of offices of physicians, health maintenance organization medical centers, and freestanding ambulatory surgical and emergency centers. [9] Consists of transient hotels, motels, other traveler accommodations, clubs, and housing at schools. [10] Consists of cosmetics and toiletries, electric appliances for personal care, hairdressing salons, and miscellaneous personal care services. [11] Consists of jewelry, watches, luggage, and similar personal items. [12] Consists of household purchases of goods and services from business, government, and nonprofit institutions providing social services and religious activities. Purchases from nonprofit establishments exclude unrelated sales, secondary sales, and sales to businesses, government, and the rest of the world, but include membership dues and fees.

Source: U.S. Bureau of Economic Analysis, *Survey of Current Business*, April 2011. See also <http://www.bea.gov/national/nipaweb/SelectTable.asp?Selected=N>.

Table 678. Personal Income and Its Disposition: 1990 to 2010

[In billions of dollars (4,847 represents $4,847,000,000,000), except as indicated. For definition of personal income and chained dollars, see text, this section]

Item	1990	2000	2005	2006	2007	2008	2009	2010
Personal income	**4,847**	**8,559**	**10,486**	**11,268**	**11,912**	**12,391**	**12,175**	**12,547**
Compensation of employees, received	3,326	5,789	7,060	7,476	7,862	8,066	7,807	7,991
Wage and salary disbursements	2,741	4,828	5,701	6,069	6,422	6,559	6,274	6,405
Supplements to wages and salaries	585	961	1,359	1,407	1,440	1,507	1,533	1,586
Proprietors' income [1]	365	818	1,070	1,133	1,090	1,102	1,012	1,055
Farm	32	30	44	29	38	51	31	45
Nonfarm	333	788	1,026	1,104	1,053	1,051	982	1,010
Rental income of persons [1]	50	215	178	147	144	222	274	301
Personal income receipts on assets	921	1,361	1,542	1,830	2,057	2,109	1,920	1,908
Personal interest income	752	984	987	1,128	1,265	1,315	1,222	1,195
Personal dividend income	169	377	555	702	792	795	697	713
Personal current transfer receipts	595	1,083	1,509	1,605	1,719	1,879	2,133	2,296
Government social benefits to persons	573	1,041	1,483	1,584	1,688	1,843	2,097	2,259
Old-age, survivors, disability, and health insurance benefits	352	621	845	943	1,003	1,068	1,165	1,214
Other current transfer receipts, from business (net)	22	42	26	21	31	37	36	37
Less: Contributions for government social insurance	410	706	873	922	960	987	970	1,004
Less: Personal current taxes	*593*	*1,232*	*1,209*	*1,352*	*1,489*	*1,438*	*1,140*	*1,167*
Equals: Disposable personal income	**4,254**	**7,327**	**9,277**	**9,916**	**10,424**	**10,953**	**11,035**	**11,380**
Less: Personal outlays	*3,977*	*7,114*	*9,150*	*9,681*	*10,209*	*10,505*	*10,380*	*10,721*
Personal consumption expenditures	3,836	6,830	8,819	9,323	9,806	10,105	10,001	10,349
Personal interest payments [2]	111	200	211	230	261	246	217	199
Personal current transfer payments	31	83	120	128	142	154	161	173
Equals: Personal saving	**277**	**213**	**128**	**235**	**215**	**448**	**655**	**659**
Personal saving as a percentage of disposable personal income	6.5	2.9	1.4	2.4	2.1	4.1	5.9	5.8
Addenda:								
Disposable personal income:								
Total, billions of chained (2005) dollars	5,896	8,162	9,277	9,651	9,874	10,043	10,100	10,241
Per capita:								
Current dollars	17,004	25,944	31,318	33,157	34,512	35,931	35,888	36,697
Chained (2005) dollars	23,568	28,899	31,318	32,271	32,693	32,946	32,847	33,025

[1] With inventory valuation adjustments and capital consumption adjustment. [2] Consists of nonmortgage interest paid by households.

Source: U.S. Bureau of Economic Analysis, *Survey of Current Business,* April 2011. See also <http://www.bea.gov/national/nipaweb/SelectTable.asp?Selected=N>.

Table 679. Selected Per Capita Income and Product Measures in Current and Chained (2005) Dollars: 1960 to 2010

[In dollars. Based on U.S. Census Bureau estimated population including Armed Forces abroad; based on quarterly averages. For explanation of chained dollars, see text, this section]

Year	Current dollars					Chained (2005) dollars			
	Gross domestic product	Gross national product	Personal income	Disposable personal income	Personal consumption expenditures	Gross domestic product	Gross national product	Disposable personal income	Personal consumption expenditures
1960	2,912	2,930	2,275	2,020	1,836	15,661	15,770	10,865	9,871
1970	5,063	5,094	4,089	3,586	3,161	20,820	20,964	15,158	13,361
1975	7,583	7,643	6,180	5,497	4,786	22,592	22,786	17,091	14,881
1980	12,243	12,394	10,107	8,794	7,710	25,640	25,967	18,863	16,538
1985	17,683	17,794	14,661	12,911	11,394	28,717	28,904	21,571	19,037
1990	23,185	23,323	19,373	17,004	15,331	32,112	32,304	23,568	21,249
1993	25,616	25,736	21,393	18,909	17,226	32,747	32,900	24,044	21,904
1994	26,893	26,985	22,299	19,678	18,033	33,671	33,784	24,517	22,466
1995	27,813	27,924	23,260	20,470	18,708	34,112	34,245	24,951	22,803
1996	29,062	29,180	24,439	21,355	19,553	34,977	35,115	25,475	23,325
1997	30,526	30,612	25,648	22,255	20,408	36,102	36,202	26,061	23,899
1998	31,843	31,905	27,251	23,534	21,432	37,238	37,312	27,299	24,861
1999	33,486	33,585	28,321	24,356	22,707	38,592	38,708	27,805	25,923
2000	35,237	35,370	30,308	25,944	24,185	39,750	39,901	28,899	26,939
2001	36,049	36,231	31,133	26,805	25,054	39,768	39,969	29,299	27,385
2002	36,935	37,106	31,444	27,799	25,819	40,096	40,283	29,976	27,841
2003	38,310	38,546	32,244	28,805	26,832	40,711	40,964	30,442	28,357
2004	40,435	40,746	33,857	30,287	28,228	41,784	42,107	31,193	29,072
2005	42,664	42,992	35,398	31,318	29,771	42,664	42,992	31,318	29,771
2006	44,805	45,047	37,679	33,157	31,174	43,391	43,625	32,271	30,341
2007	46,558	46,967	39,441	34,512	32,469	43,801	44,183	32,693	30,757
2008	47,138	47,710	40,649	35,931	33,148	43,397	43,922	32,946	30,394
2009	45,918	46,394	39,595	35,888	32,526	41,890	42,327	32,847	29,770
2010	47,275	47,883	40,459	36,697	33,373	42,722	43,272	33,025	30,034

Source: U.S. Bureau of Economic Analysis, *Survey of Current Business,* April 2011. See also <http://www.bea.gov/national/nipaweb/SelectTable.asp?Selected=N>.

Table 680. Personal Income in Current and Constant (2005) Dollars by State: 2000 to 2010

[In billions of dollars (8,554.9 represents $8,554,900,000,000). Represents a measure of income received from all sources during the calendar year by residents of each state. Data exclude federal employees overseas and U.S. residents employed by private U.S. firms on temporary foreign assignment. Totals may differ from those in Tables 673, 678, and 679]

State	Current dollars					Constant (2005) dollars [1]				
	2000	2005	2008	2009	2010, prel.	2000	2005	2008	2009	2010, prel.
United States	8,554.9	10,476.7	12,380.2	12,168.2	12,530.1	9,529.0	10,476.7	11,351.7	11,137.1	11,276.5
Alabama	107.2	135.6	158.7	157.3	162.2	119.4	135.6	145.5	144.0	146.0
Alaska	19.2	24.6	30.6	30.2	31.4	21.3	24.6	28.0	27.6	28.2
Arizona	135.7	188.2	224.0	219.0	223.7	151.1	188.2	205.4	200.5	201.3
Arkansas	60.5	77.5	93.5	93.4	96.7	67.4	77.5	85.7	85.5	87.0
California	1,135.3	1,387.7	1,604.2	1,567.0	1,605.8	1,264.6	1,387.7	1,470.9	1,434.2	1,445.1
Colorado	147.1	179.7	215.0	210.5	215.3	163.8	179.7	197.1	192.7	193.7
Connecticut	143.0	168.7	200.4	194.5	200.2	159.3	168.8	183.7	178.1	180.1
Delaware	24.4	31.1	35.6	35.0	35.9	27.2	31.1	32.7	32.1	32.3
District of Columbia	23.1	32.2	40.6	41.3	42.7	25.8	32.0	37.3	37.8	38.5
Florida	466.6	633.2	739.4	722.3	738.4	519.8	633.2	678.0	661.1	664.5
Georgia	234.8	292.6	342.9	335.5	343.8	261.6	292.6	314.4	307.0	309.4
Hawaii	35.2	45.3	54.7	54.6	55.8	39.2	45.3	50.2	50.0	50.2
Idaho	32.1	42.2	50.5	49.2	50.6	35.7	42.2	46.3	45.1	45.5
Illinois............	405.9	472.2	554.8	540.4	553.8	452.1	472.1	508.7	494.6	498.4
Indiana............	167.3	195.6	223.7	218.5	226.6	186.3	195.5	205.1	200.0	203.9
Iowa...............	79.9	95.4	114.4	113.2	116.6	89.0	95.5	104.9	103.6	104.9
Kansas............	76.7	90.9	112.0	110.4	113.4	85.4	90.9	102.7	101.1	102.0
Kentucky	100.4	119.0	138.5	139.2	144.7	111.8	119.2	127.0	127.4	130.2
Louisiana	105.3	135.3	169.8	169.0	174.3	117.3	135.3	155.7	154.7	156.9
Maine..............	34.1	42.0	48.3	48.2	49.5	38.0	42.0	44.3	44.1	44.6
Maryland	184.2	237.5	274.3	275.0	283.0	205.1	237.1	251.5	251.7	254.7
Massachusetts........	243.1	282.4	333.8	327.4	337.5	270.8	282.4	306.1	299.7	303.8
Michigan	292.6	325.7	353.1	342.1	351.8	325.9	325.7	323.8	313.1	316.6
Minnesota	160.8	193.9	226.1	220.4	227.2	179.1	194.0	207.4	201.7	204.5
Mississippi..........	61.4	77.8	90.3	89.7	92.5	68.4	77.7	82.8	82.1	83.3
Missouri...........	156.4	186.7	219.7	216.6	221.5	174.2	186.8	201.4	198.3	199.3
Montana...........	21.2	28.2	34.1	34.0	34.9	23.6	28.2	31.3	31.1	31.4
Nebraska...........	49.0	60.1	71.6	70.7	72.2	54.6	60.1	65.6	64.7	65.0
Nevada	62.5	91.8	104.7	99.6	99.9	69.7	91.8	96.0	91.1	89.9
New Hampshire.......	42.3	50.0	57.8	56.5	58.0	47.1	50.0	53.0	51.7	52.2
New Jersey	326.0	379.9	448.0	435.2	446.5	363.1	379.7	410.8	398.3	401.8
New Mexico..........	41.4	55.3	66.8	66.9	69.7	46.1	55.3	61.2	61.2	62.7
New York	657.9	786.6	937.2	909.0	946.1	732.8	786.5	859.3	832.0	851.4
North Carolina.......	225.5	277.7	330.0	327.2	339.8	251.2	277.7	302.6	299.5	305.8
North Dakota.........	16.4	20.6	26.6	26.4	27.3	18.3	20.5	24.4	24.2	24.6
Ohio...............	326.1	372.1	414.5	408.7	419.9	363.2	371.9	380.0	374.1	377.9
Oklahoma	85.0	107.6	134.5	132.1	136.6	94.7	107.6	123.3	120.9	123.0
Oregon............	98.5	117.7	139.3	138.5	142.1	109.7	117.6	127.7	126.7	127.9
Pennsylvania	369.9	432.0	508.2	506.4	522.7	412.0	432.2	466.0	463.5	470.4
Rhode Island	31.0	38.6	44.1	43.6	44.8	34.5	38.6	40.4	39.9	40.3
South Carolina........	100.9	124.4	148.9	148.3	153.4	112.4	124.4	136.5	135.7	138.0
South Dakota.........	20.0	25.8	31.7	31.2	31.6	22.2	25.8	29.1	28.5	28.5
Tennessee..........	152.2	187.6	219.2	215.8	224.1	169.6	187.7	201.0	197.5	201.6
Texas..............	597.0	756.7	968.2	956.8	993.1	665.0	756.7	887.8	875.7	893.7
Utah...............	55.0	71.5	88.8	87.9	90.1	61.3	71.5	81.4	80.5	81.1
Vermont............	17.2	20.7	24.5	24.4	25.2	19.1	20.7	22.4	22.3	22.7
Virginia............	224.8	294.2	348.3	347.3	358.1	250.4	294.7	319.3	317.9	322.3
Washington	191.6	230.0	287.0	285.7	293.0	213.4	230.1	263.2	261.5	263.6
West Virginia	40.1	48.1	57.2	58.4	60.5	44.6	48.1	52.5	53.4	54.4
Wisconsin	156.6	186.6	213.3	211.3	218.6	174.4	186.5	195.6	193.4	196.7
Wyoming	14.5	20.0	27.0	26.3	27.0	16.1	20.0	24.8	24.1	24.3

[1] Constant dollar estimates are computed by the U.S. Census Bureau using the national implicit price deflator for personal consumption expenditures from the Bureau of Economic Analysis. Any regional differences in the rate of inflation are not reflected in these constant dollar estimates.

Source: Except as noted, U.S. Bureau of Economic Analysis, *Survey of Current Business,* April 2011, and unpublished data. See also <http://www.bea.gov/regional/spi>.

Table 681. Personal Income Per Capita in Current and Constant (2005) Dollars by State: 1980 to 2010

[In dollars, except as indicated. 2010 preliminary. See headnote, Table 680]

State	Current dollars				Constant (2005) dollars [1]				Income rank	
	1980	1990	2000	2010, prel.	1980	1990	2000	2010, prel	2000	2010
United States	**10,091**	**19,354**	**30,318**	**40,584**	**21,635**	**26,826**	**33,770**	**36,524**	**(X)**	**(X)**
Alabama	7,825	15,618	24,069	33,945	16,777	21,647	26,810	30,549	44	42
Alaska	14,975	22,594	30,531	44,174	32,107	31,317	34,008	39,754	15	8
Arizona	9,484	16,806	26,262	34,999	20,334	23,294	29,252	31,497	37	40
Arkansas	7,521	14,402	22,577	33,150	16,125	19,962	25,148	29,833	48	46
California	11,928	21,380	33,398	43,104	25,574	29,634	37,201	38,792	8	12
Colorado	10,714	19,377	33,977	42,802	22,971	26,858	37,846	38,520	7	14
Connecticut	12,321	26,198	41,920	56,001	26,417	36,312	46,693	50,398	1	1
Delaware	10,756	21,209	31,007	39,962	23,061	29,397	34,538	35,964	13	20
District of Columbia	12,218	26,015	40,484	71,044	26,196	36,058	45,094	63,936	(X)	(X)
Florida	9,921	19,437	29,080	39,272	21,271	26,941	32,391	35,343	21	24
Georgia	8,408	17,563	28,531	35,490	18,027	24,343	31,780	31,939	26	37
Hawaii	11,394	21,818	29,071	41,021	24,429	30,241	32,381	36,917	22	17
Idaho	8,637	15,603	24,683	32,257	18,518	21,627	27,494	29,030	41	49
Illinois	10,980	20,835	32,636	43,159	23,542	28,879	36,352	38,841	9	11
Indiana	9,353	17,454	27,460	34,943	20,053	24,192	30,587	31,447	32	41
Iowa	9,573	17,350	27,293	38,281	20,525	24,048	30,401	34,451	33	28
Kansas	9,939	18,034	28,477	39,737	21,310	24,996	31,720	35,761	28	21
Kentucky	8,113	15,360	24,786	33,348	17,395	21,290	27,608	30,012	40	44
Louisiana	8,767	15,171	23,570	38,446	18,797	21,028	26,254	34,600	45	26
Maine	8,333	17,211	26,696	37,300	17,866	23,855	29,736	33,568	34	29
Maryland	11,164	22,681	34,681	49,025	23,936	31,437	38,630	44,120	4	4
Massachusetts	10,570	22,797	38,210	51,552	22,662	31,598	42,561	46,394	3	2
Michigan	10,291	18,719	29,392	35,597	22,064	25,946	32,739	32,036	18	36
Minnesota	10,229	19,710	32,597	42,843	21,931	27,319	36,309	38,557	10	13
Mississippi	7,005	13,117	21,555	31,186	15,019	18,181	24,009	28,066	50	50
Missouri	9,306	17,582	27,891	36,979	19,952	24,370	31,067	33,279	31	32
Montana	9,038	15,346	23,470	35,317	19,378	21,270	26,143	31,784	46	38
Nebraska	9,155	17,948	28,598	39,557	19,629	24,877	31,854	35,599	25	22
Nevada	11,679	20,042	30,986	36,997	25,040	27,779	34,514	33,296	14	31
New Hampshire	9,816	20,236	34,087	44,084	21,046	28,048	37,969	39,673	6	9
New Jersey	11,676	24,354	38,666	50,781	25,034	33,756	43,069	45,700	2	3
New Mexico	8,331	14,823	22,751	33,837	17,862	20,546	25,342	30,452	47	43
New York	10,985	23,710	34,630	48,821	23,552	32,863	38,573	43,937	5	5
North Carolina	8,183	17,194	27,914	35,638	17,545	23,832	31,093	32,073	30	35
North Dakota	7,894	15,866	25,624	40,596	16,925	21,991	28,542	36,534	38	18
Ohio	10,022	18,638	28,694	36,395	21,488	25,833	31,961	32,754	24	34
Oklahoma	9,487	16,077	24,605	36,421	20,340	22,284	27,407	32,777	42	33
Oregon	10,086	17,895	28,718	37,095	21,625	24,804	31,988	33,384	23	30
Pennsylvania	10,040	19,433	30,110	41,152	21,526	26,935	33,539	37,035	16	16
Rhode Island	9,645	19,821	29,484	42,579	20,679	27,473	32,841	38,319	17	15
South Carolina	7,736	15,844	25,081	33,163	16,586	21,961	27,937	29,845	39	45
South Dakota	8,054	16,075	26,427	38,865	17,268	22,281	29,436	34,977	36	25
Tennessee	8,227	16,574	26,691	35,307	17,639	22,973	29,730	31,775	35	39
Texas	9,870	17,260	28,504	39,493	21,162	23,923	31,750	35,542	27	23
Utah	8,492	14,847	24,517	32,595	18,207	20,579	27,309	29,334	43	48
Vermont	8,599	17,643	28,183	40,283	18,437	24,454	31,392	36,253	29	19
Virginia	10,107	20,312	31,640	44,762	21,670	28,154	35,243	40,284	12	7
Washington	10,810	19,637	32,407	43,564	23,177	27,218	36,097	39,206	11	10
West Virginia	8,066	14,436	22,174	32,641	17,294	20,009	24,699	29,375	49	47
Wisconsin	10,085	17,986	29,139	38,432	21,623	24,930	32,457	34,587	20	27
Wyoming	11,668	17,910	29,281	47,851	25,017	24,824	32,615	43,064	19	6

X Not applicable. [1] Constant dollar estimates are computed by the U.S. Census Bureau using the national implicit price deflator for personal consumption expenditures from the Bureau of Economic Analysis. Any regional differences in the rate of inflation are not reflected in these constant dollar estimates.

Source: Except as noted, U.S. Bureau of Economic Analysis, *Survey of Current Business,* April 2011, and unpublished data. See also <http://www.bea.gov/bea/regional/spi>.

Table 682. Disposable Personal Income Per Capita in Current and Constant (2005) Dollars by State: 1980 to 2010

[In dollars, except percent. 2010 preliminary. Disposable personal income is the income available to persons for spending or saving; it is calculated as personal income less personal tax and nontax payments. See headnote, Table 680]

State	Current dollars				Constant (2005) dollars [1]				Index, compared to U.S. average	
	1980	1990	2000	2010, prel.	1980	1990	2000	2010, prel.	2000	2010, prel.
United States	**8,779**	**16,985**	**25,955**	**36,808**	**18,822**	**23,542**	**28,911**	**33,125**	**100.0**	**100.0**
Alabama	6,955	13,943	21,357	31,363	14,912	19,326	23,789	28,225	82.3	85.2
Alaska	13,057	19,937	27,101	40,530	27,995	27,634	30,187	36,475	104.4	110.1
Arizona	8,418	14,932	22,939	32,443	18,048	20,697	25,551	29,197	88.4	88.1
Arkansas	6,701	12,928	20,034	30,567	14,367	17,919	22,315	27,509	77.2	83.0
California	10,420	18,614	27,664	38,674	22,341	25,800	30,814	34,805	106.6	105.1
Colorado	9,288	17,003	28,857	38,810	19,914	23,567	32,143	34,927	111.2	105.4
Connecticut	10,551	22,815	33,837	48,596	22,622	31,623	37,690	43,734	130.4	132.0
Delaware	8,977	18,262	26,427	36,171	19,247	25,312	29,436	32,552	101.8	98.3
District of Columbia	10,378	22,400	33,459	63,619	22,251	31,048	37,269	57,254	128.9	172.8
Florida	8,752	17,398	25,392	36,413	18,765	24,115	28,283	32,770	97.8	98.9
Georgia	7,397	15,424	24,606	32,519	15,859	21,379	27,408	29,266	94.8	88.3
Hawaii	9,959	18,901	25,495	37,625	21,352	26,198	28,398	33,861	98.2	102.2
Idaho	7,708	13,868	21,575	29,804	16,526	19,222	24,032	26,822	83.1	81.0
Illinois	9,439	18,180	27,877	39,097	20,238	25,199	31,051	35,185	107.4	106.2
Indiana	8,168	15,331	23,983	31,949	17,512	21,250	26,714	28,753	92.4	86.8
Iowa	8,307	15,330	24,136	35,010	17,811	21,248	26,884	31,507	93.0	95.1
Kansas	8,616	15,921	24,841	36,215	18,473	22,067	27,670	32,592	95.7	98.4
Kentucky	7,173	13,544	21,726	30,526	15,379	18,773	24,200	27,472	83.7	82.9
Louisiana	7,669	13,687	21,073	35,271	16,443	18,971	23,473	31,742	81.2	95.8
Maine	7,450	15,222	23,227	34,169	15,973	21,099	25,872	30,750	89.5	92.8
Maryland	9,488	19,420	29,231	43,753	20,343	26,917	32,560	39,376	112.6	118.9
Massachusetts	9,021	19,549	30,786	45,511	19,341	27,096	34,292	40,958	118.6	123.6
Michigan	8,961	16,368	25,285	32,728	19,213	22,687	28,164	29,454	97.4	88.9
Minnesota	8,810	17,123	27,780	38,411	18,889	23,733	30,943	34,568	107.0	104.4
Mississippi	6,303	11,938	19,491	29,155	13,514	16,547	21,710	26,238	75.1	79.2
Missouri	8,124	15,492	24,335	33,813	17,418	21,473	27,106	30,430	93.8	91.9
Montana	7,936	13,693	20,781	32,395	17,015	18,979	23,147	29,154	80.1	88.0
Nebraska	8,010	15,996	25,070	36,166	17,174	22,171	27,925	32,548	96.6	98.3
Nevada	10,279	17,562	26,882	34,313	22,039	24,342	29,943	30,880	103.6	93.2
New Hampshire	8,664	18,016	29,273	40,532	18,576	24,971	32,606	36,477	112.8	110.1
New Jersey	10,053	21,163	32,333	45,197	21,554	29,333	36,015	40,675	124.6	122.8
New Mexico	7,467	13,313	20,200	31,410	16,010	18,453	22,500	28,268	77.8	85.3
New York	9,395	20,371	28,623	42,492	20,143	28,235	31,882	38,241	110.3	115.4
North Carolina	7,160	15,145	24,253	32,567	15,351	20,992	27,015	29,309	93.4	88.5
North Dakota	6,920	14,380	23,121	36,997	14,837	19,932	25,754	33,296	89.1	100.5
Ohio	8,746	16,341	24,757	33,182	18,752	22,650	27,576	29,862	95.4	90.1
Oklahoma	8,260	14,170	21,723	33,497	17,710	19,640	24,197	30,146	83.7	91.0
Oregon	8,705	15,709	24,536	33,592	18,664	21,774	27,330	30,231	94.5	91.3
Pennsylvania	8,725	17,091	25,999	37,164	18,707	23,689	28,960	33,446	100.2	101.0
Rhode Island	8,445	17,453	25,340	38,873	18,106	24,191	28,225	34,984	97.6	105.6
South Carolina	6,840	14,044	22,165	30,713	14,665	19,466	24,689	27,640	85.4	83.4
South Dakota	7,298	14,725	23,881	36,236	15,647	20,410	26,600	32,611	92.0	98.4
Tennessee	7,374	15,004	24,011	33,146	15,810	20,796	26,745	29,830	92.5	90.1
Texas	8,553	15,463	25,166	36,354	18,338	21,433	28,032	32,717	97.0	98.8
Utah	7,575	13,131	21,454	29,823	16,241	18,200	23,897	26,839	82.7	81.0
Vermont	7,593	15,527	24,523	36,920	16,280	21,521	27,315	33,226	94.5	100.3
Virginia	8,732	17,735	26,780	40,186	18,722	24,582	29,829	36,165	103.2	109.2
Washington	9,464	17,449	27,951	40,312	20,291	24,185	31,134	36,279	107.7	109.5
West Virginia	7,077	12,908	19,815	29,977	15,173	17,891	22,071	26,978	76.3	81.4
Wisconsin	8,764	15,716	25,078	34,855	18,790	21,783	27,934	31,368	96.6	94.7
Wyoming	10,167	16,056	25,330	43,602	21,798	22,255	28,214	39,240	97.6	118.5

[1] Constant dollar estimates are computed by the Census Bureau using the national implicit price deflator for personal consumption expenditures from the Bureau of Economic Analysis. Any regional differences in the rate of inflation are not reflected in these constant dollar estimates.

Source: Except as noted, U.S. Bureau of Economic Analysis, *Survey of Current Business,* April 2011, earlier reports and unpublished data. See also <http://www.bea.gov/regional/spi>.

Table 683. Personal Income by Selected Large Metropolitan Area: 2005 to 2009

[10,476,669 represents $10,476,669,000,000. Metropolitan areas as defined December 2009. MSA = Metropolitan Statistical Area. See Appendix II. Minus sign (−) indicates decrease]

Metropolitan areas ranked by 2009 population	Personal income				Personal income per capita			
	2005 (mil. dol.)	2008 (mil. dol.)	2009 (mil. dol.)	Annual percent change, 2008–2009	2005 (dol.)	2008 (dol.)	2009 (dol.)	Index (U.S.=100), 2009
United States	10,476,669	12,380,225	12,168,161	−1.7	35,424	40,674	39,635	100.0
New York-Northern New Jersey-Long Island, NY-NJ-PA MSA	863,632	1,032,619	992,331	−3.9	45,942	54,439	52,037	131.3
Los Angeles-Long Beach-Santa Ana, CA MSA	496,595	567,707	550,832	−3.0	38,915	44,462	42,784	107.9
Chicago-Joliet-Naperville, IL-IN-WI MSA	375,515	438,902	425,178	−3.1	40,110	46,124	44,379	112.0
Dallas-Fort Worth-Arlington, TX MSA	220,482	275,258	269,280	−2.2	37,907	43,684	41,764	105.4
Philadelphia-Camden-Wilmington, PA-NJ-DE-MD MSA	236,491	277,421	274,986	−0.9	40,422	46,700	46,075	116.2
Houston-Sugar Land-Baytown, TX MSA	209,655	280,247	273,247	−2.5	39,561	48,937	46,570	117.5
Miami-Fort Lauderdale-Pompano Beach, FL MSA	210,605	244,913	237,215	−3.1	38,692	44,515	42,764	107.9
Washington-Arlington-Alexandria, DC-VA-MD-WV MSA	262,193	310,761	312,059	0.4	50,140	57,784	56,984	143.8
Atlanta-Sandy Springs-Marietta, GA MSA	179,145	209,581	203,138	−3.1	36,213	38,915	37,101	93.6
Boston-Cambridge-Quincy, MA-NH MSA	212,251	251,777	245,736	−2.4	47,602	55,400	53,553	135.1
Detroit-Warren-Livonia, MI MSA	164,087	175,014	167,009	−4.6	36,509	39,562	37,927	95.7
Phoenix-Mesa-Glendale, AZ MSA	131,597	155,067	150,352	−3.0	33,877	36,169	34,452	86.9
San Francisco-Oakland-Fremont, CA MSA	227,850	265,954	259,043	−2.6	54,909	62,427	59,993	151.4
Riverside-San Bernardino-Ontario, CA MSA	108,598	125,025	122,969	−1.6	28,124	30,547	29,680	74.9
Seattle-Tacoma-Bellevue, WA MSA	138,212	173,322	171,681	−0.9	43,159	51,636	50,378	127.1
Minneapolis-St. Paul-Bloomington, MN-WI MSA	133,840	154,421	149,795	−3.0	42,723	47,696	45,811	115.6
San Diego-Carlsbad-San Marcos, CA MSA	122,030	141,971	139,577	−1.7	41,482	47,021	45,706	115.3
St. Louis, MO-IL MSA	101,082	119,122	115,220	−3.3	36,450	42,262	40,728	102.8
Tampa-St. Petersburg-Clearwater, FL MSA	91,393	104,955	103,386	−1.5	34,634	38,445	37,632	94.9
Baltimore-Towson, MD MSA	111,453	129,323	129,704	0.3	42,064	48,296	48,201	121.6
Denver-Aurora-Broomfield, CO MSA	101,788	121,505	118,961	−2.1	43,249	48,595	46,611	117.6
Pittsburgh, PA MSA	84,956	100,276	99,611	−0.7	35,811	42,573	42,298	106.7
Portland-South Portland-Biddeford, ME MSA	74,750	88,978	87,894	−1.2	35,868	40,376	39,206	98.9
Cincinnati-Middletown, OH-KY-IN MSA	75,148	84,080	82,460	−1.9	35,744	38,950	37,967	95.8
Sacramento-Arden-Arcade-Roseville, CA MSA	75,029	86,876	85,746	−1.3	36,985	41,347	40,306	101.7
Cleveland-Elyria-Mentor, OH MSA	76,110	84,553	82,503	−2.4	35,931	40,378	39,451	99.5
Orlando-Kissimmee-Sanford, FL MSA	64,007	75,473	73,466	−2.7	32,997	36,620	35,279	89.0
San Antonio-New Braunfels, TX MSA	58,670	74,218	75,186	1.3	31,239	36,548	36,285	91.5
Kansas City, MO-KS MSA	70,738	84,584	83,610	−1.2	36,118	41,340	40,438	102.0
Las Vegas-Paradise, NV MSA	64,181	73,753	69,855	−5.3	37,558	39,249	36,711	92.6
San Jose-Sunnyvale-Santa Clara, CA MSA	89,629	105,652	101,495	−3.9	51,591	58,351	55,169	139.2
Columbus, OH MSA	60,968	68,777	68,469	−0.4	35,561	38,642	37,999	95.9
Charlotte-Gastonia-Rock Hill, NC-SC MSA	57,216	68,639	66,389	−3.3	37,656	40,223	38,034	96.0
Indianapolis-Carmel, IN MSA	60,018	68,537	67,187	−2.0	36,484	39,829	38,532	97.2
Austin-Round Rock-San Marcos, TX MSA	51,047	64,412	64,015	−0.6	34,861	38,941	37,544	94.7
Virginia Beach-Norfolk-Newport News, VA-NC MSA	56,595	66,458	66,173	−0.4	34,107	39,790	39,518	99.7
Providence-New Bedford-Fall River, RI-MA MSA	57,418	65,937	65,353	−0.9	35,670	41,228	40,829	103.0
Nashville-Davidson-Murfreesboro-Franklin, TN MSA	52,294	62,638	61,164	−2.4	36,051	40,246	38,656	97.5
Milwaukee-Waukesha-West Allis, WI MSA	58,251	66,671	65,978	−1.0	37,916	43,001	42,303	106.7
Jacksonville, FL MSA	45,618	53,381	52,297	−2.0	36,537	40,547	39,376	99.3
Memphis, TN-MS-AR MSA	44,057	50,222	49,095	−2.2	34,927	38,676	37,623	94.9
Louisville-Jefferson County, KY-IN MSA	41,228	47,793	47,433	−0.8	34,087	38,242	37,688	95.1
Richmond, VA MSA	44,587	52,001	50,966	−2.0	37,979	42,377	41,161	103.9
Oklahoma City, OK MSA	38,462	48,266	47,547	−1.5	33,298	39,971	38,742	97.7
Hartford-West Hartford-East Hartford, CT MSA	51,428	61,636	60,607	−1.7	43,636	51,744	50,675	127.9
New Orleans-Metairie-Kenner, LA MSA	43,498	51,929	50,818	−2.1	33,117	44,439	42,705	107.7
Birmingham-Hoover, AL MSA	39,199	44,868	43,650	−2.7	35,948	39,949	38,592	97.4
Salt Lake City, UT MSA	35,347	42,854	42,386	−1.1	33,830	38,552	37,500	94.6
Raleigh-Cary, NC MSA	35,209	43,320	42,789	−1.2	36,939	39,728	38,007	95.9
Buffalo-Niagara Falls, NY MSA	36,232	41,978	42,108	0.3	31,801	37,345	37,469	94.5
Rochester, NY MSA	35,256	40,693	40,424	−0.7	34,114	39,387	39,036	98.5
Tucson, AZ MSA	28,574	34,918	34,516	−1.1	30,110	34,578	33,833	85.4
Tulsa, OK MSA	30,734	38,585	37,534	−2.7	34,860	42,122	40,402	101.9
Fresno, CA MSA	24,078	28,097	28,050	−0.2	27,758	31,111	30,646	77.3
Honolulu, HI MSA	34,264	41,188	41,291	0.3	38,057	45,625	45,496	114.8
Bridgeport-Stamford-Norwalk, CT MSA	61,073	71,232	67,380	−5.4	68,543	79,642	74,767	188.6
Albuquerque, NM MSA	25,338	30,145	30,309	0.5	31,724	35,608	35,329	89.1
Albany-Schenectady-Troy, NY MSA	30,672	36,006	36,195	0.5	36,240	42,147	42,206	106.5
Omaha-Council Bluffs, NE-IA MSA	31,077	36,927	36,514	−1.1	38,343	43,999	42,982	108.4
New Haven-Milford, CT MSA	33,857	40,730	40,184	−1.3	40,334	48,169	47,387	119.6

Source: U.S. Bureau of Economic Analysis, *Survey of Current Business*, April 2011. See also <http://www.bea.gov/regional/reis>.

Income, Expenditures, Poverty, and Wealth **447**

Table 684. Average Annual Expenditures of All Consumer Units by Selected Major Types of Expenditure: 1990 to 2009

[In dollars, except as indicated (96,968 represents $96,968,000). Based on Consumer Expenditure Survey. Data are averages for the noninstitutional population. Expenditures reported here are out-of-pocket. Consumer units include families, single persons living alone or sharing a household with others but who are financially independent, or two or more persons living together who share expenses]

Type of expenditure	1990	1995	2000	2005	2006	2007	2008	2009
Number of consumer units (1,000)	96,968	103,123	109,367	117,356	118,843	120,171	120,770	120,847
Expenditures, total [1] (dol.)	**28,381**	**32,264**	**38,045**	**46,409**	**48,398**	**49,638**	**50,486**	**49,067**
Food	4,296	4,505	5,158	5,931	6,111	6,133	6,443	6,372
Food at home [1]	2,485	2,803	3,021	3,297	3,417	3,465	3,744	3,753
Meats, poultry, fish, and eggs	668	752	795	764	797	777	846	841
Dairy products	295	297	325	378	368	387	430	406
Fruits and vegetables	408	457	521	552	592	600	657	656
Other food at home	746	856	927	1,158	1,212	1,241	1,305	1,343
Food away from home	1,811	1,702	2,137	2,634	2,694	2,668	2,698	2,619
Alcoholic beverages	293	277	372	426	497	457	444	435
Housing [1]	8,703	10,458	12,319	15,167	16,366	16,920	17,109	16,895
Shelter	4,836	5,928	7,114	8,805	9,673	10,023	10,183	10,075
Utilities, fuels, and public services	1,890	2,191	2,489	3,183	3,397	3,477	3,649	3,645
Apparel and services	1,618	1,704	1,856	1,886	1,874	1,881	1,801	1,725
Transportation [1]	5,120	6,014	7,417	8,344	8,508	8,758	8,604	7,658
Vehicle purchases	2,129	2,638	3,418	3,544	3,421	3,244	2,755	2,657
Gasoline and motor oil	1,047	1,006	1,291	2,013	2,227	2,384	2,715	1,986
Other vehicle expenses	1,642	2,015	2,281	2,339	2,355	2,592	2,621	2,536
Health care	1,480	1,732	2,066	2,664	2,766	2,853	2,976	3,126
Entertainment	1,422	1,612	1,863	2,388	2,376	2,698	2,835	2,693
Reading	153	162	146	126	117	118	116	110
Tobacco products, smoking supplies	274	269	319	319	327	323	317	380
Personal insurance and pensions	2,592	2,964	3,365	5,204	5,270	5,336	5,605	5,471
Life and other personal insurance	345	373	399	381	322	309	317	309
Pensions and Social Security	2,248	2,591	2,966	4,823	4,948	5,027	5,288	5,162

[1] Includes expenditures not shown separately.

Source: U.S. Bureau of Labor Statistics, *Consumer Expenditures in 2009*, News Release, USDL-10-1390, October 2010. See also <http://stats.bls.gov/cex/home.htm>.

Table 685. Average Annual Expenditures of All Consumer Units by Metropolitan Area: 2008 to 2009

[In dollars. Covers 2-year period, 2008–2009. Metropolitan areas defined June 30, 1983: CMSA = Consolidated Metropolitan Statistical Area; MSA = Metropolitan Statistical Area; PMSA = Primary Metropolitan Statistical Area. See text, Section 1 and Appendix II. See headnote, Table 684]

Metropolitan area	Total expenditures [1]	Food	Housing Total [1]	Housing Shelter	Housing Utility, fuels [2]	Transportation Total [1]	Transportation Vehicle purchases	Transportation Gasoline and motor oil	Health care
Atlanta, GA MSA	45,941	5,375	17,072	10,639	3,899	6,760	1,597	2,631	2,417
Baltimore, MD MSA	52,452	5,931	20,795	13,617	4,209	6,621	[1] 1,452	2,444	2,973
Boston-Lawrence-Salem, MA-NH CMSA	59,227	8,167	20,802	12,857	4,248	8,591	2,818	2,125	3,453
Chicago-Gary-Lake County, IL-IN-WI CMSA	56,947	7,037	20,620	13,116	4,052	8,840	3,101	2,364	3,485
Cleveland-Akron-Lorain, OH CMSA	45,844	5,737	15,483	8,820	3,837	7,010	2,098	2,049	3,315
Dallas-Fort Worth, TX CMSA	53,886	6,734	18,198	10,253	4,275	8,689	2,877	2,616	3,032
Detroit-Ann Arbor, MI CMSA	49,397	6,412	16,344	9,635	3,791	9,463	2,793	2,624	2,672
Houston-Galveston-Brazoria, TX CMSA	59,131	7,009	18,866	10,776	4,505	10,843	3,874	2,980	3,267
Los Angeles-Long Beach, CA PMSA	56,529	7,531	21,811	14,938	3,257	8,784	2,513	2,667	2,620
Miami-Fort Lauderdale, FL CMSA	47,601	5,803	19,016	12,592	3,740	8,427	2,921	2,680	1,565
Minneapolis-St. Paul, MN-WI MSA	56,340	6,887	19,164	11,852	3,513	8,833	2,911	2,350	3,314
New York-Northern New Jersey-Long Island, NY-NJ-CT CMSA	60,273	7,420	23,624	15,482	4,309	8,495	2,321	1,943	3,027
Philadelphia-Wilmington-Trenton, PA-NJ-DE-MD CMSA	56,790	6,460	21,135	13,597	4,444	8,202	2,037	2,240	3,036
Phoenix-Mesa, AZ MSA	53,618	6,402	18,698	11,185	3,892	9,330	2,887	2,658	3,326
San Diego, CA MSA	53,820	6,541	22,207	15,146	2,989	7,171	[1] 1,941	2,412	2,249
San Francisco-Oakland-San Jose, CA CMSA	67,730	7,952	26,064	19,096	3,139	9,535	2,748	2,235	3,319
Seattle-Tacoma, WA CMSA	66,015	8,082	22,029	13,829	3,554	9,380	3,395	2,454	3,684
Washington, DC-MD-VA MSA	69,106	7,835	25,622	16,842	3,977	9,563	3,028	2,465	3,239

[1] Includes expenditures not shown separately. [2] Includes public services.

Source: U.S. Bureau of Labor Statistics, *Consumer Expenditures in 2009*, News Release, USDL-10-1390, October 2010. See also <http://stats.bls.gov/cex/home.htm>.

Table 686. Average Annual Expenditures of All Consumer Units by Race, Hispanic Origin, and Age of Householder: 2009

[In dollars. See headnote, Table 684]

Type	All consumer units [1]	White and all other races	Asian	Black or African American	Hispanic [2]	Under 25 years	65 years old and over
Expenditures, total	**49,067**	**50,723**	**56,308**	**35,311**	**41,981**	**28,119**	**37,562**
Food	6,372	6,585	7,565	4,524	6,094	4,179	4,901
Food at home	3,753	3,870	3,905	2,880	3,784	2,449	3,222
Cereals and bakery products	506	522	520	390	479	307	439
Cereals and cereal products	173	174	215	149	184	124	138
Bakery products	334	348	305	241	294	183	301
Meats, poultry, fish, and eggs [3]	841	835	966	845	955	571	720
Beef	226	233	186	191	252	146	192
Pork	168	165	172	193	202	130	145
Poultry	154	149	184	183	192	120	111
Fish and seafood	135	128	274	144	141	75	129
Dairy products	406	429	346	258	403	281	346
Fresh milk and cream	144	149	152	105	171	110	125
Other dairy products	262	280	195	153	232	171	221
Fruits and vegetables [3]	656	671	903	484	734	398	618
Fresh fruits	220	226	310	151	256	116	215
Fresh vegetables	209	213	385	136	240	130	192
Processed fruits	118	120	117	105	121	86	109
Other food at home [3]	1,343	1,412	1,169	903	1,213	891	1,100
Sugar and other sweets	141	149	106	88	109	88	127
Nonalcoholic beverages	337	351	267	253	348	232	264
Food away from home	2,619	2,715	3,660	1,645	2,310	1,731	1,679
Alcoholic beverages	435	471	350	201	267	344	292
Housing	16,895	17,224	20,395	13,503	15,983	9,735	13,196
Shelter	10,075	10,228	13,571	7,919	10,043	6,306	7,173
Owned dwellings	6,543	6,872	8,543	3,632	5,298	1,245	4,838
Mortgage interest and charges	3,594	3,713	5,349	2,220	3,454	783	1,322
Property taxes	1,811	1,917	2,334	912	1,368	324	1,793
Maintenance, repair, insurance, other expenses	1,138	1,242	860	500	476	139	1,723
Rented dwellings	2,860	2,619	4,411	4,046	4,415	4,885	1,741
Other lodging	672	737	616	241	330	176	594
Utilities, fuels, and public services	3,645	3,658	3,270	3,668	3,532	1,821	3,282
Natural gas	483	478	499	517	389	188	494
Electricity	1,377	1,379	1,056	1,462	1,339	696	1,261
Fuel oil and other fuels	141	159	[4] 48	50	47	16	186
Telephone	1,162	1,155	1,123	1,224	1,272	758	858
Water and other public services	481	488	544	415	485	163	483
Household operations	1,011	1,051	1,347	633	714	370	876
Personal services	389	392	688	281	334	156	194
Other household expenses	622	659	659	352	380	214	681
Housekeeping supplies [3]	659	696	536	429	517	309	682
Laundry and cleaning supplies	156	161	130	124	194	91	137
Postage and stationery	143	153	113	81	91	49	167
Household furnishings and equipment [3]	1,506	1,591	1,671	854	1,177	929	1,184
Household textiles	124	128	187	79	101	43	107
Furniture	343	355	304	271	331	336	209
Major appliances	194	204	183	127	146	79	159
Miscellaneous household equipment	721	772	848	319	513	427	581
Apparel and services [3]	1,725	1,704	2,150	1,755	2,002	1,396	1,068
Men and boys	383	380	427	388	432	256	215
Women and girls	678	676	913	629	693	545	456
Footwear	323	307	344	430	472	278	223
Other apparel products and services	249	248	344	231	258	163	149
Transportation	7,658	7,950	8,784	5,302	7,156	5,334	5,409
Vehicle purchases (net outlay) [3]	2,657	2,829	2,582	1,489	2,333	2,319	1,862
Cars and trucks, new	1,297	1,410	1,131	568	1,010	542	1,210
Cars and trucks, used	1,304	1,355	1,451	910	1,293	1,760	619
Gasoline and motor oil	1,986	2,045	1,871	1,618	2,104	1,483	1,241
Other vehicle expenses	2,536	2,605	3,153	1,876	2,309	1,298	1,968
Vehicle finance charges	281	290	208	242	278	180	124
Maintenance and repair	733	767	713	504	584	447	557
Vehicle insurance	1,075	1,085	1,610	859	1,049	465	972
Vehicle rental, leases, licenses, other charges	447	464	623	270	398	206	314
Public transportation	479	471	1,178	319	410	234	338
Health care [5]	3,126	3,351	2,498	1,763	1,568	676	4,846
Entertainment [6]	2,693	2,894	2,270	1,404	1,664	1,233	2,062
Personal care products and services	596	606	557	536	532	360	531
Reading	110	119	111	46	36	42	145
Education	1,068	1,080	2,327	591	707	1,910	162
Tobacco products and smoking supplies	380	413	122	230	182	330	207
Miscellaneous	816	853	611	626	544	243	663
Cash contributions	1,723	1,799	1,452	1,280	1,015	349	2,226
Personal insurance and pensions	5,471	5,674	7,117	3,550	4,230	1,988	1,856
Life and other personal insurance	309	321	283	235	119	31	320
Pensions and social security	5,162	5,353	6,834	3,315	4,111	1,957	1,537
Personal taxes	**2,104**	**2,236**	**3,526**	**743**	**745**	**173**	**807**

[1] Includes other races not shown separately. [2] People of Hispanic origin may be any race. [3] Includes other types, not shown separately. [4] Data are likely to have large sampling errors. [5] For additional health care expenditures, see Table 143. [6] For additional recreation expenditures, see Section 26.

Source: U.S. Bureau of Labor Statistics, *Consumer Expenditures in 2009*, News Release, USDL-10-1390, October 2010. See also <ftp://ftp.bls.gov/pub/special.requests/ce/standard/2009/race.txt>, <ftp://ftp.bls.gov/pub/special.requests /ce/standard/2009/hispanic.txt>, and <ftp://ftp.bls.gov/pub/special.requests/ce/standard/2009/age.txt>.

Table 687. Average Annual Expenditures of All Consumer Units by Region and Size of Unit: 2009

[In dollars. For composition of regions, see map, inside front cover. See headnote, Table 684]

Type	Region				Size of consumer unit				
	North-east	Mid-west	South	West	One person	Two persons	Three persons	Four persons	Five or more
Expenditures, total	**53,868**	**46,551**	**45,749**	**53,005**	**29,405**	**51,650**	**56,645**	**65,503**	**63,439**
Food	6,975	6,031	5,944	6,903	3,460	6,308	7,506	8,730	10,034
Food at home	4,043	3,682	3,481	4,023	1,953	3,631	4,454	5,187	6,324
Cereals and bakery products	563	510	469	516	255	470	588	719	937
Cereals and cereal products	188	176	157	182	80	156	200	258	335
Bakery products	376	334	313	334	175	314	388	460	602
Meats, poultry, fish, and eggs[1]	919	762	829	875	408	813	1,024	1,170	1,457
Beef	230	207	230	236	104	222	285	314	383
Pork	165	171	172	163	79	162	203	235	303
Poultry	169	121	158	169	71	141	188	232	279
Fish and seafood	176	103	125	150	76	132	162	176	218
Dairy products	435	419	367	432	214	391	472	568	689
Fresh milk and cream	152	140	140	148	75	129	169	207	267
Other dairy products	284	279	227	284	139	261	303	361	421
Fruits and vegetables[1]	751	616	581	740	352	664	778	860	1,048
Fresh fruits	247	210	185	262	115	226	258	284	355
Fresh vegetables	247	186	180	249	112	220	246	265	322
Processed fruits	139	114	105	126	67	110	144	161	194
Other food at home[1]	1,374	1,375	1,235	1,461	724	1,293	1,592	1,871	2,194
Sugar and other sweets	140	157	124	152	70	143	165	195	226
Nonalcoholic beverages	334	323	329	365	186	326	415	446	538
Food away from home	2,932	2,349	2,463	2,880	1,507	2,677	3,052	3,543	3,710
Alcoholic beverages	468	418	368	530	355	537	381	486	336
Housing	19,343	15,109	15,387	19,127	11,388	17,145	19,353	22,193	21,035
Shelter	11,944	8,756	8,524	12,378	7,376	10,078	11,114	13,038	12,243
Owned dwellings	7,513	6,126	5,613	7,667	3,495	6,906	7,526	9,530	8,589
Mortgage interest and charges	3,434	2,970	3,147	5,084	1,590	3,354	4,437	6,039	5,554
Property taxes	2,865	1,962	1,309	1,599	1,062	1,999	2,041	2,444	2,148
Maintenance, repair, insurance, other expenses	1,214	1,195	1,158	984	843	1,553	1,048	1,047	887
Rented dwellings	3,507	1,986	2,361	4,021	3,513	2,257	2,874	2,711	3,138
Other lodging	924	643	550	690	368	916	714	797	516
Utilities, fuels, and public services	4,095	3,421	3,741	3,343	2,298	3,740	4,233	4,658	4,951
Natural gas	719	695	266	424	314	503	528	610	667
Electricity	1,306	1,119	1,719	1,143	868	1,410	1,600	1,738	1,905
Fuel oil and other fuels	434	114	62	57	84	182	130	170	150
Telephone	1,241	1,080	1,191	1,133	722	1,155	1,431	1,529	1,549
Water and other public services	396	414	503	586	309	490	544	610	679
Household operations	1,196	780	969	1,164	548	845	1,345	1,811	1,303
Personal services	551	258	339	472	100	121	694	1,102	676
Other household expenses	645	522	630	692	448	724	650	709	628
Housekeeping supplies[1]	640	682	667	638	345	779	771	803	798
Laundry and cleaning supplies	142	163	159	155	82	159	187	205	244
Postage and stationery	139	153	123	169	83	179	154	171	142
Household furnishings and equipment[1]	1,467	1,471	1,485	1,605	821	1,702	1,891	1,884	1,741
Household textiles	126	116	122	134	55	152	169	128	161
Furniture	347	316	353	349	185	390	431	421	406
Major appliances	175	189	202	201	106	225	233	238	224
Miscellaneous household equipment	700	711	697	786	407	789	902	950	817
Apparel and services[1]	1,782	1,461	1,786	1,844	975	1,566	2,046	2,571	2,767
Men and boys	412	339	371	422	234	341	449	572	589
Women and girls	662	590	727	702	374	637	839	1,027	971
Footwear	343	251	349	336	177	285	357	463	624
Other apparel products and services	288	195	252	268	168	252	243	327	380
Transportation	8,108	7,649	7,400	7,711	4,182	8,306	8,775	10,707	9,716
Vehicle purchases (net outlay)[1]	2,754	2,921	2,612	2,380	1,441	3,039	2,659	4,004	3,065
Cars and trucks, new	1,644	1,387	1,321	881	791	1,654	1,209	1,624	1,272
Cars and trucks, used	1,089	1,468	1,211	1,468	606	1,334	1,399	2,305	1,710
Gasoline and motor oil	1,787	1,933	2,103	2,018	1,022	1,993	2,470	2,761	2,964
Other vehicle expenses	2,885	2,375	2,371	2,673	1,417	2,714	3,086	3,374	3,203
Vehicle finance charges	218	252	336	274	109	302	356	440	378
Maintenance and repair	762	706	646	876	470	812	854	874	857
Vehicle insurance	1,271	957	1,095	999	589	1,092	1,337	1,517	1,419
Vehicle rental, leases, licenses, other charges	634	460	294	524	249	507	539	543	548
Public transportation	682	420	314	640	303	559	560	568	484
Health care[2]	3,132	3,272	3,030	3,128	2,007	4,021	3,273	3,300	2,960
Entertainment[3]	2,767	2,627	2,467	3,062	1,510	2,913	2,860	3,775	3,635
Personal care products and services	601	538	593	653	345	646	719	779	717
Reading	141	112	85	121	87	136	113	100	95
Education	1,710	1,103	820	902	492	793	1,563	1,906	1,746
Tobacco products and smoking supplies	439	409	394	278	253	403	463	443	458
Miscellaneous	821	798	768	910	565	838	942	1,115	872
Cash contributions	1,568	1,684	1,692	1,941	1,268	2,028	1,776	1,718	1,964
Personal insurance and pensions	6,013	5,340	5,015	5,894	2,518	6,011	6,875	7,680	7,101
Life and other personal insurance	350	340	298	262	118	393	409	371	350
Pensions and social security	5,662	5,000	4,717	5,633	2,399	5,618	6,466	7,309	6,751
Personal taxes	**2,745**	**2,042**	**1,846**	**2,053**	**1,395**	**2,958**	**2,024**	**2,446**	**1,000**

[1] Includes other types not shown separately. [2] For additional health care expenditures, see Table 143. [3] For additional recreation expenditures, see Section 26.

Source: U.S. Bureau of Labor Statistics, *Consumer Expenditures in 2009*, News Release, USDL-10-1390, October 2010. See also <ftp://ftp.bls.gov/pub/special.requests/ce/standard/2009/region.txt> and <ftp://ftp.bls.gov/pub/special.requests/ce/standard/2009/cusize.txt>.

Table 688. Average Annual Expenditures of All Consumer Units by Income Level: 2009

[In dollars. See headnote, Table 684]

Income level	Total expendi-tures [1]	Food	Housing Total [1]	Housing Shelter	Housing Utilities, fuels [2]	Transportation Total [1]	Transportation Vehicle pur-chases	Transportation Gaso-line and motor oil	Health care	Pen-sions and social security
All consumer units	**49,067**	**6,372**	**16,895**	**10,075**	**3,645**	**7,658**	**2,657**	**1,986**	**3,126**	**5,162**
Consumer units with complete reporting:										
Less than $70,000	33,810	4,798	12,509	7,377	3,089	5,373	1,679	1,573	2,541	2,173
$70,000 to $79,999	57,833	7,818	19,127	11,393	4,188	9,880	3,410	2,470	3,679	6,536
$80,000 to $99,999	65,027	8,359	21,666	12,815	4,470	9,929	3,386	2,669	4,158	7,977
$100,000 and over	97,576	11,088	30,831	18,736	5,226	14,674	5,835	3,105	4,723	14,887
$100,000 to $119,999	76,140	9,622	23,907	14,190	4,618	12,378	4,800	2,942	4,385	10,292
$120,000 to $149,999	85,806	9,886	27,923	16,872	5,100	13,028	4,713	3,090	4,399	12,919
$150,000 and over	124,306	13,234	38,824	23,941	5,837	17,799	7,506	3,257	5,242	20,207

[1] Includes expenditures not shown separately. [2] Includes public service.

Source: U.S. Bureau of Labor Statistics, *Consumer Expenditures in 2009,* News Release, USDL-10-1390, October 2010. See also <ftp://ftp.bls.gov/pub/special.requests/ce/standard/2009/higherincome.txt>.

Table 689. Annual Expenditure Per Child by Husband-Wife Families by Family Income and Expenditure Type: 2010

[In dollars. Data are for a child in a two-child family. Excludes expenses for college. Expenditures based on before tax income data from the 2005–2006 Consumer Expenditure Survey updated to 2010 dollars using the Consumer Price Index. For more on the methodology, see report cited below]

Family income and age of child	Total	Expenditure type Housing	Expenditure type Food	Expenditure type Transpor-tation	Expenditure type Clothing	Expenditure type Health care	Expenditure type Child care and educa-tion [1]	Expenditure type Miscella-neous [2]
INCOME: LESS THAN $57,600								
Less than 2 years old	8,760	2,950	1,120	1,070	630	610	1,960	420
3 to 5 years old	8,810	2,950	1,220	1,120	490	580	1,840	610
6 to 8 years old	8,480	2,950	1,650	1,230	560	640	820	630
9 to 11 years old	9,200	2,950	1,900	1,230	570	690	1,240	620
12 to 14 years old	9,600	2,950	2,060	1,340	670	1,050	840	690
15 to 17 years old	9,630	2,950	2,050	1,490	710	980	870	580
INCOME: $57,600 TO $99,730								
Less than 2 years old	11,950	3,870	1,350	1,540	740	820	2,740	890
3 to 5 years old	11,980	3,870	1,440	1,590	600	780	2,620	1,080
6 to 8 years old	11,880	3,870	2,020	1,700	670	910	1,610	1,100
9 to 11 years old	12,660	3,870	2,310	1,700	690	970	2,030	1,090
12 to 14 years old	13,340	3,870	2,480	1,810	820	1,370	1,830	1,160
15 to 17 years old	13,830	3,870	2,470	1,960	880	1,290	2,310	1,050
INCOME: MORE THAN $99,730								
Less than 2 years old	19,820	7,010	1,830	2,330	1,030	950	4,890	1,780
3 to 5 years old	19,810	7,010	1,930	2,370	860	900	4,770	1,970
6 to 8 years old	19,770	7,010	2,540	2,490	950	1,040	3,750	1,990
9 to 11 years old	20,630	7,010	2,880	2,490	990	1,110	4,170	1,980
12 to 14 years old	21,960	7,010	3,070	2,600	1,150	1,570	4,510	2,050
15 to 17 years old	23,690	7,010	3,060	2,750	1,250	1,480	6,200	1,940

[1] Includes only families with child care and education expenses. [2] Expenses include personal care items, entertainment, and reading materials.

Source: U.S. Department of Agriculture, Center for Nutrition Policy and Promotion, *Expenditures on Children by Families, 2010,* 1528-2010, May 2011. See also <http://www.cnpp.usda.gov/Publications/CRC/crc2010.pdf>.

Table 690. Money Income of Households—Percent Distribution by Income Level, Race, and Hispanic Origin, in Constant (2009) Dollars: 1990 to 2009

[Constant dollars based on CPI-U-RS deflator. Households as of March of following year. (94,312 represents 94,312,000). Based on Current Population Survey, Annual Social and Economic Supplement (ASEC); see text, this section and Section 1, and Appendix III. For data collection changes over time, see <http://www.census.gov/hhes/www/income/histinc/hstchg.html>. For definition of median, see Guide to Tabular Presentation]

Year	Number of house-holds (1,000)	Percent distribution							Median income (dollars)
		Under $15,000	$15,000 to $24,999	$25,000 to $34,999	$35,000 to $49,999	$50,000 to $74,999	$75,000 to $99,999	$100,000 and over	
ALL HOUSEHOLDS [1]									
1990..............	94,312	14.0	11.8	11.2	15.7	20.0	12.2	15.0	47,637
2000 [2]	108,209	12.1	11.1	10.5	14.5	18.4	12.7	20.6	52,301
2008..............	117,181	13.4	12.0	11.0	14.1	17.6	11.9	19.9	50,112
2009 [3]	117,538	13.0	11.9	11.1	14.1	18.1	11.5	20.1	49,777
WHITE									
1990..............	80,968	12.0	11.5	11.1	16.0	20.6	12.9	16.0	49,686
2000 [2]	90,030	10.8	10.8	10.3	14.4	18.6	13.2	21.9	54,700
2008 [4, 5]	95,297	11.8	11.7	10.7	14.0	18.1	12.5	21.1	52,113
2009 [3, 4, 5]	95,489	11.4	11.6	10.8	14.2	18.7	12.0	21.4	51,861
BLACK									
1990..............	10,671	29.1	15.1	12.2	14.4	15.4	7.3	6.4	29,712
2000 [2]	13,174	21.0	14.4	12.9	15.4	17.2	8.8	10.3	36,952
2008 [4, 6]	14,595	23.6	15.0	13.7	15.0	14.9	8.1	9.6	34,088
2009 [3, 4, 6]	14,730	23.5	15.4	13.4	14.6	15.1	8.7	9.3	32,584
ASIAN AND PACIFIC ISLANDER									
1990..............	1,958	10.6	9.5	8.2	12.5	20.9	14.0	24.4	61,170
2000 [2]	3,963	9.3	7.7	7.4	12.4	16.9	14.8	31.5	69,448
2008 [4, 7]	4,573	12.1	8.7	8.2	12.1	15.1	12.6	31.2	65,388
2009 [3, 4, 7]	4,687	11.7	7.9	8.2	11.1	16.9	11.8	32.4	65,469
HISPANIC [8]									
1990..............	6,220	19.7	16.5	12.9	17.6	18.2	7.8	7.4	35,525
2000 [2]	10,034	14.5	15.1	12.6	17.6	18.9	10.4	11.0	41,312
2008..............	13,425	17.8	14.8	14.5	16.4	16.2	9.0	11.3	37,769
2009 [3]	13,298	16.5	15.2	14.3	15.4	17.6	9.1	11.7	38,039

[1] Includes other races not shown separately. [2] Data reflect implementation of Census 2000-based population controls and a 28,000 household sample expansion to 78,000 households. [3] Median income is calculated using $2,500 income intervals. Beginning with 2009 income data, the Census Bureau expanded the upper income intervals used to calculate medians to $250,000 or more. Medians falling in the upper open-ended interval are plugged with "$250,000." Before 2009, the upper open-ended interval was $100,000 and a plug of "$100,000" was used. [4] Beginning with the 2003 Current Population Survey (CPS), the questionnaire allowed respondents to choose more than one race. For 2002 and later, data represent persons who selected this race group only and exclude persons reporting more than one race. The CPS in prior years allowed respondents to report only one race group. See also comments on race in the text for Section 1. [5] Data represent White alone, which refers to people who reported White and did not report any other race category. [6] Data represent Black alone, which refers to people who reported Black and did not report any other race category. [7] Data represent Asian alone, which refers to people who reported Asian and did not report any other race category. [8] People of Hispanic origin may be any race.

Source: U.S. Census Bureau, *Income, Poverty and Health Insurance Coverage in the United States: 2009*, Current Population Reports, P60-238, and Historical Tables—Table H17, September 2010. See also <http://www.census.gov/hhes/www/income/income.html> and <http://www.census.gov/hhes/www/income/data/historical/household/index.html>.

Table 691. Money Income of Households—Median Income by Race and Hispanic Origin, in Current and Constant (2009) Dollars: 1980 to 2009

[In dollars. See headnote, Table 690]

Year	Median income in current dollars					Median income in constant (2009) dollars				
	All house-holds [1]	White [2]	Black [3]	Asian, Pacific Islander [4]	His-panic [5]	All house-holds [1]	White [2]	Black [3]	Asian, Pacific Islander [4]	His-panic [5]
1980.......	17,710	18,684	10,764	(NA)	13,651	43,892	46,306	26,677	(NA)	33,832
1990.......	29,943	31,231	18,676	38,450	22,330	47,637	49,686	29,712	61,170	35,525
1995 [6]	34,076	35,766	22,393	40,614	22,860	47,622	49,984	31,295	56,759	31,947
2000 [7, 8] ..	41,990	43,916	29,667	55,757	33,168	52,301	54,700	36,952	69,448	41,312
2005 [9]	46,326	48,554	30,858	61,094	35,967	50,899	53,347	33,904	67,125	39,517
2006.......	48,201	50,673	31,969	64,238	37,781	51,278	53,907	34,010	68,338	40,193
2007.......	50,233	52,115	33,916	66,103	38,679	51,965	53,912	35,086	68,382	40,013
2008.......	50,303	52,312	34,218	65,637	37,913	50,112	52,113	34,088	65,388	37,769
2009 [10] ...	49,777	51,861	32,584	65,469	38,039	49,777	51,861	32,584	65,469	38,039

NA Not available. [1] Includes other races, not shown separately. [2] Beginning with 2002, data represents White alone, which refers to people who reported White and did not report any other race category. [3] Beginning with 2002, data represents Black alone, which refers to people who reported Black and did not report any other race category. [4] Beginning with 2002, data represents Asian alone, which refers to people who reported Asian and did not report any other race category. [5] People of Hispanic origin may be any race. [6] Data reflect full implementation of the 1990 census-based sample design and metropolitan definitions, 7,000 household sample reduction, and revised race edits. [7] Implementation of Census 2000-based population controls. [8] Implementation of a 28,000 household sample expansion. [9] See footnote 3, Table 690. See also comments on race in the text for Section 1. [10] Median income is calculated using $2,500 income intervals. Beginning with 2009 income data, the Census Bureau expanded the upper income intervals used to calculate medians to $250,000 or more. Before 2009, the upper open-ended interval was $100,000 and a plug of "$100,000."

Source: U.S. Census Bureau, *Income, Poverty and Health Insurance Coverage in the United States: 2009*, Current Population Reports, P60-238, and "Historical Tables—Table H-5," September 2010. See also <http://www.census.gov/hhes/www/income/income.html> and <http://www.census.gov/hhes/www/income/data/historical/household/index.html>.

Table 692. Money Income of Households—Distribution by Income Level and Selected Characteristics: 2009

[117,538 represents 117,538,000. Households as of March of the following year. Based on Current Population Survey, Annual Social and Economic Supplement (ASEC); see text, this section and Section 1, and Appendix III. For definition of median, see Guide to Tabular Presentation. Median income is calculated using $2,500 income intervals. Beginning with 2009 income data, the Census Bureau expanded the upper income intervals used to calculate medians to $250,000 or more. Medians falling in the upper open-ended interval are plugged with "$250,000." Before 2009, the upper open-ended interval was $100,000 and a plug of "$100,000" was used]

Characteristic	Number of households (1,000)								Median house-hold income (dollars)
	Total house-holds	Under $15,000	$15,000 to $24,999	$25,000 to $34,999	$35,000 to $49,999	$50,000 to $74,999	$75,000 to $99,999	$100,000 and over	
Total	117,538	15,329	14,023	13,003	16,607	21,280	13,549	23,749	49,777
Age of householder:									
15 to 24 years	6,233	1,532	1,035	882	1,054	956	351	422	30,733
25 to 34 years	19,257	2,216	2,060	2,295	3,011	4,115	2,432	3,130	50,199
35 to 44 years	21,519	1,866	1,805	1,963	2,983	4,239	3,133	5,526	61,083
45 to 54 years	24,871	2,528	1,985	1,970	3,054	4,733	3,516	7,083	64,235
55 to 64 years	20,387	2,435	1,916	2,001	2,688	3,649	2,482	5,215	56,973
65 years and over	25,270	4,751	5,222	3,892	3,817	3,586	1,632	2,371	31,354
Region: [1]									
Northeast	21,479	2,733	2,244	2,264	2,807	3,699	2,486	5,246	53,073
Midwest	26,390	3,273	3,326	3,056	3,767	5,044	3,183	4,742	48,877
South	43,611	6,235	5,657	5,038	6,476	7,730	4,813	7,660	45,615
West	26,058	3,086	2,796	2,644	3,557	4,804	3,066	6,104	53,833
Size of household:									
One person	31,399	8,716	6,358	4,478	4,553	4,053	1,509	1,733	26,080
Two people	39,487	3,293	4,206	4,583	6,168	8,078	5,016	8,145	53,676
Three people	18,638	1,511	1,509	1,695	2,571	3,622	2,840	4,892	62,472
Four people	16,122	1,030	1,006	1,251	1,788	3,197	2,433	5,418	73,071
Five people	7,367	483	520	615	922	1,408	1,096	2,323	69,680
Six people	2,784	189	246	242	378	568	398	765	62,745
Seven or more people	1,740	108	177	137	230	353	257	479	64,667
Type of household:									
Family household	78,833	6,031	6,968	7,795	10,881	15,633	10,983	20,544	61,265
Married-couple	58,410	2,313	3,743	4,943	7,515	12,011	9,204	18,680	71,830
Male householder, spouse absent	5,580	584	651	713	951	1,246	634	799	48,084
Female householder, spouse absent	14,843	3,133	2,574	2,138	2,414	2,376	1,143	1,063	32,597
Nonfamily household	38,705	9,298	7,054	5,208	5,726	5,646	2,567	3,206	30,444
Male householder	18,263	3,462	2,766	2,483	2,959	3,053	1,535	2,002	36,611
Female householder	20,442	5,835	4,288	2,724	2,766	2,594	1,033	1,201	25,269
Educational attainment of householder: [2]									
Total	111,305	13,796	12,988	12,120	15,555	20,322	13,197	23,327	50,971
Less than 9th grade	5,091	1,753	1,131	733	599	520	190	164	21,635
9th to 12th grade (no diploma)	8,356	2,383	1,703	1,275	1,183	1,046	455	313	25,604
High school graduate	32,770	4,844	5,036	4,508	5,462	6,151	3,290	3,482	39,647
Some college, no degree	19,938	2,293	2,374	2,337	3,213	4,041	2,471	3,210	48,413
Associate's degree	10,531	862	1,040	1,100	1,534	2,262	1,606	2,125	56,789
Bachelor's degree or more . . .	34,618	1,662	1,702	2,168	3,563	6,304	5,184	14,034	82,722
Bachelor's degree	22,134	1,232	1,252	1,610	2,554	4,321	3,345	7,817	75,518
Master's degree	9,000	336	349	425	780	1,573	1,446	4,094	91,660
Professional degree	1,746	51	65	90	111	207	172	1,051	123,784
Doctoral degree	1,738	43	36	42	118	201	221	1,076	120,873
Number of earners:									
No earners	26,172	9,911	6,178	3,784	2,989	2,059	609	638	19,514
One earner	43,712	4,825	6,397	6,725	8,321	8,374	3,733	5,336	41,133
Two earners and more	47,654	591	1,446	2,494	5,297	10,847	9,207	17,772	82,165
Two earners	38,302	554	1,320	2,255	4,614	9,139	7,274	13,147	78,473
Three earners	7,023	35	104	213	594	1,377	1,519	3,180	93,835
Four earners or more	2,330	2	23	27	88	330	414	1,445	116,673
Work experience of householder:									
Total	117,538	15,329	14,023	13,003	16,607	21,280	13,549	23,749	49,777
Worked	78,888	4,583	6,498	7,614	11,384	16,522	11,458	20,828	62,508
Worked at full-time jobs	65,214	2,379	4,533	5,921	9,514	14,249	10,115	18,503	66,777
50 weeks or more	54,135	1,043	3,128	4,580	7,790	12,072	8,845	16,681	71,246
27 to 49 weeks	6,520	503	743	765	1,003	1,387	821	1,301	53,397
26 weeks or less	4,558	834	662	577	721	791	450	524	38,762
Worked at part-time jobs	13,674	2,203	1,965	1,694	1,871	2,273	1,342	2,325	41,914
50 weeks or more	7,618	912	1,058	1,003	1,073	1,326	805	1,444	46,053
27 to 49 weeks	2,836	473	449	342	358	483	251	481	40,961
26 weeks or less	3,220	821	458	349	440	465	287	401	34,395
Did not work	38,650	10,746	7,524	5,388	5,223	4,756	2,092	2,921	26,590
Tenure:									
Owner occupied	78,779	6,170	7,462	7,522	10,585	15,190	10,981	20,870	61,588
Renter occupied	37,080	8,628	6,291	5,266	5,797	5,856	2,469	2,775	31,463
Occupier paid no cash rent . .	1,679	531	271	215	225	233	98	105	26,199

[1] For composition of regions, see map, inside front cover. [2] People 25 years old and over.

Source: U.S. Census Bureau, *Income, Poverty and Health Insurance Coverage in the United States: 2009*, Current Population Reports, P60-238, and Detailed Tables—Table HINC-01, September 2010. See also <http://www.census.gov/hhes/www/cpstables/032010/hhinc/new01_000.htm>.

Income, Expenditures, Poverty, and Wealth 453

Table 693. Money Income of Households—Number and Distribution by Race and Hispanic Origin: 2009

[Households as of March of the following year. (117,538 represents 117,538,000). Based on Current Population Survey, Annual Social and Economic Supplement (ASEC); see text, this section and Section 1, and Appendix III. The 2009 CPS allowed respondents to choose more than one race. Data represent persons who selected this race group only and excludes persons reporting more than one race. See also comments on race in the text for Section 1]

Income interval	Number of households (1,000)					Percent distribution				
	All races	White alone	Black alone	Asian alone	His-panic [1]	All races	White alone	Black alone	Asian alone	His-panic [1]
All households.........	117,538	95,489	14,730	4,687	13,298	100.0	100.0	100.0	100.0	100.0
Under $10,000...........	8,570	5,787	2,128	347	1,249	7.3	6.1	14.4	7.4	9.4
$10,000 to $14,999.......	6,759	5,054	1,337	200	951	5.8	5.3	9.1	4.3	7.2
$15,000 to $19,999.......	6,924	5,389	1,181	183	989	5.9	5.6	8.0	3.9	7.4
$20,000 to $24,999.......	7,099	5,656	1,088	189	1,032	6.0	5.9	7.4	4.0	7.8
$25,000 to $29,999.......	6,633	5,255	1,020	197	963	5.6	5.5	6.9	4.2	7.2
$30,000 to $34,999.......	6,370	5,052	957	185	945	5.4	5.3	6.5	3.9	7.1
$35,000 to $39,999.......	6,033	4,886	822	192	772	5.1	5.1	5.6	4.1	5.8
$40,000 to $44,999.......	5,680	4,660	730	156	663	4.8	4.9	5.0	3.3	5.0
$45,000 to $49,999.......	4,894	4,006	594	172	617	4.2	4.2	4.0	3.7	4.6
$50,000 to $59,999.......	9,444	7,840	1,068	335	1,084	8.0	8.2	7.3	7.1	8.2
$60,000 to $74,999.......	11,836	9,987	1,152	457	1,258	10.1	10.5	7.8	9.8	9.5
$75,000 to $84,999.......	6,347	5,326	662	245	589	5.4	5.6	4.5	5.2	4.4
$85,000 to $99,999.......	7,202	6,107	625	308	626	6.1	6.4	4.2	6.6	4.7
$100,000 to $149,999......	14,034	12,081	928	790	1,042	11.9	12.7	6.3	16.9	7.8
$150,000 to $199,999......	5,209	4,505	261	362	289	4.4	4.7	1.8	7.7	2.2
$200,000 to $249,999......	2,135	1,852	79	166	115	1.8	1.9	0.5	3.5	0.9
$250,000 and above.......	2,372	2,048	95	197	116	2.0	2.1	0.6	4.2	0.9

[1] Persons of Hispanic origin may be any race.

Source: U.S. Census Bureau, *Income, Poverty and Health Insurance Coverage in the United States: 2009*, Current Population Reports, P60-238, and Detailed Tables—Table HINC-06, September 2010. See also <http://www.census.gov/hhes/www/cpstables/032010/hhinc/new06_000.htm>.

Table 694. Share of Aggregate Income Received by Each Fifth and Top 5 Percent of Households: 1970 to 2009

[Households as of March of the following year, (64,778 represents 64,778,000). Income in constant 2009 CPI-U-RS-adjusted dollars. The shares method ranks households from highest to lowest on the basis of income and then divides them into groups of equal population size, typically quintiles. The aggregate income of each group is then divided by the overall aggregate income to derive shares. Based on the Current Population Survey, Annual Social and Economic Supplement (ASEC); see text, this section and Section 1, and Appendix III. For data collection changes over time, see <http://www.census.gov/hhes/www/income/data/historical/history.html>]

Year	Number of house-holds (1,000)	Income at selected positions in constant (2009) dollars					Percent distribution of aggregate income					
		Upper limit of each fifth				Top 5 percent	Lowest 5th	Second 5th	Third 5th	Fourth 5th	Highest 5th	Top 5 percent
		Lowest	Second	Third	Fourth							
1970......	64,778	18,180	34,827	50,656	72,273	114,243	4.1	10.8	17.4	24.5	43.3	16.6
1980......	82,368	18,533	34,757	53,285	78,019	125,556	4.2	10.2	16.8	24.7	44.1	16.5
1990......	94,312	19,886	37,644	57,591	87,826	150,735	3.8	9.6	15.9	24.0	46.6	18.5
1995 [1]....	99,627	20,124	37,613	58,698	91,012	157,919	3.7	9.1	15.2	23.3	48.7	21.0
2000 [2, 3]...	108,209	22,320	41,103	64,985	101,844	180,879	3.6	8.9	14.8	23.0	49.8	22.1
2002......	111,278	21,361	39,795	63,384	100,170	178,844	3.5	8.8	14.8	23.3	49.7	21.7
2003......	112,000	20,974	39,652	63,505	101,307	179,740	3.4	8.7	14.8	23.4	49.8	21.4
2004......	113,343	20,992	39,375	62,716	99,930	178,453	3.4	8.7	14.7	23.2	50.1	21.8
2005 [4]....	114,384	21,071	39,554	63,352	100,757	182,386	3.4	8.6	14.6	23.0	50.4	22.2
2006......	116,011	21,314	40,185	63,830	103,226	185,119	3.4	8.6	14.5	22.9	50.5	22.3
2007......	116,783	20,991	40,448	64,138	103,448	183,103	3.4	8.7	14.8	23.4	49.7	21.2
2008......	117,181	20,633	38,852	62,487	99,860	179,317	3.4	8.6	14.7	23.3	50.0	21.5
2009......	117,538	20,453	38,550	61,801	100,000	180,001	3.4	8.6	14.6	23.2	50.3	21.7

[1] Data reflect full implementation of the 1990 census-based sample design and metropolitan definitions, 7,000 household sample reduction, and revised race edits. [2] Implementation of Census 2000-based population controls. [3] Implementation of a 28,000 household sample expansion. [4] Data have been revised to reflect a correction to the weights in the 2005 ASEC.

Source: U.S. Census Bureau, *Income, Poverty and Health Insurance Coverage in the United States: 2009*, Current Population Reports, P60-238, and Historical Tables—Tables H1 and H2, September 2010. See also <http://www.census.gov/hhes/www/income/income.html> and <http://www.census.gov/hhes/www/income/data/historical/household/index.html>.

Table 695. Money Income of Families—Number and Distribution by Race and Hispanic Origin: 2009

[Families as of March of the following year. (78,867 represents 78,867,000). Based on Current Population Survey, Annual Social and Economic Supplement (ASEC); see text, this section, Section 1, and Appendix III. The 2010 CPS allowed respondents to choose more than one race. Data represent persons who selected this race group only and excludes persons reporting more than one race. See also comments on race in the text for Section 1]

Income interval	Number of families (1,000)					Percent distribution				
	All races	White alone	Black alone	Asian alone	His-panic [1]	All races	White alone	Black alone	Asian alone	His-panic [1]
All families [1]	**78,867**	**64,145**	**9,367**	**3,592**	**10,422**	**100.0**	**100.0**	**100.0**	**100.0**	**100.0**
Under $10,000	4,068	2,698	1,062	156	915	5.2	4.2	11.3	4.3	8.8
$10,000 to $14,999	2,758	1,947	620	93	673	3.5	3.0	6.6	2.6	6.5
$15,000 to $19,999	3,268	2,365	687	125	754	4.1	3.7	7.3	3.5	7.2
$20,000 to $24,999	3,925	3,029	667	127	780	5.0	4.7	7.1	3.5	7.5
$25,000 to $29,999	3,984	3,067	666	145	755	5.1	4.8	7.1	4.0	7.2
$30,000 to $34,999	3,879	3,050	581	137	732	4.9	4.8	6.2	3.8	7.0
$35,000 to $39,999	3,928	3,154	545	137	633	5.0	4.9	5.8	3.8	6.1
$40,000 to $44,999	3,696	3,042	459	110	531	4.7	4.7	4.9	3.1	5.1
$45,000 to $49,999	3,274	2,661	418	128	508	4.2	4.1	4.5	3.6	4.9
$50,000 to $59,999	6,584	5,426	736	284	854	8.3	8.5	7.9	7.9	8.2
$60,000 to $74,999	8,677	7,328	803	352	1,009	11.0	11.4	8.6	9.8	9.7
$75,000 to $84,999	4,929	4,143	504	196	482	6.2	6.5	5.4	5.5	4.6
$85,000 to $99,999	5,739	4,878	489	247	510	7.3	7.6	5.2	6.9	4.9
$100,000 to $149,999	11,721	10,083	756	696	852	14.9	15.7	8.1	19.4	8.2
$150,000 to $199,999	4,467	3,852	226	321	240	5.7	6.0	2.4	8.9	2.3
$200,000 to $249,999	1,896	1,635	68	158	94	2.4	2.5	0.7	4.4	0.9
$250,000 and above	2,073	1,789	82	179	103	2.6	2.8	0.9	5.0	1.0

[1] Persons of Hispanic origin may be any race.

Source: U.S. Census Bureau, *Income, Poverty and Health Insurance Coverage in the United States: 2009*, Current Population Reports, P60-238, and Detailed Tables—Table FINC-07, September 2010. See also <http://www.census.gov/hhes/www/cpstables/032010/faminc/new07_000.htm>.

Table 696. Money Income of Families—Percent Distribution by Income Level in Constant (2009) Dollars: 1980 to 2009

[Constant dollars based on CPI-U-RS deflator. Families as of March of following year, (66,322 represents 66,322,000). Based on Current Population Survey, Annual Social and Economic Supplement (ASEC); see text, this section, Section 1, and Appendix III. For data collection changes over time, see <http://www.census.gov/hhes/www/income/data/historical/history.html>. For definition of median, see Guide to Tabular Presentation]

Year	Number of families (1,000)	Percent distribution							Median income (dollars)
		Under $15,000	$15,000 to $24,999	$25,000 to $34,999	$35,000 to $49,999	$50,000 to $74,999	$75,000 to $99,999	$100,000 and over	
ALL FAMILIES [1]									
1990	66,322	8.7	9.4	10.3	15.6	22.5	14.6	19.1	54,369
2000 [2]	73,778	7.0	8.6	9.3	14.3	19.8	15.1	26.2	61,083
2008	78,874	8.4	9.2	9.9	13.7	19.3	14.2	26.0	61,521
2009 [3]	78,867	8.7	9.1	10.0	13.8	19.4	13.5	25.6	60,088
WHITE									
1990	56,803	6.6	8.7	10.0	15.8	23.3	15.4	20.4	56,771
2000 [2]	61,330	5.7	7.9	9.0	14.2	20.1	15.8	27.7	63,849
2008 [4,5]	64,183	6.9	8.5	9.5	13.4	19.8	15.0	27.5	65,000
2009 [3,4,5]	64,145	7.2	8.4	9.5	13.8	19.9	14.1	27.0	62,545
BLACK									
1990	7,471	23.9	14.7	12.5	14.4	17.5	8.8	8.2	32,946
2000 [2]	8,731	15.7	14.0	12.8	15.8	18.7	10.3	13.0	40,547
2008 [4,6]	9,359	18.2	14.4	12.8	15.3	16.6	9.8	13.4	39,879
2009 [3,4,6]	9,367	18.0	14.5	13.3	15.2	16.4	10.6	12.1	38,409
ASIAN AND PACIFIC ISLANDER									
1990	1,536	8.1	7.8	8.2	11.6	21.2	15.0	28.5	64,969
2000 [2]	2,982	6.2	6.4	6.4	11.7	17.3	15.5	37.0	75,393
2008 [4,7]	3,494	7.7	7.2	7.6	12.8	16.0	13.0	36.6	73,578
2009 [3,4,7]	3,592	6.9	7.0	7.9	10.4	17.7	12.3	37.7	75,027
HISPANIC ORIGIN [8]									
1990	4,981	17.0	16.3	13.6	17.3	19.1	8.5	8.2	36,034
2000 [2]	8,017	12.8	14.6	13.0	18.1	19.4	10.5	12.0	41,469
2008	10,503	15.5	14.6	14.1	16.8	17.2	9.6	12.5	40,466
2009 [3]	10,422	15.2	14.7	14.3	16.0	17.9	9.5	12.4	39,730

[1] Includes other races not shown separately. [2] Data reflect implementation of Census 2000-based population controls and a 28,000 household sample expansion to 78,000 households. [3] Median income is calculated using $2,500 income intervals. Beginning with 2009 income data, the Census Bureau expanded the upper income intervals used to calculate medians to $250,000 or more. Medians falling in the upper open-ended interval are plugged with "$250,000." Before 2009, the upper open-ended interval was $100,000 and a plug of "$100,000" was used. [4] Beginning with the 2003 Current Population Survey (CPS), the questionnaire allowed respondents to choose more than one race. For 2002 and later, data represent persons who selected this race group only and excludes persons reporting more than one race. The CPS in prior years allowed respondents to report only one race group. See also comments on race in the text for Section 1. [5] Data represent White alone, which refers to people who reported White and did not report any other race category. [6] Data represent Black alone, which refers to people who reported Black and did not report any other race category. [7] Data represent Asian alone, which refers to people who reported Asian and did not report any other race category. [8] People of Hispanic origin may be any race.

Source: U.S. Census Bureau, *Income, Poverty and Health Insurance Coverage in the United States: 2009*, Current Population Reports, P60-238, and Historical Tables—Table F-23, September 2010. See also <http://www.census.gov/hhes/www/income/income.html> and <http://www.census.gov/hhes/www/income/data/historical/families/index.html>.

Income, Expenditures, Poverty, and Wealth 455

Table 697. Money Income of Families—Median Income by Race and Hispanic Origin in Current and Constant (2009) Dollars: 1990 to 2009

[In dollars. See headnote, Table 696]

Year	Median income in current dollars					Median income in constant (2009) dollars				
	All families [1]	White [2]	Black [3]	Asian, Pacific Islander [4]	His-panic [5]	All families [1]	White [2]	Black [3]	Asian, Pacific Islander [4]	His-panic [5]
1990.........	35,353	36,915	21,423	42,246	23,431	56,243	58,728	34,082	67,210	37,277
1995 [6].......	40,611	42,646	25,970	46,356	24,570	56,755	59,598	36,293	64,783	34,337
2000 [7,8]......	50,732	53,029	33,676	62,617	34,442	63,189	66,050	41,945	77,993	42,899
2004 [9,10]......	54,061	56,723	35,148	65,420	35,440	61,389	64,411	39,912	74,287	40,244
2005.........	56,194	59,317	35,464	68,957	37,867	61,741	65,172	38,965	75,764	41,605
2006.........	58,407	61,280	38,269	74,612	40,000	62,135	65,191	40,712	79,374	42,553
2007.........	61,355	64,427	40,143	77,133	40,566	63,471	66,649	41,527	79,793	41,965
2008.........	61,521	65,000	39,879	73,578	40,466	61,288	64,753	39,728	73,299	40,312
2009 [11].......	60,088	62,545	38,409	75,027	39,730	60,088	62,545	38,409	75,027	39,730

[1] Includes other races not shown separately. [2] Beginning with 2002, data represent White alone, which refers to people who reported White and did not report any other race category. [3] Beginning with 2002, data represent Black alone, which refers to people who reported Black and did not report any other race category. [4] Beginning with 2002, data represent Asian alone, which refers to people who reported Asian and did not report any other race category. [5] People of Hispanic origin may be any race. [6] Data reflect full implementation of the 1990 census-based sample design and metropolitan definitions, 7,000 household sample reduction, and revised race edits. [7] Implementation of Census 2000-based population controls. [8] Implementation of 28,000 household sample expansion. [9] See footnote 4, Table 696. See also comments on race in the text for Section 1. [10] Data have been revised to reflect a correction to the weights in the 2005 ASEC. [11] Median income is calculated using $2,500 income intervals. Beginning with 2009 income data, the Census Bureau expanded the upper income intervals used to calculate medians to $250,000 or more. Medians falling in the upper open-ended interval are plugged with "$250,000." Before 2009, the upper open-ended interval was $100,000 and a plug of "$100,000" was used.

Source: U.S. Census Bureau, *Income, Poverty and Health Insurance Coverage in the United States: 2009*, Current Population Reports, P60-238, and Historical Tables—Table F-05, September 2010. See also <http://www.census.gov/hhes/www/income /income.html> and <http://www.census.gov/hhes/www/income/data/historical/families/index.html>.

Table 698. Money Income of Families—Distribution by Family Characteristics and Income Level: 2009

[78,867 represents 78,867,000. See headnote, Table 696. Median income is calculated using $2,500 income intervals. Beginning with 2009 income data, the Census Bureau expanded the upper income intervals used to calculate medians to $250,000 or more. Medians falling in the upper open-ended interval are plugged with "$250,000." Before 2009, the upper open-ended interval was $100,000 and a plug of "$100,000" was used. For composition of regions, see map inside front cover]

Characteristic	Number of families (1,000)								Median income (dollars)
	Total	Under $15,000	$15,000 to $24,999	$25,000 to $34,999	$35,000 to $49,999	$50,000 to $74,999	$75,000 to $99,999	$100,000 and over	
All families	**78,867**	**6,827**	**7,194**	**7,863**	**10,898**	**15,260**	**10,668**	**20,157**	**60,088**
Age of householder:									
15 to 24 years old	3,405	981	505	436	531	515	197	240	29,893
25 to 34 years old	13,102	1,791	1,436	1,415	1,867	2,658	1,659	2,275	50,312
35 to 44 years old	17,067	1,345	1,336	1,450	2,232	3,288	2,554	4,863	65,196
45 to 54 years old	18,176	1,087	1,103	1,208	2,024	3,567	2,895	6,291	75,707
55 to 64 years old	13,711	777	893	1,103	1,711	2,690	2,006	4,531	71,650
65 years old and over	13,405	845	1,921	2,250	2,532	2,543	1,357	1,957	43,702
Region:									
Northeast...................	14,125	1,046	1,080	1,312	1,759	2,564	1,909	4,454	66,977
Midwest....................	17,465	1,488	1,525	1,712	2,366	3,661	2,552	4,160	60,688
South......................	29,719	2,912	3,072	3,240	4,397	5,619	3,895	6,583	54,913
West.......................	17,558	1,380	1,517	1,600	2,375	3,418	2,311	4,956	62,229
Type of family:									
Married-couple families	58,428	2,339	3,761	4,964	7,546	12,018	9,182	18,617	71,627
Male householder, no spouse present	5,582	811	740	744	969	1,095	555	668	41,501
Female householder, no spouse present...................	14,857	3,677	2,691	2,154	2,383	2,149	931	870	29,770
Unrelated subfamilies	521	223	108	69	51	47	15	8	17,447
Educational attainment of householder:									
Persons 25 years old and over, total	75,462	5,846	6,688	7,428	10,367	14,746	10,472	19,916	61,443
Less than 9th grade...............	3,323	707	787	567	502	454	167	140	27,114
9th to 12th grade (no diploma)	5,513	1,118	1,058	935	932	824	392	255	31,119
High school graduate (includes equivalency)	22,054	1,994	2,532	2,866	3,897	4,869	2,794	3,102	48,637
Some college, no degree...........	13,502	1,031	1,185	1,373	2,092	3,009	2,025	2,786	58,258
Associate's degree	7,413	422	487	621	1,060	1,697	1,286	1,840	65,248
Bachelor's degree or more	23,657	573	639	1,065	1,881	3,894	3,810	11,795	99,707
Bachelor's degree	14,956	437	490	784	1,379	2,750	2,475	6,641	90,530
Master's degree.................	6,193	106	118	217	378	892	1,054	3,426	106,931
Professional degree..............	1,265	18	12	50	60	133	119	875	150,795
Doctoral degree.................	1,244	12	19	14	63	118	160	855	135,681
Number of earners:									
No earners....................	12,205	3,410	2,498	2,167	1,871	1,355	461	445	25,740
One earner	25,981	2,966	3,636	3,806	4,712	4,865	2,313	3,681	42,010
Two earners or more	40,680	451	1,059	1,890	4,315	9,039	7,897	16,029	85,299

Source: U.S. Census Bureau, *Income, Poverty and Health Insurance Coverage in the United States: 2009*, Current Population Reports, P60-238, and Detailed Tables—Table FINC-01, September 2010. See also <http://www.census.gov/hhes/www /cpstables/032010/faminc/new01_000.htm>.

Table 699. Median Income of Families by Type of Family in Current and Constant (2009) Dollars: 1990 to 2009

[In dollars. See headnote, Table 696. For definition of median, see Guide to Tabular Presentation]

Year	Current dollars						Constant (2009) dollars					
	All families	Married-couple families			Male house-holder, no spouse present	Female house-holder, no spouse present	All families	Married-couple families			Male house-holder, no spouse present	Female house-holder, no spouse present
		Total	Wife in paid labor force	Wife not in paid labor force				Total	Wife in paid labor force	Wife not in paid labor force		
1990......	35,353	39,895	46,777	30,265	29,046	16,932	56,243	63,469	74,418	48,149	46,210	26,937
1995 [1]	40,611	47,062	55,823	32,375	30,358	19,691	56,755	65,770	78,014	45,245	42,426	27,518
2000 [2, 3] ...	50,732	59,099	69,235	39,982	37,727	25,716	63,189	73,611	86,236	49,800	46,991	32,031
2005 [4] ...	56,194	65,906	78,755	44,457	41,111	27,244	61,741	72,412	86,529	48,845	45,169	29,933
2006......	58,407	69,404	82,788	45,757	41,844	28,829	62,135	73,834	88,072	48,678	44,515	30,669
2007......	61,355	72,589	86,435	47,329	44,358	30,296	63,471	75,092	89,416	48,961	45,888	31,341
2008......	61,521	72,743	86,621	48,502	43,571	30,129	61,288	72,467	86,292	48,318	43,406	30,015
2009 [5]	60,088	71,627	85,948	47,649	41,501	29,770	60,088	71,627	85,948	47,649	41,501	29,770

[1] Data reflect full implementation of the 1990 census-based sample design and metropolitan definitions, 7,000 household sample reduction, and revised race edits. [2] Implementation of Census 2000-based population controls. [3] Implementation of a 28,000 household sample expansion. [4] Data have been revised to reflect a correction to the weights in the 2005 ASEC. [5] Median income is calculated using $2,500 income intervals. Beginning with 2009 income data, the Census Bureau expanded the upper income intervals used to calculate medians to $250,000 or more. Before 2009, the upper open-ended interval was $100,000.

Source: U.S. Census Bureau, *Income, Poverty and Health Insurance Coverage in the United States: 2009*, Current Population Reports, P60-238, and Historical Tables—Table F-7, September 2010. See also <http://www.census.gov/hhes/www/income /income.html> and <http://www.census.gov/hhes/www/income/data/historical/families/index.html>.

Table 700. Married-Couple Families—Number and Median Income by Work Experience of Husbands and Wives and Presence of Related Children: 2009

[58,428 represents 58,428,000. See headnote, Table 696. For definition of median, see Guide to Tabular Presentation]

Work experience of husband or wife	Number (1,000)					Median income (dollars)				
	All married-couple families	With no related children	One or more related children under 18 years old			All married-couple families	With no related children	One or more related children under 18 years old		
			Total	One child	Two children or more			Total	One child	Two children or more
All married-couple families ..	58,428	32,309	26,119	10,273	15,846	71,627	67,376	76,649	78,682	75,703
Husband worked	44,628	20,621	24,008	9,232	14,776	83,267	87,091	80,646	82,594	78,764
Wife worked.................	32,368	15,247	17,121	7,089	10,032	91,320	94,201	89,128	90,498	88,032
Wife did not work.............	12,261	5,374	6,887	2,142	4,745	59,686	65,642	54,532	52,094	55,666
Husband year-round, full-time worker.....................	34,828	15,321	19,507	7,482	12,024	90,459	94,269	87,091	89,620	85,785
Wife worked.................	25,579	11,668	13,911	5,768	8,142	97,488	100,124	95,646	96,699	94,895
Wife did not work.............	9,249	3,653	5,596	1,714	3,882	65,404	72,370	60,789	57,362	61,470
Husband did not work	13,800	11,688	2,111	1,041	1,070	38,565	38,971	35,881	38,842	32,444
Wife worked.................	4,569	3,271	1,297	641	656	50,854	53,705	43,612	46,467	41,679
Wife did not work.............	9,231	8,417	814	400	414	33,653	34,510	23,194	27,040	17,000

Source: U.S. Census Bureau, *Income, Poverty and Health Insurance Coverage in the United States: 2009*, Current Population Reports, P60-238, and Detailed Tables—Table FINC-04, September 2010. See also <http://www.census.gov/hhes/www /cpstables/032010/faminc/new04_000.htm>.

Table 701. Median Income of People in Constant (2009) Dollars by Sex, Race, and Hispanic Origin: 1990 to 2009

[In dollars. People as of March of following year. People 15 years old and over. Constant dollars based on CPI-U-RS deflator. Based on the Current Population Survey, Annual Social and Economic Supplement (ASEC); see text, this section and Section 1 and Appendix III. For data collection changes over time, see <http://www.census.gov/hhes/www/income/data/historical/history.html>]

Race and Hispanic Origin	Male					Female				
	1990	2000 [1]	2005 [2]	2008	2009 [3]	1990	2000 [1]	2005 [2]	2008	2009 [3]
All races [4]	**32,284**	**35,303**	**34,362**	**33,035**	**32,184**	**16,020**	**20,007**	**20,410**	**20,788**	**20,957**
White [5]	33,680	37,114	35,355	34,987	33,748	16,413	20,027	20,512	20,870	21,118
Black [6]	20,472	26,584	24,889	25,158	23,738	13,249	19,781	19,371	20,120	19,470
Asian [7]	(NA)	(NA)	37,592	36,468	37,330	(NA)	(NA)	23,777	23,021	24,343
Hispanic [8]...........	21,430	24,286	24,269	23,912	22,256	11,983	15,256	16,520	16,355	16,210
White non-Hispanic	34,933	39,245	38,834	37,267	36,785	16,833	20,757	21,371	21,666	21,939

NA Not available. [1] Implementation of Census 2000-based population controls and sample expanded by 28,000 households. [2] Beginning with the 2003 Current Population Survey (CPS), the questionnaire allowed respondents to choose more than one race. For 2005 and later, data represent persons who selected this race group only and excludes persons reporting more than one race. The CPS in prior years allowed respondents to report only one race group. See also comments on race in the text for Section 1. [3] Median income is calculated using $2,500 income intervals. Beginning with 2009 income data, the Census Bureau expanded the upper income intervals used to calculate medians to $250,000 or more. Before 2009, the upper open-ended interval was $100,000. [4] Includes other races not shown separately. [5] Beginning with 2005, data represent White alone, which refers to people who reported White and did not report any other race category. [6] Beginning with 2005, data represent Black alone, which refers to people who reported Black and did not report any other race category. [7] Beginning with 2005, data represent Asian alone, which refers to people who reported Asian and did not report any other race category. [8] People of Hispanic origin may be any race.

Source: U.S. Census Bureau, *Income, Poverty and Health Insurance Coverage in the United States: 2009,* Current Population Reports, P60-238, and Historical Tables—Table P-2, September 2010. See also <http://www.census.gov/hhes/www/income /income.html> and <http://www.census.gov/hhes/www/income/data/historical/people/index.html>.

Table 702. Money Income of People—Selected Characteristics by Income Level: 2009

[People as of March 2010 (117,728 represents 117,728,000). Covers people 15 years old and over. Median income in constant dollars based on CPI-U-RS deflator. For definition of median, see Guide to Tabular Presentation. Median income is calculated using $2,500 income intervals. Beginning with 2009 income data, the Census Bureau expanded the upper income intervals used to calculate medians to $250,000 or more. Medians falling in the upper open-ended interval are plugged with "$250,000." Before 2009, the upper open-ended interval was $100,000 and a plug of "$100,000" was used. For composition of regions, see map, inside front cover. Based on the Current Population Survey, Annual Social and Economic Supplement (ASEC), see Appendix III]

Characteristic	All persons (1,000)	People with income									Median income (current dollars)
		Total (1,000)	Number (1,000)								
			Under $5,000 [1]	$5,000 to $9,999	$10,000 to $14,999	$15,000 to $24,999	$25,000 to $34,999	$35,000 to $49,999	$50,000 to $74,999	$75,000 and over	
MALE											
Total..............	117,728	105,025	7,467	7,483	8,994	17,278	14,085	16,106	16,571	17,041	32,184
15 to 24 years old	21,403	13,280	4,148	2,476	1,723	2,477	1,156	782	392	123	10,036
25 to 34 years old	20,689	19,281	911	1,270	1,478	3,414	3,273	3,654	3,278	2,003	31,914
35 to 44 years old	20,074	19,087	609	774	1,095	2,461	2,500	3,555	3,782	4,311	42,224
45 to 54 years old	21,784	20,719	785	978	1,217	2,523	2,457	3,484	4,192	5,081	44,731
55 to 64 years old	16,985	16,252	660	809	1,248	2,242	2,043	2,420	3,029	3,803	41,296
65 years old and over	16,793	16,406	353	1,179	2,233	4,160	2,655	2,213	1,898	1,719	25,877
Region:											
Northeast..............	21,357	19,117	1,316	1,182	1,461	3,029	2,465	2,700	3,235	3,730	35,414
Midwest	25,753	23,354	1,750	1,602	1,908	3,846	3,296	3,853	3,812	3,285	32,060
South.................	42,933	37,974	2,627	3,064	3,554	6,443	5,122	5,884	5,657	5,623	31,047
West.................	27,684	24,580	1,774	1,637	2,072	3,961	3,203	3,669	3,866	4,399	33,191
Educational attainment of householder: [2]											
Total	96,325	91,745	3,319	5,008	7,271	14,801	12,930	15,324	16,177	16,916	36,801
Less than 9th grade.......	5,211	4,736	260	819	1,032	1,363	631	376	189	65	16,473
9th to 12th grade [3]	7,705	6,948	435	818	1,194	1,889	1,137	793	471	207	19,720
High school graduate [4]	30,682	28,946	1,165	1,802	2,610	6,033	5,223	5,560	4,433	2,118	30,303
Some college, no degree...	15,908	15,184	564	735	1,101	2,292	2,448	2,924	3,124	1,996	36,693
Associate's degree	7,662	7,399	231	261	394	954	1,023	1,531	1,751	1,253	42,163
Bachelor's degree											
or more..............	29,158	28,532	663	574	940	2,268	2,464	4,140	6,207	11,275	61,280
Bachelor's degree	18,674	18,205	502	421	696	1,642	1,867	2,947	4,114	6,017	54,091
Master's degree..........	6,859	6,728	120	111	176	428	441	853	1,553	3,047	69,825
Professional degree......	1,861	1,844	26	17	41	106	77	166	236	1,174	102,398
Doctoral degree........	1,763	1,755	16	26	27	90	80	175	303	1,040	89,845
Tenure:											
Owner-occupied	83,038	74,848	5,080	4,260	5,358	10,714	9,377	11,829	13,280	14,953	37,482
Renter-occupied	33,150	28,837	2,258	3,087	3,471	6,269	4,483	4,087	3,168	2,014	23,556
Occupier paid no cash rent..........	1,539	1,340	129	138	165	294	224	191	123	74	22,113
FEMALE											
Total................	124,440	106,229	12,632	14,338	13,379	19,836	14,433	13,711	10,849	7,051	20,957
15 to 24 years old	20,837	12,804	4,228	2,634	1,930	2,307	1,033	460	164	48	8,950
25 to 34 years old	20,396	17,498	1,890	1,606	1,721	3,440	2,981	2,943	1,998	916	25,236
35 to 44 years old	20,373	17,913	2,001	1,495	1,631	2,860	2,797	3,040	2,415	1,672	27,894
45 to 54 years old	22,604	20,418	1,902	1,793	1,815	3,356	3,138	3,385	2,910	2,120	28,617
55 to 64 years old	18,410	16,694	1,638	1,961	1,849	2,865	2,339	2,328	2,126	1,590	25,112
65 years old and over	21,820	20,901	972	4,847	4,434	5,012	2,143	1,556	1,234	699	15,282
Region:											
Northeast..............	23,152	20,123	2,388	2,555	2,360	3,499	2,754	2,729	2,201	1,634	22,067
Midwest	27,072	23,794	2,757	3,235	2,991	4,647	3,339	3,128	2,380	1,318	20,987
South.................	45,949	38,648	4,466	5,456	5,147	7,461	5,250	4,919	3,750	2,200	20,261
West.................	28,267	23,665	3,022	3,092	2,881	4,229	3,091	2,936	2,518	1,898	21,131
Educational attainment of householder: [2]											
Total	103,603	93,426	8,404	11,703	11,449	17,531	13,400	13,250	10,685	7,002	23,159
Less than 9th grade.......	5,240	4,036	530	1,358	1,008	781	232	56	54	17	10,516
9th to 12th grade [3]	7,555	6,175	663	1,652	1,408	1,453	558	273	128	44	12,278
High school graduate [4]	31,774	28,154	2,479	4,464	4,474	6,833	4,628	3,188	1,542	544	18,340
Some college, no degree...	17,753	16,208	1,435	1,819	1,913	3,492	2,818	2,619	1,472	639	23,107
Associate's degree	10,597	9,936	801	870	963	1,891	1,751	1,774	1,317	571	27,027
Bachelor's degree											
or more..............	30,683	28,917	2,497	1,541	1,683	3,083	3,414	5,340	6,170	5,188	40,766
Bachelor's degree	20,110	18,844	1,824	1,182	1,257	2,265	2,572	3,736	3,604	2,405	35,972
Master's degree..........	8,344	7,945	553	302	336	677	681	1,340	2,121	1,933	50,576
Professional degree......	1,213	1,142	78	23	60	99	92	142	205	442	60,259
Doctoral degree........	1,015	987	41	32	30	41	72	122	241	407	65,587
Tenure:											
Owner-occupied	86,992	75,755	8,923	9,321	8,653	13,204	10,125	10,487	8,974	6,069	22,608
Renter-occupied	35,923	29,240	3,509	4,798	4,519	6,379	4,142	3,131	1,818	944	17,204
Occupier paid no cash rent	1,525	1,234	201	217	206	255	167	93	56	40	14,762

[1] Includes persons with income deficit. [2] Persons 25 years and over. [3] No diploma attained. [4] Includes high school equivalency.
Source: U.S. Census Bureau, *Income, Poverty and Health Insurance Coverage in the United States: 2009*, Current Population Reports, P60-238, and Detailed Tables—Table PINC-01, September 2010. See also <http://www.census.gov/hhes/www/cpstables/032010/perinc/new01_000.htm>

Table 703. Average Earnings of Year-Round, Full-Time Workers by Educational Attainment: 2009

[In dollars. For people 18 years old and over as of March 2010. See headnote, Table 701]

Sex and age	All workers	Less than 9th grade	High school		College		
			9th to 12th grade (no diploma)	High school graduate [1]	Some college, no degree	Associate degree	Bachelor's degree or more
Male, total........	**62,445**	**26,604**	**33,194**	**43,140**	**52,580**	**55,631**	**92,815**
18 to 24 years old	29,599	20,041	19,556	27,822	29,564	33,915	42,299
25 to 34 years old	49,105	25,067	27,074	38,037	44,020	48,313	67,555
35 to 44 years old	66,788	26,685	39,949	43,518	55,686	58,689	98,045
45 to 54 years old	71,661	28,067	36,239	48,224	61,072	62,000	109,163
55 to 64 years old	71,222	29,648	36,837	47,164	60,230	58,176	99,572
65 years old and over ...	67,007	27,375	35,278	55,241	58,899	45,783	88,853
Female, total........	**44,857**	**19,588**	**23,478**	**32,227**	**36,553**	**42,307**	**62,198**
18 to 24 years old	24,117	(B)	16,921	22,620	21,127	26,922	32,103
25 to 34 years old	40,475	18,278	21,996	27,993	32,229	36,202	52,102
35 to 44 years old	47,260	19,963	24,218	32,947	38,057	42,092	65,881
45 to 54 years old	48,929	19,591	23,987	34,145	42,068	47,716	69,698
55 to 64 years old	48,232	20,469	26,729	34,900	41,707	45,938	67,683

B Base figure too small to meet statistical standards for reliability of derived figure. [1] Includes equivalency.
Source: U.S. Census Bureau, *Income, Poverty and Health Insurance Coverage in the United States: 2009*, Current Population Reports, series P60-238, and Detailed Tables—Table PINC-04, September 2010. See also <http://www.census.gov/hhes/www/cpstables/032010/perinc/new04_000.htm>.

Table 704. Per Capita Money Income in Current and Constant (2009) Dollars by Race and Hispanic Origin: 1990 to 2009

[In dollars. Constant dollars based on CPI-U-RS deflator. People as of March of following year. Based on the Current Population Survey, Annual Social and Economic Supplement (ASEC); see text, this section, Section 1, and Appendix III. For data collection changes over time, see <http://www.census.gov/hhes/www/income/data/historical/history.html>]

Year	Current dollars					Constant (2009) dollars				
	All races [1]	White [2]	Black [3]	Asian and Pacific Islander [4]	His-panic [5]	All races [1]	White [2]	Black [3]	Asian and Pacific Islander [4]	His-panic [5]
1990.......	14,387	15,265	9,017	(NA)	8,424	22,888	24,285	14,345	(NA)	13,402
1995 [6]	17,227	18,304	10,982	16,567	9,300	24,075	25,580	15,348	23,153	12,997
2000 [7,8]	22,346	23,582	14,796	23,350	12,651	27,833	29,373	18,429	29,084	15,757
2005 [9,10]	25,036	26,496	16,874	27,331	14,483	27,507	29,111	18,540	30,029	15,913
2006.......	26,352	27,821	17,902	30,474	15,421	28,034	29,597	19,045	32,419	16,405
2007.......	26,804	28,325	18,428	29,901	15,603	27,728	29,302	19,063	30,932	16,141
2008.......	26,964	28,502	18,406	30,292	15,674	26,862	28,394	18,336	30,177	15,615
2009 [11]	26,530	28,034	18,135	30,653	15,063	26,530	28,034	18,135	30,653	15,063

NA Not available. [1] Includes other races, not shown separately. [2] Beginning with 2003, data represents White alone, which refers to people who reported White and did not report any other race category. [3] Beginning with 2003, data represents Black alone, which refers to people who reported Black and did not report any other race category. [4] Beginning with 2003, data represents Asian alone, which refers to people who reported Asian and did not report any other race category. [5] People of Hispanic origin may be any race. [6] Data reflect full implementation of the 1990 census-based sample design and metropolitan definitions, 7,000 household sample reduction, and revised race edits. [7] Implementation of Census 2000-based population controls. [8] Implementation of a 28,000 household sample expansion. [9] See footnote 4, Table 696. See also comments on race in the text for Section 1. [10] Data have been revised to reflect a correction to the weights in the 2005 ASEC. [11] Median income is calculated using $2,500 income intervals. Beginning with 2009 income data, the Census Bureau expanded the upper income intervals used to calculate medians to $250,000 or more. Before 2009, the upper open-ended interval was $100,000.
Source: U.S. Census Bureau, *Income, Poverty and Health Insurance Coverage in the United States: 2009*, Current Population Reports, P60-238, and Historical Tables—Table P-1, September 2010. See also <http://www.census.gov/hhes/www/income/income.html> and <http://www.census.gov/hhes/www/income/data/historical/people/index.html>.

Table 705. Money Income of People—Number by Income Level and by Sex, Race, and Hispanic Origin: 2009

[In thousands (117,728 represents 117,728,000). People as of March of the following year. Based on Current Population Survey, Annual Social and Economic Supplement (ASEC); see text, this section, Section 1, and Appendix III]

Income interval	Male					Female				
	All races [1]	White alone	Black alone	Asian alone	His-panic [2]	All races [1]	White alone	Black alone	Asian alone	His-panic [2]
All households........	**117,728**	**96,190**	**13,314**	**5,287**	**17,679**	**124,440**	**99,380**	**16,054**	**5,916**	**16,609**
Under $10,000 [3]..........	27,653	20,216	5,020	1,377	5,488	45,180	35,137	6,167	2,494	8,339
$10,000 to $19,999	17,803	14,453	2,241	638	3,749	23,958	19,263	3,358	785	3,318
$20,000 to $29,999	15,585	12,913	1,686	557	2,887	16,924	13,609	2,246	671	2,013
$30,000 to $39,999	12,835	10,721	1,295	522	1,948	12,326	9,968	1,612	469	1,206
$40,000 to $49,999	10,240	8,717	943	390	1,184	8,151	6,654	970	356	620
$50,000 to $59,999	8,249	7,077	696	341	796	5,748	4,779	608	257	377
$60,000 to $74,999	8,322	7,147	632	389	666	5,101	4,187	530	301	329
$75,000 to $84,999	3,743	3,256	239	196	259	1,915	1,568	182	124	124
$85,000 to $99,999	3,456	3,020	182	208	213	1,710	1,399	134	156	77
$100,000 to $149,999	5,863	5,127	226	438	315	2,382	1,912	204	222	149
$150,000 to $199,999	1,924	1,713	69	113	83	572	495	30	43	27
$200,000 to $249,999	875	791	22	52	34	193	165	30	19	9
$250,000 and above	1,181	1,037	62	69	57	279	244	6	20	22

[1] Includes races not shown separately. [2] Persons of Hispanic origin may be of any race. [3] Includes persons without income.
Source: U.S. Census Bureau, *Income, Poverty and Health Insurance Coverage in the United States: 2009*, Current Population Reports, P60-238, and Detailed Tables—Table PINC-11, September 2010. See also <http://www.census.gov/hhes/www/cpstables/032010/perinc/new11_000.htm>.

Income, Expenditures, Poverty, and Wealth **459**

Table 706. Household Income—Distribution by Income Level and State: 2009

[In thousands (113,616 represents 113,616,000), except as indicated. The American Community Survey universe includes the household population and the population living in institutions, college dormitories, and other group quarters. Based on a sample and subject to sampling variability; see text, Section 1 and Appendix III. For definition of median, see Guide to Tabular Presentation]

State	Number of households (1,000)								Median income (dollars)
	Total	Under $25,000	$25,000 to $49,999	$50,000 to $74,999	$75,000 to $99,999	$100,000 to $149,999	$150,000 to $199,999	$200,000 or more	
United States	113,616	28,066	28,510	20,841	13,687	13,332	4,712	4,468	50,221
Alabama	1,848	592	503	314	192	161	46	39	40,489
Alaska	237	35	51	46	38	41	14	11	66,953
Arizona	2,277	562	604	435	274	256	76	69	48,745
Arkansas	1,125	381	322	197	101	83	21	20	37,823
California	12,215	2,530	2,733	2,155	1,548	1,780	748	722	58,931
Colorado	1,910	409	455	361	252	261	94	79	55,430
Connecticut	1,326	243	259	230	176	221	92	104	67,034
Delaware	327	66	77	66	44	46	16	13	56,860
District of Columbia	249	60	48	38	27	32	18	25	59,290
Florida	6,988	1,867	1,993	1,289	748	661	214	215	44,736
Georgia	3,469	933	888	632	403	367	128	119	47,590
Hawaii	446	78	97	83	67	73	28	20	64,098
Idaho	558	143	166	115	66	48	12	10	44,926
Illinois	4,757	1,095	1,118	886	619	614	214	213	53,966
Indiana..............	2,478	642	708	488	287	239	66	48	45,424
Iowa................	1,227	304	336	244	158	127	31	27	48,044
Kansas..............	1,105	277	300	214	134	111	36	32	47,817
Kentucky	1,694	547	466	294	175	143	37	32	40,072
Louisiana	1,688	519	442	282	184	167	50	43	42,492
Maine...............	545	146	150	110	64	49	14	11	45,734
Maryland	2,095	335	416	377	289	363	167	147	69,272
Massachusetts.........	2,475	507	487	423	326	407	164	162	64,081
Michigan	3,820	1,046	1,033	710	435	389	111	96	45,255
Minnesota	2,086	437	504	417	296	269	86	78	55,616
Mississippi...........	1,095	395	294	182	107	80	21	17	36,646
Missouri.............	2,340	635	643	445	270	226	65	55	45,229
Montana.............	375	108	108	71	44	31	7	6	42,322
Nebraska............	711	177	198	145	86	71	18	16	47,357
Nevada..............	966	199	251	201	128	122	36	27	53,341
New Hampshire........	506	94	116	98	72	78	28	21	60,567
New Jersey	3,155	562	617	528	428	535	239	247	68,342
New Mexico..........	742	220	201	134	81	69	21	17	43,028
New York	7,188	1,733	1,588	1,234	858	946	387	442	54,659
North Carolina........	3,646	1,036	1,005	659	403	341	104	99	43,674
North Dakota	279	71	75	55	36	28	7	7	47,827
Ohio................	4,526	1,240	1,228	857	519	445	134	104	45,395
Oklahoma............	1,430	424	403	265	154	120	33	32	41,664
Oregon..............	1,486	372	394	291	181	160	46	41	48,457
Pennsylvania	4,917	1,224	1,258	932	610	540	183	170	49,520
Rhode Island	406	97	91	74	54	55	19	16	54,119
South Carolina........	1,730	519	471	314	188	157	43	38	42,442
South Dakota.........	317	87	88	65	37	25	7	7	45,043
Tennessee...........	2,447	741	680	446	261	196	64	59	41,725
Texas...............	8,528	2,223	2,188	1,523	976	956	336	326	48,259
Utah................	863	159	227	190	121	108	33	25	55,117
Vermont.............	252	58	63	55	33	28	9	6	51,618
Virginia..............	2,971	579	678	547	383	420	183	181	59,330
Washington	2,559	522	613	492	349	360	124	99	56,548
West Virginia	749	260	212	128	70	52	14	13	37,435
Wisconsin	2,272	534	603	465	303	248	65	55	49,993
Wyoming	214	45	57	43	30	27	6	5	52,664

Source: U.S. Census Bureau, 2009 American Community Survey, B19001, "Household Income in the Past 12 Months" and B19013, "Median Household Income in the Past 12 Months (In 2009 Inflation-Adjusted Dollars)," <http://factfinder.census.gov/>, accessed January 2011.

Table 707. Family Income—Distribution by Income Level and State: 2009

[In thousands (75,531 represents 75,531,000), except as indicated. The American Community Survey universe includes the household population and the population living in institutions, college dormitories, and other group quarters. Based on a sample and subject to sampling variability; see text, Section 1 and Appendix III. For definition of median, see Guide to Tabular Presentation]

State	Total	Number of families (1,000)							Median income (dollars)
		Less than $25,000	$25,000 to $49,000	$50,000 to $74,999	$75,000 to $99,999	$100,000 to $149,999	$150,000 to $199,999	$200,000 and over	
United States	**75,531**	**12,922**	**17,708**	**14,988**	**10,852**	**11,161**	**4,041**	**3,859**	**61,082**
Alabama	1,246	278	336	244	165	144	43	36	50,779
Alaska	160	15	30	29	30	33	12	9	79,934
Arizona	1,514	272	378	316	217	208	64	59	57,855
Arkansas	768	191	220	159	88	74	20	18	46,868
California	8,366	1,348	1,776	1,494	1,137	1,399	611	601	67,038
Colorado	1,233	177	246	248	195	216	81	70	68,943
Connecticut	891	97	149	152	135	186	79	92	83,069
Delaware	221	29	48	45	35	38	14	11	67,582
District of Columbia	109	22	20	15	11	15	10	16	71,208
Florida	4,542	865	1,255	924	590	547	179	182	53,509
Georgia	2,370	474	585	457	328	311	112	102	56,176
Hawaii	310	37	59	59	54	60	24	17	75,066
Idaho	397	69	120	90	57	42	10	9	51,851
Illinois	3,120	475	666	612	483	515	187	183	66,806
Indiana	1,658	291	435	373	245	212	60	43	56,432
Iowa	798	115	197	186	135	113	28	24	61,156
Kansas	722	110	179	160	112	100	32	30	60,994
Kentucky	1,147	263	313	229	152	128	34	29	49,801
Louisiana	1,129	248	284	211	157	146	44	38	53,427
Maine	348	59	92	80	52	42	12	10	56,566
Maryland	1,392	139	234	240	212	292	143	132	84,254
Massachusetts	1,557	184	267	267	235	323	139	142	81,033
Michigan	2,524	462	641	531	361	343	101	85	56,681
Minnesota	1,349	165	283	289	237	229	77	70	69,374
Mississippi	754	205	205	146	93	70	19	15	45,601
Missouri	1,543	285	393	335	226	197	58	49	56,318
Montana	236	43	63	53	38	27	7	6	55,010
Nebraska	458	70	113	109	73	63	17	15	60,102
Nevada	632	94	157	139	94	98	28	21	60,829
New Hampshire	336	34	65	72	57	67	23	18	73,856
New Jersey	2,172	251	362	358	325	447	208	220	83,381
New Mexico	489	108	128	98	63	59	18	15	51,994
New York	4,607	780	951	826	631	750	311	358	66,891
North Carolina	2,430	488	632	497	332	303	94	85	54,288
North Dakota	172	22	41	42	31	24	6	6	63,507
Ohio	2,947	527	747	637	431	394	118	93	57,360
Oklahoma	949	194	257	205	130	106	30	28	52,403
Oregon	957	161	233	211	144	132	39	36	59,174
Pennsylvania	3,196	476	767	681	490	469	159	152	62,185
Rhode Island	258	38	54	47	43	45	16	14	69,350
South Carolina	1,164	252	302	238	160	139	39	34	52,406
South Dakota	205	34	51	52	32	23	6	7	57,764
Tennessee	1,639	356	441	343	218	172	56	52	51,344
Texas	5,956	1,202	1,445	1,118	788	819	296	289	56,607
Utah	649	80	159	153	108	95	30	23	62,935
Vermont	159	22	37	37	28	23	9	5	63,483
Virginia	1,988	257	411	376	288	338	156	160	71,270
Washington	1,651	220	350	333	265	296	103	84	68,360
West Virginia	492	113	148	101	61	47	12	11	47,659
Wisconsin	1,477	210	348	339	254	218	58	50	62,638
Wyoming	143	17	35	33	26	23	6	5	65,532

Source: U.S. Census Bureau, 2009 American Community Survey, B19101, "Family Income in the Past 12 Months" and B19113, "Median Family Income in the Past 12 Months (In 2009 Inflation-Adjusted Dollars)," <http://factfinder.census.gov/>, accessed January 2011.

Table 708. Household, Family, and Per Capita Income and Individuals, and Families Below Poverty Level by City: 2009

[The American Community Survey universe includes the household population and the population living in institutions, college dormitories, and other group quarters. Based on a sample and subject to sampling variability; see text, Section 1 and Appendix III. For definition of median, see Guide to Tabular Presentation]

City	Median household income (dol.)	Median family income (dol.)	Per capita income (dol.)	Number below poverty level [1]		Percent below poverty level [1]	
				Individuals	Families	Individuals	Families
Albuquerque, NM.............	44,594	54,819	24,597	86,771	16,149	16.6	12.3
Anaheim, CA................	55,154	60,341	21,675	48,755	8,963	14.6	12.0
Anchorage municipality, AK....	72,832	82,574	33,498	21,442	3,691	7.6	5.3
Arlington, TX	50,938	60,934	24,560	59,715	11,270	15.9	12.2
Atlanta, GA	49,981	61,658	36,912	116,092	17,208	22.5	18.6
Aurora, CO.................	45,904	55,102	21,917	54,125	10,450	16.9	13.7
Austin, TX	50,132	62,153	29,233	142,930	23,020	18.4	13.5
Bakersfield, CA	52,677	56,143	21,496	66,135	12,309	20.6	16.5
Baltimore, MD	38,772	47,160	23,267	129,796	20,348	21.0	17.0
Boston, MA	55,979	64,546	33,889	103,197	12,937	16.9	11.9
Buffalo, NY................	29,285	36,497	20,003	75,259	16,482	28.8	26.9
Charlotte, NC..............	49,779	60,798	31,270	105,805	20,325	15.3	11.5
Chicago, IL................	45,734	52,101	27,138	603,218	106,138	21.6	18.0
Cincinnati, OH	32,754	47,654	23,593	81,919	13,583	25.7	21.5
Cleveland, OH	24,687	31,159	15,583	146,122	27,344	35.0	28.8
Colorado Springs, CO	52,984	67,004	27,556	47,306	8,680	12.1	8.8
Columbus, OH	41,370	50,642	22,809	170,889	29,592	22.6	17.3
Corpus Christi, TX...........	42,157	50,746	21,088	52,984	10,639	19.0	15.5
Dallas, TX	39,829	42,699	25,941	295,464	55,029	23.2	19.5
Denver, CO	46,410	58,593	29,878	114,053	18,235	19.1	14.7
Detroit, MI	26,098	31,017	14,213	326,764	58,853	36.4	31.3
El Paso, TX	37,030	42,418	17,580	138,368	29,396	22.6	19.3
Fort Wayne, IN.............	41,038	52,144	21,145	44,801	8,958	18.1	14.4
Fort Worth, TX.............	47,634	54,404	23,399	136,577	26,492	19.0	15.2
Fresno, CA................	43,223	48,518	19,407	106,934	18,123	22.7	17.6
Honolulu, HI [2].............	57,601	75,488	30,917	38,374	6,668	10.5	7.5
Houston, TX...............	42,945	47,329	25,563	459,355	90,940	20.6	17.5
Indianapolis, IN [3]...........	40,278	50,546	23,049	159,734	29,901	20.2	16.0
Jacksonville, FL............	46,312	55,916	23,694	124,302	25,210	15.6	12.6
Kansas City, MO	41,999	55,040	25,189	79,853	13,480	16.7	11.9
Las Vegas, NV.............	50,935	58,971	24,246	83,261	14,349	14.9	10.8
Lexington-Fayette, KY	46,385	66,185	27,652	50,112	8,564	17.6	11.8
Long Beach, CA	51,379	57,196	25,791	87,465	14,862	19.3	15.8
Los Angeles, CA	48,617	52,966	26,096	744,567	128,660	19.8	16.1
Memphis, TN	34,203	40,745	19,388	173,343	32,299	26.2	21.5
Mesa, AZ.................	49,446	58,830	23,195	60,165	9,914	13.0	9.1
Miami, FL.................	28,999	34,572	19,449	112,141	19,157	26.5	20.5
Milwaukee, WI.............	34,868	39,124	18,290	158,245	27,867	27.0	22.4
Minneapolis, MN	45,538	59,498	28,131	83,562	11,127	22.6	15.2
Nashville-Davidson, TN [3].....	45,540	54,139	25,965	101,004	17,095	17.3	12.7
New Orleans, LA	36,468	43,213	23,475	82,469	13,468	23.8	18.7
New York, NY..............	50,033	56,054	30,885	1,546,046	292,822	18.7	15.8
Newark, NJ	35,963	40,359	17,396	62,973	13,103	23.9	21.2
Oakland, CA	51,473	59,306	30,327	69,706	11,679	17.2	14.5
Oklahoma City, OK	41,411	54,721	24,195	99,516	19,529	18.1	14.2
Omaha, NE	46,595	61,404	26,377	61,084	10,011	13.7	9.6
Philadelphia, PA............	37,045	45,769	21,661	374,226	61,971	25.0	19.9
Phoenix, AZ...............	47,085	53,906	22,209	331,893	53,616	21.1	16.0
Pittsburgh, PA	37,461	50,922	25,109	66,621	9,322	23.1	15.5
Plano, TX.................	77,140	96,146	37,032	22,055	4,456	8.1	6.5
Portland, OR	50,203	61,557	29,137	88,904	13,781	16.0	11.2
Raleigh, NC...............	51,969	70,998	28,775	61,333	9,446	15.9	11.0
Riverside, CA..............	56,552	63,789	22,244	43,806	6,749	15.1	10.3
Sacramento, CA............	47,107	54,296	24,471	87,870	14,284	19.2	13.7
San Antonio, TX............	42,513	51,002	21,053	261,066	47,047	19.5	15.6
San Diego, CA.............	59,901	73,648	31,140	181,891	25,241	14.3	9.1
San Francisco, CA..........	70,770	86,713	44,038	93,644	10,741	11.6	7.4
San Jose, CA..............	76,495	84,274	31,224	109,826	18,094	11.5	8.4
Santa Ana, CA.............	53,211	50,525	16,439	65,379	9,541	19.8	16.1
Seattle, WA	60,843	89,361	40,743	63,509	6,498	10.6	5.1
St. Louis, MO..............	34,801	39,483	21,208	92,032	16,983	26.7	23.9
St. Paul, MN...............	41,636	53,166	24,702	61,478	9,963	22.6	17.3
St. Petersburg, FL	41,210	52,517	25,451	36,400	6,883	15.2	12.1
Stockton, CA	45,730	49,061	19,369	62,504	11,480	22.3	17.7
Tampa, FL.................	41,605	47,440	26,154	64,742	12,037	19.2	15.3
Toledo, OH	32,325	41,568	17,816	73,755	14,521	23.8	19.6
Tucson, AZ................	35,565	45,224	19,124	123,562	18,256	23.4	16.5
Tulsa, OK.................	38,426	50,464	26,072	74,459	13,641	19.5	14.6
Virginia Beach, VA..........	59,298	67,966	29,301	27,389	5,092	6.4	4.7
Washington, DC............	59,290	71,208	40,797	104,901	15,965	18.4	14.6
Wichita, KS	44,405	56,869	23,878	57,305	11,358	15.6	12.2

[1] See headnote, Table 709. [2] Data shown for census designated place (CDP). [3] Represents the portion of a consolidated city that is not within one or more separately incorporated places.

Source: U.S. Census Bureau, 2009 American Community Survey, B19013, B19113, B19301, B17001, and B17010, <http://factfinder.census.gov/>, accessed January 2011.

U.S. Census Bureau, Statistical Abstract of the United States: 2012

Table 709. Individuals and Families Below Poverty Level—Number and Rate by State: 2000 and 2009

[In thousands (33,311 represents 33,311,000), except as indicated. Represents number and percent below poverty in the past 12 months. Prior to 2006, the American Community Survey universe was limited to the household population and excluded the population living in institutions, college dormitories, and other group quarters. Poverty status was determined for all people except institutionalized people, people in military group quarters, people in college dormitories, and unrelated individuals under 15 years old. These groups were excluded from the numerator and denominator when calculating poverty rates. Based on a sample and subject to sampling variability; see Appendix III]

| State | Number below poverty (1,000) | | | | Percent below poverty | | | |
| | Individuals | | Families | | Individuals | | Families | |
	2000	2009	2000	2009	2000	2009	2000	2009
United States	**33,311**	**42,868**	**6,615**	**7,956**	**12.2**	**14.3**	**9.3**	**10.5**
Alabama	672	805	146	167	15.6	17.5	12.4	13.4
Alaska	55	62	11	10	9.1	9.0	6.8	6.2
Arizona	780	1,070	150	175	15.6	16.5	11.6	11.6
Arkansas	439	527	96	113	17.0	18.8	13.0	14.8
California	4,520	5,129	832	887	13.7	14.2	10.7	10.6
Colorado	363	634	64	110	8.7	12.9	5.7	8.9
Connecticut	254	321	51	59	7.7	9.4	5.8	6.7
Delaware	70	93	14	16	9.3	10.8	6.7	7.1
District of Columbia	94	105	17	16	17.5	18.4	15.4	14.6
Florida	1,987	2,708	387	488	12.8	14.9	9.3	10.7
Georgia	999	1,575	206	301	12.6	16.5	10.0	12.7
Hawaii	103	131	19	23	8.8	10.4	6.8	7.5
Idaho	144	216	26	39	11.4	14.3	7.7	9.9
Illinois	1,335	1,677	262	309	11.1	13.3	8.6	9.9
Indiana	592	897	113	178	10.1	14.4	7.1	10.7
Iowa	281	343	53	61	10.0	11.8	7.0	7.7
Kansas	247	365	43	65	9.5	13.4	6.2	9.0
Kentucky	640	777	148	165	16.4	18.6	13.5	14.4
Louisiana	862	755	182	150	20.0	17.3	16.0	13.3
Maine	124	158	22	29	10.1	12.3	6.6	8.3
Maryland	477	505	89	85	9.3	9.1	6.6	6.1
Massachusetts	586	655	110	109	9.6	10.3	7.1	7.0
Michigan	975	1,577	196	292	10.1	16.2	7.7	11.6
Minnesota	328	563	66	95	6.9	11.0	5.1	7.0
Mississippi	498	624	104	131	18.2	21.9	14.2	17.3
Missouri	606	849	118	168	11.2	14.6	7.7	10.9
Montana	117	143	23	23	13.4	15.1	9.5	9.9
Nebraska	158	215	28	39	9.6	12.3	6.5	8.4
Nevada	194	322	34	57	9.9	12.4	6.9	9.0
New Hampshire	63	109	11	19	5.3	8.5	3.5	5.5
New Jersey	651	799	126	151	7.9	9.4	6.0	7.0
New Mexico	320	354	64	66	18.0	18.0	14.2	13.6
New York	2,391	2,692	491	498	13.1	14.2	10.7	10.8
North Carolina	1,018	1,478	203	289	13.1	16.3	9.6	11.9
North Dakota	71	72	14	11	11.6	11.7	8.1	6.6
Ohio	1,216	1,710	246	328	11.1	15.2	8.4	11.1
Oklahoma	459	578	100	115	13.8	16.2	11.0	12.1
Oregon	439	535	84	94	13.2	14.3	9.5	9.8
Pennsylvania	1,240	1,517	247	275	10.5	12.5	7.8	8.6
Rhode Island	108	116	23	22	10.7	11.5	8.5	8.6
South Carolina	557	754	123	150	14.4	17.1	11.7	12.9
South Dakota	83	111	16	18	11.5	14.2	8.4	9.0
Tennessee	745	1,052	158	215	13.5	17.1	10.5	13.1
Texas	3,056	4,150	639	800	15.1	17.2	12.3	13.4
Utah	192	316	40	51	8.8	11.5	7.2	7.8
Vermont	63	68	12	12	10.7	11.4	7.5	7.3
Virginia	630	803	124	148	9.2	10.5	6.8	7.5
Washington	667	804	127	133	11.6	12.3	8.6	8.1
West Virginia	327	313	72	68	18.6	17.7	14.7	13.9
Wisconsin	461	683	75	121	8.9	12.4	5.6	8.2
Wyoming	55	52	10	9	11.4	9.8	7.9	6.3

Source: U.S. Census Bureau, 2009 American Community Survey, B17001, "Poverty Status in the Past 12 Months by Sex and Age" and B17010, "Poverty Status in the Past 12 Months of Families by Family Type by Presence of Related Children under 18 Years by Age of Related Children," <http://factfinder.census.gov/>, accessed January 2011.

Table 710. Poverty Thresholds by Size of Family Unit: 1980 to 2009

[In dollars per year. For information on the official poverty thresholds; see text, this section. For more on poverty, see <http://www.census.gov/hhes/www/poverty/about/overview/measure.html>]

Size of family unit	1980	1990	1995	2000 [1]	2005	2006	2007	2008	2009
One person (unrelated individual) [2].....	4,190	6,652	7,763	8,791	9,973	10,294	10,590	10,991	10,956
Under 65 years old	4,290	6,800	7,929	8,959	10,160	10,488	10,787	11,201	11,161
65 years old and over	3,949	6,268	7,309	8,259	9,367	9,669	9,944	10,326	10,289
Two persons	5,363	8,509	9,933	11,235	12,755	13,167	13,540	14,051	13,991
Householder under 65 years old	5,537	8,794	10,259	11,589	13,145	13,569	13,954	14,417	14,366
Householder 65 years old and over....	4,983	7,905	9,219	10,418	11,815	12,201	12,550	13,014	12,968
Three persons.....................	6,565	10,419	12,158	13,740	15,577	16,079	16,530	17,163	17,098
Four persons	8,414	13,359	15,569	17,604	19,971	20,614	21,203	22,025	21,954
Five persons	9,966	15,792	18,408	20,815	23,613	24,382	25,080	26,049	25,991
Six persons	11,269	17,839	20,804	23,533	26,683	27,560	28,323	29,456	29,405
Seven persons	12,761	20,241	23,552	26,750	30,249	31,205	32,233	33,529	33,372
Eight persons....................	14,199	22,582	26,237	29,701	33,610	34,774	35,816	37,220	37,252
Nine or more persons	16,896	26,848	31,280	35,150	40,288	41,499	42,739	44,346	44,366

[1] Implementation of Census 2000-based population controls and sample expanded by 28,000 households. [2] A person living alone or with non-relatives.

Source: U.S. Census Bureau, *Income, Poverty, and Health Insurance Coverage in the United States: 2009*, Current Population Reports, P60-236, and Historical Tables—Table 1, September 2010. See also <http://www.census.gov/hhes/www/poverty/poverty .html> and <http://www.census.gov/hhes/www/poverty/data/historical/people.html>.

Table 711. People Below Poverty Level and Below 125 Percent of Poverty Level by Race and Hispanic Origin: 1980 to 2009

[29,272 represents 29,272,000. People as of March of the following year. Based on Current Population Survey, Annual Social and Economic Supplement (ASEC); see text, this section, Section 1, and Appendix III. For data collection changes over time, see <http://www.census.gov/hhes/www/income/data/historical/history.html>]

Year	Number of persons below poverty (1,000)					Percent of persons below poverty					Below 125 percent [1] of poverty level	
	All races [2]	White [3]	Black [4]	Asian and Pacific Islander [5]	His-panic [6]	All races [2]	White [3]	Black [4]	Asian and Pacific Islander [5]	His-panic [6]	Number (1,000)	Percent of total population
1980........	29,272	19,699	8,579	(NA)	3,491	13.0	10.2	32.5	(NA)	25.7	40,658	18.1
1985........	33,064	22,860	8,926	(NA)	5,236	14.0	11.4	31.3	(NA)	29.0	44,166	18.7
1988........	31,745	20,715	9,356	1,117	5,357	13.0	10.1	31.3	17.3	26.7	42,551	17.5
1989........	31,528	20,785	9,302	939	5,430	12.8	10.0	30.7	14.1	26.2	42,653	17.3
1990........	33,585	22,326	9,837	858	6,006	13.5	10.7	31.9	12.2	28.1	44,837	18.0
1991........	35,708	23,747	10,242	996	6,339	14.2	11.3	32.7	13.8	28.7	47,527	18.9
1992 [7]	38,014	25,259	10,827	985	7,592	14.8	11.9	33.4	12.7	29.6	50,592	19.7
1993 [8]	39,265	26,226	10,877	1,134	8,126	15.1	12.2	33.1	15.3	30.6	51,801	20.0
1994........	38,059	25,379	10,196	974	8,416	14.5	11.7	30.6	14.6	30.7	50,401	19.3
1995........	36,425	24,423	9,872	1,411	8,574	13.8	11.2	29.3	14.6	30.3	48,761	18.5
1996........	36,529	24,650	9,694	1,454	8,697	13.7	11.2	28.4	14.5	29.4	49,310	18.5
1997........	35,574	24,396	9,116	1,468	8,308	13.3	11.0	26.5	14.0	27.1	47,853	17.8
1998........	34,476	23,454	9,091	1,360	8,070	12.7	10.5	26.1	12.5	25.6	46,036	17.0
1999 [9]	32,791	22,169	8,441	1,285	7,876	11.9	9.8	23.6	10.7	22.7	45,030	16.3
2000 [10]	31,581	21,645	7,982	1,258	7,747	11.3	9.5	22.5	9.9	21.5	43,612	15.6
2001........	32,907	22,739	8,136	1,275	7,997	11.7	9.9	22.7	10.2	21.4	45,320	16.1
2002 [11]	34,570	23,466	8,602	1,161	8,555	12.1	10.2	24.1	10.1	21.8	47,084	16.5
2003........	35,861	24,272	8,781	1,401	9,051	12.5	10.5	24.4	11.8	22.5	48,687	16.9
2004 [12]	37,040	25,327	9,014	1,201	9,122	12.7	10.8	24.7	9.8	21.9	49,693	17.1
2005........	36,950	24,872	9,168	1,402	9,368	12.6	10.6	24.9	11.1	21.8	49,327	16.8
2006........	36,460	24,416	9,048	1,353	9,243	12.3	10.3	24.3	10.3	20.6	49,688	16.8
2007........	37,276	25,120	9,237	1,349	9,890	12.5	10.5	24.5	10.2	21.5	50,876	17.0
2008........	39,829	26,990	9,379	1,576	10,987	13.2	11.2	24.7	11.8	23.2	53,805	17.9
2009........	43,569	29,830	9,944	1,746	12,350	14.3	12.3	25.8	12.5	25.3	56,840	18.7

NA Not available. [1] Includes those in poverty, plus those who have income above poverty but less than 1.25 times their poverty threshold. [2] Includes other races, not shown separately. [3] Beginning 2002, data represent White alone, which refers to people who reported White and did not report any other race category. [4] Beginning 2002, data represent Black alone, which refers to people who reported Black and did not report any other race category. [5] Beginning 2002, data represent Asian alone, which refers to people who reported Asian and did not report any other race category. [6] People of Hispanic origin may be any race. [7] Implementation of 1990 census population controls. [8] The March 1994 income supplement was revised to allow for the coding of different income amounts on selected questionnaire items. Limits either increased or decreased in the following categories: earnings increased to $999,999; social security increased to $49,999; supplemental security income and public assistance increased to $24,999; veterans' benefits increased to $99,999; child support and alimony decreased to $49,999. [9] Implementation of Census-2000-based population controls. [10] Implementation of sample expansion by 28,000 households. [11] Beginning with the 2003 Current Population Survey (CPS), the questionnaire allowed respondents to choose more than one race. For 2002 and later, data represent persons who selected this race group only and exclude persons reporting more than one race. The CPS in prior years allowed respondents to report only one race group. See also comments on race in the text for Section 1. [12] Data have been revised to reflect a correction to the weights in the 2005 ASEC.

Source: U.S. Census Bureau, *Income, Poverty, and Health Insurance Coverage in the United States: 2009*, Current Population Reports, series P60-238, and Historical Tables—Tables 2 and 6, September 2010. See also <http://www.census.gov/hhes /www/poverty/poverty.html> and <http://www.census.gov/hhes/www/poverty/data/historical/people.html>.

Table 712. Children Below Poverty Level by Race and Hispanic Origin: 1980 to 2009

[11,114 represents 11,114,000. Persons as of March of the following year. Covers only related children in families under 18 years old. Based on Current Population Survey, Annual Social and Economic Supplement (ASEC); see text, this section, Section 1, and Appendix III. For data collection changes over time, see <http://www.census.gov/hhes/www/income/data/historical/history.html>]

Year	Number of children below poverty level (1,000)					Percent of children below poverty level				
	All races [1]	White [2]	Black [3]	Asian and Pacific Islander [4]	His-panic [5]	All races [1]	White [2]	Black [3]	Asian and Pacific Islander [4]	His-panic [5]
1980........	11,114	6,817	3,906	(NA)	1,718	17.9	13.4	42.1	(NA)	33.0
1985........	12,483	7,838	4,057	(NA)	2,512	20.1	15.6	43.1	(NA)	39.6
1990........	12,715	7,696	4,412	356	2,750	19.9	15.1	44.2	17.0	37.7
1991........	13,658	8,316	4,637	348	2,977	21.1	16.1	45.6	17.1	39.8
1992 [6].....	14,521	8,752	5,015	352	3,440	21.6	16.5	46.3	16.0	39.0
1993 [7].....	14,961	9,123	5,030	358	3,666	22.0	17.0	45.9	17.6	39.9
1994........	14,610	8,826	4,787	308	3,956	21.2	16.3	43.3	17.9	41.1
1995........	13,999	8,474	4,644	532	3,938	20.2	15.5	41.5	18.6	39.3
1996........	13,764	8,488	4,411	553	4,090	19.8	15.5	39.5	19.1	39.9
1997........	13,422	8,441	4,116	608	3,865	19.2	15.4	36.8	19.9	36.4
1998........	12,845	7,935	4,073	542	3,670	18.3	14.4	36.4	17.5	33.6
1999 [8].....	11,678	7,194	3,698	367	3,561	16.6	13.1	32.8	11.5	29.9
2000 [9].....	11,005	6,834	3,495	407	3,342	15.6	12.4	30.9	12.5	27.6
2001........	11,175	7,086	3,423	353	3,433	15.8	12.8	30.0	11.1	27.4
2002 [10]....	11,646	7,203	3,570	302	3,653	16.3	13.1	32.1	11.4	28.2
2003........	12,340	7,624	3,750	331	3,982	17.2	13.9	33.6	12.1	29.5
2004 [11]....	12,473	7,876	3,702	265	3,985	17.3	14.3	33.4	9.4	28.6
2005........	12,335	7,652	3,743	312	3,977	17.1	13.9	34.2	11.0	27.7
2006........	12,299	7,522	3,690	351	3,959	16.9	13.6	33.0	12.0	26.6
2007........	12,802	8,002	3,838	345	4,348	17.6	14.4	34.3	11.8	28.3
2008........	13,507	8,441	3,781	430	4,888	18.5	15.3	34.4	14.2	30.3
2009........	14,774	9,440	3,919	444	5,419	20.1	17.0	35.3	13.6	32.5

NA Not available. [1] Includes other races, not shown separately. [2] Beginning 2002, data represent White alone, which refers to people who reported White and did not report any other race category. [3] Beginning 2002, data represent Black alone, which refers to people who reported Black and did not report any other race category. [4] Beginning 2002, data represent Asian alone, which refers to people who reported Asian and did not report any other race category. [5] People of Hispanic origin may be of any race. [6] Implementation of 1990 census population controls. [7] The March 1994 income supplement was revised to allow for the coding of different income amounts on selected questionnaire items. Limits either increased or decreased in the following categories: earnings increased to $999,999; social security increased to $49,999; supplemental security income and public assistance increased to $24,999; veterans' benefits increased to $99,999; child support and alimony decreased to $49,999. [8] Implementation of Census 2000-based population controls. [9] Implementation of sample expansion to 28,000 households. [10] Beginning with the 2003 Current Population Survey (CPS), the questionnaire allowed respondents to choose more than one race. For 2002 and later, data represent persons who selected this race group only and excludes persons reporting more than one race. The CPS in prior years allowed respondents to report only one race group. See also comments on race in the text for Section 1. [11] Data have been revised to reflect a correction to the weights in the 2005 Annual Social and Economic Supplement (ASEC).

Source: U.S. Census Bureau, Income, Poverty, and Health Insurance Coverage in the United States: 2009, Current Population Reports, P60-238, and Historical Tables—Table 3, September 2010. See also <http://www.census.gov/hhes/www/poverty/poverty.html> and <http://www.census.gov/hhes/www/poverty/data/historical/people.html>.

Table 713. People Below Poverty Level by Selected Characteristics: 2009

[43,569 represents 43,569,000. People as of March 2010. Based on Current Population Survey (CPS); see text, this section and Section 1, and Appendix III. The 2010 CPS allowed respondents to choose more than one race. For 2009, data represent persons who selected this race group only and exclude persons reporting more than one race. The CPS in prior years allowed respondents to report only one race group. See also comments on race in the text for Section 1. For composition of regions, see map, inside front cover]

Sex, age, region, nativity	Number below poverty level (1,000)					Percent below poverty level				
	All races [1]	White alone	Black alone	Asian alone	His-panic [2]	All races [1]	White alone	Black alone	Asian alone	His-panic [2]
Total	**43,569**	**29,830**	**9,944**	**1,746**	**12,350**	**14.3**	**12.3**	**25.8**	**12.5**	**25.3**
Male	19,475	13,388	4,287	825	5,863	13.0	11.2	23.9	12.3	23.4
Female................	24,094	16,442	5,656	921	6,487	15.6	13.5	27.5	12.6	27.4
Under 18 years old	15,451	9,938	4,033	463	5,610	20.7	17.7	35.7	14.0	33.1
18 to 24 years old	6,071	4,177	1,343	294	1,440	20.7	18.4	31.2	23.9	26.3
25 to 34 years old	6,123	4,263	1,316	255	1,864	14.9	13.3	23.8	10.8	23.0
35 to 44 years old	4,756	3,415	965	210	1,495	11.8	10.7	19.0	8.9	21.2
45 to 54 years old	4,421	3,124	963	176	914	10.0	8.6	18.0	9.0	17.3
55 to 59 years old	1,792	1,294	379	57	284	9.3	8.1	18.7	7.0	15.6
60 to 64 years old	1,520	1,117	298	77	227	9.4	8.2	17.7	12.1	17.6
65 years old and over	3,433	2,501	647	213	516	8.9	7.5	19.5	15.8	18.3
65 to 74 years old	1,675	1,240	295	103	296	8.0	6.9	15.5	13.9	17.5
75 years old and over	1,758	1,261	352	110	219	10.0	8.2	24.9	18.1	19.5
Northeast...............	6,650	4,342	1,595	495	1,611	12.2	9.9	23.7	16.2	24.1
Midwest................	8,768	5,964	2,124	282	1,068	13.3	10.6	31.3	16.6	27.3
South.................	17,609	11,384	5,355	375	4,559	15.7	13.4	25.0	12.0	25.5
West	10,542	8,140	871	593	5,111	14.8	14.2	24.3	9.7	25.1
Native	36,407	24,642	9,235	632	7,748	13.7	11.3	26.3	11.8	25.2
Foreign born	7,162	5,188	709	1,114	4,603	19.0	21.1	20.5	12.9	25.5
Naturalized citizen	1,736	1,052	216	427	773	10.8	11.2	13.3	9.2	14.3
Not a citizen.............	5,425	4,136	492	686	3,830	25.1	27.1	26.9	17.3	30.2

[1] Includes other races, not shown separately. [2] Persons of Hispanic origin may be any race.

Source: U.S. Census Bureau, Income, Poverty, and Health Insurance Coverage in the United States: 2009, Current Population Reports, P60-238, and Detailed Tables—Tables POV01, POV29, and POV41. See also <http://www.census.gov/hhes/www/cpstables/032010/pov/toc.htm>.

Table 714. Work Experience of People During 2009 by Poverty Status, Sex, and Age: 2009

[99,306 represents 99,306,000. Covers only persons 16 years old and over. Based on Current Population Survey, Annual Social and Economic Supplement (ASEC); see text, this section, Section 1, and Appendix III]

| Sex and age | Worked full-time year-round | | | Did not work full-time year-round | | | Did not work | | |
| | Number (1,000) | Below poverty level | | Number (1,000) | Below poverty level | | Number (1,000) | Below poverty level | |
		Number (1,000)	Percent		Number (1,000)	Percent		Number (1,000)	Percent
BOTH SEXES									
Total...............	**99,306**	**2,641**	**2.7**	**55,466**	**8,039**	**14.5**	**83,323**	**18,944**	**22.7**
16 to 17 years old	74	2	(B)	1,863	130	7.0	6,918	1,376	19.9
18 to 64 years old	95,808	2,602	2.7	49,376	7,792	15.8	45,443	14,291	31.4
18 to 24 years old	6,372	360	5.7	12,624	2,354	18.6	10,317	3,357	32.5
25 to 34 years old	22,299	823	3.7	11,218	2,304	20.5	7,569	2,996	39.6
35 to 54 years old	50,607	1,179	2.3	18,300	2,541	13.9	15,928	5,458	34.3
55 to 64 years old	16,531	239	1.4	7,234	593	8.2	11,629	2,480	21.3
65 years old and over	3,424	38	1.1	4,228	117	2.8	30,962	3,278	10.6
MALE									
Total...............	**56,058**	**1,435**	**2.6**	**25,777**	**3,653**	**14.2**	**33,817**	**7,323**	**21.7**
16 to 17 years old	46	2	(B)	950	61	6.4	3,495	643	18.4
18 to 64 years old	53,943	1,403	2.6	22,710	3,541	15.6	17,716	5,657	31.9
18 to 24 years old	3,561	181	5.1	6,266	969	15.5	5,010	1,428	28.5
25 to 34 years old	12,628	422	3.3	5,515	1,097	19.9	2,546	1,015	39.9
35 to 54 years old	28,638	656	2.3	7,780	1,218	15.7	5,440	2,140	39.3
55 to 64 years old	9,116	143	1.6	3,149	257	8.2	4,720	1,075	22.8
65 years old and over	2,069	30	1.5	2,118	52	2.4	12,606	1,023	8.1
FEMALE									
Total...............	**43,248**	**1,207**	**2.8**	**29,689**	**4,386**	**14.8**	**49,505**	**11,622**	**23.5**
16 to 17 years old	28	–	(B)	913	69	7.5	3,423	733	21.4
18 to 64 years old	41,865	1,199	2.9	26,666	4,251	15.9	27,727	8,634	31.1
18 to 24 years old	2,811	179	6.4	6,359	1,385	21.8	5,306	1,929	36.4
25 to 34 years old	9,670	401	4.1	5,703	1,207	21.2	5,023	1,982	39.5
35 to 54 years old	21,968	523	2.4	10,520	1,322	12.6	10,488	3,318	31.6
55 to 64 years old	7,416	96	1.3	4,085	336	8.2	6,909	1,405	20.3
65 years old and over	1,355	8	0.6	2,110	66	3.1	18,356	2,255	12.3

– Represents zero. B Base figure too small to meet statistical standards for reliability of a derived figure.

Source: U.S. Census Bureau, *Income, Poverty, and Health Insurance Coverage in the United States: 2009*, Current Population Reports, P60-238, and Detailed Tables—Table POV22, September 2010. See also <http://www.census.gov/hhes/www /cpstables/032010/pov/new22_100.htm>.

Table 715. Families Below Poverty Level and Below 125 Percent of Poverty by Race and Hispanic Origin: 1980 to 2009

[6,217 represents 6,217,000. Families as of March of the following year. Based on Current Population Survey, Annual Social and Economic Supplement (ASEC); see text, this section and Section 1, and Appendix III. For data collection changes over time, see <http://www.census.gov/hhes/www/income/data/historical/history.html>]

| Year | Number of families below poverty (1,000) | | | | | Percent of persons below poverty | | | | | Below 125 percent [1] of poverty level | |
	All races [2]	White [3]	Black [4]	Asian and Pacific Islander [5]	His-panic [6]	All races [2]	White [3]	Black [4]	Asian and Pacific Islander [5]	His-panic [6]	Number (1,000)	Percent
1980.....	6,217	4,195	1,826	(NA)	751	10.3	8.0	28.9	(NA)	23.2	8,764	14.5
1985.....	7,223	4,983	1,983	(NA)	1,074	11.4	9.1	28.7	(NA)	25.5	9,753	15.3
1990.....	7,098	4,622	2,193	169	1,244	10.7	8.1	29.3	11.0	25.0	9,564	14.4
1995.....	7,532	4,994	2,127	264	1,695	10.8	8.5	26.4	12.4	27.0	10,223	14.7
2000 [7] ...	6,400	4,333	1,686	233	1,540	8.7	7.1	19.3	7.8	19.2	9,032	12.2
2001.....	6,813	4,579	1,829	234	1,649	9.2	7.4	20.7	7.8	19.4	9,525	12.8
2002 [8] ...	7,229	4,862	1,923	210	1,792	9.6	7.8	21.5	7.4	19.7	9,998	13.2
2003.....	7,607	5,058	1,986	311	1,925	10.0	8.1	22.3	10.2	20.8	10,360	13.6
2004 [9] ...	7,835	5,293	2,035	232	1,953	10.2	8.4	22.8	7.4	20.5	10,499	13.7
2005.....	7,657	5,068	1,997	289	1,948	9.9	8.0	22.1	9.0	19.7	10,442	13.5
2006.....	7,668	5,118	2,007	260	1,922	9.8	8.0	21.6	7.8	18.9	10,531	13.4
2007.....	7,623	5,046	2,045	261	2,045	9.8	7.9	22.1	7.9	19.7	10,551	13.5
2008.....	8,147	5,414	2,055	341	2,239	10.3	8.4	22.0	9.8	21.3	11,164	14.2
2009.....	8,792	5,994	2,125	337	2,369	11.1	9.3	22.7	9.4	22.7	11,620	14.7

NA Not available. [1] See footnote 1, Table 711. [2] Includes other races, not shown separately. [3] Beginning 2002, data represent White alone, which refers to people who reported White and did not report any other race category. [4] Beginning 2002, data represent Black alone, which refers to people who reported Black and did not report any other race category. [5] Beginning 2002, data represent Asian alone, which refers to people who reported Asian and did not report any other race category. [6] People of Hispanic origin may be any race. [7] Implementation of a 28,000 household sample expansion. [8] Beginning with the 2003 Current Population Survey (CPS), the questionnaire allowed respondents to choose more than one race. For 2002 and later, data represent persons who selected this race group only and excludes persons reporting more than one race. The CPS in prior years allowed respondents to report only one race group. See also comments on race in the text for Section 1, Population. [9] Data have been revised to reflect a correction to the weights in the 2005 Annual Social and Economic Supplement (ASEC).

Source: U.S. Census Bureau, *Income, Poverty, and Health Insurance Coverage in the United States: 2009*, Current Population Reports, P60-238, and Historical and Detailed Tables—Tables 4 and POV04, September 2010. See also <http://www.census.gov /hhes/www/poverty/poverty.html> and <http://www.census.gov/hhes/www/poverty/data/historical/families.html>.

Table 716. Families Below Poverty Level by Selected Characteristics: 2009

[8,792 represents 8,792,000. Families as of March 2010. Based on Current Population Survey (CPS), Annual Social and Economic Supplement (ASEC); see text, this section and Section 1, and Appendix III. The 2010 CPS allowed respondents to choose more than one race. For 2009, data represent persons who selected this race group only and exclude persons reporting more than one race. See also comments on race in the text for Section 1. For composition of regions, see map, inside front cover]

Characteristic	Number below poverty level (1,000)					Percent below poverty level				
	All races [1]	White alone	Black alone	Asian alone	His-panic [2]	All races [1]	White alone	Black alone	Asian alone	His-panic [2]
Total families	**8,792**	**5,994**	**2,125**	**337**	**2,369**	**11.1**	**9.3**	**22.7**	**9.4**	**22.7**
Age of householder:										
15 to 24 years old	1,096	708	328	26	283	34.2	30.1	52.6	21.7	36.2
25 to 34 years old	2,476	1,649	635	69	756	18.9	16.3	33.1	10.2	29.8
35 to 44 years old	2,072	1,437	491	76	681	12.1	10.7	21.9	7.9	23.5
45 to 54 years old	1,454	998	322	73	370	8.0	6.7	15.4	8.8	17.6
55 to 64 years old	894	644	192	31	154	6.5	5.6	14.2	5.5	13.4
65 years old and over	757	536	141	58	114	5.6	4.6	12.9	13.4	12.6
Region:										
Northeast.	1,314	866	329	92	335	9.3	7.4	21.2	11.8	22.5
Midwest	1,827	1,227	485	55	208	10.5	8.1	28.6	12.7	25.7
South	3,717	2,432	1,127	71	892	12.5	10.5	21.4	8.7	22.4
West.	1,934	1,470	184	120	935	11.0	10.2	21.7	7.7	22.5
Type of family:										
Married couple.	3,409	2,694	366	230	1,054	5.8	5.4	8.6	7.9	16.0
Male householder, no spouse present.	942	629	234	32	249	16.9	15.0	25.0	12.6	23.0
Female householder, no spouse present.	4,441	2,671	1,524	76	1,066	29.9	27.3	36.7	16.9	38.8

[1] Includes other races, not shown separately. [2] Hispanic persons may be any race.

Source: U.S. Census Bureau, *Income, Poverty, and Health Insurance Coverage in the United States: 2009*, Current Population Reports, P60-238, and Detailed Tables—Tables POV04 and POV44, September 2010. See also <http://www.census.gov/hhes/www/cpstables/032010/pov/toc.htm>.

Table 717. Top Wealth Holders With Gross Assets of $1.5 Million or More—Debts, Mortgages, and Net Worth: 2004

[2,728 represents 2,728,000. Net worth is defined as assets minus liabilities. Figures are estimates based on a sample of federal estate tax returns (Form 706). Based on the estate multiplier technique; for more information on this methodology, see source]

Sex and net worth	Total assets		Debts and mortgages		Net worth	
	Number of top wealth holders (1,000)	Amount [1] (mil. dol.)	Number of top wealth holders (1,000)	Amount (mil. dol.)	Number of top wealth holders (1,000)	Amount (mil. dol.)
Both sexes, total	**2,728**	**11,076,759**	**2,099**	**850,622**	**2,728**	**10,201,246**
Size of net worth:						
Under $1.5 million [2]	531	736,039	468	231,035	531	480,113
$1.5 million under $2.0 million.	746	1,386,077	544	98,187	746	1,287,890
$2.0 million under $3.5 million.	846	2,316,701	614	147,370	846	2,169,331
$3.5 million under $5.0 million.	247	1,082,889	192	58,950	247	1,023,939
$5.0 million under $10.0 million.	231	1,668,002	176	104,811	231	1,563,191
$10.0 million under $20.0 million.	79	1,155,326	64	69,849	79	1,085,477
$20.0 million or more.	47	2,731,726	40	140,421	47	2,591,305
Males, total.	**1,555**	**6,471,540**	**1,208**	**583,805**	**1,555**	**5,862,844**
Size of net worth:						
Under $1.5 million [2]	389	528,017	339	184,673	389	318,454
$1.5 million under $2.0 million.	359	675,321	258	54,149	359	621,172
$2.0 million under $3.5 million.	465	1,289,522	346	96,654	465	1,192,868
$3.5 million under $5.0 million.	131	578,304	102	37,496	131	540,808
$5.0 million under $10.0 million.	135	989,077	100	74,003	135	915,074
$10.0 million under $20.0 million.	47	679,613	38	41,466	47	638,146
$20.0 million or more.	30	1,731,686	25	95,364	30	1,636,322
Females, total.	**1,173**	**4,605,219**	**891**	**266,817**	**1,173**	**4,338,402**
Size of net worth:						
Under $1.5 million [2]	143	208,021	129	46,362	143	161,659
$1.5 million under $2.0 million.	387	710,757	286	44,038	387	666,719
$2.0 million under $3.5 million.	380	1,027,179	268	50,716	380	976,463
$3.5 million under $5.0 million.	116	504,585	89	21,454	116	483,131
$5.0 million under $10.0 million.	96	678,924	77	30,808	96	648,116
$10.0 million under $20.0 million.	33	475,713	27	28,382	33	447,331
$20.0 million or more.	18	1,000,040	15	45,057	18	954,983

[1] Includes other types of assets, not shown separately. [2] Includes individuals with zero net worth.

Source: U.S. Internal Revenue Service, Statistics of Income Division, "SOI Data Tables," July 2008, <http://www.irs.gov/taxstats/indtaxstats/article/0,,id=96426,00.html>.

Table 718. Top Wealth Holders With Gross Assets of $1.5 Million or More by Type of Property, Sex, and Size of Net Worth: 2004

[2,728 represents 2,728,000. Net worth is defined as assets minus liabilities. Figures are estimates based on a sample of federal estate tax returns (Form 706). Based on the estate multiplier technique; for more information on this methodology, see source]

Sex and net worth	Number of top wealth holders (1,000)	Assets (mil. dol.)				
		Total [1]	Personal residences	Other real estate	Closely held stock	Publicly traded stock
Both sexes, total	2,728	11,076,759	1,185,941	1,402,029	1,127,194	2,247,269
Size of net worth:						
Under $1.5 million [2]	531	736,039	176,105	134,674	42,431	63,062
$1.5 million under $2.0 million	746	1,386,077	229,369	206,626	69,066	219,818
$2.0 million under $3.5 million	846	2,316,701	342,206	329,893	141,272	415,249
$3.5 million under $5.0 million	247	1,082,889	127,444	152,634	95,958	209,459
$5.0 million under $10.0 million	231	1,668,002	148,543	230,146	165,781	373,575
$10.0 million under $20.0 million	79	1,155,326	76,472	137,770	136,144	246,824
$20.0 million or more	47	2,731,726	85,802	210,286	476,542	719,282
Males, total	1,555	6,471,540	597,971	828,055	833,929	1,140,665
Size of net worth:						
Under $1.5 million [2]	389	528,017	117,554	96,796	36,177	42,494
$1.5 million under $2.0 million	359	675,321	97,605	105,224	44,376	94,788
$2.0 million under $3.5 million	465	1,289,522	163,984	179,481	102,116	199,844
$3.5 million under $5.0 million	131	578,304	60,123	80,919	63,006	95,417
$5.0 million under $10.0 million	135	989,077	68,653	151,731	110,961	200,003
$10.0 million under $20.0 million	47	679,613	38,710	75,459	97,601	135,157
$20.0 million or more	30	1,731,686	51,342	138,446	379,692	372,962
Females, total	1,173	4,605,219	587,970	573,974	293,264	1,106,604
Size of net worth:						
Under $1.5 million [2]	143	208,021	58,550	37,879	6,255	20,568
$1.5 million under $2.0 million	387	710,757	131,764	101,402	24,690	125,030
$2.0 million under $3.5 million	380	1,027,179	178,222	150,412	39,155	215,405
$3.5 million under $5.0 million	116	504,585	67,321	71,714	32,953	114,042
$5.0 million under $10.0 million	96	678,924	79,890	78,416	54,820	173,572
$10.0 million under $20.0 million	33	475,713	37,762	62,312	38,543	111,667
$20.0 million or more	18	1,000,040	34,461	71,840	96,849	346,320

[1] Includes other types of assets, not shown separately. [2] Includes individuals with zero net worth.
Source: U.S. Internal Revenue Service, Statistics of Income Division, "SOI Data Tables," July 2008, <http://www.irs.gov/taxstats /indtaxstats/article/0,,id=96426,00.html>.

Table 719. Top Wealth Holders With Net Worth of $1.5 Million or More— Number and Net Worth by State: 2004

[2,196 represents 2,196,000. Estimates based on a sample of federal estate tax returns (Form 706). Estimates of wealth by state can be subject to significant year-to-year fluctuations and this is especially true for individuals at the extreme tail of the net worth distribution and for states with relatively small decedent populations. Based on the estate multiplier technique; for more information on this methodology, see source]

State	Number of top wealth holders (1,000)	Net worth (mil. dol.)	State	Number of top wealth holders (1,000)	Net worth (mil. dol.)
Total [1]	2,196	9,721,133	Montana	7	23,966
Alabama	18	79,123	Nebraska	13	83,265
Alaska	1	4,776	Nevada	15	80,768
Arizona	36	139,861	New Hampshire	7	27,342
Arkansas	11	94,704	New Jersey	79	324,712
California	428	1,793,642	New Mexico	9	28,107
Colorado	32	163,324	New York	168	942,812
Connecticut	47	197,801	North Carolina	59	223,408
Delaware	8	30,923	North Dakota	1	3,988
District of Columbia	7	27,850	Ohio	61	228,532
Florida	199	904,014	Oklahoma	17	58,554
Georgia	56	270,677	Oregon	15	61,328
Hawaii	7	22,552	Pennsylvania	86	399,312
Idaho	5	23,982	Rhode Island	8	30,782
Illinois	101	476,354	South Carolina	14	67,856
Indiana	32	112,272	South Dakota	6	18,850
Iowa	18	55,332	Tennessee	25	100,778
Kansas	21	65,084	Texas	108	492,663
Kentucky	18	65,404	Utah	8	52,674
Louisiana	22	92,315	Vermont	4	20,584
Maine	8	35,173	Virginia	59	223,984
Maryland	50	191,279	Washington	50	180,008
Massachusetts	83	335,482	West Virginia	12	28,415
Michigan	47	261,085	Wisconsin	26	127,515
Minnesota	33	135,682	Wyoming	5	106,698
Mississippi	8	61,786			
Missouri	33	115,716	Other areas [1]	5	28,042

[1] Includes U.S. territories and possessions.
Source: U.S. Internal Revenue Service, Statistics of Income Division, "SOI Data Tables," July 2008, <http://www.irs.gov/taxstats /indtaxstats/article/0,,id=96426,00.html>.

Table 720. Nonfinancial Assets Held by Families by Type of Asset: 2007

[221.5 represents $221,500. Families include one-person units and, as used in this table, are more comparable to the U.S. Census Bureau's household concept. Based on Survey of Consumer Finance; see Appendix III and <http://www.federalreserve.gov/pubs/oss/oss2/papers/measurement.pdf>. For definition of median, see Guide to Tabular Presentation. For data on financial assets, see Table 1170]

Family characteristic	Any financial or non-financial asset	Any non-financial asset	Vehicles	Pri-mary residence	Other resi-dential property	Equity in nonresi-dential property	Bus-iness equity	Other asset
PERCENT OF FAMILIES HOLDING ASSET								
All families, total	97.7	92.0	87.0	68.6	13.7	8.1	13.6	7.2
Age of family head:								
Under 35 years old	97.1	88.2	85.4	40.7	5.6	3.2	8.0	5.9
35 to 44 years old	96.9	91.3	87.5	66.1	12.0	7.5	18.2	5.5
45 to 54 years old	97.6	95.0	90.3	77.3	15.7	9.5	17.2	8.7
55 to 64 years old	99.1	95.6	92.2	81.0	20.9	11.5	18.1	8.5
65 to 74 years old	98.4	94.5	90.6	85.5	18.9	12.3	11.2	9.1
75 years old and over	98.1	87.3	71.5	77.0	13.4	6.8	4.5	5.8
Race or ethnicity or respondent:								
White non-Hispanic	98.9	94.6	89.6	75.6	15.3	9.0	15.8	8.4
Non-White or Hispanic........	94.9	85.8	80.9	51.9	10.0	5.9	8.2	4.3
Tenure:								
Owner occupied.............	100.0	100.0	93.8	100.0	17.5	10.8	17.5	8.0
Renter occupied or other......	92.8	74.5	72.3	(B)	5.6	2.1	5.0	5.3
MEDIAN VALUE [1] ($1,000)								
All families, total	221.5	177.4	15.5	200.0	146.0	75.0	92.2	14.0
Age of family head:								
Under 35 years old	38.8	30.9	13.3	175.0	85.0	50.0	35.0	8.0
35 to 44 years old	222.3	182.6	17.4	205.0	150.0	50.0	59.0	10.0
45 to 54 years old	306.0	224.9	18.7	230.0	150.0	80.0	76.8	15.0
55 to 64 years old	347.0	233.1	17.4	210.0	157.0	90.0	100.0	20.0
65 to 74 years old	303.3	212.2	14.6	200.0	150.0	75.0	300.0	20.0
75 years old and over	219.3	157.1	9.4	150.0	100.0	110.0	225.0	25.0
Race or ethnicity of respondent:								
White non-Hispanic	271.0	203.8	17.1	200.0	136.5	75.0	100.0	15.0
Non-White or Hispanic........	89.2	102.0	12.0	180.0	175.0	62.7	50.0	8.0
Tenure:								
Owner occupied.............	344.2	253.5	18.4	200.0	150.0	80.0	100.0	20.0
Renter occupied or other......	13.6	10.1	8.6	(B)	85.0	38.0	33.0	5.4

B Base too small to meet statistical standards for reliability of derived figure. [1] Median value of asset for families holding such assets.
Source: Board of Governors of the Federal Reserve System, "2007 Survey of Consumer Finances," May 2009, <http://www.federalreserve.gov/pubs/oss/oss2/2007/scf2007home.html>.

Table 721. Family Net Worth—Mean and Median Net Worth in Constant (2007) Dollars by Selected Family Characteristics: 1998 to 2007

[Net worth in thousands of constant (2007) dollars (359.7 represents $359,700). Constant dollar figures are based on consumer price index for all urban consumers published by U.S. Bureau of Labor Statistics. Families include one-person units and as used in this table are comparable to the U.S. Census Bureau's household concept. Based on Survey of Consumer Finance; see Appendix III. For definition of mean and median, see Guide to Tabular Presentation]

Family characteristic	1998		2001		2004		2007	
	Mean	Median	Mean	Median	Mean	Median	Mean	Median
All families	359.7	91.3	464.4	101.2	492.3	102.2	556.3	120.3
Age of family head:								
Under 35 years old	81.3	11.6	106.1	13.7	80.7	15.6	106.0	11.8
35 to 44 years old	249.9	80.8	303.7	90.7	328.6	76.2	325.6	86.6
45 to 54 years old	461.5	134.5	568.4	155.4	596.1	158.9	661.2	182.5
55 to 64 years old	677.6	162.8	856.0	216.8	926.7	273.1	935.8	253.7
65 to 74 years old	594.2	186.5	793.5	207.9	758.8	208.8	1,015.2	239.4
75 years old and over	395.7	159.9	548.6	181.6	580.0	179.1	638.2	213.5
Race or ethnicity of respondent:								
White non-Hispanic	429.5	121.9	571.2	143.0	617.0	154.5	692.2	170.4
Non-White or Hispanic........	128.0	21.2	137.4	21.0	168.2	27.2	228.5	27.8
Tenure:								
Owner occupied..............	514.7	168.2	655.5	201.8	686.3	202.6	778.2	234.2
Renter occupied or other.........	55.3	5.4	64.4	5.6	59.4	4.4	70.6	5.1

Source: Board of Governors of the Federal Reserve System, "2007 Survey of Consumer Finances," May 2009, <http://www.federalreserve.gov/pubs/oss/oss2/2007/scf2007home.html>.

Table 722. Household and Nonprofit Organization Sector Balance Sheet: 1990 to 2010

[In billions of dollars (24,220 represents $24,220,000,000,000). As of December 31. For details of financial assets and liabilities, see Table 1168]

Item	1990	1995	2000	2005	2007	2008	2009	2010
Assets	**24,220**	**32,928**	**50,047**	**71,549**	**78,546**	**65,532**	**67,690**	**70,740**
Tangible assets [1]	9,723	11,472	16,764	28,335	27,986	24,356	23,567	23,101
Real estate	7,606	8,843	13,430	24,050	23,311	19,560	18,732	18,187
Households [2,3]	6,801	8,055	12,183	22,005	20,879	17,470	17,081	16,370
Consumer durable goods [4]	2,039	2,531	3,196	4,077	4,435	4,533	4,561	4,618
Financial assets [1]	14,497	21,457	33,283	43,214	50,560	41,176	44,123	47,639
Deposits [1]	3,325	3,357	4,376	6,140	7,407	8,013	7,895	7,931
Time and savings deposits	2,490	2,300	3,033	4,914	5,889	6,083	6,172	6,422
Money market fund shares	389	472	960	949	1,348	1,582	1,313	1,131
Credit market instruments [1]	1,741	2,229	2,458	3,324	4,073	3,966	4,106	4,355
Agency and GSE-backed securities [5]	117	216	594	493	669	711	83	78
Municipal securities	648	533	531	821	896	903	1,010	1,096
Corporate and foreign bonds	238	467	551	1,298	2,017	1,956	2,081	1,919
Corporate equities [2]	1,961	4,434	8,147	8,093	9,627	5,777	7,321	8,514
Mutual fund shares [6]	512	1,253	2,704	3,669	4,597	3,326	4,178	4,708
Security credit	62	128	412	575	866	743	669	694
Life insurance reserves	392	566	819	1,083	1,202	1,180	1,242	1,329
Pension fund reserves	3,310	5,725	9,171	11,460	13,391	10,408	11,915	13,025
Equity in noncorporate business [7]	2,939	3,435	4,815	8,261	8,685	6,996	6,011	6,251
Liabilities [1]	**3,703**	**5,038**	**7,377**	**12,184**	**14,367**	**14,223**	**14,033**	**13,918**
Credit market instruments [1]	3,581	4,841	6,987	11,743	13,803	13,801	13,567	13,358
Home mortgages [8]	2,489	3,319	4,798	8,874	10,540	10,495	10,340	10,070
Consumer credit	824	1,168	1,741	2,321	2,555	2,594	2,479	2,435
Net worth	**20,517**	**27,890**	**42,670**	**59,365**	**64,179**	**51,309**	**53,657**	**56,823**
Replacement cost value of structures:								
Residential [1]	4,618	6,091	8,469	13,475	14,660	14,406	14,092	14,081
Households	4,512	5,975	8,326	13,276	14,445	14,191	13,882	13,871
Nonresidential (nonprofits)	479	600	818	1,177	1,354	1,424	1,373	1,458
Owners' equity in household real estate	4,312	4,736	7,385	13,131	10,339	6,975	6,741	6,301
Owners' equity as percentage of household real estate	63.4	58.8	60.6	59.7	49.5	39.9	39.5	38.5

[1] Includes types of assets and/or liabilities not shown separately. [2] At market value. [3] Includes all types of owner-occupied housing including farm houses and mobile homes, as well as second homes that are not rented, vacant homes for sale, and vacant land. [4] At replacement (current) cost. [5] GSE = Government-sponsored enterprises. [6] Value based on the market values of equities held and the book value of other assets held by mutual funds. [7] Net worth of noncorporate business and owners' equity in farm business and unincorporated security brokers and dealers. [8] Includes loans made under home equity lines of credit and home equity loans secured by junior liens.

Source: Board of Governors of the Federal Reserve System, "Federal Reserve Statistical Release, Z.1, Flow of Funds Accounts of the United States," March 2011, <http://www.federalreserve.gov/releases/z1/Current/>.

Table 723. Net Stock of Fixed Assets and Consumer Durable Goods in Current and Chained (2005) Dollars: 1990 to 2009

[In billions of dollars (18,307 represents $18,307,000,000,000). Estimates as of December 31. For explanation of chained dollars, see text, this section]

Item	1990	1995	2000	2005	2006	2007	2008	2009
CURRENT DOLLARS								
Net stock, total	**18,307**	**22,846**	**30,147**	**42,606**	**45,905**	**47,898**	**49,441**	**48,500**
Fixed assets	16,268	20,315	26,951	38,529	41,637	43,463	44,908	43,939
Private	12,671	15,811	21,230	30,587	32,856	33,956	34,694	33,776
Nonresidential	6,564	7,990	10,562	14,057	15,174	15,999	17,014	16,495
Equipment and software	2,507	3,100	4,134	4,931	5,243	5,461	5,685	5,611
Structures	4,057	4,890	6,429	9,127	9,931	10,539	11,329	10,885
Residential	6,107	7,821	10,668	16,530	17,682	17,956	17,680	17,281
Government	3,598	4,504	5,721	7,941	8,781	9,508	10,214	10,163
Nonresidential	3,449	4,316	5,489	7,606	8,432	9,162	9,878	9,842
Equipment and software	551	675	704	802	850	895	956	988
Structures	2,898	3,641	4,786	6,804	7,582	8,266	8,923	8,854
Residential	149	188	232	335	349	346	336	321
Federal	1,077	1,292	1,435	1,749	1,867	1,953	2,035	2,011
Defense	734	868	904	1,081	1,152	1,204	1,250	1,245
State and local	2,521	3,213	4,285	6,193	6,914	7,555	8,179	8,152
Consumer durable goods	2,039	2,531	3,196	4,077	4,268	4,435	4,533	4,561
Motor vehicles and parts	650	811	1,042	1,302	1,307	1,318	1,263	1,278
Furnishings and durable household equipment	649	787	977	1,248	1,325	1,378	1,434	1,424
Other	322	392	449	548	604	649	689	709
CHAINED (2005) DOLLARS								
Net stock, total	**(NA)**	**30,448**	**35,752**	**41,139**	**42,311**	**43,365**	**44,151**	**44,515**
Fixed assets	(NA)	28,508	32,907	37,037	37,986	38,831	39,492	39,794
Private	(NA)	22,082	25,959	29,358	30,162	30,862	31,370	31,517
Nonresidential	(NA)	10,216	12,327	13,579	13,912	14,283	14,612	14,679
Equipment and software	(NA)	3,044	4,204	4,901	5,103	5,301	5,428	5,383
Structures	(NA)	7,361	8,149	8,678	8,815	8,995	9,197	9,300
Residential	(NA)	11,898	13,626	15,780	16,249	16,578	16,751	16,831
Government	(NA)	6,430	6,949	7,678	7,825	7,971	8,122	8,266
Nonresidential	(NA)	6,149	6,648	7,357	7,503	7,646	7,795	7,935
Equipment and software	(NA)	714	734	796	824	853	891	922
Structures	(NA)	5,422	5,911	6,561	6,679	6,795	6,909	7,022
Residential	(NA)	281	302	321	323	325	327	329
Consumer durable goods	(NA)	2,175	2,943	4,102	4,332	4,556	4,689	4,754

NA Not available.

Source: U.S. Bureau of Economic Analysis, *Survey of Current Business*, August 2010. See also <http://www.bea.gov/national/FA2004/SelectTable.asp>.

The Prices section contains producer and consumer prices indexes and actual prices for selected commodities. The primary sources of the data are monthly publications of the U.S. Department of Labor, Bureau of Labor Statistics (BLS), which include *Monthly Labor Review, Consumer Price Index, Detailed Report, Producer Price Indexes*, and *U.S. Import and Export Price Indexes*. The Bureau of Economic Analysis is the source for gross domestic product measures. Cost of living data for many urban and metropolitan areas are provided by The Council for Community and Economic Research, a private organization in Arlington, VA. Table 728 on housing price indexes appears in this edition from the Office of Federal Housing Enterprise Oversight, Housing Price Index. Other commodity, housing, and energy prices may be found in the Energy and Utilities; Forestry, Fishing and Mining; and Construction and Housing sections.

Most price data is measured by an index. An index is a tool that simplifies the measurement of movements in a numerical series. An index allows you to properly compare two or more values in different time periods or places by comparing both to a base year. An index of 110, for example, means there has been a 10-percent increase in price since the reference period; similarly, an index of 90 means a 10-percent decrease. Movements of the index from one date to another can be expressed as changes in index points (simply, the difference between index levels), but it is more useful to express the movements as percent changes. This is because index points are affected by the level of the index in relation to its reference period, while percent changes are not.

Consumer price indexes (CPI)—The
CPI is a measure of the average change in prices over time in a "market basket" of goods and services purchased either by urban wage earners and clerical workers or by all urban consumers. The all urban consumer group represents 87 percent of the total U.S. population and is based on the expenditures residents of urban or metropolitan areas, including professionals, the self-employed, the poor, the unemployed, and retired people, as well as urban wage earners and clerical workers. Not included in the CPI are the spending patterns of people living in rural nonmetropolitan areas, farm families, people in the Armed Forces, and those in institutions, such as prisons and mental hospitals. Consumer inflation for all urban consumers is measured by two indexes, the Consumer Price Index for All Urban Consumers (CPI-U) and the Chained Consumer Price Index for All Urban Consumers (C-CPI-U). The broadest and most comprehensive CPI is called the All Items Consumer Price Index for All Urban Consumers (CPI-U) for the U.S. City Average. All CPI's in this section have a base of 1982–84 = 100.

The CPI is a product of a series of interrelated samples. Data from the 1990 Census of Population determines the urban areas from which data on prices are collected and the housing units within each area that are eligible for use in the shelter component of the CPI. The Census of Population also provides data on the number of consumers represented by each area selected as a CPI price collection area. A sample (of about 14,500 families each year) serves as the basis for a Point-of-Purchase Survey that identified the places where households purchased various types of goods and services. The CPI market basket is developed from detailed expenditure information provided by families and individuals on what they actually bought. In calculating the index, each item is assigned a weight to account for its relative importance in consumers' budgets. Price changes for the various items in each location are then averaged and local data are combined to obtain a U.S. city average. For the current CPI, this information was collected from the Consumer Expenditure Surveys for 2007 and 2008. In each of those years, about 7,000 families from around the country provided information each quarter on their spending habits in the interview survey. To collect information on frequently purchased items, such as food and personal care products, another 7,000 families in each of these years kept diaries listing everything they bought during a 2-week period. Over the 2 year period, then, expenditure information came from approximately 28,000 weekly diaries and 60,000 quarterly interviews used to determine the importance, or weight, of the more than 200 item categories in the CPI index structure.

The CPI represents all goods and services purchased for consumption by the reference population. BLS has classified all expenditure items into more than 200 categories, arranged into eight major groups which are food and beverages, housing, apparel, transportation, medical care, recreation, education and communication, and other goods. The CPI does not include investment items, such as stocks, bonds, real estate, and life insurance. (These items relate to savings and not to day-to-day consumption expenses.)

Producer price index (PPI)— Dating from 1890, the PPI is the oldest continuous statistical series published by BLS. The PPI is a family of indexes that measures the average change over time in the selling prices received by domestic producers of goods and services. Imports are excluded. The target set of goods and services included in the PPI is the entire marketed output of U.S. producers. The set includes both goods and services purchased by other producers as inputs to their operations or as capital investment, as well as goods and services purchased by consumers either directly from the service producer or indirectly from a retailer. Over 10,000 PPIs for individual products and groups of products are released each month.

Prices used in constructing the index are collected from sellers and generally apply to the first significant large-volume commercial transaction for each commodity. The weights used in the index represent the total net selling value of commodities produced or processed in this country. Most producer price indexes have a reference base year of 1982 = 100. The reference year of the PPI shipment weights has been taken primarily from the 2002 Census of Manufactures. For further detail regarding the PPI, see the *BLS Handbook of Methods*, Bulletin 2490 (June 2008), Chapter 14. The PPI Web page is <http://www.bls .gov/ppi/>.

BEA price indexes—BEA chain-weighted price indexes are weighted averages of the detailed price indexes used in the deflation of the goods and services that make up the gross domestic product (GDP) and its major components. Growth rates are constructed for years and quarters using quantity weights for the current and preceding year or quarter; these growth rates are used to move the index for the preceding period forward a year or quarter at a time. All chain-weighted price indexes are expressed in terms of the reference year value 2005 = 100.

Personal consumption expenditures (PCE) price and quantity indexes are based on market transactions for which there are corresponding price measures. The price index provides a measure of the prices paid by persons for domestic purchases of goods and services. PCEs are defined as market value of spending by individuals and not-for-profit institutions on all goods and services. Personal consumption expenditures also include the value of certain imputed goods and services—such as the rental value of owner-occupied homes and compensation paid in kind—such as employer-paid health and life insurance premiums. More information on this index may be found at <http://www.bea.gov /bea/mp _National.htm>.

Measures of inflation—Inflation is a period of rising price levels for goods and factors of production. Inflation results in a decline in the purchasing power of the dollar. It is suggested that changes in price levels be compared from the same month of the prior year and not as a change from the prior month. The BLS offers several indexes that measure different aspects of inflation, three of which are included in this section. The CPI measures inflation as experienced by consumers in their day-to-day living expenses. The PPI measures prices at the producer level only. The International Price Program measures change in the prices of imports and exports of nonmilitary goods between the United States and other countries.

Whereas the CPI and PPI measure a benchmark approach to price levels, the BEA's Personal Consumption Expenditures uses a chain-weight approach which links weighted averages from adjoining years.

Other measures of inflation include the futures price and spot market price indexes from the Commodity Research Bureau and the employment cost, hourly compensation, and unit labor cost indexes from the BLS. Found in Section 12, Labor Force, Employment, and Earnings, these BLS indexes are used as a measure of the change in cost of the labor factor of production and changes in long-term interest rates that are often used to measure changes in the cost of the capital factor of production.

International price indexes—The BLS International Price Program produces export and import price indexes for non-military goods traded between the United States and the rest of the world.

The export price index provides a measure of price change for all products sold by U.S. residents to foreign buyers. The import price index provides a measure of price change for goods purchased from other countries by U.S. residents. The reference period for the indexes is 2005 = 100, unless otherwise indicated. The product universe for both the import and export indexes includes raw materials, agricultural products, semifinished manufactures, and finished manufactures, including both capital and consumer goods. Price data for these items are collected primarily by mail questionnaire. In nearly all cases, the data are collected directly from the exporter or importer.

To the extent possible, the data gathered refer to prices at the U.S. border for exports and at either the foreign border or the U.S. border for imports. For nearly all products, the prices refer to transactions completed during the first week of the month. Survey respondents are asked to indicate all discounts, allowances, and rebates applicable to the reported prices, so that the price used in the calculation of the indexes is the actual price for which the product was bought or sold.

Table 724. Purchasing Power of the Dollar: 1950 to 2010

[Indexes: PPI, 1982 = $1.00; CPI, 1982-84 = $1.00. Producer prices prior to 1961, and consumer prices prior to 1964, exclude Alaska and Hawaii. Producer prices based on finished goods index. Obtained by dividing the average price index for the 1982 = 100, PPI; 1982-84 = 100, CPI base periods (100.0) by the price index for a given period and expressing the result in dollars and cents. Annual figures are based on average of monthly data]

| Year | Annual average as measured by— | | Year | Annual average as measured by— | |
	Producer prices	Consumer prices		Producer prices	Consumer prices
1950.	3.546	4.151	1981.	1.041	1.098
1952.	3.268	3.765	1982.	1.000	1.035
1953.	3.300	3.735	1983.	0.984	1.003
1954.	3.289	3.717	1984.	0.964	0.961
1955.	3.279	3.732	1985.	0.955	0.928
1956.	3.195	3.678	1986.	0.969	0.913
1957.	3.077	3.549	1987.	0.949	0.880
1958.	3.012	3.457	1988.	0.926	0.846
1959.	3.021	3.427	1989.	0.880	0.807
1960.	2.994	3.373	1990.	0.839	0.766
1961.	2.994	3.340	1991.	0.822	0.734
1962.	2.985	3.304	1992.	0.812	0.713
1963.	2.994	3.265	1993.	0.802	0.692
1964.	2.985	3.220	1994.	0.797	0.675
1965.	2.933	3.166	1995.	0.782	0.656
1966.	2.841	3.080	1996.	0.762	0.638
1967.	2.809	2.993	1997.	0.759	0.623
1968.	2.732	2.873	1998.	0.765	0.613
1969.	2.632	2.726	1999.	0.752	0.600
1970.	2.545	2.574	2000.	0.725	0.581
1971.	2.469	2.466	2001.	0.711	0.565
1972.	2.392	2.391	2002.	0.720	0.556
1973.	2.193	2.251	2003.	0.698	0.543
1974.	1.901	2.029	2004.	0.673	0.529
1975.	1.718	1.859	2005.	0.642	0.512
1976.	1.645	1.757	2006.	0.623	0.496
1977.	1.546	1.649	2007.	0.600	0.482
1978.	1.433	1.532	2008.	0.565	0.464
1979.	1.289	1.380	2009.	0.580	0.466
1980.	1.136	1.215	2010 [1]	0.556	0.459

[1] PPI data are preliminary.
Source: Bureau of Labor Statistics, CPI Detailed Report, monthly, and at <http://www.bls.gov/cpi/cpi_dr.htm>. See also Monthly Labor Review at <http://www.bls.gov/opub/mlr/welcome.htm> and Producer Price Indexes, monthly and annual.

Table 725. Consumer Price Indexes (CPI-U) by Major Groups: 1990 to 2010

[1982-84 = 100, except as indicated. Represents annual averages of monthly figures. Reflects buying patterns of all urban consumers. Minus sign (–) indicates decrease. See text, this section]

Year	All items	Com-mod-ities	Ser-vices	Food	Energy	All items less food and energy	Food and bever-ages	Hous-ing	Apparel	Trans-porta-tion	Medical care	Educa-tion and com-munica-tion [1]
1990......	130.7	122.8	139.2	132.4	102.1	135.5	132.1	128.5	124.1	120.5	162.8	(NA)
1995......	152.4	136.4	168.7	148.4	105.2	161.2	148.9	148.5	132.0	139.1	220.5	92.2
1998......	163.0	141.9	184.2	160.7	102.9	173.4	161.1	160.4	133.0	141.6	242.1	100.3
1999......	166.6	144.4	188.8	164.1	106.6	177.0	164.6	163.9	131.3	144.4	250.6	101.2
2000......	172.2	149.2	195.3	167.8	124.6	181.3	168.4	169.6	129.6	153.3	260.8	102.5
2001......	177.1	150.7	203.4	173.1	129.3	186.1	173.6	176.4	127.3	154.3	272.8	105.2
2002......	179.9	149.7	209.8	176.2	121.7	190.5	176.8	180.3	124.0	152.9	285.6	107.9
2003......	184.0	151.2	216.5	180.0	136.5	193.2	180.5	184.8	120.9	157.6	297.1	109.8
2004......	188.9	154.7	222.8	186.2	151.4	196.6	186.6	189.5	120.4	163.1	310.1	111.6
2005......	195.3	160.2	230.1	190.7	177.1	200.9	191.2	195.7	119.5	173.9	323.2	113.7
2006......	201.6	164.0	238.9	195.2	196.9	205.9	195.7	203.2	119.5	180.9	336.2	116.8
2007......	207.3	167.5	246.8	202.9	207.7	210.7	203.3	209.6	119.0	184.7	351.1	119.6
2008......	215.3	174.8	255.5	214.1	236.7	215.6	214.2	216.3	118.9	195.5	364.1	123.6
2009......	214.5	169.7	259.2	218.0	193.1	219.2	218.2	217.1	120.1	179.3	375.6	127.4
2010......	218.1	174.6	261.3	219.6	211.4	221.3	220.0	216.3	119.5	193.4	388.4	129.9
PERCENT CHANGE [2]												
1990......	5.4	5.2	5.5	5.8	8.3	5.0	5.8	4.5	4.6	5.6	9.0	(NA)
1995......	2.8	1.9	3.4	2.8	0.6	3.0	2.8	2.6	–1.0	3.6	4.5	3.8
1998......	1.6	0.1	2.7	2.2	–7.7	2.3	2.2	2.3	0.1	–1.9	3.2	1.9
1999......	2.2	1.8	2.5	2.1	3.6	2.1	2.2	2.2	–1.3	2.0	3.5	0.9
2000......	3.4	3.3	3.4	2.3	16.9	2.4	2.3	3.5	–1.3	6.2	4.1	1.3
2001......	2.8	1.0	4.1	3.2	3.8	2.6	3.1	4.0	–1.8	0.7	4.6	2.6
2002......	1.6	–0.7	3.1	1.8	–5.9	2.4	1.8	2.2	–2.6	–0.9	4.7	2.6
2003......	2.3	1.0	3.2	2.2	12.2	1.4	2.1	2.5	–2.5	3.1	4.0	1.8
2004......	2.7	2.3	2.9	3.4	10.9	1.8	3.4	2.5	–0.4	3.5	4.4	1.6
2005......	3.4	3.6	3.3	2.4	17.0	2.2	2.5	3.3	–0.7	6.6	4.2	1.9
2006......	3.2	2.4	3.8	2.4	11.2	2.5	2.4	3.8	–	4.0	4.0	2.7
2007......	2.8	2.1	3.3	4.0	5.5	2.3	3.9	3.1	–0.4	2.1	4.4	2.4
2008......	3.8	4.3	3.5	5.5	13.9	2.3	5.4	3.2	–0.1	5.9	3.7	3.4
2009......	–0.4	–2.9	1.4	1.8	–18.4	1.7	1.9	0.4	1.0	–8.3	3.2	3.0
2010......	1.6	2.9	0.8	0.8	9.5	1.0	0.8	–0.4	–0.5	7.9	3.4	2.0

– Represents zero. NA Not available. [1] Dec. 1997 = 100. [2] Change from immediate prior year. 1990 change from 1989.
Source: U.S. Bureau of Labor Statistics, *CPI Detailed Report*, monthly, <http://www.bls.gov/cpi/cpi_dr.htm>. See also *Monthly Labor Review*, <http://www.bls.gov/opub/mlr/welcome.htm>.

Table 726. Annual Percent Changes From Prior Year in Consumer Price Indexes (CPI-U)—Selected Areas: 2010

[Percent changes computed from annual averages of monthly figures published by source. Local area CPI indexes are by-products of the national CPI program. Each local index has a smaller sample size than the national index and is therefore subject to substantially more sampling and other measurement error. As a result, local area indexes show greater volatility than the national index, although their long-term trends are similar. Area definitions are those established by the Office of Management and Budget in 1983. For further detail, see the U.S. Bureau of Labor Statistics Handbook of Methods, Bulletin 2285, Chapter 19, the Consumer Price Index, and Report 751, the CPI: 1987 Revision. Minus sign (–) indicates decrease. See also text, this section and Appendix III]

Area	All items	Food and bever-age	Food	Hous-ing	Apparel	Trans-porta-tion	Medi-cal care	Fuel and other utilities
U.S. city average	**1.6**	**0.8**	**0.8**	**–0.4**	**–0.5**	**7.9**	**3.4**	**1.7**
Anchorage, AK MSA	1.8	–0.2	–0.1	0.9	3.0	4.4	5.7	–8.7
Atlanta, GA MSA	1.2	1.2	1.2	–0.6	5.8	8.8	–0.2	5.1
Boston, MA MSA	1.6	1.2	1.1	–0.8	2.2	8.8	4.3	2.1
Chicago-Gary, IL-IN CMSA	1.4	0.5	0.4	–0.2	–2.6	7.3	6.2	5.5
Cincinnati-Hamilton, OH-KY-IN CMSA	2.1	1.1	1.1	1.5	0.8	6.8	1.1	7.4
Cleveland-Akron-Lorain, OH CMSA	2.0	1.1	0.9	–0.3	7.0	7.5	4.2	2.8
Dallas-Fort Worth, TX CMSA	0.5	0.4	0.3	–2.2	–5.6	8.0	4.6	–5.7
Denver-Boulder-Greely, CO CMSA	1.9	–0.2	–0.3	0.6	–4.0	8.7	0.8	3.7
Detroit-Ann Arbor-Flint, MI CMSA	0.8	0.6	0.7	–1.4	–2.8	7.2	1.0	2.5
Honolulu, HI MSA	2.1	0.2	0.1	0.9	3.2	7.0	–0.4	16.6
Houston-Galveston-Brazoria, TX CMSA	1.9	0.1	0.1	–0.2	5.1	7.5	4.7	–4.3
Kansas City, MO-KS CMSA	2.2	2.0	2.1	0.3	2.9	7.5	2.4	4.4
Los Angeles-Anaheim-Riverside, CA CMSA	1.2	0.6	0.6	–0.5	1.0	6.9	3.1	7.7
Miami-Fort Lauderdale, FL CMSA	0.8	1.2	1.0	–1.5	–1.5	7.1	2.9	–6.6
Milwaukee, WI PMSA	3.3	1.4	1.0	1.3	0.7	9.3	7.0	5.5
Minneapolis-St. Paul, MN-WI MSA	1.8	1.6	1.0	0.7	–1.3	7.6	(NA)	4.1
New York-Northern New Jersey-Long Island, NY-NJ-CT CMSA	1.7	0.9	0.9	0.6	3.4	6.8	2.6	2.1
Philadelphia-Wilmington-Trenton, PA-NJ-DE-MD CMSA	2.0	0.8	0.9	0.9	1.4	7.8	1.6	1.8
Pittsburgh, PA MSA	1.5	1.9	2.0	(–Z)	(–Z)	6.0	5.1	–1.2
Portland, OR MSA	1.3	0.3	0.5	–0.4	1.8	7.9	3.4	–0.2
San Diego, CA MSA	1.3	0.1	(Z)	–0.8	–0.3	8.5	1.9	0.3
San Francisco-Oakland-San Jose, CA CMSA	1.4	–0.2	–0.2	–0.4	0.1	6.9	2.5	6.1
Seattle-Tacoma, WA CMSA	0.3	–0.2	–0.3	–2.3	1.0	6.9	(NA)	4.8
St. Louis-East St. Louis, MO-IL CMSA	2.4	1.8	1.5	0.6	6.1	7.0	1.6	0.8
Tampa-St. Petersburg-Clearwater, FL MSA	1.9	0.8	0.8	–1.6	–0.3	10.1	0.9	–2.1
Washington-Baltimore, DC-MD-VA-WV CMSA	1.7	0.3	0.3	0.2	–2.5	8.9	4.7	–1.5

NA Not available. Z Less than 0.05 percent.
Source: U.S. Bureau of Labor Statistics, *CPI Detailed Report*, monthly, <http://www.bls.gov/cpi/cpi_dr.htm>. See also *Monthly Labor Review*, <http://www.bls.gov/opub/mlr/welcome.htm>.

Table 727. Consumer Price Indexes for All Urban Consumers (CPI-U) for Selected Items and Groups: 2000 to 2009

[1982-84 = 100, except as noted. Annual averages of monthly figures. Minus sign (–) indicates decrease. See headnote, Table 725]

Item	2000	2005	2006	2007	2008	2009	2010	Annual percent change, 2009–2010
All items.	**172.2**	**195.3**	**201.6**	**207.3**	**215.3**	**214.5**	**218.1**	**1.6**
Food and beverages	**168.4**	**191.2**	**195.7**	**203.3**	**214.2**	**218.2**	**220.0**	**0.8**
Food	167.8	190.7	195.2	202.9	214.1	218.0	219.6	0.8
Food at home	167.9	189.8	193.1	201.2	214.1	215.1	215.8	0.3
Cereals and bakery products.	188.3	209.0	212.8	222.1	244.9	252.6	250.4	−0.8
Cereals and cereal products	175.9	186.7	187.3	194.7	214.4	221.8	217.6	−1.9
Rice, pasta, and cornmeal.	150.7	165.3	171.4	181.4	218.8	229.2	224.4	−2.4
Rice [1,2].	99.3	108.8	114.9	120.1	152.8	161.0	156.9	−2.5
Bakery products.	194.1	220.5	226.4	236.6	261.0	268.9	268.0	−0.4
Bread [2].	107.4	126.2	130.4	140.1	160.6	162.6	159.8	−1.7
Cakes, cupcakes, and cookies	187.9	209.8	214.2	221.7	239.9	250.7	251.7	0.4
Other bakery products.	191.5	211.4	215.5	220.5	236.5	245.9	247.1	0.5
Meats, poultry, fish and eggs.	154.5	184.7	186.6	195.6	204.7	203.8	207.7	1.9
Meats, poultry, and fish	155.5	186.7	188.2	195.4	203.6	204.6	208.6	1.9
Meats	150.7	187.5	188.8	195.0	201.8	200.5	206.2	2.8
Beef and veal.	148.1	200.4	202.1	211.1	220.6	218.3	224.5	2.9
Uncooked ground beef	125.2	175.1	176.3	184.3	196.4	198.5	203.6	2.6
Uncooked beef steaks [2].	109.1	145.1	146.1	151.8	155.3	150.1	153.3	2.1
Pork.	156.5	177.7	177.3	180.9	185.0	181.4	190.0	4.7
Other meats.	152.0	177.5	180.7	184.8	190.6	194.9	194.8	−0.1
Poultry.	159.8	185.3	182.0	191.4	200.9	204.2	204.0	−0.1
Chicken [2].	102.5	120.6	117.6	124.4	130.7	132.6	131.8	−0.6
Fish and seafood.	190.4	200.1	209.5	219.1	232.1	240.6	243.2	1.1
Dairy products.	160.7	182.4	181.4	194.8	210.4	197.0	199.2	1.1
Milk [2].	107.8	127.0	125.5	140.1	148.5	129.0	133.6	3.6
Cheese and related products	162.8	183.3	180.8	191.5	214.5	203.5	204.8	0.7
Ice cream and related products.	164.4	177.6	179.3	184.3	192.8	196.6	195.0	−0.8
Fruits and vegetables	204.6	241.4	252.9	262.6	278.9	272.9	273.5	0.2
Fresh fruits and vegetables	238.8	285.3	300.4	312.1	328.3	312.7	314.8	0.7
Fresh fruits.	258.3	297.4	315.2	329.5	345.4	324.4	322.3	−0.6
Fresh vegetables	219.4	271.7	284.3	293.5	309.8	299.3	305.5	2.0
Processed fruits and vegetables [2]	105.6	119.3	122.8	127.2	139.3	148.6	146.6	−1.3
Nonalcoholic beverages and beverage materials	137.8	144.4	147.4	153.4	160.0	163.0	161.6	−0.9
Juices and nonalcoholic drinks [2]	105.6	110.6	113.2	117.9	123.1	126.3	124.5	−1.4
Carbonated drinks.	123.4	131.9	134.2	140.1	147.0	154.1	154.7	0.4
Nonfrozen noncarbonated juices and drinks [2].	104.2	106.5	109.5	112.9	117.5	118.0	114.8	−2.7
Beverage materials including coffee and tea [2].	97.9	102.4	104.1	108.2	112.8	113.3	114.0	0.6
Other food at home	155.6	167.0	169.6	173.3	184.2	191.2	191.1	−0.1
Sugar and sweets	154.0	165.2	171.5	176.8	186.6	196.9	201.2	2.2
Candy and chewing gum [2].	103.8	109.5	112.2	116.1	123.2	130.2	132.5	1.8
Fats and oils	147.4	167.7	168.0	172.9	196.8	201.2	200.6	−0.3
Frozen and freeze dried prepared food	148.5	153.2	153.7	156.7	163.5	168.1	165.3	−1.7
Snacks.	166.3	178.5	181.2	184.9	199.8	213.2	216.6	1.6
Spices, seasonings, condiments, sauces	175.6	188.0	190.3	195.5	204.6	214.7	214.4	−0.1
Other miscellaneous food [2]	107.5	111.3	113.9	115.1	119.9	122.4	121.7	−0.6
Food away from home.	169.0	193.4	199.4	206.7	215.8	223.3	226.1	1.3
Full service meals and snacks [2]	106.8	121.9	125.7	130.2	135.4	139.2	141.1	1.3
Limited service meals and snacks [2].	106.3	122.4	126.0	130.6	136.9	142.6	143.9	0.9
Food at employee sites and schools [2]	104.4	118.6	122.6	126.8	131.8	137.3	141.0	2.7
Food from vending machines and mobile vendors [2].	102.4	112.6	115.1	118.3	124.1	129.7	133.1	2.6
Other food away from home [2]	109.0	131.3	136.6	144.1	150.6	155.9	159.3	2.2
Alcoholic beverages.	174.7	195.9	200.7	207.0	214.5	220.8	223.3	1.2
Alcoholic beverages at home.	158.1	172.3	174.9	179.1	184.9	190.3	191.0	0.4
Beer, ale, and other malt beverages at home	156.8	176.4	178.1	184.1	190.3	197.4	201.0	1.8
Distilled spirits at home	162.3	177.4	179.7	181.0	185.0	189.2	188.8	−0.2
Wine at home.	151.6	156.2	158.9	162.9	168.7	172.1	169.7	−1.4
Alcoholic beverages away from home	207.1	244.5	254.6	266.0	277.4	285.6	291.9	2.2
Housing	**169.6**	**195.7**	**203.2**	**209.6**	**216.3**	**217.1**	**216.3**	**−0.4**
Shelter.	193.4	224.4	232.1	240.6	246.7	249.4	248.4	−0.4
Rent of primary residence	183.9	217.3	225.1	234.7	243.3	248.8	249.4	0.2
Lodging away from home [2]	117.5	130.3	136.0	142.8	143.7	134.2	133.7	−0.4
Other lodging away from home including hotels and motels	252.4	274.2	285.6	299.9	301.0	279.2	280.4	0.4
Owners' equivalent rent of primary residence [3]	198.7	230.2	238.2	246.2	252.4	256.6	256.6	(−Z)
Tenants' and household insurance [2]	103.7	117.6	116.5	117.0	118.8	121.5	125.7	3.5
Fuels and utilities.	137.9	179.0	194.7	200.6	220.0	210.7	214.2	1.7
Household energy.	122.8	161.6	177.1	181.7	200.8	188.1	189.3	0.6
Fuel oil and other fuels	129.7	208.6	234.9	251.5	334.4	239.8	275.1	14.7
Fuel oil.	130.3	216.4	244.6	262.6	365.0	240.2	282.9	17.8
Propane, kerosene and firewood [4].	155.5	240.6	268.8	286.0	344.2	293.1	320.6	9.4

See footnotes at end of table.

U.S. Census Bureau, Statistical Abstract of the United States: 2012

Table 727. Consumer Price Indexes for All Urban, Consumers (CPI-U) for Selected Items and Groups: 2000 to 2010—Con.

[1982-84 = 100, except as noted. Annual averages of monthly figures. Minus sign (−) indicates decrease. See headnote, Table 725]

Item	2000	2005	2006	2007	2008	2009	2010	Annual percent change, 2009–2010
Energy services	**128.0**	**166.5**	**182.1**	**186.3**	**202.2**	**193.6**	**192.9**	**-0.3**
Electricity	128.5	150.8	169.2	175.8	187.1	192.7	193.1	0.2
Utility (piped) gas service	132.0	215.4	220.8	217.7	247.8	193.7	189.7	-2.1
Water and sewer and trash collection services [2]	106.5	130.3	136.8	143.7	152.1	161.1	170.9	6.0
Water and sewerage maintenance	227.5	283.4	297.2	312.6	331.3	354.4	380.7	7.4
Garbage and trash collection [5]	269.8	314.0	330.1	345.6	364.7	376.4	384.4	2.1
Household furnishings and operations	128.2	126.1	127.0	126.9	127.8	128.7	125.5	-2.5
Furniture and bedding	134.4	125.9	127.0	125.8	124.5	124.8	119.7	-4.0
Bedroom furniture	138.4	142.7	145.4	144.7	143.7	143.0	136.4	-4.6
Living room, kitchen, and dining room furniture [2]	102.4	92.7	92.8	91.6	90.5	90.7	88.9	-2.0
Appliances [2]	96.3	86.9	88.1	89.8	89.9	91.1	86.9	-4.5
Other household equipment and furnishings [2]	98.0	85.5	80.4	76.9	75.6	74.0	70.8	-4.4
Clocks, lamps, and decorator items	111.7	88.0	79.6	73.6	69.9	67.2	62.9	-6.4
Nonelectric cookware and tableware [2]	98.4	91.3	91.1	93.1	95.9	97.1	96.6	-0.5
Tools, hardware, outdoor equipment and supplies [2]	97.0	94.4	94.6	94.6	93.5	94.2	91.6	-2.7
Tools, hardware, and supplies [2]	97.3	98.1	99.4	99.7	99.0	99.2	96.5	-2.7
Outdoor equipment and supplies [2]	96.8	92.4	92.1	92.0	90.7	91.4	88.9	-2.7
Housekeeping supplies	153.4	159.9	166.6	169.4	176.5	183.1	183.3	0.1
Household cleaning products [2]	105.1	107.9	111.6	112.3	115.9	121.4	120.6	-0.7
Household paper products [2]	113.8	125.4	132.0	135.6	146.8	156.1	158.0	1.3
Miscellaneous household products [2]	104.3	106.4	111.0	113.6	116.3	116.8	116.9	0.1
Household operations [2]	110.5	130.3	136.6	140.6	147.5	150.3	150.3	(−Z)
Domestic services [2]	109.7	128.3	133.1	138.1	142.8	144.1	144.4	0.2
Gardening and lawncare services [2]	111.4	127.9	136.6	140.5	(NA)	156.5	155.3	-0.8
Apparel	**129.6**	**119.5**	**119.5**	**119.0**	**118.9**	**120.1**	**119.5**	**-0.5**
Men's and boy's apparel	129.7	116.1	114.1	112.4	113.0	113.6	111.9	-1.5
Men's apparel	133.1	121.4	119.8	118.2	118.4	118.6	117.5	-0.9
Men's shirts and sweaters [2]	98.3	84.2	84.7	82.5	80.4	81.0	78.6	-2.9
Boys' apparel	116.2	97.0	93.7	91.7	93.5	95.2	91.5	-3.8
Women's and girl's apparel	121.5	110.8	110.7	110.3	107.5	108.1	107.1	-0.9
Women's apparel	121.9	111.8	112.5	112.1	109.3	109.9	109.5	-0.4
Women's suits and separates [2]	98.2	87.3	88.2	88.9	85.7	84.9	83.9	-1.1
Women's underwear, nightwear, sportswear, and accessories [2]	101.8	95.4	94.4	91.8	90.4	93.1	96.0	3.0
Girls' apparel	119.7	105.3	101.6	101.1	98.5	99.0	95.4	-3.7
Footwear	123.8	122.6	123.5	122.4	124.2	126.9	128.0	0.9
Men's footwear	129.5	121.3	123.5	120.9	122.9	126.4	127.6	0.9
Women's footwear	119.6	121.9	122.8	122.5	122.6	123.4	125.3	1.5
Jewelry and watches [4]	137.0	127.6	130.7	137.1	146.5	149.2	152.4	2.1
Jewelry [4]	141.2	131.3	134.8	142.4	153.8	157.0	161.2	2.7
Transportation	**153.3**	**173.9**	**180.9**	**184.7**	**195.5**	**179.3**	**193.4**	**7.9**
Private transportation	149.1	170.2	177.0	180.8	191.0	174.8	188.7	8.0
New and used motor vehicles [2]	100.8	95.6	95.6	94.3	93.3	93.5	97.1	3.9
New vehicles	142.8	137.9	137.6	136.3	134.2	135.6	138.0	1.8
Used cars and trucks	155.8	139.4	140.0	135.7	134.0	127.0	143.1	12.7
Leased cars and trucks [7]	(NA)	92.7	93.1	92.6	95.1	102.4	97.0	-5.3
Motor fuel	129.3	195.7	221.0	239.1	279.7	202.0	239.2	18.4
Gasoline (all types)	128.6	194.7	219.9	238.0	277.5	201.6	238.6	18.4
Motor vehicle parts and equipment	101.5	111.9	117.3	121.6	128.7	134.1	137.0	2.2
Motor vehicle maintenance and repair	177.3	206.9	215.6	223.0	233.9	243.3	248.0	1.9
Motor vehicle insurance	256.7	329.9	331.8	333.1	341.5	357.0	375.2	5.1
Motor vehicle fees [2]	107.3	134.7	138.8	141.2	145.8	155.7	165.5	6.3
Public transportation	209.6	217.3	226.6	230.0	250.5	236.3	251.4	6.3
Airline fare	239.4	236.6	247.3	251.7	282.0	258.0	278.2	7.8
Medical care	**260.8**	**323.2**	**336.2**	**351.1**	**364.1**	**375.6**	**388.4**	**3.4**
Medical care commodities	238.1	276.0	285.9	290.0	296.0	305.1	314.7	3.1
Prescription drugs	285.4	349.0	363.9	369.2	378.3	391.1	407.8	4.3
Nonprescription drugs and medical supplies [4]	149.5	151.7	154.6	156.8	158.3	161.4	(NA)	(NA)
Medical care services	266.0	336.7	350.6	369.3	384.9	397.3	411.2	3.5
Professional medical services	237.7	281.7	289.3	300.8	311.0	319.4	328.2	2.8
Physicians' services	244.7	287.5	291.9	303.2	311.3	320.8	331.3	3.3
Dental services	258.5	324.0	340.9	358.4	376.9	388.1	398.8	2.7
Eyeglasses and eye care [4]	149.7	163.2	168.1	171.6	174.1	175.5	176.7	0.7
Services by other medical professionals [4]	161.9	186.8	192.2	197.4	205.5	209.8	214.4	2.2
Hospital and related services	317.3	439.9	468.1	498.9	534.0	567.9	607.7	7.0
Hospital services [9]	115.9	161.6	172.1	183.6	197.2	210.7	227.2	7.8

See footnotes at end of table.

476 Prices

Table 727. Consumer Price Indexes for All Urban, Consumers (CPI-U) for Selected Items and Groups: 2000 to 2010—Con.

[1982-84 = 100, except as noted. Annual averages of monthly figures. Minus sign (–) indicates decrease. See headnote, Table 725]

Item	2000	2005	2006	2007	2008	2009	2010	Annual percent change, 2009–2010
Recreation [2]	**103.3**	**109.4**	**110.9**	**111.4**	**113.3**	**114.3**	**113.3**	**–0.8**
Video and audio [2]	101.0	104.2	104.6	102.9	102.6	101.3	99.1	–2.1
Cable and satellite television and radio service [5]	266.8	331.9	344.9	351.5	359.9	367.6	372.4	1.3
Pets, pet products and services [2]	106.1	123.6	128.4	133.8	144.5	153.4	154.4	0.6
Sporting goods	119.0	115.5	117.1	116.4	118.4	119.9	118.8	–0.9
Other recreational goods [2]	87.8	69.5	67.2	64.3	62.1	60.2	57.8	–4.0
Recreation services [2]	111.7	130.5	135.1	139.4	142.9	144.6	145.1	0.3
Club membership dues and fees for participant sports [2]	108.9	117.4	121.9	123.7	125.8	125.7	123.5	–1.8
Admissions	230.5	282.3	291.9	303.8	312.3	317.8	322.8	1.6
Education and communication [2]	**102.5**	**113.7**	**116.8**	**119.6**	**123.6**	**127.4**	**129.9**	**2.0**
Education [2]	112.5	152.7	162.1	171.4	181.3	190.9	199.3	4.4
Tuition, other school fees, and childcare	324.0	440.9	468.1	494.1	522.1	549.0	573.2	4.4
College tuition and fees	331.9	475.1	507.0	538.7	572.3	606.7	638.2	5.2
Communication [2]	93.6	84.7	84.1	83.4	84.2	85.0	84.7	–0.3
Information and information processing [2]	92.8	82.6	81.7	80.7	81.4	81.9	81.5	–0.5
Telephone services [2]	98.5	94.9	95.8	98.2	100.5	102.4	102.4	(–Z)
Land-line telephone services, local charges	175.6	209.6	213.9	222.1	230.0	236.6	(NA)	(NA)
Land-line telephone services, long distance charges [2]	91.8	67.5	68.3	71.5	74.8	78.1	(NA)	(NA)
Wireless telephone services [2]	76.0	65.0	64.6	64.4	64.2	64.3	62.4	–2.9
Information technology, hardware, and services [10]	25.9	13.6	12.5	10.6	10.1	9.7	9.4	–2.7
Other goods and services	**271.1**	**313.4**	**321.7**	**333.3**	**345.4**	**368.6**	**381.3**	**3.4**
Tobacco and smoking products	394.9	502.8	519.9	554.2	588.7	730.3	807.3	10.5
Cigarettes [2]	159.9	203.5	210.4	224.8	239.0	297.4	329.0	10.6
Personal care	165.6	185.6	190.2	195.6	201.3	204.6	206.6	1.0
Personal care products	153.7	154.4	155.8	158.3	159.3	162.6	161.1	–0.9
Hair, dental, shaving, and miscellaneous personal care products [2]	103.3	101.8	102.6	103.6	104.3	105.4	104.3	–1.1
Cosmetics, perfume, bath, nail preparations and implements	166.8	171.3	173.1	177.0	178.0	183.6	182.2	–0.8
Personal care services	178.1	203.9	209.7	216.6	223.7	227.6	229.6	0.9
Haircuts and other personal care services [2]	108.7	124.4	127.9	132.1	136.5	138.9	140.1	0.9
Miscellaneous personal services	252.3	303.0	313.6	325.0	338.9	344.5	354.1	2.8
Legal services [4]	189.3	241.8	250.0	260.3	270.7	278.1	288.1	3.6
Funeral expenses [4]	187.8	228.8	240.6	252.6	265.4	275.7	282.0	2.3
SPECIAL AGGREGATE INDEXES								
Commodities	**149.2**	**160.2**	**164.0**	**167.5**	**174.8**	**169.7**	**174.6**	**2.9**
Commodities less food and beverages	137.7	142.5	145.9	147.5	153.0	144.4	150.4	4.2
Nondurables less food and beverages	147.4	168.4	176.7	182.5	196.2	179.0	189.9	6.1
Nondurables less food, beverages, and apparel	162.5	202.6	216.3	226.2	248.8	219.6	238.1	8.4
Durables	125.4	115.3	114.5	112.5	110.9	109.9	111.3	1.3
Services	195.3	230.1	238.9	246.8	255.5	259.2	261.3	0.8
Rent of shelter [3]	201.3	233.7	241.9	250.1	257.2	259.9	258.8	–0.4
Transportation services	196.1	225.7	230.8	233.7	244.1	251.0	259.8	3.5
Other services	229.9	268.4	277.5	285.6	295.8	304.0	309.6	1.8
All items less food	173.0	196.0	202.7	208.1	215.5	214.0	217.8	1.8
All items less shelter	165.7	186.1	191.9	196.6	205.5	203.3	208.6	2.6
All items less medical care	167.3	188.7	194.7	200.1	207.8	206.6	209.7	1.5
Commodities less food	139.2	144.5	148.0	149.7	155.3	147.1	153.0	4.0
Nondurables less food	149.1	170.1	178.2	184.0	197.3	181.5	191.9	5.8
Nondurables less food and apparel	162.9	201.2	213.9	223.4	244.4	218.7	235.6	7.7
Nondurables	158.2	180.2	186.7	193.5	205.9	198.5	205.3	3.4
Apparel less footwear	126.2	114.4	114.1	113.8	113.4	114.2	113.3	–0.8
Services less rent of shelter [3]	202.9	243.2	253.3	260.8	273.0	278.1	284.4	2.3
Services less medical care services	188.9	221.2	229.6	236.8	245.0	248.1	249.6	0.6
Energy	124.6	177.1	196.9	207.7	236.7	193.1	211.4	9.5
All items less energy	178.6	198.7	203.7	208.9	214.8	218.4	220.5	0.9
All items less food and energy	181.3	200.9	205.9	210.7	215.6	219.2	221.3	1.0
Commodities less food and energy commodities	144.9	140.3	140.6	140.1	140.2	142.0	143.6	1.1
Energy commodities	129.5	197.4	223.0	241.0	284.4	205.3	242.6	18.2
Services less energy services	202.1	236.6	244.7	253.1	261.0	265.9	268.3	0.9
Domestically produced farm food	170.1	195.0	198.1	206.5	220.1	220.4	221.6	0.5
Utilities and public transportation	152.6	176.6	186.7	191.3	202.8	200.3	203.1	1.4

NA Not available. Z Less than 0.05 percent. [1] Special indexes based on a substantially smaller sample. [2] December 1997=100. [3] December 1982=100. [4] December 1986=100. [5] December 1983=100. [6] December 1990=100. [7] December 2001=100. [8] December 1993=100. [9] December 1996=100. [10] December 1988=100. [11] December 2007=100.

Source: Bureau of Labor Statistics, *CPI Detailed Report*, monthly, <http://www.bls.gov/cpi/>. See also Monthly Labor Review, <http://www.bls.gov/opub/mlr/welcome.htm>.

Table 728. Cost of Living Index—Selected Urban Areas, Annual Average: 2010

[Data are for a selected urban area within the larger metropolitan area shown. Measures relative price levels for consumer goods and services in participating areas for a mid-management standard of living. The nationwide average equals 100 and each index is read as a percent of the national average. The index does not measure inflation, but compares prices at a single point in time. Excludes taxes. Metropolitan areas as defined by the Office of Management and Budget. For definitions, urban areas, and components of MSAs, see source. Beginning February 2008, data are based on an annual average survey compiled from data submitted in the first 3 quarters of the year. To calculate the annual average index, actual and estimated prices are collected to calculate an annual average price for each item used to represent the various spending categories. The share of consumer spending devoted to the category determines that category's importance, or weight, in the Index. Weights are based on the Bureau of Labor Statistics' 2009 Consumer Expenditure Survey]

Urban area	Composite index (100%)	Grocery items (13%)	Housing (29%)	Utilities (10%)	Trans- portation (12%)	Health care (4%)	Misc. goods and services (32%)
Akron, OH	100.2	105.1	99.7	107.9	107.1	86.8	96.0
Albany, GA	90.1	108.7	74.8	82.0	96.6	89.8	96.8
Amarillo, TX	89.5	89.9	89.4	80.4	92.1	95.2	90.8
Americus, GA	88.3	105.5	71.0	88.2	99.8	103.7	91.3
Anchorage, AK	128.4	134.5	142.9	94.1	122.0	135.7	124.8
Ardmore, OK	87.3	92.9	77.3	84.8	101.3	93.7	89.8
Arlington, TX	99.3	94.4	89.4	109.9	98.3	105.4	106.4
Ashland, OH	88.5	100.7	72.1	92.1	98.2	88.8	94.2
Baltimore, MD	119.4	110.8	155.4	112.5	105.3	97.9	100.0
Bellingham, WA	113.0	114.9	135.9	83.8	113.2	115.3	100.8
Bergen-Passaic, NJ	131.3	112.1	174.0	128.9	102.4	106.3	113.8
Bethesda-Gaithersburg-Frederick, MD	130.5	108.5	184.2	120.6	110.1	104.0	104.4
Boston, MA	132.5	116.7	152.7	138.6	104.5	123.5	128.6
Brazoria County, TX	89.3	87.9	75.8	100.8	96.0	95.6	95.6
Brownsville, TX	85.8	88.6	71.0	93.1	95.0	96.5	91.4
Burlington-Chittenden, Co VT	120.5	112.9	138.7	122.2	102.5	104.6	114.2
Cedar City, UT	88.7	102.5	73.9	83.7	97.8	85.5	95.5
Chapel Hill, NC	113.0	100.9	127.0	85.7	122.8	105.8	112.1
Cheyenne, WY	100.5	101.7	107.9	96.3	95.0	98.3	96.5
Chicago, IL	116.9	111.2	134.8	117.3	116.5	108.5	104.4
Cleveland, OH	101.0	108.1	93.3	109.0	101.4	104.3	102.1
Columbia, SC	100.4	105.2	82.3	109.0	102.0	106.2	110.6
Conway, AR	86.6	97.9	78.8	92.0	96.6	89.8	84.0
Cookeville, TN	85.7	86.7	71.4	82.9	87.5	87.1	98.2
Covington, KY	87.8	86.0	76.8	100.2	99.9	90.6	90.3
Decatur-Hartselle, AL	89.2	98.5	74.2	90.6	96.7	85.5	96.6
Detroit, MI	99.4	92.7	95.2	129.5	101.3	94.2	96.6
Dodge City, KS	89.3	90.0	77.6	85.5	95.6	89.9	98.5
Dothan, AL	89.8	100.3	80.1	79.7	91.8	81.7	97.9
Douglas, GA	88.6	104.1	68.5	97.9	89.3	91.3	96.6
Dover, DE	99.7	110.4	90.9	108.8	97.5	103.0	100.7
Dutchess County, NY	120.4	109.8	141.3	118.8	109.3	110.4	111.1
Dyersburg, TN	88.6	93.4	73.8	95.2	92.9	86.3	96.7
Eugene, OR	109.8	93.8	132.3	85.3	110.0	118.2	102.9
Everett, WA	111.3	112.0	128.1	85.4	110.4	129.1	102.1
Fairbanks, AK	137.4	127.9	148.5	193.1	118.7	144.9	118.8
Flagstaff, AZ	114.9	106.6	149.3	92.5	105.5	100.0	99.5
Florence, AL	90.2	96.6	79.6	91.0	94.5	84.1	96.3
Fort Lauderdale, FL	115.7	112.5	144.0	92.5	106.3	102.4	103.7
Fort Smith, AR	86.1	92.5	74.5	90.5	87.9	87.5	91.7
Framingham-Natick, MA	134.5	109.4	177.2	131.9	105.0	116.1	118.8
Fresno, CA	117.3	115.8	131.2	123.6	114.5	106.8	105.9
Gainesville, FL	99.8	106.3	101.8	99.2	103.3	92.7	95.5
Garden City KS	89.7	91.2	79.9	86.5	94.0	89.6	97.5
Glens Falls, NY	112.3	105.4	105.9	128.0	107.0	97.3	119.3
Glenwood Springs, CO	124.0	103.3	169.0	89.0	110.9	112.0	108.7
Greenville, SC	90.3	102.7	72.9	90.1	97.1	98.2	97.7
Gunnison, CO	110.0	110.6	134.5	85.7	99.0	97.3	100.6
Hampton Roads-SE Virginia, VA	111.7	106.6	121.9	108.4	104.1	109.6	108.4
Harlingen, TX	82.8	81.5	75.8	105.6	88.7	95.2	79.1
Harrisburg, PA	99.7	97.8	91.5	110.5	100.2	93.8	105.1
Hartford, CT	121.8	120.7	137.8	120.7	109.0	113.0	113.5
Hays, KS	89.4	92.0	78.8	92.4	97.5	90.7	94.2
Hilton Head Island, SC	114.1	111.4	119.8	100.4	101.6	110.7	118.5
Honolulu, HI	165.7	160.1	249.0	146.6	126.2	120.0	117.9
Indianapolis, IN	87.2	91.4	73.4	86.7	100.5	93.6	93.1
Jackson-Madison County, TN	90.2	91.1	74.2	98.9	100.0	91.5	98.1
Johnson City, TN	86.7	92.3	74.4	89.1	91.7	91.5	92.6
Jonesboro, AR	88.9	97.5	75.1	91.1	88.8	85.9	97.3
Joplin, MO	88.8	92.2	75.9	108.1	91.8	89.5	92.0
Juneau, AK	136.5	133.1	165.7	135.1	121.2	144.4	116.1
Knoxville, TN	89.4	91.4	82.0	95.1	84.2	88.4	95.1
Kodiak, AK	128.7	149.4	127.8	131.9	143.4	130.7	115.4
Lake Havasu City, AZ	111.8	107.0	139.3	95.9	93.5	98.0	101.7
Las Cruces, NM	100.6	103.7	104.4	93.7	99.0	96.5	99.1
Los Alamos, NM	109.7	97.1	128.1	91.2	110.7	102.6	104.7
Los Angeles-Long Beach, CA	136.4	106.0	207.1	101.7	113.6	109.1	107.0

See footnotes at end of table.

U.S. Census Bureau, Statistical Abstract of the United States: 2012

Table 728. Cost of Living Index—Selected Urban Areas, Annual Average: 2010—Con.

[Data are for a selected urban area within the larger metropolitan area shown. Measures relative price levels for consumer goods and services in participating areas for a mid-management standard of living. The nationwide average equals 100 and each index is read as a percent of the national average. The index does not measure inflation, but compares prices at a single point in time. Excludes taxes. Metropolitan areas as defined by the Office of Management and Budget. For definitions, urban areas, and components of MSAs, see source. Beginning February 2008, data are based on an annual average survey compiled from data submitted in the first 3 quarters of the year. To calculate the annual average index, actual and estimated prices are collected to calculate an annual average price for each item used to represent the various spending categories. The share of consumer spending devoted to the category determines that category's importance, or weight, in the Index. Weights are based on the Bureau of Labor Statistics' 2009 Consumer Expenditure Survey]

Urban area	Composite index (100%)	Grocery items (13%)	Housing (29%)	Utilities (10%)	Trans- portation (12%)	Health care (4%)	Misc. goods and services (32%)
Louisville, KY	87.7	81.6	78.7	99.1	96.9	87.2	91.9
Lubbock, TX	89.1	90.0	80.4	74.8	97.6	98.3	97.1
Madison, WI	109.8	104.8	118.0	95.0	109.5	115.2	108.6
Manchester, NH	116.8	102.3	117.0	124.5	100.1	116.1	125.0
Martinsburg-Berkeley County, WV	89.6	91.5	82.7	85.9	103.9	99.9	90.6
Martinsville-Henry County, VA	87.1	94.0	77.6	89.1	82.9	87.6	93.2
Mason City, IA	89.1	89.4	73.1	105.6	99.5	94.8	94.2
McAllen, TX	85.0	79.8	77.6	103.1	92.4	97.9	84.3
Memphis, TN	88.2	92.7	76.2	86.9	91.5	98.6	95.2
Middlesex-Monmouth, NJ	124.8	108.9	154.1	128.6	103.9	108.9	112.2
Minneapolis, MN	111.0	111.6	116.8	104.7	103.7	105.4	110.4
Minot, ND	99.9	99.3	95.9	73.5	98.2	91.0	113.6
Missoula, MT	99.4	110.2	92.2	98.3	102.2	107.2	100.1
Montgomery, AL	99.2	102.9	96.0	108.4	99.6	88.0	99.1
Morgantown, WV	100.6	93.9	111.9	89.9	100.7	96.1	97.1
Murfreesboro-Smyrna, TN	88.2	94.3	76.2	81.0	92.7	95.8	96.2
Muskogee, OK	86.0	98.0	68.3	97.5	80.8	96.7	93.5
Nashville-Franklin, TN	88.9	91.7	71.3	82.6	92.5	87.3	104.5
Nassau County, NY	145.7	123.0	206.7	140.7	113.1	119.7	115.3
New Haven, CT	122.1	117.9	134.9	123.5	106.3	112.7	117.9
New York (Brooklyn), NY	181.7	130.6	317.8	165.0	103.0	111.5	119.5
New York (Manhattan), NY	216.7	154.3	386.7	169.6	120.3	130.2	145.7
New York (Queens), NY	159.0	128.3	230.8	172.0	108.8	118.0	123.9
Newark-Elizabeth, NJ	129.7	111.6	168.5	129.2	103.9	103.1	113.9
Oakland, CA	139.1	116.8	198.8	94.7	113.6	119.9	119.0
Omaha, NE	88.3	92.0	79.3	89.9	100.0	96.8	89.7
Orange County, CA	146.4	104.5	242.8	103.2	114.6	111.6	105.2
Paducah, KY	87.3	94.8	75.8	96.5	86.6	90.3	91.3
Palm Coast-Flagler County, FL	88.2	106.9	70.0	90.4	103.6	96.5	90.6
Palm Springs, CA	121.8	111.5	154.2	112.7	110.2	100.8	106.1
Panama City, FL	99.4	93.7	101.5	99.7	108.8	94.5	97.6
Paris, TX	88.9	93.6	80.0	87.4	94.1	94.0	93.0
Philadelphia, PA	126.5	124.9	141.3	135.9	105.8	108.2	119.6
Phoenix, AZ	100.7	108.1	90.4	96.6	108.9	108.8	104.6
Pittsfield, MA	110.6	115.0	96.2	161.9	98.9	105.0	110.0
Plattsburgh, NY	100.1	98.9	95.1	119.4	105.5	113.0	95.9
Ponca City, OK	90.0	94.8	76.6	93.0	94.4	94.4	97.0
Portland, ME	116.5	101.8	143.0	102.9	111.8	109.7	105.5
Portland, OR	111.3	105.8	130.8	87.1	105.8	113.6	105.1
Providence, RI	123.3	113.4	129.0	129.0	102.5	113.2	128.1
Pryor Creek, OK	84.5	95.0	71.5	82.7	86.6	86.0	91.5
Pueblo, CO	85.6	100.5	71.5	80.1	93.8	94.1	90.1
Riverside City, CA	112.5	104.9	136.3	99.9	113.4	104.4	99.1
Rochester, NY	100.0	94.6	94.2	114.4	108.7	99.7	100.2
Round Rock, TX	89.7	81.9	78.0	107.0	87.6	96.6	97.6
Sacramento, CA	116.2	114.7	135.7	109.6	114.4	110.8	102.8
Salina, KS	86.9	86.9	76.0	87.0	94.7	94.9	93.1
Salt Lake City, UT	100.6	100.1	108.0	72.5	102.1	98.8	102.9
San Diego, CA	132.3	105.5	194.4	101.9	113.1	111.5	105.8
San Francisco, CA	164.0	111.9	281.0	94.5	113.0	117.0	124.3
San Jose, CA	156.1	115.3	260.3	137.2	114.0	119.0	103.6
Seattle, WA	121.4	115.1	140.3	85.7	118.8	119.9	119.1
Springfield, IL	85.8	89.7	70.1	79.8	104.5	106.5	91.7
Springfield, MO	88.0	93.2	76.8	83.2	96.8	95.3	93.8
St. Paul, MN	110.0	107.0	112.9	106.8	103.4	106.7	112.2
Stamford, CT	146.9	121.8	212.6	121.3	110.0	113.3	122.1
Stillwater, OK	90.1	95.5	81.2	97.9	88.8	95.7	93.1
Temple, TX	87.4	83.7	71.8	107.6	97.9	91.2	92.8
Thomasville-Lexington, NC	89.2	105.5	77.2	80.7	88.8	109.1	93.5
Truckee-Nevada County, CA	146.9	132.2	208.3	114.3	121.5	112.0	120.5
Tulsa, OK	88.4	91.9	66.5	95.2	99.1	94.6	100.5
Tupelo, MS	88.1	91.1	72.3	110.1	93.8	86.6	92.7
Waco, TX	88.9	81.8	88.5	85.3	97.6	90.9	90.5
Washington-Arlington-Alexandria, DC-VA	140.1	107.9	226.4	97.3	109.3	103.4	103.7
Wichita Falls, TX	86.5	91.9	84.0	84.4	82.5	94.5	87.4
Williamsport-Lycoming Co, PA	100.7	103.5	96.3	127.7	91.8	92.6	98.9
Youngstown-Warren, OH	90.4	92.6	77.7	110.2	92.4	86.9	94.4

Source: C2ER, Arlington, VA, ACCRA Cost of Living Index, Annual Average 2010 (copyright). See also <http://www.c2er.org>, released December 2010.

Prices 479

Table 729. Single-Family Housing Price Indexes by State: 2000 to 2010

[Index 1991, 1st quarter = 100. Data are seasonally adjusted. The index reflects average price changes in repeat sales or refinancings on the same properties. Since the data are for the fourth quarter, the index represents the annual percentage change in home values in the fourth quarter of the year shown relative to the fourth quarter of the previous year. The information is obtained by reviewing repeat mortgage transactions on single-family properties whose mortgages have been purchased or securitized by either Fannie Mae or Freddie Mac; for more information on methodology, see Appendix III. Minus sign (–) indicates decrease]

State	2000	2005	2009	2010	Percent change 2009–2010	State	2000	2005	2009	2010	Percent change 2009–2010
U.S....	**143.7**	**216.0**	**193.9**	**185.7**	**–4.2**	MO.....	150.0	197.6	193.8	181.8	–6.2
AL	142.2	182.1	197.4	176.9	–10.4	MT.....	179.5	276.9	305.7	288.5	–5.6
AK	136.5	207.6	217.0	222.9	2.7	NE	161.9	194.0	197.7	189.6	–4.1
AZ	154.9	300.7	198.6	172.6	–13.1	NV	128.0	270.0	135.0	126.1	–6.6
AR	141.2	184.9	190.7	175.2	–8.1	NH	146.7	239.0	207.0	200.4	–3.2
CA	122.8	278.5	168.1	159.2	–5.3	NJ	133.0	253.2	226.2	222.7	–1.5
CO.....	216.4	270.5	270.3	266.3	–1.5	NM.....	145.3	214.6	224.7	213.1	–5.2
CT	117.4	194.5	176.9	170.2	–3.8	NY	128.6	214.5	211.2	208.8	–1.2
DE	121.1	208.4	194.8	194.0	–0.4	NC	146.1	182.3	192.2	185.8	–3.3
DC	135.4	324.2	327.2	333.7	2.0	ND	138.2	192.2	217.0	226.5	4.4
FL	139.3	295.9	188.5	175.7	–6.8	OH	148.2	175.0	160.6	154.1	–4.0
GA	151.2	190.5	174.4	154.8	–11.2	OK	143.8	177.4	195.5	193.2	–1.2
HI	92.0	204.3	180.8	174.7	–3.3	OR	184.0	297.0	284.3	256.1	–9.9
ID......	154.2	228.3	225.8	189.6	–16.0	PA	121.4	190.3	194.0	189.2	–2.5
IL	145.5	203.8	186.6	181.5	–2.7	RI......	119.6	234.5	195.4	190.4	–2.5
IN......	142.0	165.4	160.6	159.2	–0.9	SC	144.7	184.5	191.0	179.8	–5.9
IA	157.2	191.2	198.0	195.1	–1.4	SD	160.4	209.4	226.2	220.9	–2.4
KS	152.9	187.2	196.7	191.8	–2.5	TN	146.8	185.4	190.8	183.9	–3.7
KY	150.1	183.9	190.2	189.1	–0.6	TX	142.9	172.2	191.4	188.0	–1.8
LA	156.3	211.9	231.4	227.4	–1.7	UT	194.2	255.9	266.5	249.1	–6.5
ME	133.8	221.8	211.9	209.8	–1.0	VT	126.3	206.1	208.4	205.5	–1.4
MD.....	122.0	253.0	215.4	211.2	–1.9	VA	130.9	232.9	221.5	209.6	–5.4
MA.....	157.1	254.0	221.7	221.1	–0.3	WA.....	154.4	242.4	241.9	224.7	–7.1
MI......	173.5	202.4	150.4	145.3	–3.4	WV.....	137.0	178.0	188.0	188.0	(–Z)
MN.....	172.2	253.4	219.2	209.7	–4.3	WI......	166.4	223.4	214.5	209.4	–2.4
MS.....	142.4	177.6	179.8	173.7	–3.4	WY.....	170.0	258.3	288.9	280.1	–3.0

Z Less than 0.05 percent.

Source: Federal Housing Finance Agency, *Housing Price Index, 4th quarter 2010*. See also <http://www.fhfa.gov/Default.aspx?Page=87>.

Table 730. Average Prices of Selected Fuels and Electricity: 1990 to 2010

[In dollars per unit, except electricity, in cents per kWh. Represents price to end-users, except as noted]

Item	Unit	1990	2000	2003	2004	2005	2006	2007	2008	2009	2010
Crude oil, composite [1]	Barrel........	22.22	28.26	28.53	36.98	50.24	60.24	67.94	94.74	59.29	76.69
Motor gasoline: [2]											
Unleaded regular	Gallon	1.16	1.51	1.59	1.88	2.30	2.59	2.80	3.27	2.35	2.79
Unleaded premium	Gallon	1.35	1.69	1.78	2.07	2.49	2.81	3.03	3.52	2.61	3.05
No. 2 heating oil	Gallon	0.73	0.93	0.93	1.17	1.71	1.98	2.24	2.99	1.96	2.46
No. 2 diesel fuel	Gallon	0.73	0.94	0.94	1.24	1.79	2.10	2.27	3.15	1.83	2.31
Propane, consumer grade...	Gallon	0.75	0.60	0.58	0.84	1.09	1.36	1.49	1.89	1.22	1.48
Residual fuel oil	Gallon	0.44	0.60	0.70	0.74	1.05	1.22	1.37	1.96	1.34	1.71
Natural gas, residential	1,000 cu/ft	5.80	7.76	9.63	10.75	12.70	13.73	13.08	13.89	12.14	11.20
Electricity, residential	kWh	7.83	8.24	8.72	8.95	9.45	10.40	10.65	11.26	11.51	11.58

[1] Refiner acquisition cost. [2] Average, all service.

Source: U.S. Energy Information Administration, "Monthly Energy Review," April 2011. See also <http://www.eia.gov/totalenergy/data/monthly/>.

Table 731. Retail Gasoline Prices—Selected Areas: 2000 to 2010

[In dollars per gallon. Prices are annual averages]

Area	Regular				Midgrade				Premium			
	2000	2005	2009	2010	2000	2005	2009	2010	2000	2005	2009	2010
Boston, MA	(NA)	2.26	2.31	2.74	(NA)	2.36	2.43	2.87	(NA)	2.46	2.54	2.98
Chicago, IL........	1.57	2.32	2.46	2.94	1.67	2.42	2.57	3.05	1.78	2.52	2.68	3.16
Cleveland, OH......	(NA)	2.22	2.33	2.75	(NA)	2.32	2.43	2.86	(NA)	2.43	2.54	2.96
Denver, CO	1.54	2.24	2.23	2.65	1.67	2.35	2.36	2.77	1.78	2.45	2.47	2.89
Houston, TX........	1.45	2.17	2.17	2.59	1.56	2.27	2.32	2.74	1.65	2.37	2.44	2.87
Los Angeles, CA	1.62	2.49	2.69	3.11	1.72	2.59	2.79	3.21	1.81	2.68	2.89	3.31
Miami, FL..........	(NA)	2.39	2.45	2.86	(NA)	2.49	2.60	3.01	(NA)	2.59	2.70	3.11
New York, NY.......	1.63	2.30	2.37	2.81	1.73	2.42	2.51	2.96	1.80	2.51	2.62	3.07
San Francisco, CA...	1.88	2.48	2.69	3.12	1.98	2.59	2.81	3.23	2.09	2.69	2.91	3.34
Seattle, WA	(NA)	2.36	2.56	3.00	(NA)	2.47	2.68	3.12	(NA)	2.58	2.78	3.23

NA Not available.

Source: U.S. Energy Information Administration, *Weekly U.S. Retail Gasoline Prices*, Gasoline Historical Data. See also <http://www.eia.gov/oil_gas/petroleum/data_publications/wrgp/mogas_history.html>.

Table 732. Weekly Food Cost of a Nutritious Diet by Type of Family and Individual: 2009 and 2010

[In dollars, As of December. Assumes that food for all meals and snacks is purchased at the store and prepared at home. See source for details on estimation procedures]

Family type	Thrifty plan 2009	Thrifty plan 2010	Low-cost plan 2009	Low-cost plan 2010	Moderate plan 2009	Moderate plan 2010	Liberal plan 2009	Liberal plan 2010
FAMILIES								
Family of two:								
19 to 50 years	79.80	81.10	101.70	103.40	126.70	128.40	158.60	160.80
51 to 70 years	75.70	76.90	97.60	99.20	120.50	122.60	145.00	148.00
Family of four:								
Couple, 19 to 50 years and children—								
2 to 3 and 4 to 5 years	116.20	118.10	147.50	150.20	182.70	185.50	226.30	229.90
6 to 8 and 9 to 11 years	133.40	135.60	173.40	176.60	217.50	221.00	264.10	268.50
INDIVIDUALS [1]								
Child:								
1 year	19.80	20.10	26.30	26.80	30.20	30.60	36.40	37.10
2 to 3 years	21.50	21.70	26.90	27.50	32.70	33.30	39.70	40.50
4 to 5 years	22.20	22.70	28.10	28.70	34.80	35.50	42.40	43.30
6 to 8 years	28.30	28.80	38.30	39.20	47.30	48.20	55.70	56.90
9 to 11 years	32.50	33.00	42.60	43.40	55.00	56.10	64.20	65.50
Male:								
12 to 13 years	34.60	35.10	48.70	49.50	60.70	61.70	71.50	72.70
14 to 18 years	35.60	36.20	50.10	50.80	62.90	63.80	71.90	73.40
19 to 50 years	38.40	39.00	49.50	50.30	62.10	62.90	76.10	77.10
51 to 70 years	35.10	35.60	46.80	47.60	57.50	58.60	69.70	71.10
71 years and over	35.30	35.80	46.30	47.00	57.70	58.50	71.00	71.90
Female:								
12 to 13 years	34.80	35.30	42.20	42.90	50.90	51.90	61.70	63.00
14 to 18 years	34.30	34.80	42.50	43.10	51.50	52.00	63.20	63.90
19 to 50 years	34.10	34.70	43.00	43.70	53.10	53.80	68.00	69.00
51 to 70 years	33.70	34.30	41.90	42.50	52.10	52.90	62.10	63.50
71 years and over	33.30	33.80	41.50	42.10	51.70	52.50	62.30	63.40

[1] The costs given are for individuals in 4-person families. For individuals in other size families, the following adjustments are suggested: 1-person, add 20 percent; 2-person, add 10 percent; 3-person, add 5 percent; 5- or 6-person, subtract 5 percent; 7- or more person, subtract 10 percent.

Source: U.S. Department of Agriculture, *Official USDA Food Plans: Cost of Food at Home at Four Levels*, monthly. See also <http://www.cnpp.usda.gov/Publications/FoodPlans/2010/CostofFoodDec10.pdf>.

Table 733. Food—Retail Prices of Selected Items: 2000 to 2010

[In dollars per pound, except as indicated. As of December. See Appendix III]

Food	2000	2009	2010	Food	2000	2009	2010
Cereals and bakery products:				**Fresh fruits and vegetables:**			
Flour, white, all purpose	0.28	0.46	0.44	Apples, Red Delicious	0.82	1.11	1.20
Rice, white, lg. grain, raw	(NA)	0.75	0.73	Bananas	0.49	0.57	0.59
Spaghetti and macaroni	0.88	1.17	1.19	Oranges, navel	0.62	0.93	1.02
Bread, white, pan	0.99	1.39	1.39	Grapefruit	0.58	0.88	0.99
Bread, whole wheat	1.36	1.76	1.88	Grapes, Thompson seedless	2.36	3.14	2.87
Beef:				Lemons	1.11	1.60	1.60
Ground beef, 100% beef	1.63	2.19	2.38	Pears, Anjou	(NA)	1.28	1.42
Ground chuck, 100% beef	1.98	2.83	2.93	Potatoes, white	0.35	0.56	0.58
Ground beef, lean and extra lean	2.33	3.39	3.49	Lettuce, iceberg	0.85	1.19	0.99
Round steak, USDA Choice	3.28	4.18	4.30	Tomatoes, field grown	1.57	1.96	1.59
Sirloin steak, boneless	4.81	5.68	6.07	**Processed fruits and vegetables:**			
Pork:				Orange juice, frozen concentrate,			
Bacon, sliced	3.03	3.57	4.16	12 oz. can, per 16 oz	1.88	2.53	2.46
Chops, center cut, bone-in	3.46	3.29	3.58	**Sugar and sweets:**			
Ham, boneless, excluding				Sugar, white, all sizes	0.41	0.60	0.64
canned	2.75	3.10	3.47	Sugar, white, 33–80 oz. pkg	0.40	0.57	0.62
Poultry, fish, and eggs:				**Fats and oils:**			
Chicken, fresh, whole	1.08	1.27	1.28	Margarine, stick	(NA)	1.11	1.12
Chicken legs, bone-in	1.26	1.46	1.48	Margarine, tubs, soft	0.84	1.66	1.62
Turkey, frozen, whole	0.99	1.37	1.38	Peanut butter, creamy, all sizes	1.96	2.10	1.99
Eggs, Grade A, large, (dozen)	0.96	1.77	1.79				
Dairy products:				**Nonalcoholic beverages:**			
Milk, fresh, whole, fortified				Coffee, 100% ground roast,			
(per gal.)	2.79	3.11	3.32	all sizes	3.21	3.67	4.15
Butter, salted, grade AA, stick	2.80	2.67	3.42				
American processed cheese	3.69	3.86	3.80	**Other prepared foods:**			
Cheddar cheese, natural	3.76	4.55	4.93	Potato chips, per 16 oz	3.44	4.65	4.74
Ice cream, prepack., bulk, reg.							
(1/2 gal.)	3.66	4.23	4.58				

NA Not available.

Source: U.S. Bureau of Labor Statistics, *CPI Detailed Report*, monthly, <http://www.bls.gov/cpi/cpi_dr.htm>. See also *Monthly Labor Review*, <http://www.bls.gov/opub/mlr/welcome.htm>.

Table 734. Producer Price Indexes by Stage of Processing: 1990 to 2010

Table 734. Producer Price Indexes by Stage of Processing: 1990 to 2010

[1982 = 100, except as indicated. Minus sign (–) indicates decrease. For information on producer prices, see Bureau of Labor Statistics, <http://stats.bls.gov/opub/hom/homch14_itc.htm>, and summary in Notes sheet. Also see Appendix III]

	Crude materials				Inter- mediate materi- als and supplies, compo- nents	Finished goods		Consumer foods		Finished consumer goods, excluding food
Year	Total	Food- stuffs and feed- stuffs	Fuel	Crude nonfood materials, except fuel		Con- sumer goods	Capital equip- ment	Crude	Pro- cessed	
1990........	108.9	113.1	84.8	107.3	114.5	118.2	122.9	123.0	124.4	115.3
1995........	102.7	105.8	72.1	105.8	124.9	125.6	136.7	118.8	129.8	124.0
1998........	96.8	103.9	86.7	84.5	123.0	128.9	137.6	127.2	134.8	126.4
1999........	98.2	98.7	91.2	91.1	123.2	132.0	137.6	125.5	135.9	130.5
2000........	120.6	100.2	136.9	118.0	129.2	138.2	138.8	123.5	138.3	138.4
2001........	121.0	106.1	151.4	101.5	129.7	141.5	139.7	127.7	142.4	141.4
2002........	108.1	99.5	117.3	101.0	127.8	139.4	139.1	128.5	141.0	138.8
2003........	135.3	113.5	185.7	116.9	133.7	145.3	139.5	130.0	147.2	144.7
2004........	159.0	127.0	211.4	149.2	142.6	151.7	141.4	138.2	153.9	150.9
2005........	182.2	122.7	279.7	176.7	154.0	160.4	144.6	140.2	156.9	161.9
2006........	184.8	119.3	241.5	210.0	164.0	166.0	146.9	151.3	157.1	169.2
2007........	207.1	146.7	236.8	238.7	170.7	173.5	149.5	170.2	166.7	175.6
2008........	251.8	163.4	298.3	308.5	188.3	186.3	153.8	175.5	178.6	189.1
2009........	175.2	134.5	166.3	211.1	172.5	179.1	156.7	157.8	177.3	179.4
2010[1].....	212.0	152.3	187.4	280.7	183.6	189.2	157.3	172.6	183.4	190.5
PERCENT CHANGE [2]										
1990........	5.6	1.7	–0.6	12.0	2.2	5.4	3.5	2.8	4.9	5.9
1995........	0.9	–0.7	–12.5	9.1	5.4	1.9	1.9	6.7	1.5	2.0
1998........	–12.9	–7.4	–14.4	–18.4	–2.1	–1.0	–0.4	0.5	–0.2	–1.4
1999........	1.4	–5.0	5.2	7.8	0.2	2.4	0.0	–1.3	0.8	3.2
2000........	22.8	1.5	50.1	29.5	4.9	4.7	0.9	–1.6	1.8	6.1
2001........	0.3	5.9	10.6	–14.0	0.4	2.4	0.6	3.4	3.0	2.2
2002........	–10.7	–6.2	–22.5	–0.5	–1.5	–1.5	–0.4	0.6	–1.0	–1.8
2003........	25.2	14.1	58.3	15.7	4.6	4.2	0.3	1.2	4.4	4.3
2004........	17.5	11.9	13.8	27.6	6.7	4.4	1.4	6.3	4.6	4.3
2005........	14.6	–3.4	32.3	18.4	8.0	5.7	2.3	1.4	1.9	7.3
2006........	1.4	–2.8	–13.7	18.8	6.5	3.5	1.6	7.9	0.1	4.5
2007........	12.1	23.0	–1.9	13.7	4.1	4.5	1.8	12.5	6.1	3.8
2008........	21.6	11.4	26.0	29.2	10.3	7.4	2.9	3.1	7.1	7.7
2009........	–30.4	–17.7	–44.3	–31.6	–8.4	–3.9	1.9	–10.1	–0.7	–5.1
2010[1].....	21.0	13.2	12.7	33.0	6.4	5.6	0.4	9.4	3.4	6.2

[1] Preliminary. [2] Change from immediate prior year. 1990, change from 1989.

Source: U.S. Bureau of Labor Statistics, *Producer Price Indexes*, monthly and annual. See also *Monthly Labor Review*, <http://www.bls.gov/opub/mlr/welcome.htm>.

Table 735. Commodity Research Bureau Futures Price Index: 1990 to 2010

[1967 = 100. Index computed daily. Represents unweighted geometric average of commodity futures prices (through 6 months forward) of 17 major commodity futures markets. Represents end of year index]

Commodity	1990	1995	2000	2002	2003	2004	2005	2006	2007	2008	2009	2010
All commodities......	**222.6**	**243.2**	**227.8**	**234.5**	**255.3**	**283.9**	**347.9**	**394.9**	**476.1**	**363.1**	**484.4**	**629.5**
Softs [1]	276.0	354.4	254.4	303.7	250.5	343.5	420.5	475.9	467.5	487.2	(NA)	(NA)
Industrials	245.5	272.5	211.0	176.6	256.6	232.1	302.5	368.8	418.3	475.4	(NA)	(NA)
Grains and oilseeds [2].....	171.2	218.6	174.9	188.2	225.8	177.0	193.8	279.1	427.0	545.5	(NA)	(NA)
Energy................	246.0	180.0	355.8	320.7	358.7	457.3	705.3	591.6	825.1	1,263.2	(NA)	(NA)
Oilseeds [3]	223.6	277.5	(3)	(3)	(3)	(3)	(3)	(3)	(3)	(3)	(3)	(3)
Livestock and meats	226.2	192.4	253.6	251.0	237.8	303.6	300.3	294.6	297.7	337.0	(NA)	(NA)
Metals (precious)........	257.8	276.0	265.7	289.1	364.1	396.6	478.1	611.9	773.6	894.6	(NA)	(NA)

NA Not available. [1] Prior to 1997, reported as imported. Softs include commodities that are grown and not mined such as coffee, cocoa, lumber, cotton, and sugar. [2] Prior to 1997, reported as grains. [3] Incorporated into grains and oilseeds beginning 1997.

Source: Commodity Research Bureau (CRB), Chicago, IL, *CRB Commodity Index Report*, weekly (copyright).
See also <http://www.crbtrader.com>.

Table 736. Indexes of Spot Primary Market Prices: 1990 to 2010

[1967 = 100. Represents unweighted geometric average of price quotations of 23 commodities. Computed daily and therefore much more sensitive to changes in market conditions than a monthly producer price index]

Item and number	1990	1995	2000	2002	2003	2004	2005	2006	2007	2008	2009	2010
All commodities (23)......	**258.1**	**289.1**	**224.0**	**244.3**	**283.6**	**293.0**	**303.3**	**362.4**	**413.4**	**313.0**	**424.2**	**520.3**
Foodstuffs (10)	206.4	236.4	184.7	238.1	250.2	256.0	241.7	276.0	335.9	294.2	344.7	440.3
Raw industrials (13)	301.2	332.2	255.8	248.6	309.1	321.5	354.7	437.3	477.0	326.5	489.4	583.8
Livestock and products (5)...	292.7	307.4	265.5	317.8	365.9	365.0	378.6	402.6	310.8	407.6	528.0	
Metals (5)	283.2	300.6	214.0	184.5	276.7	357.7	440.9	693.9	811.9	390.9	809.1	1,006.2
Textiles and fibers (4)	257.6	274.3	245.7	230.2	255.2	237.9	252.5	254.4	267.5	241.3	294.0	342.1
Fats and oils (4)	188.7	226.7	163.6	234.0	297.2	262.6	223.4	273.9	363.4	268.0	339.7	478.3

Source: Commodity Research Bureau, Chicago, IL, *CRB Commodity Index Report*, weekly (copyright).
See also <http://www.crbtrader.com>.

U.S. Census Bureau, Statistical Abstract of the United States: 2012

Table 737. Producer Price Indexes by Stage of Processing and Commodity: 1990 to 2010

[1982=100, except as indicated. See Appendix III]

Stage of processing	1990	1995	2000	2005	2007	2008	2009	2010 [1]
Finished goods	**119.2**	**127.9**	**138.0**	**155.7**	**166.6**	**177.1**	**172.5**	**179.9**
Finished consumer goods	**118.2**	**125.6**	**138.2**	**160.4**	**173.5**	**186.3**	**179.1**	**189.2**
Finished consumer foods	**124.4**	**129.0**	**137.2**	**155.7**	**167.0**	**178.3**	**175.5**	**182.5**
Fresh fruits and melons	118.1	85.8	91.4	102.8	123.4	122.9	110.4	123.9
Fresh and dry vegetables	118.1	144.4	126.7	142.6	165.5	172.3	162.2	178.5
Eggs for fresh use (Dec. 1991 = 100)	(NA)	86.3	84.9	79.6	132.6	152.4	123.3	123.4
Bakery products	141.0	164.3	182.3	201.1	216.6	237.5	245.8	244.9
Milled rice	102.5	113.1	101.2	120.1	155.0	251.9	205.8	183.7
Pasta products (June 1985 = 100)	114.1	125.0	121.6	127.9	136.3	183.5	180.3	170.5
Beef and veal	116.0	100.9	113.7	147.4	146.1	153.7	142.4	157.7
Pork	119.8	101.5	113.4	131.9	133.3	130.7	115.7	143.1
Processed young chickens	111.0	113.5	110.4	136.2	139.0	143.2	147.7	148.7
Processed turkeys	107.6	104.9	98.7	105.1	110.2	120.3	119.9	131.9
Finfish and shellfish	147.2	170.8	198.1	222.6	242.8	255.4	250.9	271.8
Dairy products	117.2	119.7	133.7	154.5	175.7	182.7	157.1	174.1
Processed fruits and vegetables	124.7	122.4	128.6	140.4	157.4	166.8	176.2	176.5
Soft drinks	122.3	133.1	144.1	159.1	166.7	174.9	181.8	184.1
Roasted coffee	113.0	146.5	133.5	151.1	163.7	179.0	179.2	189.5
Shortening and cooking oils	123.2	142.5	132.4	176.7	211.7	293.2	225.6	234.3
Finished consumer goods excluding foods	**115.3**	**124.0**	**138.4**	**161.9**	**175.6**	**189.1**	**179.4**	**190.5**
Alcoholic beverages	117.2	128.5	140.6	158.5	160.2	166.0	172.0	175.1
Apparel	117.5	124.2	127.4	125.6	127.0	128.0	129.3	129.4
Women's/girls/infants' cut & sew apparel (Dec. 2003 = 100)	(NA)	(NA)	(NA)	100.3	101.1	101.1	102.1	101.7
Men's and boy's cut and sew apparel Dec. 2003 = 100)	(NA)	(NA)	(NA)	98.7	98.6	99.7	101.2	101.3
Textile house furnishings	109.5	119.5	122.0	122.9	125.3	127.0	129.1	131.9
Footwear	125.6	139.2	144.9	148.1	151.6	156.9	159.9	162.4
Residential electric power (Dec. 1990 = 100)	(NA)	111.8	110.8	126.4	138.8	146.1	150.5	154.9
Residential gas (Dec. 1990 = 100)	(NA)	104.4	135.5	216.8	224.9	250.6	205.1	201.9
Gasoline	78.7	63.7	94.6	168.6	221.9	263.0	178.4	225.2
Fuel oil No. 2	73.3	56.6	93.5	178.4	223.7	305.2	162.7	207.7
Soaps and synthetic detergents	117.7	122.9	128.2	134.6	144.9	153.8	161.4	161.4
Cosmetics and other toilet preparations	121.6	129.0	137.4	143.0	147.6	147.9	148.1	149.9
Tires, tubes, and tread	96.8	100.2	93.0	108.1	118.5	128.0	131.0	138.2
Sanitary papers and health products	135.3	144.4	146.7	154.6	161.8	171.5	179.7	180.7
Sale of books	153.4	185.0	218.2	264.0	285.0	296.5	306.9	317.0
Household furniture	125.1	141.8	152.7	166.5	174.6	181.0	186.9	187.4
Floor coverings	119.0	123.7	129.6	146.4	156.6	160.6	167.5	169.4
Household appliances	110.8	112.4	107.3	103.3	105.2	107.2	111.1	110.4
Home electronic equipment	82.7	78.9	71.8	62.6	58.2	56.7	53.6	52.7
Household glassware	132.5	153.2	166.0	174.7	177.0	190.7	198.1	200.2
Household flatware	122.1	138.3	142.6	147.7	186.8	194.7	193.0	(NA)
Lawn and garden equipment, except tractors . . .	123.0	130.4	132.0	134.5	137.0	140.4	142.3	141.9
Passenger cars	118.3	134.1	132.8	131.8	126.2	128.9	130.9	129.0
Toys, games, and children's vehicles	118.1	124.3	121.9	127.0	131.0	134.3	143.1	140.7
Sporting and athletic goods	112.6	122.0	126.1	124.6	129.9	129.8	132.2	133.6
Tobacco products	221.4	231.3	397.2	457.8	489.1	508.8	539.3	570.5
Mobile homes	117.5	145.6	161.3	200.8	211.0	218.7	222.3	228.5
Jewelry, platinum, and karat gold	122.8	127.8	127.2	138.6	153.2	164.7	169.7	187.5
Costume jewelry and novelties	125.3	135.1	141.6	153.5	156.7	159.6	158.7	158.9
Capital Equipment	**122.9**	**136.7**	**138.8**	**144.6**	**149.5**	**153.8**	**156.7**	**157.3**
Agricultural machinery and equipment	121.7	142.9	153.7	174.7	184.3	192.9	199.9	203.4
Construction machinery and equipment	121.6	136.7	148.6	168.3	179.6	185.3	191.0	191.4
Metal cutting machine tools	129.8	148.0	161.9	155.1	165.8	170.3	173.8	174.6
Metal forming machine tools	128.7	145.7	161.8	178.9	184.4	192.5	198.5	200.3
Pumps, compressors, and equipment	119.2	139.4	154.1	178.5	195.0	205.4	212.6	214.9
Electronic computers (Dec. 2004 = 100)	(NA)	850.1	261.6	85.5	51.6	40.8	34.0	30.3
Textile machinery	128.8	146.7	156.2	160.5	162.5	164.9	166.3	166.0
Paper industries machinery (June 1982 = 100) . .	134.8	151.0	164.7	178.1	183.4	188.5	193.7	197.2
Printing trades machinery	124.9	133.6	142.1	144.3	150.5	152.7	157.1	155.4
Transformers and power regulators	120.9	128.9	135.8	150.3	194.9	216.2	210.6	223.0
Communication/related equip.(Dec. 1985 = 100) .	106.1	112.1	110.6	102.5	103.2	104.8	105.7	105.8
X-ray and electromedical equipment	109.8	111.8	101.5	95.7	92.8	91.6	90.1	89.5
Mining machinery and equipment	121.0	135.6	146.1	175.9	190.9	205.8	217.3	221.5
Office and store machines and equipment	109.5	111.5	112.7	115.1	114.6	122.1	123.5	121.0
Commercial furniture	133.4	148.2	158.4	172.7	181.5	190.1	196.1	196.3
Light motor trucks	130.0	159.0	157.6	148.4	145.3	146.0	151.8	153.3
Heavy motor trucks	120.3	144.1	148.0	162.4	177.2	182.2	190.3	195.7
Truck trailers	110.8	131.7	139.4	157.1	169.4	177.0	177.7	181.5
Civilian aircraft (Dec. 1985 = 100)	115.3	141.8	159.6	202.2	219.6	230.2	235.4	238.0
Ships (Dec. 1985 = 100)	110.1	132.8	146.9	176.6	192.1	199.4	210.0	215.2
Railroad equipment	118.6	134.8	135.7	160.4	176.4	180.2	181.9	184.4
Intermediate materials, supplies, and components . . .	**114.5**	**124.9**	**129.2**	**154.0**	**170.7**	**188.3**	**172.5**	**183.6**
Intermediate foods and feeds	**113.3**	**114.8**	**111.7**	**133.8**	**154.4**	**181.6**	**166.0**	**171.8**
Flour	103.6	102.3	103.8	133.6	178.4	239.8	182.9	183.7
Refined sugar	122.7	119.3	110.6	124.9	132.6	137.2	157.8	185.4
Soft drink beverage bases (December 1985 = 100)	126.2	148.3	167.1	180.4	196.0	210.3	223.5	223.1
Prepared animal feeds	107.4	109.1	102.9	115.6	142.7	182.7	175.2	171.6

See footnotes at end of table.

U.S. Census Bureau, Statistical Abstract of the United States: 2012

Table 737. Producer Price Indexes by Stage of Processing and Commodity: 1990 to 2010—Con.

[1982=100, except as indicated. See Appendix III]

Stage of processing	1990	1995	2000	2005	2007	2008	2009	2010 [1]
Intermediate materials less foods and feeds	**114.5**	**125.5**	**130.1**	**155.1**	**171.5**	**188.7**	**173.0**	**184.5**
Synthetic fibers	106.7	109.4	107.2	112.3	114.2	116.5	113.3	111.5
Processed yarns and threads	112.6	112.8	107.9	111.7	116.9	123.7	119.9	128.0
Leather	177.5	191.4	182.2	219.6	230.6	234.3	221.1	232.3
Liquefied petroleum gas	77.4	65.1	127.1	244.7	316.1	375.9	224.7	309.8
Commercial electric power	115.3	131.7	131.5	149.8	165.4	173.3	178.6	183.3
Industrial electric power	119.6	130.8	131.5	156.2	180.4	189.1	190.6	193.3
Commercial natural gas (Dec. 1990 = 100)	(NA)	96.5	134.7	232.5	235.6	272.1	211.9	208.6
Industrial natural gas (Dec. 1990 = 100)	(NA)	90.9	139.0	249.4	242.3	283.1	210.2	202.2
Natural gas to electric utilities (Dec. 1990 = 100)	(NA)	87.7	120.7	204.0	186.0	203.4	164.0	174.9
Jet fuels	76.0	55.0	88.5	169.6	211.2	300.1	169.3	225.3
No. 2 Diesel fuel	74.1	57.0	93.3	189.1	235.5	324.9	180.6	233.2
Residual fuel	57.7	52.6	84.7	148.9	173.4	229.7	156.6	213.3
Industrial chemicals	113.2	128.4	129.1	188.5	226.4	274.6	234.1	268.7
Prepared paint	124.8	142.1	160.8	187.9	208.8	223.0	236.4	236.8
Fats and oils, inedible	88.1	126.9	70.1	146.9	189.4	288.3	210.3	243.7
Mixed fertilizers	103.3	111.1	112.4	138.9	161.2	249.2	192.8	177.3
Plastic resins and materials	124.1	143.5	141.6	193.0	195.9	215.0	190.8	211.8
Synthetic rubber	111.9	126.3	119.1	151.3	169.3	206.6	185.9	215.8
Plastic construction products	117.2	133.8	135.8	158.8	179.2	185.6	186.2	190.8
Unsupported plastic film, sheet, and shapes	119.0	135.6	133.2	164.8	176.0	194.2	191.7	200.5
Plastic parts and components for manufacturing	112.9	115.9	117.3	119.8	130.0	132.8	135.8	135.7
Softwood lumber	123.8	178.5	178.6	203.6	170.5	156.3	141.4	160.9
Hardwood lumber	131.0	167.0	185.9	196.6	192.4	184.5	171.2	187.3
Plywood	114.2	165.3	157.6	186.8	176.1	174.7	163.7	176.5
Paper	128.8	159.0	149.8	159.6	169.3	184.3	179.6	182.2
Paperboard	135.7	183.1	176.7	175.5	201.7	217.9	207.2	225.3
Paper boxes and containers	129.9	163.8	172.6	183.7	197.8	208.3	211.9	219.6
Building paper and board	112.2	144.9	138.8	184.9	155.2	163.9	156.5	168.2
Commercial printing (June 1982 = 100)	128.0	144.5	155.2	161.6	166.0	169.2	167.8	168.2
Foundry and forge shop products	117.2	129.3	136.5	156.2	170.7	189.6	185.2	191.4
Primary nonferrous metals	133.4	146.8	113.6	158.2	268.6	269.1	177.6	209.2
Nonferrous wire and cable	142.6	151.5	143.7	169.4	238.7	249.2	222.4	257.7
Metal containers	114.0	117.2	106.8	123.9	133.4	144.0	155.4	159.7
Hardware	125.9	141.1	151.2	168.0	179.7	189.9	194.0	194.0
Plumbing fixtures and brass fittings	144.3	166.0	180.4	197.6	220.6	226.7	228.9	231.4
Heating equipment	131.6	147.5	155.6	179.9	195.5	208.8	219.1	221.4
Fabricated ferrous wire products (June 1982 = 100)	114.6	125.7	130.0	157.1	166.7	200.7	200.0	203.5
Mechanical power transmission equipment	125.3	146.9	163.9	189.5	205.2	219.7	231.0	232.0
Air conditioning and refrigeration equipment	122.1	130.2	135.3	146.2	157.3	162.7	164.7	163.8
Ball and roller bearings	130.6	152.0	168.8	187.1	199.8	211.9	222.8	227.0
Wiring devices	132.2	147.2	152.9	176.6	194.5	206.4	206.8	211.3
Motors, generators, motor generator sets	132.9	143.9	146.2	157.8	172.9	181.7	187.0	190.6
Switchgear and switchboard equipment	124.4	140.3	153.0	170.2	188.5	195.5	201.0	205.5
Electronic components and accessories	118.4	113.6	97.1	87.0	82.3	77.0	75.4	73.4
Internal combustion engines	120.2	135.6	143.8	147.7	154.7	157.2	162.3	161.9
Flat glass	107.5	113.2	109.7	111.0	114.2	115.9	115.0	111.3
Cement	103.7	128.1	150.1	176.4	209.7	209.7	206.8	193.9
Concrete products	113.5	129.4	147.8	177.2	203.5	210.6	214.0	210.8
Asphalt felts and coatings	97.1	100.0	104.1	130.8	145.7	187.2	220.6	222.7
Gypsum products	105.2	154.5	201.4	229.6	233.0	213.2	213.8	206.8
Glass containers	120.4	130.5	127.4	146.4	162.0	171.8	178.7	181.2
Motor vehicle parts	111.2	116.0	113.6	113.1	117.9	119.7	120.7	121.7
Aircraft engines and engine parts (Dec. 1985 = 100)	113.5	132.8	141.0	165.9	178.9	185.9	193.1	197.5
Photographic supplies	127.6	126.8	125.2	120.1	122.9	125.5	127.8	124.4
Medical/surgical/personal aid devices	127.3	141.3	146.0	159.2	163.1	165.7	167.5	168.7
Crude materials for further processing	**108.9**	**102.7**	**120.6**	**182.2**	**207.1**	**251.8**	**175.2**	**212.0**
Crude foodstuffs and feedstuffs	113.1	105.8	100.2	122.7	146.7	163.4	134.5	152.3
Wheat	87.6	118.6	80.3	102.7	172.1	235.1	149.3	157.4
Corn	100.9	109.0	76.4	75.9	141.5	199.1	146.9	160.8
Slaughter cattle	122.5	99.5	104.1	131.5	136.1	136.1	122.0	139.8
Slaughter hogs	94.1	70.2	72.7	82.7	76.1	78.1	68.9	92.6
Slaughter broilers/fryers	119.5	129.1	127.6	181.0	199.9	210.7	202.6	221.3
Slaughter turkeys	116.9	120.3	120.7	131.1	153.3	165.9	146.7	173.0
Fluid milk	100.8	93.6	92.0	113.5	143.3	137.2	95.9	121.5
Soybeans	100.8	102.2	83.4	102.6	137.9	203.9	175.9	177.1
Crude nonfood materials	101.5	96.8	130.4	223.4	246.3	313.9	197.5	249.0
Raw cotton	118.2	156.2	95.2	78.9	83.1	98.0	82.6	118.3
Coal	97.5	95.0	87.9	116.8	130.7	161.7	182.5	189.4
Natural gas	80.4	66.6	155.5	335.4	273.8	344.0	160.0	185.1
Crude petroleum	71.0	51.1	85.2	150.1	192.6	275.7	161.7	218.5
Logs and timber	142.8	220.4	196.4	197.4	217.1	216.7	187.8	213.8
Wastepaper	138.9	371.1	282.5	230.9	368.7	372.5	237.0	420.2
Iron ore	83.3	91.8	94.8	116.9	128.8	142.5	145.0	147.0
Iron and steel scrap	166.0	202.7	142.1	289.8	406.8	566.8	338.1	541.5
Nonferrous metal ores (Dec. 1983 = 100)	98.3	101.6	68.0	150.0	243.5	251.0	215.4	296.8
Copper base scrap	181.3	193.5	123.7	258.6	485.2	494.3	375.4	553.2
Aluminum base scrap	172.6	209.4	177.0	210.1	274.7	272.8	166.8	240.5
Construction sand, gravel, and crushed stone	125.4	142.3	163.1	195.8	232.4	247.7	259.1	262.2
Industrial sand	117.6	132.5	146.0	174.4	190.9	217.7	238.1	239.4

NA Not available. [1] Preliminary data.

Source: U.S. Bureau of Labor Statistics, *Producer Price Indexes*, monthly and annual. See also *Monthly Labor Review*, <http://www.bls.gov/opub/mlr/welcome.htm>. See also Monthly Labor Review at <http://www.bls.gov/opub/mlr/welcome.htm>. See also <http://www.bls.gov/ppi/>.

Table 738. Producer Price Indexes for the Net Output of Selected Industries: 2005 to 2010

[Indexes are based on selling prices reported by establishments of all sizes by probability sampling. Manufacturing industries selected by shipment value. N.e.c.= not elsewhere classified. See text, Section 22. See Appendix III]

Industry	NAICS code [1]	Index base [2]	2005	2007	2008	2009	2010 [3]
Logging industries	**113310**	**12/81**	**179.2**	**175.1**	**171.6**	**160.4**	**177.5**
Total mining industries	**21**	**12/84**	**201.0**	**220.1**	**274.7**	**178.2**	**214.7**
Crude petroleum & natural gas extraction	211111	06/02	253.5	261.5	349.2	187.6	238.3
Natural gas liquid extraction	211112	06/02	285.4	286.7	347.6	188.5	251.3
Bituminous coal & lignite surface mining	212111	12/01	111.9	120.9	140.4	149.1	156.7
Anthracite mining	212113	12/79	205.4	240.9	267.0	275.4	269.2
Iron ore mining	212210	12/84	115.7	127.5	141.0	143.5	145.5
Gold ore mining	212221	06/85	131.7	203.0	208.9	236.3	300.4
Copper ore & nickel ore mining	212234	06/88	200.8	397.8	401.7	297.1	414.3
Crushed and broken granite mining and quarrying	212313	12/83	217.3	279.3	305.1	329.1	329.5
Construction sand and gravel mining	212321	06/82	209.9	247.0	262.6	271.1	271.1
Clay and ceramic and refractory minerals mining	212325	06/84	148.3	163.4	174.2	184.5	188.7
Drilling oil and gas wells	213111	12/85	258.8	360.6	366.9	328.2	324.4
Nonmetallic minerals support activity (except fuels)	213115	06/85	127.5	140.2	146.0	148.7	148.7
Total manufacturing industries	**31–33**	**12/84**	**150.8**	**162.9**	**175.8**	**167.1**	**175.4**
Dog & cat food mfg	311111	12/85	145.8	155.2	175.3	186.2	186.5
Flour milling	311211	06/83	117.5	153.9	202.8	160.9	162.2
Rice milling	311212	06/84	102.1	129.2	209.6	170.8	152.5
Chocolate & confectionery mfg. from cacao beans	311320	06/83	157.5	166.0	181.1	194.0	198.4
Frozen fruit, juice, & vegetable mfg	311411	06/81	156.0	174.9	179.0	188.6	195.7
Frozen specialty food mfg	311412	12/82	143.6	145.5	154.1	160.3	160.0
Fruit and vegetable canning	311421	06/81	151.4	165.3	176.8	190.0	185.6
Fluid milk	311511	12/82	165.2	193.7	200.9	179.8	198.8
Ice cream and frozen dessert mfg	311520	06/83	168.2	177.7	184.5	186.1	187.3
Animal (except poultry) slaughtering	311611	12/80	141.0	142.7	149.6	135.1	157.3
Meat processed from carcasses	311612	12/82	136.6	139.5	144.7	144.2	153.3
Poultry processing	311615	12/81	135.3	139.5	145.0	148.3	150.0
Coffee and tea manufacturing	311920	06/81	161.0	173.8	189.4	191.8	199.1
Spice and extracts manufacturing	311942	12/03	99.1	102.3	108.5	115.0	115.2
Soft drinks manufacturing	312111	06/81	168.6	177.4	186.4	194.3	197.1
Bottled water manufacturing	312112	12/03	101.5	99.4	98.9	97.0	91.2
Breweries	312120	06/82	158.4	156.0	163.0	(NA)	177.2
Wineries	312130	12/83	144.8	155.7	159.3	162.3	161.8
Distilleries	312140	06/83	165.5	175.3	187.2	188.5	185.9
Tobacco stemming & redrying	312210	06/84	119.9	112.6	113.4	115.2	115.9
Cigarettes	312221	12/82	437.0	470.2	489.5	520.8	553.9
Men's/boys' cut & sew trouser/slack/jean mfg	315224	12/81	123.2	122.3	122.9	123.9	123.9
Women's/girls' cut & sew dress mfg	315233	12/80	123.7	120.8	123.0	124.6	123.7
Sawmills	321113	12/80	162.0	152.0	143.5	124.9	140.0
Wood preservation	321114	06/85	175.7	163.8	165.6	162.0	171.8
Hardwood veneer & plywood manufacturing	321211	06/85	146.2	151.1	153.0	151.5	152.3
Softwood veneer or plywood, mfg	321212	12/80	172.7	154.9	150.8	135.6	152.9
Wood window & door mfg	321911	12/03	103.1	107.3	107.7	109.2	110.5
Manufactured homes (mobile homes) mfg	321991	06/81	204.4	214.7	222.6	226.3	232.4
Paper (except newsprint) mills	322121	12/03	108.4	116.2	125.2	126.1	127.4
Newsprint mills	322122	12/03	115.7	106.8	119.4	103.9	103.5
Paperboard mills	322130	12/82	196.2	224.4	242.6	231.1	253.0
Book printing	323117	12/83	154.9	158.6	159.0	159.6	160.7
Petroleum refineries	324110	06/85	205.3	266.9	338.3	217.0	289.7
Petroleum lubricating oils and greases	324191	12/80	231.2	304.8	356.6	355.8	363.3
Industrial gas manufacturing	325120	12/03	118.3	123.3	140.9	129.1	127.2
Plastics material and resins manufacturing	325211	12/80	228.5	232.4	255.1	227.9	252.7
Synthetic rubber manufacturing	325212	06/81	150.6	170.2	214.3	203.3	236.5
Nitrogenous fertilizer manufacturing	325311	12/79	236.9	278.5	427.0	275.4	286.4
Phosphatic fertilizer manufacturing	325312	12/79	173.3	257.4	580.3	265.7	307.3
Pharmaceutical preparation mfg	325412	06/81	378.7	413.8	440.7	469.2	495.7
Plastics pipe and pipe fitting manufacturing	326122	06/93	171.9	197.2	215.0	203.0	216.7
Cement manufacturing	327310	06/82	175.2	208.4	207.8	204.3	193.2
Lime	327410	12/85	144.6	166.0	175.5	207.7	210.2
Steel investment foundries	331512	06/81	204.8	235.4	235.4	235.4	235.0
Steel foundries (except investment)	331513	06/81	160.1	183.7	193.4	191.4	198.3
Aluminum die-casting foundries	331521	06/91	116.4	126.4	133.0	119.4	127.3
Iron & steel forging	332111	12/83	128.1	140.4	150.9	148.6	150.8
Hand and edge tools, except machine tools and handsaws	332212	06/83	177.0	188.9	197.0	203.1	204.0
Saw blade & handsaw mfg	332213	06/83	146.0	152.8	158.1	165.1	162.1
Metal window and door manufacturing	332321	06/83	175.2	188.1	196.5	200.5	199.3
Sheetmetal work mfg	332322	12/82	165.6	176.8	187.6	182.5	183.7
Heating equipment (except warm air furnaces) mfg	333414	06/80	215.4	231.2	245.7	255.3	256.7
Laboratory apparatus and furniture	339111	12/91	148.1	158.8	165.3	(NA)	169.9
Surgical and medical instrument mfg	339112	06/82	135.2	134.5	136.3	137.4	138.8
Services industries:							
Beer, wine, and liquor stores	445310	06/00	111.0	113.2	120.6	119.8	125.4
Gasoline stations with convenience stores	447110	12/03	104.3	123.0	135.1	129.7	138.9
Scheduled passenger air transportation	481111	12/89	217.1	234.5	257.1	236.1	254.6
Scheduled freight air transportation	481112	12/03	104.9	109.0	127.8	119.1	129.7
General freight trucking, long-distance	484121	12/03	108.6	113.5	119.5	111.0	113.3
Pipeline transportation of crude oil	486110	06/86	125.5	138.9	152.0	156.3	201.8
Pipeline transportation of refined petroleum products	486910	06/86	120.3	131.7	139.2	147.3	153.1
Marine cargo handling	488320	12/91	115.1	122.8	124.7	127.6	131.8
United States Postal Service	491110	06/89	155.0	171.9	178.9	185.0	187.7
Nursing care facilities	623110	12/94	161.4	174.0	180.9	186.9	190.5

NA Not available. [1] North American Industry Classification System, 2002. [2] Index base year equals 100. [3] Preliminary data.
Source: U.S. Bureau of Labor Statistics, *Producer Price Indexes*, monthly and annual. See also *Monthly Labor Review*, <http://www.bls.gov/opub/mlr/welcome.htm>. For more information, see <http://www.bls.gov/ppi/>.

Prices 485

Table 739. Chain-Type Price Indexes for Personal Consumption Expenditures by Type of Expenditure: 1990 to 2009

[2005 = 100. For explanation of "chain-type", see text Section 13. See also Table 677]

Type of Expenditure	1990	1995	2000	2006	2007	2008	2009
Personal consumption expenditures	**72.1**	**82.0**	**89.8**	**102.7**	**105.6**	**109.1**	**109.3**
Household consumption expenditures [1]	71.7	82.2	89.7	102.8	105.6	109.2	109.5
Food and beverages purchased for off-premises consumption	73.9	80.9	89.5	101.7	105.7	112.1	113.5
Food and nonalcoholic beverages purchased for off-premises consumption	74.1	80.6	89.2	101.8	106.0	113.0	114.1
Alcoholic beverages purchased for off-premises consumption	72.1	83.0	91.2	101.3	103.9	107.2	110.4
Food produced and consumed on farms	93.6	81.6	78.4	96.4	104.4	103.0	89.6
Clothing, footwear, and related services	113.9	112.6	107.4	99.8	99.0	98.5	99.4
Clothing	115.8	113.7	108.7	99.6	98.8	97.9	98.7
Garments	120.1	116.6	110.6	99.4	98.4	97.1	97.6
Women's and girls' clothing	125.4	119.4	109.7	99.9	99.5	97.0	97.6
Men's and boys' clothing	113.2	113.3	111.7	98.3	96.7	97.3	97.7
Children's and infants' clothing	113.9	111.4	111.7	99.9	97.7	97.5	98.1
Footwear [2]	104.2	106.9	100.8	100.8	99.9	101.4	103.6
Housing, utilities, and fuels	64.1	73.4	84.4	104.4	108.1	112.5	113.3
Housing	64.4	74.3	86.1	103.6	107.3	110.3	112.3
Rental of tenant-occupied nonfarm housing [3]	64.2	73.5	85.1	103.6	108.0	111.8	114.3
Imputed rental of owner-occupied nonfarm housing [4]	64.6	74.4	86.3	103.5	107.0	109.7	111.5
Household utilities and fuels	61.9	69.0	76.9	108.4	112.5	123.5	117.7
Water supply and sanitation	53.8	71.0	81.4	104.9	110.3	116.8	124.0
Electricity, gas, and other fuels	64.2	68.5	75.5	109.5	113.2	125.7	115.7
Electricity	78.0	86.0	85.2	112.1	116.7	124.1	127.9
Natural gas	45.1	47.7	61.9	102.5	102.4	116.2	90.8
Fuel oil and other fuels	45.9	40.5	60.7	114.1	123.3	167.2	114.7
Furnishings, household equipment, and routine household maintenance	95.4	100.7	103.0	100.4	100.1	100.7	101.3
Furniture, furnishings, and floor coverings [5]	101.2	107.9	107.8	99.3	97.5	95.9	95.3
Household textiles	133.2	132.4	120.3	95.4	90.5	87.1	83.5
Household appliances [6]	105.7	105.7	102.7	102.7	106.2	107.7	108.9
Glassware, tableware, and household utensils [7]	111.8	115.3	111.9	96.3	94.6	95.7	95.8
Health	58.5	75.8	85.0	103.2	106.6	109.3	112.3
Medical products, appliances, and equipment	62.4	74.9	85.3	103.8	105.3	107.5	110.7
Pharmaceutical and other medical products [8]	60.1	72.7	83.9	104.0	105.5	107.9	111.4
Pharmaceutical products	59.9	72.5	83.7	104.1	105.5	108.0	111.5
Other medical products	79.1	93.2	98.6	101.5	102.4	102.7	104.1
Therapeutic appliances and equipment	74.9	87.5	94.5	102.3	104.0	105.0	106.1
Outpatient services	62.8	79.6	89.1	101.9	105.6	108.0	110.5
Physician services	65.6	85.0	92.2	101.0	105.1	106.2	108.8
Dental services	48.4	63.9	79.8	105.2	110.7	116.3	119.8
Paramedical services	65.9	78.7	88.4	101.9	104.4	107.5	109.4
Hospital and nursing home services	54.0	72.8	81.3	104.2	108.0	111.4	114.8
Hospitals	54.6	74.9	81.3	104.4	108.0	111.2	114.6
Nursing homes	52.1	64.2	81.2	103.0	107.8	112.1	115.8
Transportation	72.2	80.9	88.6	105.0	108.7	116.0	105.3
Motor vehicles	82.7	100.7	103.2	99.6	98.6	96.5	96.0
New motor vehicles	87.5	101.9	103.9	99.4	98.3	96.8	97.8
Net purchases of used motor vehicles	73.0	98.4	102.0	100.1	99.2	96.1	93.0
Motor vehicle operation	62.6	66.3	77.0	108.4	115.6	128.6	110.8
Motor vehicle parts and accessories	94.2	93.9	92.4	104.1	107.6	113.2	117.6
Motor vehicle fuels, lubricants, and fluids	51.8	51.5	66.2	112.8	123.9	144.5	105.9
Public transportation	87.2	92.0	100.4	106.1	107.5	116.0	112.4
Ground transportation	64.4	72.6	81.9	104.7	106.3	111.4	116.1
Air transportation	100.9	102.6	110.3	107.3	108.7	119.8	111.6
Water transportation	113.1	131.5	126.0	99.6	99.4	97.7	88.7
Recreation	110.1	115.2	106.5	99.1	97.8	97.8	96.5
Video and audio equipment, computers, and related services	253.5	214.3	137.6	93.9	87.6	82.7	77.1
Video and audio equipment	208.5	183.1	140.5	91.1	81.1	73.9	65.5
Sports and recreational goods and related services	112.2	118.4	109.1	99.3	97.7	97.9	97.3
Sports and recreational vehicles	84.5	93.6	97.9	102.4	101.8	102.9	103.9
Other sporting and recreational goods	123.2	128.2	113.3	98.1	96.1	96.1	95.0
Magazines, newspapers, books, and stationery	71.5	87.4	95.5	100.8	102.0	104.0	107.4
Education	40.1	56.1	71.4	106.3	112.5	119.1	125.7
Higher education	36.8	55.7	69.9	106.7	113.4	120.5	127.7
Net foreign travel and expenditures abroad by U.S. residents							
Foreign travel by U.S. residents	63.2	75.1	78.9	104.2	111.4	120.4	110.5
Less: Expenditures in the United States by nonresidents	67.4	76.5	87.7	104.7	109.0	114.2	111.3

[1] Consists of household purchases of goods and services from business, government, nonprofit institutions, and the rest of the world. [2] Consists of shoes and other footwear, and of repair and hire of footwear. [3] Consists of space rent (see footnote 4) and rent for appliances, furnishings, and furniture. [4] Consists of rent for space and for heating and plumbing facilities, water heaters, lighting fixtures, kitchen cabinets, linoleum, storm windows and doors, window screens, and screen doors, but excludes rent for appliances and furniture and purchases of fueland electricity. [5] Includes clocks, lamps, lighting fixtures, and other household decorative items;also includes repair of furniture, furnishings, and floor coverings. [6] Consists of major household appliances, small electric household appliances, and repair of household appliances. [7] Consists of dishes, flatware, and non-electric cookware and tableware. [8] Excludes drug preparations and related products dispensed by physicians, hospitals,and other medical services.

Source: U.S. Bureau of Economic Analysis, National Income and Product Accounts Table; Table 2.5.4 Price Indexes for Personal Consumption Expenditures by Function; <http://www.bea.gov/national/Index.htm\>.

Table 740. Chain-Type Price Indexes for Gross Domestic Product: 1990 to 2010

[2005 = 100. For explanation of "chain-type," see text, Section 13]

Component	1990	1995	2000	2006	2007	2008	2009	2010
Gross domestic product	**72.2**	**81.5**	**88.6**	**103.3**	**106.3**	**108.6**	**109.6**	**110.7**
Personal consumption expenditures...	**72.1**	**82.0**	**89.8**	**102.7**	**105.6**	**109.1**	**109.3**	**111.1**
Durable goods.....................	117.3	124.3	111.7	98.5	96.7	95.3	93.8	92.5
Nondurable goods.................	76.7	82.1	90.0	103.2	106.5	112.5	109.3	112.7
Services.........................	63.8	75.4	85.8	103.4	107.0	110.6	112.2	114.2
Gross private domestic investment....	**86.7**	**90.8**	**90.0**	**104.4**	**106.2**	**107.0**	**104.9**	**103.0**
Fixed investment	85.8	90.1	89.8	104.4	106.3	107.1	105.3	103.6
Nonresidential	100.8	102.2	96.2	103.5	105.5	107.0	105.7	103.7
Structures	53.5	60.6	72.3	112.9	119.8	125.5	122.2	120.5
Equipment and software	125.4	122.3	106.1	100.2	100.3	100.1	99.6	97.7
Residential......................	58.0	66.4	77.4	106.1	107.6	106.4	102.7	102.4
Net exports of goods and services:								
Exports	92.0	96.0	92.0	103.4	106.9	111.9	105.9	110.3
Goods.........................	100.2	101.4	92.9	103.3	106.8	112.0	104.4	109.4
Services.......................	74.4	83.9	89.9	103.7	107.1	111.6	109.2	112.3
Imports	93.6	95.6	90.0	104.1	107.5	118.7	106.0	112.8
Goods.........................	99.1	98.9	91.1	104.2	107.5	119.6	104.9	112.4
Services.......................	71.0	80.2	84.2	103.8	107.8	113.9	110.7	114.8
Government consumption expenditures and gross investment ..	**63.4**	**72.8**	**82.5**	**104.8**	**109.9**	**115.0**	**114.6**	**116.8**
Federal...........................	63.5	73.7	82.5	104.1	107.8	111.1	110.9	112.7
National defense	63.9	73.2	81.8	104.4	108.2	112.1	111.3	113.5
Nondefense	62.6	74.8	83.9	103.5	106.7	109.1	110.0	111.2
State and local	63.5	72.3	82.5	105.3	111.1	117.3	116.9	119.3

Source: U.S. Bureau of Economic Analysis, *Survey of Current Business*, April 2011. See also <http://www.bea.gov/national/Index.htm\>.

Table 741. Import and Export Price Indexes by End-Use Category: 1990 to 2010

[As of June. Import indexes are weighted by the 2000 Tariff Schedule of the United States Annotated, a scheme for describing and reporting product composition and value of U.S. imports. Import prices are based on U.S. dollar prices paid by importer. Export indexes are weighted by 2000 export values according to the Schedule B classification system of the U.S. Census Bureau. Prices used in these indexes were collected from a sample of U.S. manufacturers of exports and are factory transaction prices, except as noted. Minus sign (–) indicates decrease]

Year	Index (2000 = 100)						Percent change [1]					
	Imports			Exports			Imports			Exports		
	Total	Petroleum imports	Non–petroleum imports	Total	Agricultural exports	Non–agricultural exports	Total	Petroleum imports	Non–petroleum imports	Total	Agricultural exports	Non–agricultural exports
1990.....	90.8	55.4	96.4	95.1	107.7	93.5	−0.8	−13.4	0.5	−0.1	−4.0	0.5
1991.....	93.4	63.2	98.3	96.1	104.3	95.3	2.9	14.1	2.0	1.1	−3.2	1.9
1992.....	94.8	66.0	99.5	96.5	104.0	95.8	1.5	4.4	1.2	0.4	−0.3	0.5
1993.....	95.0	60.4	100.5	96.9	100.3	96.7	0.2	−8.5	1.0	0.4	−3.6	0.9
1994.....	96.3	57.6	102.6	98.5	109.3	97.5	1.4	−4.6	2.1	1.7	9.0	0.8
1995.....	101.4	62.9	107.6	104.5	117.0	103.3	5.3	9.2	4.9	6.1	7.0	5.9
1996.....	100.7	66.4	106.2	105.4	140.8	101.7	−0.7	5.6	−1.3	0.9	20.3	−1.5
1997.....	98.8	62.5	104.3	103.2	120.5	101.5	−1.9	−5.9	−1.8	−2.1	−14.4	−0.2
1998.....	93.1	44.3	100.5	99.9	110.8	98.8	−5.8	−29.1	−3.6	−3.2	−8.0	−2.7
1999.....	92.9	54.5	98.8	98.2	101.1	97.9	−0.2	23.0	−1.7	−1.7	−8.8	−0.9
2000.....	100.2	101.9	99.9	100.1	100.5	100.0	7.9	87.0	1.1	1.9	−0.6	2.1
2001.....	97.6	89.4	98.9	99.4	100.9	99.3	−2.6	−12.3	−1.0	−0.7	0.4	−0.7
2002.....	94.1	85.3	96.2	98.0	100.7	97.8	−3.6	−4.6	−2.7	−1.4	−0.2	−1.5
2003.....	96.2	96.4	97.3	99.5	110.0	98.7	2.2	13.0	1.1	1.5	9.2	0.9
2004.....	101.7	129.7	99.7	103.4	127.4	101.5	5.7	34.5	2.5	3.9	15.8	2.8
2005.....	109.2	181.5	102.0	106.7	123.9	105.4	7.4	39.9	2.3	3.2	−2.7	3.8
2006.....	117.3	242.6	104.2	111.2	124.1	110.3	7.4	33.7	2.2	4.2	0.2	4.6
2007.....	120.0	245.6	107.1	116.0	146.7	113.8	2.3	1.2	2.8	4.3	18.2	3.2
2008.....	145.5	450.3	114.9	126.1	195.2	121.2	21.3	83.3	7.3	8.7	33.1	6.5
2009.....	120.0	241.5	107.4	117.8	169.7	114.1	−17.5	−46.4	−6.5	−6.6	−13.1	−5.9
2010.....	125.2	267.4	110.7	122.2	165.3	119.1	4.3	10.7	−6.5	3.7	−2.6	4.4

[1] Percent change from immediate prior year.

Source: U.S. Bureau of Labor Statistics, *US Import and Export Price Indexes*, monthly. See also <http://www.bls.gov/web/ximpim.supp.toc.htm#long_tables>.

Table 742. Export Price Indexes—Selected Commodities: 2000 to 2010

[2000 = 100. As of June. Indexes are weighted by 2000 export values according to the Schedule B classification system of the U.S. Census Bureau. Prices used in these indexes were collected from a sample of U.S. manufacturers of exports and are factory transaction prices, except as noted]

Commodity	2000 [1]	2004	2005	2006	2007	2008	2009	2010
All commodities	100.1	103.4	106.7	111.2	116.0	126.1	117.8	122.2
Animal products	102.2	121.5	130.9	125.1	153.2	174.5	158.8	172.2
Fish	99.1	105.2	114.2	122.8	124.3	149.1	145.1	152.3
Vegetable products	100.0	140.3	130.3	131.0	159.3	239.3	205.5	177.5
Fruit and nuts	94.8	109.2	126.5	114.5	117.5	123.0	102.3	131.0
Cereals	100.0	143.3	118.1	136.9	179.2	293.6	222.1	171.4
Wheat	99.4	136.2	130.0	154.3	180.4	276.7	228.5	151.6
Corn (maize)	101.0	146.9	111.8	127.1	189.8	286.4	212.1	174.3
Oilseeds	102.8	161.0	136.2	121.5	157.4	259.3	238.1	196.2
Beverages and tobacco	100.0	110.7	110.3	112.5	120.5	136.3	142.1	139.3
Mineral products	97.8	129.7	182.3	238.4	243.4	360.5	203.9	247.9
Fuels	97.4	127.9	172.8	219.6	230.5	361.9	198.3	239.2
Chemicals and related products	100.3	115.3	122.8	130.1	131.3	142.2	135.7	144.5
Plastics and rubber products	101.5	105.7	118.4	128.7	131.3	142.2	129.8	136.8
Hides, skins, and leather products	95.7	108.6	113.0	116.8	122.6	117.3	79.1	121.2
Wood products	100.0	103.8	104.3	113.5	113.5	112.3	102.5	111.1
Woodpulp and paper products	101.6	98.1	101.9	110.6	110.6	117.5	107.3	117.6
Textiles	100.2	98.8	100.8	101.9	101.9	108.0	101.9	115.7
Stone and glass products	100.7	99.0	103.5	110.1	110.1	111.1	115.9	115.9
Gems and precious metals	98.1	101.6	106.5	162.7	162.7	183.1	171.3	211.0
Base metals	100.5	119.6	131.8	169.3	169.3	181.2	143.5	160.4
Iron and steel	101.7	152.9	164.0	173.7	209.2	243.3	150.0	194.3
Articles of iron and steel	100.2	115.3	124.8	148.5	148.5	156.6	163.6	158.1
Copper	98.7	122.7	143.1	243.9	243.9	261.2	172.0	217.0
Aluminum	98.4	107.3	113.2	149.5	149.5	150.6	100.5	117.8
Machinery	99.9	94.9	94.9	93.8	94.3	95.3	95.3	95.5
Nonelectrical machinery	100.0	99.9	100.5	101.5	102.7	103.7	105.1	106.8
Electrical machinery	99.8	89.4	88.6	85.3	85.2	86.2	84.7	83.2
Transportation equipment	100.0	106.5	108.8	111.5	113.8	116.6	120.5	121.4
Motor vehicles	100.0	102.4	103.2	104.6	105.6	106.7	107.7	108.5
Instruments	100.0	101.2	101.3	102.4	103.3	107.1	107.8	106.2
Miscellaneous manufactured articles	100.4	99.2	100.6	101.1	104.7	108.6	106.9	108.1

[1] June 2000 may not equal 100 because indexes were reweighted to an "average" trade value in 2000.
Source: U.S. Bureau of Labor Statistics, U.S. Import and Export Price Indexes, monthly. See also <http://stats.bls.gov/news .release/ximpim.toc.htm>.

Table 743. Import Price Indexes—Selected Commodities: 2000 to 2010

[2000 = 100. As of June. Indexes are weighted by the 2000 Tariff Schedule of the United States Annotated, a scheme for describing and reporting product composition and value of U.S. imports. Import prices are based on U.S. dollar prices paid by importer]

Commodity	2000 [1]	2002	2004	2005	2006	2007	2008	2009	2010
All commodities	100.2	94.1	101.7	109.2	117.1	120.0	145.5	120.0	125.2
Animal products	99.9	88.2	107.8	112.7	118.2	127.4	141.6	129.0	143.0
Meat	100.5	104.1	130.8	138.7	137.2	146.8	165.4	150.8	183.2
Fish	100.2	79.8	83.4	88.3	96.6	100.2	106.3	99.8	107.1
Vegetable products	97.1	94.7	103.0	116.9	108.6	129.3	159.5	161.2	169.5
Vegetables	93.9	106.7	113.8	136.8	143.6	175.3	202.6	293.1	326.2
Fruit and nuts	96.9	97.5	96.3	89.7	81.7	90.9	112.8	103.8	106.8
Beverages and tobacco	100.0	101.8	108.9	114.0	119.8	124.3	140.0	134.4	141.2
Mineral products	101.3	85.5	130.9	178.1	229.2	234.0	418.5	224.5	248.5
Fuels	101.3	84.4	130.0	177.5	229.0	233.7	421.6	221.3	244.9
Chemicals and related products	99.8	96.3	103.6	111.3	114.5	123.8	139.2	131.3	139.3
Organic chemicals	100.6	95.7	100.1	109.6	118.0	120.5	132.9	124.6	133.8
Pharmaceutical products	99.8	98.8	106.9	111.0	106.5	107.6	114.1	113.3	117.9
Plastics and rubber products	99.9	98.6	105.9	113.5	120.1	121.7	133.2	129.7	136.7
Hides, skins, and leather products	100.2	97.9	101.5	104.0	105.2	107.0	112.4	113.7	114.5
Wood products	100.5	99.8	129.5	124.2	120.7	113.5	118.5	110.2	134.3
Woodpulp and paper products	100.0	91.3	98.2	102.3	107.9	108.0	115.3	108.1	112.5
Textiles	99.7	98.5	100.3	100.4	100.7	102.1	103.5	102.6	103.1
Footwear and clothing accessories	99.6	99.1	99.8	99.9	100.6	101.5	105.8	108.0	106.9
Footwear	99.6	99.2	100.2	100.3	101.0	101.3	104.7	107.2	106.1
Stone and glass products	99.5	101.0	103.8	105.4	108.6	110.4	115.4	125.3	123.8
Gems and precious metals	99.3	87.5	93.5	98.3	125.1	132.8	157.1	140.6	161.5
Gold	98.3	112.3	137.1	150.7	241.2	238.2	317.4	331.7	430.5
Platinum	(NA)	111.2	116.2	125.7	230.1	257.2	368.6	196.6	292.6
Base metals	101.5	93.4	118.9	132.1	157.9	176.7	206.9	151.1	180.2
Iron and steel	104.1	94.3	155.1	170.6	173.8	206.2	308.8	174.8	238.8
Articles of iron and steel	100.6	95.6	109.0	122.7	125.1	129.0	159.7	139.6	149.9
Copper	97.2	93.0	119.0	142.7	291.6	307.5	326.2	234.8	313.8
Aluminum	97.9	97.5	110.5	113.2	150.0	146.8	155.8	105.7	132.8
Machinery	100.2	95.0	90.7	89.7	88.1	87.8	88.9	86.9	86.5
Nonelectrical machinery	99.8	94.7	90.9	90.1	88.3	88.2	89.3	87.9	87.9
Electrical machinery	100.5	95.4	90.5	89.4	87.9	87.5	88.5	85.8	85.2
Transportation equipment	100.0	100.4	102.8	104.4	104.9	105.9	109.5	109.7	109.7
Motor vehicles	100.1	100.2	102.3	103.8	104.3	105.1	108.7	108.6	108.8
Instruments	99.8	97.9	99.1	100.1	99.6	99.4	101.5	102.0	100.8
Miscellaneous manufactured articles	99.7	97.2	97.4	99.4	99.5	101.1	106.4	107.7	106.5
Furniture	99.5	97.7	99.7	103.4	103.3	104.6	111.9	112.2	109.4

NA Not available. [1] June 2000 may not equal 100 because indexes were reweighted to an "average" trade value in 2000.
Source: U.S. Bureau of Labor Statistics, U.S. Import and Export Price Indexes, monthly. See also <http://stats.bls.gov/news .release/ximpim.toc.htm>.

Business Enterprise

This section relates to the place and behavior of the business firm and to business initiative in the American economy. It includes data on the number, type, and size of businesses; financial data of domestic and multinational U.S. corporations; business investments, expenditures, and profits; and sales and inventories.

The principal sources of these data are the *Survey of Current Business*, published by the Bureau of Economic Analysis (BEA); the Web site of the Board of Governors of the Federal Reserve System at <http://www.federalreserve.gov /econresdata/default.htm>; the annual *Statistics of Income (SOI)* reports of the Internal Revenue Service (IRS); and the U.S. Census Bureau's Economic Census, *County Business Patterns, Quarterly Financial Report for Manufacturing, Mining, and Trade Corporations (QFR), Survey of Business Owners,* and *Annual Capital Expenditures Survey.*

Business firms—A firm is generally defined as a business organization under a single management and may include one or more establishments. The terms firm, business, company, and enterprise are used interchangeably throughout this section. A firm doing business in more than one industry is classified by industry according to the major activity of the firm as a whole.

The IRS concept of a business firm relates primarily to the legal entity used for tax reporting purposes. A sole proprietorship is an unincorporated business owned by one person and may include large enterprises with many employees and hired managers and part-time operators. A partnership is an unincorporated business owned by two or more persons, each of whom has a financial interest in the business. A corporation is a business that is legally incorporated under state laws. While many corporations file consolidated tax returns, most corporate tax returns represent individual corporations, some of which are affiliated through common ownership or control with other corporations filing separate returns.

Economic census—The economic census is the major source of facts about the structure and functioning of the nation's economy. It provides essential information for government, business, industry, and the general public. It furnishes an important part of the framework for such composite measures as the gross domestic product estimates, input/output measures, production and price indexes, and other statistical series that measure short–term changes in economic conditions. The Census Bureau takes the economic census every 5 years, covering years ending in "2" and "7."

The economic census is collected on an establishment basis. A company operating at more than one location is required to file a separate report for each store, factory, shop, or other location. Each establishment is assigned a separate industry classification based on its primary activity and not that of its parent company. Establishments responding to the establishment survey are classified into industries on the basis of their principal product or activity (determined by annual sales volume). The statistics issued by industry in the 2007 Economic Census are classified primarily on the 2007 North American Industry Classification System (NAICS), and, to a lesser extent, on the 2002 NAICS used in the previous census (see below).

More detailed information about the scope, coverage, methodology, classification system, data items, and publications for each of the economic censuses and related surveys is published in the 2007 *Economic Census User Guide* at <http://www.census.gov/econ/census07 /www/user_guide.html>.

Data from the 2007 Economic Census are released through the Census Bureau's American FactFinder® service on the

U.S. Census Bureau, Statistical Abstract of the United States: 2012

Census Bureau Web site. For more information, see <http://www.census.gov/econ/census07/>.

Survey of Business Owners—

The Survey of Business Owners (SBO) provides statistics that describe the composition of U.S. businesses by gender, ethnicity, race and veteran status. Data from SBO are published in a series of releases: *American Indian- and Alaska Native-Owned Firms, Asian-Owned Firms, Black-Owned Firms, Hispanic-Owned Firms, Native Hawaiian- and Other Pacific Islander-Owned Firms, Women-Owned Firms, Veteran-Owned Firms, Characteristics of Business Owners* and *Company Summary.* Data are presented by industry classifications, geographic area, and size of firm (employment and receipts). Each owner had the option of selecting more than one race and therefore is included in each race selected. For more information, see <http://www.census.gov/econ/sbo/>.

North American Industry Classification System (NAICS)—

NAICS is the standard used by federal statistical agencies in classifying business establishments for the purpose of collecting, analyzing, and publishing statistical data related to the U.S. business economy. NAICS was developed under the auspices of the Office of Management and Budget (OMB), and adopted in 1997 to replace the Standard Industrial Classification (SIC) system. The official 2007 U.S. NAICS Manual includes definitions for each industry, background information, tables showing changes between 2002 and 2007, and a comprehensive index. For more information, see <http://www.census.gov/eos/www/naics/>.

Changes between 2002 NAICS and 2007 NAICS are relatively minor, but do affect totals for sectors 52 (finance and insurance), 53 (real estate, rental, and leasing), 54 (professional, scientific, and technical services), and 56 (admin., support, waste mgt., and remediation services). Nearly all industries are comparable from 2002 to 2007 NAICS classifications. Several industries in the Information sector have been consolidated.

Quarterly Financial Report—

The Quarterly Financial Report (QFR) program publishes quarterly aggregate statistics on the financial conditions of U.S. corporations. The QFR requests companies to report estimates from their statements of income and retained earnings, and balance sheets. The statistical data are classified and aggregated by type of industry and asset size. The QFR sample includes manufacturing companies with assets of $250 thousand and above, and mining, wholesale, retail, and selected service companies with assets of $50 million and above. The data are available quarterlyin the *Quarterly Financial Report for Manufacturing, Mining, and Trade Corporations* at <http://www.census.gov/econ/qfr/index.html>.

Multinational companies—

BEA collects financial and operating data on U.S. multinational companies. These data provide a picture of the overall activities of foreign affiliates and U.S. parent companies, using a variety of indicators of their financial structure and operations. The data on foreign affiliates cover the entire operations of the affiliate, irrespective of the percentage of U.S. ownership. These data cover items such as sales, value added, employment and compensation of employees, capital expenditures, exports and imports, and research and development expenditures. Separate tabulations are available for all affiliates and for affiliates that are majority-owned by their U.S. parent(s). More information is available at <http://www.bea.gov/international/index.htm#omc>.

Statistical reliability—For a discussion of statistical collection, estimation, and sampling procedures and measures of reliability applicable to data from the Census Bureau and the Internal Revenue Service, see Appendix III.

Table 744. Number of Tax Returns, Receipts, and Net Income by Type of Business: 1990 to 2008

[14,783 represents 14,783,000. Covers active enterprises only. Figures are estimates based on sample of unaudited tax returns; see Appendix III]

Item	Number of returns (1,000)			Business receipts [1] (bil. dol.)			Net income (less loss) [2] (bil. dol.)		
	Nonfarm proprietorships	Partnerships	Corporations	Nonfarm proprietorships	Partnerships	Corporations	Nonfarm proprietorships	Partnerships	Corporations
1990	14,783	1,554	3,717	731	541	10,914	141	17	371
1991	15,181	1,515	3,803	713	539	10,963	142	21	345
1992	15,495	1,485	3,869	737	571	11,272	154	43	402
1993	15,848	1,468	3,965	757	627	11,814	156	67	498
1994	16,154	1,494	4,342	791	732	12,858	167	82	577
1995	16,424	1,581	4,474	807	854	13,969	169	107	714
1996	16,955	1,654	4,631	843	1,042	14,890	177	145	806
1997	17,176	1,759	4,710	870	1,297	15,890	187	168	915
1998	17,409	1,855	4,849	918	1,534	16,543	202	187	838
1999	17,576	1,937	4,936	969	1,829	18,009	208	228	929
2000	17,905	2,058	5,045	1,021	2,316	19,593	215	269	928
2001	18,338	2,132	5,136	1,017	2,569	19,308	217	276	604
2002	18,926	2,242	5,267	1,030	2,669	18,849	221	271	564
2003	19,710	2,375	5,401	1,050	2,818	19,755	230	301	780
2004	20,591	2,547	5,558	1,140	3,142	21,717	248	385	1,112
2005	21,468	2,764	5,671	1,223	3,719	24,060	270	546	1,949
2006	22,075	2,947	5,841	1,278	4,131	26,070	278	667	1,933
2007	23,122	3,098	5,869	1,324	4,541	27,335	281	683	1,837
2008	22,614	3,146	5,847	1,317	4,963	27,266	265	458	984

[1] Excludes investment income except for partnerships and corporations in finance, insurance, and real estate before 1998. Beginning 1998, finance and insurance, real estate, and management of companies included investment income for partnerships and corporations. Excludes investment income for S corporations; for definition, see footnote 1, Table 753. [2] Net income (less loss) is defined differently by form of organization, basically as follows: (a) Proprietorships: Total taxable receipts less total business deductions, including cost of sales and operations, depletion, and certain capital expensing, excluding charitable contributions and owners' salaries; (b) Partnerships: Total taxable receipts (including investment income except capital gains) less deductions, including cost of sales and operations and certain payments to partners, excluding charitable contributions, oil and gas depletion, and certain capital expensing; (c) Corporations: Total taxable receipts (including investment income, capital gains, and income from foreign subsidiaries deemed received for tax purposes, except for S corporations) less business deductions, including cost of sales and operations, depletion, certain capital expensing, and officers' compensation excluding S corporation charitable contributions and investment expenses; net income is before income tax.

Source: U.S. Internal Revenue Service, *Statistics of Income*, various publications.

Table 745. Number of Tax Returns and Business Receipts by Size of Receipts: 2000 to 2008

[5,045 represents 5,045,000. Covers active enterprises only. Figures are estimates based on sample of unaudited tax returns; see Appendix III. Minus sign (–) indicates loss]

Size-class of receipts	Returns (1,000)					Business receipts [1] (bil. dol.)				
	2000	2005	2006	2007	2008	2000	2005	2006	2007	2008
Corporations	**5,045**	**5,671**	**5,841**	**5,869**	**5,847**	**19,593**	**24,060**	**26,070**	**27,335**	**27,266**
Under $25,000 [2]	1,220	1,300	1,363	1,391	1,444	4	4	3	-2	-17
$25,000 to $49,999	302	340	341	356	368	10	12	13	13	14
$50,000 to $99,999	477	544	554	570	556	35	40	41	42	41
$100,000 to $499,999	1,515	1,755	1,780	1,766	1,733	397	437	443	445	432
$500,000 to $999,999	582	644	668	657	663	407	458	473	465	473
$1,000,000 or more	946	1,088	1,135	1,128	1,084	18,738	23,108	25,097	26,372	26,324
Partnerships	**2,058**	**2,764**	**2,947**	**3,098**	**3,146**	**2,316**	**3,719**	**4,131**	**4,541**	**4,963**
Under $25,000 [2]	1,105	1,465	1,568	1,650	1,705	5	5	6	6	6
$25,000 to $49,999	183	218	240	233	230	7	8	9	8	8
$50,000 to $99,999	187	233	245	275	266	13	17	18	20	19
$100,000 to $499,999	353	489	498	530	537	82	114	118	125	125
$500,000 to $999,999	92	131	149	149	147	66	92	106	107	104
$1,000,000 or more	137	227	248	261	260	2,143	3,482	3,875	4,275	4,701
Nonfarm proprietorships	**17,905**	**21,468**	**22,075**	**23,122**	**22,614**	**1,021**	**1,223**	**1,278**	**1,324**	**1,317**
Under $25,000 [2]	11,997	14,456	14,867	15,752	15,532	82	100	104	111	109
$25,000 to $49,999	2,247	2,587	2,721	2,796	2,729	80	92	96	99	97
$50,000 to $99,999	1,645	1,981	1,983	2,027	1,936	117	140	140	144	136
$100,000 to $499,999	1,733	2,091	2,139	2,173	2,051	355	425	437	440	418
$500,000 to $999,999	190	235	236	242	229	126	160	161	165	156
$1,000,000 or more	92	117	128	132	137	261	306	340	364	401

[1] Finance and insurance, real estate, and management of companies included investment income for partnerships and corporations. [2] Includes firms with no receipts.

Source: U.S. Internal Revenue Service, *Statistics of Income Bulletin* and unpublished data.

Table 746. Number of Tax Returns, Receipts, and Net Income by Type of Business and Industry: 2008

[22,614 represents 22,614,000. Covers active enterprises only. Figures are estimates based on sample of unaudited tax returns; see Appendix III. Based on the North American Industry Classification System (NAICS), 2007; see text, this section. Minus sign (–) indicates net loss]

Industry	2007 NAICS code	Number of returns (1,000)			Business receipts [1] (bil. dol.)			Net income (less loss) [2] (bil. dol.)		
		Non-farm proprietorships	Partnerships	Corporations	Non-farm proprietorships	Partnerships	Corporations	Non-farm proprietorships	Partnerships	Corporations
Total	(X)	22,614	3,146	5,847	1,317	4,963	27,266	265	458	984
Agriculture, forestry, fishing, and hunting [2]	11	307	119	137	18	28	150	(Z)	2	1
Mining	21	134	35	39	18	158	421	3	57	50
Utilities	22	13	8	7	(Z)	194	738	(Z)	2	7
Construction	23	2,822	203	767	207	268	1,459	29	–2	27
Special trade contractors	238	2,263	77	472	143	68	629	24	5	26
Manufacturing	31–33	340	46	271	28	1,032	7,555	3	37	397
Wholesale and retail trade [3]	(X)	2,601	237	986	249	1,061	7,343	12	18	137
Wholesale trade	42	326	62	381	52	659	3,881	4	15	79
Retail trade [4]	44–45	2,275	175	605	197	402	3,462	8	2	58
Motor vehicle and parts dealers	441	142	21	91	40	110	701	1	(Z)	1
Food and beverage stores	445	91	20	94	29	100	515	1	(Z)	6
Gasoline stations	447	22	8	41	29	75	338	(Z)	1	1
Transportation and warehousing	48–49	1,048	50	195	81	150	795	9	5	13
Information [4]	51	366	37	118	12	241	975	3	31	56
Broadcasting (except Internet)	515	[5] 52	6	6	[5] 3	36	113	[5] (Z)	1	6
Telecommunications	517	(5)	5	18	(5)	156	459	(5)	28	21
Finance and insurance	52	693	321	254	112	626	3,675	18	219	159
Real estate and rental and leasing	53	1,279	1,489	649	58	288	235	14	4	19
Professional, scientific, and technical services [4]	54	3,219	191	845	172	378	1,013	74	81	36
Legal services	5411	378	26	113	41	145	96	18	51	9
Accounting, tax preparation, bookkeeping, and payroll services	5412	358	21	80	13	61	37	5	12	3
Management, scientific, and technical consulting services	5416	950	52	230	47	63	212	27	9	12
Management of companies and enterprises	55	(NA)	23	46	(NA)	55	1,028	(NA)	–13	19
Administrative and support and waste management and remediation services	56	2,303	66	276	61	74	485	17	2	16
Educational services	61	620	10	52	10	4	46	3	(Z)	3
Health care and social assistance	62	1,998	69	416	119	180	619	48	23	30
Arts, entertainment, and recreation	71	1,348	67	122	33	51	96	8	–1	2
Accommodation and food services	72	434	103	293	48	148	434	1	–5	11
Accommodation	721	55	29	35	6	67	93	(Z)	–5	2
Food services and drinking places	722	380	74	258	42	81	341	1	(Z)	9
Other services [4]	81	2,606	68	371	86	26	198	20	(Z)	4
Auto repair and maintenance	8111	351	23	105	24	9	68	2	(Z)	1
Personal and laundry services	812	1,598	39	155	43	10	74	13	(Z)	2
Religious, grantmaking, civic, professional, and similar organizations	813	245	2	51	3	(Z)	12	2	(Z)	(Z)
Unclassified	(X)	484	5	2	6	(Z)	(Z)	2	(Z)	(Z)

NA Not available. X Not applicable. Z Less than $500 million. [1] Includes investment income for partnerships and corporations in finance and insurance, real estate, and management of companies' industries. Excludes investment income for S corporations; for definition, see footnote 1, Table 753. [2] See footnote 2, Table 744. [3] For corporations, represents agricultural services only. [4] For corporations, includes trade business not identified as wholesale or retail. [5] Includes other industries, not shown separately. [6] Broadcasting includes telecommunications.

Source: U.S. Internal Revenue Service, *Statistics of Income*, various publications.

U.S. Census Bureau, Statistical Abstract of the United States: 2012

Table 747. Nonfarm Sole Proprietorships—Selected Income and Deduction Items: 1990 to 2008

[In billions of dollars (731 represents $731,000,000,000), except as indicated. All figures are estimates based on samples. Tax law changes have affected the comparability of the data over time; see Statistics of Income reports for a description. See Appendix III]

Item	1990	1995	2000	2003	2004	2005	2006	2007	2008
Number of returns (1,000)	14,783	16,424	17,905	19,710	20,591	21,468	22,075	23,122	22,614
Returns with net income (1,000)	11,222	12,213	13,308	14,448	15,053	15,750	16,207	16,929	16,434
Business receipts	731	807	1,021	1,050	1,140	1,223	1,278	1,324	1,317
Income from sales and operations	719	797	1,008	1,034	1,122	1,205	1,259	1,304	1,296
Business deductions [1]	589	638	806	820	892	953	1,001	1,044	1,054
Cost of goods sold/operations [1]	291	307	387	338	371	397	410	423	435
Purchases	210	219	269	218	239	253	260	264	281
Labor costs	23	24	29	28	32	32	32	35	31
Materials and supplies	30	34	43	47	53	56	60	62	57
Advertising	(NA)	(NA)	10	12	13	14	15	16	15
Car and truck expenses	22	33	46	53	59	71	75	82	85
Commissions	9	10	12	14	13	15	16	15	13
Contract labor	(NA)	(NA)	(NA)	(NA)	25	28	35	37	35
Depreciation	24	27	32	42	43	39	39	40	41
Insurance	13	13	14	17	19	19	19	19	18
Interest paid [2]	13	10	12	11	11	12	14	15	15
Office expenses	(NA)	(NA)	10	12	12	13	13	13	13
Rent paid [3]	23	28	33	36	37	39	41	43	44
Repairs	9	10	12	13	15	15	16	16	15
Salaries and wages (net)	47	54	63	68	71	75	77	79	79
Supplies	(NA)	(NA)	22	26	27	29	32	32	32
Taxes paid	10	13	14	15	16	17	18	18	18
Utilities	14	17	19	22	21	23	24	25	25
Net income (less loss) [4]	141	169	215	230	248	270	278	281	265
Net income [4]	162	192	245	269	291	315	327	335	325
Constant (2000) Dollars [5]									
Business receipts	896	877	1,021	991	1,045	1,085	1,097	1,105	1,076
Business deductions	722	693	806	774	818	846	859	871	861
Net income (less loss)	173	184	215	217	227	239	239	234	216
Net income	198	208	245	254	266	279	280	280	266

NA Not available. [1] Includes other amounts not shown separately. [2] Interest paid includes "mortgage interest" and "other interest paid on business indebtedness." [3] Rent paid includes "Rent on machinery and equipment" and "Rent on other business property." [4] After adjustment for the passive loss carryover from prior years. Therefore, "business receipts" minus "total deductions" do not equal "net income." [5] Based on the overall implicit price deflator for gross domestic product.

Source: U.S. Internal Revenue Service, *Statistics of Income Bulletin.*

Table 748. Partnerships—Selected Income and Balance Sheet Items: 1990 to 2008

[In billions of dollars (1,735 represents $1,735,000,000,000), except as indicated. Covers active partnerships only. All figures are estimates based on samples. See Appendix III]

Item	1990	1995	2000	2003	2004	2005	2006	2007	2008
Number of returns (1,000)	1,554	1,581	2,058	2,375	2,547	2,764	2,947	3,098	3,146
Returns with net income (1,000)	854	955	1,261	1,357	1,441	1,580	1,623	1,659	1,609
Number of partners (1,000)	17,095	15,606	13,660	14,108	15,557	16,212	16,728	18,516	19,300
Assets [1,2]	1,735	2,719	6,694	9,675	11,608	13,734	17,146	20,386	19,260
Depreciable assets (net)	681	767	1,487	1,846	1,988	2,176	2,490	2,865	3,254
Inventories, end of year	57	88	150	214	276	315	446	339	431
Land	215	221	359	455	509	607	731	820	885
Liabilities [1,2]	1,415	1,886	3,696	5,303	6,248	7,483	9,350	10,440	10,167
Accounts payable	67	91	230	276	336	400	505	430	513
Short-term debt [3]	88	124	252	274	296	373	456	565	582
Long-term debt [4]	498	544	1,132	1,389	1,546	1,772	2,227	2,556	2,767
Nonrecourse loans	470	466	639	800	854	914	1,103	1,210	1,283
Partners' capital accounts [2]	320	832	2,999	4,372	5,360	6,251	7,796	9,946	9,092
Receipts [1]	566	890	2,405	2,923	3,260	3,863	4,301	4,727	5,169
Business receipts [5]	483	854	2,316	2,818	3,142	3,719	4,131	4,541	4,963
Interest received	21	31	82	71	88	134	193	260	245
Deductions [1]	550	784	2,136	2,621	2,876	3,317	3,634	4,043	4,711
Cost of goods sold/operations	243	395	1,226	1,523	1,666	1,976	2,109	2,310	2,717
Salaries and wages	56	80	201	245	269	293	332	373	403
Taxes paid	9	13	31	39	42	47	53	56	63
Interest paid	30	43	93	65	64	103	137	174	143
Depreciation	60	23	59	84	90	71	79	86	130
Net income (less loss)	17	107	269	301	385	546	667	683	458
Net income	116	179	410	469	566	724	871	976	929

[1] Includes items not shown separately. [2] Assets, liabilities, and partners' capital accounts are understated because not all partnerships file complete balance sheets. [3] Mortgages, notes, and bonds payable in less than 1 year. [4] Mortgages, notes, and bonds payable in 1 year or more. [5] Excludes investment income except for partnerships in finance, insurance, and real estate in 1995. Beginning 2000, finance and insurance, real estate, and management of companies included investment income for partnerships.

Source: U.S. Internal Revenue Service, *Statistics of Income*, various issues.

Table 749. Partnerships—Selected Items by Industry: 2008

[In billions of dollars (19,260 represents $19,260,000,000,000), except as indicated. Covers active partnerships only. Figures are estimates based on samples. Based on the North American Industry Classification System (NAICS), 2007; see text, this section. See Appendix III. Minus sign (–) indicates net loss]

Industry and year	2007 NAICS code	Number of partnerships (1,000)			Total assets [1]	Business receipts [2]	Total deductions	Net income less loss	Net income	Net loss
		Total	With net income	With net loss						
Total [3]	(X)	3,146	1,609	1,537	19,260	4,963	4,711	458.2	929.3	471.1
Agriculture, forestry, fishing, and hunting	11	119	66	54	157	28	38	1.7	10.3	8.6
Mining	21	35	23	12	328	158	119	57.3	70.5	13.3
Utilities	22	8	2	6	253	194	197	1.5	9.7	8.1
Construction	23	203	93	110	303	268	277	–2.2	18.7	20.9
Manufacturing	31–33	46	20	26	829	1,032	1,040	37.0	70.6	33.7
Wholesale trade	42	62	34	27	192	659	651	15.4	22.4	7.0
Retail trade	44–45	175	78	97	136	402	411	2.4	9.9	7.5
Transportation and warehousing	48–49	50	20	30	257	150	152	4.9	12.0	7.1
Information	51	37	14	23	581	241	239	30.7	44.4	13.7
Finance and insurance	52	321	210	111	10,400	626	407	218.7	344.9	126.2
Real estate and rental and leasing	53	1,489	720	769	4,594	288	296	4.3	142.2	137.9
Professional, scientific, and technical services	54	191	125	66	191	378	319	81.4	91.6	10.2
Management of companies and enterprises	55	23	12	11	525	55	69	–13.3	30.1	43.4
Administrative and support and waste management and remediation services	56	66	32	34	49	74	77	1.8	6.1	4.3
Educational services	61	10	6	3	3	4	4	0.4	0.8	0.4
Health care and social assistance	62	69	45	24	111	180	169	22.8	28.9	6.1
Arts, entertainment, and recreation	71	67	30	37	86	51	61	–1.5	6.0	7.5
Accommodation and food services	72	103	50	53	246	148	158	–5.0	8.5	13.5
Other services	81	68	28	40	19	26	27	–0.1	1.6	1.7

X Not applicable. [1] Total assets are understated because not all partnerships file complete balance sheets. [2] Finance and insurance, real estate, and management of companies include investment income for partnerships. [3] Includes businesses not allocable to individual industries.

Source: U.S. Internal Revenue Service, *Statistics of Income*, various issues.

Table 750. Nonfarm Noncorporate Business-Sector Balance Sheet: 1990 to 2010

[In billions of dollars (3,617 represents $3,617,000,000,000), except as noted. Represents year-end outstandings]

Item	1990	1995	2000	2005	2006	2007	2008	2009	2010
Assets	3,617	4,062	6,526	10,938	11,869	12,314	11,129	9,924	9,893
Tangible assets	3,261	3,514	5,103	8,396	8,811	8,781	7,500	6,574	6,706
Real estate [1]	2,958	3,167	4,656	7,817	8,188	8,123	6,822	5,908	6,194
Residential	2,100	2,391	3,482	6,041	6,118	5,958	4,962	4,495	4,645
Nonresidential	858	776	1,174	1,776	2,069	2,165	1,861	1,413	1,549
Equipment and software [2]	256	290	378	497	536	563	586	579	417
Residential [3]	28	32	35	43	46	47	49	46	44
Nonresidential	228	258	342	454	490	516	537	533	373
Inventories [2]	47	56	70	82	88	94	92	87	95
Financial assets	356	548	1,423	2,542	3,057	3,533	3,629	3,350	3,188
Checkable deposits and currency	71	105	164	355	429	494	498	459	437
Time and savings deposits	51	71	248	324	344	359	358	331	315
Money market fund shares	7	17	49	69	72	74	75	70	66
Treasury securities	13	24	40	56	56	59	52	48	46
Municipal securities	–	2	2	4	6	5	5	5	4
Mortgages	31	22	23	36	35	42	39	36	34
Trade receivables	98	140	342	431	471	526	523	482	459
Miscellaneous assets	86	167	554	1,266	1,644	1,973	2,079	1,919	1,827
Insurance receivables	39	44	46	65	67	69	71	71	71
Equity investment in GSEs [4]	1	1	2	2	2	2	4	5	5
Other	47	122	506	1,198	1,576	1,902	2,005	1,844	1,751
Liabilities	1,357	1,404	2,683	4,064	4,647	5,228	5,659	5,437	5,268
Credit market instruments	1,102	1,070	1,806	2,787	3,196	3,650	3,972	3,678	3,484
Bank loans n.e.c. [5]	136	165	361	630	743	882	1,000	805	728
Other loans and advances	103	100	137	150	164	175	208	199	206
Mortgages	863	805	1,308	2,008	2,289	2,593	2,764	2,674	2,550
Trade payables	60	86	260	329	349	379	367	333	314
Taxes payable	32	33	65	87	96	99	106	98	94
Miscellaneous liabilities	164	215	552	861	1,006	1,100	1,214	1,327	1,376
Net worth	2,260	2,657	3,843	6,874	7,222	7,086	5,470	4,487	4,625
Debt/net worth (percent)	48.8	40.3	47.0	40.0	44.2	51.5	72.6	82.0	75.3

– Represents or rounds to zero. [1] At market value. [2] At replacement (current) cost. [3] Durable goods in rental properties. [4] GSEs = government-sponsored enterprises. Equity in the Farm Credit System. [5] Not elsewhere classified.

Source: Board of Governors of the Federal Reserve System, "Federal Reserve Statistical Release, Z.1, Flow of Funds Accounts of the United States," March 2011, <http://www.federalreserve.gov/releases/z1/20100311/>.

Table 751. Nonfinancial Corporate Business-Sector Balance Sheet: 1990 to 2010

[In billions of dollars (9,723 represents $9,723,000,000,000). Represents year-end outstandings]

Item	1990	1995	2000	2005	2006	2007	2008	2009	2010
Assets	**9,723**	**11,514**	**19,065**	**24,626**	**27,001**	**28,813**	**26,808**	**25,165**	**27,024**
Tangible assets	6,137	6,543	9,318	12,752	14,371	15,095	13,922	11,901	12,787
Real estate [1]	3,383	3,149	4,887	7,603	8,886	9,339	8,074	6,211	6,915
Equipment and software [2]	1,852	2,325	3,109	3,592	3,821	3,961	4,103	4,033	4,076
Inventories [2]	901	1,070	1,322	1,557	1,664	1,795	1,745	1,657	1,796
Financial assets [3]	3,586	4,971	9,747	11,874	12,630	13,718	12,886	13,264	14,237
Checkable deposits and currency	166	205	246	268	151	142	33	185	354
Time and savings deposits	75	100	272	450	497	441	382	530	515
Money market fund shares	20	60	191	348	416	544	703	631	537
Treasury securities	38	57	18	52	45	38	30	45	53
Mortgages	53	58	44	68	60	41	34	26	18
Consumer credit	67	85	81	60	58	59	60	57	56
Trade receivables	967	1,185	1,939	2,108	2,090	2,253	2,081	1,963	2,056
Mutual fund shares [1]	10	46	122	140	181	191	126	190	249
Liabilities [3]	**4,729**	**6,010**	**9,611**	**11,145**	**11,782**	**12,873**	**13,173**	**13,192**	**13,863**
Credit market instruments	2,543	2,942	4,633	5,490	5,956	6,705	6,993	6,998	7,378
Commercial paper	117	157	278	90	113	124	131	58	83
Municipal securities [4]	115	135	154	177	182	190	193	198	207
Corporate bonds [5]	1,008	1,357	2,270	3,031	3,247	3,558	3,762	4,140	4,560
Bank loans n.e.c. [6]	545	602	853	509	518	610	664	543	529
Other loans and advances	482	477	726	932	1,062	1,350	1,405	1,261	1,269
Mortgages	275	213	351	751	834	873	837	798	731
Trade payables	626	877	1,541	1,699	1,813	1,899	1,669	1,612	1,795
Taxes payable	38	40	78	86	85	36	39	36	44
Net worth (market value)	**4,993**	**5,505**	**9,454**	**13,480**	**15,219**	**15,940**	**13,635**	**11,972**	**13,161**
Debt/net worth (percent)	50.9	53.4	49.0	40.7	39.1	42.1	51.3	58.5	56.1

[1] At market value. [2] At replacement (current) cost. [3] Includes items not shown separately. [4] Industrial revenue bonds. Issued by state and local governments to finance private investment and secured in interest and principal by the industrial user of the funds. [5] Through 1992, corporate bonds include net issues by Netherlands Antillean financial subsidiaries. [6] Not elsewhere classified.

Source: Board of Governors of the Federal Reserve System, "Federal Reserve Statistical Release, Z.1, Flow of Funds Accounts of the United States," March 2011, <http://www.federalreserve.gov/releases/z1/20100311/>.

Table 752. Corporate Funds—Sources and Uses: 1990 to 2010

[In billions of dollars (242 represents $242,000,000,000). Covers nonfarm nonfinancial corporate business. Minus sign (–) indicates a deficit]

Item	1990	1995	2000	2005	2006	2007	2008	2009	2010
Profits before tax	242	431	432	954	1,115	1,038	779	703	999
− Taxes on corporate income	98	140	170	271	307	293	226	170	262
− Net dividends	117	177	250	168	466	480	480	509	510
+ Capital consumption allowance [1]	365	461	636	606	636	673	854	812	753
= U.S. internal funds, book	392	575	649	1,121	978	937	927	837	980
+ Foreign earnings retained abroad	45	53	103	−18	149	169	183	198	216
+ Inventory valuation adjustment (IVA)	−13	−18	−17	−31	−38	−47	−44	12	−18
= Internal funds + IVA	424	610	735	1,089	1,089	1,058	1,069	1,049	1,181
Gross investment	374	659	916	948	975	950	169	995	1,080
Capital expenditures	433	625	953	966	1,113	1,156	1,113	804	999
Fixed investment [2]	422	580	901	919	1,040	1,130	1,137	923	942
Inventory change + IVA	12	40	53	47	60	28	−41	−125	59
Nonproduced nonfinancial assets	−1	5	−2	−1	13	−2	17	5	−3
Net financial investment	−59	33	−37	−17	−138	−207	−943	191	81
Net acquisition of financial assets [3]	124	424	1,201	944	698	1,071	−613	283	908
Foreign deposits	(Z)	2	−7	10	−14	1	−26	9	34
Checkable deposits and currency	6	4	15	74	−117	−9	−109	152	170
Time and savings deposits	−6	3	35	50	47	−56	−59	148	−15
Money market fund shares	9	23	37	40	68	128	158	−72	−93
Commercial paper	(−Z)	1	10	16	12	−53	−12	−15	17
Municipal securities	−8	−20	7	(Z)	−4	1	−3	(−Z)	(−Z)
Mortgages	−2	2	2	2	−8	−18	−8	−8	−8
Mutual fund shares	−1	5	4	1	25	(Z)	−6	40	40
Trade receivables	29	78	282	278	−18	163	−172	−118	85
Miscellaneous assets [3]	114	318	811	441	719	930	−366	131	660
U.S. direct investment abroad [4]	36	90	138	25	219	307	276	250	284
Insurance receivables	13	8	(−Z)	21	7	7	10	−2	1
Net increase in liabilities [3]	184	391	1,237	961	836	1,277	331	92	827
Net funds raised in markets	72	179	244	−18	−99	−44	−43	−69	81
Net new equity issues	−63	−58	−118	−342	−566	−787	−336	−65	−274
Credit market instruments [3]	135	237	362	324	467	743	293	−4	355
Corporate bonds [4]	47	104	164	57	216	311	205	377	420
Bank loans n.e.c [5]	3	75	44	−34	9	85	54	−131	−32
Other loans and advances [6]	55	30	84	109	133	288	55	−144	10
Mortgages	21	7	22	193	82	39	−31	−39	−76
Trade payables	28	81	313	199	110	86	−230	−57	183
Miscellaneous liabilities [3]	83	131	673	782	826	1,285	601	220	555
Foreign direct investment in U.S	59	55	249	99	191	287	235	101	169

Z Less than $500 million. [1] Consumption of fixed capital plus capital consumption adjustment. [2] Nonresidential fixed investment plus residential fixed investment. [3] Includes other items not shown separately. [4] 1990, corporate bonds include net issues by Netherlands Antillean financial subsidiaries, and U.S. direct investment abroad excludes net inflows from those bond issues. [5] Not elsewhere classified. [6] Loans from rest of the world, U.S. government, and nonbank financial institutions.

Source: Board of Governors of the Federal Reserve System, "Federal Reserve Statistical Release, Z.1, Flow of Funds Accounts of the United States," March 2011, <http://www.federalreserve.gov/releases/z1/20100311/>.

Table 753. Corporations—Selected Financial Items: 1990 to 2008

[In billions of dollars (18,190 represents $18,190,000,000,000), except as noted. Covers active corporations only. All corporations are required to file returns except those specifically exempt. See source for changes in law affecting comparability of historical data. Based on samples; see Appendix III]

Item	1990	1995	2000	2003	2004	2005	2006	2007	2008
Number of returns (1,000)........	3,717	4,474	5,045	5,401	5,558	5,671	5,841	5,869	5,847
Number with net income (1,000)....	1,911	2,455	2,819	2,932	3,116	3,324	3,367	3,368	3,184
S Corporation returns [1] (1,000).....	1,575	2,153	2,860	3,342	3,518	3,684	3,873	3,990	4,050
Assets [2]	18,190	26,014	47,027	53,645	60,118	66,445	73,081	81,486	76,799
Cash	771	962	1,820	2,120	2,730	2,823	2,902	3,625	4,384
Notes and accounts receivable	4,198	5,307	8,754	8,995	10,691	11,962	13,611	15,315	13,855
Inventories....................	894	1,045	1,272	1,267	1,386	1,505	1,613	1,656	1,619
Investments in government obligations	921	1,363	1,236	1,656	1,571	1,613	1,714	1,785	2,193
Mortgage and real estate	1,538	1,713	2,822	4,073	4,627	4,777	5,232	5,177	5,450
Other investments	4,137	7,429	17,874	20,536	22,657	25,162	27,903	30,939	27,169
Depreciable assets	4,318	5,571	7,292	7,805	7,974	8,416	8,817	9,222	9,467
Depletable assets	129	154	191	237	270	310	382	497	587
Land........................	210	242	303	342	363	407	457	493	509
Liabilities [2]	18,190	26,014	47,027	53,645	60,118	66,445	73,081	81,486	76,799
Accounts payable	1,094	1,750	3,758	4,338	5,645	6,029	7,779	7,724	6,822
Short-term debt [3]...............	1,803	2,034	4,020	4,002	4,399	4,192	4,709	4,735	4,726
Long-term debt [4]	2,665	3,335	6,184	7,384	8,154	8,332	9,399	10,786	11,062
Net worth [5]...................	4,739	8,132	17,349	18,819	20,814	23,525	25,996	28,812	25,469
Capital stock	1,585	2,194	3,966	3,151	2,308	2,482	2,513	2,775	3,184
Paid-in or capital surplus	2,814	5,446	12,265	15,258	16,160	17,828	19,142	21,792	23,574
Retained earnings [6]............	1,410	2,191	3,627	2,282	3,278	4,331	5,764	5,970	613
Receipts [2,7]	11,410	14,539	20,606	20,690	22,712	25,505	27,402	28,763	28,590
Business receipts [7,8]	9,860	12,786	17,637	18,264	19,976	21,800	23,310	24,217	24,718
Interest [9]	977	1,039	1,628	1,182	1,368	1,773	2,307	2,640	2,179
Rents and royalties	133	145	254	270	274	290	299	314	317
Deductions [2,7]	11,033	13,821	19,692	19,941	21,636	23,613	25,502	26,974	27,687
Cost of sales and operations [8]......	6,611	8,206	11,135	11,319	12,498	13,816	14,800	15,513	16,080
Compensation of officers.........	205	304	401	389	417	445	474	479	467
Rent paid on business property.....	185	232	380	407	420	439	462	477	491
Taxes paid...................	251	326	390	417	447	473	497	509	469
Interest paid..................	825	744	1,272	818	939	1,287	1,787	2,085	1,659
Depreciation	333	437	614	692	691	531	564	599	759
Advertising...................	126	163	234	225	239	253	277	277	267
Net income (less loss) [7,10]	371	714	928	780	1,112	1,949	1,933	1,837	984
Net income	553	881	1,337	1,176	1,456	2,235	2,240	2,253	1,807
Deficit.......................	182	166	409	396	344	286	306	416	823
Income subject to tax............	366	565	760	699	857	1,201	1,291	1,248	978
Income tax before credits [11].........	119	194	266	244	300	419	453	437	342
Tax credits...................	32	42	62	66	75	107	100	106	114
Foreign tax credit...............	25	30	49	50	57	82	78	87	100
Income tax after credits [12]	96	156	204	178	224	312	353	331	229

[1] Represents certain small corporations with a limit on the number of shareholders, mostly individuals, electing to be taxed at the shareholder level. [2] Includes items not shown separately. [3] Payable in less than 1 year. [4] Payable in 1 year or more. [5] Net worth is the sum of "capital stock," "additional paid-in capital," "retained earnings, appropriated," "retained earnings, unappropriated" minus "cost of treasury stock." [6] Appropriated and unappropriated and "adjustments to shareholders' equity." [7] Receipts, deductions, and net income of S corporations are limited to those from trade or business. Those from investments are excluded. [8] Includes gross sales and cost of sales of securities, commodities, and real estate by exchanges, brokers, or dealers selling on their own accounts. Excludes investment income. [9] Includes tax-exempt interest in state and local government obligations. [10] Excludes regulated investment companies. [11] Consists of regular (and alternative tax) only. [12] Includes minimum tax, alternative minimum tax, adjustments for prior year credits, and other income-related taxes.

Source: U.S. Internal Revenue Service, *Statistics of Income, Corporation Income Tax Returns*, annual.

Table 754. Corporations by Receipt-Size Class and Industry: 2008

[Number of returns in thousands (5,847 represents 5,847,000); receipts and net income in billions of dollars (27,266 represents $27,266,000,000,000). Covers active enterprises only. Figures are estimates based on a sample of unaudited tax returns; see Appendix III. Numbers in parentheses represent North American Industry Classification System 2007 codes; see text, this section. Minus sign (–) indicates a loss]

Industry	Total	Under $1 mil. [1]	$1 to $4.9 mil.	$5 to $9.9 mil.	$10 to $49.9 mil.	$50 mil. or more
Total: [2]						
Number of returns	**5,847**	4,764	787	136	126	34
Business receipts [3]	**27,266**	942	1,711	947	2,569	21,097
Net income (less loss)	**984**	-65	48	27	81	894
Agriculture, forestry, fishing, and hunting (11):						
Returns	137	119	15	2	1	(Z)
Business receipts [3]	150	21	32	13	27	56
Mining (21):						
Returns	39	29	6	2	1	(Z)
Business receipts [3]	421	5	14	11	24	367
Utilities (22):						
Returns	7	6	1	(Z)	(Z)	(Z)
Business receipts [3]	738	1	1	1	3	732
Construction (23):						
Returns	767	599	126	21	17	3
Business receipts [3]	1,459	144	272	144	344	554
Manufacturing (31–33):						
Returns	271	165	64	16	19	7
Business receipts [3]	7,555	40	149	115	391	6,862
Wholesale and retail trade (42, 44–45):						
Returns	986	668	212	46	48	12
Business receipts [3]	7,343	172	490	320	990	5,371
Transportation and warehousing (48–49):						
Returns	195	153	28	8	5	1
Business receipts [3]	795	31	62	52	93	558
Information (51):						
Returns	118	100	13	2	3	1
Business receipts [3]	975	15	31	14	59	857
Finance and insurance (52):						
Returns	254	216	24	5	6	3
Business receipts [3]	3,675	24	51	33	145	3,422
Real estate and rental and leasing (53):						
Returns	649	626	19	2	1	(Z)
Business receipts [3]	235	50	42	12	28	102
Professional, scientific, and technical services (54):						
Returns	845	743	80	12	9	2
Business receipts [3]	1,013	133	166	84	172	458
Management of companies and enterprises (55):						
Returns	46	39	2	1	2	1
Business receipts [3]	1,028	-6	6	10	46	972
Administrative and support and waste management and remediation services (56):						
Returns	276	229	39	4	3	1
Business receipts [3]	485	49	81	28	71	256
Educational services (61):						
Returns	52	48	4	(Z)	(Z)	(Z)
Business receipts [3]	46	7	7	3	6	24
Health care and social assistance (62):						
Returns	416	329	73	8	5	1
Business receipts [3]	619	99	143	56	97	224
Arts, entertainment, and recreation (71):						
Returns	122	113	8	1	1	(Z)
Business receipts [3]	96	18	17	8	14	39
Accommodation and food services (72):						
Returns	293	242	46	3	2	(Z)
Business receipts [3]	434	72	90	24	36	212
Other services (81):						
Returns	371	338	29	3	1	(Z)
Business receipts [3]	198	67	55	19	24	32

Z Less than 500 returns. [1] Includes businesses without receipts. [2] Includes businesses not allocable to individual industries. [3] Includes investment income for corporations in finance and insurance and management of companies' industries. Excludes investment income for S corporations (certain small corporations with up to 75 shareholders, mostly individuals, electing to be taxed at the shareholder level).

Source: U.S. Internal Revenue Service, *Statistics of Income, Corporation Income Tax Returns*, annual.

Table 755. Corporations by Asset-Size Class and Industry: 2008

[In billions of dollars (168 represents $168,000,000,000), except number of returns. Covers active corporations only. Excludes corporations not allocable by industry. Numbers in parentheses represent North American Industry Classification System 2007 codes; see text, this section]

Industry	Total	Asset-size class					
		Under $10 mil.[1]	$10 to $24.9 mil.	$25 to $49.9 mil.	$50 to $99.9 mil.	$100 to $249.9 mil.	$250 mil. and over
Agriculture, forestry, fishing, and hunting (11):							
Returns	137,294	136,000	838	235	112	71	38
Total receipts	168	99	15	7	9	12	25
Mining (21):							
Returns	38,506	36,654	824	372	217	180	257
Total receipts	469	46	10	11	9	16	376
Utilities (22):							
Returns	7,238	6,746	151	69	47	49	177
Total receipts	779	4	3	3	6	9	753
Construction (23):							
Returns	766,689	757,643	6,167	1,630	705	333	211
Total receipts	1,479	805	180	96	83	77	238
Manufacturing (31–33):							
Returns	270,727	254,928	7,595	3,173	1,838	1,380	1,813
Total receipts	8,181	535	224	185	193	290	6,754
Wholesale and retail trade (42, 44–45):							
Returns	986,366	967,434	11,944	3,552	1,620	922	896
Total receipts	7,507	2,000	601	389	311	394	3,814
Transportation and warehousing (48–49):							
Returns	195,228	193,101	1,246	342	207	147	184
Total receipts	822	232	40	22	26	28	474
Information (51):							
Returns	118,279	115,530	1,245	493	320	266	425
Total receipts	1,126	111	22	15	17	31	931
Finance and insurance (52):							
Returns	254,092	234,466	3,997	2,645	2,817	3,496	6,672
Total receipts	3,675	212	23	23	32	69	3,317
Real estate and rental and leasing (53):							
Returns	648,578	640,403	4,889	1,459	749	525	552
Total receipts	339	123	14	11	10	16	164
Professional, scientific, and technical services (54):							
Returns	845,356	840,495	2,740	895	527	384	315
Total receipts	1,050	540	73	40	42	60	296
Management of companies and enterprises (55):							
Returns	45,725	38,784	1,163	1,013	1,153	1,727	1,885
Total receipts	1,028	6	2	2	5	17	995
Administrative and support and waste management and remediation services (56):							
Returns	276,344	275,003	684	220	164	116	156
Total receipts	497	239	25	14	19	23	177
Educational services (61):							
Returns	52,484	52,250	104	46	33	31	20
Total receipts	48	20	2	2	3	5	15
Health care and social assistance (62):							
Returns	416,101	414,947	591	212	132	101	117
Total receipts	644	404	21	16	15	20	167
Arts, entertainment, and recreation (71):							
Returns	122,425	121,643	396	199	69	60	58
Total receipts	104	53	5	4	3	7	32
Accommodation and food services (72):							
Returns	292,901	291,455	821	266	130	89	139
Total receipts	469	213	17	12	13	20	195
Other services (81):							
Returns	371,146	370,544	385	109	57	23	27
Total receipts	204	163	8	5	6	3	20

[1] Includes returns with zero assets.
Source: U.S. Internal Revenue Service, *Statistics of Income, Corporation Income Tax Returns*, annual.

U.S. Census Bureau, Statistical Abstract of the United States: 2012

Table 756. Economic Census Summary (NAICS 2002 Basis): 2002 and 2007

[24 represents 24,000. Covers establishments with payroll. Data are based on the 2002 and 2007 economic censuses which are subject to nonsampling error. Data for the construction sector are also subject to sampling errors. For details on survey methodology and nonsampling and sampling errors, see Appendix III]

Kind of business	2002 NAICS code [1]	Establish-ments (1,000)		Sales, receipts, or shipments (bil. dol.)		Annual payroll (bil. dol.)		Paid employees [2] (1,000)	
		2002	2007	2002	2007	2002	2007	2002	2007
Mining	21	24	23	183	414	21	41	475	739
Oil & gas extraction	211	8	6	113	255	5	10	99	150
Mining (except oil & gas)	212	7	6	48	86	9	12	196	211
Mining support activities	213	9	10	22	73	7	20	180	377
Utilities	22	17	17	399	584	42	52	663	637
Construction	23	710	729	1,209	1,732	254	331	7,193	7,316
Manufacturing	31–33	351	333	3,915	5,319	568	614	14,664	13,396
Wholesale trade	42	436	435	4,635	6,516	260	336	5,878	6,227
Merchant wholesalers, durable goods	423	260	255	2,171	2,898	157	207	3,357	3,619
Merchant wholesalers, nondurable goods	424	143	135	1,980	2,991	93	116	2,273	2,320
Wholesale electronic markets and agents and brokers	425	32	45	483	627	10	13	249	289
Retail trade	44–45	1,115	1,128	3,056	3,918	302	363	14,648	15,515
Motor vehicle & parts dealers	441	125	127	802	891	65	73	1,845	1,914
Furniture & home furnishings stores	442	65	65	92	108	13	15	535	557
Electronics & appliance stores	443	47	51	82	109	9	11	391	486
Bldg. material & garden equipment & supplies dealers	444	(NA)	91	(NA)	318	(NA)	38	(NA)	1,331
Food & beverage stores	445	149	146	457	539	49	55	2,839	2,827
Health & personal care stores	446	82	88	178	234	20	28	1,024	1,068
Gasoline stations	447	121	119	249	450	14	15	927	891
Clothing & clothing accessories stores	448	150	156	168	216	21	27	1,427	1,644
Sporting goods, hobby, book, & music stores	451	62	57	73	81	9	9	611	619
General merchandise stores	452	41	46	445	577	43	54	2,525	2,763
Miscellaneous store retailers	453	129	122	91	104	13	14	792	792
Nonstore retailers	454	55	59	173	290	17	23	571	621
Transportation & warehousing [3]	48–49	200	220	382	640	116	173	3,651	4,454
Information	51	138	142	892	1,072	195	229	3,736	3,497
Publishing industries (except Internet)	511	32	31	242	282	66	81	1,090	1,093
Motion picture & sound recording industries	512	22	24	78	95	13	18	303	336
Broadcasting (except Internet)	515	10	10	74	100	14	18	291	295
Internet publishing and broadcasting	516	2	3	6	15	2	5	40	57
Telecommunications	517	49	49	412	480	72	73	1,440	1,216
Internet service providers, Web search portals, and data processing	518	19	21	75	94	26	33	514	448
Other information services	519	3	4	5	6	2	2	58	53
Finance & insurance [4]	52	440	507	2,804	3,711	378	505	6,579	6,649
Real estate & rental & leasing [4]	53	323	380	336	443	60	82	1,949	2,147
Professional, scientific, & technical services	54	771	855	887	1,258	376	505	7,244	7,908
Management of companies & enterprises	55	49	51	107	104	179	250	2,605	2,664
Admin/support waste management/remediation services	56	351	388	433	624	206	298	8,742	10,213
Administrative & support services	561	332	366	381	549	194	281	8,410	9,827
Waste management & remediation services	562	19	22	51	75	12	17	332	386
Educational services	61	49	61	31	45	10	14	430	540
Health care and social assistance	62	705	785	1,207	1,668	496	663	15,052	16,792
Ambulatory health care services	621	489	548	489	668	203	275	4,925	5,703
Hospitals	622	6	7	500	703	197	265	5,174	5,529
Nursing & residential care facilities	623	69	76	127	169	59	75	2,831	3,071
Social assistance	624	140	154	91	128	36	48	2,123	2,489
Arts, entertainment, & recreation	71	110	125	142	189	45	58	1,849	2,061
Performing arts, spectator sports, & related industries	711	38	44	58	78	21	28	423	438
Museums, historical sites, & like institutions	712	7	7	9	13	3	4	123	130
Amusement, gambling, & recreation industries	713	66	74	75	98	21	27	1,303	1,494
Accommodation & food services	72	566	634	449	614	128	171	10,121	11,601
Accommodation	721	61	63	128	180	35	46	1,813	1,971
Food services & drinking places	722	505	572	321	433	93	124	8,308	9,630
Other services (except public administration)	81	538	540	307	405	83	99	3,475	3,479
Repair & maintenance	811	231	222	118	138	35	40	1,285	1,261
Personal and laundry services	812	201	210	72	82	23	27	1,297	1,338
Religious/grantmaking/prof/like organizations	813	106	108	117	185	25	32	893	880

NA Not available. [1] Based on North American Industry Classification System, 2002; see text, this section. [2] For pay period including March 12. [3] For detailed industries, see Table 1066. [4] For detailed industries, see Table 1163.

Source: U.S. Census Bureau, "2007 Economic Census, Comparative Statistics for United States, Summary Statistics by 2002 NAICS," <http://factfinder.census.gov/>.

Table 757. Nonemployer Establishments and Receipts by Industry: 2000 to 2008

[Establishments: 16,530 represents 16,530,000. Includes only firms subject to federal income tax. Nonemployers are businesses with no paid employees. Data originate chiefly from administrative records of the Internal Revenue Service; see Appendix III. Data for 2000 based on the North American Industry Classification System (NAICS), 1997; 2007 data based on NAICS 2002; and 2008 data based on NAICS 2007. See text, this section]

Kind of business	NAICS code	Establishments (1,000)			Receipts (mil. dol.)		
		2000	2007	2008	2000	2007	2008
All industries	(X)	**16,530**	**21,708**	**21,351**	**709,379**	**991,792**	**962,792**
Forestry, fishing & hunting, & agricultural support services	113–115	223	236	231	9,196	10,963	10,883
Mining, quarrying, and oil and gas extraction	21	86	102	109	5,227	9,012	11,609
Utilities	22	14	18	18	504	728	760
Construction	23	2,014	2,657	2,528	107,538	159,042	143,954
Manufacturing	31–33	285	328	314	13,022	16,333	15,697
Wholesale trade	42	388	402	388	31,684	35,823	35,558
Retail trade	44–45	1,743	1,980	1,875	73,810	88,143	83,978
Transportation & warehousing	48–49	747	1,083	1,039	37,824	66,633	67,026
Information	51	238	307	306	7,620	10,958	11,060
Finance & insurance	52	692	764	734	49,058	54,351	56,434
Real estate & rental & leasing	53	1,696	2,327	2,130	133,398	183,264	163,461
Professional, scientific, & technical services	54	2,420	3,029	3,029	90,272	130,386	131,521
Admin/support waste mgt/remediation services	56	1,032	1,793	1,826	23,754	39,811	40,415
Educational services	61	283	528	552	3,736	7,215	7,569
Health care & social assistance	62	1,317	1,768	1,812	36,550	55,050	57,888
Arts, entertainment, & recreation	71	782	1,120	1,121	17,713	27,357	27,837
Accommodation & food services	72	218	303	308	13,418	16,071	16,100
Other services (except public administration)	81	2,350	2,965	3,029	55,056	80,653	81,042

X Not applicable.
Source: U.S. Census Bureau, "Nonemployer Statistics," June 2010, <http://www.census.gov/econ/nonemployer/>.

Table 758. Establishments, Employees, and Payroll by Employment-Size Class: 1990 to 2008

[6,176 represents 6,176,000. Excludes most government employees, railroad employees, and self-employed persons. Employees are for the week including March 12. Covers establishments with payroll. An *establishment* is a single physical location where business is conducted or where services or industrial operations are performed. For statement on methodology, see Appendix III]

Employment-size class	Unit	1990	1995	2000	2004	2005	2006	2007	2008
Establishments, total	**1,000**	**6,176**	**6,613**	**7,070**	**7,388**	**7,500**	**7,601**	**7,705**	**7,601**
Under 20 employees	1,000	5,354	5,733	6,069	6,359	6,468	6,533	6,633	6,528
20 to 99 employees	1,000	684	730	826	856	856	886	892	890
100 to 499 employees	1,000	122	135	157	154	157	163	161	164
500 to 999 employees	1,000	10	10	12	12	12	12	12	12
1,000 or more employees	1,000	6	6	7	7	7	7	7	7
Employees, total	**1,000**	**93,476**	**100,335**	**114,065**	**115,075**	**116,317**	**119,917**	**120,604**	**120,904**
Under 20 employees	1,000	24,373	25,785	27,569	28,701	28,874	29,429	30,057	29,839
20 to 99 employees	1,000	27,414	29,202	33,147	34,288	34,302	35,504	35,615	35,508
100 to 499 employees	1,000	22,926	25,364	29,736	28,976	29,591	30,616	30,453	30,850
500 to 999 employees	1,000	6,551	7,021	8,291	7,815	8,053	8,248	8,284	8,236
1,000 or more employees	1,000	12,212	12,962	15,322	15,295	15,497	16,120	16,196	16,471
Annual payroll, total	**Bil. dol.**	**2,104**	**2,666**	**3,879**	**4,254**	**4,483**	**4,792**	**5,027**	**5,131**
Under 20 employees	Bil. dol	485	608	818	926	970	1,021	1,067	1,078
20 to 99 employees	Bil. dol	547	696	1,006	1,124	1,177	1,260	1,313	1,334
100 to 499 employees	Bil. dol	518	675	1,031	1,106	1,176	1,264	1,310	1,348
500 to 999 employees	Bil. dol	174	219	336	355	376	401	428	432
1,000 or more employees	Bil. dol	381	467	690	743	784	848	910	939

Source: U.S. Census Bureau, "County Business Patterns," July 2010, <http://www.census.gov/econ/cbp/>.

Table 759. Establishments, Employees, and Payroll by Employment-Size Class and Industry: 2000 to 2008

[Establishments and employees in thousands (7,070.0 represents 7,070,000); payroll in billions of dollars. See headnote, Table 758. Data for 2000 based on the North American Industry Classification System (NAICS), 1997; 2007 data based on NAICS 2002; 2008 data based on NAICS 2007. See text, this section]

Industry	NAICS code	2000, total	2007, total	2008					
				Total	Under 20 employ-ees	20 to 99 employ-ees	100 to 499 employ-ees	500 to 999 employ-ees	1,000 or more employ-ees
Establishments, total [1]	(X)	**7,070.0**	**7,705.0**	**7,601.2**	**6,528.4**	**889.8**	**163.7**	**12.1**	**7.1**
Forestry, fishing & hunting, & ag support services	113–115	26.1	23.6	22.7	21.2	1.2	0.2	(Z)	(Z)
Mining, quarrying, and oil and gas extraction	21	23.7	26.2	27.4	21.9	4.5	1.0	0.1	(Z)
Utilities	22	17.3	16.7	17.0	11.7	3.9	1.2	0.1	(Z)
Construction	23	709.6	811.5	773.6	704.3	60.8	8.0	0.4	0.2
Manufacturing	31–33	354.5	331.4	326.2	224.5	73.7	24.7	2.3	1.0
Wholesale trade	42	446.2	434.5	429.5	364.8	55.7	8.3	0.5	0.2
Retail trade	44–45	1,113.6	1,123.6	1,100.9	945.9	127.2	27.4	0.4	(Z)
Transportation and warehousing	48–49	190.0	219.8	217.1	180.7	28.7	6.7	0.7	0.3
Information	51	133.6	143.8	141.6	113.8	21.6	5.3	0.6	0.3
Finance and insurance	52	423.7	508.1	501.9	457.6	36.0	6.7	1.0	0.6
Real estate and rental and leasing	53	300.2	380.1	365.7	349.6	14.2	1.8	0.1	(Z)
Professional, scientific, and technical services	54	722.7	867.6	848.3	783.2	55.0	9.0	0.7	0.4
Management of companies and enterprises	55	47.4	50.6	51.8	34.6	11.7	4.4	0.7	0.4
Admin/support waste mgt/remediation services	56	351.5	384.5	393.5	328.4	47.3	15.5	1.5	0.9
Educational services	61	68.0	86.9	88.6	67.9	16.5	3.4	0.4	0.4
Health care and social assistance	62	658.6	784.2	791.0	667.1	97.7	22.4	1.8	2.0
Arts, entertainment, and recreation	71	103.8	125.2	124.3	104.3	16.3	3.3	0.2	0.1
Accommodation and food services	72	542.4	632.5	636.6	452.5	172.7	10.8	0.4	0.2
Other services [2]	81	723.3	744.3	730.7	681.6	45.1	3.7	0.2	0.1
Unclassified establishments	99	99.0	10.0	12.9	12.9	(Z)	–	–	–
Employees, total [1]	(X)	**114,065**	**120,604**	**120,904**	**29,839**	**35,508**	**30,850**	**8,236**	**16,471**
Forestry, fishing & hunting, & ag support services	113–115	184	172	167	75	46	32	5	8
Mining, quarrying, and oil and gas extraction	21	456	701	629	105	182	197	63	82
Utilities	22	655	623	639	63	171	230	100	75
Construction	23	6,573	7,268	7,044	2,642	2,361	1,455	251	334
Manufacturing	31–33	16,474	13,320	13,096	1,303	3,241	4,928	1,578	2,046
Wholesale trade	42	6,112	5,965	6,165	1,773	2,188	1,550	315	340
Retail trade	44–45	14,841	15,760	15,615	5,167	5,062	5,046	247	93
Transportation and warehousing	48–49	3,790	4,395	4,439	752	1,188	1,287	468	744
Information	51	3,546	3,399	3,434	518	907	1,045	411	553
Finance and insurance	52	5,963	6,549	6,512	1,979	1,396	1,346	683	1,107
Real estate and rental and leasing	53	1,942	2,224	2,196	1,169	533	324	85	86
Professional, scientific, and technical services	54	6,816	8,180	8,033	2,699	2,147	1,712	494	980
Management of companies and enterprises	55	2,874	3,121	2,887	187	517	938	456	790
Admin/support waste mgt/remediation services	56	9,138	9,984	10,225	1,286	2,051	3,052	1,000	2,836
Educational services	61	2,532	3,039	3,141	330	698	643	296	1,174
Health care and social assistance	62	14,109	16,798	17,217	3,560	3,896	4,125	1,248	4,388
Arts, entertainment, and recreation	71	1,741	2,009	2,069	396	690	617	141	226
Accommodation and food services	72	9,881	11,565	11,926	2,910	6,589	1,692	291	445
Other services [2]	81	5,293	5,520	5,453	2,910	1,642	630	108	163
Unclassified establishments	99	144	13	15	4	1	–	–	–
Annual payroll, total [1]	(X)	**3,879**	**5,027**	**5,131**	**1,078**	**1,334**	**1,348**	**432**	**939**
Forestry, fishing & hunting, & ag support services	113–115	5	6	6	3	2	1	(Z)	(Z)
Mining, quarrying, and oil and gas extraction	21	22	40	48	7	13	16	5	7
Utilities	22	41	51	55	5	13	20	11	7
Construction	23	240	336	333	102	118	80	15	18
Manufacturing	31–33	644	627	622	49	137	226	81	130
Wholesale trade	42	270	328	353	90	119	90	22	32
Retail trade	44–45	303	375	369	116	123	120	7	4
Transportation and warehousing	48–49	126	175	176	29	46	49	18	34
Information	51	209	223	234	31	54	74	29	45
Finance and insurance	52	347	511	522	107	115	126	55	119
Real estate and rental and leasing	53	59	89	89	41	24	15	4	4
Professional, scientific, and technical services	54	362	533	539	144	149	135	40	72
Management of companies and enterprises	55	211	293	273	19	45	87	42	81
Admin/support waste mgt/remediation services	56	210	300	314	48	68	82	25	91
Educational services	61	62	94	102	8	20	21	8	45
Health care and social assistance	62	431	668	707	152	142	134	55	224
Arts, entertainment, and recreation	71	43	60	62	15	14	22	5	6
Accommodation and food services	72	126	176	183	43	90	30	8	14
Other services [2]	81	110	141	143	70	43	21	4	6
Unclassified establishments	99	4	(Z)	(Z)	(Z)	(Z)	–	–	–

– Represents zero. X Not applicable. Z Less than 50 establishments or $500 million. [1] Totals for 2000 include auxiliaries. Beginning 2007, cases previously classified under NAICS code 95 (auxiliaries) are coded in the operating NAICS sector of the establishment. [2] Except public administration.
Source: U.S. Census Bureau, "County Business Patterns," July 2010, <http://www.census.gov/econ/cbp/>.

Table 760. Employer Firms, Employment, and Annual Payroll by Employment Size of Firm and Industry: 2008

[5,930 represents 5,930,000. A firm is an aggregation of all establishments owned by a parent company (within a geographic location and/or industry) with some annual payroll. A firm may be a single location or it can include multiple locations. Employment is measured in March and payroll is annual leading to some firms with zero employment. Numbers in parentheses represent North American Industry Classification System codes, 2002; see text, this section]

Industry and data type	Unit	Total	All industries—employment size of firm						
			0 to 4	5 to 9	10 to 19	20 to 99	100 to 499	Less than 500	500 or more
Total [1]:									
Firms	1,000	5,930	3,618	1,044	633	526	90	5,912	18
Employment	1,000	120,904	6,086	6,878	8,497	20,685	17,548	59,694	61,210
Annual payroll	Bil. dol	5,131	232	223	294	775	706	2,229	2,901
Construction (23):									
Firms	1,000	761	501	125	72	56	7	760	1
Employment	1,000	7,044	810	818	959	2,116	1,219	5,921	1,122
Annual payroll	Bil. dol	333	30	29	40	102	65	265	68
Manufacturing (31–33):									
Firms	1,000	282	112	53	44	55	14	278	4
Employment	1,000	13,096	212	353	599	2,256	2,429	5,850	7,246
Annual payroll	Bil. dol	622	8	12	22	92	104	238	384
Wholesale trade (42):									
Firms	1,000	329	186	56	39	37	8	326	3
Employment	1,000	6,165	320	367	516	1,382	1,110	3,695	2,471
Annual payroll	Bil. dol	353	16	17	25	71	58	187	166
Retail trade (44–45):									
Firms	1,000	693	407	144	78	54	9	691	2
Employment	1,000	15,615	765	950	1,029	1,999	1,262	6,005	9,610
Annual payroll	Bil. dol	369	18	21	25	59	39	161	208
Transportation & warehousing (48–49):									
Firms	1,000	170	108	25	16	15	4	168	2
Employment	1,000	4,439	166	162	218	560	515	1,621	2,818
Annual payroll	Bil. dol	176	6	5	7	20	20	58	118
Information (51):									
Firms	1,000	73	42	11	8	8	2	72	1
Employment	1,000	3,434	64	72	107	323	350	917	2,518
Annual payroll	Bil. dol	234	4	3	5	19	22	53	181
Finance & insurance (52):									
Firms	1,000	253	181	36	16	15	4	252	2
Employment	1,000	6,512	316	227	209	605	738	2,094	4,417
Annual payroll	Bil. dol	522	14	12	15	45	54	139	383
Professional, scientific and technical services (54):									
Firms	1,000	772	560	105	58	40	7	769	3
Employment	1,000	8,033	850	684	766	1,492	1,118	4,910	3,122
Annual payroll	Bil. dol	539	44	33	43	99	79	298	241
Management of companies and enterprises (55):									
Firms	1,000	28	3	1	1	6	9	20	7
Employment	1,000	2,887	4	4	7	75	279	369	2,519
Annual payroll	Bil. dol	273	1	(Z)	1	5	19	25	248
Admin/support waste mgt/ remediation services (56):									
Firms	1,000	332	210	50	31	29	9	329	4
Employment	1,000	10,225	322	328	415	1,171	1,528	3,765	6,460
Annual payroll	Bil. dol	314	12	10	13	38	41	116	198
Educational services (61):									
Firms	1,000	79	39	12	10	13	3	77	1
Employment	1,000	3,141	60	81	137	562	568	1,408	1,733
Annual payroll	Bil. dol	102	2	2	3	15	18	40	62
Health care and social assistance (62):									
Firms	1,000	621	315	143	81	61	17	617	4
Employment	1,000	17,217	586	947	1,078	2,422	3,176	8,211	9,007
Annual payroll	Bil. dol	707	30	38	45	93	102	307	399
Accommodation and food services (72):									
Firms	1,000	477	198	94	87	86	9	475	2
Employment	1,000	11,926	331	630	1,178	3,202	1,664	7,005	4,921
Annual payroll	Bil. dol	183	8	8	14	44	24	98	85
Other services (except public administration) (81):									
Firms	1,000	667	420	135	66	40	4	666	1
Employment	1,000	5,453	792	882	862	1,446	633	4,615	837
Annual payroll	Bil. dol	143	18	20	21	37	20	116	27

Z Less than $500 million. [1] Includes other industries, not shown separately.
Source: U.S. Small Business Administration, Office of Advocacy, "Statistics of U.S. Businesses," <http://www.sba.gov/advo/research/data.html>, accessed May 2011.

502 Business Enterprise

Table 761. Employer Firms, Employment, and Payroll by Employment Size of Firm and State: 2000 and 2008

[5,652.5 represents 5,652,500. A firm is an aggregation of all establishments owned by a parent company (within a state) with some annual payroll. A firm may be a single location or it can include multiple locations. Employment is measured in March and payroll is annual leading to some firms with zero employment]

State	Employer firms (1,000) 2000 Total	2000 Less than 20 employees	2008 Total	2008 Less than 20 employees	2008 Less than 500 employees	Employment, 2008 (mil.) Total	Less than 20 employees	Less than 500 employees	Annual payroll, 2008 (bil. dol.) Total	Less than 20 employees	Less than 500 employees
U.S.	5,652.5	5,035.0	5,930.1	5,295.0	5,911.7	120.9	21.5	59.7	5,130.5	748.1	2,229.2
AL	79.9	68.2	79.8	67.5	77.5	1.7	0.3	0.8	59.8	8.8	27.0
AK	15.9	14.0	16.5	14.5	16.0	0.2	0.1	0.1	12.1	2.3	5.7
AZ	93.0	79.3	109.8	93.7	106.8	2.3	0.4	1.1	89.8	12.5	37.1
AR	52.4	45.4	52.7	45.2	51.0	1.0	0.2	0.5	33.8	5.2	14.3
CA	664.6	581.1	717.1	632.8	711.3	13.7	2.5	7.0	659.9	102.0	294.9
CO	116.2	101.5	130.3	114.7	127.3	2.1	0.4	1.1	91.2	15.0	40.4
CT	78.5	67.2	75.8	64.6	73.8	1.6	0.3	0.8	82.8	12.0	37.5
DE	20.2	16.6	20.4	16.3	18.9	0.4	0.1	0.2	17.6	2.3	7.0
DC	16.3	12.4	16.9	12.5	15.6	0.5	0.1	0.2	30.3	3.4	12.7
FL	354.0	319.3	414.8	376.7	410.3	7.4	1.3	3.2	267.4	43.8	110.2
GA	160.4	138.3	179.6	155.4	175.6	3.6	0.6	1.7	142.8	20.2	57.5
HI	24.3	20.8	26.4	22.3	25.5	0.5	0.1	0.3	18.5	3.2	9.6
ID	32.2	28.0	39.4	34.4	38.2	0.5	0.1	0.3	17.6	3.7	9.1
IL	254.1	218.1	260.2	225.0	255.8	5.5	0.9	2.6	250.5	34.0	106.7
IN	116.3	98.1	115.5	97.7	112.5	2.6	0.4	1.3	94.8	12.5	40.9
IA	65.6	56.2	65.0	55.5	63.2	1.3	0.2	0.7	45.2	6.4	20.7
KS	61.6	52.4	61.0	51.5	59.0	1.2	0.2	0.6	44.0	6.4	20.2
KY	72.3	61.0	71.5	60.1	69.2	1.6	0.3	0.8	54.1	7.4	23.0
LA	81.7	69.5	82.3	69.6	80.2	1.7	0.3	0.9	62.4	9.9	30.8
ME	34.1	30.1	34.9	30.7	34.0	0.5	0.1	0.3	17.7	3.5	9.5
MD	106.0	90.4	112.4	95.7	109.7	2.2	0.4	1.2	99.6	15.0	47.0
MA	148.2	127.8	141.8	122.0	138.8	3.1	0.5	1.5	161.8	21.4	68.4
MI	193.9	167.2	182.6	158.6	179.5	3.6	0.7	1.9	147.8	22.2	66.8
MN	116.2	99.4	121.0	103.9	118.4	2.5	0.4	1.2	109.4	13.7	45.1
MS	48.3	41.5	47.5	40.4	45.9	0.9	0.2	0.5	29.3	4.7	13.3
MO	118.1	101.1	120.1	102.9	117.3	2.5	0.4	1.2	93.7	12.5	38.9
MT	28.0	25.0	32.6	29.0	31.8	0.4	0.1	0.2	11.1	2.9	6.9
NE	41.4	35.5	42.3	36.1	40.9	0.8	0.1	0.4	28.2	4.0	12.5
NV	40.3	33.4	50.0	41.3	47.8	1.2	0.2	0.5	43.8	6.2	18.1
NH	32.1	27.3	32.3	27.3	31.1	0.6	0.1	0.3	25.0	4.3	12.1
NJ	202.2	178.4	202.6	178.2	199.4	3.6	0.7	1.8	185.4	28.1	80.7
NM	35.5	30.1	37.5	31.5	36.0	0.6	0.1	0.4	22.3	4.0	11.2
NY	424.8	379.2	444.0	397.5	439.7	7.6	1.5	3.9	440.6	61.0	183.6
NC	163.6	142.0	176.2	152.3	172.7	3.6	0.6	1.7	132.4	19.2	54.9
ND	17.2	14.7	17.9	15.0	17.2	0.3	0.1	0.2	10.1	1.8	5.3
OH	212.5	180.5	199.6	169.5	195.8	4.7	0.8	2.3	182.1	23.7	77.2
OK	70.2	61.0	73.3	63.1	71.3	1.3	0.3	0.7	48.0	7.8	22.7
OR	85.1	74.2	92.3	80.5	90.2	1.5	0.3	0.8	56.8	9.6	27.5
PA	237.5	204.6	237.1	203.7	233.1	5.2	0.9	2.6	215.8	29.1	92.4
RI	25.2	21.5	25.8	21.9	24.8	0.4	0.1	0.2	17.5	3.0	8.7
SC	78.4	67.2	83.4	71.3	81.1	1.7	0.3	0.8	55.1	8.9	24.2
SD	20.6	17.7	21.8	18.6	21.1	0.3	0.1	0.2	10.6	2.0	5.9
TN	102.4	86.7	102.4	86.0	99.3	2.5	0.4	1.1	90.9	12.0	38.2
TX	369.0	321.3	396.4	342.5	391.0	9.2	1.5	4.2	394.7	52.8	160.4
UT	46.2	39.3	60.3	51.9	58.4	1.1	0.2	0.5	39.4	6.0	17.6
VT	19.1	16.7	19.3	16.7	18.6	0.3	0.1	0.2	9.5	2.1	5.5
VA	139.7	120.3	154.8	133.5	151.5	3.2	0.6	1.5	138.9	19.5	60.3
WA	138.2	120.9	151.0	132.4	148.2	2.5	0.5	1.4	115.3	18.0	51.8
WV	33.5	28.8	30.9	26.0	29.7	0.6	0.1	0.3	19.2	3.0	8.9
WI	115.6	98.2	115.0	97.5	112.6	2.5	0.4	1.3	95.1	12.9	43.2
WY	15.9	13.9	18.1	15.7	17.5	0.2	0.1	0.1	8.9	2.1	5.1

Source: U.S. Small Business Administration, Office of Advocacy, "Statistics of U.S. Businesses," <http://www.sba.gov/advo/research/data.html>, accessed May 2011.

Table 762. Employer Firms, Establishments, Employment, and Annual Payroll by Firm Size: 1990 to 2008

[In thousands except as noted (5,074 represents 5,074,000). Firms are an aggregation of all establishments owned by a parent company with some annual payroll. Establishments are locations with active payroll in any quarter. This table illustrates the changing importance of enterprise sizes over time, not job growth, as enterprises can grow or decline and change enterprise size cells over time]

Item	Total	All industries—employment size of firm						
		0 to 4 [1]	5 to 9	10 to 19	20 to 99	100 to 499	Less than 500	500 or more
Firms:								
1990.................	5,074	3,021	952	563	454	70	5,060	14
1995.................	5,369	3,250	981	577	470	76	5,354	15
2000.................	5,653	3,397	1,021	617	516	84	5,635	17
2004.................	5,886	3,580	1,043	633	526	87	5,869	17
2005.................	5,984	3,678	1,050	630	521	87	5,966	17
2006.................	6,022	3,670	1,061	647	536	91	6,004	18
2007.................	6,050	3,705	1,060	645	532	89	6,031	18
2008.................	5,930	3,618	1,044	633	526	90	5,912	18
Establishments:								
1990.................	6,176	3,032	971	600	590	255	5,448	728
1995.................	6,613	3,260	998	618	639	284	5,799	814
2000.................	7,070	3,406	1,035	652	674	312	6,080	990
2004.................	7,388	3,586	1,056	667	693	330	6,331	1,056
2005.................	7,500	3,684	1,063	662	679	332	6,421	1,079
2006.................	7,601	3,677	1,073	679	698	346	6,473	1,129
2007.................	7,705	3,711	1,074	682	723	356	6,546	1,159
2008.................	7,601	3,625	1,057	667	705	360	6,414	1,187
Employment:								
1990.................	93,469	5,117	6,252	7,543	17,710	13,545	50,167	43,302
1995.................	100,315	5,395	6,440	7,734	18,422	14,660	52,653	47,662
2000.................	114,065	5,593	6,709	8,286	20,277	16,260	57,124	56,941
2004.................	115,075	5,845	6,853	8,500	20,643	16,758	58,597	56,477
2005.................	116,317	5,937	6,898	8,454	20,444	16,911	58,645	57,672
2006.................	119,917	5,960	6,974	8,676	21,077	17,537	60,224	59,693
2007.................	120,604	6,139	6,975	8,656	20,923	17,174	59,867	60,737
2008.................	120,904	6,086	6,878	8,497	20,685	17,548	59,694	61,210
Annual payroll (bil. dol.):								
1990.................	2,104	117	114	144	352	279	1,007	1,097
1995.................	2,666	142	137	175	437	361	1,252	1,414
2000.................	3,879	186	174	231	608	528	1,727	2,152
2004.................	4,254	206	196	258	670	588	1,917	2,337
2005.................	4,483	220	206	269	700	617	2,013	2,470
2006.................	4,792	230	214	282	742	661	2,129	2,664
2007.................	5,027	235	222	292	769	687	2,205	2,822
2008.................	5,131	232	223	294	775	706	2,229	2,901

[1] Employment is measured in March, thus some firms (start-ups after March, closures before March, and seasonal firms) will have zero employment and some annual payroll.

Source: U.S. Small Business Administration, Office of Advocacy, "Statistics of U.S. Businesses," <http://www.sba.gov/advo/research/data.html>, accessed May 2011.

Table 763. Number of Active Establishments by Firm Age and Size of Employer: 2009

[In thousands (2,794 represents 2,794,000). A firm may have one establishment (a single unit establishment) or many establishments (a multi-unit firm). Firms are defined at the enterprise level such that all establishments under the operational control of the enterprise are considered part of the firm. These data include nearly all nonfarm private establishments with paid employees as well as some public sector activities. The Business Dynamics Statistics data measure the net change in employment at the establishment level. Data are not to be compared with Table 760, which is shown by industry based on North American Industry Classification System codes. Data are also not comparable to U.S. Small Business Administration data (Tables 761 and 762) due to differing survey methodologies. For more information about concepts and methodology, see <http://www.ces.census.gov/index.php/bds/bds_overview>]

Firm age [1]	Firm size							Share of employment	Share of job creation	Share of job destruction
	1 to 4	5 to 9	10 to 19	20 to 99	100 to 499	Less than 500	500 or more			
Total..................	**2,794**	**1,074**	**657**	**680**	**349**	**5,554**	**1,141**	**1.00**	**1.00**	**1.00**
Startups.................	348	34	14	9	2	407	(Z)	0.06	0.16	–
1 to 5 years..............	924	295	154	112	23	1,507	10	0.23	0.16	0.20
6 to 10 years............	493	201	118	103	27	943	21	0.14	0.09	0.12
11 to 20 years...........	566	258	159	144	54	1,180	81	0.19	0.13	0.17
21 years and over.........	463	285	212	312	243	1,516	1,029	0.38	0.46	0.52
Share of employment......	0.05	0.06	0.07	0.17	0.14	0.50	0.50	(X)	(X)	(X)
Share of job creation.......	0.11	0.09	0.09	0.18	0.13	0.59	0.41	(X)	(X)	(X)

– Represents zero. X Not applicable. Z Less than 500. [1] Establishment age is computed by taking the difference between the current year of operation and the birth year. Firm age is computed from the age of the establishments belonging to that particular firm. For more information, see <http://www.ces.census.gov/index.php/bds/bds_overview>.

Source: U.S. Census Bureau, Center for Economic Studies, "Business Dynamics Statistics," <http://www.ces.census.gov/index.php/bds/bds_database_list>, accessed May 2011.

U.S. Census Bureau, Statistical Abstract of the United States: 2012

Table 764. Establishment Births, Deaths, and Employment by Sector and Firm Type—Startups, Young, and Mature Firms: 2009

[In thousands (388 represents 388,000). A firm may have one establishment (a single unit establishment) or many establishments (a multi-unit firm). Firms are defined at the enterprise level such that all establishments under the operational control of the enterprise are considered part of the firm. Sectors based on the Standard Industrial Classification System (SIC); see <http://www.osha.gov/pls/imis/sic_manual.html>. These data include nearly all nonfarm private establishments with paid employees as well as some public sector activities. The Business Dynamics Statistics data measure the net change in employment at the establishment level. Data are not comparable to Tables 760, 762, and 765, which are shown by industry based on North American Industry Classification System codes. Data are also not comparable to U.S. Small Business Administration data due to differing survey methodologies. For more information about concepts and methodology, see <http://www.ces.census.gov/index.php/bds/bds_overview>. Minus sign (–) indicates decrease]

| Sector and firm type [1] | Establishments | | | Number of employ-ees | Change in employment | | | | |
	Number	Births [2]	Deaths [3]		Net total	Due to births [2]	Due to deaths [3]	Due to birth and expan-sion [4]	Due to death and contrac-tion [4]
All sectors: [5]									
Startups [6]	388	388	–	2,218	2,218	2,126	–	2,218	–
Young firms [7]	2,443	95	500	22,048	–2,411	468	2,427	3,498	5,908
Mature firms [8]	3,771	150	276	89,140	–4,581	1,984	2,726	8,432	13,014
Agriculture:									
Startups [6]	10	10	–	42	42	42	–	42	–
Young firms [7]	60	3	13	441	–40	14	55	100	141
Mature firms [8]	53	2	5	641	–33	17	29	82	115
Mining:									
Startups [6]	2	2	–	15	15	(D)	–	15	–
Young firms [7]	9	–	1	127	–9	3	12	26	35
Mature firms [8]	15	1	1	481	–9	17	17	66	75
Construction:									
Startups [6]	19	19	–	79	79	79	–	79	–
Young firms [7]	172	8	52	1,173	–286	27	171	207	493
Mature firms [8]	252	7	34	3,678	–669	35	156	370	1,039
Transportation, communication, and utilities:									
Startups [6]	17	17	–	78	78	(D)	–	78	–
Young firms [7]	98	4	23	837	–82	23	97	139	221
Mature firms [8]	182	12	17	5,551	–273	168	190	540	813
Wholesale:									
Startups [6]	18	18	–	81	81	81	–	81	–
Young firms [7]	131	4	24	997	–100	20	105	148	248
Mature firms [8]	294	11	19	5,515	–266	132	203	562	828
Manufacturing:									
Startups [6]	11	11	–	120	120	120	–	120	–
Young firms [7]	90	3	16	1,212	–216	28	137	155	371
Mature firms [8]	202	5	14	11,580	–1,258	130	351	734	1,992
Retail:									
Startups [6]	94	94	–	742	742	742	–	742	–
Young firms [7]	511	17	104	4,920	–753	115	642	670	1,423
Mature firms [8]	877	32	48	19,116	–738	587	473	1,764	2,502
Finance, insurance, and real estate:									
Startups [6]	33	33	–	132	132	132	–	132	–
Young firms [7]	227	10	55	1,276	–157	38	193	223	379
Mature firms [8]	462	27	38	6,728	–314	232	292	749	1,062
Services:									
Startups [6]	184	184	–	931	931	931	–	931	–
Young firms [7]	1,146	44	212	11,065	–768	200	1,015	1,830	2,598
Mature firms [8]	1,435	54	100	35,850	–1,021	665	1,015	3,567	4,588

– Represents zero. D Figure withheld to avoid disclosure pertaining to a specific organization or individual. [1] Establishment type is computed by taking the difference between the current year of operation and the birth year. Firm age is computed from the age of the establishments belonging to that particular firm. For more information, see <http://www.ces.census.gov/index.php/bds/bds_overview>. [2] Birth year is defined as the year an establishment first reports positive employment. [3] Death year is defined as the year an establishment permanently shuts down. [4] For explanation of expansions and contractions, see <http://www.ces.census.gov/index.php/bds/bds_overview>. [5] Excludes government and those sectors not elsewhere classified. [6] Less than 1 year old. [7] 1–10 years old. [8] More than 10 years old.

Source: U.S. Census Bureau, Center for Economic Studies, "Business Dynamics Statistics," <http://www.ces.census.gov/index.php/bds/bds_database_list>, accessed May 2011.

Table 765. Firm Births and Deaths by Employment Size of Enterprise: 1990 to 2007

[In thousands (541.1 represents 541,100). Data represent activity from March of the beginning year to March of the ending year. Establishments with no employment in the first quarter of the beginning year were excluded. This table provides the number of births and deaths of initial establishments (based on Census ID) as an approximation of firm births and deaths]

Item	Births (initial locations)				Deaths (initial locations)			
	Total	Less than 20 employees	Less than 500 employees	500 employees or more	Total	Less than 20 employees	Less than 500 employees	500 employees or more
Firms:								
1990 to 1991	541.1	515.9	540.9	0.3	546.5	517.0	546.1	0.4
1995 to 1996	597.8	572.4	597.5	0.3	512.4	485.5	512.0	0.4
2000 to 2001	585.1	558.0	584.8	0.3	553.3	524.0	552.8	0.5
2002 to 2003 [1]	612.3	585.6	612.0	0.3	540.7	514.6	540.3	0.3
2003 to 2004	628.9	601.9	628.7	0.3	541.0	515.0	540.7	0.3
2004 to 2005	644.1	616.0	643.9	0.3	565.7	539.1	565.5	0.3
2005 to 2006	670.1	640.7	669.8	0.2	599.3	573.3	599.1	0.3
2006 to 2007	668.4	639.1	668.2	0.2	592.4	564.3	592.1	0.3
Employment:								
1990 to 1991	3,105	1,713	2,907	198	3,208	1,723	3,044	164
1995 to 1996	3,256	1,845	3,056	200	3,100	1,560	2,808	291
2000 to 2001	3,418	1,821	3,109	310	3,262	1,701	3,050	212
2002 to 2003 [1]	3,667	1,856	3,174	493	3,324	1,608	2,880	445
2003 to 2004	3,575	1,889	3,241	334	3,221	1,615	2,868	353
2004 to 2005	3,609	1,931	3,279	330	3,307	1,685	2,981	326
2005 to 2006	3,682	1,999	3,412	270	3,220	1,711	2,964	256
2006 to 2007	3,554	1,945	3,325	229	3,482	1,734	3,126	356

[1] A change in methodology ("based on Census ID" rather than "plant number") has affected the allocation of firms by employment size.

Source: U.S. Small Business Administration, Office of Advocacy, "Firm Size Data, Statistics of U.S. Businesses and Nonemployer Statistics," <http://www.sba.gov/advo/research/data.html>, accessed March 2011.

Table 766. Establishments and Employment Changes from Births, Deaths, Expansions, and Contractions by Employment Size of Enterprise: 2006 to 2007

[In thousands (6,762 represents 6,762,000), except percent. See headnote, Table 765. An establishment is a single physical location at which business is conducted or where services or industrial operations are performed. An enterprise is a business organization consisting of one or more domestic establishments under common ownership or control. Minus sign (−) indicates decrease]

Employment size of firm	Establish-ments	Births [1]	Deaths [2]	Employ-ment	Change in employ-ment	Percent change in employment due to—			
						Births [1]	Deaths [2]	Births and expan-sions [3]	Deaths and con-tractions [4]
Total.	**6,762**	**906**	**753**	**119,894**	**537**	**6.3**	**−5.0**	**16.0**	**−15.5**
1–4.	2,879	519	457	5,955	933	15.1	−11.9	39.1	−20.3
5–9.	1,073	85	77	6,969	81	7.7	−6.9	20.7	−18.5
10–19.	678	53	45	8,672	−27	7.5	−5.5	17.4	−17.1
20–99.	697	78	49	21,072	−121	6.7	−5.1	16.0	−16.6
100–499.	340	46	24	17,536	−241	5.1	−3.8	14.0	−16.5
Less than 500	5,667	782	652	60,203	625	5.5	−4.4	13.7	−13.9
500 or more.	1,095	124	101	59,691	−88	7.2	−5.6	18.3	−17.2

[1] Births are establishments that have zero employment in the first quarter of the initial year and positive employment in the first quarter of the subsequent year. [2] Deaths are establishments that have positive employment in the first quarter of the initial year and zero employment in the first quarter of the subsequent year. [3] Expansions are establishments that have positive first quarter employment in both the initial and subsequent years and increase employment during the time period between the first quarter of the initial year and the first quarter of the subsequent year. [4] Contractions are establishments that have positive first quarter employment in both the initial and subsequent years and decrease employment during the time period between the first quarter of the initial year and the first quarter of the subsequent year.

Source: U.S. Small Business Administration, Office of Advocacy, "Statistics of U.S. Businesses," <http://www.sba.gov/advo/research/data.html>, accessed March 2011.

Table 767. Small Business Administration Loans to Minority-Owned Small Businesses: 2000 to 2010

[3,675 represents $3,675,000,000. For year ending September 30. A small business must be independently owned and operated, must not be dominant in its particular industry, and must meet standards set by the Small Business Administration as to its annual receipts or number of employees]

Minority group	Number of loans					Amount (mil. dol.)				
	2000	2005	2008	2009	2010	2000	2005	2008	2009	2010
Total minority loans	**12,041**	**30,226**	**24,995**	**10,882**	**11,244**	**3,675**	**6,294**	**5,730**	**3,324**	**4,003**
African American	2,183	7,302	7,475	2,776	1,676	415	756	1,081	526	332
Asian American	5,827	13,353	10,732	5,221	5,956	2,390	4,072	3,510	2,132	2,769
Hispanic American.	3,491	8,748	6,130	2,584	3,218	767	1,341	1,027	617	812
Native American	540	823	658	301	394	102	125	112	49	90

Source: U.S. Small Business Administration, *Management Information Summary*, unpublished data.

Table 768. U.S. Firms—Ownership by Gender, Ethnicity, Race, and Veteran Status: 2007

[27,110 represents 27,110,000. Based on the 2007 Survey of Business Owners, preliminary data; see text, this section and Appendix III]

Group	All firms [1] Firms (1,000)	All firms [1] Sales and receipts (bil. dol.)	Firms with paid employees Firms (1,000)	Firms with paid employees Sales and receipts (bil. dol.)	Firms with paid employees Employees (1,000)	Firms with paid employees Annual payroll (bil. dol.)
All firms	27,110	30,181	5,753	29,209	118,669	4,887
Female.	7,793	1,193	911	1,010	7,587	218
Male.	13,911	8,513	3,237	7,944	41,582	1,534
Equally male/female	4,602	1,282	1,051	1,099	8,154	219
Hispanic [2].	2,260	345	249	275	1,936	55
Equally Hispanic [2]/non-Hispanic	243	56	47	47	379	11
Non-Hispanic.	23,804	10,586	4,903	9,732	55,009	1,906
Minority	5,763	1,029	768	864	5,917	168
Equally minority/nonminority	436	110	86	94	699	22
Nonminority	20,107	9,849	4,345	9,095	50,707	1,781
Veteran	2,449	1,233	492	1,139	5,889	214
Equally veteran/nonveteran.	1,221	422	271	373	2,486	76
Nonveteran.	22,636	9,333	4,436	8,542	48,948	1,682
White	22,600	10,270	4,647	9,435	53,138	1,851
Black or African American	1,922	137	107	99	920	24
American Indian and Alaska Native.	237	34	24	28	191	6
Asian	1,553	514	399	461	2,869	82
Native Hawaiian and Other Pacific Islander. . .	39	7	4	6	43	1
Some other race	81	18	14	15	87	2
Publicly held and other firms [3]	804	19,193	554	19,155	61,346	2,915
Classifiable firms [4]	26,306	10,988	5,199	10,053	57,323	1,972

[1] Both firms with paid employees and firms with no paid employees. [2] An Hispanic firm may be of any race and therefore may be included in more than one race group. [3] Publicly held and other firms not classifiable by gender, ethnicity, race, and veteran status. [4] All firms classifiable by gender, ethnicity, race, and veteran status.
Source: U.S. Census Bureau, 2007 Economic Census, Survey of Business Owners; <http://www.census.gov/econ/sbo/>.

Table 769. Women-Owned Firms by Kind of Business: 2007

[7,793 represents 7,793,000. See headnote, Table 768]

Kind of business	2007 NAICS code [1]	All firms [2] Firms (1,000)	All firms [2] Sales and receipts (mil. dol.)	Firms with paid employees Firms (1,000)	Firms with paid employees Sales and receipts (mil. dol.)	Firms with paid employees Employees (1,000)	Firms with paid employees Annual payroll (mil. dol.)
Total [3]	(X)	7,793	1,192,781	911	1,010,470	7,587	218,136
Forestry, fishing and hunting, and agricultural support services	113–115	27	2,053	2	1,318	10	273
Mining	21	18	11,574	2	10,725	23	1,033
Utilities.	22	4	1,928	(Z)	1,862	2	82
Construction	23	269	97,527	54	88,499	496	21,317
Manufacturing	31–33	113	109,056	34	106,787	574	20,746
Wholesale trade.	42	133	250,034	39	245,085	388	16,476
Retail trade	44–45	919	181,233	127	162,094	829	17,730
Transportation and warehousing [4]	48–49	142	32,679	19	27,723	216	7,069
Information.	51	97	26,287	9	24,214	122	6,415
Finance and insurance [5]	52	201	32,662	35	25,278	166	7,162
Real estate and rental and leasing	53	658	58,775	57	29,252	184	5,769
Professional, scientific, and technical services	54	1,096	107,619	143	77,977	642	28,870
Management of companies and enterprises	55	2	2,840	2	2,840	51	3,483
Administrative and support and waste management and remediation services	56	786	66,151	64	54,401	1,156	26,930
Educational services	61	276	9,888	17	6,886	130	2,638
Health care and social assistance.	62	1,232	93,472	128	70,353	1,141	29,415
Arts, entertainment, and recreation.	71	376	16,514	19	9,769	115	3,063
Accommodation and food services	72	192	47,491	86	44,217	967	12,384
Other services (except public administration) [6]	81	1,252	44,815	77	21,007	368	7,224
Industries not classified.	99	3	184	3	184	4	57

X Not applicable. Z Less than 500. [1] Based on the 2007 North American Industry Classification System (NAICS); see text, this section. [2] Both firms with paid employees and firms with no paid employees. [3] Firms with more than one establishment are counted in each industry in which they operate, but only once in the total. [4] Excludes scheduled passenger air transportation (NAICS 481111), rail transportation (NAICS 482), and the postal service (NAICS 491). [5] Excludes funds, trusts, and other financial vehicles (NAICS 525). [6] Excludes religious, grantmaking, civic, professional, and similar organizations (NAICS 813) and private households (NAICS 814).
Source: U.S. Census Bureau, 2007 Economic Census, Survey of Business Owners, Women-Owned Firms; <http://www.census.gov/econ/sbo/>.

Table 770. Minority-Owned Firms by Kind of Business: 2007

[1,028,595 represents $1,028,595,000,000. See headnote, Table 768. A minority-owned firm is one in which Blacks or African Americans, American Indians and Alaska Natives, Asians, Native Hawaiians and Other Pacific Islanders, and/or Hispanics own 51 percent or more of the interest or stock of the business]

Kind of business	2007 NAICS code [1]	All firms [2]		Firms with paid employees			
		Firms	Sales and receipts (mil. dol.)	Firms	Sales and receipts (mil. dol.)	Employ-ees	Annual payroll (mil. dol.)
Total [3]	(X)	5,762,940	1,028,595	768,147	864,228	5,916,651	168,215
Forestry, fishing and hunting, and agricultural support services	113–115	24,331	1,963	1,046	984	13,793	255
Mining	21	4,827	2,480	593	2,207	9,706	440
Utilities	22	3,698	521	168	448	972	48
Construction	23	551,573	96,026	62,899	74,010	430,306	15,895
Manufacturing	31–33	82,057	66,947	24,905	64,647	349,514	11,662
Wholesale trade	42	126,900	217,101	47,018	210,267	338,634	13,686
Retail trade	44–45	526,329	185,472	118,128	168,593	650,113	13,679
Transportation and warehousing [4]	48–49	432,436	43,134	23,280	20,988	155,815	4,621
Information	51	63,814	15,224	6,043	13,618	58,793	3,617
Finance and insurance [5]	52	138,241	27,021	22,111	21,004	105,366	4,593
Real estate and rental and leasing	53	346,143	28,778	25,016	13,246	91,261	2,797
Professional, scientific, and technical services	54	576,453	82,446	78,503	66,617	465,606	26,028
Management of companies and enterprises	55	1,012	2,527	1,012	2,527	30,652	1,842
Administrative and support and waste management and remediation services	56	606,877	42,842	41,125	33,007	619,334	14,613
Educational services	61	111,961	4,711	6,844	3,491	55,788	1,357
Health care and social assistance	62	755,274	84,695	104,475	70,539	811,008	27,455
Arts, entertainment, and recreation	71	196,823	9,112	6,680	5,435	48,340	1,851
Accommodation and food services	72	241,320	79,037	135,037	74,628	1,423,808	18,725
Other services (except public administration) [6]	81	973,114	38,347	63,506	17,759	255,867	5,003
Industries not classified	99	1,557	212	1,557	212	1,976	49

X Not applicable. [1] Based on the 2007 North American Industry Classification System (NAICS); see text, this section. [2] Both firms with paid employees and firms with no paid employees. [3] Firms with more than one establishment are counted in each industry in which they operate, but only once in the total. [4] Excludes scheduled passenger air transportation (NAICS 481111), rail transportation (NAICS 482), and the postal service (NAICS 491). [5] Excludes funds, trusts, and other financial vehicles (NAICS 525). [6] Excludes religious, grantmaking, civic, professional, and similar organizations (NAICS 813) and private households (NAICS 814).

Source: U.S. Census Bureau, 2007 Economic Census, *Survey of Business Owners, Minority-Owned Firms*, <http://www.census.gov/econ/sbo/>.

Table 771. Hispanic-Owned Firms by Kind of Business: 2007

[345,182 represents $345,182,000,000. See headnote, Table 768]

Kind of business	2007 NAICS code [1]	All firms [2]		Firms with paid employees			
		Firms	Sales and receipts (mil. dol.)	Firms	Sales and receipts (mil. dol.)	Employ-ees	Annual payroll (mil. dol.)
Total [3]	(X)	2,259,857	345,182	249,044	274,570	1,935,688	54,717
Forestry, fishing and hunting, and agricultural support services	113-115	10,055	919	569	591	11,115	178
Mining	21	2,335	1,031	312	910	5,467	246
Utilities	22	1,868	187	43	147	315	25
Construction	23	340,655	56,306	38,327	41,069	262,001	8,981
Manufacturing	31-33	36,582	22,711	10,557	21,559	137,535	4,514
Wholesale trade	42	43,949	64,794	13,119	62,377	99,209	3,973
Retail trade	44-45	186,461	53,790	29,743	47,598	200,899	4,807
Transportation and warehousing [4]	48-49	200,614	21,450	11,931	9,881	72,259	2,009
Information	51	21,454	3,449	2,156	2,857	14,799	738
Finance and insurance [5]	52	51,751	11,143	8,900	9,075	41,803	1,640
Real estate and rental and leasing	53	130,327	10,219	9,230	4,607	32,015	978
Professional, scientific, and technical services	54	185,375	22,395	24,751	17,139	129,920	6,347
Management of companies and enterprises	55	284	917	284	917	11,242	520
Administrative and support and waste management and remediation services	56	313,271	19,848	20,833	14,327	262,507	6,170
Educational services	61	33,113	1,372	1,605	1,011	14,005	373
Health care and social assistance	62	234,715	19,324	23,161	15,243	186,065	6,119
Arts, entertainment, and recreation	71	63,851	2,742	2,297	1,433	13,979	514
Accommodation and food services	72	65,627	18,630	31,220	17,437	357,572	4,748
Other services (except public administration) [6]	81	337,687	13,855	20,123	6,294	82,469	1,820
Industries not classified	99	432	99	432	99	513	18

X Not applicable. [1] Based on the 2007 North American Industry Classification System (NAICS); see text, this section. [2] Both firms with paid employees and firms with no paid employees. [3] Firms with more than one establishment are counted in each industry in which they operate, but only once in the total. [4] Excludes scheduled passenger air transportation (NAICS 481111), rail transportation (NAICS 482), and the postal service (NAICS 491). [5] Excludes funds, trusts, and other financial vehicles (NAICS 525). [6] Excludes religious, grantmaking, civic, professional, and similar organizations (NAICS 813) and private households (NAICS 814).

Source: U.S. Census Bureau, 2007 Economic Census, *Survey of Business Owners, Hispanic-Owned Firms*, <http://www.census.gov/econ/sbo/>.

Table 772. Black-Owned Firms by Kind of Business: 2007

[137,448 represents $137,448,000,000. See headnote, Table 768]

Kind of business	2007 NAICS code [1]	All firms [2] Firms	All firms [2] Sales and receipts (mil. dol.)	Firms with paid employees Firms	Firms with paid employees Sales and receipts (mil. dol.)	Firms with paid employees Employ-ees	Firms with paid employees Annual payroll (mil. dol.)
Total [3]	(X)	**1,921,907**	**137,448**	**106,779**	**98,840**	**920,198**	**23,899**
Forestry, fishing and hunting, and agricultural support services	113–115	4,342	336	230	137	1,256	27
Mining	21	(S)	(S)	(S)	(S)	(S)	(S)
Utilities	22	1,316	68	18	48	92	4
Construction	23	125,931	13,362	9,635	9,968	56,471	2,010
Manufacturing	31–33	16,087	6,923	1,888	6,570	29,346	1,051
Wholesale trade	42	19,410	15,163	2,328	14,509	18,300	757
Retail trade	44–45	148,245	20,736	11,241	17,709	58,680	1,456
Transportation and warehousing [4]	48–49	168,357	11,160	5,809	3,965	40,202	1,043
Information	51	23,436	2,524	1,203	2,115	11,047	727
Finance and insurance [5]	52	42,178	3,396	4,777	2,282	16,547	626
Real estate and rental and leasing	53	92,510	3,965	3,321	1,305	11,008	296
Professional, scientific, and technical services	54	163,754	13,107	12,895	9,637	81,199	3,908
Management of companies and enterprises	55	201	510	201	510	3,330	193
Administrative and support and waste management and remediation services	56	216,733	9,957	9,661	7,197	168,093	3,501
Educational services	61	47,772	1,156	1,465	709	12,252	271
Health care and social assistance	62	365,130	17,001	24,362	11,695	229,660	5,117
Arts, entertainment, and recreation	71	86,314	3,400	2,160	2,026	11,426	568
Accommodation and food services	72	41,005	6,805	7,351	6,117	140,367	1,705
Other services (except public administration) [6]	81	358,329	7,603	8,000	2,093	29,465	587
Industries not classified	99	493	42	493	42	582	14

X Not applicable. S Withheld because estimate did not meet publication standards. [1] Based on the 2007 North American Industry Classification System (NAICS); see text, this section. [2] Both firms with paid employees and firms with no paid employees. [3] Firms with more than one establishment are counted in each industry in which they operate, but only once in the total. [4] Excludes scheduled passenger air transportation (NAICS 481111), rail transportation (NAICS 482), and the postal service (NAICS 491). [5] Excludes funds, trusts, and other financial vehicles (NAICS 525). [6] Excludes religious, grantmaking, civic, professional, and similar organizations (NAICS 813) and private households (NAICS 814).

Source: U.S. Census Bureau, 2007 Economic Census, *Survey of Business Owners, Black-Owned Firms*, <http://www.census.gov/econ/sbo>.

Table 773. Asian–Owned Firms by Kind of Business: 2007

[513,871 represents $513,871,000,000. See headnote, Table 768]

Kind of business	2007 NAICS code [1]	All firms [2] Firms	All firms [2] Sales and receipts (mil. dol.)	Firms with paid employees Firms	Firms with paid employees Sales and receipts (mil. dol.)	Firms with paid employees Employ-ees	Firms with paid employees Annual payroll (mil. dol.)
Total [3]	(X)	**1,552,505**	**513,871**	**398,586**	**461,331**	**2,869,153**	**82,202**
Forestry, fishing and hunting, and agricultural support services	113–115	5,145	429	122	165	798	27
Mining	21	954	906	68	849	2,172	114
Utilities	22	484	119	65	108	379	13
Construction	23	71,103	18,647	10,660	15,972	78,820	3,425
Manufacturing	31–33	26,481	34,062	11,880	33,344	168,632	5,554
Wholesale trade	42	60,569	132,740	30,630	129,092	212,906	8,571
Retail trade	44–45	191,233	107,885	77,531	100,300	382,823	7,150
Transportation and warehousing [4]	48–49	74,244	10,348	5,298	6,726	38,259	1,412
Information	51	17,454	8,917	2,514	8,379	30,929	2,099
Finance and insurance [5]	52	42,284	11,657	7,699	8,956	41,793	2,092
Real estate and rental and leasing	53	116,225	13,332	11,515	6,498	42,433	1,298
Professional, scientific, and technical services	54	214,053	43,543	38,253	37,082	236,349	14,617
Management of companies and enterprises	55	479	1,026	479	1,026	14,675	1,029
Administrative and support and waste management and remediation services	56	75,634	11,433	9,982	9,948	158,759	4,198
Educational services	61	29,587	2,012	3,576	1,614	27,185	649
Health care and social assistance	62	164,494	45,196	55,005	40,529	367,633	14,852
Arts, entertainment, and recreation	71	40,435	2,479	1,980	1,638	20,596	599
Accommodation and food services	72	133,980	52,609	96,251	50,097	903,055	11,987
Other services (except public administration) [6]	81	287,892	16,469	35,304	8,946	140,217	2,499
Industries not classified	99	615	62	615	62	740	14

X Not applicable. [1] Based on the 2007 North American Industry Classification System (NAICS); see text, this section. [2] Both firms with paid employees and firms with no paid employees. [3] Firms with more than one establishment are counted in each industry in which they operate, but only once in the total. [4] Excludes scheduled passenger air transportation (NAICS 481111), rail transportation (NAICS 482), and the postal service (NAICS 491). [5] Excludes funds, trusts, and other financial vehicles (NAICS 525). [6] Excludes religious, grantmaking, civic, professional, and similar organizations (NAICS 813) and private households (NAICS 814).

Source: U.S. Census Bureau, 2007 Economic Census, *Survey of Business Owners, Asian–Owned Firms*, <http://www.census.gov/econ/sbo>.

Table 774. Native Hawaiian- and Other Pacific Islander-Owned Firms by Kind of Business: 2007

[6,971 represents $6,971,000,000. See headnote, Table 768]

Kind of business	2007 NAICS code [1]	All firms [2]		Firms with paid employees			
		Firms	Sales and receipts (mil. dol.)	Firms	Sales and receipts (mil. dol.)	Employ-ees	Annual payroll (mil. dol.)
Total [3]	(X)	38,881	6,971	4,386	5,840	43,187	1,432
Forestry, fishing and hunting, and agricultural support services	113–115	(S)	(S)	(S)	(S)	(S)	(S)
Mining	21	32	8	1	(D)	(4)	(D)
Utilities	22	8	2	2	(D)	(4)	(D)
Construction	23	5,072	1,573	888	1,368	6,267	288
Manufacturing	31–33	636	301	112	288	1,773	54
Wholesale trade	42	737	525	161	457	951	46
Retail trade	44–45	3,947	1,328	471	1,168	3,672	114
Transportation and warehousing [5]	48–49	2,397	259	143	158	877	31
Information	51	423	164	39	150	960	52
Finance and insurance [6]	52	(S)	(S)	(S)	(S)	(S)	(S)
Real estate and rental and leasing	53	2,745	252	215	129	715	24
Professional, scientific, and technical services	54	3,776	735	487	618	4,625	283
Management of companies and enterprises	55	14	(D)	14	(D)	(7)	(D)
Administrative and support and waste management and remediation services	56	3,586	417	298	370	8,312	182
Educational services	61	638	45	33	39	625	13
Health care and social assistance	62	3,803	373	480	307	3,323	132
Arts, entertainment, and recreation	71	2,643	111	(S)	(S)	(S)	(S)
Accommodation and food services	72	1,352	409	593	398	7,088	99
Other services (except public administration) [8]	81	5,399	176	201	63	847	19
Industries not classified	99	(S)	(S)	(S)	(S)	(S)	(S)

D Withheld to avoid disclosing data for individual companies; data are included in higher level totals. S Withheld because estimate did not meet publication standards. X Not applicable. [1] Based on the 2007 North American Industry Classification System (NAICS); see text, this section. [2] Both firms with paid employees and firms with no paid employees. [3] Firms with more than one establishment are counted in each industry in which they operate, but only once in the total. [4] 0 to 19 employees. [5] Excludes scheduled passenger air transportation (NAICS 481111), rail transportation (NAICS 482), and the postal service (NAICS 491). [6] Excludes funds, trusts, and other financial vehicles (NAICS 525). [7] 100 to 249 employees. [8] Excludes religious, grantmaking, civic, professional, and similar organizations (NAICS 813) and private households (NAICS 814).

Source: U.S. Census Bureau, 2007 Economic Census, *Survey of Business Owners, Native Hawaiian- and Other Pacific Islander-Owned Firms,* <http://www.census.gov/econ/sbo>.

Table 775. American Indian- and Alaska Native-Owned Firms by Kind of Business: 2007

[34,488 represents $34,488,000,000. See headnote, Table 768]

Kind of business	2007 NAICS code [1]	All firms [2]		Firms with paid employees			
		Firms	Sales and receipts (mil. dol.)	Firms	Sales and receipts (mil. dol.)	Employ-ees	Annual payroll (mil. dol.)
Total [3]	(X)	237,386	34,488	24,064	27,583	191,472	6,201
Forestry, fishing and hunting, and agricultural support services	113–115	5,033	292	158	95	711	28
Mining	21	834	293	159	228	1,114	43
Utilities	22	248	(D)	13	(D)	(4)	(D)
Construction	23	37,779	8,691	5,242	7,267	39,477	1,595
Manufacturing	31–33	5,018	2,969	1,045	2,865	15,059	566
Wholesale trade	42	4,871	3,204	973	3,035	7,099	295
Retail trade	44–45	19,896	5,524	2,645	4,906	19,022	417
Transportation and warehousing [5]	48–49	12,975	1,519	872	800	6,071	192
Information	51	2,981	383	261	309	2,723	88
Finance and insurance [6]	52	4,534	672	1,016	478	5,329	193
Real estate and rental and leasing	53	12,472	1,178	896	643	4,642	159
Professional, scientific, and technical services	54	23,925	2,681	2,901	1,900	14,564	730
Management of companies and enterprises	55	35	34	35	34	943	68
Administrative and support and waste management and remediation services	56	22,729	1,930	1,421	1,463	26,276	686
Educational services	61	5,252	211	179	160	1,996	59
Health care and social assistance	62	25,235	1,704	2,377	1,249	16,853	483
Arts, entertainment, and recreation	71	13,506	604	265	327	1,106	175
Accommodation and food services	72	5,431	1,200	2,058	1,119	21,737	258
Other services (except public administration) [7]	81	34,580	1,251	1,497	563	6,553	160
Industries not classified	99	132	8	132	8	121	3

D Withheld to avoid disclosing data for individual companies; data are included in higher level totals. X Not applicable. [1] Based on the 2007 North American Industry Classification System (NAICS); see text, this section. [2] Both firms with paid employees and firms with no paid employees. [3] Firms with more than one establishment are counted in each industry in which they operate, but only once in the total. [4] 20 to 99 employees. [5] Excludes scheduled passenger air transportation (NAICS 481111), rail transportation (NAICS 482), and the postal service (NAICS 491). [6] Excludes funds, trusts, and other financial vehicles (NAICS 525). [7] Excludes religious, grantmaking, civic, professional, and similar organizations (NAICS 813) and private households (NAICS 814).

Source: U.S. Census Bureau, 2007 Economic Census, *Survey of Business Owners, American Indian- and Alaska Native-Owned Firms,* <http://www.census.gov/econ/sbo>.

Table 776. Bankruptcy Petitions Filed and Pending by Type and Chapter: 1990 to 2010

[For years ending June 30. Covers only bankruptcy cases filed under the Bankruptcy Reform Act of 1978. *Bankruptcy*: legal recognition that a company or individual is insolvent and must restructure or liquidate. Petitions "filed" means the commencement of a proceeding through the presentation of a petition to the clerk of the court; "pending" is a proceeding in which the administration has not been completed]

Item	1990	1995	2000	2005	2006	2007	2008	2009	2010
Total filed	725,484	858,104	1,276,922	1,637,254	1,484,570	751,056	967,831	1,306,315	1,572,597
Business [1]	64,688	51,288	36,910	32,406	31,562	23,889	33,822	55,021	59,608
Nonbusiness [2]	660,796	806,816	1,240,012	1,604,848	1,453,008	727,167	934,009	1,251,294	1,512,989
Chapter 7 [3]	468,171	552,244	864,183	1,174,681	1,142,958	435,064	592,376	870,266	1,091,322
Chapter 11 [4]	2,116	1,755	722	847	749	540	780	1,088	1,827
Chapter 13 [5]	190,509	252,817	375,107	429,315	309,298	291,560	340,852	379,939	419,836
Voluntary	723,886	856,991	1,276,146	1,636,678	1,484,085	750,577	967,248	1,305,349	1,571,619
Involuntary	1,598	1,113	776	576	485	479	583	966	978
Chapter 7 [3]	505,337	581,390	885,447	1,196,212	1,164,815	450,332	615,748	907,603	1,133,320
Chapter 9 [6]	7	12	8	6	10	7	4	6	12
Chapter 11 [4]	19,591	13,221	9,947	6,703	6,224	5,586	7,293	13,951	14,272
Chapter 12 [7]	1,351	904	732	290	360	386	314	422	660
Chapter 13 [5]	199,186	262,551	380,770	433,945	313,085	294,693	344,421	384,187	424,242
Section 304 [8]	12	26	18	98	[9] 36	(X)	(X)	(X)	(X)
Chapter 15 [9]	(X)	(X)	(X)	(X)	40	52	51	146	91
Total pending	961,919	1,090,446	1,400,416	1,750,562	1,411,212	1,312,016	1,325,220	1,527,073	1,658,318

X Not applicable. [1] Business bankruptcies include those filed under chapters 7, 9, 11, 12, 13, or 15. [2] Includes other petitions, not shown separately. [3] Chapter 7, liquidation of nonexempt assets of businesses or individuals. [4] Chapter 11, individual or business reorganization. [5] Chapter 13, adjustment of debts of an individual with regular income. [6] Chapter 9, adjustment of debts of a municipality. [7] Chapter 12, adjustment of debts of a family farmer with regular income, effective November 26, 1986. [8] Chapter 11, U.S.C., Section 304, cases ancillary to foreign proceedings. [9] Chapter 15 was added and Section 304 was terminated by changes in the Bankruptcy Laws effective October 17, 2005.

Source: Administrative Office of the U.S. Courts, *Statistical Tables for the Federal Judiciary,* and unpublished data, <http://www.uscourts.gov/bnkrpctystats/statistics.htm>.

Table 777. Bankruptcy Cases Filed by State: 2000 to 2010

[In thousands (1,276.9 represents 1,276,900). For years ending June 30. Covers only bankruptcy cases filed under the Bankruptcy Reform Act of 1978. *Bankruptcy*: legal recognition that a company or individual is insolvent and must restructure or liquidate. Petitions "filed" means the commencement of a proceeding through the presentation of a petition to the clerk of the court]

State	2000	2005	2009	2010	State	2000	2005	2009	2010
Total [1]	1,276.9	1,637.3	1,306.3	1,572.6					
Alabama	31.4	42.6	33.6	34.9	Missouri	26.3	39.2	28.6	32.9
Alaska	1.4	1.6	1.0	1.1	Montana	3.3	4.4	2.4	3.1
Arizona	21.7	32.4	26.8	40.7	Nebraska	5.6	9.6	7.2	7.9
Arkansas	16.3	25.5	15.4	16.9	Nevada	14.3	16.3	24.4	31.0
California	160.6	122.6	171.6	242.0	New Hampshire	3.9	4.9	4.6	5.7
Colorado	15.6	30.2	24.7	31.9	New Jersey	38.7	40.7	31.6	39.7
Connecticut	11.4	11.8	9.2	11.3	New Mexico	7.1	10.1	5.3	6.6
Delaware	4.9	3.6	4.4	4.5	New York	61.7	81.7	53.2	58.2
District of Columbia . . .	2.6	1.9	1.0	1.3	North Carolina	25.8	37.5	25.5	27.7
Florida	74.0	85.8	82.9	107.4	North Dakota	2.0	2.5	1.5	1.6
Georgia	57.9	77.3	70.0	77.8	Ohio	53.6	95.8	64.5	72.9
Hawaii	5.0	3.2	2.7	3.7	Oklahoma	19.3	28.2	12.7	15.1
Idaho	7.3	9.7	6.7	8.3	Oregon	18.1	25.3	15.9	20.1
Illinois	62.3	83.6	65.0	80.8	Pennsylvania	43.8	62.3	35.6	38.8
Indiana	37.5	55.9	44.6	49.3	Rhode Island	4.8	4.4	4.9	5.4
Iowa	8.2	14.3	9.3	10.4	South Carolina	11.7	15.2	9.5	9.7
Kansas	11.4	17.3	10.1	11.4	South Dakota	2.1	2.9	1.7	2.0
Kentucky	20.8	29.2	23.6	26.0	Tennessee	47.1	60.8	52.6	52.5
Louisiana	23.1	31.1	16.8	19.5	Texas	62.9	97.5	48.8	57.8
Maine	4.1	4.7	3.5	4.1	Utah	14.4	20.5	12.1	17.0
Maryland	31.1	28.5	21.4	29.1	Vermont	1.6	1.7	1.4	1.7
Massachusetts	16.7	19.6	18.6	22.9	Virginia	37.1	38.8	33.3	37.8
Michigan	36.4	68.5	63.8	71.0	Washington	31.2	37.7	27.1	33.5
Minnesota	15.4	19.4	19.2	22.6	West Virginia	8.2	12.6	6.0	6.6
Mississippi	17.9	21.8	13.8	14.8	Wisconsin	18.0	29.0	24.7	30.0
					Wyoming	2.0	2.5	1.1	1.5

[1] Includes Island Areas, not shown separately.

Source: Administrative Office of the U.S. Courts, *Statistical Tables for the Federal Judiciary,* <http://www.uscourts.gov/bnkrpctystats/statistics.htm>.

Table 778. Patents and Trademarks: 1990 to 2010

[In thousands (99.2 represents 99,200). Calendar year data. Covers U.S. patents issued to citizens of the United States and residents of foreign countries. For data on foreign countries, see Table 1393]

Type	1990	1995	2000	2005	2006	2007	2008	2009	2010
Patents issued............	**99.2**	**113.8**	**176.0**	**157.7**	**196.4**	**182.9**	**185.2**	**191.9**	**244.3**
Inventions................	90.4	101.4	157.5	143.8	173.8	157.3	157.8	167.3	219.6
Individuals.............	17.3	17.4	22.4	14.7	16.6	14.0	12.6	12.6	16.6
Corporations:									
United States...........	36.1	44.0	70.9	65.2	78.9	70.5	70.0	74.8	97.8
Foreign [1]............	36.0	39.1	63.3	63.2	77.4	72.0	74.5	79.3	104.3
U.S. government..........	1.0	1.0	0.9	0.7	0.8	0.7	0.7	0.7	0.9
Designs.................	8.0	11.7	17.4	13.0	21.0	24.1	25.6	23.1	22.8
Botanical plants..........	0.3	0.4	0.5	0.7	1.1	1.0	1.2	1.0	1.0
Reissues................	0.4	0.3	0.5	0.2	0.5	0.5	0.6	0.5	0.9
U.S. residents	52.8	64.4	96.9	82.6	102.2	93.7	92.0	95.0	121.2
Foreign country residents	46.2	49.4	79.1	75.2	94.2	89.2	93.2	96.9	123.2
Percent of total...........	46.7	43.4	44.9	47.6	48.0	48.8	50.3	50.5	50.4
Trademarks:									
Applications filed...........	127.3	181.0	361.8	334.7	362.3	401.0	390.8	351.9	370.2
Issued...................	60.8	92.5	115.2	154.8	193.7	218.8	233.9	222.1	210.6
Trademarks.............	53.6	85.6	106.4	121.6	153.3	170.8	194.4	177.4	165.2
Trademark renewals.......	7.2	6.9	8.8	33.3	40.4	48.1	39.5	44.7	45.4

[1] Includes patents to foreign governments.

Source: U.S. Patent and Trademark Office, "Statistical Reports Available For Viewing, Calendar Year Patent Statistics," <http://www.uspto.gov/web/offices/ac/ido/oeip/taf/reports.htm> and unpublished data.

Table 779. Patents by State and Island Areas: 2010

[Includes only U.S. patents granted to residents of the United States and territories]

State	Total	Inven-tions	De-signs	Botani-cal plants	Reis-sues	State	Total	Inven-tions	De-signs	Botani-cal plants	Reis-sues
Total.............	**121,164**	**107,792**	**12,612**	**297**	**463**	Missouri.........	1,140	975	157	5	3
						Montana.........	118	105	13	–	–
Alabama	538	444	87	4	3	Nebraska.........	253	214	36	3	–
Alaska	33	28	4	–	1	Nevada	639	540	96	–	3
Arizona	2,169	1,976	179	1	13	New Hampshire...	802	725	70	–	7
Arkansas	216	144	70	2	–	New Jersey	4,345	3,874	444	7	20
California...........	30,076	27,337	2,515	101	123	New Mexico......	455	434	15	–	6
Colorado	2,435	2,135	294	1	5	New York	8,095	7,082	995	1	17
Connecticut	2,111	1,875	219	2	15	North Carolina	2,922	2,636	271	8	7
Delaware	391	367	23	–	1	North Dakota	112	107	4	–	1
District of Columbia ...	87	82	5	–	–	Ohio.............	3,983	3,230	739	2	12
Florida	3,723	2,978	670	58	17	Oklahoma	582	516	59	–	7
Georgia	2,194	1,905	257	21	11	Oregon...........	2,340	2,040	273	21	6
Hawaii	144	121	21	2	–	Pennsylvania	3,887	3,351	513	2	21
Idaho	1,162	1,095	62	–	5	Rhode Island	354	276	76	–	2
Illinois.............	4,374	3,611	739	11	13	South Carolina....	651	517	124	7	3
Indiana.............	1,697	1,492	198	1	6	South Dakota.....	82	70	12	–	–
Iowa...............	809	763	44	–	2	Tennessee	1,037	925	105	1	6
Kansas.............	728	615	108	–	5	Texas	8,026	7,545	448	5	28
Kentucky	601	536	64	–	1	Utah.............	1,145	1,017	124	–	4
Louisiana...........	355	304	48	1	2	Vermont	668	642	26	–	–
Maine..............	220	211	8	–	1	Virginia..........	1,724	1,587	131	–	6
Maryland	1,731	1,578	143	3	7	Washington	5,809	5,258	537	5	9
Massachusetts.......	5,260	4,923	315	3	19	West Virginia	134	118	14	2	–
Michigan	4,277	3,823	427	8	19	Wisconsin	2,232	1,814	404	3	11
Minnesota	4,005	3,597	390	3	15	Wyoming	89	82	7	–	–
Mississippi..........	172	145	24	3	–	Island areas......	32	27	5	–	–

– Represents zero.

Source: U.S. Patent and Trademark Office, "Statistical Reports Available For Viewing, Calendar Year Patent Statistics," <http://www.uspto.gov/web/offices/ac/ido/oeip/taf/reports.htm>.

Table 780. Copyright Registration by Subject Matter: 2000 to 2010

[In thousands (497.6 represents 497,600). For years ending September 30. Comprises claims to copyrights registered for both U.S. and foreign works. Semiconductor chips and renewals are not considered copyright registration claims]

Subject matter	2000	2005	2009	2010	Subject matter	2000	2005	2009	2010
Total copyright claims ...	**497.6**	**515.2**	**381.3**	**636.4**	Musical works [2]	138.9	133.7	93.3	124.5
Monographs [1]	169.7	191.4	133.3	247.1	Works of the visual arts [3]........	85.8	82.5	75.2	97.2
Serials	69.0	57.7	37.5	89.2	Semiconductor chip products ...	0.7	0.5	0.3	0.3
Sound recordings	34.2	49.9	42.0	78.0	Renewals.................	16.8	15.8	0.5	0.1

[1] Includes computer software and machine readable works. [2] Includes dramatic works, accompanying music, choreography, pantomimes, motion pictures, and filmstrips. [3] Two-dimensional works of fine and graphic art, including prints and art reproductions; sculptural works; technical drawings and models; photographs; commercial prints and labels; works of applied arts, cartographic works, and multimedia works.

Source: The Library of Congress, Copyright Office, *Annual Report*.

Table 781. Net Stock of Private Fixed Assets by Industry: 2000 to 2009

[In billions of dollars (21,230 represents $21,230,000,000,000). Estimates as of Dec. 31. Net stock estimates are presented in terms of current cost and cover equipment, software, and structures. Fixed assets are assets that are used repeatedly, or continuously, in processes of production for an extended period of time. (pt) = part]

Industry	NAICS code [1]	2000	2005	2008	2009
Private fixed assets	(X)	**21,230**	**30,587**	**34,694**	**33,776**
Agriculture, forestry, fishing, and hunting	11	341	442	508	493
Farms [2]	111, 112	314	407	464	449
Forestry, fishing, and related activities	113-115	27	35	44	43
Mining	21	538	1,024	1,386	1,269
Oil and gas extraction	211	403	845	1,130	1,016
Mining, except oil and gas	212	92	115	148	143
Support activities for mining	213	44	63	108	110
Utilities	22	1,039	1,402	1,828	1,824
Construction	23	174	229	288	284
Manufacturing	31-33	1,771	2,012	2,366	2,310
Durable goods	(X)	1,004	1,140	1,338	1,308
Wood products	321	32	36	41	39
Nonmetallic mineral products	327	56	65	78	75
Primary metals	331	125	129	149	146
Fabricated metal products	332	112	125	145	142
Machinery	333	142	167	201	199
Computer and electronic products	334	248	279	331	327
Electrical equipment, appliances, and components	335	45	50	59	57
Motor vehicles, bodies and trailers, and parts	3361-3363	106	122	134	128
Other transportation equipment	3364, 3365, 3369	80	96	118	116
Furniture and related products	337	16	20	22	21
Miscellaneous manufacturing	339	44	52	61	58
Nondurable goods	(X)	767	872	1,028	1,002
Food and beverage and tobacco products	311, 312	183	210	244	238
Textile mills and textile product mills	313, 314	44	43	45	42
Apparel and leather and allied products	315, 316	17	18	19	18
Paper products	322	101	102	112	107
Printing and related support activities	323	41	49	57	55
Petroleum and coal products	324	92	117	159	162
Chemical products	325	221	256	305	296
Plastics and rubber products	326	68	77	88	84
Wholesale trade	42	348	466	524	503
Retail trade	44-45	641	893	1,087	1,037
Transportation and warehousing [3]	48-49	828	982	1,122	1,106
Air transportation	481	195	244	263	255
Railroad transportation	482	283	309	338	341
Water transportation	483	40	50	59	59
Truck transportation	484	70	82	95	90
Transit and ground passenger transportation	485	37	42	47	46
Pipeline transportation	486	74	115	166	167
Warehousing and storage	493	21	29	38	37
Information	51	861	1,031	1,177	1,163
Publishing industries (includes software)	511, 516 (pt)	50	54	63	61
Motion picture and sound recording industries	512	32	36	39	36
Broadcasting and telecommunications	515, 517	760	911	1,039	1,031
Information and data processing services	516 (pt), 518, 519	20	30	36	36
Finance and insurance	52	825	1,103	1,329	1,279
Federal Reserve banks	521	11	16	19	19
Credit intermediation and related activities	522	467	614	715	683
Securities, commodity contracts, and investments	523	87	111	138	134
Insurance carriers and related activities	524	164	205	234	223
Funds, trusts, and other financial vehicles	525	96	158	223	220
Real estate and rental and leasing	53	11,535	17,710	19,082	18,601
Real estate	531	11,295	17,354	18,662	18,213
Rental and leasing services and lessors of intangible assets [4]	532, 533	239	356	420	389
Professional, scientific, and technical services [3]	54	215	318	376	372
Legal services	5411	20	26	29	28
Computer systems design and related services	5415	50	69	78	76
Management of companies and enterprises [5]	55	271	374	482	479
Admin/support waste mgt	56	151	202	235	226
Administrative and support services	561	85	124	143	139
Waste management and remediation services	562	65	78	91	88
Educational services	61	212	325	424	429
Health care and social assistance	62	690	999	1,208	1,187
Ambulatory health care services	621	210	300	363	364
Hospitals	622	426	623	756	739
Nursing and residential care facilities	623	30	43	51	49
Social assistance	624	24	33	38	36
Arts, entertainment, and recreation	71	126	190	235	226
Performing arts, spectator sports, museums, and related activities	711, 712	47	74	96	93
Amusements, gambling, and recreation industries	713	79	116	139	133
Accommodation and food services	72	340	450	545	525
Accommodation	721	180	224	267	256
Food services and drinking places	722	160	225	278	269
Other services, except government	81	328	437	494	464

X Not applicable. [1] Based on North American Industry Classification System, 2002; see text this section. [2] NAICS crop and animal production. [3] Includes other activities, not shown separately. [4] Intangible assets include patents, trademarks, and franchise agreements, but not copyrights. [5] Consists of bank and other holding companies.

Source: U.S. Bureau of Economic Analysis, "Table 3.1ES. Current-Cost Net Stock of Private Fixed Assets by Industry," August 2010, <http://www.bea.gov/national/FA2004/SelectTable.asp>.

Business Enterprise **513**

Table 782. Private Domestic Investment in Current and Chained (2005) Dollars: 1990 to 2009

[In billions of dollars (861 represents $861,000,000,000). Covers equipment, software, and structures. Minus sign (−) indicates decrease. For explanation of chained dollars; see text, Section 13]

Item	1990	2000	2004	2005	2006	2007	2008	2009
CURRENT DOLLARS								
Gross private domestic investment........	**861**	**1,772**	**1,969**	**2,172**	**2,327**	**2,295**	**2,097**	**1,589**
Less: Consumption of fixed capital	560	987	1,201	1,291	1,391	1,476	1,537	1,536
Equals: Net private domestic investment......	301	785	768	881	936	819	560	53
Fixed investment......................	846	1,718	1,904	2,122	2,267	2,266	2,138	1,716
Less: Consumption of fixed capital	560	987	1,201	1,291	1,391	1,476	1,537	1,536
Equals: Net fixed investment	286	731	703	832	876	790	601	181
Nonresidential......................	622	1,269	1,223	1,347	1,505	1,638	1,665	1,364
Residential........................	224	449	681	775	762	629	473	352
Change in private inventories	15	55	65	50	60	29	−41	−127
CHAINED (2005) DOLLARS								
Gross private domestic investment........	**994**	**1,970**	**2,058**	**2,172**	**2,230**	**2,162**	**1,957**	**1,516**
Less: Consumption of fixed capital	627	1,063	1,244	1,291	1,341	1,396	1,440	1,461
Equals: Net private domestic investment......	366	908	814	881	889	766	517	54
Fixed investment......................	987	1,914	1,993	2,122	2,171	2,133	1,997	1,631
Nonresidential......................	618	1,319	1,263	1,347	1,454	1,552	1,557	1,291
Residential........................	386	580	730	775	718	584	444	343
Change in private inventories	17	60	66	50	59	28	−38	−113

Source: U.S. Bureau of Economic Analysis, *Survey of Current Business,* April 2011. See also <http://www.bea.gov/national/nipaweb/SelectTable.asp?Selected=N>.

Table 783. Information and Communications Technology (ICT) Equipment and Computer Software Expenditures: 2008 and 2009

[In millions of dollars (91,743 represents $91,743,000,000). Covers only companies with employees. The Information and Communication Technology Survey collects noncapitalized and capitalized data on information and communication technology equipment, including computer software. This survey is sent to a sample of approximately 46,000 private nonfarm employer businesses operating in the United States]

Type of expenditure and industry	NAICS code [1]	Noncapitalized expenditures [2]		Capitalized expenditures [3]	
		2008	2009	2008	2009
Total expenditures for ICT equipment and computer software	**(X)**	**91,743**	**89,652**	**206,146**	**164,182**
Total equipment expenditures	(X)	35,496	33,131	(NA)	(NA)
Purchases	(X)	18,278	17,416	133,659	97,207
Computer and peripheral equipment.......................	(X)	12,187	11,429	65,713	48,390
Information and communication technology equipment	(X)	5,739	5,764	61,190	43,349
Electromedical and electrotherapeutic apparatus	(X)	352	224	6,756	5,468
Operating leases and rental payments	(X)	17,218	15,714	(NA)	(NA)
Computer and peripheral equipment.......................	(X)	11,823	10,518	(NA)	(NA)
Information and communication technology equipment	(X)	4,476	4,197	(NA)	(NA)
Electromedical and electrotherapeutic apparatus	(X)	920	999	(NA)	(NA)
Total computer software expenditures........................	(X)	56,247	56,521	(NA)	(NA)
Purchases and payroll for developing software	(X)	28,698	26,434	72,487	66,975
Software licensing and service/maintenance agreements	(X)	27,549	30,087	(NA)	(NA)
Forestry, fishing, and agricultural services	113–115	72	62	158	101
Mining	21	2,457	2,001	1,436	1,045
Utilities...................................	22	1,806	1,513	3,739	4,157
Construction	23	885	924	1,881	1,204
Manufacturing	31–33	16,229	14,068	19,179	15,813
Durable goods industries.....................	321, 327, 33	10,761	9,382	10,913	9,123
Nondurable goods industries..................	31, 322-326	5,467	4,687	8,266	6,690
Wholesale trade............................	42	3,076	3,023	7,000	6,582
Retail trade	44–45	4,153	4,067	14,173	10,776
Transportation and warehousing	48–49	1,804	1,721	3,522	2,905
Information................................	51	13,094	13,864	71,223	52,516
Finance and insurance	52	21,053	20,719	29,191	25,968
Real estate and rental and leasing	53	1,347	1,377	3,084	2,360
Professional, scientific, and technical services	54	11,466	10,669	15,731	11,317
Management of companies and enterprises	55	921	955	1,803	2,097
Admin/support and waste management/remediation services	56	2,221	2,413	4,732	3,901
Educational services........................	61	1,741	1,881	2,637	2,430
Health care and social assistance................	62	5,975	7,116	18,027	14,494
Arts, entertainment, and recreation..........................	71	502	500	1,174	951
Accommodation and food services	72	803	937	3,277	1,532
Other services (except public administration)	81	1,710	1,311	2,731	2,666
Equipment expenditures serving multiple industry codes	(X)	428	530	1,446	1,365

NA Not available. X Not applicable. [1] Based on North American Industry Classification System, 2002; see text, this section. [2] Expenses for ICT equipment including computer software not charged to asset accounts for which depreciation or amortization accounts are ordinarily maintained. [3] Expenses for ICT equipment including computer software chargeable to asset accounts for which depreciation or amortization accounts are ordinarily maintained.
Source: U.S. Census Bureau, "2009 Information and Communication Technology Survey," March 2011, <http://www.census.gov/econ/ict/xls/2009/full_report.html>.

Table 784. Capital Expenditures: 2000 to 2009

[In billions of dollars (1,161 represents $1,161,000,000,000). Based on a sample survey and subject to sampling error; see source for details]

Item	All companies				Companies with employees				Companies without employees			
	2000	2005	2008	2009	2000	2005	2008	2009	2000	2005	2008	2009
Capital expenditures, total ...	1,161	1,145	1,374	1,090	1,090	1,063	1,294	1,015	71	82	80	75
Structures	364	402	562	448	338	369	529	413	26	33	33	35
New	329	366	523	421	309	341	500	393	20	25	23	28
Used	35	36	39	27	29	28	29	19	6	8	10	8
Equipment and software	797	743	812	642	752	694	765	602	45	49	47	40
New	751	701	765	607	718	665	728	577	32	37	37	30
Used	46	42	47	35	34	29	37	25	12	13	10	10
Capital leases	20	18	20	17	19	18	19	17	(Z)	(Z)	1	1

Z Less than $500 million.

Source: U.S. Census Bureau, "2009 Annual Capital Expenditures Survey," February 2011, <http://www.census.gov/econ/aces/>, and earlier reports.

Table 785. Capital Expenditures by Industry: 2000 and 2009

[In billions of dollars (1,090 represents $1,090,000,000,000). Covers only companies with employees. Data for 2000 based on the North American Industry Classification System (NAICS), 1997; 2009 based on NAICS, 2007; see text this section. Based on a sample survey and subject to sampling error; see source for details]

Industry	NAICS code	2000	2009	Industry	NAICS code	2000	2009
Total expenditures	(X)	1,090	1,015				
Forestry, fishing, and agricultural services	113–115	1	2	Professional, scientific, and technical services	54	34	27
Mining	21	43	101	Management of companies and enterprises.	55	5	5
Utilities.	22	61	102	Admin/support waste mgt/remediation services	56	18	19
Construction	23	25	20	Educational services	61	18	28
Manufacturing	31–33	215	156	Health care and social assistance.	62	52	79
Durable goods	321, 327, 33	134	77	Arts, entertainment, and recreation. . . .	71	19	16
Nondurable goods	31, 322–326	81	79	Accommodation and food services	72	26	26
Wholesale trade.	42	34	25	Other services (except public administration)	81	21	29
Retail trade	44–45	70	58				
Transportation and warehousing	48–49	60	56	Structure and equipment expenditures serving multiple industry categories . .	(X)	2	3
Information.	51	160	88				
Finance and insurance	52	134	100				
Real estate and rental and leasing . . .	53	92	73				

X Not applicable.

Source: U.S. Census Bureau, "2009 Annual Capital Expenditures Survey," February 2011, <http://www.census.gov/econ/aces/>, and earlier reports.

Table 786. Business Cycle Expansions and Contractions—Months of Duration: 1945 to 2009

[A trough is the low point of a business cycle; a peak is the high point. Contraction, or recession, is the period from peak to subsequent trough; expansion is the period from trough to subsequent peak. Business cycle reference dates are determined by the National Bureau of Economic Research, Inc.]

Business cycle reference date				Contraction (Peak to trough)	Expansion (Previous trough to peak)	Length of cycle	
Peak		Trough				Trough from previous trough	Peak from previous peak
Month	Year	Month	Year				
February	1945	October	1945	8	[1] 80	[1] 88	[2] 93
November	1948	October	1949	11	37	48	45
July	1953	May	1954	10	45	55	56
August.	1957	April	1958	8	39	47	49
April	1960	February	1961	10	24	34	32
December	1969	November	1970	11	106	117	116
November	1973	March.	1975	16	36	52	47
January	1980	July	1980	6	58	64	74
July	1981	November	1982	16	12	28	18
July	1990	March.	1991	8	92	100	108
March.	2001	November	2001	8	120	128	128
December	2007	June.	2009	18	73	91	81
Average, all cycles: 1945 to 2009 (11 cycles)				11	59	73	66

[1] Previous trough: June 1938. [2] Previous peak: May 1937.

Source: National Bureau of Economic Research, Inc., Cambridge, MA, "Business Cycle Expansions and Contractions," <http://www.nber.org/cycles.html>, accessed May 2011.

Table 787. The Conference Board Leading, Coincident, and Lagging Economic Indexes: 2000 to 2010

[299.4 represents 299,400]

Item	Unit	2000	2005	2007	2008	2009	2010
The Conference Board Leading Economic Index (LEI) for the U.S., composite	2004 = 100	86.8	102.6	104.2	101.0	101.3	109.2
Average weekly hours, manufacturing	Hours	41.2	40.6	41.2	40.8	39.9	41.1
Average weekly initial claims for unemployment insurance	1,000	299.4	330.6	321.6	420.9	571.4	457.1
Manufacturers' new orders, consumer goods and materials (1982 dol.)	Mil. dol	152,036	150,268	152,102	136,427	119,598	123,972
Index of supplier deliveries— vendor performance [1]	Percent	53.4	54.1	51.2	51.6	51.5	58.1
Manufacturers' new orders, nondefense capital goods (1982 dol.)	Mil. dol	49,809	45,352	56,271	47,852	34,312	41,666
Building permits, new private housing units	1,000	1,598	2,160	1,392	896	583	594
Stock prices, 500 common stocks [1]	1941-43 = 10	1,426.8	1,207.1	1,476.7	1,220.9	946.7	1,139.3
Money supply, M2 (chain 2005 dol.)	Bil. dol	5,326	6,523	6,913	7,168	7,718	7,765
Interest rate spread, 10-year Treasury bonds less federal funds	Percent	−0.21	1.08	−0.31	1.74	3.10	3.04
Index of consumer expectations [1]	1966:1 = 100	102.7	77.4	75.6	57.3	64.1	66.0
The Conference Board Coincident Economic Index (CEI) for the U.S., composite	2004 = 100	98.2	102.4	107.0	105.7	100.0	101.0
Employees on nonagricultural payrolls	1,000	131,794	133,694	137,587	136,778	130,789	129,822
Personal income less transfer payments (chain 2005 dol.)	Bil. dol	8,327	8,981	9,650	9,634	9,196	9,224
Industrial production	2002 = 100	92.0	95.3	100.0	96.7	87.7	92.7
Manufacturing and trade sales (chain 2005 dol.)	Mil. dol	919,657	1,013,268	1,053,656	1,010,876	937,627	977,842
The Conference Board Lagging Economic Index (LAG) for the U.S., composite	2004 = 100	97.8	103.3	109.5	112.9	110.8	107.5
Average duration of unemployment	Weeks	12.7	18.4	16.9	17.8	24.3	33.1
Inventories to sales ratio, manufacturing and trade (chain 2005 dol.)	Ratio	1.36	1.31	1.33	1.39	1.40	1.34
Change in labor cost per unit of output, manufacturing (six-month change, annual rate)	Percent	2.4	−2.0	−1.5	7.3	−0.9	−1.9
Average prime rate	Percent	9.2	6.2	8.1	5.1	3.3	3.3
Commercial and industrial loans outstanding (chain 2005 dol.)	Mil. dol	980,008	669,004	805,347	889,034	791,755	662,523
Consumer installment credit to personal income ratio	Percent	18.9	21.4	20.6	20.7	20.6	19.2
Change in consumer price index for services (6-month change, annual rate)	Percent	3.8	3.5	3.3	3.6	0.8	0.9

[1] Data are from private sources and provided through the courtesy of the compilers and are subject to their copyrights: stock prices, Standard & Poor's Corporation; index of consumer expectations, University of Michigan's Survey Research Center; index of supplier deliveries, Institute for Supply Management.

Source: The Conference Board, New York, NY 10022-6601, *Business Cycle Indicators*, monthly, <http://www.conference-board.org/data/monthlybci.cfm>. Reproduced with permission from The Conference Board, Inc. 2011, The Conference Board, Inc. (copyright).

Table 788. Manufacturing and Trade—Sales and Inventories: 1992 to 2010

[In billions of dollars (541 represents $541,000,000,000), except ratios. Based on North American Industry Classification System (NAICS), 2002; see text, this section]

Year	Sales, average monthly [1]				Inventories [2]				Inventory-sales ratio [3]			
	Total	Manufacturing	Retail trade	Merchant wholesalers	Total	Manufacturing	Retail trade	Merchant wholesalers	Total	Manufacturing	Retail trade	Merchant wholesalers
1992	541	242	151	147	837	379	261	197	1.53	1.57	1.67	1.31
1993	568	252	162	154	864	380	280	205	1.50	1.50	1.68	1.30
1994	610	270	176	165	927	400	305	222	1.46	1.44	1.66	1.29
1995	655	290	185	180	986	425	323	238	1.48	1.44	1.72	1.29
1996	687	300	197	190	1,005	430	334	241	1.46	1.43	1.67	1.27
1997	724	320	206	198	1,047	444	345	259	1.42	1.37	1.64	1.26
1998	743	325	216	202	1,079	449	357	272	1.43	1.39	1.62	1.32
1999	787	336	234	217	1,139	464	385	290	1.40	1.35	1.59	1.30
2000	834	351	249	235	1,197	481	407	309	1.41	1.35	1.59	1.29
2001	819	331	256	232	1,120	428	395	298	1.43	1.38	1.58	1.32
2002	824	326	261	236	1,140	423	416	301	1.36	1.28	1.55	1.26
2003	855	335	272	248	1,149	408	432	308	1.34	1.24	1.56	1.23
2004	926	359	290	277	1,242	441	461	340	1.30	1.19	1.56	1.18
2005	1,005	395	308	301	1,313	474	472	368	1.27	1.17	1.51	1.18
2006	1,067	418	323	325	1,408	524	487	398	1.29	1.20	1.49	1.18
2007	1,126	445	334	348	1,485	563	498	423	1.29	1.22	1.48	1.18
2008	1,157	457	330	370	1,476	559	479	438	1.32	1.28	1.51	1.21
2009	999	384	306	309	1,326	510	429	387	1.37	1.36	1.45	1.30
2010	1,095	419	327	348	1,437	552	455	429	1.26	1.26	1.36	1.16

[1] Averages of monthly not-seasonally-adjusted figures. [2] Seasonally adjusted end-of-year data. [3] Averages of seasonally-adjusted monthly ratios.

Source: U.S. Council of Economic Advisors, *Economic Indicators*, May 2011.

Table 789. Industrial Production Indexes by Industry: 1990 to 2010

[2007 = 100. Except as noted, based on the North American Industry Classification System (NAICS); 2002; see text, this section]

Industry	NAICS code [1]	1990	2000	2005	2006	2007	2008	2009	2010
Total index	([2])	**62.1**	**92.1**	**95.3**	**97.4**	**100.0**	**96.3**	**85.5**	**90.1**
Manufacturing (SIC) [3]	([4])	**58.6**	**91.0**	**94.8**	**97.2**	**100.0**	**95.0**	**82.2**	**86.6**
Manufacturing (NAICS)	31–33	56.8	89.8	94.4	96.9	100.0	95.3	82.4	87.3
Durable goods	([5])	42.7	84.8	91.2	95.4	100.0	96.3	79.0	85.3
Wood products	321	81.0	99.7	105.9	106.9	100.0	85.4	65.8	69.6
Nonmetallic mineral products	327	76.0	94.7	99.4	101.1	100.0	88.3	67.5	67.6
Primary metals	331	87.1	100.3	95.2	98.0	100.0	99.7	69.5	83.3
Fabricated metal products	332	70.3	96.9	90.9	95.9	100.0	96.4	74.2	78.6
Machinery	333	72.5	98.5	92.1	96.5	100.0	97.3	75.6	80.8
Computers and electronic products	334	7.2	53.4	77.0	87.2	100.0	106.6	97.5	108.0
Electrical equipment, appliances, and components	335	82.3	114.3	95.3	96.0	100.0	96.3	76.5	78.9
Motor vehicles and parts	3361–3	54.4	97.4	102.3	100.8	100.0	80.0	59.5	76.1
Aerospace and other misc. transportation equipment	3364–9	94.5	76.1	80.2	85.2	100.0	101.9	96.1	93.7
Furniture and related products	337	75.0	102.9	104.4	102.7	100.0	90.3	66.1	65.6
Miscellaneous products	339	60.1	86.4	98.9	102.0	100.0	101.6	93.8	96.0
Nondurable goods	([6])	82.4	95.9	98.3	98.8	100.0	94.0	86.4	89.6
Food, beverage, and tobacco products	311,2	84.7	95.3	99.8	99.9	100.0	97.2	94.6	98.1
Textile and product mills	313,4	128.4	145.1	124.4	112.7	100.0	87.8	69.7	74.9
Apparel and leather	315,6	271.1	237.3	126.4	123.6	100.0	80.8	62.3	62.1
Paper	322	100.3	107.8	100.7	99.6	100.0	95.8	85.4	89.0
Printing and related support	323	98.4	108.4	98.6	97.8	100.0	93.8	79.8	76.0
Petroleum and coal products	324	77.4	85.6	95.6	97.3	100.0	95.6	94.3	96.5
Chemical	325	67.0	81.2	92.9	95.2	100.0	92.4	83.7	86.7
Plastics and rubber products	326	66.9	102.4	102.3	102.9	100.0	90.6	75.8	83.4
Other manufacturing (non-NAICS) [7]	1133, 5111	106.1	116.4	102.6	101.4	100.0	89.4	77.0	74.0
Mining	21	**106.5**	**103.0**	**97.1**	**99.5**	**100.0**	**100.8**	**95.6**	**101.3**
Utilities	2211,2	**71.9**	**89.9**	**97.3**	**96.7**	**100.0**	**99.9**	**97.3**	**101.3**
Electric power generation, transmission, and distribution	2211	69.4	87.9	97.0	97.5	100.0	99.4	96.7	100.6
Natural gas distribution	2212	87.2	100.3	98.9	93.0	100.0	102.3	100.3	104.6

[1] Based on North American Industry Classification System, 2002; see text, this section. [2] Includes NAICS codes 31–33, 1133, 5111, 21, 2211, and 2212. [3] Standard Industrial Classification (SIC); see text, this section. [4] Includes NAICS codes 31–33, 1133, and 5111. [5] Includes NAICS codes 321, 327, 331–339. [6] Includes NAICS codes 311–316, 322–326. [7] Those industries—logging and newspaper, periodical, book, and directory publishing—that have traditionally been considered to be manufacturing.
Source: Board of Governors of the Federal Reserve System, *Industrial Production and Capacity Utilization*, Statistical Release G.17, monthly. See also <http://www.federalreserve.gov/releases/g17/>.

Table 790. Index of Industrial Capacity: 1990 to 2010

[2007 output = 100. Annual figures are averages of monthly data. Capacity represents estimated quantity of output relative to output that the current stock of plant and equipment was capable of producing, as a proportion of 2007 actual output]

Year	Index of capacity		Relation of output to capacity (percent)				
	Total industry	Manufacturing	Total industry	Stage of process			Manufacturing
				Crude [1]	Primary and semifinished [2]	Finished [3]	
1990	75.3	71.8	82.5	87.6	82.7	80.8	81.7
1995	85.2	82.4	84.1	88.7	86.5	80.1	83.3
2000	113.1	114.3	81.4	88.6	83.9	76.7	79.7
2001	117.0	118.6	76.0	85.6	77.3	72.3	73.7
2002	119.1	120.1	74.8	82.9	77.0	70.7	72.9
2003	118.8	120.1	75.9	84.7	77.9	71.6	73.9
2004	118.6	119.8	77.9	86.1	79.9	73.1	76.1
2005	119.2	121.2	79.9	86.4	81.9	75.3	78.2
2006	121.2	123.6	80.4	87.8	81.4	76.1	78.6
2007	123.5	126.3	81.0	88.6	81.5	77.4	79.2
2008	123.8	126.9	77.8	87.0	76.8	74.5	74.9
2009	123.7	124.2	69.2	79.3	66.6	68.7	66.2
2010	121.0	120.8	74.5	85.3	71.8	73.4	71.7

[1] Crude processing covers a relatively small portion of total industrial capacity and consists of logging (NAICS 1133), much of mining (excluding stone, sand, and gravel mining, and oil and gas drilling, which are NAICS 21231, 21221–2, and 213111) and some basic manufacturing industries, including basic chemicals (NAICS 3251); fertilizers, pesticides, and other agricultural chemicals (NAICS 32531,2); pulp, paper, and paperboard mills (NAICS 3221); and alumina, aluminum, and other nonferrous production and processing mills (NAICS 3313,4). [2] Primary and semifinished processing loosely corresponds to the previously published aggregate, primary processing. Includes utilities and portions of several 2-digit SIC industries included in the former advanced processing group. These include printing and related support activities (NAICS 3231); paints and adhesives (NAICS 3255); and newspaper, periodical, book, and directory publishers (NAICS 5111). [3] Finished processing generally corresponds to the previously published aggregate, advanced processing. Includes oil and gas well drilling and carpet and rug mills.
Source: Board of Governors of the Federal Reserve System, *Industrial Production and Capacity Utilization*, Statistical Release G.17, monthly. (Based on data from Federal Reserve Board, U.S. Dept. of Commerce, U.S. Bureau of Labor Statistics, and McGraw-Hill Information Systems Company, New York, NY; and other sources.)

Table 791. Corporate Profits, Taxes, and Dividends: 1990 to 2010

[In billions of dollars (434 represents $434,000,000,000). Covers corporations organized for profit and other entities treated as corporations. Represents profits to U.S. residents, without deduction of depletion charges and exclusive of capital gains and losses; intercorporate dividends from profits of domestic corporations are eliminated; net receipts of dividends, reinvested earnings of incorporated foreign affiliates, and earnings of unincorporated foreign affiliates are added. CCA = capital consumption adjustment]

Item	1990	2000	2005	2007	2008	2009	2010
Corporate profits with IVA and CCA [1]	434	819	1,456	1,511	1,263	1,258	1,625
Taxes on corporate income	145	265	412	446	308	255	417
Profits after tax with IVA and CCA [1]	289	554	1,044	1,065	954	1,003	1,208
Net dividends	169	378	557	795	798	719	733
Undistributed profits with IVA and CCA [1]	120	176	486	271	157	284	476
Cash flow:							
Net cash flow with IVA and CCA [1]	493	861	1,337	1,244	1,239	1,428	1,538
Undistributed profits with IVA and CCA [1]	120	176	486	271	157	284	476
Consumption of fixed capital	373	685	863	973	1,019	1,020	1,018
Less: Inventory valuation adjustment (IVA)	−13	−17	−31	−47	−44	12	−45
Equals: Net cash flow with CCA	506	878	1,368	1,291	1,284	1,416	1,583

[1] Inventory valuation adjustment and capital consumption adjustment.
Source: U.S. Bureau of Economic Analysis, *Survey of Current Business*, April 2011. See also <http://www.bea.gov/national/nipaweb/Index.asp>.

Table 792. Corporate Profits With Inventory Valuation and Capital Consumption Adjustments—Financial and Nonfinancial Industries: 2000 to 2010

[In billions of dollars (819 represents $819,000,000,000). Based on the North American Industry Classification System, 2002; see text, this section. Minus sign (−) indicates loss. See headnote, Table 791]

Industry group	2000	2005	2007	2008	2009	2010
Corporate profits with IVA/CCA [1]	819	1,456	1,511	1,263	1,258	1,625
Domestic industries	674	1,217	1,160	852	906	1,241
Rest of the world	146	239	351	411	352	384
Corporate profits with IVA [1]	756	1,610	1,691	1,289	1,329	1,756
Domestic industries	610	1,370	1,340	878	976	1,372
Financial [2]	190	444	346	140	258	388
Nonfinancial	420	926	995	738	718	985
Utilities	26	30	50	28	30	33
Manufacturing	144	247	271	184	151	260
Wholesale trade	59	92	100	84	80	84
Retail trade	61	123	118	75	99	125
Transportation and warehousing	15	29	28	28	25	46
Information	−16	81	94	75	84	109
Other nonfinancial [3]	132	324	334	264	250	328
Rest of the world	146	239	351	411	352	384

[1] Inventory valuation adjustment and capital consumption adjustment. [2] Consists of finance and insurance and bank and other holding companies. [3] Consists of agriculture, forestry, fishing, and hunting; mining; construction; real estate and rental and leasing; professional, scientific, and technical services; administrative and waste management services; educational services; health care and social assistance; arts, entertainment, and recreation; accommodation and food services; and other services, except government.
Source: U.S. Bureau of Economic Analysis, *Survey of Current Business*, April 2011. See also <http://www.bea.gov/national/nipaweb/Index.asp>.

Table 793. Corporate Profits Before Taxes by Industry: 2000 to 2009

[In billions of dollars (772 represents $772,000,000,000). Profits are without inventory valuation and capital consumption adjustments. Minus sign (−) indicates loss. See headnote, Table 791]

Industry	2002 NAICS code [1]	2000	2005	2007	2008	2009
Corporate profits before tax	(X)	772	1,640	1,738	1,333	1,317
Domestic industries	(X)	627	1,401	1,387	922	964
Agriculture, forestry, fishing, and hunting	11	1	5	7	2	3
Mining	21	15	43	56	54	28
Utilities	221	26	31	51	29	30
Construction	23	42	85	67	41	23
Manufacturing	31-33	154	260	290	206	135
Wholesale trade	42	62	101	116	94	81
Retail trade	44–45	63	128	126	83	103
Transportation and warehousing	48–49	15	30	28	27	25
Information	51	−16	81	94	76	83
Finance and insurance	52	102	282	211	2	99
Real estate and rental and leasing	53	10	29	20	5	11
Professional, scientific, and technical services	54	2	42	55	53	51
Management of companies and enterprises [2]	551111, 551112	88	161	134	138	159
Administrative and waste management services	56	9	24	27	22	21
Educational services	61	2	5	5	5	7
Health care and social assistance	62	26	54	58	59	74
Arts, entertainment, and recreation	71	2	7	6	5	5
Accommodation and food services	72	15	22	22	13	14
Other services, except public administration	81	9	12	13	10	10
Rest of the world [3]	(X)	146	239	351	411	352

X Not applicable. [1] Based on North American Industry Classification System, 2002; see text, this section. [2] Consists of bank and other holding companies. [3] Consists of receipts by all U.S. residents, including both corporations and persons, of dividends from foreign corporations, and, for U.S. corporations, their share of reinvested earnings of their incorporated foreign affiliates, and earnings of unincorporated foreign affiliates, net of corresponding payments.
Source: U.S. Bureau of Economic Analysis, *Survey of Current Business*, April 2011. See also <http://www.bea.gov/national/nipaweb/Index.asp>.

Table 794. Manufacturing, Mining, and Trade Corporations—Profits and Stockholders' Equity by Industry: 2009 and 2010

[Averages of quarterly figures at annual rates. Manufacturing data exclude estimates for corporations with less than $250,000 in assets at time of sample selection. Mining, wholesale and retail trade data excludes estimates for corporations with less than $50 million in assets at time of sample selection. Based on sample; see source for discussion of methodology. Based on North American Industry Classification System (NAICS), 2002; see text, this section. Minus sign (–) indicates loss]

Industry	2002 NAICS code	Ratio of profits after taxes to stockholders' equity (percent)		Profits after taxes per dollar of sales (cents)		Ratio of stockholders' equity to debt	
		2009	2010	2009	2010	2009	2010
Manufacturing	31–33	10.1	15.1	5.5	8.3	1.5	1.8
Nondurable manufacturing	(X)	16.0	15.2	8.6	8.0	1.4	1.5
Food	311	17.8	16.2	5.9	5.5	1.1	1.1
Beverage and tobacco products	312	20.5	24.9	16.4	20.4	1.6	1.6
Textile mills and textile product mills	313, 314	1.0	8.6	0.4	3.7	2.1	2.2
Apparel and leather products	315, 316	13.2	19.7	5.3	7.9	2.0	2.2
Paper	322	10.9	17.1	3.4	5.6	0.7	0.9
Printing and related support activities	323	–0.5	13.9	0.0	2.9	0.4	0.5
Petroleum and coal products	324	10.5	11.9	5.2	5.0	2.4	2.5
Chemicals	325	19.9	15.2	16.8	13.4	1.3	1.4
Plastics and rubber products	326	9.3	12.6	2.9	3.7	0.9	1.1
Durable manufacturing	(X)	3.7	15.0	2.2	8.5	1.7	2.1
Wood products	321	–4.8	5.2	–2.2	1.8	1.0	1.0
Nonmetallic mineral products	327	–7.9	5.3	–5.8	3.3	1.0	1.1
Primary metals	331	–4.4	10.3	–2.9	4.8	1.8	1.9
Fabricated metal products	332	8.6	15.3	3.5	6.3	1.5	1.6
Machinery	333	7.8	14.0	4.3	7.5	1.7	2.0
Computer and electronic products	334	7.6	17.2	6.9	15.6	3.0	3.3
Electrical equipment, appliances, & components	335	9.3	11.1	8.4	10.7	3.7	4.2
Transportation equipment	336	–73.6	21.0	–3.7	5.8	0.6	1.4
Furniture and related products	337	3.1	1.3	1.0	0.5	1.0	1.1
Miscellaneous manufacturing	339	11.5	14.2	9.2	12.2	2.0	2.1
All mining	21	–1.9	11.4	–2.8	20.2	1.8	2.1
All wholesale trade	42	5.4	10.1	0.8	1.5	1.4	1.5
Durable goods	421	1.6	8.9	0.3	1.8	1.5	1.7
Nondurable goods	422	11.8	12.0	1.2	1.2	1.2	1.2
All retail trade	44–45	13.7	15.3	2.7	3.1	1.5	1.7
Food and beverage stores	445	7.1	9.5	0.9	1.1	1.1	1.1
Clothing and general merchandise stores	448, 452	15.0	17.6	3.6	4.2	1.7	1.7
All other retail trade	(X)	13.6	14.5	2.8	3.1	1.5	1.7

X Not applicable.
Source: U.S. Census Bureau, *Quarterly Financial Report for Manufacturing, Mining, and Trade Corporations*.

Table 795. Value Added, Employment, and Capital Expenditures of Nonbank U.S. Multinational Companies: 1999 to 2008

[Value added and capital expenditures in billions of dollars (2,481 represents $2,481,000,000,000); employees in thousands. See headnote, Table 796. MNC = Multinational company. MOFA = Majority-owned foreign affiliate. Minus sign (–) indicates decrease]

Item	1999	2000	2001	2002	2003	2004	2005	2006	2007	2008
VALUE ADDED										
MNCs worldwide:										
Parents and MOFAs	2,481	2,748	2,478	2,460	2,656	2,992	3,233	3,538	3,668	3,608
Parents	1,914	2,141	1,892	1,859	1,958	2,173	2,321	2,537	2,548	2,396
MOFAs	566	607	586	602	698	818	911	1,001	1,120	1,212
EMPLOYEES										
MNCs worldwide:										
Parents and all affiliates	32,227	33,598	32,539	31,894	30,762	31,245	32,094	32,766	33,281	32,983
Parents and MOFAs	30,773	32,057	30,929	30,373	29,347	29,843	30,573	31,233	31,561	31,227
Parents	23,007	23,885	22,735	22,118	21,105	21,177	21,472	21,616	21,549	21,103
Affiliates, total	9,220	9,713	9,804	9,776	9,658	10,068	10,622	11,150	11,732	11,879
MOFAs	7,766	8,171	8,194	8,256	8,242	8,667	9,101	9,617	10,012	10,124
Other	1,454	1,542	1,610	1,520	1,415	1,402	1,520	1,533	1,720	1,756
CAPITAL EXPENDITURES										
MNCs worldwide:										
Parents and all affiliates	550	(NA)	(NA)	(NA)	(NA)	487	(NA)	(NA)	(NA)	(NA)
Parents and MOFAs	519	548	561	478	444	463	507	600	666	658
Parents	406	438	450	367	335	339	377	445	495	479
Affiliates, total	144	(NA)	(NA)	(NA)	(NA)	147	(NA)	(NA)	(NA)	(NA)
MOFAs	113	111	111	110	110	123	130	155	171	179
Other	31	(NA)	(NA)	(NA)	(NA)	24	(NA)	(NA)	(NA)	(NA)

NA Not available.
Source: U.S. Bureau of Economic Analysis, *Survey of Current Business*, August 2010. See also <http: www.bea.gov /international/index.htm>.

Table 796. U.S. Multinational Companies—Selected Characteristics: 2008

[Preliminary. In billions of dollars (16,841 represents $16,841,000,000,000), except as indicated. Consists of nonbank U.S. parent companies and their nonbank foreign affiliates. U.S. parent comprises the domestic operations of a multinational and is a U.S. person that owns or controls, directly or indirectly, 10 percent or more of the voting securities of an incorporated foreign business enterprise, or an equivalent interest in an unincorporated foreign business enterprise. A U.S. person can be an incorporated business enterprise. A majority-owned foreign affiliate (MOFA) is a foreign business enterprise in which a U.S. parent company owns or controls more than 50 percent of the voting securities]

Industry	2002 NAICS code [1]	U.S. parents [2]				MOFAs [3]		
		Total assets	Capital expenditures	Value added	Employment (1,000)	Capital expenditures	Value added	Employment (1,000)
All industries	(X)	**16,841**	**478.8**	**2,396**	**21,103**	**179.1**	**1,212**	**10,124**
Mining	21	378	43.8	87	197	57.8	221	198
Utilities	22	564	37.1	73	197	3.4	9	27
Manufacturing [2]	31-33	5,315	169.3	981	7,083	63.9	517	4,600
Petroleum and coal products	324	732	35.5	118	292	4.0	75	39
Chemicals	325	1,037	22.4	187	873	14.3	110	627
Transportation equipment	336	1,329	50.5	195	1,694	11.9	62	902
Wholesale trade	42	820	34.1	137	1,049	7.7	157	797
Information [2]	51	1,455	67.1	296	1,831	7.3	46	361
Broadcasting (except Internet) and telecommunications	515, 517	1,059	56.6	199	1,122	5.2	13	88
Finance (except depository institutions) and insurance	52 exc. 521, 522	6,328	25.8	151	1,036	3.8	46	240
Professional, scientific, and technical services	54	366	8.9	158	1,192	3.8	67	679
Other industries [2]	(X)	1,614	92.6	513	8,520	31.4	147	3,222
Retail trade	44–45	404	24.3	201	4,039	7.8	53	1,063

X Not applicable. [1] Based on North American Industry Classification System, 2002; see text, this section. [2] Data are by industry of U.S. parent. [3] Data are by industry of foreign affiliate. [4] Includes other industries, not shown separately.
Source: U.S. Bureau of Economic Analysis, *Survey of Current Business*, August 2010 and unpublished data.

Table 797. U.S. Multinational Companies—Value Added: 2000 and 2008

[In billions of dollars (2,748 represents $2,748,000,000,000). See headnote, Table 796. Data are by industry of U.S. parent. Based on the North American Industry Classification System (NAICS), 2002; see text, this section]

Industry	2002 NAICS code [1]	U.S. multinationals		U.S. parents		Majority-owned foreign affiliates	
		2000	2008	2000	2008	2000	2008
All industries	(X)	**2,748**	**3,608**	**2,141**	**2,396**	**607**	**1,212**
Mining	21	39	129	28	87	11	42
Utilities	22	86	77	81	73	5	4
Manufacturing [2]	31–33	1,410	1,752	995	981	415	771
Petroleum and coal products	324	232	395	112	118	120	277
Chemicals	325	212	322	141	187	71	135
Transportation equipment	336	271	290	209	195	62	95
Wholesale trade	42	133	191	99	137	34	53
Information [2]	51	325	348	302	296	22	53
Broadcasting (except Internet) and telecommunications	515, 517	(NA)	217	(NA)	199	(NA)	18
Finance (except depository institutions) and insurance	52 exc. 521, 522	181	194	157	151	24	44
Professional, scientific, and technical services	54	141	226	101	158	41	68
Other industries [2]	(X)	433	690	379	513	54	176
Retail trade	44–45	166	240	149	201	18	39

NA Not available. X Not applicable. [1] See footnote 1, Table 796. [2] Includes other industries, not shown separately.
Source: U.S. Bureau of Economic Analysis, *Survey of Current Business*, November 2003 and August 2010.

Table 798. U.S. Majority-Owned Foreign Affiliates—Value Added by Industry of Affiliate and Country: 2008

[Preliminary. In millions of dollars (1,211,854 represents $1,211,854,000,000). See headnote, Table 796. Numbers in parentheses represent North American Industry Classification System 2002 codes; see text, this section]

Country	All industries [1]	Mining (21)	Manufacturing (31-33)			Wholesale trade (42)	Professional, scientific, and technical services (54)
			Total [1]	Chemicals (325)	Transportation equipment (336)		
All countries [2]	**1,211,854**	**221,006**	**517,133**	**110,154**	**62,050**	**157,274**	**67,463**
United Kingdom	126,352	22,515	51,164	7,597	9,451	12,073	6,935
Canada	56,712	76	30,805	6,202	2,741	7,803	3,497
Germany	94,127	1,866	61,863	8,837	11,157	10,664	5,240
France	55,561	362	28,012	15,243	83	5,848	2,403
Ireland	32,974	-1	20,347	3,065	1,041	4,906	2,229
Australia	33,296	1,120	20,087	5,245	2,547	5,291	2,533
Japan	165,991	17,589	62,612	8,472	5,415	21,739	15,141
Italy	30,753	1,753	18,141	3,441	4,924	1,584	782
Mexico	46,058	11,495	14,578	2,365	1,204	6,856	3,464
Netherlands	44,094	4	12,386	5,131	554	8,589	6,332

[1] Includes other industries, not shown separately. [2] Includes other countries, not shown separately.
Source: U.S. Bureau of Economic Analysis, *Survey of Current Business*, August 2010.

520 Business Enterprise

This section presents statistics on scientific, engineering, and technological resources, with emphasis on patterns of research and development (R&D) funding and on scientific, engineering, and technical personnel; education; and employment.

The National Science Foundation (NSF) gathers data chiefly through recurring surveys. Current NSF publications containing data on funds for research and development and on scientific and engineering personnel include detailed statistical tables; info briefs; and annual, biennial, and special reports, see <http://www.nsf.gov/statistics>. Titles or the areas of coverage of these reports include the following: *Science and Engineering Indicators; National Patterns of R&D Resources; Women, Minorities, and Persons with Disabilities in Science and Engineering, Federal Funds for Research and Development;* Federal R&D Funding by Budget Function; Federal Support to Universities, Colleges, and Selected Nonprofit Institutions; *Research and Development in Industry;* R&D expenditures and graduate enrollment and support in academic science and engineering; and characteristics of doctoral scientists and engineers and of recent graduates in the United States. Statistical surveys in these areas pose problems of concept and definition and the data should therefore be regarded as broad estimates rather than precise, quantitative statements. See sources for methodological and technical details.

The National Science Board's biennial *Science and Engineering Indicators* at <http://www.nsf.gov/statistics/seind10/> contains data and analysis of international and domestic science and technology, including measures of inputs and outputs.

Research and development outlays— NSF defines research as "systematic study directed toward fuller scientific knowledge of the subject studied" and development as "the systematic use of scientific knowledge directed toward the production of useful materials, devices, systems, or methods, including design and development of prototypes and processes."

National coverage of R&D expenditures is developed primarily from periodic surveys in four principal economic sectors: (1) *Government,* made up primarily of federal executive agencies; (2) *Industry,* consisting of manufacturing and nonmanufacturing firms and the federally funded research and development centers (FFRDCs) they administer; (3) *Universities and colleges,* composed of universities, colleges, and their affiliated institutions, agricultural experiment stations, and associated schools of agriculture and of medicine, and FFRDCs administered by educational institutions; and (4) *Other nonprofit institutions,* consisting of such organizations as private philanthropic foundations, nonprofit research institutes, voluntary health agencies, and FFRDCs administered by nonprofit organizations.

The R&D funds reported consist of current operating costs, including planning and administration costs, except as otherwise noted. They exclude funds for routine testing, mapping and surveying, collection of general purpose data, dissemination of scientific information, and training of scientific personnel.

Scientists, engineers, and technicians—Scientists and engineers are defined as persons engaged in scientific and engineering work at a level requiring a knowledge of sciences equivalent at least to that acquired through completion of a 4-year college course. Technicians are defined as persons engaged in technical work at a level requiring knowledge acquired through a technical institute, junior college, or other type of training less extensive than 4-year college training. Craftsmen and skilled workers are excluded.

Table 799. Research and Development (R&D) Expenditures by Source and Objective: 1980 to 2008

[In millions of dollars (63,224 represents $63,224,000,000), except as indicated]

Year	Total	Sources of funds					Objective (percent of total)			Character of work		
		Federal government	Industry	Universities\colleges	Non-profit	Non-federal government [1]	Defense related [2]	Space related [3]	Other	Basic research	Applied research	Development
1980.....	63,224	29,986	30,929	920	871	519	24.3	5.3	70.4	8,745	13,714	40,765
1981.....	72,292	33,739	35,948	1,058	967	581	24.4	5.2	70.4	9,658	16,329	46,305
1982.....	80,748	37,133	40,692	1,207	1,095	621	26.1	4.9	69.0	10,651	18,218	51,879
1983.....	89,950	41,451	45,264	1,357	1,220	658	27.7	4.2	68.1	11,880	20,298	57,771
1984.....	102,244	46,470	52,187	1,514	1,351	721	28.7	3.0	68.3	13,332	22,451	66,461
1985.....	114,671	52,641	57,962	1,743	1,491	834	29.9	3.1	67.0	14,748	25,401	74,522
1986.....	120,249	54,622	60,991	2,019	1,647	969	31.4	3.0	65.6	17,154	27,240	75,855
1987.....	126,360	58,609	62,576	2,262	1,849	1,065	31.7	3.2	65.1	18,481	27,951	79,929
1988.....	133,881	60,131	67,977	2,527	2,081	1,165	30.2	3.5	66.3	19,787	29,528	84,567
1989.....	141,891	60,466	74,966	2,852	2,333	1,274	27.6	3.9	68.5	21,891	32,277	87,723
1990.....	151,993	61,610	83,208	3,187	2,589	1,399	25.1	4.3	70.6	23,029	34,897	94,067
1991.....	160,876	60,783	92,300	3,458	2,852	1,483	22.4	4.5	73.1	27,140	38,631	95,105
1992.....	165,350	60,915	96,229	3,569	3,113	1,525	21.6	4.3	74.1	27,604	37,936	99,811
1993.....	165,730	60,528	96,549	3,709	3,388	1,557	21.2	4.4	74.4	28,743	37,283	99,705
1994.....	169,207	60,777	99,204	3,938	3,665	1,623	19.7	4.5	75.8	29,651	36,618	102,938
1995.....	183,625	62,969	110,871	4,110	3,925	1,751	18.6	4.5	76.9	29,610	40,936	113,079
1996.....	197,346	63,394	123,417	4,436	4,239	1,861	17.6	4.1	78.3	32,799	43,170	121,377
1997.....	212,152	64,574	136,228	4,838	4,590	1,922	16.7	4.1	79.2	36,921	46,554	128,677
1998.....	226,402	66,383	147,846	5,163	5,038	1,972	15.8	3.8	80.4	35,341	46,348	144,712
1999.....	244,922	67,055	164,660	5,619	5,489	2,098	14.6	3.2	82.2	38,887	52,006	154,029
2000.....	267,298	66,417	186,136	6,232	6,267	2,247	13.4	2.3	84.3	42,667	56,826	167,805
2001.....	277,366	72,836	188,440	6,827	6,867	2,397	14.0	2.4	83.6	47,617	64,583	165,167
2002.....	276,022	77,710	180,711	7,344	7,700	2,557	15.6	2.4	82.0	51,174	50,814	174,034
2003.....	288,324	83,618	186,174	7,650	8,140	2,742	16.5	2.3	81.2	54,375	61,563	172,386
2004.....	299,201	88,766	191,376	7,937	8,239	2,883	17.2	2.1	80.7	55,868	70,095	173,238
2005.....	322,104	93,817	207,826	8,579	8,960	2,922	17.1	2.0	80.9	59,462	70,215	192,427
2006.....	347,048	98,038	227,254	9,307	9,429	3,021	16.8	1.8	81.4	61,038	76,428	209,582
2007.....	372,535	101,772	246,927	9,993	10,593	3,249	16.2	1.5	82.3	65,988	83,214	223,333
2008 [4] ...	397,629	103,709	267,847	10,600	12,020	3,453	15.3	1.4	83.3	69,146	88,591	239,891

[1] Nonfederal R&D expenditures to university and college performers. [2] R&D spending by the Department of Defense, including space activities, and a portion of the Department of Energy funds. [3] For the National Aeronautics and Space Administration only. [4] Preliminary.
Source: U.S. National Science Foundation, *National Patterns of R&D Resources*, NSF 10-314, 2010. See also <www.nsf.gov/statistics/nsf10314/>.

Table 800. National Research and Development (R&D) Expenditures as a Percent of Gross Domestic Product by Country: 1990 to 2009

Year	United States	Japan [1]	Germany [2]	France	United Kingdom	Italy	Canada	South Korea	OECD total [3]	Russia [4]	China [5]
1990....	2.65	2.81	2.61	2.32	2.10	1.25	1.51	(NA)	2.25	2.03	(NA)
1995....	2.50	2.71	2.19	2.29	1.91	0.97	1.70	2.27	2.06	0.85	0.57
2000....	2.71	3.04	2.45	2.15	1.81	1.05	1.91	2.30	2.21	1.05	0.90
2001....	2.72	3.12	2.46	2.20	1.79	1.09	2.09	2.47	2.25	1.18	0.95
2002....	2.62	3.17	2.49	2.23	1.79	1.13	2.04	2.40	2.22	1.25	1.07
2003....	2.61	3.20	2.52	2.17	1.75	1.11	2.03	2.49	2.22	1.28	1.13
2004....	2.54	3.17	2.49	2.15	1.69	1.10	2.08	2.68	2.17	1.15	1.23
2005....	2.57	3.32	2.49	2.10	1.73	1.09	2.05	2.79	2.21	1.07	1.34
2006....	2.61	3.41	2.53	2.10	1.76	1.13	1.97	3.01	2.24	1.07	1.42
2007....	2.66	3.44	2.53	2.04	1.82	1.18	1.90	3.21	2.28	1.12	1.44
2008....	2.77	(NA)	(NA)	2.02	1.88	1.18	1.84	(NA)	(NA)	1.04	(NA)
2009....	(NA)	(NA)	2.82	2.21	1.87	1.27	1.96	(NA)	(NA)	1.24	(NA)

NA Not available. [1] Data on Japanese research and development after 1995 may not be consistent with data in earlier years because of changes in methodology. [2] Data for 1990 are for West Germany only. [3] Organization for Economic Cooperation and Development. [4] As of May 16, 2007 Russia is an OECD accession candidate country. [5] As of 2007 China is an OECD enhanced engagement country.
Source: Organization for Economic Cooperation and Development, *Main Science and Technology Indicators*, 2010/2nd edition (copyright). See also <http://www.oecd.org/>.

Table 801. Performance Sector of Research and Development (R&D) Expenditures: 2000 to 2008

[In millions of dollars (267,298 represents $267,298,000,000). For calendar year. FFRDCs are federally funded research and development centers]

Year	Total	Federal government	Industry Total	Industry: Federal government	Industry: Industry[1]	Industry FFRDC's	Univ. & colleges Total	U&C: Federal government	U&C: Non-federal government[2]	U&C: Industry	U&C: Universities & colleges	U&C: Non-profits	University & college FFRDCs[3]	Other nonprofit Total	Other nonprofit: Federal government	Other nonprofit: Industry	Other nonprofit: Non-profits
RESEARCH AND DEVELOPMENT TOTAL																	
2000	267,298	17,917	199,961	17,117	182,844	2,001	30,705	17,727	2,247	2,174	6,232	2,326	5,742	9,506	4,447	1,118	3,941
2004	299,201	22,844	208,301	20,266	188,035	2,485	43,128	27,173	2,883	2,190	7,937	2,946	7,659	12,140	5,695	1,151	5,294
2005	322,104	24,470	226,159	21,909	204,250	2,601	45,197	28,260	2,922	2,323	8,579	3,113	7,817	13,032	5,932	1,253	5,846
2006	347,048	25,556	247,669	24,304	223,365	3,122	46,983	28,815	3,021	2,515	9,307	3,325	7,306	13,469	5,992	1,374	6,103
2007	372,535	25,858	269,267	26,585	242,682	5,165	49,021	29,328	3,249	2,748	9,993	3,703	5,567	14,341	5,954	1,497	6,890
2008[4]	397,629	27,000	289,105	25,795	263,310	6,337	51,163	30,177	3,453	2,908	10,600	4,024	4,717	15,606	5,982	1,629	7,995
BASIC RESEARCH																	
2000	42,667	3,765	7,040	925	6,115	547	22,917	13,966	1,550	1,499	4,298	1,604	2,874	4,908	2,099	621	2,188
2004	55,868	4,697	7,835	1,072	6,763	175	31,994	21,154	1,958	1,488	5,392	2,002	3,730	6,366	2,788	639	2,939
2005	59,462	4,770	8,667	1,108	7,559	136	34,044	22,198	2,043	1,625	6,000	2,177	3,820	6,844	2,903	696	3,246
2006	61,038	4,716	8,384	1,444	6,940	652	35,700	22,736	2,155	1,795	6,641	2,373	3,344	7,001	2,849	763	3,389
2007	65,988	4,600	11,268	2,780	8,488	2,258	37,323	23,070	2,351	1,989	7,233	2,680	1,724	7,466	2,809	831	3,826
2008[4]	69,146	4,734	11,907	2,697	9,209	2,390	38,822	23,608	2,503	2,108	7,685	2,918	1,634	8,229	2,885	904	4,439
APPLIED RESEARCH																	
2000	56,826	6,105	39,176	2,682	36,494	269	6,617	3,315	572	553	1,585	592	1,329	3,113	1,831	283	999
2004	70,095	7,455	45,432	4,775	40,657	1,509	9,335	5,140	759	576	2,087	774	1,920	4,081	2,448	292	1,342
2005	70,215	7,557	45,284	5,289	39,995	1,492	9,333	5,158	721	573	2,114	768	1,912	4,231	2,432	318	1,482
2006	76,428	7,435	51,173	6,140	45,033	1,331	9,557	5,290	710	590	2,186	781	1,874	4,487	2,592	348	1,547
2007	83,214	7,303	57,570	8,945	48,625	1,168	10,003	5,542	736	623	2,264	839	1,354	4,722	2,596	379	1,746
2008[4]	88,591	7,573	61,437	8,679	52,758	1,998	10,556	5,824	779	656	2,390	908	713	4,985	2,546	413	2,026
DEVELOPMENT																	
2000	167,805	8,047	153,745	13,510	140,235	1,185	1,172	447	125	121	348	130	1,539	1,485	517	214	754
2004	173,238	10,692	155,034	14,419	140,615	801	1,799	878	167	126	458	170	2,008	1,692	459	220	1,013
2005	192,427	12,142	172,208	15,512	156,696	974	1,820	904	158	126	464	169	2,085	1,957	598	240	1,119
2006	209,582	13,406	188,112	16,720	171,392	1,139	1,726	789	156	130	480	171	2,088	1,981	551	263	1,168
2007	223,333	13,955	200,429	14,860	185,569	1,738	1,695	716	162	137	497	184	2,488	2,154	549	286	1,318
2008[4]	239,891	14,693	215,761	14,419	201,342	1,949	1,785	746	171	144	525	199	2,370	2,392	551	312	1,530

[1] Includes all nonfederal sources of industry R&D expenditures. [2] Preliminary. [3] Includes all R&D expenditures of FFRDCs administered by academic institutions and funded by the federal government. [2] Includes all nonfederal sources.

Source: National Science Foundation, data derived from: *Research and Development in Industry*, annual; *Academic Research and Development Expenditures*, annual; and *Federal Funds For Research and Development*, annual. See also <http://www.nsf.gov/statistics/nsf10314/>.

Table 802. Federal Obligations for Research in Current and Constant (2000) Dollars by Field of Science: 2005 to 2009

[In millions of dollars (53,738 represents $53,738,000,000). For years ending September 30. Excludes R&D plant]

Field of science	Current dollars				Constant (2000) dollars [1]			
	2005	2007	2008, prel.	2009, proj.	2005	2007	2008, prel.	2009, proj.
Research, total	53,738	54,094	55,097	54,801	47,682	45,248	45,213	44,081
Basic	27,140	26,866	27,559	28,536	24,082	22,472	22,615	22,954
Applied	26,598	27,228	27,538	26,265	23,601	22,775	22,598	21,127
Life sciences	28,128	29,464	29,675	29,299	24,958	24,645	24,351	23,567
Psychology	1,892	1,838	1,861	1,853	1,679	1,537	1,527	1,490
Physical sciences	5,494	5,136	5,249	5,593	4,875	4,296	4,308	4,499
Environmental sciences	3,503	3,171	3,315	3,352	3,108	2,652	2,720	2,697
Mathematics and computer sciences	2,983	2,946	3,285	3,333	2,647	2,464	2,696	2,681
Engineering	8,553	8,990	9,353	8,907	7,589	7,520	7,676	7,164
Social sciences	1,097	1,147	1,071	1,123	973	960	879	903
Other sciences, n.e.c. [2]	2,089	1,403	1,287	1,341	1,854	1,174	1,056	1,079

[1] Based on gross domestic product implicit price deflator. [2] Not elsewhere classified.
Source: U.S. National Science Foundation, *Federal Funds for Research and Development*, NSF 09-320, 2009. See also <http://www.nsf.gov/statistics/fedfunds/>.

Table 803. Federal Budget Authority for Research and Development (R&D) in Current and Constant (2000) Dollars by Selected Budget Functions: 2007 to 2010

[In millions of dollars (138,087 represents $138,087,000,000). For year ending September 30. Excludes R&D plant. Represents budget authority. Functions shown are those for which $1 billion or more was authorized since 2001]

Function	Current dollars				Constant (2000) dollars [1]			
	2007	2008	2009 [2]	2010 [3]	2007	2008	2009 [2]	2010 [3]
Total [4]	138,087	140,113	156,009	143,892	115,506	114,979	125,490	113,479
National defense	82,272	84,713	85,166	86,082	68,818	69,517	68,505	67,888
Health	29,461	29,063	40,389	30,976	24,643	23,849	32,488	24,429
Space research and technology	9,024	8,323	6,891	6,622	7,548	6,830	5,543	5,222
Energy	1,893	1,896	3,318	2,138	1,583	1,556	2,669	1,686
General science	7,809	8,234	11,840	9,298	6,532	6,757	9,524	7,333
Natural resources and environment	1,936	2,106	2,245	2,300	1,619	1,728	1,806	1,814
Transportation	1,361	1,394	1,440	1,427	1,138	1,144	1,158	1,125
Agriculture	1,857	1,864	2,302	2,439	1,553	1,530	1,852	1,924

[1] Based on gross domestic product implicit price deflator. [2] Includes ARRA (American Recovery and Reinvestment Act) funds. [3] Preliminary. [4] Includes other functions, not shown separately.
Source: U.S. National Science Foundation, *Federal R&D Funding by Budget Function*, NSF 10-317, 2010. See also <http://www.nsf.gov/statistics/nsf10317/>.

Table 804. Federal Research and Development (R&D) by Federal Agency: Fiscal Year (FY) 2009 and 2010

[In millions of dollars (145,605 represents $145,605,000,000). For years ending September 30. R&D refers to actual research and development activities as well as R&D facilities. R&D facilities (also known as R&D plants) includes construction, repair, or alteration of physical plant used in the conduct of R&D. Based on Office of Management and Budget data]

Federal agency	2009 [1]	2010	Federal agency	2009 [1]	2010
Total research and development	145,605	149,295	Department of Veterans Affairs	925	1,073
Defense R&D	85,309	86,756	Department of Homeland Security	943	1,034
Nondefense R&D	60,297	62,539	Department of Transportation	1,096	887
			Department of Interior	702	776
Department of Defense	81,484	82,902	U.S. Geological Survey	615	661
Science and technology	13,967	14,749	Environmental Protection Agency	563	597
All other Department of Defense R&D	67,517	68,152	Department of Education	312	353
Health and Human Services	31,058	31,458	Smithsonian	216	213
National Institute of Health	29,752	30,189	International Assistance Programs	152	121
All other Health and Human Services R&D	1,306	1,269	Department of Housing and Urban Development	58	100
Department of Energy	10,301	10,836	Department of State	101	81
Atomic Energy Defense	3,825	3,854	Nuclear Regulatory Commission	94	79
Office of Science	4,372	4,528	Department of Justice	103	73
Energy R&D	2,104	2,454	Social Security Administration	35	49
NASA	8,788	9,262	U.S. Postal Service	18	18
National Science Foundation	4,767	5,392	Tennessee Valley Authority	43	12
Department of Agriculture	2,437	2,611	Army Corps of Engineers	11	11
Department of Commerce	1,389	1,337	Telecommunications Development Agency	6	7
National Oceanic and Atmospheric Administration	785	685	Department of Labor	4	4
National Institute of Standards and Technology	553	588			

[1] Includes ARRA (American Recovery and Reinvestment Act) funds.
Source: American Association for the Advancement of Science (AAAS), AAAS Report XXXIV *Research and Development FY 2011*, annual (copyright). See also <http://www.aaas.org/spp/rd/rdreport2011/>.

Table 805. Funds for Domestic Business Research and Development (R&D) Performed by Manufacturing and Nonmanufacturing Companies by Industry: 2006 to 2008

[Based on the Survey of Industry Research and Development and the Business R&D and Innovation Survey; for information about the surveys and methodology, see http://www.nsf.gov/statistics/srvyindustry/sird.cfm]

Industry	NAICS [1] code	Total R&D funds as a percent of net sales			Company R&D funds as a percent of net sales [2]		
		2006	2007	2008	2006	2007	2008
All industries, total	(X)	3.7	3.8	3.7	3.4	3.5	3.0
All manufacturing industries, total	(X)	4.0	4.1	4.4	3.6	3.7	3.5
Food	311	0.7	(D)	0.4	0.7	0.7	0.4
Paper, printing, and support activities	322, 323	(D)	(D)	1.4	1.2	1.3	1.3
Petroleum and coal products	324	0.3	(D)	(D)	0.3	0.3	(D)
Chemicals	325	7.6	(D)	6.5	7.5	7.9	6.1
Plastic and rubber products........................	326	2.0	(D)	1.1	1.9	1.5	1.1
Nonmetallic mineral products	327	2.1	1.8	2.0	1.9	1.8	1.9
Primary metals	331	0.5	0.6	0.4	0.5	0.6	0.4
Fabricated metal products.........................	332	1.4	1.7	1.6	1.4	1.6	1.6
Machinery	333	3.6	3.7	3.6	3.6	3.7	3.5
Computer and electronic products	334	10.8	9.9	11.6	9.2	8.4	10.1
Electrical equipment, appliances, and components	335	2.6	3.1	2.9	2.5	3.0	2.7
Transportation equipment	336	(D)	(D)	5.7	2.9	3.1	2.6
All nonmanufacturing industries, total	(X)	3.2	3.4	2.8	2.9	3.0	2.2
Information...................................	51	5.3	(D)	4.9	5.2	5.1	4.8
Software publishing	5112	(D)	(D)	10.8	19.9	19.6	10.6
Internet service and data processing providers.............	518	9.6	(D)	6.3	9.4	9.6	6.2
Professional, scientific, and technical services	54	9.5	11.7	8.4	7.6	9.5	4.5
Architectural, engineering, and related services	5413	14.4	12.0	8.2	10.7	8.1	3.3
Computer systems design and related services	5415	5.3	7.0	5.9	4.9	6.6	4.2
Scientific research and development services	5417	35.1	42.0	13.2	24.2	30.0	6.4

D Figure withheld to avoid disclosure of information pertaining to a specific organization or individual. X Not applicable.
[1] North American Industry Classification System (NAICS); see text, Section 15. [2] For 2006–2007, company R&D funds included the company's own funds as well as funds from all other nonfederal sources. For 2008, company R&D funds included only the company's own funds.

Source: U.S. National Science Foundation, *Research and Development in Industry and Business Research and Development*, annual. See also <http://www.nsf.gov/statistics/>.

Table 806. Funds for Domestic Performance of Business Research and Development (R&D) in Current and Constant (2005) Dollars by Source of Funds and Selected Industries: 2005 to 2008

[In millions of dollars (226,159 represents $226,159,000,000). For calendar years. Covers basic research, applied research, and development. Based on the Survey of Industry Research and Development and the Business R&D and Innovation Survey; for information about the surveys and methodology, see http://www.nsf.gov/statistics/srvyindustry/sird.cfm]

Industry	NAICS [1] code	2005	2006	2007	2008
CURRENT DOLLARS					
Total funds	(X)	**226,159**	**247,669**	**269,267**	**290,681**
Company and other funds........................	(X)	204,250	223,365	242,682	254,321
Federal funds................................	(X)	21,909	24,304	26,585	36,360
Petroleum and coal products.......................	324	(D)	1,432	(D)	(D)
Chemicals and allied products.......................	325	42,995	46,329	(D)	58,249
Pharmaceuticals and medicines	3254	34,839	38,901	(D)	48,131
Machinery	333	8,531	9,848	9,865	10,104
Computer and electronic products....................	334	(D)	56,773	58,599	60,463
Navigational, measuring, electromedical, and control instruments	3345	15,204	18,300	20,438	15,460
Electrical equipment, appliances, and components	335	2,424	2,281	(D)	3,143
Aerospace products and parts	3364	15,055	16,367	18,436	36,941
Information..................................	51	23,836	26,883	(D)	37,964
Professional, scientific, and technical services	54	32,021	38,049	40,533	37,594
Computer systems design and related services	5415	13,592	14,841	14,407	12,146
Scientific R&D services	5417	12,299	14,525	16,849	17,913
CONSTANT (2005) DOLLARS [2]					
Total funds	(X)	**226,159**	**239,850**	**253,309**	**267,613**
Company and other funds........................	(X)	204,250	216,313	228,299	234,138
Federal funds................................	(X)	21,909	23,537	23,527	33,474
Petroleum and coal products.......................	324	(D)	1,387	(D)	(D)
Chemicals....................................	325	42,995	44,866	(D)	53,626
Pharmaceuticals and medicines	3254	34,839	37,673	(D)	44,311
Machinery	333	8,531	9,537	9,280	9,302
Computer and electronic products....................	334	(D)	54,981	55,126	55,665
Navigational, measuring, electromedical, and control instruments	3345	15,204	17,722	19,227	14,233
Electrical equipment, appliances, and components	335	2,424	2,209	(D)	2,894
Aerospace products and parts	3364	15,055	15,850	17,343	34,009
Information..................................	51	23,836	26,034	(D)	34,703
Professional, scientific, and technical services	54	32,021	36,848	38,131	34,942
Computer systems design and related services	5415	13,592	14,372	13,553	11,182
Scientific R&D services	5417	12,299	14,066	15,850	16,491

D Figure withheld to avoid disclosure of information pertaining to a specific organization or individual. X Not applicable.
[1] North American Industry Classification System; see text, Section 15. [2] Based on gross domestic product implicit price deflator.

Source: U.S. National Science Foundation, *Research and Development in Industry and Business Research and Development*, annual. See also: <http://www.nsf.gov/statistics/>

Table 807. Academic and Industrial Research and Development (R&D) Performed by State: 2007

[In millions of dollars (49,021 represents 49,021,000,000). For definition of Research and Development, see text, this section]

State	Academic R&D (mil. dol.)	Academic R&D per $1,000 of state GDP	Industry-performed R&D (mil. dol.)	Industry R&D per $1,000 of state GDP	State	Academic R&D (mil. dol.)	Academic R&D per $1,000 of state GDP	Industry-performed R&D (mil. dol.)	Industry R&D per $1,000 of state GDP
U.S.[1]	49,021	3.55	269,267	19.50	MO	941	4.11	2,736	11.95
AL	655	3.98	1,771	[2] 10.76	MT	179	5.22	134	3.91
AK	160	3.56	58	1.29	NE	365	4.54	489	6.09
AZ	783	3.18	3,846	15.64	NV	192	1.48	567	4.38
AR	240	2.52	339	3.56	NH	307	5.31	1,814	[3] 31.37
CA	6,734	3.74	64,187	35.62					
					NJ	865	1.88	17,892	38.79
CO	873	3.70	5,223	22.15	NM	410	5.45	568	7.55
CT	691	3.26	9,444	44.49	NY	3,964	3.59	10,916	9.88
DE	126	2.05	1,472	23.92	NC	1,885	4.83	6,829	17.49
DC	333	3.60	379	4.10	ND	169	5.93	126	4.42
FL	1,558	2.10	4,569	6.16					
					OH	1,807	3.91	7,265	15.71
GA	1,389	3.55	2,788	7.13	OK	299	2.19	527	3.86
HI	274	4.42	218	3.52	OR	575	3.63	3,629	[3] 22.92
ID	114	2.19	726	13.93	PA	2,438	4.57	10,387	19.48
IL	1,867	3.02	11,362	18.40	RI	230	4.93	411	8.80
IN	894	3.59	4,939	19.82					
					SC	569	3.75	1,426	9.40
IA	587	4.52	1,202	9.25	SD	82	2.33	132	3.75
KS	376	3.21	1,304	11.15	TN	761	3.10	1,638	6.68
KY	503	3.31	890	5.85	TX	3,417	2.98	13,889	12.09
LA	604	2.91	373	[2] 1.80	UT	415	3.93	1,764	16.71
ME	137	2.85	265	5.52					
					VT	115	4.67	413	16.77
MD	2,542	9.61	3,665	13.86	VA	971	2.53	4,840	12.60
MA	2,172	6.17	19,488	55.34	WA	981	3.16	12,687	40.89
MI	1,510	3.97	15,736	41.42	WV	167	2.89	233	4.03
MN	637	2.52	6,636	26.28	WI	1,067	4.57	3,411	14.61
MS	411	4.69	279	3.18	WY	80	2.54	37	[2] 1.17

[1] National totals for calendar year 2007. Includes $3.3 billion of industrial R&D expenditures that year that could not be allocated to specific states. [2] Estimated, more than 50 percent of the industrial R&D value is imputed due to raking of state data. [3] More than 50 percent of the industrial R&D value is imputed.

Source: National Science Foundation, *National Patterns of R&D Resources*, NSF-10-314, 2010. See also <http://www.nsf.gov/statistics/nsf10314/>.

Table 808. Research and Development (R&D) Expenditures in Science and Engineering at Universities and Colleges in Current and Constant (2005) Dollars: 2000 to 2009

[In millions of dollars (30,084 represents $30,084,000,000). Totals may not add due to rounding]

Characteristic	Current dollars				Constant (2005) dollars [1]			
	2000	2005	2008	2009	2000	2005	2008	2009
Total	30,084	45,799	51,934	54,935	33,844	45,799	47,655	49,746
Basic research [2]	22,547	34,368	39,408	40,955	25,365	34,367	36,161	37,087
Applied R&D [2]	7,537	11,432	12,526	13,980	8,479	11,432	11,494	12,660
Source of funds:								
Federal government	17,548	29,209	31,281	32,588	19,741	29,209	28,703	29,510
State and local government	2,200	2,940	3,452	3,647	2,475	2,940	3,168	3,303
Institutions' own funds	5,925	8,266	10,408	11,198	6,666	8,266	9,550	10,140
Industry	2,156	2,291	2,865	3,197	2,425	2,291	2,629	2,895
Other	2,255	3,093	3,928	4,305	2,537	3,093	3,604	3,898
Fields:								
Physical sciences	2,713	3,704	3,941	4,294	3,052	3,704	3,616	3,888
Environmental sciences	1,766	2,555	2,806	2,940	1,987	2,555	2,575	2,662
Mathematical sciences	342	495	620	553	384	494	569	501
Computer sciences	877	1,406	1,472	1,592	987	1,406	1,351	1,442
Life sciences	17,471	27,605	31,210	32,791	19,655	27,605	28,638	29,694
Psychology	517	826	929	979	581	826	852	887
Social sciences	1,300	1,685	1,947	2,075	1,462	1,685	1,787	1,879
Other sciences	543	778	1051	1060	611	778	964	960
Engineering	4,557	6,746	7,958	8,651	5,127	6,746	7,302	7,834

[1] Based on gross domestic product implicit price deflator (updated February 2011). [2] Basic research and applied R&D statistics were re-estimated for FY1998 and forward. These data are not directly comparable to those from earlier years.

Source: U.S. National Science Foundation, *Survey of Research and Development Expenditures at Universities and Colleges*, annual. See also <http://www.nsf.gov/statistics/srvyrdexpenditures/>.

Table 809. Federal Research and Development (R&D) Obligations to Selected Universities and Colleges: 2006 and 2007

[In millions of dollars (24,991.8 represents $24,991,800,000). For years ending September 30. For the top 40 institutions receiving federal R&D funds in 2007. Awards to the administrative offices of university systems are excluded from totals for individual institutions because that allocation of funds is unknown, but those awards are included in "total all institutions"]

Major institution ranked by total 2007 federal R&D obligations	2006	2007	Major institution ranked by total 2007 federal R&D obligations	2006	2007
Total, all institutions [1]	**24,991.8**	**24,998.0**	Cornell University	299.1	326.1
Johns Hopkins University	1,153.2	1,054.9	Pennsylvania State University	291.8	320.8
University of Washington	612.1	608.0	Case Western Reserve University	277.9	278.9
University of Michigan	516.2	501.5	University Southern California	265.5	260.3
University of Pennsylvania	497.5	498.5	University of Rochester	252.3	255.2
University of California—Los Angeles	477.6	480.0	Northwestern University	222.2	254.2
Duke University	472.5	470.7	University of Chicago	219.8	248.6
University of California—San Francisco	441.9	433.4	Emory University	228.1	247.9
University of California—San Diego	401.2	432.7	University of California—Davis	236.4	243.1
Harvard University	420.8	429.3	University of Alabama—Birmingham	235.4	235.1
University of Pittsburgh	425.4	425.9	Baylor College of Medicine	236.5	227.9
Columbia University—City of NY	467.8	425.7	University of California—Irvine	161.3	219.6
Stanford University	455.9	424.0	Ohio State University	205.9	217.2
Washington University	410.7	407.8	University of California—Berkeley	228.6	214.2
Yale University	361.7	387.3	University of Arizona	200.7	212.0
Massachusetts Institute of Technology	357.1	380.8	University of Illinois—Urbana Champaign	184.6	210.5
University of Minnesota	331.2	370.7	Boston University	204.7	208.5
University of Wisconsin—Madison	373.7	369.2	University of Iowa	193.0	208.4
University of North Carolina at Chapel Hill	343.4	353.5	The Scripps Research Institute	217.5	199.0
University of Colorado	340.1	330.0	University of Virginia	176.3	198.4
Vanderbilt University	306.4	329.6			

[1] Includes other institutions, not shown separately.

Source: U.S. National Science Foundation, *Federal S&E Support to Universities and Colleges and Nonprofit Institutions*, NSF 09-313, 2009. See also <http://www.nsf.gov/statistics/fedsupport/>.

Table 810. Graduate Science/Engineering Students in Doctorate-Granting Colleges by Characteristic and Field: 1990 to 2009

[In thousands (409.4 represents 409,400). As of fall. Includes outlying areas]

Field of science or engineering	Total			Characteristic								
				Female			Foreign			Part-time		
	1990	2000	2009	1990	2000	2009	1990	2000	2009	1990	2000	2009
Total, all surveyed fields	**409.4**	**443.5**	**573.9**	**155.5**	**201.8**	**269.7**	**103.0**	**123.3**	**163.3**	**130.8**	**123.6**	**145.0**
Science/engineering	360.6	374.8	497.2	117.9	150.3	212.1	98.9	118.0	155.1	107.5	99.3	120.7
Engineering, total	101.0	98.8	136.7	13.8	19.7	31.8	36.9	46.3	62.8	36.7	28.2	35.2
Sciences, total [1]	259.6	275.9	360.5	104.2	130.7	180.3	62.0	71.7	92.3	70.8	71.1	85.4
Physical sciences	32.9	29.6	37.1	7.7	8.8	12.2	12.2	11.5	14.8	3.9	3.5	3.4
Environmental	13.1	13.0	13.9	3.8	5.3	6.4	2.6	2.6	2.7	3.2	2.8	2.7
Mathematical sciences	18.1	14.4	20.5	5.6	5.2	7.2	6.4	5.9	8.2	4.7	3.0	4.2
Computer sciences	29.2	40.3	45.6	6.8	11.7	11.4	9.7	19.7	22.1	14.1	16.7	15.9
Agricultural sciences	11.0	11.3	14.1	3.2	4.8	6.9	3.2	2.4	3.2	2.0	2.4	3.9
Biological sciences	46.7	53.1	68.6	21.4	27.8	38.9	11.2	11.6	16.8	7.2	7.6	9.3
Psychology	38.5	40.3	46.6	25.5	29.0	34.9	1.7	2.1	2.7	12.0	10.8	12.0
Social sciences	70.0	73.9	95.2	30.1	38.1	50.5	15.0	15.8	18.7	23.8	24.3	28.1
Health fields, total	48.8	68.8	76.7	37.6	51.5	57.6	4.1	5.4	8.2	23.3	24.3	24.4

[1] For 2009, includes other sciences, not shown separately.

Source: U.S. National Science Foundation, *Survey of Graduate Science Engineering Students and Postdoctorates*, annual. See also <http://www.nsf.gov/statistics/gradpostdoc>.

Table 811. Non-U.S. Citizens Awarded Doctorates in Science and Engineering by Visa Type and Country of Citizenship: 2000 to 2009

[For description of science and engineering fields, see Table 815]

Visa and country	2000	2001	2002	2003	2004	2005	2006	2007	2008	2009
All non-U.S. citizens	**7,664**	**7,953**	**7,707**	**8,393**	**9,164**	**10,427**	**11,587**	**12,371**	**12,628**	**12,217**
Canada	243	253	251	280	337	312	315	341	355	371
Mexico	190	186	175	198	164	193	169	166	160	170
Brazil	121	130	113	99	124	140	128	111	123	121
United Kingdom	64	86	86	77	73	68	77	82	84	78
France	64	62	81	68	82	98	106	120	120	112
Germany	169	181	164	154	153	145	128	126	137	165
China	2,034	2,146	2,121	2,263	2,718	3,281	4,056	4,215	4,072	3,680
Japan	166	128	141	170	166	183	187	201	196	188
Korea	695	814	807	915	1,003	1,118	1,167	1,089	1,111	1,156
Taiwan	611	492	428	407	359	401	403	432	415	511
Thailand	149	231	258	307	263	248	194	218	273	193
India	726	717	601	688	788	1,033	1,415	1,842	2,061	2,029
Iran	40	71	35	45	45	112	124	127	129	137
Turkey	248	274	320	348	319	321	321	410	466	444
Science	5,213	5,164	5,057	5,475	5,852	6,665	7,289	7,773	8,139	8,006
Engineering	2,451	2,789	2,650	2,918	3,312	3,762	4,298	4,598	4,489	4,211
Permanent visa	1,409	1,271	1,173	1,099	1,003	1,113	1,252	1,222	(NA)	(NA)
Temporary visa	7,661	7,946	7,694	8,384	9,155	10,406	11,525	12,323	(NA)	(NA)

NA Not available.

Source: U.S. National Science Foundation, *Science and Engineering Doctorate Awards*, NSF 09-311, 2009. See also <http://www.nsf.gov/statistics/nsf09311/>.

Table 812. Science and Engineering (S&E) Degrees Awarded by Degree Level and Sex of Recipient: 1990 to 2009

[For a description of science and engineering degree categories, see source, Appendix B, <http://www.nsf.gov/statistics/nsf07307/content.cfm?pub_id=3634&id=4>]

Academic year ending	Bachelor's degree				Master's degree				Doctoral degree			
	Total S&E	Men	Women	Percent women	Total S&E	Men	Women	Percent women	Total S&E	Men	Women	Percent women
1990......	329,094	189,082	140,012	42.5	77,788	51,230	26,558	34.1	22,867	16,498	6,369	27.9
2000......	399,686	197,827	201,859	50.5	94,706	53,382	41,324	43.6	25,966	16,518	9,394	36.3
2005......	469,340	233,313	236,027	50.3	120,071	66,361	53,710	44.7	27,985	17,405	10,539	37.7
2006......	477,589	237,336	240,253	50.3	119,686	65,262	54,424	45.5	29,866	18,369	11,478	38.5
2007......	484,350	240,986	243,364	50.2	118,942	64,232	54,710	46.0	31,806	19,529	12,265	38.6
2008......	494,627	246,014	248,613	50.3	124,754	67,600	57,154	45.8	32,832	19,854	12,971	39.5
2009......	502,561	249,745	252,816	50.3	132,390	71,995	60,395	45.6	33,470	19,849	13,593	40.6

Source: U.S. National Science Foundation, *Science and Engineering Degrees: 1966–2008*, NSF-11-316, 2011, and unpublished data. See also <http://www.nsf.gov/statistics/degrees/>.

Table 813. Science and Engineering (S&E) Degrees as Share of Higher Education Degrees Conferred by State: 2007

[S&E degrees include physical, computer, agricultural, biological, earth, atmospheric, ocean, and social sciences; psychology; mathematics; and engineering]

State	S&E degrees conferred [1]	All higher education degrees [1]	S&E higher education degrees (percent)	State	S&E degrees conferred [1]	All higher education degrees [1]	S&E higher education degrees (percent)	State	S&E degrees conferred [1]	All higher education degrees [1]	S&E higher education degrees (percent)
U.S.	685,914	2,138,003	32.1	KY	7,218	27,152	26.6	ND	1,731	7,042	24.6
AL	9,920	32,207	30.8	LA	7,767	28,224	27.5	OH	24,410	82,584	29.6
AK	750	2,261	33.2	ME	2,733	8,532	32.0	OK	7,442	24,244	30.7
AZ	13,463	74,778	18.0	MD	16,932	41,936	40.4	OR	8,387	23,655	35.5
AR	3,440	14,835	23.2	MA	26,363	78,421	33.6	PA	35,314	113,396	31.1
CA	89,947	204,838	43.9	MI	23,006	75,304	30.6	RI	3,875	12,724	30.5
CO	13,729	35,981	38.2	MN	12,571	45,085	27.9	SC	7,649	25,841	29.6
CT	9,052	27,781	32.6	MS	4,294	16,438	26.1	SD	2,204	6,386	34.5
DE	2,325	7,642	30.4	MO	13,515	53,828	25.1	TN	9,272	36,576	25.3
DC	8,287	20,489	40.4	MT	2,450	6,509	37.6	TX	40,387	130,830	30.9
FL	27,510	91,561	30.0	NE	4,115	15,765	26.1	UT	8,787	23,993	36.6
GA	16,566	49,495	33.5	NV	2,267	7,279	31.1	VT	2,880	7,042	40.9
HI	2,511	7,330	34.3	NH	3,725	11,207	33.2	VA	20,679	53,981	38.3
ID	2,859	9,614	29.7	NJ	16,851	46,676	36.1	WA	14,206	37,541	37.4
IL	30,055	101,537	29.6	NM	3,302	9,748	33.9	WV	3,239	13,707	23.6
IN	14,442	51,564	28.0	NY	55,360	185,736	29.8	WI	13,691	41,842	32.7
IA	7,893	25,698	30.7	NC	19,022	55,071	34.5	WY	1,149	2,154	53.3
KS	6,552	23,943	27.4								

[1] Includes bachelor's, master's, and doctorate degrees.
Source: National Science Foundation, *Science and Engineering Indicators, 2010*, January 2010. See also <http://www.nsf.gov/statistics/seind10/>.

Table 814. Doctorates Conferred by Characteristics of Recipients: 2000 and 2009

[In percent, except as indicated. Based on the Survey of Earned Doctorate Awards. For description of methodology, see source]

Characteristic	2000, total [1]	2009									
		All fields [1]	Engineering	Physical sciences [2]	Earth sciences [3]	Mathematics	Computer sciences	Biological sciences [4]	Agricultural	Social sciences [5]	Psychology
Total conferred (number)....	41,365	49,562	7,634	4,289	877	1,554	1,611	8,026	1,166	4,842	3,471
Male...............	56.0	53.2	78.7	70.1	61.5	68.9	78.2	47.8	56.7	51.5	28.6
Female...............	43.8	46.8	21.3	29.9	38.5	31.1	21.8	52.2	43.3	48.5	71.4
RACE/ETHNICITY [6]											
Total conferred (number)....	29,936	32,231	3,148	2,351	556	772	735	5,513	668	3,026	2,896
White [7].................	79.2	74.6	69.8	79.5	86.3	76.8	72.1	74.5	81.6	73.5	76.2
Black [7].................	5.8	6.9	4.3	3.1	1.4	3.2	3.8	4.4	4.8	7.3	6.3
Asian/Pacific [7]...........	7.6	8.3	16.3	8.8	3.6	10.9	17.0	11.4	4.5	7.2	5.1
Indian/Alaskan [7]...........	0.6	0.5	0.4	0.2	0.4	0.4	0.0	0.3	0.4	0.7	0.4
Hispanic.................	4.4	5.8	5.0	4.5	4.5	4.7	2.7	5.5	4.2	6.2	7.8
Other/unknown [8]...........	2.4	3.9	4.2	3.9	3.8	4.0	4.4	3.8	4.5	5.0	4.2

[1] Includes other fields, not shown separately. [2] Astronomy, physics, and chemistry. [3] Includes earth, atmospheric and ocean sciences. [4] Biochemistry, botany, microbiology, physiology, zoology, and related fields. [5] Anthropology, sociology, political science, economics, international relations, and related fields. [6] Excludes those with temporary visas. [7] Non-Hispanic. [8] Data 2001 and after includes Native Hawaiians and Other Pacific Islanders, respondents choosing multiple races (excluding those selecting an Hispanic ethnicity), and respondents with unknown race/ethnicity.
Source: U.S. National Science Foundation, *Science and Engineering Doctorate Awards*, NSF-11-306, annual. See also <http://www.nsf.gov/statistics/doctorates/>.

Table 815. Doctorates Awarded by Field of Study and Year of Doctorate: 2000 to 2009

[Based on the Survey of Earned Doctorates; for information, see source]

Field of Study	2000	2004	2005	2006	2007	2008	2009
Total, all fields	**41,366**	**42,118**	**43,381**	**45,617**	**48,130**	**48,763**	**49,562**
Science and engineering, total	**25,966**	**26,274**	**27,986**	**29,866**	**31,806**	**32,832**	**33,470**
Engineering, total	5,323	5,777	6,427	7,185	7,745	7,859	7,634
Aeronautical/astronautical	214	201	219	238	267	266	296
Chemical	619	638	774	799	807	872	808
Civil	480	547	622	655	701	712	708
Electrical	1,330	1,389	1,547	1,786	1,968	1,887	1,694
Industrial/manufacturing	176	217	221	234	281	280	252
Materials/metallurgical	404	474	493	583	648	635	622
Mechanical	807	754	892	1,044	1,072	1,081	1,095
Other	1,293	1,557	1,659	1,846	2,001	2,126	2,159
Science, total	20,643	20,497	21,559	22,681	24,061	24,973	25,836
Biological/agricultural sciences	6,890	6,987	7,404	7,682	8,320	8,885	9192
Agricultural sciences	1,037	1,045	1,038	1,033	1,133	1,087	1,166
Biological sciences	5,853	5,942	6,366	6,649	7,187	7,798	8,026
Earth, atmospheric, and ocean sciences, total	694	686	714	757	878	865	877
Atmospheric	143	126	145	146	167	188	167
Earth/ocean sciences	551	560	569	611	711	677	710
Mathematical/computer sciences, total	1,911	2,024	2,334	2,778	3,049	3,186	3,165
Computer sciences	861	948	1,129	1,453	1,656	1,787	1,611
Mathematics	1,050	1,076	1,205	1,325	1,393	1,399	1,554
Physical sciences, total	3,378	3,335	3,643	3,927	4,101	4,082	4,289
Astronomy	185	165	186	197	223	249	262
Chemistry	1,989	1,986	2,126	2,362	2,324	2,247	2,398
Physics	1,204	1,184	1,331	1,368	1,554	1,586	1,629
Psychology	3,615	3,326	3,323	3,260	3,291	3,356	3,471
Social sciences, total	4,155	4,139	4,141	4,277	4,422	4,599	4,842
Economics	1,086	1,069	1,183	1,142	1,180	1,202	1,237
Political science	986	947	990	1,001	1,037	1,020	1,140
Sociology	617	580	536	579	576	601	664
Other social sciences	1,466	1,543	1,432	1,555	1,629	1,776	1,801
Non-science and engineering, total	**15,400**	**15,844**	**15,395**	**15,751**	**16,324**	**15,931**	**16,092**
Education	6,437	6,633	6,225	6,120	6,456	6,554	6,531
Health	1,591	1,719	1,784	1,905	2,132	2,090	2,094
Humanities	5,213	5,012	4,950	5,124	4,890	4,502	4,667
Professional/other/unknown	2,159	2,480	2,436	2,602	2,846	2,785	2,800

Source: U.S. National Science Foundation, *Science and Engineering Doctorate Awards*, annual. See also <http://www.nsf.gov/statistics/doctorates/>.

Table 816. Scientists and Engineers by Selected Demographic Characteristics: 2006

[In thousands (22,630 represents 22,630,000). Scientists and engineers refer to all persons who have received a bachelor's degree or higher in science and engineering (S&E), or S&E related field, plus persons holding a non-S&E degree or higher, employed in S&E or S&E related field]

Characteristic	Both sexes	Female	Male	Characteristic	Both sexes	Female	Male
All scientists and engineers	**22,630**	**10,230**	**12,400**	Highest degree attained:			
				Bachelor's	13,228	6,223	7,005
Age:				Master's	6,411	3,039	3,373
29 or younger	2,732	1,542	1,190	Doctorate	1,018	308	710
30-39 years	5,302	2,596	2,705	Professional	1,973	660	1,312
40-49 years	5,849	2,699	3,150				
50-59 years	5,400	2,303	3,097	Citizenship status:			
60-69 years	2,497	835	1,662	U.S. citizen, native	19,131	8,743	10,387
70 or older	851	254	596	U.S. citizen, naturalized	2,373	1,062	1,311
				Non-U.S. citizen, permanent			
Race/ethnicity:				resident	835	330	505
American Indian/Alaska Native	102	51	50	Non-U.S. citizen, temporary			
Asian	2,255	994	1,261	resident	291	95	196
Black	1,258	738	520				
Native Hawaiian/Other Pacific				Marital status:			
Islander	85	33	53	Married	16,100	6,655	9,445
White	17,420	7,670	9,751	Living in marriage-like			
Multiple race	316	156	159	relationship	892	482	410
Hispanic, any race	1,193	588	605	Widowed	356	245	111
				Separated	243	131	111
Children in the home?				Divorced	1,518	887	631
Yes	10,966	5,015	5,951	Never married	3,521	1,829	1,692
No	11,664	5,215	6,449				

Source: National Science Foundation, Division of Science Resource Statistics, Scientists and Engineers Statistical Data System (SESTAT), <http://www.nsf.gov/statistics/sestat/>, accessed March 2008.

Table 817. Civilian Employment of Scientists, Engineers, and Related Occupations by Occupation and Industry: 2008

[In thousands (293.0 represents 293,000). Standard Occupational Classification system categorize workers in 1 of 801 detailed occupations. Industry classifications correspond to 2007 North American Industry Classification (NAICS) industrial groups. For definition of scientists and engineers, see text this section]

Occupation	Total employment, all workers	Wage and salary workers						Self employed [2]
		Mining (NAICS 21) [1]	Construction (NAICS 23)	Manufacturing (NAICS 31–33)	Information (NAICS 51)	Professional, scientific and technical services (NAICS 54)	Government (NAICS 99)	
Computer and information systems managers	293.0	0.4	0.7	27.5	33.6	73.5	19.0	9.6
Engineering managers	184.0	1.8	5.0	74.9	5.2	59.2	15.7	1.1
Natural science managers	44.6	0.2	(NA)	6.9	(NA)	16.2	13.8	(NA)
Computer and mathematical scientists	3,540.4	7.6	(NA)	272.7	422.3	1,121.5	247.4	155.3
Computer specialists	3,424.3	7.1	9.8	266.1	415.7	1,096.0	228.2	154.6
Mathematical science occupations	116.1	(NA)	0.2	6.6	6.5	25.5	19.2	0.8
Surveyors, cartographers, and photogrammetrists	70.0	0.8	3.8	0.1	(NA)	50.4	10.1	1.8
Engineers [3]	1,571.9	26.1	47.7	559.6	41.5	468.8	190.3	41.8
Aerospace engineers	71.6	(NA)	(NA)	38.4	(NA)	17.8	9.5	2.4
Civil engineers	278.4	0.8	31.1	2.5	0.8	141.0	75.4	12.0
Computer and hardware engineers	74.7	(NA)	(NA)	32.1	3.5	24.5	4.7	1.0
Electrical and electronics engineers	301.5	0.3	4.8	105.3	32.4	76.9	26.4	4.8
Industrial engineers [4]	240.4	2.4	6.4	155.2	2.5	33.5	6.1	1.8
Mechanical engineers	238.7	1.3	3.1	121.2	0.2	69.7	12.3	5.5
Drafters, engineering, and mapping technicians [5]	826.2	5.3	26.0	229.8	22.4	315.0	108.5	15.1
Engineering technicians	497.3	3.9	5.1	169.5	18.9	124.3	91.7	3.6
Surveying and mapping technicians	77.0	0.6	(NA)	0.1	0.8	53.0	11.7	4.3
Life, physical, and social science occupations	1,460.8	20.1	(NA)	155.6	28.6	376.0	314.5	97.8
Life scientists	279.4	(NA)	(NA)	36.5	0.2	71.9	67.9	9.9
Physical scientists	275.5	9.4	(NA)	43.3	1.2	100.8	76.3	6.3
Social scientists and related occupations	549.4	0.3	2.6	22.3	26.7	111.0	82.6	78.2
Life, physical, and social science technicians	356.5	10.3	0.6	53.4	0.5	92.4	87.7	3.4

NA Not available. [1] Includes oil and gas extraction. [2] Includes secondary jobs and unpaid private household employment. [3] Includes kinds of engineers not shown separately. [4] Includes health and safety engineers. [5] Includes other drafters, technicians, and mapping technicians.

Source: U.S. Bureau of Labor Statistics, National Employment Matrix, December 2009 (data collected biennially). See also <http://www.bls.gov/emp/empoils.htm>.

Table 818. Employment and Earnings in Science and Engineering (S&E) Occupations by Industry: 2006

[As of May 2006. Industries ordered by Science and Engineering share of total employment]

Industry	2002 NAICS code [1]	Workers employed (number)		S&E workers as percent of all employed	Mean earnings in S&E occupations (dollars)
		All occupations	S&E occupations		
Computer systems design and related services	5415	1,254,320	609,590	48.6	75,040
Software publishers	5112	240,130	116,260	48.4	79,120
Scientific research and development services	5417	586,220	247,310	42.2	81,220
Computer and peripheral equipment manufacturing	3341	199,370	79,040	39.6	90,710
Internet service providers and Web search portals	5181	119,560	46,120	38.6	69,720
Data processing, hosting, and related services	5182	264,320	83,470	31.6	70,460
Internet publishing and broadcasting	5161	33,220	9,810	29.5	69,800
Architectural, engineering, and related services	5413	1,361,280	397,910	29.2	74,570
Communications equipment manufacturing	3342	144,200	39,270	27.2	83,400
Navigational, measuring, electromedical, and control instruments manufacturing	3345	435,510	117,950	27.1	82,190
Aerospace product and parts manufacturing	3364	464,990	114,620	24.6	80,410
Securities and commodity exchanges	5232	8,850	1,930	21.8	74,000
Semiconductor and other electronic component manufacturing	3344	452,060	93,940	20.8	83,490
Pharmaceutical and medicine manufacturing	3254	288,270	55,640	19.3	73,710
Other telecommunications	5179	5,300	980	18.5	73,820

[1] North American Industry Classification System (NAICS), 2002; see text Section 15.

Source: U.S. National Science Foundation, *Science and Engineering Indicators 2008*, January 2008. See also<http://nsf.gov/statistics/seind08/>.

530 Science and Technology

Table 819. Employment, Mean Earnings, and Growth in Science and Engineering (S&E) Occupations: 2004 to 2008

[Minus sign (–) represents a decrease. Based on data derived from Bureau of Labor Statistics' Occupational Employment Survey (OES)]

Occupation	Employment					Mean earnings	
	2004, total	2008, total	Total growth	Total growth (percent)	Average annual growth rate (percent)	2008 annual earnings (dol.)	Average annual growth rate (percent)
All occupations	**128,127,360**	**135,185,230**	**7,057,870**	**5.5**	**1.3**	**42,270**	**3.4**
STEM [1]	7,160,770	7,852,710	691,940	9.7	2.3	74,950	3.6
S&E	5,085,740	5,781,460	695,720	13.7	3.3	76,680	3.5
Engineers	1,487,810	1,626,330	138,520	9.3	2.3	84,120	3.7
Mathematical and computer scientists	2,566,170	2,972,940	406,770	15.9	3.7	74,420	3.4
Life scientists	275,500	319,520	44,020	16.0	3.8	75,130	3.7
Physical scientists	273,360	301,500	28,140	10.3	2.5	76,710	3.8
Social scientists	482,900	561,160	78,260	16.2	3.8	67,980	2.9
Technicians, programmers, and S&E managers	2,075,020	2,071,260	−3,760	−0.2	(Z)	70,170	3.6
S&E related	6,914,070	7,737,490	823,420	11.9	2.9	(NA)	(NA)
Healthcare practitioners and technicians	6,769,900	7,569,040	799,140	11.8	2.8	(NA)	(NA)
Other S&E related	144,170	168,450	24,280	16.8	4.0	(NA)	(NA)
Not STEM or S&E related	114,052,530	119,595,020	5,542,490	4.9	1.2	(NA)	(NA)

NA Not available. Z Less than 0.05. [1] STEM = science, technology, engineering, and mathematics.
Source: National Science Foundation, *Employment in Science and Engineering Occupations Reached 5.8 Million in 2008*, NSF 10-315, 2010. See also <http://www.nsf.gov/statistics/infbrief/nsf10315/>.

Table 820. Research and Development (R&D) Scientists and Engineers—Employment and Cost by Industry: 2005 to 2007

[In thousands (1,104.5 represents 1,104,500). Data are estimates on full-time-equivalent (FTE) basis. Based on the Survey of Industrial Research and Development. The Business R&D and Innovation Survey replaces the Survey of Industrial Research and Development for data available as of December 2010; see <http://www.nsf.gov/statistics/srvyindustry/about/brdis/>]

Industry	NAICS [1] code	Employed scientists and engineers [2] (1,000)			Cost per scientist or engineer, constant (2000) dollars [3,4] ($1,000)		
		2005	2006	2007	2005	2006	2007
All industries [5]	**(X)**	**1,104.5**	**1,116.6**	**1,133.0**	**192.4**	**201.6**	**211.9**
Chemicals	325	118.3	123.2	134.0	328.5	330.1	356.4
Machinery	333	61.1	62.3	61.9	125.2	141.1	144.4
Electrical equipment, appliances, and components	335	18.7	16.9	15.8	(D)	(D)	(D)
Motor vehicles, trailers, and parts	3361–3363	42.0	42.0	(NA)	(D)	(D)	(D)
Aerospace products and parts	3364	39.7	39.5	40.2	335.4	359.4	380.5
Software publishing	5112	93.4	46.5	(NA)	162.5	174.0	175.4
Architectural, engineering, and related services	5413	35.8	41.2	48.5	129.3	146.4	113.9
Computer systems design and related services	5415	82.4	93.1	88.1	158.5	157.2	160.3
Scientific R&D services	5417	43.7	44.3	50.4	264.0	298.2	308.7
NOTE: Constant 2000 dollar deflator	(X)	(X)	(X)	(X)	1.1303	1.1668	1.1982

D Withheld to avoid disclosure. NA Not available. X Not applicable. [1] North American Industry Classification System 2002 (NAICS); see text, Section 15. [2] The mean number of full-time equivalent (R&D) scientists and engineers employed in January of the year shown and the following January. [3] Based on gross domestic product implicit price deflator. [4] Represents the arithmetic mean of the numbers of R&D scientists and engineers reported in each industry for January in 2 consecutive years divided into total R&D expenditures in each industry. [5] Includes other industries not shown separately.
Source: National Science Foundation, *Research and Development in Industry*, NSF 10-319, 2010, and unpublished data. See also <http://www.nsf.gov/statistics/industry/>.

Table 821. Federal Outlays for General Science, Space, and Other Technology, 1970 to 2010, and Projections, 2011 and 2012

[In billions of dollars (4.5 represents $4,500,000,000). For fiscal years ending in year shown; see text, Section 8]

Year	Current dollars			Constant (2005) dollars		
	Total	General science/basic research	Space and other technologies	Total	General science/basic research	Space and other technologies
1970..........	4.5	0.9	3.6	22.7	4.8	17.9
1980..........	5.8	1.4	4.5	13.5	3.2	10.3
1985..........	8.6	2.0	6.6	14.7	3.4	11.3
1990..........	14.4	2.8	11.6	21.1	4.1	17.0
1995 [1]........	16.7	4.1	12.6	20.9	5.1	15.8
2000..........	18.6	6.2	12.4	21.2	7.0	14.2
2001..........	19.8	6.5	13.2	22.0	7.3	14.7
2002..........	20.7	7.3	13.5	22.7	7.9	14.7
2003..........	20.8	8.0	12.9	22.2	8.5	13.7
2004..........	23.0	8.4	14.6	23.9	8.7	15.2
2005..........	23.6	8.8	14.8	23.6	8.8	14.8
2006..........	23.6	9.1	14.5	22.8	8.8	14.0
2007..........	25.5	10.3	15.3	24.0	9.6	14.3
2008..........	27.7	10.5	17.2	25.1	9.5	15.6
2009..........	29.4	11.1	18.4	26.6	10.0	16.6
2010..........	31.0	12.7	18.4	27.5	11.2	16.3
2011, proj........	33.4	14.7	17.1	29.2	12.9	14.9
2012, proj........	32.3	14.9	17.4	27.8	12.8	15.0

[1] Due to the effects of the Credit Reform Act of 1990 on the measurement and classification of federal credit activities, the discretionary outlays for years prior to 1995 are not strictly comparable to those for 1995 and after. However, the discretionary outlays shown for 1995 are no more than $1 billion higher than they would have been if measured on the same (pre-credit reform) basis as the 1990 outlays.

Source: U.S. Office of Management and Budget, *Budget of the United States Government: Historical Tables, Fiscal Year 2012*, annual. See also <http://www.gpoaccess.gov/usbudget/fy12/hist.html>.

Table 822. Worldwide Space Launch Events: 2000 to 2010

[In millions of dollars (2,729 represents $2,729,000,000)]

Country	Non-commercial launches				Commercial launches				Launch revenues for commercial launch events (mil. dol.)			
	2000	2005	2009	2010	2000	2005	2009	2010	2000	2005	2009	2010
Total..........	50	37	54	51	35	18	24	23	2,729	1,190	2,410	2,453
United States.......	21	11	20	11	7	1	4	4	370	70	298	307
Russia............	23	18	19	18	13	8	10	13	671	350	742	826
Europe............	–	–	2	0	12	5	5	6	1,433	490	1,020	1,320
China [1]............	5	5	5	15	–	–	1	–	(X)	(X)	70	(X)
India.............	–	1	2	3	–	–	–	–	(X)	(X)	(X)	(X)
Japan.............	1	2	3	2	–	–	–	–	(X)	(X)	(X)	(X)
Israel.............	–	–	–	1	–	–	–	–	(X)	(X)	(X)	(X)
Ukraine	–	–	–	–	–	–	–	–	(X)	(X)	(X)	(X)
Iran	–	–	1	–	–	–	–	–	(X)	(X)	(X)	(X)
Brazil.............	–	–	–	–	–	–	–	–	(X)	(X)	(X)	(X)
Korea, North	–	–	1	–	–	–	–	–	(X)	(X)	(X)	(X)
Korea, South	–	–	1	1	–	–	–	–	(X)	(X)	(X)	(X)
Multinational	–	–	–	–	3	4	4	–	255	280	280	(X)

– Represents zero. X Not applicable. [1] See footnote 4, Table 1332.

Source: Federal Aviation Administration, *Commercial Space Transportation: 2010 Year in Review*, January 2011, and prior years. See also <http://www.faa.gov/about/office_org/headquarters_offices/ast/reports_studies/year_review>.

U.S. Census Bureau, Statistical Abstract of the United States: 2012

This section presents statistics on farms and farm operators; land use; farm income, expenditures, and debt; farm output, productivity, and marketings; foreign trade in agricultural products; specific crops; and livestock, poultry, and their products.

The principal sources are the reports issued by the National Agricultural Statistics Service (NASS) and the Economic Research Service (ERS) of the U.S. Department of Agriculture (USDA). The information from the 2007 Census of Agriculture is available in printed form in the Volume 1, Geographic Area Series; in electronic format on CD-ROM; and on the Internet at <http://www.agcensus.usda.gov/Publications/2007/Full_Report/index.asp>. The Department of Agriculture publishes annually *Agricultural Statistics*, a general reference book on agricultural production, supplies, consumption, facilities, costs, and returns. The ERS publishes data on farm assets, debt, and income on the Internet at <http://www.ers.usda.gov/briefing/farmincome/>. Sources of current data on agricultural exports and imports include *Outlook for U.S. Agricultural Trade,* published by the ERS; the ERS Internet site at <http://www.ers.usda.gov/briefing/AgTrade/>; and the foreign trade section of the U.S. Census Bureau Web site at <http://www.census.gov/foreign-trade/statistics/index.html>.

The field offices of the NASS collect data on crops, livestock and products, agricultural prices, farm employment, and other related subjects mainly through sample surveys. Information is obtained on crops and livestock items as well as scores of items pertaining to agricultural production and marketing. State estimates and supporting information are sent to the Agricultural Statistics Board of NASS, which reviews the estimates and issues reports containing state and national data. Among these reports are annual summaries such as *Crop Production,* *Crop Values, Agricultural Prices, and Livestock Production, Disposition and Income.*

Farms and farmland—The definitions of a farm have varied through time. Since 1850, when minimum criteria defining a farm for census purposes first were established, the farm definition has changed nine times. The current definition, first used for the 1974 census, is any place from which $1,000 or more of agricultural products were produced and sold, or normally would have been sold, during the census year.

Acreage designated as "land in farms" consists primarily of agricultural land used for crops, pasture, or grazing. It also includes woodland and wasteland not actually under cultivation or used for pasture or grazing, provided it was part of the farm operator's total operation. Land in farms includes acres set aside under annual commodity acreage programs as well as acres in the Conservation Reserve and Wetlands Reserve Programs for places meeting the farm definition. Land in farms is an operating unit concept and includes land owned and operated as well as land rented from others. All grazing land, except land used under government permits on a per-head basis, was included as "land in farms" provided it was part of a farm or ranch.

An evaluation of coverage has been conducted for each census of agriculture since 1945 to provide estimates of the completeness of census farm counts. Beginning with the 1997 Census of Agriculture, census farm counts and totals were statistically adjusted for coverage and reported at the county level. The size of the adjustments varies considerably by state. In general, farms not on the census mail list tended to be small in acreage, production, and sales of farm products. The response rate for the 2007 Census of Agriculture was 85.2 percent as compared with a response rate of 88.0 for the 2002 Census of Agriculture and 86.2 percent for the 1997 Census of Agriculture.

For more explanation about census mail list compilation, collection methods, coverage measurement, and adjustments, see Appendix A, 2007 Census of Agriculture, Volume 1 reports <http://www.agcensus.usda.gov/>.

Farm income—The final agricultural sector output comprises cash receipts from farm marketings of crops and livestock, federal government payments made directly to farmers for farm-related activities, rental value of farm homes, value of farm products consumed in farm homes, and other farm-related income such as machine hire and custom work. Farm marketings represent quantities of agricultural products sold by farmers multiplied by prices received per unit of production at the local market. Information on prices received for farm products is generally obtained by the NASS Agricultural Statistics Board from surveys of firms (such as grain elevators, packers, and processors) purchasing agricultural commodities directly from producers. In some cases, the price information is obtained directly from the producers.

Crops—Estimates of crop acreage and production by the NASS are based on current sample survey data obtained from individual producers and objective yield counts, reports of carlot shipments, market records, personal field observations by field statisticians, and reports from other sources. Prices received by farmers are marketing year averages. These averages are based on U.S. monthly prices weighted by monthly marketings during specific periods. U.S. monthly prices are state average prices weighted by marketings during the month. Marketing year average prices do not include allowances for outstanding loans, government purchases, deficiency payments or disaster payments.

All state prices are based on individual state marketing years, while U.S. marketing year averages are based on standard marketing years for each crop. For a listing of the crop marketing years and the participating states in the monthly program, see *Crop Values*. Value of production is computed by multiplying state prices by each state's production. The U.S. value of production is the sum of state values for all states. Value of production figures shown in Tables 852–856 and 858 should not be confused with cash receipts from farm marketings which relate to sales during a calendar year, irrespective of the year of production.

Livestock—Annual inventory numbers of livestock and estimates of livestock, dairy, and poultry production prepared by the Department of Agriculture are based on information from farmers and ranchers obtained by probability survey sampling methods.

Statistical reliability—For a discussion of statistical collection and estimation, sampling procedures, and measures of statistical reliability pertaining to Department of Agriculture data, see Appendix III.

Table 823. Selected Characteristics of Farms by North American Industry Classification System (NAICS): 2007

[297,220,491 represents 297,220,491,000. See text this section and Appendix III]

Industry	2007 NAICS code [1]	Farms	Land in farms (acres)	Harvested cropland (acres)	Market value of agricultural products sold (1,000) Total	Crops	Livestock [2]
Total.......................	(X)	**2,204,792**	**922,095,840**	**309,607,601**	**297,220,491**	**143,657,928**	**153,562,563**
Crop production...................	111	1,051,889	416,961,540	244,213,836	141,921,405	135,806,093	6,115,312
Oilseed and grain farming	1111	338,237	266,831,616	194,191,397	74,559,692	69,851,934	4,707,758
Soybean farming.................	11111	62,923	22,094,100	17,599,156	5,637,504	5,532,934	104,570
Oilseed (except soybean) farming....	11112	515	458,591	306,003	62,238	61,081	1,157
Dry pea and bean farming..........	11113	526	382,071	269,759	79,297	78,454	844
Wheat farming...................	11114	35,232	55,992,672	29,062,744	6,157,944	5,821,678	336,267
Corn farming....................	11115	161,874	103,071,231	86,627,715	39,675,674	38,524,804	1,150,870
Rice farming....................	11116	3,853	4,233,156	3,396,230	1,936,574	1,915,447	21,127
Other grain farming	11119	73,314	80,599,795	56,929,760	21,010,459	17,917,536	3,092,923
Vegetable and melon farming........	11121	40,589	9,272,945	6,018,702	14,975,322	14,850,087	125,235
Potato farming..................	111211	2,182	2,577,795	1,992,430	2,885,906	2,854,320	31,586
Other vegetable (except potato) and melon farming	111219	38,407	6,695,150	4,026,272	12,089,416	11,995,767	93,649
Fruit and tree nut farming	1113	98,281	12,141,683	5,339,755	18,351,629	18,225,583	126,046
Orange groves..................	11131	8,771	1,535,483	800,921	2,423,976	2,382,844	41,131
Citrus (except orange) groves.......	11132	3,429	402,617	205,522	783,426	778,099	5,326
Noncitrus fruit and tree nut farming...	11133	86,081	10,203,583	4,333,312	15,144,228	15,064,639	79,589
Apple orchards..................	111331	11,550	2,078,125	488,273	2,259,839	2,251,555	8,284
Grape vineyards.................	111332	17,036	2,067,987	1,061,070	3,890,152	3,883,341	6,811
Strawberry farming..............	111333	1,503	149,972	55,461	1,185,736	1,182,263	3,473
Berry (except strawberry) farming ...	111334	8,535	870,154	220,530	1,211,820	1,209,450	2,370
Tree nut farming	111335	22,821	3,239,199	1,652,915	3,655,251	3,626,067	29,184
Fruit and tree nut combination farming.......................	111336	995	292,842	106,488	301,611	286,946	14,666
Other noncitrus fruit farming........	111339	23,641	1,505,304	748,575	2,639,819	2,625,018	14,801
Greenhouse,nursery, and floriculture production	1114	54,889	3,974,530	1,698,564	16,967,123	16,930,975	36,147
Food crops grown under cover	11141	2,044	85,809	18,712	1,552,287	1,550,756	1,531
Nursery and floriculture production ...	11142	52,845	3,888,721	1,679,852	15,414,835	15,380,219	34,616
Nursery and tree production........	111421	34,532	3,287,008	1,505,323	8,901,860	8,875,417	26,443
Floriculture production	111422	18,313	601,713	174,529	6,512,975	6,504,801	8,173
Other crop farming	1119	519,893	124,740,766	36,965,418	17,067,639	15,947,514	1,120,126
Tobacco farming	11191	9,626	2,518,697	1,219,827	1,147,173	1,077,481	69,692
Cotton farming..................	11192	9,968	13,081,671	9,778,279	4,357,082	4,300,124	56,958
Sugarcane farming	11193	614	1,299,318	969,321	885,028	881,698	3,330
Hay farming....................	11194	254,042	49,923,443	18,606,436	6,488,172	5,807,594	680,578
All other crop farming	11199	245,643	57,917,637	6,391,555	4,190,184	3,880,617	309,568
Animal production	112	1,152,903	505,134,300	65,393,765	155,299,086	7,851,835	147,447,251
Cattle ranching and farming	1121	744,858	413,261,549	55,185,767	92,538,429	5,109,567	87,428,862
Beef cattle ranching and farming including feedlots................	11211	687,540	391,990,769	41,893,929	57,784,399	3,895,789	53,888,610
Beef cattle ranching and farming	112111	656,475	376,170,540	36,675,357	27,535,096	2,626,582	24,908,514
Cattle feedlots..................	112112	31,065	15,820,229	5,218,572	30,249,303	1,269,207	28,980,096
Dairy cattle and milk production	11212	57,318	21,270,780	13,291,838	34,754,031	1,213,778	33,540,252
Hog and pig farming	1122	30,546	6,949,176	4,747,504	18,127,114	1,614,030	16,513,083
Poultry and egg production..........	1123	64,570	7,040,000	2,140,320	37,797,542	547,736	37,249,806
Chicken egg production............	11231	35,651	2,259,774	477,371	7,546,997	104,546	7,442,452
Broilers and other meat-type chicken production	11232	17,888	3,370,828	1,209,528	22,400,358	306,268	22,094,090
Turkey production	11233	3,405	836,551	396,096	4,643,075	127,009	4,516,067
Poultry hatcheries	11234	775	69,558	9,985	2,777,612	1,790	2,775,822
Other poultry production	11239	6,851	503,289	47,340	429,499	8,124	421,375
Sheep and goat farming...........	1124	67,254	11,963,667	429,300	554,107	21,374	532,732
Sheep farming..................	11241	30,974	8,971,952	324,835	435,107	18,396	416,711
Goat farming	11242	36,280	2,991,715	104,465	119,000	2,979	116,021
Animal aquaculture...............	1125	4,777	2,451,244	70,954	1,407,750	18,384	1,389,366
Other animal production	1129	240,898	63,468,664	2,819,920	4,874,144	540,743	4,333,401
Apiculture......................	11291	7,979	503,609	92,280	263,268	19,827	243,440
Horse and other equine production...	11292	168,694	22,370,495	675,383	2,088,845	17,332	2,071,512
Fur-bearing animal and rabbit production	11293	2,252	89,224	16,894	154,325	2,744	151,581
All other animal production	11299	61,973	40,505,336	2,035,363	2,367,706	500,839	1,866,867

X Not applicable [1] North American Industry Classification System (NAICS) 2007; see text, Section 15. [2] Includes poultry, and their products sold.

Source: U.S. Department of Agriculture, National Agricultural Statistics Service, *2007 Census of Agriculture*, Vol. 1, February 2009. See also <http://www.agcensus.usda.gov/Publications/2007/Full_Report/index.asp>.

Table 824. Farms—Number and Acreage: 1990 to 2010

[As of June 1 (2,146 represents 2,146,000). Based on 1974 census definition; for definition of farms and farmland, see text, this section. Activities included as agriculture have undergone changes in recent years. Data for period 2000 to 2010 are not directly comparable with data for 1990. See source for more detail. Data for 2007 have been adjusted for underenumeration]

Year	Unit	1990	2000	2004	2005	2006	2007	2008	2009	2010
Number of farms	1,000	2,146	2,167	2,113	2,099	2,089	2,205	2,200	2,200	2,201
Land in farms	Mil. acres	987	945	932	928	926	921	920	920	920
Average per farm	Acres	460	436	441	442	443	418	418	418	418

Source: U.S. Department of Agriculture, National Agricultural Statistics Service, *Farms and Land in Farms, Final Estimates, 1988–1992; Farms and Land in Farms, Final Estimates, 1993–1997; Farm Numbers and Land in Farms, Final Estimates, 1998–2002; Farms and Land in Farms, Final Estimates, 2003-2007;* and *Farms, Land in Farms, and Livestock Operations 2010 Summary, February 2011.* See also <http://www.nass.usda.gov/Publications/index.asp>.

Table 825. Farms—Number and Acreage by State: 2000 to 2010

[As of June 1 (2,167 represents 2,167,000). See headnote, Table 824]

State	Farms (1,000) 2000	Farms (1,000) 2010	Land in farms (mil. acres) 2000	Land in farms (mil. acres) 2010	Acreage per farm 2000	Acreage per farm 2010	State	Farms (1,000) 2000	Farms (1,000) 2010	Land in farms (mil. acres) 2000	Land in farms (mil. acres) 2010	Acreage per farm 2000	Acreage per farm 2010
United States . . .	**2,167**	**2,201**	**945**	**920**	**436**	**418**							
Alabama	47	49	9	9	191	186	Montana	28	29	59	61	2,133	2,068
Alaska	1	1	1	1	1,569	1,294	Nebraska	52	47	46	46	887	966
Arizona	11	16	27	26	2,514	1,684	Nevada	3	3	6	6	2,065	1,903
Arkansas	48	49	15	14	304	278	New Hampshire . . .	3	4	(Z)	(Z)	133	113
California	83	82	28	25	337	311	New Jersey	10	10	1	1	86	71
Colorado	30	36	32	31	1,053	864	New Mexico	18	21	45	43	2,494	2,057
Connecticut	4	5	(Z)	(Z)	86	82	New York	38	36	8	7	205	193
Delaware	3	2	1	(Z)	215	198	North Carolina	56	52	9	9	166	164
Florida	44	48	10	9	236	195	North Dakota	31	32	39	40	1,279	1,241
Georgia	49	47	11	10	222	217	Ohio	79	75	15	14	187	183
Hawaii	6	8	1	1	251	148	Oklahoma	85	87	34	35	400	407
Idaho	25	26	12	11	486	444	Oregon	40	39	17	16	433	423
Illinois	77	76	28	27	357	351	Pennsylvania	59	63	8	8	130	123
Indiana	63	62	15	15	240	239	Rhode Island	1	1	(Z)	(Z)	75	57
Iowa	94	92	33	31	346	333	South Carolina	24	27	5	5	203	181
Kansas	65	66	48	46	736	705	South Dakota	32	32	44	44	1,358	1,374
Kentucky	90	86	14	14	152	163	Tennessee	88	78	12	11	134	139
Louisiana	29	30	8	8	277	268	Texas	228	248	131	130	573	527
Maine	7	8	1	1	190	167	Utah	16	17	12	11	748	669
Maryland	12	13	2	2	172	160	Vermont	7	7	1	1	192	174
Massachusetts	6	8	1	1	89	68	Virginia	49	47	9	8	180	170
Michigan	53	55	10	10	192	182	Washington	37	40	16	15	420	375
Minnesota	81	81	28	27	344	332	West Virginia	21	23	4	4	173	159
Mississippi	42	42	11	11	266	263	Wisconsin	78	78	16	15	206	195
Missouri	109	108	30	29	277	269	Wyoming	9	11	35	30	3,750	2,745

Z Less than 500,000 acres.

Source: U.S. Department of Agriculture, National Agricultural Statistics Service, *Farm Numbers and Land in Farms, Final Estimates, 1998–2002* and *Farms, Land in Farms, and Livestock Operations 2010 Summary, February 2011.* See also <http://www.nass.usda.gov/Publications/index.asp>.

Table 826. Farms by Size and Type of Organization: 1978 to 2007

[2,258 represents 2,258,000. For comments on adjustment, see text, this section]

Size and type of organization	Unit	Not adjusted for coverage 1978	Not adjusted for coverage 1982	Not adjusted for coverage 1987	Not adjusted for coverage 1992	Not adjusted for coverage 1997	Adjusted for coverage 1997[1]	Adjusted for coverage 2002[1]	Adjusted for coverage 2007[1]
Farms	1,000	2,258	2,241	2,088	1,925	1,912	2,216	2,129	2,205
Land in farms	Mil. acres	1,015	987	964	946	932	955	938	922
Average size of farm	Acres	449	440	462	491	487	431	441	418
Farms by size:									
1 to 9 acres	1,000	151	188	183	166	154	205	179	233
10 to 49 acres	1,000	392	449	412	388	411	531	564	620
50 to 179 acres	1,000	759	712	645	584	593	694	659	661
180 to 499 acres	1,000	582	527	478	428	403	428	389	368
500 to 999 acres	1,000	213	204	200	186	176	179	162	150
1,000 to 1,999 acres	1,000	98	97	102	102	101	103	99	93
2,000 acres or more	1,000	63	65	67	71	75	74	78	80
Farms by type of organization:									
Family or individual	1,000	1,966	1,946	1,809	1,653	1,643	1,923	1,910	1,906
Partnership	1,000	233	223	200	187	169	186	130	174
Corporation	1,000	50	60	67	73	84	90	74	96
Other [2]	1,000	9	12	12	12	15	17	16	28

[1] Data have been adjusted for coverage; see text, this section. [2] Cooperative, estate or trust, institutional, etc.

Source: U.S. Department of Agriculture, National Agricultural Statistics Service, *2007 Census of Agriculture,* Vol. 1. See also <http://www.agcensus.usda.gov/Publications/2007/Full_Report/index.asp>.

Table 827. Farms—Number and Acreage by Size of Farm: 2002 and 2007

[2,129 represents 2,129,000. Data have been adjusted for coverage; see text, this section]

Size of farm	Number of farms (1,000)		Land in farms (mil. acres)		Cropland harvested (mil. acres)		Percent distribution, 2007		
	2002	2007	2002	2007	2002	2007	Number of farms	All land in farms	Cropland harvested
Total...............	2,129	2,205	938.3	922.1	302.7	309.6	100.0	100.0	100.0
Under 10 acres	179	233	0.8	1.1	0.2	0.3	10.6	0.1	0.1
10 to 49 acres	564	620	14.7	15.9	4.1	4.3	28.1	1.7	1.4
50 to 69 acres	152	154	8.8	8.9	2.5	2.5	7.0	1.0	0.8
70 to 99 acres	191	192	15.7	15.8	4.7	4.5	8.7	1.7	1.5
100 to 139 acres	175	175	20.2	20.3	6.1	5.8	7.9	2.2	1.9
140 to 179 acres	142	139	22.3	22.0	7.3	6.6	6.3	2.4	2.1
180 to 219 acres	91	88	18.0	17.3	6.2	5.6	4.0	1.9	1.8
220 to 259 acres	72	68	17.1	16.3	6.5	5.7	3.1	1.8	1.9
260 to 499 acres	226	213	80.6	75.9	34.1	30.4	9.6	8.2	9.8
500 to 999 acres	162	150	112.4	104.1	56.7	51.6	6.8	11.3	16.7
1,000 to 1,999 acres	99	93	135.7	127.6	72.8	69.8	4.2	13.8	22.6
2,000 acres or more	78	80	491.9	496.9	101.6	122.5	3.6	53.9	39.6

Source: U.S. Department of Agriculture, National Agricultural Statistics Service, *2007 Census of Agriculture*, Vol. 1. See also <http://www.agcensus.usda.gov/Publications/2007/Full_Report/index.asp>.

Table 828. Farms—Number, Acreage, and Value by Tenure of Principal Operator and Type of Organization: 2002 and 2007

[2,129 represents 2,129,000. Full owners own all the land they operate. Part owners own a part and rent from others the rest of the land they operate. A principal operator is the person primarily responsible for the on-site, day-to-day operation of the farm or ranch business. Data have been adjusted for coverage; see text, this section]

Item and year	Unit	Total [1]	Tenure of operator			Type of organization		
			Full owner	Part owner	Tenant	Family or individual	Partner-ship	Corpora-tion
NUMBER OF FARMS								
2002..........................	1,000	2,129	1,428	551	150	1,910	130	74
2007..........................	1,000	2,205	1,522	542	141	1,906	174	96
Under 50 acres	1,000	853	739	70	44	774	45	26
50 to 179 acres	1,000	661	492	130	38	588	45	18
180 to 499 acres	1,000	368	198	143	27	312	34	16
500 to 999 acres	1,000	150	51	84	14	118	18	12
1,000 acres or more	1,000	173	41	114	17	114	32	24
LAND IN FARMS								
2002..........................	Mil. acres	938	357	495	87	622	146	108
2007..........................	Mil. acres	922	344	496	82	574	161	125
Value of land and buildings, 2007 [2]	Bil. dol	1,744	726	868	150	1,203	277	227
Value of farm products sold, 2007......	Bil. dol	297	117	148	32	148	62	84

[1] Includes other types, not shown separately. [2] Based on a sample of farms.

Source: U.S. Department of Agriculture, National Agricultural Statistics Service, *2007 Census of Agriculture*, Vol. 1. See also <http://www.agcensus.usda.gov/Publications/2007/Full_Report/index.asp>

Table 829. Corporate Farms—Characteristics by Type: 2007

[125.3 represents 125,300,000. Data have been adjusted for coverage; see text, this section and Appendix III]

Item	Unit	All corpora-tions	Family held corporations			Other corporations		
			Total	1 to 10 stock-holders	11 or more stock-holders	Total	1 to 10 stock-holders	11 or more stock-holders
Farms	Number	96,074	85,837	83,796	2,041	10,237	9,330	907
Percent distribution	Percent	100	89	87	2	11	10	1
Land in farms............	Mil. acres	125.3	114.3	106.4	7.8	11.1	7.7	3.3
Average per farm.........	Acres	1,304	1,331	1,270	3,834	1,080	829	3,657
Value of—								
Land and buildings [1]	Bil. dol	226.6	200.6	189.5	11.0	26.0	20.2	5.8
Average per farm.........	$1,000	2,358	2,336	2,262	5,399	2,542	2,170	6,371
Farm products sold	Bil. dol	84.1	65.8	58.9	6.9	18.3	12.2	6.2
Average per farm.........	$1,000	876	766	703	3,378	1,791	1,305	6,787

[1] Based on a sample of farms.

Source: U.S. Department of Agriculture, National Agricultural Statistics Service, *2007 Census of Agriculture*, Vol. 1. See also <http://www.agcensus.usda.gov/Publications/2007/Full_Report/index.asp>.

Agriculture 537

Table 830. Family Farm Household Income and Wealth, 2005 to 2009, and by Gross Sales, 2009

[In dollars, except for number of farms. Based on Agricultural Resource Management Survey (ARMS) Phase III. A family farm is defined as one in which the majority of the ownership of the farm business is held by related individuals. Nearly all farms (97 percent in 2009) are family farms. The farm operator is the person who runs the farm, making the day-to-day management decisions. The operator could be an owner, hired manager, cash tenant, share tenant, and/or a partner. If land is rented or worked on shares, the tenant or renter is the operator. For multiple-operator farms, a principal operator is identified as the individual making most of the day-to-day decisions about the operation. About 40 percent of farms have more than one operator, but three-quarters of these are operated by a husband-wife team. Therefore, both operators are considered part of the principal operator household. Minus sign (–) indicates loss]

Item	2005	2006	2007	2008	2009 Total	2009 Gross sales Less than $10,000 [1]	2009 Gross sales $10,000 to $249,000 [1]	2009 Gross sales $250,000 or more [2]
Number of family farms	2,034,048	2,021,903	2,143,398	2,129,869	2,131,007	1,281,788	639,270	209,949
INCOME PER FAMILY FARM HOUSEHOLD								
Net earnings from farming activities	14,227	8,541	11,364	9,764	6,866	–8,661	2,615	114,609
Off-farm income of the household . .	67,091	72,502	77,432	70,032	70,302	75,493	66,562	49,999
Earned income	46,034	51,674	58,933	50,761	50,852	56,386	44,729	35,713
Off-farm wages and salaries. . . .	34,876	38,481	48,947	42,606	43,852	50,119	37,007	26,439
Off-farm business income.	11,158	13,193	9,986	8,155	7,000	6,267	7,722	9,275
Unearned income.	35,283	20,827	18,499	19,271	19,450	19,107	21,833	14,286
Total household income, mean [3] . . .	81,317	81,043	88,796	79,796	77,169	66,832	69,177	164,609
WEALTH PER FAMILY FARM HOUSEHOLD								
Assets, mean [3].	915,210	1,026,389	1,006,020	988,156	1,031,000	(NA)	(NA)	(NA)
Farm assets.	677,118	764,485	739,905	749,190	761,894	(NA)	(NA)	(NA)
Non-farm assets	238,092	261,905	266,115	238,966	269,106	(NA)	(NA)	(NA)
Debt, mean [3]	99,345	99,766	106,874	112,705	115,981	(NA)	(NA)	(NA)
Farm debt	54,855	59,731	56,859	61,131	66,149	(NA)	(NA)	(NA)
Non-farm debt	44,491	40,035	50,015	51,574	49,832	(NA)	(NA)	(NA)
Net worth, mean [3]	815,864	926,623	899,146	875,451	915,019	(NA)	(NA)	(NA)
Farm net worth	622,264	704,754	683,046	688,059	695,745	(NA)	(NA)	(NA)
Non-farm net worth	193,601	221,869	216,101	187,392	219,274	(NA)	(NA)	(NA)

NA Not available. [1] Small family farms. Includes rural-residence family farms and intermediate family farms. [2] Large scale family farm. Includes commercial farms. [3] For definition of mean see Guide to Tabular Presentation.

Source: U.S. Department of Agriculture, Economic Research Service, *Agricultural Income and Finance Situation and Outlook*, December 2010. See also <http://usda.mannlib.cornell.edu/MannUsda/viewDocumentInfo.do?documentID=1254>.

Table 831. Farm Type, Acreage, and Production: 2000 to 2009

[(2,166 represents 2,166,000). Based on Agricultural Resource Management Survey (ARMS) Phase III]

Type of farm	Unit	2000	2002	2003	2004	2005	2006	2007	2008	2009
Total farms										
Number of farms	1,000	2,166	2,152	2,121	2,108	2,095	2,083	2,197	2,192	2,192
Total value of production . . .	Mil dol. . . .	177,286	182,461	186,644	225,698	215,295	226,045	289,530	299,066	278,051
Total acres operated	Mil.	995	955	912	990	916	893	878	894	913
Acres operated per farm . . .	Acres	459	444	430	470	437	429	400	408	417
Commercial farms [1]										
Number of farms	1,000	178	188	188	205	216	219	257	272	271
Total value of production . . .	Mil dol.	121,202	126,242	134,627	170,130	166,566	178,104	241,728	249,759	230,717
Total acres operated	Mil.	392	347	341	429	418	382	424	429	443
Acres operated per farm . . .	Acres	2,205	1,843	1,815	2,096	1,939	1,747	1,650	1,580	1,635
Intermediate farms [2]										
Number of farms	1,000	668	649	607	624	550	566	546	583	577
Total value of production . . .	Mil dol.	41,813	41,981	37,894	38,438	33,872	32,533	30,933	32,718	30,830
Total acres operated	Mil.	392	384	349	342	307	318	237	253	270
Acres operated per farm . . .	Acres	587	591	576	547	558	561	434	434	469
Rural residence farms [3]										
Number of farms	1,000	1,320	1,315	1,326	1,279	1,329	1,298	1,394	1,338	1,344
Total value of production . . .	Mil dol.	14,272	14,238	14,124	17,130	14,856	15,408	16,869	16,589	16,521
Total acres operated	Mil.	211	224	221	219	191	193	217	212	200
Acres operated per farm . . .	Acres	160	170	167	172	144	149	156	158	149

[1] Includes farms with sales of $250,000 or more. [2] Small familly farms whose operators report farming as their major occupation. [3] Includes retirement and residential farms.

Source: U.S. Department of Agriculture, Economic Research Service, ARMS Phase III—"Structural Characteristics Report," <http://www.ers.usda.gov/Data/ARMS/beta.htm>.

Table 832. Organic Agriculture—Number of Farms, Acreage, and Value of Sales: 2007

[2,577 represents 2,577,000. Data have been adjusted for coverage; see text, this section and Appendix III]

Size and usage	Number of farms	Acreage (1,000)	Sales value of organically produced commodities and commodity	Number of farms	Value (mil. dol.)
Total acres used for organic production....	20,437	2,577	Organic product sales, total...........	18,211	1,709
1 to 9 organic acres.................	9,251	29	$1 to $4,999........................	8,285	13
10 to 49 organic acres................	4,994	115	$5,000 to $9,999....................	1,935	13
50 to 179 organic acres..............	3,498	348	$10,000 to $24,999..................	2,318	37
180 to 499 organic acres.............	1,808	528	$25,000 to $49,999..................	1,515	54
500 organic acres or more............	886	1,557	$50,000 or more....................	4,158	1,593
Acres from which organic crops harvested..	16,778	1,288	Crops [1]............................	14,968	1,122
Acres of organic pastureland............	7,268	975	Livestock and poultry................	2,496	110
Acres being converted to organic production.........................	11,901	616	Livestock and poultry products.........	3,191	477

[1] Includes nursery and greenhouse crops.

Source: U.S. Department of Agriculture, National Agricultural Statistics Service, *2007 Census of Agriculture*, Vol. 1. See also <http://www.agcensus.usda.gov/Publications/2007/Full_Report/index.asp>.

Table 833. Certified Organic Farmland, Crops, and Livestock: 2000 to 2008

[1,776 represents 1,776,000. Economic Research Service collaborates with over 50 state and private certifiers to calculate U.S. and state-level estimates of certified organic acreage and livestock]

Item	Unit	2000	2001	2002	2003	2004	2005	2006	2007	2008
Farm operations [1].........	Number......	6,592	6,949	7,323	8,035	8,021	8,493	9,469	11,352	12,941
Average farm size.........	acres........	269	301	263	273	380	477	310	378	372
Total farmland............	1,000 acres...	1,776	2,094	1,926	2,197	3,045	4,054	2,936	4,290	4,816
Total cropland............	1,000 acres...	557	790	626	745	1,593	2,331	1,051	2,005	2,161
Total pasture/rangeland.....	1,000 acres...	1,219	1,305	1,300	1,452	1,452	1,723	1,885	2,285	2,655
Grains..................	1,000 acres...	416	455	496	548	491	608	624	789	908
Corn...................	1,000 acres...	78	94	96	106	99	131	138	172	195
Wheat..................	1,000 acres...	181	195	218	234	214	277	225	330	416
Oats...................	1,000 acres...	30	33	53	46	43	46	65	59	57
Beans..................	1,000 acres...	166	211	145	153	144	156	157	150	164
Soybeans...............	1,000 acres...	136	174	127	122	114	122	115	100	126
Oilseeds................	1,000 acres...	55	44	33	28	54	46	45	42	69
Hay and silage...........	1,000 acres...	231	254	268	328	357	411	508	677	793
Vegetables..............	1,000 acres...	62	72	70	79	80	99	107	132	169
Fruits..................	1,000 acres...	43	56	61	78	81	97	96	97	121
Herbs, nursery, and greenhouse.............	1,000 acres...	41	15	29	25	8	9	18	18	15
Other cropland...........	1,000 acres...	204	197	198	214	239	298	330	380	415
Livestock [2].............	1,000.......	56	72	108	124	157	197	257	363	476
Milk cows..............	1,000.......	38	49	67	74	75	87	130	166	250
Poultry [3]...............	1,000.......	3,159	5,014	6,270	8,780	7,305	13,757	9,195	12,185	15,518
Layer hens.............	1,000.......	1,114	1,612	1,052	1,591	1,788	2,415	3,072	3,872	5,538
Broilers (meat chicken)....	1,000.......	1,925	3,286	3,032	6,301	4,769	10,406	5,530	7,436	9,016

[1] Number does not include subcontracted organic farm operations. [2] Total livestock includes other and unclassified livestock animals. [3] Total poultry includes other and unclassified poultry animals.

Source: U.S. Department of Agriculture, Economic Research Service, "Briefing Rooms, Organic Agriculture," <http://www.ers.usda.gov/Briefing/Organic/>.

Table 834. Adoption of Genetically Engineered Crops: 2000 to 2010

[In percent. As of June. Based on June Agricultural Survey conducted by National Agricultural Statistical Services (NASS). Excludes conventionally bred herbicide resistant varieties. Insect resistant varieties include only those containing bacillus thuringiensis (Bt). The Bt varieties include those that contain more than one gene that can resist different types of insects. Stacked gene varieties include only those varieties containing biotech traits for both herbicide and insect resistance]

Genetically engineered crop	2000	2001	2002	2003	2004	2005	2006	2007	2008	2009	2010
Corn.........................	25	26	34	40	47	52	61	73	80	85	86
Insect resistant................	18	18	22	25	27	26	25	21	17	17	16
Herbicide resistant.............	6	7	9	11	14	17	21	24	23	22	23
Stacked gene.................	1	1	2	4	6	9	15	28	40	46	47
Cotton.......................	61	69	71	73	76	79	83	87	86	88	93
Insect resistant................	15	13	13	14	16	18	18	17	18	17	15
Herbicide resistant.............	26	32	36	32	30	27	26	28	23	23	20
Stacked gene.................	20	24	22	27	30	34	39	42	45	48	58
Soybean.....................	54	68	75	81	85	87	89	91	92	91	93
Insect resistant................	(X)	(X)	(X)	(X)	(X)	(X)	(X)	(X)	(X)	(X)	(X)
Herbicide resistant.............	54	68	75	81	85	87	89	91	92	91	93
Stacked gene.................	(X)	(X)	(X)	(X)	(X)	(X)	(X)	(X)	(X)	(X)	(X)

X Not applicable.

Source: U.S. Department of Agriculture, Economic Research Service, "Adoption of Genetically Engineered Crops in the U.S.," July 2010, <http://www.ers.usda.gov/Data/BiotechCrops/>.

Agriculture **539**

Table 835. Farms—Number, Acreage, and Value of Sales by Size of Sales: 2002 and 2007

[2,129 represents 2,129,000. Data have been adjusted for coverage; see text, this section and Appendix III]

Market value of agricultural products sold	Farms (1,000)	Acreage		Value of sales		Percent distribution		
		Total (mil.)	Average per farm	Total (mil. dol.)	Average per farm (dol.)	Farms	Acreage	Value of sales
2002								
Total...............	**2,129**	**938.3**	**441**	**200,646**	**94,244**	**100.0**	**100.0**	**100.0**
Less than $2,500.........	827	107.0	129	485	586	38.8	11.4	0.2
$2,500 to $4,999.........	213	23.1	108	763	3,582	10.0	2.5	0.4
$5,000 to $9,999.........	223	34.8	156	1,577	7,072	10.5	3.7	0.8
$10,000 to $24,999......	256	69.5	271	4,068	15,891	12.0	7.4	2.0
$25,000 to $49,999......	158	77.9	494	5,594	35,405	7.4	8.3	2.8
$50,000 to $99,999......	140	110.1	784	10,024	71,600	6.6	11.7	5.0
$100,000 to $249,999....	159	189.4	1,191	25,401	159,755	7.5	20.2	12.7
$250,000 to $499,999....	82	140.8	1,723	28,530	347,927	3.9	15.0	14.2
$500,000 to $999,999....	42	94.0	2,241	28,944	689,143	2.0	10.0	14.4
$1,000,000 or more.......	29	91.7	3,198	95,259	3,284,793	1.4	9.8	47.5
2007								
Total...............	**2,205**	**922.1**	**418**	**297,220**	**134,807**	**100.0**	**100.0**	**100.0**
Less than $2,500.........	900	121.5	135	435	483	40.8	13.2	0.1
$2,500 to $4,999.........	200	17.5	87	718	3,585	9.1	1.9	0.2
$5,000 to $9,999.........	219	27.6	126	1,553	7,104	9.9	3.0	0.5
$10,000 to $24,999......	248	65.8	265	3,960	15,949	11.3	7.1	1.3
$25,000 to $49,999......	155	59.8	386	5,480	35,419	7.0	6.5	1.8
$50,000 to $99,999......	125	78.2	623	8,961	71,429	5.7	8.5	3.0
$100,000 to $249,999....	148	147.6	1,000	24,213	164,156	6.7	16.0	8.1
$250,000 to $499,999....	93	140.7	1,507	33,410	357,811	4.2	15.3	11.2
$500,000 to $999,999....	61	119.4	1,965	42,691	702,417	2.8	13.0	14.4
$1,000,000 or more.......	56	144.0	2,593	175,800	3,167,050	2.5	15.6	59.1

Source: U.S. Department of Agriculture, National Agricultural Statistics Service, *2007 Census of Agriculture*, Vol. 1. See also <http://www.agcensus.usda.gov/Publications/2007/Full_Report/index.asp>.

Table 836. Farms—Number, Value of Sales, and Government Payments by Economic Class of Farm: 2002 and 2007

[2,129 represents 2,129,000. Economic class of farm is a combination of market value of agricultural products sold and federal farm program payments. Data have been adjusted for coverage; see text, this section and Appendix III]

Economic class	Number of farms (1,000)			Market value of agricultural products sold and government payments (mil. dol.)			
	2002, total	2007		2002, total	2007		
		Total	Receiving government payments		Total	Agricultural products sold	Government payments
Total....................	**2,129**	**2,205**	**838**	**207,192**	**305,204**	**297,220**	**7,984**
Less than $1,000.............	431	500	42	72	96	77	19
$1,000 to $2,499.............	307	271	85	508	448	332	116
$2,500 to $4,999.............	243	246	80	870	884	685	199
$5,000 to $9,999.............	247	255	87	1,746	1,811	1,488	323
$10,000 to $24,999..........	272	274	110	4,320	4,364	3,810	554
$25,000 to $49,999..........	164	164	87	5,804	5,795	5,286	508
$50,000 to $99,999..........	143	129	83	10,202	9,219	8,644	575
$100,000 to $249,999........	163	149	110	26,119	24,401	23,256	1,145
$250,000 to $499,999........	86	96	75	30,084	34,367	32,980	1,387
$500,000 to $999,999........	44	64	46	30,598	44,578	43,156	1,422
$1,000,000 to $2,499,999.....	21	42	27	31,701	62,751	61,508	1,243
$2,500,000 to $4,999,999.....	5	10	6	16,056	33,190	32,839	352
$5 million or more...........	3	6	2	49,112	83,300	83,159	141

Source: U.S. Department of Agriculture, National Agricultural Statistics Service, *2007 Census of Agriculture*, Vol. 1. See also <http://www.agcensus.usda.gov/Publications/2007/Full_Report/index.asp>.

Table 837. Farm Production Expenses: 2002 and 2007

[2,129 represents 2,129,000. Data have been adjusted for coverage; see text, this section and Appendix III]

Production expenses	2002			2007		
	Farms (1,000)	Expenses (mil. dol.)	Percent of total	Farms (1,000)	Expenses (mil. dol.)	Percent of total
Total	**2,129**	**173,199**	**100.0**	**2,205**	**241,114**	**100.0**
Fertilizer........................	1,190	9,751	5.6	1,148	18,107	7.5
Chemicals.......................	947	7,609	4.4	919	10,075	4.2
Seeds, plants, vines, and trees	875	7,599	4.4	776	11,741	4.9
Livestock and poultry [1].............	554	27,421	15.8	491	38,004	15.8
Feed	1,241	31,695	18.3	1,136	49,095	20.4
Gasoline and fuel.................	2,024	6,675	3.9	2,149	12,912	5.4
Utilities.........................	1,241	4,874	2.8	1,103	5,918	2.5
Supplies, repairs, and maintenance	1,899	13,387	7.7	1,992	15,897	6.6
Farm labor [2]....................	783	22,020	12.7	665	26,392	11.0
Customwork and custom hauling......	450	3,314	1.9	362	4,091	1.7
Cash rent for land, buildings and grazing fees.............	498	9,046	5.2	490	13,275	5.5
Rent and lease for machinery, equipment, and farm share...	151	1,468	0.8	109	1,385	0.6
Interest expense	758	9,572	5.5	667	10,881	4.5
Property taxes	1,963	5,351	3.1	1,996	6,223	2.6
Other production expenses...........	1,254	13,418	7.7	1,116	17,119	7.1

[1] Purchased or leased. 2002 does not include breeding livestock leased. [2] Includes hired and contract labor.

Source: U.S. Department of Agriculture, National Agricultural Statistics Service, *2007 Census of Agriculture*, Vol. 1. See also <http://www.agcensus.usda.gov/Publications/2007/Full_Report/index.asp>.

Table 838. Farms—Number, Acreage, and Value by State: 2002 and 2007

[2,129 represents 2,129,000. Data have been adjusted for coverage; see text, this section and Appendix III]

State	Number of farms (1,000) 2002	Number of farms (1,000) 2007	Land in farms (mil. acres) 2002	Land in farms (mil. acres) 2007	Average size of farm (acres) 2002	Average size of farm (acres) 2007	Total value of land and buildings [1] (bil. dol.) 2002	Total value of land and buildings [1] (bil. dol.) 2007	Market value of agricultural products sold and government payments, 2007 (mil. dol.)	Total number of operators, 2007 (1,000)
U.S.	2,129	2,205	938.3	922.1	441	418	1,144.9	1,744.3	305,204	3,337
AL	45	49	8.9	9.0	197	185	15.1	20.7	4,540	71
AK	1	1	0.9	0.9	1,479	1,285	0.3	0.3	59	1
AZ	7	16	26.6	26.1	3,645	1,670	10.6	19.5	3,290	26
AR	47	49	14.5	13.9	305	281	21.2	32.5	7,778	75
CA	80	81	27.6	25.4	346	313	96.1	162.5	34,125	131
CO	31	37	31.1	31.6	991	853	23.8	33.1	6,217	61
CT	4	5	0.4	0.4	85	83	3.5	5.1	556	8
DE	2	3	0.5	0.5	226	200	2.3	5.3	1,092	4
FL	44	47	10.4	9.2	236	195	29.3	52.1	7,831	73
GA	49	48	10.7	10.2	218	212	22.6	31.6	7,337	69
HI	5	8	1.3	1.1	241	149	4.6	8.6	516	11
ID	25	25	11.8	11.5	470	454	15.3	22.7	5,788	40
IL	73	77	27.3	26.8	374	348	66.7	101.5	13,816	111
IN	60	61	15.1	14.8	250	242	38.4	52.9	8,532	92
IA	91	93	31.7	30.7	350	331	64.2	104.2	21,124	136
KS	64	66	47.2	46.3	733	707	32.6	42.2	14,840	97
KY	87	85	13.8	14.0	160	164	25.5	37.5	4,928	124
LA	27	30	7.8	8.1	286	269	12.2	16.7	2,787	44
ME	7	8	1.4	1.3	190	166	2.3	3.0	626	13
MD	12	13	2.1	2.1	170	160	8.5	14.4	1,868	20
MA	6	8	0.5	0.5	85	67	4.6	6.4	494	12
MI	53	56	10.1	10.0	190	179	27.1	34.2	5,872	85
MN	81	81	27.5	26.9	340	332	41.8	69.2	13,626	120
MS	42	42	11.1	11.5	263	273	15.6	21.4	5,108	61
MO	107	108	29.9	29.0	280	269	45.3	63.2	7,832	164
MT	28	30	59.6	61.4	2,139	2,079	23.3	47.6	3,025	47
NE	49	48	45.9	45.5	930	953	35.7	52.7	15,893	72
NV	3	3	6.3	5.9	2,118	1,873	2.8	3.6	517	5
NH	3	4	0.4	0.5	132	113	1.4	2.3	202	7
NJ	10	10	0.8	0.7	81	71	7.4	11.3	994	16
NM	15	21	44.8	43.2	2,954	2,066	10.6	14.6	2,218	32
NY	37	36	7.7	7.2	206	197	12.9	16.3	4,481	58
NC	54	53	9.1	8.5	168	160	28.0	34.7	10,461	77
ND	31	32	39.3	39.7	1,283	1,241	15.8	30.6	6,444	45
OH	78	76	14.6	14.0	187	184	39.6	49.2	7,302	114
OK	83	87	33.7	35.1	404	405	23.8	40.6	6,016	131
OR	40	39	17.1	16.4	427	425	20.4	31.0	4,463	65
PA	58	63	7.7	7.8	133	124	26.3	37.3	5,885	95
RI	1	1	0.1	0.1	71	56	0.6	1.1	67	2
SC	25	26	4.8	4.9	197	189	10.1	14.0	2,420	37
SD	32	31	43.8	43.7	1,380	1,401	19.6	39.1	6,841	47
TN	88	79	11.7	11.0	133	138	28.5	37.1	2,713	117
TX	229	247	129.9	130.4	567	527	100.5	165.6	21,722	373
UT	15	17	11.7	11.1	768	664	9.0	13.9	1,438	26
VT	7	7	1.2	1.2	189	177	2.5	3.6	680	11
VA	48	47	8.6	8.1	181	171	23.3	34.1	2,961	71
WA	36	39	15.3	15.0	426	381	22.4	29.8	6,931	64
WV	21	24	3.6	3.7	172	157	4.8	8.8	595	35
WI	77	78	15.7	15.2	204	194	35.8	49.0	9,163	123
WY	9	11	34.4	30.2	3,651	2,726	10.2	15.5	1,186	19

[1] Based on reports for a sample of farms.

Source: U.S. Department of Agriculture, National Agricultural Statistics Service, *2007 Census of Agriculture*, Vol. 1. See also <http://www.agcensus.usda.gov/Publications/2007/Full_Report/index.asp>.

Table 839. Balance Sheet of the Farming Sector: 1990 to 2009

[In billions of dollars, except as indicated (841 represents $841,000,000,000). As of December 31]

Item	1990	2000	2001	2002	2003	2004	2005	2006	2007	2008	2009
Assets	841	1,203	1,256	1,260	1,383	1,588	1,779	1,924	2,055	2,023	2,057
Real estate	619	946	996	999	1,112	1,305	1,487	1,626	1,751	1,703	1,727
Livestock and poultry [1]	71	77	79	76	79	79	81	81	81	81	80
Machinery, motor vehicles [2]	86	90	93	96	100	108	113	114	115	123	126
Crops [3]	23	28	25	23	24	24	24	23	23	28	33
Purchased inputs	3	5	4	6	6	6	6	6	7	7	7
Financial assets	38	57	59	60	62	66	67	74	79	82	84
Debt [4]	131	164	171	177	164	182	196	204	214	243	245
Real estate debt	68	85	89	95	83	96	105	108	113	134	135
Farm Credit System	23	30	33	38	33	37	41	43	47	57	58
Farm Service Agency	7	3	3	3	2	2	2	2	2	2	2
Commercial banks	15	30	31	33	29	35	38	40	42	50	50
Life insurance companies	9	11	11	11	10	11	11	12	13	15	14
Individuals and others	14	11	10	10	9	11	12	10	9	10	9
Nonreal estate debt	63	79	82	82	81	86	92	96	101	109	111
Farm Credit System	10	17	20	20	20	22	24	28	32	37	40
Farm Service Agency	10	4	4	4	4	3	3	3	3	3	3
Commercial banks	31	45	45	44	44	46	48	51	54	57	57
Individuals and others	12	13	13	13	14	15	16	14	13	12	11
Equity	709	1,039	1,085	1,082	1,219	1,406	1,583	1,720	1,841	1,781	1,812
FINANCIAL RATIOS (percent)											
Farm debt/equity ratio	18.5	15.8	15.7	16.4	13.5	12.9	12.4	11.8	11.6	13.6	13.5
Farm debt/asset ratio	15.6	13.6	13.6	14.1	11.9	11.5	11.0	10.6	10.4	12.0	11.9

[1] Excludes horses, mules, and broilers. [2] Includes only farm share value for trucks and autos. [3] All non-CCC crops held on farms plus the value above loan rate for crops held under Commodity Credit Corporation (CCC). [4] Includes CCC storage and drying facility loans but excludes debt on operator dwellings and for nonfarm purposes.

Source: U.S. Department of Agriculture, Economic Research Service, "Farm Balance Sheet," <http://www.ers.usda.gov/Data/FarmBalanceSheet/>.

Table 840. Farm Sector Output and Value Added: 1990 to 2009

[In billions of dollars (179.9 represents $179,900,000,000). For definition of value added, see text, Section 13. Minus sign (−) indicates decrease]

Item	1990	2000	2001	2002	2003	2004	2005	2006	2007	2008	2009
CURRENT DOLLARS											
Farm output	**179.9**	**204.3**	**212.3**	**201.9**	**229.8**	**262.0**	**251.5**	**252.7**	**302.8**	**337.8**	**299.0**
Cash receipts from farm marketings	171.9	197.6	201.9	195.8	218.5	240.4	240.0	242.5	290.4	320.6	282.2
Farm products consumed on farms	0.6	0.3	0.3	0.3	0.3	0.3	0.3	0.4	0.4	0.4	0.4
Other farm income	4.9	8.4	9.6	9.6	10.7	12.3	11.3	13.1	12.5	14.6	12.7
Change in farm finished goods inventories	2.4	−2.0	0.6	−3.7	0.3	9.0	−0.2	−3.3	−0.5	2.1	3.8
Less: Intermediate goods and services consumed	102.6	130.7	136.1	129.6	137.4	143.7	149.5	159.6	187.9	206.7	195.1
Equals: **Gross farm value added**	77.3	73.6	76.2	72.3	92.4	118.3	102.0	93.1	114.9	131.1	104.0
Less: Consumption of fixed capital	17.9	23.3	23.9	24.7	25.8	27.4	29.5	31.3	32.9	35.0	35.9
Equals: Net farm value added	59.3	50.4	52.3	47.7	66.7	90.9	72.5	61.8	82.0	96.2	68.0
Compensation of employees	13.4	19.7	20.9	20.8	20.5	22.3	22.6	23.1	26.0	26.6	27.6
Taxes on production and imports	3.8	4.7	4.7	4.8	5.1	5.2	5.2	5.7	6.6	6.6	6.1
Less: Subsidies to operators	7.6	20.0	20.0	10.8	14.2	11.1	20.9	13.5	10.2	10.3	10.7
Net operating surplus	49.8	45.9	46.7	32.8	55.2	74.4	65.6	46.4	59.5	73.3	45.1
CHAINED (2000) DOLLARS [1]											
Farm output, total	**(NA)**	**240.6**	**237.2**	**236.2**	**246.1**	**250.2**	**251.5**	**251.9**	**255.4**	**255.0**	**260.7**
Cash receipts from farm marketings	(NA)	234.8	227.0	231.2	235.5	230.1	240.0	242.1	244.8	243.0	247.3
Farm products consumed on farms	(NA)	0.4	0.3	0.4	0.3	0.3	0.3	0.4	0.3	0.4	0.5
Other farm income	(NA)	9.3	10.3	9.9	10.6	11.7	11.3	12.3	10.1	9.8	9.3
Change in farm finished goods inventories	(NA)	−2.5	0.8	−4.5	0.4	8.1	−0.2	−3.4	−0.6	1.4	3.4
Less: Intermediate goods and services consumed	(NA)	159.2	162.1	157.2	156.0	152.7	149.5	152.6	164.7	152.3	152.6
Equals: **Gross farm value added**	**(NA)**	**83.5**	**77.7**	**81.2**	**91.6**	**97.9**	**102.0**	**99.1**	**90.3**	**102.3**	**108.5**
Less: Consumption of fixed capital	(NA)	26.0	26.3	26.9	27.7	28.5	29.5	30.3	31.0	31.8	32.3
Equals: Net farm value added	(NA)	57.8	51.6	54.5	64.1	69.4	72.5	68.7	59.2	69.7	75.5

NA Not available. [1] See text, Section 13.

Source: U.S. Bureau of Economic Analysis, *Survey of Current Business*, April 2011. See also <http://www.bea.gov/National/Index.htm>.

Table 841. Value Added to Economy by Agricultural Sector: 1990 to 2009

[In billions of dollars (188.5 represents $188,500,000,000). Data are consistent with the net farm income accounts and include income and expenses related to the farm operator dwellings. Value of agricultural sector production is the gross value of the commodities and services produced within a year. Net value-added is the sector's contribution to the National economy and is the sum of the income from production earned by all factors-of-production. Net farm income is the farm operators' share of income from the sector's production activities. The concept presented is consistent with that employed by the Organization for Economic Cooperation and Development. Minus sign (–) indicates decrease]

Item	1990	2000	2001	2002	2003	2004	2005	2006	2007	2008	2009
Value of agricultural production	**188.5**	**220.4**	**229.3**	**220.2**	**243.5**	**282.7**	**276.7**	**275.4**	**327.6**	**367.3**	**331.0**
Value of crop production	83.2	94.8	95.0	98.3	108.6	124.4	115.2	118.9	151.1	185.1	169.1
Food grains	7.5	6.5	6.4	6.8	8.0	8.9	8.6	9.1	13.6	18.7	14.4
Feed crops	18.7	20.5	21.5	24.0	24.7	27.4	24.7	29.4	42.3	58.9	50.2
Cotton	5.5	2.9	3.6	3.4	6.4	4.8	6.3	5.6	6.5	5.2	3.5
Oil crops	12.3	13.5	13.3	15.0	18.0	17.9	18.5	18.5	24.6	28.7	31.9
Fruits and tree nuts	9.4	12.4	11.9	12.6	13.4	15.5	17.4	17.3	18.7	19.3	19.0
Vegetables	11.3	15.5	15.4	17.1	16.9	16.2	17.0	18.0	19.3	21.0	20.6
All other crops	12.9	18.7	19.3	20.2	21.0	21.4	22.3	24.5	25.2	25.0	24.1
Home consumption	0.1	0.2	0.2	0.2	0.1	0.1	0.1	0.1	0.1	0.1	0.1
Value of inventory adjustment [1]	2.8	2.2	1.5	–2.9	–1.6	10.7	–0.8	–3.6	0.9	8.2	5.3
Value of livestock production	90.0	99.1	106.4	93.5	104.9	124.4	126.5	119.4	138.4	140.3	119.2
Meat animals	51.1	53.0	53.3	48.1	56.2	62.4	64.8	63.7	65.1	65.0	58.6
Dairy products	20.2	20.6	24.7	20.6	21.2	27.4	26.7	23.4	35.5	34.8	24.3
Poultry and eggs	15.3	21.9	24.6	21.1	24.0	29.5	28.7	26.7	33.1	36.8	32.5
Miscellaneous livestock	2.5	4.2	4.1	4.1	4.2	4.3	4.6	4.8	4.9	4.8	4.3
Home consumption	0.5	0.1	0.1	0.1	0.1	0.2	0.3	0.3	0.3	0.3	0.3
Value of inventory adjustment [1]	0.4	–0.6	–0.4	–0.6	–0.8	0.6	1.3	0.5	–0.4	–1.6	–0.8
Services and forestry	15.3	26.5	28.0	28.5	30.0	33.9	35.0	37.2	38.1	42.0	42.7
Machine hire and custom work	1.8	2.2	2.1	2.2	3.0	3.4	2.8	2.6	2.7	3.0	4.0
Forest products sold	1.8	2.8	2.6	2.5	2.2	2.4	2.5	0.7	0.7	0.7	0.7
Other farm income	4.5	8.7	10.1	10.2	10.5	11.3	10.9	13.2	14.2	17.7	17.3
Gross imputed rental value of farm dwellings	7.2	12.7	13.1	13.6	14.3	16.8	18.8	20.6	20.6	20.5	20.7
Less: Purchased inputs	92.2	121.8	125.7	123.3	130.3	137.4	144.0	153.7	184.3	203.0	190.0
Farm origin	39.5	47.9	48.2	48.3	53.7	57.5	56.9	61.1	73.4	79.8	77.0
Feed purchased	20.4	24.5	24.8	24.9	27.5	29.7	28.0	31.4	41.9	46.9	45.0
Livestock and poultry purchased	14.6	15.9	15.2	14.4	16.7	18.1	18.5	18.6	18.8	17.7	16.5
Seed purchased	4.5	7.5	8.2	8.9	9.4	9.6	10.4	11.0	12.6	15.1	15.5
Manufactured inputs	22.0	28.7	29.4	28.5	28.8	31.6	35.4	37.5	46.3	55.0	49.0
Fertilizers and lime	8.2	10.0	10.3	9.6	10.0	11.4	12.8	13.3	17.7	22.5	20.1
Pesticides	5.4	8.5	8.6	8.3	8.4	8.6	8.8	9.0	10.5	11.7	11.5
Petroleum fuel and oils	5.8	7.2	6.9	6.6	6.8	8.2	10.3	11.3	13.8	16.2	12.7
Electricity	2.6	3.0	3.6	3.9	3.5	3.4	3.5	3.8	4.3	4.5	4.6
Other purchased inputs	30.7	45.2	48.1	46.6	47.9	48.3	51.6	55.2	64.6	68.1	64.0
Repair and maintenance of capital items	8.6	10.9	11.2	10.5	11.0	11.9	11.9	12.5	14.3	14.8	14.7
Machine hire and custom work	3.0	4.1	4.0	4.0	3.5	3.6	3.5	3.5	3.8	4.1	3.9
Marketing, storage, and transportation expenses	4.2	7.5	7.8	7.6	7.1	7.2	8.8	9.1	10.3	10.1	10.3
Contract labor	1.6	2.7	3.1	2.7	3.3	3.1	3.1	3.0	4.4	4.7	3.9
Miscellaneous expenses	13.4	19.9	21.9	21.7	22.9	22.4	24.4	27.1	31.7	34.4	31.3
Plus: Net government transactions [2]	3.1	15.8	15.0	5.2	9.2	5.4	15.8	6.2	0.9	0.9	1.2
Direct Government payments [3]	9.3	23.2	22.4	12.4	16.5	13.0	24.4	15.8	11.9	12.2	12.3
Motor vehicle registration and licensing fees	0.4	0.5	0.5	0.4	0.5	0.5	0.6	0.6	0.6	0.6	0.6
Property taxes	5.8	6.9	6.9	6.8	6.8	7.0	8.0	9.0	10.3	10.7	10.4
Equals: Gross value added	**99.3**	**114.4**	**118.7**	**102.1**	**122.4**	**150.7**	**148.6**	**127.9**	**144.3**	**165.3**	**142.2**
Less: Capital consumption	18.1	20.1	20.6	20.9	21.4	23.1	24.9	26.2	27.0	28.7	30.1
Equals: Net value added	**81.2**	**94.3**	**98.2**	**81.1**	**100.9**	**127.6**	**123.6**	**101.7**	**117.2**	**136.6**	**112.1**
Less: Employee compensation	12.4	17.9	18.8	19.1	18.7	20.2	20.5	21.2	24.2	25.0	24.9
Less: Net rent received by nonoperator landlords	9.0	11.2	11.2	9.6	10.1	10.0	10.6	7.6	7.6	9.6	9.8
Less: Real estate and nonreal estate interest	13.5	14.6	13.3	12.8	11.6	11.6	13.2	14.4	15.1	15.4	15.2
Equals: Net farm income	**46.3**	**50.6**	**54.9**	**39.6**	**60.5**	**85.8**	**79.3**	**58.5**	**70.3**	**86.6**	**62.2**

[1] A positive value of inventory change represents current-year production not sold by December 31. A negative value is an offset to production from prior years included in current-year sales. [2] Direct government payments minus motor vehicle registration and licensing fees and property taxes. [3] Government payments reflect payments made directly to all recipients in the farm sector, including landlords. The nonoperator landlords share is offset by its inclusion in rental expenses paid to these landlords and thus is not reflected in net farm income or net cash income.

Source: U.S. Department of Agriculture, Economic Research Service, "Farm Income: Data Files—Value Added to the U.S. Economy by the Agricultural Sector via the Production of Goods and Services, 2000–2009," <http://www.ers.usda.gov/Data/FarmIncome/FinfidmuXls.htm>.

Table 842. Cash Receipts for Selected Commodities—Leading States: 2009

[In millions of dollars (43,777 represents $43,777,000,000). See headnote Table 843]

State	Value	State	Value	State	Value	State	Value
Cattle and calves	**43,777**	**Corn**	**42,035**	**Soybeans**	**30,056**	**Dairy products**	**24,342**
Texas	6,939	Iowa	7,772	Iowa	4,435	California	4,537
Nebraska	6,240	Illinois	7,534	Illinois	4,233	Wisconsin	3,271
Kansas	5,547	Nebraska	4,855	Minnesota	2,641	New York	1,685
Colorado	2,606	Minnesota	3,795	Indiana	2,516	Pennsylvania	1,510
Iowa	2,470	Indiana	3,288	Nebraska	2,256	Idaho	1,431

Source: U.S. Department of Agriculture, Economic Research Service, "Farm Income: Data Files—Cash Receipts by Commodity Groups 2000–2009," <http://www.ers.usda.gov/Data/FarmIncome/FinfidmuXls.htm>.

Agriculture 543

Table 843. Farm Income—Cash Receipts From Farm Marketings: 2000 to 2009

[In millions of dollars (192,098 represents $192,098,000,000). Represents gross receipts from commercial market sales as well as net Commodity Credit Corporation loans. The source estimates and publishes individual cash receipt values only for major commodities and major producing states. The U.S. receipts for individual commodities, computed as the sum of the reported states, may understate the value of sales for some commodities, with the balance included in the appropriate category labeled "other" or "miscellaneous." The degree of underestimation in some of the minor commodities can be substantial]

Commodities	2000	2005	2008	2009	Commodities	2000	2005	2008	2009
Total................	192,098	240,898	318,330	283,406	Broccoli	622	539	721	742
Livestock and products	99,597	124,931	141,526	119,752	Carrots..............	390	592	636	589
Meat animals..........	53,012	64,813	65,011	58,599	Corn, sweet	709	800	1,089	1,175
Cattle and calves......	40,783	49,283	48,518	43,777	Lettuce..............	1,996	1,855	1,961	2,189
Hogs	11,758	14,970	16,050	14,395	Head	1,341	1,012	1,063	1,155
Sheep and lambs......	470	560	443	427	Onions	713	810	777	807
Dairy products..........	20,587	26,705	34,849	24,342	Peppers, green, fresh ..	531	535	637	556
Poultry/eggs...........	21,854	28,834	36,832	32,463	Tomatoes.............	1,845	2,225	2,407	2,542
Broilers	13,989	20,878	23,203	21,813	Fresh	1,195	1,604	1,424	1,323
Chicken eggs.........	4,289	4,067	8,216	6,156	Misc. vegetables	2,153	2,994	3,700	3,234
Turkeys	2,771	3,026	4,477	3,573	Watermelons	240	429	500	461
Miscellaneous livestock...	4,144	4,579	4,833	4,347	Fruits/nuts	12,284	17,138	19,247	18,965
Horses/mules..........	1,218	1,104	1,158	861	Grapefruit...........	377	417	358	241
Aquaculture [1]..........	798	1,063	1,145	1,097	Lemons	267	345	511	394
Catfish.............	501	458	410	373	Oranges.............	1,775	1,901	1,978	1,993
Other livestock.........	1,970	2,219	2,262	2,152	Apples	1,466	1,712	2,664	1,986
Crops..................	92,501	115,967	176,804	163,655	Cherries	327	548	654	569
Food grains	6,525	8,611	18,708	14,384	Grapes.............	3,100	3,491	3,344	3,689
Rice	837	1,589	3,214	3,041	Wine...............	1,909	2,317	2,009	2,447
Wheat	5,672	7,005	15,456	11,315	Raisins.............	487	595	668	568
Feed crops.............	20,546	24,590	58,926	50,176	Peaches.............	470	511	546	594
Corn.................	15,162	18,486	48,596	42,035	Pears...............	288	296	388	374
Hay	3,855	4,697	7,508	5,727	Strawberries	1,045	1,399	1,919	2,124
Cotton	2,950	6,403	5,228	3,489	Blueberries	223	382	592	542
Tobacco	2,316	1,097	1,451	1,485	Raspberries	79	256	365	363
Oil crops	13,478	18,388	28,689	31,912	Almonds............	666	2,526	2,343	2,294
Peanuts	897	843	1,194	835	Pistachios	245	580	570	593
Soybeans.............	12,047	16,918	29,449	30,056	All other crops	18,645	22,449	23,538	22,650
Vegetables.............	15,758	17,291	21,017	20,593	Sugar beets	1,113	1,193	1,290	1,411
Beans, dry............	436	488	932	794	Cane for sugar........	881	815	859	864
Potatoes..............	2,369	2,655	3,651	3,396	Greenhouse/nursery ...	13,710	16,992	16,486	15,915
Beans, snap..........	393	414	486	416	Mushrooms	860	899	965	961

[1] See also Table 898.

Source: U.S. Department of Agriculture, Economic Research Service, "Farm Income: Data Files—Cash Receipts by Commodity Groups 2000–2009," <http://www.ers.usda.gov/Data/FarmIncome/FinfidmuXls.htm>.

Table 844. Value of Agricultural Production, Income, and Government Payments: 2008 and 2009

[In millions of dollars (364,879 represents $364,879,000,000). Farm income data are after inventory adjustment and include income and expenses related to the farm operator's dwelling. Minus sign (–) indicates decrease]

State	Value of agricultural production		Net farm income		Government payments, 2009	State	Value of agricultural production		Net farm income		Government payments, 2009
	2008	2009	2008	2009			2008	2009	2008	2009	
U.S.	367,324	330,931	86,598	62,187	12,263						
AL	5,490	4,967	1,283	1,019	169	MT	3,590	3,299	526	248	256
AK	38	40	5	8	6	NE	18,670	17,233	4,057	3,276	419
AZ	4,048	3,529	683	203	112	NV	679	654	161	105	11
AR	9,636	8,010	2,808	1,524	482	NH	265	231	39	19	9
CA	41,075	37,794	9,767	8,782	568	NJ	1,311	1,224	344	295	17
CO	7,080	6,640	1,179	745	192	NM	3,372	2,982	803	432	82
CT	712	649	156	116	13	NY	5,202	4,138	1,221	553	149
DE	1,212	1,173	188	193	16	NC	11,072	10,442	2,795	2,739	486
FL	8,382	7,599	1,467	1,281	80	ND	8,813	7,282	2,755	1,936	442
GA	9,033	8,136	2,974	2,359	392	OH	8,734	8,887	1,883	2,122	288
HI.......	677	650	165	133	13	OK	6,901	5,910	975	130	229
ID.......	6,863	5,898	1,806	927	140	OR	5,181	4,859	960	563	102
IL	18,268	16,285	5,503	3,641	567	PA	6,869	5,980	1,327	905	161
IN	11,100	10,539	3,203	2,540	305	RI......	88	80	16	14	6
IA	26,211	24,350	6,757	5,013	767	SC	2,839	2,559	629	531	161
KS	15,444	13,872	3,426	2,369	475	SD	9,194	8,232	2,999	2,376	256
KY	5,858	5,569	1,459	1,332	355	TN	4,032	3,899	535	613	265
LA	3,227	2,868	715	689	247	TX	22,690	20,356	3,565	2,124	1,407
ME......	749	682	166	139	20	UT	1,789	1,512	252	–52	44
MD......	2,325	2,101	365	299	53	VT	751	590	162	97	45
MA.....	714	639	156	108	16	VA	3,806	3,518	456	352	120
MI.......	7,582	6,597	1,958	1,071	180	WA	8,831	7,529	1,694	962	189
MN......	18,291	15,374	5,714	3,020	528	WV	721	655	5	–35	18
MS......	5,814	5,062	1,352	1,220	481	WI	10,826	9,275	2,044	849	406
MO.....	9,993	9,368	3,050	2,336	479	WY	1,273	1,215	92	–32	34

Source: U.S. Department of Agriculture, Economic Research Service, "Farm Income: Data Files, U.S. and State Income and Production Expenses by Category, 1949–2009," <http://www.ers.usda.gov/Data/farmincome/FinfidmuXls.htm>.

Table 845. Farm Marketings, 2008 and 2009, and Principal Commodities, 2009, by State

[In millions of dollars (324,187 represents $324,187,000,000). Cattle include calves; sheep include lambs; and greenhouse includes nursery]

State	2008 Total	2008 Crops	2008 Livestock and products	2009 Total	2009 Crops	2009 Livestock and products	State rank for total farm marketings and four principal commodities in order of marketing receipts
U.S. . .	324,187	183,096	141,090	283,406	163,655	119,752	Cattle and calves, Corn, Soybeans
AL . . .	4,464	962	3,502	4,215	880	3,335	27-Broilers, cattle and calves, chicken eggs,
AK . . .	31	25	6	32	26	6	50-Greenhouse/nursery, hay, potatoes
AZ . . .	3,465	1,959	1,505	2,943	1,766	1,178	29-Cattle and calves, dairy products, lettuce
AR . . .	8,347	3,997	4,350	7,190	3,226	3,964	12-Broilers, rice, soybeans
CA . . .	36,187	25,554	10,632	34,841	27,027	7,814	1-Dairy products, greenhouse/nursery, grapes
CO . . .	6,509	2,379	4,131	5,553	2,230	3,323	20-Cattle, corn, wheat,
CT . . .	601	413	188	536	384	152	43-Greenhouse/nursery, dairy products, chicken eggs,
DE . . .	1,095	266	828	1,010	239	771	39-Broilers, corn, soybeans
FL . . .	7,978	6,593	1,385	7,100	5,998	1,102	16-Greenhouse/nursery, oranges, tomatoes
GA . . .	7,393	2,735	4,658	6,847	2,556	4,291	18-Broilers, cotton, chicken eggs
HI	574	511	63	581	510	72	44-Other seeds, greenhouse/nursery, sugar cane
ID	6,415	3,011	3,405	5,161	2,650	2,511	21-Dairy products, cattle and calves, potatoes
IL	16,357	14,232	2,125	14,545	12,696	1,849	5-Corn, soybeans, hogs
IN	9,962	7,105	2,856	8,757	6,389	2,368	8-Corn, soybeans, hogs
IA	24,753	14,885	9,868	21,014	12,493	8,521	2-Corn, soybeans, hogs
KS . . .	13,967	6,755	7,213	12,085	5,733	6,352	7-Cattle and calves, wheat, corn
KY . . .	4,838	1,930	2,908	4,258	1,829	2,429	25-Horses, broilers, soybeans
LA . . .	3,035	1,985	1,050	2,539	1,762	778	32-sugar cane, rice, soybeans
ME . . .	676	341	335	578	320	258	42-Potatoes, dairy products, chicken eggs
MD . . .	1,965	810	1,156	1,656	751	905	36-Broilers, greenhouse/nursery, corn
MA . . .	570	454	115	481	380	101	46-Greenhouse/nursery, cranberries, dairy products
MI	6,606	4,078	2,528	5,579	3,674	1,905	19-Dairy products, corn, soybeans
MN . . .	15,838	9,752	6,087	13,325	8,423	4,902	6-Corn, soybeans, hogs
MS . . .	4,968	2,076	2,892	4,327	1,595	2,732	24-Broilers, soybeans, corn
MO . . .	8,436	4,820	3,616	7,696	4,382	3,314	11-Soybeans, corn, cattle and calves
MT . . .	2,902	1,722	1,180	2,565	1,516	1,049	34-Wheat, cattle and calves, barley
NE . . .	17,316	8,996	8,320	15,309	8,026	7,283	4-Cattle, corn, soybeans
NV . . .	572	273	299	533	257	276	45-Cattle, hay, dairy products
NH . . .	213	119	94	179	104	75	48-Greenhouse/nursery, dairy products, apples
NJ . . .	1,118	940	177	1,000	868	133	38-Greenhouse/nursery, horses/mules, blueberries
NM . . .	3,117	710	2,407	2,699	701	1,998	30-cattle and calves, dairy products, hay
NY . . .	4,694	2,011	2,683	3,676	1,680	1,996	26-Dairy products, greenhouse/nursery, corn
NC . . .	9,753	3,291	6,461	9,188	3,478	5,710	10-Broilers, hogs, greenhouse/nursery
ND . . .	7,629	6,717	912	6,352	5,581	771	17-Wheat, soybeans, corn
OH . . .	7,979	5,236	2,744	6,836	4,601	2,234	15-Soybeans, Corn, dairy products
OK . . .	5,838	1,930	3,907	4,845	1,260	3,584	23-Cattle, broilers, hogs,
OR . . .	4,375	3,234	1,141	3,893	2,995	898	28-Greenhouse/nursery, cattle and calves, dairy products
PA . . .	6,122	2,180	3,942	4,980	1,933	3,047	22-Dairy products, mushrooms/agaricus, cattle and calves
RI	68	57	10	62	53	9	49-Greenhouse/nursery, dairy products, sweet corn
SC . . .	2,360	975	1,385	2,155	907	1,248	35-Broilers, greenhouse/nursery, turkeys
SD . . .	8,048	5,366	2,681	6,861	4,499	2,362	14-Corn, cattle and calves, soybeans
TN . . .	3,116	1,780	1,336	2,841	1,705	1,137	31-Soybeans, broilers, cattle
TX . . .	19,173	8,142	11,031	16,573	5,932	10,641	3-Cattle, broilers, greenhouse/nursery
UT . . .	1,515	527	987	1,186	421	765	37-Cattle and calves, dairy products, hay
VT . . .	688	116	572	517	118	399	41-Dairy products, cattle and calves, maple products
VA . . .	2,999	1,043	1,956	2,642	1,006	1,635	33-Broilers, cattle and calves, dairy products
WA . . .	8,180	6,207	1,974	6,593	4,953	1,640	13-Apples, dairy products, potatoes
WV . . .	525	96	429	496	91	404	47-Broilers, cattle and calves, turkeys
WI . . .	9,886	3,574	6,311	7,610	2,831	4,779	9-Dairy products, corn, cattle and calves
WY . . .	974	226	748	970	224	746	40-Cattle and calves, hay, hogs

Source: U.S. Department of Agriculture, Economic Research Service, "Farm Income: Data Files, 2009 Sector Financial Indicators Cash Receipts Ranking Data," <http://www.ers.usda.gov/Data/FarmIncome/firkdmuXls.htm>.

Table 846. Indexes of Prices Received and Paid by Farmers: 2000 to 2010

[1990–1992 = 100, except as noted]

Item	2000	2005	2009	2010	Item	2000	2005	2009	2010
Prices received, all products . . .	96	114	131	145	Feed	102	117	186	180
Crops	96	110	150	156	Livestock and poultry	110	138	115	133
Food grains	85	111	186	176	Seed	124	168	299	288
Feed grains and hay	86	95	162	165	Fertilizer.	110	164	275	252
Cotton	82	70	81	117	Agricultural chemicals	120	123	150	146
Tobacco	107	94	104	103	Fuels	129	216	228	284
Oil-bearing crops	85	106	177	175	Supplies and repairs	120	140	157	160
Fruits and nuts	98	128	135	140	Autos and trucks	119	114	110	113
Commercial vegetables [1]	121	130	161	169	Farm machinery.	139	173	222	230
Potatoes and dry beans.	93	109	150	137	Building materials	121	142	163	165
All other crops	110	113	124	125	Farm services	118	133	159	161
Livestock and products	97	119	112	131	Rent.	110	129	184	191
Meat animals	94	118	106	124	Interest.	113	111	138	135
Dairy products	94	116	98	124	Taxes	123	155	204	207
Poultry and eggs	106	123	139	152	Wage rates	140	165	187	189
Prices paid, total [2]	119	142	178	182					
Production	115	140	183	187	Parity ratio (1910–14 = 100) [3] . .	39	38	35	38

[1] Excludes potatoes and dry beans. [2] Includes production items, interest, taxes, wage rates, and a family living component. The family living component is the Consumer Price Index for all urban consumers from the Bureau of Labor Statistics. See text, Section 14 and Table 724. [3] Ratio of prices received by farmers to prices paid. "

Source: U.S. Department of Agriculture, National Agricultural Statistics Service, *Agricultural Prices: Annual Summary*, and beginning 2009, "Quick Stats U.S. & All States Data—Prices," <http://quickstats.nass.usda.gov/>. "

Agriculture 545

Table 847. Civilian Consumer Expenditures for Farm Foods: 1990 to 2008

[In billions of dollars, except percent (449.8 represents $449,800,000,000). Excludes imported and nonfarm foods, such as coffee and seafood, as well as food consumed by the military, or exported]

Item	1990	1995	2000	2001	2002	2003	2004	2005	2006	2007	2008
Consumer expenditures, total .	**449.8**	**529.5**	**661.1**	**687.5**	**709.4**	**744.2**	**788.9**	**830.7**	**880.7**	**925.2**	**958.9**
Farm value, total	106.2	113.8	123.3	130.0	132.5	140.2	155.5	157.8	163.2	194.3	192.3
Marketing bill, total [1]	343.6	415.7	537.8	557.5	576.9	604.0	633.4	672.9	717.5	731.0	766.6
Percent of total consumer expenditures	76.4	78.5	81.3	81.1	81.3	81.2	80.3	81.0	81.5	79.0	79.9
At-home expenditures [2]	276.2	316.9	390.2	403.9	416.8	437.2	463.5	488.1	517.5	543.7	563.5
Farm value.	80.2	76.1	79.6	83.9	85.7	91.4	98.5	99.3	103.2	128.3	129.0
Marketing bill [1]	196.0	240.8	310.6	320.0	331.1	345.8	365.0	388.8	414.3	415.4	434.5
Away-from-home expenditures . . .	173.6	212.6	270.9	283.6	292.6	307.0	325.4	342.6	363.2	381.5	395.4
Farm value.	26.0	37.7	43.7	46.1	46.8	48.8	57.0	58.5	60.0	66.0	63.3
Marketing bill [1]	147.6	174.9	227.2	237.5	245.8	258.2	268.4	284.1	303.2	315.5	332.1
Marketing bill cost components:											
Labor cost [3]	154.0	196.6	252.9	263.8	273.1	285.9	303.7	319.8	341.0	347.4	364.3
Packaging materials	36.5	48.2	53.5	55.0	56.8	59.5	63.1	66.5	70.5	71.8	75.3
Rail and truck transport [4]	19.8	22.3	26.4	27.5	28.4	29.7	31.6	33.2	35.2	35.9	37.6
Corporate profits before taxes. . .	13.2	19.5	31.1	32.0	33.0	34.6	35.5	37.4	39.7	40.4	38.9
Fuels and electricity.	15.2	18.6	23.1	24.1	24.9	26.1	27.6	31.6	33.5	34.1	37.4
Advertising.	17.1	19.8	26.1	27.5	28.1	29.4	30.8	32.7	34.9	35.6	37.3
Depreciation	16.3	18.9	24.2	24.5	25.3	26.5	27.8	29.5	31.5	32.1	33.7
Net interest	13.5	11.6	16.9	18.6	19.2	20.1	21.1	22.4	23.9	24.3	25.5
Net rent	13.9	19.8	26.7	29.4	30.3	31.7	33.2	35.3	37.6	38.3	40.2
Repairs	6.2	7.9	10.1	10.6	10.9	11.4	12.0	12.7	13.5	13.8	14.5
Taxes	15.7	19.1	23.5	24.1	24.9	26.1	27.4	29.1	31.0	31.6	33.1
Other	22.2	13.4	23.3	20.4	22.0	23.0	19.6	22.7	25.2	25.7	28.8

[1] The difference between expenditures for domestic farm-originated food products and the farm value or payment farmers received for the equivalent farm products. [2] Food primarily purchased from retail food stores for use at home. [3] Covers employee wages and salaries and their health and welfare benefits. Also includes imputed earnings of proprietors, partners, and family workers not receiving stated remuneration. [4] Excludes local hauling.

Source: U.S. Department of Agriculture, Economic Research Service, *Food Cost Review, 1950–97*, ERS Agricultural Economic Report No. AER780, June 1999 and "ERS/USDA Briefing Room—Food marketing and price spreads: USDA marketing bill," <http://ers.usda.gov/Briefing/FoodMarketingSystem/pricespreads.htm>.

Table 848. Agricultural Exports and Imports—Volume by Principal Commodities: 1990 to 2010

[In thousands (7,703 represents 7,703,000). 1,000 hectoliters equals 264.18 gallons. Includes Puerto Rico, U.S. territories, and shipments under foreign aid programs. Excludes fish, forest products, distilled liquors, manufactured tobacco, and products made from cotton; but includes raw tobacco, raw cotton, rubber, beer and wine, and processed agricultural products]

Commodity	Unit	1990	2000	2005	2007	2008	2009	2010
EXPORTS								
Fruit juices and wine	Hectoliters	7,703	14,356	13,982	14,470	14,871	13,675	14,986
Beef, pork, lamb, and poultry meats [1]	Metric tons. . . .	1,451	4,935	4,343	5,103	6,437	6,151	6,373
Wheat, unmilled.	Metric tons. . . .	27,384	27,568	27,040	32,991	30,021	21,920	27,592
Wheat products.	Metric tons. . . .	863	844	313	448	389	404	447
Rice, paddy, milled.	Metric tons. . . .	2,534	3,241	4,388	3,477	3,800	3,426	4,490
Feed grains	Metric tons. . . .	61,066	54,946	50,865	63,215	59,659	51,388	54,794
Feed grain products.	Metric tons. . . .	1,430	2,062	3,442	4,002	1,286	1,228	1,080
Feeds and fodders [2]	Metric tons. . . .	10,974	13,065	11,422	11,823	14,372	14,594	18,925
Fresh fruits and nuts	Metric tons. . . .	2,648	3,450	3,675	3,553	4,037	4,101	4,311
Fruit products.	Metric tons. . . .	390	471	394	460	540	506	570
Vegetables, fresh	Metric tons. . . .	1,297	2,029	2,077	1,938	2,020	1,972	2,139
Vegetables, frozen and canned	Metric tons. . . .	529	1,112	1,086	1,261	1,604	1,397	1,411
Oilcake and meal.	Metric tons. . . .	5,079	6,462	6,905	8,272	8,405	9,251	10,010
Oilseeds.	Metric tons. . . .	15,820	28,017	26,462	31,077	35,011	41,210	43,297
Vegetable oils	Metric tons. . . .	1,226	2,043	1,937	2,539	2,900	3,036	3,545
Tobacco, unmanufactured	Metric tons. . . .	223	180	154	187	169	173	179
Cotton, excluding linters	Metric tons. . . .	1,696	1,485	3,405	3,258	3,001	2,540	2,961
IMPORTS								
Fruit juices.	Hectoliters	33,116	31,154	41,488	49,710	47,299	44,234	42,698
Wine	Hectoliters	2,510	4,584	7,262	8,615	8,487	9,460	9,592
Malt beverages	Hectoliters	10,382	23,464	29,947	34,749	33,668	30,278	31,605
Coffee, including products	Metric tons. . . .	1,214	1,370	1,307	1,393	1,393	1,348	1,390
Rubber and allied gums, crude	Metric tons. . . .	840	1,232	1,169	1,028	1,053	704	945
Beef, pork, lamb, and poultry meats [1]	Metric tons. . . .	1,169	1,579	1,778	1,610	1,394	1,430	1,350
Grains [3]	Metric tons. . . .	2,071	4,622	3,726	5,576	6,384	5,587	5,170
Biscuits, pasta, and noodles	Metric tons. . . .	300	711	1,001	1,084	1,038	1,019	1,097
Feeds and fodders [2]	Metric tons. . . .	959	1,224	963	1,236	1,298	1,330	1,411
Fruits, nuts, and preparations [4]	Metric tons. . . .	5,401	8,354	9,570	10,706	10,547	10,302	10,967
Vegetables, fresh or frozen	Metric tons. . . .	1,898	3,763	5,183	5,965	6,124	6,118	6,858
Tobacco, unmanufactured	Metric tons. . . .	173	216	233	243	221	199	164
Oilseeds and oilnuts	Metric tons. . . .	509	1,056	818	1,276	1,555	1,249	1,223
Vegetable oils and waxes	Metric tons. . . .	1,204	1,846	2,386	3,117	3,708	3,523	3,730
Oilcake and meal.	Metric tons. . . .	316	1,254	1,541	1,716	1,964	1,539	1,504

[1] Includes variety meats. [2] Excluding oil meal. [3] Includes wheat, corn, oats, barley, and rice. [4] Includes bananas and plantains.
Source: U.S. Department of Agriculture, Economic Research Service, "Foreign Agricultural Trade of the United States (FATUS)," <http://www.ers.usda.gov/data/fatus/> and "Global Agricultural Trade System," <http://www.fas.usda.gov/gats>.

Table 849. Agricultural Exports and Imports—Value: 1990 to 2010

[In billions of dollars, except percent (16.6 represents $16,600,000,000). Includes Puerto Rico, U.S. territories, and shipments under foreign aid programs. Excludes fish, forest products, distilled liquors, manufactured tobacco, and products made from cotton; but includes raw tobacco, raw cotton, rubber, beer and wine, and processed agricultural products]

Year	Trade balance	Exports, domestic products	Percent of all exports	Imports for consumption	Percent of all imports	Year	Trade balance	Exports, domestic products	Percent of all exports	Imports for consumption	Percent of all imports
1990....	16.6	39.5	11	22.9	5	2004....	7.4	61.4	8	54.0	4
1995....	26.0	56.3	10	30.3	4	2005....	3.9	63.2	8	59.3	4
1999....	10.7	48.4	8	37.7	4	2006....	5.6	70.9	8	65.3	4
2000....	12.3	51.3	7	39.0	3	2007....	18.1	90.0	9	71.9	4
2001....	14.3	53.7	8	39.4	3	2008....	34.3	114.8	10	80.5	4
2002....	11.2	53.1	8	41.9	4	2009....	26.8	98.5	11	71.7	5
2003....	12.0	59.4	9	47.4	4	2010....	33.9	115.8	10	81.9	4

Source: U.S. Department of Agriculture, Economic Research Service, "Foreign Agricultural Trade of the United States (FATUS)," <http://www.ers.usda.gov/data/fatus/> and U.S. Department of Agriculture, Foreign Agricultural Service, "Global Agricultural Trade System," <http://www.fas.usda.gov/gats>.

Table 850. Agricultural Imports—Value by Selected Commodity: 1990 to 2010

[In millions of dollars (22,918 represents $22,918,000,000). For calender year. Includes Puerto Rico, U.S. territories, and shipments under foreign aid programs. Excludes fish, forest products, distilled liquors, manufactured tobacco, and products made from cotton; but includes raw tobacco, raw cotton, rubber, beer and wine, and processed agricultural products]

Commodity	Value (mil. dol.)							Percent distribution		
	1990	2000	2005	2007	2008	2009	2010	1990	2000	2010
Total [1]	22,918	38,974	59,291	71,913	80,488	71,681	81,856	100.0	100.0	100.0
Cattle, live	978	1,152	1,039	1,878	1,761	1,299	1,575	4.3	3.0	2.6
Beef and veal	1,872	2,399	3,651	3,285	3,058	2,725	2,828	8.2	6.2	4.6
Pork	938	997	1,281	1,162	1,060	978	1,185	4.1	2.6	1.6
Dairy products	891	1,671	2,686	2,883	3,142	2,528	2,619	3.9	4.3	4.0
Grains and feeds	1,188	3,075	4,527	6,422	8,258	7,435	7,786	5.2	7.9	8.9
Fruits and preparations	2,167	3,851	5,842	7,439	7,899	8,210	9,174	9.5	9.9	10.3
Vegetables and preparations [2]	1,979	3,958	6,410	7,713	8,314	8,044	9,316	8.6	10.2	10.7
Sugar and related products	1,213	1,555	2,494	2,592	2,976	3,075	4,047	5.3	4.0	3.6
Wine	917	2,207	3,762	4,638	4,634	4,020	4,279	4.0	5.7	6.5
Malt beverages	923	2,179	3,096	3,625	3,668	3,339	3,507	4.0	5.6	5.0
Oilseeds and products	952	1,773	2,998	4,329	6,766	4,799	5,390	4.2	4.5	6.0
Coffee and products	1,915	2,700	2,976	3,768	4,412	4,070	4,945	8.4	6.9	5.2
Cocoa and products	1,072	1,404	2,751	2,662	3,299	3,476	4,295	4.7	3.6	3.7
Rubber, crude natural	707	842	1,552	2,119	2,857	1,274	2,820	3.1	2.2	2.9

[1] Includes other commodities, not shown separately. [2] Includes pulses.

Source: U.S. Department of Agriculture, Economic Research Service, "Foreign Agricultural Trade of the United States (FATUS)," <http://ers.usda.gov/Data/FATUS>, and U.S. Department of Agriculture, Foreign Agricultural Service, "Global Agricultural Trade System," <http://www.fas.usda.gov/gats>.

Table 851. Agricultural Imports—Value by Selected Countries of Origin: 1990 to 2010

[In millions of dollars (22,918 represents $22,918,000,000). See headnote Table 849]

Country	Value (mil. dol.)							Percent distribution		
	1990	2000	2005	2007	2008	2009	2010	1990	2000	2010
Total	22,918	38,974	59,291	71,913	80,488	71,681	81,856	100.0	100.0	100.0
Canada	3,171	8,661	12,270	15,244	18,009	14,710	16,243	13.8	22.2	19.8
European Union [1]	5,016	8,303	13,410	15,282	15,510	13,378	14,349	21.9	21.3	17.5
Mexico	2,614	5,077	8,331	10,169	10,907	11,373	13,578	11.4	13.0	16.6
China [2]	273	812	1,872	2,916	3,451	2,877	3,368	1.2	2.1	4.1
Brazil	1,563	1,144	1,952	2,644	2,615	2,433	2,892	6.8	2.9	3.5
Indonesia	683	998	1,702	2,081	2,815	1,787	2,886	3.0	2.6	3.5
Australia	1,174	1,592	2,421	2,633	2,425	2,316	2,305	5.1	4.1	2.8
Chile	481	1,026	1,521	1,837	2,049	2,145	2,293	2.1	2.6	2.8
Thailand	470	779	1,094	1,507	1,917	1,567	2,029	2.0	2.0	2.5
Colombia	790	1,123	1,437	1,539	1,769	1,772	1,978	3.4	2.9	2.4
Malaysia	308	353	666	1,139	1,867	1,295	1,729	1.3	0.9	2.1
New Zealand	855	1,132	1,712	1,733	1,833	1,608	1,665	3.7	2.9	2.0
India	285	826	923	1,166	1,601	1,236	1,592	1.2	2.1	1.9
Guatemala	497	710	920	1,064	1,314	1,297	1,386	2.2	1.8	1.7
Costa Rica	400	812	916	1,236	1,207	1,102	1,305	1.7	2.1	1.6
Argentina	389	672	831	1,079	1,257	1,091	1,160	1.7	1.7	1.4
Peru	90	196	448	683	818	807	973	0.4	0.5	1.2
Vietnam	(NA)	200	422	663	760	727	970	(NA)	0.5	1.2
Philippines	418	468	568	704	916	724	884	1.8	1.2	1.1
Ecuador	482	451	596	691	746	928	869	2.1	1.2	1.1
Rest of World	2,958	3,636	5,281	5,905	6,701	6,509	7,403	12.9	9.3	9.0

NA Not available. [1] For consistency, data for all years are shown on the basis of 27 countries in the European Union; see footnote 5, Table 1377. [2] See footnote 4, Table 1332.

Source: U.S. Department of Agriculture, Foreign Agricultural Trade of the United States(FATUS), "Global Agricultural Trade System Online (GATS)," <http://www.fas.usda.gov/gats/default.aspx>.

Table 852. Selected Farm Products—U.S. and World Production and Exports: 2000 to 2010

[In metric tons, except as indicated (60.6 represents 60,600,000). Metric ton = 1.102 short tons or .984 long tons]

Commodity	Unit	Amount United States 2000	2005	2010	Amount World 2000	2005	2010	United States as percent of world 2000	2005	2010
PRODUCTION [1]										
Wheat	Million	60.6	57.2	60.1	583.1	619.1	648.1	10.4	9.2	9.3
Corn for grain.	Million	251.9	282.3	316.2	591.4	699.7	815.3	42.6	40.3	38.8
Soybeans.	Million	75.1	83.5	90.6	175.8	220.7	262.0	42.7	37.8	34.6
Rice, milled	Million	5.9	7.1	7.6	399.4	418.2	451.6	1.5	1.7	1.7
Cotton [2]	Million bales [3]	17.2	23.9	18.1	89.1	116.4	114.6	19.3	20.5	15.8
EXPORTS [4]										
Wheat [5]	Million	28.9	27.3	34.7	101.5	117.0	124.7	28.5	23.3	27.8
Corn.	Million	49.3	54.2	48.3	76.9	81.1	90.6	64.2	66.9	53.2
Soybeans.	Million	27.1	25.6	42.2	53.7	63.4	95.6	50.5	40.3	44.1
Rice, milled basis.	Million	2.6	3.7	3.6	24.1	29.7	31.4	10.7	12.3	11.3
Cotton [2]	Million bales [3]	6.7	17.7	15.5	26.2	44.9	37.0	25.7	39.4	41.9

[1] Production years vary by commodity. In most cases, includes harvests from July 1 of the year shown through June 30 of the following year. [2] For production and trade years ending in year shown. [3] Bales of 480 lb. net weight. [4] Trade years may vary by commodity. Wheat, corn, and soybean data are for trade year beginning in year shown. Rice data are for calendar year. [5] Includes wheat flour on a grain equivalent.

Source: U.S. Department of Agriculture, Foreign Agricultural Service, "Production, Supply and Distribution Online," <http://www.fas.usda.gov/psdonline/psdhome.aspx>.

Table 853. Percent of U.S. Agricultural Commodity Output Exported: 1990 to 2009

[In percent. All export shares are estimated from export and production volumes]

Commodity group	1990 to 1994, average	1995 to 1999, average	2000 to 2004, average	2000	2005	2006	2007	2008	2009
Total agriculture [1]	**18.5**	**18.6**	**18.5**	**18.5**	**19.1**	**19.6**	**21.0**	**19.2**	**19.8**
Livestock [2]	4.2	4.5	4.6	4.6	4.4	4.6	5.6	7.7	7.8
Red meat.	4.1	7.1	8.0	8.1	7.4	8.7	9.4	11.6	12.2
Poultry	6.1	12.6	12.0	12.4	11.8	11.7	13.0	14.7	14.8
Dairy	3.5	1.4	1.2	1.2	1.2	1.3	2.3	4.5	1.4
Crops [3]	20.6	20.7	20.8	20.8	21.5	22.2	23.5	21.2	21.9
Food grains	14.5	12.8	13.3	13.3	14.1	11.8	14.6	11.1	11.9
Feed grains	21.4	21.7	19.2	20.7	20.0	20.8	20.0	15.7	15.1
Oilseeds.	29.4	31.8	33.6	33.3	28.2	32.9	40.5	40.8	45.7
Fruit and nuts.	16.2	15.9	17.5	17.6	17.2	18.9	20.6	21.9	19.9
Vegetables.	8.9	11.0	11.2	11.2	12.2	12.6	12.2	15.3	15.8
Sweeteners	5.0	4.6	4.1	3.9	5.3	6.4	7.8	7.2	8.1
Wine and beer	3.8	5.9	7.3	6.3	7.6	9.0	9.7	10.5	9.2

[1] All export shares are computed from physical weights or weight equivalents. [2] Includes animal fats; excludes live farm animals and fish/shellfish. [3] Exports include vegetable oils and oilseed meal. Excludes nursery crops.

Source: U.S. Department of Agriculture, Economic Research Service, "Food Availability (Per Capita) Data System, Food Availability: Spreadsheets," <http://www.ers.usda.gov/Data/FoodConsumption/FoodAvailSpreadsheets.htm>; USDA Foreign Agricultural Service, "Production, Supply and Distribution," <http://www.fas.usda.gov/psdonline>; and Global Agricultural Trade System, <http://www.fas.usda.gov/gats>.

Table 854. Top 10 U.S. Export Markets for Selected Commodities: 2010

[In thousands of metric tons (50,735 represents 50,735,000)]

Corn Country	Amount	Wheat [1] Country	Amount	Soybeans Country	Amount	Poultry meat Country	Amount
World, total	**50,735**	**World, total** . . .	**27,592**	**World, total**	**42,325**	**World, total**	**3,407**
Japan.	15,491	Nigeria	3,381	China [2]	24,343	Mexico	595
Mexico	7,892	Japan.	3,170	Mexico	3,587	Russia	332
Korea, South	7,005	Mexico	2,434	Japan.	2,551	Hong Kong.	209
Egypt	3,615	Philippines	1,722	Indonesia.	1,850	Canada	168
Taiwan	2,938	Egypt	1,563	Taiwan	1,441	Angola	151
Canada	1,545	Korea, South	1,528	Germany	1,171	Cuba	145
China [2]	1,455	Taiwan	819	Egypt	983	Taiwan	105
Syria	1,321	Peru.	799	Spain	788	Lithuania	94
Venezuela	1,055	Colombia	699	Korea, South	721	China [2]	90
Dominican Republic. . . .	899	Venezuela	662	Turkey	624	Georgia	89
Rest of world	7,520	Rest of world . . .	10,815	Rest of world	4,266	Rest of world	1,429

[1] Unmilled. [2] See footnote 4, Table 1332.

Source: U.S. Department of Agriculture, Foreign Agricultural Service, "Global Agricultural Trade System Online (GATS)-FATUS Commodity Aggregations," <http://www.fas.usda.gov/gats/Default.aspx>.

Table 855. Agricultural Exports—Value by Principal Commodities: 1990 to 2010

[In millions of dollars (39,495 represents $39,495,000,000). Includes Puerto Rico, U.S. territories, and shipments under foreign aid programs. Excludes fish, forest products, distilled liquors, manufactured tobacco, and products made from cotton; but includes raw tobacco, raw cotton, rubber, beer and wine, and processed agricultural products]

Commodity	Value (mil. dol.)							Percent distribution		
	1990	2000	2005	2007	2008	2009	2010	1990	2000	2010
Total agricultural exports	**39,495**	**51,265**	**63,182**	**89,990**	**114,760**	**98,453**	**115,809**	**100.0**	**100.0**	**100.0**
Animals and animal products [1]	6,636	11,600	12,226	17,188	21,304	18,046	22,351	16.8	22.6	19.3
Meat and meat products	2,558	5,276	4,299	6,122	8,269	7,722	9,338	6.5	10.3	8.1
Poultry and poultry products	910	2,235	3,138	4,092	5,051	4,774	4,812	2.3	4.4	4.2
Grains and feeds [1]	14,386	13,620	16,364	27,896	36,913	25,293	29,265	36.4	26.6	25.3
Wheat and products.	4,035	3,578	4,520	8,616	11,599	5,681	7,038	10.2	7.0	6.1
Corn.	6,037	4,469	4,789	9,763	13,431	8,746	9,835	15.3	8.7	8.5
Fruits and preparations	2,007	2,743	3,468	4,155	4,839	4,661	5,255	5.1	5.4	4.5
Nuts and preparations	978	1,322	2,992	3,387	3,780	4,075	4,795	2.5	2.6	4.1
Vegetables and preparations [2]	1,836	3,112	3,571	4,307	5,124	5,008	5,380	4.6	6.1	4.6
Oilseeds and products [1]	5,725	8,584	10,229	15,601	23,671	24,081	27,209	14.5	16.7	23.5
Soybeans.	3,550	5,258	6,274	9,992	15,431	16,423	18,557	9.0	10.3	16.0
Vegetable oils and waxes	832	1,259	1,656	2,503	3,900	3,092	3,902	2.1	2.5	3.4
Tobacco, unmanufactured	1,441	1,204	990	1,208	1,238	1,159	1,167	3.6	2.3	1.0
Cotton, excluding linters	2,783	1,873	3,921	4,578	4,798	3,316	5,746	7.0	3.7	5.0
Other	3,702	7,207	9,421	11,670	13,093	12,814	14,641	9.4	14.1	12.6

[1] Includes commodities not shown separately. [2] Includes pulses.

Source: U.S. Department of Agriculture, Economic Research Service, "Foreign Agricultural Trade of the United States (FATUS)," <http://ers.usda.gov/Data/FATUS>, and U.S. Department of Agriculture, Foreign Agricultural Service, "Global Agricultural Trade System," <http://www.fas.usda.gov/gats>.

Table 856. Agricultural Exports—Value by Selected Countries of Destination: 1990 to 2010

[(39,495 represents $39,495,000,000). Includes Puerto Rico, U.S. territories, and shipments under foreign aid programs. Excludes fish, forest products, distilled liquors, manufactured tobacco, and products made from cotton; but includes raw tobacco, raw cotton, rubber, beer and wine, and processed agricultural products]

Country	Value (mil. dol.)							Percent distribution		
	1990	2000	2005	2007	2008	2009	2010	1990	2000	2010
Total agricultural exports [1]	**39,495**	**51,265**	**63,182**	**89,990**	**114,760**	**98,453**	**115,809**	**100.0**	**100.0**	**100.0**
Canada	4,214	7,643	10,618	14,062	16,253	15,725	16,856	10.7	14.9	14.6
Mexico	2,560	6,410	9,429	12,692	15,508	12,932	14,575	6.5	12.5	12.6
Caribbean	1,015	1,408	1,913	2,575	3,592	3,082	3,192	2.6	2.7	2.8
Central America	483	1,121	1,589	2,363	3,106	2,553	2,923	1.2	2.2	2.5
South America [2]	1,063	1,704	1,943	3,510	5,334	3,459	4,243	2.7	3.3	3.7
Asia, excluding Middle East [2]	15,857	19,877	22,543	32,427	44,209	40,614	49,765	40.1	38.8	43.0
Japan.	8,142	9,292	7,931	10,159	13,223	11,072	11,819	20.6	18.1	10.2
Korea, South	2,650	2,546	2,233	3,528	5,561	3,917	5,308	6.7	5.0	4.6
Taiwan [3]	1,663	1,996	2,301	3,097	3,419	2,988	3,190	4.2	3.9	2.8
China [3,4]	818	1,716	5,233	8,314	12,115	13,109	17,522	2.1	3.3	15.1
Indonesia	275	668	958	1,542	2,195	1,796	2,246	0.7	1.3	1.9
Europe/Eurasia [2]	8,140	7,654	8,361	10,598	12,262	9,377	11,371	20.6	14.9	9.8
European Union [5]	7,474	6,515	7,052	8,754	10,080	7,445	8,894	18.9	12.7	7.7
Russia	(X)	580	972	1,329	1,838	1,429	1,141	(X)	1.1	1.0
Middle East [2]	1,728	2,323	2,844	4,952	6,650	4,745	6,021	4.4	4.5	5.2
Africa [2]	1,848	2,308	2,773	1,931	2,649	1,930	2,301	4.7	4.5	2.0
Egypt	687	1,050	819	1,801	2,050	1,354	2,092	1.7	2.0	1.8
Oceania	343	490	742	963	1,189	1,282	1,394	0.9	1.0	1.2

X Not applicable. [1] Totals include transshipments through Canada, but transshipments are not distributed by country after 2000. [2] Includes areas not shown separately. [3] See footnote 4, Table 1332. [4] China includes Macao. However Hong Kong remains separate economically until 2050 and is not included. [5] For consistency, data for all years are shown on the basis of 27 countries in the European Union; see footnote 3, Table 1377.

Source: U.S. Department of Agriculture, Economic Research Service, "Foreign Agricultural Trade of the United States (FATUS);"<http://ers.usda.gov/Data/FATUS> February 2010, and U.S. Department of Agriculture, Foreign Agricultural Service, "Global Agricultural Trade System," <http://www.fas.usda.gov/gats>.

Table 857. Cropland Used for Crops and Acreages of Crops Harvested: 1990 to 2010

[In millions of acres, except as indicated (341 represents 341,000,000)]

Item	1990	1995	2000	2004	2005	2006	2007	2008	2009	2010
Cropland used for crops	**341**	**332**	**345**	**336**	**337**	**330**	**335**	**340**	**333**	**335**
Index (1977 = 100)	90	88	91	89	89	87	89	90	88	88
Cropland harvested [1]	310	302	314	312	314	303	312	316	310	315
Crop failure	6	8	11	9	6	11	8	8	8	5
Cultivated summer fallow.	25	22	20	15	16	15	15	16	15	14
Cropland idled by all federal programs	62	55	31	35	35	37	37	35	34	31
Acres of crops harvested [2]	**322**	**314**	**325**	**321**	**321**	**312**	**322**	**325**	**319**	**322**

[1] Land supporting one or more harvested crops. [2] Area in principal crops harvested as reported by Crop Reporting Board plus acreages in fruits, vegetables for sale, tree nuts, and other minor crops. Acres are counted twice for land that is doublecropped.

Source: U.S. Department of Agriculture, Economic Research Service, "Major Uses of Land in the United States, 2002," 2006. Also in Agricultural Statistics, annual. Beginning 1991, Agricultural Resources and Environmental Indicators, periodic, and "AREI Updates: Cropland Use." See also ERS Briefing Room at <http://www.ers.usda.gov/Briefing /LandUse/majorlandusechapter.htm#trends>.

Agriculture 549

Table 858. Crops—Supply and Use: 2000 to 2010

[72.4 represents 72,400,000. Marketing year beginning January 1 for potatoes, May 1 for hay, June 1 for wheat, August 1 for cotton, September 1 for soybeans and corn. Acreage, production, and yield of all crops periodically revised on basis of census data]

Item	Unit	2000	2005	2006	2007	2008	2009	2010
CORN								
Acreage harvested	Million	72.4	75.1	70.6	86.5	78.6	79.5	81.4
Yield per acre	Bushel	136.9	147.9	149.1	150.7	153.9	164.7	152.8
Production	Mil. bu.	9,915	11,112	10,531	13,038	12,092	13,092	12,447
Imports	Mil. bu.	6.82	8.81	11.98	20.02	13.53	8.00	20.00
Total supply [1]	Mil. bu.	11,639	13,235	12,510	14,362	13,729	14,774	14,175
Ethanol	Mil. bu.	628	1,603	2,119	3,049	3,709	4,568	5,150
Exports	Mil. bu.	1,941	2,134	2,125	2,437	1,849	1,987	1,950
Total use [2]	Mil. bu.	9,740	11,268	11,207	12,737	12,056	13,066	13,500
Ending stocks	Mil. bu.	1,899	1,967	1,304	1,624	1,673	1,708	675
Price per unit [3]	Dol./bu.	1.85	2.00	3.04	4.20	4.06	3.55	5.40
Value of production	Mil. dol.	18,499	22,198	32,083	54,667	49,313	46,734	66,650
SOYBEANS								
Acreage harvested	Million	72.4	71.3	74.6	64.1	74.7	76.4	76.6
Yield per acre	Bushel	38.1	43.1	42.9	41.7	39.7	44.0	43.5
Production	Mil. bu.	2,758	3,068	3,197	2,677	2,967	3,359	3,329
Imports	Mil. bu.	4	3	9	10	13	15	15
Total supply [1]	Mil. bu.	3,052	3,327	3,655	3,261	3,185	3,512	3,495
Crushings	Mil. bu.	1,640	1,739	1,808	1,803	1,662	1,752	1,650
Exports	Mil. bu.	996	940	1,116	1,159	1,283	1,501	1,580
Total use [2]	Mil. bu.	2,804	2,878	3,081	3,056	3,047	3,361	3,355
Ending stocks	Mil. bu.	248	449	574	205	138	151	140
Price per unit [3]	Dol./bu.	4.54	5.66	6.43	10.10	9.97	9.59	11.70
Value of production	Mil. dol.	12,520	17,367	20,555	27,039	29,458	32,145	38,915
WHEAT								
Acreage harvested	Million	53.1	50.1	46.8	51.0	55.7	49.9	47.6
Yield per acre	Bushel	42.0	42.0	38.6	40.2	44.9	44.5	46.4
Production	Mil. bu.	2,228	2,103	1,808	2,051	2,499	2,218	2,208
Imports	Mil. bu.	89.8	81.4	121.9	112.6	127.0	115.0	110.0
Total supply [1,4]	Mil. bu.	3,268	2,725	2,501	2,620	2,932	2,988	3,294
Exports	Mil. bu.	1,062	1,003	908	1,263	1,015	881	1,275
Total use [2]	Mil. bu.	2,392	2,154	2,045	2,314	2,275	2,038	2,451
Ending stocks	Mil. bu.	876	571	456	306	657	950	843
Price per unit [3]	Dol./bu.	2.62	3.42	4.26	6.48	6.78	4.87	5.70
Value of production	Mil. dol.	5,782	7,171	7,695	13,289	16,626	10,654	12,992
COTTON								
Acreage harvested	Million	13.1	13.8	12.7	10.5	7.6	7.5	10.7
Yield per acre	Pounds.	632	831	814	879	813	777	811
Production [5]	Mil. bales [6]	17.2	23.9	21.6	19.2	12.8	12.2	18.1
Imports	Mil. bales [6]	–	–	–	–	–	–	–
Total supply [1]	Mil. bales [6]	21.1	29.4	27.7	28.7	22.9	18.5	21.1
Exports	Mil. bales [6]	6.7	17.5	13.0	13.7	13.3	12.0	15.8
Total use [2]	Mil. bales [6]	15.6	23.4	17.9	18.2	16.9	15.5	19.5
Ending stocks	Mil. bales [6]	6.0	6.1	9.5	10.0	6.3	3.0	1.6
Price per unit [3]	Cents/lb.	51.6	47.7	48.4	61.3	49.1	64.8	82.5
Value of production	Mil. dol.	4,260	5,695	5,013	5,653	3,021	3,788	7,318
HAY								
Acreage harvested	Million	60.4	61.6	60.6	61.0	60.2	59.8	59.9
Yield per acre	Sh. tons	2.54	2.44	2.32	2.41	2.43	2.47	2.43
Production	Mil. sh. tons	154	150	141	147	146	148	146
Price per unit [7,8]	Dol./ton	84.60	98.20	110.00	128.00	152.00	108.00	112.00
Value of production	Mil. dol.	11,557	12,534	13,634	16,842	18,639	14,716	14,401
POTATOES								
Acreage harvested	Million	1.3	1.1	1.1	1.1	1.0	1.0	1.0
Yield per acre	Cwt. [9]	381	390	393	396	396	414	395
Production	Mil. cwt. [9]	514	424	441	445	415	431	397
Price per unit [3]	Dol./cwt. [9]	5.08	7.06	7.31	7.51	9.09	8.19	8.79
Value of production	Mil. dol.	2,590	2,992	3,209	3,340	3,770	3,521	3,489

– Represents zero or rounds to less than half the unit of measurement shown. [1] Comprises production, imports, and beginning stocks. [2] Includes feed, residual, and other domestic uses not shown separately. [3] Marketing year average price. U.S. prices are computed by weighting U.S. monthly prices by estimated monthly marketings and do not include an allowance for outstanding loans and government purchases and payments. [4] Includes flour and selected other products expressed in grain-equivalent bushels. [5] State production figures, which conform with annual ginning enumeration with allowance for cross-state ginnings, rounded to thousands and added for U.S. totals. [6] Bales of 480 pounds, net weight. [7] Prices are for hay sold baled. [8] Season average prices received by farmers. U.S. prices are computed by weighting state prices by estimated sales. [9] Cwt = hundredweight (100 pounds).

Source: Production—U.S. Department of Agriculture, National Agricultural Statistics Service, *In Crop Production*, annual, and *Crop Values*, annual. Supply and disappearance—U.S. Department of Agriculture, Economic Research Service, *Feed Situation*, quarterly; *Fats and Oils Situation*, quarterly; *Wheat Situation*, quarterly; *Cotton and Wool Outlook Statistics*, periodic; and *Agricultural Supply and Demand Estimates*, periodic. All data are also in *Agricultural Statistics*, annual. See also <http://www.nass.usda.gov/Publications/Ag_Statistics/> and "Agricultural Outlook: Statistical Indicators," <http://www.ers.usda.gov /Publications/Agoutlook/AOTables/>.

Table 859. Corn—Acreage, Production, and Value by Leading States: 2008 to 2010

[78,570 represents 78,570,000. One bushel of corn (bu.) = 56 pounds]

State	Acreage harvested (1,000 acres) 2008	2009	2010	Yield per acre (bu.) 2008	2009	2010	Production (mil. bu.) 2008	2009	2010	Price per unit ($/bu) 2008	2009	2010	Value of production (mil. dol.) 2008	2009	2010
U.S.[1] . . .	78,570	79,490	81,446	154	165	153	12,092	13,092	12,447	4.06	3.55	5.40	49,313	46,734	66,650
IA	12,800	13,300	13,050	171	182	165	2,189	2,421	2,153	4.10	3.59	5.45	8,974	8,690	11,735
IL	11,900	11,800	12,400	179	174	157	2,130	2,053	1,947	4.01	3.53	5.50	8,542	7,248	10,707
NE	8,550	8,850	8,850	163	178	166	1,394	1,575	1,469	4.05	3.58	5.35	5,644	5,640	7,860
MN	7,200	7,150	7,300	164	174	177	1,181	1,244	1,292	3.92	3.47	5.20	4,629	4,317	6,719
IN	5,460	5,460	5,720	160	171	157	874	934	898	4.10	3.66	5.50	3,582	3,417	4,939
KS	3,630	3,860	4,650	134	155	125	486	598	581	4.12	3.49	5.25	2,004	2,088	3,052
SD	4,400	4,680	4,220	133	151	135	585	707	570	3.78	3.23	5.10	2,212	2,283	2,905
OH	3,120	3,140	3,270	135	174	163	421	546	533	4.21	3.55	5.55	1,773	1,940	2,958
WI	2,880	2,930	3,100	137	153	162	395	448	502	3.89	3.57	5.35	1,535	1,600	2,687
MO	2,650	2,920	3,000	144	153	123	382	447	369	4.11	3.58	5.45	1,568	1,599	2,011
MI	2,140	2,090	2,100	138	148	150	295	309	315	3.84	3.53	5.55	1,134	1,092	1,748
TX	2,030	1,960	2,080	125	130	145	254	255	302	4.82	4.01	4.90	1,223	1,022	1,478
ND	2,300	1,740	1,880	124	115	132	285	200	248	3.74	3.18	5.35	1,067	636	1,328
CO	1,010	990	1,210	137	153	151	138	151	183	4.14	3.68	5.25	573	557	959
KY	1,120	1,150	1,230	136	165	124	152	190	153	4.36	3.74	5.45	664	710	831
PA	880	920	910	133	143	128	117	132	116	4.16	3.84	5.80	487	505	676
MS	700	695	670	140	126	136	98	88	91	4.63	3.72	4.60	454	326	419
NY	640	595	590	144	134	150	92	80	89	4.32	4.02	5.20	398	321	460
NC	830	800	840	78	117	91	65	94	76	4.91	3.90	5.15	318	365	394
TN	630	590	640	118	148	117	74	87	75	4.53	3.65	4.85	337	319	363

[1] Includes other states, not shown separately.

Source: U.S. Department of Agriculture, National Agricultural Statistics Service, *Crop Production Annual Summary*, January 2011, and *Crop Values Annual Summary*, February 2011. See also <http://www.nass.usda.gov/Publications/index.asp>.

Table 860. Soybeans—Acreage, Production, and Value by Leading States: 2008 to 2010

[74,681 represents 74,681,000. One bushel of soybeans = 60 pounds]

State	Acreage harvested (1,000 acres) 2008	2009	2010	Yield per acre (bu.) 2008	2009	2010	Production (mil. bu.) 2008	2009	2010	Price per unit ($/bu.) 2008	2009	2010	Value of production (mil. dol.) 2008	2009	2010
U.S.[1] . . .	74,681	76,372	76,616	40	44	44	2,967	3,359	3,329	9.97	9.59	11.70	29,458	32,145	38,915
IA	9,670	9,530	9,730	47	51	51	450	486	496	10.20	9.52	11.70	4,586	4,627	5,806
IL	9,120	9,350	9,050	47	46	52	429	430	466	10.20	9.80	12.40	4,372	4,215	5,779
MN	6,970	7,120	7,310	38	40	45	265	285	329	10.10	9.39	11.30	2,675	2,674	3,717
NE	4,860	4,760	5,100	47	55	53	226	259	268	9.79	9.48	11.30	2,212	2,459	3,026
IN	5,430	5,440	5,330	45	49	49	244	267	259	10.20	9.80	11.80	2,492	2,612	3,050
OH	4,480	4,530	4,590	36	49	48	161	222	220	10.30	9.78	11.80	1,661	2,171	2,600
MO	5,030	5,300	5,070	38	44	42	191	231	210	9.74	9.61	12.10	1,862	2,216	2,546
SD	4,060	4,190	4,140	34	42	38	138	176	157	9.65	9.18	11.20	1,332	1,615	1,762
ND	3,760	3,870	4,070	28	30	34	105	116	138	9.71	9.26	11.30	1,022	1,075	1,564
KS	3,250	3,650	4,250	37	44	33	120	161	138	9.39	9.38	12.00	1,129	1,506	1,658
AR	3,250	3,270	3,150	38	38	35	124	123	110	9.64	9.66	11.30	1,191	1,185	1,246
MI	1,890	1,990	2,040	37	40	44	70	80	89	9.82	9.54	11.40	687	759	1,012
WI	1,590	1,620	1,630	35	40	51	56	65	82	9.80	9.62	11.40	545	623	938
MS	1,960	2,030	1,980	40	38	39	78	77	76	9.29	9.24	11.10	728	713	846

[1] Includes other states, not shown separately.

Source: U.S. Department of Agriculture, National Agricultural Statistics Service, *Crop Production Annual Summary*, January 2011, and *Crop Values Annual Summary*, February 2011. See also <http://www.nass.usda.gov/Publications/index.asp>.

Table 861. Wheat—Acreage, Production, and Value by Leading States: 2008 to 2010

[55,699 represents 55,699,000. One bushel of wheat = 60 pounds]

State	Acreage harvested (1,000 acres) 2008	2009	2010	Yield per acre (bu.) 2008	2009	2010	Production (mil. bu.) 2008	2009	2010	Price per unit ($/bu.) 2008	2009	2010	Value of production (mil. dol.) 2008	2009	2010
U.S.[1] . . .	55,699	49,893	47,637	45	45	46	2,499	2,218	2,208	6.78	4.87	5.70	16,626	10,654	12,992
ND	8,640	8,415	8,400	36	45	43	311	377	362	7.31	4.82	6.50	2,297	1,816	2,346
KS	8,900	8,800	8,000	40	42	45	356	370	360	6.94	4.79	5.20	2,471	1,770	1,872
MT	5,470	5,305	5,210	30	33	41	165	177	215	6.84	5.18	6.60	1,139	918	1,431
WA	2,255	2,225	2,285	53	55	65	119	123	148	6.26	4.85	6.75	745	594	997
TX	3,300	2,450	3,750	30	25	34	99	61	128	7.58	5.27	5.05	750	323	644
SD	3,420	3,009	2,725	51	43	45	173	129	123	6.92	5.07	6.05	1,199	663	750
OK	4,500	3,500	3,900	37	22	31	167	77	121	6.93	4.89	5.10	1,154	377	617
CO	1,936	2,479	2,377	31	41	46	60	101	108	6.62	4.57	5.60	397	460	606

[1] Includes other states, not shown separately.

Source: U.S. Department of Agriculture, National Agricultural Statistics Service, *Crop Production Annual Summary*, January 2011, and *Crop Values Annual Summary*, February 2011. See also <http://www.nass.usda.gov/Publications/index.asp>.

Agriculture 551

Table 862. Commercial Vegetable and Other Specified Crops—Area, Production, and Value, 2008 to 2010, and Leading Producing States, 2010

[289 represents 289,000. Except as noted, relates to commercial production for fresh market and processing combined. Includes market garden areas but excludes minor producing acreage in minor producing states. Excludes production for home use in farm and nonfarm gardens. Value is for season or crop year and should not be confused with calendar-year income. Hundredweight (cwt.) is the unit used for fresh market yield and production and is equal to one hundred pounds]

Crop	Area harvested (1,000 acres) [1]			Production (1,000 cwt) [2]			Value of production (mil. dol.) [3]			Leading states in order of production, 2010
	2008	2009	2010	2008	2009	2010	2008	2009	2010	
Beans, snap..........	289	285	283	21,984	21,554	20,428	485	415	447	(NA)
Fresh market........	90	92	89	5,824	5,225	5,062	308	283	304	FL, CA, GA
Processed..........	198	196	194	16,160	16,329	15,366	177	156	143	WI, OR
Beans, dry edible......	1,445	1,464	1,843	25,558	25,427	31,801	910	790	838	ND, MI, NE
Broccoli............	127	126	122	20,086	19,890	18,219	721	794	649	CA, AZ
Cabbage [4]..........	66	65	66	24,516	22,467	22,797	355	342	378	CA, NY, FL
Cantaloupes [4]........	72	75	75	19,294	19,279	18,838	357	350	314	CA, AZ, GA
Carrots.............	90	82	81	32,600	29,252	29,198	636	589	627	CA
Cauliflower...........	37	39	36	6,648	7,167	6,281	269	316	247	CA, AZ, NY
Celery.............	28	29	29	20,025	20,074	20,285	370	404	399	CA, MI
Corn, sweet.........	594	613	585	85,549	93,521	82,937	1,089	1,171	991	(NA)
Fresh market.......	233	237	247	28,899	28,839	29,149	749	846	750	FL, CA, GA
Processed..........	361	380	338	56,650	64,682	53,788	340	336	241	MN, WA, WI
Cucumbers..........	143	144	88	20,185	20,332	19,475	398	402	379	MI, FL, NC
Garlic..............	149	135	139	52,952	50,180	50,750	1,063	1,122	1,206	CA, AZ
Lettuce, head [4].......	52	49	48	12,781	11,845	11,180	412	459	429	CA, AZ
Lettuce, leaf [4]........	77	76	80	22,774	22,355	25,259	479	613	615	CA, AZ
Lettuce, Romaine [4]....	153	151	150	75,120	75,566	73,213	834	1,054	1,455	CA,AZ
Onions.............	210	205	175	8,236	8,834	7,175	148	141	105	MN, WI, WA
Peas, green [5]........	51	52	53	15,888	16,997	15,739	637	585	637	CA, FL, GA
Peppers, bell........	46	50	50	7,792	8,734	6,133	206	249	269	CA, AZ, TX
Spinach.............	42	44	44	6,687	7,219	6,542	204	203	204	MI, CA, FL
Squash.............	402	434	394	277,253	312,646	284,442	2,398	2,533	2,318	(NA)
Tomatoes............	105	109	105	31,137	33,235	28,916	1,415	1,344	1,391	CA, FL, TN
Fresh market.......	297	328	289	246,116	279,411	255,526	982	1,219	927	CA, IN, OH
Processed..........	126	124	133	40,003	38,911	41,153	500	451	492	FL, GA, CA
Watermelons [5]........	129	126	126	37,349	40,003	40,122	423	500	461	FL, CA, GA

NA Not available. [1] Area of crops for harvest for fresh market, including any partially harvested or not harvested because of low prices or other factors, plus area harvested for processing. [2] Excludes some quantities not marketed. [3] Fresh market vegetables valued at f.o.b. shipping point. Processing vegetables are equivalent returns at packinghouse door. [4] Fresh market only. [5] Processed only.

Source: U.S. Department of Agriculture, National Agricultural Statistics Service, *Vegetables 2010 Summary*, January 2011. See also <http://www.nass.usda.gov/Surveys/Guide_to_NASS_Surveys/Vegetables/index.asp>.

Table 863. Fresh Fruits and Vegetables—Supply and Use: 2000 to 2010

[In millions of pounds, except per capita in pounds (8,355 represents 8,355,000,000)]

Year	Utilized production [1]	Imports [2]	Supply, [1] total	Exports [2]	Consumption Total	Consumption Per capita [3]	Ending stocks
FRUITS							
Citrus:							
2000.....................	8,355	720	9,075	2,445	6,630	23.5	(NA)
2005.....................	7,320	1,109	8,429	2,040	6,389	21.6	(NA)
2007.....................	5,811	1,382	7,193	1,789	5,404	17.9	(NA)
2008.....................	7,315	1,322	8,637	2,362	6,275	20.6	(NA)
2009.....................	6,880	1,390	8,270	1,901	6,369	20.8	(NA)
Noncitrus: [4]							
2000.....................	13,850	11,225	25,074	3,389	21,685	77.8	(NA)
2005.....................	14,369	12,460	26,829	3,477	23,352	78.8	(NA)
2007.....................	14,016	13,437	27,453	3,329	24,125	79.8	(NA)
2008.....................	14,440	13,669	28,109	3,755	24,354	79.9	(NA)
2009.....................	15,150	13,316	28,466	3,603	24,863	80.8	(NA)
VEGETABLES AND MELONS							
2000.....................	46,995	7,231	55,570	4,200	49,147	174.6	1,266
2005.....................	46,510	9,784	57,785	4,324	51,439	173.7	1,280
2007.....................	46,608	11,157	58,927	3,878	52,704	174.5	1,472
2008.....................	45,141	11,432	58,045	4,033	51,804	170.0	1,463
2009.....................	44,396	11,753	57,612	3,802	51,529	167.6	1,555
2010.....................	44,026	13,179	58,761	3,957	52,623	169.7	1,381
POTATOES							
2000.....................	13,185	806	13,990	677	13,313	47.2	(NA)
2005.....................	12,076	788	12,863	639	12,224	41.3	(NA)
2007.....................	11,225	1,106	12,331	640	11,691	38.7	(NA)
2008.....................	10,995	1,178	12,173	642	11,531	37.8	(NA)
2009.....................	10,996	936	11,932	728	11,204	36.4	(NA)
2010.....................	10,961	916	11,877	851	11,026	35.6	(NA)

NA Not available. [1] Crop-year basis for fruits. Supply data for vegetables include ending stocks of previous year. [2] Fiscal year for fruits; calendar year for vegetables and potatoes. [3] Based on Census Bureau estimates as of April 1 for census years and estimates as of July 1 for all other years. [4] Includes bananas.

Source: U.S. Department of Agriculture, Economic Research Service, *Fruit and Tree Nuts Situation and Outlook Yearbook* and *Vegetables and Melons Situation and Outlook Yearbook*. See also <http://www.ers.usda.gov/publications/outlook/>.

Table 864. Fruits and Nuts—Utilized Production and Value, 2008 to 2010, and Leading Producing States: 2010

[4,770 represents 4,770,000]

Fruits and nuts	Unit	Utilized production [1]			Value of production (mil. dol.)			Leading states in order of production, 2010
		2008	2009	2010	2008	2009	2010	
FRUITS								
Apples [2]	1,000 tons	4,770	4,854	(NA)	2,215	2,247	(NA)	(NA)
Avocados	1,000 tons	116	299	(NA)	215	430	(NA)	(NA)
Blackberries, cultivated (OR)	1,000 tons	23	28	24	28	31	36	OR
Blueberries	1,000 tons	219	227	249	592	518	641	MI, ME, GA
Cranberries	1,000 tons	393	346	340	456	333	321	MA, WI
Dates (CA)	1,000 tons	21	24	24	26	27	28	CA
Figs (fresh) (CA)	1,000 tons	43	44	40	26	30	(NA)	CA
Grapefruit	1,000 tons	1,548	1,304	1,238	273	224	286	FL, TX, CA
Grapes (13 states)	1,000 tons	7,306	7,280	6,854	3,333	3,676	3,472	CA, WA
Kiwifruit (CA)	1,000 tons	22	25	34	20	21	(NA)	CA
Lemons	1,000 tons	619	912	882	524	335	381	CA, AZ
Nectarines	1,000 tons	303	220	235	111	139	131	CA, WA
Olives (CA)	1,000 tons	67	46	190	47	32	111	CA
Oranges [3]	1,000 tons	10,076	9,128	8,244	2,199	1,970	1,935	FL, CA
Papayas (Hawaii)	1,000 tons	17	16	14	14	14	10	HI
Peaches	1,000 tons	1,114	1,083	1,132	546	594	615	CA, SC, GA
Pears	1,000 tons	869	956	807	396	356	334	WA, CA, OR
Plums (CA)	1,000 tons	160	112	(NA)	57	58	(NA)	(NA)
Plums and prunes (fresh) [4]	1,000 tons	16	18	(NA)	6	6	(NA)	(NA)
Prunes (dried basis) (CA)	1,000 tons	368	496	(NA)	194	199	(NA)	(NA)
Raspberries	1,000 tons	75	89	76	365	362	259	CA, WA, OR
Strawberries	1,000 tons	1,266	1,401	1,425	1,918	2,130	2,245	CA, FL
Tangelos (FL)	1,000 tons	68	52	41	9	6	7	FL
Tangerines	1,000 tons	527	443	595	236	207	276	CA, FL
NUTS								
Almonds (shelled basis) (CA)	1,000 tons	1,410	1,181	(NA)	2,343	2,294	(NA)	(NA)
Hazelnuts (in the shell) (OR)	1,000 tons	32	47	(NA)	52	79	(NA)	(NA)
Macadamia nuts (HI)	1,000 tons	25	21	(NA)	34	29	(NA)	(NA)
Pecans (in the shell) (11 states)	1,000 tons	97	146	(NA)	260	417	(NA)	(NA)
Pistachios (CA)	1,000 tons	139	178	(NA)	570	593	(NA)	(NA)
Walnuts (in the shell) (CA)	1,000 tons	436	437	(NA)	558	739	(NA)	(NA)

NA Not available. [1] Excludes quantities not harvested or not marketed. Utilized production is the amount sold plus the quantities used at home or held in storage [2] Production in commercial orchards with 100 or more bearing-age trees. [3] Includes temples and Navel varieties beginning with the 2006–2007 season. [4] Idaho, Michigan, Oregon and Washington.

Source: U.S. Department of Agriculture, National Agricultural Statistics Service, *Citrus Fruits Final Estimates, 2003–2007*, December 2008; *Citrus Fruits 2010 Summary*, September 2010; and *Noncitrus Fruits and Crops 2009 Summary*, July 2010. See also <http://www.nass.usda.gov/Publications/index.asp>.

Table 865. Nuts—Supply and Use: 2000 to 2009

[In thousands of pounds (shelled) (331,466 represents 331,466,000). For marketing season beginning July 1 for almonds, hazelnuts, pecans; August 1 for walnuts; and September 1 for pistachios]

Year	Beginning stocks	Marketable production [1]	Imports	Supply, total	Consumption	Exports	Ending stocks
Total nuts: [2]							
2000	331,466	1,127,940	293,172	1,752,577	733,921	780,988	237,669
2005	262,995	1,472,240	431,881	2,167,117	779,131	1,120,833	267,153
2007	243,133	2,070,933	489,793	2,803,858	1,042,284	1,355,677	405,897
2008	405,897	2,240,219	439,516	3,085,632	1,082,566	1,460,506	405,897
2009, total [2]	**542,560**	**2,104,057**	**464,537**	**3,111,154**	**1,136,968**	**1,553,305**	**420,881**
Almonds	413,734	1,363,751	5,610	1,783,095	(NA)	1,030,403	321,255
Pecans	42,225	(NA)	80,107	249,862	139,152	71,188	39,522
Pistachios	32,922	174,769	1,297	208,988	54,701	133,075	21,211
Hazelnuts	1,127	37,425	7,987	46,539	14,331	30,621	1,587
Walnuts	52,553	381,500	3,183	437,235	170,371	229,558	37,305

NA Not available. [1] Utilized production minus inedibles and noncommercial usage. [2] Includes macadamia nuts, Brazil nuts, cashew nuts, pine nuts, chestnuts, and mixed nuts not shown separately.

Source: U.S. Department of Agriculture, Economic Research Service, *Fruit and Tree Nuts Situation and Outlook Yearbook*. See also <http://www.ers.usda.gov/publications/fts/#yearbook>.

Table 866. Honey—Number of Bee Colonies, Yield, and Production: 1990 to 2010

[Includes only beekeepers with five or more colonies. Colonies were not included if honey was not harvested]

Year	Honey-producing colonies [1] (1,000)	Yield per colony (pounds)	Production (1,000 pounds)	Average price per pound (cents)	Value of production (1,000 dollars)
1990	3,220	61.7	198,674	54	106,688
1995	2,655	79.5	211,073	69	144,585
2000	2,622	84.0	220,286	60	132,865
2005	2,409	72.5	174,614	92	160,994
2007	2,443	60.7	148,341	108	159,763
2008	2,342	69.9	163,789	142	232,744
2009	2,498	58.6	146,416	147	215,671
2010	2,684	65.5	175,904	160	281,974

[1] Honey producing colonies are the maximum number of colonies from which honey was taken during the year. It is possible to take honey from colonies which did not survive the entire year.

Source: U.S. Department of Agriculture, National Agricultural Statistics Service, *Honey*, February 2011. See also <http://www.nass.usda.gov/Surveys/Guide_to_NASS_Surveys/Bee_and_Honey/index.asp>.

Table 867. Farmers Markets Characteristics: 2005

[In percent. Based on 2006 National Farmers Market Survey. A farmers market is defined as a retail outlet in which two or more vendors sell agricultural products directly to customers through a common marketing channel. Markets included were in business in the 2005 season and conducted 51 percent of their retail sales directly with consumers]

Characteristic	Total, U.S.	Region [1]						
		North-east	Mid-Atlantic	South-east	North Central	South-west	Rocky Mountain	Far West
Number of vendors:								
Less than 10	23.9	42.4	37.4	24.1	17.8	32.3	15.9	9.4
10 to 19	25.3	27.9	28.4	22.8	29.4	29.0	19.3	12.5
20 to 39	29.0	23.6	22.6	29.7	32.3	17.7	28.4	35.6
40 or more	21.8	6.1	11.6	23.4	20.5	21.0	36.4	42.5
Vendor sales:								
$1 to $5,000	71.4	70.0	61.2	68.1	81.4	71.6	80.4	56.1
$5,001 to $25,000	22.1	26.2	22.8	25.2	15.5	23.0	18.3	31.5
$25,000 to $100,000	5.9	3.8	15.4	4.3	2.9	5.3	1.3	11.8
$100,001 and above	0.6	–	0.7	2.4	0.2	0.2	–	0.6
Months of operation:								
Year-round	12.1	3.5	13.7	19.6	4.1	17.5	4.3	35.4
Seasonal	87.9	96.5	86.3	80.4	95.9	82.5	95.7	64.6
Less than 4 months	20.0	26.3	15.5	16.9	19.2	22.2	39.6	11.4
4 to 6 months	59.5	68.0	57.4	42.6	72.0	47.6	52.7	42.9
7 to 9 months	7.6	2.3	12.9	18.2	4.6	9.5	3.3	8.6
More than 9 months	12.9	3.4	14.2	22.3	4.2	20.6	4.4	37.1
Source of goods sold:								
Grew products sold (their own products)	(NA)	65.0	72.3	69.8	76.8	78.0	60.3	68.6
Organic products	47.0	67.3	37.2	35.5	39.8	30.4	56.8	74.5
Locally grown	87.9	89.3	84.8	90.5	91.2	80.6	88.1	82.1
Pasture raised/free range	38.4	33.6	40.2	21.6	42.5	32.3	34.3	46.3
Natural	46.9	39.3	41.1	45.9	50.9	32.3	55.2	50.4
Hormone or antibiotic free	29.3	20.5	27.7	20.3	34.4	19.4	28.4	36.6
Chemical free/pesticide free	47.6	36.9	39.3	45.9	46.9	41.9	56.7	65.0
Other	12.3	13.9	13.4	12.2	7.3	19.4	16.4	17.1

– Represents zero. NA Not available. [1] Composition of regions—Northeast: Connecticut, Maine, Massachusetts, New Hampshire, New York, Rhode Island, and Vermont. Mid-Atlantic: Delaware, District of Columbia, Maryland, New Jersey, Pennsylvania, Virginia, and West Virginia. Southeast: Alabama, Florida, Georgia, Kentucky, Mississippi, North Carolina, South Carolina, and Tennessee. North Central: Illinois, Indiana, Iowa, Kansas, Minnesota, Missouri, Nebraska, North Dakota, Ohio, South Dakota, and Wisconsin. Southwest: Arkansas, Louisiana, Oklahoma, and Texas. Rocky Mountain: Arizona, Colorado, Idaho, New Mexico, Montana, Utah, and Wyoming. Far West: Alaska, California, Hawaii, Nevada, Oregon, and Washington.

Source: United States Department of Agriculture, Agricultural Marketing Service, *National Farmers Market Manager Survey 2006*, May 2009, <http://www.ams.usda.gov/AMSv1.0/FARMERSMARKETS>.

Table 868. Horticultural Specialty Crop Operations, Value of Sales, and Total land Area Used to Grow Horticultural Crops: 2009

[Horticultural specialty operation is defined as any place that produced and sold $10,000 or more of horticultural specialty products]

Item	Operations	Value of sales (1,000)	Total land area [1]			
			Green-houses (1,000 square feet)	Shade structures (1,000 square feet)	Natural shade (acres)	Area in open (acres)
Horticultural specialty crops, total [2]	**21,585**	**11,687,323**	**859,063**	**406,072**	**8,160**	**572,269**
Annual bedding/garden plants	7,989	2,305,913	258,823	13,858	140	6,815
Herbaceous perennial plants	6,416	843,788	27,101	4,330	314	3,981
Potted flowering plants for indoor or patio use	4,043	871,474	62,208	23,893	41	1,693
Foilage plants for indor or patio use	2,728	509,873	39,583	76,645	144	2,314
Cut flowers	1,703	403,254	53,495	14,248	76	12,068
Cut cultivated greens	634	84,148	5,443	152,512	2,835	2,998
Nursery stock sold	8,441	3,850,363	217,482	87,228	4,184	323,539
Propagative material [3]	1,178	601,657	29,733	3,208	53	8,169
Sod, sprigs, or plugs	1,403	876,847	419	36	(D)	85,842
Dried bulbs, corms, rhizomes, and tubers	223	48,512	183	(D)	(D)	3,736
Food crops grown under protection	1,476	553,270	61,324	1,562	19	5,863
Transplants for commercial vegetable production [4]	502	330,647	32,095	467	4	7,250
Vegetable seeds	340	89,031	163	(D)	–	38,819
Flower seeds	141	30,825	289	308	2	5,695
Aquatic plants	375	26,000	1,373	134	1	1,320
Cut Christmas trees	2,699	249,821	1,010	95	84	45,091
Other	212	11,901	68,340	27,519	227	17,075

D Withheld to avoid disclosure. – Represents zero [1] Total land area represents the land utilized on the operation as the area used for horticultural production. Includes volume of stacked benches and stacked pots and the area used to produce multiple crop types. [2] Excludes acres in production for Christmas trees or sod, sprigs, or plugs. [3] Includes cuttings, plug seedlings, liners, tissue cultured plantlets, and prefinisshed plants. [4] Includes strawberries.

Source: U.S. Department of Agriculture, National Agricultural Statistics Service, 2009 Census of Horticultural Specialties, Vol. 3, AC-07-SS-3. See also <http://www.agcensus.usda.gov/Publications/2007/Online_Highlights/Census_of_Horticulture/index.asp.

Table 869. Meat Supply and Use: 2000 to 2010

[In millions of pounds (carcass weight equivalent) (82,372 represents 82,372,000,000). Carcass weight equivalent is the weight of the animal minus entrails, head, hide, and internal organs; includes fat and bone. Covers federal and state inspected, and farm slaughtered]

Year and type of meat	Production	Imports	Supply [1]	Exports	Consump-tion [2]	Ending stocks
RED MEAT AND POULTRY						
2000.	82,372	4,136	88,480	9,344	77,067	2,069
2005.	86,781	4,846	93,807	9,275	82,334	2,199
2007.	42,143	4,298	91,608	11,203	84,008	2,151
2008.	93,460	3,646	91,520	14,352	82,590	2,451
2009.	90,493	3,735	89,659	13,498	81,327	1,994
2010.	91,639	3,439	89,524	13,977	81,120	2,114
ALL RED MEATS						
2000.	46,299	4,127	51,340	3,760	46,559	1,021
2005.	45,846	4,804	51,837	3,373	47,385	1,080
2007.	48,683	4,223	48,434	4,585	48,434	1,169
2008.	50,225	3,553	47,211	6,566	47,211	1,307
2009.	49,274	3,631	47,191	6,046	47,191	1,114
2010.	49,050	3,321	45,937	6,542	45,937	1,145
Beef:						
2000.	26,888	3,032	30,332	2,468	27,338	525
2005.	24,952	3,598	29,191	697	27,919	575
2007.	26,523	3,052	30,205	1,434	28,141	630
2008.	26,664	2,538	29,832	1,887	27,303	642
2009.	26,068	2,626	29,336	1,935	26,836	565
2010.	26,419	2,297	29,281	2,299	26,397	585
Pork:						
2000.	18,952	965	20,406	1,287	18,642	478
2005.	20,706	1,025	22,274	2,665	19,115	494
2007.	21,962	968	23,424	3,141	19,763	519
2008.	23,367	832	24,717	4,667	19,415	635
2009.	23,020	834	24,489	4,095	19,870	525
2010.	22,458	859	23,842	4,227	19,074	541
Veal:						
2000.	225	(NA)	230	(NA)	225	5
2005.	165	(NA)	169	(NA)	164	5
2007.	146	(NA)	152	(NA)	145	7
2008.	152	(NA)	159	(NA)	150	9
2009.	147	(NA)	156	(NA)	147	9
2010.	142	(NA)	151	(NA)	147	4
Lamb and mutton:						
2000.	234	130	372	5	354	13
2005.	191	180	374	9	355	10
2007.	189	203	407	18	385	13
2008.	180	183	376	18	343	21
2009.	177	171	369	18	338	15
2010.	171	165	351	18	320	15
POULTRY, TOTAL						
2000.	36,073	9	37,140	5,584	30,508	1,048
2005.	40,935	42	41,970	5,902	34,949	1,119
2007.	42,143	75	43,174	6,618	35,574	982
2008.	43,235	92	44,309	7,785	35,379	1,144
2009.	41,220	104	42,468	7,452	34,136	880
2010.	42,589	118	43,586	7,435	35,182	969
Broilers:						
2000.	30,209	6	31,011	4,918	25,295	798
2005.	34,987	33	35,721	5,203	29,608	910
2007.	35,772	61	36,565	5,904	29,942	719
2008.	36,511	79	37,309	6,961	29,603	745
2009.	35,131	86	35,961	6,818	28,527	616
2010.	36,516	98	37,230	6,773	29,684	773
Mature chicken:						
2000.	531	2	540	220	311	9
2005.	516	1	520	130	388	2
2007.	498	3	508	159	337	2
2008.	559	3	566	159	415	3
2009.	500	3	509	159	406	2
2010.	503	3	508	159	425	4
Turkeys:						
2000.	5,333	1	5,589	445	4,902	241
2005.	5,432	7	5,728	569	4,952	207
2007.	5,873	10	6,101	547	5,294	261
2008.	6,165	8	6,434	676	5,361	396
2009.	5,589	13	5,998	534	5,202	262
2010.	5,569	17	5,848	583	5,073	192

NA Not available. [1] Total supply equals production plus imports plus ending stocks of previous year. [2] Includes shipments to territories.

Source: U.S. Department of Agriculture, Economic Research Service, *Food Consumption, Prices, and Expenditures, 1970–1997* and "Agricultural Outlook: Statistical Indicators," <http://www.ers.usda.gov/publications/agoutlook/aotables/>.

Agriculture 555

Table 870. Livestock Inventory and Production: 1990 to 2010

[95.8 represents 95,800,000. Production in live weight; includes animals-for-slaughter market, younger animals shipped to other states for feeding or breeding purposes, farm slaughter and custom slaughter consumed on farms where produced, minus livestock shipped into states for feeding or breeding with an adjustment for changes in inventory]

Type of livestock	Unit	1990	1995	2000	2004	2005	2006	2007	2008	2009	2010
ALL CATTLE [1]											
Inventory: [2] Number on farms ...	Mil........	95.8	102.8	98.2	94.4	95.0	96.3	96.6	96.0	93.9	92.6
Total value............	Bil. dol.....	59.0	63.2	67.1	77.2	87.0	97.2	89.1	95.1	82.4	78.2
Value per head	Dol.	616	615	683	818	916	1,009	922	990	872	832
Production: Quantity	Bil. lb......	39.2	42.5	43.0	41.6	41.2	41.8	41.4	41.6	41.2	41.6
Beef, price per 100 pounds..........	Dol.	74.60	61.80	68.60	85.80	89.70	87.20	89.90	89.10	80.30	105.00
Calves, price per 100 pounds..........	Dol.	95.60	73.10	104.00	119.00	135.00	133.00	119.00	110.00	105.00	117.00
Value of production.....	Bil. dol.....	29.3	24.7	28.5	34.9	36.3	35.5	36.0	35.6	32.0	37.0
HOGS AND PIGS											
Inventory: [3] Number on farms ...	Mil........	53.8	59.7	59.3	60.5	61.0	61.5	62.5	68.2	67.1	64.6
Total value............	Bil. dol.....	4.3	3.2	4.3	4.0	6.3	5.8	5.6	5.0	5.4	6.8
Value per head	Dol.	79	53	72	67	103	95	90	73	83	106
Production: Quantity	Bil. lb......	21.3	24.4	25.7	26.7	27.4	28.2	29.6	31.4	31.4	30.4
Price per 100 pounds ...	Dol.	53.70	40.50	42.30	49.30	50.20	46.00	46.60	47.00	41.60	54.10
Value of production.....	Bil. dol.....	11.3	9.8	10.8	13.1	13.6	12.7	13.5	14.5	12.6	16.1
SHEEP AND LAMBS											
Inventory: [2] Number on farms ...	Mil........	11.4	9.0	7.0	6.1	6.1	6.2	6.1	6.0	5.7	5.6
Total value............	Mil. dol.....	901	663	670	720	798	872	818	823	765	761
Value per head	Dol.	79	75	95	119	130	141	134	138	133	135
Production: Quantity	Mil. lb.....	781	602	512	466	472	461	440	417	422	405
Value of production.....	Mil. dol.....	374	414	365	413	451	368	363	351	365	443

[1] Includes milk cows. [2] As of January 1. [3] As of December 1 of preceding year.

Source: U.S. Department of Agriculture, National Agricultural Statistics Service, *Meat Animals—Production, Disposition, and Income Final Estimates 1998–2002*, May 2004; *Meat Animals—Production, Disposition, and Income Final Estimates 2003–2007*, May 2009; *Meat Animals Production, Disposition, and Income 2010 Summary*, April 2011. See also <http://www.nass.usda.gov/Publications/index.asp>.

Table 871. Livestock Operations by Size of Herd: 2000 to 2010

[In thousands(1,076 represents 1,076,000). An operation is any place having one or more head on hand at any time during the year]

Size of herd	2000	2005	2009	2010	Size of herd	2000	2005	2009	2010
CATTLE [1]					MILK COWS [2]				
Total operations.....	1,076	983	946	935	Total operations.....	105	78	65	63
1 to 49 head.........	671	612	641	635	1 to 49 head.........	53	37	32	31
50 to 99 head........	186	164	131	129	50 to 99 head........	31	23	17	16
100 to 499 head......	192	178	144	141	100 head or more	21	15	16	16
500 to 999 head......	19	19	19	19					
1,000 head or more....	10	10	11	11	HOGS AND PIGS				
					Total operations.....	87	67	71	69
BEEF COWS [2]					1 to 99 head..........	50	41	50	49
Total operations.....	831	770	751	742	100 to 499 head.......	17	10	6	5
1 to 49 head.........	655	597	596	588	500 to 999 head.......	8	5	3	3
50 to 99 head........	100	95	82	82	1,000 to 1,999 head....	6	4	4	4
100 to 499 head......	71	73	67	66	2,000 to 4,999 head....	5	5	5	5
500 head or more	6	5	6	6	5,000 head or more....	2	2	3	3

[1] Includes calves. [2] Included in operations with cattle.

Source: U.S. Department of Agriculture, National Agricultural Statistics Service, *Livestock Operations Final Estimates 2003–2007*, March 2009; *Farms, Land in Farms, and Livestock Operations 2010 Summary*, February 2011. See also <http://www.nass.usda.gov/Publications/index.asp>.

Table 872. Hogs and Pigs—Number, Production, and Slaughter by States: 2008 to 2010

[Production in live weight (67,148 represents 67,148,000). See headnote Table 870]

State	Number on farms [1] (1,000)			Quantity produced (mil. lb.)			Value of production (mil. dol.)			Commercial slaughter [2] (mil. lb.)	
	2008	2009	2010	2008	2009	2010	2008	2009	2010	2009	2010
U.S [3]........	67,148	64,887	64,625	31,411	31,359	30,391	14,457	12,590	16,073	30,723	30,005
IA...........	19,900	19,000	19,000	9,428	9,608	9,255	4,040	3,580	4,527	8,682	8,144
NC..........	9,700	9,600	8,900	4,210	4,071	3,777	2,120	1,824	2,183	3,219	3,069
MN..........	7,500	7,200	7,700	3,777	3,678	3,697	1,763	1,257	1,853	2,592	2,692
IL...........	4,350	4,250	4,350	1,711	1,839	1,939	917	908	1,128	2,674	2,582
IN...........	3,550	3,600	3,650	1,726	1,739	1,754	818	728	901	2,256	2,265
NE..........	3,350	3,100	3,150	1,385	1,360	1,353	715	626	804	2,068	2,064
MO..........	3,150	3,100	2,900	1,747	1,694	1,275	765	674	705	2,229	2,196

[1] As of December 1. [2] Includes slaughter in federally inspected and other slaughter plants; excludes animals slaughtered on farms. [3] Includes other states, not shown separately.

Source: U.S. Department of Agriculture, National Agricultural Statistics Service, *Meat Animals Production, Disposition and Income 2010 Summary*, April 2011, and *Livestock Slaughter 2010 Summary*, April 2011. See also <http://www.nass.usda.gov/Publications/index.asp>.

Table 873. Cattle and Calves—Number, Production, and Value by State: 2008 to 2010

[94,521 represents 94,521,000. Includes milk cows. See headnote, Table 870]

State	Number on farms [1] (1,000)			Production (mil. lb.)			Value of production (mil. dol.)			Commercial slaughter [2] (mil. lb.)	
	2009	2010	2011	2008	2009	2010	2008	2009	2010	2009	2010
U.S. [3]	94,521	93,881	92,582	41,594	41,161	41,574	35,608	31,990	36,976	42,966	43,662
TX	13,600	13,300	13,300	7,280	6,924	6,790	6,449	5,481	6,097	8,208	8,179
NE	6,350	6,300	6,200	4,622	4,615	4,553	4,203	3,746	4,137	9,104	9,109
KS	6,300	6,000	6,300	3,892	3,916	4,090	3,321	2,965	3,444	8,175	8,347
OK	5,400	5,500	5,100	2,036	2,149	2,216	1,939	1,890	2,178	30	26
CO	2,600	2,600	2,650	1,783	1,817	1,718	1,737	1,598	1,763	3,119	3,269
IA	3,950	3,850	3,900	1,845	1,787	1,814	1,606	1,437	1,677	(4)	(4)
SD	3,700	3,800	3,700	1,490	1,471	1,481	1,401	1,326	1,559	(4)	(4)
CA	5,250	5,150	5,150	1,968	1,899	1,979	1,353	1,099	1,345	2,109	2,204
MO	4,250	4,150	3,950	1,394	1,348	1,253	1,275	1,170	1,247	108	77
MT	2,600	2,550	2,500	970	965	1,112	870	777	1,042	27	25
ID	2,110	2,170	2,200	1,140	1,047	1,171	936	800	1,028	390	346

[1] As of January 1. [2] Data cover cattle only. Includes slaughter in federally inspected and other slaughter plants; excludes animals slaughtered on farms. [3] Includes other states, not shown separately. [4] Included in U.S. total. Not printed to avoid disclosing individual operation.

Source: U.S. Department of Agriculture, National Agricultural Statistics Service, *Meat Animals—Production, Disposition and Income 2010 Summary*, April 2011, and *Livestock Slaughter 2010 Summary*, April 2011, annual. See also <http://www.nass.usda.gov/Publications/index.asp>.

Table 874. Milk Cows—Number, Production, and Value by State: 2008 to 2010

[9,315 represents 9,315,000]

State	Number on farms [1] (1,000)			Milk produced on farms [2] (mil. lb.)			Milk produced per milk cow [2]			Value of production [3] (mil. dol.)	
	2008	2009	2010	2008	2009	2010	2008	2009	2010	2009	2010
U.S [4]	9,315	9,203	9,117	189,982	189,334	192,819	20,395	20,573	21,149	24,473	31,526
CA	1,844	1,796	1,754	41,203	39,512	40,385	22,344	22,000	23,025	4,540	5,933
WI	1,252	1,257	1,262	24,472	25,239	26,035	19,546	20,079	20,630	3,306	4,192
NY	626	619	611	12,432	12,424	12,713	19,859	20,071	20,807	1,690	2,212
PA	549	545	541	10,575	10,551	10,734	19,262	19,360	19,841	1,519	1,964
ID	549	550	564	12,315	12,150	12,779	22,432	22,091	22,658	1,434	1,904
TX	418	423	413	8,416	8,840	8,828	20,134	20,898	21,375	1,176	1,510
MN	464	469	470	8,782	9,019	9,102	18,927	19,230	19,366	1,209	1,465
MI	350	355	358	7,763	7,968	8,327	22,180	22,445	23,260	1,068	1,416

[1] Average number during year. Represents cows and heifers that have calved, kept for milk; excluding heifers not yet fresh. [2] Excludes milk sucked by calves. [3] Valued at average returns per 100 pounds of milk in combined marketings of milk and cream. Includes value of milk fed to calves. [4] Includes other states, not shown separately.

Source: U.S. Department of Agriculture, National Agricultural Statistics Service, *Milk Production, Disposition, and Income 2010 Summary*, April 2011. See also <http://www.nass.usda.gov/Publications/index.asp>.

Table 875. Milk Production and Manufactured Dairy Products: 1990 to 2010

[193 represents 193,000]

Item	Unit	1990	2000	2004	2005	2006	2007	2008	2009	2010
Number of farms with milk cows	1,000	193	105	82	78	75	70	67	65	63
Cows and heifers that have calved, kept for milk [1]	Mil. head . . .	10.0	9.2	9.0	9.1	9.1	9.2	9.3	9.2	9.1
Milk produced on farms	Bil. lb.	148	167	171	177	182	186	190	189	193
Production per cow	1,000 lb.	14.8	18.2	19.0	19.6	19.9	20.2	20.4	20.6	21.1
Milk marketed by producers [1]	Bil. lb.	146	166	170	176	181	185	189	188	192
Value of milk produced	Bil. dol.	20.4	20.8	27.6	26.9	23.6	35.7	35.1	24.5	31.5
Cash receipts from marketing of milk and cream [1]	Bil. dol.	20.1	20.6	27.4	26.7	23.4	35.5	34.8	24.3	31.4
Number of dairy manufacturing plants. . . .	Number	1,723	1,164	1,093	1,088	1,094	1,123	1,125	1,248	1,273
Manufactured dairy products:										
Butter (including whey butter)	Mil. lb..	1,302	1,256	1,247	1,347	1,448	1,533	1,644	1,572	1,564
Cheese, total [2]	Mil. lb..	6,059	8,258	8,873	9,149	9,525	9,777	9,913	10,074	10,436
American (excl. full-skim American) . . .	Mil. lb..	2,894	3,642	3,739	3,808	3,913	3,877	4,109	4,203	4,275
Cream and Neufchatel.	Mil. lb.	431	687	699	715	756	773	764	767	745
All Italian varieties	Mil. lb.	2,207	3,289	3,662	3,803	3,973	4,199	4,121	4,181	4,424
Cottage cheese—creamed and lowfat. . . .	Mil. lb..	832	735	788	784	778	774	714	731	720
Nonfat dry milk [3]	Mil. lb..	902	1,457	1,412	1,210	1,244	1,298	1,519	1,512	1,563
Dry whey [4]	Mil. lb..	1,143	1,188	1,035	1,041	1,110	1,134	1,082	1,001	1,013
Yogurt, plain and fruit-flavored	Mil. lb..	(NA)	1,837	2,707	3,058	3,301	3,476	3,570	3,839	4,181
Ice cream, regular	Mil. gal..	824	980	920	960	982	956	931	918	912
Ice cream, lowfat [5]	Mil. gal..	352	373	387	360	377	383	384	400	380

NA Not available. [1] Comprises sales to plants and dealers, and retail sales by farmers direct to consumers. [2] Includes varieties not shown separately. Beginning 1974, includes full-skim. [3] Includes dry skim milk for animal feed through 2000. [4] Includes animal but excludes modified whey production. [5] Includes freezer-made milkshake in most states.

Source: U.S. Department of Agriculture, National Agricultural Statistics Service, Milk Disposition and Income Final Estimates 2003-2007, May 2009; Dairy Products 2010 Summary, April 2011; and Milk Production, Disposition, and Income 2010 Summary, April 2011. See also <http://www.nass.usda.gov/Publications/index.asp>.

Agriculture 557

Table 876. Milk Production and Commercial Use: 1990 to 2010

[In billions of pounds milkfat basis (147.7 represents 147,700,000,000) except as noted]

Year	Produc-tion	Farm use	Commercial Farm market-ings	Commercial Begin-ning stock	Imports	Com-mercial supply, total	Commercial Commodity CreditCor-poration net removals [1]	Commercial Ending stock	Exports	Disap-pear-ance [2]	Milk price per 100 pounds [3] (dollars)
1990...	147.7	2.0	145.7	4.1	2.7	152.5	8.5	5.1	(NA)	138.8	13.68
2000...	167.4	1.3	166.1	6.1	4.4	176.7	0.8	6.9	(NA)	169.0	12.40
2005...	176.9	1.1	175.8	7.2	7.5	190.5	–	8.0	3.3	179.2	15.13
2007...	185.7	1.1	184.6	9.5	7.2	201.3	–	10.4	5.7	185.2	19.13
2008...	190.0	1.1	188.9	10.4	5.3	204.6	–	10.1	8.7	185.7	18.33
2009...	189.3	1.0	188.3	10.1	5.6	204.0	0.7	11.3	4.5	187.3	12.83
2010...	192.7	1.0	191.8	11.3	4.1	207.2	0.2	10.8	8.1	188.1	16.29

– Represents zero. NA Not available. [1] Removals from commercial supply by Commodity Credit Corporation (CCC) on a fat basis. [2] Prior to 2005, disappearance represents domestic disappearance plus exports. [3] Wholesale price received by farmers for all milk delivered to plants and dealers.

Source: U.S. Department of Agriculture, Economic Research Service, "Agricultural Outlook: Statistical Indicators," <http://www.ers.usda.gov/publications/agoutlook/aotables/>.

Table 877. Broiler, Turkey, and Egg Production: 1990 to 2010

[For year ending November 30 (353 represents 353,000,000), except as noted]

Item	Unit	1990	1995	2000	2004	2005	2006	2007	2008	2009	2010
Chickens: [1]											
Number [2].........	Million	353	388	437	454	456	458	459	447	452	455
Value per head [2] ...	Dollars	2.29	2.41	2.44	2.48	2.52	2.60	2.95	3.39	3.34	3.52
Value, total [2].......	Mil. dol....	808	935	1,064	1,126	1,150	1,190	1,352	1,517	1,508	1,600
Number sold	Million	208	180	218	192	194	174	168	176	176	172
Price per pound....	Cents.....	9.6	6.5	5.7	5.8	6.5	5.9	5.6	6.6	(NA)	(NA)
Value of sales	Mil. dol....	94	60	64	58	65	54	51	62	65	72
PRODUCTION											
Broilers: [3]											
Number	Million	5,864	7,326	8,284	8,741	8,872	8,868	8,907	9,009	8,550	8,625
Weight	Bil. lb......	25.6	34.2	41.6	45.8	47.9	48.8	49.3	50.4	47.8	49.2
Price per pound....	Cents.....	32.6	34.4	33.6	44.6	43.6	36.3	43.6	(NA)	(NA)	(NA)
Production value ...	Mil. dol....	8,366	11,762	13,989	20,446	20,878	17,739	21,514	23,203	21,823	23,696
Turkeys:											
Number	Million	282	292	270	256	250	256	267	273	247	244
Weight	Bil. lb......	6.0	6.8	7.0	6.9	7.0	7.2	7.6	7.9	7.1	7.1
Price per pound....	Cents.....	39.6	41.0	40.6	41.5	44.5	48.0	52.3	56.5	(NA)	(NA)
Production value ...	Mil. dol....	2,393	2,769	2,828	2,887	3,108	3,468	3,952	4,477	3,573	4,371
Eggs:											
Average number of layers...........	Thousand..	(NA)	294,350	327,908	342,395	345,027	349,700	346,498	339,131	337,848	339,961
Eggs per layer	Number ...	(NA)	254	257	261	262	263	263	266	268	269
Total production	Billion.....	68.1	74.8	84.4	89.2	90.3	91.8	91.1	90.0	90.5	91.4
Price per dozen	Cents.....	70.8	62.5	61.6	71.3	54.0	58.3	88.5	109.0	(NA)	(NA)
Production value ...	Mil. dol....	4,021	3,893	4,346	5,303	4,067	4,460	6,719	8,216	6,166	6,518

NA Not available. [1] Excludes commercial broilers. [2] As of December 1. [3] Young chickens of the heavy breeds and other meat-type birds, to be marketed at 2–5 lbs. live weight and from which no pullets are kept for egg production. Not included in sales of chickens.

Source: U.S. Department of Agriculture, National Agricultural Statistics Service, *Poultry Production and Value Final Estimates 1998–2002*, April 2004; *Turkeys Final Estimates 1998–2002*, April 2004; *Poultry Production and Value Final Estimates 2003–2007*, May 2009; *Chickens and Eggs Final Estimates 1998–2002*, April 2004; *Chickens and Eggs Final Estimates 2003–2007*, March 2009; and *Poultry—Production and Value 2010 Summary, and Chickens and Eggs 2010 Summary*, February 2011. See also <http://www.nass.usda.gov/Publications/index.asp>.

Table 878. Broiler and Turkey Production by State: 2008 to 2010

[In millions of pounds, live weight production (50,442 represents 50,442,000,000)]

State	Broilers 2008	Broilers 2009	Broilers 2010	Turkeys 2008	Turkeys 2009	Turkeys 2010	State	Broilers 2008	Broilers 2009	Broilers 2010	Turkeys 2008	Turkeys 2009	Turkeys 2010
U.S. [1]....	50,442	47,752	49,162	7,922	7,149	7,107	MS.......	4,876	4,602	4,766	(NA)	(NA)	(NA)
AL	5,846	5,513	5,787	(NA)	(NA)	(NA)	MO.......	(NA)	(NA)	(NA)	651	611	589
AR	6,380	5,780	5,938	611	568	549	NC.......	5,493	5,317	5,419	1,208	1,090	963
CA	(NA)	(NA)	(NA)	435	390	404	OH.......	328	338	377	230	203	178
DE	1,579	1,599	1,631	(NA)	(NA)	(NA)	OK.......	1,260	1,220	1,503	(NA)	(NA)	(NA)
FL	376	252	314	(NA)	(NA)	(NA)	PA	933	875	839	216	182	159
GA	7,469	6,874	6,883	(NA)	(NA)	(NA)	SC	1,516	1,522	1,557	478	433	430
IL	(NA)	(NA)	(NA)	(NA)	(NA)	(NA)	SD	(NA)	(NA)	(NA)	189	187	193
IN........	(NA)	(NA)	(NA)	519	543	573	TN	1,019	968	987	(NA)	(NA)	(NA)
IA........	(NA)	(NA)	(NA)	360	(NA)	(NA)	TX	3,461	3,611	3,647	(NA)	(NA)	(NA)
KY	1,653	1,658	1,674	(NA)	(NA)	(NA)	UT	(NA)	(NA)	(NA)	(NA)	82	103
MD.......	1,612	1,399	1,433	(NA)	(NA)	(NA)	VA	1,252	1,204	1,292	484	449	459
MI........	(NA)	(NA)	(NA)	(NA)	(NA)	(NA)	WV.......	351	331	346	102	97	90
MN.......	238	246	231	1,306	1,161	1,208	WI	217	192	199	(NA)	(NA)	(NA)

NA Not available. [1] Includes other states, not shown separately.

Source: U.S. Department of Agriculture, National Agricultural Statistics Service, *Poultry Production and Value Final Estimates 2003–2007*, May 2009, and *Poultry—Production and Value, 2010 Summary*, April 2011. See also <http://www.nass.usda.gov/Publications/index.asp>.

Section 18
Forestry, Fishing, and Mining

This section presents data on the area, ownership, production, trade, reserves, and disposition of natural resources. Natural resources is defined here as including forestry, fisheries, and mining and mineral products.

Forestry—Presents data on the area, ownership, and timber resource of commercial timberland; forestry statistics covering the National Forests and Forest Service cooperative programs; product data for lumber, pulpwood, woodpulp, paper and paperboard, and similar data.

The principal sources of data relating to forests and forest products are *Forest Resources of the United States, 2007; Timber Demand and Technology Assessment; U.S. Timber Production, Trade, Consumption, and Price Statistics, 1965– 2005; Land Areas of the National Forest System*, issued annually by the Forest Service of the U.S. Department of Agriculture; *Agricultural Statistics* issued by the Department of Agriculture; and reports of the annual survey of manufactures, and the annual *Current Industrial Reports,* issued by the U.S. Census Bureau on the Internet and in print in the annual *Manufacturing Profiles*. Additional information is published in the monthly *Survey of Current Business* of the Bureau of Economic Analysis, and the annual *Wood Pulp and Fiber Statistics* and *The Annual Statistics of Paper, Paperboard, and Wood Pulp* of the American Forest and Paper Association, Washington, DC.

The completeness and reliability of statistics on forests and forest products vary considerably. The data for forest land area and stand volumes are much more reliable for areas that have been recently surveyed than for those for which only estimates are available. In general, more data are available for lumber and other manufactured products such as particle board and softwood panels, etc., than for the primary forest products such as poles and piling and fuelwood.

Fisheries—The principal source of data relating to fisheries is *Fisheries of the United States*, issued annually by the National Marine Fisheries Service (NMFS), National Oceanic and Atmospheric Administration (NOAA). The NMFS collects and disseminates data on commercial landings of fish and shellfish. Annual reports include quantity and value of commercial landings of fish and shellfish disposition of landings and number and kinds of fishing vessels and fishing gear. Reports for the fish-processing industry include annual output for the wholesaling and fish processing establishments, annual and seasonal employment. The principal source for these data is the annual *Fisheries of the United States.*

Mining and mineral products—Presents data relating to mineral industries and their products, general summary measures of production and employment, and more detailed data on production, prices, imports and exports, consumption, and distribution for specific industries and products. Data on mining and mineral products may also be found in Sections 19, 21, and 28 of this *Abstract;* data on mining employment may be found in Section 12.

Mining comprises the extraction of minerals occurring naturally (coal, ores, crude petroleum, natural gas) and quarrying, well operation, milling, refining and processing, and other preparation customarily done at the mine or well site or as a part of extraction activity. (Mineral preparation plants are usually operated together with mines or quarries.) Exploration for minerals is included as is the development of mineral properties.

The principal governmental sources of these data are the *Minerals Yearbook* and *Mineral Commodity Summaries*, published by the U.S. Geological Survey, U.S. Department of the Interior, and various monthly and annual publications of the Energy Information Administration, U.S.

Department of Energy. See text, Section 19, for a list of Department of Energy publications. In addition, the Census Bureau conducts a census of mineral industries every 5 years.

Nongovernment sources include the *Annual Statistical Report* of the American Iron and Steel Institute, Washington, DC; *Metals Week* and the monthly *Engineering and Mining Journal*, issued by the McGraw-Hill Publishing Co., New York, NY; *The Iron Age*, issued weekly by the Chilton Co., Philadelphia, PA; and the *Joint Association Survey of the U.S. Oil and Gas Industry*, conducted jointly by the American Petroleum Institute, Independent Petroleum Association of America, and Mid-Continent Oil and Gas Association.

Mineral statistics, with principal emphasis on commodity detail, have been collected by the U.S. Geological Survey and the former Bureau of Mines since 1880. Current data in U.S. Geological Survey publications include quantity and value of nonfuel minerals produced, sold, or used by producers, or shipped; quantity of minerals stocked; crude materials treated and prepared minerals recovered; and consumption of mineral raw materials.

The Economic Census, conducted by the Census Bureau at various intervals since 1840, collects data on mineral industries. Beginning with the 1967 census, legislation provides for a census to be conducted every 5 years for years ending in "2" and "7." The most recent results, published for 2007, are based on the North American Industry Classification System (NAICS). The censuses provide, for the various types of mineral establishments, information on operating costs, capital expenditures, labor, equipment, and energy requirements in relation to their value of shipments and other receipts.

Figure 18.1
Crude Oil Production and Imports: 1990 to 2009

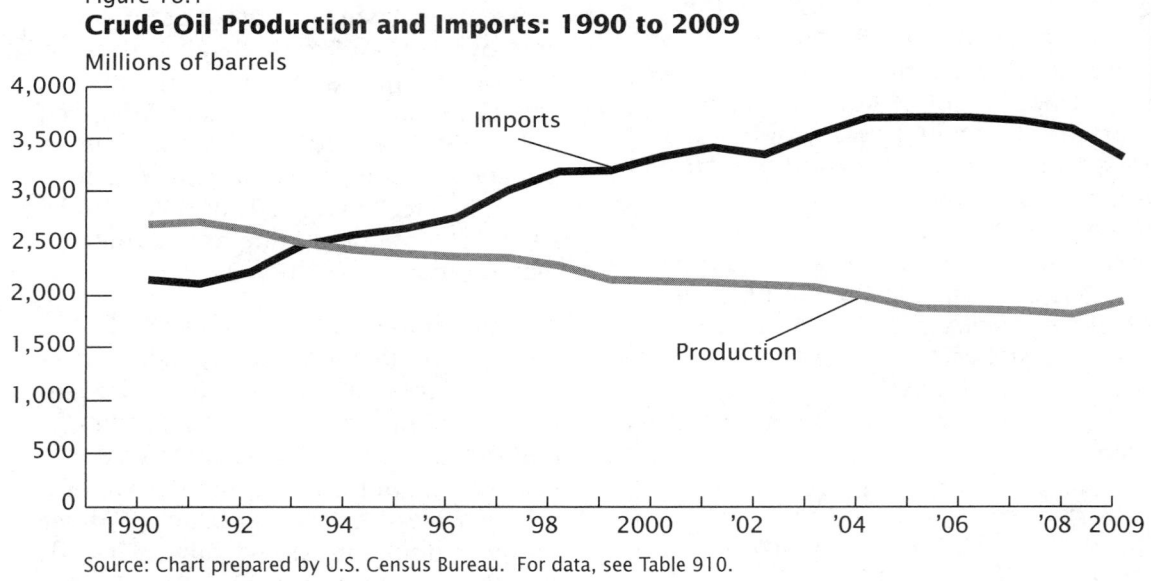

Source: Chart prepared by U.S. Census Bureau. For data, see Table 910.

U.S. Census Bureau, Statistical Abstract of the United States: 2012

Table 879. Natural Resource–Related Industries—Establishments, Sales, Payroll, and Employees by Industry: 2002 and 2007

[183 represents $183,000,000,000. Includes only establishments of firms with payroll. Data are based on the 2002 and 2007 economic censuses, which are subject to nonsampling error. For details on methodology and nonsampling and sampling errors, see Appendix III]

Industry	2002 NAICS code [1]	Establishments (number)		Value of shipments (bil. dol.)		Annual payroll (bil. dol.)		Paid employees [2] (1,000)	
		2002	2007	2002	2007	2002	2007	2002	2007
Mining............................	21	24,087	21,169	183	369	21	37	475	703
Oil & gas extraction.................	211	7,730	6,293	113	231	5	10	99	162
Mining (except oil & gas).............	212	7,253	6,465	48	81	9	11	196	220
Mining support activities.............	213	9,104	8,411	22	57	7	16	180	322
Manufacturing [3].....................	31–33	350,728	293,919	3,915	5,339	568	612	15	13
Wood product mfg...................	321	17,192	14,862	89	102	16	17	540	520
Paper mfg.........................	322	5,520	4,803	154	176	21	21	491	417
Petroleum & coal products manufacturing....	324	2,268	2,284	216	606	6	8	104	105

[1] North American Industry Classification System, 2002. [2] For pay period including March 12. [3] Includes other industries, not shown separately.

Source: U.S. Census Bureau, 2007 Economic Census, "Comparative Statistics," March 2009, <http://www.census.gov/econ/census07/www/get_data.html>.

Table 880. Natural Resource–Related Industries—Establishments, Employees, and Annual Payroll by Industry: 2000 and 2008

[1,791.3 represents 1,791,300. Excludes most government employees, railroad employees, self-employed persons, etc. See "General Explanation" in source for definitions and statement on reliability of data. An establishment is a single physical location where business is conducted or where services or industrial operations are performed. See Appendix III]

Industry	2002 NAICS Code [1]	Establishments (number)		Number of employees [2] (1,000)		Annual payroll (bil. dol.)	
		2000	2008	2000	2008	2000	2008
Natural resource–related industries, total......	(X)	**72,932**	**71,228**	**1,791.3**	**1,700.5**	**66.58**	**90.28**
Forestry, fishing, hunting, and agriculture support....	11	26,076	22,651	183.6	167.0	4.68	5.61
Forestry and logging........................	113	13,347	9,741	83.1	61.3	2.26	2.19
Timber tract operations......................	1131	469	430	3.3	2.6	0.13	0.15
Forest nurseries and gathering forest products....	1132	258	226	1.7	2.2	0.07	0.09
Logging..................................	1133	12,620	9,085	78.1	56.5	2.06	1.96
Fishing, hunting and trapping.................	114	2,671	2,292	10.0	7.5	0.34	0.36
Fishing..................................	1141	2,308	1,978	7.5	5.6	0.27	0.30
Hunting and trapping........................	1142	363	314	2.5	1.9	0.08	0.06
Agriculture and forestry support activities.........	115	10,058	10,618	90.4	98.2	2.08	3.06
Crop production support activities..............	1151	5,061	4,560	57.6	66.1	1.35	2.06
Animal production support activities............	1152	3,450	4,333	18.2	20.5	0.38	0.60
Forestry support activities....................	1153	1,547	1,725	14.7	11.7	0.35	0.40
Mining, quarrying and oil, and gas extraction.......	21	23,738	27,440	456.1	629.3	22.09	47.54
Oil and gas extraction........................	211	7,740	7,993	83.0	107.1	5.39	12.15
Mining (except oil and gas)...................	212	7,231	6,935	204.3	205.7	9.34	13.08
Coal mining...............................	2121	1,253	1,108	70.7	81.9	3.54	5.80
Metal ore mining...........................	2122	522	324	34.8	33.3	1.72	2.57
Nonmetallic mineral mining and quarrying.......	2123	5,456	5,503	98.8	90.4	4.08	4.71
Mining support activities.....................	213	8,767	12,512	168.8	316.5	7.35	22.30
Timber–related manufacturing..................	(X)	23,118	21,137	1,151.6	904.2	39.80	37.13
Wood product manufacturing..................	321	17,328	16,260	597.7	491.3	16.51	15.85
Sawmills and wood preservation...............	3211	4,695	3,902	131.4	103.5	3.78	3.47
Veneer, plywood and engineered wood product manufacturing...........................	3212	1,904	1,919	120.6	95.2	3.75	3.34
Other wood product manufacturing.............	3219	10,729	10,439	345.8	292.7	8.95	9.04
Paper manufacturing........................	322	5,790	4,877	553.9	412.9	23.29	21.29
Pulp, paper and paperboard mills..............	3221	597	504	177.1	123.4	9.48	8.16
Converted paper product manufacturing.........	3222	5,193	4,373	376.8	289.5	13.82	13.13

X Not applicable. [1] 2000 data based on North American Industry Classification System (NAICS), 2002. 2008 data based on 2007 NAICS. [2] Covers full- and part-time employees who are on the payroll in the pay period including March 12.

Source: U.S. Census Bureau, "County Business Patterns," July 2010, <http://www.census.gov/econ/cbp/index.html>.

Forestry, Fishing, and Mining 561

Table 881. Timber–Based Manufacturing Industries—Establishments, Shipments, Payroll, and Employees: 2007

[107,711,917 represents $107,711,917,000. Includes only establishments or firms with payroll. Data for industries with NAICS codes less than 6–digits were derived by summing values with the corresponding 6–digit NAICS codes. See Appendix III]

Industry	2007 NAICS code [1]	Establish-ments (number)	Value of shipments ($1,000)	Annual payroll ($1,000)	Paid employees [2]
Wood product manufacturing.	321	16,868	101,711,917	17,426,832	523,899
Sawmills and wood preservation.	3211	4,102	27,911,240	3,642,165	103,413
Sawmills	321113	3,589	22,075,666	3,144,796	90,044
Wood preservation.	321114	513	5,835,574	497,369	13,369
Veneer, plywood, and engineered wood product manufacturing	3212	1,958	22,258,829	3,829,184	106,848
Other wood product manufacturing.	3219	10,810	51,777,100	9,993,940	314,393
Millwork	32191	4,713	28,300,862	5,201,356	153,739
Wood container and pallet manufacturing	32192	2,909	7,235,876	1,519,970	58,467
All other wood product manufacturing.	32199	3,151	16,339,726	3,274,866	102,353
Paper manufacturing.	322	4,988	176,687,641	20,858,769	418,241
Pulp, paper, and paperboard mills.	3221	486	80,550,214	7,925,398	125,483
Pulp mills.	32211	39	5,027,395	504,602	7,268
Paper mills.	32212	262	49,732,085	4,919,950	80,838
Paperboard mills	32213	187	25,354,745	2,451,849	36,641
Converted paper product manufacturing.	3222	4,502	96,137,427	12,933,371	292,758
Paperboard container manufacturing	32221	2,402	50,900,190	7,387,042	165,839
Paper bag and coated and treated paper manufacturing.	32222	891	21,737,348	2,798,096	60,373
Stationery product manufacturing	32223	549	8,242,007	1,197,456	31,628
Other converted paper product manufacturing	32229	654	15,024,475	1,545,024	34,780

[1] North American Industry Classification System, 2007. [2] For pay period including March 12.

Source: U.S. Census Bureau, 2007 Economic Census, "Economy–Wide Key Statistics," August 2010. See also <http://www.census.gov/econ/census07/>.

Table 882. Timber-Based Manufacturing Industries—Employees, Payroll, and Shipments: 2009

[In thousands (11,051 represents 11,051,000). Based on the Annual Survey of Manufactures; see Appendix III]

Selected industry	2007 NAICS code [1]	All employees Number (1,000)	Payroll Total (mil. dol.)	Payroll Per employee (dol.)	Produc-tion workers, total (1,000)	Value added by manufactures Total (mil. dol.)	Value added by manufactures Per produc-tion worker (dol.)	Value of ship-ments (mil. dol.)
Manufacturing, all industries [2]	31–33	**11,051**	**534,262**	**48,344**	**7,571**	**1,978,017**	**261,261**	**4,436,196**
Timber-based manufacturing, total.	321–322	**716**	**30,867**	**43,102**	**564**	**102,431**	**181,502**	**227,256**
Percent of total manufacturing. . . .	(X)	6.48	5.78	(X)	7.45	5.18	(X)	5.12
Wood product manufacturing.	321	352	11,994	34,043	281	25,900	92,129	65,440
Sawmills and wood preservation.	3211	76	2,761	36,415	63	6,025	96,273	18,882
Veneer, plywood, and engineered wood product.	3212	63	2,297	36,565	50	4,649	93,585	12,763
Other wood product.	3219	214	6,936	32,460	169	15,225	90,166	33,795
Millwork	32191	99	3,503	35,259	80	7,687	96,550	17,361
Wood container and pallet.	32192	47	1,302	27,472	38	2,763	72,352	5,894
All other wood products.	32199	67	2,130	31,837	51	4,776	93,534	10,540
Paper manufacturing	322	364	18,873	51,875	283	76,531	270,209	161,816
Pulp, paper, and paperboard mills. . . .	3221	113	7,509	66,179	91	39,529	435,405	74,495
Pulp mills.	32211	7	465	71,378	5	1,859	348,240	4,323
Paper mills.	32212	72	4,678	64,811	59	25,704	438,369	47,066
Paperboard mills	32213	35	2,367	68,042	27	11,966	446,281	23,106
Converted paper product.	3222	250	11,364	45,392	192	37,003	192,278	87,322
Paperboard container.	32221	143	6,510	45,576	110	18,413	166,891	47,269
Paper bag and coated and treated paper.	32222	50	2,372	47,015	38	8,159	214,800	18,288
Stationery product.	32223	25	974	38,771	19	2,587	134,440	6,942
Other converted paper products	32229	32	1,507	47,211	25	7,844	315,157	14,823

X Not applicable. [1] North American Industry Classification System, 2007; see text, Section 15. [2] Includes other industries, not shown separately.

Source: U.S. Census Bureau, "Annual Survey of Manufactures, 2009," March 2011, <http://www.census.gov/manufacturing /asm/index.html>.

Table 883. Gross Domestic Product of Natural Resource-Related Industries in Current and Real (2005) Dollars by Industry: 2000 to 2010

[In billions of dollars (9,951.5 represents $9,951,500,000,000). Data are based on the 2002 North American Industry Classification System (NAICS); see text, Section 15. Data include nonfactor charges (capital consumption allowances, indirect business taxes, etc.) as well as factor charges against gross product; corporate profits and capital consumption allowances have been shifted from a company to an establishment basis]

Industry	Current dollars				Chained (2005) dollars			
	2000	2005	2009	2010	2000	2005	2009	2010
All industries, total [1]	9,951.5	12,638.4	14,119.0	14,660.4	11,226.0	12,638.4	12,880.6	13,248.2
Industries covered....................	294.5	405.9	450.9	(NA)	427.3	405.9	469.4	(NA)
Percent of all industries...............	3.0	3.2	3.2	(NA)	3.8	3.2	3.6	(NA)
Agriculture, forestry, fishing, and hunting. . .	95.6	127.1	133.1	154.1	103.7	127.1	136.2	137.3
Farms	73.6	102.0	104.0	(NA)	83.5	102.0	108.5	(NA)
Forestry, fishing, and related activities. . . .	22.0	25.1	29.2	(NA)	20.5	25.1	26.8	(NA)
Mining	108.9	192.0	240.8	281.4	232.5	192.0	263.3	271.2
Oil and gas extraction..................	67.5	128.6	141.7	(NA)	155.0	128.6	199.6	(NA)
Mining, except oil and gas	27.8	36.3	48.9	(NA)	45.4	36.3	35.6	(NA)
Support activities for mining	13.7	27.2	50.2	(NA)	29.2	27.2	35.4	(NA)
Timber-related manufacturing	90.0	86.8	77.0	(NA)	91.1	86.8	69.9	(NA)
Wood products.....................	28.3	33.0	20.9	(NA)	32.8	33.0	27.7	(NA)
Paper products	61.7	53.8	56.1	(NA)	58.3	53.8	42.2	(NA)

NA Not available. [1] Includes industries not shown separately.

Source: U.S. Bureau of Economic Analysis, *Survey of Current Business*, May 2011. See also <http://www.bea.gov/industry/gdpbyind_data.htm> .

Table 884. Forest Land and Timberland by Type of Owner and Region: 2007

[In thousands of acres (751,228 represents 751,228,000). As of January 1. Forest land is land at least 10 percent stocked by forest trees of any size, including land that formerly had such tree cover and that will be naturally or artificially regenerated. The minimum area for classification of forest land is 1 acre or strips of timber with a crown width of at least 120 feet wide. Timberland is forest land that is producing or is capable of producing crops of industrial wood and that is not withdrawn from timber utilization by statute or administrative regulation]

Region	Forest land, total	Timberland					
		Total	Federal			State, county, and municipal	Private [1]
			Total	National forest	Other		
Total................	751,228	514,213	112,733	98,721	14,015	44,994	356,485
North	172,039	164,018	11,897	10,126	1,771	25,252	126,868
Northeast............	84,796	79,803	2,971	2,401	570	9,308	67,523
North Central..........	87,243	84,215	8,926	7,725	1,201	15,944	59,345
South................	214,644	204,030	17,164	12,225	4,940	7,880	178,986
Southeast	87,889	85,665	7,559	4,970	2,590	4,689	73,417
South Central.........	126,756	118,365	9,605	7,255	2,350	3,191	105,569
Rocky Mountains.........	150,661	70,968	48,612	45,386	3,228	3,185	19,169
Great Plains...........	5,757	5,287	1,294	1,056	239	198	3,795
Intermountain	144,905	65,681	47,318	44,330	2,989	2,987	15,374
Pacific Coast	213,883	75,197	35,060	30,984	4,076	8,677	31,462
Alaska	126,869	11,865	4,750	3,772	978	4,344	2,771
Pacific Northwest.......	52,449	43,489	20,403	17,937	2,466	3,704	19,383
Pacific Southwest [2]	34,565	19,843	9,907	9,275	632	629	9,308

[1] Includes Indian lands. [2] Includes Hawaii.

Source: U.S. Forest Service, "RPA Assessment Tables," 2007, <http://www.fs.fed.us/research/rpa/>.

U.S. Census Bureau, Statistical Abstract of the United States: 2012

Table 885. National Forest System Lands by State: 2010

[In thousands of acres (246,322 represents 246,322,000). As of September 30, 2010. Data do not include Delaware, District of Columbia, Iowa, Maryland, Massachusetts, New Jersey, or Rhode Island]

State	Total lands	National Forest System lands [1]	Other lands [2]	State	Total lands	National Forest System lands [1]	Other lands [2]
U.S.	**246,322**	**206,554**	**39,768**	NE	442	352	90
				NV	6,255	5,746	509
AL	1,288	670	618	NH	829	736	93
AK	24,358	21,956	2,402	NM	10,455	9,418	1,037
AZ	11,892	11,265	627	NY	16	16	–
AR	3,553	2,599	954	NC	3,166	1,256	1,910
CA	24,444	20,822	3,622	ND	1,110	1,106	4
CO	16,021	14,521	1,500	OH	834	241	593
CT	24	24	–	OK	815	461	354
FL	1,435	1,176	259	OR	17,582	15,688	1,894
GA	1,858	867	991	PA	743	513	230
HI	1	1	–	SC	1,379	631	748
ID	21,659	20,465	1,194	SD	2,369	2,017	352
IL	924	298	626	TN	1,276	718	558
IN	644	203	441	TX	1,994	755	1,239
KS	116	108	8	UT	9,213	8,207	1,006
KY	2,208	814	1,394	VT	823	400	423
LA	1,024	604	420	VA	3,223	1,664	1,559
ME	94	54	40	WA	10,114	9,289	825
MI	4,894	2,876	2,018	WV	1,897	1,044	853
MN	5,467	2,842	2,625	WI	2,023	1,534	489
MS	2,318	1,174	1,144	WY	9,707	9,242	465
MO	16,491	14,923	1,568	PR	56	28	28
MT	19,141	17,083	2,058	VI	147	147	–

– Represents zero. [1] National Forest System is a national significant system of federally owned units of forest, range, and related land consisting of national forests, purchase units, national grasslands, land utilization project areas, experimental forest areas, experimental range areas, designated experimental areas, other land areas; water areas, and interests in lands that are administered by USDA Forest Service or designated for administration through the Forest Service. [2] Other lands are lands within the unit boundaries in private, state, county, and municipal ownership and the federal lands over which the Forest Service has no jurisdiction. Also includes lands offered to the United States and approved for acquisition and subsequent Forest Service administration, but to which title has not yet been accepted by the United States.

Source: U.S. Forest Service. U.S. Timber Production, *Trade, Consumption, and Price Statistics,* Research Paper RP-FPL-637, and unpublished data. See also <http://www.treesearch.fs.fed.us/pubs/28972>.

Table 886. Timber Volume, Growth, and Removal on Timberland by Species, Group, and Region: 2007

[932,096 represents 932,096,000,000]

Region	Net volume [1]						Timber growth [4] (mil. cu. ft.)			Timber removals [5] (mil. cu. ft.)		
	Growing stock [2] (mil. cu. ft.)			Sawtimber [3] (bil. board ft.)								
	All species	Soft-woods	Hard-woods	All species	Soft-woods	Hard-woods	All species	Soft-woods	Hard-woods	All species	Soft-woods	Hard-woods
Total	**932,096**	**529,203**	**402,893**	**1,013**	**558**	**455**	**26,744**	**15,241**	**11,503**	**15,533**	**9,859**	**5,675**
North	248,007	55,866	192,141	268	60	209	6,576	1,489	5,087	2,820	677	2,143
Northeast	137,585	34,252	103,333	146	37	109	3,249	836	2,412	1,169	353	815
North Central	110,422	21,614	88,808	122	23	99	3,327	652	2,675	1,651	324	1,328
South	288,522	118,471	170,051	325	123	202	13,272	7,632	5,640	9,696	6,317	3,379
Southeast	126,747	56,722	70,025	143	58	84	6,115	3,876	2,239	4,306	2,961	1,345
South Central	161,775	61,749	100,026	182	64	118	7,157	3,756	3,401	5,391	3,357	2,034
Rocky Mountains	137,263	124,809	12,454	159	144	15	1,761	1,577	184	543	521	22
Great Plains	4,539	1,641	2,898	7	2	5	72	27	45	41	25	16
Intermountain	132,724	123,168	9,556	153	142	11	1,689	1,550	139	502	496	6
Pacific Coast	258,304	230,057	28,247	261	232	29	5,135	4,543	593	2,474	2,344	131
Alaska	31,998	29,125	2,873	34	31	3	248	130	118	66	59	7
Pacific Northwest	158,896	146,006	12,890	159	146	13	3,340	3,039	301	1,939	1,818	121
Pacific Southwest [6]	67,410	54,926	12,484	68	55	13	1,548	1,374	174	469	466	3

[1] As of January 1. [2] Live trees of commercial species meeting specified standards of quality or vigor. Cull trees are excluded. Includes only trees 5.0-inches in diameter or larger at 4 1/2 feet above ground. [3] Live trees of commercial species containing at least one 12-foot sawlog or two noncontiguous 8-foot logs, and meeting regional specifications for freedom from defect. Softwood trees must be at least 9.0 inches in diameter and hardwood trees must be at least 11.0-inches in diameter at 4 1/2 feet above ground. [4] The net increase in the volume of trees during a specified year. Components include the increment in net volume of trees at the beginning of the specific year surviving to its end, plus the net volume of trees reaching the minimum size class during the year, minus the volume of trees that died during the year, and minus the net volume of trees that became cull trees during the year. [5] The net volume of trees removed from the inventory during a specified year by harvesting, cultural operations such as timber stand improvement, or land clearing. [6] Includes Hawaii.

Source: U.S. Forest Service, "RPA Assessment Tables," 2007, <http://www.fs.fed.us/research/rpa/>.

Table 887. Timber Removals—Roundwood Product Output by Source and Species Group: 2006

[In million cubic feet (14,990 represents 14,990,000,000)]

Source and species group	Total	Sawlogs	Pulpwood	Veneer logs	Other products [1]	Fuelwood [2]
Total................	**14,990**	**7,179**	**4,394**	**1,211**	**798**	**1,408**
Softwoods............	9,948	5,289	2,634	1,068	479	477
Hardwoods...........	5,042	1,890	1,760	143	319	931
Growing stock [3]........	13,002	6,781	3,872	1,156	703	490
Softwoods............	8,897	5,030	2,345	1,020	417	86
Hardwoods...........	4,105	1,752	1,527	136	286	404
Other sources [4]........	1,988	398	522	55	95	918
Softwoods............	1,051	260	289	48	63	391
Hardwoods...........	937	138	233	7	33	526

[1] Includes such items as cooperage, pilings, poles, posts, shakes, shingles, board mills, charcoal, and export logs. [2] Downed and dead wood volume left on the ground after trees have been cut on timberland. [3] Includes live trees of commercial species meeting specified standards of quality or vigor. Cull trees are excluded. Includes only trees 5.0-inches in diameter or larger at 4 1/2 feet above the ground. [4] Includes salvable dead trees, rough and rotten trees, trees of noncommercial species, trees less than 5.0-inches in diameter at 4 1/2 feet above the ground, tops, and roundwood harvested from nonforest land (for example, fence rows).

Source: U.S. Forest Service, "RPA Assessment Tables," 2007, <http://www.fs.fed.us/research/rpa/>.

Table 888. Timber Products—Production, Foreign Trade, and Consumption by Type of Product: 1990 to 2010

[In millions of cubic feet, roundwood equivalent (15,577 represents 15,577,000,000)]

Type of Product	1990	1995	2000	2003	2004	2005	2006	2007	2008	2009	2010
Industrial roundwood:											
Domestic production.....	15,577	15,537	15,436	14,571	15,139	15,465	14,836	13,932	12,493	11,264	11,933
Softwoods............	10,968	10,191	10,201	10,290	10,710	11,002	10,413	9,566	8,389	7,213	7,302
Hardwoods...........	4,609	5,347	5,235	4,282	4,428	4,463	4,423	4,366	4,104	4,052	4,631
Imports...............	3,091	3,907	4,529	5,096	5,805	5,802	5,292	4,147	3,065	1,986	1,722
Exports..............	2,307	2,282	1,996	1,535	1,604	1,646	1,596	1,481	1,517	1,248	1,291
Consumption..........	16,361	17,161	17,969	18,132	19,339	19,622	18,841	16,598	14,041	12,002	13,279
Softwoods............	11,779	11,961	12,659	13,398	14,357	14,652	13,732	12,009	9,845	7,941	8,451
Hardwoods...........	4,582	5,200	5,310	4,734	4,983	4,970	4,799	4,589	4,197	4,062	4,728
Lumber:											
Domestic production....	7,317	6,815	7,199	7,131	7,510	7,889	7,552	6,964	5,928	5,020	4,800
Imports...............	1,909	2,522	2,845	3,193	3,704	3,737	3,415	2,743	1,922	1,336	1,440
Exports..............	589	460	428	347	348	389	390	359	345	272	224
Consumption..........	8,637	8,877	9,616	9,977	10,866	11,237	10,577	9,347	7,506	6,084	5,906
Plywood and veneer:											
Domestic production....	1,423	1,303	1,187	1,054	1,086	1,068	1,003	912	743	617	177
Imports...............	97	107	155	240	354	373	339	265	185	177	104
Exports..............	109	89	42	35	43	37	35	40	45	37	58
Consumption..........	1,410	1,321	1,300	1,259	1,397	1,403	1,308	1,136	882	757	780
Pulp products:											
Domestic production....	5,313	6,079	5,881	5,557	5,692	5,679	5,470	5,176	4,926	4,818	4,841
Imports...............	1,038	1,248	1,459	1,579	1,669	1,570	1,440	1,071	918	434	566
Exports..............	646	905	842	643	680	708	681	526	556	423	492
Consumption..........	5,704	6,422	6,498	6,493	6,680	6,541	6,229	5,721	5,288	4,829	4,915
Logs:											
Imports...............	4	13	68	80	73	114	94	67	35	29	32
Exports..............	674	451	331	356	366	345	339	350	313	321	407
Pulpwood chips, exports...	288	377	353	155	168	166	151	205	257	195	195
Fuelwood consumption....	3,019	2,937	2,561	1,515	1,540	1,550	1,555	1,605	1,510	1,400	1,134

Source: U.S. Forest Service, *U.S. Timber Production, Trade, Consumption, and Price Statistics*, Research Paper RP-FPL-637, and unpublished data. See also <http://www.treesearch.fs.fed.us/pubs/28972>.

Table 889. Selected Timber Products—Imports and Exports: 1990 to 2010

[In million board feet (13,063 represents 13,063,000,000), except as indicated]

Product	Unit	1990	1995	2000	2005	2006	2007	2008	2009	2010
IMPORTS [1]										
Lumber, total [2]	Mil. bd. ft.	13,063	17,524	19,906	25,738	23,037	18,906	13,042	9,172	6,101
From Canada.	Percent	91	97	92	85	86	89	72	54	93
Logs, total	Mil. bd. ft. [3] . . .	23	80	435	710	585	418	253	179	198
From Canada.	Percent	84	70	96	85	85	91	(NA)	(NA)	(NA)
Paper and board [4] . . .	1,000 tons . . .	12,195	14,292	17,555	20,438	20,293	18,634	16,872	12,133	11,546
Woodpulp	1,000 tons . . .	4,893	5,969	7,227	6,762	6,939	6,793	6,272	5,044	6,136
Plywood.	Mil. sq. ft. [5] . . .	1,687	1,951	2,917	6,325	6,324	4,969	3,722	2,778	3,350
EXPORTS										
Lumber, total [2]	Mil. bd. ft.	4,623	2,958	2,700	2,348	2,359	2,193	2,148	1,690	2,133
To: Canada.	Percent	14	22	26	28	28	27	27	27	26
Japan	Percent	28	33	12	3	4	4	5	4	–
Europe	Percent	15	17	19	15	16	16	5	7	–
Logs, total	Mil. bd. ft. [3] . . .	4,213	2,820	2,068	2,157	2,120	2,189	2,240	2,005	2,541
To: Canada.	Percent	9	25	41	54	52	34	33	32	27
Japan	Percent	62	61	45	27	26	26	28	28	16
China	Percent	9	1	–	4	5	7	9	12	30
Paper and board [4] . . .	1,000 tons . . .	5,163	7,621	10,003	13,434	13,349	14,582	12,907	12,569	13,185
Woodpulp	1,000 tons . . .	5,905	8,261	6,409	6,413	6,606	6,831	7,790	7,519	8,265
Plywood.	Mil. sq. ft. [5] . . .	1,766	1,517	754	568	749	501	621	473	418

– Represents zero. NA Not available. [1] Customs value of imports; see text, Section 28. [2] Includes railroad ties. [3] Log scale. [4] Includes paper and board products. Excludes hardboard. [5] 3/8 inch basis.

Source: U.S. Forest Service, *U.S. Timber Production, Trade, Consumption, and Price Statistics*, Research Paper RP-FPL-637, and unpublished data. See also <http://www.treesearch.fs.fed.us/pubs/28972>.

Table 890. Lumber Consumption by Species Group and End Use: 1995 to 2010

[In billion board feet (59.3 represents 59,300,000,000), except per capita in board feet. Per capita consumption based on estimated resident population as of July 1]

Item	1995	2000	2002	2003	2004	2005	2006	2007	2008	2009	2010
Consumption, total	**59.3**	**66.1**	**67.5**	**67.0**	**73.1**	**75.6**	**71.3**	**62.7**	**49.7**	**40.3**	**39.6**
Per capita.	225	240	235	230	249	255	238	208	163	131	129
SPECIES GROUP											
Softwoods	47.6	54.0	56.4	56.5	62.0	64.4	60.4	52.6	40.7	31.2	33.1
Hardwoods	11.7	12.2	11.1	10.5	11.1	11.2	10.9	10.2	9.0	9.1	6.5
END USE											
New housing	18.1	21.1	22.5	24.0	25.4	27.7	23.8	17.5	11.2	(NA)	(NA)
Residential upkeep and improvements . . .	15.0	15.3	16.4	16.2	17.6	18.3	18.6	17.8	16.1	(NA)	(NA)
New nonresidential construction [1]	4.7	5.5	4.8	4.4	4.5	4.7	5.2	4.9	5.2	(NA)	(NA)
Shipping.	6.9	7.6	7.1	7.0	7.7	8.1	8.6	7.9	6.8	(NA)	(NA)
Other [2]	7.2	8.7	9.9	9.8	13.2	11.3	9.8	10.0	6.0	(NA)	(NA)

NA Not available. [1] In addition to new construction, includes railroad ties laid as replacements in existing track and lumber used by railroads for railcar repair. [2] Includes upkeep and improvement of nonresidential buildings and structures; made-at-home projects, such as furniture, boats, and picnic tables; made-on-the-job items such as advertising and display structures; and miscellaneous products and uses.

Source: U.S. Forest Service, *U.S. Timber Production, Trade, Consumption, and Price Statistics*, Research Paper RP-FPL-637, and unpublished data. See also <http://www.treesearch.fs.fed.us/pubs/28972>.

Table 891. Selected Species—Stumpage Prices in Current and Constant (1996) Dollars: 2000 to 2010

[In dollars per 1,000 board feet. Stumpage prices are based on sales of sawtimber from national forests]

Species	Current dollars				Constant (1996) dollars [1]			
	2000	2005	2009	2010	2000	2005	2009	2010
Softwoods:								
Douglas fir [2]	433	321	(NA)	(NA)	397	260	(NA)	(NA)
Southern pine [3]	258	193	105	105	237	157	71	70
Sugar pine [4]	187	114	63	100	172	93	46	50
Ponderosa pine [4, 5]	155	103	38	30	142	84	25	22
Western hemlock [6]	46	70	(NA)	(NA)	42	57	(NA)	(NA)
Hardwoods:								
All eastern hardwoods [7]	341	415	(NA)	(NA)	313	337	(NA)	(NA)
Oak, white, red, and black [7]	258	329	(NA)	(NA)	237	267	(NA)	(NA)
Maple, sugar [8]	314	648	(NA)	(NA)	288	526	(NA)	(NA)

NA Not available. [1] Deflated by the producer price index, all commodities. [2] Western Washington and western Oregon. [3] Southern region. [4] Pacific Southwest region (formerly California region). [5] Includes Jeffrey pine. [6] Pacific Northwest region. [7] Eastern and Southern regions. [8] Eastern region.

Source: U.S. Forest Service, "RPA Assessment Tables," 2007, <http://www.fs.fed.us/research/rpa/>.

Table 892. Selected Timber Products—Producer Price Indexes: 1990 to 2010

[1982 = 100. For information about producer prices, see text, Section 14]

Product	1990	1995	2000	2005	2006	2007	2008	2009	2010
Lumber and wood products [1]	**129.7**	**178.1**	**178.2**	**196.5**	**194.4**	**192.4**	**191.3**	**182.8**	**192.7**
Lumber	124.6	173.4	178.8	198.6	188.6	174.7	163.5	149.4	167.3
Softwood lumber	123.8	178.5	178.6	203.6	189.4	170.5	156.3	141.4	160.9
Hardwood lumber	131.0	167.0	185.9	196.6	195.3	192.4	184.5	171.2	187.3
Millwork [1]	130.4	163.8	176.4	197.2	201.8	201.4	204.8	205.4	206.9
General millwork	132.0	165.4	178.0	196.1	201.3	203.9	207.7	210.3	211.1
Prefabricated structural members	122.3	163.5	175.1	206.9	206.6	189.5	189.0	181.1	185.7
Plywood	114.2	165.3	157.6	186.8	172.7	176.1	174.7	163.7	176.5
Softwood plywood	119.6	188.1	173.3	223.5	190.5	197.8	193.1	171.9	196.9
Hardwood plywood and related products	102.7	122.2	130.2	138.1	(NA)	(NA)	(NA)	(NA)	(NA)
Other wood products [1]	114.7	143.7	130.5	139.2	142.8	142.1	144.7	141.8	142.6
Boxes	119.1	145.0	155.2	164.9	167.2	170.3	174.6	176.5	183.1
Pulp, paper, and allied products [1]	**141.2**	**172.2**	**183.7**	**202.6**	**209.8**	**216.9**	**226.8**	**225.6**	**236.8**
Pulp, paper, and prod., excl. bldg. paper [1]	132.9	163.4	161.4	169.8	178.4	186.7	199.1	194.1	206.6
Woodpulp	151.3	183.2	145.3	138.0	144.1	161.5	171.4	150.2	186.0
Wastepaper	138.9	371.1	282.5	230.9	234.8	368.7	372.5	237.0	420.2
Paper [1]	128.8	159.0	149.8	159.6	167.4	169.3	184.3	179.6	182.2
Writing and printing papers	129.1	158.4	146.6	156.1	162.8	166.7	181.6	180.5	179.5
Newsprint	119.6	161.8	127.5	138.5	151.8	131.6	148.0	126.4	126.1
Paperboard	135.7	183.1	176.7	175.5	192.0	201.7	217.9	207.2	225.3
Converted paper and paperboard products [1]	135.2	157.0	162.7	176.1	184.1	187.8	199.2	202.9	208.7
Office supplies and accessories	121.4	134.9	133.8	143.1	146.2	151.0	158.3	158.9	159.8
Building paper & building board mill prods.	112.2	144.9	138.8	184.9	173.0	155.2	163.9	156.5	168.2

NA Not available. [1] Includes other products not shown separately.

Source: U.S. Bureau of Labor Statistics, *Producer Price Indexes*, monthly.

Table 893. Pulpwood Consumption, Woodpulp Production, and Paper and Board Production and Consumption: 1995 to 2010

[Revised to match data from American Forest and Paper Association and American Pulpwood Association]

Item	Unit	1995	2000	2004	2005	2006	2007	2008	2009	2010
Pulpwood consumption [1]	1,000 cords [2]	97,052	95,904	87,110	88,595	86,284	84,076	77,442	70,401	72,321
Woodpulp production [3]	1,000 tons	67,103	62,758	54,301	60,267	60,568	56,636	52,899	44,990	52,607
Paper and board: [4]										
Production	1,000 tons	89,509	94,491	83,612	91,031	91,800	91,570	87,619	71,219	82,469
Consumption or new supply [5]	1,000 tons	96,126	103,147	95,068	101,864	102,948	99,825	93,640	79,141	84,968
Per capita	Pounds	731	731	627	687	688	661	613	515	548

[1] Includes changes in stocks. [2] One cord equals 128 cubic feet. [3] Excludes defibrated and exploded woodpulp used for hard pressed board. [4] Excludes hardboard. [5] Production plus imports, minus exports (excludes products); changes in inventories not taken into account.

Source: U.S. Forest Service, *U.S. Timber Production, Trade, Consumption and Price Statistics*, Research Paper FP-FPL-637, and unpublished data. See also <http://www.treesearch.fs.fed.us/pubs/28972>.

Table 894. Paper and Paperboard—Production and New Supply: 1990 to 2009

[In millions of short tons (80.45 represents 80,450,000). 1 short ton = 2,000 lbs.]

Item	1990	1995	2000	2004	2005	2006	2007	2008	2009
Production, total	**80.45**	**91.33**	**96.05**	**93.41**	**92.61**	**93.72**	**92.96**	**88.45**	**79.06**
Paper, total	39.36	42.87	45.52	41.82	41.40	41.81	41.27	38.96	33.81
Paperboard, total	39.32	46.64	48.97	50.08	49.71	50.41	50.40	48.45	44.49
Unbleached kraft	20.36	22.70	21.80	22.67	22.58	23.41	23.54	22.17	20.55
Semichemical	5.64	5.66	5.95	6.53	6.41	6.22	6.16	5.82	5.21
Bleached kraft	4.40	5.30	5.44	5.65	5.66	5.71	5.81	5.71	5.29
Recycled	8.92	12.98	15.79	15.24	15.05	15.07	14.89	14.69	13.44
Wet machine board	0.15	0.15	0.06	0.05	0.05	0.05	0.03	0.02	(NA)
Building paper	0.81	0.81	0.64	0.58	0.57	0.56	0.54	0.44	(NA)
Insulating board	0.86	0.86	0.86	0.88	0.88	0.88	0.71	0.57	(NA)
New supply, all grades, excluding products	**87.68**	**98.16**	**105.02**	**103.74**	**101.81**	**101.69**	**98.85**	**91.99**	**80.62**
Paper, total	49.49	52.77	57.13	54.88	53.69	52.97	50.88	46.71	39.37
Newsprint	13.41	12.76	12.92	10.84	10.12	9.49	8.35	7.25	5.26
Printing/writing papers	25.46	29.55	32.99	32.68	31.99	31.78	31.05	28.06	23.03
Packaging and ind. conv. papers	4.72	4.24	4.27	4.14	4.05	4.10	4.07	4.05	3.66
Tissue	5.90	6.22	6.95	7.22	7.53	7.60	7.42	7.36	7.43
Paperboard, total	36.30	43.45	46.02	47.20	46.51	47.11	46.61	44.25	40.45
Construction and other	1.90	1.95	1.88	1.66	1.61	1.62	1.36	1.03	0.79

Source: American Forest and Paper Association, Washington, DC, *Monthly Statistical Summary of Paper, Paperboard and Woodpulp*.

Table 895. Fishery Products—Domestic Catch, Imports, and Disposition: 1990 to 2009

[Live weight, in millions of pounds (16,349 represents 16,349,000,000). For data on commercial catch for selected countries, see Table 1375, Section 30]

Item	1990	1995	2000	2004	2005	2006	2007	2008	2009
Total	**16,349**	**16,484**	**17,340**	**20,412**	**20,612**	**20,960**	**20,561**	**19,199**	**18,735**
For human food	12,662	13,584	14,738	17,648	18,147	18,594	18,253	17,037	16,474
For industrial use	3,687	2,900	2,599	2,765	2,382	2,366	2,308	2,163	2,263
Domestic catch	**9,404**	**9,788**	**9,069**	**9,683**	**9,707**	**9,483**	**9,309**	**8,325**	**7,867**
For human food	7,041	7,667	6,912	7,794	7,997	7,842	7,490	6,633	6,035
For industrial use	2,363	2,121	2,157	1,889	1,710	1,641	1,819	1,692	1,833
Imports [1]	**6,945**	**6,696**	**8,271**	**10,729**	**10,905**	**11,477**	**11,252**	**10,874**	**10,868**
For human food	5,621	5,917	7,828	9,854	10,158	10,752	10,763	10,404	10,439
For industrial use [2]	1,324	779	443	875	747	725	489	471	430
Exports [1]	**4,627**	**5,166**	**5,758**	**8,203**	**8,420**	**7,710**	**7,057**	**6,353**	**5,738**
For human food	3,832	4,175	4,587	6,462	6,385	6,250	5,761	5,253	4,760
For industrial use [2]	795	991	1,171	1,741	2,035	1,459	1,296	1,100	978
Disposition of domestic catch	**9,404**	**9,788**	**9,069**	**9,683**	**9,707**	**9,483**	**9,309**	**8,325**	**7,867**
Fresh and frozen	6,501	7,099	6,657	7,488	7,776	7,627	7,450	6,538	6,040
Canned	751	769	530	552	563	573	514	336	392
Cured	126	90	119	137	160	117	121	138	103
Reduced to meal, oil, etc.	2,026	1,830	1,763	1,506	1,208	1,166	1,224	1,313	1,332

[1] Excludes imports of edible fishery products consumed in Puerto Rico; includes landings of tuna caught by foreign vessels in American Samoa. [2] Fish meal and sea herring.

Source: U.S. National Oceanic and Atmospheric Administration, National Marine Fisheries Service, *Fisheries of the United States*, annual, September 2010. See also <http://www.st.nmfs.noaa.gov/st1/fus/fus09/index.html>.

Table 896. Fisheries—Quantity and Value of Domestic Catch: 1980 to 2009

[In millions of pounds (6,482 represents 6,482,000,000), except as noted]

Year	Quantity (mil. lbs. [1])			Value (mil. dol.)	Average price per lb. (cents)	Year	Quantity (mil. lbs. [1])			Value (mil. dol.)	Average price per lb. (cents)
	Total	For human food	For industrial products [2]				Total	For human food	For industrial products [2]		
1980	6,482	3,654	2,828	2,237	34.5	2002	9,397	7,205	2,192	3,092	32.9
1985	6,258	3,294	2,964	2,326	37.2	2003	9,507	7,521	1,986	3,347	35.2
1990	9,404	7,041	2,363	3,522	37.5	2004	9,683	7,794	1,889	3,756	38.8
1995	9,788	7,667	2,121	3,770	38.5	2005	9,707	7,997	1,710	3,942	40.6
1998	9,194	7,173	2,021	3,126	34.0	2006	9,483	7,842	1,641	4,024	42.4
1999	9,339	6,832	2,507	3,467	37.1	2007	9,309	7,490	1,819	4,192	45.0
2000	9,069	6,912	2,157	3,550	39.1	2008	8,325	6,633	1,692	4,383	52.6
2001	9,489	7,311	2,178	3,218	33.9	2009	7,867	6,035	1,833	3,882	49

[1] Live weight. [2] Meal, oil, solubles, shell products, bait, and animal food.

Source: U.S. National Oceanic and Atmospheric Administration, National Marine Fisheries Service, *Fisheries of the United States*, annual, September 2010. See also <http://www.st.nmfs.noaa.gov/st1/fus/fus09/index.html>.

Table 897. Domestic Fish and Shellfish Catch and Value by Major Species Caught: 2000 to 2009

[In thousands (9,068,985 represents 9,068,985,000)]

Species	Quantity (1,000 lbs.)				Value ($1,000)			
	2000	2005	2008	2009	2000	2005	2008	2009
Total [1]	**9,068,985**	**9,707,275**	**8,325,814**	**7,867,333**	**3,549,481**	**3,942,376**	**4,383,820**	**3,882,178**
Fish, total [1]	**7,689,661**	**8,462,473**	**7,258,070**	**6,601,850**	**1,594,815**	**1,836,448**	**2,235,300**	**1,843,808**
Cod: Atlantic	25,060	13,920	19,075	19,708	26,384	20,828	30,635	25,220
Pacific	530,505	548,746	493,952	491,143	142,330	150,738	274,160	133,714
Flounder	412,723	419,430	663,116	575,119	109,910	135,176	184,211	153,261
Halibut	75,190	76,263	66,923	59,716	143,826	177,593	217,735	139,415
Herring, Atlantic	160,269	215,565	173,217	224,328	9,972	20,467	21,306	26,564
Herring, Pacific	74,835	87,295	86,219	88,723	12,043	13,799	23,794	29,759
Menhaden	1,760,498	1,243,723	1,341,413	1,404,259	112,403	62,465	90,725	89,037
Pollock, Alaska	2,606,802	3,411,307	2,276,144	1,866,203	160,525	306,972	323,212	270,597
Salmon	628,638	899,457	658,342	705,202	270,213	330,699	394,595	370,052
Tuna	50,779	44,316	47,903	49,064	95,176	85,922	107,013	96,434
Whiting (Atlantic, silver)	26,855	16,561	13,845	17,131	11,370	8,284	7,547	8,659
Whiting (Pacific, hake)	452,718	569,381	531,418	253,062	18,809	29,145	58,559	14,105
Shellfish, total [1]	**1,379,324**	**1,244,802**	**1,035,042**	**1,227,646**	**1,954,666**	**2,105,928**	**2,122,284**	**2,015,992**
Clams	118,482	105,640	107,772	101,137	153,973	173,655	186,718	191,074
Crabs	299,006	299,137	325,184	326,217	405,006	415,057	562,267	485,372
Lobsters: American	83,180	88,032	81,835	96,890	301,300	416,597	306,177	299,512
Oysters	41,146	33,963	30,162	35,571	90,667	110,679	131,590	136,493
Scallops, sea	32,747	56,702	53,527	58,000	164,609	433,512	369,860	382,217
Shrimp	332,486	260,884	256,597	301,077	690,453	406,344	441,818	370,240
Squid, Pacific	259,508	126,107	82,704	203,661	27,077	31,601	25,569	56,450

[1] Includes other species not shown separately.

Source: U.S. National Oceanic and Atmospheric Administration, National Marine Fisheries Service, *Fisheries of the United States*, annual, September 2010. See also <http://www.st.nmfs.noaa.gov/st1/fus/fus09/index.html>.

Table 898. U.S. Private Aquaculture—Trout and Catfish Production and Value: 1990 to 2010

[67.8 represents 67,800,000. Data are for calendar year and foodsize fish (those over 12 inches long)]

Item	Unit	1990	1995	2000	2005	2007	2008	2009	2010
TROUT FOODSIZE									
Number sold	Mil.	67.8	60.2	58.4	55.6	58.7	40.4	40.8	38.7
Total weight	Mil. lb.	56.8	55.6	59.0	59.9	66.9	52.4	48.7	45.2
Total value of sales	Mil. dol.	64.6	60.8	63.3	63.5	79.5	72.4	67.2	63.1
Avg. price received by processors	Dol./lb.	1.14	1.09	1.07	1.06	1.19	1.38	1.38	1.39
Percent sold to processors	Percent	58	68	70	66	64	58	63	64
CATFISH FOODSIZE									
Number sold	Mil.	272.9	321.8	420.1	395.6	365.8	304.0	266.3	263.4
Total weight	Mil. lb.	392.4	481.5	633.8	605.5	563.9	514.9	476.0	478.9
Total value of sales	Mil. dol.	305.1	378.1	468.8	427.8	423.7	389.3	352.0	375.1
Avg. price received by processors	Dol./lb.	0.78	0.79	0.74	0.71	0.75	0.76	0.74	0.78
Fish sold to processors	Mil. lb.	360.4	446.9	593.6	600.7	496.2	509.6	466.1	471.7
Avg. price paid by processors	Cents/lb.	75.8	78.6	75.1	72.5	76.7	77.6	77.1	0.8
Processor sales	Mil. lb.	183.1	227.0	297.2	300.0	252.5	251.2	229.2	231.6
Avg. price received by processors	Dol./lb.	2.24	2.40	2.36	2.29	2.44	2.44	2.53	2.50
Inventory (Jan. 1)	Mil. lb.	9.4	10.9	13.6	13.7	15.1	15.5	14.5	12.3

Source: U.S. Department of Agriculture, National Agricultural Statistics Service, *Trout Production*, February 2011; *Catfish Production*, January 2011; and *Catfish Processing*, February 2011. See also <http://www.nass.usda.gov/Publications/Reports_By_Title/index.asp/>. Also in *Agricultural Statistics*, annual.

Table 899. Supply of Selected Fishery Items: 1990 to 2009

[In millions of pounds (734 represents 734,000,000). Totals available for U.S. consumption are supply minus exports plus imports. Round weight is the complete or full weight as caught]

Species	Unit	1990	1995	2000	2004	2005	2006	2007	2008	2009
Shrimp	Heads-off weight	734	832	1,173	1,670	1,559	1,879	1,743	1,722	1,746
Tuna, canned	Canned weight	856	875	980	874	895	858	812	848	763
Snow crab	Round weight	37	42	122	168	171	187	208	197	224
Clams	Meat weight	152	144	133	132	120	125	127	121	116
Salmon, canned	Canned weight	148	147	95	98	123	56	51	26	67
American lobster	Round weight	95	94	125	138	144	150	128	144	159
Spiny lobster	Round weight	89	89	99	93	83	77	78	83	55
Scallops	Meat weight	74	62	78	94	86	94	92	88	90
Sardines, canned	Canned weight	61	44	(NA)	(NA)	(NA)	(NA)	(NA)	(NA)	(NA)
Oysters	Meat weight	56	63	71	73	65	65	70	54	59
King crab	Round weight	19	21	41	52	78	110	134	71	62
Crab meat, canned	Canned weight	9	12	29	56	59	58	66	68	59

NA Not available.

Source: U.S. National Oceanic and Atmospheric Administration, National Marine Fisheries Service, *Fisheries of the United States*, annual, September, 2010. See also <http://www.st.nmfs.noaa.gov/st1/fus/fus09/index.html>.

Table 900. Canned, Fresh, and Frozen Fishery Products—Production and Value: 1990 to 2009

[In millions of pounds (1,178 represents 1,178,000,000). Fresh fishery products exclude Alaska and Hawaii. Canned fishery products data are for natural pack only]

Product	Production (mil. lbs.)					Value (mil. dol.)				
	1990	2000	2005	2008	2009	1990	2000	2005	2008	2009
Canned, total	1,178	1,747	1,082	1,314	933	1,562	1,626	1,211	1,422	1,407
Tuna	581	671	446	474	370	902	856	628	845	757
Salmon	196	171	219	124	142	366	288	301	225	322
Clam products	110	127	123	105	100	76	120	127	95	89
Sardines, Maine	13	(Z)	(NA)	(NA)	(NA)	17	(Z)	(NA)	(NA)	(NA)
Shrimp	1	2	(D)	[1] (D)	[1] (D)	3	11	3	[1] (D)	[1] (D)
Crabs	1	(Z)	(Z)	(Z)	(Z)	4	(Z)	(Z)	(Z)	(Z)
Oysters [2]	1	(Z)	(Z)	(Z)	(Z)	1	1	(Z)	(Z)	(Z)
Other	275	776	293	611	321	193	350	152	256	239
Fish fillets and steaks [3]	441	368	615	656	508	843	823	1,136	1,392	1,206
Cod	65	56	47	39	36	132	167	116	112	102
Flounder	54	27	20	21	18	154	71	65	69	56
Haddock	7	6	24	9	14	24	24	89	44	60
Ocean perch, Atlantic	1	(Z)	1	1	1	1	1	4	3	3
Rockfish	33	11	3	2	3	53	25	8	4	6
Pollock, Atlantic	12	2	3	3	3	21	4	6	8	8
Pollock, Alaska	164	160	383	364	277	174	178	404	450	341
Other	105	106	134	218	156	284	353	444	702	630

D Figure withheld to avoid disclosure pertaining to a specific organization or individual. NA Not available. Z Less than 500,000 pounds or $500,000. [1] Includes other products not shown separately. [2] Includes oyster specialities. [3] Fresh and frozen.

Source: U.S. National Oceanic and Atmospheric Administration, National Marine Fisheries Service, *Fisheries of the United States*, annual, September 2010. See also <http://www.st.nmfs.noaa.gov/st1/fus/fus09/index.html>.

Table 901. Mineral Industries—Employment, Hours, and Earnings: 1990 to 2010

[In thousands (680 represents 680,000), except as noted. Based on the Current Employment Statistics Program, see Appendix III]

Industry and item	Unit	1990	1995	2000	2005	2007	2008	2009	2010
All mining: [1]									
All employees	1,000	680	558	520	562	664	710	643	656
Production workers	1,000	469	391	383	419	497	526	466	484
Avg. weekly hours	Number . . .	46.1	46.8	45.5	46.4	46.2	45.3	43.5	44.8
Avg. weekly earnings	Dollars . . .	630	711	771	884	989	1,043	1037	1086
Oil and gas extraction:									
All employees	1,000	190	152	125	126	146	161	160	159
Production workers	1,000	84	73	67	72	83	89	85	89
Avg. weekly hours	Number . . .	44.4	43.6	41.3	44.3	41.9	41.1	40.6	39
Avg. weekly earnings	Dollars	591	677	802	856	1,015	1,120	1119	1066
Coal mining:									
All employees	1,000	136	97	72	74	77	81	82	81
Production workers	1,000	110	78	59	61	68	71	71	70
Avg. weekly hours	Number . . .	44.7	45.7	45.6	48.5	47.9	49.0	47.8	48.4
Avg. weekly earnings	Dollars	822	929	945	1,071	1,052	1,140	1249	1366
Metal ore mining:									
All employees	1,000	53	48	38	29	36	40	35	36
Production workers	1,000	43	39	29	22	28	32	28	28
Avg. weekly hours	Number . . .	42.5	43.4	43.4	44.2	45.9	46.1	42.3	42.5
Avg. weekly earnings	Dollars	646	788	871	1,001	1,077	1,195	1,095	1,158
Nonmetallic minerals mining, and quarrying:									
All employees	1,000	113	108	115	110	110	105	92	86
Production workers	1,000	85	81	87	84	82	79	71	65
Avg. weekly hours	Number . . .	45.0	46.3	46.1	45.9	46.3	43.9	41.9	43.8
Avg. weekly earnings	Dollars	532	632	722	830	872	839	808	848

[1] Includes other industries not shown separately.

Source: U.S. Bureau of Labor Statistics, Current Employment Statistics, "Employment, Hours, and Earnings—National," <http://www.bls.gov/ces/home.htm\>, accessed May 2011.

Table 902. Mine Safety: 2000 to 2010

[Reported injury rates per 200,000 employee hours]

Item	All Mines			Coal			Metal and non-metal		
	2000	2009	2010 [1]	2000	2009	2010 [1]	2000	2009	2010 [1]
Number of mines	14,413	14,631	14,264	2,124	2,076	1,945	12,289	12,555	12,319
Number of miners	348,548	355,720	360,563	108,098	134,089	135,415	240,450	221,631	225,148
Fatalities	85	34	71	38	18	48	47	16	23
Fatal injury rate	0.03	0.01	0.02	0.04	0.01	0.04	0.02	0.01	0.01
All injury rate	5.13	3.01	2.81	6.64	3.69	3.42	4.45	2.54	2.38
Coal production (mil. tons)	1,078	1,075	1,086	1,078	1,075	1,086	(X)	(X)	(X)
Total mining area inspection hours/mine . . .	57	59	63	178	238	260	28	22	23
Citations and orders	120,269	174,354	172,035	58,394	102,458	97,082	61,875	71,896	74,953
S&S [2] citations and orders (percent)	36	32	35	42	33	35	31	31	35
Amount assessed [3] (mil. dol.)	24.7	137.0	146.4	12.0	96.4	97.8	12.7	40.6	48.6

X Not applicable. [1] Preliminary. [2] A violation that "significantly and substantially" contributes to the cause and effect of a coal or other mine safety or health hazard. [3] Government penalties or fines.

Source: U.S. Mine Safety and Health Administration, Office of Program Education and Outreach Services, "Mine Safety and Health At a Glance," May 2011, <http://www.msha.gov/MSHAINFO/FactSheets/MSHAFCT10.HTM>.

Table 903. Mining and Primary Metal Production Indexes: 1990 to 2010

[Index 2007 = 100]

Industry group	NAICS [1] code	1990	1995	2000	2005	2006	2007	2008	2009	2010
Mining [2]	**21**	**106.5**	**104.1**	**103.0**	**97.1**	**99.5**	**100.0**	**100.8**	**95.6**	**101.3**
Oil and gas extraction [2]	211	113.8	110.3	107.0	97.8	98.4	100.0	100.9	106.4	110.4
Crude oil and natural gas	211111	115.9	111.2	106.9	97.9	98.4	100.0	100.9	106.4	110.3
Coal mining	2121	94.9	93.4	95.8	99.0	101.6	100.0	101.7	93.2	94.0
Metal ore mining	2122	110.1	120.4	117.3	100.4	102.5	100.0	103.7	89.8	97.9
Iron ore	21221	107.5	119.2	119.6	103.0	100.1	100.0	101.8	51.1	95.4
Gold ore and silver ore	21222	124.5	133.2	148.4	107.2	105.4	100.0	96.4	92.3	99.5
Copper, nickel, lead, and zinc . . .	21223	119.1	136.5	119.8	96.7	100.5	100.0	108.5	98.3	93.8
Oil and gas drilling	213111	60.1	52.6	67.2	83.7	96.6	100.0	104.4	61.4	82.3
Primary metal manufacturing [2] . . .	**331**	**87.1**	**95.5**	**100.3**	**95.2**	**98.0**	**100.0**	**99.7**	**69.5**	**83.3**
Iron and steel	3311	83.8	93.1	97.1	94.3	98.4	100.0	106.4	63.1	87.7
Aluminum	3313	102.4	98.3	104.0	106.9	105.7	100.0	92.6	74.9	77.5
Nonferrous metals [2]	3314	88.7	98.6	92.1	84.2	85.4	100.0	100.7	85.8	91.6
Copper	33142	155.6	287.4	146.2	85.9	95.8	100.0	82.2	106.0	101.8

[1] Based on the 2007 North American Industry Classification System (NAICS). [2] Includes other industries not shown separately.
Source: Board of Governors of the Federal Reserve System, *The Statistical Supplement to the Federal Reserve Bulletin*, monthly, and *Industrial Production and Capacity Utilization*, Statistical Release G.17, monthly.

Table 904. Mineral Production: 1990 to 2010

[1,029.1 represents 1,029,100,000. Data represent production as measured by mine shipments, mine sales, or marketable production; see Appendix IV]

Minerals and metals	Unit	1990	2000	2008	2009	2010, est.
FUEL MINERALS						
Coal, total [1]	Mil. sh. tons	1,029.1	1,073.6	1,171.8	1,074.9	1,085.3
Bituminous [1]	Mil. sh. tons	693.2	574.3	555.3	493.7	(NA)
Subbituminous	Mil. sh. tons	244.3	409.2	539.1	504.7	(NA)
Lignite	Mil. sh. tons	88.1	85.6	75.7	72.5	(NA)
Anthracite [1]	Mil. sh. tons	3.5	4.6	1.7	1.9	(NA)
Natural gas (marketed production)	Tril. cu. ft.	18.59	20.20	21.11	21.60	22.56
Petroleum (crude)	Mil. bbl. [2]	2,685	2,131	1,812	1,938	(NA)
Uranium (recoverable content)	Mil. lb	8.9	4.0	3.9	(NA)	(NA)
NONFUEL MINERALS						
Asbestos (sales)	1,000 metric tons	(D)	5	–	–	–
Barite, primary, sold/used by producers	1,000 metric tons	430	392	648	383	670
Boron minerals, sold or used by producers	1,000 metric tons	1,090	1,070	(D)	(D)	(D)
Bromine, sold or used by producers	1,000 metric tons	177	228	(D)	(D)	(D)
Cement (excludes Puerto Rico):						
Portland [3]	Mil. metric tons	67	84	83	62	61
Masonry [3]	Mil. metric tons	3	4	3	2	2
Clays	1,000 metric tons	42,900	40,800	33,200	24,500	27,000
Diatomite	1,000 metric tons	631	677	764	575	550
Feldspar [4]	1,000 metric tons	630	790	650	[4] 550	[4] 570
Fluorspar, finished shipments	1,000 metric tons	64	–	(NA)	(NA)	(NA)
Garnet (industrial)	1,000 metric tons	47	60	63	46	54
Gypsum, crude	Mil. metric tons	15	20	14	9	9
Helium [5]	Mil. cu. meters	65	98	80	78	77
Lime, sold or used by producers	Mil. metric tons	16	20	20	16	18
Mica, scrap/flake, sold/used by producers	1,000 metric tons	109	101	84	50	53
Peat, sales by producers	1,000 metric tons	721	847	648	644	646
Perlite, processed, sold or used	1,000 metric tons	576	672	434	348	375
Phosphate rock (marketable)	Mil. metric tons	46	39	30	26	26
Potash (K2O equivalent) sales	1,000 metric tons	1,710	1,300	1,100	700	900
Pumice & pumicite, producer sales	1,000 metric tons	443	1,050	791	410	400
Salt, common, sold/used by producers	Mil. metric tons	37	46	47	46	45
Sand & gravel, sold/used by producer:	Mil. metric tons	855	1,148	1,070	869	787
Construction	Mil. metric tons	829	1,120	1,040	844	760
Industrial	Mil. metric tons	26	28	30	25	27
Silica, sales [6]	Metric tons	(NA)	312	(D)	(D)	(D)
Sodium carbonate (natural, soda ash)	1,000 metric tons	9,100	10,200	11,300	9,310	10,000
Sodium sulfate (natural and synthetic)	1,000 metric tons	349	(NA)	319	292	300
Stone: [7]	Mil. metric tons	2,230	2,810	3,240		
Crushed and broken	Mil. metric tons	1,110	1,560	1,440	1,170	1,150
Dimension [8]	1,000 metric tons	1,120	1,250	1,800	1,620	1,450
Sulfur: Total shipments	1,000 metric tons	11,500	10,700	9,430	9,670	9,800
Sulfur: Frasch mines (shipments)	1,000 metric tons	3,680	900	–	–	–
Talc and pyrophyllite, crude [9]	1,000 metric tons	1,270	851	706	511	530
Vermiculite concentrate	1,000 metric tons	209	150	100	100	100
METALS						
Antimony ore and concentrate	Metric tons	(D)	(D)	–	–	–
Aluminum	1,000 metric tons	4,048	3,668	2,658	1,727	1,720
Bauxite (dried)	1,000 metric tons	(D)	(NA)	(NA)	(NA)	(NA)
Copper (recoverable content)	1,000 metric tons	1,590	1,450	1,310	1,180	1,120
Gold (recoverable content)	Metric tons	294	353	233	223	230
Iron ore (gross weight) [10]	Mil. metric tons	57	61	54	28	50
Lead (recoverable content)	1,000 metric tons	484	449	399	406	385
Magnesium metal	1,000 metric tons	139	(D)	(D)	(D)	(D)
Manganiferous ore (gross weight) [11]	1,000 metric ton	(D)	–	(NA)	–	–
Mercury [12]	Metric tons	(NA)	(NA)	(NA)	(NA)	(NA)
Molybdenum (concentrate)	1,000 metric tons	62	41	56	48	56
Nickel ore (recovered Ni content)	1,000 metric tons	330	–	–	–	–
Palladium metal	Kilograms	5,930	10,300	11,900	12,700	11,600
Platinum metal	Kilograms	1,810	3,110	3,580	3,830	3,500
Silicon (Si content) [13]	1,000 metric tons	418	367	164	139	170
Silver (recoverable content)	Metric tons	2,120	1,860	1,230	1,250	1,280
Titanium concentrate, (TiO2 content) [14]	1,000 metric tons	(D)	300	200	200	200
Tungsten ore and concentrate [15]	Metric tons	(D)	–	(D)	(D)	(D)
Vanadium (recoverable content)	Metric tons	2,310	–	–	(D)	(D)
Zinc (recoverable content)	1,000 metric tons	508	796	748	710	699

D Withheld to avoid disclosing individual company data. NA Not available. [1] Included with bituminous. [2] 42-gal. bbl. [3] Excludes Puerto Rico. [4] Excludes attapulgite. [5] Beginning 1995, includes aplite. [6] Refined. [7] Includes grindstones, oilstones, whetstones, and deburring media. Excludes grinding pebbles and tubemill liners. [8] Includes Puerto Rico. [9] Includes only talc after 1990. [10] Represents shipments; includes byproduct ores. [11] From 5 to 35 percent manganiferous ore. [12] Mercury recovered as a byproduct of gold ores only, 1995. [13] 2006–2010 ferrosilicon only; silicon metal withheld to avoid disclosing proprietary data. [14] U.S. production rounded to one significant digit. [15] Content of ore and concentrate.

Source: Nonfuels, through 1994, U.S. Bureau of Mines, thereafter, U.S. Geological Survey, *Minerals Yearbook* and *Mineral Commodity Summaries*, annual, and *Historical Statistics for Mineral Commodities in the United States*; fuels, U.S. Energy Information Administration, *Annual Energy Review*. See also <http://www.eia.gov/totalenergy/data/annual/index.cfm>.

Table 905. Nonfuel Mineral Commodities—Summary: 2010

[1,720 represents 1,720,000. Preliminary estimates. Average price in dollars per metric tons except as noted. < = Less than]

Mineral	Unit	Mineral disposition				Average price per unit (dollars)	Employ-ment (number)
		Produc-tion	Exports	Net import reliance [1,2] (percent)	Con-sumption, apparent		
Aluminum	1,000 metric tons	1,720	1,900	38	4,610	[4] 1.02	33,500
Antimony (contained)	Metric tons	[5] –	1,900	93	21,600	[4] 3.70	15
Asbestos	1,000 metric tons	–	(A)	100	1	[6] 656	(NA)
Barite	1,000 metric tons	670	20	76	2,800	[6] 54	350
Bauxite and alumina (metal equivalent)	1,000 metric tons	(NA)	861	100	2,070	[6, 7] 27	(NA)
Beryllium (contained)	Metric tons	170	40	47	320	[4] 230	(NA)
Bismuth (contained)	Metric tons	–	350	94	910	[4] 8.22	(NA)
Boron (B$_2$O$_3$ content)	1,000 metric tons	(D)	250	[3, 8]	(D)	[6, 9] 360	1,240
Bromine (contained)	1,000 metric tons	(D)	8	<25	(D)	[10, 11] (NA)	950
Cadmium (contained)	Metric tons	[5] 650	40	[3, 12]	572	[10, 13] 3.90	(NA)
Cement	1,000 metric tons	[14] 62,800	1,000	8	69,500	[6] 92	12,000
Chromium	1,000 metric tons	[15] 160	200	56	360	[16] 230	(NA)
Clays	1,000 metric tons	[17] 27,000	4,700	[3]	23,000	(NA)	4,870
Cobalt (contained)	Metric tons	[15] 2,000	2,800	81	10,000	[4] 21	(NA)
Copper (mine, recoverable)	1,000 metric tons	1,120	77	[5] 30	1,780	[4] 3.49	8,700
Diamond (industrial)	Million carats	93	100	77	546	[18] 0.21	(NA)
Diatomite	1,000 metric tons	550	90	[3]	460	[6] 250	1,020
Feldspar	1,000 metric tons	570	13	[3]	560	[6] 64	570
Fluorspar	1,000 metric tons	(NA)	20	100	520	(NA)	(NA)
Garnet (industrial)	Metric tons	54,000	12,300	25	71,000	[6] 50–2,000	160
Gemstones	Million dollars	8.5	15,000	99	4,400	(NA)	1,100
Germanium (contained)	Kilograms	4,600	19,500	90	(NA)	[10] 940	100
Gold (contained)	Metric tons	230	380	33	(NA)	[19] 1,200	9,700
Graphite (crude)	1,000 metric tons	–	6	100	46	[6, 20] 667	(NA)
Gypsum (crude)	1,000 metric tons	9,000	360	15	19,400	[6] 6.5	4,500
Iodine	Metric tons	(D)	1,000	88	(D)	[10, 21] 24	30
Iron ore (usable)	Million metric tons	[22] 50	11	[3]	47	[6] 90	4,700
Iron and steel scrap (metal)	Million metric tons	83	19	[3]	51	[6, 23] 335	30,000
Iron and steel slag (metal)	1,000 metric tons	[24] 15	<0.1	10	15.0	[6] 20	2,100
Lead (contained)	1,000 metric tons	385	270	[3]	1,500	[4] 1.06	2,940
Lime	1,000 metric tons	18,000	150	2	18,000	[6, 25] 105	5,000
Magnesium compounds	1,000 metric tons	243	16	53	522	(NA)	300
Magnesium metal	1,000 metric tons	(D)	16	34	100	[4] 2.60	400
Manganese (gross weight)	1,000 metric tons	–	18	100	720	[26] 8	(NA)
Mercury	Metric tons	[15] (NA)	500	[3]	(NA)	[27] 900	(NA)
Mica, scrap and flake	1,000 metric tons	53	7	27	73	[6] 140	(NA)
Molybdenum (contained)	Metric tons	56,000	28,000	[3]	48,000	[10] 15.80	940
Nickel (contained) [28]	Metric tons	(D)	87,000	43	229,000	[2, 9] 21,800	(NA)
Niobium (contained)	Metric tons	–	170	100	8,300	[6] 37,500	(NA)
Nitrogen (fixed)-ammonia	1,000 metric tons	8,300	8	43	14,700	[6, 30] 390	1,050
Peat	1,000 metric tons	612	73	59	1,500	[6] 24.80	610
Perlite	1,000 metric tons	375	34	25	500	[6] 52	102
Phosphate rock	1,000 metric tons	26,100	–	15	(NA)	[6] 50	2,300
Platinum-group metals	Kilograms	[31] 15,100	54,000	[31] 94	[3] 2 (NA)	[19, 33] 1,600	1,300
Potash (K$_2$O equivalent)	1,000 metric tons	900	380	83	5,200	[6, 34] 600	1,190
Pumice and pumicite	1,000 metric tons	400	13	7	430	[6] 30	145
Salt	1,000 metric tons	45,000	1,000	24	59,000	[6, 35] 170	4,100
Silicon (contained)	1,000 metric tons	[36] (D)	[37] 130	[36] <50	[36] 290	[39] 110	(NA)
Silver (contained)	Metric tons	1,280	600	65	5,850	[19] 17.75	850
Sodium carbonate (soda ash)	1,000 metric tons	10,000	5,000	[3]	5,000	[40] 260	2,400
Sodium sulfate	1,000 metric tons	300	190	[3]	170	[41] 140	225
Stone (crushed)	Million metric tons	1,150	1	1	1,190	[6] 9.91	79,000
Sulfur (all forms)	1,000 metric tons	9,900	1,270	17	12,000	[6, 42] 40	2,600
Talc	1,000 metric tons	530	240	[3]	460	[6] 117	280
Thallium (contained)	Kilograms	–	850	100	(NA)	[10] 5,930	(NA)
Tin (contained)	Metric tons	[15] 14,100	8,400	69	38,020	[4] 10.79	(NA)
Titanium dioxide	1,000 metric tons	1,400	250	[3]	786	[6, 43] 2,187	3,400
Tungsten (contained)	Metric tons	[15] 5,300	4,400	68	14,000	[44] 180	(NA)
Vermiculite	1,000 metric tons	100	2	22	130	[6] 145	80
Zinc (contained)	1,000 metric tons	720	704	77	901	[4, 45] 1.04	1,990
Zirconium (ZrO$_2$)	Metric tons	(D)	34,000	[3]	(D)	[6, 46] 850	(NA)

– Represents or rounds to zero. D Withheld to avoid disclosing company proprietary data. NA Not available. [1] Data are rounded to no more than three significant digits; except prices. [2] Calculated as a percent of apparent consumption. [3] Net exporter. [4] Dollars per pound. [5] Refinery production. [6] Dollars per metric ton. [7] Bauxite, average value U.S. imports (f.a.s.). [8] Boric acid, gross weight. [9] Granulated pentahydrate borax in bulk, f.o.b mine. [10] Dollars per kilogram. [11] Bulk, purified bromine. [12] Metal only. [13] Average New York dealer price for 99.95% purity in 5-short-ton lots. Source: Platts Metals Week. [14] Excludes Puerto Rico. [15] Secondary production. [16] Unit value of imported chromite ore. Dollars per metric ton gross weight. [17] Excludes attapulgite. [18] Value of imports, dollars per carat. [19] Dollars per troy ounce. [20] Price of flake imports. [21] C.i.f. value, crude, per kilogram. [22] Shipments of usable ore. [23] Delivered, No. 1 Heavy Melting composite price. [24] Sales include imports and reprocessed slag from past years and decades, and only some from current production. [25] Quicklime only. [26] 46%-48% Mn metallurgical ore, per unit contained Mn, c.i.f. U.S. ports. [27] Dollars per 76-pound flask. [28] Primary and secondary materials. [29] London Metal Exchange cash price; dollars per metric ton. [30] F.o.b. Gulf Coast. [31] Platinum and palladium. [32] Platinum. [33] Dealer price of platinum. [34] Price of K2O, muriate. [35] Vacuum and open pan, bulk, pellets and packaged, f.o.b. mine and plant. [36] Silicon metal only. [37] Ferrosilicon statistics include: Production (170,000 t), exports (15,000 t), and net import reliance (44%). [38] Ferrosilicon only. [39] Ferrosilicon, 50% Si; cents per pound. [40] Quoted year-end price, dense, bulk, f.o.b. Green River, WY, dollars per short ton. [41] Quoted price, bulk, f.o.b. works, East, dollars per short ton. [42] Elemental sulfur, f.o.b. plant. [43] Year-end. Unit value based on landed-duty-paid U.S. imports for consumption of pigment with 80% or more TiO2. [44] Dollars per metric ton unit WO3 (7.93 kilograms of contained tungsten per metric ton unit). [45] Platts Metals Week North American price for Special High Grade zinc. [46] Price for domestic zircon.

Source: U.S. Geological Survey, Mineral Commodity Summaries, annual, January 2011. See also <http://minerals.er.usgs.gov/minerals/pubs/mcs/>.

572 Forestry, Fishing, and Mining

Table 906. Selected Mineral Products—Average Prices: 1990 to 2010

[Excludes Alaska and Hawaii except as noted]

Year	Nonfuels									Fuels		
	Copper, cathode [1] (cents per lb.)	Platinum [2] (dol./troy oz.)	Gold (dol./troy oz. [3])	Silver (dol./troy oz. [3])	Lead [4] (cents per lb.)	Nickel [5] (cents per pound)	Tin (New York) [5] (cents per lb.)	Zinc [6] (cents per lb.)	Sulfur, crude [7] (dol./metric ton)	Bituminous coal [8] (dol./short ton)	Crude petroleum [8] (dol./bbl.)	Natural gas [8] (dol./1,000 cu. ft.)
1990......	123	467	385	4.82	46	402	386	75	80.14	27.43	20.03	1.71
1995......	138	425	386	5.15	42	373	416	56	44.46	25.56	14.62	1.55
1997......	107	397	332	4.89	47	314	381	65	36.06	24.64	17.23	2.32
1998......	79	375	295	5.54	45	210	373	51	29.14	24.87	10.87	1.96
1999......	76	379	280	5.25	44	273	366	53	37.81	23.92	15.56	2.19
2000......	88	549	280	5.00	44	392	370	56	24.73	24.15	26.72	3.69
2001......	77	533	272	4.39	44	270	315	44	10.01	25.36	21.84	4.12
2002......	76	543	311	4.62	44	307	292	39	11.84	26.57	22.51	2.95
2003......	85	694	365	4.91	44	437	340	41	28.70	26.57	27.56	4.98
2004......	134	849	411	6.69	55	627	547	52	32.62	30.56	36.77	5.46
2005......	174	900	446	7.34	61	669	483	67	30.88	36.80	50.28	7.33
2006......	315	1,144	606	11.61	77	1,100	565	159	32.85	39.32	59.69	6.39
2007......	328	1,308	699	13.43	124	1,688	899	154	36.49	40.80	66.52	6.25
2008......	319	1,578	874	15.02	120	957	1,130	89	245.12	51.39	94.04	7.96
2009......	241	1,208	975	14.69	87	665	837	78	1.68	54.25	56.39	3.67
2010......	349	1,600	1,200	17.75	109	989	1,079	104	40.00	(NA)	74.71	4.16

NA Not available. [1] U.S. producer price. [2] Average annual dealer prices. [3] 99.95 percent purity. [4] Nationwide delivered basis. [5] Composite price. [6] Platt's Metals Week price for North American Special High Grade zinc. Average prices for 1990 are for U.S. High Grade Zinc. [7] F.o.b. (Free on Board) works. [8] Average value at the point of production or domestic first purchase price.
Source: Nonfuels, 1990, U.S. Bureau of Mines, thereafter, U.S. Geological Survey, *Minerals Yearbook* and *Mineral Commodities Summaries*, annual. See also <http://minerals.er.usgs.gov/minerals/pubs/mcs/\>. Fuels, U.S. Energy Information Administration, *Monthly Energy Review*. See also <http://www.eia.doe.gov/totalenergy/data/monthly/#prices>.

Table 907. Value of Domestic Nonfuel Mineral Production by State: 2000 to 2010

[In millions of dollars (39,400 represents $39,400,000,000). For similar data on fuels, see Table 912]

State	2000	2009	2010 [1]	State	2000	2009	2010 [1]
United States [2]	**39,400**	**71,100**	**57,100**				
Alabama	930	1,020	1,010	Montana.........	596	982	1,120
Alaska	1,140	2,620	3,240	Nebraska.........	[3] 84	248	[3] 182
Arizona	2,510	5,180	6,700	Nevada.........	2,980	6,020	7,550
Arkansas.............	484	636	630	New Hampshire....	[3] 57	108	100
California.............	3,270	3,070	2,710	New Jersey.......	[3] 291	[3] 271	[3] 233
Colorado	592	1,420	1,930	New Mexico......	786	888	1,010
Connecticut...........	[3] 112	[3] 162	[3] 142	New York........	1,020	1,370	1,290
Delaware.............	[3] 14	[3] 25	[3] 13	North Carolina.....	744	846	908
Florida.............	1,820	4,250	2,080	North Dakota......	35	[3] 51	[3] 88
Georgia.............	1,620	1,410	1,500	Ohio............	999	1,130	1,080
Hawaii	[3] 92	116	112	Oklahoma	473	675	646
Idaho	358	935	1,200	Oregon.........	299	314	292
Illinois.............	913	929	910	Pennsylvania.....	[3] 1,250	[3] 1,620	[3] 1,530
Indiana.............	695	806	837	Rhode Island......	[3] 20	[3] 44	[3] 34
Iowa.............	503	590	542	South Carolina.....	[3] 551	[3] 449	[3] 440
Kansas.............	629	953	1,040	South Dakota......	233	230	298
Kentucky	501	668	742	Tennessee........	737	675	814
Louisiana............	325	[3] 464	492	Texas............	1,950	2,650	2,560
Maine.............	96	125	114	Utah.............	1,430	3,910	4,420
Maryland	[3] 358	[3] 301	438	Vermont.........	[3] 67	[3] 122	[3] 119
Massachusetts........	[3] 200	[3] 214	[3] 194	Virginia.........	710	955	952
Michigan	1,640	1,760	1,960	Washington.......	607	650	665
Minnesota	1,460	2,050	[3] 3,860	West Virginia......	172	215	230
Mississippi...........	149	208	183	Wisconsin	[3] 372	546	651
Missouri.............	1,370	1,810	2,140	Wyoming.........	978	1,820	1,860

[1] Preliminary. [2] Includes undistributed not shown separately. [3] Partial data only; excludes values withheld to avoid disclosing individual company data.
Source: U.S. Geological Survey, *Minerals Yearbook*, annual, January 2011, and *Mineral Commodities Summaries*, annual. See also <http://minerals.er.usgs.gov/minerals/pubs/mcs/>.

Table 908. Principal Fuels, Nonmetals, and Metals—World Production and the U.S. Share: 2000 to 2010

[In millions of short tons (4,894 represents 4,894,000,000), except as indicated; see Appendix IV]

Mineral	Unit	World production				Percent U.S. of world			
		2000	2005	2009 [1]	2010 [1]	2000	2005	2009 [1]	2010 [1]
Fuels: [2]									
Coal	Mil. sh. tons	4,894	6,553	7,680	(NA)	24	19	15	(NA)
Petroleum (crude)	Bil. bbl	25.0	26.9	26.4	26.9	16	15	15	15
Natural gas (dry, marketable)	Tril. cu. ft	88.4	99.8	106.5	(NA)	31	26	27	(NA)
Natural gas plant liquids	Bil. bbl	2.4	2.8	3.0	3.1	47	36	36	36
Nonmetals:									
Asbestos	1,000 metric tons	2,110	2,210	2,070	1,970	–	–	–	–
Barite	1,000 metric tons	6,470	7,870	6,130	6,900	6	6	6	10
Cement	Mil. metric tons	(NA)	2,350	3,010	3,300	(NA)	4	2	2
Feldspar	1,000 metric tons	9,580	16,800	19,800	20,000	8	4	3	3
Fluorspar	1,000 metric tons	4,470	5,360	5,460	5,400	–	--	(NA)	(NA)
Gypsum	Mil. metric tons	106	147	148	146	19	13	6	6
Mica (incl. scrap)	1,000 metric tons	328	354	340	350	31	22	15	15
Nitrogen (N content)	Mil. metric tons	108	122	130	131	11	7	6	6
Phosphate rock (gross wt.)	Mil. metric tons	132	152	166	176	30	24	16	15
Potash (K_2O equivalent)	Mil. metric tons	27	34	21	33	4	4	3	3
Sulfur, elemental basis	Mil. metric tons	58	69	68	68	19	14	14	13
Metals, mine basis:									
Bauxite	Mil. metric tons	136	178	199	211	(NA)	(NA)	(NA)	(NA)
Copper	1,000 metric tons	13,200	15,000	15,900	16,200	11	8	7	7
Gold	Metric tons	2,590	2,470	2,450	2,500	14	10	9	9
Iron ore (gross wt.)	Mil. metric tons	1,070	1,550	2,240	2,400	6	3	1	2
Lead [3]	1,000 metric tons	3,184	3,470	3,860	4,100	15	13	11	10
Mercury	Metric tons	1,350	1,520	1,920	1,960	(NA)	(NA)	(NA)	(NA)
Molybdenum	1,000 metric tons	133	186	221	234	31	31	22	24
Nickel [3]	1,000 metric tons	1,270	1,470	1,390	1,550	(Z)	–	–	–
Silver	1,000 metric tons	18	21	22	22	11	6	6	6
Tantalum concentrates (Ta content)	Metric tons	1,040	1,380	665	670	–	–	–	–
Titanium mineral concentrates (titanium content) [4]	1,000 metric tons	(NA)	5,200	5,800	6,300	(NA)	6	3	3
Tungsten [3]	1,000 metric tons	44	59	61	61	(NA)	–	(D)	(D)
Vanadium [3]	1,000 metric tons	56	56	54	56	–	–	(D)	(D)
Zinc [3]	1,000 metric tons	8,788	10,000	11,200	12,000	10	7	7	6
Metals, smelter basis:									
Aluminum	1,000 metric tons	24,400	31,900	37,300	41,400	15	8	5	4
Cadmium	1,000 metric tons	20	20	19	22	10	7	3	3
Copper	1,000 metric tons	11,000	13,500	14,500	15,000	9	4	4	4
Iron, pig	Mil. metric tons	573	802	935	1,030	8	5	2	3
Lead [4]	1,000 metric tons	6,580	7,660	8,820	9,340	22	17	14	14
Magnesium [5], [6]	1,000 metric tons	428	622	608	760	(D)	(D)	(D)	(D)
Raw Steel	Mil. metric tons	845	1,140	1,240	1,400	12	8	5	6
Tin [7]	1,000 metric tons	271	296	260	261	2	–	–	–
Zinc	1,000 metric tons	9,137	10,300	11,400	(NA)	10	4	3	(NA)

– Represents or rounds to zero. D Withheld to avoid disclosing company data. NA Not available. Z Less than 0.05 percent.
[1] Preliminary. [2] Source: Energy Information Administration, "International Energy Statistics." [3] Content of ore and concentrate.
[4] Refinery production. [5] Primary production; no smelter processing necessary. [6] Starting 2005, excludes U.S. production.
[7] Production from primary sources only.

Source: Except as noted, Nonfuels, U.S. Geological Survey, *Minerals Yearbook*, annual, and *Mineral Commodities Summaries*, annual, January 2011, <http://minerals.er.usgs.gov/minerals/pubs/mcs/\>; and fuels, U.S. Energy Information Administration, "International Energy Statistics," <http://tonto.eia.doe.gov/cfapps/ipdbproject/IEDIndex3.cfm>, June 2011.

Table 909. Net U.S. Imports of Selected Minerals and Metals as Percent of Apparent Consumption: 1980 to 2010

[In percent. Based on net imports which equal the difference between imports and exports plus or minus government stockpile and industry stock changes]

Minerals and metals	1980	1990	1995	2000	2005	2007	2008	2009	2010 [1]
Bauxite [2]	(NA)	98	99	100	100	100	100	100	100
Fluorspar	87	91	92	100	100	100	100	100	100
Manganese	98	100	100	100	100	100	100	100	100
Strontium	100	100	100	100	100	100	100	100	100
Tantalum	90	86	80	80	100	100	100	100	100
Vanadium	35	(D)	84	100	100	100	91	81	69
Mica (sheet)	100	100	100	100	100	100	100	100	100
Platinum	(NA)	(NA)	(NA)	78	93	91	89	95	94
Tin	79	71	84	88	78	72	70	74	69
Barite	44	71	65	84	84	85	80	78	76
Zinc	60	64	71	72	67	73	72	77	77
Cobalt	93	84	79	78	83	80	81	76	81
Potash	65	68	75	80	80	81	84	73	83
Titanium	(NA)	(NA)	70	79	71	76	78	68	81
Tungsten	53	81	90	66	68	67	60	68	68
Silver	7	(NA)	(NA)	43	72	66	70	64	65
Nickel	76	64	60	54	48	17	33	21	43
Iron and steel	13	13	21	18	15	16	13	11	7
Aluminum	([3])	([3])	23	33	41	19	([2])	10	38

D Withheld to avoid disclosure. NA Not available. [1] Preliminary. [2] Includes alumina. [3] Net exporter.

Source: Through 1990, U.S. Bureau of Mines; thereafter, U.S. Geological Survey, *Mineral Commodity Summaries* and *Minerals Yearbook*, annual, and *Historical Statistics for Mineral and Material Commodities in the United States*; and import and export data from U.S. Census Bureau.

Table 910. Petroleum Industry—Summary: 1990 to 2009

[602 represents 602,000. Includes all costs incurred for drilling and equipping wells to point of completion as productive wells or abandonment after drilling becomes unproductive. Based on sample of operators of different size drilling establishments]

Item	Unit	1990	1995	2000	2005	2006	2007	2008	2009 [1]
Crude oil producing wells, (Dec. 31)	1,000	602	574	534	498	497	500	526	526
Daily output per well [2]	Bbl	12.2	11.4	10.9	10.4	10.3	10.1	9.4	10.1
Completed wells drilled, total	1,000	27.02	17.97	26.93	39.69	46.69	46.49	51.76	32.57
Crude oil	1,000	12.02	7.66	7.80	10.16	12.63	12.73	16.42	12.42
Natural gas	1,000	10.42	7.52	16.33	26.35	30.41	30.25	31.47	17.73
Dry holes	1,000	4.59	2.79	2.80	3.18	3.65	3.51	3.87	2.43
Average depth per well	Feet	4,602	5,459	4,765	5,407	5,474	5,927	6,195	6,084
Average cost per well	$1,000	384	513	755	1,721	2,102	4,172	5,136	(NA)
Average cost per foot	Dollars	76.07	87.22	142.16	306.50	378.03	688.30	782.31	(NA)
Crude oil production, total [3]	Mil. bbl	2,685	2,394	2,131	1,890	1,862	1,848	1,812	1,938
Value at wells [3, 4]	Bil. dol	53.77	35.00	56.93	95.03	111.16	122.96	170.38	109.29
Average price per barrel	Dollars	20.03	14.62	26.72	50.28	59.69	66.52	94.04	56.39
Lower 48 states [5]	Mil. bbl	2,037	1,853	1,776	1,575	1,592	1,585	1,562	1,703
Alaska	Mil. bbl	647	542	355	315	270	264	250	235
Onshore	Mil. bbl	2,290	1,838	1,482	1,265	1,241	1,244	1,310	1,256
Offshore	Mil. bbl	395	557	649	625	621	605	502	682
Imports: Crude oil [3, 6]	Mil. bbl	2,151	2,639	3,320	3,696	3,693	3,661	3,581	3,307
Refined petroleum products	Mil. bbl	775	586	874	1,310	1,310	1,255	1,146	973
Exports: Crude oil [3]	Mil. bbl	39.7	34.5	18.4	11.6	9.0	10.0	10.5	16.0
Proved reserves	Bil. bbl	26.3	22.4	22.0	21.8	21.0	21.3	19.1	(NA)
Operable refineries	Number	205	175	158	148	149	149	150	150
Capacity (Jan. 1)	Mil. bbl	5,684	5,633	6,027	6,251	6,329	6,367	6,422	6,450
Refinery input, total	Mil. bbl	5,325	5,555	5,964	6,136	6,198	6,205	6,278	6,162
Crude oil [3]	Mil. bbl	4,894	5,100	5,514	5,555	5,563	5,532	5,361	5,224
Natural gas plant liquids	Mil. bbl	171	172	139	161	183	184	178	179
Other liquids [7]	Mil. bbl	260	283	311	420	452	488	739	759
Refinery output, total [8]	Mil. bbl	5,574	5,838	6,311	6,497	6,561	6,568	6,641	6,520
Motor gasoline [9]	Mil. bbl	2,540	2,722	2,910	3,036	3,053	3,051	3,129	3,199
Jet fuel [10]	Mil. bbl	543	517	588	564	541	528	546	510
Distillate fuel oil	Mil. bbl	1,067	1,152	1,310	1,443	1,475	1,509	1,572	1,477
Residual fuel oil	Mil. bbl	347	288	255	229	232	246	227	219
Liquefied petroleum gases	Mil. bbl	182	239	258	209	229	239	230	230
Utilization rate	Percent	87.1	92.0	92.6	90.6	89.7	88.5	85.3	82.8

NA Not available. [1] Preliminary. [2] Based on number of wells producing at end of year. [3] Includes lease condensate. [4] Values based on domestic first purchase price. [5] Excluding Alaska and Hawaii. [6] Includes imports for the Strategic Petroleum Reserve. [7] Unfinished oils (net), other hydrocarbons, hydrogen, aviation and motor gasoline blending components (net). Beginning 1995, also includes oxygenates (net). [8] Includes other products not shown separately. [9] Finished motor gasoline. Beginning 1995, also includes ethanol blended into motor gasoline. [10] Prior to 2005, kerosene-type jet fuel is included with kerosene in "Other products." Beginning 2005, naphtha-type jet fuel is also included in "Other products."

Source: U.S. Energy Information Administration, *Annual Energy Review 2009*. See also <http://www.eia.doe.gov/emeu/aer /contents.html>.

Table 911. Supply, Disposition, and Ending Stocks of Crude Oil and Petroleum Products: 2010

[In millions of barrels (2,011.9 represents 2,011,900,000). Minus sign (–) indicates decrease]

Commodity	Supply				Disposition			Ending stocks
	Field production	Refinery and blender net production	Imports	Adjustments [1]	Stock change	Refinery and blender net inputs	Products Exports supplied [2]	
Crude oil	2,011.9	(X)	3,344.5	39.3	6.8	5,373.7	15.2 —	1,058.5
Commercial	2,011.9	(X)	(NA)	(NA)	6.9	(NA)	(NA) (NA)	332.0
Alaskan	218.8	(X)	(NA)	(X)	(NA)	(NA)	(NA) —	(NA)
Lower 48 states	1,793.1	(X)	(NA)	(X)	(NA)	(NA)	(NA) —	(NA)
SPR [3]	(X)	(X)	(NA)	(X)	—	(X)	(NA) (X)	726.5
Imports by SPR [3]	(X)	(X)	(NA)	(X)	(X)	(X)	(NA) (X)	(X)
Imports into SPR [3] by others	(X)	(X)	(NA)	(X)	(X)	(X)	(NA) (X)	(X)
Natural gas liquids and LRG [4]	730.4	237.6	58.4	(X)	8.1	158.9	54.7 798.2	121.3
Pentanes plus	98.8	(X)	3.5	(X)	2.0	56.8	6.7 30.4	12.5
Liquefied petroleum gases	631.7	237.6	54.8	(X)	6.1	102.1	48.1 767.8	108.8
Ethane/ethylene	304.2	7.4	0.1	(X)	3.8	(NA)	(NA) 308.0	24.7
Propane/propylene	206.2	204.0	43.9	(X)	–1.4	(NA)	39.9 415.7	49.4
Normal butane/butylene	54.0	28.3	7.4	(X)	3.6	42.1	8.2 35.9	27.7
Isobutane/isobutylene	67.2	–2.2	3.4	(X)	0.2	60.0	(NA) 8,249.0	7.1
Finished motor gasoline	(X)	3,301.7	49.3	31.9	–22.5	(X)	108.0 3,297.5	63.4
Kerosene-type jet fuel	(X)	517.4	32.8	(X)	–0.1	(X)	30.8 519.7	43.2
Distillate fuel oil [5]	(X)	1,542.4	81.4	–	–0.3	(X)	239.4 1,384.7	164.5

– Represents or rounds to zero. NA Not available. X Not applicable. [1] Includes an adjustment for crude oil, previously referred to as "Unaccounted For Crude Oil." Also included is an adjustment for motor gasoline blending components, fuel ethanol, and distillate fuel oil. See Appendix B of source for more details. [2] Products supplied is equal to field production, plus refinery and blender net production, plus imports, plus adjustments, minus stock change, minus refinery and blender net inputs, minus exports. [3] Strategic Petroleum Reserve. [4] Liquified Refinery Gases (LRGs) are liquefied petroleum gases fractionated from refinery or still gases through compression and/or refrigeration. They are retained in the liquid state. Excludes still gas. [5] Distillate stocks located in the "Northeast Heating Oil Reserve" are not included. For details, see Appendix C of source.

Source: U.S. Energy Information Administration, "Petroleum Supply Annual, Volume 1"; <http://www.eia.doe.gov/oil_gas /petroleum/data_publications/petroleum_supply_annual/psa_volume1/psa_volume1.html>.

Table 912. Crude Petroleum and Natural Gas—Production and Value by Major Producing States: 2008 to 2010

[1,812 represents 1,812,000,000 barrels]

State	Crude petroleum Quantity (mil. bbl.) 2008	2009	2010	Value (mil. dol.) 2008	2009	2010	Natural gas marketed production [1] Quantity (bil. cu. ft.) 2008	2009	2010	Value (mil. dol.) 2008	2009	2010
Total [2]	1,812	1,957	2,012	170,383	110,254	150,306	21,112	21,604	22,569	168,342	79,188	(NA)
AL	8	7	7	730	397	527	258	236	(NA)	2,490	1,021	(NA)
AK [3]	250	236	219	22,514	12,814	15,416	398	397	377	2,945	1,164	(NA)
AR	6	6	6	553	307	407	446	680	(NA)	9,642	4,812	(NA)
CA	215	207	204	19,410	11,620	15,180	296	277	(NA)	(NA)	(NA)	(NA)
CO	24	28	26	2,184	1,482	1,896	1,389	1,499	(NA)	(NA)	(NA)	(NA)
FL	2	1	2	(NA)	(NA)	(NA)	2	–	(NA)	36	20	(NA)
IL	9	9	9	881	505	657	1	1	(NA)	2,565	1,119	(NA)
IN	2	2	2	171	100	134	5	5	(NA)	961	–	(NA)
KS	40	39	40	3,645	2,147	2,928	374	354	(NA)	12,028	5,920	(NA)
KY	3	3	3	240	144	178	114	113	(NA)	(NA)	(NA)	(NA)
LA	73	69	67	7,366	4,084	5,209	1,378	1,549	2,246	862	603	(NA)
MI	6	6	7	596	333	487	153	154	(NA)	(NA)	(NA)	(NA)
MS	22	23	24	2,091	1,354	1,806	97	88	(NA)	844	310	(NA)
MT	32	28	24	(NA)	1,467	1,665	113	98	(NA)	(NA)	(NA)	(NA)
NE	2	2	2	211	114	153	3	3	(NA)	12,146	5,762	(NA)
NM	59	61	62	5,716	3,490	4,709	1,446	1,383	1,322	448	222	(NA)
NY	–	–	–	(NA)	(NA)	(NA)	50	45	(NA)	669	387	(NA)
ND	63	80	112	5,567	4,286	7,867	52	59	(NA)	14,262	6,550	(NA)
OH	6	6	6	551	329	427	85	89	(NA)	4	3	(NA)
OK	64	67	68	6,160	3,791	5,116	1,887	1,858	1,827	(NA)	(NA)	(NA)
PA	4	4	3	349	202	243	198	274	(NA)	42	21	(NA)
TX	398	404	417	38,548	23,178	31,751	6,961	6,819	6,676	(NA)	(NA)	(NA)
UT	22	23	24	1,905	1,151	1,662	434	444	(NA)	(NA)	(NA)	(NA)
WV	2	2	2	151	104	139	245	264	(NA)	(NA)	(NA)	(NA)
WY	53	51	52	4,557	2,685	3,521	2,275	2,335	2,323	16	(NA)	(NA)
Federal offshore	103	44	43	140,547	(NA)	(NA)	(NA)	(NA)	(NA)	(NA)	(NA)	(NA)
Lower 48 states	1,562	1,721	1,793	147,870	(NA)	(NA)	20,714	21,207	22,192	165,398	(NA)	(NA)

– Represents zero. NA Not available. [1] Excludes nonhydrocarbon gases. [2] Includes other states, not shown separately. State production includes state offshore production, as well as extractions from the Gulf not distributed to states. U.S. level totals shown in Tables 910 and 917 may contain revisions not carried to state level. [3] Price data are for North Slope only. Value data were calculated using price data.

Source: U.S. Energy Information Administration, "Petroleum Navigator" and "Natural Gas Navigator," <http://www.eia.gov/petroleum/index.cfm> and <http://www.eia.gov/dnav/ng/ng_sum_top.asp>, accessed May 2011.

Table 913. Crude Oil, Natural Gas, and Natural Gas Liquids—Reserves by State: 2007 to 2009

[21,317 mil. bbl. represents 21,317,000,000 bbl. As of December 31. Proved reserves are estimated quantities of the mineral, which geological and engineering data demonstrate with reasonable certainty, to be recoverable in future years from known reservoirs under existing economic and operating conditions. Based on a sample of operators of oil and gas wells]

Area	2007 Crude oil proved reserves (mil. bbl.)	Natural gas (bil. cu. ft.)	Natural gas liquids (mil. bbl.)	2008 Crude oil proved reserves (mil. bbl.)	Natural gas (bil. cu. ft.)	Natural gas liquids (mil. bbl.)	2009 Crude oil proved reserves (mil. bbl.)	Natural gas (bil. cu. ft.)	Natural gas liquids (mil. bbl.)
United States [1]	21,317	237,726	9,143	19,121	244,656	9,275	20,682	272,509	(NA)
Alabama	42	3,994	53	38	3,290	106	37	2,871	(NA)
Alaska	4,163	11,917	325	3,507	7,699	312	3,566	9,101	(NA)
Arkansas	31	3,305	3	30	5,626	2	28	10,869	(NA)
California	3,322	2,740	126	2,705	2,406	113	2,835	2,773	(NA)
Colorado	304	21,851	559	288	23,302	716	279	23,058	(NA)
Florida	32	108	2	3	1	–	9	7	(NA)
Illinois	101	(NA)	(NA)	54	(NA)	(NA)	66	–	(NA)
Indiana	17	(NA)	(NA)	15	(NA)	(NA)	8	–	(NA)
Kansas	206	3,982	198	243	3,557	181	259	3,279	(NA)
Kentucky	24	2,469	89	17	2,714	100	20	2,782	(NA)
Louisiana	458	10,045	303	388	11,573	300	370	20,688	(NA)
Michigan	55	3,630	55	48	3,174	62	33	2,763	(NA)
Mississippi	200	954	9	249	1,030	9	244	917	(NA)
Montana	410	1,052	11	321	1,000	11	343	976	(NA)
Nebraska	12	(NA)	(NA)	8	(NA)	(NA)	9	–	(NA)
New Mexico	735	17,245	844	654	16,285	804	700	15,598	(NA)
New York	(NA)	376	(NA)	(NA)	389	(NA)	(NA)	196	(NA)
North Dakota	482	511	58	573	541	55	1,046	1,079	(NA)
Ohio	48	1,027	(NA)	38	985	(NA)	38	896	(NA)
Oklahoma	530	19,031	949	581	20,845	1,034	622	22,769	(NA)
Pennsylvania	12	3,361	(NA)	14	3,577	(NA)	10	6,985	(NA)
Texas	5,122	72,091	3,658	4,555	77,546	3,560	5,006	80,424	(NA)
Utah	355	6,391	108	286	6,643	116	398	7,257	(NA)
Virginia	(NA)	2,529	(NA)	(NA)	2,378	(NA)	(NA)	3,091	(NA)
West Virginia	28	4,729	115	23	5,136	100	19	5,946	(NA)
Wyoming	690	29,710	1,032	556	31,143	1,121	583	35,283	(NA)
Federal offshore	3,905	14,439	624	3,903	13,546	548	4,129	12,552	(NA)
Lower 48 states	17,154	225,809	8,818	15,614	236,957	8,963	17,116	263,408	(NA)

– Represents zero. NA Not available. [1] Includes other states, not shown separately.

Source: U.S. Energy Information Administration, "Petroleum Navigator" and "Natural Gas Navigator," <http://www.eia.gov/dnav/pet/pet_sum_top.asp> and <http://www.eia.gov/dnav/ng/ng_sum_top.asp>, accessed March 2011.

Table 914. Federal Offshore Leasing, Exploration, Production, and Revenue: 1990 to 2010

[In millions (56.79 represents 56,790,000), except as indicated. Data presented by fiscal year. See source for explanation of terms and for reliability statement]

Item	Unit	1990	1995	2000	2005	2007	2008	2009	2010
Tracts offered.................	Number ...	10,459	10,995	7,992	11,447	4,992	19,812	9,893	6,958
Tracts leased.................	Number ...	825	835	553	989	360	2,121	483	([1])
Acres offered.................	Millions....	56.79	59.70	42.89	61.08	26.63	106.76	52.98	40
Acres leased	Millions....	4.30	4.34	2.92	5.24	2.01	11.73	2.66	([1])
New wells being drilled:									
Active.................	Number ...	120	237	236	135	115	122	54	48
Suspended	Number ...	266	155	139	59	68	67	67	76
Cumulative wells (since 1953):									
Wells completed	Number ...	13,167	13,423	13,733	13,398	12,804	12,157	11,384	10,404
Wells plugged and abandoned ...	Number ...	14,677	21,478	26,893	31,884	33,568	34,613	35,544	36,695
Revenue, total [2]	Bil. dol.....	3.4	2.7	5.2	6.3	7.0	18.0	5.8	4.8
Bonuses [3]	Bil. dol.....	0.8	0.4	0.4	0.6	0.4	9.5	1.2	1.0
Oil and gas royalties [2]	Bil. dol.....	2.6	2.1	4.1	5.5	6.4	8.3	4.4	3.6
Rentals	Bil. dol.....	0.09	0.09	0.21	0.22	0.20	0.24	0.2	0.3
Sales value [4]	Bil. dol.....	17.0	13.8	27.4	37.2	45.5	57.2	32.6	25.1
Oil	Bil. dol.....	7.0	6.3	11.5	15.4	27.8	35.9	23.5	21.3
Natural gas	Bil. dol.....	9.5	7.5	15.9	21.8	17.7	21.3	9.2	3.7
Sales volume: [5]									
Oil	Mil. bbl.....	324	409	566	332	471	358	425	261
Natural gas	Bil. cu. ft....	5,093	4,692	4,723	3,504	2,547	1,573	3,539	1,043

[1] Sale 213, Central Gulf of Mexico, was held on March 17, 2010. Forty million acres were offered for bid. Data from the sale is not yet finalized. [2] Includes condensate royalties. Excludes gas plant product royalties. [3] The 2010 bonuses include those from Sale 213, Central Gulf of Mexico, held on March 17, 2010. [4] Sales value is value at time of sale, not current value. [5] Excludes sales volumes for gas plant products and sulfur.

Source: U.S. Department of the Interior, Bureau of Ocean Energy Management, Regulation and Enforcement, *Federal Offshore Statistics*, annual; for revenue, sales value, and sales volume data after 2000, Office of Natural Resources Revenue, *Annual Reported Royalty Revenue Statistical Information*, <http://www.onrr.gov/ONRRWebStats/Home.aspx>.

Table 915. Oil and Gas Extraction Industry—Establishments, Employees, and Payroll by State: 2008

[11,367,499 represents 11,367,499,000. See headnote, Table 880]

State	Crude petroleum and natural gas extraction (211111) [1]			State	Natural gas liquid extraction (211112) [1]		
	Establish-ments	Number of employees [2]	Annual pay-roll ($1,000)		Establish-ments	Number of employees [2]	Annual pay-roll ($1,000)
United States [3] ..	**7,643**	**98,880**	**11,367,499**	**United States [3] ..**	**350**	**8,220**	**783,170**
Alabama	31	524	42,815	Alabama	2	([4])	(D)
Arkansas.........	107	1,068	91,779	Alaska	1	([4])	(D)
California........	201	4,958	687,651	Arkansas.........	2	([5])	(D)
Colorado	382	5,000	714,780	California	5	126	9,406
Florida	34	([6])	(D)	Colorado	19	1,126	173,006
Illinois...........	158	867	39,281	Florida	2	([5])	(D)
Indiana.........	42	168	6,738	Illinois...........	2	([4])	(D)
Kansas..........	409	3,018	198,163	Kansas..........	12	([7])	(D)
Kentucky	99	898	54,461	Kentucky	6	([5])	(D)
Louisiana.........	382	9,452	879,317	Louisiana.........	41	762	65,900
Michigan	94	915	88,824	Michigan	8	([4])	2,299
Mississippi.......	77	944	90,825	Minnesota	3	([5])	(D)
Montana.........	87	711	61,476	Mississippi.......	4	([4])	(D)
Nevada.........	17	([4])	6,117	Missouri	1	([5])	(D)
New Mexico	172	2,832	230,836	Montana..........	7	([4])	(D)
New York	51	289	21,371	New Mexico	17	611	52,658
North Dakota......	41	1,177	99,002	North Dakota......	6	([4])	(D)
Ohio...........	203	1,435	71,310	Ohio...........	2	([5])	(D)
Oklahoma	1,160	13,060	1,511,116	Oklahoma	50	923	88,120
Pennsylvania	175	2,067	157,641	Pennsylvania	14	([6])	(D)
Texas............	3,139	39,799	5,365,506	South Dakota......	4	([5])	(D)
Utah............	54	1,099	100,659	Texas............	101	2,347	191,044
Virginia..........	23	254	35,456	Utah............	4	65	6,443
West Virginia	219	2,845	194,455	West Virginia	7	([7])	(D)
Wyoming	164	2,694	275,784	Wyoming	23	954	91,513

D Withheld to avoid disclosing data for individual companies; data are included in higher level totals. [1] North American Industry Classification System, 2007. [2] Covers full- and part-time employees who are on the payroll in the pay period including March 12. [3] Includes other states, not shown separately. [4] 20 to 99 employees. [5] 0 to 19 employees. [6] 250 to 499 employees. [7] 100 to 249 employees.

Source: U.S. Census Bureau, "County Business Patterns," July 2009, <http://www.census.gov/econ/cbp/index.html>.

Table 916. Natural Gas Plant Liquids—Production and Value: 1990 to 2010

[Barrels of 42 gallons (569 represents 569,000,000)]

Item	Unit	1990	1995	2000	2005	2006	2007	2008	2009	2010
Field production [1]	Mil. bbl......	569	643	699	627	635	651	653	697	730
Pentanes plus	Mil. bbl......	113	122	112	97	96	96	97	99	99
Liquefied petroleum gases ...	Mil. bbl......	456	521	587	529	539	555	556	598	632
Natural gas processed.........	Tril. cu. ft....	15	17	17	15	15	16	15	(NA)	(NA)

NA Not available. [1] Includes other finished petroleum products, not shown separately.

Source: U.S. Energy Information Administration, "Petroleum Navigator" and "Natural Gas Navigator"; <http://www.eia.gov/dnav/pet/pet_sum_top.asp> and <http://www.eia.gov/dnav/ng/ng_sum_top.asp>, accessed May 2011.

Forestry, Fishing, and Mining 577

Table 917. Natural Gas—Supply, Consumption, Reserves, and Marketed Production: 1990 to 2010

[269 represents 269,000. Data are for natural gas, plus a small amount of supplemental gaseous fuels. Minus sign (−) indicates debit]

Item	Unit	1990	1995	2000	2005	2006	2007	2008	2009	2010
Producing wells (year-end)	1,000	269	299	342	426	441	453	479	493	(NA)
Production value at wells.........	Bil. of dol....	31.8	30.2	74.3	138.7	124.0	126.2	168.1	(NA)	(NA)
Avg. per 1,000 cu. ft.	Dollars	1.71	1.55	3.68	7.33	6.39	6.25	7.96	(NA)	(NA)
Proved reserves [1]	Tril. cu. ft. ...	169	165	177	204	211	238	245	(NA)	(NA)
Marketed production [2].........	**Bil. cu. ft....**	**18,594**	**19,506**	**20,198**	**18,927**	**19,410**	**20,196**	**21,112**	**21,604**	**22,569**
Minus: Extraction losses [3]	Bil. cu. ft. ...	784	908	1,016	876	906	930	953	938	(NA)
Equals: Dry production	Bil. cu. ft. ...	17,810	18,599	19,182	18,051	18,504	19,266	20,286	20,955	(NA)
Plus: Supplemental gas supplies...	Bil. cu. ft. ...	123	110	90	64	66	63	61	64	(NA)
Equals: Dry production with supplemental gas	Bil. cu. ft. ...	17,932	18,709	19,272	18,114	18,570	19,329	20,347	21,019	(NA)
Plus: Withdrawals from storage	Bil. cu. ft. ...	1,986	3,025	3,550	3,107	2,527	3,375	3,417	2,968	(NA)
Plus: Imports	Bil. cu. ft. ...	1,532	2,841	3,782	4,341	4,186	4,608	3,984	3,748	(NA)
Plus: Balancing item [4]	Bil. cu. ft. ...	307	396	−305	232	89	−209	−133	−549	(NA)
Equals: Total supply.............	Bil. cu. ft. ...	21,758	24,971	26,299	25,794	25,372	27,103	27,615	27,186	(NA)
Minus: Exports.................	Bil. cu. ft. ...	86	154	244	729	724	822	1,006	1,071	(NA)
Minus: Additions to storage [5]	Bil. cu. ft. ...	2,499	2,610	2,721	3,055	2,963	3,183	3,383	3,281	(NA)
Equals: Consumption, total	**Bil. cu. ft....**	**19,174**	**22,207**	**23,333**	**22,011**	**21,685**	**23,097**	**23,227**	**22,834**	**24,132**
Lease and plant fuel	Bil. cu. ft. ...	1,236	1,220	1,151	1,112	1,142	1,226	1,220	1,275	1,332
Pipeline fuel [6]................	Bil. cu. ft. ...	660	700	642	584	584	621	648	598	632
Residential...................	Bil. cu. ft. ...	4,391	4,850	4,996	4,827	4,368	4,722	4,892	4,778	4,952
Commercial [7].................	Bil. cu. ft. ...	2,623	3,031	3,182	2,999	2,832	3,013	3,153	3,119	3,206
Industrial	Bil. cu. ft. ...	8,255	9,384	9,293	6,597	6,512	6,648	6,661	6,167	6,600
Vehicle fuel	Bil. cu. ft. ...	(Z)	5	13	23	24	25	26	29	33
Electric power sector...........	Bil. cu. ft. ...	3,245	4,237	5,206	5,869	6,222	6,841	6,668	6,872	7,378
World production (dry)..........	Tril. cu. ft. ...	73.8	78.1	88.4	99.8	103.4	105.6	109.9	106.5	(NA)
U.S. production (dry)..........	Tril. cu. ft. ...	17.8	18.6	19.2	18.1	18.5	19.3	20.3	21.0	21.0
Percent U.S. of world..........	Percent	24.1	23.8	21.7	18.1	17.9	18.2	18.5	19.7	(NA)

NA Not available. Z Less than 500 million cubic feet. [1] Estimated, end of year. Source: U.S. Energy Information Administration, *U.S. Crude Oil, Natural Gas, and Natural Gas Liquids Reserves*, annual. [2] Marketed production includes gross withdrawals from reservoirs less quantities used for reservoir repressuring and quantities vented or flared. Excludes nonhydrocarbon gases subsequently removed. [3] Volumetric reduction in natural gas resulting from the removal of natural gas plant liquids, which are transferred to petroleum supply. [4] Quantities lost and imbalances in data due to differences among data sources. Since 1980, excludes intransit shipments that cross U.S.-Canada border (i.e., natural gas delivered to its destination via the other country). [5] Underground storage. Through 2004, includes liquefied natural gas (LNG) storage in above-ground tanks. [6] Natural gas consumed in the operation of pipelines and delivery to consumers. [7] Includes deliveries to municipalities and public authorities for institutional heating and other purposes.

Source: Except as noted, U.S. Energy Information Administration, *Annual Energy Review*; "International Energy Annual"; "U.S. Crude Oil, Natural Gas, and Natural Gas Liquids Reserves"; "Natural Gas Annual"; and "International Energy Statistics," <http://www.eia.gov>.

Table 918. Unconventional Dry Natural Gas Production and Proved Reserves: 2008 and 2009

[In billions of cubic feet (1,966 represents 1,966,000). For states not shown, no production or reserves were reported]

State	Production Coalbed methane [2] 2008	2009	Shale gas [3] 2008	2009	Proved reserves [1] Coalbed methane [2] 2008	2009	Shale gas [3] 2008	2009
U.S.	**1,966**	**1,914**	**2,022**	**3,110**	**20,798**	**18,578**	**34,428**	**60,644**
Alabama	107	105	–	–	1,727	1,342	2	–
Alaska	–	–	–	–	–	–	–	–
Arkansas	3	3	279	527	31	22	3,833	9,070
California	–	–	–	–	–	–	–	–
Colorado	497	498	–	–	8,238	7,348	–	–
Florida	–	–	–	–	–	–	–	–
Kansas..........	47	43	–	–	301	163	–	–
Kentucky	–	–	2	5	–	–	20	55
Louisiana........	1	1	23	293	9	–	858	9,307
Michigan	–	–	122	132	–	–	2,894	2,499
Mississippi.......	–	–	–	–	–	–	–	–
Montana.........	14	12	13	7	75	37	125	137
New Mexico	443	432	–	2	3,991	3,646	–	36
New York	–	–	–	–	–	–	–	–
North Dakota	–	–	3	25	–	–	24	368
Ohio............	–	–	–	–	1	–	–	–
Oklahoma	69	55	168	249	511	338	3,845	6,389
Pennsylvania	11	16	1	65	102	131	88	3,790
Texas...........	–	–	1,503	1,789	–	–	22,667	28,167
Utah............	71	71	–	–	893	725	–	–
Virginia..........	101	111	–	–	1,851	2,261	–	–
West Virginia	28	31	–	11	246	220	14	688
Wyoming	573	535	–	–	2,781	2,328	–	–

– Represents or rounds to zero. [1] Proved reserves of natural gas as of December 31 of the report year are the estimated quantities which analysis of geological and engineering data demonstrate with reasonable certainty to be recoverable in future years from known reservoirs under existing economic and operating conditions. [2] Methane is generated during coal formation and is contained in the coal microstructure. Typical recovery entails pumping water out of the coal to allow the gas to escape. Methane is the principal component of natural gas. Coal bed methane can be added to natural gas pipelines without any special treatment. [3] Natural gas produced from low permeability shale formations.

Source: U.S. Energy Information Administration, "Natural Gas Navigator," <http://www.eia.gov/dnav/ng/ng_sum_top.asp>, accessed June 2011.

Table 919. Coal Supply, Disposition, and Prices: 2000 to 2009

[In millions of short tons (1,073.6 represents 1,073,600,000). 1 short ton = 2,000 lbs.]

Item	2000	2004	2005	2006	2007	2008	2009
United States, total supply	**1,073.6**	**1,112.1**	**1,131.5**	**1,162.8**	**1,146.6**	**1,171.8**	**1,072.8**
Consumption by sector:							
Total	1,084.1	1,107.3	1,126.0	1,112.3	1,128.0	1,120.5	1,000.4
Electric power	985.8	1,016.3	1,037.5	1,026.6	1,045.1	1,040.6	936.5
Coke plants	28.9	23.7	23.4	23.0	22.7	22.1	15.3
Other industrial plants	65.2	62.2	60.3	59.5	56.6	54.4	45.4
Combined heat and power (CHP)	28.0	26.6	25.9	25.3	22.5	23.6	(NA)
Noncombined heat and power	37.2	35.6	34.5	34.2	34.1	31.0	(NA)
Residential/commercial users	4.1	5.1	4.7	3.2	3.5	3.5	3.2
Year-end coal stocks:							
Total [1]	140.0	154.0	144.3	186.9	192.8	205.1	238.8
Electric power	102.0	106.7	101.1	141.0	151.2	161.6	190.0
Coke plants	1.5	1.3	2.6	2.9	1.9	2.3	2.0
Other industrial plants	4.6	4.8	5.6	6.5	5.6	6.0	5.1
Producers/distributors	31.9	41.2	35.0	36.5	34.0	34.7	41.3
U.S. coal trade:							
Net exports [2]	46.0	20.7	19.5	13.4	22.8	47.3	36.5
Exports	58.5	48.0	49.9	49.6	59.2	81.5	59.1
Steam coal	25.7	21.2	21.3	22.1	27.0	39.0	21.8
Metallurgical coal	32.8	26.8	28.7	27.5	32.2	42.5	37.3
Imports	12.5	27.3	30.5	36.2	36.3	34.2	22.6
Average delivered price (dollars per short ton):							
Electric utilities	24.28	27.30	31.22	34.26	36.06	41.32	44.72
Independent power producers	(NA)	27.27	30.39	33.04	33.11	38.98	39.72
Coke plants	44.38	61.50	83.79	92.87	94.97	118.09	143.04
Other industrial plants	31.46	39.30	47.63	51.67	54.42	63.44	64.87
Average free alongside ship (f.a.s.):							
Exports	34.90	54.11	67.10	70.93	70.25	97.68	101.44
Steam coal	29.67	42.03	47.64	46.25	47.90	57.35	73.63
Metallurgical coal	38.99	63.63	81.56	90.81	88.99	134.62	117.73
Imports	30.10	37.52	46.71	49.10	47.64	59.83	63.91

NA Not available. [1] Includes other stocks, not shown separately. [2] Exports minus imports.

Source: U.S. Energy Information Administration, "U.S. Coal Supply and Demand: 2009 Review," annual, April 2010, <http://www.eia.doe.gov/cneaf/coal/page/special/feature.html>.

Table 920. Coal and Coke—Summary: 1990 to 2009

[In millions of short tons (1,029 represents 1,029,000,000), except as indicated. Includes coal consumed at mines. Recoverability varies between 40 and 90 percent for individual deposits; 50 percent or more of overall U.S. coal reserve base is believed to be recoverable]

Item	Unit	1990	1995	2000	2005	2006	2007	2008	2009
COAL									
Coal production, total [1,2]	Mil. sh. tons	**1,029**	**1,033**	**1,074**	**1,131**	**1,163**	**1,147**	**1,172**	**1,073**
Value [3]	Bil. dol.	22.39	19.45	18.02	26.69	29.25	30.04	36.62	35.31
Anthracite production [2]	Mil. sh. tons	3.5	4.7	4.6	1.7	1.5	1.6	1.7	1.9
Bituminous coal and lignite [4]	Mil. sh. tons	1,026	1,028	1,069	1,130	1,161	1,145	1,170	1,071
Underground	Mil. sh. tons	425	396	374	369	359	352	357	332
Surface [2]	Mil. sh. tons	605	637	700	763	804	795	815	741
Exports	Mil. sh. tons	106	89	58	50	50	59	82	59
Imports	Mil. sh. tons	3	9	13	30	36	36	34	23
Consumption [5]	Mil. sh. tons	904	962	1,084	1,126	1,112	1,128	1,121	1,000
Electric power sector [6]	Mil. sh. tons	783	850	986	1,037	1,027	1,045	1,041	937
Industrial	Mil. sh. tons	115	106	94	84	82	79	77	61
Number of mines	Number	3,243	2,104	1,453	1,415	1,438	1,374	1,458	1,407
Daily employment	1,000	131	90	72	79	83	81	87	(NA)
Production, by state: [7]									
Alabama	Mil. sh. tons	29	25	19	21	19	19	21	20
Illinois	Mil. sh. tons	60	48	33	32	33	32	33	30
Indiana	Mil. sh. tons	36	26	28	34	35	35	36	36
Kentucky	Mil. sh. tons	173	154	131	120	121	115	120	109
Montana	Mil. sh. tons	38	39	38	40	42	43	45	42
Ohio	Mil. sh. tons	35	26	22	25	23	23	26	25
Pennsylvania	Mil. sh. tons	71	62	75	67	66	65	65	60
Virginia	Mil. sh. tons	47	34	33	28	30	25	25	23
West Virginia	Mil. sh. tons	169	163	158	154	152	153	158	147
Wyoming	Mil. sh. tons	184	264	339	404	447	454	468	422
Other states	Mil. sh. tons	187	192	197	206	196	181	176	158
World production	Mil. sh. tons	5,347	5,077	4,893	6,542	6,769	7,047	7,271	(NA)
Percent U.S. of world	Percent	19.2	20.3	21.9	17.3	17.2	16.3	16.1	(NA)
COKE									
Production	Mil. sh. tons	27.6	23.7	20.8	16.7	16.4	16.2	15.6	11.1
Imports	Mil. sh. tons	0.8	3.8	3.8	3.5	4.1	2.5	3.6	0.3
Exports	Mil. sh. tons	0.6	1.4	1.1	1.7	1.6	1.4	2.0	1.3
Consumption [8]	Mil. sh. tons	27.8	25.8	23.2	18.2	18.8	17.3	17.0	10.3

NA Not available. [1] Includes bituminous coal, subbituminous coal, lignite, and anthracite. [2] Beginning 2005, includes a small amount of refuse recovery. [3] Coal values are based on free-on-board rail/barge prices, which are the free-on-board prices of coal at the point of first sale, excluding freight or shipping and insurance costs. [4] Includes subbituminous. [5] Includes some categories not shown separately. [6] Electricity-only and combined-heat-and-power (CHP) plants whose primary business is to sell electricity and/or heat to the public. [7] Source: U.S. Energy Information, "Weekly Coal Production," Original estimates, August 19, 2010. [8] Consumption is calculated as the sum of production and imports minus exports and stock change.

Source: U.S. Energy Information Administration, *Annual Energy Review*, "International Energy Annual," "Annual Coal Report," "Monthly Coal Report," and "International Energy Statistics," <http://www.eia.doe.gov>.

Forestry, Fishing, and Mining 579

Table 921. Demonstrated Coal Reserves by Major Producing State: 2008 and 2009

[In millions of short tons (487,768 represents 487,678,000,000), except as number of mines. As of January 1. The demonstrated reserve base represents the sum of coal in both measured and indicated resource categories of reliability. Measured resources of coal are estimates that have a high degree of geologic assurance from sample analyses and measurements from closely spaced and geological well-known sample sites. Indicated resources are estimates based partly from sample and analyses and measurements and partly from reasonable geologic projections]

State	2008				2009			
	Number of mines	Total reserves	Method of mining		Number of mines	Total reserves	Method of mining	
			Under-ground	Surface			Under-ground	Surface
United States [1]	1,458	487,678	332,553	155,124	1,407	486,102	331,882	154,220
Alabama	59	4,106	938	3,167	57	4,074	915	3,158
Alaska	1	6,105	5,423	682	1	6,102	5,423	680
Arkansas	2	416	272	144	2	416	272	144
Colorado	12	16,033	11,273	4,760	11	15,981	11,222	4,760
Illinois............	19	104,286	87,757	16,529	22	104,222	87,700	16,522
Indiana............	30	9,325	8,674	651	33	9,271	8,649	623
Iowa..............	(NA)	2,189	1,732	457	(NA)	2,189	1,732	457
Kansas............	2	971	(NA)	971	1	971	–	971
Kentucky	469	29,416	16,631	12,784	449	29,234	16,505	12,729
Kentucky, Eastern ...	446	10,073	902	9,171	425	9,952	828	9,124
Kentucky, Western...	23	19,342	15,729	3,613	24	19,282	15,677	3,605
Maryland	21	627	569	57	22	623	568	55
Missouri...........	2	5,988	1,479	4,509	2	5,988	1,479	4,508
Montana...........	6	119,067	70,957	48,110	6	119,017	70,955	48,062
New Mexico........	5	12,020	6,114	5,906	5	11,984	6,101	5,883
North Dakota.......	4	8,941	(NA)	8,941	4	8,903	–	8,903
Ohio..............	48	23,174	17,450	5,725	46	23,127	17,415	5,712
Oklahoma	7	1,547	1,228	319	10	1,545	1,227	318
Pennsylvania	266	27,107	22,900	4,207	244	26,998	22,802	4,195
Anthracite	66	7,192	3,842	3,350	64	7,190	3,842	3,348
Bituminous........	200	19,914	19,057	857	180	19,807	18,960	847
Tennessee.........	23	762	505	258	25	759	503	256
Texas.............	11	12,227	(NA)	12,227	12	12,183	(NA)	12,183
Utah..............	9	5,246	4,979	268	8	5,203	4,935	268
Virginia............	114	1,555	1,030	525	108	1,519	1,004	515
Washington	(NA)	1,340	1,332	8	(NA)	1,340	1,332	8
West Virginia	301	32,187	28,669	3,518	283	31,955	28,507	3,448
Wyoming	20	62,104	42,486	19,618	20	61,563	42,479	19,084

– Represents zero. NA Not available. [1] Includes other states not shown separately.

Source: U.S. Energy Information Administration, *Annual Coal Report, 2009,* September 2010. See also <http://www.eia.doe.gov/cneaf/coal/page/acr/acr_sum.html>.

Table 922. Uranium Concentrate Industry—Summary: 1990 to 2009

[In millions of feet (1.7 represents 1,700,000), except as indicated. See also Section 19, Table 938]

Item	Unit	1990	1995	2000	2004	2005	2006	2007	2008	2009
Exploration and development, surface drilling	Mil. ft..........	1.7	1.3	1.0	1.2	1.7	2.7	5.1	5.1	3.7
Expenditures	Mil. dol.........	(NA)	2.6	5.6	10.6	18.1	40.1	67.5	81.9	35.4
Number of mines operated ...	Number	39	12	10	6	10	11	12	17	20
Underground	Number	27	–	1	2	4	5	6	10	14
Openpit	Number	2	–	–	–	–	–	–	–	–
In situ leaching.	Number	7	5	4	3	4	5	5	6	4
Other sources [1]	Number	3	7	5	1	2	1	1	1	2
Mine production.	1,000 pounds...	5,876	3,528	3,123	2,452	3,045	4,692	4,541	3,879	4,145
Underground	1,000 pounds...	(D)	–	(D)	(D)	(D)	(D)	(D)	(D)	(D)
Openpit	1,000 pounds...	1,881	–	–	–	–	–	–	–	–
In situ leaching.	1,000 pounds...	(D)	3,372	2,995	(D)	2,681	4,259	(D)	(D)	(D)
Other sources [1]	1,000 pounds...	3,995	156	128	(D)	(D)	(D)	(D)	(D)	(D)
Uranium concentrate production	1,000 pounds...	8,886	6,043	3,958	2,282	2,689	4,106	4,534	3,092	3,708
Concentrate shipments from mills and plants	1,000 pounds...	12,957	5,500	3,187	2,280	2,702	3,838	4,050	4,130	3,620
Employment..............	Person-years ...	1,335	1,107	627	420	648	755	1,231	1,563	1,096

– Represents zero. D Data withheld to avoid disclosing figures for individual companies. NA Not available. [1] Includes mine water, mill site cleanup and mill tailings, and well field restoration as sources of uranium.

Source: U.S. Energy Information Administration, through 2002, *Uranium Industry,* annual. Thereafter, "Domestic Uranium Production Report" annual, July 2010. See also <http://www.eia.doe.gov/cneaf/nuclear/dupr/dupr.html>.

Section 19
Energy and Utilities

This section presents statistics on fuel resources, energy production and consumption, electric energy, hydroelectric power, nuclear power, solar and wind energy, biomass, and the electric and gas utility industries. The principal sources are the U.S. Department of Energy's Energy Information Administration (EIA), the Edison Electric Institute, Washington, DC, and the American Gas Association, Arlington, VA. The Department of Energy was created in October 1977 and assumed and centralized the responsibilities of all or part of several agencies including the Federal Power Commission (FPC), the U.S. Bureau of Mines, the Federal Energy Administration, and the U.S. Energy Research and Development Administration. For additional data on transportation, see Section 23; on fuels, see Section 18; and on energy–related housing characteristics, see Section 20.

The EIA, in its *Annual Energy Review*, provides statistics and trend data on energy supply, demand, and prices. Information is included on petroleum and natural gas, coal, electricity, hydroelectric power, nuclear power, solar, wind, wood, and geothermal energy. Among its annual reports are *Annual Energy Review*; *Electric Power Annual*; *Natural Gas Annual*; *Petroleum Supply Annual*; *State Energy Consumption, Price,* and *Expenditure Data*; *U.S. Crude Oil, Natural Gas,* and *Natural Gas Liquids Reserves*; *Electric Sales and Revenue*; *Annual Energy Outlook*; and *International Energy Statistics*. These various reports contain state, national, and international data on the production of electricity, net summer capability of generating plants, fuels used in energy production, energy sales and consumption, and hydroelectric power. The EIA also issues the *Monthly Energy Review*, which presents current supply, disposition, and price data and monthly publications on petroleum, coal, natural gas, and electric power.

Data on residential energy consumption, expenditures, and conservation activities are available from EIA's Residential Energy Consumption Survey (RECS) and are published every 4 years. The Commercial Buildings Energy Consumption Survey (CBECS), conducted on a quadrennial basis, collects information on the stock of U.S. commercial buildings, their energy-related characteristics, and their energy consumption and expenditures. Data on manufacturing energy consumption, use, and expenditures are also collected every 4 years from EIA's Manufacturing Energy Consumption Survey (MECS). Due to the long gaps between the RECS, CBECS, and MECS, tables are rotated in and out of Section 19 in an effort to keep the data as current as possible. The results from these surveys are published at <http://www.eia.gov/consumption/>.

The Edison Electric Institute's monthly bulletin and annual *Statistical Year Book of the Electric Utility Industry for the Year* contain data on the distribution of electric energy by public utilities; information on the electric power supply, expansion of electric generating facilities, and the manufacture of heavy electric power equipment is presented in the annual *Year-End Summary of the Electric Power Situation in the United States*. The American Gas Association, in its monthly and quarterly bulletins and its yearbook, *Gas Facts*, presents data on gas utilities and financial and operating statistics.

Btu conversion factors—Various energy sources are converted from original units to the thermal equivalent using British thermal units (Btu). A Btu is the amount of energy required to raise the temperature of 1 pound of water 1 degree Fahrenheit (F) at or near 39.2 degrees F. Factors are calculated annually from the latest final annual data available; some are revised as a result. The following list provides conversion factors used in 2009 for production and consumption, in that

Energy and Utilities **581**

order, for various fuels: Petroleum, 5.800 and 5.301 mil. Btu per barrel; total coal, 19.969 and 19.742 mil. Btu per short ton; and natural gas (dry), 1,025 Btu per cubic foot for both. The factors for the production of nuclear power and geothermal power were 10,460 and 21,017 Btu per kilowatt-hour, respectively. The fossil fuel steam–electric power plant generation factor of 9,760 Btu per kilowatt-hour— was used for hydroelectric power generation and for wood and waste, wind, photovoltaic, and solar thermal energy consumed at electric utilities.

Electric power industry—In recent years, EIA has restructured the industry categories it once used to gather and report electricity statistics. The electric power industry, previously divided into electric utilities and non–utilities, now consists of the Electric Power Sector, the Commercial Sector, and the Industrial Sector.

The Electric Power Sector is composed of electricity-only and combined-heat-and-power plants (CHPs) whose primary business is to sell electricity, or electricity and heat, to the public.

Electricity-only plants are composed of traditional electric utilities, and nontraditional participants, including energy service providers, power marketers, independent power producers (IPPs), and the portion of CHPs that produce only electricity.

A utility is defined as a corporation, person, agency, authority, or other legal entity or instrumentality aligned with distribution facilities for delivery of electric energy for use primarily by the public. Electric utilities include investor-owned electric utilities, municipal and state utilities, federal electric utilities, and rural electric cooperatives. In total, there are more than 3,100 electric utilities in the United States.

An independent power producer is an entity defined as a corporation, person, agency, authority, or other legal entity or instrumentality that owns or operates facilities whose primary business is to produce electricity for use by the public. They are not generally aligned with distribution facilities and are not considered electric utilities.

Combined-heat-and-power producers are plants designed to produce both heat and electricity from a single heat source. These types of electricity producers can be independent power producers or industrial or commercial establishments. As some independent power producers are CHPs, their information is included in the data for the combined-heat-and-power sector. There are approximately 2,800 unregulated independent power producers and CHPs in the United States.

The Commercial Sector consists of commercial CHPs and commercial electricity–only plants. Industrial CHPs and industrial electricity–only plants make up the Industrial Sector. For more information, please refer to the *Electric Power Annual 2009* Web site at <http://www.eia..gov/cneaf /electricity/epa/epa_sum.html>.

Table 923. Utilities—Establishments, Revenue, Payroll, and Employees by Kind of Business: 2007

[584,193 represents $584,193,000,000. Includes only establishments or firms with payroll. Data based on the 2007 Economic Census. See headnote, Table 755 and Appendix III]

Kind of business	2007 NAICS code [1]	Establish- ments (number)	Revenue Total (mil. dol.)	Revenue Per paid employee (dol.)	Annual payroll Total (mil. dol.)	Annual payroll Per paid employee (dol.)	Paid employees for pay period including March 12 (number)
Utilities..........................	22	16,578	584,193	916,744	51,654	81,057	637,247
Electric power generation, transmission, & distribution	2211	9,554	445,693	871,368	43,618	85,277	511,487
Electric power generation	22111	1,934	120,968	985,134	11,297	92,001	122,793
Hydroelectric power generation........	221111	295	2,185	534,773	290	71,092	4,086
Fossil fuel electric power generation	221112	1,248	85,362	1,140,283	6,413	85,667	74,860
Nuclear electric power generation.......	221113	79	28,996	763,603	4,083	107,525	37,972
Other electric power generation	221119	312	4,425	753,252	511	86,927	5,875
Electric power transmission, control & distribution	22112	7,620	324,726	835,428	32,321	83,153	388,694
Electric bulk power transmission & control	221121	74	4,268	697,997	543	88,795	6,114
Electric power distribution	221122	7,546	320,458	837,625	31,778	83,063	382,580
Natural gas distribution	2212	2,377	128,555	1,542,000	6,038	72,420	83,369
Water, sewage, & other systems	2213	4,647	9,944	234,582	1,998	47,125	42,391
Water supply & irrigation systems	22131	3,889	7,623	225,070	1,596	47,115	33,871
Sewage treatment facilities	22132	689	1,309	187,718	297	42,634	6,974
Steam & air-conditioning supply	22133	69	1,012	654,375	105	67,603	1,546

[1] North American Industry Classification System, 2007; see text, Section 15.

Source: U.S. Census Bureau, "2007 Economic Census." See also <http://www.census.gov/econ/census07/>, accessed September 2010.

Table 924. Utilities—Employees, Annual Payroll, and Establishments by Industry: 2008

[54,946 represents $54,946,000,000. Excludes most government employees, railroad employees, and self-employed persons, etc. An establishment is a single physical location where business is conducted or where services or industrial operations are performed. See Appendix III]

Industry	2007 NAICS code [1]	Number of employ- ees [2]	Annual payroll (mil. dol.)	Average payroll per employ- ee (dol.)	Establishments by employment size-class Total	Under 20 employ- ees	20 to 99 employ- ees	100 to 499 employ- ees	500 employ- ees and over
Utilities, total	22	639,403	54,946	85,933	16,960	11,717	3,886	1,172	185
Electric power generation, transmission and distribution	2211	510,735	46,042	90,148	9,744	5,684	2,973	918	169
Electric power generation	22111	122,610	11,910	97,140	2,087	1,256	550	231	50
Hydroelectric power generation..	221111	4,371	410	93,830	309	268	36	4	1
Fossil fuel electric power generation	221112	73,408	6,583	89,683	1,250	619	419	204	8
Nuclear electric power generation	221113	38,029	4,341	114,146	83	19	12	11	41
Other electric power generation	221119	6,802	576	84,668	445	350	83	12	–
Electric power transmission, control & distribution	22112	388,125	34,132	87,940	7,657	4,428	2,423	687	119
Electric bulk power transmission & control	221121	6,452	647	100,230	79	46	16	13	4
Electric power distribution	221122	381,673	33,485	87,732	7,578	4,382	2,407	674	115
Natural gas distribution	2212	85,542	6,709	78,428	2,400	1,618	561	207	14
Water, sewage, & other systems ...	2213	43,126	2,195	50,899	4,816	4,415	352	47	2
Water supply & irrigation systems	22131	34,724	1,761	50,715	4,082	3,785	255	40	2
Sewage treatment facilities	22132	6,363	291	45,764	663	590	69	4	–
Steam & air-conditioning supply ..	22133	2,039	143	70,047	71	40	28	3	–

– Represents zero. [1] North American Industry Classification System, 2007; see text, Section 15. [2] Covers full- and part-time employees who are on the payroll in the pay period including March 12.

Source: U.S. Census Bureau, "County Business Patterns," July 2010, <http://www.census.gov/econ/cbp/index.html>.

Energy and Utilities 583

Table 925. Energy Supply and Disposition by Type of Fuel: 1975 to 2010

[In quadrillion British thermal units (Btu) (61.32 represents 61,320,000,000,000,000). For definition of Btu, see source and text, this section]

Year	Production Total[1]	Crude oil[2]	Dry natural gas	Coal[3]	Nuclear electric power	Renewable energy[4] Total[1]	Hydroelectric power[5]	Biomass[6]	Solar/photovoltaic	Wind	Net imports, total[7]	Consumption Total[1,8]	Petroleum[9]	Dry natural gas[10]	Coal	Nuclear electric power	Renewable energy,[4] total
1975	61.32	17.73	19.64	14.96	1.90	4.69	3.16	1.50	(NA)	(NA)	11.71	71.97	32.73	19.95	12.66	1.90	4.69
1980	67.18	18.25	19.91	18.60	2.74	5.43	2.90	2.48	(NA)	(NA)	12.10	78.07	34.21	20.24	15.42	2.74	5.43
1985	67.70	18.99	16.98	19.33	4.08	6.08	2.97	3.02	(Z)	(Z)	7.58	76.39	30.93	17.70	17.48	4.08	6.08
1990	70.71	15.57	18.33	22.49	6.10	6.04	3.05	2.74	0.06	0.03	14.07	84.49	33.55	19.60	19.17	6.10	6.04
1995	71.17	13.89	19.08	22.13	7.08	6.56	3.21	3.10	0.07	0.03	17.75	91.03	34.44	22.67	20.09	7.08	6.56
1996	72.49	13.72	19.34	22.79	7.09	7.01	3.59	3.16	0.07	0.03	19.07	94.02	35.68	23.09	21.00	7.09	7.01
1997	72.47	13.66	19.39	23.31	6.60	7.02	3.64	3.11	0.07	0.03	20.70	94.60	36.16	23.22	21.45	6.60	7.02
1998	72.88	13.24	19.61	24.05	7.07	6.49	3.30	2.93	0.07	0.03	22.28	95.02	36.82	22.83	21.66	7.07	6.49
1999	71.74	12.45	19.34	23.30	7.61	6.52	3.27	2.97	0.07	0.05	23.54	96.65	37.84	22.91	21.62	7.61	6.52
2000	71.33	12.36	19.66	22.74	7.86	6.10	2.81	3.01	0.07	0.06	24.97	98.81	38.26	23.82	22.58	7.86	6.11
2001	71.74	12.28	20.17	23.55	8.03	5.16	2.24	2.62	0.06	0.07	26.39	96.17	38.19	22.77	21.91	8.03	5.16
2002	70.77	12.16	19.44	22.73	8.15	5.73	2.69	2.71	0.06	0.11	25.74	97.69	38.22	23.56	21.90	8.15	5.73
2003	70.04	12.03	19.63	22.09	7.96	5.98	2.83	2.81	0.06	0.12	27.01	97.98	38.81	22.83	22.32	7.96	5.98
2004	70.19	11.50	19.07	22.85	8.22	6.07	2.69	3.00	0.06	0.14	29.11	100.15	40.29	22.91	22.47	8.22	6.08
2005	69.43	10.96	18.56	23.19	8.16	6.23	2.70	3.10	0.06	0.18	30.15	100.28	40.39	22.56	22.80	8.16	6.24
2006	70.79	10.80	19.02	23.79	8.22	6.61	2.87	3.23	0.07	0.26	29.81	99.62	39.96	22.22	22.45	8.22	6.66
2007	71.44	10.72	19.83	23.49	8.46	6.54	2.45	3.49	0.08	0.34	29.22	101.36	39.77	23.70	22.75	8.46	6.55
2008	73.11	10.51	20.70	23.85	8.43	7.21	2.51	3.87	0.09	0.55	25.93	99.27	37.28	23.83	22.39	8.43	7.19
2009	72.60	11.35	21.10	21.63	8.36	7.60	2.67	3.92	0.10	0.72	22.74	94.48	35.40	23.34	19.69	8.36	7.59
2010[11]	75.03	11.67	22.10	22.08	8.44	8.06	2.51	4.31	0.11	0.92	21.62	98.00	35.97	24.64	20.82	8.44	8.05

NA Not available. Z Less than 5 trillion. [1] Includes other types of fuel, not shown separately. [2] Includes lease condensate. [3] Beginning 1989, includes waste coal supplied. Beginning 2001, also includes a small amount of refuse recovery. [4] Electricity net generation from conventional hydroelectric power, geothermal, solar, and wind; consumption of electricity from wood, waste, and alcohol fuels; geothermal heat pump and direct use energy; and solar thermal direct use energy. [5] Conventional hydroelectricity net generation. [6] Organic nonfossil material of biological origin constituting a renewable energy source. [7] Imports minus exports. [8] Includes coal coke net imports and electricity net imports, not shown separately. [9] Petroleum products supplied, including natural gas plant liquids and crude oil burned as fuel. Does not include biofuels that have been blended with petroleum—biofuels are included in "Renewable Energy." [10] Excludes supplemental gaseous fuels. [11] Preliminary.

Source: U.S. Energy Information Administration, "Monthly Energy Review," May 2011, <http://www.eia.gov/totalenergy/data/monthly/>.

Table 926. Energy Supply and Disposition by Type of Fuel—Estimates, 2008 and 2009, and Projections, 2010 to 2025

[Quadrillion Btu (73.80 represents 73,800,000,000,000,000) per year. Btu = British thermal unit. For definition of Btu, see source and text, this section. Mcf = 1,000 cubic feet. Projections are "reference" or mid-level forecasts. See report for methodology and assumptions used in generating projections]

Type of Fuel	2008	2009	Projections			
			2010	2015	2020	2025
Production, total	**73.80**	**73.18**	**75.64**	**78.63**	**83.42**	**87.29**
Crude oil and lease condensate	10.51	11.34	11.87	12.51	13.07	12.64
Natural gas plant liquids	2.41	2.57	2.64	2.86	3.06	3.55
Natural gas, dry	20.83	21.50	21.83	23.01	24.04	24.60
Coal [1]	23.85	21.58	22.59	20.94	22.05	23.64
Nuclear power	8.43	8.35	8.39	8.77	9.17	9.17
Renewable energy [2]	7.59	7.50	7.77	9.76	11.07	12.82
Other [3]	0.19	0.34	0.55	0.78	0.96	0.88
Imports, total	**32.76**	**29.53**	**29.16**	**29.41**	**28.57**	**28.13**
Crude oil [4]	21.39	19.70	20.19	19.25	18.46	18.35
Petroleum products [5]	6.32	5.40	4.53	5.33	5.34	5.18
Natural gas	4.08	3.82	3.89	4.01	3.80	3.20
Other imports [6]	0.96	0.61	0.55	0.82	0.98	1.39
Exports, total	**6.86**	**6.77**	**7.23**	**6.27**	**7.28**	**7.58**
Petroleum [7]	3.78	4.17	4.25	3.27	3.54	3.62
Natural gas	1.01	1.09	1.06	1.24	1.82	2.07
Coal	2.07	1.51	1.93	1.76	1.92	1.89
Consumption, total	**100.14**	**94.79**	**97.77**	**102.02**	**104.92**	**107.95**
Petroleum products [8]	38.46	36.62	36.96	39.10	39.38	39.84
Natural gas	23.85	23.31	24.45	25.77	26.00	25.73
Coal	22.38	19.69	21.05	19.73	20.85	22.61
Nuclear power	8.43	8.35	8.39	8.77	9.17	9.17
Renewable energy [9]	6.72	6.50	6.60	8.33	9.23	10.33
Other [10]	0.31	0.32	0.32	0.31	0.29	0.27
Net imports of petroleum	**23.93**	**20.93**	**20.47**	**21.31**	**20.26**	**19.91**
Prices (2006 dollars per unit):						
Imported crude oil price [11]	93.44	59.04	74.86	86.83	98.65	107.40
Gas wellhead price (dol. per 1,000 cu. ft.) [12]	8.18	3.71	4.08	4.24	4.59	5.43
Coal minemouth price (dol. per ton) [13]	31.54	33.26	36.64	32.36	32.85	33.22
Average electric price (cents per kWh)	9.80	9.80	9.60	8.90	8.80	8.90

[1] Includes waste coal. [2] Includes grid-connected electricity from conventional hydroelectric; wood and wood waste; landfill gas; municipal solid waste; other biomass; wind; photovoltaic and solar thermal sources; nonelectric energy from renewable sources, such as active and passive solar systems, and wood. Excludes electricity imports using renewable sources and nonmarketed renewable energy. [3] Includes nonbiogenic municipal solid waste, liquid hydrogen, methanol, and some domestic inputs to refineries. [4] Includes imports of crude oil for the Strategic Petroleum Reserve. [5] Includes imports of finished petroleum products, imports of unfinished oils, alcohols, ethers, blending components, and renewable fuels such as ethanol. [6] Includes coal, coal coke (net), and electricity (net). [7] Includes crude oil and petroleum products. [8] Includes petroleum-derived fuels and non-petroleum-derived fuels, such as ethanol, biodiesel, and coal-based synthetic liquids. Petroleum coke, which is a solid, is included. Also included are natural gas plant liquids, crude oil consumed as a fuel, and liquid hydrogen. [9] Includes grid-connected electricity from wood and wood waste, non-electric energy from wood, and biofuels heat and coproducts used in the production of liquid fuel, but excludes the energy content of the liquid fuels. Also includes non-biogenic municipal solid waste and net electricity imports. [10] Includes non-biogenic municipal solid waste and net electricity imports. [11] Weighted average price delivered to U.S. refiners. [12] Represents lower 48 onshore and offshore supplies. [13] Includes reported prices for both open market and captive mines.

Source: U.S. Energy Information Administration, *Annual Energy Outlook 2011,* April 2011. See also <http://www.eia.gov/forecasts/aeo/index.cfm>.

Table 927. Fossil Fuel Prices by Type of Fuel: 1980 to 2009

[In dollars per million British thermal units (Btu), except as indicated. For definition of Btu and mineral fuel conversions, see source and text, this section. All fuel prices taken as close to the point of production as possible]

Fuel	1980	1990	1995	2000	2003	2004	2005	2006	2007	2008	2009 [1]
CURRENT DOLLARS											
Composite [2]	2.04	1.84	1.47	2.60	3.09	3.61	4.74	4.73	4.95	6.52	3.97
Crude oil [3]	3.72	3.45	2.52	4.61	4.75	6.34	8.67	10.29	11.47	16.21	9.72
Natural gas [4]	1.45	1.55	1.40	3.32	4.41	4.95	6.64	5.79	5.66	7.24	3.37
Coal [5]	1.10	1.00	0.88	0.80	0.87	0.98	1.16	1.24	1.29	1.55	1.65
CONSTANT (2005) DOLLARS											
Composite [2]	4.28	2.55	1.81	2.93	3.29	3.73	4.74	4.58	4.66	6.01	3.62
Crude oil [3]	7.80	4.78	3.09	5.20	5.05	6.55	8.67	9.97	10.80	14.95	8.86
Natural gas [4]	3.03	2.14	1.72	3.75	4.69	5.11	6.64	5.61	5.33	6.67	3.07
Coal [5]	2.30	1.38	1.08	0.90	0.93	1.01	1.16	1.20	1.21	1.43	1.50

[1] Preliminary. [2] Derived by multiplying the price per Btu of each fossil fuel by the total Btu content of the production of each fossil fuel and dividing this accumulated value of total fossil fuel production by the accumulated Btu content of total fossil fuel production. [3] Domestic first purchase prices. [4] Wellhead prices. [5] Free-on-board (f.o.b.) rail/barge prices, which are the f.o.b. prices of coal at the point of first sale, excluding freight or shipping and insurance costs. Includes bituminous coal, subbituminous coal, and lignite.

Source: U.S. Energy Information Administration, *Annual Energy Review 2009,* August 2010. See also <http://www.eia.gov/totalenergy/data/annual>.

Table 928. Energy Expenditures and Average Fuel Prices by Source and Sector: 1980 to 2007

[In millions of dollars (374,346 represents $374,346,000,000), except as indicated. For definition of Btu, see text, this section. End-use sector and electric utilities exclude expenditures and prices on energy sources such as hydropower, solar, wind, and geothermal. Also excludes expenditures for reported amounts of energy consumed by the energy industry for production, transportation, and processing operations]

Source and Sector	1980	1990	1995	2000	2003	2004	2005	2006	2007
EXPENDITURES (mil. dol.)									
Total [1,2,3]	374,346	472,539	514,049	687,587	754,668	869,112	1,045,465	1,158,483	1,233,058
Natural gas [4]	51,061	65,278	75,020	119,094	144,489	162,702	200,303	190,382	196,482
Petroleum products	237,676	235,368	236,905	359,140	378,967	468,354	595,905	681,448	739,856
Motor gasoline [5]	124,408	126,558	136,647	193,947	209,592	253,218	311,094	357,129	388,561
Coal	22,607	28,602	27,431	28,080	29,402	31,764	36,932	40,005	42,673
Electricity sales	98,095	176,691	205,876	231,577	257,995	268,136	295,789	323,965	340,928
Residential sector [6]	69,418	111,097	128,388	156,061	179,288	190,120	216,016	226,255	238,695
Commercial sector [2,3]	46,932	79,288	91,788	112,870	129,458	137,903	154,558	166,899	174,108
Industrial sector [2,3]	94,316	102,411	107,060	139,810	150,740	176,639	208,248	227,319	235,692
Transportation sector [2]	163,680	179,743	186,813	278,846	295,182	364,450	466,643	538,011	584,564
Motor gasoline [5]	121,809	123,845	134,641	191,620	204,878	247,181	303,942	348,544	380,518
Electric utilities [3]	38,027	40,626	39,073	60,054	64,685	71,720	95,975	90,104	100,715
AVERAGE FUEL PRICES (dol. per mil. Btu)									
All sectors	6.89	8.25	8.28	10.31	11.38	12.87	15.52	17.34	18.23
Residential sector [6]	7.46	11.88	12.63	14.27	15.85	17.11	19.22	21.55	21.64
Commercial sector [3]	7.85	11.89	12.64	13.93	15.61	16.60	18.59	20.64	20.74
Industrial sector [3]	4.71	5.23	4.97	6.41	7.39	8.46	10.36	11.33	11.89
Transportation sector	8.60	8.27	8.08	10.78	11.20	13.36	16.84	19.10	20.58
Electric utilities [3]	1.77	1.48	1.29	1.71	1.84	2.00	2.61	2.48	2.68

[1] Includes other sources not shown separately. [2] Through 1990, total also includes ethanol blended into gasoline that is not included in motor gasoline for those years. [3] There are no direct fuel costs for hydroelectric, geothermal, wind, photovoltaic, or solar thermal energy. [4] Excludes supplemental gaseous fuels. [5] Beginning 1995, includes fuel ethanol blended into motor gasoline. [6] There are no direct fuel costs for geothermal, photovoltaic, or solar thermal energy.

Source: U.S. Energy Information Administration, "State Energy Data: Prices and Expenditures," annual, August 2009, <http://www.eia.gov/state/seds/#>.

Table 929. Energy Consumption by Mode of Transportation: 2000 to 2009

[40 represents 40,000,000,000,000. Btu = British thermal unit. For conversion rates for each fuel type, see source]

Mode	Trillion Btu			Physical units			
	2000	2005	2009	Unit	2000	2005	2009
AIR [1]							
Aviation gasoline	40	35	27	mil. gal.	333	295	227
Jet fuel	2,138	2,093	1,535	mil. gal.	14,876	14,811	12,594
HIGHWAY							
Light duty vehicle, short wheel base and motorcycle [2]	11,148	11,694	10,754	mil. gal.	89,183	93,555	86,035
Light duty vehicle, long wheel base [2]	3,613	4,298	4,470	mil. gal.	28,908	34,383	35,764
Single-unit 2-axle 6-tire or more truck	1,195	1,188	2,043	mil. gal.	9,563	9,501	16,342
Combination truck [3]	3,208	3,461	3,516	mil. gal.	25,666	27,689	28,130
Bus	139	140	234	mil. gal.	1,112	1,120	1,869
TRANSIT [4]							
Electricity	18	20	20	mil. kWh	5,382	5,765	4,695
Diesel	82	67	62	mil. gal.	591	480	449
Gasoline and other nondiesel fuels [5]	3	10	11	mil. gal.	24	81	90
Compressed natural gas	6	13	19	mil. gal.	44	94	140
RAIL [6]							
Distillate/diesel fuel	513	568	443	mil. gal.	3,700	4,098	3,192
Electricity	2	2	2	mil. kWh	470	531	565
WATER							
Residual fuel oil	960	775	680	mil. gal.	6,410	5,179	4,543
Distillate/diesel fuel oil	314	278	176	mil. gal.	2,261	2,006	1,266
Gasoline	141	158	141	mil. gal.	1,124	1,261	1,130
PIPELINE							
Natural gas	662	602	617	mil. cu. ft.	642,210	584,026	598,216

[1] Includes general aviation and certified carriers, domestic operations only. Also includes fuel used in air taxi operations, but not commuter operations. [2] Light duty vehicle, short wheel base includes passenger cars, light trucks, vans, and sport utility vehicles (SUVs) with a wheel base equal to or less than 121 inches. Light duty vehicle, long wheel base includes large passenger cars, pickup trucks, vans, and SUVs with a wheel base longer than 121 inches. [3] A power unit (truck tractor) and one or more trailing units (a semitrailer or trailer). [4] Includes light, heavy, and commuter rail; motor bus; trolley bus; van pools; automated guideway; and demand-responsive vehicles. [5] Gasoline and all other nondiesel fuels such as liquefied natural gas, methanol, and propane, except compressed natural gas. [6] Includes Amtrak and freight service carriers that have an annual operating revenue of $250 million or more.

Source: U.S. Department of Transportation, Bureau of Transportation Statistics, National Transportation Statistics, 2011. See also <http://www.bts.gov/publications/national_transportation_statistics/>, accessed May 2011.

Table 930. Energy Consumption by End-Use Sector: 1975 to 2010

[71.97 represents 71,970,000,000,000,000 Btu. Btu = British thermal units. For definition of Btu, see source and text, this section. See Appendix III. Total energy consumption in the end-use sectors consists of primary energy consumption, electricity retail sales, and electrical system energy losses]

Year	Total (quad. Btu)	Residential and commercial [1] (quad. Btu)	Industrial [2] (quad. Btu)	Transportation (quad. Btu)	Percent of total		
					Residential and commercial [1]	Industrial [2]	Transportation
1975.........	71.97	24.31	29.41	18.25	33.8	40.9	25.4
1980.........	78.07	26.33	32.04	19.70	33.7	41.0	25.2
1985.........	76.39	27.49	28.82	20.09	36.0	37.7	26.3
1990.........	84.49	30.27	31.81	22.42	35.8	37.7	26.5
1995.........	91.03	33.21	33.97	23.85	36.5	37.3	26.2
2000.........	98.81	37.60	34.66	26.55	38.1	35.1	26.9
2002.........	97.69	38.17	32.68	26.85	39.1	33.4	27.5
2003.........	97.98	38.45	32.53	26.99	39.2	33.2	27.6
2004.........	100.15	38.75	33.51	27.90	38.7	33.5	27.9
2005.........	100.28	39.48	32.44	28.35	39.4	32.4	28.3
2006.........	99.62	38.41	32.39	28.83	38.6	32.5	28.9
2007.........	101.36	39.83	32.42	29.12	39.3	32.0	28.7
2008.........	99.27	39.98	31.28	28.01	40.3	31.5	28.2
2009.........	94.48	38.96	28.51	27.00	41.2	30.2	28.6
2010 [3]......	98.00	40.36	30.14	27.51	41.2	30.8	28.1

[1] Commercial sector fuel use, including that at commercial combined-heat-and-power (CHP) and commercial electricity-only plants. [2] Industrial sector fuel use, including that at industrial combined-heat-and-power (CHP) and industrial electricity-only plants. [3] Preliminary.

Source: U.S. Energy Information Administration, "Monthly Energy Review," May 2011, <http://www.eia.gov/totalenergy/data/monthly/>.

Figure 19.1

Energy Consumption by End-Use Sector: 2010
(Quadrillion Btu)

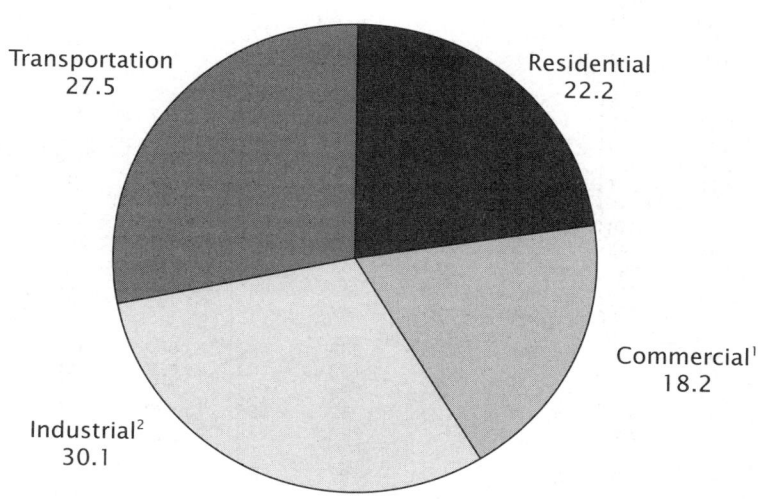

Total Consumption=98.0

Transportation 27.5

Residential 22.2

Commercial [1] 18.2

Industrial [2] 30.1

[1]Commercial sector fuel use, including that at commercial combined-heat-and-power (CHP) and comercial electricity-only plants.
[2]Industrial sector fuel use, including that at industrial combined-heat-and-power (CHP) and industrial electricity-only plants.

Source: Chart prepared by U.S. Census Bureau. For data, see Table 930.

Table 931. Energy Consumption—End-Use Sector and Selected Source by State: 2008

[In trillions of Btu (99,382 represents 99,382,000,000,000,000), except as indicated. For definition of Btu, see source and text, this section. Data are preliminary. U.S. totals may not equal sum of states due to independent rounding and/or interstate flows of electricity that are not allocated to the states. For technical notes and documentation, see source <http://www.eia.gov/state/seds/seds-technical-notes-updates.cfm>]

State	Total [1,2]	Per capita [3] (mil. Btu)	End-use sector [4]				Source				
			Resi-dential	Com-mercial	Indus-trial [2]	Trans-portation	Petro-leum [5]	Natural gas (dry) [6]	Coal	Hydro-electric power [7]	Nuclear electric power
U.S.	99,382	327	21,603	18,414	31,356	28,010	38,102	23,847	22,385	2,511	8,427
AL	2,065	441	401	279	905	480	598	420	843	60	408
AK	651	946	55	63	318	215	279	344	15	12	–
AZ	1,553	239	420	369	244	519	576	410	459	72	306
AR	1,125	392	233	167	433	292	376	238	279	46	148
CA	8,381	229	1,569	1,640	1,955	3,218	3,736	2,521	63	238	340
CO	1,498	304	350	300	412	435	504	515	385	20	–
CT	810	231	266	205	90	249	362	170	45	5	161
DE	295	337	66	58	98	73	128	50	61	–	–
DC	180	306	36	121	4	20	20	33	(Z)	–	–
FL	4,447	241	1,295	1,085	540	1,528	1,808	970	693	2	336
GA	3,015	311	745	567	812	891	1,029	437	886	21	331
HI	284	220	37	44	65	138	245	3	20	1	–
ID	529	346	128	86	187	128	159	91	9	92	–
IL	4,089	318	1,026	800	1,237	1,027	1,367	1,015	1,103	1	995
IN	2,857	447	558	377	1,302	620	836	559	1,558	4	–
IA	1,414	472	249	202	654	309	428	324	485	8	55
KS	1,136	406	233	205	420	278	408	293	372	(Z)	89
KY	1,983	462	373	258	891	461	698	233	1,025	19	–
LA	3,488	783	357	276	2,204	651	1,450	1,360	262	10	161
ME	469	356	94	79	177	119	210	65	6	44	–
MD	1,447	256	410	410	175	452	535	203	309	19	153
MA	1,475	225	431	370	185	489	657	382	107	11	61
MI	2,918	292	788	619	756	755	913	797	800	13	329
MN	1,979	378	423	362	615	579	739	410	359	7	136
MS	1,186	403	234	170	421	361	430	364	177	–	98
MO	1,937	325	531	416	406	584	716	298	793	20	98
MT	434	449	84	70	171	110	184	78	203	99	–
NE	782	439	161	141	300	180	226	169	235	3	99
NV	750	287	180	134	199	237	271	275	89	17	–
NH	311	235	90	71	44	106	168	73	40	16	98
NJ	2,637	304	596	630	391	1,020	1,300	635	98	(Z)	337
NM	693	349	115	127	245	207	267	251	284	3	–
NY	3,988	205	1,166	1,275	434	1,113	1,560	1,205	229	263	452
NC	2,702	292	715	582	628	777	953	250	795	30	416
ND	441	687	68	64	214	96	141	66	425	12	–
OH	3,987	346	952	710	1,341	984	1,300	824	1,438	4	183
OK	1,603	440	315	253	559	476	572	691	392	38	–
OR	1,105	292	276	214	283	332	374	275	41	333	–
PA	3,900	310	941	706	1,256	997	1,378	778	1,421	25	822
RI	220	209	70	56	30	65	97	91	–	(Z)	–
SC	1,660	369	362	266	585	447	560	176	445	11	541
SD	350	435	70	61	130	89	117	65	43	29	–
TN	2,261	362	543	383	720	615	763	238	644	56	283
TX	11,552	475	1,616	1,420	5,652	2,865	5,499	3,656	1,606	10	426
UT	799	293	172	156	224	247	291	237	396	7	–
VT	154	249	44	32	27	52	81	9	–	15	51
VA	2,514	322	611	598	536	768	939	311	415	10	292
WA	2,050	312	506	394	528	622	804	307	95	765	97
WV	831	458	165	112	391	163	273	120	956	12	–
WI	1,862	331	430	369	619	445	601	415	481	16	127
WY	542	1,016	48	63	302	129	179	147	500	8	–

– Represents zero. Z Less than 50 billion Btu. [1] Includes other sources, not shown separately. [2] U.S. total energy and U.S. industrial sector include 60.8 trillion Btu of net imports of coal coke that is not allocated to the states. [3] Based on estimated resident population as of July 1. [4] End-use sector data include electricity sales and associated electrical system energy losses. [5] Includes fuel ethanol blended into motor gasoline. [6] Includes supplemental gaseous fuels. [7] Conventional hydroelectric power. Does not include pumped-storage hydroelectricity.

Source: U.S. Energy Information Administration, "State Energy Data, 2008," June 2010, <http://www.eia.gov/states/seds/#>.

Table 932. Renewable Energy Consumption Estimates by Source: 1990 to 2010

[In quadrillion Btu (6.04 represents 6,040,000,000,000,000). For definition of Btu, see source and text, this section. Renewable energy is obtained from sources that are essentially inexhaustible, unlike fossil fuels of which there is a finite supply]

Source and sector	1990	2000	2005	2007	2008	2009	2010 [1]
Consumption, total	**6.04**	**6.11**	**6.24**	**6.55**	**7.19**	**7.59**	**8.05**
Conventional hydroelectric power [2]	3.05	2.81	2.70	2.45	2.51	2.67	2.51
Geothermal energy [3]	0.17	0.16	0.18	0.19	0.19	0.20	0.21
Biomass [4]	2.74	3.01	3.12	3.50	3.85	3.90	4.30
Solar energy [5]	0.06	0.07	0.06	0.08	0.09	0.10	0.11
Wind energy [6]	0.03	0.06	0.18	0.34	0.55	0.72	0.92
Residential [7]	0.64	0.49	0.50	0.52	0.56	0.55	0.55
Biomass [4]	0.58	0.42	0.43	0.43	0.45	0.43	0.42
Geothermal [3]	0.01	0.01	0.02	0.02	0.03	0.03	0.04
Solar [5]	0.06	0.06	0.06	0.07	0.08	0.09	0.10
Commercial [8]	0.10	0.13	0.12	0.12	0.13	0.13	0.13
Biomass [4]	0.09	0.12	0.11	0.10	0.11	0.11	0.11
Geothermal [3]	0.03	0.01	0.01	0.01	0.02	0.02	0.02
Hydroelectric [2]	(Z)	(Z)	(Z)	(Z)	(Z)	(Z)	(Z)
Industrial [9]	1.72	1.93	1.87	1.96	2.05	2.01	2.25
Biomass [4]	1.68	1.88	1.84	1.94	2.03	1.98	2.23
Geothermal [3]	(Z)	(Z)	(Z)	0.01	0.01	(Z)	(Z)
Hydroelectric [2]	0.03	0.04	0.03	0.02	0.02	0.02	0.02
Transportation	0.06	0.14	0.34	0.60	0.83	0.93	1.10
Fuel ethanol [10]	0.06	0.14	0.33	0.56	0.79	0.89	1.07
Biodiesel [11]	(NA)	(NA)	0.01	0.05	0.04	0.04	0.03
Electric power [12]	3.52	3.43	3.41	3.35	3.63	3.97	4.02
Biomass [4]	0.32	0.45	0.41	0.42	0.44	0.44	0.44
Geothermal [3]	0.16	0.14	0.15	0.15	0.15	0.15	0.15
Hydroelectric [2]	3.01	2.77	2.67	2.43	2.49	2.65	2.49
Solar [5]	(Z)	0.01	0.01	0.01	0.01	0.01	0.01
Wind [6]	0.03	0.06	0.18	0.34	0.55	0.72	0.92

NA Not available. Z Less than 5 trillion Btu. [1] Preliminary. [2] Power produced from natural stream flow as regulated by available storage. [3] As used at electric power plants, hot water or steam extracted from geothermal reservoirs in the Earth's crust that is supplied to steam turbines at electric power plants that drive generators to produce electricity. [4] Wood and wood-derived fuels, municipal solid waste (from biogenic sources, landfill gas, sludge waste, agricultural byproducts, and other biomass), fuel ethanol, and biodiesel. [5] The radiant energy of the sun, which can be converted into other forms of energy, such as heat or electricity. Solar thermal and photovoltaic electricity net generation and solar thermal direct use energy. [6] Energy present in wind motion that can be converted to mechanical energy for driving pumps, mills, and electric power generators. Wind pushes against sails, vanes, or blades radiating from a central rotating shaft. [7] Consists of living quarters for private households, but excludes institutional living quarters. [8] Consists of service-providing facilities and equipment of businesses, governments, and other private and public organizations. Includes institutional living quarters and sewage treatment facilities. Includes commercial combined-heat-and-power and commercial electricity-only plants. [9] Consists of all facilities and equipment used for producing, processing, or assembling goods. Includes industrial combined-heat-and-power and industrial electricity-only plants. [10] Ethanol primarily derived from corn. [11] Any liquid biofuel suitable as a diesel fuel substitute, additive, or extender. [12] Consists of electricity-only and combined-heat-and-power plants whose primary business is to sell electricity and/or heat to the public. Includes sources not shown separately.

Source: U.S. Energy Information Administration, "Monthly Energy Review," May 2011, <http://www.eia.gov/totalenergy/data/monthly/>.

Table 933. Fuel Ethanol and Biodiesel—Summary: 1990 to 2010

[110.9 represents 110,900,000,000,000. Data for 1990 are estimates. Beginning 1995, only feedstock data are estimates. Minus sign (–) indicates an excess of exports over imports, except where noted]

Fuel	1990	1995	2000	2005	2006	2007	2008	2009	2010 [1]
FUEL ETHANOL									
Feedstock [2] (tril. Btu)	110.9	197.7	233.1	552.4	687.9	914.3	1,299.5	1,517.0	1,830.0
Production:									
1,000 bbl.	17,802	32,325	38,627	92,961	116,294	155,263	221,637	260,424	315,018
Tril. Btu	63.4	115.2	137.6	331.2	414.4	553.2	789.7	928.0	1,122.0
Net imports [3] (1,000 bbl.)	(NA)	387	116	3,234	17,408	10,457	12,610	4,720	243
Stocks [4] (1,000 bbl.)	(NA)	2,186	3,400	5,563	8,760	10,535	14,226	16,594	17,940
Stock change [5] (1,000 bbl.)	(NA)	–207	–624	–439	3,197	1,775	3,691	2,368	[6] 1,229
Consumption:									
1,000 bbl.	17,802	32,919	39,367	96,634	130,505	163,945	230,556	262,776	314,032
Tril. Btu	63.4	117.3	140.3	344.3	465.0	584.1	821.5	936.0	1,118.0
BIODIESEL									
Feedstock [7] (tril. Btu)	(NA)	(NA)	(NA)	11.7	32.4	63.4	87.7	65.0	40.0
Production:									
1,000 bbl.	(NA)	(NA)	(NA)	2,162	5,963	11,662	16,145	12,054	7,401
Tril. Btu	(NA)	(NA)	(NA)	11.6	32.0	62.5	86.5	65.0	40.0
Net imports [3] (1,000 bbl.)	(NA)	(NA)	(NA)	1	242	–3,135	–8,626	–4,489	–1,958
Consumption:									
1,000 bbl.	(NA)	(NA)	(NA)	2,163	6,204	8,528	7,519	7,537	5,288
Tril. Btu	(NA)	(NA)	(NA)	11.6	33.2	45.7	40.3	40.0	28.0

NA Not available. [1] Preliminary. [2] Total corn and other biomass inputs to the production of fuel ethanol. [3] Net imports equal imports minus exports. [4] Imports minus exports. Stocks are at end of year. [5] A negative number indicates a decrease in stocks. [6] Derived using the preliminary December 2009 stock value, not the final December 2009 value shown under "Stocks." [7] Total vegetable oil and other biomass inputs to the production of biodiesel.

Source: U.S. Energy Information Administration, "Monthly Energy Review", May 2011, <http://www.eia.gov/totalenergy/data/monthly/>.

Table 934. Energy Expenditures—End-Use Sector and Selected Source by State: 2008

[In millions of dollars (1,411,922 represents $1,411,922,000,000). Data are preliminary. End-use sector and electric utilities exclude expenditures on energy sources such as hydroelectric, photovoltaic, solar thermal, wind, and geothermal. Also excludes expenditures for reported amounts of energy consumed by the energy industry for production, transportation, and processing operations. For technical notes and documentation, see source, <http://www.eia.doe.gov/emeu/states/_seds_tech_notes.html>]

State	Total [1,2]	End-use sector				Source			
		Residential	Commercial	Industrial [2]	Transportation	Petroleum products [3]	Natural gas [4]	Coal	Electricity sales
U.S.	1,411,922	256,953	192,249	272,322	690,397	874,865	229,667	49,438	360,573
AL	24,889	4,294	2,839	5,847	11,910	14,281	4,022	2,358	7,496
AK	7,509	774	777	583	5,374	6,332	550	36	921
AZ	22,610	4,340	3,349	2,363	12,558	14,200	3,777	808	6,951
AR	14,715	2,315	1,384	3,689	7,328	9,389	2,298	496	3,407
CA	136,508	20,057	19,333	17,127	79,991	86,486	23,577	169	33,180
CO	19,751	3,531	2,504	3,018	10,698	12,364	3,601	560	4,434
CT	16,460	5,273	3,317	1,357	6,513	9,410	2,196	141	5,508
DE	4,390	946	706	943	1,795	2,461	617	215	1,438
DC	2,529	487	1,525	50	468	515	475	1	1,553
FL	67,907	13,891	10,863	5,289	37,865	42,716	10,173	2,073	24,296
GA	41,568	8,066	5,190	6,718	21,595	24,456	5,595	2,739	11,951
HI	6,850	1,075	1,187	1,052	3,535	5,171	101	46	2,978
ID	6,122	1,055	597	1,237	3,232	3,964	805	21	1,361
IL	55,891	11,561	9,013	9,503	25,813	31,455	11,159	1,819	13,324
IN	33,151	5,605	3,211	8,708	15,626	19,021	5,844	3,553	7,498
IA	16,914	2,770	1,769	4,698	7,677	10,676	3,098	655	3,135
KS	14,569	2,366	1,642	3,987	6,574	9,323	2,519	530	2,923
KY	23,264	3,280	2,055	6,320	11,608	15,000	2,369	2,318	5,777
LA	38,906	3,643	2,742	18,904	13,617	24,359	9,536	620	7,215
ME	7,517	1,838	1,200	1,256	3,223	5,285	743	21	1,615
MD	24,349	5,789	5,028	2,059	11,473	13,520	2,753	1,123	8,232
MA	28,997	7,865	5,608	2,912	12,612	16,513	5,168	317	9,091
MI	39,849	9,011	5,706	6,433	18,700	22,796	8,020	1,727	9,390
MN	26,301	4,478	3,170	4,342	14,312	17,204	3,853	622	5,314
MS	15,503	2,492	1,712	2,896	8,403	9,660	3,135	577	4,183
MO	26,055	4,944	3,089	3,505	14,517	17,118	3,444	1,219	5,768
MT	5,684	911	646	1,353	2,774	3,789	698	275	1,166
NE	9,078	1,454	1,037	2,188	4,398	5,688	1,524	223	1,894
NV	11,192	2,083	1,342	1,765	6,002	6,759	2,462	197	3,417
NH	6,085	1,666	1,060	592	2,766	4,138	818	142	1,608
NJ	46,133	9,171	8,552	4,953	23,458	28,297	8,080	325	11,578
NM	8,893	1,278	1,158	1,314	5,143	6,335	1,302	567	1,796
NY	72,462	20,501	19,447	4,957	27,557	37,267	15,710	617	23,865
NC	37,854	7,406	4,823	5,375	20,249	24,306	3,230	2,602	10,356
ND	4,946	663	494	1,548	2,240	3,414	383	686	824
OH	54,144	10,791	6,949	11,224	25,180	30,461	10,165	3,173	13,254
OK	20,743	3,015	2,114	4,241	11,374	12,905	5,733	530	4,365
OR	14,882	2,516	1,673	2,048	8,645	9,609	2,429	62	3,559
PA	55,531	12,697	7,436	10,435	24,963	32,855	9,385	3,414	13,872
RI	4,223	1,282	846	398	1,698	2,408	1,115	–	1,252
SC	21,438	3,634	2,329	4,270	11,205	13,254	2,051	1,301	6,335
SD	4,233	692	463	856	2,222	2,890	568	78	784
TN	29,365	5,032	3,589	5,304	15,440	17,875	2,649	1,509	8,455
TX	165,334	20,077	14,665	64,067	66,526	113,177	27,433	3,059	37,225
UT	9,901	1,419	1,091	1,261	6,129	6,927	1,543	557	1,810
VT	3,012	831	462	303	1,416	2,177	121	–	708
VA	34,886	6,595	4,698	4,516	19,077	22,935	3,662	1,213	8,762
WA	26,669	4,319	2,962	3,122	16,265	18,312	3,101	215	5,667
WV	9,634	1,397	859	3,445	3,934	6,462	1,055	2,353	1,892
WI	25,444	5,309	3,554	4,841	11,739	14,812	4,515	989	6,262
WY	5,612	463	485	1,685	2,979	4,137	503	589	926

– Represents or rounds to zero. [1] Total expenditures are the sum of purchases for each source (including retail electricity sales) less electric power sector purchases of fuel. [2] Includes sources not shown separately, such as electricity imports and exports and coal coke net imports, which are not allocated to the states. [3] Includes fuel ethanol blended into motor gasoline. [4] Includes supplemental gaseous fuels.

Source: U.S. Energy Information Administration, "State Energy Data, 2008," June 2010, <http://www.eia.doe.gov/state/seds/index.cfm>.

Table 935. Energy Imports and Exports by Type of Fuel: 1980 to 2009

[In quadrillion of Btu. (12.10 represents 12,100,000,000,000,000 Btu). For definition of Btu, see source and text, this section]

Type of fuel	1980	1990	1995	2000	2003	2004	2005	2006	2007	2008	2009 [1]
Net imports, total [2]....	**12.10**	**14.06**	**17.75**	**24.97**	**27.01**	**29.11**	**30.15**	**29.81**	**29.24**	**25.94**	**22.85**
Coal...............	−2.39	−2.70	−2.08	−1.21	−0.49	−0.57	−0.51	−0.36	−0.60	−1.22	−0.95
Natural gas (dry).....	0.96	1.46	2.74	3.62	3.36	3.50	3.71	3.56	3.89	3.07	2.76
Petroleum [3].........	13.50	15.29	16.89	22.38	24.07	25.99	26.81	26.42	25.79	23.93	20.95
Other [4].............	0.04	0.01	0.19	0.18	0.07	0.18	0.13	0.12	0.13	0.15	0.09
Imports, total.........	15.80	18.82	22.26	28.97	31.06	33.54	34.71	34.67	34.69	32.95	29.78
Coal...............	0.03	0.07	0.24	0.31	0.63	0.68	0.76	0.91	0.91	0.86	0.57
Natural gas (dry).....	1.01	1.55	2.90	3.87	4.04	4.37	4.45	4.29	4.72	4.08	3.84
Petroleum [3].........	14.66	17.12	18.88	24.53	26.22	28.20	29.25	29.16	28.76	27.64	25.16
Other [4].............	0.10	0.08	0.24	0.26	0.17	0.29	0.24	0.25	0.24	0.28	0.19
Exports, total.........	3.69	4.75	4.51	4.01	4.05	4.43	4.56	4.87	5.45	7.02	6.93
Coal...............	2.42	2.77	2.32	1.53	1.12	1.25	1.27	1.26	1.51	2.07	1.52
Natural gas (dry).....	0.05	0.09	0.16	0.25	0.69	0.86	0.74	0.73	0.83	1.02	1.08
Petroleum..........	1.16	1.82	1.99	2.15	2.15	2.21	2.44	2.75	2.97	3.71	4.21
Other [4].............	0.07	0.07	0.05	0.08	0.10	0.11	0.11	0.12	0.10	0.13	0.09

[1] Preliminary. [2] Net imports equals imports minus exports. Minus sign (−) indicates exports are greater than imports. [3] Includes imports into the Strategic Petroleum Reserve. [4] Coal coke, small amounts of electricity transmitted across U.S. borders with Canada and Mexico, and small amounts of biodiesel.

Source: U.S. Energy Information Administration, *Annual Energy Review 2009,* August 2010. See also <http://www.eia.gov/emeu/aer/overview.html>.

Table 936. U.S. Foreign Trade in Selected Mineral Fuels: 1980 to 2010

[985 represents 985,000,000,000 cu. ft. Minus sign (−) indicates trade deficit]

Mineral fuel	Unit	1980	1990	1995	2000	2005	2007	2008	2009	2010 [1]
Natural gas:										
Imports..........	Bil. cu. ft......	985	1,532	2,841	3,782	4,341	4,608	3,984	3,751	3,737
Exports..........	Bil. cu. ft......	49	86	154	244	729	822	963	1,072	1,137
Net trade [2]........	Bil. cu. ft......	−936	−1,446	−2,687	−3,538	−3,612	−3,786	−3,021	−2,679	−2,600
Crude oil: [3]										
Imports [4]..........	Mil. bbl......	1,921	2,151	2,639	3,311	3,696	3,661	3,571	3,290	3,344
Exports..........	Mil. bbl......	105	40	35	18	12	10	11	16	15
Net trade [2]........	Mil. bbl......	−1,816	−2,112	−2,604	−3,293	−3,684	−3,651	−3,560	−3,274	−3,329
Petroleum products:										
Imports..........	Mil. bbl......	601	775	586	872	1,310	1,255	1,143	977	945
Exports..........	Mil. bbl......	94	273	312	361	414	513	647	723	829
Net trade [2]........	Mil. bbl......	−507	−502	−274	−510	−896	−742	−496	−255	−116
Coal:										
Imports..........	Mil. sh. tons...	1	3	9	13	30	36	34	23	19
Exports..........	Mil. sh. tons...	92	106	89	58	50	59	82	59	82
Net trade [2]........	Mil. sh. tons...	90.5	103.1	79.1	46.0	19.5	22.8	47.3	36.5	62.4

[1] Preliminary. [2] Exports minus imports. [3] Includes lease condensate. [4] Includes strategic petroleum reserve imports.

Source: U.S. Energy Information Administration, "Monthly Energy Review," May 2011, <http://www.eia.gov/totalenergy/data/monthly/>.

Table 937. Crude Oil Imports Into the U.S. by Country of Origin: 1980 to 2010

[In millions of barrels (1,921 represents 1,921,000,000). Barrels contain 42 gallons. Crude oil imports are reported by the Petroleum Administration for Defense (PAD) District in which they are to be processed. A PAD District is a geographic aggregation of the 50 states and D.C. into 5 districts. Includes crude oil imported for storage in the Strategic Petroleum Reserve (SPR). Total OPEC excludes, and Non-OPEC includes, petroleum imported into the United States indirectly from members of OPEC, primarily from Carribean and West European areas, as petroleum products that were refined from crude oil produced by OPEC]

Country of origin	1980	1990	1995	2000	2004	2005	2006	2007	2008	2009	2010
Total imports........	**1,921**	**2,151**	**2,639**	**3,311**	**3,674**	**3,670**	**3,685**	**3,656**	**3,571**	**3,307**	**3,344**
OPEC, total [1, 2, 3, 4].......	1,410	1,283	1,219	1,659	2,009	1,738	1,745	1,969	1,984	1,594	1,654
Algeria..............	166	23	10	(Z)	79	83	130	162	114	101	119
Angola [2]............	(NA)	86	131	108	112	164	187	181	184	164	139
Ecuador [3]............	6	(NA)	35	46	83	101	99	72	78	64	71
Iraq...............	10	188	−	226	238	190	202	177	229	164	151
Kuwait [5]..............	10	29	78	96	88	79	65	64	75	68	71
Nigeria..............	307	286	227	319	389	387	381	395	338	281	360
Saudi Arabia [5]........	456	436	460	556	547	525	519	530	551	361	394
Venezuela...........	57	243	420	446	473	449	416	420	381	352	333
Non-OPEC, total [2, 3, 4, 6]...	511	869	1,419	1,652	1,838	1,932	1,940	1,687	1,587	1,713	1,690
Brazil...............	(NA)	−	−	2	19	34	49	61	84	107	93
Canada.............	73	235	380	492	590	600	651	681	707	707	720
Colombia............	(NA)	51	76	116	51	57	52	50	65	93	124
Congo (Brazzaville) [7].....	(NA)	(NA)	(NA)	(NA)	3	9	10	23	25	24	26
Mexico.............	185	251	375	479	584	566	575	514	434	400	416
Russia..............	(NA)	(Z)	5	3	55	70	39	41	41	85	92
United Kingdom........	63	57	124	106	86	80	47	37	27	38	44

− Represents zero. NA Not available. Z Represents less than 500,000 barrels. [1] OPEC (Organization of Petroleum Exporting Countries) includes the nations shown, as well as Iran, Libya, Qatar, United Arab Emirates, and Indonesia. [2] Angola joined OPEC at the beginning of 2007. Prior to 2007, it is included in the non-OPEC total. [3] Ecuador withdrew from OPEC on Dec. 31, 1992; therefore, it is included under OPEC prior to 1995. From 1995 through 2007, it is included in the Non-OPEC total. In Nov. 2007, Ecuador rejoined OPEC; imports for 2008 are included in the OPEC total. [4] Gabon withdrew from OPEC on Dec. 31, 1994; therefore, it is included under OPEC prior to 1995. Beginning 1995, it is included in the Non-OPEC total. [5] Imports from the Neutral Zone between Kuwait and Saudi Arabia are included in Saudi Arabia. [6] Non-OPEC total includes nations not shown. [7] See footnote 5, Table 1332.

Source: U.S. Energy Information Administration, "Petroleum Supply Monthly," February 2011, <http://www.eia.gov/pub/oil_gas/petroleum/data_publications/petroleum_supply_monthly/historical/2011/2011_02/psm_2011_02.html>.

Table 938. Crude Oil and Refined Products—Summary: 1980 to 2010

[13,481 represents 13,481,000 bbl. Barrels (bbl.) of 42 gallons. Data are averages]

Year	Crude oil [1] (1,000 bbl. per day) Input to refiner-ies	Domestic produc-tion	Imports Total [3]	Imports Strategic reserve [4]	Exports	Refined oil products (1,000 bbl. per day) Domestic demand	Imports	Exports	Total oil imports [5] (1,000 bbl. per day)	Crude oil stocks [1,2] (mil. bbl.) Total	Strategic reserve [6]
1980......	13,481	8,597	5,263	44	287	17,056	1,646	258	6,909	[7] 466	108
1985......	12,002	8,971	3,201	118	204	15,726	1,866	577	5,067	814	493
1990......	13,409	7,355	5,894	27	109	16,988	2,123	748	8,018	908	586
1995......	13,973	6,560	7,230	–	95	17,725	1,605	855	8,835	895	592
2000......	15,067	5,822	9,071	8	50	19,701	2,389	990	11,459	826	541
2005......	15,220	5,178	10,126	52	32	20,802	3,588	1,133	13,714	1,008	685
2006......	15,242	5,102	10,118	8	25	20,687	3,589	1,292	13,707	1,001	689
2007......	15,156	5,064	10,031	7	27	20,680	3,437	1,405	13,468	983	697
2008......	14,648	4,950	9,783	19	29	19,498	3,132	1,773	12,915	1,028	702
2009......	14,336	5,361	9,013	56	44	18,771	2,665	1,982	11,691	1,052	727
2010......	14,722	5,512	9,163	(NA)	42	19,148	(NA)	(NA)	11,753	1,059	727

– Represents zero. NA Not available. [1] Includes lease condensate. [2] Crude oil at end of period. Includes commercial and Strategic Petroleum Reserve stocks. [3] Includes Strategic Petroleum Reserve. [4] SPR is the Strategic Petroleum Reserve. Through 2000, includes imports by SPR only; beginning in 2004, includes imports by SPR, and imports into SPR by others. [5] Crude oil (including Strategic Petroleum Reserve imports) plus refined products. [6] Crude oil stocks in the Strategic Petroleum Reserve include non-U.S. stocks held under foreign or commercial storage agreements. [7] Stocks of Alaskan crude oil in transit are included from January 1985 forward.

Source: U.S. Energy Information Administration, "Monthly Energy Review," April 2011, <http://www.eia.gov/totalenergy/data/monthly>.

Table 939. Petroleum and Coal Products Corporations—Sales, Net Profit, and Profit Per Dollar of Sales: 1990 to 2010

[318.5 represents $318,500,000,000. Represents SIC group 29 (NAICS group 324). Through 2000, based on Standard Industrial Classification (SIC) code; beginning 2003, based on North American Industry Classification System (NAICS), 1997. Profit rates are averages of quarterly figures at annual rates. Beginning 1990, excludes estimates for corporations with less than $250,000 in assets]

Item	Unit	1990	1995	2000	2003	2004	2005	2006	2007	2008	2009	2010
Sales..............	Bil. dol....	318.5	283.1	455.2	597.8	767.7	956.0	1,037.8	1,113.2	1,369.1	846.0	1,085.2
Net profit:												
Before income taxes ..	Bil. dol....	23.1	16.5	55.5	52.8	89.7	120.2	139.8	127.0	101.6	41.9	56.4
After income taxes....	Bil. dol....	17.8	13.9	42.6	43.6	71.8	96.3	111.0	105.4	81.0	43.1	54.4
Depreciation [1]	Bil. dol....	18.7	16.7	15.5	19.4	18.5	18.6	20.0	22.6	22.9	28.0	31.1
Profits per dollar of sales:												
Before income taxes ..	Cents....	7.3	5.8	12.2	8.8	11.6	12.6	13.4	11.6	5.8	5.1	5.2
After income taxes....	Cents....	5.6	4.9	9.4	7.3	9.3	10.1	10.6	9.6	4.4	5.2	5.0
Profits on stockholders' equity:												
Before income taxes ..	Percent ..	16.4	12.6	29.4	20.8	32.9	38.0	36.3	30.7	21.8	10.2	12.3
After income taxes....	Percent ..	12.7	10.6	22.6	17.1	26.3	30.4	28.8	25.5	17.3	10.5	11.9

[1] Includes depletion and accelerated amortization of emergency facilities.

Source: U.S. Census Bureau, *Quarterly Financial Report for Manufacturing, Mining and Selected Service Industries.*

Table 940. Major Petroleum Companies—Financial Summary: 1980 to 2010

[32.9 represents $32,900,000,000. Data represent a composite of approximately 42 major worldwide petroleum companies aggregated on a consolidated total company basis. Minus sign (–) indicates deficit]

Item	1980	1990	1995	2000	2005	2006	2007	2008	2009	2010
FINANCIAL DATA (bil. dol.)										
Net income	32.9	26.8	24.3	76.4	170.6	187.6	237.6	198.1	92.6	185.0
Depreciation, depletion, etc.	32.5	38.7	43.1	53.3	76.5	85.8	114.3	156.8	170.2	186.8
Cash flow [1].................	65.4	65.5	67.4	129.7	239.9	261.2	327.1	440.7	279.6	362.4
Dividends paid................	9.3	15.9	17.6	23.0	37.5	39.2	62.2	74.8	72.1	70.5
Net internal funds available for investment or debt repayment [2].................	56.1	49.6	49.8	106.7	202.4	222.0	264.9	365.9	207.5	291.9
Capital and exploratory expenditures	62.1	59.6	59.8	72.8	140.4	193.1	221.7	328.0	268.0	344.3
Long-term capitalization	211.4	300.0	304.3	516.9	800.4	910.6	1,211.8	1,362.0	1,449.3	1,621.1
Long-term debt	49.8	90.4	85.4	112.8	165.2	177.4	240.1	299.4	365.7	444.2
Preferred stock	2.0	5.2	5.7	5.4	3.5	3.4	1.9	1.4	1.2	5.0
Common stock and retained earnings [3]....	159.6	204.4	213.2	398.7	631.7	729.8	969.8	1,061.2	1,082.4	1,171.9
Excess of expenditures over cash income [4]	6.0	10.0	10.0	–33.9	–62.0	–28.9	–43.2	–37.9	60.5	52.4
RATIOS [5] (percent)										
Long-term debt to long-term capitalization ...	23.6	30.1	28.1	21.8	23.5	19.4	19.1	22.0	25.3	24.1
Net income to total average capital	17.0	9.1	8.1	15.7	23.0	22.3	21.2	15.2	6.6	10.8
Net income to average common equity	22.5	13.5	11.6	20.5	29.3	27.8	26.3	19.2	8.7	14.4

[1] Generally represents internally generated funds from operations: Sum of net income, changes in working capital and noncash items such as depreciation, depletion, amortization, impairments, and unrealized hedging gains/losses. [2] Cash flow minus dividends paid. [3] Includes common stock, capital surplus, and earned surplus accounts after adjustments. [4] Capital and exploratory expenditures plus dividends paid minus cash flow. [5] Represents approximate year-to-year comparisons because of changes in the makeup of the group due to mergers and other corporate changes.

Source: Carl H. Pforzheimer & Co., New York, NY, *Comparative Oil Company Statements*, annual.

Table 941. Nuclear Power Plants—Number, Capacity, and Generation: 1980 to 2010

[51.8 represents 51,800,000 kW]

Item	1980	1990	1995	2000	2003	2004	2005	2006	2007	2008	2009	2010
Operable generating units [1, 2]	71	112	109	104	104	104	104	104	104	104	104	104
Net summer capacity [2, 3] (mil. kW)	51.8	99.6	99.5	97.9	99.2	99.6	100.0	100.3	100.3	100.8	101.0	101.0
Net generation (bil. kWh)	251.1	576.9	673.4	753.9	763.7	788.5	782.0	787.2	806.4	806.2	798.9	807.0
Percent of total electricity net generation	11.0	19.0	20.1	19.8	19.7	19.9	19.3	19.4	19.4	19.6	20.2	19.6
Capacity factor [4] (percent)	56.3	66.0	77.4	88.1	87.9	90.1	89.3	89.6	91.8	91.1	90.3	91.2

[1] Total of nuclear generating units holding full-power licenses, or equivalent permission to operate, at the end of the year. For example, although Browns Ferry 1 was shut down in 1985, the unit remained fully licensed and thus continued to be counted as operable. It was eventually reopened in 2007. [2] As of year-end. [3] Net summer capacity is the peak steady hourly output that generating equipment is expected to supply to system load, exclusive of auxiliary and other power plant, as demonstrated by test at the time of summer peak demand. [4] Weighted average of monthly capacity factors. Monthly factors are derived by dividing actual monthly generation by the maximum possible generation for the month (number of hours in the month multiplied by the net summer capacity at the end of the month).

Source: U.S. Energy Information Administration, "Monthly Energy Review," April 2011, <http://www.eia.gov/totalenergy/data/monthly/#nuclear>.

Table 942. Nuclear Power Plants—Number of Units, Net Generation, and Net Summer Capacity by State: 2009

[798,855 represents 798,855,000,000 kWh]

State	Number of units	Nuclear net generation Total (mil. kWh)	Nuclear net generation Percent of total [1]	Nuclear net summer capability Total (mil. kW)	Nuclear net summer capability Percent of total [1]	State	Number of units	Nuclear net generation Total (mil. kWh)	Nuclear net generation Percent of total [1]	Nuclear net summer capability Total (mil. kW)	Nuclear net summer capability Percent of total [1]
U.S.	**104**	**798,855**	**20.2**	**101.0**	**9.9**	MS	1	10,999	22.6	1.3	7.9
AL	5	39,716	27.7	5.0	15.9	MO	1	10,247	11.6	1.2	5.7
AZ	3	30,662	27.4	1.8	7.0	NE	2	9,435	27.7	1.3	16.1
AR	2	15,170	26.4	3.9	25.8	NH	1	8,817	43.7	1.2	29.9
CA	4	31,761	15.5	4.4	6.7	NJ	1	34,328	55.5	4.1	22.2
CT	2	16,657	53.4	2.1	26.2	NY	6	43,485	32.7	5.3	13.3
FL	5	29,118	13.4	3.9	6.6	NC	5	40,848	34.5	5.0	18.0
GA	4	31,683	24.6	4.1	11.1	OH	3	15,206	11.2	2.1	6.4
IL	11	95,474	49.2	11.4	26.0	PA	9	77,328	35.2	9.5	20.7
IA	1	4,679	9.0	0.6	4.1	SC	7	52,150	52.1	6.5	27.1
KS	1	8,769	18.8	1.2	9.3	TN	3	26,962	33.8	3.4	16.3
LA	2	16,782	18.4	2.1	8.2	TX	4	41,498	10.4	4.9	4.8
MD	2	14,550	33.2	1.7	13.7	VT	1	5,361	73.6	0.6	55.1
MA	1	5,396	13.8	0.7	5.0	VA	4	28,212	40.3	3.4	14.3
MI	3	21,851	21.6	4.0	13.0	WA	1	6,634	6.4	1.1	3.8
MN	3	12,393	23.6	1.7	11.4	WI	3	12,683	21.2	1.6	8.9

[1] For total generation and capacity, see Table 948.

Source: U.S. Energy Information Administration, "Electric Power Annual 2009," April 2011, <http://www.eia.gov/cneaf/electricity/epa/epa_sprdshts.html>.

Table 943. Uranium Concentrate—Supply, Inventories, and Average Prices: 1990 to 2008

[8.89 represents 8,890,000 pounds (lbs.). Years ending Dec. 31. For additional data on uranium, see Section 18]

Item	Unit	1990	1995	2000	2003	2004	2005	2006	2007	2008
Production [1]	Mil. lb.	8.89	6.04	3.96	2.00	2.28	2.69	4.11	4.53	3.90
Exports [2]	Mil. lb.	2.0	9.8	13.6	13.2	13.2	20.5	18.7	14.8	17.2
Imports [2]	Mil. lb.	23.7	41.3	44.9	53.0	66.1	65.5	64.8	54.1	57.1
Electric plant purchases from domestic suppliers	Mil. lb.	20.5	22.3	24.3	21.7	28.2	27.3	27.9	18.5	20.4
Loaded into U.S. nuclear reactors [3]	Mil. lb.	(NA)	51.1	51.5	62.3	50.1	58.3	51.7	45.5	51.3
Inventories, total	Mil. lb.	129.1	72.5	111.3	85.5	95.2	93.8	106.6	112.4	108.8
At domestic suppliers	Mil. lb.	26.4	13.7	56.5	39.9	37.5	29.1	29.1	31.2	26.9
At electric plants	Mil. lb.	102.7	58.7	54.8	45.6	57.7	64.7	77.5	81.2	81.9
Average price per pound:										
Purchased imports	Dollars	12.55	10.20	9.84	10.59	12.25	14.83	19.31	34.18	41.30
Domestic purchases	Dollars	15.70	11.11	11.45	10.84	11.91	13.98	18.54	33.13	43.43

NA Not available. [1] Data are for uranium concentrate, a yellow or brown powder obtained by the milling of uranium ore, processing of in situ leach mining solutions, or as a by-product of phosphoric acid production. [2] Includes transactions by uranium buyers (consumers). Buyer imports and exports prior to 1990 are believed to be small. [3] Does not include any fuel rods removed from reactors and later reloaded into the reactor.

Source: U.S. Energy Information Administration, Annual Energy Review 2009, August 2010. See also <http://www.eia.doe.gov/emeu/aer/nuclear.html>.

Table 944. Solar Collector Shipments by Type, End Use, and Market Sector: 1980 to 2009

[Shipments in thousands of square feet (19,398 represents 19,398,000). Solar collector is a device for intercepting sunlight, converting the light to heat, and carrying the heat to where it will be either used or stored. 1985 data are not available. Based on the Annual Solar Thermal Collector Manufacturers Survey]

Year	Number of manu-facturers	Total ship-ments [1, 2, 3]	Collector type		End use			Market sector		
			Low tempera-ture [1, 2]	Medium tempera-ture, special/other [2]	Pool heating	Hot water	Space heating	Resi-dential	Com-merical	Indus-trial
1980........	233	19,398	12,233	7,165	12,029	4,790	1,688	16,077	2,417	488
1990........	51	11,409	3,645	2,527	5,016	1,091	2	5,835	294	22
1995........	36	7,666	6,813	840	6,763	755	132	6,966	604	82
2000........	26	8,354	7,948	400	7,863	367	99	7,473	810	57
2005........	25	16,041	15,224	702	15,041	640	228	14,681	1,160	31
2008........	74	16,963	14,015	2,560	11,973	1,978	186	13,000	1,294	128
2009........	88	13,798	10,511	2,307	8,934	1,992	150	10,239	974	634

[1] Includes shipments of high temperature collectors to the government, including some military, but excluding space applications. Also includes end uses such as process heating, utility, and other market sectors, not shown separately. [2] Includes imputation of shipment data to account for nonrespondents. [3] Total shipments include all domestic and export shipments and may include imported collectors that subsequently were shipped to domestic or foreign customers.

Source: U.S. Energy Information Administration, 1980–1990, "Solar Collector Manufacturing Activity", annual reports; 1995–2002, "Renewable Energy Annual"; thereafter, "Solar Thermal Collector Manufacturing Activities 2009," January 2011, <http://www.eia.gov/cneaf/solar.renewables/page/solarreport/solar.html>.

Table 945. Electricity Net Generation by Sector and Fuel Type: 1990 to 2010

[3,038.0 represents 3,038,000,000,000 kWh. Data are for fuels consumed to produce electricity. Also includes fuels consumed to produce useful thermal output at a small number of electric utility combined-heat-and-power (CHP) plants]

Source and sector	Unit	1990	1995	2000	2005	2009	2010 [1]
Net generation, total	**Bil. kWh.**	**3,038.0**	**3,353.0**	**3,802.0**	**4,055.0**	**3,950.0**	**4,120.0**
Electric power sector, total.	Bil. kWh........	2,901.3	3,194.2	3,637.5	3,902.2	3,809.8	3,971.2
Commercial sector [2]	Bil. kWh........	5.8	8.2	7.9	8.5	8.2	8.3
Industrial sector [3]	Bil. kWh........	130.8	151.0	156.7	144.7	132.3	140.5
Net generation by source, all sectors:							
Fossil fuels, total	Bil. kWh........	2,103.6	2,293.9	2,692.5	2,909.5	2,726.5	2,880.7
Coal [4]	Bil. kWh........	1,594.0	1,709.4	1,966.3	2,012.9	1,755.9	1,850.8
Petroleum [5]	Bil. kWh........	126.5	74.6	111.2	122.2	38.9	36.9
Natural gas [6]	Bil. kWh........	372.8	496.1	601.0	761.0	921.0	981.8
Other gases [7]	Bil. kWh........	10.4	13.9	14.0	13.5	10.6	11.2
Nuclear electric power	Bil. kWh........	576.9	673.4	753.9	782.0	798.9	807.0
Hydroelectric pumped storage [8]	Bil. kWh........	-3.5	-2.7	-5.5	-6.6	-4.6	-4.1
Renewable energy, total	Bil. kWh........	357.2	384.8	356.5	357.7	417.7	425.2
Conventional hydroelectric power	Bil. kWh........	292.9	310.8	275.6	270.3	273.4	257.1
Biomass, total	Bil. kWh........	45.8	56.9	60.7	54.3	54.5	56.5
Wood [9]	Bil. kWh........	32.5	36.5	37.6	38.9	36.1	38.0
Waste [10]	Bil. kWh........	13.3	20.4	23.1	15.4	18.4	18.6
Geothermal	Bil. kWh........	15.4	13.4	14.1	14.7	15.0	15.7
Solar [11]	Bil. kWh........	0.4	0.5	0.5	0.6	0.9	1.3
Wind..............................	Bil. kWh........	2.8	3.2	5.6	17.8	73.9	94.6
Other [12]	Bil. kWh........	3.8	3.6	4.7	12.4	11.6	11.2
Consumption of fuels for electricity generation:							
Coal [4]	Mil. sh. tons	792.5	860.6	994.9	1,041.4	934.7	979.6
Petroleum, total	Mil. bbl.........	218.8	132.6	195.2	206.8	67.7	64.8
Distilate fuel oil [13]	Mil. bbl.........	18.1	19.6	31.7	20.7	12.7	13.9
Residual fuel oil [14]	Mil. bbl.........	190.7	95.5	143.4	141.5	28.6	24.4
Other liquids [15]	Mil. bbl.........	0.4	0.7	1.5	3.0	2.3	1.8
Petroleum coke	Mil. sh. tons [16] ..	1.9	3.4	3.7	8.3	4.8	5.0
Natural gas [6]	Bil. cu. ft.	3.7	4.7	5.7	6.0	7.1	7.6
Other gases [7]	Tril. Btu........	0.1	0.1	0.1	0.1	0.1	0.1
Biomass.............................	Tril. Btu........	0.7	0.8	0.8	0.6	0.6	0.6
Wood [9]	Tril. Btu........	0.4	0.5	0.5	0.4	0.3	0.3
Waste [10]	Tril. Btu........	0.2	0.3	0.3	0.2	0.3	0.3
Other [12]	Tril. Btu........	0.0	0.0	0.0	0.2	0.2	0.2

[1] Preliminary. [2] Commercial combined-heat-and-power (CHP) and commercial electricity-only plants. [3] Industrial combined-heat-and-power (HCP) and industrial electricity-only plants. [4] Anthracite, bituminous coal, subbituminous coal, lignite, waste coal, and coal synfuel. [5] Distillate fuel oil, residual fuel oil, petroleum coke, jet fuel, kerosene, other petroleum, and waste oil. [6] Includes a small amount of supplemental gaseous fuels that cannot be identified separately. [7] Blast furnace gas, propane gas, and other manufactured and waste gases derived from fossil fuels. [8] Pumped storage facility production minus energy used for pumping. [9] Wood and wood-derived fuels. [10] Municipal solid waste from biogenic sources, landfill gas, sludge waste, tires, agricultural by-products, and other biomass. Through 2000, also includes nonrenewable waste (municipal solid waste from non- biogenic sources, and tire-derived fuels). [11] Solar thermal and photovoltaic energy. [12] Batteries, chemicals, hydrogen, pitch, purchased steam, sulfur, miscellaneous technologies, and beginning 2001, nonrenewable waste (municipal solid waste from nonbiogenic sources, and tire-derived fuels). [13] Fuel oil numbers 1, 2, and 4. For 1990 through 2000, electric utility data also include small amounts of kerosene and jet fuel. [14] Fuel oil numbers 5 and 6. For 1990 through 2000, electric utility data also include a small amount of fuel oil number 4. [15] Jet fuel, kerosene, other petroleum liquids, and waste oil. [16] Short tons.

Source: U.S. Energy Information Administration, "Monthly Energy Review," May 2011, <http://www.eia.gov/totalenergy /data/monthly/>.

Table 946. Total Electric Net Summer Capacity, All Sectors: 1990 to 2009

[In million kilowatts (734.1 represents 734,100,000). Data are at end of year. For plants that use multiple sources of energy, capacity is assigned to the predominant energy source]

Source	1990	1995	2000	2004	2005	2006	2007	2008	2009
Net summer capacity, total	**734.1**	**769.5**	**811.7**	**962.9**	**978.0**	**986.2**	**994.9**	**1,010.2**	**1,027.6**
Fossil fuels, total	527.8	554.2	598.9	745.4	757.1	761.6	764.0	770.2	778.2
Coal [1]	307.4	311.4	315.1	313.0	313.4	313.0	312.7	313.3	314.4
Petroleum [2]	77.9	66.6	61.8	59.1	58.5	58.1	56.1	57.4	57.0
Natural gas [3]	140.8	174.5	219.6	371.0	383.1	388.3	392.9	397.4	404.9
Dual fired [4]	113.6	122.0	149.8	172.2	174.7	(NA)	(NA)	(NA)	(NA)
Other gases [5]	1.6	1.7	2.3	2.3	2.1	2.3	2.3	2.0	2.0
Nuclear electric power	99.6	99.5	97.9	99.6	100.0	100.3	100.3	100.8	100.8
Hydroelectric pumped storage	19.5	21.4	19.5	20.8	21.3	21.5	21.9	21.9	21.9
Renewable energy, total	86.8	93.9	94.9	96.4	98.7	101.9	108.0	116.4	125.8
Conventional hydroelectric power	73.9	78.6	79.4	77.6	77.5	77.8	77.9	77.9	78.0
Biomass, total	8.1	10.3	10.0	9.7	9.8	10.1	10.8	11.1	11.4
Wood [6]	5.5	6.7	6.1	6.2	6.2	6.4	6.7	6.9	6.9
Waste [7]	2.5	3.5	3.9	3.5	3.6	3.7	4.1	4.2	4.4
Geothermal	2.7	3.0	2.8	2.2	2.3	2.3	2.2	2.3	2.4
Solar [8]	0.3	0.3	0.4	0.4	0.4	0.4	0.5	0.5	0.6
Wind	1.8	1.7	2.4	6.5	8.7	11.3	16.5	24.7	33.5
Other [9]	0.5	0.5	0.5	0.7	0.9	0.9	0.8	0.9	0.9

NA Not available. [1] Anthracite, bituminous coal, subbituminous coal, lignite, waste coal, and coal synfuel. [2] Distillate fuel oil, residual fuel oil, petroleum coke, jet fuel, kerosene, other petroleum, and waste oil. [3] Includes a small amount of supplemental gaseous fuels that cannot be identified separately. [4] Petroleum and natural gas. [5] Blast furnace gas, propane gas, and other manufactured and waste gases derived from fossil fuels. [6] Wood and wood-derived fuels. [7] Municipal solid waste from biogenic sources, landfill gas, sludge waste, tires, agricultural byproducts, and other biomass. Also includes nonrenewable waste (municipal solid waste from nonbiogenic sources, and tire-derived fuels). [8] Solar thermal and photovoltaic energy. [9] Batteries, chemicals, hydrogen, pitch, purchased steam, sulfur, and miscellaneous technologies.

Source: U.S. Energy Information Administration, *Annual Energy Review 2009,* August 2010. See also <http://www.eia.doe.gov/emeu/aer/elect.html>.

Table 947. Electricity—End Use and Average Retail Prices: 1990 to 2009

[Beginning 2004, the category "other" has been replaced by "transportation," and the categories "commercial" and "industrial" have been redefined. Data represent revenue from electricity retail sales divided by the amount of retail electricity sold (in kilowatt-hours). Prices include state and local taxes, energy or demand charges, customer service charges, environmental surcharges, franchise fees, fuel adjustments, and other miscellaneous charges applied to end-use customers during normal billing operations. Prices do not include deferred charges, credits, or other adjustments, such as fuel or revenue from purchased power, from previous reporting periods. Data are for a census of electric utilities. Beginning in 2000 data also include energy service providers selling to retail customers]

Item	1990	1995	2000	2004	2005	2006	2007	2008	2009 [1]
END USE (Billion kilowatt-hours)									
Total end use [2]	**2,837.1**	**3,164.0**	**3,592.4**	**3,715.9**	**3,811.0**	**3,816.8**	**3,923.8**	**3,906.4**	**3,741.5**
Direct use [3]	124.5	150.7	170.9	168.5	150.0	146.9	159.3	173.5	166.0
Retail sales, total [4]	**2,712.6**	**3,013.3**	**3,421.4**	**3,547.5**	**3,661.0**	**3,669.9**	**3,764.6**	**3,733.0**	**3,575.5**
Residential	924.0	1,042.5	1,192.4	1,292.0	1,359.2	1,351.5	1,392.2	1,380.0	1,362.9
Commercial [5]	838.3	953.1	1,159.3	1,230.4	1,275.1	1,299.7	1,336.3	1,336.0	1,323.0
Industrial [6]	945.5	1,012.7	1,064.2	1,017.8	1,019.2	1,011.3	1,027.8	1,009.3	881.9
Transportation [7]	4.8	5.0	5.4	7.2	7.5	7.4	8.2	7.7	7.7
AVERAGE RETAIL PRICES (Cents per kilowatt-hour)									
Total:									
Nominal	6.57	6.89	6.81	7.61	8.14	8.90	9.13	9.74	9.89
Real	9.10	8.45	7.68	7.86	8.14	8.62	8.60	8.98	9.01
Residential:									
Nominal	7.83	8.40	8.24	8.95	9.45	10.40	10.65	11.26	11.55
Real	10.84	10.30	9.30	9.25	9.45	10.07	10.03	10.38	10.52
Commercial: [8]									
Nominal	7.34	7.69	7.43	8.17	8.67	9.46	9.65	10.36	10.21
Real	10.17	9.43	8.38	8.44	8.67	9.16	9.09	9.55	9.30
Industrial: [6]									
Nominal	4.74	4.66	4.64	5.25	5.73	6.16	6.39	6.83	6.84
Real	6.57	5.72	5.23	5.43	5.73	5.97	6.02	6.30	6.23
Transportation: [7]									
Nominal	(NA)	(NA)	(NA)	7.18	8.57	9.54	9.70	10.74	11.17
Real	(NA)	(NA)	(NA)	7.42	8.57	9.24	9.13	9.90	10.18
Other: [9]									
Nominal	6.40	6.88	6.56	(X)	(X)	(X)	(X)	(X)	(X)
Real	8.86	8.44	7.40	(X)	(X)	(X)	(X)	(X)	(X)

NA Not available. X Not applicable. [1] Preliminary. [2] The sum of "total retail sales" and "direct use." [3] Use of electricity that is 1) self-generated, 2) produced by either the same entity that consumes the power or an affiliate, and 3) used in direct support of a service or industrial process located within the same facility or group of facilities that house the generating equipment. Direct use is exclusive of station use. [4] Electricity retail sales to ultimate customers reported by electric utilities and, beginning in 2000, other energy service providers. [5] Includes public street and highway lighting, interdepartmental sales, and other sales to public authorities. [6] Beginning 2003, includes agriculture and irrigation. [7] Includes sales to railroads and railways. [8] Beginning 2003, includes public street and highway lighting, interdepartmental sales, and other sales to public authorities. [9] Public street and highway lighting, interdepartmental sales, other sales to public authorities, agriculture and irrigation, and transportation including railroads and railways.

Source: U.S. Energy Information Administration, *Annual Energy Review 2009,* August 2010. See also <http://www.eia.doe.gov/emeu/aer/elect.html>.

Energy and Utilities   595

Table 948. Electric Power Industry—Net Generation and Net Summer Capacity by State: 2000 to 2009

[Capacity as of December 31. 3,802.1 represents 3,802,100,000,000. Covers utilities for public use]

State	Net generation (bil. kWh)									Net summer capacity (mil. kW)	
	2000	2005	2009							2000	2009
			Total (bil. kWh)	Petro-leum	Natural gas	Hydro-electric	Non-hydro-electric	Nuclear	Coal		
						Percent from—					
						Renewable					
U.S.	3,802.1	4,055.4	3,950.3	1.0	23.3	6.9	3.7	20.2	44.4	811.7	1,025.4
AL	124.4	137.9	143.3	0.2	22.1	8.8	2.1	27.7	38.8	23.5	31.4
AK	6.2	6.6	6.7	17.3	53.4	19.8	0.2	–	9.4	2.1	2.0
AZ	88.9	101.5	112.0	0.1	31.0	5.7	0.2	27.4	35.5	15.3	26.3
AR	43.9	47.8	57.5	0.2	19.5	7.3	2.8	26.4	43.6	9.7	15.3
CA	208.1	200.3	204.8	0.8	55.4	13.6	12.5	15.5	1.0	52.3	65.9
CO	44.2	49.6	50.6	(Z)	27.4	3.7	6.4	–	62.6	8.4	13.0
CT	33.0	33.5	31.2	1.0	31.4	1.6	2.4	53.4	7.9	6.4	8.0
DE	6.0	8.1	4.8	5.3	28.4	–	2.6	–	58.8	2.4	3.4
DC	0.1	0.2	(Z)	100.0	–	–	–	–	–	0.8	0.8
FL	191.8	220.3	218.0	4.2	54.3	0.1	2.0	13.4	24.8	41.5	59.1
GA	123.9	136.7	128.7	0.5	15.9	2.5	2.2	24.6	54.0	27.8	36.5
HI	10.6	11.5	11.0	75.3	–	1.0	6.4	–	13.6	2.4	2.6
ID	11.9	10.8	13.1	(Z)	12.5	79.6	6.6	–	0.6	3.0	3.8
IL	178.5	194.1	193.9	0.1	2.3	0.1	1.8	49.2	46.4	36.3	44.0
IN	127.8	130.4	116.7	0.1	3.3	0.4	1.5	–	92.8	23.9	27.9
IA	41.5	44.2	51.9	0.2	2.3	1.9	14.6	9.0	72.0	9.1	14.6
KS	44.8	45.9	46.7	0.3	5.7	(Z)	6.1	18.8	69.1	10.1	12.5
KY	93.0	97.8	90.6	2.2	1.0	3.7	0.4	–	92.7	16.8	20.2
LA	92.9	92.6	91.0	2.0	48.4	1.4	2.6	18.4	25.4	21.1	26.0
ME	14.0	18.8	16.3	2.7	45.0	25.8	24.1	–	0.4	4.2	4.3
MD	51.1	52.7	43.8	0.8	4.0	4.3	1.3	33.2	55.2	10.5	12.5
MA	38.7	47.5	39.0	2.3	53.9	3.1	3.2	13.8	23.2	12.4	13.7
MI	104.2	121.6	101.2	0.4	8.3	1.4	2.6	21.6	66.1	25.8	30.3
MN	51.4	53.0	52.5	0.1	5.4	1.5	12.8	23.6	55.9	10.3	14.6
MS	37.6	45.1	48.7	(Z)	47.8	–	2.9	22.6	26.6	9.0	15.8
MO	76.6	90.8	88.4	0.1	3.9	2.1	0.7	11.6	81.1	17.3	20.8
MT	26.5	27.9	26.7	1.8	0.3	35.6	3.4	–	58.4	5.2	5.8
NE	29.1	31.5	34.0	0.1	0.9	1.3	1.3	27.7	68.7	6.0	7.8
NV	35.5	40.2	37.7	(Z)	68.6	6.5	4.8	–	20.0	6.7	11.4
NH	15.0	24.5	20.2	0.9	26.5	8.3	5.9	43.7	14.3	2.9	4.2
NJ	58.1	60.5	61.8	0.5	33.4	0.1	1.6	55.5	8.3	16.6	18.5
NM	34.0	35.1	39.7	0.1	21.8	0.7	4.0	–	73.4	5.6	8.0
NY	138.1	146.9	133.2	2.0	31.4	20.7	3.4	32.7	9.6	35.6	39.7
NC	122.3	129.7	118.4	0.3	4.1	4.4	1.6	34.5	55.0	24.5	27.6
ND	31.3	31.9	34.2	0.1	(Z)	4.3	8.8	–	86.6	4.7	6.0
OH	149.1	157.0	136.1	1.0	3.4	0.4	0.5	11.2	83.6	28.5	33.5
OK	55.6	68.6	75.1	(Z)	46.1	4.7	3.9	–	45.4	14.2	20.8
OR	51.8	49.3	56.7	(Z)	28.5	58.3	7.5	–	5.6	11.3	14.0
PA	201.7	218.1	219.5	0.4	13.3	1.2	1.5	35.2	48.1	36.8	45.6
RI	6.0	6.1	7.7	0.2	97.8	0.1	1.9	–	–	1.2	1.8
SC	93.3	102.5	100.1	0.5	9.8	2.3	1.7	52.1	34.4	18.7	24.0
SD	9.7	6.5	8.2	0.1	1.0	54.1	5.2	–	39.3	2.8	3.4
TN	95.8	97.1	79.7	0.2	0.5	12.8	1.2	33.8	52.2	19.5	20.9
TX	377.7	396.7	397.2	0.4	47.6	0.3	5.3	10.4	35.0	81.9	103.0
UT	36.6	38.2	43.5	0.1	14.8	1.9	1.1	–	81.6	5.2	7.4
VT	6.3	5.7	7.3	(Z)	0.1	20.4	5.9	73.6	–	1.0	1.1
VA	77.2	78.9	70.1	1.6	17.4	2.1	3.4	40.3	36.5	19.4	23.8
WA	108.2	102.0	104.5	0.1	11.5	69.8	4.8	6.4	7.2	26.1	30.1
WV	92.9	93.6	70.8	0.2	0.2	2.3	1.0	–	96.2	15.1	16.4
WI	59.6	61.8	60.0	1.2	9.1	2.3	3.9	21.2	62.2	13.6	17.7
WY	45.5	45.6	46.0	0.1	1.1	2.1	4.8	–	91.1	6.2	7.6

– Represents zero. Z Represents less than 50 million kWh or 50,000 kW.

Source: U.S. Energy Information Administration, "Electric Power Annual 2009," January 2011, <http://www.eia.gov/cneaf/electricity/epa/epa_sprdshts.html>.

Table 949. Electric Power Industry—Capability, Peak Load, and Capacity Margin: 1980 to 2010

[558,237 represents 558,237,000 kW. Excludes Alaska and Hawaii. Capability represents the maximum kilowatt output with all power sources available and with hydraulic equipment under actual water conditions, allowing for maintenance, emergency outages, and system operating requirements. Capacity margin is the difference between capability and peak load. Minus sign (−) indicates decrease]

| Year | Capability at the time of— | | | | Noncoincident peak load | | Capacity margin | | | |
| | Summer peak load (1,000 kW) | | Winter peak load (1,000 kW) | | | | Summer | | Winter | |
	Amount	Change from prior year	Amount	Change from prior year	Summer (1,000 kW)	Winter (1,000 kW)	Amount (1,000 kW)	Percent of capability	Amount (1,000 kW)	Percent of capability
1980......	558,237	13,731	572,195	17,670	427,058	384,567	131,179	23.5	187,628	32.8
1985......	621,597	17,357	636,475	14,350	460,503	423,660	161,094	25.9	212,815	33.4
1990......	685,091	11,775	696,757	11,508	546,331	484,231	138,760	20.3	212,526	30.5
1991......	690,915	5,824	703,212	6,455	551,418	485,761	139,497	20.2	217,451	30.9
1992......	695,436	4,521	707,752	4,540	548,707	492,983	146,729	21.1	214,769	30.3
1993......	694,250	−1,186	711,957	4,205	575,356	521,733	118,894	17.1	190,224	26.7
1994......	702,985	8,735	715,090	3,133	585,320	518,253	117,665	16.7	196,837	27.5
1995......	714,222	11,237	727,679	12,589	620,249	544,684	93,973	13.2	182,995	25.1
1996......	730,376	16,154	737,637	9,958	616,790	554,081	113,586	15.6	183,556	24.9
1997......	737,855	7,479	736,666	−971	637,677	529,874	100,178	13.6	206,792	28.1
1998......	744,670	6,815	735,090	−1,576	660,293	567,558	84,377	11.3	167,532	22.8
1999......	765,744	21,074	748,271	13,181	682,122	570,915	83,622	10.9	177,356	23.7
2000......	808,054	42,310	767,505	19,234	678,413	588,426	129,641	16.0	179,079	23.3
2001......	788,990	−19,064	806,598	39,093	687,812	576,312	101,178	12.8	230,286	28.6
2002......	833,380	44,390	850,984	44,386	714,565	604,986	118,815	14.3	245,998	28.9
2003......	856,131	22,751	882,120	31,136	709,375	593,874	146,756	17.1	288,246	32.7
2004......	875,870	19,739	864,849	−17,271	704,459	618,701	171,411	19.6	246,148	28.5
2005......	882,125	6,255	878,110	13,261	758,876	626,365	123,249	14.0	251,745	28.7
2006......	891,226	9,101	899,551	21,441	789,475	640,981	101,751	11.4	258,570	28.7
2007......	914,397	23,171	913,650	14,099	782,227	637,905	132,170	14.5	275,745	30.2
2008......	909,504	−4,893	927,781	14,131	752,470	643,557	157,034	17.3	284,224	30.6
2009......	916,449	6,945	920,002	−7,779	725,958	668,818	190,491	20.8	251,184	27.3
2010 [1]	934,894	18,445	948,326	28,324	772,089	639,073	162,805	17.4	309,253	32.6

[1] Preliminary.

Source: Edison Electric Institute, Washington, DC, *Statistical Yearbook of the Electric Power Industry*, annual.

Table 950. Electric Energy Retail Sales by Class of Service and State: 2009

[In billions of kilowatt-hours (3,596.9 represents 3,596,900,000,000). Data include both bundled and unbundled consumers]

State	Total [1]	Residential	Commercial	Industrial	State	Total [1]	Residential	Commercial	Industrial
United States	3,596.9	1,364.5	1,307.2	917.4					
Alabama	82.8	31.5	21.9	29.4	Missouri.........	79.7	34.2	30.4	15.1
Alaska............	6.3	2.1	2.8	1.3	Montana.........	14.3	4.8	4.8	4.8
Arizona	73.4	32.8	29.4	11.2	Nebraska........	28.5	9.6	9.3	9.5
Arkansas	43.2	17.0	11.5	14.7	Nevada	34.3	11.9	9.0	13.4
California..........	259.6	89.8	121.1	47.8	New Hampshire...	10.7	4.4	4.4	1.8
Colorado	51.0	17.4	20.0	13.6	New Jersey	75.8	27.8	39.4	8.3
Connecticut........	29.7	12.6	13.3	3.7	New Mexico......	21.6	6.5	8.7	6.4
Delaware	11.3	4.3	4.2	2.7	New York	140.0	48.2	75.3	13.4
District of Columbia...	12.2	1.9	9.7	0.3	North Carolina....	127.7	56.3	46.2	25.1
Florida.............	224.8	115.5	92.3	16.9	North Dakota.....	12.6	4.4	4.6	3.6
Georgia	130.8	55.2	46.1	29.3	Ohio............	146.3	51.4	45.4	49.5
Hawaii	10.1	3.1	3.4	3.7	Oklahoma	54.5	21.6	18.7	14.2
Idaho.............	22.8	8.6	6.0	8.2	Oregon.........	47.6	19.8	16.0	11.8
Illinois............	136.7	44.3	50.3	41.5	Pennsylvania.....	143.7	52.9	46.4	43.6
Indiana............	99.3	32.5	23.7	43.1	Rhode Island.....	7.6	2.9	3.7	1.0
Iowa.............	43.6	13.7	11.7	18.2	South Carolina....	76.4	29.6	21.4	25.4
Kansas...........	38.2	13.1	15.0	10.1	South Dakota.....	11.0	4.5	4.2	2.3
Kentucky..........	88.8	26.5	18.7	43.6	Tennessee.......	94.7	40.1	28.0	26.6
Louisiana.........	78.7	29.7	23.3	25.6	Texas	345.3	129.8	118.5	96.9
Maine.............	11.3	4.4	4.1	2.9	Utah...........	27.6	8.7	10.2	8.6
Maryland	62.6	26.9	29.8	5.3	Vermont.........	5.5	2.1	2.0	1.4
Massachusetts.......	54.4	19.5	17.8	16.8	Virginia.........	108.5	44.8	46.8	16.7
Michigan	98.1	32.9	37.9	27.4	Washington	90.2	36.8	30.1	23.4
Minnesota.........	64.0	22.0	22.3	19.6	West Virginia	30.3	11.6	7.7	11.0
Mississippi........	46.0	18.1	13.0	14.9	Wisconsin	66.3	21.4	22.5	22.4
					Wyoming	16.6	2.7	4.3	9.6

[1] Includes transportation, not shown separately.

Source: U.S. Energy Information Administration, "Electric Sales, Revenue, and Average Price 2009," April 2011, <http://www.eia.gov/cneaf/electricity/esr/esr_sum.html>.

Table 951. Electric Energy Price by Class of Service and State: 2009

[Revenue (in cents) per kilowatt-hour (kWh). Data include both bundled and unbundled consumers]

State	Total [1]	Resi-dential	Com-mercial	Indus-trial	State	Total [1]	Resi-dential	Com-mercial	Indus-trial
United States	9.82	11.51	10.17	6.81					
					Missouri	7.35	8.54	6.96	5.42
Alabama	8.83	10.66	10.05	5.96	Montana	7.57	8.93	8.32	5.45
Alaska	15.09	17.14	14.46	13.15	Nebraska	7.21	8.52	7.33	5.75
Arizona	9.56	10.73	9.35	6.65	Nevada	10.36	12.86	10.64	7.97
Arkansas	7.57	9.14	7.56	5.76	New Hampshire . . .	15.13	16.26	14.55	13.83
California	13.24	14.74	13.42	10.07					
					New Jersey	14.52	16.31	13.83	11.81
Colorado	8.31	10.00	8.15	6.39	New Mexico	8.09	10.02	8.40	5.72
Connecticut	18.06	20.33	16.86	14.92	New York	15.52	17.50	15.51	8.98
Delaware	12.14	14.07	11.98	9.34	North Carolina	8.48	9.99	7.98	5.99
District of Columbia . . .	12.97	13.76	12.96	8.41	North Dakota	6.63	7.58	6.81	5.25
Florida	11.49	12.39	10.77	9.32					
					Ohio	9.01	10.67	9.65	6.71
Georgia	8.81	10.13	8.94	6.12	Oklahoma	6.94	8.49	6.76	4.82
Hawaii	21.21	24.20	21.86	18.14	Oregon	7.48	8.68	7.49	5.45
Idaho	6.51	7.80	6.49	5.17	Pennsylvania	9.60	11.65	9.54	7.21
Illinois	9.08	11.27	8.99	6.84	Rhode Island	14.23	15.60	13.67	12.25
Indiana	7.62	9.50	8.32	5.81					
					South Carolina	8.42	10.44	8.74	5.79
Iowa	7.37	9.99	7.55	5.27	South Dakota	7.39	8.49	7.14	5.65
Kansas	7.98	9.53	7.87	6.10	Tennessee	8.69	9.32	9.61	6.76
Kentucky	6.52	8.37	7.63	4.91	Texas	9.86	12.38	9.66	6.74
Louisiana	7.06	8.10	7.69	5.25	Utah	6.77	8.48	6.96	4.81
Maine	13.09	15.65	12.55	9.95					
					Vermont	12.75	14.90	12.93	9.21
Maryland	13.08	14.98	11.97	9.92	Virginia	8.93	10.61	8.06	6.91
Massachusetts	15.45	16.87	15.37	14.08	Washington	6.60	7.68	6.96	4.43
Michigan	9.40	11.60	9.24	6.99	West Virginia	6.65	7.90	6.77	5.24
Minnesota	8.14	10.04	7.92	6.26	Wisconsin	9.38	11.94	9.57	6.73
Mississippi	8.85	10.22	9.50	6.61	Wyoming	6.08	8.58	7.28	4.83

[1] Includes transportation, not shown separately.

Source: U.S. Energy Information Administration, "Electric Sales, Revenue, and Average Price 2009," April 2011, <http://www.eia.gov/cneaf/electricity/esr/esr_sum.html>.

Table 952. Total Electric Power Industry—Generation, Sales, Revenue, and Customers: 1990 to 2010

[2,808 represents 2,808,000,000,000 kWh. Sales and revenue are to and from ultimate customers. Commercial and Industrial are not wholly comparable on a year-to-year basis due to changes from one classification to another. For the 2005 period forward, the Energy Information Administration replaced the "Other" sector with the Transportation sector. The Transportation sector consists entirely of electrified rail and urban transit systems. Data previously reported in "Other" have been relocated to the Commercial sector, except for Agriculture (i.e., irrigation load), which have been relocated to the Industrial sector]

Class	Unit	1990	1995	2000	2005	2006	2007	2008	2009	2010 [1]
Generation [2]	Bil. kWh	2,808	3,353	3,802	4,055	4,065	4,157	4,119	3,950	4,120
Sales [3]	Bil. kWh. . . .	2,713	3,013	3,421	3,661	3,670	3,765	3,733	3,597	3,750
Residential or domestic	Bil. kWh	924	1,043	1,192	1,359	1,352	1,392	1,380	1,364	1,451
Percent of total	Percent . . .	34.1	34.6	34.9	37.1	36.8	37.0	37.0	37.9	38.7
Commercial [4]	Bil. kWh	751	863	1,055	1,275	1,300	1,336	1,336	1,307	1,329
Industrial [5]	Bil. kWh	946	1,013	1,064	1,019	1,011	1,028	1,009	917	962
Revenue [3]	Bil. dol.	178.2	207.7	233.2	298.0	326.5	343.7	363.7	353.3	370.5
Residential or domestic	Bil. dol.	72.4	87.6	98.2	128.4	140.6	148.3	155.4	157.0	168.0
Percent of total	Percent . . .	40.6	42.2	42.1	43.1	43.1	43.1	42.7	44.4	45.3
Commercial [4]	Bil. dol.	55.1	66.4	78.4	110.5	122.9	128.9	138.5	132.9	136.4
Industrial [5]	Bil. dol.	44.9	47.2	49.4	58.4	62.3	65.7	68.9	62.5	65.3
Ultimate customers, Dec. 31 [3] . . .	Million	110.6	118.3	127.6	138.4	140.4	142.1	143.3	143.5	144.2
Residential or domestic	Million	97.1	103.9	111.7	120.8	122.5	123.9	124.9	125.2	125.9
Commercial [4]	Million	12.1	12.9	14.3	16.9	17.2	17.4	17.6	17.6	17.6
Industrial [5]	Million	0.5	0.6	0.5	0.7	0.8	0.8	0.8	0.8	0.7
Avg. kWh used per customer . . .	1,000	24.5	25.5	26.8	26.5	26.1	26.5	26.1	25.1	26.0
Residential	1,000	9.5	10.0	10.7	11.3	11.0	11.2	11.0	10.9	11.5
Commercial [4]	1,000	62.2	66.6	73.5	75.6	75.7	76.9	76.1	74.4	75.6
Avg. annual bill per customer . . .	Dollar	1,612	1,756	1,828	2,154	2,325	2,418	2,538	2,462	2,570
Residential	Dollar	745	843	879	1,063	1,148	1,196	1,244	1,254	1,335
Commercial [4]	Dollar	4,562	5,124	5,464	6,551	7,158	7,418	7,884	7,570	7,754
Avg. revenue per kWh sold	Cents	6.57	6.89	6.81	8.14	8.90	9.13	9.74	9.82	9.88
Residential	Cents	7.83	8.40	8.24	9.45	10.40	10.65	11.26	11.51	11.58
Commercial [4]	Cents	7.34	7.69	7.43	8.67	9.46	9.65	10.36	10.17	10.26
Industrial [5]	Cents	4.74	4.66	4.64	5.73	6.16	6.39	6.83	6.81	6.79

[1] Preliminary. [2] "Generation" includes batteries, chemicals, hydrogen, pitch, sulfur, purchased steam, and miscellaneous technologies, which are not separately displayed. [3] Includes other types, not shown separately. Data for 1990 are as of December 31, data for following years are average yearly customers. [4] Small light and power. [5] Large light and power.

Source: Edison Electric Institute, Washington, DC, *Statistical Yearbook of the Electric Power Industry*, annual.

Table 953. Revenue and Expense Statistics for Major U.S. Investor-Owned Electric Utilities: 1995 to 2009

[In millions of nominal dollars (199,967 represents $199,967,000,000). Covers approximately 180 investor-owned electric utilities that during each of the last 3 years met any one or more of the following conditions—1 mil. megawatt-hours of total sales; 100 megawatt-hours of sales for resale, 500 megawatt-hours of gross interchange out, and 500 megawatt-hours of wheeling for other. Missing or erroneous respondent data may result in slight imbalances in some of the expense account subtotals]

Item	1995	2000	2005	2006	2007	2008	2009
Utility operating revenues	**199,967**	**233,915**	**265,652**	**275,501**	**270,964**	**298,962**	**276,124**
Electric utility	183,655	213,634	234,909	246,736	240,864	266,124	249,303
Other utility	16,312	20,281	30,743	28,765	30,100	32,838	26,822
Utility operating expenses	**165,321**	**210,250**	**236,786**	**245,589**	**241,198**	**267,263**	**244,243**
Electric utility	150,599	191,564	207,830	218,445	213,076	236,572	219,544
Operation....................	91,881	132,607	150,645	158,893	153,885	175,887	154,925
Production...................	68,983	107,554	120,586	127,494	121,700	140,974	118,816
Cost of fuel	29,122	32,407	36,106	37,945	39,548	47,337	40,242
Purchased power...........	29,981	62,608	77,902	79,205	74,112	84,724	67,630
Other	9,880	12,561	6,599	10,371	8,058	8,937	10,970
Transmission	1,425	2,713	5,664	6,179	6,051	6,950	6,742
Distribution.................	2,561	3,092	3,502	3,640	3,765	3,997	3,947
Customer accounts	3,613	4,239	4,229	4,409	4,652	5,286	5,203
Customer service	1,922	1,826	2,291	2,536	2,939	3,567	3,857
Sales	348	405	219	240	239	225	178
Administrative and general	13,028	12,768	14,130	14,580	14,346	14,718	15,991
Maintenance	11,767	12,064	12,033	12,838	13,181	14,192	14,092
Depreciation	19,885	20,636	17,123	17,373	17,936	19,049	20,095
Taxes and other	27,065	24,479	26,805	28,149	27,000	26,202	29,081
Other utility	14,722	18,686	28,956	27,143	28,122	30,692	24,698
Net utility operating income	**34,646**	**23,665**	**28,866**	**29,912**	**29,766**	**31,699**	**31,881**

Source: U.S. Energy Information Administration, "Electric Power Annual 2009," April 2011, <http://www.eia.gov/cneaf/electricity/epa/epat8p1.html>.

Table 954. Total Renewable Energy Net Generation of Electricity by Source and State: 2009

[In millions of kilowatt-hours (417,724 represents 417,724,000,000). MSW = municipal solid waste. For more on net generation, see Table 948]

State	Total [1]	Hydro-electric	Bio-mass [2]	Wind	Wood and derived fuels [3]	State	Total [1]	Hydro-electric	Bio-mass [2]	Wind	Wood and derived fuels [3]
U.S.	**417,724**	**273,445**	**18,443**	**73,886**	**36,050**	MO......	2,391	1,817	73	499	2
AL	15,585	12,535	14	(NA)	3,035	MT	10,422	9,506	(NA)	821	95
AK	1,337	1,324	7	7	(NA)	NE	883	434	66	383	(NA)
AZ	6,630	6,427	22	30	137	NV	4,269	2,461	(NA)	(NA)	1
AR	5,778	4,193	57	(NA)	1,529	NH	2,878	1,680	151	62	984
CA	53,428	27,888	2,468	5,840	3,732	NJ	992	32	928	21	(NA)
CO	5,132	1,886	56	3,164	(Z)	NM......	1,851	271	34	1,547	(NA)
CT	1,268	510	758	(NA)	1	NY	32,082	27,615	1,665	2,266	536
DE	126	(NA)	126	(NA)	(NA)	NC	7,065	5,171	131	(NA)	1,757
DC	(NA)	(NA)	(NA)	(NA)	(NA)	ND	4,484	1,475	12	2,998	(NA)
FL	4,549	208	2,377	(NA)	1,954	OH	1,161	528	210	14	410
GA	6,085	3,260	80	(NA)	2,746	OK	6,482	3,553	163	2,698	68
HI	817	113	284	251	(NA)	OR	37,306	33,034	128	3,470	674
ID	11,302	10,434	(NA)	313	478	PA	6,035	2,683	1,579	1,075	694
IL	3,666	136	710	2,820	(Z)	RI	149	5	145	(NA)	(NA)
IN	2,209	503	303	1,403	(NA)	SC	4,080	2,332	137	(NA)	1,611
IA	8,560	971	168	7,421	(Z)	SD	4,859	4,432	6	421	(NA)
KS	2,876	13	(NA)	2,863	(NA)	TN	11,162	10,212	36	52	862
KY	3,681	3,318	101	(NA)	263	TX	22,133	1,029	429	20,026	649
LA	3,600	1,236	67	(NA)	2,297	UT	1,322	835	48	160	(NA)
ME......	8,150	4,212	273	299	3,367	VT	1,915	1,486	24	12	393
MD......	2,440	1,889	376	(NA)	175	VA	3,896	1,479	709	(NA)	1,708
MA......	2,430	1,201	1,108	6	115	WA......	77,977	72,933	167	3,572	1,305
MI......	3,995	1,372	834	300	1,489	WV......	2,388	1,646	(−Z)	742	−1
MN......	7,546	809	887	5,053	796	WI	3,734	1,394	519	1,052	769
MS......	1,424	(NA)	7	(NA)	1,417	WY......	3,193	967	(NA)	2,226	(NA)

NA Not available. Z Less than 500,000 million kilowatt-hours. [1] Includes types not shown separately. [2] Includes landfill gas and municipal solid waste biogenic (paper and paper board, wood, food, leather, textiles, and yard trimmings). Also includes agriculture by-products/crops, sludge waste, and other biomass solids, liquids, and gases. Excludes wood and wood waste. [3] Black liquor and wood/woodwaste solids and liquids.

Source: Energy Information Administration, "Trends in Renewable Energy Consumption and Electricity 2009," March 2011, <http://www.eia.gov/renewable/annual/trends/>.

Table 955. Gas Utility Industry—Summary: 1990 to 2009

[54,261 represents 54,261,000. Covers natural, manufactured, mixed, and liquid petroleum gas. Based on a questionnaire mailed to all privately and municipally owned gas utilities in the United States, except those with annual revenues less than $25,000]

Item	Unit	1990	1995	2000	2005	2006	2007	2008	2009
End users [1]	**1,000**	**54,261**	**58,728**	**61,262**	**64,395**	**65,020**	**65,389**	**65,487**	**65,147**
Residential	1,000	49,802	53,955	56,494	59,569	60,147	60,534	60,654	60,344
Commercial	1,000	4,246	4,530	4,610	4,678	4,734	4,718	4,703	4,659
Industrial and other	1,000	214	242	159	147	140	137	130	144
Sales [2]	**Tril. Btu [3]**	**9,842**	**9,221**	**9,232**	**8,848**	**8,222**	**8,565**	**8,594**	**8,050**
Residential	Tril. Btu	4,468	4,803	4,741	4,516	4,117	4,418	4,541	4,387
Percent of total	Percent	45	52	51	51	50	52	53	54
Commercial	Tril. Btu	2,192	2,281	2,077	2,056	1,861	1,943	2,009	1,901
Industrial	Tril. Btu	3,010	1,919	1,698	1,654	1,576	1,522	1,410	1,193
Other	Tril. Btu	171	218	715	622	668	682	635	570
Revenues [2]	**Mil. dol.**	**45,153**	**46,436**	**59,243**	**96,909**	**91,928**	**92,131**	**102,641**	**77,675**
Residential	Mil. dol.	25,000	28,742	35,828	55,680	53,961	55,028	60,195	50,500
Percent of total	Percent	55	62	60	57	59	60	59	65
Commercial	Mil. dol.	10,604	11,573	13,339	22,653	21,557	21,248	23,592	18,451
Industrial	Mil. dol.	8,996	5,571	7,432	13,751	12,006	11,323	13,205	6,171
Other	Mil. dol.	553	549	2,645	4,825	4,405	4,533	5,649	2,553
Prices per mil. Btu [3]	**Dollars**	**4.59**	**5.05**	**6.42**	**10.95**	**11.18**	**10.76**	**11.94**	**9.65**
Residential	Dollars	5.60	6.00	7.56	12.33	13.11	12.46	13.26	11.51
Commercial	Dollars	4.84	5.07	6.42	11.02	11.58	10.93	11.75	9.71
Industrial	Dollars	2.99	2.98	4.38	8.31	7.62	7.44	9.37	5.17
Gas mains mileage	**1,000**	**1,189**	**1,278**	**1,369**	**1,438**	**1,534**	**1,520**	**1,525**	**1,526**
Field and gathering	1,000	32	31	27	23	20	19	20	20
Transmission	1,000	292	297	297	297	300	300	299	297
Distribution	1,000	865	950	1,046	1,118	1,214	1,201	1,206	1,210
Construction expenditures [4]	**Mil. dol.**	**7,899**	**10,760**	**8,624**	**10,089**	**10,218**	**10,987**	**14,090**	**12,146**
Transmission	Mil. dol.	2,886	3,380	1,590	3,368	3,316	4,327	6,388	5,377
Distribution	Mil. dol.	3,714	5,394	5,437	5,129	5,165	4,851	5,427	4,948
Production and storage	Mil. dol.	309	367	138	179	240	107	174	128
General	Mil. dol.	770	1,441	1,273	1,070	1,119	1,146	1,228	1,135
Underground storage	Mil. dol.	219	177	185	343	379	556	873	559

[1] Annual average. [2] Excludes sales for resale. [3] For definition of Btu, see text, this section. [4] Includes general.

Source: American Gas Association, Arlington, VA, *Gas Facts*, annual (copyright).

Table 956. Gas Utility Industry—Customers, Sales, and Revenues by State: 2009

[65,147 represents 65,147,000. See headnote, Table 955. For definition of Btu, see text, this section]

State	Customers [1] (1,000) Total	Resi-dential	Sales [2] (tril. Btu) Total	Resi-dential	Revenues [2] (mil. dol.) Total	Resi-dential	State	Customers [1] (1,000) Total	Resi-dential	Sales [2] (tril. Btu) Total	Resi-dential	Revenues [2] (mil. dol.) Total	Resi-dential
U.S.	**65,147**	**60,344**	**8,066**	**4,395**	**77,675**	**50,500**							
AL	853	783	95	37	1,175	652	MO	1,490	1,348	168	110	1,932	1,340
AK	133	120	62	21	499	204	MT	289	255	35	22	318	206
AZ	1,188	1,130	76	36	1,031	613	NE	483	442	65	36	521	329
AR	627	557	60	34	700	445	NV	802	760	93	40	999	511
CA	10,897	10,454	687	491	5,898	4,481	NH	112	97	14	7	200	111
							NJ	2,772	2,563	327	228	4,067	3,201
CO	1,768	1,622	198	133	1,599	1,135	NM	606	560	50	33	427	308
CT	541	489	86	44	1,005	636	NY	3,936	3,658	455	322	6,104	4,671
DE	162	149	17	10	283	179	NC	1,217	1,102	125	68	1,541	935
DC	136	130	14	11	185	143	ND	140	122	28	12	202	97
FL	702	660	42	15	591	301	OH	1,708	1,593	193	144	2,120	1,626
GA	360	324	53	17	485	221	OK	1,016	925	100	64	978	709
HI	28	25	3	1	78	19	OR	753	676	88	46	1,103	651
ID	381	342	40	26	402	269	PA	2,634	2,427	301	214	4,090	3,016
IL	3,809	3,554	511	397	4,382	3,453	RI	247	225	27	18	425	306
IN	1,711	1,569	213	135	2,068	1,415	SC	623	566	82	28	824	405
IA	974	876	126	72	1,082	689	SD	190	168	29	14	226	124
KS	938	856	103	73	1,038	789	TN	1,212	1,082	149	68	1,528	803
KY	802	721	98	51	1,006	589	TX	4,562	4,244	1,326	198	7,088	2,150
LA	948	889	219	38	1,372	480	UT	871	810	104	67	848	583
ME	28	21	5	1	63	21	VT	42	37	8	3	105	55
MD	996	939	93	71	1,152	896	VA	1,156	1,069	128	79	1,522	1,046
MA	1,522	1,361	168	117	2,314	1,688	WA	1,161	1,059	144	87	1,854	1,174
MI	3,240	3,004	435	316	4,618	3,453	WV	377	344	45	27	591	386
MN	1,557	1,424	271	138	2,133	1,199	WI	1,824	1,657	238	137	2,258	1,432
MS	488	437	52	24	493	263	WY	132	117	18	10	154	92

[1] Averages for the year. [2] Excludes sales for resale.

Source: American Gas Association, Arlington, VA, *Gas Facts*, annual (copyright).

U.S. Census Bureau, Statistical Abstract of the United States: 2012

Table 957. Privately Owned Gas Utility Industry—Balance Sheet and Income Account: 1990 to 2009

[In millions of dollars (121,686 represents $121,686,000,000). The gas utility industry consists of pipeline and distribution companies. Excludes operations of companies distributing gas in bottles or tanks]

Item	1990	1995	2000	2004	2005	2006	2007	2008	2009
COMPOSITE BALANCE SHEET									
Assets, total	**121,686**	**141,965**	**165,709**	**168,306**	**196,215**	**203,135**	**205,345**	**230,002**	**219,467**
Total utility plant	112,863	143,636	162,206	180,884	207,976	212,500	213,516	237,140	235,426
Depreciation and amortization	*49,483*	*62,723*	*69,366*	*79,889*	*91,794*	*91,804*	*86,244*	*95,211*	*91,958*
Utility plant (net)	63,380	80,912	92,839	100,996	116,183	120,696	127,272	141,929	143,468
Investment and fund accounts	23,872	26,489	10,846	12,716	16,331	17,309	13,677	11,725	9,649
Current and accrued assets	23,268	18,564	35,691	22,107	32,325	26,955	28,871	31,960	27,703
Deferred debits [1]	9,576	13,923	24,279	31,033	29,574	36,278	34,608	42,922	37,037
Liabilities, total	**121,686**	**141,965**	**165,709**	**168,709**	**196,215**	**203,135**	**205,345**	**230,002**	**219,467**
Capitalization, total	74,958	90,581	96,079	105,579	120,949	126,842	127,609	136,108	135,797
Capital stock	43,810	54,402	47,051	54,252	62,470	66,153	71,038	74,610	74,517
Long-term debts	31,148	35,548	48,267	51,327	58,264	60,632	56,538	61,498	61,280
Current and accrued liabilities	29,550	28,272	42,312	25,515	34,936	32,417	34,017	37,450	28,711
Deferred income taxes [2]	11,360	14,393	17,157	23,944	24,937	27,454	27,009	27,637	30,236
Other liabilities and credits	5,818	8,715	10,161	13,671	15,393	16,422	16,709	28,807	24,723
COMPOSITE INCOME ACCOUNT									
Operating revenues, total	**66,027**	**58,390**	**72,042**	**80,194**	**102,018**	**97,156**	**97,195**	**109,547**	**87,419**
Minus: Operating expenses [3]	*60,137*	*50,760*	*64,988*	*71,719*	*89,385*	*87,013*	*85,050*	*97,665*	*76,240*
Operation and maintenance	51,627	37,966	54,602	59,920	77,673	73,459	71,011	82,386	61,865
Federal, state, and local taxes	4,957	6,182	6,163	6,472	7,513	7,350	7,803	8,477	7,889
Equals: Operating income	5,890	7,630	7,053	8,475	12,632	10,144	12,146	11,882	11,179
Utility operating income	6,077	7,848	7,166	8,619	12,812	10,185	12,472	12,293	11,428
Income before interest charges	8,081	9,484	7,589	9,609	13,972	11,586	14,329	13,313	12,232
Net income	4,410	5,139	4,245	5,942	9,777	6,931	9,758	9,067	8,458
Dividends	3,191	4,037	3,239	2,111	2,419	2,304	2,253	2,427	2,162

[1] Includes capital stock discount and expense and reacquired securities. [2] Includes reserves for deferred income taxes.
[3] Includes expenses not shown separately.

Source: American Gas Association, Arlington, VA, *Gas Facts*, annual (copyright).

Table 958. Sewage Treatment Facilities: 2008

[Based on the North American Industry Classification System (NAICS), 2007; see text, Section 15]

State	Sewage treatment facilities (NAICS 22132)		State	Sewage treatment facilities (NAICS 22132)	
	Number of establishments	Paid employees		Number of establishments	Paid employees
U.S.	**663**	**6,363**	MO	20	98
AL	6	70	MT	3	25
AK	2	(¹)	NE	1	(¹)
AZ	15	50	NV	(NA)	(NA)
AR	2	(¹)	NH	10	(³)
CA	37	(²)	NJ	17	(²)
CO	6	28	NM	1	(¹)
CT	13	(³)	NY	31	297
DE	2	(³)	NC	26	128
DC	(NA)	(NA)	ND	1	(¹)
FL	73	837	OH	10	133
GA	8	(⁴)	OK	13	(⁴)
HI	14	(³)	OR	5	(³)
ID	6	44	PA	45	368
IL	43	379	RI	5	(³)
IN	37	479	SC	10	67
IA	4	(³)	SD	1	(¹)
KS	2	(³)	TN	10	65
KY	8	(⁴)	TX	38	309
LA	24	315	UT	1	(¹)
ME	1	(¹)	VT	2	(¹)
MD	8	34	VA	7	(³)
MA	25	(²)	WA	6	(³)
MI	21	(⁴)	WV	14	96
MN	6	(³)	WI	5	(¹)
MS	16	321	WY	2	(¹)

NA Not available. ¹ 0–19 employees. ² 250–499 employees. ³ 20–99 employees. ⁴ 100–249 employees.
Source: U.S. Census Bureau, "County Business Patterns," July 2010, <http://www.census.gov/econ/cbp/index.html>.

Table 959. Public Drinking Water Systems by Size of Community Served and Source of Water: 2009

[As of September. Covers systems that provide water for human consumption through pipes and other constructed conveyances to at least 15 service connections or serve an average of at least 25 persons for at least 60 days a year. Based on reported data in the Safe Drinking Water Information System maintained by the Environmental Protection Agency]

Type of system	Total [1]	Size of community served					Water source	
		500 or fewer persons	501 to 3,300 persons	3,301 to 10,000 persons	10,001 to 100,000 persons	100,001 persons or more	Ground water	Surface water
Total systems.....................	153,530	125,126	19,126	5,090	3,775	413	139,205	14,297
COMMUNITY WATER SYSTEMS [2]								
Number of systems..................	51,651	28,804	13,820	4,871	3,746	410	40,025	11,617
Percent of systems	100	56	27	9	7	1	78	22
Population served (1,000).............	294,340	4,821	19,807	28,403	106,857	134,453	88,032	206,264
Percent of population................	100	2	7	10	36	46	30	70
NONTRANSIENT NONCOMMUNITY WATER SYSTEM [3]								
Number of systems..................	18,395	15,619	2,625	132	18	1	17,688	702
Percent of systems	100	85	14	1	–	–	96	4
Population served (1,000).............	6,243	2,195	2,704	700	441	203	5,416	820
Percent of population................	100	35	43	11	7	3	87	13
TRANSIENT NONCOMMUNITY WATER SYSTEM [4]								
Number of systems..................	83,484	80,703	2,681	87	11	2	81,492	1,978
Percent of systems	100	97	3	–	–	–	98	2
Population served (1,000).............	13,303	7,147	2,599	472	361	2,725	10,754	2,548
Percent of population................	100	54	20	4	3	20	81	19

– Represents zero. [1] Includes a small number of systems for which the water source (ground vs. surface) is unknown. [2] A public water system that supplies water to the same population year-round. [3] A public water system that regularly supplies water to at least 25 of the same people at least 6 months per year, but not year-round. Some examples are schools, factories, and office buildings which have their own water systems. [4] A public water system that provides water in a place such as a gas station or campground where people do not remain for long periods of time and is open at least 60 day per year.

Source: U.S. Environmental Protection Agency, *Factoids: Drinking Water and Ground Water Statistics for 2009*, November 2009. See also <http://water.epa.gov/scitech/datait/databases/drink/sdwisfed/howtoaccessdata.cfm>.

Table 960. Public Drinking Water Systems—Number and Population Served by State: 2009

[306,898 represents 306,898,000. See headnote, Table 959]

State	Number of systems	Population served (1,000)				State	Number of systems	Population served (1,000)			
		Total	Commu-nity [1]	Non-tran-sient, non-com-munity [2]	Tran-sient, non-com-munity [3]			Total	Commu-nity [1]	Non-tran-sient, non-com-munity [2]	Tran-sient, non-com-munity [3]
U.S. [4]...	151,647	306,898	287,735	5,886	13,277	MO......	2,785	5,369	5,176	77	116
AL	619	5,496	5,473	16	7	MT......	2,097	972	717	79	176
AK	1,577	755	585	62	108	NE......	1,324	1,585	1,479	52	54
AZ	1,592	6,358	6,115	129	113	NV......	562	2,594	2,530	42	23
AR	1,095	2,677	2,647	9	21	NH......	2,421	1,270	855	97	319
CA	7,134	41,193	39,378	377	1,439	NJ......	3,840	9,557	8,786	354	417
CO.......	2,022	5,589	5,264	74	251	NM......	1,239	1,834	1,705	52	77
CT	2,653	2,822	2,650	114	58	NY......	9,294	21,112	17,954	313	2,845
DE	489	968	889	26	53	NC......	6,337	7,810	7,366	125	318
DC	6	607	607	(Z)	–	ND......	508	586	568	4	14
FL	5,721	19,484	18,978	251	255	OH......	5,040	11,004	10,351	228	424
GA	2,483	8,427	8,279	66	82	OK......	1,571	3,571	3,520	21	30
HI........	130	1,453	1,441	11	(Z)	OR......	2,630	3,483	3,199	72	212
ID........	1,964	1,250	1,091	52	106	PA......	9,409	12,058	10,758	521	779
IL	5,731	12,538	12,050	129	359	RI.......	443	1,053	978	26	49
IN........	4,256	5,283	4,711	195	378	SC	1,487	3,903	3,819	42	41
IA........	1,950	2,814	2,685	47	81	SD	656	718	687	8	23
KS........	1,033	2,598	2,573	21	4	TN	884	6,178	6,095	26	57
KY	479	4,469	4,451	12	6	TX	6,738	25,392	24,631	511	250
LA	1,450	5,004	4,888	56	60	UT	1,023	2,792	2,687	30	76
ME......	1,900	914	662	68	184	VT	1,366	592	452	42	98
MD......	3,527	5,523	5,146	161	216	VA	2,879	7,033	6,554	308	171
MA......	1,729	9,527	9,314	73	139	WA.....	4,148	6,710	6,172	143	395
MI.......	11,554	8,972	7,615	337	1,020	WV.....	1,076	1,570	1,498	39	33
MN......	7,262	4,806	4,191	78	536	WI......	11,482	4,914	3,988	209	717
MS......	1,277	3,169	3,083	75	10	WY.....	775	543	445	23	75

– Represents zero. Z Less than 500. [1] A public water system that supplies water to the same population year-round. [2] A public water system that regularly supplies water to at least 25 of the same people at least 6 months per year, but not year-round. Some examples are schools, factories, and office buildings which have their own water systems. [3] A public water system that provides water in a place such as a gas station or campground where people do not remain for long periods of time and is open at least 60 days per year. [4] U.S. total does not equal sum of states due to incomplete reporting of a small number of systems.

Source: U.S. Environmental Protection Agency, *Factoids: Drinking Water and Ground Water Statistics for 2009*, November 2009. See also <http://water.epa.gov/scitech/datait/databases/drink/sdwisfed/howtoaccessdata.cfm>.

Section 20
Construction and Housing

This section presents data on the construction industry and on various indicators of its activity and costs; on housing units and their characteristics and occupants; and on the characteristics and vacancy rates for commercial buildings. This edition contains data from the 2005 American Housing Survey.

The principal source of these data is the U.S. Census Bureau, which issues a variety of current publications, as well as data from the decennial census. Current construction statistics compiled by the Census Bureau appear in its *New Residential Construction* and *New Residential Sales* press releases and Web site at <http://www.census.gov/const/www/>. Statistics on expenditures by owners of residential properties are issued quarterly and annually in *Expenditures for Residential Improvements and Repairs. Value of New Construction Put in Place* presents data on all types of construction. Reports of the censuses of construction industries (see below) are also issued on various topics.

Other Census Bureau publications include the *Current Housing Reports* series, which comprise the quarterly *Housing Vacancies*, the quarterly *Market Absorption of Apartments*, the biennial *American Housing Survey* (formerly *Annual Housing Survey*), and reports of the censuses of housing and of construction industries.

Other sources include the monthly *Dodge Construction Potentials* of McGraw-Hill Construction, New York, NY, which present national and state data on construction contracts; the National Association of Home Builders with state-level data on housing starts; the NATIONAL ASSOCIATION OF REALTORS®, which presents data on existing home sales; the Bureau of Economic Analysis, which presents data on residential capital and gross housing product; and the U.S. Energy Information Administration, which provides data on commercial buildings through its periodic sample surveys.

Censuses and surveys—Censuses of the construction industry were first conducted by the Census Bureau for 1929, 1935, and 1939; beginning in 1967, a census has been taken every 5 years (through 2002, for years ending in "2" and "7"). The latest reports are part of the 2002 Economic Census. See text, Section 15, Business Enterprise.

The construction sector of the economic census, covers all employer establishments primarily engaged in (1) building construction by general contractors or operative builders; (2) heavy (nonbuilding) construction by general contractors; and (3) construction by special trade contractors. This sector includes construction management and land subdividers and developers. The 2002 census was conducted in accordance with the 2002 North American Industrial Classification System (NAICS). See text, Section 15, Business Enterprise.

From 1850 through 1930, the Census Bureau collected some housing data as part of its censuses of population and agriculture. Beginning in 1940, separate censuses of housing have been taken at 10-year intervals. For the 1970 and 1980 censuses, data on year-round housing units were collected and issued on occupancy and structural characteristics, plumbing facilities, value, and rent; for 1990, such characteristics were presented for all housing units.

The American Housing Survey (*Current Housing Reports* Series H-150 and H-170), which began in 1973, provided an annual and ongoing series of data on selected housing and demographic characteristics until 1983. In 1984, the name of the survey was changed from the Annual Housing Survey. Currently, national data are collected every other year, and data for selected metropolitan areas are collected on a rotating basis. All samples represent a cross section of the housing stock in their respective areas. Estimates are subject to both sampling and nonsampling errors; caution should therefore be used in making comparisons between years.

Data on residential mortgages were collected continuously from 1890 to 1970,

U.S. Census Bureau, Statistical Abstract of the United States: 2012

except 1930, as part of the decennial census by the Census Bureau. Since 1973, mortgage status data, limited to single family homes on less than 10 acres with no business on the property, have been presented in the American Housing Survey. Data on mortgage activity arecovered in Section 25, Banking and Finance.

Housing units—In general, a housing unit is a house, an apartment, a group of rooms or a single room occupied or intended for occupancy as separate living quarters; that is, the occupants live separately from any other individual in the building, and there is direct access from the outside or through a common hall. Transient accommodations, barracks for workers, and institutional-type quarters are not counted as housing units.

Statistical reliability—For a discussion of statistical collection and estimation, sampling procedures, and measures of statistical reliability applicable to Census Bureau data, see Appendix III.

Table 961. Construction—Establishments, Employees, and Payroll by Kind of Business (NAICS Basis): 2007 and 2008

[7,268 represents 7,268,000. Covers establishments with payroll. Excludes most government employees, railroad employees, and self-employed persons. Kind-of-business classification based on North American Industry Classification System (NAICS), 2002. For statement on methodology, see Appendix III]

Industry	2002 NAICS code [1]	Establishments		Paid employees [2] (1,000)		Annual payroll (mil. dol.)	
		2007	2008	2007	2008	2007	2008
Construction	**23**	**811,452**	**773,614**	**7,268**	**7,044**	**336,131**	**333,082**
Construction of buildings.....................	236	244,862	232,634	1,672	1,554	83,317	78,273
Residential building construction..............	2361	198,530	187,327	905	811	39,060	33,807
New single-family housing construction (except operative builders)	236115	61,613	69,206	283	276	11,889	10,675
New multifamily housing construction (except operative builders)	236116	4,373	4,035	47	49	2,466	2,963
New housing operative builders..............	236117	32,753	23,573	221	176	12,181	9,491
Residential remodelers	236118	99,791	90,513	355	309	12,523	10,678
Nonresidential building construction	2362	46,332	45,307	767	743	44,257	44,466
Industrial building construction	23621	3,963	3,572	97	78	5,057	4,401
Commercial and institutional building construction...........................	23622	42,369	41,735	670	665	39,200	40,065
Heavy and civil engineering construction	237	51,421	48,030	1,016	995	56,607	57,549
Utility system construction...................	2371	21,448	20,944	525	548	28,284	31,182
Water and sewer line and related structures	23711	13,872	13,269	207	192	10,338	9,929
Oil and gas pipeline and related structures.....	23712	1,826	1,946	122	157	7,483	10,331
Power and communication line and related structures	23713	5,750	5,729	196	199	10,463	10,923
Land subdivision	2372	12,835	10,814	77	67	3,980	3,369
Highway, street, and bridge construction........	2373	11,746	11,509	323	312	19,113	19,123
Other heavy and civil engineering construction...	2379	5,392	4,763	92	68	5,230	3,874
Specialty trade contractors	238	515,169	492,950	4,579	4,495	196,207	197,260
Foundation, structure, and building exterior contractors...........................	2381	115,764	108,067	1,103	1,024	42,369	40,354
Poured concrete foundation and structures contractors	23811	26,342	24,663	302	287	12,301	11,559
Structural steel and precast concrete contractors...........................	23812	3,697	3,743	79	84	3,844	4,135
Framing contractors.......................	23813	17,358	15,381	148	107	4,508	3,293
Masonry contractors	23814	27,122	25,022	235	212	8,426	7,742
Glass and glazing contractors...............	23815	5,584	5,541	55	60	2,472	2,912
Roofing contractors	23816	19,512	18,579	190	180	7,228	7,075
Siding contractors	23817	10,429	9,436	50	45	1,652	1,531
Other foundation, structure, and building exterior contractors......................	23819	5,720	5,702	45	49	1,938	2,106
Building equipment contractors..............	2382	187,856	184,132	1,962	2,017	93,655	98,571
Electrical contractors......................	23821	80,172	78,026	825	860	39,278	41,712
Plumbing, heating, and air-conditioning contractors...........................	23822	100,806	99,190	1,013	1,014	47,154	48,589
Other building equipment contractors	23829	6,878	6,916	124	143	7,223	8,271
Building finishing contractors.................	2383	134,306	126,100	944	878	35,164	33,075
Drywall and insulation contractors............	23831	22,458	21,268	320	291	12,655	11,961
Painting and wall covering contractors	23832	41,457	38,567	234	216	7,973	7,496
Flooring contractors.......................	23833	16,927	16,070	85	80	3,230	3,013
Tile and terrazzo contractors................	23834	11,965	11,209	71	68	2,517	2,436
Finish carpentry contractors	23835	34,263	32,054	164	150	5,908	5,383
Other building finishing contractors...........	23839	7,236	6,932	70	72	2,881	2,786
Other specialty trade contractors..............	2389	77,243	74,651	570	576	25,019	25,259
Site preparation contractors	23891	41,517	40,689	331	351	14,940	15,798
All other specialty trade contractors	23899	35,726	33,962	239	225	10,079	9,461

[1] North American Industry Classification System code, 2002. 2008 data is based on NAICS 2007; see text, Section 15.
[2] Employees on the payroll for the pay period including March 12.
Source: U.S. Census Bureau, "County Business Patterns," June 2010, <http://www.census.gov/econ/cbp>.

Table 962. Construction Materials—Producer Price Indexes: 1990 to 2010

[1982 = 100, except as noted. Data for 2010 are preliminary. For discussion of producer price indexes, see text, Section 14. This index, more formally known as the special commodity grouping index for construction materials, covers materials incorporated as integral part of a building or normally installed during construction and not readily removable. Excludes consumer durables such as kitchen ranges, refrigerators, etc. This index is not the same as the stage-of-processing index of intermediate materials and components for construction]

Commodity	1990	2000	2004	2005	2006	2007	2008	2009	2010
Construction materials	**119.6**	**144.1**	**161.5**	**169.6**	**180.2**	**183.2**	**196.4**	**189.2**	**194.6**
Interior solvent-based paint	133.0	191.1	(NA)	(NA)	(NA)	(NA)	(NA)	(NA)	(NA)
Architectural coatings	132.7	168.7	187.4	203.3	220.2	230.5	249.0	269.7	263.5
Construction products from plastics	117.2	135.8	144.6	158.8	181.8	179.2	185.6	186.2	190.8
Douglas fir, dressed	138.4	185.2	(NA)	(NA)	(NA)	(NA)	(NA)	(NA)	(NA)
Southern pine, dressed	111.2	161.0	(NA)	(NA)	(NA)	(NA)	(NA)	(NA)	(NA)
Softwood lumber	123.8	178.6	209.8	203.6	189.4	170.5	156.3	141.4	160.9
Millwork	130.4	176.4	191.9	197.2	201.8	201.4	204.8	205.4	206.9
Softwood plywood	119.6	173.3	250.9	223.5	190.5	197.8	193.1	171.9	196.9
Hardwood plywood and related products	102.7	130.2	134.4	138.1	(NA)	(NA)	(NA)	(NA)	(NA)
Hardwood veneer and plywood [1]	(NA)	(NA)	(NA)	(NA)	101.4	102.4	103.8	103.1	103.6
Softwood plywood veneer, excluding reinforced/backed	142.3	182.2	209.5	206.2	(NA)	(NA)	(NA)	(NA)	(NA)
Building paper and building board mill products	112.2	138.8	192.4	184.9	173.0	155.2	163.9	156.5	168.2
Steel pipe and tubes [2]	102.6	106.6	166.3	193.3	200.9	202.4	251.7	215.5	241.8
Builders' hardware	133.0	163.8	172.9	179.2	187.8	198.1	215.1	217.1	219.6
Plumbing fixtures and brass fittings	144.3	180.4	188.3	197.6	207.2	220.6	226.7	228.9	231.4
Heating equipment	131.6	155.6	169.5	179.9	185.7	195.5	208.8	219.1	221.4
Metal doors, sash, and trim	131.4	165.1	175.8	184.9	192.9	197.3	205.6	209.2	208.1
Siding, aluminum [3]	(NA)	142.2	(NA)	(NA)	(NA)	(NA)	(NA)	(NA)	(NA)
Sheet metal products	129.2	144.0	162.6	169.4	176.1	181.2	192.5	186.8	190.2
Outdoor lighting equipment, including parts [4]	113.0	124.7	129.4	131.8	137.7	140.1	145.3	146.6	147.3
Commercial fluorescent fixtures [5]	113.0	117.7	113.6	(NA)	(NA)	(NA)	(NA)	(NA)	(NA)
Commercial and industrial lighting fixtures	127.5	140.3	142.3	147.0	151.9	158.3	164.9	167.7	166.1
Architectural and ornamental metalwork [6]	118.7	139.8	172.5	185.4	191.5	200.1	227.0	233.1	232.7
Fabricated ferrous wire products [2]	114.6	130.0	149.3	157.1	162.6	166.7	200.7	200.0	203.5
Elevators, escalators, and other lifts	110.1	118.7	120.5	123.5	126.0	129.3	134.7	134.9	133.9
Stamped metal switch and receptacle box	158.0	183.0	205.2	(NA)	(NA)	(NA)	(NA)	(NA)	(NA)
Electrical conduit and conduit fittings [7]	(NA)	(NA)	(NA)	106.6	116.6	112.1	123.4	114.0	119.1
Other noncurrent-carrying wiring devices [7]	(NA)	(NA)	(NA)	102.3	108.0	114.3	123.2	126.2	126.4
Concrete ingredients and related products	115.3	155.6	170.4	185.3	204.9	220.2	229.7	235.7	232.9
Concrete products	113.5	147.8	161.2	177.2	195.1	203.5	210.6	214.0	210.8
Clay construction products excluding refractories	129.9	152.8	156.6	165.4	176.8	178.7	180.1	179.5	179.5
Prep asphalt and tar roofing and siding products	95.8	100.0	111.3	125.0	137.0	139.7	176.7	218.1	218.7
Gypsum products	105.2	201.4	198.8	229.6	274.9	233.0	213.2	213.8	206.8
Insulation materials	108.4	128.6	137.2	142.2	149.9	145.3	141.7	144.1	146.4
Paving mixtures and blocks	101.2	130.4	144.9	156.9	200.5	218.9	272.4	269.0	279.5

NA Not available. [1] December 2005 = 100. [2] June 1982 = 100. [3] December 1982 = 100. [4] June 1985 = 100. [5] Recessed nonair. [6] December 1983 = 100. [7] December 2004 = 100.
Source: U.S. Bureau of Labor Statistics, *Producer Price Indexes*, monthly and annual. See also <http://www.bls.gov/ppi/home.htm>.

Table 963. Value of New Construction Put in Place: 1980 to 2010

[In millions of dollars (273,936 represents $273,936,000,000). Represents value of construction put in place during year; differs from building permit and construction contract data in timing and coverage. Includes installed cost of normal building service equipment and selected types of industrial production equipment (largely site fabricated). Excludes cost of shipbuilding, land, and most types of machinery and equipment. For methodology, see Appendix III. For details, see Tables 964 and 965]

Year	Total	Private			Public		
		Total	Residential buildings	Non-residential	Total	Federal	State and local
1980	273,936	210,290	100,381	109,909	63,646	9,642	54,004
1990	476,778	369,300	191,103	178,197	107,478	12,099	95,379
1993	502,435	375,073	225,067	150,006	127,362	14,424	112,938
1994	549,420	418,999	258,561	160,438	130,421	14,440	115,981
1995	567,896	427,885	247,351	180,534	140,011	15,751	124,260
1996	623,313	476,638	281,115	195,523	146,675	15,325	131,350
1997	656,171	502,734	289,014	213,720	153,437	14,087	139,350
1998	706,779	552,001	314,607	237,394	154,778	14,318	140,460
1999	768,811	599,729	350,562	249,167	169,082	14,025	155,057
2000	831,075	649,750	374,457	275,293	181,325	14,166	167,157
2001	864,159	662,247	388,324	273,922	201,912	15,081	186,830
2002	847,873	634,435	396,696	237,739	213,438	16,578	196,860
2003	891,497	675,370	446,035	229,335	216,127	17,913	198,214
2004	991,356	771,173	532,900	238,273	220,183	18,342	201,841
2005	1,104,136	869,976	611,899	258,077	234,160	17,300	216,860
2006	1,167,222	911,837	613,731	298,105	255,385	17,555	237,831
2007	1,152,351	863,278	493,246	370,032	289,073	20,580	268,494
2008	1,067,564	758,827	350,257	408,569	308,738	23,731	285,007
2009	907,784	592,326	245,621	346,705	315,459	28,314	287,145
2010	814,532	508,240	241,690	266,550	306,293	30,800	275,493

Source: U.S. Census Bureau, "Construction Spending," <http://www.census.gov/const/www/c30index.html>.

Table 964. Value of Private Construction Put in Place: 2000 to 2010

[In millions of dollars (621,431 represents $621,431,000,000). Represents value of construction put in place during year; differs from building permit and construction contract data in timing and coverage. See Appendix III and Tables 963 and 965]

Type of construction	2000	2003	2004	2005	2006	2007	2008	2009	2010
Total construction [1]	**621,431**	**675,370**	**771,173**	**869,976**	**911,837**	**863,278**	**758,827**	**592,326**	**508,240**
Residential	346,138	446,035	532,900	611,899	613,731	493,246	350,257	245,621	241,690
New single family	236,788	310,575	377,557	433,510	415,997	305,184	185,776	105,336	112,726
New multifamily	28,259	35,116	39,944	47,297	52,803	48,959	44,338	28,246	14,022
Improvements [2]	81,091	100,344	115,399	131,092	144,931	139,103	120,144	112,038	114,942
Nonresidential	275,293	229,335	238,273	258,077	298,105	370,032	408,569	346,705	266,550
Lodging	16,304	9,930	11,982	12,666	17,624	27,481	35,364	25,350	11,014
Office [1]	52,407	30,579	32,879	37,276	45,680	53,815	55,502	37,904	24,408
General	49,637	27,380	28,679	32,962	41,085	48,945	50,137	33,861	22,154
Financial	2,689	3,174	4,186	4,285	4,542	4,785	5,054	3,822	2,215
Commercial [1]	64,055	57,505	63,195	66,584	73,368	85,858	82,654	51,286	37,998
Automotive [1]	5,967	5,039	5,235	5,614	5,528	6,281	5,640	4,487	3,392
Sales	1,629	2,099	2,443	2,834	2,285	2,571	2,430	1,513	1,305
Service/parts	3,009	1,866	1,978	1,805	2,184	2,356	1,843	2,052	1,544
Parking	1,330	1,074	814	975	1,059	1,354	1,367	923	543
Food/beverage [1]	8,786	8,369	8,232	7,795	7,442	8,046	8,029	4,869	4,525
Food	4,792	4,234	3,590	3,128	2,752	2,779	3,124	1,989	2,010
Dining/drinking	2,935	3,321	3,937	4,078	3,780	3,957	3,976	2,221	1,913
Fast food	1,058	813	705	590	910	1,310	930	660	602
Multiretail [1]	14,911	15,400	18,828	22,750	29,218	34,751	31,963	18,655	13,071
General merchandise	5,100	5,341	6,416	6,740	5,699	7,572	4,373	4,028	4,153
Shopping center	6,803	6,867	9,256	12,462	18,417	22,197	22,780	11,614	6,866
Shopping mall	2,523	2,231	2,138	2,631	3,616	4,000	4,045	2,235	1,371
Other commercial [1]	13,537	11,249	13,341	11,744	10,874	13,580	12,087	6,439	4,179
Drug store	1,682	1,790	1,427	1,315	1,238	1,500	1,967	1,920	1,066
Building supply store	2,592	2,268	2,521	2,416	2,594	3,507	2,539	1,142	800
Other stores	8,136	6,214	8,229	7,075	6,135	7,744	6,552	2,594	1,680
Warehouse	14,822	12,345	12,074	12,827	14,491	16,909	16,707	9,607	5,485
General commercial	13,511	11,004	10,830	11,468	13,493	15,641	15,482	8,621	5,018
Farm	5,988	5,103	5,485	5,854	5,817	6,292	8,227	7,230	7,346
Health care	19,455	24,217	26,272	28,495	32,016	35,588	38,437	35,651	30,758
Hospital	10,183	15,234	16,147	18,250	21,914	24,532	25,571	24,992	22,690
Medical building	5,066	6,068	7,615	8,031	7,165	7,981	9,242	7,562	5,309
Special care	4,206	2,915	2,510	2,213	2,937	3,074	3,625	3,097	2,760
Educational [1]	11,683	13,424	12,701	12,788	13,839	16,691	18,624	16,800	13,599
Preschool	770	711	674	516	487	704	746	723	437
Primary/secondary	2,948	3,204	3,202	2,718	3,240	3,968	3,919	3,381	2,376
Higher education [1]	6,333	7,259	6,496	6,946	7,611	9,424	11,587	10,739	8,612
Instructional	3,058	3,701	3,200	3,556	3,501	4,219	5,463	6,191	5,288
Dormitory	1,356	1,761	1,669	1,537	2,065	2,900	3,791	2,472	1,624
Sports/recreation	645	677	739	821	858	771	841	815	821
Other educational	1,318	1,785	1,998	2,294	2,090	2,167	1,965	1,634	1,842
Gallery/museum	920	1,371	1,335	1,745	1,697	1,939	1,708	1,382	1,670
Religious	8,030	8,559	8,153	7,715	7,740	7,522	7,197	6,190	5,260
House of worship	5,656	6,238	6,015	5,992	6,262	6,270	5,884	5,037	4,257
Other religious	2,347	2,322	2,138	1,723	1,478	1,252	1,313	1,154	1,003
Auxiliary building	1,280	1,296	1,258	1,251	1,219	1,099	1,122	1,025	769
Public safety	423	185	289	408	419	595	623	486	234
Amusement and recreation [1]	8,768	7,781	8,432	7,507	9,326	10,193	10,508	7,817	6,288
Theme/amusement park	747	270	198	200	417	522	324	269	262
Sports	1,068	1,306	900	807	959	1,902	2,280	1,601	1,721
Fitness	1,152	1,262	1,141	1,425	2,028	1,945	2,051	1,751	1,184
Performance/meeting center	732	844	1,054	1,072	737	823	1,102	781	581
Social center	2,368	1,996	2,594	1,626	1,538	1,602	1,552	1,011	771
Movie theater/studio	1,461	855	1,218	1,248	1,309	1,159	601	321	371
Transportation [1]	6,879	6,568	6,841	7,124	8,654	9,009	9,934	8,983	8,466
Air	1,804	1,012	869	748	719	732	776	531	273
Land	4,907	5,462	5,800	6,214	7,764	8,008	9,020	8,375	8,071
Railroad	4,263	4,851	5,392	5,816	7,313	7,423	8,378	7,898	7,496
Communication	18,799	14,456	15,468	18,846	22,187	27,488	26,343	19,713	17,945
Power [1]	29,344	33,619	27,603	29,210	33,654	54,115	69,242	77,622	71,375
Electricity	23,374	25,592	20,928	22,678	26,295	41,460	52,799	60,807	56,653
Gas	4,891	6,358	5,096	5,239	5,528	7,876	10,560	11,928	10,302
Oil	1,003	1,068	1,579	1,293	1,831	4,779	5,883	4,887	4,420
Sewage and waste disposal	508	278	331	240	305	408	665	488	410
Water supply	714	393	405	326	477	516	466	295	528
Manufacturing	37,583	21,434	23,219	28,413	32,264	40,215	52,754	57,976	38,105
Food/beverage/tobacco	3,985	2,695	3,094	4,446	4,330	3,794	4,514	3,291	3,578
Textile/apparel/leather & allied	413	218	185	396	133	35	260	283	527
Wood	483	376	475	933	1,350	702	352	416	317
Paper	479	818	540	442	515	450	577	519	550
Print/publishing	848	630	642	739	670	236	243	172	54
Petroleum/coal	1,255	717	1,181	734	1,650	5,061	14,724	24,743	10,030
Chemical	3,798	5,368	5,406	6,263	8,484	13,279	12,576	9,811	7,690
Plastic/rubber	1,645	659	919	834	812	974	1,035	584	575
Nonmetallic mineral	1,898	865	880	1,105	2,388	3,417	2,838	1,868	831
Primary metal	1,976	436	305	793	1,327	1,558	3,329	4,573	4,880
Fabricated metal	2,148	662	584	664	517	931	1,474	1,493	1,058
Machinery	864	707	633	872	862	489	917	1,083	944
Computer/electronic/electrical	6,392	1,444	2,779	4,039	4,001	2,556	2,129	3,756	4,565
Transportation equipment	6,318	3,314	2,562	3,518	2,422	3,218	4,537	3,642	1,957
Furniture [3]	148	278	214	91	111	160	34	(S)	(S)
Miscellaneous	4,398	2,248	2,821	2,545	2,693	3,356	3,215	1,743	551

S Suppressed because estimate does not meet publication standards. [1] Includes other types of construction, not shown separately. [2] Private residential improvement does not include expenditures on rental, vacant, or seasonal properties. [3] As of 2009, included in textile apparel/leather/furniture.

Source: U.S. Census Bureau, "Construction Spending," <http://www.census.gov/const/www/c30index.html>.

Table 965. Value of State and Local Government Construction Put in Place: 2000 to 2010

[In millions of dollars (167,157 represents $167,157,000,000). See Tables 963 and 964]

Type of construction	2000	2003	2004	2005	2006	2007	2008	2009	2010
Total construction [1]	**167,157**	**198,214**	**201,841**	**216,860**	**237,831**	**268,494**	**285,007**	**287,145**	**275,493**
Residential	2,962	3,724	4,110	4,047	4,349	5,094	4,894	5,756	7,407
Multifamily	2,945	3,593	3,956	3,740	3,990	4,476	4,072	4,840	6,343
Nonresidential	164,196	194,490	197,731	212,813	233,482	263,399	280,113	281,389	268,086
Office	4,494	6,116	6,024	5,211	5,588	7,249	8,515	9,382	8,205
Commercial [1]	1,820	2,207	1,979	1,882	1,567	1,777	1,965	2,148	1,555
Automotive	1,233	1,599	1,501	1,490	1,152	1,012	1,425	1,217	814
Parking	1,143	1,562	1,356	1,357	1,011	941	1,252	1,104	707
Warehouse	330	318	276	218	230	558	312	473	288
Health care	2,829	4,005	5,025	5,059	5,615	7,028	7,010	6,819	6,077
Hospital	1,949	2,685	3,324	3,429	4,085	5,304	5,320	5,357	4,686
Medical building	490	876	1,211	1,168	919	981	909	848	758
Special care	390	444	490	463	611	743	782	614	633
Educational [1]	46,818	59,340	59,741	65,750	69,790	78,376	84,489	83,495	71,101
Primary/secondary [1]	33,764	40,316	40,990	44,184	47,846	55,054	57,770	54,500	44,218
Elementary	12,272	13,430	14,308	14,251	13,870	16,786	18,305	17,125	13,087
Middle/junior high	5,820	7,921	8,132	9,069	10,764	11,719	10,937	10,299	6,976
High	13,326	18,561	17,950	19,892	22,631	25,887	27,985	26,673	23,840
Higher education [1]	10,749	15,451	15,864	18,033	18,961	20,556	23,542	25,064	23,879
Instructional	6,317	9,042	8,699	9,275	9,434	11,300	13,251	14,735	13,880
Parking	514	508	765	1,013	909	839	732	566	544
Administration	294	236	303	387	657	503	290	362	369
Dormitory	1,078	2,074	2,673	2,918	3,409	2,657	3,043	3,275	3,273
Library	308	544	524	588	493	700	791	862	651
Student union/cafeteria	322	702	632	880	1,028	1,547	1,398	1,408	1,128
Sports/recreation	966	1,329	1,370	1,769	1,748	1,726	2,559	2,351	2,411
Infrastructure	835	613	867	1,138	1,227	1,218	1,241	1,276	1,281
Other educational	1,645	2,687	2,357	2,735	2,312	1,890	2,485	3,074	2,268
Library/archive	976	1,815	1,501	2,098	1,857	1,287	1,557	1,875	1,424
Public safety [1]	5,854	5,844	5,477	6,013	6,608	8,423	9,666	9,426	7,594
Correctional	4,754	4,204	3,771	3,958	4,611	5,384	6,375	5,794	4,640
Detention	3,907	3,148	2,787	2,936	3,305	4,026	4,524	3,423	2,836
Police/sheriff	848	1,056	985	1,022	1,307	1,358	1,851	2,372	1,804
Other public safety	1,100	1,640	1,705	2,055	1,997	3,039	3,291	3,632	2,954
Fire/rescue	994	1,359	1,441	1,675	1,615	2,392	2,367	2,475	1,735
Amusement and recreation [1]	7,583	8,354	7,794	7,340	9,444	10,670	10,872	10,638	9,826
Sports	2,289	2,065	1,746	1,587	1,853	2,040	2,548	2,416	1,858
Performance/meeting center	2,075	2,260	2,061	1,921	2,292	1,706	1,631	1,729	1,789
Convention center	1,397	1,545	1,350	1,350	1,422	1,035	1,040	1,040	1,116
Social center	1,152	1,606	1,476	1,006	1,285	1,373	1,587	1,679	1,601
Neighborhood center	886	1,221	1,312	866	1,098	1,053	1,231	1,512	1,436
Park/camp	1,930	1,999	2,303	2,728	3,887	5,255	4,975	4,729	4,419
Transportation	13,000	16,483	16,440	16,256	17,695	21,144	23,230	27,267	29,089
Air [1]	6,700	8,146	8,715	8,993	9,676	11,390	11,579	13,299	13,002
Passenger terminal	2,930	3,778	3,972	3,310	3,766	5,224	6,164	7,211	7,059
Runway	3,196	3,793	4,049	4,861	4,898	5,164	4,551	5,228	5,210
Land [1]	5,165	7,207	6,415	5,936	6,629	7,593	9,969	12,282	14,232
Passenger terminal	1,253	2,099	1,368	907	969	1,301	2,053	2,830	3,758
Mass transit	1,484	3,160	3,067	3,208	3,228	3,587	4,371	5,938	7,098
Railroad	1,471	449	349	552	320	508	585	804	882
Water [1]	1,136	1,130	1,309	1,327	1,391	2,161	1,682	1,686	1,856
Dock/marina	863	894	1,028	930	971	1,465	1,287	1,406	1,253
Dry dock/marine terminal	236	235	281	397	420	697	395	280	603
Power	5,501	6,785	7,044	8,320	7,766	11,449	10,992	10,776	11,172
Electrical	5,257	6,041	5,851	7,091	7,195	10,176	10,192	8,306	10,407
Distribution	2,087	2,144	1,856	1,786	2,187	2,818	3,487	3,231	3,626
Highway and street [1]	51,574	56,251	57,351	63,157	71,032	75,455	80,424	81,081	82,185
Pavement	37,929	39,294	40,274	45,177	45,933	47,679	52,837	54,958	51,881
Lighting	856	1,156	1,146	1,232	1,057	1,709	1,532	1,285	2,056
Retaining wall	1,099	565	552	675	1,546	1,073	888	963	1,221
Tunnel	894	619	521	373	224	264	326	326	806
Bridge	9,302	12,980	13,150	14,244	20,057	22,827	23,690	22,125	24,459
Toll/weigh	325	180	233	320	657	421	196	270	349
Maintenance building	293	244	170	96	213	102	102	128	278
Rest facility/streetscape	878	1,213	1,306	1,042	1,347	1,424	916	1,026	1,135
Sewage and waste disposal [1]	14,000	15,625	17,084	18,336	21,524	23,323	24,102	23,229	24,132
Sewage/dry waste [1]	9,338	9,812	10,836	11,717	13,401	13,891	14,044	13,100	12,884
Plant	2,765	2,735	3,095	3,369	3,410	3,802	3,957	3,390	3,611
Line/pump station	6,326	6,934	7,574	8,243	9,820	9,784	9,823	9,396	9,151
Waste water	4,663	5,813	6,248	6,620	8,124	9,432	10,058	10,130	11,248
Plant	3,229	4,403	4,658	5,231	6,039	7,496	8,688	8,438	9,402
Line/drain	1,434	1,410	1,591	1,389	2,085	1,935	1,370	1,692	1,846
Water supply [1]	9,528	11,711	11,977	13,483	14,299	15,029	16,017	14,971	14,598
Plant	3,067	4,309	4,418	4,943	5,005	5,661	6,500	6,384	5,869
Well	378	365	318	360	623	661	460	488	385
Line	4,644	4,944	5,307	6,234	5,922	6,131	6,191	5,437	6,196
Pump station	625	767	705	776	1,285	1,124	1,293	1,383	989
Reservoir	266	450	503	502	700	586	633	351	396
Tank/tower	548	876	727	668	764	867	940	928	762
Conservation and development [1]	933	1,020	1,466	1,752	2,000	2,198	2,251	1,987	2,014
Dam/levee	303	231	297	405	591	640	772	731	731
Breakwater/jetty	270	514	654	726	809	627	645	703	708

[1] Includes other types of construction, not shown separately.

Source: U.S. Census Bureau, "Construction Spending," <http://www.census.gov/const/www/c30index.html>.

U.S. Census Bureau, Statistical Abstract of the United States: 2012

Table 966. Construction Contracts—Value of Construction and Floor Space of Buildings by Class of Construction: 1990 to 2010

[246.0 represents $246,000,000,000. Building construction includes new structures and additions; nonbuilding construction includes major alterations to existing structures which affect only valuation, since no additional floor area is created by "alteration"]

Year	Total	Resi-dential build-ings	Nonresidential buildings									Non-building con-struc-tion
			Total	Com-mer-cial [1]	Manu-factur-ing	Educa-tional [2]	Health	Public build-ings	Reli-gious	Social and recre-ational	Miscel-laneous	
VALUE (bil. dol.)												
1990............	246.0	100.9	95.4	44.8	8.4	16.6	9.2	5.7	2.2	5.3	3.1	49.7
1995............	306.5	127.9	114.2	46.6	13.8	22.9	10.8	6.3	2.8	7.1	3.8	64.4
1999............	447.2	195.0	168.7	77.2	11.3	37.1	13.6	8.2	4.5	11.6	5.1	83.5
2000............	472.9	208.3	173.3	80.9	8.9	40.9	12.4	7.5	4.6	13.8	4.4	91.3
2001............	496.5	219.7	169.1	70.2	8.0	47.0	14.4	7.8	4.8	12.0	4.8	107.7
2002............	504.0	248.7	155.1	59.6	5.5	45.3	16.1	7.3	5.1	11.5	4.7	100.2
2003............	531.7	283.4	156.1	58.8	6.9	47.7	15.8	7.1	4.5	11.0	4.3	92.3
2004............	593.2	333.1	164.4	67.3	8.0	44.0	17.6	7.2	4.5	11.6	4.4	95.6
2005............	670.2	384.0	182.4	72.2	10.1	49.1	22.3	7.9	4.1	11.7	5.0	103.8
2006............	689.5	342.1	217.3	92.9	13.7	53.8	24.3	8.2	4.1	14.3	5.9	130.1
2007............	641.0	261.6	239.4	100.9	20.8	58.1	24.4	12.4	3.8	13.5	5.5	140.1
2008............	556.4	160.9	243.0	81.6	30.8	63.8	29.9	13.3	3.6	13.5	6.5	152.5
2009............	423.4	112.0	168.2	46.9	9.7	53.7	20.2	15.4	3.3	11.5	7.5	143.3
2010............	417.2	119.7	155.0	39.2	8.5	51.4	23.0	10.2	2.3	10.9	9.5	142.5
FLOOR SPACE (mil. sq. ft.)												
1990............	3,020	1,817	1,203	694	128	152	69	47	29	51	32	(X)
1995............	3,454	2,172	1,281	700	163	186	70	40	33	56	33	(X)
1999............	5,091	3,253	1,838	1,115	141	261	98	49	48	87	39	(X)
2000............	4,982	3,113	1,869	1,180	111	273	88	44	49	94	29	(X)
2001............	4,828	3,159	1,669	988	93	295	92	44	50	81	27	(X)
2002............	4,792	3,356	1,436	810	68	277	97	37	52	71	26	(X)
2003............	5,093	3,689	1,404	794	75	270	92	35	45	67	26	(X)
2004............	5,518	4,061	1,457	875	86	231	94	34	43	68	27	(X)
2005............	5,872	4,345	1,528	927	79	246	108	33	37	67	29	(X)
2006............	5,282	3,647	1,635	1,015	83	254	110	33	35	73	33	(X)
2007............	4,316	2,647	1,669	1,054	91	247	104	51	31	66	27	(X)
2008............	2,953	1,576	1,377	772	79	253	109	49	28	59	28	(X)
2009............	1,879	1,108	771	329	37	198	68	47	25	42	26	(X)
2010............	1,790	1,146	645	263	42	169	70	33	15	34	18	(X)

X Not applicable. [1] Includes nonindustrial warehouses. [2] Includes science.
Source: McGraw-Hill Construction, a Division of the McGraw-Hill Companies, New York, NY (copyright).

Table 967. Construction Contracts—Value by Region: 2006 to 2010

[In millions of dollars (689,474 represents $689,474,000,000). Represents value of construction in regions in which work was actually done. See headnote, Table 966]

Region	2006	2007	2008	2009	2010		
					Total [1]	Residential	Nonresiden-tial
U.S.	**689,474**	**641,042**	**556,418**	**423,406**	**417,188**	**119,685**	**154,962**
New England...........	23,277	24,641	20,547	16,834	19,491	5,267	8,086
Middle Atlantic..........	67,064	65,515	64,641	51,246	51,468	9,960	26,454
East North Central.......	82,140	72,384	75,299	50,617	50,634	11,871	19,197
West North Central	40,840	43,257	33,235	30,752	31,219	8,434	10,797
South Atlantic	165,526	151,062	114,860	85,411	76,342	28,105	27,478
East South Central	39,801	36,713	37,926	25,725	25,134	8,061	8,781
West South Central	92,123	85,951	85,806	68,928	66,581	22,360	22,287
Mountain	76,382	68,082	50,912	37,400	37,027	10,583	10,315
Pacific	102,322	93,437	73,192	56,494	59,291	15,044	21,565

[1] Includes nonbuilding construction, not shown separately.
Source: McGraw-Hill Construction, a Division of the McGraw-Hill Companies, New York, NY, (copyright).

U.S. Census Bureau, Statistical Abstract of the United States: 2012

Table 968. New Privately Owned Housing Units Authorized by State: 2009 and 2010

[583.0 represents 583,000. Based on about 20,000 places in United States having building permit systems in 2009 and 2010]

State	Housing units (1,000)			Valuation (mil. dol.)			State	Housing units (1,000)			Valuation (mil. dol.)		
		2010			2010				2010			2010	
	2009	Total	1 unit	2009	Total	1 unit		2009	Total	1 unit	2009	Total	1 unit
U.S. . . .	**583.0**	**598.0**	**446.6**	**95,410**	**101,008**	**86,723**	MO. . . .	10.1	8.3	6.0	1,434	1,275	1,101
AL	13.3	10.2	8.1	1,664	1,453	1,313	MT	1.7	2.2	1.5	254	329	266
AK	0.9	0.9	0.8	195	205	184	NE	5.2	5.0	4.1	725	776	711
AZ	14.5	12.2	10.6	2,736	2,405	2,233	NV	6.8	6.4	5.4	749	827	750
AR	7.1	6.9	4.3	818	854	725	NH	2.3	2.7	2.0	421	489	424
CA	35.1	43.1	24.7	7,758	8,968	6,422	NJ	12.4	13.3	7.4	2,071	2,017	1,501
CO	9.4	11.8	9.1	2,071	2,664	2,374	NM	4.6	4.5	4.0	769	777	734
CT	3.8	3.8	2.5	715	804	629	NY	18.3	20.2	10.4	3,062	3,191	2,228
DE	3.2	3.1	2.7	361	365	338	NC	33.8	33.7	26.0	5,030	5,017	4,538
DC	1.1	0.7	0.1	131	96	21	ND	3.2	3.6	2.1	352	450	358
FL	35.3	39.5	30.9	6,789	7,843	6,957	OH	13.3	13.5	10.6	2,194	2,299	2,119
GA	18.2	17.7	15.2	2,618	2,703	2,471	OK	8.8	8.3	7.0	1,302	1,214	1,140
HI	2.6	3.4	1.9	779	769	583	OR	7.0	7.3	5.7	1,356	1,473	1,286
ID	4.9	4.6	4.0	805	774	720	PA	18.3	21.3	17.4	3,075	3,465	3,076
IL	10.9	11.6	7.9	2,101	2,360	1,726	RI	1.0	0.9	0.7	162	157	142
IN	12.6	13.0	9.9	1,933	1,988	1,757	SC	15.5	14.5	13.1	2,534	2,525	2,423
IA	7.7	7.3	5.9	1,198	1,191	1,049	SD	3.7	2.9	2.3	464	431	389
KS	6.7	4.5	3.7	881	746	681	TN	15.0	16.3	11.7	2,079	2,174	1,845
KY	7.4	6.8	5.4	923	989	825	TX	84.4	84.8	65.3	12,542	13,332	11,875
LA	12.5	11.5	10.5	1,842	1,808	1,732	UT	10.0	9.4	7.2	1,573	1,720	1,479
ME	3.1	3.0	2.7	493	480	463	VT	1.4	1.5	1.2	214	248	212
MD	11.1	12.2	8.4	2,089	1,943	1,562	VA	21.5	21.2	16.3	3,173	3,249	2,893
MA	7.9	8.6	5.5	1,554	1,683	1,371	WA	17.0	20.2	14.8	3,186	4,011	3,461
MI	6.9	9.3	7.9	1,173	1,529	1,422	WV	2.2	1.7	1.5	310	269	256
MN	9.4	9.7	6.8	1,712	1,752	1,465	WI	10.8	11.8	7.9	1,753	1,858	1,547
MS	7.0	4.8	4.0	878	646	587	WY	2.3	2.1	1.4	407	414	358

Source: U.S. Census Bureau, Construction Reports, "New Residential Construction." <http://www.census.gov/const/www/newresconstindex.html>.

Table 969. New Privately Owned Housing Units Started—Selected Characteristics: 1970 to 2010

[In thousands (1,434 represents 1,434,000). For composition of regions, see map, inside front cover]

Year	Total units	Structures with—			Region				Units for sale		
		1 unit	2 to 4 units	5 or more units	North-east	Midwest	South	West	Total	Single-family	Multi-family
1970	1,434	813	85	536	218	294	612	311	(NA)	(NA)	(NA)
1980	1,292	852	110	331	125	218	643	306	689	526	163
1983	1,703	1,068	113	522	168	218	935	382	923	713	210
1984	1,750	1,084	121	544	204	243	866	436	934	728	206
1985	1,742	1,072	93	576	252	240	782	468	867	713	154
1986	1,805	1,179	84	542	294	296	733	483	925	782	143
1987	1,621	1,146	65	409	269	298	634	420	862	732	130
1988	1,488	1,081	59	348	235	274	575	404	808	709	99
1989	1,376	1,003	55	318	179	266	536	396	735	648	87
1990	1,193	895	38	260	131	253	479	329	585	529	56
1991	1,014	840	36	138	113	233	414	254	531	490	41
1992	1,200	1,030	31	139	127	288	497	288	659	618	41
1993	1,288	1,126	29	133	127	298	562	302	760	716	44
1994	1,457	1,198	35	224	138	329	639	351	815	763	52
1995	1,354	1,076	34	244	118	290	615	331	763	712	51
1996	1,477	1,161	45	271	132	322	662	361	833	774	59
1997	1,474	1,134	45	296	137	304	670	363	843	784	59
1998	1,617	1,271	43	303	149	331	743	395	941	882	59
1999	1,641	1,302	32	307	156	347	746	392	981	912	69
2000	1,592	1,198	65	329	165	324	702	401	946	871	75
2001	1,637	1,236	66	335	160	334	730	413	990	919	71
2002	1,748	1,333	74	341	174	352	791	431	1,070	999	71
2003	1,889	1,461	83	346	182	371	849	486	1,207	1,120	87
2004	2,070	1,613	90	366	197	370	961	542	1,360	1,240	120
2005	2,155	1,682	84	389	204	354	1,039	559	1,508	1,358	150
2006	1,839	1,378	77	384	175	279	930	455	1,272	1,121	151
2007	1,398	980	60	359	151	212	692	344	875	760	115
2008	905	576	34	295	119	138	452	197	472	408	64
2009	583	441	21	121	69	100	297	117	314	297	17
2010	598	447	21	131	75	100	294	128	(NA)	(NA)	(NA)

NA Not available.
Source: U.S. Census Bureau, Construction Reports, "New Residential Construction." <http://www.census.gov/const/www/newresconstindex.html>.

Table 970. New Privately Owned Housing Units Started: 1991 to 2010

[In thousands of units (1,014 represents 1,014,000) For composition of regions, see map inside front cover]

Year	Total	1 unit	Northeast	Midwest	South	West
1991............	1,014	840	113	233	414	254
1992............	1,200	1,030	127	288	497	288
1993............	1,288	1,126	126	298	562	302
1994............	1,457	1,198	138	329	639	351
1995............	1,354	1,076	118	290	615	331
1996............	1,477	1,161	132	321	662	361
1997............	1,474	1,134	137	304	670	363
1998............	1,617	1,271	148	330	743	395
1999............	1,641	1,303	156	347	746	392
2000............	1,569	1,231	154	318	713	383
2001............	1,603	1,273	149	330	732	391
2002............	1,705	1,359	158	350	781	415
2003............	1,848	1,499	163	374	839	472
2004............	1,956	1,610	175	356	909	516
2005............	2,068	1,716	190	357	996	525
2006............	1,801	1,465	167	280	910	444
2007............	1,355	1,046	143	210	681	321
2008............	905	622	121	135	453	196
2009............	554	445	62	97	278	117
2010............	587	471	71	98	297	120

Source: U.S. Bureau of the Census, Construction Reports, Series C-20, "Housing Starts". Prepared by Economics Department, NAHB. Available at <http://www.HousingEconomics.com>.

Table 971. Characteristics of New Privately Owned One-Family Houses Completed: 1990 to 2009

[Percent distribution, except total houses. 966 represents 966,000. Data are percent distribution of characteristics for all houses completed (includes new houses completed, houses built for sale completed, contractor-built and owner-built houses completed, and houses completed for rent). Percents exclude houses for which characteristics specified were not reported]

Characteristic	1990	2000	2005	2009	Characteristic	1990	2000	2005	2009
Total houses (1,000)......	**966**	**1,242**	**1,636**	**520**	**Bedrooms..............**	**100**	**100**	**100**	**100**
Construction type	**100**	**100**	**100**	**100**	2 or less................	15	11	12	13
Site built..............	(NA)	94	96	96	3.........................	57	54	49	53
Modular...............	(NA)	3	3	2	4 or more...............	29	35	39	34
Other..................	(NA)	3	2	2	**Bathrooms..............**	**100**	**100**	**100**	**100**
Exterior wall material	**100**	**100**	**100**	**100**	1-1/2 or less	13	7	4	8
Brick...................	18	20	20	23	2.........................	42	39	36	37
Wood..................	39	14	7	9	2-1/2 or more............	45	54	59	55
Stucco.................	18	17	22	19	**Heating fuel ....**	**100**	**100**	**100**	**100**
Vinyl siding [1]	(NA)	39	34	34	Gas	59	70	66	55
Aluminum siding	5	1	(NA)	(NA)	Electricity...............	33	27	31	42
Other [1]	20	7	7	2	Oil	5	3	2	1
Floor area..............	**(NA)**	**100**	**100**	**100**	Other	3	1	1	2
Under 1,200 sq. ft	(NA)	14	10	13	**Heating system ....**	**100**	**100**	**100**	**100**
1,200 to 1,599 sq. ft.......	(NA)	22	19	20	Warm air furnace.........	65	71	67	56
1,600 to 1,999 sq. ft.......	(NA)	29	29	27	Electric heat pump........	23	23	29	37
2,000 to 2,399 sq. ft.......	(NA)	17	19	17	Other	12	6	4	7
2,400 sq. ft. and over	(NA)	18	23	23	**Central air-conditioning ...**	**100**	**100**	**100**	**100**
Average (sq. ft.)..........	2,080	2,266	2,434	2,438	With	76	85	89	88
Median (sq. ft.)..........	1,905	2,057	2,227	2,135	Without..................	24	15	11	12
Number of stories	**100**	**100**	**100**	**100**	**Fireplaces..............**	**100**	**100**	**100**	**100**
1.......................	46	47	44	47	No fireplace..............	34	40	45	49
2 or more................	49	52	55	53	1 or more................	66	59	55	51
Split level	4	1	(Z)	(Z)	**Parking facilities ....**	**100**	**100**	**100**	**100**
Foundation..............	**100**	**100**	**100**	**100**	Garage..................	82	89	91	86
Full or partial basement....	38	37	31	30	Carport	2	1	1	1
Slab..................	40	46	53	52	No garage or carport......	16	11	8	12
Crawl space............	21	17	16	18					

NA Not available. Z Less than 0.5 percent. [1] Prior to 2000, "other" includes vinyl siding.
Source: U.S. Census Bureau and U.S. Department of Housing and Urban Development "Characteristics of New Housing," <http://www.census.gov/const/www/charindex.html>.

Table 972. Housing Starts and Average Length of Time From Start to Completion of New Privately Owned One-Unit Residential Buildings: 1980 to 2010

[852 represents 852,000. For buildings started in permit issue places]

Year	Total [1]	Purpose of construction Built for sale	Contractor built	Owner built	Region [2] Northeast	Midwest	South	West
STARTS (1,000)								
1980	852	526	149	164	87	142	428	196
1990	895	529	196	147	104	193	371	226
1995	1,076	712	199	133	102	234	485	256
1998	1,271	882	209	144	122	273	574	303
1999	1,302	912	208	142	126	289	580	308
2000	1,231	871	195	128	118	260	556	297
2001	1,273	919	186	129	111	269	590	303
2002	1,359	999	198	125	118	277	628	336
2003	1,499	1,120	205	127	116	309	686	388
2004	1,611	1,240	198	130	128	306	743	433
2005	1,716	1,358	197	129	138	306	831	441
2006	1,465	1,121	189	119	118	235	757	356
2007	1,046	760	151	104	93	171	540	242
2008	622	408	107	74	63	102	324	133
2009	445	297	83	51	44	76	232	93
2010	471	306	83	54	52	79	247	93
COMPLETION (months)								
1980	6.9	6.2	5.5	10.1	7.7	8.0	6.1	7.4
1990	6.4	5.9	5.3	10.3	9.3	5.6	5.7	6.9
1995	5.9	5.2	5.8	9.5	7.4	6.0	5.4	6.0
1998	6.0	5.4	6.0	9.5	7.1	6.2	5.5	6.1
1999	6.1	5.5	6.4	9.2	7.0	6.4	5.7	6.3
2000	6.2	5.6	6.5	9.2	7.5	6.4	5.9	6.0
2001	6.2	5.6	7.0	9.2	7.6	6.5	5.8	6.3
2002	6.1	5.5	6.6	9.6	7.3	6.4	5.6	6.2
2003	6.2	5.5	6.8	9.9	7.5	6.7	5.7	6.2
2004	6.2	5.7	7.0	9.1	7.3	6.7	5.8	6.3
2005	6.4	5.9	7.6	9.8	7.7	6.6	6.0	6.8
2006	6.9	6.3	7.8	10.7	8.3	7.1	6.3	7.4
2007	7.1	6.5	7.9	10.2	8.5	7.4	6.5	8.0
2008	7.7	6.8	8.5	11.1	8.9	8.2	6.7	9.0
2009	7.9	6.6	8.7	11.9	10.7	8.2	6.7	9.0
2010	(NA)	(NA)	(NA)	(NA)	(NA)	(NA)	(NA)	(NA)

NA Not available. [1] Includes units built for rent not shown separately. [2] For composition of regions, see map, inside front cover.
Source: U.S. Census Bureau, "New Residential Construction," <http://www.census.gov/const/www/newresconstindex.html>.

Table 973. Price Indexes of New One-Family Houses Sold by Region: 1980 to 2010

[2005 = 100. Based on kinds of homes sold in 1996. Includes value of the lot. For composition of regions, see map, inside front cover]

Year	Total	Northeast	Midwest	South	West
1980	38.9	30.2	41.2	44.4	31.9
1983	43.9	36.1	46.2	51.2	34.9
1984	45.7	39.2	49.0	52.8	36.2
1985	46.2	43.1	48.2	53.9	36.4
1986	48.0	49.5	51.0	55.5	37.3
1987	50.6	56.2	54.4	57.6	39.3
1988	52.5	57.6	56.8	58.8	41.4
1989	54.6	59.2	58.1	60.5	44.0
1990	55.7	58.0	58.6	60.6	46.2
1991	56.4	56.2	60.1	61.8	46.4
1992	57.2	60.5	61.2	62.4	46.7
1993	59.4	57.4	65.2	65.5	47.8
1994	62.9	62.1	69.4	68.1	51.9
1995	64.3	62.3	70.9	70.1	52.7
1996	66.0	63.2	72.5	71.2	55.3
1997	67.5	65.9	74.3	72.7	56.5
1998	69.2	66.1	76.0	74.4	58.4
1999	72.8	69.1	79.5	78.1	62.0
2000	75.6	73.0	83.5	80.7	64.4
2001	77.9	76.7	84.4	82.8	67.1
2002	81.4	80.2	86.1	86.3	71.5
2003	86.0	84.3	90.6	89.4	78.2
2004	92.8	91.6	96.7	94.4	88.2
2005	100.0	100.0	100.0	100.0	100.0
2006	104.8	102.6	102.9	105.4	105.2
2007	104.9	101.5	102.8	107.5	102.6
2008	99.5	100.8	98.9	103.7	92.7
2009	95.1	97.1	96.0	101.1	84.8
2010	94.7	100.7	97.1	99.2	85.1

Source: U.S. Census Bureau, "Construction Price Indexes," <http://www.census.gov/const/www/constpriceindex.html>.

Table 974. New Privately Owned One-Family Houses Sold by Region and Type of Financing, 1980 to 2010, and by Sales-Price Group, 2010

[In thousands (545 represents 545,000). Based on a national probability sample of monthly interviews with builders or owners of one-family houses for which building permits have been issued or, for nonpermit areas, on which construction has started. For details, see source and Appendix III. For composition of regions, see map inside front cover. Minus sign (–) indicates decrease]

Year and sales-price group	Total sales	Region				Financing type			
		Northeast	Midwest	South	West	Conventional [1]	FHA and VA	Rural-Housing Service [2]	Cash
1980................	545	50	81	267	145	302	196	14	32
1985................	688	112	82	323	171	403	208	11	64
1990................	534	71	89	225	149	337	138	10	50
1995................	667	55	125	300	187	490	129	9	39
2000................	877	71	155	406	244	695	138	4	40
2003................	1,086	79	189	511	307	911	130	4	41
2004................	1,203	83	210	562	348	1,047	105	6	46
2005................	1,283	81	205	638	358	1,150	79	1	52
2006................	1,051	63	161	559	267	948	63	1	38
2007................	776	65	118	411	181	693	52	2	30
2008................	485	35	70	266	114	–948	–63	(NA)	23
2009................	375	31	54	202	87	234	124	(NA)	17
2010................	321	31	44	173	73	187	116	(NA)	18
Under $200,000........	134	5	23	90	18	(NA)	(NA)	(NA)	(NA)
$200,000 to $299,999....	98	8	15	46	29	(NA)	(NA)	(NA)	(NA)
$300,000 to $499,999....	63	11	6	28	19	(NA)	(NA)	(NA)	(NA)
$500,000 and over.......	25	6	1	9	8	(NA)	(NA)	(NA)	(NA)

NA Not available. [1] Includes houses reporting other types of financing. [2] Prior to 2000, the Farmers Home Administration.
Source: U.S. Census Bureau and U.S. Department of Housing and Urban Development "New Residential Sales," <http://www.census.gov/const/www/newressalesindex.html>.

Table 975. Median Sales Price of New Privately Owned One-Family Houses Sold by Region: 1980 to 2010

[In dollars. For definition of median, see Guide to Tabular Presentation. For composition of regions, see map inside front cover. See Appendix III. See also headnote, Table 974]

Year	U.S.	Northeast	Midwest	South	West	Year	U.S.	Northeast	Midwest	South	West
1980....	64,600	69,500	63,400	59,600	72,300	2004....	221,000	315,800	205,000	181,100	283,100
1985....	84,300	103,300	80,300	75,000	92,600	2005....	240,900	343,800	216,900	197,300	332,600
1990....	122,900	159,000	107,900	99,000	147,500	2006....	246,500	346,000	213,500	208,200	337,700
1995....	133,900	180,000	134,000	124,500	141,400	2007....	247,900	320,200	208,600	217,700	330,900
2000....	169,000	227,400	169,700	148,000	196,400	2008....	232,100	343,600	198,900	203,700	294,800
2002....	187,600	264,300	178,000	163,400	238,500	2009....	216,700	302,500	189,200	194,800	263,700
2003....	195,000	264,500	184,300	168,100	260,900	2010....	221,900	335,500	197,600	196,000	259,700

Source: U.S. Census Bureau and U.S. Department of Housing and Urban Development "New Residential Sales," <http://www.census.gov/const/www/newressalesindex.html>.

Table 976. New Manufactured (Mobile) Homes Placed for Residential Use and Average Sales Price by Region: 1985 to 2010

[283.4 represents 283,400. A mobile home is a moveable dwelling, 8 feet or more wide and 40 feet or more long, designed to be towed on its own chassis, with transportation gear integral to the unit when it leaves the factory, and without need of permanent foundation. Excluded are travel trailers, motor homes, and modular housing. Data are based on a probability sample and subject to sampling variability; see source. For composition of regions, see map, inside front cover]

Year	Units placed (1,000)					Average sales price (dollars)				
	Total	Northeast	Midwest	South	West	U.S.	Northeast	Midwest	South	West
1985...........	283.4	20.2	38.6	187.6	36.9	21,800	22,700	21,500	20,400	28,700
1990...........	195.4	18.8	37.7	108.4	30.6	27,800	30,000	27,000	24,500	39,300
1995...........	319.4	15.0	57.5	203.2	43.7	35,300	35,800	35,700	33,300	44,100
1997...........	336.3	14.3	55.3	219.4	47.3	39,800	41,300	40,300	38,000	47,300
1998...........	373.7	14.7	58.3	250.3	50.4	41,600	42,200	42,400	40,100	48,400
1999...........	338.3	14.1	53.6	227.2	43.5	43,300	44,000	44,400	41,900	49,600
2000...........	280.9	14.9	48.7	178.7	38.6	46,400	47,000	47,900	44,300	54,100
2001...........	196.2	12.2	37.6	116.4	30.0	48,900	50,000	49,100	46,500	58,000
2002...........	174.3	11.8	34.2	101.0	27.2	51,300	53,200	51,700	48,000	62,600
2003...........	139.8	11.2	25.2	77.2	26.1	54,900	57,300	55,100	50,500	67,700
2004...........	124.4	11.0	20.6	67.4	25.5	58,200	60,200	58,800	52,300	73,200
2005...........	122.9	9.2	17.1	68.1	28.5	62,600	67,000	60,600	55,700	79,900
2006...........	112.4	7.9	14.5	66.1	23.9	64,300	65,300	59,100	58,900	83,400
2007...........	94.8	7.0	10.8	59.4	17.7	65,400	66,100	64,900	59,900	85,500
2008...........	79.3	5.0	8.2	54.0	13.3	64,700	68,400	65,700	59,600	84,900
2009...........	52.5	3.5	5.4	36.2	7.0	63,100	61,400	65,500	59,400	82,400
2010...........	49.5	3.8	5.4	34.0	6.4	62,700	66,000	60,300	60,100	77,800

Source: U.S. Census Bureau, "Manufactured Housing," <http://www.census.gov/const/www/mhsindex.html>.

Table 977. Existing One-Family Homes Sold and Price by Region: 1990 to 2010

[2,914 represents 2,914,000. Includes existing detached single-family homes and townhomes; excludes condos and co-ops. Based on data (adjusted and aggregated to regional and national totals) reported by participating real estate multiple listing services. For definition of median, see Guide to Tabular Presentation. See Table 980 for data on condos and co-ops. For composition of regions, see map, inside front cover]

Year	Homes sold (1,000)					Median sales price (dollars)				
	U.S.	North-east	Mid-west	South	West	U.S.	North-east	Mid-west	South	West
1990.	2,914	513	804	1,008	589	97,300	146,200	76,700	86,300	141,200
1992.	3,151	577	907	1,047	620	105,500	149,000	84,600	92,900	143,300
1993.	3,427	614	961	1,167	685	109,100	149,300	87,600	95,800	144,400
1994.	3,544	618	961	1,213	752	113,500	149,300	90,900	97,200	151,900
1995.	3,519	615	940	1,212	752	117,000	146,500	96,500	99,200	153,600
1996.	3,797	656	986	1,283	872	122,600	147,800	102,800	105,000	160,200
1997.	3,964	683	1,004	1,356	921	129,000	152,400	108,900	111,300	169,000
1998.	4,495	745	1,129	1,592	1,029	136,000	157,100	116,300	118,000	179,500
1999.	4,649	728	1,145	1,704	1,072	141,200	160,700	121,600	122,100	189,400
2000.	4,603	715	1,116	1,707	1,065	147,300	161,200	125,600	130,300	199,200
2001.	4,735	710	1,154	1,795	1,076	156,600	169,400	132,300	139,600	211,700
2002.	4,974	730	1,217	1,872	1,155	167,600	190,100	138,300	149,700	234,300
2003.	5,446	770	1,323	2,073	1,280	180,200	220,300	143,700	159,700	254,700
2004.	5,958	821	1,389	2,310	1,438	195,200	254,400	151,500	171,800	289,100
2005.	6,180	838	1,411	2,457	1,474	219,000	281,600	168,300	181,100	340,300
2006.	5,677	787	1,314	2,352	1,224	221,900	280,300	164,800	183,700	350,500
2007.	4,939	723	1,181	2,053	982	217,900	288,100	161,400	178,800	342,500
2008.	4,350	623	1,022	1,721	984	196,600	271,500	150,500	169,400	276,100
2009.	4,566	641	1,067	1,745	1,113	172,100	243,200	142,900	155,000	215,400
2010.	4,308	604	984	1,669	1,051	173,100	243,900	140,800	153,700	220,700

Source: NATIONAL ASSOCIATION OF REALTORS, Washington, DC, *Real Estate Outlook; Market Trends & Insights*, monthly (copyright). See also <http://www.realtor.org/research>.

Table 978. Median Sales Price of Existing One-Family Homes by Selected Metropolitan Area: 2005 and 2010

[In thousands of dollars (219.0 represents $219,000). Includes existing detached single-family homes and townhouses. Areas are metropolitan statistical areas defined by Office of Management and Budget as of 2004, except as noted]

Metropolitan area	2005	2010	Metropolitan area	2005	2010
United States, total	**219.0**	**173.1**	NY: Nassau-Suffolk, NY.	465.2	387.0
Allentown-Bethlehem-Easton, PA-NJ	243.4	224.0	NY: Newark-Union, NJ-PA	416.8	379.2
Anaheim-Santa Ana-Irvine, CA [1]	691.9	544.7	Norwich-New London, CT	255.9	204.7
Atlantic City, NJ.	256.1	226.4	Orlando, FL	243.6	134.7
Baltimore-Towson, MD	265.3	246.1	Palm Bay-Melbourne-Titusville, FL	209.7	103.0
Barnstable Town, MA.	398.3	326.0	Philadelphia-Camden-Wilmington,		
Boston-Cambridge-Quincy, MA-NH [2].	413.2	357.3	PA-NJ-DE-MD	215.3	214.9
Boulder, CO.	348.4	358.1	Phoenix-Mesa-Scottsdale, AZ.	247.4	139.2
Bridgeport-Stamford-Norwalk, CT.	482.4	408.6	Pittsfield, MA	207.3	195.5
Cape Coral-Fort Myers, FL	269.2	88.9	Portland-South Portland-Biddeford, ME	246.6	218.0
Charleston-North Charleston, SC	197.0	200.5	Portland-Vancouver-Beaverton, OR-WA	244.9	237.3
Chicago-Naperville-Joliet, IL	264.2	191.4	Providence-New Bedford-Fall River, RI-MA. . . .	293.4	228.5
Colorado Springs, CO	205.9	195.5	Raleigh-Cary, NC.	194.9	217.6
Deltona-Daytona Beach-Ormond Beach, FL. . . .	192.5	115.6	Reno-Sparks, NV.	349.9	179.5
Denver-Aurora, CO	247.1	232.4	Richmond, VA	201.9	(NA)
Dover, DE	180.4	193.3	Riverside-San Bernardino-Ontario, CA [1]	374.2	183.0
Eugene-Springfield, OR.	197.6	196.3	Sacramento-Arden-Arcade-Roseville,CA [1]	375.9	183.6
Gainesville, FL.	184.0	161.6	Salem, OR.	177.7	173.5
Hagerstown-Martinsburg, MD-WV.	208.7	144.4	San Diego-Carlsbad-San Marcos, CA [1].	604.3	385.2
Hartford-West Hartford-East Hartford, CT.	253.3	235.8	San Francisco-Oakland-Fremont, CA [1]	715.7	525.3
Honolulu, HI.	590.0	607.6	San Jose-Sunnyvale-Santa Clara, CA [1]	744.5	602.4
Kingston, NY	251.0	213.8	Sarasota-Bradenton-Venice, FL	354.2	164.6
Las Vegas-Paradise, NV	304.7	138.0	Seattle-Tacoma-Bellevue, WA	316.8	295.7
Los Angeles-Long Beach-Santa Ana, CA [1]	529.0	316.7	Springfield, MA	201.8	190.0
Madison, WI.	218.3	217.7	Tampa-St.Petersburg-Clearwater, FL	205.3	134.2
Miami-Fort Lauderdale-Miami Beach, FL	363.9	201.9	Trenton-Ewing, NJ	261.1	250.7
Milwaukee-Waukesha-West Allis, WI.	215.7	205.9	Tucson, AZ.	231.6	156.6
Minneapolis-St. Paul-Bloomington, MN-WI	234.8	170.6	Virginia Beach-Norfolk-Newport News,		
New Haven-Milford, CT	279.1	231.0	VA-NC	197.2	205.0
New York-Northern New Jersey-Long Island,			Washington-Arlington-Alexandria,		
NY-NJ-PA.	445.2	393.7	DC-VA-MD-WV	425.8	325.3
New York-Wayne-White Plains, NY-NJ	495.2	450.0	Worcester, MA.	290.7	223.3
NY: Edison, NJ.	375.5	345.4			

NA Not available. [1] California data supplied by the California Association of REALTORS. [2] Excludes areas in New Hampshire.
Source: NATIONAL ASSOCIATION OF REALTORS, Washington, DC, *Real Estate Outlook: Market Trends & Insights*, monthly (copyright). See also <http://www.realtor.org/research\>.

Table 979. Existing Home Sales by State: 2000 to 2010

[In thousands (5,174 represents 5,174,000). Includes condos and co-ops as well as single-family homes. Data shown here reflect revisions from prior estimates]

State	2000	2005	2009	2010	State	2000	2005	2009	2010
United States	**5,174**	**7,076**	**5,156**	**4,908**	Missouri	110.2	142.9	105.9	94.6
Alabama	67.0	128.0	75.0	71.6	Montana	17.4	25.4	21.7	20.4
Alaska	14.3	24.6	22.4	22.4	Nebraska	32.3	41.2	34.7	31.9
Arizona	104.8	199.2	150.8	147.5	Nevada	44.6	98.0	104.9	97.7
Arkansas	45.0	75.3	61.8	59.9	New Hampshire	26.7	(NA)	19.6	18.9
California	573.5	601.1	510.4	468.4	New Jersey	161.1	184.4	115.3	110.0
Colorado	111.5	130.4	96.2	90.5	New Mexico	29.9	57.5	32.2	30.8
Connecticut	61.5	78.0	46.6	46.2	New York	273.3	319.8	253.8	242.0
Delaware	12.9	19.3	12.6	10.9	North Carolina	134.2	215.7	136.4	135.3
District of Columbia	10.6	12.1	8.4	8.7	North Dakota	10.8	15.8	13.1	12.5
Florida	393.6	547.1	357.8	396.5	Ohio	216.4	286.9	248.7	231.9
Georgia	143.6	242.1	176.6	162.7	Oklahoma	67.3	104.6	83.5	72.6
Hawaii	22.1	36.8	18.4	20.9	Oregon	62.6	100.5	55.0	55.2
Idaho	24.1	49.8	33.8	38.8	Pennsylvania	195.9	255.2	176.5	160.2
Illinois	246.8	315.3	184.4	176.7	Rhode Island	17.0	19.8	15.4	13.6
Indiana	111.0	138.3	104.7	97.7	South Carolina	64.3	114.6	71.1	70.7
Iowa	53.3	74.9	58.0	55.7	South Dakota	12.6	18.3	17.4	14.3
Kansas	52.6	77.9	56.5	51.8	Tennessee	100.4	170.9	107.9	101.3
Kentucky	66.0	96.2	73.8	70.3	Texas	381.8	532.5	443.3	420.5
Louisiana	66.8	87.7	54.8	51.6	Utah	35.5	51.7	31.1	28.5
Maine	27.6	33.3	23.1	22.8	Vermont	12.1	15.3	11.3	11.3
Maryland	100.5	135.5	72.5	74.5	Virginia	130.0	182.5	117.0	107.9
Massachusetts	112.3	148.6	107.9	105.3	Washington	112.4	167.8	82.3	83.7
Michigan	185.0	208.6	167.1	150.8	West Virginia	22.9	38.6	27.6	26.5
Minnesota	96.3	134.9	107.4	89.7	Wisconsin	91.6	122.8	84.5	77.7
Mississippi	38.7	61.2	41.9	42.1	Wyoming	9.6	14.3	9.1	8.5

NA Not available.

Source: NATIONAL ASSOCIATION OF REALTORS, Washington, DC, *Real Estate Outlook: Market Trends & Insights*, monthly (copyright). See also <http://www.realtor.org/research>.

Table 980. Existing Apartment Condos and Co-Ops—Units Sold and Median Sales Price by Region: 1990 to 2010

[272 represents 272,000. Data shown here reflect revisions from prior estimates. For definition of median, see Guide to Tabular Presentation. For composition of regions, see map inside front cover]

Year	Units sold (1,000)					Median sales price (dollars)				
	U.S.	Northeast	Midwest	South	West	U.S.	Northeast	Midwest	South	West
1990	272	73	55	80	64	86,900	107,500	70,200	64,200	114,600
1995	333	108	66	96	63	89,000	92,500	90,700	67,800	114,800
2000	571	197	106	160	108	114,000	108,500	121,700	84,200	149,100
2003	732	250	146	211	125	168,500	178,100	162,600	126,900	222,400
2004	820	292	161	230	137	197,100	214,100	181,000	156,600	258,000
2005	896	331	177	245	143	223,900	245,100	189,100	187,300	283,800
2006	801	299	169	211	122	221,900	249,700	190,900	184,000	264,700
2007	713	283	146	182	102	226,300	256,100	195,200	185,100	263,300
2008	563	226	107	144	86	209,800	252,500	188,200	166,800	218,500
2009	590	227	96	169	98	175,600	232,800	157,100	132,700	162,100
2010	599	213	92	191	103	171,700	242,200	150,500	118,500	154,700

Source: NATIONAL ASSOCIATION OF REALTORS, Washington, DC, *Real Estate Outlook: Market Trends & Insights*, monthly (copyright). See <http://www.realtor.org/research>.

Table 981. New Unfurnished Apartments Completed and Rented in 3 Months by Region: 2000 to 2009

[226.2 represents 226,200. Structures with five or more units, privately financed, nonsubsidized, unfurnished rental apartments. Based on sample and subject to sampling variability; see source for details. For composition of regions, see map, inside front cover]

Year and rent	Number (1,000)					Percent rented in 3 months				
	U.S.	North-east	Mid-west	South	West	U.S.	North-east	Mid-west	South	West
2000	226.2	14.8	39.5	125.9	45.9	72	85	76	67	77
2005	113.0	4.7	20.5	57.8	30.0	64	75	64	62	64
2007	104.8	5.6	9.5	61.8	28.0	55	66	58	52	58
2008	146.4	8.9	17.2	88.2	32.1	50	52	58	48	51
2009, prel.	**163.0**	**10.0**	**17.2**	**93.3**	**42.4**	**51**	**56**	**74**	**49**	**44**
Less than $950	57.3	2.7	10.2	35.7	8.8	62	85	79	58	48
$950 to $1,049	22.3	0.4	2.9	15.1	4.0	52	89	69	50	45
$1,050 to $1,149	13.3	1.1	1.0	7.3	3.9	47	57	64	50	33
$1,150 to $1,249	16.7	0.8	0.7	10.2	5.0	44	15	74	42	50
$1,250 or more	53.3	5.0	2.5	25.0	20.7	42	55	61	38	41
Median asking rent	1,063	1,250	857	1,022	1,240	(X)	(X)	(X)	(X)	(X)

X Not applicable.

Source: U.S. Census Bureau, Current Housing Reports, Series H130, *Market Absorption of Apartments*, and unpublished data. See also <http://www.census.gov/hhes/www/housing/soma/soma.html>.

Table 982. Total Housing Inventory for the United States: 1990 to 2010

[In thousands (106,283 represents 106,283,000), except percent. Based on the Current Population Survey and the Housing Vacancy Survey and subject to sampling error; see source and Appendix III for details]

Item	1990	1995	2000	2002 [1]	2005	2006	2007	2008	2009	2010
All housing units	**106,283**	**112,655**	**119,628**	**119,297**	**124,600**	**126,383**	**128,017**	**129,211**	**129,944**	**130,599**
Vacant	12,059	12,669	13,908	14,332	15,786	16,487	17,666	18,574	18,785	18,739
Year-round vacant	9,128	9,570	10,439	10,771	11,990	12,497	13,288	13,838	14,121	14,294
For rent	2,662	2,946	3,024	3,347	3,742	3,747	3,851	4,027	4,386	4,284
For sale only	1,064	1,022	1,148	1,220	1,460	1,841	2,118	2,210	2,016	1,983
Rented or sold	660	810	856	842	1,067	1,110	1,133	1,068	992	908
Held off market	4,742	4,793	5,411	5,362	5,720	5,798	6,186	6,533	6,726	7,120
Occasional use	1,485	1,667	1,892	1,819	1,896	1,866	1,995	2,056	2,064	2,241
Usual residence elsewhere	1,068	801	1,037	995	1,136	1,201	1,140	1,162	1,185	1,254
Other	2,189	2,325	2,482	2,548	2,688	2,731	3,051	3,315	3,478	3,625
Seasonal [2]	2,931	3,099	3,469	3,561	3,796	3,990	4,378	4,736	4,665	4,444
Total occupied	94,224	99,985	105,720	104,965	108,814	109,896	110,351	110,637	111,159	111,860
Owner	60,248	64,739	71,250	71,278	74,962	75,596	75,192	75,043	74,892	74,791
Renter	33,976	35,246	34,470	33,687	33,852	34,300	35,159	35,594	36,267	37,069
PERCENT DISTRIBUTION										
All housing units	100.0	100.0	100.0	100.0	100.0	100.0	100.0	100.0	100.0	100.0
Vacant	11.3	11.2	11.6	12.0	12.7	13.0	13.8	14.4	14.4	14.3
Total occupied	88.7	88.8	88.4	88.0	87.3	87.0	86.2	85.6	85.6	85.7
Owner	56.7	57.5	59.6	59.7	60.2	60.3	58.7	58.1	0.6	57.3
Renter	32.0	31.3	28.8	28.2	27.2	27.5	27.5	27.5	0.3	28.4

[1] Revised. Based on 2000 census controls. [2] Includes vacant seasonal mobile homes.
Source: U.S. Census Bureau, "Housing Vacancies and Home Ownership", <http://www.census.gov/hhes/www/housing/hvs/hvs.html>.

Table 983. Occupied Housing Inventory by Age of Householder: 1990 to 2010

[In thousands (94,224 represents 94,224,000). Based on the Current Population Survey and Housing Vacancy Survey; see source for details]

Age of householder	1990	1995	2000	2002 [1]	2005	2006	2007	2008	2009	2010
Total	**94,224**	**99,986**	**102,560**	**105,053**	**108,814**	**109,896**	**110,351**	**110,637**	**111,159**	**111,860**
Under 25 years old	5,143	5,502	5,964	6,378	6,574	6,598	6,497	6,227	6,095	6,060
25 to 29 years old	9,508	8,662	8,197	8,238	8,839	9,001	9,173	9,030	9,060	9,041
30 to 34 years old	11,213	11,206	9,939	10,184	9,636	9,451	9,352	9,278	9,314	9,477
35 to 39 years old	10,914	11,993	11,573	10,933	10,582	10,552	10,503	10,476	10,167	9,794
40 to 44 years old	9,893	11,151	12,013	11,849	11,784	11,518	11,130	10,898	10,687	10,525
45 to 49 years old	8,038	10,080	10,835	11,213	11,843	12,024	12,011	11,885	11,841	11,690
50 to 54 years old	6,532	7,882	9,414	10,132	10,651	10,927	11,086	11,336	11,586	11,721
55 to 59 years old	6,182	6,355	7,455	8,268	9,555	9,948	10,017	10,146	10,209	10,437
60 to 64 years old	6,446	5,860	6,011	6,427	7,376	7,627	8,112	8,542	8,905	9,345
65 to 69 years old	6,407	6,088	5,679	5,649	5,931	6,092	6,334	6,597	6,810	7,038
70 to 74 years old	5,397	5,693	5,420	5,142	5,043	5,071	5,066	5,079	5,280	5,449
75 years old and over	8,546	9,514	10,059	10,641	11,000	11,088	11,069	11,144	11,203	11,285

[1] Revised. Based on 2000 census controls.
Source: U.S. Census Bureau, "Housing Vacancies and Home Ownership," <http://www.census.gov/hhes/www/housing/hvs/hvs.html>.

Table 984. Vacancy Rates for Housing Units—Characteristics: 2000 to 2010

[In percent. Rate is relationship between vacant housing for rent or for sale and the total rental and homeowner supply, which comprises occupied units, units rented or sold and awaiting occupancy, and vacant units available for rent or sale. Based on the Current Population/Housing Vacancy Survey; see source for details. For composition of regions, see map, inside front cover]

Characteristic	Rental Units				Homeowner units			
	2000	2005	2009	2010	2000	2005	2009	2010
Total units	**8.0**	**9.8**	**10.6**	**10.2**	**1.6**	**1.9**	**2.6**	**2.6**
Northeast	5.6	6.5	7.2	7.6	1.2	1.5	2.0	1.7
Midwest	8.8	12.6	10.7	10.8	1.3	2.2	2.6	2.6
South	10.5	11.8	13.6	12.7	1.9	2.1	2.9	2.8
West	5.8	7.3	9.0	8.2	1.5	1.4	2.6	2.7
Units in structure:								
1 unit	7.0	9.9	9.8	9.6	1.5	1.7	2.3	2.2
2 units or more	8.7	10.0	11.3	10.8	4.7	6.2	8.7	9.2
5 units or more	9.2	10.4	12.3	11.6	5.8	6.6	8.7	9.5
Units with—								
3 rooms or less	10.3	12.1	13.3	13.4	10.4	12.0	14.2	14.9
4 rooms	8.2	9.6	10.9	10.2	2.9	3.3	5.0	5.5
5 rooms	6.9	9.3	9.7	9.1	2.0	2.2	3.1	3.0
6 rooms or more	5.2	8.1	8.3	7.7	1.1	1.4	1.8	1.7

Source: U.S. Census Bureau, "Housing Vacancies and Home Ownership," <http://www.census.gov/hhes/www/housing/hvs/hvs.html>.

Construction and Housing 615

Table 985. Housing Units and Tenure—States: 2009

[129,950 represents 129,950,000. The American Community Survey universe includes the household population and the population living in institutions, college dormitories, and other group quarters. Based on a sample and subject to sampling variability; see Appendix III]

State	Housing units						Housing tenure			
			Vacant (1,000)		Vacancy rate		Owner-occupied units		Renter-occupied units	
	Total (1,000)	Occu-pied (1,000)	Total	For sea-sonal use[1]	Hom-eowner[2]	Renter[3]	Total (1,000)	Average house-hold size	Total (1,000)	Average house-hold size
United States	129,950	113,616	16,334	4,706	2.5	8.5	74,843	2.71	38,773	2.48
Alabama	2,182	1,848	334	77	2.3	10.5	1,286	2.55	562	2.33
Alaska	284	237	47	24	1.3	6.9	154	2.98	82	2.64
Arizona	2,753	2,277	476	164	3.7	12.8	1,527	2.83	750	2.87
Arkansas	1,310	1,125	185	43	2.8	10.6	743	2.56	382	2.38
California	13,435	12,215	1,220	327	2.3	5.8	6,910	3.01	5,305	2.88
Colorado	2,168	1,910	258	104	2.6	8.1	1,280	2.64	630	2.43
Connecticut	1,446	1,326	120	26	1.4	8.0	913	2.70	413	2.26
Delaware	396	327	69	36	3.5	12.6	241	2.66	86	2.56
District of Columbia	285	249	36	3	3.7	6.1	112	2.37	138	2.17
Florida	8,848	6,988	1,861	814	4.2	13.4	4,785	2.59	2,203	2.59
Georgia	4,064	3,469	594	96	3.6	12.5	2,326	2.79	1,143	2.68
Hawaii	516	446	70	29	1.4	10.6	253	3.00	193	2.60
Idaho	648	558	89	36	2.7	8.7	399	2.73	159	2.64
Illinois	5,291	4,757	533	48	2.6	7.9	3,235	2.76	1,522	2.39
Indiana	2,809	2,478	332	36	2.5	10.7	1,745	2.60	733	2.31
Iowa	1,342	1,227	115	18	2.2	6.1	884	2.48	343	2.06
Kansas	1,232	1,105	127	16	1.9	7.5	749	2.58	356	2.27
Kentucky	1,935	1,694	241	35	2.2	10.0	1,163	2.53	531	2.35
Louisiana	1,963	1,688	275	53	2.0	8.3	1,147	2.66	541	2.44
Maine	705	545	160	110	2.3	7.4	396	2.46	149	2.05
Maryland	2,341	2,095	246	50	2.2	9.2	1,436	2.77	659	2.40
Massachusetts	2,748	2,475	273	105	1.5	5.9	1,589	2.75	886	2.23
Michigan	4,541	3,820	722	279	3.1	9.6	2,796	2.62	1,024	2.33
Minnesota	2,331	2,086	245	111	1.8	6.0	1,537	2.58	548	2.12
Mississippi	1,282	1,095	187	36	1.9	11.6	761	2.63	334	2.53
Missouri	2,682	2,340	342	77	2.5	8.3	1,616	2.59	723	2.26
Montana	441	375	66	30	2.0	6.6	260	2.60	116	2.37
Nebraska	789	711	78	14	1.8	7.5	478	2.60	233	2.15
Nevada	1,138	966	172	36	4.4	12.8	572	2.74	394	2.64
New Hampshire	600	506	94	60	1.8	7.0	367	2.69	139	2.15
New Jersey	3,525	3,155	370	127	2.1	7.7	2,087	2.82	1,068	2.46
New Mexico	878	742	136	45	2.2	9.9	515	2.71	228	2.53
New York	8,018	7,188	830	264	1.8	4.8	3,955	2.79	3,232	2.44
North Carolina	4,259	3,646	612	179	2.6	10.3	2,450	2.56	1,196	2.36
North Dakota	316	279	37	12	1.9	7.7	184	2.42	95	1.83
Ohio	5,094	4,526	568	57	2.5	9.3	3,080	2.59	1,446	2.25
Oklahoma	1,650	1,430	220	41	2.6	8.6	961	2.55	469	2.39
Oregon	1,640	1,486	154	50	2.3	6.4	937	2.59	549	2.40
Pennsylvania	5,519	4,917	602	167	2.0	6.9	3,467	2.60	1,450	2.15
Rhode Island	452	406	46	15	1.8	6.9	258	2.66	149	2.22
South Carolina	2,084	1,730	354	116	2.9	13.5	1,214	2.57	517	2.51
South Dakota	365	317	48	15	2.3	6.5	215	2.57	102	2.25
Tennessee	2,781	2,447	334	54	2.7	10.6	1,692	2.58	755	2.36
Texas	9,724	8,528	1,196	220	2.3	10.8	5,431	2.95	3,097	2.64
Utah	953	863	90	36	1.9	6.6	617	3.29	246	2.88
Vermont	314	252	63	45	1.9	7.9	179	2.51	72	2.08
Virginia	3,330	2,971	359	79	2.3	7.4	2,025	2.64	947	2.41
Washington	2,814	2,559	255	80	2.4	6.1	1,646	2.65	914	2.37
West Virginia	894	749	145	39	2.2	8.9	551	2.42	197	2.22
Wisconsin	2,584	2,272	312	154	1.8	5.9	1,567	2.54	705	2.14
Wyoming	249	214	36	17	2.2	7.2	151	2.57	62	2.25

[1] For seasonal, recreational, or occasional use. [2] Proportion of the homeowner housing inventory which is vacant for sale.
[3] Proportion of the rental inventory which is vacant for rent.

Source: U.S. Census Bureau, 2009 American Community Survey, B25002, "Occupancy Status"; B25003, "Tenure"; B25004, "Vacancy Status"; and B25010, "Average Household Size of Units by Tenure," using American FactFinder, see <http://factfinder.census.gov>, accessed March 2011.

U.S. Census Bureau, Statistical Abstract of the United States: 2012

Table 986. Homeownership and Rental Vacancy Rates by State: 2010

[The American Community Survey universe is limited to the household population and excludes the population living in institutions, college dormitories, and other group quarters. Based on a sample and subject to sampling variability, see Appendix III]

State	Homeowner vacancy rate	Rental vacancy rate	State	Homeowner vacancy rate	Rental vacancy rate	State	Homeowner vacancy rate	Rental vacancy rate
U.S.	2.6	10.2	KS	2.4	11.3	ND	1.5	7.4
			KY	2.2	10.4	OH	3.3	11.5
AL	2.9	12.1	LA	1.5	12.5	OK	2.0	10.9
AK	1.9	5.6	ME	2.2	6.2	OR	3.3	5.5
AZ	3.2	14.9	MD	2.8	10.5	PA	1.6	8.8
AR	3.1	11.4	MA	1.2	6.6	RI	1.8	7.1
CA	2.5	7.5	MI	2.7	13.1	SC	3.2	13.9
CO	2.7	7.9	MN	2.0	8.3	SD	1.5	9.5
CT	1.7	10.7	MS	2.3	15.6	TN	2.6	12.5
DE	2.4	9.9	MO	2.5	11.6	TX	2.0	13.3
DC	2.3	9.0	MT	1.6	5.7	UT	2.0	7.2
FL	4.5	15.1	NE	2.5	7.2	VT	1.9	6.1
GA	2.9	12.3	NV	4.5	13.4	VA	2.3	10.5
HI	1.9	8.1	NH	1.7	7.2	WA	2.7	7.0
ID	3.3	8.8	NJ	1.6	9.1	WV	2.1	8.2
IL	2.9	11.0	NM	1.8	6.3	WI	1.6	8.6
IN	3.0	11.8	NY	2.1	6.8	WY	2.0	8.3
IA	2.0	8.1	NC	3.4	12.0			

Source: U.S. Census Bureau, "Housing Vacancies and Home Ownership," <http://www.census.gov/hhes/www/housing/hvs/annual10/ann10ind.html>.

Table 987. Homeownership and Rental Vacancy Rates by Metropolitan Area: 2010

[Based on the Current Population Survey and the Housing Vacancy Survey, subject to sampling error; see source and Appendix III for details]

Metropolitan area	Homeowner vacancy rate	Rental vacancy rate	Metropolitan area	Homeowner vacancy rate	Rental vacancy rate
Inside Metropolitan Areas	**2.6**	**10.3**			
Akron, OH	4.1	12.5	Minneapolis-St. Paul-Bloomington, MN-WI	1.4	7.4
Albany-Schenectady-Troy, NY	1.0	8.0	Nashville-Davidson-Murfreesboro, TN	2.4	8.2
Albuquerque, NM	1.7	5.0	New Haven-Milford, CT	2.6	11.1
Allenton-Bethleham-Easton, PA-NJ	0.5	9.1	New Orleans-Metairie-Kenner, LA	2.6	15.2
Atlanta-Sandy Springs-Marietta, GA	3.0	13.8	New York-Northern New Jersey-Long Island, NY	2.1	6.6
Austin-Round Rock, TX	1.9	11.8	Oklahoma City, OK	2.7	9.6
Bakersfield, CA	1.8	6.3	Omaha-Council Bluffs, NE-IA	3.3	10.1
Baltimore-Towson, MD	2.2	11.8	Orlando, FL	5.9	19.0
Baton Rouge, LA	1.0	9.4	Oxnard-Thousand Oaks-Ventura, CA	1.1	6.4
Birmingham-Hoover, AL	2.3	8.8	Philadelphia-Camden-Wilmington, PA	1.5	11.6
Boston-Cambridge-Quincy, MA-NH	1.2	6.2	Phoenix-Mesa-Scottsdale, AZ	2.9	16.3
Bridgeport-Stamford-Norwalk, CT	1.3	8.7	Pittsburgh, PA	2.7	7.8
Buffalo-Cheektowaga-Tonawanda, NY	1.7	11.1	Portland-Vancouver-Beaverton, OR-WA	3.2	4.2
Charlotte-Gastonia-Concord, NC-SC	3.1	11.2	Poughkeepsie-Newburg-Middletown, NJ	2.0	9.5
Chicago-Naperville-Joliet, IL	3.4	12.1	Providence-New Bedford-Fall River RI-MA	1.3	7.5
Cincinnati-Middletown, OH-KY-IN	4.0	12.0	Raleigh-Cary, NC	5.0	11.4
Cleveland-Elyria-Mentor, OH	3.1	11.3	Richmond, VA	3.1	13.5
Columbia, SC	2.5	9.4	Riverside-San Bernardino-Ontario, CA	4.7	12.3
Columbus, OH	4.2	8.0	Rochester, NY	1.1	6.3
Dallas-Ft. Worth-Arlington, TX	2.3	13.5	Sacramento-Arden-Arade-Roseville, CA	2.9	8.4
Dayton, OH	3.7	18.6	St. Louis, MO-IL	2.1	11.2
Denver-Aurora, CO	1.7	8.2	Salt Lake City, UT	2.2	6.0
Detroit-Warren-Livonia, MI	2.6	16.4	San Antonio, TX	1.6	14.0
El Paso, TX	1.4	5.8	San Diego-Carlsbad-San Marcos, CA	2.9	7.8
Fresno, CA	1.6	10.1	San Francisco-Oakland-Freemont, CA	1.8	6.0
Grand Rapids-Wyoming, MI	3.6	6.9	San Jose-Sunnyvale-Santa Clara, CA	0.9	8.2
Greensboro-High Point, NC	4.1	12.8	Seattle-Bellevue-Everett, WA	3.2	7.4
Hartford-West Hartford-East Hartford, CT	1.7	11.6	Springfield, MA	0.7	7.3
Honolulu, HI	1.0	7.2	Syracuse, NY	1.3	10.6
Houston-Baytown-Sugar Land, TX	2.8	16.2	Tampa-St. Petersburg-Clearwater, FL	4.0	12.6
Indianapolis, IN	3.0	14.1	Toledo, OH	5.5	14.4
Jacksonville, FL	4.6	13.9	Tucson, AZ	3.2	11.1
Kansas City, MO-KS	2.7	14.0	Tulsa, OK	1.4	15.9
Las Vegas-Paradise, NV	5.1	13.8	Virginia Beach-Norfolk-Newport News, VA	2.8	8.8
Los Angeles-Long Beach-Santa Ana, CA	1.8	6.7	Washington-Arlington-Alexandria, DC-VA-MD-WV	2.1	8.8
Louisville, KY-IN	1.9	9.6	Worchester, MA	2.3	7.5
Memphis, TN-AR-MS	3.4	18.5			
Miami-Fort Lauderdale-Miami Beach, FL	3.5	10.1			
Milwaukee-Waukesha-West Allis, WI	1.2	7.6			

Source: U.S. Census Bureau, "Housing Vacancies and Home Ownership," <http://www.census.gov/hhes/www/housing/hvs/annual10/ann10ind.html>.

Construction and Housing 617

Table 988. Housing Units—Characteristics by Tenure and Region: 2009

[In thousands of units (130,112 represents 130,112,000), except as indicated. As of fall. Based on the American Housing Survey; see Appendix III. For composition of regions, see map, inside front cover]

Characteristic	Total housing units	Sea-sonal	Year-round units Occupied Total	Owner	Renter	North-east	Mid-west	South	West	Vacant
Total units.	**130,112**	**4,618**	**111,806**	**76,428**	**35,378**	**20,451**	**25,368**	**41,586**	**24,401**	**13,688**
Percent distribution	100.0	3.5	85.9	58.7	27.2	15.7	19.5	32.0	18.8	10.5
Units in structure:										
Single family detached	82,472	2,795	73,079	63,324	9,755	11,431	17,944	28,063	15,642	6,598
Single family attached	7,053	252	5,973	3,952	2,021	1,810	1,055	1,935	1,172	828
2 to 4 units.	10,160	167	8,350	1,353	6,998	2,571	1,792	2,096	1,892	1,643
5 to 9 units.	6,347	143	5,269	632	4,637	944	1,043	1,818	1,465	935
10 to 19 units.	5,722	127	4,661	483	4,178	741	962	1,819	1,139	934
20 or more units.	9,588	404	7,634	1,266	6,368	2,415	1,429	1,936	1,854	1,550
Manufactured/mobile home [1].	8,769	730	6,839	5,418	1,421	540	1,145	3,918	1,236	1,201
Year structure built:										
Median year.	1974	1975	1974	1975	1971	1958	1970	1979	1976	1973
1980 or later.	16,283	615	14,028	9,360	4,668	1,758	2,381	6,438	3,451	1,639
1970 to 1979.	24,799	867	21,248	13,167	8,081	2,864	4,681	8,761	4,941	2,684
1960 to 1969.	15,261	514	13,326	8,917	4,409	2,451	2,957	4,832	3,086	1,421
1950 to 1959.	41,406	1,386	35,399	23,076	12,322	10,828	9,780	8,538	6,252	4,622
Stories in structure: [2]										
1 story	41,537	1,880	35,364	26,216	9,148	1,109	4,072	19,803	10,381	4,292
2 stories.	43,447	1,145	37,867	25,210	12,657	6,291	10,192	12,065	9,320	4,435
3 stories.	27,574	542	24,508	16,721	7,787	8,689	8,530	4,611	2,678	2,524
4 or more stories	8,785	320	7,228	2,863	4,365	3,823	1,430	1,190	785	1,237
Foundation: [3]										
Full basement	29,104	490	26,713	23,821	2,892	9,022	11,276	4,269	2,145	1,902
Partial building.	8,991	170	8,208	7,350	858	2,226	3,280	1,565	1,137	613
Crawlspace	20,955	965	18,022	14,783	3,240	740	2,523	9,517	5,242	1,968
Concrete slab	28,693	1,011	24,917	20,431	4,486	1,146	1,758	13,941	8,071	2,765
Equipment:										
Lacking complete facilities	5,586	667	1,751	378	1,374	487	385	406	474	3,168
With complete facilities	124,526	3,951	110,054	76,050	34,004	19,964	24,984	41,180	23,927	10,520
Kitchen sink.	128,769	4,291	111,510	76,329	35,180	20,344	25,308	41,532	24,326	12,968
Refrigerator	126,534	4,056	111,530	76,336	35,193	20,372	25,328	41,502	24,328	10,948
Cooking stove or range	126,744	4,127	111,038	76,153	34,886	20,329	25,207	41,347	24,155	11,579
Dishwasher	82,397	2,111	73,584	57,191	16,393	11,900	15,487	28,691	17,505	6,702
Washing machine	101,387	2,482	93,372	73,826	19,545	15,327	21,537	36,611	19,896	5,534
Clothes dryer.	98,657	2,360	90,905	72,562	18,343	14,512	21,327	35,578	19,489	5,392
Disposal in kitchen sink	63,776	1,505	56,531	40,597	15,933	5,332	13,048	20,217	17,934	5,740
Safety Equipment:										
Smoke detector:										
Working	116,141	2,989	104,362	71,797	32,565	19,479	24,153	37,942	22,788	8,789
Powered by:										
Electricity	9,217	267	8,149	5,620	2,528	1,680	1,534	3,238	1,696	801
Batteries	72,868	1,547	66,536	43,210	23,326	12,985	16,379	22,831	14,341	4,785
Both.	32,128	983	28,421	22,461	5,960	4,654	5,971	11,370	6,426	2,724
Not working	9,101	824	6,157	3,686	2,472	739	974	3,045	1,399	2,119
Not reported	4,870	804	1,286	945	341	233	241	598	214	2,780
Batteries:										
Replaced in last 6 months	77,933	1,626	71,505	50,073	21,432	14,175	17,336	25,312	14,682	4,803
Not replaced in last 6 months	23,706	579	21,466	14,678	6,788	3,133	4,557	8,179	5,597	1,661
Not reported	3,357	326	1,986	920	1,066	331	457	710	488	1,045
Fire extinguisher purchased or recharged	49,902	(X)	49,902	37,922	11,980	9,405	11,183	19,118	10,196	(X)
Sprinkler system inside home.	6,401	246	5,167	2,086	3,081	938	877	1,845	1,507	988
Working carbon monoxide detector . .	43,494	673	40,698	31,691	9,007	12,483	12,688	9,927	5,600	2,123
Main heating equipment: [4]										
Warm-air furnace.	81,629	2,034	71,141	51,691	19,450	8,925	20,671	25,268	16,277	8,454
Steam or hot water system	13,969	259	12,506	7,494	5,012	9,088	2,015	592	811	1,204
Electric heat pump.	16,059	868	13,264	9,764	3,500	336	706	10,785	1,436	1,927
Built-in electric units.	5,730	320	4,761	2,120	2,641	1,159	1,134	827	1,641	649
Floor, wall, or pipeless furnace	5,525	202	4,802	2,043	2,760	435	388	1,154	2,825	520
Room heaters with flue	1,173	73	950	580	370	124	103	478	244	150
Room heaters without flue.	1,365	99	1,109	694	414	24	52	992	41	157
Portable electric heaters	1,405	107	1,167	535	632	29	65	769	304	131
Stoves	1,364	203	1,035	845	190	226	158	341	310	125
Fireplaces [5]	290	42	215	190	25	27	40	53	94	34
None	930	330	386	206	180	3	3	58	321	215
Main cooling equipment:										
Central air conditioning	88,668	2,197	78,437	59,357	19,080	6,931	18,340	39,501	13,665	8,034
One or more room units.	26,850	581	24,582	13,707	10,875	10,499	5,478	4,980	3,625	1,687
Source of water:										
Public system or private company. . .	113,489	3,238	98,027	64,372	33,655	17,101	21,435	36,594	22,897	12,224
Well serving 1 to 5 units.	15,846	1,070	13,430	11,769	1,660	3,275	3,878	4,821	1,455	1,346
Means of sewage disposal:										
Public sewer	103,155	2,596	89,467	56,736	32,732	16,263	20,432	31,288	21,484	11,092
Septic tank chemical toilet	26,662	1,800	22,307	19,667	2,640	4,185	4,930	10,279	2,913	2,555

X Not applicable. [1] Includes trailers. Includes width not reported, not shown separately. [2] Excludes mobile homes; includes basements and finished attics. [3] Limited to single-family units. [4] Includes other items, not shown separately. [5] With and without inserts.

Source: U.S. Census Bureau, Current Housing Reports, Series H150/09, *American Housing Survey for the United States: 2009*. See also <http://www.census.gov/hhes/www/housing/ahs/nationaldata.html>.

Table 989. Housing Units by Units in Structure and State: 2009

[In percent, except as indicated (129,950 represents 129,950,000). The American Community Survey universe includes the household population and the population living in institutions, college dormitories, and other group quarters. Based on a sample and subject to sampling variability; see Appendix III]

Characteristic	Total housing units (1,000)	Percent of units by units in structures—								
		1-unit detached	1-unit attached	2 units	3 or 4 units	5 or 9 units	10 or 19 units	20 or more units	Mobile homes	Boat, RV, van, etc.
U.S.	**129,950**	**61.6**	**5.8**	**3.9**	**4.5**	**4.9**	**4.6**	**9.4**	**6.5**	**0.1**
AL	2,182	67.6	1.7	2.4	3.0	4.2	3.3	7.5	14.2	0.1
AK	284	61.2	8.6	4.9	6.3	5.2	2.8	8.0	6.1	0.1
AZ	2,753	62.7	5.2	1.3	3.4	4.7	5.4	10.1	10.9	0.4
AR	1,310	69.7	1.8	3.1	3.5	3.4	3.3	6.7	12.8	0.1
CA	13,435	58.0	7.1	2.6	5.6	6.1	5.4	11.6	3.9	0.1
CO	2,168	63.2	7.0	1.5	3.5	4.9	6.1	11.0	4.6	0.1
CT	1,446	59.3	5.2	7.9	8.7	5.5	3.9	9.4	0.9	(Z)
DE	396	58.3	14.7	1.6	2.7	3.5	5.4	8.9	9.4	(Z)
DC	285	12.1	26.7	2.6	7.6	6.9	10.4	17.3	0.0	0.1
FL	8,848	53.8	6.3	2.3	3.8	5.0	6.1	11.1	9.5	0.1
GA	4,064	66.4	3.5	2.2	3.3	5.3	4.8	10.1	9.4	(Z)
HI	516	53.2	6.1	3.3	5.4	7.1	5.0	12.1	0.1	(Z)
ID	648	72.9	2.8	2.5	4.4	2.7	1.6	4.3	10.0	0.1
IL	5,291	57.8	5.8	6.0	7.0	6.4	4.1	10.5	2.8	(Z)
IN	2,809	72.4	3.4	2.6	3.7	4.8	3.8	8.6	5.3	(Z)
IA	1,342	73.5	3.5	2.6	3.6	3.8	3.6	7.5	4.2	(Z)
KS	1,232	73.2	4.6	2.5	3.4	3.8	3.4	7.3	4.9	(Z)
KY	1,935	67.0	2.3	3.3	3.9	4.9	3.5	8.4	12.3	(Z)
LA	1,963	66.1	2.7	3.8	4.1	3.4	2.8	6.2	13.3	0.2
ME	705	69.6	2.1	5.5	5.4	4.2	1.7	5.9	8.8	(Z)
MD	2,341	51.3	21.1	1.8	2.3	5.2	8.7	13.9	1.8	(Z)
MA	2,748	52.4	5.1	10.7	10.8	6.0	4.3	10.3	0.8	(Z)
MI	4,541	72.0	4.4	2.9	2.6	4.2	3.7	7.8	5.5	(Z)
MN	2,331	67.9	7.3	2.3	2.1	2.1	3.6	5.6	3.8	(Z)
MS	1,282	69.7	1.6	2.2	3.0	4.9	2.1	7.1	14.8	0.1
MO	2,682	70.2	3.5	3.6	4.8	3.8	3.3	7.0	6.7	(Z)
MT	441	68.9	2.9	3.9	4.8	2.9	1.8	4.7	11.5	0.1
NE	789	72.6	3.6	2.0	2.7	3.8	5.0	8.8	3.9	(Z)
NV	1,138	60.1	4.8	1.3	6.0	8.8	6.2	15.0	5.9	0.2
NH	600	63.1	5.2	6.2	5.5	4.7	3.3	8.0	6.1	(Z)
NJ	3,525	53.4	9.2	9.4	6.7	5.1	5.1	10.2	1.0	(Z)
NM	878	65.0	3.9	1.8	3.8	3.0	2.7	5.7	15.6	0.1
NY	8,018	41.7	4.9	10.9	7.4	5.2	4.2	9.4	2.4	(Z)
NC	4,259	64.9	3.8	2.3	2.8	4.4	4.3	8.7	13.8	(Z)
ND	316	61.7	5.0	2.0	3.7	4.6	5.8	10.4	7.2	(Z)
OH	5,094	68.3	4.7	4.6	4.5	4.9	4.0	8.9	3.8	(Z)
OK	1,650	73.3	2.1	2.1	2.6	3.7	3.5	7.2	9.1	0.1
OR	1,640	63.9	4.1	3.3	4.4	4.6	3.9	8.5	8.4	0.2
PA	5,519	57.3	18.1	4.9	4.2	3.3	2.5	5.8	4.3	(Z)
RI	452	56.6	3.5	10.8	12.1	5.5	3.6	9.1	1.1	(Z)
SC	2,084	62.5	2.4	2.3	2.9	4.8	3.6	8.4	17.7	0.1
SD	365	68.6	3.8	2.3	3.4	3.7	3.3	7.0	8.7	0.1
TN	2,781	68.5	3.1	3.0	3.0	4.6	3.7	8.3	10.1	(Z)
TX	9,724	65.2	2.6	2.1	3.3	5.0	7.0	12.0	7.3	0.2
UT	953	69.6	5.9	3.0	4.6	3.2	4.0	7.2	3.9	0.1
VT	314	65.6	3.3	6.5	6.7	5.5	2.0	7.5	7.3	(Z)
VA	3,330	62.6	10.3	1.7	2.8	4.7	5.5	10.2	5.7	(Z)
WA	2,814	63.3	3.7	2.6	3.8	5.0	5.1	10.1	7.0	0.2
WV	894	71.7	1.7	2.4	2.9	2.7	1.6	4.3	14.6	(Z)
WI	2,584	66.1	4.4	7.1	3.9	4.8	3.3	8.2	3.9	(Z)
WY	249	65.0	4.3	2.8	4.6	3.0	2.4	5.4	14.3	0.1

Z Less than .05 percent.

Source: U.S. Census Bureau, 2009 American Community Survey, B25024, "Units in Structure," <http://www.factfinder.census .gov>, accessed May 2011.

Table 990. Housing Units—Size of Units and Lot: 2009

[In thousands (130,112 represents 130,112,000), except as indicated. As of fall. Based on the American Housing Survey; see Appendix III. For composition of regions, see map, inside front cover]

Item	Total housing units	Sea-sonal	Year-round units Occupied Total	Owner	Renter	North-east	Mid-west	South	West	Vacant
Total units	**130,112**	**4,618**	**111,806**	**76,428**	**35,378**	**20,451**	**25,368**	**41,586**	**24,401**	**13,688**
Rooms:										
1 room	579	104	352	26	326	111	60	33	149	123
2 rooms	1,423	194	946	68	879	269	130	209	337	283
3 rooms	11,290	697	8,711	1,036	7,675	2,235	1,891	2,461	2,124	1,882
4 rooms	23,036	1,374	17,828	6,475	11,354	3,277	3,889	6,376	4,287	3,834
5 rooms	29,888	1,108	25,444	17,232	8,212	3,854	5,758	10,355	5,476	3,336
6 rooms	27,480	632	24,596	20,364	4,232	4,435	5,400	9,918	4,842	2,252
7 rooms	17,877	315	16,489	14,754	1,735	3,080	3,904	6,110	3,394	1,073
8 rooms or more	18,538	193	17,440	16,474	967	3,189	4,337	6,123	3,791	905
Complete bathrooms:										
No bathrooms	1,678	557	403	175	229	98	93	115	97	717
1 bathroom	46,977	1,899	38,662	15,767	22,894	9,418	9,760	11,847	7,636	6,416
1 and one-half bathrooms	17,233	363	15,656	12,081	3,575	4,066	4,770	4,217	2,603	1,214
2 or more bathrooms	64,223	1,798	57,085	48,405	8,680	6,869	10,746	25,406	14,064	5,340
Square footage of unit:										
Single detached and mobile homes	91,241	3,524	79,918	68,742	11,176	11,971	19,088	31,981	16,878	7,799
Less than 500	988	225	603	383	220	86	104	247	166	161
500 to 749	2,765	462	1,771	1,085	686	249	415	810	298	532
750 to 999	6,440	593	5,014	3,519	1,495	614	1,340	2,086	973	833
1,000 to 1,499	21,224	814	18,419	14,978	3,441	2,047	4,331	7,834	4,207	1,991
1,500 to 1,999	20,636	521	18,519	16,284	2,235	2,458	4,039	7,564	4,457	1,596
2,000 to 2,499	14,361	284	13,190	12,057	1,134	2,000	3,282	5,165	2,743	886
2,500 to 2,999	7,589	141	7,050	6,622	429	1,211	1,594	2,819	1,426	398
3,000 to 3,999	7,252	137	6,692	6,391	301	1,119	1,700	2,488	1,385	424
4,000 or more	4,456	113	4,030	3,787	243	805	994	1,519	712	313
Other [1]	5,529	234	4,630	3,638	992	1,382	1,288	1,449	510	666
Median square footage	1,700	1,150	1,800	1,800	1,300	1,900	1,800	1,700	1,700	1,500
Lot size:										
Single detached and attached units and mobile homes	95,216	3,512	83,466	70,643	12,823	13,297	19,555	33,222	17,392	8,239
Less than one-eighth acre	25,234	946	21,635	16,297	5,338	3,161	4,749	7,268	6,457	2,652
One-eighth to one-quarter acre	13,706	448	11,981	10,581	1,400	1,610	3,063	3,413	3,896	1,277
One-quarter to one-half acre	17,825	518	15,921	13,837	2,084	2,383	4,044	6,523	2,970	1,386
One-half up to one acre	11,292	372	10,036	8,874	1,162	1,974	1,964	4,945	1,153	884
1 up to 5 acres	19,172	754	17,014	14,895	2,120	3,072	3,669	8,310	1,963	1,404
5 up to 10 acres	3,104	120	2,750	2,545	205	464	737	1,106	443	234
10 acres or more	4,885	354	4,127	3,614	513	633	1,329	1,656	509	403
Median acreage	0.27	0.32	0.27	0.32	0.22	0.34	0.28	0.36	0.18	0.25

[1] Represents units not reported or size unknown.
Source: U.S. Census Bureau, Current Housing Reports, Series H150/09, *American Housing Survey for the United States: 2009,* September 2010. See also <http://www.census.gov/hhes/www/housing/ahs/nationaldata.html>.

Table 991. Occupied Housing Units—Tenure by Race of Householder: 1991 to 2009

[In thousands (93,147 represents 93,147,000), except percent. As of fall. Based on the American Housing Survey; see Appendix III]

Race of householder and tenure	1991	1995	1999	2001	2003 [1]	2005	2007	2009
ALL RACES [2]								
Occupied units, total	**93,147**	**97,693**	**102,803**	**106,261**	**105,842**	**108,871**	**110,692**	**111,806**
Owner-occupied	59,796	63,544	68,796	72,265	72,238	74,931	75,647	76,428
Percent of occupied	64.2	65.0	66.9	68.0	68.3	68.8	68.3	68.4
Renter-occupied	33,351	34,150	34,007	33,996	33,604	33,940	35,045	35,378
WHITE [3]								
Occupied units, total	**79,140**	**81,611**	**83,624**	**85,292**	**87,483**	**89,449**	**90,413**	**91,137**
Owner-occupied	53,749	56,507	60,041	62,465	63,126	65,023	65,554	65,935
Percent of occupied	67.9	69.2	71.8	73.2	72.2	72.7	72.5	72.3
Renter-occupied	25,391	25,104	23,583	22,826	24,357	24,426	24,859	25,202
BLACK [3]								
Occupied units, total	**10,832**	**11,773**	**12,936**	**13,292**	**13,004**	**13,447**	**13,856**	**13,993**
Owner-occupied	4,635	5,137	6,013	6,318	6,193	6,471	6,464	6,547
Percent of occupied	42.8	43.6	46.5	47.5	47.6	48.1	46.7	46.8
Renter-occupied	6,197	6,637	6,923	6,974	6,811	6,975	7,392	7,446
HISPANIC ORIGIN [4]								
Occupied units, total	**6,239**	**7,757**	**9,041**	**9,814**	**11,038**	**11,651**	**12,609**	**12,739**
Owner-occupied	2,423	3,245	4,087	4,731	5,106	5,752	6,364	6,439
Percent of occupied	38.8	41.8	45.2	48.2	46.3	49.4	50.5	50.5
Renter-occupied	3,816	4,512	4,955	5,083	5,931	5,899	6,244	6,300

[1] Based on 2000 census controls. [2] Includes other races not shown separately. [3] The 2003 American Housing Survey (AHS) allowed respondents to choose more than one race. Beginning in 2003, data represent householders who selected this race group only and exclude householders reporting more than one race. The AHS in prior years only allowed respondents to report one race group. See also comments on race in the text for Section 1 and the below cited source. [4] Persons of Hispanic origin may be any race.
Source: U.S. Census Bureau, Current Housing Reports, Series H150/91, H150/95RV, H150/99, H150/01, H150/03, H150/05, H150/07, and H150/09, *American Housing Survey for the United States: 2009,* September 2010. See also <http://www.census.gov/hhes/www/housing/ahs/nationaldata.html>.

Table 992. Homeownership Rates by Age of Householder and Household Type: 1990 to 2010

[In percent. Represents the proportion of owner households to the total number of occupied households. Based on the Current Population Survey and Housing Vacancy Survey; see source and Appendix III for details]

Age of householder and household type	1990	1995	2000	2004	2005	2006	2007	2008	2009	2010
United States	**63.9**	**64.7**	**67.4**	**69.0**	**68.9**	**68.8**	**68.1**	**67.8**	**67.4**	**66.9**
AGE OF HOUSEHOLDER										
Less than 25 years old	15.7	15.9	21.7	25.2	25.7	24.8	24.8	23.6	23.3	22.8
25 to 29 years old	35.2	34.4	38.1	40.2	40.9	41.8	40.6	40.0	37.7	36.8
30 to 34 years old	51.8	53.1	54.6	57.4	56.8	55.9	54.4	53.5	52.5	51.6
35 to 39 years old	63.0	62.1	65.0	66.2	66.6	66.4	65.0	64.6	63.4	61.9
40 to 44 years old	69.8	68.6	70.6	71.9	71.7	71.2	70.4	69.4	68.7	67.9
45 to 49 years old	73.9	73.7	74.7	76.3	75.0	74.9	74.0	73.6	72.3	72.0
50 to 54 years old	76.8	77.0	78.5	78.2	78.3	77.7	76.9	76.4	76.5	75.0
55 to 59 years old	78.8	78.8	80.4	81.2	80.6	80.4	79.9	79.4	78.6	77.7
60 to 64 years old	79.8	80.3	80.3	82.4	81.9	81.5	81.5	80.9	80.6	80.4
65 to 69 years old	80.0	81.0	83.0	83.2	82.8	82.4	81.7	81.6	82.0	81.6
70 to 74 years old	78.4	80.9	82.6	84.4	82.9	83.0	82.4	81.7	81.9	82.4
75 years old and over	72.3	74.6	77.7	78.8	78.4	79.1	78.7	78.6	78.9	78.9
Less than 35 years old	38.5	38.6	40.8	43.1	43.0	42.6	41.7	41.0	39.7	39.1
35 to 44 years old	66.3	65.2	67.9	69.2	69.3	68.9	67.8	67.0	66.2	65.0
45 to 54 years old	75.2	75.2	76.5	77.2	76.6	76.2	75.4	75.0	74.4	73.5
55 to 64 years old	79.3	79.5	80.3	81.9	81.2	80.9	80.6	80.1	79.5	79.0
65 years and over	76.3	78.1	80.4	81.1	80.6	80.9	80.4	80.1	80.5	80.5
TYPE OF HOUSEHOLD										
Family households:										
Married-couple families	78.1	79.6	82.4	84.0	84.2	84.1	83.8	83.4	82.8	82.1
Male householder, no spouse present	55.2	55.3	57.5	59.6	59.1	58.9	57.4	57.6	56.9	56.9
Female householder, no spouse present	44.0	45.1	49.1	50.9	51.0	51.3	49.9	49.5	49.0	48.6
Nonfamily households:										
One-person	49.0	50.5	53.6	55.8	55.6	55.7	55.2	55.0	55.1	55.3
Male householder	42.4	43.8	47.4	50.5	50.3	50.5	50.2	50.6	50.9	51.3
Female householder	53.6	55.4	58.1	59.9	59.6	59.8	59.1	58.6	58.6	58.6
Other:										
Male householder	31.7	34.2	38.0	41.7	41.7	40.8	40.0	41.3	40.2	40.7
Female householder	32.5	33.0	40.6	43.5	44.7	45.5	42.9	42.5	42.5	41.9

Source: U.S. Census Bureau, "Housing Vacancies and Home Ownership," <http://www.census.gov/hhes/www/hvs.html>.

Table 993. Homeownership Rates by State: 1990 to 2010

[In percent. See headnote, Table 992]

State	1990	2000	2005	2008	2009	2010	State	1990	2000	2005	2008	2009	2010
United States	**63.9**	**67.4**	**68.9**	**67.8**	**67.4**	**66.9**	Missouri	64.0	74.2	72.3	71.4	72.0	71.2
Alabama	68.4	73.2	76.6	73.0	74.1	73.2	Montana	69.1	70.2	70.4	70.3	70.7	68.1
Alaska	58.4	66.4	66.0	66.4	66.8	65.7	Nebraska	67.3	70.2	70.2	69.6	70.2	70.4
Arizona	64.5	68.0	71.1	69.1	68.9	66.6	Nevada	55.8	64.0	63.4	63.6	62.4	59.7
Arkansas	67.8	68.9	69.2	68.9	68.5	67.9	New Hampshire	65.0	69.2	74.0	75.0	76.0	74.9
California	53.8	57.1	59.7	57.5	57.0	56.1	New Jersey	65.0	66.2	70.1	67.3	65.9	66.5
Colorado	59.0	68.3	71.0	69.0	68.4	68.5	New Mexico	68.6	73.7	71.4	70.4	69.1	68.6
Connecticut	67.9	70.0	70.5	70.7	70.5	70.8	New York	53.3	53.4	55.9	55.0	54.4	54.5
Delaware	67.7	72.0	75.8	76.2	76.5	74.7	North Carolina	69.0	71.1	70.9	69.4	70.1	69.5
Dist. of Columbia	36.4	41.9	45.8	44.1	44.9	45.6	North Dakota	67.2	70.7	68.5	66.6	65.7	67.1
Florida	65.1	68.4	72.4	71.1	70.9	69.3	Ohio	68.7	71.3	73.3	70.8	69.7	69.7
Georgia	64.3	69.8	67.9	68.2	67.4	67.1	Oklahoma	70.3	72.7	72.9	70.4	69.6	69.2
Hawaii	55.5	55.2	59.8	59.1	59.5	56.1	Oregon	64.4	65.3	68.2	66.2	68.2	66.3
Idaho	69.4	70.5	74.2	75.0	75.5	72.4	Pennsylvania	73.8	74.7	73.3	72.6	72.2	72.2
Illinois	63.0	67.9	70.9	68.9	69.1	68.8	Rhode Island	58.5	61.5	63.1	64.5	62.9	62.8
Indiana	67.0	74.9	75.0	74.4	72.0	71.2	South Carolina	71.4	76.5	73.9	73.9	74.4	74.8
Iowa	70.7	75.2	73.9	74.0	72.4	71.1	South Dakota	66.2	71.2	68.4	70.4	69.6	70.6
Kansas	69.0	69.3	69.5	68.8	67.4	67.4	Tennessee	68.3	70.9	72.4	71.7	71.1	71.0
Kentucky	65.8	73.4	71.6	72.8	71.2	70.3	Texas	59.7	63.8	65.9	65.5	65.4	65.3
Louisiana	67.8	68.1	72.5	73.5	71.9	70.4	Utah	70.1	72.7	73.9	76.2	74.1	72.5
Maine	74.2	76.5	73.9	73.9	74.0	73.8	Vermont	72.6	68.7	74.2	72.8	74.3	73.6
Maryland	64.9	69.9	71.2	70.6	69.6	68.9	Virginia	69.8	73.9	71.2	70.6	69.7	68.7
Massachusetts	58.6	59.9	63.4	65.7	65.1	65.3	Washington	61.8	63.6	67.6	66.2	65.5	64.4
Michigan	72.3	77.2	76.4	75.9	74.5	74.5	West Virginia	72.0	75.9	81.3	77.8	78.7	79.0
Minnesota	68.0	76.1	76.5	73.1	72.9	72.6	Wisconsin	68.3	71.8	71.1	70.4	70.4	71.0
Mississippi	69.4	75.2	78.8	75.4	75.5	74.8	Wyoming	68.9	71.0	72.8	73.3	73.8	73.4

Source: U.S. Census Bureau, "Housing Vacancies and Home Ownership," <http://www.census.gov/hhes/www/hvs.html>.

Construction and Housing 621

Table 994. Occupied Housing Units—Costs by Region: 2009

[76,428 represents 76,428,000. As of fall. See headnote, Table 995, for an explanation of housing costs. Based on the American Housing Survey; see Appendix III. For composition of regions, see map, inside front cover]

Category	Number (1,000)					Percent distribution				
	Total units	North-east	Mid-west	South	West	Total units	North-east	Mid-west	South	West
OWNER-OCCUPIED UNITS										
Total..................	76,428	13,378	18,249	29,193	15,607	100.0	100.0	100.0	100.0	100.0
Monthly housing costs:										
Less than $300	2,635	192	430	1,368	647	3.4	1.4	2.4	4.7	4.1
$300 to $399	5,351	366	1,087	3,026	873	7.0	2.7	6.0	10.4	5.6
$400 to $499	6,022	653	1,549	2,835	984	7.9	4.9	8.5	9.7	6.3
$500 to $599	5,308	738	1,528	2,190	852	6.9	5.5	8.4	7.5	5.5
$600 to $699	8,141	1,682	2,093	3,261	1,105	10.7	12.6	11.5	11.2	7.1
$700 to $799	10,736	1,938	3,071	4,275	1,452	14.0	14.5	16.8	14.6	9.3
$800 to $999	14,984	2,578	4,298	5,563	2,545	19.6	19.3	23.6	19.1	16.3
$1,000 to $1,249	14,867	3,193	3,211	4,565	3,898	19.5	23.9	17.6	15.6	25.0
$1,250 to $1,499	8,383	2,039	982	2,111	3,251	11.0	15.2	5.4	7.2	20.8
Median (dol.)[1]	1,000	1,196	937	827	1,389	(X)	(X)	(X)	(X)	(X)
RENTER-OCCUPIED UNITS										
Total..................	35,378	7,073	7,119	12,392	8,794	100.0	100.0	100.0	100.0	100.0
Monthly housing costs:										
Less than $300										
$300 to $399	976	190	267	351	168	2.8	2.7	3.7	2.8	1.9
$400 to $499	1,381	357	333	408	283	3.9	5.1	4.7	3.3	3.2
$500 to $599	1,359	352	371	441	194	3.8	5.0	5.2	3.6	2.2
$600 to $699	2,094	335	616	783	360	5.9	4.7	8.7	6.3	4.1
$700 to $799	6,793	1,055	1,845	2,712	1,181	19.2	14.9	25.9	21.9	13.4
$800 to $999	9,769	1,727	2,082	3,695	2,265	27.6	24.4	29.2	29.8	25.8
$1,000 to $1,249	7,407	1,819	940	2,271	2,377	20.9	25.7	13.2	18.3	27.0
$1,250 to $1,499	2,965	727	222	648	1,368	8.4	10.3	3.1	5.2	15.6
$1,500 or more	596	169	45	137	245	1.7	2.4	0.6	1.1	2.8
No cash rent	2,037	341	398	945	352	5.8	4.8	5.6	7.6	4.0
Median (dol.)[1]	808	877	691	764	956	(X)	(X)	(X)	(X)	(X)

X Not applicable. [1] For explanation of median, see Guide to Tabular Presentation.

Source: U.S. Census Bureau, Current Housing Reports, Series H150/09, *American Housing Survey for the United States: 2009*, September 2010. See also <http://www.census.gov/hhes/www/housing/ahs/nationaldata.html>.

Table 995. Occupied Housing Units—Financial Summary by Selected Characteristics of the Householder: 2009

[In thousands of units (111,806 represents 111,806,000), except as indicated. As of fall, housing costs include real estate taxes, property insurance, utilities, fuel, water, garbage collection, homeowner association fees, mobile home fees, and mortgage. Based on the American Housing Survey; see Appendix III]

Characteristic	Total occupied units	Tenure		Black[1]		Hispanic origin[2]		Elderly[3]		Households below poverty level	
		Owner	Renter	Owner	Renter	Owner	Renter	Owner	Renter	Owner	Renter
Total units[4].............	111,806	76,428	35,378	6,547	7,446	6,439	6,300	18,472	4,623	6,405	9,334
Monthly housing costs:											
$199 or less................	3,611	2,635	976	322	370	253	132	1,119	261	727	760
$200 to $299	6,732	5,351	1,381	467	422	453	200	2,587	461	1,035	895
$300 to $399	7,381	6,022	1,359	499	357	445	172	2,897	364	818	599
$400 to $499	7,402	5,308	2,094	470	420	371	333	2,395	408	611	823
$500 to $699	14,934	8,141	6,793	801	1,569	503	1,165	3,079	827	777	1,929
$700 to $999	20,505	10,736	9,769	1,041	2,106	910	1,900	2,502	883	893	2,057
$1,000 to $1,499	22,391	14,984	7,407	1,313	1,471	1,186	1,508	1,967	533	722	1,166
$1,500 to $2,499	17,832	14,867	2,965	1,099	348	1,418	593	1,233	277	548	331
$2,500 or more	8,980	8,383	596	537	35	900	58	692	129	275	53
Median amount (dol.)[4]	909	1,000	808	901	746	1,113	854	512	640	502	629
Monthly housing costs as percent of income:[5]											
Less than 5 percent	3,065	2,903	162	133	15	171	35	594	23	8	17
5 to 9 percent	10,334	9,614	721	617	105	561	83	2,658	79	49	21
10 to 14 percent...........	13,111	11,147	1,964	842	295	711	256	2,932	170	109	47
15 to 19 percent...........	14,210	10,986	3,224	814	553	719	450	2,410	235	215	87
20 to 24 percent...........	13,271	9,589	3,682	754	697	716	603	1,966	329	191	159
25 to 29 percent...........	10,775	7,167	3,608	625	708	586	615	1,481	494	262	366
30 to 34 percent...........	8,116	5,160	2,956	488	651	579	606	1,024	370	282	360
35 to 39 percent..........	6,071	3,753	2,317	429	525	370	388	818	312	242	322
40 percent or more........	28,695	15,250	13,445	1,743	3,181	1,921	2,808	4,478	2,063	4,245	6,138
Median amount (percent)[6] ..	24	21	34	25	38	27	38	21	40	89	82

[1] For persons who selected this race group only. See footnote 3, Table 991. [2] Persons of Hispanic origin may be of any race. [3] Householders 65 years old and over. [4] Include units with no cash, not shown separately. [5] Money income before taxes. [6] For explanation of median, see Guide to Tabular Presentation.

Source: U.S. Census Bureau, Current Housing Reports, Series H150/09, *American Housing Survey for the United States: 2009*, September 2010. See also <http://www.census.gov/hhes/www/housing/ahs/nationaldata.html>.

Table 996. Owner-Occupied Housing Units—Value and Costs by State: 2009

[In percent, except as indicated (74,843 represents 74,843,000). The American Community Survey universe includes the household population and the population living in institutions, college dormitories, and other group quarters. Based on a sample and subject to sampling variability; see Appendix III. For definition of median, see Guide to Tabular Presentation]

State	Total (1,000)	Percent of units with value of—			Median value (dol.)	Median selected monthly owner costs [1] (dol.)	Selected monthly owner costs as a percent income in the past 12 months			
		$99,999 or less	$100,000 to $199,999	$200,000 or more			Less than 15 percent	15.0 to 24.9 percent	25.0 to 29.9 percent	30.0 percent or more
U.S.	74,843	23.3	30.4	46.3	185,200	1,111	16.9	32.8	12.4	37.5
AL	1,286	41.9	33.7	24.4	119,600	751	22.2	36.4	11.4	29.5
AK	154	13.1	23.8	63.1	232,900	1,384	17.3	35.6	14.0	32.8
AZ	1,527	18.3	35.7	46.0	187,700	1,158	14.6	30.9	12.8	40.9
AR	743	48.7	33.7	17.6	102,900	653	26.9	35.3	10.4	27.1
CA	6,910	7.2	12.5	80.3	384,200	1,852	10.7	24.4	12.2	52.2
CO	1,280	10.2	27.0	62.8	237,800	1,352	16.1	34.2	13.6	35.7
CT	913	3.8	19.3	76.9	291,200	1,708	13.5	32.2	13.5	40.5
DE	241	9.7	24.7	65.7	249,400	1,234	17.2	33.2	13.3	36.0
DC	112	2.2	5.0	92.7	443,700	1,841	19.6	30.9	10.0	38.9
FL	4,785	21.0	34.4	44.6	182,400	1,125	11.7	26.5	11.9	49.2
GA	2,326	23.7	39.6	36.7	162,800	1,092	17.9	33.6	12.0	35.9
HI	253	3.3	4.1	92.6	517,600	1,672	12.5	26.7	11.2	49.2
ID	399	16.7	44.6	38.8	171,700	957	16.4	34.0	12.5	36.6
IL	3,235	20.4	29.0	50.6	202,200	1,267	15.6	33.0	12.8	38.2
IN	1,745	37.2	42.2	20.6	123,100	896	22.7	37.9	11.7	27.4
IA	884	38.5	40.1	21.4	122,000	821	24.1	40.8	11.6	23.3
KS	749	39.5	36.8	23.7	125,500	883	22.6	41.0	11.0	25.2
KY	1,163	41.4	37.2	21.4	117,800	737	22.8	37.7	11.1	27.9
LA	1,147	36.8	37.0	26.2	135,400	694	26.2	34.7	10.1	28.6
ME	396	21.8	36.1	42.0	177,500	952	17.5	32.9	13.1	36.3
MD	1,436	6.2	14.2	79.6	318,600	1,689	15.6	32.1	13.5	38.5
MA	1,589	3.3	11.9	84.7	338,500	1,694	14.3	32.2	13.3	40.0
MI	2,796	34.8	39.9	25.4	132,200	1,002	16.1	33.8	12.9	36.6
MN	1,537	15.2	34.6	50.1	200,400	1,204	16.6	35.6	13.9	33.6
MS	761	50.9	30.7	18.4	98,000	654	20.8	34.4	11.2	33.1
MO	1,616	32.4	39.9	27.7	139,700	884	21.2	37.6	11.7	29.1
MT	260	25.0	32.4	42.6	176,300	783	18.2	35.0	11.6	34.7
NE	478	36.4	44.0	19.6	123,300	904	21.0	39.8	13.6	25.4
NV	572	14.1	33.5	52.4	207,600	1,471	12.0	27.0	13.3	47.1
NH	367	8.8	23.9	67.4	249,700	1,495	11.8	32.5	14.2	41.1
NJ	2,087	4.4	11.8	83.8	348,300	1,922	11.5	27.6	13.8	46.8
NM	515	28.4	35.0	36.6	160,900	763	21.9	33.2	10.2	34.2
NY	3,955	17.7	19.4	62.9	306,000	1,352	17.3	30.1	11.4	40.9
NC	2,450	27.4	38.1	34.5	155,500	940	19.7	35.6	12.0	32.3
ND	184	42.2	39.8	17.9	116,800	714	28.6	40.0	9.7	21.3
OH	3,080	31.9	43.9	24.2	134,600	975	18.6	37.3	12.7	31.1
OK	961	46.2	36.6	17.2	107,700	716	26.1	37.4	10.2	25.8
OR	937	10.8	20.5	68.7	257,400	1,246	13.3	31.0	14.0	41.5
PA	3,467	27.8	33.2	39.0	164,700	979	19.0	35.4	12.8	32.6
RI	258	4.1	19.2	76.8	267,100	1,542	12.7	30.1	13.8	43.3
SC	1,214	35.2	34.6	30.2	137,500	812	20.8	34.9	11.7	32.1
SD	215	38.4	38.8	22.8	126,200	769	22.2	38.2	13.9	25.6
TN	1,692	33.1	39.1	27.7	137,300	835	18.2	35.9	12.5	32.9
TX	5,431	37.3	38.0	24.8	125,800	1,005	20.2	36.4	11.8	31.2
UT	617	7.5	33.0	59.4	224,700	1,200	16.8	33.3	14.0	35.4
VT	179	12.3	31.5	56.2	216,300	1,183	13.6	32.9	15.0	38.1
VA	2,025	13.2	23.6	63.2	252,600	1,335	16.8	33.8	13.0	36.0
WA	1,646	8.3	18.4	73.3	287,200	1,420	13.3	31.1	14.2	40.9
WV	551	52.9	30.9	16.2	94,500	490	29.9	35.7	9.9	24.2
WI	1,567	17.7	43.5	38.8	170,800	1,109	15.4	36.5	13.4	34.5
WY	151	20.8	35.2	44.0	184,000	869	22.6	37.9	12.3	26.7

[1] For homes with a mortgage. Includes all forms of debt where the property is pledged as security for repayment of the debt, including deeds of trust, land contracts, home equity loans. Also includes cost of property insurance, utilities, real estate taxes, etc.

Source: U.S. Census Bureau, 2009 American Community Survey, B25075, "Value for Owner-Occupied Housing Units"; B25077, "Median Value for Owner-Occupied Housing Units"; B25088, "Median Selected Monthly Owner Costs by Mortgage Status"; and B25091, "Mortgage Status by Selected Monthly Owner Cost as a Percentage of Household Income," <http://factfinder.census.gov>, accessed May 2011.

Table 997. Renter-Occupied Housing Units—Gross Rent by State: 2009

[In percent, except as indicated (38,773 represents 38,773,000). The American Community Survey universe includes the household population and the population living in institutions, college dormitories, and other group quarters. Based on a sample and subject to sampling variability; see Appendix III]

State	Total [1] (1,000)	Percent of units with gross rent of— $299 or less	$300 to $499	$500 to $749	$750 to $999	$1,000 or more	Median gross rent (dol.)	Gross rent as a percent of household income in the past 12 months [2] Less than 15.0 percent	15.0 to 24.9 percent	25.0 to 29.0 percent	30.0 percent or more
U.S....	38,773	5.3	9.2	23.6	22.8	33.4	842	10.9	23.1	10.8	47.7
AL	562	7.6	16.4	31.4	20.7	12.2	657	10.7	21.2	9.5	44.2
AK	82	1.5	5.5	13.5	23.9	45.3	1,007	14.1	28.1	10.6	36.6
AZ	750	3.1	6.9	25.3	25.4	34.3	859	10.8	23.5	10.3	48.0
AR	382	9.1	19.1	36.8	16.6	8.4	606	12.6	23.9	9.1	42.8
CA	5,305	2.9	3.8	10.7	19.6	59.8	1,155	8.8	22.2	11.5	52.8
CO	630	3.6	6.4	26.5	25.6	34.1	851	9.6	23.4	11.5	49.3
CT	413	5.9	6.2	11.5	23.8	48.4	1,006	10.6	22.6	11.3	49.4
DE	86	4.4	5.7	16.1	28.1	41.3	949	11.1	23.1	10.5	49.9
DC	138	8.5	5.1	11.4	20.1	52.5	1,059	13.0	21.9	13.4	46.7
FL	2,203	3.2	4.3	17.0	28.3	41.9	952	6.5	19.8	10.6	55.9
GA	1,143	5.3	9.6	26.1	27.3	25.3	800	9.7	22.7	10.9	47.6
HI	193	3.4	3.3	9.0	13.7	64.1	1,293	8.3	20.7	10.3	52.3
ID	159	4.9	13.6	35.2	21.5	16.8	694	10.8	25.3	10.8	44.0
IL	1,522	5.3	8.9	24.1	27.7	29.6	828	12.0	22.9	10.7	47.4
IN	733	5.8	13.6	36.5	24.1	13.8	687	11.6	23.9	10.9	45.3
IA	343	7.6	20.8	38.0	17.6	9.2	611	16.0	25.6	10.0	40.2
KS	356	5.9	17.9	33.7	20.6	15.4	671	14.6	26.2	9.9	41.9
KY	531	9.6	18.6	34.6	16.8	9.7	613	13.0	22.5	9.7	41.7
LA	541	6.9	12.9	29.4	22.8	17.4	715	12.5	20.3	9.8	44.3
ME	149	8.9	12.2	28.1	22.8	19.6	722	9.4	22.5	12.1	46.5
MD	659	4.7	4.3	9.7	20.0	57.3	1,108	9.9	24.2	11.3	49.2
MA	886	8.6	8.3	13.0	19.3	47.3	988	10.9	25.0	12.8	46.3
MI	1,024	6.5	11.6	33.5	24.0	19.0	716	10.3	20.5	10.0	51.6
MN	548	7.9	10.8	27.9	23.8	24.4	757	11.0	23.8	12.1	46.8
MS	334	8.8	15.7	29.9	19.4	11.4	644	10.2	19.1	9.1	44.1
MO	723	7.1	15.3	34.9	22.1	13.7	668	13.2	24.4	10.9	43.1
MT	116	8.6	17.6	34.4	17.6	10.5	627	14.9	22.9	11.2	38.2
NE	233	6.7	17.6	37.2	20.6	10.8	644	14.4	27.9	10.4	39.1
NV	394	1.9	3.6	15.8	28.0	47.7	993	9.4	25.8	10.5	49.9
NH	139	6.4	6.6	14.5	28.4	38.6	918	9.5	25.7	12.4	45.8
NJ	1,068	5.1	3.8	8.9	20.7	58.3	1,108	10.5	24.2	10.4	49.9
NM	228	6.8	13.9	34.0	18.7	18.2	680	13.9	23.0	10.0	42.2
NY	3,232	5.9	7.7	16.6	19.2	47.0	984	12.9	22.3	10.6	48.8
NC	1,196	5.5	11.9	32.6	25.2	16.5	720	11.2	22.6	10.2	45.6
ND	95	9.7	27.4	36.0	13.0	5.9	564	19.5	26.5	8.4	36.7
OH	1,446	7.5	15.3	35.0	22.7	14.1	670	12.2	23.3	10.6	46.0
OK	469	6.1	18.3	35.1	20.0	10.8	636	14.2	23.5	9.5	41.4
OR	549	3.5	7.2	27.4	30.4	27.1	819	9.5	25.0	10.9	48.5
PA	1,450	6.9	12.3	29.2	24.1	21.4	738	12.0	24.7	11.0	44.2
RI	149	10.0	8.6	16.3	27.4	34.2	890	10.3	23.1	13.4	46.9
SC	517	5.6	12.1	32.9	23.2	16.0	706	11.4	21.3	10.0	44.9
SD	102	12.5	22.2	32.5	12.9	9.3	562	15.5	24.9	11.3	36.2
TN	755	7.2	13.7	34.2	21.7	14.5	682	10.8	22.7	10.3	45.5
TX	3,097	4.1	8.5	29.9	26.2	25.2	788	11.5	24.4	10.6	45.5
UT	246	4.3	8.3	28.9	25.4	28.2	793	11.4	25.7	10.9	45.8
VT	72	8.1	7.2	23.7	25.3	28.9	829	7.5	25.0	12.3	47.2
VA	947	4.4	6.1	17.1	20.2	46.2	989	9.4	25.7	11.5	45.6
WA	914	3.8	6.3	20.5	26.3	39.0	911	9.9	25.1	12.2	47.3
WV	197	11.1	23.6	32.0	12.5	6.3	552	13.7	19.0	10.1	40.5
WI	705	5.2	12.5	36.5	25.3	16.1	708	12.4	26.0	10.7	45.3
WY	62	6.4	14.4	30.0	22.5	15.9	700	18.6	26.3	10.3	32.8

[1] Includes units with no cash rent. [2] Does not include units "not computed."

Source: U.S. Census Bureau, 2009 American Community Survey, B25063, "Gross Rent"; B25064, "Median Gross Rent"; and B25070, "Gross Rent as a Percentage of Household Income," <http://factfinder.census.gov>, accessed May 2011.

Table 998. Mortgage Characteristics—Owner-Occupied Units: 2009

[In thousands (76,428 represents 76,428,000). As of fall. Based on the American Housing Survey; see Appendix III]

Mortgage characteristic	Total owner occupied units (1,000)	Housing unit characteristics		Household characteristics			
		New construc-tion [1]	Mobile homes	Black [2]	His-panic [3]	Elderly [4]	Below poverty level
ALL OWNERS							
Total	**76,428**	**3,830**	**5,418**	**6,547**	**6,439**	**18,472**	**6,405**
Mortgages currently on property: [5]							
None, owned free and clear	24,206	499	3,237	2,073	1,752	12,071	3,466
Regular and home equity mortgages [6]	50,300	3,251	2,107	4,338	4,525	5,804	2,710
Regular mortgage	46,703	3,174	2,002	4,153	4,325	4,604	2,509
Home equity lump sum mortgage	4,022	154	57	241	300	522	156
Home equity line of credit	9,184	297	106	426	579	1,527	334
Number of regular and home equity mortgages:							
1 mortgage	35,274	2,391	1,830	3,329	3,307	4,322	1,940
2 mortgages	10,896	621	98	646	928	833	321
3 mortgages or more	801	20	2	43	67	76	25
Type of mortgage:							
Regular and home equity lump sum	2,779	131	20	152	215	189	76
With home equity line of credit	429	11	2	16	40	52	10
No home equity line of credit	2,341	120	17	135	173	137	65
Regular no home equity lump sum	43,923	3,043	1,982	4,001	4,110	4,415	2,433
With home equity line of credit	6,153	230	36	294	407	527	189
No home equity line of credit	34,513	2,594	1,773	3,390	3,486	3,330	1,835
Home equity lump sum no regular	1,243	22	37	89	85	333	80
With home equity line of credit	248	2	–	20	17	80	14
No home equity line of credit	989	20	37	69	68	252	67
No regular or home equity lump sum	28,483	634	3,379	2,305	2,029	13,535	3,816
With home equity line of credit	2,355	54	68	96	115	867	121
No home equity line of credit	24,458	501	3,247	2,089	1,776	12,312	3,502
OWNERS WITH ONE OR MORE REGULAR OR LUMP SUM HOME EQUITY MORTGAGES							
Total	**47,945**	**3,197**	**2,039**	**4,242**	**4,410**	**4,936**	**2,589**
Type of primary mortgage:							
FHA	6,272	457	112	1,038	801	443	352
VA	3,660	273	207	316	312	356	140
RHS/RD	435	63	36	51	51	49	41
Other types	34,021	2,161	1,490	2,449	3,001	3,463	1,603
Mortgage origination:							
Placed new mortgage(s)	47,616	3,188	2,007	4,212	4,344	4,891	2,556
Primary obtained when property acquired	35,884	3,005	1,744	3,436	3,570	3,010	2,075
Obtained later	11,733	183	263	776	773	1,881	481
Assumed	259	8	28	19	51	40	25
Wrap-around	27	–	4	4	8	–	3
Combination of the above	43	–	–	7	8	5	6
Payment plan of primary mortgage:							
Fixed payment, self amortizing	40,055	2,664	1,713	3,472	3,686	3,820	1,861
Adjustable rate mortgage	1,942	80	58	201	238	187	97
Adjustable term mortgage	80	14	3	3	5	26	15
Graduated payment mortgage	523	48	–	48	62	26	17
Balloon	220	10	14	5	16	21	13
Combination of the above	169	9	–	9	14	21	5
Payment plan of secondary mortgage:							
Units with two or more mortgages	5,520	418	67	404	601	309	159
Fixed payment, self amortizing	4,514	359	58	342	482	221	117
Adjustable rate mortgage	393	15	–	32	53	32	16
Adjustable term mortgage	71	1	–	1	3	15	3
Graduated payment mortgage	71	10	–	3	16	6	–
Balloon	143	20	4	6	8	12	4
Other	2	–	–	–	–	–	–
Combination of the above	101	9	–	–	4	1	6
Reason primary refinanced:							
Units with a refinanced primary mortgage [6]	12,220	224	269	792	947	1,337	429
To get a lower interest rate	9,228	174	172	563	666	832	246
To increase payment period	180	4	9	4	16	6	11
To reduce payment period	573	5	9	25	40	37	19
To renew or extend a loan that has fallen due	123	3	2	7	15	20	8
To receive cash	1,587	16	32	147	153	265	72
Other reason	1,655	32	58	96	170	211	65
Cash received in primary mortgage refinance:							
Units receiving refinance cash	1,587	16	32	147	153	265	72
Median amount received (dol.)	30,000	(B)	(B)	18,000	40,000	50,000	25,000

– Represents or rounds to zero. B means sample too small. [1] Constructed in the past 4 years. [2] For persons who selected this race group only. See footnote 3, Table 991. [3] Persons of Hispanic origin may be any race. [4] 65 years old and over. [5] Regular mortgages include all mortgages not classified as home-equity or reverse. [6] Figures may not add to total because more than one category may apply to a unit.

Source: U.S. Census Bureau, Current Housing Reports, Series H150/09, *American Housing Survey for the United States: 2009*, September 2010. See also <http://www.census.gov/hhes/www/housing/ahs/nationaldata.html>.

Construction and Housing 625

Table 999. Home Purchase Loans by Race and Sex: 2009

[Applications in thousands (2,311 represents 2,311,000). Amount in millions of dollars (471,442 represents $471,442,000,000). Data is the final 2009 National Aggregates data]

Race and Gender [1,2,3]	Applications received		Loans originated		Applications approved not accepted		Applications denied		Applications withdrawn		Files closed for incompleteness	
	Number (1,000)	Amount (million dollars)	Number (1,000)	Amount (million dollars)	Number (1,000)	Amount (million dollars)	Number (1,000)	Amount (million dollars)	Number (1,000)	Amount (million dollars)	Number (1,000)	Amount (million dollars)
Total	2,311	471,442	1,461	309,063	168	34,704	408	66,698	220	49,116	53	11,862
White	1,718	331,865	1,121	224,268	123	23,644	287	44,572	153	32,179	34	7,203
Male	559	102,043	343	64,431	42	7,589	109	16,647	53	10,730	13	2,646
Female	362	53,925	226	35,400	26	3,775	70	8,278	32	5,251	8	1,221
Joint (male/female)	794	175,111	549	124,015	55	12,206	108	19,508	68	16,070	14	3,312
Black	90	12,256	37	5,690	8	984	35	3,739	8	1,386	3	457
Male	31	4,302	12	1,905	3	372	12	1,318	3	526	1	182
Female	39	4,488	15	2,025	3	338	16	1,491	3	473	1	162
Joint (male/female)	20	3,410	9	1,739	2	266	7	913	2	380	1	111
Asian	177	48,410	112	30,662	14	4,161	26	6,825	19	5,266	5	1,495
Male	69	17,558	43	10,848	6	1,504	11	2,640	7	1,960	2	606
Female	40	9,203	25	5,731	3	824	6	1,394	4	974	1	280
Joint (male/female)	67	21,500	44	14,010	5	1,816	9	2,762	7	2,310	2	602
Native Hawaiian/Other Pacific Islander	7	1,490	4	863	1	114	2	300	1	165	–	49
Male	3	563	1	321	–	38	1	122	–	65	–	18
Female	2	344	1	191	–	28	–	78	–	35	–	12
Joint (male/female)	2	573	1	346	–	47	–	98	–	63	–	19
American Indian/Alaska Native	13	1,717	6	858	1	123	4	396	2	281	–	60
Male	5	720	2	351	–	46	2	176	1	117	–	29
Female	4	421	1	194	–	29	1	118	–	66	–	13
Joint (male/female)	3	502	1	272	–	40	1	98	–	76	–	15
Two or more minority races	1	268	1	144	–	23	–	60	–	36	–	5
Male	0	102	–	52	–	7	–	28	–	12	–	3
Female	0	67	–	35	–	5	–	16	–	9	–	1
Joint (male/female)	0	95	–	55	–	10	–	15	–	14	–	–
Joint [4]	32	8,433	21	5,718	2	644	5	1,041	3	848	1	182
Race Not Available [5]	272	67,002	161	40,860	19	5,012	49	9,766	35	8,954	9	2,411
Male	37	8,439	19	4,613	3	730	8	1,570	5	1,245	1	281
Female	23	4,198	12	2,288	2	337	6	818	3	618	1	135
Joint (male/female)	47	13,042	29	8,322	4	996	7	1,708	6	1,686	1	330

– Rounds to zero. [1] Applicants are shown in only one race category. [2] Total includes those cases in which gender was reported and that information was not available. [3] Applicants are shown in only one gender category. [4] "Joint" means with two applicants, one reported a single designation of "White" and the other applicant reports one or more minority racial designations. [5] "Not Available" includes situations where information was reported as not provided or not applicable.

Source: Federal Financial Institutions Examination Council, "HMDA National Aggregate Report", annual, <http://www.ffiec.gov/hmdaadwebreport/nataggwelcome.aspx>.

Table 1000. Occupied Housing Units—Neighborhood Indicators by Selected Characteristics of the Householder: 2009

[In thousands (111,806 represents 111,806,000). As of fall. Based on the American Housing Survey; see Appendix III]

Characteristic	Total occupied units	Tenure		Black [1]		Hispanic origin [2]		Elderly [3]		Households below poverty level	
		Owner	Renter	Owner	Renter	Owner	Renter	Owner	Renter	Owner	Renter
Total units	**111,806**	**76,428**	**35,378**	**6,547**	**7,446**	**6,439**	**6,300**	**18,472**	**4,623**	**6,405**	**9,334**
Street noise or traffic present: Bothersome street noise or heavy traffic present [4]	111,806	76,428	35,378	6,547	7,446	6,439	6,300	18,472	4,623	6,405	9,334
Yes	25,381	15,223	10,158	1,639	2,460	1,419	1,725	3,497	1,077	1,549	3,110
No	85,122	60,264	24,858	4,836	4,895	4,972	4,545	14,744	3,498	4,692	6,119
Neighborhood crime present: Serious crime in past 12 months..................	111,806	76,428	35,378	6,547	7,446	6,439	6,300	18,472	4,623	6,405	9,334
Yes	19,299	11,649	7,650	1,428	2,045	1,223	1,403	2,105	658	951	2,254
No	90,116	63,230	26,886	4,958	5,146	5,129	4,814	15,983	3,853	5,194	6,813
Odors present .... Bothersome smoke, gas, or bad smell [4]	111,806	76,428	35,378	6,547	7,446	6,439	6,300	18,472	4,623	6,405	9,334
Yes	5,434	3,278	2,156	330	614	367	359	663	164	389	727
No	105,015	72,168	32,847	6,142	6,749	6,024	5,907	17,567	4,408	5,843	8,505
Other problems:											
Noise	2,950	1,733	1,217	176	296	165	217	382	95	156	340
Litter or housing deterioration ...	1,691	1,101	590	196	203	85	127	266	43	121	213
Poor city or county services.....	694	440	254	80	101	49	37	70	21	72	89
People	4,521	2,706	1,815	298	460	269	297	510	115	249	630
Public transportation: [4]											
With public transportation	60,257	35,616	24,641	3,719	5,856	3,998	4,996	8,283	3,245	2,815	6,562
Household uses public transportation regularly for commuting to school or work	10,212	3,817	6,395	720	1,959	569	1,682	582	564	308	2,089
Household does not use public transportation regularly for commuting to school or work.	49,681	31,606	18,075	2,963	3,838	3,411	3,285	7,679	2,670	2,473	4,427
No public transportation.	48,532	38,848	9,684	2,689	1,438	2,309	1,217	9,728	1,236	3,337	2,522
Not reported	3,017	1,964	1,053	138	152	132	88	461	142	254	250
Police protection:											
Satisfactory	101,373	69,633	31,740	5,837	6,325	5,742	5,623	16,929	4,294	5,501	8,025
Unsatisfactory	7,356	4,800	2,556	516	835	568	543	1,051	193	608	990
Secured communities: [5] Community access secured with walls or fences	10,759	5,337	5,422	367	1,371	656	1,336	1,512	827	440	1,392
Community access not secured	100,124	70,410	29,714	6,124	6,028	5,736	4,930	16,783	3,758	5,831	7,865
Secured multiunits:											
Multiunit access secured.......	7,211	1,357	5,854	106	1,301	135	998	454	1,426	118	1,503
Multiunit access not secured....	16,741	2,151	14,590	216	3,406	237	2,749	608	1,567	163	4,129
Senior citizen communities: Households with persons 55 years old and over.........	45,684	36,591	9,093	3,132	1,842	2,451	1,255	18,472	4,623	3,763	2,645
Community age restricted [6]	3,080	1,457	1,624	89	300	71	169	1,079	1,374	194	588
Access to structure:											
Enter building from outside [4,7] ...	25,915	3,734	22,181	351	5,056	401	4,212	1,142	3,314	321	6,136
Use of steps not required	9,771	1,532	8,239	91	1,915	186	1,519	565	1,780	149	2,386
Use of steps required	16,136	2,201	13,935	260	3,141	216	2,690	577	1,529	172	3,750
Enter home from outside [8]	85,891	72,694	13,197	6,196	2,391	6,038	2,089	17,330	1,309	6,084	3,198
Use of steps not required	38,011	32,654	5,357	2,706	951	3,354	950	8,253	551	2,668	1,231
Use of steps required	47,752	39,928	7,824	3,487	1,439	2,681	1,139	9,048	751	3,406	1,956
Community quality:											
Some or all activities present....	49,962	33,117	16,845	2,570	3,392	2,547	2,647	8,356	2,731	2,468	4,197
Community center or clubhouse	24,410	14,707	9,703	1,181	2,078	1,127	1,347	4,306	1,888	1,177	2,346
Golf in the community	16,709	12,762	3,947	611	471	694	499	3,410	604	832	880
Trails in the community	21,609	15,300	6,309	983	1,017	1,099	876	3,509	826	981	1,369
Shuttle bus.................	9,933	5,718	4,215	422	702	536	713	2,033	1,258	482	1,161
Daycare...................	15,883	10,633	5,249	1,157	1,297	795	934	2,392	546	822	1,568
Private or restricted beach, park, or shoreline.	21,432	15,124	6,308	925	1,053	1,158	1,145	3,327	731	964	1,466
Trash, litter, or junk on street: [9]											
None	99,010	69,415	29,595	5,639	5,764	5,752	5,211	17,001	4,172	5,507	7,264
Minor accumulation	7,250	3,491	3,759	505	1,064	342	738	673	283	396	1,366
Major accumulation	2,519	1,426	1,093	201	351	193	235	318	72	187	437

[1] For persons who selected this race group only. See footnote 3, Table 991. [2] Persons of Hispanic origin may be of any race. [3] Householders 65 years old and over. [4] Includes those not reporting. [5] Public access is restricted (walls, gates, private security). [6] At least one family member must be 55 years old or older. [7] Restricted to multiunits. [8] Restricted to single units. [9] Or on any properties within 300 feet.

Source: U.S. Census Bureau, Current Housing Reports, Series H150/09, *American Housing Survey for the United States: 2009*, September 2010. See also <http://www.census.gov/hhes/www/housing/ahs/nationaldata.html>.

Table 1001. Heating Equipment and Fuels for Occupied Units: 1995 to 2009

[97,693 represents 97,693,000. As of fall. Based on American Housing Survey. See Appendix III]

Type of equipment or fuel	Number (1,000)					Percent distribution	
	1995	2003 [1]	2005	2007	2009	2007	2009
Occupied units, total....................	**97,693**	**105,842**	**108,871**	**110,692**	**111,806**	**100.0**	**100.0**
Heating equipment:							
Warm air furnace.........................	53,165	65,380	68,275	69,582	71,141	62.9	63.6
Steam or hot water	13,669	13,257	12,880	12,760	12,506	11.5	11.2
Heat pumps	9,406	11,347	12,484	12,996	13,264	11.7	11.9
Built-in electric units....................	7,035	4,760	4,699	4,802	4,761	4.3	4.3
Floor, wall, or pipeless furnace	4,963	5,322	5,102	4,994	4,802	4.5	4.3
Room heaters with flue...................	1,620	1,432	1,294	1,135	950	1.0	0.8
Room heaters without flue.................	1,642	1,509	1,327	1,188	1,109	1.1	1.0
Fireplaces, stoves, portable heaters or other ...	5,150	2,396	2,411	2,756	2,887	2.5	2.6
None	1,044	439	399	478	386	0.4	0.3
House main heating fuel:							
Electricity..............................	26,771	32,341	34,263	36,079	37,851	32.6	33.9
Utility gas..............................	49,203	54,928	56,317	56,681	56,806	51.2	50.8
Bottled, tank, or LP gas..................	4,251	6,134	6,228	6,095	5,817	5.5	5.2
Fuel oil, kerosene, etc	12,029	10,136	9,929	9,317	8,813	8.4	7.9
Coal or coke	210	126	95	91	98	(Z)	0.1
Wood and other fuel	4,186	1,735	1,640	1,487	2,035	1.3	1.8
None	1,042	441	398	464	386	0.4	0.3
Cooking fuel:							
Electricity..............................	57,621	62,859	65,297	66,276	67,078	59.9	60.0
Gas [2]	39,218	42,612	43,316	44,194	44,477	39.9	39.8
Other fuel..............................	566	62	51	26	68	(Z)	0.1
None	287	309	206	17	183	(Z)	0.2

Z Less than 0.05 percent. [1] Based on 2000 census controls. [2] Includes utility, bottled, tank, and LP gas.
Source: U.S. Census Bureau, Current Housing Reports, Series H150/95RV, H150/03, H150/05, H150/07, and H150/09, *American Housing Survey for the United States: 2009*, September 2010. See also <http://www.census.gov/hhes/www /housing/ahs/nationaldata.html>.

Table 1002. Occupied Housing Units—Housing Indicators by Selected Characteristics of the Householder: 2009

[In thousands of units (111,806 represents 111,806,000) As of fall. Based on the American Housing Survey; see Appendix III]

Characteristic	Total occupied units (1,000)	Tenure		Black [1]		Hispanic origin [2]		Elderly [3]		Households below poverty level	
		Owner	Renter	Owner	Renter	Owner	Renter	Owner	Renter	Owner	Renter
Total units..................	**111,806**	**76,428**	**35,378**	**6,547**	**7,446**	**6,439**	**6,300**	**18,472**	**4,623**	**6,405**	**9,334**
Amenities:											
Porch, deck, balcony or patio	95,406	70,421	24,984	5,668	5,049	5,732	4,066	16,876	2,836	5,690	6,164
Telephone available	109,325	75,129	34,196	6,388	7,114	6,329	6,123	18,286	4,498	6,245	8,933
Usable fireplace.................	38,998	34,458	4,540	2,207	659	2,222	625	7,563	314	1,799	626
Separate dining room	53,676	43,717	9,959	3,975	2,298	3,372	1,780	10,171	1,012	2,982	2,163
rooms or rec. rooms	33,912	30,978	2,934	2,156	421	1,773	298	6,842	250	1,444	350
Garage or carport with home.......	74,236	60,979	13,258	4,257	1,937	5,030	2,382	14,988	1,563	4,275	2,592
Cars and trucks available:											
No cars, trucks, or vans...........	8,738	2,069	6,669	400	2,141	159	1,238	1,251	1,834	743	3,203
Other households without cars	13,421	9,006	4,415	609	674	934	974	1,789	340	999	1,082
1 car with or without trucks or vans ..	52,458	35,040	17,418	3,111	3,523	2,663	2,824	10,616	2,095	3,352	4,121
2 cars........................	28,103	22,384	5,719	1,842	951	1,843	1,027	3,935	320	1,081	791
3 or more cars	9,085	7,929	1,157	584	156	839	236	882	35	231	136
Selected deficiencies:											
Signs of rats in last 3 months	613	354	258	36	87	58	82	96	15	59	90
Signs of mice in last 3 months......	6,122	3,984	2,138	356	549	239	464	915	225	445	689
Holes in floors	1,141	581	560	78	177	61	116	115	42	119	223
Open cracks or holes............	5,517	3,101	2,416	383	617	288	402	496	149	433	862
paint (interior of unit)............	2,378	1,246	1,132	189	306	101	210	269	74	183	423
No electrical wiring	84	57	26	–	2	10	7	2	2	11	4
Exposed wiring	355	221	134	37	31	23	27	52	27	34	46
Rooms without electric outlet.......	1,274	650	624	88	187	58	121	151	56	86	232
Water leakage from inside structure [4].................	9,007	5,170	3,836	480	958	443	620	861	262	424	1,059
Water leakage from outside structure [4]..............	10,963	7,842	3,121	808	667	562	434	1,548	230	746	874

– Represents or rounds to zero. [1] For persons who selected this race group only. See footnote 3, Table 991. [2] Persons of Hispanic origin may be any race. [3] Householders 65 years old and over. [4] During the 12 months prior to the survey.
Source: U.S. Census Bureau, Current Housing Reports, Series H150/09, *American Housing Survey for the United States: 2009*, September 2010. See also <http://www.census.gov/hhes/www/housing/ahs/nationaldata.html>.

Table 1003. Home Remodeling—Number of Households With Work Done by Amount Spent: 2010

[In thousands, except percent (2,535 represents 2,535,000). As of fall 2010. For work done in the prior 12 months. Based on household survey and subject to sampling error; see source]

Remodeling project	Total households with work done [1]		Households with work done by outside contractor	Number of households by amount spent (dol.)		
	Number	Percent of households		Under $1,000	$1,000 to $2,999	Over $3,000
Conversion of garage/attic/basement into living space	2,535	1.11	706	597	410	983
Remodel bathroom	14,511	6.36	4,231	5,885	3,167	2,973
Remodel kitchen	8,452	3.71	3,097	2,732	1,240	3,062
Remodel bedroom	7,146	3.13	1,196	4,138	1,032	451
Convert room to home office	3,105	1.36	256	1,927	277	66
Convert room to home theater	723	0.32	125	268	201	103
Remodel other rooms	5,862	2.57	1,042	2,887	893	1,079
Add bathroom	1,062	0.47	205	330	132	247
Add/extend garage	481	0.21	110	141	32	164
Add other rooms—exterior addition	1,086	0.48	307	256	164	435
Add deck/porch/patio	5,414	2.37	1,654	1,633	1,433	1,315
Roofing	8,224	3.61	5,154	1,654	1,478	3,842
Siding—vinyl/metal	2,193	0.96	1,046	373	293	907
Aluminum windows	1,589	0.70	759	350	346	433
Clad-wood/wood windows	875	0.38	468	274	115	399
Vinyl windows	4,719	2.07	2,555	1,212	950	1,625
Ceramic tile floors	6,659	2.92	2,377	3,276	1,664	514
Hardwood floors	4,962	2.18	1,928	1,392	1,455	1,068
Laminate flooring	4,700	2.06	1,162	2,428	874	485
Vinyl flooring	2,785	1.22	864	1,809	239	114
Carpeting	7,189	3.15	4,126	2,399	2,147	1,057
Kitchen cabinets	4,400	1.93	1,782	1,081	792	1,420
Kitchen counter tops	4,911	2.15	2,553	1,327	983	1,456
Skylights	787	0.35	383	289	49	79
Exterior doors	5,672	2.49	2,186	3,092	1,009	273
Interior doors	4,544	1.99	1,388	2,419	676	234
Garage doors	2,649	1.16	1,500	1,188	796	54
Concrete or masonry work	3,883	1.70	1,922	1,788	734	665
Swimming pool—inground	560	0.25	277	137	36	294
Wall paneling	1,327	0.58	187	672	59	24
Ceramic wall tile	2,439	1.07	901	1,458	317	84

[1] Includes no response and amount unknown.

Source: GfK Mediamark Research & Intelligence. LLC, New York, NY, Top-Line Reports, (copyright), <http://www.gfkmri.com/>.

Table 1004. Home Improvement Loans by Race: 2009

[Applications in thousands (826.9 represents 826,900), amounts in millions of dollars (60,335.9 represents $60,335,900,000). Data is the final 2009 National Aggregates data.]

Item	Unit	Total	White, total	Black, total	Asian, total	Joint, total [1]	Race not available, total [2]
Applications received							
Number	1,000	826.9	601.7	72.7	16.9	9.2	113.8
Amount	Mil. dol.	60,335.9	45,114.6	3,185.2	2,790.9	1,023.6	7,449.7
Loans originated							
Number	1,000	388.0	317.0	20.9	7.1	4.2	35.3
Amount	Mil. dol.	32,107.4	25,611.2	859.9	1,499.2	524.8	3,363.0
Applications approved but not accepted							
Number	1,000	50.6	33.1	3.8	1.0	0.4	11.6
Amount	Mil. dol.	3,235.8	2,317.2	175.9	169.0	56.2	468.5
Applications denied							
Number	1,000	297.5	189.0	40.4	5.9	3.1	52.3
Amount	Mil. dol.	15,308.0	10,422.8	1,511.0	630.4	246.7	2,192.0
Applications withdrawn							
Number	1,000	67.6	47.2	5.0	2.0	1.1	11.2
Amount	Mil. dol.	7,251.1	5,161.7	416.4	362.8	140.0	1,054.0
Files closed for incompleteness							
Number	1,000	23.2	15.3	2.7	0.8	0.4	3.4
Amount	Mil. dol.	2,433.7	1,601.7	221.8	129.6	55.9	372.2

[1] Joint means with two applicants, one applicant reports a single designation of "White" and the other applicant reports one or more minority racial designations. [2] "Not available" includes situation where information was not provided or not applicable.

Source: Federal Financial Institutions Examination Council, "HMDA National Aggregate Report," annual. See also <http://www.ffiec.gov/hmdaadwebreport/nataggwelcome.aspx>.

Construction and Housing 629

Table 1005. Net Stock of Residential Fixed Assets: 1990 to 2009

[In billions of dollars (6,256 represents $6,256,000,000,000). End of year estimates]

Item	1990	1995	2000	2004	2005	2006	2007	2008	2009
Total residential fixed assets ...	**6,256**	**8,009**	**10,899**	**15,131**	**16,865**	**18,031**	**18,302**	**18,016**	**17,602**
By type of owner and legal form of organization:									
Private......................	6,107	7,821	10,668	14,825	16,530	17,682	17,956	17,680	17,281
Corporate	66	77	105	139	156	168	174	177	173
Noncorporate...............	6,041	7,743	10,563	14,686	16,374	17,514	17,782	17,504	17,108
Government.................	149	188	232	306	335	349	346	336	321
Federal....................	52	62	75	95	103	107	105	102	95
State and local............	97	127	156	211	232	242	241	234	226
By tenure group: [1]									
Owner-occupied	4,512	5,975	8,327	11,849	13,276	14,229	14,445	14,191	13,882
Tenant-occupied	1,719	2,005	2,537	3,234	3,537	3,747	3,801	3,769	3,665

[1] Excludes stocks of other nonfarm residential assets, which consists primarily of dormitories, and of fraternity and sorority houses.

Source: U.S. Bureau of Economic Analysis, "Table 5.1 Current-Cost Net Stock of Residential Fixed Assets by Type of Owner, Legal Form of Organization, Industry, and Tenure Group," <http://www.bea.gov/national/index.htm#fixed>.

Table 1006. Commercial Buildings—Summary: 2003

[4,645 represents 4,645,000. Excludes mall buildings. Building type based on predominant activity in which the occupants were engaged. Based on a sample survey of building representatives conducted in 2003, therefore subject to sampling variability]

Characteristic	All buildings (1,000)	Total floor-space (mil. sq. ft)	Total workers in all buildings (1,000)	Mean square foot per building [1] (1,000)	Mean square foot per worker [1]	Mean operating hours per week [1]
All buildings...............	**4,645**	**64,783**	**72,807**	**13.9**	**890**	**61**
Building floorspace (sq. ft.):						
1,001 to 5,000	2,552	6,789	9,936	2.7	683	57
5,001 to 10,000	889	6,585	7,512	7.4	877	61
10,001 to 25,000	738	11,535	10,787	15.6	1,069	67
25,001 to 50,000	241	8,668	8,881	35.9	976	72
50,001 to 100,000	129	9,057	8,432	70.4	1,074	80
100,001 to 200,000	65	9,064	11,632	138.8	779	89
200,001 to 500,000	25	7,176	6,883	289.0	1,043	100
Over 500,000.	7	5,908	8,744	896.1	676	115
Principal activity within building:						
Education.	386	9,874	12,489	25.6	791	50
Food sales.	226	1,255	1,430	5.6	877	107
Food service	297	1,654	3,129	5.6	528	86
Health care	129	3,163	6,317	24.6	501	59
Inpatient.	8	1,905	3,716	241.4	513	168
Outpatient	121	1,258	2,600	10.4	484	52
Lodging	142	5,096	2,457	35.8	2,074	167
Retail (other than mall)	443	4,317	3,463	9.7	1,246	59
Office.	824	12,208	28,154	14.8	434	55
Public assembly.	277	3,939	2,395	14.2	1,645	50
Public order and safety	71	1,090	1,347	15.5	809	103
Religious worship	370	3,754	1,706	10.1	2,200	32
Service	622	4,050	3,667	6.5	1,105	55
Warehouse and storage	597	10,078	4,369	16.9	2,306	66
Other	79	1,738	1,819	21.9	956	63
Vacant	182	2,567	(NA)	14.1	(NA)	(NA)
Energy sources: [2]						
Electricity.	4,404	63,307	72,708	14.4	871	62
Natural gas	2,391	43,468	51,956	18.2	837	65
Fuel oil.	451	15,157	19,625	33.6	772	68
District heat	67	5,443	10,190	81.4	534	79
District chilled water.	33	2,853	7,189	86.7	397	79
Propane.	502	7,076	5,858	14.1	1,208	60
Wood	62	289	262	4.6	1,105	46

NA Not available. [1] For explanation of mean, see Guide to Tabular Presentation. [2] More than one type may apply.

Source: U.S. Energy Information Administration, "2003 Commercial Buildings Energy Consumption (CBECS)," Detailed Tables, Table B1, <http://www.eia.gov/emeu/cbecs/cbecs2003/detailed_tables_2003/detailed_tables_2003.html>.

This section presents summary data for manufacturing as a whole and more detailed information for major industry groups and selected products. The types of measures shown at the different levels include data for establishments, employment and payroll, value and quantity of production and shipments, value added by manufacture, inventories, and various indicators of financial status.

The principal sources of these data are U.S. Census Bureau reports of the censuses of manufactures conducted every 5 years, the *Annual Survey of Manufactures, and Current Industrial Reports*. Reports on current activities of industries or current movements of individual commodities are compiled by such government agencies as the Bureau of Economic Analysis; Bureau of Labor Statistics; the Department of Commerce, International Trade Administration; and by private research or trade associations.

The Quarterly Financial Report publishes up-to-date aggregate statistics on the financial results and position of U.S. corporations. Based upon a sample survey, the QFR presents estimated statements of income and retained earnings, balance sheets, and related financial and operating ratios for manufacturing corporations with assets of $250,000 or over, and mining, wholesale trade and retail trade corporations with assets of $50 million and over or above industry specific receipt cut-off values. These statistical data are classified by industry and by asset size.

Several private trade associations provide industry coverage for certain sections of the economy. They include American Iron and Steel Institute (Table 1029), Consumer Electronics Association (Table 1033), and the Aerospace Industries Association (Tables 1038 and 1040).

Censuses and annual surveys—
The first census of manufactures covered the year 1809. Between 1809 and 1963,

a census was conducted at periodic intervals. Since 1967, it has been taken every 5 years (for years ending in "2" and "7"). Results from the 2002 census are presented in this section utilizing the North American Industry Classification System (NAICS). For additional information see text, Section 15, Business Enterprise, and the Census Bureau Web site at <http://www.census .gov/econ/census07/>. Census data, either directly reported or estimated from administrative records, are obtained for every manufacturing plant with one or more paid employees.

The *Annual Survey of Manufactures* (ASM), conducted for the first time in 1949, collects data for the years between censuses for the more general measure of manufacturing activity covered in detail by the censuses. The annual survey data are estimates derived from a scientifically selected sample of establishments. The Annual Survey of Manufactures is a sample survey of approximately 50,000 establishments. A new sample is selected at 5-year intervals beginning the second survey year subsequent to the Economic Census—Manufacturing. Since 2009 is the second survey year following the 2007 Economic Census, a new sample was selected based on the 2007 Economic Census—Manufacturing. The sample was supplemented by new establishments entering business in 2007 and 2008.

In 2007, there were approximately 328,500 active manufacturing establishments. For sample efficiency and cost considerations, the 2007 manufacturing population is partitioned into two groups: (1) establishments eligible to be mailed a questionnaire and (2) establishments not eligible to be mailed a questionnaire.

Establishments and classification—
Each of the establishments covered in the 2007 Economic Census—Manufacturing was classified in 1 of 480 industries (473 manufacturing industries and

U.S. Census Bureau, Statistical Abstract of the United States: 2012

7 former manufacturing industries) in accordance with the industry definitions in the 2007 NAICS manual. In the NAICS system, an industry is generally defined as a group of establishments that have similar production processes. To the extent practical, the system uses supply-based or production-oriented concepts in defining industries. The resulting group of establishments must be significant in terms of number, value added by manufacture, value of shipments, and number of employees. Establishments frequently make products classified both in their industry (primary products) and other industries (secondary products). Industry statistics (employment, payroll, value added by manufacture, value of shipments, etc.) reflect the activities of the establishments, which may make both primary and secondary products. Product statistics, however, represent the output of all establishments without regard for the classification of the producing establishment. For this reason, when relating the industry statistics, especially the value of shipments, to the product statistics, the composition of the industry's output should be considered.

Establishment—An establishment is a single physical location where business is conducted or where services or industrial operations are performed. Data in this sector includes those establishments where manufacturing is performed. A separate report is required for each manufacturing establishment (plant) with one employee or more that is in operation at any time during the year. An establishment not in operation for any portion of the year is requested to return the report form with the proper notation in the "Operational Status" section of the form. In addition, the establishment is requested to report data on any employees, capital expenditures, inventories, or shipment from inventories during the year.

Durable goods—Items with a normal life expectancy of 3 years or more. Automobiles, furniture, household appliances, and mobile homes are common examples.

Nondurable goods—Items which generally last for only a short time (3 years or less). Food, beverages, clothing, shoes, and gasoline are common examples.

Statistical reliability—For a discussion of statistical collection and estimation, sampling procedures, and measures of statistical reliability applicable to Census Bureau data, see Appendix III.

U.S. Census Bureau, Statistical Abstract of the United States: 2012

Table 1007. Gross Domestic Product in Current and Real (2005) Dollars by Industry: 2000 to 2010

[In billions of dollars (9,951.5 represents $9,951,500,000,000). Data include nonfactor charges (capital consumption allowances, indirect business taxes, etc.) as well as factor charges against gross product; corporate profits and capital consumption allowances have been shifted from a company to an establishment basis]

Industry	2002 NAICS code [1]	2000	2005	2007	2008	2009	2010
CURRENT DOLLARS							
Gross domestic product, total [2]	(X)	**9,951.5**	**12,638.4**	**14,061.8**	**14,369.1**	**14,119.0**	**14,660.4**
Private industries	(X)	8,736.1	11,052.5	12,301.9	12,514.0	12,196.5	12,696.5
Manufacturing	31–33	1,415.6	1,568.0	1,698.9	1,647.6	1,584.8	1,717.5
Durable goods	33, 321, 327	839.1	877.6	942.8	927.3	867.2	961.2
Wood products	321	28.3	33.0	28.2	25.1	20.9	(NA)
Nonmetallic mineral products	327	41.9	45.3	44.4	39.4	38.2	(NA)
Primary metals	331	46.3	53.7	59.0	61.5	43.4	(NA)
Fabricated metal products	332	120.7	120.4	134.3	135.1	121.9	(NA)
Machinery	333	110.5	109.5	125.3	125.3	112.7	(NA)
Computer and electronic products	334	172.1	183.3	196.4	204.1	206.4	(NA)
Electrical equipment, appliances, and components	335	44.1	39.9	45.8	50.6	51.7	(NA)
Motor vehicles, bodies and trailers, and parts	3361–3363	117.4	112.6	103.4	81.1	78.2	(NA)
Other transportation equipment	3364–66, 69	65.8	76.0	92.4	95.7	90.7	(NA)
Furniture and related products	337	33.8	34.3	34.7	28.8	24.2	(NA)
Miscellaneous manufacturing	339	58.3	69.6	78.8	80.6	79.0	(NA)
Nondurable goods	31, 32 (except 321 and 327)	576.5	690.4	756.1	720.3	717.6	756.3
Food and beverage and tobacco products	311, 312	164.8	172.1	179.9	181.2	206.1	(NA)
Textile mills and textile product mills	313, 314	27.9	23.5	21.7	22.4	17.6	(NA)
Apparel and leather and allied products	315, 316	21.4	16.0	14.9	13.5	11.7	(NA)
Paper products	322	61.7	53.8	58.6	53.8	56.1	(NA)
Printing and related support activities	323	40.3	37.5	38.5	37.0	32.8	(NA)
Petroleum and coal products	324	43.6	139.3	149.7	151.9	120.0	(NA)
Chemical products	325	152.2	182.7	223.2	201.1	216.5	(NA)
Plastics and rubber products	326	64.6	65.6	69.5	59.4	56.7	(NA)
CHAINED (2005) DOLLARS							
Gross domestic product, total [2]	(X)	**11,226.0**	**12,638.4**	**13,228.9**	**13,228.8**	**12,880.6**	**13,248.2**
Private industries	(X)	9,785.6	11,052.5	11,623.6	11,546.3	11,197.6	11,520.5
Manufacturing	31–33	1,396.5	1,568.0	1,690.4	1,608.6	1,469.7	1,554.4
Durable goods	33, 321, 327	747.5	877.6	972.3	982.4	857.4	942.7
Wood products	321	32.8	33.0	35.4	33.5	27.7	(NA)
Nonmetallic mineral products	327	44.7	45.3	39.4	36.7	32.1	(NA)
Primary metals	331	62.2	53.7	42.7	43.6	44.9	(NA)
Fabricated metal products	332	129.6	120.4	130.0	125.6	94.0	(NA)
Machinery	333	111.3	109.5	122.5	122.3	95.2	(NA)
Computer and electronic products	334	81.5	183.3	246.7	284.3	293.8	(NA)
Electrical equipment, appliances, and components	335	42.6	39.9	43.0	46.4	41.7	(NA)
Motor vehicles, bodies and trailers, and parts	3361–63	93.5	112.6	119.7	103.3	76.9	(NA)
Other transportation equipment	3364–66, 69	78.4	76.0	89.7	92.9	82.0	(NA)
Furniture and related products	337	35.1	34.3	33.2	27.3	19.9	(NA)
Miscellaneous manufacturing	339	60.2	69.6	77.3	79.3	73.6	(NA)
Nondurable goods	31, 32 (except 321 and 327)	649.6	690.4	719.1	634.5	613.1	618.0
Food and beverage and tobacco products	311, 312	175.7	172.1	199.6	178.5	175.4	(NA)
Textile mills and textile product mills	313, 314	27.4	23.5	21.5	21.5	15.6	(NA)
Apparel and leather and allied products	315, 316	19.6	16.0	15.0	13.6	11.7	(NA)
Paper products	322	58.3	53.8	52.9	46.0	42.2	(NA)
Printing and related support activities	323	37.5	37.5	37.5	37.3	31.8	(NA)
Petroleum and coal products	324	74.1	139.3	115.2	115.7	128.2	(NA)
Chemical products	325	169.9	182.7	216.6	170.2	164.0	(NA)
Plastics and rubber products	326	65.7	65.6	64.8	53.8	45.1	(NA)

NA Not available. X Not applicable. [1] North American Industry Classification System, 2002; see text, Section 15.
[2] Includes industries, not shown separately. For additional industries, see Table 670.

Source: U.S. Bureau of Economic Analysis, *Survey of Current Business*, May 2011, See also <http://www.bea.gov/scb/index.htm>.

Table 1008. Manufacturing—Selected Industry Statistics by State: 2007

[13,333 represents 13,333,000. Based on the 2007 Economic Census and the 2007 Nonemployer Statistics. See Appendix III]

State	Employers				Nonemployers	
	Number of establishments	Number of employees (1,000)	Annual payroll (mil. dol.)	Sales, shipments, receipts or revenue (mil. dol.)	Number of establishments	Sales, shipments, receipts or revenue (mil. dol.)
U.S.	293,919	13,333	612,474	5,339,345	328,060	16,333
AL	4,928	272	11,352	112,859	4,369	204
AK	544	13	490	8,204	1,087	33
AZ	5,074	172	8,774	57,978	6,524	318
AR	3,088	185	6,518	60,736	2,683	128
CA	44,296	1,448	71,247	491,372	43,798	2,817
CO	5,288	138	6,790	46,332	6,882	284
CT	4,924	191	10,345	58,405	3,776	250
DE	673	35	1,760	25,680	596	36
DC	137	2	81	333	185	8
FL	14,324	355	15,227	104,833	19,505	1,203
GA	8,699	411	16,128	144,281	8,891	425
HI	984	14	511	8,799	2,075	95
ID	1,942	65	2,829	18,011	2,499	91
IL	15,704	664	31,716	257,761	10,347	531
IN	9,015	537	24,475	221,878	6,650	295
IA	3,802	223	9,526	97,592	3,031	117
KS	3,170	178	7,983	76,752	2,739	106
KY	4,165	247	10,773	119,105	3,874	181
LA	3,442	148	7,565	205,055	4,001	190
ME	1,825	59	2,524	16,363	2,652	95
MD	3,680	128	6,454	41,456	4,031	197
MA	7,737	289	15,712	86,429	6,215	315
MI	13,675	582	29,910	234,456	11,725	547
MN	7,951	341	15,999	107,563	7,516	291
MS	2,598	159	5,757	59,869	2,347	103
MO	6,886	295	12,997	110,908	5,987	259
MT	1,324	20	808	10,638	1,959	67
NE	1,984	100	3,789	40,158	1,499	55
NV	2,035	52	2,291	15,736	2,217	138
NH	2,104	82	4,196	18,592	2,287	101
NJ	9,250	311	16,399	116,608	6,503	433
NM	1,574	35	1,560	17,123	3,581	103
NY	18,629	534	24,268	162,720	18,163	933
NC	10,150	506	19,590	205,867	9,828	398
NC	767	26	991	11,350	626	21
OH	16,237	760	35,485	295,891	12,782	640
OK	3,964	142	5,971	60,681	4,099	210
OR	5,717	184	8,139	66,881	6,680	258
PA	15,406	651	29,433	234,840	14,146	767
RI	1,831	54	2,375	12,062	1,290	58
SC	4,335	242	10,061	93,977	3,821	174
SD	1,052	41	1,539	13,051	877	26
TN	6,752	369	15,166	140,448	6,427	306
TX	21,115	894	42,836	593,542	28,790	1,369
UT	3,368	123	5,508	42,432	3,856	171
VT	1,108	36	1,650	10,751	1,738	54
VA	5,777	277	12,170	92,418	5,084	201
WA	7,650	270	13,275	112,053	8,599	343
WV	1,413	60	2,646	25,081	1,363	44
WI	9,659	488	21,850	163,563	6,976	312
WY	596	12	574	8,835	884	32

Source: U.S. Census Bureau, "2007 Economic Census, Geographic Area Series, Detailed Statistics for the State: 2007," April 2010, <http://www.census.gov/econ/census07/>, and "Nonemployer Statistics," August 2009, <http://www.census.gov/econ/nonemployer/index.html>.

Table 1009. Manufacturing—Establishments, Employees, and Annual Payroll by Industry: 2007 and 2008

[(120,604 represents 120,604,000). Excludes most government employees, railroad employees, and self-employed persons. See Appendix III]

Industry	2007 NAICS code [1]	Establishments 2007	Establishments 2008	Employees (1,000) [2] 2007	Employees (1,000) [2] 2008	Payroll (mil. dol.) 2007	Payroll (mil. dol.) 2008
All industries, total	(X)	7,705,018	7,601,169	120,604	120,904	5,026,778	5,130,590
Manufacturing, total	31–33	331,355	326,216	13,320	13,096	626,530	622,307
Percent of all industries	(X)	4.3	4.3	11.0	10.8	12.5	12.1
Food	311	25,796	25,760	1,439	1,467	51,002	52,653
Beverage and tobacco products	312	4,069	4,151	156	157	7,777	7,747
Textile mills	313	3,092	2,832	164	149	5,493	4,915
Textile product mills	314	6,732	7,764	153	146	4,772	4,314
Apparel manufacturing	315	10,368	7,337	197	166	5,017	4,245
Leather and allied products	316	1,392	1,315	37	33	1,134	1,035
Wood products	321	16,622	16,260	528	491	17,507	15,849
Paper	322	5,037	4,877	425	413	21,574	21,285
Printing and related support activities	323	33,281	32,697	632	627	25,436	25,194
Petroleum and coal products	324	2,408	2,373	104	104	8,510	8,357
Chemical	325	13,395	13,640	794	811	51,483	52,967
Plastics and rubber products	326	14,233	13,933	855	822	33,478	32,024
Nonmetallic mineral products	327	17,472	17,428	472	456	20,380	19,747
Primary metal	331	5,267	5,065	439	432	22,854	22,981
Fabricated metal products	332	59,637	60,086	1,566	1,588	67,401	70,734
Machinery	333	26,198	26,016	1,138	1,150	56,797	59,142
Computer and electronic products	334	14,478	14,204	1,043	1,015	72,847	69,681
Electrical equipment, appliance and components	335	6,144	6,193	406	404	18,545	18,880
Transportation equipment	336	12,857	12,800	1,574	1,527	85,876	83,573
Furniture and related products	337	21,717	20,833	517	489	17,492	16,568
Miscellaneous	339	31,160	30,652	681	650	31,153	30,415

X Not applicable. [1] North American Industry Classification System, 2002; see text, Section 15, [2] Covers full- and part-time employees who are on the payroll in the pay period including March 12.
Source: U.S. Census Bureau, "County Business Patterns," July 2010, <http://www.census.gov/econ/cbp/>.

Table 1010. Manufacturing—Establishments, Employees, and Annual Payroll by State: 2008

[(13,096 represents 13,096,000). Excludes most government employees, railroad employees, and self-employed persons. Data are for North American Industry Classification System (NAICS), 2007, codes 31–33. See Appendix III]

State	Establish-ments	Employees (1,000) [1]	Payroll (mil. dol.)	State	Establish-ments	Employees (1,000) [1]	Payroll (mil. dol.)
United States	326,216	13,096	622,307	Missouri	6,744	291	12,777
Alabama	4,926	279	11,574	Montana	1,320	20	799
Alaska	561	12	496	Nebraska	1,946	105	3,980
Arizona	4,959	166	8,696	Nevada	1,938	50	2,369
Arkansas	3,017	183	6,475	New Hampshire	2,053	83	4,860
California	43,240	1,384	74,419	New Jersey	8,957	284	15,895
Colorado	5,225	139	7,118	New Mexico	1,556	35	1,554
Connecticut	4,826	178	10,513	New York	18,251	511	24,258
Delaware	644	33	1,793	North Carolina	9,832	503	20,051
District of Columbia	123	2	84	North Dakota	759	28	1,134
Florida	13,867	342	14,829	Ohio	15,941	743	35,084
Georgia	8,571	398	15,852	Oklahoma	3,924	149	6,464
Hawaii	941	14	507	Oregon	5,648	182	8,250
Idaho	1,934	63	2,771	Pennsylvania	15,174	639	29,915
Illinois	15,378	645	32,274	Rhode Island	1,749	50	2,257
Indiana	8,867	524	23,873	South Carolina	4,373	257	10,763
Iowa	3,826	228	9,839	South Dakota	1,048	43	1,632
Kansas	3,171	183	8,442	Tennessee	6,600	364	15,388
Kentucky	4,107	248	10,587	Texas	20,820	849	43,319
Louisiana	3,485	143	7,677	Utah	3,374	124	5,588
Maine	1,773	59	2,560	Vermont	1,073	37	1,667
Maryland	3,527	122	6,503	Virginia	5,699	277	12,676
Massachusetts	7,560	264	15,390	Washington	7,561	253	13,407
Michigan	13,342	560	27,812	West Virginia	1,389	60	2,680
Minnesota	7,878	334	16,562	Wisconsin	9,583	483	22,281
Mississippi	2,565	163	6,018	Wyoming	591	11	593

[1] Covers full- and part-time employees who are on the payroll in the pay period including March 12.
Source: U.S. Census Bureau, "County Business Patterns," July 2010, <http://www.census.gov/econ/cbp/index.html\>.

Table 1011. Manufactures—Summary by Selected Industry: 2009

[11,051.3 represents 11,051,300. Based on the Annual Survey of Manufactures; see Appendix III]

Industry based on shipments	2002 NAICS code [1]	All employees			Production workers [2] (1,000)	Value added by manufactures [3] (mil. dol.)	Value of shipments [4] (mil. dol.)
		Number [2] (1,000)	Payroll				
			Total (mil. dol.)	Per employee (dol.)			
Manufacturing, total	31–33	11,051.3	534,262	48,344	7,571.0	1,978,017	4,436,196
Food [5]	311	1,394.2	51,429	36,888	1,091.4	258,615	628,566
Grain and oil seed milling	3112	51.9	2,814	54,257	38.5	31,047	86,409
Sugar and confectionery products............	3113	61.1	2,621	42,907	47.0	13,785	27,654
Fruit and vegetable preserving and specialty food	3114	167.2	6,302	37,701	139.4	29,032	64,629
Dairy products.......................	3115	131.1	6,096	46,498	94.7	28,396	84,580
Animal slaughtering and processing	3116	491.5	15,000	30,518	429.0	53,674	164,220
Bakeries and tortilla.....................	3118	257.6	9,097	35,308	171.6	35,242	59,449
Beverage and tobacco products	312	142.3	6,927	48,664	83.2	70,959	119,882
Beverage..........................	3121	128.1	5,994	46,804	72.7	45,027	88,581
Textile mills	313	108.7	3,895	35,839	90.2	11,386	26,461
Textile product mills	314	112.5	3,426	30,457	86.8	9,066	21,261
Apparel	315	113.5	2,987	26,311	90.0	6,937	14,666
Cut and sew apparel	3152	89.1	2,320	26,023	70.5	5,326	11,477
Leather and allied products...............	316	27.9	835	29,962	20.4	2,058	4,188
Wood products [5]	321	352.3	11,994	34,043	281.1	25,900	65,440
Sawmills and wood preservation...........	3211	75.8	2,761	36,415	62.6	6,025	18,882
Paper.................................	322	363.8	18,873	51,875	283.2	76,531	161,816
Pulp, paper, and paperboard mills..........	3221	113.5	7,509	66,179	90.8	39,529	74,495
Converted paper products...............	3222	250.3	11,364	45,392	192.4	37,003	87,322
Printing and related support activities	323	509.0	21,152	41,559	362.7	50,502	83,861
Petroleum and coal products...............	324	101.6	8,421	82,920	66.6	78,559	497,875
Chemical [5]	325	724.7	47,776	65,926	418.7	328,871	628,946
Basic chemical........................	3251	142.1	10,081	70,921	86.9	66,710	175,439
Pharmaceutical and medicine	3254	236.4	18,162	76,814	116.1	140,568	191,410
Soap, cleaning compound, and toilet preparation	3256	97.6	5,263	53,924	57.3	44,801	86,992
Plastics and rubber products.............	326	672.8	27,249	40,501	517.5	82,295	171,186
Plastics products	3261	549.7	21,790	39,636	422.3	67,345	138,685
Rubber product	3262	123.0	5,459	44,369	95.1	14,950	32,501
Nonmetallic mineral products	327	360.4	15,902	44,170	275.1	48,900	90,396
Glass and glass product	3272	80.8	3,804	47,086	63.5	11,043	20,403
Cement and concrete products	3273	170.0	7,260	42,700	129.7	21,642	41,393
Primary metal [5]	331	354.8	18,204	51,304	273.9	48,170	168,298
Iron and steel mills and ferroalloy	3311	98.2	6,036	61,461	78.5	14,612	63,865
Foundries............................	3315	115.5	4,976	43,097	91.5	12,112	22,793
Fabricated metal products [5]	332	1,296.6	57,606	44,429	933.3	146,876	281,317
Forging and stamping	3321	102.7	4,680	45,585	74.2	11,401	26,125
Architectural and structural metals	3323	329.4	14,165	43,001	231.5	34,030	71,022
Machine shops, turned product and screw, nut, and bolt........................	3327	321.0	14,355	44,726	239.1	30,156	48,937
Coating, engraving, heat treating, and allied activities............................	3328	111.1	4,405	39,642	83.4	11,567	20,300
Machinery [5]	333	962.1	49,079	51,014	597.1	133,057	287,634
Agriculture, construction, and mining machinery	3331	180.4	8,961	49,681	120.1	31,666	75,886
Industrial machinery	3332	110.0	6,451	58,662	53.9	12,273	26,418
Ventilation, heating, air conditioning, and commercial refrigeration equipment	3334	126.1	5,367	42,570	85.7	15,971	34,646
Metalworking machinery	3335	129.6	6,504	50,183	90.4	11,970	20,605
Computer and electronic products [5]	334	908.3	59,267	65,250	413.2	193,242	327,991
Computer and peripheral equipment..........	3341	90.4	5,152	56,992	29.7	25,974	52,530
Communications equipment	3342	115.3	8,040	69,736	46.1	24,941	45,164
Semiconductor and other electronic component..........................	3344	293.5	16,505	56,228	178.1	58,361	96,460
Navigational, measuring, medical, and control instruments	3345	375.3	27,926	74,402	138.0	79,359	125,081
Electrical equipment, appliance, and component	335	352.9	16,626	47,107	237.9	50,498	106,651
Electrical equipment	3353	124.7	6,008	48,174	80.3	17,929	36,421
Other electrical equipment and component ...	3359	131.9	6,508	49,357	84.4	18,303	39,981
Transportation equipment [5]	336	1,240.3	71,921	57,985	818.5	229,642	545,018
Motor vehicle	3361	123.5	7,927	64,195	103.3	41,968	149,900
Motor vehicle parts	3363	403.7	18,547	45,947	296.9	51,570	130,521
Aerospace product and parts	3364	429.8	31,626	73,587	222.8	99,173	178,924
Ship and boat building	3366	126.8	6,477	51,072	83.0	16,322	27,248
Furniture and related products [5]	337	360.2	12,690	35,230	269.0	32,235	60,827
Miscellaneous [5]	339	592.4	27,984	47,238	361.3	93,719	143,915
Medical equipment and supplies..............	3391	304.8	16,158	53,003	180.9	60,232	84,560

[1] North American Industrial Classification System, 2002; see text, Section 15. [2] Includes employment and payroll at administrative offices and auxiliary units. All employees represents the average of production workers plus all other employees for the payroll period ended nearest the 12th of March. Production workers represent the average of the employment for the payroll periods ended nearest the 12th of March, May, August, and November. [3] Adjusted value added; takes into account (a) value added by merchandising operations (that is, difference between the sales value and cost of merchandise sold without further manufacture, processing, or assembly), plus (b) net change in finished goods and work-in- process inventories between beginning and end of year. [4] Includes extensive and unmeasurable duplication from shipments between establishments in the same industry classification. [5] Includes industries not shown separately.

Source: U.S. Census Bureau, Annual Survey of Manufactures, "Statistics for Industry Groups and Industries: 2009 and 2008," June 2010, <http://www.census.gov/manufacturing/asm/index.html>.

Table 1012. Manufactures—Summary by State: 2009

[11,051.3 represents 11,051,300. Data are for North American Industry Classification System (NAICS) 2002 codes 31–33. Sum of state totals may not add to U.S. total because U.S. and state figures were independently derived. See Appendix III]

State	All employees [1]			Production workers [1]		Value added by manufactures [2]		Value of shipments [3] (mil. dol.)
		Payroll						
	Number (1,000)	Total (mil. dol.)	Per employee (dol.)	Number (1,000)	Wages (mil. dol.)	Total (mil. dol.)	Per production worker (dol.)	
United States	**11,051.3**	**534,262**	**48,344**	**7,571.0**	**293,251**	**1,978,017**	**261,261**	**4,436,196**
Alabama	224.0	9,747	43,513	167.6	6,269	36,184	215,889	90,531
Alaska	11.0	442	40,348	8.9	294	1,895	212,611	6,226
Arizona	134.2	7,752	57,763	77.3	3,302	23,938	309,821	47,376
Arkansas	152.3	5,720	37,566	120.4	3,946	19,208	159,553	49,324
California	1,196.0	63,629	53,200	737.4	28,681	225,082	305,224	443,487
Colorado	114.8	5,709	49,739	77.6	3,019	20,717	266,841	41,044
Connecticut	165.5	9,400	56,808	99.9	4,529	27,829	278,658	48,330
Delaware	29.3	1,501	51,145	19.1	776	6,257	327,987	19,956
District of Columbia ...	1.4	60	42,759	0.8	32	151	180,191	244
Florida	269.2	12,832	47,674	172.7	6,350	43,793	253,647	85,562
Georgia	327.4	13,617	41,584	246.3	8,499	53,437	216,985	120,614
Hawaii	11.7	455	38,957	7.3	242	1,703	233,320	5,956
Idaho	52.1	2,370	45,464	39.8	1,571	8,117	204,170	16,401
Illinois	550.2	27,012	49,090	371.8	14,220	97,756	262,928	216,068
Indiana	419.5	19,686	46,927	306.4	12,390	80,665	263,281	177,503
Iowa	191.8	8,789	45,812	137.1	5,161	35,798	261,122	82,801
Kansas	155.7	7,377	47,377	108.7	4,372	23,617	217,346	69,037
Kentucky	201.1	8,693	43,224	152.8	5,745	31,994	209,366	89,582
Louisiana	129.3	7,113	55,029	91.9	4,359	41,820	455,065	157,400
Maine	51.6	2,309	44,766	36.5	1,455	8,080	221,134	15,348
Maryland	109.9	6,043	54,986	68.9	2,830	20,848	302,588	37,713
Massachusetts	256.5	14,412	56,179	150.2	6,100	41,297	274,866	74,010
Michigan	437.9	21,623	49,383	307.3	12,894	71,019	231,085	160,063
Minnesota	297.4	14,523	48,827	192.7	7,294	46,048	238,977	99,816
Mississippi	140.7	5,496	39,054	107.6	3,581	21,223	197,254	52,483
Missouri	236.2	11,080	46,914	171.9	6,910	41,363	240,669	96,607
Montana	14.1	652	46,307	10.0	404	2,248	225,771	8,294
Nebraska	90.5	3,608	39,859	68.5	2,436	15,820	230,969	42,280
Nevada	42.1	2,132	50,682	26.4	986	7,664	290,083	14,049
New Hampshire	70.5	3,799	53,924	43.2	1,651	8,944	207,157	17,065
New Jersey	254.9	14,757	57,894	159.1	6,456	45,386	285,287	96,893
New Mexico	25.6	1,178	46,061	17.5	697	5,445	310,327	14,734
New York	446.2	21,493	48,168	291.2	10,903	80,668	277,008	145,906
North Carolina	409.0	16,748	40,952	303.8	10,247	84,451	277,947	165,971
North Dakota	22.0	894	40,717	16.2	538	3,548	218,406	9,755
Ohio	601.9	28,401	47,183	426.0	16,856	98,409	230,980	227,520
Oklahoma	127.4	5,637	44,233	92.1	3,435	22,886	248,488	56,447
Oregon	135.8	6,165	45,397	94.6	3,478	29,679	313,599	50,310
Pennsylvania	541.1	26,111	48,254	374.1	14,660	92,781	248,039	202,179
Rhode Island	39.0	1,978	50,699	24.8	953	4,632	187,114	9,622
South Carolina	196.1	8,605	43,879	146.3	5,434	31,477	215,124	73,525
South Dakota	37.9	1,467	38,746	27.4	912	4,933	180,326	12,279
Tennessee	292.8	12,595	43,014	210.8	7,589	48,282	229,043	112,861
Texas	753.7	38,493	51,070	508.2	21,266	174,881	344,139	481,827
Utah	103.4	4,970	48,047	67.1	2,625	18,962	282,543	37,783
Vermont	29.3	1,477	50,433	18.1	680	3,844	212,940	8,873
Virginia	235.4	11,039	46,891	166.5	6,425	48,658	292,224	85,107
Washington	235.3	12,493	53,089	154.8	6,777	42,628	275,408	98,090
West Virginia	50.9	2,383	46,794	37.8	1,498	9,307	246,067	21,816
Wisconsin	420.9	19,280	45,807	302.0	11,203	58,900	195,017	131,342
Wyoming	8.7	518	59,290	5.7	320	3,744	657,188	8,187

[1] Includes all full-time and part-time employees on the payrolls of operating manufacturing establishments during any part of the pay period that included the 12th of the month. Included are employees on paid sick leave, paid holidays, and paid vacations; not included are proprietors and partners of unincorporated businesses. [2] Value added is derived by subtracting the cost of materials, supplies, containers, fuel, purchased electricity, and contract work from the value of shipments (products manufactured plus receipts for services rendered). The result of this calculation is adjusted by the addition of value added by merchandising operations (i.e., the difference between the sales value and the cost of merchandise sold without further manufacture, processing, or assembly) plus the net change in finished goods and work-in-process between the beginning and end of year inventories. [3] Includes extensive and unmeasurable duplication from shipments between establishments in the same industry classification.

Source: U.S. Census Bureau, Annual Survey of Manufactures, "Geographic Area Statistics: 2008 and 2009," December 2010, <http://www.census.gov/manufacturing/asm/index.html>.

Manufactures 637

Table 1013. Manufacturing Industries—Employees by Industry: 1990 to 2010

[Annual averages of monthly figures (109,487 represents 109,487,000). Covers all full- and part-time employees who worked during, or received pay for, any part of the pay period including the 12th of the month. Minus sign (–) indicates decrease. See also head note, Table 632]

Industry	2007 NAICS code [1]	All employees (1,000)						Percent change	
		1990	2000	2005	2008	2009	2010	1990–2000	2000–2010
All industries	(X)	109,487	131,785	133,703	136,790	130,807	129,818	20.4	−1.5
Manufacturing	31–33	17,695	17,263	14,226	13,406	11,847	11,524	−2.4	−33.2
Percent of all industries	(X)	16	13	11	10	9	9	(X)	(X)
Durable goods	(X)	10,737	10,877	8,956	8,463	7,284	7,067	1.3	−35.0
Wood products [2]	321	541	613	559	456	359	341	13.4	−44.4
Sawmills & wood preservation.	3211	148	134	119	102	83	81	−9.6	−39.3
Nonmetallic mineral products [2]	327	528	554	505	465	394	372	4.9	−32.9
Cement & concrete products	3273	195	234	240	220	185	172	20.1	−26.6
Primary metals [2]	331	689	622	466	442	362	361	−9.7	−42.0
Iron & steel mills & ferroalloy production	3311	187	135	96	99	85	85	−27.7	−36.7
Steel products from purchased steel	3312	70	73	61	61	50	52	4.0	−29.1
Alumina & aluminum production	3313	108	101	73	66	56	55	−7.3	−45.4
Foundries.	3315	214	217	164	148	113	111	1.4	−49.0
Fabricated metal products [2]	332	1,610	1,753	1,522	1,528	1,312	1,285	8.9	−26.7
Architectural & structural metals	3323	357	428	398	406	345	320	20.0	−25.2
Machine shops & threaded products	3327	309	365	345	361	309	312	18.4	−14.6
Coating, engraving, & heat treating metals . .	3328	143	175	145	144	121	122	22.7	−30.2
Machinery [2]	333	1,410	1,457	1,166	1,188	1,029	993	3.3	−31.9
Agricultural, construction, & mining machinery	3331	229	222	208	242	214	208	−2.8	−6.3
HVAC & commercial refrigeration equipment	3334	165	194	154	150	129	123	17.9	−36.5
Metalworking machinery	3335	267	274	202	191	158	153	2.5	−44.0
Turbine & power transmission equipment . . .	3336	114	111	98	105	95	91	−2.4	−18.0
Other general purpose machinery	3339	336	344	269	274	237	226	2.4	−34.4
Computer & electronic products [2]	334	1,903	1,820	1,316	1,244	1,137	1,100	−4.3	−39.6
Computer & peripheral equipment.	3341	367	302	205	183	166	162	−17.8	−46.5
Communications equipment	3342	223	239	141	127	121	118	7.0	−50.5
Semiconductors & electronic components . .	3344	574	676	452	432	378	370	17.8	−45.3
Electronic instruments	3345	635	488	441	441	422	406	−23.2	−16.8
Electrical equipment & appliances [2]	335	633	591	434	424	374	361	−6.7	−39.0
Electrical equipment	3353	244	210	152	159	145	136	−13.9	−35.0
Other electrical equipment & components. . .	3359	195	191	136	137	121	118	−2.3	−38.1
Transportation equipment [2]	336	2,135	2,057	1,772	1,608	1,348	1,330	−3.6	−35.4
Motor vehicles	3361	271	291	248	192	146	151	7.4	−48.1
Motor vehicle bodies & trailers.	3362	130	183	171	140	104	108	40.8	−41.1
Motor vehicle parts	3363	653	840	678	544	414	415	28.6	−50.6
Aerospace products & parts	3364	841	517	455	507	492	477	−38.5	−7.7
Ship & boat building.	3366	174	154	154	156	131	126	−11.3	−18.6
Furniture & related products [2]	337	604	683	568	480	386	357	13.0	−47.6
Household & institutional furniture.	3371	401	443	383	307	244	223	10.6	−49.6
Miscellaneous manufacturing	339	686	728	647	629	584	568	6.2	−22.0
Medical equipment & supplies.	3391	283	305	300	311	307	302	7.7	−1.1
Other miscellaneous manufacturing	3399	403	423	347	318	278	266	5.1	−37.1
Nondurable goods	(X)	6,958	6,386	5,271	4,943	4,563	4,457	−8.2	−30.2
Food manufacturing [2].	311	1,507	1,553	1,478	1,481	1,456	1,447	3.0	−6.8
Fruit & vegetable preserving & specialty	3114	218	197	174	173	172	171	−9.5	−13.1
Dairy products	3115	145	136	132	129	131	128	−5.9	−6.0
Animal slaughtering & processing	3116	427	507	504	510	497	490	18.6	−3.3
Bakeries & tortilla manufacturing.	3118	292	306	280	281	273	276	4.9	−9.9
Beverages & tobacco products [2]	312	218	207	192	198	187	182	−4.9	−11.9
Beverages	3121	173	175	167	177	169	166	1.2	−5.1
Textile mills [2]	313	492	378	218	151	124	119	−23.1	−68.5
Fabric mills.	3132	270	192	104	66	55	53	−29.0	−72.5
Textile product mills [2]	314	236	230	176	147	126	119	−2.5	−48.4
Textile furnishings mills	3141	127	129	96	75	62	57	1.3	−55.3
Apparel [2]	315	903	484	251	199	168	158	−46.4	−67.4
Cut & sew apparel	3152	750	380	193	155	132	125	−49.3	−67.2
Leather & allied products.	316	133	69	40	33	29	28	−48.3	−59.6
Paper & paper products.	322	647	605	484	445	407	397	−6.6	−34.4
Pulp, paper, & paperboard mills	3221	238	191	142	126	117	113	−19.7	−41.1
Converted paper products	3222	409	413	343	319	290	284	1.1	−31.2
Printing & related support activities	323	809	807	646	594	522	487	−0.2	−39.7
Petroleum & coal products.	324	153	123	112	117	115	114	−19.4	−7.5
Chemicals [2]	325	1,036	980	872	847	804	784	−5.3	−20.1
Basic chemicals.	3251	249	188	150	152	145	142	−24.4	−24.4
Pharmaceuticals & medicines	3254	207	274	288	291	284	277	32.4	0.8
Soaps, cleaning compounds, and toiletries . .	3256	132	129	114	107	103	101	−2.4	−21.2
Plastics & rubber products [2]	326	825	951	802	729	625	623	15.3	−34.5
Plastics products	3261	618	737	634	585	502	500	19.2	−32.2
Rubber products	3262	207	214	168	145	123	124	3.3	−42.2

X Not applicable. [1] Based on the North American Industry Classification System, 2007 (NAICS); see text, this section and Section 15. [2] Includes other industries, not shown separately.

Source: U.S. Bureau of Labor Statistics, Current Employment Statistics Program, "Employment, Hours, and Earnings—National," March, 2011, <http://www.bls.gov/ces/home.htm\>.

Table 1014. Manufacturing Industries—Average Weekly Hours and Average Weekly Overtime Hours of Production Workers: 1990 to 2010

[Covers all full- and part-time employees who worked during, or received pay for, any part of the pay period including the 12th of the month]

Industry	2007 NAICS code [1]	Average weekly hours of production workers					Average weekly overtime hours for production workers				
		1990	1995	2000	2005	2010	1990	1995	2000	2005	2010
Total	**31–33**	**40.5**	**41.3**	**41.3**	**40.7**	**41.1**	**3.9**	**4.7**	**4.7**	**4.6**	**3.8**
Durable goods	(X)	41.1	42.1	41.8	41.1	41.3	3.9	5.0	4.8	4.6	3.8
Wood products	321	40.4	41.0	41.0	40.0	39.1	3.3	3.9	4.1	4.1	3.0
Nonmetallic mineral products	327	40.9	41.8	41.6	42.2	41.7	5.0	5.7	6.1	6.3	4.7
Primary metals	331	42.1	43.4	44.2	43.1	43.7	4.6	5.7	6.5	6.3	5.7
Fabricated metal products	332	41.0	41.9	41.9	41.0	41.4	3.9	4.8	4.9	4.6	3.8
Machinery	333	42.1	43.5	42.3	42.1	42.1	4.0	5.3	5.1	5.0	3.9
Computer and electronic products	334	41.3	42.2	41.4	40.0	40.9	3.8	4.9	4.6	3.6	2.9
Electrical equipment and appliances	335	41.2	41.9	41.6	40.6	41.1	3.0	3.5	3.7	3.8	3.6
Transportation equipment [2]	336	42.0	43.7	43.3	42.4	42.9	4.5	6.5	5.5	5.3	4.7
Furniture and related products	337	38.0	38.5	39.2	39.2	38.5	2.3	2.8	3.5	3.2	2.3
Miscellaneous manufacturing	339	39.0	39.2	39.0	38.7	38.7	3.0	3.4	3.1	3.3	2.8
Nondurable goods	(X)	39.6	40.1	40.3	39.9	40.8	3.9	4.3	4.5	4.4	3.8
Food manufacturing	311	39.3	39.6	40.1	39.0	40.7	4.4	4.6	5.0	4.7	4.5
Beverages and tobacco products	312	38.9	39.3	42.0	40.1	37.5	3.8	4.8	5.8	5.7	2.2
Textile mills	313	40.2	40.9	41.4	40.3	41.3	4.2	5.0	4.8	3.9	3.3
Textile product mills	314	38.5	38.6	38.7	38.9	39.0	2.9	3.3	3.4	4.3	2.4
Apparel	315	34.7	35.3	35.7	35.8	36.6	2.0	2.2	2.1	2.1	1.1
Leather and allied products	316	37.4	37.7	37.5	38.4	39.1	4.0	4.0	4.6	2.2	2.9
Paper and paper products	322	43.6	43.4	42.8	42.5	42.9	4.9	5.5	5.7	5.6	4.9
Printing and related support activities	323	38.7	39.1	39.2	38.4	38.2	3.6	3.8	3.7	3.3	2.2
Petroleum and coal products	324	44.4	43.7	42.7	45.5	43.0	6.2	6.3	6.5	8.5	6.4
Chemicals	325	42.8	43.3	42.2	42.3	42.2	4.9	5.6	5.0	4.7	3.6
Plastics and rubber products	326	40.6	41.1	40.8	40.0	41.9	3.4	3.9	4.0	4.0	4.0

X Not applicable. [1] Based on the North American Industry Classification System (NAICS), 2007; see text, this section and Section 15. [2] Includes railroad rolling stock manufacturing, not shown separately.

Source: U.S. Bureau of Labor Statistics, Current Employment Statistics, "Employment Hours, and Earnings—National," March 2011, <http://www.bls.gov/ces/data.htm>.

Table 1015. Indexes of Employment and Hours of All Persons in Manufacturing: 1990 to 2010

[2002 = 100. Based on Current Employment Statistics and supplemented with Current Population Survey. Employment and hours of all persons include those of paid employees, the self employed (partners and proprietors), and unpaid family workers. See text, section 12]

Industry	2007 NAICS code [1]	Employment					Hours				
		1990	1995	2000	2005	2010	1990	1995	2000	2005	2010
Food manufacturing	311	99.0	102.6	101.6	97.0	94.6	98.5	102.7	103.0	95.6	97.4
Beverage and tobacco products	312	104.3	96.5	99.1	92.2	88.3	106.0	96.7	107.6	93.9	85.6
Textile mills	313	166.1	158.4	128.0	74.2	42.6	164.4	160.6	130.3	74.0	42.8
Textile product mills	314	113.9	117.1	109.5	87.0	58.6	113.6	116.8	109.6	85.8	60.1
Apparel manufacturing	315	250.7	221.0	135.2	72.6	48.4	239.7	214.7	133.1	71.4	49.0
Leather and allied products	316	228.7	182.8	124.2	74.8	53.2	231.1	187.9	127.9	78.7	55.0
Wood product manufacturing	321	99.5	106.4	111.8	101.7	63.3	100.3	108.7	114.7	101.6	61.2
Paper manufacturing	322	118.0	116.7	110.3	88.4	72.5	122.3	120.4	112.6	89.7	74.1
Printing and related support activities	323	116.7	118.1	114.4	91.8	70.6	117.1	119.8	115.8	91.5	69.1
Petroleum and coal products	324	128.8	117.9	103.7	94.0	95.7	132.6	119.7	103.0	98.3	96.1
Chemical manufacturing	325	111.8	106.7	106.2	94.9	85.2	111.3	108.9	104.6	94.1	84.7
Plastics and rubber products	326	97.8	108.2	112.4	95.0	73.6	97.5	109.6	112.9	93.4	75.2
Nonmetallic mineral products	327	102.8	101.1	107.3	97.7	73.0	100.3	100.2	105.8	97.3	72.9
Primary metal products	331	135.7	126.3	122.0	91.8	71.0	134.7	129.6	127.2	93.8	73.2
Fabricated metal products	332	104.8	105.1	112.7	98.7	83.6	105.6	108.2	116.3	99.3	84.5
Machinery manufacturing	333	115.5	118.1	118.4	94.8	80.7	118.0	125.5	122.9	97.4	83.9
Computer and electronic products	334	127.6	113.1	121.6	87.5	73.3	132.1	120.5	126.1	88.5	75.4
Electrical equipment and appliances	335	127.7	119.4	119.0	87.9	72.8	130.9	124.8	123.4	89.1	74.6
Transportation equipment	336	116.4	107.8	112.3	96.5	72.8	115.3	110.0	114.1	96.3	73.3
Furniture and related products	337	100.3	101.1	111.1	94.9	59.5	97.3	99.5	111.0	95.3	57.8
Miscellaneous manufacturing	339	101.8	104.3	107.2	96.8	83.0	101.0	104.2	106.9	95.7	82.6

[1] North American Industry Classification System, 2007; see text, Section 15,

Source: Bureau of Labor Statistics, Labor Productivity and Costs, "Industry Employment and Hours,"<http://www.bls.gov/Lpc/iprhours10.htm>.

Table 1016. Average Hourly Earnings of Production Workers in Manufacturing Industries by State: 2007 to 2010

[In dollars. Data are based on the North American Industry Classification System (NAICS), 2007. Based on the Current Employment Statistics Program; see headnote, Table 632, and Appendix III]

State	2007	2008	2009	2010	State	2007	2008	2009	2010
United States	**17.26**	**17.75**	**18.24**	**18.61**	Missouri	16.99	17.70	18.47	18.45
Alabama	15.75	15.68	15.43	15.72	Montana	15.88	16.66	16.85	17.10
Alaska	16.37	16.39	18.57	20.45	Nebraska	15.19	15.26	16.06	16.13
Arizona	15.61	16.44	17.14	17.00	Nevada	15.54	15.53	15.61	15.51
Arkansas	14.06	14.16	14.07	13.87	New Hampshire	17.09	17.30	17.37	17.81
California	16.28	16.79	17.80	18.95	New Jersey	17.22	17.89	18.31	18.78
Colorado	17.77	19.79	21.23	22.07	New Mexico	14.40	14.72	14.59	15.76
Connecticut	20.63	21.42	23.03	23.68	New York	18.49	18.58	18.54	18.39
Delaware	17.83	17.66	17.69	16.53	North Carolina	15.08	15.49	15.88	15.85
District of Columbia	(NA)	(NA)	(NA)	(NA)	North Dakota	14.70	15.15	15.56	15.92
Florida	16.12	18.30	19.60	19.41	Ohio	19.35	19.35	18.63	18.66
Georgia	14.88	14.83	15.43	16.64	Oklahoma	14.56	14.74	14.76	14.33
Hawaii	17.06	18.93	19.06	18.58	Oregon	16.45	16.92	17.69	17.60
Idaho	19.01	19.95	20.30	20.69	Pennsylvania	15.48	15.61	16.28	16.88
Illinois	16.47	16.44	16.61	16.92	Rhode Island	13.78	13.94	14.12	14.71
Indiana	18.70	18.47	18.96	18.52	South Carolina	15.72	15.92	16.29	16.52
Iowa	16.84	16.63	16.73	16.73	South Dakota	14.27	14.64	14.82	15.28
Kansas	18.07	18.73	19.09	18.86	Tennessee	14.39	14.71	14.73	15.32
Kentucky	16.92	17.38	18.11	18.94	Texas	14.07	13.78	14.39	14.50
Louisiana	19.34	19.98	20.49	21.31	Utah	16.71	17.86	18.15	18.46
Maine	19.19	19.71	19.97	20.18	Vermont	16.49	16.51	16.41	16.63
Maryland	17.65	18.04	18.77	20.06	Virginia	17.60	18.33	18.69	19.12
Massachusetts	19.26	20.33	20.66	20.50	Washington	20.51	21.06	23.39	23.48
Michigan	22.06	22.11	21.56	21.77	West Virginia	18.71	19.02	18.69	18.11
Minnesota	17.39	17.74	18.60	18.87	Wisconsin	17.37	17.94	18.14	18.10
Mississippi	13.79	14.43	14.64	14.83	Wyoming	18.02	20.36	20.71	20.49

NA Not available.

Source: U.S. Bureau of Labor Statistics, Current Employment Statistics, "State and Metro Area Employment, Hours, and Earnings (SAE)," March, 2010, <http://www.bls.gov/sae/#data.htm>.

Table 1017. Manufacturing Full–Time Equivalent (FTE) Employees and Wages by Industry: 2000 to 2009

[123,409 represents 123,409,000. Based on National Income and Product Account tables. Full-time equivalent employees equals the number of employees on full-time schedules plus the number of employees for part-time schedules converted to full-time basis]

Industry	2002 NAICS code [1]	Full-time equivalent (FTE) employees (1,000)				Wage and salary accruals per (FTE) worker (dol.)			
		2000	2005	2008	2009	2000	2005	2008	2009
Domestic industries, total	(X)	**123,409**	**125,444**	**128,505**	**121,805**	**39,157**	**45,537**	**51,059**	**51,615**
Manufacturing	31–33	**16,948**	**13,954**	**13,149**	**11,529**	**43,933**	**50,909**	**56,373**	**57,374**
Percent of all industries	(X)	13.7	11.1	10.2	9.5	112.2	111.8	110.4	111.2
Durable goods	(X)	10,713	8,820	8,333	7,104	46,559	53,124	59,001	60,201
Wood products	321	602	549	446	348	30,350	36,003	37,586	37,899
Nonmetallic mineral products	327	549	494	456	377	38,987	45,741	48,843	49,117
Primary metals	331	611	460	434	353	45,714	53,287	60,070	57,233
Fabricated metal products	332	1,735	1,499	1,506	1,274	37,748	43,660	49,421	49,214
Machinery	333	1,427	1,142	1,167	997	46,577	53,650	59,031	59,505
Computer and electronic products	334	1,779	1,293	1,231	1,118	70,397	78,666	86,396	87,610
Electrical equipment, appliances, and components	335	583	428	413	364	40,204	48,883	55,633	56,275
Motor vehicles, bodies and trailers, and parts	3361–3363	1,301	1,095	875	665	48,846	54,026	57,157	57,483
Other transportation equipment	3364–3365	740	671	724	672	53,341	65,931	73,433	77,051
Furniture and related products	337	671	553	470	373	29,571	34,770	38,473	39,009
Miscellaneous manufacturing	339	715	636	612	562	38,724	46,725	53,433	54,597
Nondurable goods	(X)	6,235	5,134	4,816	4,425	39,423	47,103	51,824	52,838
Food and beverage and tobacco products	311–312	1,727	1,617	1,620	1,578	33,922	39,271	42,640	43,092
Textile mills and textile product mills	313–314	588	372	293	240	29,012	34,280	36,704	37,210
Apparel and leather and allied products	315	539	288	225	189	24,198	31,698	36,713	36,914
Paper products	322	598	469	430	393	45,813	53,815	58,289	59,031
Printing and related support activities	323	757	626	579	509	39,141	42,738	45,757	44,975
Petroleum and coal products	324	120	110	115	113	62,322	82,161	94,116	93,163
Chemical products	325	967	862	837	787	61,230	72,920	79,916	82,637
Plastics and rubber products	326	938	788	717	615	35,605	41,181	44,872	45,791

X Not applicable. [1] North American Industry Classification System, 2002; see text, Section 15.

Source: U.S. Bureau of Economic Analysis, *Survey of Current Business*, August 2010. See also <http://www.bea.gov/national/nipaweb/SelectTable.asp?Selected=N>.

Table 1018. Manufacturers' Shipments, Inventories, and New Orders: 1995 to 2010

[In billions of dollars (3,480 represents $3,480,000,000,000), except ratio. Based on the Manufacturers' Shipments, Inventories, and Orders (M3) survey. See source for details]

Year	Shipments	Inventories (December 31) [1]	Ratio of inventories to shipments [2]	New orders	Unfilled orders (December 31)
1995.	3,480	415	1.46	3,427	443
1996.	3,597	421	1.44	3,567	485
1997.	3,835	433	1.39	3,780	508
1998.	3,900	439	1.38	3,808	492
1999.	4,032	453	1.38	3,957	501
2000.	4,209	470	1.37	4,161	545
2001.	3,970	417	1.29	3,865	502
2002.	3,915	412	1.30	3,819	468
2003.	4,015	398	1.22	3,971	490
2004.	4,309	429	1.23	4,283	537
2005.	4,742	461	1.20	4,756	626
2006.	5,016	509	1.25	5,078	759
2007.	5,319	547	1.27	5,390	902
2008.	5,468	536	1.21	5,438	942
2009.	4,436	499	1.39	4,234	799
2010.	4,820	542	1.39	4,779	829

[1] Inventories are stated at current cost. [2] Ratio based on December seasonally adjusted inventory data.
Source: Census Bureau, Manufacturers' Shipments, Inventories, and Orders, "Historical Data," <http://www.census.gov/manufacturing/m3/historical_data/index.html>.

Table 1019. Ratios of Manufacturers' Inventories to Shipments and Unfilled Orders to Shipments by Industry Group: 2000 to 2010

[Based on the Manufacturers' Shipments, Inventories, and Orders (M3) survey. See source for details]

Industry	2007 NAICS code [1]	2000	2005	2006	2007	2008	2009	2010
INVENTORIES-TO-SHIPMENTS RATIO [2]								
All manufacturing industries	(X)	1.37	1.20	1.25	1.27	1.21	1.39	1.39
Durable goods	(X)	1.55	1.40	1.49	1.50	1.53	1.76	1.82
Wood products	321	1.32	1.28	1.26	1.37	1.40	1.47	1.54
Nonmetallic mineral products	327	1.23	1.10	1.12	1.18	1.29	1.38	1.36
Primary metals	331	1.68	1.54	1.69	1.61	1.48	1.87	1.67
Fabricated metals	332	1.56	1.53	1.61	1.56	1.56	1.67	1.79
Machinery	333	2.08	1.77	1.89	1.84	1.91	2.09	2.02
Computers and electronic products	334	1.54	1.45	1.43	1.38	1.39	1.59	1.51
Electrical equipment, appliances, and components	335	1.44	1.36	1.48	1.48	1.47	1.52	1.56
Transportation equipment	336	1.35	1.17	1.33	1.40	1.51	1.91	2.24
Furniture and related products	337	1.36	1.18	1.13	1.13	1.05	1.16	1.29
Miscellaneous products	339	1.90	1.70	1.60	1.69	1.67	1.70	1.73
Nondurable goods	(X)	1.14	0.98	1.00	1.04	0.91	1.06	1.03
Food products	311	0.88	0.75	0.81	0.83	0.76	0.79	0.79
Beverages and tobacco products	312	1.51	1.39	1.48	1.46	1.52	1.67	1.47
Textile mills	313	1.48	1.19	1.25	1.33	1.40	1.35	1.31
Textile product mills	314	1.75	1.19	1.18	1.37	1.51	1.47	1.58
Apparel	315	1.89	1.51	1.26	1.60	1.49	1.55	1.88
Leather and allied products	316	2.12	1.73	1.92	2.11	2.07	2.15	2.67
Paper products	322	1.11	1.08	1.07	1.03	1.04	1.00	0.96
Printing	323	0.80	0.80	0.80	0.79	0.79	0.76	0.78
Petroleum and coal products	324	0.71	0.75	0.72	0.87	0.55	0.95	0.88
Basic chemicals	325	1.40	1.18	1.23	1.20	1.16	1.27	1.22
Plastics and rubber products	326	1.21	1.15	1.15	1.21	1.20	1.26	1.29
UNFILLED ORDERS-TO-SHIPMENTS RATIO								
All manufacturing industries	(X)	1.57	1.59	1.82	2.04	2.07	2.17	2.07
Durable goods	(X)	2.78	3.12	3.57	4.04	4.32	4.62	4.52
Primary metals	331	2.42	1.91	1.81	1.79	1.25	1.74	1.78
Fabricated metals	332	5.58	2.55	2.61	2.60	2.47	2.58	2.59
Machinery	333	4.68	2.47	2.82	2.98	3.15	3.23	3.64
Computers and electronic products	334	5.84	3.59	3.79	3.85	3.95	4.42	4.08
Electrical equipment, appliances, and components	335	0.76	2.05	2.38	2.29	2.10	2.18	2.52
Transportation equipment	336	6.15	5.78	7.29	8.73	10.51	10.80	10.83
Furniture and related products	337	0.69	1.17	1.12	1.16	1.09	1.24	1.31
Miscellaneous products	339	0.11	0.16	0.14	0.14	0.11	0.09	0.13

X Not applicable. [1] Based on the North American Industry Classification System, 2007; see text, this section and Section 15.
[2] Ratio based on December seasonally adjusted inventory data.
Source: Census Bureau, Manufacturers' Shipments, Inventories, and Orders, "Historical Data," <http://www.census.gov/manufacturing/m3/historical_data/index.html>.

Table 1020. Value of Manufacturers' Shipments, Inventories, and New Orders by Industry: 2000 to 2010

[In billions of dollars (4,209 represents $4,209,000,000,000). Based on the Manufacturers' Shipments, Inventories, and Orders (M3) survey. See source for details]

Industry	2007 NAICS code [1]	2000	2005	2007	2008	2009	2010
SHIPMENTS							
All manufacturing industries	(X)	**4,209**	**4,742**	**5,319**	**5,468**	**4,436**	**4,820**
Durable goods	(X)	2,374	2,425	2,687	2,620	2,077	2,206
Wood products	321	94	112	102	88	65	66
Nonmetallic mineral products	327	97	115	128	115	90	92
Primary metals	331	157	203	257	283	168	221
Fabricated metals	332	268	289	345	358	281	283
Machinery	333	292	303	351	356	288	316
Computers and electronic products	334	511	373	396	384	328	364
Electrical equipment, appliances, and components	335	125	112	129	130	107	115
Transportation equipment	336	640	691	746	673	545	538
Furniture and related products	337	75	84	85	80	61	62
Miscellaneous products	339	115	143	149	153	144	150
Nondurable goods	(X)	1,835	2,317	2,632	2,848	2,359	2,614
Food products	311	435	532	590	650	629	664
Beverages and tobacco products	312	112	124	128	125	120	132
Textile mills	313	52	42	36	32	26	30
Textile product mills	314	34	35	29	27	21	22
Apparel	315	60	31	24	19	15	15
Leather and allied products	316	10	6	5	5	4	4
Paper products	322	165	162	177	179	162	172
Printing	323	104	97	103	99	84	84
Petroleum and coal products	324	235	476	615	770	498	633
Basic chemicals	325	449	611	716	739	629	677
Plastics and rubber products	326	178	200	209	204	171	182
INVENTORIES (December 31)							
All manufacturing industries	(X)	**470**	**461**	**547**	**536**	**499**	**542**
Durable goods	(X)	298	276	326	326	296	325
Wood products	321	10	12	11	10	8	8
Nonmetallic mineral products	327	10	10	12	12	10	10
Primary metals	331	22	26	34	35	26	30
Fabricated metals	332	34	36	44	46	39	41
Machinery	333	49	43	52	55	49	52
Computers and electronic products	334	63	44	44	43	43	45
Electrical equipment, appliances, and components	335	15	12	15	16	13	14
Transportation equipment	336	69	65	84	82	84	97
Furniture and related products	337	8	8	8	7	6	6
Miscellaneous products	339	18	20	20	21	20	21
Nondurable goods	(X)	172	185	221	211	203	217
Food products	311	32	33	41	41	41	44
Beverages and tobacco products	312	14	14	16	16	17	16
Textile mills	313	6	4	4	4	3	3
Textile product mills	314	5	3	3	3	3	3
Apparel	315	9	4	3	2	2	2
Leather and allied products	316	2	1	1	1	1	1
Paper products	322	15	14	15	15	13	14
Printing	323	6	6	6	6	5	5
Petroleum and coal products	324	13	27	41	32	36	43
Basic chemicals	325	52	59	70	70	65	67
Plastics and rubber products	326	18	19	21	20	18	19
NEW ORDERS							
All manufacturing industries	(X)	**4,161**	**4,756**	**5,390**	**5,438**	**4,234**	**4,779**
Durable goods	(X)	2,327	2,439	2,758	2,590	1,875	2,165
Wood products	321	94	112	102	88	65	66
Nonmetallic mineral products	327	97	115	128	115	90	92
Primary metals	331	154	209	260	274	164	229
Fabricated metals	332	270	298	351	357	268	283
Machinery	333	295	312	361	362	272	334
Computers and electronic products	334	436	302	327	313	263	296
Electrical equipment, appliances, and components	335	126	115	130	129	103	120
Transportation equipment	336	663	750	866	720	445	534
Furniture and related products	337	75	85	85	79	60	62
Miscellaneous products	339	117	142	149	153	144	151
Nondurable goods	(X)	1,835	2,317	2,632	2,848	2,359	2,614

X Not applicable. [1] Based on the North American Industry Classification System, 2007; see text, this section and Section 15.
Source: Census Bureau, Manufacturers' Shipments, Inventories, and Orders, "Historical Data," <http://www.census.gov/manufacturing/m3/historical_data/index.html>.

Table 1021. Value of Manufacturers' Shipments, Inventories, and New Orders by Market Grouping: 2000 to 2010

[In millions of dollars (4,209 represents $4,209,000,000,000). Based on the Manufacturers' Shipments, Inventories, and Orders (M3) survey. See source for details]

Market grouping	2000	2005	2006	2007	2008	2009	2010
SHIPMENTS							
All manufacturing industries	**4,209**	**4,742**	**5,016**	**5,319**	**5,468**	**4,436**	**4,820**
Consumer goods	1,501	1,895	1,980	2,106	2,253	1,845	2,040
Consumer durable goods	391	423	422	422	359	273	285
Consumer nondurable goods	1,109	1,473	1,558	1,684	1,893	1,572	1,755
Aircraft and parts	112	114	125	157	162	157	139
Defense aircraft and parts	25	37	39	43	57	63	59
Nondefense aircraft and parts	87	77	86	114	105	94	80
Construction materials and supplies	445	510	547	560	544	428	428
Motor vehicles and parts	471	501	500	501	413	302	321
Computers and related products	110	65	67	65	66	53	64
Information technology industries	400	295	320	323	315	271	292
Nondefense capital goods	808	731	795	837	839	702	754
Excluding aircraft	758	687	744	768	772	641	706
Defense capital goods	67	91	89	99	115	125	114
Durables excluding capital goods	1,498	1,603	1,678	1,751	1,666	1,250	1,339
INVENTORIES (December 31)							
All manufacturing industries	**470**	**461**	**509**	**547**	**536**	**499**	**542**
Consumer goods	128	140	148	166	154	154	166
Consumer durable goods	26	27	26	27	24	21	25
Consumer nondurable goods	102	113	122	139	130	133	142
Aircraft and parts	36	33	39	48	48	53	63
Defense aircraft and parts	9	12	12	14	12	14	14
Nondefense aircraft and parts	27	22	26	34	36	39	50
Construction materials and supplies	49	53	59	61	60	51	52
Motor vehicles and parts	22	23	26	25	22	19	23
Computers and related products	8	4	5	5	5	5	5
Information technology industries	51	38	39	38	37	37	39
Nondefense capital goods	127	108	119	128	133	128	144
Excluding aircraft	107	90	99	102	105	96	102
Defense capital goods	17	16	17	18	17	20	20
Durables excluding capital goods	154	152	174	180	176	148	162
NEW ORDERS							
All manufacturing industries	**4,161**	**4,756**	**5,078**	**5,390**	**5,438**	**4,234**	**4,779**
Consumer goods	1,502	1,894	1,979	2,106	2,251	1,844	2,040
Consumer durable goods	393	421	421	422	358	273	286
Consumer nondurable goods	1,109	1,473	1,558	1,684	1,893	1,572	1,755
Aircraft and parts	131	175	200	268	205	79	146
Defense aircraft and parts	31	34	41	45	62	56	60
Nondefense aircraft and parts	99	141	159	224	143	23	86
Construction materials and supplies	447	517	550	566	544	420	431
Motor vehicles and parts	468	503	503	499	411	300	321
Computers and related products	108	64	67	65	66	53	64
Information technology industries	410	301	334	326	315	266	296
Nondefense capital goods	831	811	888	958	878	604	774
Excluding aircraft	768	701	771	784	776	617	722
Defense capital goods	80	82	103	104	126	105	111
Durables excluding capital goods	1,416	1,547	1,635	1,696	1,586	1,166	1,280

Source: Census Bureau, Manufacturers' Shipments, Inventories, and Orders, "Historical Data," <http://www.census.gov/manufacturing/m3/historical_data/index.html>.

Table 1022. Finances and Profits of Manufacturing Corporations: 2000 to 2010

[In billions of dollars (4,548 represents $4,548,000,000,000). Data exclude estimates for corporations with less than $250,000 in assets at time of sample selection. See Table 794 for individual industry data. Minus sign (−) indicates loss]

Item	2000 [1]	2001 [1]	2001 [2]	2004 [2]	2005 [2]	2006 [2]	2007 [2]	2008 [3]	2009 [3]	2010 [3]
Net sales	4,548	4,308	4,295	4,934	5,411	5,783	6,060	6,374	5,110	5,773
Net operating profit	348	185	186	320	359	405	416	358	289	421
Net profit:										
Before taxes	381	82	83	447	524	605	603	388	361	585
After taxes	275	36	36	348	401	470	443	266	286	478
Cash dividends	132	102	103	143	179	178	178	182	172	183
Net income retained in business	143	-67	-66	205	222	292	265	84	115	295

[1] Based on the Standard Industrial Classification system. [2] Based on the North American Industry Classification System, 2002; see text, Section 15. [3] Based on the North American Industry Classification System, 2007; see text, Section 15.
Source: U.S. Census Bureau, *Quarterly Financial Report for Manufacturing, Mining, Trade, and Selected Service Industries.* See also *2010 Fourth Quarter Press Release*, March 2011, <http://www.census.gov/econ/qfr>.

Table 1023. Manufacturing Corporations—Assets and Profits by Asset Size: 1990 to 2010

[In millions of dollars (2,629,458 represents $2,629,458,000,000). Corporations and assets as of end of 4th quarter; profits for entire year. Through 2000, based on Standard Industrial Classification code (SIC); beginning 2001, based on the North American Industry Classification System; see text, Section 15. For corporations above a certain asset value based on complete canvass. The asset value for complete canvass was raised in 1988 to $50 million and in 1995 to $250 million. Asset sizes less than these values are sampled, except as noted. For details regarding Survey description, data analysis and methodology, see source, fourth quarter report. Minus sign (–) indicates loss]

Year	Total	Asset–size class						
		Under $10 million [1]	$10 to $25 million	$25 to $50 million	$50 to $100 million	$100 to $250 million	$250 million to $1 billion	$1 billion and over
Assets:								
1990......	2,629,458	142,498	74,477	55,914	72,554	123,967	287,512	1,872,536
1995......	3,345,229	155,618	87,011	68,538	87,262	159,133	370,263	2,417,403
1997......	3,746,797	167,921	87,398	76,034	85,186	157,130	397,559	2,775,570
1998......	3,967,309	170,068	87,937	69,627	86,816	148,060	419,153	2,985,647
1999......	4,382,814	170,058	85,200	67,352	97,810	138,143	398,881	3,425,370
2000......	4,852,106	171,666	85,482	72,122	90,866	149,714	389,537	3,892,720
2001 [2]	4,747,789	169,701	84,664	67,493	88,088	131,617	393,752	3,812,474
2002......	4,823,219	166,191	82,369	62,654	81,667	134,821	407,423	3,888,095
2003......	5,162,852	161,462	80,681	62,592	77,205	126,826	392,192	4,261,894
2004......	5,538,113	163,072	80,085	71,674	81,741	126,950	414,144	4,600,447
2005......	5,828,716	165,195	85,785	68,731	87,818	142,900	423,917	4,854,370
2006......	6,179,142	168,537	93,786	72,494	91,877	146,651	418,501	5,187,295
2007......	6,891,131	180,319	98,348	80,400	93,017	144,254	433,634	5,861,160
2008......	6,819,681	180,025	99,430	80,757	98,478	137,907	420,104	5,802,981
2009......	6,942,972	166,590	106,773	71,642	76,308	126,202	413,856	5,981,600
2010......	7,441,125	168,395	108,747	75,186	83,095	131,122	408,420	6,466,158
Net profit: [3]								
1990......	110,128	8,527	5,160	2,769	2,661	3,525	7,110	80,377
1995......	198,151	13,224	5,668	3,767	5,771	7,000	16,549	146,172
1997	244,505	17,948	8,383	4,153	4,675	7,074	18,433	183,836
1998......	234,386	18,350	6,421	3,790	4,681	5,610	14,364	181,170
1999......	257,805	17,398	7,618	3,504	4,798	4,795	12,756	206,934
2000......	275,313	16,578	6,820	3,403	2,742	3,510	15,121	227,136
2001 [2]	36,168	8,387	3,366	–408	403	–543	–6,782	31,746
2002......	134,686	10,003	2,784	807	1,699	3,356	–1,227	117,262
2003......	237,041	9,821	3,374	2,005	2,256	2,973	4,115	212,497
2004......	348,151	14,970	5,745	3,858	3,080	5,140	12,787	302,571
2005......	401,344	17,357	6,057	4,066	3,781	7,678	15,967	346,438
2006	470,282	22,301	8,685	5,260	4,601	8,901	21,405	399,131
2007......	442,734	22,930	9,006	4,402	6,518	8,400	17,565	373,915
2008......	266,346	18,182	7,472	5,820	3,739	3,403	2,239	225,492
2009......	286,491	9,692	5,979	4,617	2,500	2,723	2,653	258,310
2010......	477,745	17,174	9,109	4,300	5,746	5,577	19,983	415,854

[1] Excludes estimates for corporations with less than $250,000 in assets at time of sample selection. [2] Beginning 2001, data reported based on the North American Industry Classification System. [3] After taxes.
Source: U.S. Census Bureau, *Quarterly Financial Report for Manufacturing, Mining, Trade, and Selected Service Industries*. See also *2010 Fourth Quarter Press Release*, March 2011, <http://www.census.gov/econ/qfr>.

Table 1024. Manufacturing Corporations—Selected Finances: 1990 to 2010

[In billions of dollars (2,811 represents $2,811,000,000,000). Data are not necessarily comparable from year to year due to changes in accounting procedures, industry classifications, sampling procedures, etc.; for detail, see source. See head note, Table 1023. Minus sign (–) indicates loss]

Year	All manufacturing corporations			Durable goods			Nondurable goods		
	Sales	Profits [1]		Sales	Profits [1]		Sales	Profits [1]	
		Before taxes	After taxes		Before taxes	After taxes		Before taxes	After taxes
1990.......	2,811	158	110	1,357	57	41	1,454	101	69
1995.......	3,528	275	198	1,808	131	94	1,721	144	104
1996.......	3,758	307	225	1,942	147	106	1,816	160	119
1997.......	3,922	331	244	2,076	167	121	1,847	164	123
1998.......	3,949	315	234	2,169	175	128	1,781	140	107
1999.......	4,149	355	258	2,314	199	140	1,835	157	117
2000.......	4,548	381	275	2,457	191	132	2,091	190	144
2001 [2]	4,295	83	36	2,321	–69	–76	1,974	152	112
2002.......	4,217	196	135	2,261	45	21	1,955	149	113
2003.......	4,397	306	237	2,283	118	88	2,114	188	149
2004.......	4,934	447	348	2,537	200	157	2,397	248	192
2005.......	5,411	524	401	2,731	211	161	2,681	313	240
2006.......	5,783	605	470	2,910	249	193	2,873	356	278
2007.......	6,060	603	443	3,016	247	159	3,044	356	283
2008.......	6,374	388	266	2,970	98	43	3,405	290	223
2009.......	5,110	361	286	2,427	84	55	2,683	276	232
2010.......	5,773	585	478	2,719	288	233	3,054	297	245

[1] Beginning 1998, profits before and after income taxes reflect inclusion of minority stockholders' interest in net income before and after income taxes. [2] Beginning 2001, data reported based on the North American Industry Classification System.
Source: U.S. Census Bureau, *Quarterly Financial Report for Manufacturing, Mining, Trade, and Selected Service Industries*. See also *2010 Fourth Quarter Press Release*, March 2011, <http://www.census.gov/econ/qfr>.

Table 1025. Cotton, Wool, and Man-Made Fibers—Consumption by End Use: 2005 to 2009

[In millions of pounds (13,014 represents 13,014,000,000). Based on U.S. Manufactured Fiber, Cotton and Wool End Use Survey. Represents raw fiber which was put into process in order to manufacture end products manufactured by U.S. mills. Excludes glass fiber]

End use and year	Fiber con-sump-tion, total [1] (mil. lb.)	Cotton [2]		Wool [3]		Manufactured fibers					
						Manu-factured fibers con-sump-tion, total (mil. lb.)	Percent of end-use	Cellulosic [4]		Synthetic [5]	
		Cotton con-sump-tion, total (mil. lb.)	Percent of end-use	Wool con-sump-tion, total (mil. lb.)	Percent of end-use			Cel-lulosic con-sump-tion, total (mil. lb.)	Percent of end-use	Synthetic con-sump-tion, total (mil. lb.)	Percent of end-use
Total:											
2005........	13,014	2,540	19.5	95	0.7	10,379	79.8	210	1.6	10,697	82.2
2007........	10,600	1,427	13.5	91	0.9	9,082	85.7	209	2.0	8,441	79.6
2008........	9,042	1,009	11.2	77	0.9	7,956	88.0	181	2.0	7,775	86.0
2009........	7,745	784	10.1	65	0.8	6,896	89.0	159	2.1	6,737	87.0
Apparel:											
2005........	2,746	1,414	51.5	51	1.8	1,281	46.6	63	2.3	1,218	44.4
2007........	1,741	686	39.4	47	2.7	1,009	57.9	40	2.3	969	55.6
2008........	1,384	449	32.5	38	2.7	898	64.8	29	2.1	869	62.8
2009........	1,078	321	29.8	34	3.1	723	67.1	23	2.1	701	65.0
Home textiles:											
2005........	1,465	791	54.0	9	0.6	665	45.4	31	2.1	634	43.3
2007........	884	420	47.5	10	1.1	454	51.4	22	2.5	432	48.9
2008........	736	321	43.7	8	1.1	406	55.2	19	2.6	387	52.6
2009........	587	241	41.1	7	1.2	339	57.7	15	2.5	324	55.2
Floor coverings:											
2005........	4,470	32	0.7	29	0.7	4,409	98.6	–	–	4,409	98.6
2007........	3,873	32	0.8	29	0.8	3,812	98.4	–	–	3,812	98.4
2008........	3,262	27	0.8	26	0.8	3,210	98.4	–	–	3,210	98.4
2009........	2,815	22	0.8	21	0.7	2,772	98.5	–	–	2,772	98.5
Industrial: [6]											
2005........	4,333	303	7.0	5	0.1	4,025	92.9	113	2.6	3,912	90.3
2007........	4,103	290	7.1	5	0.1	3,808	92.8	147	3.6	3,661	89.2
2008........	3,660	212	5.8	5	0.1	3,443	94.1	133	3.6	3,310	90.4
2009........	3,265	199	6.1	4	0.1	3,062	93.8	122	3.7	2,940	90.1

– Represents or rounds to zero. [1] Includes other fibers such as silk, linen, jute and sisal. [2] Raw cotton. [3] Wool data includes virgin, noils, reprocessed and reused wool and is reported on clean basis. [4] Includes rayon and acetate. [5] Includes acrylic, nylon, polyester, olefin, and spandex. [6] Includes consumer-type products, such as, narrow fabrics, medical, surgical and sanitary, tires, hose, belting, felts, sewing thread, filtration etc.

Source: Fiber Economics Bureau, Inc., Arlington, VA, Fiber Organon, Vol. 81, No. 10, October 2010 (copyright).

Table 1026. Textiles—Production and Foreign Trade: 2009

[515,985 represents 515,985,000. Fabric blends as shown in the report are reported based on the chief weight of the fiber; whereas, fabrics blends as shown for imports and exports are based on the chief value of the fiber]

Product description	Unit	Quantity (1,000)			Value ($1,000)	
		Manufac-turers' produc-tion	Exports of domestic merchan-dise [1]	Imports for con-sump-tion [2]	Exports of domestic merchan-dise [1]	Imports for con-sump-tion [2, 3]
YARN						
Spun cotton yarns, carded, 85 percent or more cotton.	Kilograms....	515,985	255,368	12,355	632,805	60,167
Textured, crimped, twisted, or bulked filament yarns, nylon	Kilograms....	615,141	19,098	55,870	92,232	238,163
Textured, crimped, twisted, or bulked filament yarns, polyester	Kilograms....	247,430	23,544	32,067	72,493	67,808
BROADWOVEN FABRICS [4]						
Yarn dyed fabrics, blue denim	Sq. meters ...	127,838	108,431	30,566	215,227	79,734
85 percent or more spun yarn fabrics and blends (except yarn dyed), chiefly man made fiber, twills and sateens [5]	Sq. meters ...	135,460	(NA)	21,318	(NA)	24,853
85 percent or more filament yarn fabrics, man made, high tenacity yarn fabrics of nylon, polyester, or rayon	Sq. meters ...	115,880	21,587	13,013	69,008	44,297
85 percent or more filament yarn fabrics, man made, glass fiber fabrics.	Sq. meters ...	175,554	34,810	47,270	125,735	66,841
85 percent or more filament yarn fabrics, all other man made filament fiber fabrics, including saran, olefin, and carpet backing	Sq. meters ...	587,716	18,741	484,462	49,090	133,247
KNIT FABRICS						
Pile fabrics.	Kilograms....	8,460	(S)	116,728	(S)	147,119
Elastic fabrics (over 12 inches in width) (weight 5 percent or more elastomeric yarn or rubber thread)..	Kilograms....	8,942	(S)	19,251	(S)	159,173
Elastic fabrics (12 inches or less in width) (weight 5 percent or more elastomeric yarn or rubber thread)..	Kilograms....	4,634	(S)	658	(S)	4,982

NA Not available. S Withheld because estimate did not meet publication standards [1] Source: U.S. Census Bureau report EM 545, *U.S. Exports.* [2] Source: U.S. Census Bureau report IM 145, *U.S. Imports for Consumption.* [3] Dollar value represents the c.i.f. (cost, insurance, and freight) at the first port of entry in the United States plus calculated import duty. [4] Represents production of gray broad woven fabrics; import and export data represent gray as well as finished broad woven fabrics. [5] Total for man made fiber fabrics does not include chiefly man made/wool blends.

Source: U.S. Census Bureau, Current Industrial Reports, "Textiles," Series MQ313A, <http://www.census.gov/cir/www/313/mq313a.html>.

Table 1027. Pharmaceutical Preparations—Value of Shipments: 1990 to 2009

[In millions of dollars (33,954 represents $33,954,000,000)]

Product description	Product code	1990	2000	2005	2006	2007	2008	2009
Pharmaceutical preparations, except biologicals	(X)	33,954	79,262	118,647	123,118	(NA)	(NA)	(NA)
Affecting neoplasms, endocrine systems, and metabolic disease	3254121	2,743	9,784	23,779	25,721	28,497	33,260	33,791
Acting on the central nervous system and sense organs	3254124	7,219	18,508	25,627	29,882	28,714	26,430	29,605
Acting on the cardiovascular system	3254127	4,815	8,993	10,232	10,874	11,969	11,543	12,963
Acting on the respiratory system	325412A	3,724	10,179	16,367	18,350	16,177	16,573	16,618
Acting on the digestive system	325412D	4,840	10,046	16,829	11,775	9,822	9,949	10,983
Acting on the skin	325412G	1,558	2,941	3,657	3,303	3,498	3,635	3,797
Vitamin, nutrient, and hematitic preparations	325412L	2,588	5,676	7,556	7,711	8,062	8,749	9,033
Affecting parasitic and infective disease	325412P	5,411	11,037	11,228	11,693	11,014	9,403	10,147
Pharmaceutical preparations for veterinary use . . .	325412T	1,057	2,096	3,371	3,808	3,206	3,280	2,970

NA Not available. X Not applicable.

Source: U.S. Census Bureau, Current Industrial Reports, "Pharmaceutical Preparations, Except Biologicals," Series MA325G, <http://www.census.gov/manufacturing/cir/historical_data/ma325g/index.html>.

Table 1028. Inorganic Chemicals and Fertilizers—Production: 2000 to 2009

[In 1,000 short tons (15,809 represents 15,809,000.) 1,000 short tons = 2,000 lb.]

Product description	Product code	2000	2005	2006	2007	2008	2009
FERTILIZERS MQ325B							
Ammonia, synthetic anhydrous	3253111120	15,809	11,181	10,981	11,448	10,549	10,330
Ammonium nitrate (original melt liquor)	3253111201	7,979	7,212	7,068	8,236	7,841	6,943
Ammonium sulfate	3253111240	2,808	2,906	2,870	3,145	2,783	2,499
Urea (original melt liquor)(100%)	3253114101	7,682	5,807	5,934	6,156	5,776	5,604
Nitric acid (100%)	3253111111	8,708	7,398	7,245	8,623	7,370	6,531
Phosphoric acid (100% P2O5)	3253121111	12,492	12,621	11,797	12,081	10,158	9,542
Sulfuric acid, (100%)	3251881100	43,643	40,996	39,578	39,745	34,855	32,126
Superphosphates and other fertilizer materials (100% P2O5)	3253124102	8,899	8,141	7,184	7,241	6,014	6,142
INORGANIC CHEMICALS MQ325A							
Chlorine gas (100 percent)[1]	3251811111	14,000	10,272	12,443	11,895	10,673	9,391
Sodium hydroxide, liquid (caustic soda) (100 percent) all process: liquid [2]	3251814111	11,523	8,517	9,735	8,869	8,111	7,242
Potassium hydroxide (caustic potash) (88-92 percent) liquid [2]	3251817111	539	527	610	621	582	404
Finished sodium bicarbonate (58 percent) NaHCO3	3251817131	536	581	644	663	682	641
Hydrochloric acids (100 percent) by product and other [3]	3251884131	4,717	4,619	4,391	4,331	3,902	3,584
Aluminum oxide, except natural alumina (100 percent A12O3)	3313110100	(D)	(D)	(D)	(D)	(D)	2,918
Aluminum sulfate (commercial) (17 percent aluminum oxide) [4]	3251887151	1,076	967	1,022	967	(S)	831
Sodium chlorite (100 percent)	325188A141	940	523	615	617	607	420
Sodium silicates (soluble silicate glass, liquid and solid) (anhydrous)[5]	325188A181	1,136	1,309	1,270	1,182	1,106	981
Metasilicate anhydrous (100 percent)	325188A187	72	59	28,772	(D)	(D)	(D)
Sodium sulfate (100 percent)	325188A1A7	509	93	101	93	87	47
Granular carbons, activated (dry weight) [6,7]	325998H1E4	95	(D)	24	27	(S)	(S)
Pulverized carbons, activated, (dry weight) [6]	325998H1E7	71	(D)	64	98	(S)	(S)
Hydrogen peroxide (100 percent by weight)	325188G181	1,083	365	390	429	437	377

D Withheld to avoid disclosing data for individual companies. S Does not meet publication standards. [1] Production includes amounts liquefied. [2] Liquid production figures represent total production, including quantities later evaporated to solid caustic. [3] Includes production from salt and acid. [4] Excludes quantities produced and consumed in municipalities. [5] Excludes amounts produced and consumed in making meta, ortho, and sesquisilicates. [6] Excludes reactivated carbon. [7] Includes pelleted carbon.

Source: U.S. Census Bureau, Current Industrial Reports, "Inorganic Chemicals," Series MQ325A, July 2010, and "Fertilizers and Related Chemicals," Series MQ325B, June 2010, <http://www.census.gov/manufacturing/cir/historical_data/mq325a/index .html> and <http://www.census.gov/manufacturing/cir/historical_data/mq325b/index.html>.

Table 1029. Iron and Steel Industry—Summary: 1990 to 2010

[95.5 represents 95,500,000 tons. Comprises carbon, alloy, and stainless steel]

Item	Unit	1990	1995	2000	2005	2008	2009	2010
Steel mill products, apparent supply	Mil. tons [1]	95.5	109.6	131.9	120.8	111.0	67.1	90.2
Net shipments, total	Mil. tons [1]	85.0	97.5	109.1	105.0	98.5	62.2	83.4
STEEL MARKETS								
Automotive	Mil. tons [1]	11.1	14.6	16.1	14.5	12.8	8.0	10.6
Steel service centers, distributors	Mil. tons [1]	21.1	23.8	30.1	30.6	25.5	15.2	22.5
Construction, including maintenance [2]	Mil. tons [1]	9.2	14.9	20.3	24.0	20.4	14.8	18.0
Containers, packaging, shipping	Mil. tons [1]	4.5	4.1	3.7	3.0	2.8	2.2	2.6
Machinery, industrial equipment, tools	Mil. tons [1]	2.4	2.3	1.8	1.7	1.1	0.6	0.9
Steel for converting and processing	Mil. tons [1]	9.4	10.4	12.7	5.6	6.0	3.8	5.3
Rail transportation	Mil. tons [1]	1.1	1.4	1.3	1.3	1.5	0.9	0.9
Contractors' products	Mil. tons [1]	2.9	(2)	(2)	(2)	(2)	(2)	(2)
Oil and gas industries	Mil. tons [1]	1.9	2.6	2.9	3.1	2.4	0.9	2.1
Electrical equipment	Mil. tons [1]	2.5	2.4	2.1	1.2	0.9	0.5	0.7
Appliances, utensils, and cutlery	Mil. tons [1]	1.5	1.6	1.9	1.9	1.8	1.2	1.4
Other	Mil. tons [1]	17.4	19.3	16.2	18.3	23.3	14.1	18.5
Exports of steel mill products	Mil. tons [1]	4.3	7.1	6.5	9.4	13.5	9.3	12.1
Imports of steel mill products	Mil. tons [1]	17.2	24.4	29.4	32.1	31.9	16.2	23.9
Raw steel production [3]	Mil. tons [1]	98.9	104.9	112.2	104.6	101.3	65.5	88.7
Basic oxygen furnaces	Percent	58.5	62.5	53.0	45.0	43.1	25.0	34.3
Electric arc furnaces	Percent	36.9	42.4	47.0	55.0	58.2	40.5	54.4
Steel employment [4]	(1,000)	169	123	151	122	129	(NA)	(NA)

[1] In millions of short tons. Short ton = 2,000 lbs. [2] Beginning 1995, contractors' products included with construction. [3] Raw steel is defined as steel in the first solid state after melting suitable for further processing or sale, including ingots, steel for foundry castings and strand or pressure cast blooms, slabs or other product forms. [4] Covering only those employees engaged in the production and sale of iron and steel products, excludes mining and quarrying operations, transportation, warehousing and other non-steel producing activities.

Source: American Iron and Steel Institute, Washington, DC, Annual Statistical Report (copyright). See also <www.steel.org>.

Table 1030. Metalworking Machinery—Value of Shipments: 2005 to 2009

[In thousands of dollars (2,800,272 represents $2,800,272,000)]

Product description	Product code	2005	2006	2007	2008 [1]	2009 [1]
Metalworking machinery	(X)	**2,800,272**	**3,094,478**	**3,318,208**	**3,435,540**	**1,952,281**
Metal cutting type machine tools	333512 (pt)	2,079,874	2,293,813	2,533,389	2,650,662	1,428,386
Boring and drilling machines	333512A1	110,971	178,487	130,220	161,393	92,612
Gear cutting machines [2]	33351212	(D)	(D)	(D)	(D)	(D)
Grinding and polishing machines	33351221	265,035	259,063	237,928	270,339	165,445
Lathes [3]	33351231	248,240	295,651	375,871	396,793	204,478
Milling machines [4]	33351241	53,582	56,082	81,294	(D)	(D)
Machining centers	33351271	619,563	703,045	807,425	(D)	(D)
Station type machines [5]	33351281	104,481	79,153	(D)	(D)	114,586
Other metal cutting machine tools	33351291	431,962	464,779	585,522	543,791	289,051
Remanufactured metal cutting machine tools	3335126111	93,404	90,172	81,004	(D)	(D)
Metal forming type machine tools	333513 (pt)	720,398	800,665	784,819	784,878	523,895
Punching, shearing, bending, and forming machines	33351311	344,273	403,361	409,791	391,607	256,645
Presses (excluding forging) [6]	33351331	139,924	128,599	135,292	142,282	75,040
All other metal forming type machines [6]	33351351	206,547	228,880	209,309	231,257	163,041
Remanufactured metal forming machine tools	3335137121	(D)	15,081	10,382	19,732	(S)

D Withheld to avoid disclosing data for individual companies. S Figure does not meet publication standards. X Not applicable. [1] Data shown for years 2008 and 2009 do not include metal cutting and forming type machine tools valued under $3,025 each. [2] Data for "Gear cutting machines" are included in total "Metal cutting type." [3] Data for product code 3335123126, "Vertical NC turning machines" are included in total "Metal cutting type," but excluded from product code 33351231. [4] Data for product code 3335124101, "All milling machines valued under $3,025 each" are included in total "Metal cutting type," but excluded from product code 33351241. [5] Data for "Station type machines" are included in total "Metal cutting type." [6] Data for product codes 3335133101 "All presses valued under $3,025 each" and 3335135101 "All other metal forming type machine tools valued under $3,025 each," are included in total "Metal forming type," but excluded from product codes 33351331 and 33351351, respectively.

Source: U.S. Census Bureau, Current Industrial Reports, "Metalworking Machinery," Series MQ333W, August 2010, <http://www.census.gov/manufacturing/cir/historical_data/mq333w/index.html>.

Table 1031. Semiconductors, Electronic Components, and Semiconductor Manufacturing Equipment—Value of Shipments: 2005 to 2009

[In millions of dollars (9,728 represents $9,728,000,000)]

Product description	Product code	2005	2006	2007	2008	2009
Semiconductor machinery	3332950	9,728	12,598	13,190	9,357	5,063
Transmitting, industrial, and special purpose electron tubes [1]	3344111	652	690	734	806	773
Receiving type electron tubes [2]	3344114	621	216	(D)	(D)	(D)
Electron tubes and parts	3344117	72	49	36	31	30
Bare printed circuit boards	3344120	4,856	4,933	4,443	5,269	4,180
Integrated microcircuits [3]	3344131	61,631	54,963	49,781	51,104	40,029
Transistors	3344134	603	679	599	409	358
Diodes and rectifiers	3344137	372	467	457	458	331
Other semiconductor devices [4]	334413A	8,330	10,483	10,176	11,363	11,983
Capacitors for electronic circuitry	3344140	1,113	1,064	945	937	745
Resistors for electronic circuitry	3344150	653	660	645	622	489
Electronic coils, transformers, and other inductors	3344160	1,216	1,231	1,393	1,380	1,058
Connectors for electronic circuitry	3344170	3,589	3,980	4,189	4,065	3,036
Printed circuit assemblies, loaded boards and modules [5]	334418B	20,106	19,591	20,382	20,257	15,001
Crystals, filters, piezoelectric, and other related electronic devices [6]	3344191	779	754	689	656	552
All other miscellaneous transducers [7]	3344194	1,401	1,323	1,466	1,352	1,035
Switches, mechanical types for electronic circuitry	3344197	794	645	662	581	415
Microwave components and devices [8]	334419A	1,306	1,470	1,541	1,286	1,170
All other miscellaneous electronic components	334419E	4,040	4,346	4,831	4,772	3,889

D Figure withheld to avoid disclosure. NA Not available. [1] Except X-ray. [2] Including cathode ray (new and rebuilt). [3] Includes semiconductor networks, microprocessors, and MOS memories. [4] Includes semiconductor parts such as chips, wafers, and heat sinks. [5] Printed circuit boards with inserted electronic components. [6] Except microwave filters. [7] Includes electrical-electronic input/output transducers. [8] Except antennae, tubes, and semiconductors.

Source: U.S. Census Bureau, Current Industrial Reports, "Semiconductors, Electronic Components, and Semiconductor Manufacturing Equipment," Series MA334Q, September 2010, <http://www.census.gov/manufacturing/cir/historical_data/ma334q/index.html>.

Table 1032. Computers and Peripheral Equipment—Value of Shipments: 2004 to 2009

[In millions of dollars (37,895 represents $37,895,000,000)]

Product description	Product code	2004	2005	2006	2007	2008	2009
Electronic computers	334111	37,895	38,386	37,657	36,859	37,542	33,013
Host computers, multiusers	3341111	10,993	11,759	(D)	(D)	(D)	(D)
Single user computers, microprocessor-based, capable of supporting attached peripherals	3341117	26,309	25,906	(D)	(D)	(D)	(D)
Personal computers	3341117107	15,690	(D)	(D)	(D)	(D)	(D)
Workstations	3341117109	1,848	(D)	(D)	2,442	(D)	(D)
Mobile computers, including notebooks, subnotebooks, laptop, and tablet PCs	3341117127	8,456	(D)	(D)	(D)	(D)	(D)
Smart handheld devices	3341117129	(D)	(D)	(D)	(D)	(D)	(D)
All other single user computers	3341117130	(D)	(D)	(D)	25	(D)	(D)
Other computers (array, analog, hybrid, and special-use computers)	334111D	593	721	(D)	299	(S)	183
Computer storage devices (except parts, attachments, and accessories)	3341121	5,034	6,100	6,956	7,872	6,367	6,617
Disk subsystem and disk arrays for multiuser computer systems	3341121109	1,362	2,008	(D)	2,531	(D)	(D)
Disk drives (all sizes)	3341121112	69	11	(D)	150	201	298
Storage Area Networks(SANs)	3341121123	(D)	10	(D)	2,892	(D)	2,683
Tape drives (all sizes)	3341121138	278	289	285	239	264	194
Other computer storage devices	3341121150	(D)	3,781	3,795	2,061	1,321	(D)
Parts, attachments, and accessories for computer storage devices	3341124	1,039	1,441	1,929	1,426	1,327	740
Computer terminals (except point-of-sale and funds-transfer devices, parts, attachments, and accessories)	3341131	274	245	268	331	245	128
Parts, attachments, and accessories for computer terminals (except point-of-sale and funds-transfer devices)	3341134	2	(D)	(D)	(D)	(D)	649
All other miscellaneous computer peripheral (input/output) equipment (except parts, attachments and accessories)	3341191	4,705	4,425	4,517	4,427	4,245	3,382
Parts, subassemblies, and accessories for computer peripheral equipment	3341194	2,257	2,743	2,720	3,171	2,600	5,050
Point-of-sale terminals and funds-transfer devices	3341197	513	497	621	1,034	958	440
Parts and attachments for point-of-sale terminals and funds-transfer devices	334119D	(D)	(D)	35	12	9	(S)
Magnetic and optical recording media	3346130	1,586	1,303	1,364	1,381	(S)	841,538

D Withheld to avoid disclosing data for individual companies. S Withheld because estimates did not meet publication standards.

Source: U.S. Census Bureau, Current Industrial Reports, Computers and Peripheral Equipment, Series MA334R (beginning with 2006, MQ334R), August 2010, <http://www.census.gov/manufacturing/cir/historical_data/mq334r/index.html>.

Table 1033. U.S. Consumer Electronics Sales and Forecasts by Product Category, 2007 to 2010, and Projection, 2011

[In millions of dollars (169,110 represents $169,110,000,000). Represents shipment volumes from manufacturers to U.S. dealers. Includes both domestic production and imports of products to consumer - oriented channels, regardless of retail type, including distribution and direct-to-consumer sales]

Category	2007	2008	2009	2010	2011, proj.
Total	169,110	181,511	169,816	180,066	186,429
In home technologies, total	79,752	85,607	79,450	84,041	87,010
TV sets and displays	24,661	25,827	22,407	19,900	18,787
Digital TV sets and displays [1]	24,519	25,827	22,407	19,900	18,787
LCD flat panel	14,520	17,962	16,905	15,031	14,025
Plasma flat panel	4,488	3,689	3,316	3,451	3,334
Front projection	2,996	2,841	1,748	1,006	994
OLED	(X)	9	11	9	13
High-definition TV	19,439	23,677	21,670	19,009	17,648
Digital combinations	665	703	777	749	710
Video components [1]	4,911	6,846	7,505	6,391	6,767
Component DVD players/recorders	1,765	1,388	1,688	1,193	1,071
Next generation DVD players [2]	345	739	1,121	1,519	1,595
Set-top boxes [1]	2,798	4,719	4,696	3,679	4,101
Direct broadcast satellite (DBS) receivers	1,220	1,064	958	904	871
Cable/multi-system operator (MSO) receivers	1,085	1,300	2,090	1,733	1,637
Digital Media Adapters (DMAs)	152	563	634	645	1,112
Digital video recorders (DVRs)	1,580	3,237	2,557	2,618	3,135
Audio separates/systems detail [1]	5,003	4,483	4,223	4,362	4,485
Home technologies	203	180	139	196	284
Home information technologies and security [1]	42,933	46,400	43,355	51,822	55,730
Personal computers	21,156	23,412	21,608	28,936	32,248
Desktop computers	8,500	6,744	5,626	7,390	7,003
Notebook computers	12,656	16,668	15,982	21,546	25,246
Computer printers	2,802	3,473	2,900	3,128	3,157
Modems/broadband gateways	1,109	1,090	1,110	1,166	1,247
Other computer peripherals	5,093	5,212	5,142	5,436	5,679
Personal computer software	7,084	7,406	6,937	7,611	7,946
Home security systems	3,204	3,588	3,675	3,775	3,915
Communications [1]	2,244	2,051	1,961	1,566	1,240
Phones	576	435	433	290	253
In-vehicle technologies, total	12,257	12,802	8,167	9,111	9,301
Entertainment devices	9,501	8,711	6,004	7,275	7,644
Aftermarket autosound equipment [3]	1,974	1,521	1,230	1,368	1,362
Satellite radio receivers	156	89	64	52	45
Mobile video devices [4]	713	539	366	345	334
Factory-installed autosound	6,814	6,651	4,408	5,561	5,948
Information and security [1]	2,756	4,091	2,163	1,836	1,657
Portable and transportable navigation	2,387	3,731	1,829	1,507	1,345
Anywhere technologies, total	57,900	63,546	62,935	67,286	69,997
Digital imaging [1]	9,197	9,416	8,746	9,719	9,245
Digital cameras	6,517	6,813	6,267	7,234	6,873
All camcorders	2,112	1,885	1,709	1,802	1,745
Digital photo frames	568	718	770	683	627
Portable entertainment [1]	7,349	7,325	6,716	6,835	6,762
Portable Media/MP3 players	5,968	5,844	5,446	5,658	5,549
Electronic gaming [1]	19,738	23,558	22,752	24,224	25,118
Electronic gaming hardware	6,710	7,780	5,719	6,206	6,004
Electronic gaming software	11,154	14,166	15,582	16,517	17,508
e-toys	1,874	1,612	1,451	1,501	1,606
Portable communication [1]	21,616	23,247	24,721	26,508	28,872
Wireless communication technologies [1]	21,162	22,814	24,048	25,401	27,516
Smartphones	8,645	11,393	14,901	17,875	21,240
Consumer electronic enhancements	19,201	19,556	19,264	19,629	20,121
Accessories [1]	14,299	14,777	14,540	14,618	14,859
Primary batteries	6,421	6,565	6,489	6,320	6,372
Blank media [1]	4,902	4,779	4,724	5,011	5,261

X Not applicable. [1] Includes categories, not shown separately. [2] Includes HD-DVD. [3] Includes satellite radio receivers, satellite radio accessories and satellite radio kits, does not include Bluetooth headsets. [4] Includes all fixed navigation units.

Source: Consumer Electronics Association, Arlington, VA. U.S. Consumer Electronics Sales and Forecasts, 2006–2011, January 2011 (copyright).

Table 1034. Telecommunication Equipment—Value of Shipments: 2000 to 2009

[In millions of dollars (15,174 represents $15,174,000,000)]

Product description	Product code	2000	2005	2006	2007	2008	2009
Telephone switching and switchboard equipment	3342101	15,174	1,576	1,812	1,959	1,674	1,045
Carrier line equipment and modems	3342104	13,112	2,824	2,912	3,512	3,137	2,851
Wire line voice and data network equipment	3342107	28,971	12,289	18,563	11,181	4,574	3,191
Communication systems and equipment [1]	3342201	36,357	30,272	32,436	(NA)	(NA)	(NA)
Broadcast, studio, and related electronic equipment	3342202	4,029	3,289	3,653	3,350	4,110	4,237
Wireless networking equipment	3342203	(NA)	(NA)	(NA)	6,159	4,845	4,219
Radio station equipment	3342205	(NA)	(NA)	(NA)	17,824	16,456	16,449
Other communications systems equipment	3342209	(NA)	(NA)	(NA)	6,355	10,882	10,705
Alarm systems [2]	3342901	2,755	1,910	1,526	2,044	2,090	1,663
Vehicular and pedestrian traffic control equipment [3]	3342902	838	1,020	1,048	1,239	1,231	(S)
Intercommunications systems [4]	3342903	447	416	433	438	458	389
Modems, consumer type	3344184	95	98	79	82	87	(D)

D Withheld to avoid disclosing data of individual companies. NA Not available. S Estimates did not meet publication standards. [1] Includes microwave and space satellites. [2] Includes electric sirens and horns. [3] Includes electrical railway signals and attachments. [4] Includes inductive paging systems (selective calling), except telephone and telegraph.

Source: U.S. Census Bureau, Current Industrial Reports, "Telecommunications," Series MQ334P, <http://www.census.gov/manufacturing/cir/historical_data/mq334p/index.html>.

Table 1035. Motor Vehicle Manufactures—Summary by Selected Industry: 2009

[29,994 represents $29,994,000,000. Based on the Annual Survey of Manufactures; see Appendix III]

Industry	2002 NAICS code [1]	All employees [2]			Produc- tion workers [2]	Value of ship- ments [3] (mil. dol.)
		Number	Payroll			
			Total (mil. dol.)	Payroll per employee (dol.)		
Motor vehicle manufacturing, total...........	3361–3363	**616,156**	**29,994**	**48,679**	**467,652**	**301,710**
Motor vehicle, total............................	3361	123,484	7,927	64,195	103,349	149,900
Automobile and light duty motor vehicle	33611	101,510	6,838	67,362	86,354	134,129
Automobile.............................	336111	51,440	3,359	65,291	43,762	53,724
Light truck and utility vehicle	336112	50,070	3,479	69,491	42,592	80,405
Heavy duty truck...........................	33612	21,974	1,089	49,564	16,995	15,771
Motor vehicle body and trailer	3362	89,012	3,520	39,542	67,390	21,289
Motor vehicle body and trailer manufacturing	33621	89,012	3,520	39,542	67,390	21,289
Motor vehicle body	336211	37,561	1,578	42,003	27,494	9,571
Truck trailer	336212	17,781	647	36,386	13,785	4,095
Motor home...............................	336213	6,889	262	38,001	4,983	1,716
Travel trailer and camper	336214	26,781	1,033	38,583	21,128	5,908
Motor vehicle parts.............................	3363	403,660	18,547	45,947	296,913	130,521
Motor vehicle gasoline engine and engine parts....	33631	43,338	2,184	50,389	32,486	16,123
Motor vehicle electrical and electronic equipment...	33632	51,816	2,554	49,281	35,021	13,796
Motor vehicle steering and suspension...........	33633	33,338	1,340	40,198	24,697	8,093
Motor vehicle brake system....................	33634	20,021	796	39,741	14,436	7,541
Motor vehicle transmission and power train parts ...	33635	46,946	2,855	60,813	35,772	21,047
Motor vehicle seating and interior trim...........	33636	37,555	1,562	41,599	26,570	12,942
Motor vehicle metal stamping	33637	65,146	3,074	47,189	49,922	17,739
Other motor vehicle parts.....................	33639	105,501	4,183	39,646	78,009	33,241

[1] North American Industry Classification System, 2002; see text, Section 15, [2] Includes all full-time and part-time employees on the payrolls of operating manufacturing establishments during any part of the pay period that included the 12th of the month specified on the report form. Included are employees on paid sick leave, paid holidays, and paid vacations; not included are proprietors and partners of unincorporated businesses. [3] Includes extensive and unmeasurable duplication from shipments between establishments in the same industry classification.

Source: U.S. Census Bureau, Annual Survey of Manufactures, "Statistics for Industry Groups and Industries: 2009 and 2008," December 2010, <http://www.census.gov/manufacturing/asm/index.html>.

Table 1036. Motor Vehicle Manufactures—Employees, Payroll, and Shipments by Major State: 2009

[7,927,052 represents 7,927,052,000. Industry based on the 2002 North American Industry Classification System (NAICS); see text, Section 15. See footnote 3, Table 1035 for information regarding shipments. Based on the Annual Survey of Manufactures; see Apppendix III]

State	Motor vehicle manufacturing (NAICS 3361)			Motor vehicle parts manufacturing (NAICS 3363)		
	Employees	Payroll (1,000 dol.)	Value of shipments (1,000 dol.)	Employees	Payroll (1,000 dol.)	Value of shipments (1,000 dol.)
United States [1]...........	**123,484**	**7,927,052**	**149,900,446**	**403,660**	**18,547,126**	**130,520,776**
Alabama	10,289	661,398	11,554,222	14,471	611,344	5,962,628
Arizona	–	–	–	2,307	102,689	570,954
Arkansas	–	–	–	4,064	137,529	817,939
California	5,224	381,065	6,755,286	18,332	758,901	5,425,380
Connecticut	–	–	–	(3)	(D)	(D)
Florida	–	–	–	3,183	131,803	702,470
Georgia	1,782	90,625	(D)	6,705	286,178	2,327,290
Illinois.................	3,903	195,086	3,139,563	17,648	757,313	4,787,208
Indiana.................	10,892	714,699	14,626,216	44,537	2,359,643	14,094,643
Iowa.................	–	–	–	3,048	117,320	764,286
Kansas.................	(3)	(D)	(D)	1,658	(D)	(D)
Kentucky	12,013	737,890	(D)	22,931	940,443	8,898,952
Louisiana	(2)	(D)	(D)	1,208	41,884	(D)
Massachusetts.............	–	–	–	1,428	94,053	795,638
Michigan	21,474	1,466,854	31,088,278	79,144	3,939,554	26,291,309
Minnesota	1,759	87,765	(D)	2,134	82,754	428,587
Mississippi.................	(3)	(D)	(D)	2,311	104,485	(D)
Missouri.................	5,353	397,349	(D)	9,001	358,149	2,853,154
Nebraska.................	–	–	–	3,506	125,736	822,248
New Hampshire.............	–	–	–	1,023	30,342	169,833
New York	–	–	–	11,245	623,879	2,838,979
North Carolina.............	(2)	(D)	(D)	12,741	586,175	4,920,321
Ohio.................	14,862	977,473	16,264,699	53,649	2,668,740	16,721,596
Oklahoma	(2)	(D)	(D)	3,025	103,104	623,652
Oregon.................	–	–	–	1,194	55,633	241,980
Pennsylvania.............	–	–	–	8,451	341,234	2,070,884
South Carolina.............	4,041	(D)	(D)	12,032	543,432	5,077,128
South Dakota.............	–	–	–	–	–	–
Tennessee................	(4)	(D)	(D)	23,837	942,561	9,289,397
Texas.................	4,601	331,774	11,296,033	10,098	433,933	3,036,744
Utah.................	–	–	–	2,971	135,311	1,065,081
Virginia.................	(2)	(D)	(D)	4,718	199,758	1,149,559
Washington	–	–	–	2,090	86,161	(D)
West Virginia	–	–	–	1,658	94,180	(D)
Wisconsin	(3)	(D)	(D)	9,423	353,341	2,486,211

– Represents zero. D Withheld to avoid disclosing data on individual companies. [1] Includes states not shown separately.
[2] Employee class size of 1,000 to 2,499. [3] Employee class size of 2,500 to 4,999. [4] Employee class size of 5,000 to 9,999.

Source: U.S. Census Bureau, Annual Survey of Manufactures, "Geographic Area Statistics: Statistics for all Manufacturing by State: 2009 and 2008," December 2010, <http://www.census.gov/manufacturing/asm/index.html>.

Table 1037. Aerospace—Sales, New Orders, and Backlog: 2000 to 2009

[In billions of dollars (109.3 represents $109,300,000,000), except as indicated. Reported by establishments in which the principal business is the development and/or production of aerospace products]

Item	2000	2004	2005	2006	2007	2008	2009
Net sales..........................	109.3	124.3	124.2	155.9	126.8	135.2	145.8
U.S. government net sales.............	41.0	64.2	62.8	69.7	48.4	59.5	59.4
Percent U.S. government..............	37.5	51.7	50.6	44.7	38.2	44.0	40.7
Complete aircraft and parts.............	57.2	49.6	49.9	(D)	(D)	(D)	(D)
Aircraft engines and parts.............	12.5	16.1	18.5	28.6	15.5	(D)	(D)
Missiles and space vehicles, parts	15.6	14.2	(S)	(D)	(D)	(D)	(D)
Other products, services...............	24.0	44.4	45.8	(D)	43.70	(D)	(D)
Net, new orders.....................	140.1	131.7	186.4	202.8	231.6	189.3	107.1
Backlog, December 31	215.0	234.3	290.0	334.5	437.1	482.1	430.7

D Withheld to avoid disclosing data of individual companies. S Does not meet publication standards.

Source: U.S. Census Bureau, Current Industrial Reports, "Civil Aircraft and Aircraft Engines; and Aerospace Industry," Series MA336G, June 2010 ,<http://www.census.gov/manufacturing/cir/historical_data/ma336g/index.html>.

Table 1038. Net Orders for U.S. Civil Jet Transport Aircraft: 1990 to 2010

[1990 data are net new firm orders; beginning 2000, net announced orders. Minus sign (–) indicates net cancellations. In 1997, Boeing acquired McDonnell Douglas]

Type of aircraft and customer	1990	2000	2005	2006	2007	2008	2009	2010
Total number [1]	670	585	1,004	1,058	1,417	662	142	530
U.S. customers	259	412	220	321	281	112	24	232
Foreign customers	411	193	811	737	1,136	550	118	298
Boeing 737, total	189	378	571	739	846	484	178	486
U.S. customers	38	302	152	242	164	107	34	206
Foreign customers	151	86	439	497	682	377	144	280
Boeing 747, total	153	24	43	72	25	3	2	–1
U.S. customers	24	1	13	18	–	–	–2	–2
Foreign customers	129	18	30	54	25	3	4	1
Boeing 757, total	66	43	–	–	–	–	–	–
U.S. customers	33	38	–	–	–	–	–	–
Foreign customers	33	14	–	–	–	–	–	–
Boeing 767, total	60	6	15	10	36	28	2	3
U.S. customers	23	–2	–	–	27	–	–1	–
Foreign customers	37	14	20	10	9	28	3	3
Boeing 777, total	34	113	154	76	141	54	19	46
U.S. customers	34	60	10	35	23	11	–7	3
Foreign customers..................	–	53	146	41	118	43	26	43
Boeing 787, total	–	–	235	161	369	93	–59	–4
U.S. customers	–	–	45	26	67	–6	–	25
Foreign customers..................	–	–	190	135	302	99	–59	–29
McDonnell Douglas MD-11, total..........	52	–	–	–	–	–	–	–
U.S. customers	16	–	–	–	–	–	–	–
Foreign customers	36	–	–	–	–	–	–	–
McDonnell Douglas MD-80/90, total	116	–	–	–	–	–	–	–
U.S. customers	91	–	–	–	–	–	–	–
Foreign customers	25	–	–	–	–	–	–	–
McDonnell Douglas MD-95, total..........	–	21	–	–	–	–	–	–
U.S. customers	–	13	–	–	–	–	–	–
Foreign customers	–	8	–	–	–	–	–	–

– Represents zero. [1] Beginning 2000, includes unidentified customers.

Source: Aerospace Industries Association of America, Washington, DC, "Orders: U.S. Civil Jet Transport Aircraft," Statistical Series 22, <http://www.aia-aerospace.org/industry_information/economics/aerospace_statistics/>.

Table 1039. U.S. Aircraft Shipments: 1990 to 2010

[Value in millions of dollars (38,585 represents $38,585,000,000)]

Year	Total		Civil						Military	
			Large transports		General aviation [1]		Rotocraft			
	Units	Value	Units	Value	Units	Value	Units	Value	Units	Value
1990	3,321	38,585	521	22,215	1,144	2,007	603	254	1,053	14,109
1995........	2,441	33,658	256	15,263	1,077	2,842	292	194	816	15,359
1996........	2,220	37,518	269	18,915	1,115	3,048	278	193	558	15,363
1997........	2,780	43,652	374	26,929	1,549	4,593	346	231	511	11,899
1998........	3,534	53,728	559	35,663	2,193	5,534	363	252	419	12,280
1999........	3,797	56,692	620	38,171	2,475	6,803	345	200	357	11,518
2000........	4,113	50,289	485	30,327	2,802	8,040	493	270	333	11,652
2001........	3,904	56,221	526	34,155	2,616	7,991	415	247	347	13,828
2002........	3,252	49,361	379	27,547	2,196	7,261	318	157	359	14,396
2003........	3,261	42,431	281	21,033	2,080	6,205	517	366	383	14,827
2004........	3,802	43,555	283	20,484	2,296	6,918	805	515	418	15,639
2005........	4,677	51,190	290	22,116	2,853	8,632	947	816	587	19,626
2006........	5,426	55,472	398	25,875	3,134	9,550	898	843	996	19,204
2007........	5,350	68,823	441	29,160	3,279	11,941	1,009	1,330	1,062	26,392
2008........	5,263	72,892	375	24,076	3,079	13,348	1,084	1,486	725	33,982
2009........	3,399	71,272	381	27,350	1,585	9,082	564	972	869	33,868
2010........	2,842	71,831	459	29,265	1,334	7,875	249	791	800	33,900

[1] Excludes off-the-shelf military aircraft.

Source: U.S. Department of Commerce, International Trade Administration, "Shipments of Complete U.S. Aircraft, 1971–2010," <http://trade.gov/mas/manufacturing/OAAI/aero_stats.asp\>.

Manufactures 651

Table 1040. Aerospace Industry Sales by Product Group and Customer: 1990 to 2010

[In billions of dollars (134.4 represents $134,400,000,000). Due to reporting practices and tabulatimg methods, figures may differ from those in Table 1038]

Group	1990	2000	2005 [1]	2006	2007	2008	2009	2010
CURRENT DOLLARS								
Total sales.	**134.4**	**144.7**	**167.3**	**182.8**	**197.0**	**200.3**	**211.9**	**214.5**
Product group:								
Aircraft, total	71.4	81.6	86.7	98.3	105.2	102.7	110.8	112.3
Civil [2]	31.3	47.6	37.2	45.8	52.6	48.2	51.1	47.9
Military	40.1	34.0	49.5	52.4	52.7	54.5	59.7	64.5
Missiles	14.2	9.3	18.4	20.3	22.2	23.4	25.8	26.9
Space	26.4	29.7	36.7	37.6	39.9	43.4	45.5	45.9
Related products and services [3]	22.4	24.1	25.5	26.7	29.6	30.8	29.9	29.3
Customer group:								
Aerospace products and services, total	112.0	120.6	141.8	156.2	167.3	169.5	182.1	185.1
DOD [4]	60.5	47.5	75.6	77.6	80.7	84.9	95.4	102.1
NASA [5] and other agencies	11.1	13.4	17.3	17.2	18.7	21.3	22.5	22.1
Other customers [6]	40.4	59.7	48.9	61.3	68.0	63.4	64.2	60.9
Related products and services [3]	22.4	24.1	25.5	26.7	29.7	30.7	32.5	31.4
CONSTANT (2000) DOLLARS [7]								
Total sales.	**123.5**	**144.7**	**146.0**	**154.0**	**160.9**	**157.8**	**162.9**	**162.9**
Product group:								
Aircraft, total	65.6	81.6	75.6	82.8	86.0	80.9	85.2	85.3
Civil [2]	28.7	47.6	32.4	38.6	42.9	38.0	39.3	36.3
Military	36.8	34.0	43.2	44.2	43.0	43.0	45.9	49.0
Missiles	13.0	9.3	16.1	17.1	18.1	18.5	19.8	20.4
Space	24.3	29.7	32.0	31.7	32.6	34.2	35.0	34.9
Related products and services [3]	20.6	24.1	22.3	22.5	24.2	24.3	23.0	22.3
Customer group:								
Aerospace products and services, total	102.9	120.6	123.7	131.5	136.7	133.5	140.0	140.8
DOD [4]	55.6	47.5	66.0	65.4	65.9	66.8	73.3	77.7
NASA [5] and other agencies	10.2	13.4	15.1	14.5	15.2	16.8	17.3	16.8
Other customers [6]	37.1	59.7	42.7	51.6	55.6	49.9	49.4	46.3
Related products and services [3]	20.6	24.1	22.3	22.5	24.3	24.2	25.0	23.9

[1] Beginning in 2005, sales numbers for individual product groups are not comparable to figures in prior years due to revised survey methodology. However, total annual sales data remain comparable across all years of the time series. [2] All civil sales of aircraft (domestic and export sales of jet transports, commuters, business, and personal aircraft and helicopters). [3] Electronics, software, and ground support equipment, plus sales of non-aerospace products which are produced by aerospace-manufacturing use technology, processes, and materials derived from aerospace products. [4] Department of Defense. [5] National Aeronautics and Space Administration. [6] Includes civil aircraft sales (see footnote 4), commercial space sales, all exports of military aircraft and missiles and related propulsion and parts. [7] Based on Aerospace Industry Association's aerospace composite price deflator (200=100).

Source: Aerospace Industries Association of America, Inc., Washington, DC, "2010 Year-end Review and Forecast," December 2010, <http://www.aia-aerospace.org/economics/year_end_review_and_forecast>.

Table 1041. Major Household Appliances—Value of Shipments: 2000 to 2009

[In millions of dollars (2,170 represents $2,170,000,000)]

Product description	Product code	2000	2005	2006	2007	2008	2009
Electric household ranges, ovens and surface cooking units, equipment and parts	3352211	2,170	2,577	2,541	2,736	2,506	2,062
Gas household ranges, ovens, and surface cooking units, equipment and parts	3352213	779	1,392	1,363	1,541	1,473	1,126
Other household ranges, cooking equipment and outdoor cooking equipment [1]	3352215	1,251	965	784	491	510	485
Household refrigerators, including combination refrigerator-freezers	3352221	5,396	5,405	5,427	5,440	5,891	5,189
Parts and attachments for household refrigerators and freezers	3352223	(D)	(D)	(D)	159	107	92
Household laundry machines and parts	3352240	4,047	5,236	5,184	5,232	5,835	4,820
Water heaters, electric	3352281	573	638	652	950	953	869
Water heaters, except electric	3352283	844	970	903	1,572	1,547	1,452
Household appliances, n.e.c and parts [2]	3352285	2,066	2,433	2,413	2,717	2,602	2,126

D Withheld to avoid disclosing data of individual companies. [1] Includes parts and accessories. [2] n.e.c. means not elsewhere classified.

Source: U.S. Census Bureau, Current Industrial Reports, "Major Household Appliances," Series MA335F, <http://www.census.gov/manufacturing/cir/historical_data/mq335f/index.html>.

Section 22
Wholesale and Retail Trade

This section presents statistics relating to the distributive trades, specifically wholesale trade and retail trade. Data shown for the trades are classified by kind of business and cover sales, establishments, employees, payrolls, and other items. The principal sources of these data are from the U.S. Census Bureau and include the *2007 Economic Census*, annual and monthly surveys, and the *County Business Patterns* program. These data are supplemented by several tables from trade associations, such as the National Automobile Dealers Association (Table 1057). Several notable research groups are also represented, such as Nielsen Claritas (Table 1059).

Data on wholesale and retail trade also appear in several other sections. For instance, labor force employment and earnings data appear in Section 12, Labor Force, Employment, and Earnings; gross domestic product of the industry (Table 653) appears in Section 13, Income, Expenditures, Poverty, and Wealth; and financial data (several tables) from the quarterly *Statistics of Income Bulletin,* published by the Internal Revenue Service, appear in Section 15, Business Enterprise.

Censuses—Censuses of wholesale trade and retail trade have been taken at various intervals since 1929. Beginning with the 1967 census, legislation provides for a census of each area to be conducted every 5 years (for years ending in "2" and "7"). For more information on the most recent census, see the *Guide to the 2007 Economic Census* found at <http://www .census.gov/econ/census07 /www/user_guide.html>. The industries covered in the censuses and surveys of business are defined in the *North American Industry Classification System*, (NAICS). Retail trade refers to places of business primarily engaged in retailing merchandise to the general public; and *wholesale trade*, to establishments primarily engaged in selling goods to other businesses and normally operating from a warehouse or office that have little

or no display of merchandise.

Many Census Bureau tables in this section utilize the 2002 NAICS codes, which replaced the Standard Industrial Classification (SIC) system. NAICS made substantial structural improvements and identifies over 350 new industries. At the same time, it causes breaks in time series far more profound than any prior revision of the previously used SIC system. For information on this system and how it affects the comparability of wholesale and retail statistics historically, see text, Section 15, Business Enterprise, and especially the Census Bureau Web site at <http://www.census.gov/eos/www /naics>. In general, the 2007 Economic Census has three series of publications for these two sectors: 1) subject series with reports such as product lines and establishment and firm sizes, 2) geographic reports with individual reports for each state, and 3) industry series with individual reports for industry groups. For information on these series, see the Census Bureau Web site at <http://www .census.gov/econ/census07/>.

Current surveys—Current sample surveys conducted by the Census Bureau cover various aspects of wholesale and retail trade. Its *Monthly Retail Trade and Food Services* release at <http://www .census.gov/retail> contains monthly estimates of sales, inventories, and inventory/sales ratios for the United States, by kind of business. Annual figures on retail sales, year-end inventories, purchases, accounts receivable, and gross margins by kind of business are located on the Census Bureau Web site at <http://www.census.gov/econ/retail .htm>. Additionally, annual data for accommodation and food services are located at the same site.

Statistics from the Census Bureau's monthly wholesale trade survey include national estimates of sales, inventories, and inventory/sales ratios for merchant wholesalers excluding manufacturers' sales branches and offices. Data are

Wholesale and Retail Trade 653

presented by major summary groups "durable and nondurable," and 4-digit NAICS industry groups. Merchant wholesalers excluding manufacturers' sales branches and offices are those wholesalers who take title to the goods they sell (e.g., jobbers, exporters, importers, industrial distributors). These data, based on reports submitted by a sample of firms, appear in the *Monthly Wholesale Trade Report* at <http://www.census.gov/wholesale>. This report, along with monthly sales, inventories, and inventories/sales ratios, also provides data on annual sales, inventories, and year-end inventories/sales ratios. The Annual Wholesale Trade Survey provides data on merchant wholesalers excluding manufacturer sales branches and offices as well as summary data for all merchant wholesalers. This report also provides separate data for manufacturer sales branches and offices, and electronic markets, agents, brokers, and commission merchants. Also included in the *Monthly Wholesale Trade Report are* data on annual sales, year-end inventories, inventories/sales ratios, operating expenses, purchases, and gross margins. Data are presented by major summary groups "durable and nondurable" and 4-digit NAICS industry groups for sales,

end-of-year inventories, and operating expenses. The reports are available as documents on the Census Bureau Web site at <http://www.census.gov/econ /wholesale.htm>.

E-commerce—Electronic commerce (or e-commerce) is sales of goods and services over the Internet and extranet, electronic data interchange (EDI), or other online systems. Payment may or may not be made online. E-commerce data were collected in four separate Census Bureau surveys. These surveys used different measures of economic activity such as shipments for manufacturing, sales for wholesale and retail trade, and revenues for service industries. Consequently, measures of total economic and e-commerce activity vary by economic sector, are conceptually and definitionally different, and therefore, are not additive. This edition has several tables on e-commerce sales, such as Tables 1045, 1055, and 1056 in this section; and 1278 in Section 27, Accommodation, Food Services, and Other Services.

Statistical reliability—For a discussion of statistical collection and estimation, sampling procedures, and measures of statistical reliability applicable to Census Bureau data, see Appendix III.

Table 1042. Wholesale and Retail Trade—Establishments, Sales, Payroll, and Employees: 2002 and 2007

[435.5 represents $435,500. Covers establishments with payroll. For statement on methodology, see Appendix III]

Kind of business	2002 NAICS code [1]	Establishments (1,000)		Sales (bil. dol.)		Annual payroll (bil. dol.)		Paid employees (1,000)	
		2002	2007	2002	2007	2002	2007	2002	2007
Wholesale trade	**42**	**435.5**	**435.0**	**4,635**	**6,516**	**260**	**336**	**5,878**	**6,227**
Wholesale trade, durable goods	423	260.4	255.0	2,171	2,898	157	207	3,357	3,619
Wholesale trade, nondurable goods	424	142.7	134.6	1,980	2,991	93	116	2,273	2,320
Wholesale electronic markets and agents and brokers	425	32.4	45.4	483	627	10	13	249	289
Retail trade	**44–45**	**1,114.6**	**1,128.1**	**3,056**	**3,918**	**302**	**363**	**14,648**	**15,515**
Motor vehicle and parts dealers	441	125.1	126.8	802	891	65	73	1,845	1,914
Furniture and home furnishings stores	442	65.2	65.1	92	108	13	15	535	557
Electronics and appliance stores	443	46.8	50.8	82	109	9	11	391	486
Building material and garden equipment and supplies dealers	444	(NA)	91.1	(NA)	318	(NA)	38	(NA)	1,331
Food and beverage stores	445	148.8	146.1	457	539	49	55	2,839	2,827
Health and personal care stores	446	81.8	88.5	178	234	20	28	1,024	1,068
Gasoline stations	447	121.4	118.8	249	450	14	15	927	891
Clothing and clothing accessories stores	448	149.8	156.5	168	216	21	27	1,427	1,644
Sporting goods, hobby, book, and music stores	451	62.2	57.4	73	81	9	9	611	619
General merchandise stores	452	40.7	45.9	445	577	43	54	2,525	2,763
Miscellaneous store retailers	453	129.5	121.9	91	104	13	14	792	792
Nonstore retailers	454	54.9	59.4	173	290	17	23	571	621

NA Not available. [1] North American Industrial Classification System; see text, Section 15.

Source: U.S. Census Bureau, "2007 Economic Census, Comparative Statistics for the United States, (2002 NAICS Basis): 2007 and 2002," July 2010, <http://www.census.gov/econ/census07/>.

Table 1043. Wholesale Trade—Nonemployer Firms and Receipts by Industry Type: 2008

[35,558,379 represents $35,558,379,000. Includes only firms subject to federal income tax. Nonemployers are businesses with no paid employees. A firm is a single physical location where business is conducted or services or industrial operations are performed. Each distinct business income tax return filed by a nonemployer business is counted as a firm. Based on NAICS 2007, see text, Section 15]

Industy type	2007 NAICS code [1]	Firms				Receipts ($1,000)
		Total	Corpora-tions [2]	Individual proprietor-ships [3]	Partner-ships [4]	
Wholesale trade, total	**42**	**388,298**	**68,723**	**303,783**	**15,792**	**35,558,379**
Durable goods merchant wholesalers	**423**	**194,592**	**38,172**	**147,832**	**8,588**	**19,478,901**
Motor vehicle and motor vehicle parts and supplies merchant wholesalers	4231	16,324	3,545	12,080	699	2,457,040
Furniture and home furnishing merchant wholesalers	4232	13,853	2,230	11,028	595	1,141,288
Lumber and other construction materials merchant wholesalers	4233	8,557	1,884	6,124	549	989,129
Professional and commercial equipment and supplies merchant wholesalers	4234	10,513	2,123	7,891	499	1,119,132
Metal and mineral (except petroleum) merchant wholesalers	4235	3,231	737	2,345	149	520,663
Electrical and electronic goods merchant wholesalers	4236	10,768	2,987	7,231	550	1,252,357
Hardware and plumbing and heating equipment and supplies merchant wholesalers	4237	4,962	1,160	3,561	241	538,545
Machinery, equipment, and supplies merchant wholesalers	4238	19,010	5,249	12,817	944	2,691,743
Miscellaneous durable goods merchant wholesalers	4239	107,374	18,257	84,755	4,362	8,769,004
Nondurable goods merchant wholesalers	**424**	**145,715**	**25,597**	**114,097**	**6,021**	**12,972,847**
Paper and paper product merchant wholesalers	4241	6,729	1,139	5,352	238	542,368
Drugs and druggists' sundries merchant wholesalers	4242	2,796	644	2,026	126	232,209
Apparel, piece goods, and notions merchant wholesalers	4243	22,681	4,262	17,374	1,045	1,664,534
Grocery and related products merchant wholesalers	4244	27,181	5,008	21,169	1,004	3,765,473
Farm product raw material merchant wholesalers	4245	4,544	648	3,713	183	542,500
Chemical and allied products merchant wholesalers	4246	3,661	1,138	2,266	257	432,324
Petroleum and petroleum products merchant wholesalers	4247	2,316	481	1,698	137	326,312
Beer, wine, and distilled alcoholic beverage merchant wholesalers	4248	4,058	777	2,908	373	363,536
Miscellaneous nondurable goods merchant wholesalers	4249	71,749	11,500	57,591	2,658	5,103,591
Wholesale electronic markets and agents and brokers	**425**	**47,991**	**4,954**	**41,854**	**1,183**	**3,106,631**
Business to business electronics markets	42511	6,965	778	5,953	234	448,048

[1] North American Industry Classification System, 2007. See text, Section 15. [2] A legally incorporated business under state laws. [3] Also referred to as "sole proprietorship," an unincorporated business with a sole owner. Includes self-employed persons. [4] An unincorporated business where two or more persons join to carry on a trade or business with each having a shared financial interest in the business.

Source: U.S. Census Bureau, "Nonemployer Statistics," June 2010, <http://www.census.gov/econ/nonemployer/index.html>.

Wholesale and Retail Trade 655

Table 1044. Wholesale Trade—Establishments, Employees, and Payroll: 2007 and 2008

[434.5 represents 434,500. Covers establishments with payroll. Excludes self-employed individuals, employees of private households, railroad employees, agricultural production employees, and most government employees. For statement on methodology, see Appendix III]

Kind of business	2002 NAICS code [1]	Establishments (1,000)		Employees [2] (1,000)		Payroll (bil. dol.)	
		2007	2008	2007	2008	2007	2008
Wholesale trade, total	42	434.5	429.5	5,965	6,165	328.0	353.1
Merchant wholesalers, durable goods.	423	247.3	248.5	3,395	3,553	197.1	215.8
Motor vehicle/motor vehicle parts and supply merchant wholesalers.	4231	24.5	26.0	356	395	15.9	17.9
Furniture and home furnishing merchant wholesalers	4232	12.7	13.6	154	169	7.4	8.2
Lumber and other construction materials merchant wholesalers.	4233	19.6	19.4	264	256	12.5	12.1
Professional and commercial equipment and supplies merchant wholesalers.	4234	36.1	35.0	706	724	49.8	55.8
Metal and mineral (except petroleum) merchant wholesalers.	4235	10.7	11.1	160	169	9.4	10.0
Electrical goods merchant wholesalers.	4236	29.4	30.0	450	510	34.3	41.2
Hardware, plumbing and heating equipment and supplies merchant wholesalers	4237	20.1	20.2	232	244	11.9	12.7
Machinery, equipment, and supplies merchant wholesalers.	4238	59.7	59.5	724	738	39.8	41.4
Miscellaneous durable goods merchant wholesalers	4239	34.5	33.6	350	349	16.2	16.6
Merchant wholesalers, nondurable goods.	424	130.6	129.8	2,228	2,313	113.6	122.3
Paper and paper product merchant wholesalers.	4241	11.4	11.5	172	171	8.8	8.6
Drugs and druggists' sundries merchant wholesalers.	4242	7.6	8.6	248	274	19.9	22.6
Apparel, piece goods and notions merchant wholesalers. . .	4243	16.2	16.5	197	211	10.3	10.9
Grocery and related product merchant wholesalers	4244	33.6	33.0	768	796	34.2	36.2
Farm product raw material merchant wholesalers.	4245	6.6	6.3	61	61	2.5	2.9
Chemical and allied products merchant wholesalers	4246	12.5	12.8	139	150	8.6	9.8
Petroleum and petroleum products merchant wholesalers . .	4247	7.0	7.3	95	105	5.6	6.3
Beer, wine, and distilled alcoholic beverages	4248	4.2	4.2	179	184	9.1	9.7
Miscellaneous nondurable goods merchant wholesalers . . .	4249	31.4	29.6	368	362	14.7	15.3
Wholesale electronic markets and agents and brokers.	425	56.5	51.2	342	299	17.2	15.0

[1] North American Industry Classification System, 2002; data for 2008 based on NAICS 2007. See text, Section 15.
[2] Covers full- and part-time employees who are on the payroll in the pay period including March 12.
Source: U.S. Census Bureau, "County Business Patterns," July 2010, <http://www.census.gov/econ/cbp/index.html>.

Table 1045. Merchant Wholesale Trade Sales—Total and E-Commerce: 2009

[3,706,945 represents $3,706,945,000,000. Covers only businesses with paid employees. Excludes manufacturers' sales branches and offices. Based on the Annual Wholesale Trade Survey, see Appendix III]

Kind of business	2002 NAICS code [1]	2009			
		Value of sales (mil. dol.)		E-commerce as percent of total sales	Percent distribution of E-commerce sales
		Total	E-commerce		
Total merchant wholesale trade	42	3,706,945	728,663	19.7	100.0
Durable goods.	423	1,679,308	281,951	16.8	38.7
Motor vehicles, parts and supplies	4231	250,762	94,762	37.8	13.0
Furniture and home furnishings.	4232	51,098	6,866	13.4	0.9
Lumber and other construction materials	4233	90,203	4,806	5.3	0.7
Professional and commercial equipment and supplies . . .	4234	335,642	93,022	27.7	12.8
Computer, peripheral equipment, and software.	42343	166,788	56,723	34.0	0.8
Metals and minerals (except petroleum)	4235	104,115	2,717	2.6	0.4
Electrical goods.	4236	312,648	38,196	12.2	5.2
Hardware, and plumbing and heating equipment and supplies.	4237	90,039	9,617	10.7	1.3
Machinery, equipment and supplies	4238	275,201	10,625	3.9	1.5
Miscellaneous durable goods	4239	169,600	21,340	12.6	2.9
Nondurable goods.	424	2,027,637	446,712	22.0	61.3
Paper and paper products.	4241	81,581	14,748	18.0	2.0
Drugs and druggists' sundries.	4242	376,102	281,205	74.8	38.6
Apparel, piece goods and notions	4243	123,854	31,523	25.5	4.3
Groceries and related products.	4244	475,893	67,791	14.2	9.3
Farm product raw materials.	4245	164,757	(S)	(S)	(S)
Chemical and allied products	4246	90,290	4,494	5.0	0.6
Petroleum and petroleum products	4247	404,997	(S)	(S)	(S)
Beer, wine, and distilled alcoholic beverages	4248	107,842	(S)	(S)	(S)
Miscellaneous nondurable goods	4249	202,591	27,180	13.4	3.7

S Figure does not meet publication standards. [1] North American Industry Classification System, 2002. See text, Section 15.
Source: U.S. Census Bureau, "E-Stats, 2009 E-commerce Multi-sector Report," May 2011, <http://www.census.gov/econ/estats/>.

Table 1046. Merchant Wholesalers—Summary: 2000 to 2009

[In billions of dollars (2,814.6 represents $2,814,600,000,000), except ratios. Inventories and inventories/sales ratios, as of December, not seasonally adjusted. Excludes manufacturers' sales branches and offices. Data adjusted using final results of the 2007 Economic Census. Based on data from the Annual Wholesale Trade Survey and the Monthly Wholesale Trade Survey; see Appendix III]

Kind of business	2002 NAICS code [1]	2000	2004	2005	2006	2007	2008	2009
SALES								
Merchant wholesalers	42	**2,814.6**	**3,320.0**	**3,615.4**	**3,904.0**	**4,174.3**	**4,435.2**	**3,706.9**
Durable goods	423	**1,486.7**	**1,682.1**	**1,815.5**	**1,983.7**	**2,074.5**	**2,079.4**	**1,679.3**
Motor vehicles, parts, and supplies	4231	222.2	284.2	304.5	336.1	341.2	308.1	250.8
Furniture and home furnishings	4232	52.7	59.8	63.1	69.1	69.1	64.1	51.1
Lumber and other construction materials	4233	87.2	127.2	138.7	141.6	126.5	116.1	90.2
Professional, commercial equipment and supplies	4234	282.2	300.8	316.3	330.0	354.3	359.3	335.6
Computer, peripheral equipment and software	42343	174.8	157.2	162.5	160.9	171.3	176.2	166.8
Metal and mineral (except petroleum)	4235	93.8	121.0	136.3	158.4	165.9	177.9	104.1
Electrical and electronic goods	4236	260.0	266.1	285.1	320.2	349.0	354.2	312.6
Hardware, plumbing, heating equipment and supplies	4237	72.1	84.0	94.7	108.5	112.2	108.3	90.0
Machinery, equipment, and supplies	4238	256.1	260.2	288.3	312.8	328.8	351.7	275.2
Miscellaneous durable goods	4239	160.3	178.6	188.6	207.0	227.4	239.8	169.6
Nondurable goods	424	**1,327.9**	**1,637.9**	**1,799.8**	**1,920.3**	**2,099.8**	**2,355.8**	**2,027.6**
Paper and paper products	4241	77.8	81.7	86.8	89.9	91.3	90.9	81.6
Drugs and druggists' sundries	4242	176.0	293.8	324.5	341.9	351.8	369.2	376.1
Apparel, piece goods, and notions	4243	96.5	114.9	123.1	131.5	139.7	136.9	123.6
Grocery and related products	4244	374.7	402.3	418.6	434.4	475.8	488.9	475.9
Farm product raw materials	4245	102.7	115.4	106.0	111.3	145.8	197.4	164.8
Chemical and allied products	4246	62.3	79.5	92.1	95.8	102.3	116.1	90.3
Petroleum and petroleum products	4247	195.8	284.1	368.7	425.9	486.9	631.6	405.0
Beer, wine, and distilled alcoholic beverages	4248	71.3	86.9	92.3	98.5	103.8	106.9	107.8
Miscellaneous nondurable goods	4249	170.9	179.4	187.8	191.2	202.5	217.9	202.6
INVENTORIES								
Merchant wholesalers	42	**309.4**	**341.3**	**368.8**	**399.3**	**425.0**	**439.7**	**389.2**
Durable goods	423	**198.6**	**213.9**	**233.1**	**255.9**	**262.5**	**276.5**	**227.3**
Motor vehicles, parts, and supplies	4231	28.8	33.9	37.8	40.4	42.1	46.1	35.2
Furniture and home furnishings	4232	6.4	7.2	7.8	8.4	8.5	8.1	6.4
Lumber and other construction materials	4233	8.4	13.3	14.2	14.5	13.7	13.0	10.4
Professional, commercial equipment and supplies	4234	27.8	26.4	27.3	29.5	30.2	30.6	27.9
Computer, peripheral equipment and software	42343	12.1	10.1	10.1	10.6	10.4	10.5	10.2
Metal and mineral (except petroleum)	4235	13.4	20.1	21.1	26.6	25.2	28.9	19.0
Electrical and electronic goods	4236	31.1	28.1	30.5	34.4	37.0	38.4	32.9
Hardware, plumbing, heating equipment and supplies	4237	11.5	13.5	15.3	17.2	18.1	17.3	15.2
Machinery, equipment, and supplies	4238	51.2	50.3	56.3	61.4	64.5	69.7	59.5
Miscellaneous durable goods	4239	20.1	21.2	22.8	23.5	23.1	24.3	21.0
Nondurable goods	424	**110.9**	**127.4**	**135.6**	**143.4**	**162.5**	**163.2**	**161.8**
Paper and paper products	4241	6.7	6.6	7.1	7.2	7.3	7.7	6.9
Drugs and druggists' sundries	4242	24.1	31.7	29.7	30.6	31.7	32.0	32.2
Apparel, piece goods, and notions	4243	13.7	15.5	17.2	17.7	18.1	19.3	15.6
Grocery and related products	4244	20.4	20.5	22.4	24.1	26.6	28.6	27.1
Farm product raw materials	4245	11.6	10.0	11.2	14.3	20.5	17.4	19.6
Chemical and allied products	4246	6.0	7.4	8.4	8.6	9.7	10.5	8.9
Petroleum and petroleum products	4247	5.2	9.5	12.2	13.1	17.1	13.0	19.9
Beer, wine, and distilled alcoholic beverages	4248	6.5	7.7	8.4	9.1	10.2	11.0	10.5
Miscellaneous nondurable goods	4249	16.6	18.4	19.1	18.9	21.4	23.7	21.3
INVENTORIES/SALES RATIO								
Merchant wholesalers	42	**1.03**	**1.03**	**1.02**	**1.02**	**1.02**	**0.99**	**1.05**
Durable goods	423	**1.27**	**1.27**	**1.28**	**1.29**	**1.27**	**1.33**	**1.35**
Motor vehicles, parts, and supplies	4231	1.19	1.19	1.24	1.20	1.23	1.50	1.40
Furniture and home furnishings	4232	1.20	1.20	1.24	1.22	1.23	1.27	1.24
Lumber and other construction materials	4233	1.04	1.04	1.02	1.02	1.08	1.12	1.15
Professional, commercial equipment and supplies	4234	0.88	0.88	0.86	0.89	0.85	0.85	0.83
Computer, peripheral equipment and software	42343	0.64	0.64	0.62	0.66	0.61	0.60	0.61
Metal and mineral (except petroleum)	4235	1.66	1.66	1.55	1.68	1.52	1.62	1.82
Electrical and electronic goods	4236	1.05	1.05	1.07	1.07	1.06	1.08	1.05
Hardware, plumbing, heating equipment and supplies	4237	1.61	1.61	1.62	1.58	1.61	1.60	1.69
Machinery, equipment, and supplies	4238	1.93	1.93	1.95	1.96	1.96	1.98	2.16
Miscellaneous durable goods	4239	1.18	1.18	1.21	1.13	1.02	1.01	1.24
Nondurable goods	424	**0.83**	**0.78**	**0.75**	**0.75**	**0.77**	**0.69**	**0.80**
Paper and paper products	4241	0.86	0.80	0.82	0.80	0.80	0.84	0.84
Drugs and druggists' sundries	4242	1.37	1.08	0.92	0.89	0.90	0.87	0.86
Apparel, piece goods, and notions	4243	1.42	1.35	1.40	1.34	1.29	1.41	1.26
Grocery and related products	4244	0.54	0.51	0.54	0.55	0.56	0.58	0.57
Farm product raw materials	4245	1.13	0.87	1.05	1.28	1.40	0.88	1.19
Chemical and allied products	4246	0.97	0.93	0.91	0.90	0.95	0.90	0.98
Petroleum and petroleum products	4247	0.26	0.33	0.33	0.31	0.35	0.21	0.49
Beer, wine, and distilled alcoholic beverages	4248	0.91	0.89	0.91	0.92	0.99	1.03	0.97
Miscellaneous nondurable goods	4249	0.97	1.03	1.01	0.99	1.05	1.09	1.05

[1] North American Industry Classification System, 2002. See text, Section 15.

Source: U.S. Census Bureau, "2009 Annual Wholesale Trade Report," February 2011, <http://www.census.gov/wholesale/>.

Wholesale and Retail Trade 657

Table 1047. Wholesale and Retail Trade—Establishments, Employees, and Payroll by State: 2007 and 2008

[5,965 represents 5,965,000. Covers establishments with payroll. Excludes most government employees, railroad employees, and self-employed persons. Based on North American Industry Classification System (NAICS) 2002; data for 2008 based on NAICS 2007. See text, Section 15. For statement on methodology, see Appendix III]

State	Wholesale trade (NAICS 42)						Retail trade (NAICS 44, 45)					
	Establishments		Employees [1] (1,000)		Annual payroll (mil. dol.)		Establishments		Employees [1] (1,000)		Annual payroll (mil. dol.)	
	2007	2008	2007	2008	2007	2008	2007	2008	2007	2008	2007	2008
U.S.	434,464	429,463	5,965	6,165	327,991	353,061	1,123,629	1,100,943	15,760	15,615	375,200	369,289
AL	5,669	5,621	80	80	3,606	3,722	19,670	19,131	245	244	5,293	5,246
AK	741	761	9	9	456	469	2,668	2,578	35	35	974	971
AZ	6,965	6,933	99	101	5,239	5,295	19,341	19,112	342	343	8,241	7,891
AR	3,561	3,459	47	47	2,009	2,040	11,795	11,467	143	142	3,019	3,024
CA	60,805	60,768	820	888	50,591	58,314	114,025	111,200	1,713	1,669	46,059	43,881
CO	7,423	7,410	99	105	5,834	6,429	19,368	18,990	262	262	6,630	6,641
CT	4,644	4,579	75	78	4,984	5,563	13,688	13,485	198	193	5,322	5,176
DE	984	1,021	18	19	1,374	1,444	3,920	3,804	57	55	1,394	1,321
DC	420	414	5	5	335	360	1,870	1,821	20	20	529	521
FL	32,283	31,713	320	318	15,148	15,215	73,529	72,118	1,028	996	24,721	23,662
GA	14,273	13,888	206	205	11,200	11,614	35,920	35,371	486	476	11,149	10,641
HI	1,886	1,829	21	21	870	875	5,051	4,891	71	71	1,782	1,786
ID	2,076	2,094	24	26	1,036	1,116	6,379	6,225	83	82	1,936	1,892
IL	20,023	19,756	303	318	17,664	19,575	42,892	41,743	667	653	16,202	15,722
IN	8,283	8,034	115	117	5,326	5,415	23,446	22,936	334	331	7,273	7,122
IA	4,911	4,929	64	66	2,713	2,927	13,285	12,780	180	180	3,672	3,753
KS	4,555	4,501	57	61	2,683	3,079	11,306	10,978	150	151	3,201	3,261
KY	4,521	4,428	67	75	2,929	3,674	16,254	16,024	216	230	4,578	5,204
LA	5,621	5,579	74	77	3,487	3,797	17,037	16,866	234	234	5,247	5,239
ME	1,632	1,606	18	19	791	838	6,951	6,775	84	85	1,921	1,931
MD	5,970	5,905	95	98	5,522	5,640	19,566	19,088	301	294	7,582	6,999
MA	8,720	8,647	143	143	10,021	10,289	25,666	25,121	367	361	9,291	9,176
MI	11,972	11,806	167	171	9,404	9,723	37,709	36,381	475	466	10,288	10,359
MN	8,618	8,462	137	138	8,442	8,721	20,741	20,206	316	304	7,056	6,787
MS	2,913	2,890	36	37	1,449	1,504	12,379	12,148	144	145	2,993	2,965
MO	8,393	8,268	126	131	5,719	6,118	23,148	22,577	323	319	7,181	7,127
MT	1,522	1,451	14	15	556	600	5,224	5,137	60	60	1,356	1,380
NE	3,037	3,014	38	42	1,745	2,052	7,865	7,623	109	109	2,260	2,323
NV	3,001	3,009	40	40	2,058	2,038	8,570	8,387	144	142	3,852	3,681
NH	1,951	1,860	24	26	1,441	1,692	6,569	6,473	101	102	2,427	2,437
NJ	16,005	15,724	269	270	18,078	19,783	34,544	33,564	467	465	12,200	12,386
NM	2,011	2,028	22	23	927	1,012	7,242	7,107	100	101	2,377	2,306
NY	34,609	34,112	390	394	22,961	23,764	76,516	75,853	899	892	23,016	23,090
NC	12,200	12,070	174	181	8,956	9,920	36,329	35,676	475	477	10,770	10,549
ND	1,483	1,513	17	19	728	851	3,376	3,294	46	45	951	966
OH	15,396	15,026	233	232	11,799	12,060	39,832	38,650	593	585	12,885	13,062
OK	4,617	4,602	59	62	2,744	3,002	13,446	13,218	176	178	3,778	3,844
OR	5,767	5,730	78	77	3,990	4,106	14,699	14,486	208	206	5,081	4,951
PA	15,875	15,559	237	248	12,820	14,049	46,328	45,583	682	677	15,291	15,249
RI	1,468	1,464	21	21	1,107	1,062	4,168	4,017	55	50	1,497	1,229
SC	4,980	5,033	64	67	2,999	3,256	18,893	18,461	238	237	5,082	5,019
SD	1,389	1,403	16	16	607	689	4,172	4,069	51	51	1,075	1,063
TN	7,496	7,291	123	127	6,234	6,289	24,047	23,568	326	327	7,519	7,310
TX	32,075	31,815	467	491	26,701	28,811	78,111	77,669	1,156	1,171	27,330	27,484
UT	3,681	3,631	50	56	2,397	2,715	8,874	8,955	142	148	3,356	3,471
VT	859	851	11	11	488	509	3,791	3,734	41	41	964	964
VA	7,795	7,659	116	114	6,080	6,200	29,382	28,872	440	434	10,315	9,894
WA	9,656	9,717	129	138	6,923	7,698	22,990	22,481	328	332	8,712	8,701
WV	1,610	1,576	20	21	845	907	7,003	6,846	95	93	1,842	1,847
WI	7,325	7,194	114	115	5,560	5,796	21,065	20,542	322	319	6,946	6,984
WY	794	830	8	8	412	445	2,989	2,862	33	33	783	800

[1] Covers full- and part-time employees who are on the payroll in the pay period including March 12.

Source: U.S. Census Bureau, "County Business Patterns," July 2010, <http://www.census.gov/econ/cbp/index.html>.

Table 1048. Retail Trade—Establishments, Employees, and Payroll: 2007 and 2008

[1,123.6 represents 1,123,600. Covers establishments with payroll. Excludes most government employees, railroad employees, and self-employed persons. For statement on methodology, see Appendix III]

Kind of business	2002 NAICS code [1]	Establishments (1,000)		Employees [2] (1,000)		Payroll (bil. dol.)	
		2007	2008	2007	2008	2007	2008
Retail trade, total	44–45	1,123.6	1,100.9	15,760	15,615	375.2	369.3
Motor vehicle and parts dealers	441	127.3	122.4	1,938	1,884	74.7	69.1
Automobile dealers	4411	51.2	49.5	1,274	1,254	55.4	51.1
New car dealers	44111	24.4	24.2	1,138	1,125	50.9	47.2
Used car dealers	44112	26.9	25.3	136	129	4.5	4.0
Other motor vehicle dealers	4412	17.0	16.7	169	165	6.1	5.6
Recreational vehicle dealers	44121	3.0	3.0	43	40	1.7	1.4
Motorcycle and boat and other motor vehicle dealers	44122	14.0	13.8	126	124	4.4	4.2
Motorcycle dealers	441221	6.0	6.0	69	70	2.4	2.3
Automotive parts, accessories, and tire stores	4413	59.1	56.1	496	466	13.2	12.3
Automotive parts, accessories and tire stores	44131	39.6	37.6	329	303	7.8	7.2
Tire dealers	44132	19.5	18.5	166	163	5.5	5.1
Furniture and home furnishing stores	442	65.5	61.7	597	533	15.6	13.9
Furniture stores	4421	29.2	27.3	272	253	8.3	7.4
Home furnishings stores	4422	36.2	34.4	325	281	7.3	6.5
Floor covering stores	44221	14.6	13.9	95	84	3.5	3.0
Other home furnishings stores	44229	21.6	20.5	230	196	3.8	3.5
Window treatment stores	442291	3.1	2.5	16	8	0.4	0.2
Electronics and appliance stores	443	18.6	18.1	214	188	3.5	3.3
Appliance, TV, and all other electronics stores	44311	52.5	49.2	501	465	12.5	11.2
Household appliance stores	443111	38.3	37.1	387	364	9.4	8.5
Radio, television, and other electronics stores	443112	9.0	8.9	69	69	2.1	2.1
Computer and software stores	44312	29.3	28.2	318	295	7.3	6.4
Bldg. material & garden equip. & supp. dealers	444	12.1	10.2	100	88	2.6	2.3
Building material & supplies dealers [3]	4441	67.9	69.4	1,202	1,171	34.9	34.1
Home centers	44411	7.2	7.0	(NA)	(NA)	(D)	(D)
Hardware stores	44413	14.2	16.0	140	143	3.0	3.3
Lawn & garden equip, & supplies stores [3]	4442	20.4	19.8	172	164	4.6	4.3
Nursery and garden centers	44422	16.1	15.6	145	137	3.8	3.6
Food & beverage stores	445	151.0	143.7	2,882	2,862	56.3	56.7
Grocery stores	4451	92.3	89.1	2,565	2,571	50.6	51.5
Supermarkets & grocery (except convenience) stores	44511	64.1	63.4	2,425	2,450	48.4	49.5
Convenience stores	44512	28.2	25.7	140	121	2.2	1.9
Specialty food stores	4452	28.3	23.9	175	145	3.0	2.4
Beer, wine, & liquor stores [4]	4453	30.4	30.7	143	146	2.7	2.8
Health & personal care stores [3]	446	89.4	88.4	1,069	1,025	32.0	31.3
Pharmacies & drug stores	44611	42.3	42.0	798	756	24.9	24.7
Cosmetics, beauty supplies, & perfume stores	44612	14.2	14.0	91	95	1.7	1.6
Optical goods stores	44613	12.9	13.2	71	74	1.9	2.0
Gasoline stations	447	115.5	114.1	889	897	14.9	15.3
Gasoline stations with convenience stores	44711	95.4	95.1	725	725	11.5	11.8
Other gasoline stations	44719	20.1	19.1	164	171	3.4	3.5
Clothing & clothing accessories stores	448	155.4	155.6	1,648	1,648	27.5	26.7
Clothing stores [3]	4481	99.3	99.5	1,279	1,287	19.7	19.2
Men's clothing stores	44811	8.6	8.1	66	58	1.5	1.4
Women's clothing stores	44812	35.6	36.0	342	343	5.3	5.2
Children's & infants' clothing stores	44813	7.0	7.3	94	91	1.0	1.1
Family clothing stores	44814	27.3	28.4	635	662	9.4	9.3
Shoe stores	4482	27.2	28.2	206	208	3.3	3.3
Jewelry, luggage, & leather goods stores	4483	28.8	27.9	163	153	4.5	4.2
Jewelry stores	44831	27.5	26.7	154	146	4.2	4.0
Sporting goods, hobby, book, & music stores	451	60.1	55.8	640	618	10.2	10.0
Sporting goods/hobby/musical instrument stores [3]	4511	43.5	40.9	456	432	7.5	7.4
Sporting goods stores	45111	23.8	22.1	236	228	4.3	4.2
Hobby, toy, and game stores	45112	9.5	9.2	136	124	1.9	1.8
Book, periodical, & music stores [3]	4512	16.6	14.9	184	186	2.6	2.6
Book stores	451211	10.6	9.7	145	152	1.9	2.0
Prerecorded tape, CD, & record stores	45122	4.5	3.7	31	27	0.6	0.4
General merchandise stores	452	47.5	45.7	2,897	2,977	56.7	59.2
Department stores	4521	10.1	8.8	1,620	1,292	30.4	24.0
Other general merchandise stores	4529	37.3	36.9	1,278	1,685	26.3	35.2
Warehouse clubs & superstores	45291	3.3	4.4	961	1,374	21.9	30.7
All other general merchandise stores	45299	34.1	32.5	316	311	4.4	4.4
Miscellaneous store retailers [3]	453	123.4	117.2	814	779	15.6	14.7
Florists	4531	19.8	18.5	94	90	1.4	1.3
Office supplies, stationery, and gift stores	4532	40.7	38.8	315	305	5.4	5.0
Office supplies and stationery stores	45321	9.8	9.4	122	114	2.8	2.4
Gift, novelty, and souvenir stores	45322	30.9	29.4	193	191	2.7	2.6
Used merchandise stores	4533	17.7	17.7	134	135	2.3	2.3
Other miscellaneous store retailers [3]	4539	45.2	42.2	271	250	6.4	6.0
Nonstore retailers [3]	454	47.7	57.9	512	592	19.9	22.9
Electronic shopping & mail-order houses	4541	16.7	21.9	268	332	11.5	14.2
Direct selling establishments	4543	25.9	31.1	194	212	7.0	7.4
Fuel dealers	45431	10.5	10.0	91	84	3.5	3.2

D Figure withheld to avoid disclosure. NA Not available. [1] Based on North American Industry Classification System 2002; 2008 data based on NAICS 2007. See text, Section 15. [2] See footnote 2, Table 1044. [3] Includes other kinds of business, not shown separately. [4] Includes government employees.

Source: U.S. Census Bureau, "County Business Patterns," July 2010, <http://www.census.gov/econ/cbp/index.html>.

Table 1049. Retail Trade—Nonemployer Firms and Receipts by Industry Type: 2008

[83,978,402 represents $83,978,402,000. See headnote, Table 1043]

Industy type	2007 NAICS code [1]	Firms				Receipts ($1,000)
		Total	Corpora-tions [2]	Individual proprietor-ships [3]	Partner-ships [4]	
Retail trade, total..........................	44–45	1,875,425	118,666	1,709,868	46,891	83,978,402
Motor vehicle & parts dealers..................	441	168,009	16,311	146,743	4,955	19,585,681
Furniture & home furnishings stores.............	442	44,547	6,224	36,107	2,216	2,782,601
Electronics and appliance stores.................	443	30,712	3,925	25,773	1,014	1,704,534
Bldg material & garden equip. & supplies dealers....	444	38,337	4,125	32,853	1,359	2,840,241
Building material & supplies dealers.............	4441	27,247	3,243	22,977	1,027	2,186,846
Food & beverage stores........................	445	104,026	13,306	85,875	4,845	9,362,717
Grocery stores.............................	4451	45,523	5,467	38,308	1,748	4,511,595
Specialty food stores.......................	4452	46,482	5,646	38,566	2,270	2,884,105
Health & personal care stores..................	446	138,800	6,120	130,912	1,768	3,340,730
Gasoline stations............................	447	9,454	1,737	7,195	522	1,406,670
Clothing & clothing accessories stores...........	448	136,888	9,712	122,798	4,378	5,590,143
Clothing stores.............................	4481	88,025	6,679	78,098	3,248	3,522,343
Jewelry, luggage, and leather goods stores.......	4483	43,845	2,478	40,426	941	1,772,173
Sporting goods, hobby, book, & music stores.......	451	84,151	6,041	74,900	3,210	3,730,729
Book, periodical, and music stores.............	4512	26,125	1,452	23,901	772	841,282
General merchandise stores....................	452	32,978	2,971	28,798	1,209	1,573,593
Miscellaneous store retailers..................	453	277,169	22,967	243,559	10,643	13,001,983
Office supplies, stationery, and gift stores........	4532	59,783	4,788	52,526	2,469	2,154,284
Nonstore retailers...........................	454	810,354	25,227	774,355	10,772	19,058,780
Electronic shopping & mail-order houses.........	4541	82,784	5,885	74,300	2,599	3,291,510
Direct selling establishments..................	4543	699,975	17,171	675,764	7,040	14,904,094

[1] North American Industry Classification System, 2007. See text, Section 15. [2] A legally incorporated business under state laws. [3] Also referred to as "sole proprietorship," an unincorporated business with a sole owner. Includes self-employed persons. [4] An unincorporated business where two or more persons join to carry on a trade or business with eachhaving a shared financial interest in the business.

Source: U.S. Census Bureau, "Nonemployer Statistics," June 2010, <http://www.census.gov/econ/nonemployer/index.html>.

Table 1050. Retail Industries—Employees, Average Weekly Hours, and Average Hourly Earnings: 2000 to 2010

[Annual averages of monthly figures (15,280 represents 15,280,000). Covers all full- and part-time employees who worked during, or received pay for, any part of the pay period including the 12th of the month]

Industry	2007 NAICS code [1]	Employees (1,000)			Average weekly hours			Average hourly earnings (dol.)	
		2000	2005	2010	2000	2005	2010	2000	2010
Retail trade, total......................	44,45	15,280	15,280	14,414	30.7	30.6	30.2	10.86	13.24
Motor vehicle and parts dealers [2]...............	441	1,847	1,919	1,625	35.9	35.8	36.5	14.94	17.06
Automobile dealers........................	4411	1,217	1,261	1,006	35.1	35.8	36.7	16.95	18.23
Other motor vehicle dealers................	4412	132	166	128	35.1	34.7	33.6	12.35	17.22
Auto parts, accessories, and tire stores.........	4413	499	491	490	38.2	36.0	36.9	11.04	14.54
Automotive parts and accessories...........	44131	339	329	323	38.6	34.8	36.6	10.67	14.03
Furniture and home furnishings stores [2].........	442	544	576	436	31.2	30.7	29.2	12.33	15.25
Furniture stores...........................	4421	289	298	217	31.7	31.7	33.8	13.37	16.17
Home furnishings stores...................	4422	254	278	220	30.7	29.5	24.7	11.06	14.04
Electronics and appliance stores [2]..............	443	564	536	498	31.4	32.8	32.0	13.67	16.99
Building material and garden supply stores [2].......	444	1,142	1,276	1,126	35.7	36.8	33.9	11.25	14.11
Building material and supplies dealers..........	4441	982	1,134	1,001	36.2	37.3	34.2	11.30	14.12
Home centers..........................	44411	479	637	621	36.5	37.8	32.7	10.97	12.85
Lawn and garden equipment and supplies stores...	4442	160	142	125	32.5	32.6	31.7	10.89	13.99
Food and beverage stores [2]....................	445	2,993	2,818	2,811	31.7	30.1	29.0	9.76	12.04
Grocery stores.............................	4451	2,582	2,446	2,464	31.9	30.0	29.0	9.71	12.12
Supermarkets and other grocery stores.........	44511	2,438	2,301	2,327	31.9	30.0	28.9	9.84	12.27
Specialty food stores......................	4452	270	236	211	31.6	33.0	29.7	9.97	11.13
Health and personal care stores [2]..............	446	928	954	979	29.8	29.3	29.4	11.68	16.99
Pharmacies and drug stores.................	44611	677	695	714	29.7	28.9	29.3	11.89	17.59
Gasoline stations [2].........................	447	936	871	816	31.6	31.6	30.7	8.05	10.24
Gasoline stations with convenience stores......	44711	787	751	719	31.3	31.3	30.4	7.87	9.99
Clothing and clothing accessories stores [2].........	448	1,322	1,415	1,377	24.9	24.4	21.2	9.96	11.57
Clothing stores.............................	4481	954	1,066	1,063	24.4	23.1	20.1	9.88	10.90
Jewelry, luggage, and leather goods stores......	4483	175	169	131	27.7	31.9	28.1	11.48	15.57
Sporting goods, hobby, book, and music stores [2]....	451	686	647	601	26.4	23.3	23.4	9.33	11.67
Sporting goods and musical instrument stores.....	4511	437	447	460	27.0	23.5	23.8	9.55	11.82
Book, periodical, and music stores.............	4512	249	200	140	25.4	23.0	22.0	8.91	11.11
General merchandise stores....................	452	2,820	2,934	2,971	27.8	29.4	31.7	9.22	10.98
Miscellaneous store retailers [2].................	453	1,007	900	760	29.2	28.5	28.0	10.20	12.50
Office supplies, stationary, and gift stores........	4532	471	391	305	29.7	27.8	27.1	10.46	13.06
Gift, novelty, and souvenir stores.............	45322	266	213	159	26.0	24.3	23.2	8.28	10.86
Used merchandise stores...................	4533	107	113	124	26.7	27.8	29.5	8.07	10.72
Pet and pet supplies stores.................	45391	72	88	99	27.0	28.9	27.4	9.78	12.83
Nonstore retailers [2]........................	454	492	435	416	35.4	34.5	36.3	13.22	17.71
Electronic shopping and mail-order houses.......	4541	257	240	244	36.2	33.0	35.9	13.38	18.19
Direct selling establishments.................	4543	169	145	132	34.1	36.0	37.1	13.70	17.16
Fuel dealers.............................	45431	106	94	81	37.6	38.2	38.6	13.79	17.13

[1] Based on the North American Industry Classification System (NAICS), 2007; see text, this section and Section 15. [2] Includes other kind of businesses, not shown separately.

Source: U.S. Bureau of Labor Statistics, Current Employment Statistics, "Employment, Hours, and Earnings—National," <http://www.bls.gov/ces/data.htm>.

Table 1051. Retail Trade and Food Services—Sales by Kind of Business: 2000 to 2010

[In billions of dollars (3,294.1 represents $3,294,100,000,000)]

Kind of Business	2007 NAICS code [1]	2000	2005	2006	2007	2008	2009	2010
Retail sales and food services, total	44, 45, 722	**3,294.1**	**4,094.1**	**4,304.2**	**4,451.7**	**4,409.5**	**4,091.7**	**4,355.4**
Retail sales, total	44, 45	**2,988.8**	**3,696.7**	**3,880.1**	**4,005.8**	**3,952.9**	**3,638.5**	**3,889.5**
GAFO, total [2]	(X)	863.9	1,061.9	1,113.5	1,148.9	1,144.7	1,099.0	1,132.0
Motor vehicle and parts dealers	441	797.6	890.1	901.7	911.8	788.7	676.8	744.3
Automobile and other motor vehicle dealers	4411, 4412	733.9	819.6	829.0	836.7	712.1	602.3	667.1
Automobile dealers	4411	688.7	754.2	761.9	768.5	652.0	556.9	621.4
New car dealers.	44111	630.1	682.0	685.6	687.7	576.6	488.2	546.8
Auto parts, accessories, and tire stores	4413	63.7	70.4	72.6	75.1	76.6	74.5	77.2
Furniture, home furnishings, electronics and appliance stores	442, 443	173.7	210.8	220.8	222.2	208.8	185.0	188.7
Furniture and home furnishings stores	442	91.3	109.4	113.0	111.3	99.9	86.7	88.2
Furniture stores	4421	50.7	58.8	60.1	59.4	53.2	46.6	47.7
Home furnishings stores	4422	40.6	50.6	52.8	52.0	46.7	40.1	40.6
Electronics and appliance stores [3]	443	82.4	101.4	107.8	110.8	108.9	98.4	100.5
Appliances, televisions, and other electronics stores	44311	58.3	78.3	84.2	86.3	84.6	75.9	75.5
Building materials, garden equipment, and supply stores [3]	444	229.3	321.4	334.5	321.3	305.1	268.2	284.0
Hardware stores	44413	16.2	18.9	20.0	20.6	20.3	19.0	19.3
Food and beverage stores [3]	445	445.7	509.0	526.2	548.9	571.2	570.6	583.3
Grocery stores.	4451	403.0	457.6	472.1	491.8	512.1	510.6	521.7
Supermarkets and other grocery (except convenience) stores.	44511	(NA)	435.3	448.9	468.6	488.0	487.4	496.4
Beer, wine and liquor stores	4453	28.7	33.8	36.2	38.3	39.9	40.8	42.1
Health and personal care stores	446	155.4	210.4	223.6	237.4	247.0	253.2	263.0
Pharmacies and drug stores	44611	130.9	179.2	191.0	202.3	211.0	217.4	222.3
Gasoline stations.	447	250.0	379.2	422.3	452.0	502.5	388.5	453.3
Clothing and clothing access, stores [3]	448	168.0	201.3	213.4	221.6	216.1	204.9	213.9
Clothing stores [3]	4481	118.2	145.7	154.6	161.8	158.1	152.2	158.8
Women's clothing stores	44812	31.5	37.0	38.7	40.3	38.4	35.8	37.0
Shoe stores [3]	4482	22.9	25.3	26.7	26.8	26.7	25.0	26.4
Jewelry stores	44831	25.0	28.6	30.3	31.0	29.3	25.7	26.7
Sporting goods, hobby, book & music stores [3]	451	76.1	81.2	83.5	85.0	84.3	81.4	84.5
Sporting goods stores	45111	25.4	30.8	34.0	35.9	37.2	37.2	39.1
Hobby, toy, and game stores	45112	17.0	16.4	16.1	16.4	16.3	15.8	17.5
General merchandise stores	452	404.3	528.5	554.4	578.7	596.5	592.0	609.8
Department stores (excluding L.D.) [4]	4521	232.5	215.3	213.2	209.4	198.7	187.6	186.2
Discount department stores	452112	96.3	84.8	80.3	76.9	70.9	62.8	64.0
Department stores (including L.D.) [4]	4521	239.9	220.7	218.1	213.9	202.9	190.8	188.9
Discount department stores	452112	100.3	87.5	82.7	79.0	72.8	64.4	65.4
Warehouse clubs and superstores	45291	139.6	271.9	298.0	325.0	352.1	356.5	370.8
Miscellaneous store retailers.	453	108.1	108.8	115.1	117.8	113.2	105.4	112.1
Office supplies, stationery, and gift stores	4532	41.8	40.0	41.5	41.4	39.0	35.7	35.1
Office supplies and stationery stores	45321	22.8	22.3	22.9	23.2	21.9	20.3	20.2
Used merchandise stores	4533	10.1	9.5	10.5	11.1	11.2	10.9	12.8
Nonstore retailers [3]	454	180.7	256.1	284.8	309.1	319.6	312.5	352.8
Electronic shopping and mail-order houses	4541	113.9	175.9	202.4	223.9	228.5	234.7	270.7
Fuel dealers.	45431	26.7	34.5	35.5	37.4	44.0	34.8	38.7
Food services and drinking places [5]	722	**305.4**	**397.4**	**424.0**	**445.9**	**456.6**	**453.3**	**466.0**

X Not applicable. NA Not available. [1] North American Industry Classification System, 2007; see text, Section 15. [2] GAFO (General Merchandise, Apparel, Furniture, and Office Supplies) represents stores classified in the following NAICS codes: 442, 443, 448, 451, 452, and 4532. [3] Includes other kinds of businesses, not shown separately. [4] L.D. represents leased departments. [5] See also Table 1281.

Source: U.S. Census Bureau, "Annual Revision of Monthly Retail and Food Services: Sales and Inventories—January 1992 Through March 2010," March 2011, <http://www.census.gov/retail/index.html>.

Table 1052. Retail Trade Corporations—Sales, Net Profit, and Profit Per Dollar of Sales: 2009 and 2010

[Represents North American Industry Classification System, 2007 (NAICS) groups 44 and 45. Profit rates are averages of quarterly figures at annual rates. Covers corporations with assets of $50,000,000 or more]

Item	Unit	Total retail trade		Food and beverage stores (NAICS 445)		Clothing and general merchandise stores (NAICS 448, 452)		All other retail stores	
		2009	2010	2009	2010	2009	2010	2009	2010
Sales	Bil. dol . . .	2,032	2,159	389	398	746	773	897	988
Net profit:									
Before income taxes	Bil. dol . . .	84.1	100.1	6.2	7.3	40.0	48.4	38.0	44.4
After income taxes.	Bil. dol . . .	56.2	68.2	3.3	4.3	27.1	33.0	25.8	31.0
Profits per dollar of sales:									
Before income taxes	Cents	4.1	4.6	1.6	1.8	5.2	6.2	4.2	4.5
After income taxes.	Cents	2.7	3.1	0.9	1.1	3.5	4.2	2.8	3.1
Profits on stockholders' equity:									
Before income taxes	Percent . .	20.5	22.5	13.4	16.0	22.2	25.9	20.5	20.8
After income taxes.	Percent . .	13.6	15.3	7.1	9.5	15.0	17.6	13.6	14.5

Source: U.S. Census Bureau, *Quarterly Financial Report for Manufacturing, Mining and Trade Corporations*, annual, <http://www.census.gov/econ/qfr/>.

Wholesale and Retail Trade 661

Table 1053. Retail Trade and Food Services—Estimated Per Capita Sales by Selected Kind of Business: 2000 to 2009

[Estimates are shown in dollars and are based on data from the Annual Retail Trade Survey and the Census Bureau's Population Estimates Program. Based on estimated resident population estimates as of July 1. For additional information, see <http://www.census.gov/popest/estimates.php>. For statement on methodology, see Appendix III]

Kind of business	2007 NAICS code [1]	2000	2004	2005	2006	2007	2008	2009
Retail and food service sales	**44–45,722**	**11,674**	**13,160**	**13,849**	**14,423**	**14,770**	**14,497**	**13,343**
Retail sales, total	**44–45**	**10,592**	**11,881**	**12,505**	**13,002**	**13,291**	**12,996**	**11,865**
Total (excluding motor vehicle and parts dealers)	44–45 ex 441	7,766	8,918	9,494	9,980	10,266	10,403	9,658
Motor vehicle and parts dealers	441	2,827	2,964	3,011	3,021	3,025	2,593	2,207
Furniture and home furnishings stores	442	324	355	370	379	369	328	283
Electronics and appliance stores	443	292	323	343	361	368	358	321
Building material and garden equipment and supplies dealers	444	813	1,010	1,087	1,121	1,066	1,003	875
Food and beverage stores	445	1,579	1,676	1,722	1,763	1,821	1,878	1,861
Health and personal care stores	446	551	682	712	749	788	812	826
Gasoline stations	447	886	1,107	1,283	1,415	1,500	1,652	1,267
Clothing and clothing accessories stores	448	595	650	681	715	735	710	668
Sporting goods, hobby, book, and music stores	451	270	272	275	280	282	277	265
General merchandise stores	452	1,433	1,698	1,788	1,858	1,920	1,961	1,931
Miscellaneous store retailers	453	383	361	368	386	391	372	344
Nonstore retailers	454	640	783	866	954	1,026	1,051	1,019
Food services and drinking places, total	**722**	**1,082**	**1,279**	**1,344**	**1,421**	**1,479**	**1,501**	**1,478**

[1] North American Industry Classification System, 2007; see text, Section 15.
Source: U.S. Census Bureau, "2009 Annual Retail Trade Survey," March 2011 <http://www.census.gov/retail/>.

Table 1054. Retail Trade—Merchandise Inventories and Inventory/Sales Ratios by Kind of Business: 2000 to 2010

[Inventories in billions of dollars (406.8 represents $406,800,000,000). As of Dec. 31, seasonally adjusted. Estimates exclude food services. Includes warehouses. Adjusted for seasonal variations. Sales data also adjusted for holiday and trading-day differences. Based on data from the Monthly Retail Trade Survey, Annual Retail Trade Survey, and administrative records; see Appendix III. Data have been adjusted using results of the 2007 Economic Census]

Kind of business	2007 NAICS code [1]	Inventories				Inventory/sales ratio			
		2000	2005	2009	2010	2000	2005	2009	2010
Retail Inventories, total [2]	**44–45**	**406.8**	**472.2**	**429.2**	**455.5**	**1.62**	**1.50**	**1.38**	**1.35**
Total excluding motor vehicle and parts dealers	44–45 ex 441	278.5	319.2	315.8	327.4	1.49	1.33	1.24	1.21
Motor vehicle and parts dealers	441	128.3	153.0	113.4	128.1	2.02	2.08	1.96	1.92
Furniture, home furnishings, electronics, and appliance stores	442, 443	25.7	30.8	26.5	27.9	1.85	1.72	1.71	1.78
Building material and garden equipment and supplies dealers	444	34.3	45.1	43.0	43.8	1.75	1.64	1.97	1.79
Food and beverage stores	445	32.2	33.8	37.2	37.7	0.85	0.78	0.77	0.77
Clothing and clothing accessories stores	448	36.8	43.3	41.8	43.1	2.61	2.51	2.44	2.39
General merchandise stores	452	65.0	74.2	69.9	73.7	1.87	1.65	1.40	1.44
Department stores	4521	42.7	38.0	30.9	31.1	2.17	2.13	1.98	2.02

[1] North American Industry Classification System, 2007; see text, Section 15. [2] Includes other kind of businesses, not shown separately.
Source: U.S. Census Bureau, "Annual Revision of Monthly Retail and Food Services: Sales and Inventories—January 1992 Through March 2010," March 2011, <http://www.census.gov/retail/index.html>.

Table 1055. Retail Trade Sales—Total and E-Commerce by Kind of Business: 2009

[3,638,471 represents $3,638,471,000,000. Covers retailers with and without payroll. Based on the Annual Retail Trade Survey; see Appendix III]

Kind of business	2007 NAICS code [1]	Value of sales (mil. dol.)		E-commerce as percent of total sales	Percent distribution of E-commerce sales
		Total	E-commerce		
Retail trade, total [2]	**44-45**	**3,638,471**	**145,214**	**4.0**	**100.0**
Motor vehicle and parts dealers	441	676,801	17,201	2.5	11.8
Electronics and appliance stores	443	98,384	1,140	1.2	0.8
Building material and garden equipment and supplies stores	444	268,206	477	0.2	0.3
Food and beverage stores	445	570,581	883	0.2	0.6
Health and personal care stores	446	253,243	177	0.1	0.1
Clothing and clothing accessories stores	448	204,866	2,965	1.4	2.0
Sporting goods, hobby, book, and music stores	451	81,373	1,865	2.3	1.3
General merchandise stores	452	592,009	220	(Z)	0.2
Miscellaneous store retailers	453	105,366	2,360	2.2	1.6
Nonstore retailers	454	312,470	116,543	37.3	80.3
Electronic shopping and mail-order houses	45411	234,667	112,791	48.1	77.7

Z Less than 0.05 percent. [1] North American Industry Classification System, 2007; see text, Section 15 . [2] Includes other kinds of businesses, not shown separately.
Source: U.S. Census Bureau, "E-Stats, 2009 E-commerce Multi-sector Report," May 2011,<http://www.census.gov/econ/estats/>.

Table 1056. Electronic Shopping and Mail-Order Houses—Total and E-Commerce Sales by Merchandise Line: 2008 and 2009

[228,545 represents $228,545,000,000. Represents North American Industry Classification System code 454110 which comprises establishments primarily engaged in retailing all types of merchandise using nonstore means, such as catalogs, toll-free telephone numbers, or electronic media, such as interactive television or computer. Covers businesses with and without paid employees. Based on the Annual Retail Survey; see Appendix III]

Merchandise lines	Value of sales, 2008 (mil. dol.)	2009 Value of sales (mil. dol.)		E-commerce as percent of total sales	2009 Percent distribution	
		Total	E-commerce		Total	E-commerce
Total	**228,545**	**234,667**	**112,791**	**48.1**	**100.0**	**100.0**
Books and magazines	7,059	6,824	5,214	76.4	2.9	4.6
Clothing and clothing accessories (includes footwear)	24,570	26,047	19,507	74.9	11.1	17.3
Computer hardware	23,154	22,088	11,026	49.9	9.4	9.8
Computer software	4,990	5,608	3,092	55.1	2.4	2.7
Drugs, health aids, beauty aids	66,421	71,329	5,994	8.4	30.4	5.3
Electronics and appliances	16,780	17,684	14,211	80.4	7.5	12.6
Food, beer, and wine	3,846	3,667	2,244	61.2	1.6	2.0
Furniture and home furnishings	13,363	13,158	9,894	75.2	5.6	8.8
Music and videos	5,877	6,396	5,351	83.7	2.7	4.7
Office equipment and supplies	8,466	7,953	5,736	72.1	3.4	5.1
Sporting goods	6,477	7,030	4,820	68.6	3.0	4.3
Toys, hobby goods, and games	6,022	5,926	3,604	60.8	2.5	3.2
Other merchandise [1]	29,574	29,167	14,096	48.3	12.4	12.5
Nonmerchandise receipts [2]	11,946	11,790	8,002	67.9	5.0	7.1

[1] Includes jewelry, collectibles, souvenirs, auto parts and accessories, hardware, and lawn and garden equipment and supplies.
[2] Includes auction commissions, shipping and handling, customer training, customer support, and advertising.
Source: U.S. Census Bureau, "E-Stats, 2009 E-commerce Multi-sector Report," May 2011, <http://www.census.gov/econ /estats/>.

Table 1057. Franchised New Car Dealerships—Summary: 1990 to 2010

[316 represents $316,000,000,000]

Item	Unit	1990	2000	2003	2004	2005	2006	2007	2008	2009	2010
Dealerships [1]	Number	24,825	22,250	21,650	21,640	21,495	21,200	20,770	20,010	18,460	17,700
Sales	Bil. dol.	316	650	699	714	699	675	693	571	492	553
New cars sold [2]	Millions	9.3	8.8	7.6	7.5	7.7	7.8	7.6	6.8	5.5	5.7
Used vehicles sold	Millions	14.2	20.5	19.5	19.7	19.7	19.2	18.5	15.0	14.9	15.3
Employment	1,000	924	1,114	1,130	1,130	1,138	1,120	1,115	1,057	913	892
Dealer pretax profits as a percentage of sales	Percent	1.0	1.6	1.7	1.7	1.6	1.5	1.5	1.0	1.5	2.1
Inventory: [3]											
Domestic: [4]											
Total	1,000	2,537	3,183	3,085	3,267	2,991	2,943	2,712	2,478	1,697	1,687
Days' supply	Days	73	68	63	75	70	71	67	80	72	60
Imported: [4]											
Total	1,000	707	468	618	646	566	605	619	687	519	494
Days' supply	Days	72	50	49	59	52	51	51	65	61	55

[1] At end of year. [2] Data provided by Ward's Automotive Reports. [3] Annual average. Includes light trucks. [4] Classification based on where automobiles are produced (i.e., automobiles manufactured by foreign companies but produced in the U.S., Canada, and Mexico are classified as domestic).
Source: National Automobile Dealers Association, McLean, VA, *NADA Data*, annual. See also <http://www.nada.org /Publications/NADADATA>.

Table 1058. Retail Sales and Leases of New and Used Vehicles: 1990 to 2009

[In thousands, except as noted (52,484 represents 52,484,000)]

Item	1990	2000	2003	2004	2005	2006	2007	2008	2009
Vehicle sales and leases, total (number of vehicles)	**52,484**	**64,320**	**63,644**	**62,839**	**64,626**	**62,744**	**61,562**	**52,845**	**48,545**
New vehicle sales and leases	14,954	22,700	20,072	20,294	20,488	20,178	20,143	16,315	13,053
New vehicle sales	13,890	17,410	16,670	16,850	16,990	16,460	16,230	13,300	10,550
New vehicle leases	1,064	5,290	3,402	3,444	3,498	3,718	3,913	3,015	2,503
Used vehicle sales [1]	37,530	41,620	43,572	42,545	44,138	42,566	41,419	36,530	35,492
Vehicle sales, total value (bil. dol.) [2]	**447**	**736**	**738**	**765**	**776**	**786**	**774**	**643**	**575**
New vehicle sales (bil. dol.)	227	380	382	407	421	445	435	351	274
Used vehicle sales (bil. dol.)	220	356	356	358	355	341	339	292	301
Average price (current dol.): [2]									
New vehicle sales	16,350	21,850	22,894	24,082	24,796	26,854	26,950	26,477	26,245
Used vehicle sales	5,857	8,547	8,180	8,410	8,036	8,009	8,186	7,986	8,483

[1] Used car sales include sales from franchised dealers, independent dealers, and casual sales. [2] Includes leased vehicles.
Source: U.S. Bureau of Transportation Statistics, "National Transportation Statistics," <http://www.bts.gov/publications /national_transportation_statistics/>.

Table 1059. Retail Trade and Food Services—Sales by Type of Store and State: 2009

[In millions of dollars (4,320,921 represents $4,320,921,000,000). Retail Market Power is based on the Census of Retail Trade (CRT), in addition to monthly and annual surveys of retail trade data from the Bureau of the Census and Claritas' current-year demographic estimates. Sales data is calculated by using business sales estimates, business locations, and employee counts. Sales at the national level by NAICS code are validated against the 2002 Economic Census (NAICS Majors only) and County Business Patterns data provided by the Census Bureau. Based on North American Industry Classification System (NAICS), 2002; see text, Section 15]

State	Total retail sales plus food services and drinking places (NAICS 44–45, 722)	All retail stores [1] (NAICS 44–45)	Motor vehicle and parts dealers (NAICS 441)	Furniture and home furnishings (NAICS 442)	Electronics and appliances (NAICS 443)	Building and material supply (NAICS 444)	Food and beverage stores (NAICS 445)	Health and personal care (NAICS 446)
U.S.	4,320,921	3,862,237	703,512	92,650	101,451	430,041	589,554	255,813
AL	65,008	59,475	11,511	1,373	1,408	7,702	6,968	4,624
AK	10,966	9,742	1,589	208	173	981	1,681	180
AZ	93,053	83,872	14,690	1,993	3,114	8,240	12,112	4,273
AR	38,330	35,248	7,496	652	1,038	4,380	3,779	2,391
CA	519,572	458,979	79,126	11,009	17,065	44,951	78,820	28,483
CO	75,326	66,795	13,090	1,934	2,044	7,599	11,238	2,531
CT	54,372	48,951	8,299	1,300	1,235	6,002	8,324	3,662
DE	15,502	13,960	2,638	467	400	1,883	2,476	993
DC	6,443	3,885	59	173	88	136	1,214	672
FL	282,928	250,252	49,908	7,425	5,973	23,114	37,840	18,572
GA	130,325	115,515	22,075	2,989	2,775	14,991	16,480	8,028
HI	21,626	18,257	2,622	357	376	1,578	3,270	1,348
ID	21,888	20,139	4,342	558	316	2,617	2,604	753
IL	178,910	157,961	26,198	3,305	4,057	16,330	21,607	8,843
IN	85,301	76,262	14,334	1,558	1,805	9,305	8,798	5,290
IA	40,305	36,856	6,998	759	705	5,367	5,413	1,945
KS	34,823	31,504	5,967	647	686	3,391	5,436	1,726
KY	54,696	49,377	8,213	1,017	768	6,352	6,723	4,153
LA	64,296	58,331	11,018	1,464	1,333	7,672	6,562	4,132
ME	21,639	19,827	3,222	298	328	2,587	3,485	1,010
MD	82,402	73,007	14,219	2,000	1,784	8,751	14,352	4,159
MA	96,567	83,651	14,154	2,331	1,868	9,721	16,679	7,668
MI	128,859	115,837	22,906	2,346	2,932	14,088	14,698	9,053
MN	76,969	69,188	11,589	1,513	2,139	8,819	10,433	3,767
MS	37,956	34,738	6,108	698	514	4,696	3,740	2,652
MO	86,051	77,439	13,510	1,349	1,922	8,605	9,145	4,817
MT	16,919	15,527	2,830	425	460	2,312	1,996	559
NE	26,964	24,724	4,628	563	471	2,999	2,667	1,263
NV	44,768	38,721	6,235	729	1,134	2,923	5,196	1,634
NH	27,433	25,354	4,414	433	811	3,267	4,762	1,132
NJ	131,207	117,522	22,115	2,969	3,123	11,436	25,159	9,195
NM	27,657	24,906	4,598	487	512	2,503	2,542	1,072
NY	267,671	238,440	33,783	6,472	9,058	24,907	41,669	25,298
NC	128,140	115,219	22,563	3,244	2,287	15,817	15,235	8,521
ND	11,602	10,840	2,284	187	249	1,597	1,218	573
OH	145,059	127,801	23,385	2,464	2,901	13,821	20,854	8,451
OK	47,207	42,802	9,429	957	612	5,067	3,973	2,552
OR	54,704	48,539	8,687	1,128	1,563	5,135	8,215	2,113
PA	174,483	157,876	27,985	3,234	2,800	16,439	25,208	12,040
RI	13,968	12,077	1,980	272	182	1,192	3,447	1,532
SC	60,305	53,934	9,322	1,123	768	6,976	7,895	4,389
SD	13,759	12,754	2,604	204	312	1,888	1,278	535
TN	89,524	80,700	14,358	1,786	1,861	9,888	10,778	7,156
TX	336,509	301,778	66,232	8,291	7,244	32,075	42,883	14,208
UT	40,796	38,012	7,352	1,129	878	4,147	4,919	1,004
VT	10,471	9,666	1,664	184	187	1,378	1,728	633
VA	119,784	107,250	18,514	2,743	2,906	12,282	17,666	6,079
WA	97,464	88,375	14,311	2,147	1,936	9,586	13,315	3,985
WV	24,338	22,227	3,870	330	335	2,665	2,593	1,857
WI	76,252	69,110	12,610	1,282	1,839	8,755	9,502	4,096
WY	9,824	9,036	1,879	144	174	1,126	978	213

See footnotes at end of table.

U.S. Census Bureau, Statistical Abstract of the United States: 2012

Table 1059. Retail Trade and Food Services—Sales by Type of Store and State: 2009—Con.

[See headnote page 664]

State	Gasoline service stations (NAICS 447)	Clothing and clothing accessories (NAICS 448)	Sporting goods, hobby, book & music stores (NAICS 451)	General merchandise (NAICS 452)	Miscellaneous stores (NAICS 453)	Nonstore retailers (NAICS 454)	Food services & drinking places (NAICS 722)
U.S.	372,452	210,534	87,343	597,752	114,232	306,904	458,684
AL	6,742	2,777	1,131	11,228	1,565	2,445	5,533
AK	734	391	348	2,479	380	598	1,224
AZ	8,443	3,591	1,674	15,273	2,289	8,178	9,181
AR	4,191	1,262	623	7,377	1,160	900	3,083
CA	36,327	28,033	11,049	71,851	13,002	39,263	60,593
CO	5,202	3,006	2,298	11,315	2,187	4,351	8,531
CT	3,492	3,539	1,237	5,197	1,221	5,442	5,421
DE	926	792	319	1,798	614	655	1,542
DC	167	492	189	287	99	309	2,558
FL	20,663	16,306	5,206	38,553	7,037	19,656	32,675
GA	13,495	6,310	2,305	18,223	3,343	4,501	14,810
HI	1,239	2,269	451	3,660	789	296	3,369
ID	2,548	587	670	3,318	665	1,160	1,749
IL	13,288	8,194	3,477	25,244	4,034	23,383	20,949
IN	9,428	3,765	1,753	13,485	2,353	4,388	9,040
IA	5,059	1,148	693	5,911	710	2,149	3,448
KS	3,692	1,295	674	5,487	808	1,695	3,319
KY	6,630	1,852	847	9,791	1,684	1,345	5,319
LA	7,486	2,741	1,218	10,696	2,084	1,926	5,965
ME	2,268	818	393	2,558	540	2,318	1,812
MD	5,073	4,787	1,775	9,564	1,754	4,790	9,395
MA	6,002	5,598	2,285	7,742	1,952	7,650	12,916
MI	11,010	5,436	2,780	20,330	3,839	6,420	13,021
MN	7,101	3,001	1,570	11,487	1,674	6,095	7,780
MS	5,177	1,783	578	7,131	1,089	573	3,218
MO	10,394	2,911	1,452	13,191	2,339	7,805	8,612
MT	2,659	408	488	2,425	541	423	1,393
NE	2,815	737	714	3,685	501	3,682	2,240
NV	3,167	3,431	789	6,164	1,355	5,964	6,047
NH	1,842	1,164	618	3,299	595	3,018	2,078
NJ	7,791	8,022	2,967	11,005	3,073	10,667	13,685
NM	3,409	854	447	5,178	1,135	2,169	2,751
NY	14,092	23,275	5,981	25,141	10,732	18,033	29,231
NC	12,562	5,054	2,002	17,810	3,277	6,847	12,920
ND	1,771	321	245	1,559	283	553	762
OH	14,727	4,970	2,725	18,675	3,407	11,420	17,258
OK	6,889	1,739	826	8,191	1,877	691	4,405
OR	3,636	2,042	1,400	9,245	1,723	3,652	6,166
PA	14,852	7,245	3,236	20,781	4,542	19,513	16,608
RI	859	608	206	715	298	785	1,892
SC	7,024	3,182	1,008	9,412	1,693	1,140	6,371
SD	1,737	282	211	1,726	292	1,685	1,005
TN	9,542	4,220	1,537	13,396	2,224	3,953	8,824
TX	29,686	15,503	6,808	48,757	8,120	21,972	34,731
UT	3,845	1,356	1,076	5,782	869	5,655	2,784
VT	1,239	328	265	597	316	1,147	806
VA	11,716	5,761	2,400	17,918	2,866	6,401	12,534
WA	6,036	3,742	2,249	15,335	2,699	13,032	9,089
WV	3,076	583	323	4,955	627	1,013	2,111
WI	8,774	2,837	1,642	11,404	1,636	4,732	7,142
WY	1,931	183	185	1,418	339	466	788

[1] Excluding food services and drinking places (NAICS 722). Includes other types of stores, not shown separately.
Source: Nielsen Claritas Retail Market Power, 2010 (copyright).

U.S. Census Bureau, Statistical Abstract of the United States: 2012

Table 1060. New Motor Vehicle Sales and Car Production: 1990 to 2010

[In thousands (14,137 represents 14,137,000). Includes leases]

Type of vehicle	1990	2000	2005	2006	2007	2008	2009	2010
New motor vehicle sales	**14,137**	**17,806**	**17,445**	**17,049**	**16,460**	**13,494**	**10,601**	**11,772**
New-car sales and leases	9,300	8,852	7,720	7,821	7,618	6,814	5,456	5,729
Domestic	6,897	6,833	5,533	5,476	5,253	4,535	3,619	3,885
Import	2,403	2,019	2,187	2,345	2,365	2,278	1,837	1,844
New-truck sales and leases	4,837	8,954	9,725	9,228	8,842	6,680	5,145	6,044
Light	4,560	8,492	9,228	8,683	8,471	6,382	4,945	5,826
Domestic	3,957	7,651	8,013	7,337	7,083	5,285	4,061	4,927
Import	603	841	1,216	1,347	1,388	1,097	884	899
Other	278	462	497	544	371	299	200	218
Domestic-car production	6,231	5,542	4,321	4,367	3,924	3,777	2,247	2,840
Average expenditure per new car [1] (dol.)	14,371	21,041	23,017	23,634	23,892	23,441	23,276	24,296
Domestic (dol.)	13,936	19,586	21,593	22,166	22,284	22,204	22,148	23,095
Import (dol.)	15,510	25,965	26,621	27,062	27,465	25,903	25,499	26,808

[1] Estimate based on the manufacturer's suggested retail price.
Source: U.S. Bureau of Economic Analysis, "Auto and Truck Seasonal Adjustment," April 2011, <http://www.bea.gov /national/xls/gap_hist.xls>. Data are mainly from "Ward's Automotive Reports," published by Ward's Communications, Southfield, MI.

Table 1061. Shopping Centers—Number and Gross Leasable Area: 1990 to 2010

[As of December 31. A shopping center is a group of architecturally unified commercial establishments built on a site that is planned, developed, owned, and managed as an operating unit related in its location, size, and type of shops to the trade area that the unit serves. The unit provides on-site parking in definite relationship to the types and total size of the stores. The data base attempts to include all centers with three or more stores. Estimates are based on a sample of data available on shopping center properties; for details, contact source]

Year	Total	Gross leasable area (square feet)					
		Less than 100,001	100,001 to 200,000	200,001 to 400,000	400,001 to 800,000	800,001 to 1,000,000	More than 1,000,000
NUMBER							
1990	76,397	64,149	7,775	3,046	857	204	366
1995	81,563	67,681	8,629	3,590	1,049	220	394
2000	88,859	73,157	9,548	4,159	1,306	249	440
2005	98,888	81,324	10,366	4,823	1,614	275	486
2006	101,924	83,935	10,536	4,985	1,691	284	493
2007	104,606	86,214	10,692	5,152	1,760	291	497
2008	106,617	87,842	10,849	5,280	1,839	306	501
2009	107,514	88,549	10,940	5,335	1,879	307	504
2010	107,773	88,757	10,967	5,352	1,885	307	505
Gross Leasable Area (mil. sq. ft.)							
1990	4,731	1,678	1,090	814	472	183	495
1995	5,279	1,799	1,213	963	576	197	531
2000	5,956	1,967	1,342	1,123	709	222	593
2005	6,713	2,177	1,458	1,309	871	245	653
2006	6,902	2,238	1,482	1,353	912	254	663
2007	7,072	2,291	1,504	1,400	949	260	668
2008	7,234	2,334	1,527	1,437	991	273	672
2009	7,308	2,353	1,540	1,452	1,013	274	677
2010	7,326	2,358	1,543	1,457	1,016	274	678

Source: CoStar Group, Inc., Washington, DC (copyright).

Table 1062. Food and Alcoholic Beverage Sales by Sales Outlet: 1990 to 2009

[In billions of dollars (553.4 represents $553,400,000,000)]

Sales outlet	1990	2000	2003	2004	2005	2006	2007	2008	2009
Food sales, total [1]	**553.4**	**814.6**	**920.1**	**966.1**	**1,021.2**	**1,084.8**	**1,139.3**	**1,172.1**	**1,182.0**
Food at home	305.3	423.2	476.4	494.5	520.9	552.3	578.4	596.7	607.4
Food stores [2]	256.4	303.5	323.8	334.0	347.3	359.9	377.4	397.4	397.4
Other stores [3]	32.3	89.4	122.6	129.4	142.4	160.4	167.3	165.1	176.4
Home-delivered, mail order	5.3	19.2	18.3	18.9	19.5	20.3	21.0	21.0	19.9
Farmers, manufacturers, wholesalers	3.5	4.6	4.8	4.9	5.2	5.4	6.0	6.2	6.5
Home production and donations	7.7	6.5	6.8	7.2	6.5	6.5	6.7	6.9	7.2
Food away from home [4]	248.1	391.5	443.7	471.6	500.3	532.4	560.9	575.4	574.5
Alcoholic beverage sales, total	**72.7**	**111.9**	**126.9**	**139.4**	**146.4**	**159.2**	**167.3**	**168.3**	**167.0**
Packaged alcoholic beverages	38.0	52.7	57.5	59.8	62.3	69.4	72.6	72.5	75.4
Liquor stores	18.6	24.5	26.0	27.7	29.4	31.0	32.6	34.3	35.3
Food stores	10.8	15.9	17.8	18.5	19.3	20.0	20.9	22.0	22.0
All other	8.6	12.3	13.7	13.6	13.6	18.4	19.0	16.2	18.2
Alcoholic drinks away from home	34.7	59.2	69.4	79.6	84.1	89.8	94.7	95.9	91.6
Eating and drinking places [5]	26.7	41.9	45.0	53.0	55.6	59.6	62.5	63.5	65.8
Hotels and motels [5]	3.4	9.9	15.9	17.4	18.8	20.0	21.2	21.2	21.1
All other	4.6	7.4	8.6	9.2	9.6	10.2	10.9	11.2	4.7

[1] Includes taxes and tips. [2] Excludes sales to restaurants and institutions. [3] Includes eating and drinking establishments, trailer parks, commissary stores, and military exchanges. [4] Includes food furnished and donations. [5] Includes tips.
Source: U.S. Department of Agriculture, Economic Research Service, "Food CPI, Prices, and Expenditures: Food Expenditure Tables," June 2010, <http://www.ers.usda.gov/briefing/CPIFoodAndExpenditures/Data>.

Section 23
Transportation

This section presents data on civil air transportation, both passenger and cargo, and on water transportation, including inland waterways, oceanborne commerce, the merchant marine, cargo, and vessel tonnages.

This section also presents statistics on revenues, passenger and freight traffic volume, and employment in various revenue-producing modes of the transportation industry, including motor vehicles, trains, and pipelines. Data are also presented on highway mileage and finances, motor vehicle travel, accidents, and registrations; and characteristics of public transit, railroads, and pipelines.

Principal source of transportation data is the annual *National Transportation Statistics* publication of the U.S. Bureau of Transportation Statistics. Principal sources of air and water transportation data are the *Annual Report* issued by the Air Transport Association of America, Washington, DC and the annual *Waterborne Commerce of the United States* issued by the Corps of Engineers of the Department of Army. In addition, the U.S. Census Bureau in its commodity flow survey (part of the census of transportation, taken every 5 years through 2007, for years ending in "2" and "7") provides data on the type, weight, and value of commodities shipped by manufacturing establishments in the United States, by means of transportation, origin, and destination. The advance reports for 2007 are part of the 2007 Economic Census. This census was conducted in accordance with the 2002 North American Industry Classification System (NAICS). See text, Section 15, Business Enterprise, for a discussion of the Economic Census and NAICS.

The Bureau of Transportation Statistics (BTS) was established within the U.S. Department of Transportation (USDOT) in 1992 to collect, report, and analyze transportation data. Today, BTS is a component of the USDOT Research and Innovative Technology Administration (RITA). BTS products include reports to Congress, the Secretary of Transportation, and stakeholders in the nation's transportation community. These stakeholders include: federal agencies, state and local governments, metropolitan planning organizations, universities, the private sector and general public. Congress requires the BTS to report (congressional mandate, laid out in 49 U.S.C. 111 (1)) on transportation statistics to the President and Congress. *The Transportation Statistics Annual Report* (TSAR), provides a data overview of U.S. transportation issues. As required by Congress, each TSAR has two essential components: a review of the state of transportation statistics with recommendations for improvements and a presentation of the data. The BTS publication *National Transportation Statistics (NTS)*, a companion report to the TSAR, has more comprehensive and longer time-series data. NTS presents information on the U.S. transportation system, including its physical components, safety record, economic performance, energy use, and environmental impacts. The BTS publication *State Transportation* Statistics presents a statistical profile of transportation in the 50 states and the District of Columbia. This profile includes infrastructure, freight movement and passenger travel, system safety, vehicles, transportation-related economy and finance, energy usage and the environment.

The principal compiler of data on public roads and on operation of motor vehicles is the U.S. Department of Transportation's (DOT) Federal Highway Administration (FHWA). These data appear in FHWA's annual *Highway Statistics* and other publications.

The U.S. National Highway Traffic Safety Administration (NHTSA), through its *Traffic Safety Facts FARS/GES Annual Report*, presents descriptive statistics about traffic crashes of all severities, from those that result in property damage to those that result in the loss of human life. The data for this report is a compilation of motor vehicle crash data from the *Fatality Analysis Reporting System (FARS)* and the *General Estimates System (GES)*. For other publications and reports, go to the National Center for Statistics and Analysis (NCSA), Publications and Data Request. The Web site is located at <http://wwnrd .nhtsa.dot.gov/CAT/index.aspx>. DOT's Federal Railroad Administration (FRA), Office of Safety Analysis presents railroad safety information including accidents and incidents, inspections and highway-rail crossing data in its annual report *Railroad Safety Statistics*. The Web site is located at <http://safetydata.fra .dot.gov /officeofsafety>.

Data are also presented in many nongovernment publications. Among them are the weekly and annual *Cars of Revenue Freight Loaded* and the annual *Yearbook of Railroad Facts*, both published by the Association of American Railroads, Washington, DC; *Public Transportation Fact Book*, containing electric railway and motorbus statistics, published annually by the American Public Transportation Association, Washington, DC; and *Injury Facts*, issued by the National Safety Council, Chicago, IL.

Civil aviation—Federal promotion and regulation of civil aviation have been carried out by the Federal Aviation Administration (FAA) and the Civil Aeronautics Board (CAB). The CAB promoted and regulated the civil air transportation industry within the United States and between the United States and foreign countries. The Board granted licenses to provide air transportation service, approved or disapproved proposed rates and fares, and approved or disapproved proposed agreements and corporate relationships involving air carriers. In December 1984, the CAB ceased to exist as an agency. Some of its functions were transferred to the DOT, as outlined below. The responsibility for investigation of aviation accidents resides with the National Transportation Safety Board.

The Office of the Secretary, DOT aviation activities include: negotiation of international air transportation rights, selection of U.S. air carriers to serve capacity-controlled international markets, oversight of international rates and fares, maintenance of essential air service to small communities, and consumer affairs. DOT's Bureau of Transportation Statistics (BTS) handles aviation information functions formerly assigned to CAB. Prior to BTS, the Research and Special Programs Administration handled these functions.

The principal activities of the FAA include: the promotion of air safety; controlling the use of navigable airspace; prescribing regulations dealing with the competency of airmen, airworthiness of aircraft and air traffic control; operation of air route traffic control centers, airport traffic control towers, and flight service stations; the design, construction, maintenance, and inspection of navigation, traffic control, and communications equipment; and the development of general aviation.

The CAB published monthly and quarterly financial and traffic statistical data for the certificated route air carriers. BTS continues these publications, including both certificated and noncertificated (commuter) air carriers. The FAA annually publishes data on the use of airway facilities; data related to the location of airmen, aircraft, and airports; the volume of activity in the field of nonair carrier (general aviation) flying; and aircraft production and registration.

General aviation comprises all civil flying (including such commercial operations as small demand air taxis, agriculture application, powerline patrol, etc.) but excludes certificated route air carriers, supplemental operators, large-aircraft commercial operators, and commuter airlines.

Air carriers and service—The CAB previously issued "certificates of public convenience and necessity" under Section 401 of the Federal Aviation Act of 1958 for scheduled and nonscheduled (charter) passenger services and cargo services. It also issued certificates under Section 418 of the Act to cargo air carriers for domestic all-cargo service only. The DOT Office of the Secretary now issues the certificates under a "fit, willing, and able" test of air carrier operations. Carriers operating only a 60-seat-or-less aircraft are given exemption authority to carry passengers, cargo, and mail in scheduled and nonscheduled service under Part 298 of the DOT (formerly CAB) regulations. Exemption authority carriers who offer scheduled passenger service to an essential air service point must meet the "fit, willing, and able" test.

Vessel shipments, entrances, and clearances—Shipments by dry cargo vessels comprise shipments on all types of watercraft, except tanker vessels; shipments by tanker vessels comprise all types of cargo, liquid and dry, carried by tanker vessels. A vessel is reported as entered only at the first port which it enters in the United States, whether or not cargo is unloaded at that port.

A vessel is reported as cleared only at the last port at which clearance is made to a foreign port, whether or not it takes on cargo. Army and Navy vessels entering or clearing without commercial cargo are not included in the figures.

Units of measurement—Cargo (or freight) tonnage and shipping weight both represent the gross weight of the cargo including the weight of containers, wrappings, crates, etc. However, shipping weight excludes lift and cargo vans and similar substantial outer containers. Other tonnage figures generally refer to stowing capacity of vessels, 100 cubic feet being called 1 ton. Gross tonnage comprises the space within the frames and the ceiling of the hull, together with those closed-in spaces above deck available for cargo, stores, passengers, or crew, with certain minor exceptions. Net or registered tonnage is the gross tonnage less the spaces occupied by the propelling machinery, fuel, crew quarters, master's cabin, and navigation spaces. Substantially, it represents space available for cargo and passengers. The net tonnage capacity of a ship may bear little relation to weight of cargo. Deadweight tonnage is the weight in long tons required to depress a vessel from light water line (that is, with only the machinery and equipment on board) to load line. It is, therefore, the weight of the cargo, fuel, etc., which a vessel is designed to carry with safety.

Federal-aid highway systems—
The Intermodal Surface Transportation Efficiency Act (ISTEA) of 1991 eliminated the historical Federal-Aid Highway Systems and created the National Highway System (NHS) and other federal-aid highway categories. The final NHS was approved by Congress in December of 1995 under the National Highway System Designation Act.

Functional systems—Roads and streets are assigned to groups according to the character of service intended. The functional systems are (1) arterial highways that generally handle the long trips, (2) collector facilities that collect and disperse traffic between the arterials and the lower systems, and (3) local roads and streets that primarily serve direct access to residential areas, farms, and other local areas.

Regulatory bodies— The Federal Energy Regulatory Commission (FERC) is an independent agency that regulates the interstate transmission of electricity, natural gas, and oil. FERC also reviews proposals to build liquefied natural gas (LNG) terminals and interstate natural gas pipelines as well as licensing hydropower projects. The Energy Policy Act of 2005 gave FERC additional responsibilities such as regulating the transmission and wholesale sales of electricity in interstate commerce. See source for more details.

Railroads—The Surface Transportation Board (STB) was created in the Interstate Commerce Commission Termination Act of 1995, Pub. L. No.104-88, 109 Stat. 803 (1995) (ICCTA), and is the successor agency to the Interstate Commerce Commission. The STB is an economic regulatory agency that Congress charged with the fundamental missions of resolving railroad rate and service disputes and reviewing proposed railroad mergers. The STB is decisionally independent, although it is administratively affiliated with the Department of Transportation.

The STB serves as both an adjudicatory and a regulatory body. The agency has jurisdiction over railroad rate and service issues and rail restructuring transactions (mergers, line sales, line construction, and line abandonment); certain trucking company, moving van, and noncontiguous ocean shipping company rate matters; certain intercity passenger bus company structure, financial, and operational matters; and rates and services of certain pipelines not regulated by the Federal Energy Regulatory Commission. Other ICC regulatory functions were either eliminated or transferred to the Federal Highway Administration or the Bureau of Transportation Statistics within DOT.

Class I Railroads are regulated by the STB and subject to the Uniform System of Accounts and required to file annual and periodic reports. Railroads are classified based on their annual operating revenues. The class to which a carrier belongs is determined by comparing its adjusted operating revenues for 3 consecutive years to the following scale: Class I, $250 million or more; Class II, $20 million to $250 million; and Class III, $0 to $20 million. Operating revenue dollar ranges are indexed for inflation.

Postal Service—The U.S. Postal Service provides mail processing and delivery services within the United States. The Postal Accountability and Enhancement Act of 2006 was the first major legislative change to the Postal Service since 1971 when the Postal Reorganization Act of 1970 created the Postal Service as an independent establishment of the Federal Executive Branch. The Act of 2006 changed the way the U.S. Postal Service operates and conducts business. Now annual rate increases for market

dominant products are linked to the Consumer Price Index and the Postal Service has more flexibility for pricing competitive products, enabling it to respond to dynamic market conditions and changing customer needs.

Revenue and cost analysis describes the Postal Service's system of attributing revenues and costs to classes of mail and service. This system draws primarily upon probability sampling techniques to develop estimates of revenues, volumes, and weights, as well as costs by class of mail and special service. The costs attributed to classes of mail and special services are primarily incremental costs which vary in response to changes in volume; they account for roughly 60 percent of the total costs of the Postal Service. The balance represents "institutional costs." Statistics on revenues, volume of mail, and distribution of expenditures are presented in the Postal Service's annual report, *Cost and Revenue Analysis*, and its *Annual Report of the Postmaster General* and its annual *Comprehensive Statement on Postal Operations*.

Statistical reliability—For a discussion of statistical collection and estimation, sampling procedures, and measures of statistical reliability applicable to Census Bureau data, see Appendix III.

Table 1063. Transportation-Related Components of U.S. Gross Domestic Product: 2000 to 2009

[In billions of dollars (1,045.3 represents $1,045,300,000,000), except percent. For explanation of chained dollars, see Section 13 text. Minus sign (–) indicates a decrease]

Item	2000	2005	2006	2007	2008	2009
CURRENT DOLLARS						
Total transportation-related final demand [1]	**1,045.3**	**1,266.1**	**1,325.8**	**1,406.6**	**1,393.3**	**1,225.9**
Total gross domestic product (GDP)	9,951.5	12,638.4	13,398.9	14,061.8	14,369.1	14,119.0
Transportation as a percent of GDP	10.5	10.0	9.9	10.0	9.7	8.7
Personal consumption of transportation	798.4	979.3	1,008.8	1,052.6	1,033.4	890.6
Motor vehicles and parts	363.2	409.6	397.1	402.5	343.2	319.7
Gasoline and oil	172.9	283.8	314.7	343.0	383.3	280.8
Transportation services	262.3	285.9	297.0	307.1	306.9	290.1
Gross private domestic investment	177.6	188.8	206.9	199.2	157.1	85.4
Transportation structures	6.8	7.1	8.7	9.0	9.9	9.0
Transportation equipment	170.8	181.7	198.2	190.2	147.2	76.4
Net exports of transportation-related goods and service [2]	−109.0	−136.6	−137.8	−112.8	−82.3	−37.5
Exports (+)	179.0	216.6	240	260.2	270.6	218.3
Civilian aircraft, engines, and parts	48.1	55.9	64.5	73.0	74.0	74.8
Automotive vehicles, engines, and parts	80.4	98.4	107.3	121.3	121.5	81.7
Passenger fares	20.7	21.0	22.0	25.6	31.4	26.4
Other transportation	29.8	41.3	46.2	40.3	43.7	35.4
Imports (−)	288.0	353.2	377.8	373	352.9	255.8
Civilian aircraft, engines, and parts	26.4	25.8	28.4	34.4	35.4	30.6
Automotive vehicles, engines, and parts	195.9	239.4	256.6	256.7	231.2	157.6
Passenger fares	24.3	26.1	27.5	28.4	32.6	26.0
Other transportation	41.4	61.9	65.3	53.5	53.7	41.6
Government transportation-related purchases	178.3	234.6	247.9	267.6	285.1	287.4
Federal purchases [3]	19.3	30.1	32.0	32.0	34.8	36.4
State and local purchases [3]	150.0	188.6	201.0	215.9	232.3	236.7
Defense-related purchases [4]	9.0	15.9	14.9	19.7	18.0	14.3
CHAINED (2005) DOLLARS						
Total transportation-related final demand [1]	**1,211.8**	**1,266.1**	**1,254.6**	**1,273.4**	**1,182.6**	**1,104.4**
Total gross domestic product (GDP)	11,226.0	12,638.4	12,976.2	13,228.9	13,228.8	12,880.6
Transportation as a percent of GDP	10.8	10.0	9.7	9.6	8.9	8.6
Personal consumption of transportation	903.6	979.3	960.5	968.7	886.6	840.2
Motor vehicles and parts	356.1	409.6	396.6	403.9	348.2	324.0
Gasoline and oil	261.3	283.8	278.9	276.8	265.3	265.3
Transportation services	286.2	285.9	285.0	288.0	273.1	250.9
Gross private domestic investment	194.1	188.8	204.9	194.3	152.1	77.5
Transportation structures	7.9	7.1	8.4	8.5	9.1	8.1
Transportation equipment	186.2	181.7	196.5	185.8	143.0	69.4
Net exports of transportation-related goods and service [2]	−109.3	−136.6	−140.9	−118.5	−83.3	−42.0
Exports (+)	204.5	216.6	233.8	246.8	246.0	198.2
Civilian aircraft, engines, and parts	58.4	55.9	62.0	67.1	64.9	62.5
Automotive vehicles, engines, and parts	83.2	98.4	106.0	118.4	117.2	78.4
Passenger fares	28.6	21.0	21.9	23.4	25.9	24.9
Other transportation	34.3	41.3	43.9	37.9	38.0	32.4
Imports (−)	313.8	353.2	374.7	365.3	329.3	240.2
Civilian aircraft, engines, and parts	30.7	25.8	27.3	31.5	30.5	25.0
Automotive vehicles, engines, and parts	202.9	239.4	255.6	253.1	222.4	150.4
Passenger fares	29.1	26.1	26.1	25.1	25.0	21.6
Other transportation	51.1	61.9	65.7	55.6	51.4	43.2
Government transportation-related purchases	223.4	234.6	230.1	228.9	227.2	228.7
Federal purchases [3]	23.1	30.1	30.8	29.6	31.5	32.5
State and local purchases [3]	189.1	188.6	184.9	180.5	180.3	183.2
Defense-related purchases [4]	11.2	15.9	14.4	18.8	15.4	13.0

[1] Sum of total personal consumption of transportation, total gross private domestic investment, net exports of transportation-related goods and services, and total government transportation-related purchases. [2] Exports minus imports.
[3] Federal purchases and state and local purchases are the sum of consumption expenditures and gross investment.
[4] Defense-related purchases are the sum of transportation of material and travel.

Source: U.S. Bureau of Transportation Statistics, "National Transportation Statistics," <http://www.bts.gov/publications/national_transportation_statistics/>

Table 1064. Employment in Transportation and Warehousing: 1990 to 2010

[In thousands (3,476 represents 3,476,000). Annual average of monthly figures. Based on Current Employment Statistics program; see Appendix III]

Industry	NAICS code [1]	1990	1995	2000	2005	2008	2009	2010
Transportation and warehousing	**48–49**	**3,476**	**3,838**	**4,410**	**4,361**	**4,508**	**4,236**	**4,184**
Air transportation	481	529	511	614	501	491	463	464
Rail transportation	482	272	233	232	228	231	218	215
Water transportation	483	57	51	56	61	67	63	63
Truck transportation	484	1,122	1,249	1,406	1,398	1,389	1,268	1,244
Transit and ground	485	274	328	372	389	423	422	432
Pipeline transportation	486	60	54	46	38	42	43	42
Scenic and sightseeing	487	16	22	28	29	28	28	27
Support activities	488	364	430	537	552	592	549	540
Couriers and messengers	492	375	517	605	571	573	546	527
Warehousing and storage	493	407	444	514	595	672	637	628

[1] North American Industry Classification System 2007, see text, Sections 12 and 15.
Source: U.S. Bureau of Labor Statistics, Current Employment Statistics, National, "Employment, Hours, and Earnings," <http://www.bls.gov/ces/data.htm/>.

Table 1065. Transportation and Warehousing—Establishments, Employees, and Payroll by Kind of Business (NAICS Basis): 2007 and 2008

[4,395.4 represents 4,395,400. Covers establishments with payroll. Excludes self-employed individuals, railroad employees, and most government employees. For statement on methodology, see Appendix III. County Business Patterns excludes rail transportation (NAICS 482) and the National Postal Service (NAICS 491)]

Industry	NAICS code [1]	Establishments		Paid employees (1,000)		Annual payroll (mil. dol.)	
		2007	2008	2007	2008	2007	2008
Transportation & warehousing	**48–49**	**219,806**	**217,083**	**4,395.4**	**4,438.9**	**175,479.8**	**176,164.6**
Air transportation	481	5,730	5,558	480.6	485.7	25,787.0	24,863.5
Scheduled air transportation	4811	3,084	3,036	435.9	445.3	23,042.9	22,168.5
Scheduled passenger air transportation	481111	2,585	2,556	417.1	423.1	22,329.8	21,266.3
Scheduled freight air transportation	481112	499	480	(NA)	22.2	713.1	902.2
Nonscheduled air transportation	4812	2,646	2,522	44.8	40.4	2,744.1	2,694.9
Water transportation	483	1,928	1,748	68.9	69.0	4,467.1	4,763.1
Deep sea, coastal, & Great Lakes water transportation	4831	1,255	1,126	48.2	49.4	3,285.6	3,549.2
Inland water transportation	4832	673	622	20.8	19.6	1,181.5	1,213.8
Inland water freight transportation	483211	411	364	17.4	16.9	1,029.8	1,098.8
Inland water passenger transportation	483212	262	258	3.4	2.8	151.7	115.1
Truck transportation	484	121,419	115,321	1,476.4	1,426.9	58,867.8	56,703.2
General freight trucking	4841	68,494	65,196	998.7	947.2	40,934.5	38,417.1
General freight trucking, local	48411	28,595	27,113	211.9	176.8	7,903.9	6,276.6
General freight trucking, long distance	48412	39,899	38,083	786.8	770.4	33,030.6	32,140.5
Specialized freight trucking	4842	52,925	50,125	477.7	479.6	17,933.3	18,286.1
Used household & office goods moving	48421	8,502	8,059	105.4	97.8	3,365.0	3,117.1
Specialized freight (except used goods) trucking, local	48422	32,125	31,483	207.0	207.0	7,814.9	7,952.8
Specialized freight (except used goods) trucking, long-distance	48423	12,298	10,583	165.4	174.9	6,753.4	7,216.2
Transit & ground passenger transportation	485	18,322	18,011	440.6	449.4	10,019.2	10,057.9
Urban transit systems	4851	932	871	52.9	47.8	1,837.1	1,792.7
Mixed mode systems	485111	67	36	1.5	(NA)	45.8	(D)
Commuter rail	485112	26	22	0.7	(NA)	38.0	175.5
Bus and other motor vehicle mode systems	485113	795	806	47.6	41.8	1,601.5	1,499.8
Other	485119	44	7	3.1	(NA)	151.8	(D)
Interurban & rural bus transportation	4852	508	487	17.4	15.0	469.8	421.9
Taxi & limousine service	4853	7,493	7,413	72.5	71.0	1,652.5	1,626.6
Taxi service	48531	2,993	2,897	33.4	29.7	658.8	625.5
Limousine service	48532	4,500	4,516	39.1	41.4	993.7	1,001.1
School & employee bus transportation	4854	4,673	4,501	206.8	219.6	3,896.5	3,886.8
Charter bus industry	4855	1,247	1,335	28.4	30.7	666.2	757.0
Other transit & ground passenger transportation	4859	3,469	3,404	62.6	65.3	1,497.1	1,572.7
Special needs transportation	485991	2,337	2,396	47.7	52.2	1,169.6	1,278.5
Pipeline transportation	486	2,775	2,871	42.4	40.2	3,675.3	3,568.8
Pipeline transportation of crude oil	4861	374	370	8.3	6.1	850.3	661.0
Pipeline transportation of natural gas	4862	1,479	1,638	24.7	24.0	2,063.5	2,125.6
Other pipeline transportation	4869	922	863	9.4	10.0	761.5	782.3
Scenic & sightseeing transportation	487	2,781	2,589	27.5	23.0	808.4	678.8
Scenic & sightseeing transportation, land	4871	698	643	9.7	9.6	247.0	242.6
Scenic & sightseeing transportation, water	4872	1,880	1,747	15.6	11.4	479.4	354.0
Scenic & sightseeing transportation, other	4879	203	199	2.2	2.1	82.0	82.2
Support activities for transportation	488	38,566	42,296	610.6	645.7	26,400.8	28,169.7
Support activities for air transportation	4881	5,430	5,785	165.3	174.4	6,229.3	6,770.8
Airport operations	48811	1,748	2,048	73.0	89.5	1,981.3	2,528.1
Air traffic control	488111	223	202	2.2	2.0	84.1	122.6
Other support activities for air transportation	48819	3,682	3,737	92.3	84.9	4,248.0	4,242.7
Support activities for rail transportation	4882	1,018	1,023	28.6	25.8	1,155.6	990.7
Support activities for water transportation	4883	2,330	2,462	93.4	93.7	5,027.8	4,907.9
Port and harbor operations	48831	223	268	6.6	5.6	318.6	282.7
Marine cargo handling	48832	552	532	62.9	63.7	3,428.1	3,272.7
Navigational services to shipping	48833	830	868	13.0	13.4	756.6	847.9
Other	48839	725	794	10.9	10.9	524.6	504.5
Support activities for road transportation	4884	10,178	10,112	76.5	78.0	2,393.8	2,311.1
Motor vehicle towing	48841	8,267	8,400	53.2	55.3	1,617.9	1,629.5
Freight transportation arrangement	4885	17,903	21,418	212.2	246.1	10,157.2	11,970.4
Other support activities for transportation	4889	1,707	1,496	34.7	27.6	1,437.0	1,218.9
Couriers & messengers	492	13,845	14,339	569.2	596.3	21,479.1	21,568.3
Couriers	4921	9,116	9,717	528.2	559.1	20,385.4	20,624.0
Local messengers & local delivery	4922	4,729	4,622	41.0	37.1	1,093.7	944.3
Warehousing & storage	493	14,440	14,350	679.1	702.8	23,975.2	25,791.3

NA Not available. D Data withheld to avoid disclosure. [1] Based on the North American Industry Classification System (NAICS), 2002; data for 2008 based on NAICS 2007, see text, Section 15.

Source: U.S. Census Bureau, "County Business Patterns" July 2010, <http://www.census.gov/econ/cbp/index.html>.

Table 1066. Transportation and Warehousing—Establishments, Revenue, Payroll, and Employees by Industry: 2002 and 2007

[382,152 represents $382,152,000,000. For establishments with payroll. Based on the 2002 and 2007 Economic Censuses. Paid employees for pay period including March 12. See Appendix III]

Kind of business	NAICS code [1]	Number of establish-ments	Revenue (mil. dol.)	Annual payroll (mil. dol.)	Paid employees (1,000)
Transportation and warehousing total, 2002....	**48–49**	**199,618**	**382,152**	**115,989**	**3,650.9**
Air transportation [2]	481	3,847	19,735	3,805	99.1
Water transportation	483	1,890	23,331	3,194	66.2
Truck transportation	484	112,642	164,219	47,750	1,435.2
Transit and ground passenger transportation [3]	485	17,260	18,850	7,675	398.4
Pipeline transportation [3]	486	2,188	22,031	2,477	36.8
Scenic and sightseeing transportation	487	2,523	1,859	526	22.5
Support activities for transportation [3]	488	33,942	57,414	16,202	465.6
Couriers and messengers	492	12,655	58,165	17,175	561.5
Warehousing and storage	493	12,671	16,548	17,183	565.5
Transportation and warehousing total, 2007....	**48–49**	**219,706**	**639,916**	**173,183**	**4,454.4**
Air transportation [2]	481	5,661	146,612	26,120	478.2
Water transportation	483	1,721	34,447	4,544	76.0
Truck transportation	484	120,390	217,833	58,266	1,507.9
Transit and ground passenger transportation [3]	485	17,791	26,465	9,844	444.9
Pipeline transportation [3]	486	2,529	25,718	3,219	37.0
Scenic and sightseeing transportation	487	2,542	2,448	653	24.4
Support activities for transportation [3]	488	42,130	86,596	24,579	608.4
Couriers and messengers	492	13,004	77,877	20,431	557.2
Warehousing and storage	493	13,938	21,921	25,526	720.5

[1] 2002 Data based on the North American Industry Classification System (NAICS), 2007 data are based on the 2002 NAICS; see text, Section 15. [2] Excludes large certificated passenger carriers that do not report to the Office of Airline Information, U.S. Department of Transportation. [3] Includes other industries not shown separately.

Source: U.S. Census Bureau, 2007 Economic Census, EC0748A2, "Transportation and Warehousing: Geographic Area Series: Comparative Statistics for the United States, (2002 NAICS Basis): 2007 and 2002," <http://factfinder.census.gov/>, accessed March 2011.

Table 1067. Transportation and Warehousing—Nonemployer Establishments and Receipts by Kind of Business: 2006 to 2008

[1,002.0 represents 1,002,000. Includes only firms subject to federal income tax. Nonemployers are businesses with no paid employees. Data originate chiefly from administrative records of the Internal Revenue Service; see Appendix III]

Kind of Business	NAICS code [1]	Establishments (1,000)			Receipts (mil. dol.)		
		2006	2007	2008	2006	2007	2008
Transportation and warehousing	**48–49**	**1,002.0**	**1,083.1**	**1,039.5**	**62,928**	**66,633**	**67,026**
Air transportation	481	21.0	21.0	20.5	1,303	1,347	1,349
Water transportation	483	6.7	6.5	6.4	548	516	538
Truck transportation	484	531.8	542.5	508.0	46,653	47,927	47,880
General freight trucking	4841	485.3	489.2	459.5	42,781	43,816	43,936
General freight trucking, local	48411	194.2	193.1	180.2	14,075	14,263	13,873
General freight trucking, long-distance	48412	291.1	296.1	279.3	28,705	29,553	30,063
Specialized freight trucking	4842	46.5	53.3	48.6	3,872	4,111	3,944
Transit and ground passenger transportation	485	193.6	202.1	207.1	6,266	6,759	7,256
Urban transit system	4851	1.1	1.2	1.2	41	43	48
Interurban and rural bus transportation	4852	1.7	1.7	1.6	76	77	78
Taxi and limousine service	4853	151.6	161.4	166.8	4,803	5,270	5,726
School and employee bus transportation	4854	7.3	7.2	6.9	197	202	214
Charter bus industry	4855	4.1	3.8	3.8	187	194	182
Other transit and ground passenger transportation	4859	27.8	26.8	26.8	962	973	1,009
Pipeline transportation	486	0.8	0.8	0.8	81	75	81
Scenic and sightseeing transportation	487	3.9	5.1	4.7	167	197	185
Support activities for transportation	488	63.2	106.3	102.2	3,387	4,759	4,821
Couriers and messengers	492	172.8	190.5	180.9	3,995	4,513	4,362
Warehousing and storage	493	8.1	8.3	8.7	529	542	553

[1] Based on the 2007 North American Industry Classification System (NAICS); see text, Section 15.

Source: U.S. Census Bureau, "Nonemployer Statistics," June 2010, <http://www.census.gov/econ/nonemployer/index.html>.

Table 1068. Transportation System Mileage Within the United States: 1980 to 2009

[3,860 represents 3,860,000. Numbers, except where indicated]

System	Unit	1980	1985	1990	1995	2000	2005	2007	2008	2009
Highway [1]	1,000	3,860	3,864	3,867	3,912	3,936	3,996	4,032	4,043	4,051
Class 1 rail [2]	Number	164,822	145,764	119,758	108,264	99,250	95,664	94,313	94,082	93,921
Amtrak	Number	24,000	24,000	24,000	24,000	23,000	22,007	21,708	21,178	21,178
Transit: [3]										
Commuter rail [4]	Number	(NA)	3,574	4,132	4,160	5,209	7,118	7,135	7,261	7,561
Heavy rail [5]	Number	(NA)	1,293	1,351	1,458	1,558	1,622	1,623	1,623	1,623
Light rail [6]	Number	(NA)	384	483	568	834	1,188	1,341	1,397	1,477
Navigable channels	Number	26,000	26,000	26,000	26,000	26,000	26,000	25,320	25,320	25,320
Oil pipeline [7]	Number	218,393	213,605	208,752	181,912	176,996	162,919	166,256	169,586	172,048
Gas pipeline [8]	1,000	1,052	1,111	1,270	1,332	1,377	1,484	1,523	1,533	1,540

NA Not available. [1] All public road and street mileage in the 50 states and the District of Columbia. [2] Data represent miles of road owned (aggregate length of road, excluding yard tracks, sidings, and parallel lines). [3] Transit system length is measured in directional route-miles; see source. [4] Also called metropolitan rail or regional rail. [5] Also called metro, subway, rapid transit, or rapid rail. [6] Also called streetcar, tramway, or trolley. [7] Includes trunk and gathering lines for crude-oil pipeline. [8] Excludes service pipelines.

Source: U.S. Bureau of Transportation Statistics, "National Transportation Statistics," <http://www.bts.gov/publications/national_transportation_statistics>.

Table 1069. U.S. Aircraft, Vehicles, and Other Conveyances: 2000 to 2009

[178,099 represents 178,099]

System	2000	2002	2003	2004	2005	2006	2007	2008	2009
Air:									
Air carrier [1]	8,055	8,194	8,176	8,186	8,225	8,089	8,044	7,856	(NA)
General aviation [2] (active fleet)	217,533	211,244	209,708	219,426	224,352	221,943	231,607	228,663	223,877
Highway, registered vehicles (1,000): [3]									
Light duty vehicle, short wheel base [4]	178,099	183,162	185,392	189,462	191,223	194,295	196,491	196,763	193,980
Motorcycle	4,346	5,004	5,370	5,781	6,227	6,679	7,138	7,753	7,930
Light duty vehicle, long wheel base [4]	33,642	36,319	35,772	37,412	39,279	38,715	39,187	39,685	40,488
Truck [5]	8,988	9,378	9,451	9,574	9,884	10,334	10,752	10,873	10,973
Bus	746	761	777	795	807	822	834	843	842
Transit:									
Motor bus	58,578	60,719	61,659	61,318	62,284	64,025	63,359	63,151	63,343
Light rail cars [6]	1,306	1,448	1,482	1,622	1,645	1,801	1,802	1,948	2,059
Heavy rail cars [7]	10,311	10,849	10,754	10,858	11,110	11,052	11,222	11,377	11,461
Trolley bus	652	616	672	597	615	609	559	590	531
Commuter rail cars and locomotives	5,497	5,631	5,866	6,130	6,290	6,300	6,279	6,494	6,722
Demand response	22,087	24,808	25,873	26,333	28,346	29,406	29,433	30,773	34,235
Other [8]	7,705	8,033	8,626	10,544	11,622	12,454	12,953	14,953	17,766
Rail:									
Class I, freight cars (1,000)	560	478	467	474	475	475	460	450	416
Class I, locomotive	20,028	20,506	20,774	22,015	22,779	23,732	24,143	24,003	24,045
Nonclass I freight cars	132,448	130,590	124,580	120,169	120,195	120,688	120,463	109,487	108,233
Car companies' and shippers' freight cars	688,194	691,329	687,337	693,978	717,211	750,404	805,074	833,188	839,020
Amtrak, passenger train car	1,894	2,896	1,623	1,211	1,186	1,191	1,164	1,177	1,214
Amtrak, locomotive	378	372	442	276	258	319	270	278	274
Water:									
Non-self-propelled vessels [9]	31,360	32,381	31,335	31,296	33,152	32,211	31,654	31,238	31,008
Self-propelled vessels [10]	8,202	8,621	8,648	8,994	8,976	8,898	9,041	9,063	9,101
Ocean-going self-propelled vessels (1,000 gross tons and over)	454	426	418	423	366	344	275	272	196
Recreational boats (1,000)	12,782	12,854	12,795	12,781	12,942	12,746	12,873	12,693	12,722

NA Not available. [1] Air carrier aircraft are those carrying passengers or cargo for hire under 14 CFR 121 and 14 CFR 135. [2] Includes air taxi aircraft. [3] FHWA updated VM-1 from 2000 to 2009 using an enhanced methodology implemented in March 2011. [4] Light Duty Vehicles Short Wheel Base - passenger cars, light trucks, vans and sport utility vehicles with a wheelbase (WB) equal to or less than 121 inches. Light Duty Vehicles Long Wheel Base - large passenger cars, vans, pickup trucks, and sport/utility vehicles with wheelbases (WB) larger than 121 inches. [5] Includes combinations. [6] Fixed rail streetcar or trolley, for example. [7] Metro, subway, or rapid transit, for example. [8] Includes aerial tramway, automated guideway transit, cablecar, ferry boat, inclined plane, monorail, and vanpool. [9] Includes dry-cargo barges, tank barges, and railroad-car floats. [10] Includes dry-cargo and/or passenger, offshore supply vessels, railroad-car ferries, tankers, and towboats.

Source: U.S. Bureau of Transportation Statistics, "National Transportation Statistics," <http://www.bts.gov/publications/national_transportation_statistics/>.

Table 1070. Shipment Characteristics by Mode of Transportation: 2002 and 2007

[8,397,210 represents $8,397,210,000,000 (except as indicated otherwise). For business establishments in mining, manufacturing, wholesale trade, and selected retail industries. 2007 industries classified by the 2002 North American Industry Classification (NAICS). 2002 industries classified by the 1997 North American Industry Classification. Selected auxiliary establishments are also included. Based on the 2007 Economic Census; see Appendix III]

Mode of transportation	Value (mil. dol.)		Tons (1,000)		Ton-miles (mil.)		Average miles per shipment	
	2002	2007	2002	2007	2002	2007	2002	2007
All modes	8,397,210	11,684,872	11,667,919	12,543,425	3,137,898	3,344,658	546	619
Single modes	7,049,383	9,539,037	11,086,660	11,698,128	2,867,938	2,894,251	240	234
Truck [1]	6,235,001	8,335,789	7,842,836	8,778,713	1,255,908	1,342,104	173	206
For-hire truck	3,757,114	4,955,700	3,657,333	4,075,136	959,610	1,055,646	523	599
Private truck.............	2,445,288	3,380,090	4,149,658	4,703,576	291,114	286,457	64	57
Rail.............	310,884	436,420	1,873,884	1,861,307	1,261,612	1,344,040	807	728
Water.............	89,344	114,905	681,227	403,639	282,659	157,314	568	520
Shallow draft	57,467	91,004	458,577	343,307	211,501	117,473	450	144
Great lakes	843	(S)	38,041	17,792	13,808	6,887	339	657
Deep draft	31,034	23,058	184,610	42,540	57,350	32,954	664	923
Air (includes truck and air).......	264,959	252,276	3,760	3,611	5,835	4,510	1,919	1,304
Pipeline [2]	149,195	399,646	684,953	650,859	(S)	(S)	(S)	(S)
Multiple modes	1,079,185	1,866,723	216,686	573,729	225,715	416,642	895	975
Parcel, U.S. Postal Service or courier	987,746	1,561,874	25,513	33,900	19,004	27,961	894	975
Truck and rail	69,929	187,248	42,984	225,589	45,525	196,772	1,413	1,007
Truck and water	14,359	58,389	23,299	145,521	32,413	98,396	1,950	1,429
Rail and water	3,329	13,892	105,107	54,878	114,986	47,111	957	1,928
Other multiple modes	3,822	45,320	19,782	113,841	13,788	46,402	(S)	1,182
Other and unknown modes ...	268,642	279,113	364,573	271,567	44,245	33,764	130	116

S Data do not meet publication standards due to high sampling variability or other reasons. [1] Truck as a single mode includes shipments that went by private truck only, for-hire truck only, or a combination of private truck and for-hire truck. [2] Commodity Flow Survey data exclude shipments of crude oil.

Source: U.S. Department of Transportation, Research and Innovative Technology Administration, Bureau of Transportation Statistics, and U.S. Department of Commerce, U.S. Census Bureau, 2007 Commodity Flow Survey, <http://factfinder.census.gov/>, accessed April 2011.

Table 1071. Hazardous Shipments—Value, Tons, and Ton-Miles: 2002 and 2007

[660,181 represents $660,181,000,000. For business establishments in mining, manufacturing, wholesale trade, and selected retail industries. 2007 industries classified by the 2002 North American Industry Classification (NAICS). 2002 industries classified by the 1997 North American Industry Classification. Selected auxiliary establishments are also included. Based on the 2007 Economic Census; see Appendix III]

Mode of transportation	Value (mil. dol.)		Tons (1,000)		Ton-miles (mil.)		Average miles per shipment	
	2002	2007	2002	2007	2002	2007	2002	2007
All modes	660,181	1,448,218	2,191,519	2,231,133	326,727	323,457	136	96
Single modes	644,489	1,370,615	2,158,533	2,111,622	311,897	279,105	105	65
Truck [1]	419,630	837,074	1,159,514	1,202,825	110,163	103,997	86	59
For-hire truck	189,803	358,792	449,503	495,077	65,112	63,288	285	214
Private truck........................	226,660	478,282	702,186	707,748	44,087	40,709	38	32
Rail............................	31,339	69,213	109,369	129,743	72,087	92,169	695	578
Water............................	46,856	69,186	228,197	149,794	70,649	37,064	(S)	383
Air (includes truck and air)................	1,643	1,735	64	(S)	85	(S)	2,080	1,095
Pipeline [2]	145,021	393,408	661,390	628,905	(S)	(S)	(S)	(S)
Multiple modes	9,631	71,069	18,745	111,022	12,488	42,886	849	834
Parcel, U.S. Postal Service or courier	4,268	7,675	245	236	119	151	837	836
Other multiple modes	5,363	63,394	18,500	110,786	12,369	42,735	1,371	2,749
Other and unknown modes	6,061	6,534	14,241	8,489	2,342	1,466	57	58
Class of material	660,181	1,448,218	2,191,519	2,231,133	326,727	323,457	136	96
Class 1, Explosives	7,901	11,754	5,000	3,047	1,568	911	651	738
Class 2, Gasses	73,932	131,810	213,358	250,506	37,262	55,260	95	51
Class 3, Flammable and combustible liquid ...	490,238	1,170,455	1,788,986	1,752,814	218,574	181,615	106	91
Class 4, Flammable solid; spontaneously combustible material; dangerous when wet material........................	6,566	4,067	11,300	20,408	4,391	5,547	158	309
Class 5, Oxidizers and organic peroxides	5,471	6,695	12,670	14,959	4,221	7,024	407	361
Class 6, Toxic materials and infectious substances	8,275	21,198	8,459	11,270	4,254	5,667	626	467
Class 7, Radioactive materials	5,850	20,633	57	515	44	37	(S)	(S)
Class 8, Corrosive materials	38,324	51,475	90,671	114,441	36,260	44,395	301	208
Class 9, Miscellaneous hazardous material ...	23,625	30,131	61,018	63,173	20,153	23,002	368	484

S Data do not meet publication standards due to high sampling variability or other reasons. [1] Truck as a single mode includes shipments that went by private truck only, for-hire truck only, or a combination of private truck and for-hire truck. [2] Commodity Flow Survey Data exclude shipments of crude oil.

Source: U.S. Department of Transportation, Research and Innovative Technology Administration, Bureau of Transportation Statistics, and U.S. Department of Commerce, U.S. Census Bureau, 2007 Commodity Flow Survey, <http://factfinder.census.gov/>, accessed April 2011.

Table 1072. Transportation Accidents, Deaths, and Injuries: 1990 to 2009

[6,471 represents 6,471,000. Number, except as indicated]

Mode	Accidents					Deaths					Injuries				
	1990	1995	2000	2005	2009	1990	1995	2000	2005	2009	1990	1995	2000	2005	2009
Transit type:															
Air:															
Air carrier [1]	24	36	56	40	30	39	168	92	22	52	29	25	31	14	23
Commuter [2]	15	12	12	6	2	6	9	5	–	–	11	17	7	–	1
On-demand [3]	107	75	80	65	47	51	52	71	18	17	36	14	12	20	4
General aviation	2,242	2,056	1,837	1,670	1,474	770	735	596	563	474	409	396	309	271	274
Land:															
Highway crashes (1,000) [4]	6,471	6,699	6,394	6,159	5,505	44.6	41.8	41.9	43.5	33.8	3,231	3,465	3,189	2,699	2,217
Passenger car occupants	5,561	5,594	4,926	4,499	(NA)	24.1	22.4	20.7	18.5	13.1	2,376	2,469	2,052	1,573	1,216
Motorcyclists	103	66	69	101	(NA)	3.2	2.2	2.9	4.6	4.5	84	57	58	87	90
Light truck occupants	2,152	2,750	3,208	3,382	(NA)	8.6	9.6	11.5	13.0	10.3	505	722	887	872	759
Large truck occupants	372	363	438	423	(NA)	0.7	0.6	0.8	0.8	0.5	42	30	31	27	17
Bus occupants	60	59	56	50	(NA)	(Z)	(Z)	(Z)	0.1	(Z)	33	19	18	11	12
Pedestrians	(NA)	(NA)	(NA)	(NA)	(NA)	6.5	5.6	4.8	4.9	4.1	105	86	78	64	59
Pedacyclists	(NA)	(NA)	(NA)	(NA)	(NA)	0.9	0.8	0.7	0.8	0.6	75	67	51	45	51
Other	(NA)	(NA)	(NA)	(NA)	(NA)	0.6	0.5	0.6	0.8	0.7	11	14	15	18	14
Railroad [5]	8,594	7,092	6,485	6,331	3,807	1,297	1,146	937	884	695	25,143	14,440	11,643	9,550	7,925
Highway-rail grade crossing	5,715	4,633	3,502	3,066	1,917	698	579	425	359	247	2,407	1,894	1,219	1,053	738
Railroad	2,879	2,459	2,983	3,265	1,890	599	567	512	525	448	22,736	12,546	10,424	8,497	7,187
Transit [6]	58,002	25,683	24,261	8,151	5,360	339	274	295	236	230	54,556	57,196	56,697	18,131	(NA)
Waterborne:															
Waterborne (vessel related) [7]	3,613	5,349	5,403	4,977	4,458	85	53	53	78	57	175	154	150	140	(NA)
Recreational boating [8]	6,411	8,019	7,740	4,969	4,730	865	829	701	697	736	3,822	4,141	4,355	3,451	3,358
Pipeline: [9]	379	349	380	495	405	9	21	38	14	14	76	64	81	48	67
Hazard liquid	180	188	146	143	116	3	3	1	2	4	7	11	4	2	4
Gas	199	161	234	352	289	6	18	37	12	10	69	53	77	46	63
Hazardous materials [10, 11]	8,879	14,853	17,557	15,929	14,822	8	7	16	34	12	77	53	77	915	201

– Represents or rounds to zero. NA Not available. Z Less than 50. [1] See footnote 1, Table 1078. Injuries classified as serious. [2] See footnote 2, Table 1078. Injuries classified as serious. [3] See footnote 3, Table 1078. Injuries classified as serious. [4] Data on deaths are from U.S. National Highway Traffic Safety Administration and are based on deaths within 30 days of the accident. Includes only police reported crashes. For more details, see Table 1103. [5] Accidents which result in damages to railroad property. Grade crossing accidents are also included when classified as a train accident. Deaths exclude fatalities in railroad-highway grade crossing accidents. [6] Includes motor bus, commuter rail, heavy rail, light rail, demand response, van pool, and automated guideway. Starting with 2002, only injuries requiring immediate medical treatment away from the scene now qualify as reportable. [7] Accidents resulting in death, injury, or requiring medical treatment beyond first aid; damages exceeding $500; or a person's disappearance. [8] Covers accidents involving commercial vessels which must be reported to U.S. Coast Guard if there is property damage exceeding $25,000; material damage affecting the seaworthiness or efficiency of a vessel; stranding or grounding; loss of life; or injury causing a person's incapacity for more than 3 days. [9] Beginning 1990, pipeline accidents/incidents are credited to year of occurrence; prior data are credited to the year filed. [10] Incidents, deaths, and injuries involving hazardous materials cover all types of transport, exclude pipelines and bulk, nonpackaged water incidents. [11] The data reported under accident are incident numbers.

Source: U.S. Bureau of Transportation Statistics, "National Transportation Statistics," <http://www.bts.gov/publications/national_transportation_statistics/>.

Table 1073. U.S. Scheduled Airline Industry—Summary: 1995 to 2009

[For calendar years or December 31, (547.8 represents 547,800,000). For domestic and international operations. Covers carriers certificated under Section 401 of the Federal Aviation Act. Table data have been revised for 2000 through 2008. Minus sign (–) indicates loss]

Item	Unit	1995	2000	2004	2005	2006	2007	2008	2009
SCHEDULED SERVICE									
Revenue passengers enplaned	Mil	547.8	666.1	703.7	738.6	744.7	769.6	743.3	703.9
Revenue passenger miles	Bil	540.7	692.8	734.0	779.0	797.4	829.4	812.4	769.5
Available seat miles	Bil	807.1	957.0	971.9	1,003.3	1,006.3	1,037.7	1,021.3	957.2
Revenue passenger load factor	Percent	67.0	72.4	75.5	77.6	79.2	79.9	79.5	80.4
Mean passenger trip length [1]	Miles	987	1,040	1,043	1,055	1,071	1,078	1,093	1,093
Cargo ton miles	Mil	16,921	23,888	27,978	28,037	29,339	29,570	28,375	25,002
Aircraft departures	1,000	8,062	9,035	11,429	11,564	11,268	11,399	10,896	10,132
FINANCES [2]									
Total operating revenue [3]	Mil. dol.	95,117	130,248	134,660	151,544	165,532	174,696	186,119	154,719
Passenger revenue	Mil. dol.	69,835	93,622	85,669	93,500	101,419	107,678	111,542	91,331
Cargo revenue	Mil. dol.	9,882	14,456	17,146	20,704	22,848	24,531	29,192	22,914
Charter revenue	Mil. dol.	3,742	4,913	5,503	6,074	6,026	5,544	4,338	3,709
Total operating expense	Mil. dol.	89,266	123,234	136,150	151,097	157,892	165,353	189,466	152,310
Operating profit (or loss)	Mil. dol.	5,852	7,014	−1,490	448	7,640	9,344	−3,348	2,409
Interest income (or expense)	Mil. dol.	−2,426	−2,193	−3,715	−4,209	−4,150	−3,915	−3,769	−4,267
Net profit (or loss)	Mil. dol.	2,314	2,533	−9,104	−27,220	18,186	7,691	−23,747	−2,528
Revenue per passenger mile	Cents	12.9	13.5	11.7	12.0	12.7	13.0	13.7	11.9
Operating profit margin	Percent	6.2	5.4	−1.1	0.3	4.6	5.3	−1.8	1.6
Net profit margin	Percent	2.4	1.9	−6.8	−18.0	11.0	4.4	−12.8	−1.6
Adjusted Net Profit (or loss) [4]	Percent	2.4	1.9	−6.8	−18.0	11.0	4.4	−12.8	−1.6
EMPLOYEES [5]									
Total	1,000	547.0	679.7	585.2	576.2	565.0	576.0	559.6	536.2
Pilots and copilots	1,000	55.4	78.4	75.2	78.4	77.8	76.6	77.1	74.8

[1] For definition of mean, see Guide to Tabular Presentation. [2] 2009 data are preliminary. [3] Includes other types of revenues, not shown separately. [4] Excludes special items: bankruptcy-related reorganization charges and fresh-start accounting gains, and special goodwill charges. [5] Average full-time equivalents.

Source: Air Transport Association of America, Washington, DC, *Air Transport Annual Report*.

Table 1074. Airline Cost Indexes: 1980 to 2009

[2000 = 100. To be included in the cost index, carriers must have met the following criteria on an annual basis: 1) must report both passenger revenue and revenue passenger miles (RPMs) and 2) passenger revenue must be greater than or equal to 25 percent of total operating revenue. Data prior to 1990 excludes passenger airlines with annual revenue less than $100 million]

Index	1980	1990	1995	2000	2001	2002	2003	2004	2005	2006	2007	2008	2009
Composite index [1]	77.4	101.1	99.0	100.0	108.5	113.6	122.8	149.1	177.9	195.8	199.8	262.0	197.3
Labor costs	52.0	73.1	91.3	100.0	107.8	118.7	122.7	122.3	117.3	119.0	119.1	119.8	127.4
Fuel	113.7	98.1	69.7	100.0	98.6	89.9	107.9	144.1	206.6	242.8	258.0	374.2	234.9
Aircraft ownership [2]	33.5	71.1	83.0	100.0	102.3	105.2	101.8	103.4	99.1	98.9	94.3	91.0	93.0
Nonaircraft ownership	40.4	88.1	103.3	100.0	139.4	113.0	111.4	104.1	106.1	104.2	106.6	118.8	114.8
Professional services	27.0	67.5	85.4	100.0	102.8	97.3	98.4	103.4	105.5	111.2	115.8	125.4	118.5
Food and beverage	88.5	125.5	106.9	100.0	100.5	87.2	74.6	67.1	61.3	57.9	57.8	60.0	59.7
Landing fees	49.2	81.0	95.8	100.0	109.2	125.2	130.8	131.2	130.7	135.6	136.7	148.6	158.9
Maintenance material	73.3	119.2	94.0	100.0	96.3	84.1	67.3	64.8	59.1	62.2	69.9	77.0	83.3
Aircraft insurance	246.1	161.0	341.5	100.0	163.5	271.0	180.9	174.3	157.1	181.0	152.3	124.0	150.8
Nonaircraft insurance	73.3	68.2	223.8	100.0	171.3	573.7	450.9	373.7	319.9	259.3	222.1	195.4	184.4
Passenger commissions	121.5	227.0	184.8	100.0	86.4	57.8	41.9	37.2	31.6	29.2	28.2	27.0	26.7
Communication	50.3	85.7	86.5	100.0	109.6	102.6	82.0	76.1	73.3	68.5	71.2	79.2	77.1
Advertising and promotion	112.9	165.0	107.8	100.0	93.0	74.7	69.1	77.8	75.5	80.9	67.3	59.0	61.7
Utilities and office supplies	67.9	97.7	87.0	100.0	103.6	92.3	81.0	81.3	87.6	94.3	102.2	108.8	99.8
Transportation-related expenses	46.0	55.0	57.5	100.0	119.1	132.3	256.4	397.4	475.0	508.4	506.7	604.5	524.9
Other operating expenses	56.0	87.4	74.1	100.0	126.4	106.5	94.9	94.3	108.6	108.1	116.1	156.8	123.8
Interest [3]	160.7	182.0	174.6	100.0	98.1	98.8	93.3	96.3	120.6	133.5	120.3	105.6	118.7

[1] Weighted average of all components, including interest. [2] Includes lease, aircraft and engine rentals, depreciation, and amortization. [3] Interest on long-term debt and capital and other interest expense.

Source: Air Transport Association of America, Washington, DC, *U.S. Passenger Airline Cost Index*. See also <http://www.airlines.org/economics/>.

Table 1075. Top 40 Airports in 2009—Passengers Enplaned: 1999 and 2009

[In thousands (611,582 represents 611,582,000), except rank. For calendar year. Airports ranked by total passengers enplaned by large certificated air carriers on scheduled and nonscheduled operations, 2009]

Airport	1999 Rank	1999 Total	2009 Rank	2009 Total	Airport	1999 Rank	1999 Total	2009 Rank	2009 Total
All airports	(X)	611,582	(X)	663,173	Fort Lauderdale-Hollywood Intl, FL.	32	6,224	24	9,568
Total, top 40	(X)	468,471	(X)	507,289	Washington, DC (Ronald Reagan Washington Natl.) . .	30	6,663	25	8,414
Atlanta, GA (Hartsfield Intl)	1	37,232	1	41,876	San Diego, CA (Lindbergh Field).	27	7,253	26	8,380
Chicago, IL (O'Hare Intl)	2	31,658	2	28,994	Chicago, IL (Midway)	33	6,138	27	8,224
Dallas/Ft. Worth Intl, TX.	3	27,593	3	26,333	Tampa Intl, FL	28	6,912	28	8,082
Denver, Intl, CO.	5	17,502	4	23,722	Honolulu Intl, HI.	23	8,576	29	7,548
Los Angeles, Intl, CA	4	24,044	5	21,677	Portland Intl, OR	31	6,541	30	6,351
Houston, Intercontinental, TX . .	13	14,735	6	18,610	St. Louis, MO (Lambert-St Louis Intl)	11	14,930	31	6,069
Phoenix Sky Harbor Intl, AZ . . .	8	16,090	7	18,329	Cincinnati, OH (Cincinnati Northern Kentucky Intl).	26	7,616	32	5,193
Las Vegas, NV (McCarran Intl) .	10	15,367	8	18,314	Memphis Intl, TN	39	4,534	33	5,054
Charlotte-Douglas Intl, NC.	21	9,442	9	17,078	Kansas City Intl, MO	35	5,601	34	4,909
New York, NY (JFK Intl)	20	10,138	10	16,192	Cleveland, OH (Cleveland-Hopkins Intl)	34	5,921	35	4,694
San Francisco Intl, CA.	7	16,563	11	15,997	Oakland Intl, CA	37	4,738	36	4,570
Minneapolis-St. Paul Intl, MN. . .	9	15,391	12	15,506	Raleigh, NC (Raleigh-Durham Intl)	43	4,026	37	4,408
Newark Intl, NJ	12	14,912	13	15,209	Sacramento Intl, CA	45	3,658	38	4,406
Orlando Intl, FL	16	12,564	14	15,063	Nashville, TN (Nashville Intl) . .	42	4,064	39	4,369
Detroit, MI (Wayne County)	6	16,570	15	15,042	Santa Ana, CA (John Wayne-Orange County)	46	3,643	40	4,311
Seattle-Tacoma Intl, WA	19	13,064	16	14,720					
Philadelphia, Intl, PA.	14	10,347	17	14,714					
Miami Intl, FL.	15	12,764	18	13,390					
Boston, MA (Logan Intl).	17	11,091	19	11,378					
New York, NY (La Guardia)	18	10,805	20	10,751					
Baltimore, MD (BWI Intl)	25	8,004	21	10,228					
Salt Lake City Intl, UT	22	8,718	22	9,903					
Washington, DC (Dulles Intl) . . .	29	6,839	23	9,714					

X Not applicable.
Source: U.S. Bureau of Transportation Statisics, Office of Airline Information, BTS Form 41, Schedule T-3, unpublished data.

Table 1076. Domestic Airline Markets: 2009

[In thousands (4,106 represents 4,106,000). For calendar year. Data are for the 25 top markets and include all commercial airports in each metro area. Data represent origin and final destination of travel]

Market	Passengers	Market	Passengers
Los Angeles-New York.	4,106	Las Vegas-San Francisco	1,727
Fort Lauderdale-New York	4,093	Orlando-Philadelphia.	1,708
Chicago-New York	3,914	Chicago-Orlando	1,703
New York-Orlando	3,675	Dallas/Fort Worth-Houston	1,694
New York-San Francisco	3,140	Dallas/Fort Worth-New York.	1,684
New York-Atlanta	3,086	Chicago-Las Vegas	1,674
Los Angeles-San Francisco.	2,564	Chicago-Washington.	1,664
Miami-New York.	2,225	New York-San Juan	1,577
Las Vegas-New York	2,186	Los Angeles-Washington.	1,550
New York-West Palm Beach	1,951	Atlanta-Washington	1,544
New York-Tampa	1,815	Chicago-Phoenix	1,520
Chicago-Los Angeles	1,784	Las Vegas-Seattle	1,514
Boston-New York.	1,751		

Source: Air Transport Association of America, Washington, DC, *Annual Report*.

Table 1077. Worldwide Airline Fatalities: 1990 to 2008

[For scheduled air transport operations. Excludes accidents due to acts of unlawful interference]

Year	Fatal accidents	Passenger deaths	Death rate [1]	Year	Fatal accidents	Passenger deaths	Death rate [1]
1990	27	544	0.05	2000	18	757	0.04
1992	28	1,070	0.09	2001	13	577	0.03
1993	33	864	0.07	2002	14	791	0.04
1994	27	1,170	0.09	2003	7	466	0.02
1995	25	711	0.05	2004	9	203	0.01
1996	24	1,146	0.07	2005	17	712	0.03
1997	25	921	0.06	2006	23	755	0.02
1998	20	904	0.05	2007	11	587	0.01
1999	21	499	0.03	2008	11	439	0.01

[1] Rate per 100 million passenger kilometers performed. Passenger-kilometers performed (PKPs) is the number of passengers multiplied by the number of kilometers travelled.

Source: International Civil Aviation Organization, Montreal, Canada, *Civil Aviation Statistics of the World*, annual.

Table 1078. Aircraft Accidents: 1990 to 2010

[For years ending December 31]

Item	Unit	1990	1995	2000	2005	2008	2009	2010, prel.
Air carrier accidents, all services [1]	Number	24	36	56	40	28	30	28
Fatal accidents	Number	6	3	3	3	2	2	1
Fatalities	Number	39	168	92	22	3	52	2
Aboard	Number	12	162	92	20	1	51	2
Rates per 100,000 flight hours:								
Accidents	Rate	0.198	0.267	0.306	0.206	0.147	0.167	0.159
Fatal accidents	Rate	0.049	0.022	0.016	0.015	0.010	0.011	0.006
Commuter air carrier accidents [2]	Number	15	12	12	6	7	2	6
Fatal accidents	Number	3	2	1	–	–	–	–
Fatalities	Number	6	9	5	–	–	–	–
Aboard	Number	4	9	5	–	–	–	–
Rates per 100,000 flight hours:								
Accidents	Rate	0.641	0.457	3.247	2.002	2.385	0.685	1.899
Fatal accidents	Rate	0.128	0.076	0.271	–	–	–	–
On-demand air taxi accidents [3]	Number	107	75	80	65	58	47	31
Fatal accidents	Number	29	24	22	11	20	2	6
Fatalities	Number	51	52	71	18	69	17	17
Aboard	Number	49	52	68	16	69	14	17
Rates per 100,000 flight hours:								
Accidents	Rate	4.76	3.02	2.04	1.70	1.81	1.63	1.05
Fatal accidents	Rate	1.29	0.97	0.56	0.29	0.62	0.07	0.20
General aviation accidents [4]	Number	2,242	2,056	1,837	1,670	1,569	1,480	1,435
Fatal accidents	Number	444	413	345	321	275	275	267
Fatalities	Number	770	735	596	563	494	478	450
Aboard	Number	765	728	585	558	485	469	447
Rates per 100,000 flight hours:								
Accidents	Rate	7.85	8.21	6.57	7.20	6.86	7.08	6.86
Fatal accidents	Rate	1.55	1.63	1.21	1.38	1.21	1.32	1.27

– Represents zero. [1] U.S. air carriers operating under 14 CFR 121. Beginning 2000, includes aircraft with 10 or more seats, previously operating under 14 CFR 135. [2] All scheduled service of U.S. air carriers operating under 14 CFR 135. Beginning 2000, only aircraft with fewer than 10 seats. [3] All nonscheduled service of U.S. air carriers operating under 14 CFR 135. [4] U.S. civil registered aircraft not operated under 14 CFR 121 or 135.

Source: U.S. National Transportation Safety Board, "Aviation Accident Statistics," <http://www.ntsb.gov/aviation/stats.htm>, accessed June 2011.

Table 1079. U.S. Carrier Delays, Cancellations, and Diversions: 1995 to 2009

[In thousands (5,327.4 represents 5,327,400). For calendar year. See headnote, Table 1080]

Item	1995	2000	2002	2003	2004	2005	2006	2007	2008	2009
Total operations	**5,327.4**	**5,683.0**	**5,271.4**	**6,488.5**	**7,129.3**	**7,140.6**	**7,141.9**	**7,455.5**	**7,009.7**	**6,450.3**
Delays:										
Late departures [1]	827.9	1,131.7	717.4	834.4	1,187.6	1,279.4	1,424.8	1,573.0	1,327.2	1,084.3
Late arrivals [2]	1,039.3	1,356.0	868.2	1,057.8	1,421.4	1,466.1	1,615.5	1,804.0	1,524.7	1,218.3
Cancellations [3]	91.9	187.5	65.1	101.5	127.8	133.7	121.9	160.8	137.4	89.4
Diversions [4]	10.5	14.3	8.4	11.4	13.8	14.0	16.2	17.2	17.3	15.5

[1] Late departures comprise flights departing 15 minutes or more after the scheduled departure time. [2] Late arrivals comprise flights arriving 15 minutes or more after the scheduled arrival time. [3] A cancelled flight is one that was not operated, but was listed in a carrier's computer reservation system within seven days of the scheduled departure. [4] A diverted flight is one that left from the scheduled departure airport but flew to a destination point other than the scheduled destination point.

Source: U.S. Bureau of Transportation Statistics, "National Transportation Statistics," <http://www.bts.gov/publications/national_transportation_statistics/>.

Table 1080. On-Time Flight Arrivals and Departures at Major U.S. Airports: 2010

[In percent. Quarterly, based on gate arrival and departure times for domestic scheduled operations of U.S. major airlines. All U.S. airlines with 1 percent or more of total U.S. domestic scheduled airline passenger revenues are required to report on-time data. A flight is considered on time if it operated less than 15 minutes after the scheduled time shown in the carrier's computerized reservation system. See source for data on individual airlines]

Airport	On-time arrivals				On-time departures			
	1st quarter	2nd quarter	3rd quarter	4th quarter	1st quarter	2nd quarter	3rd quarter	4th quarter
Total, all airports	**77.9**	**80.5**	**81.0**	**79.6**	**79.5**	**81.8**	**82.1**	**80.6**
Atlanta, Hartsfield	75.8	79.5	78.9	80.6	78.0	80.1	78.5	79.6
Boston, Logan International	70.4	81.7	77.7	75.3	77.2	84.9	82.2	80.0
Baltimore/Washington International..........	74.3	81.6	81.3	81.2	71.1	78.0	77.0	75.1
Charlotte, Douglas......................	79.3	84.9	84.3	83.2	79.9	84.6	83.5	85.4
Washington, Reagan National..............	74.6	80.2	79.5	82.1	78.7	84.4	83.4	85.6
Denver International	83.4	82.5	85.1	83.5	80.4	79.7	80.9	80.1
Dallas-Fort Worth International	78.6	80.6	81.9	87.5	75.4	77.1	78.3	84.6
Detroit, Metro Wayne County..............	76.0	77.5	78.2	79.3	77.1	77.4	78.2	80.8
Newark International	65.9	76.0	76.0	69.5	70.1	78.7	78.9	76.0
Fort Lauderdale-Hollywood International	73.5	82.8	79.7	78.0	75.3	82.5	82.0	79.2
Washington/Dulles......................	74.0	82.7	82.6	84.1	76.1	82.9	83.9	85.2
Houston, George Bush	80.7	80.9	81.3	86.3	81.5	83.3	82.0	86.1
New York, JFK International................	70.8	77.2	76.1	74.9	73.1	76.1	73.6	76.3
Las Vegas, McCarran International	84.3	82.7	84.5	78.9	81.0	80.3	81.1	74.5
Los Angeles International	83.1	82.6	82.9	78.1	83.2	83.3	83.9	79.2
New York, La Guardia	69.7	77.8	74.5	72.4	76.2	83.6	81.0	80.0
Orlando International......................	75.8	83.8	81.8	81.8	76.7	82.8	81.9	82.6
Chicago, Midway	79.4	81.2	83.4	77.0	70.6	72.0	74.5	63.2
Miami International	73.6	76.5	78.1	83.5	71.6	73.8	75.2	82.0
Minneapolis-St. Paul International...........	81.0	77.8	79.4	76.3	80.4	80.6	79.4	78.6
Chicago, O'Hare	76.4	73.5	81.5	80.4	75.9	74.1	80.4	79.7
Portland International	86.2	84.9	84.9	78.9	89.3	89.5	88.9	83.2
Philadelphia International	69.8	81.3	81.3	79.5	74.5	83.6	82.6	80.7
Phoenix, Sky Harbor International...........	86.1	86.5	87.3	80.7	83.8	84.5	85.0	80.1
San Diego, Lindbergh Field...............	83.6	82.5	84.2	75.8	83.4	85.2	85.7	77.2
Seattle-Tacoma International..............	87.0	87.0	85.6	80.9	89.5	89.8	88.0	84.7
San Francisco International................	68.9	73.2	73.6	69.4	73.1	77.5	77.4	73.3
Salt Lake City International	85.8	85.0	84.0	75.7	88.0	87.0	85.5	79.1
Tampa, Tampa International	77.0	83.2	81.7	82.0	78.6	84.3	83.6	83.4

Source: U.S. Department of Transportation, Aviation Consumer Protection Division, *Air Travel Consumer Report*, monthly. See also <http://airconsumer.ost.dot.gov>.

Table 1081. Consumer Complaints Against U.S. Airlines: 1990 to 2010

[Calendar year data. Represents complaints filed by consumers to the U.S. Department of Transportation, Aviation Consumer Protection Division, regarding service problems with air carrier personnel. See source for data on individual airlines]

Complaint category	1990	2000	2004	2005	2006	2007	2008	2009	2010
Total...........	**7,703**	**20,564**	**5,839**	**6,900**	**6,452**	**10,960**	**10,643**	**8,821**	**10,985**
Flight problems [1]	3,034	8,698	1,462	1,942	1,845	4,097	3,247	2,041	3,336
Customer service [2] ...	758	4,074	742	800	870	1,214	1,333	1,103	1,344
Baggage	1,329	2,753	1,085	1,586	1,400	2,154	2,081	1,607	1,937
Ticketing/boarding [3]...	624	1,405	637	679	708	1,136	1,404	1,583	1,510
Refunds............	701	803	376	530	485	745	803	669	730
Fares [4]	312	708	180	219	173	315	389	436	465
Disability [5]	(NA)	612	467	430	368	428	474	519	572
Oversales [6]	399	759	263	284	275	420	432	370	544
Discrimination [7]	(NA)	(NA)	96	100	90	82	115	131	143
Advertising..........	96	42	41	45	30	34	39	53	77
Tours	29	25	[8]	[8]	[8]	[8]	[8]	[8]	[8]
Animals	(NA)	1	3	3	3	7	5	5	8
Smoking............	74	[9]	[9]	[9]	[9]	[9]	[9]	[9]	[9]
Credit..............	5	[9]	[9]	[9]	[9]	[9]	[9]	[9]	[9]
Other..............	342	684	487	282	205	328	321	304	319

NA Not available. [1] Cancellations, delays, etc., from schedule. [2] Unhelpful employees, inadequate meals or cabin service, treatment of delayed passengers. [3] Errors in reservations and ticketing; problems in making reservations and obtaining tickets. Includes disability compliants prior to 1998. [4] Incorrect or incomplete information about fares, discount fare conditions, and availability, etc. [5] Prior to 2000, included in ticketing/boarding. [6] All bumping problems, whether or not airline complied with DOT regulations. [7] Allegations of discrimination by airlines due to factors other than disability, such as race, religion, national origin or sex. [8] Included in "Other" beginning 2002. [9] Included in "Other" beginning 2000.

Source: U.S. Department of Transportation, Aviation Consumer Protection Division, *Air Travel Consumer Report*, monthly. See also <http://airconsumer.ost.dot.gov>.

Table 1082. Commuter/Regional Airline Operations Summary: 2005 to 2009

[154.2 represents 154,200,000. Calendar year data. Commuter/regional airlines operate primarily aircraft of predominately 75 passengers or less and 18,000 pounds of payload capacity serving short haul and small community markets. Represents operations within all North America by U.S. Regional Carriers. Averages are means. For definition of mean, see Guide to Tabular Presentation]

Item	Unit	2005	2006	2007	2008	2009
Passenger carriers operating.............	Number	75	71	72	(NA)	62
Passengers enplaned	Millions......	154.2	153.9	159.0	(NA)	159.5
Average passengers enplaned per carrier...	1,000	2,055.6	2,168.0	2,208.5	(NA)	(NA)
Revenue passenger miles (RPM)	Billions	73.8	70.8	73.8	(NA)	72.9
Average RPMs per carrier...............	Millions......	983.7	997.2	1,024.7	(NA)	(NA)
Available seat miles	Billions	104.8	94.8	99.0	(NA)	97.6
Average load factor	Percent	70.4	74.7	74.6	(NA)	74.7
Departures completed..................	Millions......	5.3	5.0	5.0	(NA)	4.1
Airports served	Number	846	688	666	(NA)	644
Average trip length....................	Miles	478.5	460.0	464.0	(NA)	457.0
Average seating capacity (seats)..........	Number	54.4	51.0	52.4	(NA)	55.0
Fleet flying hours....................	1,000	7,333.0	7,133.1	7,306.7	(NA)	5,146.0

NA Not available.

Source: Compiled by the Regional Airline Association and BACK Aviation from DOT Form 41 data, *Annual Report of the Regional Airline Industry* (copyright). See also <http://www.raa.org/>.

Table 1083. Airports, Aircraft, and Airmen: 1980 to 2009

[As of December 31 or for years ending December 31]

Item	1980	1990	1995	2000	2005	2007	2008	2009
Airports, total [1]..............	**15,161**	**17,490**	**18,224**	**19,281**	**19,854**	**20,341**	**19,930**	**19,750**
Public [1]......................	4,814	5,589	5,415	5,317	5,270	5,221	5,202	5,178
Percent—with lighted runways ...	66.2	71.4	74.3	75.9	76.8	(NA)	(NA)	(NA)
With paved runways...........	72.3	70.7	73.3	74.3	74.8	(NA)	(NA)	(NA)
Private......................	10,347	11,901	12,809	13,964	14,584	14,839	14,451	14,298
Percent—with lighted runways ...	15.2	7.0	6.4	7.2	9.2	(NA)	(NA)	(NA)
With paved runways...........	13.3	31.5	33.0	32.0	33.2	(NA)	(NA)	(NA)
Certificated [2]	730	680	667	651	575	565	560	559
Civil	(X)	(X)	572	563	575	(NA)	(NA)	(NA)
Civil military	(X)	(X)	95	88	(NA)	(NA)	(NA)	(NA)
General aviation	14,431	16,810	17,557	18,630	19,279	19,776	19,370	19,191
Active air carrier fleet [3]............	3,805	6,083	7,411	8,055	8,225	8,044	7,856	(NA)
Fixed wing	3,803	6,072	7,293	8,016	8,182	7,998	7,808	(NA)
Helicopter	2	11	118	39	43	46	48	(NA)
General aviation fleet [4]............	211,043	198,000	188,089	217,533	224,352	231,607	228,663	223,877
Fixed-wing....................	200,094	184,500	162,342	183,276	185,373	186,806	182,961	177,446
Turbojet.....................	2,992	4,100	4,559	7,001	9,823	10,385	11,042	11,268
Turboprop....................	4,089	5,300	4,995	5,762	7,942	9,514	8,906	9,055
Piston......................	193,013	175,200	152,788	170,513	167,608	166,907	163,013	157,123
Rotocraft	6,001	6,900	5,830	7,150	8,728	9,567	9,876	9,984
Other........................	4,945	6,600	4,741	6,700	6,454	5,940	5,652	5,480
Gliders......................	(X)	(X)	2,182	2,041	2,074	1,947	1,914	1,808
Lighter than air................	(X)	(X)	2,559	4,660	4,380	3,993	3,738	3,672
Experimental	(X)	(X)	15,176	20,407	23,627	23,228	23,364	24,419
Airman certificates held: [5]								
Pilot, total....................	827,071	702,659	639,184	625,581	609,737	590,349	613,746	594,285
Women	52,902	40,515	38,032	36,757	36,584	35,784	37,981	36,808
Student	199,833	128,663	101,279	93,064	87,213	84,339	80,989	72,280
Recreational	(X)	87	232	340	278	239	252	234
Airplane:								
Private.....................	357,479	299,111	261,399	251,561	228,619	211,096	222,596	211,619
Commercial	183,442	149,666	133,980	121,858	120,614	115,127	124,746	125,738
Air transport.................	69,569	107,732	123,877	141,596	141,992	143,953	146,838	144,600
Rotocraft only [6]	6,030	9,567	7,183	7,775	9,518	12,290	14,647	15,298
Glider only	7,039	7,833	11,234	9,387	21,369	21,274	21,055	21,268
Flight instructor certificates	60,440	63,775	77,613	80,931	90,555	92,175	93,202	94,863
Instrument ratings	260,462	297,073	298,798	311,944	311,828	309,865	325,247	323,495
Nonpilot [7].....................	368,356	492,237	651,341	547,453	644,016	666,559	678,181	682,315
Mechanic.....................	250,157	344,282	405,294	344,434	320,293	322,852	326,276	329,027
Repairmen....................	(X)	(X)	61,233	38,208	40,030	40,277	41,056	41,389
Parachute rigger...............	9,547	10,094	11,824	10,477	8,150	8,186	8,248	8,362
Ground instructor...............	61,550	66,882	96,165	72,326	74,378	74,544	74,983	75,461
Dispatcher....................	6,799	11,002	15,642	16,340	18,079	19,043	19,590	20,132
Flight navigator	1,936	1,290	916	570	298	250	222	181
Flight engineer.................	38,367	58,687	60,267	65,098	57,756	54,394	53,135	51,022

NA Not available. X Not applicable. [1] Existing airports, heliports, seaplane bases, etc. recorded with Federal Aviation Administration (FAA). Includes civil and joint-use civil-military airports, heliports, STOL (short takeoff and landing) ports, and seaplane bases in the United States and its territories. Sole-use military airports are included beginning in 2007. Includes U.S. outlying areas. Airport-type definitions: Public—publicly owned and under control of a public agency; private—owned by a private individual or corporation. May or may not be open for public use. [2] Certificated airports serve air-carriers with aircraft seating more than 9 passengers. As of 2005, the Federal Aviation Administration (FAA) no longer certificates military airports. [3] Air-carrier aircraft are aircraft carrying passengers or cargo for hire under 14 CFR 121 (large aircraft—more than 30 seats) and 14 CFR 135 (small aircraft--30 seats or fewer). Beginning in 1990, the number of aircraft is the monthly average reported in use for the last three months of the year. Prior to 1990, it was the number of aircraft reported in use during December of a given year. [4] 2000 dip in helicopters due to estimating methods. [5] Beginning 1995 excludes commuters. [6] Data for 1980 are for helicopters only. [7] All certificates on record. No medical examination required.

Source: U.S. Bureau of Transportation Statistics, National Transportation Statistics, annual. See also <http://www.bts.gov/publications/national_transportation_statistics/>. Airmen certificates held: U.S. Federal Aviation Administration, <http://www.faa.gov/data_research/aviation_data_statistics/civil_airmen_statistics/>. Prior to 2000: FAA Statistical Handbook of Aviation, annual.

Table 1084. Freight Carried on Major U.S. Waterways: 1990 to 2009

[In millions of tons (4.2 represents 4,200,000)]

Item	1990	1995	2000	2005	2006	2007	2008	2009
Atlantic intracoastal waterway . . .	4.2	3.5	3.1	2.7	2.6	2.5	2.9	2.5
Great Lakes.	167.1	177.8	187.5	169.4	173.0	161.0	152.4	108.7
Gulf intracoastal waterway.	115.4	118.0	113.8	116.1	122.6	125.1	115.9	108.1
Mississippi River system [1]	659.1	707.2	715.5	678.0	702.1	699.0	681.6	622.1
Mississippi River main stem . . .	475.3	520.3	515.6	464.6	497.7	500.5	486.8	447.7
Ohio River system [2]	260.0	267.6	274.4	280.1	270.7	260.2	259.2	229.5
Columbia River	51.4	57.1	55.2	51.5	52.3	58.1	54.8	46.0
Snake River	4.8	6.8	6.7	5.3	5.2	5.4	3.7	4.4

[1] Main channels and all tributaries of the Mississippi, Illinois, Missouri, and Ohio Rivers. [2] Main channels and all navigable tributaries and embayments of the Ohio, Tennessee, and Cumberland Rivers.

Source: U.S. Army Corps of Engineers, *Waterborne Commerce of the United States*, annual. See also <http://www.iwr.usace.army.mil/ndc/wcsc/wcsc.htm>, accessed April 2011.

Table 1085. Waterborne Commerce by Type of Commodity: 1995 to 2009

[In millions of short tons (2,240.4 represents 2,240,400,000). One short ton equals 2,000 pounds. Domestic trade includes all commercial movements between United States ports and on inland rivers, Great Lakes, canals, and connecting channels of the United States, Puerto Rico, and Virgin Islands]

Commodity	1995	2000	2005	2009 Total	2009 Domestic	2009 Foreign imports	2009 Foreign exports
Total.	2,240.4	2,424.6	2,527.6	2,210.8	857.1	858.9	494.8
Coal.	324.5	297.0	316.6	291.0	210.7	22.9	57.4
Petroleum and petroleum products	907.1	1,044.0	1,111.4	1,016.4	319.7	582.2	114.5
Crude petroleum	504.6	571.4	602.7	515.3	64.2	451.1	–
Petroleum products [1]	402.5	472.4	508.8	501.1	255.5	131.1	114.5
Gasoline	114.4	125.2	156.1	143.6	68.4	50.6	24.6
Distillate fuel oil	76.7	91.7	141.1	171.0	75.7	55.7	39.6
Residual fuel oil	111.9	131.6	96.1	81.3	69.0	4.6	7.7
Chemicals and related products	153.7	172.4	174.9	154.9	62.2	36.8	55.9
Fertilizers.	35.7	35.1	34.5	27.4	11.3	5.2	10.9
Other chemicals and related products	118.0	137.3	140.4	127.6	50.9	31.7	45.0
Crude material, inedible.	381.7	380.3	386.0	280.9	143.0	74.6	63.3
Forest products, wood and chips.	47.2	33.1	29.4	16.9	5.0	3.6	8.3
Pulp and waste paper	14.9	13.6	18.7	21.8	–	1.6	20.2
Soil, sand, gravel, rock, and stone [1].	152.5	165.0	177.9	120.9	89.4	28.5	3.0
Limestone	54.0	67.4	73.5	56.2	40.0	13.8	2.4
Phosphate rock	10.7	3.4	6.0	4.6	2.4	2.2	–
Sand & gravel	77.0	79.0	80.2	51.9	44.4	6.9	0.5
Iron ore and scrap	104.9	97.9	85.7	60.0	30.3	6.1	23.6
Marine shells	0.5	0.3	–	–	–	–	–
Nonferrous ores and scrap	27.9	29.2	29.2	20.8	5.5	12.9	2.5
Sulphur, clay, and salt	23.4	11.3	8.7	6.4	0.5	1.1	4.7
Slag	1.9	4.0	6.0	3.3	1.4	1.7	0.2
Other nonmetal minerals	8.4	25.9	30.4	30.9	10.8	19.2	0.9
Primary manufactured goods	106.3	153.0	166.4	89.6	24.2	44.3	21.2
Papers products.	13.1	12.1	13.7	12.3	0.1	4.8	7.3
Lime, cement, and glass	33.9	55.9	62.4	24.9	12.4	11.3	1.2
Primary iron and steel products.	44.1	57.1	52.1	25.0	6.7	14.9	3.3
Primary nonferrous metal products	12.3	25.5	33.5	25.3	4.9	11.3	9.1
Primary wood products	2.9	2.5	4.8	2.2	0.1	1.8	0.3
Food and farm products	303.2	283.3	251.3	279.0	81.2	37.1	160.7
Fish	3.6	2.4	3.0	2.9	0.1	1.8	1.0
Grain [1]	167.9	145.2	124.0	121.6	44.4	1.8	75.4
Wheat	48.5	43.4	36.4	32.5	8.9	0.7	22.9
Corn.	105.0	88.2	75.2	79.7	32.9	0.1	46.7
Oilseeds.	46.1	57.6	47.2	74.8	25.5	0.3	49.0
Soybeans.	42.0	47.3	40.8	65.0	22.2	0.1	42.7
Vegetables products	9.0	8.9	8.3	10.7	1.3	5.0	4.4
Processed grain and animal feed	33.0	23.1	18.4	17.4	4.6	0.7	12.1
Other agricultural products	43.5	46.1	50.5	51.5	5.3	27.4	18.8
All manufactured equip, machinery and products . . .	57.0	83.6	110.3	89.6	14.1	57.3	18.1
Waste and scrap, n.e.c. [2]	5.4	4.3	2.0	1.8	1.8	–	–
Unknown or not elsewhere classified	1.6	6.8	8.7	7.5	0.1	3.8	3.6

– Represents or rounds to zero. [1] Includes commodities not shown separately. [2] Not elsewhere classified.

Source: U.S. Army Corps of Engineers, *Waterborne Commerce of the United States*, annual. See also <http://www.iwr.usace.army.mil/ndc/wcsc/wcsc.htm>, accessed April 2011.

Table 1086. Top U.S. Ports by Tons of Traffic: 2009

[In thousands of short tons (30,136 represents 30,136,000), except rank. One short ton equals 2,000 lbs. For calendar year for the top 30 ports. Represents tons of cargo shipped from or received by the specified port. Excludes cargo carried on general ferries; coal and petroleum products loaded from shore facilities directly onto bunkers of vessels for fuel; and amounts of less than 100 tons of government-owned equipment in support of Corps of Engineers projects]

Port name	Rank	Total	Foreign Total	Inbound	Outbound	Domestic
Baltimore, MD	26	30,136	20,253	10,472	9,781	9,883
Baton Rouge, LA	13	51,918	17,834	11,225	6,609	34,084
Beaumont, TX	7	67,715	43,287	36,873	6,413	24,429
Corpus Christi, TX	5	68,240	50,804	39,674	11,131	17,436
Duluth-Superior, MN and WI	25	30,226	7,755	509	7,246	22,471
Freeport, TX	27	27,363	23,338	21,094	2,244	4,025
Houston, TX	2	211,341	147,969	84,630	63,340	63,372
Huntington-Tristate [1]	8	59,172	–	–	–	59,172
Lake Charles, LA	11	52,252	32,622	27,565	5,057	19,630
Long Beach, CA	4	72,500	58,573	37,283	21,289	13,928
Los Angeles, CA	9	58,406	51,400	31,279	20,121	7,006
Marcus Hook, PA	30	24,569	16,439	16,159	280	8,130
Mobile, AL	12	52,219	27,836	15,595	12,241	24,383
New Orleans, LA	6	68,126	31,058	14,144	16,914	37,068
New York, NY and NJ	3	144,690	83,469	64,032	19,437	61,221
Norfolk Harbor, VA	15	40,326	33,724	8,193	25,531	6,602
Pascagoula, MS	16	36,618	28,210	21,507	6,703	8,408
Paulsboro, NJ	24	30,258	18,901	16,905	1,997	11,357
Philadelphia, PA	22	31,751	20,319	19,900	419	11,432
Pittsburgh, PA	20	32,891	–	–	–	32,891
Plaquemines, LA, Port of	14	50,869	16,161	2,215	13,946	34,708
Port Arthur, TX	19	33,804	24,385	14,441	9,945	9,419
Richmond, CA	28	25,363	14,371	12,385	1,986	10,992
Savannah, GA	21	32,339	30,389	16,694	13,694	1,950
Seattle, WA	29	24,608	19,445	6,882	12,563	5,163
South Louisiana, LA, Port of	1	212,581	103,077	36,017	67,061	109,503
St. Louis, MO and IL	23	31,337	–	–	–	31,337
Tampa, FL	17	34,888	12,084	5,768	6,316	22,804
Texas City, TX	10	52,632	36,476	31,701	4,775	16,157
Valdez, AK	18	34,473	8	8	–	34,465

– Represents zero. [1] The Port of Huntington is the largest inland shipping port in the United States.
Source: U.S. Army Corps of Engineers, *Waterborne Commerce of the United States, annual.* See also <http://www.iwr.usace.army.mil/ndc/wcsc/wcsc.htm>, accessed April 2011.

Table 1087. Top U.S. Ports/Waterways by Container Traffic: 2009

[In thousands of twenty-foot equivalent units (TEUS), (28,746.4 represents 28,746,400). For calendar year. For the 30 leading ports/waterways in total TEUS. A TEUS is a measure of containerized cargo capacity equal to 1 standard 20 foot length by 8 foot width by 8 foot 6 inch height container]

Port/waterway name	Rank	Total loaded	Domestic loaded Total [1]	Inbound	Outbound	Foreign loaded Total	Inbound
Total [2]	(X)	28,746.4	4,418.6	1,860.4	1,860.4	24,746.4	14,517.3
Anchorage, AK	17	254.0	257.2	211.3	42.7	–	–
Apra Harbor, GU	28	59.2	68.8	51.1	8.1	–	–
Baltimore, MD	16	453.1	70.0	25.0	26.5	401.7	226.5
Boston, MA	22	158.8	19.2	6.1	5.6	147.1	83.4
Camden-Gloucester, NJ	26	94.1	52.2	18.3	33.6	42.2	32.3
Charleston, SC	10	941.1	–	–	–	941.1	493.7
Freeport, TX	29	57.3	–	–	–	57.3	35.1
Gulfport, MS	23	156.5	–	–	–	156.5	100.2
Honolulu, HI	12	686.2	870.0	445.0	211.8	29.4	17.4
Houston, TX	7	1,262.8	36.5	14.3	18.1	1,230.4	479.6
Jacksonville, FL	13	631.4	448.4	74.0	374.0	183.3	76.2
Kahului, Maui, HI	30	54.4	85.9	42.5	11.9	–	–
Long Beach, CA	2	4,063.8	331.4	49.4	237.3	3,777.1	2,549.2
Los Angeles, CA	1	4,919.2	–	–	–	4,919.2	3,430.9
Miami, FL	14	622.6	–	–	–	622.6	285.7
Mobile, AL	27	86.1	–	–	–	86.1	34.5
New Orleans, LA	18	231.6	11.8	6.3	2.9	222.3	73.3
New York (NY and NJ)	3	3,761.3	226.9	84.0	113.9	3,563.4	2,332.9
Norfolk Harbor, VA	6	1,413.2	70.0	26.5	25.0	1,361.8	673.0
Oakland, CA	5	1,542.9	223.9	26.6	143.6	1,372.7	636.8
Palm Beach, FL	25	109.4	–	–	–	109.4	26.2
Philadelphia, PA	24	153.6	–	–	–	153.6	117.2
Port Everglades, FL	15	531.5	8.6	–	8.6	522.9	218.8
Portland, OR	21	162.1	9.7	4.8	3.4	153.9	68.7
San Juan, PR	11	809.5	600.9	479.1	121.1	209.3	150.4
Savannah, GA	4	1,898.7	–	–	–	1,898.7	906.7
Seattle, WA	8	1,219.3	270.7	41.5	133.5	1,044.4	583.7
Tacoma, WA	9	1,150.7	269.3	49.3	219.2	882.2	481.4
Wilmington, DE	20	164.0	–	–	–	164.0	130.5
Wilmington, NC	19	184.3	–	–	–	184.3	96.6

– Represents zero. X Not applicable. [1] Includes empty TEUS. [2] Includes other ports/waterways not shown separately.
Source: U.S. Army Corps of Engineers, *U.S. Waterborne Container Traffic for U.S. Port/Waterway in 2008.*
See also <http://www.iwr.usace.army.mil/ndc/wcsc/wcsc.htm>, accessed April 2011.

Table 1088. Highway Mileage—Urban and Rural by Ownership: 1990 to 2008

[In thousands (3,880 represents 3,880,000). As of Dec. 31. Includes Puerto Rico beginning 2000]

Type and Control	1990	1995	2000	2003	2004	2005	2006	2007	2008
Total mileage [1]	3,880	3,912	3,951	3,991	3,997	4,012	4,033	4,032	4,059
Urban mileage [2]	757	819	859	954	994	1,023	1,043	1,044	1,079
Under state control	96	112	112	127	130	144	148	145	152
Under local control [1]	661	706	746	828	862	874	890	894	920
Rural mileage	3,123	3,093	3,092	3,036	3,003	2,989	2,990	2,988	2,980
Under state control	703	691	664	653	650	637	635	634	633
Under local control [1]	2,242	2,231	2,311	2,263	2,236	2,228	2,231	2,228	2,223
Under federal control	178	170	117	120	118	123	123	126	124

[1] Includes state park, state toll, other state agency, other local agency and other roadways not identified by ownership.
[2] Roadways in federal parks, forest, and reservations that are not part of the state and local highway system.
Source: U.S. Federal Highway Administration, *Highway Statistics*, annual. See also <http://www.fhwa.dot.gov/policy/ohpi/hss/index.cfm>.

Table 1089. Highway Mileage by State—Functional Systems and Urban/Rural: 2009

[As of Dec. 31. Excludes Puerto Rico. For definition of functional systems, see text, this section]

State	Total	Functional systems					Urban	Rural
		Interstate	Other freeways and expressways	Arterial	Collector	Local		
U.S.	4,050,717	46,720	12,287	402,648	793,249	2,795,813	1,081,371	2,969,346
AL [1]	93,820	867	31	8,281	18,054	66,587	20,536	73,283
AK	15,719	1,082	–	1,555	2,791	10,291	2,419	13,300
AZ [2]	60,440	1,168	176	5,730	8,132	45,234	22,917	37,523
AR	100,100	655	252	6,988	21,089	71,116	12,845	87,255
CA	171,874	2,460	1,537	27,423	32,251	108,203	90,043	81,831
CO	88,278	952	314	8,936	16,275	61,801	19,375	68,903
CT	21,407	346	240	2,758	3,206	14,857	15,162	6,245
DE	6,302	41	30	643	1,046	4,542	2,993	3,309
DC	1,505	13	17	268	157	1,050	1,505	–
FL	121,447	1,471	771	12,779	14,409	92,017	81,040	40,407
GA	121,631	1,242	148	14,059	22,915	83,267	38,608	83,023
HI	4,371	55	34	754	832	2,696	2,319	2,052
ID	48,180	612	–	4,150	10,380	33,038	5,743	42,437
IL	139,577	2,182	99	14,646	21,793	100,857	41,433	98,144
IN [3]	95,679	1,171	164	8,536	22,351	63,457	26,778	68,901
IA	114,347	781	–	9,754	31,557	72,255	11,355	102,992
KS	140,753	874	188	9,525	33,541	96,625	12,932	127,821
KY	78,963	762	67	5,872	16,133	56,129	12,583	66,380
LA	61,335	905	51	5,527	10,038	44,814	16,339	44,996
ME	22,839	367	21	2,178	5,930	14,343	2,996	19,843
MD	31,461	482	294	3,797	5,052	21,836	17,389	14,072
MA	36,177	573	312	6,162	4,830	24,300	28,197	7,980
MI	121,651	1,242	329	14,679	24,446	80,955	35,860	85,791
MN	137,932	917	178	13,420	30,478	92,939	20,802	117,130
MS	74,985	699	67	7,551	15,509	51,159	11,025	63,960
MO	130,359	1,180	408	10,276	24,896	93,599	23,592	106,767
MT	73,627	1,192	–	6,036	16,214	50,185	3,075	70,552
NE	93,631	481	32	8,097	20,760	64,261	6,414	87,217
NV	34,844	571	69	3,081	4,996	26,127	7,283	27,561
NH	16,041	225	73	1,521	2,743	11,479	4,928	11,113
NJ	38,835	431	404	5,757	4,151	28,092	31,557	7,278
NM	68,384	1,000	5	5,111	8,535	53,733	7,993	60,391
NY	114,546	1,705	789	13,852	20,685	77,515	48,431	66,115
NC	105,317	1,140	497	9,554	17,397	76,729	35,867	69,450
ND	86,843	571	–	5,919	11,814	68,539	1,898	84,945
OH	123,024	1,572	483	10,978	22,737	87,255	44,783	78,242
OK	115,851	933	191	10,931	25,301	78,495	18,774	97,077
OR	59,128	729	58	7,041	17,671	33,629	12,894	46,234
PA [4]	121,780	1,792	897	12,932	19,824	86,335	45,302	76,478
RI	6,400	71	90	835	887	4,517	5,188	1,212
SC	66,263	843	91	7,147	15,088	43,094	16,422	49,841
SD	82,354	679	11	6,422	19,021	56,221	2,986	79,368
TN	93,252	1,104	153	9,064	17,899	65,032	23,658	69,594
TX	310,850	3,233	1,486	31,645	64,729	209,757	97,117	213,733
UT	44,877	936	21	3,706	8,132	32,082	11,146	33,731
VT	14,436	320	20	1,302	3,123	9,671	1,424	13,012
VA	74,182	1,119	292	8,381	14,135	50,255	23,795	50,387
WA	83,507	764	379	7,786	17,224	57,354	23,191	60,316
WV	38,598	555	10	3,476	8,609	25,948	5,366	33,232
WI	114,910	743	505	12,217	22,310	79,135	22,380	92,530
WY	28,105	913	3	3,610	11,173	12,406	2,713	25,392

– Represents zero. [1] 2008 data used for the rural minor collector, and rural and urban local functional systems. [2] 2008 data.
[3] Excludes 823 miles of Federal agency owned roads plus 71 miles of other non-Federal agency owned roads. [4] 2008 data used for the rural minor collector, and rural and urban local functional systems.
Source: U.S. Federal Highway Administration, *Highway Statistics*, annual. See also <http://www.fhwa.dot.gov/policy/ohpi/hss/index.cfm>.

Table 1090. Bridge Inventory—Total Deficient and Obsolete: 1996 to 2010, and by State, 2010

[As of December 2010. Based on the National Bridge Inventory program; for details, see source]

| State and year | Number of bridges | Deficient and obsolete | | | | | |
| | | Total | | Structurally deficient [1] | | Functionally obsolete [2] | |
		number	Percent	Number	Percent	Number	Percent
1996..............	581,862	182,726	31.4	101,518	17.4	81,208	14.0
1997..............	582,751	175,885	30.2	98,475	16.9	77,410	13.3
1998..............	582,984	172,582	29.6	93,076	16.0	79,506	13.6
1999..............	585,542	170,050	29.0	88,150	15.1	81,900	14.0
2000..............	587,755	167,993	28.6	87,106	14.8	80,887	13.8
2001..............	590,066	165,099	28.0	83,630	14.2	81,469	13.8
2002..............	591,220	163,010	27.6	81,437	13.8	81,573	13.8
2003..............	592,246	160,819	27.2	79,811	13.5	81,008	13.7
2004..............	593,885	158,318	26.7	77,758	13.1	80,560	13.6
2005..............	594,616	156,177	26.3	75,871	12.8	80,306	13.5
2006..............	596,842	153,990	25.8	73,764	12.4	80,226	13.4
2007..............	599,766	152,316	25.4	72,524	12.1	79,792	13.3
2008..............	601,411	151,391	25.2	71,469	11.9	79,922	13.3
2009..............	603,245	149,647	24.8	71,179	11.8	78,468	13.0
U.S. total, 2010.......	**604,474**	**146,633**	**24.3**	**69,223**	**11.5**	**77,410**	**12.8**
Alabama	16,018	3,676	22.9	1,592	9.9	2,084	13.0
Alaska	1,134	280	24.7	138	12.2	142	12.5
Arizona	7,578	903	11.9	230	3.0	673	8.9
Arkansas	12,587	2,814	22.4	930	7.4	1,884	15.0
California	24,557	7,091	28.9	3,135	12.8	3,956	16.1
Colorado	8,506	1,399	16.4	578	6.8	821	9.7
Connecticut	4,191	1,411	33.7	383	9.1	1,028	24.5
Delaware	861	161	18.7	50	5.8	111	12.9
District of Columbia	244	158	64.8	30	12.3	128	52.5
Florida	11,912	1,883	15.8	290	2.4	1,593	13.4
Georgia	14,670	2,729	18.6	941	6.4	1,788	12.2
Hawaii	1,137	507	44.6	141	12.4	366	32.2
Idaho	4,132	787	19.0	373	9.0	414	10.0
Illinois..............	26,337	4,002	15.2	2,239	8.5	1,763	6.7
Indiana.............	18,548	4,003	21.6	1,975	10.6	2,028	10.9
Iowa................	24,731	6,599	26.7	5,372	21.7	1,227	5.0
Kansas..............	25,329	4,899	19.3	2,816	11.1	2,083	8.2
Kentucky	13,849	4,311	31.1	1,311	9.5	3,000	21.7
Louisiana	13,361	3,829	28.7	1,722	12.9	2,107	15.8
Maine...............	2,393	771	32.2	369	15.4	402	16.8
Maryland	5,195	1,322	25.4	364	7.0	958	18.4
Massachusetts..........	5,113	2,548	49.8	558	10.9	1,990	38.9
Michigan	10,928	2,726	24.9	1,437	13.1	1,289	11.8
Minnesota	13,108	1,537	11.7	1,149	8.8	388	3.0
Mississippi	17,065	4,019	23.6	2,650	15.5	1,369	8.0
Missouri.............	24,245	7,021	29.0	4,075	16.8	2,946	12.2
Montana.............	5,119	877	17.1	391	7.6	486	9.5
Nebraska............	15,376	3,794	24.7	2,797	18.2	997	6.5
Nevada	1,753	208	11.9	39	2.2	169	9.6
New Hampshire.........	2,409	747	31.0	371	15.4	376	15.6
New Jersey	6,520	2,280	35.0	674	10.3	1,606	24.6
New Mexico...........	3,903	642	16.4	330	8.5	312	8.0
New York	17,365	6,467	37.2	2,088	12.0	4,379	25.2
North Carolina	18,099	4,976	27.5	2,353	13.0	2,623	14.5
North Dakota	4,418	943	21.3	710	16.1	233	5.3
Ohio................	28,033	6,598	23.5	2,742	9.8	3,856	13.8
Oklahoma	23,692	6,811	28.7	5,212	22.0	1,599	6.7
Oregon..............	7,255	1,650	22.7	456	6.3	1,194	16.5
Pennsylvania	22,359	9,608	43.0	5,906	26.4	3,702	16.6
Rhode Island	757	396	52.3	163	21.5	233	30.8
South Carolina.........	9,252	1,995	21.6	1,210	13.1	785	8.5
South Dakota..........	5,891	1,425	24.2	1,193	20.3	232	3.9
Tennessee	19,892	3,856	19.4	1,225	6.2	2,631	13.2
Texas...............	51,440	9,133	17.8	1,618	3.1	7,515	14.6
Utah................	2,911	420	14.4	130	4.5	290	10.0
Vermont.............	2,712	861	31.7	326	12.0	535	19.7
Virginia.............	13,522	3,429	25.4	1,267	9.4	2,162	16.0
Washington	7,755	1,971	25.4	394	5.1	1,577	20.3
West Virginia	7,069	2,543	36.0	1,018	14.4	1,525	21.6
Wisconsin	13,982	1,861	13.3	1,142	8.2	719	5.1
Wyoming	3,060	661	21.6	395	12.9	266	8.7
Puerto Rico	2,201	1,095	49.8	225	10.2	870	39.5

[1] Bridges are structurally deficient if they have been restricted to light vehicles, require immediate rehabilitation to remain open, or are closed. [2] Bridges are functionally obsolete if they have deck geometry, load carrying capacity, clearance or approach roadway alignment that no longer meet the criteria for the system of which the bridge is carrying a part.

Source: U.S. Federal Highway Administration, Office of Bridge Technology, "National Bridge Technology," <http://www.fhwa.dot.gov/bridge/nbi.htm>.

Table 1091. Funding for Highways and Disposition of Highway–User Revenue: 1990 to 2008

[In millions of dollars (75,444 represents $75,444,000,000). Data compiled from reports of state and local authorities]

Type	1990	1995	2000	2003	2004	2005	2006	2007	2008
Total receipts	**75,444**	**96,269**	**131,115**	**139,246**	**145,315**	**154,690**	**165,443**	**192,714**	**192,718**
Current income	69,880	87,620	119,815	124,593	129,521	137,668	147,615	167,983	172,785
Highway-user revenues	44,346	59,331	81,335	79,280	83,006	90,343	93,648	97,916	94,152
Other taxes and fees	19,827	21,732	31,137	37,783	38,956	39,214	44,455	55,584	61,163
Investment income, other receipts. . .	5,707	6,557	7,342	7,530	7,560	8,111	9,512	14,484	17,471
Bond issue proceeds [1]	5,564	8,649	11,301	14,654	15,794	17,022	17,828	24,730	19,933
Funds drawn from or placed in reserves [2]	−36	−2,791	−8,418	4,359	2,174	−1,990	−4,382	−20,961	−10,660
Total funds available	75,408	93,478	122,697	143,605	147,489	152,700	161,061	171,753	182,058
Total disbursements	**75,408**	**93,478**	**122,697**	**143,605**	**147,489**	**152,700**	**161,061**	**171,753**	**182,058**
Current disbursements	72,457	88,994	117,592	136,213	139,478	144,629	153,413	163,721	173,869
Capital outlay.	35,151	44,228	61,323	70,004	70,274	75,162	78,676	81,098	91,144
Maintenance and traffic services. . . .	20,365	24,319	30,636	35,011	36,327	37,882	40,426	45,759	44,972
Administration and research	6,501	8,419	10,020	11,986	12,737	11,126	13,189	14,370	14,711
Highway law enforcement and safety.	7,235	8,218	11,031	13,501	14,322	14,066	14,482	15,074	14,565
Interest on debt	3,205	3,810	4,583	5,711	5,819	6,392	6,639	7,420	8,477
Bond retirement [1]	2,951	4,484	5,105	7,393	8,011	8,071	7,648	8,032	8,189

[1] Proceeds and redemptions of short-term notes and refunding issues are excluded. [2] Negative numbers indicate that funds were placed in reserves.
Source: U.S. Federal Highway Administration, *Highway Statistics*, annual. See also <http://www.fhwa.dot.gov/policy/ohpi/hss/index.cfm>.

Table 1092. Federal Aid to State and Local Governments for Highway Trust Fund by State: 2009

[Year ending Sept. 30. (35,607 represents $35,607,000,000)]

State	Total (mil. dol.)	Per capita (dol.) [1]	State	Total (mil. dol.)	Per capita (dol.) [1]	State	Total (mil. dol.)	Per capita (dol.) [1]	State	Total (mil. dol.)	Per capita (dol.) [1]
U.S. [2]	**35,607**	**114**	ID	258	167	MT	387	397	RI	189	179
U.S. [3]	**34,733**	**113**	IL	1,370	106	NE	275	153	SC	476	104
AL	725	154	IN	942	147	NV	374	141	SD	226	279
AK	335	480	IA	453	151	NH	178	134	TN	634	101
AZ	605	92	KS	383	136	NJ	791	91	TX	2,503	101
AR	419	145	KY	505	117	NM	277	138	UT	317	114
CA	2,494	67	LA	619	138	NY	1,779	91	VT	137	220
CO	470	94	ME	148	112	NC	1,117	119	VA	845	107
CT	487	138	MD	497	87	ND	245	379	WA	640	96
DE	181	205	MA	866	131	OH	1,181	102	WV	475	261
DC	133	222	MI	1,100	110	OK	798	217	WI	806	143
FL	1,518	82	MN	563	107	OR	416	109	WY	226	416
GA	1,265	129	MS	430	146	PA	1,478	117			
HI	214	165	MO	981	164						

[1] Based on estimated population as of July 1. [2] Includes outlying areas and undistributed funds, not shown separately. [3] For the 50 states and the District of Columbia.
Source: U.S. Census Bureau, *Federal Aid to States for Fiscal Year, 2009,* August 2010. See also <http://www.census.gov/prod/www/abs/fas.html>.

Table 1093. State Motor Fuel Tax Receipts, 2008 and 2009, and Gasoline Tax Rates, 2009

[666 represents $666,000,000. Federal tax rate is 18.4 cents a gallon]

State	Net receipts (mil. dol.) 2008	Net receipts (mil. dol.) 2009	Tax rate, [1] 2009	State	Net receipts (mil. dol.) 2008	Net receipts (mil. dol.) 2009	Tax rate, [1] 2009	State	Net receipts (mil. dol.) 2008	Net receipts (mil. dol.) 2009	Tax rate, [1] 2009
AL	666	635	18.00	KY	609	621	24.10	ND	144	143	23.00
AK	30	7	8.00	LA	598	598	20.00	OH	1,840	1,707	28.00
AZ	708	633	18.00	ME	240	229	29.50	OK	371	438	17.00
AR	464	446	21.50	MD	752	734	23.50	OR	398	421	24.00
CA	3,254	3,025	18.00	MA	665	653	21.00	PA	2,106	2,040	30.00
CO	555	542	22.00	MI	972	947	19.00	RI	146	0	30.00
CT	678	614	25.00	MN	664	751	27.10	SC	521	502	16.00
DE	118	115	23.00	MS	419	407	18.40	SD	129	128	22.00
DC	23	24	23.50	MO	710	681	17.00	TN	833	818	20.00
FL	2,215	2,149	16.00	MT	194	177	27.75	TX	3,043	3,001	20.00
GA	997	467	7.50	NE	304	314	26.80	UT	364	334	24.50
HI	85	73	17.00	NV	308	453	24.00	VT	88	80	20.00
ID	219	216	25.00	NH	153	145	19.63	VA	935	897	17.50
IL	1,314	1,260	19.00	NJ	588	559	10.50	WA	1,168	1,165	37.50
IN	856	918	18.00	NM	[2] 289	321	18.88	WV	359	339	32.20
IA	435	428	21.00	NY	1,607	1,625	25.15	WI	980	949	30.90
KS	424	414	24.00	NC	1,573	1,505	30.15	WY	106	87	14.00

[1] State gasoline tax rates in cents per gallon. In effect December 31. [2] 2007 data.
Source: U.S. Federal Highway Administration, *Highway Statistics*, annual. See also <http://www.fhwa.dot.gov/policy/ohpi/hss/index.cfm>.

Table 1094. Public Obligations for Highways—Changes in Indebtedness During the Year: 1995 to 2009

[In millions of dollars (37,449 represents $37,449,000,000). Table summarizes state indebtedness from all state bond issues, including the toll facility issues and the state issues for local roads. This table is compiled from reports of state authorities. Table also summarizes the change in status of the highway obligations of local governments including toll authorities]

Item	1995	2000	2004	2005	2006	2007	2008	2009
STATE GOVERNMENT								
Obligations outstanding, beginning of year . . .	37,449	56,264	80,513	82,476	89,642	89,899	102,039	111,600
Obligations issued	4,718	9,067	13,344	19,784	15,651	20,924	20,769	22,372
Obligations retired	2,940	3,897	8,291	14,072	8,780	7,108	12,183	8,326
Obligations outstanding, end of year	39,228	61,434	85,565	88,187	96,513	103,715	110,625	125,646
LOCAL GOVERNMENT [1,2]								
Obligations outstanding, beginning of year . . .	26,393	34,904	42,733	44,406	47,346	50,092	52,478	(NA)
Bonds outstanding, beginning of year	25,613	34,229	41,979	43,403	46,344	48,854	51,103	(NA)
Bonds outstanding, end of year	29,505	34,949	44,368	46,168	49,130	51,049	53,895	(NA)
Obligations outstanding, end of year	30,295	35,557	45,331	47,170	50,366	52,336	55,414	(NA)

NA Not available. [1] Short-term notes data not shown. The data are included in beginning and ending year obligations. [2] The number of local government data estimated varied year to year.

Source: U.S. Federal Highway Administration, *Highway Statistics*, annual. See also <http://www.fhwa.dot.gov/policy/ohpi/hss/index.cfm>.

Table 1095. State Disbursements for Highways by State: 1995 to 2009

[In millions of dollars (67,615 represents $67,615,000,000). Comprise disbursements from current revenues or loans for construction, maintenance, interest and principal payments on highway bonds, transfers to local units, and miscellaneous. Includes transactions by state toll authorities. Excludes amounts allocated for collection expenses and nonhighway purposes, and mass transit]

State	1995	2000	2004	2005	2006	2007	2008	2009
United States	**67,615**	**89,832**	**104,677**	**116,517**	**117,048**	**130,306**	**139,584**	**143,767**
Alabama	1,002	1,246	1,562	1,519	1,684	1,752	1,916	1,969
Alaska	438	501	623	643	654	710	730	935
Arizona	1,199	2,040	2,569	2,458	2,662	2,335	2,806	2,988
Arkansas	666	817	1,219	1,078	1,134	1,036	1,051	1,072
California	5,966	6,750	7,967	8,308	10,571	13,288	14,697	21,808
Colorado	922	1,392	1,870	1,652	1,490	1,601	1,695	1,906
Connecticut	1,153	1,304	1,677	1,434	1,223	1,265	1,370	2,175
Delaware	441	595	798	1,104	804	676	683	711
District of Columbia	140	244	369	327	287	334	335	469
Florida	3,421	4,208	5,804	7,369	7,725	8,069	8,698	7,194
Georgia	1,437	1,567	1,935	2,070	2,655	2,878	3,817	3,506
Hawaii	360	272	314	506	323	352	444	504
Idaho	350	492	568	608	622	758	802	890
Illinois	3,006	3,447	4,289	4,201	4,974	5,424	6,299	5,385
Indiana	1,433	1,932	2,578	2,235	2,416	3,251	3,280	3,280
Iowa	1,078	1,494	1,401	1,392	1,515	1,564	1,505	1,721
Kansas	1,019	1,206	1,387	1,394	1,521	1,414	1,487	1,464
Kentucky	1,397	1,651	1,907	1,723	1,635	2,194	2,404	2,522
Louisiana	1,198	1,301	1,576	1,387	1,866	1,923	2,488	3,480
Maine	379	488	702	616	628	584	739	652
Maryland	1,289	1,599	1,831	2,049	2,304	2,689	2,747	2,800
Massachusetts	2,501	3,524	3,612	3,196	2,723	2,815	2,898	2,810
Michigan	1,974	2,748	2,930	3,561	3,263	3,240	3,269	3,178
Minnesota	1,210	1,692	1,995	2,131	2,143	2,168	2,352	2,365
Mississippi	662	1,039	1,087	1,081	1,272	1,647	1,346	1,301
Missouri	1,313	1,818	2,135	2,069	2,430	3,955	2,545	2,846
Montana	388	474	657	664	696	622	651	708
Nebraska	578	745	859	876	882	1,436	1,352	1,398
Nevada	484	651	1,045	865	1,144	1,063	906	1,221
New Hampshire	328	387	389	389	524	693	681	641
New Jersey	2,102	4,503	3,849	7,119	5,561	4,018	3,921	4,222
New Mexico	535	1,162	1,164	911	942	942	860	1,272
New York	4,584	5,307	6,094	9,638	5,659	7,459	7,537	6,977
North Carolina	1,871	2,621	3,557	3,698	3,330	3,385	3,584	3,659
North Dakota	270	385	388	456	506	441	471	478
Ohio	2,637	3,351	3,657	4,040	4,251	4,418	4,631	4,852
Oklahoma	828	1,417	1,175	1,163	2,001	1,282	1,634	1,765
Oregon	888	1,010	1,000	1,628	1,254	1,736	1,364	1,395
Pennsylvania	3,153	4,517	4,283	4,567	5,537	5,999	5,956	6,979
Rhode Island	290	256	373	407	488	494	419	389
South Carolina	668	970	1,254	1,360	1,476	1,472	1,470	1,353
South Dakota	286	466	455	466	491	402	451	500
Tennessee	1,230	1,440	1,549	1,718	1,658	1,657	1,771	1,936
Texas	3,593	5,665	7,134	8,918	9,101	13,136	15,948	9,883
Utah	431	1,072	1,871	986	1,128	1,335	1,229	1,855
Vermont	194	287	297	310	335	368	395	400
Virginia	2,107	2,678	3,002	3,384	3,195	3,228	3,875	3,572
Washington	1,909	1,871	2,469	2,625	2,656	3,057	3,901	3,807
West Virginia	781	1,170	1,056	1,425	1,117	1,057	1,208	1,410
Wisconsin	1,252	1,663	1,942	2,363	2,161	2,279	2,392	2,549
Wyoming	272	396	458	429	434	484	574	611

Source: U.S. Federal Highway Administration, *Highway Statistics*, annual. See also <http://www.fhwa.dot.gov/policy/ohpi/hss/index.cfm>.

U.S. Census Bureau, Statistical Abstract of the United States: 2012

Table 1096. State Motor Vehicle Registrations: 1990 to 2009

[In thousands (188,798 represents 188,798,000). Compiled principally from information obtained from state authorities, but it was necessary to draw on other sources and to make numerous estimates in order to complete series. Excludes motorcycles; see Table 1098]

Type	1990	1995	2000	2005	2007	2008	2009
All motor vehicles.........	**188,798**	**201,530**	**221,475**	**241,194**	**247,265**	**248,165**	**246,283**
Private and commercial.......	185,541	197,941	217,567	237,140	243,094	243,953	242,058
Publicly owned.............	3,257	3,589	3,908	4,054	4,170	4,212	4,225
Automobiles [1]...............	133,700	128,387	133,621	136,568	135,933	137,080	134,880
Private and commercial.......	132,164	126,900	132,247	135,192	134,510	135,638	133,438
Publicly owned.............	1,536	1,487	1,374	1,376	1,423	1,442	1,442
Buses......................	627	686	746	807	834	843	842
Private and commercial.......	275	288	314	331	345	350	351
Publicly owned.............	351	398	432	476	490	493	491
Trucks [1]	54,470	72,458	87,108	103,819	110,497	110,242	110,561
Private and commercial.......	53,101	70,754	85,005	101,616	108,239	107,965	108,269
Publicly owned.............	1,369	1,704	2,103	2,203	2,258	2,277	2,292

[1] Trucks include pickups, panels, and delivery vans. Personal passenger vans, passenger minivans, and utility-type vehicles are no longer included in automobiles but are included in trucks.

Source: U.S. Federal Highway Administration, *Highway Statistics*, annual. See also <http://www.fhwa.dot.gov/policy/ohpi/hss/index.cfm>.

Table 1097. Alternative Fueled Vehicles and Estimated Consumption of Vehicle Fuels by Fuel Type: 2005 to 2009

[In thousands, (420,778 represents 420,778,000). Vehicles in use do not include concept and demonstration vehicles that are not ready for delivery to end users. Vehicles in use represent accumulated acquisitions, less retirements, as of the end of each calendar year]

Vehicles and fuel consumption	Unit	2005	2007	2008	2009
ALTERNATIVE FUELED VEHICLES IN USE					
Total...........................	Number	592,125	695,766	775,667	826,318
Compressed Natural Gas (CNG).........	Number	117,699	114,391	113,973	114,270
Electric [1]............................	Number	51,398	55,730	56,901	57,185
Ethanol, 85 percent (E85) [2, 3].............	Number	246,363	364,384	450,327	504,297
Hydrogen.........................	Number	119	223	313	357
Liquefied Natural Gas (LNG).............	Number	2,748	2,781	3,101	3,176
Liquefied Petroleum Gas (LPG)...........	Number	173,795	158,254	151,049	147,030
Other fuels [4].......................	Number	3	3	3	3
FUEL CONSUMPTION					
Alternative fuels:	1,000 gal.(g-e-g) [5] ...	420,778	414,715	430,329	431,107
Compressed Natural Gas (CNG).........	1,000 gal.(g-e-g) [5] ...	166,878	178,565	189,358	199,513
Electric [1]...........................	1,000 gal.(g-e-g) [5] ...	5,219	5,037	5,050	4,956
Ethanol, 85 percent (E85) [2].............	1,000 gal.(g-e-g) [5] ...	38,074	54,091	62,464	71,213
Hydrogen.........................	1,000 gal.(g-e-g) [5] ...	25	66	117	140
Liquefied Natural Gas (LNG).............	1,000 gal.(g-e-g) [5] ...	22,409	24,594	25,554	25,652
Liquefied Petroleum Gas (LPG)...........	1,000 gal.(g-e-g) [5] ...	188,171	152,360	147,784	129,631
Other fuels [4]........................	1,000 gal.(g-e-g) [5] ...	2	2	2	2
Biodiesel	1,000 gal.(g-e-g) [5] ...	93,281	367,764	324,329	325,102
Oxygenates:					
Methyl Tertiary Butyl Ether (MTBE)........	1,000 gal.(g-e-g) [5] ...	1,654,500	–	–	–
Ethanol in Gasohol	1,000 gal.(g-e-g) [5] ...	2,756,663	4,694,304	6,442,781	7,343,133
Total alternative and replacement fuels......	1,000 gal.(g-e-g) [5] ...	4,925,222	5,476,783	7,197,439	8,099,342
FUEL CONSUMPTION IN NATIVE UNITS					
Alternative fuels:					
Compressed Natural Gas (CNG).........	million cubic feet	20,106	21,514	22,814	24,038
Electric [1]...........................	1,000 kwh	173,967	167,900	168,333	165,200
Ethanol, 85 percent (E85) [2].............	1,000 gallons.......	52,881	75,126	86,756	98,907
Hydrogen.........................	1,000 kilograms.....	23	60	107	128
Liquefied Natural Gas (LNG).............	1,000 gallons.......	33,953	37,264	38,718	38,867
Liquefied Petroleum Gas (LPG)...........	1,000 gallons.......	254,285	205,892	199,708	175,177
Biodiesel	1,000 gallons.......	90,827	358,156	315,796	316,549
Oxygenates:					
Methyl Tertiary Butyl Ether (MTBE)........	1,000 gallons.......	2,035,320	–	–	–
Ethanol in Gasohol	1,000 gallons.......	4,013,679	6,885,690	9,435,428	10,753,990

– Represents zero. X Not applicable. [1] Excludes gasoline-electric and diesel-electric hybrids because the input fuel is gasoline or diesel rather than an alternative transportation fuel. [2] The remaining portion of E85 percent ethanol is gasoline. Consumption data include the gasoline portion of the fuel. [3] For 2009, the EIA estimates that the number of E85 vehicles that are capable of operating on E85, gasoline, or both, is about 10 million. Many of these alternative-fueled vehicles (AFVs) are sold and used as traditional gasoline-powered vehicles. In this table, AFVs in use include only those E85 vehicles believed to be used as AFVs. These are primarily fleet-operated vehicles. [4] May include P-Series fuel or any other fuel designated by the Secretary of Energy as an alternative fuel in accordance with the Energy Policy Act of 1995. [5] Gasoline equivalent gallons.

Source: U.S. Energy Information Administration, "Alternatives to Traditional Transportation Fuels," <http://www.eia.gov/renewable/data.cfm>.

Table 1098. State Motor Vehicle Registrations, 1990 to 2009, Motorcycle Registrations and Licensed Drivers by State: 2009

[In thousands (188,798 represents 188,798,000). Motor vehicle registrations cover publicly, privately, and commercially owned vehicles. For uniformity, data have been adjusted to a calendar-year basis as registration years in states differ; figures represent net numbers where possible, excluding reregistrations and nonresident registrations. See also Table 1096]

State	Motor vehicle registrations [1]						2009		Motor cycle registra- tions, [2] 2009	Licensed drivers, 2009
	1990	1995	2000	2005	2007	2008	Total	Auto mobiles (incl. taxis)		
U.S.	188,798	201,530	221,475	241,194	247,265	248,165	246,283	134,880	7,883	209,618
AL	3,744	3,553	3,960	4,545	4,678	4,730	4,611	2,172	122	3,782
AK	477	542	594	673	680	691	695	236	29	508
AZ	2,825	2,873	3,795	3,972	4,372	4,373	4,358	2,228	138	4,403
AR	1,448	1,613	1,840	1,940	2,010	2,041	2,037	947	76	2,065
CA	21,926	22,432	27,698	32,487	33,935	33,483	34,433	19,973	759	23,681
CO	3,155	2,812	3,626	1,808	1,707	1,618	1,429	641	95	3,705
CT	2,623	2,622	2,853	3,059	3,047	3,094	3,072	1,983	65	2,916
DE	526	592	630	737	851	868	843	464	26	700
DC	262	243	242	237	218	224	218	167	1	376
FL	10,950	10,369	11,781	15,691	16,474	16,462	15,315	7,598	663	14,005
GA	5,489	6,120	7,155	8,063	8,513	8,570	8,507	4,134	196	6,315
HI	771	802	738	948	993	945	895	449	49	890
ID	1,054	1,043	1,178	1,374	1,282	1,318	1,375	563	56	1,055
IL	7,873	8,973	8,973	9,458	9,757	9,794	9,891	5,824	349	8,301
IN	4,366	5,072	5,571	4,955	4,956	5,848	5,848	3,136	204	5,550
IA	2,632	2,814	3,106	3,398	3,360	3,431	3,363	1,736	184	2,145
KS	2,012	2,085	2,296	2,368	2,429	2,449	2,425	875	85	2,045
KY	2,909	2,631	2,826	3,428	3,547	3,604	3,585	1,952	68	2,939
LA	2,995	3,286	3,557	3,819	3,927	3,979	4,033	1,941	70	3,086
ME	977	967	1,024	1,075	1,080	1,074	1,056	538	55	1,014
MD	3,607	3,654	3,848	4,322	4,510	4,525	4,484	2,598	83	3,905
MA	3,726	4,502	5,265	5,420	5,367	5,328	5,262	3,128	158	4,630
MI	7,209	7,674	8,436	8,247	8,192	7,945	7,913	4,372	266	7,083
MN	3,508	3,882	4,630	4,647	4,756	4,783	4,796	2,506	251	3,245
MS	1,875	2,144	2,289	1,978	2,008	2,035	2,026	1,156	28	1,931
MO	3,905	4,255	4,580	4,589	4,917	4,866	4,904	2,560	104	4,218
MT	783	968	1,026	1,009	949	927	925	370	126	738
NE	1,384	1,467	1,619	1,703	1,739	1,757	1,793	784	50	1,349
NV	853	1,047	1,220	1,349	1,424	1,417	1,397	707	68	1,690
NH	946	1,122	1,052	1,174	1,185	1,214	1,212	640	81	1,034
NJ [3]	5,652	5,906	6,390	6,262	6,247	6,247	6,114	3,705	157	5,924
NM	1,301	1,484	1,529	1,548	1,599	1,570	1,621	698	54	1,378
NY	10,196	10,274	10,235	11,863	11,495	11,089	11,245	8,726	345	11,329
NC	5,162	5,682	6,223	6,148	6,317	6,249	6,047	3,451	128	6,504
ND	630	695	694	695	711	717	722	347	32	477
OH	8,410	9,810	10,467	10,634	10,848	10,933	11,022	6,319	386	7,937
OK	2,649	2,856	3,014	3,725	3,225	3,292	3,396	1,670	124	2,321
OR	2,445	2,785	3,022	2,897	3,088	3,106	3,046	1,440	104	2,842
PA	7,971	8,481	9,260	9,864	9,938	10,366	9,857	5,818	409	8,687
RI	672	699	760	812	797	794	789	482	34	746
SC	2,521	2,833	3,095	3,339	3,521	3,604	3,614	1,974	106	3,268
SD	704	709	793	854	865	907	926	402	62	602
TN	4,444	5,400	4,820	4,980	5,340	5,098	5,140	2,855	162	4,477
TX	12,800	13,682	14,070	17,470	18,072	18,208	18,208	8,831	435	15,374
UT	1,206	1,447	1,628	2,210	2,320	2,439	2,454	1,217	59	1,720
VT	462	492	515	508	565	581	557	292	29	507
VA	4,938	5,613	6,046	6,591	6,614	6,526	6,302	3,732	79	5,348
WA	4,257	4,503	5,116	5,598	5,758	5,980	5,581	3,102	228	5,027
WV	1,225	1,425	1,442	1,352	1,413	1,402	1,412	700	49	1,329
WI	3,815	3,993	4,366	4,725	5,018	4,999	4,874	2,527	365	4,105
WY	528	601	586	646	652	664	652	214	30	411

[1] Automobiles, trucks, and buses (excludes motorcycles). Excludes vehicles owned by military services. [2] Private and commercial. [3] State did not provide current data. Table displays 2007 private and commercial and state, county and municipal vehicles.

Source: U.S. Federal Highway Administration, *Highway Statistics*, annual. See also <http://www.fhwa.dot.gov/policy/ohpi/hss/index.cfm>.

Transportation 689

Table 1099. Roadway Congestion by Urbanized Area: 2009

[14,779 represents 14,779,000. Various federal, state, and local information sources were used to develop the database with the primary source being the Federal Highway Administration's Highway Performance Monitoring System]

Urbanized area	Freeway daily vehicle miles of travel		Annual person hours of delay		Annual congestion cost [1]		
	Total miles (1,000)	Per lane—mile of freeway	Total hours (1,000)	Per person [2]	Per person (dol.)	Delay and fuel cost (mil. dol.)	Fuel wasted (gal. per person)
Total, average	**14,779**	**15,391**	**41,808**	**25**	**591**	**994**	**20**
Akron, OH	5,156	11,853	6,713	11	239	148	8
Albany-Schenectady, NY	6,761	10,993	7,844	13	310	190	11
Albuquerque, NM	4,886	14,585	10,798	18	467	286	14
Allentown-Bethlehem, PA-NJ	4,637	11,173	9,998	16	377	237	13
Atlanta, GA	45,862	18,199	112,262	27	649	2,727	22
Austin, TX	11,960	14,585	30,272	24	553	691	21
Baltimore, MD	25,516	16,356	82,836	33	810	2,024	28
Beaumont, TX	2,909	12,121	3,536	15	357	86	15
Birmingham, AL	9,263	13,622	16,227	19	447	380	16
Boston, MA-NH-RI	39,805	15,610	118,707	28	633	2,691	21
Bridgeport-Stamford, CT-NY	10,025	16,570	20,972	23	548	507	20
Buffalo, NY	6,397	9,842	11,660	11	267	280	10
Cape Coral, FL	1,637	14,882	7,465	16	394	183	13
Charleston-North, Charleston, SC	3,595	13,315	9,189	18	445	227	16
Charlotte, NC-SC	11,539	14,072	17,207	17	435	437	14
Chicago, IL-IN	54,415	18,018	372,755	44	1,112	9,476	33
Cincinnati, OH-KY-IN	17,766	14,385	21,391	13	309	525	10
Cleveland, OH	16,628	11,793	21,859	13	286	489	11
Colorado Springs, CO	3,872	11,558	12,074	22	493	266	18
Columbus, OH	14,313	14,909	14,282	11	257	323	10
Dallas-Fort, Worth-Arlington, TX	62,777	17,199	159,654	32	728	3,649	25
Dayton, OH	6,909	11,810	7,479	10	228	170	8
Denver-Aurora, CO	19,697	15,388	75,196	33	758	1,711	27
Detroit, MI	29,406	15,356	87,996	23	521	2,032	17
El Paso, TX-NM	5,522	12,409	10,020	14	340	242	12
Fresno, CA	3,857	12,857	6,669	10	247	165	9
Grand Rapids, MI	4,850	10,778	8,131	13	318	193	13
Hartford, CT	10,457	13,237	14,072	16	357	321	13
Honolulu, HI	5,873	14,152	14,394	20	460	326	17
Houston, TX	54,290	16,653	144,302	37	868	3,403	33
Indianapolis, IN	13,060	14,119	20,164	17	419	503	13
Jackson, MS	4,717	12,923	5,607	13	385	161	13
Jacksonville, FL	11,701	14,811	18,481	17	420	445	15
Kansas City, MO-KS	20,692	10,777	22,172	14	348	538	14
Las Vegas, NV	10,481	18,716	30,077	21	481	673	18
Los Angeles-Long Beach-Santa Ana, CA .	131,537	23,447	514,955	40	921	11,997	31
Louisville, KY-IN	11,808	14,227	16,019	15	365	389	13
Memphis, TN-MS-AR	8,192	12,603	17,639	17	411	430	15
Miami, FL	39,243	18,001	140,972	26	612	3,272	20
Milwaukee, WI	10,194	13,683	24,113	16	384	570	13
Minneapolis-St. Paul, MN	27,970	16,262	74,070	27	626	1,689	24
Nashville-Davidson, TN	14,430	13,486	25,443	23	567	624	18
New Haven, CT	7,275	13,857	11,956	19	463	285	17
New Orleans, LA	4,776	12,736	19,867	20	506	511	15
New York-Newark, NY-NJ-CT	113,607	15,735	454,443	24	580	10,878	19
Oklahoma City, OK	9,472	12,301	16,335	17	396	376	14
Omaha, NE-IA	3,999	12,900	8,737	14	292	184	11
Orlando, FL	13,199	14,504	39,185	27	673	962	22
Oxnard-Ventura, CA	6,958	17,615	8,921	13	310	216	13
Pensacola, FL-AL	1,303	8,687	4,715	13	303	108	11
Philadelphia, PA-NJ-DE-MD	34,956	14,505	136,429	26	613	3,274	20
Phoenix, AZ	29,872	19,027	80,390	23	611	2,161	20
Pittsburgh, PA	11,524	9,003	39,718	23	548	965	19
Portland, OR-WA	12,991	16,549	40,554	22	515	958	18
Providence, RI-MA	10,771	11,644	15,679	13	278	343	10
Raleigh-Durham, NC	11,408	13,113	18,541	17	431	472	15
Richmond, VA	11,398	10,804	12,895	14	292	279	12
Riverside-San Bernardino, CA	23,212	20,818	39,008	20	501	976	17
Sacramento, CA	15,166	18,383	28,461	15	363	671	14
Salem, OR	1,358	10,864	4,119	17	420	100	14
Salt Lake City, UT	7,576	13,291	18,789	19	418	415	15
San Antonio, TX	19,562	15,650	29,446	19	435	664	18
San Diego, CA	37,196	18,645	71,034	23	549	1,672	20
San Francisco-Oakland, CA	47,967	19,110	121,117	30	698	2,791	24
San Jose, CA	16,170	17,867	42,313	24	526	937	20
Sarasota-Bradenton, FL	2,323	14,079	8,563	13	292	198	10
Seattle, WA	29,645	15,981	86,549	27	665	2,119	22
St. Louis, MO-IL	28,630	12,209	48,777	21	531	1,238	18
Tampa-St. Petersburg, FL	13,532	15,290	54,130	23	529	1,239	18
Toledo, OH-MI	3,695	11,030	4,427	9	197	102	6
Tucson, AZ	3,632	14,528	11,282	16	453	317	12
Tulsa, OK	6,997	9,329	8,621	12	289	202	12
Virginia Beach, VA	12,907	13,658	33,469	22	461	714	17
Washington, DC-VA-MD	37,450	18,048	180,970	41	913	4,066	33
Worcester, MA	5,658	11,666	6,051	14	305	135	11

[1] Value of extra time (delay) and the extra fuel consumed by vehicles traveling at slower speeds. Fuel cost per gallon is the average price for each state. [2] The hours of extra travel time divided by the number of urban area peak period travelers. This is an annual measure indicating the sum of all extra travel time that would occur during the year for the average traveler.

Source: Texas Transportaton Institute, College Station, Texas, *2010 Urban Mobility Study*, Summer 2010 (copyright). See also <http://mobility.tamu.edu/ums/>.

Table 1100. Commuting to Work by State: 2009

[In percent, except as indicated (138,592 represents 138,592,000). For workers 16 years old and over. The American Community Survey universe includes the household population and the population living in institutions, college dormitories, and other group quarters. Based on a sample and subject to sampling variability; see Appendix III]

State	Total workers (1,000)	Commuted by car, truck, or van		Used public transpor- tation [1]	Walked	Used other means [2]	Worked at home	Mean travel time to work (min.)
		Drove alone	Car- pooled	Percent of workers who—				
U.S.	138,592	76.1	10.0	5.0	2.9	1.7	4.3	25.1
AL	1,960	84.4	10.3	0.4	1.3	1.0	2.5	23.6
AK	335	68.2	13.3	1.4	8.0	4.5	4.6	17.7
AZ	2,752	75.9	11.8	2.1	2.4	2.7	5.2	24.3
AR	1,223	81.1	11.6	0.4	1.9	1.6	3.5	21.1
CA	16,146	73.0	11.6	5.2	2.8	2.3	5.2	26.6
CO	2,465	74.3	10.1	3.3	3.0	2.6	6.7	24.5
CT	1,708	78.9	8.4	4.5	2.9	1.2	4.1	24.3
DE	413	80.5	8.9	3.8	2.4	1.2	3.3	23.6
DC	291	36.5	6.7	37.1	11.1	3.5	5.2	29.2
FL	7,893	79.3	10.4	1.9	1.5	2.2	4.8	25.4
GA	4,290	78.4	11.0	2.5	1.7	1.7	4.8	26.9
HI	638	67.7	14.0	6.0	4.5	3.2	4.5	25.5
ID	675	77.5	11.0	1.0	2.6	2.8	5.1	19.8
IL	5,918	73.5	9.0	8.8	3.2	1.7	3.9	28.0
IN	2,875	83.0	9.2	1.1	2.2	1.2	3.3	22.9
IA	1,526	78.9	9.8	1.2	4.0	1.2	4.9	18.5
KS	1,369	81.2	9.5	0.4	2.8	1.8	4.3	18.5
KY	1,825	81.5	10.6	1.2	2.4	1.2	3.1	22.6
LA	1,962	81.8	10.6	1.3	2.0	1.9	2.5	24.7
ME	636	78.3	10.1	0.7	4.2	1.5	5.3	22.9
MD	2,840	73.4	10.0	8.8	2.6	1.1	4.1	31.3
MA	3,232	71.9	8.2	9.4	4.7	1.6	4.2	27.3
MI	4,136	82.6	9.0	1.3	2.4	1.2	3.6	23.7
MN	2,658	78.0	9.2	3.4	2.9	1.5	4.9	22.5
MS	1,187	83.5	10.7	0.4	1.7	1.1	2.6	23.6
MO	2,752	81.0	10.0	1.5	2.0	1.3	4.3	23.2
MT	458	75.3	9.8	0.8	5.4	2.8	5.9	16.8
NE	921	80.4	10.2	0.6	3.3	1.1	4.4	17.9
NV	1,203	79.2	10.3	3.1	2.1	1.8	3.4	23.1
NH	679	82.2	8.0	0.6	2.8	1.1	5.2	25.7
NJ	4,099	71.4	8.7	10.6	3.4	2.0	4.0	29.8
NM	863	77.9	11.5	1.1	2.4	1.8	5.2	21.6
NY	8,906	54.0	7.4	26.6	6.4	1.7	3.9	31.4
NC	4,152	80.8	10.7	1.0	2.0	1.1	4.4	23.2
ND	345	78.5	10.6	0.3	3.6	1.3	5.7	16.6
OH	5,166	83.0	8.4	1.8	2.3	0.9	3.6	22.8
OK	1,645	82.0	11.0	0.4	1.9	1.4	3.4	20.5
OR	1,705	72.0	10.4	4.1	3.9	3.3	6.4	22.1
PA	5,750	76.8	9.0	5.3	4.0	1.3	3.7	25.4
RI	501	80.3	9.0	2.8	3.2	1.2	3.6	23.2
SC	1,961	82.0	10.0	0.6	1.9	1.5	3.9	23.2
SD	413	77.3	10.2	0.5	4.3	1.7	6.0	16.7
TN	2,720	83.4	9.8	0.8	1.4	1.1	3.4	24.0
TX	11,074	79.6	11.4	1.6	1.7	1.9	3.8	24.6
UT	1,258	76.1	11.7	2.4	2.9	2.0	4.8	21.0
VT	317	74.8	10.0	0.9	5.4	1.7	7.2	21.9
VA	3,823	77.5	10.4	4.4	2.2	1.3	4.1	27.2
WA	3,093	72.1	11.3	5.9	3.4	2.1	5.3	25.4
WV	745	81.7	10.3	0.9	2.8	1.0	3.4	25.1
WI	2,815	79.8	9.2	1.9	3.4	1.6	4.1	21.2
WY	277	77.2	10.9	1.4	3.4	1.9	5.2	18.0

[1] Excluding taxicabs. [2] Includes taxicabs, motorcycles, bicycles, and other means.

Source: U.S. Census Bureau, 2009 American Community Survey, B08006, "Sex of Worker by Means of Transportation to Work" and R0801, "Mean Travel Time to Work of Workers 16 Years Old and Over Who Did Not Work At Home (minutes)," <http://factfinder.census.gov/>, accessed January 2011.

U.S. Census Bureau, Statistical Abstract of the United States: 2012

Table 1101. Motor Vehicle Distance Traveled by Type of Vehicle: 1970 to 2009

[1,110 represents 1,110,000,000,000. The travel data by vehicle type and stratification of trucks are estimated by the Federal Highway Administration (FHWA)]

Year	Vehicle—miles of travel (bil.) [1]					Average miles traveled per vehicle (1,000) [1]				
	Total [2]	Light duty vehicle short WB [2,3]	Buses [4]	Light duty vehicle long WB [3]	Trucks [5,6]	Total [2]	Light duty vehicle short WB [2,3]	Buses [4]	Light duty vehicle long WB [3]	Trucks [5,6]
1970.........	1,110	920	4.5	123	62	10.0	10.0	12.0	8.7	13.6
1980.........	1,527	1,122	6.1	291	108	9.5	8.8	11.5	10.4	18.7
1985.........	1,775	1,256	4.5	391	124	10.0	9.4	7.5	10.5	20.6
1990.........	2,144	1,418	5.7	575	146	11.1	10.3	9.1	11.9	23.6
1991.........	2,172	1,367	5.8	649	150	11.3	10.3	9.1	12.2	24.2
1992.........	2,247	1,381	5.8	707	153	11.6	10.6	9.0	12.4	25.4
1993.........	2,296	1,385	6.1	746	160	11.6	10.5	9.4	12.4	26.3
1994.........	2,358	1,416	6.4	765	170	11.7	10.8	9.6	12.2	25.8
1995.........	2,423	1,438	6.4	790	178	11.8	11.2	9.4	12.0	26.5
1996.........	2,486	1,470	6.6	817	183	11.8	11.3	9.4	11.8	26.1
1997.........	2,562	1,503	6.8	851	191	12.1	11.6	9.8	12.1	27.0
1998.........	2,632	1,550	7.0	868	196	12.2	11.8	9.8	12.2	25.4
1999.........	2,691	1,569	7.7	901	203	12.2	11.9	10.5	12.0	26.0
2000.........	2,747	1,967	14.8	491	262	12.2	11.0	19.8	14.6	29.1
2001.........	2,796	1,987	13.0	512	272	11.9	10.7	17.3	14.7	28.9
2002.........	2,856	2,036	13.3	520	276	12.2	11.1	17.5	14.3	29.4
2003.........	2,890	2,051	13.4	528	286	12.2	11.1	17.2	14.8	30.3
2004.........	2,965	2,083	13.5	569	284	12.2	11.0	17.0	15.2	29.7
2005.........	2,989	2,096	13.2	581	285	12.1	11.0	16.3	14.8	28.8
2006.........	3,014	2,048	14.0	633	301	12.0	10.5	17.1	16.3	29.1
2007.........	3,031	2,104	14.5	587	304	11.9	10.7	17.4	15.0	28.3
2008.........	2,977	2,025	14.8	605	311	11.6	10.3	17.6	15.3	28.6
2009.........	2,954	2,013	14.4	617	288	11.6	10.4	17.1	15.2	26.2

[1] FHWA updated VM-1 from 2000 to 2009 using on an enhanced methodology implemented in March 2011. Prior to 2000, "Light Duty Vehicles Short WB" were categorized as "Cars"; "Light Duty Vehicles Long WB" were categorized as "Vans, pickups, sport utility vehicles." [2] Motorcycles included with "Cars" through 1994; thereafter in total, not shown separately. [3] Light Duty Vehicles Short WB—passenger cars, light trucks, vans and sport utility vehicles with a wheelbase (WB) equal to or less than 121 inches. Light Duty Vehicles Long WB—large passenger cars, vans, pickup trucks, and sport/utility vehicles with wheelbases (WB) larger than 121 inches. [4] Includes school buses. [5] Includes combinations. [6] 2000 to 2009: Single-Unit—single frame trucks that have 2-Axles and at least 6 tires or a gross vehicle weight rating exceeding 10,000 lbs.

Source: U.S. Federal Highway Administration, *Highway Statistics*, annual. See also <http://www.fhwa.dot.gov/policy/ohpi/hss/index.cfm>.

Table 1102. Domestic Motor Fuel Consumption by Type of Vehicle: 1970 to 2009

[92.3 represents 92,300,000,000. Comprises all fuel types used for propulsion of vehicles under state motor fuels laws. Excludes federal purchases for military use. Minus sign (–) indicates decrease]

Year	Annual fuel consumption (bil. gal.) [1]						Average miles per gallon [1]				
	All vehicles [2]	Annual percent change [3]	Light duty vehicle short WB [2,4]	Buses [5]	Light duty vehicle long WB [4]	Trucks [6,7]	All vehicles [2]	Light duty vehicle short WB [2,4]	Buses [5]	Light duty vehicle long WB [4]	Trucks [6,7]
1970.......	92.3	4.8	67.8	0.8	12.3	11.3	12.0	13.5	5.5	10.0	5.5
1980.......	115.0	–5.9	70.2	1.0	23.8	20.0	13.3	16.0	6.0	12.2	5.4
1985.......	121.3	2.2	71.7	0.8	27.4	21.4	14.6	17.5	5.4	14.3	5.8
1990.......	130.8	–0.8	69.8	0.9	35.6	24.5	16.4	20.3	6.4	16.1	6.0
1991.......	128.6	–1.7	64.5	0.9	38.2	25.0	16.9	21.2	6.7	17.0	6.0
1992.......	132.9	3.3	65.6	0.9	40.9	25.5	16.9	21.0	6.6	17.3	6.0
1993.......	137.3	3.3	67.2	0.9	42.9	26.2	16.7	20.6	6.6	17.4	6.1
1994.......	140.8	2.5	68.1	1.0	44.1	27.7	16.7	20.8	6.6	17.3	6.1
1995.......	143.8	2.1	68.1	1.0	45.6	29.0	16.8	21.1	6.6	17.3	6.1
1996.......	147.4	2.5	69.2	1.0	47.4	29.6	16.9	21.2	6.6	17.2	6.2
1997.......	150.4	2.0	69.9	1.0	49.4	29.9	17.0	21.5	6.7	17.2	6.4
1998.......	155.4	3.3	71.7	1.1	50.5	32.0	16.9	21.6	6.7	17.2	6.1
1999.......	161.4	3.9	73.2	1.1	52.8	33.9	16.7	21.4	6.7	17.0	6.0
2000.......	162.5	0.7	88.9	2.2	28.9	42.0	16.9	22.1	6.7	17.0	6.2
2001.......	163.5	0.6	87.8	1.9	30.1	43.0	17.1	22.6	6.8	17.0	6.3
2002.......	168.7	3.2	91.5	1.9	30.8	43.3	17.0	22.3	6.9	16.9	6.4
2003.......	170.0	0.8	91.6	1.9	31.3	44.8	17.0	22.4	7.1	16.9	6.4
2004.......	173.5	2.1	93.4	1.9	33.8	44.4	17.1	22.3	7.1	16.9	6.4
2005.......	174.8	0.7	93.2	1.9	34.4	44.5	17.2	22.5	7.1	16.9	6.4
2006.......	175.0	0.1	88.6	2.0	37.0	46.4	17.2	23.1	7.1	17.1	6.5
2007.......	176.2	0.7	89.6	2.0	36.9	47.2	17.2	22.9	7.2	17.1	6.4
2008.......	170.8	–3.1	85.6	2.1	34.9	47.7	17.4	23.7	7.2	17.3	6.5
2009.......	168.1	–1.6	85.6	1.9	35.8	44.5	17.6	23.8	7.2	17.4	6.5

[1] See footnote 1, Table 1101. [2] Motorcycles included with "Cars" through 1994; thereafter in total, not shown separately. [3] Change from immediate prior year. [4] Light Duty Vehicles Short WB—passenger cars, light trucks, vans and sport utility vehicles with a wheelbase (WB) equal to or less than 121 inches. Light Duty Vehicles Long WB—large passenger cars, vans, pickup trucks, and sport/utility vehicles with wheelbases (WB) larger than 121 inches. [5] Includes school buses. [6] Includes combinations. [7] 2000 to 2009: Single-Unit—single frame trucks that have 2-Axles and at least 6 tires or a gross vehicle weight rating exceeding 10,000 lbs.

Source: U.S. Federal Highway Administration, *Highway Statistics*, annual. See also <http://www.fhwa.dot.gov/policy/ohpi/hss/index.cfm>.

Table 1103. Motor Vehicle Accidents—Number and Deaths: 1990 to 2009

[11.5 represents 11,500,000]

Item	Unit	1990	1995	2000	2004	2005	2006	2007	2008	2009
ACCIDENTS										
Motor vehicle accidents [1]	Million ...	11.5	10.7	13.4	10.9	10.7	10.4	10.6	10.2	10.8
DEATHS										
Motor vehicle deaths within 1 yr. [2]	1,000	46.8	43.4	43.4	44.9	45.3	45.3	43.9	39.7	35.9
Noncollision accidents	1,000	4.9	4.4	4.8	5.1	5.3	5.4	5.2	4.5	4.0
Collision accidents:										
With other motor vehicles	1,000	19.9	19.0	19.1	19.6	19.0	18.5	17.7	15.4	13.9
With pedestrians	1,000	7.3	6.4	5.9	6.0	6.1	6.2	6.0	5.7	5.3
With fixed objects	1,000	13.1	12.1	12.3	13.0	13.6	13.9	13.8	12.9	11.6
Deaths within 30 days [3]	1,000	44.6	41.8	41.9	42.8	43.5	42.7	41.3	37.4	33.8
Occupants	1,000	33.9	33.1	33.5	33.3	33.1	32.1	30.5	26.8	24.5
Passenger cars	1,000	24.1	22.4	20.7	19.2	18.5	17.9	16.6	14.6	13.1
Light trucks [4]	1,000	8.6	9.6	11.5	12.7	13.0	12.8	12.5	10.8	10.3
Large trucks [4]	1,000	0.7	0.6	0.8	0.8	0.8	0.8	0.8	0.7	0.5
Buses	1,000	(Z)	(Z)	(Z)	(Z)	0.1	(Z)	(Z)	0.1	(Z)
Other/unknown	1,000	0.5	0.4	0.5	0.6	0.7	0.6	0.6	0.6	0.6
Motorcycle riders [5]	1,000	3.2	2.2	2.9	4.0	4.6	4.8	5.2	5.3	4.5
Nonoccupants	1,000	7.5	6.5	5.6	5.5	5.9	5.8	5.6	5.3	4.9
Pedestrians	1,000	6.5	5.6	4.8	4.7	4.9	4.8	4.7	4.4	4.1
Pedalcyclist	1,000	0.9	0.8	0.7	0.7	0.8	0.8	0.7	0.7	0.6
Other/unknown	1,000	0.1	0.1	0.1	0.1	0.2	0.2	0.2	0.2	0.2
Traffic death rates: [3, 6]										
Per 100 million vehicle miles	Rate....	2.1	1.7	1.5	1.4	1.5	1.4	1.4	1.3	1.1
Per 100,000 licensed drivers	Rate....	26.7	23.7	22.0	21.5	21.7	21.1	20.1	18.0	(NA)
Per 100,000 registered vehicles	Rate....	24.2	21.2	19.3	18.0	17.7	17.0	16.1	14.5	(NA)
Per 100,000 resident population	Rate....	17.9	15.9	14.9	14.6	14.7	14.3	13.7	12.3	11.0

NA Not available. Z Fewer than 50. [1] Covers only accidents occurring on the road. Data are estimated. Year-to-year comparisons should be made with caution. [2] Deaths that occur within 1 year of accident. Includes collision categories, not shown separately. [3] Within 30 days of accident. Source: U.S. National Highway Traffic Safety Administration, *Traffic Safety Facts*, annual; and unpublished data. See Internet site <http://www-nrd.nhtsa.dot.gov/CATS/index.aspx>. [4] See footnotes 2 and 3 in Table 1107. [5] Includes motorized cycles. [6] Based on 30-day definition of traffic deaths.

Source: Except as noted, National Safety Council, Itasca, IL, *Injury Facts*, annual (copyright). See also <http://www.nsc.org/>.

Table 1104. Traffic Fatalities by State: 1990 to 2009

[For deaths within 30 days of the accident]

State	1990	2000	2005	2009	Fatality rate [1] 1990	Fatality rate [1] 2009	State	1990	2000	2005	2009	Fatality rate [1] 1990	Fatality rate [1] 2009
U.S.	44,599	41,945	43,510	33,808	2.1	1.1	MO.	1,097	1,157	1,257	878	2.2	1.3
AL	1,121	996	1,148	848	2.6	1.5	MT	212	237	251	221	2.5	2.0
AK	98	106	73	64	2.5	1.3	NE	262	276	276	223	1.9	1.2
AZ	869	1,036	1,179	807	2.5	1.3	NV	343	323	427	243	3.4	1.2
AR	604	652	654	585	2.9	1.8	NH	158	126	166	110	1.6	0.9
CA	5,192	3,753	4,333	3,081	2.0	1.0	NJ	886	731	747	583	1.5	0.8
CO	544	681	606	465	2.0	1.0	NM	499	432	488	361	3.1	1.4
CT	385	341	278	223	1.5	0.7	NY	2,217	1,460	1,434	1,156	2.1	0.9
DE	138	123	133	116	2.1	1.3	NC	1,385	1,557	1,547	1,314	2.2	1.3
DC	48	48	48	29	1.4	0.8	ND	112	86	123	140	1.9	1.7
FL	2,891	2,999	3,518	2,558	2.6	1.3	OH	1,638	1,366	1,321	1,021	1.8	0.9
GA	1,562	1,541	1,729	1,284	2.2	1.2	OK	641	650	803	738	1.9	1.6
HI	177	132	140	109	2.2	1.1	OR	579	451	487	377	2.2	1.1
ID	244	276	275	226	2.5	1.5	PA	1,646	1,520	1,616	1,256	1.9	1.2
IL	1,589	1,418	1,363	911	1.9	0.9	RI	84	80	87	83	1.1	1.0
IN	1,049	886	938	693	2.0	0.9	SC	979	1,065	1,094	894	2.8	1.8
IA	465	445	450	372	2.0	1.2	SD	153	173	186	131	2.2	1.4
KS	444	461	428	386	1.9	1.3	TN	1,177	1,307	1,270	989	2.5	1.4
KY	849	820	985	791	2.5	1.7	TX	3,250	3,779	3,536	3,071	2.1	1.3
LA	959	938	963	821	2.5	1.8	UT	272	373	282	244	1.9	0.9
ME	213	169	169	159	1.8	1.1	VT	90	76	73	74	1.5	1.0
MD	707	588	614	547	1.7	1.0	VA	1,079	929	947	757	1.8	0.9
MA	605	433	441	334	1.3	0.6	WA	825	631	649	492	1.8	0.9
MI	1,571	1,382	1,129	871	1.9	0.9	WV	481	411	374	356	3.1	1.8
MN	566	625	559	421	1.5	0.7	WI	769	799	815	561	1.7	1.0
MS	750	949	931	700	3.1	1.7	WY	125	152	170	134	2.1	1.4

[1] Deaths per 100 million vehicle miles traveled.

Source: U.S. National Highway Traffic Safety Administration, *Traffic Safety Facts*, annual. See also <http://www-nrd.nhtsa.dot.gov/CATS/index.aspx>.

Table 1105. Fatal Motor Vehicle Accidents—National Summary: 1990 to 2009

[Based on data from the Fatality Analysis Reporting System (FARS). FARS gathers data on accidents that result in loss of human life. FARS is operated and maintained by National Highway Traffic Safety Administration's (NHTSA), National Center for Statistics and Analysis (NCSA). FARS data are gathered on motor vehicle accidents that occurred on a roadway customarily open to the public, resulting in the death of a person within 30 days of the accident. Collection of these data depend on the use of police, hospital, medical examiner/coroner, and Emergency Medical Services reports; state vehicle registration, driver licensing, and highway department files; and vital statistics documents and death certificates. See source for further detail]

Item	1990	1995	2000	2005	2006	2007	2008	2009
Fatal crashes, total	**39,836**	**37,241**	**37,526**	**39,252**	**38,648**	**37,435**	**34,172**	**30,797**
One vehicle involved	23,445	21,250	21,117	22,678	22,701	22,167	20,644	18,745
Two or more vehicles involved	16,391	15,991	16,409	16,574	15,947	15,268	13,528	12,052
Persons killed in fatal crashes [1]	**44,599**	**41,817**	**41,945**	**43,510**	**42,708**	**41,259**	**37,423**	**33,808**
Occupants	33,890	33,064	36,348	33,070	32,119	30,527	26,791	24,474
Drivers	22,854	22,370	25,567	23,237	22,831	21,717	19,279	17,640
Passengers	10,931	10,576	10,695	9,750	9,187	8,716	7,441	6,770
Other	105	118	86	83	101	94	71	64
Motorcyclists	3,244	2,227	2,897	4,576	4,837	5,174	5,312	4,462
Nonoccupants	7,465	6,526	5,597	5,864	5,752	5,558	5,320	4,872
Pedestrians	6,482	5,584	4,763	4,892	4,795	4,699	4,414	4,092
Pedalcyclists	859	833	693	786	772	701	718	630
Other	124	109	141	186	185	158	188	150
Occupants killed by vehicle type:								
Passenger cars	24,092	22,423	20,699	18,512	17,925	16,614	14,646	13,095
Mini-compact (95 inches)	3,556	2,207	1,113	452	416	347	270	212
Subcompact (95 to 99 inches)	4,753	4,584	3,660	2,536	2,228	1,931	1,667	1,333
Compact (100 to 104 inches)	5,310	6,899	7,022	6,288	6,105	5,538	4,780	4,128
Intermediate (105 to 109) inches	4,849	4,666	5,204	5,571	5,461	5,243	4,763	4,393
Full-size (110 to 114) inches	2,386	2,116	2,287	2,491	2,520	2,410	2,210	2,175
Largest (115 inches and over)	2,249	1,297	897	796	773	780	755	674
Unknown	989	654	516	378	422	365	201	180
Motorcycles and Other Motorized Cycles	3,129	2,114	2,897	4,576	4,837	5,174	5,312	4,462
Motorcycles	3,014	2,001	2,783	4,418	4,679	4,986	5,060	4,222
Other motorized cycles	115	113	114	158	158	188	252	240
Light trucks [2]	8,601	9,568	11,526	13,037	12,761	12,458	10,816	10,287
Pickup	5,979	5,938	6,003	6,067	5,993	5,847	5,097	4,792
Utility	1,214	1,935	3,358	4,831	4,928	4,834	4,214	4,091
Van	1,154	1,639	2,129	2,112	1,815	1,764	1,492	1,394
Other	254	56	36	27	25	13	13	10
Large trucks [3]	705	648	754	804	805	805	682	503
Medium trucks	134	96	106	118	107	112	91	81
Heavy trucks	571	552	648	686	698	693	592	422
Buses	32	33	22	58	27	36	67	26
Other vehicles	296	307	401	492	500	540	523	481
Unknown	164	85	49	167	101	74	57	82
Persons involved in fatal crashes	**107,777**	**102,102**	**100,716**	**101,262**	**98,356**	**94,338**	**84,510**	**76,309**
Occupants	99,297	94,621	94,325	94,614	91,860	88,136	78,500	70,845
Drivers	58,893	56,164	57,280	59,220	57,846	56,019	50,416	45,230
Passengers	40,229	38,252	36,889	35,231	33,826	31,919	27,924	25,470
Other	175	205	156	163	188	198	160	145
Nonoccupants	8,480	7,481	6,391	6,648	6,496	6,202	6,010	5,464
Vehicle miles traveled (VMT) [4] (bil.)	2,144	2,423	2,747	2,989	3,014	3,031	2,977	2,954
Licensed drivers (1,000)	167,015	176,628	190,625	200,549	202,810	205,742	208,321	209,618
Registered vehicles (1,000)	184,275	197,065	217,028	247,031	252,930	257,472	259,360	258,958
Percent distribution of fatal accidents by the highest driver (BAC) in accident: [5]								
0.00 percent	54.0	62.1	62.7	63.3	62.6	62.4	63.1	62.3
0.01 to 0.07 percent	6.3	5.5	5.6	5.4	5.7	5.9	5.6	5.6
0.08 percent and over	39.4	32.1	31.4	31.1	31.4	31.5	31.1	31.9
Percent distribution of fatal accidents by the highest (BAC) in accident: [5]								
0.00 percent	49.5	57.7	58.7	59.5	58.4	58.4	58.6	58.0
0.01 to 0.07 percent	6.5	5.7	5.9	5.6	6.0	6.1	5.8	5.7
0.08 percent and over	44.0	36.7	35.4	34.9	35.6	35.6	35.5	36.3
Fatalities per 100,000 resident population								
Under 5 years old	4.90	4.30	3.70	2.94	2.81	2.44	1.95	2.02
5 to 9 years old	5.14	4.48	3.55	3.00	2.62	2.36	1.95	1.84
10 to 15 years old	7.60	7.23	5.65	4.67	4.33	4.27	3.41	3.02
16 to 20 years old	36.66	31.59	29.38	27.48	26.63	24.97	20.78	18.08
21 to 24 years old	33.47	29.68	27.02	27.73	27.78	26.74	23.25	19.11
25 to 34 years old	22.78	19.44	17.29	17.82	17.99	16.92	15.66	13.69
35 to 44 years old	16.11	15.10	15.08	15.08	14.78	14.27	12.88	11.62
45 to 54 years old	14.83	13.39	13.79	14.59	14.47	14.06	13.07	12.10
55 to 64 years old	15.00	13.92	13.61	13.88	13.31	12.61	12.03	10.87
65 to 74 years old	17.03	16.64	15.29	15.16	13.82	13.46	12.26	11.42
75 years old and over	25.45	26.09	23.29	20.47	18.76	18.17	16.56	15.52
Fatalities per 100 million VMT [4]	2.08	1.73	1.53	1.46	1.42	1.36	1.26	1.14
Fatalities per 100,000 licensed drivers	26.70	23.68	22.00	21.70	21.06	20.05	17.96	16.13
VMT [5] per registered vehicle	11,637	12,294	12,657	12,100	11,916	11,772	11,478	11,407
Fatalities per 100,000 registered vehicles	24.20	21.22	19.33	17.61	16.89	16.02	14.43	13.06
Fatal crashes per 100 million VMT [4]	2.08	1.73	1.53	1.46	1.42	1.36	1.26	1.14
Fatalities per 100,000 resident population	17.88	15.91	14.87	14.71	14.30	13.68	12.30	11.01

[1] Deaths within 30 days of the accident. Starting with 1995, total does not include motorcyclist data. [2] Trucks with a gross vehicle weight rating of 10,000 pounds or less, including pickups, vans, truck-based station wagons, and utility vehicles. [3] Trucks with a gross vehicle weight rating of over 10,000 pounds. [4] VMT = vehicle miles of travel. [5] BAC = blood alcohol concentration.
Source: U.S. National Highway Traffic Safety Administration, Fatality Analysis Reporting System, annual. See also <http://www-nrd.nhtsa.dot.gov/CATS/index.aspx>.

Table 1106. Motor Vehicle Occupants and Nonoccupants Killed and Injured: 1980 to 2009

[For deaths within 30 days of the accident. (3,231 represents 3,231,000)]

Year	Total	Occupants							Nonoccupants			
		Total	Passenger cars	Light trucks [1]	Large trucks [1]	Buses	Other/ unknown [2]	Motorcycle riders [3]	Total	Pedestrian	Pedal-cyclist	Other/ unknown [2]
KILLED												
1980.........	51,091	36,783	27,449	7,486	1,262	46	540	5,144	9,164	8,070	965	129
1985.........	43,825	31,479	23,212	6,689	977	57	544	4,564	7,782	6,808	890	84
1990.........	44,599	33,890	24,092	8,601	705	32	460	3,244	7,465	6,482	859	124
1995.........	41,817	33,064	22,423	9,568	648	33	392	2,227	6,526	5,584	833	109
1998.........	41,501	33,088	21,194	10,705	742	38	409	2,294	6,119	5,228	760	131
1999.........	41,717	33,392	20,862	11,265	759	59	447	2,483	5,842	4,939	754	149
2000.........	41,945	33,451	20,699	11,526	754	22	450	2,897	5,597	4,763	693	141
2001.........	42,196	33,243	20,320	11,723	708	34	458	3,197	5,756	4,901	732	123
2002.........	43,005	34,105	20,569	12,274	689	45	528	3,270	5,630	4,851	665	114
2003.........	42,884	33,627	19,725	12,546	726	41	589	3,714	5,543	4,774	629	140
2004.........	42,836	33,276	19,192	12,674	766	42	602	4,028	5,532	4,675	727	130
2005.........	43,510	33,070	18,512	13,037	804	58	659	4,576	5,864	4,892	786	186
2006.........	42,708	32,119	17,925	12,761	805	27	601	4,837	5,752	4,795	772	185
2007.........	41,259	30,527	16,614	12,458	805	36	614	5,174	5,558	4,699	701	158
2008.........	37,423	26,791	14,646	10,816	682	67	580	5,312	5,320	4,414	718	188
2009.........	33,808	24,474	13,095	10,287	503	26	563	4,462	4,872	4,092	630	150
INJURED (1,000)												
1990.........	3,231	2,960	2,376	505	42	33	4	84	187	105	75	7
1995.........	3,465	3,246	2,469	722	30	19	4	57	162	86	67	10
1998.........	3,192	3,012	2,201	763	29	16	4	49	131	69	53	8
1999.........	3,236	3,047	2,138	847	33	22	7	50	140	85	51	3
2000.........	3,189	2,997	2,052	887	31	18	10	58	134	78	51	5
2001.........	3,033	2,841	1,927	861	29	15	9	60	131	78	45	8
2002.........	2,926	2,735	1,805	879	26	19	6	65	126	71	48	7
2003.........	2,889	2,697	1,756	889	27	18	7	67	124	70	46	8
2004.........	2,788	2,594	1,643	900	27	16	7	76	118	68	41	9
2005.........	2,699	2,494	1,573	872	27	11	10	87	118	64	45	8
2006.........	2,575	2,375	1,475	857	23	10	11	88	112	61	44	7
2007.........	2,491	2,264	1,379	841	23	12	8	103	124	70	43	10
2008.........	2,346	2,120	1,340	768	23	15	9	96	130	69	52	9
2009.........	2,217	2,011	1,216	759	17	12	7	90	116	59	51	7

[1] See footnotes 2 and 3, Table 1107. [2] Includes combination trucks. [3] Includes motorized cycles.
Source: U.S. National Highway Traffic Safety Administration, *Traffic Safety Facts*, annual, and unpublished data.
See also <http://www-nrd.nhtsa.dot.gov/CATS/index.aspx>.

Table 1107. Vehicles Involved in Crashes by Vehicle Type, Rollover Occurrence, and Crash Severity: 2009

[9,534.4 represents 9,534,400. Excludes motorcycles]

Crash severity by vehicle type	Total		Rollover occurrence			
			Yes		No	
	Number (1,000)	Percent	Number (1,000)	Percent	Number (1,000)	Percent
Vehicles involved in all crashes [1]	**9,534.4**	**100.0**	**230.1**	**2.4**	**9,304.3**	**97.6**
Passenger cars	5,211.0	100.0	83.6	1.6	5,127.4	98.4
Light trucks: [2]						
Pickup	1,386.5	100.0	52.0	3.8	1,334.5	96.2
Utility	1,642.8	100.0	66.4	4.0	1,576.4	96.0
Van...........................	630.0	100.0	9.7	1.5	620.3	98.5
Other..........................	290.8	100.0	4.6	1.6	286.2	98.4
Large truck [3]	295.9	100.0	9.8	3.3	286.1	96.7
Bus	57.6	100.0	(Z)	(Z)	57.6	100.0
Other/unknown	19.9	100.0	4.0	20.1	15.9	79.9
Fatal crashes....................	40.8	100.0	8.7	21.4	32.1	78.6
Passenger cars	18.4	100.0	3.0	16.4	15.3	83.6
Light trucks: [2]						
Pickup	8.5	100.0	2.4	28.1	6.1	71.9
Utility	6.9	100.0	2.2	32.3	4.7	67.7
Van...........................	2.5	100.0	0.4	17.0	2.1	83.0
Other..........................	(Z)	100.0	(Z)	18.8	(Z)	81.3
Large truck [3]	3.2	100.0	0.4	13.1	2.8	86.9
Bus	0.2	100.0	(Z)	3.2	0.2	96.8
Other/unknown	1.2	100.0	0.2	21.1	0.9	78.9

Z less than 50 or 0.05. [1] Includes injury and property-only crashes, not shown separately. [2] Trucks of 10,000 pounds gross vehicle weight rating or less, including pickups, vans, truck-based station wagons and utility vehicles. [3] Trucks over 10,000 pounds gross vehicle weight rating.
Source: U.S. National Highway Traffic Safety Administration, *Traffic Safety Facts*, annual. See also <http://www-nrd.nhtsa.dot.gov/CATS/index.aspx>.

Transportation 695

Table 1108. Speeding-Related Traffic Fatalities by Road Type, Speed Limit, and State: 2009

[Speeding consists of exceeding the posted speed limit or driving too fast for the road conditions or any speed-related violation charged (racing, driving above speed limit, speed greater than reasonable, exceeding special speed limit)]

State	Traffic fatalities, total	Speeding-related fatalities by road type and speed limit								
			Interstate		Noninterstate					
		Total [1]	Over 55 mph	At or under 55 mph	55 mph	50 mph	45 mph	40 mph	35 mph	Under 35 mph
United States	33,808	10,591	964	287	2,701	465	1,508	724	1,279	1,277
Alabama	848	327	21	2	75	10	100	24	27	27
Alaska	64	26	5	5	8	1	6	–	1	–
Arizona	807	283	54	6	23	20	61	13	25	33
Arkansas	585	105	19	2	39	3	11	4	12	11
California	3,081	1,087	145	18	266	39	100	100	161	119
Colorado	465	171	17	8	21	14	11	21	21	23
Connecticut	223	103	10	6	6	4	13	15	7	40
Delaware	116	44	5	1	8	14	6	3	2	3
District of Columbia	29	10	–	1	–		1	–	–	8
Florida	2,558	535	56	17	78	19	127	36	73	85
Georgia	1,284	238	17	13	54	10	42	12	47	30
Hawaii	109	59	–	5	2	1	10	1	20	20
Idaho	226	81	8	–	15	8	8	–	4	7
Illinois.	911	325	41	10	113	5	23	15	27	64
Indiana.	693	174	20	3	53	8	27	16	19	25
Iowa	372	62	5	3	28	4	3	1	8	8
Kansas.	386	103	9	–	43	3	6	5	5	15
Kentucky	791	154	7	3	85	4	18	–	24	11
Louisiana	821	288	30	1	115	8	49	5	35	19
Maine.	159	61	2	2	10	7	18	4	7	5
Maryland	547	184	10	21	15	39	11	37	18	28
Massachusetts.	334	76	13	4	4	3	4	4	9	30
Michigan	871	205	16	2	95	7	16	7	17	34
Minnesota	421	95	5	5	48	4	2	2	1	20
Mississippi	700	106	9	1	24	4	25	4	18	10
Missouri	878	379	26	12	124	23	29	19	54	38
Montana.	221	86	15	1	5	1	5	–	6	8
Nebraska	223	30	7	–	1	7	1	2	1	2
Nevada	243	91	12	2	11	–	23	–	20	8
New Hampshire	110	39	3	1	2	6	1	1	14	11
New Jersey	583	95	2	3	5	24	8	4	13	29
New Mexico	361	69	5	5	9	1	4	5	6	11
New York	1,156	368	6	8	142	11	32	22	20	57
North Carolina	1,314	517	32	2	270	9	125	8	49	13
North Dakota	140	32	4	1	10	–	3	–	1	2
Ohio.	1,021	287	22	4	129	11	21	12	55	25
Oklahoma	738	234	26	2	25	7	83	18	8	14
Oregon.	377	125	7	1	55	3	16	6	8	8
Pennsylvania	1,256	634	19	37	152	12	131	94	116	54
Rhode Island	83	28	–	5	–	2	–	–	4	9
South Carolina.	894	337	37	1	99	9	84	29	43	22
South Dakota	131	41	12	–	19	2	2	–	2	–
Tennessee	989	209	10	10	35	10	48	30	29	30
Texas	3,071	1,228	106	37	149	40	116	104	132	140
Utah	244	104	23	5	9	9	5	12	10	10
Vermont.	74	22	1	–	2	8	–	2	5	3
Virginia.	757	147	8	8	45	3	20	8	27	18
Washington	492	208	16	–	15	22	15	10	41	44
West Virginia	356	120	20	1	44	2	13	5	11	8
Wisconsin	561	203	8	2	105	–	21	3	14	36
Wyoming	134	56	13	–	11	4	4	1	2	2

– Represents zero. [1] Includes fatalities that occurred on roads for which the speed limit was unknown.

Source: U.S. National Highway Traffic Safety Administration, *Traffic Safety Facts, Speeding*, annual. See also <http://www-nrd.nhtsa.dot.gov/CATS/index.aspx>.

Table 1109. Distracted Drivers—Crashes/Road Fatalities and Injuries: 2005 to 2009

["Distraction" is defined as a specific type of inattention that occurs when drivers divert their attention from the driving task to focus on some other activity instead. It is worth noting that "distraction" is a subset of "inattention" (which also includes fatigue, physical conditions of the driver, and emotional conditions of the driver). For more information, see the appendices of the report at <http://www-nrd.nhtsa.dot.gov/Pubs/811379.pdf>]

Description	2005	2008	2009	Description	2005	2008	2009
Fatal crashes [1]				Drivers	4,217	5,477	5,084
				Percentage	7	11	11
Overall:				Fatalities	4,472	5,838	5,474
Crashes	39,252	34,172	30,797	Percentage	10	16	16
Drivers	59,220	50,416	45,230	People injured in crashes: [3]			
Fatalities	43,510	37,423	33,808	Overall	2,699,000	2,346,000	2,217,000
Involving driver distraction: [2]				Involving distraction:			
Crashes	4,026	5,307	4,898	Estimate.	604,000	466,000	448,000
Percentage	10	16	16	Percentage of total.	22	20	20

[1] Source: NHTSA's Fatality Analysis Reporting System (FARS). [2] For multi-vehicle crashes, the crash was reported as a distracted-driving crash if at least one driver was reported as distracted. In some of these multi-vehicle crashes, multiple drivers were reported as distracted. [3] Source: National Automotive Sampling System (NASS) General Estimates System (GES).

Source: U.S. National Highway Traffic Safety Administration, *Traffic Safety Facts*, Research Note, "An Examination of Driver Distraction as Recorded in the NHTSA Databases." See also <http://www-nrd.nhtsa.dot.gov/CATS/index.aspx>.

Table 1110. Fatalities by Highest Driver Blood Alcohol Concentration (BAC) in the Crash: 1990 to 2009

[g/dl means grams per deciliter. A motor vehicle crash is considered to be alcohol-impaired if at least one driver involved in the crash is determined to have had a BAC of .08 g/dL or higher. Thus, any fatality that occurs in an alcohol-impaired crash is considered an alcohol-impaired-driving fatality. The term "alcohol-impaired" does not indicate that a crash or fatality was caused by the presence of alcohol. A person is considered to be legally impaired with a BAC of .08 g/dl or more]

Item	1990	1995	2000	2005	2006	2007	2008	2009
Total Fatalities [1]	**44,599**	**41,817**	**41,945**	**43,510**	**42,708**	**41,259**	**37,423**	**33,808**
BAC=.00								
Number	23,823	25,768	26,082	27,423	26,633	25,611	23,499	20,961
Percent	53.4	61.6	62.2	63.0	62.4	62.1	62.8	62.0
BAC=.01–.07								
Number	2,901	2,416	2,422	2,404	2,479	2,494	2,115	1,905
Percent	6.5	5.8	5.8	5.5	5.8	6.0	5.7	5.6
Alcohol-Impaired-Driving Fatalities BAC=.08+								
Number	17,705	13,478	13,324	13,582	13,491	13,041	11,711	10,839
Percent	39.7	32.2	31.8	31.2	31.6	31.6	31.3	32.1

[1] Total fatalities include those in which there was no driver or motorcycle rider present.
Source: U.S. National Highway Traffic Safety Administration, *Traffic Safety Facts*, annual; and unpublished data. See also <http://www-nrd.nhtsa.dot.gov/CATS/index.aspx>.

Table 1111. Traffic Fatalities by State and Highest Driver Blood Alcohol Concentration (BAC) in the Crash: 2009

[See headnote, Table 1110]

State	Traffic fatalities, total [1]	(BAC=.00) Number	(BAC=.00) Percent	(BAC=.01–.07) Number	(BAC=.01–.07) Percent	Alcohol impaired driving fatalities (BAC=.08 or more) Number	Alcohol impaired driving fatalities (BAC=.08 or more) Percent	(BAC=.01 or more) Number	(BAC=.01 or more) Percent
United States	**33,808**	**20,961**	**62**	**1,905**	**6**	**10,839**	**32**	**12,744**	**38**
Alabama	848	522	62	46	5	280	33	325	38
Alaska	64	42	65	3	4	20	31	22	35
Arizona	807	514	64	42	5	219	27	260	32
Arkansas	585	372	64	43	7	168	29	211	36
California	3,081	1,956	63	168	5	950	31	1,118	36
Colorado	465	285	61	20	4	158	34	178	38
Connecticut	223	109	49	15	7	99	44	114	51
Delaware	116	68	58	4	3	45	38	48	42
District of Columbia	29	17	59	2	7	10	35	12	41
Florida	2,558	1,649	64	134	5	770	30	904	35
Georgia	1,284	885	69	63	5	331	26	394	31
Hawaii	109	51	47	6	6	52	48	59	54
Idaho	226	160	71	7	3	58	26	65	29
Illinois.	911	530	58	62	7	319	35	381	42
Indiana.	693	443	64	39	6	210	30	249	36
Iowa	372	254	68	22	6	96	26	118	32
Kansas.	386	208	54	23	6	154	40	177	46
Kentucky	791	550	70	45	6	194	25	239	30
Louisiana	821	455	55	72	9	295	36	366	45
Maine.	159	106	67	6	4	47	29	53	33
Maryland	547	354	65	32	6	162	30	194	35
Massachusetts.	334	201	60	23	7	108	32	130	39
Michigan	871	579	66	45	5	246	28	291	33
Minnesota	421	289	69	23	5	108	26	131	31
Mississippi	700	436	62	30	4	234	33	264	38
Missouri	878	518	59	58	7	300	34	358	41
Montana.	221	129	58	11	5	81	36	92	42
Nebraska	223	135	61	22	10	66	30	88	39
Nevada	243	152	63	22	9	68	28	90	37
New Hampshire	110	73	66	7	6	30	27	36	33
New Jersey	583	397	68	36	6	149	25	185	32
New Mexico	361	232	64	15	4	114	32	129	36
New York	1,156	766	66	68	6	321	28	388	34
North Carolina	1,314	879	67	67	5	363	28	430	33
North Dakota	140	81	58	6	4	54	38	59	42
Ohio.	1,021	643	63	54	5	324	32	378	37
Oklahoma	738	473	64	30	4	235	32	265	36
Oregon.	377	235	62	26	7	115	30	141	37
Pennsylvania	1,256	783	62	64	5	406	32	470	37
Rhode Island	83	43	52	7	8	34	40	40	48
South Carolina	894	468	52	47	5	377	42	423	47
South Dakota	131	69	53	6	5	53	40	59	45
Tennessee	989	642	65	42	4	303	31	345	35
Texas	3,071	1,628	53	202	7	1,235	40	1,437	47
Utah.	244	190	78	14	6	40	16	54	22
Vermont	74	46	62	4	6	23	32	28	37
Virginia.	757	476	63	34	5	243	32	278	37
Washington	492	259	53	26	5	206	42	232	47
West Virginia	356	221	62	19	5	115	32	134	38
Wisconsin	561	308	55	38	7	213	38	251	45
Wyoming	134	81	60	7	5	47	35	54	40

[1] Total fatalities include those in which there was no driver or motorcycle rider present.
Source: U.S. National Highway Traffic Safety Administration, *Traffic Safety Facts*, annual. See also <http://www-nrd.nhtsa.dot.gov/CATS/index.aspx>.

Transportation 697

Table 1112. Crashes by Crash Severity: 1990 to 2009

[6,471 represents 6,471,000. A crash is a police-reported event that produces injury and/or property damage, involves a vehicle in transport and occurs on a trafficway or while the vehicle is in motion after running off the trafficway]

Item	1990	1995	2000	2004	2005	2006	2007	2008	2009
Crashes (1,000)	**6,471**	**6,699**	**6,394**	**6,181**	**6,159**	**5,973**	**6,024**	**5,811**	**5,505**
Fatal..................	39.8	37.2	37.5	38.4	39.3	38.6	37.4	34.2	30.8
Nonfatal injury	2,122	2,217	2,070	1,862	1,816	1,746	1,711	1,630	1,517
Property damage only	4,309	4,446	4,286	4,281	4,304	4,189	4,275	4,146	3,957
Percent of total crashes:									
Fatal..................	0.6	0.6	0.6	0.6	0.6	0.6	0.6	0.6	0.6
Nonfatal injury	32.8	33.1	32.4	30.1	29.5	29.2	28.4	28.1	27.6
Property damage only	66.6	66.4	67.0	69.3	69.9	70.1	71.0	71.4	71.9

Source: U.S. National Highway Safety Traffic Administration, *Traffic Safety Facts*, annual. See also <http://www-nrd.nhtsa.dot .gov/CATS/index.aspx>.

Table 1113. Alcohol Involvement for Drivers in Fatal Crashes: 1999 and 2009

[BAC = blood alcohol concentration]

Age, sex, and vehicle type	1999		2009	
	Number of drivers	Percentage with BAC of .08% or greater	Number of drivers	Percentage with BAC of .08% or greater
Total drivers involved in fatal crashes [1]	**56,502**	**20.3**	**45,230**	**22.3**
Drivers by age group:				
Under 16 years old	333	9.6	181	7.2
16 to 20 years old	7,985	16.9	5,051	18.8
21 to 24 years old	5,639	31.4	4,597	34.5
25 to 34 years old	11,763	27.6	8,610	31.6
35 to 44 years old	11,059	24.8	7,757	25.9
45 to 54 years old	7,708	17.1	7,664	22.1
55 to 64 years old	4,608	10.8	5,276	12.7
65 to 74 years old	3,251	6.9	2,868	6.9
75 years old and over	3,346	3.7	2,547	3.3
Drivers by sex:				
Male..................................	41,012	23.4	32,807	25.4
Female................................	14,835	11.6	11,825	13.7
Drivers by vehicle type:				
Passenger cars	27,878	21.3	18,279	23.2
Light trucks [2]	19,865	22.3	17,822	23.2
Large trucks [2].........................	4,868	1.5	3,187	1.7
Motorcycles............................	2,528	32.8	4,593	28.6
Buses................................	318	0.9	221	–

– Represents zero. [1] Includes age and sex unknown, and other and unknown types of vehicles. [2] See footnotes 2 and 3, Table 1107.

Source: U.S. National Highway Traffic Safety Administration, *Traffic Safety Facts*, annual. See also <http://www-nrd.nhtsa.dot .gov/CATS/index.aspx>.

Table 1114. Licensed Drivers and Number in Accidents by Age: 2009

[211,000 represents 211,000,000]

Age group	Licensed drivers		Drivers in accidents				Accident rates per number of drivers	
			Fatal		All			
	Number (1,000)	Percent	Number	Percent	Number (1,000)	Percent	Fatal [1]	All [2]
Total.................	**211,000**	**100.0**	**48,000**	**100.0**	**16,500**	**100.0**	**23**	**8**
19 years old and under	10,326	4.9	3,900	8.1	2,020	12.2	38	20
Under 16 years old	658	0.3	200	0.4	250	1.5	(3)	(3)
16 years old..............	1,311	0.6	500	1.0	300	1.8	38	23
17 years old..............	2,145	1.0	700	1.5	420	2.5	33	20
18 years old..............	2,854	1.4	1,200	2.5	530	3.2	42	19
19 years old..............	3,358	1.6	1,300	2.7	520	3.1	39	15
20 to 24 years old	17,465	8.3	6,300	13.1	2,480	15.0	36	14
20 years old..............	3,404	1.6	1,400	2.9	500	3.0	41	15
21 years old..............	3,447	1.6	1,400	2.9	490	3.0	41	14
22 years old..............	3,444	1.6	1,200	2.5	470	2.8	35	14
23 years old..............	3,551	1.7	1,200	2.5	620	3.7	34	17
24 years old..............	3,619	1.7	1,100	2.3	400	2.4	30	11
25 to 34 years old	36,694	17.4	8,800	18.3	3,270	19.8	24	9
35 to 44 years old	38,424	18.2	7,500	15.6	2,910	17.6	20	8
45 to 54 years old	41,921	19.9	8,300	17.3	2,750	16.7	20	7
55 to 64 years old	33,271	15.8	5,900	12.3	1,710	10.4	18	5
65 to 74 years old	19,135	9.1	3,500	7.3	820	5.0	18	4
75 years old and over	13,764	6.5	3,800	7.9	540	3.3	28	4

[1] Per 100,000 licensed drivers. [2] Per 100 licensed drivers. [3] Rates for drivers under age 16 are substantially overstated due to the high proportion of unlicensed drivers involved.

Source: National Safety Council, Itasca, IL, *Injury Facts, annual* (copyright). See also <http://www.nsc.org/>.

Table 1115. Passenger Transit Industry—Summary: 1990 to 2009

[16,053 represents $16,053,000,000. Includes Puerto Rico. Includes aggregate information for all transit systems in the United States. Excludes nontransit services such as taxicab, school bus, unregulated jitney (a small bus or automobile that transport passengers on a route for a small fare), sightseeing bus, intercity bus, and special application mass transportation systems (e.g., amusement parks, airports, island, and urban park ferries). Includes active vehicles only]

Item	Unit	1990	1995	2000	2005	2007	2008	2009
Operating systems.............	Number	5,078	5,973	6,000	6,429	7,700	7,700	7,200
Motor bus systems	Number	2,688	2,250	2,262	1,500	1,200	1,100	1,088
Revenue vehicles, active	Number	93,553	116,473	131,918	150,827	163,973	169,436	172,893
Motor bus.................	Number	58,714	67,107	75,013	82,027	65,249	66,506	64,832
Commuter rail	Number	5,007	5,164	5,498	6,392	6,391	6,617	6,941
Demand response [1]..........	Number	16,471	29,352	33,080	41,958	64,865	65,799	68,957
Heavy rail..................	Number	10,419	10,157	10,591	11,110	11,222	11,377	11,461
Light rail...................	Number	913	999	1,577	1,645	1,810	1,969	2,068
Trolley bus	Number	832	885	951	615	559	590	531
Other	Number	1,197	2,809	5,208	7,080	13,877	16,578	18,103
Operating funding, total	Mil. dol	16,053	18,241	24,243	31,708	35,541	37,975	38,918
Agency funds..............	Mil. dol	6,786	8,069	11,004	12,559	13,473	14,304	14,549
Passenger funding..........	Mil. dol	5,891	6,801	8,746	10,269	11,145	11,860	12,273
Other	Mil. dol	895	1,268	2,258	2,290	2,328	2,444	2,276
Government funds [2]..........	Mil. dol	9,267	10,172	13,239	19,149	22,068	23,671	24,369
Directly generated [3]........	Mil. dol	([4])	1,544	1,959	2,694	2,698	2,448	2,543
Local	Mil. dol	5,327	3,981	5,319	6,658	8,322	8,754	8,763
State	Mil. dol	2,970	3,830	4,967	7,495	8,371	9,795	9,857
Federal.................	Mil. dol	970	817	994	2,303	2,678	2,674	3,207
Operating expense	Mil. dol	15,742	17,849	22,646	30,295	33,877	36,398	37,245
Vehicle operations	Mil. dol	6,654	8,282	10,111	13,793	15,560	16,780	16,997
Maintenance	Mil. dol	4,631	5,047	6,445	8,259	9,136	9,651	9,693
General administration	Mil. dol	3,450	2,590	3,329	4,075	4,779	4,983	5,330
Purchased transportation	Mil. dol	1,008	1,930	2,761	4,168	4,402	4,983	5,225
Capital expenditures	Mil. dol	(NA)	7,230	9,587	12,383	14,528	17,765	17,919
Vehicle-miles operated	Million	3,242	3,550	4,081	4,601	5,038	5,204	5,219
Motor bus.................	Million	2,130	2,184	2,315	2,485	2,302	2,377	2,332
Trolley bus	Million	14	14	14	13	11	12	13
Heavy rail.................	Million	537	537	595	646	657	674	685
Light rail..................	Million	24	35	53	69	84	88	91
Commuter rail	Million	213	238	271	303	326	339	344
Demand response [1]..........	Million	306	507	759	978	1,471	1,495	1,529
Other	Million	18	37	74	107	186	219	227
Trips taken	Million	8,799	7,763	9,363	9,815	10,247	10,521	10,381
Motor bus.................	Million	5,677	4,848	5,678	5,855	5,413	5,573	5,452
Trolley bus	Million	126	119	122	107	97	101	104
Heavy rail.................	Million	2,346	2,033	2,632	2,808	3,460	3,547	3,490
Light rail..................	Million	175	251	320	381	419	454	465
Commuter rail	Million	328	344	413	423	459	472	468
Demand response [1]..........	Million	68	88	105	125	209	191	190
Other	Million	79	80	93	117	190	183	212
Avg. fare per trip	Cents	67	88	93	102	109	113	118
Employees, number (avg.) [5]	1,000	273	311	360	367	383	400	403
Payroll, employee	Mil. dol	7,226	8,213	10,400	12,177	13,205	13,914	14,212
Fringe benefits, employee	Mil. dol	3,986	4,484	5,413	8,093	9,092	9,366	9,927

NA Not available. [1] This operation (also called paratransit or dial-a-ride) is comprised of passenger cars, vans or small buses operating in response to calls from passengers or their agents to the transit operator, who then dispatches a vehicle to pick up the passengers and transport them to their destinations. [2] Represents the sum of federal, state, and local assistance, and that portion of directly generated funds that accrue from tax collections, toll transfers from other sectors of operations, and bond proceeds. [3] These are any funds generated from taxes controlled by the transit agency. [4] Funds data are included in local government data through 1993. [5] Through 1990, represents employee equivalents of 2,080 hours = one employee; beginning 1995, equals actual employees.

Source: American Public Transportation Association, Washington, DC, *Public Transportation Fact Book*, annual. See also <http://www.apta.com/resources/statistics/Pages/default.aspx>.

Table 1116. Top Twenty Cities—Transit Savings: 2011

[Individuals who ride public transportation can save on average $10,116 annually based on the April 13, 2011 national average gas price and the national unreserved monthly parking rate. On a per month basis, transit riders can save on average $843 per month. See the monthly press release "Riding Public Transit Saves Individuals" dated April 13 at <http://www.apta.com/mediacenter/pressreleases/2011/Pages/default.aspx>. This release and other monthly "Transit Savings" releases contain information and methodology on how savings are calculated. The cities with the highest transit ridership are ranked in order of their transit savings based on the purchase of a monthly public transit pass and factoring in local gas prices for and the local monthly unreserved parking rate]

City	Savings (dollars)		City	Savings (dollars)	
	Monthly	Annual		Monthly	Annual
New York	1,213	14,561	Portland..........	862	10,345
Boston	1,114	13,368	Denver...........	859	10,311
San Francisco	1,106	13,268	Cleveland.........	853	10,230
Chicago	1,016	12,192	Washington D.C....	850	10,202
Seattle	990	11,875	Baltimore	848	10,176
Philadelphia.......	974	11,684	Miami............	831	9,973
Honolulu	964	11,562	Dallas............	797	9,564
Los Angeles.......	912	10,939	Pittsburgh	796	9,558
Minneapolis.......	893	10,715	Atlanta...........	786	9,431
San Diego	883	10,592	Las Vegas	780	9,361

Source: American Public Transportation Association, Media Center, Press Releases. See also <http://www.apta.com/resources/statistics/Pages/default.aspx>.

Table 1117. Characteristics of Rail Transit by Transit Authority: 2009

Mode and transit agency	Primary city served	States served	Direc-tional route—miles [1,2]	Number of high-way-rail cross-ings [1]	Number of stations	Number of ADA acces-sible stations [3]
Total [4]	37	33	11,601.2	6,408	3,085	2,014
Heavy rail	11	17	1,602.8	27	1,025	499
Chicago Transit Authority.......................	Chicago	IL, IN	207.8	25	143	89
Greater Cleveland Regional Transit Authority	Cleveland	OH	38.1	–	18	13
L.A. County Metropolitan Transportation Authority	Los Angeles	CA	31.9	–	16	16
Maryland Transit Administration...................	Baltimore	MD	29.4	–	14	14
Massachusetts Bay Transportation Authority.........	Boston	MA, NH, RI	76.3	–	53	49
Metropolitan Atlanta Rapid Transit Authority	Atlanta	GA	96.1	–	38	38
Miami-Dade Transit Agency......................	Miami	FL	45.0	–	22	22
MTA New York City Transit.......................	New York	NY, NJ, CT	493.8	–	468	83
Port Authority Trans-Hudson Corporation	New York	NY, NJ, CT	28.6	2	13	7
Port Authority Transit Corporation	Philadelphia	PA, NJ, DE	31.5	–	13	5
San Francisco Bay Area Rapid Transit District	San Francisco	CA	209.0	–	43	43
Southeastern Pennsylvania Transportation Authority ..	Philadelphia	PA	74.9	–	75	29
Staten Island Rapid Transit Operating Authority	New York	NY, CT	28.6	–	23	5
Washington Metropolitan Area TransitAuthority.......	Washington	DC, MD, VA	211.8	–	86	86
Commuter rail [5]	21	25	8,521.1	3,337	1,224	794
Alaska Railroad Corporation	Anchorage	AK	959.9	133	10	10
Altamont Commuter Express.....................	San Jose	CA	172.0	127	10	10
Central Puget Sound Regional Transit Authority	Seattle	WA	146.9	44	10	10
Connecticut Department of Transportation	Hartford	CT	101.2	3	9	8
Dallas Area Rapid Transit	Dallas	TX	29.0	24	5	5
Fort Worth Transportation Authority...............	Fort Worth	TX	43.3	19	5	5
Maryland Transit Administration...................	Baltimore	MD	400.4	40	42	24
Massachusetts Bay Transportation Authority.........	Boston	MA, NH, RI	737.5	257	133	95
Metro Transit	Minneapolis	MN	77.9	36	6	6
MTA Long Island Rail Road	New York	NY, NJ, CT	638.2	343	124	104
MTA Metro-North Commuter Railroad Co	New York	NY, NJ, CT	545.7	158	110	43
New Jersey Transit Corporation..................	New York	NY, NJ, CT	996.8	317	164	70
North County Transit District	San Diego	CA	82.2	34	8	8
NE Illinois Regional Commuter Rail Corporation......	Chicago	IL, WI	980.4	578	240	168
Northern Indiana Commuter Transportation District ...	Chicago	IL, IN	179.8	117	20	13
Northern New England Passenger Rail Authority	Boston	MA, ME, NH	230.4	65	10	10
Peninsula Corridor Joint Powers Board.............	San Francisco	CA	153.7	46	32	26
Pennsylvania Department of Transportation	Philadelphia	PA	144.4	7	12	4
Regional Transportation Authority	Nashville	TN	62.8	35	6	6
Rio Metro Regional Transit District	Albuquerque	NM	193.1	86	10	10
South Florida Regional Transportation Authority......	Miami	FL	142.2	73	18	18
Southeastern Pennsylvania Transportation Authority ..	Philadelphia	PA	446.9	283	154	55
Southern California Regional Rail Authority	Los Angeles	CA	777.8	436	55	55
Tri-County Metropolitan Transportation District of Oregon	Portland	OR	29.2	27	5	5
Utah Transit Authority	Salt Lake City	UT	87.7	29	8	8
Virginia Railway Express.......................	Washington	DC, VA, MD	161.5	20	18	18

– Represents zero. [1] Vehicles operated in maximum services (VOMS) include directly operated (DO) and Purchase Transportation (PT) by mode. [2] The mileage in each direction over which public transportation vehicles travel while in revenue service. The mileage is computed without regard to the number of traffic lanes or rail tracks existing in the right-of-way. [3] Number of stations that comply with the American with Disabilities Act of 1992 (ADA). Additional stations may be wheelchair accessible but not comply with other provisions of the ADA. [4] Includes light rail, not shown separately. [5] Excludes commuter-type services operated independently by Amtrak.

Source: U.S. Bureau of Transportation Statistics, *State Transportation Statistics, 2010*. See also <http://www.bts.gov/publications/state_transportation_statistics/>. National Transit database; Access NTD data; "Top transit cities." See also <http://www.ntdprogram.gov/ntdprogram/data.htm>.

U.S. Census Bureau, Statistical Abstract of the United States: 2012

Table 1118. Transit Ridership in Selected Urbanized Areas: 2009

Urbanized areas	Annual unlinked passenger trips [1] (1,000)	Area rank based on trips per capita [2]	Unlinked passenger trips per capita	Percent distribution				
				Motor bus	Heavy rail [3]	Light rail [4]	Commuter rail [5]	Other [6]
U.S. urbanized areas	10,063,138	(X)	51.9	53.0	34.6	4.6	4.6	3.1
Atlanta, GA	168,714	26	48.2	49.5	49.4	–	–	1.1
Austin, TX	39,439	27	43.7	97.4	–	–	–	2.6
Baltimore, MD	125,162	17	60.3	74.5	10.8	7.1	6.5	1.2
Boston, MA-NH-RI.	375,540	8	93.1	28.8	39.6	18.8	10.9	1.8
Chicago, IL-IN	633,465	11	76.2	55.1	32.0	–	11.9	0.9
Cincinnati, OH-KY-IN.	27,106	95	18.0	98.3	–	–	–	1.7
Cleveland, OH	46,457	63	26.0	83.5	9.7	5.1	–	1.8
Dallas-Fort Worth-Arlington, TX.	73,616	99	17.8	66.4	–	25.8	3.7	4.1
Denver-Aurora, CO	98,356	25	49.6	78.5	–	20.1	–	1.4
Detroit, MI	54,590	127	14.0	94.1	–	–	–	5.9
Houston, TX.	88,734	73	23.2	82.2	–	13.1	–	4.7
Indianapolis, IN	8,450	231	6.9	97.0	–	–	–	3.0
Kansas City, MO-KS	16,093	154	11.8	96.2	–	–	–	3.8
Las Vegas, NV.	67,126	24	51.1	98.5	–	–	–	1.5
Los Angeles-Long Beach-Santa Ana, CA.	704,768	18	59.8	83.6	6.7	6.5	1.7	1.5
Miami, FL.	159,650	48	32.5	78.4	11.4	–	2.6	7.6
Milwaukee, WI	49,597	36	37.9	97.2	–	–	–	2.8
Minneapolis-St. Paul, MN	89,624	38	37.5	86.6	–	11.0	0.1	2.3
New York-Newark, NY-NJ-CT	4,019,430	1	225.8	31.1	60.8	0.6	6.5	1.0
Philadelphia, PA-NJ-DE-MD	368,902	13	71.6	51.5	28.5	8.0	9.8	2.2
Phoenix-Mesa, AZ.	78,135	60	26.9	90.0	–	7.1	–	2.9
Pittsburgh, PA	70,309	32	40.1	85.0	–	10.4	–	4.5
Portland, OR-WA.	115,380	12	72.9	64.6	–	34.1	0.1	1.2
Providence, RI-MA	21,487	93	18.3	96.2	–	–	–	3.8
Riverside-San Bernardino, CA.	24,159	107	16.0	95.8	–	–	–	4.2
Sacramento, CA	39,933	55	28.7	55.5	–	43.4	–	1.1
San Antonio, TX.	44,500	44	33.5	97.3	–	–	–	2.7
San Diego, CA.	106,735	33	39.9	59.3	–	36.7	1.4	2.7
San Francisco-Oakland, CA	443,459	2	137.4	41.0	25.9	11.4	2.6	19.1
San Jose, CA.	46,600	51	30.3	74.6	–	23.1	–	2.3
Seattle, WA	189,536	15	69.9	69.7	–	2.0	1.3	26.9
St. Louis, MO-IL.	55,500	61	26.7	62.9	–	35.0	–	2.1
Tampa-St. Petersburg, FL	27,001	141	13.1	96.3	–	1.9	–	1.8
Virginia Beach, VA.	18,907	135	13.6	96.0	–	–	–	4.0
Washington, DC-VA-MD	495,268	3	125.9	38.7	59.9	–	0.8	0.5

– Represents zero. X Not applicable. [1] The number of times passengers board public transportation vehicles. A passenger is counted each time he or she boards a vehicle even if the boarding is part of the same journey from origin to destination. [2] As of April 1. Based on the decennial census. [3] Also called metro, subway, rapid transit, or rapid rail. [4] Also called streetcar, tramway, or trolley. [5] Also called metropolitan rail or regional rail. [6] Includes such modes as trolley bus, ferry, cable car, vanpool, automated Guideway, monorail, publico, inclined plane and demand response (see footnote 1, Table 1115).

Source: U.S. Department of Transportation, Federal Transit Administration, National Transit Database; Access NTD data, Historical Data Files, <http://www.ntdprogram.gov/ntdprogram/data.htm>.

Table 1119. Federal Aid to State and Local Governments for Federal Transit Administration (FTA) by State: 2009

[Year ending Sept. 30. (11,298 represents $11,298,000,000)]

State	Total (mil. dol.)	Per capita [1] (dol.)	State	Total (mil. dol.)	Per capita [1] (dol.)	State	Total (mil. dol.)	Per capita [1] (dol.)	State	Total (mil. dol.)	Per capita [1] (dol.)
U.S. [2] . . .	11,298	36	ID.	12	8	MT	19	19	RI.	44	42
U.S. [3] . . .	11,012	36	IL	732	57	NE	16	9	SC	35	8
AL	67	14	IN.	105	16	NV	93	35	SD	20	24
AK	77	110	IA.	49	16	NH	16	12	TN	85	14
AZ	218	33	KS	22	8	NJ	683	78	TX	618	25
AR	27	9	KY	59	14	NM.	59	30	UT	281	101
CA.	1,459	39	LA.	94	21	NY	2,003	103	VT	21	34
CO.	167	33	ME.	18	14	NC	105	11	VA.	190	24
CT	156	44	MD.	223	39	ND	14	21	WA.	347	52
DE	26	30	MA.	274	42	OH	246	21	WV.	26	14
DC	398	664	MI.	154	15	OK	39	11	WI	77	14
FL	231	12	MN.	189	36	OR.	248	65	WY.	9	17
GA.	189	19	MS.	20	7	PA	515	41			
HI.	54	42	MO.	184	31						

[1] Based on estimated population as of July 1. [2] Includes outlying areas and undistributed funds, not shown separately. [3] For the 50 states and the District of Columbia.

Source: U.S. Census Bureau, Federal, State, and Local Governments, *Federal Aid to States for Fiscal Year, 2009,* published August 2010. See <http://www.census.gov/prod/www/abs/fas.html>.

Transportation 701

Table 1120. Truck Transportation, Couriers and Messengers, and Warehousing and Storage—Estimated Revenue: 2004 to 2009

[In millions of dollars (266,251 represents $266,251,000,000). For taxable employer firms. Estimates have been adjusted to the results of the 2007 Economic Census]

Kind of business	NAICS code [1]	2004	2005	2006	2007	2008	2009
Selected transportation and warehousing industries	**48, 49**	**266,251**	**285,603**	**306,700**	**317,631**	**324,890**	**273,246**
Truck transportation	484	182,518	200,519	213,327	217,833	222,529	180,663
General freight trucking	4841	121,760	133,740	141,037	142,508	146,199	117,578
General freight trucking, local	48411	18,661	20,038	21,783	21,174	21,601	17,704
General freight trucking, long-distance	48412	103,099	113,702	119,254	121,334	124,598	99,874
General freight trucking, long-distance, truckload	484121	72,713	79,548	82,481	83,386	86,673	70,368
General freight trucking, long-distance, less than truckload	484122	30,386	34,154	36,773	37,948	37,925	29,506
Specialized freight trucking	4842	60,758	66,779	72,290	75,325	76,330	63,085
Used household and office goods moving	48421	13,707	14,836	15,079	14,549	14,226	11,947
Specialized freight (except used goods) trucking, local	48422	24,921	27,206	29,951	31,549	32,058	26,397
Specialized freight (except used goods) trucking, long-distance	48423	22,130	24,737	27,260	29,227	30,046	24,741
Couriers and messengers	492	65,343	66,468	72,874	77,877	78,839	69,834
Couriers	4921	62,031	63,313	69,650	74,392	75,594	67,138
Local messengers and local delivery	4922	3,312	3,155	3,224	3,485	3,245	2,696
Warehousing and storage	493	18,390	18,616	20,499	21,921	23,522	22,749
General warehousing and storage	49311	11,693	12,303	13,985	15,187	16,409	15,883
Refrigerated warehousing and storage	49312	3,291	3,011	3,156	3,391	3,483	3,484
Farm product warehousing and storage	49313	757	747	775	864	899	798
Other warehousing and storage	49319	2,649	2,555	2,583	2,479	2,731	2,584

[1] Data are based on 2002 NAICS. Data for 2009 are based on 2007 NAICS; see text, this section and Section 15.
Source: U.S. Census Bureau, "Service Annual Survey: 2009, Truck Transportation, Messenger Services and Warehousing," January 2011, <http://www.census.gov/services/index.html>.

Table 1121. Truck Transportation—Summary: 2005 to 2009

[In millions of dollars (200,519 represents $200,519,000,000), except where noted. For taxable and tax-exempt employer firms. Covers NAICS 484. Estimates have been adjusted to the results of the 2007 Economic Census. Data are based on the 2002 North American Industry Classification System (NAICS). Data for 2009 are based on 2007 NAICS; see text, this section and Section 15]

Item	2005	2006	2007	2008	2009
Total operating revenue	**200,519**	**213,327**	**217,833**	**222,529**	**180,663**
Total motor carrier revenue	187,996	199,747	204,211	208,835	169,489
Local trucking [1]	61,810	66,820	69,367	70,608	61,149
Long-distance trucking [1]	126,186	132,927	134,844	138,227	108,340
Size of shipments:					
Less-than-truckload	43,102	52,211	53,411	53,909	43,303
Truckload	144,894	147,536	150,800	154,926	126,186
Commodities handled:					
Agricultural and fish products	16,853	17,660	17,853	18,575	18,585
Grains, alcohol, and tobacco products	6,803	8,635	9,509	10,001	8,933
Stone, nonmetallic minerals, and metallic ores	13,071	15,050	16,135	15,425	12,664
Coal and petroleum products	6,820	7,373	7,990	9,075	7,754
Pharmaceutical and chemical products	10,252	10,791	11,750	11,688	9,893
Wood products, textiles, and leathers	16,705	16,826	17,686	18,720	14,344
Base metal and machinery	15,909	17,570	17,934	18,173	13,689
Electronic, motorized vehicles, and precision instruments	14,856	15,529	14,744	15,095	11,553
Used household and office goods	11,574	11,994	12,458	11,933	9,794
New furniture and miscellaneous manufactured products	21,509	21,544	19,957	20,962	16,271
Other goods	53,644	56,775	58,195	59,188	46,009
Hazardous materials	15,837	(S)	14,545	14,224	12,679
Origin and destination of shipments:					
U.S. to U.S.	180,804	191,751	195,667	200,111	162,482
U.S. to Canada	1,546	1,804	1,954	2,218	1,652
U.S. to Mexico	1,587	1,617	1,563	1,552	1,100
Canada to U.S.	1,284	1,293	1,177	1,316	1,050
Mexico to U.S	1,321	1,718	(S)	1,760	1,538
All other destinations	1,454	1,564	1,908	1,878	1,667
Inventory of revenue-generating equipment (1,000):					
Trucks	216	238	243	246	237
Owned and/or leased with drivers	190	211	215	223	214
Leased without drivers	26	27	28	23	23
Truck-tractors	854	866	884	858	792
Owned and/or leased with drivers	722	723	739	724	678
Leased without drivers	132	143	145	134	114
Trailers	1,903	1,910	1,927	1,943	1,827
Owned and/or leased with drivers	1,560	1,579	1,593	1,630	1,535
Leased without drivers	343	331	334	313	292
Highway miles traveled (mil.):					
Total	88,067	88,320	88,061	85,924	75,211
By loaded or partially loaded vehicles	71,096	71,151	71,215	69,106	60,236
By empty vehicles	16,971	17,169	16,846	16,818	14,975

S Estimate does not meet publication standards. [1] Local trucking is the carrying of goods within a single metro area and its adjacent nonurban areas; long-distance trucking is the carrying of goods between metro areas.
Source: U.S. Census Bureau, "Service Annual Survey, 2009: Truck Transportation, Messenger Services and Warehousing," January 2011, <http://www.census.gov/services/index.html>.

Table 1122. Railroads, Class I—Summary: 1990 to 2009

[As of December 31, or calendar year data, except as noted (216 represents 216,000). Compiled from annual reports of Class I railroads only, except where noted. Minus sign (–) indicates deficit]

Item	Unit	1990	2000	2004	2005	2006	2007	2008	2009
Class I line-hauling companies [1]	Number	14	8	7	7	7	7	7	7
Employees [2]	1,000	216	168	158	162	168	167	164	152
Compensation	Mil. dol.	8,654	9,623	10,337	10,879	11,419	11,599	11,977	10,960
Average per hour	Dollars	15.8	21.5	24.2	25.7	26.0	27.3	28.9	29.8
Average per year	Dollars	39,987	57,157	65,550	66,975	68,141	69,367	72,836	72,153
Mileage:									
Railroad line owned [3]	1,000	146	121	123	121	120	120	119	119
Railroad track owned [4]	1,000	244	205	211	208	207	207	206	206
Equipment:									
Locomotives in service	Number	18,835	20,028	22,015	22,779	23,730	24,143	23,999	24,040
Average horsepower	1,000 lb.	2,665	3,261	3,458	3,467	3,485	3,518	3,601	3,598
Cars in service:									
Freight train [5]	1,000	1,212	1,381	1,288	1,312	1,347	1,386	1,393	1,363
Freight cars [6]	1,000	659	560	474	475	475	460	450	416
Average capacity	Tons	87.5	92.3	94.3	95.1	96.0	96.7	97.7	98.0
Income and expenses:									
Operating revenues	Mil. dol.	28,370	34,102	40,517	46,118	52,152	54,600	61,243	47,849
Operating expenses	Mil. dol.	24,652	29,040	35,107	37,843	40,980	42,747	47,348	37,225
Net revenue from operations	*Mil. dol.*	*3,718*	*5,062*	*5,410*	*8,275*	*11,172*	*11,852*	*13,895*	*10,624*
Income before fixed charges	Mil. dol.	4,627	5,361	5,523	8,361	11,276	12,084	13,863	11,167
Provision for taxes [7]	Mil. dol.	1,088	1,430	1,543	2,224	3,643	4,108	4,645	3,576
Ordinary income	Mil. dol.	1,961	2,501	2,867	4,917	6,482	6,797	8,102	6,423
Net income	Mil. dol.	1,977	2,500	2,867	4,917	6,482	6,797	8,102	6,423
Net railway operating income	Mil. dol.	2,648	3,924	4,147	6,075	7,560	7,765	9,248	7,045
Total taxes [8]	Mil. dol.	3,780	4,379	4,480	5,176	6,830	7,272	8,069	6,519
Indus. return on net investment	Percent	8.1	6.5	6.1	8.5	10.2	9.9	10.7	8.0
Gross capital expenditures	Mil. dol.	3,591	5,290	6,345	7,068	8,159	9,853	10,189	9,701
Equipment	Mil. dol.	996	1,508	1,301	1,026	1,470	2,213	2,315	2,597
Roadway and structures	Mil. dol.	2,644	4,549	4,941	5,364	6,982	6,944	7,907	7,352
Other	Mil. dol.	–49	–767	102	678	-293	696	-33	-248
Balance sheet:									
Total property investment	Mil. dol.	70,348	106,136	135,941	141,400	148,320	156,666	164,286	171,769
Accrued depreciation and amortization	Mil. dol.	22,222	23,989	29,771	32,508	35,763	38,702	41,187	44,195
Net investment	Mil. dol.	48,126	82,147	106,170	108,892	112,556	117,963	123,099	127,574
Shareholder's equity	Mil. dol.	23,662	32,401	51,955	55,828	58,901	59,300	62,787	67,826
Net working capital	Mil. dol.	–3,505	–5,783	–5,171	–4,729	–4,461	–5,482	–3,592	–1,033
Cash dividends	Mil. dol.	2,074	819	1,888	1,267	1,089	6,427	3,345	1,377
Amtrak passenger traffic:									
Passenger revenue	Mil. dol.	941.9	1,201.6	1,432.6	1,461.7	1,606.0	1,774.7	1,964.7	1,819.6
Revenue passengers carried	1,000	22,382	22,985	25,215	25,076	24,549	26,550	28,705	27,279
Revenue passenger miles	Million	6,125	5,574	5,511	5,381	5,410	5,784	6,179	5,914
Averages:									
Revenue per passenger	Dollars	42.1	52.3	56.8	58.3	65.4	66.8	68.4	66.7
Revenue per passenger mile	Cents	15.4	21.6	26.0	27.2	27.2	30.7	31.8	30.8
Freight service:									
Freight revenue	Mil. dol.	24,471	33,083	39,131	44,457	50,315	52,932	59,409	46,127
Per ton-mile	Cents	2.7	2.3	2.4	2.6	2.8	3.0	3.3	3.0
Per ton originated	Dollar	19.3	19.0	21.2	23.4	25.7	27.3	30.7	27.7
Revenue-tons originated	Million	1,425	1,738	1,844	1,899	1,957	1,940	1,934	1,668
Revenue-tons carried	Million	2,024	2,179	2,398	2,448	2,517	2,431	2,420	2,058
Tons carried one mile	Billion	1,034	1,466	1,663	1,696	1,772	1,771	1,777	1,532
Average miles of road operated	1,000	133	121	121	121	120	120	119	119
Revenue ton-miles per mile of road	1,000	7,763	12,156	13,695	14,071	14,805	14,801	14,887	12,857
Revenue per ton-mile	Cents	3	2	2	3	3	3	3	3
Train miles	Million	380	504	535	548	563	543	524	436
Net ton-miles per train-mile [9]	Number	2,755	2,923	3,126	3,115	3,163	3,274	3,414	3,548
Net ton-miles per loaded car-mile [9]	Number	69.1	73.1	78.5	79.0	82	84	87	88
Train-miles per train-hour	Miles	24	21	19	19	18	19	19	21
Haul per ton, U.S. as a system	Miles	726	843	902	893	906	913	919	918
Accidents/incidents: [10]									
Casualties—all railroads:									
Persons killed	Number	1,297	937	891	884	903	851	804	695
Persons injured	Number	25,143	11,643	9,194	9,550	8,795	9,639	9,019	7,940
Class I railroads: [11]									
Persons killed	Number	1,166	778	784	745	788	714	652	(NA)
Persons injured	Number	19,284	7,655	6,298	6,414	5,817	6,254	5,684	(NA)

NA Not available. [1] See text, this section, for definition of Class I. [2] Average midmonth count. [3] Represents the aggregate length of roadway of all line-haul railroads. Excludes yard tracks, sidings, and parallel lines. (Includes estimate for Class II and III railroads). [4] Includes multiple main tracks, yard tracks, and sidings owned by both line-haul and switching and terminal. (Includes estimate for Class II and III railroads). [5] Includes cars owned by all railroads, private car companies, and shippers. [6] Class I railroads only. [7] Includes state income taxes. [8] Includes payroll, income, and other taxes. [9] Revenue and nonrevenue freight. [10] Source: Federal Railroad Administration, *Railroad Safety Statistics*, <http://www.fra.dot.gov/>. [11] Includes Amtrak data. Includes highway grade crossing casualties.

Source: Except as noted, Association of American Railroads, Washington, DC, *Industry Information, Industry Statistics, Railroad Statistics*. See also <http://www.aar.org/StatisticsandPublications.aspx>.

Table 1123. Railroads, Class-I Line-Haul-Revenue Freight Originated by Commodity Group: 1990 to 2010

[21,401 represents 21,401,000]

Commodity group	1990	1995	2000	2005	2006	2007	2008	2009	2010
Carloads (1,000) [1]	**21,401**	**23,726**	**27,763**	**31,142**	**32,114**	**31,459**	**30,625**	**26,005**	**28,491**
Farm products	1,689	1,692	1,437	1,510	1,590	1,681	1,726	1,531	1,685
Metallic ores	508	463	322	662	674	662	671	527	829
Coal	5,912	6,095	6,954	7,202	7,574	7,480	7,713	6,842	6,859
Nonmetallic minerals	1,202	1,159	1,309	1,488	1,470	1,398	1,325	1,054	1,203
Food and kindred products	1,307	1,377	1,377	1,448	1,487	1,493	1,501	1,462	1,585
Lumber and wood products	780	719	648	611	548	456	391	285	312
Pulp, paper, allied products	611	628	633	679	671	652	666	546	620
Chemicals, allied products	1,531	1,642	1,820	1,937	1,943	2,050	2,040	1,895	2,185
Petroleum and coal products	573	596	565	689	689	691	578	494	539
Stone, clay, and glass products	539	516	541	603	570	513	467	371	413
Primary metal products	477	575	723	680	728	666	634	354	514
Fabricated metal products	31	32	30	36	50	55	58	62	84
Machinery, exc. electrical	39	41	35	42	43	40	44	38	46
Transportation equipment	1,091	1,473	1,984	1,923	1,871	1,810	1,521	1,105	1,321
Waste and scrap materials	439	623	619	706	701	726	729	568	622
Tons (mil.) [1]	**1,425**	**1,550**	**1,738**	**1,899**	**1,957**	**1,940**	**1,934**	**1,668**	**1,803**
Farm products	147	154	136	140	149	152	156	137	153
Metallic ores	47	44	32	60	61	59	60	44	70
Coal	579	627	758	804	852	850	879	787	790
Nonmetallic minerals	109	110	126	146	141	138	132	105	121
Food and kindred products	81	91	94	102	105	105	105	101	107
Lumber and wood products	53	51	49	48	43	36	31	22	24
Pulp, paper, allied products	33	36	36	38	37	35	34	28	30
Chemicals, allied products	126	138	155	165	167	176	175	162	183
Petroleum and coal products	40	43	42	57	57	57	46	39	43
Stone, clay, and glass products	44	43	48	55	52	48	45	35	39
Primary metal products	38	47	60	57	61	56	54	30	43
Fabricated metal products	1	1	1	1	1	1	1	1	1
Machinery, exc. electrical	1	1	1	1	1	1	1	1	1
Transportation equipment	23	30	42	38	36	34	27	19	24
Waste and scrap materials	28	38	40	47	48	48	49	37	42
Gross revenue (mil. dol.) [1]	**29,775**	**33,782**	**36,331**	**46,743**	**52,639**	**54,637**	**60,513**	**48,041**	**55,932**
Farm products	2,422	3,020	2,673	3,628	4,205	4,529	5,403	4,413	5,050
Metallic ores	408	394	338	485	529	542	637	403	590
Coal	6,954	7,356	7,794	9,393	10,821	11,471	14,200	12,052	13,530
Nonmetallic minerals	885	875	969	1,293	1,462	1,527	1,749	1,320	1,780
Food and kindred products	2,188	2,464	2,424	3,253	3,730	4,041	4,610	4,261	4,681
Lumber and wood products	1,390	1,385	1,524	2,278	2,335	1,987	1,684	1,095	1,226
Pulp, paper, allied products	1,486	1,543	1,526	1,953	2,124	2,100	2,228	1,656	1,855
Chemicals, allied products	3,933	4,553	4,636	5,432	6,049	6,830	7,655	6,781	7,996
Petroleum and coal products	918	997	1,010	1,500	1,722	1,853	1,930	1,590	1,776
Stone, clay, and glass products	931	1,044	1,113	1,505	1,664	1,607	1,636	1,215	1,398
Primary metal products	979	1,199	1,371	1,734	2,157	2,267	2,572	1,312	1,930
Fabricated metal products	42	44	48	55	79	86	92	77	114
Machinery, exc. electrical	67	69	61	91	109	126	166	116	130
Transportation equipment	3,100	3,269	3,843	3,960	4,228	4,292	3,964	2,677	3,647
Waste and scrap materials	504	685	706	1,070	1,190	1,276	1,415	1,022	1,187

[1] Includes commodity groups and small packaged freight shipments, not shown separately.

Source: Association of American Railroads, Washington, DC, *Freight Commodity Statistics*, annual. See also <http://www.aar.org/NewsAndEvents.asp>.

U.S. Census Bureau, Statistical Abstract of the United States: 2012

Table 1124. Railroads, Class-I Cars of Revenue Freight Loaded, 1990 to 2010, and by Commodity Group, 2009 and 2010

[In thousands (16,177 represents 16,177,000). Figures are 52-week totals]

Year	Car-loads [1]	Commodity group	Carloads 2009 [2]	Carloads 2010 [2,3]	Commodity group	Carloads 2009 [2]	Carloads 2010 [2,3]
1990.....	16,177	Coal....................	6,580	6,674	Metals and products.........	315	456
2000 [2]....	16,354	Metallic ores...............	101	230	Stone, clay, and glass products.	327	352
2004 [2]....	16,600	Chemicals, allied products.....	1,353	1,483	Crushed stone, gravel, sand...	700	809
2005 [2]....	16,691	Grain......................	1,038	1,150	Nonmetallic minerals.........	243	253
2006 [2]....	16,936	Motor vehicles and equipment..	535	627	Waste and scrap materials...	359	407
2007 [2]....	16,564	Pulp, paper, allied products....	294	299	Lumber, wood products.......	119	132
2008 [2]....	16,208	Primary forest products.......	79	83	Coke.....................	139	171
2009 [2]....	13,563	Food and kindred products....	396	407	Petroleum products..........	278	294
2010 [2,3]....	14,562	Grain mill products..........	426	435	All other carloads...........	240	252

[1] Excludes intermodal. [2] Excludes 3 Class I railroads. See text this section for definition of class 1 railroads. [3] 2010 data preliminary.

Source: Association of American Railroads, Washington, DC, *Weekly Railroad Traffic*, annual. See also <http://www.aar.org/NewsAndEvents.aspx>.

Table 1125. Petroleum Pipeline Companies—Characteristics: 1980 to 2009

[173 represents 173,000. Covers pipeline companies operating in interstate commerce and subject to the jurisdiction of the Federal Energy Regulatory Commission]

Item	Unit	1980	1985	1990	1995	2000	2005	2007	2008	2009
Miles of pipeline, total...	1,000.........	173	171	168	177	152	131	147	147	149
Gathering lines.......	1,000.........	36	35	32	35	18	14	15	12	11
Trunk lines...........	1,000.........	136	136	136	142	134	118	132	135	137
Total deliveries........	Mil. Bbl.......	10,600	10,745	11,378	12,862	14,450	12,732	13,934	12,972	12,791
Crude oil...........	Mil. Bbl.......	6,405	6,239	6,563	6,952	6,923	6,675	7,038	6,858	6,431
Products...........	Mil. Bbl.......	4,195	4,506	4,816	5,910	7,527	6,057	6,896	6,114	6,360
Total trunk line traffic....	Bil. Bbl. miles...	3,405	3,342	3,500	3,619	3,508	3,485	3,459	3,438	3,337
Crude oil...........	Bil. Bbl. miles...	1,948	1,842	1,891	1,899	1,602	1,571	1,451	1,581	1,462
Products...........	Bil. Bbl. miles...	1,458	1,500	1,609	1,720	1,906	1,914	2,008	1,856	1,875
Carrier property value...	Mil. dol.......	19,752	21,605	25,828	27,460	29,648	29,526	35,863	39,069	41,565
Operating revenues.....	Mil. dol.......	6,356	7,461	7,149	7,711	7,483	7,917	8,996	9,244	9,987
Net income...........	Mil. dol.......	1,912	2,431	2,340	2,670	2,705	3,076	3,757	3,932	4,131

Source: PennWell Publishing Co., Houston, Texas, *Oil & Gas Journal*, annual (copyright).

Table 1126. U.S. Postal Service Rates for Letters and Postcards: 1991 to 2011

[In dollars. International rates exclude Canada and Mexico]

Domestic mail date of rate change	Letters First ounce	Letters Each added ounce	Post-cards	Express mail— first 1/2 pound	International air mail date of rate change	Letters— first ounce [1]	Post-cards	Aero-grammes
1991 (Feb. 3)...........	0.29	0.23	0.19	9.95	**First 1/2 ounce**			
1995 (Jan. 1)..........	0.32	0.23	0.20	10.75	1991 (Feb. 3).......	0.50	0.40	0.45
1999 (Jan. 10)..........	0.33	0.22	0.20	11.75	1995 (July 9).......	0.60	0.40	0.45
2001 (Jan. 7)..........	0.34	0.21	0.20	12.25	1999 (Jan. 10)......	0.60	0.50	0.50
2001 (July 1)...........	0.34	0.23	0.21	12.45	**First ounce** [1]			
2002 (June 30).........	0.37	0.23	0.23	13.65	2001 (Jan. 7).......	0.80	0.70	0.70
2006 (Jan. 8)..........	0.39	0.24	0.24	14.40	2006 (Jan. 8).......	0.84	0.75	0.75
2007 (May 14).........	0.41	0.17	0.26	16.25	2007 (May 14)......	0.90	0.90	[2]
2008 (May 12).........	0.42	0.17	0.27	[3] 12.60	2008 (May 12)......	0.94	0.94	[2]
2009 (May 11).........	0.44	0.17	0.28	[4] 13.05	2009 (May 11)......	0.98	0.98	[2]
2010 (January 4)........	0.44	0.17	0.28	[5] 13.65	2010 (no change)...	0.98	0.98	[2]
2011 (April 17)..........	0.44	0.20	0.29	[6] 13.25	2011 (no change)...	0.98	0.98	[2]

[1] International letter prices after the first ounce vary according to the price group that is applicable to each destination country.
[2] Aerogrammes were discontinued on May 14, 2007. [3] On May 12, 2008, the Postal Service initiated a zoned pricing structure for Express Mail. Prices for a mail piece weighing up to a half-pound range from $12.60 to zones 1 and 2 to $19.50 to zone 8.
[4] Express Mail prices increased on January 18, 2009. Prices for a mail piece weighing up to a half-pound range from $13.05 to zones 1 and 2 to $21.20 to zone 8. [5] Express Mail prices increased on January 4, 2010. Prices for a mail piece weighing up to a half-pound range from $13.65 to zones 1 and 2 to $22.20 to zone 8. [6] Express Mail prices changed on January 2, 2011. Prices for a mail piece weighing up to a half-pound range from $13.25 to zones 1 and 2 to $26.65 to zone 8.
Source: U.S. Postal Service, *United States Domestic Postage Rate: Recent History* and unpublished data.
See also <http://www.usps.com/prices/welcome.htm>.

Table 1127. U.S. Postal Service—Summary: 1990 to 2010

[166,301 represents 166,301,000,000 except as indicated. For years ending September 30. Includes Puerto Rico and all outlying areas. See text, this section]

Item	1990	1995	2000	2005	2008	2009	2010
Offices, stations, and branches	**40,067**	**39,149**	**38,060**	**37,142**	**36,723**	**36,496**	**36,222**
Number of post offices	28,959	28,392	27,876	27,385	27,232	27,161	27,077
Number of stations and branches	11,108	10,757	10,184	9,757	9,491	9,335	9,145
Delivery Points (mil.)	(NA)	(NA)	135.9	144.3	149.0	150.1	150.9
Residential	(NA)	(NA)	123.9	131.3	135.7	136.6	137.5
City	(NA)	(NA)	76.1	78.5	79.8	80.2	80.5
P.O. Box	(NA)	(NA)	15.9	15.6	15.6	15.6	15.7
Rural/highway contract	(NA)	(NA)	31.9	37.2	40.2	40.8	41.2
Business	(NA)	(NA)	12.1	13.0	13.5	13.5	13.3
Pieces of mail handled (mil.)	**166,301**	**180,734**	**207,882**	**211,743**	**202,703**	**176,744**	**170,574**
Domestic	165,503	179,933	206,782	210,891	201,128	175,363	169,154
First class mail [1]	89,270	96,296	103,526	98,071	91,697	83,776	78,203
Priority mail [2,6]	518	869	1,223	888	[2]	[2]	[2]
Express mail [2,7]	59	57	71	56	[2]	[2]	[2]
Periodicals (formerly 2d class)	10,680	10,194	10,365	9,070	8,605	7,901	7,269
Standard Mail (formerly Standard A)	63,725	71,112	90,057	100,942	99,084	82,448	82,525
Package Services (formerly Standard B)	663	936	1,128	1,166	846	731	658
U.S. Postal Service	538	412	363	621	824	455	431
Free for the blind	35	52	47	76	72	62	68
Shipping Services Volume [2]	(X)	(X)	(X)	(X)	1,575	1,381	1,420
International economy mail (surface) [2]	166	106	79	23	[2]	[2]	[2]
International airmail [2]	632	696	1,021	829	[2]	[2]	[2]
Employees, total (1,000)	**843**	**875**	**901**	**803**	**765**	**712**	**672**
Career	761	753	788	705	663	623	584
Headquarters	2	2	2	3	3	3	3
Headquarters support	6	4	6	4	4	4	5
Inspection Service	4	4	4	3	3	3	2
Inspector General	(X)	(X)	1	1	1	1	1
Field Career	749	743	775	693	652	612	573
Postmasters	27	27	26	25	25	24	23
Supervisors/managers	43	35	39	33	32	29	28
Professional, administrative, and technical	10	11	10	9	8	6	6
Clerks	290	274	282	222	195	178	157
Mail handlers	51	57	61	56	56	53	49
City carriers	236	240	241	228	212	201	192
Motor vehicle operators	7	8	9	9	9	8	7
Rural carriers	42	46	57	64	69	68	67
Special delivery messengers	2	2	(X)	(X)	(X)	(X)	(X)
Building and equipment maintenance	33	38	42	40	40	40	37
Vehicle maintenance	5	5	6	5	5	5	5
Other [3]	1	2	2	2	1	1	1
Noncareer	83	122	114	98	102	89	88
Casuals	27	26	30	19	12	4	7
Transitional	(X)	32	13	8	18	17	16
Rural substitutes	43	50	58	57	58	55	52
Relief/Leave replacements	12	13	12	12	12	11	11
Nonbargaining temporary	(Z)	1	1	1	1	2	2
Compensation and employee benefits (mil. dol.)	34,214	41,931	49,532	53,932	60,992	56,544	60,348
Avg. salary per employee (dol.) [4]	37,570	45,001	50,103	62,635	67,076	70,140	72,099
Pieces of mail per employee, (1,000)	197	207	231	264	265	248	254
Total revenue (mil. dol.) [5]	**40,074**	**54,509**	**64,540**	**69,993**	**74,968**	**68,116**	**67,077**
Operating postal revenue	39,201	54,176	64,476	69,798	74,829	68,043	66,963
Mail revenue	37,892	52,490	62,284	66,649	71,261	65,064	63,285
First class mail	24,023	31,955	35,516	36,062	38,179	35,883	34,026
Priority mail [2,6]	1,555	3,075	4,837	4,634	[2]	[2]	[2]
Express mail [2,7]	630	711	996	872	[2]	[2]	[2]
Periodicals (formerly 2d class)	1,509	1,972	2,171	2,161	2,295	2,038	1,879
Standard Mail (formerly Standard A)	8,082	11,792	15,193	18,954	20,586	17,345	17,331
Package Services (formerly Standard B)	919	1,525	1,912	2,201	1,845	1,684	1,516
Shipping Services [2]	(X)	(X)	(X)	(X)	8,355	8,112	8,533
International economy mail (surface) [2]	222	205	180	134	[2]	[2]	[2]
International airmail [2]	941	1,254	1,477	1,631	[2]	[2]	[2]
Service revenue	1,310	1,687	2,191	3,150	3,671	3,028	3,767
Registry [8]	174	118	98	77	57	50	48
Certified [8]	310	560	385	601	718	731	752
Insurance [8]	47	52	109	132	145	129	126
Collect-on-delivery	26	21	22	9	(NA)	(NA)	(NA)
Money orders	155	196	235	208	205	190	182
Other [8]	592	737	1,342	2,122	2,547	1,928	2,659
Operating expenses (million dollars) [9]	40,490	50,730	62,992	68,283	77,738	71,830	75,426

NA Not available. X Not applicable. Z Fewer than 500. [1] Items mailed at 1st class rates and weighing 11 ounces or less. [2] "Volume" and "Mailing & Shipping Revenue" restructured for the "Postal Accountability and Enhancement Act (PAEA) of 2006." [3] Includes discontinued operations, area offices, and nurses. [4] For career bargaining unit employees. Includes fringe benefits. [5] Net revenues after refunds of postage. Includes operating reimbursements, stamped envelope purchases, indemnity claims, and miscellaneous revenue and expenditure offsets. Shown in year which gave rise to the earnings. [6] Provides 2 to 3 day delivery service. [7] Overnight delivery of packages weighing up to 70 pounds. [8] Beginning 2000, return receipt revenue broken out from registry, certified, and insurance and included in "other." [9] Shown in year in which obligation was incurred.

Source: U.S. Postal Service, *Annual Report of the Postmaster General and Comprehensive Statement on Postal Operations*, annual, and unpublished data.

This section presents statistics on the various information and communications media: publishing, including newspapers, periodicals, books, and software; motion pictures, sound recordings, broadcasting, and telecommunications; and information services, such as libraries. Statistics on computer use and Internet access are also included. Data on the usage, finances, and operations of the U.S. Postal Service previously shown in this section are now presented in Section 23, Transportation.

Information industry—

The U.S. Census Bureau's *Service Annual Survey, Information Services Sector,* provides estimates of operating revenue of taxable firms and revenues and expenses of firms exempt from federal taxes for industries in the information sector of the economy. Similar estimates were previously issued in the *Annual Survey of Communications Services.* Data are based on the North American Industry Classification System (NAICS). The information sector is a newly created economic sector. It comprises establishments engaged in the following processes: (a) producing and distributing information and cultural products, (b) providing the means to transmit or distribute these products as well as data or communications, and (c) processing data. It includes establishments previously classified in the Standard Industrial Classification (SIC) in manufacturing (publishing); transportation, communications, and utilities (telecommunications and broadcasting); and services (software publishing, motion picture production, data processing, online information services, and libraries).

This new sector is comprised of industries which existed previously, were revised from previous industry definitions, or are completely new industries. Among those which existed previously are newspaper publishers, motion picture and video production, and online information services. Revised industries include book pulishers, libraries, and archives.

Newly created industries include database and directory publishers, record production, music publishers, sound recording studios, cable networks, wired telecommunications carriers, paging, and satellite telecommunications.

Data from 1998 to 2003 are based on the 1997 NAICS; beginning 2004, data are based on the 2002 NAICS. Major revisions in many communications industries affect the comparability of these data. The following URL contains detailed information about NAICS, see <http://www.census.gov/eos/www/naics/>. See also the text in Section 15, Business Enterprise.

Several industries in the information sectors have been consolidated: paging is now included in Wireless Telecommunications Carriers (except Satellite). Cable and other program distribution and most Internet service providers are now included in Wired Telecommunications Carriers.

The 1997 Economic Census was the first economic census to cover the new information sector of the economy. The census, conducted every 5 years, for the years ending "2" and "7," provides information on the number of establishments, receipts, payroll, and paid employees for the United States and various geographic levels. The most recent reports are from the 2007 Economic Census. This census was conducted in accordance with the 2007 NAICS.

The Federal Communications Commission (FCC), established in 1934, regulates wire and radio communications. Only the largest carriers and holding companies file annual financial reports which are publically available. The FCC has jurisdiction over interstate and foreign communication services but not over intrastate or local services. Also, the gross operating revenues of the telephone carriers reporting publically available data annually to the FCC are estimated to

Information and Communications 707

cover about 90 percent of the revenues of all U.S. telephone companies. Data are not service comparable with Census Bureau's *Annual Survey* because of coverage and different accounting practices for those telephone companies which report to the FCC.

Reports filed by the broadcasting industry cover all radio and television stations operating in the United States. The private radio services represent the largest and most diverse group of licensees regulated by the FCC. These services provide voice, data communications, point-to-point, and point-to-multipoint radio communications for fixed and mobile communicators. Major users of these services are small businesses, the aviation industry, the maritime trades, the land transportation industry, the manufacturing industry, state and local public safety and govern-mental authorities, emergency medical service providers, amateur radio operators, and personal radio operations (CB and the General Mobile Radio Service). The FCC also licenses entities as private and common carriers. Private and common carriers provide fixed and land mobile communications service on a for-profit basis. Principal sources of wire, radio, and television data are the FCC's Annual Report and its annual *Statistics of Communications Common Carriers* at <http://fcc.gov/wcb/iatd /stats.html/>.

Statistics on publishing are available from the Census Bureau, as well as from various private agencies. Editor & Publisher Co., New York, NY, presents annual data on the number and circulation of daily and Sunday newspapers in its *International Year Book*. The Book Industry Study Group, New York, NY, collects data on books sold and domestic consumer expenditures. Data on academic and public libraries are collected by the Institute of Museums and Library Services. Data on Internet use by adults are collected by the Pew Internet and American Life Project, Washington, DC, and Mediamark Research, Inc., New York, NY.

Advertising—Data on advertising previously shown in this section are now presented in Section 27, Accommodation, Food Services, and Other Services.

Statistical reliability—For a discussion of statistical collection and estimation, sampling procedures, and measures of statistical reliability applicable to Census Bureau data, see Appendix III.

Table 1128. Information Industries—Type of Establishment, Employees, and Payroll: 2008

[(3,434.2 represents 3,434,200). Excludes self-employed individuals employees on private households, railroad employees, agricultural production employees, and most government employees. For more information see source and Appendex III]

Industry	2007 NAICS code [1]	Establishments				Employ-ees [6] (1,000)	Annual payroll (mil. dol.)
		Total [2]	Corpora-tions [3]	Sole proprietor-ships [4]	Non profits [5]		
Information industries.	**51**	**141,554**	**76,024**	**8,288**	**5,130**	**3,434.2**	**233,641**
Publishing industries	511	30,418	14,152	1,725	872	1,059.1	81,127
Newspaper, periodical, book, and database publishers	5111	22,321	8,945	1,583	853	672.7	34,494
Newspaper publishers	51111	8,375	3,992	772	187	346.4	13,983
Periodical publishers	51112	8,000	2,690	441	372	157.0	10,147
Book publishers	51113	3,097	1,045	221	258	95.2	5,994
Database and directory publishers	51114	1,760	911	68	9	52.5	3,284
Other publishers	51119	1,089	307	81	27	21.6	1,086
Greeting card publishers	511191	107	32	4	(X)	11.7	623
All other publishers	511199	982	275	77	27	9.9	464
Software publishers	5112	8,097	5,207	142	19	386.4	46,633
Motion picture and sound recording industries	512	24,353	7,844	1,438	530	351.5	16,485
Motion picture and video industries	5121	20,533	6,789	1,123	438	327.3	14,447
Motion picture and video production	51211	12,396	3,573	595	234	156.2	10,259
Motion picture and video distribution	51212	544	217	14	14	8.9	839
Motion picture and video exhibition	51213	5,140	2,275	376	179	134.7	1,405
Motion picture theaters (except drive-ins)	512131	4,872	2,207	312	178	133.6	1,381
Drive-in motion picture theaters	512132	268	68	64	1	1.2	24
Post production and other motion picture and video industries	51219	2,453	724	138	11	27.5	1,944
Teleproduction and other postproduction services	512191	2,183	637	114	6	24.1	1,722
Other motion picture and video industries	512199	270	87	24	5	3.4	222
Sound recording industries	5122	3,820	1,055	315	92	24.3	2,038
Record production	51221	374	101	27	4	1.1	93
Integrated record production/distribution	51222	445	151	30	7	8.1	1,054
Music publishers	51223	723	245	62	7	5.8	446
Sound recording studios	51224	1,793	427	166	8	5.9	286
Other sound recording industries	51229	485	131	30	66	3.4	159
Broadcasting (except Internet)	515	10,065	4,811	378	1,191	291.6	18,380
Radio and television broadcasting	5151	9,416	4,582	359	1,035	250.3	14,306
Radio broadcasting	51511	7,181	3,393	283	731	123.5	6,195
Radio networks	515111	1,020	298	73	179	14.3	944
Radio stations	515112	6,161	3,095	210	552	109.2	5,251
Television broadcasting	51512	2,235	1,189	76	304	126.8	8,110
Cable and other subscription programming	5152	649	229	19	156	41.2	4,074
Telecommunications	517	53,722	37,029	4,000	313	1,200.5	78,583
Wired telecommunications carriers	5171	34,382	30,798	287	241	844.0	55,853
Wireless telecommunications carriers (except satellite)	5172	12,807	3,826	3,362	28	286.3	17,796
Satellite telecommunications	5174	709	293	63	6	9.9	836
Other telecommunications	5179	5,824	2,112	288	38	60.2	4,097
Telecommunications resellers	517911	2,503	913	98	3	27.3	1,563
Data processing, hosting, and related services	518	15,642	9,723	426	101	392.0	27,198
Other information services	519	7,354	2,465	321	2,123	139.6	11,868
News syndicates	51911	604	431	17	9	9.2	823
Libraries and archives	51912	2,291	78	93	2,026	29.9	810
Internet publishing and broadcasting and Web search portals	51913	3,785	1,741	159	80	88.7	9,618
All other information services	51919	674	215	52	8	11.8	618

X Not applicable. [1] 2007 North American Industry Classification System; see text, this section and Section 15. [2] Includes other types of establsihments, not shown separately. [3] An incorporated business that is granted a charter recognizing it as a separate legal entity having its own privileges, and liabilities distinct from those of its members. [4] An unincorporated business with a sole owner. [5] An organization that does not distribute surplus funds to its owners or shareholders, but instead uses surplus funds to help pursue its goals. Most non-profit organizations are exempt from income taxes. [6] For employees on the payroll for the pay period including March 12.

Source: U.S. Census Bureau, "County Business Patterns," July 2010, <http://www.census.gov/econ/cbp/index.html>.

Table 1129. Information Sector Services—Estimated Revenue and Expenses: 2007 to 2009

[In millions of dollars (1,072,341 represents $1,072,341,000), except percent. For taxable and tax-exempt employer firms. Estimates have been adjusted to the results of the 2002 Economic Census. Based on the Service Annual Survey and administrative data; see Appendix III]

Industry	2002 NAICS [1] code	Operating revenue			Operating expenses		
		2007	2008	2009	2007	2008	2009
Information industries.	**51**	**1,072,341**	**1,107,368**	**1,076,833**	**842,145**	**860,986**	**843,965**
Publishing industries (except Internet)	511	282,223	284,242	263,689	203,614	203,031	187,222
Newspaper, periodical, book, and directory publishers.	5111	146,822	141,896	124,975	111,805	109,206	97,786
Newspaper publishers.	51111	47,563	43,919	36,338	41,998	40,380	34,413
Periodical publishers	51112	46,003	44,985	39,060	35,716	33,539	30,360
Book publishers.	51113	27,807	28,032	27,222	16,265	17,413	16,405
Directory and mailing list publishers	51114	18,515	18,371	16,670	13,281	13,633	12,755
Other publishers	51119	6,934	6,589	5,685	4,545	4,241	3,853
Greeting card publishers	511191	4,479	4,443	3,862	2,923	2,573	2,410
All other publishers	511199	2,155	2,146	1,823	1,622	1,668	1,443
Software publishers	5112	135,401	142,346	138,714	91,809	93,825	89,436
Motion picture and sound recording industries . . .	512	94,986	95,359	90,946	78,231	80,874	78,227
Motion picture and video industries.	5121	79,797	80,089	76,098	66,783	70,178	67,919
Motion picture and video production and distribution.	51211,12	61,911	62,161	58,010	51,812	55,036	52,767
Motion picture and video exhibition	51213	12,705	12,782	13,262	10,624	10,739	10,844
Motion picture theaters (except drive-ins)	512131	12,609	12,687	13,167	10,573	10,687	10,773
Drive-in motion picture theaters.	512132	96	(S)	(S)	(S)	(S)	(S)
Postproduction services and other motion picture and video industries.	51219	5,181	5,146	4,826	4,347	4,403	4,308
Teleproduction and other post-production services	512191	4,379	4,363	4,136	3,824	3,890	3,824
Other motion picture and video industries . . .	512199	802	783	690	(S)	513	484
Sound recording industries	5122	15,189	15,270	14,848	11,448	10,696	10,308
Record production.	51221	338	351	417	323	268	319
Integrated record production/distribution.	51222	9,082	8,953	8,665	7,316	6,968	6,757
Music publishers	51223	4,466	4,715	4,593	2,685	2,354	2,202
Sound recording studios	51224	854	810	748	757	743	667
Other sound recording industries	51229	449	(S)	425	(S)	(S)	363
Broadcasting (except Internet)	515	99,919	103,798	98,919	74,048	75,543	71,767
Radio and television broadcasting.	5151	54,993	54,229	47,367	44,975	44,132	40,327
Radio broadcasting	51511	18,995	18,253	15,952	16,006	15,390	13,608
Radio networks	515111	4,124	4,295	4,259	4,941	4,667	4,072
Radio stations	515112	14,871	13,958	11,693	11,065	10,723	9,536
Television broadcasting	51512	35,998	35,976	31,415	28,969	28,742	26,719
Cable and other subscription programming.	5152	44,926	49,569	51,552	29,073	31,411	31,440
Internet publishing and broadcasting.	516	15,035	17,760	19,504	13,211	15,453	17,080
Telecommunications	517	480,030	498,068	494,337	392,516	396,893	400,980
Wired telecommunications carriers	5171	186,060	184,197	172,093	156,397	153,890	152,713
Wireless telecommunications carriers (except satellite)	5172	170,583	181,418	185,584	134,902	136,322	138,020
Paging	517211	889	846	742	653	654	550
Cellular and other wireless telecommunications.	517212	169,694	180,572	184,842	134,249	135,668	137,470
Telecommunications resellers	5173	11,853	11,105	9,990	7,333	6,754	6,526
Satellite telecommunications	5174	4,450	4,796	5,265	3,386	3,633	4,212
Cable and other program distribution	5175	100,416	109,351	114,284	84,863	90,568	93,983
Other telecommunications.	5179	6,668	(S)	7,121	5,635	(S)	5,526
Internet service providers, Web search portals, and data processing services	518	93,804	101,465	102,821	75,656	83,959	83,464
Internet service providers and Web search portals.	5181	27,152	29,702	29,057	15,888	17,347	17,560
Internet service providers.	518111	11,093	10,603	10,340	7,777	8,117	8,969
Web search portals.	518112	16,059	19,099	18,717	8,111	9,230	8,591
Data processing, hosting, and related services.	5182	66,652	71,763	73,764	59,768	66,612	65,904
Other information services	519	6,344	6,676	6,617	4,869	5,233	5,225
News syndicates	51911	2,140	2,092	1,960	1,711	1,719	1,597
Libraries and archives	51912	1,854	2,034	2,039	1,626	1,725	1,801
Other information services	51919	2,350	2,550	2,618	1,532	1,789	1,827

S Data do not meet publication standards. [1] North American Industry Classification System (NAICS), 2002; see text, Section 15.

Source: U.S. Census Bureau, "Service Annual Survey 2009: Information Sector Services," January 2011, <http://www.census.gov/econ/www/servmenu.html>.

Table 1130. Information Industries—Establishments, Revenue, Payroll, and Employees by Kind of Business: 2007

[For establishments with payroll. (1,072,343, represents $1,072,343,000,000). Based on the 2007 Economic Census; see Appendix III]

Kind of business	2007 NAICS code [1]	Establishments	Receipts (mil. dol.)	Annual payroll (mil. dol.)	Paid employees (1,000)
Information industries.	51	141,566	1,072,343	228,837	3,497
Publishing industries (except Internet)	511	30,958	282,224	80,867	1,093
Newspaper, periodical, book, & directory publishers.	5111	22,683	146,823	34,504	706
Software publishers.	5112	8,275	135,401	46,363	387
Motion picture & sound recording industries	512	23,891	94,986	17,635	336
Motion picture & video industries.	5121	20,164	79,797	15,494	309
Sound recording industries	5122	3,727	15,189	2,142	27
Broadcasting (except Internet)	515	10,188	99,919	18,076	295
Cable & other subscription programming	5152	717	44,926	3,751	46
Telecommunications	517	51,999	491,124	75,401	1,251
Wired telecommunications carriers	5171	33,548	290,781	54,192	885
Wireless telecommunications carriers (except satellite)	5172	11,973	170,584	16,201	289
Satellite telecommunications	5174	823	4,450	793	10
Other telecommunications.	5179	5,655	25,309	4,216	67
Data processing, hosting, and related services.	518	17,129	66,652	26,428	394
Other information services	519	7,401	37,438	10,428	128

[1] North American Industry Classification System, 2007; see text, this section and Section 15.

Source: U.S. Census Bureau, "2007 Economic Census; Geographic Area Series: Summary Statistics for the United States, EC0751A1, (2007 NAICS Basis)," June 2010, <http://www.census.gov/econ/census07/>.

Table 1131. Information Industries—Establishments, Employees, and Payroll by State: 2007

[Based on 2007 NAICS code Economic Census and the 2007 Nonemployer statistics. Data are for North American Industry Classification System (NAICS) 2007 code 51]

State	Establishments	Annual payroll (mil. dol)	Paid employees [1]	Non-employer establishments	State	Establishments	Annual payroll (mil. dol)	Paid employees [1]	Non employer establishments
U.S . . .	**141,566**	**228,837**	**3,496,773**	**307,143**	MO. . . .	2,627	3,880	73,040	4,563
AL	1,700	1,875	40,054	2,760	MT	638	343	9,500	940
AK	407	374	6,754	527	NE	957	984	20,217	1,299
AZ	2,275	3,006	52,573	5,325	NV	1,109	973	17,914	3,121
AR	1,034	1,343	26,074	1,618	NH	790	1,149	15,482	1,542
CA	21,068	48,147	556,535	54,910	NJ	4,092	8,950	134,356	9,712
CO. . . .	3,183	5,663	84,564	7,036	NM. . . .	828	495	13,987	1,606
CT	1,834	2,556	40,345	4,036	NY	11,326	22,538	301,340	27,846
DE	383	457	8,565	683	NC	3,481	4,263	76,413	7,368
DC. . . .	749	2,129	24,499	1,359	NC	367	332	7,124	411
FL	8,296	9,663	175,382	20,284	OH	4,199	5,178	97,360	9,042
GA	4,328	8,156	122,496	9,370	OK	1,585	1,463	32,481	2,740
HI	622	510	10,083	1,234	OR	1,992	2,055	39,258	4,139
ID	717	528	15,163	1,318	PA	5,302	7,774	137,115	10,094
IL	5,696	8,630	136,589	11,757	RI	394	416	8,059	964
IN	2,282	2,089	45,786	4,510	SC	1,410	1,581	33,052	2,945
IA	1,590	1,426	34,397	2,168	SD	437	313	7,296	588
KS	1,502	3,064	52,737	2,047	TN	2,491	2,370	50,778	6,142
KY	1,594	1,252	33,996	2,648	TX	9,541	15,460	250,410	21,144
LA	1,455	1,361	30,537	2,695	UT	1,412	1,762	33,310	3,409
ME. . . .	777	523	13,520	1,260	VT	514	255	6,048	839
MD. . . .	2,571	3,764	63,081	6,993	VA	4,064	7,533	104,147	7,545
MA. . . .	3,772	8,623	110,038	7,997	WA. . . .	3,301	11,277	111,840	6,557
MI	3,791	4,314	77,639	7,800	WV. . . .	679	387	10,285	897
MN. . . .	2,772	4,232	70,314	5,642	WI	2,286	2,625	54,179	3,889
MS. . . .	1,017	646	15,902	1,367	WY. . . .	329	151	4,159	457

[1] Number of paid employees for pay period including March 12

Source: U.S. Census Bureau, "2007 Economic Census, Geographic Area Series," April 2010, <http://www.census.gov/econ/census07/>, and "Nonemployer Statistics," August 2009, <http://www.census.gov/econ/nonemployer/index.html>.

Table 1132. Utilization and Number of Selected Media: 2000 to 2009

[100.2 represents 100,200,000]

Media	Unit	2000	2002	2003	2004	2005	2006	2007	2008	2009
Households with—										
Telephones [1]	Millions	100.2	104.0	107.1	106.4	107.0	108.8	112.2	112.7	114.0
Telephone service [1]	Percent	94.1	95.3	94.7	93.5	92.9	93.4	94.9	95.0	95.7
Land line households with										
wireless telephone [2]	Percent	(X)	(X)	(X)	(X)	42.4	45.6	58.9	58.5	59.4
Wireless-only [2]	Percent	(X)	(X)	(X)	(X)	7.3	10.5	13.6	17.5	22.7
Radio [3]	Millions	100.5	105.1	106.7	108.3	109.9	110.5	110.5	115.6	114.0
Percent of total households	Percent	99.0	99.0	99.0	99.0	99.0	99.0	99.0	99.0	99.0
Average number of sets	Number	5.6	5.6	8.0	8.0	8.0	8.0	8.0	8.0	8.0
Total broadcast stations [4,5]	Number	(NA)	26,319	26,613	26,254	27,354	27,807	29,593	29,832	30,503
Radio stations	Number	(NA)	13,331	13,563	13,525	13,660	13,837	13,977	14,253	14,420
AM stations	Number	4,685	4,804	4,794	4,774	4,757	4,754	4,776	4,786	4,790
FM commercial	Number	5,892	6,173	6,217	6,218	6,231	6,266	6,309	6,427	6,479
FM educational	Number	(NA)	2,354	2,552	2,533	2,672	2,817	2,892	3,040	3,151
Television stations [4]	Number	1,663	1,719	1,733	1,748	1,750	1,756	1,759	1,759	1,782
Commercial	Number	1,288	1,338	1,352	1,366	1,370	1,376	1,379	1,378	1,392
VHF TV band	Number	567	583	585	589	588	587	583	582	373
UHF TV band	Number	721	755	767	777	782	789	796	796	1,019
Educational	Number	(NA)	381	381	382	380	380	380	381	390
VHF TV band	Number	(NA)	127	127	125	126	128	128	129	107
UHF TV band	Number	(NA)	254	254	257	252	252	252	252	283
Cable television systems [6]	Number	10,400	9,900	9,400	8,875	7,926	7,090	6,635	6,101	6,203
Cable subscribers	Millions	66.1	64.6	64.8	65.3	65.3	64.9	65.9	66.2	65.8
Cable availability (passed by cable)	Millions	91.7	90.7	90.8	91.6	92.6	94.1	95.1	95.4	95.5
Broadband subscribers: [7]										
Total fixed broadband [8]	Millions	6.8	19.4	27.7	37.4	47.8	60.2	70.2	75.7	80.7
Mobile broadband	Millions	(NA)	(NA)	(NA)	(NA)	(NA)	(NA)	(NA)	25.0	52.5

NA Not available. [1] As of November. Based on Current Population Survey. For occupied housing units. Source: Federal Communications Commission, *Telephone Subscribership in the United States*, February 2010. See also <www.fcc.gov/wcb/iatd/stats.html/>. [2] From January to June. Based on *National Health Interview Survey* for families living in the same housing unit. Source: National Center for Health Statistics, *Wireless Substitution: Early Release of Estimates From the National Health Interview Survey*, July–December 2010. See also <http://www.cdc.gov/nchs/nhis/releases.htm>, December 2009, and <www.cdc.gov/nchs/data/nhis/earlyrelease/wireless200905.htm#Methods\>. A "family" can be an individual or a group of two or more related persons living together in the same housing unit (a "household"). [3] Source: Radio Advertising Bureau New York, NY, *Radio Marketing Guide*, annual (copyright) [4] As of December, 31. Source: Federal Communications Commission, *Broadcast Station Totals Index*, <http://www.fcc.gov/mb/audio/totals/index.html>. [5] Includes Class A, Low Power TV, UHF and VHF Translators; FM Translators and Boosters; and Low Power FM stations. [6] As of January 1. Source: Warren Communications News, Washington DC, *Television and Cable Factbook* (copyright). [7] As of December. Connections over 200kbps in at least one direction. Source: Federal Communications Commission, Wireline Competition Bureau, *High-Speed Services for Internet Access: December 31, 2008*, February 2010. FCC Form 477 gathers standardized information about subscribership to high-speed Internet access services from telephone companies, cable system operators, terrestrial wireless service providers, satellite service providers, and any other facilities-based providers of advanced telecommunications capability Includes wireline, cable modem, and satellite and fixed wireless. [8] includes aDSl, sDSL, cable modem, FTTP, satellite, fixed wireless, power line, and other.
Source: Compiled from sources mentioned in footnotes.

Table 1133. Multimedia Audiences—Summary: 2010

[In percent, except total (228,112 represents 228,112,000). As of fall 2010. For persons 18 years old and over. Represents the percent of persons participating during the prior week, except as indicated. Based on sample and subject to sampling error; see source for details]

Item	Total population (1,000)	Television viewing	Television prime time viewing	Cable viewing [1]	Radio listening	Newspaper reading	Accessed Internet [2]
Total	**228,112**	**92.91**	**83.06**	**82.61**	**82.14**	**67.19**	**77.31**
18 to 24 years old	28,815	89.61	71.88	77.62	85.67	58.66	92.70
25 to 34 years old	40,710	89.57	77.47	77.77	86.42	58.37	88.35
35 to 44 years old	41,552	92.42	83.47	83.04	86.84	65.49	85.17
45 to 54 years old	44,605	93.94	85.44	84.64	86.48	70.48	80.02
55 to 64 years old	34,456	94.31	87.41	85.85	82.26	72.50	76.12
65 years old and over	37,973	97.07	90.34	85.76	64.55	76.33	43.10
Male	110,308	93.02	82.65	82.40	83.56	66.71	77.07
Female	117,804	92.81	83.44	82.80	80.81	67.65	77.54
Not high school graduate	32,211	92.91	82.14	72.90	74.00	49.17	42.40
High school graduate	70,358	94.20	85.00	83.58	80.26	66.99	67.43
Attended college	63,819	93.05	82.08	85.03	85.52	69.01	88.33
College graduate	61,723	91.30	82.33	84.06	85.04	74.96	95.40
Household income:							
Less than $10,000	11,226	89.85	78.81	64.48	72.50	54.76	44.66
$10,000 to $19,999	19,365	92.31	82.91	70.33	72.39	58.16	46.84
$20,000 to $29,999	22,396	92.06	81.81	74.18	73.75	62.49	56.40
$30,000 to $34,999	11,098	93.72	83.59	80.49	77.12	62.54	62.51
$35,000 to $39,999	10,938	92.70	85.00	80.08	79.87	63.83	68.91
$40,000 to $49,999	20,079	92.92	83.92	80.96	81.23	66.11	73.65
$50,000 to $74,999	43,492	93.31	83.58	84.92	84.19	69.74	84.11
$75,000 to $99,999	31,643	93.63	83.99	88.21	88.15	69.65	91.12
$100,000 or more	57,875	93.23	82.75	90.14	87.41	73.10	94.97

[1] In the past 7 days. [2] In the last 30 days.
Source: GfK Mediamark Research & Intelligence, LLC, New York, NY, Multimedia Audiences, fall 2010 (copyright). See <http://www.gfkmri.com>.

Table 1134. Publishing Industries—Estimated Revenue by Source and Media Type: 2005 to 2009

[In millions of dollars (260,956 represents $260,956,000,000). For taxable and tax-exempt employer firms. Covers NAICS 5111. Estimates have been adjusted to the results of the 2002 Economic Census. Based on the North American Industry Classification System (NAICS), 2002. See text, this section, and Section 15 and Appendix III]

Source of revenue and media type	2005	2006	2007	2008	2009
Publishing industries (except Internet) [1]	**260,956**	**269,890**	**282,223**	**284,242**	**263,689**
Newspaper publishers	**49,401**	**48,949**	**47,563**	**43,919**	**36,338**
General newspapers	42,405	41,963	39,947	36,808	29,633
Subscription and sales	8,708	8,674	8,288	8,323	8,105
Advertising space	33,697	33,289	31,659	28,485	21,528
Specialized newspapers	1,836	1,877	2,091	2,029	1,829
Subscription and sales	(S)	(S)	(S)	(S)	(S)
Advertising space	1,559	1,538	1,724	1,678	1,488
Other operating revenue	5,160	5,109	5,525	5,082	4,876
Printing services	1,525	1,401	1,371	1,271	1,246
Distribution services	2,135	2,009	1,956	1,681	1,546
All other	1,500	1,699	2,198	2,130	2,084
Print newspapers	42,102	41,756	39,874	36,473	29,885
Online newspapers	1,537	1,449	1,655	2,045	1,320
Other media newspapers	602	635	509	319	257
Periodical publishers	**42,778**	**44,757**	**46,003**	**44,985**	**39,060**
General interest periodicals	21,270	22,592	22,516	20,802	17,097
Subscription and sales	7,191	7,445	7,730	6,795	6,179
Advertising space	14,079	15,147	15,146	14,007	10,918
Professional and academic periodicals	7,990	7,955	8,156	7,510	6,308
Subscription and sales	4,793	4,830	4,781	4,166	4,061
Advertising space	3,197	3,125	3,375	3,344	2,247
Other periodicals	2,624	2,651	3,029	2,853	2,516
Subscription and sales	1,176	1,172	998	819	681
Advertising space	1,448	1,479	2,031	2,034	1,835
Other operating revenue	10,894	11,559	12,302	13,820	13,139
Printing services for others	1,237	1,183	1,183	1,179	1,018
Licensing of rights to content	374	426	451	442	409
All other	9,283	9,950	10,668	12,199	11,712
Print	29,170	29,697	30,047	26,974	22,030
Online	2,191	2,893	2,780	3,237	2,906
Other media	523	608	874	954	985
Book publishers	**27,006**	**26,701**	**27,807**	**28,032**	**27,222**
Books, print	23,356	22,995	23,580	23,825	22,738
Textbooks	9,977	10,126	10,697	11,162	9,891
Children's books	2,604	2,388	2,627	2,515	2,522
General reference books	1,017	860	792	751	625
Professional, technical, and scholarly books	2,979	2,997	2,916	3,127	3,838
Adult trade books	6,779	6,624	6,548	6,270	5,862
All other operating revenue	3,650	3,706	4,227	4,207	4,484
Print books	21,618	21,255	21,526	21,592	20,597
Online books	(S)	862	1,005	1,139	1,286
Other media books	860	878	1,049	1,094	855
Directory and mailing list publishers	**18,461**	**17,617**	**18,515**	**18,371**	**16,670**
Directories	13,110	12,594	12,632	11,730	10,136
Subscription and sales	332	318	315	330	274
Advertising space	12,778	12,276	12,317	11,400	9,862
Database and other collections	3,247	3,068	3,779	4,121	4,282
Subscription and sales	2,590	2,416	2,884	2,946	2,950
Advertising space	657	652	895	1,175	1,332
Other operating revenue	2,104	1,955	2,104	2,520	2,252
Rental or sale of mailing lists	566	542	693	705	625
All other	1,538	1,413	(S)	1,815	(S)
Print directories, databases, and other collections of information	12,431	12,126	12,153	11,349	9,843
Online directories, databases, and other collections of information	3,134	2,767	3,390	3,805	3,908
Other media directories, databases, and other collections of information	792	769	868	697	667

S Figure does not meet publication standards. [1] Includes other industries not shown separately.
Source: U.S. Census Bureau, "Service Annual Survey 2009: Information Sector Services," January 2011, <http://www.census.gov/econ/www/servmenu.html>.

Table 1135. Daily and Sunday Newspapers—Number and Circulation: 1970 to 2009

[Number of newspapers as of February 1 the following year. Circulation figures as of September 30 of year shown (62.1 represents 62,100,000). For English language newspapers only]

Type	1970	1980	1990	2000	2002	2003	2004	2005	2006	2007	2008	2009
NUMBER												
Daily: Total [1]	1,748	1,745	1,611	1,480	1,457	1,456	1,457	1,452	1,437	1,422	1,408	1,397
Morning	334	387	559	766	777	787	814	817	833	867	872	869
Evening	1,429	1,388	1,084	727	692	680	653	645	614	565	546	528
Sunday	586	736	863	917	913	917	915	914	907	907	902	919
NET PAID CIRCULATION (mil.)												
Daily: Total [1]	62.1	62.2	62.3	55.8	55.2	55.2	54.6	53.3	52.3	50.7	48.6	46.3
Morning	25.9	29.4	41.3	46.8	46.6	46.9	46.9	46.1	45.4	44.5	42.8	40.8
Evening	36.2	32.8	21.0	9.0	8.6	8.3	7.7	7.2	6.9	6.2	5.8	5.5
Sunday	49.2	54.7	62.6	59.4	58.8	58.5	57.8	55.3	53.2	51.2	49.1	46.8
PER CAPITA CIRCULATION [2]												
Daily: Total [1]	0.30	0.27	0.25	0.20	0.19	0.19	0.19	0.18	0.18	0.17	0.16	0.15
Morning	0.13	0.13	0.17	0.17	0.16	0.16	0.16	0.16	0.15	0.15	0.14	0.13
Evening	0.18	0.14	0.08	0.03	0.03	0.03	0.03	0.02	0.02	0.02	0.02	0.02
Sunday	0.24	0.24	0.25	0.21	0.20	0.20	0.20	0.19	0.18	0.17	0.16	0.15

[1] All-day newspapers are counted in both morning and evening columns but only once in total. Circulation is divided equally between morning and evening. [2] Based on U.S. Census Bureau estimated resident population as of July 1.

Source: Editor & Publisher Co., New York, NY, *Editor & Publisher International Year Book*, annual (copyright). See also <http://www.editorandpublisher.com/Resources/Resources.aspx>.

Table 1136. Daily and Sunday Newspapers—Number and Circulation, 1991 to 2009, and by State, 2009

[Number of newspapers as of February 1 the following year. Circulation as of September 30 (60,687 represents 60,687,000). For English language newspapers only. California, New York, Massachusetts, and Virginia Sunday newspapers include national circulation]

State	Daily Number	Daily Circulation [1] Net paid (1,000)	Daily Circulation [1] Per capita [2]	Sunday Number	Sunday Net paid circulation [1] (1,000s)	State	Daily Number	Daily Circulation [1] Net paid (1,000)	Daily Circulation [1] Per capita [2]	Sunday Number	Sunday Net paid circulation [1] (1,000s)
Total, 1991	1,586	60,687	0.24	875	62,068	KY	22	486	0.11	14	528
Total, 1992	1,570	60,164	0.23	891	62,160	LA	24	530	0.12	18	579
Total, 1993	1,556	59,812	0.23	884	62,566	ME	7	186	0.14	4	151
Total, 1994	1,548	59,305	0.23	886	62,294	MD	10	390	0.07	8	527
Total, 1995	1,533	58,193	0.22	888	61,529	MA	32	1,073	0.16	16	1,026
Total, 1996	1,520	56,983	0.21	890	60,798	MI	48	1,372	0.14	28	1,660
Total, 1997	1,509	56,728	0.21	903	60,484	MN	25	754	0.14	15	926
Total, 1998	1,489	56,182	0.20	898	60,066	MS	22	293	0.10	19	305
Total, 1999	1,483	55,979	0.20	905	59,894	MO	42	747	0.12	22	1,000
Total, 2000	1,480	55,773	0.20	917	59,421	MT	11	172	0.18	7	172
Total, 2001	1,468	55,578	0.19	913	59,090	NE	15	348	0.19	6	322
Total, 2002	1,457	55,186	0.19	913	58,780	NV	6	248	0.09	5	281
Total, 2003	1,456	55,185	0.19	917	58,495	NH	9	163	0.12	8	184
Total, 2004	1,457	54,626	0.19	915	57,753	NJ	17	906	0.10	14	1,103
Total, 2005	1,452	53,345	0.18	914	55,270	NM	17	244	0.12	12	243
Total, 2006	1,437	52,329	0.18	907	53,175	NY	60	5,981	0.31	44	4,374
Total, 2007	1,422	50,742	0.17	907	51,246	NC	46	1,042	0.11	38	1,193
Total, 2008	1,408	48,598	0.16	902	49,115	ND	10	146	0.23	7	147
						OH	82	1,836	0.16	42	2,106
Total, 2009	**1,397**	**46,278**	**0.15**	**919**	**46,895**	OK	37	485	0.13	30	580
AL	24	537	0.11	20	605	OR	18	541	0.14	12	560
AK	7	87	0.12	4	89	PA	80	2,349	0.19	43	2,600
AZ	16	579	0.09	12	733	RI	6	142	0.14	3	173
AR	25	421	0.15	15	485	SC	16	499	0.11	14	585
CA	83	6,041	0.16	59	4,737	SD	11	132	0.16	4	110
CO	29	779	0.16	15	840	TN	26	731	0.12	19	851
CT	17	526	0.15	13	614	TX	81	2,105	0.08	78	2,714
DE	1	105	0.12	2	130	UT	6	307	0.11	6	355
DC	2	650	1.08	2	868	VT	9	104	0.17	4	82
FL	37	2,660	0.14	36	3,347	VA	26	2,937	0.37	20	861
GA	34	753	0.08	29	1,022	WA	22	645	0.10	17	1,303
HI	4	235	0.18	6	252	WV	20	334	0.18	15	424
ID	11	187	0.12	9	261	WI	33	724	0.13	17	870
IL	63	1,753	0.14	30	1,980	WY	9	82	0.15	5	67
IN	67	1,082	0.17	27	1,118						
IA	37	518	0.17	13	553						
KS	35	331	0.12	13	297						

[1] Circulation figures based on the principal community served by a newspaper which is not necessarily the same location as the publisher's office. [2] Per capita based on estimated resident population as of July 1.

Source: Editor & Publisher Co., New York, NY, *Editor & Publisher International Year Book*, annual (copyright). See also <http://www.editorandpublisher.com/Resources/Resources.aspx>.

U.S. Census Bureau, Statistical Abstract of the United States: 2012

Table 1137. Book Publishers' Net Shipments: 2007 to 2010

[In millions (3,126.8 represents 3,126,800,000). Represents net publishers' shipments after returns. Includes all titles released by publishers in the United States and imports which appear under the imprints of American publishers. Multivolume sets, such as encyclopedias, are counted as one unit. Due to changes in methodology and scope, these data are not comparable to those previously published]

Type of publication	2007, est.	2008, est.	2009, proj.	2010, proj.
Total.	3,126.8	3,078.9	3,101.3	3,168.9
Trade	2,281.7	2,237.7	2,248.3	2,294.3
Adult	1,380.8	1,348.5	1,360.8	1,393.4
Juvenile	900.9	889.2	887.5	900.8
Religious	274.5	247.1	239.2	246.8
Professional.	245.9	255.8	264.5	269.0
Scholarly	72.1	74.9	76.2	77.5
Elementary and high school	175.0	182.3	188.7	194.1
College	77.6	81.1	84.5	87.2

Source: Book Industry Study Group, Inc., New York, NY, *Book Industry Trends 2009*, annual (copyright).

Table 1138. Software Publishers—Estimated Revenue by Source of Revenue and Software Type: 2005 to 2009

[In millions of dollars (116,643 represents $116,643,000,000). For taxable and tax-exempt employer firms. Covers NAICS 5111. Estimates have been adjusted to the results of the 2002 Economic Census. Based on the North American Industry Classification System (NAICS), 2002. See text, this section, and Section 15, See also Appendix III]

Item	2005	2006	2007	2008	2009
Operating revenue.	**116,643**	**125,203**	**135,401**	**142,346**	**138,714**
Source of revenue:					
System software publishing [1]	42,876	44,166	49,038	52,406	48,843
Operating system software	15,905	15,434	17,759	18,620	17,931
Network software.	12,196	12,869	13,857	14,665	12,457
Database management software.	6,962	8,275	9,337	10,205	9,465
Development tools and programming languages software	3,253	3,059	2,987	3,035	3,011
Application software publishing [1]	41,800	43,301	45,445	45,442	47,101
General business productivity and home use applications	19,834	18,956	19,311	19,807	23,067
Cross-industry application software.	11,307	12,751	12,949	12,223	11,354
Vertical market application software	6,721	6,787	7,378	7,285	6,399
Utilities application software	1,144	1,372	1,459	1,566	1,687
Other services [1]	31,967	37,736	40,918	44,498	42,770
Customization and integration of packaged software	4,796	4,705	4,077	5,243	4,644
Information technology technical consulting services	4,435	5,421	6,064	5,815	5,606
Application service provisioning	(S)	(S)	(S)	(S)	(S)
Resale of computer hardware and software	2,177	3,115	3,993	4,769	4,146
Information technology-related training services.	1,475	1,662	1,712	1,839	1,381
Breakdown of revenue by software sales type:					
System software	42,876	44,166	49,038	52,406	48,843
Personal computer software	14,564	14,441	17,348	18,217	17,391
Enterprise or network software	15,964	17,407	17,644	18,274	16,536
Mainframe computer software	8,831	9,246	9,679	10,503	9,592
Other system software.	3,517	3,072	4,367	5,412	5,324
Application software	41,800	43,301	45,445	45,442	47,101
Personal computer software	20,404	(S)	19,348	19,696	21,194
Enterprise or network software	14,672	16,236	18,357	17,970	17,848
Mainframe computer software	2,645	2,548	2,525	2,144	2,139
Other application software.	4,079	5,118	5,215	(S)	5,920

S Data do not meet publication standards. [1] Includes other sources of revenue and other expenses, not shown separately.
Source: U.S. Census Bureau, "Service Annual Survey 2009: Information Sector Services," January 2011, <http://www.census.gov/econ/www/servmenu.html>.

U.S. Census Bureau, Statistical Abstract of the United States: 2012

Table 1139. Motion Picture and Sound Recording Industries—Estimated Revenue and Sources of Revenue: 2005 to 2009

[In millions of dollars (88,931 represents $88,931,000,000). For taxable and tax-exempt employer firms. Covers NAICS 512. Estimates have been adjusted to the results of the 2002 Economic Census. Based on the North American Industry Classification System (NAICS), 2002. See text Section 15 and Appendix III]

Kind of business	2005	2006	2007	2008	2009
Operating revenue	88,931	93,214	94,986	95,359	90,946
Motion picture and video industries	**72,991**	**76,394**	**79,797**	**80,089**	**76,098**
Motion picture and video production and distribution [1]	56,826	59,170	61,911	62,161	58,010
Domestic licensing of rights to motion picture films	15,076	15,231	14,939	13,337	12,747
Domestic licensing of rights to television programs	9,408	9,156	10,085	9,395	9,979
International licensing of rights to motion picture films	6,205	7,017	7,456	7,093	6,488
International licensing of rights to television programs	3,111	2,873	2,977	3,490	3,359
Sale of audiovisual works for wholesale, retail, and rental markets	7,560	10,360	12,313	12,254	10,499
Motion picture and video exhibition [1]	11,654	12,326	12,705	12,782	13,262
Feature film exhibition revenue	7,757	8,108	8,483	8,545	8,947
Admissions to domestic films	7,558	8,059	8,421	8,476	8,868
Admissions to foreign films	199	(S)	62	69	79
Food and beverage sales	3,284	3,543	3,711	3,722	3,808
Postproduction services and other motion picture and video industries [1]	4,511	4,898	5,181	5,146	4,826
Audiovisual postproduction services	2,362	2,607	2,736	2,674	2,643
Motion picture film laboratory services	453	(S)	436	420	324
Duplication and copying services	(S)	1,045	(S)	1,091	1,157
Sound recording industries	**15,940**	**16,820**	**15,189**	**15,270**	**14,848**
Integrated record production and distribution [1]	10,110	10,642	9,082	8,953	8,665
Licensing revenue	(S)	1,512	1,299	1,441	1,392
Sales of recordings	(S)	(S)	7,454	6,917	6,496
Music publishers [1]	4,335	4,645	4,466	4,715	4,593
Licensing of rights to use musical compositions	2,207	2,322	(S)	2,887	2,862
Print music	1,771	1,926	1,667	1,254	(S)
Sound recording studios [1]	703	831	854	810	748
Studio recording	461	509	508	505	445

S Data do not meet publication standards. [1] Includes other sources of revenue not shown separately.

Source: U.S. Census Bureau, "Service Annual Survey 2009: Information Sector Services," January 2011, <http://www.census.gov/econ/www/servmenu.html>.

Table 1140. Recording Media—Manufacturers' Shipments and Value: 2000 to 2010

[1,079.2 represents 1,079,200,000. Based on reports of Recording Industry Association of America members companies who distributed about 85 percent of the prerecorded music in 2010. These data are supplemented by other sources]

Medium	2000	2003	2004	2005	2006	2007	2008	2009	2010
UNIT SHIPMENTS (mil.)									
Total [1]	1,079.2	798.4	958.0	1,301.8	1,588.5	1,774.3	1,919.2	1,851.8	1,726.3
Physical:									
Compact disks [2]	942.5	746.0	767.0	705.4	619.7	511.1	368.4	292.9	225.8
Music video [3]	18.2	19.9	32.8	33.8	23.2	27.5	25.1	23.0	17.8
Other albums [4]	78.2	3.2	2.5	2.0	1.3	1.7	3.0	3.2	4.0
Other singles [5]	40.3	12.1	6.6	5.1	3.2	3.2	1.1	1.2	1.5
Digital:									
Download single	(X)	(X)	139.4	366.9	586.4	809.9	1,042.7	1,138.3	1,162.4
Download album	(X)	(X)	4.6	13.6	27.6	42.5	63.6	76.4	83.1
Kiosk [6]	(X)	(X)	(X)	0.7	1.4	1.8	1.6	1.7	1.7
Music video	(X)	(X)	(X)	1.9	9.9	14.2	20.8	20.4	18.1
Mobile [7]	(X)	(X)	(X)	170.0	315.3	361.0	405.1	305.8	220.5
Subscription [8]	(X)	(X)	(X)	1.3	1.7	1.8	1.6	1.2	1.5
VALUE (mil. dol.)									
Total [1]	14,323.7	11,854.4	12,345.0	12,296.9	11,758.2	10,372.1	8,768.4	7,683.9	6,850.1
Physical:									
Compact disks [2]	13,214.5	11,232.9	11,446.5	10,520.2	9,372.6	7,452.3	5,471.3	4,274.1	3,361.3
Music video [3]	281.9	399.9	607.2	602.2	451.1	484.9	434.6	418.9	354.1
Other albums [4]	653.7	164.2	66.1	48.5	22.1	29.3	57.6	60.2	87.0
Other singles [5]	173.6	57.5	34.9	24.1	17.6	16.2	6.4	5.6	5.5
Digital:									
Download single	(X)	(X)	138.0	363.3	580.6	801.8	1,032.2	1,220.3	1,366.8
Download album	(X)	(X)	45.5	135.7	275.9	424.9	635.3	763.4	828.8
Kiosk [6]	(X)	(X)	(X)	1.0	1.9	2.6	2.6	6.3	6.4
Music video	(X)	(X)	(X)	3.7	19.7	28.2	41.3	40.6	36.1
Mobile [7]	(X)	(X)	(X)	421.6	774.5	878.9	977.1	728.8	526.7
Subscription [8]	(X)	(X)	(X)	149.2	206.2	200.9	221.4	213.1	200.9

X Not applicable [1] Net, after returns. [2] Includes DualDisc. [3] Includes DVD video. [4] Includes cassette, LP/EP, DVD audio, and super audio CD (SACD). [5] Includes CD single and vinyl single. [6] Includes singles and albums. [7] Includes master ringtones, ringbacks, music videos, full length downloads and other mobile. [8] Weighted annual average. Number of units not included in total.

Source: Recording Industry Association of America, Washington, DC, *2010 Year-end Statistics* (copyright). See also <http://www.riaa.com/keystatistics.php>.

Table 1141. Radio and Television Broadcasting—Estimated Revenue and Expenses: 2008 and 2009

[In millions of dollars (4,295 represents $4,295,000,000). For taxable and tax-exempt employer firms. Estimates have been adjusted to the results of the 2002 Economic Census. Based on the North American Industry Classification System (NAICS), 2002. See text, Section 15 and Appendix III]

Item	Radio networks (NAICS 515111)		Radio stations (NAICS 515112)		TV broadcasting (NAICS 51512)	
	2008	2009	2008	2009	2008	2009
Operating revenue	**4,295**	**4,259**	**13,958**	**11,693**	**35,976**	**31,415**
Air time	927	826	12,029	9,823	28,117	23,796
National/regional air time	472	411	3,143	2,482	17,438	15,319
Local air time	455	415	8,886	7,341	10,679	8,477
Other operating revenue	3,368	3,433	1,929	1,870	7,859	7,619
Network compensation	164	183	357	351	1,390	1,311
Public and noncommercial programming services	363	366	(S)	(S)	2,154	1,922
All other operating revenue	2,841	2,884	900	888	4,315	4,386
Operating expenses	**4,667**	**4,072**	**10,723**	**9,536**	**28,742**	**26,719**
Personnel costs	962	849	5,584	4,857	8,677	7,935
Gross annual payroll	789	733	4,739	4,075	7,322	6,761
Employer's cost for fringe benefits	131	92	667	641	1,225	1,073
Temporary staff and leased employee expense	42	(S)	178	141	130	101
Expensed materials, parts and supplies (not for resale)	27	26	99	99	251	219
Expensed equipment	10	10	36	40	79	75
Expensed purchase of other materials, parts and supplies	17	16	63	59	172	144
Expensed purchased services	(S)	287	1,129	979	1,980	1,668
Expensed purchases of software	23	21	46	44	158	116
Purchased electricity and fuels (except motor fuel)	19	24	189	192	292	259
Lease and rental payments	99	134	406	416	505	428
Purchased repair and maintenance	21	25	79	76	211	190
Purchased advertising and promotional services	(S)	83	409	251	814	675
Other operating expenses	3,304	2,910	3,911	3,601	17,834	16,897
Broadcast rights and music license fees	613	583	847	747	10,401	10,389
Network compensation fees (networks only)	164	159	74	75	389	317
Depreciation and amortization charges	396	341	612	663	1,800	1,658
Governmental taxes and license fees	16	23	91	83	150	164
All other operating expenses	2,115	1,804	2,287	2,033	5,094	4,369

S Data do not meet publication standards.
Source: U.S. Census Bureau, "Service Annual Survey 2009: Information Sector Services," January 2011, <http://www.census.gov/econ/www/servmenu.html>.

Table 1142. Cable and Premium TV—Summary: 1980 to 2010

[17,500 represents 17,500,000. Cable TV for calendar year. Premium TV as of December 31 of year shown]

Year	Cable TV				Premium TV					
	Average basic sub-scribers (1,000)	Average monthly basic rate (dol.)	Revenue [1]		Units [2]			Monthly rate [4]		
			Total (mil. dol.)	Basic (mil. dol.)	Total premium [3] (1,000)	Premium cable (1,000)	Non-cable delivered premium (1,000)	All premium weighted average [5] (dollars)	Premium cable (dollars)	Non-cable delivered premium (dollars)
1980	17,500	7.69	2,609	1,615	8,581	7,336	(NA)	8.91	8.62	(NA)
1985	35,440	9.73	8,831	4,138	29,885	29,418	(NA)	10.29	10.25	(NA)
1990	50,520	16.78	17,582	10,174	39,902	39,751	(NA)	10.35	10.30	(NA)
1995	60,550	23.07	24,137	16,763	60,098	46,600	8,725	8.32	8.54	6.99
1997	63,600	26.48	28,931	20,213	72,910	51,450	17,500	8.33	8.43	8.00
1998	64,650	27.81	31,191	21,574	79,483	54,410	21,355	8.60	8.74	8.22
1999	65,500	28.92	34,095	22,732	84,234	56,985	25,532	8.75	8.85	8.50
2000	66,250	30.37	36,427	24,142	94,100	62,618	30,158	8.72	8.81	8.48
2001	66,732	32.87	41,847	26,324	101,676	68,353	32,780	8.97	9.10	8.66
2002	66,472	34.71	47,989	27,690	109,046	71,637	37,024	9.19	9.29	9.00
2003	66,050	36.59	53,242	29,000	108,522	71,740	36,364	9.38	9.45	9.23
2004	65,727	38.14	58,586	30,080	118,151	76,844	40,892	9.91	9.92	9.88
2005	65,337	39.63	64,891	31,075	126,067	81,790	43,780	9.95	9.97	9.93
2006	65,319	41.17	71,887	32,274	132,951	85,055	47,514	10.01	10.02	9.98
2007	65,141	42.72	78,937	33,393	143,009	90,878	51,595	10.05	10.06	10.02
2008	64,274	44.28	85,232	34,151	149,749	92,364	56,825	10.08	10.10	10.06
2009	62,874	46.13	89,479	34,804	150,111	85,818	64,293	10.12	10.13	10.09
2010	60,958	47.89	93,368	35,031	166,241	88,359	77,882	10.15	10.17	10.13

NA Not available. [1] Includes installation revenue, subscriber revenue, and nonsubscriber revenue; excludes telephony and high-speed access. [2] Individual program services sold to subscribers. [3] Includes multipoint distribution service (MDS), satellite TV (STV), multipoint multichannel distribution service (MMDS), satellite master antenna TV (SMATV), C-band satellite, DBS satellite and Telco Video for full- and mini-premium services. [4] Weighted average representing 8 months of unregulated basic rate and 4 months of FCC rolled-back rate. [5] Includes average premium unit price based on data for major premium movie services.
Source: SNL Kagan, a division of SNL Financial LC. From the Broadband Cable Financial Databook, annual (copyright); the Cable Program Investor and Cable TV Investor: Deals & Finance newsletters (monthly); and various other SNL Kagan publications.

Table 1143. Cable and Other Subscription Programming—Estimated Revenue and Expenses: 2005 to 2009

[In millions of dollars (37,370 represents $37,370,000,000). For taxable and tax-exempt employer firms. Covers NAICS 51521. Estimates have been adjusted to the results of the 2002 Economic Census. Based on the North American Industry Classification System (NAICS), 2002. See text, Section 15 and Appendix III]

Item	2005	2006	2007	2008	2009
Operating revenue	**37,370**	**40,907**	**44,926**	**49,569**	**51,552**
Source of revenue:					
Licensing of rights to broadcast specialty programming [1]	19,279	21,196	23,563	26,183	28,746
Air time	16,061	17,107	18,605	19,958	19,921
All other operating services revenue	2,030	2,604	2,758	3,428	2,885
Operating expenses	**24,538**	**26,463**	**29,073**	**31,411**	**31,440**
Personnel costs	4,831	4,754	5,592	5,894	6,104
Gross annual payroll	3,894	3,726	4,192	4,496	4,640
Employer's cost for fringe benefits	608	610	874	868	974
Temporary staff and leased employee expense	329	418	526	530	490
Expensed materials, parts and supplies (not for resale)	143	138	137	171	148
Expensed equipment	55	50	67	80	70
Expensed purchase of other materials, parts and supplies	88	88	70	91	78
Expensed purchased services	2,306	2,789	2,460	3,282	3,231
Expensed purchases of software	32	40	49	157	60
Purchased electricity and fuels (except motor fuel)	39	39	40	69	70
Lease and rental payments	551	494	473	550	576
Purchased repair and maintenance	86	81	64	118	122
Purchased advertising and promotional services	1,598	2,135	1,834	2,388	2,403
Other operating expenses	17,258	18,782	20,884	22,064	21,957
Depreciation and amortization charges	(S)	2,662	2,885	3,307	3,326
Government taxes and license fees	112	79	65	66	65
Program and production costs	11,086	12,202	13,804	14,263	14,413
All other operating expenses	3,450	3,839	4,130	4,428	4,153

S Data do not meet publication standards. [1] Protected by copyright.
Source: U.S. Census Bureau, "Service Annual Survey 2009: Information Sector Services," January 2011, <http://www.census.gov/econ/www/servmenu.html>.

Table 1144. Internet Publishing and Broadcasting—Estimated Revenue and Expenses: 2005 to 2009

[In millions of dollars (9,378 represents $9,378,000,000). For taxable and tax-exempt employer firms. Covers NAICS 516. Establishments engaged in publishing and/or broadcasting on the Internet exclusively. Estimates have been adjusted to the results of the 2002 Economic Census. Based on the North American Industry Classification System (NAICS), 2002. See text,Section 15, and Appendix III]

Item	2005	2006	2007	2008	2009
Operating revenue	**9,378**	**11,510**	**15,035**	**17,760**	**19,504**
Source of revenue:					
Publishing and broadcasting of content on the Internet	5,498	6,316	7,576	8,894	(S)
Online advertising space	1,812	2,579	3,469	4,298	4,957
Licensing of rights to use intellectual property	372	442	486	495	560
All other operating revenue	1,696	(S)	(S)	4,073	3,710
Breakdown of revenue by type of customer:					
Government	(S)	(S)	(S)	(S)	(S)
Business firms and not-for-profit organizations	6,615	7,894	9,784	12,061	13,454
Household consumers and individual users	2,227	2,991	4,344	4,527	4,825
Operating expenses	**8,202**	**10,102**	**13,211**	**15,453**	**17,080**
Personnel	3,563	4,398	5,648	6,790	6,855
Gross annual payroll	2,842	3,513	4,189	5,094	5,085
Employer's cost for fringe benefits	507	636	892	(S)	(S)
Temporary staff and leased employee expense	214	249	(S)	(S)	(S)
Expensed materials, parts and supplies (not for resale)	286	322	(S)	(S)	(S)
Expensed equipment	121	123	(S)	(S)	(S)
Expensed purchase of other materials, parts and supplies	165	199	(S)	235	388
Expensed purchased services	1,396	1,789	(S)	2,774	3,387
Expensed purchases of software	176	245	(S)	307	(S)
Purchased electricity and fuels (except motor fuel)	14	22	(S)	(S)	(S)
Lease and rental payments	310	343	(S)	537	(S)
Purchased repair and maintenance	90	96	(S)	(S)	(S)
Purchased advertising and promotional services	806	1,083	1,366	1,757	(S)
Other operating expenses	2,957	3,593	(S)	5,449	6,192
Depreciation and amortization charges	716	811	(S)	1,272	(S)
Government taxes and license fees	56	66	(S)	83	111

S Data do not meet publication standards.
Source: U.S. Census Bureau, "Service Annual Survey 2009: Information Sector Services," January 2011, <http://www.census.gov/econ/www/servmenu.html>.

Table 1145. Telecommunications Industry—Carriers and Revenue: 2000 to 2008

[Revenue in millions of dollars (292,762 represents $292,762,000,000). Based on annual Telecommunications Reporting Worksheets (FCC Form 499-A) filed by telecommunications providers. Revenues are categorized as those billed to universal service contributors for resale (carrier's carrier revenues); and, those billed to telecommunication providers with annual contributions less than $10,000 and end users (end user revenues). Does not include any revenues, such as from Internet access or other information services, customer premises equipment, inside wiring, or published directories, that are not assessable for contributions to universal service support and cost recovery mechanisms]

Category	Carriers (number)				Telecommunications revenue (mil. dol.)			
	2000	2005	2007	2008	2000	2005	2007	2008
Total [1]	4,879	5,005	5114	5,354	292,762	297,921	299,451	297,365
Local service providers (fixed local & pay phone)	2,641	2,922	3,048	3,168	128,075	122,609	115,963	116,447
Incumbent local exchange carriers (ILECs)	1,335	1,303	1.304	1,297	116,158	103,561	93,885	89,732
Competitors of Incumbent local exchange carriers	607	1,043	1,312	1,462	10,945	18,568	21,690	26,440
CAPs and CLECs [2]	479	734	774	813	9,814	16,930	17,476	20,980
Interconnected VoIP providers [3]	(NA)	(NA)	251	334	(NA)	(NA)	2,394	3,541
Private carriers	(4)	(4)	(4)	(4)	39	770	1,031	1,051
Wireless service providers [5]	1,430	905	874	870	63,280	108,809	117,752	128,314
Telephony [6]	783	402	428	412	59,823	107,834	116,971	127,730
Paging service providers	425	300	238	229	3,102	579	555	426
Toll service providers	808	1,178	1,192	1,316	101,407	66,503	59,611	52,604
Interexchange carriers	212	262	250	237	87,311	46,856	44,083	37,358
Operator service providers	20	23	23	31	635	548	631	1,063
Prepaid service providers	23	69	93	121	727	1,828	1,713	1,999
Satellite service carriers	25	40	41	45	336	714	444	860
Toll resellers	493	721	693	654	10,641	13,362	9,943	8,256
Other toll carriers, including VoIP [3]	35	63	92	228	1,758	3,195	2,798	3,068

NA Not available. [1] Revenue data include adjustments, not shown separately. [2] Competitive access providers (CAPs) and competitive local exchange carriers (CLECs). [3] Voice Over Internet Protocol. [4] Data not available separately. [5] Includes specialized mobile radio services and other services, not shown separately. [6] Cellular service, personal communications service, and specialized mobile radio.

Source: U.S. Federal Communications Commission, Wireline Competition Bureau, Telecommunications Industry Revenues and Trends in Telephone Service. See also <http://www.fcc.gov/wcb/iatd/stats.html\>.

Table 1146. Wired and Wireless Telecommunications Carriers—Estimated Revenue: 2005 to 2009

[In millions of dollars (204,455 represents $204,455,000,000). For taxable and tax-exempt employer firms. Covers NAICS 5171 Wired Telecommunications and NAICS 517211 Paging and NAICS 517212 Cellular and Other Wireless. Estimates have been adjusted to the results of the 2002 Economic Census. Based on the North American Industry Classification System (NAICS), 2002. See text Section 15 and Appendix III]

Item	2005	2006	2007	2008	2009
Wired telecommunications carriers operating revenue	204,455	193,434	186,060	184,197	172,093
Fixed services	95,475	89,791	87,307	84,109	73,098
Fixed local	58,676	57,429	56,088	53,473	46,435
Fixed long-distance	33,719	30,917	29,717	29,430	25,658
Fixed all distance [1]	3,080	1,445	1,502	1,206	1,005
Other telecommunication services	93,184	88,182	86,057	87,299	85,154
Carrier services	34,372	30,131	25,163	23,221	20,973
Private network services	26,525	23,238	22,460	22,641	21,747
Subscriber line charges	8,195	7,587	5,856	5,109	4,072
Internet access services	14,315	15,272	20,045	22,468	25,007
Intrernet telephony	1,189	1,826	2,049	2,333	2,303
Telecommunications network installation services	(S)	5,876	6,142	7,062	7,626
Reselling services for telecommunications equipment, retail	3,550	3,320	3,256	3,307	2,533
Rental of telecommunications equipment	(S)	(S)	323	271	343
Repair and maintenance services for telecommunications equipment	791	729	763	887	914
All other operating revenue	15,796	15,461	12,696	12,789	13,841
Wireless telecommunications carriers operating revenue [2]	138,375	154,719	169,694	180,572	184,842
Paging	1,545	1,294	889	846	742
Messaging (paging) services	1,212	1,031	708	688	587
Mobile services	115,535	127,210	136,135	144,622	145,183
Mobile telephony	59,103	55,592	55,575	59,575	58,120
Mobile long distance	4,551	4,950	5,436	4,865	4,672
Mobile all-distance	443,818	(S)	59,218	57,458	58,345
Other mobile services	8,063	(S)	(S)	22,724	24,046
Other telecommunications services	9,946	12,278	15,013	17,543	19,808
Internet access services	1,148	2,565	4,621	6,991	10,101
Installation services for telecommunications networks	(S)	153	189	327	222
Reselling services for telecommunications equipment, retail	7,963	8,557	9,008	8,994	8,281
Rental of telecommunications equipment	(S)	(S)	72	(D)	(D)
Repair and maintenance services for telecommunications equipment	545	(S)	(S)	(D)	(D)
All other operating revenue	12,894	(S)	(S)	18,407	19,851

D Data withheld to avoid disclosure. S Estimate does not meet publication standard. [1] No distinction between local or long distance.

Source: U.S. Census Bureau, "Service Annual Survey 2009: Information Sector Services," January 2011, <http://www.census.gov/econ/www/servmenu.html>.

Table 1147. Telephone Systems—Summary: 1990 to 2008

[130 represents 130,000,000. Covers principal carriers filing annual reports with Federal Communications Commission]

Item	Unit	1990	1995	2000	2002 [1]	2003 [1]	2004 [1]	2005 [1]	2006 [1]	2007 [1]	2008 [1]
LOCAL EXCHANGE CARRIERS											
Carriers [2]	Number ..	51	53	52	53	54	56	56	56	55	55
Access lines [3]	Millions...	130	166	245	264	275	286	349	379	424	(NA)
Operating revenues [4]	Bil. dol ...	84	96	117	111	109	107	106	105	103	(NA)
Average monthly residential local telephone rate [4]	Dollars ...	19.24	20.01	20.78	24.07	24.52	24.52	24.64	25.26	25.62	(NA)
Average monthly single-line business telephone rate [4]	Dollars ...	41.21	41.80	41.80	41.95	41.96	43.49	43.75	45.32	48.17	(NA)
INTERNATIONAL TELEPHONE SERVICE [5]											
Number of U.S. billed minutes	Millions...	8,030	15,889	30,135	35,988	45,904	63,653	70,064	72,440	69,975	74,934
Revenue from private-line service	Mil. dol ...	201	514	1,502	988	899	711	738	792	717	817
Revenue from resale service	Mil. dol ...	167	1,756	7,367	5,101	5,760	5,226	5,750	6,077	6,959	8,459

NA Not available. [1] Beginning 2001, detailed financial data are only filed by Regional Bell Operating Companies (RBOCs). Access lines and calls reported by all subject reporting companies. [2] Beginning 1985, the number of carriers dropped due to a change in the reporting threshold for carriers from $1 million to $100 million in annual operating revenue. [3] Beginning 2008, carriers no longer report this data to the Federal Communications Commission. [4] Gross operating revenues, gross plant, and total assets of reporting carriers estimated at more than 90 percent of total industry. New accounting rules became effective in 1988; prior years may not be directly comparable on a one-to-one basis. Includes Virgin Islands, and prior to 1991, Puerto Rico. Beginning 2008, carriers no longer report this data to the Federal Communications Commission. [5] Beginning 1991, data are for all U.S. points, and include calls to and from Alaska, Hawaii, Puerto Rico, Guam, the U.S. Virgin Islands, and offshore U.S. points. Beginning 1991, carriers first started reporting traffic to and from Canada and Mexico. Data for Canada and Mexico in prior years are staff estimates. Beginning 2004, revenue from private-line service includes non-confidential private line service revenue and the total of private line and miscellaneous service revenue for carriers requesting confidential treatment for international telephone service

Source: U.S. Federal Communications Commission, *Statistics of Communications Common Carriers, Trends in Telephone Service,* and *Trends in the International Telecommunications Industry.* See also <http://www.fcc.gov/wcb/iatd/stats.html>.

Table 1148. Average Annual Telephone Service Expenditures by All Consumer Units: 2001 to 2009

[In dollars except percent distribution. Based on Consumer Expenditure Survey. A consumer unit is defined as members of a household related by blood, marriage, adoption, or some other legal arrangement; a single person living alone or sharing a household with others, but who is financially independent; or two or more persons living together who share responsibility for at least two out of the three major types of expenses: food, housing, and other expenses]

Year	Average annual telephone service (dol.)				Percent distribution			
	Total telephone services	Residential telephone/ pay phone	Cellular phone service	Other services [1]	Total telephone services	Residential telephone/ pay phone	Cellular phone service	Other services [1]
2001	914	686	210	19	100.0	75.0	23.0	2.0
2002	957	641	294	22	100.0	67.0	30.7	2.3
2003	956	620	316	20	100.0	64.8	33.1	2.1
2004	990	592	378	20	100.0	59.8	38.2	2.0
2005	1,048	570	455	23	100.0	54.4	43.4	2.2
2006	1,087	542	524	21	100.0	49.9	48.2	2.0
2007	1,110	482	608	20	100.0	43.4	54.8	1.8
2008	1,127	467	643	17	100.0	41.4	57.1	1.5
2009	1,162	434	712	16	100.0	37.3	61.3	1.4

[1] Phone cards, pager services, and beginning in 2007, Voice over Internet Protocol, known as VoIP.

Source: Bureau of Labor Statistics, "Consumer Expenditures in 2009," News Release, UDDL-10-1390, October 2010. See also <http://www.bls.gov/news.release/cesan.htm>.

Table 1149. Cellular Telecommunications Industry: 1990 to 2010

[Calendar year data, except as noted (5,283 represents 5,283,000). Based on a survey sent to facilities-based commercial mobile radio service providers, including cellular, personal communications services, advanced wireless service, mobile WiMAX, and enhanced special mobile radio (ESMR) systems. The number of operational systems beginning 2000 differs from that reported for previous periods as a result of the consolidated operation of ESMR systems in a broader service area instead of by a city-to-city basis]

Item	Unit	1990	2000	2005	2006	2007	2008	2009	2010
Subscribers	1,000	5,283	109,478	207,896	233,041	255,396	270,334	285,646	302,859
Cell sites [1]	Number ..	5,616	104,288	183,689	195,613	213,299	242,130	247,081	253,086
Employees	Number ..	21,382	184,449	233,067	253,793	266,782	268,528	249,247	250,393
Service revenue	Mil. dol ...	4,548	52,466	113,538	125,457	138,869	148,084	152,552	159,930
Roamer revenue [2]	Mil. dol ...	456	3,883	3,786	3,494	3,742	3,739	3,061	3,026
Capital investment [3]	Mil. dol ...	6,282	89,624	199,025	223,449	244,591	264,761	285,122	310,015
Average monthly bill [4]	Dollars ...	80.90	45.27	49.98	50.56	49.79	50.07	48.16	47.21
Average length of call [4]	Minutes ..	2.20	2.56	3.00	3.03	(NA)	2.27	1.81	1.79
Number of text messages [5]	Billions...	(NA)	(Z)	9.8	18.7	48.1	110.4	152.7	187.7
Number of MMS [5,6]	Billions...	(NA)	(NA)	0.2	0.3	0.8	1.6	5.1	4.3

NA Not available. Z Entry less than half the unit of measurement shown. [1] The basic geographic unit of a wireless PCS or cellular system. [2] Service revenue generated by subscribers' calls outside of their system areas. [3] Beginning 2005, cumulative capital investment figure reached by summing the incremental capital investment in year shown with cumulative capital investment of prior year. [4] As of December 31. [5] Number of messages in final month of survey, (December). [6] Multimedia Messaging Service.

Source: CTIA-The Wireless Association, Washington, DC, *Semi-annual Wireless Survey,* (copyright).

Table 1150. Cable and Other Programming Distribution—Estimated Revenue: 2005 to 2009

[In millions of dollars (79,723 represents $79,723,000,000). For taxable and tax-exempt employer firms. Covers NAICS 5175. Estimates have been adjusted to the results of the 2002 Economic Census. Based on the North American Industry Classification System (NAICS), 2002. See text, Section 15 and Appendix III]

Item	2005	2006	2007	2008	2009
Operating revenue	79,723	88,474	100,416	109,351	114,284
Sources of revenue:					
Multichannel programming distribution services	51,737	55,564	60,529	64,556	66,884
Basic programming package	39,524	42,294	45,468	47,913	49,847
Premium programming package	9,573	10,159	11,441	12,837	13,312
Pay-per-view	2,640	3,111	3,620	3,806	3,725
Other revenue	27,986	32,910	39,887	44,795	47,400
Air time	3,501	3,878	3,936	4,076	3,617
Rental and reselling services for program distribution equipment	2,511	3,152	3,910	4,381	5,076
Installation services for connections to program distribution networks	641	723	931	963	946
Internet access services	11,568	13,736	16,281	18,070	19,325
Internet telephony	518	1,577	3,433	5,167	6,286
Fixed local telephony	1,737	2,134	2,614	2,818	3,091
Fixed long-distance telephony	639	414	194	177	205
All other operating revenue	6,871	7,296	8,588	9,143	8,854
Type of customer:					
Government	546	522	581	660	711
Business firms and not for profit organizations	6,626	6,971	8,682	8,598	9,601
Household customers and individual customers	72,551	80,981	91,153	100,093	103,972

Source: U.S. Census Bureau, "Service Annual Survey 2009: Information Sector Services," January 2011, <http://www.census.gov/econ/www/servmenu.html>.

Table 1151. Internet Service Providers and Data Processing, Hosting, and Related Services—Estimated Revenue: 2005 to 2009

[In millions of dollars (13,760 represents $13,760,000,000). For taxable and tax-exempt employer firms. Estimates have been adjusted to the results of the 2002 Economic Census. Based on the North American Industry Classification System (NAICS), 2002. See text, Section 15, and Appendix III]

Item	Internet service providers (NAICS 518111)			Data processing, hosting, and related services (NAICS 5182)		
	2005	2008	2009	2005	2008	2009
Operating revenue	13,760	10,603	10,340	(X)	(X)	(X)
Internet access service	10,079	5,837	5,292	(X)	(X)	(X)
Online advertising space	1,285	2,146	2,118	(X)	(X)	(X)
Internet backbone services	(S)	(S)	(S)	(X)	(X)	(X)
Internet telephony	(S)	(S)	(S)	(X)	(X)	(X)
Web site hosting services	655	503	490	(X)	(X)	(X)
Information technology design and development services	(S)	(S)	(S)	(X)	(X)	(X)
All other operating revenue	1,362	(S)	(S)	(X)	(X)	(X)
Operating revenue	(X)	(X)	(X)	58,915	71,763	73,764
Data processing IT infrastructure provisioning, and hosting services	(X)	(X)	(X)	29,715	38,015	39,446
Business processing management services	(X)	(X)	(X)	15,198	18,566	19,150
Data management services	(X)	(X)	(X)	6,013	7,181	6,709
Application service provisioning	(X)	(X)	(X)	5,298	8,435	8,988
Web site hosting services	(X)	(X)	(X)	(S)	1,695	1,900
Collocation services	(X)	(X)	(X)	(S)	(S)	(S)
Other operating revenue	(X)	(X)	(X)	29,200	33,748	(S)
IT design and development services	(X)	(X)	(X)	6,438	(S)	(S)
IT technical support services	(X)	(X)	(X)	1,429	1,742	2,144
IT technical consulting services	(X)	(X)	(X)	2,222	2,771	2,565
Information and document transformation services	(X)	(X)	(X)	3,068	3,429	3,176
Software publishing	(X)	(X)	(X)	1,677	2,412	2,535
Reselling services for computer hardware and software, retail	(X)	(X)	(X)	1,252	2,083	(S)
All other operating revenue	(X)	(X)	(X)	13,114	15,326	14,644

S Data do not meet publication standards. X Not applicable.

Source: U.S. Census Bureau, "2008 Service Annual Survey 2009: Information Sector Services," January 2011, <http://www.census.gov/econ/www/servmenu.html>.

Table 1152. Public Libraries, Selected Characteristics: 2008

[11,391 represents $11,391,000,000. Based on survey of public libraries. Data are for public libraries in the 50 states and the District of Columbia. The response rates for these items are between 97 and 100 percent. See source for details]

| Population of service area | Number of— | | Operating income | | | Paid staff [3] | | Average number of public use Internet computers per stationary outlet [5] |
| | Public libraries | Stationary outlets [1] | Total [2] (mil. dol.) | Source | | Total | Librarians with ALA-MLS [4] | |
				State government (percent)	Local government (percent)			
Total..............	9,221	16,671	11,391	8.7	82.7	145,244	32,562	13.2
1,000,000 or more.....	27	1,126	1,764	6.4	82.8	18,678	4,782	24.0
500,000 to 999,000	57	1,156	1,766	8.5	83.8	20,309	4,991	21.6
250,000 to 499,999	106	1,141	1,352	11.0	81.4	16,578	4,083	18.6
100,000 to 249,999	337	2,010	1,791	8.6	84.2	23,134	4,980	17.1
50,000 to 99,999	557	1,646	1,443	10.6	82.1	18,873	4,301	16.2
25,000 to 49,999	967	1,705	1,394	8.2	83.9	18,435	4,364	14.7
10,000 to 24,999	1,763	2,275	1,158	8.2	82.5	16,468	3,531	12.0
5,000 to 9,999	1,497	1,647	422	9.1	79.4	6,873	1,054	8.5
2,500 to 4,999	1,340	1,372	174	7.0	77.1	3,176	315	6.2
1,000 to 2,499	1,573	1,594	100	5.8	75.4	2,050	132	4.6
Fewer than 1,000......	997	999	28	11.1	69.5	671	30	3.5

[1] The sum of central and branch libraries. The total number of central libraries was 9,042; the total of branch libraries was 7,629. [2] Includes income from the federal government (0.4%) and other sources (8.2%), not shown separately. [3] Full-time equivalents. [4] Librarians with master's degrees from a graduate library education program accredited by the American Library Association (ALA). Total librarians, including those without ALA-MLS, were 47,926. [5] The average per stationary outlet was calculated by dividing the total number of public use Internet computers in central and branch outlets by the total number of such outlets.

Source: Institute of Museum and Library Services, "Public Libraries Survey: Fiscal Year 2008," (IMLS-2010–PLS-02), June 2010. See also <http://harvester.census.gov/imls/pubs/pls/index.asp>.

Table 1153. Number of Public Libraries and Library Services by State: 2008

[For Fiscal Year. 1,504,861 represents 1,504,861,000. Based on Public Libraries Survey. Public libraries can have one or more outlets that provide direct service to the public. The three types of outlets include central libraries, branch libraries, and bookmobiles]

State	Number of public libraries [1]	Library visits (1,000s)	Per capita visits [2]	Per capita circulation of materials [2]	Average number of public use Internet computers per stationary outlet [3]	State	Number of public libraries [1]	Library visits (1,000s)	Per capita visits [2]	Per capita circulation of materials [2]	Average number of public use Internet computers per stationary outlet [3]
U.S.	9,221	1,504,861	5.1	7.7	13.2	MO......	152	28,353	5.5	9.4	12.8
AL	210	15,477	3.5	4.4	15.4	MT......	80	4,063	4.5	6.5	7.8
AK	86	3,473	5.1	6.3	5.5	NE......	270	8,983	6.9	10.5	6.6
AZ	86	26,196	4.0	7.3	17.8	NV......	22	10,956	4.0	6.5	12.7
AR	51	9,909	3.7	4.9	8.6	NH......	231	7,302	5.6	8.4	4.9
CA......	181	171,873	4.5	5.8	15.7	NJ	303	49,289	5.9	7.3	14.4
CO......	115	30,666	6.3	12.0	15.9	NM......	91	7,487	4.8	6.3	11.9
CT	195	23,775	6.8	9.4	14.2	NY......	755	117,214	6.2	8.2	13.7
DE	21	4,361	5.5	10.4	13.9	NC......	77	37,600	4.1	5.8	15.7
DC......	1	2,705	4.6	3.0	12.0	ND......	81	2,426	4.3	7.2	5.6
FL	80	84,363	4.5	6.2	25.5	OH......	251	92,280	8.0	16.7	15.8
GA......	59	36,980	4.0	4.7	16.4	OK......	115	14,551	4.9	7.0	10.6
HI.......	1	5,891	4.6	5.5	10.4	OR......	126	22,267	6.6	15.4	10.6
ID.......	104	8,550	6.4	9.4	8.9	PA	457	48,315	4.0	5.8	11.4
IL.......	634	77,553	6.6	9.0	13.3	RI.......	48	6,330	6.0	7.0	14.2
IN.......	238	41,168	7.2	13.7	16.0	SC	42	16,770	3.8	5.4	16.0
IA.......	539	18,534	6.3	9.6	6.4	SD	114	3,922	5.6	8.4	6.1
KS	327	14,671	6.2	11.4	8.0	TN	187	20,454	3.4	4.1	13.6
KY	116	18,512	4.4	6.7	16.7	TX	561	74,221	3.3	4.9	17.2
LA	68	14,632	3.3	4.0	13.1	UT......	69	17,487	6.7	13.0	13.2
ME.....	272	7,188	5.9	7.7	5.2	VT	183	3,893	6.4	7.7	5.0
MD.....	24	32,814	5.9	9.9	20.7	VA	91	39,888	5.2	9.2	15.0
MA.....	370	42,169	6.5	8.4	10.6	WA......	64	42,271	6.5	12.1	13.4
MI.......	384	54,390	5.5	8.0	14.8	WV......	97	6,008	3.3	4.2	7.0
MN.....	138	28,793	5.5	10.7	12.4	WI	381	35,467	6.3	10.9	9.9
MS.....	50	8,859	3.0	2.9	8.6	WY......	23	3,560	6.8	9.0	9.4

[1] Of the 9,221 public libraries, 7,469 were single outlet libraries and 1,752 were multiple outlet libraries. Single outlet libraries are a central library, bookmobile, or books by mail only outlet. Multiple outlet libraries have to or more direct service outlets including some combination of single outlet libraries. [2] Per capita rate and per 1,000 population based on total unduplicated population of legal service area given by the state library agency of each state. [3] The average per stationary outlet was calculated by dividing the total number of public use Internet computers in central and branch outlets by the total number of such outlets.

Source: Institute of Museum and Library Services, "Public Libraries Survey: Fiscal Year 2008," (IMLS-2010–PLS-02), June 2010. See also <http://harvester.census.gov/imls/pubs/pls/index.asp>.

Table 1154. Public Library Use of the Internet: 2009 and 2010

[In percent, except number of outlets. As of spring. Based on sample survey; see source for details]

Item	2009				2010			
		Metropolitan status [1]				Metropolitan status [1]		
	Total	Urban	Suburban	Rural	Total	Urban	Suburban	Rural
Total libraries [2]	**16,620**	**2,940**	**5,421**	**8,259**	**16,802**	**2,898**	**5,841**	**8,063**
Connected with public access	99.0	99.0	99.4	98.7	99.3	99.5	99.4	99.3
Average number of workstations	14.2	25.4	15.8	9.2	16.0	28.0	19.6	9.6
Speed of access:								
Less than 256 kbps	3.4	[3]	1.0	3.6	1.4	[3]	[3]	2.3
257 kbps to 768 kbps	9.2	1.9	5.0	8.5	5.0	[3]	4.2	6.9
769 kbps to 1.4 mbps	9.3	2.1	5.8	8.3	5.6	1.4	4.2	5.8
1.5 mbps	25.5	15.8	25.8	32.6	22.7	9.8	21.1	28.0
1.6 mbps to 3 mbps	10.0	11.0	8.4	12.9	12.0	11.1	9.9	13.7
3.1 mbps to 6 mbps	11.2	10.1	9.9	10.2	11.3	12.2	10.7	11.5
6.1 mbps to 10 mbps	11.0	19.0	15.9	7.4	12.1	16.3	14.6	9.0
10.1mbps to 20mbps	(X)	16.4	9.2	3.7	10.8	22.2	12.3	6.1
20.1mbps to 30mbps	(X)	2.3	1.2	[3]	2.0	2.7	2.4	1.4
30.1mbps to 40mbps	(X)	3.6	1.3	[3]	1.4	1.0	2.1	1.1
Greater than 40mbps.	(X)	14.8	9.5	4.5	10.7	20.8	13.1	5.8
Don't know.	8.1	2.2	6.9	6.8	5.0	1.4	4.7	6.3
Public library availability of wireless Internet access:								
Currently available	82.2	87.5	87.3	76.5	85.7	91.5	89.3	81.2
Plan to make available within the next year......................	6.8	6.0	6.9	15.0	5.9	4.9	4.4	7.2

[1] Urban = inside central city; Suburban = In metro area, outside of a central city; Rural = outside a metro area.
[2] Central libraries and branches; excludes bookmobiles. [3] Less than 1 percent.
Source: Information Policy and Access Center, College of Information Studies, University of Maryland, College Park, MD, 2010–2011 Public Library Funding and Technology Access Survey: Survey Findings and Results by John Carlo Bertot, et al., University of Maryland, College Park, MD. Study funded by the American Library Association.

Table 1155. Household Internet Usage In and Outside of the Home by Selected Characteristics: 2010

[In thousands except percent. (119,545 represents 119,545,000). As of October. Internet Use Supplement 2010. Excludes GPS devices, digital music players, and devices with only limited computing capabilities, for example: household appliances. Based on the Current Population Survey. See text, Section 1 and Appendix III]

Characteristics	Total house-holds	In the home			Anywhere		No internet use	
		Percent						
		All house-holds	Dial-up	Broad-band	Total house-holds	Percent of house-holds	Total house-holds	Percent of house-holds
All households.	**119,545**	**71.06**	**2.82**	**68.24**	**95,907**	**80.23**	**23,638**	**19.77**
Age of householder:								
Under 25 years old	6,575	70.35	1.80	68.54	5,722	87.03	853	12.97
25 to 34 years old	19,838	77.45	1.23	76.22	17,815	89.81	2,022	10.19
35 to 44 years old	21,595	81.53	1.95	79.58	19,771	91.55	1,825	8.45
45 to 54 years old	24,704	77.27	2.92	74.35	21,353	86.43	3,352	13.57
55 years and older.	46,833	60.36	3.98	56.38	31,246	66.72	15,586	33.28
Sex of householder:								
Male.	60,064	73.96	2.78	71.18	49,215	81.94	10,849	18.06
Female.	59,481	68.13	2.85	65.28	46,691	78.50	12,789	21.50
Race and ethnicity of householder: [1]								
White	83,613	74.86	3.02	71.83	68,766	82.24	14,847	17.76
Black	14,863	57.83	2.38	55.45	10,797	72.64	4,067	27.36
American Indian/Alaskan Native	731	56.82	4.55	52.28	531	72.64	200	27.36
Asian	4,667	82.77	1.86	80.91	4,084	87.51	583	12.49
Hispanic.	14,142	59.11	2.21	56.90	10,437	73.80	3,705	26.20
Educational attainment of householder:								
Elementary	5,309	29.41	2.25	27.16	2,197	41.38	3,112	58.62
Some high school	8,870	39.49	2.70	36.79	4,864	54.84	4,006	45.16
High school diploma/GED	34,947	60.33	3.43	56.89	25,049	71.68	9,898	28.32
Some college.	34,168	77.42	3.10	74.32	29,783	87.17	4,385	12.83
Bachelor's degree or more	36,251	89.24	2.07	87.17	34,014	93.83	2,238	6.17
Family income of householder: [1]								
Less than $15,000.	15,369	39.58	2.87	36.71	8,797	57.24	6,572	42.76
15,000 to 24,999	11,116	52.61	3.40	49.21	7,380	66.39	3,736	33.61
25,000 to 34,999	11,971	63.27	3.38	59.89	9,097	75.99	2,874	24.01
35,000 to 49,999	13,333	77.88	3.37	74.51	11,615	87.11	1,718	12.89
50,000 to 74,999	16,391	87.14	2.83	84.31	15,327	93.51	1,064	6.49
75,000 to 99,999	9,785	93.84	2.13	91.71	9,513	97.22	272	2.78
100,000 to 149,000	8,685	96.38	1.57	94.81	8,531	98.22	154	1.78
150,000 and over.	5,961	97.99	0.68	97.31	5,899	98.97	61	1.03

[1] Includes other groups, not shown separately.
Source: U.S. Department of Commerce, National Telecommunications and Information Administration, "Digital Nation: Expanding Internet Usage," February 2011, <http://www.ntia.doc.gov/reports.html>.

Table 1156. Household Internet Usage In and Outside of the Home by State: 2010

[In percent. As of October. See headnote, Table 1155]

State	Any-where	In the home			No Internet use	State	Any-where	In the home			No Internet use
		Total	Broad-band	Dial-up				Total	Broad-band	Dial-up	
U.S.	80.23	71.06	2.82	68.24	19.77	MO.	78.21	67.82	3.47	64.35	21.79
AL	74.18	60.03	4.51	55.52	25.82	MT	75.74	65.33	3.96	61.37	24.26
AK	88.64	78.67	5.30	73.37	11.36	NE	82.54	71.25	2.33	68.92	17.46
AZ	83.46	75.50	1.30	74.20	16.54	NV	84.33	76.58	2.37	74.20	15.67
AR	70.87	58.76	6.38	52.38	29.13	NH	86.35	80.98	3.15	77.82	13.65
CA	84.19	75.86	2.75	73.11	15.81	NJ	82.86	74.76	1.49	73.28	17.14
CO.	82.68	74.78	3.14	71.63	17.32	NM	76.77	62.60	4.90	57.70	23.23
CT	81.95	76.49	1.65	74.84	18.05	NY	79.30	71.06	2.05	69.01	20.70
DE	79.08	71.72	3.37	68.35	20.92	NC	76.53	68.42	3.29	65.14	23.47
DC	80.95	73.40	1.71	71.69	19.05	ND	79.87	73.13	2.25	70.88	20.13
FL	79.93	72.02	1.83	70.19	20.07	OH	78.44	67.47	3.58	63.89	21.56
GA	79.89	70.43	1.82	68.60	20.11	OK	77.30	66.20	3.74	62.46	22.70
HI	78.57	71.09	1.93	69.15	21.43	OR	86.18	78.31	3.59	74.72	13.82
ID	84.12	75.54	3.55	71.98	15.88	PA	78.13	70.21	2.85	67.36	21.87
IL	79.85	70.71	2.04	68.67	20.15	RI	79.84	72.08	1.33	70.75	20.16
IN	74.73	61.29	2.44	58.85	25.27	SC	74.38	63.77	4.25	59.52	25.62
IA	79.45	70.70	3.24	67.46	20.55	SD	80.97	69.04	3.50	65.54	19.03
KS	84.78	76.38	1.75	74.63	15.22	TN	72.20	63.29	3.80	59.49	27.80
KY	72.02	61.27	3.52	57.75	27.98	TX	80.23	69.51	2.67	66.84	19.77
LA	74.94	62.81	2.35	60.47	25.06	UT	90.10	82.31	2.64	79.67	9.90
ME	81.72	73.36	5.99	67.36	18.28	VT	83.52	74.69	5.47	69.21	16.48
MD	83.25	76.34	2.23	74.11	16.75	VA	79.84	72.99	3.47	69.51	20.16
MA	83.82	77.53	1.64	75.89	16.18	WA	88.37	79.70	3.00	76.70	11.63
MI	80.81	69.76	3.43	66.34	19.19	WV	72.87	65.12	5.98	59.13	27.13
MN	83.44	73.65	3.08	70.56	16.56	WI	83.15	73.69	3.17	70.52	16.85
MS	71.43	57.66	5.98	51.68	28.57	WY	84.35	74.40	1.46	72.94	15.65

Source: U.S. Department of Commerce, National Telecommunications and Information Administration, "Digital Nation: Expanding Internet Usage," February 2011,<http://www.ntia.doc.gov/reports.html>.

Table 1157. Internet Access by Selected Characteristics: 2010

[For persons 18 years old and over (228,112 represents 228,112,000). As of fall 2010. Based on sample and subject to sampling error; see source for details]

Characteristic	Total adults	Accessed the Internet					
		At home	At work	At school or a library	At another place	Using a cellphone or mobile device	Using WIFI or wireless connection outside of home
Total adults, (1,000) [1]	228,112	156,039	77,760	20,199	31,052	63,718	40,280
PERCENT DISTRIBUTION							
Total	100.00	100.00	100.00	100.00	100.00	100.00	100.00
Age:							
18 to 34 years old	30.48	33.34	31.74	58.92	51.45	52.81	44.61
35 to 54 years old	37.77	41.31	50.09	29.93	33.17	37.64	40.49
55 years old and over	31.75	25.35	18.18	11.16	15.38	9.55	14.91
Sex:							
Male.	48.36	48.35	50.18	45.25	50.55	52.82	54.76
Female.	51.64	51.65	49.82	54.75	49.45	47.18	45.24
Census region: [2]							
Northeast.	18.28	19.52	19.62	18.43	18.77	19.10	19.23
Midwest	21.92	21.55	22.09	23.32	19.98	20.54	21.43
South	36.96	34.57	34.24	32.85	33.42	36.68	33.47
West.	22.84	24.36	24.05	25.40	27.82	23.68	25.87
Household size:							
1 to 2 persons	45.92	41.42	40.88	32.56	37.83	33.82	37.93
3 to 4 persons	37.21	41.50	44.42	47.48	44.00	45.77	44.72
5 or more persons	16.87	17.08	14.70	19.95	18.17	20.41	17.35
Any child in household.	40.63	44.25	46.26	44.30	46.87	51.71	46.09
Marital status:							
Single.	26.05	26.25	23.93	53.62	40.20	40.71	35.27
Married	55.07	59.86	62.96	36.18	46.13	48.60	53.90
Other	18.89	13.88	13.11	10.20	13.67	10.69	10.83
Educational attainment:							
Graduated college plus	27.06	36.21	47.89	34.49	34.85	37.78	47.59
Attended college	27.98	32.07	30.89	40.77	32.62	33.77	31.03
Did not attend college	44.96	31.71	21.21	24.74	32.53	28.45	21.39
Employed full-time	48.00	55.21	86.38	38.65	51.29	63.91	63.24
Employed part-time	12.12	13.34	13.21	23.89	16.57	13.75	15.23
Household income:							
Less than $50,000	41.69	27.82	15.67	38.58	33.56	26.86	21.77
$50,000 to $74,999	19.07	20.98	20.32	16.78	16.75	17.44	17.04
$75,000 to $149,999	28.58	36.64	44.25	31.21	33.24	36.87	38.46
$150,000 or more	10.66	14.57	19.76	13.43	16.45	18.83	22.73

[1] Includes other labor force status not shown separately. [2] For composition of regions, see map, inside front cover.
Source: Mediamark Research & Intelligence, LLC, New York, NY, CyberStats, fall 2010 (copyright). See <http://www.gfkmri.com>.

U.S. Census Bureau, Statistical Abstract of the United States: 2012

1158. Adult Computer and Adult Internet Users by Selected Characteristics: 2000 to 2011

[Percent of persons 18 years old and over. Represents persons who use a computer or the Internet at a workplace, school, home, or anywhere else, on at least an occasional basis. Based on telephone surveys of persons with land-line telephones unless otherwise noted. In May 2011, 2,277 persons were interviewed including 755 cell phone users. The response rate for the landline sample was 13.6 percent. The response rate for the cellular sample was 11.5 percent. This survey includes interviews conducted in English and Spanish. In May 2010, 2,252 persons were interviewed including 744 cell phone users. In 2009, 2,253 persons were interviewed including 651 cell phone users. For 2000, Internet users include persons who ever go online to access the Internet or World Wide Web or to send and receive e-mail. For 2005, 2009, 2010 and 2011, Internet users include those who at least occasionally use the Internet or send and receive e-mail]

Characteristic	Adult computer users				Adult Internet users				All adults, by type of home connection, 2011[1]	
	2000	2005	2009	2010	2000	2005	2010	2011[1]	Broad-band	Dial-up
Total adults.............	**65**	**71**	**78**	**77**	**53**	**69**	**79**	**78**	**61**	**4**
Age:										
18 to 29 years old	82	83	88	89	72	82	95	95	74	2
30 to 49 years old	76	81	87	86	62	80	87	87	73	4
50 to 64 years old	61	72	78	78	48	68	78	74	57	6
65 years old and over	21	31	42	42	15	28	42	42	29	3
Sex:										
Male..................	66	72	78	78	56	70	79	78	61	4
Female................	64	70	77	76	51	67	79	78	62	4
Race/ethnicity:										
White, non-Hispanic........	66	72	78	79	55	70	80	79	66	3
Black, non-Hispanic........	59	60	66	72	42	54	71	67	51	4
English-speaking Hispanic ...	64	75	84	74	48	73	82	78	47	7
Educational attainment:										
Less than high school	28	36	47	43	19	35	52	42	23	3
High school graduate [2]	56	63	67	67	41	59	67	69	49	5
Some college.............	80	81	89	88	69	80	90	89	73	2
College graduate or higher ...	88	90	94	96	79	88	96	94	83	4
Annual household income:										
Less than $30,000..........	48	52	56	58	35	50	63	63	41	5
$30,000 to $49,999	74	76	82	82	61	74	84	85	72	4
$50,000 to $74,999	85	88	93	89	74	86	89	89	79	2
$75,000 or more	90	92	95	96	81	91	95	96	88	2

[1] 2011 survey includes interviews conducted in English and Spanish. [2] Includes those with a GED certificate.

Source: Pew Internet & American Life Project Surveys from September-December 2000; September and December of 2005; April 2009; May 2010 and May 2011,<http://www.pewinternet.org>.

Table 1159. Internet Activities of Adults by Geographic Community Type: 2011

[In percent. For Internet users 18 years old and over. Represents persons who have ever performed the activity. Based on telephone surveys of persons with land-line telephones and cell phones. See headnote, Table 1160]

Activity	Survey date (month, year)	Total adults	Internet users performing activity			
			Total	Urban	Suburban	Rural
Buy a product online	May, 2011 ..	55	71	73	72	70
Buy or make a reservation for travel	May, 2011 ..	51	65	66	66	60
Categorize or tag online content like a photo, news story or blog post	Sept, 2010..	24	33	37	32	25
Create or work on your own online journal or blog	May, 2011 ..	11	14	16	13	11
Do any banking online..................	May, 2011 ..	47	61	68	60	50
Look for health or medical information online	May, 2011 ..	55	71	72	69	81
Look for news or information about politics	May, 2011 ..	47	61	64	61	48
Look online for info about a job	May, 2011 ..	44	56	63	56	45
Make a donation to a charity online..............	May, 2011 ..	19	25	31	26	15
Make a phone call online, using a service such as Skype or Vonage	May, 2011 ..	18	24	25	27	13
Pay bills online......................	Sept, 2010..	42	57	55	62	45
Pay to access or download digital content online (e.g. newspaper article)...................	Sept, 2010..	32	43	47	43	35
Play online games....................	Sept, 2010..	27	36	36	38	34
Post a comment or review online	Sept, 2010..	24	32	34	35	24
Research a product or service online	Sept, 2010..	58	78	79	79	77
Search online for a map or driving directions	Sept, 2010..	60	82	84	83	79
Send instant messages..................	Nov, 2010...	34	46	49	47	42
Send or read e-mail....................	Nov, 2010...	68	92	93	93	90
Take part in chat rooms or online discussions with other people	Sept, 2010..	17	22	25	21	20
Use a search engine to find information	May, 2011 ..	71	92	90	93	89
Use a social networking site like MySpace, Facebook or LinkedIn	May, 2011 ..	50	65	67	65	61
Use Twitter......................	May, 2011 ..	10	13	15	14	7
Visit a local, state, or federal government Web site.....	May, 2011 ..	52	67	68	69	61
Watch a video on a video-sharing site..............	May, 2011 ..	55	71	72	71	68

Source: Pew Internet & American Life Project Surveys, <http://www.pewinternet.org>.

Information and Communications 725

1160. Typical Daily Internet Activities of Adult Internet Users: 2011

[Percent of Internet users 18 years old and over. Represents persons who reported doing the activity "yesterday." Based on telephone surveys of persons with land-line telephones and cell phones. In May 2011, 2,277 persons were interviewed including 755 cell phone users. The response rate for the landline sample was 13.6 percent. The response rate for the cellular sample was 11.5 percent. In November 2010, 2,257 persons were interviewed including 755 cell phone users. The response rate for the landline sample was 13.7 percent. The response rate for the cellular sample was 15 percent. In September 2010, 3,001 persons were interviewed including 1,000 cell phone users. The response rate for the landline sample was 13.6 percent. The response rate for the cellular sample was 17 percent]

Activity	Survey date (month/year)	Total Internet users	Age 18 to 29 years old	Age 30 to 49 years old	Age 50 to 64 years old	Age 65 years old and over	Sex Male	Sex Female
Buy a product online	May, 2011	6	7	5	7	7	7	5
Buy or make a reservation for travel	May, 2011	4	4	4	3	1	4	3
Categorize or tag online content like a photo, news story or blog post	Sept, 2010	11	18	12	5	4	12	10
Create or work on your own online journal or blog	May, 2011	4	4	6	3	2	6	3
Do any banking online	May, 2011	24	19	28	27	15	24	23
Look for health or medical information online	May, 2011	10	8	9	11	10	8	11
Look for news or information about politics	May, 2011	30	27	34	34	19	36	26
Look online for info about a job	May, 2011	11	15	12	9	1	11	11
Make a donation to a charity online	May, 2011	1	1	1	2	1	1	1
Make a phone call online, using a service such as Skype or Vonage	May, 2011	5	6	5	5	2	6	4
Pay bills online	Sept, 2010	15	14	19	11	11	15	15
Pay to access or download digital content online (e.g. newspaper article)	Sept, 2010	10	13	9	12	3	13	8
Play online games	Sept, 2010	13	16	15	10	9	13	13
Post a comment or review online	Sept, 2010	4	6	5	2	3	5	4
Research a product or service online	Sept, 2010	28	27	32	26	16	31	24
Search online for a map or driving directions	Sept, 2010	14	15	17	12	7	16	12
Send instant messages	Nov, 2010	18	29	17	13	4	18	18
Send or read e-mail	Nov, 2010	61	64	63	61	46	59	64
Take part in chat rooms or online discussions with other people	Sept, 2010	7	9	9	5	2	8	6
Use a search engine to find information	May, 2011	59	66	64	52	37	61	57
Use a social networking site like MySpace, Facebook or LinkedIn	May, 2011	43	61	46	32	15	38	48
Use Twitter	May, 2011	4	8	5	2	–	5	4
Visit a local, state, or federal government Web site	May, 2011	13	11	15	13	6	14	12
Watch a video on a video-sharing site	May, 2011	28	47	27	20	11	32	25

– Rounds to less than half the unit of measurement shown.
Source: Pew Internet & American Life Project Surveys, <http://www.pewinternet.org>.

1161. Online News Consumption by Selected Characteristics: 2000 to 2011

[Percent of Internet users 18 years old and over. Represents persons who report getting news online "ever" or "yesterday." Based on telephone surveys of persons with land-line telephones, unless otherwise noted. In April 2009, 2,253 persons were interviewed, including 561 cell phone users. The response rate for the landline sample was 20.6 percent and 18.2 percent for the cell sample. In May 2010, 2,252 persons were interviewed including 744 cell phone users. The response rate for the landline sample was 21.8 percent. The response rate for the cellular sample was 19.3 percent. In May 2011, 2,277 persons were interviewed including 755 cell phone users. The response rate for the landline sample was 13.6 percent. The response rate for the cellular sample was 11.5 percent. This survey includes interviews conducted in English and Spanish]

Characteristic	"Ever" get news online 2000	2009	2010	2011 [1]	Got news online "yesterday" 2000	2009	2010	2011 [1]
Total adult Internet users	**60**	**72**	**75**	**76**	**22**	**38**	**43**	**45**
Age:								
18 to 29 years old	56	74	75	72	16	35	44	43
30 to 49 years old	63	76	78	83	25	44	45	51
50 to 64 years old	57	71	76	77	25	37	42	44
65 years old and over	53	56	62	60	28	28	34	32
Sex:								
Male	66	73	77	77	29	42	48	52
Female	53	72	74	76	16	35	38	39
Race/ethnicity:								
White, non-Hispanic	60	73	75	76	23	40	43	46
Black, non-Hispanic	63	72	72	77	13	32	42	34
English-speaking Hispanic	57	67	73	72	23	34	35	40
Annual household income:								
Less than $30,000	55	59	64	65	21	28	28	31
$30,000 to $49,999	57	69	74	79	20	33	35	44
$50,000 to $74,999	63	75	78	82	22	40	47	52
$75,000 or more	69	84	84	88	31	53	60	62
Frequency of Internet use:								
Daily	66	81	82	(NA)	33	50	54	(NA)
Several times per week	59	59	64	(NA)	17	13	14	(NA)
Less Often	51	30	38	(NA)	12	2	5	(NA)

NA Not available. [1] Includes interviews conducted in English and Spanish.
Source: Pew Internet & American Life Project Surveys from March 2000, April 2009, May 2010 and May 2011, <http://www.pewinternet.org>.

Section 25
Banking, Finance, and Insurance

This section presents data on the nation's finances, various types of financial institutions, money and credit, securities, insurance, and real estate. The primary sources of these data are publications of several departments of the federal government, especially the U.S. Treasury Department, and independent agencies such as the Federal Deposit Insurance Corporation, the Board of Governors of the Federal Reserve System, and the Securities and Exchange Commission. National data on insurance are available primarily from private organizations, such as the American Council of Life Insurers and the Insurance Information Institute.

Flow of funds—The flow of funds accounts of the Federal Reserve Board bring together statistics on all of the major forms of financial instruments to present an economy-wide view of asset and liability relationships. In flow form, the accounts relate borrowing and lending to one another and to the nonfinancial activities that generate income and production. Each claim outstanding is included simultaneously as an asset of the lender and as a liability of the debtor. The accounts also indicate the balance between asset totals and liability totals over the economy as a whole. Several publications of the Federal Reserve Board contain information on the flow of funds accounts: Summary data on flows and outstandings, in the statistical release *Flow of Funds Accounts of the United States* (quarterly); and concepts and organization of the accounts in *Guide to the Flow of Funds Accounts* (2000). Data are also available on the Federal Reserve Board's Web site at <http://www.federalreserve.gov/>.

Survey of Consumer Finances (SCF)— The Federal Reserve Board, in cooperation with the Treasury Department, sponsors this survey, which is conducted every 3 years to provide detailed information on the finances of U.S. families. Among the topics covered are the balance sheet, pension, income, and other demographic characteristics of U.S. families. The survey also gathers information on the use of financial institutions. Since 1992, data for the SCF have been collected by the National Organization for Research at the University of Chicago. Data and information on the survey are available on the Federal Reserve Board's Web site at <http://www.federalreserve.gov/pubs /oss/oss2/scfindex.html>.

Banking system—Banks in this country are organized under the laws of both the states and the federal government and are regulated by several bank supervisory agencies. National banks are supervised by the Comptroller of the Currency. *Reports of Condition* have been collected from national banks since 1863. Summaries of these reports are published in the Comptroller's *Annual Report*, which also presents data on the structure of the national banking system.

The Federal Reserve System was established in 1913 to exercise central banking functions, some of which are shared with the U.S. Treasury. It includes national banks and such state banks that voluntarily join the system. Statements of state bank members are consolidated by the Federal Reserve Board with data for national banks collected by the Comptroller of the Currency into totals for all member banks of the system. Balance sheet data for member banks and other commercial banks are available on the Federal Reserve Board's Web site at <http://www .federalreserve.gov/econresdata/releases /statisticsdata.htm>.

The Federal Deposit Insurance Corporation (FDIC), established in 1933, insures each depositor up to $250,000. Major item balance sheet and income data for all insured financial institutions are published in the *FDIC Quarterly Banking Profile*. This publication is also available on the Internet at the following address: <http://www.fdic.gov>. Quarterly financial information for individual institutions is available through the FDIC and Federal

Financial Institutions Examination Council Web sites at <http://www.fdic.gov> and <http://www.ffiec.gov>.

Credit unions—Federally chartered credit unions are under the supervision of the National Credit Union Administration. State-chartered credit unions are supervised by the respective state supervisory authorities. The administration publishes comprehensive program and statistical information on all federal and federally insured state credit unions in the *Annual Report of the National Credit Union Administration.*

Other credit agencies—Insurance companies, finance companies dealing primarily in installment sales financing, and personal loan companies represent important sources of funds for the credit market. Statistics on loans, investments, cash, etc., of life insurance companies are published principally by the American Council of Life Insurers in its *Life Insurers Fact Book.* Consumer credit data are available on the Federal Reserve Board's Web site at <http://www.federalreserve .gov/econresdata/releases/statisticsdata .htm>. Government corporations and credit agencies make available credit of specified types or to specified groups of private borrowers, either by lending directly or by insuring or guaranteeing loans made by private lending institutions. Data on operations of government credit agencies, along with other government corporations, are available in reports of individual agencies.

Securities—The Securities and Exchange Commission (SEC) was established in 1934 to protect the interests of the public and investors against malpractices in the securities and financial markets and to provide the fullest possible disclosure of information regarding securities to the investing public.

Data on the securities industry and securities transactions are also available from a number of private sources. The Securities Industry and Financial Markets Association, New York, NY, <http://www.sifma .org/>, publishes the *Securities Industry Fact Book* and *Securities Industry Yearbook.* The Investment Company Institute, Washington, DC, <http://www.ici.org/>, publishes a reference book, research newsletters, and a variety of research reports that examine the industry, its shareholders, or industry issues. The annual *Mutual Fund Fact Book* is a guide to trends and statistics observed in the investment company industry. *Fundamentals* is a newsletter summarizing the findings of major Institute research projects. Institute research reports provide a detailed examination of shareholder demographics and other aspects of fund ownership.

Among the many sources of data on stock and bond prices and sales are the New York Stock Exchange, New York, NY, <http://www.nyse.com/>; NASDAQ, Washington, DC, <http://www.nasdaq.com/>; Global Financial Data, Los Angeles, CA, <http://www.globalfinancialdata.com/>; and Dow-Jones & Company, Inc., New York, NY, <http://www.djindexes.com>.

Insurance—Insuring companies, which are regulated by the various states or the District of Columbia, are classified as either life or property. Both life and property insurance companies may underwrite health insurance. Insuring companies, other than those classified as life, are permitted to underwrite one or more property lines provided they are so licensed and have the necessary capital or surplus. There are a number of published sources for statistics on the various classes of insurance—life, health, fire, marine, and casualty. Organizations representing certain classes of insurers publish reports for these classes. The American Council of Life Insurers publishes statistics on life insurance purchases, ownership, benefit payments, and assets in its *Life Insurers Fact Book.*

Statistical reliability—For a discussion of statistical collection, estimation, and sampling procedures and measures of reliability applicable to data from the Census Bureau and the Federal Reserve Board's Survey of Consumer Finances, see Appendix III.

Figure 25.1
Interest Rates and Bond Yields: 1990 to 2010
(Annual averages)

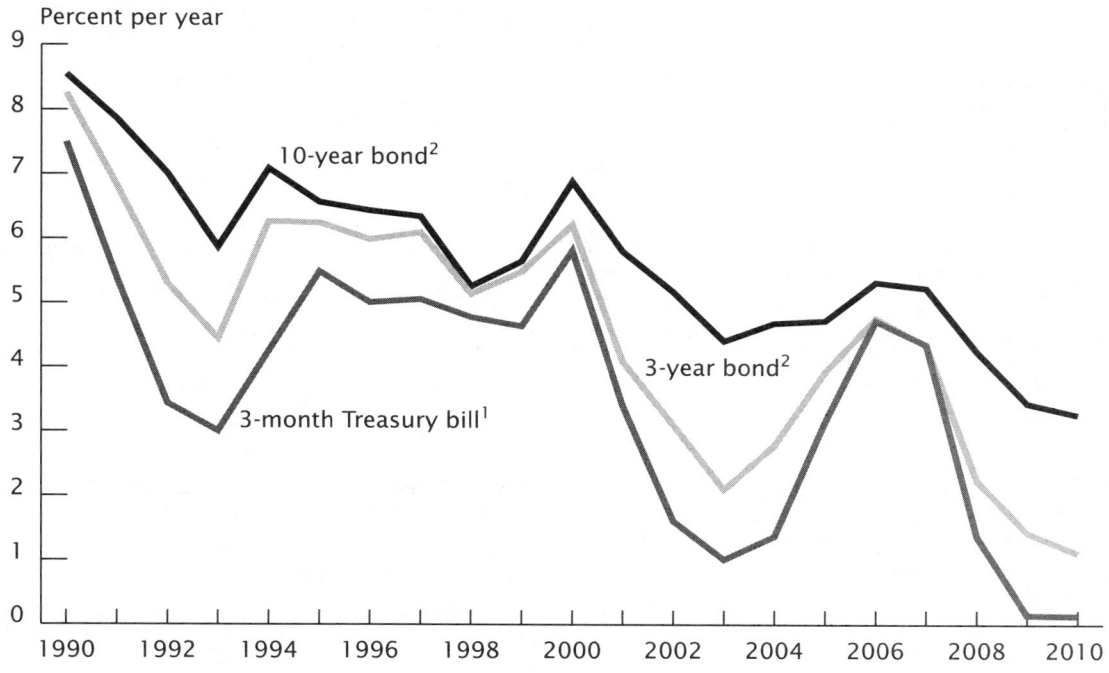

Percent per year

10-year bond[2]

3-month Treasury bill[1]

3-year bond[2]

[1]New issues.   [2]U.S. Treasury, constant maturities.

Source: Chart prepared by U.S. Census Bureau. For data, see Tables 1197 and 1198.

Figure 25.2
Foreign Holdings of U.S. Treasury Securities by Country: 2010
(In billions of dollars)

Total = 4,385.3

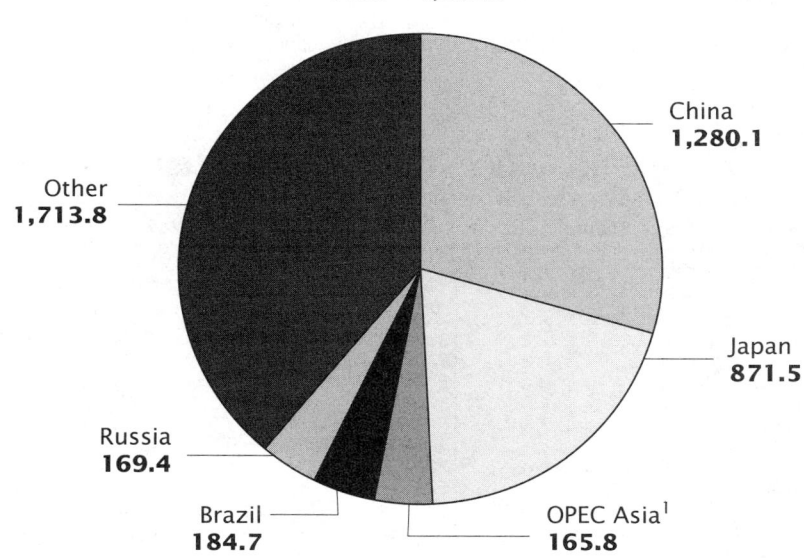

China
1,280.1

Other
1,713.8

Japan
871.5

Russia
169.4

Brazil
184.7

OPEC Asia[1]
165.8

[1]Comprises Iran, Iraq, Kuwait, Qatar, Saudi Arabia, and the United Arab Emirates.

Source: Chart prepared by U.S. Census Bureau. For data, see Table 1206.

Banking, Finance, and Insurance 729

Table 1162. Gross Domestic Product in Finance, Insurance, Real Estate, Rental and Leasing in Current and Chained (2005) Dollars: 2000 to 2010

[In billions of dollars, except percent (762 represents $762,000,000,000.) Represents value added by industry. Data for 2000 based on the 1997 North American Classification System (NAICS); beginning 2005 based on 2002 NAICS. See text, Section 15. For definition of gross domestic product and explanation of chained dollars, see text, Section 13, Income]

Industry	NAICS code	Current Dollars				Chained (2005) dollars			
		2000	2005	2009	2010	2000	2005	2009	2010
Finance & insurance, total	52	**762**	**1,029**	**1,172**	**1,235**	**841**	**1,029**	**1,094**	**1,129**
Percent of gross domestic product		7.7	8.1	8.3	8.4	7.5	8.1	8.5	8.5
Monetary authorities–central bank, credit intermediation, and related activities. . . .	521,522	338	471	514	(NA)	371	471	492	(NA)
Security, commodity contracts, & investment activities.	523	126	183	175	(NA)	124	183	149	(NA)
Insurance carriers & related activities	524	274	338	425	(NA)	339	338	404	(NA)
Funds, trusts, & other financial vehicles (part).	525	24	37	58	(NA)	20	37	57	(NA)
Real estate & rental & leasing, total. . .	53	**1,236**	**1,578**	**1,869**	**1,859**	**1,422**	**1,578**	**1,701**	**1,713**
Percent of gross domestic product		12.4	12.5	13.2	12.7	12.7	12.5	13.2	12.9
Real estate	531	1,098	1,425	1,687	(NA)	1,266	1,425	1,533	(NA)
Rental & leasing services and lessors of other nonfinancial intangible assets [1] . . .	532,533	138	153	182	(NA)	156	153	168	(NA)

NA Not available. [1] Includes lessors of other nonfinancial intangible assets.

Source: U.S. Bureau of Economic Analysis, *Survey of Current Business*, July 2011, <http://www.bea.gov/Industry/Index.htm>.

Table 1163. Finance and Insurance/Real Estate and Rental and Leasing—Establishments, Revenue, Payroll, and Employees by Kind of Business (2002 NAICS Basis): 2002 and 2007

[2,804 represents $2,804,000,000,000. For establishments with payroll. Based on the 2002 and 2007 Economic Censuses; see Appendix III]

Kind of business	2002 NAICS code [1]	Number of establishments		Revenue (bil. dol.)		Annual payroll (bil. dol.)		Paid employees (1,000)	
		2002	2007	2002	2007	2002	2007	2002	2007
Finance & insurance [2]	52	**440,268**	**506,507**	**2,804**	**3,711**	**377.8**	**505.2**	**6,579**	**6,649**
Monetary authorities—central bank.	521	47	47	29	45	1.2	1.3	22	19
Credit intermediation & related activities.	522	196,451	231,439	1,056	1,343	151.2	180.9	3,300	3,280
Security, commodity contracts, & like activity	523	72,338	85,475	316	612	103.4	166.3	832	885
Insurance carriers & related activities	524	169,520	184,752	1,380	1,669	120.6	153.9	2,406	2,423
Real estate & rental & leasing	53	**322,815**	**379,503**	**336**	**452**	**60.2**	**85.2**	**1,949**	**2,249**
Real estate	531	256,086	308,004	224	289	41.7	58.6	1,305	1,487
Rental & leasing services	532	64,344	65,120	95	122	16.9	21.1	617	630
Lessors of other nonfinancial intangible assets. . .	533	2,385	2,447	17	33	1.7	2.3	27	29

[1] Based on the North American Industry Classification System (NAICS); see text, Section 15. [2] Total does not include NAICS 525, Funds, trusts, and other financial vehicles, not published in the 2007 Economic Census.

Source: U.S. Census Bureau, "2007 Economic Census; Core Business Statistics Series: Advance Comparative Statistics for the United States (2002 NAICS Basis): 2007 and 2002," June 2010, see <http://www.census.gov/econ/census07/www/get_data/index.html>.

Table 1164. Finance and Insurance—Nonemployer Establishments and Receipts by Kind of Business: 2006 to 2008

[758.2 represents 758,167. Includes only firms subject to federal income tax. Nonemployers are businesses with no paid employees. Data originate chiefly from administrative records of the Internal Revenue Service; see Appendix III]

Kind of business	NAICS code [1]	Establishments (1,000)			Receipts (mil. dol.)		
		2006	2007	2008	2006	2007	2008
Finance and insurance	52	**758.2**	**763.5**	**733.5**	**52,768**	**54,351**	**56,434**
Credit intermediation & related activities	522	89.7	92.7	72.8	4,983	4,591	3,394
Depository credit intermediation	5221	7.4	7.6	7.4	232	228	202
Nondepository credit intermediation	5222	30.3	31.7	27.0	2,489	2,376	1,900
Activities related to credit intermediation.	5223	51.9	53.4	38.4	2,262	1,986	1,292
Security, commodity contracts, & like activity	523	280.3	281.7	270.9	28,113	29,618	32,752
Securities & commodity contracts interm & brokerage . . .	5231	32.9	32.6	30.8	4,983	5,496	6,631
Investment banking and securities dealing	52311	8.3	8.1	7.4	1,480	1,596	2,175
Securities brokerage	52312	19.6	19.8	19.0	2,829	2,977	3,360
Commodity contracts dealing	52313	1.3	1.4	1.3	169	412	582
Commodity contracts brokerage	52314	3.7	3.4	3.1	506	511	514
Securities & commodity exchanges.	5232	2.1	1.9	1.9	529	578	846
Other financial investment activities	5239	245.3	247.1	238.2	22,600	23,544	25,276
Insurance carriers & related activities	524	388.3	389.2	389.8	19,672	20,143	20,288
Insurance carriers	5241	0.5	2.9	3.1	32	189	191
Agencies & other insurance-related activities	5242	387.8	386.2	386.7	19,640	19,954	20,097
Insurance agencies & brokerages	52421	263.0	268.5	267.1	14,593	15,016	14,977
Other insurance related activities	52429	125.2	117.7	119.6	5,047	4,938	5,119

[1] Based on 2002 NAICS for 2006 data; data for 2007 and 2008, 2007 North American Industry Classification System (NAICS). For more information, see text, Section 15.

Source: U.S. Census Bureau, "Nonemployer Statistics," June 2010, <http://www.census.gov/econ/nonemployer/index.html>.

Table 1165. Finance and Insurance—Establishments, Employees, and Payroll: 2007 and 2008

[508.1 represents 508,091. Covers establishments with payroll. Employees are for the week including March 12. Excludes most government employees, railroad employees, and self-employed persons. For statement on methodology, see Appendix III]

Kind of business	NAICS code [1]	Establishments (1,000)		Employees (1,000)		Payroll (bil.dol.)	
		2007	2008	2007	2008	2007	2008
Finance & insurance, total [2]	52	**508.1**	**501.9**	**6,549**	**6,512**	**510.6**	**522.3**
Monetary authorities—central bank	521	0.1	0.1	20	19	1.4	1.4
Credit intermediation & related activities	522	232.7	225.0	3,226	3,077	182.5	175.3
Depository credit intermediation [2]	5221	127.2	129.8	2,138	2,135	121.2	119.4
Commercial banking	52211	93.0	95.6	1,640	1,644	99.0	97.1
Savings institutions	52212	15.9	16.1	248	235	12.4	12.3
Credit unions	52213	18.0	18.0	242	253	9.2	9.8
Nondepository credit intermediation [2]	5222	58.8	51.0	747	645	44.8	41.9
Real estate credit	522292	26.3	20.4	369	276	20.9	18.0
Activities related to credit intermediation	5223	46.8	44.3	341	297	16.5	13.9
Security, commodity contracts & like activity	523	90.1	92.7	942	974	172.3	184.3
Security & commodity contracts intermediation & brokerage [2]	5231	39.7	42.3	529	534	101.7	104.5
Investment banking & securities dealing	52311	9.3	4.5	184	137	46.1	46.9
Securities brokerage	52312	27.7	35.4	323	375	52.1	53.8
Securities & commodity exchanges	5232	(NA)	0.1	(NA)	(NA)	(NA)	(NA)
Other financial investment activities	5239	49.9	50.2	404	432	69.2	78.8
Insurance carriers & related activities	524	181.5	183.2	2,327	2,432	151.0	159.9
Insurance carriers [2]	5241	33.6	35.7	1,424	1,518	100.7	108.8
Direct life insurance carriers	524113	8.3	8.6	359	399	28.2	31.3
Direct health & medical insurance carriers	524114	4.1	4.7	414	469	27.8	30.7
Direct property & casualty insurance carriers	524126	13.2	15.3	533	549	36.1	39.2
Agencies & other insurance-related activities [2]	5242	147.9	147.5	903	914	50.3	51.1
Insurance agencies & brokerages	52421	134.3	134.6	698	696	38.5	38.8

NA Not available. [1] 2008 data use 2007 North American Industry Classification System (NAICS). 2007 data use NAICS 2002. For more information, see text, Section 15. [2] Includes industries not shown separately.

Source: U.S. Census Bureau, "County Business Patterns," July 2010, <http://www.census.gov/econ/cbp/index.html>.

Table 1166. Flow of Funds Accounts—Financial Assets of Financial and Nonfinancial Institutions by Holder Sector: 1990 to 2010

[In billions of dollars (35,754 represents $35,754,000,000,000). As of Dec. 31]

Sector	1990	1995	2000	2004	2005	2006	2007	2008	2009	2010
All sectors	**35,754**	**53,444**	**90,208**	**113,297**	**124,107**	**138,822**	**150,786**	**138,747**	**144,395**	**150,927**
Households [1]	14,497	21,457	33,283	39,138	43,214	47,975	50,560	41,176	44,123	47,639
Nonfinancial business	3,981	5,568	11,227	13,083	14,483	15,761	17,330	16,596	16,698	17,511
Farm business	38	49	57	66	67	74	79	82	84	86
Nonfarm noncorporate	356	548	1,423	2,106	2,542	3,057	3,533	3,629	3,350	3,188
Nonfinancial corporations	3,586	4,971	9,747	10,912	11,874	12,630	13,718	12,886	13,264	14,237
State and local government	1,020	1,122	1,662	2,030	2,247	2,461	2,591	2,509	2,598	2,739
U.S. Government	442	432	570	641	644	641	687	1,268	1,380	1,650
Monetary authorities	342	472	636	841	879	908	951	2,271	2,267	2,453
Commercial banking	3,338	4,499	6,709	9,058	9,844	10,886	11,879	14,056	14,288	14,402
U.S.-chartered commercial banks	2,644	3,322	4,999	6,865	7,393	8,189	8,841	10,248	10,045	10,076
Foreign banking offices in U.S.	367	671	805	664	818	828	1,048	1,625	1,268	1,338
Bank-holding companies	298	467	842	1,429	1,524	1,760	1,883	2,079	2,877	2,906
Banks in U.S.-affiliated areas	28	39	63	100	109	108	108	105	99	83
Savings institutions	1,323	1,013	1,218	1,650	1,789	1,715	1,815	1,524	1,254	1,244
Credit unions	217	311	441	655	686	716	759	812	883	911
Life insurance companies	1,351	2,064	3,136	4,130	4,351	4,685	4,950	4,515	4,824	5,177
Property-casualty insurance companies	533	740	858	1,159	1,246	1,336	1,386	1,309	1,388	1,403
Private pension funds	1,629	2,899	4,468	4,922	5,389	6,083	6,411	4,553	5,471	6,080
Defined benefit plans	900	1,466	1,979	2,132	2,281	2,530	2,596	1,853	2,105	2,215
Defined contribution plans	729	1,433	2,489	2,790	3,107	3,553	3,815	2,699	3,366	3,865
State and local government employee retirement funds	730	1,327	2,293	2,578	2,721	3,090	3,199	2,325	2,674	2,928
Federal government retirement funds	340	541	797	1,023	1,072	1,141	1,197	1,221	1,324	1,415
Money market mutual funds	493	741	1,812	1,880	2,007	2,312	3,033	3,757	3,258	2,755
Mutual funds	608	1,853	4,433	5,436	6,049	7,068	7,829	5,435	6,962	7,963
Closed-end funds	53	136	142	246	271	294	317	205	231	246
Exchange-traded funds	−	1	66	227	301	423	608	531	773	986
Government-sponsored enterprises (GSE)	478	897	1,965	2,883	2,819	2,873	3,174	3,400	3,014	6,591
Agency- and GSE-backed mortgage pools	1,020	1,571	2,493	3,384	3,548	3,841	4,464	4,961	5,376	1,166
Asset-backed securities issuers	268	663	1,497	2,657	3,388	4,196	4,541	4,132	3,347	2,454
Finance companies	596	705	1,213	1,858	1,857	1,891	1,911	1,852	1,662	1,595
Real estate investment trusts	28	33	65	251	305	344	317	254	255	274
Security brokers and dealers	262	568	1,221	1,845	2,127	2,742	3,092	2,217	2,084	2,075
Funding corporations	236	366	1,165	1,184	1,341	1,460	1,851	2,859	2,443	2,316
Rest of the world	1,967	3,466	6,841	10,539	11,530	13,980	15,935	15,008	15,816	16,952

− Represents zero. [1] Includes nonprofit organizations.

Source: Board of Governors of the Federal Reserve System, "Federal Reserve Statistical Release, Z.1, Flow of Funds Accounts of the United States," March 2011, <http://www.federalreserve.gov/releases/z1/20100311>.

Table 1167. Flow of Funds Accounts—Credit Market Debt Outstanding: 1990 to 2010

[In billions of dollars (13,767 represents $13,767,000,000,000). As of December 31. Excludes corporate equities and mutual fund shares. Represents credit market debt owed by sectors shown]

Item	1990	1995	2000	2004	2005	2006	2007	2008	2009	2010
Credit market debt................	13,767	18,469	27,138	37,816	41,276	45,352	50,043	52,433	52,261	52,636
Domestic nonfinancial................	10,835	13,667	18,165	24,442	26,767	29,178	31,699	33,601	34,629	36,296
Households [1]....................	3,581	4,841	6,987	10,570	11,743	12,930	13,803	13,801	13,567	13,358
Corporations....................	2,543	2,942	4,633	5,167	5,490	5,956	6,705	6,993	6,998	7,378
Nonfarm noncorporate business.........	1,102	1,070	1,806	2,455	2,787	3,196	3,650	3,972	3,678	3,484
Farm business..................	124	131	156	173	190	204	219	223	221	225
State and local government............	987	1,047	1,198	1,683	1,855	2,008	2,199	2,251	2,360	2,465
U.S. government..................	2,498	3,637	3,385	4,395	4,702	4,885	5,122	6,362	7,805	9,386
Rest of the world....................	318	568	815	1,439	1,514	1,883	2,126	1,709	2,014	2,104
Financial sectors..................	2,614	4,234	8,158	11,936	12,996	14,291	16,217	17,123	15,618	14,236
Commercial banking...............	198	251	509	739	824	1,002	1,263	1,425	1,666	1,855
Savings institutions..............	140	115	301	405	427	319	423	356	152	114
Credit unions...................	–	1	3	11	15	19	32	41	27	26
Life insurance companies...........	–	1	2	11	11	14	29	55	48	45
Government-sponsored enterprises (GSE)..	399	807	1,826	2,676	2,592	2,628	2,910	3,182	2,707	6,379
Agency- and GSE-backed mortgage pools..	1,020	1,571	2,493	3,384	3,548	3,841	4,464	4,961	5,376	1,166
Asset-backed securities issuers..........	269	666	1,504	2,662	3,392	4,199	4,544	4,135	3,350	2,456
Finance companies..............	398	500	807	1,130	1,109	1,144	1,280	1,200	1,044	964
Real estate investment trusts...........	28	45	168	340	395	411	421	373	339	351
Brokers and dealers...............	15	29	41	62	62	69	65	143	93	130
Funding corporations................	147	249	503	515	620	645	786	1,253	817	751

– Represents or rounds to zero. [1] Includes nonprofit organizations.
Source: Board of Governors of the Federal Reserve System, "Federal Reserve Statistical Release, Z.1, Flow of Funds Accounts of the United States," March 2011, <http://www.federalreserve.gov/releases/z1/20100311>.

Table 1168. Flow of Funds Accounts—Financial Assets and Liabilities of Foreign Sector: 1990 to 2010

[In billions of dollars (1,967 represents $1,967,000,000,000). As of December 31. Minus sign (–) indicates loss]

Type of instrument	1990	1995	2000	2004	2005	2006	2007	2008	2009	2010
Total financial assets [1]..........	1,967	3,466	6,841	10,539	11,530	13,980	15,935	15,008	15,816	16,952
Net interbank assets................	53	229	161	118	106	97	–57	363	70	20
U.S. checkable deposits and currency....	86	158	236	285	300	312	306	370	361	390
U.S. time deposits..................	40	40	102	149	156	167	208	273	230	233
Net security RPs [2].................	20	68	91	186	231	365	338	115	31	–98
Credit market instruments [1]...........	882	1,465	2,451	4,635	5,191	6,200	7,273	7,503	7,785	8,437
Open market paper..............	11	43	114	230	240	286	278	233	192	192
Treasury securities.................	438	817	1,021	1,814	1,984	2,126	2,376	3,251	3,697	4,394
Official.....................	286	490	640	1,252	1,341	1,558	1,737	2,401	2,871	3,258
Private.....................	152	327	382	562	644	568	640	851	826	1,136
Agency- and GSE-backed securities [3]...	49	123	348	875	1,013	1,264	1,582	1,407	1,189	1,186
Official.....................	5	18	116	373	487	695	954	941	761	681
Private.....................	44	106	232	503	526	568	628	466	427	504
U.S. corporate bonds [4].............	209	355	842	1,559	1,763	2,321	2,719	2,354	2,468	2,430
Loans to U.S. corporate business......	172	122	117	131	163	169	271	207	182	161
U.S. corporate equities..............	243	485	1,483	1,905	2,039	2,448	2,812	1,807	2,436	3,091
Mutual fund shares................	–	60	149	196	242	317	373	256	322	368
Trade receivables..................	46	49	49	49	57	63	84	90	95	114
Miscellaneous assets...............	591	900	2,101	2,986	3,178	3,978	4,544	4,154	4,360	4,283
Foreign direct investment in U.S. [5]......	505	680	1,421	1,743	1,906	2,154	2,411	2,521	2,673	2,866
Other.......................	85	220	680	1,243	1,272	1,824	2,134	1,633	1,687	1,417
Total liabilities................	1,437	2,144	3,579	5,611	6,088	7,234	8,482	8,379	8,689	8,999
U.S. official foreign exchange and net IMF [6]......................	72	75	57	76	54	55	60	67	120	121
U.S. official reserve assets............	298	419	803	957	998	1,085	1,342	940	768	850
Credit market instruments [1]...........	318	568	815	1,439	1,514	1,883	2,126	1,709	2,014	2,104
Commercial paper...............	75	56	121	345	384	482	413	342	401	396
Bonds......................	145	413	573	985	1,012	1,276	1,587	1,237	1,494	1,571
Bank loans n.e.c. [7]...............	19	35	71	70	84	98	103	108	97	115
Trade payables....................	29	47	51	48	54	61	73	63	61	95
Miscellaneous liabilities [1]............	720	1,036	1,854	3,092	3,468	4,151	4,882	5,601	5,726	5,829
U.S. equity in IBRD, [8] etc..............	20	27	35	42	43	45	47	48	50	53
Nonofficial foreign currencies.........	1	2	3	3	1	1	24	554	11	1
U.S. direct investment abroad [4, 5].......	630	886	1,532	2,498	2,652	2,948	3,553	3,743	4,051	4,380

– Represents zero. [1] Includes other items not shown separately. [2] Repurchase agreements. [3] GSE = Government-sponsored enterprises. [4] Through 1992, corporate bonds include net issues by Netherlands Antillean financial subsidiaries; U.S. direct investment abroad excludes net inflows from those bond issues. [5] Direct investment is valued on a current-cost basis.
[6] IMF = International Monetary Fund. [7] Not elsewhere classified. [8] International Bank for Reconstruction and Development.
Source: Board of Governors of the Federal Reserve System, "Federal Reserve Statistical Release, Z.1, Flow of Funds Accounts of the United States," March 2011, <http://www.federalreserve.gov/releases/z1/20100311>.

Table 1169. Flow of Funds Accounts—Assets of Households and Nonprofit Organizations: 1990 to 2010

[As of December 31 (14,497 represents $14,497,000,000,000). See also Table 722]

Type of instrument	Total (billion dollars)							Percent distribution		
	1990	2000	2005	2007	2008	2009	2010	1990	2000	2010
Total financial assets	**14,497**	**33,283**	**43,214**	**50,560**	**41,176**	**44,123**	**47,639**	**100.0**	**100.0**	**100.0**
Deposits	3,325	4,376	6,140	7,407	8,013	7,895	7,931	22.9	13.1	16.6
Foreign deposits	13	48	60	81	56	46	51	0.1	0.1	0.1
Checkable deposits and currency	433	335	217	90	292	363	327	3.0	1.0	0.7
Time and savings deposits	2,490	3,033	4,914	5,889	6,083	6,172	6,422	17.2	9.1	13.5
Money market fund shares	389	960	949	1,348	1,582	1,313	1,131	2.7	2.9	2.4
Credit market instruments	1,741	2,458	3,324	4,073	3,966	4,106	4,355	12.0	7.4	9.1
Open-market paper	94	97	98	107	6	35	63	0.6	0.3	0.1
Treasury securities	504	579	464	256	248	770	1,079	3.5	1.7	2.3
Agency and GSE-backed securities [1]	117	594	493	669	711	83	78	0.8	1.8	0.2
Municipal securities	648	531	821	896	903	1,010	1,096	4.5	1.6	2.3
Corporate and foreign bonds	238	551	1,298	2,017	1,956	2,081	1,919	1.6	1.7	4.0
Other loans and advances [2]	–	2	9	18	30	24	28	–	–	0.1
Mortgages	141	103	139	110	112	102	92	1.0	0.3	0.2
Corporate equities [3]	1,961	8,147	8,093	9,627	5,777	7,321	8,514	13.5	24.5	17.9
Mutual fund shares	512	2,704	3,669	4,597	3,326	4,178	4,708	3.5	8.1	9.9
Security credit	62	412	575	866	743	669	694	0.4	1.2	1.5
Life insurance reserves	392	819	1,083	1,202	1,180	1,242	1,329	2.7	2.5	2.8
Pension fund reserves [4]	3,310	9,171	11,460	13,391	10,408	11,915	13,025	22.8	27.6	27.3
Equity in noncorporate business	2,939	4,815	8,261	8,685	6,996	6,011	6,251	20.3	14.5	13.1
Miscellaneous assets	254	379	609	712	766	787	834	1.8	1.1	1.8

– Represents or rounds to zero. [1] GSE = government-sponsored enterprises. [2] Syndicated loans to nonfinancial corporate business by nonprofits and domestic hedge funds. [3] Only those directly held and those in closed-end and exchange-traded funds. Other equities are included in mutual funds and life insurance and pension reserves. [4] See also Table 1217.

Source: Board of Governors of the Federal Reserve System, "Federal Reserve Statistical Release, Z.1, Flow of Funds Accounts of the United States," March 2011, <http://www.federalreserve.gov/releases/z1/20100311>.

Table 1170. Financial Assets Held by Families by Type of Asset: 2004 and 2007

Median value in thousands of constant 2007 dollars (25.3 represents $25,300). All dollar figures are adjusted to 2007 dollars using the "current methods" version of the consumer price index for all urban consumers published by U.S. Bureau of Labor Statistics. Families include one-person units; for definition of family, see text, Section 1. Based on Survey of Consumer Finances; see Appendix III]

Age of family head and family income	Any financial asset [1]	Trans-action accounts [2]	Certifi-cates of deposit	Savings bonds	Stocks [3]	Pooled invest-ment funds [4]	Retire-ment accounts [5]	Life insur-ance [6]	Other man-aged [7]
PERCENT OF FAMILIES OWNING ASSET									
2004, total	93.8	91.3	12.7	17.6	20.7	15.0	49.7	24.2	7.3
2007, total	**93.9**	**92.1**	**16.1**	**14.9**	**17.9**	**11.4**	**52.6**	**23.0**	**5.8**
Under 35 years old	89.2	87.3	6.7	13.7	13.7	5.3	41.6	11.4	(B)
35 to 44 years old	93.1	91.2	9.0	16.8	17.0	11.6	57.5	17.5	2.2
45 to 54 years old	93.3	91.7	14.3	19.0	18.6	12.6	64.7	22.3	5.1
55 to 64 years old	97.8	96.4	20.5	16.2	21.3	14.3	60.9	35.2	7.7
65 to 74 years old	96.1	94.6	24.2	10.3	19.1	14.6	51.7	34.4	13.2
75 years old and over	97.4	95.3	37.0	7.9	20.2	13.2	30.0	27.6	14.0
Percentiles of income: [8]									
Less than 20	79.1	74.9	9.4	3.6	5.5	3.4	10.7	12.8	2.7
20 to 39.9	93.2	90.1	12.7	8.5	7.8	4.6	35.6	16.4	4.7
40 to 59.9	97.2	96.4	15.4	15.2	14.0	7.1	55.2	21.6	5.3
60 to 79.9	99.7	99.3	19.3	20.9	23.2	14.6	73.3	29.4	5.7
80 to 89.9	100.0	100.0	19.9	26.2	30.5	18.9	86.7	30.6	7.6
90 to 100	100.0	100.0	27.7	26.1	47.5	35.5	89.6	38.9	13.6
MEDIAN VALUE [9]									
2004, total	25.3	4.1	16.5	1.1	16.5	44.4	38.7	6.6	49.4
2007, total	**28.8**	**4.0**	**20.0**	**1.0**	**17.0**	**56.0**	**45.0**	**8.0**	**70.0**
Under 35 years old	6.8	2.4	5.0	0.7	3.0	18.0	10.0	2.8	(B)
35 to 44 years old	25.8	3.4	5.0	1.0	15.0	22.5	36.0	8.3	24.0
45 to 54 years old	54.0	5.0	15.0	1.0	18.5	50.0	67.0	10.0	45.0
55 to 64 years old	72.4	5.2	23.0	1.9	24.0	112.0	98.0	10.0	59.0
65 to 74 years old	68.1	7.7	23.2	1.0	38.0	86.0	77.0	10.0	70.0
75 years old and over	41.5	6.1	30.0	20.0	40.0	75.0	35.0	5.0	100.0

B Base figure too small. [1] Includes other types of financial assets, not shown separately. [2] Checking, savings, and money market deposit accounts, money market mutual funds, and call accounts at brokerages. [3] Covers only those stocks and bonds that are directly held by families outside mutual funds, retirement accounts, and other managed assets. [4] Excludes money market mutual funds and indirectly held mutual funds and includes all other types of directly held pooled investment funds, such as traditional open-ended and closed-end mutual funds, real estate investment trusts, and hedge funds. [5] The tax-deferred retirement accounts consist of IRAs, Keogh accounts, and certain employer-sponsored accounts. Employer-sponsored accounts include 401(k), 403(b), and thrift saving accounts from current or past jobs; other current job plans from which loans or withdrawals can be made; and accounts from past jobs from which the family expects to receive the account balance in the future. [6] The value of such policies according to their current cash value, not their death benefit. [7] Includes personal annuities and trusts with an equity interest and managed investment accounts. [8] Percentiles of income distribution in 2007 dollars: 20th: $20,600; 40th: $36,500; 60th: $59,600; 80th: $98,200; 90th: $140,900. Percentiles of distribution of net worth in 2007 dollars: 25th: $14,100; 50th: $120,300; 75th: $372,000; 90th: $908,200. Percentile: A value on a scale of zero to 100 that indicates the percent of a distribution that is equal to or below it. [9] Median value of financial asset for families holding such assets.

Source: Board of Governors of the Federal Reserve System, "2007 Survey of Consumer Finances," February 2009, <http://www.federalreserve.gov/pubs/oss/oss2/2007/scf2007home.html>.

Banking, Finance, and Insurance 733

Table 1171. Flow of Funds Accounts—Liabilities of Households and Nonprofit Organizations: 1990 to 2010

[As of December 31 (3,703 represents $3,703,000,000,000). See also Table 722]

Type of instrument	Total (bil. dol.)							Percent distribution		
	1990	2000	2005	2007	2008	2009	2010	1990	2000	2010
Total liabilities	**3,703**	**7,377**	**12,184**	**14,367**	**14,223**	**14,033**	**13,918**	**100.0**	**100.0**	**100.0**
Credit market instruments	3,581	6,987	11,743	13,803	13,801	13,567	13,358	94.7	96.4	96.0
Home mortgages [1]	2,489	4,798	8,874	10,540	10,495	10,340	10,070	65.0	72.8	72.4
Consumer credit	824	1,741	2,321	2,555	2,594	2,479	2,435	23.6	19.0	17.5
Municipal securities	86	138	205	241	249	264	268	1.9	1.7	1.9
Bank loans, not elsewhere classified. ..	18	64	36	100	118	148	269	0.9	0.3	1.9
Other loans and advances.	82	119	119	127	133	134	136	1.6	1.0	1.0
Commercial mortgages	83	127	187	240	212	203	180	1.7	1.5	1.3
Security credit	39	235	232	326	165	203	278	3.2	1.9	2.0
Trade payables	67	135	186	215	230	241	259	1.8	1.5	1.9
Unpaid life insurance premiums [2]	16	20	22	24	27	22	22	0.3	0.2	0.2

[1] Includes loans made under home equity lines of credit and home equity loans secured by junior liens. [2] Includes deferred premiums.

Source: Board of Governors of the Federal Reserve System, "Federal Reserve Statistical Release, Z.1, Flow of Funds Accounts of the United States," March 2011, <http://www.federalreserve.gov/releases/z1/20100311>.

Table 1172. Financial Debt Held by Families by Type of Debt: 2004 and 2007

[Median debt in thousands of constant 2007 dollars (60.7 represents $60,700). See headnote, Table 1170]

Age of family head and family income	Any debt	Secured by residential property		Lines of credit not secured by residential property	Installment loans	Credit card balances [2]	Other [3]
		Primary residence [1]	Other				
PERCENT OF FAMILIES HOLDING DEBT							
2004, total	76.4	47.9	4.0	1.6	46.0	46.2	7.6
2007, total	**77.0**	**48.7**	**5.5**	**1.7**	**46.9**	**46.1**	**6.8**
Under 35 years old	83.5	37.3	3.3	2.1	65.2	48.5	5.9
35 to 44 years old	86.2	59.5	6.5	2.2	56.2	51.7	7.5
45 to 54 years old	86.8	65.5	8.0	1.9	51.9	53.6	9.8
55 to 64 years old	81.8	55.3	7.8	1.2	44.6	49.9	8.7
65 to 74 years old	65.5	42.9	5.0	1.5	26.1	37.0	4.4
75 years old and over	31.4	13.9	0.6	(B)	7.0	18.8	1.3
Percentiles of income: [4]							
Less than 20	51.7	14.9	1.1	(B)	27.8	25.7	3.9
20 to 39.9.	70.2	29.5	1.9	1.8	42.3	39.4	6.8
40 to 59.9.	83.8	50.5	2.6	(B)	54.0	54.9	6.4
60 to 79.9.	90.9	69.7	6.8	2.1	59.2	62.1	8.7
80 to 89.9.	89.6	80.8	8.5	(B)	57.4	55.8	9.6
90 to 100	87.6	76.4	21.9	2.1	45.0	40.6	7.0
MEDIAN DEBT [5]							
2004, total	60.7	104.3	95.6	3.3	12.7	2.4	4.4
2007, total	**67.3**	**107.0**	**100.0**	**3.8**	**13.0**	**3.0**	**5.0**
Under 35 years old	36.2	135.3	78.0	1.0	15.0	1.8	4.5
35 to 44 years old	106.2	128.0	101.6	4.6	13.5	3.5	5.0
45 to 54 years old	95.9	110.0	82.0	6.0	12.9	3.6	4.5
55 to 64 years old	60.3	85.0	130.0	10.0	10.9	3.6	6.0
65 to 74 years old	40.1	69.0	125.0	30.0	10.3	3.0	5.0
75 years old and over	13.0	40.0	50.0	(B)	8.0	0.8	4.5

B Base figure too small. [1] First and second mortgages and home equity loans and lines of credit secured. [2] Families that had an outstanding balance on any of their credit cards after paying their most recent bills. [3] Includes loans on insurance policies, loans against pension accounts, borrowing on margin accounts and unclassified loans. [4] See footnote 8, Table 1170. [5] Median amount of financial debt for families holding such debts.

Source: Board of Governors of the Federal Reserve System, "2007 Survey of Consumer Finances," February 2009, <http://www.federalreserve.gov/pubs/oss/oss2/2007/scf2007home.html>.

Table 1173. Amount of Debt Held by Families—Percent Distribution: 2004 and 2007

[See headnote, Table 1170]

Type of debt	2004	2007	Purpose of debt	2004	2007	Type of lending institution	2004	2007
Total.	**100.0**	**100.0**	**Total. ....**	**100.0**	**100.0**	**Total. ....**	**100.0**	**100.0**
Secured by residential property:			Primary residence:				35.1	37.3
Primary residence	75.2	74.7	Purchase	70.2	69.5	Commercial bank.	7.3	4.2
Other	8.5	10.1	Improvement	1.9	2.3	Thrift institution	3.6	4.2
Lines of credit not secured by residential property	0.7	0.4	Other residential property	9.5	10.8	Credit union .... Finance or loan company	4.1	3.4
Installment loans	11.0	10.2	Investments, excluding real estate	2.2	1.6	Brokerage	2.5	1.6
Credit card balances ...	3.0	3.5	Vehicles	6.7	5.5	Real estate lender [1] ...	39.4	41.6
Other	1.6	1.1	Goods and services.	6.0	6.2	Individual lender	1.7	1.4
			Education.	3.0	3.6	Other nonfinancial	2.0	2.0
			Other loans	0.6	0.5	Government.	0.7	0.4
						Credit card issuer	3.0	3.6
						Other type of lender. ..	0.5	0.4

[1] Includes mortgage lender.

Source: Board of Governors of the Federal Reserve System, "2007 Survey of Consumer Finances," February 2009, <http://www.federalreserve.gov/pubs/oss/oss2/2007/scf2007home.html>.

734 Banking, Finance, and Insurance

Table 1174. Ratios of Debt Payments to Family Income: 2001 to 2007

[In percent. All dollar figures are adjusted to 2007 dollars using the "current methods" version of the consumer price index for all urban consumers published by U.S. Bureau of Labor Statistics. Families include one-person units; for definition of family, see text, Section 1. Based on Survey of Consumer Finance; see Appendix III. For definition of median, see Guide to Tabular Presentation]

Age of family head and family income (constant [2007] dollars)	Ratio of debt payments to family income						Percent of debtors with—					
	Aggregate			Median for debtors			Ratios above 40 percent			Any payment 60 days or more past due		
	2001	2004	2007	2001	2004	2007	2001	2004	2007	2001	2004	2007
All families	**12.9**	**14.4**	**14.5**	**16.7**	**18.0**	**18.6**	**11.8**	**12.2**	**14.7**	**7.0**	**8.9**	**7.1**
Under 35 years old	17.2	17.8	19.7	17.7	18.0	17.5	12.0	12.8	15.1	11.9	13.7	9.4
35 to 44 years old	15.1	18.2	18.5	17.8	20.6	20.3	10.1	12.5	12.7	5.9	11.7	8.6
45 to 54 years old	12.8	15.3	14.9	17.4	18.4	19.3	11.6	13.1	16.0	6.2	7.6	7.3
55 to 64 years old	10.9	11.5	12.5	14.3	15.7	17.5	12.3	10.2	14.5	7.1	4.2	4.9
65 to 74 years old	9.2	8.7	9.6	16.0	15.6	17.9	14.7	11.6	15.6	1.5	3.4	4.4
75 years old and over	3.9	7.1	4.4	8.0	12.8	13.0	14.6	10.7	13.9	0.8	3.9	1.0
Percentiles of income: [1]												
Less than 20	16.1	18.2	17.6	19.2	19.7	19.0	29.3	26.8	26.9	13.4	15.9	15.1
20 to 39.9	15.8	16.6	17.2	16.7	17.4	17.0	16.6	18.5	19.5	11.7	13.8	11.5
40 to 59.9	17.1	19.4	19.8	17.6	19.5	20.3	12.3	13.7	14.5	7.9	10.4	8.3
60 to 79.9	16.8	18.5	21.7	18.1	20.6	21.9	6.5	7.1	12.7	4.0	7.1	4.1
80 to 89.9	17.0	17.3	19.7	17.2	18.1	19.3	3.5	2.4	8.1	2.6	2.3	2.1
90 to 100	8.1	9.3	8.4	11.2	12.7	12.5	2.0	1.8	3.8	1.3	0.3	0.2

[1] See footnote 8, Table 1170.
Source: Board of Governors of the Federal Reserve System, "2007 Survey of Consumer Finances," February 2009, <http://www.federalreserve.gov/pubs/oss/oss2/2007/scf2007home.html>.

Table 1175. Household Debt-Service Payments and Financial Obligations as a Percentage of Disposable Personal Income: 1990 to 2010

[As of end of year, seasonally adjusted. Household debt service ratio is an estimate of the ratio of debt payments to disposable personal income. Debt payments consist of the estimated required payments on outstanding mortgage and consumer debt. The financial obligations ratio adds automobile lease payments, rental payments on tenant-occupied property, homeowners' insurance, and property tax payments to the debt service ratio]

Year	Household debt service ratio	Financial obligations ratio			Year	Household debt service ratio	Financial obligations ratio		
		Total	Renter	Home-owner			Total	Renter	Home-owner
1990	12.03	17.46	24.85	15.57	2006	13.87	18.65	25.38	17.33
1995	11.67	17.10	26.67	14.80	2007	13.89	18.76	25.02	17.48
2000	12.59	17.66	30.44	15.13	2008	13.51	18.43	25.24	17.05
2004	13.31	17.93	25.41	16.46	2009	12.67	17.63	24.76	16.16
2005	13.77	18.46	25.19	17.12	2010	11.75	16.64	23.88	15.13

Source: Board of Governors of the Federal Reserve System, "Household Debt Service and Financial Obligations Ratios," <http://www.federalreserve.gov/releases/housedebt/default.htm\>.

Table 1176. FDIC-Insured Financial Institutions—Deposit Insurance Fund (DIF): 1990 to 2010

[In billions of dollars, except as indicated (4,735 represents $4,735,000,000,000). As of December 31. Includes Island Areas. Includes insured branches of foreign banks. Minus sign (–) indicates decrease]

Item	1990	2000	2004	2005	2006	2007	2008	2009	2010
Number of institutions	15,369	9,920	8,988	8,845	8,691	8,544	8,314	8,021	7,666
Assets, total [1]	4,735	7,472	10,117	10,895	11,882	13,051	13,894	13,112	13,352
Domestic deposits, total [2]	3,415	4,212	5,725	6,230	6,640	6,922	7,505	7,705	7,888
Estimated insured deposits [3]	2,697	3,055	3,622	3,891	4,154	4,292	4,751	5,408	6,221
DIF balance (BIF/SAIF prior to 2006) . . .	4	42	48	49	50	52	17	–21	–7
Reserve ratio [4]	0.15	1.36	1.31	1.25	1.21	1.22	0.36	–0.39	–0.12
Number of problem institutions	1,496	94	80	52	50	76	252	702	884
Assets of problem institutions	646.8	23.8	28.2	6.6	8.3	22.2	159.4	402.8	390.0
Number of assisted institutions	1	–	–	–	–	–	5	8	–
Assets of assisted institutions	(Z)	–	–	–	–	–	1,306.0	1,917.5	–
Number of failed institutions	381	7	4	–	–	3	25	140	157
Assets of assisted institutions	146.6	0.4	0.2	–	–	2.6	371.9	169.7	92.1

– Represents zero. Z Less than $50 million. [1] Does not include foreign branch assets. [2] Excludes foreign office deposits, which are uninsured. [3] In general, insured deposits are total domestic deposits minus estimated uninsured deposits. Prior to September 30, 2009 insured deposits included deposits in accounts of $100,000 or less, beginning September 30, 2009, insured deposits include deposits in accounts of $250,000 or less. The Dodd-Frank Wall Street Reform and Consumer Protection Act temporarily provides unlimited coverage for noninterest bearing transaction accounts for two years begining December 31, 2010. Begining in the fourth quarter of 2010, estimates of insured deposits include the entire balance of noninterest bearing transaction accounts. [4] DIF balance as percent of DIF-insured deposits.
Source: U.S. Federal Deposit Insurance Corporation, *The FDIC Quarterly Banking Profile*.

Table 1177. FDIC-Insured Financial Institutions—Number, Assets, and Liabilities: 1990 to 2010

[In billions of dollars, except as indicated (4,649 represents $4,649,000,000,000). As of December 31. 2010 data preliminary. Includes Island Areas. Excludes insured branches of foreign banks. Except as noted, includes foreign branches of U.S. banks]

Item	1990	2000	2004	2005	2006	2007	2008	2009	2010
Commercial bank offices, total [1]	**63,205**	**73,174**	**78,473**	**80,967**	**83,860**	**86,398**	**89,975**	**95,056**	**94,399**
Number of main offices	12,347	8,315	7,631	7,526	7,401	7,283	7,086	6,995	6,676
Number of branches	50,858	64,859	70,842	73,441	76,459	79,115	82,889	88,061	87,723
Savings institutions offices, total [2]	**2,815**	**1,589**	**1,345**	**1,307**	**1,279**	**1,251**	**1,219**	**1,180**	**1,128**
Number of financial institutions reporting	15,162	9,905	8,976	8,833	8,680	8,534	8,305	8,012	7,657
Assets, total [3]	**4,649**	**7,462**	**10,106**	**10,878**	**11,862**	**13,034**	**13,841**	**13,087**	**13,321**
Net loans and leases	2,867	4,576	6,037	6,640	7,156	7,804	7,700	7,053	7,145
Real estate loans	1,612	2,396	3,680	4,141	4,508	4,782	4,705	4,462	4,267
1–4 family residential mortgages	859	1,340	1,833	2,042	2,735	2,853	2,713	2,577	2,534
Commercial real estate	(NA)	873	1,299	1,509	1,712	1,867	1,934	1,813	1,656
Construction and development	171	197	338	450	590	629	591	451	322
Home equity loans [4]	86	151	491	534	559	611	668	662	637
Commercial and industrial loans	646	1,086	968	1,086	1,215	1,439	1,494	1,222	1,186
Loans to individuals	451	672	930	949	955	1,058	1,089	1,058	1,318
Credit cards and related plans	142	266	399	396	385	422	445	421	702
Farm loans	33	49	49	52	54	57	60	60	59
Other loans and leases	218	448	496	494	504	573	529	483	548
Less: Reserve for losses	65	71	82	77	78	103	174	228	231
Less: Unearned income	29	3	3	3	2	2	3	4	2
Securities	890	1,361	1,860	1,893	1,981	1,954	2,035	2,500	2,668
Domestic office assets	4,259	6,702	9,160	9,824	10,557	11,475	12,321	11,651	11,695
Foreign office assets	390	760	945	1,054	1,304	1,559	1,520	1,437	1,626
Liabilities and capital, total	**4,649**	**7,462**	**10,106**	**10,878**	**11,862**	**13,034**	**13,841**	**13,087**	**13,321**
Noninterest-bearing deposits	511	802	1,173	1,267	1,270	1,260	1,481	1,618	1,774
Interest-bearing deposits	3,127	4,113	5,412	5,874	6,555	7,156	7,554	7,609	7,649
Other borrowed funds	569	1,467	1,905	2,063	2,121	2,517	2,570	1,782	1,718
Subordinated debt	28	90	119	131	161	185	185	157	147
Other liabilities	128	356	459	424	507	569	759	476	520
Equity capital	286	634	1,039	1,119	1,248	1,347	1,291	1,424	1,487
Domestic office deposits	3,344	4,208	5,719	6,221	6,631	6,913	7,496	7,697	7,873
Foreign office deposits	293	707	866	921	1,194	1,503	1,539	1,530	1,550

NA Not available. [1] Includes insured branches of foreign banks that file a Call Report. [2] Main offices. [3] Includes other items not shown separately. [4] For one- to four-family residential properties.

Source: U.S. Federal Deposit Insurance Corporation, *The FDIC Quarterly Banking Profile, Historical Statistics on Banking*, annual; *Statistics on Banking*, annual; and *FDIC Quarterly Banking Profile Graph Book*.

Table 1178. FDIC-Insured Financial Institutions—Income and Selected Measures of Financial Condition: 1990 to 2010

[In billions of dollars, except as indicated (437.7 represents $437,700,000,000). 2010 data preliminary. Includes Island Areas. Includes foreign branches of U.S. banks. Minus sign (–) indicates decrease]

Item	1990	2000	2004	2005	2006	2007	2008	2009	2010
Interest income	437.7	511.9	417.5	522.0	643.5	724.8	603.2	541.1	537.0
Interest expense	295.9	276.6	123.3	205.0	313.4	372.1	245.6	145.5	107.0
Net interest income	141.8	235.3	294.1	317.0	330.1	352.7	357.7	395.8	430.1
Provisions for loan losses	41.4	32.1	29.0	29.8	29.6	69.3	176.2	249.5	157.0
Noninterest income	62.2	165.6	203.6	223.4	240.4	233.1	207.7	260.4	236.8
Net operating revenue	204.0	401.0	497.8	130.3	141.4	102.4	9.5	–6.1	81.6
Percent of net operating revenue [1]	23.3	33.7	62.8	58.3	59.7	53.9	4.9	–1.5	34.4
Noninterest expense	144.2	242.3	295.5	317.4	332.3	367.0	368.3	405.3	392.7
Income taxes	9.1	43.6	58.5	64.6	68.1	46.4	6.3	5.7	37.8
Net income	11.3	81.5	122.2	133.8	145.2	100.0	4.5	–10.6	87.5
PERFORMANCE RATIOS									
Return on assets [2] (percent)	0.24	1.14	1.28	1.28	1.28	0.81	0.03	–0.08	0.66
Return on equity [3] (percent)	3.95	13.53	13.2	12.43	12.3	7.75	0.35	–0.77	5.99
Net interest margin [4] (percent)	3.47	3.77	3.52	3.47	3.31	3.29	3.16	3.47	3.76
Net charge-offs [5]	34.80	26.30	32.02	31.59	27.02	44.11	100.36	188.80	187.10
Net charge-offs to loans and leases, total (percent)	1.19	0.59	0.56	0.49	0.39	0.59	1.29	2.52	2.54
Net charge-off rate, credit card loans (percent)	3.39	4.36	4.99	4.74	3.44	4.06	5.44	9.26	10.08
CONDITION RATIOS									
Equity capital to assets (percent)	6.16	8.49	10.28	10.28	10.52	10.34	9.33	10.88	11.16
Noncurrent assets plus other real estate owned to assets [6] (percent)	3.16	0.71	0.53	0.50	0.54	0.95	1.91	3.36	3.11

[1] Net operating revenue equals net interest income plus noninterest income. Net operating revenue equals income excluding discretionary transactions such as gains or losses on the sale of investment securities and extraordinary items. Income taxes subtracted from operating income have been adjusted to exclude the portion applicable to securities gains or losses. [2] Net income (including securities transactions and nonrecurring items) as a percentage of average total assets. [3] Net income as a percentage of average total equity capital. [4] Interest income less interest expense as a percentage of average earning assets (i.e. the profit margin a bank earns on its loans and investments). [5] Total loans and leases charged off (removed from balance sheet because of uncollectibility), less amounts recovered on loans and leases previously charged off. [6] Noncurrent assets: the sum of loans, leases, debt securities and other assets that are 90 days or more past due, or in nonaccrual status. Other real estate owned, primarily foreclosed property.

Source: U.S. Federal Deposit Insurance Corporation, *Annual Report*; *Statistics on Banking*, annual; and *FDIC Quarterly Banking Profile*.

Table 1179. FDIC-Insured Financial Institutions by Asset Size: 2010

[12,067.6 represents $12,067,600,000,000. Preliminary. Minus sign (−) indicates loss. See headnote, Table 1178]

Item	Unit	Total	Less than $100 mil.	$100 mil. to $1 bil.	$1 bil. to $10 bil.	Greater than $10 bil.
COMMERCIAL BANKS						
Institutions reporting	Number	6,529	2,325	3,694	424	86
Assets, total........................	Bil. dol......	12,067.6	131.9	1,058.6	1,090.4	9,786.6
Deposits...........................	Bil. dol......	8,514.3	112.0	884.0	841.9	6,676.3
Net income	Bil. dol......	79.2	(Z)	3.4	2.0	73.1
Return on assets	Percent	0.66	0.36	0.34	0.19	0.75
Return on equity	Percent	5.99	3.06	3.35	1.67	6.78
Equity capital to assets	Percent	11.10	11.42	10.04	11.29	11.19
Noncurrent assets plus other real estate owned to assets.................	Percent	3.12	2.35	3.53	3.91	3.00
Net charge-offs to loans and leases	Percent	2.67	0.80	1.14	1.96	3.00
Percentage of banks losing money	Percent	20.63	20.69	20.49	23.35	11.63
SAVINGS INSTITUTIONS						
Institutions reporting	Number	1,128	297	674	21	136
Assets, total........................	Bil. dol......	1,253.8	16.5	233.1	662.9	341.3
Deposits...........................	Bil. dol......	908.7	13.2	184.7	450.3	260.5
Net income	Bil. dol......	8.3	(Z)	0.7	6.2	1.4
Return on assets	Percent	0.67	0.08	0.29	0.95	0.42
Return on equity	Percent	5.92	0.58	2.71	8.15	3.83
Equity capital to assets	Percent	11.75	14.36	10.99	12.29	11.07
Noncurrent assets plus other real estate owned to assets.................	Percent	3.07	2.56	2.96	3.32	2.66
Net charge-offs to loans and leases	Percent	1.47	0.55	0.80	1.90	1.24
Percentage of banks losing money	Percent	23.23	32.66	20.18	14.29	19.12

Z Less than $500 million.

Source: U.S. Federal Deposit Insurance Corporation, *Annual Report*; *Statistics on Banking*, annual; and *FDIC Quarterly Banking Profile*. See also <http://www.fdic.gov/bank/index.html>.

Table 1180. FDIC-Insured Financial Institutions—Number and Assets by State and Island Areas: 2010

[In billions of dollars, except as indicated (13,321.4 represents $13,321,400,000,000). As of December 31. Information is obtained primarily from the Federal Financial Institutions Examination Council (FFIEC) Call Reports and the Office of Thrift Supervision's Thrift Financial Reports. Data are based on the location of each reporting institution's main office. Reported data may include assets located outside of the reporting institution's home state]

State or Island Area	Number of institutions	Total	Less than $1 bil.	$1 bil. to $10 bil.	Greater than $10 bil.	State or Island Area	Number of institutions	Total	Less than $1 bil.	$1 bil. to $10 bil.	Greater than $10 bil.
Total...	**7,657**	**13,321.4**	**1,440.2**	**1,431.7**	**10,449.5**	NV.....	29	1,247.4	3.7	20.0	1,223.7
AL.....	144	225.3	28.3	5.3	191.7	NH.....	24	9.9	8.9	1.1	−
AK.....	6	5.0	1.2	3.8	−	NJ.....	117	174.4	29.1	54.2	91.1
AZ.....	40	13.8	6.2	7.6	−	NM.....	53	18.9	11.0	7.9	−
AR.....	130	58.2	25.5	21.2	11.5	NY.....	186	643.7	47.1	123.1	473.5
CA.....	272	473.7	61.9	89.8	322.0	NC.....	100	1,728.4	24.8	25.0	1,678.6
CO.....	117	49.2	19.7	19.1	10.4	ND.....	92	24.8	13.3	11.5	−
CT.....	54	82.9	15.6	25.5	41.8	OH.....	239	2,285.9	42.8	33.1	2,210.0
DE.....	27	960.8	3.4	26.1	931.4	OK.....	248	79.6	33.2	18.1	28.2
DC.....	6	1.7	1.7	−	−	OR.....	34	38.2	5.8	6.8	25.6
FL.....	247	151.2	56.0	59.9	35.3	PA.....	216	281.2	59.5	91.2	130.5
GA.....	268	270.0	51.9	26.1	192.0	RI.....	14	136.1	2.5	5.6	128.0
HI.....	9	39.9	1.4	10.2	28.3	SC.....	83	38.2	21.8	16.4	−
ID.....	18	8.1	4.5	3.5	−	SD.....	83	1,287.8	11.2	13.5	1,263.1
IL.....	607	327.3	100.0	69.1	158.2	TN.....	191	86.6	45.2	16.9	24.5
IN.....	146	66.3	29.0	37.3	−	TX.....	615	374.8	109.2	106.3	159.3
IA.....	360	66.1	49.2	16.9	−	UT.....	57	346.3	11.2	45.4	289.6
KS.....	326	63.0	40.1	22.9	−	VT.....	14	5.7	4.2	1.5	−
KY.....	198	54.7	34.9	19.8	−	VA.....	115	492.0	28.5	39.0	424.5
LA.....	156	62.7	34.3	16.7	11.8	WA.....	79	66.1	17.1	35.6	13.4
ME.....	29	29.3	11.0	7.2	11.1	WV.....	65	25.4	11.1	14.3	−
MD.....	87	34.4	21.7	12.7	−	WI.....	276	148.2	55.9	21.5	70.7
MA.....	165	256.6	43.3	57.8	155.5	WY.....	37	7.6	7.6	−	−
MI.....	136	68.1	28.2	26.3	13.6						
MN.....	404	61.3	51.8	9.4	−	AS	1	0.1	0.1	−	−
MS.....	91	59.2	20.2	25.4	13.6	GU....	1	0.1	0.1	−	−
MO.....	336	129.3	56.2	44.1	29.0	FM....	3	1.3	1.3	−	−
MT.....	73	22.1	10.2	11.9	−	PR....	7	77.9	−	33.2	44.7
NE.....	224	54.1	26.1	14.9	13.1	VI.....	2	0.2	0.2	−	−

− Represents zero. AS—American Samoa, GU—Guam, FM—Federated States of Micronesia, PR—Puerto Rico. VI—Virgin Islands.

Source: U.S. Federal Deposit Insurance Corporation, *Statistics on Banking*, annual.

Table 1181. FDIC-Insured Financial Institutions—Number of Offices and Deposits by State: 2009

[As of June 30 (7,675.6 represents $7,675,620,000,000). Includes insured U.S. branches of foreign banks. The term "offices" includes both main offices and branches. "Banking office" is defined to include all offices and facilities that actually hold deposits, and does not include loan production offices, computer centers, and other nondeposit installations, such as automated teller machines (ATMs). Several institutions have designated home offices that do not accept deposits; these have been included to provide a more complete listing of all offices. The figures for each geographical area only include deposits of offices located within that area. Based on the Summary of Deposits survey]

State	Number of offices	Total deposits (bil. dol.)	State	Number of offices	Total deposits (bil. dol.)	State	Number of offices	Total deposits (bil. dol.)
Total [1] ..	98,517	7,675.62	KS	1,561	60.03	ND	444	17.58
U.S.....	97,952	7,620.69	KY	1,827	68.87	OH.....	4,014	226.33
AL	1,578	82.06	LA	1,650	82.82	OK.....	1,411	69.04
AK	133	8.91	ME.....	511	27.60	OR.....	1,124	53.66
AZ	1,381	86.15	MD.....	1,804	112.80	PA	4,719	285.87
AR	1,483	50.88	MA.....	2,217	205.20	RI......	259	39.83
CA	7,176	845.91	MI......	3,008	155.70	SC	1,458	70.25
CO.....	1,662	91.23	MN.....	1,842	129.66	SD	487	107.44
CT.....	1,296	95.72	MS.....	1,209	45.12	TN	2,298	114.69
DE	274	290.21	MO.....	2,436	128.96	TX	6,965	499.04
DC	244	27.36	MT	392	17.55	UT	602	271.95
FL	5,666	409.89	NE	1,092	43.03	VT	266	10.63
GA	2,758	180.86	NV	550	183.50	VA	2,684	214.27
HI......	284	28.35	NH	433	26.37	WA.....	1,891	109.22
ID......	541	18.66	NJ	3,338	246.49	WV.....	664	28.78
IL......	4,942	361.76	NM.....	514	25.79	WI	2,351	126.66
IN.....	2,400	98.45	NY	5,478	853.67	WY.....	235	12.03
IA......	1,621	66.49	NC	2,779	207.41			

Source: U.S. Federal Deposit Insurance Corporation, Bank and Thrift Branch Office Data Book, annual. For more information: <http://www.fdic.gov/bank/index.html>.

Table 1182. U.S. Banking Offices of Foreign Banks—Summary: 1990 to 2010

[In billions of dollars, except as indicated (834 represents $834,000,000,000). As of December. Covers the U.S. offices of foreign banking organizations that are located in the 50 states and the District of Columbia. Offices located in Puerto Rico, American Samoa, Guam, the Virgin Islands and other U.S.-affiliated insular areas are excluded. Foreign-owned institutions are those owned by a bank located outside of the United States and its affiliated insular areas. The U.S. offices of foreign banking organizations consist of U.S. branches and agencies of foreign banks and bank subsidiaries of foreign banking organizations. The latter are U.S. commercial banks of which more than 25 percent are owned by a foreign banking organization or where the relationship is reported as being a controlling relationship by the filer of the FR Y-10 (Report of Changes in Organizational Structure) report form]

Item	1990	2000	2005	2006	2007	2008	2009	2010	Share [1]			
									1990	2000	2005	2010
Assets	834	1,358	2,123	2,515	2,871	3,032	2,872	2,839	20.9	18.9	20.6	20.5
Loans, total	412	557	802	913	1,055	1,167	1,022	961	17.2	13.5	14.1	13.7
Business	199	309	276	342	412	483	384	327	27.7	25.0	24.5	25.1
Deposits.........	425	770	1,162	1,375	1,629	1,606	1,795	1,752	14.6	16.5	17.3	18.3

[1] Foreign owned banks plus U.S. branches and offices of foreign banks as percent of all banks in the United States.
Source: Board of Governors of the Federal Reserve System, "Share Data for U.S. Offices of Foreign Banks," March 2011, <http://www.federalreserve.gov/Releases/iba/fboshr.htm>.

Table 1183. Federal and State-Chartered Credit Unions—Summary: 1990 to 2010

[Except as noted, as of December 31 (36,241 represents 36,241,000). Federal data include District of Columbia, Puerto Rico, Guam, and Virgin Islands. Excludes state-insured, privately insured, and noninsured state-chartered credit unions and corporate central credit unions, which have mainly other credit unions as members]

Year	Operating credit unions		Number of failed institutions [1]	Members (1,000)		Assets (mil. dol.)		Loans outstanding (mil. dol.)		Savings (mil. dol.)	
	Federal	State		Federal	State	Federal	State	Federal	State	Federal	State
1990........	8,511	4,349	164	36,241	19,454	130,073	68,133	83,029	44,102	117,892	62,082
2000........	6,336	3,980	29	43,883	33,705	242,881	195,363	163,851	137,485	210,188	169,053
2003........	5,776	3,593	13	46,153	36,287	336,611	273,572	202,898	173,236	291,484	236,856
2004........	5,572	3,442	21	46,858	36,710	358,701	288,294	223,878	190,376	308,317	247,804
2005........	5,393	3,302	27	47,612	36,895	377,804	300,868	249,515	208,728	321,820	255,804
2006........	5,189	3,173	22	48,262	37,487	394,125	315,817	270,420	223,917	333,914	267,275
2007........	5,036	3,065	12	48,474	38,363	417,578	335,885	289,169	237,755	349,100	283,298
2008........	4,847	2,959	19	49,129	39,437	447,024	364,043	309,276	256,719	373,369	307,762
2009........	4,714	2,840	31	49,599	40,333	482,612	401,993	311,146	261,367	408,832	343,836
2010........	4,589	2,750	29	50,081	40,447	500,075	414,395	306,276	258,555	427,603	358,877

[1] 1990 for year ending September 30; beginning 2000, reflects calendar year. A failed institution is defined as a credit union which has ceased operation because it was involuntarily liquidated or merged with assistance from the National Credit Union Share Insurance Fund.
Source: National Credit Union Administration, Annual Report of the National Credit Union Administration, and unpublished data.

Table 1184. Noncash Payments by Method of Payment and ATM Cash Withdrawals: 2006 and 2009

[95.2 represents 95,200,000,000. Based on two data collection efforts to estimate the annual number and value of significant types of noncash Estimates of check payments and ATM withdrawals were based on findings from the payments. Depository Institutions Based on two data collection efforts to estimate the annual number and value of significant types of noncash payments. Estimates of check payments and ATM withdrawals were based on findings from the Depository Institutions Payments Study (2010 DI study). Electronic payments volume estimates were based on findings from the Electronic Payments Study and supplemented by the 2010 DI study. The Depository Institutions Payments Study collected the number and value of different types of payments from deposit accounts at a representative, random sample of depository institutions. A total of 1,311 depository institutions (commercial banks, savings institutions, and credit unions) from a stratified random sample of 2,700 institutions provided data for the survey. The Electronic Payments Study estimated the number and value of electronic payments in the United States for calendar year 2009. Data were collected by surveying payment networks and card issuers. Of the 116 organizations asked to participate, 94 of the largest organizations provided data. Respondents to this study collectively accounted for an estimated 95.5 percent of the electronic transactions and 99.6 percent of the electronic payments value in the United States]

Method of payment	Transactions (billions)		Value (trillion dollars)		Average value per transaction (dollars)	
	2006	2009	2006	2009	2006	2009
Noncash payments, total	**95.2**	**109.0**	**75.7**	**72.2**	**796**	**663**
Checks (paid)	30.5	24.5	41.6	31.6	1,363	1,292
Commercial checks	30.1	24.1	41.4	31.2	1,371	1,295
Commercial banks	25.1	20.7	39.0	29.2	1,550	1,414
Credit unions	2.7	2.1	0.8	0.7	288	352
Savings institutions	2.3	1.3	1.6	1.3	696	973
U.S. Treasury checks	0.2	0.2	0.2	0.3	1,203	1,545
Postal money orders	0.2	0.1	(Z)	(Z)	164	183
Electronic payments	64.7	84.5	34.1	40.6	544	480
Automated Clearing House (ACH)......	14.6	19.1	31.0	37.2	2,122	1,946
Debit cards	25.0	37.9	1.0	1.4	39	38
Signature [1]	15.7	23.4	0.6	0.9	40	37
PIN [2]	9.4	14.5	0.3	0.6	37	39
Credit cards [3]	21.7	21.6	2.1	1.9	98	89
Prepaid and EBT [4]	3.3	6.0	0.1	0.1	23	24
Memo:						
ATM cash withdrawals	**5.8**	**6.0**	**0.6**	**0.6**	**100**	**108**
Checks (written) [5]	33.1	27.8	42.3	32.4	1,277	1,165
Checks converted to ACH	2.6	3.3	0.7	0.8	267	227

Z Less than $50 billion. [1] Signature debit card payments are made like credit card payments, but use funds from transaction deposit accounts. [2] PIN debit card payments also use funds from transaction deposit accounts and typically require the entry of the same personal identification number (PIN) used to access automated teller machines (ATMs). Excludes a portion estimated to have been returned to the customer as cash. [3] Credit cards include both general purpose and private-label cards. [4] Includes general purpose and private label prepaid cards, which use funds from a nontraditional prefunded transaction account, as well as electronic benefit transfers. [5] Includes the use of checks as source documents to initiate electronic payments.

Source: Board of Governors of the Federal Reserve System "The 2010 Federal Reserve Payments Study, Noncash Payment Trends in the United States: 2006–2009"; April 2011; <http://www.frbservices.org/files/communications/pdf/research/2010_payments_study.pdf>; "Recent Payment Trends in the United States," *Federal Reserve Bulletin*, October 2008, <http://www.federalreserve.gov/pubs/bulletin/2008/default.htm>, and "The 2007 Federal Reserve Payments Study," December 2007, <http://www.frbservices.org/files/communications/pdf/research/2007_payments_study.pdf>.

Table 1185. Percentage of Households Using Selected Electronic Banking Technologies: 1995 to 2007

[Covers only those households that access services (other than by check or credit card) at a bank, thrift institution, or credit union. Based on sample surveys. For details on the Survey of Consumer Finances, see Appendix III and the Federal Reserve Board, <www.federalreserve.gov/boarddocs/surveys\>. The Reuters/University of Michigan Surveys of Consumers is based on data from approximately 1,000 respondents. For details, see the University of Michigan Survey Research Center, <http://www.sca.isr.umich.edu/>]

Technology	Survey of Consumer Finances					Reuters/University of Michigan Surveys of Consumers		
	1995	1998	2001	2004	2007	1999	2003	2006
ELECTRONIC								
Direct deposit of any type	53	67	71	75	80	65	70	77
ATM card	35	55	57	65	76	59	65	69
Debit card [1]	20	37	50	62	71	(NA)	54	62
Preauthorized debts	25	40	43	50	49	31	46	57
Automated phone system	(NA)	26	22	20	25	40	44	46
Computer banking...........	4	7	19	34	53	10	32	51
Smart card [2]	1	2	3	(NA)	(NA)	(NA)	6	12
Prepaid card [3]	(NA)	(NA)	(NA)	(NA)	(NA)	(NA)	73	73
NONELECTRONIC								
In person	87	81	78	78	85	(NA)	(NA)	(NA)
Mail	59	55	51	51	59	(NA)	(NA)	(NA)
Phone (talk in person)	(NA)	43	42	42	57	(NA)	(NA)	(NA)

NA Not available. [1] A debit card is a card that automatically deducts the amount of a purchase from the money in an account. [2] A smart card is a type of payment card containing a computer chip which is set to hold a sum of money. As the card is used, purchases are subtracted from that sum. [3] Prepaid cards are cards that contain a stored value, or a value that has been paid up-front, allowing you to use the card much like cash. As you use the card, the prepaid value is drawn down. Examples are phone cards and gift cards. Smart cards are different from prepaid cards in that you can add money to the card at special machines designed for smart cards or sometimes at ATMs.

Source: Board of Governors of the Federal Reserve System, *Federal Reserve Bulletin*, July 2009, and unpublished data.

Banking, Finance, and Insurance **739**

Table 1186. Percent of U.S. Households That Use Selected Payment Instruments: 2001 and 2007

[In percent. Based on Survey of Consumer Finances conducted by the Board of Governors of the Federal Reserve System; see Appendix III]

Characteristic of head of household	Any of these instruments		ATM [1]		Debit card		Direct deposit		Automatic bill paying		Software [2]	
	2001	2007	2001	2007	2001	2007	2001	2007	2001	2007	2001	2007
All households	**88.9**	**91.8**	**69.8**	**79.7**	**47.0**	**67.0**	**67.3**	**74.9**	**40.3**	**45.5**	**18.0**	**19.1**
Under 30 years old	83.8	88.6	78.1	84.8	60.6	78.3	48.8	61.3	32.1	35.7	17.0	21.4
30 to 60 years old	89.9	92.4	76.8	85.9	53.4	74.9	64.8	72.6	44.1	48.8	22.0	21.6
61 years old and over	89.4	92.1	48.9	63.5	24.6	43.9	83.2	86.4	35.9	42.9	9.0	12.3
Household income: [3]												
Low income	74.3	79.7	46.8	58.8	29.2	48.1	51.9	60.5	18.2	23.8	6.1	7.7
Moderate income.	88.6	91.1	67.4	78.5	46.3	68.0	63.1	68.5	35.1	37.8	10.7	10.7
Middle income	92.5	96.4	75.2	87.5	50.0	75.0	65.7	76.8	45.1	50.2	16.3	18.8
Upper income	97.1	98.4	83.7	91.0	57.8	75.8	80.2	86.6	55.2	61.6	29.9	30.5
No college degree	85.1	88.4	63.7	74.0	42.3	63.7	61.8	68.9	33.7	38.0	10.9	11.9
College degree	96.4	98.2	81.6	90.3	56.2	72.9	78.0	85.9	53.2	59.3	31.8	32.2

[1] The question on ATM cards asked whether any member of the household had an ATM card, not whether the member used it. The other questions asked about usage of other instruments. [2] The question on software asked whether the respondent or spouse/partner uses any type of computer software to help in managing their money. [3] Low income is defined as less than 50 percent of the median household income; moderate income is 50 to 80 income is 80 to 120 percent of the median; and upper income is greater than 120 percent of the median. Each survey refers to income in the previous year. Median income was $41,990 in 2000 and $48,201 in 2006.

Source: Mester, Loretta J., "Changes in the Use of Electronic Means of Payment: 1995-2007," Business Review, Third Quarter 2009, published by Federal Reserve Bank of Philadelphia. See also <http://www.philadelphiafed.org/research-and-data/publications/business-review/2009/q3/brq309_changes-in-electronic-payment.pdf>.

Table 1187. Debit Cards—Holders, Number, Transactions, and Volume, 2000 and 2009, and Projections, 2012

[160 represents 160,000,000]

Type of debit card	Cardholders (mil.)			Number of cards (mil.)			Number of point-of-sale transactions (mil.)			Purchase volume (bil. dol.)		
	2000	2009	2012, proj.	2000	2009	2012, proj.	2000	2009	2012, proj.	2000	2009	2012, proj.
Total [1]	**160**	**183**	**191**	**235**	**509**	**530**	**8,291**	**38,541**	**52,620**	**311**	**1,449**	**2,089**
Bank [2]	137	162	165	137	466	484	5,290	32,244	44,351	210	1,209	1,784
EFT systems [3]	159	182	189	223	279	291	2,979	6,269	8,223	100	238	303
Other [4]	11	12	14	14	12	14	22	27	44	1	1	2

[1] Cardholders may hold more than one type of card. Bank cards and EFT cards are the same pieces of plastic that carry multiple brands. The total card figure shown does not include any duplication. [2] Visa and Master Card debit cards. For 2006 and later, includes Interlink & Master Card PIN debit. [3] Cards issued by financial institution members of regional and national switches such as Star, Interlink (before 2006), Pulse, Nyce, etc. EFT = Electronic funds transfer. [4] Retail cards such as those issued by supermarkets.

Source: The Nilson Report, Carpinteria, CA, Twice-monthly (copyright, used by permission).

Table 1188. Credit Cards—Holders, Number, Spending, and Debt, 2000 and 2009, and Projections, 2012

[159 represents 159,000,000]

Type of credit card	Cardholders (mil.)			Number of cards (mil.)			Credit card purchase volume (bil. dol.)			Credit card debt outstanding (bil. dol.)		
	2000	2009	2012, proj.	2000	2009	2012, proj.	2000	2009	2012, proj.	2000	2009	2012, proj.
Total [1]	**159**	**156**	**160**	**1,425**	**1,245**	**1,167**	**1,242**	**1,944**	**2,378**	**680**	**886**	**870**
Visa	93	100	107	255	270	261	487	764	932	268	366	359
Master Card.	86	80	84	200	203	174	281	477	524	212	268	255
Store	114	100	96	597	470	455	120	132	135	92	102	94
Oil company.	76	58	56	98	61	60	45	45	52	5	8	9
Discover.	36	40	43	50	54	59	69	100	127	48	53	54
American Express . . .	23	34	37	33	49	52	221	420	603	50	87	97
The Rest [2]	133	105	81	192	137	106	5	5	5	5	3	2

[1] Cardholders may hold more than one type of card. [2] Includes Universal Air Travel Plan (UATP), phone cards, automobile rental, and miscellaneous cards; credit card purchase volume and cardholders excludes phone cards.

Source: The Nilson Report, Carpinteria, CA, Twice-monthly newsletter (copyright, used by permission).

Table 1189. Usage of General Purpose Credit Cards by Families: 1995 to 2007

[General purpose credit cards include Master Card, Visa, Optima, and Discover cards. Excludes cards used only for business purposes. All dollar figures are given in constant 2007 dollars based on consumer price index data as published by U.S. Bureau of Labor Statistics. Families include one-person units; for definition of family, see text, Section 1. Based on Survey of Consumer Finances; see Appendix III. For definition of median, see Guide to Tabular Presentation]

Age of family head, family income, and housing tenure	Percent having a general purpose credit card	Median number of cards	Median new charges on last month's bill (dollars)	Percent having a balance after last month's bill	Median balance [1] (dollars)	Percent of card holding families who—		
						Almost always pay off the balance	Sometimes pay off the balance	Hardly ever pay off the balance
1995, total	66.4	2	200	56.0	2,000	52.4	20.1	27.5
2001, total	72.7	2	200	53.6	2,100	55.3	19.1	25.6
2004, total	71.5	2	300	56.2	2,300	55.7	20.3	24.0
2007, total	**70.2**	**2**	**300**	**58.3**	**3,000**	**55.3**	**19.4**	**25.4**
Under 35 years old	58.9	2	100	70.9	2,000	47.1	22.9	30.0
35 to 44 years old	68.1	2	300	68.2	3,400	46.9	22.5	30.6
45 to 54 years old	74.3	2	300	64.6	4,000	48.8	19.4	31.8
55 to 64 years old	78.9	3	300	58.6	3,500	56.0	20.0	24.0
65 to 74 years old	79.5	2	300	39.9	3,900	70.4	16.7	12.9
75 years old and over	66.0	1	200	23.9	900	80.8	8.8	10.4
Less than $10,000.	27.7	2	200	56.8	1,200	59.2	20.7	20.1
$10,000 to $24,999	44.5	2	100	55.9	1,000	54.4	19.4	26.2
$25,000 to $49,999	66.4	2	100	60.3	2,100	49.7	20.5	29.8
$50,000 to $99,999	85.8	2	200	66.2	3,900	50.4	20.7	29.0
$100,000 and more	94.3	3	1,000	47.1	6,000	67.3	16.3	16.3
Owner occupied.	81.5	2	300	55.3	4,000	57.5	19.4	23.1
Renter occupied or other.	45.4	2	100	70.2	1,400	46.6	19.2	34.2

[1] Among families having a balance.

Source: Board of Governors of the Federal Reserve System, unpublished data.

Table 1190. Consumer Credit Outstanding and Finance Rates: 1990 to 2010

[In billions of dollars (808 represents $808,000,000,000), except percent. Covers most short- and intermediate-term credit extended to individuals, excluding loans secured by real estate. Estimated amounts of seasonally adjusted credit outstanding as of end of year; finance rates, annual averages]

Type of credit	1990	2000	2003	2004	2005	2006	2007	2008	2009	2010
Total.	**808**	**1,717**	**2,077**	**2,192**	**2,291**	**2,385**	**2,522**	**2,561**	**2,449**	**2,408**
Revolving.	239	683	768	800	830	871	942	958	866	801
Nonrevolving [1]	570	1,034	1,309	1,393	1,461	1,514	1,580	1,604	1,584	1,607
FINANCE RATES (percent)										
Commercial banks:										
New automobiles (48 months).	11.78	9.34	6.94	6.60	7.07	7.72	7.77	7.02	6.72	6.21
Other consumer goods (24 months) . . .	15.46	13.90	11.96	11.89	12.06	12.41	12.38	11.37	11.10	10.87
Credit card plans	18.17	15.78	12.30	12.72	12.51	13.21	13.30	12.08	13.40	13.78
Finance companies:										
New automobiles	12.54	6.85	3.81	4.92	6.02	4.99	4.87	5.52	3.82	4.26
Used automobiles	15.99	13.47	9.86	8.81	8.81	9.61	9.24	8.74	9.41	8.16

[1] Comprises automobile loans and all other loans not included in revolving credit, such as loans for mobile homes, education, boats, trailers, or vacations. These loans may be secured or unsecured.

Source: Board of Governors of the Federal Reserve System, "Consumer Credit-G.19," April 2011, <http://www.federalreserve.gov/releases/g19/current/g19.htm> and "Finance Companies-G.20," April 2011, <http://www.federalreserve.gov/releases/g20/current/g20.htm>.

Table 1191. Consumer Credit by Type of Holder: 1990 to 2010

[In billions of dollars (824 represents $824,000,000,000). As of December 31. Not seasonally adjusted]

Type of holder	1990	2000	2003	2004	2005	2006	2007	2008	2009	2010
Total.	**824**	**1,741**	**2,103**	**2,220**	**2,321**	**2,416**	**2,555**	**2,594**	**2,479**	**2,435**
Nonfinancial corporations	67	81	59	59	60	58	59	60	57	56
U.S. government	–	60	82	86	90	92	98	111	186	317
Commercial banking	382	551	669	704	707	741	804	879	855	1,099
Savings institutions	50	65	78	91	109	96	91	86	78	87
Credit unions	92	184	206	215	229	235	236	236	237	226
Government-sponsored enterprises . . .	19	37	21	–	–	–	–	–	–	–
Asset-backed securities issuers	77	528	595	572	610	661	684	646	578	131
Finance companies	138	234	393	492	517	534	584	576	488	519

– Represents or rounds to zero.

Source: Board of Governors of the Federal Reserve System, "Federal Reserve Statistical Release, Z.1, Flow of Funds Accounts of the United States," March 2011, <http://www.federalreserve.gov/releases/z1/20100311>.

Table 1192. Mortgage Debt Outstanding by Type of Property and Holder: 1990 to 2010

[In billions of dollars (3,781 represents $3,781,000,000,000). As of December 31]

Type of property and holder	1990	2000	2003	2004	2005	2006	2007	2008	2009	2010
Total mortgages [1]	**3,781**	**6,753**	**9,377**	**10,637**	**12,070**	**13,462**	**14,516**	**14,605**	**14,316**	**13,833**
Home [2]	2,606	5,107	7,240	8,268	9,382	10,456	11,167	11,069	10,859	10,546
Multifamily residential	287	402	557	605	667	708	787	837	848	841
Commercial	820	1,160	1,497	1,668	1,916	2,191	2,449	2,565	2,474	2,313
Farm	68	85	83	96	105	108	113	134	135	133
Household sector.	141	103	121	131	139	122	110	112	102	92
State and local government.	110	131	133	141	152	166	173	170	179	184
Commercial banking	849	1,660	2,256	2,596	2,958	3,403	3,644	3,841	3,819	3,651
Savings institutions [3]	802	723	871	1,057	1,153	1,077	1,094	861	633	615
Credit unions	33	104	160	188	220	250	282	315	318	319
Life insurance companies	268	236	261	273	285	304	326	342	326	318
Government-sponsored enterprises (GSE). . .	156	264	622	629	589	607	643	701	708	5,020
Agency- and GSE-backed mortgage pools. . .	1,020	2,493	3,343	3,384	3,548	3,841	4,464	4,961	5,376	1,166
Asset-backed securities issuers	66	604	1,009	1,443	2,128	2,760	2,936	2,584	2,200	1,887
Finance companies	114	238	370	476	541	594	532	448	397	340
Real estate investment trusts	8	17	49	118	146	136	121	76	59	51
HOME MORTGAGES [2]										
Total [1]	**2,606**	**5,107**	**7,240**	**8,268**	**9,382**	**10,456**	**11,167**	**11,069**	**10,859**	**10,546**
State and local government.	61	67	68	72	77	85	89	87	92	94
Commercial banking	433	970	1,360	1,582	1,792	2,082	2,211	2,248	2,261	2,207
Savings institutions [3]	600	594	703	874	954	868	879	666	449	430
Credit unions	33	104	160	188	220	250	282	315	318	319
Government-sponsored enterprises (GSE). . .	119	210	519	509	454	458	448	456	444	4,705
Agency- and GSE-backed mortgage pools. . .	991	2,426	3,234	3,277	3,446	3,749	4,372	4,864	5,267	1,094
Asset-backed securities issuers	55	385	666	1,049	1,622	2,141	2,177	1,865	1,529	1,266
Finance companies	80	187	320	422	490	538	473	375	328	277
Memo:										
Home equity loans included above [1, 4]	215	408	593	776	915	1,066	1,131	1,114	1,032	949
Commercial banking	115	235	366	484	549	654	692	776	762	710
Savings institutions [3]	60	73	96	121	152	138	180	119	80	74
Credit unions	20	41	52	64	76	87	94	99	95	88

[1] Includes other holders not shown separately. [2] Mortgages on one- to four-family properties including mortgages on farm houses. [3] Federal Home Loan Bank loans to savings institutions are included in other loans and advances. [4] Loans made under home equity lines of credit and home equity loans secured by junior liens. Excludes home equity loans held by individuals.

Source: Board of Governors of the Federal Reserve System, "Federal Reserve Statistical Release, Z.1, Flow of Funds Accounts of the United States," March 2011, <http://www.federalreserve.gov/releases/z1/20100311>.

Table 1193. Characteristics of Conventional First Mortgage Loans for Purchase of Single-Family Homes: 2000 to 2010

[In percent, except as indicated (for purchase price, 234.9 represents $234,900). Annual averages. Covers fully amortized conventional mortgage loans used to purchase single-family nonfarm homes. Excludes refinancing loans, nonamortized and balloon loans, loans insured by the Federal Housing Administration, and loans guaranteed by the Veterans Administration. Based on a sample of mortgage lenders, including savings and loans associations, savings banks, commercial banks, and mortgage companies]

Loan characteristics	New homes						Previously occupied homes					
	2000	2005	2007	2008	2009	2010	2000	2005	2007	2008	2009	2010
Contract interest rate, all loans [1]	7.4	5.9	6.3	5.9	5.0	4.7	7.9	5.8	6.5	6.1	5.1	4.8
Fixed-rate loans.	8.0	6.1	6.3	5.9	5.0	4.7	8.2	6.0	6.5	6.1	5.1	4.9
Adjustable-rate loans [2]. . . .	6.5	5.3	6.2	5.7	([5])	4.3	7.2	5.6	6.3	5.7	([5])	4.2
Initial fees, charges [3]	0.69	0.54	0.81	0.84	1.00	0.82	0.66	0.33	0.40	0.46	0.55	0.71
Effective interest rate, all loans [4]	7.5	5.9	6.4	6.1	5.1	4.8	8.1	5.9	6.5	6.2	5.1	4.9
Fixed-rate loans.	8.2	6.2	6.4	6.1	5.2	4.8	8.3	6.0	6.5	6.2	5.2	5.0
Adjustable-rate loans [2]. . . .	6.5	5.3	6.3	5.8	([5])	4.4	7.2	5.6	6.4	5.8	([5])	4.3
Term to maturity (years).	29.2	29.2	29.4	29.1	28.8	28.5	28.6	28.3	29.3	28.3	28.1	27.5
Purchase price ($1,000)	234.9	328.5	360.4	350.6	332.3	335.3	191.8	291.3	286.2	296.4	303.6	297.7
Loan-to-price ratio	77.4	75.2	77.1	76.2	73.9	73.4	77.9	74.6	79.9	77.0	74.6	74.2
Percent of number of loans with adjustable rates	40	29	11	4	([5])	3	21	30	11	8	([5])	5

[1] Initial interest rate paid by the borrower as specified in the loan contract. [2] Loans with a contractual provision for periodic adjustments in the contract interest rate. [3] Includes all fees, commissions, discounts, and "points" paid by the borrower, or seller, in order to obtain the loan. Excludes those charges for mortgage, credit, life, or property insurance; for property transfer; and for title search and insurance. [4] Contract interest rate plus fees and charges amortized over a ten year period. [5] Insufficient data to report meaningful numbers.

Source: U.S. Federal Housing Finance Agency, *Monthly Interest Rate Survey*, Historical Summary Table, <http://www.fhfa.gov/Default.aspx?Page=252>.

Table 1194. Mortgage Originations and Delinquency and Foreclosure Rates: 1990 to 2010

[In percent, except as indicated (459 represents $459,000,000,000). Covers one- to four-family residential nonfarm mortgage loans. Mortgage origination is the making of a new mortgage, including all steps taken by a lender to attract and qualify a borrower, process the mortgage loan, and place it on the lender's books. Based on the National Delinquency Survey which covers 45 million loans on one- to four-unit properties, representing between 80 to 85 percent of all 'first-lien' residential mortgage loans outstanding. Loans surveyed were reported by approximately 120 lenders, including mortgage bankers, commercial banks, and thrifts]

Item	1990	2000	2004	2005	2006	2007	2008	2009	2010
MORTGAGE ORIGINATIONS									
Total (bil. dol.)	**459**	**1,139**	**2,773**	**2,908**	**2,726**	**2,306**	**1,509**	**1,995**	**1,572**
Purchase (bil. dol.)	389	905	1,309	1,512	1,399	1,140	731	664	473
Refinance (bil. dol.)	70	234	1,463	1,397	1,326	1,166	777	1,331	1,099
DELINQUENCY RATES [1]									
Total	**4.7**	**4.4**	**4.5**	**4.5**	**4.6**	**5.4**	**6.9**	**9.4**	**9.3**
Prime conventional loans	(NA)	2.3	2.3	2.3	2.4	2.9	4.3	6.5	6.5
Subprime conventional loans	(NA)	11.9	10.8	10.8	12.3	15.6	19.9	25.5	25.9
Federal Housing Administration loans	6.7	9.1	12.2	12.5	12.7	12.7	13.0	14.0	12.8
Veterans Administration loans	6.3	6.8	7.3	7.0	6.7	6.4	7.2	7.9	7.5
FORECLOSURE RATES									
Total loans in foreclosure process [2]	**0.9**	**1.2**	**1.2**	**1.0**	**1.2**	**2.0**	**3.3**	**4.3**	**4.6**
Prime conventional loans	(NA)	0.4	0.5	0.4	0.5	1.0	1.9	3.0	3.5
Subprime conventional loans	(NA)	9.4	3.8	3.3	4.5	8.7	13.7	15.1	14.5
Federal Housing Administration loans	1.3	1.7	2.7	2.3	1.9	2.3	2.4	3.2	3.5
Veterans Administration loans	1.2	1.2	1.5	1.1	1.0	1.1	1.7	2.2	2.4
Loans entering foreclosure process [3]	1.2	1.5	1.7	1.6	1.9	2.8	4.2	5.4	5.0
Prime conventional loans	(NA)	0.6	0.8	0.7	0.8	1.3	2.4	4.0	4.0
Subprime conventional loans	(NA)	9.2	5.9	5.6	7.3	11.7	16.5	16.2	12.9
Federal Housing Administration loans	1.7	2.3	3.9	3.4	3.3	3.6	3.8	4.8	4.7
Veterans Administration loans	1.6	1.5	2.0	1.5	1.4	1.6	2.3	3.1	3.3

NA Not available. [1] Number of loans delinquent 30 days or more as percentage of mortgage loans serviced in survey. Annual average of quarterly figures. Delinquency rate does not include loans in the process of foreclosure. [2] Percentage of loans in the foreclosure process at year-end, not seasonally adjusted. [3] Percentage of loans entering foreclosure process at year-end, not seasonally adjusted.

Source: Mortgage Bankers Association of America, Washington, DC, "MBA Mortgage Originations Estimates," National Delinquency Survey, quarterly, <http://www.mortgagebankers.org/>; and unpublished data.

Table 1195. Delinquency Rates and Charge-Off Rates on Loans at Insured Commercial Banks: 1990 to 2010

[In percent. Annual averages of quarterly figures, not seasonally adjusted. Delinquent loans are those past due 30 days or more and still accruing interest as well as those in nonaccrual status. They are measured as a percentage of end-of-period loans. Charge-offs, which are the value of loans removed from the books and charged against loss reserves, are measured net of recoveries as a percentage of average loans and annualized. Includes only U.S.-chartered commercial banks]

Type of loan	1990	2000	2004	2005	2006	2007	2008	2009	2010
DELINQUENCY RATES									
Total loans	**5.33**	**2.18**	**1.80**	**1.57**	**1.57**	**2.06**	**3.67**	**6.56**	**6.97**
Real estate	6.10	1.89	1.44	1.37	1.49	2.27	4.67	8.46	9.70
Residential [1]	(NA)	2.11	1.55	1.55	1.73	2.55	5.01	9.14	10.84
Commercial [2]	(NA)	1.49	1.20	1.07	1.12	1.94	4.44	7.90	8.52
Consumer	3.83	3.55	3.08	2.81	2.90	3.13	3.76	4.70	4.15
Credit cards	(NA)	4.50	4.11	3.70	4.01	4.25	5.02	6.52	4.90
Other	(NA)	2.98	2.46	2.24	2.21	2.46	3.00	3.57	3.33
Leases	1.97	1.59	1.34	1.28	1.26	1.20	1.58	2.30	1.89
Commercial and industrial	5.34	2.22	2.18	1.51	1.27	1.22	1.88	3.90	3.44
Agricultural	3.84	2.54	1.68	1.30	1.11	1.21	1.19	2.37	3.05
CHARGE-OFF RATES									
Total loans	**1.44**	**0.66**	**0.60**	**0.54**	**0.42**	**0.61**	**1.43**	**2.66**	**2.65**
Real estate	0.85	0.10	0.09	0.06	0.09	0.23	1.21	2.29	2.15
Residential [1]	(NA)	0.12	0.10	0.08	0.11	0.26	1.28	2.36	2.12
Commercial [2]	(NA)	0.05	0.07	0.05	0.06	0.20	1.20	2.36	2.32
Consumer	1.82	2.36	2.68	2.75	2.05	2.49	3.53	5.49	5.87
Credit cards	3.46	4.46	5.04	4.84	3.64	4.00	5.52	9.40	9.34
Other	1.03	1.14	1.31	1.38	1.06	1.58	2.34	3.05	2.05
Leases	0.66	0.31	0.42	0.58	0.17	0.24	0.54	1.29	0.72
Commercial and industrial	1.29	0.76	0.53	0.26	0.29	0.49	0.98	2.30	1.69
Agricultural	0.21	0.25	0.19	0.07	0.10	0.10	0.17	0.51	0.80

NA Not available. [1] Residential real estate loans include loans secured by one- to four-family properties, including home equity lines of credit, booked in domestic offices, only. [2] Commercial real estate loans include construction and land development loans, loans secured by multifamily residences, and loans secured by nonfarm, nonresidential real estate, booked in domestic offices, only.

Source: Federal Financial Institutions Examination Council (FFIEC), *Consolidated Reports of Condition and Income* (1990–2000: FFIEC 031 through 034; beginning 2004: FFIEC 031 & 041).

Table 1196. Money Stock: 1990 to 2010

[In billions of dollars (825 represents $825,000,000,000). As of December. Seasonally adjusted averages of daily figures]

Item	1990	2000	2003	2004	2005	2006	2007	2008	2009	2010
M1, total	**825**	**1,087**	**1,306**	**1,376**	**1,375**	**1,366**	**1,374**	**1,603**	**1,694**	**1,831**
Currency [1]	246	531	663	698	724	750	760	815	862	916
Travelers' checks [2]	8	8	8	8	7	7	6	6	5	5
Demand deposits [3]	277	310	326	343	324	304	300	469	441	508
Other checkable deposits [4]	294	238	310	328	319	306	307	313	386	402
M2, total	**3,277**	**4,916**	**6,065**	**6,409**	**6,674**	**7,066**	**7,495**	**8,248**	**8,531**	**8,817**
M1	825	1,087	1,306	1,376	1,375	1,366	1,374	1,603	1,694	1,831
Non-M1 components of M2	2,453	3,829	4,758	5,032	5,300	5,700	6,121	6,646	6,837	6,986
Retail money funds	356	905	778	696	700	800	974	1,084	823	706
Savings deposits (including MMDAs)	923	1,878	3,163	3,509	3,606	3,695	3,873	4,106	4,837	5,357
Commercial banks	581	1,424	2,338	2,633	2,777	2,911	3,045	3,335	3,997	4,437
Thrift institutions	342	454	825	876	829	783	828	772	840	920
Small time deposits [5]	1,173	1,046	818	828	993	1,205	1,275	1,456	1,177	923
Commercial banks	611	701	542	552	646	780	858	1,077	858	652
Thrift institutions	563	345	276	276	347	425	417	379	319	271

[1] Currency outside U.S. Treasury, Federal Reserve Banks and the vaults of depository institutions. [2] Outstanding amount of U.S. dollar-denominated travelers' checks of nonbank issuers. Travelers' checks issued by depository institutions are included in demand deposits. [3] Demand deposits at domestically chartered commercial banks, U.S. branches and agencies of foreign banks, and Edge Act corporations (excluding those amounts held by depository institutions, the U.S. government, and foreign banks and official institutions) less cash items in the process of collection and Federal Reserve float. [4] Negotiable order of withdrawal (NOW) and automatic transfer service (ATS) balances at domestically chartered commercial banks, U.S. branches and agencies of foreign banks, Edge Act corporations, and thrift institutions, credit union share draft balances, and demand deposits at thrift institutions. [5] Small-denomination time deposits are those issued in amounts of less than $100,000. All Individual Retirement Account (IRA) and Keogh account balances at commercial banks and thrift institutions are subtracted from small time deposits.

Source: Board of Governors of the Federal Reserve System, Federal Reserve Statistical Release H.6, weekly. See also <http://www.federalreserve.gov/rnd.htm>.

Table 1197. Money Market Interest Rates and Mortgage Rates: 1990 to 2010

[Percent per year. Annual averages of monthly data, except as indicated]

Type	1990	1995	2000	2003	2004	2005	2006	2007	2008	2009	2010
Federal funds, effective rate	8.10	5.83	6.24	1.13	1.35	3.22	4.97	5.02	1.92	0.16	0.18
Prime rate charged by banks	10.01	8.83	9.23	4.12	4.34	6.19	7.96	8.05	5.09	3.25	3.25
Discount rate [1]	6.98	5.21	5.73	2.12	2.34	4.19	5.96	5.86	2.39	0.50	0.72
Eurodollar deposits, 3-month	8.16	5.93	6.45	1.14	1.55	3.51	5.19	5.32	3.31	1.03	0.45
Large negotiable CDs:											
3-month, secondary market	8.15	5.92	6.46	1.15	1.57	3.51	5.16	5.27	2.97	0.55	0.31
6-month, secondary market	8.17	5.98	6.59	1.17	1.74	3.73	5.24	5.23	3.14	0.87	0.44
Taxable money market funds [2]	7.82	5.48	5.89	0.64	0.82	2.66	4.51	4.70	2.05	0.18	0.04
Tax-exempt money market funds [2]	5.45	3.39	3.54	0.53	0.66	1.87	2.90	3.13	1.77	0.19	0.04
Certificates of deposit (CDs): [3]											
6-month	7.79	4.92	5.09	1.02	1.14	2.37	3.29	3.46	2.12	0.86	0.39
1-year	7.92	5.39	5.46	1.20	1.45	2.77	3.64	3.65	2.36	1.16	0.65
2-year	7.96	5.69	5.64	1.77	2.21	3.18	3.75	3.65	2.43	1.43	0.98
5-year	8.06	6.00	5.97	2.93	3.34	3.75	4.02	3.89	3.17	2.21	1.88
U.S. government securities:											
Secondary market: [4]											
3-month Treasury bill	7.50	5.49	5.82	1.01	1.37	3.15	4.73	4.36	1.37	0.15	0.14
6-month Treasury bill	7.46	5.56	5.90	1.05	1.58	3.39	4.81	4.44	1.62	0.28	0.20
Auction average: [5]											
3-month Treasury bill	7.51	5.51	5.85	1.02	1.38	3.16	4.73	4.41	1.48	0.16	0.14
Home mortgages:											
New-home mortgage yields [6]	10.05	7.87	7.52	5.80	5.77	5.94	6.63	6.41	6.05	5.14	4.80
Conventional, 15 yr. fixed [3]	9.73	7.39	7.76	5.25	5.23	5.50	6.13	6.11	5.83	4.83	4.27
Conventional, 30 yr. fixed [3]	9.97	7.86	8.08	5.89	5.86	5.93	6.47	6.40	6.23	5.38	4.86

[1] Rate for the Federal Reserve Bank of New York. Beginning 2003, the rate charged for discounts made and advances extended under the Federal Reserve's primary credit discount window program, which became effective January 9, 2003. The rate replaced that for adjustment credit, which was discontinued after January 8, 2003. [2] 12-month return for period ending December 31. Source: iMoneyNet, Inc., Westborough, MA, Money Market Insight, monthly, (copyright), <http://www.imoneynet.com>. [3] Annual averages. Source: Bankrate, Inc., North Palm Beach, FL, Bank Rate Monitor, weekly (copyright), <http://www.bankrate.com>. [4] Averages based on daily closing bid yields in secondary market, bank discount basis. [5] Averages computed on an issue-date basis; bank discount basis. Source: U.S. Council of Economic Advisors, Economic Indicators, monthly. [6] Effective rate (in the primary market) on conventional mortgages, reflecting fees and charges as well as contract rate and assumed, on the average, repayment at end of ten years. Source: U.S. Federal Housing Finance Board, Terms on Conventional Single-Family Mortgages, Annual National Averages, All Homes.

Source: Except as noted, Board of Governors of the Federal Reserve System, "H15, Selected Interest Rates," <http://www.federalreserve.gov/releases/h15/data.htm>.

Table 1198. Bond Yields: 1990 to 2010

[Percent per year. Annual averages of daily figures, except as indicated]

Type	1990	2000	2003	2004	2005	2006	2007	2008	2009	2010
U.S. Treasury, constant maturities: [1, 2]										
1-year	7.89	6.11	1.24	1.89	3.62	4.94	4.53	1.83	0.47	0.32
2-year	8.16	6.26	1.65	2.38	3.85	4.82	4.36	2.01	0.96	0.70
3-year	8.26	6.22	2.10	2.78	3.93	4.77	4.35	2.24	1.43	1.11
5-year	8.37	6.16	2.97	3.43	4.05	4.75	4.43	2.80	2.20	1.93
7-year	8.52	6.20	3.52	3.87	4.15	4.76	4.51	3.17	2.82	2.62
10-year	8.55	6.89	4.41	4.69	4.73	5.33	5.24	4.25	3.44	3.26
20-year	(NA)	6.23	4.96	5.04	4.64	5.00	4.91	4.36	4.11	4.03
State and local govt. bonds, Aaa rating [3]	6.96	5.58	4.52	4.51	4.28	4.15	4.13	4.58	4.27	3.90
State and local govt. bonds, Baa rating [3]	7.30	6.19	5.20	5.09	4.86	4.71	4.59	5.64	6.34	5.63
Municipal (Bond Buyer, 20 bonds)	7.27	5.71	4.75	4.68	4.40	4.40	4.40	4.85	4.62	4.30
High-grade municipal bonds (Standard & Poor's) [4]	7.25	5.77	4.73	4.63	4.29	4.42	4.42	4.80	4.64	4.16
Corporate Aaa rating seasoned [3, 5]	9.32	7.62	5.66	5.63	5.23	5.59	5.56	5.63	5.31	4.94
Corporate Baa rating seasoned [3]	10.36	8.37	6.76	6.39	6.06	6.48	6.48	7.44	7.29	6.04
Corporate seasoned, all industries [3]	9.77	7.98	6.24	6.00	5.57	5.98	6.01	6.44	6.12	5.40

NA Not available. [1] Yields on actively traded non-inflation-indexed issues adjusted to constant maturities. Data from U.S. Treasury. [2] Through 1995, yields are based on closing bid prices quoted by at least five dealers. Beginning 2000, yields are based on closing indicative prices quoted by secondary market participants. [3] Data from Moody's Investors Service, New York, NY. [4] Source: U.S. Council of Economic Advisors, *Economic Indicators*, monthly. [5] Moody's Aaa rates through December 6, 2001, are average of Aaa utility and Aaa industrial bond rates. As of December 7, 2001, these rates are averages of Aaa industrial bonds only.

Source: Except as noted, Board of Governors of the Federal Reserve System, "H15, Selected Interest Rates," <http://www.federalreserve.gov/releases/h15/data.htm>.

Table 1199. Volume of Debt Markets by Type of Security: 1990 to 2010

[In billions of dollars (1,081 represents $1,081,000,000,000). Covers debt markets as represented by the source]

Type of security	1990	2000	2005	2006	2007	2008	2009	2010
NEW ISSUE VOLUME [1]								
Total	**1,081**	**2,489**	**5,512**	**5,824**	**5,947**	**4,620**	**6,806**	**6,637**
U.S. Treasury securities [2]	398	312	746	789	752	1,037	2,185	2,304
Federal agency securities [3]	55	447	669	747	942	985	1,117	1,033
Municipal	128	201	408	387	429	390	410	433
Mortgage-backed securities [4]	380	660	2,182	2,089	2,186	1,362	2,041	1,742
Asset-backed securities [5]	44	282	754	754	510	139	151	109
Corporate debt [6]	77	588	753	1,059	1,128	707	902	1,015
DAILY TRADING VOLUME								
Total	**111.2**	**357.6**	**918.7**	**893.1**	**1,014.9**	**1,033.6**	**814.6**	**949.8**
U.S. Treasury securities [2, 7]	111.2	206.5	554.5	524.7	570.2	553.1	407.9	528.2
Federal agency securities [7]	(NA)	72.8	78.8	74.4	83.0	104.5	77.7	71.5
Municipal [8]	(NA)	8.8	16.9	22.5	25.1	19.4	12.5	13.3
Mortgage-backed securities [4, 7]	(NA)	69.5	251.8	254.6	320.1	344.9	299.9	320.6
Corporate debt [6]	(NA)	(NA)	16.7	16.9	16.4	11.8	16.8	16.3
VOLUME OF SECURITIES OUTSTANDING								
Total	**7,657**	**16,925**	**26,569**	**29,475**	**31,775**	**33,434**	**34,425**	**35,969**
U.S. Treasury securities [2]	2,196	2,952	4,166	4,323	4,517	5,774	7,261	8,853
Federal agency securities	422	1,854	2,616	2,634	2,906	3,211	2,727	2,728
Municipal	1,179	1,481	2,226	2,403	2,619	2,680	2,809	2,925
Mortgage-backed securities [4]	1,278	3,566	7,213	8,635	9,143	9,102	9,188	8,912
Asset-backed securities [5]	76	1,052	1,950	2,127	2,472	2,672	2,429	2,150
Money market instruments [9]	1,157	2,663	3,434	4,009	4,171	3,791	3,127	2,865
Corporate debt [6]	1,350	3,358	4,965	5,344	5,947	6,204	6,884	7,536

NA Not available. [1] Covers only long-term issuance. [2] Marketable public debt. [3] Includes overnight discount notes. Beginning 2004, excludes Sallie Mae. [4] Includes only Government National Mortgage Association (GNMA), Federal National Mortgage Association (FNMA), Federal Home Loan Mortgage Corporation (FHLMC) mortgage-backed securities (MBS) and collateralized mortgage obligations (CMOs) and private-label MBS/CMOs. Beginning with 2004, Sallie Mae has been excluded from "Issuance in the U.S. Bond Market" data. [5] Includes auto, credit card, home equity, manufacturing, student loans, and other. [6] Includes nonconvertible corporate debt, Yankee bonds, and MTNs (Medium-Term Notes), but excludes all issues with maturities of one year or less, agency debt, and all certificates of deposit. [7] Primary dealer transactions. [8] Beginning 2000, includes customer-to-dealer and dealer-to-dealer transactions. [9] Commercial paper, bankers acceptances, and large time deposits.

Source: The Securities Industry and Financial Markets Association, New York, NY, copyright, <http://www.sifma.org/research/research.aspx?ID=10806>. Based on data supplied by Board of Governors of the Federal Reserve System, U.S. Department of Treasury, Thomson Reuters, FHLMC, FNMA, GNMA, Federal Home Loan Banks, Student Loan Marketing Association, Federal Farm Credit Banks, Tennessee Valley Authority, Bloomberg, Loan Performance, Dealogic and Municipal Securities Rulemaking Board.

Banking, Finance, and Insurance 745

Table 1200. Total Returns of Stocks, Bonds, and Treasury Bills: 1980 to 2010

[In percent. Average annual percent change. Stock return data are based on the Standard & Poor's 500 index. Minus sign (–) indicates loss]

| Period | Stocks | | | | Treasury bills, total return | Bonds (10-year), total return |
	Total return before inflation	Capital gains	Dividends and reinvestment	Total return after inflation		
1980 to 1989	17.55	12.59	4.40	11.85	9.13	13.01
1990 to 1999	18.21	15.31	2.51	14.85	4.95	8.02
2000 to 2009	−0.45	−2.73	2.27	−3.39	2.74	6.63
2001.	−11.89	−13.04	1.32	−13.68	3.32	5.53
2002.	−22.10	−23.37	1.65	−23.91	1.61	15.37
2003.	28.68	26.38	1.82	26.31	1.03	0.46
2004.	10.88	8.99	1.73	7.38	1.43	4.61
2005.	4.91	3.00	1.85	1.45	3.30	3.09
2006.	15.80	13.62	1.91	11.97	4.97	2.21
2007.	5.49	3.53	1.89	1.35	4.52	10.54
2008.	−37.00	−38.49	1.88	−37.10	1.24	20.23
2009.	26.25	23.45	2.44	23.11	0.15	−9.50
2010.	15.06	12.78	2.02	13.36	0.03	7.26

Source: Global Financial Data, Los Angeles, CA, "GFD Guide to Total Returns," <http://www.globalfinancialdata.com>, and unpublished data (copyright).

Table 1201. Equities, Corporate Bonds, and Treasury Securities— Holdings and Net Purchases by Type of Investor: 2000 to 2010

[In billions of dollars (17,575 represents $17,575,000,000,000). Holdings as of December 31. Minus sign (–) indicates net sales]

| Type of investor | Holdings | | | | | Net purchases | | | | |
	2000	2005	2008	2009	2010	2000	2005	2008	2009	2010
EQUITIES [1]										
Total [2]	**17,575**	**20,636**	**15,678**	**20,003**	**23,293**	**5.6**	**−76.6**	**263.4**	**313.4**	**−9.3**
Household sector [3]	8,147	8,093	5,777	7,321	8,514	−637.5	−372.5	−112.4	111.2	−89.9
Rest of the world [4]	1,483	2,039	1,807	2,436	3,091	199.7	56.9	104.7	131.8	93.2
Life insurance companies	892	1,162	1,002	1,208	1,423	111.3	65.9	81.8	33.4	45.6
Private pension funds	1,971	2,442	1,600	1,836	1,983	62.8	−42.0	−184.6	−175.6	−111.1
State and local government retirement funds	1,299	1,716	1,238	1,550	1,779	11.6	−5.6	1.2	−17.3	−25.8
Mutual funds	3,227	4,176	3,014	4,136	4,801	193.1	129.6	−38.1	86.3	37.7
Exchange-traded funds	66	286	474	670	854	42.4	50.0	154.2	70.5	88.2
CORPORATE & FOREIGN BONDS										
Holdings, total	**4,826**	**8,694**	**11,016**	**11,434**	**11,440**	**358.6**	**864.2**	**−227.6**	**−68.2**	**−109.6**
Household sector [3]	551	1,298	1,956	2,081	1,919	84.3	119.6	−213.3	−146.7	−331.9
Rest of the world [4]	842	1,763	2,354	2,468	2,430	168.2	328.5	−21.8	−139.4	−42.6
Commercial banking	266	687	980	868	750	56.0	123.4	1.7	−114.2	−95.2
Property-casualty insurance companies	188	263	268	298	299	6.4	17.5	−15.4	30.8	24.3
Life insurance companies	1,215	1,825	1,817	1,915	2,023	47.9	74.7	−45.5	97.6	102.3
Private pension funds	266	290	400	443	482	−76.3	22.2	42.7	42.8	40.6
State and local government retirement funds	314	228	313	309	312	4.2	14.5	15.9	−4.3	**3.8**
Mutual funds	338	663	960	1,106	1,255	−10.6	65.9	69.9	146.2	147.0
Government-sponsored enterprises . . .	131	466	387	311	296	19.1	50.9	−77.7	−33.8	−16.9
Funding corporations.	25	67	667	710	760	−8.9	−29.4	497.3	43.6	51.9
TREASURY SECURITIES										
Holdings, total	**3,358**	**4,678**	**6,338**	**7,782**	**9,361**	**−294.9**	**307.3**	**1,239.0**	**1,443.7**	**1,579.6**
State and local governments.	310	481	486	506	520	5.5	92.3	−48.6	20.1	11.1
Rest of the world [4]	1,021	1,984	3,251	3,697	4,394	−75.2	245.1	710.1	583.9	680.5
Monetary authority.	512	744	476	777	1,021	33.7	26.4	−264.7	300.7	244.9
Money market mutual funds	92	89	578	406	335	−12.9	−9.6	399.5	−171.3	−71.0

– Represents zero. [1] Excludes mutual fund shares; see Table 1215. [2] Includes other types, not shown separately. [3] Includes nonprofit organizations. [4] Holdings and net purchases of U.S. issues by foreign residents.
Source: Board of Governors of the Federal Reserve System, "Federal Reserve Statistical Release, Z.1, Flow of Funds Accounts of the United States," March 2011, <http://www.federalreserve.gov/releases/z1/20100311>.

Table 1202. New Security Issues of Corporations by Type of Offering: 2000 to 2010

[In billions of dollars (1,075 represents $1,075,000,000,000). Represents gross proceed of issues maturing in more than one year. Figures are the principal amount or the number of units multiplied by the offering price. Excludes secondary offerings, employee stock plans, investment companies other than closed-end, intracorporate transactions, Yankee bonds, and private placements listed. Stock data include ownership securities issued by limited partnerships]

Type of Offering	2000	2005	2009	2010	Type of Offering	2000	2005	2009	2010
Total.	**1,075**	**2,362**	**1,181**	**1,002**	Nonfinancial.	360	211	479	489
					Financial	679	2,036	468	382
Bonds, total	940	2,247	947	871	Stocks, total	135	115	234	131
Sold in the U.S.	827	2,115	784	589	Nonfinancial.	118	55	63	61
Sold abroad	112	131	163	282	Financial	17	61	171	70

Source: Source: Board of Governors of the Federal Reserve System, "New Security Issues, U.S. Corporations," <http://www.federalreserve.gov/econresdata/releases/corpsecure/current.htm>.

Table 1203. U.S. Purchases and Sales of Foreign Bonds and Stocks, 1990 to 2010, and by Selected Country, 2010

[In billions of dollars (31.2 represents $31,200,000,000). Covers transactions in all types of long-term foreign securities by foreigners as reported to the Treasury International Capital Reporting System by banks, brokers, and other entities in the United States. Data cover new issues of securities, transactions in outstanding issues, and redemptions of securities. Includes transactions executed in the United States for the account of foreigners, and transactions executed abroad for the account of reporting institutions and their domestic customers. Data by country show the country of location of the foreign buyers and sellers who deal directly with reporting institutions in the United States. The data do not necessarily indicate the country of beneficial owner or issuer. The term "foreigner" covers all institutions and individuals domiciled outside the United States, including U.S. citizens domiciled abroad, and the foreign branches, subsidiaries, and other affiliates abroad of U.S. banks and businesses; the central governments, central banks, and other official institutions of foreign countries; and international and regional organizations. "Foreigner" also includes persons in the United States to the extent that they are known by reporting institutions to be acting on behalf of foreigners. Excludes acquisitions of foreign stocks through mergers that involve stock swaps. Including stock swaps, net sales of foreign securities was $163 billion in 2010. Minus sign (−) indicates net sales by U.S. investors or a net inflow of capital into the United States]

Year and country	Net Purchases			Total transactions [1]			Bonds		Stocks	
	Total	Bonds	Stocks	Total	Bonds	Stocks	Purchases	Sales	Purchases	Sales
1990................	31.2	21.9	9.2	907	652	255	337	315	132	123
2000................	17.1	4.1	13.1	5,539	1,922	3,617	963	959	1,815	1,802
2003................	56.5	−32.0	88.6	5,580	2,883	2,698	1,425	1,457	1,393	1,305
2004................	152.8	67.9	85.0	6,399	2,986	3,413	1,527	1,459	1,749	1,664
2005................	172.4	45.1	127.3	7,572	2,965	4,608	1,505	1,460	2,367	2,240
2006................	250.9	144.5	106.5	11,283	3,904	7,379	2,024	1,880	3,743	3,636
2007................	229.2	133.9	95.3	16,604	6,078	10,527	3,107	2,973	5,311	5,216
2008................	−86.9	−66.4	−20.4	15,332	4,475	10,856	2,218	2,272	5,423	5,443
2009................	197.6	138.2	59.3	10,442	4,042	6,400	2,079	1,952	3,229	3,170
2010, [2] total.......	147.6	86.8	60.9	14,801	7,394	7,407	3,740	3,654	3,734	3,673
United Kingdom.......	−10.3	−6.5	−3.8	5,318	3,028	2,289	1,511	1,517	1,143	1,147
Cayman Islands.......	2.4	−3.5	5.9	2,746	1,454	1,293	725	729	649	643
Canada...............	52.6	49.9	2.8	1,159	668	491	359	309	247	244
Hong Kong...........	18.2	−7.8	26.0	682	69	612	31	39	319	293
Japan................	19.8	6.5	13.4	501	127	374	67	60	194	180
Bermuda.............	2.7	1.5	1.1	743	551	192	277	275	97	95
France...............	−8.6	−4.8	−3.8	403	190	213	93	97	105	108
Australia.............	17.3	17.2	0.2	255	101	154	59	42	77	77
Germany.............	−36.0	−32.7	−3.3	226	150	75	59	92	36	39
British Virgin Islands ...	−3.6	0.5	−4.1	243	54	189	27	27	92	97
Netherlands...........	−7.3	−7.3	–	158	63	95	28	35	48	48
Bahamas, The........	−0.7	1.2	−1.9	178	57	121	29	28	60	61
Switzerland...........	−0.4	5.7	−6.2	165	34	131	20	14	62	68
Brazil................	21.8	0.8	21.0	180	66	114	33	33	67	47

– Represents zero. [1] Total purchases plus total sales. [2] Includes other countries not shown separately.
Source: U.S. Department of Treasury, *Treasury Bulletin*, quarterly, Capital Movements Tables (Section IV).
See <http://www.fms.treas.gov/bulletin/index.html>.

Table 1204. U.S. Holdings of Foreign Stocks and Bonds by Country: 2008 to 2010

[In billions of dollars (2,748.4 represents $2,748,400,000,000). See also Table 1289]

Country	Stocks			Country	Bonds		
	2008	2009	2010, prel.		2008	2009	2010, prel.
Total holdings.............	2,748.4	3,995.3	4,485.6	Total holdings.............	1,237.3	1,570.3	1,737.3
Europe [1].................	1,378.9	1,961.9	2,031.8	Europe [1].................	571.2	741.4	771.7
United Kingdom.......	393.3	592.4	638.7	United Kingdom..............	189.0	254.4	244.7
Switzerland...........	214.3	298.3	328.2	Belgium & Luxembourg.......	43.4	64.6	123.0
France...............	212.2	250.7	235.9	Germany...................	74.9	106.2	109.0
Germany.............	159.9	192.7	205.7	Netherlands................	75.9	76.1	79.2
Netherlands...........	76.6	108.8	111.1	France....................	52.7	76.0	46.1
Spain................	63.3	87.4	70.4	Ireland...................	22.6	25.8	38.1
Ireland...............	22.3	79.2	62.2	Sweden...................	20.2	25.5	33.0
Sweden..............	30.3	44.0	58.4	Canada...................	165.9	219.5	283.9
Belgium and Luxembourg.....	31.6	59.8	56.4	Caribbean financial centers [1]....	227.2	251.0	265.9
Canada.................	180.2	295.1	359.5	Cayman Islands.............	202.4	217.5	226.6
Caribbean financial centers [1]....	283.1	334.7	377.4	Bermuda.................	19.2	26.8	29.9
Bermuda.............	143.3	121.1	132.1	Latin America, excluding			
Cayman Islands...........	95.2	147.5	168.1	Caribbean financial centers [1] ...	65.9	94.2	114.5
Latin America, excluding				Mexico..................	19.0	22.6	34.5
Caribbean financial centers [1] ...	137.3	276.6	331.5	Asia [1]..................	98.9	101.0	109.6
Brazil................	72.1	180.3	211.4	Japan...................	39.7	26.6	34.9
Mexico...............	46.0	65.1	82.9	Africa...................	6.4	9.3	11.6
Asia [1].................	659.2	929.3	1,153.5	Other countries [1]...........	97.7	153.9	180.0
Japan................	347.6	370.8	441.1	Australia.................	71.0	107.3	131.7
Hong Kong............	61.5	91.4	138.6				
China [2].............	53.3	101.6	104.4				
Korea, South..........	45.3	87.9	122.4				
Taiwan [2]............	41.2	76.6	97.5				
Africa [1].............	35.6	58.0	72.8				
South Africa..........	29.6	49.5	66.0				
Other countries [1]......	74.1	139.8	159.2				
Australia.............	65.2	127.9	144.2				

[1] Includes other countries, not shown separately. [2] See footnote 3, Table 1206.
Source: U.S. Bureau of Economic Analysis, *Survey of Current Business*, July 2011.

Table 1205. Foreign Purchases and Sales of U.S. Securities by Type of Security, 1990 to 2010, and by Selected Country, 2010

[In billions of dollars (18.7 represents $18,700,000,000). Covers transactions in all types of long-term domestic securities by foreigners as reported as reported to the Treasury International Capital Reporting System by banks, brokers, and other entities in the United States (except nonmarketable U.S. Treasury notes, foreign series; and nonmarketable U.S. Treasury bonds and notes, foreign currency series). Data by country show the country of domicile of the foreign buyers and sellers of the securities; in the case of outstanding issues, this may differ from the country of the original issuer. Excludes U.S. equities acquired through mergers and reincorporations that involve stock swaps and principal repayment flows on foreign holdings of U.S. government agency and corporate asset-backed securities (ABS). Including stock swaps and accounting for ABS repayment flows, net purchases of U.S. securities was $716 billion in 2010. Minus sign (–) indicates net sales by foreigners or a net outflow of capital from the United States]

Year and country	Net purchases					Total transactions [1]				
	Total	Treasury bonds and notes [2]	U.S. government corporations [3] bonds	Corporate bonds [4]	Corporate stocks	Total	Treasury bonds and notes [2]	U.S. government corporations [3] bonds	Corporate bonds [4]	Corporate stocks
1990.	18.7	17.9	6.3	9.7	−15.1	4,204	3,620	104	117	362
2000.	457.8	−54.0	152.8	184.1	174.9	16,910	7,795	1,305	775	7,036
2002.	547.6	119.9	195.1	182.3	50.2	25,498	14,409	3,261	1,459	6,369
2003.	719.9	263.6	155.8	265.7	34.7	26,332	15,739	2,725	1,694	6,174
2004.	916.5	352.1	226.4	309.5	28.5	29,441	17,520	2,192	2,033	7,696
2005.	1,011.5	338.1	219.3	372.2	82.0	33,303	19,764	1,976	2,182	9,382
2006.	1,143.2	195.5	286.5	510.8	150.4	41,011	21,720	2,858	2,846	13,587
2007.	1,005.8	198.0	219.0	393.4	195.5	58,455	30,057	3,882	3,433	21,083
2008.	414.9	314.9	−38.7	93.9	44.8	61,035	28,944	5,219	2,841	24,031
2009.	638.9	538.4	−11.5	−40.8	152.7	40,321	22,648	2,098	2,420	13,155
2010, total [5].	**933.9**	**707.9**	**115.0**	**−1.8**	**112.8**	**49,041**	**31,623**	**1,997**	**2,035**	**13,386**
United Kingdom	397.9	343.6	31.5	−5.0	27.8	17,585	14,629	405	708	1,843
Cayman Islands.	59.9	18.4	7.1	18.3	16.1	8,698	3,392	329	465	4,513
France	27.9	−5.0	16.4	−6.4	23.0	7,720	5,896	62	38	1,725
Canada	95.8	80.2	7.8	1.6	6.2	2,194	1,296	69	97	732
Japan	200.8	124.1	68.0	4.1	4.6	2,096	1,535	362	67	133
Bermuda	15.0	3.1	4.6	1.7	5.5	1,250	186	96	72	896
Bahamas, The	−8.8	−8.8	0.7	−0.9	0.1	927	432	9	128	358
British Virgin Islands . . .	−2.2	−4.4	0.3	0.3	1.6	1,094	568	4	41	482
Anguilla	−0.2	−1.4	0.0	0.7	1.4	1,003	43	0	2	958
China [6].	24.3	51.2	−29.3	−0.4	2.8	505	356	103	8	38
Israel	4.5	3.4	0.6	0.2	0.4	297	259	5	4	29
Ireland	−9.1	−3.1	−4.0	−3.0	1.0	458	278	70	40	70

[1] Total purchases plus total sales. [2] Marketable bonds and notes. [3] Includes federally sponsored agencies. [4] Includes transactions in directly placed issues abroad by U.S. corporations and issues of states and municipalities. [5] Includes other countries, not shown separately. [6] See footnote 3, Table 1206.

Source: U.S. Department of Treasury, *Treasury Bulletin*, quarterly, Capital Movements Tables (Section IV). See <http://www.fms.treas.gov/bulletin/index.html>.

Table 1206. Foreign Holdings of U.S. Securities by Country: 2008 to 2010

[In billions of dollars (3,253.0 represents $3,253,000,000,000). Covers only private holdings of U.S. securities, except as noted. See also Table 1289]

Country	2008	2009	2010, prel.	Country	2008	2009	2010, prel.
U.S. Treasury securities [1, 2]. . . .	**3,253.0**	**3,671.4**	**4,385.3**	Japan.	265.2	261.2	270.5
China [3].	808.3	1,036.4	1,280.1	Taiwan [3].	36.4	43.5	52.2
Japan.	660.1	750.2	871.5	Hong Kong.	23.4	24.6	31.9
OPEC Asia [4].	180.6	166.1	165.8	Africa.	3.4	2.7	2.4
Brazil	140.1	170.3	184.7	Other countries [2]	48.2	48.9	43.5
Russia	133.8	156.3	169.4	Australia.	28.9	25.7	23.5
Hong Kong.	78.2	145.9	133.5				
Taiwan [3].	94.5	125.8	153.7	**Corporate stocks. . . . .**	**1,850.1**	**2,494.3**	**2,991.6**
Belgium and Luxembourg	112.9	111.3	117.7	Europe [2].	964.4	1,281.1	1,550.4
Switzerland	73.6	91.0	105.5	United Kingdom	282.7	372.0	451.8
United Kingdom.	84.7	29.7	98.5	Belgium and Luxembourg	147.4	197.6	231.6
				Switzerland	118.0	166.0	202.7
Corporate and agency bonds. .	**2,770.6**	**2,825.6**	**2,868.5**	Netherlands	124.6	159.5	179.9
Europe [2].	1,753.3	1,782.6	1,762.2	France	87.3	116.1	163.6
Belgium and Luxembourg	668.9	705.7	677.2	Ireland	56.0	78.3	95.3
United Kingdom.	566.0	546.4	549.6	Germany	45.3	57.2	67.4
Ireland	153.0	154.5	151.0	Sweden	31.4	46.0	57.9
Switzerland	98.8	113.4	121.2	Canada	234.1	306.0	365.7
Germany	90.5	85.5	83.7	Caribbean financial centers [2].	305.0	424.2	511.2
Netherlands	84.7	73.7	66.8	Cayman Islands.	214.9	299.2	357.8
France	41.0	49.0	59.8	Latin America, excluding			
Canada	63.8	70.1	87.7	Caribbean financial centers	39.1	54.5	65.4
Caribbean financial centers [2].	480.2	516.8	536.9	Mexico.	10.3	14.5	20.8
Cayman Islands.	336.8	354.1	363.8	Asia [2].	239.6	336.4	391.3
Bermuda	109.5	124.1	131.4	Japan.	161.9	231.2	275.0
Latin America, excluding Caribbean				Africa.	5.1	5.9	6.6
financial centers [2].	33.8	26.6	32.2	Other countries [2]	62.8	86.2	101.0
Asia [2].	387.9	377.9	403.6	Australia.	57.3	77.5	91.5

[1] Includes foreign official holdings. [2] Includes other countries not shown separately. [3] With the establishment of diplomatic relations with China on January 1, 1979, the U.S. government recognized the People's Republic of China as the sole legal government of China and acknowledged the Chinese position that there is only one China and that Taiwan is part of China. [4] Comprises Indonesia, Iran, Iraq, Kuwait, Qatar, Saudi Arabia, and the United Arab Emirates.

Source: U.S. Bureau of Economic Analysis, *Survey of Current Business*, July 2011.

Table 1207. Stock Prices and Yields: 2000 to 2010

[Closing values as of end of December, except as noted]

Index	2000	2005	2006	2007	2008	2009	2010
STOCK PRICES							
Standard & Poor's indices: [1]							
S&P 500 composite (1941–43 = 10)	1,320	1,248	1,418	1,468	903	1,115	1,257
S&P 400 MidCap Index (1982 = 100)	517	738	804	858	538	727	907
S&P 600 SmallCap Index (Dec. 31, 1993 = 100)	220	351	400	395	269	333	416
S&P 500 Citigroup Value Index (Dec. 31, 1974 = 35)	636	648	764	761	447	525	590
S&P 500 Citigroup Growth Index (Dec. 31, 1974 = 35) . . .	688	597	653	703	451	582	659
Russell indices: [2]							
Russell 1000 (Dec. 31, 1986 = 130)	700	679	770	800	488	612	697
Russell 2000 (Dec. 31, 1986 = 135)	484	673	788	766	499	625	784
Russell 3000 (Dec. 31, 1986 = 140)	726	723	822	849	521	653	749
N.Y. Stock Exchange common stock index:							
Composite (Dec. 31, 2002 = 5000)	6,946	7,754	9,139	9,740	5,757	7,185	7,964
Yearly high	7,165	7,868	9,188	10,387	9,713	7,288	7,983
Yearly low	6,095	6,903	7,708	8,344	4,607	4,182	6,356
American Stock Exchange Composite Index (Dec. 29, 1995 = 550)	898	1,759	2,056	2,410	1,398	1,825	2,208
NASDAQ Composite Index (Feb. 5, 1971 = 100)	2,471	2,205	2,415	2,653	1,577	2,269	2,653
Nasdaq-100 (Jan. 31, 1985 = 125)	2,342	1,645	1,757	2,085	1,212	1,860	2,218
Industrial (Feb. 5, 1971 = 100).	1,483	1,860	2,090	2,179	1,191	1,748	2,184
Banks (Feb. 5, 1971 = 100)	1,939	3,078	3,417	2,663	2,026	1,651	1,847
Computers (Oct. 29, 1993 = 200)	1,295	992	1,053	1,283	684	1,168	1,372
Transportation (Feb. 5, 1971 = 100).	1,160	2,438	2,582	2,673	1,885	1,951	2,562
Telecommunications (Oct. 29, 1993 = 200)	463	184	235	257	146	217	226
Biotech (Oct. 29, 1993 = 200)	1,085	790	798	835	730	844	970
Dow-Jones and Co., Inc.:							
Composite (65 stocks).	3,317	3,638	4,121	4,394	3,086	3,567	4,033
Industrial (30 stocks)	10,787	10,718	12,463	13,265	8,776	10,428	11,578
Transportation (20 stocks)	2,947	4,196	4,560	4,571	3,537	4,100	5,107
Utility (15 stocks)	412	405	457	533	371	398	405
Dow-Jones Wilshire 5000 Composite Index [3] (December 31, 1980 = 1,405) [3]	12,176	12,518	14,258	14,820	9,087	11,497	13,290
COMMON STOCK YIELDS (percent)							
Standard & Poor's Composite Index (500 stocks): [4]							
Dividend-price ratio [5]	1.15	1.83	1.87	1.86	2.37	2.01	1.81
Earnings-price ratio [6]	3.63	5.36	5.78	5.29	3.54	4.55	5.93

[1] Standard & Poor's Indices are market-value weighted and are chosen for market size, liquidity, and industry group representation. The S&P 500 index represents 500 large publicly-traded companies. The S&P MidCap Index tracks mid-cap companies. The S&P SmallCap Index consists of 600 domestic small-cap stocks. [2] The Russell 1000 and 3000 indices show respectively the 1000 and 3000 largest capitalization stocks in the United States. The Russell 2000 index shows the 2000 largest capitalization stocks in the United States after the first 1000. [3] Dow-Jones Wilshire 5000 Composite Index (full-cap) measures the performance of all U.S. headquartered equity securities with readily available prices. Source: Dow-Jones & Company, Inc., New York, NY, Dow-Jones Indexes, (copyright). [4] Source: U.S. Council of Economic Advisors, Economic Indicators, monthly. [5] Aggregate cash dividends (based on latest known annual rate) divided by aggregate market value based on Wednesday closing prices. Averages of monthly figures. [6] Averages of quarterly ratios which are ratio of earnings (after taxes) for 4 quarters ending with particular quarter-to-price index for last day of that quarter.

Source: Except as noted, Global Financial Data, Los Angeles, CA, (copyright), <http://www.globalfinancialdata.com/>.

Table 1208. Dow Jones U.S. Total Market Index by Industry: 2000 to 2010

[As of end of year]

Industry	2000	2005	2006	2007	2008	2009	2010
U.S. Total Market Index, total . . .	**306.88**	**302.37**	**343.25**	**357.48**	**219.66**	**276.57**	**316.56**
Basic materials	154.49	205.79	236.22	307.92	147.91	239.44	309.95
Consumer goods	219.82	265.88	298.60	320.39	231.71	278.07	323.20
Consumer services	279.11	298.62	338.32	310.76	211.93	278.96	340.32
Oil and gas	272.96	422.12	510.72	679.31	429.60	494.01	580.28
Financial	440.91	510.02	592.98	474.23	226.52	258.79	287.09
Health care	360.18	315.50	332.38	354.89	268.73	320.51	328.59
Industrials	276.11	280.72	314.41	351.44	207.77	255.47	315.97
Technology	749.01	513.48	561.85	645.98	365.85	595.55	664.45
Telecommunications	210.38	126.90	168.11	179.65	115.34	119.63	133.50
Utilities	177.80	152.41	178.78	204.52	137.79	148.29	153.14

Source: Dow-Jones & Company, Inc., New York, NY, Dow-Jones Indexes (copyright).

Table 1209. Transaction Activity in Equities, Options, and Security Futures, 1990 to 2010, and by Exchange, 2010

[In billions of dollars (2,229 represents $2,229,000,000,000). Market value of all sales of equities and options listed on an exchange or subject to last-sale reporting. Also reported are the value of such options that were exercised and the value of single-stock futures that were delivered. Excludes options and futures on indexes]

Year and exchange	Market value of sales (billion dollars)			
	Total	Equity trading	Option trading	Option exercises and futures deliveries
1990.	2,229	2,154	27	48
2000.	36,275	35,557	485	233
2003.	22,737	22,292	164	282
2004.	27,876	27,158	223	495
2005.	34,568	33,223	350	995
2006.	43,941	41,798	531	1,611
2007.	66,136	63,064	861	2,211
2008.	82,012	78,653	1,096	2,264
2009.	59,850	57,556	710	1,574
2010, total [1]	**64,008**	**61,146**	**725**	**2,137**
BATS (Better Alternative Trading System)				
Echange, Inc..	6,779	6,764	3	11
Chicago Board Options Exchange, Inc..	687	112	144	432
EDGX Exchange, Inc.	1,101	1,101	–	–
FINRA, Inc. [2]	18,120	18,120	–	–
International Securities Exchange, LLC	883	410	120	352
NASDAQ OMX BX.	1,625	1,565	16	45
The Nasdaq Stock Market LLC	13,433	13,317	27	89
National Stock Exchange	331	331	–	–
New York Stock Exchange, Inc..	8,403	8,403	–	–
NYSE Arca, Inc. [3].	10,024	9,670	91	263

– Represents zero. [1] Includes other exchanes not shown separately. [2] Financial Industry Regulatory Authority. [3] NYSE Euronext completed its acquisition of the American Stock Exchange (Amex) on October 1, 2008. Post merger, the Amex equities business was branded NYSE Alternext US.

Source: U.S. Securities and Exchange Commission, "Select SEC and Market Data." For more information, see <http://www.sec.gov>.

Table 1210. Volume of Trading on New York Stock Exchange: 1990 to 2010

[39,946 represents 39,946,000,000. Round lot: A unit of trading or a multiple thereof. On the NYSE the unit of trading is generally 100 shares in stocks. For some inactive stocks, the unit of trading is 10 shares. Odd lot: An amount of stock less than the established 100-share unit or 10-share unit of trading]

Item	Unit	1990	2000	2004	2005 [1]	2006	2007	2008	2009	2010
Shares traded.	**Million . . . .**	**39,946**	**265,499**	**372,718**	**523,811**	**597,720**	**671,402**	**806,883**	**738,193**	**601,275**
Round lots	Million	39,665	262,478	367,099	516,743	588,127	664,020	802,170	738,193	601,275
Average daily shares . . .	Million	157	1,042	1,457	2,051	2,343	2,645	3,171	2,929	2,386
High day	Million	292	1,561	2,690	3,628	3,853	5,505	7,342	5,043	5,557
Low day	Million	57	403	509	694	797	917	849	585	849
Odd lots	Million	282	3,021	5,619	7,068	9,593	7,383	4,713	([2])	([2])
Value of shares traded	**Bil. dol. . . .**	**1,336**	**11,205**	**11,841**	**18,174**	**22,247**	**28,805**	**28,272**	**17,562**	**17,852**
Round lots	Bil. dol. . . .	1,325	11,060	11,618	17,858	21,790	28,428	28,080	17,562	17,852
Odd lots	Bil. dol. . . .	11	145	223	316	458	378	192	([2])	([2])

[1] Beginning 2005, reflects trades of NYSE Group. [2] This is a discontinued data series and is no longer collected due to the rescinding of the rules 440F & 440G.

Source: New York Stock Exchange, Inc., New York, NY, "Facts & Figures," <http://www.nyxdata.com/factbook> (copyright).

Table 1211. Stock Ownership by Age of Head of Family and Family Income: 2001 to 2007

[Median value in thousands of constant 2007 dollars (40.4 represents $40,400). Constant dollar figures are based on consumer price index data published by U.S. Bureau of Labor Statistics. Families include one-person units; for definition of family, see text, Section 1. Based on Survey of Consumer Finance; see Appendix III. For definition of median, see Guide to Tabular Presentation]

Age of family head and family income (constant (2007) dollars)	Families having direct or indirect stock holdings [1] (percent)			Median value among families with holdings			Stock holdings share of total financial assets (percent)		
	2001	2004	2007	2001	2004	2007	2001	2004	2007
All families.	**52.2**	**50.2**	**51.1**	**40.4**	**35.7**	**35.0**	**56.1**	**51.3**	**53.3**
Under 35 years old	49.0	40.8	38.6	8.2	8.8	7.0	52.5	40.3	44.3
35 to 44 years old	59.5	54.5	53.5	32.2	22.0	26.0	57.2	53.5	53.7
45 to 54 years old	59.3	56.5	60.4	58.5	54.9	45.0	59.1	53.8	53.0
55 to 64 years old	57.4	62.8	58.9	94.2	78.0	78.0	56.2	55.0	55.0
65 to 74 years old	40.0	46.9	52.1	175.8	76.9	57.0	55.4	51.5	55.3
75 years old and over . . .	35.7	34.8	40.1	128.7	94.3	41.0	51.8	39.3	48.1
Percentiles of income: [2]									
Less than 20	12.9	11.7	13.6	8.8	8.2	6.5	37.4	32.0	39.0
20 to 39.9	34.1	29.6	34.0	9.1	11.0	8.8	35.6	30.9	34.3
40 to 59.9	52.5	51.7	49.5	17.5	16.5	17.7	46.8	43.4	38.3
60 to 79.9	75.7	69.9	70.5	33.5	28.7	34.1	52.0	41.7	52.5
80 to 89.9	82.0	83.8	84.4	75.6	60.9	62.0	57.3	48.8	49.3
90 to 100	89.7	92.7	91.0	289.7	225.2	219.0	60.5	57.5	57.6

[1] Indirect holdings are those in retirement accounts and other managed assets. [2] See footnote 8, Table 1170.

Source: Board of Governors of the Federal Reserve System, "2007 Survey of Consumer Finances," February 2009, <http://www.federalreserve.gov/pubs/oss/oss2/2007/scf2007home.html\>.

Table 1212. Households Owning Mutual Funds by Age and Income: 2000 and 2010

[In percent. Ownership includes money market, stock, bond, and hybrid mutual funds, variable annuities, and mutual funds owned through Individual Retirement Accounts (IRAs), Keoghs, and employer-sponsored retirement plans. In 2010, an estimated 51,600,000 households own mutual funds. A mutual fund is an open-end investment company that continuously issues and redeems shares that represent an interest in a pool of financial assets]

Age of household head and household income [1, 2]	Percent distribution, 2010	As a percent of all households		Age of household head and household income [1, 2]	Percent distribution, 2010	As a percent of all households	
		2000	2010			2000	2010
Total..................	**100**	**45**	**44**	Less than $25,000........	6	13	10
Less than 35 years old	15	36	31	$25,000 to $34,999.......	6	33	26
35 to 44 years old	20	55	47	$35,000 to $49,999.......	13	46	40
45 to 54 years old	27	59	56	$50,000 to $74,999.......	20	66	48
55 to 64 years old	20	50	51	$75,000 to $99,999.......	19	75	71
65 years old and over	18	26	37	$100,000 to $199,999.....	29	84	78
				$200,000 and over........	7	56	81

[1] Age is based on the sole or co-decision maker for household saving and investing. [2] Total reported is household income before taxes in prior year.

Source: Investment Company Institute, Washington, DC, *Research Fundamentals*, Vol. 19, No. 6, September 2010 (copyright).

Table 1213. Characteristics of Mutual Fund Owners: 2010

[In percent, except as indicated. Mutual fund ownership includes holdings of money market, stock, bond, and hybrid mutual funds; and funds owned through variable annuities, Individual Retirement Accounts (IRAs), Keoghs, and employer-sponsored retirement plans. Based on a national probability sample of 1,805 primary financial decision-makers in households with mutual fund investments. For definition of mutual fund, see headnote, Table 1214. For definition of median, see Guide to Tabular Presentation]

Characteristic	Total	Age			Household income			
		Under 40 years old	40 to 64 years old	65 years old and over	Less than $50,000	$50,000 to $99,000	$100,000 to $149,000	$150,000 or more
Median age [1] (years)	50	33	51	72	53	50	48	50
Median household income [2] (dol.) ...	80,000	75,000	87,500	53,500	35,000	72,000	119,900	188,200
Median household financial assets [3] (dollars)	200,000	50,000	250,000	300,000	75,000	125,000	270,000	500,000
Own an IRA....................	68	59	70	72	58	64	77	83
Household with defined contribution retirement plan(s) [4]	77	85	84	45	60	79	85	88
401(k) plan..................	65	74	72	27	49	66	71	75
403(b), state, local, or federal government plan	33	36	34	24	23	33	43	36
Median mutual fund assets (dol.) ...	100,000	25,000	130,000	150,000	40,000	75,000	175,000	300,000
Own:								
Equity funds..................	80	77	83	74	73	79	84	87
Bond funds	53	47	56	48	38	53	60	64

[1] See Table 1212, footnote 1. [2] See Table 1212, footnote 2. [3] Includes assets in employer-sponsored retirement plans but excludes value of primary residence. [4] For definition of defined contribution plan, see headnote, Table 552.

Source: Investment Company Institute, Washington, DC, *Profile of Mutual Fund Shareholders, 2011*, Winter 2011 (copyright).

Table 1214. Mutual Funds—Summary: 1990 to 2010

[Number of funds and assets as of December 31 (1,065 represents $1,065,000,000,000). A mutual fund is an open-end investment company that continuously issues and redeems shares that represent an interest in a pool of financial assets. Excludes data for funds that invest in other mutual funds. Minus sign (−) indicates net redemptions]

Type of fund	Unit	1990	2000	2004	2005	2006	2007	2008	2009	2010
Number of funds, total	**Number**...	**3,079**	**8,155**	**8,040**	**7,974**	**8,118**	**8,027**	**8,022**	**7,685**	**7,581**
Equity funds.................	Number ...	1,099	4,385	4,547	4,586	4,769	4,764	4,827	4,653	4,585
Hybrid funds	Number ...	193	523	509	504	507	488	492	471	478
Bond funds	Number ...	1,046	2,208	2,042	2,014	1,995	1,970	1,920	1,857	1,866
Money market funds, taxable [1]	Number ...	506	704	637	593	573	545	534	476	442
Money market funds, tax-exempt [2] ...	Number ...	235	335	305	277	274	260	249	228	210
Assets, total..................	**Bil. dol.**....	**1,065**	**6,965**	**8,095**	**8,891**	**10,398**	**12,002**	**9,604**	**11,120**	**11,821**
Equity funds.................	Bil. dol.....	239	3,962	4,387	4,943	5,914	6,519	3,706	4,957	5,667
Hybrid funds	Bil. dol.....	36	346	517	564	650	717	498	639	741
Bond funds	Bil. dol.....	291	811	1,290	1,357	1,495	1,681	1,568	2,208	2,608
Money market funds, taxable [1]	Bil. dol.....	415	1,611	1,589	1,690	1,969	2,618	3,339	2,917	2,474
Money market funds, tax-exempt [2] ...	Bil. dol.....	84	234	312	336	369	468	494	399	330
Net sales:										
Equity, hybrid and bond funds	Bil. dol....	51	300	293	303	369	405	−9	512	392
Money market funds, taxable [1]	Bil. dol.....	36	192	−157	64	255	623	605	−424	−450
Money market funds, tax-exempt [2] ...	Bil. dol.....	7	31	16	25	33	90	25	−88	−67

[1] Funds invest in short-term, high-grade securities sold in the money market. [2] Funds invest in municipal securities with relatively short maturities.

Source: Investment Company Institute, Washington, DC, *Mutual Fund Fact Book*, annual (copyright).

Table 1215. Mutual Fund Shares—Holdings and Net Purchases by Type of Investor: 2000 to 2010

[In billions of dollars (4,433 represents $4,433,000,000,000). Holdings as of Dec. 31. For definition of mutual fund, see headnote, Table 1214. Excludes money market mutual funds. Minus sign (–) indicates net sales]

Type of investor	Holdings					Net purchases				
	2000	2005	2008	2009	2010	2000	2005	2008	2009	2010
Total................................	4,433	6,049	5,435	6,962	7,963	237.6	260.2	31.0	490.5	376.4
Households, nonprofit organizations.........	2,704	3,669	3,326	4,178	4,708	76.3	173.5	15.2	363.7	286.4
Nonfinancial corporate business.............	122	140	126	190	249	3.5	1.5	–6.1	39.9	39.9
State and local governments...............	31	30	33	35	38	1.2	0.8	14.3	–7.2	–2.3
Rest of the world........................	149	242	256	322	368	–9.2	32.2	–2.0	17.7	17.4
Commercial banking......................	15	17	20	46	45	2.5	–1.8	1.3	14.8	–5.9
Credit unions..........................	2	2	2	1	2	–0.3	–1.0	0.0	–0.7	0.2
Property-casualty insurance companies.......	3	6	4	5	6	0.4	0.3	–0.4	0.1	–0.1
Life insurance companies.................	97	109	121	141	156	5.6	–9.9	–10.7	–	1.0
Private pension funds....................	1,132	1,585	1,366	1,817	2,132	107.7	70.0	20.5	64.8	42.6
State and local government retirement funds...	178	248	181	227	262	49.9	–5.5	–1.1	–2.5	–2.8

– Represents or rounds to zero.

Source: Board of Governors of the Federal Reserve System, "Federal Reserve Statistical Release, Z.1, Flow of Funds Accounts of the United States," March 2011, <http://www.federalreserve.gov/releases/z1/20100311>.

Table 1216. Retirement Assets by Type of Asset: 1990 to 2010

[In billions of dollars, except as indicated (3,923 represents $3,923,000,000,000). As of December 31]

Institution	1990	2000	2005	2006	2007	2008	2009	2010
Retirement assets, total	3,923	11,696	14,863	16,730	17,945	13,892	16,022	17,488
IRA assets.................................	636	2,629	[1] 3,652	[2] 4,207	[2] 4,784	[1] 3,585	[1] 4,251	[1] 4,710
Bank and thrift deposits [3].................	266	250	278	313	340	391	431	460
Life insurance companies [4]..............	40	203	308	318	[1] 1,327	[1] 1,316	[1] 1,320	[1] 1,337
Mutual funds...........................	142	1,256	1,709	2,036	2,311	1,604	1,974	2,222
Securities held in brokerage accounts [5]	188	920	[1] 1,357	[2] 1,541	[2] 1,806	[1] 1,274	[1] 1,526	[1] 1,690
Traditional	(NA)	2,407	[1] 3,259	[2] 3,722	[2] 4,223	[1] 3,173	[1] 3,743	[1] 4,121
Roth.................................	(X)	78	[1] 160	[2] 196	[2] 233	[1] 173	[1] 215	[1] 265
SEP and SAR-SEP [6]....................	(NA)	134	[1] 191	[2] 236	[2] 266	[1] 193	[1] 235	[1] 260
SIMPLE [7]	(X)	10	[1] 42	[2] 52	[2] 63	[1] 46	[1] 58	[1] 64
Defined contribution plans...............	892	2,970	3,623	4,147	4,444	3,416	4,084	4,525
401(k) plans...........................	(NA)	1,725	2,396	2,768	2,982	2,230	[1] 2,725	[1] 3,056
403(b) plans...........................	(NA)	518	617	689	734	619	700	750
457 plans.............................	(NA)	110	143	158	173	140	169	[1] 189
Other defined contribution plans [8]........	(NA)	618	466	531	555	427	490	530
State and local government pension plans ...	742	2,340	2,763	3,157	3,298	2,415	2,760	3,021
Private defined benefit plans..............	922	2,009	2,310	2,557	2,621	1,880	2,132	2,242
Federal pension plans [9]..................	340	797	1,072	1,141	1,197	1,221	1,324	1,415
Annuities [10]	391	951	1,443	1,521	1,600	1,376	1,471	1,576
Memo:								
Mutual fund retirement assets............	208	2,558	3,574	4,228	4,769	3,287	4,138	4,687
Percent of total retirement assets..........	5	22	24	25	27	24	26	27
Percent of all mutual funds	20	37	40	41	40	34	37	40

NA Not available. X Not applicable. [1] Data are estimated. [2] Data are preliminary. [3] Includes Keogh deposits. [4] Annuities held by IRAs, excluding variable annuity mutual fund IRA assets. [5] Excludes mutual fund assets held through brokerage accounts, which are included in mutual funds. [6] Simplified Employee Pension IRAs and salary reduction (SAR) SEP IRAs. [7] Savings Incentive Match Plan for Employees (SIMPLE) IRAs. [8] Includes Keoghs and other defined contribution plans (profit-sharing, thrift-savings, stock bonus, and money purchase) without 401(k) features. [9] Federal pension plans include U.S. Treasury security holdings of the civil service retirement and disability fund, the military retirement fund, the judicial retirement funds, the Railroad Retirement Board, and the foreign service retirement and disability fund. These plans also include securities held in the National Railroad Retirement Investment Trust and Federal Employees Retirement System (FERS) Thrift Savings Plan (TSP). [10] Annuities include all fixed and variable annuity reserves at life insurance companies less annuities held by IRAs, 403(b) plans, 457 plans, and private pension funds. Some of these annuity reserves represent assets of individuals held outside retirement plan arrangements and IRAs; however, information to separate out such reserves is not available.

Source: Investment Company Institute, "The U.S. Retirement Market, Fourth Quarter 2010," April 2011, <http://www.ici.org/info/ret_10_q4_data.xls>.

Table 1217. Assets of Private and Public Pension Funds by Type of Fund: 1990 to 2010

[In billions of dollars (3,269 represents $3,269,000,000,000). As of end of year. Except for corporate equities, represents book value. Excludes social security trust funds; see Table 547]

Type of pension fund	1990	2000	2004	2005	2006	2007	2008	2009	2010
Total, all types	**3,269**	**9,084**	**10,551**	**11,379**	**12,646**	**13,257**	**10,283**	**11,792**	**12,896**
Private funds	2,199	5,994	6,950	7,586	8,415	8,861	6,737	7,794	8,552
Insured [1]	570	1,526	2,028	2,197	2,332	2,451	2,185	2,323	2,473
Noninsured [2, 3]	1,629	4,468	4,922	5,389	6,083	6,411	4,553	5,471	6,080
Credit market instruments [3]	464	622	655	700	758	861	951	1,063	1,170
Agency- and GSE-backed securities [4]	133	197	235	252	269	297	318	269	171
Corporate and foreign bonds	158	266	268	290	318	357	400	443	482
Corporate equities	606	1,971	2,338	2,442	2,725	2,673	1,600	1,836	1,983
Mutual fund shares	40	1,132	1,278	1,585	1,880	2,111	1,366	1,817	2,132
Unallocated insurance contracts [5]	215	308	328	338	388	431	318	413	451
State and local government employee retirement funds [3]	730	2,293	2,578	2,721	3,090	3,199	2,325	2,674	2,928
Credit market instruments [3]	402	743	675	693	808	820	834	825	816
Agency- and GSE-backed securities [4]	63	179	259	258	308	331	337	307	285
Corporate and foreign bonds	142	314	213	228	283	297	313	309	312
Corporate equities	285	1,299	1,601	1,716	1,926	2,014	1,238	1,550	1,779
Federal government retirement funds [6]	340	797	1,023	1,072	1,141	1,197	1,221	1,324	1,415

[1] Annuity reserves held by life insurance companies, excluding unallocated contracts held by private pension funds. [2] Private defined benefit plans and defined contribution plans (including 401(k) type plans). [3] Includes other types of assets not shown separately. [4] GSE = Government-sponsored enterprises. [5] Assets held at life insurance companies (e.g., guaranteed investment contracts (GICs), variable annuities). [6] Includes the Federal Employees Retirement System Thrift Savings Plan, the National Railroad Retirement Investment Trust, and nonmarketable government securities held by federal government retirement funds.
Source: Board of Governors of the Federal Reserve System, "Federal Reserve Statistical Release, Z.1, Flow of Funds Accounts of the United States," March 2011, <http://www.federalreserve.gov/releases/z1/20100311>.

Table 1218. Annual Revenues of Selected Securities Industries: 2004 to 2009

[In millions of dollars (375,111 represents $375,111,000,000). Covers taxable and tax-exempt employer firms only. Based on Service Annual Survey. Estimates have been adjusted to the results of the 2007 Economic Census. See Appendix III]

Kind of business	NAICS code [1]	2004	2005	2006	2007	2008	2009
Total	**523x**	**375,111**	**429,316**	**532,727**	**572,358**	**393,986**	**462,333**
Securities and commodity contracts intermediation and brokerage	5231	263,373	295,804	366,975	371,500	202,520	286,348
Investment banking and securities dealing	52311	135,697	155,507	201,501	203,139	120,461	158,694
Securities brokerage	52312	120,303	131,831	154,982	155,797	69,056	115,370
Commodity contracts dealing	52313	3,713	4,941	5,884	6,981	6,114	7,049
Commodity contracts brokerage	52314	(S)	3,525	4,608	5,583	6,889	5,235
Other financial investment activities [2]	5239x	111,738	133,512	165,752	200,858	191,466	175,985
Portfolio management	52392	95,253	114,641	143,900	177,941	169,593	151,268
Investment advice	52393	16,485	18,871	21,852	22,917	21,873	24,717

S Estimate does not meet publication standards. [1] Data is based on 2002 NAICS; see text, this section and Section 15. [2] Excludes NAICS 52391 (miscellaneous intermediation) and NAICS 52399 (all other financial investment activities).
Source: U.S. Census Bureau, "Service Annual Survey: 2009," January 2011, <http://www.census.gov/services/index.html>.

Table 1219. Securities Industry—Financial Summary: 1990 to 2009

[In billions of dollars, except as indicated. (71.4 represents $71,400,000,000). Minus sign (–) indicates negative loss]

Type	1990	2000	2003	2004	2005	2006	2007	2008	2009
Number of firms	8,437	7,258	6,565	6,284	6,016	5,808	5,562	5,178	5,063
Revenues, total	**71.4**	**349.5**	**219.0**	**242.9**	**332.5**	**458.5**	**496.5**	**296.6**	**288.1**
Commissions	12.0	54.1	45.5	47.6	46.8	49.7	54.4	55.2	49.0
Trading/investment gains	15.7	70.8	38.8	30.7	30.7	55.2	4.1	-55.3	45.3
Underwriting profits	3.7	18.7	17.2	19.1	19.9	23.6	26.5	16.3	22.6
Margin interest	3.2	24.5	5.3	7.0	13.3	23.7	32.3	18.1	4.5
Mutual fund sales	3.2	19.4	16.2	18.5	20.7	23.3	26.2	22.1	17.2
Other	33.4	161.9	96.0	120.1	201.2	282.9	353.0	240.2	149.5
Expenses, total	**70.6**	**310.4**	**193.3**	**219.7**	**311.3**	**419.9**	**491.5**	**320.1**	**212.4**
Interest expense	28.1	131.9	44.4	59.7	140.2	226.1	282.2	122.7	21.9
Compensation	22.9	95.2	77.4	83.5	88.8	103.4	106.3	95.0	95.9
Commissions/clearance paid	3.0	15.5	16.3	17.4	18.6	22.0	25.9	26.4	23.3
Other	16.6	67.8	55.1	59.2	63.6	68.4	77.0	76.0	71.3
Net income, pretax	**0.8**	**39.1**	**25.7**	**23.2**	**21.2**	**38.6**	**5.1**	**–23.6**	**75.7**
Pre-tax profit margin (percent)	1.1	11.2	11.7	9.5	6.4	8.4	1.0	-7.9	26.3
Pre-tax return on equity (percent)	2.2	31.1	17.6	15.0	13.1	22.1	2.7	-12.8	38.3
Assets	657	2,866	3,980	4,831	5,215	6,222	6,777	4,441	4,345
Liabilities	623	2,728	3,831	4,671	5,051	6,037	6,591	4,261	4,131
Ownership equity	34	138	149	160	164	185	186	181	215

Source: U.S. Securities and Exchange Commission, "Select SEC and Market Data Fiscal 2010", <http://www.sec.gov/about/secstats2010.pdf>.

Table 1220. Life Insurance in Force and Purchases in the United States—Summary: 1990 to 2009

[As of December 31 or calendar year, as applicable (389 represents 389,000,000). Covers life insurance with life insurance companies only. Data represents all life insurance in force on lives of U.S. residents whether issued by U.S. or foreign companies]

Year	Life insurance in force — Number of policies, total (millions)	Life insurance in force — Value (bil. dol.) Total [2]	Life insurance in force — Value (bil. dol.) Individual	Life insurance in force — Value (bil. dol.) Group	Life insurance purchases [1] — Number (1,000) Total	Life insurance purchases [1] — Number (1,000) Individual	Life insurance purchases [1] — Number (1,000) Group	Life insurance purchases [1] — Amount (bil. dol.) Total	Life insurance purchases [1] — Amount (bil. dol.) Individual	Life insurance purchases [1] — Amount (bil. dol.) Group
1990.........	389	9,393	5,391	3,754	28,791	14,199	14,592	1,529	1,070	459
2000.........	369	15,953	9,376	6,376	34,882	13,345	21,537	2,515	1,594	921
2003.........	379	17,044	9,655	7,236	35,767	13,821	21,946	2,823	1,773	1,050
2004.........	373	17,508	9,717	7,631	38,453	12,581	25,872	2,948	1,846	1,102
2005.........	373	18,399	9,970	8,263	34,519	11,407	23,112	2,836	1,796	1,040
2006.........	375	19,112	10,057	8,906	29,287	10,908	18,378	2,835	1,813	1,022
2007.........	374	19,539	10,232	9,158	30,788	10,826	19,962	2,994	1,891	1,103
2008.........	335	19,120	10,254	8,717	28,599	10,207	18,392	2,943	1,870	1,073
2009.........	291	18,138	10,324	7,688	29,190	10,139	19,051	2,900	1,744	1,156

[1] Excludes revivals, increases, dividend additions, and reinsurance acquired. Includes long-term credit insurance (life insurance on loans of more than 10 years' duration). [2] Includes other types of policies not shown separately.

Source: American Council of Life Insurers, Washington, DC, *Life Insurers Fact Book*, annual (copyright).

Table 1221. U.S. Life Insurance Companies—Summary: 1990 to 2009

[As of December 31 or calendar year, as applicable (402.2 represents $402,200,000,000). Covers domestic and foreign business of U.S. companies. Beginning in 2000, includes annual statement data for companies that primarily are health insurance companies. Beginning in 2003, includes fraternal benefit societies]

Item	Unit	1990	2000	2003	2004	2005	2006	2007	2008	2009
U.S. companies [1]	Number ...	2,195	1,269	1,227	1,179	1,119	1,072	1,009	976	946
Income	**Bil. dol. ....**	**402.2**	**811.5**	**727.0**	**756.8**	**779.0**	**883.6**	**950.4**	**940.6**	**781.4**
Life insurance premiums	Bil. dol.....	76.7	130.6	127.3	139.7	142.3	149.2	142.7	147.2	124.6
Annuity considerations [2]	Bil. dol.....	129.1	306.7	268.6	276.7	277.1	302.7	314.2	328.1	231.6
Health insurance premiums.....	Bil. dol.....	58.3	105.6	115.8	125.8	118.3	141.2	151.5	165.0	166.2
Investment and other..........	Bil. dol.....	138.2	268.5	215.3	214.7	241.4	290.4	342.0	300.3	259.1
Payments under life insurance and annuity contracts	Bil. dol.....	88.4	375.2	307.1	331.7	365.7	422.7	461.0	445.1	374.9
Payments to life insurance beneficiaries	Bil. dol.....	24.6	44.1	51.7	51.6	53.0	55.7	58.0	59.9	59.5
Surrender values under life insurance [3]	Bil. dol.....	18.0	27.2	35.9	35.5	39.2	38.5	47.7	58.6	48.1
Surrender values under. annuity contracts [3, 4]	Bil. dol.....	(NA)	214.0	140.3	162.9	190.3	237.8	262.3	236.7	182.7
Policyholder dividends..........	Bil. dol.....	12.0	20.0	20.8	19.0	17.9	18.4	19.5	19.1	16.2
Annuity payments [4]	Bil. dol.....	32.6	68.7	57.1	61.2	63.9	71.1	72.3	69.6	67.1
Matured endowments	Bil. dol.....	0.7	0.6	0.6	0.6	0.6	0.6	0.6	0.6	0.6
Other payments..............	Bil. dol.....	0.6	0.6	0.7	0.9	0.7	0.6	0.6	0.6	0.8
Health insurance benefit payments.................	Bil. dol.....	40.0	78.8	81.9	88.5	79.6	97.0	106.1	118.9	122.0
BALANCE SHEET										
Assets...................	**Bil. dol. ....**	**1,408**	**3,182**	**3,887**	**4,253**	**4,482**	**4,823**	**5,092**	**4,648**	**4,959**
Government bonds	Bil. dol.....	211	364	538	563	590	579	580	634	685
Corporate securities	Bil. dol.....	711	2,238	2,666	2,965	3,136	3,413	3,662	3,104	3,436
Percent of total assets.......	Percent ...	50	70	69	70	70	71	71	67	69
Bonds	Bil. dol.....	583	1,241	1,644	1,785	1,850	1,882	1,991	1,968	2,050
Stocks	Bil. dol.....	128	997	1,022	1,180	1,285	1,531	1,670	1,136	1,386
Mortgages.................	Bil. dol.....	270	237	269	283	295	314	336	353	336
Real estate	Bil. dol.....	43	36	31	31	33	33	35	32	28
Policy loans	Bil. dol.....	63	102	107	109	110	113	117	122	123
Other....................	Bil. dol.....	110	204	276	303	319	371	362	402	350
Interest earned on assets [5]	Percent ...	8.89	7.05	5.03	4.80	4.90	5.35	5.71	5.70	4.60
Obligations and surplus funds [6]...	Bil. dol.....	1,408	3,182	3,888	4,253	4,482	4,823	5,092	4,648	4,959
Policy reserves	**Bil. dol. ...**	**1,197**	**2,712**	**2,895**	**3,160**	**3,360**	**3,608**	**3,791**	**3,471**	**3,812**
Annuities [7]	Bil. dol.....	798	1,841	1,835	2,024	2,174	2,328	2,458	2,137	2,422
Group.................	Bil. dol.....	516	960	662	712	758	807	843	716	798
Individual..............	Bil. dol.....	282	881	1,173	1,312	1,415	1,521	1,615	1,422	1,624
Supplementary contracts [8].....	Bil. dol.....	17	34	15	16	16	17	18	13	16
Life insurance	Bil. dol.....	349	742	921	988	1,029	1,110	1,148	1,134	1,178
Health insurance	Bil. dol.....	33	96	123	134	141	153	166	186	196
Liabilities for deposit-type contracts [9]	Bil. dol.....	18	21	405	445	456	487	517	454	416
Capital and surplus	Bil. dol.....	91	188	231	250	256	266	282	263	301

NA Not available. [1] Beginning 2000, includes life insurance companies that sell accident and health insurance. [2] Beginning 2003, excludes certain deposit-type funds from income due to codification. [3] Beginning with 2000, "surrender values" include annuity withdrawals of funds, which were not included in 1990. [4] Beginning 2003, excludes payments under deposit-type contracts. [5] Net rate. [6] Includes other obligations not shown separately. [7] Beginning 2003, excludes reserves for guaranteed interest contracts (GICs). [8] Through 2000, includes reserves for contracts with and without life contingencies; beginning 2003, includes only reserves for contracts with life contingencies. [9] Policyholder dividend accumulations for all years. Beginning 2003, also includes liabilities for guaranteed interest contracts, supplementary contracts without life contingencies, and premium and other deposits.

Source: American Council of Life Insurers, Washington, DC, *Life Insurers Fact Book*, annual (copyright).

Table 1222. Property and Casualty Insurance—Summary: 2000 to 2009

[In billions of dollars (305.1 represents $305,100,000,000). Minus sign (−) indicates loss]

Item	2000	2004	2005	2006	2007	2008	2009
Premiums, net written [1]	305.1	425.7	427.6	447.8	446.7	439.9	422.9
Automobile, private [2]	120.0	157.6	159.6	160.5	159.7	158.6	157.4
Automobile, commercial [2]	19.8	26.7	26.8	26.7	25.6	23.8	21.9
Homeowners' multiple peril	32.7	50.0	53.0	55.8	55.6	56.4	57.7
Commercial multiple peril	(NA)	29.1	29.7	31.9	31.2	30.2	28.9
Marine, inland and ocean	8.3	10.8	11.2	12.3	13.0	12.5	11.6
Workers' compensation	26.2	36.7	39.7	41.8	40.6	36.5	32.0
Medical malpractice	(NA)	9.1	9.7	10.4	10.0	9.5	9.2
Other liability [3]	(NA)	39.8	39.4	42.2	41.2	38.5	36.0
Reinsurance	(NA)	13.7	6.6	12.9	13.1	13.8	12.6
Losses and expenses	321.3	407.7	421.4	401.0	417.1	457.6	424.4
Underwriting gain/loss	−27.3	6.0	−3.7	34.5	21.6	−19.6	1.6
Net investment income	42.0	40.0	49.7	52.3	56.5	53.1	48.3
Operating earnings after taxes	4.4	29.4	34.4	62.2	53.6	22.8	36.3

NA Not available. [1] Excludes state funds. Includes other lines of insurance not shown separately. [2] Includes premiums for automobile liability and physical damage. [3] Coverages protecting against legal liability resulting from negligence, carelessness, or failure to act.

Source: Insurance Information Institute, New York, NY, *The III Insurance Fact Book*, annual; and *Financial Services Fact Book*, annual (copyright). Data from ISO and Highline Data LLC. See also <http://www.iii.org>.

Table 1223. Automobile Insurance—Average Expenditures Per Insured Vehicle by State: 2000 and 2008

[In dollars. Average expenditure equals total premiums written divided by liability car-years. A car-year is equal to 365 days of insured coverage for a single vehicle. The average expenditures for automobile insurance in a state are affected by a number of factors, including the underlying rate structure, the coverages purchased, the deductibles and limits selected, the types of vehicles insured, and the distribution of driver characteristics. The NAIC does not rank state average expenditures and does not endorse any conclusions drawn from this data]

State	2000	2008	State	2000	2008	State	2000	2008	State	2000	2008
U.S.	690	789	ID	505	562	MO	612	657	PA	699	817
AL	594	667	IL	652	720	MT	530	667	RI	825	986
AK	770	904	IN	570	612	NE	533	547	SC	620	751
AZ	792	858	IA	479	519	NV	829	970	SD	482	520
AR	606	653	KS	540	576	NH	665	727	TN	592	641
CA	672	776	KY	616	699	NJ	977	1,081	TX	678	854
CO	755	729	LA	806	1,105	NM	674	728	UT	620	709
CT	871	950	ME	528	600	NY	939	1,044	VT	568	653
DE	849	1,007	MD	757	922	NC	564	595	VA	576	663
DC	996	1,126	MA	946	903	ND	477	503	WA	722	840
FL	781	1,055	MI	702	907	OH	579	617	WV	680	808
GA	674	765	MN	696	698	OK	603	663	WI	545	581
HI	702	816	MS	654	654	OR	625	727	WY	496	632

Source: National Association of Insurance Commissioners (NAIC), Kansas City, MO, Auto Insurance Database Report, annual (copyright). Reprinted with permission of the NAIC. Further reprint or distribution strictly prohibited without prior written permission of the NAIC.

Table 1224. Renters and Homeowners Insurance—Average Premiums by State: 2008

[In dollars. Average premium equals premiums divided by exposure per house-years. A house-year is equal to 365 days of insured coverage for a single dwelling and is the standard measurement for homeowners insurance. The NAIC does not rank state average expenditures and does not endorse any conclusions drawn from these data]

State	2008 Renters [1]	2008 Home-owners [2]	State	2008 Renters [1]	2008 Home-owners [2]	State	2008 Renters [1]	2008 Home-owners [2]
U.S.	176	791	KY	149	601	ND	112	808
AL	199	845	LA	228	1,155	OH	163	565
AK	178	856	ME	130	572	OK	218	1,048
AZ	202	628	MD	132	637	OR	153	439
AR	203	788	MA	218	1,026	PA	123	586
CA	224	911	MI	174	715	RI	149	897
CO	177	842	MN	141	845	SC	173	789
CT	194	980	MS	272	980	SD	113	609
DE	134	535	MO	165	788	TN	195	692
DC	151	926	MT	154	721	TX [3]	216	1,460
FL	207	1,390	NE	140	814	UT	134	432
GA	218	749	NV	205	692	VT	149	650
HI	202	862	NH	134	647	VA	131	604
ID	152	387	NJ	140	691	WA	172	471
IL	154	628	NM	186	703	WV	173	638
IN	169	658	NY	216	983	WI	123	503
IA	132	612	NC	130	683	WY	155	676
KS	166	916						

[1] Based on the HO-4 renters insurance policy for tenants. Includes broad named-peril coverage for the personal property of tenants. [2] Based on the HO-3 homeowner package policy for owner-occupied dwellings, 1–4 family units. Provides "all risks" coverage (except those specifically excluded in the policy) on buildings, broad named-peril coverage on personal property, and is the most common package written. [3] The Texas Insurance Commissioner promulgates residential policy forms which are similar but not identical to the standard forms.

Source: National Association of Insurance Commissioners (NAIC), Kansas City, MO, Dwelling Fire, Homeowners Owner-Occupied, and Homeowners Tenant and Condominium/Cooperative Unit Owners Insurance (copyright). Reprinted with permission of the NAIC. Further reprint or distribution strictly prohibited without prior written permission of the NAIC.

Banking, Finance, and Insurance 755

Table 1225. Real Estate and Rental and Leasing—Nonemployer Establishments and Receipts by Kind of Business: 2006 to 2008

[2,420.9 represents 2,420,900. Includes only firms subject to federal income tax. Nonemployers are businesses with no paid employees. Data originate chiefly from administrative records of the Internal Revenue Service; see Appendix III]

Kind of business	NAICS code [1]	Establishments (1,000)			Receipts (mil. dol.)		
		2006	2007	2008	2006	2007	2008
Real estate & rental & leasing, total............	**53**	**2,420.9**	**2,327.1**	**2,130.4**	**193,105**	**183,264**	**163,461**
Real estate	531	2,338.3	2,243.5	2,049.7	186,400	176,526	156,793
Lessors of real estate	5311	804.1	780.0	731.1	105,927	102,825	94,785
Offices of real estate agents & brokers	5312	829.9	790.7	700.3	36,214	31,460	24,935
Activities related to real estate...................	5313	704.4	672.8	618.4	44,259	42,242	37,073
Rental & leasing services	532	81.1	81.8	79.1	6,564	6,583	6,516
Automotive equipment rental & leasing.............	5321	19.8	20.3	19.7	1,023	1,057	1,059
Consumer goods rental..........................	5322	18.1	18.5	17.9	862	898	881
General rental centers...........................	5323	3.9	3.9	4.0	358	348	347
Commercial/industrial equipment rental & leasing	5324	39.3	39.1	37.4	4,320	4,280	4,230
Lessors of other nonfinancial intangible assets........	533	1.5	1.7	1.6	141	154	152

[1] Data use 2007 North American Industry Classification System (NAICS). For more information, see text, Section 15. 2006 data are 2002 NAICS. 2007 and 2008 are 2007 NAICS.

Source: U.S. Census Bureau, "Nonemployer Statistics," June 2010, <http://www.census.gov/econ/nonemployer/index.html>.

Table 1226. Real Estate and Rental and Leasing—Establishments, Employees, and Payroll: 2007 and 2008

[(380.1 represents 380,100). Covers establishments with payroll. Employees are for the week including March 12. Most government employees are excluded. For statement on methodology, see Appendix III]

Kind of business	NAICS code [1]	Establishments (1,000)		Employees (1,000)		Payroll (bil. dol.)	
		2007	2008	2007	2008	2007	2008
Real estate & rental & leasing, total................	**53**	**380.1**	**365.7**	**2,224.2**	**2,196.3**	**89.0**	**88.8**
Real estate	531	312.5	298.8	1,554.2	1,528.3	64.5	63.9
Lessors of real estate	5311	115.3	115.7	539.2	539.9	18.2	19.8
Offices of real estate agents & brokers	5312	111.0	99.9	367.1	342.3	17.8	15.8
Activities related to real estate...................	5313	86.2	83.2	647.9	646.0	28.6	28.3
Rental & leasing services	532	65.0	64.4	638.3	636.1	21.9	22.5
Automotive equipment rental & leasing...............	5321	13.5	13.9	199.9	191.2	6.6	6.5
Passenger car rental & leasing.................	53211	7.2	7.5	144.7	(3)	4.4	4.3
Truck, utility trailer & RV rental & leasing.............	53212	6.3	6.3	55.2	54.8	2.1	2.2
Consumer goods rental [2].........................	5322	31.3	31.6	237.1	236.6	5.2	5.6
Video tape & disc rental.......................	53223	16.3	14.3	127.5	113.7	1.7	1.6
General rental centers............................	5323	5.4	4.6	35.5	43.5	1.2	1.5
Commercial/industrial equipment rental & leasing	5324	14.8	14.4	165.8	164.7	8.9	8.9
Lessors of other nonfinancial intangible assets............	533	2.6	2.4	31.7	32.0	2.6	2.4

[1] 2008 data use 2007 North American Industry Classification System (NAICS). 2007 data use NAICS 2002. For more information, see text, Section 15. [2] Includes industries not shown separately. [3] Over 100,000 employees.

Source: U.S. Census Bureau, "County Business Patterns," July 2010, <http://www.census.gov/econ/cbp/>.

Table 1227. Rental and Leasing Services—Revenue by Kind of Business: 2004 to 2009

[In millions of dollars (102,208 represents $102,208,000). Covers taxable and tax-exempt employer firms. Estimates have been adjusted using the results of the 2002 Economic Census. Based on Service Annual Survey; see Appendix III]

Kind of business	NAICS code [1]	2004	2005	2006	2007	2008	2009
Rental & leasing services.................	**532**	**102,208**	**107,495**	**117,285**	**121,685**	**123,569**	**110,222**
Automotive equipment rental & leasing.........	5321	40,347	42,305	44,591	44,982	46,093	41,990
Passenger car rental & leasing	53211	25,033	26,302	28,180	29,222	30,299	28,540
Truck, utility trailer, & RV rental & leasing	53212	15,314	16,003	16,411	15,760	15,794	13,450
Consumer goods rental [2]....................	5322	23,425	22,818	23,677	24,750	24,139	22,088
Video tape & disc rental....................	53223	10,284	9,022	9,193	9,262	8,475	7,352
General rental centers......................	5323	3,831	3,547	3,925	4,249	4,195	3,737
Commercial/industrial equip. rental & leasing	5324	34,605	38,825	45,092	47,704	49,142	42,407

[1] Data are based on 2002 NAICS; see text, this section and Section 15. [2] Includes other kinds of business, not shown separately.

Source: U.S. Census Bureau, "Service Annual Survey: 2009," January 2011, <http://www.census.gov/services/index.html>.

Arts, Recreation, and Travel

This section presents data on the arts, entertainment, and recreation economic sector of the economy, and personal recreational activities, the arts and humanities, and domestic and foreign travel.

Arts, Entertainment, and Recreation Industry—The U.S. Census Bureau surveys—*County Business Patterns, Economic Census, Nonemployer Statistics* and *Service Annual Survey,* provide data on the *Arts, Entertainment, and Recreation Sector.* The County Business Patterns annual data includes number of establishments, number of employees, first quarter and annual payrolls, and number of establishments by employment size class. The Economic Census, conducted every five years for the years ending '2' and '7,' provides information on the number of establishments, receipts, payroll, and paid employees for the United States and various geographic levels. Nonemployer statistics are an annual tabulation of economic data by industry for active businesses without paid employees that are subject to federal income tax. The Service Annual Survey provides estimates of operation revenue of taxable firms and revenues and expenses of firms exempt from federal taxes for industries in this sector of the economy. See Appendix III for more details.

Recreation and leisure activities— Data on the participation in various recreation and leisure time activities are based on several sample surveys. Data on the public's involvement with arts events and activities are published by the National Endowment for Arts (NEA). The NEA's Survey of Public Participation in the Arts remains the largest periodic study of arts participation in the United States. The most recent data are from the 2008 survey. Data on participation in

fishing, hunting, and other forms of wildlife associated recreation are published periodically by the U.S. Department of Interior, Fish and Wildlife Service. The most recent data are from the 2006 survey. Data on participation in various sports recreation activities are published by the National Sporting Goods Association. Mediamark, Inc. also conducts periodic surveys on sports and leisure activities, as well as other topics.

Parks and recreation— The Department of the Interior has responsibility for administering the national parks. The National Park Service publishes information on visits to national park areas in its annual report, *National Park Statistical Abstract. The National Parks*: Index (year) is an annual report which contains brief descriptions, with acreages and visits for each area administered by the service, plus certain "related" areas. This information can be found at: <http://www.nature .nps.gov/stats>. Statistics for state parks are compiled by the National Association of State Park Directors.

Travel—Statistics on arrivals and departures to the United States, cities and states visited by overseas travelers, and tourism sales and employment are reported by the International Trade Administration (ITA), Office of Travel & Tourism Industries (OTTI). Data on domestic travel and travel expenditures are published by the research department of the U.S. Travel Association. Other data on household transportation characteristics are in Section 23, Transportation.

Statistical reliability—For a discussion of statistical collection and estimation, sampling procedures, and measures of statistical reliability applicable to Census Bureau data, see Appendix III.

Arts, Recreation, and Travel 757

Table 1228. Arts, Entertainment, and Recreation Services—Estimated Revenue: 2004 to 2009

[In millions of dollars (157,914 represents $157,914,000,000). For taxable and tax-exempt employer firms. Except where indicated, estimates adjusted using the results of the 2007 Economic Census. Based on the Service Annual Survey, see Appendix III]

Industry	2002 NAICS Code [1]	2004	2005	2006	2007	2008	2009
Arts, entertainment, and recreation	71	**157,914**	**167,055**	**178,478**	**189,418**	**193,016**	**188,436**
Performing arts, spectator sports, and related industries	711	63,433	65,910	72,769	77,772	80,399	80,232
Performing arts companies	7111	12,157	13,143	13,492	13,573	13,758	14,143
Spectator sports	7112	23,904	24,850	27,493	30,403	31,824	31,690
Sports teams and clubs	711211	14,391	14,564	16,401	18,794	20,251	20,642
Racetracks	711212	7,027	7,366	7,968	8,197	7,701	7,201
Other spectator sports	711219	2,486	2,920	3,124	3,412	3,872	3,847
Promoters of performing arts, sports, and similar events	7113	12,485	12,875	15,059	16,122	16,382	16,435
Agents and managers for artists, athletes, entertainers and other public figures	7114	4,065	4,176	4,521	4,919	5,206	4,933
Independent artists, writers, and performers	7115	10,822	10,866	12,204	12,755	13,229	13,031
Museums, historical sites, and similar institutions	712	9,663	12,471	11,982	13,286	12,520	11,539
Amusement, gambling, and recreation industries	713	84,818	88,674	93,727	98,360	100,097	96,665
Amusement parks and arcades	7131	11,027	11,926	12,417	13,544	14,110	13,358
Amusement and theme parks	71311	9,720	10,491	10,816	11,890	12,307	11,624
Amusement arcades	71312	1,307	1,435	1,601	1,654	1,803	1,734
Gambling industries	7132	23,416	24,040	25,175	25,135	25,602	25,091
Casinos (except casino hotels)	71321	15,442	15,753	16,505	16,557	16,874	16,410
Other gambling industries	71329	7,974	8,287	8,670	8,578	8,728	8,681
Other amusement and recreation industries	7139	50,375	52,708	56,135	59,681	60,385	58,216
Golf courses and country clubs	71391	18,469	19,356	20,523	21,195	21,044	20,326
Skiing facilities	71392	1,956	1,989	2,178	2,257	2,476	2,438
Marinas	71393	3,316	3,530	3,805	4,042	3,764	3,305
Fitness and recreational sports centers	71394	17,174	18,286	19,447	21,416	22,336	21,907
Bowling centers	71395	3,379	3,232	3,094	3,403	3,338	3,114
All other amusement and recreation industries	71399	6,081	6,315	7,088	7,368	7,427	7,126

[1] Based on 2002 North American Industry Classification System (NAICS); see text, this section and Section 15.
Source: U.S. Census Bureau, Service Annual Survey: 2009, January 2011, <http://www.census.gov/services/index.html>.

Table 1229. Arts, Entertainment, and Recreation—Establishments, Revenue, Payroll, and Employees by Kind of Business: 2002 and 2007

[For establishments with payroll (141,904 represents $141,904,000,000). Includes only establishments of firms with payroll. Definition of paid employees varies among NAICS sectors. Data are based on the 2002 and 2007 economic censuses which are subject to nonsampling error. For details on survey methodology, sampling and nonsampling errors, see Appendix III]

Kind of business	2002 NAICS code [1]	Number of establishments		Revenue (mil. dol.)		Annual payroll (mil. dol.)		Paid employees (1,000)	
		2002	2007	2002	2007	2002	2007	2002	2007
Arts, entertainment, and recreation, total	71	**110,313**	**124,620**	**141,904**	**189,417**	**45,169**	**58,359**	**1,849**	**2,061**
Performing arts, spectator sports, and related industries [2]	711	37,735	43,868	58,286	77,773	21,231	27,839	423	438
Performing arts companies	7111	9,303	8,838	10,864	13,574	3,267	3,980	138	128
Spectator sports	7112	4,072	4,237	22,313	30,403	10,206	14,136	108	121
Promoters of performing arts, sports and similar events	7113	5,236	6,647	12,169	16,122	2,184	2,957	102	121
Agents and managers for artists, athletes, entertainers and others	7114	3,262	3,534	3,602	4,919	1,251	1,694	17	19
Museums, historical sites, and similar institutions [2]	712	6,663	7,125	8,608	13,285	2,935	3,662	123	130
Amusement, gambling, and recreation industries [2]	713	65,915	73,627	75,010	98,359	21,002	26,859	1,303	1,494
Amusement parks and arcades	7131	3,015	3,145	9,443	13,544	2,069	2,802	122	134
Gambling industries	7132	2,072	2,327	18,893	25,135	3,596	4,566	158	170
Other amusement and recreation services	7139	60,828	68,155	46,674	59,680	15,337	19,490	1,023	1,190

[1] Based on 2002 North American Industry Classification System (NAICS); see text, this section and section 15. [2] Includes other industries not shown separately.
Source: U.S. Census Bureau, 2007 Economic Census, Core Business Statistics, *Comparative Statistics 2007 and 2002, Arts, Entertainment and Recreation,* accessed January 2011, <http://www.census.gov/econ/census07/www/using_american_factfinder/index.html>.

Table 1230. Arts, Entertainment, and Recreation—Nonemployer Establishments and Receipts by Kind of Business (NAICS Basis): 2006 to 2008

[(1,001.8 represents 1,001,800). Includes only firms subject to federal income tax. Nonemployers are businesses with no paid employees]

Kind of business	2007 NAICS code [1]	Firms (1,000)			Receipts (mil.dol.)		
		2006	2007	2008	2006	2007	2008
Arts, entertainment, and recreation	**71**	**1,001.8**	**1,119.6**	**1,121.4**	**24,782**	**27,357**	**27,837**
Performing arts, spectator sports, and related industries	711	855.7	967.4	970.8	18,733	20,841	21,226
Performing arts companies	7111	41.7	53.4	55.6	944	1,132	1,163
Spectator sports	7112	95.6	141.6	143.7	1,993	2,532	2,552
Promoters of performing arts, sports, and similar events	7113	37.8	39.8	40.8	1,475	1,584	1,631
Agents/managers for artists, athletes, and other public figures	7114	33.7	33.8	34.2	1,253	1,294	1,326
Independent artists, writers, and performers	7115	646.9	698.9	696.5	13,067	14,299	14,555
Museums, historical sites, and similar institutions	712	5.9	6.2	6.3	88	103	102
Amusement, gambling, and recreation industries	713	140.1	145.9	144.3	5,961	6,413	6,509
Amusement parks and arcades	7131	5.6	5.5	5.2	337	330	322
Gambling industries	7132	8.8	10.4	10.3	1,122	1,278	1,334
Other amusement and recreation services	7139	125.6	130.0	128.8	4,503	4,805	4,852

[1] Data for 2006 and 2007 based on the 2002 North American Industry Classification System (NAICS), 2008 data is based on 2007 NAICS; see text, Section 15.

Source: U.S. Census Bureau, Nonemployer Statistics, released June 2010, <http://www.census.gov/econ/nonemployer>.

Table 1231. Arts, Entertainment, and Recreation—Establishments, Employees, and Payroll by Kind of Business (NAICS Basis): 2007 to 2008

[(2,008.6 represents 2,008,600). Covers establishments with paid employees. Excludes self-employed individuals, employees of private households, railroad employees, agricultural production employees and most government employees. For statement on methodology, see Appendix III. County Business Patterns excludes rail transportation (NAICS 482) National Postal Service (NAICS 491) and other NAICS industries]

Kind of business	2007 NAICS code [1]	Establishments		Employees [2] (1,000)		Payroll (mil. dol)	
		2007	2008	2007	2008	2007	2008
Arts, entertainment, & recreation	**71**	**125,222**	**124,279**	**2,008.6**	**2,069.3**	**60,357**	**62,343**
Performing arts, spectator sports	711	44,260	44,477	436.1	452.2	28,932	30,495
Performing arts companies	7111	9,453	8,911	134.4	131.3	4,243	4,269
Theater companies & dinner theaters	71111	3,553	3,418	69.7	71.7	2,038	2,142
Dance companies	71112	703	647	9.5	8.9	250	237
Musical groups & artists	71113	4,612	4,438	43.3	41.1	1,584	1,607
Other performing arts companies	71119	585	408	12.0	9.5	371	283
Spectator sports	7112	4,631	4,416	126.1	127.3	14,591	15,438
Sports teams & clubs	711211	819	850	52.8	56.4	12,186	12,981
Racetracks	711212	733	718	51.2	50.7	1,389	1,397
Other spectator sports	711219	3,079	2,848	22.1	20.2	1,017	1,060
Promoters of performing arts, sports, and similar events	7113	6,367	6,649	112.4	129.8	2,992	3,090
Promoters of performing arts, sports, & similar events with facilities	71131	2,580	2,665	85.8	103.1	1,782	2,039
Promoters of performing arts, sports, & similar events without facilities	71132	3,787	3,984	26.6	26.7	1,210	1,051
Agents/managers for artists, athletes, and other public figures	7114	3,722	3,558	17.4	18.9	1,709	1,944
Independent artists, writers, & performers	7115	20,087	20,943	45.8	45.0	5,397	5,756
Museums, historical sites, & similar institutions	712	7,312	7,272	128.5	133.5	3,597	3,845
Museums	71211	4,920	4,723	83.7	85.3	2,404	2,527
Historical sites	71212	1,051	1,222	9.8	10.4	228	250
Zoos & botanical gardens	71213	595	600	28.5	31.4	784	882
Nature parks & other similar institutions	71219	746	727	6.6	6.4	180	186
Amusement, gambling, & recreation industries	713	73,650	72,530	1,444.0	1,483.7	27,828	28,002
Amusement parks & arcades	7131	3,097	3,144	128.4	142.4	2,755	2,864
Amusement & theme parks	71311	634	524	101.2	110.3	2,391	2,450
Amusement arcades	71312	2,463	2,620	27.1	32.1	364	414
Gambling industries	7132	2,729	2,481	205.3	174.3	5,851	4,960
Casinos (except casino hotels)	71321	488	349	136.9	114.4	4,099	3,417
Other gambling industries	71329	2,241	2,132	68.4	59.8	1,753	1,544
Other amusement & recreation services	7139	67,824	66,905	1,110.3	1,166.9	19,221	20,178
Golf courses & country clubs	71391	11,851	12,059	316.4	322.6	8,059	8,378
Skiing facilities	71392	402	373	75.7	78.4	651	681
Marinas	71393	4,085	3,972	28.8	28.7	945	954
Fitness & recreational sports centers	71394	31,453	30,961	514.5	563.1	6,617	7,232
Bowling centers	71395	4,571	4,492	80.5	81.3	997	1,021
All other amusement & recreation industries	71399	15,462	15,048	94.4	92.8	1,951	1,912

[1] 2007 data based on the 2002 North American Industry Classification System (NAICS), 2008 data based on 2007 NAICS; see text, this section and Section 15. [2] For employees on the payroll for the period including March 12.

Source: U.S. Census Bureau, "County Business Patterns," released July 2010, <http://www.census.gov/econ/cbp/index.html>.

Table 1232. Expenditures Per Consumer Unit for Entertainment and Reading: 1985 to 2009

[Data are annual averages. In dollars, except as indicated. Based on Consumer Expenditure Survey (CE). For description of survey, see text, Section 13; also see headnote, Table 686. For composition of regions, see map, inside front cover]

Year and characteristic	Entertainment and reading		Entertainment				
	Total	Percent of total expenditures	Total	Fees and admissions	Audio and visual equipment and services	Other entertainment, supplies, and equipment services [1]	Reading
1985.	1,311	5.6	1,170	320	371	479	141
1990.	1,575	5.6	1,422	371	454	597	153
1994.	1,732	5.5	1,567	439	533	595	165
1995.	1,775	5.5	1,612	433	542	637	163
1996.	1,993	5.9	1,834	459	561	814	159
1997.	1,977	5.7	1,813	471	577	766	164
1998.	1,907	5.4	1,746	449	535	762	161
1999.	2,050	5.5	1,891	459	608	824	159
2000.	2,009	5.3	1,863	515	622	727	146
2001.	2,094	5.3	1,953	526	660	767	141
2002.	2,218	5.5	2,079	542	692	845	139
2003.	2,187	5.4	2,060	494	730	835	127
2004.	2,348	5.4	2,218	528	788	903	130
2005.	2,514	5.4	2,388	588	888	912	126
2006.	2,493	5.2	2,376	606	906	863	117
2007.	2,816	5.7	2,698	658	987	1,053	118
2008.	2,951	5.8	2,835	616	1,036	1,183	116
2009, total	**2,803**	**5.7**	**2,693**	**628**	**975**	**1,090**	**110**
Age of reference person:							
Under 25 years old	1,275	4.5	1,233	234	574	425	42
25 to 34 years old	2,573	5.5	2,504	521	1,018	965	69
35 to 44 years old	3,402	5.9	3,317	917	1,111	1,289	85
45 to 54 years old	3,295	5.6	3,176	811	1,065	1,300	119
55 to 64 years old	3,053	5.8	2,906	629	1,024	1,253	147
65 to 74 years old	2,652	6.2	2,498	497	934	1,067	154
75 years old and over	1,721	5.4	1,587	266	669	652	134
Hispanic or Latino Origin of reference person:							
Hispanic.	1,700	4.0	1,664	302	818	544	36
Non-Hispanic.	2,948	5.9	2,829	671	996	1,162	119
Race of reference person:							
White, Asian, and all other races.	2,987	5.9	2,869	684	994	1,192	118
Black	1,450	4.1	1,404	223	840	341	46
Region of residence:							
Northeast.	2,908	5.4	2,767	780	1,003	984	141
Midwest.	2,739	5.9	2,627	573	927	1,127	112
South.	2,552	5.6	2,467	508	993	966	85
West.	3,183	6.0	3,062	751	970	1,340	121
Size of consumer unit:							
One person	1,597	5.4	1,510	307	661	541	87
Two or more persons	3,289	5.8	3,170	757	1,102	1,311	119
Two persons.	3,049	5.9	2,913	642	1,042	1,230	136
Three persons	2,973	5.2	2,860	599	1,053	1,209	113
Four persons	3,875	5.9	3,775	1,058	1,242	1,476	100
Five persons or more.	3,730	5.9	3,635	956	1,179	1,501	95
Income before taxes:							
Quintiles of income:							
Lowest 20 percent	1,063	4.9	1,015	143	524	348	48
Second 20 percent	1,740	5.5	1,668	247	747	673	72
Third 20 percent.	2,197	5.3	2,106	372	926	808	91
Fourth 20 percent	3,316	5.8	3,197	648	1,128	1,420	119
Highest 20 percent	5,691	6.0	5,474	1,729	1,548	2,197	217
Education:							
Less than a high school graduate	1,446	4.8	1,406	151	639	616	40
High school graduate.	2,254	5.8	2,184	332	880	973	70
High school graduate with some college.	2,724	6.1	2,626	539	978	1,109	98
Associate's degree	2,955	5.9	2,848	596	1,037	1,215	107
Bachelor's degree	3,615	5.5	3,458	1,030	1,142	1,286	157
Master's, professional, doctoral degree.	4,453	5.9	4,212	1,468	1,285	1,459	241

[1] Other equipment and services include pets, toys, hobbies, and playground equipment; and other entertainment supplies, equipment, and services.

Source: U.S. Bureau of Labor Statistics, Consumer Expenditure Survey, "Consumer Expenditures in 2009," October 2010. See also <http://www.bls.gov/cex/home.htm#tables>.

Table 1233. Personal Consumption Expenditures for Recreation: 1990 to 2009

[In billions of dollars (314.7 represents $314,700,000,000), except percent. Represents market value of purchases of goods and services by individuals and nonprofit institutions. Table data have been revised, along with changes to "Type of products and services." These changes resulted from BEA's 13th comprehensive NIPA revision released in July 2009. For more on these changes and revisions, see <http://www.bea.gov/scb/pdf/2009/03%20March/0309_nipa_preview.pdf>]

Type of product or service	1990	2000	2005	2006	2007	2008	2009
Total recreation expenditures	**314.7**	**639.9**	**807.4**	**859.1**	**905.8**	**916.0**	**897.1**
Percent of total personal consumption [1]	8.2	9.4	9.2	9.2	9.2	9.1	9.0
Video and audio equipment, computers, and related services	81.1	184.4	239.4	256.1	269.5	273.3	265.2
Video and audio equipment	43.7	83.1	107.8	114.6	116.0	115.6	107.1
Information processing equipment	9.6	44.1	55.9	60.4	65.6	65.8	64.7
Services related to video and audio goods and computers	27.8	57.2	75.7	81.1	87.9	92.0	93.4
Sports and recreational goods and related services	74.2	147.9	188.4	199.6	207.6	203.0	196.9
Sports and recreational vehicles	16.6	34.9	47.7	49.7	50.4	44.8	41.7
Other sporting and recreational goods	55.4	108.7	135.2	144.2	151.0	152.3	150.0
Maintenance and repair of recreational vehicles and sports equipment	2.1	4.2	5.4	5.8	6.2	5.8	5.2
Membership clubs, sports centers, parks, theaters, and museums	49.7	91.9	110.6	117.8	124.7	129.3	126.5
Membership clubs and participant sports centers	14.3	26.4	30.5	31.9	33.8	34.2	32.7
Amusements parks, campgrounds, and related recreational services	19.2	31.1	34.9	37.4	40.6	43.0	41.8
Admissions to specified spectator amusements	14.4	30.6	39.2	42.1	44.1	45.6	45.6
Motion picture theaters	5.1	8.6	9.1	9.4	9.6	9.7	10.4
Live entertainment, excluding sports	4.5	10.4	13.8	14.9	15.0	15.4	14.5
Spectator sports	4.8	11.6	16.3	17.8	19.5	20.5	20.7
Museums and libraries	1.9	3.8	5.9	6.4	6.2	6.5	6.4
Magazines, newspapers, books, and stationery	47.3	81.0	93.1	98.2	103.2	104.9	105.1
Gambling	23.7	67.6	95.6	103.9	110.9	111.9	109.3
Pets, pet products, and related services	18.8	39.7	53.1	56.9	61.8	65.7	67.1
Photographic goods and services	16.7	19.7	18.7	18.2	19.0	18.9	17.7
Package tours [2]	3.2	7.8	8.5	8.3	9.1	9.0	9.2

[1] See Table 677. [2] Consists of tour operators' and travel agents' margins. Purchases of travel and accommodations included in tours are accounted for separately in other personal consumption expenditures categories.

Source: U.S. Bureau of Economic Analysis, National Economic Accounts, *National Income and Product Account Tables, Table 2.5.5*, August 2010. See also <http://www.bea.gov/national/nipaweb/Index.asp>.

Table 1234. Performing Arts—Selected Data: 1990 to 2009

[Sales, receipts, and expenditures in millions of dollars (282 represents $282,000,000). For season ending in year shown, except as indicated]

Item	1990	1995	2000	2003	2004	2005	2006	2007	2008	2009
Legitimate theater: [1]										
Broadway shows:										
New productions	40	33	37	36	39	39	39	35	36	43
Attendance (mil.)	8.0	9.0	11.4	11.4	11.6	11.5	12.0	12.3	12.3	12.2
Playing weeks [2, 3]	1,070	1,120	1,464	1,544	1,451	1,494	1,501	1,509	1,560	1,548
Gross ticket sales	282	406	603	721	771	769	862	939	938	943
Broadway road tours: [4]										
Attendance (mil.)	11.1	15.6	11.7	12.4	12.9	18.2	17.1	16.7	15.3	14.3
Playing weeks	944	1,242	888	877	1,060	1,389	1,377	1,400	1,138	1,112
Gross ticket sales	367	701	572	642	714	934	915	950	956	883
Nonprofit professional theatres: [5]										
Companies reporting [6]	185	215	262	1,274	1,477	1,490	1,893	1,910	1,919	1,825
Gross income	308	444	791	1,481	1,571	1,647	1,791	1,881	1,884	1,779
Earned income	188	281	466	787	856	845	923	962	955	811
Contributed income	119	163	325	694	715	802	868	919	929	968
Gross expenses	306	445	708	1,476	1,464	1,530	1,667	1,742	1,860	1,892
Productions	2,265	2,646	3,241	13,000	11,000	12,000	14,000	17,000	15,000	17,000
Performances	46,131	56,608	66,123	170,000	169,000	169,000	172,000	197,000	202,000	187,000
Total attendance (mil.)	15.2	18.6	22.0	34.3	32.1	32.5	30.5	31.0	32.0	30.0
OPERA America professional member companies: [7]										
Number of companies reporting [8]	98	88	98	91	95	93	94	97	85	84
Expenses [8]	321	435	637	692	678	742	752	872	826	816
Performances [9]	2,336	2,120	1,768	1,741	1,946	1,893	1,851	1,961	1,753	1744
Total attendance (mil.) [9, 10]	7.5	4.1	6.2	5.8	5.1	5	5.3	5.3	5.1	4.3
Main season attendance (mil.) [9, 11]	4.1	3.9	3.8	3.1	3.4	3.3	3.4	3.6	3.1	2.9
Symphony orchestras: [12]										
Concerts	18,931	29,328	33,154	38,182	37,263	37,196	36,731	37,169	33,029	32,813
Attendance (mil.)	24.7	30.9	31.7	27.8	27.7	26.5	29.1	28.8	28.7	25.4
Gross revenue	378	536	734	781	827	812	945	1,052	992	969
Operating expenses	622	859	1,126	1,315	1,483	1,513	1,603	1,808	1,862	1,864
Support	258	351	521	576	639	626	713	721	785	726

[1] Source: The Broadway League, New York, NY. For season ending in year shown. [2] All shows (new productions and holdovers from previous seasons). [3] Eight performances constitute one playing week. [4] North American Tours include U.S. and Canadian companies. [5] Source: Theatre Communications Group, New York, NY. For years ending on or prior to Aug. 31. [6] Beginning in 2002, nonprofit theatre data is based on survey responses and extrapolated data from IRS Form 990. [7] Source: OPERA America, New York, NY. For years ending on or prior to Aug 31. [8] U.S. companies. [9] Prior to 1993, and for 1999, U.S. and Canadian companies; 1993 to 1998 and 2000 to 2009, U.S. companies only. [10] Includes educational performances, outreach, etc. [11] For paid performances. [12] Source: League of American Orchestras, New York, NY. For years ending Aug. 31. Prior to 1995, represents 254 U.S. orchestras; beginning 1995, represents all U.S. orchestras, excluding college/university and youth orchestras. Also, beginning 1995, data based on 1,200 orchestras.

Source: Compiled from sources listed in footnotes. See also <http://www.livebroadway.com/>; <http://www.tcg.org/>; <http://www.operaamerica.org/>; and <http://www.americanorchestras.org/>.

Arts, Recreation, and Travel 761

Table 1235. Arts and Humanities—Selected Federal Aid Programs: 1990 to 2009

[In millions of dollars (170.8 represents $170,800,000), except as indicated. For fiscal year ending September 30. FY 2009 includes funds from the American Recovery and Reinvestment Act]

Type of fund and program	1990	1995	2000	2004	2005	2006	2007	2008	2009
National Endowment for the Arts:									
Funds available [1]	170.8	152.1	85.2	105.5	108.8	112.8	111.7	129.3	186.8
Program appropriation [2]	152.3	138.1	79.6	99.3	99.5	100.7	100.3	119.6	178.1
Grants awarded (number) [3]	4,252	3,534	1,906	2,150	2,161	2,293	2,158	2,219	3,075
Funds obligated [4, 5]	157.6	147.9	83.5	102.6	104.4	107.0	106.5	125.5	176.2
National Endowment for the Humanities:									
Funds available [1]	140.6	152.3	102.6	127.1	119.8	121.5	122.3	128.6	134.5
Program appropriation	114.2	125.7	82.7	98.7	99.9	102.2	102.2	105.7	114.7
Matching funds [6]	26.3	25.7	15.1	15.9	15.9	15.2	15.2	14.3	14.3

[1] Includes other program funds not shown separately. Excludes administrative funds. [2] FY 1990–FY 1996 include Regular Program Funds, Treasury Funds, Challenge Grant Funds, and Policy, Planning, and Research Funds. FY 1997 includes Regular Program Funds, Matching Grant Funds, and Policy, Research and Technology Funds. FY 1998–FY 2000 includes Regular Program Funds and Matching Grant Funds. [3] Excludes cooperative agreements and interagency agreements. [4] Includes obligations for new grants, supplemental awards on previous years' grants, cooperative agreements, and interagency agreements. [5] Beginning with 1997 data, the grantmaking structure changed from discipline-based categories to thematic ones. [6] Represents federal funds obligated only upon receipt or certification by endowment of matching nonfederal gifts. Funds for matching grants are not allocated by program area because they are awarded on a grant-by-grant basis.

Source: U.S. National Endowment for the Arts, *Annual Report*, and U.S. National Endowment for the Humanities, *Annual Report*. See also <http://arts.endow.gov/> and <http://www.neh.gov/>.

Table 1236. Total State Arts Agency Legislative Appropriations: 2010 to 2011

[In thousands of dollars (293,188 represents 293,188,000). For fiscal year ending September 30. The National Assembly of State Arts Agencies (NASAA) is the membership organization of the nations' state and jurisdictional arts agencies. Legislative appropriations include funds designated to the state arts agency by state legislatures. These include line items, which are not controlled by the agency but passed through to designated entities. State arts agencies also receive monies from other sources including other state funds, the federal government (primarily the National Endowment for the Arts), private funds, and legislative earmarks. Minus sign (–) indicates decrease in spending]

State	Legislative appropriations including line items 2010	Legislative appropriations including line items 2011	Percent change, 2010 to 2011	State	Legislative appropriations including line items 2010	Legislative appropriations including line items 2011	Percent change, 2010 to 2011	State	Legislative appropriations including line items 2010	Legislative appropriations including line items 2011	Percent change, 2010 to 2011
U.S. [1]	293,188	272,045	−7.2	KY	3,186	3,070	−3.7	OH	6,594	6,594	−
AL	4,626	4,626	−	LA	5,579	3,925	−29.7	OK	4,764	4,407	−7.5
AK	684	693	1.2	ME	695	654	−5.8	OR	2,088	1,917	−8.2
AZ	823	666	−19.1	MD	13,312	13,267	−0.3	PA	11,992	8,400	−30.0
AR	1,657	2,098	26.6	MA	9,693	9,099	−6.1	RI	2,352	2,103	−10.6
CA	4,123	4,312	4.6	MI	1,417	1,417	−	SC	2,454	2,051	−16.4
CO	1,200	1,122	−6.5	MN	30,015	29,990	−0.1	SD	526	669	27.0
CT	6,262	6,112	−2.4	MS	1,727	1,682	−2.6	TN	8,383	8,106	−3.3
DE	1,740	1,683	−3.3	MO	10,427	7,612	−27.0	TX	7,033	6,075	−13.6
DC	5,849	5,126	−12.4	MT	466	440	−5.4	UT	2,911	2,815	−3.3
FL	5,218	6,357	21.8	NE	1,489	1,433	−3.7	VT	508	508	−
GA	2,320	791	−65.9	NV	1,094	1,106	1.2	VA	4,421	3,795	−14.2
HI	6,160	5,080	−17.5	NH	515	462	−10.3	WA	1,844	1,347	−27.0
ID	788	716	−9.1	NJ	17,075	20,699	21.2	WV	2,501	2,488	−0.5
IL	7,577	9,472	25.0	NM	1,958	1,779	−9.1	WI	2,418	2,418	−
IN	3,202	3,202	−	NY	52,032	41,522	−20.2	WY	1,144	1,295	13.3
IA	1,024	1,024	−	NC	8,678	8,651	−0.3				
KS	1,138	812	−28.7	ND	684	684	−				

− Represents zero. [1] Includes U.S. territories.

Source: National Assembly of State Arts Agencies, "Legislative Appropriations Annual Survey," February 2011, <http://www.nasaa-arts.org/>.

Table 1237. Personal Participation in Various Arts or Creative Activities: 2008

[In percent, except as indicated (224.8 represents 224,800,000). For persons 18 years old and over. Represents participation at least once in the prior 12 months]

Item	Adult population (millions)	Classical music [1]	Painting [2]	Pottery	Sewing [3]	Photography	Creative writing	Purchased art [4]	Choir/chorale
Total	224.8	3.1	9.0	6.0	13.1	14.7	6.9	28.7	5.2
Sex: Male	108.5	3.0	7.1	4.5	2.3	13.3	6.2	29.6	3.9
Female	116.3	3.2	10.7	7.4	23.2	16.1	7.5	27.9	6.3
Race and ethnicity:									
White alone	154.5	3.5	9.4	6.9	15.5	16.1	7.0	29.6	4.9
African American alone	25.6	2.0	6.8	3.5	7.6	10.0	7.5	20.1	10.3
Other alone	14.3	4.7	11.9	6.1	10.2	16.2	8.2	16.5	5.5
Hispanic	30.4	1.1	7.4	3.6	7.1	10.9	5.3	30.6	2.2
Age: 18 to 24 years old	28.9	5.9	14.7	6.4	9.0	17.8	11.3	37.2	6.1
25 to 34 years old	39.9	3.7	11.3	6.1	10.0	16.1	9.7	38.8	3.8
35 to 44 years old	41.8	3.0	9.9	7.5	11.4	18.6	6.2	27.1	4.3
45 to 54 years old	43.9	2.5	7.4	7.0	15.4	14.6	6.4	28.0	6.8
55 to 64 years old	33.3	2.4	6.8	5.4	15.7	13.0	4.4	25.6	5.3
65 to 74 years old	19.9	1.8	5.0	4.1	17.7	10.4	5.2	28.7	6.2
75 years old and older	17.1	1.4	4.4	2.1	15.4	5.5	3.1	14.2	3.6

[1] Of those who reported playing a musical instrument in the last 12 months. [2] Includes painting, drawing, sculpture, and printmaking. [3] Includes weaving, crocheting, quilting, needlepoint, and sewing. [4] Of those who reported owning original art.

Source: U.S. National Endowment for the Arts, "2008 Survey of Public Participation in the Arts," <http://www.nea.gov/pub/>.

Table 1238. Attendance/Participation Rates for Various Arts Activities: 2008

[In percent, except as indicated (224.8 represents 224,800,000). For persons 18 years old and over. Represents attending, visiting, or reading at least once in the prior twelve months. Excludes elementary and high school performances]

Item	Adult population (million)	Jazz concert	Classical music concert	Musicals	Non-musical plays	Art museums/ galleries	Craft/ visual art festivals	Parks/ historic buildings [1]	Read literature [2]
Total	**224.8**	**7.8**	**9.3**	**16.7**	**9.4**	**22.7**	**24.5**	**24.9**	**50.2**
Sex:									
Male	108.5	7.7	8.5	14.4	8.2	21.4	20.5	24.4	41.9
Female	116.3	7.9	10.0	18.9	10.6	24.0	28.3	25.4	58.0
Race and Ethnicity:									
White alone	154.5	8.8	11.3	20.0	11.4	26.0	29.3	29.5	55.7
African American alone	25.6	8.6	4.3	8.6	5.5	12.0	12.2	12.6	42.6
Other alone	14.3	4.0	8.8	13.4	6.1	23.4	17.0	20.0	43.9
Hispanic	30.4	3.9	3.8	8.1	4.3	14.5	13.7	14.0	31.9
Age:									
18 to 24 years old	28.9	7.3	6.9	14.5	8.2	22.9	17.8	21.9	51.7
25 to 34 years old	39.9	7.7	7.0	16.0	9.2	24.3	22.7	25.7	50.1
35 to 44 years old	41.8	7.2	8.9	18.2	8.9	25.7	27.2	26.8	50.8
45 to 54 years old	43.9	9.8	10.2	17.4	8.7	23.3	29.1	28.0	50.3
55 to 64 years old	33.3	9.7	11.6	19.5	12.3	24.3	28.9	27.6	53.1
65 to 74 years old	19.9	6.1	12.2	18.0	11.0	19.9	24.8	24.1	49.1
75 years old and older	17.1	4.0	9.7	10.0	7.4	10.5	12.7	11.2	42.3
Education:									
Grade school	11.2	1.5	1.8	1.7	0.7	3.8	4.9	3.8	18.5
Some high school	22.1	2.4	2.3	5.2	2.8	9.2	11.2	9.1	34.3
High school graduate	68.3	3.9	3.1	8.1	4.0	9.6	17.3	14.6	39.1
Some college	61.4	8.1	9.1	17.1	9.0	23.8	27.5	28.4	56.2
College graduate	41.3	13.7	16.7	30.1	17.5	40.6	35.8	39.4	66.6
Graduate school	20.5	17.4	27.1	37.9	24.3	52.2	41.6	48.1	71.2
Income: [3]									
Less than $10,000	11.6	4.3	4.0	6.6	4.2	9.4	10.7	10.3	38.6
$10,000 to $19,999	19.3	3.6	3.9	6.3	3.7	10.3	13.0	11.4	38.3
$20,000 to $29,999	23.4	4.1	4.4	7.7	4.1	11.9	15.5	13.9	41.7
$30,000 to $39,999	22.6	7.1	6.8	11.0	6.7	16.3	21.8	19.9	43.2
$40,000 to $49,999	18.8	8.9	8.7	15.4	7.4	20.2	24.7	23.2	51.9
$50,000 to $74,999	40.7	7.6	9.5	15.4	8.6	23.9	26.2	26.8	50.1
$75,000 to $99,999	27.2	8.7	11.7	21.8	13.4	31.3	33.8	32.6	59.1
$100,000 to $149,999	21.4	13.4	14.8	32.0	14.1	34.4	34.5	41.2	62.1
$150,000 and over	16.0	15.4	22.8	40.1	24.2	51.9	34.5	47.3	71.2

[1] Visiting historic parks or monuments or touring buildings or neighborhoods for the historic or design value.
[2] Literature is defined as poetry, novels, short stories, or plays. [3] Excludes results for respondents who did not report income.
Source: U.S. National Endowment for the Arts, "2008 Survey of Public Participation in the Arts," <http://www.nea.gov/pub/>.

Table 1239. Attendance/Participation in Various Leisure Activities: 2008

[In percent, except as indicated (224.8 represents 224,800,000). See headnote, Table 1237]

Item	Adult population (mil.)	Attendance at—		Participation in—					
		Movies	Sports events	Exercise	Playing sports	Outdoor activities	Gardening	Volunteering/ charity work	Community activities
Total	**224.8**	**53.3**	**30.6**	**52.9**	**26.3**	**28.2**	**41.6**	**32.0**	**27.8**
Sex:									
Male	108.5	52.7	34.9	52.1	33.2	31.1	33.6	28.9	26.2
Female	116.3	54.0	26.6	53.6	20.0	25.4	48.9	34.9	29.3
Race and Ethnicity:									
White alone	154.5	55.7	34.0	57.4	29.2	16.9	47.2	35.8	31.8
African American alone	25.6	47.4	24.5	42.6	21.0	7.2	24.4	27.0	21.9
Other alone	14.3	49.3	21.8	48.6	23.5	26.1	40.1	25.7	22.7
Hispanic	30.4	48.1	22.1	40.7	17.9	17.3	28.0	20.1	14.7
Age:									
18 to 24 years old	28.9	74.2	37.4	57.4	42.0	34.8	15.1	27.2	19.4
25 to 34 years old	39.9	64.5	37.3	57.5	34.9	35.7	34.8	29.4	23.5
35 to 44 years old	41.8	59.5	36.7	59.5	32.0	34.3	43.9	37.6	33.2
45 to 54 years old	43.9	52.6	31.3	51.8	23.9	29.0	49.1	35.7	31.8
55 to 64 years old	33.3	46.2	25.9	51.8	17.1	22.4	52.4	33.4	29.7
65 to 74 years old	19.9	31.7	18.2	47.6	13.3	17.9	54.5	30.2	30.9
75 years old and over	17.1	18.9	10.3	30.0	6.4	6.3	41.0	23.2	21.5
Education:									
Grade school	11.2	15.9	6.6	21.1	6.7	8.2	30.3	11.4	8.4
Some high school	22.1	37.9	17.8	35.7	19.0	17.8	29.5	17.7	14.8
High school graduate	68.3	42.5	22.8	40.0	17.4	20.8	37.7	20.9	18.3
Some college	61.4	60.8	33.7	58.5	29.1	30.9	43.2	35.6	29.5
College graduate	41.3	68.8	44.9	70.8	38.9	39.8	49.0	48.1	42.6
Graduate school	20.5	71.6	44.2	77.1	40.0	42.3	53.3	51.5	48.0
Income: [1]									
Less than $10,000	11.6	32.3	14.9	35.6	15.9	14.6	25.3	16.0	15.0
$10,000 to $19,999	19.3	32.4	13.4	35.3	14.5	15.3	30.4	18.8	14.8
$20,000 to $29,999	23.4	38.2	21.1	40.4	14.9	18.3	35.4	19.6	18.1
$30,000 to $39,999	22.6	48.6	22.3	46.8	23.3	24.2	37.7	29.2	22.9
$40,000 to $49,999	18.8	54.0	28.7	54.9	26.5	28.7	44.9	31.5	25.9
$50,000 to $74,999	40.7	58.5	33.3	55.6	26.0	31.6	42.8	32.2	27.5
$75,000 or more	27.2	67.5	42.2	66.2	37.0	40.9	50.2	42.0	35.0
$100,000 to $149,999	21.4	71.4	46.8	73.3	39.1	39.7	54.0	49.6	47.2
$150,000 and over	16.0	76.7	53.1	73.2	46.0	43.9	50.9	49.0	43.9

[1] Excludes results for respondents who did not report income.
Source: U.S. National Endowment for the Arts, "2008 Survey of Public Participation in the Arts," <http://www.nea.gov/pub/>.

Table 1240. Adult Participation in Selected Leisure Activities by Frequency: 2010

[In thousands (16,640 represents 16,640,000), except percent. For fall 2010. Percent is based on total projected population of 228,112,000. Based on sample and subject to sampling error; see source]

Activity	Participated in the last 12 months [1]		Freqency of participation							
			Two or more times a week		Once a week		Two to three times a month		Once a month	
	Number	Percent	Number	Percent	Number	Percent	Number	Percent	Number	Percent
Adult education courses	16,640	7.3	3,116	1.4	1,973	0.9	762	0.3	1,312	0.6
Attend auto shows.	19,346	8.5	313	0.1	337	0.2	557	0.2	721	0.3
Attend art galleries or shows	20,985	9.2	78	(Z)	215	0.1	879	0.4	2,272	1.0
Attend classical music/opera performances.	9,715	4.3	99	(Z)	65	(Z)	409	0.2	900	0.4
Attend country music performances . . .	11,266	4.9	67	(Z)	125	0.1	239	0.1	458	0.2
Attend dance performances	10,010	4.4	122	0.1	162	0.1	335	0.2	403	0.2
Attend horse races	6,654	2.9	159	0.1	177	0.1	155	0.1	379	0.2
Attend other music performances [2]	26,536	11.6	135	0.1	332	0.2	1,120	0.5	2,129	0.9
Attend rock music performances	25,176	11.0	187	0.1	173	0.1	730	0.3	1,136	0.5
Backgammon.	4,234	1.9	435	0.2	366	0.2	416	0.2	486	0.2
Baking	57,703	25.3	10,394	4.6	8,482	3.7	12,482	5.5	9,321	4.1
Barbecuing	79,119	34.7	12,497	5.5	12,939	5.7	18,871	8.3	10,473	4.6
Billiards/pool	19,468	8.5	975	0.4	1,432	0.6	2,125	0.9	2,063	0.9
Bird watching	13,793	6.1	6,101	2.7	1,338	0.6	1,169	0.5	876	0.4
Board games.	37,993	16.7	2,890	1.3	3,134	1.4	6,574	2.9	7,759	3.4
Book clubs.	5,747	2.5	285	0.1	234	0.1	419	0.2	2,732	1.2
Chess	6,896	3.0	549	0.2	533	0.2	823	0.4	576	0.3
Concerts on radio	6,441	2.8	1,308	0.6	747	0.3	548	0.2	572	0.3
Cooking for fun	50,243	22.0	19,162	8.4	7,495	3.3	6,795	3.0	4,415	1.9
Crossword puzzles	29,996	13.2	12,866	5.6	3,136	1.4	2,811	1.2	2,674	1.2
Dance/go dancing	20,995	9.2	1,636	0.7	2,162	1.0	2,728	1.2	2,964	1.3
Dining out	112,477	49.3	20,158	8.8	25,173	11.0	26,644	11.7	15,686	6.9
Entertain friends or relatives at home . .	87,455	38.3	6,976	3.1	9,139	4.0	18,565	8.1	19,611	8.6
Fantasy sports league	8,969	3.9	2,855	1.3	1,559	0.7	372	0.2	330	0.1
Furniture refinishing.	6,292	2.8	201	0.1	79	(Z)	359	0.2	406	0.2
Go to bars/night clubs	43,513	19.1	3,133	1.4	4,846	2.1	7,428	3.3	6,430	2.8
Go to beach.	58,670	25.7	3,303	1.5	2,018	0.9	4,875	2.1	5,428	2.4
Go to live theater	30,547	13.4	333	0.2	256	0.1	896	0.4	3,331	1.5
Go to museums	32,960	14.5	121	0.1	198	0.1	1,171	0.5	3,317	1.5
Home decoration and furnishing	22,781	10.0	890	0.4	977	0.4	1,861	0.8	4,178	1.8
Karaoke	8,186	3.6	460	0.2	401	0.2	665	0.3	904	0.4
Painting, drawing	13,791	6.1	2,360	1.0	1,288	0.6	1,625	0.7	1,609	0.7
Photo album/scrap book	15,284	6.7	1,237	0.5	743	0.3	1,973	0.9	2,332	1.0
Photography	26,173	11.5	4,358	1.9	3,310	1.5	5,332	2.3	3,508	1.5
Picnic.	26,321	11.5	281	0.1	591	0.3	1,672	0.7	3,780	1.7
Play bingo	10,271	4.5	754	0.3	1,095	0.5	811	0.4	1,342	0.6
Play cards	46,190	20.3	5,679	2.5	4,969	2.2	6,400	2.8	7,567	3.3
Play musical instrument.	18,078	7.9	7,435	3.3	2,096	0.9	1,959	0.9	1,211	0.5
Reading books.	86,540	37.9	47,483	20.8	8,298	3.6	7,513	3.3	6,312	2.8
Reading comic books	5,557	2.4	1,161	0.5	636	0.3	886	0.4	527	0.2
Sodoku puzzles	26,540	11.6	10,265	4.5	2,505	1.1	3,159	1.4	2,495	1.1
Trivia games	11,872	5.2	1,891	0.8	1,327	0.6	1,397	0.6	1,490	0.7
Woodworking.	10,202	4.5	1,714	0.8	965	0.4	1,631	0.7	1,443	0.6
Word games	22,147	9.7	7,768	3.4	2,709	1.2	2,817	1.2	1,899	0.8
Zoo attendance	28,148	12.3	189	0.1	239	0.1	632	0.3	2,112	0.9

Z represents less than 0.05. [1] Includes those participating less than once a month not shown separately. [2] Excluding country and rock.

Source: GfK Mediamark Research & Intelligence, LLC, New York, NY, *Top-line Reports* (copyright). See also <http://www.gfkmri.com/>.

Table 1241. Household Pet Ownership: 2006

[In percent, except as indicated (72.1 represents 72,100,000). Based on a sample survey of 47,000 households in 2006]

Item	Dogs	Cats	Birds	Horses
Total companion pet population (millions) [1]	72.1	81.7	11.2	7.3
Number of households owning pets (millions)	43.0	37.5	4.5	2.1
Percent of households owning companion pets [1]	37.2	32.4	3.9	1.8
Average number owned per household	1.7	2.2	2.5	3.5
PERCENT OF HOUSEHOLDS OWNING PETS				
Annual household income:				
Under $20,000.	30.7	30.1	4.4	1.5
$20,000 to $34,999	37.3	33.6	4.2	1.7
$35,000 to $54,999	39.8	34.1	4.4	2.1
$55,000 to $84,999	42.8	35.5	3.7	1.9
$85,000 and over.	42.1	33.3	3.7	2.3
Household size: [1]				
One person	21.9	24.7	2.1	0.8
Two persons.	37.6	33.4	3.9	1.7
Three persons	47.5	39.1	5.1	2.3
Four persons	51.9	38.5	5.4	2.7
Five or more persons	54.3	40.0	6.6	3.6

[1] As of December 31, 2006.

Source: American Veterinary Medical Association, Schaumburg, IL, *U.S. Pet Ownership and Demographics Sourcebook, 2007*, (copyright). See also <http://www.avma.org/reference/marketstats/sourcebook.asp>.

Table 1242. Retail Sales and Household Participation in Lawn and Garden Activities: 2005 to 2010

[(35,208 represents $35,208,000,000). For calendar year. Subject to sampling variability; see source]

Activity	Retail sales (mil. dol.)					Percent households engaged in activity				
	2005	2007	2008	2009	2010	2005	2007	2008	2009	2010
Total...............	35,208	35,102	36,060	30,121	28,409	83	71	70	72	68
Lawn care..............	9,657	10,754	9,638	8,075	7,765	54	48	46	46	45
Indoor houseplants.......	1,464	988	1,177	1,081	920	42	31	31	30	29
Flower gardening.........	3,003	2,386	2,679	2,299	1,933	41	30	32	31	28
Insect control............	1,869	2,103	1,734	1,567	1,350	30	25	25	22	22
Shrub care..............	1,109	913	746	623	930	31	23	22	21	20
Vegetable gardening......	1,154	1,421	1,402	1,762	1,701	25	22	23	27	26
Tree care..............	2,820	2,192	2,473	1,743	2,086	26	18	20	19	16
Landscaping............	9,078	9,874	11,712	8,418	7,232	31	27	28	27	24
Flower bulbs............	945	811	796	748	660	29	20	20	19	18
Fruit trees..............	507	477	538	575	702	13	10	10	11	10
Container gardening......	1,295	927	1,003	994	836	26	18	19	19	17
Raising transplants [1]......	237	320	220	241	286	11	7	8	9	8
Herb gardening..........	371	451	391	423	428	17	13	12	14	15
Growing berries.........	151	144	138	229	159	8	5	6	8	8
Ornamental gardening.....	678	561	424	445	504	12	6	6	6	6
Water gardening.........	870	780	989	898	917	11	11	10	11	12

[1] Starting plants in advance of planting in ground.
Source: The National Gardening Association, Burlington, VT, *National Gardening Survey*, annual (copyright). See also <http://www.garden.org/>.

Table 1243. Selected Recreational Activities: 1990 to 2010

[21,000 represents 21,000,000]

Activity	Unit	1990	1995	2000	2005	2006	2007	2008	2009	2010
Golf facilities [1]...........	Number...	12,846	14,074	15,489	16,052	15,990	15,970	15,979	15,979	15,890
Tennis players: [2].........	1,000.....	21,000	17,820	22,900	24,720	24,200	25,130	26,880	30,130	27,810
Skiing: [3]										
Skier visits [4]............	Million....	50.0	52.7	52.2	56.9	58.9	55.1	60.5	57.4	59.8
Operating resorts........	Number...	591	520	503	492	478	481	473	471	471
Motion picture screens [5]...	1,000.....	24	28	37	39	40	40	40	40	40
Receipts, box office......	Mil. dol....	4,428	5,269	7,511	8,821	9,180	9,632	9,635	10,610	10,579
Attendance............	Million....	1,048	1,211	1,393	1,376	1,401	1,399	1,341	1,415	1,341
Boating: [6]										
People participating in reational boating [7].......	Million....	67.4	70.0	67.5	57.9	60.2	66.4	70.1	65.9	75.0
Retail expenditures on boating [8].............	Mil. dol....	13,731	17,226	27,065	37,317	39,493	37,416	33,624	30,821	30,434
Recreational boats in use by boat type [9].............	Million....	16.0	15.4	16.8	17.7	16.8	16.9	16.8	16.8	16.7
Outboard.............	Million....	(NA)	(NA)	8.3	8.5	8.3	8.3	8.3	8.3	8.2
Inboard..............	Million....	(NA)	(NA)	1.0	1.1	1.1	1.1	1.1	1.1	1.1
Sterndrive...........	Million....	(NA)	(NA)	1.6	1.7	1.6	1.7	1.6	1.6	1.5
Personal Watercraft.....	Million....	(NA)	(NA)	1.2	1.2	1.2	1.2	1.2	1.3	1.3
Sailboat..............	Million....	(NA)	(NA)	1.6	1.6	1.6	1.6	1.5	1.5	1.5
Other...............	Million....	(NA)	(NA)	3.1	3.6	3.1	3.1	3.1	3.0	3.0

NA Not available. [1] Source: National Golf Foundation, Jupiter, FL. [2] Source: Tennis Industry Association, Hilton Head, SC. Based on a nationwide telephone survey of households, in which all household members ages 6 and up are enumerated with data on tennis participation collected for each person. [3] Source: National Ski Areas Association, Kottke National End of Season Survey Report (copyright). [4] Represents one person visiting a ski area for all or any part of a day or night, and includes full-and half-day, night, complimentary, adult, child, season, and other types of tickets. Data are estimated and are for the season ending in the year shown. [5] Source: Motion Picture Association of America, Inc., Encino, CA. [6] Source: National Marine Manufacturers Association, Chicago, IL. (copyright). [7] People participating is now measured as adults 18 years and older. [8] Represents estimated expenditures for new and used boats, motors and engines, accessories, safety equipment, fuel, insurance, docking, maintenance, launching, storage, repairs, and other expenses. [9] 2010 data are estimated.
Source: Compiled from sources listed in footnotes.

Table 1244. College and Professional Football Summary: 1990 to 2010

[35,330 represents 35,330,000. For definition of median, see Guide to Tabular Presentation]

Sport	Unit	1990	1995	2000	2005	2007	2008	2009	2010
NCAA college: [1]									
Teams	Number ...	533	565	606	615	619	628	630	639
Attendance	1,000	35,330	35,638	39,059	43,487	48,752	48,839	48,285	49,671
National Football League: [2]									
Teams	Number ...	28	30	31	32	32	32	32	32
Attendance, total [3]	1,000	17,666	19,203	20,954	21,792	22,256	21,859	21,285	21,107
Regular season	1,000	13,960	15,044	16,387	17,012	17,345	17,057	16,651	16,570
Average per game	Number ..	62,321	62,682	66,078	66,455	67,755	66,629	65,043	64,978
Postseason games [4]	1,000	848	(NA)	809	802	792	807	824	800
Players' salaries: [5]									
Average	$1,000 ...	354	584	787	1,400	1,750	1,824	1,896	2,000
Median base salary	$1,000 ...	275	301	441	569	772	788	790	906

NA Not available. [1] Source: National Collegiate Athletic Association, Indianapolis, IN, <http://www.ncaa.org/wps/portal> (copyright). [2] Source: National Football League, New York, NY, <http://www.nfl.com/>. [3] Preseason attendance data are not shown. [4] Includes Pro Bowl (a nonchampionship game) and Super Bowl. [5] Source: National Football League Players Association, Washington, DC, <http://www.nflpa.org/>.

Source: Compiled from sources listed in footnotes.

Table 1245. Selected Spectator Sports: 1990 to 2010

[55,512 represents 55,512,000]

Sport	Unit	1990	1995	2000	2005	2006	2007	2008	2009	2010
Baseball, major leagues: [1]										
Attendance	1,000	55,512	51,288	74,339	76,286	77,524	80,803	79,975	74,823	74,499
Regular season	1,000	54,824	50,469	72,748	74,926	76,043	79,503	78,588	73,368	73,054
National League	1,000	24,492	25,110	39,851	41,644	44,085	44,114	41,579	41,128	40,890
American League	1,000	30,332	25,359	32,898	33,282	34,503	35,390	34,464	32,239	32,164
Playoffs [2]	1,000	479	533	1,314	1,191	1,218	1,083	1,167	1,166	1,210
World Series	1,000	209	286	277	168	225	173	219	289	244
Players' salaries: [3]										
Average	$1,000 ...	598	1,111	1,896	2,476	2,699	2,825	2,926	2,996	3,015
Basketball: [4, 5]										
NCAA—Men's college:										
Teams	Number ...	767	868	932	983	984	982	1,017	1,017	1,033
Attendance	1,000	28,741	28,548	29,025	30,569	30,940	32,836	33,396	33,111	32,821
NCAA—Women's college:										
Teams	Number ...	782	864	956	1,036	1,018	1,003	1,013	1,032	1,037
Attendance [6]	1000	2,777	4,962	8,698	9,940	9,903	10,878	11,121	11,160	11,135
National hockey league [7]:										
Regular season attendance	1,000	12,580	9,234	18,800	([8])	20,854	20,862	21,236	21,475	20,996
Playoffs attendance	1,000	1,356	1,329	1,525	([8])	1,530	1,497	1,587	1,640	1,702
Professional rodeo: [9]										
Rodeos	Number ...	754	739	688	662	649	592	609	560	570
Performances	Number ...	2,159	2,217	2,081	1,940	1,884	1,733	1,861	1,656	1,671
Members	Number ...	5,693	6,894	6,255	6,127	5,892	5,528	5,825	5,653	5,323
Permit-holders (rookies)	Number ...	3,290	3,835	3,249	2,701	2,468	2,186	2,233	2,042	1,881
Total prize money	Mil. dol..	18.2	24.5	32.3	36.6	36.2	40.5	39.1	38.0	39.9

[1] Source: Major League Baseball (previously, The National League of Professional Baseball Clubs), New York, NY, National League Green Book, and The American League of Professional Baseball Clubs, New York, NY, American League Red Book. [2] Beginning 1995, two rounds of playoffs were played. Prior years had one round. [3] Source: Major League Baseball Players Association, New York, NY. [4] Season ending in year shown. [5] Source: National Collegiate Athletic Association, Indianapolis, IN (copyright). [6] For women's attendance total, excludes double-headers with men's teams. [7] For season ending in year shown. Source: National Hockey League, Montreal, Quebec. [8] In September 2004, franchise owners locked out their players upon the expiration of the collective bargaining agreement. The entire season was cancelled in February 2005. [9] Source: Professional Rodeo Cowboys Association, Colorado Springs, CO., Official Professional Rodeo Media Guide, annual (copyright).

Source: Compiled from sources listed in footnotes.

Table 1246. Adult Attendance at Sports Events by Frequency: 2010

[In thousands (557 represents 557,000), except percent. For fall 2010. Percent is based on total projected population of 228,112,000. Data not comparable to previous years. Based on survey and subject to sampling error; see source]

Event	Attend regularly		Attend on occasion		Event	Attend regularly		Attend on occasion	
	Number	Percent	Number	Percent		Number	Percent	Number	Percent
Auto racing—NASCAR	557	0.24	5,759	2.52	NFL weekend games	1,377	0.60	9,644	4.23
Baseball:					NFL playoffs/Super Bowl	829	0.36	2,827	1.24
College	500	0.22	2,674	1.17	Golf—professional (PGA,				
Professional (MLB)	2,172	0.95	22,217	9.74	LPGA) and other	528	0.23	2,698	1.18
Basketball:					High school sports	5,043	2.21	7,414	3.25
College	1,149	0.50	7,059	3.09	Horse racing	193	0.08	2,327	1.02
Professional (NBA, WNBA)	1,052	0.46	7,596	3.33	Ice hockey—professional				
Bowling	299	0.13	1,116	0.49	(NHL)	875	0.38	5,705	2.50
Boxing	404	0.18	1,171	0.51	Mixed martial arts (MMA)	288	0.13	1,279	0.56
Bull riding—professional	138	0.06	1,482	0.65	Motorcycle racing	248	0.11	1,543	0.68
Equestrian events	386	0.17	1,213	0.53	Rodeo	320	0.14	2,578	1.13
Figure skating	128	0.06	882	0.39	Soccer—professional (MLS)				
Fishing	649	0.28	1,739	0.76	and World Cup	362	0.16	2,167	0.95
Football:					Tennis—men's and women's	264	0.12	1,511	0.66
College	3,043	1.33	11,139	4.88	Wrestling—professional	218	0.10	1,716	0.75
Professional (NFL) Monday or Thursday night games	1,119	0.49	5,454	2.39					

Source: GfK Mediamark Research & Intelligence. LLC, New York, NY, Top-line Reports copyright). See <http://www.gfkmri.com>.

Table 1247. Participation in NCAA Sports by Sex: 2009 to 2010

[For the academic year]

Sport	Males			Females		
	Teams	Athletes	Average squad	Teams	Athletes	Average squad
Total.	**8,530**	**249,307**	**(X)**	**9,660**	**186,460**	**(X)**
Archery [1]	(X)	(X)	(X)	(X)	(X)	(X)
Badminton [1]	(X)	(X)	(X)	(X)	(X)	(X)
Baseball.	910	30,365	33.4	(X)	(X)	(X)
Basketball	1,038	17,008	16.4	1,059	15,423	14.6
Bowling	1	40	40	57	507	8.9
Cross country [2]	928	13,476	14.5	1,005	14,551	14.5
Equestrian [1,2]	5	8	1.6	47	1,508	32.1
Fencing [2]	34	633	18.6	41	688	16.8
Field hockey.	(X)	(X)	(X)	262	5,634	21.5
Football	633	66,313	104.8	(X)	(X)	(X)
Golf [2]	798	8,385	10.5	557	4,455	8.0
Gymnastics	17	333	19.6	83	1,417	17.1
Ice hockey	136	3,945	29.0	84	1,941	23.1
Lacrosse	262	9,844	37.6	344	7,683	22.3
Rifle [2]	31	243	7.8	36	190	5.3
Rowing.	61	2,276	37.3	143	6,999	48.9
Rugby [1]	1	63	63.0	4	146	36.5
Sailing [1]	24	587	24.5	(X)	(X)	(X)
Skiing [2]	34	493	14.5	38	499	13.1
Soccer	782	21,770	27.8	967	23,650	24.5
Softball.	(X)	(X)	(X)	957	17,726	18.5
Squash [1]	29	458	15.8	28	380	13.6
Swimming/diving [2]	399	9,025	22.6	512	11,769	23.0
Synchronized swimming [1]	(X)	(X)	(X)	(X)	(X)	(X)
Tennis	752	7,940	10.6	912	8,895	9.8
Track, indoor [2]	601	22,064	36.7	673	22,074	32.8
Track, outdoor [2]	706	25,349	35.9	767	24,028	31.3
Volleyball	90	1,367	15.2	1,025	15,133	14.8
Water polo	41	925	22.6	59	1,164	19.7
Wrestling	217	6,397	29.5	(X)	(X)	(X)

X Not applicable. [1] Sport recognized by the NCAA but does not have an NCAA championship. [2] Co-ed championship sport.
Source: The National Collegiate Athletic Association (NCAA), Indianapolis, IN, *2009–2010 Participation study* (copyright), <http://www.ncaa.publications.com>.

Table 1248. Participation in High School Athletic Programs by Sex: 1980 to 2010

[Data based on number of state associations reporting and may underrepresent the number of schools with and participants in athletic programs]

Year	Participant [1]		Sex and sport	Most popular sports, 2009–2010 [2]	
	Males	Females		Schools	Participants
1980–81.	3,503,124	1,853,789	MALE		
1985–86.	3,344,275	1,807,121	Football (11-player)	14,226	1,109,278
1988–89.	3,416,844	1,839,352	Track & field (outdoor)	16,011	572,123
1989–90.	3,398,192	1,858,659	Basketball	17,969	540,207
1990–91.	3,406,355	1,892,316	Baseball.	15,786	472,644
1991–92.	3,429,853	1,940,801	Soccer	11,375	391,839
1992–93.	3,416,389	1,997,489	Wrestling	10,363	272,890
1993–94.	3,472,967	2,130,315	Cross country	13,942	239,608
1994–95.	3,536,359	2,240,461	Tennis	9,916	162,755
1995–96.	3,634,052	2,367,936	Golf	13,693	157,756
1996–97.	3,706,225	2,474,043	Swimming & diving	6,820	131,376
1997–98.	3,763,120	2,570,333			
1998–99.	3,832,352	2,652,726			
1999–20.	3,861,749	2,675,874	FEMALE		
2000–01.	3,921,069	2,784,154	Track & field (outdoor)	15,923	469,177
2001–02.	3,960,517	2,806,998	Basketball	17,711	439,550
2002–03.	3,988,738	2,856,358	Volleyball	15,382	403,985
2003–04.	4,038,253	2,865,299	Softball (fast pitch).	15,298	378,211
2004–05.	4,110,319	2,908,390	Soccer.	10,901	356,116
2005–06.	4,206,549	2,953,355	Cross country	13,809	201,968
2006–07.	4,321,103	3,021,807	Tennis	10,166	182,395
2007–08.	4,372,115	3,057,266	Swimming & diving	7,171	158,419
2008–09.	4,422,662	3,114,091	Competitive spirit squads	4,879	123,644
2009–10.	4,455,740	3,172,637	Golf	9,651	70,872

[1] A participant is counted in the number of sports participated in. [2] Ten most popular sports for each sex in terms of number of participants.
Source: National Federation of State High School Associations, Indianapolis, IN, *The 2009–2010 High School Athletics Participation Survey* (copyright), <http://www.nfhs.org/>.

Arts, Recreation, and Travel 767

Table 1249. Participation in Selected Sports Activities: 2009

[In thousands (269,988 represents 269,988,000), except rank. Data are based on a questionnaire mailed to 10,000 households. The questionnaire asked the male and female heads of households and up to two other household members who were at least seven years of age to indicate their age, the sports in which they participated in 2009, and the number of days of participation in 2009. A participant is defined as an individual seven years of age or older who participates in a sport more than once a year. See source for methodology]

Activity	All persons Number	Sex		Age								Household income (dollars)						
		Male	Female	7–11 years	12–17 years	18–24 years	25–34 years	35–44 years	45–54 years	55–64 years	65 and over	Under 15,000	15,000–24,999	25,000–34,999	35,000–49,999	50,000–74,999	75,000–99,999	100,000 and over
SERIES I SPORTS																		
Total............	269,988	132,437	137,551	19,892	25,056	29,526	40,018	43,475	43,208	31,556	37,257	25,568	24,659	27,297	39,689	54,549	41,485	56,740
Number participated in—																		
Aerobic exercising [1]	33,138	9,519	23,619	1,285	1,960	4,215	8,332	7,286	4,626	2,824	2,611	1,760	2,076	2,443	3,748	7,437	6,287	9,387
Backpacking [2]	12,281	7,043	5,238	1,617	1,750	1,903	2,208	2,526	1,497	582	197	1,325	764	1,218	1,770	2,724	1,613	2,867
Baseball...........	11,507	9,314	2,193	3,971	2,727	1,078	776	1,412	727	502	316	573	456	1,076	1,772	2,473	2,366	2,791
Basketball.........	24,410	16,904	7,506	4,802	6,482	4,249	2,860	3,214	1,998	513	292	1,816	1,078	1,852	3,702	5,069	4,739	6,154
Bicycle riding [1]	38,139	21,265	16,874	6,801	6,395	3,066	5,345	6,937	4,835	2,853	1,906	2,433	1,894	2,529	5,266	8,321	6,859	10,837
Billiards...........	28,172	17,583	10,589	1,183	2,306	5,678	7,546	5,598	3,857	1,301	702	2,763	1,624	2,300	4,397	5,961	4,863	6,265
Bowling...........	44,972	23,507	21,465	5,976	6,428	8,325	7,635	8,223	4,565	2,285	1,536	3,337	2,414	3,241	6,867	10,415	8,422	10,275
Camping [3]	50,863	26,353	24,510	5,942	7,212	5,572	8,759	9,434	7,187	4,050	2,707	4,119	2,685	3,833	7,520	13,219	8,808	10,678
Exercise walking [1]	93,359	37,093	56,266	3,573	5,520	8,200	16,045	17,803	17,330	12,595	12,294	6,855	7,061	7,911	12,813	19,961	16,814	21,944
Exercising with equipment [1]	57,206	27,815	29,391	960	4,015	7,420	13,104	11,438	9,659	5,090	5,519	2,917	2,885	4,423	8,112	12,161	10,707	16,001
Fishing (net)......	32,876	22,714	10,162	3,146	3,508	2,577	6,114	6,327	5,241	3,553	2,409	2,539	2,152	2,775	5,821	7,500	5,359	6,729
Fishing—fresh water	28,996	20,290	8,706	3,038	3,101	2,470	5,429	5,806	4,195	3,043	1,913	2,327	1,869	2,635	5,350	6,552	4,429	5,834
Fishing—salt water	8,195	5,807	2,387	529	949	513	1,121	1,248	1,952	986	896	453	435	453	768	2,056	1,765	2,265
Football—tackle....	8,890	7,912	978	1,672	3,435	2,032	497	635	205	184	232	952	1,247	881	1,335	1,640	1,282	1,553
Golf.............	22,317	16,893	5,424	1,276	1,660	1,763	4,131	4,208	4,168	2,823	2,288	606	675	1,078	3,061	4,614	4,589	7,693
Hiking...........	34,013	17,397	16,616	3,093	3,828	3,650	6,570	6,527	5,853	2,690	1,804	2,294	1,858	2,126	4,234	7,587	6,726	9,189
Running/jogging [1]	32,212	17,736	14,476	2,672	4,975	5,451	8,332	5,531	3,719	1,024	507	1,189	1,784	2,033	4,340	5,787	7,970	9,109
Soccer...........	13,578	7,732	5,846	5,129	3,228	1,692	1,223	1,398	608	171	130	956	539	727	1,644	2,527	2,603	4,583
Softball..........	11,829	5,977	5,852	1,821	2,226	1,910	2,239	1,771	1,271	430	160	1,055	536	874	2,165	2,658	2,354	2,186
Swimming [1]	50,226	23,816	26,410	8,296	8,108	4,604	7,863	8,053	6,484	3,889	2,929	3,171	2,313	4,125	3,442	11,031	8,918	14,227
Tennis...........	10,818	5,656	5,163	1,443	1,535	970	2,216	2,366	1,540	482	267	411	436	509	1,301	2,149	1,955	4,058
Volleyball.........	10,733	4,303	6,430	1,337	3,147	1,975	1,757	1,190	865	298	164	707	651	447	1,917	2,014	1,969	3,027
Weightlifting.......	34,505	23,387	11,118	347	3,702	4,900	10,329	6,963	5,098	1,818	1,348	2,029	2,123	2,330	5,224	6,976	7,192	8,631
Yoga............	15,738	3,241	12,497	357	705	2,449	4,507	3,672	2,028	1,163	858	1,025	1,013	1,254	1,885	3,524	2,574	4,462

See footnotes at end of table.

U.S. Census Bureau, Statistical Abstract of the United States: 2012

Table 1249. Participation in Selected Sports Activities: 2009—Con.

[See headnote, page 768]

Activity	All persons Number	Sex Male	Sex Female	Age 7–11 years	Age 12–17 years	Age 18–24 years	Age 25–34 years	Age 35–44 years	Age 45–54 years	Age 55–64 years	Age 65 and over	Income Under 15,000	Income 15,000–24,999	Income 25,000–34,999	Income 35,000–49,999	Income 50,000–74,999	Income 75,000–99,999	Income 100,000 and over
Total	269,988	132,436	137,552	19,893	25,055	29,526	40,018	43,475	43,208	31,556	37,257	23,091	25,508	28,537	37,918	64,447	39,400	51,086
SERIES II SPORTS																		
Number participated in—																		
Archery	7,106	5,025	2,081	1,158	1,302	658	1,930	931	745	218	163	544	662	415	1,005	2,028	1,257	1196
Boating-motor/power	23,959	13,641	10,318	1,480	2,761	3,047	3,647	4,803	4,125	2,197	1,899	820	1,482	1,979	3,279	5,143	4,743	6,514
Hockey (ice)	3,057	2,228	829	536	588	312	460	628	211	208	113	46	117	252	88	1,217	452	885
Hunting with bow and arrow	6,187	5,362	825	128	510	914	1,534	1,368	973	435	324	464	508	467	1,687	1,390	807	862
Hunting with firearms	18,816	15,835	2,981	389	1,788	2,377	3,904	3,169	3,651	2,099	1,440	1,279	1,635	2,123	3,328	4,737	2,317	3,398
In-line roller skating	7,874	3,896	3,978	2,089	1,848	1,108	910	1,238	499	124	59	233	443	1,044	1,495	1,718	1,541	1,401
Mountain biking—off road	8,368	4,986	3,382	819	732	793	1,964	1,990	1,346	451	272	404	361	609	863	2,044	1,342	2,745
Muzzleloading	3,797	3,234	563	–	290	581	754	633	795	482	262	227	408	362	822	906	607	466
Paintball games	6,271	5,215	1,056	398	1,867	2,084	607	780	407	126	–	524	539	787	533	1,380	950	1,559
Scooter riding	8,114	4,549	3,566	4,384	2,097	166	324	330	380	181	252	290	381	707	795	2,443	1,373	2,126
Skateboarding	8,418	6,298	2,121	2,752	3,255	1,580	414	328	36	8	44	600	442	879	1,181	1,814	1,216	2,287
Skiing—alpine	6,992	4,384	2,608	546	910	902	1,384	1,308	1,080	586	276	61	566	468	494	1,089	1,086	3,227
Skiing—cross country	1,695	888	807	60	233	91	160	458	342	272	78	73	49	107	77	620	353	416
Snowboarding	6,189	4,314	1,876	504	1,554	1,614	1,605	697	73	85	58	91	150	826	583	1,358	1,415	1,767
Table tennis/ping pong	13,306	7,596	5,710	1,418	2,353	1,992	2,751	2,049	1,863	442	439	362	963	1,069	997	4,297	2,391	3,228
Target shoot	19,776	15,054	4,722	1,079	1,993	2,688	4,331	3,276	3,323	1,770	1,316	1,325	1,912	2,263	3,070	4,316	2,813	4,058
Target shoot—airgun	5,167	4,228	938	559	1,449	852	469	643	559	341	293	470	444	620	675	1,406	975	577
Water skiing	5,191	2,826	2,364	362	678	1,175	1,158	1,016	625	154	12	186	106	257	697	907	873	2,165
Work out at club	38,320	17,597	20,723	394	2,123	6,387	8,837	7,242	6,072	3,588	3,674	1,315	1,600	3,114	4,107	9,731	6,817	11,635

– Represents zero. [1] Participant engaged in activity at least six times in the year. [2] Includes wilderness camping. [3] Vacation/overnight.

Source: National Sporting Goods Association, Mt. Prospect, IL, *Sports Participation in 2009: Series 1 and Series II*, (copyright). See <http://www.nsga.org/i4a/pages/index.cfm?pageid=3346>.

Arts, Recreation, and Travel 769

Table 1250. Sporting Goods Sales by Product Category: 1990 to 2009, and Projection, 2010

[In millions of dollars (50,725 represents $50,725,000,000), except percent. Based on a sample survey of consumer purchases of 80,000 households, (100,000 beginning 2000), except recreational transport, which was provided by industry associations. Excludes Alaska and Hawaii. Minus sign (–) indicates decrease]

Selected product category	1990	2000	2004	2005	2006	2007	2008	2009	2010, proj.
Sales, all products	**50,725**	**74,442**	**85,811**	**88,434**	**90,472**	**91,423**	**80,431**	**70,856**	**75,666**
Annual percent change [1]	(NA)	4.6	7.6	3.1	2.3	1.1	-12.0	-11.9	6.8
Percent of retail sales	(NA)	2.5	2.5	2.4	2.3	2.3	2.0	1.9	1.9
Athletic and sport clothing	10,130	11,030	11,201	10,898	10,580	10,834	10,113	9,246	9,665
Athletic and sport footwear [2]	11,654	13,026	14,752	15,719	16,910	17,524	17,190	17,069	17,282
Aerobic shoes	611	292	237	261	262	280	260	223	216
Basketball shoes	918	786	877	878	964	892	718	741	735
Cross training shoes	679	1,528	1,327	1,437	1,516	1,584	1,626	1,531	1,527
Golf shoes	226	226	230	259	232	244	239	202	195
Gym shoes, sneakers	2,536	1,871	2,221	2,314	2,434	2,699	2,639	2,539	2,593
Jogging and running shoes	1,110	1,638	1,989	2,157	2,260	2,193	2,301	2,363	2,423
Tennis shoes	740	533	508	528	505	452	467	396	380
Walking shoes	2,950	3,317	3,496	3,673	4,091	4,197	4,204	4,416	4,543
Athletic and sport equipment [2]	14,439	21,608	23,328	23,735	24,497	25,061	24,862	24,421	24,568
Archery	265	259	332	372	396	396	394	379	383
Baseball and softball	217	319	352	372	388	401	396	374	378
Billiards and indoor games	192	516	622	572	574	531	396	312	300
Camping	1,072	1,354	1,531	1,447	1,526	1,453	1,461	1,496	1,526
Exercise	1,824	3,610	5,074	5,177	5,239	5,500	5,328	5,301	5,354
Fishing tackle	1,910	2,030	2,026	2,139	2,218	2,247	2,067	1,859	1,861
Golf	2,514	3,805	3,198	3,466	3,669	3,722	3,495	2,836	2,864
Hunting and firearms	2,202	2,274	3,175	3,563	3,732	3,942	4,548	5,199	5,165
Optics	438	729	859	887	1,014	1,019	1,024	1,070	1,091
Skin diving and scuba	294	355	351	358	369	376	373	343	350
Snow skiing [3]	475	495	452	643	501	531	482	502	516
Tennis	333	383	362	397	418	440	387	368	364
Recreational transport	14,502	28,779	36,531	38,082	38,485	38,003	28,266	20,120	24,151
Bicycles and supplies	2,423	5,131	4,898	5,343	5,161	5,393	5,285	4,471	5,200
Pleasure boats, motors, accessories	7,644	13,224	16,054	17,634	17,907	17,473	13,679	9,097	10,781
Recreational vehicles	4,113	9,529	14,753	14,366	14,732	14,505	8,758	6,118	7,648
Snowmobiles	322	894	826	739	685	632	544	435	522

NA Not available. [1] Represents change from immediate prior year. [2] Includes other products not shown separately. [3] Data through 2004 categorized as "Skiing Downhill."

Source: National Sporting Goods Association, Mt. Prospect, IL, *The Sporting Goods Market in 2010* and prior issues, (copyright). See <http://www.nsga.org/i4a/pages/index.cfm?pageid=3345>.

Table 1251. Consumer Purchases of Sporting Goods by Consumer Characteristics: 2009

[In percent. Based on sample survey of consumer purchases of 100,000 households. Excludes Alaska and Hawaii]

Characteristic	Total	Footwear					Equipment				
		Aerobic shoes	Fitness shoes	Gym shoes/ sneak- ers	Jog- ging/ running shoes	Walking shoes	Multi pur- pose home gyms	Rod/ reel combi- nation	Golf club sets	Rifles	Soccer balls
Total	**100**	**100**	**100**	**100**	**100**	**100**	**100**	**100**	**100**	**100**	**100**
Age of user:											
Under 14 years old	18.7	7.2	10.0	44.7	9.4	5.5	–	6.2	1.5	5.4	53.4
14 to 17 years old	5.6	4.5	2.6	7.9	6.4	2.9	1.5	1.3	0.9	1.1	15.8
18 to 24 years old	9.8	5.0	4.8	5.0	6.0	2.2	1.3	5.1	2.3	3.8	8.5
25 to 34 years old	13.4	22.0	30.2	10.3	25.9	8.5	50.8	11.7	15.9	10.6	11.5
35 to 44 years old	14.0	14.3	15.4	11.3	24.0	13.0	17.9	19.7	17.9	18.6	2.7
45 to 64 years old	25.7	35.4	32.7	15.7	24.5	45.6	27.4	49.1	39.3	52.4	6.6
65 years old and over	12.8	11.6	4.3	5.1	3.8	22.3	1.1	6.9	22.2	8.1	0.5
Multiple ages	–	–	–	–	–	–	–	–	–	–	1.0
Sex of user:											
Male	49.3	26.6	37.1	52.9	44.6	36.7	77.2	78.4	66.8	85.9	62.5
Female	50.7	73.4	62.9	47.1	55.4	63.3	21.4	16.2	33.2	10.3	36.0
Household use	–	–	–	–	–	–	1.4	5.4	–	3.8	1.5
Annual household income:											
Under $15,000	11.4	7.5	3.6	6.8	3.2	8.2	1.5	9.2	–	6.1	4.4
$15,000 to $24,999	12.2	11.2	6.5	7.6	4.7	8.5	4.1	8.2	5.6	2.4	7.5
$25,000 to $34,999	12.3	11.9	8.1	9.4	8.0	11.5	13.2	12.1	4.1	7.3	9.1
$35,000 to $49,999	14.9	12.4	16.5	15.3	14.1	15.8	17.9	9.0	3.7	22.1	15.8
$50,000 to $74,999	18.4	16.3	21.2	21.5	19.5	19.8	27.8	18.9	22.9	20.7	15.9
$75,000 to $99,999	14.9	15.8	19.3	16.8	19.5	16.9	15.1	17.8	38.4	13.6	23.7
$100,000 and over	15.9	24.9	24.8	22.6	31.0	19.3	20.4	24.8	25.3	27.8	23.6
Education of household head:											
Less than high school	5.9	2.6	2.7	3.7	1.5	6.1	2.0	7.5	–	2.8	2.5
High school	22.4	19.7	13.7	22.3	9.5	19.9	4.3	23.7	5.2	13.6	10.8
Some college	36.0	28.2	40.0	32.7	30.9	36.8	35.1	41.1	29.2	38.8	36.5
College graduate	35.7	49.5	43.6	41.3	58.1	37.2	58.6	27.7	65.6	44.8	50.2

– Represents or rounds to zero.
Source: National Sporting Goods Association, Mt. Prospect, IL, *The Sporting Goods Market in 2010*, (copyright). See <http://www.nsga.org.public/pages/index.cfm?pageid=869\>.

Table 1252. National Park System—Summary: 1990 to 2009

[For year ending September 30, except as noted. (986 represents $986,000,000). Includes data for five areas in Puerto Rico and Virgin Islands, one area in American Samoa, and one area in Guam]

Item	1990	1995	2000	2005	2006	2007	2008	2009
Finances (mil. dol.): [1]								
Expenditures reported....................	986	1,445	1,833	2,451	2,463	2,412	2,614	2,888
Salaries and wages.................	459	633	799	984	998	1,005	1,066	1,143
Improvements, maintenance.............	160	234	299	361	389	381	428	466
Construction.....................	109	192	215	381	300	280	303	354
Other.........................	259	386	520	725	776	746	817	925
Funds available.......................	1,506	2,225	3,316	4,218	4,242	4,266	4,537	5,416
Appropriations...................	1,053	1,325	1,881	2,425	2,450	2,484	2,636	3,467
Other [2].........................	453	900	1,435	1,793	1,792	1,782	1,901	1,949
Revenue from operations	79	106	234	286	308	346	404	352
Recreation visits (millions): [3]								
All areas........................	258.7	269.6	285.9	273.5	272.6	275.6	274.9	285.6
National parks [4].................	57.7	64.8	66.1	63.5	60.4	62.3	61.2	63.0
National monuments	23.9	23.5	23.8	20.9	19.6	19.7	20.2	22.6
National historical, commemorative, archaeological [5]..................	57.5	56.9	72.2	74.9	73.6	75.1	76.2	82.6
National parkways.................	29.1	31.3	34.0	31.7	32.6	31.1	30.2	29.9
National recreation areas [4]	47.2	53.7	50.0	46.8	47.8	48.9	49.6	50.9
National seashores and lakeshores	23.3	22.5	22.5	21.7	19.6	19.9	19.3	20.6
National Capital Parks.............	7.5	5.5	5.4	4.3	6.2	4.9	5.1	4.8
Recreation overnight stays (millions)........	17.6	16.8	15.4	13.5	13.2	13.8	13.7	14.6
In commercial lodgings	3.9	3.8	3.7	3.4	3.4	3.6	3.6	3.5
In Park Service campgrounds...........	7.9	7.1	5.9	5.2	5.0	5.1	5.0	5.4
In backcountry......................	1.7	2.2	1.9	1.7	1.7	1.7	1.8	1.9
Other............................	4.2	3.7	3.8	3.2	3.1	3.4	3.3	3.8
Land (1,000 acres): [6, 7]								
Total............................	76,362	77,355	78,153	79,048	78,810	78,845	78,859	80,442
Parks..........................	46,089	49,307	49,785	49,910	49,912	49,911	49,916	50,592
Recreation areas..................	3,344	3,353	3,388	3,391	3,391	3,413	3,413	3,414
Other..........................	26,929	24,695	24,980	25,747	25,507	25,521	25,530	26,436
Acquisition, net	21	27	186	17	54	23	9	18

[1] Financial data are those associated with the National Park System. Certain other functions of the National Park Service (principally the activities absorbed from the former Heritage Conservation and Recreation Service in 1981) are excluded. [2] Includes funds carried over from prior years. [3] For calendar year. Includes other areas, not shown separately. [4] For 1990, combined data for North Cascades National Park and two adjacent National Recreation Areas are included in National Parks total. [5] Includes military areas. [6] Federal land only, as of Dec. 31. Federal land acreages, in addition to National Park Service administered lands, also include lands within national park system area boundaries but under the administration of other agencies. Year-to-year changes in the federal lands figures includes changes in the acreages of these other lands and hence often differ from "net acquisition." [7] The decrease in the 2006 land total reflects corrected acreage by the Bureau of Land Management, and not by the National Park Service lands.

Source: U.S. National Park Service, *National Park Statistical Abstract*, annual, and unpublished data. See also <http://www2.nature.nps.gov/stats/>.

Table 1253. State Parks and Recreation Areas by State: 2010

[For year ending June 30 (13,997 represents 13,997,000). Data are shown as reported by state park directors. In some states, park agency has forests, fish and wildlife areas, and/or other areas under its control. In other states, park agency is responsible for state parks only]

State	Acreage (1,000)	Visitors (1,000)[1]	Revenue Total ($1,000)	Revenue Percent of operating expenditures	State	Acreage (1,000)	Visitors (1,000)[1]	Revenue Total ($1,000)	Revenue Percent of operating expenditures
United States ...	**13,997**	**740,733**	**980,205**	**50.1**	Missouri.........	204	16,215	9,084	34.6
					Montana.........	46	1,896	1,448	19.9
Alabama	48	3,839	28,414	89.0	Nebraska........	135	11,144	17,959	77.0
Alaska	3,387	5,405	2,940	35.1	Nevada	146	3,046	2,586	25.3
Arizona	64	2,267	9,947	52.6	New Hampshire...	233	1,586	15,719	118.0
Arkansas	54	8,831	22,549	44.2	New Jersey	437	17,164	11,622	32.8
California	1,571	65,036	94,836	26.7	New Mexico	99	4,769	5,800	27.6
Colorado	225	12,285	27,000	48.9	New York	1,354	56,322	85,558	39.6
Connecticut	207	8,209	6,466	34.5	North Carolina....	211	14,899	6,200	18.1
Delaware	26	4,947	13,079	63.3	North Dakota	20	1,086	1,670	45.4
Florida	704	20,110	52,706	65.3	Ohio............	174	53,814	27,268	42.3
Georgia	87	9,722	32,552	66.3	Oklahoma	72	11,088	29,980	94.9
Hawaii	34	10,425	2,334	28.5	Oregon..........	103	43,755	16,112	32.1
Idaho	46	4,649	6,184	38.5	Pennsylvania	294	38,523	19,527	25.2
Illinois...........	488	42,294	7,475	12.3	Rhode Island	9	5,872	5,247	58.3
Indiana..........	180	15,846	44,568	83.5	South Carolina....	85	8,197	19,493	77.2
Iowa............	69	14,374	4,108	30.8	South Dakota.....	103	7,786	14,140	85.4
Kansas	33	7,800	6,583	55.6	Tennessee.......	181	29,919	33,661	43.2
Kentucky	45	7,013	52,427	60.1	Texas...........	615	7,474	37,667	48.8
Louisiana........	44	2,069	7,709	25.6	Utah............	151	4,683	12,090	40.2
Maine...........	97	2,602	3,463	40.9	Vermont.........	69	758	10,969	142.2
Maryland	134	10,132	13,924	41.8	Virginia	70	7,463	14,888	51.0
Massachusetts....	350	35,271	12,644	19.5	Washington	109	44,135	20,478	31.0
Michigan	285	21,167	40,770	88.7	West Virginia	177	7,171	21,094	58.1
Minnesota	284	8,922	18,126	29.0	Wisconsin	293	14,470	18,886	82.7
Mississippi.......	24	1,217	8,618	51.9	Wyoming	120	3,066	1,636	19.3

[1] Includes overnight visitors.

Source: The National Association of State Park Directors, Raleigh, NC, *2009–2010 Annual Information Exchange*, February 2011. See <http://www.naspd.org/>.

Table 1254. National Park Service (NPS) Visits and Acreage by State: 2010

State	Recreation visits [1]	Gross area acres	Federal land			Nonfederal land	
			NPS fee acres [2]	NPS/OTFED less than fee acres [3]	Other federal fee acres [4]	Other public acres	Private acres
Total............	279,337,864	84,324,776	79,700,359	354,976	426,013	1,177,511	2,665,916
Alabama	781,550	22,737	16,714	202	–	3,296	2,525
Alaska	2,274,843	54,654,000	52,620,395	105,940	8	187,513	1,740,145
Arizona	10,546,150	2,962,853	2,618,748	115	76,937	57,067	209,986
Arkansas	3,125,664	104,977	98,320	3,395	20	2,761	482
California	34,915,676	8,111,386	7,576,590	22,456	11,250	318,671	182,420
Colorado	5,635,307	673,589	609,880	6,859	42,451	862	13,537
Connecticut	19,313	7,782	5,719	1,055	–	874	133
District of Columbia ...	33,140,005	7,090	6,942	12	5	126	4
Florida	9,222,981	2,638,389	2,437,504	1,330	45,839	129,202	24,514
Georgia	6,776,556	63,420	39,761	125	1,461	16,900	5,173
Hawaii	4,493,123	369,124	357,772	1	22	11,228	100
Idaho	530,977	518,033	507,713	1,138	3,960	901	4,320
Illinois	354,125	115	12	–	–	17	86
Indiana	2,395,485	15,378	10,598	499	–	3,287	995
Iowa	222,295	2,713	2,708	–	–	5	1
Kansas	100,361	11,636	461	269	–	39	10,866
Kentucky	1,797,894	95,416	94,395	137	–	832	52
Louisiana	496,329	24,107	17,531	–	–	2,476	4,101
Maine	2,504,208	90,285	66,903	11,146	22	10,648	1,566
Maryland	3,541,570	73,388	40,543	5,938	480	23,806	2,621
Massachusetts	9,913,501	57,962	32,946	1,030	44	21,919	2,023
Michigan	1,796,006	718,228	631,718	731	42	58,515	27,222
Minnesota	540,195	301,343	139,570	3,193	142	98,801	59,637
Mississippi	6,588,026	118,733	104,004	5,232	–	69	9,428
Missouri	4,140,544	83,475	54,382	9,262	–	14,070	5,760
Montana	4,584,011	1,274,374	1,214,184	1,233	6,137	1,464	51,355
Nebraska	290,323	45,735	5,650	494	981	386	38,223
Nevada	5,399,439	778,512	774,751	–	2,508	81	1,172
New Hampshire	30,941	21,889	13,168	1,556	5,772	162	1,232
New Jersey	5,858,443	99,206	35,362	140	3,208	59,000	1,497
New Mexico	1,657,550	391,364	376,862	39	2,715	3,365	8,384
New York	17,506,353	72,898	33,504	3,920	164	19,938	15,372
North Carolina	17,093,464	406,268	363,169	12,272	20,782	3,289	6,757
North Dakota	659,927	72,579	71,250	256	151	56	867
Ohio	2,738,275	34,150	19,421	1,329	84	8,205	5,110
Oklahoma	1,266,189	10,241	10,008	9	189	8	27
Oregon	888,358	199,095	192,020	1,404	4,975	183	513
Pennsylvania	8,970,475	137,663	50,861	2,582	387	19,627	64,207
Rhode Island	51,559	5	5	–	–	–	–
South Carolina	1,529,172	32,184	31,538	61	5	51	530
South Dakota	4,199,267	297,413	141,312	122,326	–	78	33,697
Tennessee	7,898,557	385,805	357,610	1,679	9,629	3,616	13,272
Texas	5,495,156	1,245,085	1,201,669	85	1,013	5,079	37,240
Utah	8,975,525	2,117,043	2,097,106	833	1,142	12,803	5,160
Vermont	31,209	23,193	8,830	3,874	8,809	544	1,135
Virginia	22,708,338	363,664	304,289	6,842	24,914	7,001	20,619
Washington	7,281,785	1,967,436	1,834,321	2,147	100,187	12,799	17,982
West Virginia	1,811,722	92,670	65,044	326	314	6,894	20,092
Wisconsin	251,145	133,754	61,744	11,484	802	47,624	12,102
Wyoming	6,307,997	2,396,390	2,344,852	21	48,462	1,380	1,675

– Represents zero. [1] See footnotes, Table 1255.
Source: U.S. National Park Service, Land Resource Board, and unpublished data. See also <http://www2.nature.nps.gov /stats/>.

Table 1255. National Park Service (NPS) Visits and Acreage by Type of Area: 2010

[Includes data for five areas in Puerto Rico and Virgin Islands, one area in American Samoa, and one area in Guam]

Type of area	Recreation visits [1]	Gross area acres	Federal land			Non-federal land	
			NPS fee acres [2]	NPS/OTFED less than fee acres [3]	Other federal fee acres [4]	Other public acres	Private acres
Total [5]	281,303,769	84,383,361	79,715,228	354,979	456,856	1,183,700	2,672,598
National historic sites.......	9,747,040	34,174	21,353	783	51	947	11,039
National historical parks	28,135,991	183,932	132,135	3,580	364	28,722	19,132
National memorials	30,799,674	10,745	9,421	9	162	81	1,072
National monuments	23,012,207	2,027,071	1,841,318	14,830	43,612	5,901	121,410
National parks	64,623,855	52,094,660	50,387,537	226,558	47,595	497,320	935,651
National recreation areas ...	49,044,088	3,700,824	3,151,111	23,735	243,101	110,228	172,649
National seashores	18,118,155	596,562	404,436	14,947	61,226	106,668	9,284
National parkways	28,576,098	178,166	158,450	9,108	213	303	10,092

[1] Recreation visit represents the entry of a person onto lands or waters administered by the National Park Service (NPS) for recreational purposes excluding government personnel, through traffic (commuters), trades-persons, and persons residing within park boundaries. [2] Fee represents complete Federal ownership of all rights in the land. [3] Represents Federal ownership of some rights in the land. [4] NPS acreage lies under the jurisdiction of another federal agency (such as Bureau of Land Management). [5] Includes other "type of areas," not shown separately.
Source: U.S. National Park Service, Land Resource Board, and unpublished data. See also <http://www2.nature.nps.gov /stats/>.

Table 1256. Participants in Wildlife-Related Recreation Activities: 2006

[In thousands (33,916 represents 33,916,000). For persons 16 years old and over engaging in activity at least once in 2006. Based on survey and subject to sampling error; see source for details]

Participant	Number	Days of participation	Trips	Participant	Number	Days of participation
Total sportspersons [1] ..	**33,916**	**736,707**	**588,891**	Wildlife watchers [1]	71,132	(X)
Total anglers	29,952	516,781	403,492	Away from home [2]	22,977	352,070
Freshwater.	25,431	433,337	336,528	Observe wildlife [2]	21,546	291,027
Excluding Great Lakes ..	25,035	419,942	323,265	Photograph wildlife	11,708	103,872
Great Lakes.	1,420	18,016	13,264	Feed wildlife.	7,084	77,329
Saltwater	7,717	85,663	66,963	Around the home [3]	67,756	(X)
Total hunters	12,510	219,925	185,399	Observe wildlife	44,467	(X)
Big game	10,682	164,061	115,255	Photograph wildlife	18,763	(X)
Small game	4,797	52,395	40,856	Feed wildlife.	55,512	(X)
Migratory birds.	2,293	19,770	16,390	Visit public parks	13,271	(X)
Other animals	1,128	15,205	12,898	Maintain plantings or natural areas	14,508	(X)

X Not applicable. [1] Detail does not add to total due to multiple responses and nonresponse. [2] Persons taking a trip of at least 1 mile from home for activity. [3] Activity within 1 mile of home.

Source: U.S. Fish and Wildlife Service, *2006 National Survey of Fishing, Hunting, and Wildlife Associated Recreation*, October 2007. See also <http://wsfrprograms.fws.gov/Subpages/NationalSurvey/nat_survey2006_final.pdf>.

Table 1257. Expenditures for Wildlife-Related Recreation Activities: 2006

[(42,011 represents $42,011,000,000). For persons 16 years old and over. Based on survey and subject to sampling error; see source for details]

Expenditure item	Fishing Expenditures (mil. dol.)	Fishing Spenders Number (1,000)	Fishing Spenders Percent of anglers	Hunting Expenditures (mil. dol.)	Hunting Spenders Number (1,000)	Hunting Spenders Percent of hunters	Wildlife watching Expenditures (mil. dol.)	Wildlife watching Spenders Number (1,000)	Wildlife watching Spenders Percent of watch-ers [2]
Total, all items [1]	**42,011**	**28,307**	**95**	**22,893**	**12,153**	**97**	**45,655**	**55,979**	**79**
Total trip-related [3].	17,879	26,318	88	6,679	10,828	87	12,875	19,443	85
Food and lodging.	6,303	22,572	75	2,791	9,567	76	7,516	16,415	71
Food	4,327	22,415	75	2,177	9,533	76	4,298	16,261	71
Lodging	1,975	5,304	18	614	1,599	13	3,218	6,624	29
Transportation	4,962	22,361	75	2,697	10,064	80	4,456	18,329	80
Public.	524	1,163	4	214	401	3	1,567	2,902	13
Private	4,438	21,979	73	2,483	9,982	80	2,889	17,447	76
Other trip costs	6,614	22,275	74	1,190	3,416	27	903	7,681	33
Total equipment and other expenditures.	24,133	25,355	85	16,215	11,745	94	32,780	52,178	73
Equipment [4]	5,332	19,082	64	5,366	9,287	74	9,870	49,040	69
Auxiliary equipment.	779	3,837	13	1,330	4,196	34	1,033	4,848	7
Special equipment [5]	12,646	1,818	6	4,035	505	4	12,271	1,914	3
Other expenditures [6]	5,375	20,638	69	5,483	10,632	85	9,606	19,070	27
Magazines, books	115	2,944	10	84	1,767	14	360	9,490	13
Licenses, stamps, tags, and permits	503	16,259	54	743	9,862	79	(X)	(X)	(X)

X Not applicable. [1] Total not adjusted for multiple responses or nonresponse. [2] Percent of wildlife-watching participants column is based on away-from-home participants for trip-related expenditures. For equipment and other expenditures the percent of wildlife-watching participants is based on total participants. [3] Information on trip-related expenditures for wildlife watching was collected for away-from-home participants only. Equipment and other expenditures for wildlife watching are based on information collected from both away-from-home and around-the-home participants. [4] Includes fishing, hunting, and wildlife-watching. [5] Special equipment includes boats, campers, cabins, trail bikes, etc. [6] Other expenditures not shown.

Source: U.S. Fish and Wildlife Service, *2006 National Survey of Fishing, Hunting, and Wildlife Associated Recreation*, October 2007. See <http://wsfrprograms.fws.gov/Subpages/NationalSurvey/nat_survey2006_final.pdf>.

Table 1258. Tribal Gaming Revenues: 2004 to 2009

[In millions (19,479 represents $19,479,000,000). For year ending September 30]

Region	2004 Number of operations	2004 Revenue	2005 Number of operations	2005 Revenue	2006 Number of operations	2006 Revenue	2007 Number of operations	2007 Revenue	2008 Number of operations	2008 Revenue	2009 Number of operations	2009 Revenue
Total [1]	**375**	**19,479**	**392**	**22,579**	**394**	**24,889**	**391**	**26,143**	**405**	**26,739**	**419**	**26,482**
Region I	45	1,602	49	1,829	46	2,080	46	2,264	47	2,376	49	2,521
Region II	54	5,822	57	6,993	56	7,675	58	7,796	59	7,363	62	6,970
Region III. . . .	45	2,160	48	2,529	45	2,719	46	2,874	46	2,774	47	2,600
Region IV. . . .	117	3,816	118	3,984	122	4,070	111	4,225	115	4,402	120	4,384
Region V	87	1,259	92	1,730	98	2,126	102	2,584	110	3,047	113	3,225
Region VI. . . .	27	4,821	28	5,514	27	6,219	28	6,400	28	6,776	28	6,783

[1] Portland (Region 1): Alaska, Idaho, Oregon, and Washington. Sacramento (Region 2): California, and Northern Nevada. Phoenix (Region 3): Arizona, Colorado, New Mexico, and Southern Nevada. St Paul (Region 4): Iowa, Michigan, Minnesota, Montana, North Dakota, Nebraska, South Dakota, Wisconsin, and Wyoming. Data for Montana not included for 2004. Oklahoma City (Region 5): Western Oklahoma, and Texas. Tulsa (Region 5): Kansas and Eastern Oklahoma. Washington (Region 6): Alabama, Connecticut, Florida, Louisiana, Mississippi, North Carolina, and New York.

Source: National Indian Gaming Commission, *Gaming Revenue* reports. See also <http://www.nigc.gov>.

U.S. Census Bureau, Statistical Abstract of the United States: 2012

Table 1259. Gaming Revenue by Industry: 2000 to 2009

[In millions of dollars (62,154 represents $62,154,000,000). Data shown are for gross revenue. Gross gambling revenue (GGR) is the amount wagered minus the winnings returned to players, a true measure of the economic value of gambling. GGR is the figure used to determine what an operation earns before taxes, salaries, and other expenses are paid]

Industry	2000	2003	2004	2005	2006	2007	2008	2009
Total [1]	**62,154**	**73,036**	**78,589**	**84,433**	**90,931**	[2] **92,272**	[2,3] **92,157**	[2,3] **89,262**
Card rooms	949	979	989	1,025	1,104	[3] 1,180	[3] 1,282	[3] 1,232
Commercial casinos	26,455	[2] 28,669	[2] 30,595	[2] 31,775	[2] 34,113	[3] 34,407	[2,3] 33,031	[2,3] 31,379
Charitable games and bingo	2,466	2,331	2,336	[3] 2,338	[3] 2,237	[3] 2,220	[3] 2,131	[3] 2,067
Legal bookmaking	131	128	116	130	192	168	136	136
Lotteries	17,277	20,283	21,405	22,898	24,631	24,780	25,698	25,139
Parimutuel wagering	3,935	3,821	3,750	3,683	3,677	[3] 3,529	[3] 3,141	[3] 2,827

[1] Includes industry not shown separately. [2] Amount includes deepwater cruise ships, cruises-to-nowhere and noncasino devices. [3] Data are estimated.

Source: Christiansen Capital Advisors, LLC. Prepared for the American Gaming Association (AGA). Industry Information, Fact Sheets, *Gaming Revenue: Current-Year Data* (copyright), <http://www.americangaming.org/Industry/factsheets/index.cfm> and <www.cca-i.com>.

Table 1260. North America Cruise Industry in the United States: 2005 to 2009

[The North American passenger cruise industry is defined as those cruise lines that primarily market their cruises in North America. These cruise lines offer cruises with destinations throughout the globe. While most of these cruises originate in ports throughout North America, cruises also originate at ports in other continents]

Item	Unit	2005	2006	2007	2008	2009
Capacity Measures:						
Number of ships	Number	145	151	159	161	167
Lower berths [1]	Number	225,364	244,271	259,973	270,664	284,754
Passenger embarkations, global [2]	**1,000**	**11,500**	**12,000**	**12,562**	**13,006**	**13,442**
United States	1,000	8,612	9,001	9,184	8,958	8,904
Florida	1,000	4,875	4,994	4,977	5,110	5,257
California	1,000	1,301	1,241	1,334	1,436	1,266
New York	1,000	382	512	537	524	420
Other U.S. ports	1,000	2,054	2,254	2,336	1,888	1,961
Canada	1,000	455	423	477	427	450
San Juan	1,000	581	555	534	521	507
Rest of world	1,000	1,852	2,021	2,367	3,100	3,581
United States expenditures of the North American cruise industry [3,4]	**Bil. dol.**	**16.18**	**17.64**	**18.70**	**19.07**	**17.15**
U.S. purchases of the cruise lines	Bil. dol.	11.76	12.89	13.74	14.40	12.67
Passenger and crew	Bil. dol.	3.23	3.48	3.63	3.40	3.31
Wages & taxes paid by cruise lines	Bil. dol.	1.19	1.27	1.33	1.27	1.17

[1] Single beds. [2] Port of departure. [3] See details in the report for the sources of U.S. expenditures of the North American cruise industry. [4] Includes wages and salaries paid to U.S. employees of the cruise lines.

Source: Business Research & Economic Advisors (BREA), Exton, PA. The Contribution of the North American Cruise Industry to the U.S. Economy in 2009. Prepared for the Cruise Lines International Association, June 2010, <http://www.cruising.org>.

Table 1261. Top States and Cities Visited by Overseas Travelers: 2000 to 2010

[25,975 represents 25,975,000. Includes travelers for business and pleasure, international travelers in transit through the United States, and students. Excludes travel by international personnel and international businessmen employed in the United States. Starting with the 2006 data, the statistical policy for visitation estimates of international visitation requires a minimum sample of 400 respondents. States and cities are ranked by the latest overseas visitors data.]

State and other area	Overseas visitors [1] (1,000)				City	Overseas visitors [1] (1,000)			
	2000	2005	2009	2010		2000	2005	2009	2010
Total overseas travelers [2,3]	**25,975**	**21,679**	**23,756**	**26,363**	New York City, NY [4]	5,714	5,810	7,792	8,462
New York	5,922	6,092	8,006	8,647	Los Angeles, CA	3,533	2,580	2,518	3,348
Florida	6,026	4,379	5,274	5,826	Miami, FL	2,935	2,081	2,661	3,111
California	6,364	4,791	4,632	5,615	Orlando, FL	3,013	2,016	2,399	2,715
Nevada	2,364	1,821	1,900	2,504	San Francisco, CA	2,831	2,124	2,233	2,636
Hawaiian Islands	2,727	2,255	1,853	2,135	Las Vegas, NV	2,260	1,778	1,853	2,425
Guam	1,325	1,127	1,140	1,318	Washington, DC	1,481	1,106	1,544	1,740
Massachusetts	1,429	867	1,259	1,292	Oahu/Honolulu, HI	2,234	1,821	1,497	1,634
Illinois	1,377	1,149	1,164	1,186	Boston, MA	1,325	802	1,140	1,186
Texas	1,169	954	903	1,028	Chicago, IL	1,351	1,084	1,117	1,134
New Jersey	909	997	926	975	San Diego, CA	701	499	618	765
Pennsylvania	649	629	879	923	Atlanta, GA	701	564	570	712
Georgia	805	650	689	817	Philadelphia, PA	390	434	594	633
Arizona	883	564	665	765	Flagstaff, AZ [5]	(B)	(B)	428	501
Washington	468	369	380	501	Seattle, WA	416	347	356	475
Utah	(B)	(B)	(B)	475	Houston, TX	442	(B)	428	448
Virginia	364	(B)	380	369	Anaheim-Santa Ana	494	390	309	369
Colorado	519	(B)	333	343	Tampa/St. Petersburg, FL	519	455	404	343
North Carolina	416	(B)	309	343	Dallas-Plano-Irving, TX	494	(B)	285	343

B Figure too small to meet statistical standards for reliability of a derived figure. [1] Excludes Canada and Mexico. [2] A person is counted in each area visited, but only once in the total. [3] Includes other states and cities, not shown separately. [4] Data include New York City-White Plains-Wayne, NY-NJ grouped together. [5] Data include Flagstaff, Grand Canyon and Sedona grouped together.

Source: U.S. Department of Commerce, International Trade Administration, Office of Travel and Tourism, June 2011, <http://www.tinet.ita.doc.gov/outreachpages/inbound.general_information.inbound_overview.html>.

Table 1262. Real Tourism Output: 2000 to 2009

[In millions of dollars (574,304 represents 574,304,000,000)]

Commodity	Direct output (current dollars)			Real output (chained 2005 dollars)		
	2000	2005	2009	2000	2005	2009
Total	**574,304**	**692,605**	**699,098**	**640,882**	**692,605**	**631,366**
Traveler accommodations	103,122	123,831	130,915	116,936	123,831	122,717
Food services and drinking places	86,964	112,962	111,706	100,240	112,962	96,272
Domestic passenger air transportation services	71,255	68,916	67,210	64,556	68,916	60,245
International passenger air transportation services	29,142	39,059	45,404	36,997	39,059	41,489
Passenger rail transportation services	1,045	1,178	1,540	1,034	1,178	1,303
Passenger water transportation services	6,348	10,420	10,890	5,056	10,420	12,317
Interurban bus transportation	1,362	1,738	1,888	1,619	1,738	1,580
Interurban charter bus transportation	1,614	1,781	1,443	1,888	1,781	1,302
Urban transit systems and other transportation services	3,147	3,631	3,805	3,785	3,631	3,375
Taxi service	3,710	3,929	4,611	4,637	3,929	4,014
Scenic and sightseeing transportation services	2,549	2,873	2,887	2,980	2,873	2,605
Automotive rental	25,759	26,632	30,626	28,454	26,632	23,601
Other vehicle rental	622	634	585	660	634	525
Automotive repair services	11,516	11,561	14,692	13,440	11,561	12,491
Parking lots and garages	1,262	2,099	1,929	1,579	2,099	1,581
Highway tolls	506	685	691	618	685	562
Travel arrangement and reservation services	29,579	30,987	34,733	28,742	30,987	32,592
Motion pictures and performing arts	10,332	12,798	11,834	12,233	12,798	10,613
Spectator sports	5,515	7,128	6,522	6,924	7,128	5,545
Participant sports	9,177	11,004	10,383	9,895	11,004	9,951
Gambling	25,620	35,904	41,365	29,055	35,904	37,617
All other recreation and entertainment	13,988	17,583	16,608	16,548	17,583	14,733
Gasoline	37,495	57,808	51,217	56,869	57,808	48,942
Nondurable PCE [1] commodities other than gasoline	92,675	107,463	95,615	98,346	107,463	86,994

[1] Personal consumption expenditures.

Source: U.S. Bureau of Economic Analysis, "Industry Economic Accounts, U.S. Travel and Tourism Satellite Accounts for 2005–2009," <http://www.bea.gov/industry/>.

Table 1263. Domestic Travel Expenditures by State: 2009

[610,200 represents $610,200,000,000. Represents U.S. spending on domestic overnight trips and day trips of 50 miles or more, one way, away from home. Excludes spending by foreign visitors and by U.S. residents in U.S. territories and abroad]

State	Total (mil. dol.)	Percent distribu-tion	Rank	State	Total (mil. dol.)	Percent distribu-tion	Rank	State	Total (mil. dol.)	Percent distribu-tion	Rank
U.S. total	**610,200**	**100.0**	**(X)**	KS	5,094	0.8	37	ND	1,853	0.3	47
				KY	7,107	1.2	30	OH	14,451	2.4	12
AL	7,123	1.2	29	LA	8,673	1.4	24	OK	5,834	1.0	33
AK	1,721	0.3	48	ME	2,490	0.4	43	OR	7,229	1.2	28
AZ	11,448	1.9	18	MD	11,675	1.9	17	PA	17,889	2.9	7
AR	5,237	0.9	36	MA	12,419	2.0	15	RI	1,579	0.3	50
CA	75,514	12.4	1	MI	14,148	2.3	13	SC	8,938	1.5	22
CO	12,028	2.0	16	MN	9,887	1.6	21	SD	2,126	0.3	46
CT	8,611	1.4	26	MS	5,842	1.0	32	TN	12,927	2.1	14
DE	1,334	0.2	51	MO	11,351	1.9	19	TX	43,328	7.1	3
DC	5,631	0.9	34	MT	2,757	0.5	42	UT	5,038	0.8	38
FL	48,394	7.9	2	NE	3,639	0.6	39	VT	1,678	0.3	49
GA	17,570	2.9	9	NV [1]	22,883	3.8	6	VA	17,705	2.9	8
HI	8,631	1.4	25	NH	2,955	0.5	40	WA	10,667	1.7	20
ID	2,889	0.5	41	NJ	16,824	2.8	10	WV	2,352	0.4	44
IL	25,134	4.1	5	NM	5,317	0.9	35	WI	8,744	1.4	23
IN	8,362	1.4	27	NY	35,904	5.9	4	WY	2,345	0.4	45
IA	6,056	1.0	31	NC	15,613	2.6	11				

X Not applicable. [1] Estimate is not comparable to previous years due to a change in source data.

Source: U.S. Travel Association, Washington, DC, *Impact of Travel on State Economies, 2009* (copyright). See also <http://www.ustravel.org/index.html>.

Table 1264. Travel Forecast Summary: 2008 to 2014

[In billions of dollars (13,229 represents $13,229,000,000,000)]

Measurement	Unit	2008	2009	2010 [1]	2011 [2]	2012 [2]	2013 [2]	2014 [2]
Real GDP	Billions	13,229	12,881	13,248	13,606	14,039	14,546	15,051
Unemployment rate	Percent	5.8	9.3	9.6	8.8	8.2	7.1	6.2
Consumer price index (CPI) [3]	Percent	215.3	214.5	218.1	224.3	228.5	235.3	239.9
Travel price index (TPI) [3]	Percent	257.7	241.5	250.8	265.9	272.3	281.2	284.9
Total travel expenditures in US	Billions	772.5	704.4	758.7	817.0	851.1	892.5	933.4
U.S. residents	Billions	662.4	610.2	655.6	703.6	727.8	761.7	796.5
International visitors [4]	Billions	110.0	93.9	103.1	113.4	123.3	130.8	136.8
Total international visitors to the United States	Millions	57.9	55.0	59.7	61.8	64.9	67.9	70.7
Total domestic person trips [5]	Millions	1,964.9	1,897.8	1,964.6	2,005.9	2,043.1	2,089.2	2,137.1

[1] Projected. [2] Forecast. [3] 1982 through 1984 = 100. [4] Excludes international visitors' spending on traveling to the U.S. on U.S. flag carriers, and other misc. transportation. [5] One person on one trip 50 miles or more, one way, away from home or including one or more nights away from home.

Source: U.S. Travel Association's Travel Forecast Model, Bureau of Labor Statistics, Department of Commerce, Bureau of Economic Analysis, Office of Travel and Tourism Industries. See <http://www.ustravel.org/index.html>.

Table 1265. Chain-Type Price Indexes for Direct Tourism Output: 2000 to 2010

[Index numbers, 2005=100. See headnote, Table 1266. For explanation of chain-type price indexes, see text, Section 13]

Tourism goods and services group	2000	2002	2003	2004	2005	2006	2007	2008	2009	2010
Traveler accommodations	88.2	92.0	92.7	95.1	100.0	103.6	108.1	110.2	106.7	107.9
Transportation	90.3	85.6	89.6	92.8	100.0	107.0	111.5	122.1	111.0	119.3
Passenger air transportation	99.7	90.1	92.9	93.6	100.0	106.7	109.7	121.0	110.7	120.8
All other transportation-related commodities	83.9	82.4	87.1	92.2	100.0	107.3	112.8	122.9	111.0	118.1
Food services and drinking places	86.8	92.0	94.0	96.9	100.0	103.2	107.0	111.9	116.0	117.6
Recreation, entertainment, and shopping	90.8	94.3	95.8	97.8	100.0	102.4	105.0	108.8	110.2	111.2
Recreation and entertainment	86.6	91.7	94.5	96.9	100.0	103.2	106.5	110.1	110.6	111.5
Shopping	94.2	96.3	96.8	98.5	100.0	101.7	103.9	107.8	109.9	111.1
All tourism goods and services	89.6	90.1	92.6	95.3	100.0	104.5	108.3	114.5	110.7	114.8

Source: U.S. Department of Commerce, Bureau of Economic Analysis, Office of Travel and Tourism Industries, *United States Travel and Tourism Satellite Accounts (TTSAs)*, <http://www.bea.gov/bea/dn2/home/tourism.htm>.

Table 1266. Tourism Sales by Commodity Group and Tourism Employment by Industry Group: 2005 to 2010

[Sales in billions of dollars (693 represents $693,000,000,000). Employment in thousands (5,876 represents 5,876,000). Direct tourism-related sales comprise all output consumed directly by visitors (e.g., traveler accommodations, passenger air transportation, souvenirs). Direct tourism-related employment comprises all jobs where the workers are engaged in the production of direct tourism-related output (e.g., hotel staff, airline pilots, and souvenir sellers)]

Tourism commodity group	Direct tourism sales (bil. dol.)				Tourism industry group	Direct tourism employment (1,000)			
	2005	2008	2009	2010		2005	2008	2009	2010
All commodities [1]	693	798	699	746	All industries	5,876	5,885	5,406	5,330
Traveler accommodations	124	151	131	140	Traveler accommodations	1,334	1,355	1,250	1,240
Transportation	264	316	274	310	Transportation	1,158	1,147	1,087	1,071
Passenger air transportation	108	131	113	134	Air transportation services	487	481	453	444
All other transportation-related commodities	156	185	162	176	All other transportation-related industries	672	666	635	627
Food services and drinking places	113	124	112	114	Food and beverage services	1,878	1,937	1,716	1,691
					Recreation, entertainment, and shopping	1,254	1,203	1,120	1,099
Recreation, entertainment, and shopping	192	207	182	182	Recreation and entertainment	651	637	586	570
Recreation and entertainment	84	94	87	86	Shopping	604	566	534	530
Shopping	107	113	96	96	All other industries	251	243	233	229

[1] Commodities that are typically purchased by visitors from the producer: such as airline passenger fares, meals, or hotel services.

Source: U.S. Bureau of Economic Analysis, "Industry Economic Accounts, Satellite Industry Accounts, Travel and Tourism." See <http://www.bea.gov/bea/dn2/home/tourism.htm>.

Table 1267. International Travelers and Payments: 1990 to 2010

[(47,880 represents $47,880,000,000). For coverage, see Table 1268. Some traveler data revised since originally issued]

Year	Travel and passenger fare (mil. dol.)				U.S. net travel and passenger receipts (mil. dol)	U.S. travelers to international countries (1,000)	International travelers to the U.S. (1,000)
	Payments by U.S. travelers		Receipts from international visitors				
	Total [1]	Travel payments	Total [1]	Travel receipts			
1990.........	47,880	37,349	58,305	43,007	10,425	44,624	39,363
1995.........	59,579	44,916	82,304	63,395	22,725	51,285	43,318
2000.........	88,979	65,366	103,088	82,891	14,109	61,327	51,238
2004.........	90,468	66,738	93,397	75,465	2,929	61,809	46,086
2005.........	95,119	69,930	102,769	82,160	7,650	63,503	49,206
2006.........	99,605	72,959	107,825	86,187	8,220	63,662	50,977
2007.........	104,808	77,127	122,542	97,355	17,734	64,028	55,979
2008.........	112,335	80,494	141,380	110,423	29,045	63,564	57,937
2009.........	99,255	74,118	120,294	94,191	21,039	61,419	54,958
2010 [2]........	102,786	75,507	134,436	103,505	31,650	(NA)	59,745

NA Not available. [1] Includes passenger fares, not shown separately. [2] Preliminary estimates for the receipts payment figures, and U.S. travelers to international countries.

Source: U.S. Department of Commerce, International Trade Administration, Office of Travel and Tourism Industries, and the Bureau of Economic Analysis (BEA), June 2011, <http://www.tinet.ita.doc.gov>.

Table 1268. International Travel: 1990 to 2010

[In thousands (44,619 represents 44,619,000). U.S. travelers cover residents of the United States, its territories and possessions. International travelers to the U.S. include travelers for business and pleasure, excludes travel by international personnel and international businessmen employed in the United States. Some traveler data revised since originally issued]

Item and area	1990	1995	2000	2005	2006	2007	2008	2009	2010
U.S. travelers to international countries [1]....	**44,619**	**51,285**	**61,327**	**63,503**	**63,662**	**64,028**	**63,564**	**61,419**	**(NA)**
Canada....................	12,252	13,005	15,189	14,391	13,855	13,375	12,504	11,667	(NA)
Mexico....................	16,377	18,771	19,285	20,325	19,659	19,425	20,271	19,452	(NA)
Total overseas.............	15,990	19,059	26,853	28,787	30,148	31,228	30,789	30,300	(NA)
Europe..................	8,043	8,596	13,373	11,976	12,029	12,304	11,238	10,635	(NA)
International travelers to the U.S.........	**39,363**	**43,318**	**51,238**	**49,206**	**50,977**	**55,979**	**57,937**	**54,958**	**59,745**
Canada....................	17,263	14,663	14,667	14,862	15,992	17,760	18,910	17,973	19,959
Mexico....................	7,041	8,016	10,596	12,665	13,317	14,327	13,686	13,229	13,423
Total overseas.............	15,059	20,639	25,975	21,679	21,668	23,892	25,341	23,756	26,363
Europe..................	6,659	8,793	11,597	10,313	10,136	11,406	12,783	11,550	11,985
Asia....................	4,360	6,616	7,554	6,198	6,152	6,377	6,179	5,669	7,020
South America............	1,328	2,449	2,941	1,820	1,928	2,274	2,556	2,742	3,250
Caribbean	1,137	1,044	1,331	1,135	1,198	1,317	1,201	1,206	1,201
Oceania.................	662	588	731	737	756	834	852	872	1,095
Central America..........	412	509	822	696	694	786	776	758	760
Middle East.............	365	454	702	527	553	620	681	666	736
Africa..................	137	186	295	252	253	278	315	294	316

NA Not available. [1] A person is counted in each area visited but only once in the total.

Source: U.S. Department of Commerce, International Trade Administration, Office of Travel and Tourism, June 2011, <http://www.tinet.ita.doc.gov>

Table 1269. Top 20 U.S. Gateways for Nonstop International Air Travel: 2008 and 2009

[160,589 represents 160,589,000. International passengers are residents of any country traveling nonstop to and from the United States on U.S. and foreign carriers. The data cover all passengers arriving and departing from U.S. airports on nonstop commercial international flights with 60 seats or more]

Gateway airport	2008 [1]	2009	Percent change 2008–2009	Gateway airport	2008 [1]	2009	Percent change 2008–2009
Total.....................	**160,589**	**151,096**	**-5.9**	Washington (Dulles), DC....	6,020	5,999	-0.3
Total, top 20	**140,336**	**133,759**	**-4.7**	Dallas–Ft. Worth, TX......	4,949	4,662	-5.8
Top 20, percentage of total ...	**87.4**	**88.5**	**1.1**	Philadelphia, PA...........	3,724	3,739	0.4
				Boston, MA	3,573	3,493	-2.2
New York (JFK), NY...........	21,983	21,423	-2.5	Honolulu, HI..............	3,414	3,276	-4.0
Miami, FL...................	15,957	15,715	-1.5	Fort Lauderdale, FL........	3,073	2,933	-4.6
Los Angeles, CA..............	16,225	14,727	-9.2	Orlando, FL	2,588	2,905	12.3
Newark, NJ	10,959	10,583	-3.4	Detroit, MI	3,805	2,738	-28.0
Chicago (O'Hare), IL...........	11,125	10,204	-8.3	Seattle–Tacoma, WA........	2,802	2,528	-9.8
Atlanta, GA	9,255	8,765	-5.3	Charlotte, NC.............	2,303	2,344	1.8
San Francisco, CA.............	8,331	7,905	-5.1	Minneapolis–St. Paul, MN ...	2,563	2,214	-13.6
Houston (G. Bush), TX.........	7,687	7,606	-1.1	Las Vegas, NV.............	2,235	2,153	-3.7

[1] Data have been revised.

Source: U.S. Department of Transportation, Research and Innovative Technology Administration, Bureau of Transportation Statistics, Office of Airline Information, T-100 Segment data, September 2010, <http://www.bts.gov/publications>.

Table 1270. Selected U.S.-Canadian and U.S.-Mexican Border Land—Passenger Gateways: 2010

[(28,875 represents 28,875,000)]

Item and gateway	Entering the U.S. (1,000)	Item and gateway	Entering the U.S. (1,000)
All U.S.-Canadian land gateways [1]		**All U.S.-Mexican land gateways [1]**	
Personal vehicles	28,875	Personal vehicles	64,045
Personal vehicle passengers	56,769	Personal vehicle passengers	125,750
Buses	116	Buses	219
Bus passengers	2,451	Bus passengers	2,680
Train passengers	255	Train passengers	3
Pedestrians	395	Pedestrians	39,915
Selected top five gateways:		**Selected top five gateways:**	
Personal vehicles		Personal vehicles	
Buffalo-Niagara Falls, NY	5,478	San Ysidro, CA	13,348
Detroit, MI	4,051	El Paso, TX	9,968
Blaine, WA	3,366	Hidalgo, TX	5,604
Port Huron, MI	1,651	Laredo, TX	4,864
Calais, ME	1,055	Brownsville, TX	4,640
Personal vehicle passengers		Personal vehicle passengers	
Buffalo-Niagara Falls, NY	11,918	San Ysidro, CA	23,601
Detroit, MI	7,218	El Paso, TX	17,920
Blaine, WA	6,996	Laredo, TX	10,858
Port Huron, MI	3,443	Hidalgo, TX	10,692
Champlain-Rouses Point, NY	2,239	Brownsville, TX	9,292
Pedestrians		Pedestrians	
Buffalo-Niagara Falls, NY	259	El Paso, TX	6,930
Sumas, WA	28	San Ysidro, CA	6,440
International Falls, MN	22	Calexico, CA	4,587
Detroit, MI	17	Nogales, AZ	3,971
Point Roberts, WA	14	Laredo, TX	3,588

[1] Data reflect all personal vehicles and buses, passengers, and pedestrians entering the U.S.-Canadian border and U.S.-Mexican border, regardless of nationality.

Source: U.S. Department of Transportation, Bureau of Transportation Statistics, based on data from the Department of Homeland Security, U.S. Customs and Border Protection, Office of Field Operations, Operations Management Reporting system. See also <http://www.transtats.bts.gov/BorderCrossing.aspx/>.

Table 1271. Foreign Visitors for Pleasure Admitted by Country of Citizenship: 2000 to 2008

[In thousands (30,511 represents 30,511,000). For years ending September 30. Represents non-U.S. citizens (also known as nonimmigrants) admitted to the country for a temporary period of time]

Country	2000 [1]	2005	2007	2008	Country	2000 [1]	2005	2007	2008
All countries [2]	**30,511**	**23,815**	**27,486**	**29,442**	Thailand	76	37	46	48
					Turkey	93	57	64	71
					United Arab Emirates	36	3	4	5
Europe [3]	11,806	10,016	10,703	12,558	Africa [3]	327	212	228	253
Austria	182	116	124	154	Egypt	44	19	24	27
Belgium	254	154	175	231	Nigeria	27	40	41	54
Czech Republic	44	26	30	36	South Africa	114	64	67	65
Denmark	150	153	191	236	Oceania [3]	748	723	823	878
Finland	95	76	78	100	Australia	535	527	623	672
France	1,113	1,007	1,073	1,345	New Zealand	170	184	188	195
Germany	1,925	1,248	1,315	1,579	North America [3, 5]	6,501	5,546	8,071	7,867
Greece	60	40	42	52	Canada	277	23	36	43
Hungary	58	30	32	34	Mexico	3,972	4,070	6,326	6,112
Iceland	27	34	44	49	Caribbean	1,404	876	1,081	1,049
Ireland	325	398	501	585	Bahamas, The	24	257	334	302
Italy	626	636	700	884	Dominican Republic	195	189	228	207
Netherlands	559	483	515	638	Haiti	72	65	82	93
Norway	144	117	143	184	Jamaica	240	152	205	200
Poland	116	119	121	125	Trinidad and Tobago	133	106	122	128
Portugal	86	81	98	114	Central America	792	578	628	663
Russia	74	53	72	94	Costa Rica	172	109	122	138
Spain	370	402	533	699	El Salvador	175	147	141	129
Sweden	321	249	282	356	Guatemala	177	135	148	161
Switzerland	400	207	232	267	Honduras	87	75	90	101
United Kingdom	4,671	4,232	4,211	4,568	Nicaragua	47	33	37	40
Asia [3]	7,853	5,688	5,745	5,693	Panama	106	64	72	77
China [4]	656	221	278	319	South America [3]	2,867	1,498	1,856	2,114
India	253	247	379	421	Argentina	515	145	214	261
Indonesia	62	42	45	45	Bolivia	48	18	23	25
Israel	319	220	241	254	Brazil	706	385	491	600
Japan	4,946	3,758	3,446	3,266	Chile	194	82	98	106
Korea, South	606	528	625	600	Colombia	411	282	353	379
Malaysia	64	32	34	37	Ecuador	122	119	137	132
Pakistan	47	34	32	35	Peru	190	142	135	148
Philippines	163	144	156	170	Uruguay	66	24	27	28
Saudi Arabia	67	10	13	19	Venezuela	570	270	348	404
Singapore	131	57	64	77					

[1] Due to the temporary expiration of the Visa Waiver Program from May through October 2000, data for business and pleasure not available separately for 2000 and 2001. [2] Total includes unknown visitors by country of citizenship. [3] Total includes other countries, not shown separately. [4] See Table 1332, footnote 4. [5] The majority of short-term admissions from Canada and Mexico are excluded.

Source: U.S. Dept. of Homeland Security, Office of Immigration Statistics, *2008 Yearbook of Immigration Statistics*. See also <http://www.dhs.gov/ximgtn/statistics/publications/yearbook.shtm>.

This section presents statistics relating to services other than those covered in the previous few sections (22 to 26) on wholesale and retail trade, transportation, communications, financial services, and recreation services. Data shown for services are classified by kind of business and cover sales or receipts, establishments, employees, payrolls, and other items.

The principal sources of these data are from the U.S. Census Bureau and include the *2007 Economic Census,* annual surveys, and the *County Business Patterns* program. These data are supplemented by data from several sources such as the National Restaurant Association on food and drink sales (Table 1283), the American Hotel & Lodging Association on lodging (Table 1282), and Magna Global on advertising (Table 1279).

Data on these services also appear in several other sections. For instance, labor force employment and earnings data appear in Section 12, Labor Force, Employment, and Earnings; gross domestic product of the industry (Table 670) appears in Section 13, Income, Expenditures, Poverty, and Wealth; and financial data (several tables) from the quarterly *Statistics of Income Bulletin,* published by the Internal Revenue Service, appear in Section 15, Business Enterprise.

Censuses—Limited coverage of the service industries started in 1933. Beginning with the 1967 census, legislation provides for a census of each area to be conducted every 5 years (for years ending in "2" and "7"). For more information on the most current census, see the Economic Census, *Guide to Economic Census,* found at <http://www.census.gov/econ/census /guide/index.html>. The industries covered in the censuses and surveys of business are defined in the *North American Industry Classification System* (NAICS). For information on NAICS, see the Census Web site at <http://www .census.gov/epcd/www/naics.html>.

In general, the 2007 Economic Census has two final series of publications for these sectors: 1) subject series with reports such as product lines, and establishment and firm sizes and 2) geographic reports with individual reports for each state. For information on these series, see the Census Bureau Web site at <http://www .census.gov/econ/census07>.

Current surveys—The Service Annual Survey provides annual estimates of nationwide receipts for selected personal, business, leasing and repair, amusement and entertainment, social and health, and other professional service industries in the United States. For selected social, health, and other professional service industries, separate estimates are developed for receipts of taxable firms and revenue and expenses for firms and organizations exempt from federal income taxes. Several service sectors from this survey are covered in other sections of this publication. The estimates for tax exempt firms in these industries are derived from a sample of employer firms only. Estimates obtained from annual and monthly surveys are based on sample data and are not expected to agree exactly with results that would be obtained from a complete census of all establishments. Data include estimates for sampling units not reporting.

Statistical reliability—For a discussion of statistical collection and estimation, sampling procedures, and measures of statistical reliability applicable to Census Bureau data, see Appendix III.

Table 1272. Selected Service-Related Industries—Establishments, Sales, Payroll, and Employees by Kind of Business: 2007

[1,251,004 represents $1,251,004,000,000. Covers only establishments with payroll. For statement on methodology, see Appendix III]

Kind of business	2007 NAICS code [1]	Establish-ments, (number)	Sales or receipts (mil. dol.)	Annual payroll (mil. dol.)	Paid employ-ees [2] (1,000)
Professional, scientific, and technical services	54	**847,492**	**1,251,004**	**502,074**	**7,870**
Professional, scientific, and technical services	541	847,492	1,251,004	502,074	7,870
Management of companies and enterprises.	55	**51,451**	**104,443**	**249,511**	**2,664**
Administrative and support and waste management and remediation services	56	**395,292**	**630,771**	**301,450**	**10,251**
Administrative and support services.	561	373,505	555,583	284,603	9,865
Waste management and remediation services.	562	21,787	75,188	16,848	386
Accommodation and food services.	72	**634,361**	**613,796**	**170,827**	**11,601**
Accommodation.	721	62,740	180,391	46,393	1,971
Food services and drinking places	722	571,621	433,405	124,434	9,630
Other services (except public administration)	81	**540,148**	**405,284**	**99,123**	**3,479**
Repair and maintenance.	811	222,151	137,733	40,070	1,261
Personal and laundry services	812	210,151	82,105	26,759	1,338
Religious, grantmaking, civic, professional, and similar organizations.	813	107,846	185,447	32,294	880

[1] North American Industrial Classification System, 2007; see text, Section 15. [2] For employees on the payroll during the pay period including March 12.

Source: U.S. Census Bureau, 2007 Economic Census, "Economy-Wide Key Statistics," <http://factfinder.census.gov>, accessed July 2011.

Table 1273. Selected Service-Related Industries—Nonemployer Establishments and Receipts by Kind of Business: 2006 to 2008

[2,904 represents 2,904,000. Includes only firms subject to federal income tax. Nonemployers are businesses with no paid employees. Data originate chiefly from administrative records of the Internal Revenue Service; see Appendix III]

Kind of business	2007 NAICS code [1]	Firms (1,000)			Receipts (mil. dol.)		
		2006	2007	2008	2006	2007	2008
Professional, scientific, and technical services	54	**2,904**	**3,029**	**3,029**	**124,237**	**130,386**	**131,521**
Professional, scientific, and technical services [2]	541	2,904	3,029	3,029	124,237	130,386	131,521
Legal services	5411	254	256	255	15,390	15,744	15,923
Accounting, tax preparation, bookkeeping, and payroll services	5412	348	355	350	7,714	8,103	8,233
Architectural, engineering [3]	5413	238	232	226	11,308	11,420	11,197
Management, scientific and technical consulting	5416	536	642	641	25,653	29,011	29,722
Scientific research and development services	5417	31	35	35	1,086	1,196	1,263
Administrative and support and waste management and remediation services	56	**1,482**	**1,793**	**1,826**	**34,989**	**39,811**	**40,415**
Administrative and support services [2]	561	1,463	1,771	1,806	33,569	38,280	38,737
Office administrative services	5611	190	198	204	2,923	3,191	3,250
Business support services.	5614	193	224	219	5,521	5,969	5,927
Services to buildings and dwellings.	5617	850	1,047	1,083	17,702	20,625	21,110
Waste management and remediation services	562	19	21	21	1,421	1,531	1,678
Accommodation and food services.	72	**287**	**303**	**308**	**15,694**	**16,071**	**16,100**
Accommodation.	721	55	55	54	3,660	3,592	3,484
Food services and drinking places	722	232	249	254	12,034	12,479	12,616
Full-service restaurants.	7221	38	40	42	3,972	4,005	4,075
Limited-service eating places	7222	48	49	48	3,376	3,456	3,425
Special food services.	7223	122	133	137	3,085	3,352	3,438
Drinking places (alcoholic beverages)	7224	25	26	27	1,601	1,666	1,679
Other services (except public administration)	81	**2,931**	**2,965**	**3,029**	**77,986**	**80,653**	**81,042**
Repair and maintenance [2]	811	693	704	699	27,276	28,183	27,567
Automotive repair and maintenance	8111	289	305	302	13,987	14,634	14,334
Personal and household goods repair [4]	8114	303	297	297	8,765	8,853	8,616
Personal and laundry services	812	2,047	2,054	2,124	47,776	49,282	50,257
Personal care services	8121	870	911	967	19,266	20,661	21,680
Death care services.	8122	15	16	16	802	856	886
Drycleaning and laundry services	8123	35	35	34	1,966	2,004	1,978
Other personal services	8129	1,128	1,093	1,108	25,742	25,760	25,713
Religious, grantmaking, civic, professional, and similar organizations.	813	190	206	206	2,933	3,189	3,218

[1] North American Industry Classification System, see text, Section 15. Data for 2002-2007 based on NAICS 2002; beginning 2008 Nonemployer data is based on NAICS 2007. [2] Includes other kinds of business not shown separately. [3] Includes related services. [4] Includes maintenance.

Source: U.S. Census Bureau, "Nonemployer Statistics," June 2010, <http://www.census.gov/econ/nonemployer/index.html>.

Table 1274. Selected Service-Related Industries—Establishments, Employees, and Payroll by Industry: 2007 and 2008

[868 represents 868,000. Covers establishments with paid employees. Excludes most government employees, railroad employees, and self-employed persons. For statement on methodology, see Appendix III]

Kind of business	2007 NAICS code [1]	Establishments (1,000)		Employees [2] (1,000)		Annual payroll (bil. dol.)	
		2007	2008	2007	2008	2007	2008
Professional, scientific, & technical services	**54**	**868**	**848**	**8,180**	**8,033**	**533.0**	**539.1**
Professional, scientific, & technical services	541	868	848	8,180	8,033	533.0	539.1
Legal services	5411	191	188	1,207	1,199	89.7	91.8
Offices of lawyers	54111	176	173	1,110	1,110	85.4	88.3
Accounting, tax preparation, bookkeeping, and payroll services	5412	123	123	1,357	1,319	55.9	56.8
Tax preparation services	541213	25	25	216	213	2.7	2.1
Architectural, engineering, & related services [3]	5413	117	115	1,435	1,458	98.6	103.1
Architectural services	54131	25	25	207	210	14.2	14.2
Engineering services	54133	58	59	961	998	71.4	76.4
Specialized design services [3]	5414	35	33	135	130	6.8	6.7
Graphic design services	54143	17	16	64	60	3.2	2.9
Computer systems design & related services [3]	5415	117	119	1,298	1,325	101.7	107.7
Custom computer programming services	541511	53	55	537	586	43.3	48.0
Computer systems design services	541512	49	48	540	499	41.5	40.6
Management, scientific, & technical consulting services [3]	5416	152	142	1,015	870	72.1	63.0
Management consulting services	54161	117	108	830	703	60.6	51.9
Environmental consulting services	54162	9	10	69	72	3.8	4.3
Scientific research & development services	5417	18	16	688	634	61.8	59.8
Research & development in the physical engineering & life sciences	54171	15	14	631	594	57.6	57.1
Advertising & related services [3]	5418	40	41	446	479	25.3	27.5
Advertising agencies	54181	14	14	173	165	12.5	12.4
Direct mail advertising	54186	3	3	73	73	3.0	3.1
Other professional, scientific, & tech services	5419	74	72	600	620	21.1	22.6
Veterinary services	54194	28	29	294	302	8.7	9.2
Management of companies and enterprises	**55**	**51**	**52**	**3,121**	**2,887**	**292.7**	**273.3**
Administrative and support and waste management and remediation services	**56**	**385**	**394**	**9,984**	**10,225**	**299.9**	**313.9**
Administrative & support services [3]	561	363	372	9,628	9,857	284.2	297.0
Employment services	5613	44	54	5,131	5,231	143.3	153.0
Temporary help services	56132	30	34	2,901	2,875	65.5	68.5
Business support services [3]	5614	36	36	766	828	22.9	24.2
Telephone call centers	56142	5	5	386	429	9.6	9.2
Collection agencies	56144	5	5	141	151	4.7	4.9
Credit bureaus	56145	1	1	25	21	1.8	1.8
Travel arrangement & reservation services	5615	22	22	244	259	12.5	12.7
Travel agencies	56151	16	16	123	123	6.5	6.8
Investigation & security services	5616	25	26	778	832	20.0	21.3
Investigation, guard, & armored car services	56161	15	15	658	710	15.1	16.3
Security systems services	56162	10	10	120	122	4.9	5.0
Services to buildings & dwellings	5617	180	177	1,723	1,702	40.4	40.7
Waste management & remediation services	562	21	22	355	367	15.7	16.9
Waste collection	5621	10	10	185	195	8.1	8.7
Waste treatment & disposal	5622	3	3	57	50	2.8	2.6
Remediation & other waste mgmt services	5629	9	9	113	122	4.8	5.6
Accommodation & food services	**72**	**632**	**637**	**11,565**	**11,926**	**176.3**	**183.2**
Accommodation	721	64	63	1,908	1,976	46.2	48.0
Traveler accommodation	7211	54	54	1,856	1,926	44.9	46.8
Hotels (except casino hotels) & motels	72111	49	49	1,454	1,489	32.4	33.3
RV (recreational vehicle) parks & recreational camps	7212	7	7	40	40	1.1	1.1
Rooming & boarding houses	7213	2	2	12	11	0.2	0.2
Food services & drinking places	722	569	574	9,657	9,950	130.2	135.2
Full-service restaurants	7221	219	221	4,580	4,708	67.1	68.9
Limited-service eating places	7222	267	269	4,137	4,225	47.9	49.6
Special food services	7223	35	38	576	661	10.6	12.1
Drinking places (alcoholic beverages)	7224	47	45	365	356	4.6	4.6
Other services (except public administration)	**81**	**744**	**731**	**5,520**	**5,453**	**140.7**	**143.1**
Repair & maintenance [3]	811	226	217	1,323	1,272	43.8	41.8
Automotive repair & maintenance	8111	166	161	893	866	25.6	25.1
Personal & household goods repair & maintenance	8114	23	21	95	82	2.8	2.3
Personal & laundry services [3]	812	213	209	1,380	1,368	28.3	28.2
Personal care services	8121	113	113	617	637	10.7	11.4
Death care services	8122	21	21	137	136	4.2	4.2
Drycleaning & laundry services	8123	41	39	374	331	8.3	7.6
Religious/grantmaking/civic/professional [4]	813	306	304	2,817	2,813	68.6	73.1
Religious organizations	8131	180	180	1,691	1,699	30.5	31.7
Grantmaking & giving services	8132	16	17	147	192	6.9	9.6
Social advocacy organizations	8133	15	16	129	140	4.7	5.3
Civic & social organizations	8134	30	29	330	263	5.4	4.5
Business/professional/labor/political [4]	8139	64	62	520	519	21.1	22.0
Labor unions [4]	81393	16	15	173	173	5.0	5.2

[1] North American Industry Classification System, 2007; data for 2007 based on 2002 NAICS. See text, section 15.
[2] Includes employees on the payroll for the pay period including March 12. [3] Includes other kinds of business, not shown separately.
[4] And similar organizations.

Source: U.S. Census Bureau, "County Business Patterns," July 2010, <http://www.census.gov/econ/cbp/index.html>.

Table 1275. Employed Persons—Sex, Race, and Hispanic or Latino Origin by Industry: 2010

[15,253 represents 15,253,000. Civilian noninstitutional population 16 years and older. Based on the Current Population Survey; see text, Sections 1 and 13, and Appendix III. For information on employees in other sectors, see Tables 616 and 632]

Industry	2007 NAICS code [1]	Total employed (1,000)	Percent of total			
			Female	Black [2]	Asian [2]	Hispanic or Latino [3]
Professional and business services	(X)	15,253	41.3	8.7	5.7	14.5
Professional and technical services	54	9,115	43.2	5.6	7.8	7.1
Legal services	5411	1,592	54.8	5.8	3.0	6.9
Accounting, tax preparation, bookkeeping, & payroll services	5412	961	62.9	6.4	6.4	7.7
Architectural, engineering, and related services	5413	1,474	24.7	5.4	6.0	7.9
Specialized design services	5414	356	58.5	3.2	5.6	8.7
Computer systems design & related services	5415	1,905	26.4	5.3	17.3	5.1
Management, scientific, and technical consulting services	5416	1,177	42.6	6.1	5.2	5.6
Scientific research & development services	5417	536	43.5	6.7	12.0	8.4
Advertising and related services	5418	498	48.3	4.7	2.8	7.4
Other professional, scientific, and technical services [4]	5419	330	56.3	7.8	6.7	12.0
Veterinary services	54194	287	78.3	2.7	1.2	10.5
Management, administrative, and waste services . .	55–56	6,138	38.6	13.2	2.5	25.5
Management of companies and enterprises	55	74	48.7	8.2	7.1	8.0
Employment services	5613	913	52.2	18.2	3.1	21.1
Business support services	5614	736	61.8	13.7	2.4	12.4
Travel arrangement & reservation services	5615	263	63.3	8.4	7.4	12.7
Investigations & security services	5616	814	23.5	25.0	3.1	15.2
Services to buildings and dwellings [5]	5617	1,383	52.8	10.0	2.0	35.6
Landscaping services	56173	1,180	9.0	6.0	0.8	41.5
Other administrative and support services	5611,2,9	295	43.7	12.4	4.1	14.4
Waste management and remediation services	562	478	15.6	13.6	1.3	19.2
Accommodation and food services.	72	9,564	52.9	11.2	6.8	22.2
Accommodation.	721	1,419	56.2	13.8	9.0	22.9
Traveler accommodation	7211	1,309	56.9	14.7	9.5	24.4
Recreational vehicle parks and camps, and rooming and board houses.	7212,3	110	48.5	3.7	3.0	5.1
Food services and drinking places	722	8,146	52.4	10.7	6.4	22.0
Restaurants and other food services [6]	722	7,897	52.4	10.9	6.5	22.3
Drinking places, alcoholic beverages	7224	249	51.6	6.7	2.4	14.3
Other services	81	6,769	51.6	9.2	6.3	16.8
Other services (except private households)	81	6,102	47.3	9.3	6.6	14.3
Repair and maintenance	811	1,985	11.6	6.2	3.4	21.0
Automotive repair and maintenance [7]	8111	1,180	8.7	6.3	2.4	20.6
Car washes	811192	159	14.9	12.5	4.4	34.8
Electronic & precision equipment repair and maintenance	8112	167	16.7	4.6	6.6	14.3
Commercial and industrial machinery & equipment repair and maintenance.	8113	275	7.2	5.0	2.0	19.6
Personal and household goods repair and maintenance [8]	8114	199	27.6	3.5	7.0	18.8
Footwear and leather goods repair	81143	4	(Z)	(Z)	(Z)	(Z)
Personal and laundry services	812	2,278	72.5	10.6	12.5	13.9
Barber shops	812111	107	25.2	34.0	1.1	11.7
Beauty salons	812112	957	90.5	9.9	6.2	12.1
Nail salons and other personal care services	812113,81219	412	77.9	4.7	36.2	7.9
Drycleaning & laundry services.	8123	347	56.3	13.5	16.4	28.5
Funeral homes, cemeteries, and crematories	8122	134	37.4	10.1	1.6	7.7
Other personal services	8129	322	60.0	9.5	4.7	14.3
Membership associations and organizations.	813	1,839	54.7	11.0	2.7	7.8
Religious organizations	8131	1,034	48.3	10.7	3.1	6.5
Civic, social, advocacy organizations, grantmaking & giving services	8132,3,4	583	64.8	13.7	2.8	9.1
Business, professional, political, and similar organizations [9].	8139	160	65.7	3.6	1.2	8.3
Labor unions	81393	61	37.8	9.8	0.7	14.9
Private households	814	667	90.9	8.7	3.3	39.5

X Not applicable. Z Base less than 50,000. [1] Based on the North American Industry Classification System, 2007; see Section 15. [2] The Current Population Survey (CPS) allows respondents to choose more than one race. Data represents persons who selected this race group only and exclude persons reporting more than one race. See also comments on race in text for Section 1. [3] Persons of Hispanic or Latino ethnicity may be any race. [4] Excludes NAICS 54194 (veterinary services). [5] Excludes NAICS 56173 (landscaping services). [6] Excludes NAICS 7224 (drinking places, alcoholic beverages). [7] Excludes NAICS 811192 (car washes). [8] Excludes NAICS 81143 (footwear and leather goods repair). [9] Excludes NAICS 81393 (labor unions).

Source: U.S. Bureau of Labor Statistics, "Employment and Earnings Online," <http://www.bls.gov/opub/ee/home.htm> and <http://www.bls.gov/cps/home.htm>.

U.S. Census Bureau, Statistical Abstract of the United States: 2012

Table 1276. Selected Service-Related Industries—Establishments, Employees, and Annual Payroll by State: 2008

[8,033 represents 8,033,000. Covers establishments with paid employees. Excludes most government employees, railroad employees, and self-employed persons. For statement on methodology, see Appendix III]

State	Professional, scientific, and technical services (NAICS 54) [1]			Administrative and support and waste management and remediation services (NAICS 56) [1]			Accommodation and food services (NAICS 72) [1]		
	Establish-ments	Employ-ees [2] (1,000)	Annual payroll (mil. dol.)	Establish-ments	Employ-ees [2] (1,000)	Annual payroll (mil. dol.)	Establish-ments	Employ-ees [2] (1,000)	Annual payroll (mil. dol.)
United States	848,309	8,033	539,067	393,538	10,225	313,933	636,586	11,926	183,228
Alabama	9,425	96	5,430	4,213	132	3,089	8,080	160	1,899
Alaska	1,860	13	868	1,084	22	1,028	2,013	25	573
Arizona	16,583	127	7,275	8,535	253	8,519	11,603	260	3,960
Arkansas	5,788	34	1,511	2,502	59	1,382	5,178	94	1,075
California..........	112,737	1,189	87,854	43,355	1,131	37,253	76,110	1,409	24,265
Colorado	23,261	165	11,219	8,565	207	7,728	12,230	238	3,742
Connecticut	9,806	100	7,410	5,494	104	3,725	7,930	138	2,500
Delaware	2,406	24	1,796	1,400	30	993	1,873	34	519
District of Columbia ...	4,607	89	9,815	1,101	38	1,366	2,219	54	1,374
Florida	68,559	438	25,464	32,848	1,394	43,641	35,110	769	12,131
Georgia	27,908	229	13,857	12,495	348	9,873	18,770	371	5,022
Hawaii	3,297	24	1,316	1,890	48	1,304	3,539	100	2,310
Idaho	4,243	32	1,571	2,221	38	918	3,507	57	699
Illinois............	38,988	375	27,247	17,140	523	14,473	26,580	479	7,389
Indiana............	12,997	103	5,210	7,419	171	4,626	12,770	260	3,347
Iowa..............	6,263	47	2,132	3,624	76	1,876	6,903	115	1,372
Kansas............	7,133	57	2,904	3,587	74	2,097	5,843	108	1,272
Kentucky	8,184	66	2,894	4,039	97	2,101	7,366	157	1,914
Louisiana	11,354	88	4,658	4,491	111	3,195	8,216	186	2,790
Maine.............	3,497	23	1,195	1,949	23	654	3,934	48	807
Maryland	19,317	237	17,440	8,151	194	6,508	10,879	202	3,190
Massachusetts.......	21,721	259	22,830	9,845	204	7,667	16,062	264	4,664
Michigan	22,341	256	16,397	12,277	306	8,999	19,623	340	4,453
Minnesota	16,554	147	8,563	7,199	141	4,429	11,183	222	3,134
Mississippi	4,761	32	1,420	2,237	51	1,118	4,864	123	1,899
Missouri...........	13,516	144	8,327	7,497	164	4,419	12,215	247	3,319
Montana...........	3,545	18	753	1,699	20	472	3,349	47	610
Nebraska	4,245	50	2,312	2,611	60	1,749	4,257	70	795
Nevada	7,982	58	3,356	4,221	104	2,797	5,776	312	8,466
New Hampshire......	3,992	30	1,697	2,252	44	1,619	3,508	56	848
New Jersey	30,811	331	24,865	13,731	294	9,617	19,421	291	5,463
New Mexico........	4,812	43	2,697	1,992	44	1,131	4,060	81	1,148
New York	58,518	583	45,524	25,251	519	20,934	44,492	626	12,234
North Carolina.......	22,442	190	11,581	11,667	282	7,666	18,494	363	4,747
North Dakota	1,508	11	477	898	13	286	1,838	32	380
Ohio..............	24,790	236	13,400	14,083	346	9,164	23,525	435	5,301
Oklahoma	9,210	69	3,380	4,388	102	2,711	6,988	134	1,582
Oregon............	11,634	89	5,312	5,435	92	2,450	10,353	156	2,322
Pennsylvania........	29,723	314	21,131	15,026	307	8,677	27,264	432	6,025
Rhode Island	3,056	24	1,581	1,747	25	705	2,961	44	665
South Carolina.......	9,732	80	4,167	5,642	132	3,310	9,372	193	2,499
South Dakota.......	1,782	11	413	1,024	13	289	2,385	37	463
Tennessee..........	11,273	109	5,528	6,711	209	5,639	11,707	247	3,195
Texas.............	58,176	602	41,360	25,854	945	27,933	43,907	909	12,766
Utah..............	8,435	72	3,422	3,964	120	3,203	4,692	97	1,265
Vermont...........	2,149	20	997	1,081	9	223	1,943	31	470
Virginia............	27,539	392	30,645	10,629	254	9,098	15,982	312	4,532
Washington	19,659	164	11,098	9,129	173	6,782	16,080	244	3,942
West Virginia	2,920	29	954	1,451	32	774	3,649	63	758
Wisconsin	11,322	103	5,391	6,960	140	3,534	14,251	227	2,664
Wyoming	1,948	9	425	934	7	193	1,732	29	469

[1] North American Industry Classification System, 2007. See text, section 15. [2] For employees on the payroll for the pay period including March 12.

Source: U.S. Census Bureau, "County Business Patterns," July 2010, <http://www.census.gov/econ/cbp/index.html>.

Table 1277. Professional, Scientific, and Technical Services—Estimated Revenue: 2004 to 2009

[In millions of dollars (963,369 represents $963,369,000,000). For taxable employer firms. Estimates have been adjusted to the results of the 2007 Economic Census. Based on the Service Annual Survey and administrative data; see Appendix III]

Kind of business	2002 NAICS code [1]	2004	2005	2006	2007	2008	2009
Professional, scientific, and technical services (except notaries)	**54**	**963,369**	**1,045,367**	**1,123,407**	**1,227,445**	**1,293,177**	**1,222,629**
Legal services (except notaries)	5411	204,833	213,942	224,842	236,689	241,612	234,113
Offices of lawyers	54111	193,499	201,717	212,524	225,060	229,871	223,006
Other legal services	54119	11,334	12,225	12,318	11,629	11,741	11,107
Accounting, tax preparation, bookkeeping and payroll services	5412	90,665	97,358	103,787	114,110	119,645	118,013
Offices of certified public accountants	541211	51,809	56,285	60,244	66,588	69,233	68,974
Tax preparation services	541213	4,462	4,663	4,890	5,251	5,503	5,710
Payroll services	541214	23,109	24,336	25,969	28,916	30,493	28,617
Other accounting services	541219	11,285	12,074	12,684	13,355	14,416	14,712
Architectural, engineering, & related services	5413	189,110	213,247	232,296	254,201	268,111	235,426
Architectural services	54131	27,688	30,186	32,587	37,150	37,759	29,887
Landscape architectural services	54132	3,423	3,711	4,085	4,365	4,365	3,406
Engineering services	54133	139,452	159,245	173,861	187,532	200,123	178,810
Testing laboratories	54138	9,416	9,605	10,093	12,387	13,469	12,701
Other related services	54134,5,6,7	9,131	10,500	11,670	12,767	12,395	10,622
Specialized design services	5414	17,914	18,761	19,548	20,554	20,009	16,231
Interior design services	54141	7,560	8,040	8,899	9,799	9,282	6,783
Graphic design services	54143	7,953	8,328	8,342	8,281	8,340	7,215
All other design services	54142,9	2,401	2,393	2,307	2,474	2,387	2,233
Computer systems design and services	5415	179,229	196,050	213,359	244,389	265,719	259,200
Custom computer programming services	541511	60,279	67,163	72,232	84,896	92,246	89,766
Computer systems design services	541512	80,425	89,144	98,047	110,159	116,817	110,053
Computer facilities management services	541513	24,363	24,473	26,368	30,133	35,778	38,153
Other computer-related services	541519	14,162	15,270	16,712	19,201	20,878	21,228
Management, scientific, and technical consulting services	5416	117,234	129,104	135,783	146,814	154,006	141,597
Management consulting services	54161	98,900	109,069	114,349	122,380	128,011	115,540
Environmental consulting services	54162	8,169	8,322	9,225	10,423	11,125	10,856
Other scientific and technical consulting services	54169	10,165	11,713	12,209	14,011	14,870	15,201
Scientific research and development services	5417	51,620	55,881	62,355	66,657	74,830	76,609
Research and development in physical, engineering and life sciences	54171	49,748	54,029	60,776	65,047	73,132	74,875
Research and development in social sciences and humanities	54172	1,872	1,852	1,579	1,610	1,698	1,734
Advertising and related services	5418	65,931	71,194	79,107	87,434	88,878	80,799
Advertising agencies	54181	24,570	25,425	27,879	30,666	31,886	29,843
Public relations agencies	54182	6,951	7,542	8,630	9,279	9,174	8,380
Media buying agencies	54183	2,078	2,689	3,696	4,606	4,955	4,327
Media representatives	54184	2,522	2,892	3,231	3,577	3,691	3,316
Display advertising	54185	5,933	7,015	7,842	9,111	9,142	7,595
Direct mail advertising	54186	11,491	12,342	12,464	12,360	11,514	9,996
All other advertising	54187,9	12,386	13,289	15,365	17,835	18,516	17,342
Other professional, scientific, and technical services	5419	46,833	49,830	52,330	56,597	60,367	60,641
Marketing research and public opinion polling	54191	12,417	13,186	14,337	15,493	16,223	15,277
Photographic services	54192	6,647	6,735	6,688	6,767	7,016	6,417
Photography studios, portrait	541921	4,808	4,904	4,856	5,055	5,139	4,976
Commercial photography	541922	1,839	1,831	1,832	1,712	1,877	1,441
Translation and interpretation services	54193	1,231	1,354	1,505	1,895	2,122	(S)
Veterinary services	54194	19,145	20,703	22,372	24,568	25,794	25,642
All other professional, scientific, and technical services	54199	7,393	7,852	7,428	7,874	9,212	10,216

S Data did not meet publication standards. [1] Based on the North American Industry Classification System, 2002; see Section 15.

Source: U.S. Census Bureau, "Service Annual Survey 2009: Professional, Scientific, and Technical Sector Services," January 2011, <http://www.census.gov/services/index.html>.

Table 1278. Selected Service Industries—E-Commerce Revenue: 2008 and 2009

[149,668 represents $149,668,000,000. Includes data only for businesses with paid employees, except for accommodation and food services, which also includes businesses with and without paid employees. Except as noted, based on the Service Annual Survey]

Kind of business	2002 NAICS code [1]	E-commerce revenue (mil. dol.) 2008	E-commerce revenue (mil. dol.) 2009	E-commerce as percent of total revenue, 2009	E-commerce revenue, percent distribution, 2009
Selected service industries, total	(X)	**149,668**	**153,007**	**2.3**	**100.0**
Selected transportation and warehousing [2]	(X)	7,945	6,912	2.5	2.8
Truck transportation	484	7,736	6,711	3.7	2.8
Couriers and messengers	492	(S)	107	0.2	(Z)
Warehousing and storage	493	(S)	(S)	(S)	(S)
Information.	51	50,975	53,791	5.0	22.1
Publishing industries	511	19,427	21,180	8.0	8.7
Online information services.	51811	(S)	7,062	24.3	2.9
Selected finance [3]	(X)	14,022	12,635	2.7	5.2
Securities and commodity contracts intermediation and brokerage	5231	13,556	12,040	4.2	4.9
Rental and leasing services	532	8,484	9,593	8.7	3.9
Selected professional, scientific, and technical services [4]	54	21,748	23,608	1.9	9.7
Computer systems design and related services	5415	5,130	5,089	2.0	2.1
Administrative and support and waste management and remediation services	56	17,140	17,351	2.9	7.1
Travel arrangements and reservation services.	5615	8,144	7,358	22.4	3.0
Health care and social assistance services.	62	1,023	1,428	0.1	0.6
Arts, entertainment, and recreation services.	71	4,203	4,204	2.2	1.7
Accommodation and food services [5]	72	16,712	15,876	2.6	6.5
Selected other services [6].	81	7,416	7,609	2.1	3.1
Repair and maintenance	811	1,039	1,030	0.8	0.4
Religious, grantmaking, civic, professional, and similar organizations	813	4,889	4,822	3.1	2.0

X Not applicable. S Data do not meet publication standards. Z Less than 0.05. [1] North American Industry Classification System (NAICS), 2002; see text Section 15. [2] Excludes NAICS 481 (air transportation), 482 (rail transportation), 483 (water transportation), 485 (transit and ground passenger transportation), 486 (pipeline transportation), 487 (scenic and sightseeing transportation), 488 (support activities for transportation) and 491 (postal service). [3] Excludes NAICS 521 (monetary authorities-central bank), 522 (credit intermediation and related activities), 5232 (securities and commodity exchanges), NAICS 52391 (miscellaneous intermediation), 52399 (all other financial investment activities), 524 (insurance carriers and related activities) and 525 (funds and trusts). [4] Excludes NAICS 54112 (offices of notaries). [5] Based on 2008 Annual Retail Trade Survey. [6] Excludes NAICS 81311 (religious organizations), 81393 (labor and similar organizations), 81394 (political organizations) and 814 (private households).

Source: U.S. Census Bureau, "E-Stats," <http://www.census.gov/econ/estats/>.

Table 1279. Forecast Summary—Media Supplier Advertising Revenues: 2000 to 2010

[In millions of dollars (177,500 represents $177,500,000,000). See source for definitions of types of advertising]

Media supplier	2000	2004	2005	2006	2007	2008	2009	2010
Total supplier ad revenue	**177,500**	**188,942**	**196,668**	**204,889**	**205,847**	**194,328**	**163,184**	**170,456**
Total [1]	**175,535**	**186,979**	**196,398**	**202,701**	**205,523**	**191,951**	**162,744**	**167,936**
Direct.	31,108	39,688	42,477	45,882	48,680	48,190	42,444	42,484
Direct mail	18,250	22,559	23,085	24,478	24,890	23,459	19,853	20,604
Direct online [2]	560	4,440	6,371	8,785	11,355	13,554	13,656	15,022
Directories [3]	12,299	12,689	13,021	12,619	12,435	11,177	8,934	6,858
National	53,494	55,699	59,200	61,858	64,498	63,132	56,797	61,009
National television [3, 4]	25,574	31,452	33,231	33,712	34,820	35,141	33,723	36,210
Magazines [3]	19,025	17,961	19,351	20,373	20,975	19,533	15,554	15,623
National digital/online [5]	5,665	3,541	3,931	5,067	6,098	6,057	5,549	7,144
Network and satellite radio	1,065	1,175	1,161	1,178	1,226	1,220	1,100	1,145
National newspapers [3].	2,165	1,570	1,527	1,527	1,379	1,180	873	887
Local	90,933	91,591	94,721	94,961	92,345	80,630	63,504	64,443
Local newspapers [3]	46,506	45,133	45,880	45,074	40,830	33,559	23,949	21,909
Local TV [3, 6]	18,530	20,047	21,281	21,023	22,001	19,706	16,995	18,670
Local radio [3]	18,819	18,932	19,018	19,031	18,476	16,536	13,203	13,847
Emerging outdoor	195	377	425	545	741	914	920	1,146
Other outdoor	5,040	5,457	5,876	6,260	6,542	6,077	4,980	4,997
Local digital/online [5].	1,843	1,645	2,241	3,028	3,755	3,837	3,456	3,874
Political [7]	1,180	1,259	270	1,538	324	1,777	439	2,033
Olympics [8]	785	704	–	650	–	600	–	488

– Represents zero. [1] Excludes political and olympic revenue. [2] Includes paid search, lead generation and Internet yellow pages. [3] Excludes Internet-based advertising revenues. [4] Includes English and Spanish-language network TV, national cable and national syndication. Excludes incremental olympic revenues. [5] Includes rich/online video, Internet classifieds, e-mail, digital display and mobile. [6] Includes local broadcast and local cable TV. Excludes local political advertising revenues. [7] Total political advertising revenue on local broadcast and local cable TV. [8] Incremental advertising revenue from olympics on network TV.

Source: MAGNAGLOBAL, New York, NY, (copyright), <http://www.magnaglobal.com>.

Table 1280. Administrative and Support and Waste Management and Remediation Services—Estimated Revenue: 2004 to 2009

[In millions of dollars (494,684 represents $494,684,000,000). Taxable employer firms. For taxable and tax-exempt employer firms. Estimates have been adjusted to results of the 2007 Economic Census. Based on the Service Annual Survey and administrative data; see Appendix III]

Kind of business	2002 NAICS code [1]	2004	2005	2006	2007	2008	2009
Administrative and support and waste management and remediation services	**56**	**494,684**	**542,574**	**585,113**	**623,761**	**639,287**	**592,846**
Administrative and support services	561	434,472	477,336	513,280	548,574	560,435	520,340
Office administrative services	56111	35,039	38,180	38,699	39,295	41,036	42,417
Facilities support services	56121	15,195	18,246	21,746	25,735	28,994	29,280
Employment services	5613	153,300	171,183	188,935	202,682	204,142	183,069
Employment placement agencies	56131	7,756	8,788	10,115	11,786	12,418	10,429
Temporary help services	56132	81,286	90,654	98,710	105,691	103,640	85,196
Professional employer organizations	56133	64,258	71,741	80,110	85,205	88,084	87,444
Business support services	5614	50,718	54,836	59,723	62,297	62,813	59,599
Document preparation services	56141	2,643	2,881	3,193	3,404	3,286	2,865
Telephone call centers	56142	14,305	15,138	16,370	16,955	17,156	16,753
Telephone answering services	561421	1,827	1,988	1,962	2,289	2,327	2,260
Telemarketing bureaus	561422	12,478	13,150	14,408	14,666	14,829	14,493
Business service centers	56143	9,499	9,970	9,676	10,368	10,335	9,183
Private mail centers	561431	2,141	2,022	2,108	2,149	2,147	1,958
Other business service centers (including copy shops)	561439	7,358	7,948	7,568	8,219	8,188	7,225
Collection agencies	56144	10,933	11,557	11,704	12,245	11,986	11,139
Credit bureaus	56145	5,464	6,246	8,063	8,191	7,860	7,759
Other business support services	56149	7,874	9,044	10,717	11,134	12,190	11,900
Repossession services	561491	551	608	643	717	806	884
Court reporting and stenotype services	561492	1,859	1,953	2,175	2,248	2,210	2,210
All other business support services	561499	5,464	6,483	7,899	8,169	9,174	8,806
Travel arrangement and reservation services	5615	29,420	30,974	33,332	37,112	37,026	32,907
Travel agencies	56151	11,760	12,989	14,827	17,289	16,808	14,237
Tour operators	56152	3,640	3,811	3,842	4,397	4,584	4,448
Other travel arrangement and reservation services. . . .	56159	14,020	14,174	14,663	15,426	15,634	14,222
Convention and visitors bureaus	561591	1,208	1,239	1,302	1,503	1,559	1,482
All other travel arrangement and reservation services	561599	12,812	12,935	13,361	13,923	14,075	12,740
Investigation and security services	5616	34,022	37,529	38,140	40,904	42,944	41,912
Investigation, guard, and armored car services	56161	21,260	23,578	23,682	24,911	25,683	25,143
Investigation services	561611	3,287	3,575	3,461	3,887	3,700	3,630
Security guards and patrol services	561612	15,840	17,836	17,980	18,799	19,618	19,128
Armored car services	561613	2,133	2,167	2,241	2,225	2,365	2,385
Security systems services	56162	12,762	13,951	14,458	15,993	17,261	16,769
Security systems services (except locksmiths)	561621	11,384	12,474	12,853	14,360	15,624	15,312
Locksmiths	561622	1,378	1,477	1,605	1,633	1,637	1,457
Services to buildings and dwellings	5617	84,583	90,859	96,432	103,364	105,358	97,832
Exterminating and pest control services	56171	7,645	8,100	8,473	8,693	8,932	9,114
Janitorial services	56172	29,041	29,779	30,116	33,021	34,887	32,372
Landscaping services	56173	41,319	45,856	50,398	53,910	53,200	48,328
Carpet and upholstery cleaning services	56174	2,619	2,913	2,920	2,962	3,106	2,884
Other services to buildings and dwellings	56179	3,959	4,211	4,525	4,778	5,233	5,134
Other support services	5619	32,195	35,529	36,273	37,185	38,122	33,324
Packaging and labeling services	56191	4,613	5,097	5,050	5,050	5,341	4,526
Convention and trade show organizers	56192	9,455	10,625	11,264	11,238	11,998	9,618
All other support services	56199	18,127	19,807	19,959	20,897	20,783	19,180
Waste management and remediation services	562	60,212	65,238	71,833	75,187	78,852	72,506
Waste collection	5621	33,108	34,936	38,857	40,462	43,276	40,028
Solid waste collection	562111	30,913	32,534	35,910	36,999	39,495	36,797
Hazardous waste collection	562112	1,548	1,547	1,728	1,857	1,986	1,824
Other waste collection	562119	647	855	1,219	1,606	1,795	1,407
Waste treatment and disposal	5622	11,742	13,104	14,096	14,264	14,496	13,172
Hazardous waste treatment and disposal	562211	3,773	4,532	5,138	5,864	5,972	5,945
Solid waste landfill	562212	5,800	5,858	5,902	5,648	5,695	4,951
Solid waste combustors and incinerators	562213	1,578	2,051	2,348	2,081	2,123	1,729
Other nonhazardous waste treatment and disposal . . .	562219	591	663	708	671	706	547
Remediation and other waste management services . . .	5629	15,362	17,198	18,880	20,461	21,080	19,306
Remediation services	56291	9,172	10,776	11,950	12,424	12,544	12,020
Materials recovery facility	56292	3,021	2,984	3,264	4,072	4,636	3,679
All other waste management services	56299	3,169	3,438	3,666	3,965	3,900	3,607
Septic tank and related services	562991	2,072	2,277	2,428	2,553	2,573	2,403
All other miscellaneous waste management services	562998	1,097	1,161	1,238	1,412	1,327	1,204

[1] North American Industry Classification System, 2002; see text, Section 15.

Source: U.S. Census Bureau, "Service Annual Survey 2009: Administrative and Support and Waste Management and Remediation Sector Services," January 2011, <http://www.census.gov/services/index.html>.

Table 1281. Estimated Accommodation and Food Services Sales by Kind of Business: 2000 to 2009

[In millions of dollars (443,558 represents $443,558,000,000). Estimates are based on data from the Annual Retail Trade Survey and administrative records and have been adjusted to the preliminary results of the 2007 Economic Census]

Kind of business	2007 NAICS code [1]	2000	2004	2005	2006	2007	2008	2009
Accommodation and food services, total	**72**	**443,558**	**525,834**	**560,037**	**597,771**	**629,864**	**640,699**	**616,268**
Accommodation	721	138,181	151,225	162,676	173,734	183,983	184,131	163,016
Traveler accommodation	7211	133,582	146,270	157,494	168,070	178,040	178,044	156,992
RV parks and recreational camps	7212	3,608	3,955	4,130	4,532	4,760	4,885	4,781
Rooming and boarding houses	7213	991	1,000	1,052	1,132	1,183	1,202	1,243
Food services and drinking places [2]	722	305,377	374,609	397,361	424,037	445,881	456,568	453,252
Full service restaurants	7221	134,204	165,871	174,864	186,845	196,262	196,929	195,349
Limited service eating places	7222	127,879	158,632	169,033	178,523	186,404	194,629	195,155
Drinking places	7224	15,415	17,675	18,120	19,426	19,984	19,973	20,011

[1] North American Industry Classification System, 2007; see text, Section 15. [2] Includes other kinds of business not shown separately.

Source: U.S. Census Bureau, "Annual Accommodation and Food Services—2009," <http://www.census.gov/retail/>.

Table 1282. Lodging Industry Summary: 1990 to 2009

Year	Average occupancy rate (percent)	Average room rate (dol.)	Room size of property	2009		Item	2009	
				Establish-ments	Rooms (mil.)		Business traveler	Leisure traveler
1990	63.3	57.96	Total	50,800	4.8	Typical night:		
1995	65.5	66.65				Made reservations		
2000	63.7	85.89	Percent:			(percent)	91	87
2005	63.1	90.88	Under 75 rooms	55.6	25.5	Amount paid (dol.)	$123.00	$105.00
2006	63.3	97.78	75–149 rooms	32.6	36.6	Length of stay:		
2007	63.1	103.87	150–299 rooms	8.6	18.4	One night:	36	48
2008	60.4	106.84	300–500 rooms	2.2	8.8	Two nights	22	25
2009	54.7	97.85	Over 500 rooms	1.0	10.7	Three or more	42	27

Source: American Hotel & Lodging Association, Washington, DC Lodging Industry Profile, annual (copyright). See also <http://www.ahla.com>.

Table 1283. Commercial and Noncommercial Groups—Food and Drink Establishments and Sales: 1990 to 2011

[In millions of dollars (238,149 represents $238,149,000,000). Excludes military. Data refer to sales to consumers of food and alcoholic beverages. Sales are estimated. For details, see source]

Type of group	Establish-ments, 2008	Sales (mil. dol.)						
		1990	1995	2000	2005	2009	2010	2011 [1]
Total	**957,354**	**238,149**	**294,631**	**377,652**	**486,494**	**567,787**	**581,065**	**601,816**
Commercial restaurant services [2,3]	753,197	211,606	265,910	345,345	445,078	519,845	531,732	550,826
Eating places [2]	507,507	155,552	198,293	259,743	329,598	383,960	391,423	404,491
Full-service restaurants	222,070	77,811	96,396	133,834	165,170	185,918	188,706	194,556
Limited-service restaurants [4]	213,835	[5] 69,798	[5] 92,901	107,147	136,903	159,010	162,350	167,707
Snack and nonalcoholic beverage bars	53,678	(5)	(5)	12,867	17,150	24,529	25,309	26,413
Bars and taverns [6]	46,624	9,533	9,948	12,412	15,002	17,408	17,722	18,289
Managed services [2]	23,250	14,149	18,186	24,841	32,030	39,296	40,331	42,081
Manufacturing and industrial plants	(NA)	3,856	4,814	6,223	6,570	6,686	6,696	6,907
Colleges and universities	(NA)	2,788	3,989	5,879	9,283	12,912	13,097	13,700
Lodging places	11,620	13,568	15,561	19,438	23,854	25,763	27,167	28,698
Retail hosts [2,7]	132,792	9,513	12,589	14,869	22,502	29,481	30,774	32,051
Department store restaurants	2,222	876	1,038	903	490	(NA)	(NA)	(NA)
Grocery store restaurants [7]	54,397	5,432	6,624	7,116	12,032	(NA)	(NA)	(NA)
Gasoline service stations	59,087	1,718	2,520	4,693	6,137	(NA)	(NA)	(NA)
Recreation and sports	24,942	2,871	3,866	4,772	11,397	12,212	12,679	13,249
Noncommercial restaurant services [2]	204,157	26,543	28,722	32,307	41,416	47,942	49,333	50,990
Employee restaurant services	3,003	1,864	1,364	986	548	417	406	417
Industrial, commercial organizations	765	1,603	1,129	717	260	(NA)	(NA)	(NA)
Educational restaurant services	106,224	7,671	9,059	9,977	11,007	12,180	12,787	13,125
Elementary and secondary schools	101,957	3,700	4,533	5,039	5,320	6,011	6,243	6,423
Hospitals	5,799	8,968	9,219	9,982	12,332	14,535	15,611	16,251
Miscellaneous	52,448	2,892	3,673	4,898	9,703	10,522	11,167	11,449
Clubs	29,246	1,993	2,278	3,164	7,555	8,480	9,000	9,212

NA Not available. [1] Projection. [2] Includes other types of groups, not shown separately. [3] Data for establishments with payroll. [4] Fast-food restaurants. [5] Snack and nonalcoholic beverage bars included in limited service restaurants, prior to 1997. [6] For establishments serving food. [7] Includes a portion of delicatessen sales in grocery stores.

Source: National Restaurant Association, *Restaurant Numbers: 25 Year History, 1970–1995*, Washington, DC, 1998; *Restaurant Industry in Review*, annual; and *National Restaurant Association 2011 Restaurant Industry Forecast*, December 2010, (copyright).

Table 1284. Other Services—Estimated Revenue for Employer Firms by Kind of Business: 2006 to 2009

[In millions of dollars (375,355 represents $375,355,000,000). For employer firms. Estimates have been adjusted to the results of the 2007 Economic Census. Based on the Service Annual Survey; see Appendix III]

Kind of business	2002 NAICS code [1]	2006	2007	2008	2009
Other services [2]	**81**	**375,355**	**405,282**	**384,813**	**364,372**
Repair and maintenance [3]	811	134,143	137,732	136,692	127,383
Automotive repair and maintenance	8111	85,050	85,887	84,428	79,487
Automotive mechanical and electrical repair and maintenance	81111	42,972	43,555	42,381	40,036
General automotive repair	811111	36,911	37,722	36,845	34,636
Automotive body, paint, interior, and glass repair	81112	29,736	30,006	29,933	27,711
Automotive body, paint, and interior repair and maintenance	811121	25,824	26,413	26,151	24,443
Other automotive repair and maintenance	81119	12,342	12,326	12,114	11,740
Electronic and precision equipment repair and maintenance	8112	18,554	19,327	18,816	18,803
Commercial and industrial machinery and equipment (except automotive and electronic) repair and maintenance	8113	23,663	25,962	26,794	23,041
Personal and household goods repair and maintenance	8114	6,876	6,556	6,654	6,052
Home and garden equipment and appliance repair and maintenance	81141	2,789	2,595	2,615	2,488
Personal and laundry services [3]	812	79,890	82,105	83,749	81,618
Personal care services	8121	25,092	26,304	27,277	26,887
Hair, nail, and skin care services	81211	20,150	20,903	21,391	21,170
Barber shops	812111	527	568	593	596
Beauty salons	812112	18,411	19,010	19,231	18,913
Nail salons	812113	1,212	1,325	1,567	1,661
Other personal care services	81219	4,942	5,401	5,886	5,717
Death care services	8122	15,309	15,293	15,487	15,194
Funeral homes and funeral services	81221	11,909	11,943	12,384	12,214
Cemeteries and crematories	81222	3,400	3,350	3,103	2,980
Drycleaning and laundry services	8123	22,769	23,234	23,056	22,232
Coin-operated laundries and drycleaners	81231	3,259	3,354	3,340	3,300
Drycleaning and laundry services (except coin-operated)	81232	7,925	8,086	8,187	7,929
Linen and uniform supply	81233	11,585	11,794	11,529	11,003
Pet care (except veterinary) services	81291	2,181	2,346	2,505	2,551
Photofinishing	81292	2,027	2,025	1,964	1,912
Parking lots and garages	81293	8,000	8,276	8,510	8,491
All other personal services	81299	4,512	4,627	4,950	4,351
Religious, grantmaking, civic, professional, and similar organizations (except religious, labor, and political organizations) [4]	813	161,322	185,445	164,372	155,371
Grantmaking and giving services	8132	74,987	93,275	70,486	60,644
Social advocacy organizations	8133	17,680	19,729	21,130	21,218
Civic and social organizations	8134	15,073	15,444	15,227	15,071
Business, professional, and other organizations (except labor and political organizations)	8139	53,582	56,997	57,529	58,438

[1] Based on the North American Industry Classification System, 2002; see Section 15. [2] Except public administration, religious, labor, and political organizations, and private households. [3] For taxable firms only. [4] For tax-exempt firms only.

Source: U.S. Census Bureau, "Service Annual Survey 2009: Other Sector Services," January 2011, <http://www.census.gov/services/index.html>.

Table 1285. National Nonprofit Associations—Number by Type: 1980 to 2010

[Data compiled during last few months of year previous to year shown and the beginning months of year shown]

Type	1980	1990	2000	2004	2005	2006	2007 [1]	2008	2009	2010
Total	**14,726**	**22,289**	**21,840**	**22,659**	**22,720**	**23,772**	**25,048**	**25,176**	**24,100**	**23,983**
Trade, business, commercial	3,118	3,918	3,880	3,812	3,789	3,942	4,072	4,003	3,840	3,761
Agriculture and environment	677	940	1,103	1,140	1,170	1,286	1,353	1,439	1,365	1,442
Legal, governmental, public admin., military	529	792	790	839	868	887	938	951	927	913
Scientific, engineering, technical	1,039	1,417	1,302	1,354	1,354	1,396	1,505	1,588	1,549	1,563
Educational	[2]2,376	1,291	1,297	1,313	1,318	1,365	1,471	1,530	1,462	1,444
Cultural	([2])	1,886	1,786	1,735	1,733	1,782	1,881	1,896	1,761	1,717
Social welfare	994	1,705	1,829	1,972	2,072	2,218	2,307	2,582	2,531	2,673
Health, medical	1,413	2,227	2,495	2,921	2,982	3,089	3,383	3,552	3,460	3,481
Public affairs	1,068	2,249	1,776	1,881	1,854	1,938	1,951	1,842	1,769	1,734
Fraternal, nationality, ethnic	435	573	525	547	550	567	580	523	482	461
Religious	797	1,172	1,123	1,157	1,147	1,162	1,204	1,146	1,101	1,056
Veteran, hereditary, patriotic	208	462	835	803	774	790	774	645	602	585
Hobby, avocational	910	1,475	1,330	1,449	1,433	1,525	1,615	1,511	1,421	1,374
Athletic sports	504	840	717	755	762	863	960	1,008	972	946
Labor unions	235	253	232	213	208	209	227	212	195	188
Chambers of Commerce [3]	105	168	143	136	135	137	169	162	147	142
Greek and non-Greek letter societies	318	340	296	305	349	302	335	325	309	305
Fan clubs	(NA)	581	381	327	314	314	323	261	207	198

NA Not available. [1] The increase in the number of associations comes from the increase in newly discovered and established associations. [2] Data for cultural associations included with educational associations. [3] National and binational. Includes trade and tourism organizations.

Source: Gale, Cengage Learning, Farmington Hills, MI, compiled from *Encyclopedia of Associations*, annual (copyright).

This section presents data on the flow of goods, services, and capital between the United States and other countries; changes in official reserve assets of the United States; international investments; and foreign assistance programs.

The Bureau of Economic Analysis publishes current figures on U.S. international transactions and the U.S. international investment position in its monthly Survey of *Current Business. Statistics* for the foreign aid programs are presented by the Agency for International Development (AID) in its annual U.S. *Overseas Loans and Grants and Assistance from International Organizations.*

The principal source of merchandise import and export data is the U.S. Census Bureau. Current data are presented monthly in *U.S. International Trade in Goods and Services report Series FT 900.* The *Guide to Foreign Trade Statistics*, found on the Census Bureau Web site at <http://www.census.gov /foreign-trade/guide/index.html>, lists the Census Bureau's monthly and annual products and services in this field. In addition, the International Trade Administration and the Bureau of Economic Analysis present summary as well as selected commodity and country data for U.S. foreign trade on their Web sites: <http://ita.doc.gov/td/industry /otea/> and <http://www.bea.gov /international/index>, respectively. The merchandise trade data published by the Bureau of Economic Analysis in the *Survey of Current Business* and on the Web include balance of payments adjustments to the Census Bureau data. The U.S. Treasury Department's *Monthly Treasury Statement of Receipts and Outlays of the United States Government* contains information on import duties. The International Trade Commission, U.S. Department of Agriculture (agricultural products), U.S. Department of Energy (mineral fuels, like petroleum and coal), and the U.S. Geological Survey (minerals)

release various reports and specialized products on U.S. trade.

International accounts—
The international transactions tables (Tables 1286 to 1288) show, for given time periods, the transfer of goods, services, grants, and financial assets and liabilities between the United States and the rest of the world. The international investment position table (Table 1289) presents, for specific dates, the value of U.S. investments abroad and of foreign investments in the United States. The movement of foreign and U.S. capital as presented in the balance of payments is not the only factor affecting the total value of foreign investments. Among the other factors are changes in the valuation of assets or liabilities, including changes in prices of securities, defaults, expropriations, and write-offs.

Direct investment abroad means the ownership or control, directly or indirectly, by one person of 10 percent or more of the voting securities of an incorporated business enterprise or an equivalent interest in an unincorporated business enterprise. Direct investment position is the value of U.S. parents' claims on the equity of and receivables due from foreign affiliates, less foreign affiliates' receivables due from their U.S. parents. Income consists of parents' shares in the earnings of their affiliates plus net interest received by parents on intercompany accounts, less withholding taxes on dividends and interest.

Foreign aid—Foreign assistance is divided into three major categories— grants (military supplies and services and other grants), credits, and other assistance (through net accumulation of foreign currency claims from the sale of agricultural commodities). *Grants* are transfers for which no payment is expected (other than a limited percentage of the foreign currency "counterpart" funds generated by the grant), or which at most involve an obligation on the part of the receiver to extend aid to the United States or other countries to achieve a common objective. *Credits* are loan disbursements or transfers under other agreements which give rise to specific obligations to repay, over a period of years, usually with interest. All known returns to the U.S. government stemming from grants and credits (reverse grants, returns of grants, and payments of principal) are taken into account in net grants and net credits, but no allowance is made for interest or commissions. *Other assistance* represents the transfer of U.S. farm products in exchange for foreign currencies (plus, since enactment of Public Law 87-128, currency claims from principal and interest collected on credits extended under the farm products program), less the government's disbursements of the currencies as grants, credits, or for purchases. The net acquisition of currencies represents net transfers of resources to foreign countries under the agricultural programs, in addition to those classified as grants or credits.

In 1952, economic, technical, and military aid programs were combined under the Mutual Security Act, which in turn was followed by the Foreign Assistance Act passed in 1961. Appropriations to provide military assistance were also made in the Department of Defense Appropriation Act (rather than the Foreign Assistance Appropriation Act) beginning in 1966 for certain countries in Southeast Asia and in other legislation concerning programs for specific countries (such as Israel). Figures on activity under the Foreign Assistance Act as reported in the *Foreign Grants and Credits* series differ from data published by AID or its immediate predecessors, due largely to differences in reporting, timing, and treatment of particular items.

Exports—The Census Bureau compiles export data primarily from Shipper's Export Declarations required to be filed with customs officials for shipments leaving the United States. They include U.S. exports under mutual security programs and exclude shipments to U.S. Armed Forces for their own use.

The value reported in the export statistics is generally equivalent to a free alongside ship (f.a.s.) value at the U.S. port of export, based on the transaction price, including inland freight, insurance, and other charges incurred in placing the merchandise alongside the carrier at the U.S. port of exportation. This value, as defined, excludes the cost of loading merchandise aboard the exporting carrier and also excludes freight, insurance, and any other charges or transportation and other costs beyond the U.S. port of exportation. The country of destination is defined as the country of ultimate destination or country where the merchandise is to be consumed, further processed, or manufactured, as known to the shipper at the time of exportation. When ultimate destination is not known, the shipment is statistically credited to the last country to which the shipper knows the merchandise will be shipped in the same form as exported.

Effective January 1990, the United States began substituting Canadian import statistics for U.S. exports to Canada. As a result of the data exchange between the United States and Canada, the United States has adopted the Canadian import exemption level for its export statistics based on shipments to Canada.

Data are estimated for shipments valued under $2,501 to all countries, except Canada, using factors based on the ratios of low-valued shipments to individual country totals.

Prior to 1989, exports were based on Schedule B, Statistical Classification of Domestic and Foreign Commodities Exported from the United States. Beginning in 1989, Schedule B classifications are based on the Harmonized System and coincide with the Standard International Trade Classification, Revision 3. This revision will affect the comparability of most export series beginning with the 1989 data for commodities.

Imports—The Census Bureau compiles import data from various customs forms required to be filed with customs officials. Data on import values are presented on two valuations bases in this section: The c.i.f. (cost, insurance, and freight) and the customs import value (as appraised by the U.S. Customs Service in accordance with legal requirements of the Tariff Act of 1930, as amended). This latter valuation, primarily used for collection of import duties, frequently does not reflect the actual transaction value. Country of origin is defined as country where the merchandise was grown, mined, or manufactured. If country of origin is unknown, country of shipment is reported.

Imports are classified either as "General imports" or "Imports for consumption." *General imports* are a combination of entries for immediate consumption, entries into customs bonded warehouses, and entries into U.S. Foreign Trade Zones, thus generally reflecting total arrivals of merchandise. *Imports for consumption* are a combination of entries for immediate consumption, withdrawals from warehouses for consumption, and entries of merchandise into U.S. customs territory from U.S. Foreign Trade Zones, thus generally reflecting the total of the commodities entered into U.S. consumption channels.

Beginning in 1989, import statistics are based on the Harmonized Tariff Schedule of the United States, which coincides with import Standard International Trade Classification, Revision 3. This revision will affect the comparability of most import series beginning with the 1989 data.

Area coverage—Except as noted, the geographic area covered by the export and import trade statistics is the United States Customs area (includes the 50 states, the District of Columbia, and Puerto Rico), the U.S. Virgin Islands (effective January 1981), and U.S. Foreign Trade Zones (effective July 1982). Data for selected tables and total values for 1980 have been revised to reflect the U.S. Virgin Islands' trade with foreign countries, where possible.

Statistical reliability—For a discussion of statistical collection and estimation, sampling procedures, and measures of statistical reliability applicable to Census Bureau data, see Appendix III.

Table 1286. U.S. International Transactions by Type of Transaction: 1990 to 2010

[In millions of dollars (706,975 represents $706,975,000,000). Minus sign (–) indicates debits]

Type of transaction [1]	1990	1995	2000	2003	2004	2005	2006	2007	2008	2009	2010
Exports of goods and services and income receipts	**706,975**	**1,004,631**	**1,425,260**	**1,345,930**	**1,578,939**	**1,824,780**	**2,144,443**	**2,488,394**	**2,656,585**	**2,174,533**	**2,500,817**
Exports of goods and services	535,233	794,387	1,072,782	1,023,519	1,163,146	1,287,441	1,459,823	1,654,561	1,842,682	1,575,037	1,837,577
Goods, balance of payments basis [2]	387,401	575,204	784,781	729,816	821,986	911,686	1,039,406	1,163,957	1,307,499	1,069,491	1,288,699
Services [3]	147,832	219,183	288,002	293,703	341,160	375,755	420,417	490,604	535,183	505,547	548,878
Transfers under U.S. military agency sales contracts [4]	9,932	14,643	6,210	5,918	8,751	12,082	15,587	17,091	14,711	16,611	17,483
Travel	43,007	63,395	82,891	65,159	75,465	82,160	86,187	97,355	110,423	94,191	103,505
Passenger fares	15,298	18,909	20,197	15,091	17,932	20,609	21,638	25,187	30,957	26,103	30,931
Other transportation	22,042	26,081	25,562	26,354	29,791	32,013	35,824	40,638	44,016	35,533	39,936
Royalties and license fees [5]	16,634	30,289	51,808	56,813	67,094	74,448	83,549	97,803	102,125	97,183	105,583
Other private services [5]	40,251	65,048	100,792	123,799	141,465	153,665	176,798	211,641	232,019	234,858	250,320
U.S. government miscellaneous services	668	818	542	567	663	778	834	890	933	1,069	1,121
Income receipts	171,742	210,244	352,478	322,411	415,793	537,339	684,620	833,834	813,903	599,495	663,240
Income receipts on U.S.-owned assets abroad	170,570	208,065	348,083	317,740	411,059	532,542	679,608	828,732	808,721	594,319	657,963
Direct investment receipts	65,973	95,260	151,839	186,417	250,606	294,538	324,816	370,758	413,739	356,203	432,000
Other private receipts	94,072	108,092	192,398	126,529	157,313	235,120	352,122	455,436	389,881	233,324	224,469
U.S. government receipts	10,525	4,713	3,846	4,794	3,140	2,884	2,670	2,538	5,101	4,792	1,494
Compensation of employees	1,172	2,179	4,395	4,671	4,734	4,796	5,012	5,102	5,182	5,176	5,278
Imports of goods and services and income payments	**-759,290**	**-1,080,124**	**-1,782,832**	**-1,793,223**	**-2,119,214**	**-2,464,813**	**-2,853,549**	**-3,083,637**	**-3,207,834**	**-2,427,804**	**-2,835,620**
Imports of goods and services	-616,097	-890,771	-1,449,532	-1,514,503	-1,768,502	-1,996,065	-2,213,111	-2,351,288	-2,541,020	-1,956,310	-2,337,604
Goods, balance of payments basis [2]	-498,438	-749,374	-1,230,568	-1,270,225	-1,485,492	-1,692,416	-1,875,095	-1,982,843	-2,137,608	-1,575,400	-1,934,555
Services [3]	-117,659	-141,397	-218,964	-244,278	-283,010	-303,649	-338,016	-368,446	-403,413	-380,909	-403,048
Direct defense expenditures	-17,531	-10,043	-12,698	-22,978	-26,110	-27,676	-27,330	-27,917	-28,311	-30,474	-30,391
Travel	-37,349	-44,916	-65,366	-58,311	-66,738	-69,930	-72,959	-77,127	-80,494	-74,118	-75,507
Passenger fares	-10,531	-14,663	-23,613	-20,125	-23,730	-25,189	-26,646	-27,681	-31,841	-25,137	-27,279
Other transportation	-24,966	-27,034	-37,209	-40,619	-48,945	-54,212	-55,320	-55,773	-56,696	-42,591	-51,202
Royalties and license fees [5]	-3,135	-6,919	-16,606	-19,259	-23,691	-25,577	-25,038	-26,479	-29,623	-29,849	-33,450
Other private services [5]	-22,229	-35,199	-61,085	-80,300	-90,622	-97,720	-127,308	-149,848	-172,543	-174,325	-180,598
U.S. government miscellaneous services	-1,919	-2,623	-2,386	-2,686	-3,175	-3,345	-3,415	-3,621	-3,905	-4,415	-4,621
Income payments	-143,192	-189,353	-333,300	-278,721	-350,712	-468,748	-640,438	-732,349	-666,814	-471,494	-498,016
Income payments on foreign-owned assets in the United States	-139,728	-183,090	-322,345	-266,743	-337,691	-453,800	-624,912	-717,623	-650,880	-457,261	-483,504
Direct investment payments	-3,450	-30,318	-56,910	-73,750	-99,754	-121,333	-150,770	-126,174	-129,447	-94,025	-151,361
Other private payments	-95,508	-97,149	-180,918	-119,051	-155,266	-228,408	-338,897	-426,796	-354,609	-218,881	-196,004
U.S. government payments	-40,770	-55,623	-84,517	-73,942	-82,671	-104,059	-135,245	-164,653	-166,824	-144,355	-136,139
Compensation of employees	-3,464	-6,263	-10,955	-11,978	-13,021	-14,948	-15,526	-14,725	-15,934	-14,233	-14,512
Unilateral current transfers, net	**-26,654**	**-38,074**	**-58,767**	**-71,796**	**-88,243**	**-105,741**	**-91,515**	**-115,061**	**-125,885**	**-123,280**	**-136,095**
U.S. government grants [4]	-10,359	-11,190	-16,836	-22,175	-23,704	-33,615	-27,767	-34,567	-36,461	-42,221	-44,717
U.S. government pensions and other transfers	-3,224	-3,451	-4,705	-5,341	-6,264	-6,303	-6,508	-7,323	-8,390	-8,874	-10,365
Private remittances and other transfers [6]	-13,070	-23,433	-37,226	-44,280	-58,275	-65,822	-57,240	-73,170	-81,034	-72,185	-81,013

See footnotes at end of table.

U.S. Census Bureau, Statistical Abstract of the United States: 2012

Table 1286. U.S. International Transactions by Type of Transaction: 1990 to 2010—Con.

[In millions of dollars (706,975 represents $706,975,000,000). Minus sign (–) indicates debits]

Type of transaction[1]	1990	1995	2000	2003	2004	2005	2006	2007	2008	2009	2010
Capital account transactions, net	-7,220	-222	-1	-1,821	3,049	13,116	-1,788	384	6,010	-140	-152
U.S.-owned assets abroad, excl. financial derivatives (increase/financial outflow (–))	-81,234	-352,264	-560,523	-325,424	-1,000,870	-546,631	-1,285,729	-1,453,604	332,109	-139,330	-1,005,182
U.S. official reserve assets	-2,158	-9,742	-290	1,523	2,805	14,096	2,374	-122	-4,848	-52,256	-1,834
Special drawing rights	**-192**	**-808**	**-722**	**601**	**-398**	**4,511**	**-223**	**-154**	**-106**	**-48,230**	**-31**
Reserve position in the International Monetary Fund	731	-2,466	2,308	1,494	3,826	10,200	3,331	1,021	-3,473	-3,357	-1,293
Foreign currencies	-2,697	-6,468	-1,876	-572	-623	-615	-734	-989	-1,269	-669	-510
U.S. government assets, other than official reserve assets	2,317	-984	-941	537	1,710	5,539	5,346	-22,273	-529,615	541,342	7,540
U.S. credits and other long-term assets	-8,410	-4,859	-5,182	-7,279	-3,044	-2,255	-2,992	-2,475	-2,202	-4,069	-4,976
Repayments on U.S. credits and other long-term assets[7]	10,856	4,125	4,265	7,981	4,716	5,603	8,329	4,104	2,354	2,133	2,408
U.S. foreign currency holdings and U.S. short-term assets	-130	-250	-24	-165	38	2,191	9	-23,902	-529,766	543,278	10,108
U.S. private assets	-81,393	-341,538	-559,292	-327,484	-1,005,385	-566,266	-1,293,449	-1,431,209	866,571	-628,417	-1,010,888
Direct investment	-37,183	-98,750	-159,212	-149,564	-316,223	-36,235	-244,922	-414,039	-329,081	-303,606	-351,350
Foreign securities	-28,765	-122,394	-127,908	-146,722	-170,549	-251,199	-365,129	-366,512	197,347	-226,813	-151,916
U.S. claims on unaffiliated foreigners reported by U.S. nonbanking concerns	-27,824	-45,286	-138,790	-18,184	-152,566	-71,207	-181,299	-928	456,177	144,867	7,421
U.S. claims reported by U.S. banks and securities brokers	12,379	-75,108	-133,382	-13,014	-366,047	-207,625	-502,099	-649,730	542,128	-242,865	-515,043
Foreign-owned assets in the United States, excluding financial derivatives (increase/financial inflow (+))	139,357	435,102	1,038,224	858,303	1,533,201	1,247,347	2,065,169	2,064,642	431,406	335,793	1,245,736
Foreign official assets in the United States	33,910	109,880	42,758	278,069	397,755	259,268	487,939	481,043	554,634	480,237	349,754
U.S. government securities											
U.S. Treasury securities	29,576	68,977	-5,199	184,931	273,279	112,841	208,564	98,432	548,653	569,893	397,797
Other	667	3,735	40,909	39,943	41,662	100,493	219,837	171,465	42,728	-132,569	-80,817
Other U.S. government liabilities	1,868	-105	-1,825	-723	-134	-421	2,816	5,436	9,029	58,182	12,124
U.S. liabilities reported by U.S. banks and securities brokers	3,385	34,008	5,746	48,643	69,245	26,260	22,365	109,019	-149,676	-68,873	-9,375
Other foreign official assets	-1,586	3,265	3,127	5,275	13,703	20,095	34,357	96,691	103,900	53,604	30,025
Other foreign assets in the United States	105,447	325,222	995,466	580,234	1,135,446	988,079	1,577,230	1,583,599	-123,228	-144,444	895,982
Direct investment	48,494	57,776	321,274	63,750	145,966	112,638	243,151	221,166	310,092	158,581	236,226
U.S. Treasury securities	-2,534	91,544	-69,983	91,455	93,608	132,300	-58,229	66,845	162,944	-14,937	256,428
U.S. securities other than U.S. Treasury securities	1,592	77,249	459,889	220,705	381,493	450,386	683,245	605,414	-165,639	3,955	120,453
U.S. currency	16,586	8,840	-3,357	10,591	13,301	8,447	2,227	-10,675	29,187	12,632	28,319
U.S. liabilities to unaffiliated foreigners reported by U.S. nonbanking concerns	45,133	59,637	170,672	96,526	165,872	69,572	244,793	183,221	-31,475	12,404	77,456
U.S. liabilities reported by U.S. banks and securities brokers	-3,824	30,176	116,971	97,207	335,206	214,736	462,043	517,628	-428,337	-317,079	177,100
Financial derivatives, net	(NA)	(NA)	(NA)	(NA)	(NA)	(NA)	29,710	6,222	-32,947	49,456	13,735
Statistical discrepancy	28,066	30,951	-61,361	-11,969	93,138	31,942	-6,742	92,660	-59,443	130,773	216,761
Balance on goods	-111,037	-174,170	-445,787	-540,409	-663,507	-780,730	-835,689	-818,886	-830,109	-505,910	-645,857
Balance on services	30,173	77,786	69,038	49,425	58,150	72,106	82,402	122,158	131,770	124,637	145,830
Balance on goods and services	**-80,864**	**-96,384**	**-376,749**	**-490,984**	**-605,356**	**-708,624**	**-753,288**	**-696,728**	**-698,338**	**-381,272**	**-500,027**
Balance on income	*28,550*	*20,891*	*19,178*	*43,691*	*65,081*	*68,591*	*44,182*	*101,485*	*147,089*	*128,001*	*165,224*
Unilateral current transfers, net	-26,654	-38,074	-58,767	-71,796	-88,243	-105,741	-91,515	-115,061	-125,885	-123,280	-136,095
Balance on current account	-78,968	-113,567	-416,338	-519,089	-628,519	-745,774	-800,621	-710,303	-677,135	-376,551	-470,898

NA Not available. [1] Credits, +: Exports of goods and services and income receipts; unilateral current transfers to the United States; capital account transactions receipts; financial inflows—increase in foreign-owned assets (U.S. liabilities) or decrease in U.S.-owned assets (U.S. claims). Debits, –: Imports of goods and services and income payments; unilateral current transfers to foreigners; capital account transactions payments; financial outflows—decrease in foreign-owned assets (U.S. liabilities) or increase in U.S.-owned assets (U.S. claims). [2] See Table 2 footnotes for explanations of the various balance of payments adjustments made to convert goods on a Census-basis to goods on a balance of payments basis. The adjustments are made to improve coverage, eliminate duplication and align the goods data with national and international accounting guidelines. [3] Includes some goods: Mainly military equipment and supplies in lines 5 and 22 that are commingled in the source data and cannot be separately identified. Beginning with statistics for 1999, line 5 excludes equipment and supplies exported under the U.S. Foreign Military Sales program that can be separately identified, and line 22 excludes petroleum purchases abroad by U.S. military agencies that can be separately identified. [4] Includes transfers of goods and services under U.S. military grant programs. [5] Beginning in 1982, these lines are presented on a gross basis. The definition of exports is revised to exclude U.S. parents' payments to foreign affiliates and to include U.S. affiliates' receipts from foreign parents. [6] Beginning in 1982, the definition of imports is revised to include U.S. parents' payments to foreign affiliates and to exclude U.S. affiliates' receipts from foreign parents. [6] Beginning in 1982, the "other transfers" component includes taxes paid by U.S. private residents to foreign governments and taxes paid by private nonresidents to the U.S. Government. [7] Includes sales of foreign obligations to foreigners.

Source: U.S. Bureau of Economic Analysis, Survey of Current Business, July 2011. See also <http://www.bea.gov/scb/index.html>.

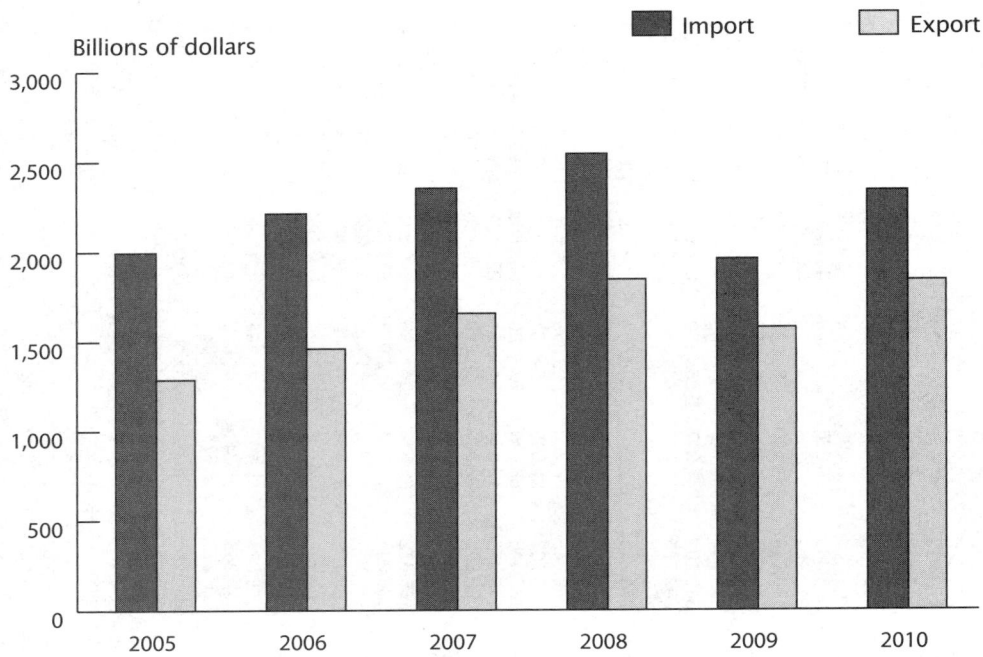

Figure 28.1
U.S. International Trade in Goods and Services: 2005 to 2010

Source: Chart prepared by U.S. Census Bureau. For data, see Table 1300.

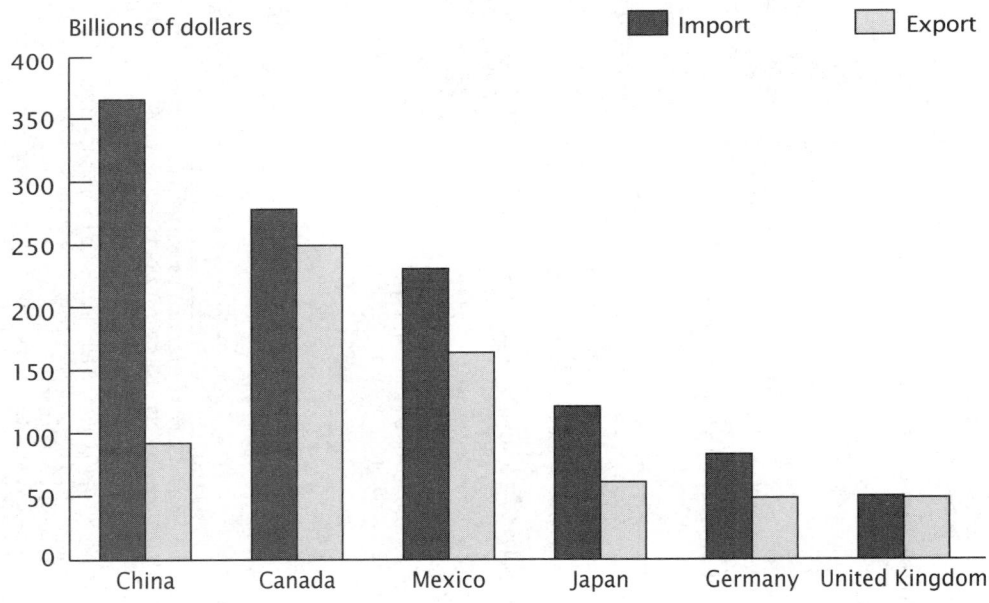

Figure 28.2
Top U.S. Trading Partners—Imports, Exports: 2010

Source: Chart prepared by U.S. Census Bureau. For data, see Table 1307.

U.S. Census Bureau, Statistical Abstract of the United States: 2012

Table 1287. U.S. Balances on International Transactions by Area and Selected Country: 2009 and 2010

[In millions of dollars (–505,910 represents –$505,910,000,000). Minus sign (–) indicates debits]

Area or Country	2009, balance on—				2010, balance on—			
	Goods [1]	Services	Income	Current account	Goods [1]	Services	Income	Current account
All areas	**–505,910**	**124,637**	**128,001**	**–376,551**	**–645,857**	**145,830**	**165,224**	**–470,898**
Europe	–69,203	38,144	63,475	23,270	–95,829	35,720	57,086	–13,468
European Union	–58,165	35,115	53,709	27,588	–79,724	31,783	42,348	–10,701
Euro Area [2]	–48,951	21,138	58,399	26,908	–66,240	19,891	52,138	2,102
Germany	–27,736	–7,026	–3,236	–38,501	–34,328	–6,217	–6,696	–46,804
Italy	–14,259	496	3,246	–10,869	–14,382	299	356	–14,083
Netherlands	16,518	5,823	39,073	61,039	15,740	4,601	41,007	60,093
United Kingdom	–954	10,451	–3,415	7,245	–1,672	8,030	–7,532	–1,418
Canada	–21,718	20,102	16,201	11,662	–31,719	24,639	25,643	15,570
Latin America, other Western Hemisphere	–49,422	12,595	54,247	–10,358	–62,263	20,579	69,179	–4,095
Mexico	–50,711	9,391	–3,277	–57,358	–69,322	10,227	–134	–72,159
Venezuela	–18,812	4,388	2,994	–11,436	–22,178	4,277	1,870	–16,124
Asia and Pacific	–312,062	45,254	–42,944	–338,601	–371,829	56,236	–31,879	–381,118
Australia	11,479	6,664	6,671	24,916	12,980	7,693	9,504	29,626
China [3]	–227,164	7,781	–41,355	–263,548	–273,038	11,140	–35,394	–300,348
Hong Kong	18,045	–136	926	18,672	22,771	–1,054	1,345	22,966
India	–4,856	–2,512	2,286	–9,566	–10,346	–3,309	3,503	–14,918
Japan [4]	–44,817	17,443	–22,637	–50,588	–61,339	19,219	–32,563	–75,692
Korea, South	–10,215	4,513	1,449	–5,309	–9,739	4,742	1,033	–4,991
Singapore	6,331	3,660	6,331	16,263	10,657	6,053	13,476	30,119
Taiwan [3]	–9,335	1,573	–4,169	–12,424	–9,204	3,158	–3,755	–10,349
Middle East	–15,581	2,732	–3,368	–28,427	–27,371	3,430	2,294	–32,255
Africa	–37,923	3,744	5,388	–42,008	–56,846	4,079	7,810	–59,235
International and unallocated	(X)	2,067	35,003	7,911	(X)	1,146	35,090	3,705

X Not applicable. [1] Adjusted to balance of payments basis. [2] See footnote 3, table 1354. [3] See footnote 4, Table 1332. [4] Includes Ryukyu Islands.

Source: U.S. Bureau of Economic Analysis, *Survey of Current Business*, July 2011. See also <http://www.bea.gov/scb/index.htm>.

Table 1288. Private International Service Transactions by Selected Type of Service and Selected Country: 2000 to 2010

[In millions of dollars (281,249 represents $281,249,000,000). For all transactions, see Table 1286]

Type of Service and country	Exports				Imports			
	2000	2005	2009	2010	2000	2005	2009	2010
Private services, total	281,249	362,895	487,867	530,274	203,880	272,627	346,020	368,036
TYPE OF SERVICE								
Travel	82,891	82,160	94,191	103,505	65,366	69,930	74,118	75,507
Passenger fares	20,197	20,609	26,103	30,931	23,613	25,189	25,137	27,279
Other transportation	25,562	32,013	35,533	39,936	37,209	54,212	42,591	51,202
Freight	12,791	16,261	17,466	19,768	27,885	44,193	29,795	37,915
Port services	12,771	15,752	18,067	20,168	9,324	10,019	12,797	13,288
Royalties and license fees	51,808	74,448	97,183	105,583	16,606	25,577	29,849	33,450
Other private services	100,792	153,665	234,858	250,320	61,085	97,720	174,325	180,598
By type: [1]								
Education	10,348	14,021	19,948	21,291	2,032	3,992	5,357	5,677
Financial services	(NA)	(NA)	62,444	66,387	(NA)	(NA)	13,597	13,803
Insurance services	3,631	7,566	14,427	14,605	11,284	28,710	63,614	61,767
AREA AND COUNTRY								
Europe	106,296	150,571	198,729	200,616	88,741	120,254	147,560	151,769
European Union	93,103	131,216	170,096	169,098	76,840	103,436	123,124	125,399
Euro Area	56,036	76,089	106,952	106,113	45,039	59,599	74,686	75,262
Belgium	2,591	3,184	3,653	3,777	2,039	2,169	3,275	3,713
Luxembourg	6,83	1,568	2,899	3,841	289	504	839	957
France	10,474	12,646	16,150	15,843	10,498	11,931	14,575	15,067
Germany	15,595	20,449	24,089	24,118	12,240	18,512	23,040	22,476
Italy	5,403	7,031	8,307	8,349	5,059	5,973	6,400	6,666
Netherlands	6,975	8,481	13,212	12,874	5,559	7,450	7,346	8,215
United Kingdom	31,706	44,793	49,067	48,535	27,869	34,736	37,920	39,652
Canada	24,613	32,719	42,644	50,521	17,875	21,977	22,295	25,579
Latin America, other Western Hemisphere	55,633	63,355	95,949	105,723	37,607	51,062	83,183	85,460
Mexico	15,532	22,192	23,080	24,110	10,780	14,177	13,538	13,730
Asia and Pacific	77,560	95,946	122,165	143,069	49,620	65,091	77,352	87,558
Australia	5,541	7,558	12,024	13,168	3,412	4,583	5,352	5,600
China [2]	5,020	8,403	15,971	21,135	3,171	6,146	8,161	9,967
India	2,563	5,081	9,831	10,319	1,887	4,964	12,359	13,661
Japan	32,843	40,517	40,049	44,750	16,387	20,483	20,990	23,541
Korea, South	6,924	9,565	12,758	15,105	4,587	5,875	6,384	7,756
Taiwan [2]	4,616	5,795	6,459	9,292	4,154	6,415	5,125	6,330
Middle East	6,753	8,939	15,541	16,903	3,380	5,239	8,596	9,329
Africa	4,997	6,247	10,578	11,208	2,708	3,919	6,766	7,104
South Africa	1,483	1,553	2,347	2,476	805	923	1,481	1,714
International organizations and unallocated	5,396	5,117	2,260	2,231	3,949	5,085	268	1,237

NA not available. [1] Royalties and license fees and "other private services" by detailed type of service include both affiliated and unaffiliated transactions. Additional historical estimates for royalties and license fees and "other private services" by detailed type that include only unaffiliated transactions are available in table 3b. [2] See footnote 4, Table 1332.

Source: U.S. Bureau of Economic Analysis, *Survey of Current Business*, July 2011. See also <http://www.bea.gov/scb/index.htm>.

Table 1289. International Investment Position by Type of Investment: 2000 to 2010

[In billions of dollars (−1,337 represents −$1,337,000,000,000). Estimates for end of year; subject to considerable error due to nature of basic data. Unless otherwise specified, types below refer to current-cost method. For information on current-cost method and market value, see article cited in source]

Type of investment	2000	2005	2006	2007	2008	2009	2010, prel.
Net international investment position	**−1,337**	**−1,932**	**−2,192**	**−1,796**	**−3,260**	**−2,396**	**−2,471**
Financial derivatives, net [1]	(X)	58	60	71	160	135	110
Net international investment position, excluding financial derivatives	−1,337	−1,990	−2,251	−1,867	−3,420	−2,531	−2,581
U.S.-owned assets abroad	**6,239**	**11,962**	**14,428**	**18,400**	**19,465**	**18,487**	**20,315**
Financial derivatives (gross positive fair value) [1]	(X)	1,190	1,239	2,559	6,127	3,501	3,653
U.S.-owned assets abroad, excluding financial derivatives	6,239	10,772	13,189	15,840	13,337	14,986	16,662
U.S. official reserve assets	128	188	220	277	294	404	489
Gold [2]	72	134	165	218	227	284	368
Special drawing rights	11	8	9	9	9	58	57
Reserve position in the International Monetary Fund	15	8	5	4	8	11	12
Foreign currencies	31	38	41	45	49	50	52
U.S. government assets, other than official reserve assets	85	78	72	94	624	83	75
U.S. credits and other long-term assets [3]	83	77	72	70	70	72	74
U.S. foreign currency holdings and U.S. short-term assets [4]	3	1	1	24	554	11	1
U.S. private assets	6,025	10,506	12,897	15,469	12,419	14,500	16,099
Direct investment at current cost	1,532	2,652	2,948	3,553	3,749	4,068	4,429
Foreign securities	2,426	4,329	5,604	6,835	3,986	5,566	6,223
Bonds	573	1,012	1,276	1,587	1,237	1,570	1,737
Corporate stocks	1,853	3,318	4,329	5,248	2,748	3,995	4,486
U.S. claims on unaffiliated foreigners [2]	837	1,018	1,184	1,233	931	862	874
U.S. claims reported by U.S. banks	1,232	2,507	3,160	3,847	3,754	4,005	4,573
Foreign-owned assets in the United States	**7,576**	**13,894**	**16,620**	**20,196**	**22,725**	**20,883**	**22,786**
Financial derivatives (gross negative fair value) [1]	(X)	1,132	1,179	2,488	5,968	3,366	3,542
Foreign-owned assets in the Unites States, excluding financial derivatives	7,576	12,762	15,441	17,708	16,757	17,517	19,244
Foreign official assets in the United States	1,037	2,313	2,833	3,412	3,944	4,403	4,864
U.S. government securities	756	1,725	2,167	2,540	3,264	3,589	3,957
U.S. Treasury securities	640	1,341	1,558	1,737	2,401	2,880	3,321
Other	116	385	609	803	864	709	637
Other U.S. government liabilities	26	23	26	32	41	99	110
U.S. liabilities reported by U.S. banks	153	297	297	406	256	187	178
Other foreign official assets	102	269	343	434	383	528	618
Other foreign assets	6,539	10,448	12,608	14,296	12,813	13,115	14,380
Direct investment at current cost	1,421	1,906	2,154	2,346	2,397	2,442	2,659
U.S. Treasury securities	382	644	568	640	852	792	1,065
U.S. securities other than U.S. Treasury securities	2,623	4,353	5,372	6,190	4,621	5,320	5,860
Corporate and other bonds	1,069	2,243	2,825	3,289	2,771	2,826	2,868
Corporate stocks	1,554	2,110	2,547	2,901	1,850	2,494	2,992
U.S. currency	205	280	283	272	301	314	342
U.S. liabilities to unaffiliated foreigners	739	658	799	863	741	707	748
U.S. liabilities reported by U.S. banks	1,169	2,607	3,431	3,985	3,901	3,540	3,707
Memoranda:							
Direct investment abroad at market value	2,694	3,638	4,470	5,275	3,102	4,331	4,843
Direct investment in the United States at market value	2,783	2,818	3,293	3,551	2,486	3,027	3,451

X Not applicable. [1] A break in series in 2005 reflects the introduction of U.S. Department of the Treasury data on financial derivatives. [2] U.S. official gold stock is valued at market price. [3] Also includes paid-in capital subscriptions to international financial institutions and resources provided to foreigners under foreign assistance programs requiring repayment over several years. Excludes World War I debts that are not being serviced. [4] Beginning in 2007, includes foreign-currency-denominated assets obtained through temporary reciprocal currency arrangements between the Federal Reserve System and foreign central banks.

Source: U.S. Bureau of Economic Analysis, *Survey of Current Business*, July 2011. See also <http://www.bea.gov/scb.index.htm>.

Table 1290. U.S. Reserve Assets: 1990 to 2010

[In billions of dollars (83.3 represents $83,300,000,000). As of end of year]

Type	1990	2000	2004	2005	2006	2007	2008	2009	2010
Total	**83.3**	**67.6**	**86.8**	**65.1**	**65.9**	**70.6**	**77.6**	**130.8**	**132.4**
Gold stock	11.1	11.0	11.0	11.0	11.0	11.0	11.0	11.0	11.0
Special drawing rights	11.0	10.5	13.6	8.2	8.9	9.5	9.3	57.8	56.8
Foreign currencies	52.2	31.2	42.7	37.8	40.9	45.8	49.6	50.5	52.1
Reserve position in IMF [1]	9.1	14.8	19.5	8.0	5.0	4.2	7.7	11.4	12.5

[1] International Monetary Fund.

Source: U.S. Department of the Treasury, *Treasury Bulletin*, quarterly. See also <http://www.fms.treas.gov/bulletin/index.html>.

Table 1291. Foreign Direct Investment Position in the United States on a Historical-Cost Basis by Selected Country, 2000 to 2010, and by Industry, 2010

[In millions of dollars (1,256,867 represents $1,256,867,000,000). Foreign direct investment is defined as the ownership or control, directly or indirectly, by one foreign entity (as used here, "entity" is synonymous with "person" as the term is used in a broad legal sense including any individual, branch, partnership, association, trust, corporation, or government) of 10 percent or more of the voting interest of a U.S. business enterprise. Data are based on surveys of U.S. affiliates of foreign companies]

Country	2000	2005	2008	2009	2010 Total[1]	2010 Manufacturing	2010 Wholesale trade	2010 Finance[2] and insurance
All countries................	**1,256,867**	**1,634,121**	**2,046,662**	**2,114,501**	**2,342,829**	**748,279**	**330,889**	**356,781**
Canada.......................	114,309	165,667	168,746	202,303	206,139	35,728	5,491	65,214
Europe[3]......................	887,014	1,154,048	1,477,896	1,516,268	1,697,196	585,004	189,346	284,260
Austria......................	3,007	2,425	4,251	4,455	4,353	2,234	418	2
Belgium.....................	14,787	10,024	23,379	37,820	43,236	20,662	7,151	(D)
Denmark....................	4,025	6,117	5,537	6,383	9,285	3,027	(D)	1
Finland......................	8,875	5,938	7,613	7,293	6,558	4,241	1,775	(Z)
France......................	125,740	114,260	141,922	157,921	184,762	71,286	18,827	22,469
Germany...................	122,412	177,176	173,843	191,461	212,915	69,222	16,601	41,631
Ireland.....................	25,523	17,465	21,270	24,217	30,583	18,382	(D)	5,429
Italy........................	6,576	7,725	19,466	14,979	15,689	6,844	1,254	(D)
Luxembourg................	58,930	79,680	130,020	146,580	181,203	65,996	4,586	42,315
Netherlands................	138,894	156,602	179,938	199,906	217,050	78,003	24,638	47,849
Norway.....................	2,665	9,810	11,511	9,951	10,356	445	4,855	91
Spain.......................	5,068	7,472	30,037	38,812	40,723	4,592	55	2,437
Sweden.....................	21,991	22,269	32,578	35,598	40,758	25,386	10,602	142
Switzerland................	64,719	133,387	157,121	140,745	192,231	85,074	11,799	45,348
United Kingdom............	277,613	371,350	447,529	416,139	432,488	93,705	82,168	73,662
Other.......................	6,188	32,348	91,878	84,008	75,006	35,906	(D)	29
Latin America and other Western								
Hemisphere[3]...............	53,691	57,175	56,538	48,300	60,074	15,454	6,649	−17,868
South and Central America[3].....	13,384	22,507	13,581	14,699	19,206	7,357	2,119	548
Brazil......................	882	2,051	16	−1,651	1,093	−1,003	1,169	(D)
Mexico.....................	7,462	3,595	8,420	11,492	12,591	4,937	832	(D)
Panama....................	3,819	10,983	916	1,101	1,485	632	−39	7
Venezuela.................	792	5,292	2,402	2,599	2,857	(D)	−3	2
Other Western Hemisphere[3]....	40,307	34,668	42,957	33,601	40,869	8,097	4,529	−18,416
Bermuda...................	18,336	2,147	13,703	2,175	5,142	3,131	(D)	−19,757
Netherlands Antilles.........	3,807	5,531	6,351	8,024	3,680	(D)	291	32
U.K. Islands, Caribbean.......	15,191	23,063	27,799	25,120	31,150	4,424	3,335	1,283
Other......................	1,719	3,277	−5,132	−2,411	768	(D)	462	30
Africa.......................	2,700	2,341	1,817	1,205	2,010	135	530	−7
Middle East[3]................	6,506	8,306	16,233	16,949	15,407	3,536	6,013	(D)
Israel......................	3,012	4,231	6,752	7,109	7,231	3,582	485	(D)
Saudi Arabia...............	(D)	(D)	(D)	(D)	(D)	−55	(D)	(Z)
Asia and Pacific[3].............	192,647	246,585	325,431	329,475	362,003	108,421	122,860	(D)
Australia...................	18,775	36,392	37,399	41,289	49,543	5,263	75	4,348
Hong Kong.................	1,493	3,467	4,217	4,172	4,272	(D)	1,538	12
India.......................	96	1,497	2,820	2,375	3,344	381	20	(Z)
Japan......................	159,690	189,851	234,748	239,312	257,273	80,739	104,009	19,313
Korea, South...............	3,110	6,077	12,859	13,503	15,213	2,460	12,300	161
Singapore..................	5,087	3,338	25,801	20,658	21,831	(D)	975	(D)
Taiwan[4]....................	3,174	3,731	4,462	4,516	5,180	1,935	1,674	−114

D Suppressed to avoid disclosure of data of individual companies. Z Less than $500,000. [1] Includes other industries, not shown separately. [2] Excludes depository institutions [3] Includes other countries, not shown separately. [4] See footnote 4, Table 1332.
Source: U.S. Bureau of Economic Analysis, *Survey of Current Business*, July 2011, and previous issues.
See <http://www.bea.gov/scb/index.htm>.

Table 1292. U.S. Majority-Owned Affiliates of Foreign Companies—Selected Financial and Operating Data by Industry of Affiliate: 2008

[In millions of dollars, except as indicated (11,671,560 represents $11,671,560,000,000). Preliminary. A majority-owned U.S. affiliate is a U.S. business enterprise in which a foreign entity (as used here, "entity" is synonymous with "person" as the term is used in a broad legal sense including any individual, branch, partnership, association, trust, corporation, or government) has a direct or indirect voting interest greater than 50 percent]

Industry	2007 NAICS Code	Total assets	Sales	Employment (1,000)	Employee compensation	Gross property, plant, and equipment	Merchandise exports	Merchandise imports
All industries..............	**(X)**	**11,671,560**	**3,448,568**	**5,593.5**	**408,453**	**1,442,375**	**232,413**	**566,925**
Manufacturing[1].................	31–33	1,500,219	1,288,552	2,115.5	166,749	558,736	131,300	223,993
Petroleum and coal products.......	324	115,965	226,817	38.1	5,216	69,207	(D)	63,080
Chemicals................	325	375,916	267,418	305.8	35,027	127,734	30,048	46,827
Computers and electronic products..	334	99,150	60,476	164.7	11,071	20,915	13,229	12,823
Transportation equipment.........	336	245,902	219,616	420.5	29,132	88,517	26,574	54,218
Wholesale trade.................	42	695,840	1,019,137	648.8	55,753	287,568	89,824	322,319
Retail trade...................	44–45	68,003	120,905	464.4	14,469	41,430	700	7,303
Information...................	51	254,337	101,672	249.1	23,517	53,351	968	644
Finance and insurance.........	52, exc.	8,111,541	494,441	407.5	56,720	75,019	(D)	(Z)
Real estate and rental and leasing ...	53	140,526	24,925	39.4	2,759	109,793	(D)	(D)
Professional, scientific, and technical								
services.....................	54	120,883	78,727	248.3	22,525	14,631	565	348
Other industries.................	(X)	780,211	320,210	1,420.5	65,960	301,848	(D)	(D)

X Not applicable. D Suppressed to avoid disclosure of data of individual companies. Z Less than $500,000. [1] Includes industries not shown separately.
Source: U.S. Bureau of Economic Analysis, *Survey of Current Business*, November 2010, and *Foreign Direct Investment in the United States: Operations of U.S. Affiliates of Foreign Companies, Preliminary 2008 Estimates*. For more information, see <http://www.bea.gov/international/di1fdiop.htm>.

Foreign Commerce and Aid 797

Table 1293. Foreign Direct Investment in the United States—Property, Plant, and Equipment and Employment of Majority-Owned U.S. Affiliates of Foreign Companies by State: 2002 to 2008

[Gross book value of property, plant, and equipment in millions of dollars (1,035,916 represents $1,035,916,000,000); employment in thousands (5,570.4 represents 5,570,400). A U.S. majority-owned affiliate is a U.S. business enterprise in which a foreign entity (as used here, "entity" is synonymous with "person" as the term is used in a broad legal sense including any individual, branch, partnership, association, trust, corporation, or government) has a direct or indirect voting interest greater than 50 percent.]

State and other area	Gross book value of property, plant, and equipment (mil. dol.)		Employment		
				2008	
	2002	2007	2002 (1,000)	Total (1,000)	Percentage of total employment in the state or area [1]
Total.................	1,035,916	1,283,009	5,570.4	5,593.5	4.7
Alabama	15,520	21,965	75.1	78.4	4.8
Alaska	30,052	34,336	12.6	12.5	5.1
Arizona	(D)	13,119	57.6	76.5	3.4
Arkansas.................	4,872	5,041	35.7	33.3	3.3
California.................	89,193	110,214	635.3	594.1	4.6
Colorado	13,026	(D)	77.7	85.4	4.3
Connecticut.................	(D)	13,615	(D)	104.6	7.1
Delaware	6,252	4,337	23.6	30.8	8.2
District of Columbia..........	5,135	5,489	17.5	15.9	3.3
Florida.................	28,993	33,647	258.3	254.0	3.8
Georgia.................	(D)	(D)	191.4	179.8	5.2
Hawaii	(D)	6,167	(D)	30.6	6.1
Idaho.................	2,131	2,035	12.5	17.5	3.2
Illinois..................	41,862	49,207	281.5	273.3	5.3
Indiana..................	27,991	(D)	133.3	141.6	5.5
Iowa..................	5,776	8,406	36.6	48.2	3.7
Kansas..................	5,238	8,011	34.9	53.5	4.6
Kentucky	24,091	28,272	88.4	95.2	6.1
Louisiana.................	26,993	30,701	50.5	48.1	3.0
Maine..................	5,511	6,252	31.7	30.7	6.0
Maryland	(D)	13,538	(D)	108.6	5.1
Massachusetts..............	(D)	26,272	(D)	188.9	6.4
Michigan	(D)	22,681	(D)	150.6	4.2
Minnesota	9,805	16,276	88.1	97.2	4.1
Mississippi.................	5,097	10,962	25.8	26.8	2.9
Missouri..................	14,484	(D)	91.5	91.3	3.8
Montana..................	1,824	3,194	5.9	7.2	2.0
Nebraska.................	1,840	(D)	18.7	25.2	3.1
Nevada	(D)	9,681	25.9	37.3	3.3
New Hampshire..............	(D)	5,131	(D)	40.4	7.2
New Jersey	30,956	38,811	230.1	230.0	6.7
New Mexico	(D)	4,054	13.0	18.7	2.9
New York	68,310	82,623	440.8	417.0	5.7
North Carolina..............	(D)	29,553	(D)	206.7	5.9
North Dakota..............	1,100	1,461	7.4	10.1	3.4
Ohio..................	32,124	42,938	214.2	231.6	5.0
Oklahoma	7,434	10,142	33.9	36.8	2.9
Oregon..................	(D)	10,142	51.3	46.9	3.2
Pennsylvania..............	(D)	37,822	(D)	263.5	5.1
Rhode Island..............	(D)	5,350	(D)	21.3	5.1
South Carolina..............	21,573	(D)	133.1	107.2	6.7
South Dakota..............	685	1,184	7.6	8.8	2.6
Tennessee.................	16,795	22,467	130.7	130.6	5.4
Texas..................	88,116	119,255	353.0	439.4	4.9
Utah..................	10,612	6,413	32.3	32.5	3.0
Vermont..................	1,286	1,456	11.1	10.5	4.1
Virginia..................	(D)	(D)	142.2	159.7	5.2
Washington	(D)	22,400	84.7	91.2	3.7
West Virginia	7,388	6,605	22.7	22.0	3.7
Wisconsin	16,103	14,520	107.1	84.3	3.4
Wyoming	10,551	11,497	8.5	10.6	4.6
Puerto Rico	2,583	2,974	19.8	20.4	(NA)
Other U.S. areas	(D)	73,480	10.2	14.8	(NA)
Foreign	2,328	2,394	0.3	1.3	(NA)
Unspecified [2]...............	66,341	92,253	(NA)	(NA)	(NA)

D Suppressed to avoid the disclosure of data of individual companies. NA Not available. [1] The data on total employment in the state or area that is used to calculate the shares shown in this table are equal to employment in private industries less employment of private households. For consistency with the coverage of the private-industry employment data, U.S.-affiliate employment in Puerto Rico, in "other U.S. areas," and in "foreign" was excluded from the U.S.-affiliate employment total when the percentage shares were computed. 1. The data on total employment in the state or area that is used to calculate the shares shown in this table are equal to employment in private industries less employment of private households. For consistency with the coverage of the private-industry employment data, U.S.-affiliate employment in Puerto Rico, in "other U.S. areas," and in "foreign" was excluded from the U.S.-affiliate employment total when the percentage shares were computed. [2] Includes aircraft, railroad rolling stock, satellites, undersea cable, and trucks engaged in interstate transportation.

Source: U.S. Bureau of Economic Analysis, *Survey of Current Business*, November 2010, and *Foreign Direct Investment in the United States: Operations of U.S. Affiliates of Foreign Companies, Preliminary 2008 Estimates.* See also <http://www.bea.gov/international/di1fdiop.htm>.

Table 1294. U.S. Businesses Acquired or Established by Foreign Direct Investors—Investment Outlays by Industry of U.S. Business Enterprise and Country of Ultimate Beneficial Owner: 2000 to 2008

[In millions of dollars (335,629 represents $335,629,000,000). Foreign direct investment is the ownership or control directly or indirectly, by one foreign individual branch, partnership, association, trust, corporation, or government of 10 percent or more of the voting securities of a U.S. business enterprise or an equivalent interest in an unincorporated one. Data represent number and full cost of acquisitions of existing U.S. business enterprises, including business segments or operating units of existing U.S. business enterprises and establishments of new enterprises. Investments may be made by the foreign direct investor itself, or indirectly by an existing U.S. affiliate of the foreign direct investor. Covers investments in U.S. business enterprises with assets of over $1 million, or ownership of 200 acres of U.S. land]

Industry and country	2000	2003	2004	2005	2006	2007	2008, prel.
Total [1]	**335,629**	**63,591**	**86,219**	**91,390**	**165,603**	**251,917**	**260,362**
By type of investment:							
U.S. businesses acquired	322,703	50,212	72,738	73,997	148,604	223,616	242,799
U.S. businesses established	12,926	13,379	13,481	17,393	16,999	28,301	17,564
By type of investor:							
Foreign direct investors	105,151	27,866	34,184	40,304	44,129	88,337	47,078
U.S. affiliates	230,478	35,725	52,035	51,086	121,474	163,580	213,284
INDUSTRY [2]							
Manufacturing	143,285	10,750	18,251	34,036	56,330	118,370	141,079
Wholesale trade	8,561	1,086	(D)	3,489	8,273	5,631	3,977
Retail trade	1,672	941	3,073	1,262	1,295	6,867	2,775
Information	67,932	9,236	4,315	8,487	10,341	8,585	22,214
Depository institutions	2,636	4,864	(D)	7,973	7,547	12,307	15,996
Finance (except depository institutions) and insurance	44,420	23,511	26,234	5,529	33,776	27,497	29,584
Real estate and rental and leasing	4,526	2,817	6,335	8,756	12,441	17,852	3,796
Professional, scientific, and technical services	32,332	1,955	(D)	6,407	8,923	9,018	15,167
Other industries	30,264	8,429	10,121	15,453	26,677	45,790	25,775
COUNTRY [3]							
Canada	28,346	9,157	31,502	13,640	12,121	38,502	25,181
Europe [1]	249,167	39,024	43,815	56,416	106,732	132,454	157,853
France	26,149	2,955	6,415	5,608	18,140	14,307	16,565
Germany	18,452	8,830	4,788	7,239	20,514	15,831	12,823
Netherlands	47,686	1,077	461	2,609	4,769	8,357	12,545
Switzerland	22,789	649	6,505	2,332	12,401	6,501	9,041
United Kingdom	110,208	20,373	23,288	30,420	26,261	56,051	19,657
Latin America and other Western Hemisphere	15,400	1,607	2,629	5,042	(D)	(D)	18,259
South and Central America	5,334	182	1,382	980	2,273	(D)	3,551
Other Western Hemisphere	10,066	1,425	1,247	4,062	(D)	1,933	14,708
Africa	(D)	(D)	(D)	(D)	(D)	(D)	129
Middle East	947	1,738	1,318	5,068	11,755	21,882	12,263
Asia and Pacific [1]	40,282	11,469	6,015	10,924	15,759	34,408	44,863
Australia	(D)	9,032	3,850	4,713	5,650	12,983	10,522
Japan	26,044	1,544	1,027	4,245	8,350	7,928	28,041

D Suppressed to avoid disclosure of data of individual companies. [1] Includes other countries, not shown separately. [2] Based on 1997 North American Industry Classification System (NAICS). Beginning 2002, based on NAICS 2002; see text, Section 15. [3] For investments in which more than one investor participated, each investor and each investor's outlays are classified by country of each ultimate beneficial owner.

Source: U.S. Bureau of Economic Analysis, *Survey of Current Business*, June 2009. See also <http://www.bea.gov/bea/index.htm>.

Table 1295. U.S. Direct Investment Position Abroad, Capital Outflows, and Income by Industry of Foreign Affiliates: 2000 to 2010

[In millions of dollars (1,316,247 represents $1,316,247,000,000). See headnote, Table 1296]

Industry	Direct investment position on a historical-cost basis			Capitol outflows [inflows(–)]			Income [1]		
	2000	2009	2010	2000	2009	2010	2000	2009	2010
All industries, total [2]	1,316,247	3,547,038	3,908,231	142,627	282,686	328,905	133,692	335,283	409,555
Mining	72,111	163,467	175,532	2,174	17,784	12,637	13,164	24,953	29,675
Manufacturing [2]	343,899	526,705	585,789	43,002	47,126	61,149	42,230	42,115	63,246
Food	23,497	44,780	46,441	2,014	3,166	4,669	2,681	2,907	3,558
Chemicals	75,807	121,900	140,884	3,812	16,487	19,500	(D)	13,668	15,904
Primary and fabricated metals	21,644	21,218	22,129	1,233	429	1,300	1,536	947	1,553
Machinery	22,229	39,755	43,881	2,659	3,377	3,762	2,257	2,450	4,322
Computer and electronic products	59,909	68,720	81,968	17,303	−1,350	11,175	8,860	7,008	10,833
Electrical equipment, appliances, and components	10,005	22,482	23,635	2,100	821	2,087	1,079	1,558	1,696
Transportation equipment	49,887	48,567	50,332	7,814	4,873	1,033	4,107	−1,114	6,638
Wholesale trade	93,936	181,186	193,531	11,938	15,532	17,064	14,198	21,440	25,828
Information	52,345	144,562	161,723	16,531	11,680	13,137	−964	14,647	17,409
Depository institutions	40,152	121,340	133,602	−1,274	−16,399	2,194	2,191	2,350	5,933
Finance and insurance	217,086	761,279	802,960	21,659	49,691	13,506	15,210	41,465	40,241
Professional, scientific, and technical services	32,868	76,118	84,658	5,441	4,030	7,441	3,548	6,495	7,442
Holding companies (nonbank)	(NA)	1,351,158	1,538,617	(NA)	140,858	184,277	(NA)	166,191	198,633

D Withheld to avoid disclosure of individual company data. NA Not available. [1] For 2006, income is shown gross of withholding taxes. [2] Includes other industries, not shown separately.

Source: U.S. Bureau of Economic Analysis, *Survey of Current Business*, July 2011. For most recent copy and historical issues, see <http://www.bea.gov/scb/index.htm>.

Table 1296. U.S. Direct Investment Position Abroad on a Historical-Cost Basis by Selected Country: 2000 to 2010

[In millions of dollars (1,316,247 represents $1,316,247,000,000). U.S. investment abroad is the ownership or control by one U.S. person of 10 percent or more of the voting securities of an incorporated foreign business enterprise or an equivalent interest in an unincorporated foreign business enterprise. Negative position can occur when a U.S. parent company's liabilities to the foreign affiliate are greater than its equity in and loans to the foreign affiliate]

Country	2000	2004	2005	2006	2007	2008	2009	2010
All countries	1,316,247	2,160,844	2,241,656	2,477,268	2,993,980	3,232,493	3,547,038	3,908,231
Canada	132,472	214,931	231,836	205,134	250,642	246,483	266,577	296,691
Europe [1]	687,320	1,180,130	1,210,679	1,397,704	1,682,023	1,844,182	2,005,931	2,185,898
Austria	2,872	9,264	11,236	14,897	14,646	13,546	15,628	16,876
Belgium	17,973	41,840	49,306	51,862	62,491	65,279	70,697	73,526
Czech Republic	1,228	2,444	2,729	3,615	4,066	5,053	5,355	5,909
Denmark	5,270	6,815	6,914	5,849	8,950	10,481	9,790	9,828
Finland..................	1,342	2,208	1,950	2,107	2,202	2,012	1,988	1,472
France	42,628	63,359	60,526	63,008	74,179	84,409	89,249	92,820
Germany	55,508	79,467	100,473	93,620	100,601	107,833	110,958	105,828
Greece	795	1,899	1,884	1,804	2,179	2,092	1,995	1,798
Hungary..................	1,920	3,024	2,795	2,602	6,457	3,737	3,914	4,863
Ireland	35,903	72,907	55,173	86,372	117,708	150,131	160,232	190,478
Italy	23,484	25,184	24,528	25,435	28,216	27,663	29,861	29,015
Luxembourg...............	27,849	83,634	79,937	125,146	144,180	172,251	206,133	274,923
Netherlands...............	115,429	219,384	240,205	279,373	412,122	423,059	481,140	521,427
Norway..................	4,379	8,491	8,533	9,667	12,188	24,706	27,652	33,843
Poland	3,884	7,256	5,575	6,934	15,614	12,489	13,455	12,684
Portugal.................	2,664	1,915	2,138	2,832	2,991	3,006	2,667	2,639
Russia	1,147	6,088	9,363	11,371	15,029	19,777	19,945	9,880
Spain...................	21,236	48,409	50,197	49,356	61,093	54,194	57,357	58,053
Sweden	25,959	29,730	30,153	33,857	36,615	35,876	35,846	29,444
Switzerland	55,377	121,790	100,692	102,022	94,675	133,222	149,772	143,627
Turkey	1,826	2,682	2,563	3,141	5,584	4,542	5,042	5,693
United Kingdom.............	230,762	330,416	351,513	406,358	426,357	448,412	458,536	508,369
Latin America and other								
Western Hemisphere..........	266,576	351,709	379,582	418,429	556,160	588,992	676,183	724,405
South America [1]	84,220	68,685	73,311	80,477	104,732	98,603	120,545	136,401
Argentina.................	17,488	9,201	10,103	13,174	13,692	12,197	14,328	12,111
Brazil...................	36,717	29,485	30,882	33,504	48,807	43,953	55,176	66,021
Chile	10,052	10,804	11,127	10,927	16,337	16,286	21,549	26,260
Colombia.................	3,693	2,991	4,292	3,799	4,552	5,028	6,176	6,574
Ecuador..................	832	881	941	904	1,007	1,098	1,209	1,250
Peru....................	3,130	4,773	5,542	5,561	5,964	4,448	5,594	7,907
Venezuela	10,531	9,109	8,934	10,922	12,871	13,545	14,242	13,693
Central America [1]...........	73,841	73,214	82,496	91,811	102,472	101,291	103,510	104,127
Costa Rica................	1,716	2,687	1,598	2,105	2,267	2,414	1,712	1,651
Honduras.................	399	755	821	864	626	809	870	1,027
Mexico..................	39,352	63,384	73,687	82,965	91,046	87,443	89,419	90,304
Panama..................	30,758	4,919	4,826	4,636	6,171	5,963	6,871	6,040
Other Western Hemisphere [1]	108,515	209,810	223,775	246,142	348,956	389,098	452,128	483,877
Bahamas, The	3,291	11,255	13,451	13,703	16,567	23,127	28,167	31,488
Barbados.................	2,141	3,249	3,881	4,831	2,136	3,154	4,068	5,710
Bermuda	60,114	100,856	113,222	133,480	211,708	207,547	254,541	264,442
Dominican Republic..........	1,143	1,028	815	789	712	806	1,105	1,344
Jamaica..................	2,483	3,551	1,018	940	801	940	708	678
Netherlands Antilles..........	3,579	4,712	5,607	3,924	6,483	13,314	17,036	22,935
Trinidad and Tobago..........	1,550	2,577	2,219	2,940	3,916	5,109	6,323	7,653
U.K. Islands, Caribbean.......	33,451	82,159	83,164	84,817	105,829	134,298	139,880	149,039
Africa [1]	11,891	20,356	22,756	28,158	32,607	36,746	43,575	53,522
Egypt...................	1,998	4,526	5,475	5,564	7,023	7,804	9,149	11,746
Nigeria..................	470	1,936	1,105	1,677	1,584	3,254	4,971	5,224
South Africa	3,562	3,913	3,969	3,980	5,240	4,999	6,107	6,503
Middle East [1]	10,863	18,963	21,115	24,206	28,448	31,294	36,257	36,573
Israel...................	3,735	6,171	7,978	9,168	9,487	9,444	9,273	9,694
Saudi Arabia	3,661	3,657	3,830	4,410	5,012	5,126	8,023	8,005
United Arab Emirates	683	2,962	2,285	2,670	2,967	3,337	4,195	4,271
Asia and Pacific [1]............	207,125	374,754	375,689	403,637	444,101	484,796	518,516	611,143
Australia.................	34,838	(D)	75,669	67,632	84,331	92,668	109,827	133,990
China [2].................	11,140	17,616	19,016	26,459	29,710	53,927	49,799	60,492
Hong Kong................	27,447	32,735	36,415	39,636	40,720	40,042	49,152	54,035
India....................	2,379	7,658	7,162	9,746	14,622	18,354	20,894	27,066
Indonesia................	8,904	(D)	8,603	9,484	14,978	16,273	15,645	15,502
Japan...................	57,091	71,005	81,175	84,428	85,224	99,803	96,015	113,263
Korea, South	8,968	17,747	19,760	27,299	23,558	22,426	26,813	30,165
Malaysia.................	7,910	8,909	11,097	11,185	12,140	12,243	13,235	15,982
New Zealand	4,271	4,620	5,191	5,933	5,527	4,451	6,270	6,872
Philippines...............	3,638	6,176	6,522	6,948	6,953	5,505	5,908	6,579
Singapore	24,133	61,076	76,390	81,879	93,529	83,169	88,925	106,042
Taiwan [2]	7,836	(D)	14,356	16,999	15,807	18,053	19,237	20,977
Thailand.................	5,824	7,499	10,352	10,642	10,284	9,162	9,776	12,701

D Suppressed to avoid disclosure of data of individual companies. [1] Includes other countries, not shown separately.
[2] See footnote 4, Table 1332.

Source: U.S. Bureau of Economic Analysis, *Survey of Current Business*, July 2011. For most recent copy and historical issues, see http://www.bea.gov/pubs.htm>.

U.S. Census Bureau, Statistical Abstract of the United States: 2012

Table 1297. U.S. Government Foreign Grants and Credits by Type and Country: 2000 to 2010

[In millions of dollars. (1,500 represents 1,500,000,000) See text, this section. Negative figures (–) occur when the total of grant returns, principal repayments, and/or foreign currencies disbursed by the U.S. Government exceeds new grants and new credits utilized and/or acquisitions of foreign currencies through new sales of farm products]

Country	2000	2004	2005	2006	2007	2008	2009	2010
Investment in financial institutions	1,500	1,994	1,263	2,024	1,651	1,385	1,676	2,337
Western Europe [1]	**429**	**346**	**327**	**60**	**182**	**225**	**253**	**340**
Ireland	–	50	–	30	–	34	7	14
Spain	–19	–19	–19	–205	(Z)	(Z)	(Z)	(Z)
Yugoslavia [2]	1	13	4	–73	–2	3	–5	–2
Bosnia and Hercegovina	52	66	72	49	45	29	27	41
Macedonia	50	42	68	31	1	35	21	29
Former Yugoslavia - Regional [2]	63	38	66	120	45	53	168	83
Other [3] and unspecified [4]	478	47	29	5	5	18	4	5
Eastern Europe [1]	**2,270**	**1,276**	**–95**	**266**	**1,089**	**2,010**	**1,644**	**1,490**
Albania	26	43	54	31	43	38	32	29
Romania	38	35	59	42	41	9	12	24
Newly Independent States of the former Soviet Union:								
Armenia	20	66	85	62	74	87	71	34
Azerbaijan	8	47	74	51	44	36	29	34
Belarus	1	1	2	4	6	8	10	4
Georgia	36	113	131	85	104	421	232	67
Kazakhstan	42	57	69	41	42	44	41	158
Kyrgyzstan	15	39	60	50	26	40	44	41
Moldova	32	27	39	26	21	53	43	19
Russia	797	251	–681	–920	–41	403	331	223
Tajikistan	8	40	61	35	33	24	33	32
Turkmenistan	4	4	13	3	(Z)	–9	11	9
Ukraine	138	114	147	120	72	83	112	125
Uzbekistan	22	53	52	23	13	11	9	5
Former Soviet Union—Regional [4]	501	372	456	470	461	508	535	485
Other [3] and unspecified [4]	419	105	153	73	73	76	73	100
Near East and South Asia [1]	**3,378**	**3,135**	**5,515**	**4,767**	**9,947**	**9,038**	**11,780**	**14,413**
Afghanistan	5	1,382	2,304	3,807	7,541	6,125	8,555	10,862
Bangladesh	43	50	52	44	81	76	53	71
Egypt	3,139	2,689	2,827	149	1,766	1,797	1,749	1,216
Greece	–149	–457	–114	–103	–74	–66	–74	–76
India	–64	–40	–69	63	46	28	28	41
Nepal	15	37	51	58	64	64	80	57
Pakistan	366	–341	532	712	527	688	1,254	1,528
Turkey	–80	–298	–225	–191	–296	–43	–28	46
UNRWA [5]	97	27	57	137	135	–	–	–
Other and unspecified [3]	21	79	54	47	117	310	141	635
Africa [1]	**1,054**	**2,228**	**2,120**	**1,261**	**3,546**	**4,778**	**6,425**	**7,315**
Algeria	–53	–145	–173	–1,324	–18	–18	–11	–13
Burundi	3	27	6	37	18	16	32	27
Cameroon	1	2	7	10	5	6	7	11
Cape Verde	1	4	4	9	7	28	38	2
Congo, Democratic Republic of the (former Zaire) [6]	(Z)	(Z)	17	1	10	11	12	7
Ethiopia	142	234	308	233	278	447	440	550
Ghana	40	67	53	57	65	87	157	123
Guinea	19	33	36	29	15	75	31	20
Kenya	44	82	96	187	179	284	390	340
Liberia	19	50	40	61	81	261	142	135
Madagascar	21	34	42	45	60	82	68	64
Malawi	45	54	46	68	75	88	95	92
Mali	50	46	55	57	55	58	114	94
Mozambique	119	105	65	98	111	152	192	146
Nigeria	–17	41	67	–178	123	200	211	255
Rwanda	26	36	49	55	70	93	111	103
Senegal	27	53	40	39	40	70	73	106
Somalia	7	16	10	33	40	168	108	35
South Africa	68	332	103	106	155	242	360	266
Sudan	17	120	130	390	364	529	513	521
Tanzania	15	66	65	76	114	129	207	215
Uganda	92	120	149	154	184	194	228	237
Zambia	44	56	91	91	119	164	151	121
Zimbabwe	23	31	27	32	59	141	153	113
Other and unspecified [4]	164	407	513	621	1,070	767	1,826	3,102
Far East and Pacific [1]	**551**	**–133**	**67**	**–93**	**144**	**696**	**621**	**865**
Cambodia	23	44	58	56	61	60	66	90
Hong Kong	–15	–28	–28	–28	–28	–23	–16	–15
Indonesia	272	–157	–3	–68	–14	–84	–46	66
Korea, Republic of	–132	–110	–43	–43	–40	182	–68	–67
Laos	5	5	2	1	1	3	5	6
Malaysia	134	–45	–40	–41	–185	2	2	4
Philippines	22	–14	–31	–25	51	143	128	133
Thailand	–99	8	9	–62	1	19	8	14
Pacific Islands, Trust Territory of the Pacific Island [7]	145	204	190	174	195	211	348	185
Other and unspecified [4]	19	40	47	37	182	200	215	214

See footnotes at end of table.

Table 1297. U.S. Government Foreign Grants and Credits by Type and Country: 2000 to 2010—Con.

[In millions of dollars. See headnote, page 801]

Country	2000	2004	2005	2006	2007	2008	2009	2010
Western Hemisphere [1].............	1,621	1,907	2,096	1,512	1,398	2,087	4,311	2,977
Bolivia.............	136	217	159	142	155	135	139	79
Brazil.............	195	−136	−93	−344	−181	−166	−87	−303
Colombia.............	33	467	598	620	771	914	1,223	642
Ecuador.............	14	37	60	80	73	52	60	47
El Salvador.............	27	103	51	28	42	58	100	48
Guatemala.............	49	40	21	34	25	55	66	68
Haiti.............	63	83	118	154	164	192	232	1,047
Honduras.............	100	83	71	63	87	100	133	56
Mexico.............	−123	14	40	30	51	52	1,277	418
Nicaragua.............	53	28	37	56	75	97	91	37
Panama [8].............	−13	14	8	11	6	9	7	9
Peru.............	87	168	127	71	−258	128	539	188
Other [9] and unspecified [4].............	1,100	725	745	471	407	366	426	439
Other international organizations.............	2,837	3,015	4,608	4,114	4,857	5,348	7,908	8,652
Middle East.............	4,345	8,413	16,705	10,220	10,195	10,801	9,608	9,028
Iraq [10].............	(Z)	5,040	10,857	9,157	7,039	6,228	5,269	2,942
Israel.............	3,932	2,163	4,953	390	2,373	2,955	1,994	2,692
Jordan.............	317	801	583	463	422	643	687	802
Lebanon.............	22	29	37	46	147	253	244	119
Yemen.............	16	31	25	30	40	22	31	48
West Bank-Gaza Regional.............	64	171	179	128	152	474	812	687

− Represents zero. Z Less than $500,000. [1] Includes other countries, not shown separately. [2] In 1992, some successor countries assumed portions of outstanding credits of the former Yugoslavia (assignment of the remaining portions is pending). Subsequent negative totals reflect payments to the United States on these assumed credits which were greater than the extension of new credits and grants to these countries. [3] Includes European Atomic Energy Community, European Coal and Steel Community, European Payments Union, European Productivity Agency, North Atlantic Treaty Organization, and Organization for European Economic Cooperation. [4] In recent years, significant amounts of foreign assistance has been reported on a regional, inter-regional, and worldwide basis. Country totals in this table may understate actual assistance to many countries. [5] United Nations Relief and Works Agency for Palestine refugees. [6] See footnote 5, table 1332. [7] Excludes transactions with Commonwealth of the Northern Mariana Islands after October 1986; includes transactions with Federated States of Micronesia, Republic of the Marshall Islands, and Republic of Palau. [8] Includes transfer of Panama Canal to the Republic of Panama on Dec. 1999. [9] Includes Andean Development Corporation, Caribbean Development Bank, Central American Bank for Economic Integration, Eastern Caribbean Central Bank, Inter-American Institute of Agricultural Science, Organizations of American States, and Pan American Health Organization. [10] Foreign assistance to Iraq in 1991−96 was direct humanitarian assistance to ethnic minorities of Northern Iraq after the conflict in the Persian Gulf. Foreign assistance to Iraq in 2003 thru 2009 includes Iraq Reconstruction and humanitarian assistance.

Source: U.S. Bureau of Economic Analysis, press releases, and unpublished data. See <http://www.bea.gov/scb/index.htm>.

Table 1298. U.S. Foreign Economic and Military Aid Programs: 1980 to 2009

[In millions of dollars (9,694 represents $9,694,000,000). For years ending September 30. Total aid programs are the sum of economic and military assistance. Major components in recent years include U.S. Agency for International Development (USAID), U.S. Department of Agriculture (USDA), State Department and voluntary contributions to international financial institutions. Annual figures are in obligations]

Year and Region	Total foreign assistance	Military assistance	Economic assistance, by funding agency					
			Total	USAID	USDA	State Department	Other U.S. agencies	Multilateral organizations
1980.............	9,694	2,122	7,572	4,062	1,437	459	137	1,478
1985.............	18,128	5,801	12,327	8,132	2,052	431	164	1,548
1990.............	16,015	4,971	11,044	6,964	1,643	590	377	1,469
1995.............	16,398	4,165	12,232	7,281	1,401	763	1,006	1,781
2000.............	18,101	4,876	13,224	5,907	2,567	2,486	1,154	1,110
2004.............	33,507	6,144	27,363	11,330	2,150	4,018	6,980	2,885
2005.............	37,076	7,352	29,724	10,102	2,318	5,020	10,626	1,659
2006.............	39,407	12,287	27,120	9,618	2,033	5,347	8,630	1,492
2007.............	40,857	13,203	27,655	11,414	1,835	5,634	7,038	1,733
2008.............	48,923	15,899	33,024	9,426	2,792	9,733	9,188	1,884
2009, total.............	**44,957**	**11,010**	**33,947**	**11,763**	**2,571**	**11,391**	**5,895**	**2,327**
Asia.............	12,307	6,215	6,092	3,190	299	1,373	1,093	137
Central Asia.............	1,913	148	1,764	665	18	234	847	−
Eastern Europe.............	498	87	411	208	−	86	117	−
Latin America and Caribbean....	3,027	127	2,900	880	133	1,247	595	45
Middle East and North Africa.....	9,460	4,051	5,409	3,189	32	1,524	664	−
Oceania.............	222	1	221	23	−	3	196	−
Sub-Saharan Africa.............	10,088	260	9,828	2,155	2,042	4,175	1,303	153
Western Europe.............	97	5	93	41	−	16	35	−
Canada.............	26	−	26	−	−	−	26	−
World, not specified.............	7,318	116	7,202	1,411	47	2,732	1,018	1,993

− Represents or rounds to zero.

Source: U.S. Agency for International Development (USAID), *U.S. Overseas Loans and Grants: Obligations and Loan Authorizations*, annual. See also <http://gbk.eads.usaidallnet.gov>.

Table 1299. U.S. Foreign Economic and Military Aid by Major Recipient Country: 2001 to 2009

[In millions of dollars (16,836 represents $16,836,000,000). For years ending September 30. Annual figures are in obligations]

Region/Country	2001	2005	2007	2008	2009 Total	2009 Economic aid	2009 Military aid
Total [1]	**16,836**	**37,176**	**40,857**	**48,923**	**44,957**	**33,947**	**11,010**
Afghanistan	106	2,252	5,813	8,892	8,764	3,046	5,718
Albania	55	43	35	46	37	34	3
Angola	88	67	49	58	55	54	1
Armenia	92	76	81	215	63	60	3
Azerbaijan	29	64	56	37	48	44	4
Bangladesh	162	84	93	171	172	171	1
Bolivia	203	162	181	128	101	101	–
Bosnia and Herzegovina	160	47	42	37	46	42	5
Bulgaria	60	44	27	26	21	12	9
Burundi	35	59	38	46	63	63	1
Cambodia	45	98	75	76	83	80	4
Chad	9	63	98	127	222	222	–
Colombia	264	824	497	888	895	839	57
Comoros	–	1	–	2	–	–	–
Congo (Kinshasa) [2]	99	121	150	260	349	325	23
Ecuador	65	87	66	52	46	45	1
Egypt	1,716	1,563	1,972	1,492	1,785	483	1,301
El Salvador	139	59	252	223	156	145	11
Eritrea	80	133	13	15	17	17	–
Ethiopia	212	693	463	996	940	939	2
Georgia	97	106	97	274	622	609	13
Ghana	70	72	431	230	175	174	1
Guatemala	80	96	84	111	141	140	1
Haiti	94	224	210	310	369	366	3
Honduras	52	271	63	74	42	42	–
India	222	214	161	148	133	132	1
Indonesia	195	588	236	208	226	209	17
Iraq	–	9,482	7,959	7,506	2,256	2,253	3
Israel	2,839	2,714	2,510	2,425	2,432	52	2,380
Jamaica	35	66	36	22	28	26	1
Jordan	272	683	542	879	816	578	238
Kazakhstan	47	66	105	112	91	86	5
Kenya	155	262	515	718	918	917	1
Kosovo	105	43	–	207	136	133	2
Liberia	54	148	257	312	225	173	52
Macedonia	64	48	35	32	33	29	3
Madagascar	50	89	67	119	68	68	–
Malawi	39	84	105	103	135	135	–
Mali	48	55	381	142	222	222	–
Marshall Islands	41	44	48	48	49	49	–
Mexico	55	102	89	95	499	466	34
Micronesia, Federated States of	82	94	100	79	108	108	–
Morocco	42	55	82	525	244	236	8
Mozambique	214	127	237	799	325	325	–
Namibia	16	50	91	131	396	396	–
Nepal	51	73	81	106	89	89	1
Nicaragua	67	96	58	145	46	44	1
Nigeria	98	151	340	485	501	498	2
Pakistan	188	758	975	963	1,783	1,354	429
Peru	216	191	165	159	149	148	1
Philippines	151	167	169	161	185	155	30
Poland	18	93	32	31	79	49	29
Romania	67	63	35	26	21	8	14
Russia	541	1,585	1,593	1,261	479	396	83
Rwanda	39	83	122	172	170	169	–
Senegal	41	48	72	78	144	143	1
Serbia	205	90	119	58	51	49	2
South Africa	70	187	399	568	571	570	1
Sri Lanka	28	160	44	69	90	82	8
Sudan	96	1,043	1,180	1,416	1,213	1,174	39
Tajikistan	62	64	33	70	48	47	1
Tanzania	107	137	233	1,056	377	377	–
Turkey	7	54	30	21	19	15	4
Uganda	95	291	366	456	474	470	4
Ukraine	146	149	165	111	167	158	9
Uzbekistan	60	42	17	14	12	12	–
West Bank/Gaza [3]	240	350	165	575	1,039	1,039	–
Zambia	51	144	204	263	292	292	–
Zimbabwe	23	61	141	234	286	286	–

– Represents or rounds to zero. [1] Includes other countries, not shown separately. [2] See footnote 5, Table 1332.
[3] See footnote 7, Table 1332.

Source: U.S. Agency for International Development, *U.S. Overseas Loans and Grants: Obligations and Loan Authorizations*, annual. See also <http://gbk.eads.usaidallnet.gov>.

Table 1300. U.S. International Trade in Goods and Services: 2000 to 2010

[In millions of dollars (–376,749 represents –$376,749,000,000). Data presented on a balance of payments basis and will not agree with the following merchandise trade tables in this section]

Category	2000	2004	2005	2006	2007	2008	2009	2010
TRADE BALANCE								
Total.	**–376,749**	**–605,357**	**–708,624**	**–753,288**	**–696,728**	**–698,338**	**–381,272**	**–500,027**
Goods	–445,787	–663,507	–780,730	–835,689	–818,886	–830,109	–505,910	–645,857
Services.	69,038	58,150	72,106	82,401	122,158	131,770	124,637	145,830
Travel	17,525	8,727	12,230	13,228	20,228	29,929	20,073	27,998
Passenger fares.	–3,416	–5,798	–4,580	–5,008	–2,494	–884	966	3,652
Other transportation	–11,647	–19,154	–22,199	–19,496	–15,135	–12,680	–7,058	–11,266
Royalties, license fees. . . .	35,202	43,403	48,871	58,511	71,324	72,502	67,334	72,133
Other private services	39,707	50,843	55,945	49,490	61,793	59,476	–13,863	–163,115
Other [1]	–6,488	–17,359	–15,594	–11,743	–10,826	–13,600	–3,346	–29,270
U.S. govt misc. services. . . .	–1,844	–2,512	–2,567	–2,581	–2,731	–2,972	–3,346	–3,500
EXPORTS								
Total.	**1,072,783**	**1,163,146**	**1,287,441**	**1,459,823**	**1,654,561**	**1,842,682**	**1,575,037**	**1,837,577**
Goods	784,781	821,986	911,686	1,039,406	1,163,957	1,307,499	1,069,491	1,288,699
Services.	288,002	341,160	375,755	420,417	490,604	535,183	505,547	548,878
Travel	82,891	75,465	82,160	86,187	97,355	110,423	94,191	103,505
Passenger fares.	20,197	17,932	20,609	21,638	25,187	30,957	26,103	30,931
Other transportation	25,562	29,791	32,013	35,824	40,638	44,016	35,533	39,936
Royalties, license fees. . . .	51,808	67,094	74,448	83,549	97,803	102,125	97,183	105,583
Other private services	100,792	141,465	153,665	176,798	211,641	232,019	234,858	250,320
Other [1]	6,210	8,751	12,082	15,587	17,091	14,711	16,611	17,483
U.S. govt misc. services. . . .	542	663	778	834	890	933	1,069	1,121
IMPORTS								
Total.	**1,449,532**	**1,768,502**	**1,996,065**	**2,213,111**	**2,351,289**	**2,541,020**	**1,956,310**	**2,337,604**
Goods	1,230,568	1,485,492	1,692,416	1,875,095	1,982,843	2,137,608	1,575,400	1,934,555
Services.	218,964	283,010	303,649	338,016	368,446	403,413	380,909	403,048
Travel	65,366	66,738	69,930	72,959	77,127	80,494	74,118	75,507
Passenger fares.	23,613	23,730	25,189	26,646	27,681	31,841	25,137	27,279
Other transportation	37,209	48,945	54,212	55,320	55,773	56,696	42,591	51,202
Royalties, license fees. . . .	16,606	23,691	25,577	25,038	26,479	29,623	29,849	33,450
Other private services	61,085	90,622	97,720	127,308	149,848	172,543	174,325	180,598
Other [1]	12,698	26,110	27,676	27,330	27,917	28,311	30,474	30,391
U.S. govt misc. services. . . .	2,386	3,175	3,345	3,415	3,621	3,905	4,415	4,621

[1] Represents transfers under U.S. military sales contracts for exports and direct defense expenditures for imports.
Source: U.S. Census Bureau, U.S. International Trade in Goods and Services, Annual Revision for 2010, Series FT-900(11-04) and previous reports. See also <http://www.census.gov/foreign-trade/Press-Release/2010pr/final_revisions/>.

Table 1301. U.S. International Trade in Goods by Related Parties: 2000 to 2010

[In millions of dollars (1,205,339 represents $1,205,339,000,000). "Related party trade" is trade by U.S. companies with their subsidiaries abroad as well as trade by U.S. subsidiaries of foreign companies with their parent companies. Based on the North American Industry Classification System (NAICS), 2002; see text, Section 15]

Country and commodity	2002 NAICS code	2000	2005	2008	2009	2010
IMPORTS FOR CONSUMPTION						
Total imports	(X)	1,205,339	1,662,380	2,090,483	1,549,163	1,898,610
Related party trade, total [1]	**(X)**	**563,084**	**775,730**	**975,096**	**740,481**	**922,202**
Canada	(X)	100,689	127,719	156,666	107,315	138,222
Japan.	(X)	108,290	108,322	111,898	73,859	93,892
Mexico	(X)	89,068	99,709	111,979	100,935	135,984
China [2]	(X)	18,061	62,716	89,339	84,829	107,038
Germany	(X)	37,781	51,870	64,058	45,000	53,951
Transportation equipment	336	161,150	188,445	189,984	132,812	179,516
Computer & electronic products	334	166,279	176,719	182,337	163,662	203,900
Chemicals	325	45,452	84,459	137,095	118,149	134,065
Machinery, except electrical	333	39,918	56,804	62,192	42,216	53,747
Oil & gas	211	13,241	48,725	104,091	61,700	80,071
EXPORTS						
Total exports	(X)	780,418	803,992	1,300,136	1,056,932	1,277,504
Related party trade, domestic exports, total [1] . . .	**(X)**	**196,596**	**245,712**	**373,646**	**261,332**	**314,489**
Canada	(X)	64,133	76,331	89,928	71,478	88,689
Mexico	(X)	34,249	44,570	51,789	39,653	49,313
Japan.	(X)	20,313	17,427	18,825	15,038	16,718
Netherlands.	(X)	6,845	9,308	16,364	15,784	15,070
Germany	(X)	6,751	9,250	18,275	11,902	12,588
Transportation equipment	336	46,288	52,513	63,946	43,758	55,400
Chemicals	325	26,376	48,121	61,497	54,655	64,548
Computer & electronic products	334	51,210	41,882	47,027	36,405	42,689
Machinery, except electrical	333	19,831	25,473	32,978	26,418	32,301
Electrical equipment, appliances & components. . . .	335	7,575	9,888	11,806	8,624	10,494

X Not applicable. [1] Includes other countries and other commodities, not shown separately. [2] See footnote 4, Table 1332.
Source: U.S. Census Bureau, "Related Party Trade—2010." See <http://www.census.gov/foreign-trade/Press-Release/2010pr/aip/related_party/rp10.pdf>.

Table 1302. U.S. Freight Gateways—Value of Shipments: 2009

[In billions of dollars, except as indicated (2,615.7 represents $2,615,700,000,000). For the top 50 gateways ranked by value of shipments. Trade does not include low value shipments. In general, these are imports of less than $1,250, exports less than $2,500, and intransit shipments]

Port	Mode	Rank	Total trade	Exports	Imports	Exports as a percent of total
Total U.S. merchandise trade	(X)	(X)	2,615.7	1,056.0	1,559.6	40.4
Top 50 gateways	(X)	(X)	2,067.5	810.4	1,257.1	39.2
As a percent of total	(X)	(X)	79.0	76.7	80.6	(X)
Port of Los Angeles, CA	Water	1	195.6	28.0	167.7	14.3
Port of New York and New Jersey, NY and NJ	Water	2	142.8	38.3	104.5	26.8
JFK International Airport, NY	Air	3	127.0	65.8	61.2	51.8
Port of Houston, TX..................	Water	4	106.1	57.7	48.4	54.4
Port of Laredo, TX	Land	5	95.1	45.3	49.8	47.7
Chicago, IL........................	Air	6	90.8	31.0	59.8	34.1
Port of Detroit, MI	Land	7	85.0	47.7	37.2	56.2
Port of Long Beach, CA..............	Water	8	68.5	24.2	44.4	35.2
Port of Los Angeles, CA	Air	9	63.1	30.9	32.2	49.0
Port of Buffalo-Niagara Falls, NY	Land	10	61.0	33.2	27.8	54.5
Port of Huron, MI	Land	11	58.5	28.4	30.1	48.5
Port of Savannah, GA	Water	12	46.6	18.9	27.7	40.5
New Orleans, LA	Air	13	44.9	19.2	25.7	42.8
Port of Charleston, SC.	Water	14	44.9	16.3	28.6	36.4
Port of Norfolk Harbor, VA	Water	15	43.0	18.9	24.0	44.0
Port of El Paso, TX	Land	16	42.3	17.9	24.4	42.3
San Francisco International Airport......	Air	17	39.8	21.0	18.8	52.8
Miami International Airport, FL	Air	18	39.1	27.5	11.7	70.2
Dallas-Forth Worth Airport, TX	Air	19	35.8	14.9	20.9	41.6
Anchorage, AK	Air	20	34.7	8.4	26.2	24.3
Port of Oakland, CA.................	Water	21	33.8	12.7	21.1	37.6
Port of Seattle, WA	Water	22	33.4	7.9	25.5	23.8
Port of New Orleans, LA	Water	23	32.9	18.5	14.4	56.4
Atlanta, GA	Air	24	32.3	11.5	20.8	35.6
Port of Baltimore, MD	Water	25	30.1	10.7	19.4	35.6
Port of Otay Mesa Station, CA.	Land	26	28.6	9.4	19.2	32.9
Cleveland, OH.....................	Air	27	26.8	15.7	11.2	58.3
Port of Tacoma, WA.................	Water	28	25.2	6.0	19.2	23.8
Port of Philadelphia, PA..............	Water	29	23.3	2.8	20.5	11.9
San Juan International Airport, PR	Air	30	21.9	13.7	8.3	62.3
Washington Dulles Airport, DC	Air	31	20.4	5.8	14.5	28.6
Annapolis, MD.....................	Water	32	19.4	–	19.4	
Port of Champlain-Rouses Pt., NY	Land	33	19.2	7.9	11.3	41.3
Port of Hidalgo, TX..................	Land	34	19.1	8.5	10.6	44.5
Port of Corpus Christi, TX	Water	35	18.7	4.0	14.7	21.3
Port of Miami, FL...................	Water	36	18.5	9.1	9.5	49.0
Port of Morgan City, LA	Water	37	17.1	0.2	16.8	1.4
Port of Port Everglades, FL	Water	38	16.3	9.5	6.8	58.5
Port of Nogales, AZ.................	Land	39	16.2	5.9	10.3	36.7
Port of Gramery, LA.................	Water	40	16.1	9.7	6.4	60.1
Port of Pembina, ND	Land	41	15.3	8.7	6.6	56.7
Blaine, WA	Land	42	14.6	9.1	5.5	62.6
Chicago, IL.	Land	43	14.0	–	14.0	–
Port of Jacksonville, FL	Water	44	13.5	6.0	7.5	44.4
Texas City, Texas	Water	45	13.3	2.7	10.6	20.6
Port Arthur, TX.....................	Water	46	13.1	2.3	10.8	17.8
Houston Intercontinental Airport, TX	Air	47	12.7	7.2	5.5	56.7
Eagle Pass, TX	Land	48	12.5	4.6	7.9	36.6
Newark, NJ	Air	49	12.4	4.1	8.3	32.9
Beaumont, TX.....................	Water	50	12.2	2.5	9.7	20.4

– Represents zero. X Not applicable.

Source: Air and Water: U.S. Department of Commerce, U.S. Census Bureau, Foreign Trade Division, USA Trade Online, special tabulation, available at <http://data.usatradeonline.gov/> as of December 2010. Air and Water: U.S. Department of Commerce, U.S. Census Bureau, Foreign Trade Division, USA Trade Online, special tabulation, available at <http://data.usatradeonline.gov/> as of December 2010. Land: U.S. Department of Transportation, Research and Innovative Technology Administration, Bureau of Transportation Statistics, TransBorder Freight Data, special tabulation, available at <http://www.bts.gov/programs/international/transborder/> as of March 2011.

Table 1303. U.S. Exports and Imports for Consumption of Merchandise by Customs District: 2000 to 2010

[In billions of dollars (780.0 represents $780,000,000,000). Exports are f.a.s. (free alongside ship) value all years; imports are on customs-value basis. These data may differ from those in Tables 1301, 1307, and 1308. For methodology, see Foreign Trade Statistics in Appendix III]

Customs district	Exports					Imports for consumption				
	2000	2005	2008	2009	2010	2000	2005	2008	2009	2010
Total [1]	780.0	901.1	1,287.4	1,056.0	1,278.3	1,205.6	1,673.5	2,103.6	1,559.6	1,913.2
Anchorage, AK	5.9	12.1	13.5	11.9	14.5	13.4	10.4	10.7	12.4	16.2
Baltimore, MD	6.2	9.0	16.5	11.2	14.7	18.6	29.6	31.3	21.0	28.8
Boston, MA	7.0	10.4	11.9	8.3	8.2	18.7	21.7	24.4	17.4	19.2
Buffalo, NY	38.2	35.0	43.5	35.7	40.4	38.4	42.6	46.0	31.6	39.2
Charleston, SC [2]	12.6	16.2	22.3	16.4	19.5	16.9	31.9	36.5	26.3	29.4
Chicago, IL	21.7	29.9	36.6	31.5	35.8	51.1	78.7	116.9	96.7	125.6
Cleveland, OH	22.7	20.8	23.8	21.4	25.3	36.5	49.0	70.4	55.8	69.2
Dallas/Fort Worth, TX	11.5	17.8	19.8	17.4	18.1	18.8	31.8	37.1	30.8	38.4
Detroit, MI	79.4	106.9	119.1	89.6	113.3	97.6	123.1	117.4	81.3	106.1
Duluth, MN	1.5	1.9	3.2	2.3	2.6	7.0	9.3	8.5	5.8	6.8
El Paso, TX	18.0	19.9	21.1	19.8	29.3	24.1	28.0	32.4	30.4	44.1
Great Falls, MT	5.0	9.8	18.0	15.3	17.4	14.3	27.1	34.9	21.7	26.3
Honolulu, HI	0.7	2.4	5.6	5.8	7.4	2.9	3.7	6.0	3.8	4.6
Houston/Galveston, TX	29.7	47.0	89.9	75.1	94.6	40.9	89.4	151.0	92.4	116.8
Laredo, TX	57.7	60.5	79.6	66.8	81.3	62.7	78.7	95.1	80.0	104.2
Los Angeles, CA	77.6	78.4	110.0	86.1	105.2	150.1	215.5	247.1	196.4	242.7
Miami, FL	31.0	34.1	54.9	49.5	58.8	23.3	31.8	35.4	29.6	36.6
Milwaukee, WI	0.1	0.1	0.2	0.1	0.1	1.5	1.3	1.1	0.7	0.9
Minneapolis, MN	1.4	2.3	2.3	2.0	2.6	4.3	6.9	16.6	11.4	13.6
Mobile, AL [2]	4.0	5.0	8.5	7.3	8.8	7.9	14.3	24.7	17.3	20.8
New Orleans, LA	35.9	32.6	65.6	57.0	68.1	54.0	97.8	151.3	94.2	125.3
New York, NY	79.5	90.9	143.7	110.9	136.3	145.6	176.7	209.5	155.6	190.5
Nogales, AZ	7.3	6.9	9.2	7.6	8.8	14.1	13.0	16.8	14.0	17.4
Norfolk, VA [2]	12.4	16.8	25.8	19.8	21.1	13.6	23.5	29.6	21.6	23.9
Ogdensburg, NY	12.4	13.3	16.5	13.5	16.2	23.7	28.2	33.0	23.9	27.8
Pembina, ND	8.7	13.6	22.0	16.9	21.3	11.0	12.8	17.4	12.5	14.7
Philadelphia, PA	6.0	10.2	19.4	13.1	14.3	28.3	47.8	73.3	49.2	56.9
Port Arthur, TX	1.2	2.1	5.3	4.9	6.5	10.9	20.9	32.4	20.1	26.4
Portland, ME	2.6	2.8	4.8	4.2	4.4	8.7	11.2	11.6	10.0	9.8
Portland, OR	7.2	6.3	14.3	10.3	12.3	12.5	14.2	16.9	11.0	12.2
Providence, RI	(Z)	0.1	0.3	0.2	0.3	1.3	4.4	5.7	4.0	5.8
San Diego, CA	12.7	15.0	16.6	14.0	16.2	22.2	28.4	37.4	30.4	32.4
San Francisco, CA	58.3	36.6	43.7	37.0	47.1	68.6	62.4	71.6	49.7	60.6
San Juan, PR	4.8	9.7	17.2	18.8	20.7	11.8	19.5	21.6	18.9	19.4
Savannah, GA	15.9	24.7	38.3	33.8	41.1	26.1	47.9	62.7	53.4	68.0
Seattle, WA	40.4	44.1	59.9	53.9	58.6	40.5	51.7	60.7	47.7	52.6
St. Albans, VT	4.5	4.3	3.8	2.9	3.3	9.4	12.6	10.2	7.6	6.9
St. Louis, MO	1.3	1.3	2.8	1.6	1.0	7.9	9.7	12.7	10.1	11.5
Tampa, FL	4.8	10.1	18.1	10.4	14.4	14.7	19.3	22.2	13.6	16.4
Virgin Islands, U.S.	0.3	0.5	2.7	1.2	1.9	4.8	9.1	16.6	9.2	10.5
Washington, DC	2.8	3.7	5.7	6.0	6.0	2.6	3.7	8.8	10.2	8.2
Wilmington, NC	2.5	2.2	3.2	4.0	5.3	10.6	15.4	15.3	12.9	12.8

Z Less than $50 million. [1] Totals shown for exports reflect the value of estimated parcel post and Special Category shipments, and adjustments for undocumented exports to Canada, which are not distributed by customs district. The value of bituminous coal exported through Norfolk, VA; Charleston, SC; and Mobile, AL is reflected in the total but not distributed by district. [2] Excludes exports of bituminous coal, which are included in "Total."

Source: U.S. Census Bureau, U.S. Highlights of Export and Import Trade, series FT 990; U.S. Merchandise Trade: Selected Highlights, series FT 920; 1991-2004, U.S. Export History and U.S. Import History on compact disc; 2005-2010, U.S. Merchandise Trade: Selected Highlights, December issues, series FT920. See also <http://www.census.gov/foreign-trade/Press-Release/ft920_index.html>.

Table 1304. Export and Import Unit Value Indexes—Selected Countries: 2006 to 2010

[Indexes in U.S. dollars, 2005 = 100. A unit value is an implicit price derived from value and quantity data]

Country	Export unit value					Import unit value				
	2006	2007	2008	2009	2010	2006	2007	2008	2009	2010
United States	103.6	108.6	115.2	109.8	115.2	104.9	109.3	121.9	107.9	115.3
Australia	114.0	127.4	159.6	138.4	169.1	102.7	109.5	119.8	111.3	123.9
Belgium	105.2	119.7	133.0	118.6	122.3	105.9	118.0	132.7	114.5	120.6
Canada	107.2	115.4	126.9	107.0	120.1	107.2	111.8	120.0	111.6	120.8
France	100.4	109.5	115.3	(NA)	(NA)	102.0	112.4	120.1	(NA)	(NA)
Germany	101.7	113.4	122.2	113.1	(NA)	104.7	116.1	128.3	112.1	(NA)
Greece	105.7	118.8	135.3	120.6	125.1	105.1	117.7	134.9	125.7	127.8
Ireland	100.8	107.1	110.9	105.7	(NA)	103.8	113.3	122.3	111.2	(NA)
Italy	106.1	121.6	137.4	127.8	129.3	110.5	124.1	144.8	123.5	130.0
Japan	97.7	98.6	105.6	104.3	108.2	108.0	114.6	141.8	116.9	133.3
Korea, South	100.6	103.8	108.4	90.5	101.2	107.7	114.0	138.1	104.9	117.7
Netherlands	104.2	115.3	129.1	112.3	114.3	104.6	116.0	129.9	113.8	116.6
Norway	120.1	131.7	164.8	120.3	135.2	104.9	119.4	129.3	115.1	118.6
Spain	105.7	118.2	128.9	113.9	111.3	103.9	114.9	127.6	108.1	108.4
Sweden	105.4	119.4	125.7	111.1	116.7	107.2	119.6	130.3	111.3	118.1
Switzerland	102.7	111.6	127.8	130.7	136.2	104.5	113.6	126.2	120.3	125.5
United Kingdom	103.7	113.0	118.2	102.9	107.8	104.7	114.8	118.9	104.4	109.9

NA Not available.

Source: International Monetary Fund, Washington, DC, International Financial Statistics, monthly, (copyright).

U.S. Census Bureau, Statistical Abstract of the United States: 2012

Table 1305. U.S. Exports of Goods by State of Origin: 2000 to 2010

[In millions of dollars (782,429 represents $782,429,000,000), except as indicated. Exports are on a f.a.s. (free along ship) value basis. Exports are based on origin of movement]

State and other areas	Exports 2000	Exports 2009	2010 Total	2010 Rank	State and other areas	Exports 2000	Exports 2009	2010 Total	2010 Rank
Total.............	782,429	1,056,043	1,278,263	(X)	Nebraska...........	2,511	4,873	5,820	35
					Nevada	1,482	5,672	5,912	34
United States	712,055	1,000,266	1,207,883	(X)	New Hampshire.....	2,373	3,061	4,367	40
Alabama	7,317	12,355	15,502	25	New Jersey........	18,638	27,244	32,154	11
Alaska............	2,464	3,270	4,155	42	New Mexico........	2,391	1,270	1,541	46
Arizona...........	14,334	14,023	15,636	24	New York..........	42,846	58,743	69,696	3
Arkansas..........	2,599	5,267	5,219	37	North Carolina......	17,946	21,793	24,905	16
California..........	119,640	120,080	143,192	2	North Dakota.......	626	2,193	2,536	44
Colorado..........	6,593	5,867	6,727	32	Ohio..............	26,322	34,104	41,494	8
Connecticut	8,047	13,979	16,056	23	Oklahoma	3,072	4,415	5,353	36
Delaware..........	2,197	4,312	4,966	39	Oregon............	11,441	14,907	17,671	21
District of Columbia...	1,003	1,091	1,501	47	Pennsylvania.......	18,792	28,381	34,928	10
Florida............	26,543	46,888	55,365	4	Rhode Island.......	1,186	1,496	1,949	45
Georgia...........	14,925	23,743	28,950	12	South Carolina......	8,565	16,488	20,329	17
Hawaii............	387	563	684	51	South Dakota.......	679	1,011	1,259	49
Idaho.............	3,559	3,877	5,157	38	Tennessee.........	11,592	20,484	25,943	15
Illinois............	31,438	41,626	50,058	6	Texas.............	103,866	162,995	206,961	1
Indiana............	15,386	22,907	28,745	13	Utah..............	3,221	10,337	13,809	26
Iowa..............	4,466	9,042	10,880	28	Vermont...........	4,097	3,219	4,277	41
Kansas............	5,145	8,917	9,905	30	Virginia...........	11,698	15,052	17,163	22
Kentucky	9,612	17,650	19,343	19	Washington	32,215	51,851	53,353	5
Louisiana..........	16,814	32,616	41,356	9	West Virginia	2,219	4,826	6,449	33
Maine.............	1,779	2,231	3,164	43	Wisconsin	10,508	16,725	19,790	18
Maryland	4,593	9,225	10,163	29	Wyoming	503	926	983	50
Massachusetts.......	20,514	23,593	26,304	14					
Michigan	33,845	32,655	44,768	7	Puerto Rico	9,735	20,937	22,784	(X)
Minnesota	10,303	15,532	18,904	20	Virgin Islands	174	1,217	1,899	(X)
Mississippi	2,726	6,316	8,229	31	Other [1]...........	60,810	33,620	45,698	(X)
Missouri	6,497	9,522	12,926	27	Timing adjustments ..	-346	(X)	(X)	(X)
Montana...........	541	1,053	1,389	48					

X Not applicable. [1] Includes unreported, not specified, special category, estimated shipments, and re-exports.
Source: U.S. Census Bureau, *U.S. International Trade in Goods and Services*, December issues, series FT-900.
See <http://www.census.gov/foreign-trade/Press-Release/2010pr/12/>.

Table 1306. U.S. Agricultural Exports by State: 2000 to 2009

[In millions of dollars (50,762 represents $50,762,000,000). For years ending September 30]

State	2000	2005	2007	2008	2009	State	2000	2005	2007	2008	2009
U.S.........	50,762	62,516	82,217	115,305	96,632						
AL	401	563	626	994	867	NE	2,816	2,821	4,063	5,930	4,826
AK	2	3	4	5	5	NV	39	44	45	60	72
AZ	391	412	496	746	626	NH..........	14	15	20	24	23
AR	1,210	1,713	2,123	3,200	2,616	NJ..........	150	193	244	334	311
CA	6,298	9,354	11,313	13,353	12,499	NM..........	82	143	271	383	262
CO	894	632	1,018	1,235	1,113	NY	515	626	836	1,163	928
CT	140	171	257	377	339	NC	1,525	1,802	2,068	3,107	2,879
DE	127	136	162	247	236	ND..........	1,475	1,705	2,545	3,949	3,186
FL	1,469	1,546	1,925	2,188	2,060	OH..........	1,348	1,579	2,202	2,840	2,671
GA	908	1,118	1,438	2,057	1,841	OK..........	534	761	890	1,632	982
HI	81	95	88	100	102	OR	749	912	1,194	1,551	1,340
ID..........	803	905	1,203	1,815	1,484	PA	989	1,151	1,516	1,941	1,732
IL	2,951	3,281	4,723	7,560	5,538	RI..........	7	11	13	15	16
IN..........	1,501	1,821	2,436	3,805	3,140	SC	333	344	390	663	550
IA..........	2,944	4,002	5,259	7,870	6,486	SD..........	1,094	1,236	1,864	3,054	2,327
KS	2,929	2,910	3,883	5,930	4,705	TN	561	817	785	1,365	1,202
KY	806	1,085	1,237	1,662	1,485	TX	2,877	3,626	5,210	6,042	4,747
LA	426	568	733	953	838	UT	246	249	334	462	374
ME	61	73	105	122	112	VT	14	75	119	155	130
MD..........	273	286	362	487	439	VA	490	513	548	825	718
MA	120	73	105	121	119	WA..........	1,595	1,942	2,665	3,174	2,968
MI.	813	1,044	1,372	1,924	1,552	WV..........	36	40	49	70	67
MN..........	2,230	2,768	3,619	5,469	4,284	WI	1,283	1,512	2,090	3,014	2,238
MS..........	571	956	1,176	1,707	1,275	WY	48	51	62	114	104
MO..........	1,204	1,361	2,024	3,195	2,706						
MT..........	319	585	739	1,257	929	Unallocated ...	2,072	2,882	3,825	5,171	4,689

Source: U.S. Department of Agriculture, Economic Research Service, "State Export Data," <http://www.ers.usda.gov/data/stateexports/>.

Table 1307. U.S. Exports, Imports, and Merchandise Trade Balance by Country: 2005 to 2010

[In millions of dollars (901,082 represents $901,082,000,000). Includes silver ore and bullion. Country totals include exports of special category commodities, if any. Data include nonmonetary gold and include trade of Virgin Islands with foreign countries. For methodology, see Foreign Trade Statistics in Appendix III. Minus sign (–) denotes an excess of imports over exports]

Country	Exports, domestic and foreign					General imports [1]					Merchandise trade balance				
	2005	2007	2008	2009	2010	2005	2007	2008	2009	2010	2005	2007	2008	2009	2010
Total [1]	901,082	1,148,199	1,287,442	1,056,043	1,278,263	1,673,455	1,956,962	2,103,641	1,559,625	1,913,160	-772,373	-808,763	-816,199	-503,582	-634,897
Afghanistan	262	495	482	1,509	2,156	67	74	85	116	85	195	421	397	1,392	2,071
Albania	19	34	40	48	46	37	10	12	15	30	-19	24	28	33	16
Algeria	1,106	1,652	1,243	1,108	1,195	10,446	17,816	19,355	10,718	14,518	-9,340	-16,164	-18,112	-9,610	-13,323
Angola	929	1,242	2,019	1,423	1,294	8,484	12,508	18,911	9,339	11,940	-7,555	-11,266	-16,892	-7,916	-10,646
Anguilla	32	93	81	53	36	4	5	4	6	3	28	88	77	47	33
Antigua and Barbuda	190	240	183	157	158	4	8	5	9	5	186	232	178	148	153
Argentina	4,122	5,856	7,536	5,569	7,395	4,584	4,487	5,822	3,890	3,803	-462	1,369	1,714	1,679	3,592
Armenia	65	111	151	77	113	46	33	43	78	75	19	78	109	–	38
Aruba	559	529	680	446	541	2,920	2,995	3,179	1,278	19	-2,361	-2,466	-2,499	-833	522
Australia	15,589	19,178	22,219	19,599	21,798	7,342	8,615	10,589	8,012	8,583	8,246	10,563	11,630	11,588	13,215
Austria	2,544	3,110	2,649	2,537	2,428	6,103	10,669	8,457	6,379	6,835	-3,558	-7,559	-5,808	-3,842	-4,407
Azerbaijan	132	178	239	185	253	45	1,887	4,361	1,973	1,989	87	-1,710	-4,122	-1,787	-1,736
Bahamas, The	1,787	2,468	2,760	2,504	3,178	700	504	604	819	807	1,087	1,965	2,155	1,685	2,371
Bahrain	351	591	830	667	1,250	432	625	539	463	420	-81	-33	291	204	830
Bangladesh	320	456	468	435	578	2,693	3,432	3,748	3,699	4,294	-2,373	-2,976	-3,280	-3,264	-3,716
Barbados	395	457	497	405	397	32	38	40	33	43	363	419	457	372	354
Belarus	35	102	134	137	133	345	1,033	1,070	574	175	-310	-932	-935	-437	-42
Belgium	18,691	25,259	28,903	21,608	25,456	13,023	15,281	17,308	13,826	15,552	5,668	9,977	11,595	7,782	9,904
Belize	218	234	353	253	289	98	105	154	100	120	119	129	199	153	169
Benin	72	289	846	397	463	1	5	31	–	–	72	284	815	397	463
Bermuda	490	660	822	807	637	87	24	140	13	22	403	636	682	794	615
Bolivia	219	278	389	431	507	293	363	511	504	680	-74	-85	-122	-73	-173
Bosnia and Herzegovina	18	20	34	21	26	70	25	25	25	26	-53	-5	9	-4	0
Botswana	67	54	62	93	48	178	187	219	132	170	-111	-134	-157	-39	-122
Brazil	15,372	24,172	32,299	26,095	35,425	24,436	25,644	30,453	20,070	23,958	-9,064	-1,472	1,846	6,026	11,467
Brunei	50	140	112	100	124	563	405	114	42	12	-513	-265	-3	59	112
Bulgaria	268	306	509	224	171	454	426	391	228	260	-186	-120	119	-4	-89
Cambodia	70	139	154	127	154	1,767	2,463	2,412	1,924	2,301	-1,697	-2,325	-2,257	-1,797	-2,147
Cameroon	117	133	125	154	132	158	297	614	250	297	-41	-164	-489	-96	-165
Canada	211,899	248,888	261,150	204,658	249,105	290,384	317,057	339,491	226,248	277,647	-78,486	-68,169	-78,342	-21,590	-28,542
Cayman Islands	681	640	746	643	582	53	21	14	14	11	627	619	732	630	571
Chad	54	66	63	63	88	1,498	2,145	3,334	1,984	2,044	-1,444	-2,079	-3,272	-1,921	-1,956
Chile	5,134	8,148	11,857	9,346	10,905	6,664	8,999	8,196	5,949	7,009	-1,531	-851	3,661	3,396	3,896
China [2]	41,192	62,937	69,733	69,497	91,881	243,470	321,443	337,773	296,374	364,944	-202,278	-258,506	-268,040	-226,877	-273,063
Colombia	5,462	8,558	11,437	9,451	12,069	8,849	9,434	13,093	11,323	15,659	-3,387	-876	-1,656	-1,872	-3,590
Congo (Brazzaville) [3]	104	140	185	277	254	1,623	3,071	5,074	3,105	3,316	-1,519	-2,931	-4,889	-2,828	-3,062
Congo (Kinshasa) [3]	65	113	130	79	93	264	206	266	331	528	-199	-94	-136	-251	-435
Costa Rica	3,599	4,580	5,680	4,700	5,180	3,415	3,942	3,938	5,612	8,697	183	639	1,742	-912	-3,517
Cote d'Ivoire	124	162	254	206	163	1,198	600	1,092	745	1,177	-1,074	-439	-838	-539	-1,014
Croatia	159	247	467	202	312	364	332	271	251	333	-206	-85	196	-49	-21
Cuba	369	447	712	533	368	–	–	–	–	–	369	447	711	533	368
Cyprus	84	169	217	179	134	31	17	14	53	11	54	152	204	126	123
Czech Republic	1,054	1,262	1,378	970	1,411	2,193	2,431	2,569	1,933	2,450	-1,139	-1,168	-1,190	-964	-1,039

See footnotes at end of table.

Table 1307. U.S. Exports, Imports, and Merchandise Trade Balance by Country: 2005 to 2010—Con.

[See headnote, page 808]

Country	Exports, domestic and foreign					General imports [1]					Merchandise trade balance				
	2005	2007	2008	2009	2010	2005	2007	2008	2009	2010	2005	2007	2008	2009	2010
Total [1]	**901,082**	**1,148,199**	**1,287,442**	**1,056,043**	**1,278,263**	**1,673,455**	**1,956,962**	**2,103,641**	**1,559,625**	**1,913,160**	**-772,373**	**-808,763**	**-816,199**	**-503,582**	**-634,897**
Denmark	1,918	2,890	2,711	2,056	2,133	5,144	6,064	6,446	5,511	6,011	-3,226	-3,175	-3,735	-3,454	-3,878
Djibouti	48	59	141	196	123	1	4	7	3	3	46	54	134	194	120
Dominica	62	84	105	77	73	3	2	2	3	2	58	82	103	74	71
Dominican Republic	4,719	6,084	6,594	5,269	6,579	4,604	4,216	3,978	3,329	3,672	115	1,868	2,617	1,939	2,907
Ecuador	1,964	2,936	3,450	3,938	5,410	5,759	6,135	9,048	5,273	7,451	-3,795	-3,199	-5,598	-1,335	-2,041
Egypt	3,159	5,259	6,002	5,253	6,835	2,091	2,377	2,370	2,058	2,238	1,068	2,883	3,632	3,195	4,597
El Salvador	1,854	2,313	2,462	2,019	2,433	1,989	2,044	2,228	1,822	2,206	-134	270	234	197	227
Equatorial Guinea	281	236	185	306	272	1,561	1,777	3,367	2,489	2,214	-1,280	-1,541	-3,183	-2,184	-1,942
Estonia	145	242	226	189	188	511	296	392	162	698	-366	-54	-167	27	-510
Ethiopia	456	167	302	267	773	62	88	152	113	128	394	79	149	154	645
Fiji	28	30	55	31	44	169	153	162	144	179	-141	-123	-107	-113	-135
Finland	2,254	3,133	3,761	1,662	2,181	4,342	5,266	5,903	3,985	3,884	-2,088	-2,133	-2,142	-2,323	-1,703
France	22,259	26,676	28,840	26,493	26,969	33,842	41,553	44,049	34,236	38,355	-11,583	-14,877	-15,209	-7,743	-11,386
French Guiana	27	31	18	17	36	—	—	—	—	—	27	31	18	17	36
French Polynesia	112	124	130	113	122	60	62	72	29	53	52	62	58	83	69
Gabon	99	478	284	171	243	2,816	2,182	2,279	1,231	2,212	-2,716	-1,704	-1,995	-1,060	-1,969
Georgia	214	364	586	364	301	194	212	208	70	198	20	153	379	294	103
Germany	34,184	49,420	54,505	43,306	48,161	84,751	94,164	97,497	71,498	82,429	-50,567	-44,744	-42,991	-28,192	-34,268
Ghana	337	416	608	716	989	158	199	222	135	273	179	218	386	581	716
Gibraltar	163	594	2,641	1,087	1,494	5	3	1	1	1	159	591	2,639	1,086	1,493
Greece	1,192	2,110	1,932	2,487	1,108	884	1,192	999	841	798	309	918	933	1,647	310
Grenada	82	83	84	59	71	6	8	7	6	8	77	75	77	53	63
Guadeloupe	55	139	384	206	365	2	5	7	2	2	52	134	377	204	363
Guatemala	2,835	4,065	4,718	3,875	4,478	3,137	3,026	3,463	3,148	3,193	-302	1,039	1,256	727	1,285
Guinea	94	74	102	95	85	75	99	106	67	69	19	-26	-5	28	16
Guyana	177	188	289	260	290	120	123	146	173	299	57	65	143	87	-9
Haiti	710	680	944	790	1,209	447	488	450	552	551	262	192	494	238	658
Honduras	3,254	4,461	4,846	3,368	4,606	3,749	3,912	4,041	3,319	3,932	-495	549	805	48	674
Hong Kong	16,351	19,902	21,499	21,051	26,570	8,892	7,026	6,483	3,571	4,296	7,459	12,876	15,015	17,480	22,274
Hungary	1,023	1,292	1,431	1,233	1,290	2,561	2,828	3,103	2,223	2,489	-1,538	-1,536	-1,672	-991	-1,199
Iceland	512	630	470	350	325	269	206	241	179	201	243	424	229	170	124
India	7,919	14,969	17,682	16,441	19,250	18,804	24,073	25,704	21,166	29,533	-10,886	-9,104	-8,022	-4,725	-10,283
Indonesia	3,054	3,970	5,644	5,107	6,946	12,014	14,301	15,799	12,939	16,478	-8,960	-10,332	-10,155	-7,832	-9,532
Iran	96	145	683	280	208	174	173	104	65	95	-79	-28	579	216	113
Iraq	1,374	1,560	2,070	1,772	1,642	9,054	11,396	22,080	9,263	12,143	-7,680	-9,835	-20,010	-7,491	-10,501
Ireland	8,447	7,777	7,611	7,465	7,276	28,733	30,445	31,346	28,101	33,848	-20,286	-22,668	-23,736	-20,636	-26,572
Israel	9,737	12,887	14,487	9,559	11,294	16,830	20,794	22,336	18,744	20,982	-7,093	-7,907	-7,849	-9,185	-9,688
Italy	11,524	14,150	15,461	12,268	14,219	31,009	35,028	36,135	26,430	28,505	-19,485	-20,878	-20,674	-14,162	-14,286
Jamaica	1,701	2,316	2,643	1,441	1,662	376	720	729	468	328	1,325	1,596	1,915	973	1,334
Japan	54,681	61,160	65,142	51,134	60,486	138,004	145,463	139,262	95,804	120,545	-83,323	-84,304	-74,120	-44,669	-60,059
Jordan	644	856	940	1,192	1,174	1,267	1,329	1,137	924	974	-623	-473	-197	268	200
Kazakhstan	538	753	986	603	730	1,101	1,252	1,603	1,544	1,872	-563	-499	-618	-940	-1,142
Kenya	573	520	442	654	375	348	325	344	281	311	225	195	99	373	64
Korea, South	27,572	34,402	34,669	28,612	38,846	43,781	47,562	48,069	39,216	48,875	-16,210	-13,161	-13,400	-10,604	-10,029

See footnotes at end of table.

U.S. Census Bureau, Statistical Abstract of the United States: 2012

Table 1307. U.S. Exports, Imports, and Merchandise Trade Balance by Country: 2005 to 2010—Con.

[See headnote, page 808]

Country	Exports, domestic and foreign					General imports [1]					Merchandise trade balance				
	2005	2007	2008	2009	2010	2005	2007	2008	2009	2010	2005	2007	2008	2009	2010
Kuwait	1,975	2,484	2,719	1,951	2,774	4,335	4,118	7,093	3,783	5,382	-2,360	-1,634	-4,374	-1,831	-2,608
Kyrgyzstan	31	49	44	57	79	5	2	2	6	4	27	47	42	51	75
Latvia	178	381	394	289	345	362	334	228	142	193	-185	47	166	147	152
Lebanon	466	826	1,464	1,852	2,009	86	104	99	77	84	379	722	1,365	1,775	1,925
Lesotho	4	8	1	17	11	404	443	374	304	299	-400	-436	-373	-288	-288
Liberia	69	76	157	95	191	91	115	143	80	180	-22	-39	13	14	11
Libya	84	511	721	666	666	1,590	3,385	4,179	1,919	2,117	-1,506	-2,874	-3,458	-1,253	-1,451
Liechtenstein	20	16	29	23	29	296	284	245	180	213	-276	-268	-216	-156	-184
Lithuania	390	720	831	399	628	634	456	750	590	637	-244	265	81	-191	-9
Luxembourg	711	926	988	1,292	1,439	389	526	536	443	451	323	399	452	849	988
Macau	102	226	307	209	225	1,249	1,095	915	237	141	-1,147	-869	-609	-28	84
Macedonia	32	34	36	35	34	48	73	78	44	37	-17	-39	-42	-9	-3
Madagascar	28	32	71	106	116	324	338	324	253	108	-295	-306	-254	-148	8
Malawi	28	51	45	40	37	116	59	65	63	72	-87	-8	-20	-23	-35
Malaysia	10,461	11,680	12,949	10,403	14,080	33,685	32,629	30,736	23,283	25,900	-23,224	-20,948	-17,787	-12,879	-11,820
Mali	32	32	31	37	37	4	9	5	4	6	-89	22	26	33	31
Malta	194	207	253	208	457	283	329	279	219	262	13	-121	-25	-10	195
Martinique	35	194	289	263	297	22	7	8	5	23	85	186	281	258	274
Mauritania	86	103	107	56	83	1	1	46	35	53	102	102	60	22	30
Mauritius	31	50	51	70	40	222	187	176	169	196	-191	-138	-125	-99	-156
Mexico	120,248	135,918	151,220	128,892	163,473	170,109	210,714	215,942	176,654	229,908	-49,861	-74,796	-64,722	-47,762	-66,435
Moldova	40	53	66	27	38	50	23	12	8	12	-10	30	54	18	26
Monaco	17	43	63	18	49	37	21	22	39	24	-21	21	40	-21	25
Mongolia	22	26	57	41	115	144	83	53	15	12	-122	-57	4	26	103
Morocco	481	1,294	1,436	1,630	1,947	446	610	879	468	685	35	684	557	1,162	1,262
Mozambique	63	115	213	190	224	12	5	17	39	65	51	110	197	151	159
Namibia	112	128	280	202	111	130	220	301	329	195	-17	-92	-21	-126	-84
Nepal	25	29	29	31	28	111	90	85	55	61	-87	-61	-56	-24	-33
Netherlands	26,468	32,837	39,719	32,242	34,939	14,862	18,403	21,123	16,098	19,055	11,606	14,434	18,597	16,143	15,884
Netherlands Antilles	1,138	2,082	2,952	2,056	2,943	922	782	809	476	1,026	215	1,300	2,142	1,580	1,917
New Caledonia	38	58	89	78	108	27	79	50	27	71	11	-22	39	51	37
New Zealand	2,592	2,718	2,534	2,159	2,819	3,155	3,113	3,171	2,558	2,762	-563	-396	-637	-399	57
Nicaragua	625	890	1,094	715	981	1,181	1,604	1,704	1,612	2,007	-555	-714	-609	-897	-1,026
Niger	79	69	50	58	49	66	10	44	106	27	13	60	6	-48	22
Nigeria	1,620	2,778	4,102	3,687	4,068	24,239	32,770	38,068	19,128	30,516	-22,620	-29,992	-33,966	-15,441	-26,448
Norway	1,942	3,040	3,292	2,790	3,099	6,776	7,318	7,315	5,688	6,950	-4,834	-4,277	-4,023	-2,898	-3,851
Oman	571	1,059	1,382	1,126	1,105	555	1,041	852	907	773	16	18	530	219	332
Pakistan	1,252	1,944	1,898	1,618	1,901	3,253	3,578	3,591	3,163	3,509	-2,002	-1,634	-1,693	-1,545	-1,608
Panama	2,162	3,669	4,887	4,293	6,063	327	365	379	302	381	1,835	3,304	4,508	3,991	5,682
Papua New Guinea	55	66	70	218	186	58	109	106	103	97	-3	-43	-36	115	89
Paraguay	896	1,237	1,610	1,355	1,810	52	68	78	56	62	844	1,169	1,532	1,299	1,748
Peru	2,309	4,120	6,183	4,919	6,754	5,119	5,272	5,812	4,223	5,057	-2,810	-1,152	371	696	1,697
Philippines	6,895	7,712	8,295	5,766	7,376	9,250	9,408	8,713	6,794	7,982	-2,355	-1,696	-418	-1,028	-606
Poland	1,268	3,123	4,131	2,302	2,982	1,949	2,226	2,587	2,038	2,964	-681	897	1,544	263	18
Portugal	1,132	2,478	2,646	1,085	1,058	2,329	3,049	2,451	1,577	2,141	-1,197	-571	195	-492	-1,083
Qatar	987	2,524	2,716	2,713	3,160	448	477	484	506	466	539	2,046	2,232	2,207	2,694
Romania	609	677	1,048	672	730	1,208	1,054	1,107	752	1,008	-599	-378	-58	-80	-278

See footnotes at end of table.

U.S. Census Bureau, Statistical Abstract of the United States: 2012

Table 1307. U.S. Exports, Imports, and Merchandise Trade Balance by Country: 2005 to 2010—Con.

[See headnote, page 808]

Country	Exports, domestic and foreign					General imports [1]					Merchandise trade balance				
	2005	2007	2008	2009	2010	2005	2007	2008	2009	2010	2005	2007	2008	2009	2010
Russia	3,962	7,283	9,335	5,332	6,006	15,307	19,314	26,783	18,200	25,691	-11,344	-12,031	-17,448	-12,868	-19,685
Saudi Arabia	6,805	10,396	12,484	10,792	11,556	27,193	35,626	54,747	22,053	31,413	-20,387	-25,230	-42,263	-11,261	-19,857
Senegal	141	150	137	176	218	4	19	18	7	5	138	132	119	169	213
Serbia and Montenegro	132	–	–	–	–	55	–	–	–	–	78	–	–	–	–
Sierra Leone	38	55	59	43	61	9	48	48	24	29	29	7	12	18	32
Singapore	20,466	25,619	27,854	22,232	29,017	15,110	18,394	15,885	15,705	17,427	5,356	7,225	11,969	6,527	11,590
Slovakia	150	503	548	210	256	961	1,505	1,301	628	1,073	-811	-1,002	-754	-418	-817
Slovenia	234	297	310	244	328	413	488	467	388	465	-179	-192	-157	-144	-137
South Africa	3,907	5,521	6,490	4,453	5,631	5,886	9,054	9,948	5,879	8,220	-1,979	-3,533	-3,458	-1,426	-2,589
Spain	6,839	9,766	12,190	8,717	10,178	8,615	10,498	11,094	7,857	8,553	-1,776	-732	1,096	860	1,625
Sri Lanka	198	227	283	230	179	2,083	2,065	1,962	1,593	1,748	-1,885	-1,838	-1,679	-1,363	-1,569
St. Kitts and Nevis	94	111	124	108	131	50	54	54	48	51	44	57	70	60	80
St. Lucia	135	165	241	136	401	32	33	26	18	18	103	132	215	119	383
St. Vincent and the Grenadines	45	69	83	75	86	16	1	1	1	2	30	68	82	74	84
Sudan	108	79	143	78	116	14	7	5	10	8	95	72	138	69	108
Suriname	246	304	406	380	362	165	130	127	139	191	80	174	280	241	171
Swaziland	12	29	12	15	24	199	145	134	110	121	-187	-116	-122	-95	-97
Sweden	3,715	4,473	5,018	4,561	4,706	13,821	13,024	12,498	8,186	10,495	-10,106	-8,551	-7,480	-3,625	-5,789
Switzerland	10,718	17,039	22,024	17,504	20,687	13,000	14,760	17,782	16,053	19,136	-2,282	2,279	4,242	1,451	1,551
Syria	155	361	409	304	503	324	111	352	303	429	-169	251	57	1	74
Taiwan [2]	21,614	25,829	24,926	18,486	26,043	34,826	38,278	36,326	28,362	35,846	-13,211	-12,449	-11,400	-9,877	-9,803
Tajikistan	29	53	51	41	57	241	1	8	9	2	-212	52	43	33	55
Tanzania	96	174	169	158	164	34	46	56	49	43	63	128	114	109	121
Thailand	7,257	8,336	9,067	6,918	8,977	19,890	22,755	23,538	19,082	22,693	-12,633	-14,418	-14,472	-12,164	-13,716
Togo	28	288	117	125	158	6	5	11	7	9	21	283	106	118	149
Trinidad and Tobago	1,417	1,780	2,250	1,988	1,926	7,891	8,790	9,030	5,180	6,613	-6,474	-7,010	-6,780	-3,192	-4,687
Tunisia	261	403	502	501	571	264	458	644	326	405	-3	-55	-142	176	166
Turkey	4,239	6,499	9,959	7,095	10,546	5,182	4,601	4,642	3,662	4,207	-943	1,898	5,317	3,433	6,339
Turkmenistan	215	127	60	60	40	135	219	140	93	48	80	-92	-80	-33	-8
Turks and Caicos Islands	238	396	434	294	190	9	13	10	57	12	228	383	424	237	178
Uganda	63	80	89	119	94	26	26	53	31	58	37	54	36	88	36
Ukraine	533	1,342	1,868	887	1,359	1,098	1,220	2,340	495	1,078	-565	122	-472	392	281
United Arab Emirates	8,120	10,787	14,417	12,211	11,673	1,468	1,337	1,286	1,498	1,145	6,651	9,449	13,131	10,713	10,528
United Kingdom	38,568	49,981	53,599	45,704	48,414	51,033	56,858	58,587	47,480	49,775	-12,465	-6,876	-4,988	-1,776	-1,361
Uruguay	357	641	893	745	975	732	492	244	239	235	-376	149	649	506	740
Uzbekistan	74	89	301	98	101	96	165	292	89	68	-22	-76	8	8	33
Venezuela	6,421	10,201	12,610	9,315	10,649	33,978	39,910	51,424	28,059	32,707	-27,557	-29,709	-38,814	-18,744	-22,058
Vietnam	1,193	1,903	2,789	3,097	3,709	6,631	10,633	12,901	12,288	14,868	-5,438	-8,730	-10,112	-9,191	-11,159
Virgin Islands, British	125	176	310	233	146	34	43	11	6	19	91	133	299	227	127
Yemen	219	642	401	381	391	279	292	8	7	181	-60	350	393	374	210
Zambia	29	69	79	57	56	32	49	51	9	30	-7	21	27	49	26
Zimbabwe	46	105	93	85	68	94	73	112	22	59	-48	33	-19	63	9

– Represents or rounds to zero. [1] Includes timing adjustment and unidentified countries, not shown separately. [2] See footnote 4, Table 1332. [3] See footnote 5, Table 1332. See also<http://www.census.gov/foreign-trade/Press-Release/2010pr /final_revisions/>, released June 9, 2011.

Source: U.S. Census Bureau, U.S. International Trade in Goods and Services, Series FT-900(07-04), and previous final reports.

Table 1308. U.S. Exports and General Imports by Selected SITC Commodity Groups: 2000 to 2010

[In millions of dollars (781,918 represents $781,918,000,000). SITC = Standard International Trade Classification. For methodology, see Foreign Trade Statistics in Appendix III. N.e.s. = not elsewhere specified]

Selected commodity	Exports [1]				General imports [2]			
	2000	2008	2009	2010	2000	2008	2009	2010
Total....................	781,918	1,287,442	1,056,043	1,278,263	1,218,022	2,103,641	1,559,625	1,913,160
Agricultural commodities [3]....	51,296	115,248	98,423	115,786	39,186	80,662	71,849	82,015
Animal feeds...............	3,780	7,610	7,763	8,996	597	1,258	1,162	1,349
Cereal flour..............	1,310	2,870	2,957	3,037	1,753	4,268	4,161	4,519
Corn.....................	4,695	13,931	9,146	10,181	160	350	283	300
Cotton, raw and linters....	1,893	4,812	3,365	5,896	28	12	1	8
Meat and preparations.......	7,004	12,584	11,618	13,216	3,841	5,046	4,598	5,071
Soybeans.................	5,284	15,455	16,443	18,589	31	182	210	220
Vegetables and fruits.........	7,477	14,040	14,014	15,712	9,286	19,145	18,571	20,915
Wheat...................	3,374	11,294	5,380	6,769	229	1,080	698	563
Manufactured goods [3]........	625,894	912,382	743,321	873,246	1,012,855	1,490,383	1,185,889	1,438,617
ADP equipment, office machinery...............	46,595	28,639	21,282	22,238	92,133	96,526	91,098	113,476
Airplane parts..............	15,062	(X)	(X)	(X)	5,572	(X)	(X)	(X)
Airplanes..................	24,777	(X)	(X)	(X)	12,412	(X)	(X)	(X)
Alcoholic beverages, distilled...	424	1,049	1,007	1,126	2,946	5,478	5,011	5,608
Aluminum.................	3,780	6,204	4,291	5,171	6,949	13,429	8,679	10,815
Artwork/antiques...........	1,387	5,409	4,605	3,034	5,864	7,513	5,031	6,268
Basketware, etc.............	3,309	7,692	8,068	8,360	4,840	12,196	11,530	13,316
Chemicals, cosmetics........	5,292	11,534	11,120	12,488	3,539	9,577	8,396	9,564
Chemicals, dyeing...........	4,089	6,238	5,546	7,407	2,667	3,073	2,424	3,105
Chemicals, fertilizers........	2,249	6,540	3,475	3,731	1,684	8,377	4,156	6,647
Chemicals, inorganic........	5,359	12,846	10,203	11,806	6,108	16,826	10,790	13,833
Chemicals, medicinal........	12,893	37,379	41,809	41,960	14,685	59,212	60,002	65,170
Chemicals, n.e.s............	12,264	25,287	20,428	24,136	5,725	12,713	9,582	11,379
Chemicals, organic..........	17,990	34,256	27,779	37,494	28,578	47,802	42,183	45,792
Chemicals, plastics.........	19,519	40,281	33,078	42,019	10,647	18,912	13,694	17,825
Clothing..................	8,191	3,169	2,919	3,197	64,296	78,893	69,326	78,518
Copper...................	1,425	3,439	2,375	3,496	4,471	10,358	5,596	7,821
Cork, wood, lumber........	4,320	4,241	3,495	4,732	8,227	5,704	3,574	4,479
Crude fertilizers............	1,724	2,428	1,765	2,367	1,401	2,966	1,682	2,257
Electrical machinery.........	89,917	82,049	63,964	77,019	108,747	112,623	91,683	119,634
Fish and preparations........	2,806	4,017	3,763	4,223	9,907	13,994	12,982	14,576
Footwear.................	663	673	620	728	14,842	19,545	17,523	20,902
Furniture and bedding........	4,744	5,170	4,023	4,821	18,923	31,371	24,588	31,124
Gem diamonds.............	1,289	5,943	2,156	2,862	12,068	19,744	12,736	18,599
General industrial machinery...	33,094	55,192	45,034	51,793	34,667	66,910	50,181	60,426
Glass....................	2,502	3,317	2,828	3,380	2,248	2,653	2,117	2,588
Gold, nonmonetary..........	5,898	18,714	13,898	17,458	2,657	6,120	8,810	12,491
Iron and steel mill products....	5,715	18,493	12,022	15,720	15,807	38,910	18,230	24,440
Jewelry..................	1,574	4,834	4,322	4,848	6,459	9,615	8,676	10,085
Lighting, plumbing..........	1,384	2,516	2,141	2,509	5,104	7,767	6,120	7,397
Metal manufactures, n.e.s.....	13,453	18,743	14,669	17,491	16,204	30,403	21,414	25,913
Metal ores; scrap..........	4,234	29,431	20,058	28,366	3,817	9,309	5,460	7,293
Metalworking machinery......	6,191	6,074	4,294	5,330	7,726	8,548	4,961	5,565
Nickel...................	401	1,567	931	1,130	1,425	3,430	1,665	2,976
Optical goods.............	3,246	2,860	2,773	3,278	4,019	5,090	4,513	5,507
Paper and paperboard........	10,640	14,668	12,891	14,920	15,185	18,073	14,463	15,285
Photographic equipment......	4,236	3,595	3,211	3,345	6,896	2,489	1,776	2,048
Plastic articles, n.e.s........	7,607	9,511	8,224	9,710	8,034	15,793	13,743	16,042
Platinum..................	888	1,161	844	1,370	5,566	7,115	2,982	4,146
Power generating machinery...	32,743	33,658	28,056	33,013	33,773	48,187	36,181	42,465
Printed materials...........	4,776	6,355	5,601	5,879	3,680	5,372	4,231	4,585
Pulp and waste paper........	4,576	7,744	6,694	8,640	3,381	4,004	2,441	3,887
Records/magnetic media......	5,395	5,250	4,413	4,424	5,172	6,735	5,183	5,296
Rubber articles, n.e.s........	1,673	1,915	1,625	2,049	1,962	3,169	2,481	3,310
Rubber tires and tubes.......	2,379	3,981	3,641	4,159	4,785	9,705	8,136	10,673
Scientific instruments.........	30,984	42,588	38,105	44,276	22,007	37,275	31,975	37,795
Ships, boats...............	1,070	3,114	1,917	2,498	1,178	1,675	1,267	1,588
Specialized industrial machinery...............	30,959	51,928	36,956	46,754	22,711	35,574	24,235	30,912
Television, VCR, etc..........	27,921	24,379	19,992	21,511	70,468	133,187	119,392	137,305
Textile yarn, fabric..........	10,534	11,860	9,288	11,384	15,171	21,854	18,232	22,120
Toys/games/sporting goods....	3,609	4,697	4,170	4,245	20,011	32,617	27,918	30,630
Travel goods...............	351	463	449	463	4,430	7,986	6,444	8,012
Vehicles..................	57,421	98,871	65,288	88,119	161,544	190,799	127,863	178,946
Watches/clocks/parts.........	348	416	356	379	3,481	4,340	3,065	3,747
Wood manufactures..........	1,842	2,270	1,725	2,053	7,228	8,446	6,230	6,920
Mineral fuel [3]...............	13,179	76,075	54,536	80,460	135,367	491,885	271,739	354,968
Coal.....................	2,162	8,196	6,162	10,100	805	3,958	1,766	2,018
Crude oil.................	463	2,270	1,618	1,368	89,876	353,537	194,603	260,105
Petroleum preparations.......	5,746	51,384	36,351	53,528	25,673	87,103	52,584	67,409
Liquified propane/butane......	663	1,011	1,409	2,448	1,508	4,755	2,202	2,541
Natural gas...............	411	4,879	3,271	4,921	12,594	34,423	16,056	17,402
Mineral fuels, other mineral....	3,734	7,030	5,131	7,434	4,911	4,452	2,444	3,410
Reexports.................	68,203	131,066	120,345	155,847	(X)	(X)	(X)	(X)

X Not applicable. [1] Free Alongside Ship (FAS) basis. Exports by commodity are only for domestic exports. [2] Customs value basis. [3] Includes other commodities, not shown separately.

Source: U.S. Census Bureau, *U.S. International Trade in Goods and Services*, Series FT 900 (07-04), and previous final reports. See also <http://www.census.gov/foreign-trade/Press-Release/2010pr/final_revisions/>, released June 9, 2011.

Table 1309. U.S. Total and Aerospace Foreign Trade: 1990 to 2010

[In millions of dollars (−101,718 represents −$101,718,000,000), except percent. Data are reported as exports of domestic merchandise, including Department of Defense shipments and undocumented exports to Canada, f.a.s. (free alongside ship) basis, and imports for consumption, customs value basis. Minus sign (−) indicates deficit]

Year	U.S. Merchandise Trade			Aerospace Trade						
						Exports				
								Civil		
	Trade balance[1]	Imports	Exports	Trade balance	Imports	Total	Percent of U.S. exports	Total	Transports	Total military
1990......	−101,718	495,311	393,592	27,282	11,801	39,083	9.9	31,517	16,691	7,566
1994......	−150,630	663,256	512,626	25,010	12,363	37,373	7.3	30,050	15,931	7,322
1995......	−158,801	743,543	584,742	21,562	11,509	33,071	5.7	25,079	10,606	7,991
1996......	−170,214	795,289	625,075	26,602	13,668	40,270	6.4	29,477	13,624	10,792
1997......	−180,522	869,704	689,182	32,240	18,134	50,374	7.3	40,075	21,028	10,299
1998......	−229,758	911,896	682,138	40,961	23,110	64,071	9.4	51,999	29,168	12,072
1999......	−328,821	1,024,618	695,797	37,381	25,063	62,444	9.0	50,624	25,672	11,820
2000......	−436,104	1,218,022	781,918	26,735	27,944	54,679	7.0	45,566	19,615	9,113
2001......	−411,899	1,140,999	729,100	26,035	32,473	58,508	8.0	49,371	22,151	9,137
2002......	−468,263	1,161,366	693,103	29,533	27,242	56,775	8.2	47,348	21,626	9,427
2003......	−532,350	1,257,121	724,771	27,111	25,393	52,504	7.2	44,366	19,149	8,138
2004......	−654,830	1,469,704	814,875	31,002	25,815	56,817	7.0	47,772	18,577	9,045
2005......	−772,373	1,673,455	901,082	39,783	27,649	67,433	7.5	57,587	21,888	9,845
2006......	−827,971	1,853,938	1,025,967	54,809	30,453	85,262	8.3	71,857	32,897	13,404
2007......	−808,763	1,956,962	1,148,199	60,614	36,610	97,224	8.5	83,977	40,297	13,247
2008......	−816,199	2,103,641	1,287,442	57,389	37,694	95,082	7.4	82,264	33,326	12,819
2009......	−503,582	1,559,625	1,056,043	56,034	25,132	81,166	7.7	70,500	(NA)	10,666
2010......	−633,903	1,912,041	1,278,139	51,152	26,351	77,503	6.1	67,128	(NA)	10,375

NA Not available. [1] Exports minus imports.

Source: Aerospace Industries Association of America, Washington, DC, *Aerospace Facts and Figures*, annual, <http://www.aia-aerospace.org/resource-center/economics>.

Table 1310. U.S. High Technology Exports by Industry and Selected Major Country: 2000 to 2009

[In billions of dollars (222.5 represents $222,500,000,000)]

Selected industry	2000	2008	2009	Selected country	2000	2008	2009
Total exports..............	**222.5**	**218.8**	**187.7**	**Total exports.........**	**222.5**	**218.8**	**187.7**
Computers and office equipment...	57.8	47.0	38.3	Canada................	34.4	29.1	37.3
Consumer electronics...........	10.0	8.6	7.6	China [1]...............	4.6	15.0	28.1
Communications equipment......	26.9	32.6	29.6	Japan.................	19.9	10.9	28.0
Electronic components..........	22.1	17.5	16.3	Korea, South..........	12.1	7.5	14.0
Semiconductors................	60.0	50.2	43.6	Malaysia..............	7.8	8.3	9.0
Industrial electronics...........	30.5	38.7	28.3	Mexico................	30.0	27.7	7.2
Electromedical equipment........	8.1	18.3	20.2	Taiwan [1]..............	10.4	8.0	7.0
Photonics.....................	7.1	5.9	3.9	European Union 27.....	51.5	46.9	7.0

[1] See footnote 2, Table 1332.

Source: TechAmerica Foundation Trade in the Cyberstates 2010, annual (copyright). See also <http://www.techamericafoundation.org>.

Table 1311. U.S. Exporting Companies Profile by Employment-Size Class: 2000 and 2009

[(668,310 represents $668,310,000,000). Based on data from export trade documents and the Business Register. For information on data limitations, see the Technical Documentation in the source]

Employment-size class	Number of exporters		Known export value [1] (mil. dol.)		Percent of—			
					Number of exporters		Known export value	
	2000	2009	2000	2009	2000	2009	2000	2009
All companies, total.......	**246,452**	**275,843**	**668,310**	**938,794**	**100.0**	**100.0**	**100.0**	**100.0**
No employees..............	74,772	99,305	47,024	83,161	30.3	36.0	7.0	8.9
1 to 19 employees...........	96,268	107,482	45,272	68,360	39.1	39.0	6.8	7.3
20 to 49 employees..........	31,362	30,582	21,262	37,633	12.7	11.1	3.2	4.0
50 to 99 employees..........	16,988	15,603	19,711	32,572	6.9	5.7	2.9	3.5
100 to 249 employees........	13,685	11,910	32,192	51,186	5.6	4.3	4.8	5.5
250 to 499 employees........	5,454	4,387	27,397	35,111	2.2	1.6	4.1	3.7
500 or more employees.......	7,923	6,574	475,453	630,770	3.2	2.4	71.1	67.2

[1] Known value is defined as the value of exports by known exporters, i.e., those export transactions that could be matched to specific companies. Export values are on f.a.s. or "free alongside ship basis."

Source: U.S. Census Bureau, *A Profile of U.S. Exporting Companies, 2000 and 2008–2009*, <http://www.census.gov/foreign-trade/Press-Release/edb/2009/edbrel.pdf>.

Foreign Commerce and Aid 813

Table 1312. Domestic Exports and Imports for Consumption of Merchandise by Selected NAICS Product Category: 2000 to 2010

[In millions of dollars (712,285 represents $712,285,000,000). Includes nonmonetary gold. For methodology, see Foreign Trade Statistics in Appendix III. NAICS = North American Industry Classification System; see text, Section 15]

Product category	2000	2005	2007	2008	2009	2010
Domestic exports, total...................	**712,285**	**798,997**	**1,031,022**	**1,156,376**	**935,698**	**1,122,416**
Agricultural, forestry, and fishery products	29,153	37,109	53,517	68,233	55,552	65,737
Agricultural products, total....................	23,596	30,683	46,436	61,073	49,069	58,009
Livestock and livestock products..................	1,255	1,118	1,362	1,520	1,409	1,540
Forestry products, not elsewhere specified...........	1,644	1,686	1,925	1,894	1,622	2,178
Fish, fresh or chilled, and other marine products	2,658	3,622	3,795	3,746	3,452	4,010
Mining, total........................	6,187	12,629	17,013	24,751	17,332	26,234
Oil and gas........................	1,706	4,547	5,689	8,706	6,570	9,090
Minerals and ores.....................	4,481	8,082	11,324	16,045	10,762	17,144
Manufacturing, total....................	644,440	708,205	897,516	987,582	802,183	952,409
Food and kindred products	24,966	28,937	38,793	48,476	43,843	50,910
Beverages and tobacco products	5,568	3,423	4,193	4,793	4,373	5,341
Textiles and fabrics...................	7,010	8,483	8,251	8,213	6,434	7,832
Textile mill products...................	2,236	2,344	2,651	2,611	2,276	2,582
Apparel and accessories..................	8,104	4,075	3,133	3,055	2,812	3,071
Leather and allied products...............	2,322	2,300	2,355	2,266	1,876	2,420
Wood products.....................	4,854	4,463	4,973	5,041	3,976	5,073
Paper products...................	15,539	16,640	19,738	21,713	19,175	22,962
Printed, publishing, & similar products	4,869	5,526	6,321	6,504	5,747	6,020
Petroleum and coal products...............	8,862	17,979	30,976	58,440	41,494	61,003
Chemicals	77,649	114,821	147,596	166,249	145,896	171,443
Plastics and rubber products..............	16,970	18,784	22,041	23,403	20,340	24,255
Nonmetallic mineral products..............	7,830	6,663	8,372	8,927	7,482	9,223
Primary metal products..................	20,126	27,455	44,623	54,713	38,173	49,708
Fabricated metal products................	21,737	23,370	29,878	32,483	27,737	32,667
Machinery, except electrical	85,038	97,001	122,669	134,117	104,139	126,040
Computers and electronic products............	161,449	122,744	135,429	134,757	106,782	121,111
Electrical equipment, appliances and components	25,401	26,457	33,422	34,548	26,498	30,998
Transportation equipment	121,701	144,985	190,474	192,296	154,120	176,397
Furniture and fixtures	2,882	2,844	3,511	3,999	3,525	3,980
Miscellaneous manufactured commodities	19,327	28,909	38,117	40,978	35,486	39,373
Special classification provisions	32,505	41,055	62,069	75,010	59,866	77,186
Waste & scrap	4,948	10,389	22,020	28,943	21,784	29,411
Used or second-hand merchandise.............	1,950	2,570	5,708	7,326	6,005	4,712
Goods returned or reimported...............	333	65	36	47	31	29
Special classification provision, not elsewhere specified.................	25,274	28,030	34,305	38,693	32,046	43,034
Imports for consumption, total	**1,205,339**	**1,664,497**	**1,946,341**	**2,093,578**	**1,551,063**	**1,899,886**
Agricultural, forestry, and fishery products	24,378	30,761	37,678	41,068	36,802	42,683
Agricultural products, total....................	11,771	15,818	19,677	22,477	21,508	24,014
Livestock and livestock products..................	3,085	3,277	4,691	4,435	3,600	4,115
Forestry products, not elsewhere specified...........	1,409	2,250	2,745	3,417	1,773	3,356
Fish, fresh or chilled, and other marine products	8,113	9,416	10,565	10,739	9,920	11,198
Mining, total........................	79,841	192,115	241,494	341,123	184,585	235,394
Oil and gas	76,166	185,621	233,384	329,397	177,929	228,066
Minerals and ores	3,675	6,494	8,110	11,726	6,655	7,328
Manufacturing, total....................	1,040,329	1,372,004	1,585,062	1,627,042	1,260,343	1,549,521
Food and kindred products	18,944	29,779	34,706	39,987	36,131	41,037
Beverages and tobacco products	8,350	12,849	15,937	15,877	14,454	15,514
Textiles and fabrics...................	7,042	7,450	7,451	6,943	5,283	6,524
Textile mill products...................	7,347	13,508	15,410	14,984	13,227	15,824
Apparel and accessories..................	62,928	74,478	78,947	76,182	66,818	75,407
Leather and allied products...............	21,463	26,559	29,400	29,479	25,548	30,857
Wood products.....................	15,388	23,654	18,540	14,142	9,746	11,363
Paper products	19,080	22,094	23,472	24,014	18,514	21,029
Printed, publishing, & similar products	4,197	5,599	6,347	6,170	4,890	5,323
Petroleum and coal products...............	40,156	81,359	102,303	130,639	75,139	102,161
Chemicals	76,606	131,936	160,297	195,731	162,366	187,631
Plastics and rubber products..............	17,362	28,072	32,039	33,006	27,749	34,363
Nonmetallic mineral products..............	14,740	18,445	19,683	18,070	13,081	16,078
Primary metal products..................	43,833	64,666	88,928	99,327	55,412	79,025
Fabricated metal products................	27,974	41,026	50,011	51,934	39,780	46,691
Machinery, except electrical	79,366	109,619	121,276	123,669	86,832	104,797
Computers and electronic products............	250,694	269,921	312,769	300,391	265,557	324,372
Electrical equipment, appliances and components	39,567	55,179	67,115	67,758	55,519	68,462
Transportation equipment	213,110	251,386	277,450	254,296	180,256	239,809
Furniture and fixtures	15,607	25,096	27,674	26,321	21,566	25,702
Miscellaneous manufactured commodities	56,577	79,329	95,307	98,121	82,475	97,552
Special classification provisions	60,791	69,617	82,054	84,308	69,301	72,253
Waste & scrap	1,875	3,207	5,031	5,669	3,459	5,260
Used or second-hand merchandise.............	6,345	6,026	8,994	7,757	5,205	6,403
Goods returned or reimported...............	33,851	37,024	39,494	40,134	38,101	40,985
Special classification provision, not elsewhere specified.........................	18,720	23,359	28,535	30,747	22,535	19,605

Source: U.S. Census Bureau, *U.S. International Trade in Goods and Services*, Series FT-900, December 2010, <http://www.census.gov/foreign-trade/Press-Release/2010pr/12/>.

Section 29
Puerto Rico and the Island Areas

This section presents summary economic and social statistics for Puerto Rico, the U.S. Virgin Islands, Guam, American Samoa, and the Northern Mariana Islands. Primary sources are the decennial censuses of population and housing, County Business Patterns, and the Puerto Rico Community Survey conducted by the U.S. Census Bureau; the annual *Vital Statistics of the United States*, issued by the National Center for Health Statistics; and the annual *Income and Product* of the Puerto Rico Planning Board.

Jurisdiction—The United States gained jurisdiction over these areas as follows: the islands of *Puerto Rico* and *Guam*, surrendered by Spain to the United States in December 1898, were ceded to the United States by the Treaty of Paris, ratified in 1899. Puerto Rico became a commonwealth on July 25, 1952, thereby achieving a high degree of local autonomy under its own constitution. The *U.S. Virgin Islands*, comprising 50 islands and cays, was purchased by the United States from Denmark in 1917. *American Samoa*, a group of seven islands, was acquired by the United States in accordance with a convention among the United States, Great Britain, and Germany, ratified in 1900 (Swains Island was annexed in 1925). By an agreement approved by the Security Council and the United States, the Northern Mariana Islands, previously under Japanese mandate, was administered by the United States between 1947 and 1986 under the United Nations trusteeship system. The Northern Mariana Islands became a commonwealth in 1986.

Censuses—Because characteristics of Puerto Rico and the Island Areas differ, the presentation of census data for them is not uniform. The 1960 Census of Population covered all of the places listed above except the Northern Mariana Islands (their census was conducted in April 1958 by the Office of the High Commissioner), while the 1960 Census of Housing excluded American Samoa. The 1970, 1980, 1990, 2000, and 2010. Censuses of Population and Housing covered all five areas. Beginning in 1967, Congress authorized the economic censuses, to be taken at 5-year intervals, for years ending in "2" and "7." Prior economic censuses were conducted in Puerto Rico for 1949, 1954, 1958, and 1963 and in Guam and the U.S. Virgin Islands for 1958 and 1963. In 1967, the census of construction industries was added for the first time in Puerto Rico; in 1972, the U.S. Virgin Islands and Guam were covered; and in 1982, the economic census was taken for the first time for the Northern Mariana Islands.

Puerto Rico Community Survey—The Puerto Rico Community Survey (PRCS) began in 2005 and was a critical element in the Census Bureau's reengineered 2010 census plan. The American Community Survey is the equivalent of the PRCS for the United States (50 states and District of Columbia). The PRCS collects and produces population and housing information every year instead of every 10 years. About 36,000 households are surveyed each year from across every municipio in Puerto Rico.

Information in other sections—In addition to the statistics presented in this section, other data are included as integral parts of many tables showing distribution by states in various sections of the *Abstract*. See "Puerto Rico and the Island Areas" in the Index. For definition and explanation of terms used, see Sections 1, 2, 4, 17, 20, 21, and 22.

U.S. Census Bureau, Statistical Abstract of the United States: 2012

Selected Island Areas of the United States

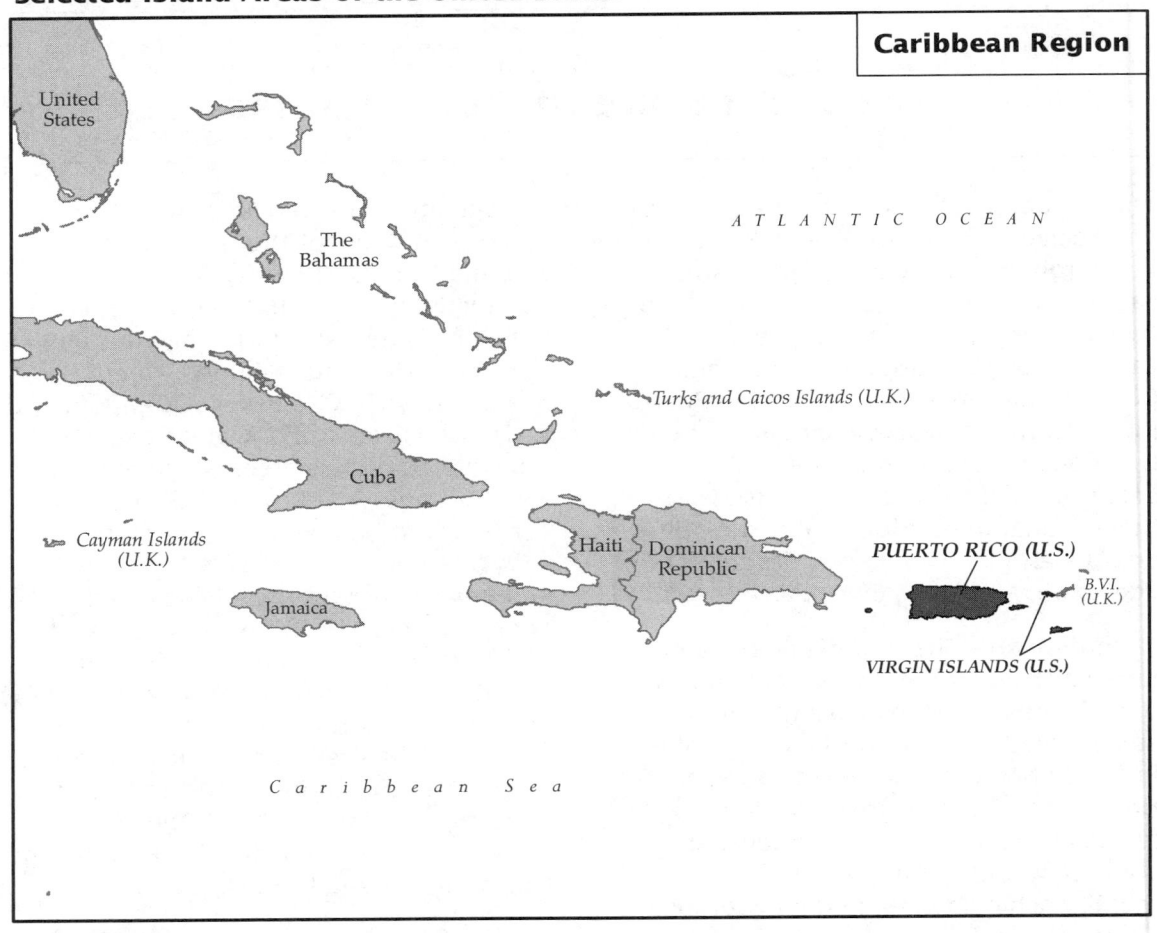

Caribbean Region

United States

ATLANTIC OCEAN

The Bahamas

Turks and Caicos Islands (U.K.)

Cuba

Cayman Islands (U.K.)

Haiti

Dominican Republic

PUERTO RICO (U.S.)

B.V.I. (U.K.)

VIRGIN ISLANDS (U.S.)

Jamaica

C a r i b b e a n   S e a

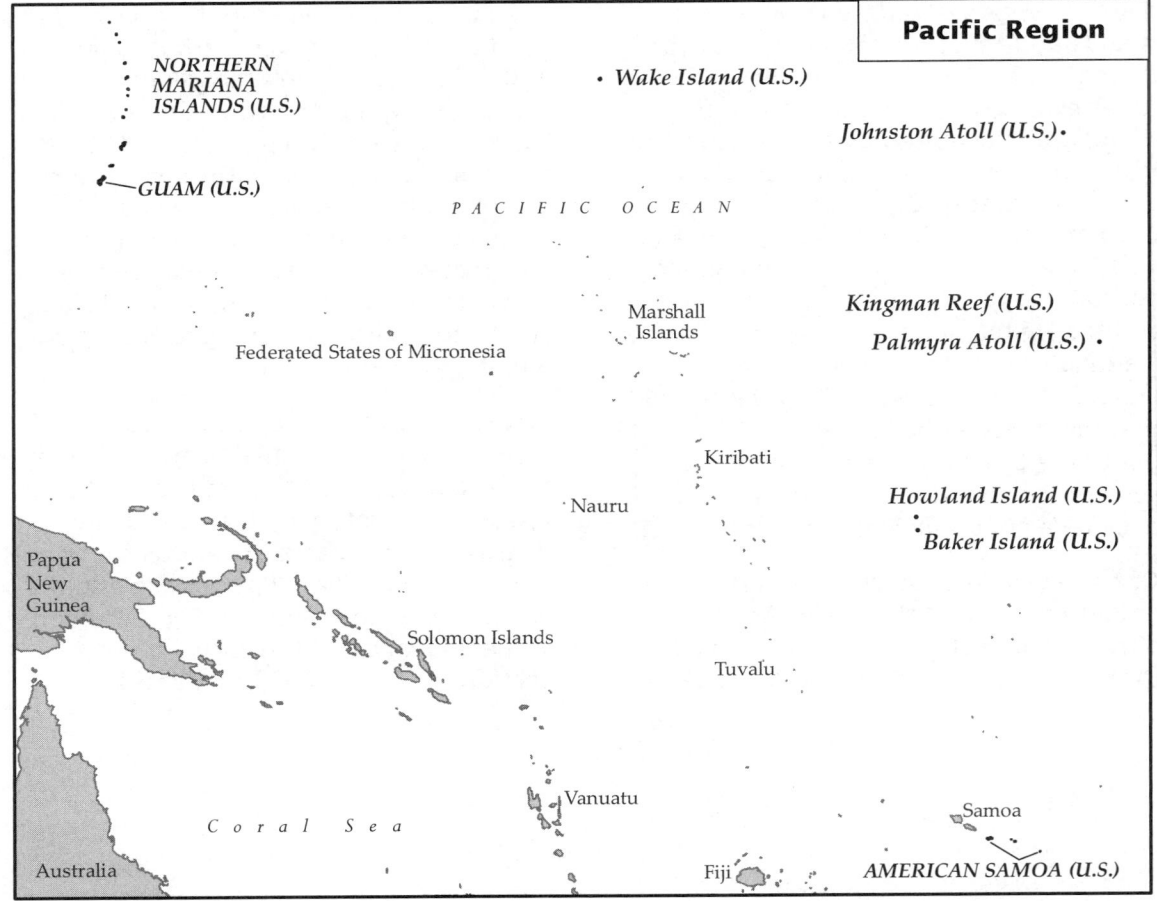

Pacific Region

NORTHERN MARIANA ISLANDS (U.S.)

• **Wake Island (U.S.)**

Johnston Atoll (U.S.)•

—**GUAM (U.S.)**

P A C I F I C   O C E A N

Marshall Islands

Kingman Reef (U.S.)

Federated States of Micronesia

Palmyra Atoll (U.S.) •

Kiribati

Nauru

Howland Island (U.S.)

•**Baker Island (U.S.)**

Papua New Guinea

Solomon Islands

Tuvalu

Vanuatu

Samoa

C o r a l   S e a

Fiji

AMERICAN SAMOA (U.S.)

Australia

U.S. Census Bureau, Statistical Abstract of the United States: 2012

Table 1313. Estimated Resident Population With Projections: 1990 to 2025

[In thousands (3,537 represents 3,537,000). Population as of July 1. Population data generally are de-facto figures for the present territory. Data for 1990 to 2000 are adjusted to the 2000 Census of Population for Puerto Rico only. See text, Section 30, for general comments regarding the data. For details of methodology, coverage, and reliability, see source]

Area	1990	2000	2005	2007	2008	2009	2010	Projected		
								2015	2020	2025
Puerto Rico	3,537	3,814	3,911	3,941	3,955	3,967	3,979	4,024	4,051	4,055
American Samoa...........	47	58	62	64	65	66	66	71	75	79
Guam.....................	134	155	169	174	176	178	181	193	204	214
Virgin Islands.............	104	109	110	110	110	110	110	109	108	107
Northern Mariana Islands	44	70	71	59	55	51	48	44	49	53

Source: U.S. Census Bureau, International Data Base, <http://www.census.gov/ipc/www/idb/>, accessed June 2010.

Table 1314. Vital Statistics—Specified Areas: 1990 to 2008

[Births, deaths, and infant deaths by place of residence. Rates for 1990 and 2000 based on population enumerated as of April 1; for other years, on population estimated as of July 1]

Area and year	Births		Deaths		Infant deaths	
	Number	Rate [1]	Number	Rate [1]	Number	Rate [2]
Puerto Rico:						
1990.................	66,417	18.8	25,957	7.3	888	13.4
1995.................	63,425	17.0	30,032	8.1	804	12.7
2000.................	59,333	15.2	28,369	7.2	574	9.7
2005.................	50,564	12.9	29,531	7.5	466	9.2
2006.................	48,597	12.4	28,206	7.2	426	8.8
2007.................	46,642	11.8	29,169	7.4	394	8.5
2008.................	45,620	11.5	(NA)	(NA)	(NA)	(NA)
Guam:						
1990.................	3,839	28.6	520	3.9	31	8.1
1995.................	4,180	29.0	592	4.1	38	9.4
2000.................	3,766	24.4	648	4.2	22	5.8
2005.................	3,187	18.9	677	4.0	34	10.7
2006.................	3,391	19.8	679	4.0	45	13.3
2007.................	3,483	20.1	778	4.5	36	10.3
2008.................	3,457	19.6	(NA)	(NA)	(NA)	(NA)
Virgin Islands:						
1990.................	2,267	21.8	480	4.6	33	14.6
1995.................	2,063	18.1	664	5.8	34	16.6
2000.................	1,564	12.9	641	5.3	21	13.4
2005.................	1,605	14.8	663	6.1	11	(B)
2006.................	1,687	15.5	624	5.7	9	(B)
2007.................	1,697	15.5	703	6.4	12	(B)
2008.................	1,784	16.2	(NA)	(NA)	(NA)	(NA)
American Samoa:						
2000.................	1,731	26.4	219	3.3	11	(NA)
2005.................	1,720	27.6	272	4.4	12	(B)
2007.................	1,288	20.1	250	3.9	11	(B)
2008.................	1,332	20.5	(NA)	(NA)	(NA)	(NA)
Northern Marianas:						
2000.................	1,431	19.9	136	1.9	11	(NA)
2005.................	1,335	16.6	186	2.3	6	(B)
2007.................	1,387	16.4	137	1.6	5	(B)
2008.................	1,265	22.9	(NA)	(NA)	(NA)	(NA)

NA Not available. B Base figure too small to meet statistical standards of reliability. [1] Per 1,000 population. [2] Rates are infant deaths (under 1 year) per 1,000 live births.
Source: U.S. National Center for Health Statistics, National Vital Statistics Reports (NVSR), *Births: Final Data for 2008*, Vol. 59, No. 1, December 2010, and *Deaths: Final Data for 2007*, Vol. 58, No. 19, May 2011. See also <http://www.cdc.gov/nchs/nvss.htm>.

Table 1315. Public Elementary and Secondary Schools by Area: 2008

[For school year ending in year shown, unless otherwise indicated. (3,413,884 represents $3,413,884,000)]

Item	Puerto Rico	Guam	U.S. Virgin Islands	American Samoa	Northern Marianas	Item	Puerto Rico	Guam	U.S. Virgin Islands	American Samoa	Northern Marianas
Enrollment, fall.....	503,635	(NA)	15,768	(NA)	10,913	Teachers	39,356	(NA)	1,331	(NA)	514
						Student support staff	3,828	(NA)	275	(NA)	30
Elementary (pre-kindergarten–grade 8)	355,115	(NA)	10,567	(NA)	7,816	Other support services staff ..	16,225	(NA)	165	(NA)	91
Secondary (grades 9–12 and secondary ungraded)	148,520	(NA)	5,201	(NA)	3,097	Current expenditures [1] ($1,000)......	3,413,884	229,243	196,533	63,105	51,241
Staff, fall..........	70,034	(NA)	2,472	(NA)	1,043	Per pupil [2] (dol.)	6,898	8,084	12,358	4,309	5,162
School district staff	3,182	(NA)	133	(NA)	70						
School staff	46,799	(NA)	1,899	(NA)	852						

NA Not available. [1] Public elementary and secondary day schools. [2] Per pupil expenditures include current expenditures, capital expenditures, and interest on school debt and excludes "other current expenditures" such as community services, private school programs, adult education, and other programs not allocable to expenditures per pupil in public schools.
Source: U.S. National Center for Education Statistics, *Digest of Education Statistics*, annual. See also <http://nces.ed.gov/annuals>.

Table 1316. Occupational Employment and Average Annual Wages in Guam, Puerto Rico, and Virgin Islands: 2010

[The Occupational Employment Survey (OES) program conducts a semiannual mail survey designed to produce estimates of employment and wages for specific occupations. For more details on the survey, see <http://www.bls.gov/oes/oes_emp.htm#scope>]

Selected occupation	SOC code [1]	Guam		Puerto Rico		Virgin Islands	
		Employ-ment	Average annual wages [2]	Employ-ment	Average annual wages [2]	Employ-ment	Average annual wages [2]
Total, all occupations [3, 4]	(X)	59,560	31,250	950,570	26,870	42,700	37,130
Management	11	5,370	57,180	36,110	67,740	2,430	76,880
Business and financial operations	13	2,250	47,650	41,980	36,430	1,390	51,250
Computer and mathematical	15	620	43,030	9,360	41,350	370	56,330
Architecture and engineering	17	860	53,550	12,150	50,440	330	66,220
Life, physical, and social science	19	350	43,100	7,160	41,800	380	48,670
Community and social services	21	620	35,840	18,730	28,420	590	44,010
Legal	23	230	67,600	4,640	58,900	460	92,540
Education, training, and library	25	(NA)	(NA)	(NA)	31,320	3,170	39,420
Arts, design, entertainment sports	27	660	27,970	6,590	29,960	390	40,080
Healthcare practitioner and technical	29	1,500	61,470	45,600	33,250	1,170	58,370
Healthcare support	31	860	24,110	13,980	18,700	550	27,180
Protective service	33	2,640	30,250	62,320	25,350	2,720	32,870
Food preparation and serving related	35	6,380	17,990	66,730	17,740	4,010	22,350
Buildings and grounds cleaning and maintenance	37	3,000	18,800	44,760	18,090	2,530	22,860
Personal care and service	39	1,410	22,620	11,840	19,800	910	21,680
Sales and related occupations	41	4,270	20,870	101,910	21,960	4,800	26,540
Office and administrative support	43	10,760	26,620	178,450	23,300	8,240	31,610
Farming, fishing, and forestry	45	(NA)	(NA)	1,340	24,930	40	31,940
Construction and extraction	47	5,080	26,700	39,500	20,740	2,160	42,970
Installation, maintenance, and repair	49	3,150	29,650	31,120	27,510	2,390	43,410
Production	51	1,650	26,160	68,700	22,360	1,640	43,500
Transportation and material moving	53	3,630	28,460	55,050	20,660	2,040	29,870

NA Not available. X Not applicable. [1] Office of Management and Budget's Standard Occupational Classification (SOC) is used to define occupations. SOC categorizes workers into 1 of 801 detailed occupations and aggregates; the detailed occupations into 23 major occupational groups. [2] Annual wages have been calculated by multiplying the hourly mean wage by a "year-round, full-time" hours figure of 2,080 hours; for those occupations where there is not an hourly mean wage published, the annual wage has been directly calculated from the reported survey data. [3] Estimates for detailed occupations do not sum to the totals because the totals include occupations not shown separately. [4] Estimates do not include self-employed workers.

Source: U.S. Bureau of Labor Statistics, "Occupational Employment Statistics," <http://www.bls.gov/oes/data.htm>, accessed May 2011.

Table 1317. Prisoners in Custody of Correctional Authorities in U.S. Territories and Commonwealths: 2007 and 2008

[As of December 31. Minus sign (–) indicates decrease]

Jurisdiction	Total inmates			Sentenced to more than 1 year			
	2007	2008	Percent change 2007–2008	2007	2008	Percent change 2007–2008	Incar-ceration rate, 2008 [1]
Total [2]	14,678	13,576	–7.5	11,465	10,346	–9.8	237
American Samoa	236	132	–44.1	122	48	–60.7	74
Guam [2]	535	578	8.1	320	304	–5.0	173
Northern Mariana Islands	137	124	–9.5	78	78	0.0	141
Puerto Rico	13,215	12,130	–8.2	10,553	9,642	–8.6	244
U.S. Virgin Islands	555	612	10.3	392	274	–30.1	249

[1] The number of prisoners with a sentence of more than 1 year per 100,000 persons in the resident population. [2] Data for Guam 2008 are estimates.

Source: U.S. Bureau of Justice Statistics, *Prisoners in 2008*, NCJ 228417, December 2009. See also <http://bjs.ojp.usdoj.gov/index.cfm?ty=pbdetail&iid=1763>.

Table 1318. Federal Direct Payments: 2008

[In thousands of dollars (6,944,719 represents $6,944,719,000). For fiscal years ending September 30]

Selected program payment	Puerto Rico	Guam	Virgin Islands	American Samoa	Northern Mariana Islands
Direct payments to individuals for retirement and disability [1]	6,944,719	244,794	202,372	52,434	30,254
Social security:					
Retirement insurance	2,960,862	92,355	122,871	14,108	7,617
Survivors' insurance	1,278,912	41,239	30,993	13,931	5,590
Disability insurance	1,893,913	22,944	24,384	12,586	2,005
Federal retirement and disability:					
Civilian [2]	268,565	56,130	17,308	1,685	7,489
Military	21,381	8,217	1,772	1,808	899
Veterans benefits:					
Service-connected disability	308,938	19,765	2,999	7,045	957
Other benefit payments	181,969	3,311	694	1,082	120
Other	30,179	833	1,352	190	23

[1] Includes other payments, not shown separately. [2] Includes retirement and disability payments to former U.S. Postal Service employees.

Source: U.S. Census Bureau, Consolidated Federal Funds Reports, *Consolidated Federal Funds Report for Fiscal Year, 2008*, CFFR/08, July 2009. See also <http://www.census.gov/govs/cffr/>.

Table 1319. Selected Social, Demographic, and Housing Characteristics in Puerto Rico: 2009

[The Puerto Rico Community Survey universe includes the household population and the population living in institutions, college dormitories, and other group quarters. Based on a sample and subject to sampling variability; see text, this section and Appendix III]

Characteristic	Estimate	Percent	Characteristic	Estimate	Percent
Total.	**3,967,288**	**100.0**	**Females 15 years and over**	1,678,925	100.0
			Never married	589,767	35.1
SEX AND AGE			Now married, except separated	601,349	35.8
Male	1,905,314	48.0	Separated	63,688	3.8
Female	2,061,974	52.0	Widowed	178,326	10.6
			Divorced	245,795	14.6
Under 5 years	233,657	5.9			
5 to 9 years	250,900	6.3	HOUSEHOLDS		
10 to 14 years	300,475	7.6	**Total households**	**1,181,112**	**100.0**
15 to 19 years	304,511	7.7	Family households (families)	877,711	74.3
20 to 24 years	282,238	7.1	With own children under 18 years	356,561	30.2
25 to 34 years	541,548	13.7	Married-couple families	517,026	43.8
35 to 44 years	533,184	13.4	With own children under 18 years	181,410	15.4
45 to 54 years	510,276	12.9	Male householder, no wife present	69,665	5.9
55 to 59 years	225,347	5.7	With own children under 18 years	30,896	2.6
60 to 64 years	225,750	5.7	Female householder, no husband present	291,020	24.6
65 to 74 years	314,267	7.9	With own children under 18 years	144,255	12.2
75 to 84 years	173,673	4.4	Nonfamily households	303,401	25.7
85 years and over	71,462	1.8	Householder living alone	268,774	22.8
			65 years and over	114,276	9.7
MARITAL STATUS					
Males 15 years and over	**1,503,331**	**100.0**	Average household size	3.32	(X)
Never married	660,765	44.0	Average family size	3.96	(X)
Now married, except separated	589,141	39.2			
Separated	42,309	2.8	DISABILITY STATUS OF THE CIVILIAN NONINSTITUTIONALIZED POPULATION		
Widowed	44,317	2.9			
Divorced	166,799	11.1	Population 5 years and over	3,705,320	100.0
			With a disability	809,016	21.8

X Not applicable.

Source: U.S. Census Bureau, 2009 Puerto Rico Community Survey, DP-2 PR, "Selected Social Characteristics Puerto Rico: 2009," <http://factfinder.census.gov/>, accessed February 2011.

Table 1320. Tenure by Household Type in Puerto Rico: 2009

[The Puerto Rico Community Survey universe includes the household population and the population living in institutions, college dormitories, and other group quarters. Based on a sample and subject to sampling variability; see text, this section and Appendix III]

Household Type	Owner occupied	Renter occupied	Household Type	Owner occupied	Renter occupied
Total households	**844,860**	**336,252**	Householder 15 to 34 years	17,162	48,434
Family households	646,413	231,298	Householder 35 to 64 years	101,580	65,600
Married-couple family	433,826	83,200	Householder 65 years and over	49,995	8,249
Householder 15 to 34 years	34,628	23,959	Nonfamily households	198,447	104,954
Householder 35 to 64 years	274,841	50,069	Householder living alone	179,289	89,485
Householder 65 years and over	124,357	9,172	Householder 15 to 34 years	9,228	12,241
Other family	212,587	148,098	Householder 35 to 64 years	83,483	49,546
Male householder, no wife present	43,850	25,815	Householder 65 years and over	86,578	27,698
Householder 15 to 34 years	5,134	10,794	Householder not living alone	19,158	15,469
Householder 35 to 64 years	26,891	13,110	Householder 15 to 34 years	1,318	5,412
Householder 65 years and over	11,825	1,911	Householder 35 to 64 years	12,192	8,129
Female householder, no husband present	168,737	122,283	Householder 65 years and over	5,648	1,928

Source: U.S. Census Bureau, 2009 Puerto Rico Community Survey, B25011, "Tenure by Household Type and Age of Householder," <http://factfinder.census.gov/>, accessed February 2011.

U.S. Census Bureau, Statistical Abstract of the United States: 2012

Table 1321. Puerto Rico—Summary: 1990 to 2010

[3,512.4 represents 3,512,400]

Item	Unit	1990	2000	2005	2006	2007	2008	2009	2010
POPULATION									
Total [1]	1,000	3,512.4	3,808.0	3,903.5	3,919.9	3,934.6	3,947.7	3,960.7	3,973.0
Persons per family	Number	3.7	3.4	3.3	3.2	3.2	3.2	3.2	3.1
EDUCATION [2]									
Enrollment, total	1,000	953.0	971.5	958.7	1,017.7	1,000.5	964.1	951.3	952.4
Public (except public colleges or universities)	1,000	651.2	612.3	575.6	564.3	540.5	526.5	503.7	493.3
College and university	1,000	156.0	175.5	208.0	209.5	224.0	227.5	235.6	249.4
Expenses	Mil. dol	1,686.4	4,254.1	5,902.4	6,353.4	6,588.5	6,852.6	7,331.7	7,371.7
As percent of GNP	Percent	7.8	10.3	11.0	11.2	11.1	11.1	11.2	11.6
Public	Mil. dol	1,054.2	3,160.4	4,274.6	4,533.9	4,811.9	5,026.3	5,403.1	5,416.1
Private	Mil. dol	644.2	1,093.7	1,627.8	1,819.5	1,776.6	1,826.3	1,928.6	1,955.6
LABOR FORCE [3]									
Total [4]	1,000	1,124	1,303	1,385	1,422	1,409	1,368	1,349	1,313
Employed [5]	1,000	963	1,159	1,238	1,256	1,263	1,218	1,168	1,103
Agriculture [6]	1,000	36	24	26	22	16	15	19	17
Manufacturing	1,000	168	159	138	136	135	129	112	102
Trade	1,000	185	239	261	271	260	257	244	240
Government	1,000	222	249	274	280	296	279	271	261
Unemployed	1,000	161	143	147	166	147	151	181	210
Unemployment rate [7]	Rate	14.0	11.0	10.6	11.7	10.4	11.0	13.4	16.0
Compensation of employees	Mil. dol	13,639	23,504	29,372	30,027	30,234	30,869	30,743	29,894
Average compensation	Dollar	14,854	20,280	23,725	23,907	23,938	25,344	26,321	27,102
Salary and wages	Mil. dol	13,639	23,504	25,393	25,844	26,102	26,700	26,510	25,807
INCOME [8]									
Personal income:									
Current dollars	Mil. dol	21,105	38,856	48,820	50,842	52,110	56,124	58,562	60,401
Constant (1954) dollars	Mil. dol	5,551	8,491	9,611	9,555	9,542	9,761	9,791	9,850
Disposable personal income:									
Current dollars	Mil. dol	19,914	36,239	45,488	47,333	48,752	53,075	55,639	57,547
Constant (1954) dollars	Mil. dol	5,238	7,919	8,955	8,896	8,927	9,230	9,303	9,385
Average family income:									
Current dollars	Dollar	22,232	34,693	41,273	41,505	42,381	45,494	47,315	47,129
Constant (1954) dollars	Dollar	5,847	7,581	8,125	7,800	7,761	7,926	7,911	7,700
BANKING [9]									
Assets	Mil. dol	27,902	58,813	109,292	112,658	109,320	110,558	106,960	82,851
TOURISM [8]									
Number of visitors	1,000	3,426	4,566	5,073	5,022	5,062	5,213	4,783	4,872
Visitor expenditures	Mil. dol	1,366	2,388	3,239	3,369	3,414	3,535	3,473	3,598
Average per visitor	Dollar	399	523	638	671	674	678	726	738
Net income from tourism	Mil. dol	383	615	771	806	(NA)	(NA)	(NA)	(NA)

NA Not available. [1] 1990 and 2000 enumerated as of April 1; all other years estimated as of July 1. [2] Enrollment for the first school month. Expenses for school year ending in year shown. "Public" includes: Public Preschool, Public Elementary, Public Intermediate, Public High School, Public Post-High School, Public Technological, Public Adult Education, Public Vocational Education, and Public Special Education. "College and university" includes both public and private colleges and universities. [3] Annual average of monthly figures. For fiscal years. [4] For population 16 years old and over. [5] Includes other employment not shown separately. [6] Includes forestry and fisheries. [7] Percent unemployed of the labor force. [8] For fiscal years. [9] As of June 30. Does not include federal savings banks and international banking entities.
Source: Puerto Rico Planning Board, San Juan, PR, *Economic Report of the Governor*, annual. See also <http://www.gobierno.pr/gprportal/inicio>.

Table 1322. Puerto Rico—Economic Summary by Industry: 2008

[In thousands of dollars (16,969,984 represents $16,969,984,000). Covers establishments with payroll. Excludes self-employed individuals, employees of private households, railroad employees, agricultural production employees, and most government employees. For statement on methodology, see Appendix III]

Industry	2007 NAICS code [1]	Establishments	Employees [2]	Annual payroll (1,000)
Total, all industries [3]	(X)	**46,348**	**748,838**	**16,969,984**
Construction	23	2,716	55,402	980,540
Manufacturing	31–33	2,064	106,132	3,526,855
Wholesale trade	42	2,338	36,360	1,218,421
Retail trade	44–45	10,811	131,689	2,126,121
Transportation and warehousing	48–49	1,093	16,798	419,811
Information	51	448	20,862	768,028
Finance and insurance	52	2,178	40,710	1,565,957
Real estate and rental and leasing	53	1,716	14,848	304,631
Professional, scientific, and technical services	54	4,235	30,341	960,700
Management of companies and enterprises	55	100	5,986	253,552
Admin/support waste mgt/remediation services	56	1,741	69,968	1,050,359
Educational services	61	769	35,306	696,622
Health care and social assistance	62	7,117	79,624	1,651,276
Arts, entertainment, and recreation	71	447	4,082	72,815
Accommodation and food services	72	4,300	74,733	914,630

X Not applicable. [1] 2007 North American Industry Classification System. See text, section 15. [2] Covers full- and part-time employees who are on the payroll in the pay period including March 12. [3] Includes other industries, not shown separately.
Source: U.S. Census Bureau, "County Business Patterns," August 2010, <http://www.census.gov/econ/cbp/index.html>.

Table 1323. Puerto Rico—Gross Product and Net Income: 1990 to 2010

[In millions of dollars (21,619 represents $21,619,000,000). For fiscal years ending June 30. Data for 2010 are preliminary. Minus sign (–) indicates decrease]

Item	1990	1995	2000	2005	2008	2009	2010
Gross product	**21,619**	**28,452**	**41,419**	**53,752**	**61,665**	**62,678**	**63,292**
Agriculture	434	318	407	499	519	506	553
Manufacturing	12,126	17,867	24,489	35,581	40,234	44,019	44,641
Contract construction and mining [1]	720	1,006	2,157	2,155	2,032	1,818	1,658
Transportation & other public services [2]	2,468	3,276	2,579	2,841	3,097	2,881	2,835
Trade	4,728	5,989	6,093	7,368	7,520	7,549	7,708
Finance, insurance, real estate	3,896	5,730	10,511	14,694	19,185	18,206	18,862
Services	3,015	4,724	9,987	11,520	11,258	11,186	11,728
Government	3,337	4,440	5,478	8,151	8,762	9,047	8,276
Commonwealth	2,884	3,793	4,601	7,032	7,350	7,567	6,740
Municipalities	453	647	877	1,118	1,412	1,480	1,536
Rest of the world	−8,985	−14,195	−20,283	−29,056	−30,941	−32,534	−32,969
Statistical discrepancy	−121	−703	585	141	−312	−512	−340
Net income	**17,941**	**23,653**	**32,610**	**43,484**	**48,993**	**49,989**	**49,547**
Agriculture	486	442	385	479	519	506	554
Manufacturing	11,277	16,685	22,627	33,427	37,299	40,974	41,356
Mining	26	30	34	42	36	28	27
Contract construction	679	903	1,764	1,718	1,661	1,473	1,305
Transportation & other public services [2]	1,778	2,360	1,961	2,075	2,382	2,134	2,044
Trade	3,420	4,108	4,995	6,043	6,162	6,180	6,232
Finance, insurance, and real estate	3,280	4,735	8,175	11,634	13,909	12,803	13,051
Services	2,643	4,146	7,475	8,972	9,202	9,377	9,671
Commonwealth government [3]	3,337	4,440	5,478	8,151	8,762	9,047	8,276
Rest of the world	−8,985	−14,195	−20,283	−29,056	−30,941	−32,534	−32,969

[1] Mining includes only quarries. [2] Includes warehousing and other public utilities. [3] Includes all other services not elsewhere classified.

Source: Puerto Rico Planning Board, San Juan, PR, *Economic Report of the Governor*, annual. See also <http://www.gobierno.pr/gprportal/inicio>.

Table 1324. Puerto Rico—Transfer Payments: 1990 to 2010

[In millions of dollars (4,871 represents $4,871,000,000). Data represent transfer payments between federal and state governments and other nonresidents. Data for 2010 are preliminary]

Item	1990	1995	2000	2005	2008	2009	2010
Total receipts	**4,871**	**6,236**	**8,659**	**10,551**	**13,985**	**15,445**	**17,259**
Federal government	4,649	5,912	7,966	9,673	12,858	14,192	16,325
Transfers to individuals [1]	4,577	5,838	7,868	9,547	12,672	13,978	16,082
Veterans benefits	349	440	491	491	609	518	778
Medicare	368	661	1,196	1,825	2,306	2,461	2,510
Old age, disability, survivors (social security)	2,055	2,912	3,863	5,118	6,134	6,620	6,829
Nutritional assistance	880	1,063	1,193	1,306	1,513	1,547	1,605
Industry subsidies	72	74	98	127	185	213	243
U.S. state governments	18	18	15	15	24	36	45
Other nonresidents	205	307	679	863	1,103	1,217	890
Total payments	**1,801**	**2,301**	**2,763**	**3,583**	**3,655**	**4,050**	**4,349**
Federal government	1,756	2,132	2,693	3,516	3,588	3,883	4,132
Transfers from individuals	817	1,052	1,326	1,792	1,834	1,866	1,871
Contribution to Medicare	97	162	191	303	393	441	449
Employee contribution for social security	720	888	1,133	1,483	1,436	1,421	1,419
Transfers from industries	16	49	51	74	104	101	98
Unemployment insurance	247	184	234	221	252	534	782
Employer contribution for social security	675	847	1,081	1,429	1,398	1,382	1,381
Other nonresidents [2]	45	164	70	67	67	167	217
Net balance	**3,070**	**3,935**	**5,897**	**6,968**	**10,330**	**11,394**	**12,911**
Federal government	2,893	3,780	5,273	6,157	9,270	10,308	12,193
U.S. state governments	16	13	10	10	21	32	40
Other nonresidents	162	143	614	801	1,040	1,055	677

[1] Includes other receipts and payments not shown separately. [2] Includes U.S. state governments.

Source: Puerto Rico Planning Board, San Juan, PR, *Economic Report of the Governor*, annual. See also <http://www.gobierno.pr/gprportal/inicio>.

Table 1325. Puerto Rico—Merchandise Imports and Exports: 1980 to 2010

[In millions of dollars (9,018 represents $9,018,000,000). Imports are imports for consumption; see text, Section 28]

Item	1980	1985	1990	1995	2000	2004	2005	2006	2007	2008	2009	2010
Imports	9,018	10,162	16,200	18,969	27,006	37,335	40,499	42,380	44,107	41,409	38,922	39,999
From U.S.	5,345	6,130	10,792	12,213	15,172	18,124	20,994	21,982	22,402	19,777	20,038	20,641
From other	3,673	4,032	5,408	6,756	11,834	19,211	19,505	20,398	21,705	21,632	18,884	19,358
Exports	6,576	11,087	20,402	23,573	43,191	54,997	56,836	59,219	62,401	63,658	59,594	68,337
To U.S.	5,643	9,873	17,915	20,986	38,335	45,311	47,121	47,452	47,507	46,439	40,779	47,630
To other	933	1,214	2,487	2,587	4,856	9,686	9,715	11,767	14,894	17,219	18,815	20,707

Source: U.S. Census Bureau, *Foreign Commerce and Navigation U.S. Trade with Puerto Rico and U.S. Possessions*, FT 895, and unpublished data. See also <http://www.census.gov/foreign-trade/statistics/index.html>. Beginning 2009, *USATradeOnline*, <http://www.usatradeonline.gov/>.

Table 1326. Puerto Rico—Agricultural Summary: 2002 and 2007

[1 cuerda = .97 acre]

All farms	Unit	2002	2007	All farms	Unit	2002	2007
Farms	Number ...	17,659	15,745	Tenants	Number ...	1,636	2,425
Farm land	Cuerdas...	690,687	557,530	Farms by type of			
Average size of farm	Cuerdas...	39.1	35.4	organization:			
Approximate land area	Cuerdas...	2,254,365	2,254,365	Individual or family	Number ...	15,843	13,958
Proportion in farms	Percent ...	30.6	24.7	Partnership	Number ...	162	49
Farms by size:				Corporation	Number ...	595	575
Less than 10 cuerdas	Number ...	7,943	7,502	Other	Number ...	1,059	1,163
10 to 19 cuerdas	Number ...	3,847	3,545	Farms by value of sales:			
20 to 49 cuerdas	Number ...	3,228	2,680	Less than $1,000	Number ...	3,977	4,442
50 to 99 cuerdas	Number ...	1,282	865	$1,000 to $2,499	Number ...	3,471	2,771
100 to 174 cuerdas	Number ...	590	524	$2,500 to $4,499	Number ...	3,044	2,428
175 to 259 cuerdas	Number ...	281	207	$5,000 to $7,499	Number ...	1,575	1,206
260 cuerdas or more	Number ...	488	422	$7,500 to $9,999	Number ...	1,087	882
Tenure of operator:				$10,000 to $19,999	Number ...	1,781	1,497
Operators	Number ...	17,659	15,745	$20,000 to $39,999	Number ...	1,062	1,030
Full owners	Number ...	13,693	11,402	$40,000 to $59,999	Number ...	375	281
Part owners	Number ...	2,330	1,918	$60,000 or more	Number ...	1,287	1,208

Source: U.S. Department of Agriculture, National Agricultural Statistics Service, *2007 Census of Agriculture—Geographic Area Series Part 52, Puerto Rico*, Vol. 1, 2009. See also <http://www.agcensus.usda.gov/Publications/2007/Full_Report/index.asp>.

Table 1327. Puerto Rico—Farms and Market Value of Agricultural Products Sold: 2007

[515,686 represents $515,686,000]

Type of product	Number of farms	Market value ($1,000)	Average value per farm (dol.)	Type of product	Number of farms	Market value ($1,000)	Average value per farm (dol.)
Total	**15,745**	**515,686**	**32,752**	Horticultural specialties	524	44,576	85,068
Crops, including horticultural				Grasses and other crops	256	13,372	52,236
specialties	10,206	218,835	(NA)				
Coffee	5,678	41,824	7,366	Livestock, poultry, and their			
Pineapples	53	527	9,942	products	5,662	296,850	52,428
Plantains	3,756	44,875	11,947	Cattle and calves	3,568	33,005	9,250
Bananas	1,980	10,082	5,092	Poultry and poultry products	1,079	63,574	58,919
Grains	969	1,553	1,603	Dairy products	354	184,543	521,307
Root crops or tubers	1,691	6,683	3,952	Hogs and pigs	1,075	6,239	5,803
Fruits and coconuts	2,350	19,904	8,470	Aquaculture	40	833	20,818
Vegetables and melons [1]	1,007	35,440	35,194	Other	787	8,657	11,000

NA Not available. [1] Includes hydroponic crops.

Source: U.S. Department of Agriculture, National Agricultural Statistics Service, *2007 Census of Agriculture—Geographic Area Series Part 52, Puerto Rico*, Vol. 1, 2009. See also <http://www.agcensus.usda.gov/Publications/2007/Full_Report/index.asp>.

Table 1328. Guam, Virgin Islands, and Northern Mariana Islands—Economic Summary: 2007

[Sales and payroll in millions of dollars (6,244 represents $6,244,000,000). Based on the 2007 Economic Census; see Appendix III. Selected kinds of businesses displayed]

Selected kinds of business	Guam	Virgin Islands	Northern Mariana Islands	Selected kinds of business	Guam	Virgin Islands	Northern Mariana Islands
Total:				Paid employees [2]	2,394	797	872
Establishments [1]	3,143	2,583	1,191	Retail trade:			
Sales	6,244	19,479	1,284	Establishments	660	641	255
Annual payroll	1,101	1,085	246	Sales	1,618	1,397	272
Paid employees [2]	52,394	35,300	22,622	Annual payroll	150	146	29
Construction:				Paid employees [2]	8,219	6,773	2,770
Establishments	317	195	50	Professional, scientific, and			
Sales	579	352	31	technical services:			
Annual payroll	121	115	7	Establishments	227	257	87
Paid employees [2]	6,011	3,388	528	Sales	231	284	25
Manufacturing:				Annual payroll	77	60	9
Establishments	63	70	59	Paid employees [2]	2,217	1,370	404
Sales	167	(D)	190	Accommodation & Food			
Annual payroll	39	(D)	57	Services:			
Paid employees [2]	1,495	([3])	7,094	Establishments	429	255	140
Wholesale trade:				Sales	635	461	173
Establishments	191	58	72	Annual payroll	155	130	45
Sales	800	288	143	Paid employees [2]	11,477	6,146	4,772
Annual payroll	56	25	10				

D Withheld to avoid disclosing data for individual companies; data are included in higher level totals. [1] Includes other industries, not shown separately. [2] For pay period including March 12. [3] 1,000 to 2,499 employees.

Source: U.S. Census Bureau, 2007 Economic Census of the Island Areas, "General Statistics for Island Areas: 2007," <http://factfinder.census.gov/>, accessed August 2010.

This section presents statistics for the world as a whole and for many countries on a comparative basis with the United States. Data are shown for population, births and deaths, social and industrial indicators, finances, agriculture, communication, and military affairs.

Statistics of the individual nations may be found primarily in official national publications, generally in the form of yearbooks, issued by most of the nations at various intervals in their own national languages and expressed in their own or customary units of measure. (For a listing of selected publications, see Guide to Sources.) For handier reference, especially for international comparisons, the United Nations Statistics Division compiles data as submitted by member countries and issues a number of international summary publications, generally in English and French. Among these are the *Statistical Yearbook;* the *Demographic Yearbook; International Trade Statistics Yearbook; National Accounts Statistics: Main Aggregates* and *Detailed Tables; Population and Vital Statistics Reports, semi-annually;* the *Monthly Bulletin of Statistics;* and *the Energy Statistics Yearbook.* Specialized agencies of the United Nations also issue international summary publications on agricultural, labor, health, and education statistics. Among these are the *Production Yearbook* and *Trade Yearbook* issued by the Food and Agriculture Organization, the *Yearbook of Labour Statistics* issued by the International Labour Office and *World Health Statistics* issued by the World Health Organization, and the *Statistical Yearbook* issued by the Educational, Scientific, and Cultural Organization.

The U.S. Census Bureau publishes estimates and projections of key demographic measures for countries and regions of the world in its International Data Base at <http://www.census.gov/ipc/www/idb/>.

The International Monetary Fund (IMF) and the Organization for Economic Cooperation and Development (OECD) also compile data on international statistics. The IMF publishes a series of reports relating to financial data. These include *International Financial Statistics, Direction of Trade,* and *Balance of Payments Yearbook,* published in English, French, and Spanish. The OECD publishes a vast number of statistical publications in various fields such as economics, health, and education. Among these are *OECD in Figures, Main Economic Indicators, Economic Outlook, National Accounts, Labour Force Statistics, OECD Health Data,* and *Education at a Glance.*

Statistical coverage, country names, and classifications—Problems of space and availability of data limit the number of countries and the extent of statistical coverage shown. The list of countries included and the spelling of country names are based almost entirely on the list of independent nations, dependencies, and areas of special sovereignty provided by the U.S. Department of State.

In the last quarter-century, several important changes took place in the status of the world's nations. In 1991, the Soviet Union broke up into 15 independent countries: Armenia, Azerbaijan, Belarus, Estonia, Georgia, Kazakhstan, Kyrgyzstan, Latvia, Lithuania, Moldova, Russia, Tajikistan, Turkmenistan, Ukraine, and Uzbekistan. In the South Pacific, the Marshall Islands, Micronesia, and Palau gained independence from the United States in 1991. Following the breakup of the Socialist Federal Republic of Yugoslavia in 1992, the United States recognized Bosnia and Herzegovina, Croatia, Slovenia, and Macedonia as independent countries.

The Treaty of Maastricht created the European Union (EU) in 1992 with 12 member countries. The EU is not a state intended to replace existing states, but it is more than just an international organization. Its member states have set up common institutions to which they delegate some of their sovereignty so that decisions on specific matters of joint interest can be made democratically at a European level. This pooling of sovereignty is also called "European integration." The EU has grown in size with successive waves of accessions in 1995, 2004, and 2007. The 27 current members of the EU are: Austria, Belgium, Bulgaria, Cyprus, Czech Republic, Denmark, Estonia, Finland, France, Germany, Greece, Hungary, Ireland, Italy, Latvia, Lithuania, Luxembourg, Malta, the Netherlands, Poland, Portugal, Romania, Slovakia, Slovenia, Spain, Sweden, and the United Kingdom.

In 1992, the EU decided to establish an economic and monetary union (EMU), with the introduction of a single European currency managed by a European Central Bank. The single currency—the euro—became a reality on January 1, 2002, when euro notes and coins replaced national currencies in 12 of the then 15 countries of the European Union (Belgium, Germany, Greece, Spain, France, Ireland, Italy, Luxembourg, the Netherlands, Austria, Portugal, and Finland). Since then, 12 countries have become members of the EU, but Slovakia, Slovenia, Malta, Cyprus, and Estonia have been the only new members of the EU to adopt the euro as the national currency.

On January 1, 1993, Czechoslovakia was succeeded by two independent countries: the Czech Republic and Slovakia. Eritrea announced its independence from Ethiopia in April 1993 and was subsequently recognized as an independent nation by the United States. In May of 2002, Timor-Leste won independence from Indonesia.

Serbia and Montenegro, both former republics of Yugoslavia, became independent of one another on May 31, 2006. This separation is seen in the population estimates tables (Tables 1332, 1358, and 1404), but some tables may still show both countries as combined. On February 17, 2008, Kosovo declared its independence from Serbia, making it the world's newest independent state. The Netherlands Antilles dissolved on October 10, 2010. As a result, Cuaçao and Sint

Moortan became autonomous territories of the Netherlands.

The population estimates and projections used in Tables 1329–1332, 1334, and 1339 were prepared by the Census Bureau. For each country, available data on population, by age and sex, fertility, mortality, and international migration were evaluated and, where necessary, adjusted for inconsistencies and errors in the data. In most instances, comprehensive projections were made by the cohort-component method, resulting in distributions of the population by age and sex and requiring an assessment of probable future trends of fertility, mortality, and international migration.

Economic associations—
The Organization for European Economic Co–operation (OEEC), a regional grouping of Western European countries established in 1948 for the purpose of harmonizing national economic policies and conditions, was succeeded on September 30, 1961, by the Organization for Economic Cooperation and Development (OECD). The member nations of the OECD are Australia, Austria, Belgium, Canada, Chile, Czech Republic, Denmark, Estonia, Finland, France, Germany, Greece, Hungary, Iceland, Ireland, Israel, Italy, Japan, Luxembourg, Mexico, the Netherlands, New Zealand, Norway, Poland, Portugal, Slovakia, Slovenia, South Korea, Spain, Sweden, Switzerland, Turkey, the United Kingdom, and the United States.

Quality and comparability of the data—The quality and comparability of the data presented here are affected by a number of factors:

(1) The year for which data are presented may not be the same for all subjects for a particular country or for a given subject for different countries, though the data shown are the most recent available. All such variations have been noted. The data shown are for calendar years except as otherwise specified.

(2) The bases, methods of estimating, methods of data collection, extent of coverage, precision of definition, scope of territory, and margins of error may vary for different items within a particular country, and for like items for different

U.S. Census Bureau, Statistical Abstract of the United States: 2012

countries. Footnotes and headnotes to the tables give a few of the major time periods and coverage qualifications attached to the figures; considerably more detail is presented in the source publications. Many of the measures shown are, at best, merely rough indicators of magnitude.

(3) Figures shown in this section for the United States may not always agree with figures shown in the preceding sections. Disagreements may be attributable to the use of differing original sources, a difference in the definition of geographic limits (the 50 states, conterminous United States only, or the United States including certain outlying areas and possessions), or to possible adjustments made in the United States' figures by other sources to make them more comparable with figures from other countries.

International comparisons of national accounts data—To compare national accounts data for different countries, it is necessary to convert each country's data into a common unit of currency, usually the U.S. dollar. The market exchange rates, which often are used in converting national currencies, do not necessarily reflect the relative purchasing power in the various countries. It is necessary that the goods and services produced in different countries be valued consistently if the differences observed are meant to reflect real differences in the volumes of goods and services produced. The use of purchasing power parities (see Tables 1347, 1348, and 1394) instead of exchange rates is intended to achieve this objective.

The method used to present the data shown in Table 1348 is to construct volume measures directly by revaluing the goods and services sold in different countries at a common set of international prices. By dividing the ratio of the gross domestic products of two countries expressed in their own national currencies by the corresponding ratio calculated at constant international prices, it is possible to derive the implied purchasing power

parity (PPP) between the two currencies concerned. PPPs show how many units of currency are needed in one country to buy the same amount of goods and services that one unit of currency will buy in the other country. For further information, see *National Accounts, Main Aggregates, Volume I*, issued annually by the Organisation for Economic Cooperation and Development, Paris, France.

International Standard Industrial Classification—The original version of the International Standard Industrial Classification of All Economic Activities (ISIC) was adopted in 1948. A number of countries have utilized the ISIC as the basis for devising their industrial classification scheme.

Substantial comparability has been attained between the industrial classifications of many other countries, including the United States and the ISIC by ensuring, as far as practicable, that the categories at detailed levels of classification in national schemes fit into only one category of the ISIC. The United Nations, the International Labour Organization, the Food and Agriculture Organization, and other international bodies use the ISIC in publishing and analyzing statistical data. Revisions of the ISIC were issued in 1958, 1968, 1989, 2002, and 2008.

International maps—A series of regional world maps is provided on pages 826–834. References are included in Table 1331 for easy location of individual countries on the maps. The Robinson map projection is used for this series of maps. A map projection is used to portray all or part of the round Earth on a flat surface, but this cannot be done without some distortion. For the Robinson projection, distortion is very low along the Equator and within 45 degrees of the center but is greatest near the poles. For additional information on map projections and maps, please contact the Earth Science Information Center, U.S. Geological Survey, 507 National Center, Reston, VA 22092.

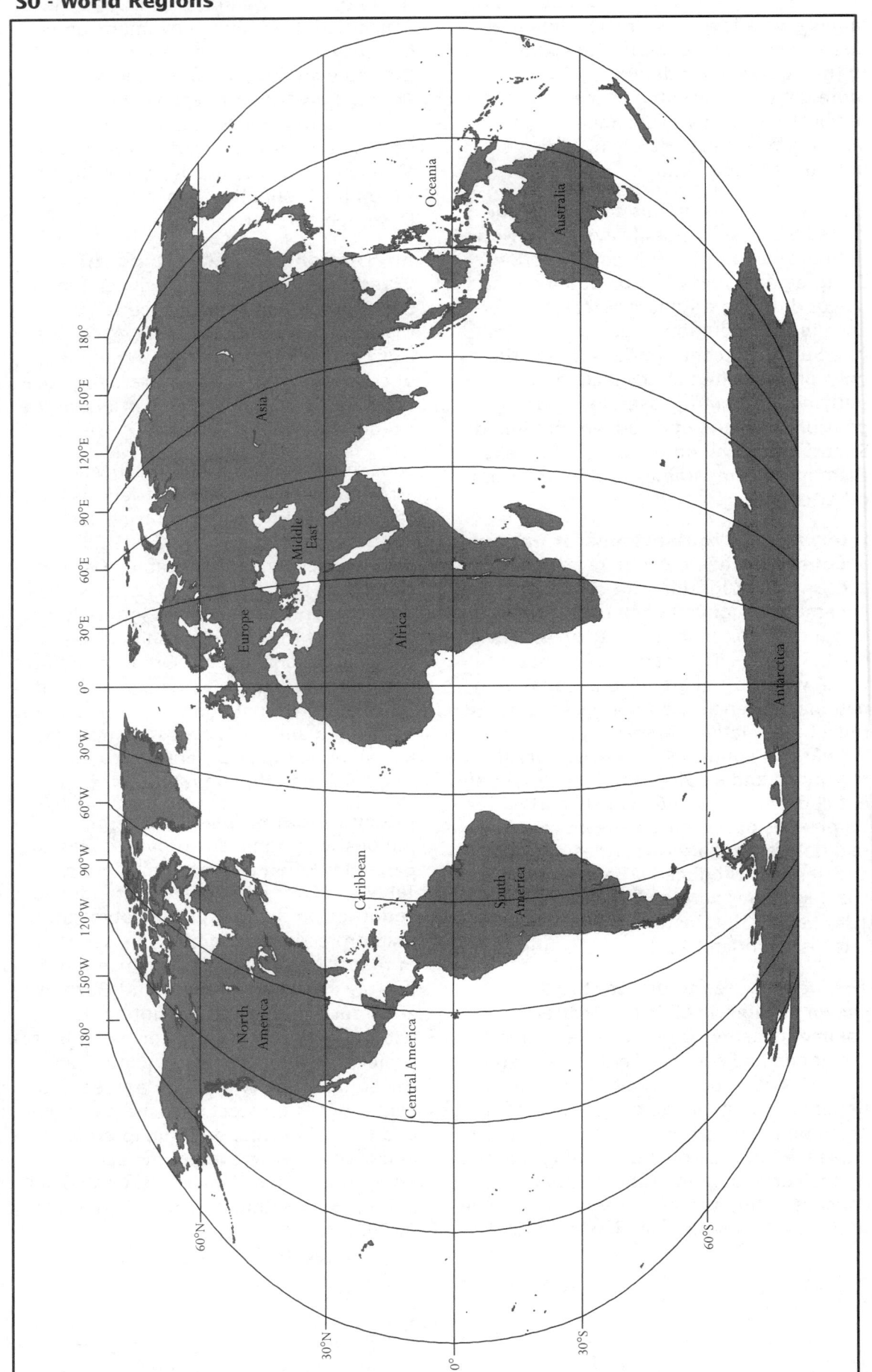

U.S. Census Bureau, Statistical Abstract of the United States: 2012

U.S. Census Bureau, Statistical Abstract of the United States: 2012

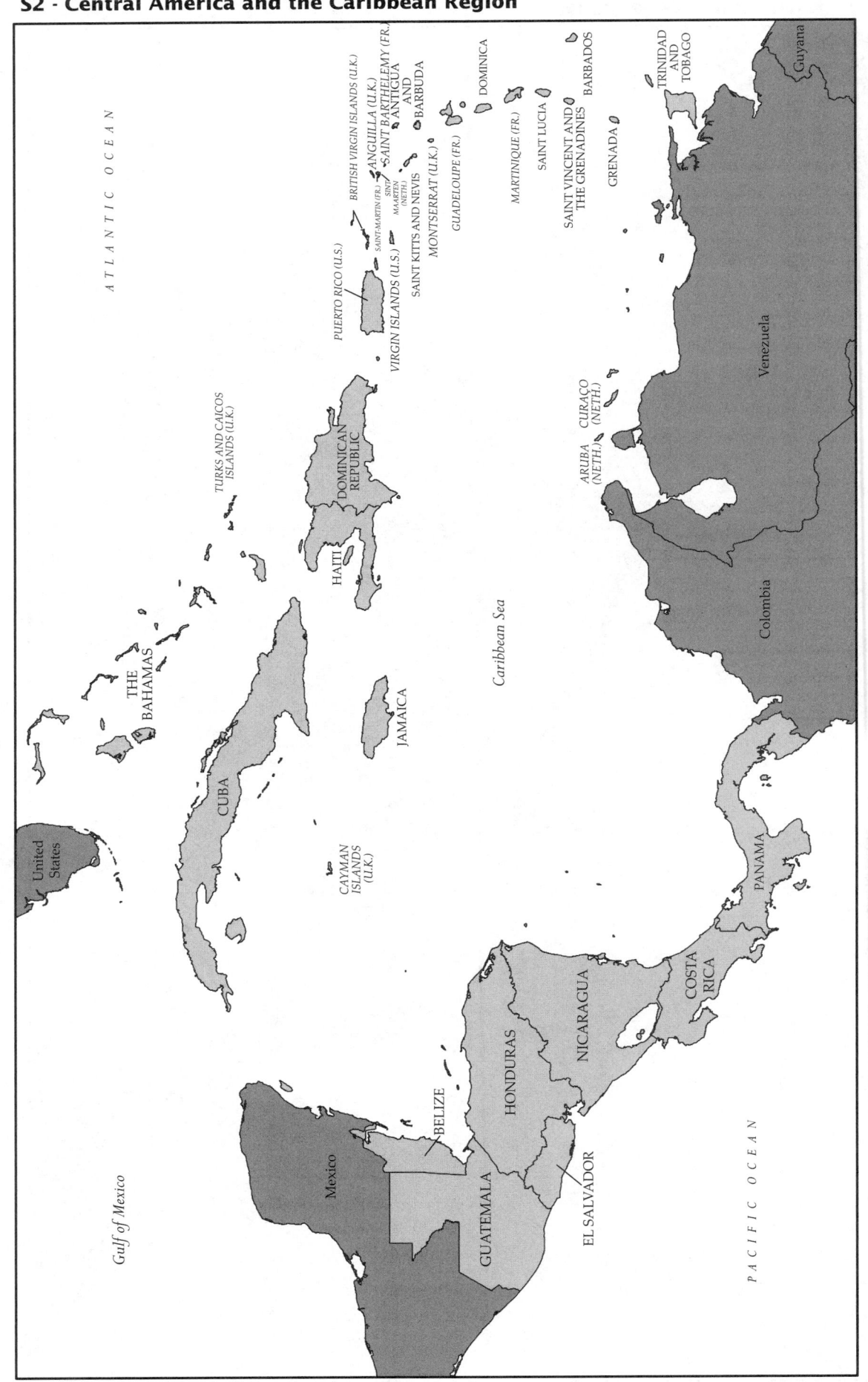

U.S. Census Bureau, Statistical Abstract of the United States: 2012

Caribbean Sea

ATLANTIC OCEAN

VENEZUELA

SURINAME

GUYANA

FRENCH GUIANA (FR.)

COLOMBIA

ECUADOR

PERU

BRAZIL

BOLIVIA

CHILE

PARAGUAY

PACIFIC OCEAN

ARGENTINA

URUGUAY

FALKLAND ISLANDS (U.K.)

SOUTH GEORGIA AND SOUTH SANDWICH ISLANDS (U.K.)

U.S. Census Bureau, Statistical Abstract of the United States: 2012

U.S. Census Bureau, Statistical Abstract of the United States: 2012

U.S. Census Bureau, Statistical Abstract of the United States: 2012

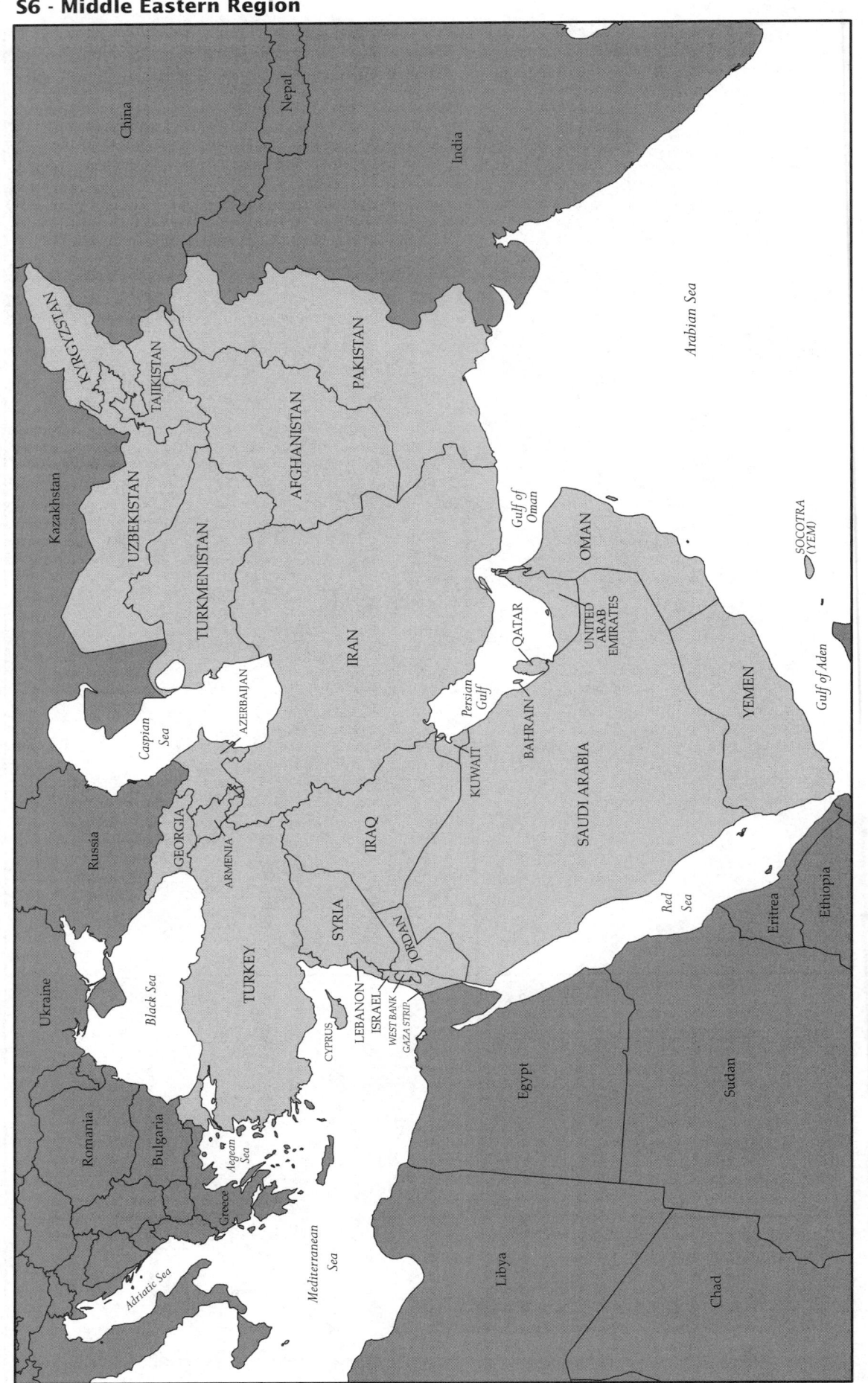

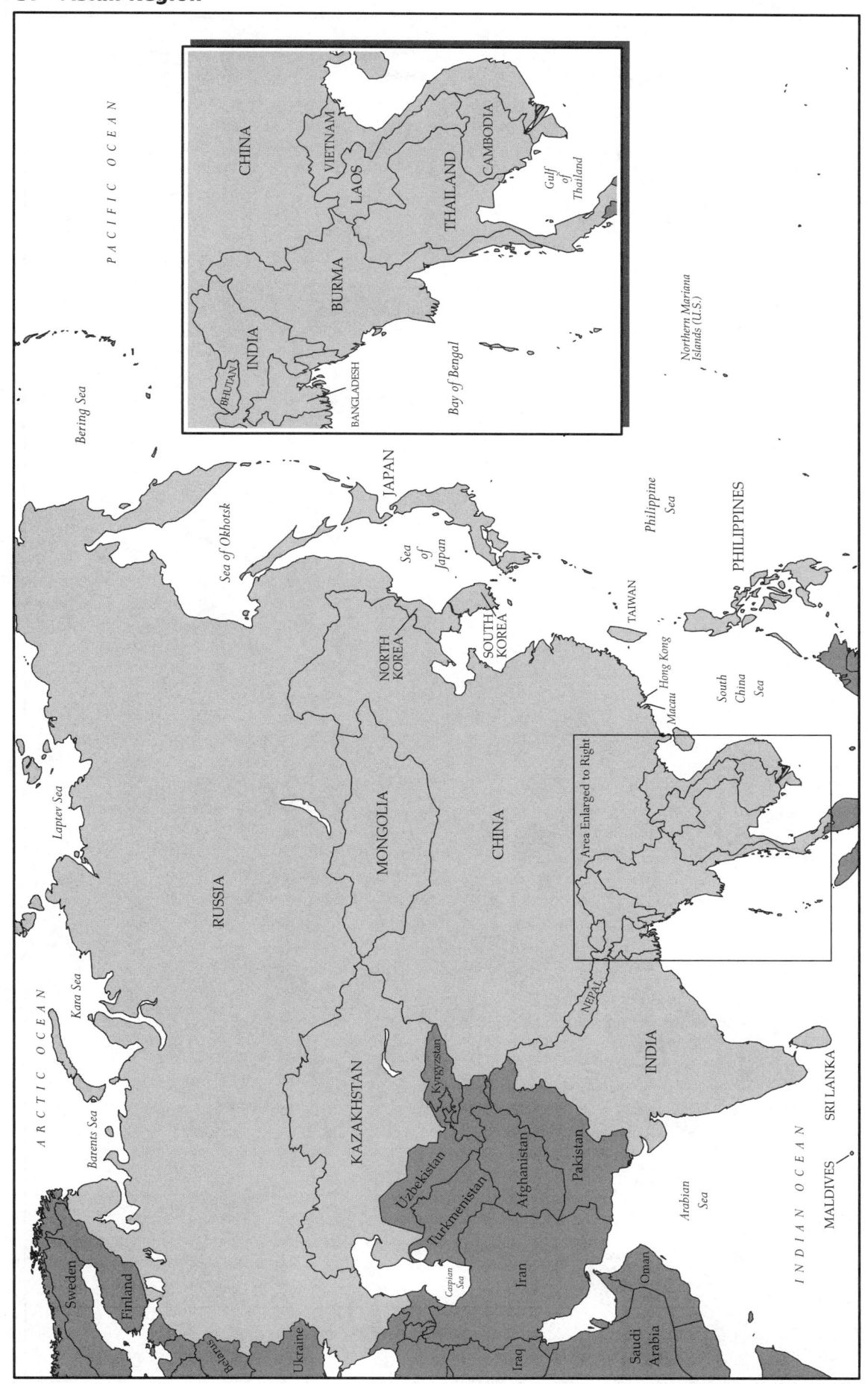

PACIFIC OCEAN

CHINA

VIETNAM

LAOS

THAILAND

CAMBODIA

Gulf of Thailand

BURMA

INDIA

BHUTAN

BANGLADESH

Bay of Bengal

Northern Mariana Islands (U.S.)

Bering Sea

Sea of Okhotsk

JAPAN

Sea of Japan

Philippine Sea

PHILIPPINES

NORTH KOREA

SOUTH KOREA

TAIWAN

Hong Kong

Macau

South China Sea

Laptev Sea

Kara Sea

RUSSIA

MONGOLIA

CHINA

Area Enlarged to Right

ARCTIC OCEAN

Barents Sea

KAZAKHSTAN

NEPAL

INDIA

SRI LANKA

Kyrgyzstan

Uzbekistan

Turkmenistan

Afghanistan

Pakistan

Arabian Sea

INDIAN OCEAN

MALDIVES

Caspian Sea

Iran

Oman

Sweden

Finland

Belarus

Ukraine

Iraq

Saudi Arabia

U.S. Census Bureau, Statistical Abstract of the United States: 2012

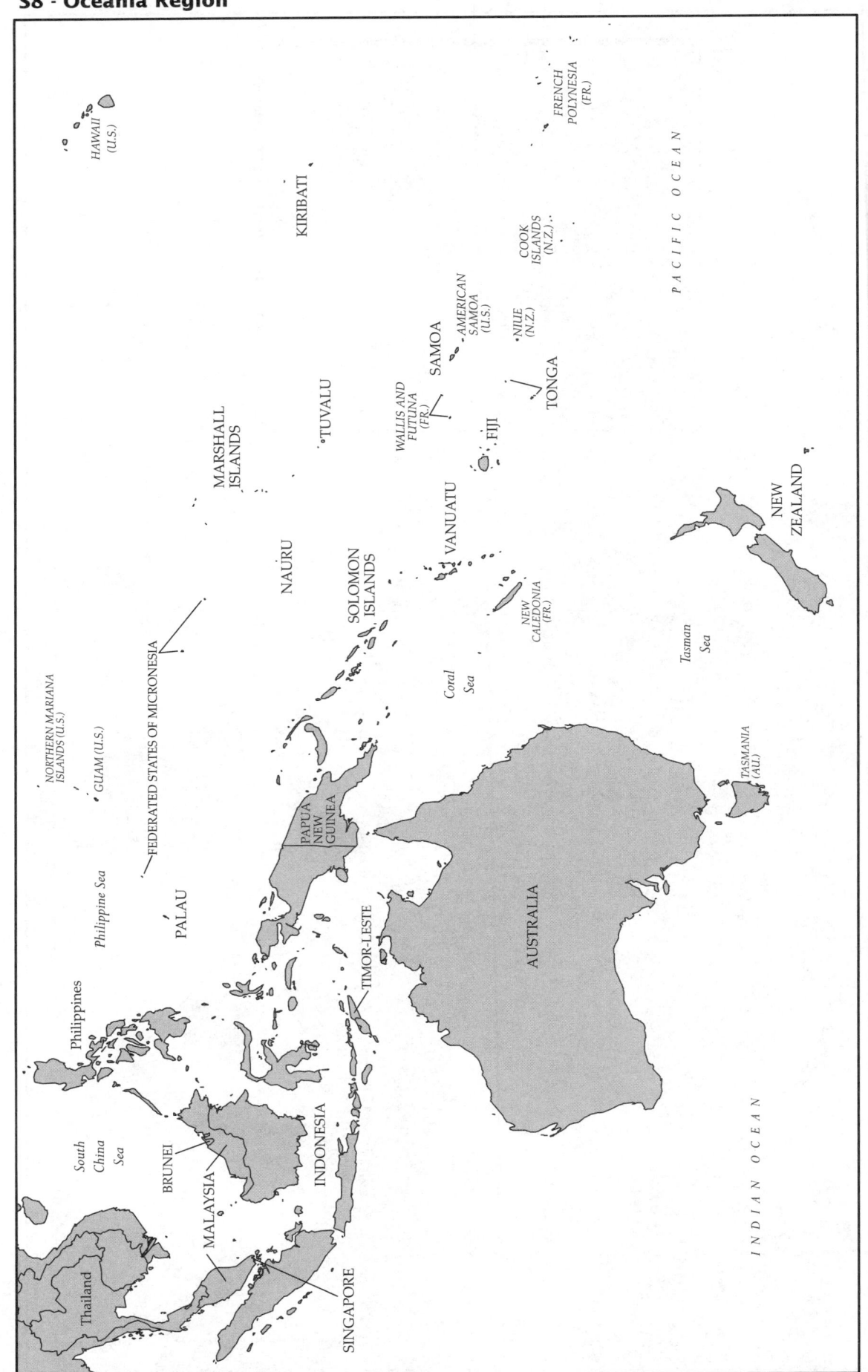

U.S. Census Bureau, Statistical Abstract of the United States: 2012

Table 1329. Total World Population: 1980 to 2050

[As of midyear (4,453 represents 4,453,000,000)]

Year	Population (mil.)	Average annual [1] Growth rate (percent)	Average annual [1] Population change (mil.)	Year	Population (mil.)	Average annual [1] Growth rate (percent)	Average annual [1] Population change (mil.)
1980........	4,453	1.8	82.7	2015........	7,231	1.0	74.7
1985........	4,858	1.7	83.7	2020........	7,597	0.9	70.8
1990........	5,289	1.6	83.0	2025........	7,941	0.8	65.6
1995........	5,700	1.4	80.1	2030........	8,259	0.7	60.4
2007........	6,624	1.2	77.2	2035........	8,551	0.6	55.5
2008........	6,701	1.1	76.2	2040........	8,820	0.6	50.8
2009........	6,777	1.1	76.1	2045........	9,064	0.5	45.9
2010........	6,853	1.1	76.1	2050........	9,284	(NA)	(NA)

NA Not available. [1] Represents change from year shown to immediate succeeding year.
Source: U.S. Census Bureau, International Data Base, <http://www.census.gov/ipc/www/idb/>, accessed June 2010.

Table 1330. Population by Continent: 1980 to 2050

[In millions, except percent (4,453 represents 4,453,000,000). As of midyear]

Year	World	Africa [1]	North America [1]	South America [1]	Asia	Europe [1]	Oceania
1980....................	4,453	479	371	242	2,644	695	23
1990....................	5,289	630	424	297	3,189	723	26
2000....................	6,089	803	486	348	3,691	730	30
2010....................	6,853	1,015	539	396	4,133	734	35
2020....................	7,597	1,261	595	440	4,531	731	39
2030....................	8,259	1,532	648	477	4,841	718	43
2040....................	8,820	1,827	695	504	5,049	698	46
2050....................	9,284	2,138	739	520	5,167	671	49
PERCENT DISTRIBUTION							
1980....................	100.0	10.7	8.3	5.4	59.4	15.6	0.5
2000....................	100.0	13.2	8.0	5.7	60.6	12.0	0.5
2050....................	100.0	23.0	8.0	5.6	55.7	7.2	0.5

[1] Estimates and projections for France include the four overseas departments of French Guiana, Guadeloupe, Martinique, and Reunion in the national total. These areas are included in the same regions as France (Europe). Saint Barthelemy and Saint Martin recently voted to become French overseas collectivities apart from Guadeloupe and are included in the totals for North America.
Source: U.S. Census Bureau, International Data Base, <http://www.census.gov/ipc/www/idb/>, accessed June 2010.

Table 1331. Population and Population Change by Development Status: 1950 to 2050

[(2,557 represents 2,557,000,000). As of midyear. Minus sign (–) indicates decrease. The "less developed" countries include all of Africa, all of Asia except Japan, the Transcaucasian and Central Asian republics of the New Independent States, all of Latin America and the Caribbean, and all of Oceania except Australia, New Zealand, and Hawaii. This category matches the "less developed country" classification employed by the United Nations]

Year	Number (mil.) World	Number (mil.) Less developed countries [1]	Number (mil.) More developed countries [1]	Percent of world Less developed countries [1]	Percent of world More developed countries [1]
POPULATION					
1950..............	2,557	1,749	807	68.4	31.6
1960..............	3,042	2,132	911	70.1	29.9
1970..............	3,713	2,709	1,004	73.0	27.0
1980..............	4,453	3,371	1,082	75.7	24.3
1990..............	5,289	4,145	1,144	78.4	21.6
2000..............	6,089	4,895	1,193	80.4	19.6
2010..............	6,853	5,622	1,231	82.0	18.0
2020..............	7,597	6,338	1,259	83.4	16.6
2030..............	8,259	6,984	1,275	84.6	15.4
2040..............	8,820	7,539	1,281	85.5	14.5
2050..............	9,284	8,005	1,279	86.2	13.8
POPULATION CHANGE					
1950–1960.........	486	382	104	78.7	21.3
1960–1970.........	670	578	93	86.2	13.8
1970–1980.........	740	662	78	89.4	10.6
1980–1990.........	836	774	62	92.5	7.5
1990–2000.........	800	751	49	93.8	6.2
2000–2010.........	764	727	38	95.1	4.9
2010–2020.........	744	716	28	96.2	3.8
2020–2030.........	662	646	16	97.6	2.4
2030–2040.........	561	555	6	99.0	1.0
2040–2050.........	464	466	–2	100.3	–0.3

[1] See footnote 1, Table 1330.
Source: U.S. Census Bureau, International Data Base, <http://www.census.gov/ipc/www/idb/>, accessed June 2010.

Table 1332. Population by Country or Area: 1990 to 2020

[5,288,828 represents 5,288,828,000. Covers countries or areas with populations of 5,000 or more in 2010. Population data generally are de facto figures for the present territory. Population estimates were derived from information available as of spring 2010. See text of this section for general comments concerning the data. For details of methodology, coverage, and reliability, see source. Minus sign (–) indicates decrease]

Country or area	Map refer- ence [1]	Mid-year population (1,000)				Popula- tion rank, 2010	Annual rate of growth,[2] 2010 to 2020 (percent)	Popula- tion per sq. mile, 2010	Area [3] (sq. mile)
		1990	2000	2010	2020, proj.				
World	S0	5,288,828	6,088,684	6,853,019	7,597,239	(X)	1.0	134	50,972,239
Afghanistan	S6	13,449	22,021	29,121	35,975	41	2.1	116	251,826
Albania	S4	3,245	3,158	2,987	3,075	135	0.3	282	10,578
Algeria	S5	25,089	30,429	34,586	38,594	35	1.1	38	919,591
Andorra	S4	53	65	85	86	199	0.1	468	181
Angola	S5	8,297	10,377	13,068	15,898	70	2.0	27	481,351
Antigua and Barbuda	S2	64	75	87	98	198	1.2	508	171
Argentina	S3	33,036	37,336	41,343	45,379	32	0.9	39	1,056,637
Armenia	S6	3,377	3,043	2,967	3,017	137	0.2	272	10,889
Australia	S8	16,956	19,053	21,516	23,939	54	1.1	7	2,966,138
Austria	S4	7,723	8,113	8,214	8,220	92	(Z)	258	31,832
Azerbaijan	S6	7,200	7,809	8,304	9,058	91	0.9	260	31,903
Bahamas, The	S2	245	283	310	338	177	0.8	80	3,865
Bahrain	S6	501	635	738	827	163	1.1	2,580	286
Bangladesh	S7	112,213	132,151	156,118	183,109	7	1.6	3,106	50,258
Barbados	S2	262	274	286	295	180	0.3	1,721	166
Belarus	S4	10,201	10,034	9,613	9,249	88	–0.4	123	78,340
Belgium	S4	9,969	10,264	10,423	10,465	79	(Z)	892	11,690
Belize	S2	191	248	315	380	176	1.9	36	8,805
Benin	S5	4,705	6,619	9,056	11,956	90	2.8	212	42,711
Bhutan	S7	615	606	700	782	164	1.1	47	14,824
Bolivia	S3	6,574	8,195	9,947	11,640	84	1.6	24	418,263
Bosnia and Herzegovina	S4	4,424	4,035	4,622	4,592	120	–0.1	234	19,763
Botswana	S5	1,265	1,680	2,029	2,312	144	1.3	9	218,815
Brazil	S3	151,170	176,320	201,103	222,608	5	1.0	62	3,266,183
Brunei	S8	253	325	395	464	175	1.6	194	2,033
Bulgaria	S4	8,894	7,818	7,149	6,569	98	–0.8	171	41,888
Burkina Faso	S5	8,361	11,588	16,242	21,978	61	3.0	154	105,714
Burma	S7	40,464	47,439	53,414	59,126	24	1.0	212	252,320
Burundi	S5	5,536	6,823	9,863	13,429	85	3.1	995	9,915
Cambodia	S7	9,368	12,351	14,454	16,927	66	1.6	212	68,152
Cameroon	S5	11,884	15,343	19,294	23,471	58	2.0	106	182,513
Canada	S1	27,791	31,100	33,760	36,387	36	0.7	10	3,511,006
Cape Verde	S5	340	430	509	583	169	1.4	327	1,557
Central African Republic	S5	3,085	3,980	4,845	5,991	116	2.1	20	240,534
Chad	S5	5,841	7,943	10,543	12,756	78	1.9	22	486,177
Chile	S3	13,129	15,156	16,746	18,058	60	0.8	58	287,186
China [4]	S7	1,148,364	1,263,638	1,330,141	1,384,545	1	0.4	360	3,694,942
Colombia	S3	33,147	38,910	44,205	49,085	29	1.0	103	428,225
Comoros	S5	429	579	773	1,001	160	2.6	896	863
Congo (Brazzaville) [5]	S5	2,266	3,104	4,126	5,444	126	2.8	31	131,853
Congo (Kinshasa) [5]	S5	39,047	51,849	70,916	95,605	19	3.0	81	875,308
Costa Rica	S2	3,023	3,883	4,516	5,098	122	1.2	229	19,714
Cote d'Ivoire	S5	12,491	16,885	21,059	25,504	57	1.9	172	122,781
Croatia	S4	4,508	4,411	4,487	4,427	123	–0.1	208	21,612
Cuba	S2	10,513	11,106	11,477	11,647	73	0.1	271	42,402
Cyprus	S6	745	920	1,103	1,267	157	1.4	309	3,568
Czech Republic	S4	10,310	10,270	10,202	10,013	81	–0.2	342	29,825
Denmark	S4	5,141	5,337	5,516	5,642	109	0.2	337	16,384
Djibouti	S5	499	669	741	922	162	2.2	83	8,950
Dominica	S2	70	71	73	74	201	0.2	251	290
Dominican Republic	S2	7,084	8,469	9,824	11,109	86	1.2	527	18,656
Ecuador	S3	10,318	12,446	14,791	16,905	65	1.3	138	106,888
Egypt	S5	54,907	65,159	80,472	96,260	16	1.8	209	384,344
El Salvador	S2	5,110	5,850	6,052	6,217	106	0.3	756	8,000
Equatorial Guinea	S5	371	491	651	836	166	2.5	60	10,830
Eritrea	S5	3,138	4,197	5,793	7,260	108	2.3	149	38,996
Estonia	S4	1,569	1,380	1,291	1,203	154	–0.7	79	16,366
Ethiopia	S5	48,397	64,165	88,013	120,420	14	3.1	228	386,100
Fiji	S8	740	805	876	936	158	0.7	124	7,056
Finland	S4	4,986	5,169	5,255	5,272	112	(Z)	45	117,303
France	S4	58,168	61,137	64,768	67,518	21	0.4	262	247,125
Gabon	S5	938	1,236	1,545	1,877	151	1.9	16	99,485
Gambia, The	S5	949	1,368	1,824	2,317	147	2.4	472	3,861
Georgia	S6	5,426	4,777	4,601	4,440	121	–0.4	171	26,911
Germany [6]	S4	79,380	82,188	82,283	81,422	15	–0.1	611	134,622
Ghana	S5	15,408	19,752	24,340	28,784	47	1.7	277	87,851
Greece	S4	10,130	10,559	10,750	10,742	75	(–Z)	213	50,443
Grenada	S2	94	102	108	113	191	0.5	812	133
Guatemala	S2	8,966	11,085	13,550	16,264	68	1.8	328	41,374
Guinea	S5	6,118	8,350	10,324	13,420	80	2.6	109	94,871
Guinea-Bissau	S5	996	1,279	1,565	1,893	150	1.9	144	10,857
Guyana	S3	772	786	748	754	161	0.1	10	76,003
Haiti	S2	6,798	8,413	9,649	10,693	87	1.0	907	10,641
Honduras	S2	4,794	6,359	7,989	9,465	93	1.7	185	43,201
Hungary	S4	10,372	10,147	9,992	9,772	83	–0.2	289	34,598
Iceland	S1	255	281	309	329	178	0.6	8	38,707
India	S7	838,159	1,006,300	1,173,108	1,326,093	2	1.2	1,022	1,147,951
Indonesia	S8	181,770	213,829	242,968	267,532	4	1.0	347	699,447
Iran	S6	58,100	68,632	76,923	86,543	18	1.2	130	591,349

See footnotes at end of table.

U.S. Census Bureau, Statistical Abstract of the United States: 2012

Country or area	Map refer- ence [1]	Mid-year population (1,000)				Popula- tion rank, 2010	Annual rate of growth, [2] 2010 to 2020 (percent)	Popula- tion per sq. mile, 2010	Area [3] (sq. mile)
		1990	2000	2010	2020, proj.				
Iraq	S6	18,140	22,679	29,672	36,889	40	2.2	176	168,868
Ireland	S4	3,508	3,822	4,623	5,177	119	1.1	174	26,596
Israel	S6	4,478	6,115	7,354	8,479	96	1.4	880	8,356
Italy	S4	56,743	57,719	58,091	57,028	23	−0.2	512	113,568
Jamaica	S2	2,347	2,616	2,847	3,051	138	0.7	681	4,182
Japan	S7	123,537	126,729	126,804	121,633	10	−0.4	901	140,728
Jordan	S6	3,267	4,688	6,407	7,278	102	1.3	187	34,286
Kazakhstan	S7	16,398	15,032	15,460	15,977	63	0.3	15	1,042,355
Kenya	S5	23,354	30,508	40,047	48,319	33	1.9	182	219,745
Kiribati	S8	71	85	99	112	195	1.2	318	313
Korea, North	S7	20,019	21,263	22,757	23,433	50	0.3	490	46,490
Korea, South	S7	42,869	46,839	48,636	49,362	26	0.1	1,300	37,421
Kosovo	S4	1,862	1,700	1,815	1,933	148	0.6	432	4,203
Kuwait	S6	2,142	1,974	2,789	3,744	139	2.9	405	6,880
Kyrgyzstan	S6	4,382	4,851	5,509	6,314	110	1.4	74	74,054
Laos	S7	4,210	5,397	6,368	7,447	104	1.6	71	89,112
Latvia	S4	2,664	2,376	2,218	2,077	141	−0.7	92	24,034
Lebanon	S6	3,440	3,791	4,125	4,243	127	0.3	1,044	3,950
Lesotho	S5	1,703	1,916	1,920	1,969	146	0.3	164	11,720
Liberia	S5	2,139	2,601	3,685	4,727	129	2.5	99	37,189
Libya	S5	4,146	5,125	6,461	7,759	101	1.8	10	679,359
Liechtenstein	S4	29	32	35	37	211	0.5	567	62
Lithuania	S4	3,695	3,654	3,545	3,435	130	−0.3	146	24,201
Luxembourg	S4	383	439	498	556	170	1.1	498	998
Macedonia	S4	1,861	2,015	2,072	2,113	143	0.2	211	9,820
Madagascar	S5	11,633	15,742	21,282	28,374	56	2.9	95	224,533
Malawi	S5	9,546	11,802	15,448	20,204	64	2.7	425	36,324
Malaysia	S8	17,882	23,151	28,275	32,652	43	1.4	223	126,895
Maldives	S7	217	300	396	392	174	−0.1	3,439	115
Mali	S5	8,327	10,621	13,796	17,890	67	2.6	29	471,116
Malta	S4	359	390	407	419	173	0.3	3,334	122
Marshall Islands	S8	46	53	66	78	204	1.7	942	70
Mauritania	S5	1,925	2,501	3,205	4,005	133	2.2	8	397,954
Mauritius	S5	1,062	1,186	1,294	1,379	153	0.6	1,651	784
Mexico	S1	84,924	99,927	112,469	124,654	11	1.0	150	750,558
Micronesia, Federated States of	S8	109	108	107	102	192	−0.5	395	271
Moldova	S4	4,394	4,391	4,317	4,267	124	−0.1	340	12,699
Monaco	S4	30	32	31	31	213	0.1	39,609	1
Mongolia	S7	2,218	2,664	3,087	3,535	134	1.4	5	599,828
Montenegro	S4	583	732	667	639	165	−0.4	128	5,194
Morocco	S5	24,000	28,113	31,627	34,956	38	1.0	184	172,317
Mozambique	S5	12,667	18,125	22,061	26,480	52	1.8	73	303,622
Namibia	S5	1,471	1,893	2,128	2,263	142	0.6	7	317,873
Nauru	S8	9	10	9	10	223	0.5	1,143	8
Nepal	S7	18,918	24,818	28,952	34,209	42	1.7	523	55,348
Netherlands	S4	14,952	15,908	16,783	17,332	59	0.3	1,283	13,086
New Zealand	S8	3,414	3,802	4,252	4,615	125	0.8	41	103,363
Nicaragua	S2	3,685	4,935	5,996	7,030	107	1.6	129	46,328
Niger	S5	7,842	10,951	15,878	22,749	62	3.6	32	489,073
Nigeria	S5	96,604	123,179	152,217	182,344	8	1.8	433	351,648
Norway	S4	4,242	4,492	4,676	4,836	118	0.3	40	117,483
Oman	S6	1,794	2,432	2,968	3,635	136	2.0	25	119,498
Pakistan	S6	118,816	152,429	184,405	213,719	6	1.5	620	297,635
Palau	S8	15	19	21	22	218	0.4	118	177
Panama	S2	2,393	2,900	3,411	3,894	132	1.3	119	28,703
Papua New Guinea	S8	3,683	4,813	6,065	7,259	105	1.8	35	174,849
Paraguay	S3	4,200	5,418	6,376	7,192	103	1.2	42	153,398
Peru	S3	21,600	26,087	29,907	33,230	39	1.1	61	494,207
Philippines	S7	65,088	81,222	99,900	119,329	12	1.8	868	115,124
Poland	S4	38,119	38,654	38,464	37,949	34	−0.1	327	117,473
Portugal	S4	9,923	10,336	10,736	10,842	76	0.1	304	35,317
Qatar	S6	446	627	841	905	159	0.7	188	4,473
Romania	S4	22,866	22,447	21,959	21,303	53	−0.3	247	88,761
Russia	S7	147,973	146,710	139,390	132,242	9	−0.5	22	6,323,451
Rwanda	S5	6,999	8,398	11,056	14,327	74	2.6	1,161	9,524
Saint Kitts and Nevis	S2	42	46	50	54	208	0.8	495	101
Saint Lucia	S2	138	153	161	166	188	0.3	688	234
Saint Vincent and the Grenadines	S2	107	108	104	101	194	−0.3	694	150
Samoa	S8	163	176	192	204	185	0.6	176	1,089
San Marino	S4	23	27	31	34	212	0.8	1,336	24
Sao Tome and Principe	S5	116	141	176	211	187	1.8	472	372
Saudi Arabia	S6	16,061	21,312	25,732	29,819	46	1.5	31	829,996
Senegal	S5	7,348	9,469	12,323	15,736	71	2.4	166	74,336
Serbia	S4	7,786	7,604	7,345	7,012	97	−0.5	246	29,913
Seychelles	S5	71	79	88	96	197	0.8	503	176
Sierra Leone	S5	4,228	3,809	5,246	6,625	113	2.3	190	27,653
Singapore	S8	3,047	4,037	4,701	5,015	117	0.6	17,723	265
Slovakia	S4	5,263	5,400	5,470	5,494	111	(Z)	295	18,573
Slovenia	S4	1,991	2,011	2,003	1,951	145	−0.3	257	7,780
Solomon Islands	S8	321	434	559	685	168	2.0	52	10,805
Somalia	S5	6,692	7,386	10,112	13,272	82	2.7	42	242,215

See footnotes at end of table.

U.S. Census Bureau, Statistical Abstract of the United States: 2012

Country or area	Map reference [1]	Mid-year population (1,000)				Population rank, 2010	Annual rate of growth, [2] 2010 to 2020 (percent)	Population per sq. mile, 2010	Area [3] (sq. mile)
		1990	2000	2010	2020, proj.				
South Africa	S5	38,476	45,064	49,109	48,530	25	−0.1	105	468,907
Spain	S4	39,351	40,589	46,506	50,016	27	0.7	241	192,656
Sri Lanka	S7	17,365	19,436	21,514	23,112	55	0.7	862	24,954
Sudan	S5	25,888	34,109	43,940	56,292	30	2.5	48	917,374
Suriname	S3	395	432	487	537	172	1.0	8	60,232
Swaziland	S5	882	1,144	1,354	1,513	152	1.1	204	6,642
Sweden	S4	8,601	8,924	9,074	9,245	89	0.2	57	158,430
Switzerland	S4	6,837	7,267	7,623	7,751	94	0.2	494	15,443
Syria	S6	12,500	16,471	22,198	24,744	51	1.1	313	70,900
Tajikistan	S6	5,272	6,230	7,487	8,874	95	1.7	137	54,637
Tanzania	S5	25,214	33,712	41,893	49,989	31	1.8	122	342,008
Thailand	S7	55,197	62,157	67,090	70,768	20	0.5	340	197,255
Timor-Leste	S8	746	847	1,155	1,389	156	1.8	201	5,743
Togo	S5	3,721	4,992	6,587	8,608	100	2.7	314	20,998
Tonga	S8	92	102	123	141	189	1.4	443	277
Trinidad and Tobago	S2	1,255	1,252	1,229	1,209	155	−0.2	621	1,980
Tunisia	S5	8,211	9,568	10,589	11,559	77	0.9	177	59,985
Turkey	S6	56,561	67,329	77,804	86,757	17	1.1	262	297,155
Turkmenistan	S6	3,658	4,385	4,941	5,529	115	1.1	27	181,440
Tuvalu	S8	9	10	10	11	222	0.8	1,043	10
Uganda	S5	17,456	23,956	33,399	47,691	37	3.6	439	76,100
Ukraine	S4	51,622	49,005	45,416	42,561	28	−0.6	203	223,679
United Arab Emirates	S6	1,826	3,219	4,976	6,495	114	2.7	154	32,278
United Kingdom	S4	57,411	59,140	62,348	65,761	22	0.5	667	93,409
United States	S1	**249,623**	**282,172**	**310,233**	**341,387**	**3**	**1.0**	**88**	**3,537,438**
Uruguay	S3	3,110	3,328	3,510	3,653	131	0.4	52	67,573
Uzbekistan	S6	20,530	25,042	27,866	30,565	44	0.9	170	164,247
Vanuatu	S8	154	190	222	251	184	1.2	47	4,706
Venezuela	S3	19,325	23,493	27,223	31,276	45	1.4	80	340,560
Vietnam	S7	67,258	79,178	89,571	98,721	13	1.0	748	119,718
Yemen	S6	12,416	17,407	23,495	29,727	48	2.4	115	203,849
Zambia	S5	7,858	10,345	13,460	18,065	69	2.9	47	287,026
Zimbabwe	S5	10,156	11,820	11,652	15,832	72	3.1	78	149,362
OTHER									
Taiwan [4]	S7	20,278	22,183	23,025	23,278	49	0.1	1,849	12,456
AREAS OF SPECIAL SOVEREIGNTY AND DEPENDENCIES									
American Samoa	S8	47	58	66	75	203	1.2	865	77
Anguilla	S1	8	11	15	18	220	2.0	420	35
Aruba	S1	63	90	105	119	193	1.3	1,505	69
Bermuda	S1	58	63	68	72	202	0.5	3,274	21
Cayman Islands	S1	26	38	50	62	207	2.1	493	102
Cook Islands	S8	18	16	11	9	221	−2.9	126	91
Faroe Islands	S4	47	46	49	52	209	0.5	91	538
French Polynesia	S8	202	249	291	329	179	1.2	197	1,478
Gaza Strip [7]	S6	646	1,130	1,604	2,121	149	2.8	11,542	139
Gibraltar	S4	29	27	29	30	215	0.2	11,506	3
Greenland	S1	56	57	58	58	206	(−Z)	(Z)	160,075
Guam	S8	134	155	181	204	186	1.2	861	210
Guernsey	S4	63	62	65	67	205	0.3	2,151	30
Hong Kong	S7	5,688	6,659	7,090	7,328	99	0.3	17,422	407
Isle of Man	S4	69	76	84	90	200	0.8	380	221
Jersey	S4	84	87	93	101	196	0.8	2,085	45
Macau	S7	352	432	568	614	167	0.8	52,163	11
Mayotte	S5	90	156	231	312	182	3.0	1,601	144
Montserrat	S2	11	4	5	5	227	0.5	130	39
Netherlands Antilles [8]	S2	189	210	229	243	183	0.6	740	309
New Caledonia	S8	169	211	252	290	181	1.4	36	7,056
Northern Mariana Islands	S8	44	70	48	49	210	0.1	270	179
Puerto Rico	S2	3,537	3,814	3,979	4,051	128	0.2	1,162	3,425
Saint Barthelemy	S2	5	7	7	7	225	−0.4	913	8
Saint Helena	S5	7	7	8	8	224	0.2	64	119
Saint Martin	S2	30	28	30	33	214	0.7	1,439	21
Saint Pierre and Miquelon	S1	6	6	6	5	226	−1.1	64	93
Turks and Caicos Islands	S2	12	18	24	29	217	2.2	64	366
Virgin Islands	S2	104	109	110	108	190	−0.1	822	134
Virgin Islands, British	S2	16	20	25	29	216	1.5	428	58
Wallis and Futuna	S8	13	15	15	16	219	0.3	280	55
West Bank [7]	S6	1,253	1,980	2,515	3,058	140	2.0	1,155	2,178
Western Sahara	S5	217	336	492	652	171	2.8	5	102,703

X Not applicable. Z Less than 0.05 percent or less than one person per square mile. [1] See maps on pp. 826–834 for geographic locations. [2] Computed by the exponential method. For explanation of average annual percent change, see Guide to Tabular Presentation. [3] Source: Central Intelligence Agency, "CIA World Factbook," accessed August 2010. (Data converted from square kilometers to square miles). [4] With the establishment of diplomatic relations with China on January 1, 1979, the U.S. government recognized the People's Republic of China as the sole legal government of China and acknowledged the Chinese position that there is only one China and that Taiwan is part of China. [5] "Congo" is the official short-form name for both the Republic of Congo and the Democratic Republic of the Congo. To distinguish one from the other the U.S. Department of State adds the capital in parentheses. This practice is unofficial and provisional. [6] Data for 1990 are for former West Germany and East Germany combined. [7] The Gaza Strip and West Bank are Israeli occupied with interim status subject to Israeli/Palestinian negotiations. The final status is yet to be determined. [8] See footnote 4, Table 1398.

Source: Except as noted, U.S. Census Bureau, International Data Base, <http://www.census.gov/ipc/www/idb/>, accessed June 2010.

Table 1333. Foreign or Foreign-Born Population, Labor Force, and Net Migration in Selected OECD Countries: 2000 and 2007

[31,108 represents 31,108,000. In Australia and the United States, the data refer to people present in the country who are foreign born. In the European countries and Japan, they generally refer to foreigners and represent the nationalities of residents. Minus sign (–) indicates net loss]

Country	Foreign population [1]				Foreign labor force [2]				Average net migration 1990–2007 [3] (per 1,000 population)
	Number (1,000)		Percent of total population		Number (1,000)		Percent of total population		
	2000	2007	2000	2007	2000	2007	2000	2007	
United States	**31,108**	**41,100**	**11.0**	**13.6**	**18,029**	**24,778**	**12.9**	**16.3**	**4.0**
Australia	4,412	5,254	23.0	25.0	2,373	2,827	24.7	25.8	5.7
Austria	702	840	8.7	10.1	346	452	10.6	13.1	3.9
Belgium	862	971	8.4	9.1	388	449	8.6	9.5	3.2
Denmark	259	299	4.8	5.5	97	127	3.4	4.4	2.2
France	(NA)	(NA)	(NA)	(NA)	1,578	1,486	6.0	5.4	1.3
Germany	7,297	6,745	8.9	8.2	3,546	3,874	8.8	9.4	3.0
Italy [4]	1,380	3,433	2.4	5.8	838	1,638	3.9	6.6	3.8
Japan [5]	1,686	2,151	1.3	1.7	155	194	0.2	0.3	–0.1
Luxembourg	165	206	37.3	43.2	153	222	58.0	66.6	9.8
Netherlands	668	688	4.2	4.2	300	314	3.9	3.6	1.8
Spain [6]	1,371	5,221	3.4	11.6	455	1,981	2.5	9.0	7.0
Sweden	477	525	5.4	5.7	222	(NA)	5.0	(NA)	3.0
Switzerland [7]	1,384	1,571	19.3	20.8	717	876	20.1	21.3	4.3
United Kingdom [8]	2,342	3,824	4.0	6.5	1,107	2,035	4.0	7.2	0.7

NA Not available. [1] Data are from population registers of foreigners except for France, Greece, Mexico, and Poland (census), Ireland and the United Kingdom (Labour Force Survey), Portugal (residence permits), Australia (inter- and post-censal estimates), and the United States (Current Population Survey). [2] Includes unemployed except for Belgium, Greece, Norway, Luxembourg, Netherlands, and the United Kingdom. Germany, Luxembourg, and Netherlands include cross-border workers. Belgium and Italy include the self-employed. Data for Austria, Germany, and Luxembourg are from social security registers, and for Denmark, from the register of population. Data for Italy, Spain, and Switzerland are from residence or work permits. Figures for Japan and Netherlands are estimates. Data for other countries are from labor force surveys. [3] Or latest period available. [4] Children under 18 who are registered on their parents' permit are not counted. [5] Data are based on registered foreign nationals which include foreigners staying in Japan for more than 90 days. [6] Number of foreigners with a residence permit. Permits of short duration (less than 6 months) as well as students are excluded. [7] Number of foreigners with an annual residence permit or with a settlement permit (permanent permit). Seasonal and frontier workers are excluded. [8] Estimated from the annual labour force survey. Fluctuations from year to year may be due to sampling error.

Source: Organization for Economic Cooperation and Development (OECD), 2010, "International migration database", OECD International Migration Statistics database and "Population and vital statistics," Labour Force Statistics database (copyright), <http://dx.doi.org/10.1787/data-00287-en> and <http://dx.doi.org/10.1787/data-00342-en>, accessed May 2010.

Table 1334. Age Distribution by Country or Area: 2010 and 2020

[In percent. Covers countries with 13 million or more population in 2010]

Country or area	2010		2020, proj.		Country or area	2010		2020, proj.	
	Under 15 years old	65 years old and over	Under 15 years old	65 years old and over		Under 15 years old	65 years old and over	Under 15 years old	65 years old and over
World	**26.5**	**7.8**	**24.6**	**9.6**	Madagascar	43.3	3.0	41.4	3.3
					Malawi	45.3	2.7	43.1	2.8
Afghanistan	42.9	2.4	38.2	2.7	Malaysia	29.9	4.8	26.8	6.9
Algeria	24.7	5.1	21.9	6.9	Mali	47.5	3.0	44.9	2.9
Angola	43.4	2.7	41.5	2.5	Mexico	28.7	6.4	25.0	8.3
Argentina	25.5	10.9	23.7	12.4	Morocco	28.2	6.0	24.9	7.5
Australia	18.4	13.7	17.6	17.0	Mozambique	44.1	2.9	42.1	3.1
Bangladesh	34.8	4.6	28.3	5.8	Nepal	35.6	4.3	27.6	5.1
Brazil	26.5	6.6	23.6	8.8	Netherlands	17.2	15.2	15.5	19.4
Burkina Faso	46.0	2.5	44.3	2.4	Niger	49.7	2.3	48.4	2.3
Burma	27.9	5.0	24.7	6.2	Nigeria	41.2	3.1	37.9	3.4
Cambodia	32.5	3.7	30.2	4.6	Pakistan	36.1	4.2	29.7	4.8
Cameroon	40.7	3.3	37.4	3.7	Peru	28.5	5.8	24.4	7.6
Canada	15.9	15.5	15.4	20.1	Philippines	34.9	4.2	31.6	5.4
Chile	22.7	9.3	19.9	12.4	Poland	14.8	13.5	14.6	18.6
China [1]	17.9	8.6	17.0	12.4	Romania	14.9	14.8	14.1	17.6
Colombia	27.2	6.0	23.3	8.4	Russia	15.0	13.3	16.3	16.0
Congo (Kinshasa) [2]	46.7	2.5	44.4	2.6	Saudi Arabia	30.1	2.9	25.0	3.8
Cote d'Ivoire	40.2	2.9	35.6	3.7	South Africa	28.6	5.5	26.9	7.4
Ecuador	30.6	6.3	25.8	8.1	Spain	15.0	16.9	15.0	18.5
Egypt	32.8	4.4	30.3	6.0	Sri Lanka	23.6	8.3	21.1	11.5
Ethiopia	46.2	2.7	45.4	2.7	Sudan	42.5	2.6	39.6	3.1
France	18.6	16.5	17.8	20.0	Syria	35.8	3.7	30.0	4.6
Germany	13.5	20.4	12.9	22.6	Taiwan [1]	16.2	10.8	12.9	15.5
Ghana	36.8	3.6	32.4	4.0	Tanzania	42.5	2.9	36.4	3.3
Guatemala	38.7	3.8	33.0	4.9	Thailand	20.1	8.9	17.9	12.3
India	30.1	5.3	26.3	6.7	Turkey	26.9	6.2	23.4	8.1
Indonesia	27.7	6.1	23.8	7.7	Uganda	50.0	2.1	49.5	1.9
Iran	24.4	5.0	23.3	6.1	Ukraine	13.7	15.5	14.5	17.8
Iraq	38.4	3.1	33.7	3.9	United Kingdom	17.4	16.3	17.6	18.5
Italy	13.4	20.3	12.0	23.1	**United States**	**20.1**	**13.0**	**20.0**	**16.1**
Japan	13.3	22.6	11.3	28.3	Uzbekistan	27.3	4.7	23.2	5.9
Kazakhstan	21.6	7.6	22.2	9.5	Venezuela	30.0	5.3	26.1	7.4
Kenya	42.3	2.7	36.4	3.3	Vietnam	25.6	5.5	22.6	6.9
Korea, North	20.9	9.6	19.6	10.6	Yemen	43.5	2.6	37.3	3.0
Korea, South	16.2	11.1	12.6	15.6	Zambia	46.7	2.5	46.2	2.5

[1] See footnote 4, Table 1332. [2] See footnote 5, Table 1332.
Source: U.S. Census Bureau, International Data Base, <http://www.census.gov/ipc/www/idb/>, accessed June 2010.

Table 1335. Births to Unmarried Women by Country: 1980 to 2008

[Percent of all live births]

Country	1980	1990	2000	2005	2006	2007	2008
United States	**18.4**	**28.0**	**33.2**	**36.9**	**38.5**	**39.7**	**40.6**
Canada	12.8	24.4	28.3	25.6	27.1	27.3	(NA)
Japan.................	0.8	1.1	1.6	2.0	2.1	(NA)	(NA)
Denmark	33.2	46.4	44.6	45.7	46.4	46.1	46.2
France	11.4	30.1	43.6	48.4	50.5	51.7	52.6
Germany [1]	(X)	15.1	23.4	29.2	30.0	30.8	32.1
Ireland	5.9	14.6	31.5	31.8	32.7	(NA)	(NA)
Italy	4.3	6.5	9.7	15.2	16.2	17.7	(NA)
Netherlands...........	4.1	11.4	24.9	34.9	37.1	39.5	41.2
Spain	3.9	9.6	17.7	26.6	28.4	30.2	31.7
Sweden	39.7	47.0	55.3	55.4	55.5	54.8	54.7
United Kingdom	11.5	27.9	39.5	42.9	43.7	(NA)	(NA)

NA Not available. X Not applicable. [1] Data are for 1991 instead of 1990.
Source: U.S. Bureau of Labor Statistics, updated and revised from "Families and Work Transition in 12 Countries, 1980–2001," *Monthly Labor Review*, September 2003, with national sources, some of which may be unpublished.

Table 1336. Marriage and Divorce Rates by Country: 1980 to 2008

[Per 1,000 population aged 15–64 years]

Country	Marriage rate				Divorce rate			
	1980	1990	2000	2008	1980	1990	2000	2008
United States [1]	**15.9**	**14.9**	**12.5**	**10.6**	**7.9**	**7.2**	**6.2**	**5.2**
Canada	11.5	10.0	7.5	6.4	3.7	4.2	3.4	(NA)
Japan.................	9.8	8.4	9.2	(NA)	1.8	1.8	3.1	(NA)
Denmark	8.0	9.1	10.8	10.3	4.1	4.0	4.0	4.1
France	9.7	7.7	7.9	6.6	2.4	2.8	3.0	(NA)
Germany [2]	(X)	8.2	7.6	6.9	(X)	2.5	3.5	3.5
Ireland [3]	10.9	8.3	7.6	(NA)	(NA)	(NA)	1.0	(NA)
Italy	8.7	8.2	7.3	6.3	0.3	0.7	1.0	1.3
Netherlands...........	9.6	9.4	8.2	6.7	2.7	2.8	3.2	2.9
Spain	9.4	8.5	7.9	6.2	(NA)	0.9	1.4	3.5
Sweden	7.1	7.4	7.0	8.3	3.7	3.5	3.8	3.5
United Kingdom	11.6	10.0	8.0	(NA)	4.1	4.1	4.0	(NA)

NA Not available. X Not applicable. [1] Divorce rates exclude data for California, Georgia, Hawaii, Indiana, Louisiana, and Minnesota in 2008. [2] Data are for 1991 instead of 1990. [3] Divorce not allowed by law prior to 1997.
Source: U.S. Bureau of Labor Statistics, updated and revised from "Families and Work in Transition in 12 Countries, 1980–2001," *Monthly Labor Review*, September 2003, with national sources, some of which may be unpublished.

Table 1337. Single-Parent Households: 1980 to 2009

[In thousands (6,061 represents 6,061,000), except for percent. For the United Kingdom in 1981, children are defined as those under 15 and those who are 15, 16, or 17 and attended school full-time; for later years, children are defined as those under 16 and those who are 16 or 17 and attend school full-time. For Ireland, children are defined as those under 15. For Denmark for 2009 and France, children are defined as those under 25. For Canada for 2001 onward and for Germany for 1995 onward, children are of all ages. For Germany in 1991 and all other countries, children are defined as those under 18 living at home, or away at school. Data are generally for the entire year, but in some instances they are only for a particular month within the year]

Country and year	Number (1,000)	Percent of all households with children	Country and year	Number (1,000)	Percent of all households with children
United States:			Germany:		
1980.................	6,061	19.5	1991.................	1,429	15.2
1990.................	7,752	24.0	1995 [1]	2,496	18.8
2000.................	9,357	27.0	2000 [1]	2,274	17.6
2008.................	10,536	29.5	2008.................	2,616	21.7
Canada:			Ireland: [2]		
1981.................	437	12.7	1981.................	30	7.2
1991.................	572	16.2	1991.................	44	10.7
2001 [1]	1,184	23.5	2002.................	50	17.4
2006.................	1,276	24.6	2006.................	78	22.6
Japan:			Netherlands:		
1980.................	796	4.9	1988.................	179	9.6
1990.................	934	6.5	2000.................	240	13.0
2000.................	996	8.3	2009 [1]	310	16.0
2005.................	1,163	10.2	Sweden:		
Denmark: [2]			1985.................	117	11.2
1980.................	99	13.4	1995 [1]	189	17.4
1990.................	117	17.8	2000.................	233	21.4
2001.................	120	18.4	2008.................	200	18.7
2009 [1]	165	21.7	United Kingdom: [3]		
France:			1981.................	1,010	13.9
1982.................	887	10.2	1991.................	1,344	19.4
1990.................	1,175	13.2	2000.................	1,434	20.7
1999.................	1,494	17.4	2008.................	1,750	25.0
2005 [1]	1,725	19.8			

[1] Break in series. [2] Data are from family-based, rather than household-based, statistics. [3] Great Britain only (excludes Northern Ireland).
Source: U.S. Bureau of Labor Statistics, updated and revised from "Families and Work in Transition in 12 Countries, 1980–2001," *Monthly Labor Review*, September 2003, with national sources, some of which may be unpublished.

Table 1338. Percent Distribution of Households by Type and Country: 1980 to 2009

[Data are generally for the entire year, but in some instances they are only for a particular month within the year]

Year	Total	Married-couple households [1]			Single parent [2]	One person	Other [3]
		Total	With children [2]	Without children [2]			
United States:							
1980............	100.0	60.8	30.9	29.9	7.5	22.7	9.0
1990............	100.0	56.0	26.3	29.8	8.3	24.6	11.0
1995............	100.0	54.4	25.5	28.9	9.1	25.0	11.5
2000............	100.0	52.8	24.1	28.7	8.9	25.5	12.7
2008............	100.0	50.0	21.6	28.4	9.0	27.5	13.5
Canada:							
1981............	100.0	66.8	36.3	30.5	5.3	20.3	7.6
1991............	100.0	62.8	29.6	33.2	5.7	22.9	8.6
2001 [4].........	100.0	58.5	33.4	25.2	10.2	25.7	5.5
2006............	100.0	57.4	31.4	26.1	10.3	26.8	5.5
Japan:							
1980............	100.0	68.4	42.9	25.6	2.2	19.8	9.5
1990............	100.0	65.2	33.1	32.1	2.3	23.1	9.4
1995............	100.0	62.8	27.4	35.4	2.0	25.6	9.6
2000............	100.0	60.3	23.6	36.7	2.1	27.6	10.0
2005............	100.0	57.6	20.8	36.8	2.4	29.5	10.5
Denmark: [5]							
1980............	100.0	50.3	25.0	25.3	3.9	44.9	1.0
1990............	100.0	45.6	19.5	26.1	4.2	49.6	0.6
1995............	100.0	44.9	18.2	26.6	4.2	50.4	0.5
2001............	100.0	45.7	18.5	27.2	4.2	49.6	0.6
2009 [4].........	100.0	47.4	21.2	26.1	5.9	46.2	0.6
France:							
1982............	100.0	67.5	39.8	27.7	4.5	24.6	3.4
1990............	100.0	64.0	35.9	28.1	5.5	27.1	3.4
1999............	100.0	59.3	29.9	29.4	6.3	31.0	3.4
2005 [4].........	100.0	56.4	27.2	29.2	6.7	32.8	4.1
Germany:							
1991............	100.0	55.3	31.6	23.7	7.1	33.6	4.0
1995............	100.0	53.3	29.2	24.0	6.8	34.9	5.1
2000 [4].........	100.0	56.8	28.0	28.8	6.0	36.1	1.2
2005............	100.0	54.7	25.5	29.1	6.4	37.5	1.4
2008............	100.0	52.6	23.6	29.0	6.5	39.4	1.5
Ireland:							
1981............	100.0	(NA)	(NA)	(NA)	(NA)	16.9	(NA)
1991............	100.0	61.6	47.9	13.7	10.6	20.2	7.6
1996............	100.0	59.6	44.5	15.1	11.2	21.5	7.7
2002............	100.0	59.2	41.4	17.7	11.7	21.6	7.6
2006............	100.0	57.3	37.4	20.0	11.6	22.4	8.7
Netherlands:							
1988............	100.0	64.7	37.3	27.4	5.4	28.7	1.2
1993............	100.0	63.1	33.3	29.9	5.0	30.9	1.0
2000 [4].........	100.0	60.2	30.6	29.6	5.6	33.4	0.7
2005............	100.0	58.5	29.4	29.1	6.3	34.5	0.7
2007............	100.0	57.7	28.7	28.9	6.4	35.3	0.7
2009............	100.0	57.0	28.1	28.9	6.5	35.8	0.7
Sweden:							
1985............	100.0	54.8	23.8	31.0	3.2	36.1	5.9
1990............	100.0	52.1	21.9	30.2	3.9	39.6	4.4
1995 [4].........	100.0	50.7	21.2	29.4	4.6	42.3	2.4
2000............	100.0	45.8	19.1	26.7	5.3	46.5	2.3
2008............	100.0	44.5	18.6	25.9	4.4	48.1	3.0
United Kingdom: [6]							
1981............	100.0	65.0	31.0	34.0	5.0	22.0	8.0
1991............	100.0	61.0	25.0	36.0	6.0	27.0	6.0
1994–95.........	100.0	58.0	25.0	33.0	7.0	27.0	8.0
2000............	100.0	58.0	23.0	35.0	6.0	29.0	7.0
2008............	100.0	56.0	21.0	35.0	7.0	30.0	7.0

NA Not available. [1] May include unmarried cohabiting couples. Such couples are explicitly included under married couples in Canada, Denmark, Ireland, France, the Netherlands, Sweden, and the United Kingdom. In Germany, cohabitants are grouped with married couples beginning in 2000. In other countries, some unmarried cohabitants are included as married couples, while some are classified under "other households." [2] Children are defined as unmarried children living at home according to the following age limits: under 18 years old in the United States, Canada (1981–96), Japan, Denmark (1980–2007), Sweden, and the United Kingdom, except that the United Kingdom includes 15-, 16-, and 17-year-olds in 1981 and 16- and 17-year-olds thereafter only if they are attending school full-time; under 25 years old in Denmark (2009 only) and France; and children of all ages in Canada (2001 onward), Germany, Ireland, and the Netherlands. [3] Includes both family and nonfamily households not elsewhere classified. These households comprise, for example, siblings residing together, other households composed of relatives, and households made up of roommates. Some unmarried cohabiting couples may also be included in the "other" group. See footnote 1. [4] Break in series. [5] From family-based statistics. However, one person living alone constitutes a family in Denmark. In this respect, the Danish data are closer to household statistics. [6] Great Britain only (excludes Northern Ireland).

Source: U.S. Bureau of Labor Statistics, updated and revised from "Families and Work in Transition in 12 Countries, 1980–2001," *Monthly Labor Review*, September 2003, with national sources, some of which may be unpublished.

Table 1339. Births, Deaths, and Life Expectancy by Country or Area: 2010 and 2020

[Covers countries with 13 million or more population in 2010]

Country or area	Crude birth rate [1] 2010	Crude birth rate [1] 2020, proj.	Crude death rate [2] 2010	Crude death rate [2] 2020, proj.	Expectation of life at birth (years) 2010	Expectation of life at birth (years) 2020, proj.	Infant mortality rate [3] 2010	Infant mortality rate [3] 2020, proj.	Total fertility rate per woman [4] 2010	Total fertility rate per woman [4] 2020, proj.
United States	13.8	13.5	8.4	8.5	78.2	79.5	6.1	5.4	2.06	2.06
Afghanistan	38.1	34.4	17.7	15.2	44.7	48.3	151.5	129.1	5.50	4.38
Algeria	16.7	14.9	4.7	5.0	74.3	76.5	26.8	18.7	1.76	1.70
Angola	43.3	39.1	23.7	20.5	38.5	41.4	178.1	156.0	6.05	5.16
Argentina	17.8	15.6	7.4	7.3	76.8	78.5	11.1	8.5	2.33	2.15
Australia	12.4	11.9	6.8	7.5	81.7	82.5	4.7	4.1	1.78	1.76
Bangladesh	23.4	19.5	5.8	5.6	69.4	72.4	52.5	36.8	2.65	2.24
Brazil	18.1	15.5	6.4	6.6	72.3	74.8	21.9	15.9	2.19	2.06
Burkina Faso	44.0	39.9	13.0	10.6	53.3	56.9	83.0	67.8	6.21	5.49
Burma	19.5	17.3	8.2	7.9	64.5	68.0	50.8	37.2	2.28	2.09
Cambodia	25.6	21.3	8.2	7.3	62.3	65.9	56.9	43.7	2.90	2.39
Cameroon	33.6	28.3	12.0	10.7	54.0	57.0	62.2	50.4	4.25	3.47
Canada	10.3	10.1	7.9	9.0	81.3	82.2	5.0	4.4	1.58	1.61
Chile	14.5	13.2	5.9	6.7	77.5	79.2	7.5	6.0	1.90	1.77
China [5]	12.2	11.0	6.9	8.3	74.5	76.0	16.5	12.6	1.54	1.58
Colombia	17.8	15.4	5.2	5.6	74.3	76.6	16.9	12.3	2.18	1.94
Congo (Kinshasa) [6]	42.3	37.7	11.4	9.4	54.7	58.1	79.4	61.8	6.11	5.16
Cote d'Ivoire	31.5	26.1	10.4	9.1	56.2	59.9	66.4	51.6	4.01	3.15
Ecuador	20.3	17.0	5.0	5.2	75.5	77.5	20.3	15.0	2.46	2.09
Egypt	25.0	20.8	4.9	4.8	72.4	74.9	26.2	17.9	3.01	2.67
Ethiopia	43.3	39.8	11.3	9.1	55.8	59.4	79.0	61.7	6.07	5.53
France	12.4	11.3	8.7	9.6	81.1	82.0	3.3	3.1	1.97	1.90
Germany	8.2	8.4	11.0	12.2	79.4	80.7	4.0	3.6	1.42	1.49
Ghana	28.1	22.7	8.9	7.3	60.6	65.3	49.9	38.1	3.57	2.75
Guatemala	27.4	22.7	5.0	4.6	70.6	73.4	26.9	19.2	3.36	2.57
India	21.3	18.2	7.5	7.3	66.5	69.7	49.1	35.4	2.65	2.35
Indonesia	18.5	15.6	6.3	6.6	71.1	73.7	28.9	20.4	2.28	2.04
Iran	18.5	16.2	5.9	6.0	69.8	72.4	43.5	33.6	1.89	1.81
Iraq	29.4	23.4	4.9	4.3	70.3	73.1	43.2	30.3	3.76	2.96
Italy	8.0	7.3	10.8	12.0	80.3	81.4	5.4	4.6	1.32	1.42
Japan	7.4	6.7	9.8	12.5	82.2	82.9	2.8	2.7	1.20	1.30
Kazakhstan	16.7	14.1	9.4	9.1	68.2	71.2	24.9	18.2	1.87	1.83
Kenya	35.1	20.8	9.3	7.9	58.8	61.8	53.5	42.4	4.38	2.57
Korea, North	14.6	13.1	10.6	11.2	64.1	67.6	50.2	38.0	1.94	1.82
Korea, South	8.7	8.2	6.2	7.6	78.8	81.1	4.2	3.6	1.22	1.29
Madagascar	37.9	33.8	8.0	6.4	63.3	66.8	52.8	40.2	5.09	4.44
Malawi	41.3	36.5	13.7	10.9	50.9	55.3	83.5	63.1	5.51	4.68
Malaysia	21.4	18.3	4.9	5.3	73.6	75.9	15.5	11.4	2.70	2.43
Mali	46.1	41.0	14.6	11.4	52.2	56.6	113.7	91.9	6.54	5.51
Mexico	19.4	17.0	4.8	5.3	76.3	78.1	17.8	13.2	2.31	2.14
Morocco	19.4	16.9	4.7	5.0	75.7	77.7	28.6	19.5	2.23	2.07
Mozambique	37.8	36.2	19.8	18.2	41.4	43.2	103.8	86.2	5.13	4.58
Nepal	22.4	19.7	6.9	6.4	65.8	69.2	46.0	33.2	2.53	2.11
Netherlands	10.3	10.3	8.8	9.6	79.6	80.8	4.7	4.1	1.66	1.67
Niger	51.1	46.7	14.5	11.3	53.0	57.0	114.5	92.9	7.68	6.79
Nigeria	36.1	30.6	16.3	14.1	47.2	50.5	93.0	78.7	4.82	3.92
Pakistan	25.3	20.7	7.1	6.2	65.6	69.0	65.3	47.2	3.28	2.42
Peru	19.0	16.3	6.1	6.3	71.0	73.7	27.7	20.2	2.32	2.00
Philippines	25.7	22.2	5.1	4.9	71.4	74.0	19.9	14.7	3.23	2.83
Poland	10.0	8.8	10.1	10.8	75.9	77.8	6.7	5.6	1.29	1.39
Romania	9.6	8.5	11.8	12.0	73.7	76.0	11.3	8.7	1.27	1.38
Russia	11.1	9.3	16.0	15.6	66.2	68.6	10.3	8.6	1.41	1.48
Saudi Arabia	19.4	17.8	3.3	3.4	73.9	76.1	16.7	12.0	2.35	2.04
South Africa	19.6	18.1	17.0	17.3	49.2	51.4	43.8	36.8	2.33	2.12
Spain	10.9	8.7	8.7	9.3	81.1	82.0	3.4	3.2	1.47	1.51
Sri Lanka	15.9	13.3	6.2	6.8	75.3	77.3	18.1	13.2	1.96	1.85
Sudan	36.6	31.2	11.7	6.9	54.2	64.4	72.4	38.9	4.93	4.04
Syria	24.4	19.7	3.7	3.7	74.5	76.6	16.1	11.7	3.02	2.34
Taiwan [5]	9.0	8.2	6.9	8.2	78.2	79.7	5.3	4.6	1.15	1.23
Tanzania	33.4	25.6	12.3	11.2	52.5	54.9	68.1	56.4	4.31	3.00
Thailand	13.0	11.7	6.5	7.5	75.0	77.1	16.7	12.3	1.65	1.68
Turkey	18.3	15.1	6.1	6.3	72.2	74.8	24.8	17.3	2.18	1.96
Uganda	47.6	45.4	11.9	10.3	53.0	55.2	63.7	51.7	6.73	6.31
Ukraine	9.6	8.5	15.7	15.4	68.5	70.7	8.7	7.3	1.27	1.35
United Kingdom	12.3	11.9	9.3	9.5	79.9	81.1	4.7	4.1	1.92	1.86
Uzbekistan	17.5	16.1	5.3	5.4	72.2	74.8	22.7	16.3	1.92	1.74
Venezuela	20.3	18.1	5.1	5.6	73.8	75.3	21.1	17.0	2.45	2.22
Vietnam	17.3	14.5	6.0	6.0	71.9	74.4	21.6	15.7	1.93	1.77
Yemen	34.4	25.6	7.2	5.7	63.4	66.9	56.8	41.9	4.81	3.20
Zambia	44.6	38.9	12.8	11.0	52.0	54.1	68.4	50.6	6.07	5.26

[1] Number of births during 1 year per 1,000 persons (based on midyear population). [2] Number of deaths during 1 year per 1,000 persons (based on midyear population). [3] Number of deaths of children under 1 year of age per 1,000 live births in a calendar year. [4] Average number of children that would be born if all women lived to the end of their childbearing years and, at each year of childbearing age, they experienced the birth rates occurring in the specified year. [5] See footnote 4, Table 1332. [6] See footnote 5, Table 1332.

Source: U.S. Census Bureau, International Data Base, <http://www.census.gov/ipc/www/idb/>, accessed June 2010.

Table 1340. Life Expectancy at Birth and at Age 65 by Sex—Selected Countries: 1990 and 2008

Country	Life expectancy at birth (years)				Life expectancy at age 65 (years)			
	Females		Males		Females		Males	
	1990	2008	1990	2008	1990	2008	1990	2008
United States [1]	**78.8**	**80.3**	**71.8**	**75.3**	**18.9**	**19.8**	**15.1**	**17.1**
Australia	80.1	83.7	73.9	79.2	19.0	21.6	15.2	18.6
Austria	79.0	83.3	72.3	77.8	18.1	21.1	14.4	17.7
Belgium	79.5	(NA)	72.7	(NA)	18.8	(NA)	14.3	(NA)
Canada	80.8	(NA)	74.4	(NA)	19.9	(NA)	15.7	(NA)
Czech Republic	75.5	80.5	67.6	74.1	15.3	18.8	11.7	15.3
Denmark	77.8	81.0	72.0	76.5	17.9	19.5	14.0	16.6
Finland	79.0	83.3	71.0	76.5	17.8	21.4	13.8	17.5
France	80.9	84.3	72.8	77.6	19.8	(NA)	15.5	(NA)
Germany	78.5	82.7	72.0	77.6	17.7	20.7	14.0	17.6
Greece	79.5	82.5	74.6	77.5	18.0	19.9	15.7	17.7
Hungary	73.7	77.8	65.1	69.8	15.3	17.5	12.0	13.6
Iceland	80.5	83.0	75.4	79.6	19.5	20.5	16.2	18.2
Ireland	77.7	82.3	72.1	77.5	17.0	20.4	13.3	17.2
Italy	80.3	(NA)	73.8	(NA)	19.0	(NA)	15.2	(NA)
Japan	81.9	86.1	75.9	79.3	20.0	23.6	16.2	18.6
Korea, South	75.5	83.3	67.3	76.5	16.3	21.0	12.4	16.6
Mexico	73.5	77.5	67.7	72.7	17.8	18.3	16.0	16.8
Netherlands	80.1	82.3	73.8	78.0	18.9	20.5	14.4	17.0
New Zealand	78.4	82.4	72.5	78.4	18.3	20.8	14.6	18.3
Norway	79.8	83.0	73.4	78.3	18.6	20.5	14.6	17.5
Poland	75.2	80.0	66.2	71.3	16.1	19.0	12.4	14.7
Portugal	77.5	82.4	70.6	76.2	17.1	20.3	14.0	16.9
Slovakia	75.4	78.7	66.6	70.9	15.7	17.5	12.2	13.8
Spain	80.6	84.3	73.4	78.0	19.3	21.9	15.5	18.0
Sweden	80.4	83.2	74.8	79.1	19.0	20.8	15.3	17.9
Switzerland	80.9	84.6	74.0	79.8	19.7	22.3	15.3	18.9
Turkey	69.5	75.8	65.4	71.4	14.3	15.8	12.8	14.0
United Kingdom	78.5	(NA)	72.9	(NA)	17.9	(NA)	14.0	(NA)

NA Not available. [1] Source of 2008 life expectancy data: U.S. National Center for Health Statistics, National Vital Statistics Reports (NVSR), "United States Life Tables," Vol. 58, No. 21, June 2010, and unpublished data.

Source: Except as noted, Organization for Economic Cooperation and Development (OECD), 2011, "OECD Health Data," OECD Health Statistics database (copyright), <http://www.oecd.org/health/healthdata>, accessed April 2011.

Table 1341. People Infected With HIV and AIDS-Related Deaths by Region: 2001 and 2008

[In thousands (29,000 represents 29,000,000), except percent. Estimates are based on ranges, called 'plausibility bounds,' which reflect the certainty associated with each estimate and define the boundaries within which the actual numbers lie]

Region	Adults and children living with HIV		Adults and children newly infected with HIV		Adult (15–49 yrs.) prevalence (percent)		Adult and child deaths due to AIDS	
	2001	2008	2001	2008	2001	2008	2001	2008
Total	**29,000**	**33,400**	**3,200**	**2,700**	**0.8**	**0.8**	**1,900**	**2,000**
Sub-Saharan Africa	19,700	22,400	2,300	1,900	5.8	5.2	1,400	1,400
North Africa and Middle East	200	310	30	35	0.2	0.2	11	20
South and South-East Asia	4,000	3,800	310	280	0.3	0.3	260	270
East Asia	560	850	99	75	(Z)	(Z)	22	59
Oceania	36	59	6	4	0.2	0.3	(Z)	2
Latin America	1,600	2,000	150	170	0.5	0.6	66	77
Caribbean	220	240	21	20	1.1	1.0	20	12
Eastern Europe and Central Asia	900	1,500	280	110	0.5	0.7	26	87
Western and Central Europe	660	850	40	30	0.2	0.3	8	13
North America	1,200	1,400	52	55	0.6	0.6	19	25

Z Less than 0.1 percent or 1,000 deaths.

Source: Joint United Nations Programme on HIV/AIDS (UNAIDS) and World Health Organization (WHO), *AIDS Epidemic Update: December 2009* (copyright). See also <http://www.unaids.org/en/KnowledgeCentre/HIVData/EpiUpdate/EpiUpdArchive/2009/default.asp>.

Table 1342. Percentage of the Adult Population Considered to Be Obese: 2008

[Obesity rates are defined as the percentage of the population with a Body Mass Index (BMI) over 30 kg/m². The BMI is a single number that evaluates an individual's weight status in relation to height (weight/height ², with weight in kilograms and height in meters). For the United States, Australia, Canada, Ireland, Japan, South Korea, Luxembourg, Mexico, New Zealand, and the United Kingdom, figures are based on health examinations, rather than self-reported information. Obesity estimates derived from health examinations are generally higher and more reliable than those coming from self-reports because they preclude any misreporting of people's height and weight. However, health examinations are only conducted regularly in a few countries. For more information on methods by country, see <http://www.irdes.fr/EspaceAnglais/home.html>]

Country	2008	Country	2008	Country	2008
United States	**33.8**	France	11.2	Luxembourg	[1] 20.0
Australia	[1] 24.8	Germany	[3] 13.6	Mexico	[2] 30.0
Austria	[2] 12.4	Greece	18.1	New Zealand	[1] 26.5
Belgium	13.8	Hungary	[4] 18.8	Norway	10.0
Canada	24.2	Ireland	[1] 23.0	Spain	[2] 14.9
Czech Republic	17.1	Italy	9.9	Sweden	10.0
Denmark	[3] 11.4	Japan	3.4	Switzerland	[1] 8.1
Finland	15.7	Korea, South	3.8	United Kingdom	24.5

[1] 2007 data. [2] 2006 data. [3] 2005 data. [4] 2003 data.

Source: Except as noted, Organization for Economic Cooperation and Development (OECD), 2011, "OECD Health Data," OECD Health Statistics database (copyright), accessed April 2011. See also <http://www.oecd.org>.

Table 1343. Daily Tobacco Consumption by Country and Sex: 1990 and 2009

[Daily smokers as percent of population. Includes tobacco forms consumed by smoking only]

Country	Total		Females		Males	
	1990	2009	1990	2009	1990	2009
United States	**25.5**	**[1] 16.5**	**22.8**	**[1] 15.1**	**28.4**	**[1] 17.9**
Australia.	[2] 28.6	[3] 16.6	[2] 27.0	[3] 15.2	[2] 30.2	[3] 18.0
Canada	28.2	[1] 17.5	26.7	[1] 15.1	29.8	[1] 19.9
Denmark	44.5	16.0	42.0	14.0	47.0	18.0
Finland.	25.9	[1] 20.4	20.0	[1] 17.6	32.4	[1] 24.0
France	30.0	[1] 26.2	20.0	[1] 22.3	38.0	[1] 30.6
Greece.	38.5	[1] 39.7	26.0	[1] 33.5	51.0	[1] 46.3
Iceland.	30.3	15.8	29.9	15.7	30.8	15.9
Ireland	30.0	[3] 29.0	29.0	[3] 27.0	31.0	[3] 31.0
Italy	27.8	23.3	17.8	17.1	37.8	29.9
Japan.	37.4	24.9	14.3	11.9	60.5	38.9
Luxembourg.	[4] 33.0	[1] 20.0	[4] 25.0	[1] 18.0	[4] 41.0	[1] 23.0
Netherlands.	37.0	28.0	32.0	24.0	43.0	32.0
New Zealand	28.0	[3] 18.1	27.0	[3] 17.0	28.0	[3] 19.3
Norway.	35.0	21.0	33.0	20.0	36.0	21.0
Poland	(NA)	[5] 26.3	(NA)	[5] 19.3	(NA)	[5] 33.9
Sweden	25.8	[1] 14.0	25.9	[1] 15.7	25.8	[1] 12.2
United Kingdom	30.0	[1] 22.0	30.0	[1] 21.0	31.0	[1] 22.0

NA Not available. [1] 2008 data. [2] 1989 data. [3] 2007 data. [4] 1987 data. [5] 2004 data.

Source: Organization for Economic Cooperation and Development (OECD), 2011, "OECD Health Data," OECD Health Statistics database (copyright), <http://www.oecd.org/health/healthdata>, accessed April 2011.

Table 1344. Road Fatalities by Country: 1990 to 2009

[Fatalities include any person killed immediately or dying within 30 days as a result of an injury accident. For countries that do not apply the threshold of 30 days, conversion coefficients are estimated so that comparisons on the basis of the 30 day-definition can be made]

Country	1990	2000	2005	2008	2009	Country	1990	2000	2005	2008	2009
United States [1]	**44,599**	**41,945**	**43,443**	**37,261**	**33,808**	Japan.	14,595	10,403	7,931	6,023	5,772
Australia.	2,331	1,817	1,627	1,441	1,502	Korea, South	14,174	10,236	6,376	5,870	(NA)
Austria	1,391	976	768	679	633	Luxembourg.	71	76	47	35	48
Belgium	1,976	1,470	1,089	944	(NA)	Mexico.	5,469	5,224	4,710	5,379	4,870
Canada	3,963	2,927	2,905	2,729	(NA)	Netherlands.	1,376	1,166	817	750	720
Czech Republic	(NA)	1,486	1,286	1,076	901	New Zealand	729	462	405	366	384
Denmark [2]	634	498	331	406	303	Norway.	332	341	224	255	212
Estonia.	436	204	170	132	100	Poland	7,333	6,294	5,444	5,437	4,572
Finland.	649	396	379	344	279	Portugal.	2,646	1,857	1,247	885	737
France [3]	11,215	8,079	5,318	4,275	4,273	Russia	35,366	29,594	33,957	29,936	26,084
Germany	7,906	7,503	5,361	4,477	4,152	Slovakia	(NA)	648	600	606	384
Greece.	1,737	2,037	1,658	1,553	(NA)	Slovenia	517	313	258	214	171
Hungary.	2,432	1,200	1,278	996	(NA)	Spain	6,948	5,776	3,857	3,100	2,714
Iceland.	24	32	19	12	17	Sweden	772	591	440	397	358
India.	(NA)	78,911	94,968	(NA)	(NA)	Switzerland	954	592	409	357	349
Ireland	478	415	396	279	(NA)	Turkey	6,317	5,510	4,505	4,236	4,300
Italy	7,151	7,061	5,818	4,731	(NA)	United Kingdom . . .	5,402	3,580	3,336	2,645	2,337

NA Not available. [1] As of July 1. [2] As of January 1. [3] Data on January 1 of the following year.

Source: Organization for Economic Cooperation and Development (OECD), 2011, "Road Injury Accidents," *Transport Statistics*, OECD Publishing (copyright). See also <http://stats.oecd.org//Index.aspx?QueryId=28912>.

Table 1345. Suicide Rates by Sex and Country: 2008

[Per 100,000 persons. Data are for 2008, except as indicated]

Country	Total	Men	Women	Country	Total	Men	Women
OECD average [1] . .	**11.1**	**17.6**	**5.2**	Italy [4]	4.9	8.0	2.1
United States [2]	**10.1**	**16.6**	**4.0**	Japan.	19.4	28.3	10.7
Australia [1]	7.5	11.9	3.3	Korea [1]	21.5	32.0	13.2
Austria	11.9	19.6	5.3	Luxembourg [1]	12.0	18.6	6.2
Belgium [3]	16.3	24.8	8.4	Mexico [4]	4.3	7.5	1.4
Canada [3]	10.2	15.7	4.9	Netherlands [4]	7.1	10.1	4.2
Czech Republic	11.0	18.9	3.8	New Zealand [1]	12.3	18.6	6.3
Denmark [1]	9.9	15.0	5.3	Norway [4]	9.6	13.5	5.7
Finland.	17.3	27.1	7.8	Poland	12.9	23.2	3.5
France	13.5	21.1	6.8	Portugal [5]	8.7	14.6	3.8
Germany [1]	9.1	14.5	4.3	Slovakia [2]	10.9	20.0	2.9
Greece.	2.6	4.5	0.9	Spain [2]	6.3	10.0	2.9
Hungary.	19.6	33.8	7.8	Sweden [4]	10.6	15.2	6.1
Iceland.	11.2	15.3	6.7	Switzerland [4]	14.3	20.6	8.7
Ireland	9.1	14.3	4.0	United Kingdom [4] . .	5.8	9.2	2.5

[1] 2006 data. [2] 2005 data. [3] 2004 data. [4] 2007 data. [5] 2003 data.

Source: Organization for Economic Cooperation and Development (OECD), 2011, "OECD Health Data," *OECD Health Statistics* database (copyright), <http://www.oecd.org/health/healthdata>.

Table 1346. Health Expenditures by Country: 1980 to 2008

[In percent. GDP = gross domestic product; for explanation, see text, Section 13]

Country	Total expenditures on health (percent of GDP)					Public expenditures on health (percent of total)				
	1980	1990	2000	2005	2008	1980	1990	2000	2005	2008
United States	**9.0**	**12.2**	**13.4**	**15.4**	**16.0**	**40.8**	**39.2**	**43.2**	**44.4**	**46.5**
Australia.	6.1	6.7	8.0	8.4	(NA)	62.6	66.2	66.8	66.9	(NA)
Austria	7.4	8.3	9.9	10.4	10.5	68.8	73.4	76.8	76.1	76.9
Belgium	6.3	7.2	9.0	10.6	11.1	(NA)	(NA)	(NA)	(NA)	(NA)
Canada	7.0	8.9	8.8	9.9	10.4	75.6	74.5	70.4	70.3	70.2
Czech Republic	(NA)	4.7	6.5	7.2	7.1	96.8	97.4	90.3	87.3	82.5
Denmark	8.9	8.3	8.3	9.5	(NA)	87.8	82.7	82.4	83.7	(NA)
Finland.	6.3	7.7	7.2	8.4	8.4	79.0	80.9	71.1	73.5	74.2
France	7.0	8.4	10.1	11.1	11.2	80.1	76.6	79.4	79.3	77.8
Germany [1]	8.4	8.3	10.3	10.7	10.5	78.7	76.2	79.8	76.8	76.8
Greece.	5.9	6.6	7.9	9.5	(NA)	55.6	53.7	60.0	60.1	(NA)
Hungary.	(NA)	(NA)	7.0	8.3	7.3	(NA)	(NA)	70.7	72.3	71.0
Iceland.	6.3	7.8	9.5	9.4	9.1	88.2	86.6	81.1	81.4	83.2
Ireland	8.2	6.1	6.1	7.5	8.7	82.0	71.7	75.3	76.6	76.9
Italy	(NA)	7.7	8.1	8.9	9.1	(NA)	79.5	72.5	76.2	77.2
Japan.	6.5	6.0	7.7	8.2	(NA)	71.3	77.6	81.3	82.7	(NA)
Korea, South	3.9	4.2	4.8	5.7	6.5	20.0	36.3	45.5	52.1	55.3
Luxembourg.	5.2	5.4	7.5	7.9	6.8	92.8	93.1	85.1	84.9	84.1
Mexico	(NA)	4.4	5.1	5.9	5.9	(NA)	40.4	46.6	45.0	46.9
Netherlands	7.4	8.0	8.0	9.8	9.9	69.4	67.1	63.1	(NA)	(NA)
New Zealand	5.9	6.9	7.7	8.9	9.9	88.0	82.4	78.0	77.1	80.4
Norway.	7.0	7.6	8.4	9.1	8.5	85.1	82.8	82.5	83.5	84.2
Poland	(NA)	4.8	5.5	6.2	7.0	(NA)	91.7	70.0	69.3	72.2
Portugal	5.3	5.9	8.8	10.2	(NA)	64.3	65.5	72.5	71.8	(NA)
Slovakia	(NA)	(NA)	5.5	7.0	8.0	(NA)	(NA)	89.4	74.4	67.8
Spain	5.3	6.5	7.2	8.3	9.0	79.9	78.7	71.6	70.6	72.5
Sweden	8.9	8.2	8.2	9.2	9.4	92.5	89.9	84.9	81.6	81.9
Switzerland	7.3	8.2	10.2	11.2	10.7	(NA)	52.4	55.4	59.5	59.1
Turkey	2.4	2.7	4.9	5.4	6.2	29.4	61.0	62.9	67.8	71.2
United Kingdom	5.6	5.9	7.0	8.3	8.7	89.4	83.6	79.3	81.9	82.6

NA Not available. [1] Data prior to 1991 are for former West Germany.
Source: Organization for Economic Cooperation and Development (OECD), 2011, "OECD Health Data," OECD Health Statistics database (copyright), <http://www.oecd.org/health/healthdata>, accessed April 2011.

Table 1347. Physicians and Inpatient Care—Selected Countries: 2000 to 2008

Country	Practicing physicians per 1,000 population			Acute inpatient care					
				Beds per 1,000 population			Average length of stay (days)		
	2000	2005	2008	2000	2005	2008	2000	2005	2008
United States	**2.3**	**2.4**	**2.4**	**2.9**	**2.7**	**[1] 2.7**	**5.8**	**5.6**	**5.5**
Australia.	2.5	2.8	[1] 3.0	3.6	3.5	(NA)	6.1	6.0	(NA)
Austria	3.9	4.3	4.6	6.2	5.8	5.6	7.6	6.9	6.8
Belgium	3.9	4.0	3.0	4.7	4.4	4.3	7.7	7.7	[1] 7.0
Canada	(NA)	(NA)	(NA)	3.2	2.9	[1] 2.7	7.2	7.2	[1] 7.5
Czech Republic	3.4	3.6	3.6	5.7	5.3	5.2	8.7	8.0	7.4
Denmark	2.9	3.3	[1] 3.4	3.5	3.2	3.0	3.8	3.5	(NA)
Finland.	2.5	2.6	2.7	2.4	2.2	1.9	5.7	5.5	5.5
France	(NA)	(NA)	(NA)	4.1	3.7	3.5	5.6	5.4	5.2
Germany	3.3	3.4	3.6	6.4	5.9	5.7	9.2	8.1	7.6
Greece.	(NA)	(NA)	(NA)	3.7	3.9	4.0	6.2	5.6	(NA)
Hungary.	2.7	2.8	3.1	5.8	5.5	4.1	7.1	6.5	6.0
Iceland.	3.4	3.7	3.7	(NA)	(NA)	(NA)	6.1	5.4	5.6
Ireland	(NA)	(NA)	(NA)	2.8	2.8	[1] 2.7	6.4	6.5	6.2
Italy	(NA)	(NA)	(NA)	4.1	3.3	3.0	7.0	6.7	[1] 6.7
Japan.	1.9	(NA)	2.2	9.6	8.2	8.1	24.8	19.8	18.8
Korea, South	1.3	1.6	1.9	3.9	4.6	5.4	11.0	(NA)	(NA)
Luxembourg.	2.2	2.4	[1] 2.8	(NA)	4.5	4.5	7.5	7.6	[1] 7.3
Mexico	1.6	1.8	2.0	1.8	1.7	1.6	4.0	4.0	3.9
Netherlands	(NA)	(NA)	(NA)	3.2	3.1	2.9	9.0	7.2	5.9
New Zealand	2.2	2.1	2.5	(NA)	(NA)	2.2	4.3	5.4	(NA)
Norway.	(NA)	3.6	4.0	3.1	2.9	2.5	6.0	5.2	4.8
Poland	2.2	2.1	2.2	5.2	4.7	4.4	8.9	6.5	5.7
Portugal	(NA)	(NA)	(NA)	3.1	2.9	2.8	7.7	7.1	[1] 6.8
Slovakia	3.2	(NA)	[1] 3.0	5.7	5.0	4.9	8.5	7.3	6.9
Spain	3.3	3.8	3.6	2.8	2.6	2.6	7.1	6.7	6.5
Sweden	3.1	3.5	(NA)	2.4	2.2	(NA)	5.0	4.6	[1] 4.5
Switzerland	(NA)	(NA)	3.8	4.1	3.6	3.3	9.3	8.5	7.7
Turkey	(NA)	(NA)	(NA)	1.9	2.1	2.2	5.4	5.1	4.3
United Kingdom	2.0	2.4	2.6	3.1	3.0	2.7	8.2	7.9	7.1

NA Not available. [1] 2007 data.
Source: Organization for Economic Cooperation and Development (OECD), 2011, "OECD Health Data," OECD Health Statistics database (copyright); <http://www.oecd.org/health/healthdata>, accessed April 2011.

Table 1348. Gross National Income (GNI) by Country: 2000 and 2009

[49 represents $49,000,000,000. GNI measures the total domestic and foreign value added claimed by residents. GNI comprises GDP plus net receipts of primary income (compensation of employees and property income) from nonresident sources]

Country	Gross national income [1]				GNI on purchasing power parity basis [2]			
	Total (bil. dol.)		Per capita (dol.)		Total (bil. dol.)		Per capita (dol.)	
	2000	2009	2000	2009	2000	2009	2000	2009
Algeria............	49	154	1,610	4,420	156	283	5,410	8,110
Argentina..........	276	304	7,460	7,550	328	568	8,560	14,090
Australia...........	407	958	21,260	43,770	492	842	26,740	38,510
Bangladesh.........	50	93	350	580	115	251	870	1,550
Belarus............	14	54	1,380	5,560	52	123	5,600	12,740
Belgium............	260	488	25,400	45,270	290	395	28,930	36,610
Brazil..............	674	1,564	3,870	8,070	1,189	1,968	6,920	10,160
Bulgaria...........	13	46	1,640	6,060	50	101	6,870	13,260
Burkina Faso.......	3	8	250	510	9	18	850	1,170
Cambodia..........	4	10	280	650	11	27	940	1,820
Cameroon..........	10	23	620	1,190	24	43	1,620	2,190
Canada............	681	1,416	22,130	41,980	851	1,258	28,440	37,280
Chile..............	75	161	4,840	9,470	137	228	9,310	13,420
China [3]...........	1,169	4,856	930	3,650	2,949	9,170	2,560	6,890
Colombia...........	94	228	2,350	4,990	228	392	5,840	8,600
Congo (Kinshasa) [4]...	4	11	80	160	10	20	200	300
Cote d'Ivoire.......	11	23	620	1,070	25	34	1,450	1,640
Czech Republic.....	60	182	5,800	17,310	151	251	15,630	23,940
Ecuador...........	16	54	1,340	3,970	55	110	4,850	8,100
Egypt..............	97	172	1,390	2,070	251	471	3,720	5,680
Ethiopia...........	8	27	130	330	30	77	500	930
France............	1,482	[5] 2,751	24,450	[5] 42,620	1,556	2,191	27,070	33,950
Germany...........	2,097	3,476	25,510	42,450	2,113	3,017	26,590	36,850
Ghana.............	6	28	330	1,190	18	37	940	1,530
Greece............	137	328	12,560	29,040	202	325	20,050	28,800
Guatemala.........	19	37	1,730	2,650	39	64	3,560	4,570
Hong Kong.........	177	221	26,570	31,570	177	312	27,530	44,540
Hungary...........	48	130	4,700	12,980	120	191	12,910	19,090
India..............	458	1,406	450	1,220	1,576	3,786	1,650	3,280
Indonesia..........	119	471	580	2,050	452	855	2,260	3,720
Iran...............	107	331	1,670	4,530	435	836	7,110	11,470
Italy..............	1,190	2,114	20,890	35,110	1,446	1,919	26,950	31,870
Japan.............	4,393	4,857	34,620	38,080	3,292	4,265	26,630	33,440
Kazakhstan........	19	110	1,260	6,920	66	164	5,260	10,320
Kenya.............	13	30	420	760	35	62	1,160	1,570
Korea, South.......	466	967	9,910	19,830	804	1,328	18,110	27,240
Madagascar........	4	9	250	430	12	19	840	990
Malawi............	2	4	150	290	7	12	520	780
Malaysia..........	80	202	3,450	7,350	195	377	8,500	13,710
Mexico............	501	962	5,110	8,960	878	1,506	9,090	14,020
Montenegro........	(NA)	4	(NA)	6,650	4	8	6,580	13,110
Morocco...........	38	90	1,310	2,770	73	143	2,730	4,400
Mozambique.......	4	10	230	440	8	20	460	880
Nepal.............	5	13	220	440	20	35	840	1,180
Niger.............	2	5	170	340	6	10	550	680
Nigeria............	33	185	270	1,190	141	321	1,220	2,070
Pakistan...........	68	170	490	1,000	233	455	1,720	2,680
Peru..............	53	122	2,050	4,200	124	237	4,820	8,120
Philippines.........	76	165	970	1,790	178	326	2,340	3,540
Poland............	177	468	4,590	12,260	403	698	10,920	18,290
Portugal...........	123	233	12,070	21,910	178	256	17,990	24,080
Romania...........	38	179	1,690	8,330	126	312	6,370	14,540
Russia............	250	1,324	1,710	9,340	974	2,599	7,260	18,330
Saudi Arabia.......	168	437	8,150	17,210	362	610	17,550	24,020
Senegal...........	5	13	510	1,040	13	23	1,330	1,810
Serbia [6]..........	11	44	1,400	6,000	44	86	6,230	11,700
Singapore.........	94	186	23,350	37,220	133	248	32,080	49,780
South Africa.......	134	284	3,050	5,760	291	496	6,750	10,050
Spain.............	621	1,476	15,420	32,120	851	1,447	22,230	31,490
Sri Lanka..........	16	40	880	1,990	50	96	2,680	4,720
Sudan.............	11	52	320	1,220	37	84	1,150	1,990
Sweden............	262	454	29,500	48,840	246	354	28,030	38,050
Switzerland........	289	506	40,280	65,430	245	364	33,840	47,100
Syria..............	16	51	960	2,410	52	97	3,330	4,620
Tanzania..........	10	21	300	500	25	58	800	1,360
Thailand...........	122	255	1,960	3,760	303	518	4,970	7,640
Turkey............	265	652	3,990	8,720	580	1,010	8,110	13,500
Uganda............	7	15	270	460	16	39	700	1,190
Ukraine...........	34	129	700	2,800	156	284	3,630	6,180
United Kingdom......	1,526	2,558	25,910	41,370	1,532	2,217	27,740	35,860
United States	**9,846**	**14,234**	**34,890**	**46,360**	**10,071**	**14,011**	**36,440**	**45,640**
Uzbekistan.........	15	31	630	1,100	35	81	1,490	2,910
Venezuela..........	100	286	4,100	10,090	204	347	8,660	12,220
Vietnam...........	30	88	390	1,000	108	244	1,510	2,790
Yemen............	7	25	400	1,060	31	55	1,750	2,330
Zimbabwe..........	6	5	480	360	(NA)	(NA)	(NA)	(NA)

NA Not available. [1] Gross national income calculated using the World Bank Atlas method; for details, see source.
[2] For explanation of Purchasing Power Parity, see headnote, Table 1349. [3] See footnote 4, Table 1332. [4] See footnote 5, Table 1332. [5] Includes the French overseas departments of French Guiana, Guadeloupe, Martinique, and Reunion.
[6] See footnote 4, Table 1404.

Source: The World Bank, Washington, DC, *World Development Indicators*, annual (copyright). See also <http://data.worldbank.org\>, accessed May 2011

Table 1349. Real Gross Domestic Product (GDP) Per Capita and Per Employed Persons by Country: 1990 to 2009

[U.S. figures based on the System of National Income and Product Accounts (NIPA) from the Bureau of Economic Analysis. All other countries, based on the 1993 United Nations System of National Accounts. Per capita data based on total resident population. Real GDP is a macroeconomic measure of the size of an economy adjusted for price changes and inflation. Employment data include people serving in the armed forces for some countries. Real dollars are calculated based on 2009 Purchasing Power Parities (PPPs). PPPs are currency conversion rates used to convert GDPs expressed in different currencies to a common value (U.S. dollars in this case). A PPP for a given country is the number of national currency units needed to buy the specific basket of goods and services that one dollar will buy in the United States. See text, this section]

Country	Real GDP per capita (2009 U.S. dollars)				Real GDP per employed person (2009 U.S. dollars)			
	1990	2000	2008	2009	1990	2000	2008	2009
United States	**35,200**	**43,571**	**47,570**	**45,918**	**72,804**	**88,961**	**98,671**	**99,763**
Canada	29,718	35,766	39,385	37,946	62,435	73,938	76,349	75,676
Australia.	27,345	34,270	39,497	39,178	58,736	72,613	78,404	79,188
Japan.	28,560	31,270	34,198	32,445	54,884	60,792	68,017	65,507
Korea, South	11,627	19,961	27,194	27,169	27,561	44,353	56,063	56,342
Austria.	28,834	32,458	40,314	38,701	61,905	74,987	81,623	79,381
Belgium	27,957	33,832	37,504	36,161	72,472	84,403	89,894	87,515
Denmark	29,003	36,086	38,913	36,813	57,145	71,021	73,652	72,551
France	27,681	32,252	34,779	33,679	70,431	80,491	86,185	84,978
Germany [1]	29,397	34,643	38,229	36,452	61,149	72,737	77,940	74,120
Italy	28,544	33,276	33,820	31,887	71,606	82,635	80,107	77,363
Netherlands.	29,449	37,756	42,726	40,839	69,252	76,383	81,776	78,542
Norway.	37,504	50,962	57,300	55,653	77,264	98,671	104,489	103,156
Spain	23,763	30,215	34,044	32,565	61,467	70,812	72,247	74,616
Sweden	28,803	34,198	40,310	37,919	53,601	70,549	81,228	78,646
United Kingdom.	26,908	33,595	38,669	36,528	57,315	71,981	80,620	77,878

[1] Prior to 1991, data are for the former West Germany.

Source: U.S. Bureau of Labor Statistics, "International Comparisons of GDP per Capita and per Hour, 1960–2009," October 2010, <http://www.bls.gov/fls/intl_gdp_capita_gdp_hour.htm>.

Table 1350. Average Annual Percent Changes in International Economic Composite Indexes by Country: 1990 to 2010

[Change from previous year; derived from indexes with base 2000 = 100. The coincident index changes are for calendar years and the leading index changes are for years ending June 30 because they lead the coincident indexes by about 6 months, on average. The G-7 countries are United States, Canada, France, Germany, Italy, United Kingdom, and Japan. Minus sign (–) indicates decrease]

Country	Leading index						Coincident index					
	1990	2000	2005	2008	2009	2010	1990	2000	2005	2008	2009	2010
Total, 13 countries.	**2.1**	**6.3**	**5.1**	**0.4**	**–10.9**	**8.1**	**4.5**	**5.0**	**2.1**	**–2.3**	**–13.2**	**2.8**
12 countries, excluding U.S.	3.8	7.7	5.5	0.8	–7.0	4.3	6.8	5.4	1.7	–0.2	–12.0	4.1
G-7 countries.	2.0	6.0	5.0	–	–11.5	8.0	4.5	4.8	1.9	–2.6	–13.7	2.3
North America	–0.9	4.1	4.3	–	–16.3	14.0	–0.2	4.8	2.8	–5.2	–14.5	0.6
United States	**–1.0**	**3.9**	**4.4**	**–0.3**	**–17.4**	**15.1**	**–0.1**	**4.4**	**2.6**	**–5.8**	**–15.2**	**0.2**
Canada	–1.1	7.1	3.1	3.2	–4.7	3.0	–1.7	9.7	4.7	–0.3	–11.4	5.0
Four European countries.	1.8	4.4	4.1	1.1	–7.6	6.0	5.9	9.8	2.0	1.2	–10.1	3.0
France	1.5	1.5	6.4	–0.7	–8.0	11.9	5.7	14.4	2.1	–1.9	–14.2	0.3
Germany	4.5	6.2	4.4	1.6	–7.0	4.1	7.2	7.9	–0.5	5.0	–7.4	7.1
Italy	0.2	7.2	2.4	–2.0	–9.4	4.9	9.3	16.2	5.3	–2.1	–15.4	0.9
United Kingdom.	–0.3	2.5	2.4	5.3	–6.8	3.0	0.9	4.0	3.4	1.5	–4.6	2.8
Seven Pacific region countries	6.1	11.2	6.9	0.2	–6.7	2.9	8.1	1.2	1.2	–1.6	–13.9	5.1
Australia.	–1.4	8.2	5.3	4.7	–7.8	4.6	–0.4	5.1	3.7	2.0	–1.8	3.4
Taiwan [1]	4.9	8.5	6.5	2.6	–0.8	10.7	5.1	4.9	4.8	–0.8	–7.1	12.2
Thailand.	12.1	9.5	5.5	6.7	–0.6	9.6	11.6	9.4	6.5	3.1	–1.8	10.0
Japan.	6.6	11.3	7.1	–1.4	–7.6	1.2	8.6	–0.5	0.3	–2.6	–16.6	4.6
Korea, South	6.5	15.9	7.3	10.0	–0.7	11.9	9.9	13.7	4.7	2.9	0.2	7.4
Malaysia	5.0	19.8	8.4	12.7	–3.8	15.9	9.1	11.1	3.1	0.4	–6.3	6.5
New Zealand	0.8	4.6	1.2	1.1	–1.9	7.1	–1.2	2.7	6.0	–1.6	–6.2	3.2

– Represents zero. [1] See footnote 4, Table 1332.

Source: Foundation for International Business and Economic Research, New York, NY, *International Economic Indicators*, monthly.

Table 1351. Sectoral Contributions to Gross Value Added: 2000 and 2010

[In percent. According to the 1993 System of National Accounts (SNA) and the International Standard Industrial Classification (ISIC), Revision 3 (1990). Value added is estimated at basic prices and includes financial intermediation services indirectly measured (FISIM). Value added represents an industry's contribution to national GDP and is calculated as the difference between production and intermediate inputs. Value added comprises labor costs, consumption of fixed capital, indirect taxes less subsidies, and net operating surplus and mixed income]

Country	Agriculture [1]		Industry				Services	
			Total		Manufacturing			
	2000	2010	2000	2010	2000	2010	2000	2010
United States [2]	1.2	[3] 1.0	23.4	[3] 20.0	15.9	[3] 12.7	75.4	[3] 79.0
Australia.	3.9	[4] 2.6	25.9	[4] 27.1	12.2	[4] 9.4	70.2	[4] 70.3
Austria	2.0	1.5	30.8	29.2	20.6	19.2	67.2	69.3
Belgium	1.4	0.7	27.0	21.9	19.3	[3] 14.0	71.6	77.4
Canada	2.3	[5] 1.7	33.2	[5] 31.5	19.2	[5] 13.4	64.5	[5] 66.8
Czech Republic	3.9	[3] 2.3	38.1	[3] 37.7	26.8	[3] 23.6	58.0	[3] 60.0
Denmark	2.6	1.3	26.8	22.1	16.2	12.4	70.6	76.7
Finland.	3.5	2.9	34.7	29.0	26.5	18.8	61.8	68.1
France	2.8	[3] 1.8	22.9	[3] 19.0	16.0	[3] 10.7	74.4	[3] 80.2
Germany	1.3	0.9	30.3	27.9	22.9	20.7	68.5	71.3
Greece.	6.6	3.3	21.0	17.9	11.1	10.8	72.5	78.8
Hungary.	5.4	3.5	31.7	30.7	23.0	23.0	62.9	65.8
Iceland [2].	9.1	[3] 7.2	26.1	[3] 25.2	13.9	[3] 15.2	64.8	[3] 67.6
Ireland	3.2	[3] 1.0	41.8	[3] 31.9	32.7	[3] 24.2	55.0	[3] 67.1
Italy	2.8	1.9	28.4	25.3	21.0	16.8	68.8	72.8
Japan [6].	1.7	[3] 1.4	31.1	[3] 26.0	21.3	[3] 17.6	67.2	[3] 72.6
Korea	4.6	2.6	38.1	39.3	28.3	30.6	57.3	58.2
Luxembourg.	0.7	0.3	18.4	13.0	11.3	6.8	81.0	86.7
Mexico	4.2	[3] 3.6	35.8	[3] 33.8	21.6	[3] 17.7	61.5	[3] 62.6
Netherlands.	2.6	1.9	24.9	23.7	15.6	13.2	72.4	74.3
New Zealand [7].	8.5	[8] 5.4	24.2	[8] 23.8	16.1	[8] 14.3	67.3	[8] 70.8
Norway.	2.1	1.6	42.0	40.8	10.6	9.2	56.0	57.6
Poland	5.0	3.5	31.7	31.7	18.5	18.6	63.3	64.8
Portugal	3.7	2.4	28.0	23.0	17.5	13.5	68.3	74.5
Slovakia.	4.5	3.8	36.2	34.8	24.7	20.6	59.3	61.4
Spain	4.4	2.7	29.2	25.7	18.6	[3] 12.7	66.4	71.7
Sweden	2.1	1.9	28.8	26.6	22.0	16.4	69.1	71.6
Switzerland	1.6	1.1	27.3	27.2	19.0	19.1	71.1	71.7
Turkey	10.8	9.4	30.0	26.1	21.4	14.5	59.2	64.5
United Kingdom	1.0	0.7	27.3	21.8	17.4	11.5	71.7	77.4

[1] Includes forestry, fishing, and hunting. [2] Value added is estimated at factor cost. [3] 2009 data. [4] 2008 data. [5] 2007 data. [6] Value added is estimated approximately at market prices. [7] Value added is estimated at producer's prices. [8] 2006 data.
Source: Organization for Economic Cooperation and Development (OECD), 2011, "National Accounts at a Glance," OECD National Accounts Statistics database (copyright),<http://dx.doi.org/10.1787/data-00369-en>, accessed April 2010.

Table 1352. Index of Industrial Production by Country: 1990 to 2010

[Annual averages of monthly data. Industrial production index measures output in the manufacturing, mining, electric, gas, and water utilities industries. Minus sign (–) indicates decrease]

Country	Index (2005 = 100)								Annual percent change				
									2000 to 2001	2005 to 2006	2007 to 2008	2008 to 2009	2009 to 2010
	1990	1995	2000	2005	2007	2008	2009	2010					
OECD, total.	73.0	78.7	94.9	100.0	107.2	105.0	92.1	99.4	–2.2	3.8	–2.1	–12.2	7.9
Australia.	73.2	81.2	94.1	100.0	105.3	108.0	106.2	111.0	1.0	2.2	2.6	–1.6	4.4
Austria	59.7	64.5	85.4	100.0	113.8	116.0	103.1	110.0	3.0	7.7	1.9	–11.1	6.7
Belgium [1]	82.3	82.9	95.8	100.0	108.0	106.8	93.1	99.7	–1.0	5.0	–1.1	–12.9	7.1
Canada [2]	68.3	77.7	98.9	100.0	98.6	93.1	83.1	87.9	–4.0	–0.6	–5.6	–10.7	5.8
Czech Republic [1]	89.9	67.9	74.9	100.0	119.8	117.7	101.6	111.7	10.0	8.3	–1.8	–13.6	10.0
Denmark	72.1	82.3	96.5	100.0	102.1	101.0	85.8	87.3	1.4	4.1	–1.1	–15.0	1.8
Finland.	58.9	66.6	91.2	100.0	114.6	115.5	94.6	100.4	0.7	9.6	0.8	–18.1	6.1
France	88.5	88.2	99.4	100.0	102.0	99.5	87.0	91.7	0.9	0.6	–2.4	–12.6	5.4
Germany [3]	85.7	82.5	93.9	100.0	113.5	113.7	94.1	105.0	0.4	6.2	0.2	–17.3	11.6
Greece.	83.7	82.1	100.6	100.0	102.6	102.4	92.4	87.0	–1.8	0.6	–0.3	–9.7	–5.8
Hungary [1].	51.9	45.6	76.0	100.0	118.5	118.5	97.6	107.8	3.5	9.9	–0.1	–17.6	10.4
Ireland	23.6	37.5	74.9	100.0	108.5	106.1	101.4	108.8	11.0	3.1	–2.2	–4.5	7.4
Italy	90.2	96.9	104.3	100.0	105.4	101.7	82.6	87.9	–1.3	3.5	–3.5	–18.8	6.4
Japan [1].	96.9	94.0	98.4	100.0	107.2	103.8	81.7	94.8	–6.3	4.3	–3.2	–21.3	16.0
Korea, South [1]	31.7	47.9	74.3	100.0	115.9	119.8	119.7	139.1	0.6	8.4	3.4	–0.1	16.2
Luxembourg.	66.5	68.1	83.7	100.0	101.9	96.3	80.5	89.5	3.1	2.1	–5.5	–16.4	11.2
Mexico [4].	67.1	70.2	99.7	100.0	107.9	107.7	99.5	105.5	–3.5	5.7	–0.1	–7.6	6.0
Netherlands.	77.9	84.4	95.2	100.0	103.8	105.3	97.6	104.5	0.5	1.5	1.5	–7.4	7.0
New Zealand	73.0	83.3	88.0	100.0	97.6	96.8	88.9	90.1	–0.2	–3.8	–0.8	–8.1	1.3
Norway.	74.2	93.7	104.5	100.0	96.7	97.1	93.3	88.1	–0.7	–2.2	0.5	–3.9	–5.6
Poland	47.3	53.6	76.8	100.0	122.5	125.8	121.0	134.4	0.9	12.0	2.7	–3.8	11.1
Portugal	93.3	90.7	107.1	100.0	103.0	98.8	90.6	92.1	3.1	3.1	–4.0	–8.3	1.7
Spain	79.1	82.0	97.8	100.0	106.0	98.4	82.8	83.5	–1.5	3.9	–7.3	–15.8	0.8
Sweden [5,6].	64.3	77.0	92.3	100.0	107.7	104.5	85.9	93.3	–0.5	3.6	–3.0	–17.8	8.7
Switzerland	78.3	81.3	99.0	100.0	118.1	119.6	110.1	117.0	–0.7	7.8	1.3	–7.9	6.2
Turkey	57.0	66.6	80.8	100.0	114.8	114.2	102.9	116.4	–8.7	7.3	–0.6	–9.9	13.1
United Kingdom	91.5	97.2	104.2	100.0	100.5	97.5	87.6	89.5	–1.4	0.2	–2.9	–10.1	2.1
United States	65.2	75.1	96.6	100.0	104.9	101.0	89.7	94.5	–3.4	2.2	–3.7	–11.2	5.3

[1] Not adjusted for unequal number of working days in the month. [2] Gross domestic product in industry at factor cost and 1986 prices. [3] Data prior to 1991 are for former West Germany. [4] Including construction. [5] Mining and manufacturing. [6] Annual figures correspond to official annual figures and differ from the average of the monthly figures.
Source: Organization for Economic Cooperation and Development (OECD), 2011, "Production and sales," Main Economic Indicators database (copyright), <http://dx.doi.org/10.1787/data-00048-en>, accessed April 2011.

Table 1353. Selected Indexes of Manufacturing Activity by Country: 1990 to 2009

[2002 = 100. Data relate to employees (wage and salary earners) in Belgium, and to all employed persons (employees, self-employed workers, and unpaid family workers) in the other countries. Minus sign (−) indicates decrease. For explanation of average annual percent change, see Guide to Tabular Presentation]

Index	United States	Canada	Japan	Belgium	France	Germany [1]	Italy	Netherlands	Norway	Sweden	United Kingdom
Output per hour:											
1990	58.1	70.7	70.9	74.5	63.6	69.8	78.1	68.3	87.8	49.4	70.1
1995	68.5	83.4	83.4	86.7	75.2	80.6	94.2	82.1	88.1	64.9	81.7
2000	88.8	100.7	98.5	97.8	94.0	96.5	100.9	96.6	94.6	91.6	93.5
2005	122.8	104.8	121.7	107.5	112.3	112.1	100.8	113.9	119.1	128.0	115.8
2008	135.7	104.0	127.9	114.1	115.1	122.4	99.4	121.5	117.2	137.5	124.0
2009	146.2	105.0	113.3	115.8	106.8	111.0	93.5	116.1	118.1	127.5	119.8
Average annual percent change:											
1990–2000	4.3	3.6	3.3	2.8	4.0	3.3	2.6	3.5	0.7	6.4	2.9
2007–2008	0.4	−2.4	0.2	1.0	−0.9	−0.2	−3.6	−2.3	0.9	−3.0	0.2
2008–2009	7.7	1.0	−11.4	1.5	−7.2	−9.3	−5.9	−4.4	0.8	−7.3	−3.4
Compensation per hour, national currency basis: [2]											
1990	62.1	68.3	77.4	69.9	64.3	59.7	61.3	61.8	58.5	61.0	58.4
1995	73.4	81.6	92.4	84.3	79.8	81.2	82.5	77.0	69.2	71.7	71.6
2000	91.3	94.2	98.0	93.2	91.8	94.7	94.1	90.9	89.0	90.6	90.2
2005	112.5	112.8	99.6	105.4	109.3	104.1	110.8	110.0	112.6	111.0	116.1
2008	123.2	121.7	98.8	116.9	119.7	112.3	120.3	121.0	132.1	124.0	129.3
2009	129.6	121.4	97.8	124.5	121.8	118.0	126.7	125.4	139.4	129.0	132.8
Average annual percent change:											
1990–2000	3.9	3.3	2.4	2.9	3.6	4.7	4.4	3.9	4.3	4.0	4.4
2007–2008	4.0	0.2	1.9	3.3	2.7	2.6	3.4	3.8	5.7	3.2	2.0
2008–2009	5.2	−0.2	−1.0	6.5	1.8	5.1	5.3	3.6	5.5	4.0	2.7
Real hourly compensation: [3]											
1990	82.9	87.4	82.7	89.2	79.6	78.2	93.4	85.1	77.0	80.8	81.6
1995	86.0	93.5	92.3	95.3	88.0	89.5	98.1	92.2	80.9	78.4	84.6
2000	95.4	98.6	96.5	97.0	95.1	97.9	99.1	97.8	92.9	95.0	93.4
2005	103.7	105.3	100.2	98.9	102.7	99.8	103.6	104.7	107.7	107.9	106.5
2008	102.9	106.4	97.7	101.3	106.0	101.1	104.6	109.3	118.2	109.5	106.1
2009	108.7	105.5	98.1	107.9	107.6	105.7	109.4	112.0	122.1	114.3	109.5
Average annual percent change:											
1990–2000	1.4	1.2	1.6	0.8	1.8	2.3	0.6	1.4	1.9	1.6	1.4
2007–2008	0.1	−2.1	0.5	−1.2	−0.1	0.1	−	1.3	1.8	−2.5	−1.9
2008–2009	5.6	−0.8	0.4	6.5	1.5	4.5	4.6	2.5	3.3	4.4	3.2
Unit labor costs, national currency: [2]											
1990	107.0	96.6	109.2	93.8	101.2	85.5	78.6	90.5	66.6	123.4	83.2
1995	107.1	97.9	110.8	97.2	106.1	100.8	87.7	93.8	78.5	110.4	87.6
2000	102.8	93.5	99.5	95.3	97.6	98.1	93.2	94.1	94.1	98.9	96.5
2005	91.6	107.6	81.8	98.0	97.4	92.9	110.0	96.6	94.5	86.7	100.2
2008	90.7	117.0	77.2	102.5	103.9	91.8	121.0	99.6	112.8	90.2	104.3
2009	88.7	115.7	86.3	107.6	114.0	106.3	135.5	108.0	118.0	101.2	110.9
Average annual percent change:											
1990–2000	−0.4	−0.3	−0.9	0.2	−0.4	1.4	1.7	0.4	3.5	−2.2	1.5
2007–2008	3.5	2.7	1.6	2.3	3.7	2.8	7.2	6.2	4.7	6.4	1.9
2008–2009	−2.2	−1.1	11.8	5.0	9.7	15.8	12.0	8.4	4.6	12.2	6.3
Unit labor costs, U.S. dollar basis: [2, 4]											
1990	107.0	130.1	94.3	119.7	128.9	109.4	134.3	115.9	85.0	202.6	98.8
1995	107.1	112.1	147.7	140.7	147.6	145.6	110.2	136.3	98.9	150.4	92.1
2000	102.8	98.8	115.6	93.0	95.3	95.8	91.0	91.9	85.2	104.8	97.3
2005	91.6	139.5	93.0	129.1	128.2	122.3	144.8	127.2	117.2	112.8	121.4
2008	90.7	172.4	93.5	159.6	161.9	143.0	188.5	155.1	159.7	133.2	128.7
2009	88.7	159.2	115.4	158.5	168.1	156.7	199.8	159.1	149.8	128.5	115.6
Average annual percent change:											
1990–2000	−0.4	−2.7	2.1	−2.5	−3.0	−1.3	−3.8	−2.3	−	−6.4	−0.2
2007–2008	3.5	3.4	15.7	9.8	11.4	10.5	15.1	14.0	8.7	9.1	−5.7
2008–2009	−2.2	−7.7	23.4	−0.7	3.8	9.6	6.0	2.6	−6.2	−3.5	−10.2
Employment:											
1990	116.1	98.7	128.7	118.3	117.0	131.2	110.8	111.4	102.2	119.9	134.5
1995	113.3	91.7	120.1	106.0	103.0	106.1	100.6	102.6	104.1	100.3	116.4
2000	113.0	102.2	108.0	102.8	101.4	101.9	99.4	103.0	105.0	101.3	110.0
2005	93.5	98.3	94.9	94.1	92.3	94.4	99.1	91.3	92.6	91.7	86.6
2008	88.1	90.2	95.1	92.1	88.7	96.3	99.9	91.7	102.4	92.6	80.3
2009	78.4	81.1	89.2	87.6	84.9	93.7	95.2	88.8	98.1	83.4	75.4
Average annual percent change:											
1990–2000	−0.3	0.3	−1.7	−1.4	−1.4	−2.5	−1.1	−0.8	0.3	−1.7	−2.0
2007–2008	−3.6	−3.3	−1.9	0.1	−1.3	1.6	−0.8	0.5	1.9	−0.4	−2.9
2008–2009	−11.0	−10.1	−6.2	−4.9	−4.3	−2.7	−4.7	−3.2	−4.2	−9.9	−6.1
Aggregate hours:											
1990	116.5	97.2	139.6	116.4	128.2	135.4	113.0	112.8	104.1	110.2	135.2
1995	115.9	91.8	122.0	103.1	111.3	111.7	101.6	103.7	107.3	101.3	118.9
2000	115.1	102.7	109.0	102.7	105.4	104.0	100.5	103.6	107.1	103.8	110.8
2005	93.5	97.9	96.3	95.3	93.7	95.0	97.0	91.6	95.8	94.3	87.8
2008	88.9	89.4	95.6	93.0	90.7	95.6	98.8	92.1	106.3	94.3	81.3
2009	77.7	78.6	84.2	83.6	86.8	86.2	88.4	87.9	99.3	83.4	75.1
Average annual percent change:											
1990–2000	−0.1	0.6	−2.4	−1.2	−1.9	−2.6	−1.2	−0.8	0.3	−0.6	−2.0
2007–2008	−4.0	−3.8	−3.3	−1.3	−1.2	0.7	−1.3	0.3	1.7	0.1	−3.1
2008–2009	−12.6	−12.1	−11.9	−10.1	−4.3	−9.8	−10.5	−4.6	−6.6	−11.6	−7.6

− Represents or rounds to zero. [1] Data prior to 1991 are for the former West Germany. [2] In Canada, France, Sweden, and the United Kingdom, compensation adjusted for employment taxes and government subsidies to estimate the actual cost to employers. [3] Index of hourly compensation divided by the index of consumer prices to adjust for changes in purchasing power. [4] Indexes in national currency adjusted for changes in prevailing exchange rates.

Source: U.S. Bureau of Labor Statistics, *International Comparisons of Manufacturing Productivity and Unit Labor Cost Trends 2009, Supplementary Tables 1950–2009*, December 2010. See also <http://www.bls.gov/ilc>.

Table 1354. Indexes of Hourly Compensation Costs for All Employees in Manufacturing by Country: 2000 to 2009

[United States = 100. Compensation costs include pay for time worked, other direct pay (including holiday and vacation pay, bonuses, other direct payments, and the cost of pay in kind), employer expenditures for legally required insurance programs and contractual and private benefit plans, and for some countries, other labor taxes. Data adjusted for exchange rates. Area averages are trade-weighted to account for difference in countries' relative importance to U.S. trade in manufactured goods. The trade weights used to compute the average compensation cost measures for selected economic groups are based on the relative dollar value of U.S. trade in manufactured commodities (exports plus imports) with each country or area in 2009; see source for detail]

Area or country	2000	2005	2007	2008	2009	Area or country	2000	2005	2007	2008	2009
United States	**100**	**100**	**100**	**100**	**100**	Ireland	65	98	111	122	116
Total [1]	**66**	**76**	**83**	**86**	**79**	Israel	53	47	51	61	55
OECD [2]	70	82	88	92	84	Italy	67	93	102	111	104
Europe	86	111	121	129	118	Japan.	103	86	76	86	91
Euro Area [3]	87	113	123	134	125	Korea, South	40	51	62	50	42
Eastern Europe [4]	13	21	27	32	28	Mexico	18	18	19	19	16
East Asia [4]	35	38	43	41	36	Netherlands	85	117	126	139	130
Argentina	33	18	25	31	30	New Zealand	38	56	61	59	52
Australia.	68	97	108	115	103	Norway.	102	144	168	181	161
Austria.	98	122	135	148	143	Philippines	4	4	4	5	4
Belgium	104	134	144	158	147	Poland	14	18	24	29	22
Brazil	18	17	23	26	25	Portugal	24	31	35	38	36
Canada	76	90	101	101	88	Singapore	48	45	50	58	52
Czech Republic	14	24	31	38	33	Slovakia	11	20	27	34	34
Denmark	95	127	145	155	148	Spain	50	70	78	86	83
Finland.	81	113	125	139	131	Sweden	96	119	134	137	119
France	87	109	121	131	120	Switzerland	101	121	123	136	132
Germany	103	128	139	150	139	Taiwan [5]	30	27	26	27	23
Hungary.	12	23	28	30	26	United Kingdom	83	106	117	111	92

[1] Trade-weighted measure includes all 32 foreign economies. [2] Organization for Economic Cooperation and Development; see text, this section. [3] Euro area refers to European Union member countries that have adopted the Euro as the common currency as of January 1, 2011 (Austria, Belgium, Cyprus, Estonia, Finland, France, Germany, Greece, Ireland, Italy, Luxembourg, Malta, Netherlands, Portugal, Slovakia, Slovenia, and Spain). [4] Czech Republic, Hungary, Poland, and Slovakia. [5] Excludes Japan. [6] See footnote 4, Table 1332.

Source: U.S. Bureau of Labor Statistics, *International Comparisons of Hourly Compensation Costs in Manufacturing, 2009,* March 2011. See also <http://www.bls.gov/ilc/>.

Table 1355. Annual Percent Change in Labor Productivity and Hours Worked by Country: 1995 to 2009

[Change for period shown. For Advanced, Other Advanced, and Eastern European countries, labor productivity growth refers to the growth in gross domestic product per hour worked. Data are derived from The Conference Board Total Economy Database, in association with the Groningen Growth and Development Centre at the University of Groningen, Netherlands. Growth for regional aggregates is based on the weighted sum of country labor productivity growth, with the weight calculated as the two-period average of country share in PPP adjusted nominal GDP, plus a reallocation term. Gross domestic product for each country is measured in constant 2010 U.S. dollars, using GDP deflator changes. Minus sign (−) indicates decrease]

Country	Labor productivity		Total hours worked		Country	Labor productivity		Total hours worked	
	1995 to 2000	2000 to 2009	1995 to 2000	2000 to 2009		1995 to 2000	2000 to 2009	1995 to 2000	2000 to 2009
Advanced Economies [1] . .	2.4	1.4	0.9	(Z)	Israel	1.2	1.2	3.7	1.7
United States	**2.5**	**1.7**	**1.7**	**−0.1**	New Zealand	1.5	0.9	1.1	1.4
Japan.	2.0	1.5	−1.1	−1.0	Norway.	2.3	0.8	1.4	0.9
European Union					Singapore	2.1	0.1	4.2	3.6
(EU-15, old) [2]	1.8	0.9	1.1	0.3	South Korea	5.4	3.9	−0.4	−0.1
Austria	1.8	1.2	1.2	0.3	Switzerland	1.6	0.5	0.4	1.0
Belgium	2.0	0.4	0.8	0.9	Taiwan [4]	4.6	3.0	0.5	0.1
Denmark	1.1	0.3	1.7	0.3					
Finland.	2.8	1.4	1.9	0.2	Addenda:				
France	2.1	0.8	0.7	0.3	European Union				
Germany	2.0	0.9	(Z)	−0.3	(EU-12, new) [5]	3.2	3.3	−0.2	0.4
Greece	4.0	2.3	−0.6	0.8	Bulgaria	2.1	2.8	−2.5	1.7
Ireland	5.0	2.3	4.3	0.6	Cyprus.	2.0	1.0	1.7	1.9
Italy	0.9	−0.2	1.0	0.4	Czech Republic	1.9	3.5	−0.4	−0.3
Luxembourg.	2.6	0.9	3.4	2.0	Estonia	8.1	4.6	−1.7	−0.8
Netherlands	1.7	1.1	2.2	0.2	Hungary.	2.2	3.0	1.4	−1.1
Portugal	1.3	0.8	2.8	−0.2	Latvia.	4.4	5.0	0.8	−1.0
Spain	0.2	1.1	3.8	1.2	Lithuania	4.2	4.4	0.1	0.2
Sweden	2.6	1.5	0.8	0.2	Malta	2.2	1.1	0.7	0.5
United Kingdom	2.5	1.2	0.9	0.2	Poland	5.3	1.6	(Z)	2.3
Other Advanced					Romania	−1.2	6.2	(Z)	−1.7
Economies [3]	3.3	2.1	0.9	0.7	Slovakia	4.8	4.7	−1.5	0.1
Australia.	2.3	1.4	1.5	1.5	Slovenia.	4.8	2.2	−0.6	0.6
Canada	2.1	0.7	2.0	1.0					
Hong Kong.	0.7	2.7	2.0	0.9	European Union				
Iceland.	2.3	3.1	2.5	−0.3	(EU-27, enlarged) [6] . . .	2.1	1.1	0.8	0.3

Z Less than 0.05 percent. [1] "Advanced" includes the U.S., EU-15, Japan, and "Other Advanced." [2] Referring to all members of the European Union until 30 April 2004. See footnote 2, Table 1378 for list of EU-15 countries. [3] "Other Advanced" includes Australia, Canada, Hong Kong, Iceland, Israel, New Zealand, Norway, South Korea, Singapore, Switzerland, and Taiwan, province of China. [4] See footnote 4, Table 1332. [5] Referring to new membership of the European Union as of 1 May 2004. [6] Referring to membership of the European Union. See footnote 5, Table 1377 for list of EU-27 countries.

Source: The Conference Board, New York, NY, The Conference Board, Total Economy Database," January 2011, <http://www.conference-board.org/economics/database.cfm>. Reproduced with permission from The Conference Board, Inc., 2011, The Conference Board, Inc.

Table 1356. Annual Percent Changes in Consumer Prices by Country: 2000 to 2010

[Change from previous year. See text, this section, for general comments concerning the data. For additional qualifications of the data for individual countries, see source. Minus sign (–) indicates decrease]

Country	2000	2005	2008	2009	2010
United States	**3.4**	**3.4**	**3.8**	**–0.4**	**1.6**
Argentina	–0.9	9.6	8.6	6.3	10.8
Australia	4.5	2.7	4.4	1.8	2.8
Austria	2.4	2.3	3.2	0.5	1.8
Bangladesh	2.2	7.0	8.9	5.4	8.1
Belgium	2.5	2.8	4.5	–0.1	2.2
Bolivia	4.6	5.4	14.0	3.3	2.5
Brazil	7.0	6.9	5.7	4.9	5.0
Canada	2.7	2.2	2.4	0.3	1.8
Chile	3.8	3.1	8.7	1.5	1.4
Colombia	9.2	5.0	7.0	4.2	2.3
Ecuador	96.1	2.4	8.4	5.2	3.6
Egypt	2.7	4.9	18.3	11.8	11.3
France	1.7	1.7	2.8	0.1	1.5
Germany	1.5	1.6	2.6	0.3	1.1
Ghana	25.2	15.1	16.5	19.3	10.7
Greece	3.2	3.5	4.2	1.2	4.7
Guatemala	6.0	8.4	12.6	1.9	3.9
India	4.0	4.2	8.4	10.9	12.0
Indonesia	3.7	10.5	11.1	2.8	7.0
Iran	14.5	13.4	25.5	13.5	10.1
Israel	1.1	1.3	4.6	3.3	2.7
Italy	2.5	2.0	3.4	0.8	1.5
Japan	–0.7	–0.3	1.4	–1.4	–0.7
Kenya	10.0	10.3	26.2	9.2	4.0
Korea, South	2.3	2.8	4.7	2.8	2.9
Malaysia	1.5	3.0	5.4	0.6	1.7
Mexico	9.5	4.0	5.1	5.3	4.2
Netherlands	2.3	1.7	2.5	1.2	1.3
Nigeria	6.9	17.9	11.6	11.5	13.7
Norway	3.1	1.5	3.8	2.2	2.4
Pakistan	4.4	9.1	20.3	13.6	13.9
Peru	3.8	1.6	5.8	2.9	1.5
Philippines	4.0	7.6	9.3	3.2	3.8
Portugal	2.8	2.3	2.6	–0.8	1.4
Romania	45.7	9.0	7.8	5.6	6.1
Russia	20.8	12.7	14.1	11.7	6.9
South Africa	5.3	3.4	11.5	7.1	4.3
Spain	3.4	3.4	4.1	–0.4	1.9
Sri Lanka	6.2	11.6	22.6	3.4	5.9
Sweden	1.0	0.5	3.4	–0.3	1.3
Switzerland	1.5	1.2	2.4	–0.5	0.7
Thailand	1.6	4.5	5.4	–0.9	3.3
Turkey	54.9	10.1	10.4	6.3	8.6
United Kingdom	2.9	2.8	4.0	–0.6	4.6
Venezuela	16.2	16.0	31.4	28.6	29.1

Source: International Monetary Fund, Washington, DC, *International Financial Statistics,* monthly (copyright).

Table 1357. Comparative Price Levels—Selected OECD Countries: 2011

[Purchasing power parities (PPPs) are the rates of currency conversion that eliminate the differences in price levels between countries. Comparative price levels are defined as the ratios of PPPs to exchange rates. The PPPs are given in national currency units per U.S. dollar. The table is to be read vertically. Each column shows the number of specified monetary units needed in each of the countries listed to buy the same representative basket of consumer goods and services. In each case the representative basket costs a hundred units in the country whose currency is specified. Example of data: An item that costs $1.00 in the United States would cost $1.46 (U.S. dollars) in Japan]

Country	United States (U.S. dollar)	Canada (Canadian dollar)	Mexico (Mexican peso)	Japan (Yen)	France (Euro)	Germany (Euro)	Italy (Euro)	United Kingdom (Pound)
United States	**100**	**73**	**132**	**69**	**75**	**81**	**87**	**79**
Australia [1]	168	123	222	115	126	136	146	132
Austria	128	94	170	88	96	104	112	101
Belgium	134	98	177	91	100	108	116	105
Canada	137	100	181	94	102	111	119	107
Czech Republic	89	65	118	61	67	72	77	70
Denmark	171	125	227	117	128	139	149	135
Finland	145	106	193	100	109	118	127	114
France	134	98	177	91	100	108	116	105
Germany	123	90	163	84	92	100	107	97
Greece	115	84	153	79	86	94	100	91
Hungary	86	63	114	59	64	70	75	68
Iceland	128	93	169	87	96	104	111	100
Ireland	144	105	191	99	108	117	125	113
Italy	115	84	152	79	86	93	100	90
Japan	146	107	193	100	109	118	127	115
Korea, South	86	63	113	59	64	69	75	67
Luxembourg	141	103	187	97	106	115	123	111
Mexico	76	55	100	52	57	61	66	59
Netherlands	128	94	169	88	96	104	111	100
New Zealand [1]	128	94	170	88	96	104	112	101
Norway	178	130	236	122	133	144	155	140
Poland	75	55	99	51	56	61	65	59
Portugal	112	82	149	77	84	91	98	88
Slovakia	87	63	115	59	65	70	75	68
Spain	116	85	154	80	87	94	101	91
Sweden	147	107	194	101	110	119	128	115
Switzerland	188	138	249	129	141	153	164	148
Turkey	70	51	93	48	52	57	61	55
United Kingdom	127	93	169	87	95	103	111	100

[1] Estimates based on quarterly consumer prices.

Source: Organization for Economic Cooperation and Development (OECD), 2011, "Prices: Comparative Price Levels," Main Economic Indicators database (copyright), <http://dx.doi.org/10.1787/data-00536-en>, accessed April 2011.

Table 1358. Indexes of Living Costs Abroad: 2011

[As of January 2011. Washington, DC=100. Indexes compare the costs in dollars of representative goods and services (excluding housing and education) purchased at the foreign location and the cost of comparable goods and services in the Washington, DC area. The indexes are computed for private American employees and exclude special advantages that may be available only to U.S. Government employees. The indexes are place-to-place comparisons at specific times and currency exchange rates. They cannot be used for measuring cost changes over time at a foreign location. Since the indexes reflect only the expenditure pattern and living costs of American families, they should not be used to compare living costs of Americans in the United States with the living costs of foreign nationals living in their own country]

Country/Territory	City	Survey date	Local index [1]	Country/Territory	City	Survey date	Local index [1]
Algeria	Algiers	2/16/2009	127	Kenya	Nairobi	5/19/2008	143
Angola	Luanda	5/21/2008	190	Korea	Seoul	2/16/2010	140
Argentina	Buenos Aires	5/2/2010	126	Kuwait	Kuwait City	11/21/2009	136
Armenia	Yerevan	3/14/2010	113	Laos	Vientiane	12/30/2005	107
Australia	Canberra	7/29/2010	135	Latvia	Riga	5/30/2007	139
Austria	Vienna	3/11/2008	186	Lebanon	Beirut	4/18/2010	121
Azerbaijan	Baku	2/1/2009	156	Liberia	Monrovia	8/14/2009	149
Bahamas	Nassau	6/24/2009	143	Lithuania	Vilnius	5/22/2010	122
Bahrain	Bahrain	11/3/2009	123	Luxembourg	Luxembourg	12/9/2009	162
Bangladesh	Dhaka	3/6/2006	88	Macedonia	Skopje	4/23/2007	135
Belarus	Minsk	3/15/2007	136	Madagascar	Antananarivo	1/23/2008	128
Belgium	Brussels	5/12/2010	179	Malaysia	Kuala Lumpur	8/24/2008	121
Belize	Belmopan	4/6/2008	132	Mexico	Mexico City	3/6/2009	99
Bolivia	La Paz	7/1/2009	110	Moldova	Chisinau	2/23/2010	115
Bosnia-Herzegovina	Sarajevo	8/6/2009	126	Mongolia	Ulaanbaatar	1/16/2009	136
Botswana	Gaborone	6/16/2009	119	Morocco	Rabat	9/15/2010	142
Brazil	Rio de Janeiro	12/29/2009	156	Mozambique	Maputo	8/16/2009	141
Bulgaria	Sofia	5/11/2010	135	Namibia	Windhoek	11/23/2009	138
Burma	Rangoon	10/22/2008	142	Nepal	Kathmandu	9/22/2009	103
Burundi	Bujumbura	7/7/2009	135	Netherlands	The Hague	4/23/2009	152
Cambodia	Phnom Penh	2/8/2009	122	New Zealand	Wellington	9/27/2010	159
Cameroon	Yaounde	4/25/2010	158	Nicaragua	Managua	4/15/2008	113
Canada	Montreal	1/12/2007	134	Niger	Niamey	6/7/2010	124
Central African				Nigeria	Abuja	11/12/2008	161
Republic	Bangui	8/13/2008	189	Norway	Oslo	1/26/2009	176
Chad	Ndjamena	8/26/2009	176	Oman	Muscat	5/17/2010	131
Chile	Santiago	10/22/2010	135	Pakistan	Islamabad	12/10/2004	102
China [2]	Beijing	5/17/2010	138	Panama	Panama City	7/31/2008	119
Colombia	Bogota	1/4/2008	109	Paraguay	Asuncion	1/16/2008	114
Congo [3]	Kinshasa	7/16/2008	167	Peru	Lima	1/14/2010	142
Costa Rica	San Jose	12/10/2009	123	Philippines	Manila	5/4/2010	108
Cote d'Ivoire	Abidjan	12/21/2008	129	Poland	Warsaw	9/17/2009	130
Croatia	Zagreb	5/31/2010	132	Portugal	Lisbon	2/28/2008	148
Cuba	Havana	4/30/2010	146	Qatar	Doha	5/12/2010	149
Cyprus	Nicosia	5/17/2010	156	Romania	Bucharest	11/25/2008	134
Czech Republic	Prague	9/15/2005	130	Russia	Moscow	2/26/2009	154
Denmark	Copenhagen	3/30/2009	190	Rwanda	Kigali	11/16/2008	136
Djibouti	Djibouti City	4/10/2004	161	Saudi Arabia	Riyadh	4/9/2010	122
Ecuador	Quito	8/10/2009	120	Serbia	Belgrade	3/17/2009	99
Egypt	Cairo	3/13/2006	96	Sierra Leone	Freetown	6/15/2009	131
El Salvador	San Salvador	2/8/2009	123	Singapore	Singapore	4/19/2009	133
Estonia	Tallinn	7/6/2010	116	Slovakia	Bratislava	12/7/2009	172
Ethiopia	Addis Ababa	4/17/2010	115	South Africa	Johannesburg	9/30/2010	143
Finland	Helsinki	4/14/2009	171	Spain	Madrid	4/11/2010	160
France	Paris	10/11/2009	201	Sri Lanka	Colombo	3/17/2010	105
Gabon	Libreville	11/16/2008	157	Sudan	Khartoum	11/14/2008	139
Georgia	Tbilisi	4/14/2009	140	Sweden	Stockholm	5/13/2010	185
Germany	Berlin	6/23/2010	168	Switzerland	Geneva	5/21/2008	235
Ghana	Accra	1/20/2010	138	Syria	Damascus	3/26/2008	96
Greece	Athens	9/4/2008	171	Taiwan [2, 3]	Taipei	2/24/2009	145
Guatemala	Guatemala City	6/4/2009	106	Tajikistan	Dushanbe	4/18/2010	105
Guinea	Conakry	10/29/2008	162	Tanzania	Dar es Salaam	11/16/2009	117
Guyana	Georgetown	7/28/2009	150	Thailand	Bangkok	2/26/2008	126
Haiti	Port-au-Prince	9/29/2008	129	Timor-Leste	Timor Leste	7/11/2007	128
Honduras	Tegucigalpa	8/11/2010	99	Turkey	Istanbul	4/29/2010	151
Hong Kong	Hong Kong	6/7/2009	156	Turkmenistan	Ashgabat	11/17/2009	130
Hungary	Budapest	5/7/2008	163	Uganda	Kampala	6/7/2010	124
Iceland	Reykjavik	5/17/2010	148	Ukraine	Kyiv	10/5/2008	131
India	New Delhi	11/20/2008	107	United Arab Emirates	Dubai	6/9/2009	117
Indonesia	Jakarta	6/17/2009	116	United Kingdom	London	4/16/2009	159
Ireland	Dublin	7/7/2010	164	Uruguay	Montevideo	2/18/2009	136
Israel	Tel Aviv	6/8/2010	146	Uzbekistan	Tashkent	4/7/2009	107
Italy	Rome	3/31/2009	183	Venezuela	Caracas	9/23/2010	180
Jamaica	Kingston	6/24/2009	112	Vietnam	Hanoi	5/5/2008	113
Japan	Okinawa	5/2/2009	175	Yemen	Sanaa	4/25/2009	92
Jordan	Amman	4/14/2008	130	Zambia	Lusaka	7/1/2009	130
Kazakhstan	Astana	5/22/2008	148	Zimbabwe	Harare	1/14/2008	243

[1] Also called the "local index," the living cost index measures living costs for private American citizens. The local index is a comparison of prices at the foreign post and in Washington, DC, with the price ratios weighted by the expenditure pattern of American employees living at the foreign post. It is, thereby, a measure of the cost of living for Americans at the foreign post compared with the cost of living in Washington, DC. This is the index most appropriate for use by business firms and other private organizations to establish cost-of-living allowances for their American employees stationed abroad. [2] See footnote 4, Table 1332. [3] There are no U.S. Government employees in Taiwan. The figures listed in this column represent a living cost comparison for American employees of the American Institute in Taiwan, who have some duty-free and other special benefits that may not be available to other Americans in Taiwan.

Source: U.S. Department of State, Bureau of Administration, "Indexes of Living Costs Abroad, Quarters Allowances, and Hardship Differentials," January 2011, <http://aoprals.state.gov/content.asp?content_id=186&menu_id=81>.

Table 1359. Percent of Household Final Consumption Expenditures Spent on Food, Alcohol, and Tobacco Consumed at Home by Selected Countries: 2009

Country/Territory	Food [1]	Alcoholic beverages and tobacco	Country/Territory	Food [1]	Alcoholic beverages and tobacco
United States [2]	6.8	1.9	Latvia	21.8	6.6
			Lithuania	31.5	3.4
Algeria	43.8	2.0	Malaysia	24.0	2.5
Australia	10.5	4.0	Mexico	40.4	1.3
Austria	11.1	3.3	Morocco	11.5	2.9
Azerbaijan	46.9	2.4	Netherlands	12.1	4.3
Belarus	43.2	6.0	New Zealand	39.9	2.5
Belgium	13.0	3.8	Nigeria	12.9	4.5
Bolivia	28.2	2.2	Norway	45.5	2.5
Brazil	24.7	2.0	Pakistan	29.0	2.0
Bulgaria	18.2	3.7	Peru	36.7	1.7
Canada	9.1	3.9	Philippines	20.3	6.6
Chile	23.3	0.8	Poland	15.6	3.5
China [3]	32.9	2.9	Portugal	12.7	0.3
Colombia	27.6	4.7	Romania	28.0	2.7
Croatia	25.8	3.3	Russia	23.7	1.3
Czech Republic	15.6	7.7	Saudi Arabia	8.0	2.4
Ecuador	19.0	1.9	Singapore	16.6	4.8
Egypt	38.1	2.3	Slovakia	15.0	4.5
Estonia	14.6	8.0	Slovenia	19.8	4.6
Finland	11.9	5.0	South Africa	15.1	2.6
France	13.5	3.1	Spain	13.2	3.1
Germany	11.4	3.6	Sweden	11.5	3.7
Hong Kong	12.2	0.8	Switzerland	10.2	3.6
Hungary	16.3	8.1	Taiwan [3]	24.0	2.1
Indonesia	43.0	6.3	Thailand	24.8	5.6
Ireland	7.2	5.4	Tunisia	35.7	1.0
Israel	17.7	1.6	Turkey	24.4	4.1
Italy	14.2	2.7	Turkmenistan	27.1	3.0
Japan	14.2	3.2	Ukraine	42.1	6.4
Jordan	40.7	4.8	United Arab Emirates	8.7	0.4
Kazakhstan	34.9	3.7	United Kingdom	8.8	3.7
Korea, South	14.5	1.6	Venezuela	29.1	3.1
Kuwait	19.0	6.6	Vietnam	38.1	2.8

[1] Includes nonalcoholic beverages. [2] 2008 data. [3] See footnote 4, Table 1332.
Source: U.S. Department of Agriculture, Economic Research Service; "Food, CPI, Prices and Expenditures: Food Expenditure Tables," July 2011, <http://www.ers.usda.gov/Briefing/CPIFoodAndExpenditures/Data/>.

Table 1360. Gross Public Debt, Expenditures, and Receipts by Country: 1990 to 2011

[Percent of nominal gross domestic product. Gross debt includes one-off revenues from the sale of the mobile telephone licenses. Expenditures and receipts refer to the general government sector, which is a consolidation of accounts for the central, state, and local governments plus social security. Expenditures, or total outlays, are defined as current outlays plus capital outlays. Receipts cover current receipts, but exclude capital receipts. Nontax receipts consist of property income (including dividends and other transfers from public enterprises), fees, charges, sales, fines, capital transfers received by the general government, etc. Minus sign (–) indicates deficit]

Country	Gross debt			Expenditures			Receipts		
	1990	2000	2011	1990	2000	2011	1990	2000	2011
United States [1]	−4.3	1.5	−9.4	37.2	33.9	40.9	32.9	35.4	31.5
Australia	−2.0	0.9	−2.6	35.8	35.2	36.1	33.7	36.1	33.5
Austria	−2.5	−1.9	−5.8	51.5	52.2	52.8	49.0	50.3	47.1
Belgium	−6.8	−0.1	−5.2	52.3	49.2	54.0	45.5	49.1	48.8
Canada	−5.8	2.9	−4.5	48.8	41.1	42.9	43.0	44.1	38.4
Czech Republic	(X)	−3.7	−5.0	(X)	41.6	45.4	(X)	37.9	40.3
Denmark	−1.3	2.3	−4.0	55.9	53.3	58.4	54.6	55.5	54.4
Finland	5.4	6.9	−5.2	47.9	48.3	58.1	53.3	55.2	52.9
France	−2.4	−1.5	−8.0	49.4	51.6	54.8	47.0	50.1	46.8
Germany	(X)	1.3	−4.6	(X)	45.1	47.6	(X)	46.4	42.9
Greece	−14.0	−3.7	−10.0	44.9	46.7	50.1	30.8	43.0	40.1
Hungary	(NA)	−3.0	−3.6	(NA)	46.9	48.8	(NA)	43.9	45.2
Iceland	−3.3	1.7	−5.8	38.9	41.9	49.2	35.6	43.6	43.4
Ireland	−2.8	4.8	−11.6	42.8	31.3	45.8	40.0	36.1	34.3
Italy	−11.4	−0.9	−5.1	52.9	46.1	50.6	41.5	45.3	45.5
Japan [2]	2.0	−7.6	−9.4	31.6	39.0	42.2	33.6	31.4	32.7
Korea, South	3.1	5.4	1.1	19.0	22.4	30.9	22.1	27.9	32.0
Netherlands	−5.3	2.0	−5.3	54.9	44.2	51.1	49.6	46.1	45.7
New Zealand	−4.5	1.9	−3.9	53.2	39.2	43.7	48.7	41.1	39.8
Norway	2.2	15.4	10.8	53.3	42.3	44.1	55.5	57.7	54.9
Portugal	−6.1	−3.0	−7.8	40.5	43.1	51.3	34.5	40.2	43.5
Spain	−4.1	−1.0	−7.7	42.8	39.1	46.6	38.7	38.1	38.9
Sweden	3.4	3.7	−2.0	60.1	57.0	55.2	63.4	60.7	53.2
United Kingdom	−2.0	3.7	−12.5	41.5	36.6	53.2	39.4	40.3	40.7

NA Not available. X Not applicable. [1] Receipts exclude the operating surpluses of public enterprises, while expenditures include them. [2] The 2000 expenditures include capital transfers to the Deposit Insurance Company. Receipts include deferred tax payments on postal savings accounts in 2000.
Source: Organization for Economic Cooperation and Development (OECD), 2011, OECD Economic Outlook, Vol. 2010/2 (copyright), OECD Publishing. See also <http://dx.doi.org/10.1787/eco_outlook-v2010-2-en>.

U.S. Census Bureau, Statistical Abstract of the United States: 2012

Table 1361. Percent Distribution of Tax Receipts by Country: 1990 to 2008

Country	Total [1]	Income and profits taxes [2]			Social security contributions			Taxes on goods and services [5]		
		Total [3]	Individual	Corporate	Total [4]	Employees	Employers	Total [3]	General consumption taxes [6]	Taxes on specific goods, services [7]
United States:										
1990.........	100.0	46.0	37.1	8.9	25.1	11.0	12.9	17.4	8.0	7.0
2000.........	100.0	50.7	41.9	8.7	23.2	10.4	11.6	16.1	7.6	6.3
2008.........	100.0	46.8	37.9	8.9	24.5	10.8	12.4	17.0	7.8	6.2
Canada:										
1990.........	100.0	48.6	40.8	7.0	12.1	4.4	7.6	25.8	14.1	10.3
2000.........	100.0	50.1	36.8	12.2	13.6	5.5	7.8	24.2	14.2	8.6
2008.........	100.0	49.5	37.3	10.7	14.5	5.8	8.3	23.4	13.2	8.5
France:										
1990.........	100.0	16.1	10.7	5.3	44.1	13.2	27.2	28.4	18.8	8.7
2000.........	100.0	24.9	18.0	6.9	36.0	8.9	24.8	25.7	16.9	8.2
2008.........	100.0	24.1	17.4	6.8	37.2	9.2	25.3	24.5	16.8	6.9
Germany:										
1990.........	100.0	32.4	27.6	4.8	37.5	16.2	19.1	26.7	16.6	9.2
2000.........	100.0	30.1	25.3	4.8	39.0	17.2	19.2	28.1	18.4	8.8
2008.........	100.0	31.9	26.8	5.2	36.4	15.9	17.2	28.9	19.4	8.5
Italy:										
1990.........	100.0	36.5	26.3	10.0	32.9	6.3	23.6	28.0	14.7	10.6
2000.........	100.0	33.1	24.8	6.9	28.6	5.4	19.9	27.9	15.4	9.6
2008.........	100.0	34.6	26.8	8.6	31.1	5.5	21.2	24.4	13.7	8.3
Japan:										
1990.........	100.0	50.2	27.8	22.4	26.4	10.6	12.7	13.7	4.4	7.5
2000.........	100.0	34.8	21.1	13.8	35.2	14.7	16.4	19.3	9.1	8.0
2008.........	100.0	55.4	32.6	22.8	(NA)	(NA)	(NA)	29.1	14.5	11.2
United Kingdom:										
1990.........	100.0	39.3	29.4	9.9	17.0	6.6	9.9	31.1	16.9	12.6
2000.........	100.0	39.1	29.3	9.8	17.0	6.8	9.6	31.9	18.1	12.4
2008.........	100.0	39.9	29.9	9.9	19.2	7.9	10.8	28.8	17.8	9.8

NA Not available. [1] Includes property taxes, employer payroll taxes other than social security contributions, and miscellaneous taxes, not shown separately. [2] Includes taxes on capital gains. [3] Includes other taxes, not shown separately. [4] Includes contributions of self-employed, not shown separately. [5] Taxes on the production, sales, transfer, leasing, and delivery of goods and services and rendering of services. [6] Primary value-added and sales taxes. [7] For example, excise taxes on alcohol, tobacco, and gasoline.

Source: Organization for Economic Cooperation and Development (OECD), 2010, "Comparative Tables," Taxing Wages database (copyright), <http://dx.doi.org/10.1787/data-00265-en>, accessed May 2010.

Table 1362. Household Tax Burden by Country: 2008

[Percent of gross wage earnings of the average production worker. The tax burden reflects income tax plus employee social security contributions less cash benefits. Minus sign (–) indicates tax credit]

Country	Single person without children	One earner family with two children	Country	Single person without children	One earner family with two children
United States	**22.4**	**5.2**	Japan...........	20.1	13.8
Australia.........	22.0	8.6	Korea, South	11.8	9.1
Austria..........	32.7	18.1	Luxembourg.......	26.4	0.9
Belgium..........	41.5	20.2	Mexico...........	5.3	5.3
Canada..........	22.8	8.8	Netherlands.......	31.8	22.6
Czech Republic....	22.2	−6.5	New Zealand......	18.4	0.6
Denmark.........	39.4	28.8	Norway..........	29.3	21.8
Finland..........	29.2	22.6	Poland..........	24.3	17.8
France..........	27.7	17.1	Portugal..........	22.3	8.7
Germany.........	41.3	20.8	Slovakia..........	21.3	2.4
Greece..........	25.1	25.4	Spain...........	19.7	12.0
Hungary..........	38.2	25.3	Sweden.........	25.3	17.9
Iceland..........	23.9	3.0	Switzerland	21.5	8.1
Ireland..........	20.9	2.2	Turkey	27.2	25.7
Italy............	29.3	15.1	United Kingdom....	25.3	18.5

Source: Organization for Economic Cooperation and Development (OECD), 2010, "Comparative Tables," Taxing Wages database (copyright), <http://dx.doi.org/10.1787/data-00265-en>, accessed May 2010.

Table 1363. Household Net Saving Rates by Country: 1995 to 2008

[As a percentage of household disposable income. Household savings are estimated by subtracting household consumption expenditure from household disposable income, plus the change in net equity of households in pension funds. Households include households plus nonprofit institutions serving households. Net saving rates are measured after deducting consumption of fixed capital (depreciation), with respect to assets used in enterprises operated by households, as well as owner-occupied dwellings. The household saving rate is calculated as the ratio of household savings to household disposable income (plus the change in net equity of households in pension funds). Minus sign (–) indicates an excess of expenditures over income]

Country	1995	2000	2002	2003	2004	2005	2006	2007	2008
United States	**5.7**	**3.0**	**3.7**	**3.8**	**3.4**	**1.5**	**2.5**	**1.7**	**2.7**
EU-27 [1]	(NA)	6.6	7.4	7.3	6.6	6.4	5.8	5.5	5.8
Australia [2]	6.4	2.2	-2.7	-3.2	-2.1	-0.2	0.8	(NA)	(NA)
Austria	11.8	9.2	8.0	9.2	9.4	9.7	10.9	11.4	12.0
Belgium	16.4	12.3	12.9	12.2	10.8	10.0	10.9	11.2	11.5
Canada	9.4	4.8	3.5	2.7	3.2	2.2	3.6	2.6	3.8
Chile	(NA)	6.5	6.8	6.4	7.2	7.1	7.7	7.7	(NA)
Czech Republic	10.0	3.3	3.0	2.4	0.5	3.2	4.8	6.3	5.8
Denmark	1.3	-1.9	4.1	4.1	0.7	-1.5	0.4	-1.0	-0.3
Finland	3.9	-0.1	0.6	1.4	2.5	0.7	-1.4	-1.2	-1.0
France	12.7	11.8	13.7	12.5	12.4	11.4	11.4	12.0	11.6
Germany	11.0	9.2	9.9	10.3	10.4	10.5	10.5	10.8	11.2
Greece	(NA)	-6.0	-8.0	-7.3	-7.2	-8.0	-7.3	(NA)	(NA)
Ireland	(NA)	(NA)	5.4	5.4	8.3	5.6	3.8	2.7	4.1
Italy	17.0	8.4	11.2	10.3	10.2	9.9	9.1	8.2	8.6
Japan	(NA)	8.9	5.1	3.9	3.6	3.8	3.6	3.8	(NA)
Korea, South	(NA)	9.3	0.4	5.2	9.2	7.2	5.2	2.9	2.8
Netherlands	14.0	6.7	8.4	7.5	7.3	6.3	6.0	8.1	6.8
Norway	4.8	4.3	8.2	8.9	7.2	10.1	0.1	-1.2	(NA)
Poland	14.6	10.3	8.3	7.8	8.0	7.1	6.8	7.4	(NA)
Russia	(NA)	(NA)	12.8	13.2	11.8	12.0	12.6	(NA)	(NA)
Slovakia	5.2	6.1	3.5	1.2	0.5	1.2	0.5	2.5	1.8
Slovenia	(NA)	7.0	9.9	7.6	9.2	11.1	11.2	10.5	(NA)
Spain	(NA)	5.9	5.6	6.0	4.9	4.7	4.2	3.6	6.1
Sweden	9.5	4.8	9.1	9.0	7.7	6.8	7.8	9.1	12.1
Switzerland	12.7	11.7	10.7	9.4	9.0	10.1	11.4	12.7	(NA)
United Kingdom	6.9	0.1	-0.1	0.4	-1.7	-1.3	-2.9	-4.3	-4.5

NA Not available. [1] See footnote 5, Table 1377 for list of EU-27 countries. [2] Data refer to fiscal year.

Source: Organization for Economic Cooperation and Development (OECD), 2010, *OECD Factbook 2010: Economic, Environmental and Social Statistics*, OECD Publishing (copyright). See also <http://www.oecd-ilibrary.org/content/serial/18147364>.

Table 1364. Insurance and Pensions by Country: 1999 and 2009

Country	Insurance						Pension, [1] 2009		
	Direct gross premiums (percent of GDP)		2009 premiums (mil. U.S. dol.)		Financial assets [2] (mil. U.S. dol.)		Financial assets (mil. U.S. dol.)	Contributions to pension funds (percent of GDP)	Benefits paid by pension funds (percent of GDP)
	1999	2009	Life	Non-life	1999	2009			
United States	**10.5**	**11.4**	**802,310**	**1,222,375**	**3,334,437**	**628,045**	**9,603,619**	**[3] 3.4**	**[3] 4.5**
Australia	8.8	[4] 5.6	31,995	25,435	133,167	[4] 209,523	808,224	8.9	4.9
Austria	5.4	6.0	[4] 10,576	[4] 15,705	[5] 45,066	101,436	18,987	[4] 0.4	[4] 0.2
Belgium	6.9	8.2	25,650	13,927	(NA)	(NA)	19,165	0.4	0.3
Canada	6.4	7.3	38,478	74,215	190,851	388,908	806,350	3.2	2.7
Czech Republic	3.0	3.9	3,162	4,405	3,620	15,915	11,332	0.9	0.4
Denmark	6.4	[4] 9.5	[4] 21,948	[4] 10,551	[6] 60,856	(NA)	133,980	0.6	0.7
Finland	4.4	3.9	4,654	4,816	25,186	63,633	182,286	9.8	10.5
France	8.3	10.4	50,763	95,777	115,468	2,094,590	[4] 21,931	(NA)	(NA)
Germany	6.6	[4] 6.6	114,003	132,765	777,311	258,647	173,810	0.3	0.2
Greece	2.0	[4] 2.2	3,316	3,900	[7] 3,351	11,032	63	(Z)	(Z)
Iceland	2.6	2.3	26	251	577	(NA)	14,351	6.6	5.0
Ireland	14.0	20.3	37,759	8,902	[5] 23,251	58,922	100,278	(NA)	(NA)
Italy	5.5	7.7	115,096	51,748	[7] 156,926	517,175	86,818	0.6	0.2
Japan	7.4	[4] 8.3	376,297	96,709	1,923,772	[4] 3,045,193	[8] 301,994	[8] 0.4	[8] 0.2
Korea, South	11.6	11.1	61,514	37,629	98,057	2,586	29,632	0.2	0.3
Luxembourg	27.5	44.1	21,502	1,562	22,130	[9] 67,921	1,171	0.9	0.1
Mexico	1.7	[4] 1.7	7,719	9,821	(NA)	33,888	107,135	0.6	0.2
Netherlands	9.3	7.9	34,142	33,027	257,354	323,717	997,922	5.3	3.9
Norway	4.5	5.6	[4] 14,186	9,287	[7] 51,063	[4] 14,053	27,852	0.5	0.3
Poland	2.7	3.8	9,708	6,772	6,097	30,185	58,143	1.6	(Z)
Portugal	5.6	8.2	13,957	5,770	20,515	73,573	30,441	0.6	0.7
Slovakia	2.8	3.3	1,487	1,401	878	6,295	5,508	6.2	(NA)
Spain	5.5	5.7	40,563	44,605	(NA)	225,037	118,159	0.6	0.4
Sweden	6.8	5.8	12,933	12,536	211,523	328,973	33,435	(NA)	(NA)
Switzerland	12.5	10.0	27,341	29,958	(NA)	371,870	551,450	8.4	5.5
Turkey	1.4	[3] 1.3	1,439	7,032	1,984	7,299	14,017	[9] 0.3	0.1
United Kingdom	13.9	[4] 14.5	[4] 282,776	[4] 116,853	1,473,777	[4] 2,385,748	1,753,016	2.7	3.2

NA Not available or not applicable. Z Less than 0.05 percent. [1] All types of plans are included (occupational and personal, mandatory and voluntary) covering both public and private sector workers. Further details can be found at <www.oecd.org/daf/pensions/gps>. [2] Investments by direct insurance companies. [3] 2007 data. [4] 2008 data. [5] 1996 data. [6] 1993 data. [7] 1997 data. [8] 2005 data. [9] 2006 data.

Source: Organization for Economic Cooperation and Development (OECD), 2011, *OECD Insurance Statistics* database (copyright), <http://stats.oecd.org//Index.aspx?QueryId=29073>, accessed April 2011.

International Statistics **855**

U.S. Census Bureau, Statistical Abstract of the United States: 2012

Table 1365. Civilian Labor Force, Employment, and Unemployment by Country: 1990 to 2010

[125,840 represents 125,840,000. Data based on U.S. labor force definitions (see source) except that minimum age for population base varies as follows: United States, Canada, France, Sweden, and United Kingdom, 16 years; Australia, Japan, Netherlands, Germany, and Italy (beginning 1993), 15 years; and Italy (prior to 1993), 14 years]

Year	United States	Canada	Australia	Japan	France	Germany [1]	Italy	Netherlands	Sweden	United Kingdom
Civilian labor force (1,000):										
1990	125,840	14,047	8,440	62,990	24,867	29,412	22,670	6,767	4,597	28,766
2000	[2] 142,583	15,632	9,590	66,710	26,193	[2] 39,302	[2] 23,361	[2] 8,008	4,490	28,962
2005	[2] 149,320	17,056	10,529	65,386	27,061	[2] 40,696	24,179	[2] 8,400	[2] 4,693	30,137
2009	154,142	18,058	11,602	65,362	27,972	41,507	24,705	8,716	4,888	31,274
2010	153,889	18,263	11,868	65,100	28,067	41,189	24,741	8,654	4,942	31,421
Labor force participation rate: [3]										
1990	66.5	67.4	64.7	62.6	57.4	55.0	47.2	57.0	67.4	64.3
2000	[2] 67.1	66.0	64.4	61.7	56.8	[2] 56.7	[2] 48.1	[2] 63.0	63.7	62.8
2005	66.0	67.3	65.4	59.5	56.2	[2] 57.5	48.7	[2] 64.2	[2] 64.8	63.1
2009	65.4	67.2	66.7	59.3	56.6	58.5	48.4	65.2	64.8	63.3
2010	64.7	67.0	66.5	59.0	56.5	58.1	48.2	64.3	64.7	63.1
Civilian employment (1,000):										
1990	118,793	12,964	7,877	61,710	22,872	27,952	21,080	6,251	4,513	26,713
2000	[2] 136,891	14,677	8,989	63,790	23,928	[2] 36,236	[2] 20,973	[2] 7,762	4,230	27,375
2005	[2] 141,730	16,032	9,998	62,910	24,632	[2] 36,123	22,290	[2] 7,959	[2] 4,334	28,674
2009	139,877	16,732	10,953	62,242	25,395	38,279	22,760	8,389	4,486	28,880
2010	139,064	16,969	11,247	62,000	25,423	38,209	22,621	8,264	4,534	28,944
Employment-population ratio: [4]										
1990	62.8	62.2	60.4	61.3	52.8	52.3	43.9	52.7	66.1	59.8
2000	[2] 64.4	62.0	60.3	59.0	51.9	[2] 52.2	[2] 43.2	[2] 61.1	60.1	59.4
2005	62.7	63.3	62.1	57.3	51.2	[2] 51.1	44.9	[2] 60.9	[2] 59.9	60.0
2009	59.3	62.2	62.9	56.4	51.4	54.0	44.6	62.8	59.5	58.5
2010	58.5	62.3	63.0	56.2	51.2	53.9	44.1	61.4	59.3	58.2
Unemployment rate:										
1990	5.6	7.7	6.7	2.0	8.0	5.0	7.0	7.6	1.8	7.1
2000	[2] 4.0	[2] 6.1	6.3	4.4	8.6	[2] 7.8	[2] 10.2	[2] 3.1	5.8	5.5
2005	5.1	6.0	[2] 5.0	3.8	9.0	[2] 11.2	7.8	[2] 5.3	[2] 7.7	4.9
2009	9.3	7.3	5.6	4.8	9.2	7.8	7.9	3.7	8.2	7.7
2010	9.6	7.1	5.2	4.8	9.4	7.2	8.6	4.5	8.3	7.9
Under 25 years old	18.4	13.6	11.5	9.0	24.1	10.2	28.0	8.8	24.8	19.8
Teenagers [5]	25.9	18.6	16.8	9.7	28.7	11.0	44.6	11.4	35.4	29.6
20 to 24 years old	15.5	10.7	8.1	8.8	23.2	9.9	25.1	6.7	20.3	15.0
25 years old and over	8.2	5.9	3.8	4.4	7.9	6.9	7.2	3.7	5.9	5.8

[1] Unified Germany for 1991 onward. Prior to 1991, data relate to the former West Germany. [2] Break in series. Data not comparable with prior years. [3] Civilian labor force as a percent of the civilian working-age population. Germany and Japan include the institutionalized population as part of the working-age population. [4] Civilian employment as a percent of the civilian working-age population. Germany and Japan include the institutionalized population as part of the working-age population. [5] 16 to 19-year-olds in the United States, Canada, France, Sweden, and the United Kingdom; 15 to 19-year-olds in Australia, Japan, Germany, Italy, and the Netherlands.

Source: U.S. Bureau of Labor Statistics, *International Comparisons of Annual Labor Force Statistics, Adjusted to U.S. Concepts, 10 Countries, 1970–2010,* March 2011. See also <http://www.bls.gov/fls/flscomparelf.htm>.

Table 1366. Unemployment Rates by Country: 2000 to 2010

[Annual averages. The standardized unemployment rates shown here are calculated as the number of unemployed persons as a percentage of the civilian labor force. The unemployed are persons of working age who, in the reference period, are without work, available for work, and have taken specific steps to find work]

Country	2000	2005	2009	2010	Country	2000	2005	2009	2010
OECD, total	6.2	6.8	[1] 6.0	[1] 6.0	Ireland	4.4	4.4	11.8	13.6
EU-27 [2]	9.2	8.9	9.0	9.6	Italy	10.2	7.7	7.8	8.4
					Japan	4.7	4.4	5.1	5.1
United States	**4.0**	**5.1**	**9.3**	**9.6**	Korea, South	4.4	3.7	3.7	3.7
Australia	6.3	5.0	5.6	5.2	Netherlands	3.0	4.7	3.5	4.5
Austria	3.5	5.2	4.8	4.4	New Zealand	6.2	3.8	6.1	6.5
Belgium	7.0	8.5	7.9	8.3	Norway	3.5	4.6	3.2	3.6
Canada	6.8	6.8	8.3	8.0	Poland	16.1	17.8	8.2	9.6
Czech Republic	8.9	7.9	6.7	7.3	Portugal	3.9	7.6	9.5	10.8
Denmark	4.6	4.8	6.0	7.4	Spain	13.9	9.2	18.0	20.1
Finland	9.8	8.4	8.2	8.4	Sweden	4.7	7.1	8.3	8.4
France	(NA)	8.9	9.1	9.3	Switzerland	2.5	4.2	4.1	4.2
Germany	7.8	11.1	7.7	7.1	United Kingdom	5.4	4.9	7.6	7.9
Hungary	6.4	7.2	10.0	11.2					

NA Not available. [1] 2008 data. [2] See footnote 5, Table 1377.

Source: Organization for Economic Cooperation and Development (OECD), 2011, "Labour: Labour Force Statistics," Main Economic Indicators database (copyright); <http://dx.doi.org/10.1787/data-00046-en>, accessed April 2011.

Table 1367. Percent of Persons Not in Education or at Work: 2008

[Represents those persons not in education and either unemployed or not in the labor force]

Country	15 to 19 years old			20 to 24 years old		
	Total	Unemployed	Not in the labor force	Total	Unemployed	Not in the labor force
Australia............	6.3	3.0	3.3	10.5	3.7	6.8
Belgium.............	5.5	1.9	3.6	14.2	7.8	6.4
Brazil..............	13.8	3.7	10.1	22.5	7.6	14.9
Canada.............	7.3	2.9	4.4	13.0	5.6	7.4
Czech Republic.......	2.7	1.6	1.1	10.6	4.1	6.5
Denmark...........	2.8	1.1	1.7	7.7	2.8	4.9
Finland............	5.1	1.9	3.2	12.0	5.5	6.5
France.............	5.3	2.6	2.7	13.8	8.3	5.5
Germany...........	3.7	2.0	1.7	14.0	7.0	7.0
Greece.............	8.4	2.3	6.1	17.1	9.9	7.2
Hungary...........	5.7	1.6	4.1	18.4	7.5	10.9
Israel..............	22.3	1.2	21.1	37.5	5.3	32.2
Italy...............	9.6	2.7	6.9	22.0	8.3	13.7
Mexico.............	23.2	2.8	20.4	(NA)	(NA)	(NA)
Poland............	2.3	0.7	1.6	15.6	7.1	8.5
Portugal...........	7.1	3.7	3.4	13.4	8.2	5.2
Spain..............	10.6	5.4	5.2	19.5	10.4	9.1
Sweden............	4.4	1.8	2.6	12.9	6.5	6.4
Switzerland.........	9.4	2.4	7.0	9.1	3.7	5.4
United States........	**7.3**	**2.4**	**4.9**	**17.2**	**6.4**	**10.8**

NA Not available.

Source: Organization for Economic Cooperation and Development (OECD), 2010, "How successful are students in moving from education to work?," Education at a Glance 2010: OECD Indicators, OECD Publishing (copyright). See also <http://dx.doi.org/10.1787/eag-2010-24-en>, accessed April 2011.

Table 1368. Female Labor Force Participation Rates by Country: 1980 to 2010

[In percent. Female labor force of all ages divided by female population 15–64 years old]

Country	1980	1990	2000	2009	2010	Country	1980	1990	2000	2009	2010
OECD, total...........	**(NA)**	**(NA)**	**60.7**	**63.2**	**(NA)**	Japan..............	54.8	60.3	64.0	68.5	(NA)
						Korea, South........	46.1	51.2	54.9	58.3	56.7
EU–27 [1].............	(NA)	(NA)	61.0	65.3	(NA)	Luxembourg.........	39.9	50.3	69.4	95.7	(NA)
Australia.............	52.5	62.2	66.1	71.4	71.6	Mexico.............	34.0	23.4	43.3	47.0	48.3
Austria..............	48.7	55.4	62.2	70.3	(NA)	Netherlands.........	35.5	53.0	65.5	74.2	(NA)
Belgium.............	46.9	52.4	56.6	61.5	(NA)	New Zealand........	44.5	65.4	68.0	74.0	74.1
Canada	57.3	67.5	69.8	74.3	74.4	Norway.............	62.3	71.2	76.2	78.0	77.1
Czech Republic........	(X)	69.1	64.2	62.3	62.3	Poland.............	(NA)	(NA)	60.5	57.1	58.4
Denmark............	71.1	78.2	75.6	76.7	76.1	Portugal...........	54.6	62.4	67.3	73.1	(NA)
Finland.............	70.1	73.8	72.2	74.1	73.3	Slovakia............	(X)	(X)	63.0	60.7	61.5
France	54.0	59.6	64.5	66.1	(NA)	Spain..............	32.4	41.5	52.0	65.0	66.1
Germany [2]	52.8	56.7	63.6	71.0	(NA)	Sweden............	74.3	80.9	75.0	77.7	77.8
Greece..............	33.0	43.6	49.5	55.0	(NA)	Switzerland	54.3	65.7	76.8	82.8	(NA)
Hungary............	(NA)	(NA)	52.1	54.9	56.4	Turkey.............	(NA)	36.8	30.3	28.8	(NA)
Iceland.............	(NA)	(NA)	82.8	80.5	(NA)	United Kingdom.......	58.2	66.4	67.8	70.4	70.5
Ireland.............	36.3	43.8	56.9	63.7	63.4	**United States........**	**59.5**	**68.6**	**70.8**	**70.2**	**(NA)**
Italy	39.6	45.9	46.8	51.5	51.5						

NA Not available. X Not applicable. [1] See footnote 5, Table 1377. [2] Prior to 1991, data are for former West Germany.

Source: Organization for Economic Cooperation and Development (OECD), 2011, "Labour Market Statistics: Labour Force Statistics by Sex and Age: Indicators," OECD Employment and Labour Market Statistics database (copyright); <http://dx.doi.org/10.1787/data-00310-en>, accessed April 2011.

Table 1369. Civilian Employment-Population Ratio: 1990 to 2010

[Civilian employment as a percent of the civilian working-age population. See headnote, Table 1365]

Country	Women					Men				
	1990	1995	2000	2009	2010	1990	1995	2000	2009	2010
United States [1]............	**54.3**	**55.6**	**57.5**	**54.4**	**53.6**	**72.0**	**70.8**	**71.9**	**64.5**	**63.7**
Canada.................	54.1	52.7	56.0	58.7	58.5	70.6	66.1	68.2	65.9	66.2
Australia................	49.5	50.5	52.5	56.9	56.6	71.4	68.2	68.4	69.1	69.5
Japan..................	48.0	47.7	46.4	45.7	45.7	75.4	75.0	72.5	68.0	67.5
France.................	43.2	43.4	45.0	46.8	46.6	63.5	59.4	59.5	56.5	56.3
Germany [1, 2, 3, 4]	40.5	42.7	44.4	48.3	48.1	65.6	63.1	60.6	59.9	60.1
Italy [1]	29.2	29.1	31.6	34.7	34.5	60.0	56.2	60.6	55.3	54.5
Netherlands [1, 3, 4]	39.4	44.4	51.7	57.1	56.2	66.5	66.7	70.8	68.6	66.7
Sweden [4]	61.8	54.7	56.1	56.0	55.5	70.6	62.0	64.2	63.0	63.3
United Kingdom...........	50.3	49.8	52.5	53.1	52.8	70.0	64.7	66.9	64.2	63.8

[1] Break in series between 1990 and 1995. [2] Unified Germany for 1991 onward. Prior to 1991, data relate to the former West Germany. [3] Break in series between 1995 and 2000. [4] Break in series between 2000 and 2009.

Source: U.S. Bureau of Labor Statistics, International Comparisons of Annual Labor Force, Adjusted to U.S. Concepts, 10 Countries, 1970–2010, March 2011. See also <http://www.bls.gov/fls/flscomparelf.htm>.

Table 1370. Civilian Employment by Industry and Country: 2000 and 2010

[136,891 represents 136,891,000. Civilian employment approximating U.S. concepts. See headnote, Table 1365]

Industry	United States [1,2]	Canada [1]	Australia	Japan	France [2]	Germany [2]	Italy [2]	Sweden [2]	United Kingdom
TOTAL EMPLOYMENT (1,000)									
2000, total	136,891	14,677	8,989	63,790	23,928	36,236	20,973	4,230	27,375
Agriculture, forestry, fishing [3] . . .	2,464	479	442	3,070	1,095	959	1,120	122	330
Industry [4]	30,050	3,204	1,856	19,710	5,861	11,898	6,634	1,000	6,632
Manufacturing	19,644	2,240	1,083	13,180	4,222	8,647	4,944	762	4,425
Services [5]	104,377	10,994	6,691	41,010	16,972	23,379	13,219	3,108	20,413
2010, total	139,064	16,969	11,247	62,000	25,423	38,209	22,621	4,534	28,944
Agriculture, forestry, fishing [3] . . .	2,206	369	373	2,390	723	850	863	95	363
Industry [4]	23,889	3,216	2,220	15,440	5,228	10,716	6,267	886	5,231
Manufacturing	14,081	1,743	1,000	10,460	3,332	8,095	4,255	575	2,882
Services [5]	112,969	13,384	8,654	44,170	19,472	26,643	15,491	3,553	23,350
PERCENT DISTRIBUTION [6]									
2000, total	100.0	100.0	100.0	100.0	100.0	100.0	100.0	100.0	100.0
Agriculture, forestry, fishing [3] . . .	1.8	3.3	4.9	4.8	4.6	2.6	5.3	2.9	1.2
Industry [4]	22.0	21.8	20.6	30.9	24.5	32.8	31.6	23.6	24.2
Manufacturing	14.4	15.3	12.0	20.7	17.6	23.9	23.6	18.0	16.2
Services [5]	76.2	74.9	74.4	64.3	70.9	64.5	63.0	73.5	74.6
2010, total	100.0	100.0	100.0	100.0	100.0	100.0	100.0	100.0	100.0
Agriculture, forestry, fishing [3] . . .	1.6	2.2	3.3	3.9	2.8	2.2	3.8	2.1	1.3
Industry [4]	17.2	19.0	19.7	24.9	20.6	28.0	27.7	19.5	18.1
Manufacturing	10.1	10.3	8.9	16.9	13.1	21.2	18.8	12.7	10.0
Services [5]	81.2	78.9	76.9	71.2	76.6	69.7	68.5	78.4	80.7

[1] Data for the United States and Canada are based on the 2002 North American Industry Classification System (NAICS).
[2] Break in series between 2000 and 2010. [3] Includes hunting. [4] Includes manufacturing, mining, and construction. [5] Transportation, communication, public utilities, trade, finance, public administration, private household services, and miscellaneous services.
[6] Civilian employment as a percent of the civilian working-age population.
Source: U.S. Bureau of Labor Statistics, *International Comparisons of Annual Labor Force Statistics, Adjusted to U.S. Concepts, 10 Countries, 1960–2010,* March 2011. See also <http://www.bls.gov/fls/flscomparelf.htm>.

Table 1371. Educational Performance: 2008 and 2009

[Tertiary-type A includes education leading to a BA, Master's, or equivalent degree, and advanced research programs. Performance figures were gathered from the Program for International Student Assessment (PISA), an internationally standardized assessment jointly developed by participating countries, which takes place in 3-year cycles. To implement PISA, each of the participating countries selects a nationally representative sample of 15-year-olds, regardless of grade level. Tests are typically administered to between 4,500 and 10,000 students in each country]

Country	Student performance on the combined reading, scientific, and mathematical literacy scales, 2009			Educational attainment of adult population and current graduation rates, 2008 (percent)	
	Mean score on the combined reading literacy scale [1]	Mean score on the mathematical literacy scale [2]	Mean score on the scientific literacy scale [3]	Upper secondary or higher attainment (25 to 64 years old) [4]	Tertiary-type A attainment (25 to 64 years old) [5]
Australia.	515	514	527	70	26
Austria	470	496	494	81	11
Canada	524	527	529	87	25
Czech Republic	478	493	500	91	14
Finland.	536	541	554	81	22
France	496	497	498	70	16
Germany	497	513	520	85	16
Greece.	483	466	470	61	17
Italy	486	483	489	53	14
Japan.	520	529	539	(NA)	24
Korea.	539	546	538	79	26
Luxembourg.	472	489	484	68	20
Mexico	425	419	416	34	15
Poland	500	495	508	87	20
Spain	481	483	488	51	20
Sweden	497	494	495	85	23
Switzerland	501	534	517	87	23
United Kingdom	494	492	514	70	24
United States	**500**	**487**	**502**	**89**	**32**
OECD mean	493	496	501	71	21

NA Not available. [1] Reading literacy is understanding, using, and reflecting on written texts in order to achieve one's goals, to develop one's knowledge and potential, and to participate in society. [2] Mathematical literacy is an individual's capacity to identify and understand the role that mathematics plays in the world, to make well-founded judgements, and to use and engage with mathematics in ways that meet the needs of that individual's life. [3] Scientific literacy is the capacity to use scientific knowledge to identify questions and to draw evidence-based conclusions in order to understand and help make decisions about the natural world and the changes made to it through human activity. [4] Excluding ISCED 3C short programs. [5] Includes advanced research programs.
Source: Organization for Economic Cooperation and Development (OECD), 2010, *Education at a Glance 2010: OECD Indicators,* OECD Publishing (copyright). See also <http://www.pisa.oecd.org>.

Table 1372. World Supply and Utilization of Major Crops, Livestock, and Products: 2003 to 2010

[In millions of units (215.0 represents 215,000,000). For major crops, data ending in year shown. For meat and dairy, calendar year data, selected countries]

Commodity	2003	2004	2005	2006	2007	2008	2009	2010 [1]
Wheat:								
Area (hectares)	215.0	210.0	217.2	219.7	213.0	218.2	224.7	277.1
Production (metric tons)	568.6	554.8	626.7	619.1	596.3	612.1	682.2	683.8
Exports (metric tons) [2]	105.7	108.7	111.8	117.0	111.8	117.3	143.7	135.8
Consumption (metric tons) [3]	604.3	589.3	607.6	622.1	616.1	616.8	641.5	652.8
Ending stocks (metric tons) [4]	168.8	134.3	153.4	150.5	130.6	125.9	166.7	197.9
Coarse grains:								
Area (hectares)	291.4	305.8	300.4	300.9	305.0	318.3	313.0	310.2
Production (metric tons)	873.4	915.9	1,015.4	979.5	987.6	1,080.0	1,110.2	1,108.3
Exports (metric tons) [2]	102.2	103.2	101.0	107.3	117.8	127.2	113.0	123.2
Consumption (metric tons) [3]	901.0	944.8	978.5	993.4	1,012.6	1,056.1	1,079.5	1,107.0
Ending stocks (metric tons) [4]	171.9	143.0	179.9	166.0	141.0	164.9	195.6	196.9
Rice, milled:								
Area (hectares)	146.4	148.9	151.3	153.4	154.2	155.1	157.8	156.2
Production (metric tons)	379.0	392.7	401.3	418.6	420.3	433.6	448.1	440.4
Exports (metric tons) [2]	28.7	27.4	28.2	29.7	31.4	31.2	28.9	30.8
Consumption (metric tons) [3]	408.9	414.1	409.0	416.1	421.7	428.1	436.9	438.0
Ending stocks (metric tons) [4]	102.9	81.5	73.7	76.2	74.8	80.3	91.5	93.8
Total grains: [5]								
Area (hectares)	652.8	664.7	669.0	674.0	672.2	691.6	695.5	693.5
Production (metric tons)	1,821.0	1,863.3	2,043.4	2,017.3	2,004.1	2,125.7	2,240.5	2,232.5
Exports (metric tons) [2]	236.6	239.4	241.0	253.9	261.0	275.7	285.6	289.8
Consumption (metric tons) [3]	1,914.2	1,948.1	1,995.2	2,031.6	2,050.4	2,100.9	2,157.8	2,197.6
Ending stocks (metric tons) [4]	443.5	358.8	407.0	392.7	346.4	371.1	453.8	488.7
Oilseeds:								
Crush (metric tons)	269.4	279.7	302.2	319.5	328.6	339.9	338.7	357.3
Production (metric tons)	331.5	335.8	381.3	391.3	403.5	391.4	396.3	441.6
Exports (metric tons)	70.0	66.8	74.4	75.4	82.8	91.8	94.2	108.2
Ending stocks (metric tons)	49.1	45.0	57.8	64.5	72.6	60.2	55.0	70.3
Meals: [6]								
Production (metric tons)	185.6	190.9	206.5	217.1	224.5	231.9	228.9	243.6
Exports (metric tons)	54.1	59.1	61.3	66.6	69.6	72.3	69.3	72.0
Oils: [7]								
Production (metric tons)	96.1	102.9	111.7	118.9	121.8	128.6	133.5	140.1
Exports (metric tons)	36.0	39.3	42.9	47.8	49.2	53.9	56.0	58.3
Cotton:								
Area (hectares)	30.7	32.3	35.7	34.7	34.6	32.9	30.6	30.2
Production (bales) [8]	91.0	96.7	121.6	116.4	121.8	119.7	107.1	101.3
Exports (bales) [8]	30.5	33.2	35.0	44.9	37.5	39.0	30.1	35.6
Consumption (bales) [8]	97.6	97.2	107.9	115.0	122.0	121.2	107.4	118.5
Ending stocks (bales) [8]	47.6	48.1	60.6	61.9	62.3	60.7	60.5	44.0
Beef and Pork:								
Production (metric tons)	144.5	147.0	150.3	153.5	152.8	156.6	157.9	158.3
Consumption (metric tons)	144.4	146.5	149.4	152.4	152.2	156.0	157.1	157.6
Exports (metric tons) [2]	10.7	11.4	12.3	12.7	12.7	13.6	13.0	13.3
Broilers and Turkeys:								
Production (metric tons)	63.2	64.8	68.2	69.5	73.6	76.9	77.0	79.4
Consumption (metric tons)	62.7	64.0	67.5	69.3	73.3	75.9	76.2	78.2
Exports (metric tons) [2]	6.5	6.6	7.4	7.1	8.0	9.1	9.0	9.2
Dairy:								
Milk production (metric tons)	409.6	415.6	421.4	427.7	436.8	435.0	435.5	440.3

[1] Forecast for crops, preliminary for meat and dairy. [2] Excludes intra-EU (European Union) trade but includes intra-FSU (Former Soviet Union) trade. [3] Where stocks data are not available, consumption includes stock changes. [4] Stocks data are based on differing marketing years and do not represent levels at a given date. Data not available for all countries. [5] Wheat, coarse grains, and rice. [6] Includes the following types of meals: copra, cottonseed, fishmeal, palm kernel, rapeseed, sunflower, soybean, and peanut. [7] Includes the following types of oils: coconut, cottonseed, olive, palm, palm kernel, peanut, sunflower, rapeseed, and soybean. [8] 480-pound bales.

Source: U.S. Department of Agriculture, Economic Research Service, "Agricultural Outlook: Statistical Indicators," February 2011, <http://www.ers.usda.gov/publications/agoutlook/aotables/>.

Table 1373. World Crop Production Summary: 2009 to 2011

[In millions of metric tons, (648.2 represents 648,200,000), except as indicated]

Country	Wheat 2009–2010	Wheat 2010–2011 prel.	Coarse grains 2009–2010	Coarse grains 2010–2011 prel.	Rice (milled) 2009–2010	Rice (milled) 2010–2011 prel.	Oilseeds [1] 2009–2010	Oilseeds [1] 2010–2011 prel.	Cotton 2009–2010	Cotton 2010–2011 prel.
World.........	648.2	648.1	1,109.6	1,084.6	440.1	451.6	442.4	449.3	101.4	114.6
United States	60.4	60.1	348.8	330.2	7.1	7.6	98.9	100.4	12.2	18.1
Canada	26.8	23.2	22.5	22.1	(2)	(2)	16.0	16.3	(2)	(2)
Mexico..........	4.1	3.7	27.3	29.5	0.2	0.2	0.6	0.6	0.4	0.7
EU-27 [3]	138.6	135.8	155.3	139.6	1.9	1.9	29.7	28.9	1.1	1.1
Russia	61.8	41.5	31.8	16.4	0.6	0.7	8.0	7.2	(2)	(2)
Ukraine	20.9	16.8	24.1	21.4	0.1	0.1	9.3	9.9	(2)	(2)
China..........	115.1	115.0	163.6	174.2	136.6	139.3	57.8	56.8	32.0	30.5
India..........	80.7	80.8	33.9	40.4	89.1	94.5	32.4	34.4	23.0	24.0
Indonesia	(2)	(2)	6.9	6.8	36.4	36.9	9.4	9.8	–	–
Pakistan........	24.0	23.9	3.6	3.6	6.8	4.7	5.2	4.8	9.6	8.7
Thailand.........	(2)	(2)	4.2	4.1	20.3	20.3	0.6	0.6	–	–
Argentina	11.0	15.0	28.0	28.5	0.7	1.1	57.9	54.4	1.0	1.3
Brazil	5.0	5.9	58.4	57.3	7.7	9.5	71.5	76.9	5.5	9.3
Australia.........	21.9	26.0	11.1	13.6	0.1	0.6	2.6	3.7	1.8	4.4
South Africa......	2.0	1.5	13.9	12.4	(2)	(2)	1.2	1.7	–	0.1
Turkey	18.5	17.0	11.2	10.1	0.4	0.5	1.5	1.8	1.8	2.1
All others	93.4	82.0	165.0	174.4	132.2	133.9	39.6	41.0	13.1	14.4

– Represents zero. [1] Includes soybean, cottonseed, peanut (in shell), sunflower seed, rapeseed for individual countries. Copra and palm kernel are added to world totals. [2] Indicates no reported or insignificant production. [3] See footnote 5, Table 1377.
Source: U.S. Department of Agriculture, Foreign Agricultural Service, *World Agricultural Production*, May 2011. See also <http://www.fas.usda.gov/wap_arc.asp>.

Table 1374. Wheat, Rice, and Corn—Exports and Imports of Leading Countries: 2000 to 2010

[In thousands of metric tons (28,904 represents 28,904,000). Wheat data are for trade year beginning in July of year shown; rice data are for calendar year; corn data are for trade year beginning in October of year shown. Countries listed are the ten leading exporters or importers in 2010]

Leading exporters	Exports 2000	Exports 2005	Exports 2010 [1]	Leading importers	Imports 2000	Imports 2005	Imports 2010 [1]
WHEAT				**WHEAT**			
United States	**28,904**	**27,291**	**34,700**	Egypt...........	6,050	7,771	10,000
EU-27 [2]	15,675	15,701	22,000	Brazil...........	7,177	6,235	6,500
Canada	17,316	16,020	17,000	Indonesia........	4,069	5,072	5,600
Australia...........	15,930	16,012	14,500	Algeria..........	5,600	5,483	5,300
Argentina..........	11,325	9,635	8,500	Japan...........	5,885	5,469	5,200
Kazakhstan	3,972	3,817	5,000	EU-27 [2]	3,536	6,755	4,500
Russia	696	10,664	4,000	Korea, South	3,127	3,884	4,200
Ukraine	78	6,461	3,500	Morocco.........	3,632	2,390	3,900
Turkey	1,601	3,214	3,000	Nigeria..........	1,913	3,679	3,700
Brazil	3	807	1,700	Mexico..........	3,066	3,549	3,500
RICE				**RICE**			
Thailand............	7,521	7,376	10,000	Nigeria..........	1,250	1,650	1,900
Vietnam...........	3,528	4,705	6,000	Indonesia........	1,500	539	1,750
United States	**2,583**	**3,623**	**3,565**	EU-27 [2]	1,310	1,124	1,350
Pakistan...........	2,429	3,664	2,650	Bangladesh	672	514	1,350
India.............	1,685	4,688	2,400	Philippines.......	1,410	1,622	1,200
Cambodia	–	350	1200	Iran	765	1,500	1,200
Uruguay...........	736	834	900	Iraq	959	1,306	1,150
Argentina..........	381	485	625	Saudi Arabia	992	1,357	1,069
China [3]............	1,847	1,216	600	Malaysia	596	751	907
Brazil	22	274	600	Cote d'Ivoire......	496	775	900
CORN				**CORN**			
United States	**49,313**	**54,201**	**49,532**	Japan...........	16,340	16,617	16,100
Argentina..........	9,676	9,464	14,500	Mexico..........	6,017	6,787	9,000
Brazil	6,261	4,524	8,500	Korea, South	8,728	8,483	8,000
Ukraine	397	2,464	5,500	EU-27 [2]	3,689	2,673	6,500
India.............	95	521	2,500	Egypt...........	5,268	4,397	5,400
South Africa........	1,281	548	2,000	Taiwan [3]	4,924	4,533	4,700
Serbia	(X)	(X)	1,700	Colombia........	1,857	3,151	3,600
Paraguay	564	1,911	1,700	Iran	1,265	2,300	3,200
EU-27 [2]	585	449	1,000	Malaysia	2,588	2,517	2,800
Canada	122	253	1,000	Algeria..........	1,600	2,026	2,400

– Represents or rounds to zero. X Not applicable. [1] Estimates. [2] See footnote 5, Table 1377. [3] See footnote 4, Table 1332.
Source: U.S. Department of Agriculture, Economic Research Service, unpublished data from the PS&D (Production, Supply, and Distribution) database.

Table 1375. Fisheries—Commercial Catch by Country: 1990 to 2008

[In thousands of metric tons, live weight (97,852 represents 97,852,000). Catch of fish, crustaceans, and mollusks. Includes aquaculture (the farming of aquatic organisms), but not marine mammals and aquatic plants]

Country	1990	2000	2005	2008	Country	1990	2000	2005	2008
World [1]	97,852	130,957	142,691	142,287	Russia	7,604	4,048	3,312	3,499
					Philippines	2,209	2,291	2,803	3,302
China [2]	31,136	41,568	49,469	47,527	Norway	1,754	3,191	3,055	3,275
India	3,800	5,609	6,653	7,584	Burma	743	1,169	2,217	3,169
Peru	6,874	10,665	9,415	7,406	Korea, South	2,843	2,118	2,076	2,418
Indonesia	3,022	4,909	5,893	6,647	Bangladesh	846	1,661	2,216	2,563
United States [3]	5,871	5,174	5,385	4,850	Malaysia	1,005	1,441	1,390	1,639
Japan	10,361	5,751	4,836	4,981	Mexico	1,383	1,369	1,438	1,740
Chile	5,195	4,692	5,027	4,398	Taiwan [2]	1,444	1,338	1,322	1,340
Vietnam	939	1,949	3,367	4,549	Iceland	1,508	1,986	1,673	1,289
Thailand	2,790	3,736	4,118	3,831	Canada	1,685	1,125	1,235	(NA)

[1] Includes other countries not shown separately. [2] See footnote 4, Table 1332. [3] The weight of clams, oysters, scallops, and other mollusks includes the shell weight.

Source: U.S. National Oceanic and Atmospheric Administration, National Marine Fisheries Service, *Fisheries of the United States*, annual. Data from Food and Agriculture Organization of the United Nations, Rome, Italy.

Table 1376. Meat Production by Type and Country: 2009 and 2010

[In thousands of metric tons (57,356 represents 57,356,000). Carcass weight basis for beef, veal, and pork. Broiler (chicken, 16-week-old) weight based on ready-to-cook equivalent]

Country	Beef and veal [1]		Country	Pork		Country	Broiler meat [2]	
	2009	2010, prel.		2009	2010, prel.		2009	2010, prel.
World [3]	57,356	57,323	World [3]	100,399	103,223	World [3]	72,293	75,991
United States	11,891	12,048	China [4]	48,905	51,070	United States	15,935	16,563
Brazil	8,935	9,115	EU-27 [5]	22,434	23,000	China [4]	12,100	12,550
EU-27 [5]	7,913	8,085	United States	10,442	10,187	Brazil	11,023	12,312
China [4]	5,764	5,600	Brazil	3,130	3,195	EU-27 [5]	8,756	9,095
India	2,514	2,830	Russia	1,844	1,920	Mexico	2,781	2,809
Argentina	3,380	2,600	Vietnam	1,850	1,870	India	2,550	2,650
Australia	2,129	2,087	Canada	1,789	1,772	Russia	2,060	2,310
Mexico	1,700	1,751	Japan	1,310	1,291	Argentina	1,500	1,600
Pakistan	1,457	1,486	Philippines	1,240	1,255	Iran	1,525	1,600
Russia	1,460	1,435	Mexico	1,162	1,165	Thailand	1,200	1,280
Canada	1,252	1,272	Taiwan [4]	779	768	South Africa	1,250	1,290

[1] May include meat of other bovines. [2] Excludes chicken paws. [3] Includes other countries, not shown separately. [4] See footnote 4, Table 1332. [5] See footnote 5, Table 1377.

Source: U.S. Department of Agriculture, Foreign Agricultural Service, *Livestock and Poultry: World Markets and Trade*, annual. See also <http://www.fas.usda.gov/currwmt.asp>.

Table 1377. Meat Consumption by Type and Country: 2009 and 2010

[In thousands of metric tons (56,668 represents 56,668,000). Carcass weight basis for beef, veal, and pork. Broiler (chicken, 16-week-old) weight based on ready-to-cook equivalent]

Country	Beef and veal [1]		Country	Pork		Country	Broiler [2]	
	2009	2010 [3]		2009	2010 [3]		2009	2010 [3]
World	56,668	56,544	World	100,268	102,953	World	71,860	75,127
United States	12,239	12,040	China [4]	48,823	51,097	United States	12,940	13,463
EU-27 [5]	8,262	8,185	EU-27 [5]	21,057	21,271	China [4]	12,210	12,457
Brazil	7,374	7,592	United States	9,013	8,653	Brazil	8,032	9,132
China [4]	5,749	5,589	Russia	2,688	2,773	EU-27 [5]	8,692	8,779
Russia	2,347	2,307	Brazil	2,423	2,577	Mexico	3,264	3,344
Argentina	2,727	2,305	Japan	2,467	2,485	Russia	2,966	2,923
India [6]	1,905	1,930	Vietnam	1,876	1,881	India	2,549	2,649
Mexico	1,971	1,944	Mexico	1,770	1,774	Japan	1,978	2,063
Pakistan	1,461	1,491	Korea, South	1,480	1,539	Iran	1,542	1,660
Japan	1,211	1,224	Philippines	1,298	1,358	South Africa	1,443	1,514
Canada	1,016	999	Ukraine	713	795	Argentina	1,327	1,395
Other countries	10,406	10,938	Other countries	6,660	6,750	Other countries	14,917	15,748

[1] May include meat of other bovines. [2] Excludes chicken paws. [3] Preliminary data. [4] See footnote 4, Table 1332. [5] European Union-27: Austria, Belgium, Bulgaria, Cyprus, Czech Republic, Denmark, Estonia, Finland, France, Germany, Greece, Hungary, Ireland, Italy, Latvia, Lithuania, Luxembourg, Malta, Netherlands, Poland, Portugal, Romania, Slovakia, Slovenia, Spain, Sweden, and United Kingdom. [6] Includes buffalo.

Source: U.S. Department of Agriculture, Foreign Agricultural Service, *Livestock and Poultry: World Markets and Trade*, annual. See also <http://www.fas.usda.gov/currwmt.asp>.

Table 1378. EU and U.S. Organic Land, Farm Sector, and Sales: 2007 and 2008

[EU numbers for land and farms include those certified organic and in-conversion; U.S. numbers include only certified organic farms and land. "Certified organic" means that agricultural products have been grown and processed according to USDA's national organic standards and certified by USDA-accredited state and private certification organizations. 1 hectare = 2.47 acres]

Country	2007 Total organic land (hectares)	2007 Organic farms (number)	2007 Farmland under organic production (percent)	2008 Total organic land (hectares)	2008 Organic farms (number)	2008 Farmland under organic production (percent)	2008 Retail sales (million Euros) [1]
United States	1,736,825	11,352	(NA)	1,949,781	12,941	0.6	16,529
Austria	372,026	19,997	13.4	491,825	19,961	17.4	810
Belgium	32,628	821	2.4	35,721	901	2.6	305
Denmark	145,393	2,835	5.5	150,104	2,753	4.6	724
Finland.	148,760	4,406	6.5	150,374	3,991	6.6	74
France	557,133	11,978	1.9	580,956	13,298	2.1	2,591
Germany	865,336	18,703	5.1	907,786	19,813	5.4	5,850
Greece.	278,397	23,769	3.3	317,824	24,057	3.8	58
Ireland	41,122	1,134	1.0	44,751	1,220	1.1	104
Italy	1,150,253	45,231	9.1	1,002,414	44,371	7.9	1,970
Luxembourg.	3,380	81	2.6	3,535	85	2.7	41
Netherlands.	47,019	1,374	2.5	50,434	1,402	2.6	537
Portugal	233,475	1,949	6.4	229,717	1,949	6.6	70
Spain	988,323	18,226	3.9	1,129,844	21,291	4.5	350
Sweden	248,104	3,028	8.0	336,439	3,686	10.8	623
United Kingdom.	660,200	5,506	4.2	737,631	5,383	4.6	2,494
EU-15 [2]	5,771,549	159,038	(NA)	6,169,355	164,161	(NA)	16,601

NA Not available. [1] U.S. dollars converted using average exchange rate for 2008, 0.78 euro per dollar. [2] European Union-15: Austria, Belgium, Denmark, Finland, France, Germany, Greece, Ireland, Italy, Luxembourg, Netherlands, Portugal, Spain, Sweden, and United Kingdom.

Source: U.S. Department of Agriculture, Economic Research Service, "Market-Led Versus Government-Facilitated Growth: Development of the U.S. and EU Organic Agricultural Sectors," August 2005, and unpublished data. See also <http://www.ers.usda.gov/Publications/WRS0505/>.

Table 1379. World Production of Major Mineral Commodities: 1990 to 2010

[5,347 represents 5,347,000,000]

Commodity	Unit	1990	2000	2009	2010, prel.	Leading producers, 2009
MINERAL FUELS						
Coal.	Mil. short tons	5,347	4,894	7,680	(NA)	China, [3] United States, India
Dry natural gas	Tril. cu. ft.	73.8	88.4	106.5	(NA)	United States, Russia, Canada
Natural gas plant liquids [1]	Mil. barrels [2].	1,694	2,359	2,957	3,062	United States, Saudi Arabia, Canada
Petroleum, crude	Mil. barrels [2].	22,079	25,000	26,374	27,026	Russia, Saudi Arabia, United States
NONMETALLIC MINERALS						
Cement, hydraulic	Mil. metric tons.	1,160	1,600	3,010	3,300	China, [3] India, United States
Diamond, gem and industrial. . .	Mil. carats	111	(NA)	129	125	Russia, Botswana, Congo (Kinshasa) [4]
Nitrogen in ammonia	Mil. metric tons. . . .	97.5	109.0	130.0	131.0	China, [3] India, Russia
Phosphate rock, marketable . . .	Mil. metric tons. . . .	162	133	166	176	China, [3] United States, Morocco, Western Sahara
Potash, marketable	Mil. metric tons. . . .	28.0	25.3	21.0	33.0	Canada, Russia, Belarus
Salt	Mil. metric tons. . . .	183	214	276	270	China, [3] United States, Germany
Sulfur, elemental basis	Mil. metric tons. . . .	58.0	57.2	68.0	68.0	United States, China, [3] Russia
METALS						
Aluminum [5]	Mil. metric tons. . . .	19.3	24.0	37.0	41.0	China, [3] Russia, Canada
Bauxite, gross weight	Mil. metric tons. . . .	113	135	199	211	Australia, China, [3] Brazil
Chromite, gross weight	1,000 metric tons. . .	13,200	14,400	19,300	22,000	South Africa, India, Kazakhstan
Copper, metal content [6].	1,000 metric tons. . .	8,950	13,200	15,900	16,200	Chile, Peru, United States
Gold, metal content	Metric tons.	2,180	2,550	2,450	2,500	China, [3] United States, Australia
Iron ore, gross weight [7]	Mil. metric tons. . . .	983	1,060	2,240	2,400	China, [3] Australia, Brazil
Lead, metal content [6].	1,000 metric tons. . .	3,370	3,100	3,860	4,100	China, [3] Australia, United States
Nickel, metal content [6].	1,000 metric tons. . .	974	1,250	1,390	1,550	Russia, Indonesia, Australia
Tin, metal content [6]	1,000 metric tons. . .	220	238	260	261	China, [3] Indonesia, Peru

NA Not available. [1] Excludes China. [2] 42-gallon barrels. [3] See footnote 4, Table 1332. [4] See footnote 5, Table 1332. [5] Unalloyed ingot metal. [6] Mine output. [7] Includes iron ore concentrates and iron ore agglomerates.

Source: Mineral fuels, U.S. Energy Information Administration, International Energy Statistics database, <http://tonto.eia.doe.gov/cfapps/ipdbproject/IEDIndex3.cfm>, accessed April 2011; nonmetallic minerals and metals, 1990, U.S. Bureau of Mines, thereafter, U.S. Geological Survey, *Minerals Yearbook*; *Annual Reports*; and *Mineral Commodity Summaries*, 2010.

Table 1380. World Primary Energy Production by Region and Type: 1980 to 2008

[In quadrillion Btu (287.5 represents 287,500,000,000,000,000). Btu = British thermal unit. For Btu conversion factors, see source]

Region and type	1980	1990	1995	2000	2003	2004	2005	2006	2007	2008 [1]
World total [2]	**287.5**	**349.9**	**363.5**	**394.3**	**421.1**	**444.5**	**457.7**	**467.2**	**475.2**	**491.4**
North America	83.2	92.0	96.2	98.9	98.7	99.0	98.5	100.5	100.9	101.7
United States	**67.2**	**70.9**	**71.3**	**71.5**	**70.3**	**70.4**	**69.6**	**71.0**	**71.6**	**73.4**
Central and South America	12.1	16.7	21.1	26.0	25.7	27.0	28.0	29.0	29.0	29.6
Europe	40.2	46.9	49.0	50.6	50.3	50.3	48.6	47.3	46.3	46.5
Eurasia [3]	56.5	72.1	51.9	55.5	62.6	65.7	67.5	69.3	70.8	71.7
Middle East	42.3	41.0	48.3	57.5	57.6	62.2	65.3	65.3	64.5	68.2
Africa	17.4	21.6	24.1	27.8	30.2	32.1	34.7	35.4	36.5	37.5
Asia and Oceania	35.8	59.6	72.9	78.0	96.0	108.2	115.1	120.4	127.0	136.3
Petroleum [4]	133.1	136.2	136.6	151.7	154.6	162.4	164.7	164.9	164.0	166.0
Dry natural gas	54.8	76.1	80.4	91.0	97.7	99.9	102.9	106.6	108.9	113.2
Coal	71.2	90.9	88.0	89.1	105.3	116.6	123.2	127.6	134.0	142.0
Hydroelectric power	17.9	22.3	25.3	26.7	26.7	27.9	28.9	29.7	29.6	30.7
Nuclear electric power	7.6	20.4	23.3	25.7	26.4	27.3	27.5	27.8	27.1	27.2
Geothermal, solar, wind, wood, and waste	0.5	1.6	2.1	3.0	3.7	4.0	4.4	4.7	5.3	5.9

[1] Preliminary. [2] Includes geothermal, solar, and wood and waste energy produced in the United States and not used for generating electricity, not shown separately by type. [3] Prior to 1992, data were for the former U.S.S.R. only. [4] Includes only crude oil, including lease condensate and natural gas plant liquids.

Source: U.S. Energy Information Administration, International Energy Statistics database, <http://www.eia.gov/cfapps/ipdbproject/IEDIndex3.cfm>, accessed April 2011.

Table 1381. World Primary Energy Consumption by Region and Type: 1980 to 2008

[In quadrillion Btu (283.2 represents 283,200,000,000,000,000). Btu = British thermal unit. For Btu conversion factors, see source]

Region and type	1980	1990	1995	2000	2003	2004	2005	2006	2007	2008 [1]
World total [2,3]	**283.2**	**347.7**	**365.4**	**397.5**	**425.7**	**448.9**	**461.6**	**470.9**	**482.3**	**493.0**
North America	91.6	100.7	109.3	119.3	118.8	121.3	122.0	121.7	123.9	121.9
United States	**78.1**	**85.0**	**91.8**	**99.8**	**98.7**	**101.0**	**101.0**	**100.5**	**102.5**	**100.6**
Central and South America	11.5	14.5	17.6	20.8	21.6	22.4	23.1	24.3	24.6	25.8
Europe	71.8	76.3	76.7	81.2	83.9	85.4	85.8	86.4	85.8	85.7
Eurasia [4]	46.7	61.0	42.2	40.4	42.8	44.1	44.6	43.8	45.4	45.8
Middle East	5.8	11.2	13.8	17.3	19.8	21.0	22.9	23.9	23.9	25.5
Africa	6.8	9.5	10.7	12.0	13.3	14.0	14.5	14.6	15.2	16.1
Asia and Oceania	48.9	74.5	95.1	106.5	125.5	140.7	148.5	156.1	163.5	(NA)
Petroleum [5]	131.0	136.6	143.1	156.4	161.9	167.6	170.7	171.5	172.8	172.2
Dry natural gas	53.9	75.4	81.1	90.9	98.2	101.7	105.0	107.4	111.1	114.4
Coal	69.9	89.1	87.9	92.4	106.6	118.0	122.5	127.1	133.5	139.2

NA Not available. [1] Preliminary. [2] See footnote 2, Table 1380. [3] Includes hydroelectric power, nuclear electric power, and geothermal, solar, wind, wood, and waste, not shown separately. [4] Prior to 1992, data were for the former U.S.S.R. only. [5] Includes all refined petroleum products.

Source: U.S. Energy Information Administration, International Energy Statistics database, <http://www.eia.gov/cfapps/ipdbproject/IEDIndex3.cfm>, accessed April 2011.

Table 1382. World Energy Consumption by Region and Energy Source, 2005 to 2007, and Projections, 2015 to 2030

[In quadrillion Btu (472.7 represents 472,700,000,000,000,000). Btu = British thermal units. For Btu conversion factors, see source. Energy totals include net imports of coal coke and electricity generated from biomass in the United States. Totals may not equal sum of components due to independent rounding. The electricity portion of the national consumption values consists of generation for domestic use plus an adjustment for electricity trade based on a fuel's share of total generation in the exporting country]

Region and energy source	2005	2006	2007	Projections			
				2015	2020	2025	2030
World, total	**472.7**	**483.1**	**495.2**	**543.5**	**590.5**	**638.7**	**686.5**
North America	122.4	121.8	123.7	124.3	129.4	134.9	140.2
United States	**100.5**	**99.8**	**101.7**	**101.6**	**105.0**	**108.3**	**111.2**
Western Europe	82.4	82.9	82.3	82.0	83.0	85.0	86.5
Industrialized Asia	39.0	39.5	39.7	39.7	41.8	43.3	44.8
Eastern Europe and former Soviet Union	50.4	51.0	51.5	52.4	54.2	56.2	57.8
Developing Asia	112.6	119.6	127.1	159.3	187.8	217.0	246.9
Middle East	22.8	23.9	25.1	32.9	36.5	39.1	41.8
Africa	17.2	17.3	17.8	20.8	22.5	24.6	26.5
Central and South America	26.0	27.1	28.0	32.1	35.5	38.7	42.2
Oil	170.4	172.8	174.7	179.3	186.0	197.2	210.0
Natural gas	106.3	108.3	112.1	129.1	141.2	150.2	155.8
Coal	122.3	126.4	132.4	139.1	152.4	167.8	185.6
Nuclear	27.5	27.8	27.1	32.2	37.4	41.1	43.9
Other	46.2	47.9	48.8	63.8	73.4	82.4	91.2

Source: U.S. Energy Information Administration, International Energy Outlook 2010, July 2010. See also <http://www.eia.gov/oiaf/ieo/ieorefcase.html>.

Table 1383. Energy Consumption by Country: 2000 and 2008

[397.5 represents 397,500,000,000,000,000. See text of this section for general comments about the data. For data qualifications for countries and Btu conversion factors, see source]

Country	Total (quad. Btu) 2000	Total (quad. Btu) 2008	Per capita (mil. Btu) 2000	Per capita (mil. Btu) 2008	Country	Total (quad. Btu) 2000	Total (quad. Btu) 2008	Per capita (mil. Btu) 2000	Per capita (mil. Btu) 2008
World, total	**397.5**	**493.0**	**65.3**	**73.6**	Japan	22.4	21.9	177.0	171.8
United States	**99.8**	**100.6**	**353.8**	**330.4**	Korea, North	0.9	0.9	40.4	39.2
Algeria	1.2	1.7	40.7	50.6	Korea, South	7.8	9.9	167.4	204.3
Argentina	2.7	3.3	71.5	81.4	Kuwait	0.9	1.2	460.8	459.2
Australia	4.8	5.8	253.6	273.8	Libya	0.6	0.8	122.9	126.7
Austria	1.4	1.5	171.6	185.1	Malaysia	2.0	2.5	85.4	89.6
Bahrain	0.4	0.5	574.7	762.4	Mexico	6.4	7.3	63.8	66.5
Bangladesh	0.5	0.9	3.8	5.8	Morocco	0.4	0.6	15.9	18.1
Belarus	1.1	1.2	104.9	119.7	Netherlands	3.8	4.1	238.5	248.6
Belgium	2.7	2.9	266.3	280.0	New Zealand	0.8	0.9	223.2	211.5
Brazil	8.5	10.6	48.4	54.1	Nigeria	0.8	1.1	6.6	7.4
Bulgaria	0.9	0.8	111.0	114.8	Norway	2.0	1.9	436.1	418.4
Burma	0.2	0.3	3.3	5.1	Pakistan	1.9	2.5	12.2	13.9
Canada	13.1	14.0	420.0	422.4	Peru	0.5	0.7	20.3	23.8
Chile	1.0	1.2	67.2	73.9	Philippines	1.3	1.3	15.4	13.5
China [1]	36.4	85.1	28.8	64.6	Poland	3.6	3.9	93.8	101.0
Colombia	1.2	1.4	30.1	31.8	Portugal	1.1	1.1	103.6	99.3
Congo (Kinshasa) [2]	0.1	0.1	1.8	1.6	Romania	1.6	1.7	70.7	76.0
Cuba	0.5	0.4	41.2	36.4	Russia	27.2	30.4	185.5	216.2
Czech Republic	1.4	1.6	135.9	158.0	Saudi Arabia	4.9	6.7	227.7	270.0
Denmark	0.9	0.8	163.7	152.5	Serbia	(X)	0.7	(X)	79.1
Ecuador	0.3	0.5	27.7	34.6	South Africa	4.6	5.7	101.7	117.1
Egypt	2.0	3.2	30.8	41.0	Spain	5.5	6.5	136.3	141.7
Finland	1.2	1.3	234.9	246.3	Sweden	2.3	2.2	254.2	245.3
France	10.9	11.3	181.7	180.3	Switzerland	1.3	1.3	177.3	173.1
Germany	14.3	14.4	173.5	174.3	Syria	0.8	0.8	47.5	39.2
Greece	1.3	1.5	126.7	137.1	Taiwan [1]	3.8	4.6	171.6	199.0
Hong Kong	0.8	1.1	121.0	153.9	Thailand	2.6	4.0	41.5	59.8
Hungary	1.0	1.1	100.8	110.4	Trinidad and Tobago	0.4	0.9	336.0	720.6
India	13.5	20.0	13.4	17.5	Tunisia	0.3	0.3	31.5	33.6
Indonesia	3.9	5.8	18.3	24.5	Turkey	3.2	4.3	47.0	56.8
Iran	5.0	8.1	73.1	108.2	Ukraine	5.8	6.3	117.4	137.0
Iraq	1.1	1.4	47.8	48.2	United Arab Emirates	1.9	3.3	579.7	704.9
Ireland	0.6	0.7	157.0	152.7	United Kingdom	9.7	9.3	163.8	151.0
Israel	0.8	0.9	132.7	120.9	Venezuela	2.8	3.2	117.9	120.9
Italy	7.6	7.9	132.2	135.7	Vietnam	0.7	1.6	9.3	18.3

X Not applicable. [1] See footnote 4, Table 1332. [2] See footnote 5, Table 1332.

Source: U.S. Energy Information Administration, International Energy Statistics database, <http://www.eia.gov/cfapps/ipdbproject/IEDIndex3.cfm> accessed April 2011.

Table 1384. World Daily Crude Oil Production by Major Producing Country: 1980 to 2010

[In thousands of barrels per day (59,558 barrels represents 59,558,000 barrels)]

Country	1980	1990	1995	2000	2005	2007	2008	2009	2010
World, total [1]	**59,558**	**60,492**	**62,385**	**68,492**	**73,712**	**72,986**	**73,655**	**72,259**	**74,043**
United States	**8,597**	**7,355**	**6,560**	**5,822**	**5,178**	**5,064**	**4,950**	**5,361**	**5,512**
Algeria	1,106	1,175	1,202	1,254	1,797	1,834	1,825	1,741	1,729
Angola	150	475	646	746	1,250	1,744	1,981	1,907	1,939
Argentina	491	483	715	761	704	679	661	654	641
Australia	380	575	562	722	446	465	477	475	436
Brazil	182	631	695	1,269	1,634	1,748	1,812	1,950	2,055
Canada	1,435	1,553	1,805	1,977	2,369	2,628	2,579	2,579	2,734
China [2]	2,114	2,774	2,990	3,249	3,609	3,729	3,790	3,799	4,076
Colombia	126	440	585	691	526	531	588	671	786
Ecuador	204	285	392	395	532	511	505	486	486
Egypt	595	873	920	768	658	637	581	539	523
India	182	660	703	646	665	698	694	680	752
Indonesia	1,577	1,462	1,503	1,428	1,067	964	972	946	943
Iran	1,662	3,088	3,643	3,696	4,139	3,912	4,050	4,037	4,080
Iraq	2,514	2,040	560	2,571	1,878	2,086	2,375	2,391	2,399
Kazakhstan	(X)	(X)	414	718	1,288	1,360	1,345	1,455	1,525
Kuwait	1,656	1,175	2,057	2,079	2,529	2,464	2,586	2,350	2,300
Libya	1,787	1,375	1,390	1,410	1,633	1,702	1,736	1,650	1,650
Malaysia	283	619	682	690	631	588	609	578	554
Mexico	1,936	2,553	2,618	3,012	3,334	3,076	2,792	2,601	2,576
Nigeria	2,055	1,810	1,993	2,165	2,627	2,350	2,165	2,208	2,455
Norway	486	1,630	2,766	3,222	2,698	2,270	2,182	2,067	1,869
Oman	282	685	851	970	774	710	757	813	865
Qatar	472	406	442	737	835	851	924	927	1,127
Russia	(X)	(X)	5,995	6,479	9,043	9,437	9,357	9,495	9,674
Saudi Arabia	9,900	6,410	8,231	8,404	9,550	8,722	9,261	8,250	8,900
United Arab Emirates	1,709	2,117	2,233	2,368	2,535	2,603	2,681	2,413	2,415
United Kingdom	1,622	1,820	101	68	34	26	26	24	20
Venezuela	2,168	2,137	2,750	3,155	2,565	2,433	2,394	2,239	2,146
Yemen	–	193	345	438	400	319	298	285	257

– Represents zero. X Not applicable. [1] Includes countries not shown separately. [2] See footnote 4, Table 1332.

Source: U.S. Energy Information Administration, International Energy Statistics database, <http://www.eia.gov/cfapps/ipdbproject/IEDIndex3.cfm>, accessed April 2011.

Table 1385. World Dry Natural Gas Production by Major Producing Country: 1980 to 2009

[In trillion cubic feet (53.37 represents 53,370,000,000,000)]

Country	Natural gas production								
	1980	1990	2000	2004	2005	2006	2007	2008	2009
World, total [1]	**53.37**	**73.79**	**88.40**	**97.03**	**99.79**	**103.42**	**105.63**	**109.92**	**106.47**
United States	**19.40**	**17.81**	**19.18**	**18.59**	**18.05**	**18.50**	**19.27**	**20.29**	**20.96**
Russia	(X)	(X)	20.63	22.39	22.62	23.17	23.06	23.39	20.61
Canada	2.76	3.85	6.47	6.48	6.56	6.55	6.42	6.05	5.63
Iran	0.25	0.84	2.13	2.96	3.66	3.84	3.95	4.11	4.63
Norway	0.92	0.98	1.87	2.95	3.07	3.09	3.17	3.50	3.65
Qatar	0.18	0.28	1.03	1.38	1.62	1.79	2.23	2.72	3.15
China [2]	0.51	0.51	0.96	1.44	1.76	2.07	2.45	2.69	2.93
Algeria	0.41	1.79	2.94	2.83	3.15	3.08	3.00	3.05	2.88
Netherlands	3.40	2.69	2.56	3.04	2.77	2.73	2.69	2.96	2.79
Saudi Arabia	0.33	1.08	1.76	2.32	2.52	2.59	2.63	2.84	2.77
Indonesia	0.65	1.60	2.24	2.03	2.00	2.20	2.42	2.47	2.56
Egypt	0.03	0.29	0.65	1.15	1.50	1.60	1.64	2.08	2.21
Uzbekistan	(X)	(X)	1.99	2.11	2.11	2.22	2.30	2.39	2.17
United Kingdom	1.32	1.75	3.83	3.43	3.12	2.82	2.55	2.47	2.09
Malaysia	0.06	0.65	1.60	1.90	1.97	1.97	1.96	2.16	2.07
Mexico	0.90	0.90	1.31	1.25	1.35	1.74	1.68	1.69	1.77
United Arab Emirates	0.20	0.78	1.36	1.63	1.66	1.72	1.78	1.77	1.72
Australia	0.31	0.72	1.16	1.31	1.44	1.51	1.55	1.58	1.67
Argentina	0.28	0.63	1.32	1.58	1.61	1.63	1.58	1.56	1.46
Trinidad and Tobago	0.08	0.18	0.49	0.99	1.07	1.29	1.38	1.39	1.43
India	0.05	0.40	0.79	1.00	1.06	1.09	1.11	1.14	1.42
Pakistan	0.29	0.48	0.86	0.97	1.09	1.28	1.30	1.34	1.36
Turkmenistan	(X)	(X)	1.64	2.07	2.22	2.23	2.43	2.49	1.35
Thailand	–	0.21	0.66	0.79	0.84	0.86	0.92	1.02	1.09
Oman	0.03	0.10	0.32	0.61	0.70	0.84	0.85	0.85	0.87
Nigeria	0.04	0.13	0.44	0.77	0.79	1.01	1.15	1.16	0.82
Ukraine	(X)	(X)	0.64	0.68	0.69	0.69	0.69	0.70	0.72
Bangladesh	0.05	0.16	0.34	0.46	0.49	0.54	0.57	0.63	0.70
Venezuela	0.52	0.76	0.96	0.96	0.83	0.92	0.73	0.73	0.65
Azerbaijan	(X)	(X)	0.20	0.18	0.21	0.24	0.38	0.59	0.58

– Represents or rounds to zero. X Not applicable. [1] Includes countries not shown separately. [2] See footnote 4, Table 1332.
Source: U. S. Energy Information Administration, International Energy Statistics database, <http://www.eia.gov/cfapps /ipdbproject/IEDIndex3.cfm>, accessed April 2011.

Table 1386. World Coal Production by Major Producing Country: 1980 to 2009

[In millions of short tons (4,181.9 represents 4,181,900,000)]

Country	1980	1990	2000	2004	2005	2006	2007	2008	2009
World, total [1]	**4,181.9**	**5,346.7**	**4,893.7**	**6,222.8**	**6,553.2**	**6,773.3**	**7,088.0**	**7,504.5**	**7,679.8**
China [2]	683.6	1,190.4	1,271.5	2,299.7	2,500.9	2,573.9	2,781.1	3,086.5	3,362.0
United States	**829.7**	**1,029.1**	**1,073.6**	**1,112.1**	**1,131.5**	**1,162.7**	**1,146.6**	**1,171.8**	**1,072.8**
India	125.8	247.6	370.0	446.7	473.3	500.2	531.5	568.4	611.4
Australia	115.2	225.5	338.1	388.2	404.9	405.0	430.1	438.5	440.1
Indonesia	0.6	11.6	84.5	157.2	188.2	249.7	287.2	301.6	332.4
Russia	(X)	(X)	264.9	285.4	311.8	313.7	318.6	336.2	327.1
South Africa	131.9	193.2	248.9	267.7	270.1	269.8	273.0	278.1	272.6
Germany	(X)	(X)	226.0	232.7	227.0	220.6	225.5	214.3	203.7
Poland	253.5	237.1	179.2	178.3	175.0	171.1	159.8	158.0	148.3
Kazakhstan	(X)	(X)	85.4	95.8	95.4	106.1	107.8	122.4	111.9
Central African Republic	12.1	32.9	58.8	72.9	80.6	88.5	92.6	97.7	98.5
Colombia	4.5	22.6	42.0	59.2	65.1	72.3	77.1	81.0	80.9
Turkey	20.8	52.3	69.7	51.1	64.3	70.8	83.1	87.5	79.8
Greece	25.6	57.2	70.4	77.2	76.5	71.4	73.1	72.4	71.3
Canada	40.4	75.3	76.2	72.7	72.0	72.8	76.5	74.7	69.4
Czech Republic	(X)	(X)	71.8	68.1	68.4	69.3	69.0	66.4	62.2
Ukraine	(X)	(X)	68.8	65.7	66.5	68.0	65.0	65.7	60.6
Vietnam	5.7	5.1	12.8	28.1	35.7	42.9	46.9	44.8	48.4
Serbia	(X)	(X)	(X)	(X)	(X)	40.5	40.9	42.7	42.2
Korea, North	48.6	51.0	32.8	35.0	38.2	38.7	33.4	35.6	41.3
Romania	38.8	42.1	32.3	35.0	34.3	38.5	39.4	39.5	33.7
Bulgaria	33.3	34.9	29.2	29.2	27.2	28.3	31.4	31.7	30.0
United Kingdom	143.8	104.1	33.7	27.0	22.1	19.9	18.2	19.4	19.7
Thailand	1.6	13.7	19.6	22.1	23.0	21.0	20.1	20.2	19.4
Estonia	(X)	(X)	12.9	15.4	16.1	15.5	18.2	17.8	16.5
Mongolia	5.3	7.9	5.7	7.6	8.3	9.2	10.4	11.3	12.3
Mexico	4.0	8.6	12.5	10.9	11.9	12.7	13.8	12.7	11.6
Bosnia and Herzegovina	(X)	(X)	8.2	9.8	10.1	11.2	11.7	12.9	10.5
Spain	30.9	39.2	25.9	22.6	21.5	20.3	18.9	11.2	10.4
Hungary	28.7	19.7	15.5	12.4	10.5	11.0	10.8	10.4	9.9

X Not applicable. Z Less than 50,000 short tons. [1] Includes countries not shown separately. [2] See footnote 4, Table 1332.
Source: U.S. Energy Information Administration, International Energy Statistics database, <http://www.eia.gov/cfapps /ipdbproject/IEDIndex3.cfm>, accessed April 2011.

Table 1387. Net Electricity Generation by Type and Country: 2008

[19,103.2 represents 19,103,200,000,000. kWh = kilowatt hours]

Country	Total[1] (bil. kWh)	Percent distribution Thermal[2]	Hydro	Nuclear	Country	Total[1] (bil. kWh)	Percent distribution Thermal[2]	Hydro	Nuclear
World, total[3]	**19,103.2**	**67.4**	**16.3**	**13.6**	Norway	139.7	0.4	98.9	–
					Thailand	139.0	91.6	5.1	–
United States	**4,119.4**	**71.0**	**6.2**	**19.6**	Egypt	123.9	87.6	11.7	–
China[4]	3,221.2	81.3	16.2	2.0	Venezuela	118.1	26.6	73.4	–
Japan	1,015.2	65.8	7.4	24.2	Argentina	115.4	66.9	26.0	6.0
Russia	984.5	67.6	16.6	15.7	Netherlands	101.3	85.6	0.1	3.9
India	785.5	82.0	14.4	1.7	Malaysia	91.9	92.0	8.0	–
Canada	632.2	24.2	59.9	14.1	Pakistan	87.7	66.7	31.4	2.0
Germany	594.7	61.3	3.5	23.7	United Arab Emirates	81.1	100.0	–	–
France	541.9	9.5	11.6	77.0	Belgium	78.4	38.7	0.5	55.2
Brazil	454.8	12.2	80.4	3.1	Czech Republic	78.4	63.4	2.6	32.2
Korea, South	418.2	64.8	0.7	34.3	Kazakhstan	75.9	90.3	9.7	–
United Kingdom	361.8	80.4	1.4	13.8	Finland	73.6	33.2	23.0	29.6
Italy	295.0	80.5	14.0	–	Vietnam	70.0	63.2	36.8	–
Spain	293.5	60.7	7.9	19.1	Switzerland	64.4	1.3	55.4	40.9
Mexico	245.5	77.3	15.8	3.8	Romania	62.0	55.3	27.4	17.2
Australia	242.2	92.7	4.9	–	Austria	61.9	29.4	60.7	–
South Africa	238.3	95.0	0.5	4.7	Chile	60.3	55.9	39.2	–
Taiwan[4]	221.4	78.8	1.9	17.7	Greece	59.0	91.1	5.6	–
Iran	201.7	97.6	2.3	–	Philippines	57.4	65.8	17.0	–
Saudi Arabia	191.9	100.0	–	–	Paraguay	54.9	(Z)	100.0	–
Turkey	188.8	81.6	17.4	–	Israel	53.0	99.6	(Z)	–
Ukraine	181.3	47.3	6.2	46.5	Colombia	51.0	14.3	84.5	–
Poland	146.1	95.8	1.5	–	Uzbekistan	47.0	76.1	23.9	–
Sweden	145.1	2.4	47.1	41.8	Portugal	43.0	66.7	15.6	–
Indonesia	141.2	86.3	8.1	–	Bulgaria	41.7	58.3	6.7	35.3

– Represents zero. Z Less than 0.05 percent. [1] Includes thermal, hydro, nuclear, and geothermal, solar, wind, and wood and waste generation, some of which are not shown separately. [2] Electricity generated from coal, oil, and gas. [3] Includes countries not shown separately. [4] See footnote 4, Table 1332.

Source: U.S. Energy Information Administration, International Energy Statistics database, <http://www.eia.gov/cfapps/ipdbproject/IEDIndex3.cfm>, accessed April 2011.

Table 1388. Commercial Nuclear Power Generation by Country: 1990 to 2010

[Generation for calendar years; other data as of December (1,743.9 represents 1,743,900,000,000). kWh = kilowatt-hours. kW = kilowatts]

Country	Reactors 1990	2000	2009	2010	Gross electricity generated (bil. kWh) 1990	2000	2009	2010	Gross capacity (1,000 kW) 1990	2000	2009	2010
Total	**368**	**433**	**441**	**441**	**1,743.9**	**2,540.5**	**2,546.6**	**2,591.9**	**301,745**	**373,804**	**397,295**	**396,693**
United States	112	104	104	104	606.4	789.1	833.6	864.1	105,998	103,129	107,023	107,642
Argentina	2	2	2	2	7.0	6.2	8.2	7.1	1,005	1,005	1,005	1,005
Armenia	(X)	1	1	1	(X)	(NA)	2.5	2.4	(X)	408	408	408
Belgium	7	7	7	7	42.7	48.2	47.2	47.9	5,740	5,995	6,207	6,211
Brazil	1	2	2	2	2.0	6.1	12.9	14.5	657	1,966	2,007	2,007
Bulgaria	(X)	6	2	2	(X)	(NA)	15.3	15.2	(X)	3,760	2,000	2,000
Canada	19	21	21	19	74.0	73.8	90.9	52.2	13,855	15,795	15,367	14,331
China[1]	(NA)	2	11	13	(NA)	14.7	(NA)	(NA)	(NA)	1,968	9,014	10,744
Czech Republic	(X)	4	6	6	(X)	13.6	27.1	27.8	(X)	1,760	3,876	3,892
Finland	4	4	4	4	18.9	22.5	23.5	22.8	2,400	2,760	2,800	2,820
France	58	57	58	58	314.1	395.7	410.0	428.2	58,862	62,920	65,880	65,880
Germany	22	19	17	17	147.2	169.7	134.9	140.5	23,973	22,234	21,497	21,517
Great Britain	42	33	19	19	68.8	83.6	(NA)	(NA)	15,274	15,272	12,540	11,709
Hungary	4	4	4	4	13.6	14.1	15.4	15.7	1,760	1,851	2,000	2,000
India	6	13	17	19	6.0	15.5	17.0	23.3	1,330	2,960	4,120	4,560
Italy	2	(NA)	(NA)	(NA)	–	(NA)	(NA)	(NA)	1,132	(NA)	(NA)	(NA)
Japan	40	52	56	54	191.9	319.8	272.3	292.3	31,645	45,082	50,492	48,847
Korea, South	9	16	20	20	52.8	108.9	147.8	149.7	7,616	13,768	18,393	18,509
Lithuania	(X)	2	1	–	(X)	7.8	11.6	–	(X)	3,000	1,300	–
Mexico	1	2	2	2	2.1	8.2	10.5	5.8	675	1,350	1,364	1,502
Netherlands	2	1	1	1	3.4	3.9	4.2	3.9	540	480	515	515
Pakistan	1	1	2	2	0.4	0.4	2.9	2.7	137	137	462	462
Romania	(X)	1	2	2	(X)	5.5	11.7	11.6	(X)	706	1,412	1,412
Russia	(X)	29	31	32	(X)	128.9	163.3	167.8	(X)	21,266	23,242	24,242
Slovakia	(X)	6	4	4	(X)	16.5	(NA)	(NA)	(X)	2,640	1,894	1,894
Slovenia	1	1	1	1	4.6	4.8	5.7	5.6	664	664	727	727
South Africa	2	2	2	2	8.9	13.6	12.1	13.5	1,930	1,930	1,930	1,930
Spain	10	9	8	8	54.3	62.2	52.9	61.9	7,984	7,808	7,735	7,800
Sweden	12	11	10	10	68.2	57.3	52.3	58.2	10,344	9,844	9,685	9,743
Switzerland	5	5	5	5	23.6	26.3	27.5	26.5	3,079	3,322	3,370	3,405
Taiwan[1]	6	6	6	6	32.9	38.5	41.6	41.6	5,146	5,144	5,144	5,144
Ukraine	(X)	14	15	15	(X)	77.3	82.2	89.1	(X)	12,880	13,880	13,835

– Represents zero. NA Not available. X Not applicable. [1] See footnote 4, Table 1332.

Source: Platts Energy, A Division of The McGraw-Hill Companies Inc., New York, NY, *Nucleonics Week*, February issue (copyright).

Table 1389. Carbon Dioxide Emissions From Consumption of Fossil Fuels by Country: 1990 to 2009

[In million metric tons of carbon dioxide (21,616.0 represents 21,616,000,000). Includes carbon dioxide emissions from the consumption of petroleum, natural gas, coal, and the flaring of natural gas]

Region/Country	1990	1995	2000	2005	2006	2007	2008	2009
World, total [1]	**21,616.0**	**22,150.1**	**23,803.6**	**28,366.2**	**28,939.2**	**29,724.5**	**30,399.5**	**30,313.2**
United States	**5,041.0**	**5,319.9**	**5,861.8**	**5,991.5**	**5,913.7**	**6,018.1**	**5,833.1**	**5,424.5**
Australia	267.6	289.1	356.3	397.2	400.9	410.4	425.3	417.7
Brazil	237.3	289.1	344.4	369.7	383.1	400.4	426.5	425.2
Canada	470.6	508.7	573.3	623.4	597.2	610.0	598.5	541.0
China [2]	2,269.7	2,861.7	2,849.7	5,512.7	5,817.1	6,256.7	6,800.5	7,706.8
France	367.7	372.5	401.7	414.0	416.4	423.1	428.5	396.7
Germany	(X)	890.8	854.7	847.4	850.6	827.2	823.1	765.6
India	578.6	870.2	1,003.0	1,183.3	1,282.7	1,368.4	1,463.3	1,591.1
Indonesia	156.0	214.8	266.3	330.6	360.3	390.2	405.4	414.9
Iran	202.1	262.2	320.6	449.2	475.8	489.3	512.1	528.6
Italy	415.4	431.4	447.7	471.9	467.5	459.5	449.7	407.9
Japan	1,047.0	1,116.2	1,201.4	1,241.3	1,239.9	1,254.4	1,215.5	1,098.0
Korea, South	242.1	381.4	438.8	493.8	484.2	503.1	521.8	528.1
Mexico	302.2	321.4	383.0	397.8	437.0	444.3	452.1	443.6
Netherlands	211.1	222.6	246.3	268.5	269.9	258.1	249.5	248.9
Poland	333.8	308.2	292.6	287.6	299.1	295.9	294.8	285.8
Russia	(X)	1,603.1	1,556.1	1,652.7	1,675.5	1,627.2	1,672.0	1,556.7
Saudi Arabia	208.0	235.3	290.5	405.5	406.1	396.5	425.7	438.2
South Africa	298.0	347.5	386.0	432.5	444.6	463.7	483.7	451.2
Spain	224.1	243.4	317.5	382.9	376.1	387.9	360.1	329.9
Taiwan [2]	118.3	182.4	256.1	288.8	297.1	293.7	290.4	279.1
Thailand	83.9	145.1	161.8	241.8	237.2	247.4	255.0	254.9
Turkey	129.5	153.2	201.9	230.9	251.0	280.2	272.9	253.1
Ukraine	(X)	421.4	324.9	353.6	333.3	354.1	352.8	252.5
United Kingdom	601.8	560.1	560.3	583.1	585.5	569.9	563.9	519.9

X Not applicable. [1] Includes other countries not shown separately. [2] See footnote 4, Table 1332.
Source: U.S. Energy Information Administration, International Energy Statistics database, <http://www.eia.gov/cfapps /ipdbproject/IEDIndex3.cfm>, accessed April 2011.

Table 1390. Average Temperatures and Precipitation—Selected International Cities

[In degrees Fahrenheit, except as noted. Data are generally based on a standard 30-year period; for details, see source. For data on U.S. cities, see Tables 391–396. Minus sign (–) indicates degrees below zero]

City	January					July				
	Average high	Average low	Warmest	Coldest	Average precipitation (inches)	Average high	Average low	Warmest	Coldest	Average precipitation (inches)
Amsterdam, Netherlands	41	34	57	3	3.1	69	55	90	39	2.9
Athens, Greece	55	44	70	28	1.9	89	73	108	61	0.2
Baghdad, Iraq	58	38	75	25	1.1	110	78	122	61	–
Bangkok, Thailand	89	71	95	54	0.4	90	78	99	72	6.2
Beijing, China	34	17	54	1	0.2	86	72	104	63	8.8
Berlin, Germany	35	26	58	–11	(NA)	73	56	95	41	(NA)
Bogota, Colombia	66	43	84	27	1.9	64	47	82	32	1.8
Brasilia, Brazil	81	64	95	54	(NA)	79	52	97	37	(NA)
Buenos Aires, Argentina	85	64	104	44	4.2	58	41	88	23	2.3
Cairo, Egypt	65	49	86	32	0.2	93	72	108	63	–
Frankfurt, Germany	38	30	56	–4	1.8	75	57	97	38	2.4
Geneva, Switzerland	39	29	57	–2	2.2	77	56	96	41	2.8
Hong Kong, China	67	58	79	43	1.1	89	81	97	70	14.3
Istanbul, Turkey	46	37	64	16	3.7	82	66	100	50	0.7
Jakarta, Indonesia	83	75	92	72	(NA)	88	74	92	67	(NA)
Karachi, Pakistan	76	55	93	39	0.3	89	83	109	68	3.5
Lagos, Nigeria	82	79	93	64	(NA)	79	76	88	70	(NA)
London, England	45	36	61	15	2.4	72	56	93	45	1.8
Madrid, Spain	51	32	68	14	1.8	90	61	104	46	0.4
Manila, Philippines	86	71	95	61	0.8	88	76	99	70	15.9
Mexico City, Mexico	70	45	86	26	0.3	74	56	86	37	5.1
Montreal, Canada	21	7	52	–31	2.8	79	61	93	43	3.4
Moscow, Russia	21	11	46	–33	1.4	71	55	95	41	3.2
Nairobi, Kenya	77	58	88	45	1.8	71	54	85	43	0.5
New Delhi, India	68	48	85	32	0.9	93	81	111	70	7.9
Paris, France	43	34	59	1	(NA)	75	58	95	41	(NA)
Rio De Janeiro, Brazil	91	74	109	64	5.3	81	64	102	52	1.8
Rome, Italy	55	39	64	19	3.2	83	66	100	55	0.6
Seoul, Korea	33	21	55	–1	(NA)	82	71	97	55	(NA)
Singapore, Singapore	85	73	100	66	9.4	86	76	99	70	5.9
Sydney, Australia	79	65	109	49	4.0	62	44	80	32	2.5
Tel Aviv, Israel	62	46	84	32	(NA)	87	69	100	50	(NA)
Tokyo, Japan	48	35	66	25	2.0	82	71	95	55	5.3
Toronto, Canada	28	15	59	–24	1.9	79	60	99	45	2.8

– Represents zero. NA Not available.
Source: U.S. National Oceanic and Atmospheric Administration, *Climates of the World*. See also <http://www.ncdc.noaa.gov /oa/oldpubs/>.

Table 1391. Key Global Telecom Indicators for the World Telecommunication Service Sector: 2005 to 2010

[In millions (1,259 represents 1,259,000,000), except as indicated]

Indicators	2005	2007	2008	2009	2010
NUMBER (mil.)					
Fixed telephone lines [1]	1,259	1,271	1,240	1,215	1,197
Mobile cellular subscribers	2,217	3,354	4,012	4,652	5,282
Internet users	1,036	1,393	1,611	1,858	2,084
Fixed broadband subscriptions	216	351	413	471	555
Mobile broadband subscriptions	73	307	458	703	940
PER 100 INHABITANTS					
Fixed telephone lines [1]	19.3	19.0	18.3	17.7	17.3
Mobile cellular subscriptions	33.9	50.1	59.3	67.9	76.2
Internet users	15.9	20.8	23.8	27.1	30.1
Fixed broadband subscriptions	3.3	5.2	6.1	6.9	8.0
Mobile broadband subscriptions	1.1	4.6	6.8	10.3	13.6

[1] See footnote 1, Table 1392.

Source: ITU World Telecommunication/ICT Indicators Database, <http://www.itu.int/ITU-D/ict/statistics/at_glance /KeyTelecom.html>. Reproduced with the kind permission of ITU.

Table 1392. Telephones, Cellular Phones, and Internet Use by Country: 2009

[Rates per 100 persons, except as indicated. For data qualifications for countries, see source]

Country	Telephone main lines [1]	Cellular phone sub- scribers	Internet users (percent of population)	Country	Telephone main lines [1]	Cellular phone sub- scribers	Internet users (percent of population)
Afghanistan	0.46	42.63	3.5	Iran	34.78	70.83	11.1
Australia	42.36	113.75	74.3	Italy	36.24	147.01	48.8
Azerbaijan	15.86	87.83	27.4	Japan	34.08	91.46	78.0
Belize	10.16	52.74	11.7	Korea, South	53.69	100.70	81.5
Brazil	21.42	89.79	39.2	Mali	0.65	34.17	1.9
Bulgaria	29.23	140.18	45.0	Mexico	17.64	76.20	28.3
Cambodia	0.37	42.34	0.5	Morocco	10.99	79.11	41.3
Canada	52.50	70.92	80.3	Namibia	6.54	56.05	5.9
China [3]	23.31	55.52	28.9	Nicaragua	4.44	55.80	3.5
Colombia	16.37	92.33	49.4	Pakistan	1.95	52.18	11.3
Cuba	9.99	5.54	14.3	Portugal	39.74	148.77	48.3
Denmark	37.69	124.97	86.8	Romania	25.02	119.39	36.6
Dominican Republic	9.57	85.53	26.8	Russia	32.21	163.62	29.0
Egypt	12.42	66.69	24.3	Saudi Arabia	16.22	174.43	38.0
Estonia	36.77	202.99	72.5	Serbia	31.53	100.63	41.7
Ethiopia	1.10	4.89	0.5	Singapore	40.65	145.24	68.3
France	56.94	95.51	71.6	Slovakia	22.56	101.70	75.2
Gambia	2.87	84.04	7.6	Slovenia	51.19	103.98	64.3
Georgia	14.55	66.59	30.5	Spain	45.28	113.76	62.6
Germany	59.27	127.79	79.3	Sweden	55.69	125.87	90.8
Greece	47.02	119.12	44.5	Switzerland	61.75	122.30	81.3
Haiti	1.08	36.36	10.0	Syria	17.67	45.57	20.4
Honduras	9.59	112.39	9.8	Taiwan [2]	63.19	116.70	69.9
Hong Kong, China	60.91	179.39	69.4	Turkey	22.10	83.91	36.4
Hungary	30.71	118.01	61.8	United Kingdom	52.17	130.55	83.6
India	3.09	43.83	5.1	**United States**	**44.81**	**90.78**	**78.0**
Indonesia	14.77	69.25	8.7	Venezuela	24.02	98.39	31.2

[1] A fixed telephone line (previously called main telephone line in operation) is an active line (those that have registered an activity in the past three months) connecting the subscriber's terminal equipment to the public switched telephone network (PSTN) and which has a dedicated port in the telephone exchange equipment. This term is synonymous with the terms main station or Direct Exchange Line (DEL) that are commonly used in telecommunication documents. It may not be the same as an access line or a subscriber. This should include the active number of analog fixed telephone lines, ISDN channels, fixed wireless (WLL), public payphones and VoIP subscriptions. Fixed telephone lines per 100 inhabitants is calculated by dividing the number of fixed telephone lines by the population and multiplying by 100. [2] See footnote 4, Table 1332.

Source: ITU World Telecommunication/ICT Indicators Database; <http://www.itu.int/ITU-D/ict/statistics/at_glance /KeyTelecom.html>. Reproduced with the kind permission of ITU.

Table 1393. Patents by Country: 2010

[Includes only U.S. patents granted to residents of areas outside of the United States and its territories. See also Table 778]

Country	Total [1]	Inventions	Designs	Country	Total [1]	Inventions	Designs
Total	**123,177**	**111,822**	**10,187**	Netherlands	1,919	1,614	113
				Australia	2,079	1,748	282
Japan	46,978	44,814	1,910	Switzerland	1,889	1,608	276
Germany	13,633	12,363	1,070	Israel	1,917	1,819	79
Korea, South	12,508	11,671	769	Sweden	1,594	1,434	150
Taiwan [2]	9,635	8,238	1,348	Finland	1,232	1,143	82
Canada	5,511	4,852	635	Belgium	896	820	62
United Kingdom	5,038	4,302	665	Austria	905	727	177
France	5,100	4,450	586	Denmark	766	605	134
Italy	2,254	1,798	439	Other countries	9,323	7,816	1,410

[1] Includes patents for botanical plants and reissues, not shown separately. [2] See footnote 4, Table 1332.

Source: U.S. Patent and Trademark Office, Technology Assessment and Forecast Database.

Table 1394. Dow Jones Global Index by Country and Industry: 2000 to 2010

[Index figures shown are as of December 31. 1991 = 100. Based on share prices denominated in U.S. dollars. Stocks in countries that impose significant restrictions on foreign ownership are included in the world index in the same proportion that shares are available to foreign investors]

Country and industry	2000	2005	2009	2010	Country and industry	2000	2005	2009	2010
World, total	**210.9**	**234.1**	**226.9**	**253.9**	Asia/Pacific	93.0	132.0	123.0	142.5
Americas	299.1	307.3	296.5	340.9	Australia	156.0	312.5	389.7	436.9
United States	**306.9**	**302.4**	**276.6**	**316.6**	Hong Kong	245.6	273.6	420.8	479.6
Canada	225.3	365.4	433.9	526.6	Indonesia	31.2	79.0	152.1	210.4
Mexico	132.2	360.1	495.9	626.8	Japan	88.3	113.5	80.6	91.8
Europe	241.2	264.8	264.2	270.2	Malaysia	88.5	119.5	186.9	254.0
Austria	86.2	335.5	253.9	277.4	New Zealand	96.7	227.3	173.9	181.9
Belgium	196.9	321.2	323.6	337.0	Singapore	135.2	176.3	266.3	327.6
Denmark	220.1	375.1	435.1	556.0	Thailand	27.2	76.7	97.2	152.1
Finland	1,537.8	948.5	843.1	936.0					
France	252.9	273.3	286.0	269.0	Basic materials	117.6	213.8	301.0	373.9
Germany	219.1	224.3	264.9	282.7	Consumer goods	183.8	241.9	272.2	318.4
Ireland	312.3	470.4	216.9	189.9	Consumer services	192.8	214.4	200.4	238.5
Italy	192.2	213.8	166.0	135.1	Oil and Gas	230.7	383.3	444.0	485.9
Netherlands	335.7	309.6	281.7	279.8	Financial	207.1	259.8	173.7	182.0
Norway	151.8	276.1	344.0	388.7	Healthcare	329.9	310.6	320.0	328.1
Spain	193.5	288.6	374.6	282.2	Industrial	167.1	192.4	188.4	228.8
Sweden	339.0	378.3	410.7	544.6	Technology	552.7	375.1	402.6	450.3
Switzerland	388.8	452.5	514.2	572.9	Telecommunications	273.3	201.6	219.5	234.5
United Kingdom	199.8	217.6	198.1	211.7	Utilities	156.0	176.9	198.3	195.1

Source: CME Group Index Services, LLC, New York, NY, Dow Jones Indexes, (copyright).

Table 1395. Foreign Stock Market Activity—Morgan Stanley Capital International Indexes: 2000 to 2010

[Index figures shown are as of December 31. January 1, 1970 = 100, except as noted. Minus sign (–) indicates decrease. Based on share prices denominated in U.S. dollars. EM = Emerging Markets]

Index and country	Index 2000	Index 2009	Index 2010	Percent change[1] 2009	Percent change[1] 2010	Index and country	Index 2000	Index 2009	Index 2010	Percent change[1] 2009	Percent change[1] 2010
ALL COUNTRY (AC) INDEXES						Hong Kong	5,475.0	7,289.8	8,724.0	55.2	19.7
AC World index[2]	290.1	299.4	330.6	31.5	10.4	Japan	2,552.0	2,201.7	2,495.8	4.4	13.4
AC World index except USA[2]	193.5	242.9	263.4	37.4	8.4	Singapore	2,081.0	3,555.7	4,211.7	67.3	18.4
AC Asia Pacific[2]	89.6	120.5	137.7	34.5	14.3	**EMERGING MARKETS**					
AC Europe[2]	376.5	400.2	406.7	32.9	1.6						
European Union[2]	361.5	365.4	364.7	32.0	–0.2	**EM**					
						Far East index[4]	127.9	348.9	405.2	66.3	16.1
DEVELOPED MARKETS						China[6],[7]	22.6	64.8	66.3	58.8	2.3
						India[6]	114.5	468.5	559.4	100.5	19.4
						Indonesia	77.8	634.6	832.6	120.8	31.2
World index	1,221.0	1,168.5	1,280.1	27.0	9.6	Korea, South	78.7	327.1	409.9	69.4	25.3
EAFE® index[3]	1,492.0	1,580.8	1,658.3	27.7	4.9	Malaysia	160.7	341.8	452.9	47.8	32.5
Europe index	1,378.0	1,442.1	1,456.8	31.2	1.0	Pakistan[6]	44.6	82.0	98.0	78.1	19.5
Pacific index	1,832.0	2,006.5	2,268.9	21.1	13.1	Philippines	146.7	269.0	350.5	60.2	30.3
Far East index	2,583.0	2,373.9	2,709.9	10.4	14.2	Sri Lanka[6]	36.3	167.4	287.8	184.2	71.9
						Taiwan[7]	191.7	264.2	312.6	75.1	18.3
United States	**1,250.0**	**1,061.1**	**1,201.0**	**24.2**	**13.2**	Thailand	58.9	225.8	340.5	70.0	50.8
Canada	832.5	1,574.2	1,860.7	52.7	18.2	**EM**					
						Latin America	915.6	4,116.7	4,613.7	98.1	12.1
Australia	317.7	804.1	884.4	68.8	10.0	Argentina	1,233.0	2,101.0	3,573.0	61.1	70.1
New Zealand[4]	56.4	96.4	99.4	43.0	3.2	Brazil	763.2	3,624.5	3,761.4	121.3	3.8
Austria	708.3	1,406.0	1,509.3	38.4	7.3	Chile	604.7	2,051.6	2,909.6	81.4	41.8
Belgium	1,222.0	1,074.5	1,050.5	54.3	–2.2	Colombia[6]	42.1	790.5	1,112.6	76.5	40.8
Denmark	2,201.0	4,232.7	5,494.4	35.2	29.8	Mexico	1,464.9	5,138.1	6,473.4	53.1	26.0
Finland[4]	921.8	460.2	492.7	7.2	7.1	Peru[6]	125.0	1,217.7	1,817.4	69.3	49.2
France	1,509.0	1,599.6	1,491.8	27.6	–6.7	Venezuela[6]	106.1	(NA)	(NA)	(NA)	(NA)
Germany	1,436.0	1,613.4	1,710.5	21.3	6.0	Czech Republic[8]	79.9	544.6	504.3	19.6	–7.4
Greece[4]	475.8	418.3	224.4	22.6	–46.4	Hungary[8]	233.6	742.7	663.2	73.9	–10.7
Ireland[4]	308.4	132.4	106.3	9.9	–19.7	Jordan	55.1	149.9	131.9	–7.7	–12.0
Italy	447.2	383.5	315.9	22.6	–17.6	Poland[6]	499.0	902.4	1,016.4	37.3	12.6
Luxembourg[5]	491.9	(NA)	(NA)	(NA)	(NA)	Russia[8]	155.2	795.3	932.0	100.3	17.2
Netherlands	2,177.0	2,010.9	1,998.4	37.9	–0.6	South Africa[6]	157.6	468.0	611.6	53.4	30.7
Norway	1,181.0	2,760.6	2,965.0	82.5	7.4	Turkey	247.7	528.1	625.1	92.0	18.4
Portugal[4]	127.8	146.8	125.4	35.4	–14.6						
Spain	347.1	672.4	501.7	36.5	–25.4						
Sweden	4,240.0	5,247.0	6,888.0	60.2	31.3						
Switzerland	2,695.0	3,564.5	3,915.2	22.9	9.8						
United Kingdom	1,146.0	1,081.9	1,137.8	37.3	5.2						

NA Not available. [1] Percent change during calendar year (e.g., December 31, 2009 through December 31, 2010). Adjusted for foreign exchange fluctuations relative to U.S. dollar. [2] January 1, 1988 = 100. [3] Europe, Australasia, Far East Index. Comprises all European and Far East countries listed under developed markets plus Australia, New Zealand, and Israel (reclassified May 2010). [4] January 1, 1988 = 100. Reclassified to Developed Markets on May 2010. [5] MSCI Luxembourg Index discontinued as of March 29, 2002. [6] January 1, 1993 = 100. [7] See footnote 4, Table 1332. [8] January 1, 1995 = 100.

Source: MSCI Barra, <http://www.mscibarra.com/about/indexdata_tou.jsp?/products/indices/stdindex/performance.jsp>, (copyright). The MSCI data contained herein is the property of MSCI Inc. (MSCI). MSCI, its affiliates and information providers make no warranties with respect to any such data. The MSCI data contained herein is used under license and may not be further used, distributed, or disseminated without the express written consent of MSCI.

International Statistics 869

Table 1396. Foreign Stock Market Indices: 1980 to 2010

[As of year end. The DAX-30 index is a total return index which includes dividends, whereas the other foreign indices are price indices which exclude dividends]

Year	London FTSE 100	Tokyo Nikkei 225	Hong Kong Hang Seng	Germany DAX-30	Paris CAC-40	Dow Jones Europe STOXX 50
1980.........	647	7,116	1,477	481	(X)	(X)
1985.........	1,413	13,113	1,752	1,366	(X)	(X)
1990.........	2,144	23,849	3,025	1,398	1,518	835
1995.........	3,689	19,868	10,073	2,254	1,872	1,538
1997.........	5,136	15,259	10,723	4,250	2,999	2,634
1998.........	5,883	13,842	9,507	5,002	3,943	3,320
1999.........	6,930	18,934	16,962	6,958	5,958	4,742
2000.........	6,223	13,786	15,096	6,434	5,926	4,557
2001.........	5,217	10,543	11,397	5,160	4,625	3,707
2002.........	3,940	8,579	9,321	2,893	3,064	2,408
2003.........	4,477	10,677	12,576	3,965	3,558	2,660
2004.........	4,814	11,489	14,230	4,256	3,821	2,775
2005.........	5,619	16,111	14,876	5,408	4,715	3,349
2006.........	6,221	17,226	19,965	6,597	5,542	3,697
2007.........	6,457	15,308	27,813	8,067	5,614	3,684
2008.........	4,434	8,860	14,388	4,810	3,218	2,065
2009.........	5,413	10,546	21,873	5,957	3,936	2,579
2010.........	5,900	10,229	23,035	6,914	3,805	2,586

X Not applicable.

Source: Global Financial Data, Los Angeles, CA, <http://www.globalfinancialdata.com>, unpublished data (copyright).

Table 1397. U.S. and Foreign Stock Markets—Market Capitalization and Value of Shares Traded: 2000 to 2010

[In billions of U.S. dollars (15,104.0 represents $15,104,000,000,000). Market capitalization is the market value of all domestic listed companies at the end of the year. The market value of a company is the share price times the number of shares outstanding. Value of shares traded is the annual total turnover of listed company shares]

Country	Market capitalization				Value of shares traded			
	2000	2005	2009	2010	2000	2005	2009	2010
United States	**15,104.0**	**16,970.9**	**15,077.3**	**17,139.0**	**31,862.5**	**21,510.0**	**46,735.9**	**30,454.8**
Argentina..........	166.1	61.5	48.9	63.9	6.0	16.4	2.7	2.6
Australia...........	372.8	804.1	1,258.5	1,454.5	226.3	616.1	761.8	1,221.9
Austria............	29.9	124.4	53.6	121.8	9.4	45.9	25.5	48.1
Belgium...........	182.5	288.5	261.4	269.3	38.0	125.7	127.8	111.5
Brazil	226.2	474.6	1,167.3	1,545.6	101.3	154.2	649.2	901.1
Canada	841.4	1,480.9	1,681.0	2,160.2	634.7	845.0	1,239.6	1,365.7
Chile	60.4	136.4	209.5	341.6	6.1	18.9	37.6	54.3
China [1]...........	581.0	780.8	5,007.6	4,762.8	721.5	586.3	8,956.2	8,030.0
Denmark	107.7	178.0	186.9	231.7	91.6	152.0	148.3	144.6
Egypt.............	28.7	79.7	90.0	82.5	11.1	25.4	52.8	37.1
Finland............	293.6	209.5	91.0	212.7	206.6	273.5	91.2	178.7
France	1,446.6	1,758.7	1,972.0	1,926.5	1,083.3	1,526.1	1,365.8	1,452.9
Germany	1,270.2	1,221.3	1,297.6	1,429.7	1,069.1	1,763.2	1,288.9	1,405.0
Greece	110.8	145.0	54.7	72.6	95.1	65.3	51.7	43.1
Hong Kong.........	623.4	1,055.0	2,291.6	2,711.3	377.9	460.1	1,489.6	1,597.5
India.............	148.1	553.1	1,179.2	1,615.9	509.8	433.9	1,088.9	1,056.8
Indonesia..........	26.8	81.4	178.2	360.4	14.3	41.9	115.3	129.5
Iran	34.0	38.7	63.3	86.6	5.0	8.2	17.1	17.1
Ireland	81.9	114.1	29.9	60.7	14.4	64.7	18.5	29.5
Israel	64.1	120.1	182.1	218.1	23.4	59.9	88.3	133.4
Italy	768.4	798.2	317.3	570.3	778.4	1,115.2	459.7	946.3
Japan	3,157.2	4,736.5	3,377.9	4,099.6	2,693.9	4,997.4	4,192.6	4,280.4
Korea, South	171.6	718.2	836.5	1,089.2	1,067.7	1,203.0	1,581.5	1,626.6
Luxembourg........	34.0	51.3	105.6	101.1	1.2	0.2	0.3	0.2
Malaysia	116.9	181.2	256.0	410.5	58.5	50.0	73.0	90.2
Mexico	125.2	239.1	340.6	454.3	45.3	52.7	77.1	108.5
Morocco...........	10.9	27.2	62.9	69.2	1.1	4.1	0.3	10.8
Netherlands........	640.5	592.9	542.5	661.2	677.2	835.8	604.2	592.1
New Zealand	18.6	43.4	67.1	36.3	10.8	17.4	37.2	10.7
Norway............	65.0	191.0	227.2	250.9	60.1	194.8	247.8	217.1
Philippines.........	51.6	40.2	80.1	157.3	8.2	7.0	3.1	26.8
Poland	31.3	93.9	135.3	190.2	14.6	30.0	17.2	77.5
Portugal...........	60.7	67.0	98.6	82.0	54.4	41.6	45.8	54.8
Russia	38.9	548.6	861.4	1,004.5	20.3	159.3	1.9	799.7
Saudi Arabia	67.2	646.1	318.8	353.4	17.3	1,103.5	682.5	203.2
Singapore	152.8	316.7	310.8	370.1	91.5	119.8	252.3	282.1
Sweden	328.3	403.9	432.3	581.2	390.0	464.0	390.3	439.6
Switzerland	792.3	938.6	1,070.7	1,229.4	609.1	883.3	795.6	869.4
Taiwan [1]..........	247.6	516.0	695.9	804.1	983.5	716.5	1,066.1	892.6
Thailand...........	29.5	124.9	138.2	277.7	23.3	89.3	134.9	217.9
Turkey	69.7	161.5	225.7	307.7	179.2	201.3	243.5	421.6
United Kingdom......	2,580.0	3,058.2	2,796.4	3,107.0	1,835.3	4,167.0	3,402.5	3,006.7

[1] See footnote 4, Table 1332.

Source: Standard and Poor's, New York, NY, *Standard & Poor's Global Stock Markets Factbook 2011* (copyright).

Table 1398. Foreign Exchange Rates: 2010

[Foreign currency units per U.S. dollar. Rates shown include market, official, principal, and secondary rates]

Country	Currency	2010	Country	Currency	2010
Afghanistan [1]	Afghanis	46.45	Kyrgyzstan	Soms	46.34
Albania	Leks	104.08	Laos	Kip	8,320.27
Algeria	Algerian dinars	76.00	Latvia	Lats	0.54
Antigua and Barbuda	E. Caribbean dollars	2.70	Lebanon	Lebanese pounds	1,507.50
Argentina	Argentine pesos	3.90	Lesotho	Maloti	7.90
Armenia	Drams	374.29	Liberia	Liberian dollars	(NA)
Aruba	Aruban guilders	(NA)	Libya [1]	Libyan dinars	1.26
Australia	Australian dollars	1.09	Lithuania	Litai	2.66
Austria	Euro	0.76	Luxembourg	Euro	0.76
Bahamas, The	Bahamian dollars	1.00	Macedonia	Denars	46.43
Bahrain	Bahrain dinars	0.38	Madagascar	Malagasy ariary	2,062.50
Bangladesh	Taka	70.59	Malaysia	Ringgit	3.04
Barbados	Barbadian dollars	(NA)	Mali	CFA francs	495.28
Belarus	Belarusian rubel	3,019.90	Malta	Euro	0.76
Belgium	Euro	0.76	Mauritania	Ouguiyas	261.50
Belize	Belizean dollars	2.00	Mauritius	Mauritian rupees	30.99
Benin	CFA francs	495.28	Mexico	Mexican pesos	12.69
Bolivia	Bolivianos	7.04	Moldova	Lei	12.37
Botswana	Pula	6.74	Mongolia	Togrogs	1,357.50
Brazil	Reals	1.77	Morocco	Dirhams	8.36
Bulgaria	Leva	1.51	Mozambique	Meticais	35.00
Burkina Faso	CFA francs	495.28	Namibia	Namibia dollars	7.57
Burma [1]	Kyats	966.00	Nepal	Nepalese rupees	72.56
Cambodia	Riel	4,145.00	Netherlands	Euro	0.76
Cameroon	CFA francs	495.28	New Zealand	New Zealand dollars	1.39
Canada	Canadian dollars	1.03	Nicaragua	Cordobas	21.35
Central African Republic	CFA francs	495.28	Niger	CFA francs	495.28
Chad	CFA francs	495.28	Nigeria	Naira	150.88
Chile	Chilean pesos	525.34	Norway	Norwegian kroner	6.04
China [2]	Yuan	6.79	Oman	Rials omani	0.38
Colombia	Colombian pesos	1,869.90	Pakistan	Pakistan rupees	85.27
Comoros	Comorian francs	(NA)	Panama	Balboas	1.00
Congo (Brazzaville) [3]	CFA francs	507.71	Papua New Guinea	Kina	2.75
Costa Rica	Colones	583.00	Paraguay	Guaranies	4,767.60
Cote d'Ivoire	CFA francs	495.28	Peru	Nuevos soles	2.82
Croatia	Kunas	5.64	Philippines	Philippine pesos	45.11
Curaçao [4]	Guilders	1.79	Poland	Zlotych	3.07
Cyprus	Euro	0.76	Portugal	Euro	0.76
Czech Republic	Koruny	19.11	Qatar	Qatar riyals	3.64
Denmark	Kroner	5.62	Romania	Lei	3.20
Djibouti	Djibouti francs	(NA)	Russia	Russian rubles	30.00
Dominica	E. Caribbean dollars	2.70	Rwanda	Rwanda francs	586.25
Dominican Republic	Dominican pesos	36.92	Saint Kitts and Nevis	E. Caribbean dollars	2.70
Ecuador	U.S. dollars	1.00	Saint Lucia	E. Caribbean dollars	2.70
Egypt	Egyptian pounds	5.61	Saint Vincent and the		
El Salvador	U.S. dollars	(NA)	Grenadines	E. Caribbean dollars	2.70
Equatorial Guinea	CFA francs	495.28	Saudi Arabia	Saudi Arabian riyals	3.75
Estonia	Krooni	11.80	Senegal	CFA francs	495.28
Ethiopia [1]	Birr	14.40	Sierra Leone	Leones	(NA)
Fiji	Fiji dollars	(NA)	Singapore	Singapore dollar	1.37
Finland	Euro	0.76	Slovakia	Koruny	0.76
France	Euro	0.76	Slovenia	Euro	0.76
Gabon	CFA francs	495.28	South Africa	Rand	7.38
Georgia	Lari	1.80	Spain	Euro	0.76
Germany	Euro	0.76	Sri Lanka	Sri Lanka rupees	113.36
Greece	Euro	0.77	Sudan	Sudanese dinars	2.36
Guatemala	Quetzales	8.08	Suriname [1]	Suriname dollar	2.75
Guyana	Guyana dollars	204.07	Swaziland	Emalangeni	7.57
Haiti	Gourdes	40.15	Sweden	Swedish kronor	7.51
Honduras	Lempiras	18.90	Switzerland	Swiss francs	1.04
Hong Kong	Hong Kong dollars	7.78	Syria	Syrian pounds	46.46
Hungary	Forint	206.15	Tanzania	Tanzania shillings	1,423.30
Iceland	Kronur	139.32	Thailand	Baht	31.66
India	Indian rupees	46.16	Togo	CFA francs	495.28
Indonesia	Rupiah	9,169.50	Trinidad and Tobago	Tt dollars	6.33
Iran	Rials	10,308.20	Tunisia	Tunisian dinars	1.44
Iraq	Dinars	1,170.00	Turkey	Liras	1.52
Ireland	Euro	0.76	Uganda	Uganda shillings	2,166.00
Israel	New sheqalim	3.74	Ukraine	Hryvnias	7.91
Italy	Euro	0.77	United Arab Emirates	Dirhams	3.67
Jamaica	Jamaica dollars	87.41	United Kingdom	Pounds sterling	0.64
Japan	Yen	87.78	Uruguay	Uruguayan pesos	20.05
Jordan	Jordanian dinars	0.71	Vanuatu	Vatu	(NA)
Kazakhstan	Tenge	147.28	Venezuela	Bolivares	4.30
Kenya	Kenya shillings	79.22	Yemen	Yemeni rials	220.05
Korea, South	Won	1,153.77	Zambia	Zambian kwacha	4,823.60
Kuwait	Kuwaiti dinars	0.29	Zimbabwe	Zimbabwe dollar	234.25

NA Not available. [1] End-of-year values were used if annual averages were unavailable. Some values were estimated using partial year data. [2] See footnote 4, Table 1332. [3] See footnote 5, Table 1332. [4] The Netherlands Antilles dissolved on October 10, 2010. Curaçao and Sint Maarten became autonomous territories of the Kingdom of the Netherlands.

Source: Central Intelligence Agency, *The World Factbook*, <https://www.cia.gov/library/publications/the-world-factbook/index.html/>, accessed May 2011.

Table 1399. Reserve Assets and International Transaction Balances by Country: 2000 to 2010

[In millions of U.S. dollars (43,442 represents $43,442,000,000). Assets include holdings of convertible foreign currencies, special drawing rights, and reserve position in International Monetary Fund and exclude gold holdings. Minus sign (–) indicates debits]

Country	Total reserve assets		2010		Current account balance			Merchandise trade balance		
	2000	2009	Total	Currency holdings [1]	2000	2009	2010	2000	2009	2010
United States	43,442	76,366	78,824	33,814	–416,374	–378,435	(NA)	–444	–503,578	(NA)
Algeria	9,229	95,070	105,592	104,263	(NA)	160	(NA)	(NA)	7,784	(NA)
Argentina	19,301	29,402	32,294	30,272	–8,981	8,373	(NA)	2,452	18,528	(NA)
Australia	13,906	24,846	25,103	21,294	–14,763	–43,836	(NA)	–4,862	–4,406	(NA)
Austria	10,990	5,176	6,290	4,073	–1,339	10,995	(NA)	–3,978	–3,258	(NA)
Bangladesh	1,141	6,518	6,860	6,431	–306	3,345	(NA)	–1,654	–4,693	(NA)
Belgium [2]	7,671	10,147	10,714	5,117	(NA)	3,522	(NA)	(NA)	–2,939	(NA)
Brazil	24,894	151,410	186,396	182,185	–24,225	–24,302	(NA)	–698	25,290	(NA)
Burma	171	(NA)	(NA)	(NA)	–212	(NA)	(NA)	–504	(NA)	(NA)
Cameroon	163	2,345	(NA)	(NA)	–249	–1,137	(NA)	502	–326	(NA)
Canada	24,639	34,597	37,011	29,148	19,622	–38,380	(NA)	45,047	–4,246	(NA)
Chile	11,540	16,128	18,062	17,089	–898	4,217	(NA)	2,119	13,982	(NA)
China [3]	129,155	1,541,150	1,861,050	1,848,880	20,518	297,142	(NA)	34,474	249,509	(NA)
Colombia	6,843	15,786	18,030	17,110	795	–5,001	(NA)	2,670	2,546	(NA)
Congo (Brazzaville) [4]	170	2,428	(NA)	(NA)	648	(NA)	(NA)	2,037	(NA)	(NA)
Cote d'Ivoire	513	2,084	(NA)	(NA)	–241	1,670	(NA)	1,486	4,185	(NA)
Denmark	11,596	47,389	47,728	45,671	2,262	11,222	(NA)	6,641	8,103	(NA)
Ecuador	727	1,833	932	898	926	–268	(NA)	1,399	78	(NA)
Egypt	10,068	20,574	21,825	21,007	–971	–3,349	(NA)	–8,321	–16,818	(NA)
Finland	6,122	6,194	4,758	3,195	10,526	6,814	(NA)	13,684	4,790	(NA)
France	28,428	29,747	36,233	23,513	19,674	–51,858	(NA)	–3,173	–61,965	(NA)
Germany	43,664	38,225	40,450	24,257	–32,279	165,471	(NA)	55,466	188,348	(NA)
Ghana	178	(NA)	(NA)	(NA)	–387	–1,198	(NA)	–830	–2,207	(NA)
Greece	10,303	[5] 992	850	70	–9,820	–35,913	(NA)	–20,239	–42,836	(NA)
Hungary	8,588	28,114	29,122	28,299	–4,004	–699	(NA)	–2,913	4,756	(NA)
India	29,091	169,154	178,748	173,902	–4,601	–26,626	(NA)	–10,641	–78,816	(NA)
Indonesia	21,876	40,546	60,329	58,421	7,992	10,192	6,294	25,042	30,147	31,093
Ireland	4,114	1,238	1,196	326	–516	–6,488	(NA)	25,010	44,960	(NA)
Israel	17,869	38,663	46,043	44,976	–2,209	7,592	(NA)	–3,857	–96	(NA)
Italy	19,623	29,196	30,963	23,167	–5,781	–66,199	(NA)	9,549	3,259	(NA)
Japan	272,392	652,065	689,266	672,880	119,660	142,194	(NA)	116,716	43,632	(NA)
Kenya	689	2,455	2,805	2,585	–199	–1,661	(NA)	–1,262	–4,989	(NA)
Korea, South	73,781	172,185	189,276	186,312	12,251	32,791	28,213	16,954	37,862	41,876
Kuwait	5,436	12,928	13,790	12,093	14,672	28,605	(NA)	13,027	33,263	(NA)
Malaysia	21,744	60,874	68,088	66,426	8,488	31,801	(NA)	20,827	40,254	(NA)
Mexico	27,254	63,526	78,092	74,598	–18,767	–6,303	–5,703	–8,337	–4,602	–3,121
Morocco	3,702	14,542	14,668	14,115	–501	–5,362	(NA)	–3,235	–16,364	(NA)
Nepal	726	(NA)	(NA)	(NA)	–299	–256	(NA)	–814	–3,461	(NA)
Netherlands	7,401	11,399	11,994	5,780	7,264	36,581	(NA)	17,800	51,066	(NA)
Nigeria	7,607	28,553	22,675	20,999	7,427	21,659	(NA)	10,415	29,042	(NA)
Norway	21,181	31,166	34,324	32,338	25,079	50,122	(NA)	25,908	54,405	(NA)
Pakistan	1,162	7,220	9,315	8,516	–85	–3,993	(NA)	–1,157	–10,270	(NA)
Peru	6,427	20,420	27,693	27,047	–1,546	247	(NA)	–403	5,873	(NA)
Philippines	10,047	24,739	35,949	35,059	–2,228	8,788	(NA)	–5,971	–8,863	(NA)
Poland	20,387	48,430	57,675	56,049	–10,343	–9,598	(NA)	–12,307	–4,355	(NA)
Portugal	6,838	1,566	2,371	1,307	–12,189	–23,952	(NA)	–15,156	–24,410	(NA)
Romania	1,896	25,998	28,156	27,469	–1,355	–6,955	–6,744	–1,684	–9,606	–7,749
Saudi Arabia	15,032	261,336	288,775	280,575	14,317	20,955	(NA)	49,777	105,230	(NA)
Singapore	61,532	119,796	146,565	145,380	10,178	32,628	(NA)	13,678	30,231	(NA)
South Africa	4,669	22,477	24,789	22,999	–191	–11,327	(NA)	4,698	534	(NA)
Spain	23,784	11,613	12,433	8,640	–23,185	–80,375	(NA)	–37,087	–62,833	(NA)
Sri Lanka	797	2,944	(NA)	(NA)	–1,044	–292	(NA)	–1,044	–2,101	(NA)
Sudan	106	698	(NA)	(NA)	–557	–3,908	(NA)	440	–694	(NA)
Sweden	11,407	27,339	27,639	24,622	6,617	31,460	(NA)	15,215	14,015	(NA)
Switzerland	24,769	62,640	145,114	141,132	32,830	38,972	(NA)	2,064	1,391	(NA)
Thailand	24,573	86,422	108,784	107,567	9,313	21,861	(NA)	11,701	32,691	(NA)
Trinidad and Tobago	1,064	5,854	(NA)	(NA)	544	(NA)	(NA)	969	(NA)	(NA)
Turkey	17,260	45,209	52,410	51,327	–9,920	–13,991	–48,561	–22,057	–24,850	–56,354
United Kingdom . . .	29,759	35,532	44,379	32,035	–38,800	–37,051	(NA)	–49,850	–128,558	(NA)
Venezuela	10,046	13,844	8,530	5,969	11,853	8,561	(NA)	16,664	19,153	(NA)

NA Not available. [1] Holdings of convertible foreign currencies. [2] Balance of payments current account and trade balance data for 2000 are for Belgium-Luxembourg. Thereafter, data is for Belgium only. [3] See footnote 4, Table 1332. [4] See footnote 5, Table 1332. [5] Break in series. Data not comparable to earlier years.

Source: International Monetary Fund, Washington, DC, *International Financial Statistics*, monthly, (copyright).

Table 1400. International Tourism Arrivals, Expenditures, and Receipts—Leading Countries: 2000 to 2009

[Arrivals in thousands of nonresident tourists at national borders, except as noted (77,190 represents 77,190,000); expenditures and receipts in millions of dollars. Receipts are dollars spent by foreign tourists on travel inside the country shown. Expenditures are dollars visitors (same-day visitors and tourists) from a given country of origin spend on travel outside their country of residence. Excludes international transport receipts]

Country	Arrivals (1,000)					Expenditures (mil. dol.)				Receipts (mil. dol.)				
	2000	2005	2007	2008	2009, prel.	2000	2005	2008	2009, prel.	2000	2005	2007	2008	2009, prel.
France	77,190	74,988	80,853	79,218	76,800	22,533	31,727	41,570	38,575	32,855	43,954	54,209	57,236	49,450
United States	51,238	49,206	55,979	57,937	54,884	67,043	73,320	85,323	79,222	97,943	102,070	119,586	134,972	121,131
Spain	46,403	55,914	58,666	57,192	52,178	5,922	15,046	20,363	16,911	29,802	47,789	57,734	61,978	53,337
China [1]	31,229	46,809	54,720	53,049	50,875	13,114	21,759	36,157	43,702	16,231	29,296	37,233	40,843	39,675
Italy [1]	41,181	36,513	43,654	42,734	43,239	15,685	22,370	30,927	27,864	27,493	35,319	42,660	46,192	40,311
United Kingdom [2]	25,209	29,970	32,778	31,888	29,889	38,262	59,532	69,792	50,559	21,769	30,573	38,698	36,424	30,498
Hong Kong [2]	13,059	23,359	28,169	29,507	29,591	12,502	13,305	16,095	15,960	5,868	10,179	13,566	15,018	16,020
Turkey	9,586	20,273	22,248	24,994	25,994	1,713	2,872	3,506	4,147	7,636	18,152	18,487	21,951	21,250
Germany [3]	18,983	21,500	24,421	24,884	24,220	52,824	74,189	91,598	81,044	18,611	29,121	36,101	40,021	34,781
Russia [2]	21,169	22,201	22,909	23,676	(NA)	8,848	17,314	23,778	20,763	3,429	5,870	9,447	11,795	9,297
Malaysia	10,222	16,431	20,973	22,052	23,646	2,075	3,711	6,709	6,508	5,011	8,846	14,050	15,293	15,798
Mexico [3]	20,641	21,915	21,370	22,637	21,454	5,499	7,600	8,526	7,134	8,294	11,803	12,852	13,289	11,275
Austria [3]	17,982	19,952	20,773	21,935	21,355	6,232	9,316	11,432	10,817	9,899	16,243	18,559	21,630	19,176
Ukraine	6,431	17,631	23,122	25,449	20,798	470	2,805	4,203	3,330	394	3,125	4,597	5,768	3,576
Canada	19,627	18,771	17,935	17,142	15,737	12,438	18,017	27,210	24,169	10,778	13,768	15,568	15,668	13,707
Greece	13,096	14,765	16,165	15,939	14,915	4,558	3,039	3,930	3,381	9,219	13,334	15,550	17,416	14,681
Thailand	9,579	11,567	14,464	14,584	14,150	2,772	3,800	5,003	4,343	7,483	9,577	16,667	18,163	15,665
Egypt	5,116	8,244	10,610	12,296	11,914	1,072	1,629	2,915	2,538	4,345	6,851	9,303	10,985	10,755
Poland	17,400	15,200	14,975	12,960	11,890	3,315	5,548	9,903	7,327	5,677	6,274	10,599	11,768	9,011
Saudi Arabia [4]	6,585	8,037	11,531	14,757	10,897	(NA)	9,087	15,129	18,814	(NA)	4,626	5,972	5,910	5,964
Macao [4]	5,197	9,014	12,942	10,610	10,402	(NA)	358	554	510	(NA)	7,759	13,076	16,761	17,886
Portugal	12,097	10,612	12,321	(NA)	(NA)	2,228	3,050	4,328	3,776	5,243	7,676	10,175	10,980	9,707
South Africa	5,872	7,369	9,091	9,592	9,934	2,085	3,374	4,404	4,151	2,677	7,516	8,779	7,956	7,624
Netherlands [3]	10,003	10,012	11,008	10,104	9,921	12,191	16,140	21,825	20,757	7,197	10,450	13,339	13,346	12,408
Croatia [3]	5,831	8,467	9,307	9,415	9,335	568	754	1,113	1,013	2,758	7,370	9,233	11,280	9,000
Hungary	(NA)	9,978	8,638	8,814	9,058	1,651	2,382	4,037	3,638	3,733	4,120	4,739	6,033	5,712
Denmark [3]	3,535	9,178	9,284	9,016	8,547	4,669	6,850	9,678	(NA)	3,671	5,293	5,976	6,242	5,679
Morocco	4,278	5,843	7,408	7,879	8,341	425	612	1,090	1,106	2,039	4,610	7,181	7,221	6,625
Switzerland [5]	7,821	7,229	8,448	8,608	8,294	5,419	8,782	10,923	10,628	6,652	10,041	12,183	14,458	13,816
Korea, South [2]	5,322	6,023	6,448	6,891	7,818	7,132	15,406	19,065	13,330	6,834	5,806	6,138	9,774	9,442
Romania [2]	5,264	5,839	6,891	8,862	7,575	425	925	2,176	1,473	359	1,052	1,610	1,991	1,228
Singapore	6,062	7,079	7,722	7,778	7,489	4,535	10,070	15,136	15,808	5,142	6,205	9,083	10,719	9,200
Ireland	6,646	7,333	7,957	8,026	7,189	2,525	6,074	10,413	8,773	2,615	4,782	6,074	6,356	4,894
United Arab Emirates [5,6]	3,907	7,126	8,332	(NA)	(NA)	3,019	6,186	13,288	(NA)	1,063	3,218	6,072	7,162	(NA)
Tunisia	5,058	6,378	6,762	7,050	6,901	263	374	458	415	1,682	2,143	2,575	2,953	2,773
Belgium [3]	6,457	6,747	7,045	7,165	6,815	9,429	14,948	19,822	17,923	6,592	9,845	11,017	11,801	9,967
Japan [2]	4,757	6,728	8,347	8,351	6,790	31,884	37,565	27,901	25,199	3,373	12,430	9,345	10,820	10,329
Indonesia	5,064	5,002	5,506	6,234	6,324	3,197	3,584	5,554	5,165	4,975	4,522	5,346	7,377	6,318
Syria [3]	2,100	3,571	4,158	5,430	6,092	669	550	800	(NA)	1,082	1,944	2,884	3,150	(NA)
Czech Republic [3]	4,773	6,336	6,680	6,649	6,032	1,276	2,405	4,585	4,077	2,973	4,676	6,388	7,204	6,477

NA Not available. [1] See footnote 4, Table 1332. [2] Arrivals are of nonresident visitors at national borders. [3] Arrivals are of nonresident tourists in all types of accommodation establishments. [4] Receipts include both travel and passenger transport. [5] Arrivals of nonresident tourists in hotels and similar establishments. [6] Expenditures and receipts include both travel and passenger transport.

Source: World Tourism Organization, Madrid, Spain, World Tourism Barometer, April 2011 (copyright).

Table 1401. Research and Development (R&D) Expenditures by Country

[Figures are for 2007, except as noted, or latest year available. GDP = gross domestic product; for explanation, see text, Section 13]

Country	Gross domestic expenditure on R&D (GERD)				Higher education expenditure on R&D (HERD)	
		Percent financed by—		Per capita at current U.S. dollars, PPPs [1]		
	Percent of GDP	Government	Industry		Percent of GERD	Percent of GDP
OECD total	**2.29**	**28.56**	**63.79**	**748**	**16.8**	**0.38**
EU-15 [2]	1.90	33.36	55.60	635	21.6	0.41
EU-27 [3]	1.77	34.11	54.98	530	21.8	0.39
Australia [4]	2.01	38.37	57.23	716	25.7	0.52
Austria [4]	2.56	35.60	47.68	952	24.1	0.62
Belgium	1.87	24.65	59.68	662	21.8	0.41
Brazil	1.02	57.88	39.38	92	(NA)	(NA)
Canada [4]	1.88	31.42	49.40	724	33.7	0.63
China [5,6]	1.49	24.62	70.37	77	8.5	0.13
Czech Republic	1.54	41.19	53.96	369	16.9	0.26
Denmark	2.55	27.58	59.53	917	27.5	0.70
Finland	3.47	24.05	68.20	1,206	18.7	0.65
France	2.08	38.42	52.44	680	19.2	0.40
Germany	2.54	27.76	68.07	874	16.3	0.41
Greece	0.57	46.82	31.06	163	50.4	0.29
Hungary	0.97	44.41	43.86	181	23.4	0.23
Iceland	2.75	38.80	50.35	980	25.1	0.69
India	0.71	80.81	16.11	13	4.9	0.03
Ireland	1.31	30.13	59.26	591	26.4	0.35
Italy	1.13	48.32	40.42	334	30.3	0.34
Japan [4]	3.44	15.63	77.71	1,157	12.6	0.43
Korea	3.47	24.80	73.65	861	10.7	0.37
Luxembourg	1.63	16.61	79.72	1,300	3.0	0.05
Mexico	0.46	45.34	46.49	57	27.4	0.13
Netherlands	1.70	36.23	51.06	669	26.6	0.45
New Zealand	1.21	42.66	40.14	325	30.1	0.36
Norway	1.64	44.87	45.25	878	31.4	0.51
Poland	0.57	58.61	34.26	91	33.9	0.19
Portugal	1.18	55.20	36.27	269	29.9	0.35
Russia	1.12	62.62	29.45	165	6.3	0.07
Slovakia	0.46	53.92	35.60	92	25.0	0.11
South Africa	0.92	38.19	43.87	76	19.3	0.18
Spain	1.27	42.49	47.07	401	26.4	0.33
Sweden	3.60	24.43	63.86	1,320	21.3	0.77
Switzerland	2.90	22.71	69.73	1,003	22.9	0.66
Turkey	0.71	47.07	48.45	92	48.2	0.34
United Kingdom	1.79	29.33	47.19	640	24.5	0.44
United States [4,7,8]	**2.68**	**27.73**	**66.44**	**1,221**	**13.3**	**0.36**

NA Not available or not applicable. [1] Purchasing power parities. See headnote, Table 1349. [2] See footnote 2, Table 1378.
[3] See footnote 5, Table 1377. [4] Government budget appropriations for R&D: federal government only. [5] See footnote 4, Table 1332.
[6] Percent of GERD/BERD financed by government or industry: the sum of the breakdown does not add to the total. [7] GERD, BERD: Excluding most or all capital expenditures. [8] HERD: Excluding most or all capital expenditures.
Source: Organization for Economic Cooperation and Development (OECD), 2010, "Main Science and Technology Indicators," *OECD Science, Technology and R&D Statistics* database (copyright), <http://dx.doi.org/10.1787/data-00182-en>, accessed May 2010.

Table 1402. Development Assistance by Country: 2009

[119,782 represents $119,782,000,000]

Country	Official development aid (ODA)			Multilateral ODA (mil. U.S. dol.)	Net private grants (mil. U.S. dol.)
	Mil. U.S. dollars	Percent of GNI [1]	Percent of total DAC[2] ODA		
DAC [2] total	119,782	0.31	100.0	36,278	22,047
EU-15 [3]	67,211	0.44	56.1	26,226	3,328
United States	**28,831**	**0.21**	**24.1**	**3,658**	**16,288**
Australia	2,762	0.29	2.3	450	(NA)
Austria	1,142	0.30	1.0	635	140
Belgium	2,610	0.55	2.2	1,025	377
Canada	4,000	0.30	3.3	859	1,338
Denmark	2,810	0.88	2.3	904	116
Finland	1,290	0.54	1.1	499	17
France	12,602	0.47	10.5	5,581	(NA)
Germany	12,079	0.35	10.1	4,983	1,369
Greece	607	0.19	0.5	310	2
Ireland	1,006	0.54	0.8	313	182
Italy	3,297	0.16	2.8	2,423	162
Japan	9,457	0.18	7.9	3,290	533
Korea	816	0.10	0.7	235	156
Luxembourg	415	1.04	0.3	149	13
Netherlands	6,426	0.82	5.4	1,628	542
New Zealand	309	0.28	0.3	83	46
Norway	4,086	1.06	3.4	918	(NA)
Portugal	513	0.23	0.4	236	4
Spain	6,584	0.46	5.5	2,111	(NA)
Sweden	4,548	1.12	3.8	1,539	74
Switzerland	2,310	0.45	1.9	559	357
United Kingdom	11,283	0.51	9.4	3,891	329

NA Not available. [1] Gross national income. See headnote, Table 1348. [2] DAC: OECD Development Assistance Committee.
[3] See footnote 2, Table 1378.
Source: Organization for Economic Cooperation and Development (OECD), 2011, "Aggregate Aid Statistics: ODA by donor," *OECD International Development Statistics* database (copyright); <http://stats.oecd.org//Index.aspx?QueryId=29354>, accessed April 2011.

Table 1403. Net Flow of Financial Resources to Developing Countries and Multilateral Organizations: 1995 to 2009

[167,206 represents $167,206,000,000. Net flow covers loans, grants, and grant-like flows minus amortization on loans. Military flows are excluded. The Development Assistance Committee (DAC) determines those countries that are to be considered "developing." GNI = gross national income. For explanation of GNI, see headnote, Table 1348. Minus sign (−) indicates net inflow]

Country	Amount (mil. dol.)				Percent of GNI			
	1995	2000	2008	2009	1995	2000	2008	2009
DAC total [1]	167,206	134,239	275,776	377,724	0.73	0.55	0.68	0.98
United States	46,984	25,252	13,678	115,276	0.65	0.25	0.09	0.82
Australia.	2,536	1,961	3,997	3,188	0.73	0.53	0.43	0.34
Austria	958	1,135	10,831	3,273	0.41	0.61	2.71	0.87
Belgium	−234	2,281	4,425	3,224	−0.09	1.00	0.89	0.68
Canada	5,724	6,483	24,069	7,340	1.04	0.95	1.63	0.56
Denmark	1,799	2,176	5,150	3,757	1.07	1.39	1.50	1.18
Finland.	604	1,087	−222	3,185	0.48	0.91	−0.08	1.34
France	12,477	5,557	40,641	38,420	0.81	0.41	1.44	1.43
Germany	21,197	12,331	35,727	29,130	0.87	0.66	0.98	0.86
Greece.	(NA)	229	1,166	850	(NA)	0.20	0.35	0.26
Ireland	247	740	6,101	4,188	0.46	0.93	2.71	2.27
Italy	2,800	10,846	5,581	5,569	0.26	1.01	0.25	0.27
Japan.	42,295	11,423	31,805	45,444	0.79	0.24	0.63	0.88
Korea.	1,973	44	10,700	6,442	0.38	0.01	1.14	0.77
Luxembourg.	72	129	426	428	0.40	0.73	0.99	1.08
Netherlands	6,795	6,947	−14,022	6,045	1.71	1.85	−1.61	0.77
New Zealand	166	142	433	387	0.31	0.32	0.38	0.35
Norway.	1,670	1,437	3,759	4,089	1.15	0.87	0.83	1.06
Portugal	395	4,622	1,528	−1,060	0.38	4.45	0.67	−0.48
Spain.	2,025	23,471	30,087	13,233	0.37	4.25	1.96	0.92
Sweden	2,224	3,952	5,896	7,164	1.00	1.76	1.22	1.77
Switzerland	1,118	1,765	12,141	9,106	0.35	0.68	2.63	1.77
United Kingdom	13,382	10,230	41,878	69,045	1.19	0.72	1.57	3.11

NA Not available. [1] DAC: OECD Development Assistance Committee.
Source: Organization for Economic Cooperation and Development (OECD), 2011, "Official and private flows," OECD International Development Statistics database (copyright), <http://dx.doi.org/10.1787/data-00072-en>, accessed April 2011.

Table 1404. External Debt by Country: 1990 to 2009

[In billions of dollars (28.1 represents $28,100,000,000). Total external debt is debt owed to nonresidents repayable in foreign currency, goods, or services. Total external debt is the sum of public, publicly guaranteed, and private nonguaranteed long-term debt, use of IMF credit, and short-term debt. Short-term debt includes all debt having an original maturity of one year or less and interest in arrears on long-term debt]

Country	1990	2000	2008	2009	Country	1990	2000	2008	2009
Algeria	28.1	25.4	5.8	5.3	Montenegro	(NA)	(NA)	1.5	2.3
Angola	8.6	9.4	15.1	16.7	Morocco.	25.0	20.7	20.8	23.8
Argentina	62.2	140.9	118.9	120.2	Nepal	1.6	2.9	3.7	3.7
Bangladesh	12.3	15.5	22.9	23.8	Nigeria	33.4	31.4	11.5	7.8
Brazil	119.7	241.5	262.1	276.9	Pakistan	20.6	32.7	48.5	53.7
Bulgaria	10.9	11.2	39.8	40.6	Panama	6.5	6.6	10.7	12.4
Cameroon	6.6	10.3	2.8	2.9	Peru	20.0	28.6	27.9	29.6
Chile	19.2	37.3	64.3	71.6	Philippines	30.6	58.3	64.9	62.9
China [1]	55.3	145.7	378.2	428.4	Poland	(NA)	(NA)	(NA)	(NA)
Colombia	17.2	33.9	46.6	52.2	Romania	1.1	11.2	102.5	117.5
Congo (Kinshasa) [2] . . .	10.3	11.7	12.2	12.2	Russia [3]	(NA)	160.0	402.5	381.3
Cote d'Ivoire	17.3	12.1	12.6	11.7	Serbia [4]	17.8	11.5	30.7	33.4
Ecuador	12.1	13.3	17.3	12.9	Sierra Leone	1.2	1.2	0.4	0.4
Egypt	33.0	29.0	33.4	33.3	South Africa	(NA)	24.9	41.9	42.1
Ethiopia	8.6	5.5	2.9	5.0	Sri Lanka	5.9	9.1	15.6	17.2
Ghana	3.7	6.1	4.9	5.7	Sudan	14.8	16.0	19.5	20.1
Guatemala	2.8	3.9	14.8	13.8	Tanzania	6.4	7.1	6.0	7.3
India.	85.7	100.2	224.7	237.7	Thailand.	28.1	79.7	54.9	58.8
Indonesia	69.9	143.4	146.2	157.5	Tunisia	7.7	11.3	20.8	21.7
Iran	9.0	7.7	14.0	13.4	Turkey	49.4	116.6	263.5	251.4
Jamaica	4.8	4.7	10.3	11.0	Ukraine	(NA)	12.2	93.1	93.2
Jordan	8.3	7.4	6.6	6.6	Uruguay	4.4	8.4	11.0	12.2
Kazakhstan	(NA)	12.4	107.3	109.9	Venezuela	33.2	42.3	50.2	54.5
Lebanon.	1.8	10.2	24.3	24.9	Vietnam	23.3	12.8	25.0	28.7
Malaysia	15.3	41.9	66.2	66.4	Zimbabwe	3.3	3.8	5.3	5.0
Mexico.	104.4	150.9	203.6	192.0					

NA Not available. [1] See footnote 4, Table 1332. [2] See footnote 5, Table 1332. [3] The debt of the former Soviet Union is included in Russia's data after 1990 on the assumption that 100 percent of all outstanding external debt as of December 1991 has become a liability of Russia. Beginning in 2000, the data for Russia has also been revised to include obligations to members of the former Council for Mutual Economic Assistance and other countries in the form of trade-related credits amounting to $15.4 billion as of the end of 1996. [4] In June 2006, Serbia and Montenegro became separate countries (formerly Yugoslavia). Data for 2000 are for Serbia and Montenegro. Starting 2006, data excludes Montenegro. External debt obligations—excluding IBRD, IMF, and short-term—of Bosnia and Herzegovina before 2000 are included under Serbia and Montenegro. Data from 2000 onwards are estimates and also reflect borrowing by the former Yugoslavia that are not yet allocated to the successor republics.
Source: Source: The World Bank, Washington, DC, World Development Indicators 2011 database (copyright). See also <http://data.worldbank.org/>.

Table 1405. Foreign Direct Investment Flows in OECD Countries: 2000 to 2009

[In billions of dollars (314.0 represents $314,000,000,000). Data are converted to U.S. dollars using the yearly average exchange rate]

Country	Inflows			Cumulative 1990 to 2009	Outflows			Cumulative 1990 to 2009
	2000	2008	2009 [1]		2000	2008	2009 [1]	
United States	**314.0**	**324.6**	**129.9**	**2,689.8**	**142.6**	**330.5**	**248.1**	**2,908.8**
Australia	6.8	46.6	(NA)	224.4	1.1	35.8	(NA)	116.0
Austria	8.8	6.8	8.6	112.6	5.7	29.4	6.5	148.9
Belgium	(NA)	109.9	−39.8	350.8	(NA)	131.9	−77.4	302.8
Canada	66.8	55.2	18.7	514.8	44.7	80.8	38.9	558.2
Czech Republic	5.0	6.4	2.7	79.8	(Z)	4.3	1.3	11.0
Denmark	33.0	2.2	3.0	112.2	25.0	14.1	6.9	137.1
Finland	8.8	−1.0	(−Z)	75.4	24.0	9.3	3.8	110.4
France	42.9	62.1	59.6	806.0	175.6	160.8	147.2	1,514.8
Germany	198.3	26.4	38.8	735.6	56.6	134.3	61.1	1,125.2
Greece	(NA)	4.5	2.4	25.6	(NA)	2.4	2.1	17.6
Hungary	2.8	66.0	3.1	201.2	0.6	63.7	3.2	159.2
Iceland	0.2	0.9	0.1	16.9	0.4	−4.3	4.5	27.2
Ireland	26.5	−16.4	24.6	104.0	4.6	18.9	23.9	145.6
Italy	13.4	17.0	30.5	262.7	12.4	43.8	43.9	415.7
Japan	29.0	2.4	11.9	219.4	49.8	128.0	74.7	1,032.5
Korea, South	8.6	7.6	6.6	78.2	3.5	17.3	20.3	103.0
Luxembourg	(NA)	103.3	194.9	1,016.4	(NA)	132.7	222.3	1,167.5
Mexico	17.8	22.5	14.5	290.3	(NA)	(NA)	(NA)	(NA)
Netherlands	63.9	−0.1	32.6	525.8	75.7	67.2	28.9	824.0
New Zealand	1.4	2.2	−1.3	43.6	0.6	−0.4	−0.3	8.5
Norway	6.0	10.4	(NA)	66.1	8.3	26.0	(NA)	120.9
Poland	9.3	14.9	13.7	150.1	(Z)	4.5	5.2	29.6
Portugal	6.6	4.7	2.9	66.9	8.1	2.7	1.3	59.5
Spain	39.6	73.4	8.1	468.1	58.2	75.4	10.3	685.3
Sweden	23.2	33.7	10.9	299.1	40.6	27.8	30.3	346.4
Switzerland	19.3	15.1	27.0	201.2	44.7	55.3	33.3	516.2
Turkey	1.0	18.3	8.4	97.5	0.9	2.5	1.6	11.8
United Kingdom	118.8	89.5	71.3	1,252.5	233.5	181.9	33.1	1,723.2

NA Not available. Z Less than $50 million. [1] Preliminary.

Source: Organization for Economic Cooperation and Development (OECD), 2011, "Foreign Direct Investment: Flows by Partner Country," OECD International Direct Investment Statistics database (copyright); <http://dx.doi.org/10.1787/data-00335-en>, accessed April 2011.

Table 1406. Military Expenditures, 2009, and Manpower, 2010, by Country

[120,022 represents 120,022,000. Manpower covers males and females deemed fit for military service, ages 16–49, and who are not otherwise disqualified for health reasons]

Country	Expenditures (percent of GDP [1])	Manpower (1,000)	Country	Expenditures (percent of GDP [1])	Manpower (1,000)
United States	[2] **4.1**	**120,022**	Ireland	[2] 0.9	1,944
Afghanistan	1.9	7,847	Israel	[3] 7.3	2,964
Algeria	[3] 3.3	17,249	Italy	[2] 1.8	22,596
Argentina	0.8	16,873	Japan	[3] 0.8	43,931
Australia	3.0	8,652	Kazakhstan	[7] 1.1	6,438
Austria	0.8	3,134	Korea, North	(NA)	10,067
Belgium	[2] 1.3	3,812	Korea, South	[3] 2.7	21,033
Bolivia	1.3	3,776	Lebanon	[2] 3.1	1,863
Brazil	1.7	83,836	Libya	[2] 3.9	2,970
Bulgaria	[2] 2.6	2,659	Malaysia	[2] 2.0	12,423
Burma	[2] 2.1	21,633	Mexico	[3] 0.5	48,882
Cambodia	[2] 3.0	5,603	Morocco	[8] 5.0	14,403
Canada	[2] 1.1	13,023	Netherlands	[2] 1.6	6,324
Chile	[3] 2.7	7,183	Nicaragua	[3] 0.6	2,563
China [4]	[3] 4.3	618,589	Nigeria	[3] 1.5	40,708
Colombia	[2] 3.4	19,012	Norway	[2] 1.9	1,754
Congo (Brazzaville) [5]	0.9	1,145	Pakistan	[6] 3.0	75,327
Cote d'Ivoire	1.5	6,556	Peru	[3] 1.5	12,354
Cuba	[3] 3.8	4,822	Philippines	[2] 0.9	41,571
Czech Republic	[6] 1.5	4,061	Poland	[2] 1.7	15,584
Denmark	[6] 1.3	2,018	Russia	[2] 3.9	46,813
Ecuador	0.9	6,104	Saudi Arabia	[2] 10.0	13,043
Egypt	[2] 3.4	35,305	South Africa	[3] 1.7	14,093
El Salvador	0.6	2,452	Spain	[2] 1.2	18,721
Ethiopia	1.2	24,757	Sudan	[2] 3.0	13,316
France	[2] 2.6	23,747	Sweden	[2] 1.5	3,359
Germany	[2] 1.5	29,538	Syria	[2] 5.9	9,940
Greece	[2] 4.3	4,049	Thailand	[2] 1.8	27,491
Hungary	[2] 1.8	3,800	Turkey	[2] 5.3	35,005
India	[3] 2.5	489,571	Ukraine	[2] 1.4	15,686
Indonesia	[2] 3.0	107,539	United Kingdom	[2] 2.4	24,035
Iran	[3] 2.5	39,566	Venezuela	[2] 1.2	11,690
Iraq	[3] 8.6	13,013	Vietnam	[2] 2.5	41,504

NA Not available. [1] GDP calculated on an exchange rate basis. [2] 2005 data. [3] 2006 data. [4] See footnote 4, Table 1332. [5] See footnote 5, Table 1332. [6] 2007 data. [7] 2010 data. [8] 2003 data.

Source: Central Intelligence Agency, *The World Factbook*, <https://www.cia.gov/library/publications/the-world-factbook/index.html>, accessed June 2011.

Appendix I
Guide to Sources of Statistics, State Statistical Abstracts, and Foreign Statistical Abstracts

Alphabetically arranged, this guide contains references to important primary sources of statistical information for the United States and other countries. Secondary sources have been included if the information contained in them is presented in a particularly convenient form or if primary sources are not readily available. Nonrecurrent publications presenting compilations or estimates for years later than 2000, or types of data not available in regular series, are also included. Data are also available in press releases.

Valuable information may also be found in state reports, foreign statistical abstracts, which are included at the end of this appendix, and in reports for particular commodities, industries, or similar segments of our economic and social structures, many of which are not included here.

Publications listed under each subject are divided into two main groups: "U.S. Government" and "Nongovernment." The location of the publisher of each report is given except for federal agencies located in Washington, DC. Most federal publications may be purchased from the Superintendent of Documents, U.S. Government Printing Office, Washington, DC, tel. 202–512–1800, (Web site<http://bookstore.gpo.gov>). In some cases, federal publications may be obtained from the issuing agency.

Title	Frequency	Paper	Internet PDF	Internet Other formats
U.S. GOVERNMENT				
Administrative Office of the United States Courts <http://www.uscourts.gov>				
Calendar Year Reports on Authorized Wiretaps (state and federal)	Annual	X	X	X
Federal Court Management Statistics	Annual	X		X
Federal Judicial Caseload Statistics	Annual	X		
Judicial Business of the United States Courts	Annual	X	X	
Statistical Tables for the Federal Judiciary	Semiannual	X		X
Agency for International Development <http://www.usaid.gov>				
U.S. Overseas Loans and Grants: Obligations and Loan Authorizations	Annual		X	X
Army Corps of Engineers <http://www.usace.army.mil>				
Waterborne Commerce of the United States (in five parts)	Annual	X		X
Board of Governors of the Federal Reserve System <http://www.federalreserve.gov>				
Assets and Liabilities of Commercial Banks in the United States H.8	Weekly	X	X	X
Consumer Credit G.19	Monthly	X	X	X
Federal Reserve Bulletin	Annual	X	X	X
Foreign Exchange Rates H.10	Weekly			X
Flow of Funds Accounts of the United States Z.1	Quarterly	X	X	X
Industrial Production and Capacity Utilization G.17	Monthly	X	X	X
Money Stock and Debt Measures H.6	Weekly	X	X	X
Statistical Supplement to the Federal Reserve Bulletin	Monthly	X	X	X
Bureau of Economic Analysis <http://www.bea.gov>				
Survey of Current Business	Monthly	X	X	X
Bureau of Justice Statistics <http://www.ojp.usdoj.gov/bjs>				
American Indians and Crime: A BJS Statistical Profile, December 2004	Periodic	X	X	X
Background Checks for Firearm Transfers	Annual	X	X	X
Capital Punishment, 2006, December 2007	Annual		X	X
Carjacking, 1993–2002, July 2004	Periodic		X	X
Census of Publicly Funded Forensic Crime Laboratories, February 2005	Periodic	X	X	X
Census of State and Federal Correctional Facilities, 2000, August 2003	Periodic	X	X	X
Civil Rights Complaints in U.S. District Courts, July 2002	Periodic	X	X	X
Civil Trial Cases and Verdicts in Large Counties, 2001, April 2004	Periodic	X	X	X
Compendium of Federal Justice Statistics, 2004, December 2006	Annual	X	X	X
Contacts Between Police and Public: Findings from the 2005 National Survey, April 2007	Periodic	X	X	X

Title	Frequency	Paper	Internet PDF	Internet Other formats

Title	Frequency	Paper	PDF	Other formats
Bureau of Justice Statistics—Con.				
Contract Trials and Verdicts in Large Counties, 2001, February 2005	Periodic	X	X	X
Crime and the Nation's Households, 2005, April 2007	Annual	X	X	X
Crimes Against Persons Age 65 or Older, 1993–2002, January 2005	Periodic	X	X	X
Criminal Victimization in the United States, 2006, December 2007	Annual	X	X	X
Cross-National Studies in Crime and Justice, September 2004	Periodic	X	X	X
Defense Counsel in Criminal Cases, November 2000	Periodic	X	X	X
Education and Correctional Populations, January 2003	Periodic	X	X	X
Family Violence Statistics	Periodic	X	X	X
Federal Criminal Case Processing, 2002, January 2005	Periodic	X	X	X
Federal Law Enforcement Officers, 2004, August 2006	Biennial	X	X	X
Felony Defendants in Large Urban Counties, 2004, April 2008	Biennial		X	X
Felony Sentences in State Courts, 2004, July 2007	Biennial		X	X
Firearm Use by Offenders, November 2001	Periodic	X	X	X
Hepatitis Testing and Treatment in State Prisons, April 2004	Periodic	X	X	X
Hispanic Victims of Violent Crime, 1993–2000, April 2002	Periodic	X	X	X
HIV in Prisons 2006	Annual		X	X
Homicide Trends in the United States	Annual	X	X	X
Identity Theft, 2005, November 2007	Periodic	X	X	X
Immigration Offenders in the Federal Criminal Justice System, August 2002	Periodic	X	X	X
Incarcerated Parents and Their Children, August 2000	Periodic	X	X	X
Indicators of School Crime and Safety	Annual	X	X	X
Intimate Partner Violence, 1993 to 2001, February 2003	Periodic	X	X	X
Jails in Indian Country, 2004, November 2006	Annual	X	X	X
Justice Expenditure and Employment Extract Series, 2005, August 2007	Annual			X
Juvenile Offenders and Victims	Periodic	X	X	X
Juvenile Victimization and Offending, 1993–2003	Periodic	X	X	X
Law Enforcement Management and Administrative Statistics 2000: Data for Individual State and Local Agencies with 100 or More Officers	Periodic	X	X	X
Local Police Departments, 2003, May 2006	Periodic	X	X	X
Medical Malpractice Trials and Verdicts in Large Counties, April 2004	Periodic	X	X	X
Money Laundering Offenders, 1994–2001, July 2003	Periodic	X	X	X
Prevalence of Imprisonment in the U.S. Population, 1974–2001, August 2003	Periodic	X	X	X
Prison and Jail Inmates at Midyear, 2006, June 2007	Annual	X	X	X
Prisoners in 2006, December 2007	Annual	X	X	X
Probation and Parole in the United States	Annual	X	X	X
Profile of Jail Inmates, 2002, July 2004	Periodic	X	X	X
Prosecutors in State Courts, 2001, May 2002	Biennial	X	X	X
Rape and Sexual Assault: Reporting to Police and Medical Attention, August 2002	Periodic	X	X	X
Reentry Trends in the United States Current Data Electronic	Periodic		X	X
Sheriff's Offices, 2003, April 2006	Periodic		X	X
Sourcebook of Criminal Justice Statistics	Annual	X	X	X
State Court Prosecutors in Large Districts, December 2001	Periodic	X	X	X
State Court Prosecutors in Small Districts, 2001, January 2003	Periodic	X	X	X
State Court Sentencing of Convicted Felons, 2004, July 2007	Biennial		X	X
State Prison Expenditures, 2001, June 2004	Periodic	X	X	X
Summary of State Sex Offender Registries, 2001, March 2002	Periodic	X	X	X
Survey of DNA Crime Laboratories, 2001, January 2002	Periodic	X	X	X
Survey of State Criminal History Information Systems, September 2003	Biennial	X	X	X
Survey of State Procedures Related to Firearm Sales, 2005, November 2006	Periodic	X	X	X
Tort Trials and Verdicts in Large Counties, November 2004	Periodic	X	X	X
Traffic Stop Data Collection Policies for State Police, 2004, June 2005	Periodic	X	X	X
Violent Victimization of College Students, 1995–2002, January 2005	Periodic	X	X	X
Weapon Use and Violent Crime, 1993–2001, September 2003	Periodic	X	X	X
Bureau of Labor Statistics <http://www.bls.gov>				
100 Years of U.S. Consumer Spending: Data for the Nation, New York City, and Boston, Report 991	Periodic	X	X	
College Enrollment and Work Activity of High School Graduates	Annual	X	X	
Comparative Labor Force Statistics, Ten Countries	Semiannual	X	X	X
Compensation and Working Conditions	Quarterly		X	X
Consumer Expenditure Survey, Integrated Diary and Interview Survey data	Annual	X	X	X
Consumer Prices: Energy and Food	Monthly	X	X	X
Consumer Price Index (CPI) Detailed Report	Monthly		X	X
Employer Costs for Employee Compensation	Annual	X	X	X
Employment and Earnings	Monthly		X	X
Employment and Wages	Annual	X	X	X
Employment Characteristics of Families	Annual	X	X	X
Employment Cost Index	Quarterly	X	X	X
Employment Cost Indexes and Levels	Annual	X	X	X
The Employment Situation	Monthly	X	X	X
Geographic Profile of Employment and Unemployment	Annual	X	X	X
International Comparisons of Hourly Compensation Costs for Production Workers in Manufacturing	Annual	X	X	X
International Comparisons of Manufacturing Productivity and Unit Labor Cost Trends	Annual	X	X	X
Metropolitan Area Employment and Unemployment	Monthly	X	X	X
Monthly Labor Review	Monthly		X	X
National Compensation Survey	Annual	X	X	X
Occupational Injuries and Illnesses in the United States by Industry	Annual	X	X	X
Occupational Projections and Training Data	Biennial	X	X	X
Producer Price Indexes Detailed Report	Monthly		X	X
Productivity and Costs by Industry	Periodic	X	X	X
Selected Service-Providing and Mining Industries, 2005	Annual	X	X	X
Manufacturing, 2005	Annual	X	X	X

878 Appendix I

Title	Frequency	Paper	Internet	
			PDF	Other formats
Bureau of Labor Statistics—Con.				
Wholesale Trade, Retail Trade, and Food Services and Drinking Places, 2005	Annual	X	X	X
Real Earnings	Monthly	X	X	X
Regional and State Employment and Unemployment	Monthly	X	X	X
Relative Importance of Components in the Consumer Price Indexes	Annual	X	X	X
Union Members	Annual	X	X	X
U.S. Import and Export Price Indexes	Monthly	X	X	X
Usual Weekly Earnings of Wage and Salary Workers	Quarterly	X	X	X
Work Experience of the Population	Annual	X	X	X
Bureau of Land Management				
<http://www.blm.gov/wo/st/en.html>				
Public Land Statistics	Annual	X	X	
Census Bureau				
<http://www.census.gov>				
2007 Economic Census:				
Comparative Statistics	Quinquennial	X	X	X
Bridge Between North American Industry Classification System (NAICS) and Standard Industrial Classification (SIC)	Quinquennial	X	X	X
Business Expenses	Quinquennial	X	X	X
Industry/Geography	Quinquennial		X	X
2007 Economic Census, Company Statistics Series, Survey of Business Owners.......	Quinquennial	X	X	X
American Indian- and Alaska Native-Owned Firms	Quinquennial	X	X	X
Asian-Owned Firms	Quinquennial	X	X	X
Black-Owned Firms	Quinquennial	X	X	X
Hispanic-Owned Firms	Quinquennial	X	X	X
Native Hawaiian- and Other Pacific Islander-Owned Firms	Quinquennial	X	X	X
American Community Survey Annual Earnings and Poverty Report............	Annual	X	X	
Annual Revision of Monthly Retail and Food Services: Sales and Inventories	Annual		X	
Annual Revision of Monthly Wholesale Distributors: Sales and Inventories	Annual		X	X
Census of Housing Decennial (2000, most recent)......................	Decennial	X	X	X
Census of Population Decennial (2000, most recent)	Decennial	X	X	X
County Business Patterns....................................	Annual		X	X
Current Construction Reports:				
New Residential Construction and New Residential Sales	Annual		X	
Value of Construction Put in Place, C30........................	Monthly		X	
Residential Improvements and Repairs, C50	Monthly		X	
Current Housing Reports:				
Housing Vacancies, H111....................................	Quarterly		X	X
Who Can Afford to Buy a House, H121	Occasional	X	X	X
Survey of Market Absorption of Apartments (SOMA).................	Quarterly		X	X
Characteristics of Apartments Completed, H131...................	Annual	X	X	X
American Housing Survey for the United States, H150	Biennial	X	X	X
American Housing Survey for Selected Metropolitan Areas, H170	Biennial	X	X	X
Current Industrial Reports	Annual		X	
Current Population Reports (Series P20 and P23)......................	Annual	X	X	X
Consumer Income and Poverty, P60, and Household Economic Studies, P70	Periodic	X	X	
Alternative Poverty Estimates in the United States: 2003	Periodic	X	X	
Alternative Income Estimates in the United States: 2003	Periodic	X	X	
Income, Poverty, and Health Insurance Coverage in the United States, 2007	Annual	X	X	X
Economic Census of Outlying Areas..............................	Quinquennial	X	X	
Global Population Profile: 2002 (Series WP)........................	Periodic	X	X	X
International Briefs (Series IB)	Annual	X	X	
International Data Base...............................	Annual			X
International Population Reports (Series P95)	Annual	X	X	
Manufacturer's Shipments, Inventories, and Orders	Monthly		X	
Manufacturer's Shipments, Inventories, and Orders: 1992–2005	Annual		X	
New York City Housing and Vacancy Survey, 2005....................	Every 3 years		X	X
Nonemployer Statistics	Annual		X	X
Population Estimates and Projections............................	Annual			X
Quarterly Financial Report for Manufacturing, Mining, and Trade Corporations	Quarterly		X	
Residential Finance Survey, 2001..............................	Every 10 years	X	X	X
Service Annual Survey Report	Annual		X	
Survey of Plant Capacity Utilization (Current Industrial Reports MQ-C1).............	Annual		X	
U.S. International Trade in Goods and Services: includes cumulative data	Annual		X	X
U.S. Trade with Puerto Rico and U.S. Possessions (FT 895)......................	Monthly		X	
Vehicle Inventory and Use Survey (discontinued)	Quinquennial	X	X	X
Centers for Disease Control and Prevention, Atlanta, Georgia				
<http://www.cdc.gov>				
CDC Injury Fact Book	Periodic	X	X	X
Morbidity and Mortality Weekly Report	Annual	X	X	X
Centers for Medicare and Medicaid Services (CMS)				
<http://www.cms.hhs.gov>				
CMS Statistics....................................	Annual	X	X	
Data Compendium...................................	Annual	X	X	
Health Care Financing Review. Medicare and Medicaid Statistical Supplement	Annual	X	X	
Health Care Financing Review	Quarterly	X	X	
Trustees Report.....................................	Annual	X	X	
Wallet Card	Annual	X	X	
Central Intelligence Agency				
<http://www.cia.gov>				
World Factbook	Annual	X	X	X
Coast Guard (See Department of Homeland Security)				

Title	Frequency	Paper	Internet PDF	Internet Other formats
Comptroller of the Currency <http://www.occ.treas.gov>				
Quarterly Journal.	Quarterly		X	X
Office of the Clerk U.S. House of Representatives <http://clerk.house.gov>				
Statistics of the Presidential and Congressional Election	Biennial		X	X
Council of Economic Advisers <http://www.whitehouse.gov>				
Economic Indicators	Monthly	X	X	X
Economic Report of the President	Annual	X	X	
Department of Agriculture, Economic Research Service <http://www.ers.usda.gov>				
Agricultural Income and Finance (Situation and Outlook Report)	Annual	X	X	X
Amber Waves	Periodic	X	X	X
Cotton and Wool Yearbook	Annual			X
Dairy Yearbook	Annual			X
Feedgrains Yearbook.	Annual		X	
Food Spending in American Households	Annual	X	X	
Fruit and Tree Nut Yearbook.	Annual		X	
Oil Crops Yearbook	Annual		X	X
Poultry Yearbook	Annual			X
Red Meat Yearbook	Annual			X
Rice Yearbook	Annual		X	X
Sugar and Sweeteners Yearbook	Periodic			X
Situation and Outlook Reports. Issued for agricultural exports, cotton and wool, dairy, feed, fruit and tree nuts, agricultural resources, livestock and poultry, oil crops, rice, aquaculture, sugar and sweeteners, tobacco, vegetables, wheat, and world agriculture	Periodic	X	X	
Vegetable and Melons Yearbook	Annual			X
World Agricultural Supply and Demand Estimates	Monthly	X	X	X
Department of Agriculture, Food and Nutrition Service <http://www.fns.usda.gov/fns/default.htm>				
Characteristics of Food Stamp Households	Annual	X	X	
Food and Consumer Service Programs	Monthly			X
Department of Agriculture, Foreign Agricultural Service <http://www.fas.usda.gov>				
Livestock and Poultry World Markets and Trade	Biannual	X	X	
Department of Agriculture, National Agricultural Statistics Service <http://www.nass.usda.gov>				
Agricultural Chemical Usage.	Periodic			X
Agricultural Statistics.	Annual	X	X	
Catfish Production	Annual	X	X	X
Cattle.	Biennial	X	X	X
Census of Agriculture	Quinquennial	X	X	X
Cherry Production	Annual	X	X	X
Chickens and Eggs	Annual	X	X	X
Citrus Fruits	Annual	X	X	X
Cranberries	Annual	X	X	X
Crop Production Reports.	Monthly	X	X	X
Crop Progress	Weekly	X	X	X
Crop Values Report	Annual	X	X	X
Dairy Products.	Annual	X	X	X
Farm Labor	Quarterly	X	X	X
Farms, Land in Farms, and Livestock Operations	Annual	X	X	X
Floriculture Crops	Annual	X	X	X
Agricultural Land Values and Cash Rents	Monthly	X	X	X
Livestock Slaughter	Annual	X	X	X
Meat Animals: Production, Disposition, and Income	Annual	X	X	X
Milk Production	Annual	X	X	X
Noncitrus Fruits and Nuts	Biennial	X	X	X
Poultry: Production and Value Summary	Annual	X	X	X
Stock Reports. Stocks of grain, peanuts, potatoes, and rice	Periodic	X	X	X
Trout Production	Annual	X	X	X
Turkeys: Hatchery and Raised.	Annual	X	X	X
Usual Planting and Harvesting Dates	Periodic	X	X	X
Vegetable Reports.	Periodic	X	X	X
Weekly Weather and Crop Bulletin Report	Weekly	X	X	
Winter Wheat Seedlings	Annual	X	X	X
Department of Agriculture, Natural Resources and Conservation Service <http://www.nrcs.usda.gov>				
National Resources Inventory	Periodic	X		X
Department of Defense <http://www.defenselink.mil/pubs>				
Foreign Military Sales and Military Assistance Facts	Annual			X
Personnel Statistics	Annual		X	
Department of Education <http://www.ed.gov/index.jhtml>				

Title	Frequency	Paper	PDF	Other formats
Department of Education, Rehabilitation Services Administration				
Caseload Statistics of State Vocational Rehabilitation Agencies in Fiscal Year	Annual	X	X	X
Department of Health and Human Services <http://www.hhs.gov>				
Annual Report	Annual	X		
Department of Homeland Security <http://www.dhs.gov/index.shtm>				
Budget in Brief	Annual	X	X	
Department of Homeland Security, Coast Guard <http://www.uscg.mil/default.asp>				
Fact File	Periodic	X	X	X
Department of Homeland Security, Office of Immigration Statistics <http://www.dhs.gov/ximgtn/statistics/>				
Yearbook of Immigration Statistics	Annual	X	X	
Department of Housing and Urban Development <http://www.hud.gov>				
Survey of Mortgage Lending Activity	Monthly	X		X
Department of Justice, Bureau of Alcohol, Tobacco Tax, Firearms and Explosives <http://www.atf.treas.gov>				
Alcohol and Tobacco Summary Statistics	Annual	X		
Tobacco Products Monthly Statistical Releases	Monthly	X		
Department of Labor <http://www.dol.gov>				
Annual Report of the Secretary	Annual	X	X	X
Department of State <http://www.state.gov>				
United States Contribution to International Organizations	Annual			X
Department of Transportation <http://www.dot.gov>				
Air Travel Consumer Report	Monthly	X	X	X
Airport Activity Statistics of Certified Route Air Carriers	Annual	X		X
Transportation Safety Information Report	Quarterly	X		X
U.S. International Air Travel Statistics	Quarterly	X	X	X
Wage Statistics of Class I Railroads in the United States	Annual	X	X	
Department of the Treasury, Bureau of Public Debt <http://www.publicdebt.treas.gov>				
Monthly Statement of the Public Debt of the United States	Monthly	X	X	X
Department of the Treasury, Financial Management Services <http://www.fms.treas.gov>				
Active Foreign Credits of the United States Government	Quarterly	X		
Combined Statement of Receipts, Outlays, and Balances	Annual	X	X	
Monthly Treasury Statement of Receipts and Outlays of the United States Government	Monthly	X	X	X
Treasury Bulletin	Quarterly	X	X	X
Financial Report of the United States Government	Annual	X	X	
Department of Veterans Affairs <http://www.va.gov>				
Disability Compensation, Pension, and Death Pension Data	Annual			X
Government Life Insurance Programs for Veterans and Members of the Service	Annual			X
Selected Compensation and Pension Data by State of Residence	Annual			X
Veterans Affairs Annual Accountability Report	Annual	X	X	X
Drug Enforcement Administration <http://www.whitehousedrugpolicy.gov>				
Drug Abuse and Law Enforcement Statistics	Irregular	X	X	X
Employment and Training Administration <http://www.doleta.gov>				
Unemployment Insurance Claims	Weekly			X
Energy Information Administration <http://www.eia.gov>				
Annual Energy Outlook	Annual	X	X	X
Annual Energy Review	Annual	X	X	X
Annual Coal Report	Annual		X	X
Electric Power Annual	Annual		X	X
Electric Power Monthly	Monthly		X	X
Electric Sales, Revenue and Retail Price	Annual			X
Emissions of Greenhouse Gases in the U.S.	Annual		X	X
International Energy Statistics portal	On going		X	X
International Energy Outlook	Annual		X	X
Monthly Energy Review	Monthly		X	X
Performance Profiles of Major Energy Producers	Annual		X	X
Petroleum Marketing Annual	Annual		X	X
Petroleum Marketing Monthly	Monthly		X	X
Petroleum Supply Annual Volume 1	Annual		X	X
Petroleum Supply Annual Volume 2	Annual		X	X
Petroleum Supply Monthly	Monthly		X	X
Quarterly Coal Report	Quarterly		X	X
Renewable Energy Annual	Annual		X	
Residential Energy Consumption Survey	Quadrennial		X	X

U.S. Census Bureau, Statistical Abstract of the United States: 2012

Title	Frequency	Paper	Internet PDF	Internet Other formats
Energy Information Administration—Con.				
State Electricity Profiles..	Annual		X	X
State Energy Data Report.......................................	Annual		X	X
State Energy Price and Expenditure Report	Annual		X	X
U.S. Crude Oil, Natural Gas, and Natural Gas Liquids Reserves	Annual		X	X
Weekly Coal Production	Weekly		X	X
Environmental Protection Agency				
<http://www.epa.gov/>				
Air Quality Data..	Annual			X
Drinking Water Infrastructure Needs Survey	Periodic	X	X	
Needs Survey, Conveyance and Treatment of Municipal Wastewater Summaries of				
Technical Data	Biennial		X	
Toxics Release Inventory.......................................	Annual		X	X
National Water Quality Inventory: 2000 Report (EPA-841-T-01-001)..	Biennial	X	X	
Export-Import Bank of the United States				
<http://www.exim.gov/>				
Annual Report..	Annual	X	X	
Report to the U.S. Congress on Export Credit Competition and the Export-Import Bank				
of the United States	Annual	X	X	
Farm Credit Administration.				
<http://www.fca.gov/FCA-HomePage.htm>				
Annual Report on the Farm Credit System	Annual	X	X	
Federal Bureau of Investigation				
<http://www.fbi.gov/ucr/ucr.htm>				
Crime in the United States.....................................	Annual		X	X
Hate Crime Statistics..	Annual		X	X
Law Enforcement Officers Killed and Assaulted	Annual		X	X
Federal Communications Commission				
<http://www.fcc.gov/>				
Annual Assessment of the Status of Competition in the Market for the				
Delivery of Video Programming	Annual	X	X	
Annual Report	Annual	X	X	
High-Speed Services for Internet Access	Semiannual		X	
Statistics of Communications Common Carriers...................	Discontinued			
Telecommunications Industry Revenue...........................	Annual	X	X	
Trends in Telephone Service....................................	Annual		X	
Trends in the International Telecommunications Industry	Annual	X	X	
Federal Deposit Insurance Corporation				
<http://www.fdic.gov/>				
Annual Report..	Annual	X	X	X
FDIC Quarterly	Quarterly	X	X	X
Historical Statistics on Banking................................	Annual			X
Quarterly Banking Profile	Quarterly	X	X	X
Statistics on Banking..	Quarterly			X
Summary of Deposits	Annual			X
Federal Highway Administration				
<http://www.fhwa.dot.gov>				
Highway Statistics	Annual	X	X	
Federal Railroad Administration				
<http://www.fra.dot.gov>				
<http://safetydata.fra.dot.gov/officeofsafety>				
Railroad Safety Statistics......................................	Annual	X	X	X
Fish and Wildlife Service				
<http://www.fws.gov/>				
Federal Aid in Fish and Wildlife Restoration	Annual	X	X	
National Survey of Fishing, Hunting, and Wildlife Associated Recreation.............	Quinquennial	X	X	
Forest Service				
<http://www.fs.fed.us/>				
An Analysis of the Timber Situation in the United States 1996–2050	Periodic			X
Land Areas of the National Forest System	Annual	X		X
U.S. Timber Production, Trade, Consumption, and Price Statistics 2001	Biennial	X	X	
RPA Assessment Tables	Periodic			X
General Services Administration				
<http://www.gsa.gov/>				
Federal Real Property Profile	Annual		X	X
Geological Survey				
<http://minerals.usgs.gov/minerals>				
Mineral Commodity Summaries	Annual	X	X	
Mineral Industry Surveys......................................	Monthly & Qtrly		X	X
Minerals Yearbook..	Annual	X	X	X
Internal Revenue Service				
<http://www.irs.gov/taxstats>				
Corporation Income Tax Returns...............................	Annual	X	X	X
Individual Income Tax Returns.................................	Annual	X	X	X
IRS Data Book..	Annual	X	X	X
Statistics of Income Bulletin...................................	Quarterly	X	X	X

Title	Frequency	Paper	PDF	Other formats
International Trade Administration, Office of Travel and Tourism Industries <http://www.tinet.ita.doc.gov>				
U.S. Travel and Tourism Statistics	Annual	X		X
International Trade Commission <http://www.usitc.gov>				
Recent Trends in U.S. Services	Periodic	X	X	
Synthetic Organic Chemicals, U.S. Production and Sales	Annual	X	X	
Library of Congress <http://www.loc.gov/index.html>				
Annual Report	Annual	X	X	
Maritime Administration <http://www.marad.dot.gov>				
Annual Report	Annual	X	X	
Cargo-Carrying U.S. Flag Fleet by Area of Operation	Semiannual	X	X	X
Merchant Fleet Ocean-Going Vessels 1,000 Gross Tons and Over	Quarterly			X
Seafaring Wage Rates	Biennial	X	X	
Mine Safety and Health Administration <http://www.msha.gov>				
Informational Reports by Mining Industry: Coal; Metallic Minerals; Nonmetallic Minerals (except stone and coal); Stone, Sand, and Gravel	Annual			X
Mine Injuries and Worktime (Some preliminary data)	Quarterly	X		X
National Aeronautics and Space Administration <http://ifmp.nasa.gov>				
Annual Procurement Report	Annual	X	X	
National Center for Education Statistics <http://nces.ed.gov>				
Characteristics of the 100 Largest Public Elementary and Secondary School Districts in the United States	Annual	X	X	X
Characteristics of Private Schools in the United States, 2005–2006	Annual	X	X	X
College and University Library Survey	Triennial			X
Computer and Internet Use by Children and Adolescents	Biennial	X	X	
The Condition of Education	Annual	X	X	
Digest of Education Statistics	Annual	X	X	
Enrollment in Postsecondary Institutions, Graduation Rates, and Financial Statistics	Annual		X	
Indicators of School Crime and Safety	Annual	X	X	
National Education Statistics Quarterly (last edition 4th quarter 2005)	Quarterly			X
The Nation's Report Card: Mathematics Highlights 2007	Periodic	X	X	
The Nation's Report Card: Reading Highlights 2007	Periodic	X	X	
The Nation's Report Card: Science 2005	Periodic	X	X	
The Nation's Report Card: History 2006	Periodic	X	X	
The Nation's Report Card: Writing 2007	Periodic	X	X	
Projections of Education Statistics	Annual	X	X	X
School and Staffing Survey	Quadrennial			X
Characteristics of Schools, Districts, Teachers, Principals, and School Libraries in the United States	Annual	X	X	
Status and Trends in the Education of Racial and Ethnic Minorities	Irregular	X	X	
National Center for Health Statistics <http://www.cdc.gov/nchs/>				
Ambulatory Care Visits to Physician Offices, Hospital Outpatient Departments, and Emergency Departments	Annual	X	X	
Health: United States	Annual	X	X	
Health Characteristics of Adults 55 Years of Age and Over	Periodic	X	X	
Fertility, Family Planning, and Reproductive Health of U.S. Women: Data from the 2002 National Survey of Family Growth	Periodic		X	X
National Hospital Discharge Survey: Annual Summary	Annual		X	
National Vital Statistics Reports (NVRS)	Monthly		X	
Vital and Health Statistics:				
Series 10: Health Interview Survey Statistics	Annual	X	X	
Series 11: Health and Nutrition Examination Survey Statistics	Irregular	X	X	
Series 13: Data from National Health Care Survey	Irregular	X	X	
Series 14: Data on Health Resources: Manpower and Facilities	Irregular	X	X	
Series 20: Mortality Data	Irregular	X	X	
Series 21: Natality, Marriage, and Divorce Data	Irregular	X	X	
Series 23: Data from the National Survey of Family Growth	Irregular	X	X	
National Credit Union Administration <http://www.ncua.gov>				
Annual Report	Annual	X	X	
Yearend Statistics	Annual	X	X	
National Endowment for the Arts <http://www.nea.gov>				
National Endowment for the Arts, Annual Report	Annual			X
The Performing Arts in the GDP, 2002	Periodic	X	X	
Artist Labor Force by State, 2000	Periodic	X	X	
Artist Employment, 2000–2002	Periodic	X	X	
The Arts in the GDP	Periodic	X	X	
Demographic Characteristics of Art Attendance, 2002	Periodic	X	X	
2002 Survey of Public Participation in the Arts	Periodic	X	X	

Title	Frequency	Paper	Internet PDF	Internet Other formats
National Endowment for the Humanities <http://www.neh.gov>				
Budget Request	Annual	X		X
National Guard Bureau <http://www.ngb.army.mil/default.aspx>				
Annual Review of the Chief	Annual	X	X	
National Highway Traffic Safety Administration <http://www.nhtsa.dot.gov>				
Traffic Safety Facts	Annual	X	X	
National Oceanic and Atmospheric Administration <http://www.lib.noaa.gov>				
Climates of the World, HCS 6-4	Monthly			X
Comparative Climatic Data	Annual		X	X
Daily Normals of Temp, Precip, HDD, & CDD/Clim 84	Periodic			X
Fisheries of the United States	Annual	X	X	
General Summary of Tornadoes	Annual			X
Hourly Precipitation Data. Monthly with annual summary; for each state	Monthly			X
Local Climatological Data. Monthly with annual summary; for major cities	Monthly			X
Monthly Climatic Data for the World	Monthly			X
Monthly Normals of Temp, Precip, HDD, & CDD/Clim 84	Periodic		X	X
Our Living Oceans	Periodic	X	X	
Storm Data	Monthly			X
U.S. Climate Normals	Daily	X	X	X
Weekly Weather and Crop Bulletin National summary	Weekly	X	X	
National Park Service <http://www.nps.gov/>				
Federal Recreation Fee Report	Annual	X		
National Park Statistical Abstract	Annual	X	X	
National Science Foundation <http://www.nsf.gov/statistics>				
Academic Institutional Profiles	Annual		X	X
Academic Research and Development Expenditures	Annual		X	X
Characteristics of Doctoral Scientists and Engineers in the United States	Biennial		X	X
Characteristics of Recent Science/Engineering Graduates	Biennial		X	X
Federal Funds for Research and Development	Annual		X	X
Federal Research and Development Funding by Budget Function Report	Annual		X	X
Federal Science and Engineering Support to Universities, Colleges, and Nonprofit Institutions: Detailed Statistical Tables	Annual		X	X
Graduate Students and Postdoctorates in Science and Engineering	Annual		X	X
National Patterns of Research and Development Resources	Annual		X	X
Research and Development in Industry	Annual		X	X
Science and Engineering Degrees	Annual		X	X
Science and Engineering Degrees, by Race/Ethnicity of Recipients	Annual		X	X
Science and Engineering Doctorate Awards	Annual		X	X
Science and Engineering Indicators	Biennial	X	X	X
Science and Engineering State Profiles	Annual		X	X
Scientific and Engineering Research Facilities at Universities and Colleges	Biennial		X	X
Women, Minorities, and Persons with Disabilities in Science and Engineering	Biennial		X	X
National Transportation Safety Board <http://www.ntsb.gov>				
Annual Review of Aircraft Accident Data: U.S. Air Carrier Operations	Annual		X	
Annual Review of Aircraft Accident Data: US General Aviation	Annual		X	
Office of Juvenile Justice and Delinquency Prevention <http://ojjdp.ncjrs.org/>				
Highlights of the 2006 National Youth Gang Survey (FS-200805)	Annual		X	X
Juvenile Arrests 2004 (Bulletin, NCJ 214563)	Annual	X	X	X
Victims of Violent Juvenile Crime (Bulletin, NCJ 201628)	Periodic	X	X	X
Office of Management and Budget <http://www.whitehouse.gov/omb>				
The Budget of the United States Government	Annual	X	X	
Office of Personnel Management <http://www.opm.gov>				
Demographic Profile of the Federal Workforce	Biennial		X	X
Employment and Trends	Bimonthly		X	X
The Fact Book	Annual		X	X
Statistical Abstract for the Federal Employee Benefit Programs	Annual			X
Work Years and Personnel Costs	Annual		X	X
Patent and Trademark Office <http://www.uspto.gov>				
Technology Assessment and Forecast Reports	Periodic	X	X	X
All Technologies (Utility Patents)	Annual	X	X	X
Patent Counts by Country/State and Year, Utility Patents Report	Annual	X	X	X
Patenting Trends in the United States	Annual	X		
Railroad Retirement Board, Chicago, Illinois <http://www.rrb.gov/default.asp>				
Annual Report	Annual		X	
Quarterly Benefit Statistics	Quarterly	X		X

884 Appendix I

Title	Frequency	Paper	Internet PDF	Internet Other formats
Securities and Exchange Commission <http://www.sec.gov/about.shtml>				
Select SEC and Market Data.............................	Annual		X	
Small Business Administration <http://www.sba.gov/advocacy>				
Annual Report.............................	Annual	X		X
Quarterly Indicators.........................	Annual	X	X	X
Small Business and Micro Business Lending.................	Annual	X	X	X
State and Territory Small Business Profiles..............	Annual	X	X	X
The Small Business Economy......................	Annual	X	X	X
Social Security Administration <http://www.ssa.gov>				
Annual Statistical Report on the Social Security Disability Insurance Program	Annual	X	X	X
Annual Statistical Supplement to the Social Security Bulletin..................	Annual	X	X	X
Children Receiving Social Security Income (SSI)	Annual	X	X	X
Congressional Statistics	Annual	X	X	X
Fast Facts & Figures about Social Security.............	Annual	X	X	X
Income of the Population 55 and over...............	Biennially	X	X	X
OASDI Beneficiaries by State and County	Annual	X	X	X
Social Security Bulletin......................	Quarterly	X	X	X
SSI Annual Statistical Report	Annual	X	X	X
SSI Disabled Recipients Who Work..................	Annual	X	X	X
SSI Recipients by State and County	Annual	X	X	X
State Assistance Programs for SSI Recipients	Annual	X	X	X
Substance Abuse and Mental Health Services Administration <http://www.samhsa.gov>				
National Survey on Drug Use and Health	Annual	X	X	X
National Survey on Substance Abuse Treatment Services (N-SSATS)...............	Annual	X	X	X
U.S. Copyright Office <http://www.copyright.gov>				
Annual Report.............................	Annual	X	X	
NONGOVERNMENT				
Aerospace Industries Association, Washington, DC <http://www.aia-aerospace.org>				
Aerospace Facts and Figures	Annual	X	X	X
Aerospace Industry Year-End Review and Forecast..............	Annual		X	
Commercial Helicopter Shipments	Annual		X	
Employment in the Aerospace Industry................	Quarterly		X	
Exports of Aerospace Products.....................	Quarterly		X	
Imports of Aerospace Products.....................	Quarterly		X	
Manufacturing Production, Capacity, and Utilization in Aerospace and Aircraft and parts	Quarterly		X	
Orders, Shipments, Backlog and Inventories for Aircraft, Missiles, and Parts...........	Quarterly		X	
Air Transport Association of America, Incorporated, Washington, DC <http://www.airlines.org>				
Air Transport Association, Annual Report	Annual		X	
The Alan Guttmacher Institute, New York, NY <http://www.guttmacher.org>				
Perspectives on Sexual and Reproductive Health.................	Quarterly	X	X	X
American Bureau of Metal Statistics, Incorporated, Secaucus, NJ <http://www.abms.com>				
Non-Ferrous Metal Yearbook....................	Annual	X		X
American Council of Life Insurers, Washington, DC <http://www.acli.com>				
Life Insurers Fact Book	Annual	X	X	
American Dental Association, Chicago, IL <http://www.ada.org>				
Dental Students' Register	Annual	X		
Distribution of Dentists in the United States by Region and State..................	Triennial	X		
Survey of Dental Practice	Annual	X		
American Forest and Paper Association, Washington, DC <http://www.afandpa.org>				
Annual Statistical Summary of Recovered Paper Utilization.....................	Annual	X	X	
Statistics of Paper, Paperboard, and Wood Pulp..............	Monthly	X	X	
American Gas Association, Washington, DC <http://www.aga.org>				
Gas Facts	Annual	X	X	
American Iron and Steel Institute, Washington, DC <http://www.steel.org/AM/Template.cfm?Section=Home>				
Annual Statistical Report........................	Annual	X		
American Medical Association, Chicago, IL <http://www.ama-assn.org>				
Physician Characteristics and Distribution in the U.S...............	Annual	X		
State Medical Licensure Statistics, and License Requirements	Annual	X		

Title	Frequency	Paper	PDF	Other formats
			Internet	

Title	Frequency	Paper	PDF	Other formats
American Osteopathic Association, Chicago, IL <http://www.osteopathic.org/index.cfm>				
American Osteopathic Association Fact Sheet	Biennial	X	X	
American Petroleum Institute, Washington, DC <http://www.api.org>				
The Basic Petroleum Data Book (online subscription)	Annual	X		
Joint Association Survey on Drilling Costs (JA5)............................	Annual	X		
Petroleum Industry Environmental Report...............................	Annual	X		X
Quarterly Well Completion Report (online subscription)	Quarterly	X	X	
American Public Transportation Association, Washington, DC <http://www.apta.com>				
Public Transportation Fact Book	Annual	X	X	
Association for Manufacturing Technology, McLean, VA <http://www.amtonline.org>				
Economic Handbook of the Machine Tool Industry 2003–2004. (Online version by subscription only.)...	Annual		X	
Association of American Railroads, Washington, DC <http://www.aar.org>				
Analysis of Class I Railroads..	Annual	X	X	X
Cars of Revenue Freight Loaded.......................................	Weekly		X	X
Freight Commodity Statistics, Class I Railroads in the United States	Annual	X	X	X
Yearbook of Railroad Facts	Annual	X	X	
Association of Racing Commissioners International, Incorporated, Lexington, KY <http://www.arci.com>				
Statistical Reports on Greyhound Racing in the United States...................	Annual	X		
Statistical Reports on Horse Racing in the United States......................	Annual	X		
Statistical Reports on Jai Alai in the United States	Annual	X		
Book Industry Study Group, Inc., New York, NY <http://www.bisg.org>				
Book Industry Trends..	Annual	X		
Used-Book Sales...	Periodic	X		
Boy Scouts of America, Irving, TX <http://www.scouting.org>				
Annual Report	Annual	X		X
The Bureau of National Affairs, Incorporated, Washington, DC <http://www.bna.com>				
Basic Patterns in Union Contracts.....................................	Annual	X		
BNA's Employment Outlook	Quarterly	X		
BNA's Job Absence and Turnover......................................	Quarterly	X		
Directory of U.S. Labor Organizations..................................	Annual	X		
National Labor Relations Board Election Statistics	Annual	X		
Union Membership and Earnings Data Book	Annual	X		
Source Book on Collective Bargaining	Annual	X		
Carl H. Pforzheimer and Company, New York, NY				
Comparative Oil Company Statistics Annual...............................	Annual	X		
Chronicle of Higher Education, Incorporated, Washington, DC <http://chronicle.com>				
Almanac...	Annual	X		X
College Board, New York, NY <http://www.collegeboard.com>				
2007 College-Bound Seniors Total Group Profile Report	Annual	X	X	
Commodity Research Bureau, Barchart.com, Inc., Chicago, IL <http://www.crbtrader.com>				
Commodity Year Book Update CD......................................	Discontinued			
CRB Commodity Index Report	Weekly		X	
CRB Commodity Year Book..	Annual	X		
CRB Encyclopedia of Historical Commodity and Financial Prices	Biennial	X		
CRB Futures Perspective	Weekly	X	X	
Final Markets-End-of-day Data	Daily			X
Futures Market Service...	Daily		X	X
Trends in Futures (Electronic Futures Trend Analyzer)	Daily			X
The Conference Board, New York, NY <http://www.conference-board.org>				
Business Cycle Indicators...	Monthly	X	X	
Corporate Contributions	Annual	X	X	
Productivity, Employment, and Income in the World's Economies	Annual	X	X	
Congressional Quarterly (CQ) Press, Washington, DC <http://www.cqpress.com/gethome.asp>				
America Votes...	Biennial	X		
Consumer Electronics Association (Electronic Industries Alliance), Arlington, VA <http://www.ce.org>				
Consumer Electronics Association (CEA) Sales and Forecasts	Semiannual	X	X	
The Council of State Governments, Lexington, KY				

886 Appendix I

Title	Frequency	Paper	Internet PDF	Internet Other formats
<http://www.c+sg.org>				
The Book of the States	Annual	X	X	
State Administrative Officials Classified by Function	Annual	X		
State Elective Officials and the Legislatures	Annual	X		
State Legislative Leadership, Committees, and Staff	Annual	X		
Credit Union National Association, Incorporated, Madison, WI				
<http://www.cuna.org>				
The Credit Union Ranking Report	Annual	X		
Credit Union Services Profile	Annual	X		
Operating Ratios and Spreads	Semiannual	X		
Dow Jones and Company, New York, NY				
<http://online.wjs.com/public/us?>				
Wall Street Journal	Daily	X		X
Edison Electric Institute, Washington, DC				
<http://www.eei.org>				
Statistical Yearbook of the Electric Power Industry	Annual	X	X	X
Editor and Publisher Company, New York, NY				
<http://www.editorandpublisher.com/eandp/index.jsp>				
Editor and Publisher	Monthly	X		
International Year Book	Annual	X		X
Market Guide	Annual	X		
Euromonitor International, London, England				
<http://www.euromonitor.com>				
Consumer Asia	Annual	X		
Consumer China	Annual	X		
Consumer Eastern Europe	Annual	X		
Consumer Europe	Annual	X		
Consumer International	Annual	X		
Consumer Latin America	Annual	X		
European Marketing Data and Statistics	Annual	X		
International Marketing Data and Statistics	Annual	X		
Latin America Marketing Data and Statistic	Annual	X		
World Consumer Expenditure Patterns	Annual	X		
World Consumer Income Patterns	Annual	X		
World Economic Factbook	Annual	X		
World Retail Data and Statistics	Annual	X		
Federal National Mortgage Association, Washington, DC				
<http://www.fanniemae.com>				
Annual Report	Annual	X	X	
Food and Agriculture Organization of the United Nations, Rome, Italy				
<http://www.fao.org>				
Fertilizer Yearbook	Annual	X		
Production Yearbook	Annual	X		
Trade Yearbook	Annual	X		
Yearbook of Fishery Statistics	Annual	X		
Yearbook of Forest Products	Annual	X		
The Foundation Center, New York, NY				
<http://www.foundationcenter.org>				
Foundation Yearbook	Annual	X		
FC Stats	Annual			X
General Aviation Manufacturers Association, Washington, DC				
<http://www.gama.aero/home.php>				
Shipment Report	Quarterly	X		X
Statistical Databook	Annual	X	X	
Girl Scouts of the USA, New York, NY				
<http://www.girlscouts.org>				
Annual Report	Annual	X	X	
Giving USA Foundation, Indianapolis, IN				
<http://www.aafrc.org>				
Giving USA	Annual			X
Health Forum, an American Hospital Association Company, Chicago, IL				
<http://www.healthforum.com>				
Annual Report	Annual	X		
AHA Hospital Statistics	Annual	X		X
Independent Petroleum Association of America, Washington, DC				
<http://www.ipaa.org>				
Domestic Oil and Gas Trends	Monthly	X		
Oil and Natural Gas Production in Your State	Annual	X	X	X
U.S. Petroleum Statistics	Annual	X	X	X
Information Today, Incorporated, Medford, NJ				
<http://www.infotoday.com>				
American Library Directory	Annual	X		
Bowker Annual Library and Book Trade Almanac	Annual	X		
Institute for Criminal Justice Ethics, New York, NY				
<http://www.lib.jjay.cuny.edu/cje>				
Criminal Justice Ethics	Semiannual	X		
Insurance Information Institute, New York, NY				

Title	Frequency	Paper	Internet PDF	Internet Other formats
<http://www.iii.org> The I.I.I. Insurance Fact Book	Annual	X	X	X
The Financial Services Fact Book (published jointly with the Financial Services Roundtable)	Annual	X		X
Inter-American Development Bank, Washington, DC <http://www.iadb.org> Annual Report	Annual	X	X	
Economic and Social Progress in Latin America	Annual	X		
International Air Transport Association <http://www.iata.org/index.htm> World Air Transport Statistics	Annual	X	X	X
International City Management Association, Washington, DC <http://www.icma.org> Compensation: An Annual Report on Local Government Executive Salaries and Fringe Benefits	Annual			X
Municipal Year Book	Annual	X		
International Labour Organization, Geneva, Switzerland <http://www.ilo.org> Yearbook of Labour Statistics	Annual	X		X
International Monetary Fund, Washington, DC <http://www.imf.org> Annual Report	Annual	X	X	X
Balance of Payments Statistics	Monthly	X		
Direction of Trade Statistics	Monthly	X		
Government Finance Statistics Yearbook	Annual	X		
International Financial Statistics	Monthly	X		
International Telecommunication Union, Geneva Switzerland <http://www.itu.int/home/index.html> ITU Yearbook of Statistics	Annual	X		
World Telecommunication Indicators	Annual	X		
Investment Company Institute, Washington, DC <http://www.ici.org> Mutual Fund Fact Book	Annual	X	X	X
Jane's Information Group, Coulsdon, United Kingdom and Alexandria, VA <http://www.janes.com> Jane's Air-Launched Weapons	Monthly	X		X
Jane's All the World's Aircraft	Annual	X		X
Jane's Armour and Artillery	Annual	X		X
Jane's Avionics	Annual	X		X
Jane's Fighting Ships	Annual	X		X
Jane's Infantry Weapons	Annual	X		X
Jane's Merchant Ships	Annual	X		X
Jane's Military Communications	Annual	X		X
Jane's Military Logistics	Annual	X		X
Jane's Military Training Systems	Annual	X		X
Jane's NATO Handbook	Annual	X		X
Jane's Spaceflight Directory	Annual	X		X
Joint Center for Housing Studies, Cambridge, MA <http://www.jchs.harvard.edu> The State of the Nation's Housing	Annual	X	X	X
Joint Center for Political and Economic Studies, Washington, DC <http://www.jointcenter.org> Black Elected Officials (BEO) Roster	Continually updatedl		X	
McGraw-Hill Construction Dodge, a Division of the McGraw-Hill Companies, New York, NY <http://www.construction.com> <http://www.dodge.construction.com/Analytics/> Dodge Construction Potential (online subscription)	Monthly	X	X	X
National Academy of Sciences, Washington, DC <http://www.pnas.org> Summary Report. Doctorate Recipients from United States' Universities	Annual	X		
National Academy of Social Insurance, Washington, DC <http://www.nasi.org> Workers Compensation, Benefits, Coverage, and Costs	Annual	X	X	
National Association of Home Builders, Washington, DC <http://www.nahb.org> Home Builders Forecast (online subscription)	Monthly			X
Housing Economics (online subscription)	Monthly			X
Housing Market Statistics (online subscription)	Monthly			X
National Association of Latino Elected and Appointed Officials, Washington, DC <http://www.naleo.org> National Directory of Latino Elected Officials	Annual		X	X
National Association of Realtors, Washington, DC <http://www.realtor.org> Economist's Commentary	Daily			X

Title	Frequency	Paper	Internet PDF	Other formats
Investment and Vacation Home Buyers Survey	Annual		X	
NAR Member Survey	Annual	X		
Profile of Home Buyer and Sellers	Annual	X		
Real Estate Insights	Monthly			
Research Update	Annual	X		
National Association of State Budget Officers, Washington, DC <http://www.nasbo.org>				
State Expenditure Report	Annual	X	X	
Fiscal Survey of the States	Semiannual	X	X	
National Association of State Park Directors, Raleigh, NC <http://www.naspd.org>				
Annual Information Exchange	Annual		X	X
National Catholic Educational Association, Washington, DC <http://www.ncea.org>				
Catholic Schools in America	Annual		X	X
United States Catholic Elementary and Secondary Schools Staffing and Enrollment	Annual	X		X
U.S. Catholic Elementary Schools and their Finances	Biennial			
U.S. Catholic Secondary Schools and their Finances	Biennial	X		
National Council of Churches USA, New York, NY <http://www.ncccusa.org>				
Yearbook of American and Canadian Churches	Annual	X		X
National Education Association, Washington, DC <http://www.nea.org/index.html>				
Rankings of the States and Estimates of School Statistics	Annual	X	X	
Status of the American Public School Teacher, 2000–2001	Quinquennial	X	X	
National Fire Protection Association, Quincy, MA <http://www.nfpa.org>				
NFPA Journal	Bimonthly			X
National Golf Foundation, Jupiter, FL <http://www.ngf.org/cgi/home.asp>				
Golf Consumer Profile	Annual		X	
Golf Facilities in the U.S.	Annual	X	X	
National Marine Manufacturers Association, Chicago, IL <http://www.nmma.org>				
Boating (A Statistical Report on America's Top Family Sport)	Annual	X	X	X
U.S. Recreational Boat Registration Statistics	Annual	X	X	
National Restaurant Association, Washington, DC <http://www.restaurant.org>				
Hourly Wages for Food Service Occupations	Annual	X	X	
Quick-Service Restaurant Trends	Annual	X	X	
Restaurant Economic Trends (online subscriptions)	Monthly			X
Restaurant Industry Forecast	Annual	X	X	
Restaurant Industry in Review	Annual	X	X	
Restaurant Industry Operations Report	Annual	X	X	
Restaurant Industry Pocket Factbook	Annual			X
Restaurant Performance Index	Monthly	X		X
Restaurant Spending	Annual	X	X	
State of the Restaurant Industry Work Force	Annual	X	X	
Tableservice Restaurant Trends	Annual	X	X	
National Safety Council, Itasca, IL <http://www.nsc.org>				
Injury Facts	Annual	X		X
National Sporting Goods Association, Mount Prospect, IL <http://www.nsga.org>				
The Sporting Goods Market in 2009	Annual	X	X	
Sports Participation in 2009	Annual	X	X	
New York Stock Exchange, Inc., New York, NY <http://www.nyse.com>				
Fact Book (online subscription)	Annual	X	X	
The New York Times Almanac, 2008	Annual	X		
North American Jewish Data Bank, New York, NY <http://jewishdatabank.org>				
Jewish Population of the United States	Annual		X	X
Organization for Economic Cooperation and Development, Paris, France <http://www.oecd.org>				
OECD-FAO Agricultural Outlook	Annual	X		X
Bank Profitability: Financial Statements of Banks, 1924–2003	Biannual	X		X
Central Government Debt: Statistical Yearbook, 1996–2005	Annual	X		X
Coal Information	Annual	X		X
CO2 Emissions From Fuel Combustion, 1971–2004	Annual	X		X
Communications Outlook	Biannual	X		X
DAC Journal	Quarterly	X	X	
Education at a Glance: OECD Indicators	Annual	X		X
Electricity Information	Annual	X		X
Energy Balances of Non-OECD Countries	Annual	X		X
Energy Balances of OECD Countries	Annual	X		X
Energy Prices and Taxes	Quarterly	X	X	
Energy Statistics of Non-OECD Countries	Annual	X	X	X

Title	Frequency	Paper	PDF	Other formats
Energy Statistics of OECD Countries	Annual	X	X	X
Environmental Data Compendium	Annual	X		X
Environmental Outlook	Sporadic	X	X	
Financial Market Trends	Triennial	X	X	
Geographical Distribution of Financial Flows to Aid Recipients	Annual	X		
Organization for Economic Cooperation and Development, Paris, France—Con.				
Historical Statistics, 1970–2000. 2001 Edition	Discontinued	X	X	X
Information Technology Outlook, 2002 Edition	Biennial	X	X	X
Insurance Statistics Yearbook	Annual	X	X	X
International Development Statistics	Annual			X
Internal Migration Outlook	Annual	X	X	
International Trade by Commodity Statistics	Annual	X	X	
Iron and Steel Industry in 2002, 2004 Edition	Annual			
Labor Force Statistics	Annual	X	X	
Main Economic Indicators	Monthly	X	X	
Main Science and Technology Indicators, Vol. 2003	Biennial	X	X	
Measuring Globalisation: The Role of Multinationals in Organisation for Economic Cooperation and Development (OECD) Countries	One time			
Monthly Statistics of International Trade	Monthly	X	X	
National Accounts of OECD Countries	Annual	X	X	X
Natural Gas Information	Annual	X	X	X
Nuclear Energy Data	Annual	X		
OECD Economic Outlook	Biennial	X		X
OECD Economic Studies	Annual	X		X
OECD Economic Surveys	Annual	X		X
OECD Employment Outlook	Annual	X		X
OECD Factbook	Annual	X	X	X
OECD Health Data	Annual	X	X	X
OECD Science, Technology, and Industry Outlook	Biennial	X	X	X
OECD Territorial Reviews	Quarterly	X	X	
OECD in Figures	Bimonthly	X		X
Oil Information 2003 Edition	Annual	X	X	
Oil, Gas, Coal, and Electricity Quarterly Statistics	Quarterly	X	X	
Quarterly Labour Force Statistics (discontinued as of 4th quarter 2004)	Quarterly	X	X	
Quarterly National Accounts	Quarterly	X	X	X
Research and Development Statistics	Annual	X	X	
Revenue Statistics 1965–2005, 2006 Edition	Annual	X	X	
Review of Fisheries in OECD Member Countries	Annual	X	X	
Structural Statistics for Industry and Services	Annual	X	X	
Taxing Wages	Annual	X	X	
Trends in International Migration 2004 Edition	Annual	X	X	
Trends in the Transport Sector	Annual	X	X	
Uranium Resources Production and Demand, 2001	Biennial	X	X	
World Energy Outlook	Annual	X	X	
PennWell Corporation, Tulsa, OK <http://www.pennwell.com>				
Offshore (online subscription)	Monthly	X	X	
Oil and Gas Journal (online subscription)	Weekly	X	X	
Puerto Rico Planning Board, San Juan, PR <http://www.jp.gobierno.pr>				
Activity Index	Monthly	X		X
Balance of Payments Puerto Rico	Annual	X		
Economic Report to the Governor	Annual	X		
External Trade Statistics	Annual	X		X
Income and Product	Annual	X		
Projections	Annual	X		
Selected Statistics on Construction Industry	Annual	X		
Selected Statistics on Puerto Rico's External Trade	Annual	X		X
Statistical Appendix-Economic Report to the Governor	Annual	X		X
Radio Advertising Bureau, New York, NY <http://www.rab.com>				
Media Facts	Annual		X	
Radio Marketing Guide and Fact Book	Quarterly		X	
Reed Business Information, New York, NY <http://www.reedbusiness.com/index.html>				
Library Journal	Semimonthly	X		
Publishers Weekly	Weekly	X		X
School Library Journal	Monthly	X		X
Regional Airline Association, Washington, DC <http://www.raa.org>				
Statistical Report	Annual	X	X	
Securities Industry and Financial Markets Association, New York, NY <http://www.sifma.com>				
Foreign Activity Report	Quarterly	X		
Securities Industry Trends	Periodic	X		
Securities Industry Yearbook	Annual	X		X
Standard and Poor's Corporation, New York, NY <http://www.standardandpoors.com>				
Analysts' Handbook	Monthly	X		
Corporation Records	Daily	X		
Daily Stock Price Records	Quarterly	X		

890 Appendix I

Title	Frequency	Paper	Internet PDF	Internet Other formats
Standard and Poor's Global Stock Market Factbook	Annual	X		
United Nations Statistics Division, New York, NY <http://unstats.un.org/unsd/default.htm>				
Compendium of Human Settlements Statistics (Series N)	Annual	X		
United Nations Statistics Division, New York, NY—Con.				
Demographic Yearbook (Series R)	Annual	X	X	X
Energy Balances and Electricity Profiles (Series W)........................	Annual	X	X	
Energy Statistics Yearbook (Series J)	Annual	X	X	
Industrial Statistics Yearbook: (Series P)..............................	Annual	X		X
Commodity Production Statistics	Annual	X		
International Trade Statistics Yearbook (Series G).........................	Annual	X		
Monthly Bulletin of Statistics (Series Q)	Monthly	X		
National Accounts Statistics (Series X)	Annual	X		X
Main Aggregates and Detailed Tables.................................	Annual	X		
....	Annual	X		
Population and Vital Statistics Report (Series A).........................	Quarterly	X		
Social Statistics and Indicators (Series K).............................	Occasional	X		X
The World's Women: Trends and Statistics	Quinquennial	X	X	X
Statistical Yearbook (Series; also available in CD-ROM, Series S/CD)	Annual	X		X
World Statistics Pocketbook (Series V)	Annual	X		
United Nations Conference on Trade and Development,				
Development and Globalization: Facts and Figures	Annual	X	X	X
....	Annual	X	X	X
United States Telecom Association, Washington, DC				
Statistics of the Local Exchange Carriers	Annual		X	X
University of Michigan, Center for Political Studies, Institute for Social Research, Ann Arbor, MI				
National Election Studies Cumulative Datafile............................	Biennial	X		X
Warren Communications News, Washington, DC <http://www.warren-news.com>				
Cable and Station Coverage Atlas....................................	Annual			X
Television and Cable Factbook	Annual	X		X
World Almanac, New York, NY <http://www.worldalmanac.com>				
The World Almanac and Book of Facts	Annual	X		X
The World Bank Group, Washington, DC				
	Annual	X	X	
Global Development Finance, 2008	Annual	X	X	
	Annual	X	X	
World Development Indicators, 2008...................................	Annual	X		X
World Health Organization, Geneva, Switzerland				
....	Annual	X	X	
....	Annual	X	X	
....	Annual	X	X	X

Guide to State Statistical Abstracts

This bibliography includes the most recent statistical abstracts for states published since 2000, plus those that will be issued in late 2011. For some states, a near equivalent has been listed in substitution for, or in addition to, a statistical abstract. All sources contain statistical tables on a variety of subjects for the state as a whole, its component parts, or both. Internet sites also contain statistical data.

Alabama

University of Alabama, Center for Business and Economic Research, Box 870221, Tuscaloosa, AL 35487-0221. 205-348-6191. Fax: 205-348-2951. Internet site <http://cber.cba.ua.edu/>.

Alabama Economic Outlook, 2011. Revised annually.

Alaska

Department of Commerce, Community and Economic Development, 550 West 7th Avenue, Suite 1770, Anchorage, AK 99501. 907-269-8100. Fax 907-269-8125. Internet site <http://www.dced.state .ak.us/dca/misc_resources.htm>.

The Alaska Economic Performance Report, 2006. Online.

Arizona

University of Arizona, Economic and Business Research Center, Eller College of Management, 1130 East Helen Street, McClelland Hall, Rm. 103, P.O. Box 210108, Tucson, AZ 85721-0108. 520-621-2155. Fax: 520-621-2150. Internet site <http://www.ebr.eller.arizona.edu/>.

Arizona Statistical Abstract, 2003.

Arizona's Economy. Quarterly Online, 2011. Online.

Arizona Economic Indicators Databook, 2009. Semiannual. Online.

Arkansas

University of Arkansas at Little Rock, Institute for Economic Advancement, Economic Research, 2801 South University Avenue, Little Rock, AR 72204-1099. 501-569-8519. Fax: 501-569-8538. Internet site <http://www.iea.ualr.edu>.

Arkansas State and County Economic Data, 2010.

Arkansas Personal Income Handbook, 2010.

Arkansas Statistical Abstract, 2008. Revised biennially.

California

Department of Finance, 915 L Street, Sacramento, CA 95814. 916-445-3878. Internet site <http://www.dof.ca.gov/>.

California Statistical Abstract, 2009. Annual. Online only.

Colorado

University of Colorado at Boulder, Government Publications Library, University Libraries, 184 UCB, 1720 Pleasant Street, Boulder, CO 80309-0184. 303-492-8705. Internet site <http:/ucblibraries.colorado .edu/>.

Colorado by the Numbers. Online only.

Colorado Office of Economic Development and International Trade, 1625 Broadway, Suite 2700, Denver, CO 80202. 303-892-3840. Fax: 303-892-3848. Internet site <http://www.colorado.gov/cs/Satellite /OEDIT/1162927366334>.

Colorado Data Book, 2010–11. Online only.

Connecticut

Connecticut Department of Economic and Community Development, 505 Hudson Street, Hartford, CT 06106-7106. 860-270-8000. Internet site <http://www. ct.gov/ecd/site /default.asp>.

Connecticut Town Profiles, 2011.

Delaware

Delaware Economic Development Office, 99 Kings Highway, Dover, DE 19901-7305. 302-739-4271. Fax: 302-739-5749. Internet site <http://dedo.delaware.gov>.

Delaware Statistical Overview, 2008. Online only.
Delaware Data Book, 2011.

District of Columbia

Business Resource Center, John A. Wilson Building, 1350 Pennsylvania Avenue, NW, Washington, DC 20004. 202-727-1000. Internet site. <http://brc.dc.gov/resources /facts.asp>.

Market Facts and Statistics. Online only.

Florida

University of Florida, Bureau of Economic and Business Research, P.O. Box 117145, 221 Matherly Hall, Gainesville, FL 32611-7145. 352-392-0171, ext. 219. Fax: 352-392-4739. Internet site <http://www.bebr.ufl .edu>.

Florida Statistical Abstract, 2010. Annual. Also available on CD-ROM.

Florida County Perspective, 2010. One profile for each county. Annual. Also available on CD-ROM.

Florida County Rankings, 2010. Annual. Also available on CD-ROM.

Georgia

University of Georgia, Terry College of Business, Selig Center for Economic Growth, Athens, GA 30602-6254. 706-542-8100. Fax: 706-542-3835 Internet site <http://www.selig.uga.edu/>.

Georgia Statistical Abstract, 2008-09.

University of Georgia, Center for Agribusiness and Economic Development, 301 Lumpkin House, Athens, GA 30602-7509. 706-542-2434. Fax: 706-542-0770. Internet site <http://www.georgiastats.uga.edu/>.

The Georgia County Guide, 2010. Annual.

Hawaii

Hawaii State Department of Business, Economic Development & Tourism, Research and Economic Analysis Division, Statistics and Data Support Branch, P.O. Box 2359, Honolulu, HI 96804. 808-586-2423. Fax: 808-587-2790. Internet site <http://www.hawaii.gov/dbedt/>.

The State of Hawaii Data Book 2009. Annual. Periodically updated.

Idaho

State of Idaho Department of Labor, 317 West Main St., Boise, ID 83735. 208-332-3570. Fax: 208-334-6430. Internet site <http://labor.idaho.gov/dnn/default .aspx?alias=labor.idaho.gov/dnn/idl/>.

County Profiles Idaho. Online.

Idaho Community Profiles. Online.

Illinois

The Institute of Government and Public Affairs, University of Illinois, 1007 W. Nevada Street, Urbana, IL 61801, MC-037. 217-333-3340. Fax: 217-244-4817. Internet site <http://www.igpa.uiuc.edu/>.

Indiana

Indiana University, Kelley School of Business, Indiana Business Research Center, 100 South Avenue, Suite 240, Bloomington, IN 47404. 812-855-5507. Internet site <http://www.ibrc.indiana.edu/>.

STATS Indiana. Online only.

Iowa

Iowa State University, Office of Social and Economic Trend Analysis, 303 East Hall, Ames, IA 50010-1070. 515-294-9903. Fax: 515-294-0592. Internet site <http://www.seta.iastate.edu/>.

State Library of Iowa, State Data Center, Ola Babcock Miller Building, 1112 East Grand, Des Moines, IA 50319-0233. 800-248-4483. Fax: 515-242-6543. Internet site <http://www.iowadatacenter.org>.

Kansas

University of Kansas, Policy Research Institute, 1541 Lilac Lane, 607 Blake Hall, Lawrence, KS 66045-3129. 785-864-3701. Fax: 785-864-3683. Internet site <http://www.ipsr.ku.edu/>.

Kansas Statistical Abstract, 2009. 44th ed. Online only.

Kentucky

Kentucky Cabinet for Economic Development, Old Capitol Annex, 300 West Broadway, Frankfort, KY 40601. 800-626-2930. Fax: 502-564-3256. Internet site <http://www.thinkkentucky.com/>.

Louisiana

Louisiana State Census Data Center, Office of Electronic Services, 1201 N. Third Street, Suite. 7-210, Baton Rouge, LA, 70802. Fax: 225-219-4027. Internet site <http://www.louisiana.gov/Explore /Demographics_and_Geography/>.

Maine

Maine State Planning Office, 38 State House Station, 19 Union Street, Augusta, ME 04333-0038. 800-662-4545. Fax: 207-287-6077. Internet site <http://www.maine.gov/spo/>.

Maryland

RESI, Towson University, 7400 York Road, Suite 200, Towson, MD 21252-0001. 410-704-7374. Fax: 410-704-4115. Internet site <http://wwwnew.towson.edu/>.

Maryland Statistical Abstract, 2006.

Massachusetts

MassCHIP, Massachusetts Department of Public Health, 250 Washington Street, Boston, MA 02108-4619. 617-624-6000. Internet site <http://masschip.state.ma.us/>.

Instant Topics. Online only.

Michigan

Michigan Economic Development Corporation, 300 North Washington Square, Lansing, MI 48913. 1-888-522-0103. Internet site <http://www.michigan.org /medc/miinfo>.

Minnesota

Minnesota Department of Employment and Economic Development, 1st National Bank Building, 332 Minnesota Street Suite E200, Saint Paul, MN 55101-1351. 800-657-3858. Internet site <http://www.deed.state .mn.us/facts/index.htm>.

Compare Minnesota: Profiles of Minnesota's Economy & Population. Online only.

Minnesota State Demographic Center, 658 Cedar Street Room 300, Saint Paul, MN 55155, 651-296-2557. Internet site <http://www.demography.state.mn.us/>.

Mississippi

Mississippi State University, College of Business and Industry, Office of Business Research and Services, P.O. Box 5288, Mississippi State, MS 39762. 662-325-2850. Fax: 662-325-2410. Internet site <http://www.cbi.msstate.edu/dept /bizserv/abstract/>

Mississippi Statistical Abstract, 2007.
40th ed. Also available on CD-ROM.

Missouri

University of Missouri–Columbia, Economic and Policy Analysis Research Center, 10 Professional Building, Columbia, MO 65211. 573-882-4805. Fax: 573-882-5563. Internet site <http://eparc.mirrouri.edu/>.

Missouri Statistical Data Archive. Online only.

Montana

Montana Department of Commerce, Census and Economic Information Center, 301 S. Park Ave., P.O. Box 200505, Helena, MT 59620-0505, 406-841-2740. Fax: 406-841-2731. Internet site <http://ceic.mt.gov/>.

Nebraska

Nebraska Department of Economic Development, P. O. Box 94666, 301 Centenial Mall South, Lincoln, NE 68509-4666. 800-426-6505. Fax: 402-471-3778. Internet site <http://info.neded.org/>.

Nevada

Nevada Department of Administration, Budget and Planning Division, 209 East Musser Street, Room 200, Carson City, NV 89701-4298. 775-684-0222. Fax: 775-684-0260. Internet site <http://www.budget.state.nv.us/>.

Nevada Statistical Abstract. Online only.

New Hampshire

New Hampshire Office of Energy and Planning, 4 Chenell Drive, Concord, NH 03301-8501. 603-271-2155. Fax: 603-271-2615. Internet site <http://www.nh.gov/oep/index.htm>.

New Jersey

New Jersey State Data Center, NJ Department of Labor and Workforce Development, 1 John Fitch Plaza, P.O. Box 110 Trenton, NJ 08625-0110. 609-984-2595. Fax: 609-984-6833. Internet site <http://www.state.nj.us/labor/lra/>.

Labor Market Information, 2008. Online only.

New Mexico

University of New Mexico, Bureau of Business and Economic Research, MSC06 3510, 1 University of New Mexico, Albuquerque, NM 87131-0001. 505-277-6626. Fax: 505-277-2773. Internet site <http://bber.unm.edu/>.

New Mexico Business, Current Economic Report Monthly.

FOR-UNM Bulletin. Quarterly.

New York

Nelson A. Rockefeller Institute of Government, 411 State Street, Albany, NY 12203-1003. 518-443-5522. Fax: 518-443-5788. Internet site <http://www.rockinst.org/>.

New York State Statistical Yearbook, 2009 34th ed.

North Carolina

Office of State Budget and Management, 116 West Jones Street, Raleigh, NC 27603-8005. 919-807-4700. Fax: 919-733-0640. Internet site <http://www.osbm.state.nc.us/osbm/>.

How North Carolina Ranks, 2010. Online only.

North Dakota

University of North Dakota, Bureau of Business and Economic Research, P.O. Box 8098, Grand Forks, ND 58202-8098. 800-225-5863. Fax: 701-777-2019. Internet site <http://business.und.edu/>.

North Dakota Statistical Abstract. Online only.

Ohio

Office of Strategic Research, Ohio Department of Development, 77 South High Street, P.O. Box 1001, Columbus, OH 43216-1001. 614-466-2116. Fax: 614-466-9697. Internet site <http://www.odod.state.oh.us/research>.

Research products and services. Updated continuously.

Ohio County Profiles, 2009.

Ohio County Indicators. Updated periodically.

Oklahoma

University of Oklahoma, Center for Economic and Management Research, Michael F. Price College of Business, 307 West Brooks, Suite 4, Norman OK 73019-4004. 405-325-2931. Fax: 405-325-7688. Internet site <http://www.ou.edu/price/cemr.html/>.

Statistical Abstract of Oklahoma, 2010.

Oregon

Secretary of State, Archives Division, Archives Bldg., 800 Summer Street, NE, Salem, OR 97310. 503-373-0701 ext.1. Fax: 503-378-4118. Internet site <http://www.sos.state.or.us/bbook>.

Oregon Blue Book. 2011 Centennial. Biennial.

Pennsylvania

Pennsylvania State Data Center, Institute of State and Regional Affairs, Penn State Harrisburg, 777 West Harrisburg Pike, Middletown, PA 17057-4898. 717-948-6336. Fax: 717-948-6754. Internet site <http://pasdc.hbg.psu.edu>.

Pennsylvania Statistical Abstract, 2010. Also Available on CD-Rom.

Rhode Island

Rhode Island Economic Development Corporation, 315 Iron Horse Way, Suite 101,

Providence, RI 02908. 401–278–9100. Fax: 401–273–8270. Internet site <http://www.riedc.com/>.

RI Databank. Online only.

South Carolina

Budget and Control Board, Office of Research and Statistics, 1919 Blanding Street, Columbia 29201. 803–898–9960. Internet site <http://www.ors2.state.sc.us /abstract/index.asp>.

South Carolina Statistical Abstract, 2009. Also available on CD-Rom.

South Dakota

University of South Dakota, State Data Center, Business Research Bureau, The University of South Dakota, 414 E. Clark Street, Vermillion, SD 57069. 605–677–5708. Fax: 605–677–5427. Internet site <http://www.usd.edu/>.

2006 South Dakota Community Abstracts.

Tennessee

College of Business Administration, The University of Tennessee, 916 Volunteer Blvd., 716 Stokely Management Center, Knoxville, Tennessee 37996–0570. 865–974–5441. Fax: 865–974–3100. Internet site <http://cber.bus.utk.edu/Default.htm>.

Tennessee Statistical Abstract, 2003. Last printed edition. Biennial.

Texas

Dallas Morning News, Communications Center, P.O. Box 655237, Dallas, TX 75265–5237. 214–977–8262. Internet site <http://www.texasalmanac.com/>.

Texas Almanac, 2010-2011. 64th ed.

Texas State Data Center and Office of the State Demographer, Institute for Demographic and Socioeconomic Research (IDSER), 501 West Durango Blvd., San Antonio, TX 78207–4415. 210–458–6543. Fax: 210–458–6541. Internet site <http://txsdc.utsa.edu/>.

Utah

Governor's Office of Planning and Budget, Demographic & Economic Analysis, Suite 150, P.O. Box 132210, Salt Lake City, UT 84114–2210. 801–538–1027. Fax: 801–538–1547. Internet site <http://www. governor.utah.gov/dea>.

2011 Economic Report to the Governor. Annual.

Utah Data Guide Newsletter, 2010. Quarterly. Also available online.

Vermont

Department of Labor, Labor Market Information, 3 Green Mountain Drive, P.O. Box 488, Montpelier, VT 05601–0488. 802–828–4202. Fax: 802–828–4050. Internet site <http://www.vtlmi.info/>.

Vermont Economic-Demographic Profile, 2010. Annual.

Virginia

University of Virginia, Weldon Cooper Center for Public Service, 2400 Old Ivy Road P.O. Box 400206, Charlottesville, VA 22904–4206. 434–982–5522. Fax: 434–982–5524. Internet site <http://www.coopercenter.org/>.

Stat Chat. Online only.

Washington

Washington State Office of Financial Management, Forecasting Division, P.O. Box 43113, Olympia, WA 98504–3113. 360–902–0555. Internet site <http://www.ofm. wa.gov/>.

Washington State Data Book, 2009. Online only.

West Virginia

West Virginia University, College of Business and Economics, Bureau of Business and Economic Research, 1601 University Ave, P.O. Box 6025, Morgantown, WV 26506–6025. 304–293–4092. Fax: 304–293–5652. Internet site <http://www.be.wvu.edu /bber/index.htm>.

2009 West Virginia County Data Profiles. Also available on CD-Rom.

West Virginia Economic Outlook, 2011. Annual. Also available on CD-Rom.

Wisconsin

Wisconsin Legislative Reference Bureau, One East Main Street, Suite 200, Madison, WI 53701–2037. 608–266–0341. Internet site <http://www.legis.state.wi.us/lrb/pubs /bluebook.htm/>.

2009–2010 Wisconsin Blue Book. Biennial.

Wyoming

Department of Administration and Information, Economic Analysis Division, 2800 Central Avenue, Suite 206, Cheyenne, WY 82002–0060. 307–777–7504. Fax: 307–632–1819. Internet site <http://eadiv.state.wy.us/>.

The Equality State Almanac, 2009.

Guide to Foreign Statistical Abstracts

This bibliography presents recent statistical abstracts for member nations of the Organization for Economic Cooperation and Development and Russia. All sources contain statistical tables on a variety of subjects for the individual countries. Many of the following publications provide text in English as well as in the national language(s). For further information on these publications, contact the named statistical agency which is responsible for editing the publication.

Australia
Australian Bureau of Statistics, Canberra. <http://www.abs.gov.au>.
Year Book Australia. Annual. 2008. (In English.)

Austria
Statistik Austria, 1110 Wien. <http://www.statistik.at/index.shtml>.
Statistisches Jahrbuch Osterreichs. Annual. 2010. With CD-ROM. (In German.) With English translations of table headings.

Belgium
L'Institut National de Statistique, Rue de Louvain; 44–1000 Bruxelles. <http://statbel.fgov.be/info/links_en.asp>.
Annuaire statistique de la Belgique. Annual. 1995. (In French.)

Canada
Statistics Canada, Ottawa, Ontario, KIA OT6. <http://www.statcan.ca/start.html>.
Canada Year book. 2001. (In English.)

Czech Republic
Czech Statistical Office, Na padesatem 81, Praha 10. <http://www.czso.cz/>.
Statisticka Rocenka Ceske Republiky 2010. With CD-ROM. (In English and Czech.)

Denmark
Danmarks Statistik, Sejrogade 11, 2100 Kobenhavn O. <http://www.dst.dk>.
Statistisk ARBOG. 2010. Annual. English version available only on internet and is free of charge at: <www.dst.dk/yearbook>. (Printed version— In Danish only.)

Finland
Statistics Finland, Helsinki. <http://www.stat.fi/comment>.
Statistical Yearbook of Finland, Annual. 2010. With CD-ROM. (In English, Finnish, and Swedish.)

France
Institut National de la Statistique et des Etudes Economiques, Paris 18, Bld. Adolphe Pinard, 75675 Paris (Cedex 14). <http://www.insee.fr/fr/home/home_page.asp>.
Annuaire Statistique de la France. Annual. 2003. (In French.) 2005 CD-ROM only.

Germany
Statistisches Bundesamt, Wiesbaden. <http://www.destatis.de/contact>.
Statistisches Jahrbuch fur die Bundesrepublic Deutschland. Annual. 2010. (In German.) *Statistisches Jahrbuch fur das Ausland.* 2006.
Statistisches Jahrbuch 2005 *Fur die Bundesreublik Deutschland und fur das ausland* CD-ROM.

Greece
Hellenic Statistica Authority. <http:// www.statistics.gr/>.
Concise Statistical Yearbook 2009. (In English and Greek.)
Statistical Yearbook of Greece. Annual. 2008. (In English and Greek.)

Hungary
Hungarian Central Statistical Office, 1024 Budapest. <http://www.ksh.hu>.
Statistical Yearbook of Hungary, 2009. With CD-ROM. (In English and Hungarian.)

Iceland
Hagstofa Islands/Statistics Iceland. <http://www.hagstofa.is>.
Statistical Yearbook of Iceland. 2010. (In English and Icelandic.)

Ireland
Central Statistics Office, Skehard Road, Cork. <http://www.cso.ie>.
Statistical Yearbook of Ireland. Annual. 2008. (In English.)

Italy
Istituto Nazionale Statistica. Via Cesare Balbo 16 Roma. <http://www.istat.it>.
*Annuario Statistico Italia*no. Annual. 2008. With CD-ROM. (In Italian.)

Japan

Statistics Bureau, Ministry of Internal Affairs and Communications, Statistical Research and Training Institute, Ministry of Internal Affairs and Communications, Japan. <http://www.stat.go.jp/english/data/index.htm>.

Japan Statistical Yearbook. Annual. 2011. (In English and Japanese.)

Korea, South

Statistics Korea, Daejeon Government, #920 Dunsan-dong Seo-gu, Daejeon, Korea 302 701. <http://www.nso.go.kr/>.

Korea Statistical Yearbook. Annual. 2010. (In Korean and English.)

Luxembourg

Statec Centre Administratif Pierre Werner, 13 rue Erasme, B.P. 304, L-2013, Luxembourg. <www.statec.lu/>.

Annuaire Statistique du Luxembourg. 2010. (In French.) (Alphabetical numbering system).

Mexico

Instituto Nacional de Estadistica Geografia e Informatica, Av. Heroe Nacozari Num. 2301 Sur Fracc. Jardines del Parque, CP 20270 Aguascalientes, Ags. <http://www.inegi.gob.mx/difusion/ingles/fiest.html>.

Anuario estadistico de los Estados Unidos Mexicanos. Annual. 1998. Also on disc. (In Spanish.) Agenda Estadistica 1999.

Netherlands

Statistics Netherlands, Henri Faasdreef 312, 2492 JP The Hague. <http://www.cbs.nl/en/>.

Statistical Yearbook 2009 of the Netherlands. (In English.)

Statistisch Jaarboek 2010.

New Zealand

Statistics, New Zealand, Wellington. <http://www.stats.govt.nz/>.

New Zealand Official Yearbook. Annual. 2010. (In English.)

Norway

Statistics Norway, Oslo/Kongsvinger. <http://www.ssb.no/en/>.

Statistical Yearbook. Annual. 2010. (In English.)

Poland

Central Statistical Office al. Niepodleglosci 208, 00-925 Warsaw. <http://www.stat.gov.pl/english/index.htm>.

Concise Statistical Yearbook of Poland. 2010 With CD-ROM. (In Polish and English.)

Statistical Yearbook of the Republic of Poland 2007. CD-ROM only. (In Polish and English.)

Portugal

INE (Instituto Nacional de Estatistica.) Av. Antonio Jose de Almeida P-1000-043 Lisboa. <http://www.ine.pt/index_eng.htm>.

Anuario Estatistico de Portugal. 2001. (In Portuguese and English.)

Russia

State Committee of Statistics of Russia, Moscow. <http://www.gks.ru/eng/>.

Statistical Yearbook. 2010. With CD-ROM (In Russian.)

Slovakia

Statistical Office of the Slovak Republic, Postovy Priecinok 2, 845 02 Bratislava 45. <http://www.statistics.sk/webdata/english/index2_a.htm>.

Statisticka Rocenka Slovenskej Republiky. 2010. (In English and Slovak.) With CD-ROM.

Spain

INE (Instituto Nacional de Estadistica); Paseo de la Castellana, 183, Madrid 16. <http://www.ine.es/welcoing.htm>.

Anuario Estadistico de Espana. 2011. CD-ROM only. (In Spanish.)

Sweden

Statistics Sweden, SE-104 51 Stockholm. <http://www.scb.se/indexeng.asp>.

Statistisk Arsbok for Sverige. Annual. 2009. (In English and Swedish.)

Switzerland

Bundesamt fur Statistik, Hallwylstrasse 15, CH-3003, Bern.

Statistisches Jahrbuch der Schweiz. Annual. 2011. With CD-ROM. (In French and German.)

Turkey

State Institute of Statistics, Prime Ministry, Necatibey Cad/Ankara. No. 114 06100.

Statistical Yearbook of Turkey. 2004. With CD-ROM. (In English and Turkish.)

Turkey in Statistics. 1999. (In English only.)

United Kingdom

The Stationary Office; P.O. Box 29, Norwich, NR3 1GN. <http://www.statistics.gov.uk/>.

Annual Abstract of Statistics. Annual. 2002. (In English.)

The United States Office of Management and Budget (OMB) defines metropolitan and micropolitan statistical areas according to published standards that are applied to U.S. Census Bureau data. The general concept of a metropolitan or micropolitan statistical area is that of a core area containing a substantial population nucleus, together with adjacent communities having a high degree of economic and social integration with that core. Currently defined metropolitan and micropolitan statistical areas are based on application of 2000 standards (which appeared in the Federal Register on December 27, 2000) to 2000 decennial census data. Current metropolitan and micropolitan statistical area definitions were announced by OMB effective June 6, 2003, and subsequently updated as of December 2003, November 2004, December 2005, December 2006, November 2007, November 2008, and December 2009.

Standard definitions of metropolitan areas were first issued in 1949 by the then Bureau of the Budget (predecessor of OMB), under the designation "standard metropolitan area" (SMA). The term was changed to "standard metropolitan statistical area" (SMSA) in 1959 and to "metropolitan statistical area" (MSA) in 1983. The term "metropolitan area" (MA) was adopted in 1990 and referred collectively to metropolitan statistical areas (MSAs), consolidated metropolitan statistical areas (CMSAs), and primary metropolitan statistical areas (PMSAs). The term "core-based statistical area" (CBSA) became effective in 2000 and refers collectively to metropolitan and micropolitan statistical areas.

OMB has been responsible for the official metropolitan areas since they were first defined, except for the period 1977 to 1981, when they were the responsibility of the Office of Federal Statistical Policy and Standards, U.S. Department of Commerce. The standards for defining metropolitan areas were modified in 1958, 1971, 1975, 1980, 1990, and 2000.

Defining Metropolitan and Micropolitan Statistical Areas—

The 2000 standards provide that each CBSA must contain at least one urban area of 10,000 or more population. Each metropolitan statistical area must have at least one urbanized area of 50,000 or more inhabitants. Each micropolitan statistical area must have at least one urban cluster of at least 10,000 but less than 50,000 population.

Under the standards, the county (or counties) in which at least 50 percent of the population resides within urban areas of 10,000 or more population, or that contain at least 5,000 people residing within a single urban area of 10,000 or more population, is identified as a "central county" (counties). Additional "outlying counties" are included in the CBSA if they meet specified requirements of commuting to or from the central counties. Counties or equivalent entities form the geographic "building blocks" for metropolitan and micropolitan statistical areas throughout the United States and Puerto Rico.

If specified criteria are met, a metropolitan statistical area containing a single core with a population of 2.5 million or more may be subdivided to form smaller groupings of counties referred to as "metropolitan divisions."

As of December 2009, there are 366 metropolitan statistical areas and 576 micropolitan statistical areas in the United States. In addition, there are eight metropolitan statistical areas and five micropolitan statistical areas in Puerto Rico.

Principal Cities and Metropolitan and Micropolitan Statistical Area Titles—

The largest city in each metropolitan or micropolitan statistical area is designated a "principal city." Additional cities qualify if specified requirements are met concerning population size and employment. The title of each metropolitan or micropolitan statistical area consists of the names of up to three of its principal cities and the name of each state into which the metropolitan or micropolitan statistical area extends. Titles of metropolitan divisions also typically are based on principal city names, but in certain cases consist of county names.

Defining New England City and Town Areas—In view of the importance of cities and towns in New England, the 2000 standards also provide for a set of geographic areas that are defined using cities and towns in the six New England states. The New England city and town areas (NECTAs) are defined using the same criteria as metropolitan and micropolitan statistical areas and are identified as either metropolitan or micropolitan, based, respectively, on the presence of either an urbanized area of 50,000 or more population or an urban cluster of at least 10,000 but less than 50,000 population. If the specified criteria are met, a NECTA containing a single core with a population of at least 2.5 million may be subdivided to form smaller groupings of cities and towns referred to as New England city and town area divisions.

Changes in Definitions Over Time—Changes in the definitions of these statistical areas since the 1950 census have consisted chiefly of (1) the recognition of new areas as they reached the minimum required city or urbanized area population and (2) the addition of counties (or cities and towns in New England) to existing areas as new decennial census data showed them to qualify.

In some instances, formerly separate areas have been merged, components of an area have been transferred from one area to another, or components have been dropped from an area. The large majority of changes have taken place on the basis of decennial census data. However, Census Bureau data serve as the basis for intercensal updates in specified circumstances.

Because of these historical changes in geographic definitions, users must be cautious in comparing data for these statistical areas from different dates. For some purposes, comparisons of data for areas as defined at given dates may be appropriate; for other purposes, it may be preferable to maintain consistent area definitions. Historical metropolitan area definitions are available for 1999, 1993, 1990, 1983, 1981, 1973, 1970, 1963, 1960, and 1950.

Excluding Tables 20 through 24 in the Population section; Table 595 in the Labor Force section; Table 683 in the Income section, and the tables that follow in this appendix, the tables presenting data for metropolitan areas in this edition of the Statistical Abstract are based on the 1999 or earlier metropolitan area definitions. For a list of component counties according to the 1999 definition, see Appendix II in the 2002 edition of the Statistical Abstract or <http://www.census.gov /population/www/estimates /pastmetro.html>.

Figure A1
Metropolitan and Micropolitan Statistical Areas of the United States
As defined by the U.S. Office of Management and Budget, December 2009

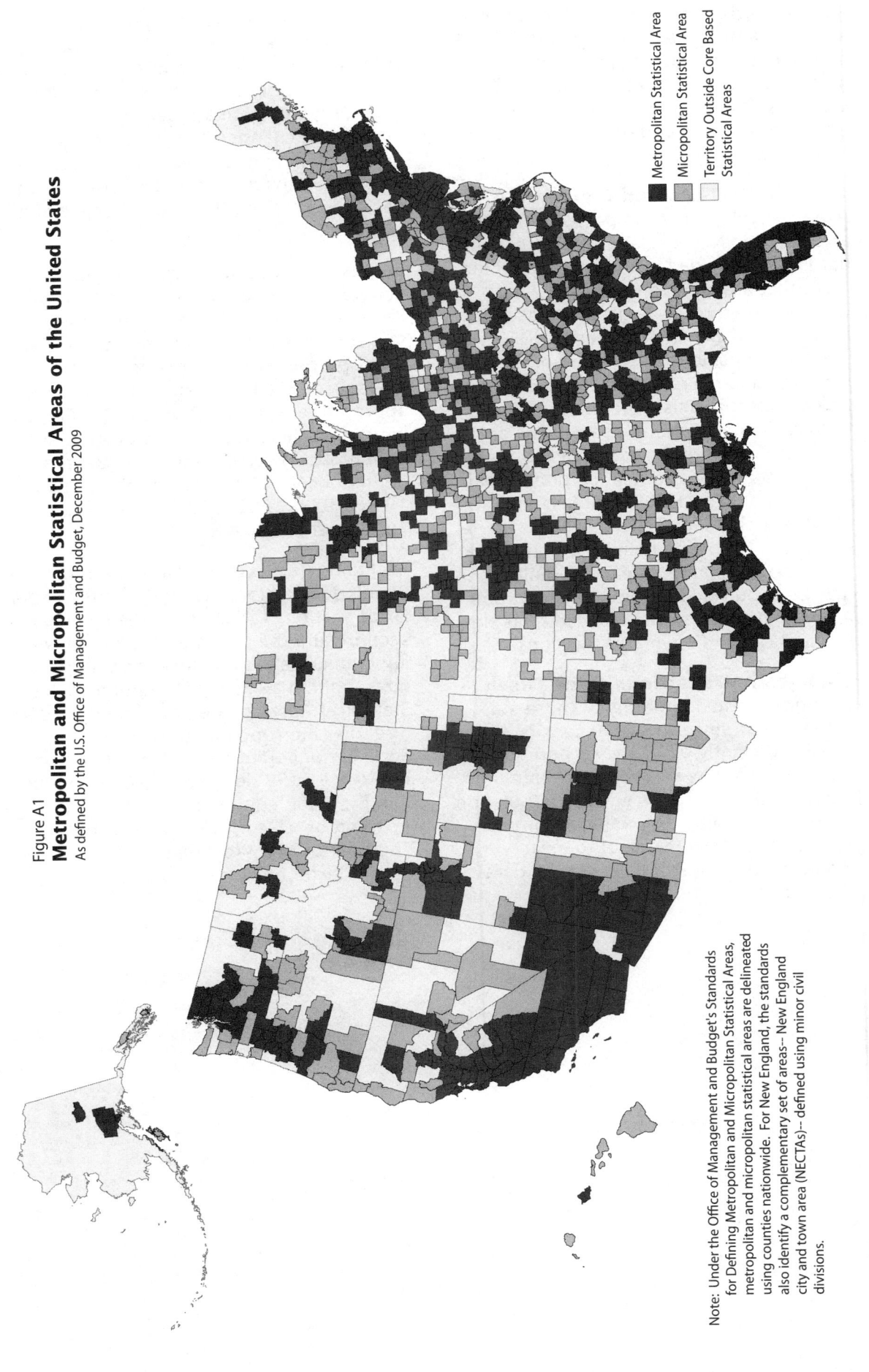

Metropolitan Statistical Area

Micropolitan Statistical Area

Territory Outside Core Based
Statistical Areas

Note: Under the Office of Management and Budget's Standards
for Defining Metropolitan and Micropolitan Statistical Areas,
metropolitan and micropolitan statistical areas are delineated
using counties nationwide. For New England, the standards
also identify a complementary set of areas-- New England
city and town area (NECTAs)-- defined using minor civil
divisions.

Metropolitan and Micropolitan New England City and Town Areas (NECTAs)
As defined by the U.S. Office of Management and Budget, December 2009

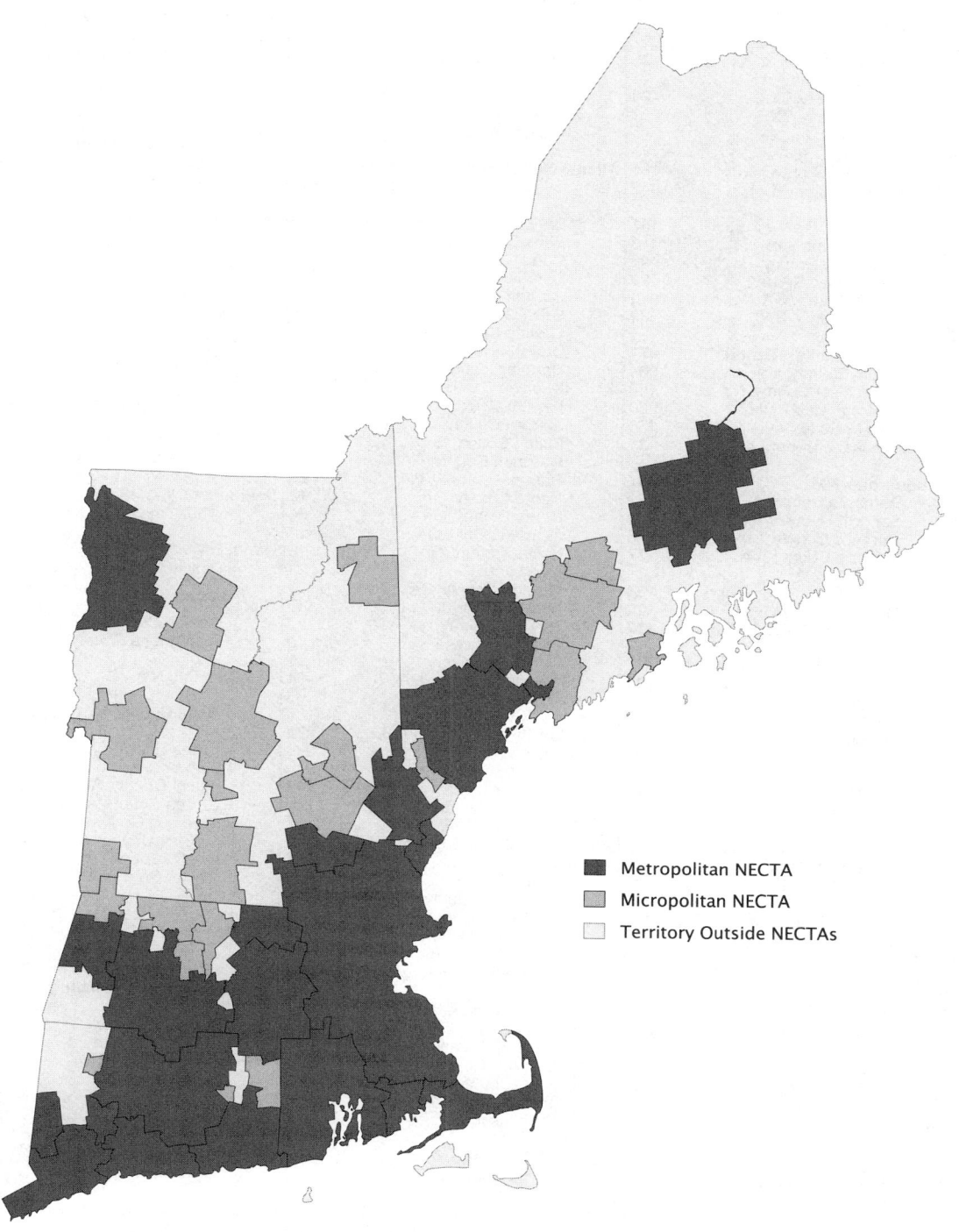

Metropolitan NECTA

Micropolitan NECTA

Territory Outside NECTAs

Note: Under the Office of Management and Budget's Standards for Defining Metropolitan and Micropolitan Statistical Areas, metropolitan and micropolitan statistical areas are delineated using counties nationwide. For New England, the standards also identify a complementary set of areas-- New England city and town area (NECTAs)-- defined using minor civil divisions.

Table A. Metropolitan Statistical Areas and Components—Population: 2010

[Population as of April 2010. (165 represents 165,000). Metropolitan statistical areas as defined by the U.S. Office of Management and Budget as of December 2009. All metropolitan statistical areas are arranged alphabetically]

Metropolitan statistical area / Metropolitan division / Component county	Population, 2010 (1,000)	Metropolitan statistical area / Metropolitan division / Component county	Population, 2010 (1,000)	Metropolitan statistical area / Metropolitan division / Component county	Population, 2010 (1,000)
Abilene, TX	**165**	**Athens-Clarke County, GA**	**193**	East Baton Rouge Parish, LA	440
Callahan County, TX	14	Clarke County, GA	117	East Feliciana Parish, LA.	20
Jones County, TX	20	Madison County, GA	28	Iberville Parish, LA	33
Taylor County, TX	132	Oconee County, GA	33	Livingston Parish, LA	128
		Oglethorpe County, GA	15	Pointe Coupee Parish, LA	23
Akron, OH	**703**			St. Helena Parish, LA	11
Portage County, OH	161	**Atlanta-Sandy Springs-Marietta, GA**	**5,269**	West Baton Rouge Parish, LA	24
Summit County, OH	542	Barrow County, GA	69	West Feliciana Parish, LA	16
		Bartow County, GA	100		
Albany, GA	**157**	Butts County, GA	24	**Battle Creek, MI**	**136**
Baker County, GA	3	Carroll County, GA	111	Calhoun County, MI	136
Dougherty County, GA.	95	Cherokee County, GA	214		
Lee County, GA	28	Clayton County, GA	259	**Bay City, MI**	**108**
Terrell County, GA	9	Cobb County, GA	688	Bay County, MI	108
Worth County, GA	22	Coweta County, GA	127		
		Dawson County, GA	22	**Beaumont-Port Arthur, TX**	**389**
Albany-Schenectady-Troy, NY	**871**	DeKalb County, GA	692	Hardin County, TX	55
Albany County, NY	304	Douglas County, GA	132	Jefferson County, TX	252
Rensselaer County, NY	159	Fayette County, GA	107	Orange County, TX	82
Saratoga County, NY	220	Forsyth County, GA	176		
Schenectady County, NY.	155	Fulton County, GA	921	**Bellingham, WA**	**201**
Schoharie County, NY	33	Gwinnett County, GA.	805	Whatcom County, WA	201
		Haralson County, GA	29		
Albuquerque, NM	**887**	Heard County, GA	12	**Bend, OR**	**158**
Bernalillo County, NM	663	Henry County, GA	204	Deschutes County, OR	158
Sandoval County, NM	132	Jasper County, GA	14		
Torrance County, NM	16	Lamar County, GA	18	**Billings, MT**	**158**
Valencia County, NM	77	Meriwether County, GA	22	Carbon County, MT	10
		Newton County, GA	100	Yellowstone County, MT	148
Alexandria, LA	**154**	Paulding County, GA	142		
Grant Parish, LA	22	Pickens County, GA	29	**Binghamton, NY**	**252**
Rapides Parish, LA	132	Pike County, GA	18	Broome County, NY	201
		Rockdale County, GA	85	Tioga County, NY	51
Allentown-Bethlehem-Easton, PA-NJ	**821**	Spalding County, GA	64		
Warren County, NJ	109	Walton County, GA	84	**Birmingham-Hoover, AL**	**1,128**
Carbon County, PA	65			Bibb County, AL	23
Lehigh County, PA	349	**Atlantic City-Hammonton, NJ**	**275**	Blount County, AL	57
Northampton County, PA	298	Atlantic County, NJ	275	Chilton County, AL	44
				Jefferson County, AL	658
Altoona, PA	**127**	**Auburn-Opelika, AL**	**140**	St. Clair County, AL	84
Blair County, PA	127	Lee County, AL	140	Shelby County, AL	195
				Walker County, AL	67
Amarillo, TX	**250**	**Augusta-Richmond County, GA-SC**	**557**		
Armstrong County, TX	2	Burke County, GA	23	**Bismarck, ND**	**109**
Carson County, TX	6	Columbia County, GA	124	Burleigh County, ND	81
Potter County, TX	121	McDuffie County, GA	22	Morton County, ND	27
Randall County, TX	121	Richmond County, GA	201		
		Aiken County, SC	160	**Blacksburg-Christiansburg-Radford, VA**	**163**
Ames, IA	**90**	Edgefield County, SC.	27	Giles County, VA	17
Story County, IA	90			Montgomery County, VA	94
		Austin-Round Rock-San Marcos, TX	**1,716**	Pulaski County, VA	35
Anchorage, AK	**381**	Bastrop County, TX	74	Radford city, VA	16
Anchorage Municipality, AK	292	Caldwell County, TX	38		
Matanuska-Susitna Borough, AK	89	Hays County, TX	157	**Bloomington, IN**	**193**
		Travis County, TX	1,024	Greene County, IN	33
Anderson, IN	**132**	Williamson County, TX	423	Monroe County, IN	138
Madison County, IN	132			Owen County, IN	22
		Bakersfield-Delano, CA	**840**		
Anderson, SC	**187**	Kern County, CA	840	**Bloomington-Normal, IL**	**170**
Anderson County, SC	187			McLean County, IL	170
		Baltimore-Towson, MD	**2,710**		
Ann Arbor, MI	**345**	Anne Arundel County, MD	538	**Boise City-Nampa, ID**	**617**
Washtenaw County, MI	345	Baltimore County, MD	805	Ada County, ID	392
		Carroll County, MD	167	Boise County, ID	7
Anniston-Oxford, AL	**119**	Harford County, MD	245	Canyon County, ID	189
Calhoun County, AL	119	Howard County, MD	287	Gem County, ID	17
		Queen Anne's County, MD	48	Owyhee County, ID	12
Appleton, WI	**226**	Baltimore city, MD	621		
Calumet County, WI	49			**Boston-Cambridge-Quincy, MA-NH**	**4,552**
Outagamie County, WI	177	**Bangor, ME**	**154**	**Boston-Quincy, MA**	**1,888**
		Penobscot County, ME	154	Norfolk County, MA	671
Asheville, NC	**425**			Plymouth County, MA	495
Buncombe County, NC	238	**Barnstable Town, MA**	**216**	Suffolk County, MA	722
Haywood County, NC	59	Barnstable County, MA	216		
Henderson County, NC	107				
Madison County, NC	21	**Baton Rouge, LA**	**802**		
		Ascension Parish, LA	107		

U.S. Census Bureau, Statistical Abstract of the United States: 2012

Metropolitan statistical area / Metropolitan division / Component county	Population, 2010 (1,000)
Cambridge-Newton-Framingham, MA	**1,503**
Middlesex County, MA....	1,503
Peabody, MA.	**743**
Essex County, MA.......	743
Rockingham County-Strafford County, NH	**418**
Rockingham County, NH ..	295
Strafford County, NH	123
Boulder, CO	**295**
Boulder County, CO......	295
Bowling Green, KY	**126**
Edmonson County, KY....	12
Warren County, KY	114
Bremerton-Silverdale, WA	**251**
Kitsap County, WA.......	251
Bridgeport-Stamford-Norwalk, CT	**917**
Fairfield County, CT......	917
Brownsville-Harlingen, TX	**406**
Cameron County, TX.....	406
Brunswick, GA	**112**
Brantley County, GA	18
Glynn County, GA.......	80
McIntosh County, GA.....	14
Buffalo-Niagara Falls, NY	**1,136**
Erie County, NY.........	919
Niagara County, NY......	216
Burlington, NC	**151**
Alamance County, NC....	151
Burlington-South Burlington, VT	**211**
Chittenden County, VT....	157
Franklin County, VT......	48
Grand Isle County, VT	7
Canton-Massillon, OH	**404**
Carroll County, OH.......	29
Stark County, OH........	376
Cape Coral-Fort Myers, FL	**619**
Lee County, FL..........	619
Cape Girardeau-Jackson, MO-IL	**96**
Alexander County, IL.....	8
Bollinger County, MO.....	12
Cape Girardeau County, MO.	76
Carson City, NV	**55**
Carson City, NV.........	55
Casper, WY	**75**
Natrona County, WY	75
Cedar Rapids, IA	**258**
Benton County, IA	26
Jones County, IA	21
Linn County, IA	211
Champaign-Urbana, IL	**232**
Champaign County, IL....	201
Ford County, IL	14
Piatt County, IL	17
Charleston, WV	**304**
Boone County, WV	25
Clay County, WV	9
Kanawha County, WV	193
Lincoln County, WV	22
Putnam County, WV	55
Charleston-North Charleston-Summerville, SC	**665**
Berkeley County, SC	178
Charleston County, SC ...	350
Dorchester County, SC ...	137
Charlotte-Gastonia-Rock Hill, NC-SC	**1,758**
Anson County, NC.......	27
Cabarrus County, NC....	178
Gaston County, NC	206
Mecklenburg County, NC..	920
Union County, NC	201
York County, SC.........	226
Charlottesville, VA	**202**
Albemarle County, VA	99
Fluvanna County, VA	26
Greene County, VA	18
Nelson County, VA.......	15
Charlottesville city, VA	43
Chattanooga, TN-GA	**528**
Catoosa County, GA	64
Dade County, GA........	17
Walker County, GA	69
Hamilton County, TN	336
Marion County, TN.......	28
Sequatchie County, TN ...	14
Cheyenne, WY	**92**
Laramie County, WY	92
Chicago-Joliet-Naperville, IL-IN-WI	**9,461**
Chicago-Joliet-Naperville, IL	**7,883**
Cook County, IL.........	5,195
DeKalb County, IL.......	105
DuPage County, IL.......	917
Grundy County, IL.......	50
Kane County, IL.........	515
Kendall County, IL.......	115
McHenry County, IL......	309
Will County, IL	678
Gary, IN	**708**
Jasper County, IN	33
Lake County, IN........	496
Newton County, IN.......	14
Porter County, IN........	164
Lake County-Kenosha County, IL-WI	**870**
Lake County, IL	703
Kenosha County, WI	166
Chico, CA	**220**
Butte County, CA........	220
Cincinnati-Middletown, OH-KY-IN	**2,130**
Dearborn County, IN	50
Franklin County, IN	23
Ohio County, IN	6
Boone County, KY	119
Bracken County, KY......	8
Campbell County, KY.....	90
Gallatin County, KY	9
Grant County, KY	25
Kenton County, KY	160
Pendleton County, KY	15
Brown County, OH.......	45
Butler County, OH	368
Clermont County, OH	197
Hamilton County, OH	802
Warren County, OH	213
Clarksville, TN-KY	**274**
Christian County, KY	74
Trigg County, KY	14
Montgomery County, TN ..	172
Stewart County, TN	13
Cleveland, TN	**116**
Bradley County, TN	99
Polk County, TN.........	17
Cleveland-Elyria-Mentor, OH	**2,077**
Cuyahoga County, OH....	1,280
Geauga County, OH	93
Lake County, OH........	230
Lorain County, OH.......	301
Medina County, OH......	172
Coeur d'Alene, ID	**138**
Kootenai County, ID......	138
College Station-Bryan, TX	**229**
Brazos County, TX.......	195
Burleson County, TX.....	17
Robertson County, TX....	17
Colorado Springs, CO	**646**
El Paso County, CO.......	622
Teller County, CO........	23
Columbia, MO	**173**
Boone County, MO.......	163
Howard County, MO	10
Columbia, SC	**768**
Calhoun County, SC	15
Fairfield County, SC......	24
Kershaw County, SC	62
Lexington County, SC	262
Richland County, SC	385
Saluda County, SC	20
Columbus, GA-AL	**295**
Russell County, AL	53
Chattahoochee County, GA	11
Harris County, GA	32
Marion County, GA	9
Muscogee County, GA....	190
Columbus, IN	**77**
Bartholomew County, IN ..	77
Columbus, OH	**1,837**
Delaware County, OH	174
Fairfield County, OH......	146
Franklin County, OH......	1,163
Licking County, OH	166
Madison County, OH	43
Morrow County, OH	35
Pickaway County, OH	56
Union County, OH	52
Corpus Christi, TX	**428**
Aransas County, TX......	23
Nueces County, TX	340
San Patricio County, TX...	65
Corvallis, OR	**86**
Benton County, OR	86
Crestview-Fort Walton Beach-Destin, FL	**181**
Okaloosa County, FL.....	181
Cumberland, MD-WV	**103**
Allegany County, MD	75
Mineral County, WV......	28
Dallas-Fort Worth-Arlington, TX	**6,372**
Dallas-Plano-Irving, TX	**4,236**
Collin County, TX........	782
Dallas County, TX........	2,368
Delta County, TX	5
Denton County, TX.......	663
Ellis County, TX	150
Hunt County, TX.........	86
Kaufman County, TX	103
Rockwall County, TX	78
Fort Worth-Arlington, TX	**2,136**
Johnson County, TX......	151
Parker County, TX	117
Tarrant County, TX.......	1,809
Wise County, TX	59

U.S. Census Bureau, Statistical Abstract of the United States: 2012

Metropolitan statistical area / Metropolitan division / Component county	Population, 2010 (1,000)	Metropolitan statistical area / Metropolitan division / Component county	Population, 2010 (1,000)	Metropolitan statistical area / Metropolitan division / Component county	Population, 2010 (1,000)
Dalton, GA	**142**	**Durham-Chapel Hill, NC**	**504**	**Fort Smith, AR-OK**	**299**
Murray County, GA	40	Chatham County, NC	64	Crawford County, AR	62
Whitfield County, GA	103	Durham County, NC	268	Franklin County, AR	18
		Orange County, NC	134	Sebastian County, AR	126
Danville, IL	**82**	Person County, NC	39	Le Flore County, OK	50
Vermilion County, IL	82			Sequoyah County, OK	42
		Eau Claire, WI	**161**		
Danville, VA	**107**	Chippewa County, WI	62	**Fort Wayne, IN**	**416**
Pittsylvania County, VA . . .	64	Eau Claire County, WI	99	Allen County, IN	355
Danville city, VA	43			Wells County, IN	28
		El Centro, CA	**175**	Whitley County, IN	33
Davenport-Moline-Rock Island,		Imperial County, CA	175		
IA-IL	**380**			**Fresno, CA**	**930**
Henry County, IL	50	**Elizabethtown, KY**	**120**	Fresno County, CA	930
Mercer County, IL	16	Hardin County, KY	106		
Rock Island County, IL. . . .	148	Larue County, KY	14	**Gadsden, AL**	**104**
Scott County, IA	165			Etowah County, AL	104
		Elkhart-Goshen, IN	**198**		
Dayton, OH	**842**	Elkhart County, IN	198	**Gainesville, FL**	**264**
Greene County, OH	162			Alachua County, FL	247
Miami County, OH	103	**Elmira, NY**	**89**	Gilchrist County, FL	17
Montgomery County, OH . .	535	Chemung County, NY	89		
Preble County, OH	42			**Gainesville, GA**	**180**
		El Paso, TX	**801**	Hall County, GA	180
Decatur, AL	**154**	El Paso County, TX	801		
Lawrence County, AL	34			**Glens Falls, NY**	**129**
Morgan County, AL	119	**Erie, PA**	**281**	Warren County, NY	66
		Erie County, PA	281	Washington County, NY . . .	63
Decatur, IL	**111**				
Macon County, IL	111	**Eugene-Springfield, OR**	**352**	**Goldsboro, NC**	**123**
		Lane County, OR	352	Wayne County, NC	123
Deltona-Daytona Beach-					
Ormond Beach, FL	**495**	**Evansville, IN-KY**	**359**	**Grand Forks, ND-MN**	**98**
Volusia County, FL	495	Gibson County, IN	34	Polk County, MN	32
		Posey County, IN	26	Grand Forks County, ND . .	67
Denver-Aurora-Broomfield,		Vanderburgh County, IN . .	180		
CO	**2,543**	Warrick County, IN	60	**Grand Junction, CO**	**147**
Adams County, CO	442	Henderson County, KY . . .	46	Mesa County, CO	147
Arapahoe County, CO	572	Webster County, KY	14		
Broomfield County, CO . . .	56			**Grand Rapids-Wyoming, MI**	**774**
Clear Creek County, CO . .	9	**Fairbanks, AK**	**98**	Barry County, MI	59
Denver County, CO	600	Fairbanks North Star		Ionia County, MI	64
Douglas County, CO	285	Borough, AK	98	Kent County, MI	603
Elbert County, CO	23			Newaygo County, MI	48
Gilpin County, CO	5	**Fargo, ND-MN**	**209**		
Jefferson County, CO	535	Clay County, MN	59	**Great Falls, MT**	**81**
Park County, CO	16	Cass County, ND	150	Cascade County, MT	81
Des Moines-West Des Moines,		**Farmington, NM**	**130**	**Greeley, CO**	**253**
IA	**570**	San Juan County, NM	130	Weld County, CO	253
Dallas County, IA	66				
Guthrie County, IA	11	**Fayetteville, NC**	**366**	**Green Bay, WI**	**306**
Madison County, IA	16	Cumberland County, NC . .	319	Brown County, WI	248
Polk County, IA	431	Hoke County, NC	47	Kewaunee County, WI	21
Warren County, IA	46			Oconto County, WI	38
		Fayetteville-Springdale-Rogers,			
Detroit-Warren-Livonia, MI	**4,296**	**AR-MO**	**463**	**Greensboro-High Point, NC**	**724**
Detroit-Livonia-Dearborn, MI	**1,821**	Benton County, AR	221	Guilford County, NC	488
Wayne County, MI	1,821	Madison County, AR	16	Randolph County, NC	142
Warren-Troy-Farmington		Washington County, AR. . .	203	Rockingham County, NC . .	94
Hills, MI	**2,476**	McDonald County, MO. . . .	23		
Lapeer County, MI	88			**Greenville, NC**	**190**
Livingston County, MI	181	**Flagstaff, AZ**	**134**	Greene County, NC	21
Macomb County, MI	841	Coconino County, AZ	134	Pitt County, NC	168
Oakland County, MI	1,202				
St. Clair County, MI	163	**Flint, MI**	**426**	**Greenville-Mauldin-Easley, SC** . .	**637**
		Genesee County, MI	426	Greenville County, SC	451
Dothan, AL	**146**			Laurens County, SC	67
Geneva County, AL	27	**Florence, SC**	**206**	Pickens County, SC	119
Henry County, AL	17	Darlington County, SC. . . .	69		
Houston County, AL	102	Florence County, SC	137	**Gulfport-Biloxi, MS**	**249**
				Hancock County, MS	44
Dover, DE	**162**	**Florence-Muscle Shoals, AL**	**147**	Harrison County, MS	187
Kent County, DE	162	Colbert County, AL	54	Stone County, MS	18
		Lauderdale County, AL . . .	93		
Dubuque, IA	**94**			**Hagerstown-Martinsburg,**	
Dubuque County, IA.	94	**Fond du Lac, WI**	**102**	**MD-WV**	**269**
		Fond du Lac County, WI . .	102	Washington County, MD . .	**147**
Duluth, MN-WI	**280**			Berkeley County, WV	104
Carlton County, MN	35	**Fort Collins-Loveland, CO**	**300**	Morgan County, WV	18
St. Louis County, MN	200	Larimer County, CO.	300		
Douglas County, WI	44			**Hanford-Corcoran, CA**	**153**
				Kings County, CA.	153

U.S. Census Bureau, Statistical Abstract of the United States: 2012

Metropolitan statistical area / Metropolitan division / Component county	Population, 2010 (1,000)	Metropolitan statistical area / Metropolitan division / Component county	Population, 2010 (1,000)	Metropolitan statistical area / Metropolitan division / Component county	Population, 2010 (1,000)
Harrisburg-Carlisle, PA	549	**Iowa City, IA**	153	**Killeen-Temple-Fort Hood, TX** . . .	405
Cumberland County, PA . . .	235	Johnson County, IA	131	Bell County, TX	310
Dauphin County, PA	268	Washington County, IA . . .	22	Coryell County, TX	75
Perry County, PA	46	**Ithaca, NY**	102	Lampasas County, TX	20
		Tompkins County, NY	102		
Harrisonburg, VA	125			**Kingsport-Bristol-Bristol, TN-VA**	310
Rockingham County, VA . .	76	**Jackson, MI**	160	Hawkins County, TN	57
Harrisonburg city, VA	49	Jackson County, MI	160	Sullivan County, TN	157
				Scott County, VA	23
Hartford-West Hartford-East Hartford, CT	1,212	**Jackson, MS**	539	Washington County, VA . . .	55
Hartford County, CT	894	Copiah County, MS	29	Bristol city, VA	18
Middlesex County, CT	166	Hinds County, MS	245		
Tolland County, CT	153	Madison County, MS	95	**Kingston, NY**	182
		Rankin County, MS	142	Ulster County, NY	182
Hattiesburg, MS	143	Simpson County, MS	28		
Forrest County, MS	75	**Jackson, TN**	115	**Knoxville, TN**	698
Lamar County, MS	56	Chester County, TN	17	Anderson County, TN	75
Perry County, MS	12	Madison County, TN	98	Blount County, TN	123
				Knox County, TN	432
Hickory-Lenoir-Morganton, NC . .	365	**Jacksonville, FL**	1,346	Loudon County, TN	49
Alexander County, NC	37	Baker County, FL	27	Union County, TN	19
Burke County, NC	91	Clay County, FL	191		
Caldwell County, NC	83	Duval County, FL	864	**Kokomo, IN**	99
Catawba County, NC	154	Nassau County, FL	73	Howard County, IN	83
		St. Johns County, FL	190	Tipton County, IN	16
Hinesville-Fort Stewart, GA	78				
Liberty County, GA	63	**Jacksonville, NC**	178	**La Crosse, WI-MN**	134
Long County, GA	14	Onslow County, NC	178	Houston County, MN	19
				La Crosse County, WI	115
Holland-Grand Haven, MI	264	**Janesville, WI**	160		
Ottawa County, MI	264	Rock County, WI	160	**Lafayette, IN**	202
				Benton County, IN	9
Honolulu, HI	953	**Jefferson City, MO**	150	Carroll County, IN	20
Honolulu County, HI	953	Callaway County, MO	44	Tippecanoe County, IN . . .	173
		Cole County, MO	76		
Hot Springs, AR	96	Moniteau County, MO	16	**Lafayette, LA**	274
Garland County, AR	96	Osage County, MO	14	Lafayette Parish, LA	222
				St. Martin Parish, LA	52
Houma-Bayou Cane-Thibodaux, LA	208	**Johnson City, TN**	199		
Lafourche Parish, LA	96	Carter County, TN	57	**Lake Charles, LA**	200
Terrebonne Parish, LA	112	Unicoi County, TN	18	Calcasieu Parish, LA	193
		Washington County, TN . . .	123	Cameron Parish, LA	7
Houston-Sugar Land-Baytown, TX	5,947	**Johnstown, PA**	144	**Lake Havasu City-Kingman, AZ**	200
Austin County, TX	28	Cambria County, PA	144	Mohave County, AZ	200
Brazoria County, TX	313				
Chambers County, TX	35	**Jonesboro, AR**	121	**Lakeland-Winter Haven, FL**	602
Fort Bend County, TX	585	Craighead County, AR	96	Polk County, FL	602
Galveston County, TX	291	Poinsett County, AR	25		
Harris County, TX	4,092			**Lancaster, PA**	519
Liberty County, TX	76	**Joplin, MO**	176	Lancaster County, PA	519
Montgomery County, TX . . .	456	Jasper County, MO	117		
San Jacinto County, TX . . .	26	Newton County, MO	58	**Lansing-East Lansing, MI**	464
Waller County, TX	43			Clinton County, MI	75
		Kalamazoo-Portage, MI	327	Eaton County, MI	108
Huntington-Ashland, WV-KY-OH	288	Kalamazoo County, MI	250	Ingham County, MI	281
Boyd County, KY	50	Van Buren County, MI	76		
Greenup County, KY	37			**Laredo, TX**	250
Lawrence County, OH	62	**Kankakee-Bradley, IL**	113	Webb County, TX	250
Cabell County, WV	96	Kankakee County, IL	113		
Wayne County, WV	42			**Las Cruces, NM**	209
		Kansas City, MO-KS	2,035	Doña Ana County, NM	209
Huntsville, AL	418	Franklin County, KS	26		
Limestone County, AL	83	Johnson County, KS	544	**Las Vegas-Paradise, NV**	1,951
Madison County, AL	335	Leavenworth County, KS . .	76	Clark County, NV	1,951
		Linn County, KS	10		
Idaho Falls, ID	130	Miami County, KS	33	**Lawrence, KS**	111
Bonneville County, ID	104	Wyandotte County, KS	158	Douglas County, KS	111
Jefferson County, ID	26	Bates County, MO	17		
		Caldwell County, MO	9	**Lawton, OK**	124
Indianapolis-Carmel, IN	1,756	Cass County, MO	99	Comanche County, OK . . .	124
Boone County, IN	57	Clay County, MO	222		
Brown County, IN	15	Clinton County, MO	21	**Lebanon, PA**	134
Hamilton County, IN	275	Jackson County, MO	674	Lebanon County, PA	134
Hancock County, IN	70	Lafayette County, MO	33		
Hendricks County, IN	145	Platte County, MO	89	**Lewiston, ID-WA**	61
Johnson County, IN	140	Ray County, MO	23	Nez Perce County, ID	39
Marion County, IN	903	**Kennewick-Pasco-Richland, WA**	253	Asotin County, WA	22
Morgan County, IN	69	Benton County, WA	175		
Putnam County, IN	38	Franklin County, WA	78	**Lewiston-Auburn, ME**	108
Shelby County, IN	44			Androscoggin County, ME	108

Metropolitan statistical area / Metropolitan division / Component county	Population, 2010 (1,000)
Lexington-Fayette, KY	**472**
Bourbon County, KY	20
Clark County, KY	36
Fayette County, KY	296
Jessamine County, KY	49
Scott County, KY	47
Woodford County, KY	25
Lima, OH	**106**
Allen County, OH	106
Lincoln, NE	**302**
Lancaster County, NE	285
Seward County, NE	17
Little Rock-North Little Rock-Conway, AR	**700**
Faulkner County, AR	113
Grant County, AR	18
Lonoke County, AR	68
Perry County, AR	10
Pulaski County, AR	383
Saline County, AR	107
Logan, UT-ID	**125**
Franklin County, ID	13
Cache County, UT	113
Longview, TX	**214**
Gregg County, TX	122
Rusk County, TX	53
Upshur County, TX	39
Longview, WA	**102**
Cowlitz County, WA	102
Los Angeles-Long Beach-Santa Ana, CA	**12,829**
Los Angeles-Long Beach-Glendale, CA	**9,819**
Los Angeles County, CA	9,819
Santa Ana-Anaheim-Irvine, CA	**3,010**
Orange County, CA	3,010
Louisville/Jefferson County, KY-IN	**1,284**
Clark County, IN	110
Floyd County, IN	75
Harrison County, IN	39
Washington County, IN	28
Bullitt County, KY	74
Henry County, KY	15
Jefferson County, KY	741
Meade County, KY	29
Nelson County, KY	43
Oldham County, KY	60
Shelby County, KY	42
Spencer County, KY	17
Trimble County, KY	9
Lubbock, TX	**285**
Crosby County, TX	6
Lubbock County, TX	279
Lynchburg, VA	**253**
Amherst County, VA	32
Appomattox County, VA	15
Bedford County, VA	69
Campbell County, VA	55
Bedford city, VA	6
Lynchburg city, VA	76
Macon, GA	**232**
Bibb County, GA	156
Crawford County, GA	13
Jones County, GA	29
Monroe County, GA	26
Twiggs County, GA	9
Madera-Chowchilla, CA	**151**
Madera County, CA	151
Madison, WI	**569**
Columbia County, WI	57
Dane County, WI	488
Iowa County, WI	24
Manchester-Nashua, NH	**401**
Hillsborough County, NH	401
Manhattan, KS	**127**
Geary County, KS	34
Pottawatomie County, KS	22
Riley County, KS	71
Mankato-North Mankato, MN	**97**
Blue Earth County, MN	64
Nicollet County, MN	33
Mansfield, OH	**124**
Richland County, OH	124
McAllen-Edinburg-Mission, TX	**775**
Hidalgo County, TX	775
Medford, OR	**203**
Jackson County, OR	203
Memphis, TN-MS-AR	**1,316**
Crittenden County, AR	51
DeSoto County, MS	161
Marshall County, MS	37
Tate County, MS	29
Tunica County, MS	11
Fayette County, TN	38
Shelby County, TN	928
Tipton County, TN	61
Merced, CA	**256**
Merced County, CA	256
Miami-Fort Lauderdale-Pompano Beach, FL	**5,565**
Fort Lauderdale-Pompano Beach-Deerfield Beach, FL	**1,748**
Broward County, FL	1,748
Miami-Miami Beach-Kendall, FL	**2,496**
Miami-Dade County, FL	2,496
West Palm Beach-Boca Raton-Boynton Beach, FL	**1,320**
Palm Beach County, FL	1,320
Michigan City-La Porte, IN	**111**
LaPorte County, IN	111
Midland, TX	**137**
Midland County, TX	137
Milwaukee-Waukesha-West Allis, WI	**1,556**
Milwaukee County, WI	948
Ozaukee County, WI	86
Washington County, WI	132
Waukesha County, WI	390
Minneapolis-St. Paul-Bloomington, MN-WI	**3,280**
Anoka County, MN	331
Carver County, MN	91
Chisago County, MN	54
Dakota County, MN	399
Hennepin County, MN	1,152
Isanti County, MN	38
Ramsey County, MN	509
Scott County, MN	130
Sherburne County, MN	88
Washington County, MN	238
Wright County, MN	125
Pierce County, WI	41
St. Croix County, WI	84
Missoula, MT	**109**
Missoula County, MT	109
Mobile, AL	**413**
Mobile County, AL	413
Modesto, CA	**514**
Stanislaus County, CA	514
Monroe, LA	**176**
Ouachita Parish, LA	154
Union Parish, LA	23
Monroe, MI	**152**
Monroe County, MI	152
Montgomery, AL	**375**
Autauga County, AL	55
Elmore County, AL	79
Lowndes County, AL	11
Montgomery County, AL	229
Morgantown, WV	**130**
Monongalia County, WV	96
Preston County, WV	34
Morristown, TN	**137**
Grainger County, TN	23
Hamblen County, TN	63
Jefferson County, TN	51
Mount Vernon-Anacortes, WA	**117**
Skagit County, WA	117
Muncie, IN	**118**
Delaware County, IN	118
Muskegon-Norton Shores, MI	**172**
Muskegon County, MI	172
Myrtle Beach-North Myrtle Beach-Conway, SC	**269**
Horry County, SC	269
Napa, CA	**136**
Napa County, CA	136
Naples-Marco Island, FL	**322**
Collier County, FL	322
Nashville-Davidson—Murfreesboro—Franklin, TN	**1,590**
Cannon County, TN	14
Cheatham County, TN	39
Davidson County, TN	627
Dickson County, TN	50
Hickman County, TN	25
Macon County, TN	22
Robertson County, TN	66
Rutherford County, TN	263
Smith County, TN	19
Sumner County, TN	161
Trousdale County, TN	8
Williamson County, TN	183
Wilson County, TN	114
New Haven-Milford, CT	**862**
New Haven County, CT	862
New Orleans-Metairie-Kenner, LA	**1,168**
Jefferson Parish, LA	433
Orleans Parish, LA	344
Plaquemines Parish, LA	23
St. Bernard Parish, LA	36
St. Charles Parish, LA	53
St. John the Baptist Parish, LA	46
St. Tammany Parish, LA	234
New York-Northern New Jersey-Long Island, NY-NJ-PA	**18,897**
Edison-New Brunswick, NJ	**2,340**
Middlesex County, NJ	810
Monmouth County, NJ	630
Ocean County, NJ	577
Somerset County, NJ	323

U.S. Census Bureau, Statistical Abstract of the United States: 2012

Metropolitan statistical area / Metropolitan division / Component county	Population, 2010 (1,000)
Nassau-Suffolk, NY	**2,833**
Nassau County, NY	1,340
Suffolk County, NY	1,493
Newark-Union, NJ-PA	**2,148**
Essex County, NJ	784
Hunterdon County, NJ	128
Morris County, NJ	492
Sussex County, NJ	149
Union County, NJ	536
Pike County, PA	57
New York-White Plains-Wayne, NY-NJ	**11,576**
Bergen County, NJ	905
Hudson County, NJ	634
Passaic County, NJ	501
Bronx County, NY	1,385
Kings County, NY	2,505
New York County, NY	1,586
Putnam County, NY	100
Queens County, NY	2,231
Richmond County, NY	469
Rockland County, NY	312
Westchester County, NY	949
Niles-Benton Harbor, MI	**157**
Berrien County, MI	157
North Port-Bradenton-Sarasota, FL	**702**
Manatee County, FL	323
Sarasota County, FL	379
Norwich-New London, CT	**274**
New London County, CT	274
Ocala, FL	**331**
Marion County, FL	331
Ocean City, NJ	**97**
Cape May County, NJ	97
Odessa, TX	**137**
Ector County, TX	137
Ogden-Clearfield, UT	**547**
Davis County, UT	306
Morgan County, UT	9
Weber County, UT	231
Oklahoma City, OK	**1,253**
Canadian County, OK	116
Cleveland County, OK	256
Grady County, OK	52
Lincoln County, OK	34
Logan County, OK	42
McClain County, OK	35
Oklahoma County, OK	719
Olympia, WA	**252**
Thurston County, WA	252
Omaha-Council Bluffs, NE-IA	**865**
Harrison County, IA	15
Mills County, IA	15
Pottawattamie County, IA	93
Cass County, NE	25
Douglas County, NE	517
Sarpy County, NE	159
Saunders County, NE	21
Washington County, NE	20
Orlando-Kissimmee-Sanford, FL	**2,134**
Lake County, FL	297
Orange County, FL	1,146
Osceola County, FL	269
Seminole County, FL	423
Oshkosh-Neenah, WI	**167**
Winnebago County, WI	167
Owensboro, KY	**115**
Daviess County, KY	97
Hancock County, KY	9
McLean County, KY	10
Oxnard-Thousand Oaks-Ventura, CA	**823**
Ventura County, CA	823
Palm Bay-Melbourne-Titusville, FL	**543**
Brevard County, FL	543
Palm Coast, FL	**96**
Flagler County, FL	96
Panama City-Lynn Haven-Panama City Beach, FL	**169**
Bay County, FL	169
Parkersburg-Marietta-Vienna, WV-OH	**162**
Washington County, OH	62
Pleasants County, WV	8
Wirt County, WV	6
Wood County, WV	87
Pascagoula, MS	**162**
George County, MS	23
Jackson County, MS	140
Pensacola-Ferry Pass-Brent, FL	**449**
Escambia County, FL	298
Santa Rosa County, FL	151
Peoria, IL	**379**
Marshall County, IL	13
Peoria County, IL	186
Stark County, IL	6
Tazewell County, IL	135
Woodford County, IL	39
Philadelphia-Camden-Wilmington, PA-NJ-DE-MD	**5,965**
Camden, NJ	1,251
Burlington County, NJ	449
Camden County, NJ	514
Gloucester County, NJ	288
Philadelphia, PA	4,009
Bucks County, PA	625
Chester County, PA	499
Delaware County, PA	559
Montgomery County, PA	800
Philadelphia County, PA	1,526
Wilmington, DE-MD-NJ	706
New Castle County, DE	538
Cecil County, MD	101
Salem County, NJ	66
Phoenix-Mesa-Glendale, AZ	**4,193**
Maricopa County, AZ	3,817
Pinal County, AZ	376
Pine Bluff, AR	**100**
Cleveland County, AR	9
Jefferson County, AR	77
Lincoln County, AR	14
Pittsburgh, PA	**2,356**
Allegheny County, PA	1,223
Armstrong County, PA	69
Beaver County, PA	171
Butler County, PA	184
Fayette County, PA	137
Washington County, PA	208
Westmoreland County, PA	365
Pittsfield, MA	**131**
Berkshire County, MA	131
Pocatello, ID	**91**
Bannock County, ID	83
Power County, ID	8
Portland-South Portland-Biddeford, ME	**514**
Cumberland County, ME	282
Sagadahoc County, ME	35
York County, ME	197
Portland-Vancouver-Hillsboro, OR-WA	**2,226**
Clackamas County, OR	376
Columbia County, OR	49
Multnomah County, OR	735
Washington County, OR	530
Yamhill County, OR	99
Clark County, WA	425
Skamania County, WA	11
Port St. Lucie, FL	**424**
Martin County, FL	146
St. Lucie County, FL	278
Poughkeepsie-Newburgh-Middletown, NY	**670**
Dutchess County, NY	297
Orange County, NY	373
Prescott, AZ	**211**
Yavapai County, AZ	211
Providence-New Bedford-Fall River, RI-MA	**1,601**
Bristol County, MA	548
Bristol County, RI	50
Kent County, RI	166
Newport County, RI	83
Providence County, RI	627
Washington County, RI	127
Provo-Orem, UT	**527**
Juab County, UT	10
Utah County, UT	517
Pueblo, CO	**159**
Pueblo County, CO	159
Punta Gorda, FL	**160**
Charlotte County, FL	160
Racine, WI	**195**
Racine County, WI	195
Raleigh-Cary, NC	**1,130**
Franklin County, NC	61
Johnston County, NC	169
Wake County, NC	901
Rapid City, SD	**126**
Meade County, SD	25
Pennington County, SD	101
Reading, PA	**411**
Berks County, PA	411
Redding, CA	**177**
Shasta County, CA	177
Reno-Sparks, NV	**425**
Storey County, NV	4
Washoe County, NV	421
Richmond, VA	**1,258**
Amelia County, VA	13
Caroline County, VA	29
Charles City County, VA	7
Chesterfield County, VA	316
Cumberland County, VA	10
Dinwiddie County, VA	28
Goochland County, VA	22
Hanover County, VA	100
Henrico County, VA	307
King and Queen County, VA	7
King William County, VA	16
Louisa County, VA	33
New Kent County, VA	18
Powhatan County, VA	28
Prince George County, VA	36
Sussex County, VA	12

U.S. Census Bureau, Statistical Abstract of the United States: 2012

Metropolitan statistical area / Metropolitan division / Component county	Population, 2010 (1,000)
Colonial Heights city, VA	17
Hopewell city, VA	23
Petersburg city, VA	32
Richmond city, VA	204
Riverside-San Bernardino-Ontario, CA	**4,225**
Riverside County, CA	2,190
San Bernardino County, CA	2,035
Roanoke, VA	**309**
Botetourt County, VA	33
Craig County, VA	5
Franklin County, VA	56
Roanoke County, VA	92
Roanoke city, VA	97
Salem city, VA	25
Rochester, MN	**186**
Dodge County, MN	20
Olmsted County, MN	144
Wabasha County, MN	22
Rochester, NY	**1,054**
Livingston County, NY	65
Monroe County, NY	744
Ontario County, NY	108
Orleans County, NY	43
Wayne County, NY	94
Rockford, IL	**349**
Boone County, IL	54
Winnebago County, IL	295
Rocky Mount, NC	**152**
Edgecombe County, NC	57
Nash County, NC	96
Rome, GA	**96**
Floyd County, GA	96
Sacramento—Arden-Arcade—Roseville, CA	**2,149**
El Dorado County, CA	181
Placer County, CA	348
Sacramento County, CA	1,419
Yolo County, CA	201
Saginaw-Saginaw Township North, MI	**200**
Saginaw County, MI	200
St. Cloud, MN	**189**
Benton County, MN	38
Stearns County, MN	151
St. George, UT	**138**
Washington County, UT	138
St. Joseph, MO-KS	**127**
Doniphan County, KS	8
Andrew County, MO	17
Buchanan County, MO	89
DeKalb County, MO	13
St. Louis, MO-IL [1]	**2,813**
Bond County, IL	18
Calhoun County, IL	5
Clinton County, IL	38
Jersey County, IL	23
Madison County, IL	269
Monroe County, IL	33
St. Clair County, IL	270
Franklin County, MO	101
Jefferson County, MO	219
Lincoln County, MO	53
St. Charles County, MO	360
St. Louis County, MO	999
Warren County, MO	33
Washington County, MO	25
St. Louis city, MO	319
Salem, OR	**391**
Marion County, OR	315
Polk County, OR	75
Salinas, CA	**415**
Monterey County, CA	415
Salisbury, MD	**125**
Somerset County, MD	26
Wicomico County, MD	99
Salt Lake City, UT	**1,124**
Salt Lake County, UT	1,030
Summit County, UT	36
Tooele County, UT	58
San Angelo, TX	**112**
Irion County, TX	2
Tom Green County, TX	110
San Antonio-New Braunfels, TX	**2,143**
Atascosa County, TX	45
Bandera County, TX	20
Bexar County, TX	1,715
Comal County, TX	108
Guadalupe County, TX	132
Kendall County, TX	33
Medina County, TX	46
Wilson County, TX	43
San Diego-Carlsbad-San Marcos, CA	**3,095**
San Diego County, CA	3,095
Sandusky, OH	**77**
Erie County, OH	77
San Francisco-Oakland-Fremont, CA	**4,335**
Oakland-Fremont-Hayward, CA	**2,559**
Alameda County, CA	1,510
Contra Costa County, CA	1,049
San Francisco-San Mateo-Redwood City, CA	**1,776**
Marin County, CA	252
San Francisco County, CA	805
San Mateo County, CA	718
San Jose-Sunnyvale-Santa Clara, CA	**1,837**
San Benito County, CA	55
Santa Clara County, CA	1,782
San Luis Obispo-Paso Robles, CA	**270**
San Luis Obispo County, CA	270
Santa Barbara-Santa Maria-Goleta, CA	**424**
Santa Barbara County, CA	424
Santa Cruz-Watsonville, CA	**262**
Santa Cruz County, CA	262
Santa Fe, NM	**144**
Santa Fe County, NM	144
Santa Rosa-Petaluma, CA	**484**
Sonoma County, CA	484
Savannah, GA	**348**
Bryan County, GA	30
Chatham County, GA	265
Effingham County, GA	52
Scranton—Wilkes-Barre, PA	**564**
Lackawanna County, PA	214
Luzerne County, PA	321
Wyoming County, PA	28
Seattle-Tacoma-Bellevue, WA	**3,440**
Seattle-Bellevue-Everett, WA	**2,645**
King County, WA	1,931
Snohomish County, WA	713
Tacoma, WA	**795**
Pierce County, WA	795
Sebastian-Vero Beach, FL	**138**
Indian River County, FL	138
Sheboygan, WI	**116**
Sheboygan County, WI	116
Sherman-Denison, TX	**121**
Grayson County, TX	121
Shreveport-Bossier City, LA	**399**
Bossier Parish, LA	117
Caddo Parish, LA	255
De Soto Parish, LA	27
Sioux City, IA-NE-SD	**144**
Woodbury County, IA	102
Dakota County, NE	21
Dixon County, NE	6
Union County, SD	14
Sioux Falls, SD	**228**
Lincoln County, SD	45
McCook County, SD	6
Minnehaha County, SD	169
Turner County, SD	8
South Bend-Mishawaka, IN-MI	**319**
St. Joseph County, IN	267
Cass County, MI	52
Spartanburg, SC	**284**
Spartanburg County, SC	284
Spokane, WA	**471**
Spokane County, WA	471
Springfield, IL	**210**
Menard County, IL	13
Sangamon County, IL	197
Springfield, MA	**693**
Franklin County, MA	71
Hampden County, MA	463
Hampshire County, MA	158
Springfield, MO	**437**
Christian County, MO	77
Dallas County, MO	17
Greene County, MO	275
Polk County, MO	31
Webster County, MO	36
Springfield, OH	**138**
Clark County, OH	138
State College, PA	**154**
Centre County, PA	154
Steubenville-Weirton, OH-WV	**124**
Jefferson County, OH	70
Brooke County, WV	24
Hancock County, WV	31
Stockton, CA	**685**
San Joaquin County, CA	685
Sumter, SC	**107**
Sumter County, SC	107
Syracuse, NY	**663**
Madison County, NY	73
Onondaga County, NY	467
Oswego County, NY	122
Tallahassee, FL	**367**
Gadsden County, FL	46

U.S. Census Bureau, Statistical Abstract of the United States: 2012

Metropolitan statistical area / Metropolitan division / Component county	Population, 2010 (1,000)
Jefferson County, FL	15
Leon County, FL	275
Wakulla County, FL	31
Tampa-St. Petersburg-Clearwater, FL	**2,783**
Hernando County, FL	173
Hillsborough County, FL	1,229
Pasco County, FL	465
Pinellas County, FL	917
Terre Haute, IN	**172**
Clay County, IN	27
Sullivan County, IN	21
Vermillion County, IN	16
Vigo County, IN	108
Texarkana, TX-Texarkana, AR	**136**
Miller County, AR	43
Bowie County, TX	93
Toledo, OH	**651**
Fulton County, OH	43
Lucas County, OH	442
Ottawa County, OH	41
Wood County, OH	125
Topeka, KS	**234**
Jackson County, KS	13
Jefferson County, KS	19
Osage County, KS	16
Shawnee County, KS	178
Wabaunsee County, KS	7
Trenton-Ewing, NJ	**367**
Mercer County, NJ	367
Tucson, AZ	**980**
Pima County, AZ	980
Tulsa, OK	**937**
Creek County, OK	70
Okmulgee County, OK	40
Osage County, OK	47
Pawnee County, OK	17
Rogers County, OK	87
Tulsa County, OK	603
Wagoner County, OK	73
Tuscaloosa, AL	**219**
Greene County, AL	9
Hale County, AL	16
Tuscaloosa County, AL	195
Tyler, TX	**210**
Smith County, TX	210
Utica-Rome, NY	**299**
Herkimer County, NY	65
Oneida County, NY	235
Valdosta, GA	**140**
Brooks County, GA	16
Echols County, GA	4
Lanier County, GA	10
Lowndes County, GA	109
Vallejo-Fairfield, CA	**413**
Solano County, CA	413
Victoria, TX	**115**
Calhoun County, TX	21
Goliad County, TX	7
Victoria County, TX	87
Vineland-Millville-Bridgeton, NJ	**157**
Cumberland County, NJ	157
Virginia Beach-Norfolk-Newport News, VA-NC	**1,672**
Currituck County, NC	24
Gloucester County, VA	37
Isle of Wight County, VA	35
James City County, VA	67
Mathews County, VA	9
Surry County, VA	7
York County, VA	65
Chesapeake city, VA	222
Hampton city, VA	137
Newport News city, VA	181
Norfolk city, VA	243
Poquoson city, VA	12
Portsmouth city, VA	96
Suffolk city, VA	85
Virginia Beach city, VA	438
Williamsburg city, VA	14
Visalia-Porterville, CA	**442**
Tulare County, CA	442
Waco, TX	**235**
McLennan County, TX	235
Warner Robins, GA	**140**
Houston County, GA	140
Washington-Arlington-Alexandria, DC-VA-MD-WV	**5,582**
Bethesda-Rockville-Frederick, MD	**1,205**
Frederick County, MD	233
Montgomery County, MD	972
Washington-Arlington-Alexandria, DC-VA-MD-WV	**4,377**
District of Columbia, DC	602
Calvert County, MD	89
Charles County, MD	147
Prince George's County, MD	863
Arlington County, VA	208
Clarke County, VA	14
Fairfax County, VA	1,082
Fauquier County, VA	65
Loudoun County, VA	312
Prince William County, VA	402
Spotsylvania County, VA	122
Stafford County, VA	129
Warren County, VA	38
Alexandria city, VA	140
Fairfax city, VA	23
Falls Church city, VA	12
Fredericksburg city, VA	24
Manassas city, VA	38
Manassas Park city, VA	14
Jefferson County, WV	53
Waterloo-Cedar Falls, IA	**168**
Black Hawk County, IA	131
Bremer County, IA	24
Grundy County, IA	12
Wausau, WI	**134**
Marathon County, WI	134
Wenatchee-East Wenatchee, WA	**111**
Chelan County, WA	72
Douglas County, WA	38
Wheeling, WV-OH	**148**
Belmont County, OH	70
Marshall County, WV	33
Ohio County, WV	44
Wichita, KS	**623**
Butler County, KS	66
Harvey County, KS	35
Sedgwick County, KS	498
Sumner County, KS	24
Wichita Falls, TX	**151**
Archer County, TX	9
Clay County, TX	11
Wichita County, TX	132
Williamsport, PA	**116**
Lycoming County, PA	116
Wilmington, NC	**362**
Brunswick County, NC	107
New Hanover County, NC	203
Pender County, NC	52
Winchester, VA-WV	**128**
Frederick County, VA	78
Winchester city, VA	26
Hampshire County, WV	24
Winston-Salem, NC	**478**
Davie County, NC	41
Forsyth County, NC	351
Stokes County, NC	47
Yadkin County, NC	38
Worcester, MA	**799**
Worcester County, MA	799
Yakima, WA	**243**
Yakima County, WA	243
York-Hanover, PA	**435**
York County, PA	435
Youngstown-Warren-Boardman, OH-PA	**566**
Mahoning County, OH	239
Trumbull County, OH	210
Mercer County, PA	117
Yuba City, CA	**167**
Sutter County, CA	95
Yuba County, CA	72
Yuma, AZ	**196**
Yuma County, AZ	196

[1] The portion of Sullivan city in Crawford County, Missouri, is legally part of the St. Louis, MO-IL Metropolitan Statistical Area. The estimate shown here for the St. Louis, MO-IL Metropolitan Statistical Area does not include this area.

Source: U.S. Census Bureau, 2010 Census, <http://2010.census.gov/2010census/data/>.

Table B. Microbiopolitan Statistical Areas and Components—Population: 2010

[Population as of April 2010. (58 represents 58,000). Micropolitan statistical areas as defined by the U.S. Office of Management and Budget as December 2009. All metropolitan statistical areas are arranged alphabetically]

Micropolitan statistical area Component county	Population, 2010 (1,000)	Micropolitan statistical area Component county	Population, 2010 (1,000)	Micropolitan statistical area Component county	Population, 2010 (1,000)
Abbeville, LA	58	**Arkadelphia, AR**	23	**Bemidji, MN**	44
Vermilion Parish, LA	58	Clark County, AR	23	Beltrami County, MN	44
Aberdeen, SD	41	**Ashland, OH**	53	**Bennettsville, SC**	29
Brown County, SD	37	Ashland County, OH	53	Marlboro County, SC	29
Edmunds County, SD	4	**Ashtabula, OH**	101	**Bennington, VT**	37
Aberdeen, WA	73	Ashtabula County, OH	101	Bennington County, VT	37
Grays Harbor County, WA	73	**Astoria, OR**	37	**Berlin, NH-VT**	39
Ada, OK	37	Clatsop County, OR	37	Coos County, NH	33
Pontotoc County, OK	37	**Atchison, KS**	17	Essex County, VT	6
Adrian, MI	100	Atchison County, KS	17	**Big Rapids, MI**	43
Lenawee County, MI	100	**Athens, OH**	65	Mecosta County, MI	43
Alamogordo, NM	64	Athens County, OH	65	**Big Spring, TX**	35
Otero County, NM	64	**Athens, TN**	52	Howard County, TX	35
Albany-Lebanon, OR	117	McMinn County, TN	52	**Bishop, CA**	19
Linn County, OR	117	**Athens, TX**	79	Inyo County, CA	19
Albemarle, NC	61	Henderson County, TX.	79	**Blackfoot, ID**	46
Stanly County, NC	61	**Auburn, IN**	42	Bingham County, ID.	46
Albert Lea, MN	31	DeKalb County, IN	42	**Bloomsburg-Berwick, PA**	86
Freeborn County, MN	31	**Auburn, NY**	80	Columbia County, PA.	67
Albertville, AL	93	Cayuga County, NY	80	Montour County, PA.	18
Marshall County, AL.	93	**Augusta-Waterville, ME**	122	**Bluefield, WV-VA**	107
Alexander City, AL	53	Kennebec County, ME.	122	Tazewell County, VA.	45
Coosa County, AL	12	**Austin, MN**	39	Mercer County, WV	62
Tallapoosa County, AL.	42	Mower County, MN	39	**Blytheville, AR**	46
Alexandria, MN	36	**Bainbridge, GA**	28	Mississippi County, AR	46
Douglas County, MN	36	Decatur County, GA.	28	**Bogalusa, LA**	47
Alice, TX	41	**Baraboo, WI**	62	Washington Parish, LA	47
Jim Wells County, TX	41	Sauk County, WI	62	**Bonham, TX**	34
Allegan, MI	111	**Barre, VT**	60	Fannin County, TX	34
Allegan County, MI.	111	Washington County, VT	60	**Boone, IA**	26
Alma, MI	42	**Bartlesville, OK**	51	Boone County, IA.	26
Gratiot County, MI	42	Washington County, OK	51	**Boone, NC**	51
Alpena, MI	30	**Bastrop, LA**	28	Watauga County, NC	51
Alpena County, MI	30	Morehouse Parish, LA	28	**Borger, TX**	22
Altus, OK	26	**Batavia, NY**	60	Hutchinson County, TX	22
Jackson County, OK	26	Genesee County, NY	60	**Bozeman, MT**	90
Americus, GA	38	**Batesville, AR**	37	Gallatin County, MT.	90
Schley County, GA.	5	Independence County, AR. . . .	37	**Bradford, PA**	43
Sumter County, GA	33	**Bay City, TX**	37	McKean County, PA.	43
Amsterdam, NY	50	Matagorda County, TX.	37	**Brainerd, MN**	91
Montgomery County, NY	50	**Beatrice, NE**	22	Cass County, MN.	29
Andrews, TX	15	Gage County, NE.	22	Crow Wing County, MN	63
Andrews County, TX	15	**Beaver Dam, WI**	89	**Branson, MO**	84
Angola, IN	34	Dodge County, WI	89	Stone County, MO	32
Steuben County, IN	34	**Beckley, WV**	79	Taney County, MO	52
Arcadia, FL	35	Raleigh County, WV	79	**Brenham, TX**	34
DeSoto County, FL	35	**Bedford, IN**	46	Washington County, TX	34
Ardmore, OK	57	Lawrence County, IN	46	**Brevard, NC**	33
Carter County, OK	48	**Beeville, TX**	32	Transylvania County, NC	33
Love County, OK	9	Bee County, TX	32	**Brigham City, UT**	50
		Bellefontaine, OH	46	Box Elder County, UT	50
		Logan County, OH	46	**Brookhaven, MS**	35
				Lincoln County, MS	35

U.S. Census Bureau, Statistical Abstract of the United States: 2012

Micropolitan statistical area Component county	Population, 2010 (1,000)	Micropolitan statistical area Component county	Population, 2010 (1,000)	Micropolitan statistical area Component county	Population, 2010 (1,000)
Brookings, OR	22	**Chester, SC**	33	**Coshocton, OH**	37
Curry County, OR	22	Chester County, SC	33	Coshocton County, OH	37
Brookings, SD	32	**Chillicothe, OH**	78	**Crawfordsville, IN**	38
Brookings County, SD	32	Ross County, OH	78	Montgomery County, IN	38
Brownsville, TN	19	**Claremont, NH**	44	**Crescent City, CA**	29
Haywood County, TN	19	Sullivan County, NH	44	Del Norte County, CA	29
Brownwood, TX	38	**Clarksburg, WV**	94	**Crossville, TN**	56
Brown County, TX	38	Doddridge County, WV	8	Cumberland County, TN	56
Bucyrus, OH	44	Harrison County, WV	69	**Crowley, LA**	62
Crawford County, OH	44	Taylor County, WV	17	Acadia Parish, LA	62
Burley, ID	43	**Clarksdale, MS**	26	**Cullman, AL**	80
Cassia County, ID	23	Coahoma County, MS	26	Cullman County, AL	80
Minidoka County, ID	20	**Clearlake, CA**	65	**Culpeper, VA**	47
Burlington, IA-IL	48	Lake County, CA	65	Culpeper County, VA	47
Henderson County, IL	7	**Cleveland, MS**	34	**Danville, KY**	53
Des Moines County, IA	40	Bolivar County, MS	34	Boyle County, KY	28
Butte-Silver Bow, MT	34	**Clewiston, FL**	39	Lincoln County, KY	25
Silver Bow County, MT	34	Hendry County, FL	39	**Daphne-Fairhope-Foley, AL**	182
Cadillac, MI	48	**Clinton, IA**	49	Baldwin County, AL	182
Missaukee County, MI	15	Clinton County, IA	49	**Decatur, IN**	34
Wexford County, MI	33	**Clovis, NM**	48	Adams County, IN	34
Calhoun, GA	55	Curry County, NM	48	**Defiance, OH**	39
Gordon County, GA	55	**Coffeyville, KS**	35	Defiance County, OH	39
Cambridge, MD	33	Montgomery County, KS	35	**Del Rio, TX**	49
Dorchester County, MD	33	**Coldwater, MI**	45	Val Verde County, TX	49
Cambridge, OH	40	Branch County, MI	45	**Deming, NM**	25
Guernsey County, OH	40	**Columbia, TN**	81	Luna County, NM	25
Camden, AR	31	Maury County, TN	81	**DeRidder, LA**	36
Calhoun County, AR	5	**Columbus, MS**	60	Beauregard Parish, LA	36
Ouachita County, AR	26	Lowndes County, MS	60	**Dickinson, ND**	25
Campbellsville, KY	25	**Columbus, NE**	32	Billings County, ND	1
Taylor County, KY	25	Platte County, NE	32	Stark County, ND	24
Cañon City, CO	47	**Concord, NH**	146	**Dillon, SC**	32
Fremont County, CO	47	Merrimack County, NH	146	Dillon County, SC	32
Canton, IL	37	**Connersville, IN**	24	**Dixon, IL**	36
Fulton County, IL	37	Fayette County, IN	24	Lee County, IL	36
Carbondale, IL	60	**Cookeville, TN**	106	**Dodge City, KS**	34
Jackson County, IL	60	Jackson County, TN	12	Ford County, KS	34
Carlsbad-Artesia, NM	54	Overton County, TN	22	**Douglas, GA**	51
Eddy County, NM	54	Putnam County, TN	72	Atkinson County, GA	8
Cedar City, UT	46	**Coos Bay, OR**	63	Coffee County, GA	42
Iron County, UT	46	Coos County, OR	63	**Dublin, GA**	58
Cedartown, GA	41	**Corbin, KY**	36	Johnson County, GA	10
Polk County, GA	41	Whitley County, KY	36	Laurens County, GA	48
Celina, OH	41	**Cordele, GA**	23	**DuBois, PA**	82
Mercer County, OH	41	Crisp County, GA	23	Clearfield County, PA	82
Central City, KY	31	**Corinth, MS**	37	**Dumas, TX**	22
Muhlenberg County, KY	31	Alcorn County, MS	37	Moore County, TX	22
Centralia, IL	39	**Cornelia, GA**	43	**Duncan, OK**	45
Marion County, IL	39	Habersham County, GA	43	Stephens County, OK	45
Centralia, WA	75	**Corning, NY**	99	**Dunn, NC**	115
Lewis County, WA	75	Steuben County, NY	99	Harnett County, NC	115
Chambersburg, PA	150	**Corsicana, TX**	48	**Durango, CO**	51
Franklin County, PA	150	Navarro County, TX	48	La Plata County, CO	51
Charleston-Mattoon, IL	65	**Cortland, NY**	49	**Durant, OK**	42
Coles County, IL	54	Cortland County, NY	49	Bryan County, OK	42
Cumberland County, IL	11				

Micropolitan statistical area Component county	Population, 2010 (1,000)	Micropolitan statistical area Component county	Population, 2010 (1,000)	Micropolitan statistical area Component county	Population, 2010 (1,000)
Dyersburg, TN	38	**Farmington, MO**	65	**Georgetown, SC**	60
Dyer County, TN	38	St. Francois County, MO	65	Georgetown County, SC	60
Eagle Pass, TX	54	**Fergus Falls, MN**	57	**Gettysburg, PA**	101
Maverick County, TX	54	Otter Tail County, MN.	57	Adams County, PA.	101
East Liverpool-Salem, OH	108	**Fernley, NV**	52	**Gillette, WY**	46
Columbiana County, OH	108	Lyon County, NV	52	Campbell County, WY	46
Easton, MD.	38	**Findlay, OH**	75	**Glasgow, KY**.	52
Talbot County, MD	38	Hancock County, OH.	75	Barren County, KY.	42
East Stroudsburg, PA	170	**Fitzgerald, GA**	27	Metcalfe County, KY	10
Monroe County, PA	170	Ben Hill County, GA.	18	**Gloversville, NY**	56
Edwards, CO	60	Irwin County, GA	10	Fulton County, NY	56
Eagle County, CO	52	**Forest City, NC**	68	**Granbury, TX**.	60
Lake County, CO	7	Rutherford County, NC	68	Hood County, TX	51
Effingham, IL	34	**Forrest City, AR**	28	Somervell County, TX	8
Effingham County, IL	34	St. Francis County, AR.	28	**Grand Island, NE**	73
El Campo, TX	41	**Fort Dodge, IA**	38	Hall County, NE	59
Wharton County, TX	41	Webster County, IA	38	Howard County, NE	6
El Dorado, AR.	42	**Fort Leonard Wood, MO**	52	Merrick County, NE	8
Union County, AR	42	Pulaski County, MO	52	**Grants, NM**	27
Elizabeth City, NC	64	**Fort Madison-Keokuk, IA-MO** . .	43	Cibola County, NM.	27
Camden County, NC	10	Lee County, IA	36	**Grants Pass, OR**	83
Pasquotank County, NC	41	Clark County, MO	7	Josephine County, OR.	83
Perquimans County, NC	13	**Fort Morgan, CO**	28	**Great Bend, KS**	28
Elk City, OK	22	Morgan County, CO	28	Barton County, KS.	28
Beckham County, OK	22	**Fort Payne, AL**	71	**Greeneville, TN**	69
Elko, NV	51	DeKalb County, AL	71	Greene County, TN	69
Elko County, NV.	49	**Fort Polk South, LA**	52	**Greensburg, IN**.	26
Eureka County, NV	2	Vernon Parish, LA	52	Decatur County, IN	26
Ellensburg, WA.	41	**Fort Valley, GA**	28	**Greenville, MS**	51
Kittitas County, WA	41	Peach County, GA	28	Washington County, MS	51
Emporia, KS	36	**Frankfort, IN**	33	**Greenville, OH**	53
Chase County, KS	3	Clinton County, IN	33	Darke County, OH	53
Lyon County, KS	34	**Frankfort, KY**	71	**Greenwood, MS**	43
Enid, OK	61	Anderson County, KY	21	Carroll County, MS.	11
Garfield County, OK.	61	Franklin County, KY	49	Leflore County, MS	32
Enterprise-Ozark, AL	100	**Fredericksburg, TX**	25	**Greenwood, SC**	70
Coffee County, AL	50	Gillespie County, TX	25	Greenwood County, SC	70
Dale County, AL.	50	**Freeport, IL**.	48	**Grenada, MS**.	22
Escanaba, MI	37	Stephenson County, IL	48	Grenada County, MS.	22
Delta County, MI	37	**Fremont, NE**	37	**Guymon, OK**.	21
Espanola, NM.	40	Dodge County, NE.	37	Texas County, OK	21
Rio Arriba County, NM.	40	**Fremont, OH**	61	**Hammond, LA**	121
Eufaula, AL-GA	30	Sandusky County, OH	61	Tangipahoa Parish, LA	121
Barbour County, AL	27	**Gaffney, SC**.	55	**Hannibal, MO**	39
Quitman County, GA	3	Cherokee County, SC	55	Marion County, MO	29
Eureka-Arcata-Fortuna, CA. . . .	135	**Gainesville, TX**	38	Ralls County, MO.	10
Humboldt County, CA	135	Cooke County, TX	38	**Harriman, TN**	54
Evanston, WY.	21	**Galesburg, IL**	71	Roane County, TN	54
Uinta County, WY	21	Knox County, IL	53	**Harrisburg, IL**	25
Fairmont, MN	21	Warren County, IL	18	Saline County, IL	25
Martin County, MN.	21	**Gallup, NM**	71	**Harrison, AR**.	45
Fairmont, WV	56	McKinley County, NM	71	Boone County, AR.	37
Marion County, WV	56	**Garden City, KS**	37	Newton County, AR	8
Fallon, NV.	25	Finney County, KS.	37	**Hastings, NE**.	38
Churchill County, NV	25	**Gardnerville Ranchos, NV**.	47	Adams County, NE	31
Faribault-Northfield, MN	64	Douglas County, NV	47	Clay County, NE	7
Rice County, MN	64			**Havre, MT**	16
				Hill County, MT	16

U.S. Census Bureau, Statistical Abstract of the United States: 2012

Micropolitan statistical area Component county	Population, 2010 (1,000)	Micropolitan statistical area Component county	Population, 2010 (1,000)	Micropolitan statistical area Component county	Population, 2010 (1,000)
Hays, KS	28	**Jacksonville, IL**	41	**La Follette, TN**	41
Ellis County, KS	28	Morgan County, IL	36	Campbell County, TN	41
		Scott County, IL	5		
Heber, UT	24			**La Grande, OR**	26
Wasatch County, UT	24	**Jacksonville, TX**	51	Union County, OR	26
		Cherokee County, TX	51		
Helena, MT	75			**LaGrange, GA**	67
Jefferson County, MT	11	**Jamestown, ND**	21	Troup County, GA	67
Lewis and Clark County, MT	63	Stutsman County, ND	21		
				Lake City, FL	68
Helena-West Helena, AR	22	**Jamestown-Dunkirk-Fredonia, NY**	135	Columbia County, FL	68
Phillips County, AR	22	Chautauqua County, NY	135		
				Lamesa, TX	14
Henderson, NC	45	**Jasper, IN**	55	Dawson County, TX	14
Vance County, NC	45	Dubois County, IN	42		
		Pike County, IN	13	**Lancaster, SC**	77
Hereford, TX	19			Lancaster County, SC	77
Deaf Smith County, TX	19	**Jennings, LA**	32		
		Jefferson Davis Parish, LA	32	**Laramie, WY**	36
Hilo, HI	185			Albany County, WY	36
Hawaii County, HI	185	**Jesup, GA**	30		
		Wayne County, GA	30	**Las Vegas, NM**	29
Hilton Head Island-Beaufort, SC	187			San Miguel County, NM	29
Beaufort County, SC	162	**Juneau, AK**	31		
Jasper County, SC	25	Juneau City and Borough, AK	31	**Laurel, MS**	85
				Jasper County, MS	17
Hobbs, NM	65	**Kahului-Wailuku, HI**	155	Jones County, MS	68
Lea County, NM	65	Maui County, HI	155		
				Laurinburg, NC	36
Homosassa Springs, FL	141	**Kalispell, MT**	91	Scotland County, NC	36
Citrus County, FL	141	Flathead County, MT	91		
				Lawrenceburg, TN	42
Hood River, OR	22	**Kapaa, HI**	67	Lawrence County, TN	42
Hood River County, OR	22	Kauai County, HI	67		
				Lebanon, MO	36
Hope, AR	32	**Kearney, NE**	53	Laclede County, MO	36
Hempstead County, AR	23	Buffalo County, NE	46		
Nevada County, AR	9	Kearney County, NE	6	**Lebanon, NH-VT**	175
				Grafton County, NH	89
Houghton, MI	39	**Keene, NH**	77	Orange County, VT	29
Houghton County, MI	37	Cheshire County, NH	77	Windsor County, VT	57
Keweenaw County, MI	2				
		Kendallville, IN	48	**Levelland, TX**	23
Hudson, NY	63	Noble County, IN	48	Hockley County, TX	23
Columbia County, NY	63				
		Kennett, MO	32	**Lewisburg, PA**	45
Humboldt, TN	50	Dunklin County, MO	32	Union County, PA	45
Gibson County, TN	50				
		Kerrville, TX	50	**Lewisburg, TN**	31
Huntingdon, PA	46	Kerr County, TX	50	Marshall County, TN	31
Huntingdon County, PA	46				
		Ketchikan, AK	13	**Lewistown, PA**	47
Huntington, IN	37	Ketchikan Gateway Borough, AK	13	Mifflin County, PA	47
Huntington County, IN	37				
		Key West, FL	73	**Lexington, NE**	26
Huntsville, TX	68	Monroe County, FL	73	Dawson County, NE	24
Walker County, TX	68			Gosper County, NE	2
		Kill Devil Hills, NC	34		
Huron, SD	17	Dare County, NC	34	**Lexington Park, MD**	105
Beadle County, SD	17			St. Mary's County, MD	105
		Kingsville, TX	32		
Hutchinson, KS	65	Kenedy County, TX	(Z)	**Liberal, KS**	23
Reno County, KS	65	Kleberg County, TX	32	Seward County, KS	23
Hutchinson, MN	37	**Kinston, NC**	59	**Lincoln, IL**	30
McLeod County, MN	37	Lenoir County, NC	59	Logan County, IL	30
Indiana, PA	89	**Kirksville, MO**	30	**Lincolnton, NC**	78
Indiana County, PA	89	Adair County, MO	26	Lincoln County, NC	78
		Schuyler County, MO	4		
Indianola, MS	29			**Lock Haven, PA**	39
Sunflower County, MS	29	**Klamath Falls, OR**	66	Clinton County, PA	39
		Klamath County, OR	66		
Iron Mountain, MI-WI	31			**Logansport, IN**	39
Dickinson County, MI	26	**Kodiak, AK**	14	Cass County, IN	39
Florence County, WI	4	Kodiak Island Borough, AK	14		
				London, KY	59
Jackson, WY-ID	31	**Laconia, NH**	60	Laurel County, KY	59
Teton County, ID	10	Belknap County, NH	60		
Teton County, WY	21			**Los Alamos, NM**	18
				Los Alamos County, NM	18

Micropolitan statistical area / Component county	Population, 2010 (1,000)	Micropolitan statistical area / Component county	Population, 2010 (1,000)	Micropolitan statistical area / Component county	Population, 2010 (1,000)
Lufkin, TX	87	**McComb, MS**	54	**Mount Airy, NC**	74
Angelina County, TX	87	Amite County, MS	13	Surry County, NC	74
Lumberton, NC	134	Pike County, MS	40	**Mount Pleasant, MI**	70
Robeson County, NC	134	**McMinnville, TN**	40	Isabella County, MI	70
Macomb, IL	33	Warren County, TN	40	**Mount Pleasant, TX**	32
McDonough County, IL	33	**McPherson, KS**	29	Titus County, TX	32
Madison, IN	32	McPherson County, KS	29	**Mount Sterling, KY**	44
Jefferson County, IN	32	**Meadville, PA**	89	Bath County, KY	12
Madisonville, KY	47	Crawford County, PA	89	Menifee County, KY	6
Hopkins County, KY	47	**Menomonie, WI**	44	Montgomery County, KY	26
Magnolia, AR	25	Dunn County, WI	44	**Mount Vernon, IL**	47
Columbia County, AR	25	**Meridian, MS**	107	Hamilton County, IL	8
Malone, NY	52	Clarke County, MS	17	Jefferson County, IL	39
Franklin County, NY	52	Kemper County, MS	10	**Mount Vernon, OH**	61
Manitowoc, WI	81	Lauderdale County, MS	80	Knox County, OH	61
Manitowoc County, WI	81	**Merrill, WI**	29	**Murray, KY**	37
Marble Falls, TX	43	Lincoln County, WI	29	Calloway County, KY	37
Burnet County, TX	43	**Mexico, MO**	26	**Muscatine, IA**	54
Marinette, WI-MI	66	Audrain County, MO	26	Louisa County, IA	11
Menominee County, MI	24	**Miami, OK**	32	Muscatine County, IA	43
Marinette County, WI	42	Ottawa County, OK	32	**Muskogee, OK**	71
Marion, IN	70	**Middlesborough, KY**	29	Muskogee County, OK	71
Grant County, IN	70	Bell County, KY	29	**Nacogdoches, TX**	65
Marion, OH	67	**Midland, MI**	84	Nacogdoches County, TX	65
Marion County, OH	67	Midland County, MI	84	**Natchez, MS-LA**	53
Marion-Herrin, IL	66	**Milledgeville, GA**	55	Concordia Parish, LA	21
Williamson County, IL	66	Baldwin County, GA	46	Adams County, MS	32
Marquette, MI	67	Hancock County, GA	9	**Natchitoches, LA**	40
Marquette County, MI	67	**Minden, LA**	41	Natchitoches Parish, LA	40
Marshall, MN	26	Webster Parish, LA	41	**New Bern, NC**	127
Lyon County, MN	26	**Mineral Wells, TX**	28	Craven County, NC	104
Marshall, MO	23	Palo Pinto County, TX	28	Jones County, NC	10
Saline County, MO	23	**Minot, ND**	70	Pamlico County, NC	13
Marshall, TX	66	McHenry County, ND	5	**Newberry, SC**	38
Harrison County, TX	66	Renville County, ND	2	Newberry County, SC	38
Marshalltown, IA	41	Ward County, ND	62	**New Castle, IN**	49
Marshall County, IA	41	**Mitchell, SD**	23	Henry County, IN	49
Marshfield-Wisconsin Rapids, WI	75	Davison County, SD	20	**New Castle, PA**	91
Wood County, WI	75	Hanson County, SD	3	Lawrence County, PA	91
Martin, TN	35	**Moberly, MO**	25	**New Iberia, LA**	73
Weakley County, TN	35	Randolph County, MO	25	Iberia Parish, LA	73
Martinsville, VA	68	**Monroe, WI**	37	**New Philadelphia-Dover, OH**	93
Henry County, VA	54	Green County, WI	37	Tuscarawas County, OH	93
Martinsville city, VA	14	**Montrose, CO**	41	**Newport, TN**	36
Maryville, MO	23	Montrose County, CO	41	Cocke County, TN	36
Nodaway County, MO	23	**Morehead City, NC**	66	**Newton, IA**	37
Mason City, IA	52	Carteret County, NC	66	Jasper County, IA	37
Cerro Gordo County, IA	44	**Morgan City, LA**	55	**New Ulm, MN**	26
Worth County, IA	8	St. Mary Parish, LA	55	Brown County, MN	26
Mayfield, KY	37	**Moscow, ID**	37	**Nogales, AZ**	47
Graves County, KY	37	Latah County, ID	37	Santa Cruz County, AZ	47
Maysville, KY	31	**Moses Lake, WA**	89	**Norfolk, NE**	48
Lewis County, KY	14	Grant County, WA	89	Madison County, NE	35
Mason County, KY	17	**Moultrie, GA**	45	Pierce County, NE	7
McAlester, OK	46	Colquitt County, GA	45	Stanton County, NE	6
Pittsburg County, OK	46	**Mountain Home, AR**	42	**North Platte, NE**	38
		Baxter County, AR	42	Lincoln County, NE	36
		Mountain Home, ID	27	Logan County, NE	1
		Elmore County, ID	27	McPherson County, NE	1

U.S. Census Bureau, Statistical Abstract of the United States: 2012

Micropolitan statistical area / Component county	Population, 2010 (1,000)	Micropolitan statistical area / Component county	Population, 2010 (1,000)	Micropolitan statistical area / Component county	Population, 2010 (1,000)
North Vernon, IN	29	**Paragould, AR**	42	**Prineville, OR**	21
Jennings County, IN	29	Greene County, AR	42	Crook County, OR	21
North Wilkesboro, NC	69	**Paris, TN**	32	**Pullman, WA**	45
Wilkes County, NC	69	Henry County, TN	32	Whitman County, WA	45
Norwalk, OH	60	**Paris, TX**	50	**Quincy, IL-MO**	77
Huron County, OH	60	Lamar County, TX	50	Adams County, IL	67
Oak Harbor, WA	79	**Parsons, KS**	22	Lewis County, MO	10
Island County, WA	79	Labette County, KS	22	**Raymondville, TX**	22
Oak Hill, WV	46	**Payson, AZ**	54	Willacy County, TX	22
Fayette County, WV	46	Gila County, AZ	54	**Red Bluff, CA**	63
Ocean Pines, MD	51	**Pecos, TX**	14	Tehama County, CA	63
Worcester County, MD	51	Reeves County, TX	14	**Red Wing, MN**	46
Ogdensburg-Massena, NY	112	**Pella, IA**	33	Goodhue County, MN	46
St. Lawrence County, NY	112	Marion County, IA	33	**Rexburg, ID**	51
Oil City, PA	55	**Pendleton-Hermiston, OR**	87	Fremont County, ID	13
Venango County, PA	55	Morrow County, OR	11	Madison County, ID	38
Okeechobee, FL	40	Umatilla County, OR	76	**Richmond, IN**	69
Okeechobee County, FL	40	**Peru, IN**	37	Wayne County, IN	69
Olean, NY	80	Miami County, IN	37	**Richmond-Berea, KY**	100
Cattaraugus County, NY	80	**Phoenix Lake-Cedar Ridge, CA**	55	Madison County, KY	83
Oneonta, NY	62	Tuolumne County, CA	55	Rockcastle County, KY	17
Otsego County, NY	62	**Picayune, MS**	56	**Rio Grande City-Roma, TX**	61
Ontario, OR-ID	54	Pearl River County, MS	56	Starr County, TX	61
Payette County, ID	23	**Pierre, SD**	20	**Riverton, WY**	40
Malheur County, OR	31	Hughes County, SD	17	Fremont County, WY	40
Opelousas-Eunice, LA	83	Stanley County, SD	3	**Roanoke Rapids, NC**	77
St. Landry Parish, LA	83	**Pierre Part, LA**	23	Halifax County, NC	55
Orangeburg, SC	93	Assumption Parish, LA	23	Northampton County, NC	22
Orangeburg County, SC	93	**Pittsburg, KS**	39	**Rochelle, IL**	53
Oskaloosa, IA	22	Crawford County, KS	39	Ogle County, IL	53
Mahaska County, IA	22	**Plainview, TX**	36	**Rockingham, NC**	47
Ottawa-Streator, IL	155	Hale County, TX	36	Richmond County, NC	47
Bureau County, IL	35	**Platteville, WI**	51	**Rockland, ME**	40
LaSalle County, IL	114	Grant County, WI	51	Knox County, ME	40
Putnam County, IL	6	**Plattsburgh, NY**	82	**Rock Springs, WY**	44
Ottumwa, IA	36	Clinton County, NY	82	Sweetwater County, WY	44
Wapello County, IA	36	**Plymouth, IN**	47	**Rolla, MO**	45
Owatonna, MN	37	Marshall County, IN	47	Phelps County, MO	45
Steele County, MN	37	**Point Pleasant, WV-OH**	58	**Roseburg, OR**	108
Owosso, MI	71	Gallia County, OH	31	Douglas County, OR	108
Shiawassee County, MI	71	Mason County, WV	27	**Roswell, NM**	66
Oxford, MS	47	**Ponca City, OK**	47	Chaves County, NM	66
Lafayette County, MS	47	Kay County, OK	47	**Ruidoso, NM**	20
Paducah, KY-IL	99	**Pontiac, IL**	39	Lincoln County, NM	20
Massac County, IL	15	Livingston County, IL	39	**Russellville, AR**	84
Ballard County, KY	8	**Poplar Bluff, MO**	43	Pope County, AR	62
Livingston County, KY	10	Butler County, MO	43	Yell County, AR	22
McCracken County, KY	66	**Portales, NM**	20	**Ruston, LA**	63
Pahrump, NV	44	Roosevelt County, NM	20	Jackson Parish, LA	16
Nye County, NV	44	**Port Angeles, WA**	71	Lincoln Parish, LA	47
Palatka, FL	74	Clallam County, WA	71	**Rutland, VT**	62
Putnam County, FL	74	**Portsmouth, OH**	79	Rutland County, VT	62
Palestine, TX	58	Scioto County, OH	79	**Safford, AZ**	46
Anderson County, TX	58	**Pottsville, PA**	148	Graham County, AZ	37
Pampa, TX	23	Schuylkill County, PA	148	Greenlee County, AZ	8
Gray County, TX	23	**Price, UT**	21	**St. Marys, GA**	51
Roberts County, TX	1	Carbon County, UT	21	Camden County, GA	51

Micropolitan statistical area / Component county	Population, 2010 (1,000)	Micropolitan statistical area / Component county	Population, 2010 (1,000)	Micropolitan statistical area / Component county	Population, 2010 (1,000)
St. Marys, PA	32	**Sikeston, MO**	39	**Talladega-Sylacauga, AL**	82
Elk County, PA	32	Scott County, MO	39	Talladega County, AL	82
Salina, KS	62	**Silver City, NM**	30	**Tallulah, LA**	12
Ottawa County, KS	6	Grant County, NM	30	Madison Parish, LA	12
Saline County, KS	56	**Silverthorne, CO**	28	**Taos, NM**	33
Salisbury, NC	138	Summit County, CO	28	Taos County, NM	33
Rowan County, NC	138	**Snyder, TX**	17	**Taylorville, IL**	35
Sanford, NC	58	Scurry County, TX	17	Christian County, IL	35
Lee County, NC	58	**Somerset, KY**	63	**The Dalles, OR**	25
Sault Ste. Marie, MI	39	Pulaski County, KY	63	Wasco County, OR	25
Chippewa County, MI.	39	**Somerset, PA**	78	**The Villages, FL**	93
Sayre, PA	63	Somerset County, PA	78	Sumter County, FL	93
Bradford County, PA.	63	**Southern Pines-Pinehurst, NC** .	88	**Thomaston, GA**	27
Scottsbluff, NE	38	Moore County, NC	88	Upson County, GA.	27
Banner County, NE	1	**Spearfish, SD**	24	**Thomasville, GA**	45
Scotts Bluff County, NE	37	Lawrence County, SD	24	Thomas County, GA	45
Scottsboro, AL	53	**Spencer, IA**	17	**Thomasville-Lexington, NC** . . .	163
Jackson County, AL	53	Clay County, IA	17	Davidson County, NC	163
Scottsburg, IN	24	**Spirit Lake, IA**	17	**Tiffin, OH**	57
Scott County, IN.	24	Dickinson County, IA	17	Seneca County, OH.	57
Seaford, DE	197	**Starkville, MS**	48	**Tifton, GA**	40
Sussex County, DE	197	Oktibbeha County, MS.	48	Tift County, GA	40
Searcy, AR	77	**Statesboro, GA**	70	**Toccoa, GA**	26
White County, AR	77	Bulloch County, GA	70	Stephens County, GA	26
Sebring, FL	99	**Statesville-Mooresville, NC**	159	**Torrington, CT**	190
Highlands County, FL	99	Iredell County, NC	159	Litchfield County, CT	190
Sedalia, MO	42	**Staunton-Waynesboro, VA**	119	**Traverse City, MI**	143
Pettis County, MO	42	Augusta County, VA	74	Benzie County, MI	18
Selinsgrove, PA	40	Staunton city, VA	24	Grand Traverse County, MI . . .	87
Snyder County, PA.	40	Waynesboro city, VA	21	Kalkaska County, MI	17
Selma, AL	44	**Stephenville, TX**	38	Leelanau County, MI	22
Dallas County, AL	44	Erath County, TX	38	**Troy, AL**	33
Seneca, SC	74	**Sterling, CO**	23	Pike County, AL.	33
Oconee County, SC.	74	Logan County, CO	23	**Truckee-Grass Valley, CA**	99
Seneca Falls, NY	35	**Sterling, IL**	58	Nevada County, CA	99
Seneca County, NY	35	Whiteside County, IL	58	**Tullahoma, TN**	100
Sevierville, TN	90	**Stevens Point, WI**	70	Coffee County, TN	53
Sevier County, TN	90	Portage County, WI	70	Franklin County, TN	41
Seymour, IN	42	**Stillwater, OK**	77	Moore County, TN	6
Jackson County, IN	42	Payne County, OK	77	**Tupelo, MS**	136
Shawnee, OK	69	**Storm Lake, IA**	20	Itawamba County, MS	23
Pottawatomie County, OK	69	Buena Vista County, IA	20	Lee County, MS.	83
Shelby, NC	98	**Sturgis, MI**	61	Pontotoc County, MS.	30
Cleveland County, NC	98	St. Joseph County, MI	61	**Tuskegee, AL**	21
Shelbyville, TN	45	**Sulphur Springs, TX**	35	Macon County, AL	21
Bedford County, TN	45	Hopkins County, TX.	35	**Twin Falls, ID**	100
Shelton, WA	61	**Summerville, GA**	26	Jerome County, ID.	22
Mason County, WA	61	Chattooga County, GA.	26	Twin Falls County, ID	77
Sheridan, WY	29	**Sunbury, PA**	95	**Ukiah, CA**	88
Sheridan County, WY	29	Northumberland County, PA . .	95	Mendocino County, CA	88
Show Low, AZ	107	**Susanville, CA**	35	**Union, SC**	29
Navajo County, AZ.	107	Lassen County, CA	35	Union County, SC	29
Sidney, OH	49	**Sweetwater, TX**	15	**Union City, TN-KY**	39
Shelby County, OH	49	Nolan County, TX.	15	Fulton County, KY	7
Sierra Vista-Douglas, AZ	131	**Tahlequah, OK**	47	Obion County, TN	32
Cochise County, AZ	131	Cherokee County, OK	47	**Urbana, OH**	40
				Champaign County, OH.	40
				Uvalde, TX	26
				Uvalde County, TX.	26

U.S. Census Bureau, Statistical Abstract of the United States: 2012

Micropolitan statistical area Component county	Population, 2010 (1,000)	Micropolitan statistical area Component county	Population, 2010 (1,000)	Micropolitan statistical area Component county	Population, 2010 (1,000)
Valley, AL	34	**Warrensburg, MO**	53	**Willimantic, CT**	118
Chambers County, AL	34	Johnson County, MO	53	Windham County, CT	118
Van Wert, OH	29	**Warsaw, IN**	77	**Williston, ND**	22
Van Wert County, OH	29	Kosciusko County, IN	77	Williams County, ND	22
Vermillion, SD	14	**Washington, IN**	32	**Willmar, MN**	42
Clay County, SD	14	Daviess County, IN	32	Kandiyohi County, MN	42
Vernal, UT	33	**Washington, NC**	48	**Wilmington, OH**	42
Uintah County, UT	33	Beaufort County, NC	48	Clinton County, OH	42
Vernon, TX	14	**Washington Court House, OH** .	29	**Wilson, NC**	81
Wilbarger County, TX	14	Fayette County, OH	29	Wilson County, NC	81
Vicksburg, MS	49	**Watertown, SD**	33	**Winfield, KS**	36
Warren County, MS	49	Codington County, SD	27	Cowley County, KS	36
		Hamlin County, SD	6		
Vidalia, GA	36			**Winona, MN**	51
Montgomery County, GA	9	**Watertown-Fort Atkinson, WI** . .	84	Winona County, MN	51
Toombs County, GA	27	Jefferson County, WI	84		
				Woodward, OK	20
Vincennes, IN	38	**Watertown-Fort Drum, NY**	116	Woodward County, OK	20
Knox County, IN	38	Jefferson County, NY	116		
				Wooster, OH	115
Wabash, IN	33	**Wauchula, FL**	28	Wayne County, OH	115
Wabash County, IN	33	Hardee County, FL	28		
				Worthington, MN	21
Wahpeton, ND-MN	23	**Waycross, GA**	55	Nobles County, MN	21
Wilkin County, MN	7	Pierce County, GA	19		
Richland County, ND	16	Ware County, GA	36	**Yankton, SD**	22
				Yankton County, SD	22
Walla Walla, WA	59	**Weatherford, OK**	27		
Walla Walla County, WA	59	Custer County, OK	27	**Yazoo City, MS**	28
				Yazoo County, MS	28
Walterboro, SC	39	**West Plains, MO**	40		
Colleton County, SC	39	Howell County, MO	40	**Zanesville, OH**	86
				Muskingum County, OH	86
Wapakoneta, OH	46	**West Point, MS**	21		
Auglaize County, OH	46	Clay County, MS	21		
Warren, PA	42	**Whitewater, WI**	102		
Warren County, PA	42	Walworth County, WI	102		

Z Less than 500.

Source: U.S. Census Bureau, 2010 Census, <http://2010.census.gov/2010census/data/>.

Appendix III
Limitations of the Data

Introduction– The data presented in this *Statistical Abstract* came from many sources. The sources include not only federal statistical bureaus and other organizations that collect and issue statistics as their principal activity, but also governmental administrative and regulatory agencies, private research bodies, trade associations, insurance companies, health associations, and private organizations such as the National Education Association and philanthropic foundations. Consequently, the data vary considerably as to reference periods, definitions of terms and, for ongoing series, the number and frequency of time periods for which data are available.

The statistics presented were obtained and tabulated by various means. Some statistics are based on complete enumerations or censuses while others are based on samples. Some information is extracted from records kept for administrative or regulatory purposes (school enrollment, hospital records, securities registration, financial accounts, social security records, income tax returns, etc.), while other information is obtained explicitly for statistical purposes through interviews or by mail. The estimation procedures used vary from highly sophisticated scientific techniques, to crude "informed guesses."

Each set of data relates to a group of individuals or units of interest referred to as the *target universe* or *target population,* or simply as the *universe* or *population.*

Prior to data collection the target universe should be clearly defined. For example, if data are to be collected for the universe of households in the United States, it is necessary to define a "household." The target universe may not be completely tractable. Cost and other considerations may restrict data collection to a *survey universe* based on some available list, such list may be inaccurate or out of date. This list is called a *survey frame* or *sampling frame.*

The data in many tables are based on data obtained for all population units, *a census,* or on data obtained for only a portion, or *sample,* of the population units. When the data presented are based on a sample, the sample is usually a scientifically selected *probability sample.* This is a sample selected from a list or sampling frame in such a way that every possible sample has a known chance of selection and usually each unit selected can be assigned a number, greater than zero and less than or equal to one, representing its likelihood or probability of selection.

For large-scale sample surveys, the probability sample of units is often selected as a multistage sample. The first stage of a multistage sample is the selection of a probability sample of large groups of population members, referred to as primary sampling units (PSUs). For example, in a national multistage household sample, PSUs are often counties or groups of counties. The second stage of a multistage sample is the selection, within each PSU selected at the first stage, of smaller groups of population units, referred to as secondary sampling units. In subsequent stages of selection, smaller and smaller nested groups are chosen until the ultimate sample of population units is obtained. To qualify a multistage sample as a probability sample, all stages of sampling must be carried out using probability sampling methods.

Prior to selection at each stage of a multistage (or a single stage) sample, a list of the sampling units or sampling frame for that stage must be obtained. For example, for the first stage of selection of a national household sample, a list of the counties and county groups that form the PSUs must be obtained. For the final stage of selection, lists of households, and sometimes persons within the households, have to be compiled in the field. For surveys of economic entities and for the economic censuses the U.S. Census Bureau generally uses a frame constructed from the

Bureau's Business Register. The Business Register contains all establishments with payroll in the United States including small single establishment firms as well as large multi-establishment firms.

Wherever the quantities in a table refer to an entire universe, but are constructed from data collected in a sample survey, the table quantities are referred to as *sample estimates.* In constructing a sample estimate, an attempt is made to come as close as is feasible to the corresponding universe quantity that would be obtained from a complete census of the universe. Estimates based on a sample will, however, generally differ from the hypothetical census figures. Two classifications of errors are associated with estimates based on sample surveys:

(1) *sampling error*—the error arising from the use of a sample, rather than a census, to estimate population quantities and

(2) *nonsampling error*—those errors arising from nonsampling sources. As discussed below, the magnitude of the sampling error for an estimate can usually be estimated from the sample data. However, the magnitude of the nonsampling error for an estimate can rarely be estimated. Consequently, actual error in an estimate exceeds the error that can be estimated.

The particular sample used in a survey is only one of a large number of possible samples of the same size which could have been selected using the same sampling procedure. Estimates derived from the different samples would, in general, differ from each other. The *standard error* (SE) is a measure of the variation among the estimates derived from all possible samples. The standard error is the most commonly used measure of the sampling error of an estimate. Valid estimates of the standard errors of survey estimates can usually be calculated from the data collected in a probability sample. For convenience, the standard error is sometimes expressed as a percent of the estimate and is called the relative standard error or *coefficient of variation* (CV). For example, an estimate of 200 units with an estimated standard error of 10 units has an estimated CV of 5 percent.

A sample estimate and an estimate of its standard error or CV can be used to construct interval estimates that have a prescribed confidence that the interval includes the average of the estimates derived from all possible samples with a known probability. To illustrate, if all possible samples were selected under essentially the same general conditions, and using the same sample design, and if an estimate and its estimated standard error were calculated from each sample, then: 1) approximately 68 percent of the intervals from one standard error below the estimate to one standard error above the estimate would include the average estimate derived from all possible samples; 2) approximately 90 percent of the intervals from 1.6 standard errors below the estimate to 1.6 standard errors above the estimate would include the average estimate derived from all possible samples; and 3) approximately 95 percent of the intervals from two standard errors below the estimate to two standard errors above the estimate would include the average estimate derived from all possible samples.

Thus, for a particular sample, one can say with the appropriate level of confidence (e.g., 90 percent or 95 percent) that the average of all possible samples is included in the constructed interval. Example of a confidence interval: An estimate is 200 units with a standard error of 10 units. An approximately 90 percent confidence interval (plus or minus 1.6 standard errors) is from 184 to 216.

All surveys and censuses are subject to nonsampling errors. Nonsampling errors are of two kinds—*random* and *nonrandom.* Random nonsampling errors arise because of the varying interpretation of questions (by respondents or interviewers) and varying actions of coders, keyers, and other processors. Some randomness is also introduced when respondents must estimate. Nonrandom nonsampling errors result from total nonresponse (no usable data obtained for a sampled unit), partial or item nonresponse (only a portion of a response may be usable), inability or unwillingness on the part of respondents to provide correct information, difficulty interpreting questions, mistakes in recording or keying data, errors of collection or processing, and coverage problems (overcoverage and undercoverage of the target universe). Random nonresponse errors usually, but not always, result in an understatement of sampling errors and thus an overstatement of the precision of survey estimates. Estimating the magnitude of nonsampling errors would require special experiments or access to independent data and, consequently, the magnitudes are seldom available.

Nearly all types of nonsampling errors that affect surveys also occur in complete censuses. Since surveys can be conducted on a smaller scale than censuses, nonsampling errors can presumably be controlled more tightly. Relatively more funds and effort can perhaps be expended toward eliciting responses, detecting and correcting response error, and reducing processing errors. As a result, survey results can sometimes be more accurate than census results.

To compensate for suspected nonrandom errors, adjustments of the sample estimates are often made. For example, adjustments are frequently made for nonresponse, both total and partial. Adjustments made for either type of nonresponse are often referred to as *imputations*. Imputation for total nonresponse is usually made by substituting for the questionnaire responses of the nonrespondents the "average" questionnaire responses of the respondents. These imputations usually are made separately within various groups of sample members, formed by attempting to place respondents and nonrespondents together that have "similar" design or ancillary characteristics. Imputation for item nonresponse is usually made by substituting for a missing item the response to that item of a respondent having characteristics that are "similar" to those of the nonrespondent.

For an estimate calculated from a sample survey, the *total error* in the estimate is composed of the sampling error, which can usually be estimated from the sample, and the nonsampling error, which usually cannot be estimated from the sample. The total error present in a population quantity obtained from a complete census is composed of only nonsampling errors. Ideally, estimates of the total error associated with data given in the *Statistical Abstract* tables should be given. However, due to the unavailability of estimates of nonsampling errors, only estimates of the levels of sampling errors, in terms of estimated standard errors or coefficients of variation, are available. To obtain estimates of the estimated standard errors from the sample of interest, obtain a copy of the referenced report which appears at the end of each table.

Source of Additional Material: The Federal Committee on Statistical Methodology (FCSM) is an interagency committee dedicated to improving the quality of federal statistics <http://www.fcsm.census.gov>.

Principal data bases—Beginning below are brief descriptions of 35 of the sample surveys and censuses that provide a substantial portion of the data contained in this *Abstract*.

U.S. DEPARTMENT OF AGRICULTURE, National Agriculture Statistics Service

Census of Agriculture

Universes, Frequency, and Types of Data: Complete count of U.S. farms and ranches conducted once every 5 years with data at the national, state, and county level. Data published on farm numbers and related items/characteristics.

Type of Data Collection Operation: Complete census for number of farms; land in farms; farm income; agriculture products sold; farms by type of organization; total cropland; irrigated land; farm operator characteristics; livestock and poultry inventory and sales; and selected crops harvested. Market value of land, buildings, and products sold, total farm production expenses, machinery and equipment, and fertilizer and chemicals.

Data Collection and Imputation Procedures: Data collection is by mailing questionnaires to all farmers and ranchers. Producers can return their forms by mail or online. Nonrespondents are contacted by telephone and correspondence follow-ups. Imputations were made for all nonresponse item/characteristics and coverage adjustments were made to account for missed farms and ranches. The response rate for the 2007 Census was 85.2 percent.

Estimates of Sampling Error: Weight adjustments were made to account for the undercoverage and whole-unit nonresponse of farms on the Census Mail List (CML). These were treated as sampling errors.

Other (nonsampling) Errors: Nonsampling errors are due to incompleteness of the census mailing list, duplications on the list, respondent reporting errors, errors in editing reported data, and in imputation for missing data. Evaluation studies are conducted to measure certain nonsampling errors such as list coverage and classification error. It is a reasonable assumption that the net effect of non measurable errors is zero (the positive errors cancel the negative errors).

Sources of Additional Material:
U.S. Department of Agriculture (NASS), 2007 Census of Agriculture, Appendix A-1 Census of Agriculture Methodology, Appendix B-1 General Explanation and Census of Agriculture Report Form.

Basic Area Frame Sample

Universe, Frequency, and Types of Data: The June Agricultural Survey collects data on planted acreage and livestock inventories on all land in the 48 contiguous states and Hawaii. The survey also serves to measure list incompleteness and is subsampled for multiple frame surveys.

Type of Data Collection Operation: Stratified probability sample of about 11,000 land area units of about 1 sq. mile (range from 0.1 sq. mile in cities to several sq. miles in open grazing areas). Sample represents 42,000 operating arrangements. About 20 percent of the sample replaced annually.

Data Collection and Imputation Procedures: Data collection is by personal enumeration. Imputation is based on enumerator observation or data reported by respondents having similar agricultural characteristics.

Estimates of Sampling Error: Estimated CVs range from 1 percent to 2 percent for regional estimates to 3 percent to 6 percent for state estimates of major crop acres and livestock inventories.

Other (nonsampling) Errors: Minimized through rigid quality controls on the collection process and careful review of all reported data.

Sources of Additional Material:
U.S. Department of Agriculture, National Agricultural Statistics Service, USDA's National Agricultural Statistics Service: The Fact Finders of Agriculture, March 2007.

Multiple Frame Surveys

Universe, Frequency, and Types of Data: Surveys of U.S. farm operators to obtain data on major livestock inventories, selected crop acreage and production, grain stocks, and farm labor characteristics, farm economic data, and chemical use data. Estimates are made quarterly, semi-annually, or annually depending on the data series.

Type of Data Collection Operation: Primary frame is obtained from general or special purpose lists, supplemented by a probability sample of land areas used to estimate for list incompleteness.

Data Collection and Imputation Procedures: Mail, telephone, or personal interviews used for initial data collection. Mail nonrespondent follow-up by phone and personal interviews. Imputation based on average of respondents.

Estimates of Sampling Error: Estimated CVs range from 1 percent to 2 percent at the U.S. level for crop and livestock data series and 3 to 5 percent for economic data. Regional CVs range from 3 to 6 percent, while state estimate CVs run 5 to 10 percent.

Other (nonsampling) Errors: In addition to above, replicated sampling procedures used to monitor effects of changes in survey procedures.

Sources of Additional Material: U.S. Department of Agriculture, National Agricultural Statistics Service), USDA's National Agricultural Statistics Service: The Fact Finders of Agriculture, March 2007.

Objective Yield Surveys

Universe, Frequency, and Types of Data: Monthly surveys during the growing season of corn, cotton, potatoes, soybeans, and winter wheat fields in top producing states for forecasting and estimating yield per acre.

Type of Data Collection Operation: Random location of plots in probability sample. Corn, cotton, and soybeans, are selected in June from Basic Area Frame Sample (see above). Winter wheat and potatoes are selected from March and June multiple frame surveys, respectively.

Data Collection and Imputation Procedures: Enumerators count and measure plant characteristics in sample fields. Production is measured from plots at harvest. Harvest loss is measured from post harvest gleanings.

Estimates of Sampling Error: CVs for national estimates of production are about 2 to 3 percent.

Other (nonsampling) Errors: In addition to above, replicated sampling procedures are used to monitor effects of changes in survey procedures.

Sources of Additional Material: U.S. Department of Agriculture, National Agricultural Statistics Service), USDA's National Agricultural Statistics Service: The Fact Finders of Agriculture, March 2007.

U.S. BUREAU OF JUSTICE STATISTICS (BJS)

National Crime Victimization Survey

Universe, Frequency, and Types of Data: Monthly survey of individuals and households in the United States to obtain data on criminal victimization of those units for compilation of annual estimates.

Type of Data Collection Operation: National probability sample survey of about 46,000 interviewed households in 203 PSUs every 6 months selected from a list of addresses from the 2000 census, supplemented by new construction permits and an area sample where permits are not required.

Data Collection and Imputation Procedures: Interviews are conducted every 6 months for 3 years for each household in the sample; 7,700 households are interviewed monthly. Personal interviews are used in the first interview; the intervening interviews are conducted by telephone whenever possible.

Estimates of Sampling Error: CVs for 2009 are 4 percent for crimes of violence; 19.1 percent for estimate of rape/sexual assault counts; 10.2 percent for robbery counts; 4.7 percent for assault counts; 18.6 percent for purse snatching/pocket picking; 2.2 percent for property crimes; 4.2 percent for burglary counts; 2.5 percent for theft (of property); and 7.3 percent for motor vehicle theft counts.

Other (nonsampling) Errors: Respondent recall errors which may include reporting incidents for other than the reference period; interviewer coding and processing errors; and possible mistaken reporting or classifying of events. Adjustment is made for a household noninterview rate of about 8 percent and for a within-household noninterview rate of 13 percent.

Sources of Additional Material: U.S. Bureau of Justice Statistics, *Criminal Victimization in the United States,* annual.

U.S. BUREAU OF LABOR STATISTICS

Consumer Expenditure Survey (CE)

Universe, Frequency and Types of Data: Consists of two continuous components: a quarterly interview survey and a weekly diary or recordkeeping survey. They are nationwide surveys that collect data on consumer expenditures, income, characteristics, and assets and liabilities. Samples are national probability samples of households that are representative of the civilian noninstitutional population. The surveys have been ongoing since 1980.

Type of Data Collection Operation: The Interview Survey is a panel rotation survey. Each panel is interviewed for five quarters and then dropped from the survey. About 15,000 consumer units are interviewed each quarter. The Diary Survey sample is new each year and consists of about 3,200 consumer units. Data are collected on an ongoing basis in 91 areas of the country.

Data Collection and Imputation Procedures: For the Interview Survey, data are collected by personal interview with each consumer unit interviewed once per quarter for five consecutive quarters. Designed to collect information that respondents can recall for 3 months or longer, such as large or recurring expenditures. For the Diary Survey, respondents record all their expenditures in a self-reporting diary for two consecutive one-week periods. Designed to pick up items difficult to recall over a long period, such as detailed food expenditures. Missing or invalid attributes, expenditures, or incomes are imputed. Assets and liabilities are not imputed. The U.S. Census Bureau collects the data for the Bureau of Labor Statistics.

Estimates of Sampling Error: Standard error tables are available since 2000.

Other (nonsampling) Errors: Includes incorrect information given by respondents, data processing errors, interviewer errors, and so on. They occur regardless of whether data are collected from a sample or from the entire population.

Sources of Additional Material: Bureau of Labor Statistics, see Internet site <http://www.bls.gov/cex>.

Consumer Price Index (CPI)

Universe, Frequency, and Types of Data: A monthly survey of price changes of all types of consumer goods and services purchased by urban wage earners and clerical workers prior to 1978, and urban consumers thereafter. Both indexes continue to be published.

Type of Data Collection Operation: Prior to 1978, and since 1998, sample of various consumer items in 87 urban areas; from 1978-1997, in 85 PSUs, except from January 1987 through March 1988, when 91 areas were sampled.

Data Collection and Imputation Procedures: Prices of consumer items are obtained each month from about 25,500 retail outlets and from about 4,000 housing units in 87 areas. Prices of food, fuel, and a few other items are obtained monthly; prices of most other commodities and services are collected every month in the three largest geographic areas and every other month in others.

Estimates of Sampling Error: Estimates of standard errors are available.

Other (nonsampling) Errors: Errors result from inaccurate reporting, difficulties in defining concepts and their operational implementation, and introduction of product quality changes and new products.

Sources of Additional Material: U.S. Bureau of Labor Statistics, Internet site <http://www.bls.gov/cpi/home.htm> and BLS Handbook of Methods, Chapter 17, see Internet site <http://www.bls.gov/opub/hom/pdf/homch17.pdf>.

Current Employment Statistics (CES) Program

Universe, Frequency, and Types of Data: Monthly survey drawn from a sampling frame of roughly 8.9 million unemployment insurance tax accounts in order to obtain data by industry on employment, hours, and earnings.

Type of Data Collection Operation: In 2009, the CES sample included about 140,000 businesses and government agencies, which represent approximately 410,000 individual worksites.

Data Collection and Imputation Procedures: Each month, the state agencies cooperating with BLS, as well as BLS Data Collection Centers, collect data through various automated collection modes and mail. BLS Washington staff prepares national estimates of employment, hours, and earnings while states use the data to develop state and area estimates.

Estimates of Sampling Errors: The relative standard error for total nonfarm employment is 0.1 percent. From April 2008 to March 2009, the cumulative net birth/death model added 779,000.

Other (nonsampling) Errors: Estimates of employment adjusted annually to reflect complete universe. Average adjustment is 0.3 percent over the last decade, with an absolute range from than 0.1 percent to 0.7 percent.

Sources of Additional Material: U.S. Bureau of Labor Statistics, Employment and Earnings, monthly, Explanatory Notes and Estimates of Errors, Tables 2-A through 2-F. See <http://www.bls.gov/web/cestntab.htm>.

National Compensation Survey (NCS)

Universe, Frequency, and Types of Data: NCS collects data from establishments of all employment-size classes in private industries as well as state and local governments. The survey stratifies its data by geographic area and industry. NCS collects data on work schedules, wages, salaries, and employer costs for employee benefits. For approximately 80 metropolitan areas and the nation, NCS produces information on workers' earnings and benefits in a variety of occupations at different work levels. NCS is also responsible for two quarterly releases: the Employment Cost Index (ECI), which measures percent changes in the cost of employment, and the Employer Costs for Employee Compensation (ECEC), which measures costs per hour worked for individual benefits. The survey provides data by industry sector, industry division, occupational group, bargaining status, metropolitan area status, census region, and census division. ECEC also provides data by establishment-size class.

Type of Data Collection Operation: Establishments are selected for the survey based on a probability–proportionate-to-employment technique. NCS replaces its sample on a continual basis. Private industry establishments are in the survey for approximately 5 years.

Data Collection and Imputation Procedures: A personal visit to the establishment is the initial source for collecting data. Communication via mail, fax, and telephone provide quarterly updates. Imputation is done for individual benefits.

Estimates of Sampling Error: NCS uses standard errors to evaluate published series. These standard errors are available at <http://www.bls.gov/ncs/ect/home.htm>.

Other (nonsampling) Errors: Nonsampling errors have a number of potential sources. The primary sources are (1) survey nonresponse and (2) data collection and processing errors. Nonsampling errors are not measured. The use of quality assurance programs reduces the potential for nonsampling errors. These programs include the use of reinterviews, interview observations, and the systematic professional review of reports. The programs also serve as a training device that provides feedback on errors for field economists (or data collectors). Quality assurance programs also provide information on sources of error. This information is used to improve procedures that result in fewer errors. NCS also conducts extensive training of field economists to maintain high standards in data collection.

Sources of Additional Material: Bureau of Labor Statistics, *BLS Handbook of methods,* Chapter 8 <http://www.bls.gov/opub/hom//pdf/homch8.pdf>.

Producer Price Index (PPI)

Universe, Frequency, and Types of Data: Monthly survey of producing companies to determine price changes of all commodities and services produced in the United States for sale in commercial transactions. Data on agriculture, forestry, fishing, manufacturing, mining, gas, electricity, construction, public utilities, wholesale trade, retail trade, transportation, healthcare, and other services.

Type of Data Collection Operation: Probability sample of approximately 30,000 establishments that result in about 120,000 price quotations per month.

Data Collection and Imputation Procedures: Data are collected by mail and facsimile. Missing prices are estimated by those received for similar products or services. Some prices are obtained from trade publications, organized exchanges, and government agencies. To calculate index, price changes are multiplied by their relative weights taken from the Census Bureau's 2002 shipment values from their Census of Industries.

Estimates of Sampling Error: Not applicable.

Other (nonsampling) Errors: Not available at present.

Sources of Additional Material: U.S. Bureau of Labor Statistics, *BLS Handbook of Methods,* Chapter 14, Bulletin 2490. U.S. Bureau of Labor Statistics Internet site <http://stats.bls.gov/ppi>.

BOARD OF GOVERNORS OF THE FEDERAL RESERVE SYSTEM

Survey of Consumer Finances

Universe, Frequency, and Types of Data: Periodic sample survey of families. In this survey a given household is divided into a primary economic unit and other economic units. The primary economic unit, which may be a single individual, is generally chosen as the person or couple who either holds the title to the home or is listed on the lease, along with all other people in the household who are financially interdependent with that person or couple. The primary economic unit is used as the reference family. The survey collects detailed data on the composition of family balance sheets, the terms of loans, and relationships with financial institutions. It also gathers information on the employment history and pension rights of the survey respondent and the spouse or partner of the respondent.

Type of Data Collection Operation: The survey employs a two-part strategy for sampling families. Some families are selected by standard multistage area probability sampling methods applied to all 50 states. The remaining families in the survey are selected using statistical records derived from tax returns, under the strict rules governing confidentiality and the rights of potential respondents to refuse participation.

Data Collection and Imputation Procedures: National Opinion Research Center (NORC) at the University of Chicago has collected data for the survey since 1992. Since 1995, the survey has used computer-assisted personal interviewing. Adjustments for nonresponse are made through multiple imputation of unanswered questions and through weighting adjustments based on data used in the sample design for families that refused participation.

Estimates of Sampling Error: Because of the complex design of the survey, the estimation of potential sampling errors is not straightforward. A replicate-based procedure is available.

Other (nonsampling) Errors: The survey aims to complete 4,500 interviews, with about two thirds of that number deriving from the area–probability sample. The response rate is typically about 70 percent for the area–probability sample and about 35 percent over all strata in the tax–data sample. Proper training and monitoring of interviewers, careful design of questionnaires, and systematic editing of the resulting data were used to control inaccurate survey responses.

Sources of Additional Material: Board of Governors of the Federal Reserve System, "Recent Changes in U.S. Family Finances: Evidence from the Survey of Consumer Finances," *Federal Reserve Bulletin*, 2010, <http://www.federalreserve.gov /Pubs/Bulletin>.

U.S. CENSUS BUREAU

2007 Economic Census

(Industry Series, Geographic Area Series and Subject Series Reports) (for NAICS sectors 21 to 81).

Universe, Frequency, and Types of Data: Conducted every 5 years to obtain data on number of establishments, number of employees, payroll, total sales/ receipts/revenue, and other industry-specific statistics. The universe is all establishments with paid employees excluding agriculture, forestry, fishing and hunting, and government. (Non-employer Statistics, discussed separately, covers those establishments without paid employees.)

Changes for 2007 included tabulations to include Census designated places (unincorporated places), expanded Survey of Business Owners data, data on franchising for more industries, and complete implementation of the North American Product Classification System (NAPCS).

Type of Data Collection Operation: All large employer firms were surveyed (i.e., all employer firms above payroll-size cutoffs established to separate large from small employers) plus,

in most sectors, a sample of the small employer firms.

Data Collection and Imputation Procedures: Mail questionnaires were used with both mail and telephone follow–ups for nonrespondents. Businesses also had the option to respond electronically. Data for nonrespondents and for small employer firms not mailed a questionnaire were obtained from administrative records of other federal agencies or imputed.

Estimates of Sampling Error: Not applicable for basic data such as sales, revenue, receipts, payroll, etc. for sectors other than Construction (NAICS 23). Estimates of sampling error for construction industries are included with the data as published on the Census Bureau web site. Other (nonsampling) errors: establishment response rates by NAICS sector in 2002 ranged from 80 percent to 89 percent. Nonsampling errors may occur during the collection, reporting, keying, and classification of the data.

Sources of Additional Material: U.S. Census Bureau, see <http://www.census.gov/econ /census07/www/methodology/>.

American Community Survey (ACS)

Universe, Frequency, and Types of Data: Nationwide survey to obtain annual data about demographic, social, economic, and housing characteristics of housing units and the people residing in them. It covers the household population and, beginning in 2006, also includes the group quarter population living in correctional facilities, skilled-nursing homes, military barracks, college residence halls, and other group quarters.

Type of Data Collection Operation: Housing unit address sampling is performed twice a year in both August and January. First-phase of sampling defines the universe for the second stage of sampling through two steps. First, all addresses that were eligible for the second-phase sampling within the past four years are excluded from eligibility.

This ensures that no address is in sample more than once in any 5-year period. The second step is to select a 20 percent systematic sample of "new" units, i.e. those units that have never appeared on a previous Master Address File (MAF) extract. All new addresses are systematically assigned to either the current year or to one of four back-samples. This procedure maintains five equal partitions of the universe. The second-phase sampling is done on the current year's partition and results in approximately 3,000,000 housing unit addresses in the U.S. and 36,000 in Puerto Rico (PR). **Group quarter sampling** is performed separately from the housing unit sampling. The sampling begins with separating the small (15 persons or fewer) and the large (more than 15 persons) group quarters. The target sampling rate for both groups is a 2.5% sample of the group quarters population. It results in approximately 200,000 group quarter residents being selected in the U.S., and an additional 1,000 in Puerto Rico.

Data Collection and Imputation Procedures: The American Community Survey is conducted every month on independent samples. The data collection operation for housing units (HUs) consists of three modes or phases: mail, telephone, and personal visit. For the first phase, each housing unit in the independent monthly samples is mailed a pre-notice letter announcing the selection of the address to participate, a survey questionnaire package, and a reminder postcard. These sample units addresses receive a second (replacement) questionnaire package if the initial questionnaire has not been returned by mid-month. The second phase is for sample addresses for which a questionnaire is not returned in the mail and a telephone number is available is forwarded to telephone centers is available, is forwarded to telephone centers for follow-up. Interviewers attempt to contact and interview these mail nonresponse cases by telephone. The third phase is for sample addresses that are still unresponsive after two months of attempts are forwarded for a possible personal visit. Mailable addresses with neither a response to the mailout nor a telephone interview are sampled at a rate of 1 in 2, 2 in 5, or 1 in 3 based on the expected rate of completed interviews at the tract level. Unmailable addresses are sampled at a rate of 2 in 3. Those addresses selected through this process are assigned to Field Representatives (FRs), who visit the addresses, verify their existence, determine their occupancy status, and conduct interviews. **Collection of group quarters** data is conducted by FR's only. Their methods include completing the questionnaire while speaking to the resident in person or over the telephone, or leaving paper questionnaires for residents to complete for themselves and then pick them up later. This last option is used for data collection in federal prisons. If needed, a personal interview can be conducted with a proxy, such as a relative or guardian. After data collection is completed, any remaining incomplete or inconsistent information on the questionnaire are imputed during the final automated edit of the collected data.

Estimates of Sampling Error: The data in the ACS products are estimates and can vary from the actual values that would have been obtained by conducting a census of the entire population. The estimates from the chosen sample addresses can also vary from those that would have been obtained from a different set of addresses. This variation causes uncertainty, which can be measured using statistics such as standard error, margin of error, and confidence interval. All ACS estimates are accompanied by margin of errors to assist users.

Other (nonsampling) Errors: Nonsampling Error—In addition to sampling error, data users should realize that other types of errors may be introduced during any of the various complex operations used to select, collect and process survey data. An important goal of the ACS is to minimize the amount of nonsampling error introduced through coverage issues in the sample list, nonresponse from sample housing units, and transcribing or editing data.

One way of accomplishing this is by finding additional sources of addresses, following up on nonrespondents and maintaining quality control systems.

Sources of Additional Material:
U.S. Census Bureau, American Community Survey Web site available on the Internet, <http://www.census.gov/acs /www/index.html> U.S. Census Bureau, American Community Survey Accuracy of the Data documents available on the Internet, <http://www.census.gov/acs /www/data_documentation /documentation_main/>.

American Housing Survey

Universe, Frequency, and Types of Data:
Conducted nationally in odd numbered years to obtain data on the approximately 124 million occupied or vacant housing units in the United States (group quarters are excluded). Data include characteristics of occupied housing units, vacant units, new housing and mobile home units, financial characteristics, recent mover households, housing and neighborhood quality indicators, and energy characteristics.

Type of Data Collection Operation: The national sample was a multistage probability sample with about 57,000 units eligible for interview in 2005. Sample units, selected within 394 PSUs, were surveyed over a 4-month period.

Data Collection and Imputation Procedures: For 2005, the survey was conducted by personal interviews. The interviewers obtained the information from the occupants or, if the unit was vacant, from informed persons such as landlords, rental agents, or knowledgeable neighbors.

Estimates of Sampling Error: For the national sample, illustrations of the Standard Error (SE) of the estimates are provided in the Appendix D of the 2005 report.

Other (nonsampling) Errors: Response rate was about 90 percent. Nonsampling errors may result from incorrect or incomplete responses, errors in

coding and recording, and processing errors. Appendix D of the 2005 report has a complete discussion of the errors.

Sources of Additional Material:
U.S. Census Bureau, *Current Housing Reports,* Series H–150 and H–170, *American Housing Survey see* <http://www.census.gov/hhes/www /ahs.html>.

Annual Survey of Government Employment and Payroll

Universe, Frequency, and Types of Data:
The survey measures the number of state, local and federal civilian government employees and their gross payrolls for the pay period including March 12. The survey is conducted annually except in years ending in '2' and '7', when a census of all state and local governments is done. The survey provides data on full-time and part-time employment, part-time hours worked, full-time equivalent employment, and payroll statistics by governmental function (elementary and secondary education, higher education, police protection, fire protection, financial administration, central staff services, judicial and legal, highways, public welfare, solid waste management, sewerage, parks and recreation, health, hospitals, water supply, electric power, gas supply, transit, natural resources, correction, libraries, air transportation, water transport and terminals, other education, state liquor stores, social insurance administration, and housing and community development).

Type of Data Collection Operations: The survey sample was taken from the 2002 Census of Governments and contains approximately 11,000 local government units. These units were sampled from a sampling frame that contained 83,767 local governments (county, city, township, special district, and school districts) in addition to 50 state governments and the District of Columbia. This frame was slightly different from the Annual Finance Survey sampling frame. Forty-two of the state governments provided data from central payroll records for all or most of their agencies/institutions. Data for agencies and institutions for the remaining state governments were obtained by mail canvass questionnaires. Local governments were also canvassed using a mail questionnaire. However, elementary and secondary school system data in Florida, North Dakota, and Washington were supplied by special arrangements with the state education agency in each of these states. All respondents receiving the mail questionnaire had the option of responding using the Employment Web site developed for reporting data. Approximately 26% of the state agency and local government respondents chose to respond on the Web.

Editing and Imputation Procedures: Editing is a process that ensures survey data are accurate, complete, and consistent. Efforts are made at all phases of collection, processing, and tabulation to minimize errors. Although some edits are built into the Internet data collection instrument and the data entry programs, the majority of the edits are performed after the case has been loaded into the Census Bureau's database. Edits consist primarily of two types: consistency and a ratio of the current years reported value to the prior year's value. The consistency edits check the logical relationships of data items reported on the form. For example, if a value exists for employees for a function then a value must exist for payroll also. If part-time employees and payroll are reported then part-time hours must be reported and vice versa. The current year/prior year edits compare data for the number of employees, the function reported for the employees, and the average salary between reporting years. If data fall outside of acceptable tolerance levels, the item is flagged for review. Some additional checks are made comparing data from the Annual Finance Survey to data reported on the Annual Survey of Government Employment and Payroll to verify that employees reported on the Annual Survey of Government Employment and Payroll at a particular function

have a corresponding expenditure on the Finance Survey. For both types of edits, the edit results are reviewed by analysts and adjusted when needed. When the analyst is unable to resolve or accept the edit failure, contact is made with the respondent to verify or correct the reported data.

Imputation: Not all respondents answer every item on the questionnaire. There are also questionnaires that are not returned despite efforts to gain a response. Imputation is the process of filling in missing or invalid data with reasonable values in order to have a complete data set. For general purpose governments and for schools, the imputations were based on recent historical data from either a prior year annual survey or the most recent Census of Governments, if it was available. These data were adjusted by a growth rate that was determined by the growth of units that were similar (in size, geography, and type of government) to the nonrespondent. If there was no recent historical data available, the imputations were based on the data from a randomly selected donor that was similar to the nonrespondent. This donor's data were adjusted by dividing each data item by the population (or enrollment) of the donor and multiplying the result by the nonrespondent's population (or enrollment). For special districts, if prior year data are available, the data are brought forward with a national level growth rate applied. Otherwise, the data are imputed to be zero. In cases where good secondary data sources exist, the data from those sources were used.

Estimates of Sampling Error: For intercensal surveys, estimated coefficients of variation for all variables are given in tabulations on the Website. For U.S. and state-and-local government-level estimates of total full-time equivalents and total payroll, most relative standard errors are generally less than one percent, but vary considerably for detailed characteristics.

Other (nonsampling) Errors: Although every effort is made in all phases of collection, processing, and tabulation

U.S. Census Bureau, Statistical Abstract of the United States: 2012

to minimize errors, the sample data are subject to nonsampling errors such as inability to obtain data for every variable from all units in the sample, inaccuracies in classification, response errors, misinterpretation of questions, mistakes in keying and coding, and coverage errors. These same errors may be evident in census collections and may affect the Census of Governments data used to adjust the sample during the estimation phase and used in the imputation process.

Sources of Additional material: <http://www.census.gov/govs/www/apes/index.html> and <http://www.census.gov/govs/www/apesstl06.html>.

Annual Survey of Government Finances

Universe, Frequency, and Types of Data: The United States Census Bureau conducts an Annual Survey of Government Finances, as authorized by law under Title 13, United States Code, Section 182. Alternatively, every 5 years, in years ending in a '2' or '7', a Census of Governments, including a Finance portion, is conducted under Title 13, Section 161. The survey coverage includes all state and local governments in the United States. For both the Census and annual survey, the finance detail data is equivalent, encompassing the entire range of government finance activities—revenue, expenditure, debt, and assets.

Type of Data Collection Operations: The data collection phase for the annual survey made use of three methods to obtain data: mail canvass, internet collection, and central collection from State sources. In 28 states, all or part of the general purpose finance data for local governments was obtained from cooperative arrangements between the Census Bureau and a state government agency. These usually involved a data collection effort carried out to meet the needs of both agencies—the state agency for purposes of audit, oversight, or information, and the Census Bureau for statistical purposes. Data for the balance of local governments

in this annual survey were obtained via mail questionnaires sent directly to county, municipal, township, special district, and school district governments. School district data were collected via cooperative arrangements with state education agencies. Data for state governments were compiled by analysts of the Census Bureau, usually with the cooperation and assistance of state officials. The data were compiled from state government audits, budgets, and other financial reports, either in printed or electronic format. The compilation generally involved recasting the state financial records into the classification categories used for reporting by the Census Bureau.

Data Collection and Imputation Procedures: Survey is conducted by mail with mail follow-ups of nonrespondents. Imputation for all nonresponse items is based on previous year reports or, for new governments, on data from similar donors.

Estimates of Sampling Error: The local government statistics in the intercensal survey years are developed from a sample survey. Therefore, the local totals, as well as aggregates of state and local government data, are considered estimated amounts subject to sampling error. State government finance data are not subject to sampling. Consequently, State-local aggregates shown here have a relative standard error less than or equal to the local government estimates they include. Estimates of major United States totals for local governments are subject to a computed sampling variability of less than one-half of 1 percent. State and local government totals are generally subject to sampling variability of less than 3 percent.

Other (nonsampling) Errors: The estimates are also subject to inaccuracies in classification, response, and processing. Efforts were made at all phases of collection, processing, and tabulation to minimize errors. However, the data are still subject to errors from imputations for missing data, errors from misreported data, errors from miscoding, and difficulties in identifying every unit that should be included in the report. Every effort was made to keep such errors to a minimum through care in examining, editing, and tabulating the data reported by government officials.

Sources of Additional Material: <http://www.census.gov/govs/index.html> and <http://www.census.gov/govs/state/index.html>.

Annual Survey of Manufactures (ASM)

Universe, Frequency, and Types of Data: The Annual Survey of Manufactures is conducted annually, except for years ending in '2' and '7' for all manufacturing establishments having one or more paid employees. The purpose of the ASM is to provide key intercensal measures of manufacturing activity, products, and location for the public and private sectors. The ASM provides statistics on employment, payroll, worker hours, payroll supplements, cost of materials, value added by manufacturing, capital expenditures, inventories, and energy consumption. It also provides estimates of value of shipments for 1,800 classes of manufactured products.

Type of Data Collection Operation: The ASM includes approximately 50,000 establishments selected from the census universe of 346,000 manufacturing establishments. Approximately 24,000 large establishments are selected with certainty, and the remaining 26,000 other establishments are selected with probability proportional to a composite measure of establishment size. The survey is updated from two sources: Internal Revenue Service administrative records are used to include new single-unit manufacturers and the Company Organization Survey identifies new establishments of multiunit forms.

Data Collection and Imputation Procedures: Survey is conducted by mail with phone and mail follow-ups of nonrespondents. Imputation (for all nonresponse items) is based on previous year reports, or for new establishments in survey, on industry averages.

Estimates of Sampling Error: Estimated relative standard errors for number of employees, new expenditures, and for value added totals are given in annual publications. For U.S. level industry statistics, most estimated relative standard errors are 2 percent or less, but vary considerably for detailed characteristics.

Other (nonsampling) Errors: The unit response rate is about 85 percent. Nonsampling errors include those due to collection, reporting, and transcription errors, many of which are corrected through computer and clerical checks.

Sources of Additional Material: U.S. Census Bureau, *Annual Survey of Manufactures,* and Technical Paper 24.

Census of Population

Universe, Frequency, and Types of Data: Complete count of U.S. population conducted every 10 years since 1790. Data obtained on number and characteristics of people in the United States.

Type of Data Collection Operation: In the 1990, 2000, and 2010 censuses the 100 percent items included: age, date of birth, sex, race, Hispanic origin, and relationship to householder. In 1980, approximately 19 percent of the housing units were included in the sample; in 1990 and 2000, approximately 17 percent.

Data Collection and Imputation Procedures: In 1980, 1990, 2000, and 2010 mail questionnaires were used extensively with personal interviews in the remainder. Extensive telephone and personal follow-up for nonrespondents was done in the censuses. Imputations were made for missing characteristics.

Estimates of Sampling Error: Sampling errors for data are estimated for all items collected by sample and vary by characteristic and geographic area. The coefficients of variation (CVs) for national and state estimates are generally very small.

Other (nonsampling) Errors: Since 1950, evaluation programs have been conducted to provide information on the magnitude of some sources of nonsampling errors such as response bias and undercoverage in each census. Results from the evaluation program for the 1990 census indicated that the estimated net undercoverage amounted to about 1.5 percent of the total resident population. For Census 2000, the evaluation program indicated a net overcount of 0.5 percent of the resident population.

Sources of Additional Material:
U.S. Census Bureau, The Coverage of Population in the 1980 Census, PHC80-E4; *Content Reinterview Study: Accuracy of Data for Selected Population and Housing Characteristics as Measured by Reinterview*, PHC80-E2; *1980 Census of Population*, Vol. 1, (PC80-1), Appendixes B, C, and D. *Content Reinterview Survey: Accuracy of Data for Selected Population and Housing Characteristics as Measured by Reinterview*, 1990, CPH-E-1; Effectiveness of Quality Assurance, CPH-E-2; Programs to Improve Coverage in the 1990 Census, 1990, CPH-E-3. For Census 2000 evaluations, see <http://www.census.gov/pred/www>.

County Business Patterns

Universe, Frequency, and Types of Data: County Business Patterns is an annual tabulation of basic data items extracted from the Business Register, a file of all known single- and multi-location employer companies maintained and updated by the U.S. Census Bureau. Data include number of establishments, number of employees, first quarter and annual payrolls, and number of establishments by employment size class. Data are excluded for self-employed individuals, private households, railroad employees, agricultural production workers, and most government employees.

Type of Data Collection Operation: The annual Company Organization Survey and the Economic Census provide individual establishment data for multilocation companies. Data for single establishment companies are obtained from various Census Bureau programs, such as the Annual Survey of Manufactures and Current Business Surveys, as well as from administrative records of the Internal Revenue Service, the Social Security Administration, and the Bureau of Labor Statistics.

Estimates of Sampling Error: Not applicable.

Other (nonsampling) Errors: The data are subject to nonsampling errors, such as inability to identify all cases in the universe; definition and classification difficulties; differences in interpretation of questions; errors in recording or coding the data obtained; and estimation of employers who reported too late to be included in the tabulations and for records with missing or misreported data.

Sources of Additional Material:
U. S. Census Bureau, County Business Patterns <http://www.census.gov/econ/cbp/index.html>

Current Population Survey (CPS)

Universe, Frequency, and Types of Data: Nationwide monthly sample designed primarily to produce national and state estimates of labor force characteristics of the civilian noninstitutionalized population 16 years of age and older.

Type of Data Collection Operation: Multistage probability sample that currently includes 72,000 households from 824 sample areas. Sample size increased in some states to improve data reliability for those areas on an annual average basis. A continual sample rotation system is used. Households are in sample 4 months, out for 8 months, and in for 4 more. Month-to-month overlap is 75 percent; year-to-year overlap is 50 percent.

Data Collection and Imputation Procedures: For first and fifth months that a household is in sample, personal interviews; other months, approximately 85 percent of the data collected by phone. Imputation is done for item nonresponse. Adjustment for total nonresponse is done by a predefined cluster of units, by state, metropolitan status and CBSA size; for item nonresponse imputation varies by subject matter.

Estimates of Sampling Error: The national total estimates of the civilian labor force and of employment have monthly CVs of about 0.2 percent and annual average CVs of about 0.1 percent. Unemployment is a much smaller characteristic and consequently has substantially larger CVs than the civilian labor force or employment. The national unemployment rate, the most important CPS statistic, has a monthly CV of about 2 percent and an annual average CV of about 1 percent. Assuming a 6 percent unemployment rate, states have annual average CVs of about 8 percent. The estimated CVs for family income and poverty rate for all persons in 2005 are 0.4 percent and 1.2 percent, respectively. CVs for subnational areas, such as states, tend to be larger and vary by area.

Other (nonsampling) Errors: Estimates of response bias on unemployment are available. Estimates of unemployment rate from reinterviews range from −2.4 percent to 1.0 percent of the basic CPS unemployment rate (over a 30-month span from January 2004 through June 2006). Eligible CPS households are approximately 82 percent of the assigned households, with a corresponding response rate of 92 percent.

Sources of Additional Material: U.S. Census Bureau and Bureau of Labor Statistics, Current Population Survey: Design and Methodology, (Technical Paper 66), available on the Internet <http://www.census.gov/prod/2006pubs/tp-66.pdf> and the Bureau of Labor Statistics, <http://www.bls.gov/cps/> and the *BLS Handbook of Methods*, Chapter 1, available on the Internet at <http://www.bls.gov/opub/hom/homch1_a.htm>.

Foreign Trade—Export Statistics

Universe, Frequency, and Types of Data: As of October 1, 2008, the Shipper's Export Declaration (SED) Form 7525-V became obsolete. Electronic Export Information (EEI) replaced the SED and all export information must be filed through the Automated Export System (AES) by either a United States Principal Party in Interest (USPPI) or an Authorized U.S. agent. The EEI filings are processed each month to obtain data on the movement of U.S. merchandise exports to foreign countries. Data obtained include value, quantity, and shipping weight of exports by commodity, country of destination, district of exportation, and mode of transportation.

Type of Data Collection Operation: USPPIs or Authorized U.S. Agents are required to submit EEI for exportation of merchandise valued over $2,500. Data for shipments valued under $2,501 are estimated, based on established percentages of individual country totals.

Data Collection and Imputation Procedures: The EEI filings are received on a daily basis from ports throughout the country and subjected to a monthly processing cycle. They are fully processed to the extent they reflect items valued over $2,500. Estimates for shipments valued at $2,500 or less are made, based on established percentages of individual country totals.

Estimates of Sampling Error: Not applicable.

Other (nonsampling) Errors: The goods data are a complete enumeration of EEI reported in AES and are not subject to sampling errors; but they are subject to several types of nonsampling errors. Quality assurance procedures are performed at every stage of collection, processing and tabulation; however the data are still subject to several types of nonsampling errors. The most significant of these include reporting errors, undocumented shipments, timeliness, data capture errors, and errors in the estimation of low-valued transactions. The number of data errors and the overall data quality are expected to improve due to the elimination of paper SEDs and the mandatory filing of export data through the AES. Additional information on errors affecting export data can be found at <http://www.census.gov /foreign-trade/Press-release /current_press_release/explain.pdf>.

Sources of Additional Material: Effect of Mandatory Electronic Filing on Export data, <http://www.census.gov /foreign-trade/aip /mandatoryelectronicfiling.html\>, U.S. Census Bureau, FT 900 U.S. International Trade in Goods and Services, FT 925 (discounted after 1996), U.S. Merchandise Trade, FT 895 U.S. Trade with Puerto Rico and U.S. Possessions, FT 920 U.S. Merchandise trade: selected highlights, and Information Section on Goods and Services at <http://www.census .gov/ft900>.

Foreign Trade—Import Statistics

Universe, Frequency, and Types of Data: The import entry documents collected by U.S. Customs and Border Protection are processed each month to obtain data on the movement of merchandise imported into the United States. Data obtained include value, quantity, and shipping weight by commodity, country of origin, district of entry, and mode of transportation.

Type of Data Collection Operation: Import entry documents, either paper or electronic, are required to be filed for the importation of goods into the United States valued over $2,000 or for articles which must be reported on formal entries. U.S. Bureau of Customs and Border Protection officials collect and transmit statistical copies of the documents to the Census Bureau on a flow basis for data compilation. Estimates for shipments valued under $2,001 and not reported on formal entries are based on estimated established percentages for individual country totals.

Data Collection and Imputation Procedures: Statistical copies of import entry documents, received on a daily basis from ports of entry throughout the country, are subjected to a monthly processing cycle. They are

fully processed to the extent they reflect items valued at $2,001 and over or items which must be reported on formal entries.

Estimates of Sampling Error: Not applicable.

Other (nonsampling) Errors: The goods data are a complete enumeration of documents collected by the U.S. Customs and Border Protection and are not subject to sampling errors; but they are subject to several types of nonsampling errors. Quality assurance procedures are performed at every stage of collection, processing, and tabulation; however the data are still subject to several types of nonsampling errors. The most significant of these include reporting errors, undocumented shipments, timeliness, data capture errors, and errors in the estimation of low-valued transactions. Additional information on errors affecting import data can be found at <http://www.census.gov /foreign-trade/Press-Release /current_press_release/explain.pdf>.

Sources of Additional Material: U.S. Census Bureau, FT 900 U.S. International Trade in Goods and Services, FT 925 (discounted after 1996), U.S. Merchandise Trade, FT 895 U.S. Trade with Puerto Rico and U.S. Possessions, FT920 U.S. Merchandise Trade: selected highlights, and Information Section on Goods and Services at <http://www.census.gov /ft900>.

Monthly Retail Trade and Food Service Survey

Universe, Frequency, and Types of Data: Provides monthly estimates of retail and food service sales by kind of business and end of month inventories of retail stores.

Type of Data Collection Operation: Probability sample of all firms from a list frame. The list frame is the Bureau's Business Register updated quarterly for recent birth Employer Identification (EI) Numbers issued by the Internal Revenue Service and assigned a kind of business code by the Social Security

Administration. The largest firms are included monthly; a sample of others is included every month also.

Data Collection and Imputation Procedures: Data are collected by mail questionnaire with telephone follow-ups and fax reminders for nonrespondents. Imputation is made for each nonresponse item and each item failing edit checks.

Estimates of Sampling Error: For the 2006 monthly surveys, CVs are about 0.4 percent for estimated total retail sales and 0.7 percent for estimated total retail inventories. Sampling errors are shown in monthly publications.

Other (nonsampling) Errors: Imputation rates are about 22 percent for monthly retail and food service sales, and 29 percent for monthly retail inventories.

Sources of Additional Material: U.S. Census Bureau, Current Business Reports, Annual Revision of Monthly Retail and Food Services: Sales and Inventories.

Monthly Survey of Construction

Universe, Frequency, and Types of Data: Survey conducted monthly of newly constructed housing units (excluding mobile homes). Data are collected on the start, completion, and sale of housing. (Annual figures are aggregates of monthly estimates.)

Type of Data Collection Operation: A multistage probability sample of approximately 900 of the 20,000 permit-issuing jurisdictions in the U.S. was selected. Each month in each of these permit offices, field representatives list and select a sample of permits for which to collect data. To obtain data in areas where building permits are not required, a multistage probability sample of 80 land areas (census tracts or subsections of census tracts) was selected. All roads in these areas are canvassed and data are collected on all new residential construction found. Sampled buildings are followed up until they are completed (and sold, if for sale).

Data Collection and Imputation Procedures: Data are obtained by telephone inquiry and/or field visit. Nonresponse/undercoverage adjustment factors are used to account for late reported data.

Estimates of Sampling Error: Estimated CV of 5 percent to 6 percent for estimates of national totals of units started, but may be higher than 20 percent for estimated totals of more detailed characteristics, such as housing units in multiunit structures.

Other (nonsampling) Errors: Response rate is over 90 percent for most items. Nonsampling errors are attributed to definitional problems, differences in interpretation of questions, incorrect reporting, inability to obtain information about all cases in the sample, and processing errors.

Sources of Additional Material: All data are available on the Internet at <http://www.census.gov/starts>, <http://www.census.gov/newhome-sales> or <http://www.census.gov/const/www/newsresconstindex.html>. Further documentation of the survey is also available at those sites.

Nonemployer Statistics

Universe, Frequency, and Types of Data: Nonemployer statistics are an annual tabulation of economic data by industry for active businesses without paid employees that are subject to federal income tax. Data showing the number of firms and receipts by industry are available for the U.S., states, counties, and metropolitan areas. Most types of businesses covered by the Census Bureau's economic statistics programs are included in the nonemployer statistics. Tax-exempt and agricultural-production businesses are excluded from nonemployer statistics.

Type of Data Collection Operation: The universe of nonemployer firms is created annually as a byproduct of the Census Bureau's Business Register processing for employer establishments. If a business is active but without paid employees, then it becomes part of the potential nonemployer universe. Industry classification and receipts are available for each potential nonemployer business. These data are obtained primarily from the annual business income tax returns of the Internal Revenue Service (IRS). The potential nonemployer universe undergoes a series of complex processing, editing, and analytical review procedures at the Census Bureau to distinguish nonemployers from employers, and to correct and complete data items used in creating the data tables.

Estimates of Sampling Error:
Not applicable.

Other (nonsampling) Errors:
The data are subject to nonsampling errors, such as industry misclassification as well as errors of response, keying, nonreporting, and coverage.

Sources of Additional Material:
U. S. Census Bureau, Nonemployer Statistics at <http://www.census.gov /epcd/nonemployer/index.html>.

Service Annual Survey

Universe, Frequency, and Types of Data:
The U.S. Census Bureau conducts the Service Annual Survey (SAS) to provide nationwide estimates of revenues and expenses for selected service industries. Estimates are summarized by industry classification based on the 2002 North American Industry Classification System (NAICS). The SAS was expanded in 2009. Selected service industries covered by the Service Annual Survey include all or part of the following NAICS sectors: Utilities (NAICS 22), Transportation and Warehousing (NAICS 48-49); Information (NAICS 51); Finance and Insurance (NAICS 52); Real Estate and Rental and Leasing (NAICS 53); Professional, Scientific, and Technical Services (NAICS 54); Administrative and Support and Waste Management and Remediation Services (NAICS 56); Educational Services (NAICS 61); Health Care and Social Assistance (NAICS 62); Arts, Entertainment, and Recreation (NAICS 71); and Other Services, except Public Administration (NAICS 81). Data

collected include total revenue, total expenses, detailed expenses, revenue from e-commerce transactions; and for selected industries, revenue from detailed service products, revenue from exported services, and inventories. For industries with a significant nonprofit component, separate estimates are developed for taxable firms and firms and organizations exempt from federal income taxes. Questionnaires are mailed in January and request annual data for the prior year. Estimates are published approximately 12 months after the initial survey mailing.

Type of Data Collection Operation:
The Service Annual Survey estimates are developed from a probability sample of employer firms and administrative records for nonemployers. Service Annual Survey questionnaires are mailed to a probability sample that is periodically reselected from a universe of firms located in the United States and having paid employees. The sample includes firms of all sizes and covers both taxable firms and firms exempt from federal income taxes. Updates to the sample are made on a quarterly basis to account for new businesses. Firms without paid employees, or nonemployers, are included in the estimates through imputation and/or administrative records data provided by other federal agencies. Links to additional information about confidentiality protection, sampling error, nonsampling error, sample design, definitions, and copies of the questionnaires may be found at <http://www.census.gov/services /index.html>.

Estimates of Sampling Error: The full 2007 Service Annual Survey results, including coefficients of variations (CVs), can be found at <http://www.census.gov/services /index.html>. Links to additional information regarding sampling error may be found at <http://www.census.gov /services/sas/cv.html>.

Other (Nonsampling) Errors: Data are imputed for unit nonresponse, item nonresponse, and for reported data that fails edits. The percent of imputed data for total revenue for the 2009 Service Annual Survey estimates range from 6.5 percent to 19.3 percent for total revenue estimates computed at the NAICS sector (2-digit NAICS code) level.

Sources of Additional Material:
U.S. Census Bureau, Current Business Reports, *Service Annual Survey*, Census Bureau Web site: <http://www.census.gov/services /index.html>.

Survey of Business Owners (SBO)

Universe, Frequency, and Types of Data: The Survey of Business Owners (SBO), formerly known as the Surveys of Minority- and Women-Owned Business Enterprises (SMOBE/SWOBE), provides statistics that describe the composition of U.S. businesses by gender, ethnicity, race, and veteran status. Data are presented for businesses owned by American Indians and Alaska Natives, Asians, Blacks, Hispanics, Native Hawaiians and Other Pacific Islanders, Veterans, and Women. All U.S. firms operating during 2007 with receipts of $1,000 or more, which are classified by the North American Industry Classification System (NAICS) codes 11 through 99, are represented, except for the following: NAICS 111, 112, 4811 (part), 481111, 482, 491, 525, 813, 814, and 92. The lists of all firms (or sample frames) are compiled from a combination of business tax returns and data collected on other economic census reports. The published data include the number of firms, sales and receipts, number of paid employees, and annual payroll. Data are presented by industry classifications, geographic area (states, metropolitan and micropolitan statistical areas, counties, and corporate municipalities [places] including cities, towns, townships, villages, and boroughs), and size of firm (employment and receipts).

Type of Data Collection Operation: The survey is based on a stratified probability sample of approximately 2.3 million firms from a universe of approximately 27.1 million firms. There were 5.7 million firms with paid employees and 21.4 million firms with no paid employees.

Data Collection and Imputation Procedures: Data were collected through a mailout/mailback operation. Compensation for missing data is addressed through reweighting, edit correction, and standard statistical imputation methods.

Estimates of Sampling Error: Sampling error is present in these estimates because they are based on the results of a sample survey and not on an enumeration of the entire universe. Since these estimates are based on a probability sample, it is possible to estimate the sampling variability of the survey estimates. The standard error (SE) provides a measure of the variation. The relative standard error (RSE) or coefficient of variation (CV) provides a measure of the magnitude of the variation relative to the estimate and is calculated as 100 multiplied by the ratio of the estimate to the SE. The CVs for number of firms and receipts at the national level typically range from 0 to 4 percent.

Other (Nonsampling) Error: Nonsampling errors are attributed to many sources: inability to obtain information for all cases in the universe, adjustments to the weights of respondents to compensate for nonrespondents, imputation for missing data, data errors and biases, mistakes in recording or keying data, errors in collection or processing, and coverage problems. Explicit measures of the effects of these nonsampling errors are not available. However, it is believed that most of the important operational and data errors were detected and corrected through an automated data edit designed to review the data for reasonableness and consistency. Quality control techniques were used to verify that operating procedures were carried out as specified.

Sources of Additional Materials:
U.S. Census Bureau, Survey of Business Owners, <http://www.census .gov/econ/sbo/> U.S. Census Bureau, 2007 Economic Census User Guide:

<http://www.census.gov/econ/census07/www/user_guide.html>

U.S. DEPARTMENT OF EDUCATION National Center for Education Statistics

Integrated Postsecondary Education Data Survey (IPEDS), Completions

Universe, Frequency, and Types of Data: Annual survey of all Title IV (federal financial aid) eligible postsecondary institutions to obtain data on enrollments; faculty and staff finances; institutional prices; financial aid; and earned degrees and other formal awards, conferred by field of study, level of degree, sex, and by racial/ethnic characteristics (every other year prior to 1989, then annually).

Type of Data Collection Operation: Complete census.

Data Collection and Imputation Procedures: Data are collected through a Web-based survey in the fall of every year. Missing data are imputed by using data of similar institutions.

Estimates of Sampling Error: Not applicable.

Other (nonsampling Errors): For 2009-10, the response rate for degree-granting institutions was 100.0 percent.

Sources of Additional Material: U.S. Department of Education, National Center for Education Statistics, *Postsecondary Institutions and Price of Attendance in the United States: Fall 2009 and Degrees and Other Awards Conferred: 2008–09 and 12-month enrollment, 2008–09.*
See <http://www.nces.ed.gov/ipeds/>.

National Household Education Surveys (NHES) Program

Universe, Frequency, and Types of Data: The National Household Education Surveys Program is a system of telephone surveys of the noninstitutionalized civilian population of the United States. Surveys in NHES have varying universes of interest depending on the particular survey. Specific topics covered by each survey are at the NHES Web site <http://nces.ed.gov/nhes>. A list of the surveys fielded as part of NHES, each universe, and the years they were fielded is provided below.

1) Adult Education—Interviews were conducted with a representative sample of civilian, noninstitutionalized persons aged 16 and older who were not enrolled in grade 12 or below (1991, 1995, 1999, 2001, 2003, 2005).

2) Before- and After-School Programs and Activities—Interviews were conducted with parents of a representative sample of students in grades K through 8 (1999, 2001, 2005).

3) Civic Involvement—Interviews were conducted with representative samples of parents, youth, and adults (1996, 1999).

4) Early Childhood Program Participation—Interviews were conducted with parents of a representative sample of children from birth through grade 3, with the specific age groups varying by survey year (1991, 1995, 1999, 2001, 2005).

5) Household and Library Use—Interviews were conducted with a representative sample of U.S. households (1996).

6) Parent and Family Involvement in Education—Interviews were conducted with parents of a representative sample of children age three through grade 12 or in grades K through 12 depending on the survey year (1996, 1999, 2003, and 2007).

7) School Readiness—Interviews were conducted with parents of a representative sample of 3-7 year-old children (1993 and 1999) and of 3-5 year old children, not yet in kindergarten, 2007).

8) School Safety and Discipline—Interviews were conducted with a representative sample of students in grades 6-12, their parents, and the

parents of a representative sample of students in grades 3-12 (1993).

Type of Data Collection Operation: NHES uses telephone interviews to collect data.

Data Collection and Imputation Procedures: Telephone numbers are selected using random digit dialing (RDD) techniques. Approximately 45,000 to 64,000 households are contacted in order to identify persons eligible for the surveys. Data are collected using computer-assisted telephone interviewing (CATI) procedures. Missing data are imputed using hot-deck imputation procedures.

Estimates of Sampling Error: Unweighted sample sizes range between 2,250 and 55,708. The average root design effects of the surveys in NHES range from 1.1 to 1.5, except for the Adult Education survey of 1991. In 1991, average root design effects for the Adult Education survey ranged from 2.3 to 4.5.

Other (nonsampling) Errors: Because of unit nonresponse and because the samples are drawn from households with telephone instead of all households, nonresponse and/or coverage bias may exist for some estimates. However, both sources of potential bias are adjusted for in the weighting process. Analyses of both potential sources of bias in the NHES collections have been studied and no significant bias has been detected.

Sources of Additional Material: Please see the NHES Web site at <http://nces.ed.gov/nhes>.

Schools and Staffing Survey (SASS)

Universe, Frequency and Types of Data: NCES designed the SASS survey system to emphasize teacher demand and shortage, teacher and administrator characteristics, school programs, and general conditions in schools. SASS also collects data on many other topics, including principals' and teachers' perceptions of school climate and problems in their schools; teacher compensation; district hiring practices; basic characteristics of the student population; and for the first time, instructional time and teacher and school performance. The SASS has had four core components: the School Questionnaire, the Teacher Questionnaire, the Principal Questionnaire, and the School District Questionnaire. For the 2007-08 SASS, a sample of public charter schools is included in the sample as part of the public school questionnaire. Since 1987-88, the SASS is the largest, most extensive survey of K through 12 school districts, schools, teachers, and administrators in the U.S. Surveys have been conducted every 3 to 4 years depending on budgetary constraints. The SASS includes data from public, private, and Bureau of Indian Education (BIE) school sectors. Therefore, the SASS provides a multitude of opportunities for analysis and reporting on elementary and secondary educational issues.

Type of Data Collection Operation: The U.S. Census Bureau performs the data collection and begins by sending advance letters to the sampled Local Education Agencies (LEAs) and schools in August and September of collection years. Beginning in October, questionnaires are delivered by U.S. Census Bureau field representatives. The sampling frame for the public school sample is the most recent Common Core of Data (CCD) school file. CCD is a universe file that includes all elementary and secondary schools in the United States. Schools operated by the Department of Defense or those that offered only kindergarten or pre-kindergarten or adult education were excluded from the SASS sample. The list frame used for the private school sample is the most recent Private School Universe Survey (PSS) list, updated with association lists. An area frame supplement is based on the canvassing of private schools within specific geographical areas. A separate universe of schools funded by the Bureau of Indian Education (BIE) is drawn from the Program Education Directory maintained by the BIE. To avoid duplicates in the BIE files, BIE schools in the CCD school file are treated as public schools.

U.S. Census Bureau, Statistical Abstract of the United States: 2012

Estimates of Sampling Error: Sample errors can be calculated using replicate weights and Balanced Repeated Replication complex survey design methodology. Errors depend on cell sizes and range from less than 1 percent to over 5 percent (for reasonable cell sizes).

Other (nonsampling) Errors: Because of unit nonresponse, bias may exist in some sample cells. However, bias has been adjusted for in the weighting process. Analysis of bias has been studied and no significant bias has been detected.

Sources of Additional Material: Please see the SASS Web site at <http://nces.ed.gov/surveys/sass/>.

U.S. DEPARTMENT OF JUSTICE, FEDERAL BUREAU OF INVESTIGATION

Uniform Crime Reporting (UCR) Program

Universe, Frequency, and Types of Data: Monthly reports on the number of criminal offenses that become known to law enforcement agencies. Data are also collected on crimes cleared by arrest or exceptional means; age, sex, and race of arrestees and for victims and offenders for homicides, number of law enforcement employees, on fatal and nonfatal assaults against law enforcement officers, and on hate crimes reported.

Type of Data Collection Operation: Crime statistics are based on reports of crime data submitted either directly to the FBI by contributing law enforcement agencies or through cooperating state UCR Programs.

Data Collection and Imputation Procedures: States with UCR programs collect data directly from individual law enforcement agencies and forward reports, prepared in accordance with UCR standards, to the FBI. Accuracy and consistency edits are performed by the FBI.

Estimates of Sampling Error: Not applicable.

Other (nonsampling) Errors: During 2008, law enforcement agencies active in the UCR Program represented 94.9 percent of the total population. The coverage amounted to 96.0 percent of the United States population in Metropolitan Statistical Areas, 87.6 percent of the population in cities outside metropolitan areas, and 90.0 percent in nonmetropolitan counties.

Sources of Additional Material: U.S. Department of Justice, Federal Bureau of Investigation, *Crime in the United States,* annual, *Hate Crime Statistics,* annual, *Law Enforcement Officers Killed and Assaulted,* annual, <http://www.fbi.gov/ucr/ucr.htm>.

U.S. INTERNAL REVENUE SERVICE

Corporation Income Tax Returns

Universe, Frequency, and Types of Data: Annual study of unaudited corporation income tax returns, Forms 1120, 1120–A, 1120–F, 1120–L, 1120–PC, 1120–REIT, 1120–RIC, and 1120S, filed by corporations or businesses legally defined as corporations. Data provided on various financial characteristics by industry and size of total assets, and business receipts.

Type of Data Collection Operation: Stratified probability sample of approximately 112,000 returns for Tax Year 2008, allocated to sample classes which are based on type of return, size of total assets, size of net income or deficit, and selected business activity. Sampling rates for sample classes varied from 0.25 percent to 100 percent.

Data Collection and Imputation Procedures: Computer selection of sample of tax return records. Data adjusted during editing for incorrect, missing, or inconsistent entries to ensure consistency with other entries on return and to comply with statistical definitions.

Estimates of Sampling Error: Estimated CVs for Tax Year 2008: Coefficients of variation are published in the 2008 Statistics of Income

Corporation Income Tax Returns, Table 1, by industry group. Sampling rates are contained in Section 3 of the same report.

Other (nonsampling) Errors: Nonsampling errors include coverage errors, processing errors, and response errors.

Sources of Additional Material: U.S. Internal Revenue Service, *Statistics of Income, Corporation Income Tax Returns,* annual.

Individual Income Tax Returns

Universe, Frequency, and Types of Data: Annual study of unaudited individual income tax returns, Forms 1040, 1040A, and 1040EZ, filed by U.S. citizens and residents. Data provided on various financial characteristics by size of adjusted gross income, marital status, and by taxable and nontaxable returns. Data by state, based on the population of returns filed, also include returns from 1040NR, filed by nonresident aliens plus certain self employment tax returns.

Type of Data Collection Operation: Stratified probability sample of 328,630 returns for tax year 2008. The sample is classified into sample strata based on the larger of total income or total loss amounts, the size of business plus farm receipts, and other criteria such as the potential usefulness of the return for tax policy modeling. Sampling rates for sample strata varied from 0.10 percent to 100 percent.

Data Collection and Imputation Procedures: Computer selection of sample of tax return records. Data adjusted during editing for incorrect, missing, or inconsistent entries to ensure consistency with other entries on return.

Estimates of Sampling Error: Estimated CVs for tax year 2008: Adjusted gross income less deficit 0.08 percent; salaries and wages 0.16 percent; and tax exempt interest received 1.07 percent. (State data not subject to sampling error.)

Other (nonsampling) Errors: Processing errors and errors arising from the use of tolerance checks for the data.

Sources of Additional Material: U.S. Internal Revenue Service, *Statistics of Income, Individual Income Tax Returns,* annual, (Publication 1304).

Partnership Income Tax Returns

Universe, Frequency, and Types of Data: Annual study of preaudited income tax returns of partnerships related to financial and tax–related activity during calendar year 2008 and reported on Forms 1065 and 1065B to the IRS in calendar year 2009. Data are provided by industry, based on the NAICS industry coding used by IRS.

Type of Data Collection Operation: Stratified probability sample of approximately 34,496 partnership returns from a population of 3.3 million filed during calendar year 2009. The sample is classified based on combinations of industry code, gross receipts, net income or loss, and total assets. Sampling rates vary from 0.04 percent to 100 percent.

Data Collection and Imputation Procedures: The sample of tax return records are selected via computer after data are transcribed by IRS and placed on an administrative file. Data are manually adjusted during editing for incorrect, missing, or inconsistent entries to ensure consistency with other entries on return. Data not available due to regulations are handled with weighting adjustments.

Estimates of Sampling Error: Some of the estimated Coefficients of Variation (the estimated standard error of the total divided by the estimated total) for tax year 2008: For number of partnerships, 0.36 percent; business receipts, 2.63 percent; net income, 2.83 percent; and ordinary business income, 2.23 percent.

Other (nonsampling) Errors: The potential exists for coverage error due to unavailable returns; processing errors; and taxpayer reporting errors, since data are preaudit.

Sources of Additional Material:
U.S. Internal Revenue Service, *Statistics of Income, Partnership Returns* and *Statistics of Income Bulletin,* Vol. 28, No. 2 (Fall 2009).

Sole Proprietorship Income Tax Returns

Universe, Frequency, and Types of Data: Annual study of unaudited income tax returns of nonfarm sole proprietorships, Form 1040 with business schedules. Data provided on various financial characteristics by industry.

Type of Data Collection Operation: Stratified probability sample of roughly 90,000 sole proprietorships for tax year 2008. The sample is classified based on presence or absence of certain business schedules; the larger of total income or loss; size of business plus farm receipts, and other criteria such as the potential usefulness of the return for tax policy modeling. Sampling rates vary from 0.1 percent to 100 percent.

Data Collection and Imputation Procedures: Computer selection of sample of tax return records. Data adjusted during editing for incorrect, missing, or inconsistent entries to ensure consistency with other entries on return.

Estimates of Sampling Error: Estimated CVs for tax year 2008 are available. For sole proprietorships, total business receipts, 0.53 percent; depreciation 1.21 percent.

Other (nonsampling) Errors: Processing errors and errors arising from the use of tolerance checks for the data.

Sources of Additional Material:
U.S. Internal Revenue Service, *Statistics of Income, Sole Proprietorship Returns* (for years 1980 through 1983) and *Statistics of Income Bulletin,* Vol. 28, No. 2 (Fall 2008, as well as bulletins for earlier years).

U.S. NATIONAL CENTER FOR HEALTH STATISTICS (NCHS)

National Health Interview Survey (NHIS)

Universe, Frequency, and Types of Data: Continuous data collection covering the civilian noninstitutional population to obtain information on demographic characteristics, conditions, injuries, impairments, use of health services, health behaviors, and other health topics.

Type of Data Collection Operation: Multistage probability sample of 49,000 households (in 198 PSUs) from 1985 to 1994; 36–40,000 households (358 design PSUs or 449 effective PSUs when divided by state boundaries) from 1995 to 2005; an estimated completed 35,000 households (428 effective PSUs) beginning in 2006.

Data Collection and Imputation Procedures: Some missing data items (e.g., race, ethnicity) are imputed using a hot deck imputation value. Sequential regression models are used to create multiple imputation files for family income. Unit nonresponse is compensated for by an adjustment to the survey weights.

Estimates of Sampling Error: For 2008, medically attended injury episodes rates (crude) in the past 12 months by falling for: females 50.43 (4.30) and males 34.87 (3.73) per 1,000 population; for 2008, injury episodes rates (crude) during the past 12 months inside the home—27.90 (2.28) per 1,000 population.

Other (nonsampling) Errors: The response rate was 93.8 percent in 1996; in 2008, the total household response rate was 84.9 percent, with the final family response rate of 84.5 percent, and the final sample adult response rate of 62.6 percent. (Note: the NHIS questionnaire was redesigned in 1997, and a new sample design was instituted in 2006).

Sources of Additional Material: National Center for Health Statistics, Summary Health Statistics for the U.S. Population: National Health Interview Survey, 2009, Vital and Health Statistics, Series 10, No. 248; National Center for Health Statistics, Summary Health Statistics for U.S. Children: National Health Interview Survey, 2009, Vital and Health Statistics, Series 10, No. 247; National Center for Health Statistics, Summary Health Statistics for U.S. Adults: National Health Interview Survey, 2009, Vital and Health Statistics, Series 10, No. 249; U.S. National Center for Health Statistics, Design and Estimation for the National Health Interview Survey, 1995-2004, Vital and Health Statistics, Series 2, No. 130.

National Survey of Family Growth (NSFG)

Universe, Frequency, and Types of Data: Periodic survey of men and women 15-44 years of age in the household population of the United States. Interviews were conducted in 2002 in person by trained female interviewers. Interview topics covered include births and pregnancies, marriage, divorce, and cohabitation, sexual activity, contraceptive use, and medical care. For men, data on father involvement with children were collected. The most sensitive data—on sexual behavior related to HIV and Sexually Transmitted Disease risk—were collected in a self-administered form in which the data are entered into a computer.

Type of Data Collection Operation: In the 2002 (Cycle 6) NSFG, the sample was a multistage area probability sample of men and women 15-44 years of age in the household population of the United States. Only one person 15-44 was selected from households with one or more persons 15-44. Data were collected and entered into laptop (notebook) computers. In the self-administered portion, the respondent entered his or her own answers into the computer. Sample included 12,571 interviews. The response rate was 79 percent. Hispanic and Black persons, as well as those 15-19 years of age, were sampled at higher rates than White adults. All percentages and other statistics shown for the NSFG are weighted to make national estimates. The weights adjust for the different rates of sampling for each group, and for nonresponse.

Data Collection and Imputation Procedures: When interviews are received, they are reviewed for consistency and quality, and analysis variables (recodes) are created. Missing data on these recodes were imputed using multiple regression techniques and checked again for consistency. Variables indicating whether a value has been imputed ("imputation flags") are included on the data file.

Estimates of Sampling Error: Sampling error codes are included on the data file so that users can estimate sampling errors for their own analyses. Sampling error estimates for nine illustrative analyses are shown on the NSFG Web site at <http://www.cdc.gov/nchs/nsfg.htm>. Sampling error estimates are also shown in most NCHS reports.

Other (nonsampling) Errors: In any survey, errors can occur because the respondent (the person being interviewed) does not recall the specific fact or event being asked about. The NSFG questionnaire in 2002 was programmed to check the consistency of many variables during the interview, so that the interviewer and respondent had a chance to correct any inconsistent information. Further checking occurred after the interview and during recoding and imputation. Typically, less than 1 percent of cases need imputation because of missing data.

Sources of Additional Material: The following references can be found at <http://www.cdc.gov/nchs/nsfg.htm>. "National Survey of Family Growth, Cycle 6: Sample Design, Weighting, and Variance Estimation." *Vital and Health Statistics,* Series 2, Number 142, July 2006. "Plan and Operation of Cycle 6 of the National Survey of Family Growth." *Vital and Health Statistics,* Series 1, No. 42. August 2005. "Sexual Behavior and

Selected Health Measures: Men and Women 15–44 Years of Age, United States, 2002." *Advance Data from Vital and Health Statistics*, No. 362, Sept 15, 2005.

National Vital Statistics System

Universe, Frequency, and Types of Data: Annual data on births and deaths in the United States.

Type of Data Collection Operation: Mortality data based on complete file of death records, except 1972, based on 50 percent sample. Natality statistics 1951–1971, based on 50 percent sample of birth certificates, except a 20 percent to 50 percent sample in 1967, received by NCHS.

Data Collection and Imputation Procedures: Reports based on records from registration offices of all states, District of Columbia, New York City, Puerto Rico, Virgin Islands, Guam, American Samoa, and Northern Marianas.

Estimates of Sampling Error: For recent years, there is no sampling for these files; the files are based on 100 percent of events registered.

Other (nonsampling) Errors: It is believed that more than 99 percent of the births and deaths occurring in this country are registered.

Sources of Additional Material: U.S. National Center for Health Statistics, *Vital Statistics of the United States,* Vol. I and Vol. II, annual, and the *National Vital Statistics Reports.* See the NCHS Web site at <http://www.cdc.gov/nchs/nvss.htm>.

National Highway Traffic Safety Administration (NHTSA)

Fatality Analysis Reporting System (FARS)

Universe, Frequency, and Types of Data: FARS is a census of all fatal motor vehicle traffic crashes that occur throughout the United States including the District of Columbia and Puerto Rico on roadways customarily open to the public. The crash must be reported to the state/jurisdiction and at least one directly related fatality must occur within thirty days of the crash.

Type of Data Collection Operation: One or more analysts, in each state, extract data from the official documents and enter the data into a standardized electronic database.

Data Collection and Imputation Procedures: Detailed data describing the characteristics of the fatal crash, the vehicles and persons involved are obtained from police crash reports, driver and vehicle registration records, autopsy reports, highway department, etc. Computerized edit checks monitor the accuracy and completeness of the data. The FARS incorporates a sophisticated mathematical multiple imputation procedure to develop a probability distribution of missing blood alcohol concentration (BAC) levels in the database for drivers, pedestrians, and cyclists.

Estimates of Sampling Error: Since this is census data, there are no sampling errors.

Other (nonsampling) Errors: FARS represents a census of all police-reported crashes and captures all data reported at the state level. FARS data undergo a rigorous quality control process to prevent inaccurate reporting. However, these data are highly dependent on the accuracy of the police accident reports. Errors or omissions within police accident reports may not be detected.

Sources of Additional Material: The FARS Coding and Validation Manual, ANSI D16.1 Manual on Classification of Motor Vehicle Traffic Accidents (Sixth Edition).

Appendix IV
Weights and Measures

For assistance on metric usage, call or write:

Elizabeth J. Gentry
National Institute of Standards and Technology (NIST)
Weights and Measures Division
100 Bureau Drive – Mail Stop 2600
Gaithersburg, MD 20899-2600

Telephone: 301-975-3690 or 4004   FAX: 301-975-8091

E-mail: TheSI@nist.gov

Internet site: <http://ts.nist.gov/WeightsAndMeasures/Metric/mpo_home.cfm>

[Conversions provided in table are approximate]

Symbol	When you know conventional	Multiply by	To find metric	Symbol
in	inches	2.54	centimeters	cm
ft	feet	30.48	centimeters	cm
yd	yards	0.91	meters	m
mi	miles	1.61	kilometers	km
in^2	square inches	6.45	square centimeters	cm^2
ft^2	square feet	0.09	square meters	m^2
yd^2	square yards	0.84	square meters	m^2
mi^2	square miles	2.59	square kilometers	km^2
	acre	0.41	hectare	ha
oz	ounces [1]	28.35	grams	g
lb	pounds [1]	0.45	kilograms	kg
oz (troy)	ounces [2]	31.10	grams	g
	short tons (2,000 lb)	0.91	metric tons	t
	long tons (2,240 lb)	1.02	metric tons	t
fl oz	fluid ounces	29.57	milliliters	mL
c	cups	0.24	liters	L
pt	pints	0.47	liters	L
qt	quarts	0.95	liters	L
gal	gallons	3.78	liters	L
ft^3	cubic feet	0.03	cubic meters	m^3
yd^3	cubic yards	0.76	cubic meters	m^3
°F	degrees Fahrenheit (subtract 32)	0.55	degrees Celsius	°C

Symbol	When you know metric	Multiply by	To find conventional	Symbol
cm	centimeters	0.39	inches	in
cm	centimeters	0.03	feet	ft
m	meters	1.09	yards	yd
km	kilometers	0.62	miles	mi
cm^2	square centimeters	0.15	square inches	in^2
m^2	square meters	10.76	square feet	ft^2
m^2	square meters	1.20	square yards	yd^2
km^2	square kilometers	0.39	square miles	mi^2
ha	hectares	2.47	acre	
g	grams	0.04	ounces [1]	oz
kg	kilograms	2.21	pounds [2]	lb
g	grams	0.04	ounces [2]	oz (troy)
t	metric tons	1.10	short tons (2,000 lb)	
t	metric tons	0.98	long tons (2,240 lb)	
mL	milliliters	0.03	fluid ounces	fl oz
L	liter	4.23	cups	c
L	liters	2.13	pints (liquid)	pt
L	liters	1.05	quarts (liquid)	qt
L	liters	0.26	gallons	gal
m^3	cubic meters	35.32	cubic feet	ft^3
m^3	cubic meters	1.32	cubic yards	yd^3
°C	degrees Celsius (after multiplying, add 32)	1.80	degrees Fahrenheit	°F

[1] For weighing ordinary commodities.   [2] For weighing precious metals, jewels, etc.

U.S. Census Bureau, Statistical Abstract of the United States: 2012

Appendix V
Tables Deleted From the
2011 Edition of the Statistical Abstract

U.S. Census Bureau, Statistical Abstract of the United States: 2012

Index

NOTE: Index citations refer to **table** numbers, not **page** numbers.

NOTE: Index citations refer to **table** numbers, not **page** numbers.

NOTE: Index citations refer to **table** numbers, not **page** numbers.

NOTE: Index citations refer to **table** numbers, not **page** numbers.

U.S. Census Bureau, Statistical Abstract of the United States: 2012

NOTE: Index citations refer to **table** numbers, not **page** numbers.

U.S. Census Bureau, Statistical Abstract of the United States: 2012

NOTE: Index citations refer to **table** numbers, not **page** numbers.

NOTE: Index citations refer to **table** numbers, not **page** numbers.

NOTE: Index citations refer to **table** numbers, not **page** numbers.

NOTE: Index citations refer to **table** numbers, not **page** numbers.

U.S. Census Bureau, Statistical Abstract of the United States: 2012

Coal (see also Petroleum and coal product manufacturing and Coal mining):—Con.
   Consumption, 919, 925, 926, 931, 934, 945, 1381, 1382
   Emissions, 375, 376
   Expenditures, 928
   Foreign trade, 919, 920, 926, 935, 936, 1308
   Freight, on waterways, 1084
   Net generation, 945
   Net summer capacity, 946
   Prices, 737, 906, 919, 920
   Production, 920, 925, 926
      World production, 908, 920, 1379, 1380, 1386
   Reserves, 921, 922
Coal bed methane, 918
Coal mining:
   Earnings, 880, 901
   Employment, 880, 901, 902, 920
   Establishments, 880
   Fatalities, 902
   Gross domestic product, 670
   Injuries, 902
   Inspections, 902
   Mines, 902, 920
   Output, 903, 925
   Productivity, 903, 920
   Safety, 902
   Shipments, 901
   Supply, 919
Coast Guard, 386, 534
Coastal population, 25, 26, 362
Coastlines, 362, 364
Cobalt, 905
Cocaine (see also Drugs (illegal), and Arrests), 207, 327, 328
Cocoa, 217, 850
Cod, 897, 900
Coffee:
   Consumption, 215, 217
   Foreign trade, 848, 850
   Price indexes, 727
   Prices, 727, 733, 737
Cogeneration of electricity (combined–heat–and–power), 930, 945
Cohabitation, unmarried, 63, 90, 95
Coke. (See Coal.)
College:
   Costs, 288, 289
   Enrollment, 219, 225, 226, 227, 277, 278, 279, 280, 282, 283, 284, 287
   Federal obligations, 809
   Freshmen, 286
   Price index, 290, 727
   Research & development, 808
   Science & engineering, 810, 812, 813
   State appropriations, 292
   Tuition, 293
Colleges and universities. (See Education, and Higher education institutions.)
Colombia. (See Foreign countries.)
Colorado. (See State data.)
Commerce:
   Domestic, by rail, 1123, 1124
   Domestic, by water, 1084, 1085
   Foreign. (See Foreign trade.)
Commercial buildings:
   Characteristics, 1006

Commercial buildings:—Con.
   Construction value, 966
   Crime incidents, 317
   Floorspace, 966
Commercial energy, 928, 930, 931, 932, 934, 947, 950, 951, 952, 955
Commodities. (See individual types of commodities.)
Commodity flow, 1071
Communicable diseases, 184
Communications:
   Degrees conferred, 301, 302, 303
   Price indexes, 725
Communications equipment manufacturing:
   Earnings, 632, 818, 1009, 1011
   Employees, 632, 818, 1009, 1011
   Establishments, 1009
   Foreign trade, 1310
   Inventories, 1020
   Productivity, 641
   Shipments, 1011, 1020, 1034
Communications industry. (See Information industry.)
Community development, 454, 473
Community food, housing services, 576
Community service, 585
Commuting to work, 656, 1100
Complementary and alternative medicine, 167
Comoros. (See Foreign countries.)
Compact disks, 1140
Computers:
   Broadband, 1132, 1151, 1154, 1156, 1157, 1158, 1391
   Consumer expenditures, 739
   Cyber–bullying, 251
   Foreign trade, 1301, 1310, 1312
   Injuries associated with, 201
   Sales, 783, 1056
   Use, 251, 264, 1132, 1133, 1157, 1158, 1159, 1160, 1161, 1391, 1392
Computer programming and data processing services, 632
Computer sales, 1033
Computer specialists:
   Degrees conferred, 301, 302, 303, 810, 814, 815
   Labor force, 616, 618, 817
   Research & development, 802, 805, 808, 820
   Salary offers, 298
Computer systems design:
   Capital, 781
   Earnings, 1274
   Employees, 1274
   Establishments, 1274
   Gross domestic product, 670
   Receipts, 1277
   Research and development, 805, 806
Computerized axial tomography (CAT scans), 171
Computers and electronic product manufacturing:
   Capital, 781
   Earnings, 632, 818, 1009, 1011
   Employees, 632, 818, 1009, 1011, 1013
   Establishments, 1009
   Finances, 794
   Foreign trade, 1312
   Gross domestic product, 670

NOTE: Index citations refer to **table** numbers, not **page** numbers.

U.S. Census Bureau, Statistical Abstract of the United States: 2012

NOTE: Index citations refer to **table** numbers, not **page** numbers.

NOTE: Index citations refer to **table** numbers, not **page** numbers.

NOTE: Index citations refer to **table** numbers, not **page** numbers.

U.S. Census Bureau, Statistical Abstract of the United States: 2012

NOTE: Index citations refer to **table** numbers, not **page** numbers.

NOTE: Index citations refer to **table** numbers, not **page** numbers.

NOTE: Index citations refer to **table** numbers, not **page** numbers.

NOTE: Index citations refer to **table** numbers, not **page** numbers.

NOTE: Index citations refer to **table** numbers, not **page** numbers.

U.S. Census Bureau, Statistical Abstract of the United States: 2012

NOTE: Index citations refer to **table** numbers, not **page** numbers.

NOTE: Index citations refer to **table** numbers, not **page** numbers.

U.S. Census Bureau, Statistical Abstract of the United States: 2012

NOTE: Index citations refer to **table** numbers, not **page** numbers.

NOTE: Index citations refer to **table** numbers, not **page** numbers.

U.S. Census Bureau, Statistical Abstract of the United States: 2012

Graphite, 905
Great Britain. (See Foreign countries.)
Great Lakes, 359, 360, 361, 1084
Greece. (See Foreign countries.)
Greenhouse and nursery crops, 843
Greenhouse gases, 375, 376
Greenland. (See Foreign countries.)
Grenada. (See Foreign countries.)
Grocery stores (See also Food and beverage
    stores), 632, 641, 1048, 1051, 1059
Gross domestic product (GDP):
    Components, annual growth rates, 667, 668,
        669, 1064
    Foreign countries, 1349
    Implicit price deflators for, 667
    Industry, 670
    National defense outlays, 503
    Per capita, 679, 1349
    Per employed person, 1349
    Price indexes, 740
    Relation to national and personal income, 673
    Sectoral contributions, 1351
    State, 671, 672
Gross national product, 679, 1348
Gross private domestic investment, 667, 668,
    740
Gross value added, 1351
Ground water used, 371
Group quarters population, 74
Guadeloupe. (See Foreign countries.)
Guam. (See Island areas of the U.S.)
Guamanian population, 1313
Guatemala. (See Foreign countries.)
Guernsey. (See Foreign countries.)
Guinea. (See Foreign countries.)
Guinea–Bissau. (See Foreign countries.)
Guns. (See Firearms.)
Guyana. (See Foreign countries.)
Gymnastics, 1208
Gypsum and gypsum products, 737, 904, 905,
    908, 962

H
Haddock, 900
Haiti. (See Foreign countries.)
Halibut, 897
Hallucinogenic drugs, 207
Handguns, 310, 329
Handicapped. (See Disability.)
Harrasment victimization, 319
Hate crimes, 322, 323
Hawaii. (See State data.)
Hawaiian population. (See Native Hawaiian and
    Other Pacific Islander population.)
Hay, 843, 858
Hazardous waste/materials, 384, 385, 1033,
    1071
Hazelnuts (filberts), 864, 865
Head Start program, 574
Health and education service industries, 631,
    665
Health and personal care stores:
    Earnings, 632, 756, 1048
    Employees, 632, 756, 1048
    Establishments, 756, 1048, 1049
    Nonemployers, 1049
    Productivity, 641
    Sales, 756, 1049, 1051, 1053, 1054

Health care and social assistance industry:
    Capital, 781, 783
    Earnings, 630, 643, 756, 759, 760, 769, 770,
        771, 772, 773, 774, 775, 1274
    Electronic commerce, 1278
    Employees, 160, 630, 756, 769, 770, 771,
        772, 773, 774, 775, 1274
    Equipment and software expenditures, 759,
        760, 783
    Establishments, 756, 757
    Finances, 746, 749
    Gross domestic product, 670
    Hires and separations, 637
    Hours, 611
    Nonemployers, 757
    Profits, 793
    Receipts, 746, 749, 754, 755, 756, 757, 769,
        770, 771, 772, 773, 774, 775
Health insurance (see also Health services,
    Insurance carriers, Medicaid, Medicare,
    and SCHIP):
    Contributions, 158
    Coverage, 145, 148, 155, 156, 157, 158
    Enrollment and payments, 145, 147, 151,
        152, 153, 154
    Expenditures, 134, 135, 136, 137, 138, 139,
        140, 141, 143, 145, 158, 538, 684, 685,
        686, 687, 688, 739
    Premiums and policy reserves, life insurance
        companies, 1221
    State Children's Health Insurance program,
        145
Health insurance industry, employment, 162
Health maintenance organizations (HMO), 154
Health sciences, degrees conferred, 301, 302,
    303, 304
Health services:
    Buildings and floor space, 1006
    Charitable contributions, 580, 583
    Construction, value, 964, 965
    Coverage, 146, 147, 148, 152, 155, 524
    Expenditures, 134, 135, 136, 137, 139, 140,
        141, 143, 435, 436, 443, 451, 454, 458,
        460, 686, 1346
    Government employment and payrolls, 462
    Government, federal expenditures, 141, 432,
        434, 474
    Hospitals, 172, 173, 174, 175, 176, 178, 179
    Industry, 162, 632, 660, 781
    Medicaid, 141, 148, 151, 152, 153, 155, 432,
        474
    Medicare, 135, 138, 141, 144, 146, 147, 149,
        150, 155, 474, 547
    Nursing homes, 136, 137, 140
    Occupations, 164, 165, 616
    Philanthropy, 580
    Price indexes, 142, 727
    Veterans' health care, 135, 138
    Volunteers, 585
Heart disease, 124, 169, 179
    Deaths, 117, 118, 119, 121, 122, 123
Heating and plumbing equipment, 944, 971,
    988
Heating oil, 730
Heavy and civil engineering construction, 632,
    660, 961
HVAC and commercial refrigeration equipment
    manufacturing, 632
Height, average, 209

NOTE: Index citations refer to **table** numbers, not **page** numbers.

U.S. Census Bureau, Statistical Abstract of the United States: 2012

NOTE: Index citations refer to **table** numbers, not **page** numbers.

U.S. Census Bureau, Statistical Abstract of the United States: 2012

NOTE: Index citations refer to **table** numbers, not **page** numbers.

U.S. Census Bureau, Statistical Abstract of the United States: 2012

NOTE: Index citations refer to **table** numbers, not **page** numbers.

NOTE: Index citations refer to **table** numbers, not **page** numbers.

Injuries, 115, 130, 170, 179, 200, 201, 202, 1070, 1114, 1121(see also Accidents, and Occupational safety)
  Crime victimization, 315
  Industrial, 657, 658, 659, 660, 902
Inmates (see also Correctional institutions and Prisons and prisoners), 349, 350
Installment loans (see also Loans and mortgages), 1172, 1173, 1190
Institutional care facilities (see also Hospitals, and Nursing and residential care facilities), 172, 175
Instruments and related products, manufacturing:
  Earnings, 632, 1017
  Employees, 632, 1017
  Foreign trade, 742, 743, 1312
  Gross domestic product, 1007
  Productivity, 641
  Profits, 794
  Toxic chemical releases, 382
Insurance. (See individual forms of insurance.)
Insurance agents, brokers, and service:
  Earnings, 1165
  Employees, 1165
  Establishments, 1165, 1177
  Finances, 1201, 1222
  Gross domestic product, 1162
  Prices, 727, 739
Insurance carriers:
  Capital, 781
  Earnings, 632, 1163, 1165
  Employees, 632, 1163, 1165
  Establishments, 1163, 1164, 1165
  Finances, 1166, 1222
  Gross domestic product, 1162
  Nonemployers, 1164
  Occupational safety, 660
  Profits, 1222
  Receipts, 1163, 1164
Insurance, government. (See Social insurance.)
Insurance, medical care, 135, 139, 140, 1364
Intentional self-harm. (See Suicide.)
Interest:
  Payments, federal government, 473
  Persons receiving income, 542
  Receipts, by source:
    Individual income tax returns, 483
    National and personal income component, 678
Interest rates, 1193, 1197
Intermediate goods, price indexes, producer, 737
Internal revenue collections (see also Tax receipts), 480
Internal waterways, traffic, 1084
International affairs:
  Charitable organizations, 583
  Commerce, 1303, 1304, 1307, 1325
  Development aid, 1402, 1403, 1405
  Federal outlays, 473
  Foreign exchange rates, 1398
  Foreign investments in U.S., 1205, 1206, 1289, 1291
  International transactions, U.S., 1286, 1287, 1288, 1289, 1290
  U.S. government aid, 1297, 1298, 1299
  U.S. investments, 1203, 1204, 1286, 1296

International data (See Foreign countries, or World summary statistics.)
International investment position, U.S., 1286, 1289, 1296
International mail (U.S. postal), 1126
Internet access/use, 1132, 1133, 1157, 1240, 1391
  Activities, 1159, 1160, 1161
  Connection type, 1156, 1158, 1161
  Public libraries, 1154
  Schools, 251, 264
Internet publishing and broadcasting:
  Earnings, 632, 756, 1128
  Employees, 632, 756, 1128
  Establishments, 756, 1128
  Finances, 1129
  Revenue, 756, 1129, 1144
Internet service providers, Web search portals, data processing:
  Earnings, 632, 756, 1128
  Employees, 632, 756, 1128
  Establishments, 756, 1128
  Finances, 1129
  Revenue, 756, 1129, 1151
Interracial married couples, 60
Inventories (see also commodities, and Stocks), 667, 1018, 1019, 1020, 1021, 1046, 1054, 1057
Investments (see also Capital stock, and Securities):
  Foreign, in U.S., 1205, 1206, 1286, 1289, 1291, 1293, 1294, 1295, 1405
  Private domestic, gross, 667, 674, 740
  U.S. government obligations, 1177
  U.S. international, 1203, 1204, 1286, 1289, 1296
Iowa. (See State data.)
Iran. (See Foreign countries.)
Iraq. (See Foreign countries.)
Ireland. (See Foreign countries.)
Iron, nutritional, 216
Iron (see also Steel):
  Foreign trade, 909, 1308
  Mining industry, 641, 901
  Prices, 737, 905
  Production, 904, 905, 908, 977, 1379
Iron and steel mills (see also Primary metal manufacturing):
  Capital, 1030
  Earnings, 632, 1009, 1011
  Employees, 632, 1009, 1011, 1030
  Establishments, 1009
  Foreign trade, 1030
  Shipments, 1011, 1030
Iron and steel products, 742, 743, 904, 905, 908, 909, 1308
Irrigation, 371
Islamic population. (See Religions.)
Island Areas of the U.S.:
  Agriculture, 1326, 1327
  Aid by U.S. government, 1318
  Area, 358
  Banks and banking, 1321
  Births, 82, 1314
  Climate (Puerto Rico), 393, 394, 395, 396
  Commerce, 1323, 1325
  Deaths, 113, 116, 123
  Economic summary, 1322, 1328
  Education, 1315, 1321

NOTE: Index citations refer to **table** numbers, not **page** numbers.

NOTE: Index citations refer to **table** numbers, not **page** numbers.

NOTE: Index citations refer to **table** numbers, not **page** numbers.

NOTE: Index citations refer to **table** numbers, not **page** numbers.

NOTE: Index citations refer to **table** numbers, not **page** numbers.

NOTE: Index citations refer to **table** numbers, not **page** numbers.

NOTE: Index citations refer to **table** numbers, not **page** numbers.

U.S. Census Bureau, Statistical Abstract of the United States: 2012

NOTE: Index citations refer to **table** numbers, not **page** numbers.

NOTE: Index citations refer to **table** numbers, not **page** numbers.

U.S. Census Bureau, Statistical Abstract of the United States: 2012

NOTE: Index citations refer to **table** numbers, not **page** numbers.

NOTE: Index citations refer to **table** numbers, not **page** numbers.

U.S. Census Bureau, Statistical Abstract of the United States: 2012

NOTE: Index citations refer to **table** numbers, not **page** numbers.

U.S. Census Bureau, Statistical Abstract of the United States: 2012

Professional, scientific and technical services:—Con.
  Employees, 630, 632, 756, 759, 760, 769, 770, 771, 772, 773, 774, 775, 1272, 1273, 1274, 1275, 1276
  Equipment and software expenditures, 783
  Establishments, 756, 757, 759, 1272, 1273, 1276
  Finances, 746, 749
  Gross domestic product, 670
  Hours, 630
  Multinational companies, 796, 797, 798
  Nonemployers, 757, 1273
  Occupational safety, 660
  Profits, 793
  Sales, receipts, 746, 749, 754, 755, 756, 757, 769, 770, 771, 772, 773, 774, 775, 1272, 1273, 1277
Profits, 753, 1057, 1178, 1179, 1219, 1222
  Corporations, 674, 744, 791, 792, 793, 794, 1022
  Partnerships and proprietorships, 744, 747, 748
Projections:
  Births, 1339
  College enrollment, 219, 221
  Deaths, 1339
  Degrees conferred, 221
  Employment, 618, 621
  Energy, 926
  High school graduates, 221
  Island areas, 1313
  Labor force, 587, 618, 621
  Life expectancy, 104, 1339
  Population, 3, 9, 12, 1313, 1329, 1330, 1331, 1332
  School enrollment, 219, 221
  Teachers, 221
Propane, 876
Property and casualty insurance, 1201, 1215, 1222
  Fire losses, 354, 356, 357
Property crime, 306, 307, 308, 309, 320, 321
Property tax, 436, 451
  Rates, selected cities, 448
  State and local government, 435, 436
Proprietors' income, 678
Proprietorships, 744, 746, 747
Propylene, 911
Protective service workers. (See Public safety.)
Protein, available for consumption, 216
Protestants. (See Religions.)
Psychiatric care and institutions. (See Mental hospitals.)
Psychology:
  Degrees conferred, 301, 302, 303, 814, 815
  Employment, 616
  Enrollment, 810
  Research, U.S. government obligations for, 802
Psychotherapeutic drugs, nonmedical use, 207
Public administration. (See Government.)
Public aid, assistance:
  Benefits paid, 538, 564
  Federal aid to state and local governments, 432, 433, 434
  Federal expenditures, 135, 136, 138, 139, 147, 151, 152, 565, 566
  Homeless, 575

Public aid, assistance:—Con.
  Means-tested, 543
  Program participation of household, 543
  Recipients, 542, 564, 565, 566
Public domain. (See Public lands.)
Public housing, 434, 546, 575
Public lands (see also Forests):
  Area, 367, 369, 884, 1254, 1255
  Leases, permits, licenses, 914
  National forests, 884
  National park system, 1252, 1254, 1255
  Ownership, 884
  Recreation, 1252, 1254, 1255
  States, 1253
Public officials, prosecutions, 338
Public roads. (See Highways.)
Public safety (see also Law enforcement):
  Employment, 616
    City government, 467
    Fire protection, 355, 462, 465
    Police protection and correction, 462, 465
  Expenditures:
    City government, 458
    Construction, value, 964, 965
    County government, 460
    Local government, 456
    State and local government, 435, 471
    State government, 451, 454
  Volunteers, 585
Public schools. (See Education.)
Public transportation, 686, 687, 727
Public utilities, 924, 955, 956, 958, 959, 960
Publishing. (see also Books, Newspapers, and Printing.):
  Books, 737, 1128, 1129, 1134
  Newspapers, 1128, 1129, 1134, 1135, 1136
  Periodicals, 1128, 1129, 1134
  Directory and mailing list, 1128, 1129, 1134
Publishing industry:
  Capital, 781
  Earnings, 632, 756, 1128, 1130
  Employees, 632, 756, 1128, 1130
  Establishments, 756, 1128, 1130
  Finances, 794, 1129
  Gross domestic product, 670, 1007
  Industrial production index, 789
  Profit, 794
  Receipts, revenue, 756, 1129, 1130
Puerto Rican population (see also Hispanic origin population):
  Agriculture, 1326, 1327
  Births, 79, 86, 1315
  Deaths, 113, 116, 123, 1315
  Educational attainment, 230
  Households, 1319, 1320
  Labor force, 564, 593
  Population, 37, 1281, 1314
  Summary, 1321
  Tenure, 1319
Puerto Rico. (See Island areas of the U.S.)
Pulmonary diseases (see also Respiratory diseases), 117, 118, 119, 120, 121, 123, 179, 184
Pulp manufacturing, 880, 881, 882
Pulpwood, 887, 888, 889, 893
Pulses, 218
Pumice and pumicite, 904, 905
Purchasing power of the dollar, 724
Pyrites, 906

NOTE: Index citations refer to **table** numbers, not **page** numbers.

NOTE: Index citations refer to **table** numbers, not **page** numbers.

U.S. Census Bureau, Statistical Abstract of the United States: 2012

NOTE: Index citations refer to **table** numbers, not **page** numbers.

S

Safety and security measures, 250, 660, 902
Sailing, 1249
Saint Kitts and Nevis. (See Foreign countries.)
Saint Lucia. (See Foreign countries.)
Saint Vincent and the Grenadines. (See Foreign countries.)
Salad and cooking oils, consumption, 217
Salaries and wages. (See Earnings.)
Sales. (See individual commodities and industries.)
Salesworkers, 616, 626, 634, 642
Salmon, 897, 899, 900
Salmonellosis, 184
Salt (common), production/value, 904, 905, 1379
Samoa. (See Foreign countries.)
Samoa, American. (See Island areas of the U.S.)
Samoan population, 1313
San Marino. (See Foreign countries.)
Sand and gravel industry (see also Mining industry), 737, 904
Sanitation. (See Health and Sewage treatment.)
Sao Tome and Principe. (See Foreign countries.)
Sardines, 900
Saudi Arabia. (See Foreign countries.)
Savings:
  Credit unions, 1183
  Deposits, 675, 1169
  Gross savings, sources and uses, 674
  Personal, 674, 678
  Rates, 1363. (See Savings institutions.)
Savings banks. (See Savings institutions.)
Savings bonds, 478, 1170
Savings institutions:
  Consumer credit, 1191
  Debt held by families, 1173
  Earnings, 1165
  Employees, 1165
  Establishments, 1165, 1177
  Finances, 1166, 1167, 1176, 1179, 1192, 1196
  Individual Retirement Accounts (IRAs), 1216
  Service charges, 677
Saw logs, 888, 892
Saw mills, 880, 881, 882
Scallops, 897, 899
Scenic and sightseeing transportation industry, 632, 1063, 1065, 1066
SCHIP (See Children's Health Insurance Program.)
Scholastic Assessment Test (SAT), 267
Schools (see also Education):
  After-school activities, 252
  Alternative, 244, 263
  Boards, elected officials, 421
  Bullying, 251
  Charter schools, 239, 263
  Choice, 238
  Computer use, 264
  Districts, 242, 429
  Dress code, 250
  Drug testing, 250
  Fundraising, 252
  Homeschooling, 240
  Libraries, 264, 265
  Lunch programs, 263, 570
  Magnet schools, 263
  Number, 241, 265, 278, 280

Parent participation, 252
Schools (see also Education):—Con.
  Parent Teacher Association (PTA), 252
  Parent Teacher Organization (PTO), 252
  Safety and security, 250
  Special education, 189, 190, 244, 263
  Types, 239, 241, 244, 263
  Vocational, 244, 263
  Volunteers, 252
  Weapons, 249
Science, literacy, 1371
Scientific instruments. (See Instruments.)
Scientific research. (See Research and development.)
Scientists and engineers (see also individual fields):
  Characteristics, 816
  Degrees conferred, 301, 302, 303, 811, 812, 813, 814, 815
  Employment, 616, 817, 819, 820
  Non U.S. citizens, 811, 814, 816
  Occupation, 800, 812, 817
Scrap metal. (See individual commodities.)
Scuba diving, 1249, 1250
Seafood, 897, 899, 900
Securities:
  Brokerage charges, 677
  Foreign holdings, 1168, 1206, 1286, 1289, 1397
  Foreign purchases and sales, 1203, 1205, 1394, 1395, 1397
  Government, 440, 750, 751, 1168, 1199, 1205, 1206
  Held by life insurance, 1221
  Holdings of banks, 750, 751, 1177
  Holdings of individuals and businesses, 1169
  New issues, 1199, 1202
  Prices, indexes, yields, and issues, 1198, 1207, 1208, 1395
  Sales, stocks and bonds, 1199, 1203, 1205, 1394, 1395, 1397
  Savings of individuals, 675
  State and local government, 440, 722, 750, 751, 1199
Securities, commodity contracts, and investments (industry):
  Capital, 781
  Earnings, 632, 1163, 1165
  Electronic commerce, 1278
  Employees, 632, 1163, 1165
  Establishments, 1163, 1164, 1165
  Finances, 1166, 1218, 1219
  Gross domestic product, 1162
  Nonemployers, 1164
  Profits, 1219
  Receipts, 1163, 1164
Sedatives, persons using, 207
Seeds, 841
Selenium, dietary, 216
Self-employed, 605, 606, 817
Semiconductors (see also Computer and electronic product components), 818, 1031, 1310
Senators, U.S., 407, 412, 413
Senegal. (See Foreign countries.)
Septicemia, 117, 118, 119, 120, 121, 122
Serbia. (See Foreign countries.)
Service industries (see also specific sectors):
  Capital, 781, 783

NOTE: Index citations refer to **table** numbers, not **page** numbers.

U.S. Census Bureau, Statistical Abstract of the United States: 2012

NOTE: Index citations refer to **table** numbers, not **page** numbers.

NOTE: Index citations refer to **table** numbers, not **page** numbers.

NOTE: Index citations refer to **table** numbers, not **page** numbers.

NOTE: Index citations refer to **table** numbers, not **page** numbers.

U.S. Census Bureau, Statistical Abstract of the United States: 2012

NOTE: Index citations refer to **table** numbers, not **page** numbers.

NOTE: Index citations refer to **table** numbers, not **page** numbers.

U.S. Census Bureau, Statistical Abstract of the United States: 2012

NOTE: Index citations refer to **table** numbers, not **page** numbers.

Tuna, 897, 899, 900
Tungsten, 904, 905, 908, 909
Tunisia. (See Foreign countries.)
Turbines. (See Steam engines.)
Turkey. (See Foreign countries.)
Turkeys, 733, 737, 843, 869, 878
Turkmenistan. (See Foreign countries.)
Turks and Caicos Islands. (See Foreign countries.)
Tuvalu. (See Foreign countries.)
Typhoid fever, 184

U

Uganda (See Foreign countries.)
Ukraine (See Foreign countries.)
Ulcers, 196
Ultrasound, diagnostic, 171
Unemployment. (See Labor force, unemployed workers.)
Unemployment insurance:
  Beneficiaries, 542, 558, 559, 629
  Coverage, workers and earnings, 559
  Governmental finances, 435, 451, 475
  Payments, 538, 539, 540, 541, 558, 559
Union membership, 664, 665, 666
United Arab Emirates. (See Foreign countries.)
United Kingdom. (See Foreign countries.)
United States securities (see also Debt), 1169, 1177, 1197, 1198, 1199, 1201, 1205, 1206
Universities. (See Education, higher education institutions.)
Unpaid work, 639
Uranium (see also Nuclear power), 904, 922, 943
Urban population, 29
Urban transit systems industry, 1066
Uruguay. (See Foreign countries.)
Utah. (See State data.)
Utilities (see also Electric light power industry, and Gas utility industry.):
  Capital, 781, 783, 785, 924, 955, 956, 958, 959, 960
  Cost of living, 728
  Customers and bills, 952
  Earnings, 630, 632, 643, 644, 756, 759, 760, 769, 770, 771, 772, 773, 774, 775, 923, 924
  Electric, 949
  Employees, 630, 632, 756, 759, 769, 770, 771, 772, 773, 774, 775, 923, 924
  Equipment and software expenditures, 783
  Establishments, 756, 757, 759, 924
  Expense, 953
  Finances, 746, 749
  Gross domestic product, 670
  Gas, 955, 956, 957
  Hours, 630
  Income, 953
  Industrial production index, 789
  Industry, 756, 923, 924, 949
  Investor owned, 953
  Multinational companies, 796, 797
  Net generation, 949, 952
  Net summer capacity, 949
  Nonemployers, 757
  Occupational safety, 660
  Price indexes, 726
  Productivity, 641

Utilities (see also Electric light power industry, and Gas utility industry.):—Con.
  Revenue, 952, 953
  Sales, 746, 749, 754, 755, 756, 757, 769, 770, 771, 772, 773, 774, 775
  Sewage treatment, 924, 958
  States, 951
  Water, 924, 959, 960
Uzbekistan. (See Foreign countries.)

V

Vacancy rates, housing, 982, 984, 985, 986, 987
Vanadium, 908, 909
Vanuatu. (See Foreign countries.)
Veal (see also Beef, Meat, and meat products), 217, 737, 869, 1377
Vegetable oils. (See Oils.)
Vegetables (see also individual commodities):
  Acreage, 862
  Consumer expenditures, 686, 687
  Consumption, 218, 863
  Farm marketings, sales, 841, 843
  Foreign trade, 848, 850, 853, 855, 863, 1308
  Gardens, 1242
  Organic, 833
  Prices, 727, 737, 738, 742, 846
  Production, 862, 863
Vehicles. (See Motor vehicles.)
Veneer, wood products, 880, 881, 882, 895
Venereal diseases (see also AIDS), 184
Venezuela. (See Foreign countries.)
Vermiculite, 904, 905
Vermont. (See State data.)
Vessels. (See Ships.)
Veterans:
  Business owners, 768
  Characteristics, 522
  Employment, 590
  Number, 520
  Pensions and other benefits:
    Service-connected compensation, 523, 524
    Disbursements, 503, 524, 538, 540
    Federal aid to state and local governments, 432
    Federal payments, 474
    Health expenditures, 135, 138
    Veterans or dependents receiving, 523, 542
Veterans Affairs, Dept. of:
  Expenditures, 135, 138, 523, 524, 539, 540, 541
  Home loans, 1194
Vetoed bills, Congressional, 415
Victimizations, criminal, 315, 316, 317, 318, 319, 320, 321, 322, 323
Vietnam. (See Foreign countries.)
Violent crime, (see also Crime), 306, 307, 308, 309, 310, 318.
Virgin Islands. (See Island areas of the U.S.)
Virginia. (See State data.)
Visa holders, doctorates, 811
Vital statistics. (See Births and birth rates, Deaths and death rates, Divorces, and Marriages.):
Vitamins, 216
Vocational rehabilitation, 135, 576
Volleyball, 1247, 1248, 1249

NOTE: Index citations refer to **table** numbers, not **page** numbers.

U.S. Census Bureau, Statistical Abstract of the United States: 2012

NOTE: Index citations refer to **table** numbers, not **page** numbers.

NOTE: Index citations refer to **table** numbers, not **page** numbers.

U.S. Census Bureau, Statistical Abstract of the United States: 2012

NOTE: Index citations refer to **table** numbers, not **page** numbers.